BASEBALL PROSPECTUS 2021

The Essential Guide to the 2021 Season

Edited by R.J. Anderson, Patrick Dubuque, and Craig Goldstein

Nathalie Alonso, Lucas Apostoleris, Rob Arthur, Darius Austin, Emma Baccellieri, Bill Baer, Mark Barry, Sydney Bergman, Nathan Bishop, Grant Brisbee, Craig Brown, Adrian Burgos Jr., Craig Calcaterra, Russell A. Carleton, Ben Carsley, Alexis Collins, Zach Crizer, Bradford William Davis, James Fegan, Noah Frank, Bailey Freeman, Ken Funck, Brendan Gawlowski, Mike Gianella, Steven Goldman, Bryan Grosnick, Jon Hegglund, Kamila Hinkson, Kendra James, Alex Kirshner, Justin Klugh, Keanan Lamb, Tom Ley, Rob Mains, Rachael McDaniel, Kelsey McKinney, Jake Mintz, Emily Nemens, Marc Normandin, Eric Nusbaum, Robert O'Connell, Sridhar Pappu, Jeffrey Paternostro, Kate Preusser, Tommy Rancel, David Roth, Jon 'Boog' Sciambi, Ginny Searle, Jarrett Seidler, Stephanie Springer, Elizabeth Strom, Matt Sussman, Jon Tayler, Luis Torres, Matt Trueblood, Collin Whitchurch, Randy Wilkins, Jasmyn Wimbish, Jeffrey Wiser, Kazuto Yamazaki, Clinton Yates

Craig Brown and Bret Sayre, Associate Editors
Robert Au, Harry Pavlidis and Amy Pircher, Statistics Editors

Library of Congress Cataloging-in-Publication Data:
paperback
ISBN-10: 1950716848
ISBN-13: 978-1950716845

Project Credits
Cover Design: Ginny Searle
Interior Design and Production: Amy Pircher, Robert Au
Layout: Amy Pircher, Robert Au

Cover Photos
Front Cover: Mookie Betts. © Tim Heitman-USA TODAY Sports

Baseball icon courtesy of Uberux, from https://www.shareicon.net/author/uberux

Manufactured in the United States of America
10 9 8 7 6 5 4 3 2 1

This book is dedicated to our friend Rob McQuown.

Thanks for the research, and for everything else.

Table of Contents

Foreword

by Jon "Boog" Sciambi

About a decade ago, in what now feels like medieval times, I was asked to write a piece about broadcasting and analytics for Baseball Prospectus—and that's the inelegant tapestry I wove, if indeed a tapestry can be woven by typing with fat, freckled sausage fingers. Honestly, I think I wrote it just as an excuse to tell the Chipper Jones story. But here we are, after 10 years of evolution and, at the risk of sounding like the needy Mayor Of Baseball Broadcasterville, I ask you, "How are we doing?!?!"[1]

Much has changed since I wrote that article, revolutionary and evolutionary progress having been made. Too much, some might say, as data and shifts and all-or-nothing swings have altered the baseball viewing experience in a way many of us who love baseball consider troublesome. In general, though, the game has become even more analytically inclined since then, almost every team investing in "new-age information." So you can say without equivocation that baseball—front offices, media, players and fans—has never been more informed than it is today. Never been smarter, in other words. And sites like BP are partially to thank.

When I look back at what I wrote, a number of things jump out. First, I stole the "OBP is life" joke from BP alum Joe Sheehan, and I never gave him proper credit because I'm a dirty thief with no accountability or originality. Also, I need to copyright "more accurate and therefore more delicious," and sell it for millions of dollars (though I'd settle for BP using it as the subheading for the site because I'm too lazy to go to the copyright office).

I still think "erasing the noise" is as important as ever. I know some will stay married to triple crown stats and wins—and that's fine—but there's an important reason to go light on that stuff: accuracy. The lowest standard to reach for a broadcaster is to simply stay out of the way and to be accurate. Being inaccurate and calling unnecessary attention to yourself are directly proportional. If teams are evaluating players and making in-game decisions based on certain types of information and statistics, it's incumbent on us as chroniclers to speak in those terms as well. If teams aren't using RBI or winning percentage as a way to measure and evaluate performance, we probably shouldn't be, either. If the game is smarter, and the broadcast is smarter, then the curious customer becomes smarter. We are there to frame the picture, and a stained frame distracts from the art we are all there to admire.

The trick is in finding the balance somewhere between accuracy and coma-inducing. As White Sox radio broadcaster Len Kasper says, "One criticism of advanced stats is that some fans don't want to feel like they're attending a math class when they watch a game." Formulas and lectures are not why people choose the escape hatch of entertainment. But, when used properly, advanced stats can actually help broadcasters tell the story more completely.

For example, a team that leads the league in defensive efficiency "converts a lot of outs on balls in play." That concise description is often all that is needed to make the point without boring the customers who are there for the delicious hot dog with too many details on how the sausage is made. As Brewers announcer Brian Anderson says, "We apply more journalism when using analytics. It's important to be curious as to why decisions are made...we can still analyze whether something is right or wrong, that is always fun, but it is important to 'report' first so we can serve the audience better in a more applicable way. Beware not to choke the entertainment out of the process."

I think the broadcasting landscape has improved over the last 10 years as it relates to advanced stats. On ESPN, Jason Benetti[2], Mike Petriello and Eduardo Perez do a magnificent job with the Statcast broadcasts. By definition, there is a specialization to that show, but those guys have mastered the magical combination of informing and entertaining. Those things don't have to be mutually exclusive, but too often are. On our standard ESPN broadcasts, I'd prefer to see slash stats rather than OPS; for pitchers, I'd prefer more rate stats—K%, BB% and HR% . I still think that if we keep these concepts relatively simple we can[3] support *and illuminate*. Context is crucial, so i think it's important for broadcasters to consistently cite the league-average on-base or slugging percentage, or the standard strikeout rate. We've spent so much time explaining what these things are over the last 10 years that we can now just reference them without the explanation—that in itself is a marked evolution, waves lapping upon the shore so consistently over the last 10 years that it has changed the lay of the coast.

I think one of the other points to be made about broadcasting in 2020 is that there is more time to fill—despite all the efforts to speed the game up, the average time of a nine-inning game last year was about 17 minutes longer than in 2010. The ball is in play less frequently and the amount of time between pitches has grown. That means there is more time for broadcasters to say dumb s@#%. It's up to us to use that space better. For all the overanalysis that can consume the game, sometimes the bar doesn't need to be any higher than "don't say dumb s@#%." Thirty years in this business, and that's my life advice as a philosopher. Vin Scully, I ain't.

Back to the top. How are we doing? Here's the hope and goal for me: Smart. Fun. Interesting. Accurate.

Some nights we do it, some nights we don't. But I'm out there busting my buns every night. Tell your old man to drag Lanier and Walton up and down the court for 48 minutes. (Wait, was that my out loud voice?)

In all seriousness, I am indebted to the folks at BP for the education over the years, for making me a smarter baseball fan and, hopefully, a better broadcaster. Each year my prep for the season includes going through every page of the BP Annual and clipping notes that I can use for broadcast.

If it is your first time reading an Annual, just know it is delivered with love. Because if there's one thing people might not fully get about the stathead community, it's that we love this game. Can I say 'we?' I'm saying we. We are just like every other fan, in love and curious. We can be yellers and screamers and fist-pumpers and remote-control throwers and criers when our team loses. We wear jerseys, too. We love this game that is so unbelievably interesting and fun. This book only enhances that experience. Delicious. ▪

—Jon "Boog" Sciambi is a play-by-play announcer for the Chicago Cubs and ESPN.

To read Boog's original article on building a better broadcast, visit: https://www.baseballprospectus.com/fantasy/article/10101/analyze-this-building-a-better-broadcast/

---

1. Ed Koch was New York City mayor in the 70s/80s who when walking around the city would interact with people by using his catch phrase, "how am I doing??"

2. Editors note—Jason Benetti once read Infinite Jest by David Foster Wallace, although the first 300 pages were read improperly.

3. Aaron Goldsmith told me to use this quote. While it is usually attributed to Vin Scully it was actually Andrew Lang who said "Most people use statistics like a drunk man uses a lamppost; more for support than illumination." I don't know who he is.

Statistical Introduction

by Bryan Grosnick

Sports are, fundamentally, a blend of athletic endeavor and storytelling. Baseball, like any other sport, tells its stories in so many ways: in the arc of a game from the stands or a season from the box scores, in photos, or even in numbers. At Baseball Prospectus, we understand that statistics don't replace observation or any of baseball's stories, but complement everything else that makes the game so much fun.

What stats help us with is with patterns and precision, variance and value. This book can help you learn things you may not see from watching a game or hundred, whether it's the path of a career over time or the breadth of the entire MLB. We'd also never ask you to choose between our numbers and the experience of viewing a game from the cheap seats or the comfort of your home; our publication combines running the numbers with observations and wisdom from some of the brightest minds we can find. But if you *do* want to learn more about the numbers beyond what's on the backs of player jerseys, let us help explain.

Offense

We've revised our methodology for determining batting value. Long-time readers of the book will notice that we've retired True Average in favor of a new metric: Deserved Runs Created Plus (DRC+). Developed by Jonathan Judge and our stats team, this statistic measures everything a player does at the plate–reaching base, hitting for power, making outs, and moving runners over–and puts it on a scale where 100 equals league-average performance. A DRC+ of 150 is terrific, a DRC+ of 100 is average and a DRC+ of 75 means you better be an excellent defender.

DRC+ also does a better job than any of our previous metrics in taking contextual factors into account. The model adjusts for how the park affects performance, but also for things like the talent of the opposing pitcher, value of different types of batted-ball events, league, temperature and other factors. It's able to describe a player's expected offensive contribution than any other statistic we've found over the years, and also does a better job of predicting future performance as well.

The other aspect of run-scoring is baserunning, which we quantify using Baserunning Runs. BRR not only records the value of stolen bases (or getting caught in the act), but also accounts for all the stuff that doesn't show up on the back of a baseball card: a runner's ability to go first to third on a single, or advance on a fly ball.

Defense

Where offensive value is *relatively* easy to identify and understand, defensive value is ... not. Over the past dozen years, the sabermetric community has focused mostly on stats based on zone data: a real-live human person records the type of batted ball and estimated landing location, and models are created that give expected outs. From there, you can compare fielders' actual outs to those expected ones. Simple, right?

Unfortunately, zone data has two major issues. First, zone data is recorded by commercial data providers who keep the raw data private unless you pay for it. (All the statistics we build in this book and on our website use public data as inputs.) That hurts our ability to test assumptions or duplicate results. Second, over the years it has become apparent that there's quite a bit of "noise" in zone-based fielding analysis. Sometimes the conclusions drawn from zone data don't hold up to scrutiny, and sometimes the different data provided by different providers don't look anything alike, giving wildly different results. Sometimes the hard-working professional stringers or scorers might unknowingly inflict unconscious bias into the mix: for example good fielders will often be credited with more expected outs despite the data, and ballparks with high press boxes tend to score more line drives than ones with a lower press box.

Enter our Fielding Runs Above Average (FRAA). For most positions, FRAA is built from play-by-play data, which allows us to avoid the subjectivity found in many other fielding metrics. The idea is this: count how many fielding plays are made by a given player and compare that to expected plays for an average fielder at their position (based on pitcher ground ball tendencies and batter handedness). Then we adjust for park and base-out situations.

When it comes to catchers, our methodology is a little different thanks to the laundry list of responsibilities they're tasked with beyond just, well, catching and throwing the ball. By now you've probably heard about "framing" or the art of making umpires more likely to call balls outside the strike zone for strikes. To put this into one tidy number, we incorporate pitch tracking data (for the years it exists) and adjust for important factors like pitcher, umpire, batter and home-field advantage using a mixed-model approach. This grants us a number for how many strikes the catcher is personally adding to (or subtracting from) his pitchers' performance ... which we then convert to runs added or lost using linear weights.

Framing is one of the biggest parts of determining catcher value, but we also take into account blocking balls from going past, whether a scorer deems it a passed ball or a wild pitch. We use a similar approach—one that really benefits from the pitch tracking data that tells us what ends up in the dirt and what doesn't. We also include a catcher's ability to prevent stolen bases and how well they field balls in play, and *finally* we come up with our FRAA for catchers.

Pitching

Both pitching and fielding make up the half of baseball that isn't run scoring: run prevention. Separating pitching from fielding is a tough task, and most recent pitching analysis has branched off from Voros McCracken's famous (and controversial) statement, "There is little if any difference among major-league pitchers in their ability to prevent hits on balls hit in the field of play." The research of the analytic community has validated this to some extent, and there are a host of "defense-independent" pitching measures that have been developed to try and extract the effect of the defense behind a hurler from the pitcher's work.

Our solution to this quandary is Deserved Run Average (DRA), our core pitching metric. DRA seeks to evaluate a pitcher's performance, much like earned run average (ERA), the tried-and-true pitching stat you've seen on every baseball broadcast or box score from the past century, but it's very different. To start, DRA takes an event-by-event look at what the pitchers does, and adjusts the value of that event based on different environmental factors like park, batter, catcher, umpire, base-out situation, run differential, inning, defense, home field advantage, pitcher role and temperature. That mixed model gives us a pitcher's expected contribution, similar to what we do for our DRC+ model for hitters and FRAA model for catchers. (Oh, and we also consider the pitcher's effect on basestealing and on balls getting past the catcher.)

DRA is set to the scale of runs allowed per nine innings (RA9) instead of ERA, which makes DRA's scale slightly higher than ERA's. Because of this, for ease of use, we're supplying DRA-, which is much easier for the reader to parse. As with DRC+, DRA- is an "index" stat, meaning instead of using some arbitrary and shifting number to denote what's "good," average is always 100. The reason that it uses a minus rather than a plus is because like ERA, a lower number is better. Therefore a 75 DRA- describes a performance 25 percent better than average, whereas a 150 DRA- means that either a pitcher is getting extremely lucky with their results, or getting ready to try a new pitch.

Since the last time you picked up an edition of this book, we've also made a few minor changes to DRA to make it better. Recent research into "tunneling"—the act of throwing consecutive pitches that appear similar from a batter's point of view until after the swing decision point–data has given us a new contextual factor to account for in DRA: plate distance. This refers to the distance between successive pitches as they approach the plate, and while it has a smaller effect than factors like velocity or whiff rate, it still can help explain pitcher strikeout rate in our model.

Recently Added Descriptive Statistics

Returning to our 2021 edition of the book are a few figures which recently appeared. These numbers may be a little bit more familiar to those of you who have spent some time investigating baseball statistics.

Fastball Percentage

Our fastball percentage (FA%) statistic measures how frequently a pitcher throws a pitch classified as a "fastball," measured as a percentage of overall pitches thrown. We qualify three types of fastballs:

1. The traditional four-seam fastball;
2. The two-seam fastball or sinker;
3. "Hard cutters," which are pitches that have the movement profile of a cut fastball and are used as the pitcher's primary offering or in place of a more traditional fastball.

For example, a pitcher with a FA% of 67 throws any combination of these three pitches about two-thirds of the time.

Whiff Rate

Everybody loves a swing and a miss, and whiff rate (Whiff%) measures how frequently pitchers induce a swinging strike. To calculate Whiff%, we add up all the pitches thrown that ended with a swinging strike, then divide that number by a pitcher's total pitches thrown. Most often, high whiff rates correlate with high strikeout rates (and overall effective pitcher performance).

Called Strike Probability

Called Strike Probability (CSP) is a number that represents the likelihood that all of a pitcher's pitches will be called a strike while controlling for location, pitcher and batter handedness, umpire and count. Here's how it works: on each pitch, our model determines how many times (out of 100) that a similar pitch was called for a strike given those factors mentioned above, and when normalized for each batter's strike zone. Then we average the CSP for all pitches thrown by a pitcher in a season, and that gives us the yearly CSP percentage you see in the stats boxes.

As you might imagine, pitchers with a higher CSP are more likely to work in the zone, where pitchers with a lower CSP are likely locating their pitches outside the normal strike zone, for better or for worse.

Projections

Many of you aren't turning to this book just for a look at what a player has done, but for a look at what a player is going to do: the PECOTA projections. PECOTA, initially developed by Nate Silver (who has moved on to greater fame as a political analyst), consists of three parts:

1. Major-league equivalencies, which use minor-league statistics to project how a player will perform in the major leagues;

2. Baseline forecasts, which use weighted averages and regression to the mean to estimate a player's current true talent level; and

3. Aging curves, which uses the career paths of comparable players to estimate how a player's statistics are likely to change over time.

With all those important things covered, let's take a look at what's in the book this year.

Team Prospectus

Most of this book is composed of team chapters, with one for each of the 30 major-league franchises. On the first page of each chapter, you'll see a box that contains some of the key statistics for each team as well as a very inviting stadium diagram. (You can see an example of this for the Los Angeles Dodgers on this very page!)

We start with the team name, their unadjusted 2020 win-loss record, and their divisional ranking. Beneath that are a host of other team statistics. **Pythag** presents an adjusted 2020 winning percentage, calculated by taking runs scored per game (**RS/G**) and runs allowed per game (**RA/G**) for the team, and running them through a version of Bill James' Pythagorean formula that was refined and improved by David Smyth and Brandon Heipp. (The formula is called "Pythagenpat," which is equally fun to type and to say.)

Next up is **DRC+**, described earlier, to indicate the overall hitting ability of the team either above or below league-average. Run prevention on the pitching side is covered by **DRA** (also mentioned earlier) and another metric: Fielding Independent Pitching (**FIP**), which calculates another ERA-like statistic based on strikeouts, walks, and home runs recorded. Defensive Efficiency Rating (**DER**) tells us the percentage of balls in play turned into outs for the team, and is a quick fielding shorthand that rounds out run prevention.

After that, we have several measures related to roster composition, as opposed to on-field performance. **B-Age** and **P-Age** tell us the average age of a team's batters and pitchers, respectively. **Payroll** is the combined team payroll for all on-

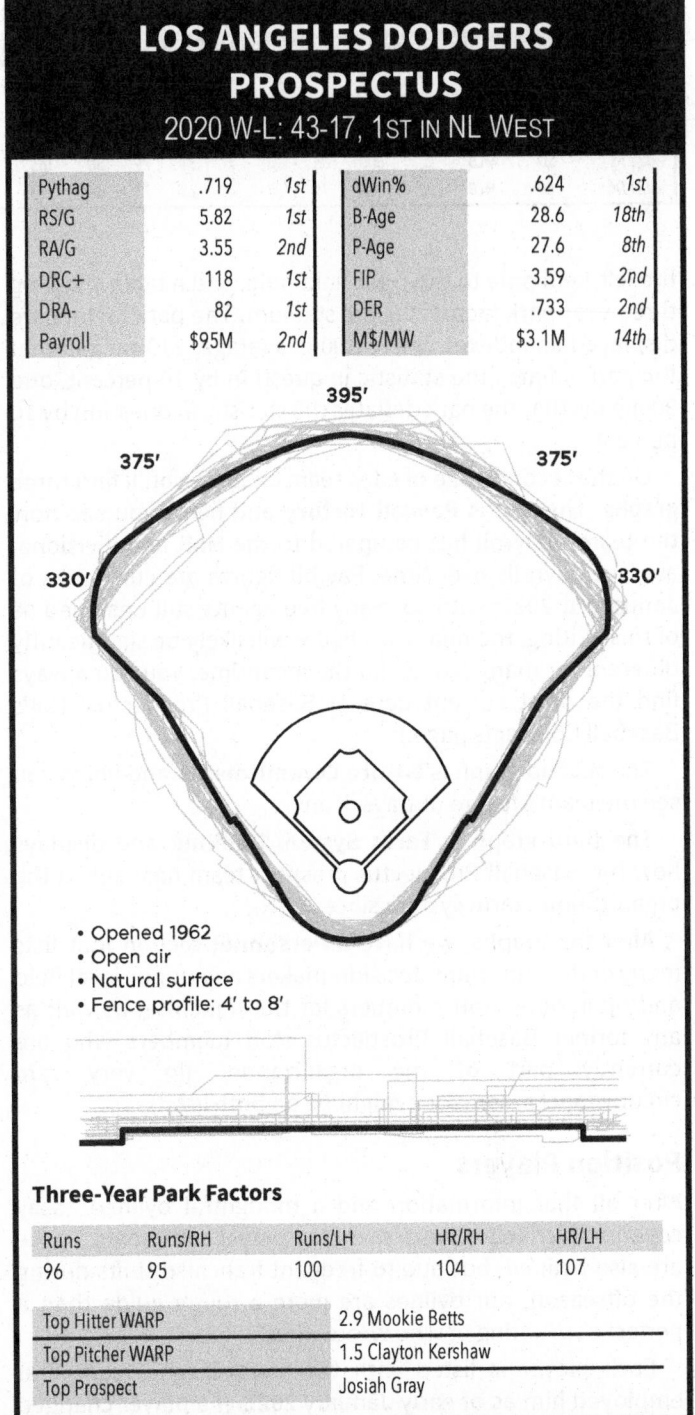

LOS ANGELES DODGERS PROSPECTUS

2020 W-L: 43-17, 1ST IN NL WEST

Pythag	.719	1st	dWin%	.624	1st
RS/G	5.82	1st	B-Age	28.6	18th
RA/G	3.55	2nd	P-Age	27.6	8th
DRC+	118	1st	FIP	3.59	2nd
DRA-	82	1st	DER	.733	2nd
Payroll	$95M	2nd	M$/MW	$3.1M	14th

- Opened 1962
- Open air
- Natural surface
- Fence profile: 4' to 8'

Three-Year Park Factors

Runs	Runs/RH	Runs/LH	HR/RH	HR/LH
96	95	100	104	107

Top Hitter WARP	2.9 Mookie Betts
Top Pitcher WARP	1.5 Clayton Kershaw
Top Prospect	Josiah Gray

field players, and Doug Pappas' Marginal Dollars per Marginal Win (**M$/MW**) tells us how much money a team spent to earn production above replacement level.

Next to each of these stats, we've listed each team's MLB rank in that category from first to 30th. In this, first always indicates a positive outcome and 30th a negative outcome, except in the case of salary—first is highest.

After the franchise statistics, we share a few items about the team's home ballpark. There's the aforementioned diagram of the park's dimensions (including distances to the outfield wall), a graphic showing the height of the wall from

Fernando Tatis Jr. SS Born: 01/02/99 Age: 22 Bats: R Throws: R Height: 6'3" Weight: 217 Origin: International Free Agent, 2015

YEAR	TEAM	LVL	AGE	PA	R	2B	3B	HR	RBI	BB	K	SB	CS	Whiff%	AVG/OBP/SLG	DRC+	BABIP	BRR	FRAA	WARP
2018	SA	AA	19	394	77	22	4	16	43	33	109	16	5		.286/.355/.507	136	.370	3.0	SS(83): -1.9	2.4
2019	SD	MLB	20	372	61	13	6	22	53	30	110	16	6	35.3%	.317/.379/.590	118	.410	7.1	SS(83): 0.9	3.4
2020	SD	MLB	21	257	50	11	2	17	45	27	61	11	3	28.2%	.277/.366/.571	126	.306	0.7	SS(57): -5.5	0.9
2021 FS	SD	MLB	22	600	85	22	4	31	79	50	165	20	8	31.6%	.254/.323/.487	121	.306	1.7	SS 0, 2B 0	3.7
2021 DC	SD	MLB	22	554	79	21	4	28	73	46	153	18	7	31.6%	.254/.323/.487	121	.306	1.5	SS 0	3.4

Comparables: Darryl Strawberry, Bo Bichette, Ronald Acuña Jr.

the left-field pole to the right-field pole, and a table showing three-year park factors for the stadium. The park factors are displayed as indexes where 100 is average, 110 means that the park inflates the statistic in question by 10 percent, and 90 means that the park deflates the statistic in question by 10 percent.

On the second page of each team chapter, you'll find three graphs. The first is **Payroll History** and helps you see how the team's payroll has compared to the MLB and divisional average payrolls over time. Payroll figures are current as of January 1, 2021; with so many free agents still unsigned as of this writing, the final 2021 figure will likely be significantly different for many teams. (In the meantime, you can always find the most current data at Baseball Prospectus' Cot's Baseball Contracts page.)

The second graph is **Future Commitments** and helps you see the team's future outlays, if any.

The third graph is **Farm System Ranking** and displays how the Baseball Prospectus prospect team has ranked the organization's farm system since 2007.

After the graphs, we have a **Personnel** section that lists many of the important decision-makers and upper-level field and operations staff members for the franchise, as well as any former Baseball Prospectus staff members who are currently part of the organization. (In very rare circumstances, someone might be on both lists!)

Position Players

After all that information and a thoughtful bylined essay covering each team, we present our player comments. These are also bylined, but due to frequent franchise shifts during the offseason, our bylines are more a rough guide than a perfect accounting of who wrote what.

Each player is listed with the major-league team that employed him as of early January 2021. If a player changed teams after that point via free agency, trade, or any other method, you'll be able to find them in the chapter for their previous squad.

As an example, take a look at the player comment for Padres shortstop Fernando Tatis Jr.: the stat block that accompanies his written comment is at the top of this page. First we cover biographical information (age is as of June 30, 2021) before moving onto the stats themselves. Our statistic columns include standard identifying information like **YEAR**, **TEAM**, **LVL** (level of affiliated play) and **AGE** before getting

into the numbers. Next, we provide raw, untranslated numbers like you might find on the back of your dad's baseball cards: **PA** (plate appearances), **R** (runs), **2B** (doubles), **3B** (triples), **HR** (home runs), **RBI** (runs batted in), **BB** (walks), **K** (strikeouts), **SB** (stolen bases) and **CS** (caught stealing).

Following the basic stats is **Whiff%** (whiff rate), which denotes how often, when a batter swings, he fails to make contact with the ball. Another way to think of this number is an inverse of a hitter's contact rate.

Next, we have unadjusted "slash" statistics: **AVG** (batting average), **OBP** (on-base percentage) and **SLG** (slugging percentage). Following the slash line is **DRC+** (Deserved Runs Created Plus), which we described earlier as total offensive expected contribution compared to the league average.

BABIP (batting average on balls in play) tells us how often a ball in play fell for a hit, and can help us identify whether a batter may have been lucky or not ... but note that high BABIPs also tend to follow the great hitters of our time, as well as speedy singles hitters who put the ball on the ground.

The next item is **BRR** (Baserunning Runs), which covers all of a player's baserunning accomplishments including (but not limited to) swiped bags and failed attempts. Next is **FRAA** (Fielding Runs Above Average), which also includes the number of games previously played at each position noted in parentheses. Multi-position players have only their two most frequent positions listed here, but their total FRAA number reflects all positions played.

Our last column here is **WARP** (Wins Above Replacement Player). WARP estimates the total value of a player, which means for hitters it takes into account hitting runs above average (calculated using the DRC+ model), BRR and FRAA. Then, it makes an adjustment for positions played and gives the player a credit for plate appearances based upon the difference between "replacement level"—which is derived from the quality of players added to a team's roster after the start of the season–and the league average.

The final line just below the stats box is **PECOTA** data, which is discussed further in a following section.

Catchers

Catchers are a special breed, and thus they have earned their own separate box which displays some of the defensive metrics that we've built just for them. As an example, let's check out Yasmani Grandal.

Yasmani Grandal

YEAR	TEAM	P. COUNT	FRM RUNS	BLK RUNS	THRW RUNS	TOT RUNS
2018	LAD	16816	15.7	0.8	0.1	16.5
2019	MIL	18740	19.4	1.8	-0.1	21.1
2020	CHW	4830	3.7	0.3	-0.2	3.8
2021	CHW	14430	16.7	0.4	1.0	18.0

The **YEAR** and **TEAM** columns match what you'd find in the other stat box. **P. COUNT** indicates the number of pitches thrown while the catcher was behind the plate, including swinging strikes, fouls and balls in play. **FRM RUNS** is the total run value the catcher provided (or cost) his team by influencing the umpire to call strikes where other catchers did not. **BLK RUNS** expresses the total run value above or below average for the catcher's ability to prevent wild pitches and passed balls. **THRW RUNS** is calculated using a similar model as the previous two statistics, and it measures a catcher's ability to throw out basestealers but also to dissuade them from testing his arm in the first place. It takes into account factors like the pitcher (including his delivery and pickoff move) and baserunner (who could be as fast as Billy Hamilton or as slow as Yonder Alonso). **TOT RUNS** is the sum of all of the previous three statistics.

Pitchers

Let's give our pitchers a turn, using 2020 AL Cy Young winner Shane Bieber as our example. Take a look at his stat block: the first line and the **YEAR**, **TEAM**, **LVL** and **AGE** columns are the same as in the position player example earlier.

Here too, we have a series of columns that display raw, unadjusted statistics compiled by the pitcher over the course of a season: **W** (wins), **L** (losses), **SV** (saves), **G** (games pitched), **GS** (games started), **IP** (innings pitched), **H** (hits allowed) and **HR** (home runs allowed). Next we have two statistics that are rates: **BB/9** (walks per nine innings) and **K/9** (strikeouts per nine innings), before returning to the unadjusted K (strikeouts).

Next up is **GB%** (ground ball percentage), which is the percentage of all batted balls that were hit on the ground, including both outs and hits. Remember, this is based on observational data and subject to human error, so please approach this with a healthy dose of skepticism.

BABIP (batting average on balls in play) is calculated using the same methodology as it is for position players, but it often tells us more about a pitcher than it does a hitter. With pitchers, a high BABIP is often due to poor defense or bad luck, and can often be an indicator of potential rebound, and a low BABIP may be cause to expect performance regression. (A typical league-average BABIP is close to .290-.300.)

The metrics **WHIP** (walks plus hits per inning pitched) and **ERA** (earned run average) are old standbys: WHIP measures walks and hits allowed on a per-inning basis, while ERA measures earned runs on a nine-inning basis. Neither of these stats are translated or adjusted.

DRA- (Deserved Run Average) was described at length earlier, and measures how the pitcher "deserved" to perform compared to other pitchers. Please note that since we lack all the data points that would make for a "real" DRA for minor-league events, the DRA- displayed for minor league partial-seasons is based off of different data. (That data is a modified version of our cFIP metric, which you can find more information about on our website.)

Just like with hitters, **WARP** (Wins Above Replacement Player) is a total value metric that puts pitchers of all stripes on the same scale as position players. We use DRA as the primary input for our calculation of WARP. You might notice that relief pitchers (due to their limited innings) may have a lower WARP than you were expecting or than you might see in other WARP-like metrics. WARP does not take leverage into account, just the actions a pitcher performs and the expected value of those actions ... which ends up judging high-leverage relief pitchers differently than you might imagine given their prestige and market value.

MPH gives you the pitcher's 95th percentile velocity for the noted season, in order to give you an idea of what the *peak* fastball velocity a pitcher possesses. Since this comes from our pitch-tracking data, it is not publicly available for minor-league pitchers.

Finally, we display the three new pitching metrics we described earlier. **FB%** (fastball percentage) gives you the percentage of fastballs thrown out of all pitches. **WHF** (whiff rate) tells you the percentage of swinging strikes induced out of all pitches. **CSP** (called strike probability) expresses the likelihood of all pitches thrown to result in a called strike, after controlling for factors like handedness, umpire, pitch type, count and location.

Shane Bieber RHP   Born: 05/31/95   Age: 26   Bats: R   Throws: R   Height: 6'3"   Weight: 200   Origin: Round 4, 2016 Draft (#122 overall)

YEAR	TEAM	LVL	AGE	W	L	SV	G	GS	IP	H	HR	BB/9	K/9	K	GB%	BABIP	WHIP	ERA	DRA-	WARP	MPH	FA%	Whiff%	CSP
2018	AKR	AA	23	3	0	0	5	5	31	26	1	0.3	8.7	30	47.3%	.278	0.87	1.16	61	0.9				
2018	COL	AAA	23	3	1	0	8	8	48^2	30	3	1.1	8.7	47	52.0%	.227	0.74	1.66	69	1.2				
2018	CLE	MLB	23	11	5	0	20	19	114^2	130	13	1.8	9.3	118	46.2%	.356	1.33	4.55	74	2.6	94.7	57.4%	26.2%	51.3%
2019	CLE	MLB	24	15	8	0	34	33	214^1	186	31	1.7	10.9	259	44.4%	.298	1.05	3.28	75	4.9	94.4	45.8%	30.8%	44.9%
2020	CLE	MLB	25	8	1	0	12	12	77^1	46	7	2.4	14.2	122	48.4%	.267	0.87	1.63	53	2.6	95.3	53.6%	40.7%	39.6%
2021 FS	CLE	MLB	26	10	6	0	26	26	150	120	18	2.1	11.9	197	45.5%	.296	1.04	2.66	65	4.0	94.7	50.0%	33.2%	44.2%
2021 DC	CLE	MLB	26	13	9	0	30	30	196	157	24	2.1	11.9	258	45.5%	.296	1.04	2.66	65	5.7	94.7	50.0%	33.2%	44.2%

Comparables: Luis Severino, Danny Salazar, Joe Musgrove

PECOTA

All players have PECOTA projections for 2021, as well as a set of other numbers that describe the performance of comparable players according to PECOTA. All projections for 2021 are for the player at the date we went to press in early January and are projected into the league and park context as indicated by the team abbreviation. (Note that players at very low levels of the minors are too unpredictable to assess using these numbers.) All PECOTA projected statistics represent a player's projected major-league performance.

How we're doing that is a little different this season. There are really two different values that go into the final stat line that you see for PECOTA: How a player performs, and how much playing time he'll be given to perform it. In the past we've estimated playing time based on each team's roster and depth charts, and we'll continue to do that. These projections are denoted as **2021 DC**.

But in many cases, a player won't be projected for major-league playing time; most of the time this is because they aren't projected to be major-league players at all, but still developing as prospects. Or perhaps a player will provide Triple-A depth, only to have an opportunity open up because of injury. For these purposes, we're also supplying a second projection, labeled **2021 FS**, or full season. This is what we would project the player to provide in 600 plate appearances or 150 innings pitched.

Below the projections are the player's three highest-scoring comparable players as determined by PECOTA. All comparables represent a snapshot of how the listed player was performing at the same age as the current player, so if a 23-year-old pitcher is compared to Bartolo Colón, he's actually being compared to a 23-year-old Colón, not the version that pitched for the Rangers in 2018, nor to Colón's career as a whole.

A few points about pitcher projections. First, we aren't yet projecting peak velocity, so that column will be blank in the PECOTA lines. Second, projecting DRA is trickier than evaluating past performance, because it is unclear how deserving each pitcher will be of his anticipated outcomes. However, we know that another DRA-related statistic–contextual FIP or cFIP–estimates future run scoring very well. So for PECOTA, the projected DRA- figures you see are based on the past cFIPs generated by the pitcher and comparable players over time, along with the other factors described above.

If you're familiar with PECOTA, then you'll have noticed that the projection system often appears bullish on players coming off a bad year and bearish on players coming off a good year. (This is because the system weights several previous seasons, not just the most recent one.) In addition, we publish the 50th percentile projections for each player–which is smack in the middle of the range of projected production—which tends to mean PECOTA stat lines don't often have extreme results like 40 home runs or 250 strikeouts in a given season. In essence, PECOTA doesn't project very many extreme seasons.

Managers

After all those wonderful team chapters, we've got statistics for each big-league manager, all of whom are organized by alphabetical order. Here you'll find a block including an extraordinary amount of information collected from each manager's entire career. For more information on the acronyms and what they mean, please visit the Glossary at www.baseballprospectus.com.

There is one important metric that we'd like to call attention to, and you'll find it next to each manager's name: **wRM+** (weighted reliever management plus). Developed by Rob Arthur and Rian Watt, wRM+ investigates how good a manager is at using their best relievers during the moments of highest leverage, using both our proprietary DRA metric as well as Leverage Index. wRM+ is scaled to a league average of 100, and a wRM+ of 105 indicates that relievers were used approximately five percent "better" than average. On the other hand, a wRM+ of 95 would tell us the team used its relievers five percent "worse" than the average team.

While wRM+ does not have an extremely strong correlation with a manager, it is statistically significant; this means that a manager is not *entirely* responsible for a team's wRM+, but does have some effect on that number.

A Taxonomy of 2020 Abnormalities

by Rob Mains

I'm going to start this with a trivia question. Trust me, it's relevant. Don't bother skipping to the end of the article to find the answer, it's not there.

Only five players have appeared in 140 or more games for 16 straight seasons. Who are they?

It's a trivia question starting off an essay, so you know how this works: Whatever you guessed, you're wrong. It's okay. As someone who purchased this book, chances are good that you're an educated baseball fan. But the circumstances behind 2020 force us to abandon, or at least seriously question, some of our favorite patterns and crutches for evaluating the game we love.

We just completed what was undoubtedly the strangest season in MLB history. No fans, geographically limited schedule, universal DH, seven-inning twin bills, runners on second in extra innings, a 16-team postseason, a club playing at a Triple-A stadium. Some of these changes will likely persist (sorry), but we've never had so many tweaks dumped on us all at once, at least not since they figured out how many balls were in a walk.

And the biggest, of course, was the 60-game season. The 19th century was dotted with teams that went bankrupt before the season ended, but the lone season with only 60 scheduled games was 1877. That year there were only six teams, the league rostered a total of 77 players (just 16 more than the 2020 Marlins), and batters called for pitches to be thrown high or low by the pitcher, who was 50 feet away. We can say the 2020 season was easily the shortest ever for recognizable baseball.

As such, it'll stand out. Few abbreviated seasons do. Just about everybody reading this knows the 1994 season ended after Seattle's Randy Johnson struck out Oakland's Ernie Young for the last out of the Mariners-A's game on August 11. The ensuing player strike wiped out the rest of the season and the postseason. Teams played only 112-117 games that year.

And many of you know that a strike in the middle of the 1981 season split the season in two, resulting in the only Division Series until 1995. Teams played only 103-111 games that year, the shortest regular season since 1885.

Those two seasons are memorable. So when we see that nobody drove in 100 runs in 1981, or that Greg Maddux was the only pitcher with 180 or more innings pitched in 1994, we think, "Of course. Strike year."

But we don't remember other short years. You might not recall that the 1994 strike spilled into the next year, chopping 18 games off the 1995 schedule. You might've read that the 1918 season, played during the last pandemic, ended after Labor Day due to the government's World War I "work or fight" order. A strike erased the first week and a half of the 1972 season, but that year's best known as the last time pitchers batted in the American League.

The point is, while we don't remember small changes to the schedule, we remember the big ones. The 1981 mid-season strike. The 1994 season- and Series-ending strike. And, of course, the pandemic-shortened 2020 season. We won't need a reminder why Marcell Ozuna's 18 homers were the fewest to lead the National League in a century. (Literally; Cy Williams led with 15 in 1920.)

Now, about that trivia question. The five players are Hank Aaron, Brooks Robinson, Pete Rose, Ichiro Suzuki, and Johnny Damon. The one nobody gets, of course, is Damon, and a lot of people miss Ichiro, whose last season of 140-plus games came garbed in the red-orange and ocean blue of Miami when he was 42. That's half of what makes it a good question. The other half is the two guys whom many think made the list but didn't. Lou Gehrig? His streak started in the Yankees' 42nd game of the 1925 season and lasted only 13 seasons after that. And everybody assumes Cal Ripken Jr. did it, having played 2,632 straight games over 17 seasons. But one of those 17 seasons was 1994, when the Orioles played only 112 games.

My point? *I just told you* everybody remembers the 1994 strike year, but everybody forgets it fell in the middle of Ripken's streak, separating the first twelve years from the last four. Just because we recall something doesn't mean it's always at the front of our minds.

Nobody is going to forget 2020, and baseball is obviously not the main reason. But there will come a time in the future when you're looking at a player's or a team's record, and there will be baffling numbers there for 2020, and you'll think, "I wonder what happened." (Not to mention the missing line for minor league players.) Just like you forgot that the 1994 strike limited Ripken to 112 games.

Try not to forget it, though. The 2020 season resulted in weird statistical results for several reasons.

There were only 60 games.

I know, duh. But that had impacts beyond counting stats like Ozuna's home run total or Yu Darvish and Shane Bieber leading the majors with eight wins. (I know, pitcher wins, but still.)

The 162-game season is the longest among major North American sports, and that duration gives us a gift. Over the course of a long season, small variations tend to even out. A player who has a ten-game hot streak will probably have a ten-game cold streak. A team that starts the year losing a bunch of close games will probably win a bunch of them. We get regression to the mean. Statistics stabilize.

Consider flipping a coin. Over the long run, we expect it to come up heads about half the time. But the fewer flips, the more variation there'll be. If you flip a coin six times, probability theory tells us you'll get at least two-third heads about 34 percent of the time. Flip it 30 times, your chance of two-thirds heads drops to five percent.

Or, relevant to this case, if you flip a coin 60 times, your chance of getting at least 36 heads—that's 60 percent—is 7.75 percent. Expand the coin-flipping to 162 times, and the chance of getting 60 percent heads drops to 0.73 percent.

In other words, the odds of an outcome that's 20 percent better (or worse) than expected is *more than ten times higher* when you flip your coin 60 times than when you do it 162 times. Call it small sample size, call lack of mean reversion, or call it luck not evening out, 162 is a lot more predictive than 60. You get much more variation over 60 games than over 162. Bieber's 1.63 ERA and 0.87 FIP aren't something we'd see over a full season, and neither is Javier Baéz's .203/.238/.360.

Some players' lines in 2020 look normal. Brian Anderson had an .811 OPS in 2019 and an .810 OPS in 2020. (He probably would have gotten that last point if he'd been given enough time.) But there are many like Bieber and Baéz, some of them from young players still establishing their talent levels. The answer to the question, "What went right or wrong for that guy in 2020?" is most likely "Nothing, it was just a 2020 thing."

Preseason training was abbreviated for hitters.

Every year, spring training drags. Players get tired of it, fans get tired of it, and you sure can tell sportswriters get tired of it. Yes, something to get everyone into shape is necessary, but does it really have to drag on for over a month? Can't we shorten it?

The 2020 season answered in the negative, at least for hitters. Warren Spahn is credited with saying that hitting is timing and pitching is upsetting timing. It appears nobody had his timing down after the abbreviated July summer camp. Through August 9—18 games into the season—MLB batters were hitting .230/.311/.395 with a .275 BABIP. That BABIP, had it held, would have been the lowest since 1968, the Year of the Pitcher. In recent years it's hovered around .300.

It didn't hold. Play returned to more normal levels the rest of the year: .249/.325/.425 with a .297 BABIP starting August 10. But batters whose play concentrated in those first two weeks wound up with ugly lines. Andrew Benintendi went on the injured list with a season-ending rib cage strain on August 11. His final line: .103/.314/.128 in 14 games. Franchy Cordero went on the IL with a hamate bone fracture on August 9 and a .154/.185/.231 line. Even though he came back strong in a late September return, it was too late to repair his full-season numbers.

Preseason training was abbreviated for pitchers.

Every year, spring training drags. Players get tired of it, fans get tired of it … wait, I already said that. But the abbreviated preseason was tough on pitchers, too. As noted, they had the upper hand coming out of the gate. But then they lost that hand. And then their arms, too.

The 2020 season was spread over 67 days. During those 67 days, 237 pitchers hit the Injured List, compared to 135 in the first 67 days of 2019. A lot of those IL stints, though, were COVID-19-related. Still, over the first 67 days of the 2019 season, there were 72 pitchers on the IL with arm injuries. That figure jumped to 110 in 2020, a 53 percent increase.

There are a number of factors contributing to pitcher arm injuries, ranging from usage to velocity, but it appears that attenuated preseason training played a role. A lot of pitchers had super-short seasons due to arm woes. Corey Kluber, Roberto Osuna, and Shohei Ohtani combined for seven innings, none after August 8. All suffered arm injuries. We'll never know whether they'd have fared better with a longer preseason, but we can guess how they probably feel.

Everybody played.

Rosters were set to expand from 25 to 26 in 2020, so even if we'd had a normal season, we'd have likely seen 2019's record of 1,410 players on MLB rosters broken. But due to the pandemic, rosters started the year at 30 and were cut to only 28. Add multiple COVID-19 absences and the revolving door caused by poor starts by hitters and a rash of pitcher arm injuries, and 1,289 players appeared in MLB games in 2020. The comparable figure over the first 67 days of the 2019 season was 1,109. That 16 percent increase works out to an average of six more players per team in 2020 compared to a similar slice of 2019. A future look back at 2020 rosters will include a lot of unfamiliar names.

Plus became a minus.

In advanced metrics, we adjust batter and pitcher performance for park and league/era variations. A plus sign appended to the end of a measure means that it's adjusted for park and league. It's scaled to an average of 100, with higher figures above average and lower figures below average. (Similarly, a metric with a minus is also park- and league-adjusted and scaled to 100, with lower values better.)

Here at BP, our advanced measure of offensive performance is DRC+. Baseball-Reference has OPS+ and FanGraphs has wRC+.

Using park and league adjustments, we can compare Dante Bichette's 1995 Steroid Era season at pre-humidor Coors Field (.340/.364/.620, 40 homers, 128 RBI, MVP runner-up) with Jim Wynn's 1968 Year of the Pitcher season at the cavernous Astrodome (.269/.376/.474, 26 homers, 67 RBI, no MVP votes). It's not close. DRC+, OPS+, and wRC+ all give the nod to Wynn, handily. This is a useful tool. As my Baseball Prospectus colleague Patrick Dubuque tweeted last fall, "Please note that when I ask how you are, I am already adjusting for era."

The 2020 season messes up plus (and minus) stats for two reasons. First, the park adjustment was based on only 30 home games instead of the usual 81. Everything noted above regarding the short season applies, literally doubly, to park effect calculations. DRC+ uses a single-season park factor. OPS+ uses a three-year average and wRC+ five years. The figure for 2020 is suspect.

Second, OPS+ and wRC+ adjust for league: American and National. (DRC+ adjusts for opponent, regardless of league.) While there were two leagues in 2020, they were an artificial construct. To reduce travel, teams played opponents geographically, not based on league. There weren't two leagues, American and National. There were three, Western, Central, and Eastern.

That makes a difference because teams in the same league played in different run-scoring environments. AL teams scored 4.58 runs per game, NL teams 4.71. That's a small difference. But teams in the East scored 0.21 more runs per game (4.95) than teams in the West (4.74), and they both scored a lot more than Central teams (4.25). Adjusting for league misses that difference, so this book will be safe in that regard, but other sources may be distorted somewhat.

Not every game was a "game."

In 2020, the rising tide of strikeouts was finally stemmed. Strikeouts per team per game fell from 8.8 in 2019 to 8.7 in 2020. That marked the first decline after 14 straight annual increases.

In 2020, the rising tide of strikeouts rose higher. Batters struck out in 23.4 percent of plate appearances compared to 23.0 percent in 2019. That marked the 15th straight annual increase.

Both are true statements.

Because of two rule changes—seven-inning doubleheaders and runners on second in extra innings—games in 2020 were unprecedented in their brevity. There were 37.0 plate appearances per game in 2020. The only years with fewer were 1904 and 1906-1909. The average game in 2020 entailed 8.61 innings pitched, the fewest since 1899.

So when you see any per-game stats for 2020, you need to increase them by 3 or 4 percent to get them on equal footing with recent years.

Or, better, just ignore them. Last year happened. There were major league games contested between major league teams. But when you're looking at those physical or electronic baseball cards, when you're weaving narratives over why this young player's inevitable rise to stardom fell apart or why that old veteran rekindled his magic, don't linger on the 2020 line. It was just too weird. ▪

Thanks to Lucas Apostoleris for research assistance.

—Rob Mains is an author of Baseball Prospectus.

2020's Labor Battle Was Just the Beginning

by Marc Normandin

Last year at this time, in this same space, we posed a couple of questions following a quick history lesson of labor relations in Major League Baseball. "It's 1972 and 1994 (and '73, and '76, and '80, '81, '85 and 1990) all over again. Will the MLBPA prevail, as they (mostly) did in those instances? Or will this be the time that MLB's owners break the union and send the rights of labor into the past once more?"

The questions focused around the labor battle that was expected to begin between the MLB Players Association and MLB's owners in earnest during the 2021 season, with the Collective Bargaining Agreement set to expire afterward. What was unknown at the time was that the world—and especially the United States, for reasons we don't have the space to get into here—would be ravaged by a global pandemic. The emergence and spread of this novel coronavirus at first delayed the start of the 2020 MLB season, and then resulted in a shortened, 60-game campaign with an expanded postseason to help make up a fraction of the television revenue and a nearly empty set of ballparks.

Before that shortened season began, though, we bore witness to a potential answer to the questions posed in last year's essay. Major League Baseball, seeing an opportunity to ram through as many points on their preexisting agenda as possible while attention was elsewhere mid-pandemic, went ahead and advanced their plan to disaffiliate dozens of minor-league teams, lay off hundreds and hundreds and hundreds of talent evaluators and player development types, shrink the Rule 4 draft to an eighth of its former size, and established an early tone for the upcoming bargaining negotiations by crying poor. Anonymous executives leaked to high-profile reporters that it would be at least three years before MLB was able to meaningfully recover on a financial level from having to miss part of the 2020 season, their citations always needed, with others saying that hey, maybe collective bargaining should just be pushed off until we can all sort out this new normal.

All of this, though, was in the background of MLB's most egregious attempted power grab of 2020. The league and the MLBPA began working on a plan for how a 2020 season could even happen during a pandemic shortly after the season's start was delayed. In what would come to be known as The March Agreement, the two sides worked out a basic framework for a season, on points like how service time

would work should there be no season at all, and what kind of pay the players could expect if there was a shortened season.

Well, there was *supposedly* an agreement on that last point. While the MLBPA walked away from the meeting believing that the two sides had agreed that the players would simply be paid pro rata—their agreed-upon salary, but on a rate basis calculated from how many scheduled games the 2020 season would have—MLB would claim that this was only the plan in a situation where fans were in attendance. A mass public relations campaign to smear the MLBPA and its players as greedy liars trying to keep baseball from the general public was launched, and it was as embarrassing as it was intense. The league demanded that the players make sacrifices by accepting further pay cuts, but the PA stood firm, and eventually leaked their own proof that MLB was well aware that they had no grounds to ask for a second pay cut once it was clear that the league wasn't going to drop the issue unless forced.

Before this leak, though, came the PA's request that, should MLB believe a second pay cut was necessary in order for a shortened season to work, all they had to do was open their books and prove that this was the case. This whole event was eye-opening. For players who suddenly didn't have baseball to focus on and could see MLB's owners for who they are; for fans who maybe weren't aware that the revenue figures MLB reports out aren't the real ones; for those who didn't think that the modern PA had it in them to so aggressively stand their ground against the unceasing demands of MLB.

In the end, it was the PA's own power play that made a 60-game season happen with pro rata salaries. The union let it be known they were considering a grievance against MLB for not doing their best to have as long (and therefore as profitable) a season as would be possible. The possible grievance was, at the time, estimated to be worth around $1 billion in damages. Major League Baseball quickly, in comparison to their previous movements in these discussions, put forth a 60-game season with March's pro rata pay scale.

This was a pivotal moment: the PA told MLB to show their work and where to shove their books if they wouldn't open up, and the league at first didn't know how to react. They kept pushing, as they often do in these cases, hoping that their press releases and leaks would be enough to turn fan and media opinion against the players. After all, there was cause to believe in this tactic; fans have long flocked to the banner of owners over greedy players, in part because those millions of the latter were public record, while the billions earned by owners went unreported, invisible.

The league had pushed too far, though, showing themselves unable to respond to what should have been a simple request, and against a union that, comparatively, looked like they were amenable to having a baseball season with their "tell us when and where to play" public approach. The owners, on the other hand, came off like a group hoping there wouldn't be a season at all, and more because they were hoping to use this moment to damage the union—from a financial standpoint, from a solidarity standpoint, from a public relations standpoint—a year before the next round of CBA negotiations were set to begin.

The Players Association did not allow themselves to be broken, not even when MLB pushed to break them a year earlier than expected. The players had, for all intents and purposes, their first major labor victory since the end of the 1994-1995 strike—that's a few lifetimes, in labor years, especially given the rate of successes in the first 30-odd years in the union's history. Bartolo Colón's entire MLB career happened in between those milestone Ws, with buffer years on each end to boot!

Yes, standing firm against MLB was monumental and a good sign for the fight still to come, but that's the thing: There is still a whole lot of labor battle left. And not even in the way that's usually implied, in that boss vs. worker is an eternal struggle until there is no more boss to struggle against. The PA proved to MLB that they are not the pushovers that MLB was expecting after two decades of slowly diminishing labor's gains. The current iteration of the PA, now armed with new chief negotiator Bruce Meyer—already hated by MLB's attorneys—and players angrier than they've been in decades, is in a position to fight back. To what end, remains to be seen: How far they are willing to push is up to them. They passed their first test, though, by putting MLB in a position where they had to either give up information they absolutely did not want to give up, acquiesce to the PA's demand that the original agreement be honored, or just blow up the entire 2020 season and risk seeing their public relations strategy similarly get shot to hell.

A lockout that keeps MLB from opening in 2022 remains a very real possibility. MLB's losses from the 2020 season are nowhere near what they have reported them to be, and franchise valuations actually rose during the 2020 season, as owning a piece of an MLB team remains a sound investment. These deep pockets, and expanding revenue streams—streams they are trying to grow further still by attempting to permanently expand the postseason, a move that would only further encourage teams to avoid spending and not bother to try to build a winner on purpose thanks to the lower threshold for postseason entry—keep them in a position where they can still attempt to outlast the players, who as a group made less than they expected in 2020, in any protracted negotiation.

And, make no mistake, there are entire classes of players who will be hurt by a lockout following a shortened 2020 season. The players MLB's 2021 austerity measures will impact the most include those whose 2021 options were declined, the arbitration-eligible players who were non-tendered, and everyone on a pre-arbitration contract who is still trying to pay away whatever debt and disarray their years of poverty-level minor-league wages created. As with the mid-80s and early 90s, MLB's owners will surely hope to pit the well-off veterans against those with less experience and lower earnings. Which is just one more reason why the PA should focus on spreading out player earnings more evenly in the next round of collective bargaining by significantly raising the minimum salary, as it will make it easy for players of all experience and salary levels to understand just what it is they are hoping to achieve by resisting whatever MLB's next awful proposal includes.

Regardless of which hill the union chooses to defend in the coming labor battle, though, what matters is that they're prepared to die on it. Metaphorically speaking, of course: you have to make those sorts of distinctions clear coming off of a season played during a global pandemic. MLB, like they did in 2020's surprise, pandemic-inspired negotiations, is going to want to break the union. They are going to want to tell the Players Association that it's the owners' way or no way at all, and they're going to have more conviction this time around than they did in 2020. That's because 2021 into 2022 was always the plan, and because now they're aware that the PA is capable of fighting back against the league's demands. The attempt to break the union, to impose whatever drastic measure will be required, from the league's view, to Save Baseball, is coming. Whatever commissioner Rob Manfred and the owners come up with—a salary cap? further harm to amateurs, minor-league players, and pre-arbitration players?—you know that the end goal will be to do away with "Marvin Miller's financial system," as Manfred put it not that long ago.

As the league did this time last year, they want to further impose their will, and lessen the power of the players. There is more power in those players than was imagined last spring, though, and the way the MLBPA handled negotiating what a mid-pandemic season would look like—and pay like—is your proof. We still don't have answers to all of the questions related to what still feels like an inevitable lockout of the 2022 season. We do know, though, that the players are willing to fight in a way they haven't for a long time. And that's going to be necessary in order to make it through what's yet to come. ▪

—Marc Normandin is an editor of Baseball Prospectus.

ATLANTA BRAVES

Essay by Kelsey McKinney

Player comments by Jon Tayler and BP staff

By the third inning of the fifth game of the National League Championship Series, it felt as inevitable as a playoff game can feel. Atlanta was up 3-1 in the series, and they looked good. The bats were hot, the fielding was quick, the energy in the dugout was dry kindling just waiting for a match to explode in a roar that would take down the Dodgers once again, and propel Atlanta into the World Series. The inning started with promise. The Braves were up by two runs already and bing, bang, boom the first two runners hit singles. A ground out moved them to second and third. Isn't that beautiful? When good baseball is played, and a professional sacrifices being the hero to move his buddies into scoring position. It felt good.

I sat up from my reclined position on my couch, moved the scorebook I'd been using all season to try and focus on the games to the coffee table, and leaned forward, elbows on my knees. It just needed a match. One measly match. You could feel it in the air, even through the television. You could see it in the quick bounce of Dansby Swanson's batting stance. Did he feel it too? He must, because here came the first pitch out of Joe Kelly's hand, swirling down toward the plate, and he had the green light. Swanson swung and his bat arced through the zone, no radiation on his hands, all firm contact on that breaking pitch, so that it ricocheted away from the batter's box and far over Kelly's head. A Texas Leaguer! It was falling so quickly, popping right into that no man's land that no shift can fully cover between the infield and the outfield. A softball slap of a hit, rocketing right toward the ground. I sat up straighter.

But he was gaining ground quickly: the new Dodger, Mookie Betts. His arms unfurl somehow has his legs sprint, faster, faster, toward the infield. He throws the arm with his glove down toward the green turf, his legs still moving him forward, and somehow the ball plops right into the leather, the force of it throwing him a bit off-balance as he continues to run. "Oh shit!" I yelled on my couch, because on the other side of that gray Dodgers jersey is the even more terrifying right arm, which was plucking the ball from the lattice of the glove and side arming it in a perfect arc to the plate where it arrived … late. "SAFE!" I yelled, throwing my arms out to the side and almost knocking over my beer bottle. And he was safe. He'd beaten the ball with plenty of time.

ATLANTA BRAVES PROSPECTUS
2020 W-L: 35-25, 1ST IN NL EAST

Pythag	.592	6th	dWin%	.562	4th
RS/G	5.80	2nd	B-Age	28.7	11th
RA/G	4.80	15th	P-Age	28.9	12th
DRC+	115	2nd	FIP	4.42	13th
DRA-	98	14th	DER	.693	21st
Payroll	$58M	14th	M$/MW	$2.4M	10th

- Opened 2017
- Open air
- Natural surface
- Fence profile: 6' to 16'

Three-Year Park Factors

Runs	Runs/RH	Runs/LH	HR/RH	HR/LH
102	101	105	94	100

Top Hitter WARP	2.6 Freddie Freeman
Top Pitcher WARP	1.5 Max Fried
Top Prospect	Ian Anderson

Payroll History (in millions)

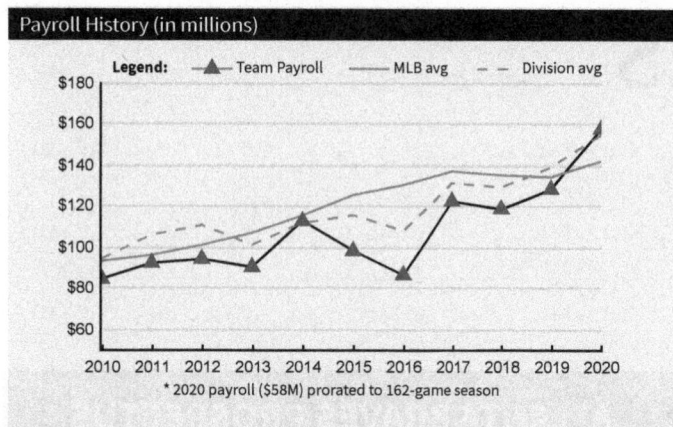

Legend: ▲ Team Payroll — MLB avg -- Division avg

* 2020 payroll ($58M) prorated to 162-game season

Future Commitments (in millions)

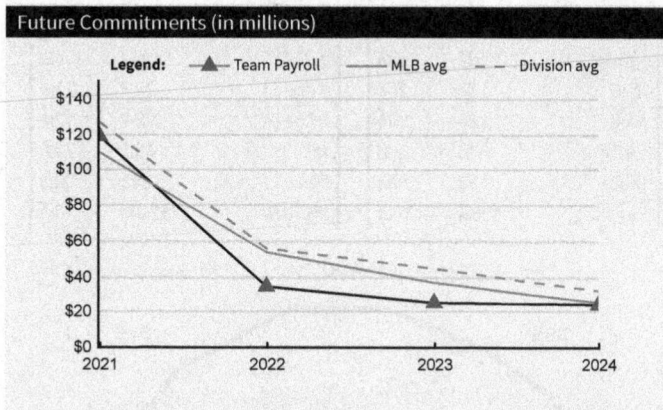

Legend: ▲ Team Payroll — MLB avg -- Division avg

Farm System Ranking

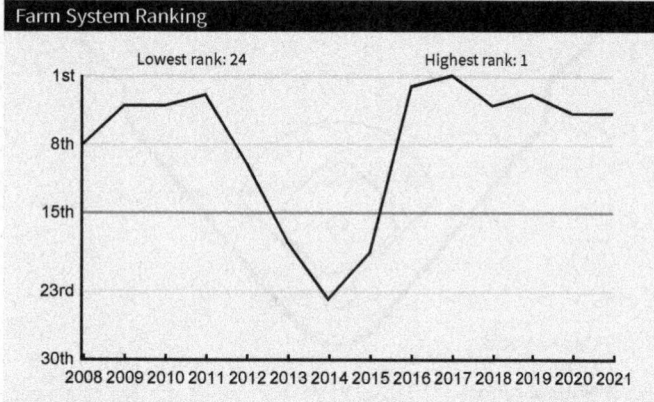

Lowest rank: 24   Highest rank: 1

Personnel

Executive Vice President, General Manager
Alex Anthopoulos

Assistant General Manager, Research and Development
Jason Paré

Assistant General Manager, Player Development
Ben Sestanovich

Special Assistant to the General Manager
Mike Fast

Manager
Brian Snitker

BP Alumni
Mike Fast
Jason Paré
Ronit Shah
Noah Woodward
Colin Wyers

Except Betts was walking toward the dugout and several people were morphing their hands around invisible baseballs and pressing them into their ears emphatically, their fingers poking their heads. They wanted a review, and they got one. The video replay showed that Betts was simply too fast, and Ozuna from the other side of the field, timed his tag incorrectly. He had been several feet off the third base bag when Betts made his catch, and so it was a double play. The inning was over, the kindling doused with water.

I marked it as a baserunning error in my scorebook that I'd started keeping for televised games. It was October, but it didn't feel like it. The players were in Texas in a dome and not wearing jackets and I was on my couch like I had been for (at that point) seven months. What I wanted more than anything was to escape into the play. I wanted to get mad about a slider that hung, to scream about a bunt that popped right up into the pitcher's mitt. I wanted to roll my eyes at a poorly timed throw over to first or a kicked ground ball. My own team (the Washington Nationals) had proven to be a ball of trash rolling downhill since early August, so I decided to pick the good team in the division. I chose Atlanta.

Really, I chose Atlanta because they seemed like they were having fun and I wanted to have fun. On October 8, in the middle of game three of the NLDS, Ronald Acuña Jr. danced his way to the dugout between innings. He held his hands over his head, the ball in one, and shimmied his hips. He spun in a circle at the top of the dugout steps. His teeth are so white and so straight, his smile as bright as the full moon. I forgot for a moment that all of the fans behind him were cardboard cutouts. I smiled back at him from my couch. This was nice. This was what baseball should be. Smile at your teammates, baby, because you're going to the NLCS. In interviews, the Atlanta players said they were dancing in the dugout, that no one could talk because the music was so loud.

I miss that, not being able to talk because it is so loud and everyone is having so much fun. I miss the feeling of a friend's hand cupped around my ear screaming something I still can't hear. I miss being able to celebrate successes, to dance around and spray champagne. Maybe, I thought, the Atlanta players could be my friends. They had something I didn't have, but I'd watched them absolutely ruin the Nationals all year. They were scrappy and smart. They had an energy that felt wholesome but mature. There were no ethical concerns for me about them being underpaid. This would work, I told myself going into the NLCS. I would yet again pick the World Series winning team for my essay in *Baseball Prospectus*. I was the good luck charm. Atlanta was going to WIN. IT. ALL.

You know how it went, but let's relive it anyway. Atlanta defeated the pesky Marlins easily in the Division Series. Three games in a row, and none of them felt like a problem. Only Game 2 even felt close. By the time Acuña Jr. was dancing on the top step of the dugout, an Atlanta win felt as sure as the sun setting. But even though I couldn't focus on the 2020 season at all, I was pretty sure that the Dodgers were a different animal. The Dodgers are shiny. They have players whose names people who don't watch baseball know. They all seem to have necklaces that have been very recently polished. They are Los Angeles. They are tan. They are not so easy to beat.

But Atlanta showed up. Hell yeah. They won Game 1 by four runs: no problem. Then they won Game Two. Lost Game 3, sure, that's fine. Won Game 4. Atlanta was up 3-1. That's a hitter's count. If I were the manager (which I am not) I would tell everyone to calm down. Just play smart, good baseball. Don't do anything stupid, and we'll win this. All we have to do is win one of three games. In fact, I did tell the team this. I told it to them through my television. I was invested now. I applauded.

But as you already know, they didn't play smart, and they didn't play carefully. Immediately after Mookie Betts made his incredible catch and Ozuna made his silly error, Corey Seager came up to bat in the fourth and absolutely smashed a home run. Atlanta was still up 2-1, but something had shifted. They managed to score a run in the eighth, but it never felt hopeful. They lost game five and game six and now the odds were much worse.

By the beginning of Game 7, I could barely see the embers of the team I'd lost in Game 5. But all they had to do was win this one. Win one game. We know, of course, that they did not. We also know that it was the baserunning that got them again. But I would have sworn, before I started writing this piece and looked up the details of that dreaded play, that the baserunning error that soaked the Atlanta team with a firehose and ruined their chances for good came in the eighth or ninth inning. That's how absolutely damning it felt to me.

I remembered it wrong. Memory is a funny thing: superimposing what we know is coming on top of what we know happened. In reality, it was only the fourth inning. The game was tied 2-2. Dodgers relief pitcher Tony Gonsolin led off the fourth inning by walking two batters and giving up an RBI single. There was optimism streaming through the television screen. Maybe my new adopted team could still pull it off. You could see the players sitting up a little bit taller in the dugout.

But the players were distracted. Or maybe they were given bad signals by coaches. With runners on second and third, Justin Turner easily scooped up a rocket of a grounder at third and when he looked up (probably to check on the runners) Dansby Swanson was halfway down the baseline. His head wasn't tucked down. He was running, but it didn't even really seem like he was sprinting. Did he think there was someone on first and he had to? I stood up from my couch with my hands on my head.Turner side-armed it to the plate and began a textbook rundown with the catcher, Swanson

shuffling sideways between them down the baseline. Turner stretched, and with Swanson just out of reach dove. He was out. An error. But what's this? Turner hops up from his belly where he landed to his knees, pivots toward third and rockets the ball to the bag. Austin Riley, for some unknown reason, had decided to also make a baserunning error. On the replay, you can see Riley hesitate. He's going toward third, then he's not. He's halfway down the baseline and he chickens out, swallows some bravery and tries again. But he didn't commit soon enough. Riley tucked his legs in a figure four. He didn't even slide face first into the third out of the inning. 5-2-5-6. The inning was over. Atlanta was up by a run, but they might as well have handed the trophy to the Dodgers then.

I wanted to be mad at him. I wanted so, so badly to be mad. Were this a normal year, I would have been yelling at the television. Who cares that this was a team I adopted for the playoffs! They were making silly, little league mistakes in not one but two games, and giving up a 3-1 lead in the series. It was only the fourth inning. I should have been furious, but optimistic and instead I just felt defeated. It was hard for me to feel mad at Swanson for taking off from the bag when he didn't need to, or at Riley for stealing during a risky rundown. It was hard for me to even feel mad at the coaches. They showed the replay over and over again. Swanson was just out of reach and then Turner dove, laid himself all the way out to brush the pant leg with his glove. It was an incredible effort, and one I could barely believe. Who had that kind of energy in this kind of year, to do something unbelievable?

When I think about the playoffs, I think about those two plays. I'm sure the players do too. The frustration of those plays is that we, the fans, (even me a temporary one) know that the team is better than that. They know it too.

I've thought a lot about those two innings since they happened, replaying the failure in my mind, but that's not really fair. The Atlanta players had a hell of a season. They had a 58.3 win percentage. They won the National League East by four games and crushed the next best team (the Marlins) immediately in the playoffs. Without the errors, they looked good on the field and in the batter's box. Those two mistakes loom large because of their consequences, but they don't define that team. There were five more innings after that baserunning error to come back and win the game. I can't blame them for not being able to mount a comeback. This is a hard year to do anything! In the back of my mind all season I've heard a low but constant hum reminding me that this was just a game in a year where games felt frivolous and unnecessary and dangerous. There will be an asterisk next to this short, weird, awful season for all of history. Those mistakes don't really matter, after all.

This is a year for giving grace where we can afford to. Everyone is working really hard. Everyone is trying their best. Everyone is being given less to work with than a normal year and asked for the same output in return. Sure, there were two mistakes in that series that could have saved Atlanta, but they did have a good season. They had optimism, and dance moves, and only lost to the World Series champions because of mental errors. That's a team that under more normal circumstances, will thrive. And I for one, am really looking forward to watching them again and feeling just a little bit more.

—*Kelsey McKinney is a co-owner at Defector.com.*

HITTERS

Ronald Acuña Jr. LF Born: 12/18/97 Age: 23 Bats: R Throws: R Height: 6'0" Weight: 205 Origin: International Free Agent, 2014

YEAR	TEAM	LVL	AGE	PA	R	2B	3B	HR	RBI	BB	K	SB	CS	Whiff%	AVG/OBP/SLG	DRC+	BABIP	BRR	FRAA	WARP
2018	GWN	AAA	20	101	9	2	0	1	3	11	25	5	1		.211/.297/.267	78	.281	1.0	LF(18): -3.1, CF(2): -0.6, RF(1): -0.3	-0.5
2018	ATL	MLB	20	487	78	26	4	26	64	45	123	16	5	26.7%	.293/.366/.552	137	.352	3.1	LF(101): -10.8, CF(13): 1.0, RF(3): 0.3	2.9
2019	ATL	MLB	21	715	127	22	2	41	101	76	188	37	9	27.8%	.280/.365/.518	129	.337	8.6	CF(100): -3.2, LF(46): 5.0, RF(35): 0.9	6.1
2020	ATL	MLB	23	202	46	11	0	14	29	38	60	8	1	29.9%	.250/.406/.581	138	.302	1.8	CF(34): 1.2, RF(28): 1.3	1.8
2021 FS	ATL	MLB	23	600	92	23	3	30	70	71	172	25	8	28.1%	.264/.361/.495	135	.336	3.9	RF -5, LF -3	4.0
2021 DC	ATL	MLB	23	569	87	22	2	28	67	67	163	24	8	28.1%	.264/.361/.495	135	.336	3.7	RF -4, LF -3	3.5

Comparables: Eric Davis, Kyle Schwarber, Yasiel Puig

The unfair thing about being Ronald Acuña Jr. is putting up a 6-WARP campaign as a 21-year-old and being expected to be even better the next year. The amazing thing about Acuña is that he was. The Braves' superstar finished in the top 15 in the majors in DRC+ and WARP, nearly doubled his walk rate, was caught just once in nine stolen base attempts, posted a career-high ISO, hard-hit rate and average exit velocity and ranked as one of the fastest runners and better outfielders in the game. The only stumble was a relatively pedestrian .250 batting average, and if that's what you care about, Baseball Prospectus has a wealth of reading material for you.

In a world without Freddie Freeman, Acuña is Atlanta's MVP, if not the National League's. In a world without fellow second-generation freak Fernando Tatis Jr., Acuña is the easy pick for the best under-25 player in baseball. In a world without Mike Trout, Acuña might be the best player in baseball, full stop. The sky isn't the limit for him; the edge of our known solar system is.

Ozzie Albies 2B Born: 01/07/97 Age: 24 Bats: S Throws: R Height: 5'8" Weight: 165 Origin: International Free Agent, 2013

YEAR	TEAM	LVL	AGE	PA	R	2B	3B	HR	RBI	BB	K	SB	CS	Whiff%	AVG/OBP/SLG	DRC+	BABIP	BRR	FRAA	WARP
2018	ATL	MLB	21	684	105	40	5	24	72	36	116	14	3	22.2%	.261/.305/.452	106	.285	5.9	2B(157): 7.0	4.0
2019	ATL	MLB	22	702	102	43	8	24	86	54	112	15	4	23.0%	.295/.352/.500	119	.325	4.4	2B(158): -0.4	4.4
2020	ATL	MLB	23	124	21	5	0	6	19	5	30	3	1	24.8%	.271/.306/.466	109	.317	0.6	2B(29): 0.2	0.6
2021 FS	ATL	MLB	24	600	71	27	5	19	73	42	122	13	3	23.0%	.261/.318/.433	107	.304	6.4	2B 2, SS 0	3.7
2021 DC	ATL	MLB	24	569	67	25	4	18	69	39	116	12	3	23.0%	.261/.318/.433	107	.304	6.1	2B 2	3.5

Comparables: Enrique Hernández, Scooter Gennett, Bobby Grich

A right wrist contusion robbed Albies of about five weeks in an already short season, and hampered him significantly in the few games he played before hitting the injured list in early August. The good news is that, once back, he swung a bat made out of titanium, slashing .338/.372/.581 in September. Before chalking up Albies' overall mediocre season to that balky wrist, though, keep in mind that he took a significant step back in walk rate, going from 7.7 percent in 2019 to a more Rougned Odor-adjacent 4.2 percent this year. Nor can that be blamed entirely on the wrist: Amid that torrid and healthy September, Albies drew a mere three free passes in 78 plate appearances.

Given his average defense and unexceptional base running, Albies' status as a building block for the Braves rests on him figuring out how to take a walk every now and then in addition to his superb power. He did it the year prior, and given that his underlying swing stats didn't nosedive, the safe bet is that Albies finds his way to first more often in 2021.

Abraham Almonte RF Born: 06/27/89 Age: 32 Bats: S Throws: R Height: 5'10" Weight: 223 Origin: International Free Agent, 2005

YEAR	TEAM	LVL	AGE	PA	R	2B	3B	HR	RBI	BB	K	SB	CS	Whiff%	AVG/OBP/SLG	DRC+	BABIP	BRR	FRAA	WARP
2018	KC	MLB	29	151	15	1	2	3	9	15	36	2	2	29.8%	.179/.260/.284	68	.219	1.1	CF(35): 0.2, RF(3): 0.0, LF(1): -0.1	0.0
2019	RNO	AAA	30	382	78	33	4	17	59	60	70	12	3		.270/.382/.558	119	.294	0.5	CF(58): -2.9, RF(31): -1.6, LF(4): 1.2	1.8
2019	ARI	MLB	30	38	11	3	1	1	4	7	8	0	0	24.3%	.290/.421/.548	93	.364	2.1	RF(9): 0.2, CF(3): -0.2	0.3
2020	SD	MLB	31	13	0	0	0	0	0	2	4	1	1	23.8%	.091/.231/.091	92	.143	-0.4	LF(2): 0.3, CF(1): -0.0	0.0
2021 FS	ATL	MLB	32	600	58	20	3	15	60	63	152	7	2	27.5%	.208/.295/.347	80	.261	3.4	RF -6, LF 3	0.2
2021 DC	ATL	MLB	32	334	32	11	2	8	33	35	85	4	1	27.5%	.208/.295/.347	80	.261	1.9	RF -3, LF 2	0.0

Comparables: Cameron Maybin, Pete Whisenant, Corey Patterson

The Padres decided to bring back Almonte for a second stint, perhaps with the hope that his hot September the previous year was an indication of improved plate discipline and power. It wasn't; though, to be fair, the Padres barely gave him a chance to do much of anything. Almonte signed with the Braves before Halloween, suggesting he's comfortable with prioritizing a ring over swings.

Johan Camargo 3B Born: 12/13/93 Age: 27 Bats: S Throws: R Height: 6'0" Weight: 195 Origin: International Free Agent, 2010

YEAR	TEAM	LVL	AGE	PA	R	2B	3B	HR	RBI	BB	K	SB	CS	Whiff%	AVG/OBP/SLG	DRC+	BABIP	BRR	FRAA	WARP
2018	GWN	AAA	24	36	6	2	0	3	7	3	9	0	0		.303/.361/.636	129	.333	0.3	SS(4): -0.5, 3B(3): -0.2, 2B(1): -0.0	0.2
2018	ATL	MLB	24	524	63	27	1	19	76	51	108	1	1	26.5%	.272/.349/.457	115	.315	-1.6	3B(114): -9.8, SS(18): -1.5, 2B(3): -0.1	1.6
2019	GWN	AAA	25	64	10	6	0	2	15	5	12	0	0		.483/.531/.690	185	.591	-1.9	3B(7): -0.6, SS(4): 0.3, 2B(3): -0.6	0.6
2019	ATL	MLB	25	248	31	12	1	7	32	15	43	1	0	25.2%	.233/.279/.384	80	.258	0.2	SS(25): 0.5, 3B(18): -0.2, LF(11): 0.3	0.3
2020	ATL	MLB	27	127	16	8	0	4	9	6	35	0	0	33.9%	.200/.244/.367	80	.247	0.2	2B(21): -1.9, 3B(10): 2.5	0.1
2021 FS	ATL	MLB	27	600	60	27	2	16	68	39	143	1	0	28.2%	.234/.289/.383	84	.286	0.2	3B -3, 2B 0	0.1
2021 DC	ATL	MLB	27	535	54	24	2	14	60	34	127	1	0	28.2%	.234/.289/.383	84	.286	0.2	3B -3, 2B 0	-0.1

Comparables: Kevin Kouzmanoff, Jim Morrison, Mickey Klutts

It's been a frustrating two years for Camargo, who went from breakout star in 2018 to utility player and Josh Donaldson backup in '19 to… this. His offense disappeared alongside his starting role, and neither reappeared in 2020, as the Braves committed to letting Austin Riley cook at third base, and Camargo wasn't able to steal the job back despite Riley's struggles. Nor did time spent filling in for Albies at second base go any better. The gains he made in 2018 haven't stuck, as Camargo's contact rates and plate discipline have eroded, leaving him decidedly below league-average offensively. His first year of arbitration eligibility arrives in 2021, meaning his paychecks are about to start getting bigger—as will the pressure to prove that 2018 wasn't a fluke.

William Contreras C Born: 12/24/97 Age: 23 Bats: R Throws: R Height: 6'0" Weight: 180 Origin: International Free Agent, 2015

YEAR	TEAM	LVL	AGE	PA	R	2B	3B	HR	RBI	BB	K	SB	CS	Whiff%	AVG/OBP/SLG	DRC+	BABIP	BRR	FRAA	WARP
2018	ROM	LO-A	20	342	54	17	1	11	39	29	73	1	1		.293/.360/.463	134	.351	-0.9	C(43): -0.3	1.6
2018	FLO	HI-A	20	90	3	7	0	0	10	6	16	0	0		.253/.300/.337	102	.309	-0.3	C(20): -0.4	0.1
2019	FLO	HI-A	21	207	26	11	0	3	22	14	44	0	0		.263/.324/.368	112	.329	-0.2	C(43): -0.8	1.0
2019	MIS	AA	21	209	24	9	0	3	17	15	40	0	0		.246/.306/.340	99	.295	0.8	C(53): -1.1	0.9
2020	ATL	MLB	23	10	0	1	0	0	1	0	4	0	0	40.9%	.400/.400/.500	83	.667	-0.3	C(4): 0.2	0.0
2021 FS	ATL	MLB	23	600	59	22	1	14	58	38	167	0	0	40.9%	.222/.278/.347	71	.291	-0.1	C -5	-0.3
2021 DC	ATL	MLB	23	133	13	4	0	3	13	8	37	0	0	40.9%	.222/.278/.347	71	.291	0.0	C -1	-0.1

Comparables: Bryan Anderson, Austin Romine, Miguel Perez

YEAR	TEAM	P. COUNT	FRM RUNS	BLK RUNS	THRW RUNS	TOT RUNS
2020	ATL	404	0.0	0.0	0.0	0.0
2021	ATL	4810	-0.6	-0.6	0.0	-1.2

Willson's little brother remains one of the more intriguing catching prospects in baseball, but without a minor league season to show off his stuff, he spent most of the year at the Braves' alternate site. He did get to make his MLB debut, though his time in the majors amounted to all of 10 plate appearances over four games in late July while Travis d'Arnaud and Tyler Flowers were both unavailable. The strong work of those two kept Contreras from claiming any larger role in Atlanta, but his time is coming: Flowers is a free agent this winter, and d'Arnaud has just one year left on his contract.

Travis d'Arnaud C Born: 02/10/89 Age: 32 Bats: R Throws: R Height: 6'2" Weight: 210 Origin: Round 1, 2007 Draft (#37 overall)

YEAR	TEAM	LVL	AGE	PA	R	2B	3B	HR	RBI	BB	K	SB	CS	Whiff%	AVG/OBP/SLG	DRC+	BABIP	BRR	FRAA	WARP
2018	NYM	MLB	29	16	1	0	0	1	3	1	5	0	0	25.0%	.200/.250/.400	79	.222	-0.1	C(4): 1.0	0.1
2019	LAD	MLB	30	1	0	0	0	0	0	0	0	0	0	0.0%	.000/.000/.000	105	.000			0.0
2019	NYM	MLB	30	25	2	0	0	0	2	2	5	0	0	30.8%	.087/.160/.087	70	.111	0.4	C(9): 0.1	0.1
2019	TB	MLB	30	365	50	16	0	16	67	30	80	0	1	26.1%	.263/.323/.459	103	.295	0.4	C(76): -2.2, 1B(21): -1.6	1.4
2020	ATL	MLB	31	184	19	8	0	9	34	16	49	1	0	30.9%	.321/.386/.533	110	.407	-0.8	C(35): -1.0	0.9
2021 FS	ATL	MLB	32	600	71	25	1	22	80	48	147	1	0	28.2%	.261/.327/.437	110	.319	-1.0	C 7, 1B 0	3.7
2021 DC	ATL	MLB	32	468	55	20	1	17	62	37	115	1	0	28.2%	.261/.327/.437	110	.319	-0.7	C 7	3.0

Comparables: Jody Davis, Mike Macfarlane, Ryan Doumit

YEAR	TEAM	P. COUNT	FRM RUNS	BLK RUNS	THRW RUNS	TOT RUNS
2018	NYM	694	1.0	0.1	0.0	1.0
2019	NYM	899	0.2	0.0	0.0	0.0
2019	TB	9708	1.8	-2.4	0.1	-0.6
2020	ATL	5251	3.1	-0.2	0.2	3.1
2021	ATL	13228	8.3	-1.1	-0.5	6.7

Perhaps the platonic ideal of a Wilpon-era Mets rage DFA, d'Arnaud split time with three different teams in 2019 (though if you blinked, you missed his stint with the Dodgers), excelled in Tampa Bay and turned that into a two-year, $16 million deal with Atlanta. That was a shrewd investment, as d'Arnaud put up his best season ever at the dish and ranked as one of the better backstops in the league with the glove. Not that there aren't red flags in his profile: His strikeout rate ballooned to 27.2 percent, and despite a drop in contact rates, his BABIP was more peak Ichiro than 31-year-old catcher. A sky-high hard-hit rate of 57.2 percent makes that figure a little more palatable if not probable, but it's unlikely that he can replicate this kind of performance next year.

Adam Duvall LF   Born: 09/04/88   Age: 32   Bats: R   Throws: R   Height: 6'1"   Weight: 215   Origin: Round 11, 2010 Draft (#348 overall)

YEAR	TEAM	LVL	AGE	PA	R	2B	3B	HR	RBI	BB	K	SB	CS	Whiff%	AVG/OBP/SLG	DRC+	BABIP	BRR	FRAA	WARP
2018	ATL	MLB	29	57	8	0	0	0	0	3	17	0	0	31.9%	.132/.193/.151	82	.194	0.6	LF(12): -0.0, RF(2): -0.0	0.1
2018	CIN	MLB	29	370	40	19	0	15	61	34	100	2	2	28.0%	.205/.286/.399	80	.244	-0.6	LF(89): 6.9, 1B(10): 0.3, 3B(1): -0.0	0.7
2019	GWN	AAA	30	429	74	20	4	32	93	48	86	1	0		.266/.364/.602	134	.261	0.2	LF(51): 4.7, RF(26): 1.5	3.1
2019	ATL	MLB	30	130	17	4	1	10	19	7	39	0	0	28.3%	.267/.315/.567	104	.306	0.4	LF(31): 1.8, RF(2): -0.5	0.6
2020	ATL	MLB	32	209	34	8	0	16	33	15	54	0	0	27.1%	.237/.301/.532	121	.240	0.2	LF(45): 0.5, RF(17): -1.6, CF(1): -0.0	0.8
2021 FS	ATL	MLB	32	600	75	24	2	35	95	43	174	4	1	27.8%	.232/.299/.484	112	.269	-0.6	LF 1, RF -1	2.6

Comparables: Henry Rodriguez, Geoff Jenkins, Bo Jackson

Birthed fully formed from the forehead of Mark Trumbo, Duvall represents a dying breed of hack-happy sluggers who offer virtually nothing else in terms of value. The former All-Star never met a breaking pitch he wouldn't swing at (and over), is fine defensively so long as you don't ask him to do anything beyond the bare minimum, and won't embarrass himself on the basepaths (though he won't win you any games there either). But what Duvall can do is destroy fastballs from those pitchers stupid or stubborn enough to challenge him with heat, and he's a valuable platoon piece as someone who mashes lefties. That should be enough to keep him employed and above league average offensively, despite a toolbox that has only a hammer and a broken tape measure in it. It wasn't, as he found himself one of the autumn's more surprising non-tenders.

Tyler Flowers C   Born: 01/24/86   Age: 35   Bats: R   Throws: R   Height: 6'4"   Weight: 260   Origin: Round 33, 2005 Draft (#1007 overall)

YEAR	TEAM	LVL	AGE	PA	R	2B	3B	HR	RBI	BB	K	SB	CS	Whiff%	AVG/OBP/SLG	DRC+	BABIP	BRR	FRAA	WARP
2018	ATL	MLB	32	296	34	9	0	8	30	35	76	0	0	29.0%	.227/.341/.359	100	.292	0.3	C(76): 13.2	2.9
2019	ATL	MLB	33	310	36	11	3	11	34	31	105	0	0	36.7%	.229/.319/.413	79	.325	-3.7	C(83): 10.3	1.4
2020	ATL	MLB	34	80	5	6	0	1	5	8	34	0	0	36.5%	.217/.325/.348	73	.412	0.7	C(22): -0.1	0.2
2021 FS	ATL	MLB	35	600	66	22	1	17	63	54	208	1	0	34.6%	.225/.321/.370	95	.337	-0.6	C 19	4.0

Comparables: David Ross, Jason LaRue, Todd Pratt

YEAR	TEAM	P. COUNT	FRM RUNS	BLK RUNS	THRW RUNS	TOT RUNS
2018	ATL	10295	13.7	-0.4	-0.2	13.1
2019	ATL	11730	15.3	-3.8	-0.6	11.0
2020	ATL	3036	1.6	0.0	0.1	1.7
2021	ATL	16650	20.2	1.0	-0.4	20.7

Flowers' unexpected 2017 breakout continues to recede further and further into the distance, as his offense never found that level again and, in some cases, hit new lows, like a grotesque 42.5 percent strikeout rate. Entering 2021, it'd be pointless to expect anything more of Flowers than backup catcher-level offense, because, well, that's what he is: a backup catcher, and a glove-first one at that. The good thing for Flowers is that his blocking, framing and pitch-calling skills all remain above average, and as his skill with the bat decays, the average offensive production of catchers leaguewide plummets to match it. He should always be able to find a home as a clubhouse leader who can make a couple of starts a week, work with a young pitcher and run into a fastball every now and then.

Freddie Freeman 1B   Born: 09/12/89   Age: 31   Bats: L   Throws: R   Height: 6'5"   Weight: 220   Origin: Round 2, 2007 Draft (#78 overall)

YEAR	TEAM	LVL	AGE	PA	R	2B	3B	HR	RBI	BB	K	SB	CS	Whiff%	AVG/OBP/SLG	DRC+	BABIP	BRR	FRAA	WARP
2018	ATL	MLB	28	707	94	44	4	23	98	76	132	10	3	24.3%	.309/.388/.505	136	.358	-1.7	1B(161): 3.5	4.4
2019	ATL	MLB	29	692	113	34	2	38	121	87	127	6	3	24.4%	.295/.389/.549	141	.318	0.6	1B(158): -7.5	4.0
2020	ATL	MLB	31	262	51	23	1	13	53	45	37	2	0	20.1%	.341/.462/.640	172	.366	-2.1	1B(58): -0.2	2.6
2021 FS	ATL	MLB	31	600	90	26	2	28	85	84	116	7	2	23.2%	.279/.390/.510	146	.312	0.6	1B 0, 3B 0	4.6
2021 DC	ATL	MLB	31	569	85	25	2	27	80	79	110	7	2	23.2%	.279/.390/.510	146	.312	0.6	1B 0	4.3

Comparables: Mark Teixeira, Adrián González, Harmon Killebrew

A picture may not be worth a thousand words, but in the case of Freeman, a glance at his Brooks Baseball visualizations would tell you the secret to his brilliant 2020: Don't miss the ball when you swing at it, and hit the living crap out of it when you connect. A paragon of consistency, Freeman found new heights by cutting his whiff rate and upping his contact and hard-hit rates (as well as putting the ball on the ground less). That he leveled up at the age of 31 and after 10 years of already excellent results is a testament to the kind of player he is, and a terrifying thought for the rest of the NL East. The future in Atlanta was supposed to be Acuña and Albies. It wasn't supposed to be that plus Freeman morphing into Peak Todd Helton in Coors, and a Coors he can somehow take along on the road.

Adeiny Hechavarría 2B   Born: 04/15/89   Age: 32   Bats: R   Throws: R   Height: 6'0"   Weight: 195   Origin: International Free Agent, 2010

YEAR	TEAM	LVL	AGE	PA	R	2B	3B	HR	RBI	BB	K	SB	CS	Whiff%	AVG/OBP/SLG	DRC+	BABIP	BRR	FRAA	WARP
2018	NYY	MLB	29	37	3	0	0	2	2	1	10	1	0	29.3%	.194/.216/.361	88	.208	0.1	SS(16): -1.4, 3B(4): -0.3	-0.1
2018	TB	MLB	29	237	29	7	0	3	26	12	37	1	0	19.3%	.258/.289/.332	88	.290	1.5	SS(61): -1.3	0.8
2018	PIT	MLB	29	47	2	4	0	1	3	3	11	0	0	25.6%	.233/.277/.395	87	.281	-1.3	SS(15): -1.1	-0.1
2019	SYR	AAA	30	102	15	9	0	0	17	6	14	2	1		.348/.382/.446	122	.395	0.3	SS(14): 1.9, 3B(13): -1.1, 2B(2): 0.3	0.8
2019	ATL	MLB	30	70	14	5	1	4	15	6	15	0	0	26.4%	.328/.400/.639	132	.372	0.4	SS(12): -0.2, 2B(3): -0.4, 3B(1): -0.1	0.6
2019	NYM	MLB	30	151	20	7	0	5	18	8	33	3	1	23.3%	.204/.252/.359	72	.231	-1.8	2B(26): -1.6, SS(15): -0.2, 3B(8): -0.6	-0.4
2020	ATL	MLB	31	63	7	3	0	0	2	4	12	0	0	20.4%	.254/.302/.305	81	.319	-1.0	2B(12): -0.4, 3B(8): -0.4, SS(4): 0.0	-0.2
2021 FS	ATL	MLB	32	600	58	24	2	11	60	34	120	4	1	22.5%	.238/.286/.355	76	.284	1.2	SS -1, 2B -1	0.0

Comparables: Kiko Garcia, Bill Almon, Curtis Wilkerson

Hechavarría would've been perfectly at home in the 1970s as one of the decade's many all-glove infielders, a society of men whose on-base percentage and slugging percentage both floated in the low .300s. He's no fit at all for this modern era that requires you to, you know, hit.

Ender Inciarte CF Born: 10/29/90 Age: 30 Bats: L Throws: L Height: 5'11" Weight: 190 Origin: International Free Agent, 2008

YEAR	TEAM	LVL	AGE	PA	R	2B	3B	HR	RBI	BB	K	SB	CS	Whiff%	AVG/OBP/SLG	DRC+	BABIP	BRR	FRAA	WARP
2018	ATL	MLB	27	660	83	27	6	10	61	49	86	28	14	14.8%	.265/.325/.380	94	.293	2.3	CF(155): 9.6	3.1
2019	GWN	AAA	28	30	5	1	0	0	1	4	3	0	1		.231/.333/.269	85	.261	0.3	CF(5): 0.1	0.1
2019	ATL	MLB	28	230	30	11	2	5	24	26	41	7	1	20.6%	.246/.343/.397	95	.286	0.4	CF(63): 4.5	1.2
2020	ATL	MLB	30	131	17	2	1	1	10	12	25	4	1	23.9%	.190/.262/.250	81	.228	-1.1	CF(46): -4.3	-0.5
2021 FS	ATL	MLB	30	600	62	23	3	10	57	47	101	17	7	19.1%	.254/.318/.365	88	.296	0.3	CF 8	1.9
2021 DC	ATL	MLB	30	401	41	15	2	6	38	31	68	11	4	19.1%	.254/.318/.365	88	.296	0.2	CF 5, LF 0	1.3

Comparables: Bobby Tolan, Marquis Grissom, Mike Kingery

Ender's game has long been his glove, and that leather had to speak for the dead in 2020, as his offense slipped to nigh-unplayable levels. Then again, it's hard to imagine any level of defense being good enough to make up for a year where you're 74 percent below league average at the plate, as Inciarte was. It's just fortunate the pitcher wasn't hitting behind him. Already no one's idea of a slugger, his power completely dried up, with just four extra-base hits all season and a hard-hit rate of 6.4 percent. Inciarte can still draw a walk, steal a bag and play the outfield well, making him the quintessential backup outfielder. Unless his bat rebounds next year (a definite possibility, given the small sample size monster that ate a lot of seasons), that's his new ceiling, too.

Alex Jackson C Born: 12/25/95 Age: 25 Bats: R Throws: R Height: 6'2" Weight: 215 Origin: Round 1, 2014 Draft (#6 overall)

YEAR	TEAM	LVL	AGE	PA	R	2B	3B	HR	RBI	BB	K	SB	CS	Whiff%	AVG/OBP/SLG	DRC+	BABIP	BRR	FRAA	WARP
2018	MIS	AA	22	252	27	12	1	5	24	20	78	0	0		.200/.282/.329	69	.280	-0.9	C(61): -2.1	-0.4
2018	GWN	AAA	22	125	15	11	2	3	17	12	42	0	0		.204/.296/.426	86	.292	0.2	C(29): 2.7	0.5
2019	GWN	AAA	23	345	52	9	0	28	65	20	118	1	0		.229/.313/.533	105	.261	-2.8	C(78): 17.9	3.1
2019	ATL	MLB	23	15	0	0	0	0	0	1	5	0	0	45.5%	.000/.133/.000	76	.000		C(4): 0.5	0.1
2020	ATL	MLB	25	7	0	1	0	0	0	0	4	0	0	61.5%	.286/.286/.429	68	.667	-0.2	C(4): -0.0	0.0
2021 FS	ATL	MLB	25	600	59	23	1	16	56	37	233	0	0	53.6%	.190/.266/.331	66	.296	-0.2	C -2	-0.4
2021 DC	ATL	MLB	25	167	16	6	0	4	15	10	64	0	0	53.6%	.190/.266/.331	66	.296	0.0	C -1	-0.1

Comparables: Kyle Skipworth, Greg Halman, Pete Alonso

YEAR	TEAM	P. COUNT	FRM RUNS	BLK RUNS	THRW RUNS	TOT RUNS
2019	ATL	534	0.3	0.1		0.4
2020	ATL	332	-0.1	0.0	0.0	-0.1
2021	ATL	6012	-1.2	0.7	0.2	-0.3

Like fellow catching prospect Contreras, Jackson lost some sorely-needed reps last summer, hanging out at the Braves' alternate site aside from three days in late July and two in late August with the big club. What strides he made weren't documented, but the safe bet is that Atlanta focused on his bat-to-ball skills and his plate discipline, the two bugaboos in his game. The power, though, is there, and while he's a safer bet to spend 2021 in the minors than with the Braves, the world will always welcome both lovers and backup catchers who can swat.

★ ★ ★ *2021 Top 101 Prospect* **#81** ★ ★ ★

Shea Langeliers C Born: 11/18/97 Age: 23 Bats: R Throws: R Height: 6'0" Weight: 205 Origin: Round 1, 2019 Draft (#9 overall)

YEAR	TEAM	LVL	AGE	PA	R	2B	3B	HR	RBI	BB	K	SB	CS	Whiff%	AVG/OBP/SLG	DRC+	BABIP	BRR	FRAA	WARP
2019	ROM	LO-A	21	239	27	13	0	2	34	17	55	0	0		.255/.310/.343	100	.325	-1.3	C(42): 0.8	0.9
2021 FS	ATL	MLB	23	600	54	25	2	9	52	37	190	1	0		.213/.267/.318	64	.305	0.2	C 1	-0.2

Comparables: Josh Phegley, José Briceño, Kyle Higashioka

For as much as everyone talks about the Braves growing pitching prospects on trees, they're equally flush in catching talent. Langeliers is the best defender of the bunch and good enough to catch in the majors right now. He is not good enough to DH in the majors right now, as his stat line proves, but he has an excess of raw power to tap into as he climbs the proverbial ladder. The defense and leadership skills alone make Langeliers and his Zane Grey-caliber name one of the safest prospects in the low minors to bet on, but the bat may take a while.

Nick Markakis RF Born: 11/17/83 Age: 37 Bats: L Throws: L Height: 6'1" Weight: 210 Origin: Round 1, 2003 Draft (#7 overall)

YEAR	TEAM	LVL	AGE	PA	R	2B	3B	HR	RBI	BB	K	SB	CS	Whiff%	AVG/OBP/SLG	DRC+	BABIP	BRR	FRAA	WARP
2018	ATL	MLB	34	705	78	43	2	14	93	72	80	1	1	11.4%	.297/.366/.440	116	.318	-1.6	RF(158): 6.9, LF(3): -0.4	3.5
2019	ATL	MLB	35	469	61	25	2	9	62	47	59	2	0	13.2%	.285/.356/.420	105	.310	-2.8	RF(103): -11.5, LF(9): 3.4	0.4
2020	ATL	MLB	37	141	15	15	0	1	15	10	23	0	1	12.7%	.254/.312/.392	91	.302	-1.6	RF(29): -2.4, LF(7): 0.7	-0.3
2021 FS	ATL	MLB	37	600	60	31	1	10	62	57	106	1	0	12.5%	.255/.332/.378	97	.301	-1.9	RF -7, LF 0	0.2

Comparables: Paul O'Neill, George Hendrick, Orlando Merced

Markakis was set to sit out the 2020 season, opting out in early July over the COVID-19 pandemic, only to change course three weeks later and join the Braves after all. That return didn't show up in the box scores, as Markakis posted one of his weakest seasons at the plate in his long career, but despite that, he led the team in starts in right field. The Braves are seemingly content to keep him around until he doesn't want to be there (and then welcome him back when he does), and truthfully, you could do worse in terms of reserve outfield options, particularly when they have the Veteran Intangibles that Markakis does. The trick for the Braves will be to reduce his playing time; at 37, leadership and the occasional start or two every week is just about all Markakis has to offer at this point.

Jack Mayfield 2B Born: 09/30/90 Age: 30 Bats: R Throws: R Height: 5'11" Weight: 190 Origin: Undrafted Free Agent, 2013

YEAR	TEAM	LVL	AGE	PA	R	2B	3B	HR	RBI	BB	K	SB	CS	Whiff%	AVG/OBP/SLG	DRC+	BABIP	BRR	FRAA	WARP
2018	FRE	AAA	27	479	66	31	1	16	66	33	92	5	4		.270/.324/.457	109	.304	-0.2	2B(62): -6.3, SS(48): -8.9, 3B(4): -0.7	0.1
2019	RR	AAA	28	431	78	26	1	26	79	37	78	7	1		.287/.350/.566	117	.291	0.0	SS(43): -1.5, 2B(33): 2.9, 3B(24): -1.5	2.5
2019	HOU	MLB	28	65	8	5	0	2	5	1	16	0	0	28.2%	.156/.169/.328	72	.174	-0.6	SS(21): 0.2, 2B(5): -0.2, 3B(1): -0.0	0.0
2020	HOU	MLB	30	47	5	1	0	0	3	2	14	0	0	29.7%	.190/.239/.214	66	.276	-0.1	3B(8): 0.4, SS(6): -0.5, 2B(5): -0.1	-0.2
2021 FS	ATL	MLB	30	600	66	25	1	23	73	38	165	1	0	29.0%	.224/.280/.402	86	.274	-0.5	2B -2, SS -6	0.0
2021 DC	ATL	MLB	30	100	11	4	0	3	12	6	27	0	0	29.0%	.224/.280/.402	86	.274	-0.1	2B 0, SS -1	0.0

Comparables: Josh Barfield, Chris Valaika, Whit Merrifield

Mayfield is an unfortunate surname for a baseball player. Something definitive like Jack Willfield would be more reassuring. Nominative determinism aside, it turns out that Jack can field but can't hit, at least at the major-league level. He should return to producing above-average slash lines at Triple-A with the occasional foray onto the big-league bench.

Marcell Ozuna LF Born: 11/12/90 Age: 30 Bats: R Throws: R Height: 6'1" Weight: 225 Origin: International Free Agent, 2008

YEAR	TEAM	LVL	AGE	PA	R	2B	3B	HR	RBI	BB	K	SB	CS	Whiff%	AVG/OBP/SLG	DRC+	BABIP	BRR	FRAA	WARP
2018	STL	MLB	27	628	69	16	2	23	88	38	110	3	0	24.2%	.280/.325/.433	109	.309	2.6	LF(147): -2.2	2.4
2019	STL	MLB	28	549	80	23	1	29	89	62	114	12	2	27.7%	.241/.328/.472	111	.257	3.1	LF(129): -11.2	1.5
2020	ATL	MLB	30	267	38	14	0	18	56	38	60	0	0	31.4%	.338/.431/.636	151	.391	-0.2	LF(19): 3.1, RF(2): -0.2	2.4
2021 FS	ATL	MLB	30	600	83	23	2	30	94	59	139	4	2	28.1%	.280/.354/.504	135	.325	-1.3	LF -9, CF 0	3.4

Comparables: Jason Kubel, Rondell White, David Murphy

Like the Pirates used to be with starters on their last legs, the Braves have established themselves as the softest of pillows for sluggers who earned a frosty reception in free agency. Josh Donaldson turned his one-year deal with Atlanta in 2019 into a 5-WARP season and a four-year contract with the Twins. Ozuna is likely to be the next beneficiary of the Braves' single-season signings program, putting up his best season ever as he led the NL in homers, RBI and total bases. Ozuna's putrid defense and mediocre base running suggest that he might not age particularly gracefully. But it's okay to swing through strike one as long as you obliterate strike two, and his 2020 results will net him some long-term security somewhere.

───────────── ★ ★ ★ *2021 Top 101 Prospect* **#18** ★ ★ ★ ─────────────

Cristian Pache CF Born: 11/19/98 Age: 22 Bats: R Throws: R Height: 6'2" Weight: 215 Origin: International Free Agent, 2015

YEAR	TEAM	LVL	AGE	PA	R	2B	3B	HR	RBI	BB	K	SB	CS	Whiff%	AVG/OBP/SLG	DRC+	BABIP	BRR	FRAA	WARP
2018	FLO	HI-A	19	387	46	20	5	8	40	15	69	7	6		.285/.311/.431	113	.330	-1.1	CF(93): 3.9	1.3
2018	MIS	AA	19	109	10	3	1	1	7	5	28	0	2		.260/.294/.337	71	.347	-0.5	CF(28): 1.3	-0.1
2019	MIS	AA	20	433	50	28	8	11	53	34	104	8	11		.278/.340/.474	139	.351	-1.7	CF(58): 1.6, RF(23): 3.3, LF(22): 0.0	3.3
2019	GWN	AAA	20	105	13	8	1	1	8	9	18	0	0		.274/.337/.411	90	.329	-0.9	CF(23): -3.2, RF(3): 3.3	0.2
2020	ATL	MLB	22	4	0	0	0	0	0	0	2	0	0	33.3%	.250/.250/.250	83	.500		LF(2): 0.2	0.0
2021 FS	ATL	MLB	22	600	57	19	5	11	56	35	160	11	5	33.3%	.231/.279/.350	72	.302	1.2	CF 2, RF 4	0.5
2021 DC	ATL	MLB	22	535	50	17	5	10	50	31	142	9	5	33.3%	.231/.279/.350	72	.302	1.1	CF 2, RF 4	0.3

Comparables: Felix Pie, Greg Halman, Anthony Gose

The man (barely; he just turned 22 in November) atop Atlanta's prospect lists got more playing time in October than the regular season, as Pache was thrust into action after Adam Duvall pulled an oblique in Game 1 of the NLCS. He quickly showed just why scouts and analysts alike have drooled over him, displaying dizzying speed on the bases and elite defense in center field. It's the offense that still needs the most work: Pache has yet to display much if any power and has a ways to go with his selectivity. If nothing else, though, the defense is enough to make him a regular. Barring some surprise (or some unsurprising service time manipulation), he'll be on the Opening Day roster and a starter in his own right.

Austin Riley 3B Born: 04/02/97 Age: 24 Bats: R Throws: R Height: 6'3" Weight: 240 Origin: Round 1, 2015 Draft (#41 overall)

YEAR	TEAM	LVL	AGE	PA	R	2B	3B	HR	RBI	BB	K	SB	CS	Whiff%	AVG/OBP/SLG	DRC+	BABIP	BRR	FRAA	WARP
2018	MIS	AA	21	109	17	10	3	6	20	8	28	0	0		.333/.394/.677	175	.415	1.0	3B(27): 1.2	1.3
2018	GWN	AAA	21	324	41	17	0	12	47	26	95	1	0		.282/.346/.464	122	.374	1.1	3B(71): -0.3	1.5
2019	GWN	AAA	22	194	39	13	0	15	41	20	39	0	0		.293/.366/.626	138	.300	0.2	3B(30): -0.9, LF(7): -0.8, 1B(4): 0.2	1.3
2019	ATL	MLB	22	297	41	11	1	18	49	16	108	0	2	38.4%	.226/.279/.471	89	.293	-0.4	LF(58): 2.0, 1B(6): -0.8, 3B(5): -0.3	0.4
2020	ATL	MLB	23	206	24	7	1	8	27	16	49	0	0	30.1%	.239/.301/.415	91	.280	-0.2	3B(46): 1.2, 1B(4): 0.3, LF(4): -0.0	0.3
2021 FS	ATL	MLB	24	600	69	22	2	27	80	45	177	0	0	34.1%	.235/.300/.433	100	.294	0.4	3B -1, 1B 0	1.1
2021 DC	ATL	MLB	24	569	65	21	2	25	75	42	167	0	0	34.1%	.235/.300/.433	100	.294	0.3	3B -1, 1B 0	1.0

Comparables: Pete Incaviglia, Frank Howard, Pat Burrell

To get a sense of the kind of hitter Riley is, here are his monthly splits in 2020 by OPS: .371 (July), .875 (August), .669 (September), .489 (October). Tiny sample sizes abound in those cutoffs, but the point is that Atlanta's young third baseman is as streaky as they come. Not that this should come as a surprise, blessed as Riley is with prodigious power yet cursed at the same time with the plate discipline of a blindfolded Mark Reynolds. On the plus side, he did substantially cut down his strikeout rate from 2019 to '20; on the less positive side, it's still triple his anemic walk rate. At age 23, he remains a work in progress both with the bat and the glove, and one who needs to take a significant step forward with both in 2021 to remain part of Atlanta's long-term plans.

Pablo Sandoval 3B Born: 08/11/86 Age: 34 Bats: S Throws: R Height: 5'10" Weight: 268 Origin: International Free Agent, 2003

YEAR	TEAM	LVL	AGE	PA	R	2B	3B	HR	RBI	BB	K	SB	CS	Whiff%	AVG/OBP/SLG	DRC+	BABIP	BRR	FRAA	WARP
2018	SF	MLB	31	252	22	10	1	9	40	19	52	0	0	21.7%	.248/.310/.417	95	.282	-2.8	3B(36): -1.8, 1B(24): -1.4, 2B(2): -0.6	-0.1
2019	SF	MLB	32	296	42	23	0	14	41	18	67	1	0	26.7%	.268/.313/.507	97	.304	0.0	3B(45): -4.1, 1B(23): 0.1, P(1): -0.0	0.4
2020	ATL	MLB	34	4	0	0	0	0	0	2	1	0	0	50.0%	.000/.500/.000		.000	0.0	3B(1): 0.1	
2020	SF	MLB	34	90	5	1	0	1	6	6	18	0	0	29.7%	.220/.278/.268	82	.266	-0.5	1B(8): 0.3, 3B(4): -0.3	-0.1
2021 FS	ATL	MLB	34	600	60	26	1	16	68	40	135	1	0	26.4%	.228/.286/.372	84	.271	-0.7	3B -12, 1B -1	-1.5

Comparables: *Adrián Beltré, Sean Berry, Tim Wallach*

For all of the imperfections in Sandoval's game, getting bat to ball—whether at eye- or shoetop-level—was both his calling card and *raison d'être*. With that skill in free-fall, there seems little left to sustain a relatively brief, but extremely storied, career. His three-homer World Series Game One against the Tigers in 2012 and his 2014 World Series-clinching catch, plopping on his backside in foul ground with Sal Perez's popout safely stowed, remain the Panda's iconic moments. The fact that he may have played his final postseason in an Atlanta uniform will be the answer to a trivia question decades hence, but no matter his past, present, or future shape, he'll always be a Giant.

Braden Shewmake SS Born: 11/19/97 Age: 23 Bats: L Throws: R Height: 6'4" Weight: 190 Origin: Round 1, 2019 Draft (#21 overall)

YEAR	TEAM	LVL	AGE	PA	R	2B	3B	HR	RBI	BB	K	SB	CS	Whiff%	AVG/OBP/SLG	DRC+	BABIP	BRR	FRAA	WARP
2019	ROM	LO-A	21	226	37	18	2	3	39	21	29	11	3		.318/.389/.473	162	.359	3.5	SS(39): -0.0	2.5
2019	MIS	AA	21	52	7	0	0	0	1	4	11	2	0		.217/.288/.217	58	.278	0.7	SS(14): 1.8	0.3
2021 FS	ATL	MLB	23	600	52	27	2	10	56	39	141	10	3		.230/.287/.345	74	.291	2.6	SS 7	0.9

Comparables: *Max Schrock, Stephen Piscotty, Garin Cecchini*

Atlanta's first-round pick in 2019 tore up Low-A before a brief yet rocky stint in Double-A, but with no minor league season in '20, Shewmake was left to continue his development away from the prying eyes of scouts and analysts. What he showed in his draft summer at the plate and in the field was enough to get him into the Braves' Top 10 list; the trick will be developing power and showing enough offense to keep that spot in a deep and competitive system and escape a future as a utility player. Well, that and finding the missing R from his last name.

Dansby Swanson SS Born: 02/11/94 Age: 27 Bats: R Throws: R Height: 6'1" Weight: 190 Origin: Round 1, 2015 Draft (#1 overall)

YEAR	TEAM	LVL	AGE	PA	R	2B	3B	HR	RBI	BB	K	SB	CS	Whiff%	AVG/OBP/SLG	DRC+	BABIP	BRR	FRAA	WARP
2018	ATL	MLB	24	533	51	25	4	14	59	44	122	10	4	25.3%	.238/.304/.395	90	.290	0.9	SS(136): 5.4	2.5
2019	ATL	MLB	25	545	77	26	3	17	65	51	124	10	5	27.5%	.251/.325/.422	97	.300	1.6	SS(126): 1.3	2.7
2020	ATL	MLB	26	264	49	15	0	10	35	22	71	5	0	31.6%	.274/.345/.464	107	.350	2.1	SS(60): -2.3	1.0
2021 FS	ATL	MLB	27	600	70	23	2	17	64	56	156	7	2	28.4%	.241/.319/.394	99	.307	1.3	SS -2, 2B 0	1.8
2021 DC	ATL	MLB	27	602	70	23	2	17	65	56	156	7	2	28.4%	.241/.319/.394	99	.307	1.3	SS -2	1.8

Comparables: *Jose Valentin, Julio Lugo, Alex Gonzalez*

Following a sophomore slump that stretched all the way through his senior year, Swanson looked like nothing more than a nice head of hair and disarmingly attractive face attached to a solid glove, a noodle bat and a name that's exceedingly fun to say in a syrupy, deep Southern accent. Yet the Man Who Would Be Waffle House King (and favorite son of Cobb County dads who tuck their golf shirts into their khaki shorts) showed his no. 1 pick bona fides in 2020, with a career-best DRC+ and what likely would've been a 3-WARP campaign over a full year. The concern is that Swanson built that success on a foundation of sand, as none of his swing or contact rates took any noticeable tick in the right direction; in fact, his whiffs went up, as did his strikeouts. A high BABIP papered over those issues, as did the numbers he put up on fastballs (a .588 slugging percentage and eight of his 10 homers), though he continued to flail against everything else. What gains he made seem easily reversible if they exist at all; 2021 will be in many ways a make-or-break season for the Georgia native.

★　★　★ *2021 Top 101 Prospect* **#40** ★　★　★

Drew Waters CF Born: 12/30/98 Age: 22 Bats: S Throws: R Height: 6'2" Weight: 185 Origin: Round 2, 2017 Draft (#41 overall)

YEAR	TEAM	LVL	AGE	PA	R	2B	3B	HR	RBI	BB	K	SB	CS	Whiff%	AVG/OBP/SLG	DRC+	BABIP	BRR	FRAA	WARP
2018	ROM	LO-A	19	365	58	32	6	9	36	21	72	20	5		.303/.353/.513	139	.362	3.9	CF(83): -0.6	2.4
2018	FLO	HI-A	19	133	14	7	3	0	3	8	33	3	0		.268/.316/.374	92	.363	0.0	CF(30): -1.5, RF(1): -0.1	-0.1
2019	MIS	AA	20	454	63	35	9	5	41	28	121	13	6		.319/.366/.481	143	.436	-3.3	LF(55): 6.3, CF(38): 7.0, RF(18): -1.2	4.2
2019	GWN	AAA	20	119	17	5	0	2	11	11	43	3	0		.271/.336/.374	79	.429	0.7	RF(16): 2.1, LF(7): 0.4, CF(3): 0.8	0.3
2021 FS	ATL	MLB	22	600	58	26	5	11	58	37	210	9	3		.225/.280/.354	74	.338	4.1	LF 10, CF 1	1.5
2021 DC	ATL	MLB	22	468	45	20	4	9	45	29	163	7	2		.225/.280/.354	74	.338	3.2	LF 8, CF 0	0.9

Comparables: *Cristian Pache, Felix Pie, Fernando Tatis Jr.*

The other precocious outfielder in Atlanta's system, Waters offers more offensive upside than Pache, but is a step down in terms of defense and also carries a ton of swing-and-miss in his game. That plate discipline will be the deciding factor as to whether Waters is a first-division regular or a guy who bounces around the league as a toolsy reserve who can't quite put it all together. His glove and his speed are enough to contend for a bench spot now, if nothing else. Like everyone else in the Braves' system, he's preposterously young, and there's still plenty of time to develop. If and when that time comes, he, Pache and Acuña are going to make for an outfield where no ball falls in and one that leads the league in panache.

PITCHERS

★ ★ ★ *2021 Top 101 Prospect* **#5** ★ ★ ★

Ian Anderson **RHP** Born: 05/02/98 Age: 23 Bats: R Throws: R Height: 6'3" Weight: 170 Origin: Round 1, 2016 Draft (#3 overall)

YEAR	TEAM	LVL	AGE	W	L	SV	G	GS	IP	H	HR	BB/9	K/9	K	GB%	BABIP	WHIP	ERA	DRA-	WARP	MPH	FA%	Whiff%	CSP
2018	FLO	HI-A	20	2	6	0	20	20	100	73	2	3.6	10.6	118	44.9%	.285	1.13	2.52	68	2.3				
2018	MIS	AA	20	2	1	0	4	4	19¹	14	0	4.2	11.2	24	43.5%	.311	1.19	2.33	67	0.5				
2019	MIS	AA	21	7	5	0	21	21	111	82	8	3.8	11.9	147	44.4%	.290	1.16	2.68	78	1.6				
2019	GWN	AAA	21	1	2	0	5	5	24²	23	5	6.6	9.1	25	37.1%	.277	1.66	6.57	100	0.4				
2020	ATL	MLB	22	3	2	0	6	6	32¹	21	1	3.9	11.4	41	53.1%	.250	1.08	1.95	65	0.9	95.9	48.5%	29.0%	46.4%
2021 FS	ATL	MLB	23	9	8	0	26	26	150	131	19	4.3	10.2	169	45.8%	.292	1.36	4.09	95	1.5	95.9	48.5%	29.0%	46.4%
2021 DC	ATL	MLB	23	8	9	0	27	27	148	129	19	4.3	10.2	167	45.8%	.292	1.36	4.09	95	1.9	95.9	48.5%	29.0%	46.4%

Comparables: Archie Bradley, Henry Owens, Dustin May

Tasked with helping save a Braves rotation taking on more water than the *Titanic*, the 22-year-old Anderson did just that, shouldering the team by giving up two runs in four postseason starts. Not bad for a rookie just four years removed from facing 16-year-olds in upstate New York. Anderson marries quality velocity with a devastating changeup that batters simply can't touch: They hit .104 against it with a whiff rate of 39.8 percent. The next step for him is tightening up his control and continuing to refine his curveball, which was more of a show-me pitch than a showstopper in his debut season. Still, he's already displayed a mid-rotation floor with ace upside and is the latest victory for Atlanta's impressive player development system (and the team cloning machine that's set exclusively to "Dansby Swanson").

Jhoulys Chacín **RHP** Born: 01/07/88 Age: 33 Bats: R Throws: R Height: 6'3" Weight: 215 Origin: International Free Agent, 2004

YEAR	TEAM	LVL	AGE	W	L	SV	G	GS	IP	H	HR	BB/9	K/9	K	GB%	BABIP	WHIP	ERA	DRA-	WARP	MPH	FA%	Whiff%	CSP
2018	MIL	MLB	30	15	8	0	35	35	192²	153	18	3.3	7.3	156	41.2%	.254	1.16	3.50	100	1.8	92.2	48.1%	21.4%	48.8%
2019	MIL	MLB	31	3	10	0	19	19	88²	99	19	4.0	8.1	80	36.6%	.312	1.56	5.79	142	-1.2	91.8	43.5%	20.1%	47.4%
2019	BOS	MLB	31	0	2	0	6	5	14²	16	6	4.3	12.9	21	38.5%	.303	1.57	7.36	83	0.3	91.8	44.3%	24.6%	46.9%
2020	ATL	MLB	32	1	0	0	2	0	5	6	1	5.4	5.4	3	16.7%	.294	1.80	7.20	128	0.0	92.4	42.4%	0.0%	49.4%
2021 FS	ATL	MLB	33	2	3	0	57	0	50	51	9	3.9	8.0	44	39.0%	.294	1.46	5.11	118	-0.4	92.0	45.5%	20.2%	48.0%

Comparables: Edwin Jackson, Trevor Cahill, Kyle Gibson

One of the many disposable veterans signed as depth for Atlanta's pitching staff, Chacín lived up to that tag as well as anyone, throwing five unremarkable innings in relief before getting the boot.

Tucker Davidson **LHP** Born: 03/25/96 Age: 25 Bats: L Throws: L Height: 6'2" Weight: 215 Origin: Round 19, 2016 Draft (#559 overall)

YEAR	TEAM	LVL	AGE	W	L	SV	G	GS	IP	H	HR	BB/9	K/9	K	GB%	BABIP	WHIP	ERA	DRA-	WARP	MPH	FA%	Whiff%	CSP
2018	FLO	HI-A	22	7	10	0	24	24	118¹	120	5	4.4	7.5	99	46.7%	.334	1.50	4.18	91	1.2				
2019	MIS	AA	23	7	6	0	21	21	110²	88	5	3.7	9.9	122	48.6%	.311	1.20	2.03	91	0.7				
2019	GWN	AAA	23	1	1	0	4	4	19	20	0	4.3	5.7	12	49.2%	.345	1.53	2.84	112	0.2				
2020	ATL	MLB	24	0	1	0	1	1	1²	3	1	21.6	10.8	2	28.6%	.333	4.20	10.80	119	0.0	93.9	75.5%	16.7%	42.0%
2021 FS	ATL	MLB	25	1	1	0	57	0	50	48	7	5.4	8.2	45	45.6%	.292	1.57	5.20	114	-0.3	93.9	75.5%	16.7%	42.0%
2021 DC	ATL	MLB	25	1	1	0	4	4	19	18	2	5.4	8.2	17	45.6%	.292	1.57	5.20	114	0.1	93.9	75.5%	16.7%	42.0%

Comparables: Bernardo Flores Jr., Robert Dugger, Ryan Helsley

Davidson is no leviathan, but Thomas Hobbes nailed his MLB debut: nasty, brutish and short. He remains one of Atlanta's top pitching prospects, though, thanks to premium velocity and a high-spin curveball.

Grant Dayton **LHP** Born: 11/25/87 Age: 33 Bats: L Throws: L Height: 6'2" Weight: 210 Origin: Round 11, 2010 Draft (#347 overall)

YEAR	TEAM	LVL	AGE	W	L	SV	G	GS	IP	H	HR	BB/9	K/9	K	GB%	BABIP	WHIP	ERA	DRA-	WARP	MPH	FA%	Whiff%	CSP
2019	GWN	AAA	31	0	1	0	22	0	26²	20	6	1.4	13.8	41	38.6%	.280	0.90	3.04	51	1.0				
2019	ATL	MLB	31	0	1	0	14	0	12	12	4	3.0	10.5	14	39.4%	.276	1.33	3.00	82	0.2	92.5	76.5%	26.2%	49.8%
2020	ATL	MLB	32	2	1	0	18	0	27¹	22	4	3.6	10.5	32	26.0%	.265	1.21	2.30	107	0.1	92.0	62.9%	29.6%	42.2%
2021 FS	ATL	MLB	33	2	2	0	57	0	50	37	7	3.0	10.4	57	33.0%	.258	1.09	2.91	73	0.9	92.1	65.8%	28.9%	43.9%
2021 DC	ATL	MLB	33	2	2	0	45	0	48	36	6	3.0	10.4	55	33.0%	.258	1.09	2.91	73	1.0	92.1	65.8%	28.9%	43.9%

Comparables: Justin Miller, Oliver Drake, Ryan Tepera

A broken toe cost Dayton a bigger role in Atlanta's bullpen in 2019, but given a new opportunity in 2020, he was one of Brian Snitker's better southpaw options, viciously handcuffing left-handed batters to the tune of a .398 OPS. That lefty-on-lefty success was about all Dayton had going for him, though. Right-handed hitters crushed him, his velocity is subpar and his stuff grades out as average. Despite throwing his curveball more often and with more break, the results were mediocre at best, with a .289 batting average against and a 22.7 percent whiff rate. Middle relief is almost certainly his ceiling, and he should be personally lobbying Rob Manfred to undo the three-batter minimum.

Jasseel De La Cruz RHP Born: 06/26/97 Age: 24 Bats: R Throws: R Height: 6'1" Weight: 195 Origin: International Free Agent, 2015

YEAR	TEAM	LVL	AGE	W	L	SV	G	GS	IP	H	HR	BB/9	K/9	K	GB%	BABIP	WHIP	ERA	DRA-	WARP	MPH	FA%	Whiff%	CSP
2018	ROM	LO-A	21	3	4	0	15	13	69	65	6	4.4	8.5	65	62.4%	.309	1.43	4.83	88	0.8				
2019	ROM	LO-A	22	0	1	0	4	4	18	19	1	2.5	11.0	22	51.1%	.391	1.33	2.50	96	0.1				
2019	FLO	HI-A	22	3	1	0	4	4	28	12	0	2.2	8.4	26	52.2%	.174	0.68	1.93	50	0.9				
2019	MIS	AA	22	4	7	0	17	16	87	71	7	3.8	7.6	73	45.4%	.263	1.24	3.83	96	0.3				
2021 FS	ATL	MLB	24	2	3	0	57	0	50	50	8	5.4	7.9	44	42.4%	.291	1.60	5.64	127	-0.6				
2021 DC	ATL	MLB	24	0	0	0	11	0	12	12	2	5.4	7.9	10	42.4%	.291	1.60	5.64	127	-0.1				

Comparables: Chad Bettis, Braden Shipley, John Gant

A live-armed righty with control issues, De La Cruz never got a chance to show his stuff in Atlanta after a solid 2019 despite being on the team's 40-man roster, spending all summer at the Braves' alternate site. A strong spring training likely lands him in the Opening Day bullpen.

Mike Foltynewicz RHP Born: 10/07/91 Age: 29 Bats: R Throws: R Height: 6'4" Weight: 195 Origin: Round 1, 2010 Draft (#19 overall)

YEAR	TEAM	LVL	AGE	W	L	SV	G	GS	IP	H	HR	BB/9	K/9	K	GB%	BABIP	WHIP	ERA	DRA-	WARP	MPH	FA%	Whiff%	CSP
2018	ATL	MLB	26	13	10	0	31	31	183	130	17	3.3	9.9	202	43.0%	.252	1.08	2.85	76	3.9	98.6	56.3%	25.4%	49.0%
2019	GWN	AAA	27	5	1	0	10	10	51¹	49	1	3.0	7.9	45	39.2%	.318	1.29	3.86	75	1.5				
2019	ATL	MLB	27	8	6	0	21	21	117	109	23	2.8	8.1	105	36.9%	.270	1.25	4.54	89	1.8	97.3	52.2%	23.5%	50.5%
2020	ATL	MLB	28	0	1	0	1	1	3¹	4	3	10.8	8.1	3	44.4%	.167	2.40	16.20	138	0.0	92.5	44.3%	14.3%	49.6%
2021 FS	ATL	MLB	29	2	2	0	57	0	50	46	7	3.4	8.6	47	39.0%	.283	1.31	4.11	99	0.2	97.7	53.7%	24.1%	49.8%

Comparables: Kevin Gausman, Trevor Williams, Jon Gray

On October 4, 2019, Foltynewicz shut out the Cardinals over seven innings, striking out seven, to win Game 2 of the NLDS. After that date, he was obliterated in that series' Game 5, giving up seven runs in the first inning; was hit hard in spring training and then again in summer camp; made all of one 2020 start in which he was hammered for six runs in 3⅓ innings and struggled to crack 90 mph with a fastball that once averaged 96 and was subsequently designated for assignment and banished to the Braves' alternate site. There he spent the remainder of the season, watching as his team traded for Tommy Milone for rotation help. Life, as the saying goes, comes at you fast, and in Foltynewicz's case, it ran into him like a freight train going light speed. Where he goes from here is anyone's guess.

Max Fried LHP Born: 01/18/94 Age: 27 Bats: L Throws: L Height: 6'4" Weight: 190 Origin: Round 1, 2012 Draft (#7 overall)

YEAR	TEAM	LVL	AGE	W	L	SV	G	GS	IP	H	HR	BB/9	K/9	K	GB%	BABIP	WHIP	ERA	DRA-	WARP	MPH	FA%	Whiff%	CSP
2018	MIS	AA	24	1	0	0	2	2	11¹	4	0	3.2	12.7	16	66.7%	.190	0.71	0.00	69	0.3				
2018	GWN	AAA	24	2	6	0	13	13	66¹	66	4	4.1	9.6	71	56.2%	.346	1.45	4.61	88	0.9				
2018	ATL	MLB	24	1	4	0	14	5	33²	26	3	5.3	11.8	44	50.0%	.324	1.37	2.94	73	0.7	96.3	58.7%	34.3%	48.1%
2019	ATL	MLB	25	17	6	0	33	30	165²	174	21	2.6	9.4	173	52.8%	.338	1.33	4.02	70	4.2	96.3	56.9%	26.0%	48.4%
2020	ATL	MLB	26	7	0	0	11	11	56	42	2	3.1	8.0	50	52.3%	.268	1.09	2.25	81	1.1	95.6	51.9%	25.6%	47.2%
2021 FS	ATL	MLB	27	9	8	0	26	26	150	141	18	3.6	9.5	157	52.8%	.304	1.34	4.12	95	1.5	96.1	55.5%	26.4%	48.0%
2021 DC	ATL	MLB	27	9	9	0	27	27	156	146	18	3.6	9.5	163	52.8%	.304	1.34	4.12	95	2.0	96.1	55.5%	26.4%	48.0%

Comparables: Anthony Banda, Chase De Jong, Eduardo Rodriguez

Fun fact: Fried's middle name is Dorian, which suggests that there's a ghastly portrait of him somewhere in the bowels of an abandoned Turner Field getting visibly older and uglier with every curveball he flicks. Set to turn 27 in January, Fried is somehow the grizzled veteran in Atlanta's rotation of baby geniuses, despite having thrown fewer innings in his career than Charlie Hough did in 1987. He was also one of the few reliable presences in a battered rotation, chipping in five or more innings each turn with regularity. Fried doesn't get the whiffs you want to see in a frontline pitcher thanks to his pedestrian fastball, but he's a master at avoiding hard contact and getting weak ground balls, and that curve remains a work of art.

Shane Greene RHP Born: 11/17/88 Age: 32 Bats: R Throws: R Height: 6'4" Weight: 200 Origin: Round 15, 2009 Draft (#465 overall)

YEAR	TEAM	LVL	AGE	W	L	SV	G	GS	IP	H	HR	BB/9	K/9	K	GB%	BABIP	WHIP	ERA	DRA-	WARP	MPH	FA%	Whiff%	CSP
2018	DET	MLB	29	4	6	32	66	0	63¹	68	12	2.7	9.2	65	41.1%	.311	1.37	5.12	87	0.7	96.0	50.8%	21.9%	51.1%
2019	DET	MLB	30	0	2	22	38	0	38	21	5	2.8	10.2	43	52.6%	.180	0.87	1.18	65	0.9	94.4	49.4%	26.6%	52.9%
2019	ATL	MLB	30	0	1	1	27	0	24²	25	3	1.8	7.7	21	38.4%	.314	1.22	4.01	89	0.3	93.6	43.3%	25.8%	49.2%
2020	ATL	MLB	31	1	0	0	28	0	27²	22	2	2.9	6.8	21	42.9%	.270	1.12	2.60	95	0.3	93.5	39.4%	20.0%	47.0%
2021 FS	ATL	MLB	32	2	2	0	57	0	50	46	7	3.1	8.5	47	44.2%	.286	1.27	3.93	97	0.2	94.5	45.8%	23.3%	50.1%

Comparables: Alex Colomé, Andrew Miller, Brandon Workman

No longer a closer and never blessed with the premium velocity that most closers have, Greene appears to have embraced his transition into middle relief by abandoning the results that made him a ninth-inning option in the first place. His strikeout rate of 19.3 percent landed him in the bottom fifth among qualified relievers, and his swinging-strike rate was a mere 7.5 percent. That decline in whiffs plus his age as he reaches free agency is like stripping the tires off of a used car, but Greene succeeded anyway thanks to a changeup he infrequently fiddled with in 2019 but used routinely in '20. That pitch was a winner: a .167 batting average against, a .227 expected wOBA and a 28 percent whiff rate. That'll help him keep hard contact away and, along with his ability to stymie righties, secure a spot as a sixth- or seventh-inning guy—his spiritual home all this time, as it turns out.

Cole Hamels   LHP   Born: 12/27/83   Age: 37   Bats: L   Throws: L   Height: 6'4"   Weight: 205   Origin: Round 1, 2002 Draft (#17 overall)

YEAR	TEAM	LVL	AGE	W	L	SV	G	GS	IP	H	HR	BB/9	K/9	K	GB%	BABIP	WHIP	ERA	DRA-	WARP	MPH	FA%	Whiff%	CSP
2018	CHC	MLB	34	4	3	0	12	12	76¹	61	6	2.7	8.7	74	46.2%	.288	1.10	2.36	77	1.6	94.5	67.8%	27.0%	46.3%
2018	TEX	MLB	34	5	9	0	20	20	114¹	115	23	3.3	9.0	114	44.3%	.296	1.37	4.72	115	0.2	93.4	60.3%	27.1%	45.8%
2019	CHC	MLB	35	7	7	0	27	27	141²	141	17	3.6	9.0	142	45.4%	.319	1.39	3.81	99	1.4	93.0	66.3%	27.5%	47.5%
2020	ATL	MLB	36	0	1	0	1	1	3¹	3	0	2.7	5.4	2	36.4%	.273	1.20	8.10	124	0.0	90.3	55.8%	28.0%	48.1%
2021 FS	ATL	MLB	37	8	9	0	26	26	150	148	23	4.1	8.6	143	44.8%	.297	1.44	4.76	111	0.2	93.3	64.9%	27.4%	46.9%

Comparables: Zack Greinke, Aníbal Sánchez, Justin Verlander

All we saw and heard of Hamels in 2020—and likely the entirety of his Braves career—were intermittent appearances at training camp and one 3⅓ inning start in September. Tendinitis in his left triceps was the persistent bugaboo, and worrisomely, it morphed into shoulder fatigue that put an end to his season before it ever got a chance to begin. A full offseason of rest can only help, but at 37 years old and with stuff and peripherals on the decline, Hamels will have to prove he can handle the burdens of a rotation spot before he'll be given another one.

Félix Hernández   RHP   Born: 04/08/86   Age: 35   Bats: R   Throws: R   Height: 6'3"   Weight: 208   Origin: International Free Agent, 2002

YEAR	TEAM	LVL	AGE	W	L	SV	G	GS	IP	H	HR	BB/9	K/9	K	GB%	BABIP	WHIP	ERA	DRA-	WARP	MPH	FA%	Whiff%	CSP
2018	SEA	MLB	32	8	14	0	29	28	155²	159	27	3.4	7.2	125	46.5%	.288	1.40	5.55	118	0.0	91.1	43.3%	19.8%	45.3%
2019	SEA	MLB	33	1	8	0	15	15	71²	85	17	3.1	7.2	57	48.5%	.311	1.53	6.40	145	-1.0	91.4	39.5%	21.8%	49.6%
2021 FS	ATL	MLB	35	2	3	0	57	0	50	49	7	3.4	8.0	44	47.3%	.293	1.36	4.46	106	0.0	91.2	41.4%	20.8%	47.4%

Comparables: Jake Peavy, Josh Beckett, Cole Hamels

We never got a chance to see what Hernández was capable of in his first season outside of Seattle, as the former Cy Young winner opted out of the season owing to COVID-19 concerns. That's probably for the best: The thought of him in a non-Mariners uniform is genuinely upsetting.

Luke Jackson   RHP   Born: 08/24/91   Age: 29   Bats: R   Throws: R   Height: 6'2"   Weight: 210   Origin: Round 1, 2010 Draft (#45 overall)

YEAR	TEAM	LVL	AGE	W	L	SV	G	GS	IP	H	HR	BB/9	K/9	K	GB%	BABIP	WHIP	ERA	DRA-	WARP	MPH	FA%	Whiff%	CSP
2018	GWN	AAA	26	2	1	0	10	1	21¹	11	0	4.2	14.3	34	42.1%	.289	0.98	1.69	38	0.8				
2018	ATL	MLB	26	1	2	1	35	0	40²	41	3	4.6	10.2	46	47.8%	.342	1.52	4.43	129	-0.4	96.1	41.7%	25.2%	42.7%
2019	ATL	MLB	27	9	2	18	70	0	72²	76	10	3.2	13.1	106	59.1%	.388	1.40	3.84	65	1.7	97.4	37.9%	36.8%	42.1%
2020	ATL	MLB	28	2	0	0	19	0	26¹	39	2	4.4	6.8	20	61.9%	.389	1.97	6.84	84	0.5	95.8	37.4%	23.2%	42.7%
2021 FS	ATL	MLB	29	2	2	0	57	0	50	46	5	3.8	9.3	51	53.9%	.300	1.35	3.97	92	0.3	96.7	38.3%	30.7%	42.4%
2021 DC	ATL	MLB	29	2	2	0	45	0	48	44	5	3.8	9.3	49	53.9%	.300	1.35	3.97	92	0.5	96.7	38.3%	30.7%	42.4%

Comparables: Austin Brice, Kevin McCarthy, Michael Lorenzen

Jackson has both the name and appearance of a guy who writes mildly popular songs about how relationships are like busting horses or fixing tractors that slot somewhere in the 20s on Billboard's country charts. Given how badly things went last season, he may want to consider picking up a six-string and seeing what he can eke out of it. An out-of-nowhere relief ace for the first half of 2019, Jackson slammed back to earth after the beginning of July and continued drilling through the soil in 2020, with equally huge drops in strikeout rate and fastball velocity. He can still get the ground balls, but that's it; that outstanding whiff rate that elevated his game in 2019 looks like the outlier. He's a mediocre middle reliever until proven otherwise, or until he teams up with Brooks and Dunn to record a new Braves team anthem.

Chris Martin   RHP   Born: 06/02/86   Age: 35   Bats: R   Throws: R   Height: 6'8"   Weight: 225   Origin: Round 21, 2005 Draft (#627 overall)

YEAR	TEAM	LVL	AGE	W	L	SV	G	GS	IP	H	HR	BB/9	K/9	K	GB%	BABIP	WHIP	ERA	DRA-	WARP	MPH	FA%	Whiff%	CSP
2018	TEX	MLB	32	1	5	0	46	0	41²	46	5	1.1	8.0	37	40.9%	.323	1.22	4.54	118	-0.2	96.8	72.3%	20.4%	50.8%
2019	TEX	MLB	33	0	2	4	38	0	38	35	8	0.9	10.2	43	50.0%	.293	1.03	3.08	66	0.9	97.4	82.4%	25.5%	55.1%
2019	ATL	MLB	33	1	1	0	20	0	17²	17	1	0.5	11.2	22	52.2%	.356	1.02	4.08	58	0.5	96.8	70.6%	28.0%	49.5%
2020	ATL	MLB	34	1	1	1	19	0	18	8	1	1.5	10.0	20	38.1%	.171	0.61	1.00	82	0.3	95.4	63.3%	26.7%	48.6%
2021 FS	ATL	MLB	35	2	2	3	57	0	50	45	6	1.8	9.3	51	44.1%	.292	1.11	3.20	80	0.7	96.7	73.2%	25.2%	51.5%
2021 DC	ATL	MLB	35	2	2	3	51	0	54	49	6	1.8	9.3	55	44.1%	.292	1.11	3.20	80	0.9	96.7	73.2%	25.2%	51.5%

Comparables: Javy Guerra, Dan Otero, David Hernandez

Most people come back from vacations toting souvenirs; Martin returned stateside in 2018 with a splitter, and it's proven to be a valuable acquisition. His path to success is simple: Keep the ball down and avoid walks. Martin executed that to perfection last season, making him a valuable setup piece. Good luck sorting out his arsenal, but it's clear there's no need to fix him. (Sorry, I'm sorry, I'm trying to remove it.)

Tyler Matzek LHP Born: 10/19/90 Age: 30 Bats: L Throws: L Height: 6'3" Weight: 230 Origin: Round 1, 2009 Draft (#11 overall)

YEAR	TEAM	LVL	AGE	W	L	SV	G	GS	IP	H	HR	BB/9	K/9	K	GB%	BABIP	WHIP	ERA	DRA-	WARP	MPH	FA%	Whiff%	CSP
2019	GWN	AAA	28	0	0	0	5	0	10	10	1	4.5	11.7	13	48.1%	.360	1.50	9.00	79	0.2				
2020	ATL	MLB	29	4	3	0	21	0	29	23	1	3.1	13.3	43	45.5%	.338	1.14	2.79	59	0.9	96.4	70.8%	27.6%	47.4%
2021 FS	ATL	MLB	30	2	2	1	57	0	50	41	6	5.0	11.3	62	44.5%	.294	1.38	4.14	94	0.3	96.4	70.8%	27.6%	47.4%
2021 DC	ATL	MLB	30	2	2	1	45	0	48	39	5	5.0	11.3	60	44.5%	.294	1.38	4.14	94	0.4	96.4	70.8%	27.6%	47.4%

Comparables: Kevin Gausman, Allen Webster, Erasmo Ramírez

Prior to 2020, the last time anyone had seen Matzek on a major league mound was five years ago, when he made five starts for the Rockies and walked 19 batters in 15 innings. Injuries, struggles with an anxiety disorder and a long slow bounce around the pros followed, including two separate stints with the indy league Texas AirHogs. Most busted first-round picks see their story end there, but Matzek proved such an exemplary AirHog that he landed a minor league deal with Atlanta in 2019, then completed his improbable resurrection by making the Braves' roster out of summer camp and dominating as a setup man. With newfound velocity and a slider-first approach, he's a ghost who found his way back to the land of the living, and one of the best success stories of the last decade. Kudos to him.

Mark Melancon RHP Born: 03/28/85 Age: 36 Bats: R Throws: R Height: 6'1" Weight: 215 Origin: Round 9, 2006 Draft (#284 overall)

YEAR	TEAM	LVL	AGE	W	L	SV	G	GS	IP	H	HR	BB/9	K/9	K	GB%	BABIP	WHIP	ERA	DRA-	WARP	MPH	FA%	Whiff%	CSP
2018	SF	MLB	33	1	4	3	41	0	39	48	2	3.2	7.2	31	50.8%	.365	1.59	3.23	80	0.6	92.9	68.3%	23.2%	46.2%
2019	SF	MLB	34	4	2	1	43	0	46¹	49	3	3.1	8.5	44	60.2%	.354	1.40	3.50	90	0.5	93.4	68.8%	24.8%	44.7%
2019	ATL	MLB	34	1	0	11	23	0	21	22	1	0.9	10.3	24	61.9%	.339	1.14	3.86	44	0.7	93.4	61.2%	27.9%	44.9%
2020	ATL	MLB	35	2	1	11	23	0	22²	22	1	2.8	5.6	14	58.3%	.300	1.28	2.78	89	0.3	93.3	57.9%	19.6%	46.6%
2021 FS	ATL	MLB	36	2	2	0	57	0	50	49	5	2.9	7.2	40	56.1%	.296	1.32	3.77	92	0.3	93.3	64.5%	23.7%	45.5%

Comparables: Luke Gregerson, Mariano Rivera, Will Harris

A philosophical quandary for you: Can you be a successful closer if you don't strike anyone out? Like a tree falling in an empty forest, Melancon is a conundrum. On the one hand, his strikeout rate dropped to a preposterously low 14.7 percent last season, seventh-worst in the majors among qualified relievers. On the other, he gave up a single home run all season and was scored upon in just five of 23 appearances. Melancon leans on a cutter that's far too hittable, but also throws a curveball that no one can touch. Now a free agent, general managers will pore over his seemingly contradictory stats to see if they can figure out how to get this particular goose out of the bottle. Easy, Melancon would retort: Just say, it's out.

Tommy Milone LHP Born: 02/16/87 Age: 34 Bats: L Throws: L Height: 6'0" Weight: 215 Origin: Round 10, 2008 Draft (#301 overall)

YEAR	TEAM	LVL	AGE	W	L	SV	G	GS	IP	H	HR	BB/9	K/9	K	GB%	BABIP	WHIP	ERA	DRA-	WARP	MPH	FA%	Whiff%	CSP
2018	SYR	AAA	31	7	4	0	20	20	109²	101	11	2.0	9.3	113	35.1%	.304	1.14	4.19	69	2.6				
2018	WAS	MLB	31	1	1	0	5	4	26¹	37	7	0.3	7.9	23	26.9%	.357	1.44	5.81	103	0.2	88.5	58.9%	23.3%	46.9%
2019	TAC	AAA	32	4	2	0	9	8	49¹	49	7	2.2	7.8	43	38.3%	.286	1.24	3.83	62	1.7				
2019	SEA	MLB	32	4	10	0	23	6	111²	102	24	1.9	7.6	94	36.8%	.252	1.12	4.76	116	-0.3	88.3	43.7%	22.2%	46.0%
2020	ATL	MLB	33	1	4	0	9	9	39	55	9	1.4	9.2	40	33.8%	.374	1.56	6.69	122	-0.1	87.5	45.3%	27.7%	45.8%
2021 FS	ATL	MLB	34	2	3	0	57	0	50	50	9	1.8	7.9	43	36.1%	.290	1.22	4.08	102	0.1	88.0	45.4%	24.3%	46.0%

Comparables: Homer Bailey, Wade Miley, Iván Nova

Spiritually a member of the Orioles for the last five years or so, Milone finally realized his destiny by joining Baltimore's patchwork rotation (and made a bid to become the internet's favorite pitcher by changing his uniform number to 69). Unfortunately, this match made in heaven was broken up by Atlanta's desperate need for starters, but Milone was unable to replicate his surprising success in Charm City with the Braves, getting torched for 16 runs in 9⅔ frames before a sore left elbow landed him on the injured list. The solution here is clear: Return Milone to where he belongs, which is throwing five mediocre innings per start as an Oriole until the sky collapses, and restore order to this particular slice of the universe.

A.J. Minter LHP Born: 09/02/93 Age: 27 Bats: L Throws: L Height: 6'0" Weight: 215 Origin: Round 2, 2015 Draft (#75 overall)

YEAR	TEAM	LVL	AGE	W	L	SV	G	GS	IP	H	HR	BB/9	K/9	K	GB%	BABIP	WHIP	ERA	DRA-	WARP	MPH	FA%	Whiff%	CSP
2018	ATL	MLB	24	4	3	15	65	0	61¹	57	3	3.2	10.1	69	37.7%	.331	1.29	3.23	76	1.1	98.3	49.0%	32.0%	47.9%
2019	GWN	AAA	25	2	2	5	20	0	22²	24	4	1.2	11.9	30	37.7%	.351	1.19	3.57	55	0.8				
2019	ATL	MLB	25	3	4	5	36	0	29¹	36	3	7.1	10.7	35	38.6%	.393	2.01	7.06	122	-0.2	97.5	39.3%	30.5%	45.3%
2020	ATL	MLB	26	1	1	0	22	0	21²	15	1	3.7	10.0	24	48.1%	.280	1.11	0.83	80	0.4	97.0	38.8%	29.1%	46.4%
2021 FS	ATL	MLB	27	2	2	3	57	0	50	42	6	3.8	10.7	59	40.4%	.290	1.27	3.65	88	0.5	97.6	42.0%	30.5%	46.5%
2021 DC	ATL	MLB	27	2	2	3	45	0	48	40	6	3.8	10.7	56	40.4%	.290	1.27	3.65	88	0.6	97.6	42.0%	30.5%	46.5%

Comparables: Aaron Bummer, Keynan Middleton, Edubray Ramos

A wild burst of, well, wildness dropped A.J. Minter from Craig Kimbrel's heir as unhittable closer in Atlanta to low-leverage project and Triple-A outcast in 2019. The lefty responded to that year from hell by pretending it never happened, quietly returning to effective setup reliever status. Buoyed by better command of his cutter and four-seamer, Minter sliced his walk rate and got more ground balls. That sets him up well to realize the role he was initially pegged for when he burst onto the scene in 2017—assuming, that is, that he doesn't flip back into the 2019 version of himself that couldn't throw a strike to save his life.

Charlie Morton RHP Born: 11/12/83 Age: 37 Bats: R Throws: R Height: 6'5" Weight: 215 Origin: Round 3, 2002 Draft (#95 overall)

YEAR	TEAM	LVL	AGE	W	L	SV	G	GS	IP	H	HR	BB/9	K/9	K	GB%	BABIP	WHIP	ERA	DRA-	WARP	MPH	FA%	Whiff%	CSP
2018	HOU	MLB	34	15	3	0	30	30	167	130	18	3.4	10.8	201	47.8%	.284	1.16	3.13	82	3.1	97.5	63.5%	28.7%	48.3%
2019	TB	MLB	35	16	6	0	33	33	194²	154	15	2.6	11.1	240	47.8%	.299	1.08	3.05	60	5.9	96.1	50.2%	29.6%	50.0%
2020	TB	MLB	36	2	2	0	9	9	38	43	4	2.4	9.9	42	42.1%	.355	1.39	4.74	80	0.7	95.6	56.4%	25.0%	52.1%
2021 FS	*ATL*	*MLB*	*37*	*9*	*8*	*0*	*26*	*26*	*150*	*135*	*17*	*3.1*	*9.8*	*163*	*46.1%*	*.299*	*1.25*	*3.80*	*90*	*1.9*	*96.3*	*54.6%*	*28.6%*	*50.0%*
2021 DC	*ATL*	*MLB*	*37*	*8*	*8*	*0*	*25*	*25*	*137*	*124*	*16*	*3.1*	*9.8*	*148*	*46.1%*	*.299*	*1.25*	*3.80*	*90*	*2.2*	*96.3*	*54.6%*	*28.6%*	*50.0%*

Comparables: Aníbal Sánchez, Kyle Lohse, Aaron Sele

Morton had an eventful few weeks last fall. He started Game 7 of the ALCS, guiding the Rays to their second pennant in franchise history. He then had his club option declined, at which point the Rays and the Braves engaged in a bidding war for his services. The Braves won that by paying him the exact amount the Rays refused to ($15 million). As a result, it appears that he'll finish his career in Atlanta, right where it started. Morton's velocity dipped last season as he battled shoulder woes, and it's worth wondering how much he has left. That being said, few active pitchers are as intelligent or thoughtful about their craft as he is, so rest assured that he'll get the most of whatever the amount is.

──────────── ★ ★ ★ *2021 Top 101 Prospect* **#62** ★ ★ ★ ────────────

Kyle Muller LHP Born: 10/07/97 Age: 23 Bats: R Throws: L Height: 6'7" Weight: 250 Origin: Round 2, 2016 Draft (#44 overall)

YEAR	TEAM	LVL	AGE	W	L	SV	G	GS	IP	H	HR	BB/9	K/9	K	GB%	BABIP	WHIP	ERA	DRA-	WARP	MPH	FA%	Whiff%	CSP
2018	ROM	LO-A	20	3	0	0	6	6	30	24	3	2.4	6.9	23	50.0%	.256	1.07	2.40	99	0.2				
2018	FLO	HI-A	20	4	2	0	14	14	80²	80	2	3.6	8.8	79	39.6%	.355	1.39	3.24	98	0.5				
2018	DAY	HI-A	20	2	0	0	2	2	13	10	0	2.8	11.1	16		.357	1.08	0.00						
2018	MIS	AA	20	4	1	0	5	5	29	22	3	1.9	8.4	27	35.8%	.247	0.97	3.10	89	0.4				
2019	MIS	AA	21	7	6	0	22	22	111²	81	5	5.5	9.7	120	39.2%	.286	1.33	3.14	99	0.1				
2021 FS	*ATL*	*MLB*	*23*	*1*	*1*	*0*	*57*	*0*	*50*	*47*	*8*	*5.3*	*8.6*	*48*	*38.3%*	*.289*	*1.55*	*5.22*	*121*	*-0.5*				
2021 DC	*ATL*	*MLB*	*23*	*1*	*1*	*0*	*4*	*4*	*19*	*18*	*3*	*5.3*	*8.6*	*18*	*38.3%*	*.289*	*1.55*	*5.22*	*121*	*0.0*				

Comparables: Rony García, Luis Severino, Jayson Aquino

Part of the same draft class that produced Ian Anderson, Muller wasn't able to replicate his erstwhile teammate's major league success, remaining at the Braves' alternate site all summer. For most teams, the alternate site was a source of mystery, but with Atlanta bleeding out pitchers over the fall, any in-house option that failed to escape its gravitational pull has to be treated with some suspicion. Some daylight and game experience can only help the lefty on his quest to join the rotation alongside Anderson, as opposed to pre-2020 projections that had him in the bullpen long-term as a power arm from the left side.

Sean Newcomb LHP Born: 06/12/93 Age: 28 Bats: L Throws: L Height: 6'5" Weight: 255 Origin: Round 1, 2014 Draft (#15 overall)

YEAR	TEAM	LVL	AGE	W	L	SV	G	GS	IP	H	HR	BB/9	K/9	K	GB%	BABIP	WHIP	ERA	DRA-	WARP	MPH	FA%	Whiff%	CSP
2018	ATL	MLB	25	12	9	0	31	30	164	137	18	4.4	8.8	160	42.7%	.275	1.33	3.90	85	2.8	95.4	62.4%	24.9%	46.3%
2019	GWN	AAA	26	2	1	0	4	3	20²	14	1	2.2	8.7	20	45.5%	.241	0.92	2.18	45	0.9				
2019	ATL	MLB	26	6	3	1	55	4	68¹	61	8	3.8	8.6	65	49.5%	.282	1.32	3.16	84	1.0	96.6	65.2%	22.9%	48.9%
2020	ATL	MLB	27	0	2	0	4	4	13²	20	4	4.0	6.6	10	35.3%	.340	1.90	11.20	143	-0.2	95.0	54.0%	20.3%	44.0%
2021 FS	*ATL*	*MLB*	*28*	*2*	*2*	*0*	*57*	*0*	*50*	*46*	*6*	*4.7*	*8.8*	*49*	*43.5%*	*.290*	*1.46*	*4.61*	*104*	*0.0*	*95.8*	*62.2%*	*23.5%*	*47.0%*
2021 DC	*ATL*	*MLB*	*28*	*2*	*2*	*0*	*31*	*3*	*43*	*40*	*5*	*4.7*	*8.8*	*42*	*43.5%*	*.290*	*1.46*	*4.61*	*104*	*0.2*	*95.8*	*62.2%*	*23.5%*	*47.0%*

Comparables: Nick Pivetta, Jordan Montgomery, Cody Reed

What does the future hold for Newcomb? A switch in 2019 from the rotation to the bullpen led to solid results; going back into the rotation this season was a full-on disaster. The biggest culprit is a fastball that was tagged for a .759 slugging percentage, offsetting all the good done by his increased usage of his changeup to go with the curveball that put him on the prospect map. None of those secondary pitches matter if your heater is getting blasted, though, and now the question becomes whether Newcomb gets one more shot as a starter or is bullpen-bound for good. His 2020 numbers don't suggest he's suited for anything other than relief.

Darren O'Day RHP Born: 10/22/82 Age: 38 Bats: R Throws: R Height: 6'4" Weight: 220 Origin: Undrafted Free Agent, 2006

YEAR	TEAM	LVL	AGE	W	L	SV	G	GS	IP	H	HR	BB/9	K/9	K	GB%	BABIP	WHIP	ERA	DRA-	WARP	MPH	FA%	Whiff%	CSP
2018	BAL	MLB	35	0	2	2	20	0	20	18	3	1.8	12.2	27	24.5%	.326	1.10	3.60	82	0.3	88.1	52.1%	25.9%	51.5%
2019	ATL	MLB	36	0	0	0	8	0	5¹	3	0	1.7	10.1	6	23.1%	.231	0.75	1.69	103	0.0	87.8	55.1%	35.0%	47.8%
2020	ATL	MLB	37	4	0	0	19	0	16¹	8	1	2.8	12.1	22	27.0%	.194	0.80	1.10	90	0.2	87.2	57.1%	31.9%	43.7%
2021 FS	*ATL*	*MLB*	*38*	*3*	*2*	*0*	*57*	*0*	*50*	*39*	*6*	*2.5*	*10.7*	*59*	*33.8%*	*.273*	*1.07*	*2.84*	*74*	*0.9*	*87.5*	*55.6%*	*30.8%*	*46.2%*

Comparables: Kyle Farnsworth, Dan Plesac, Pat Neshek

The year is 2048. Across the irradiated plains of the United States, desperate bands of survivors cling together and fight over access to water in the parched deserts of the Midwest. In the bombed-out remains of Washington, D.C., Emperor Barron Trump issues a decree condemning all haters and losers to death. Resistance fighters are preparing an offensive from New New York to overthrow his despotic regime. O'Day is wrapping up his 41st season on his 23rd different team as a middle reliever who handcuffs right-handers. His fastball now travels 72 mph. Opposing hitters bat .128 against it.

Jared Shuster **LHP**   Born: 08/03/98   Age: 22   Bats: L   Throws: L   Height: 6'3"   Weight: 210   Origin: Round 1, 2020 Draft (#25 overall)

A somewhat underslot pick out of Wake Forest, Shuster employed a dominant 2019 stint in the Cape and a strong 2020 college season to force his way up draft boards. He found his way into the first round after looking good in four starts for the Demon Deacons before the college season came to an early end, showing improved velocity and stuff. The lefty's problem as a freshman and sophomore was walks—58 free passes in 102 innings over those two seasons—so it's encouraging to see that he handed out just five walks in seven starts in the Cape Cod League in 2019, then walked only four batters in 26⅓ innings in his final year at Wake Forest. Assuming the 2021 season is something closer to normal, he'll likely head to Single-A next spring to work on developing his secondary pitches and showing that his newfound control is no fluke.

Will Smith **LHP**   Born: 07/10/89   Age: 31   Bats: R   Throws: L   Height: 6'5"   Weight: 255   Origin: Round 7, 2008 Draft (#229 overall)

YEAR	TEAM	LVL	AGE	W	L	SV	G	GS	IP	H	HR	BB/9	K/9	K	GB%	BABIP	WHIP	ERA	DRA-	WARP	MPH	FA%	Whiff%	CSP
2018	SAC	AAA	28	0	0	0	6	0	5²	2	0	0.0	12.7	8	27.3%	.182	0.35	0.00	73	0.1				
2018	SF	MLB	28	2	3	14	54	0	53	37	3	2.5	12.1	71	38.7%	.286	0.98	2.55	74	1.0	94.3	46.1%	31.9%	50.7%
2019	SF	MLB	29	6	0	34	63	0	65¹	46	10	2.9	13.2	96	42.1%	.277	1.03	2.76	58	1.8	94.3	47.0%	34.4%	45.4%
2020	ATL	MLB	30	2	2	0	18	0	16	11	7	2.2	10.1	18	30.0%	.121	0.94	4.50	122	0.0	94.3	45.2%	36.7%	44.3%
2021 FS	ATL	MLB	31	2	2	28	57	0	50	39	6	3.0	11.5	63	38.7%	.280	1.11	2.94	74	0.9	94.3	46.4%	34.3%	46.3%
2021 DC	ATL	MLB	31	2	2	28	51	0	54	42	7	3.0	11.5	68	38.7%	.280	1.11	2.94	74	1.1	94.3	46.4%	34.3%	46.3%

Comparables: Jeurys Familia, Erasmo Ramírez, Trevor May

Smith probably wishes he'd stayed in the wild wild NL West for his entire career (sorry). One of the first major free agents off the board last winter, his transition from San Francisco to Atlanta didn't go off all that well; the velocity was fine, and the swings-and-misses were there. His slider wasn't, losing a lot of its sharpness and downward tilt, as opposing batters slugged a Bonds-ian .737 on that pitch despite a whiff rate of 55 percent, suggesting that both they and Smith had about the same idea of where his breaker was going once it left his hand. Add that to fewer first-pitch strikes, more fly balls and fewer swings outside the strike zone, and you can see why Smith's hard-hit rate was a not-so-jiggy 45 percent. (Again, sorry.) There's a lot in there to tweak and fix for Smith to resume being a trustworthy setup man.

Drew Smyly **LHP**   Born: 06/13/89   Age: 32   Bats: L   Throws: L   Height: 6'2"   Weight: 188   Origin: Round 2, 2010 Draft (#68 overall)

YEAR	TEAM	LVL	AGE	W	L	SV	G	GS	IP	H	HR	BB/9	K/9	K	GB%	BABIP	WHIP	ERA	DRA-	WARP	MPH	FA%	Whiff%	CSP
2019	SA	AAA	30	1	0	0	3	3	12²	10	2	2.1	12.8	18	27.6%	.308	1.03	4.97	51	0.5				
2019	PHI	MLB	30	3	2	0	12	12	62²	62	13	3.0	9.8	68	39.3%	.310	1.32	4.45	104	0.4	93.3	43.1%	27.9%	44.3%
2019	TEX	MLB	30	1	5	1	13	9	51¹	64	19	6.0	9.1	52	28.0%	.310	1.91	8.42	198	-2.2	92.5	52.8%	23.9%	48.7%
2020	SF	MLB	31	0	1	0	7	5	26¹	20	2	3.1	14.4	42	41.7%	.310	1.10	3.42	64	0.7	95.4	45.6%	34.7%	50.1%
2021 FS	ATL	MLB	32	9	8	0	26	26	150	124	24	3.5	11.2	185	34.9%	.283	1.22	3.61	87	2.2	93.6	47.4%	28.2%	47.4%
2021 DC	ATL	MLB	32	4	4	0	14	14	72	59	11	3.5	11.2	89	34.9%	.283	1.22	3.61	87	1.3	93.6	47.4%	28.2%	47.4%

Comparables: Tyler Thornburg, Anthony Bass, Alex Colomé

There's a narrative beat in many superhero films when the protagonist who discovers superpowers shortly thereafter finds out about a weakness, limit or downside to those powers: Superman, meet Kryptonite. Avengers, sorry about that Thanos snap. Between the moment of discovery and the reassertion of vulnerability exists a giddy state of euphoria: Could this be real? Is it me doing these things? We shouldn't blame the injury-plagued Smyly if he feels that way after rediscovering a fastball that tickles the mid-90s, which he mainly paired with his looping, 80 mph curve to devastating effect. For his brief time on the mound in 2020, this late-career velocity surge helped turn him into a dominant whiff-machine. It's all-too easy to see the foreshadowing of the coming *hamartia* in Smyly's checkered injury past, or in his difficulty navigating through an opposing lineup a third time. His recent powers, however, should be enough to merit the free agent a look by any team whose rotation is more *Galaxy Quest* than *Justice League*.

Chad Sobotka **RHP**   Born: 07/10/93   Age: 27   Bats: R   Throws: R   Height: 6'7"   Weight: 225   Origin: Round 4, 2014 Draft (#133 overall)

YEAR	TEAM	LVL	AGE	W	L	SV	G	GS	IP	H	HR	BB/9	K/9	K	GB%	BABIP	WHIP	ERA	DRA-	WARP	MPH	FA%	Whiff%	CSP
2018	FLO	HI-A	24	2	0	2	13	1	20¹	9	0	3.1	12.4	28	37.5%	.225	0.79	2.21	43	0.7				
2018	MIS	AA	24	2	3	6	22	0	28	16	1	4.2	11.9	37	30.0%	.259	1.04	1.93	45	0.9				
2018	GWN	AAA	24	0	0	3	9	0	9¹	5	0	8.7	11.6	12	38.1%	.238	1.50	1.93	75	0.1				
2018	ATL	MLB	24	1	0	0	14	0	14¹	5	2	5.7	13.2	21	28.6%	.120	0.98	1.88	53	0.4	98.1	63.6%	30.7%	47.2%
2019	GWN	AAA	25	2	1	2	17	0	20²	23	3	1.7	13.9	32	46.2%	.408	1.31	4.79	64	0.6				
2019	ATL	MLB	25	0	0	0	32	0	29	28	6	5.9	11.8	38	44.6%	.324	1.62	6.21	92	0.3	97.9	56.6%	35.1%	41.7%
2020	ATL	MLB	26	0	0	0	4	0	3²	6	0	4.9	4.9	2	18.8%	.375	2.18	12.27	131	0.0	96.1	62.5%	12.1%	48.9%
2021 FS	ATL	MLB	27	1	1	0	57	0	50	42	7	5.2	10.6	58	38.9%	.286	1.44	4.61	104	0.0	97.7	58.5%	31.0%	43.6%
2021 DC	ATL	MLB	27	1	1	0	34	0	36	30	5	5.2	10.6	42	38.9%	.286	1.44	4.61	104	0.1	97.7	58.5%	31.0%	43.6%

Comparables: Keynan Middleton, James Norwood, Edubray Ramos

Given that 2020 was a leap year, it's understandable that everyone might have one day they'd like to remove to return to a more standard 365. Sobotka would pick September 5, when he gave up five earned runs in two-thirds of an inning, moving his season ERA from a pristine 0.00 to 12.27. He didn't pitch again the rest of the way.

Mike Soroka RHP   Born: 08/04/97   Age: 23   Bats: R   Throws: R   Height: 6'5"   Weight: 225   Origin: Round 1, 2015 Draft (#28 overall)

YEAR	TEAM	LVL	AGE	W	L	SV	G	GS	IP	H	HR	BB/9	K/9	K	GB%	BABIP	WHIP	ERA	DRA-	WARP	MPH	FA%	Whiff%	CSP
2018	GWN	AAA	20	2	1	0	5	5	27	20	0	2.0	10.3	31	70.1%	.299	0.96	2.00	59	0.8				
2018	ATL	MLB	20	2	1	0	5	5	25²	30	1	2.5	7.4	21	43.5%	.349	1.44	3.51	103	0.2	94.4	68.9%	22.2%	48.8%
2019	GWN	AAA	21	1	0	0	2	2	9¹	5	1	1.0	9.6	10	72.7%	.190	0.64	3.86	45	0.4				
2019	ATL	MLB	21	13	4	0	29	29	174²	153	14	2.1	7.3	142	50.6%	.282	1.11	2.68	66	4.8	94.5	63.3%	22.7%	47.7%
2020	ATL	MLB	22	0	1	0	3	3	13²	11	0	4.6	5.3	8	61.0%	.268	1.32	3.95	94	0.2	94.3	59.3%	22.6%	47.2%
2021 FS	ATL	MLB	23	9	8	0	26	26	150	151	18	2.9	7.6	127	51.5%	.300	1.33	4.21	98	1.2	94.5	63.3%	22.7%	47.7%
2021 DC	ATL	MLB	23	9	10	0	27	27	156	157	18	2.9	7.6	132	51.5%	.300	1.33	4.21	98	1.8	94.5	63.3%	22.7%	47.7%

Comparables: Brett Anderson, Madison Bumgarner, Roger Clemens

Soroka, we hardly knew ya: The breakout star of Atlanta's 2019 campaign made it all of three starts into 2020 before he tore his right Achilles tendon in early August, knocking him out for the rest of the year. It's not worth reading into his results too much, given how puny a sample size we're talking about; more important is that his stuff looked much the same as they did the year prior (though his fastball remains alarmingly straight). Assuming a full recovery from surgery, the baby-faced Canadian will resume his place atop the Braves' rotation alongside fellow tots Anderson and Fried. Still just 23, his future remains incandescent so long as he avoids further injury.

Josh Tomlin RHP   Born: 10/19/84   Age: 36   Bats: R   Throws: R   Height: 6'1"   Weight: 190   Origin: Round 19, 2006 Draft (#581 overall)

YEAR	TEAM	LVL	AGE	W	L	SV	G	GS	IP	H	HR	BB/9	K/9	K	GB%	BABIP	WHIP	ERA	DRA-	WARP	MPH	FA%	Whiff%	CSP
2018	COL	AAA	33	0	1	0	3	3	9¹	19	3	0.0	7.7	8	34.2%	.457	2.04	6.75	102	0.1				
2018	CLE	MLB	33	2	5	0	32	9	70¹	92	25	1.5	5.9	46	31.7%	.286	1.48	6.14	153	-1.4	89.5	72.5%	19.3%	50.0%
2019	ATL	MLB	34	2	1	2	51	1	79¹	82	14	0.8	5.8	51	33.2%	.279	1.12	3.74	108	0.1	90.5	74.0%	19.9%	47.4%
2020	ATL	MLB	35	2	2	0	17	5	39²	40	6	1.8	8.2	36	38.1%	.306	1.21	4.76	94	0.5	89.3	70.1%	22.9%	49.0%
2021 FS	ATL	MLB	36	2	3	0	57	0	50	54	10	1.6	7.1	39	36.5%	.294	1.26	4.59	110	-0.1	89.9	72.4%	20.8%	48.5%
2021 DC	ATL	MLB	36	2	3	0	43	3	55	59	11	1.6	7.1	43	36.5%	.294	1.26	4.59	110	0.1	89.9	72.4%	20.8%	48.5%

Comparables: Ian Kennedy, Jason Vargas, Jason Hammel

That Tomlin finished second on the Braves in innings pitched in 2020 is as easy a way as any to show how utterly pear-shaped things got for them, pitching-wise. That he was one of their more reliable arms gets the point across too. The veteran righty wasn't able to keep up the entirety of the late-career resurgence that was his 2019 in Atlanta, though the fact that he's still contributing at age 35 and with a fastball that putters in at 88 mph is something of a miracle on its own. Perhaps aware that you can't live life in the slow lane, Tomlin threw more cutters and curveballs into the mix, but his gains—a big spike in strikeout rate—were offset by poor results on those pitches anyway, particularly the curve. There's value in what he offers, which is to say gobbling up innings like Mr. Creosote, but league-average work is the best you can hope for.

Touki Toussaint RHP   Born: 06/20/96   Age: 25   Bats: R   Throws: R   Height: 6'3"   Weight: 215   Origin: Round 1, 2014 Draft (#16 overall)

YEAR	TEAM	LVL	AGE	W	L	SV	G	GS	IP	H	HR	BB/9	K/9	K	GB%	BABIP	WHIP	ERA	DRA-	WARP	MPH	FA%	Whiff%	CSP
2018	MIS	AA	22	4	6	0	16	16	86	66	7	3.8	11.2	107	46.5%	.286	1.19	2.93	84	1.4				
2018	GWN	AAA	22	5	0	0	8	8	50¹	35	0	3.0	10.0	56	43.2%	.280	1.03	1.43	73	1.1				
2018	ATL	MLB	22	2	1	0	7	5	29	18	1	6.5	9.9	32	45.6%	.258	1.34	4.03	104	0.2	95.7	53.4%	27.4%	43.6%
2019	GWN	AAA	23	1	6	0	10	10	39²	51	5	6.4	10.0	44	41.8%	.393	1.99	7.49	140	0.0				
2019	ATL	MLB	23	4	0	0	24	1	41²	44	5	5.6	9.7	45	42.5%	.345	1.68	5.62	98	0.3	95.6	49.2%	29.8%	41.4%
2020	ATL	MLB	24	0	2	0	7	5	24¹	27	7	5.9	11.1	30	37.7%	.328	1.77	8.88	113	0.1	96.3	41.1%	31.9%	42.1%
2021 FS	ATL	MLB	25	1	2	0	57	0	50	46	7	5.6	9.7	53	41.5%	.298	1.55	5.25	113	-0.2	95.9	46.4%	30.3%	42.0%
2021 DC	ATL	MLB	25	1	2	0	26	3	37	34	5	5.6	9.7	39	41.5%	.298	1.55	5.25	113	0.0	95.9	46.4%	30.3%	42.0%

Comparables: Sean Reid-Foley, Zack Littell, Robert Stephenson

Toussaint's 2020 was so ghastly and depressing that it should qualify for pandemic assistance. Putting up the equivalent of Dylan Cease's year but without any of Cease's luck, Toussaint made it past the fourth inning in exactly one of his five starts, while the slider he started throwing in place of his non-competitive sinker was hit so hard that he basically abandoned it by season's end. On the plus side, his four-seamer still sits at 94 mph (albeit with below-average spin and movement), and his curveball and splitter are true weapons. The talent is still there. It just looks more and more like said talent will be making a home for itself in the bullpen.

Jacob Webb RHP   Born: 08/15/93   Age: 27   Bats: R   Throws: R   Height: 6'2"   Weight: 210   Origin: Round 18, 2014 Draft (#553 overall)

YEAR	TEAM	LVL	AGE	W	L	SV	G	GS	IP	H	HR	BB/9	K/9	K	GB%	BABIP	WHIP	ERA	DRA-	WARP	MPH	FA%	Whiff%	CSP
2018	MIS	AA	24	1	2	7	21	0	22²	16	4	4.8	13.9	35	39.2%	.273	1.24	3.18	58	0.6				
2018	GWN	AAA	24	2	2	11	30	0	31²	20	3	3.1	9.7	34	40.7%	.218	0.98	3.13	62	0.7				
2019	GWN	AAA	25	0	1	1	10	0	10¹	9	1	7.8	10.5	12	50.0%	.296	1.74	6.97	91	0.2				
2019	ATL	MLB	25	4	0	2	36	0	32¹	24	4	3.3	7.8	28	38.9%	.235	1.11	1.39	100	0.2	96.3	54.5%	26.2%	46.6%
2020	ATL	MLB	26	0	0	0	8	0	10	7	0	4.5	9.0	10	60.0%	.280	1.20	0.00	85	0.2	94.5	52.4%	32.9%	46.6%
2021 FS	ATL	MLB	27	2	2	0	57	0	50	41	6	4.1	9.7	53	42.5%	.277	1.30	3.77	89	0.4	95.7	53.8%	28.4%	46.6%
2021 DC	ATL	MLB	27	2	2	0	45	0	48	40	6	4.1	9.7	51	42.5%	.277	1.30	3.77	89	0.6	95.7	53.8%	28.4%	46.6%

Comparables: Sam Tuivailala, Edubray Ramos, Jensen Lewis

There's something to be said about being the guy your team turns to when nothing matters anymore. That was Webb, whose eight September appearances had an average leverage index of .08—the statistical definition of "no pressure, kid."

Patrick Weigel RHP Born: 07/08/94 Age: 26 Bats: R Throws: R Height: 6'6" Weight: 240 Origin: Round 7, 2015 Draft (#210 overall)

YEAR	TEAM	LVL	AGE	W	L	SV	G	GS	IP	H	HR	BB/9	K/9	K	GB%	BABIP	WHIP	ERA	DRA-	WARP	MPH	FA%	Whiff%	CSP
2018	BRA	ROK	23	0	0	0	4	3	4	2	0	0.0	13.5	6	33.3%	.333	0.50	0.00	18	0.2				
2019	MIS	AA	24	0	1	0	7	7	15²	8	0	5.2	9.2	16	53.8%	.205	1.09	1.72	66	0.3				
2019	GWN	AAA	24	6	1	0	21	11	63¹	42	9	4.5	7.8	55	36.3%	.214	1.17	2.98	62	2.2				
2020	ATL	MLB	25	0	0	0	1	0	0²	2	0	40.5	0.0	0	25.0%	.500	7.50	27.00	99	0.0	95.6	58.3%	0.0%	43.6%
2021 FS	ATL	MLB	26	1	1	0	57	0	50	50	8	5.2	8.1	45	40.0%	.293	1.58	5.67	122	-0.5	95.6	58.3%	0.0%	43.6%
2021 DC	ATL	MLB	26	1	1	0	18	1	24	24	4	5.2	8.1	21	40.0%	.293	1.58	5.67	122	-0.1	95.6	58.3%	0.0%	43.6%

Comparables: Ryan Helsley, Chase De Jong, Brady Lail

Tommy John surgery in 2017 couldn't slow Weigel, a fastball-slider righty who can touch 99 mph and generally sits 95. What has kept him in neutral is a total lack of control. Still, his 2020 easily beat his 2019, when he got called up to the bigs three different times without actually making it into a game.

Bryse Wilson RHP Born: 12/20/97 Age: 23 Bats: R Throws: R Height: 6'2" Weight: 225 Origin: Round 4, 2016 Draft (#109 overall)

YEAR	TEAM	LVL	AGE	W	L	SV	G	GS	IP	H	HR	BB/9	K/9	K	GB%	BABIP	WHIP	ERA	DRA-	WARP	MPH	FA%	Whiff%	CSP
2018	FLO	HI-A	20	2	0	0	5	5	26²	16	0	2.4	8.8	26	57.1%	.229	0.86	0.34	80	0.5				
2018	MIS	AA	20	3	5	0	15	15	77	77	3	3.0	10.4	89	41.7%	.354	1.34	3.97	83	1.3				
2018	GWN	AAA	20	3	0	0	5	3	22	20	6	1.2	11.5	28	42.9%	.280	1.05	5.32	68	0.5				
2018	ATL	MLB	20	1	0	0	3	1	7	8	0	7.7	7.7	6	28.6%	.381	2.00	6.43	120	0.0	96.4	71.1%	30.4%	45.2%
2019	GWN	AAA	21	10	7	0	21	21	121	120	12	1.9	8.8	118	44.7%	.315	1.21	3.42	67	4.0				
2019	ATL	MLB	21	1	1	0	6	4	20	26	5	4.5	7.2	16	31.3%	.350	1.80	7.20	149	-0.3	96.7	72.8%	20.5%	48.0%
2020	ATL	MLB	22	1	0	1	6	2	15²	18	2	5.2	8.6	15	43.8%	.348	1.72	4.02	105	0.1	95.7	81.8%	21.2%	46.8%
2021 FS	ATL	MLB	23	2	2	0	57	0	50	50	9	3.2	8.2	45	41.0%	.291	1.36	4.75	110	-0.2	96.1	77.4%	21.6%	47.1%
2021 DC	ATL	MLB	23	2	2	0	37	3	46	46	8	3.2	8.2	42	41.0%	.291	1.36	4.75	110	0.1	96.1	77.4%	21.6%	47.1%

Comparables: Lucas Giolito, Jaime Barria, David Holmberg

Like the rest of us, Wilson clearly spent his quarantine trying to learn how to bake, and like the rest of us, the results were mixed. The fastball that is his bread and butter didn't spend enough time proofing, with opposing batters slugging .607 against it. His attempts to refine his slider went over about as well as your attempt to make a sourdough starter. His control—summarized by a walk rate of 12.3 percent—needed more time in the oven. But despite all those issues, Wilson soldiered through a solid-enough season split between the rotation and bullpen and capped it all off with a stellar start against the Dodgers in the NLCS, holding the eventual champs to one run over six innings. That'll earn him a Paul Hollywood handshake and likely a chance to win a spot in the back of the rotation, if Atlanta doesn't fill that hole this winter.

Kyle Wright RHP Born: 10/02/95 Age: 25 Bats: R Throws: R Height: 6'4" Weight: 215 Origin: Round 1, 2017 Draft (#5 overall)

YEAR	TEAM	LVL	AGE	W	L	SV	G	GS	IP	H	HR	BB/9	K/9	K	GB%	BABIP	WHIP	ERA	DRA-	WARP	MPH	FA%	Whiff%	CSP
2018	MIS	AA	22	6	8	0	20	20	109¹	103	6	3.5	8.6	105	53.1%	.317	1.34	3.70	82	1.9				
2018	GWN	AAA	22	2	1	0	7	4	28²	15	2	2.5	8.8	28	49.3%	.186	0.80	2.51	82	0.5				
2018	ATL	MLB	22	0	0	0	4	0	6	4	2	9.0	7.5	5	41.2%	.133	1.67	4.50	111	0.0	95.3	51.6%	28.9%	37.3%
2019	GWN	AAA	23	11	4	0	21	21	112¹	107	13	2.8	9.3	116	47.3%	.314	1.26	4.17	72	3.4				
2019	ATL	MLB	23	0	3	0	7	4	19²	24	4	5.9	8.2	18	41.0%	.351	1.88	8.69	129	-0.1	96.5	54.4%	23.8%	43.0%
2020	ATL	MLB	24	2	4	0	8	8	38	35	7	5.7	7.1	30	44.7%	.262	1.55	5.21	124	-0.2	96.3	48.4%	24.0%	43.7%
2021 FS	ATL	MLB	25	9	9	0	26	26	150	144	21	4.4	8.2	136	45.8%	.290	1.45	4.71	106	0.6	96.3	50.1%	24.2%	43.2%
2021 DC	ATL	MLB	25	2	3	0	9	9	45	43	6	4.4	8.2	40	45.8%	.290	1.45	4.71	106	0.3	96.3	50.1%	24.2%	43.2%

Comparables: Reynaldo López, Mitch Keller, Zack Littell

Remember sitting in math class in high school, looking around as your friends breezed through trigonometry and calculus problem, and then wondering why your own homework was such a mess? That was Wright, glumly trying to remember the quadratic formula as his fellow former first-round rotation-mates all mastered sine curves and tangents. It's an especially confounding state of affairs given that Wright throws 95 mph with an easy, simple delivery. The problem is that 95 doesn't mean much if your fastball has no action behind it, and his heater is as bland and hittable as they come. Understandably, Wright swapped his four-seamer for his sinker, which proved harder to square up, but his strikeout rate remained anemic, and there's not much daylight between it and his walk rate. Given that his postseason offered no real clues to his future, better control and adjustments to the fastball are paramount to Wright passing this particular class.

Huascar Ynoa RHP   Born: 05/28/98   Age: 23   Bats: R   Throws: R   Height: 6'2"   Weight: 220   Origin: International Free Agent, 2014

YEAR	TEAM	LVL	AGE	W	L	SV	G	GS	IP	H	HR	BB/9	K/9	K	GB%	BABIP	WHIP	ERA	DRA-	WARP	MPH	FA%	Whiff%	CSP
2018	ROM	LO-A	20	7	8	0	18	18	91²	69	7	4.1	9.8	100	46.3%	.264	1.21	3.63	84	1.3				
2018	FLO	HI-A	20	1	4	0	6	6	24²	33	1	4.4	11.3	31	44.6%	.444	1.82	8.03	80	0.4				
2019	FLO	HI-A	21	0	1	0	3	3	11	10	0	4.9	13.1	16	59.3%	.370	1.45	3.27	80	0.2				
2019	MIS	AA	21	1	2	1	6	0	13²	17	2	3.3	9.9	15	65.1%	.375	1.61	5.27	112	-0.1				
2019	GWN	AAA	21	3	5	0	17	14	72²	80	14	4.2	9.8	79	42.7%	.332	1.57	5.33	104	1.1				
2019	ATL	MLB	21	0	0	0	2	0	3	6	1	3.0	9.0	3	41.7%	.455	2.33	18.00	137	0.0	98.8	60.6%	24.1%	38.4%
2020	ATL	MLB	22	0	0	0	9	5	21²	23	2	5.4	7.1	17	55.9%	.318	1.66	5.82	90	0.3	97.4	44.3%	25.5%	46.0%
2021 FS	*ATL*	*MLB*	*23*	*2*	*2*	*0*	*57*	*0*	*50*	*48*	*6*	*4.9*	*8.3*	*46*	*47.9%*	*.295*	*1.51*	*5.02*	*111*	*-0.2*	*97.5*	*45.9%*	*25.4%*	*45.2%*
2021 DC	*ATL*	*MLB*	*23*	*2*	*2*	*0*	*37*	*3*	*49*	*47*	*6*	*4.9*	*8.3*	*45*	*47.9%*	*.295*	*1.51*	*5.02*	*111*	*0.1*	*97.5*	*45.9%*	*25.4%*	*45.2%*

Comparables: Luis Severino, Pedro Avila, Rony García

One of the many young arms pressed into service by Atlanta's rash of pitching injuries, Ynoa didn't make the most of his opportunity in the rotation. To be fair, the Braves used him more as an opener than a traditional starter, but you have to squint to find much good in those outings. Like Toussaint, Wilson and Wright, Ynoa needs to work on his control and do something about a fastball that sits at 95 mph but elicits no swings and misses. His slider produced better returns, but there's no consistent third pitch, as he threw his changeup just 33 times all season. Everything about Ynoa's profile screams "middle reliever, and not a particularly good one," and the Braves have so many of those arms that he's going to have a tough time emerging from a crowded group.

MIAMI MARLINS

Essay by Emma Baccellieri

Player comments by Jarrett Seidler and BP staff

The 2020 baseball season was built to erase its own context.

It all looked ridiculous, of course, through a lens that looked either backward or forward: *What would you think if you saw this last year?* ("Ah, yeah, this is just the 60-game scramble-season we're playing amid a global pandemic.") How would you read this in the history books? ("After months on pause, some entertainment industries resumed with modifications, such as baseball stadiums filled with cardboard cutouts instead of fans.") But watching through the lens of someone who was there in real time, against the backdrop of real life, it looked … like baseball. If you wanted, or needed, to forget everything else, you could. The broadcast was aimed squarely on the field with little reference to the stuffed animals in the seats. The video-game soundtrack seemed normal after a brief period of adjustment. The new rules and abbreviated doubleheaders could be discussed as on-the-field matters with minimal reference to why they were necessary. And so it went—an elbow bump doesn't look so different from a handshake, and a neck gaiter isn't weird in Ohio in April, so really, how much magical thinking does it take to get used to it in Texas in July? It was baseball. All the rest was only as noticeable as you wanted it to be.

That the season can be viewed as just baseball is obvious in the fact that any version of this book can exist at all. But the ability to view it this way falls apart when it comes to the Marlins. From start to finish, their season was shaped by these external forces, providing their central conflict, the scrambled outline of their schedule, the emotional thrust for their eventual playoff berth. The Marlins were the first North American major professional sports team to experience an in-season outbreak of the coronavirus and therefore also the first to see the other side of that. There can be no honest attempt to view any of this as strictly baseball. So how are you supposed to remember the 2020 Miami Marlins?

⚾   ⚾   ⚾

The place to begin is probably the hotel. (As it happens, the hotel is also the place where it almost ended, but that is neither here nor there.) In late July and early August, the

MIAMI MARLINS PROSPECTUS
2020 W-L: 31-29, 2ND IN NL EAST

Pythag	.431	24th	dWin%	.431	20th
RS/G	4.38	21st	B-Age	29.4	20th
RA/G	5.07	22nd	P-Age	27.4	2nd
DRC+	94	22nd	FIP	5.00	25th
DRA-	101	17th	DER	.688	25th
Payroll	$42M	23rd	M$/MW	$1.9M	6th

400'
386'   387'
344'   335'

- Opened 2012
- Retractable roof
- Synthetic surface
- Fence profile: 7' to 11'6"

Three-Year Park Factors

Runs	Runs/RH	Runs/LH	HR/RH	HR/LH
95	95	94	87	91

Top Hitter WARP	1.5 Miguel Rojas
Top Pitcher WARP	1.9 Pablo López
Top Prospect	Sixto Sánchez

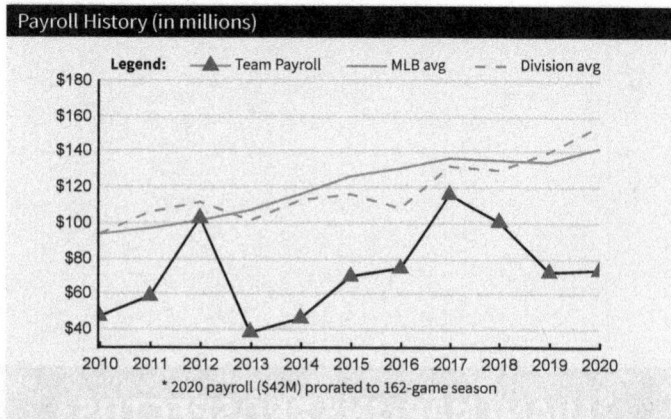

Payroll History (in millions)

Legend: ▲ Team Payroll — MLB avg -- Division avg

* 2020 payroll ($42M) prorated to 162-game season

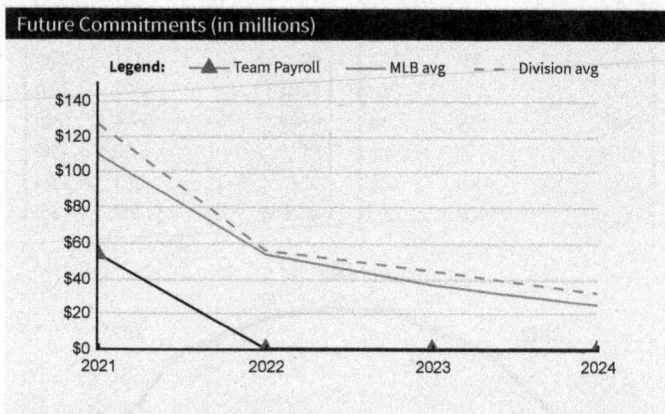

Future Commitments (in millions)

Legend: ▲ Team Payroll — MLB avg -- Division avg

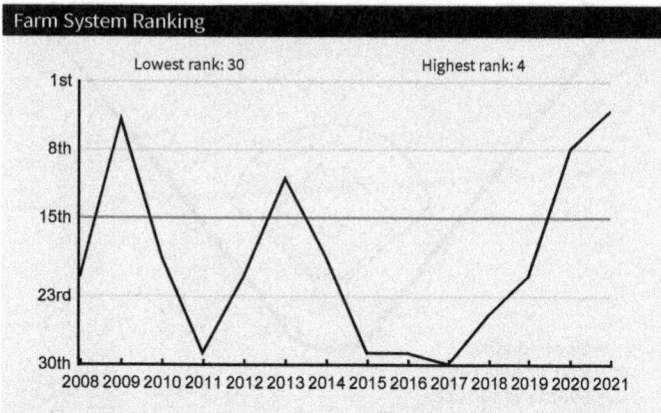

Farm System Ranking

Lowest rank: 30   Highest rank: 4

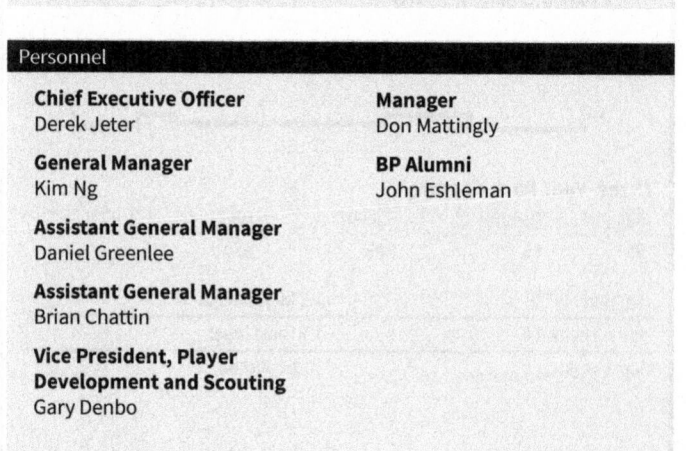

Personnel

Chief Executive Officer
Derek Jeter

General Manager
Kim Ng

Assistant General Manager
Daniel Greenlee

Assistant General Manager
Brian Chattin

Vice President, Player Development and Scouting
Gary Denbo

Manager
Don Mattingly

BP Alumni
John Eshleman

Marlins spent more than a week at the Rittenhouse Hotel in Philadelphia, isolated both from baseball and from the rest of the world with an outbreak of COVID-19.

The Marlins had arrived at the hotel before their Opening Day game against the Phillies on July 24. By July 26, four players learned that they had tested positive for the coronavirus, including scheduled starter José Ureña. The team made a few substitutions and played anyway. By July 27, the number of positive tests in their traveling party had hit 13, which would soon be 17, which would soon be 21. The Marlins stopped playing. Instead, they stayed in the hotel, left to wait without much sense of just what they were waiting for.

They were waiting as sickness requires anyone to wait—waiting to learn just who had been infected and hoping for health to be restored. But they were also waiting to be able to play baseball again, and on this point, there was no clarity. While MLB's detailed handbook of coronavirus protocol offered how to flush an airplane toilet (be sure to shut it first), and how to label the hand sanitizer in the dugout ("conspicuous signage"), it did not share anything specific on how to navigate an outbreak. There was no threshold at which a team's season would be cancelled and no timeline for when its season could restart. If half your roster was out—and, for the Marlins, *more* than half the roster was—you'd simply have to build a new one. If your schedule was wrecked, you'd build a new one of those, too. Or maybe you wouldn't. Maybe it would all go the other way—no roster, no schedule, no season. Who could tell? There was no specific marker to count down to or count up for and no idea of which way to look.

Instead, there was the hotel. There was the wait.

There has been some academic debate on the subject of whether hotels qualify as liminal spaces. A liminal space is designed for transition; it's a hallway, a waiting room, a highway rest stop. These are places that you are meant to pass through rather than stay inside. A hotel *can* fit this definition—your stay is meant to be temporary—but the fit is not ideal. A hotel is not so explicitly transitory as those other locations: it's part of the destination rather than the journey, and sometimes, it *is* the destination. A hotel may not have a particularly strong sense of place, but it will still feel like *a* place, in a way that a transitional area like a corridor will not.

This makes a hotel a curious space to wait for something. It's a comfortable place to stay, of course, because it has to be. But so much of that comfort is dependent on the knowledge of a checkout time. An indefinite wait on terms that no one knows over a process that cannot be controlled? That's not meant for a hotel.

The French anthropologist Marc Augé suggested a different category of space for a hotel—not a liminal space but a "non-place." His distinction is a very academic one (Augé introduced the idea in a 1995 essay titled "Non-Places: An Introduction to Supermodernity") but the core of it feels relevant here:

"The space of non-place creates neither singular identity nor relations; only solitude, and similitude. There is no room for history unless it has been transformed into an element of spectacle, usually in allusive texts. What reigns there is actuality, the urgency of the present moment. Since non-places are there to be passed through, they are measured in units of time."

This feels closer to the Marlins' stay in the Rittenhouse Hotel: waiting in a non-place, in their non-season, for this non-baseball.

The baseball season has little use for traditional units of time. "An hour" does not mean as much as "three innings"; a few days does not mean as much as a series; a week does not mean as much as a road trip. An off day is not defined by "day" so much as it is by "off." The schedule is its own calendar. In the hotel, however, all this was useless. Here, the Marlins were stuck in "actuality, the urgency of the present moment"—a non-place, just passing through, without a timeline or deadline or lifeline.

"I don't put this in the nightmare category," Commissioner Rob Manfred would tell ESPN in the middle of the hotel stay. "It's not a positive thing, but I don't see it as a nightmare."

The statement justifiably received a little scorn. (One shudders to think of Manfred's dreams if "Miami Marlins indefinitely stranded in makeshift quarantine unit due to viral outbreak" does not qualify as a nightmare.) But the assessment of the situation was more accurate than it might have sounded initially. An extended stay in a liminal space, passing through a non-place, isn't a *nightmare*. There are no horror-film jump cuts or physical frights here. But it does not feel like anything you could find in regular waking life, and if it's dreamlike, it's certainly not enjoyable.

⚾   ⚾   ⚾

The Marlins checked out and left Philadelphia in early August. The team arranged a set of sleeper buses for the infected players to make the 17-hour drive back to Miami; if the question of who would drive these buses seems important, much like the question of who had been asked to work in the hotel that had unexpectedly become a quarantine unit, it was never centered as such. Instead, the center of the situation was now baseball, and all the rest was only as noticeable as you wanted it to be.

If it feels like it would be difficult *not* to notice all the rest under these circumstances—well, again, this was a season built to erase its own context. The Marlins tried to proceed as normally as a team possibly could. They needed a new roster, so they promoted some players from the alternate training site and picked up a few more on waivers and selected the contracts of some others. They needed to play 57 games in 55 days, so they got a new schedule that would allow them to do just that, crammed with abbreviated doubleheaders. Thusly, Miami set out to contend for its first playoff berth

in more than a decade, a goal that had been made newly feasible by the news that the postseason would conveniently expand this year.

This was ridiculous. All of it—absurd, an affront to any principle of competitive integrity and to the general idea that a season like this could be pulled off convincingly. If you were trying to maintain the illusion that this was just baseball, cropping out the empty stadiums and papering over the adjusted schedule, that illusion shattered with the Marlins. Their situation could not be ignored. If you were turning to this season in search of normal baseball, and therefore normal life, you instead would see only a joke. (Whether the joke was funny or in poor taste was a matter of interpretation.) You would instead see these Marlins.

They were not quite a *team*, at least not as the term is typically understood, with 61 players needed to make it through 60 games. There was no sense of narrative cohesion around these moves; Miami swapped guys out with abandon, spinning through the injured list, picking up other clubs' flotsam while it waited to retrieve its own jetsam. If you were devoted to trying to view this season logically, you would probably assume that this went rather poorly, given everything known about every variable involved. And, of course, you would be wrong. This was a playoff team! How could it be anything else?

The Marlins' postseason chances had been clocked at next to zero at the start of the season, and after their indefinite break and roster remodel, they played roughly as originally expected, with below-average team performances for both offense and pitching. Their -41 run differential would be the worst of any playoff team in history. So, naturally, despite all this, they won and kept winning. They worked to win even more with the deadline acquisition of Starling Marte. (Another surprise that could not be easily dismissed—"What are the Marlins more likely to do next season, trade for the most desirable hitter available on the market, or charter a special plague bus to drive down the East Coast?" might have been a genuinely difficult question to answer in December 2019.) They made the postseason comfortably, not squeaking in as the eighth seed but instead grabbing the sixth, even advancing to the next round. Here was another illusion shattered—there was no sanctity to these playoffs. The baseball was not normal and neither was it particularly rational.

It was baseball, but *not*, generally taking the right shape but hitting the wrong notes and missing the typical relationships to space and identity and logic. It would have been unthinkable looking forward and might eventually be horrific looking backward, but when you were looking at it head on in actuality, in the urgency of the present moment, it was simply weird. The Marlins had passed through a non-place and ended up playing non-baseball. It was a joke that you were not supposed to get. It wasn't a nightmare, but it wasn't much of anything else, either.

Which is all to say—it was baseball. All the rest was only as noticeable as you wanted it to be. ∎

—Emma Baccellieri is an author at Sports Illustrated.

HITTERS

Jesús Aguilar 1B   Born: 06/30/90   Age: 31   Bats: R   Throws: R   Height: 6'3"   Weight: 277   Origin: International Free Agent, 2007

YEAR	TEAM	LVL	AGE	PA	R	2B	3B	HR	RBI	BB	K	SB	CS	Whiff%	AVG/OBP/SLG	DRC+	BABIP	BRR	FRAA	WARP
2018	MIL	MLB	28	566	80	25	0	35	108	58	143	0	0	28.7%	.274/.352/.539	135	.309	-1.1	1B(132): 3.6, 3B(5): 0.0	3.6
2019	TB	MLB	29	107	13	3	0	4	16	12	22	0	0	23.2%	.261/.336/.424	104	.290	-1.7	1B(15): -0.0	0.1
2019	MIL	MLB	29	262	26	9	0	8	34	31	59	0	0	27.4%	.225/.320/.374	93	.264	-1.9	1B(60): 0.1, 3B(2): -0.0	0.1
2020	MIA	MLB	30	216	31	10	0	8	34	23	40	0	1	22.3%	.277/.352/.457	115	.306	-0.6	1B(31): -0.3, 3B(1): -0.0	0.5
2021 FS	MIA	MLB	31	600	74	24	1	24	78	58	143	0	0	25.6%	.243/.325/.432	107	.288	-0.8	1B 1, 3B 0	1.5
2021 DC	MIA	MLB	31	467	58	19	1	19	61	45	111	0	0	25.6%	.243/.325/.432	107	.288	-0.6	1B 1	1.3

Comparables: Tony Clark, Justin Bour, Steve Balboni

Miami plucked Aguilar off waivers last offseason from Tampa Bay's carousel of cheap first basemen, hoping he'd bounce back from a troubled 2019. He didn't quite make it all the way back to his homer-fueled All-Star level of production, but he did hit the ball on the ground less and that pushed his output to the middle of the two poles. That made him a perfectly fine first base option, and the surprise introduction of the designated hitter to the National League gave the Marlins a new place to work his bat in. As a free talent pickup, that's as good as you can ask for.

Jorge Alfaro C   Born: 06/11/93   Age: 28   Bats: R   Throws: R   Height: 6'3"   Weight: 230   Origin: International Free Agent, 2010

YEAR	TEAM	LVL	AGE	PA	R	2B	3B	HR	RBI	BB	K	SB	CS	Whiff%	AVG/OBP/SLG	DRC+	BABIP	BRR	FRAA	WARP
2018	PHI	MLB	25	377	35	16	2	10	37	18	138	3	0	42.4%	.262/.324/.407	84	.406	0.5	C(104): 12.2, 3B(1): -0.0	2.5
2019	MIA	MLB	26	465	44	14	1	18	57	22	154	4	4	38.5%	.262/.312/.425	86	.364	-2.1	C(118): -2.0, 1B(1): -0.0	1.1
2020	MIA	MLB	27	100	12	2	0	3	16	4	36	2	0	41.7%	.226/.280/.344	69	.333	-0.1	C(29): -0.3, RF(1): -0.1	-0.4
2021 FS	MIA	MLB	28	600	64	23	2	19	69	28	215	2	1	39.9%	.241/.299/.399	92	.358	0.1	C 1, 1B 0	2.0
2021 DC	MIA	MLB	28	433	46	17	1	14	50	20	155	2	0	39.9%	.241/.299/.399	92	.358	0.1	C 0	1.4

Comparables: David Ross, John Russell, Mike Zunino

YEAR	TEAM	P. COUNT	FRM RUNS	BLK RUNS	THRW RUNS	TOT RUNS
2018	PHI	14249	12.3	-2.4	0.0	9.9
2019	MIA	16970	-1.7	-3.5	0.1	-5.2
2020	MIA	3746	-3.1	0.0	0.0	-3.1
2021	MIA	15632	-0.3	-1.9	0.0	-2.1

Over the past five seasons, Alfaro has swung at a higher percentage of pitches than any player in baseball and had the third-worst contact rate on them (min. 500 PA). It's a credit to his massive underlying hitting talent that he's only been mediocre in that time frame instead of the worst hitter in baseball. The former seven-time Top 101 prospect strikes out far too much, walks far too little and doesn't lift the ball enough when he does make contact, which means much of his hard contact is on the ground. He hasn't been lighting the world on fire defensively either, despite flashing top-notch framing ability in 2018 to pair with his great agility and arm strength. We've seen enough catchers develop in their late-20s to retain hope that he can all put it together entering his age-28 season but the flashes of supreme upside are starting to look more like embers of what might've been instead of the sparks that will ignite a legendary flame.

Eddy Alvarez SS   Born: 01/30/90   Age: 31   Bats: S   Throws: R   Height: 5'9"   Weight: 185   Origin: Undrafted Free Agent, 2014

YEAR	TEAM	LVL	AGE	PA	R	2B	3B	HR	RBI	BB	K	SB	CS	Whiff%	AVG/OBP/SLG	DRC+	BABIP	BRR	FRAA	WARP
2018	CHA	AAA	28	364	52	26	3	8	37	43	79	5	3		.253/.348/.435	113	.314	1.7	2B(67): 2.3, SS(31): -3.8, 3B(1): 0.3	1.3
2019	NO	AAA	29	271	45	18	2	12	43	30	53	12	3		.323/.407/.570	129	.374	3.6	3B(33): -2.0, SS(19): 0.5, 2B(10): -1.2	2.0
2020	MIA	MLB	30	41	6	1	0	0	2	3	16	2	0	33.7%	.189/.268/.216	58	.333	1.4	2B(9): -0.7, 3B(3): 0.3, SS(1): 0.2	0.1
2021 FS	MIA	MLB	31	600	60	23	2	13	59	59	174	3	1	33.7%	.222/.306/.349	83	.304	0.6	SS 4, 2B -2	1.0

Comparables: Tyler Greene, Danny Klassen, Josh Rutledge

Way back in 2014, Eddy the Jet won an Olympic silver medal in short track speed skating. What happened next might be an even unlikelier outcome—he retired from the ice and signed with the White Sox as a 24-year-old undrafted free agent, three years removed from his last baseball experience as a community college walk-on. It wasn't an easy road, and at times it certainly looked like Alvarez wasn't going to make it, but six years and a trade to Miami later he joined Jim Thorpe as the second Olympic medalist from a different sport to play Major League Baseball. He promptly collected his first two major-league hits off Jacob deGrom while filling in around the Marlins infield after their COVID outbreak. The poetic ending would've seen him glide away with a regular job as the Marlins rolled to playoff glory; the real ending is that he's an up-and-down utility player who passed through waivers in September. Life is bittersweet.

Brian Anderson 3B   Born: 05/19/93   Age: 28   Bats: R   Throws: R   Height: 6'3"   Weight: 208   Origin: Round 3, 2014 Draft (#76 overall)

YEAR	TEAM	LVL	AGE	PA	R	2B	3B	HR	RBI	BB	K	SB	CS	Whiff%	AVG/OBP/SLG	DRC+	BABIP	BRR	FRAA	WARP
2018	MIA	MLB	25	670	87	34	4	11	65	62	129	2	4	24.3%	.273/.357/.400	108	.332	2.3	RF(91): -1.1, 3B(71): -9.0	1.8
2019	MIA	MLB	26	520	57	33	1	20	66	44	114	5	1	27.4%	.261/.342/.468	107	.305	2.0	3B(67): 1.1, RF(55): 6.3	3.1
2020	MIA	MLB	27	229	27	7	1	11	38	22	66	0	0	34.6%	.255/.345/.465	106	.323	0.8	3B(56): 7.5, 1B(1): -0.1, 2B(1): -0.0	1.4
2021 FS	MIA	MLB	28	600	72	26	2	21	80	55	162	2	1	28.6%	.255/.341/.438	115	.327	0.2	3B -1, RF 0	2.4
2021 DC	MIA	MLB	28	567	68	25	2	20	76	52	153	2	0	28.6%	.255/.341/.438	115	.327	0.2	3B -1	2.2

Comparables: Fernando Tatis, Corey Koskie, Howard Johnson

Anderson doesn't do anything particularly well with the stick yet but does absolutely everything well enough, leading to solidly above-average offensive performance every year. His ability to play the outfield when called upon has been masking his stellar infield glove for a few years, and left alone at the hot corner, he snagged a 2020 Gold Glove nomination and led the majors in third base FRAA. He's a very good baseball player without the flash, panache or high-profile posting needed to be a star.

Jon Berti 2B Born: 01/22/90 Age: 31 Bats: R Throws: R Height: 5'10" Weight: 190 Origin: Round 18, 2011 Draft (#559 overall)

YEAR	TEAM	LVL	AGE	PA	R	2B	3B	HR	RBI	BB	K	SB	CS	Whiff%	AVG/OBP/SLG	DRC+	BABIP	BRR	FRAA	WARP
2018	NH	AA	28	316	55	13	7	8	42	29	46	21	9		.314/.399/.498	152	.354	0.6	3B(27): -0.8, 2B(20): -0.1, CF(7): 0.9	2.2
2018	COL	AAA	28	73	10	1	0	0	3	9	13	8	1		.217/.333/.233	77	.271	-0.5	LF(11): -1.5, 2B(6): -0.2, 3B(4): -0.7	-0.4
2018	TOR	MLB	28	15	2	1	1	0	2	0	4	1	0	23.1%	.267/.267/.467	85	.364	0.6	2B(4): -0.6	0.0
2019	NO	AAA	29	79	14	1	0	4	8	15	11	5	0		.290/.430/.500	132	.292	1.2	3B(9): -0.4, CF(6): 1.2, SS(5): 0.6	0.8
2019	MIA	MLB	29	287	52	14	1	6	24	24	73	17	3	24.6%	.273/.348/.406	87	.360	5.0	SS(32): -1.4, CF(21): -1.2, 3B(20): 1.5	1.1
2020	MIA	MLB	30	149	21	5	0	2	14	23	37	9	2	19.6%	.258/.388/.350	87	.354	0.5	2B(21): -0.4, CF(9): -1.6, RF(7): -0.6	0.2
2021 FS	MIA	MLB	31	600	69	24	4	11	54	60	155	32	6	22.5%	.247/.338/.373	100	.330	14.6	2B 7, 3B 0	4.0
2021 DC	MIA	MLB	31	567	66	23	3	10	51	56	146	31	6	22.5%	.247/.338/.373	100	.330	13.8	2B 6, 3B 0	3.6

Comparables: Jose Valentin, Dale Sveum, Ian Desmond

Just a few minutes before August 25th turned to August 26th, Berti began a great adventure. The Marlins were deep into their second doubleheader in four days, holding a 2-0 lead against the Mets in the sixth inning of the second game, a "home" game played at Citi Field. Berti walked on five pitches against Mets reliever Jeurys Familia, and that's when the Yakety Sax music started. On the very next pitch, Berti scampered off for second and the ball clanked off Ali Sánchez's glove. A batter later, Berti took off for third; the throw would've beaten him if third baseman J.D. Davis had been anywhere near the bag, but he failed to cover in time and Berti was safe again. With Berti now 90 feet away, Sánchez made several casual lobs back to Familia on the mound, and Berti eventually timed one of them and took off on a delayed steal of home. It was a heads-up play, except for the part where Berti tripped halfway down the line. Now stumbling home, he would've been easily out at the plate but for the part where Sánchez dropped the ball *again*. Berti became the first player in franchise history to steal three bases in one inning. And then the clock struck midnight.

★ ★ ★ 2021 Top 101 Prospect #33 ★ ★ ★

JJ Bleday RF Born: 11/10/97 Age: 23 Bats: L Throws: L Height: 6'3" Weight: 205 Origin: Round 1, 2019 Draft (#4 overall)

YEAR	TEAM	LVL	AGE	PA	R	2B	3B	HR	RBI	BB	K	SB	CS	Whiff%	AVG/OBP/SLG	DRC+	BABIP	BRR	FRAA	WARP
2019	JUP	HI-A	21	151	13	8	0	3	19	11	29	0	0		.257/.311/.379	105	.306	-1.1	RF(32): -0.9	0.1
2021 FS	MIA	MLB	23	600	55	26	2	13	60	39	168	1	0		.232/.286/.361	78	.308	0.2	RF -14	-1.7

The first full professional season for a top college hitting prospect like Bleday usually tells us so much. By now, we very well could have seen him emerge into an elite prospect, or even quickly ascend to the majors like Alex Bregman or Andrew Benintendi did. Instead, he played a bunch of simulated games behind closed doors at the alternate site and instructs. There are no stats to analyze and no first-hand reports to ponder, only rumblings that he performed well. It can be inferred from the lack of a call-up that he probably wasn't an absolute wrecking ball, and if there were major warning signs we'd have probably heard about those, too. Where he fits in the space between, well ... maybe we'll get that figured out in 2021.

Lewis Brinson CF Born: 05/08/94 Age: 27 Bats: R Throws: R Height: 6'5" Weight: 212 Origin: Round 1, 2012 Draft (#29 overall)

YEAR	TEAM	LVL	AGE	PA	R	2B	3B	HR	RBI	BB	K	SB	CS	Whiff%	AVG/OBP/SLG	DRC+	BABIP	BRR	FRAA	WARP
2018	JAX	AA	24	26	1	0	0	1	1	3	5	1	0		.130/.231/.261	59	.118	-0.1	CF(8): -1.0	-0.2
2018	NO	AAA	24	27	0	1	1	0	3	0	6	0	0		.222/.222/.333	61	.286	0.0	CF(5): -1.6	-0.2
2018	MIA	MLB	24	406	31	10	5	11	42	17	120	2	1	34.4%	.199/.240/.338	64	.257	-0.9	CF(106): 3.3	-0.1
2019	NO	AAA	25	339	56	15	4	16	56	32	100	16	5		.270/.361/.510	106	.356	2.3	CF(50): 4.4, RF(27): 5.1, LF(6): -0.6	2.2
2019	MIA	MLB	25	248	15	9	1	0	15	13	73	1	1	32.8%	.173/.236/.221	42	.253	1.5	CF(60): 6.4, RF(11): 0.7	-0.1
2020	MIA	MLB	26	112	14	6	0	3	12	6	30	4	0	30.8%	.226/.268/.368	83	.288	1.5	RF(31): -0.8, LF(21): 0.3, CF(7): 0.2	0.0
2021 FS	MIA	MLB	27	600	57	23	4	15	63	39	174	7	2	32.8%	.211/.274/.355	70	.279	3.1	RF 3, LF 0	0.1
2021 DC	MIA	MLB	27	267	25	10	1	6	28	17	77	3	1	32.8%	.211/.274/.355	70	.279	1.4	RF 1, LF 0	-0.1

Comparables: Todd Dunwoody, Jason Romano, Ron LeFlore

It's hard for some people to move on from the glories of their past. Imagine how hard it must be to move on from the glories of one's past's future, coming to terms with what you haven't become. Brinson was a top-30 prospect three times as a member of three different organizations (Rangers, Brewers, Marlins). As a prospect, Brinson had a habit of flatlining upon promotion before electroshocking back to life after an adjustment period, but his bat has been fairly unresponsive to medical intervention as a big-leaguer. As it stands, Brinson's legs and glove should keep him on the fringes of the majors as long as he's cheap, and he's not threatening to get expensive with the way he's swinging. His best hope for changing what lies ahead might be to accept what doesn't.

Francisco Cervelli C Born: 03/06/86 Age: 35 Bats: R Throws: R Height: 6'0" Weight: 220 Origin: International Free Agent, 2003

YEAR	TEAM	LVL	AGE	PA	R	2B	3B	HR	RBI	BB	K	SB	CS	Whiff%	AVG/OBP/SLG	DRC+	BABIP	BRR	FRAA	WARP
2018	PIT	MLB	32	404	39	15	3	12	57	51	84	2	3	25.4%	.259/.378/.431	116	.308	0.7	C(94): -3.9, 1B(5): -0.1	2.4
2019	ATL	MLB	33	37	4	5	1	2	7	4	10	0	0	23.8%	.281/.378/.688	94	.350	0.8	C(9): -0.6, 1B(2): -0.1	0.1
2019	PIT	MLB	33	123	11	3	0	1	5	9	31	1	0	25.0%	.193/.279/.248	73	.260	-0.3	C(32): 0.3, 1B(1): -0.0	0.2
2020	MIA	MLB	34	62	10	2	0	3	7	8	14	1	0	30.0%	.245/.355/.453	101	.278	-0.6	C(16): 0.3	0.3
2021 FS	MIA	MLB	35	600	62	22	2	13	59	69	146	5	2	26.0%	.235/.344/.364	100	.305	-0.3	C 0, 1B 0	2.5

Comparables: Hank Foiles, Steve Yeager, Ray Noble

Cervelli retired in October to protect his health after suffering a season-ending concussion in August, his seventh reported concussion in the last decade. A year earlier, he'd briefly given up catching following his sixth head injury, which he told Jason Mackey of the *Pittsburgh Post-Gazette* had brought on panic attacks, violent mood swings, vertigo, and fogginess. For a short time in the mid-2010s, Cervelli emerged as baseball's newest two-way catching star, a venerable pitch framer with on-base skills who blossomed when he finally got a full-time job with the Pirates. The concussions robbed him of both skill and playing time over the past half-decade, and ultimately took away his ability to play at all, but even more worrisome are the potential long-term effects on Cervelli's health. We wish him all the best in his post-playing career.

YEAR	TEAM	P. COUNT	FRM RUNS	BLK RUNS	THRW RUNS	TOT RUNS
2018	PIT	13280	-5.8	-1.1	0.6	-6.3
2019	ATL	835	0.0	-0.7	0.1	-0.6
2019	PIT	4334	0.0	-1.1	0.1	-1.0
2020	MIA	2102	-0.1	0.0	0.0	-0.1
2021	*MIA*	*16650*	*-4.0*	*1.4*	*-0.2*	*-2.7*

★ ★ ★ *2021 Top 101 Prospect* **#58** ★ ★ ★

Jazz Chisholm SS Born: 02/01/98 Age: 23 Bats: L Throws: R Height: 5'11" Weight: 184 Origin: International Free Agent, 2015

YEAR	TEAM	LVL	AGE	PA	R	2B	3B	HR	RBI	BB	K	SB	CS	Whiff%	AVG/OBP/SLG	DRC+	BABIP	BRR	FRAA	WARP
2018	KC	LO-A	20	341	52	17	4	15	43	30	97	8	2		.244/.311/.472	101	.303	-1.4	SS(75): -0.3	0.9
2018	VIS	HI-A	20	160	27	6	2	10	27	9	52	9	2		.329/.369/.597	138	.443	0.5	SS(36): -0.7	0.9
2019	JXN	AA	21	364	51	6	5	18	44	41	123	13	4		.204/.305/.427	108	.261	2.9	SS(88): -5.8	1.7
2019	JAX	AA	21	94	6	4	2	3	10	11	24	3	0		.284/.383/.494	103	.370	-0.5	SS(22): -1.8	0.4
2020	MIA	MLB	22	62	8	1	1	2	6	5	19	2	2	25.7%	.161/.242/.321	74	.200	-0.4	2B(13): -1.7, SS(9): -0.1	-0.2
2021 FS	*MIA*	*MLB*	*23*	*600*	*59*	*24*	*5*	*17*	*63*	*47*	*218*	*10*	*3*	*25.7%*	*.208/.277/.366*	*75*	*.310*	*5.8*	*SS -2*	*0.4*
2021 DC	*MIA*	*MLB*	*23*	*267*	*26*	*10*	*2*	*7*	*28*	*21*	*97*	*4*	*1*	*25.7%*	*.208/.277/.366*	*75*	*.310*	*2.6*	*2B 0, SS -1*	*0.2*

Comparables: Yu Chang, Cameron Maybin, Trevor Story

Ideally, Chisholm's big-league debut wouldn't have involved being rushed into a late-season semi-regular role bouncing between shortstop, his natural position, and second. But 2020 wasn't ideal for anyone. Chisholm just wasn't prepared to hit major-league pitching after a season struggling to make contact at Double-A. He was overmatched, even while flashing the elite bat speed that makes him one of the top middle-infield prospects around. Even if it didn't quite go as planned, the Nassau native made history as the seventh Bahamian player to reach the bigs, the first of a new wave of impact prospects from one of baseball's emerging hotbeds.

Griffin Conine OF Born: 07/11/97 Age: 23 Bats: L Throws: R Height: 6'1" Weight: 213 Origin: Round 2, 2018 Draft (#52 overall)

YEAR	TEAM	LVL	AGE	PA	R	2B	3B	HR	RBI	BB	K	SB	CS	Whiff%	AVG/OBP/SLG	DRC+	BABIP	BRR	FRAA	WARP
2018	BLU	ROK	20	9	1	1	0	0	3	1	2	0	0		.375/.444/.500	126	.500		RF(2): 2.3	0.2
2018	VAN	SS	20	230	24	14	2	7	30	19	63	5	0		.238/.309/.427	93	.304	-1.5	RF(46): 10.1	0.4
2019	LAN	LO-A	21	348	59	19	2	22	64	38	125	2	0		.283/.371/.576	155	.405	2.8	RF(74): 6.2	3.7
2021 FS	*MIA*	*MLB*	*23*	*600*	*48*	*27*	*2*	*12*	*55*	*39*	*244*	*2*	*0*		*.189/.249/.314*	*53*	*.309*	*0.9*	*RF 10*	*-1.1*

Comparables: Jaylin Davis, Zoilo Almonte, Jesús Aguilar

It was always destiny, wasn't it? The son of "Mr. Marlin" Jeff Conine was born in 1997 in South Florida, when his pops manned first base for a Marlins squad about to go on a magical World Series run. Twenty-three summers later, he came home in the Jonathan Villar deal. Like his dad, Griffin is a bat-first corner type; he projects to hit for more power than Jeff did, but also has a long way to go before you can project him to play in the bigs for 17 years. It's got the potential to be a great story if his hit tool can live up to it.

Garrett Cooper 1B Born: 12/25/90 Age: 30 Bats: R Throws: R Height: 6'5" Weight: 235 Origin: Round 6, 2013 Draft (#182 overall)

YEAR	TEAM	LVL	AGE	PA	R	2B	3B	HR	RBI	BB	K	SB	CS	Whiff%	AVG/OBP/SLG	DRC+	BABIP	BRR	FRAA	WARP
2018	NO	AAA	27	34	2	1	0	1	5	3	5	0	0		.300/.382/.433	115	.333	-0.5	1B(5): 0.3, LF(4): 0.5	0.1
2018	MIA	MLB	27	38	2	1	0	0	2	4	12	0	0	35.1%	.212/.316/.242	66	.333	0.4	LF(6): 0.7, 1B(4): 1.1, RF(3): -0.1	0.1
2019	MIA	MLB	28	421	52	16	1	15	50	33	109	0	0	23.4%	.281/.344/.446	101	.355	-0.4	1B(73): -0.2, RF(31): 5.1	1.2
2020	MIA	MLB	30	133	20	8	0	6	20	11	31	0	0	22.2%	.283/.353/.500	110	.337	-0.8	1B(15): 0.6	0.4
2021 FS	*MIA*	*MLB*	*30*	*600*	*69*	*25*	*1*	*21*	*76*	*48*	*155*	*0*	*0*	*23.4%*	*.261/.330/.430*	*109*	*.329*	*-0.5*	*1B 2, LF 0*	*1.9*
2021 DC	*MIA*	*MLB*	*30*	*534*	*62*	*22*	*1*	*18*	*68*	*43*	*137*	*0*	*0*	*23.4%*	*.261/.330/.430*	*109*	*.329*	*-0.4*	*1B 2*	*1.7*

Comparables: Brian Daubach, Andres Galarraga, Mark Trumbo

Cooper hit by far the biggest home run of his short career in Game 2 of the NL Wild Card Series, mashing a Yu Darvish hanging breaker over the ivy and out of the Friendly Confines of Wrigley. The dinger broke a 7th-inning scoreless tie and pushed the Marlins out of the three-game melee and into the divisional round. Cooper broke camp as the primary designated hitter, and for the first time in his Miami tenure, he wasn't forced to roam around the outfield in search of playing time that wasn't available at first base. Despite missing a month on the COVID-IL, he seems to have finally bridged the gap between Quad-A slugger and starting major-league player.

José Devers SS Born: 12/07/99 Age: 21 Bats: L Throws: R Height: 6'0" Weight: 174 Origin: International Free Agent, 2016

YEAR	TEAM	LVL	AGE	PA	R	2B	3B	HR	RBI	BB	K	SB	CS	Whiff%	AVG/OBP/SLG	DRC+	BABIP	BRR	FRAA	WARP
2018	GBO	LO-A	18	362	46	12	4	0	24	15	49	13	6		.273/.313/.332	92	.318	-2.6	SS(58): 2.2, 2B(15): 0.0	0.2
2019	MRL	ROK	19	46	7	3	1	0	2	4	4	3	1		.275/.370/.400	83	.306	1.5	SS(1): -0.1	0.1
2019	JUP	HI-A	19	138	13	3	1	0	3	8	20	5	0		.325/.384/.365	128	.387	-1.8	SS(32): -1.9	0.6
2021 FS	*MIA*	*MLB*	*21*	*600*	*49*	*26*	*3*	*6*	*51*	*32*	*143*	*12*	*4*		*.237/.288/.334*	*71*	*.307*	*2.5*	*SS -4, 2B 1*	*-0.3*

Comparables: Ketel Marte, Cole Tucker, Sergio Alcántara

Best remembered for who he isn't—Giancarlo Stanton, for whom he was traded, and his cousin Rafael—Devers is an interesting prospect in his own right. He's smooth with his glove at an up-the-middle position and last we saw him on a minor-league field, he even hit a little bit. That was back in 2019, but Devers did spend the summer at the alternate site, developing in front of the watchful eyes of the Marlins professional staff. Despite only 35 career games in High-A, it's possible Devers is on the fast track, given that the Marlins snuck him on to their taxi squad when they made the playoffs.

Isan Díaz 2B Born: 05/27/96 Age: 25 Bats: L Throws: R Height: 5'11" Weight: 201 Origin: Round 2, 2014 Draft (#70 overall)

YEAR	TEAM	LVL	AGE	PA	R	2B	3B	HR	RBI	BB	K	SB	CS	Whiff%	AVG/OBP/SLG	DRC+	BABIP	BRR	FRAA	WARP
2018	JAX	AA	22	355	44	19	1	10	42	53	95	10	3		.245/.364/.418	121	.325	0.0	2B(82): 2.1	1.4
2018	NO	AAA	22	155	19	4	4	3	14	15	45	4	0		.204/.281/.358	65	.278	0.8	2B(35): -1.6	-0.4
2019	NO	AAA	23	435	89	21	2	26	70	49	96	5	4		.305/.395/.578	132	.349	0.7	2B(99): 0.8	3.1
2019	MIA	MLB	23	201	17	5	2	5	23	19	59	0	3	28.2%	.173/.259/.307	62	.224	0.1	2B(48): 0.0	-0.3
2020	MIA	MLB	24	22	3	0	0	0	1	0	7	0	0	32.4%	.182/.182/.182	77	.267	0.0	2B(7): 0.8	0.1
2021 FS	MIA	MLB	25	600	65	23	3	23	73	58	195	3	1	28.8%	.220/.303/.406	93	.298	0.5	2B -1, SS 0	1.7
2021 DC	MIA	MLB	25	333	36	12	1	12	40	32	108	1	0	28.8%	.220/.303/.406	93	.298	0.3	2B 0	0.9

Comparables: Ernie Fazio, Jerry Buchek, Garrett Hampson

While quarantined in Philadelphia after 18 of his teammates came down with COVID, Díaz opted out of the 2020 season. Even though he quite understandably opted out in the middle of the league's worst outbreak of 2020, the Marlins placed him on the restricted list without pay or service time, a patently ludicrous bit of "business" that will gain them an extra year of team control down the line. He ultimately opted back into the season around the trade deadline, spurring Miami to deal Jonathan Villar, and promptly suffered a season-ending groin injury upon his return from the alternate site. Through it all, he remains a promising young hitter with major power potential, though a season of lost reps clouds his long-term development.

Lewin Díaz 1B Born: 11/19/96 Age: 24 Bats: L Throws: L Height: 6'4" Weight: 217 Origin: International Free Agent, 2013

YEAR	TEAM	LVL	AGE	PA	R	2B	3B	HR	RBI	BB	K	SB	CS	Whiff%	AVG/OBP/SLG	DRC+	BABIP	BRR	FRAA	WARP
2018	FTM	HI-A	21	310	21	11	3	6	35	10	56	1	0		.224/.255/.344	67	.255	-1.8	1B(74): 2.7	-1.3
2019	FTM	HI-A	22	234	34	11	1	13	36	14	40	0	0		.290/.333/.533	157	.297	-1.3	1B(52): 4.9	2.0
2019	JAX	AA	22	129	16	6	0	8	14	11	28	0	1		.200/.279/.461	122	.188	-0.2	1B(30): -2.2	0.5
2019	PNS	AA	22	138	12	16	1	6	26	8	23	0	0		.302/.341/.587	130	.320	-0.6	1B(31): -0.2	0.9
2020	MIA	MLB	24	41	2	2	0	0	3	2	12	0	0	23.4%	.154/.195/.205	73	.222	-0.1	1B(11): 0.9	0.0
2021 FS	MIA	MLB	24	600	63	24	2	23	78	36	166	0	0	23.4%	.227/.280/.409	85	.279	1.0	1B 4	0.2
2021 DC	MIA	MLB	24	133	14	5	0	5	17	8	36	0	0	23.4%	.227/.280/.409	85	.279	0.2	1B 1	0.0

Comparables: Kendrys Morales, Russ Canzler, Ben Paulsen

Díaz was a nice get for Sergio Romo at the 2019 trade deadline, having been in the midst of a breakout season in which his power was finally showing up in games. He was brought up a year early out of brief necessity and didn't stick, but it's safe to assume he'll be ready for a longer look next year.

Corey Dickerson OF Born: 05/22/89 Age: 32 Bats: L Throws: R Height: 6'1" Weight: 200 Origin: Round 8, 2010 Draft (#260 overall)

YEAR	TEAM	LVL	AGE	PA	R	2B	3B	HR	RBI	BB	K	SB	CS	Whiff%	AVG/OBP/SLG	DRC+	BABIP	BRR	FRAA	WARP
2018	PIT	MLB	29	533	65	35	7	13	55	21	80	8	3	22.0%	.300/.330/.474	105	.333	-4.1	LF(124): 10.7	2.4
2019	IND	AAA	30	38	4	1	0	0	4	3	8	0	0		.182/.237/.212	60	.222	0.2	LF(7): 0.6	0.0
2019	PHI	MLB	30	137	13	10	2	8	34	3	33	0	0	26.2%	.293/.307/.579	105	.333	-3.1	LF(32): -1.2	0.0
2019	PIT	MLB	30	142	20	18	0	4	25	13	23	1	0	28.3%	.315/.373/.551	107	.353	-0.1	LF(33): -0.7	0.5
2020	MIA	MLB	31	210	25	5	1	7	17	15	35	1	1	25.7%	.258/.311/.402	99	.283	1.0	LF(46): -3.0, RF(1): -0.0	0.3
2021 FS	MIA	MLB	32	600	68	31	3	18	68	35	129	4	2	25.1%	.251/.298/.416	92	.297	-0.1	LF 10	2.2
2021 DC	MIA	MLB	32	500	57	26	3	15	57	29	108	3	1	25.1%	.251/.298/.416	92	.297	-0.1	LF 9	1.8

Comparables: Alfonso Soriano, Starling Marte, Yoenis Céspedes

One of the most consistent hitters in baseball, Dickerson put up his sixth consecutive season with a DRC+ between 100 and 109 for his fifth different team in that span. He took his talents to South Beach as the nominal big fish in Miami's offseason consignment store shopping, signing a two-year, $17.5 million bargain. After a typically steady performance in the regular season, he delivered one of the biggest hits in recent franchise history when he bopped a three-run go-ahead homer against the Cubs in Game 1 of the NL Wild Card Series. Dickerson has his flaws—he can't hit lefties well and doesn't get on base quite as much as you'd like—but adding a few average-caliber regulars like him lifted the Marlins out of their rebuild a year or two ahead of schedule. More teams should try trying.

Jerar Encarnación RF Born: 10/22/97 Age: 23 Bats: R Throws: R Height: 6'5" Weight: 239 Origin: International Free Agent, 2015

YEAR	TEAM	LVL	AGE	PA	R	2B	3B	HR	RBI	BB	K	SB	CS	Whiff%	AVG/OBP/SLG	DRC+	BABIP	BRR	FRAA	WARP
2018	BAT	SS	20	190	30	14	2	4	24	4	57	1	1		.284/.305/.448	87	.390	-0.3	RF(37): 9.8	0.5
2018	GBO	LO-A	20	59	3	0	0	0	2	5	23	0	0		.074/.153/.074	-3	.129	-0.2	RF(12): 5.7, 1B(1): -0.0	-0.1
2019	CLI	LO-A	21	281	34	16	0	10	43	23	69	3	1		.298/.363/.478	141	.375	-1.6	RF(63): 7.2	2.3
2019	JUP	HI-A	21	272	27	10	1	6	28	17	71	3	2		.253/.298/.372	101	.326	-1.9	RF(31): 5.8, LF(23): -1.1, 1B(3): -0.0	0.8
2021 FS	MIA	MLB	23	600	54	26	2	16	63	33	230	2	1		.218/.267/.362	69	.336	-0.1	RF 10, LF 1	0.2

Comparables: Jorge Oña, Socrates Brito, Rymer Liriano

Encarnacion was a surprise inclusion on Miami's summer camp roster. He's a massive man with light tower power and questionable bat-to-ball ability, so a summer's worth of reps against advanced pitching was certainly better than hitting off a JUGS machine.

Monte Harrison CF   Born: 08/10/95   Age: 25   Bats: R   Throws: R   Height: 6'3"   Weight: 225   Origin: Round 2, 2014 Draft (#50 overall)

YEAR	TEAM	LVL	AGE	PA	R	2B	3B	HR	RBI	BB	K	SB	CS	Whiff%	AVG/OBP/SLG	DRC+	BABIP	BRR	FRAA	WARP
2018	JAX	AA	22	583	85	20	3	19	48	44	215	28	9		.240/.316/.399	96	.368	3.6	CF(120): -8.0, RF(14): 0.4	0.1
2019	NO	AAA	23	244	41	7	2	9	24	25	73	20	2		.274/.357/.451	93	.373	3.2	CF(32): 2.6, RF(19): -2.4, LF(3): 0.8	0.9
2020	MIA	MLB	25	51	8	1	0	1	3	4	26	6	0	42.5%	.170/.235/.255	51	.350	0.1	CF(16): 1.5, RF(13): 0.4	0.0
2021 FS	MIA	MLB	25	600	59	23	2	14	55	44	256	15	3	42.5%	.204/.279/.338	70	.354	5.1	CF 0, LF -2	-0.4
2021 DC	MIA	MLB	25	166	16	6	0	4	15	12	70	4	1	42.5%	.204/.279/.338	70	.354	1.4	CF 0, LF -1	-0.1

Comparables: Dave Krynzel, Jai Miller, Greg Halman

There were a lot of overmatched Marlins prospects pressed into duty in 2020, but Harrison was at the head of the class. He struck out over half the time in his debut season, amplifying severe swing-and-miss issues that have threatened his hit tool ever since he came over from Milwaukee. When he did hit it, he didn't hit it that hard: He averaged 81.7 mph in terms of exit velocity, near the very bottom of the majors. Harrison has tried all kinds of swing changes to increase his ability to make contact, but he hasn't found a bat path that has consistently gotten him to strike the ball hard yet. Unlike some of the other emergency Marlins, Harrison had enough high-minors experience (192 games) that he shouldn't have been quite this overwhelmed by major-league pitching. He needs to find a swing and setup that will actually work, lest he find himself in the same position as outfield-mate Lewis Brinson.

Matt Joyce LF   Born: 08/03/84   Age: 36   Bats: L   Throws: R   Height: 6'2"   Weight: 194   Origin: Round 12, 2005 Draft (#360 overall)

YEAR	TEAM	LVL	AGE	PA	R	2B	3B	HR	RBI	BB	K	SB	CS	Whiff%	AVG/OBP/SLG	DRC+	BABIP	BRR	FRAA	WARP
2018	NAS	AAA	33	35	4	3	0	0	3	3	5	0	0		.281/.343/.375	101	.333	-0.3	LF(6): 0.0	0.0
2018	OAK	MLB	33	246	34	9	0	7	15	35	53	0	2	25.5%	.208/.322/.353	98	.242	0.1	LF(49): 2.0, RF(6): -0.3, CF(3): -0.1	0.7
2019	ATL	MLB	34	238	32	10	0	7	23	38	45	0	0	25.5%	.295/.408/.450	123	.351	1.4	RF(33): 0.7, LF(4): -0.6	1.5
2020	MIA	MLB	36	148	16	4	0	2	14	20	41	1	0	33.0%	.252/.351/.331	93	.353	-0.1	RF(27): -1.3, LF(15): -0.9	-0.1
2021 FS	MIA	MLB	36	600	67	23	1	15	63	82	163	3	1	28.3%	.228/.340/.370	100	.305	-1.0	RF 0, LF 2	1.6

Comparables: Shin-Soo Choo, Andre Ethier, Jeromy Burnitz

Because Joyce missed the team outbreak in Philadelphia while recovering from his own summer bout with COVID, the sweet-swinging lefty was one of the few incumbent Marlins ready to roll when the club resumed play on August 4th. From there, he started more often than not against righties, rotating through both outfield corners and DH. Joyce has run some of the most extreme platoon splits in baseball for his entire career; if you can make sure he never, ever sees a southpaw like Don Mattingly was able to, you can still squeeze a little value out of his bat.

Starling Marte CF   Born: 10/09/88   Age: 32   Bats: R   Throws: R   Height: 6'1"   Weight: 195   Origin: International Free Agent, 2007

YEAR	TEAM	LVL	AGE	PA	R	2B	3B	HR	RBI	BB	K	SB	CS	Whiff%	AVG/OBP/SLG	DRC+	BABIP	BRR	FRAA	WARP
2018	PIT	MLB	29	606	81	32	5	20	72	35	109	33	14	24.3%	.277/.327/.460	107	.312	0.1	CF(139): 7.0	3.4
2019	PIT	MLB	30	586	97	31	6	23	82	25	94	25	6	25.2%	.295/.342/.503	107	.319	3.9	CF(130): 2.3	3.4
2020	MIA	MLB	32	112	13	6	0	4	13	2	22	5	0	23.5%	.245/.286/.415	98	.275	0.1	CF(28): -1.8	0.2
2020	ARI	MLB	32	138	23	8	1	2	14	10	19	5	2	27.1%	.311/.384/.443	100	.353	1.0	CF(33): -0.6, LF(1): 0.0	0.4
2021 FS	MIA	MLB	32	600	72	27	3	16	70	30	119	33	9	25.1%	.267/.327/.419	105	.315	7.4	CF -2, LF 0	2.9
2021 DC	MIA	MLB	32	567	68	25	3	15	66	28	112	31	9	25.1%	.267/.327/.419	105	.315	7.0	CF -2	2.7

Comparables: Al Martin, Jeffrey Leonard, Matt Diaz

Consider Marte as representative of the game of baseball and state of things more broadly in 2020. He opened the year by getting traded to Arizona for a pair of high-upside, intriguing prospects—the quality of which reflected not only Marte's on-field prowess but the affordable team option on him for 2021, as well. He suffered unfathomable personal loss during baseball's interregnum when his wife Noelia Brazoban suffered a fatal heart attack in May. He decided to play once baseball returned in late July, but found himself changing teams once again at the deadline, that affordable option now rendered as a burden due to Arizona's so-called economic headwinds. Marte was a salve for an experienced and strikeout-prone outfield in Miami and helped spur the team to their playoff entry, though he missed most of the postseason with a broken finger. The Marlins rewarded him and themselves by exercising their option for next year. In a year where March stretched on for years, Marte's 61 games played in a 60-game schedule was truly emblematic.

Kameron Misner OF   Born: 01/08/98   Age: 23   Bats: L   Throws: L   Height: 6'4"   Weight: 218   Origin: Round 1, 2019 Draft (#35 overall)

YEAR	TEAM	LVL	AGE	PA	R	2B	3B	HR	RBI	BB	K	SB	CS	Whiff%	AVG/OBP/SLG	DRC+	BABIP	BRR	FRAA	WARP
2019	MRL	ROK	21	38	2	2	0	0	4	9	7	3	0		.241/.421/.310	138	.318	0.4	CF(5): -0.1, RF(3): -0.2	0.2
2019	CLI	LO-A	21	158	25	7	0	2	20	21	35	8	0		.276/.380/.373	136	.357	2.2	CF(32): 7.1	2.0
2021 FS	MIA	MLB	23	600	55	26	2	11	57	52	186	11	1		.225/.298/.345	79	.320	5.1	CF 19, RF 0	2.8

A 2019 SEC first-rounder would seem to be a lock to show up at the alternate site at some point, but Miami never invited Misner, which can't be a good sign for his development track. He did participate in the fall instructional league, so at least we know he's healthy.

Harold Ramirez CF Born: 09/06/94 Age: 26 Bats: R Throws: R Height: 5'10" Weight: 232 Origin: International Free Agent, 2011

YEAR	TEAM	LVL	AGE	PA	R	2B	3B	HR	RBI	BB	K	SB	CS	Whiff%	AVG/OBP/SLG	DRC+	BABIP	BRR	FRAA	WARP
2018	NH	AA	23	505	60	37	0	11	70	27	88	16	2		.320/.365/.471	131	.371	2.5	RF(61): -2.7, LF(18): -0.5	1.7
2019	NO	AAA	24	120	19	12	1	4	14	6	19	1	1		.355/.408/.591	122	.402	-2.3	LF(16): -0.2, RF(8): 0.1	0.4
2019	MIA	MLB	24	446	54	20	3	11	50	18	91	2	1	25.7%	.276/.312/.416	84	.328	-0.2	LF(61): 4.1, RF(55): -2.5, CF(27): 2.2	0.7
2020	MIA	MLB	26	11	2	0	0	0	1	1	2	0	1	29.2%	.200/.273/.200	79	.250		RF(2): -0.1, LF(1): 0.0	0.0
2021 FS	MIA	MLB	26	600	61	26	3	14	70	30	130	3	1	25.9%	.257/.308/.392	92	.314	0.9	LF 8, RF -2	1.7
2021 DC	MIA	MLB	26	100	10	4	0	2	11	5	21	0	0	25.9%	.257/.308/.392	92	.314	0.2	LF 1, RF 0	0.3

Comparables: Todd Hollandsworth, Alfonso Soriano, Mark Brouhard

The Opening Day right fielder looked poised to play a big role in the outfield; he missed time with COVID and then suffered a season-ending hamstring injury in his first game after recovering.

Miguel Rojas SS Born: 02/24/89 Age: 32 Bats: R Throws: R Height: 6'0" Weight: 188 Origin: International Free Agent, 2005

YEAR	TEAM	LVL	AGE	PA	R	2B	3B	HR	RBI	BB	K	SB	CS	Whiff%	AVG/OBP/SLG	DRC+	BABIP	BRR	FRAA	WARP
2018	MIA	MLB	29	528	44	13	0	11	53	24	69	6	3	15.5%	.252/.297/.346	90	.272	-2.5	SS(83): 5.4, 1B(49): -0.3, 3B(39): -1.0	1.6
2019	MIA	MLB	30	526	52	29	1	5	46	32	61	9	5	16.6%	.284/.331/.379	93	.313	-1.7	SS(125): -4.8, 1B(6): -0.1, 2B(3): -0.1	1.4
2020	MIA	MLB	31	143	20	10	1	4	20	16	18	5	1	17.3%	.304/.392/.496	123	.330	-0.6	SS(39): 6.4, 1B(1): -0.0, 3B(1): 0.0	1.5
2021 FS	MIA	MLB	32	600	61	27	1	10	60	41	86	7	3	16.4%	.260/.321/.372	92	.293	-0.9	SS 1, 1B 0	1.2
2021 DC	MIA	MLB	32	534	54	24	1	9	53	36	77	6	2	16.4%	.260/.321/.372	92	.293	-0.8	SS 1	1.2

Comparables: Kevin Elster, Larry Brown, Marco Scutaro

Far too many people in power around the world abdicated their responsibility in 2020, in baseball and beyond. The abdication of power by Major League Baseball and commissioner Rob Manfred enveloped the entire season, starting when the league frittered away weeks and weeks of time and planning in a futile attempt to pay players less than pro rata. It continued to the very end, when the league failed to keep a COVID-positive player away from the on-field celebration at the end of the World Series. The worst example was in the middle, in the handling of Miami's team outbreak in late July. It may not have been foreseeable that it would be the Marlins who would have an outbreak, and it may not have been foreseeable that it would be on the very first weekend of the season, but it was completely foreseeable that an outbreak would happen somewhere, sometime. And Major League Baseball had no real response for it, initially leaving the decision about whether or not to forge ahead in the face of multiple positive tests up to the Marlins players. There were no protocols on when to hit pause, on how long to wait, on what to do; just an operational manual filled with much of the same virus theater that has permeated all aspects of our society, along with a broader idea that if the players did everything "right," nothing bad would happen. Of course, since everything in baseball is part of the greater labor fight now, when things went wrong, the answer was to blame the players for getting sick. It may have been Miguel Rojas who led Miami's decision to play on July 26th as the unofficial team leader, but it never should've been his call to make. Rojas was ultimately one of over a dozen Marlins to test positive; he would homer in his return four weeks later and lead the team to the playoffs.

Jesús Sánchez RF Born: 10/07/97 Age: 23 Bats: L Throws: R Height: 6'3" Weight: 222 Origin: International Free Agent, 2014

YEAR	TEAM	LVL	AGE	PA	R	2B	3B	HR	RBI	BB	K	SB	CS	Whiff%	AVG/OBP/SLG	DRC+	BABIP	BRR	FRAA	WARP
2018	CHA	HI-A	20	378	56	24	2	10	64	15	71	6	3		.301/.331/.462	133	.350	-1.5	RF(78): 1.8, CF(7): -1.4	1.2
2018	MTG	AA	20	110	14	8	0	1	11	11	21	1	1		.214/.300/.327	93	.263	0.7	RF(26): -0.8, CF(1): -0.0	-0.1
2019	MTG	AA	21	316	32	11	1	8	49	24	65	5	4		.275/.332/.404	121	.327	0.1	RF(72): 0.0	1.4
2019	NO	AAA	21	78	11	1	0	4	9	9	15	0	0		.246/.338/.446	73	.250	0.3	CF(8): -1.6, RF(8): 3.6	0.2
2019	DUR	AAA	21	71	6	2	1	1	5	6	20	0	0		.206/.282/.317	52	.279	-0.3	RF(15): 0.7	-0.2
2020	MIA	MLB	23	29	1	1	0	0	2	4	11	0	0	25.0%	.040/.172/.080	81	.071	0.0	RF(10): 0.4	0.0
2021 FS	MIA	MLB	23	600	60	26	4	16	65	40	172	2	0	25.0%	.234/.289/.387	82	.309	1.7	RF -1, CF -4	0.0
2021 DC	MIA	MLB	23	200	20	8	1	5	21	13	57	0	0	25.0%	.234/.289/.387	82	.309	0.6	RF 0, CF -1	0.0

Comparables: Brandon Moss, Tyler Austin, Jeff Francoeur

The Marlins gave Sánchez a clean shot to win the right field job in late-August. He looked completely overmatched at the plate, losing his starting spot in a week and his roster spot just a few days later, never to return. He has the barrel control and swing to project a plus hit tool and substantial raw power, but it just hasn't clicked yet. It's been years now since we've seen the whole package work together. Hitters hit, and Sánchez hasn't hit anywhere since A-ball.

Connor Scott OF Born: 10/08/99 Age: 21 Bats: L Throws: L Height: 6'3" Weight: 187 Origin: Round 1, 2018 Draft (#13 overall)

YEAR	TEAM	LVL	AGE	PA	R	2B	3B	HR	RBI	BB	K	SB	CS	Whiff%	AVG/OBP/SLG	DRC+	BABIP	BRR	FRAA	WARP
2018	MRL	ROK	18	119	15	1	4	0	8	14	29	8	5		.223/.319/.311	89	.307	-1.2	CF(22): -1.6	-0.4
2018	GBO	LO-A	18	89	4	2	0	1	5	10	27	1	3		.211/.295/.276	58	.300	-1.9	CF(22): -3.0	-0.8
2019	CLI	LO-A	19	413	56	24	4	4	36	31	91	21	9		.251/.311/.368	98	.322	1.6	CF(85): -2.6, LF(1): -0.1	1.1
2019	JUP	HI-A	19	111	12	4	1	1	5	11	26	2	1		.235/.306/.327	85	.301	0.9	CF(24): -1.5	0.1
2021 FS	MIA	MLB	21	600	48	27	4	8	52	42	199	12	8		.213/.272/.322	63	.317	-6.1	CF -4, LF 0	-1.9

Comparables: Mickey Moniak, Rey Fuentes, Derrick Robinson

Scott is fast and can glove it in center. The bat projection is there, somewhere—you don't get drafted that high without offensive projection—but it hasn't shown up as a pro yet, although he's had challenging assignments thus far.

Magneuris Sierra CF Born: 04/07/96 Age: 25 Bats: L Throws: L Height: 5'11" Weight: 178 Origin: International Free Agent, 2012

YEAR	TEAM	LVL	AGE	PA	R	2B	3B	HR	RBI	BB	K	SB	CS	Whiff%	AVG/OBP/SLG	DRC+	BABIP	BRR	FRAA	WARP
2018	NO	AAA	22	367	48	12	5	2	17	13	73	14	5		.260/.287/.341	60	.322	3.2	CF(81): 5.8, RF(1): 0.7	0.2
2018	MIA	MLB	22	156	10	3	0	0	7	6	39	3	2	26.0%	.190/.222/.211	39	.259	-0.4	CF(32): -0.3, RF(19): -0.1	-0.8
2019	JAX	AA	23	197	21	8	2	1	7	13	32	7	1		.282/.337/.365	109	.338	1.8	CF(21): 0.7, RF(15): 4.2, LF(4): 1.7	1.6
2019	NO	AAA	23	352	56	11	7	6	21	15	58	26	10		.271/.304/.399	61	.312	3.7	CF(32): -0.7, LF(24): -1.4, RF(23): 1.5	-0.3
2019	MIA	MLB	23	42	5	1	1	0	1	2	7	3	3	10.7%	.350/.381/.425	81	.424	-0.7	CF(9): 3.3, RF(5): 0.4	0.3
2020	MIA	MLB	24	53	8	3	1	0	7	5	9	4	1	17.1%	.250/.333/.364	102	.306	-0.3	CF(11): 1.4, LF(5): 0.8, RF(4): 0.1	0.3
2021 FS	MIA	MLB	25	600	55	24	5	6	51	30	141	17	7	19.4%	.239/.282/.337	67	.308	0.3	RF 5, CF -3	-0.5
2021 DC	MIA	MLB	25	133	12	5	1	1	11	6	31	3	1	19.4%	.239/.282/.337	67	.308	0.1	RF 1, CF -1	-0.1

Comparables: Brady Anderson, Eddie Miller, Joey Gathright

Sierra might finally be settling in as a nifty slash-and-burn fourth outfielder, which is an upgrade from the past few seasons where it looked like his offensive profile had been slashed and burned.

Chad Wallach C Born: 11/04/91 Age: 29 Bats: R Throws: R Height: 6'2" Weight: 246 Origin: Round 5, 2013 Draft (#142 overall)

YEAR	TEAM	LVL	AGE	PA	R	2B	3B	HR	RBI	BB	K	SB	CS	Whiff%	AVG/OBP/SLG	DRC+	BABIP	BRR	FRAA	WARP
2018	NO	AAA	26	174	20	7	0	3	16	20	47	0	1		.224/.324/.333	83	.300	-2.6	C(40): 8.1	0.8
2018	MIA	MLB	26	52	4	1	0	1	5	4	23	0	0	42.0%	.178/.275/.267	54	.333	0.1	C(14): 2.6	0.3
2019	MIA	MLB	27	54	4	3	0	1	3	6	12	0	0	27.6%	.250/.333/.375	96	.314	-0.1	C(14): -0.7	0.2
2020	MIA	MLB	29	48	4	3	0	1	6	3	12	0	0	29.5%	.227/.277/.364	81	.290	-0.4	C(15): -0.3	0.0
2021 FS	MIA	MLB	29	600	63	23	1	17	62	54	181	1	0	31.0%	.211/.293/.359	80	.282	-0.7	C 7, 1B 0	1.5
2021 DC	MIA	MLB	29	233	24	9	0	6	24	20	70	0	0	31.0%	.211/.293/.359	80	.282	-0.3	C 4	0.7

Comparables: Juan Brito, Guillermo Quiroz, Max Stassi

Catching admittedly remains a bit of a mystery box to baseball analysts, even with pitch framing solved. The Marlins love what Wallach brings to the table as a staff leader and game caller—soft factors we can't quantify well—so much so that they ran him out in every postseason game. From one vantage point, he's a generic no-hit backup catcher with a decent but unspectacular glove and a well-respected last name. But he keeps moving up in the world despite that, from waiver claim to up-and-down third catcher to backup to playoff starter. Perhaps his virtue falls in the presently unquantifiable space between.

YEAR	TEAM	P. COUNT	FRM RUNS	BLK RUNS	THRW RUNS	TOT RUNS
2018	MIA	2036	2.2	0.3	0.1	2.6
2019	MIA	1947	0.4	-1.5	0.0	-1.1
2020	MIA	1950	0.0	0.2	0.0	0.2
2021	MIA	8418	1.9	1.1	0.2	3.2

PITCHERS

Sandy Alcantara RHP Born: 09/07/95 Age: 25 Bats: R Throws: R Height: 6'5" Weight: 200 Origin: International Free Agent, 2013

YEAR	TEAM	LVL	AGE	W	L	SV	G	GS	IP	H	HR	BB/9	K/9	K	GB%	BABIP	WHIP	ERA	DRA-	WARP	MPH	FA%	Whiff%	CSP
2018	JUP	HI-A	22	0	0	0	3	3	11¹	10	0	4.0	6.4	8	61.8%	.294	1.32	3.97	132	-0.1				
2018	NO	AAA	22	6	3	0	19	19	115²	107	10	3.0	6.8	88	48.7%	.284	1.25	3.89	89	1.8				
2018	MIA	MLB	22	2	3	0	6	6	34	25	3	6.1	7.9	30	47.3%	.256	1.41	3.44	124	-0.1	98.0	60.0%	27.1%	45.2%
2019	MIA	MLB	23	6	14	0	32	32	197¹	179	23	3.7	6.9	151	44.1%	.274	1.32	3.88	93	2.6	97.7	57.0%	23.8%	49.0%
2020	MIA	MLB	24	3	2	0	7	7	42	35	4	3.2	8.4	39	49.6%	.277	1.19	3.00	85	0.7	98.4	60.0%	24.1%	51.6%
2021 FS	MIA	MLB	25	9	9	0	26	26	150	143	20	4.3	8.3	137	46.0%	.292	1.43	4.64	103	0.8	97.9	57.9%	24.1%	49.3%
2021 DC	MIA	MLB	25	8	10	0	27	27	159	152	21	4.3	8.3	145	46.0%	.292	1.43	4.64	103	1.4	97.9	57.9%	24.1%	49.3%

Comparables: Lucas Giolito, Tyler Mahle, Luis Severino

Alcantara may never turn out to be the ace that his velocity and stuff portends, but he is plenty good in his current form. He's already driven past many of the roadblocks that force hard-throwing starting prospects into the 'pen. Alcantara is durable and turning into quite the innings eater, missed time in 2020 due to COVID notwithstanding. He's now a five-pitch starter, throwing a two-seam fastball, four-seam fastball, slider, changeup and curveball. And he pounds the strike zone, belying earlier command concerns from his days as a top prospect. If you can throw enough innings, pitches and strikes to stay in the rotation, and you have an arm as good as Alcantara's, you're not that far off from a high-end outcome.

Alcantara needs a more consistent swing-and-miss offering to take the last big step towards the top of the rotation. He started getting more whiffs on his fastball in 2020 thanks to a tick more heat but it remains to be seen if that will hold throughout a full season. There's no true out pitch at present, just a variety of above-average or plus that will occasionally flash bigger. Until that happens, he's "only" going to be a mid-rotation stalwart.

Richard Bleier LHP Born: 04/16/87 Age: 34 Bats: L Throws: L Height: 6'3" Weight: 215 Origin: Round 6, 2008 Draft (#183 overall)

YEAR	TEAM	LVL	AGE	W	L	SV	G	GS	IP	H	HR	BB/9	K/9	K	GB%	BABIP	WHIP	ERA	DRA-	WARP	MPH	FA%	Whiff%	CSP
2018	BAL	MLB	31	3	0	0	31	0	32²	36	0	1.1	4.1	15	57.5%	.319	1.22	1.93	113	-0.1	89.9	60.8%	19.1%	53.5%
2019	BAL	MLB	32	3	0	4	53	1	55¹	65	6	1.3	4.9	30	59.6%	.317	1.32	5.37	107	0.1	90.8	64.7%	17.1%	53.2%
2020	MIA	MLB	33	1	1	0	21	0	16²	14	0	2.2	5.9	11	70.6%	.275	1.08	2.16	65	0.5	90.4	53.2%	17.0%	47.8%
2021 FS	MIA	MLB	34	2	2	6	57	0	50	54	5	2.1	5.8	32	62.0%	.303	1.33	4.37	101	0.1	90.6	61.2%	17.4%	51.9%
2021 DC	MIA	MLB	34	2	2	6	53	0	57	62	6	2.1	5.8	36	62.0%	.303	1.33	4.37	101	0.3	90.6	61.2%	17.4%	51.9%

Comparables: Tommy Hunter, Chris Rusin, Luis García

Bleier was a reinforcement Marlin, picked up from the Orioles during the COVID layoff for a PTBNL that turned out to be a rookie-ball flier. Baltimore general manager Mike Elias said Miami had prior interest in Bleier, though, and he hung around as a setup option even after the cavalry returned. He's a no-true-outcomes leftballer, hurling up a mix of low-velocity slop that rarely strikes anyone out, while being stingy with the walks and homers—generally hoping to induce batters to hit 'em where they are. He's just good enough against righties that the anti-LOOGY rule changes didn't kill his career. Honestly, one would have expected a "break glass in case of emergency" pickup out of the Orioles bullpen to do far worse.

Brad Boxberger RHP Born: 05/27/88 Age: 33 Bats: R Throws: R Height: 5'10" Weight: 211 Origin: Round 1, 2009 Draft (#43 overall)

YEAR	TEAM	LVL	AGE	W	L	SV	G	GS	IP	H	HR	BB/9	K/9	K	GB%	BABIP	WHIP	ERA	DRA-	WARP	MPH	FA%	Whiff%	CSP
2018	ARI	MLB	30	3	7	32	60	0	53¹	44	9	5.4	12.0	71	45.8%	.292	1.43	4.39	114	-0.1	93.4	66.3%	27.1%	46.7%
2019	HBG	AA	31	1	1	1	8	0	8²	6	0	3.1	11.4	11	38.1%	.286	1.04	1.04	71	0.1				
2019	LOU	AAA	31	0	0	0	5	0	5¹	10	2	8.4	13.5	8	16.7%	.500	2.81	11.81	179	-0.1				
2019	KC	MLB	31	1	3	1	29	0	26²	25	3	5.7	9.1	27	39.0%	.297	1.57	5.40	126	-0.2	91.6	47.0%	29.0%	45.8%
2020	MIA	MLB	32	1	0	0	23	0	18	17	3	4.0	9.0	18	50.0%	.286	1.39	3.00	83	0.3	94.1	55.2%	24.2%	49.0%
2021 FS	MIA	MLB	33	2	2	0	57	0	50	41	6	4.4	9.8	54	42.3%	.280	1.33	3.70	89	0.4	93.1	56.1%	26.7%	47.2%

Comparables: Mike Dunn, Jeremy Jeffress, Santiago Casilla

Boxberger looked utterly cooked at the end of 2019, a season in which he was released from not only Kansas City's major-league club, but Cincinnati's Triple-A team and Washington's Double-A team. It wasn't a tough diagnosis: He could ill afford a full grade of command, nor either of the ticks he lost on his heater. His career seemed, well, done. Miami picked him up for a no-risk look-see on a late non-roster invite, the type of deal thrown at former All-Star closers to see if there's something to fix. In a bit of a surprise, some juice remained. Boxberger's velocity was back and he made the team, quickly establishing himself as The Eighth-Inning Guy, performing well during the regular season and playoff run. He might not be a closer anymore and he's certainly not an All-Star, but it's not a bad second act.

Jeff Brigham RHP Born: 02/16/92 Age: 29 Bats: R Throws: R Height: 6'0" Weight: 195 Origin: Round 4, 2014 Draft (#129 overall)

YEAR	TEAM	LVL	AGE	W	L	SV	G	GS	IP	H	HR	BB/9	K/9	K	GB%	BABIP	WHIP	ERA	DRA-	WARP	MPH	FA%	Whiff%	CSP
2018	JAX	AA	26	4	1	0	7	7	38	27	1	2.1	9.7	41	40.9%	.299	0.95	1.18	91	0.4				
2018	NO	AAA	26	5	2	0	9	9	52¹	53	7	2.2	8.3	48	28.1%	.319	1.26	3.44	85	0.9				
2018	MIA	MLB	26	0	4	0	4	4	16¹	16	2	7.2	6.6	12	18.0%	.292	1.78	6.06	160	-0.4	94.9	61.1%	19.9%	47.4%
2019	NO	AAA	27	0	1	2	17	0	24	9	0	3.0	11.2	30	40.8%	.184	0.71	1.50	20	1.2				
2019	MIA	MLB	27	3	2	1	32	0	38¹	36	8	3.3	9.2	39	32.7%	.283	1.30	4.46	97	0.3	98.0	51.5%	25.4%	49.6%
2020	MIA	MLB	28	0	0	0	1	0	1	2	0	0.0	0.0	0	0.0%	.400	2.00	9.00	112	0.0	95.0	68.2%	0.0%	57.3%
2021 FS	MIA	MLB	29	2	2	0	57	0	50	45	8	3.4	9.0	50	32.8%	.275	1.28	4.30	101	0.1	97.3	53.9%	23.4%	49.5%
2021 DC	MIA	MLB	29	2	2	0	33	3	44	39	7	3.4	9.0	44	32.8%	.275	1.28	4.30	101	0.3	97.3	53.9%	23.4%	49.5%

Comparables: Alec Mills, Kelvin Marte, Glenn Sparkman

We can all relate to Brigham's 2020, a tale of fleeting hope sandwiched by lengthy disappointments. Sidelined in the preseason by a biceps injury, he would have missed months of action—if there had been any. COVID-19 gave him time to recover and return for a single inning, then ended his season with a positive test.

★ ★ ★ *2021 Top 101 Prospect* **#45** ★ ★ ★

Edward Cabrera RHP Born: 04/13/98 Age: 23 Bats: R Throws: R Height: 6'5" Weight: 217 Origin: International Free Agent, 2015

YEAR	TEAM	LVL	AGE	W	L	SV	G	GS	IP	H	HR	BB/9	K/9	K	GB%	BABIP	WHIP	ERA	DRA-	WARP	MPH	FA%	Whiff%	CSP
2018	GBO	LO-A	20	4	8	0	22	22	100¹	105	11	3.8	8.3	93	43.4%	.329	1.47	4.22	139	-1.7				
2019	JUP	HI-A	21	5	3	0	11	11	58	37	1	2.8	11.3	73	47.3%	.281	0.95	2.02	62	1.4				
2019	JAX	AA	21	4	1	0	8	8	38²	28	6	3.0	10.0	43	48.5%	.242	1.06	2.56	70	0.7				
2021 FS	MIA	MLB	23	1	2	0	57	0	50	47	7	4.0	8.7	48	44.3%	.292	1.40	4.74	112	-0.2				
2021 DC	MIA	MLB	23	1	2	0	6	6	27	25	4	4.0	8.7	26	44.3%	.292	1.40	4.74	112	0.1				

Comparables: Jonathan Hernández, Gerrit Cole, Frankie Montas

Most top pitching prospects with upper-minors experience debuted in 2020 as compressed schedules forced nearly every team's hand. Despite Miami's pressing pitching needs, Cabrera did not. He suffered from minor arm issues towards the end of summer camp and the Marlins handled his ramp-up very carefully at the alternate site. By the time the playoffs rolled around he was throwing simulated games as part of the taxi squad, and he very well might've shown up if the team had advanced a little further. We're still in on him, even if major question marks remain about whether he's a starter or reliever long-term.

Daniel Castano LHP   Born: 09/17/94   Age: 26   Bats: L   Throws: L   Height: 6'3"   Weight: 231   Origin: Round 19, 2016 Draft (#586 overall)

YEAR	TEAM	LVL	AGE	W	L	SV	G	GS	IP	H	HR	BB/9	K/9	K	GB%	BABIP	WHIP	ERA	DRA-	WARP	MPH	FA%	Whiff%	CSP
2018	MRL	ROK	23	0	1	0	2	1	9	10	0	0.0	8.0	8	58.6%	.345	1.11	4.00	39	0.4				
2018	GBO	LO-A	23	4	3	0	8	8	50	48	10	0.7	9.4	52	62.0%	.288	1.04	2.70	79	0.8				
2018	JUP	HI-A	23	5	8	0	14	14	76	95	3	2.8	6.6	56	54.2%	.359	1.57	4.74	81	1.2				
2019	JUP	HI-A	24	0	2	0	12	0	33	33	2	1.9	8.5	31	61.8%	.316	1.21	3.82	96	0.0				
2019	JAX	AA	24	7	2	0	18	11	86	82	2	1.7	7.6	73	48.5%	.308	1.14	3.35	94	0.3				
2020	MIA	MLB	25	1	2	0	7	6	29²	30	3	3.3	3.6	12	46.6%	.270	1.38	3.03	127	-0.2	92.0	50.2%	19.7%	50.6%
2021 FS	MIA	MLB	26	2	3	0	57	0	50	55	7	2.6	6.0	33	45.6%	.299	1.39	4.85	112	-0.2	92.0	50.2%	19.7%	50.6%
2021 DC	MIA	MLB	26	2	3	0	45	3	57	62	8	2.6	6.0	38	45.6%	.299	1.39	4.85	112	0.0	92.0	50.2%	19.7%	50.6%

Comparables: Gregory Soto, Cody Stashak, Joe Palumbo

Soft-tossing lefty Castano was called upon to take a few starts in August when nobody else in the organization could. While his ERA sparkled enough to get some additional work later in the season, his DRA and peripherals tell the story of an overmatched Quad-A pitcher walking a very tight rope.

Adam Cimber RHP   Born: 08/15/90   Age: 30   Bats: R   Throws: R   Height: 6'3"   Weight: 195   Origin: Round 9, 2013 Draft (#268 overall)

YEAR	TEAM	LVL	AGE	W	L	SV	G	GS	IP	H	HR	BB/9	K/9	K	GB%	BABIP	WHIP	ERA	DRA-	WARP	MPH	FA%	Whiff%	CSP
2018	CLE	MLB	27	0	3	0	28	0	20	26	3	3.1	3.1	7	66.2%	.329	1.65	4.05	137	-0.3	89.4	73.5%	12.8%	50.3%
2018	SD	MLB	27	3	5	0	42	0	48¹	42	2	1.9	9.5	51	51.9%	.317	1.08	3.17	87	0.6	88.7	75.8%	24.2%	59.1%
2019	CLE	MLB	28	6	3	1	68	0	56²	56	6	3.0	6.5	41	55.0%	.289	1.32	4.45	107	0.1	87.8	67.8%	20.3%	50.1%
2020	CLE	MLB	29	0	1	0	14	0	11¹	13	1	1.6	4.0	5	52.4%	.293	1.32	3.97	100	0.1	87.5	50.8%	22.2%	52.7%
2021 FS	MIA	MLB	30	2	2	0	57	0	50	52	5	2.0	6.7	37	53.5%	.302	1.28	4.07	96	0.2	88.0	67.1%	20.6%	52.4%
2021 DC	MIA	MLB	30	2	2	0	53	0	57	59	6	2.0	6.7	42	53.5%	.302	1.28	4.07	96	0.5	88.0	67.1%	20.6%	52.4%

Comparables: James Russell, Jay Ritchie, Nick Wittgren

Is Cimber the solution to the three-true-outcome problem in baseball? A mere 16 percent of the batters he faced walked, homered or struck out, the lowest rate among all hurlers with double-digit frames. Given Cimber's middling career rates, this was probably a small-sample fluke than the new normal. Still, if he keeps it up for much longer Rob Manfred might get some ideas—like, say, forcing every pitcher to rely on mid-80s velocity and a mound-scraping release point. In an alternate reality, there are cardboard cutouts of a mid-delivery Cimber in every bullpen, with signage that instructs "You must release the ball from this low to enter the game." In this reality, he's just trying to stay on the roster for another year.

Ross Detwiler LHP   Born: 03/06/86   Age: 35   Bats: R   Throws: L   Height: 6'5"   Weight: 210   Origin: Round 1, 2007 Draft (#6 overall)

YEAR	TEAM	LVL	AGE	W	L	SV	G	GS	IP	H	HR	BB/9	K/9	K	GB%	BABIP	WHIP	ERA	DRA-	WARP	MPH	FA%	Whiff%	CSP
2018	TAC	AAA	32	2	5	0	16	13	84²	94	10	2.7	5.5	52	40.9%	.318	1.41	4.89	96	1.0				
2018	SEA	MLB	32	0	1	0	1	0	6	8	1	3.0	3.0	2	52.6%	.389	1.67	4.50	144	-0.1	91.0	52.6%	15.0%	56.3%
2019	CHA	AAA	33	1	2	0	8	8	43	44	11	2.3	7.3	35	50.0%	.287	1.28	3.98	76	1.2				
2019	CHW	MLB	33	3	5	0	18	12	69²	86	20	3.5	5.9	46	50.6%	.304	1.62	6.59	165	-1.8	93.2	51.5%	16.2%	50.9%
2020	CHW	MLB	34	1	1	0	16	0	19²	19	2	2.3	6.9	15	58.3%	.293	1.22	3.20	86	0.3	93.4	56.9%	27.9%	47.2%
2021 FS	MIA	MLB	35	2	2	0	57	0	50	53	7	3.5	6.6	36	49.3%	.300	1.47	5.14	114	-0.3	93.2	53.1%	19.5%	50.0%
2021 DC	MIA	MLB	35	2	2	0	53	0	57	61	8	3.5	6.6	42	49.3%	.300	1.47	5.14	114	-0.1	93.2	53.1%	19.5%	50.0%

Comparables: Javy Guerra, Homer Bailey, Johnny Cueto

When he's a promising 21-year-old left-hander selected sixth overall out of Missouri State—Potential Hoss Ross.

During his standalone full (mostly), healthy and above-average year in a major league rotation back in 2012 with the Nationals—Big Boss Ross.

When he's pitching in the Atlantic League at the start of 2019, five MLB organizations later—A Rolling Stone Gathers No Moss Ross.

When he's sopping up innings as a mop-up man for the White Sox later that same year, piling up ghastly statistics while pitching through an obvious hip injury—Operating at a Loss Ross.

Living a second (third? fourth?) life as a decently effective reliever, throwing sinkers in 2020—Saucy Rossy

Getting DFA'd at the end of the year anyway—To Live is to Mourn Loss Ross

Catching on with Miami—Live Más Ross

Dax Fulton LHP   Born: 10/16/01   Age: 19   Bats: L   Throws: L   Height: 6'6"   Weight: 230   Origin: Round 2, 2020 Draft (#40 overall)

One of the best prep pitchers in the 2020 Draft, Fulton was still available to the Marlins at the 40th pick because of September 2019 Tommy John surgery. They gave him first-round money to eschew his commitment to Vanderbilt. He's quite a few years away, but his talent is promising.

Yimi García RHP Born: 08/18/90 Age: 30 Bats: R Throws: R Height: 6'2" Weight: 228 Origin: International Free Agent, 2009

YEAR	TEAM	LVL	AGE	W	L	SV	G	GS	IP	H	HR	BB/9	K/9	K	GB%	BABIP	WHIP	ERA	DRA-	WARP	MPH	FA%	Whiff%	CSP
2018	OKC	AAA	27	1	0	1	14	0	14²	16	2	0.0	8.6	14	37.8%	.341	1.09	4.30	49	0.5				51.4%
2018	LAD	MLB	27	1	2	0	25	0	22¹	29	7	1.6	7.7	19	35.5%	.319	1.48	5.64	138	-0.3	96.6	56.4%	21.9%	51.4%
2019	LAD	MLB	28	1	4	0	64	0	62¹	40	15	2.0	9.5	66	29.2%	.172	0.87	3.61	88	0.7	96.3	46.0%	26.7%	48.3%
2020	MIA	MLB	29	3	0	1	14	0	15	9	0	3.0	11.4	19	47.2%	.250	0.93	0.60	75	0.3	96.2	49.4%	29.2%	47.2%
2021 FS	MIA	MLB	30	3	2	27	57	0	50	41	7	2.4	9.8	54	34.5%	.270	1.11	3.36	84	0.6	96.3	48.0%	26.7%	48.4%
2021 DC	MIA	MLB	30	3	2	27	59	0	63	52	9	2.4	9.8	68	34.5%	.270	1.11	3.36	84	0.9	96.3	48.0%	26.7%	48.4%

Comparables: Nick Wittgren, Shawn Armstrong, Emilio Pagán

The Dodgers non-tendered García last winter after a frustratingly homer-prone run. Miami quickly pounced with a major-league contract, reuniting him with manager Don Mattingly, whose last season in Los Angeles coincided with García's best. Mattingly used García as a high-leverage fireman when he was available and García rewarded him with the best 15 innings of his career, without allowing a single homer. There's some reason to believe there were real adjustments buried in the small-sample size here; he's decreased the usage of his fastball rather substantially since returning from Tommy John surgery several years ago, and he induced a lot more grounders than he has in the past.

Braxton Garrett LHP Born: 08/05/97 Age: 23 Bats: L Throws: L Height: 6'2" Weight: 202 Origin: Round 1, 2016 Draft (#7 overall)

YEAR	TEAM	LVL	AGE	W	L	SV	G	GS	IP	H	HR	BB/9	K/9	K	GB%	BABIP	WHIP	ERA	DRA-	WARP	MPH	FA%	Whiff%	CSP
2019	JUP	HI-A	21	6	6	0	20	20	105	92	13	3.2	10.1	118	53.9%	.294	1.23	3.34	99	0.2				
2019	JAX	AA	21	0	1	0	1	1	1²	4	0	16.2	5.4	1	55.6%	.444	4.20	16.20	209	-0.1				
2020	MIA	MLB	22	1	1	0	2	2	7²	8	3	5.9	9.4	8	61.9%	.278	1.70	5.87	103	0.1	90.9	48.9%	23.1%	37.0%
2021 FS	MIA	MLB	23	1	1	0	57	0	50	47	6	5.7	8.7	48	50.4%	.295	1.57	4.98	109	-0.1	90.9	48.9%	23.1%	37.0%
2021 DC	MIA	MLB	23	1	1	0	4	4	19	17	2	5.7	8.7	18	50.4%	.295	1.57	4.98	109	0.1	90.9	48.9%	23.1%	37.0%

Comparables: Pedro Avila, Trevor Rogers, Jonathan Hernández

Garrett tore his UCL only four games into his pro career back in 2017, which cost him nearly all of his first two full seasons. He took the ball on his regular turn in 2019, reestablishing his health and a solid level of performance. What he didn't quite have was his best fastball velocity, but that sometimes lags a year behind the return to the field. He didn't get the expected chance to establish his best fastball in the minors in 2020, and when called upon for a pair of spot starts in the majors it was still hovering right around 90. While Garrett still has a plus curveball and a strong command profile, he's going to have a hard time missing many bats without a little more oomph on the fastball and better velocity separation between his heater and change. We remain hopeful that will all come around with a better foundation; he's still only 129 2/3 innings into his pro career, after all.

Jorge Guzman RHP Born: 01/28/96 Age: 25 Bats: R Throws: R Height: 6'1" Weight: 246 Origin: International Free Agent, 2014

YEAR	TEAM	LVL	AGE	W	L	SV	G	GS	IP	H	HR	BB/9	K/9	K	GB%	BABIP	WHIP	ERA	DRA-	WARP	MPH	FA%	Whiff%	CSP
2018	JUP	HI-A	22	0	9	0	21	21	96	84	7	6.0	9.5	101	37.9%	.308	1.54	4.03	101	0.5				
2019	JAX	AA	23	7	11	0	25	24	138²	96	13	4.6	8.2	127	31.7%	.244	1.20	3.50	85	1.3				
2020	MIA	MLB	24	0	0	0	1	0	1	2	2	9.0	0.0	0	20.0%	.000	3.00	18.00	131	0.0	98.8	63.2%	0.0%	47.0%
2021 FS	MIA	MLB	25	1	2	0	57	0	50	50	9	6.0	8.2	45	32.7%	.293	1.68	6.09	128	-0.7	98.8	63.2%	0.0%	47.0%
2021 DC	MIA	MLB	25	1	2	0	33	3	44	44	8	6.0	8.2	40	32.7%	.293	1.68	6.09	128	-0.3	98.8	63.2%	0.0%	47.0%

Comparables: Matt Hall, Mauricio Llovera, Keury Mella

Guzman popped up for an emergency August cameo by virtue of already being on the 40-man roster, where he showed off the good (upper-90s heater and two viable secondary offerings) and bad (poor command) in his lone relief appearance. He appears headed down the bullpen path long-term.

Elieser Hernandez RHP Born: 05/03/95 Age: 26 Bats: R Throws: R Height: 6'0" Weight: 214 Origin: International Free Agent, 2011

YEAR	TEAM	LVL	AGE	W	L	SV	G	GS	IP	H	HR	BB/9	K/9	K	GB%	BABIP	WHIP	ERA	DRA-	WARP	MPH	FA%	Whiff%	CSP
2018	JUP	HI-A	23	0	1	0	2	2	6	9	2	6.0	7.5	5	68.2%	.350	2.17	6.00	92	0.1				
2018	JAX	AA	23	0	0	0	2	2	9	7	3	4.0	10.0	10	22.7%	.211	1.22	4.00	89	0.1				
2018	MIA	MLB	23	2	7	0	32	6	65²	68	11	3.7	6.2	45	27.6%	.291	1.45	5.21	134	-0.7	92.7	62.2%	21.3%	49.8%
2019	NO	AAA	24	3	1	0	9	9	48	35	0	2.6	12.9	69	32.4%	.315	1.02	1.12	29	2.4				
2019	MIA	MLB	24	3	5	0	21	15	82¹	76	20	2.8	9.3	85	33.5%	.267	1.24	5.03	98	0.9	92.9	55.3%	25.3%	49.2%
2020	MIA	MLB	25	1	0	0	6	6	25²	21	5	1.8	11.9	34	33.8%	.267	1.01	3.16	83	0.5	93.4	58.9%	29.2%	55.8%
2021 FS	MIA	MLB	26	9	8	0	26	26	150	128	24	3.1	10.2	169	33.1%	.280	1.20	3.94	93	1.7	93.0	57.6%	25.4%	51.0%
2021 DC	MIA	MLB	26	8	9	0	25	25	137	117	22	3.1	10.2	155	33.1%	.280	1.20	3.94	93	1.9	93.0	57.6%	25.4%	51.0%

Comparables: Anthony Bass, Alex Reyes, Antonio Senzatela

Miami plucked Hernandez out of the lower levels of Houston's minors via the Rule 5 draft back in 2018. Two years later he looks to be a viable back-end starter with a fastball-slider repertoire who'll give up his fair share of dingers. In other words, a developmental win.

James Hoyt RHP Born: 09/30/86 Age: 34 Bats: R Throws: R Height: 6'6" Weight: 230 Origin: Undrafted Free Agent, 2013

YEAR	TEAM	LVL	AGE	W	L	SV	G	GS	IP	H	HR	BB/9	K/9	K	GB%	BABIP	WHIP	ERA	DRA-	WARP	MPH	FA%	Whiff%	CSP
2018	FRE	AAA	31	0	3	5	25	0	28	19	2	2.6	10.6	33	50.0%	.262	0.96	2.25	59	0.8				
2018	HOU	MLB	31	0	0	0	1	0	0¹	1	0	27.0	0.0	0	100.0%	.500	6.00	0.00	46	0.0	94.8	66.7%	25.0%	33.6%
2019	COL	AAA	32	2	0	4	40	2	42	46	3	4.3	10.3	48	52.5%	.374	1.57	3.43	103	0.5				
2019	CLE	MLB	32	0	0	0	8	0	8¹	6	2	2.2	10.8	10	45.0%	.222	0.96	2.16	105	0.0	95.2	42.3%	40.0%	43.5%
2020	MIA	MLB	33	2	0	0	24	0	14²	9	1	4.9	12.3	20	45.5%	.250	1.16	1.23	81	0.3	90.8	30.6%	35.3%	41.8%
2021 FS	MIA	MLB	34	2	2	0	57	0	50	42	6	3.8	10.5	58	45.2%	.290	1.26	3.65	85	0.5	92.0	34.0%	36.3%	42.1%
2021 DC	MIA	MLB	34	2	2	0	41	0	44	36	5	3.8	10.5	51	45.2%	.290	1.26	3.65	85	0.6	92.0	34.0%	36.3%	42.1%

Comparables: Oliver Drake, Luis García, Chris Hatcher

Formerly a bog-standard 95-and-a-slider up-and-down type who now has a hard time touching 90 mph, Hoyt emerged as a surprisingly reliable option in Miami's 'pen—after his emergency purchase out of DFA limbo—by spamming his slider over two-thirds of the time.

Brandon Kintzler RHP Born: 08/01/84 Age: 36 Bats: R Throws: R Height: 5'10" Weight: 200 Origin: Round 40, 2004 Draft (#1182 overall)

YEAR	TEAM	LVL	AGE	W	L	SV	G	GS	IP	H	HR	BB/9	K/9	K	GB%	BABIP	WHIP	ERA	DRA-	WARP	MPH	FA%	Whiff%	CSP
2018	CHC	MLB	33	2	1	0	25	0	18	27	3	4.5	6.0	12	53.0%	.381	2.00	7.00	142	-0.3	94.4	85.8%	19.0%	45.4%
2018	WAS	MLB	33	1	2	2	45	0	42²	40	2	2.7	6.5	31	48.4%	.304	1.24	3.59	142	-0.7	93.9	84.0%	16.2%	49.1%
2019	CHC	MLB	34	3	3	1	62	0	57	45	5	2.1	7.6	48	55.6%	.255	1.02	2.68	78	1.0	94.4	73.3%	18.6%	49.3%
2020	MIA	MLB	35	2	3	12	24	0	24¹	21	3	4.1	5.2	14	56.6%	.247	1.32	2.22	106	0.1	93.0	75.8%	15.2%	49.9%
2021 FS	MIA	MLB	36	2	3	0	57	0	50	52	6	2.8	6.6	36	54.2%	.298	1.36	4.36	105	0.0	93.9	77.0%	17.3%	49.1%

Comparables: Luis Ayala, Joe Smith, Tony Castillo

For the second time in his career, Kintzler stepped into a closer's job for lack of any particular better options and, just like the first time around, it went just fine. The itinerant sinkerballer lingered on the free agent market until Miami gobbled him up as part of its late splurge on useful veteran spare parts. For $3.25 million, they rented an adequate closer for a year. Kintzler still doesn't strike anyone out, but he does consistently put up shiny ERAs and had previous late-game experience—sometimes, just enough actually is enough.

Brandon Leibrandt LHP Born: 12/13/92 Age: 28 Bats: L Throws: L Height: 6'4" Weight: 190 Origin: Round 6, 2014 Draft (#172 overall)

YEAR	TEAM	LVL	AGE	W	L	SV	G	GS	IP	H	HR	BB/9	K/9	K	GB%	BABIP	WHIP	ERA	DRA-	WARP	MPH	FA%	Whiff%	CSP
2018	LHV	AAA	25	4	1	0	20	6	50²	34	1	1.8	5.7	32	46.6%	.229	0.87	1.42	83	0.7				
2020	MIA	MLB	27	0	0	0	5	0	9	3	0	7.0	3.0	3	38.5%	.115	1.11	2.00	127	-0.1	90.6	47.3%	14.7%	50.5%
2021 FS	MIA	MLB	28	2	3	0	57	0	50	52	8	3.5	6.8	37	40.6%	.290	1.43	4.83	112	-0.2	90.6	47.3%	14.7%	50.5%

Comparables: Andrew Suárez, William Cuevas, Tyler Wilson

The Marlins looked absolutely everywhere for major-league ready players after they lost most of their roster to COVID. They found Leibrandt pitching for the New Jersey Blasters, a Washington Generals-style house opponent the Somerset Patriots formed to have a team to play against in the absence of an Atlantic League season. After years of struggling with injuries, the former Phillies prospect made the majors just a few short weeks later, although the story has an unhappy ending—he went down for the season with another elbow injury after just five appearances.

Pablo López RHP Born: 03/07/96 Age: 25 Bats: L Throws: R Height: 6'4" Weight: 225 Origin: International Free Agent, 2012

YEAR	TEAM	LVL	AGE	W	L	SV	G	GS	IP	H	HR	BB/9	K/9	K	GB%	BABIP	WHIP	ERA	DRA-	WARP	MPH	FA%	Whiff%	CSP
2018	JAX	AA	22	1	2	0	8	8	43²	30	3	1.6	10.5	51	41.6%	.248	0.87	0.62	76	0.9				
2018	NO	AAA	22	1	1	0	4	4	18²	16	3	1.9	7.2	15	44.8%	.241	1.07	3.38	87	0.3				
2018	MIA	MLB	22	2	4	0	10	10	58²	56	8	2.8	7.1	46	49.2%	.282	1.26	4.14	102	0.5	94.7	60.4%	24.3%	46.5%
2019	NO	AAA	23	0	0	0	2	2	9¹	10	0	2.9	9.6	10	61.5%	.385	1.39	1.93	92	0.2				
2019	MIA	MLB	23	5	8	0	21	21	111¹	111	15	2.2	7.7	95	47.3%	.303	1.24	5.09	85	1.9	95.6	58.7%	23.7%	49.0%
2020	MIA	MLB	24	6	4	0	11	11	57¹	50	4	2.8	9.3	59	52.8%	.293	1.19	3.61	72	1.4	95.4	63.1%	26.5%	47.4%
2021 FS	MIA	MLB	25	9	8	0	26	26	150	141	17	2.6	8.6	143	48.9%	.296	1.24	3.78	89	2.0	95.4	60.6%	24.8%	48.1%
2021 DC	MIA	MLB	25	8	8	0	25	25	137	129	16	2.6	8.6	131	48.9%	.296	1.24	3.78	89	2.2	95.4	60.6%	24.8%	48.1%

Comparables: Joe Ross, Luke Weaver, Lance McCullers Jr.

One of the catalysts for Miami's sudden playoff surge was López pitching like an ace. Long a command-and-control specialist, López has picked up a couple ticks of velocity in the majors while altering his pitch mix. He ratcheted up his changeup usage in 2020, throwing his best offspeed pitch nearly 30 percent of the time, and developed a new cutter that gave him an additional glove-side look on top of his curveball. He pitched at a Cy Young level through his first six starts, and while he wasn't able to keep it up through September by traditional metrics, his seasonal DRA was still creeping towards elite. If he keeps striking batters out and suppressing hard contact like he did in 2020, he's only a couple hundred innings away from being talked about as one of the best young pitchers in the game, even though he isn't the best young pitcher on the Marlins.

─────────────── ★ ★ ★ *2021 Top 101 Prospect* **#51** ★ ★ ★ ───────────────

Max Meyer RHP Born: 03/12/99 Age: 22 Bats: L Throws: R Height: 6'0" Weight: 196 Origin: Round 1, 2020 Draft (#3 overall)

With great rotation upside comes great bullpen risk. The Marlins bypassed safer options like Texas A&M lefty Asa Lacy and Vanderbilt slugger Austin Martin with the third pick last summer in favor of Meyer's venomous two-pitch combo. The converted closer was hitting triple digits as a starter with his lively fastball during the abbreviated 2020 college season, and his hard slider has as much bite as any in the game. The changeup needs work—he didn't need it a whole lot as a Minnesota Golden Gopher—and if it doesn't get there he's going back into the bullpen-verse sooner or later. Frankly, we half-expected to see him slinging webs out of the 'pen in the playoffs a la Garrett Crochet. He's a kingpin-in-waiting if he can stick as a starter, and you know, one grade of changeup really can make a difference.

Nick Neidert RHP Born: 11/20/96 Age: 24 Bats: R Throws: R Height: 6'1" Weight: 202 Origin: Round 2, 2015 Draft (#60 overall)

YEAR	TEAM	LVL	AGE	W	L	SV	G	GS	IP	H	HR	BB/9	K/9	K	GB%	BABIP	WHIP	ERA	DRA-	WARP	MPH	FA%	Whiff%	CSP
2018	JAX	AA	21	12	7	0	26	26	152²	142	17	1.8	9.1	154	45.0%	.311	1.13	3.24	80	2.8				
2019	JUP	HI-A	22	0	1	0	2	2	9¹	10	1	3.9	5.8	6	29.0%	.300	1.50	4.82	110	0.0				
2019	NO	AAA	22	3	4	0	9	9	41	45	4	4.8	8.1	37	23.8%	.339	1.63	5.05	117	0.4				
2020	MIA	MLB	23	0	0	0	4	0	8¹	10	1	2.2	4.3	4	60.7%	.333	1.44	5.40	94	0.1	93.2	60.3%	12.9%	52.4%
2021 FS	MIA	MLB	24	3	4	0	57	0	50	53	8	3.3	6.9	38	40.8%	.300	1.44	5.13	115	-0.3	93.2	60.3%	12.9%	52.4%
2021 DC	MIA	MLB	24	3	4	0	42	6	64	69	10	3.3	6.9	49	40.8%	.300	1.44	5.13	115	0.0	93.2	60.3%	12.9%	52.4%

Comparables: Beau Burrows, Aaron Sanchez, Archie Bradley

A low-90s fastball. A changeup-first offspeed repertoire. Two breaking balls, technically distinguishable but neither distinguished. All of this plus strike-throwing ability and some funk in the delivery. It's a Kyle Hendricks starter kit, right? Kyle Hendricks starter kits are never Kyle Hendricks though, and Neidert is no different. It all adds up to a back of the rotation starter, with the potential for less.

─────────────── ★ ★ ★ *2021 Top 101 Prospect* **#94** ★ ★ ★ ───────────────

Trevor Rogers LHP Born: 11/13/97 Age: 23 Bats: L Throws: L Height: 6'5" Weight: 217 Origin: Round 1, 2017 Draft (#13 overall)

YEAR	TEAM	LVL	AGE	W	L	SV	G	GS	IP	H	HR	BB/9	K/9	K	GB%	BABIP	WHIP	ERA	DRA-	WARP	MPH	FA%	Whiff%	CSP
2018	GBO	LO-A	20	2	7	0	17	17	72²	86	4	3.3	10.5	85	46.7%	.398	1.56	5.82	94	0.6				
2019	JUP	HI-A	21	5	8	0	18	18	110¹	97	7	2.0	10.0	122	40.8%	.307	1.10	2.53	80	1.5				
2019	JAX	AA	21	1	2	0	5	5	26	25	3	3.1	9.7	28	28.8%	.319	1.31	4.50	102	0.0				
2020	MIA	MLB	22	1	2	0	7	7	28	32	4	4.2	12.5	39	46.1%	.380	1.61	6.11	80	0.6	95.8	60.0%	30.1%	47.2%
2021 FS	MIA	MLB	23	9	8	0	26	26	150	140	21	3.5	9.4	156	42.5%	.299	1.33	4.20	97	1.3	95.8	60.0%	30.1%	47.2%
2021 DC	MIA	MLB	23	4	6	0	21	21	84	78	11	3.5	9.4	87	42.5%	.299	1.33	4.20	97	1.0	95.8	60.0%	30.1%	47.2%

Comparables: Kris Bubic, Brock Burke, Patrick Sandoval

Pay attention to the DRA on this one. The tall lefty substantially outpitched his ghastly ERA last year, inducing whiffs and managing contact well with both a high-spin fastball and a nasty, sinking changeup. He had one nightmare start where he was torched for nine runs; that hurts more in an abbreviated season. Rogers was a year ahead of schedule reaching the majors with very limited high-minors experience and he was ready for the assignment. He's already come very far over the past two seasons, and further development of his slider and command could vault him further up the major-league rotation.

─────────────── ★ ★ ★ *2021 Top 101 Prospect* **#4** ★ ★ ★ ───────────────

Sixto Sánchez RHP Born: 07/29/98 Age: 22 Bats: R Throws: R Height: 6'0" Weight: 234 Origin: International Free Agent, 2015

YEAR	TEAM	LVL	AGE	W	L	SV	G	GS	IP	H	HR	BB/9	K/9	K	GB%	BABIP	WHIP	ERA	DRA-	WARP	MPH	FA%	Whiff%	CSP
2018	CLR	HI-A	19	4	3	0	8	8	46²	39	1	2.1	8.7	45	51.5%	.295	1.07	2.51	76	0.9				
2019	JUP	HI-A	20	0	2	0	2	2	11	14	1	1.6	4.9	6	60.5%	.351	1.45	4.91	117	-0.1				
2019	JAX	AA	20	8	4	0	18	18	103	87	5	1.7	8.5	97	47.3%	.288	1.03	2.53	83	1.1				
2020	MIA	MLB	21	3	2	0	7	7	39	36	3	2.5	7.6	33	58.0%	.303	1.21	3.46	79	0.8	100.1	47.0%	24.9%	50.1%
2021 FS	MIA	MLB	22	9	8	0	26	26	150	150	17	2.8	8.2	136	50.7%	.306	1.31	4.09	95	1.5	100.1	47.0%	24.9%	50.1%
2021 DC	MIA	MLB	22	7	9	0	25	25	134	134	16	2.8	8.2	121	50.7%	.306	1.31	4.09	95	1.7	100.1	47.0%	24.9%	50.1%

Comparables: Brett Anderson, David Holmberg, Jack Flaherty

An answer in the form of a question. The Final Jeopardy category is EMERGING BASEBALL SUPERSTARS.

ANSWER: This short and stout Miami hurler burst on the national scene in 2020. He was immediately one of the hardest-throwing starting pitchers in the majors. He continued to throw a veritable potpourri of offspeed pitches, as he'd done throughout his minor-league career. His changeup has the speed of a normal pitcher's fastball to go along with filthy movement. He rips off visually stunning breaking balls. His command is present most of the time. He's been an ace-in-waiting since he was a teenager in the Phillies system. He's almost there already.

QUESTION: Who is Sixto Sánchez, Alex?

Josh D. Smith LHP   Born: 10/11/89   Age: 31   Bats: L   Throws: L   Height: 6'3"   Weight: 200   Origin: Round 25, 2012 Draft (#766 overall)

YEAR	TEAM	LVL	AGE	W	L	SV	G	GS	IP	H	HR	BB/9	K/9	K	GB%	BABIP	WHIP	ERA	DRA-	WARP	MPH	FA%	Whiff%	CSP
2018	WOR	AAA	28	9	5	0	28	14	98²	85	4	3.9	8.8	97	43.2%	.301	1.30	3.01	88	1.2				
2019	COL	AAA	29	8	1	6	41	0	52²	32	7	4.1	12.6	74	38.5%	.229	1.06	2.73	49	1.9				
2019	CLE	MLB	29	0	0	0	8	0	8¹	8	0	8.6	13.0	12	38.1%	.381	1.92	5.40	103	0.0	92.4	62.8%	21.3%	48.2%
2019	MIA	MLB	29	0	0	0	6	0	4¹	3	0	6.2	4.2	2	26.7%	.200	1.38	8.31	161	-0.1	91.4	61.8%	21.6%	54.9%
2020	MIA	MLB	30	0	0	0	2	0	1²	2	1	5.4	21.6	4	33.3%	.500	1.80	10.80	70	0.0	90.5	67.4%	30.8%	43.6%
2021 FS	MIA	MLB	31	2	3	0	57	0	50	46	7	5.1	10.2	56	40.0%	.304	1.49	5.09	113	-0.2	92.0	63.4%	23.2%	49.1%

Comparables: Adam Kolarek, Cole Sulser, Gregory Infante

On August 19th, 2020, lefty Josh A. Smith relieved righty Josh D. Smith for Miami, repeating a trick the early-2000s Mets used to pull off where you pull one bad pitcher for another who has the same name but throws with the opposite arm. Unlike the Bobbies Jones, it doesn't seem like these two are going to stay in the majors long enough to pull it off again.

Alex Vesia LHP   Born: 04/11/96   Age: 25   Bats: L   Throws: L   Height: 6'1"   Weight: 209   Origin: Round 17, 2018 Draft (#507 overall)

YEAR	TEAM	LVL	AGE	W	L	SV	G	GS	IP	H	HR	BB/9	K/9	K	GB%	BABIP	WHIP	ERA	DRA-	WARP	MPH	FA%	Whiff%	CSP
2018	MRL	ROK	22	1	0	0	4	0	8²	4	0	3.1	7.3	7	52.2%	.174	0.81	0.00	84	0.1				
2018	BAT	SS	22	3	0	0	10	0	24²	27	1	1.5	11.3	31	31.3%	.394	1.26	1.82	191	-1.1				
2019	CLI	LO-A	23	1	2	3	19	1	31²	24	1	4.8	14.5	51	27.3%	.359	1.29	2.56	71	0.5				
2019	JUP	HI-A	23	4	0	1	10	0	18²	12	2	0.5	11.6	24	43.2%	.244	0.70	1.93	49	0.5				
2019	JAX	AA	23	2	0	1	9	0	16¹	8	0	0.6	13.8	25	41.4%	.286	0.55	0.00	53	0.4				
2020	MIA	MLB	24	0	1	0	5	0	4¹	7	3	14.5	10.4	5	20.0%	.333	3.23	18.69	161	-0.1	93.1	72.9%	28.3%	46.7%
2021 FS	MIA	MLB	25	2	2	0	57	0	50	46	7	4.3	9.6	53	37.3%	.295	1.40	4.58	105	0.0	93.1	72.9%	28.3%	46.7%
2021 DC	MIA	MLB	25	2	2	0	47	0	50	46	7	4.3	9.6	53	37.3%	.295	1.40	4.58	105	0.2	93.1	72.9%	28.3%	46.7%

Comparables: Aaron Fletcher, Phillip Diehl, Alex Reyes

When they said the majors were going to be tough, they probably didn't mean this. Vesia started his debut season by taking the loss on the weekend that COVID-19 sidelined half of the Marlins roster and ended it by giving up five runs in a game Miami was already losing by 11.

Nick Vincent RHP   Born: 07/12/86   Age: 34   Bats: R   Throws: R   Height: 5'10"   Weight: 185   Origin: Round 18, 2008 Draft (#555 overall)

YEAR	TEAM	LVL	AGE	W	L	SV	G	GS	IP	H	HR	BB/9	K/9	K	GB%	BABIP	WHIP	ERA	DRA-	WARP	MPH	FA%	Whiff%	CSP
2018	SEA	MLB	31	4	4	0	62	1	56¹	50	7	2.4	8.9	56	29.7%	.274	1.15	3.99	79	0.9	90.7	96.0%	24.4%	51.0%
2019	LHV	AAA	32	0	0	0	10	0	12¹	9	1	0.7	9.5	13	35.3%	.242	0.81	1.46	47	0.5				
2019	PHI	MLB	32	1	2	0	14	0	14	11	1	2.6	10.9	17	35.3%	.303	1.07	1.93	83	0.2	90.0	96.6%	21.3%	51.7%
2019	SF	MLB	32	0	2	0	18	1	30²	36	7	2.3	8.8	30	39.2%	.322	1.43	5.58	115	-0.1	90.4	94.8%	25.5%	48.5%
2020	MIA	MLB	33	1	2	3	21	0	22¹	23	5	2.4	6.9	17	33.8%	.286	1.30	4.43	129	-0.2	90.3	87.9%	21.1%	52.6%
2021 FS	MIA	MLB	34	2	2	0	57	0	50	46	7	2.2	8.0	44	35.2%	.277	1.17	3.60	90	0.4	90.4	93.3%	23.4%	50.7%

Comparables: Fernando Salas, Huston Street, Keith Foulke

In an age of high-velocity fastball/slider arms, Vincent has carved out a long career with one weird trick: using lots of fastballs and cutters mostly in the high-80s, less frequently in the low-90s. He's somehow been effective more often than not, even through the peripatetic NRI phase of his career. The margins are thin for Vincent as an increasingly dinger-prone pitcher heading into his mid-30s, but he's been beating the odds since 2012.

Jordan Yamamoto RHP   Born: 05/11/96   Age: 25   Bats: R   Throws: R   Height: 6'0"   Weight: 185   Origin: Round 12, 2014 Draft (#356 overall)

YEAR	TEAM	LVL	AGE	W	L	SV	G	GS	IP	H	HR	BB/9	K/9	K	GB%	BABIP	WHIP	ERA	DRA-	WARP	MPH	FA%	Whiff%	CSP
2018	MRL	ROK	22	1	0	0	3	3	11	5	1	1.6	12.3	15	59.1%	.190	0.64	2.45	36	0.5				
2018	JUP	HI-A	22	4	1	0	7	7	40²	26	0	1.8	10.4	47	41.2%	.271	0.84	1.55	60	1.1				
2018	JAX	AA	22	1	0	0	3	3	17	12	1	2.1	12.2	23	45.0%	.282	0.94	2.12	84	0.3				
2019	JAX	AA	23	3	5	0	12	12	65¹	53	7	3.4	8.8	64	46.0%	.275	1.19	3.58	93	0.3				
2019	MIA	MLB	23	4	5	0	15	15	78²	54	11	4.1	9.4	82	36.6%	.225	1.14	4.46	72	1.9	93.6	67.9%	22.7%	46.9%
2020	MIA	MLB	24	0	1	0	4	3	11¹	27	8	5.6	10.3	13	31.9%	.487	3.00	18.26	182	-0.4	92.2	61.1%	19.8%	46.5%
2021 FS	MIA	MLB	25	2	3	0	57	0	50	48	8	4.5	9.0	50	36.1%	.292	1.46	5.04	113	-0.2	93.2	66.3%	22.1%	46.8%
2021 DC	MIA	MLB	25	2	3	0	40	4	57	54	9	4.5	9.0	57	36.1%	.292	1.46	5.04	113	0.0	93.2	66.3%	22.1%	46.8%

Comparables: Mitch Keller, Albert Abreu, Robert Dugger

There were hidden costs to the way the 2020 season unfolded. Yamamoto seemed to be emerging as a viable mid-rotation option in 2019 and everything looked fine in spring. By the time summer camp rolled around, he just wasn't the same pitcher. His grip on a rotation spot quickly slipped away and he ended up at the alternate site to rebuild arm strength. When called upon later in the season, it became clear why the Marlins had lost confidence in him. His velocity was consistently down a couple ticks and he got various levels of lit up in every game he pitched in, culminating in a 13-run relief bombing. He'll be hoping a more normal offseason can get things back on track.

NEW YORK METS

Essay by Jarrett Seidler

Player comments by Bryan Grosnick and BP staff

The nicest thing you can say about the Wilpons is that they always tried to win. The second nicest thing you can say is that they weren't very good at it.

Fred and Jeff Wilpon controlled the New York Mets for 17 seasons. They expected to make the playoffs each year, every summer serving as a perpetual push toward October no matter the circumstances. It was a relentlessly optimistic, borderline delusional mindset, one that demanded every player stay healthy and perform at peak level.

The Wilpon-led Mets made the postseason three times.

In 2006, hedge fund billionaire Steve Cohen agreed to purchase Picasso's "Le Rêve" for $139 million from casino tycoon Steve Wynn. Before the transaction was completed, Wynn inadvertently put his elbow through the painting's canvas while showing it off to a group of friends (including Nora Ephron and Barbara Walters). He decided that the mishap was a sign that he was supposed to keep the painting, and he had it restored instead of selling it.

Seven years later, Wynn decided to ignore the sign and move on from his damaged Picasso after all. Once again, Cohen was the buyer. He paid $155 million, considerably more than he was going to cough up for the piece in its original mint condition.

The Mets may not be a Picasso, but the Wilpons did enough damage to the franchise to give Cohen a healthy sense of déjà vu.

There's a famous scene from the 1980s that was immortalized in John Helyar's *Lords of the Realm*. Legend has it that then-commissioner Peter Ueberroth admonished the assembled group of MLB owners for wanting to hit a metaphorical red button that would win them the World Series at a deficit instead of hitting a black button that would make them a profit. In the ensuing decades, more and more owners have prioritized the black button, profits over pennants.

NEW YORK METS PROSPECTUS

2020 W-L: 26-34, 4th in NL East

Pythag	.464	20th	dWin%	.549	6th
RS/G	4.77	13th	B-Age	28.2	16th
RA/G	5.13	23rd	P-Age	29.6	23rd
DRC+	105	6th	FIP	4.47	15th
DRA-	91	9th	DER	.669	27th
Payroll	$80M	3rd	M$/MW	$7.8M	28th

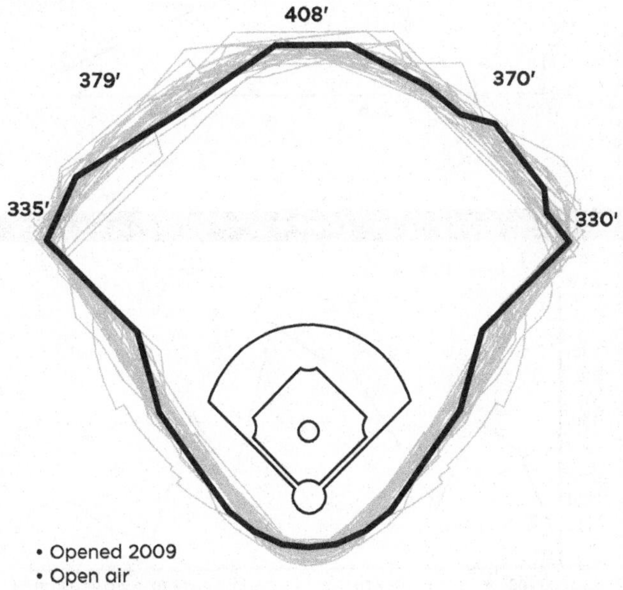
408'
379'
370'
335'
330'

- Opened 2009
- Open air
- Natural surface
- Fence profile: 8'

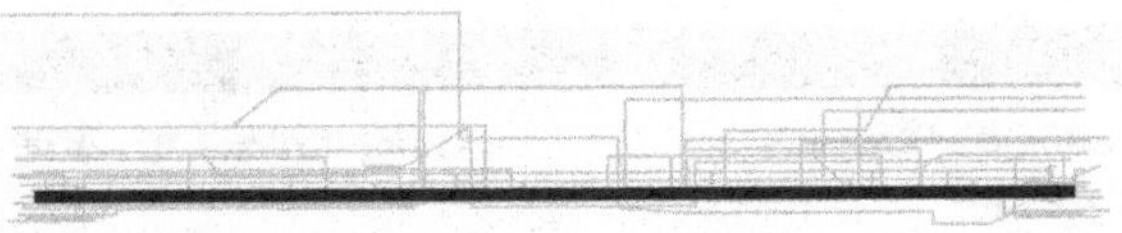

Three-Year Park Factors

Runs	Runs/RH	Runs/LH	HR/RH	HR/LH
94	93	95	98	95

Top Hitter WARP	1.1 Jeff McNeil
Top Pitcher WARP	2.3 Jacob deGrom
Top Prospect	Ronny Mauricio

Payroll History (in millions)

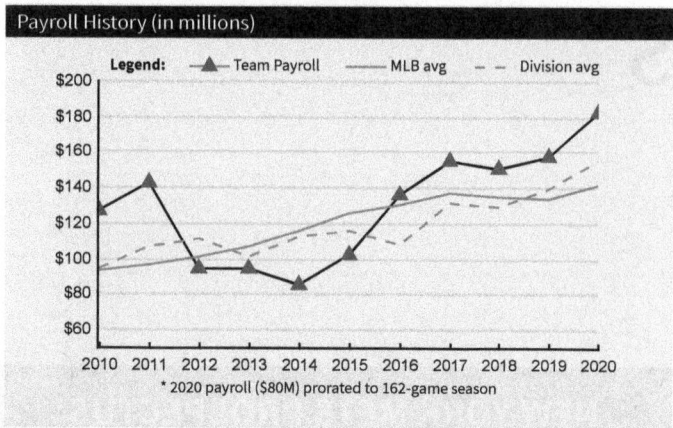

Legend: ▲ Team Payroll — MLB avg - - Division avg

* 2020 payroll ($80M) prorated to 162-game season

Future Commitments (in millions)

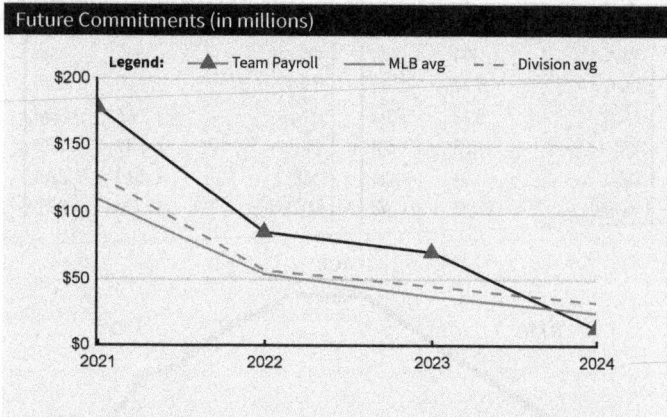

Legend: ▲ Team Payroll — MLB avg - - Division avg

Farm System Ranking

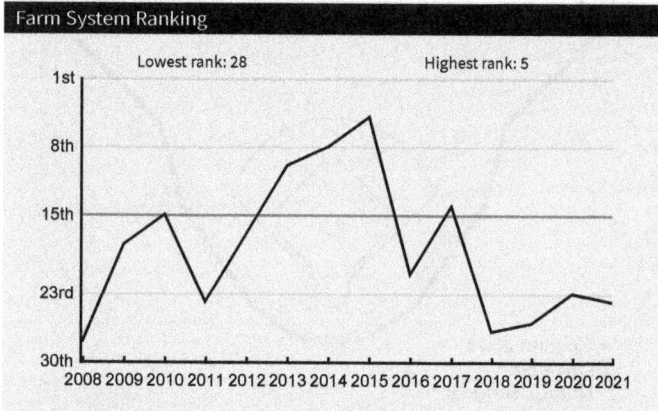

Lowest rank: 28   Highest rank: 5

Personnel

President of BasebalL Operations
Sandy Alderson

General Manager
Jared Porter

Vice President, Assistant General Manager
Zack Scott

Vice President, International & Amateur Scouting
Tommy Tanous

Senior Director, Baseball Operations
Ian Levin

Manager
Luis Rojas

BP Alumni
Josh Turner

In 1986, just weeks after the Mets won their most recent World Series, Fred Wilpon and his brother-in-law Saul Katz raised their stake in the franchise from a small minority share to half the team. For the next 15 years, the Brooklyn-born real estate investors tenuously existed as equal co-owners alongside publishing heir Nelson Doubleday. Wilpon ran the day-to-day operations of the team as CEO, while Doubleday influenced some larger moves, like the Mike Piazza trade.

By 2001, Doubleday wanted out. He decided to sell his half to the Wilpons in a deal that went through only after a messy public split, a lawsuit and intervention from then-MLB commissioner Bud Selig. Shortly after vacating his ownership perch, Doubleday told *The Star-Ledger* that Jeff Wilpon, since installed as Mets COO by his father, "has decided that he's going to learn how to run a baseball team and take over at the end of the year. Run for the hills, boys."

For a few years after taking full control, the Wilpons were red button owners. They ran a top-five payroll from 2003 to 2009, signing high-end free agents like Carlos Beltrán and Pedro Martinez, and trading for expensive stars like Johan Santana and Carlos Delgado. Sure, there were warning signs—Martinez recounted in his autobiography how Jeff Wilpon pressured him to pitch with an injured toe to protect a big gate—and gossip about the Wilpons' meddling and micromanagement became frequent tabloid and talk radio fodder. But baseball fans can generally be mollified if you spend some money and contend for the playoffs, and the Wilpons did the bare minimum.

Then, close friend of the family Bernie Madoff got busted for running the largest Ponzi scheme in history. The Wilpons had around $500 million caught up in the con, and by the time the 2000s were over it was clear that their ability to play big-market baseball owners had been propped up by fictitious profits from the scam. When that house of cards crumbled, so too did the baseball team living in the penthouse.

⚾   ⚾   ⚾

General manager Sandy Alderson got to deal with the Madoff mess on the other side. Hired in 2010 at the urging of Selig to stabilize the front office, the longtime baseball consigliere tried to build a winner under the worst of circumstances. Despite constant proclamations from ownership that baseball operations wouldn't be affected by the Madoff scandal, payroll plummeted, from second in the majors at the start of the 2009 season to 25th six years later. Every now and again, you would hear that the team was just about to turn the corner, to go back to being a big spender. It never happened. Worse, it wasn't always clear how much the team had to spend at any given time, as debt service and financial restructuring took priority over the on-field product, leading to a scattershot decision-making process. The Wilpons still wanted to win and forced short-sighted moves towards contention, but they couldn't or wouldn't hit the red button anymore.

As the analytics boom of the 2010s progressed, the Mets were left on the sidelines. They forewent major technology spending, passing on investments like motion capture, TrackMan and high-speed cameras as other teams bet on their futures. They ran one of the smallest research-and-development shops in the game, employing only a handful of analysts at any given time as other front offices staffed up by the dozen. They fell years behind the analytics curve, even as they employed some of the brightest minds in the game. Their player development and acquisitions suffered for it.

Even though he was still heavily involved in the team, Fred Wilpon all but disappeared from the public eye after a disastrous 2011 profile in *The New Yorker*, rarely answering questions from the media. That left his son as the face of ownership, a scowling presence hovering over everything from big baseball moves like the Yoenis Céspedes trade—which Alderson sought his approval on before consummating minutes before the 2015 deadline—to minutiae like the wording of press releases about injuries. In a 2014 lawsuit, former Mets senior vice president Leigh Castergine alleged that, before she was fired, Jeff Wilpon told a meeting of Castergine and six male team executives that he was "as morally opposed to putting an e-cigarette sign in my ballpark as I am to Leigh having this baby without being married." The case was settled out of court before trial.

In the midst of the chaos, Alderson built a pennant winner in 2015 around homegrown pitching. But as the fates foretold, the LOLMets returned with new twists on classic hits; you may remember such tunes as "James Loney starting against Madison Bumgarner in the 2016 Wild Card Game" (that one ended in a shutout) and "we liked Eric Campbell's exit velocity, but it took us almost 200 games to notice he was smashing the ball into the ground, directly at fielders" (that one ended in a DFA after the 2016 season). Alderson's influence waned when the team went 70-92 in 2017; he took a medical leave of absence in June 2018, and the hiatus soon became permanent.

To replace one of the most accomplished front-office luminaries of his generation, the Mets hired agent Brodie Van Wagenen of CAA. He had no front office experience. As best as anyone could tell, his prime qualification for GM was that Jeff Wilpon liked talking baseball with him. Van Wagenen quickly proclaimed a fourth-place team as the divisional favorites, pawning off 2018 first-rounder Jarred Kelenic—now the No. 6 prospect in baseball—to bring in aging former client Robinson Canó and closer Edwin Díaz for a quick fix. After signing Jed Lowrie—another ex-client who would go on to total eight plate appearances during a two-year contract—Van Wagenen brashly told the rest of the NL East to "come get us."

They did.

Ⓜ   Ⓜ   Ⓜ

The high-water mark for the 2020 Mets was the night of August 28. As Game 2 of a seven-inning doubleheader at Yankee Stadium was underway, word leaked that Steve Cohen had, for the second time in less than a year, agreed to buy the team.

The prior December, Cohen had preliminarily agreed to purchase 80 percent of the Mets at a valuation of $2.6 million, with Fred Wilpon remaining the team's control person and Jeff staying on as COO for five more years. By February, the deal had fallen apart, or so it seemed. The *New York Post* reported that the Wilpons sought to retain more control over the team than Cohen was comfortable with, not just during the transition period but even beyond. The Wilpons re-opened the bidding, queuing up a months-long circus that included a bid from global pop icon Jennifer Lopez and fiancé/ESPN analyst/disgraced baseball legend Alex Rodriguez.

Cohen ended up with the team anyway, by virtue of being the richest person involved. Put simply, he wanted to buy his favorite baseball team, and he had the financial wherewithal to outbid all comers. But, instead of paying a little more the second time around, the way he did with the Picasso, this time Cohen paid a little less, just a hair under $2.5 billion—and, as a bonus, he immediately assumed full control of the team, without the five-year transitionary period from the original negotiations.

About an hour after the Cohen news broke, Amed Rosario walked off Aroldis Chapman to sweep the doubleheader. For several beats, nobody on the field realized it was a walkoff, since it was the seventh inning in the wrong ballpark. Such was baseball in 2020.

The win pulled the Mets into a playoff spot despite a middling 15-16 record. After further depleting a mediocre farm system for marginal upgrades around the edges, the team would sputter down the stretch one last time under Wilpon ownership. They would be eliminated on the last Saturday in September, in a season in which the playoff field was expanded and a .500 record would've earned entry as a wild card. At least the sun was finally, at last, rising over Citi Field again.

Ⓜ   Ⓜ   Ⓜ

More than a month before officially assuming control of the team, Cohen announced that he was bringing Alderson back as team president, picking a decorated baseball executive to helm his franchise instead of a mediocre family member. Less than two hours after the sale closed in November, Alderson fired Van Wagenen.

Cohen and Alderson aimed high to replace the ousted ex-agent, initially seeking a big-name president of baseball operations. Cohen later admitted that they couldn't get permission from other teams to interview many of their top candidates. (Theo Epstein, the most sought-after unemployed executive in baseball, decided to take some time off.) So, they pivoted to finding a general manager to work under Alderson, eventually landing Arizona senior VP and assistant GM Jared Porter.

In Porter, they found a respected baseball lifer who embodies everything Van Wagenen was not. He has a long resume working in some of the best front offices in the game, winning four World Series rings under Epstein in both Boston and Chicago, the last two as pro scouting director. Where Van Wagenen's hiring was met with a collective LOLMets, Porter's was met with resounding praise from the baseball community.

⚾   ⚾   ⚾

The literal translation of "Le Rêve" is "the dream." Steve Cohen has an ambitious one: to win a World Series in the next three to five years.

Cohen has vowed to smash Ueberroth's red button in search of that dream—a welcome departure not only from the Wilpons, but the other owners who prefer the black button. The increased budget has already manifested across the organization, from small, subtle moves, like signing pitching prospect Sam McWilliams to the largest major-league contract ever given to a minor-league free agent with no service time, to early shopping in the free-agent gourmet aisle, as seen when they inked catcher James McCann to a four-year deal.

The Wilpons built Citi Field as a shrine to Branch Rickey's Brooklyn Dodgers, Fred's childhood favorite team. Cohen has instead pointed to the modern Dodgers—who have spent the better part of a decade building up a scouting, player development and analytics machine—as his artistic inspiration. The first step on that path is building a talented front office, and then stepping back and letting them do their jobs without the ownership interference that has long plagued the team. In the early going, Cohen has made all the right moves there; he's acted more like a passionate baseball fan, handing out bobbleheads and trading barbs on Twitter about bringing back Piazza-era black alternate jerseys and Old Timers' Day, than a micromanager who swears he knows better than the field staff and the front office.

It is said that Picasso painted "Le Rêve" in a day. The ball Mookie Wilson hit between Bill Buckner's legs—another piece in Cohen's collection and the closest thing to fine art the Mets have ever produced—was immortalized in an instant. Steve Cohen's dream to fly a World Series banner above Citi Field may take a little longer than either, but for now, anyway, it looks worth the wait. ◼

—*Jarrett Seidler is an author of Baseball Prospectus.*

HITTERS

Pete Alonso 1B Born: 12/07/94   Age: 26   Bats: R   Throws: R   Height: 6'3"   Weight: 245   Origin: Round 2, 2016 Draft (#64 overall)

YEAR	TEAM	LVL	AGE	PA	R	2B	3B	HR	RBI	BB	K	SB	CS	Whiff%	AVG/OBP/SLG	DRC+	BABIP	BRR	FRAA	WARP
2018	BNG	AA	23	273	42	12	0	15	52	43	50	0	2		.314/.440/.573	177	.344	-1.6	1B(51): 1.8	2.2
2018	LV	AAA	23	301	50	19	1	21	67	33	78	0	1		.260/.355/.585	121	.284	1.2	1B(59): 5.0	1.4
2019	NYM	MLB	24	693	103	30	2	53	120	72	183	1	0	28.2%	.260/.358/.583	140	.280	0.5	1B(156): 6.1	5.3
2020	NYM	MLB	26	239	31	6	0	16	35	24	61	1	0	30.4%	.231/.326/.490	106	.242	-2.3	1B(39): -4.3	0.1
2021 FS	NYM	MLB	26	600	84	24	1	41	96	61	161	0	0	28.9%	.256/.352/.543	136	.292	-0.7	1B 5	4.1
2021 DC	NYM	MLB	26	588	82	23	1	40	94	60	158	0	0	28.9%	.256/.352/.543	136	.292	-0.7	1B 5	4.1

Comparables: Fred McGriff, Ryan Howard, Matt Olson

At first glance, Alonso appears to have been the victim of the dreaded sophomore slump: A handful of his doubles transformed into singles, a few of his singles morphed into pop-ups, and his slash line looked more like that of Mike Napoli than Mark McGwire. But by the end of the shortened season, the Polar Bear looked like he was back in his element: outstanding power, a careful eye, and, *y'know, maybe we should mention that power again?* He even started making slightly more consistent contact on pitches in the zone, making it safe to assume that he'll be a dynamic middle-of-the-order slugger going forward.

★ ★ ★ *2021 Top 101 Prospect* **#84** ★ ★ ★

Francisco Alvarez C Born: 11/19/01   Age: 19   Bats: R   Throws: R   Height: 5'11"   Weight: 220   Origin: International Free Agent, 2018

YEAR	TEAM	LVL	AGE	PA	R	2B	3B	HR	RBI	BB	K	SB	CS	Whiff%	AVG/OBP/SLG	DRC+	BABIP	BRR	FRAA	WARP
2019	MTS	ROK	17	31	8	4	0	2	10	4	4	0	1		.462/.548/.846	224	.500	-0.3	C(4): 0.3	0.4
2019	KNG	ROK+	17	151	24	6	0	5	16	17	33	1	1		.289/.385/.453	127	.356	-1.4		0.9
2021 FS	NYM	MLB	19	600	49	26	2	9	53	36	194	2	1		.219/.273/.324	64	.318	-1.1	C 0	-0.4

The missed development time for Alvarez, already considered an "advanced" catching prospect in most circles, might be less of a factor than for most backstop prospects. While losing a full season of pro ball and the opportunity to build on his outstanding performance as a 17-year-old, Alvarez still has all the tools (and time) to develop into an offense-first backstop with the athleticism and frame to stick behind the plate. He signed with the Sydney Blue Sox to get some reps over the winter but never made it on the field, so the few weeks he had at the Mets' alternate site and fall instructs were the only chance he had in the back half of 2020 to build on the electric start to his pro career.

Brett Baty 3B   Born: 11/13/99   Age: 21   Bats: L   Throws: R   Height: 6'3"   Weight: 210   Origin: Round 1, 2019 Draft (#12 overall)

YEAR	TEAM	LVL	AGE	PA	R	2B	3B	HR	RBI	BB	K	SB	CS	Whiff%	AVG/OBP/SLG	DRC+	BABIP	BRR	FRAA	WARP
2019	MTS	ROK	19	25	5	3	0	1	8	5	6	0	0		.350/.480/.650	148	.462	0.2	3B(4): -0.2	0.2
2019	KNG	ROK+	19	186	30	12	2	6	22	24	56	0	0		.226/.344/.445	108	.312	-0.4		0.6
2019	BRK	SS	19	17	2	1	0	0	3	6	3	0	0		.200/.529/.300	173	.286	-0.3	3B(2): -0.2	0.1
2021 FS	NYM	MLB	21	600	47	27	2	8	48	50	231	1	0		.186/.262/.291	53	.306	0.7	3B 0	-2.3

Baty's lost season at least ended on a high note: he was added to the Mets' player pool in late August, just in time to get a few reps with the pro staff before the season came to a close. He'll never be Brett *Glovey*, so the big Texan has to develop his hit tool to support his big-time raw power; despite admiring Adrian Beltre as a youngster, the chances of becoming a gloveman like his Hall-of-Fame-bound hero are markedly low. Already entering his age-21 season and with only 211 plate appearances beyond high school, Baty remains a high-variance prospect who needs far more time facing professional breaking pitches than just the handful he experienced this past September.

Robinson Canó 2B   Born: 10/22/82   Age: 38   Bats: L   Throws: R   Height: 6'0"   Weight: 212   Origin: International Free Agent, 2001

YEAR	TEAM	LVL	AGE	PA	R	2B	3B	HR	RBI	BB	K	SB	CS	Whiff%	AVG/OBP/SLG	DRC+	BABIP	BRR	FRAA	WARP
2018	SEA	MLB	35	348	44	22	0	10	50	32	47	0	0	18.3%	.303/.374/.471	124	.329	-0.4	2B(69): -2.5, 1B(14): 0.3, 3B(2): 0.1	1.8
2019	NYM	MLB	36	423	46	28	0	13	39	25	69	0	0	19.4%	.256/.307/.428	89	.280	-0.7	2B(99): -7.4	0.0
2020	NYM	MLB	38	182	23	9	0	10	30	9	24	0	0	19.8%	.316/.352/.544	113	.319	-1.2	2B(34): -0.9	0.6
2021 FS	NYM	MLB	38	600	67	30	0	21	80	39	105	0	0	19.3%	.272/.328/.449	107	.303	-1.7	2B -8, 1B 0	1.7

Comparables: Jeff Kent, Ian Kinsler, Chase Utley

This was supposed to be the place where you read about Canó's late-career resurgence in Queens. You know, a couple of quick sentences espousing how his bat looked more like Year Five than Year 15 of his no-doubt Hall of Fame career, and maybe a quick hit on his well-documented clubhouse presence. Instead, another PED suspension will cost the veteran second-sacker his 2021 season, $24 million dollars, and quite possibly his plaque in Cooperstown. While Sandy Alderson's new front office might enjoy being able to reinvest some of Canó's immediate salary, there's no silver lining for the player himself. Though he has done a remarkable job of keeping his skills sharp to this point, he'll likely be returning in 2022 for his age-39 season while trying to shake off the rust of a lost year and the bad feelings of a jilted New York fanbase.

Yoenis Céspedes LF   Born: 10/18/85   Age: 35   Bats: R   Throws: R   Height: 5'11"   Weight: 225   Origin: International Free Agent, 2012

YEAR	TEAM	LVL	AGE	PA	R	2B	3B	HR	RBI	BB	K	SB	CS	Whiff%	AVG/OBP/SLG	DRC+	BABIP	BRR	FRAA	WARP
2018	NYM	MLB	32	157	20	6	0	9	29	13	50	3	0	28.3%	.262/.325/.496	99	.333	0.5	LF(35): 1.8	0.6
2020	NYM	MLB	35	34	3	1	0	2	4	2	15	0	0	33.3%	.161/.235/.387	75	.214	0.0		0.0
2021 FS	NYM	MLB	35	600	68	24	1	29	80	44	174	3	1	30.4%	.240/.306/.451	102	.297	-1.0	LF 2, 1B 0	1.9

Comparables: Frank Howard, Willie Horton, Alfonso Soriano

Legendary even before he played his first game in America, and so improbable that he may as well have been written by Terry Pratchett, of course *La Potencia* made an unlikely return to the Mets during the bizarre, abbreviated season we all just witnessed. Blessed by the advent of the National League DH, Céspedes took on the role of *Casey at the Bat* for the Amazins, struggling mightily for eight games–but hammering two dingers–before opting out of his return engagement. In a world where every player has been scouted since the womb, and where the reams of performance data drown us in terabytes, Céspedes was the last tall tale. He leaves the Mets, and maybe the major leagues, much the way he came to us: unpredictable, compelling, charismatic, and almost downright fictional.

Robinson Chirinos C   Born: 06/05/84   Age: 37   Bats: R   Throws: R   Height: 6'1"   Weight: 220   Origin: International Free Agent, 2000

YEAR	TEAM	LVL	AGE	PA	R	2B	3B	HR	RBI	BB	K	SB	CS	Whiff%	AVG/OBP/SLG	DRC+	BABIP	BRR	FRAA	WARP
2018	TEX	MLB	34	426	48	15	1	18	65	45	140	2	0	33.6%	.222/.338/.419	106	.304	-1.4	C(108): -10.8	1.2
2019	HOU	MLB	35	437	57	22	1	17	58	51	125	1	2	33.9%	.238/.347/.443	100	.306	-0.1	C(112): 3.0	2.6
2020	TEX	MLB	36	49	3	1	0	0	2	5	12	0	0	33.3%	.119/.224/.143	69	.161	-0.5	C(13): 0.3	-0.2
2020	NYM	MLB	36	33	1	2	0	1	5	1	9	0	0	29.2%	.219/.242/.375	73	.273	0.0	C(12): -0.2	-0.1
2021 FS	NYM	MLB	37	600	64	22	1	20	62	60	184	2	1	33.4%	.205/.310/.369	86	.275	-1.1	C -13	-0.1

Comparables: Doug Mirabelli, David Ross, Jason Varitek

YEAR	TEAM	P. COUNT	FRM RUNS	BLK RUNS	THRW RUNS	TOT RUNS
2018	TEX	15216	-11.2	0.7	-0.8	-11.3
2019	HOU	15758	-3.5	5.8	-0.5	1.9
2020	TEX	1958	-1.1	0.0	0.1	-1.1
2020	NYM	1580	-0.9	0.0	0.0	-0.9
2021	NYM	16650	-14.8	1.7	-0.4	-13.5

After half a decade as one of the game's most underrated offensive catchers, Chirinos' career took a sharp downward turn upon his return to his old Arlington stomping grounds. *Pelo Buche* may have value to some teams as a clubhouse presence and wearer-of-pads, but this looks like the end of the road.

Michael Conforto RF   Born: 03/01/93   Age: 28   Bats: L   Throws: R   Height: 6'1"   Weight: 215   Origin: Round 1, 2014 Draft (#10 overall)

YEAR	TEAM	LVL	AGE	PA	R	2B	3B	HR	RBI	BB	K	SB	CS	Whiff%	AVG/OBP/SLG	DRC+	BABIP	BRR	FRAA	WARP
2018	NYM	MLB	25	638	78	25	1	28	82	84	159	3	4	27.9%	.243/.350/.448	112	.289	-4.2	LF(84): 1.1, CF(58): -7.3, RF(13): 0.1	1.8
2019	NYM	MLB	26	648	90	29	1	33	92	84	149	7	2	26.9%	.257/.363/.494	122	.290	-0.3	RF(132): 10.0, CF(39): -3.7	4.1
2020	NYM	MLB	27	233	40	12	0	9	31	24	57	3	3	26.0%	.322/.412/.515	120	.412	-0.5	RF(52): -3.1	0.9
2021 FS	NYM	MLB	28	600	83	25	1	28	81	71	152	4	2	26.9%	.267/.368/.488	130	.328	-1.4	RF 7, LF 0	4.7
2021 DC	NYM	MLB	28	588	81	24	1	28	80	70	149	4	1	26.9%	.267/.368/.488	130	.328	-1.4	RF 7	4.3

Comparables: Pat Burrell, Dan Pasqua, Phil Plantier

A few years ago, it was opined that "every team has a Michael Conforto." *They should be so lucky.* In 2020, Conforto stayed healthy and was the lifeblood of the Mets' offense. Not only did he lead the team in games played and plate appearances while poking around near the top of several NL offensive leaderboards, he showed off his glove as an outstanding right fielder. (Seriously. Go check out his balletic catch on September 9 that ended up as one of the team's top defensive plays for the season.) No longer a quiet star, Conforto plays louder than his soft-spoken demeanor. With free agency impending at the end of the 2021 season and a prime platform year looming, all those teams that don't have a Michael Conforto may want to shell out big bucks to get one of their own.

Pete Crow-Armstrong OF   Born: 03/25/02   Age: 19   Bats: L   Throws: L   Height: 6'1"   Weight: 180   Origin: Round 1, 2020 Draft (#19 overall)

Crow-Armstrong, a prep center fielder from the prestigious Harvard-Westlake High School in California, is the son of two actors who had recurring roles on the mid-aughts NBC TV series *Heroes*. Rather appropriately, the 19th-overall pick in the 2020 draft has his own superpower: he's already an outstanding defender in center field, with above-average skills across the board, plus speed, and a preternatural ability to read the ball off the bat and run stellar routes. Like with every other prep hitter, the bat will be a question mark until it isn't, and he may never develop even average game power. The hope is that he'll develop into a tremendous defensive asset who hits for average and corks a few line drives over the fence, but we'll either have to wait four years or steal Hiro Nakamura's time travel powers to find out if he'll reach that potential.

J.D. Davis LF   Born: 04/27/93   Age: 28   Bats: R   Throws: R   Height: 6'3"   Weight: 218   Origin: Round 3, 2014 Draft (#75 overall)

YEAR	TEAM	LVL	AGE	PA	R	2B	3B	HR	RBI	BB	K	SB	CS	Whiff%	AVG/OBP/SLG	DRC+	BABIP	BRR	FRAA	WARP
2018	FRE	AAA	25	377	56	25	2	17	81	36	69	3	0		.342/.406/.583	162	.385	0.0	3B(51): 4.2, LF(11): -0.8, RF(11): -0.3	3.6
2018	HOU	MLB	25	113	9	2	0	1	5	10	29	0	0	31.4%	.175/.248/.223	67	.233	-0.5	3B(23): 0.9, 1B(13): 0.0, LF(5): 0.6	0.0
2019	NYM	MLB	26	453	65	22	1	22	57	38	97	3	0	28.1%	.307/.369/.527	121	.355	0.4	LF(79): -4.9, 3B(31): -0.5	2.1
2020	NYM	MLB	27	229	26	9	0	6	19	31	56	0	0	29.3%	.247/.371/.389	103	.318	-0.5	3B(34): -0.2, LF(8): -0.4	0.4
2021 FS	NYM	MLB	28	600	75	24	1	25	76	57	161	1	0	28.8%	.249/.332/.445	109	.310	-0.9	3B 6, LF -3	2.1
2021 DC	NYM	MLB	28	588	73	23	1	25	75	56	157	1	0	28.8%	.249/.332/.445	109	.310	-0.9	3B 5, LF -3	2.1

Comparables: Fernando Tatis, Dean Palmer, Hank Blalock

When the Mets move a defensively-challenged hitter into left field to shoehorn them into the lineup, the outcomes typically range somewhere between unintentionally hilarious (Todd Hundley) or downright sad (Lucas Duda). While both Davis and Dominic Smith served some time in the Hundley-Duda Memorial Pit of Despair, Davis not only showed his limitations on the grass, but also saw his offensive production peter out as well. At his best, his right-handed batted ball profile and production make for a valuable lineup cog, but he'll be best served at a position where he can focus on what he does well offensively, not how much work he needs with a glove. Still, he's proven that he can be an adequate big-league regular, provided his time in left field is minimal.

Todd Frazier 3B   Born: 02/12/86   Age: 35   Bats: R   Throws: R   Height: 6'3"   Weight: 220   Origin: Round 1, 2007 Draft (#34 overall)

YEAR	TEAM	LVL	AGE	PA	R	2B	3B	HR	RBI	BB	K	SB	CS	Whiff%	AVG/OBP/SLG	DRC+	BABIP	BRR	FRAA	WARP
2018	NYM	MLB	32	472	54	18	0	18	59	48	112	9	4	24.2%	.213/.303/.390	99	.241	2.5	3B(109): 5.9	2.5
2019	STL	HI-A	33	43	3	0	0	1	8	6	8	0	1		.216/.326/.297	116	.250	0.1	3B(10): 1.1, 1B(5): -0.1, SS(3): -0.1	0.3
2019	NYM	MLB	33	499	63	19	2	21	67	40	106	1	2	25.6%	.251/.329/.443	103	.284	0.0	3B(120): 6.5, 1B(3): 0.1	2.7
2020	TEX	MLB	34	121	11	7	1	2	7	10	26	1	1	26.1%	.241/.322/.380	93	.300	-0.2	1B(16): -0.6, 3B(15): -0.7	-0.1
2020	NYM	MLB	34	51	5	2	0	2	5	1	16	0	0	28.7%	.224/.255/.388	98	.290	0.3	3B(14): 1.2, P(1): -0.0	0.3
2021 FS	NYM	MLB	35	600	65	23	1	23	72	55	155	7	3	25.6%	.218/.305/.396	89	.263	-1.5	3B 6, 1B 0	0.8

Comparables: Dean Palmer, Casey Blake, Eric Hinske

For someone nicknamed "The ToddFather," Frazier sure seems to have difficulty ordering hits these days.

Robel García 2B   Born: 03/28/93   Age: 28   Bats: S   Throws: R   Height: 6'0"   Weight: 195   Origin: International Free Agent, 2010

YEAR	TEAM	LVL	AGE	PA	R	2B	3B	HR	RBI	BB	K	SB	CS	Whiff%	AVG/OBP/SLG	DRC+	BABIP	BRR	FRAA	WARP
2019	TNS	AA	26	92	12	5	0	6	26	12	22	1	1		.295/.391/.590	171	.333	-0.7	3B(18): 0.4, 2B(4): 0.6, SS(1): -0.0	1.1
2019	IOW	AAA	26	296	51	12	2	21	52	30	98	3	3		.281/.361/.585	125	.364	2.8	2B(29): 0.8, LF(21): 2.9, 3B(19): -2.3	2.1
2019	CHC	MLB	26	80	8	2	2	5	11	7	35	0	0	45.3%	.208/.275/.500	71	.303	-0.4	2B(18): -1.0, LF(5): -0.2, RF(1): -0.1	-0.2
2021 FS	NYM	MLB	28	600	64	22	2	22	66	51	226	0	0	45.3%	.211/.287/.388	82	.313	1.1	2B -1, 3B -2	0.2
2021 DC	NYM	MLB	28	311	33	11	1	11	34	26	117	0	0	45.3%	.211/.287/.388	82	.313	0.6	2B -1, 3B -1	0.0

Comparables: David Bote, Mitch Walding, Jai Miller

García has serious power for a second baseman but has to sell out so fully to reach it that even Gene Simmons gives him the side eye.

Luis Guillorme SS
Born: 09/27/94 Age: 26 Bats: L Throws: R Height: 5'10" Weight: 190 Origin: Round 10, 2013 Draft (#296 overall)

YEAR	TEAM	LVL	AGE	PA	R	2B	3B	HR	RBI	BB	K	SB	CS	Whiff%	AVG/OBP/SLG	DRC+	BABIP	BRR	FRAA	WARP
2018	LV	AAA	23	281	41	15	2	3	33	30	39	2	1		.304/.380/.417	106	.350	0.3	SS(54): 1.9, 2B(9): -1.4, 3B(5): 1.0	1.3
2018	NYM	MLB	23	74	4	2	0	0	5	7	3	1	0	10.0%	.209/.284/.239	92	.219	0.7	3B(14): -1.8, 2B(8): -0.5	0.0
2019	SYR	AAA	24	278	33	12	0	7	32	39	42	4	4		.307/.412/.452	130	.346	0.7	2B(30): -0.3, SS(26): -0.9, 3B(13): 0.1	1.9
2019	NYM	MLB	24	70	8	4	0	1	3	7	14	0	0	19.7%	.246/.324/.361	85	.304	0.4	2B(8): 0.0, SS(8): -0.2, 3B(5): -0.0	0.2
2020	NYM	MLB	26	68	6	6	0	0	9	10	17	2	0	20.7%	.333/.426/.439	90	.463	0.0	2B(17): 0.2, 3B(4): -0.3, SS(3): 0.0	0.1
2021 FS	NYM	MLB	26	600	62	28	1	8	56	66	118	0	0	18.7%	.261/.347/.368	99	.323	-1.0	2B 1, 3B -5	1.2
2021 DC	NYM	MLB	26	484	50	23	1	6	45	53	95	0	0	18.7%	.261/.347/.368	99	.323	-0.8	2B 1, 3B -4	0.9

Comparables: Gordon Beckham, Bret Barberie, Brent Gates

The most dextrous defender in blue and orange since Rey Ordoñez, Guillorme used his limited 2020 playing time to do something he'd never managed in his previous cups of coffee with the big club: string together more than a handful of hits and post the sort of snazzy batting average that transforms a high-minors depth profile into that of a valuable utility infielder. Perhaps the new Mets regime will value infield defense more than the prior ones, but given the surfeit of bodies on the left side of the infield, Guillorme is likely to find playing time only if he skips town, despite his most impressive all-around season to date.

Guillermo Heredia CF
Born: 01/31/91 Age: 30 Bats: R Throws: L Height: 5'10" Weight: 195 Origin: International Free Agent, 2016

YEAR	TEAM	LVL	AGE	PA	R	2B	3B	HR	RBI	BB	K	SB	CS	Whiff%	AVG/OBP/SLG	DRC+	BABIP	BRR	FRAA	WARP
2018	TAC	AAA	27	37	4	1	0	0	2	4	3	2	1		.286/.432/.321	113	.308	0.9	LF(6): 1.0, CF(5): -0.5	0.3
2018	SEA	MLB	27	337	29	14	1	5	19	32	52	2	4	17.1%	.236/.318/.342	88	.270	0.0	CF(89): -6.5, LF(32): 3.1, RF(2): -0.1	0.3
2019	DUR	AAA	28	30	3	1	0	1	4	1	10	0	1		.214/.267/.357	66	.294	0.0	CF(8): -0.2	0.0
2019	TB	MLB	28	231	31	13	0	5	20	18	60	2	2	27.4%	.225/.306/.363	76	.293	2.0	CF(41): 0.5, RF(28): 0.8, LF(14): -0.0	0.4
2020	PIT	MLB	29	18	2	0	0	0	2	2	4	1	0	18.8%	.188/.278/.188	92	.250	-0.1	RF(5): 0.4, CF(2): 0.1	0.3
2020	NYM	MLB	29	18	4	0	0	2	3	1	5	0	0	21.4%	.235/.278/.588	90	.200	-0.1	CF(7): 0.4	0.0
2021 FS	NYM	MLB	30	600	64	26	1	14	63	53	124	4	3	22.8%	.248/.334/.385	100	.299	-4.1	LF 3, CF 0	1.8
2021 DC	NYM	MLB	30	277	29	12	0	6	29	24	57	2	1	22.8%	.248/.334/.385	100	.299	-1.9	LF 2, CF 0	0.7

Comparables: Rusty Kuntz, Jeff Barry, Dave Stegman

If archetypal fourth outfielder Heredia was going to find more playing time, the 2020 Pirates outfield seemed like the perfect opportunity. Unfortunately, he didn't even last the short season on the roster and found his way to the best offensive outfield in the majors, paving the way for a 2021 return as—you guessed it—a fourth outfielder.

Juan Lagares CF
Born: 03/17/89 Age: 32 Bats: R Throws: R Height: 6'2" Weight: 219 Origin: International Free Agent, 2006

YEAR	TEAM	LVL	AGE	PA	R	2B	3B	HR	RBI	BB	K	SB	CS	Whiff%	AVG/OBP/SLG	DRC+	BABIP	BRR	FRAA	WARP
2018	NYM	MLB	29	64	9	1	1	0	6	3	9	3	1	23.6%	.339/.375/.390	88	.392	1.0	CF(20): 1.5	0.4
2019	NYM	MLB	30	285	38	12	1	5	27	22	75	4	1	25.6%	.213/.279/.326	61	.279	3.3	CF(125): -5.7	-0.6
2020	NYM	MLB	31	0	0	0	0	0	0	0	0	0	0		None/None/None				CF(2): 0.1	
2021 FS	NYM	MLB	32	600	57	26	2	11	57	34	142	11	4	25.4%	.230/.284/.350	72	.290	1.0	CF -9	-1.1

Comparables: Pete Whisenant, Randy Kutcher, John Shelby

The former all-world gloveman briefly escaped from Queens to sunny San Diego, but couldn't find purchase either with the Padres or in a brief reunion with the Mets. Now seven years removed from his Gold Glove, teams would rather employ younger, faster, and cheaper center fielders who also can't hit.

Francisco Lindor SS
Born: 11/14/93 Age: 27 Bats: S Throws: R Height: 5'11" Weight: 190 Origin: Round 1, 2011 Draft (#8 overall)

YEAR	TEAM	LVL	AGE	PA	R	2B	3B	HR	RBI	BB	K	SB	CS	Whiff%	AVG/OBP/SLG	DRC+	BABIP	BRR	FRAA	WARP
2018	CLE	MLB	24	745	129	42	2	38	92	70	107	25	10	17.3%	.277/.352/.519	127	.279	-0.5	SS(157): 5.9	6.5
2019	CLE	MLB	25	654	101	40	2	32	74	46	98	22	5	16.9%	.284/.335/.518	117	.291	-2.3	SS(137): -4.8	3.8
2020	CLE	MLB	27	266	30	13	0	8	27	24	41	6	2	20.4%	.258/.335/.415	120	.280	-0.4	SS(58): -0.2	1.4
2021 FS	NYM	MLB	27	600	79	33	1	25	79	52	98	16	5	18.1%	.274/.344/.482	123	.294	1.0	SS 1	3.9
2021 DC	NYM	MLB	27	588	78	32	1	24	77	51	96	15	5	18.1%	.274/.344/.482	123	.294	1.0	SS 1	3.9

Comparables: Aledmys Díaz, Cal Ripken Jr., Troy Tulowitzki

Shortly after Cleveland's playoff exit, Lindor was asked whether they could afford to extend him. The response? "Of course. It's a billion-dollar team." There was a wry smile on his face, conscious of the cartoonish predictability of the team's financial decisions; he might as well be asking Scrooge McDuck for a deal. Lindor shares the youthful, exuberant spirit of Huey, Dewey and Louie, but he hasn't melted the hearts of ownership. On *DuckTales*, this particular adventure would end with Lindor landing the treasure he so richly deserves and reuniting with his baseball family. If you head down to Progressive Field over the offseason, you might instead catch the bespectacled Dolan clan, complete with top hats and spats, performing a surprisingly passable synchronized backstroke through the mounds of cash saved by not extending their franchise shortstop. Cleveland fans might wish that were so anyway; humor has a way of softening the edges of disappointment.

The owner of Lindor's new squad has a bigger vat of cash to swim through and doesn't seem to mind spending some of it on a competitive baseball team. Cleveland fans are going to need to hire personal comedians to follow them around if they want humor to dull the pain of watching Lindor flash his trademark smile all year in New York.

Jed Lowrie 2B Born: 04/17/84 Age: 37 Bats: S Throws: R Height: 6'0" Weight: 180 Origin: Round 1, 2005 Draft (#45 overall)

YEAR	TEAM	LVL	AGE	PA	R	2B	3B	HR	RBI	BB	K	SB	CS	Whiff%	AVG/OBP/SLG	DRC+	BABIP	BRR	FRAA	WARP
2018	OAK	MLB	34	680	78	37	1	23	99	78	128	0	0	20.3%	.267/.353/.448	125	.304	-3.0	2B(136): -0.4, 3B(14): -0.5	3.9
2019	SYR	AAA	35	48	7	1	0	2	3	4	12	0	0		.250/.312/.409	92	.300	0.5	2B(5): -0.5, 3B(5): -0.9, SS(1): -0.1	0.0
2019	NYM	MLB	35	8	0	0	0	0	0	1	4	0	0	40.0%	.000/.125/.000	70	.000	0.1		0.0
2021 FS	NYM	MLB	37	600	67	25	1	17	64	59	133	0	0	20.8%	.245/.326/.395	97	.295	-1.1	2B -4, 3B -1	1.3

Comparables: Miguel Tejada, Rich Aurilia, Jhonny Peralta

For the second consecutive season, Jed Lowrie teased the Mets with the possibility of bringing his potent bat into the lineup, only to have an injury claim his season. This time, it was his balky left knee that brought a new injury term, "*PCL laxity*", into the Mets' increasingly robust medical lexicon.

Jake Marisnick CF Born: 03/30/91 Age: 30 Bats: R Throws: R Height: 6'4" Weight: 220 Origin: Round 3, 2009 Draft (#104 overall)

YEAR	TEAM	LVL	AGE	PA	R	2B	3B	HR	RBI	BB	K	SB	CS	Whiff%	AVG/OBP/SLG	DRC+	BABIP	BRR	FRAA	WARP
2018	FRE	AAA	27	82	18	8	2	4	13	6	17	3	1		.342/.402/.671	168	.396	-0.5	CF(12): -2.3, RF(6): 0.9	0.5
2018	HOU	MLB	27	235	34	8	1	10	28	15	84	6	2	34.8%	.211/.275/.399	79	.292	2.3	CF(96): -5.7, LF(1): -0.0, RF(1): -0.0	-0.1
2019	HOU	MLB	28	318	46	16	3	10	34	17	95	10	3	29.2%	.233/.289/.411	67	.310	0.8	CF(109): 7.7	0.7
2020	NYM	MLB	29	34	4	3	0	2	5	1	10	0	0	32.4%	.333/.353/.606	87	.429	-0.1	CF(16): 1.5	0.1
2021 FS	NYM	MLB	30	600	62	23	2	23	70	37	196	16	6	30.8%	.217/.280/.396	79	.290	0.1	CF -4, RF 0	-0.1

Comparables: Brandon Barnes, Michael A. Taylor, Laynce Nix

Acquired in the offseason to be something of a platoon partner for Brandon Nimmo, Marisnick's combination of outstanding defense and occasional ability to punish a left-handed pitcher should have balanced out the lineup while providing sorely needed outs for the pitching staff. Instead, the team saw precious little of their new addition's glove (and flow) as hamstring injuries limited him to just 16 games. He put up outstanding numbers in his limited game action last season thanks to a power surge, but the underlying strikeout issues probably make him most desirable in a role similar to the one he had on the Astros: the fourth or fifth outfielder on a good team.

★ ★ ★ *2021 Top 101 Prospect* **#42** ★ ★ ★

Ronny Mauricio SS Born: 04/04/01 Age: 20 Bats: S Throws: R Height: 6'3" Weight: 166 Origin: International Free Agent, 2017

YEAR	TEAM	LVL	AGE	PA	R	2B	3B	HR	RBI	BB	K	SB	CS	Whiff%	AVG/OBP/SLG	DRC+	BABIP	BRR	FRAA	WARP
2018	MTS	ROK	17	212	26	13	3	3	31	10	31	1	6		.279/.307/.421	124	.310	-0.3	SS(45): 0.3	0.7
2018	KNG	ROK	17	35	6	3	0	0	4	3	9	1	0		.233/.286/.333	74	.304	0.5	SS(8): -0.1	0.0
2019	COL	LO-A	18	504	62	20	5	4	37	23	99	6	10		.268/.307/.357	100	.330	2.9	SS(106): -0.1	2.3
2021 FS	NYM	MLB	20	600	45	26	3	7	50	30	168	3	4		.220/.263/.318	57	.301	-5.0	SS 2	-1.6

Comparables: Cole Tucker, Alcides Escobar, Andrew Velazquez

One of the biggest baseball-related disappointments of 2020 was the loss of the minor-league season. That meant losing out on the opportunity to watch the growth and development of players like Mauricio, who live in that special place far enough away from the majors to never have disappointed us, yet are starting to flash world-class skills that wouldn't be out of place on an All-Star team. Success isn't remotely assured for the rangy shortstop—he'll need to grow into some power and prove his hit tool against tougher pitching—but even after the lost season, he still remains in that sweet spot between "too far away" and "yeah, we know him." There's been a litany of hyped Mets shortstop prospects over the past two decades, but Mauricio still retains the possibility of being the best of the bunch.

James McCann C Born: 06/13/90 Age: 31 Bats: R Throws: R Height: 6'3" Weight: 220 Origin: Round 2, 2011 Draft (#76 overall)

YEAR	TEAM	LVL	AGE	PA	R	2B	3B	HR	RBI	BB	K	SB	CS	Whiff%	AVG/OBP/SLG	DRC+	BABIP	BRR	FRAA	WARP
2018	DET	MLB	28	457	31	16	0	8	39	26	116	0	3	26.6%	.220/.267/.314	72	.282	-4.2	C(114): -5.0	-0.3
2019	CHW	MLB	29	476	62	26	1	18	60	30	137	4	1	28.7%	.273/.328/.460	95	.359	-0.1	C(106): -10.2	1.0
2020	CHW	MLB	30	111	20	3	0	7	15	8	30	1	1	29.2%	.289/.360/.536	112	.339	-0.5	C(30): 0.1	0.7
2021 FS	NYM	MLB	31	600	62	24	1	22	73	38	169	2	1	28.3%	.243/.303/.413	90	.311	-1.1	C -7	0.9
2021 DC	NYM	MLB	31	484	50	19	1	18	59	31	136	2	0	28.3%	.243/.303/.413	90	.311	-0.9	C -6	0.5

Comparables: Randy Knorr, Nick Hundley, Damian Miller

YEAR	TEAM	P. COUNT	FRM RUNS	BLK RUNS	THRW RUNS	TOT RUNS
2018	DET	16729	-2.3	-1.4	1.1	-2.6
2019	CHW	15359	-8.0	-0.9	0.9	-8.0
2020	CHW	4053	1.5	0.0	0.0	1.5
2021	NYM	14430	-3.2	-0.3	0.2	-3.3

In a masterstroke of innovation, the Tigers non-tendered McCann, their former second-round pick, at the end of the 2018 season. The massive insult of being cast off by a horrid rebuilding team spurred McCann to the best offensive season of his career in 2019, and his first All-Star Game appearance. Tapping into the power of injustice, the White Sox insulted McCann again, signing Yasmani Grandal in November of 2019 and handing him McCann's starting job. In a heavily-used backup role, McCann improved even more offensively, and arrested career-long struggles at pitch-framing to boot. After inking him to a four-year, $40 million deal, the Mets will receive an increasingly solid all-around backstop, but will be wasting their money if they do not seek out a new, galling way to draw his ire and fuel his hunger for a revenge tour. If a club unceremoniously releases him in spring training, it may well produce an MVP campaign, just, you know, for another team.

Jeff McNeil 3B Born: 04/08/92 Age: 29 Bats: L Throws: R Height: 6'1" Weight: 195 Origin: Round 12, 2013 Draft (#356 overall)

YEAR	TEAM	LVL	AGE	PA	R	2B	3B	HR	RBI	BB	K	SB	CS	Whiff%	AVG/OBP/SLG	DRC+	BABIP	BRR	FRAA	WARP
2018	BNG	AA	26	241	49	16	3	14	43	22	23	3	0		.327/.402/.626	174	.316	1.7	2B(47): 3.9, 3B(9): -0.6, SS(3): -0.3	2.9
2018	LV	AAA	26	143	23	10	2	5	28	14	19	3	0		.368/.427/.600	156	.394	0.4	2B(24): -3.3, 3B(3): -0.1, LF(2): 0.1	0.9
2018	NYM	MLB	26	248	35	11	6	3	19	14	24	7	1	16.3%	.329/.381/.471	118	.359	0.8	2B(54): -2.6, 3B(4): 0.3	1.2
2019	NYM	MLB	27	567	83	38	1	23	75	35	75	5	6	20.0%	.318/.384/.531	128	.337	-2.7	LF(71): -5.2, RF(42): -1.2, 2B(37): -2.8	2.5
2020	NYM	MLB	28	209	19	14	0	4	23	20	24	0	2	17.5%	.311/.383/.454	117	.335	-1.4	LF(28): -1.5, 2B(12): 0.7, 3B(9): 2.5	1.1
2021 FS	NYM	MLB	29	600	77	30	2	20	73	44	86	7	2	18.8%	.292/.362/.471	125	.318	1.7	2B -5, LF -6	2.7
2021 DC	NYM	MLB	29	588	76	29	2	20	72	44	84	7	2	18.8%	.292/.362/.471	125	.318	1.7	2B -5, LF -6	2.6

Comparables: Ian Kinsler, Chase Utley, Jose Altuve

While filling in across the diamond and jump-starting the team's offense, the Mets' resident Swiss Army knife also does the little things well. McNeil endeared himself to fans by adopting puppies and giving Joe West the business, and won over his teammates by talking up his manager and putting his body on the line to make ill-conceived, Kool-Aid Man-adjacent catches in the outfield. But for all the little things, McNeil's bread and butter is still one very, very big thing: He reaches base almost 40 percent of the time, making hard contact while hardly ever striking out. After three years of continued production (and a hot September waylaying a cold August's concerns), Six has established himself as perhaps the most important factor among the team's position players, the one thing they should never leave Queens without.

Tomás Nido C Born: 04/12/94 Age: 27 Bats: R Throws: R Height: 6'0" Weight: 211 Origin: Round 8, 2012 Draft (#260 overall)

YEAR	TEAM	LVL	AGE	PA	R	2B	3B	HR	RBI	BB	K	SB	CS	Whiff%	AVG/OBP/SLG	DRC+	BABIP	BRR	FRAA	WARP
2018	BNG	AA	24	228	23	18	1	5	30	7	36	0	0		.274/.298/.437	110	.303	-2.0	C(48): 8.5	1.6
2018	NYM	MLB	24	90	10	3	0	1	9	4	27	0	0	36.8%	.167/.200/.238	58	.224	0.2	C(30): 3.4	0.3
2019	SYR	AAA	25	40	3	1	0	0	4	1	13	0	0		.289/.300/.316	79	.423	-1.2	C(11): 1.4	0.1
2019	NYM	MLB	25	144	9	5	0	4	14	7	37	0	0	37.1%	.191/.231/.316	58	.232	-1.5	C(48): 5.1	0.3
2020	NYM	MLB	26	26	4	1	0	2	6	2	6	0	0	32.7%	.292/.346/.583	102	.312	0.0	C(7): -0.1	0.1
2021 FS	NYM	MLB	27	600	59	28	1	17	63	32	157	0	0	36.2%	.226/.272/.374	73	.282	-0.8	C 16	1.9
2021 DC	NYM	MLB	27	173	17	8	0	5	18	9	45	0	0	36.2%	.226/.272/.374	73	.282	-0.2	C 6	0.7

Comparables: Chris Krug, Jim Campbell, John Orton

After starting the season firmly ensconced as the Mets' reserve catcher, Tomas Nido promptly did something nearly no one thought he would do: he hit. Of course it was a small sample size, even by backup catcher standards, but it included a charmed two-homer game and a solid line drive off of Aaron Nola. Even a little bit of offensive efficacy could make the talented receiver a major-league regular for the next decade, but unfortunately his chance for a breakout was cut short after he contracted COVID-19, ending his season. Given his previous role as Noah Syndergaard's personal catcher, the Mets are likely to keep him around as James McCann's backup in the hopes that his surge with the bat in 2020 was a sign of things to come.

YEAR	TEAM	P. COUNT	FRM RUNS	BLK RUNS	THRW RUNS	TOT RUNS
2018	NYM	3483	3.5	-0.1	0.0	3.4
2018	BNG	6635	7.7	0.0	0.5	8.0
2019	NYM	5589	5.3	0.4	-0.6	5.1
2019	SYR	1379	1.2	0.1	0.1	1.4
2020	NYM	1049	0.8	0.1	0.0	0.9
2021	NYM	6012	5.7	0.4	0.0	6.1

Brandon Nimmo CF Born: 03/27/93 Age: 28 Bats: L Throws: R Height: 6'3" Weight: 206 Origin: Round 1, 2011 Draft (#13 overall)

YEAR	TEAM	LVL	AGE	PA	R	2B	3B	HR	RBI	BB	K	SB	CS	Whiff%	AVG/OBP/SLG	DRC+	BABIP	BRR	FRAA	WARP
2018	NYM	MLB	25	535	77	28	8	17	47	80	140	9	6	26.6%	.263/.404/.483	122	.351	5.1	RF(62): 0.1, CF(44): -0.9, LF(32): 2.1	3.6
2019	SYR	AAA	26	44	10	2	0	1	6	8	8	3	0		.200/.364/.343	100	.231	0.2	CF(8): 0.4, LF(2): -0.2	0.2
2019	NYM	MLB	26	254	34	11	1	8	29	46	71	3	0	27.7%	.221/.375/.407	100	.293	1.0	CF(43): -0.0, LF(38): -0.8, RF(6): 0.5	0.9
2020	NYM	MLB	27	225	33	8	3	8	18	33	43	1	2	21.8%	.280/.404/.484	123	.326	-1.5	CF(44): 0.0, LF(22): -2.2, RF(10): 0.1	0.9
2021 FS	NYM	MLB	28	600	85	26	4	19	58	85	143	5	2	25.0%	.260/.383/.445	128	.329	2.3	CF -5, RF 1	3.7
2021 DC	NYM	MLB	28	588	83	26	4	18	57	83	140	5	1	25.0%	.260/.383/.445	128	.329	2.3	CF -5, RF 1	3.8

Comparables: B.J. Upton, Jose Cruz, Don Lock

Trout, Soto, Votto, Freeman … Nimmo. Since his debut in 2016, the Mets' center fielder has the fifth-highest on-base percentage among consistent MLB regulars, and the names most adjacent to him on this list are a veritable who's who of MVPs and All-Stars. The only thing he lacks compared to all the other names on the top 10 OBP list–which continues with the names Judge, Goldschmidt, Yelich, Harper, and Rendon–is power production; in that regard Nimmo remains miles away from his peers. Nevertheless, the man with the million-dollar smile remains an underrated offensive catalyst despite his limitations when it comes to speed, defense, and power. When he's able to put the ball in play regularly, such as during his healthy the 2018 and 2020 seasons, he's an outstanding regular, no matter where he's slotted in an outfield.

Eduardo Núñez 2B   Born: 06/15/87   Age: 34   Bats: R   Throws: R   Height: 6'0"   Weight: 195   Origin: International Free Agent, 2004

YEAR	TEAM	LVL	AGE	PA	R	2B	3B	HR	RBI	BB	K	SB	CS	Whiff%	AVG/OBP/SLG	DRC+	BABIP	BRR	FRAA	WARP
2018	BOS	MLB	31	502	56	23	3	10	44	16	69	7	2	15.8%	.265/.289/.388	83	.290	-2.6	2B(74): -2.0, 3B(45): 1.2	0.2
2019	BOS	MLB	32	174	13	7	0	2	20	4	27	5	1	17.2%	.228/.243/.305	58	.257	1.7	2B(31): 1.3, 3B(8): -0.5, SS(6): -0.5	-0.2
2020	NYM	MLB	33	2	0	0	0	0	0	0	0	1	0	33.3%	.500/.500/.500	96	.500		RF(1): 0.1	0.0
2021 FS	*NYM*	*MLB*	*34*	*600*	*58*	*27*	*1*	*13*	*70*	*26*	*102*	*22*	*7*	*16.4%*	*.258/.297/.382*	*83*	*.295*	*1.8*	*2B -2, 3B 0*	*0.5*

Comparables: Clete Boyer, Bill Stein, Terry Pendleton

It only took two big-league plate appearances before Núñez's long-standing knee issues hobbled him and brought his season (and likely his career) to a close. Without his signature speed and the defensive flexibility that comes with it, he's likely played the last meaningful major-league game of a solid career.

José Peraza SS   Born: 04/30/94   Age: 27   Bats: R   Throws: R   Height: 6'0"   Weight: 210   Origin: International Free Agent, 2010

YEAR	TEAM	LVL	AGE	PA	R	2B	3B	HR	RBI	BB	K	SB	CS	Whiff%	AVG/OBP/SLG	DRC+	BABIP	BRR	FRAA	WARP
2018	CIN	MLB	24	683	85	31	4	14	58	29	75	23	6	14.1%	.288/.326/.416	101	.307	2.4	SS(156): -3.4, RF(1): -0.0	3.1
2019	CIN	MLB	25	403	37	18	2	6	33	17	58	7	6	16.7%	.239/.285/.346	78	.268	2.7	2B(78): 1.0, SS(39): 0.3, LF(33): -2.2	0.5
2020	BOS	MLB	26	120	13	8	1	1	8	5	18	1	1	21.6%	.225/.275/.342	93	.258	0.0	2B(27): 1.6, LF(5): -0.6, SS(3): -0.0	0.3
2021 FS	*NYM*	*MLB*	*27*	*600*	*60*	*27*	*2*	*10*	*59*	*27*	*90*	*19*	*8*	*16.7%*	*.254/.299/.367*	*82*	*.286*	*-1.2*	*2B 2, CF -2*	*0.5*
2021 DC	*NYM*	*MLB*	*27*	*242*	*24*	*10*	*1*	*4*	*24*	*10*	*36*	*7*	*3*	*16.7%*	*.254/.299/.367*	*82*	*.286*	*-0.5*	*2B 1, CF -1*	*0.1*

Comparables: Bill Spiers, Jean Segura, Yuniesky Betancourt

There's nothing worse than grabbing the wrong tool for the job. Ever try to use a Phillips head to fasten a straight screw? Build Ikea furniture with the wrong size Allen wrench? Use your plus-plus speed without knowing how to get on base? It's a terrible feeling. Though he was offered a clear path to consistent playing time, Peraza proved ill-equipped to get the job done. He did not hit well or field well, and he's never been known to pack a power tool. Peraza is mighty fast, it's true, but if you're only bringing one tool to the party, you better be able to put it to good use. Peraza does not, which makes him a "utility infielder" in name only, no matter which half of that designation you focus on.

Wilson Ramos C   Born: 08/10/87   Age: 33   Bats: R   Throws: R   Height: 6'1"   Weight: 245   Origin: International Free Agent, 2004

YEAR	TEAM	LVL	AGE	PA	R	2B	3B	HR	RBI	BB	K	SB	CS	Whiff%	AVG/OBP/SLG	DRC+	BABIP	BRR	FRAA	WARP
2018	TB	MLB	30	315	30	14	0	14	53	22	61	0	0	24.4%	.297/.346/.488	121	.335	-4.4	C(73): -0.8	1.8
2018	PHI	MLB	30	101	9	8	1	1	17	10	19	0	0	24.9%	.337/.396/.483	122	.408	-2.6	C(23): -0.0	0.5
2019	NYM	MLB	31	524	52	19	0	14	73	44	69	1	0	20.5%	.288/.351/.416	100	.310	-4.6	C(124): -6.7	1.6
2020	NYM	MLB	33	155	13	6	0	5	15	10	31	0	0	25.9%	.239/.297/.387	87	.271	-0.6	C(41): -0.9	-0.1
2021 FS	*NYM*	*MLB*	*33*	*600*	*65*	*25*	*0*	*19*	*72*	*40*	*123*	*0*	*0*	*22.7%*	*.261/.315/.418*	*97*	*.304*	*-1.3*	*C -4*	*1.6*

Comparables: Matt Wieters, Ryan Doumit, Terry Kennedy

YEAR	TEAM	P. COUNT	FRM RUNS	BLK RUNS	THRW RUNS	TOT RUNS
2018	TB	9962	0.2	0.3	-0.2	0.3
2018	PHI	3155	0.1	-0.3	0.2	0.0
2019	NYM	17269	-4.7	-0.5	-3.3	-8.6
2020	NYM	5757	-0.4	-0.5	0.2	-0.8
2021	*NYM*	*16650*	*-3.7*	*-1.1*	*-0.1*	*-4.9*

While PECOTA projected a small decline for Ramos in the 2020 season, the reality was a bit harsher than what our beloved projection system posited. Unfortunately for both Ramos and the Mets, without substantially above-average offensive production, the Buffalo isn't a starting-caliber catcher due to his intolerable defense. (Just one example: a brilliant relay throw could've saved the Mets' August 14 game against the Phillies, but Ramos couldn't lay down a tag at the plate.) Without positive framing numbers, a high-end arm, or other defensive charms, a significant bounce-back at the plate is required to keep Ramos in a starting role, rather than as a bat-first reserve catcher.

René Rivera C   Born: 07/31/83   Age: 37   Bats: R   Throws: R   Height: 5'10"   Weight: 215   Origin: Round 2, 2001 Draft (#49 overall)

YEAR	TEAM	LVL	AGE	PA	R	2B	3B	HR	RBI	BB	K	SB	CS	Whiff%	AVG/OBP/SLG	DRC+	BABIP	BRR	FRAA	WARP
2018	IE	HI-A	34	25	4	0	0	2	3	3	5	0	0		.286/.400/.571	131	.286	0.1	C(4): -0.0	0.1
2018	LAA	MLB	34	87	8	4	0	4	11	4	32	0	0	34.4%	.244/.287/.439	74	.348	-1.1	C(26): 0.5, 1B(2): -0.0	0.1
2018	ATL	MLB	34	4	0	0	0	0	0	0	3	0	0	60.0%	.000/.000/.000	72	.000		C(3): 0.2	0.0
2019	SYR	AAA	35	396	53	13	0	25	73	31	103	0	0		.254/.319/.501	105	.281	-2.0	C(80): 5.1, 1B(2): -0.1, P(1): -0.0	2.2
2019	NYM	MLB	35	20	2	0	0	1	3	3	4	0	0	21.6%	.235/.350/.412	90	.250		C(8): -0.6	0.0
2020	NYM	MLB	37	4	0	0	0	0	0	0	3	0	0	33.3%	.250/.250/.250	89	1.000		C(1): -0.0	0.0
2021 FS	*NYM*	*MLB*	*37*	*600*	*71*	*23*	*0*	*29*	*72*	*36*	*209*	*1*	*0*	*31.3%*	*.234/.291/.436*	*92*	*.319*	*-1.5*	*C 4, 1B 0*	*2.1*

Comparables: Tim Laker, Mike Rivera, Sandy Martinez

YEAR	TEAM	P. COUNT	FRM RUNS	BLK RUNS	THRW RUNS	TOT RUNS
2018	ATL	136	0.1	0.2	-0.1	0.2
2018	LAA	3346	1.6	-1.6	0.2	0.1
2019	NYM	858	0.1	-0.7	-0.1	-0.7
2019	SYR	11258	1.4	0.0	3.2	4.5
2020	NYM	135	0.0	0.0	0.0	0.0
2021	*NYM*	*16650*	*3.3*	*-1.1*	*0.6*	*2.7*

A full 16 years after his MLB debut, veteran backstop Rene Rivera leveraged every team's need for an everyday third catcher into two appearances with the Mets. Unfortunately, his season ended early due to elbow surgery in his non-throwing arm, leaving his status as a preeminent defense-first Triple-A safety valve in jeopardy.

Ali Sánchez C   Born: 01/20/97   Age: 24   Bats: R   Throws: R   Height: 6'1"   Weight: 200   Origin: International Free Agent, 2013

YEAR	TEAM	LVL	AGE	PA	R	2B	3B	HR	RBI	BB	K	SB	CS	Whiff%	AVG/OBP/SLG	DRC+	BABIP	BRR	FRAA	WARP
2018	COL	LO-A	21	205	26	11	1	4	22	10	23	1	1		.259/.293/.389	118	.274	0.4	C(36): 1.4	1.0
2018	STL	HI-A	21	142	11	9	0	2	16	5	15	1	1		.274/.296/.385	98	.292	-0.9	C(27): -0.1	0.1
2019	BNG	AA	22	294	28	13	0	1	30	23	52	1	0		.278/.337/.337	116	.341	-1.9	C(65): 1.2	1.7
2019	SYR	AAA	22	65	5	4	0	0	3	5	11	0	1		.179/.277/.250	57	.217	-0.5	C(20): 1.2	0.1
2020	NYM	MLB	23	10	0	0	0	0	0	1	3	0	0	43.5%	.111/.200/.111	84	.167	0.2	C(5): -0.1	0.1
2021 FS	NYM	MLB	24	600	53	23	1	9	50	37	135	1	0	43.5%	.225/.277/.321	63	.281	-1.1	C -3	-0.9
2021 DC	NYM	MLB	24	103	9	4	0	1	8	6	23	0	0	43.5%	.225/.277/.321	63	.281	-0.2	C -1	-0.2

Comparables: *Austin Romine, Gary Sánchez, Meibrys Viloria*

YEAR	TEAM	P. COUNT	FRM RUNS	BLK RUNS	THRW RUNS	TOT RUNS
2019	SYR	2336	0.9	0.0	0.3	1.1
2019	BNG	9109	-1.7	0.0	2.0	0.3
2020	NYM	539	0.0	0.0	0.0	0.0
2021	NYM	2405	-0.1	-0.3	-0.1	-0.5

Sanchez made his debut in 2020, but is far more likely to be a Triple-A mainstay than to see any extended action in the big leagues. HIs defense may be rock-solid, but his bat is mostly vapor.

Dominic Smith 1B   Born: 06/15/95   Age: 26   Bats: L   Throws: L   Height: 6'0"   Weight: 239   Origin: Round 1, 2013 Draft (#11 overall)

YEAR	TEAM	LVL	AGE	PA	R	2B	3B	HR	RBI	BB	K	SB	CS	Whiff%	AVG/OBP/SLG	DRC+	BABIP	BRR	FRAA	WARP
2018	LV	AAA	23	375	52	21	1	6	41	34	76	3	0		.258/.328/.380	81	.315	1.9	1B(53): 6.5, LF(22): -0.2, RF(4): 2.2	0.5
2018	NYM	MLB	23	149	14	11	1	5	11	4	47	0	0	27.8%	.224/.255/.420	76	.297	0.3	1B(28): -0.5, LF(13): -1.9	-0.4
2019	NYM	MLB	24	197	35	10	0	11	25	19	44	1	2	26.2%	.282/.355/.525	111	.320	2.8	1B(36): -0.6, LF(32): -1.0, RF(1): -0.1	0.9
2020	NYM	MLB	25	199	27	21	1	10	42	14	45	0	0	26.0%	.316/.377/.616	120	.368	0.5	1B(25): -1.0, LF(23): -4.7	0.5
2021 FS	NYM	MLB	26	600	68	28	1	25	80	47	146	1	0	26.3%	.248/.315/.446	101	.295	-0.5	LF -2, 1B 2	1.1
2021 DC	NYM	MLB	26	588	67	28	1	25	79	46	143	1	0	26.3%	.248/.315/.446	101	.295	-0.5	LF -2, 1B 2	1.4

Comparables: *Tony Clark, Mike Jacobs, Carlos Delgado*

Four years into his major-league career, Smith still hasn't eclipsed the 90-game mark in a season—though it's a good bet he would have given a standard-length 2020. Smith fought to establish himself as one of the best hitters in the National League while playing out of position, during a pandemic, with a compressed schedule, on a team that didn't truly support him when he took a knee for the national anthem during the Black Lives Matter protests. He stepped up as a leader as well, doing the hard work of following up a rare dismal offensive performance by holding court for an emotional press conference, explaining for reporters, teammates and the world just what the social justice movement is about for him. For a guy that couldn't seem to regularly crack a lineup until this year, it looks like Smith is just about everything you'd want in a ballplayer.

Mallex Smith CF   Born: 05/06/93   Age: 28   Bats: L   Throws: R   Height: 5'10"   Weight: 180   Origin: Round 5, 2012 Draft (#165 overall)

YEAR	TEAM	LVL	AGE	PA	R	2B	3B	HR	RBI	BB	K	SB	CS	Whiff%	AVG/OBP/SLG	DRC+	BABIP	BRR	FRAA	WARP
2018	TB	MLB	25	544	65	27	10	2	40	47	98	40	12	25.5%	.296/.367/.406	98	.366	4.4	CF(71): -7.0, RF(47): -1.9, LF(38): -1.2	0.9
2019	TAC	AAA	26	48	8	3	0	1	6	3	4	7	0		.333/.375/.467	107	.350	0.6	CF(10): 0.2	0.3
2019	SEA	MLB	26	566	70	19	9	6	37	42	140	46	9	28.6%	.227/.300/.335	73	.301	6.8	CF(106): -5.9, RF(28): 2.5, LF(5): 0.0	0.3
2020	SEA	MLB	27	47	2	2	0	0	3	2	13	2	0	26.9%	.133/.170/.178	63	.188	0.0	RF(12): -1.1, CF(3): -0.2	-0.3
2021 FS	NYM	MLB	28	600	59	24	6	7	52	51	146	37	11	27.6%	.233/.307/.343	80	.306	9.0	CF -8, RF 0	0.2

Comparables: *Cesar Geronimo, Herm Winningham, Cecil Espy*

After years and years (and years) of utter developmental failure, the Mariners appear to be turning the corner. Unfortunately, it would appear ending the curse that has plagued Mariner minor leaguers for a decade, scattering them to Japan and to culinary schools, required one final blood sacrifice. Alas, Smith drew the short straw for being tossed into the volcano. The speedy outfielder's game disintegrated; he set career lows in practically every category except errors and saw himself reduced to wandering around the Tacoma intramural expo that served at the minor leagues in 2020. He's still only 28 and a couple years removed from his breakout year in Tampa Bay. When he bounces back to be a productive regular for the Mets in 2021, remember for all that fanbase's kvetching that it turns out the real Mets were the Mariners, all along.

Mark Vientos 3B   Born: 12/11/99   Age: 21   Bats: R   Throws: R   Height: 6'4"   Weight: 185   Origin: Round 2, 2017 Draft (#59 overall)

YEAR	TEAM	LVL	AGE	PA	R	2B	3B	HR	RBI	BB	K	SB	CS	Whiff%	AVG/OBP/SLG	DRC+	BABIP	BRR	FRAA	WARP
2018	KNG	ROK	18	262	32	12	0	11	52	37	43	1	0		.287/.389/.489	148	.312	-3.0	3B(54): -1.7	0.7
2019	COL	LO-A	19	454	48	27	1	12	62	22	110	1	4		.255/.300/.411	122	.311	-5.2	3B(100): -3.0	1.5
2021 FS	NYM	MLB	21	600	51	27	1	13	58	38	186	0	0		.210/.266/.336	64	.291	-1.4	3B 0, SS 0	-1.7

Comparables: *Nick Castellanos, Neftali Soto, Rio Ruiz*

Even at the age of 20, Vientos can muscle the ball out of a park going the other way and he performed well enough in 2019 to spark visions of a bright future. Filling out and figuring out the holes in his swing are the next steps.

PITCHERS

★ ★ ★ *2021 Top 101 Prospect* **#79** ★ ★ ★

Matthew Allan **RHP** Born: 04/17/01 Age: 20 Bats: R Throws: R Height: 6'3" Weight: 225 Origin: Round 3, 2019 Draft (#89 overall)

YEAR	TEAM	LVL	AGE	W	L	SV	G	GS	IP	H	HR	BB/9	K/9	K	GB%	BABIP	WHIP	ERA	DRA-	WARP	MPH	FA%	Whiff%	CSP
2019	MTS	ROK	18	1	0	0	5	4	8¹	5	0	4.3	11.9	11	31.6%	.263	1.08	1.08	48	0.3				
2019	BRK	SS	18	0	0	0	1	1	2	5	0	4.5	13.5	3	42.9%	.714	3.00	9.00	136	0.0				
2021 FS	NYM	MLB	20	2	3	0	57	0	50	51	8	6.2	8.7	48	35.6%	.308	1.72	6.20	141	-1.0				

Instead of spending a full season hewing through Low-A hitters in Columbia or St. Lucie, the Mets' top pitching prospect joined the team's 60-man player pool in the middle of August, returning to the same Brooklyn field where he had such success during the previous season's New York-Penn League playoffs. While Allan was facing the team's other top prospects and a few major-league quality hitters, one of the goals was to convert his changeup from what he previously called a "slow fastball" to a different offering with more break and greater separation from his heater. If he can build up a third plus pitch to go with his fastball and curveball, he'll be facing (and beating) more high-minors hitters by the end of next season.

Jacob Barnes **RHP** Born: 04/14/90 Age: 31 Bats: R Throws: R Height: 6'2" Weight: 231 Origin: Round 14, 2011 Draft (#431 overall)

YEAR	TEAM	LVL	AGE	W	L	SV	G	GS	IP	H	HR	BB/9	K/9	K	GB%	BABIP	WHIP	ERA	DRA-	WARP	MPH	FA%	Whiff%	CSP
2018	RMV	AAA	28	1	0	2	11	0	11²	5	0	6.2	7.7	10	58.1%	.167	1.11	1.54	89	0.1				
2018	MIL	MLB	28	0	1	2	49	0	48²	51	4	4.3	8.7	47	49.0%	.331	1.52	3.33	78	0.8	97.4	50.5%	30.1%	44.6%
2019	SA	AAA	29	2	0	1	14	0	14	14	3	1.3	9.6	15	50.0%	.282	1.14	4.50	60	0.4				
2019	MIL	MLB	29	1	1	0	18	1	19²	22	3	5.0	10.1	22	46.8%	.322	1.68	6.86	113	0.0	95.3	46.4%	21.8%	41.9%
2019	KC	MLB	29	0	4	0	15	0	13	14	4	7.6	6.9	10	50.0%	.250	1.92	8.31	147	-0.3	96.1	50.4%	25.2%	41.2%
2020	LAA	MLB	30	0	2	0	18	0	18	19	1	2.0	12.0	24	39.6%	.391	1.28	5.50	73	0.4	97.3	46.6%	34.2%	42.0%
2021 FS	NYM	MLB	31	1	1	0	57	0	50	44	6	3.9	9.6	53	45.8%	.293	1.32	3.94	89	0.4	96.6	48.3%	28.4%	42.6%
2021 DC	NYM	MLB	31	1	1	0	22	0	24	21	3	3.9	9.6	25	45.8%	.293	1.32	3.94	89	0.3	96.6	48.3%	28.4%	42.6%

Comparables: Kelvin Herrera, Hunter Strickland, Paul Sewald

Occasionally, diagnosing the source of a pitcher's woes are easy: No need to get Freudian or Jungian when you can break out the velocity charts. These ink blots are clearer, but wringing solutions from them is rarely simple when *pitch harder* is as unhelpful a refrain as *be happier* is in a different sort of analysis. Barnes enlisted self-help as best he could and restored some of his velocity and results in 2020, but only enough to be cut from one team instead of two. Now, he'll try to achieve inner peace with the Mets.

Dellin Betances **RHP** Born: 03/23/88 Age: 33 Bats: R Throws: R Height: 6'8" Weight: 265 Origin: Round 8, 2006 Draft (#254 overall)

YEAR	TEAM	LVL	AGE	W	L	SV	G	GS	IP	H	HR	BB/9	K/9	K	GB%	BABIP	WHIP	ERA	DRA-	WARP	MPH	FA%	Whiff%	CSP
2018	NYY	MLB	30	4	6	4	66	0	66²	44	7	3.5	15.5	115	43.7%	.319	1.05	2.70	48	2.1	99.7	47.8%	37.4%	47.0%
2019	NYY	MLB	31	0	0	0	1	0	0²	0	0	0.0	27.0	2		.000	0.00	0.00	208	0.0	95.3	62.5%	0.0%	52.3%
2020	NYM	MLB	32	0	1	0	15	0	11²	12	0	9.3	8.5	11	41.2%	.353	2.06	7.71	108	0.1	95.8	49.0%	21.4%	45.5%
2021 FS	NYM	MLB	33	2	2	0	57	0	50	39	5	5.6	12.0	66	44.7%	.297	1.41	4.06	89	0.4	98.2	48.4%	30.9%	46.5%
2021 DC	NYM	MLB	33	2	2	0	45	0	48	37	5	5.6	12.0	63	44.7%	.297	1.41	4.06	89	0.6	98.2	48.4%	30.9%	46.5%

Comparables: Craig Kimbrel, Kenley Jansen, Brad Lidge

The Mets' biggest free agent pitching acquisition prior to the 2020 season ended up as a pretty good avatar for the way many of us experienced this past calendar year. After all, Betances' season was littered with health scares, possessed of several false starts, and punctuated by moments of abysmal failure. Even his celebrated fastball did an effective impression of time during quarantine by crawling to a standstill. After picking up his pricey $6.8 million player option, he and the Mets will both hope to turn the page on a remarkably bad year by healing up and starting over. Like many people, he'll hope to go back to the way things were, in 2021, but he may not be able to do so

Brad Brach **RHP** Born: 04/12/86 Age: 35 Bats: R Throws: R Height: 6'6" Weight: 215 Origin: Round 42, 2008 Draft (#1275 overall)

YEAR	TEAM	LVL	AGE	W	L	SV	G	GS	IP	H	HR	BB/9	K/9	K	GB%	BABIP	WHIP	ERA	DRA-	WARP	MPH	FA%	Whiff%	CSP
2018	BAL	MLB	32	1	2	11	42	0	39	50	4	4.4	8.8	38	46.9%	.374	1.77	4.85	95	0.3	95.4	61.4%	29.5%	44.5%
2018	ATL	MLB	32	1	2	1	27	0	23²	22	1	3.4	8.4	22	45.8%	.296	1.31	1.52	75	0.4	96.0	52.3%	28.6%	41.7%
2019	CHC	MLB	33	4	3	0	42	0	39²	42	3	6.4	10.2	45	39.3%	.375	1.76	6.13	109	0.0	95.7	60.5%	27.5%	44.5%
2019	NYM	MLB	33	1	1	0	16	0	14²	15	1	1.8	9.2	15	34.9%	.341	1.23	3.68	77	0.2	95.4	71.0%	26.4%	53.5%
2020	NYM	MLB	34	1	0	0	14	0	12¹	8	2	10.2	10.2	14	34.5%	.222	1.78	5.84	131	-0.1	91.8	68.7%	31.9%	38.9%
2021 FS	NYM	MLB	35	2	2	0	57	0	50	45	7	4.8	8.9	49	39.8%	.284	1.44	4.51	99	0.1	94.8	62.5%	28.7%	44.1%
2021 DC	NYM	MLB	35	2	2	0	51	0	54	49	7	4.8	8.9	53	39.8%	.284	1.44	4.51	99	0.3	94.8	62.5%	28.7%	44.1%

Comparables: Steve Cishek, Tyler Clippard, Brian Fuentes

Credit Brach with trying to make the best of a bad situation over 12 ⅓ miserable innings. Just two years removed from his peak with Baltimore, he's shifted from "wildly underrated" to just plain wild, as he now has to focus on keeping hitters from squaring up his diminished fastball. He's moved to relying on his cutter more frequently, but take a look at that stat line and let us know if it helped. Even when he could locate the erratic pitch, opposing hitters pounced on it for a .583 slugging percentage. At this point, he might be more of a righty specialist, and that makes him more of a sixth-inning situational arm than the slick setup man he once was.

Carlos Carrasco RHP Born: 03/21/87 Age: 34 Bats: R Throws: R Height: 6'4" Weight: 224 Origin: International Free Agent, 2003

YEAR	TEAM	LVL	AGE	W	L	SV	G	GS	IP	H	HR	BB/9	K/9	K	GB%	BABIP	WHIP	ERA	DRA-	WARP	MPH	FA%	Whiff%	CSP
2018	CLE	MLB	31	17	10	0	32	30	192	173	21	2.0	10.8	231	47.2%	.317	1.12	3.38	65	5.3	95.6	44.9%	33.5%	45.9%
2019	CLE	MLB	32	6	7	1	23	12	80	92	18	1.8	10.8	96	41.0%	.357	1.35	5.29	111	0.2	95.6	46.0%	31.2%	46.6%
2020	CLE	MLB	33	3	4	0	12	12	68	55	8	3.6	10.9	82	46.2%	.294	1.21	2.91	81	1.3	95.6	39.6%	32.7%	44.7%
2021 FS	NYM	MLB	34	10	7	0	26	26	150	132	22	2.6	10.6	176	45.2%	.298	1.18	3.45	81	2.6	95.6	43.2%	32.6%	45.6%
2021 DC	NYM	MLB	34	9	8	0	27	27	156	138	22	2.6	10.6	183	45.2%	.298	1.18	3.45	81	3.2	95.6	43.2%	32.6%	45.6%

Comparables: Corey Kluber, Zack Greinke, Johnny Cueto

A year after being diagnosed with leukemia, Carrasco took every turn in the rotation until it was time to rest for the final weekend ahead of the playoffs—and he did so with aplomb. He made a few tweaks along the way: leaning on his changeup at a career-high rate, and swapping his sinker for a curveball. Other than a few more walks, the results were as good as we've come to expect. Any scenario that saw Carrasco making a full return would've been heartening, but this one seems particularly so. Good on you, Cookie.

Miguel Castro RHP Born: 12/24/94 Age: 26 Bats: R Throws: R Height: 6'7" Weight: 205 Origin: International Free Agent, 2012

YEAR	TEAM	LVL	AGE	W	L	SV	G	GS	IP	H	HR	BB/9	K/9	K	GB%	BABIP	WHIP	ERA	DRA-	WARP	MPH	FA%	Whiff%	CSP
2018	BAL	MLB	23	2	7	0	63	1	86¹	75	9	5.2	5.9	57	48.5%	.259	1.45	3.96	145	-1.5	98.3	58.1%	23.6%	47.8%
2019	BAL	MLB	24	1	3	2	65	0	73¹	63	10	5.0	8.7	71	48.3%	.269	1.42	4.66	82	1.1	99.0	49.1%	27.6%	46.0%
2020	NYM	MLB	25	2	2	1	26	0	24²	28	4	4.7	13.9	38	52.4%	.407	1.66	4.01	68	0.6	99.8	50.7%	30.9%	46.4%
2021 FS	NYM	MLB	26	2	2	0	57	0	50	44	6	5.0	9.8	54	48.1%	.292	1.44	4.44	97	0.2	99.0	52.0%	27.4%	46.6%
2021 DC	NYM	MLB	26	2	2	0	45	0	48	42	6	5.0	9.8	52	48.1%	.292	1.44	4.44	97	0.4	99.0	52.0%	27.4%	46.6%

Comparables: Ryan Perry, Ed Nunez, Dave Beard

Little changed in his peripherals, but the start of his age-25 season looked to be something of a long-awaited coming out party for Castro. Since his teens, he had the raw heat on his fastball to be an oohs-and-ahs relief prospect, but his gangly mechanics commonly resulted in too many free passes. With only a brief uptick in velocity on his secondaries and a slight rise in whiff rate, Castro strung together 15 glorious innings of strikeout after strikeout, punctuated by far fewer free passes. The magic wore off after his midseason trade to the Mets, but he remains tantalizing due to his high-end velocity and the possibility that, for a few weeks at a time, at least, he can smooth things out enough to be a force in the middle innings.

Jacob deGrom RHP Born: 06/19/88 Age: 33 Bats: L Throws: R Height: 6'4" Weight: 180 Origin: Round 9, 2010 Draft (#272 overall)

YEAR	TEAM	LVL	AGE	W	L	SV	G	GS	IP	H	HR	BB/9	K/9	K	GB%	BABIP	WHIP	ERA	DRA-	WARP	MPH	FA%	Whiff%	CSP
2018	NYM	MLB	30	10	9	0	32	32	217	152	10	1.9	11.2	269	46.2%	.283	0.91	1.70	46	8.0	98.2	52.1%	31.5%	48.4%
2019	NYM	MLB	31	11	8	0	32	32	204	154	19	1.9	11.2	254	43.6%	.284	0.97	2.43	46	7.8	98.8	49.3%	31.9%	46.2%
2020	NYM	MLB	32	4	2	0	12	12	68	47	7	2.4	13.8	104	42.5%	.288	0.96	2.38	57	2.2	100.3	44.9%	41.0%	44.0%
2021 FS	NYM	MLB	33	10	6	0	26	26	150	114	16	2.2	11.8	197	43.1%	.288	1.01	2.33	57	4.7	99.0	48.8%	34.2%	46.2%
2021 DC	NYM	MLB	33	13	6	0	29	29	180	137	20	2.2	11.8	236	43.1%	.288	1.01	2.33	57	6.0	99.0	48.8%	34.2%	46.2%

Comparables: Corey Kluber, Kenta Maeda, Max Scherzer

Few pitchers continue to add velocity in their early 30s, but BP's Rob Arthur discovered that deGrom truly is in a class of his own: Only two starting pitchers since 2008 have added as much oomph to their fastball during the middle of their career, and both of those pitchers were injury-riddled hurlers, not an established star like deGrom. He's now the hardest-throwing starter in baseball over the age of 30, and he's complemented that by becoming more unpredictable in his pitch selection, often working his devastating slider out of the zone in hitters' counts instead of leaning into his heater. So even though the shortened season saw him down to a mere Cy Young finalist rather than Cy Young winner, there's reason to believe that deGrom will extend his peak even once his fastball velocity inevitably plateaus.

Edwin Díaz RHP Born: 03/22/94 Age: 27 Bats: R Throws: R Height: 6'3" Weight: 165 Origin: Round 3, 2012 Draft (#98 overall)

YEAR	TEAM	LVL	AGE	W	L	SV	G	GS	IP	H	HR	BB/9	K/9	K	GB%	BABIP	WHIP	ERA	DRA-	WARP	MPH	FA%	Whiff%	CSP
2018	SEA	MLB	24	0	4	57	73	0	73¹	41	5	2.1	15.2	124	46.6%	.281	0.79	1.96	39	2.7	99.3	62.5%	39.8%	48.3%
2019	NYM	MLB	25	2	7	26	66	0	58	58	15	3.4	15.4	99	36.4%	.381	1.38	5.59	60	1.5	99.6	66.1%	37.9%	46.9%
2020	NYM	MLB	26	2	1	6	26	0	25²	18	2	4.9	17.5	50	45.5%	.381	1.25	1.75	45	1.0	99.6	61.9%	48.2%	43.8%
2021 FS	NYM	MLB	27	2	2	33	57	0	50	33	5	3.5	14.6	81	41.2%	.297	1.06	2.40	57	1.3	99.5	63.9%	41.5%	46.3%
2021 DC	NYM	MLB	27	2	2	33	51	0	54	35	5	3.5	14.6	87	41.2%	.297	1.06	2.40	57	1.5	99.5	63.9%	41.5%	46.3%

Comparables: José Leclerc, Michael Feliz, Francisco Rodríguez

It took until September of his second season with the Mets, but Díaz is finally starting to resemble the pitcher the team thought they were acquiring in their blockbuster trade, instead of the combustible reliever they received in 2019. The signs that his first season in Queens could have been a fluke were always there, but after being gently worked back into high-leverage situations, Díaz turned up the heat and struck out 45.5 percent of the batters he faced in 2020. He ended his season with a dominant stretch that reaffirmed his grasp on the closer role and as the anchor of the bullpen.

Jerad Eickhoff RHP Born: 07/02/90 Age: 31 Bats: R Throws: R Height: 6'4" Weight: 246 Origin: Round 15, 2011 Draft (#474 overall)

YEAR	TEAM	LVL	AGE	W	L	SV	G	GS	IP	H	HR	BB/9	K/9	K	GB%	BABIP	WHIP	ERA	DRA-	WARP	MPH	FA%	Whiff%	CSP
2018	CLR	HI-A	27	0	1	0	3	3	9	3	2	4.0	10.0	10	36.8%	.062	0.78	3.00	70	0.2				
2018	LHV	AAA	27	0	0	0	4	4	18²	17	1	3.9	4.8	10	52.5%	.267	1.34	2.41	99	0.1				
2018	PHI	MLB	27	0	1	0	3	1	5¹	10	1	0.0	18.6	11	20.0%	.643	1.88	6.75	68	0.1	92.0	52.0%	42.2%	49.1%
2019	REA	AA	28	0	1	0	2	2	7¹	8	2	3.7	7.4	6	22.7%	.300	1.50	9.82	119	-0.1				
2019	LHV	AAA	28	3	1	0	4	4	17¹	13	3	4.2	8.3	16	25.0%	.227	1.21	4.67	85	0.4				
2019	PHI	MLB	28	3	4	1	12	10	58¹	58	18	2.8	7.7	50	35.1%	.260	1.30	5.71	125	-0.3	91.2	39.1%	26.7%	47.8%
2021 FS	NYM	MLB	30	2	3	0	57	0	50	51	10	3.4	8.3	45	36.1%	.295	1.42	5.11	116	-0.3	91.2	39.7%	27.4%	47.9%

Comparables: Kevin Gausman, Nick Tropeano, Anthony DeSclafani

LeBron to Cleveland, Griffey to Seattle, Odysseus to Ithaca. And after five years in Philadelphia, Eickhoff triumphantly returned to the organization that drafted him, signing with the Rangers midseason. Even if he technically never took the field, 2020 wasn't a total loss; after serving up a home run on nearly a quarter of his fly balls in 2019, it had to be comforting to watch so many snagged at the warning track at Globe Life Field. Eickhoff has since joined the Mets, ending his Texas reunion with a whimper.

Jeurys Familia RHP Born: 10/10/89 Age: 31 Bats: R Throws: R Height: 6'3" Weight: 240 Origin: International Free Agent, 2007

YEAR	TEAM	LVL	AGE	W	L	SV	G	GS	IP	H	HR	BB/9	K/9	K	GB%	BABIP	WHIP	ERA	DRA-	WARP	MPH	FA%	Whiff%	CSP
2018	OAK	MLB	28	4	2	1	30	0	31¹	24	2	4.0	11.5	40	40.3%	.293	1.21	3.45	68	0.7	98.5	66.8%	35.4%	47.3%
2018	NYM	MLB	28	4	4	17	40	0	40²	36	1	3.1	9.5	43	50.9%	.315	1.23	2.88	103	0.1	97.8	70.2%	26.7%	49.7%
2019	NYM	MLB	29	4	2	0	66	0	60	62	7	6.3	9.4	63	50.0%	.350	1.73	5.70	120	-0.3	97.8	65.8%	28.6%	47.0%
2020	NYM	MLB	30	2	0	0	25	0	26²	20	2	6.4	7.8	23	60.0%	.247	1.46	3.71	90	0.4	98.5	59.7%	27.8%	46.2%
2021 FS	NYM	MLB	31	2	2	0	57	0	50	44	5	5.2	9.0	50	53.5%	.291	1.47	4.49	97	0.2	98.1	64.7%	28.9%	47.2%
2021 DC	NYM	MLB	31	2	2	0	51	0	54	48	6	5.2	9.0	54	53.5%	.291	1.47	4.49	97	0.4	98.1	64.7%	28.9%	47.2%

Comparables: Kelvin Herrera, Mychal Givens, Randy Myers

There were a few hints that the stalwart of the Mets' bullpen might be rounding into form during the abbreviated 2020 season: He started strong in July, and his velocity improved as the short season wore on, but by the end of the year it seemed clear that 2019 wasn't just a fluke. Familia couldn't translate the improved giddyup on his sinker and slider into whiffs, instead working to keep the ball in the infield. Back when he was a top-flight reliever, Familia could do both: induce grounders but also punch hitters out with regularity. In his present form, he's more of a fringy setup option; though the uniform remains the same, he's a different pitcher than in his prime.

J.T. Ginn RHP Born: 05/20/99 Age: 22 Bats: R Throws: R Height: 6'2" Weight: 200 Origin: Round 2, 2020 Draft (#52 overall)

Usually a Mets pitcher experiences a severe elbow injury after they make it to the big leagues, but this time perhaps the team is skipping to the middle of the story instead of starting on page one? Ginn turned down an overslot offer from the Dodgers back in the first round of the 2018 draft, and despite the elbow injury sustained during his second year at Mississippi State, the decision has turned out to make good financial sense for the former SEC Freshman of the Year. The Mets bet big on his ability to rebound from surgery to reclaim his lively fastball and ripping slider, but the early returns on this investment might not be clear until 2022.

Robert Gsellman RHP Born: 07/18/93 Age: 27 Bats: R Throws: R Height: 6'4" Weight: 200 Origin: Round 13, 2011 Draft (#402 overall)

YEAR	TEAM	LVL	AGE	W	L	SV	G	GS	IP	H	HR	BB/9	K/9	K	GB%	BABIP	WHIP	ERA	DRA-	WARP	MPH	FA%	Whiff%	CSP
2018	NYM	MLB	24	6	3	13	68	0	80	76	8	3.1	7.9	70	50.4%	.294	1.30	4.28	97	0.5	96.1	62.8%	22.4%	49.3%
2019	NYM	MLB	25	2	3	1	52	0	63²	64	7	3.3	8.5	60	43.6%	.317	1.37	4.66	99	0.3	97.1	51.8%	26.4%	47.2%
2020	NYM	MLB	26	0	0	0	6	4	14	22	4	5.1	5.8	9	41.5%	.367	2.14	9.64	130	-0.1	95.8	64.0%	16.9%	45.3%
2021 FS	NYM	MLB	27	3	3	0	57	0	50	52	8	3.7	7.5	41	45.0%	.302	1.47	5.22	112	-0.2	96.6	57.5%	23.4%	47.5%
2021 DC	NYM	MLB	27	3	3	0	44	4	61	64	9	3.7	7.5	51	45.0%	.302	1.47	5.22	112	0.0	96.6	57.5%	23.4%	47.5%

Comparables: Reynaldo López, Chase De Jong, Joe Ross

Gsellman's 2020 had more false starts than an elementary school track meet. First a triceps injury set his debut back, then he had just one appearance in the bullpen before getting shifted into the starting rotation. That went just about as badly as it could have; he exceeded two innings as a starter just once, and not because he was designed to be an opener. After one final bullpen appearance, he hit the injured list again, this time with a fractured rib, and his season was over. It's hard to be surprised at the terrible stat line, given his medical issues and the surprise shift in role mid-season, but Gsellman should be counted on to return to his role as a sixth- or seventh-inning relief arm, not as a swingman or back-end starter. Despite his wide assortment of pitches and prospect pedigree, he's best served in a mid-leverage relief role without being asked to do much more.

Jared Hughes RHP Born: 07/04/85 Age: 36 Bats: R Throws: R Height: 6'7" Weight: 240 Origin: Round 4, 2006 Draft (#110 overall)

YEAR	TEAM	LVL	AGE	W	L	SV	G	GS	IP	H	HR	BB/9	K/9	K	GB%	BABIP	WHIP	ERA	DRA-	WARP	MPH	FA%	Whiff%	CSP
2018	CIN	MLB	32	4	3	7	72	0	78²	57	4	2.6	6.8	59	63.6%	.254	1.02	1.94	102	0.3	93.5	86.0%	25.4%	42.2%
2019	PHI	MLB	33	2	1	0	25	0	23	16	7	3.1	7.8	20	53.2%	.167	1.04	3.91	94	0.2	93.1	79.9%	24.0%	37.8%
2019	CIN	MLB	33	3	4	1	47	0	48¹	41	6	3.5	6.3	34	59.7%	.259	1.24	4.10	94	0.4	92.9	81.1%	22.1%	37.9%
2020	NYM	MLB	34	1	2	0	18	0	22¹	23	3	5.6	8.5	21	56.5%	.303	1.66	4.84	95	0.3	93.3	59.4%	32.3%	40.2%
2021 FS	NYM	MLB	35	2	3	0	57	0	50	48	6	3.8	7.3	40	57.6%	.289	1.40	4.39	101	0.1	93.2	76.2%	26.0%	39.6%

Comparables: Javy Guerra, Javier López, Cory Gearrin

Five unearned runs made Hughes' first (and likely last) season in New York look more palatable than his ERA would suggest. His velocity never rebounded to where it was prior to 2019, so his ceiling is probably now that of a league-average reliever.

Ariel Jurado RHP Born: 01/30/96 Age: 25 Bats: R Throws: R Height: 6'2" Weight: 240 Origin: International Free Agent, 2002

YEAR	TEAM	LVL	AGE	W	L	SV	G	GS	IP	H	HR	BB/9	K/9	K	GB%	BABIP	WHIP	ERA	DRA-	WARP	MPH	FA%	Whiff%	CSP
2018	FRI	AA	22	5	3	0	16	16	101²	107	12	1.5	5.1	58	51.0%	.291	1.22	3.28	126	-1.0				
2018	TEX	MLB	22	5	5	0	12	8	54²	66	7	3.0	3.5	21	51.7%	.304	1.54	5.93	155	-1.1	93.3	70.4%	10.4%	51.2%
2019	NAS	AAA	23	3	0	0	4	4	22²	29	1	0.8	8.7	22	38.0%	.400	1.37	3.57	99	0.4				
2019	TEX	MLB	23	7	11	0	32	18	122¹	148	21	2.6	6.0	81	46.0%	.322	1.50	5.81	147	-2.0	94.2	64.2%	18.1%	49.1%
2020	NYM	MLB	24	0	0	0	1	1	4	9	1	0.0	4.5	2	31.6%	.471	2.25	11.25	110	0.0	93.2	50.0%	22.0%	40.2%
2021 FS	NYM	MLB	25	2	3	0	57	0	50	57	9	2.6	6.3	34	45.6%	.305	1.45	5.37	119	-0.4	94.0	64.5%	17.0%	49.0%

Comparables: Antonio Senzatela, Sean Reid-Foley, Zach Eflin

After eight years in the Rangers' system, Texas finally gave up on the swing-starter and former top prospect. After getting dealt to the Mets, Jurado made one terribly ill-fated start before setting out in search of the third organization of his career.

Franklyn Kilome RHP Born: 06/25/95 Age: 26 Bats: R Throws: R Height: 6'6" Weight: 175 Origin: International Free Agent, 2013

YEAR	TEAM	LVL	AGE	W	L	SV	G	GS	IP	H	HR	BB/9	K/9	K	GB%	BABIP	WHIP	ERA	DRA-	WARP	MPH	FA%	Whiff%	CSP
2018	REA	AA	23	4	6	0	19	19	102	96	7	4.5	7.3	83	44.8%	.309	1.44	4.24	99	0.8				
2018	BNG	AA	23	0	3	0	7	7	38	31	3	2.4	9.9	42	41.0%	.289	1.08	4.03	94	0.4				
2020	NYM	MLB	25	0	1	1	4	0	11¹	14	5	7.1	10.3	13	34.3%	.310	2.03	11.12	138	-0.1	96.4	53.7%	30.2%	44.6%
2021 FS	NYM	MLB	26	1	1	0	57	0	50	49	8	5.3	8.4	46	40.0%	.291	1.57	5.62	118	-0.4	96.4	53.7%	30.2%	44.6%
2021 DC	NYM	MLB	26	1	1	0	34	0	36	35	6	5.3	8.4	33	40.0%	.291	1.57	5.62	118	-0.1	96.4	53.7%	30.2%	44.6%

Comparables: Bryan Mitchell, Adrian Houser, Myles Jaye

While there were signs Kilomé could eventually contribute at the major-league level, he gave up at least two runs in each of his four relief appearances during his post-TJS debut season. Suffice to say he's not guaranteed a big-league spot in 2021.

Seth Lugo RHP Born: 11/17/89 Age: 31 Bats: R Throws: R Height: 6'4" Weight: 225 Origin: Round 34, 2011 Draft (#1032 overall)

YEAR	TEAM	LVL	AGE	W	L	SV	G	GS	IP	H	HR	BB/9	K/9	K	GB%	BABIP	WHIP	ERA	DRA-	WARP	MPH	FA%	Whiff%	CSP
2018	NYM	MLB	28	3	4	3	54	5	101¹	81	9	2.5	9.1	103	45.8%	.270	1.08	2.66	85	1.4	96.5	48.6%	23.3%	50.1%
2019	NYM	MLB	29	7	4	6	61	0	80	56	8	1.8	11.7	104	43.4%	.267	0.90	2.70	55	2.3	96.7	56.7%	26.6%	51.2%
2020	NYM	MLB	30	3	4	3	16	7	36²	40	8	2.5	11.5	47	50.5%	.344	1.36	5.15	76	0.8	96.2	55.4%	30.1%	47.6%
2021 FS	NYM	MLB	31	4	3	0	57	0	50	42	6	2.6	10.5	58	46.1%	.287	1.13	3.23	75	0.8	96.5	54.1%	26.8%	49.8%
2021 DC	NYM	MLB	31	4	3	0	52	6	77	65	10	2.6	10.5	89	46.1%	.287	1.13	3.23	75	1.6	96.5	54.1%	26.8%	49.8%

Comparables: Matt Andriese, Zack Godley, Erasmo Ramírez

Lugo may have established himself as a very effective reliever during 2019 and the start of 2020, but he's always stated a preference to return to the rotation. In August he got his wish, as Steven Matz was bumped and Lugo earned his chance to start again. The results were … let's just say mixed, as he balanced five fair-to-good starts with two absolute disasters. His velocity only dipped a smidge in his move to the rotation, but he got battered during his second time through opposing lineups, struggling to limit his walks and looking less than comfortable while dealing with his midseason role change. It can be tough to balance Lugo's established dominance as a reliever against the potential for him to emerge as a mid-rotation starter, but either way he'd benefit greatly from having a defined role and sticking with it all season long, instead of being shifted after just a handful of appearances.

Steven Matz LHP Born: 05/29/91 Age: 30 Bats: R Throws: L Height: 6'2" Weight: 201 Origin: Round 2, 2009 Draft (#72 overall)

YEAR	TEAM	LVL	AGE	W	L	SV	G	GS	IP	H	HR	BB/9	K/9	K	GB%	BABIP	WHIP	ERA	DRA-	WARP	MPH	FA%	Whiff%	CSP
2018	NYM	MLB	27	5	11	0	30	30	154	134	25	3.4	8.9	152	47.9%	.270	1.25	3.97	80	3.0	95.1	60.0%	23.3%	52.7%
2019	NYM	MLB	28	11	10	0	32	30	160¹	163	27	2.9	8.6	153	46.3%	.304	1.34	4.21	90	2.4	95.0	50.6%	23.0%	50.5%
2020	NYM	MLB	29	0	5	0	9	6	30²	42	14	2.9	10.6	36	33.3%	.346	1.70	9.68	146	-0.5	96.1	53.9%	23.4%	47.3%
2021 FS	NYM	MLB	30	9	8	0	26	26	150	145	23	3.0	9.2	153	43.4%	.301	1.31	4.24	96	1.4	95.2	53.8%	23.2%	50.5%
2021 DC	NYM	MLB	30	7	6	0	22	22	108	104	16	3.0	9.2	110	43.4%	.301	1.31	4.24	96	1.4	95.2	53.8%	23.2%	50.5%

Comparables: Andrew Heaney, Kevin Gausman, Anthony DeSclafani

Every time Matz threw a pitch in 2020, it seemed to be heading over the outfield wall. Giving up two home runs per nine innings is usually a cry for help, but Matz's rate of 4.11 homers per nine was so far beyond the pale that it dwarfed the numbers for every other starting pitcher in the league. Given that it's hardly possible for things to get worse from a performance perspective, and that he was a perfectly fine starter the two previous years, the Mets tendered him a contract for the 2021 season in the hopes that he can right the ship since his velocity and movement didn't change dramatically. If he can keep even a few more balls inside the stadium, he'll go back to being a decent starting pitcher—all the other tools are there.

Trevor May   RHP   Born: 09/23/89   Age: 31   Bats: R   Throws: R   Height: 6'5"   Weight: 240   Origin: Round 4, 2008 Draft (#136 overall)

YEAR	TEAM	LVL	AGE	W	L	SV	G	GS	IP	H	HR	BB/9	K/9	K	GB%	BABIP	WHIP	ERA	DRA-	WARP	MPH	FA%	Whiff%	CSP
2018	ROC	AAA	28	0	4	2	13	4	27	24	2	5.3	8.3	25	39.0%	.293	1.48	4.00	76	0.5				
2018	MIN	MLB	28	4	1	3	24	1	25¹	21	4	1.8	12.8	36	37.7%	.309	1.03	3.20	66	0.6	95.5	59.2%	32.7%	46.5%
2019	MIN	MLB	29	5	3	2	65	0	64¹	43	8	3.6	11.1	79	34.2%	.233	1.07	2.94	81	1.0	97.5	62.9%	30.1%	46.4%
2020	MIN	MLB	30	1	0	2	24	0	23¹	20	5	2.7	14.7	38	25.5%	.326	1.16	3.86	85	0.4	97.9	51.7%	43.0%	44.6%
2021 FS	NYM	MLB	31	2	2	11	57	0	50	40	8	3.2	11.9	66	33.2%	.286	1.17	3.59	82	0.6	97.4	59.0%	34.3%	45.9%
2021 DC	NYM	MLB	31	2	2	11	51	0	54	44	9	3.2	11.9	71	33.2%	.286	1.17	3.59	82	0.8	97.4	59.0%	34.3%	45.9%

Comparables: Erasmo Ramírez, Matt Andriese, Alex Colomé

May's a valedictorian, electronic music artist, relief pitcher, occasional writer at MLB Trade Rumors and Twitch streamer—and judging by his Twitter metrics, it's the last of those he's most famous for. On the field, @IamTrevorMay is your prototypical modern-day reliever: He strikes out a lotta dudes but gives up too many homers to be more than a solid option in middle relief. If there's a path forward, it might be by becoming a bit more of a throwback. Like just about everyone, he increased the usage of his slider at the expense of his fastball last season. Unlike everyone, it's unclear that this tradeoff benefits DJ HEYBEEF. He's steadily added velocity to his heater in recent years, and now sits comfortably in the mid-90s. Moreover, he's adept at locating his high-spinner up in the zone, where he notched a very high 22 percent whiff rate last year—better than any of his offspeed pitches. Perhaps he can share his thoughts on that over a game of Call of Duty?

Corey Oswalt   RHP   Born: 09/03/93   Age: 27   Bats: R   Throws: R   Height: 6'5"   Weight: 250   Origin: Round 7, 2012 Draft (#230 overall)

YEAR	TEAM	LVL	AGE	W	L	SV	G	GS	IP	H	HR	BB/9	K/9	K	GB%	BABIP	WHIP	ERA	DRA-	WARP	MPH	FA%	Whiff%	CSP
2018	LV	AAA	24	4	4	0	11	11	52¹	58	9	3.4	8.9	52	43.9%	.331	1.49	6.02	136	-0.5				
2018	NYM	MLB	24	3	3	0	17	12	64²	69	14	2.8	6.3	45	40.8%	.278	1.38	5.85	128	-0.4	92.5	67.0%	16.6%	47.8%
2019	BRK	SS	25	0	0	0	2	2	6	6	0	4.5	10.5	7	27.8%	.333	1.50	1.50	107	0.0				
2019	SYR	AAA	25	10	4	0	16	16	86²	84	9	1.6	8.2	79	43.8%	.305	1.14	2.91	65	3.0				
2019	NYM	MLB	25	0	1	0	2	0	6²	9	1	8.1	6.8	5	34.8%	.364	2.25	12.15	115	0.0	93.8	65.7%	15.8%	42.1%
2020	NYM	MLB	26	0	0	0	4	1	13	14	3	1.4	7.6	11	36.6%	.289	1.23	4.85	114	0.0	93.8	53.4%	29.7%	40.9%
2021 FS	NYM	MLB	27	2	2	0	57	0	50	50	9	2.7	8.0	44	40.8%	.292	1.32	4.64	103	0.0	93.2	62.2%	20.9%	44.7%
2021 DC	NYM	MLB	27	2	2	0	27	4	43	43	7	2.7	8.0	37	40.8%	.292	1.32	4.64	103	0.3	93.2	62.2%	20.9%	44.7%

Comparables: Luis Perdomo, Chase De Jong, Luis Cessa

The New York Mets' injury-prone starting rotation has often led the team to look for a proverbial "break-glass-in-case-of-emergency" fire extinguisher in human form. Enter Oswalt, ideally that man-shaped fire extinguisher, but instead of being full of suppressant, he's filled to the brim with hanging sliders, the pitching equivalent of butane.

David Peterson   LHP   Born: 09/03/95   Age: 25   Bats: L   Throws: L   Height: 6'6"   Weight: 240   Origin: Round 1, 2017 Draft (#20 overall)

YEAR	TEAM	LVL	AGE	W	L	SV	G	GS	IP	H	HR	BB/9	K/9	K	GB%	BABIP	WHIP	ERA	DRA-	WARP	MPH	FA%	Whiff%	CSP
2018	COL	LO-A	22	1	4	0	9	9	59¹	46	1	1.7	8.6	57	65.0%	.285	0.96	1.82	72	1.2				
2018	STL	HI-A	22	6	6	0	13	13	68²	74	1	2.5	7.6	58	60.3%	.340	1.35	4.33	83	1.0				
2019	BNG	AA	23	3	6	0	24	24	116	119	9	2.9	9.5	122	52.0%	.342	1.34	4.19	116	-1.0				
2020	NYM	MLB	24	6	2	0	10	9	49²	36	5	4.3	7.2	40	44.2%	.233	1.21	3.44	110	0.2	94.2	53.2%	26.2%	44.8%
2021 FS	NYM	MLB	25	9	9	0	26	26	150	144	22	4.6	8.1	135	46.3%	.288	1.48	4.93	105	0.6	94.2	53.2%	26.2%	44.8%
2021 DC	NYM	MLB	25	4	4	0	12	12	67	64	10	4.6	8.1	60	46.3%	.288	1.48	4.93	105	0.5	94.2	53.2%	26.2%	44.8%

Comparables: Nick Margevicius, Josh Fleming, Eric Lauer

Jumping from Double-A to the majors isn't the great leap that it used to be, but it's still quite the gap to cover, even if you're a high-floor left-handed starting pitcher with a deep enough arsenal to make it through the order a couple of times. But Peterson's wiles and his slider proved enough to get by at the back of the Mets' rotation, even if he couldn't approximate his minor-league ground ball or strikeout rates in his first go-round in the majors. The two strong starts to close out the year and the sharp ERA are tantalizing, but the lack of dominant stuff means that his ceiling probably isn't much higher than that of a fourth starter.

Rick Porcello   RHP   Born: 12/27/88   Age: 32   Bats: R   Throws: R   Height: 6'5"   Weight: 205   Origin: Round 1, 2007 Draft (#27 overall)

YEAR	TEAM	LVL	AGE	W	L	SV	G	GS	IP	H	HR	BB/9	K/9	K	GB%	BABIP	WHIP	ERA	DRA-	WARP	MPH	FA%	Whiff%	CSP
2018	BOS	MLB	29	17	7	0	33	33	191¹	177	27	2.3	8.9	190	44.0%	.286	1.18	4.28	89	2.8	92.8	50.0%	20.4%	48.9%
2019	BOS	MLB	30	14	12	0	32	32	174¹	198	31	2.3	7.4	143	38.0%	.310	1.39	5.52	124	-0.5	92.5	56.5%	18.0%	49.1%
2020	NYM	MLB	31	1	7	0	12	12	59	74	5	2.3	8.2	54	40.5%	.373	1.51	5.64	83	1.1	92.6	53.2%	15.5%	49.2%
2021 FS	NYM	MLB	32	9	9	0	26	26	150	157	27	2.2	7.8	130	39.7%	.300	1.30	4.49	103	0.8	92.6	54.0%	18.0%	49.1%

Comparables: Frank Viola, Brad Radke, Scott Baker

Given the Mets' injury issues and Porcello's New Jersey roots, it seemed like only a matter of time before the veteran right-hander found his way to his hometown team. But Porcello was paid more like a mid-rotation starter than the back-of-the-rotation profile he's shown since his Cy Young win in Boston. He leaned harder on his slider than usual, and there was some weirdness in his batted ball profile: He was top-five in the majors in both line drive percentage (bad!) and infield fly percentage (good!), but was worst in the National League at stranding a runner once they reached base. Overall, it was a bust of a year for the local kid, and his next free agent contract is much more likely to reflect his diminished standing than his previous one.

Erasmo Ramírez RHP Born: 05/02/90 Age: 31 Bats: R Throws: R Height: 6'0" Weight: 220 Origin: International Free Agent, 2007

YEAR	TEAM	LVL	AGE	W	L	SV	G	GS	IP	H	HR	BB/9	K/9	K	GB%	BABIP	WHIP	ERA	DRA-	WARP	MPH	FA%	Whiff%	CSP
2018	TAC	AAA	28	0	2	0	5	5	18²	14	1	1.4	8.2	17	44.4%	.250	0.91	2.41	79	0.4				
2018	SEA	MLB	28	2	4	0	10	10	45²	52	14	2.4	6.5	33	39.6%	.271	1.40	6.50	146	-0.7	91.9	40.8%	19.5%	49.5%
2019	WOR	AAA	29	6	8	0	27	24	125¹	125	18	3.1	6.8	95	47.0%	.285	1.34	4.74	94	2.5				
2019	BOS	MLB	29	0	0	0	1	0	3	4	2	3.0	3.0	1	41.7%	.222	1.67	12.00	143	-0.1	92.0	53.7%	22.2%	47.2%
2020	NYM	MLB	30	0	0	1	6	0	14¹	8	1	2.5	5.7	9	42.5%	.179	0.84	0.63	107	0.1	92.1	44.6%	21.3%	45.9%
2021 FS	NYM	MLB	31	2	3	0	57	0	50	51	8	2.9	7.1	39	44.5%	.290	1.36	4.70	106	-0.1	92.0	43.1%	20.4%	47.9%

Comparables: Nathan Eovaldi, Matt Andriese, Justin Germano

Houdini's got nothing on Ramirez, who popped up with the Mets in September and performed one of the great magic tricks of the 2020 season. The well-traveled reliever was asked to serve five innings in relief on September 7, gave up a solo homer to J.T. Realmuto, and never looked back, refusing to concede a run for the rest of the season. Was there some dramatic change in his delivery or velocity that allowed for this dramatic change in his performance from the fringy major leaguer he was over the past several seasons? Nah, there were no tricks up his sleeve. He didn't strike out many hitters or induce ground balls, but lucked into a .179 batting average on balls in play, and a correspondingly shiny ERA. He's likely to regress back to no. 7 starter or long reliever, but at least for a brief moment he was able to be the star of the show.

Chasen Shreve LHP Born: 07/12/90 Age: 30 Bats: L Throws: L Height: 6'4" Weight: 195 Origin: Round 11, 2010 Draft (#344 overall)

YEAR	TEAM	LVL	AGE	W	L	SV	G	GS	IP	H	HR	BB/9	K/9	K	GB%	BABIP	WHIP	ERA	DRA-	WARP	MPH	FA%	Whiff%	CSP
2018	STL	MLB	27	1	2	0	20	0	14²	14	3	5.5	9.8	16	20.0%	.297	1.57	3.07	120	-0.1	93.3	56.1%	31.0%	42.5%
2018	NYY	MLB	27	2	2	1	40	0	38	39	8	4.3	10.9	46	48.6%	.320	1.50	4.26	63	0.9	93.4	52.9%	33.1%	39.2%
2019	MEM	AAA	28	2	2	3	51	0	60	45	6	3.9	10.1	67	29.7%	.273	1.18	3.45	52	2.1				
2019	STL	MLB	28	1	0	0	3	0	2	2	0	4.5	9.0	2	0.0%	.333	1.50	9.00	121	0.0	91.3	66.7%	10.5%	34.5%
2020	NYM	MLB	29	1	0	0	17	0	25	17	4	4.3	12.2	34	39.3%	.250	1.16	3.96	81	0.5	92.9	51.2%	37.8%	40.6%
2021 FS	NYM	MLB	30	2	2	0	57	0	50	42	8	4.5	10.7	59	36.5%	.283	1.34	4.11	94	0.3	93.1	52.8%	34.6%	40.2%

Comparables: Shawn Armstrong, Nick Wittgren, Tommy Kahnle

Shreve made the most of his NRI and nailed down the "second lefty" spot on the Mets' roster, which seems to be about right for someone with his profile. With him, there tends to be a little too much of everything: too many homers and walks for his team's liking, to go with plenty of strikeouts for the opposing hitters. Though his effectiveness waned in September, he was one of the Mets' most reliable relief arms during the short season. Despite more strikeouts than any reliever except Edwin Díaz and the third-most innings of anyone in the New York bullpen, the Mets non-tendered him in the offseason because of another too much: his price tag in arbitration.

Marcus Stroman RHP Born: 05/01/91 Age: 30 Bats: R Throws: R Height: 5'7" Weight: 180 Origin: Round 1, 2012 Draft (#22 overall)

YEAR	TEAM	LVL	AGE	W	L	SV	G	GS	IP	H	HR	BB/9	K/9	K	GB%	BABIP	WHIP	ERA	DRA-	WARP	MPH	FA%	Whiff%	CSP
2018	TOR	MLB	27	4	9	0	19	19	102¹	115	9	3.2	6.8	77	62.6%	.328	1.48	5.54	93	1.3	93.7	49.3%	22.4%	47.3%
2019	TOR	MLB	28	6	11	0	21	21	124²	118	10	2.5	7.1	99	54.8%	.293	1.23	2.96	76	2.8	93.9	36.9%	24.2%	45.3%
2019	NYM	MLB	28	4	2	0	11	11	59²	65	8	3.5	9.1	60	48.0%	.339	1.47	3.77	79	1.2	93.4	44.1%	25.5%	43.9%
2021 FS	NYM	MLB	30	9	8	0	26	26	150	150	20	3.4	8.2	136	54.1%	.302	1.38	4.41	98	1.2	93.7	41.5%	24.2%	45.3%
2021 DC	NYM	MLB	30	9	8	0	25	25	142	142	19	3.4	8.2	128	54.1%	.302	1.38	4.41	98	1.6	93.7	41.5%	24.2%	45.3%

Comparables: Sonny Gray, Kevin Gausman, Kyle Hendricks

Already dealing with a torn calf muscle, Stroman made the choice to opt out of the 2020 season, dealing a serious blow to the Mets' already-thin rotation. His second important choice of the calendar year, the decision to accept the team's qualifying offer of $18.9 million and return for the 2021 season, was just as surprising but much more welcome for the Flushing Faithful. Stroman's sinker-slider-cutter pitch mix isn't a perfect fit for the Mets' unexceptional infield defense, but his attitude towards the club—including an enthusiastic approval of new owner Steve Cohen—and New York roots make him a logical fit in Queens. Given that the Mets rotation tends towards the extremes: the highs of deGrom and Syndergaard and the lows of … most everybody else, Stroman's solid third-starter profile is a most welcome return.

Noah Syndergaard RHP Born: 08/29/92 Age: 28 Bats: L Throws: R Height: 6'6" Weight: 242 Origin: Round 1, 2010 Draft (#38 overall)

YEAR	TEAM	LVL	AGE	W	L	SV	G	GS	IP	H	HR	BB/9	K/9	K	GB%	BABIP	WHIP	ERA	DRA-	WARP	MPH	FA%	Whiff%	CSP
2018	NYM	MLB	25	13	4	0	25	25	154¹	148	9	2.3	9.0	155	48.5%	.323	1.21	3.03	55	5.0	99.3	53.7%	28.4%	47.5%
2019	NYM	MLB	26	10	8	0	32	32	197²	194	24	2.3	9.2	202	47.3%	.315	1.23	4.28	69	5.1	99.3	59.2%	27.0%	50.0%
2021 FS	NYM	MLB	28	10	7	0	26	26	150	135	17	2.6	9.7	160	47.0%	.299	1.19	3.34	78	2.9	99.3	57.6%	27.4%	49.3%
2021 DC	NYM	MLB	28	6	5	0	19	19	97	87	11	2.6	9.7	104	47.0%	.299	1.19	3.34	78	2.1	99.3	57.6%	27.4%	49.3%

Comparables: Stephen Strasburg, Aaron Nola, Clayton Kershaw

Try to imagine what it's like to have ulnar collateral ligament surgery, the kind that cost Syndergaard his season. It's the middle of March, 2020. You've found out that, though no fault of your own, so much of your world is about to change abruptly. Your health has to be a primary focus, and you'll spend the next several months poring over every small change in feeling, hoping that it's not a sign something went wrong. Time will slow down, and you'll become physically limited in what you can or can't do. Your normal routines will break down, and you may even find yourself with odd pockets of spare time and no idea what to do with it. You'll become physically disconnected from your co-workers and/or friends, people you're used to spending time with on a regular basis. There's pain, and boredom, and work, but eventually a light at the end of the tunnel. Summer 2021. There's a chance that things could go back to some kind of normal. It may not be exactly the same; it may take some time to get back to where you were. Maybe it won't work out. Maybe things could even get better. Can you imagine it?

Thomas Szapucki LHP Born: 06/12/96 Age: 25 Bats: R Throws: L Height: 6'2" Weight: 181 Origin: Round 5, 2015 Draft (#149 overall)

YEAR	TEAM	LVL	AGE	W	L	SV	G	GS	IP	H	HR	BB/9	K/9	K	GB%	BABIP	WHIP	ERA	DRA-	WARP	MPH	FA%	Whiff%	CSP
2019	COL	LO-A	23	0	0	0	11	8	21²	14	1	4.2	10.8	26	33.3%	.260	1.11	2.08	74	0.4				
2019	STL	HI-A	23	1	3	0	9	9	36	33	1	3.8	10.5	42	48.5%	.337	1.33	3.25	96	0.1				
2021 FS	NYM	MLB	25	1	1	0	57	0	50	45	7	5.0	9.0	50	38.8%	.286	1.47	4.86	110	-0.2				
2021 DC	NYM	MLB	25	1	1	0	14	3	25	22	3	5.0	9.0	25	38.8%	.286	1.47	4.86	110	0.1				

Comparables: Domingo Germán, Alex Reyes, John Gant

Instead of getting a clear picture of what post-Tommy John life might be like for Szapucki after a taste of facing upper-minors bats, the one-time top prospect faced another delay in a career already chock full of them. While somewhat effective in his 2019 stint in the low minors, it's entirely possible that his stuff will never return to the heights he flashed back in 2016. Maybe 2021 will finally be the show-me year for the star-crossed southpaw: either he'll be able to build up enough arm strength to remain a solid starting pitching prospect, or it will be time to downshift him into a bullpen role.

Nick Tropeano RHP Born: 08/27/90 Age: 30 Bats: R Throws: R Height: 6'4" Weight: 205 Origin: Round 5, 2011 Draft (#160 overall)

YEAR	TEAM	LVL	AGE	W	L	SV	G	GS	IP	H	HR	BB/9	K/9	K	GB%	BABIP	WHIP	ERA	DRA-	WARP	MPH	FA%	Whiff%	CSP
2018	IE	HI-A	27	1	1	0	2	2	9	9	1	1.0	9.0	9	26.9%	.320	1.11	2.00	59	0.2				
2018	LAA	MLB	27	5	6	0	14	14	76	68	16	3.7	7.6	64	37.9%	.256	1.30	4.74	106	0.5	92.0	47.5%	27.4%	45.2%
2019	SL	AAA	28	4	6	0	17	15	79²	90	12	3.5	9.6	85	34.6%	.351	1.52	5.87	87	1.9				
2019	LAA	MLB	28	0	1	0	3	1	13²	18	6	4.0	6.6	10	25.0%	.286	1.76	9.88	187	-0.5	92.2	46.5%	27.0%	45.7%
2020	PIT	MLB	29	1	0	0	7	0	15²	14	1	2.3	10.9	19	29.3%	.325	1.15	1.15	89	0.2	92.2	30.2%	33.3%	45.9%
2021 FS	NYM	MLB	30	2	3	0	57	0	50	47	9	3.8	9.2	51	33.9%	.287	1.37	4.66	105	0.0	92.1	42.1%	29.1%	45.5%

Comparables: Kevin Gausman, Jake Odorizzi, Dan Straily

After escaping the Angels' pitching ranks and sheltering for a while among the Yankees' reserves, Tropeano was plucked from the waiver wire by the Pirates and proceeded to have his best season as a pro. Pittsburgh encouraged him to throw his split finger more than ever before, resulting in him almost doubling his strikeout percentage from last season. While initially picked up to cover innings after Joe Musgrove's injury, Tropeano pitched effectively out of the bullpen as a long reliever for Pittsburgh's mercurial pitching staff. After being waived and non-tendered in a single weary autumn, he'll enter 2021 forced to prove himself all over again, this time with the Mets.

Justin Wilson LHP Born: 08/18/87 Age: 33 Bats: L Throws: L Height: 6'2" Weight: 205 Origin: Round 5, 2008 Draft (#144 overall)

YEAR	TEAM	LVL	AGE	W	L	SV	G	GS	IP	H	HR	BB/9	K/9	K	GB%	BABIP	WHIP	ERA	DRA-	WARP	MPH	FA%	Whiff%	CSP
2018	CHC	MLB	30	4	5	0	71	0	54²	45	5	5.4	11.4	69	35.8%	.310	1.43	3.46	103	0.2	96.1	75.4%	26.8%	52.0%
2019	NYM	MLB	31	4	2	4	45	0	39	33	4	4.4	10.2	44	50.5%	.299	1.33	2.54	71	0.8	96.6	52.4%	25.6%	49.5%
2020	NYM	MLB	32	2	1	0	23	0	19²	18	1	4.1	10.5	23	43.4%	.333	1.37	3.66	79	0.4	96.6	59.4%	24.7%	50.3%
2021 FS	NYM	MLB	33	2	2	0	57	0	50	41	5	4.4	10.4	57	44.4%	.288	1.31	3.50	83	0.6	96.4	61.4%	25.7%	50.5%

Comparables: Jeremy Jeffress, Bryan Shaw, Anthony Bass

A bastion of consistency in a New York bullpen that was anything but, Wilson put up another solid season, putting aside both the notions that his 2018 run with the Cubs was anything but a fluke, or that he'll ever return to the role of top-flight closer rather than a well-rounded fireman. He's settled as a southpaw without big splits and enough minor injury flags to warrant judicious use, but remains more effective and reliable than many of the boom-or-bust relief options floating about the majority of the majors.

PHILADELPHIA PHILLIES

Essay by Bill Baer

Player comments by Justin Klugh and BP staff

In Texas Hold'em, the most popular variant of poker, players love to play 10-9, especially when both cards share a suit. To many players, a hand like this represents potential, the ability to sneak in and steal the pot away from a much more powerful starting hand like pocket aces. Along with winning a minority of hands by making one or two pairs, "suited connectors" as they're known, can, with luck, lead to straights and flushes which offer greater payouts against strong two- or three-card hands.

The Phillies are the player at the table who got 10-9 and decided to gamble. From 2013-17, they never won more than 73 games. In the latter half of that era, they went into a rebuilding phase, pawning off the last of their remaining veterans for prospects under new front office leadership. Their poor finishes led to high draft picks, which led to a minor league system that slowly but surely rose through the ranks. The Phillies both acquired and developed a plethora of intriguing prospects, including Aaron Nola and Scott Kingery, as well as Jerad Eickhoff, Nick Williams, Adam Haseley, Cornelius Randolph and Mickey Moniak, among others.

By the time 2018 came around, the Phillies were ready to return to competing. They didn't quite get there, finishing 80-82. With one of the National League's more inconsistent offenses, it became obvious what the Phillies needed: an impact hitter to complement one of their developmental successes, Rhys Hoskins. After the 2018 season, owner John Middleton said, "We're going into this [offseason] expecting to spend money and maybe even be a little bit stupid about it." The free agent market was slow to develop, but the Phillies ultimately got their guy, signing superstar outfielder Bryce Harper to a 13-year, $330 million contract. Matt Klentak, then the GM, complemented Harper by signing veteran outfielder Andrew McCutchen and closer David Robertson, while also pulling off trades for catcher J.T. Realmuto and shortstop Jean Segura.

Let's imagine the NL East at this point as a poker hand.

Note: In poker, hands are described by the card followed by its suit. For instance, an ace of spades would be written "As." Additionally, there are two "blinds," or forced bets as a hand starts, known as "big" [BB] and "small" [SB]. Bets are often

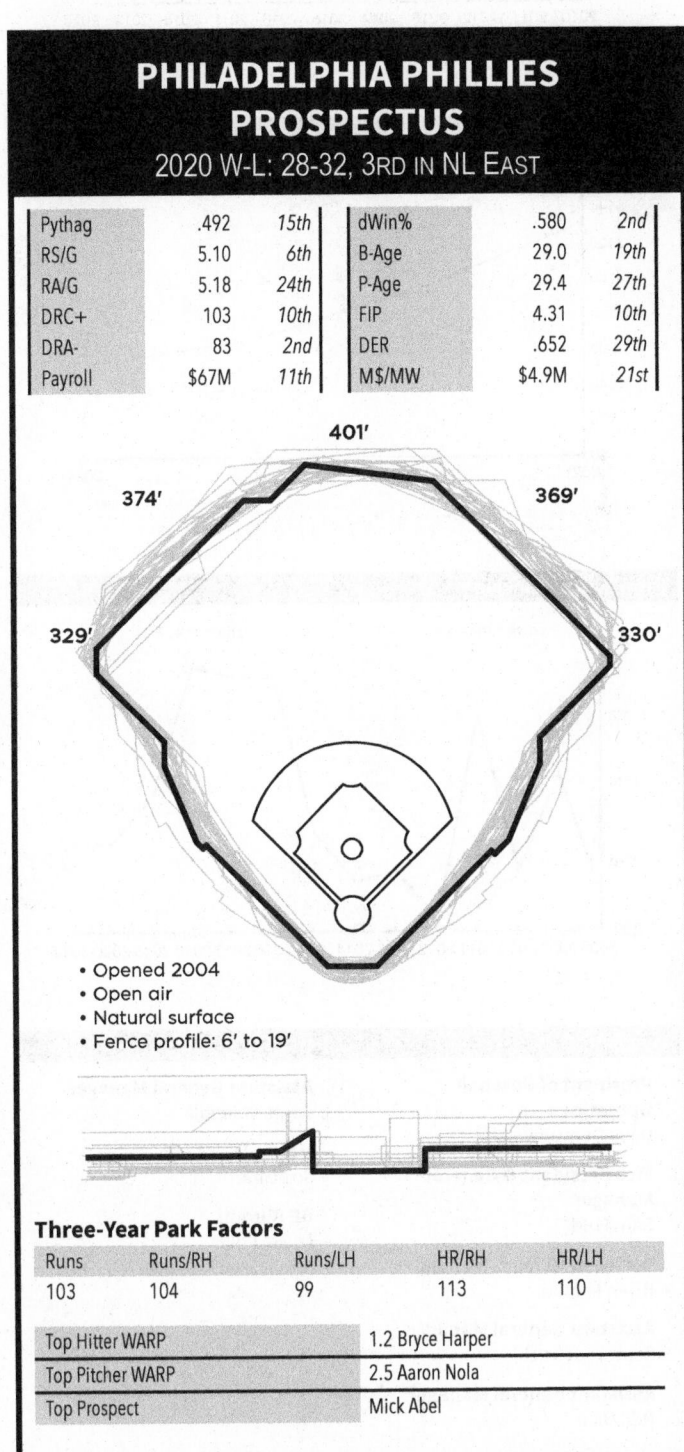

PHILADELPHIA PHILLIES PROSPECTUS
2020 W-L: 28-32, 3RD IN NL EAST

Pythag	.492	15th	dWin%	.580	2nd
RS/G	5.10	6th	B-Age	29.0	19th
RA/G	5.18	24th	P-Age	29.4	27th
DRC+	103	10th	FIP	4.31	10th
DRA-	83	2nd	DER	.652	29th
Payroll	$67M	11th	M$/MW	$4.9M	21st

401'
374'
369'
329'
330'

• Opened 2004
• Open air
• Natural surface
• Fence profile: 6' to 19'

Three-Year Park Factors

Runs	Runs/RH	Runs/LH	HR/RH	HR/LH
103	104	99	113	110

Top Hitter WARP	1.2 Bryce Harper
Top Pitcher WARP	2.5 Aaron Nola
Top Prospect	Mick Abel

Payroll History (in millions)

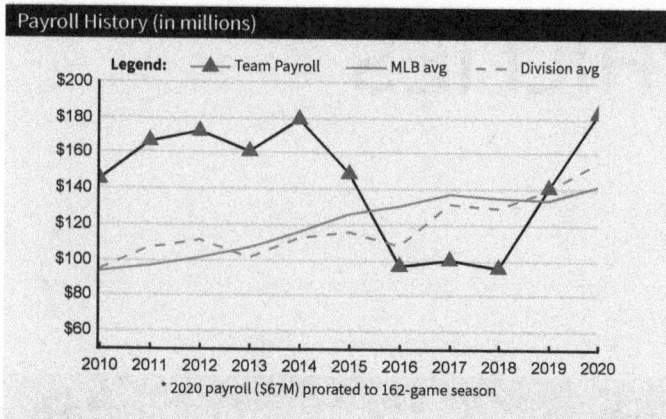

Legend: —▲— Team Payroll —— MLB avg – – – Division avg

* 2020 payroll ($67M) prorated to 162-game season

Future Commitments (in millions)

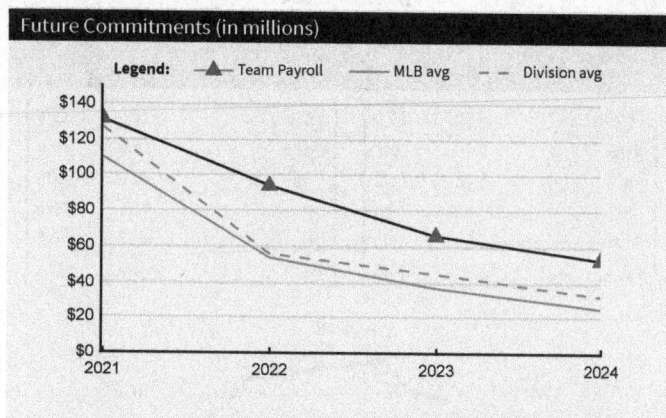

Legend: —▲— Team Payroll —— MLB avg – – – Division avg

Farm System Ranking

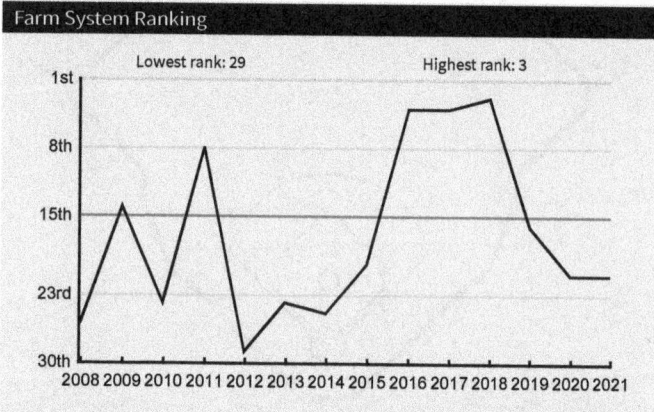

Lowest rank: 29   Highest rank: 3

Personnel

President of Baseball Operations
Dave Dombrowski

Vice President & General Manager
Sam Fuld

Assistant General Manager
Brian Minniti

Assistant General Manager
Scott Proefrock

Assistant General Manager
Ned Rice

Assistant General Manager
Jorge Velandia

Manager
Joe Girardi

BP Alumni
Lewie Pollis
Alex Rosen

---

made in multiples of the big blind before any community cards are seen. Once the community cards come out (the flop, turn, and river), bets are often made in multiples of the "pot," or the collection of chips all players have bet throughout the hand.

Pre-Flop

Braves [Ks, Kh] raise 3.5x BB. Nationals [Jc, Jh] call. Mets [Ad, 10c] call. Phillies [10d, 9d] call. Marlins [7s, 7h] call.

In this hand, you can see that the Braves feel pretty confident about their starting hand and for good reason. You can visualize Ronald Acuña Jr. as one king and Freddie Freeman as the other. The Nationals have a powerful hand of their own and certainly want to jump into the fray to at least see some community cards before reevaluating where they stand. They are, after all, weak to the three higher-ranking starting hand pairs, and can be beaten by hands like AK, and AQ as well. But if a jack comes up, or no face cards at all, they're in a strong position. The Mets don't exactly have the best starting hand and probably shouldn't gamble, but it has some potential if everything breaks their way. The Phillies are far behind, but stand to win a lot of money by hitting big on the community cards. The Marlins were mathematically priced in, seeing at least a four-to-one return on their initial investment if they hit one of the two remaining 7s.

The Braves remained powerful in 2019. The Nationals shocked everyone and won the World Series. The Mets treaded water, while the Marlins were, well, the Marlins, finishing a distant fifth at 57-105. The Phillies showed flashes of competitiveness but fell apart late in the season. Harper was solid, but did not quite live up to the lofty expectations everyone had set for him.

Outside of Nola and to a lesser extent Rhys Hoskins and Scott Kingery, none of the prospects the Phillies had did much of anything. Williams, entering his third season, put up a .442 OPS over 67 games. Haseley slugged below .400 in 67 games of his own. Vince Velasquez, once a prized pitching prospect, continued to struggle, allowing 69 runs in 117 1/3 innings. The pitching was an enormous problem for the Phillies, as Eickhoff and Nick Pivetta couldn't hang in the majors either. If you view prospects as outs in a poker hand, as one avenue for a hand to pan out, it's worth noting that the Phillies haven't done a good job of either accruing those possibilities or actually hitting on them.

That being said, the Phillies got a great season out of Héctor Neris, who saved 28 games with a 2.93 ERA across 68 appearances. Nola wasn't quite Cy Young caliber the way he was in 2018, but his 3.87 ERA in 202 1/3 innings was more than acceptable. Along with Harper, Realmuto, and a veteran core that included the likes of McCutchen, Jay Bruce, and Jake Arrieta, there was enough promise here to think things might pay off in 2020. Like a 10-9 starting hand, the Phillies' roster had potential but wasn't quite strong enough on its own.

The Flop and Post-Flop Betting

Flop: Jd, 8s, 3d. Braves bet 75 percent of the pot. Nationals call. Mets call. Phillies call. Marlins fold.

The Phillies hit a flop that didn't give them a hand, but did give them plenty of potential. They had a flush draw as well as an "open-ended" straight draw, meaning either a Queen or a 7 would have made them a straight, plus only one overcard.

Since the Phillies can't know for sure what's in the other players' hands, it appears as if they have at least 17 outs: eight cards for the straight (four Queens, four sevens) and nine cards for the flush (the remaining diamonds). Since there are 52 cards in the deck and they have seen five of them, 17 outs with 47 unknown cards gives them 36 percent odds to win the hand, they believe. That's a lot of incentive to stay the course and keep investing in the hand.

Going into 2020, the Phillies made another big splash, adding starter Zack Wheeler on a five-year, $118 million contract, giving them a terrific no. 2 starter behind Nola. The Phillies also signed shortstop Didi Gregorius to a one-year, $14 million deal. Unfortunately, the COVID-19 pandemic complicated things for everybody across Major League Baseball. The season was suspended in March, then reformed into a 60-game season that began in mid-July and ran through the end of September. The schedule involved teams mostly playing against their division rivals.

Nevertheless, the Phillies were expected to compete and they kind of did. They hit their stride from late August through early September, going on two separate five-game winning streaks that took them from five games under .500 to four games over. After a doubleheader split with the Red Sox on September 8, the Phillies were only 1.5 games out of first place in the NL East. The wheels quickly fell off. From September 13 through the end of the season on the 27th, the Phillies went 5-12, finishing the year 28-32, barely ahead of the last place Nationals and Mets.

The Phillies' relievers were the biggest issue, combining for a league-worst 7.06 ERA. They even tried to supplement the bullpen with mid-season additions of David Phelps, Brandon Workman, and Heath Hembree, but those three struggled mightily in their new uniforms. Other things that went wrong included Kingery not hitting (.511 OPS) and the back of the rotation being unreliable (Arrieta 5.08 ERA, Velasquez 5.56, prospect Spencer Howard 5.92). Segura, who had hit .300 or better in each of the previous three seasons, batted a meager .266.

2020 wasn't without promise, however. Hoskins hit well. Third baseman Alec Bohm finished second in NL Rookie of the Year balloting with a .338/.400/.481 line across 44 games. Wheeler outpitched even Nola, 2.92 to 3.28 in terms of ERA. Zach Eflin posted the best ERA of his five-year career at 3.97. Harper was excellent, slugging .542 with a .420 on-base percentage, smacking 13 homers and knocking 33 runs in 244 plate appearances.

Take the good with the bad and the Phillies' position becomes clearer. There is clear potential with this hand (Harper, Wheeler, Nola, Hoskins, etc.) but it isn't what you'd term a "made hand." If the hand was declared over *right now*, they'd lose to even the Mets just based on high card or the Marlins' weak pair. Still, you'd favor them against the Marlins because of how many outs they have remaining in the deck, knowing there are two cards to come.

The Turn

Turn: [Kc]. Braves bet the size of the pot. Nationals call. Mets rattle their chips ostentatiously, then call.

Here's where the Phillies are at right now. The Braves just hit three of a kind. The Phillies have invested a large portion of their stack into this hand, and still stand to win a lot of money if they continue playing, especially since so many other players are still in the hand. While the flop strengthened their hand, the turn didn't, leaving them just one final card to see. They still have 17 outs out of 46 cards, or 37 percent.

The Phillies have to be mindful of the "sunk cost fallacy," which is essentially a warning against throwing good money after bad. For example, you may have spent upwards of $10,000 repairing your old, beat-up car over the years, but there will come a point where you just have to get a new car. You're never going to see that $10,000 again, but you can stop investing money into a lost cause and instead put it towards a more worthwhile cause.

In poker, there's a term known as "pot committed." It's surprisingly nuanced, especially beyond what you might hear from your average player playing a casual poker game at home with their buddies. Generally speaking, "pot committed" means the ratio of chips in the pot and the chips you have remaining outweigh your odds of winning. In other words, if there are $60 in chips in the pot and you have only $12 remaining (20 percent of the pot), and your odds of winning are 25 percent, you are theoretically pot committed. You should be willing to wager the rest of your remaining chips at this point.

(Because team ownerships, with the exception of the publicly-traded Braves under Liberty Global, keep their books closed, we don't quite know how many chips each team had entering the hand, though we can make educated guesses.)

The Phillies are at a crossroads. With one more card left to see (the river), they can decide they're pot committed, seeing their $200+ million payroll to the very end even if it means wagering the remainder of their chips. They can also decide that this roster is a sunk cost, folding their hand to keep their few remaining chips, waiting for other opportunities. They had an interesting hand with a lot of potential. No one would fault them for wanting to gamble with it. They could, however, be faulted for wanting to continue gambling with it.

Their offseason moves, as disjointed as they appeared from the outside, might signal how they plan to proceed. Hiring Dave Dombrowski as the head of their baseball operations department is as big a tell as there is in baseball. The longtime organizational architect has a reputation for pushing his chips to the middle, and for coming out the other side a winner, taking home World Series titles with Boston and Florida, while establishing competitive teams in both Detroit and Montreal. To pair with the 64-year-old Dombrowski, the Phillies have elevated 39-year-old Sam Fuld from director of integrative baseball performance to general manager. A player as recently as 2015, what Fuld brings to the table is a bit hazier than Dombrowski, but his reputation within the game is pristine and his ascension gives the Phillies front office a long-term component that it otherwise lacked.

The club has in essence asked the two men to take over their hand, mid turn and see it through. We know Dombrowski's tendencies at the table, but we don't know how Fuld will influence his direction. We do know the decision that's staring down the barrel at them: hold 'em or fold 'em. What would you do? ∎

—Bill Baer is the author of the Baer in Mind newsletter.

HITTERS

Alec Bohm 3B
Born: 08/03/96   Age: 24   Bats: R   Throws: R   Height: 6'5"   Weight: 218   Origin: Round 1, 2018 Draft (#3 overall)

YEAR	TEAM	LVL	AGE	PA	R	2B	3B	HR	RBI	BB	K	SB	CS	Whiff%	AVG/OBP/SLG	DRC+	BABIP	BRR	FRAA	WARP
2018	PHW	ROK	21	27	8	1	1	0	3	2	0	2	0		.391/.481/.522	147	.391	-1.6	3B(5): 1.3	0.1
2018	PHE	ROK	21	10	0	0	0	0	2	0	4	0	0		.222/.200/.222	148	.333	0.0	3B(4): 0.2	0.1
2018	WIL	SS	21	121	9	5	1	0	12	10	19	1	0		.224/.314/.290	89	.273	-0.9	3B(20): -2.7	-0.6
2019	JS	LO-A	22	93	13	9	0	3	11	12	14	3	0		.367/.441/.595	212	.406	-0.8	3B(14): -0.8, 1B(5): -0.1	1.1
2019	CLR	HI-A	22	177	25	10	3	4	27	17	21	1	2		.329/.395/.506	172	.358	0.8	3B(25): 1.1, 1B(7): 0.6	2.0
2019	REA	AA	22	270	38	11	1	14	42	28	38	2	2		.269/.344/.500	154	.265	-0.7	3B(44): 0.0, 1B(12): -0.8	2.1
2020	PHI	MLB	24	180	24	11	0	4	23	16	36	1	1	25.2%	.338/.400/.481	100	.410	0.5	3B(38): 0.3, 1B(7): -1.0	0.3
2021 FS	PHI	MLB	24	600	71	29	2	18	74	48	127	1	0	25.2%	.281/.345/.446	117	.337	0.0	3B -1, 1B 0	2.3
2021 DC	PHI	MLB	24	577	68	28	2	17	71	46	123	1	0	25.2%	.281/.345/.446	117	.337	0.0	3B -1	2.3

Comparables: Brandon Laird, Abraham Toro, Josh Bell

Given how little has come out of the Phillies' farm system since 2012 and how passionate fans are about the success of the 2007-11 teams, it makes sense for Phillies fans to linger in the past like it's a parking lot outside Citizens Bank Park. Understandable, then, that Bohm, the rookie with the shaggy mane, long stride, massive hands, and relentless clutchness (.452 BA with RISP in 52 PA) evoked memories of Jayson Werth, gliding over the base paths and cursing out fans. Yet there was a key difference between Werth and Bohm: Bohm is a part of the Phillies' *future*. Ignoring some disastrous innings at third, Bohm never looked uncomfortable as a major leaguer, sliding right into the NL Rookie of the Year race as comfortably as he put on pants specially-made for a human giant. By late September, when the Phillies were at peak disappointment, there were only seven players in the NL East who were hitting over .300, and the only Phillie of the bunch was the third baseman of the future who reminded everybody of the right fielder of the past.

Jay Bruce RF
Born: 04/03/87   Age: 34   Bats: L   Throws: L   Height: 6'3"   Weight: 230   Origin: Round 1, 2005 Draft (#12 overall)

YEAR	TEAM	LVL	AGE	PA	R	2B	3B	HR	RBI	BB	K	SB	CS	Whiff%	AVG/OBP/SLG	DRC+	BABIP	BRR	FRAA	WARP
2018	STL	HI-A	31	27	3	1	0	1	2	2	6	0	0		.360/.407/.520	134	.444	0.0	1B(3): 0.2, RF(3): -0.4	0.1
2018	NYM	MLB	31	361	31	18	1	9	37	41	75	2	3	28.8%	.223/.310/.370	91	.263	-1.8	RF(64): -0.6, 1B(21): -0.2	0.0
2019	PHI	MLB	32	149	16	6	0	12	31	3	29	0	0	29.6%	.221/.235/.510	96	.190	0.1	LF(31): 3.6	0.7
2019	SEA	MLB	32	184	27	11	0	14	28	16	53	1	0	31.5%	.212/.283/.533	114	.210	0.6	RF(24): -1.5, 1B(16): 0.5, LF(6): 3.0	1.0
2020	PHI	MLB	33	103	11	4	2	6	14	7	24	0	0	29.1%	.198/.252/.469	95	.197	-0.7	LF(11): 1.2, RF(6): -0.3, 1B(2): -0.2	0.3
2021 FS	PHI	MLB	34	600	69	25	2	31	85	51	154	3	1	29.8%	.223/.294/.453	97	.250	0.0	RF -1, 1B 1	1.1

Comparables: Cody Ross, Corey Hart, Carlos González

Typically, a team puts Bruce in their lineup for a variety of reasons: homers. Bombs. Dongs. Round-trippers. Four-baggers. Deep flies. Big flies. Wallops. Moonshots. Yardwork. When the Phillies traded for Bruce in 2019 out of a sudden need for outfield depth, they got 12 of them in 51 games, including five in his first seven appearances. But that's just about all they got, except for the second year of his contract. A left quad issue cut into Bruce's usefulness, and for regular Jay Bruce player comment-readers, that likely indicates a theme. Point to a tendon on Bruce and it either has been strained or was just strained by you pointing at it. Fortunately, he doesn't need them all working properly to serve as a powerful pinch hitter or ornamental outfielder.

Arquímedes Gamboa SS
Born: 09/23/97   Age: 23   Bats: S   Throws: R   Height: 6'0"   Weight: 190   Origin: International Free Agent, 2014

YEAR	TEAM	LVL	AGE	PA	R	2B	3B	HR	RBI	BB	K	SB	CS	Whiff%	AVG/OBP/SLG	DRC+	BABIP	BRR	FRAA	WARP
2018	CLR	HI-A	20	497	49	14	4	2	37	53	111	6	4		.214/.304/.279	74	.281	-1.0	SS(109): -2.0	-0.6
2019	REA	AA	21	421	35	10	5	3	28	59	112	21	8		.188/.305/.270	73	.264	2.1	SS(102): -2.2, 3B(3): -0.2, 2B(2): -0.7	0.6
2021 FS	PHI	MLB	23	600	56	24	3	10	52	55	180	7	2		.210/.285/.324	69	.294	1.8	SS -3, 3B 0	-0.5

Comparables: Tyler Wade, Cristhian Adames, Cole Tucker

Having been on the 40-man for quite some time, the question loomed: How much longer would Gamboa's flashy speed, plus glove, and excellent full name keep him in the mix? In search of roster space, the Phillies answered that question by designating him for assignment in late July.

Luis Garcia SS Born: 10/01/00 Age: 20 Bats: S Throws: R Height: 5'11" Weight: 170 Origin: International Free Agent, 2017

YEAR	TEAM	LVL	AGE	PA	R	2B	3B	HR	RBI	BB	K	SB	CS	Whiff%	AVG/OBP/SLG	DRC+	BABIP	BRR	FRAA	WARP
2018	PHW	ROK	17	187	33	11	3	1	32	15	21	12	8		.369/.433/.488	196	.418	-0.1	SS(42): -2.1	1.6
2019	JS	LO-A	18	524	36	14	3	4	36	44	132	9	8		.186/.261/.255	57	.247	-5.0	SS(72): -0.2, 2B(55): -5.3	-1.4
2021 FS	PHI	MLB	20	600	46	25	3	7	50	33	174	10	6		.216/.265/.315	57	.299	-6.2	SS -2, 2B -4	-2.5

Comparables: Leury García, Juan Lagares, Andrew Velazquez

Garcia didn't have a great time at High-A Lakewood in 2019, but it was widely expected that the shortstop would continue to develop as the intelligent line drive-hitter, slick defender and accurate thrower promised when *Baseball America* named him the best player in the 2018 Gulf Coast League. Now all of 20 years old, Garcia missed out on a second crack at Lakewood in 2020, and a chance to dispel doubts about his previous struggles and small stature. The year in limbo provided different challenges and opportunities for everyone: For Garcia, the time off made him a prime candidate to pack on some muscle.

Phil Gosselin 2B Born: 10/03/88 Age: 32 Bats: R Throws: R Height: 6'1" Weight: 188 Origin: Round 5, 2010 Draft (#164 overall)

YEAR	TEAM	LVL	AGE	PA	R	2B	3B	HR	RBI	BB	K	SB	CS	Whiff%	AVG/OBP/SLG	DRC+	BABIP	BRR	FRAA	WARP
2018	GWN	AAA	29	311	38	18	2	5	36	28	59	0	2		.251/.319/.384	97	.300	1.0	2B(63): -2.6, 1B(5): -0.7, 3B(4): -0.2	0.1
2018	CIN	MLB	29	28	5	0	0	1	2	4	8	0	0	21.6%	.125/.250/.250	77	.133	0.3	3B(8): 0.2, 1B(1): -0.0, 2B(1): -0.0	0.0
2019	LHV	AAA	30	353	54	20	5	8	47	46	61	3	2		.314/.405/.497	136	.365	-0.3	2B(58): 1.7, 1B(7): 0.4, 3B(6): 0.1	2.5
2019	PHI	MLB	30	68	5	3	0	0	7	3	16	0	0	23.3%	.262/.294/.308	74	.347	0.3	LF(6): -0.0, SS(5): -0.5, 3B(1): 0.0	0.0
2020	PHI	MLB	32	102	14	5	0	3	12	10	27	0	0	25.0%	.250/.324/.402	89	.323	0.7	1B(8): -0.1, LF(7): -0.6, RF(7): -0.5	0.0
2021 FS	PHI	MLB	32	600	55	21	2	12	58	46	151	1	0	24.3%	.227/.292/.341	73	.292	0.5	2B -1, 3B 0	-0.3

Comparables: Gordon Beckham, Iván De Jesús Jr., Matt Kata

"THE GOOSE IS LOOSE," they'd yell in Philly as another Gosselin knock would land on the outfield grass. Largely a spare piece filed away in the minors, the 31-year-old found himself on the big club as he filled the new DH and various infield roles until Rhys Hoskins' injury offered him regular time at first. Gosselin smacked two home runs in his season debut and was hitting .327 with a .944 OPS at the end of August, but fell victim to a September chill with only six hits in 45 plate appearances. "THE GOOSE WAS LOOSE," the people of Philly sadly chanted as his numbers regressed to a far less thrilling slash line and the team drifted out of contention. In another, better season, a player like Gosselin sells T-shirts. In 2020, he supplied another dose of baseball's cruel reality.

Didi Gregorius SS Born: 02/18/90 Age: 31 Bats: L Throws: R Height: 6'3" Weight: 205 Origin: International Free Agent, 2007

YEAR	TEAM	LVL	AGE	PA	R	2B	3B	HR	RBI	BB	K	SB	CS	Whiff%	AVG/OBP/SLG	DRC+	BABIP	BRR	FRAA	WARP
2018	NYY	MLB	28	569	89	23	5	27	86	48	69	10	6	19.7%	.268/.335/.494	121	.259	2.3	SS(132): 0.4	4.4
2019	NYY	MLB	29	344	47	14	2	16	61	17	53	2	1	22.9%	.238/.276/.441	96	.237	1.0	SS(80): -7.3	0.8
2020	PHI	MLB	30	237	34	10	2	10	40	15	28	3	2	19.0%	.284/.339/.488	112	.285	0.9	SS(59): -4.9	0.5
2021 FS	PHI	MLB	31	600	68	26	2	24	83	35	90	6	2	20.6%	.259/.313/.449	104	.271	0.3	SS 1	2.4

Comparables: Michael Young, Rich Aurilia, Asdrúbal Cabrera

While a man rode in circles around Citizens Bank Park bearing a message of "SIGN J.T.", there was another impending free agent playing a key role for the Phillies offense. Gregorius' narrative coming into the 2020 season was one of bouncing back from Tommy John surgery at age 30, but he quickly re-wrote that story, leading the team in hits. The Phillies have tried to get creative with their playing structure in the past few seasons, jamming parts in there and hoping an infield would just kind of happen, but Gregorius was right where he was supposed to be: playing smooth, buttery defense at shortstop and adding some left-handed beef to the middle of the order. He never led the team in home runs or extra-base hits, but while players like Rhys Hoskins or Bryce Harper missed time due to injury or slumps, there Didi was, consistently hitting line drives and making seamless stops. It's the kind of shortstop performance the Phillies have been lacking since the days of Jimmy Rollins.

Bryce Harper RF Born: 10/16/92 Age: 28 Bats: L Throws: R Height: 6'3" Weight: 210 Origin: Round 1, 2010 Draft (#1 overall)

YEAR	TEAM	LVL	AGE	PA	R	2B	3B	HR	RBI	BB	K	SB	CS	Whiff%	AVG/OBP/SLG	DRC+	BABIP	BRR	FRAA	WARP
2018	WAS	MLB	25	695	103	34	0	34	100	130	169	13	3	31.6%	.249/.393/.496	125	.289	-3.2	RF(116): -12.1, CF(63): -0.1, 1B(1): -0.0	2.5
2019	PHI	MLB	26	682	98	36	1	35	114	99	178	15	3	34.0%	.260/.372/.510	122	.313	-1.4	RF(152): 3.7	3.7
2020	PHI	MLB	28	244	41	9	2	13	33	49	43	8	2	28.7%	.268/.420/.542	147	.279	-0.3	RF(48): -5.7, CF(3): -0.2	1.2
2021 FS	PHI	MLB	28	600	91	26	1	30	83	112	129	13	4	32.1%	.265/.409/.517	152	.302	0.4	RF -11, 1B 0	4.4
2021 DC	PHI	MLB	28	577	87	25	1	29	80	108	124	13	4	32.1%	.265/.409/.517	152	.302	0.3	RF -11	4.1

Comparables: Tim Salmon, Danny Tartabull, Darryl Strawberry

Harper is a member of the Phillies now, an adopted Pennsylvanian with a swing as violent and righteous as stomping on a lanternfly. We're two years into his forever in Philadelphia, and he seems as invested in the team's future as anybody in the front office. The challenge with Harper isn't his performance, but the post-holiday-season letdown following the buzz of his arrival and the team built for him to carry. He knows who he is, the Phillies know who he is, and we know who he is. By the time the superstar was hacking his hair off in frustration amidst a midseason slump, the 2020 squad had made it clear they didn't have the bullpen to back him up. Regardless, he's made it clear: Harper will give you a solid BA, a bunch of homers, team-carrying intensity and the desire to play through an injury—in this case, a back issue that became public in late September. Everybody knows who Harper is. The question is now on the Phillies: Who else is going to show up?

Adam Haseley CF Born: 04/12/96 Age: 25 Bats: L Throws: L Height: 6'1" Weight: 190 Origin: Round 1, 2017 Draft (#8 overall)

YEAR	TEAM	LVL	AGE	PA	R	2B	3B	HR	RBI	BB	K	SB	CS	Whiff%	AVG/OBP/SLG	DRC+	BABIP	BRR	FRAA	WARP
2018	CLR	HI-A	22	354	54	13	5	5	38	19	54	7	3		.300/.343/.415	109	.346	2.9	LF(39): -2.5, CF(30): -2.2, RF(12): 3.4	0.7
2018	REA	AA	22	159	23	4	0	6	17	16	19	0	1		.316/.403/.478	133	.327	-0.5	CF(28): -2.3, LF(5): -0.5, RF(5): -0.5	0.4
2019	REA	AA	23	190	30	8	2	8	21	21	35	4	2		.267/.353/.485	119	.290	2.1	RF(23): 1.3, CF(19): -1.8, LF(2): -0.1	1.0
2019	LHV	AAA	23	78	8	6	0	2	9	8	14	1	1		.294/.377/.471	116	.346	-0.8	CF(12): -0.4, LF(5): 0.1, RF(1): -0.0	0.3
2019	PHI	MLB	23	242	30	14	0	5	26	14	60	4	0	28.9%	.266/.324/.396	70	.344	1.1	CF(40): -3.9, LF(22): 2.0, RF(10): 0.6	-0.2
2020	PHI	MLB	24	92	7	5	0	0	13	7	17	0	0	15.2%	.278/.348/.342	87	.349	0.0	CF(24): -2.1, LF(11): -0.6, RF(9): -0.6	-0.3
2021 FS	PHI	MLB	25	600	66	27	2	14	63	45	136	3	1	23.9%	.258/.325/.401	98	.319	-0.4	CF -8, LF 1	0.9
2021 DC	PHI	MLB	25	475	52	22	2	11	50	36	107	2	1	23.9%	.258/.325/.401	98	.319	-0.3	CF -7, LF 1	0.7

Comparables: Brian Anderson, Ryan Christenson, Ryan Kalish

After a little over 100 games in the big leagues, the Phillies' top draft pick of 2017 has "fourth outfielder" written all over him. Rob Manfred has yet to introduce the idea of 10 men on the field (though we can assume it's in a packed folder in his desk labeled 'why not??'), so this is not ideal for Haseley's development. The 24-year-old continued to convert major league pitches into ground balls at the highest rate of any Phillies outfielder with significant playing time, was spritzed with a water bottle any time he touched a bat when a lefty was pitching and suffered a wrist injury in the middle of the shortened season, giving Roman Quinn got the majority of the playing time in center. Haseley's lack of home run power and speed made him a lot less useful than the center fielder of the future the Phillies hoped they'd drafted. They may have to settle for "first sub," which is disappointing, especially since they're called hoagies around here.

Rhys Hoskins 1B Born: 03/17/93 Age: 28 Bats: R Throws: R Height: 6'4" Weight: 245 Origin: Round 5, 2014 Draft (#142 overall)

YEAR	TEAM	LVL	AGE	PA	R	2B	3B	HR	RBI	BB	K	SB	CS	Whiff%	AVG/OBP/SLG	DRC+	BABIP	BRR	FRAA	WARP
2018	PHI	MLB	25	660	89	38	0	34	96	87	150	5	3	22.0%	.246/.354/.496	129	.272	0.2	LF(135): -0.7, 1B(17): 0.2	3.9
2019	PHI	MLB	26	705	86	33	5	29	85	116	173	2	2	23.2%	.226/.364/.454	114	.267	-2.3	1B(158): 2.6	2.4
2020	PHI	MLB	27	185	35	9	0	10	26	29	43	1	0	26.6%	.245/.384/.503	127	.276	0.5	1B(40): -3.5	0.5
2021 FS	PHI	MLB	28	600	88	25	1	29	77	87	149	2	1	23.6%	.239/.363/.476	129	.279	-0.3	1B 0, LF 0	3.4
2021 DC	PHI	MLB	28	577	84	24	1	28	74	83	143	2	1	23.6%	.239/.363/.476	129	.279	-0.3	1B 0	3.0

Comparables: Jim Thome, Mike Napoli, Fred McGriff

Hoskins' prolific 2017 debut season, in which he became the fastest player in history to hit nine, 10, and 11 home runs, has left the stat box above. Yet here we are, still using it as a reference point for Hoskins' potential, because we don't have a lot of alternatives. There's a spot for Hoskins in the Phillies' lineup, if he wants it. There's a place in Phillies history for him, too. But the 27-year-old first baseman has yet to find consistency. Vast cold stretches and health issues have kept him from being the slugger he appears to be during several spasms of homering. That continued in 2020, when his attempt to revamp his swing was disrupted by the spring sabbatical and he didn't hit a home run until 17 games into the season. Then, he hit eight in thirteen games. His last one came on September 11, a few days before a UCL issue ended his year. A slow start and an abrupt end answered exactly none of the questions the Phillies had about him, and Hoskins will begin 2021 a year older, still hoping to string a few of the streaks together into one long one. If they don't, he's still working walks, though; his 29 free passes and .384 OBP in 41 games both ranked second on the team to Bryce Harper.

Scott Kingery 3B Born: 04/29/94 Age: 27 Bats: R Throws: R Height: 5'10" Weight: 180 Origin: Round 2, 2015 Draft (#48 overall)

YEAR	TEAM	LVL	AGE	PA	R	2B	3B	HR	RBI	BB	K	SB	CS	Whiff%	AVG/OBP/SLG	DRC+	BABIP	BRR	FRAA	WARP
2018	PHI	MLB	24	484	55	23	2	8	35	24	126	10	3	29.1%	.226/.267/.338	69	.291	2.1	SS(119): -3.9, 3B(10): -0.2, 2B(4): -0.1	0.2
2019	PHI	MLB	25	500	64	34	4	19	55	34	147	15	4	31.9%	.258/.315/.474	93	.337	3.1	CF(65): -2.2, 3B(41): 1.4, SS(18): 2.0	1.9
2020	PHI	MLB	26	124	12	5	0	3	6	9	35	0	0	31.7%	.159/.228/.283	66	.200	-0.6	2B(29): -2.9, CF(9): -1.8, SS(1): -0.0	-0.7
2021 FS	PHI	MLB	27	600	60	24	3	18	65	37	166	12	3	31.1%	.221/.278/.377	76	.281	4.0	2B 3, CF 0	0.8
2021 DC	PHI	MLB	27	577	58	23	2	17	63	35	160	12	3	31.1%	.221/.278/.377	76	.281	3.8	2B 3, CF 0	0.9

Comparables: Orlando Miller, Dale Sveum, Andujar Cedeno

The six-year contract that Kingery signed before his major league debut imbued him with a certain level of destiny. Everything that's happened since has been a refutation of that destiny. At times he's performed without direction, or without a home, and now he enters 2021 without momentum. Kingery contracted COVID-19 at a team training facility and his quest to become an in-house Ben Zobrist fell apart. As the Phillies re-evaluate their extensive collection of veterans, Kingery may finally find a home at second base, as he grows perilously near becoming a veteran himself. The expectations of the teams and fans would be best served to ignore the numbers, leave him at the keystone and see what fate has in store.

Andrew Knapp C Born: 11/09/91 Age: 29 Bats: S Throws: R Height: 6'1" Weight: 189 Origin: Round 2, 2013 Draft (#53 overall)

YEAR	TEAM	LVL	AGE	PA	R	2B	3B	HR	RBI	BB	K	SB	CS	Whiff%	AVG/OBP/SLG	DRC+	BABIP	BRR	FRAA	WARP
2018	LHV	AAA	26	25	2	1	0	0	1	5	6	0	0		.250/.400/.300	112	.357	-0.2	C(4): 0.2, 3B(1): -0.6, LF(1): -0.4	0.0
2018	PHI	MLB	26	215	19	6	2	4	15	24	75	1	0	34.7%	.198/.294/.316	68	.303	1.2	C(53): -5.4, 1B(1): -0.0	-0.3
2019	PHI	MLB	27	160	12	9	0	2	8	18	51	0	0	31.2%	.213/.318/.324	69	.325	1.4	C(43): -0.4, 1B(1): -0.1	0.2
2020	PHI	MLB	29	89	9	4	1	2	15	15	19	0	0	30.4%	.278/.404/.444	109	.346	0.5	C(29): 0.2, 1B(1): -0.0	0.3
2021 FS	PHI	MLB	29	600	61	22	2	12	56	70	176	1	0	31.9%	.219/.318/.344	87	.303	0.4	C -10, 1B 0	0.5
2021 DC	PHI	MLB	29	407	41	14	1	8	38	47	119	1	0	31.9%	.219/.318/.344	87	.303	0.2	C -8	0.2

Comparables: David Ross, Marcus Jensen, Kelly Stinnett

Knapp was likely most famous in Phillies circles for two things before 2020: GIFs of him dancing in the dugout, and the steep drop-off between him and the Phillies' starting catcher, J.T. Realmuto. The comparison wasn't fair; being a backup isn't easy, especially a backup to the best-hitting catcher in baseball, and the inconsistency in playing time doesn't help. But Knapp didn't look like a big-league ballplayer for most of his career ... until 2020. Maybe it was the knowledge that the Phillies could have a job opening at catcher soon, maybe it was the shortened season, maybe it was the fact that even the light-hitting Knapp is still a career .300 hitter in the month of August and the 2020 season was mostly August. Probably the second. His work with a triumvirate of catching experts among the Phillies coaching staff boosted his defense, as well, and Knapp was able to use the tight schedule to take his always-present catching IQ to a whole new level. Progress aside, Philly fans would be pretty upset to see Knapp starting on Opening Day in 2021, not because of who *he* is, but because of who he's not.

YEAR	TEAM	P. COUNT	FRM RUNS	BLK RUNS	THRW RUNS	TOT RUNS
2018	PHI	6695	-3.5	-0.4	-0.3	-4.2
2019	PHI	4955	-0.2	-0.6	0.1	-0.7
2020	PHI	3132	-1.7	0.0	0.0	-1.7
2021	*PHI*	*14430*	*-7.0*	*0.1*	*0.2*	*-6.6*

Rafael Marchan C Born: 02/25/99 Age: 22 Bats: S Throws: R Height: 5'9" Weight: 170 Origin: International Free Agent, 2015

YEAR	TEAM	LVL	AGE	PA	R	2B	3B	HR	RBI	BB	K	SB	CS	Whiff%	AVG/OBP/SLG	DRC+	BABIP	BRR	FRAA	WARP
2018	WIL	SS	19	210	28	8	2	0	12	11	18	9	6		.301/.343/.362	134	.330	0.3	C(47): 2.7	1.2
2019	JS	LO-A	20	265	21	16	0	0	20	24	31	1	3		.271/.347/.339	130	.311	0.7	C(48): 1.8	2.1
2019	CLR	HI-A	20	86	6	4	0	0	3	6	8	1	2		.231/.291/.282	84	.254	-0.4	C(22): -0.3	0.2
2020	PHI	MLB	21	9	3	0	0	1	3	1	2	0	0	33.3%	.500/.556/.875	90	.600	-0.3	C(3): 0.1	0.0
2021 FS	*PHI*	*MLB*	*22*	*600*	*56*	*24*	*2*	*8*	*54*	*31*	*108*	*6*	*3*	*33.3%*	*.245/.289/.343*	*73*	*.289*	*-2.5*	*C -1*	*0.0*
2021 DC	*PHI*	*MLB*	*22*	*271*	*25*	*11*	*0*	*3*	*24*	*14*	*49*	*2*	*1*	*33.3%*	*.245/.289/.343*	*73*	*.289*	*-1.1*	*C -1*	*0.0*

Comparables: Travis d'Arnaud, Rob Brantly, Tucker Barnhart

One of the best moments of the Phillies' 2020 season was Marchan hitting his first big league home run, because it was also his first professional home run since joining the organization in 2016. His notoriety is based less on his performance than the fact that, as the Phillies entered the 2020-21 offseason, he was the only major-league catcher signed to a contract.

YEAR	TEAM	P. COUNT	FRM RUNS	BLK RUNS	THRW RUNS	TOT RUNS
2020	PHI	432	-0.1	0.0	0.0	-0.1
2021	*PHI*	*9620*	*-2.2*	*1.2*	*-0.4*	*-1.4*

Nick Maton SS Born: 02/18/97 Age: 24 Bats: L Throws: R Height: 6'2" Weight: 178 Origin: Round 7, 2017 Draft (#203 overall)

YEAR	TEAM	LVL	AGE	PA	R	2B	3B	HR	RBI	BB	K	SB	CS	Whiff%	AVG/OBP/SLG	DRC+	BABIP	BRR	FRAA	WARP
2018	JS	LO-A	21	466	52	26	5	8	51	43	103	5	3		.256/.330/.404	102	.318	1.6	SS(110): 7.4, 2B(3): -0.3	2.2
2019	CLR	HI-A	22	384	35	14	3	5	45	41	71	11	8		.276/.358/.380	126	.335	-5.9	SS(65): -2.0, 2B(15): -0.1, 3B(8): -0.1	1.6
2019	REA	AA	22	72	6	3	0	2	6	9	14	1	1		.210/.306/.355	94	.234	0.1	2B(11): -0.1, SS(8): -0.2	0.2
2021 FS	*PHI*	*MLB*	*24*	*600*	*61*	*26*	*3*	*14*	*59*	*48*	*170*	*5*	*3*		*.228/.296/.365*	*81*	*.305*	*-1.9*	*2B -2, SS 2*	*0.3*
2021 DC	*PHI*	*MLB*	*24*	*203*	*20*	*8*	*1*	*4*	*20*	*16*	*57*	*1*	*1*		*.228/.296/.365*	*81*	*.305*	*-0.7*	*2B -1, SS 1*	*0.1*

Comparables: Nick Ahmed, Tyler Smith, Todd Frazier

The middle infield has been a fluid place for the Phillies in the last few years: unproven rookies, pricy veterans, deck chairs arranged tastefully. At 23, Maton's whole career is still in front of him, but thus far he has put out the kind of numbers the Phillies are used to seeing from their farm system. Light bat, low speed, but a steady, versatile glove. He'll go well with the existing décor.

Andrew McCutchen LF Born: 10/10/86 Age: 34 Bats: R Throws: R Height: 5'11" Weight: 195 Origin: Round 1, 2005 Draft (#11 overall)

YEAR	TEAM	LVL	AGE	PA	R	2B	3B	HR	RBI	BB	K	SB	CS	Whiff%	AVG/OBP/SLG	DRC+	BABIP	BRR	FRAA	WARP
2018	NYY	MLB	31	114	18	2	1	5	10	22	22	1	3	20.8%	.253/.421/.471	121	.279	0.3	RF(15): -1.9, LF(12): -0.0	0.4
2018	SF	MLB	31	568	65	28	2	15	55	73	123	13	6	22.9%	.255/.357/.415	115	.309	-3.7	RF(128): -4.9	1.4
2019	PHI	MLB	32	262	45	12	1	10	29	43	55	2	1	25.5%	.256/.378/.457	107	.299	0.0	LF(52): -0.8, CF(15): -0.7	0.9
2020	PHI	MLB	34	241	32	9	0	10	34	22	48	4	0	22.0%	.253/.324/.433	110	.281	-0.7	LF(39): -4.8	0.2
2021 FS	*PHI*	*MLB*	*34*	*600*	*83*	*22*	*1*	*23*	*60*	*71*	*136*	*9*	*4*	*23.2%*	*.252/.350/.441*	*117*	*.298*	*-3.8*	*LF -5, CF 0*	*2.1*
2021 DC	*PHI*	*MLB*	*34*	*577*	*80*	*22*	*1*	*23*	*58*	*68*	*130*	*8*	*4*	*23.2%*	*.252/.350/.441*	*117*	*.298*	*-3.6*	*LF -5*	*1.9*

Comparables: Jimmy Wynn, Dale Murphy, Larry Doby

The best news about McCutchen's 2020 season is that it continued past June. Of course, so did just about everyone else's. The delayed season gave McCutchen's torn ACL ample time to heal, and he returned to the top of the Phillies lineup ready to do more than offer quiet leadership and look fly as hell in a throwback. Still, he hit fewer ground balls and more fly balls, hammered lefties and missed more pitches against righties. Perhaps most notably, he traded patience for contact, swinging (and connecting) more often and earlier in the count than ever. And when a Philly writer accidentally called him "Lawrence McCutcheon," Cutch turned it into a whole second personality. After the Phillies were hit by bad luck and their legendarily terrible bullpen, they needed their leadoff hitter to be more than a delight. Cutch, his once league-best skills having eroded, was at least reliable, which was more than the Phillies could say about several other key elements.

Mickey Moniak CF Born: 05/13/98 Age: 23 Bats: L Throws: R Height: 6'2" Weight: 195 Origin: Round 1, 2016 Draft (#1 overall)

YEAR	TEAM	LVL	AGE	PA	R	2B	3B	HR	RBI	BB	K	SB	CS	Whiff%	AVG/OBP/SLG	DRC+	BABIP	BRR	FRAA	WARP
2018	CLR	HI-A	20	465	50	28	3	5	55	22	100	6	5		.270/.304/.383	85	.334	-0.1	CF(99): -7.3, LF(9): -0.3, RF(2): -0.5	-1.1
2019	REA	AA	21	504	63	28	13	11	67	33	111	15	3		.252/.303/.439	96	.307	1.4	CF(94): -2.2, RF(24): 0.5	1.3
2020	PHI	MLB	22	18	3	0	0	0	0	4	6	0	0	50.0%	.214/.389/.214	83	.375	0.2	LF(5): 0.5, RF(1): 0.1	0.1
2021 FS	PHI	MLB	23	600	56	23	5	13	56	37	178	7	3	50.0%	.215/.270/.347	65	.292	2.6	LF -4, RF 1	-0.9
2021 DC	PHI	MLB	23	237	22	9	2	5	22	14	70	2	1	50.0%	.215/.270/.347	65	.292	1.0	LF -2, RF 0	-0.5

Comparables: Brett Phillips, Dustin Fowler, Carlos Tocci

When Atlanta rookie hurler Ian Anderson started Game 2 of the NLDS against the Marlins, it was a big moment for Phillies fans: Finally, someone from the 2016 draft class had achieved enough success to complain that the Phillies had taken Moniak instead of him. Until then, the reasoning had been the Phillies' 1:1 pick had come in a thin year for the draft; owner John Middleton called it "skim milk" (though he might have also just been ordering a warm glass of his favorite drink). Moniak has struggled with pitch recognition, hitting against lefties and getting his swing right, giving the Phillies ... another fourth outfielder. That the 22-year-old was pressed into big league service in 2020—and just simply did not look like a big leaguer, at least not yet—is a statement on how many Phillies outfielders' bodies had piled up on the injured list.

Roman Quinn CF Born: 05/14/93 Age: 28 Bats: S Throws: R Height: 5'10" Weight: 175 Origin: Round 2, 2011 Draft (#66 overall)

YEAR	TEAM	LVL	AGE	PA	R	2B	3B	HR	RBI	BB	K	SB	CS	Whiff%	AVG/OBP/SLG	DRC+	BABIP	BRR	FRAA	WARP
2018	LHV	AAA	25	107	14	2	3	2	11	8	19	13	1		.296/.349/.439	104	.351	3.5	CF(21): 0.3, RF(2): -0.2, LF(1): 0.1	0.6
2018	PHI	MLB	25	143	13	6	4	2	12	10	35	10	4	28.9%	.260/.317/.412	82	.340	-0.9	CF(30): 0.9, RF(5): 1.3, LF(4): 0.0	0.3
2019	CLR	HI-A	26	25	6	3	0	1	3	3	6	2	0		.500/.565/.800	198	.692	0.3	CF(5): 0.3	0.4
2019	PHI	MLB	26	122	18	3	1	4	11	12	34	8	0	31.6%	.213/.298/.370	67	.271	0.3	CF(34): -0.6, P(2): -0.0	-0.1
2020	PHI	MLB	27	116	14	3	1	2	7	5	39	12	0	30.0%	.213/.261/.315	49	.313	1.2	CF(37): -4.3, RF(2): -0.1	-0.5
2021 FS	PHI	MLB	28	600	59	19	5	13	56	46	183	28	8	30.3%	.227/.293/.354	78	.316	10.9	CF 2, 1B 0	1.5
2021 DC	PHI	MLB	28	407	40	13	3	8	38	31	124	19	5	30.3%	.227/.293/.354	78	.316	7.4	CF 1	1.0

Comparables: Johnny Jeter, Manny Martinez, Cesar Geronimo

Time-wise, the shortened schedule didn't really change much for Quinn, who played in no more than fifty games in both 2018 and 2019. So the 41 games he had to make an impression in 2020 was about typical for him, only this time, he got there by staying fairly healthy. The speedy Quinn had a center field job to win and being deployed more often than Adam Haseley seemed to indicate that the team liked him out there. No indication was made as to why. On the field, he made some strange decisions on routes, and his bat didn't benefit from the regular playing time everyone long assumed he needed. He still has his speed, but in keeping with his skill set, the longtime prospect enigma appears to have supplied equally speedy closure.

J.T. Realmuto C Born: 03/18/91 Age: 30 Bats: R Throws: R Height: 6'1" Weight: 212 Origin: Round 3, 2010 Draft (#104 overall)

YEAR	TEAM	LVL	AGE	PA	R	2B	3B	HR	RBI	BB	K	SB	CS	Whiff%	AVG/OBP/SLG	DRC+	BABIP	BRR	FRAA	WARP
2018	MIA	MLB	27	531	74	30	3	21	74	38	104	3	2	22.4%	.277/.340/.484	121	.312	4.1	C(112): 3.7, 1B(13): 0.6	4.8
2019	PHI	MLB	28	593	92	36	3	25	83	41	123	9	1	23.8%	.275/.328/.493	105	.309	2.1	C(133): 19.5, 1B(4): 0.0	5.6
2020	PHI	MLB	29	195	33	6	0	11	32	16	48	4	1	29.8%	.266/.349/.491	107	.307	-0.5	C(36): -0.5, 1B(6): -0.2	0.9
2021 FS	PHI	MLB	30	600	73	29	2	24	85	40	137	8	2	25.0%	.268/.329/.463	114	.317	1.0	C 9, 1B 1	4.6

Comparables: Lance Parrish, Javy Lopez, Hector Villanueva

YEAR	TEAM	P. COUNT	FRM RUNS	BLK RUNS	THRW RUNS	TOT RUNS
2018	MIA	16598	-0.4	0.9	0.1	0.6
2019	PHI	19208	10.5	4.8	4.7	20.0
2020	PHI	5047	1.8	0.6	0.1	2.4
2021	PHI	16650	2.6	2.8	-0.2	5.1

Despite only wearing a Phillies uniform for 1.(pandemic) seasons, the Phillies' All-Star catcher became the fulcrum on which the team's near future was to rest. Would Matt Klentak sign the career .278/.329/.457-slasher, skilled pitching staff manager and stolen base-sniper to an extension? Or would he let Realmuto and his nascent hip issues go play for another team and wind up with nothing to show for three Phillies prospects, including Sixto Sánchez? All the 29-year-old could do was smile politely and offer vague platitudes about his openness to being in Philadelphia while continuing his stellar career, with both his on-base and slugging percentages significantly increasing. The season closed with the future unclear, for both player and team, an unsatisfying conclusion to an unsatisfying chapter of Phillies baseball.

Jean Segura SS Born: 03/17/90 Age: 31 Bats: R Throws: R Height: 5'10" Weight: 220 Origin: International Free Agent, 2007

YEAR	TEAM	LVL	AGE	PA	R	2B	3B	HR	RBI	BB	K	SB	CS	Whiff%	AVG/OBP/SLG	DRC+	BABIP	BRR	FRAA	WARP
2018	SEA	MLB	28	632	91	29	3	10	63	32	69	20	11	12.7%	.304/.341/.415	104	.327	-1.0	SS(144): 3.4	3.5
2019	PHI	MLB	29	618	79	37	4	12	60	30	73	10	2	14.7%	.280/.323/.420	86	.302	2.5	SS(142): -3.8	1.7
2020	PHI	MLB	30	217	28	5	2	7	25	23	45	2	2	22.4%	.266/.347/.422	94	.314	1.3	2B(32): 4.6, 3B(24): 0.2, SS(4): 0.4	1.1
2021 FS	PHI	MLB	31	600	62	26	2	14	69	36	111	18	6	16.3%	.272/.325/.408	101	.317	1.3	SS -3	1.8
2021 DC	PHI	MLB	31	543	56	24	2	13	62	33	101	16	6	16.3%	.272/.325/.408	101	.317	1.2	SS -3, 2B 0	1.7

Comparables: Erick Aybar, Michael Young, Mike Aviles

The Phillies' Opening Day third baseman rolled into training camp a little fitter than last year, accrediting his weight loss to the fact that he'd cut out whiskey. This was ironic, as much of the Phillies' 2020 output had fans reaching for a drink. Segura saved most of his frantic production for the back-end of the abbreviated schedule, improving his OPS by more than 100 points in the second half. Due to injuries across the diamond and the promotion of third base prospect Alec Bohm, Segura wound up in a utility role by offering more utility than Scott Kingery. Unlike Kingery, Segura was a casualty not of the pandemic, but of a schedule that came to an abrupt, unsatisfying end. Segura had four multi-hit games in the 10 days leading up to the Phillies' elimination from an expanded playoff field, ending with a line parallel to his usual, excellent career production, minus the bounce-back narrative.

Bryson Stott SS Born: 10/06/97 Age: 23 Bats: L Throws: R Height: 6'3" Weight: 200 Origin: Round 1, 2019 Draft (#14 overall)

YEAR	TEAM	LVL	AGE	PA	R	2B	3B	HR	RBI	BB	K	SB	CS	Whiff%	AVG/OBP/SLG	DRC+	BABIP	BRR	FRAA	WARP
2019	PHE	ROK	21	11	3	1	1	1	3	2	0	0	0		.667/.727/1.333	262	.625	0.4	SS(4): 0.1	0.3
2019	WIL	SS	21	182	27	8	2	5	24	22	39	5	3		.274/.370/.446	149	.336	1.1	SS(34): -1.0, 2B(2): -0.1, 3B(2): -0.1	1.4
2021 FS	PHI	MLB	23	600	56	26	3	14	62	40	180	9	3		.228/.286/.368	81	.311	1.6	SS 1, 2B 0	0.7

In the world we once knew, Stott would have started the season in Low-A Lakewood. But given the ominous cloud one experiences just by opening the front door, the Phillies safely stationed their top 2019 draft pick in Allentown, where practice games saw him get six or seven at-bats a contest. The 23-year-old shortstop put together a solid slash line in his first 48 games in the minors last year; his speed is an asset, his defensive instincts are sharp and his hitting skills have been called "advanced." And is it a coincidence that the Phillies drafted a player whose first name starts with the letters "B-R-Y" and who was born in Las Vegas? Yes, entirely. But with Alec Bohm and Spencer Howard in the majors, Stott is near the top of the list of Phillies prospects, and his raw talent is calibrating to each new level with every at-bat.

PITCHERS

★ ★ ★ *2021 Top 101 Prospect* #54 ★ ★ ★

Mick Abel RHP Born: 08/18/01 Age: 19 Bats: R Throws: R Height: 6'5" Weight: 190 Origin: Round 1, 2020 Draft (#15 overall)

Gatorade's 2020 Oregon Baseball Player of the Year was rewarded with more than just orange drink at the MLB Draft. The Phillies selected Abel with the 15th overall pick after he spent his canceled senior season throwing bullpens. The plus fastball is said to have only improved with command that has sharpened throughout his young career; the slider lives in the mid-80s, unlike Abel himself, who was somehow born in 2001. (For the best, because otherwise he might have had to face Matt Cain.) After the draft, the young man spent the year pitching from home in Oregon, sending footage back to the big club for evaluation. He was the only pitcher of note in the organization who didn't pitch at Citizens Bank Park this season, and as the Phillies are desperate for help from within, Abel may represent a change in the team's luck.

José Alvarado LHP Born: 05/21/95 Age: 26 Bats: L Throws: L Height: 6'2" Weight: 245 Origin: International Free Agent, 2012

YEAR	TEAM	LVL	AGE	W	L	SV	G	GS	IP	H	HR	BB/9	K/9	K	GB%	BABIP	WHIP	ERA	DRA-	WARP	MPH	FA%	Whiff%	CSP
2018	TB	MLB	23	1	6	8	70	0	64	42	1	4.1	11.2	80	55.6%	.273	1.11	2.39	59	1.7	99.4	70.5%	32.1%	48.9%
2019	TB	MLB	24	1	6	7	35	1	30	29	2	8.1	11.7	39	46.2%	.360	1.87	4.80	116	-0.1	100.0	79.5%	31.1%	42.6%
2020	TB	MLB	25	0	0	0	9	0	9	9	2	6.0	13.0	13	41.7%	.318	1.67	6.00	97	0.1	98.6	76.8%	28.0%	43.9%
2021 FS	PHI	MLB	26	2	2	4	57	0	50	42	5	5.7	10.7	59	48.6%	.296	1.48	4.35	96	0.2	99.5	75.6%	30.8%	45.2%
2021 DC	PHI	MLB	26	2	2	4	52	0	55	46	6	5.7	10.7	65	48.6%	.296	1.48	4.35	96	0.5	99.5	75.6%	30.8%	45.2%

Comparables: Tanner Scott, José Leclerc, Alex Reyes

Two years prior to Alvarado's breakout 2018 season, he was throwing hard but walking too many to have a certain big-league future. Two years after Alvarado's breakout 2018, he was throwing hard but walking too many to have a certain big-league future—oh, and he was dealing with a shoulder injury. Beats us as to what comes next, though there's a fair chance it involves an upper-90s sinker that misses the zone.

Victor Arano RHP Born: 02/07/95 Age: 26 Bats: R Throws: R Height: 6'2" Weight: 228 Origin: International Free Agent, 2013

YEAR	TEAM	LVL	AGE	W	L	SV	G	GS	IP	H	HR	BB/9	K/9	K	GB%	BABIP	WHIP	ERA	DRA-	WARP	MPH	FA%	Whiff%	CSP
2018	PHI	MLB	23	1	2	3	60	0	59¹	54	6	2.6	9.1	60	38.7%	.296	1.20	2.73	79	0.9	95.7	40.4%	32.2%	45.6%
2019	PHI	MLB	24	1	0	0	3	0	4²	2	1	3.9	13.5	7	28.6%	.167	0.86	3.86	102	0.0	96.0	38.8%	51.4%	38.3%
2021 FS	PHI	MLB	26	2	2	0	57	0	50	42	7	4.0	10.1	56	38.5%	.281	1.29	3.90	90	0.4	95.8	40.2%	34.6%	44.7%
2021 DC	PHI	MLB	26	2	2	0	40	0	43	36	6	4.0	10.1	48	38.5%	.281	1.29	3.90	90	0.5	95.8	40.2%	34.6%	44.7%

Comparables: Roberto Osuna, Paco Rodríguez, Keynan Middleton

The idea of a second spring training must have been terrifying to Arano, who strained his shoulder the first time around and spent the rest of the year, summer camp included, not quite getting back up to speed. Having lost most of 2019 to bone spurs, the fastball-slider reliever will enter next spring as a bit of a forgotten man; given what transpired to the corps in his absence, the anonymity could work to his advantage.

Jake Arrieta RHP Born: 03/06/86 Age: 35 Bats: R Throws: R Height: 6'4" Weight: 230 Origin: Round 5, 2007 Draft (#159 overall)

YEAR	TEAM	LVL	AGE	W	L	SV	G	GS	IP	H	HR	BB/9	K/9	K	GB%	BABIP	WHIP	ERA	DRA-	WARP	MPH	FA%	Whiff%	CSP
2018	PHI	MLB	32	11	11	0	32	32	179²	171	21	3.0	7.2	143	50.8%	.290	1.28	3.81	91	2.4	94.8	55.8%	19.3%	50.1%
2019	PHI	MLB	33	8	8	0	24	24	135²	149	21	3.4	7.3	110	51.4%	.320	1.47	4.64	111	0.5	94.1	56.2%	18.3%	47.0%
2020	PHI	MLB	34	4	4	0	9	9	44¹	51	6	3.2	6.5	32	51.8%	.333	1.51	5.08	96	0.5	93.7	52.4%	19.0%	47.1%
2021 FS	PHI	MLB	35	9	9	0	26	26	150	149	19	3.4	7.2	119	50.9%	.290	1.37	4.23	100	1.1	94.2	55.2%	18.7%	48.0%

Comparables: Johnny Cueto, Aníbal Sánchez, Homer Bailey

As the season began, many Philly fans were simply waiting for the veteran Arrieta's contract to come off the books. By the time it did, it felt momentous. Out of nine starts, Arrieta pitched through the seventh only once, a bounce-back game from the worst start of his career on August 30, when he allowed nine baserunners and seven earned runs in 1⅓ innings. His velocity has dropped, his command isn't helpful and he doesn't strike anyone out. For the $75 million the Phillies gave him over three years, 64 starts and a lot of grumbling, they got back one season of league-average production and a near-constant conversation about how they had to improve their rotation despite having signed an All-Star Cy Young-winner to do just that. The most valuable thing Arrieta gave the Phillies in 2020 was the gift of not having to think about him anymore.

Connor Brogdon RHP   Born: 01/29/95   Age: 26   Bats: R   Throws: R   Height: 6'6"   Weight: 205   Origin: Round 10, 2017 Draft (#293 overall)

YEAR	TEAM	LVL	AGE	W	L	SV	G	GS	IP	H	HR	BB/9	K/9	K	GB%	BABIP	WHIP	ERA	DRA-	WARP	MPH	FA%	Whiff%	CSP
2018	JS	LO-A	23	5	3	5	31	7	69¹	59	3	2.1	10.3	79	33.3%	.316	1.08	2.47	77	1.1				
2019	CLR	HI-A	24	2	0	0	10	0	20	11	1	2.2	10.3	23	32.6%	.222	0.80	1.80	51	0.5				
2019	REA	AA	24	1	1	2	15	0	23²	12	4	2.7	14.8	39	28.6%	.216	0.80	2.66	50	0.6				
2019	LHV	AAA	24	3	1	2	26	0	32¹	23	4	3.3	12.2	44	38.2%	.268	1.08	3.06	59	1.0				
2020	PHI	MLB	25	1	0	0	9	0	11¹	5	3	4.0	13.5	17	36.4%	.105	0.88	3.97	85	0.2	97.1	64.7%	32.6%	41.8%
2021 FS	PHI	MLB	26	2	2	0	57	0	50	41	7	4.6	11.3	62	36.5%	.289	1.35	4.17	94	0.3	97.1	64.7%	32.6%	41.8%
2021 DC	PHI	MLB	26	2	2	0	46	0	49	41	7	4.6	11.3	61	36.5%	.289	1.35	4.17	94	0.4	97.1	64.7%	32.6%	41.8%

Comparables: Kodi Whitley, Phil Maton, Bryan Garcia

Having surged from Single to Triple-A in 2019, Brogdon was sent to the pen in Lehigh Valley due to a packed rotation. There, he was able to develop a taste for power pitching as opposed to balancing stamina to go deep into a game, crafting a mid-90s heater and a weaponized changeup. When the Phillies needed fast bullpen help, they tabbed Brogdon in August 2020. He gave up three home runs in his debut, and it looked like he would fit right in and have no trouble making friends through relatable experiences. But the 26-year-old wound up being one of the Phillies' rare bullpen success stories, allowing only one more home run in his eight remaining appearances, culminating in a 1.80 ERA and 3.75 K/BB ratio through that stretch. No word on whether Brogdon's performance led to alienation.

Enyel De Los Santos RHP   Born: 12/25/95   Age: 25   Bats: R   Throws: R   Height: 6'3"   Weight: 235   Origin: International Free Agent, 2014

YEAR	TEAM	LVL	AGE	W	L	SV	G	GS	IP	H	HR	BB/9	K/9	K	GB%	BABIP	WHIP	ERA	DRA-	WARP	MPH	FA%	Whiff%	CSP
2018	LHV	AAA	22	10	5	0	22	22	126²	104	12	3.1	7.8	110	40.6%	.267	1.16	2.63	79	2.3				
2018	PHI	MLB	22	1	0	0	7	2	19	19	2	3.8	7.1	15	47.4%	.315	1.42	4.74	111	0.0	97.0	60.3%	22.0%	50.2%
2019	LHV	AAA	23	5	7	0	19	19	94	81	16	3.4	7.9	83	37.7%	.255	1.23	4.40	82	2.5				
2019	PHI	MLB	23	0	1	0	5	1	11	13	4	4.1	7.4	9	37.5%	.321	1.64	7.36	97	0.1	95.8	59.1%	25.9%	53.5%
2021 FS	PHI	MLB	25	2	3	0	57	0	50	49	7	3.6	8.1	44	39.9%	.293	1.39	4.58	106	0.0	96.4	59.7%	24.0%	51.9%

Comparables: Yusmeiro Petit, Jake Thompson, Jake Odorizzi

Traded twice in his youth as the quintessential "live arm," the disappearance of De Los Santos left many searching for proof of said life. He resurfaced in August as a replacement when Reggie McLain went on paternity leave, but then was released and cleared waivers without appearing in a game. It's fair to say that he's no longer part of the team's plans. Live arms generally become relievers; it's part of the circle of life. Sometimes, though, they just become arms.

Kyle Dohy LHP   Born: 09/17/96   Age: 24   Bats: L   Throws: L   Height: 6'2"   Weight: 202   Origin: Round 16, 2017 Draft (#473 overall)

YEAR	TEAM	LVL	AGE	W	L	SV	G	GS	IP	H	HR	BB/9	K/9	K	GB%	BABIP	WHIP	ERA	DRA-	WARP	MPH	FA%	Whiff%	CSP
2018	JS	LO-A	21	3	3	7	24	0	33²	16	1	4.5	16.8	63	40.0%	.319	0.98	0.80	33	1.3				
2018	CLR	HI-A	21	2	1	2	7	0	11	5	1	2.5	14.7	18	44.4%	.222	0.73	1.64	25	0.5				
2018	REA	AA	21	2	5	1	18	0	22²	13	3	8.7	11.9	30	30.6%	.227	1.54	5.56	101	0.1				
2019	REA	AA	22	1	0	2	6	0	11	2	0	4.1	18.0	22	58.3%	.167	0.64	0.82	46	0.3				
2019	LHV	AAA	22	6	5	1	41	0	56²	57	4	8.6	13.2	83	36.1%	.373	1.96	6.19	119	0.2				
2021 FS	PHI	MLB	24	1	1	0	57	0	50	40	8	8.1	12.4	69	38.3%	.298	1.71	5.66	122	-0.5				
2021 DC	PHI	MLB	24	1	1	0	23	0	24	19	3	8.1	12.4	33	38.3%	.298	1.71	5.66	122	-0.1				

Comparables: Kyle Nelson, José Castillo, Patrick Sandoval

In so many of these descriptions of young pitchers, we always end up saying, "There's raw talent there, clearly, but the command is the issue." Dohy has no track record of hitting his targets in the same way that a freshman in undergrad has no track record of cooking for themselves. Sometimes, they end up a major-league reliever. Sometimes they spend their twenties eating a lot of Hot Pockets.

Seranthony Domínguez RHP   Born: 11/25/94   Age: 26   Bats: R   Throws: R   Height: 6'1"   Weight: 225   Origin: International Free Agent, 2011

YEAR	TEAM	LVL	AGE	W	L	SV	G	GS	IP	H	HR	BB/9	K/9	K	GB%	BABIP	WHIP	ERA	DRA-	WARP	MPH	FA%	Whiff%	CSP
2018	REA	AA	23	1	2	0	8	0	13	8	0	1.4	12.5	18	51.9%	.296	0.77	2.08	65	0.3				
2018	PHI	MLB	23	2	5	16	53	0	58	32	4	3.4	11.5	74	55.7%	.220	0.93	2.95	66	1.3	99.5	66.6%	34.9%	49.2%
2019	PHI	MLB	24	3	0	0	27	0	24²	24	3	4.4	10.6	29	52.9%	.328	1.46	4.01	86	0.3	98.8	61.2%	30.7%	46.9%
2021 FS	PHI	MLB	26	2	2	0	57	0	50	41	5	4.7	10.4	57	50.1%	.291	1.34	3.79	86	0.5	99.1	63.9%	32.8%	48.0%
2021 DC	PHI	MLB	26	0	0	0	11	0	12	9	1	4.7	10.4	13	50.1%	.291	1.34	3.79	86	0.2	99.1	63.9%	32.8%	48.0%

Comparables: Victor Arano, Roberto Osuna, Trevor Rosenthal

Folks, we haven't seen Seranthony-adjacent arms mismanaged like this since the Suez Crisis. The Phillies shut Domínguez down midway through the 2019 season with a partially torn UCL. The initial hope was that PRP injection and rest would do the job, but said ligament was damaged enough by the spring to necessitate Tommy John surgery, which means we may not get to watch Domínguez dominate again until 2022.

Zach Eflin   RHP   Born: 04/08/94   Age: 27   Bats: R   Throws: R   Height: 6'6"   Weight: 220   Origin: Round 1, 2012 Draft (#33 overall)

YEAR	TEAM	LVL	AGE	W	L	SV	G	GS	IP	H	HR	BB/9	K/9	K	GB%	BABIP	WHIP	ERA	DRA-	WARP	MPH	FA%	Whiff%	CSP
2018	LHV	AAA	24	2	2	0	4	4	20	20	0	2.2	6.8	15	46.0%	.317	1.25	4.05	81	0.3				
2018	PHI	MLB	24	11	8	0	24	24	128	130	16	2.6	8.6	123	40.0%	.313	1.30	4.36	104	1.0	96.4	58.2%	24.0%	51.4%
2019	PHI	MLB	25	10	13	0	32	28	163¹	172	28	2.6	7.1	129	43.3%	.295	1.35	4.13	105	1.1	95.4	55.5%	20.3%	48.7%
2020	PHI	MLB	26	4	2	0	11	10	59	60	8	2.3	10.7	70	46.5%	.347	1.27	3.97	66	1.6	95.5	61.1%	24.0%	48.8%
2021 FS	PHI	MLB	27	9	8	0	26	26	150	140	21	2.5	8.9	149	45.6%	.292	1.21	3.73	87	2.1	95.6	57.6%	22.1%	49.3%
2021 DC	PHI	MLB	27	8	8	0	27	27	134	125	19	2.5	8.9	133	45.6%	.292	1.21	3.73	87	2.3	95.6	57.6%	22.1%	49.3%

Comparables: José Berríos, Reynaldo López, Zach Davies

Eflin has been a fluid project in Philadelphia: arriving as a sinkerballer, adapting to Gabe Kapler and Chris Young's system, then abandoning it to go back to what felt comfortable, all while moving from the rotation to the pen and back again. He starts and finishes strong every season, but the problem is, hitters keep figuring him out in the middle. In his final appearance of 2020, his singular one in relief, a broadcaster used the last few minutes of the game to play up how great it was that Eflin had gotten his ERA under 4.00 after it had soared to over 5.00 by mid-September. This qualifies as a "success story" for the Phillies, and in truth, it is a bit of one: Eflin's overall 2020 output is acceptable for the no. 4 or 5 pitcher he always was, no matter what costume he wore. He's just supposed to be it all year long.

David Hale   RHP   Born: 09/27/87   Age: 33   Bats: R   Throws: R   Height: 6'2"   Weight: 210   Origin: Round 3, 2009 Draft (#87 overall)

YEAR	TEAM	LVL	AGE	W	L	SV	G	GS	IP	H	HR	BB/9	K/9	K	GB%	BABIP	WHIP	ERA	DRA-	WARP	MPH	FA%	Whiff%	CSP
2018	SWB	AAA	30	3	2	0	11	11	55²	58	5	2.7	7.1	44	46.6%	.306	1.35	4.20	76	1.1				
2018	MIN	MLB	30	0	0	0	1	0	3	4	1	12.0	6.0	2	40.0%	.333	2.67	12.00	131	0.0	93.1	45.6%	22.2%	38.3%
2018	NYY	MLB	30	0	0	0	3	0	10²	12	2	0.8	5.1	6	42.1%	.278	1.22	2.53	135	-0.1	93.3	49.1%	23.6%	48.6%
2019	SWB	AAA	31	3	2	0	7	7	32²	36	3	2.8	8.3	30	50.5%	.333	1.41	4.13	90	0.7				
2019	NYY	MLB	31	3	0	2	20	0	37²	39	2	1.7	5.5	23	50.8%	.298	1.22	3.11	94	0.3	95.2	59.8%	17.4%	47.3%
2020	PHI	MLB	32	0	0	1	11	2	17	23	2	2.1	7.4	14	50.9%	.382	1.59	3.71	77	0.4	94.6	53.2%	22.8%	49.9%
2021 FS	PHI	MLB	33	2	2	0	57	0	50	50	7	2.9	7.1	39	48.2%	.287	1.32	4.38	100	0.1	94.8	56.1%	20.1%	48.1%
2021 DC	PHI	MLB	33	2	2	0	40	0	43	43	6	2.9	7.1	33	48.2%	.287	1.32	4.38	100	0.2	94.8	56.1%	20.1%	48.1%

Comparables: Tommy Hunter, Trevor Cahill, Chris Rusin

Not sure if you've heard about this, but that 2020 Phillies bullpen had some problems. But none of those problems were named David Hale until August 21, when he was traded to the Phillies from the Yankees for minor leaguer Addison Russ. The first of several panic moves by the Phillies front office to fortify its continually imploding bullpen, the veteran Hale did very little to avert the crisis, allowing multiple base runners in five out of six of his relief appearances with the team. The Phillies' injury woes even forced Hale to make a spot start late in the year, through which he threw three scoreless innings before running into trouble. The small sample size makes a lot of conclusions feel unfair, but in a season of subpar relief work for the Phillies, Hale fit right in.

Ian Hamilton   RHP   Born: 06/16/95   Age: 26   Bats: R   Throws: R   Height: 6'1"   Weight: 200   Origin: Round 11, 2016 Draft (#326 overall)

YEAR	TEAM	LVL	AGE	W	L	SV	G	GS	IP	H	HR	BB/9	K/9	K	GB%	BABIP	WHIP	ERA	DRA-	WARP	MPH	FA%	Whiff%	CSP
2018	BIR	AA	23	2	1	12	21	0	25¹	20	0	4.3	12.1	34	45.2%	.328	1.26	1.78	73	0.4				
2018	CHA	AAA	23	1	1	10	22	0	26¹	18	2	1.4	9.6	28	46.2%	.262	0.84	1.71	74	0.4				
2018	CHW	MLB	23	1	2	0	10	0	8	6	2	2.2	5.6	5	48.0%	.174	1.00	4.50	75	0.1	98.1	70.1%	23.7%	46.2%
2019	CHA	AAA	24	0	2	3	16	0	16¹	28	4	1.7	11.0	20	50.9%	.480	1.90	9.92	134	0.0				
2020	CHW	MLB	25	0	0	0	4	0	4	4	0	11.2	9.0	4	27.3%	.364	2.25	4.50	107	0.0	95.8	74.7%	36.4%	45.2%
2021 FS	PHI	MLB	26	1	1	0	57	0	50	44	7	4.1	9.0	49	43.9%	.282	1.35	4.18	95	0.3	96.5	73.2%	32.3%	45.6%
2021 DC	PHI	MLB	26	1	1	0	29	0	31	27	4	4.1	9.0	30	43.9%	.282	1.35	4.18	95	0.3	96.5	73.2%	32.3%	45.6%

Comparables: Edubray Ramos, Jake Newberry, Thyago Vieira

As far as Hamiltons go, Ian's luck with flying objects at his face is at least a grade better than others. But while he's re-emerged from a spring training car accident and a foul ball that struck him in the dugout, breaking his jaw and ending his 2019 season, the high-90s velocity he once touted to paper over other irregularities has not. At 93-95 mph, a lot of Hamilton's quirks—a crossfire throwing motion with a unique arm action, his slider a bizarre product of an old attempt to teach himself a changeup and acts accordingly strange—turned into warts, and he found himself bouncing along the waiver wire, from the White Sox to the Mariners and then to the Phillies. Hamilton is a plus athlete, whose washboard abs still stack well against any other reliever, and those sorts of guys often figure it out with time, patience and recovery. But something will need to change in his recent trendline for Hamilton to appear in the next version of this book.

Heath Hembree   RHP   Born: 01/13/89   Age: 32   Bats: R   Throws: R   Height: 6'4"   Weight: 220   Origin: Round 5, 2010 Draft (#168 overall)

YEAR	TEAM	LVL	AGE	W	L	SV	G	GS	IP	H	HR	BB/9	K/9	K	GB%	BABIP	WHIP	ERA	DRA-	WARP	MPH	FA%	Whiff%	CSP
2018	BOS	MLB	29	4	1	0	67	0	60	53	10	4.0	11.4	76	39.7%	.295	1.33	4.20	86	0.7	96.5	55.0%	31.6%	45.2%
2019	BOS	MLB	30	1	0	2	45	0	39²	34	7	4.1	10.4	46	23.6%	.273	1.31	3.86	134	-0.5	95.8	69.8%	27.5%	45.3%
2020	PHI	MLB	31	3	0	0	22	0	19	26	9	3.8	9.5	20	31.7%	.333	1.79	9.00	169	-0.5	95.7	57.6%	26.9%	46.1%
2021 FS	PHI	MLB	32	2	2	0	57	0	50	43	9	3.6	9.4	52	32.8%	.270	1.27	4.07	96	0.2	96.0	61.6%	28.6%	45.5%

Comparables: Hunter Strickland, Fernando Abad, Jeremy Jeffress

The best thing to happen to Hembree in 2020 was being paired with Brandon Workman in his trade from Boston to Philadelphia, so that his inability to retire hitters was overshadowed by Workman's even greater passion for not doing so.

★ ★ ★ *2021 Top 101 Prospect* **#65** ★ ★ ★

Spencer Howard RHP Born: 07/28/96 Age: 24 Bats: R Throws: R Height: 6'3" Weight: 210 Origin: Round 2, 2017 Draft (#45 overall)

YEAR	TEAM	LVL	AGE	W	L	SV	G	GS	IP	H	HR	BB/9	K/9	K	GB%	BABIP	WHIP	ERA	DRA-	WARP	MPH	FA%	Whiff%	CSP
2018	JS	LO-A	21	9	8	0	23	23	112	101	6	3.2	11.8	147	37.8%	.351	1.26	3.78	73	2.3				
2019	PHE	ROK	22	0	0	0	1	1	2¹	3	1	3.9	11.6	3	71.4%	.333	1.71	11.57	98	0.0				
2019	PHW	ROK	22	0	0	0	1	1	3	1	0	3.0	15.0	5	60.0%	.200	0.67	0.00	103	0.0				
2019	CLR	HI-A	22	2	1	0	7	7	35	19	1	1.3	12.3	48	44.3%	.261	0.69	1.29	46	1.2				
2019	REA	AA	22	1	0	0	6	6	30²	20	2	2.6	11.2	38	42.5%	.254	0.95	2.35	60	0.8				
2020	PHI	MLB	23	1	2	0	6	6	24¹	30	6	3.7	8.5	23	38.0%	.329	1.64	5.92	108	0.1	96.0	56.5%	25.7%	52.3%
2021 FS	PHI	MLB	24	9	8	0	26	26	150	138	23	3.0	9.3	155	37.2%	.289	1.26	4.00	93	1.7	96.0	56.5%	25.7%	52.3%
2021 DC	PHI	MLB	24	6	6	0	22	22	102	94	16	3.0	9.3	105	37.2%	.289	1.26	4.00	93	1.5	96.0	56.5%	25.7%	52.3%

Comparables: Dylan Cease, Archie Bradley, Cristian Javier

Promoting Howard in early August was supposed to bolster the Phillies' two-deep rotation, but after six starts, his potential success story became something of a nightmare. His bloated DRA helped him fit right in with the Phillies' pitching staff, as did his inability to push deep into games, failing to pitch into the sixth inning in any of his starts. After the rough start, any potential bounceback or adjustment was curtailed by a shoulder injury that shelved him the rest of the year. The contact-based peripherals were a little kinder on Howard's performance than the statistical ones, and his pedigree is exemplary, standing as BP's no. 2 prospect in the system next year. It'll be worthwhile to monitor the shoulder as spring approaches, but 2021 will prove to be just the second of what will likely be many chances to succeed.

Tommy Hunter RHP Born: 07/03/86 Age: 35 Bats: R Throws: R Height: 6'3" Weight: 250 Origin: Round 1, 2007 Draft (#54 overall)

YEAR	TEAM	LVL	AGE	W	L	SV	G	GS	IP	H	HR	BB/9	K/9	K	GB%	BABIP	WHIP	ERA	DRA-	WARP	MPH	FA%	Whiff%	CSP
2018	PHI	MLB	31	5	4	4	65	0	64	65	6	2.1	7.2	51	50.7%	.304	1.25	3.80	101	0.3	97.2	86.0%	21.2%	49.0%
2019	PHI	MLB	32	0	0	0	5	0	5¹	2	0	0.0	8.4	5	30.8%	.154	0.38	0.00	105	0.0	95.1	86.1%	28.1%	46.0%
2020	PHI	MLB	33	0	1	1	24	0	24²	22	2	2.2	9.1	25	41.2%	.308	1.14	4.01	81	0.5	94.0	76.8%	25.7%	43.4%
2021 FS	PHI	MLB	34	2	2	0	57	0	50	47	6	2.3	8.4	46	45.6%	.291	1.21	3.62	90	0.4	95.4	81.2%	24.0%	45.8%

Comparables: Anthony Swarzak, Glen Perkins, Casey Janssen

Hunter's most memorable moment of the 2020 season was a press conference in late August, when criticism of the Phillies bullpen had reached its peak. Hunter, sick of the comments and flexing his biceps, lamented that "baseball is so messed up," and assured people that Phillies' pitchers were "giving everything we have." It was a big moment, and narratively, a potential turnaround for the bullpen and Hunter specifically, who was in a stretch of eight scoreless starts. Unfortunately, the lively presser didn't do much for his on-field work, as Hunter wound up with a 10.33 ERA with RISP, as batters hit .304 against him at Citizens Bank Park. Hunter has always been capable of spurts of shutdown success—but rarely more than that, and the shortened season did not allow him room to schedule many.

Cole Irvin LHP Born: 01/31/94 Age: 27 Bats: L Throws: L Height: 6'4" Weight: 217 Origin: Round 5, 2016 Draft (#137 overall)

YEAR	TEAM	LVL	AGE	W	L	SV	G	GS	IP	H	HR	BB/9	K/9	K	GB%	BABIP	WHIP	ERA	DRA-	WARP	MPH	FA%	Whiff%	CSP
2018	LHV	AAA	24	14	4	0	26	25	161¹	135	11	2.0	7.3	131	46.0%	.273	1.05	2.57	75	3.3				
2019	LHV	AAA	25	6	1	0	17	16	93²	113	13	1.3	6.2	65	40.6%	.328	1.36	3.94	93	1.9				
2019	PHI	MLB	25	2	1	1	16	3	41²	45	7	2.8	6.7	31	33.6%	.302	1.39	5.83	139	-0.6	93.3	50.5%	20.7%	48.5%
2020	PHI	MLB	26	0	1	0	3	0	3²	11	1	2.5	9.8	4	35.3%	.625	3.27	17.18	96	0.0	94.2	52.4%	14.0%	49.0%
2021 FS	PHI	MLB	27	8	9	0	26	26	150	161	27	2.5	7.0	117	39.1%	.297	1.35	4.84	110	0.2	93.4	50.8%	19.6%	48.6%
2021 DC	PHI	MLB	27	2	3	0	31	8	53	57	9	2.5	7.0	41	39.1%	.297	1.35	4.84	110	0.2	93.4	50.8%	19.6%	48.6%

Comparables: Dillon Peters, Jalen Beeks, Ryan Borucki

The 27-year-old Irvin threw a scoreless inning of relief against Atlanta, one proud, glorious frame in which no disasters happened whatsoever. There were other appearances, but it feels rude to mention them. Irvin was optioned off the roster in late August, as middle relievers who get hit hard tend to be.

Damon Jones LHP Born: 09/30/94 Age: 26 Bats: L Throws: L Height: 6'5" Weight: 233 Origin: Round 18, 2017 Draft (#533 overall)

YEAR	TEAM	LVL	AGE	W	L	SV	G	GS	IP	H	HR	BB/9	K/9	K	GB%	BABIP	WHIP	ERA	DRA-	WARP	MPH	FA%	Whiff%	CSP
2018	JS	LO-A	23	10	7	0	23	22	113¹	105	7	4.0	9.8	123	55.8%	.329	1.37	3.41	83	1.6				
2019	CLR	HI-A	24	4	3	0	11	11	58¹	38	3	3.7	13.6	88	56.9%	.315	1.06	1.54	64	1.4				
2019	REA	AA	24	1	0	0	4	4	22	9	0	3.7	12.7	31	52.5%	.225	0.82	0.82	54	0.6				
2019	LHV	AAA	24	0	1	0	8	8	34	27	4	6.9	8.7	33	51.6%	.258	1.56	6.62	103	0.6				
2021 FS	PHI	MLB	26	8	10	0	26	26	150	134	24	6.5	10.4	174	46.4%	.293	1.61	5.44	119	-0.5				
2021 DC	PHI	MLB	26	1	2	0	8	8	35	31	5	6.5	10.4	40	46.4%	.293	1.61	5.44	119	0.0				

Comparables: Anthony Kay, Alex Reyes, Gregory Soto

Jones was old for a prospect before the Year That Wasn't, and he's even older for one now. There's enough life in his fastball and enough bite in his slider that they could, theoretically, still combine to make a starting pitcher; before you get too excited, it's probably the same kind of not-quite-five-and-dive starters that have made a home in the back of Philly's rotation the last couple of years.

Mauricio Llovera RHP   Born: 04/17/96   Age: 25   Bats: R   Throws: R   Height: 5'11"   Weight: 224   Origin: International Free Agent, 2014

YEAR	TEAM	LVL	AGE	W	L	SV	G	GS	IP	H	HR	BB/9	K/9	K	GB%	BABIP	WHIP	ERA	DRA-	WARP	MPH	FA%	Whiff%	CSP
2018	CLR	HI-A	22	8	7	0	23	22	121	100	14	2.5	10.2	137	40.7%	.281	1.11	3.72	70	2.7				
2019	REA	AA	23	3	4	0	14	12	65¹	60	7	3.9	9.9	72	39.4%	.310	1.35	4.55	96	0.2				
2020	PHI	MLB	24	0	0	0	1	0	1	5	0	9.0	9.0	1	42.9%	.714	6.00	36.00	82	0.0	94.9	46.3%	10.5%	42.8%
2021 FS	PHI	MLB	25	2	2	0	57	0	50	49	8	4.1	8.7	48	40.6%	.296	1.44	5.11	111	-0.2	94.9	46.3%	10.5%	42.8%
2021 DC	PHI	MLB	25	2	2	0	32	3	43	42	7	4.1	8.7	41	40.6%	.296	1.44	5.11	111	0.1	94.9	46.3%	10.5%	42.8%

Comparables: Jorge Alcala, Ryan Helsley, Hunter Wood

Statistics are complicated things, whispering lies and half-truths. But when you see a guy pitch one inning and strike out 10 percent of the batters he faced, it's pretty certain he had a bad time. It's likely that Llovera's high-nineties fastball makes him too titillating to forget entirely, but he's going to need to make some adjustments to his delivery and control.

Adonis Medina RHP   Born: 12/18/96   Age: 24   Bats: R   Throws: R   Height: 6'1"   Weight: 187   Origin: International Free Agent, 2014

YEAR	TEAM	LVL	AGE	W	L	SV	G	GS	IP	H	HR	BB/9	K/9	K	GB%	BABIP	WHIP	ERA	DRA-	WARP	MPH	FA%	Whiff%	CSP
2018	CLR	HI-A	21	10	4	0	22	21	111¹	103	11	2.9	9.9	123	49.7%	.318	1.25	4.12	95	0.9				
2019	REA	AA	22	7	7	0	22	21	105²	103	11	3.5	7.0	82	45.3%	.291	1.36	4.94	123	-1.3				
2020	PHI	MLB	23	0	1	0	1	1	4	3	0	6.8	9.0	4	81.8%	.273	1.50	4.50	80	0.1	93.6	53.6%	29.7%	41.9%
2021 FS	PHI	MLB	24	8	10	0	26	26	150	152	23	4.5	7.7	128	45.7%	.294	1.51	5.45	118	-0.4	93.6	53.6%	29.7%	41.9%
2021 DC	PHI	MLB	24	1	2	0	8	8	32	32	5	4.5	7.7	27	45.7%	.294	1.51	5.45	118	0.0	93.6	53.6%	29.7%	41.9%

Comparables: Paul Blackburn, Alex Cobb, Jonathan Hernández

Medina climbed up through the Phillies farm system until reaching Double-A in 2019, when his wobbly control and inconsistent velocity caught up with him. That didn't matter in 2020, though, because the Phillies needed pitchers, and Medina was certifiably one of those. The 24-year-old made his debut in a four-inning start that was exactly what you'd expect for a young pitcher struggling with command: full of hits and walks and a hit batsman. It would be his sole appearance with the big club, because it turned out the team didn't need pitchers *that* badly. He spent most of his summer at the alternate site in Lehigh Valley, honing his control on a fastball with some zip.

Francisco Morales RHP   Born: 10/27/99   Age: 21   Bats: R   Throws: R   Height: 6'4"   Weight: 185   Origin: International Free Agent, 2016

YEAR	TEAM	LVL	AGE	W	L	SV	G	GS	IP	H	HR	BB/9	K/9	K	GB%	BABIP	WHIP	ERA	DRA-	WARP	MPH	FA%	Whiff%	CSP
2018	WIL	SS	18	4	5	0	13	13	56¹	54	6	5.3	10.9	68	40.9%	.324	1.54	5.27	283	-5.1				
2019	JS	LO-A	19	1	8	1	27	15	96²	82	8	4.3	12.0	129	44.5%	.325	1.32	3.82	90	0.7				
2021 FS	PHI	MLB	21	2	3	0	57	0	50	47	9	6.3	9.5	52	37.8%	.290	1.64	5.72	129	-0.7				

Comparables: Lucas Sims, Aaron Sanchez, Lance McCullers Jr.

The broad view is that the Phillies, after a five-year rebuild, have little talent to work with in the minor leagues. But if you lean in close and plug your ears to drown out the screams of Phillies fans, you'll find a series of teenage international signees have been quietly developing in the depths of the system. Morales, a 21-year-old with a mid-nineties heater and a slider that hates right-handed hitters, qualifies for this category, and was targeted by analysts as being a breakout candidate for 2020. Then, of course, it was 2020 itself that broke, and Morales had to figure out a different way to iron out his command issues. Legend has it he's out there somewhere, using his raw stuff to chuck baseballs into space with no idea how to control them. Assuming he doesn't kill a god with an errant pitch, the future is bright for this young high-ceiling starter.

Adam Morgan LHP   Born: 02/27/90   Age: 31   Bats: L   Throws: L   Height: 6'1"   Weight: 200   Origin: Round 3, 2011 Draft (#120 overall)

YEAR	TEAM	LVL	AGE	W	L	SV	G	GS	IP	H	HR	BB/9	K/9	K	GB%	BABIP	WHIP	ERA	DRA-	WARP	MPH	FA%	Whiff%	CSP
2018	PHI	MLB	28	0	2	1	67	0	49¹	49	5	4.0	9.1	50	51.8%	.324	1.44	3.83	96	0.4	95.7	34.7%	28.7%	48.3%
2019	PHI	MLB	29	3	3	0	40	0	29²	20	4	3.0	8.8	29	41.0%	.216	1.01	3.94	87	0.4	93.8	28.1%	33.3%	47.1%
2020	PHI	MLB	30	0	1	0	17	0	13	14	3	4.2	11.1	16	47.2%	.333	1.54	5.54	80	0.3	93.5	33.8%	33.3%	44.9%
2021 FS	PHI	MLB	31	2	2	0	57	0	50	45	7	3.2	9.4	52	42.6%	.287	1.26	3.84	93	0.3	94.4	31.9%	31.7%	46.9%

Comparables: Matt Andriese, Neil Ramírez, Mike Montgomery

The Phillies planned for Morgan to be one of their impact arms in the pen this year, given a solid 2019 cut short by a flexor strain. The injury took some bite off his fastball, so he started relying on it less and his off-speed stuff more. That led to pumping his slider in there with career-high frequency in 2020, keeping lefties hitting only .200 against him. Unfortunately, the approach left him naked against right-handers, who battered his weak changeup and sent liners whizzing past him to the tune of a .364 BAA. It was an unfortunate year to pick to become a LOOGY. Morgan had elbow surgery on that pesky flexor tendon at the end of the season, in hopes of being back to 100 percent in 2021, but there's no surgical procedure to keep him from having to face righties.

Héctor Neris RHP   Born: 06/14/89   Age: 32   Bats: R   Throws: R   Height: 6'2"   Weight: 227   Origin: International Free Agent, 2010

YEAR	TEAM	LVL	AGE	W	L	SV	G	GS	IP	H	HR	BB/9	K/9	K	GB%	BABIP	WHIP	ERA	DRA-	WARP	MPH	FA%	Whiff%	CSP
2018	LHV	AAA	29	2	0	1	19	0	18²	9	0	3.4	14.9	31	42.9%	.265	0.86	1.45	55	0.5				
2018	PHI	MLB	29	1	3	11	53	0	47²	46	11	3.0	14.3	76	30.0%	.361	1.30	5.10	52	1.4	96.6	47.1%	41.8%	46.5%
2019	PHI	MLB	30	3	6	28	68	0	67²	45	10	3.2	11.8	89	44.9%	.241	1.02	2.93	59	1.8	95.8	34.5%	38.7%	39.3%
2020	PHI	MLB	31	2	2	5	24	0	21²	24	0	5.4	11.2	27	39.7%	.381	1.71	4.57	80	0.4	95.4	51.9%	39.1%	41.5%
2021 FS	PHI	MLB	32	2	2	29	57	0	50	41	7	4.3	11.0	61	40.2%	.287	1.31	3.91	89	0.4	95.8	41.8%	39.4%	41.3%
2021 DC	PHI	MLB	32	2	2	29	52	0	55	45	7	4.3	11.0	67	40.2%	.287	1.31	3.91	89	0.6	95.8	41.8%	39.4%	41.3%

Comparables: Pedro Báez, Danny Farquhar, Nate Jones

They've tried to give Neris a nickname a couple of times in Philadelphia, like "Happy Héctor," or "Héctor the Protector." They never stick, because there's always some rough stretch where they feel too ironic. And yet, despite his inconsistency, his apparent desire to pitch with runners on base, and his splitter occasionally going from an out pitch to out-of-the-park pitch, he's remained in a consistent late relief role for the Phillies since 2016. In 2019, that worked in the Phillies' favor; in 2020, Neris lost sight of the strike zone, and while he didn't cough up any home runs, leaving runners on base for other Philly relievers wasn't much of a different result (as seen by the 59.5 percent strand rate). In one overwritten scene, he literally dropped the ball while on the mound, balking what became the winning run into scoring position.

Aaron Nola RHP Born: 06/04/93 Age: 28 Bats: R Throws: R Height: 6'2" Weight: 200 Origin: Round 1, 2014 Draft (#7 overall)

YEAR	TEAM	LVL	AGE	W	L	SV	G	GS	IP	H	HR	BB/9	K/9	K	GB%	BABIP	WHIP	ERA	DRA-	WARP	MPH	FA%	Whiff%	CSP
2018	PHI	MLB	25	17	6	0	33	33	212¹	149	17	2.5	9.5	224	49.8%	.254	0.97	2.37	58	6.6	94.6	49.5%	27.8%	48.4%
2019	PHI	MLB	26	12	7	0	34	34	202¹	176	27	3.6	10.2	229	49.6%	.297	1.27	3.87	70	5.1	95.0	46.2%	26.7%	44.8%
2020	PHI	MLB	27	5	5	0	12	12	71¹	54	9	2.9	12.1	96	48.8%	.283	1.08	3.28	58	2.2	94.4	46.0%	31.3%	43.1%
2021 FS	PHI	MLB	28	10	6	0	26	26	150	118	17	2.8	11.3	188	48.0%	.287	1.10	2.79	68	3.8	94.8	46.9%	28.1%	45.2%
2021 DC	PHI	MLB	28	12	8	0	29	29	186	146	21	2.8	11.3	233	48.0%	.287	1.10	2.79	68	5.1	94.8	46.9%	28.1%	45.2%

Comparables: Cole Hamels, Gerrit Cole, Jake Peavy

As players establish their careers, we come to refer to them by their year-to-year performances as though they're different people. There's a 2018 Nola who was crisp, effective, an All-Star with his whole future ahead of him. Then there's a 2019 Aaron Nola, who lost the bite on his best pitches as he was occasionally asked to follow instructions that made no sense. And now there's a 2020 Aaron Nola, who looked like the dominant 2018 version through August, posting a 2.35 ERA in five starts … until the month of September arrived and Nola's annual struggles began. In his career, the 27-year-old has a 4.28 ERA with 27 home runs surrendered in the regular season's final month, as opposed to the 3.28 ERA and average of 13 home runs in every other month combined. For most of the season, Nola is a shining beacon of in-house talent capable of deep starts, missing bats, preventing runs, and leading a rotation. If the Phillies ever find themselves playing important September baseball in the near future, they'll need the 2018 and August 2020 Aaron Nolas to hang around as long as they can.

Blake Parker RHP Born: 06/19/85 Age: 36 Bats: R Throws: R Height: 6'3" Weight: 225 Origin: Round 16, 2006 Draft (#479 overall)

YEAR	TEAM	LVL	AGE	W	L	SV	G	GS	IP	H	HR	BB/9	K/9	K	GB%	BABIP	WHIP	ERA	DRA-	WARP	MPH	FA%	Whiff%	CSP
2018	LAA	MLB	33	2	1	14	67	0	66¹	63	12	2.6	9.5	70	34.8%	.297	1.24	3.26	115	-0.2	94.0	58.1%	25.1%	46.5%
2019	PHI	MLB	34	2	1	0	23	2	25	19	6	2.2	11.2	31	28.3%	.250	1.00	5.04	60	0.7	92.0	47.9%	29.2%	45.4%
2019	MIN	MLB	34	1	2	10	37	0	36¹	34	7	4.0	8.4	34	43.8%	.276	1.38	4.21	108	0.0	92.9	55.5%	26.2%	44.6%
2020	PHI	MLB	35	3	0	0	14	1	16	12	2	5.1	14.1	25	37.1%	.303	1.31	2.81	76	0.3	92.0	41.3%	29.4%	42.6%
2021 FS	PHI	MLB	36	2	2	0	57	0	50	42	8	3.7	10.6	58	38.4%	.282	1.26	3.74	89	0.4	92.9	51.5%	27.2%	44.8%

Comparables: Shawn Kelley, Tyler Clippard, Mark Melancon

There was a moment in 2020 when Parker appeared to be on verge of completely liquefying on the mound. Fluid poured out of him, dripped off his fingertips and saturated his uniform, to the point that the cameras zoomed in to show anyone watching that a man was about to be soaked into the mound. Though moist, Parker made his splitter effective again for the month of August—fortunate, given that he went back to it a little more than in 2019. Parker was typically good for allowing a baserunner or two, but he set himself apart from the rest of the Phillies bullpen by allowing only a single unearned run in his first eight appearances. His formula of never throwing hittable pitches, striking out everyone he didn't walk, actually did the job. The rest of the year was a bit more of an adventure, with a couple of relief disasters that helped him blend right in, especially on nights he followed the walks with home runs. Still, opposing hitters could only touch him for a .200 BA, the best rate of his career, so whatever he was sweating out, he didn't miss.

David Parkinson LHP Born: 12/14/95 Age: 25 Bats: R Throws: L Height: 6'2" Weight: 210 Origin: Round 12, 2017 Draft (#353 overall)

YEAR	TEAM	LVL	AGE	W	L	SV	G	GS	IP	H	HR	BB/9	K/9	K	GB%	BABIP	WHIP	ERA	DRA-	WARP	MPH	FA%	Whiff%	CSP
2018	JS	LO-A	22	8	1	0	17	17	95¹	74	4	2.5	10.9	115	45.0%	.299	1.05	1.51	65	2.4				
2018	CLR	HI-A	22	3	0	0	5	4	29	17	1	2.8	8.1	26	40.3%	.229	0.90	1.24	80	0.4				
2019	REA	AA	23	10	9	0	22	22	119	107	10	2.9	8.9	118	36.1%	.310	1.23	4.08	100	0.1				
2021 FS	PHI	MLB	25	2	3	0	57	0	50	48	7	4.1	8.7	48	37.1%	.294	1.41	4.48	110	-0.2				

Comparables: David Peterson, Nick Margevicius, Josh Fleming

The Phillies' 2018 Minor League Pitcher of the Year, Parkinson was left off the 60-man roster for 2020. It was particularly frustrating for the 25-year-old, who, after being promoted to Double-A, struggled to hit 90 mph with his fastball. He'd reportedly taken a new approach to his strength training over the winter and gotten the Phillies to send him to Driveline in an attempt to see better results on the mound. We'll soon see if it worked.

David Phelps RHP Born: 10/09/86 Age: 34 Bats: R Throws: R Height: 6'2" Weight: 198 Origin: Round 14, 2008 Draft (#440 overall)

YEAR	TEAM	LVL	AGE	W	L	SV	G	GS	IP	H	HR	BB/9	K/9	K	GB%	BABIP	WHIP	ERA	DRA-	WARP	MPH	FA%	Whiff%	CSP
2019	CHC	MLB	32	2	1	1	24	0	17	17	2	5.3	9.5	18	45.8%	.326	1.59	3.18	99	0.1	94.6	45.5%	23.7%	44.1%
2019	TOR	MLB	32	0	0	0	17	1	17¹	14	3	3.6	9.3	18	31.1%	.262	1.21	3.63	121	-0.1	93.6	39.7%	15.7%	42.3%
2020	PHI	MLB	33	2	4	0	22	0	20²	19	7	2.2	13.5	31	47.9%	.293	1.16	6.53	78	0.4	95.3	46.5%	26.8%	45.4%
2021 FS	PHI	MLB	34	2	2	0	57	0	50	44	7	3.1	9.9	54	42.9%	.291	1.23	3.55	86	0.5	94.9	44.5%	23.2%	44.2%

Comparables: Wade Davis, Brandon Morrow, Daniel Hudson

Seventeen times, Phelps threw a pitch that resulted in a flyball. Seven of those cleared the fence, and of those seven, six were left up; five topped 103 mph in exit velocity; four gave the opponents the lead; three lead to audible swearing on the broadcast; and two were described by broadcasters as moonshots. Two years removed from Tommy John, Phelps rediscovered his velocity but the command is in another castle. He's still worth a roster spot, but he might want to look for it somewhere besides Philadelphia.

David Robertson RHP Born: 04/09/85 Age: 36 Bats: R Throws: R Height: 5'11" Weight: 195 Origin: Round 17, 2006 Draft (#524 overall)

YEAR	TEAM	LVL	AGE	W	L	SV	G	GS	IP	H	HR	BB/9	K/9	K	GB%	BABIP	WHIP	ERA	DRA-	WARP	MPH	FA%	Whiff%	CSP
2018	NYY	MLB	33	8	3	5	69	0	69²	46	7	3.4	11.8	91	44.0%	.252	1.03	3.23	67	1.5	94.2	42.5%	32.6%	43.3%
2019	PHI	MLB	34	0	1	0	7	0	6²	8	1	8.1	8.1	6	33.3%	.350	2.10	5.40	144	-0.1	93.7	57.4%	28.8%	42.6%
2021 FS	PHI	MLB	36	2	2	0	57	0	50	43	7	3.9	9.9	55	42.0%	.285	1.30	3.84	91	0.4	94.1	45.3%	31.9%	43.2%

Comparables: Billy Wagner, Francisco Rodríguez, Brad Lidge

Rumor had it Robertson could finally return to the mound for the Phillies late in the 2020 season, thanks to the ample recovery time from Tommy John surgery following a grade-1 flexor strain. But in late August, the 35-year-old suffered a setback and that idea was scuttled. Could they have used a veteran arm to rack up some scoreless late innings, cutter after cutter? More than anything in the world, yes; but it seems likely that Robertson's two-year, $23 million deal with the Phillies will end with him having made merely seven appearances and seemingly scaring the front office away from paying for high-end relief help in the near future. It's a shame; Robertson was a consistently effective closer and the deal was fair; but this just wasn't a time in which the Phillies could have nice things.

JoJo Romero LHP Born: 09/09/96 Age: 24 Bats: L Throws: L Height: 5'11" Weight: 200 Origin: Round 4, 2016 Draft (#107 overall)

YEAR	TEAM	LVL	AGE	W	L	SV	G	GS	IP	H	HR	BB/9	K/9	K	GB%	BABIP	WHIP	ERA	DRA-	WARP	MPH	FA%	Whiff%	CSP
2018	REA	AA	21	7	6	0	18	18	106²	97	13	3.5	8.4	100	51.8%	.289	1.29	3.80	95	1.1				
2019	REA	AA	22	4	4	0	11	11	57²	58	4	1.9	8.1	52	47.7%	.325	1.21	4.84	102	0.0				
2019	LHV	AAA	22	3	5	0	13	13	53²	68	8	5.9	6.7	40	49.5%	.347	1.92	6.88	163	-0.6				
2020	PHI	MLB	23	0	0	0	12	0	10²	13	1	1.7	8.4	10	48.5%	.387	1.41	7.59	78	0.2	97.0	56.5%	28.6%	47.9%
2021 FS	PHI	MLB	24	2	2	5	57	0	50	50	7	4.3	7.5	41	46.6%	.293	1.48	5.04	110	-0.2	97.0	56.5%	28.6%	47.9%
2021 DC	PHI	MLB	24	2	2	5	52	0	55	55	8	4.3	7.5	46	46.6%	.293	1.48	5.04	110	0.0	97.0	56.5%	28.6%	47.9%

Comparables: Logan Allen, Génesis Cabrera, Drew Anderson

Even among the concrete rubble and twisted rebar that was the Phillies' bullpen, there is an instinctive need to look for bright spots. Many innings, a few roster moves and a couple of trades later, Phillies fans were still squinting. Fortunately, Romero was promoted in late August and made four appearances for the big club before he allowed a run in relief. In this setting, that was enough to make him the alpha, culminating in an appearance in late September in which cameras caught the 24-year-old chugging an energy drink, crushing the can against his own arm and then running into the game to pitch two scoreless innings. That kind of energy was sorely missing from Phillies relief pitching in 2020. Unfortunately, not long after, Romero succumbed to the same brain fungus that had infected the rest of the pen and finished the season with the numbers you see above.

Ramón Rosso RHP Born: 06/09/96 Age: 25 Bats: R Throws: R Height: 6'4" Weight: 240 Origin: International Free Agent, 2015

YEAR	TEAM	LVL	AGE	W	L	SV	G	GS	IP	H	HR	BB/9	K/9	K	GB%	BABIP	WHIP	ERA	DRA-	WARP	MPH	FA%	Whiff%	CSP
2018	JS	LO-A	22	5	1	0	12	12	67²	45	3	2.7	10.8	81	48.1%	.278	0.96	1.33	67	1.6				
2018	CLR	HI-A	22	6	2	0	11	10	55²	49	1	3.2	9.4	58	48.3%	.322	1.24	2.91	78	1.0				
2019	REA	AA	23	3	2	0	10	10	54¹	46	8	2.5	8.6	52	32.4%	.273	1.12	3.15	90	0.4				
2019	LHV	AAA	23	2	4	0	14	14	68²	67	13	4.1	8.4	64	39.7%	.283	1.43	5.50	93	1.4				
2020	PHI	MLB	24	0	1	0	7	1	9²	9	1	7.4	10.2	11	15.4%	.320	1.76	6.52	126	0.0	96.7	69.1%	31.2%	43.6%
2021 FS	PHI	MLB	25	2	3	0	57	0	50	48	9	5.1	9.0	50	33.6%	.290	1.54	5.60	120	-0.4	96.7	69.1%	31.2%	43.6%
2021 DC	PHI	MLB	25	2	3	0	39	4	57	55	11	5.1	9.0	57	33.6%	.290	1.54	5.60	120	-0.2	96.7	69.1%	31.2%	43.6%

Comparables: Hunter Harvey, Mike Shawaryn, Ryan Helsley

The idea was that 24-year-old Rosso, another right-handed power pitcher starting in the minors, could translate those skills into a competent relief pitcher out of training camp. The Phillies found themselves gouged by the exchange rate, however, as the young man left his fastball command on the train.

Ranger Suárez LHP Born: 08/26/95 Age: 25 Bats: L Throws: L Height: 6'1" Weight: 217 Origin: International Free Agent, 2012

YEAR	TEAM	LVL	AGE	W	L	SV	G	GS	IP	H	HR	BB/9	K/9	K	GB%	BABIP	WHIP	ERA	DRA-	WARP	MPH	FA%	Whiff%	CSP
2018	REA	AA	22	4	3	0	12	12	75	64	2	2.4	6.5	54	48.9%	.284	1.12	2.76	97	0.6				
2018	LHV	AAA	22	2	0	0	9	9	49¹	48	2	2.7	5.7	31	47.1%	.299	1.28	2.74	85	0.7				
2018	PHI	MLB	22	1	1	0	4	3	15	21	3	3.6	6.6	11	50.0%	.375	1.80	5.40	127	-0.1	93.7	60.4%	17.9%	51.1%
2019	LHV	AAA	23	2	2	0	7	7	38	41	8	2.4	7.6	32	54.3%	.306	1.34	5.68	105	0.6				
2019	PHI	MLB	23	6	1	0	37	0	48²	52	6	2.2	7.8	42	54.7%	.326	1.32	3.14	86	0.6	94.0	52.6%	22.5%	43.9%
2020	PHI	MLB	24	0	1	0	3	0	4	10	1	9.0	2.2	1	45.0%	.474	3.50	20.25	128	0.0	92.6	60.6%	21.4%	38.5%
2021 FS	PHI	MLB	25	1	2	0	57	0	50	53	7	3.7	6.9	38	50.2%	.303	1.48	5.02	111	-0.2	93.8	54.6%	21.8%	43.9%
2021 DC	PHI	MLB	25	1	2	0	40	0	43	46	6	3.7	6.9	33	50.2%	.303	1.48	5.02	111	0.0	93.8	54.6%	21.8%	43.9%

Comparables: Devin Smeltzer, Cionel Pérez, Lewis Thorpe

My god, a left-handed pitcher! And in a Phillies uniform! Is he the last of his kind? Not quite, but Suárez would have found himself with some big league innings this year, or possibly even a rotation spot, if not for a move to the COVID-19 list early in the season. He didn't pitch for the big club until September, and the catastrophic disruption to Suárez's usual training schedule was apparent. When a pitcher unable to rely on his velocity starts having command issues, things get ugly fast: In four nonconsecutive innings, Suárez allowed a total of 15 base runners and nine earned runs. There's a good chance, if MLB offers something closer to a normal season, he shows a little more usefulness in his next campaign.

Vince Velasquez RHP   Born: 06/07/92   Age: 29   Bats: R   Throws: R   Height: 6'3"   Weight: 212   Origin: Round 2, 2010 Draft (#58 overall)

YEAR	TEAM	LVL	AGE	W	L	SV	G	GS	IP	H	HR	BB/9	K/9	K	GB%	BABIP	WHIP	ERA	DRA-	WARP	MPH	FA%	Whiff%	CSP
2018	PHI	MLB	26	9	12	0	31	30	146²	138	16	3.6	9.9	161	37.6%	.322	1.34	4.85	93	1.9	96.2	64.0%	27.3%	50.3%
2019	PHI	MLB	27	7	8	0	33	23	117¹	120	26	3.3	10.0	130	33.9%	.308	1.39	4.91	112	0.4	96.3	66.7%	25.9%	46.8%
2020	PHI	MLB	28	1	1	0	9	7	34	36	5	4.5	12.2	46	43.2%	.373	1.56	5.56	78	0.7	95.8	58.5%	26.8%	48.3%
2021 FS	PHI	MLB	29	9	8	0	26	26	150	132	24	3.7	10.4	174	38.1%	.290	1.30	4.19	96	1.4	96.2	64.1%	26.5%	48.1%
2021 DC	PHI	MLB	29	7	7	0	48	19	124	109	20	3.7	10.4	143	38.1%	.290	1.30	4.19	96	1.4	96.2	64.1%	26.5%	48.1%

Comparables: Jon Gray, Kevin Gausman, Mike Foltynewicz

Asking "Is this the year Velasquez puts it all together?" has become as wistful a springtime tradition in Philadelphia as demanding baseball come back and then hating it. Every year, Velasquez just hasn't quite gotten there, but his plus fastball and raw talent are just too darn tantalizing—and the Phillies farm system just too shallow—to let him go. So, 2020 brought us another year of Velasquez starting 10-15 percent of the Phillies' games; another 4-5.00 ERA; another string of pitch counts that typically hit 60 or 70 by the third frame. Velasquez had some better outings when he pitched to contact, and his role became even more important in September when Jake Arrieta and Spencer Howard went down with injuries. But if there's anything the Phillies do know after four full seasons of this, it's what Velasquez is capable of: long starts—but not deep ones—that usually unravel somewhere around the middle innings when he stops being able to find the zone or miss bats. And 2020 was pretty much just nine more appearances and seven more starts of that.

Zack Wheeler RHP   Born: 05/30/90   Age: 31   Bats: L   Throws: R   Height: 6'4"   Weight: 195   Origin: Round 1, 2009 Draft (#6 overall)

YEAR	TEAM	LVL	AGE	W	L	SV	G	GS	IP	H	HR	BB/9	K/9	K	GB%	BABIP	WHIP	ERA	DRA-	WARP	MPH	FA%	Whiff%	CSP
2018	NYM	MLB	28	12	7	0	29	29	182¹	150	14	2.7	8.8	179	43.5%	.284	1.12	3.31	67	4.8	98.3	58.3%	24.8%	48.2%
2019	NYM	MLB	29	11	8	0	31	31	195¹	196	22	2.3	9.0	195	42.9%	.316	1.26	3.96	77	4.2	98.7	59.0%	23.0%	50.6%
2020	PHI	MLB	30	4	2	0	11	11	71	67	3	2.0	6.7	53	56.1%	.308	1.17	2.92	75	1.6	98.6	65.7%	22.7%	49.1%
2021 FS	PHI	MLB	31	9	8	0	26	26	150	142	17	2.7	7.9	132	50.1%	.291	1.25	3.74	87	2.1	98.6	60.6%	23.3%	49.7%
2021 DC	PHI	MLB	31	10	8	0	27	27	159	151	18	2.7	7.9	140	50.1%	.291	1.25	3.74	87	2.7	98.6	60.6%	23.3%	49.7%

Comparables: Chris Archer, Sonny Gray, Kyle Hendricks

Entering 2020, the Phillies needed rotation depth; the front office said, "Okay," and signed Wheeler. Afterward, the Phillies still needed more rotation depth; the front office said, "No," and that was that. Fortunately, Wheeler had a solid first season with the Phillies, including a league-best HR/9. When he typically ran into trouble, it was in his third trip through the order, when hitters hit .303 against him. But it's important to remember that this is true of any starter, and doubly important to remember that any inning that wasn't pitched by the Phillies bullpen was a valuable one. Then, the unthinkable happened: Wheeler attempted to put on a pair of pants, somehow did it wrong and egregiously injured his fingernail. Still, in September, Matt Klentak said he liked the Phillies' chances in the playoffs with Aaron Nola and Wheeler at the top of their rotation, which was a hell of a statement to hear if you were someone who believed the architect of the 2020 Phillies bullpen still had any credibility by September.

Brandon Workman RHP   Born: 08/13/88   Age: 32   Bats: R   Throws: R   Height: 6'5"   Weight: 235   Origin: Round 2, 2010 Draft (#57 overall)

YEAR	TEAM	LVL	AGE	W	L	SV	G	GS	IP	H	HR	BB/9	K/9	K	GB%	BABIP	WHIP	ERA	DRA-	WARP	MPH	FA%	Whiff%	CSP
2018	WOR	AAA	29	2	1	1	17	0	30	21	3	1.5	10.2	34	38.2%	.247	0.87	3.90	70	0.6				
2018	BOS	MLB	29	6	1	0	43	0	41¹	34	6	3.5	8.1	37	45.6%	.259	1.21	3.27	138	-0.6	93.4	38.9%	27.0%	48.2%
2019	BOS	MLB	30	10	1	16	73	0	71²	29	1	5.7	13.1	104	51.1%	.211	1.03	1.88	58	1.9	94.8	33.8%	34.8%	41.0%
2020	PHI	MLB	31	1	4	9	21	0	19²	31	4	5.9	10.5	23	47.7%	.443	2.24	5.95	113	0.0	94.1	26.3%	25.6%	44.0%
2021 FS	PHI	MLB	32	2	2	0	57	0	50	42	6	4.8	10.3	57	45.7%	.285	1.38	3.98	93	0.3	94.4	32.5%	31.1%	42.9%

Comparables: Shane Greene, Alex Colomé, Joe Kelly

No statistic could convey how miserable Workman made Phillies fans in 2020, but if you listen closely, even now, the echoes of screamed curses can still be heard across the Delaware Valley. Workman was the worst part of the worst bullpen in baseball—and the worst Phillies relief corps since 1940—and he had plenty of competition. On key pitches during crucial at bats, Workman would throw a pitch two feet out of the strike zone. His specialty, a breaking pitch that dropped directly into the hitter's favorite spot, was great for opposing team morale. By season's end, Workman had faced 101 batters. Forty-six of them reached base. That didn't stop Joe Girardi from sending him out there 14 times in what we can only assume was an experiment to see if he'd allow a ball to be hit so hard that it would create a renewable energy source to replace the sun.

WASHINGTON NATIONALS

Essay by Clinton Yates

Player comments by Sydney Bergman, Jon Tayler and BP staff

The year 2021 marks the beginning of the rest of Washington Nationals fans' lives.

When the team first arrived at RFK Stadium back in the day, they delivered an improbable 81-81 record, with manager Frank Robinson at the helm and Vinny Castilla at third base. The team's lodging under that sagging halo allowed them to capitalize on the nostalgia from the franchises that played there before, and when they moved into Nationals Park, fandom became an odd process of self-identification in the nation's capital.

People didn't demand culture, they just wanted to see baseball in a new park, eat some hot dogs and catch some organ music, but the team was bad. Unwatchably bad. Sure, Mr. National Ryan Zimmerman plugged along, and we got fan favorites like Chad Cordero, Dmitri Young and personal fav Ronnie Beliiard. But until they got back-to-back top picks in the draft, and hauled in Strasburg and Harper (and Rendon the year after at number six), it was a wasteland, best defined by the time the team took the field wearing jerseys missing a letter, reading "Natinals" instead of Nationals. The vibe fit.

When Zim went yard to inaugurate the new stadium on Sunday Night Baseball remains the greatest moment in franchise history, but those achievements occurred amidst consecutive 100-loss seasons. In a lot of ways, he was the facelessness of the franchise. When a hot first half landed him an All-Star berth in 2017, everyone realized: That was only his *second*? One Gold Glove, no Top-10 MVP finishes? All that greatness, just vanished with the newsprint.

Then, the organization was sprinkled with a little stardust that changed the trajectory of the franchise.

It served as a headfirst dive into How To Build A Baseball Town 101. They drafted Stephen Strasburg and his development was A1 news from the jump. The fans who dug themselves into the trenches of the Nationals internet circles were people who paid close attention to his ins and outs, because that was the only way to care about baseball in D.C. What the Nationals provided for many in the area, was a local sports team that didn't demand a lot of travel. Locals either had renounced fandom after the Senators left, or had latched on to the Orioles and were switching over. The new team felt like it was wedged in between the Orioles and Braves.

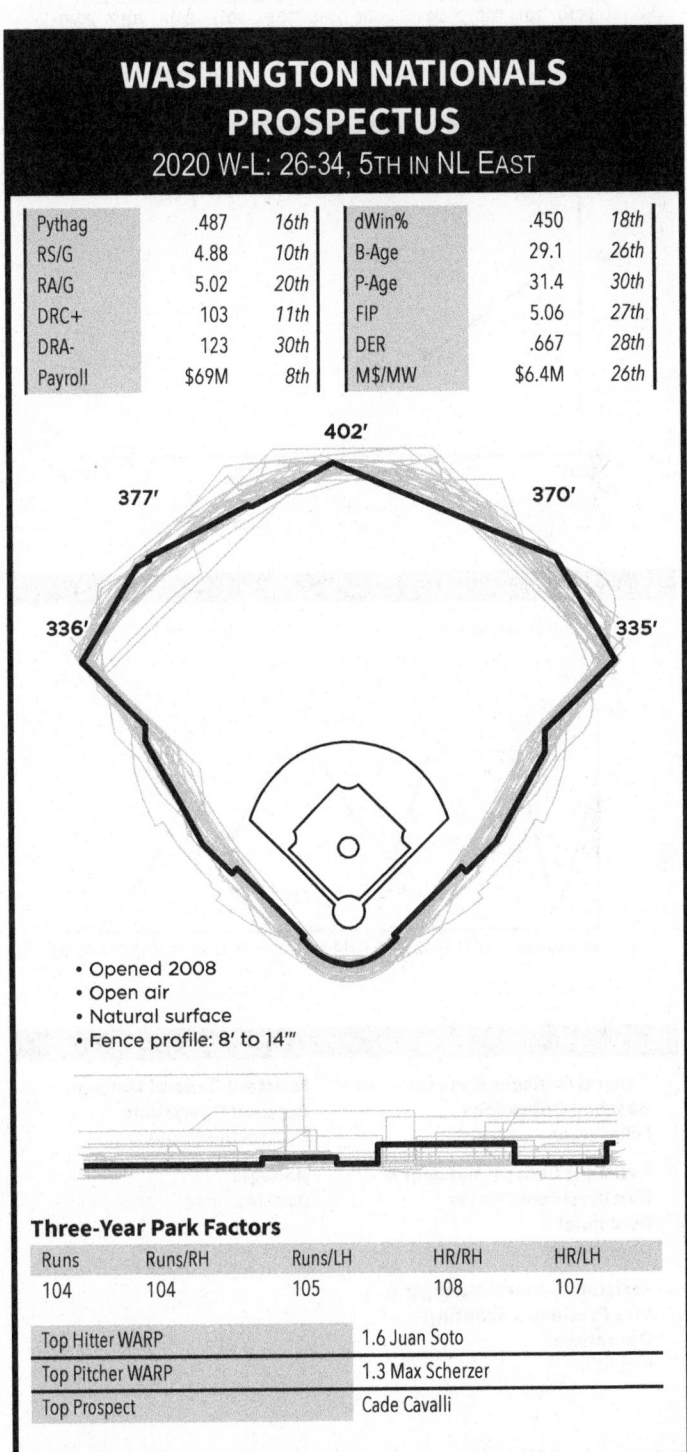

WASHINGTON NATIONALS PROSPECTUS
2020 W-L: 26-34, 5TH IN NL EAST

Pythag	.487	16th	dWin%	.450	18th
RS/G	4.88	10th	B-Age	29.1	26th
RA/G	5.02	20th	P-Age	31.4	30th
DRC+	103	11th	FIP	5.06	27th
DRA-	123	30th	DER	.667	28th
Payroll	$69M	8th	M$/MW	$6.4M	26th

- Opened 2008
- Open air
- Natural surface
- Fence profile: 8' to 14'"

Three-Year Park Factors

Runs	Runs/RH	Runs/LH	HR/RH	HR/LH
104	104	105	108	107

Top Hitter WARP	1.6 Juan Soto
Top Pitcher WARP	1.3 Max Scherzer
Top Prospect	Cade Cavalli

5

Payroll History (in millions)

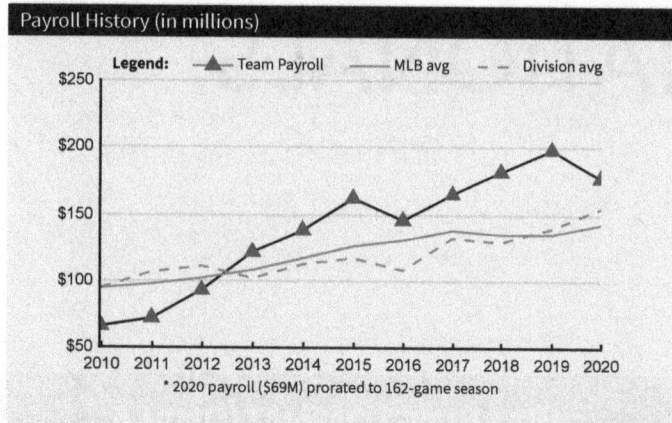

Legend: ▲ Team Payroll — MLB avg - - Division avg

* 2020 payroll ($69M) prorated to 162-game season

Future Commitments (in millions)

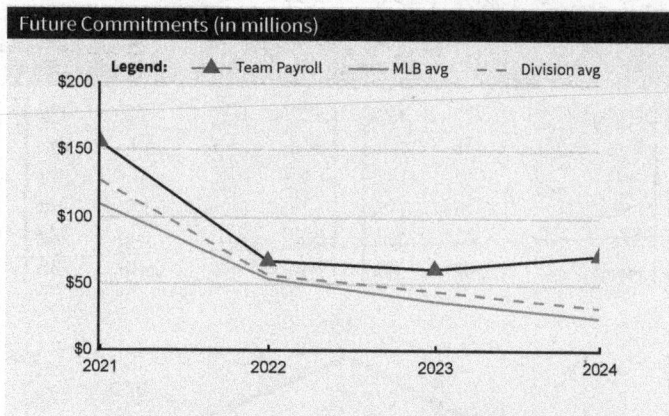

Legend: ▲ Team Payroll — MLB avg - - Division avg

Farm System Ranking

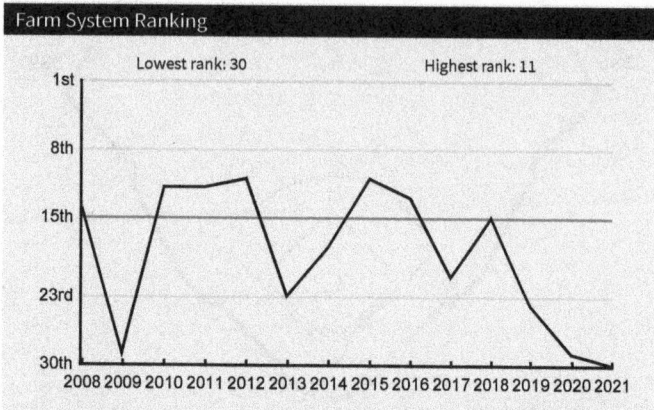

Lowest rank: 30   Highest rank: 11

Personnel

General Manager & President of Baseball Operations
Mike Rizzo

Assistant General Manager & Vice President, Player Personnel
Doug Harris

Assistant General Manager & Vice President, Scouting Operations
Kris Kline

Assistant General Manager, Baseball Operations
Michael DeBartolo

Manager
Dave Martinez

Because the Nats were so new, there was something of an expectations-free ease to the fandom, at least until Strasburg arrived in the big leagues.

Strasmas was real. His debut was televised nationally: a Tuesday night game against the Pirates at Nationals Park, the night before the anniversary of his selection in the draft. Seven innings. Two runs. Fourteen strikeouts and zero walks. The Pirates may as well have been the Washington Generals. Grown folks who'd spent a lot of time being extremely rational about a young man making his way to the bigs were suddenly agog, rightfully so, after one start. The whole beginning of his career led to a level of high-volume feelings that are almost too intense to revisit in detail.

Tommy John. The "shutdown." Inverted W's. It was like watching your kid take dishes out of the dishwasher. For something so early in the franchise's history, it was one of the more exhausting exercises in team support, even for the most intense baseball fans, much less ones who had gravitated towards the team in a low-stakes environment. Fandom didn't mean rooting for the team, it meant having an opinion on it. The feel-good, show-up-and-watch-a-game era was over. All of a sudden you had to pick a side. It was annoying.

Point being, everyone got to learn how much they were going to care, long before the team started contending. Those years fans spend investing, soaking it in, getting used to the idea of caring, all came crashing down in a single wave. Everything that had to happen, did. They signed Jayson Werth to a deal that people knew was likely to be overvalued in terms of money, but if that's what it took to land him, so be it. And to an extent, it worked. Random free agent veteran to bring attitude and leadership and energy to the team just like in the movies? Check.

Bryce Harper, Rookie of the Century comes along, wins Rookie of the Year, they make the playoffs, Davey Johnson won Manager of the Year award and three separate guys won Silver Slugger (including Strasburg).

Okay now it's time to start winning.

Don't hold your breath. They lost to the Cardinals that year. The next year Bryce Harper won seemingly every award known to humankind and they didn't even make the playoffs. Whatever, it was a fun year!

Okay, NOW it's time to start winning?

The next year, Daniel Murphy showed up, Anthony Rendon was a beacon, and Max Scherzer won the Cy Young Award two years after signing an eye-popping $210M contract.

Surely, now it was REALLY time to start winning, no?

No. They lost to the Dodgers in the NLDS.

By this point, we've had enough case law to show the many different facets of Nats fans. The ones who think this team's cheapness with managers is coming back to haunt them. The ones who buy into some absurd curse for shutting down Stras back when they thought the team really had a chance to win something years back, god knows what. The fan base was officially self-identifying as "short-suffering."

The idea being that even if the team wasn't, say, the Cubs, the nature of the collapses was no less devastating, considering the circumstances. Some Cleveland fan might say they'd been suffering for 70 years and be 25 years old. Time wipes away the old pain, but in terms of new pain, no one had Nats fans beat. It's a "what have you done to me lately" mentality, and it leaves scars. Shit, Pete Kozma showed up in the Australian League world series a couple seasons back and I instantly got tight about it.

The honeymoon period was over. They'd thrown too much money around, received too much love and were too well-liked for the "aw shucks our guys didn't get it done this year" stuff to work. 2017 suddenly became a sort of understated World Series or bust year, and Scherzer won the Cy Young Award AGAIN. They won the division by 20 games.

NOW, IT IS DEFINITELY TIME TO F***ING WIN SOMETHING.

They didn't make it out of the NLDS.

The images of Willson Contreras backpicking guys all series, eventually ending the best threat the Nationals had to take the series is still burned in this author's brain. Dusty Baker, a surefire Hall of Famer and previous Manager of the Year (three times!) was shown the door. The franchise had gone from teenage youthful enthusiasm to grown-man grizzled goonery in the time it took for Jose Lobaton's ankle to flex, straighten, and then return to the bag (he was safe, by the way).

They didn't even make the playoffs the next year. They missed the postseason with a manager who thought bringing camels to spring training was a good idea, to you know, get over the hump. I'm sure it sounded good on paper. The Nationals were now officially a bit of a circus. Honestly, they got bailed out because the Capitals, a team that spent its own 40 days in the desert, won the Stanley Cup and the catharsis was so intense nobody cared about anything for the rest of the year.

Then 2019 happened. Bryce Harper, once the past, present and future was gone to Philly. After a godawful start that we all remember, they actually won the whole damn thing. Not exactly out of nowhere, but certainly not expected the way things started. It was as if they'd broken the pattern. As Strasburg, the World Series MVP, himself said, "sometimes you're the buzzsaw." Somehow Gerardo Parra's walkup song "Baby Shark" became the theme of the season, after the veteran landed with the Nats about a week after the Giants released him. Fourth outfielders are supposed to, on some level, be good clubhouse presences, but they're not supposed to win over an entire fanbase. When they won it was surreal, to say the least.

Then, before the next season even got started, a pandemic broke out, and suddenly the Nationals championship victory lap was cut short. Of course, the 2020 season did eventually happen. But at that point, a team that had literally built itself from the ground up was a shell of itself. The magic had worn off guys like Aníbal Sánchez and Howie Kendrick, who just looked old. Zimmerman opted out entirely and Strasburg shut it down early with a hand injury.

After literal generations without a team, a decade plus of well-earned heartbreak and then a completely insane title run, we only had ourselves to really celebrate it with. Literally, inside of our homes. The season after a championship is supposed to be one long parade: Disappointing season? Blame it on the hangover from the champagne. But the time off was long enough for everyone to sober up, and 2020 became more like cleaning up the plastic cups after a house party.

Why does all that matter? Because the Nationals have an identity to sort out. They're no longer the plucky new kids. They're no longer the kinda embarrassing middle schoolers. They're far from the overly cocky high school kids who thought their whole lives were ahead of them. We've moved past the existential dread of disappointment through repeated failure. They won the World Series! Then we all forgot about everything.

The main question becomes what is acceptable from a year-to-year standpoint. Are they going to do that thing where they act like "Champion" is their only identity? Are they going to hit reset and start the whole thing over, go back to the early Zimmerman days? Or are they going to be who they should be, and just continue to grow and build the game from a fan standpoint?

When pitchers and catchers report to West Palm Beach in 2021, the Nationals will be back to being just another team, oddly enough. A decent team, a longshot, but a shot. The team has their trophy, and we got our parade, but we missed the victory lap—the season-long celebration of each other, of the investment everyone made.

The MLS' Seattle Sounders were technically the last team awarded a trophy before it all came down, but it wasn't that franchise's first time. This was different. And as we came to find out, the Nats beat a team of cheats. In many ways, they kind of saved baseball, nevermind themselves. If you thought MLB was under the microscope following the revelation that the Astros had a coordinated sign-stealing scheme, think about the level of scandal it would be if they'd just claimed their second title in three seasons. There was no saving baseball, or any sport, from the fire that was a worldwide pandemic, but the Nationals pulled MLB out of the frying pan it almost found itself in. But the fact of the matter is that the 2019 Nationals will probably never get the credit they deserve. Fans will only get over that if the franchise does too. What fans expect or even want from this team in 2021, nevermind the franchise going forward, will be fascinating to see.

Luckily, there is one person that every Nationals fan can throw all their efforts toward. Not merely a star—stars litter the night's sky—the man they call Childish Bambino is the

Nationals' sun; as long as he's in their orbit, there will be light. Already a champion, Juan Soto is the past, the present and the future. ■

—Clinton Yates is a columnist for The Undefeated and panelist on Around The Horn.

HITTERS

Yasel Antuna SS Born: 10/26/99 Age: 21 Bats: S Throws: R Height: 6'0" Weight: 170 Origin: International Free Agent, 2016

YEAR	TEAM	LVL	AGE	PA	R	2B	3B	HR	RBI	BB	K	SB	CS	Whiff%	AVG/OBP/SLG	DRC+	BABIP	BRR	FRAA	WARP
2018	HAG	LO-A	18	362	44	14	2	6	27	32	79	8	7		.220/.293/.331	83	.269	-0.6	SS(67): -8.8, 2B(9): 0.2	-0.9
2021 FS	WAS	MLB	21	600	51	26	3	11	56	41	172	8	5		.218/.276/.337	69	.295	-4.9	SS -10, 3B 0	-2.0

Comparables: Andrew Velazquez, Juan Diaz, Delino DeShields

Impressive reports from their alternate site and the sweet siren song of upside led the Nats to add Antuna to their 40-man despite the 370 plate appearances he's managed since the start of 2018. He could still be a future star, a lesson in sunk costs or anything in between.

Josh Bell 1B Born: 08/14/92 Age: 28 Bats: S Throws: R Height: 6'4" Weight: 250 Origin: Round 2, 2011 Draft (#61 overall)

YEAR	TEAM	LVL	AGE	PA	R	2B	3B	HR	RBI	BB	K	SB	CS	Whiff%	AVG/OBP/SLG	DRC+	BABIP	BRR	FRAA	WARP
2018	PIT	MLB	25	583	74	31	4	12	62	77	104	2	5	24.5%	.261/.357/.411	100	.305	-0.8	1B(137): -6.8	0.1
2019	PIT	MLB	26	613	94	37	3	37	116	74	118	0	1	25.5%	.277/.367/.569	130	.288	-3.1	1B(134): -11.1	2.0
2020	PIT	MLB	28	223	22	3	0	8	22	22	59	0	0	33.6%	.226/.305/.364	83	.273	-0.4	1B(35): -0.0	-0.1
2021 FS	WAS	MLB	28	600	72	25	3	22	76	69	140	2	1	27.4%	.248/.340/.435	110	.298	-1.1	1B -6	1.0
2021 DC	WAS	MLB	28	576	69	24	2	21	73	66	134	2	1	27.4%	.248/.340/.435	110	.298	-1.1	1B -6	1.0

Comparables: Logan Morrison, Lucas Duda, Derrek Lee

Bell is built like a hybrid of Optimus Prime and an old-growth sequoia, so it's frustrating the power has been just average. It looked like a power surge was coming in 2019, when he dialed up his launch angle and started barreling the ball more, swinging more often at pitches in the zone while smoothing out an idiosyncratic approach at the plate. That method regressed in 2020, as he continued to swing at strikes but also swung through them, costing him the hit tool that was his calling card throughout the minors. A defensive liability even at first, without a universal DH it's hard to find a place for him, and he's still got two more years before free agency. That primed the pump for a trade to the Nationals, where he will try to rediscover his power stroke from 2019.

Emilio Bonifácio OF Born: 04/23/85 Age: 36 Bats: S Throws: R Height: 5'10" Weight: 200 Origin: International Free Agent, 2001

YEAR	TEAM	LVL	AGE	PA	R	2B	3B	HR	RBI	BB	K	SB	CS	Whiff%	AVG/OBP/SLG	DRC+	BABIP	BRR	FRAA	WARP
2019	DUR	AAA	34	288	48	19	3	8	36	25	63	15	6		.286/.353/.475	101	.351	2.9	CF(31): -2.8, LF(22): 1.5, SS(12): -0.6	1.1
2020	WAS	MLB	35	3	1	0	0	0	0	0	2	0	1	28.6%	.000/.000/.000	107	.000	0.0	LF(1): 0.2	0.0
2021 FS	WAS	MLB	36	600	52	15	2	10	49	40	174	17	5	28.6%	.207/.266/.299	55	.283	5.2	CF -9, LF 0	-2.2

Comparables: Rich Thompson, Kazuo Matsui, Omar Infante

Bonifácio unexpectedly resurfaced in the majors after three years of bouncing between the minors and the Atlantic League. His return was even shorter than his annual April hot streaks.

Asdrúbal Cabrera 3B Born: 11/13/85 Age: 35 Bats: S Throws: R Height: 6'0" Weight: 205 Origin: International Free Agent, 2002

YEAR	TEAM	LVL	AGE	PA	R	2B	3B	HR	RBI	BB	K	SB	CS	Whiff%	AVG/OBP/SLG	DRC+	BABIP	BRR	FRAA	WARP
2018	PHI	MLB	32	185	20	13	0	5	17	12	38	0	0	25.5%	.228/.286/.392	107	.266	0.5	SS(31): -0.6, 3B(22): -0.5, 2B(2): 0.1	0.8
2018	NYM	MLB	32	407	48	23	1	18	58	29	81	0	0	21.6%	.277/.329/.488	104	.309	1.9	2B(90): -10.8	0.6
2019	WAS	MLB	33	146	24	10	1	6	40	19	18	0	0	17.9%	.323/.404/.565	137	.330	-1.2	2B(31): -1.6, 3B(5): -0.3, 1B(3): 0.3	0.9
2019	TEX	MLB	33	368	45	15	0	12	51	38	85	4	0	21.8%	.235/.318/.393	94	.278	0.2	3B(93): 6.0	1.8
2020	WAS	MLB	35	213	23	9	3	8	31	19	39	0	0	20.6%	.242/.305/.447	103	.259	0.5	1B(25): -0.9, 3B(17): -1.3	0.3
2021 FS	WAS	MLB	35	600	67	30	1	19	76	49	128	3	1	21.2%	.249/.317/.419	99	.292	-0.7	2B -6, 3B 0	1.0

Comparables: Jhonny Peralta, J.J. Hardy, Rich Aurilia

The Nationals found treasure in the scrapheap in 2019, signing Cabrera for a paltry sum after his release from the Rangers and receiving All-Star production from him during the run up to the postseason. Like the Nationals, he failed to repeat the same kind of magic last season, putting up numbers more similar to the ones he posted in Texas. The only glimmers of good fortune present in his season came versus lefties (against whom he put up an OPS above 1.000), and three of the four other members of the NL East. (He was, improbably, stymied by Philadelphia pitching.) Cabrera's competence against southpaws, combined with defensive versatility, should ensure him at least another season as a back-up infielder.

Starlin Castro 2B Born: 03/24/90 Age: 31 Bats: R Throws: R Height: 6'2" Weight: 220 Origin: International Free Agent, 2006

YEAR	TEAM	LVL	AGE	PA	R	2B	3B	HR	RBI	BB	K	SB	CS	Whiff%	AVG/OBP/SLG	DRC+	BABIP	BRR	FRAA	WARP
2018	MIA	MLB	28	647	76	32	2	12	54	48	124	6	4	22.8%	.278/.329/.400	101	.330	0.3	2B(150): -6.2	1.6
2019	MIA	MLB	29	676	68	31	4	22	86	28	111	2	2	19.2%	.270/.300/.436	90	.293	-1.8	2B(117): -6.2, 3B(45): -0.3, SS(3): -0.2	0.6
2020	WAS	MLB	30	63	9	3	1	2	4	3	13	0	0	22.0%	.267/.302/.450	103	.311	-0.3	2B(16): 0.2	0.2
2021 FS	WAS	MLB	31	600	64	25	1	17	72	31	126	3	1	20.5%	.258/.301/.403	92	.304	-0.6	2B -9, 3B 0	0.5
2021 DC	WAS	MLB	31	542	58	23	1	15	65	28	114	3	1	20.5%	.258/.301/.403	92	.304	-0.5	2B -8	0.5

Comparables: Mike Aviles, Jordy Mercer, Ian Desmond

It's not the years; it's the miles. Castro will be entering his 11th season in the bigs, with almost 1,500 games—including a pair of 162-appearance seasons—to show for his efforts. Despite being on the younger side (especially in an aging Nationals lineup), there isn't much intrigue left here. Castro's best skill is, arguably, his durability—or, at least, it *was*, until he suffered a fractured wrist on a diving attempt a few weeks into the season. Heading forward, he should continue to hit decently, walk infrequently and—most importantly of all—be available almost every day.

Wilmer Difo 2B Born: 04/02/92 Age: 29 Bats: S Throws: R Height: 5'11" Weight: 200 Origin: International Free Agent, 2010

YEAR	TEAM	LVL	AGE	PA	R	2B	3B	HR	RBI	BB	K	SB	CS	Whiff%	AVG/OBP/SLG	DRC+	BABIP	BRR	FRAA	WARP
2018	WAS	MLB	26	456	55	14	7	7	42	39	82	10	3	23.2%	.230/.298/.350	78	.269	-1.5	2B(112): 4.7, 3B(20): -0.8, SS(9): 0.8	0.6
2019	FRE	AAA	27	261	48	14	3	4	30	25	51	13	5		.300/.369/.438	94	.369	3.7	SS(32): -1.9, 2B(20): 1.4, 3B(10): -0.0	1.2
2019	WAS	MLB	27	144	15	2	0	2	8	12	29	0	1	27.3%	.252/.315/.313	74	.310	1.0	SS(33): -1.5, 3B(6): -0.3, 2B(2): 0.1	0.1
2020	WAS	MLB	28	18	1	0	0	0	1	3	4	0	0	23.8%	.071/.222/.071	96	.091	0.2	2B(4): -0.1, SS(4): -0.2, 3B(2): -0.0	0.0
2021 FS	WAS	MLB	29	600	59	24	3	11	57	45	135	13	5	24.7%	.236/.299/.353	79	.294	1.2	SS 5, 2B 5	1.5

Comparables: Emilio Bonifácio, Tony Womack, Bobby Knoop

Handed the keys to the second base job in 2018 after Daniel Murphy's departure, Difo promptly drove the car into a ditch, then spent the next season futilely trying to reverse out of it. For 2020, he didn't even bother getting behind the wheel, collecting a single hit in 18 plate appearances and getting designated for assignment in early September. Bereft of power and merely average defensively, Difo's career now has the trajectory of "light-hitting utility infielder," a kind of player that fell out of vogue years ago (though Tony La Russa is probably barking at someone to get Difo as you read this). That all doesn't bode well for him getting back into the driver's seat, or even squeezing into the middle seat in the back.

Luis García SS Born: 05/16/00 Age: 21 Bats: L Throws: R Height: 6'2" Weight: 211 Origin: International Free Agent, 2016

YEAR	TEAM	LVL	AGE	PA	R	2B	3B	HR	RBI	BB	K	SB	CS	Whiff%	AVG/OBP/SLG	DRC+	BABIP	BRR	FRAA	WARP
2018	HAG	LO-A	18	323	48	14	4	3	31	19	49	8	5		.297/.335/.402	109	.343	0.7	3B(36): -4.6, SS(27): 0.4, 2B(11): -1.2	0.4
2018	FBG	HI-A	18	221	34	7	2	4	23	12	33	4	1		.299/.338/.412	115	.337	-0.3	SS(40): -2.7	0.4
2019	HBG	AA	19	553	66	22	4	4	30	17	86	11	5		.257/.280/.337	69	.299	3.1	SS(93): -3.9, 2B(38): 0.4	0.5
2020	WAS	MLB	20	139	18	6	0	2	16	5	29	1	1	29.1%	.276/.302/.366	64	.340	-0.8	2B(37): -11.3, SS(3): 0.0	-1.4
2021 FS	WAS	MLB	21	600	52	28	3	8	59	21	133	6	2	29.1%	.253/.283/.359	71	.317	0.9	2B -2, SS 0	-0.5
2021 DC	WAS	MLB	21	237	20	11	1	3	23	8	52	2	0	29.1%	.253/.283/.359	71	.317	0.4	2B -1, SS 0	-0.2

Comparables: Ramiro Pena, Elvis Andrus, Rubén Tejada

García has a good claim as Washington's top prospect, though that's in a system so thin you can practically see through it. Regardless, he has a solid hit tool and should grow into his power (he didn't turn 20 until May). While shortstop may ultimately be too tough for him, he'll find a comfortable home at second base. He even managed to hold his own in a brief MLB stint, though walking just five times in 40 games suggests there's more work to do. García should keep developing in Triple-A to begin 2021, and then take over the keystone in D.C. when he's ready, maybe around June. "Soon," Nationals fans whisper, casting a worried glance at Starlin Castro and Carter Kieboom.

Yan Gomes C Born: 07/19/87 Age: 33 Bats: R Throws: R Height: 6'2" Weight: 215 Origin: Round 10, 2009 Draft (#310 overall)

YEAR	TEAM	LVL	AGE	PA	R	2B	3B	HR	RBI	BB	K	SB	CS	Whiff%	AVG/OBP/SLG	DRC+	BABIP	BRR	FRAA	WARP
2018	CLE	MLB	30	435	52	26	0	16	48	21	119	0	0	29.4%	.266/.313/.449	102	.336	-1.1	C(111): 9.1	3.1
2019	WAS	MLB	31	358	36	16	0	12	43	38	84	2	0	25.6%	.223/.316/.389	91	.265	0.1	C(93): -1.6, 1B(1): -0.0	1.3
2020	WAS	MLB	33	119	14	6	1	4	13	6	22	1	0	22.4%	.284/.319/.468	108	.314	-0.5	C(30): 0.7	0.4
2021 FS	WAS	MLB	33	600	61	25	1	20	70	37	157	1	0	26.1%	.225/.288/.385	83	.279	-1.0	C -5, 1B 0	0.5
2021 DC	WAS	MLB	33	542	55	23	1	18	63	34	142	1	0	26.1%	.225/.288/.385	83	.279	-0.9	C -6, 1B 0	0.2

Comparables: Adam Melhuse, Damian Miller, Welington Castillo

YEAR	TEAM	P. COUNT	FRM RUNS	BLK RUNS	THRW RUNS	TOT RUNS
2018	CLE	15311	7.5	1.7	0.0	9.3
2019	WAS	13282	-4.3	2.8	0.7	-0.9
2020	WAS	4477	-1.6	0.3	0.2	-1.1
2021	WAS	16835	-6.6	2.1	-0.5	-5.1

For the last two seasons, Gomes has been half of Washington's solution to the loss of Wilson Ramos, pairing up with Kurt Suzuki to form a catcher tandem that was occasionally good and mostly adequate. At catcher, that's basically free real estate. Suzuki heading to free agency leaves Gomes atop the depth chart, but he shouldn't get cozy up there. Set to turn 34 in July and boasting a ceiling of "league average" at the plate and behind it, the Brazilian veteran is better suited staying in a part-time role or becoming the veteran backup to an up-and-coming youngster. The Nationals don't have one of those in stock, so until they do, expect Gomes to keep his part-time role alongside another older backstop looking for a place to crash for the next season or two. Yan's a pretty good roommate.

Josh Harrison 2B   Born: 07/08/87   Age: 34   Bats: R   Throws: R   Height: 5'8"   Weight: 190   Origin: Round 6, 2008 Draft (#191 overall)

YEAR	TEAM	LVL	AGE	PA	R	2B	3B	HR	RBI	BB	K	SB	CS	Whiff%	AVG/OBP/SLG	DRC+	BABIP	BRR	FRAA	WARP
2018	PIT	MLB	30	374	41	13	1	8	37	18	68	3	0	23.5%	.250/.293/.363	87	.286	0.5	2B(87): -5.6, 3B(2): -0.0	0.0
2019	TOL	AAA	31	29	2	1	0	0	3	6	4	0	0		.174/.345/.217	105	.211	-0.9	2B(4): -0.1	0.0
2019	DET	MLB	31	147	10	7	1	1	8	6	27	4	2	26.5%	.175/.218/.263	63	.207	-1.1	2B(34): 2.7	-0.1
2020	WAS	MLB	33	91	11	2	0	3	14	6	12	1	2	22.7%	.278/.352/.418	118	.288	-0.4	2B(12): -0.5, 3B(10): -0.7, LF(5): 0.7	0.3
2021 FS	WAS	MLB	33	600	59	25	2	13	64	30	112	12	4	24.1%	.247/.304/.374	87	.288	1.5	RF -2, 3B 0	0.9
2021 DC	WAS	MLB	33	407	40	17	1	9	44	20	76	8	2	24.1%	.247/.304/.374	87	.288	1.0	RF -2, 3B 0	0.2

Comparables: Omar Infante, Adam Kennedy, Brandon Phillips

It's been a long time since Harrison was anything more than a likable yet below-average player, and a rough final season in Pittsburgh in 2018 plus a short and ugly stint with Detroit in '19 suggested that even those days were dead and gone. But like a phoenix rising from Arizona, he popped up on Washington's roster as part of a rotating infield carousel and posted a career-high on-base percentage and his best DRC+ figure since 2014. More walks, fewer strikeouts and better performance against fastballs (a .371 batting average and .657 slugging percentage) were the keys to his resurgence and earned him a one-year deal to stick around as a backup. The fun times likely won't last, but at least he's getting a happier sendoff than before.

Brock Holt 2B   Born: 06/11/88   Age: 33   Bats: L   Throws: R   Height: 5'10"   Weight: 180   Origin: Round 9, 2009 Draft (#265 overall)

YEAR	TEAM	LVL	AGE	PA	R	2B	3B	HR	RBI	BB	K	SB	CS	Whiff%	AVG/OBP/SLG	DRC+	BABIP	BRR	FRAA	WARP
2018	BOS	MLB	30	367	41	18	2	7	46	37	73	7	7	16.7%	.277/.362/.411	101	.337	-1.9	2B(56): -5.3, SS(23): -2.0, RF(11): -0.7	0.1
2019	WOR	AAA	31	37	7	2	0	1	3	8	12	1	0		.250/.432/.429	107	.400	0.0	SS(3): 1.1, 2B(2): -0.3	0.2
2019	BOS	MLB	31	295	38	14	2	3	31	28	57	1	0	18.9%	.297/.369/.402	97	.365	-1.1	2B(60): 3.7, 1B(11): 1.7, SS(6): 0.6	1.3
2020	MIL	MLB	32	36	1	0	0	0	1	4	9	0	0	19.4%	.100/.222/.100	77	.136	0.1	3B(13): -0.5, LF(3): 0.2, RF(1): -0.1	0.0
2020	WAS	MLB	32	70	11	6	0	0	4	5	15	1	0	19.8%	.262/.314/.354	77	.340	1.3	LF(6): -0.4, 3B(5): 0.0, 1B(4): 0.5	0.0
2021 FS	WAS	MLB	33	600	59	23	1	9	55	59	138	8	3	18.5%	.240/.326/.345	87	.310	-0.5	2B 0, SS 1	0.9

Comparables: Dick Green, Randy Velarde, Tony Graffanino

Holt is the second do-it-all late-season pickup to experience the Nationals utilityman bump. In 2019, Asdrúbal Cabrera went from meh to machine after being DFA by the Rangers. Holt was similarly flailing, coming off a 3-for-30 stretch with Milwaukee, when he joined the Nats as part of their attempts to patchwork one (1) competent infielder from a scrapheap of designated hitters. Holt's offense returned, albeit over a small sample, and he'll likely continue as a fielding skeleton key who can also sometimes make good contact.

Howie Kendrick 2B   Born: 07/12/83   Age: 37   Bats: R   Throws: R   Height: 5'11"   Weight: 225   Origin: Round 10, 2002 Draft (#294 overall)

YEAR	TEAM	LVL	AGE	PA	R	2B	3B	HR	RBI	BB	K	SB	CS	Whiff%	AVG/OBP/SLG	DRC+	BABIP	BRR	FRAA	WARP
2018	WAS	MLB	34	160	17	14	0	4	12	5	29	1	1	21.5%	.303/.331/.474	94	.350	-3.1	2B(33): -2.7, LF(6): -0.1, 1B(2): 0.0	-0.2
2019	WAS	MLB	35	370	61	23	1	17	62	27	48	2	1	17.0%	.344/.395/.572	132	.358	-2.6	1B(48): 1.8, 2B(23): 0.7, 3B(15): -1.4	2.3
2020	WAS	MLB	37	100	11	4	0	2	14	7	17	0	0	20.7%	.275/.320/.385	93	.311	-0.3	1B(6): -0.0	0.0
2021 FS	WAS	MLB	37	600	65	28	1	15	72	40	125	9	3	18.5%	.267/.325/.406	100	.322	-0.5	2B -1, LF 0	1.7

Comparables: Brandon Phillips, Bret Boone, Randy Velarde

Sometimes, glory days, they pass you by. In Kendrick's case, they went by quickly. Less than a year after playing the hero throughout the Nationals' championship run—and then returning despite having a richer offer on the table from the Rays—he had one of the worst seasons of his career. Compared to 2019, he struck out more frequently and walked and made quality contact less frequently. Kendrick turned 37 in July, and while the normal sample-size caveats apply to his 2020, it's probably fair to say this professional hitter has seen his finest hours.

Carter Kieboom SS   Born: 09/03/97   Age: 23   Bats: R   Throws: R   Height: 6'2"   Weight: 210   Origin: Round 1, 2016 Draft (#28 overall)

YEAR	TEAM	LVL	AGE	PA	R	2B	3B	HR	RBI	BB	K	SB	CS	Whiff%	AVG/OBP/SLG	DRC+	BABIP	BRR	FRAA	WARP
2018	FBG	HI-A	20	285	48	15	0	11	46	36	50	6	1		.298/.386/.494	156	.332	0.5	SS(56): -0.4	2.3
2018	HBG	AA	20	273	36	16	1	5	23	22	59	3	1		.262/.326/.395	106	.324	0.5	SS(62): 2.6	1.3
2019	FRE	AAA	21	494	79	24	3	16	79	68	100	5	2		.303/.409/.493	126	.362	1.4	SS(62): -3.7, 2B(41): 3.2, 3B(10): -0.1	3.5
2019	WAS	MLB	21	43	4	0	0	2	2	4	16	0	0	26.7%	.128/.209/.282	61	.143	0.1	SS(10): -1.0	-0.1
2020	WAS	MLB	23	122	15	1	0	0	9	17	33	0	1	25.6%	.202/.344/.212	85	.299	1.4	3B(31): 3.7	0.5
2021 FS	WAS	MLB	23	600	62	22	2	16	64	59	171	1	0	25.8%	.232/.320/.375	91	.312	0.4	3B -5, 2B 0	0.8
2021 DC	WAS	MLB	23	542	56	20	1	14	58	53	154	1	0	25.8%	.232/.320/.375	91	.312	0.4	3B -5	0.1

Comparables: B.J. Upton, Willy Adames, Corey Seager

Many of us learned how to bake bread during quarantine, and that means that we also learned that the loaf doesn't always turn out how you wanted it to—especially when you're a novice. Kieboom is starting to look like one of those March loaves. He's now more than 150 at-bats into his big-league career, and neither his bat nor his glove have proven worthy of his lofty prospect status. He did field better in 2020 than he had during his initial cup-of-coffee cameo in 2019, but his bat played so light as to be captured in a single statistic: he had one extra base hit in 99 at-bats. One. Another rotten year and it'll be time to wonder if Kieboom will ever rise, or if the Nationals should give up baking and stick to buying their bread from the store.

Victor Robles CF   Born: 05/19/97   Age: 24   Bats: R   Throws: R   Height: 6'0"   Weight: 205   Origin: International Free Agent, 2013

YEAR	TEAM	LVL	AGE	PA	R	2B	3B	HR	RBI	BB	K	SB	CS	Whiff%	AVG/OBP/SLG	DRC+	BABIP	BRR	FRAA	WARP
2018	NAT	ROK	21	27	7	1	0	0	1	7	4	4	1		.333/.556/.389	200	.429	1.9	CF(7): -0.3	0.4
2018	SYR	AAA	21	182	25	9	1	2	10	18	26	14	6		.278/.356/.386	100	.318	1.2	CF(39): -0.8	0.4
2018	WAS	MLB	21	66	8	3	1	3	10	4	12	3	2	24.1%	.288/.348/.525	103	.311	0.7	CF(14): 0.1, LF(2): 0.0, RF(2): -0.2	0.3
2019	WAS	MLB	22	617	86	33	3	17	65	35	140	28	9	23.5%	.255/.326/.419	84	.310	5.6	CF(141): 6.6, RF(15): 1.1	2.3
2020	WAS	MLB	23	189	20	5	1	3	15	9	53	4	1	27.8%	.220/.293/.315	72	.298	2.8	CF(52): 0.4	0.2
2021 FS	WAS	MLB	24	600	68	26	4	15	61	38	152	24	9	24.9%	.245/.327/.396	100	.315	0.1	CF 3, LF 0	2.3
2021 DC	WAS	MLB	24	576	65	25	3	14	59	37	146	23	9	24.9%	.245/.327/.396	100	.315	0.1	CF 3	2.2

Comparables: Dale Murphy, Chris Young, Adam Jones

Poor Robles, who went from crown prince in D.C. as the top prospect and heir apparent to Bryce Harper in the outfield to having Juan Soto steal every last ounce of his thunder. Not that he's earning himself any spotlights after cratering offensively in 2020, when a total lack of plate discipline and power combined to make him Jeff Mathis But Fast. The good news is there's nowhere to go from there but up, and given that he's still just 24 with loud tools, the Nationals can wait and see whether he can climb out of his hole. If nothing else, he's still a great defender and baserunner. It's adjusting to major-league pitching that's been the hardest part, and Robles hasn't shown any consistent signs of figuring things out; if anything, he's going backwards. Heavy is the head that wears the crown, even briefly.

Adrían Sanchez SS   Born: 08/16/90   Age: 30   Bats: R   Throws: R   Height: 6'0"   Weight: 208   Origin: International Free Agent, 2007

YEAR	TEAM	LVL	AGE	PA	R	2B	3B	HR	RBI	BB	K	SB	CS	Whiff%	AVG/OBP/SLG	DRC+	BABIP	BRR	FRAA	WARP
2018	SYR	AAA	27	295	21	15	2	4	27	16	42	10	6		.234/.281/.349	69	.260	0.3	SS(29): 2.0, 3B(23): -1.9, 2B(19): 1.1	-0.1
2018	WAS	MLB	27	59	8	2	1	0	3	1	8	0	0	20.7%	.276/.288/.345	87	.320	1.0	2B(13): -1.1, 3B(7): -0.2	0.1
2019	HBG	AA	28	282	43	19	1	6	36	19	39	11	5		.316/.365/.469	156	.349	2.3	2B(33): -0.8, 3B(21): 0.3, SS(18): 1.8	3.0
2019	WAS	MLB	28	32	3	0	0	0	1	1	10	0	0	28.1%	.226/.250/.226	60	.333	0.6	3B(6): 0.0, 2B(4): -0.0, SS(2): -0.0	0.0
2021 FS	WAS	MLB	30	600	56	26	2	11	57	30	136	5	1	24.8%	.230/.275/.343	69	.285	0.7	SS 6, 2B 0	0.3

Comparables: Rey Navarro, Melvin Dorta, Niuman Romero

Now 30 years old with all of 166 career major league plate appearances, Sanchez is the ghost that hangs over Wilmer Difo's shoulder, rattling his glove and wailing about a life spent stapled to the bench as a backup infielder with no standout skill beyond being cheap.

Kyle Schwarber LF   Born: 03/05/93   Age: 28   Bats: L   Throws: R   Height: 6'0"   Weight: 225   Origin: Round 1, 2014 Draft (#4 overall)

YEAR	TEAM	LVL	AGE	PA	R	2B	3B	HR	RBI	BB	K	SB	CS	Whiff%	AVG/OBP/SLG	DRC+	BABIP	BRR	FRAA	WARP
2018	CHC	MLB	25	510	64	14	3	26	61	78	140	4	3	30.2%	.238/.356/.467	111	.288	-3.4	LF(120): 2.7	1.9
2019	CHC	MLB	26	610	82	29	3	38	92	70	156	2	3	28.1%	.250/.339/.531	120	.276	-5.0	LF(140): -0.6, C(1): 0.1	2.7
2020	CHC	MLB	27	224	30	6	0	11	24	30	66	1	0	28.2%	.188/.308/.393	96	.219	-0.8	LF(48): -0.5	0.3
2021 FS	WAS	MLB	28	600	78	22	2	31	85	82	180	3	1	28.6%	.229/.343/.466	119	.287	0.0	LF -6, C 0	2.5

Comparables: Jonny Gomes, Jason Michaels, Pat Burrell

The key to Schwarber's success is simple: hit the ball hard, hit the ball high and let physics do its thing. He used that philosophy to good effect during his career-year in 2019, and it seemed to carry over to the start of 2020. Through the end of August, he was hitting a Schwarberian .228/.333/.500 with nine home runs. But while Schwarber was hitting the ball hard, he wasn't hitting it all that high. A career-worst launch angle precipitated a September that probably left him humming a certain Green Day song while in the batter's box. Maybe it's unfair to read too much into a month-long slump during a shortened season, but it felt like the progress he had made came undone. Schwarber is now entering his walk year, and if there's one piece of advice we'd give him, it's this: lift and separate.

Juan Soto LF   Born: 10/25/98   Age: 22   Bats: L   Throws: L   Height: 6'1"   Weight: 220   Origin: International Free Agent, 2015

YEAR	TEAM	LVL	AGE	PA	R	2B	3B	HR	RBI	BB	K	SB	CS	Whiff%	AVG/OBP/SLG	DRC+	BABIP	BRR	FRAA	WARP
2018	HAG	LO-A	19	74	12	5	3	5	24	14	13	2	0		.373/.486/.814	214	.405	0.3	RF(14): 1.1, CF(2): 0.2	1.1
2018	FBG	HI-A	19	73	17	3	1	7	18	11	8	0	1		.371/.466/.790	250	.340	1.4	RF(14): 1.0, LF(1): 0.0	1.4
2018	HBG	AA	19	35	4	2	0	2	10	4	7	1	0		.323/.400/.581	113	.364	0.0	LF(4): 0.6, RF(4): -0.5	0.1
2018	WAS	MLB	19	494	77	25	1	22	70	79	99	5	2	22.2%	.292/.406/.517	125	.338	-0.5	LF(114): 2.7	3.0
2019	WAS	MLB	20	659	110	32	5	34	110	108	132	12	1	24.0%	.282/.401/.548	135	.312	1.4	LF(150): -0.8	4.9
2020	WAS	MLB	22	196	39	14	0	13	37	41	28	6	2	21.5%	.351/.490/.695	170	.363	-1.0	LF(36): -2.8, RF(6): -0.6	1.6
2021 FS	WAS	MLB	22	600	91	28	3	27	87	98	109	8	2	23.0%	.292/.411/.528	157	.327	2.2	LF 1, RF -1	6.3
2021 DC	WAS	MLB	22	610	92	28	3	28	88	100	111	8	2	23.0%	.292/.411/.528	157	.327	2.2	LF 1, RF -1	6.3

Comparables: Adam Dunn, Carlos May, Curt Blefary

Soto continued to do Soto things: hit, hit for power, take his walks and even field a competent left field. Despite Soto's narrative parallels with a certain other highly touted former Nationals outfielder, he's closer to Anthony Rendon as a player. He walks far more than he strikes out, he chases little and wastes rarely and he smiles with his teeth. The Nationals found a diamond: the challenge now is to rebuild around him and to not let him walk out the door in a few years' time, the way Rendon and that other guy have the past couple winters.

Andrew Stevenson LF   Born: 06/01/94   Age: 27   Bats: L   Throws: L   Height: 6'0"   Weight: 192   Origin: Round 2, 2015 Draft (#58 overall)

YEAR	TEAM	LVL	AGE	PA	R	2B	3B	HR	RBI	BB	K	SB	CS	Whiff%	AVG/OBP/SLG	DRC+	BABIP	BRR	FRAA	WARP
2018	SYR	AAA	24	331	40	10	1	6	28	31	75	12	6		.235/.318/.338	84	.296	-1.0	CF(49): -8.3, LF(25): 1.4, RF(4): -0.4	-0.9
2018	WAS	MLB	24	86	9	2	0	1	13	6	23	1	1	36.0%	.253/.306/.320	69	.333	0.4	LF(16): -1.4, CF(3): -0.3, RF(1): -0.1	-0.2
2019	HBG	AA	25	88	12	4	0	1	5	3	24	3	0		.250/.284/.333	16	.339	1.1	LF(10): 2.5, CF(8): -0.9	-0.1
2019	FRE	AAA	25	333	50	17	8	6	44	24	76	10	4		.334/.383/.503	98	.428	1.5	CF(52): -10.5, LF(12): -1.1, RF(9): 1.1	0.3
2019	WAS	MLB	25	37	4	1	1	0	0	6	11	0	1	29.7%	.367/.486/.467	75	.579	-0.2	LF(5): -0.7	-0.1
2020	WAS	MLB	26	47	11	7	1	2	12	5	11	2	0	27.7%	.366/.447/.732	111	.464	-0.4	LF(9): 0.5, RF(4): 0.1, CF(1): 0.1	0.1
2021 FS	WAS	MLB	27	600	64	24	4	10	50	45	160	9	3	30.5%	.239/.303/.359	80	.319	2.8	LF 1, CF -4	0.3
2021 DC	WAS	MLB	27	542	58	22	4	9	46	41	144	8	3	30.5%	.239/.303/.359	80	.319	2.5	LF 1, CF -4	0.1

Comparables: Greg Golson, Choo Freeman, Eric Reed

It took him a while to get going, and the sample size is miniscule, but Stevenson is finally beginning to show the skills that made him a second-round pick. It's not his fault that playing time has been hard to come by, owing to Washington's crowded outfield and propensity for lining the bench with mid-tier veterans, but he hadn't forced the issue either, falling mostly flat when given playing time. That's likely changed after he spent 2020 hitting the ball with real authority, including an enormous jump in exit velocity and hard-hit rate. Granted, we're talking about results from all of 47 plate appearances across 15 games, but with Adam Eaton gone, it would behoove the Nationals to give Stevenson some rope and see what's fact and what's fiction, and whether he can hack it as a regular.

Kurt Suzuki C   Born: 10/04/83   Age: 37   Bats: R   Throws: R   Height: 5'11"   Weight: 210   Origin: Round 2, 2004 Draft (#67 overall)

YEAR	TEAM	LVL	AGE	PA	R	2B	3B	HR	RBI	BB	K	SB	CS	Whiff%	AVG/OBP/SLG	DRC+	BABIP	BRR	FRAA	WARP
2018	ATL	MLB	34	388	45	24	0	12	50	22	43	0	0	16.9%	.271/.332/.444	115	.275	-2.0	C(93): -5.5	1.8
2019	WAS	MLB	35	309	37	11	0	17	63	20	36	0	1	18.7%	.264/.324/.486	115	.248	0.4	C(75): -8.6	1.4
2020	WAS	MLB	37	129	15	8	0	2	17	11	19	1	0	16.9%	.270/.349/.396	112	.301	-1.5	C(30): -0.7	0.0
2021 FS	WAS	MLB	37	600	65	26	0	19	75	37	98	1	0	17.7%	.249/.316/.409	98	.272	-1.6	C -8	1.3

Comparables: Ramon Hernandez, Yadier Molina, Jamie Burke

Are you in the market for second base? Well, good news—you too can swipe a bag off Suzuki. (Does it matter if you're a catcher, you might ask? No, no, as J.T. Realmuto proved by stealing off Suzuki twice in a single game.) While Suzuki empowers thieves, he himself isn't one, as evidenced by his bottom-scraping framing metrics. He can still hit a little, but given his defensive shortcomings, any team who is willingly playing Suzuki behind the plate is probably losing value.

YEAR	TEAM	P. COUNT	FRM RUNS	BLK RUNS	THRW RUNS	TOT RUNS
2018	ATL	12636	-7.5	1.5	-0.4	-6.4
2019	WAS	10655	-5.9	-1.7	-1.3	-8.9
2020	WAS	4520	-3.6	-0.1	0.1	-3.6
2021	WAS	16650	-11.9	1.6	-0.5	-10.7

Trea Turner SS   Born: 06/30/93   Age: 28   Bats: R   Throws: R   Height: 6'2"   Weight: 185   Origin: Round 1, 2014 Draft (#13 overall)

YEAR	TEAM	LVL	AGE	PA	R	2B	3B	HR	RBI	BB	K	SB	CS	Whiff%	AVG/OBP/SLG	DRC+	BABIP	BRR	FRAA	WARP
2018	WAS	MLB	25	740	103	27	6	19	73	69	132	43	9	20.4%	.271/.344/.416	106	.314	2.7	SS(159): 7.1	5.0
2019	WAS	MLB	26	569	96	37	5	19	57	43	113	35	5	23.4%	.298/.353/.497	107	.348	4.1	SS(122): 3.8	4.0
2020	WAS	MLB	27	259	46	15	4	12	41	22	36	12	4	19.6%	.335/.394/.588	137	.353	5.0	SS(59): -7.8	1.5
2021 FS	WAS	MLB	28	600	84	29	5	20	69	49	110	36	9	21.4%	.287/.349/.475	124	.327	11.7	SS 7	5.8
2021 DC	WAS	MLB	28	610	85	30	5	21	70	50	112	37	9	21.4%	.287/.349/.475	124	.327	11.9	SS 7	5.8

Comparables: Brad Miller, Stephen Drew, Derek Jeter

Those middling two seasons that had some folks questioning Turner's 2016 breakout are starting to look less like red flags and more like a hyper-talented young hitter figuring things out. He put together his best year since that aforementioned 73-game '16 campaign, posting a career-high DRC+ and leading the majors in hits, to make it two straight seasons of above-average offense. Even better, this one was fueled by fewer strikeouts, fewer swings and misses—particularly on the breaking balls that had been eating him alive—and more walks than 2019; he went from 91st in strikeout percentage to 22nd. That's the kind of jump that you just love to see, and coupled with an uptick in exit velocity and hard-hit rate that's stuck, plus his Olympic-caliber speed and good defense, it turns Turner into a dark horse NL MVP pick for 2021.

Ryan Zimmerman 1B   Born: 09/28/84   Age: 36   Bats: R   Throws: R   Height: 6'3"   Weight: 215   Origin: Round 1, 2005 Draft (#4 overall)

YEAR	TEAM	LVL	AGE	PA	R	2B	3B	HR	RBI	BB	K	SB	CS	Whiff%	AVG/OBP/SLG	DRC+	BABIP	BRR	FRAA	WARP
2018	WAS	MLB	33	323	33	21	2	13	51	30	55	1	1	22.8%	.264/.337/.486	111	.284	-0.5	1B(73): 1.4	1.0
2019	WAS	MLB	34	190	20	9	0	6	27	17	39	0	0	26.6%	.257/.321/.415	93	.297	-0.9	1B(44): 1.2	0.2
2021 FS	WAS	MLB	36	600	68	29	1	20	70	47	150	2	0	24.9%	.240/.307/.409	97	.295	-1.2	1B -1	0.4

Comparables: Eric Chavez, Casey Blake, Adrián Beltré

In 2019, Zimmerman finally got the ending he deserved: the long-elusive World Series title to cap off a 15-year career in which he kept watching everyone else end their drought. That he didn't retire despite a bunch of back problems and an upcoming 35th birthday was a mild surprise, though you can imagine that he very much wanted a chance to take a victory lap, celebrate on Opening Day, do the ring ceremony, all that good stuff. And like everyone else, all his fun 2020 plans were ruined by the COVID-19 pandemic, as he opted out of the season and stayed home with his family. Assuming he decides to come back to baseball in 2021 (and assuming the Nationals re-sign him), this is probably his last hurrah, so while he missed out on the post-title party, hopefully he gets the other ending he deserves: a chance to say goodbye to the fans of the only franchise he's ever known.

PITCHERS

Dakota Bacus RHP Born: 04/02/91   Age: 30   Bats: R   Throws: R   Height: 6'2"   Weight: 220   Origin: Round 9, 2012 Draft (#289 overall)

YEAR	TEAM	LVL	AGE	W	L	SV	G	GS	IP	H	HR	BB/9	K/9	K	GB%	BABIP	WHIP	ERA	DRA-	WARP	MPH	FA%	Whiff%	CSP
2018	HBG	AA	27	2	1	2	26	0	37	36	1	3.2	11.7	48	53.7%	.372	1.32	3.89	50	1.1				
2019	FRE	AAA	28	5	5	9	46	0	55¹	50	3	4.6	8.5	52	40.4%	.301	1.41	3.58	70	1.5				
2020	WAS	MLB	29	0	0	0	11	0	11¹	14	1	7.1	5.6	7	46.3%	.325	2.03	7.94	120	0.0	92.3	34.2%	24.0%	46.1%
2021 FS	*WAS*	*MLB*	*30*	*2*	*2*	*0*	*57*	*0*	*50*	*49*	*7*	*4.7*	*7.9*	*43*	*44.8%*	*.292*	*1.51*	*4.98*	*109*	*-0.1*	*92.3*	*34.2%*	*24.0%*	*46.1%*
2021 DC	*WAS*	*MLB*	*30*	*2*	*2*	*0*	*48*	*0*	*51*	*50*	*7*	*4.7*	*7.9*	*44*	*44.8%*	*.292*	*1.51*	*4.98*	*109*	*0.0*	*92.3*	*34.2%*	*24.0%*	*46.1%*

Comparables: Jacob Barnes, Cole Sulser, Sam Selman

Bacus' name makes him sound like a tertiary Kurt Vonnegut character, a four-year starting linebacker on a mid-tier MAC football team or a grizzled rodeo champion. No one's going to mistake him for a major league-caliber reliever after the year he had.

Aaron Barrett RHP Born: 01/02/88   Age: 33   Bats: R   Throws: R   Height: 6'3"   Weight: 230   Origin: Round 9, 2010 Draft (#266 overall)

YEAR	TEAM	LVL	AGE	W	L	SV	G	GS	IP	H	HR	BB/9	K/9	K	GB%	BABIP	WHIP	ERA	DRA-	WARP	MPH	FA%	Whiff%	CSP
2018	AUB	SS	30	2	0	0	20	0	20²	13	0	3.5	11.3	26	55.8%	.255	1.02	1.74	253	-1.6				
2019	HBG	AA	31	0	2	31	50	0	52¹	39	6	2.8	10.7	62	51.1%	.258	1.05	2.75	71	0.7				
2019	WAS	MLB	31	0	0	0	3	0	2¹	5	1	15.4	3.9	1	27.3%	.400	3.86	15.43	85	0.0	92.6	70.6%	15.0%	36.5%
2020	WAS	MLB	32	0	0	0	2	0	1²	2	0	10.8	5.4	1	60.0%	.400	2.40	10.80	99	0.0	91.2	45.2%	0.0%	41.3%
2021 FS	*WAS*	*MLB*	*33*	*2*	*3*	*0*	*57*	*0*	*50*	*47*	*7*	*5.3*	*9.1*	*50*	*44.5%*	*.295*	*1.53*	*5.02*	*111*	*-0.2*	*92.0*	*60.3%*	*8.9%*	*38.5%*

Comparables: Brad Boxberger, Nick Vincent, Steve Cishek

Barrett was the feel-good story of the 2019 Nationals, so, if nothing else, he'll always have that moment. He's a slider-sinker guy now after ditching a four-seamer that had nothing on it any more, but how well that works is still TBD.

Ben Braymer LHP Born: 04/28/94   Age: 27   Bats: L   Throws: L   Height: 6'2"   Weight: 220   Origin: Round 18, 2016 Draft (#544 overall)

YEAR	TEAM	LVL	AGE	W	L	SV	G	GS	IP	H	HR	BB/9	K/9	K	GB%	BABIP	WHIP	ERA	DRA-	WARP	MPH	FA%	Whiff%	CSP
2018	HAG	LO-A	24	3	0	0	7	0	25²	18	2	1.8	8.8	25	50.8%	.262	0.90	1.75	76	0.4				
2018	FBG	HI-A	24	6	3	2	21	11	89	73	4	2.9	9.4	93	38.0%	.296	1.15	2.43	81	1.5				
2019	HBG	AA	25	4	4	0	13	13	79	56	7	2.4	7.9	69	31.1%	.228	0.97	2.51	67	1.6				
2019	FRE	AAA	25	0	6	0	13	13	60	81	18	5.2	7.0	47	33.0%	.346	1.93	7.20	189	-1.4				
2020	WAS	MLB	26	1	0	0	3	1	7¹	7	0	6.1	9.8	8	28.6%	.333	1.64	1.23	113	0.0	90.1	53.9%	20.7%	40.2%
2021 FS	*WAS*	*MLB*	*27*	*3*	*4*	*0*	*57*	*0*	*50*	*51*	*9*	*4.3*	*8.1*	*44*	*32.8%*	*.294*	*1.50*	*5.38*	*118*	*-0.4*	*90.1*	*53.9%*	*20.7%*	*40.2%*
2021 DC	*WAS*	*MLB*	*27*	*3*	*4*	*0*	*42*	*6*	*66*	*67*	*12*	*4.3*	*8.1*	*59*	*32.8%*	*.294*	*1.50*	*5.38*	*118*	*-0.1*	*90.1*	*53.9%*	*20.7%*	*40.2%*

Comparables: Caleb Baragar, Dillon Maples, Locke St. John

Despite being a soft-tossing lefty, Braymer racked up a fair number of strikeouts and also handed out far too many walks, defying all our beliefs of what it means to be a crafty southpaw.

Cade Cavalli RHP Born: 08/14/98   Age: 22   Bats: R   Throws: R   Height: 6'4"   Weight: 226   Origin: Round 1, 2020 Draft (#22 overall)

Tabbed with the 22nd pick of the 2020 draft, Cavalli—a former two-way player who converted to pitching full-time as a sophomore—boasts a lot of upside thanks to a big body and power stuff, including a fastball that touches 98 mph and a pair of plus breaking balls in his curveball and slider. The question will be whether the right-hander can find consistent command and control, as he battled wildness in his first two seasons at Oklahoma before tightening things up in his shortened junior year. That will go a long way toward determining whether Cavalli's future is in the rotation or the bullpen. Washington will almost certainly let him start for now, but future struggles with walks or a pressing need in relief could force the team's hand.

Patrick Corbin LHP Born: 07/19/89   Age: 31   Bats: L   Throws: L   Height: 6'3"   Weight: 210   Origin: Round 2, 2009 Draft (#80 overall)

YEAR	TEAM	LVL	AGE	W	L	SV	G	GS	IP	H	HR	BB/9	K/9	K	GB%	BABIP	WHIP	ERA	DRA-	WARP	MPH	FA%	Whiff%	CSP
2018	ARI	MLB	28	11	7	0	33	33	200	162	15	2.2	11.1	246	48.5%	.304	1.05	3.15	61	5.9	93.4	48.6%	34.7%	41.7%
2019	WAS	MLB	29	14	7	0	33	33	202	169	24	3.1	10.6	238	48.7%	.295	1.18	3.25	63	5.9	94.0	53.6%	31.8%	42.4%
2020	WAS	MLB	30	2	7	0	11	11	65²	85	10	2.5	8.2	60	45.2%	.362	1.57	4.66	98	0.6	92.3	52.2%	23.7%	46.6%
2021 FS	*WAS*	*MLB*	*31*	*9*	*8*	*0*	*26*	*26*	*150*	*146*	*21*	*3.0*	*9.1*	*151*	*47.0%*	*.305*	*1.31*	*4.12*	*95*	*1.5*	*93.5*	*52.0%*	*30.5%*	*43.3%*
2021 DC	*WAS*	*MLB*	*31*	*10*	*10*	*0*	*29*	*29*	*169*	*164*	*23*	*3.0*	*9.1*	*170*	*47.0%*	*.305*	*1.31*	*4.12*	*95*	*2.2*	*93.5*	*52.0%*	*30.5%*	*43.3%*

Comparables: Jake Odorizzi, Sonny Gray, Nathan Eovaldi

There is something up—or, rather, down—with Corbin's fastball velocity. Corbin's never been a flamethrower; he's instead relied on his devastating slider and how it plays off his low-90s heat. His velocity dipped a full two miles per hour to career-low marks in 2020. His slider's efficacy went down with his oomph, as it drew a career-low whiff rate. It remains to be seen if Corbin's dipping velocity was caused by the unusual season, aging, conditioning, an unreported (or undiagnosed) injury or some combination thereof. Whatever the case, the Nationals have more than 106 million reasons to hope that it was a one-year aberration.

Sean Doolittle   LHP   Born: 09/26/86   Age: 34   Bats: L   Throws: L   Height: 6'2"   Weight: 204   Origin: Round 1, 2007 Draft (#41 overall)

YEAR	TEAM	LVL	AGE	W	L	SV	G	GS	IP	H	HR	BB/9	K/9	K	GB%	BABIP	WHIP	ERA	DRA-	WARP	MPH	FA%	Whiff%	CSP
2018	WAS	MLB	31	3	3	25	43	0	45	21	3	1.2	12.0	60	31.6%	.196	0.60	1.60	66	1.0	95.7	88.8%	33.8%	50.9%
2019	WAS	MLB	32	6	5	29	63	0	60	63	11	2.2	9.9	66	24.9%	.315	1.30	4.05	100	0.3	95.2	88.2%	23.5%	50.7%
2020	WAS	MLB	33	0	2	0	11	0	7²	9	3	4.7	7.0	6	3.8%	.273	1.70	5.87	166	-0.2	92.2	81.9%	18.7%	49.6%
2021 FS	WAS	MLB	34	3	2	0	57	0	50	41	8	2.0	8.8	48	27.3%	.258	1.05	2.94	77	0.8	95.0	87.5%	25.0%	50.6%

Comparables: Nick Vincent, Kirby Yates, Tommy Hunter

We hear drums, drums in the deep. Sliders are coming. Doolittle is best known as a one-pitch pitcher—you don't need a trash can to know he's probably going to throw a low-to-mid-90s fastball high in the zone. He hasn't thrown a curveball since 2014, and his slider and changeup usage each lingered in single digits throughout his big-league career. With his velocity dipping in 2020, Doolittle threw more sliders, and to decent effect (albeit over a small sample). There are two obvious paths forward ahead of him: one involves regaining his velocity, the other entails improving his slider to give him another weapon. We'll see which way Doolittle goes; we just hope that one of the most likable players in the game can find a way to enjoy more success heading forward.

Roenis Elías   LHP   Born: 08/01/88   Age: 32   Bats: L   Throws: L   Height: 6'1"   Weight: 205   Origin: International Free Agent, 2011

YEAR	TEAM	LVL	AGE	W	L	SV	G	GS	IP	H	HR	BB/9	K/9	K	GB%	BABIP	WHIP	ERA	DRA-	WARP	MPH	FA%	Whiff%	CSP
2018	WOR	AAA	29	1	0	1	4	0	7¹	2	1	2.5	11.0	9	46.7%	.071	0.55	1.23	60	0.2				
2018	TAC	AAA	29	2	4	0	10	7	33²	32	1	4.0	8.3	31	43.0%	.316	1.40	4.54	94	0.4				
2018	SEA	MLB	29	3	1	0	23	4	51	46	1	2.8	6.0	34	34.6%	.285	1.22	2.65	119	-0.2	95.7	54.9%	20.7%	46.9%
2019	WAS	MLB	30	0	0	0	4	0	3	5	2	3.0	6.0	2	30.0%	.375	2.00	9.00	258	-0.2	95.7	60.0%	20.0%	57.0%
2019	SEA	MLB	30	4	2	14	44	0	47	41	8	3.3	8.6	45	35.0%	.252	1.23	3.64	102	-0.2	95.5	57.3%	26.9%	51.1%
2021 FS	WAS	MLB	32	2	3	0	57	0	50	52	9	3.7	8.1	44	37.1%	.300	1.47	5.24	119	-0.4	95.6	56.6%	24.5%	49.8%

Comparables: Anthony DeSclafani, Erasmo Ramírez, Chad Bettis

Elias has pitched all of three innings since the Nationals got him at the 2019 trade deadline, including time missed this year with forearm pain, potentially undoing what had looked like a career-saving conversion to relief.

Erick Fedde   RHP   Born: 02/25/93   Age: 28   Bats: R   Throws: R   Height: 6'4"   Weight: 200   Origin: Round 1, 2014 Draft (#18 overall)

YEAR	TEAM	LVL	AGE	W	L	SV	G	GS	IP	H	HR	BB/9	K/9	K	GB%	BABIP	WHIP	ERA	DRA-	WARP	MPH	FA%	Whiff%	CSP
2018	SYR	AAA	25	3	3	0	13	13	67¹	78	3	2.4	9.4	70	48.7%	.393	1.43	4.41	83	1.1				
2018	WAS	MLB	25	2	4	0	11	11	50¹	55	8	3.9	8.2	46	53.0%	.336	1.53	5.54	108	0.3	95.9	54.9%	23.3%	43.8%
2019	HBG	AA	26	2	0	0	5	4	24²	18	2	1.8	9.9	27	50.8%	.262	0.93	2.55	64	0.5				
2019	FRE	AAA	26	1	1	0	2	2	10	19	5	3.6	9.0	10	36.1%	.452	2.30	12.60	185	-0.2				
2019	WAS	MLB	26	4	2	0	21	12	78	81	11	3.8	4.7	41	48.8%	.288	1.46	4.50	128	-0.5	94.3	55.2%	16.8%	46.3%
2020	WAS	MLB	27	2	4	0	11	8	50¹	47	10	3.9	5.0	28	55.0%	.234	1.37	4.29	118	0.0	95.0	55.5%	15.3%	46.2%
2021 FS	WAS	MLB	28	8	9	0	26	26	150	156	22	3.5	6.9	114	51.9%	.295	1.44	4.92	110	0.2	94.8	55.3%	17.2%	45.9%
2021 DC	WAS	MLB	28	3	5	0	16	16	68	71	10	3.5	6.9	52	51.9%	.295	1.44	4.92	110	0.3	94.8	55.3%	17.2%	45.9%

Comparables: Daniel Mengden, Jeff Hoffman, Luis Perdomo

Fedde. /FEH-dee/. Noun. A bendy pitch not otherwise categorized as a slider, curve or slurve.

Origin: The "Fedde" as a pitch type came into common usage circa 2019-20, with Nationals pitcher Erick Fedde, who began classifying his sliderish curve (or curvish slider) as, simply, his "breaking ball."

Usage: Opponents either feasted or starved against the Fedde in 2019-20, depending on how it's classified. If combined into a single pitch, the Fedde was its namesake's most effective pitch over the two-year period. If separated, the more slider-ish Fedde held opponents to a sub-.200 batting average against, as opposed to the .341 average they posted against the more curve-ish variety.

Alternative usage: If a certain pitcher wants to stick on a big-league staff heading forward, then he should consider mastering throwing the sharper Fedde more frequently.

Kyle Finnegan   RHP   Born: 09/04/91   Age: 29   Bats: R   Throws: R   Height: 6'2"   Weight: 200   Origin: Round 6, 2013 Draft (#191 overall)

YEAR	TEAM	LVL	AGE	W	L	SV	G	GS	IP	H	HR	BB/9	K/9	K	GB%	BABIP	WHIP	ERA	DRA-	WARP	MPH	FA%	Whiff%	CSP
2018	MID	AA	26	1	1	13	21	0	25	18	0	4.0	10.1	28	62.5%	.286	1.16	2.16	66	0.5				
2018	NAS	AAA	26	0	2	1	13	0	17²	22	2	3.6	8.7	17	39.7%	.357	1.64	7.13	80	0.3				
2019	MID	AA	27	0	1	9	21	0	22²	16	0	2.8	14.3	36	54.2%	.333	1.01	1.59	51	0.6				
2019	LV	AAA	27	3	1	5	21	0	28	23	3	3.9	11.6	36	40.9%	.323	1.25	2.89	50	1.0				
2020	WAS	MLB	28	1	0	0	25	0	24²	21	2	4.7	9.5	26	50.0%	.292	1.38	2.92	85	0.4	96.6	70.4%	28.3%	51.1%
2021 FS	WAS	MLB	29	2	2	0	57	0	50	42	5	4.7	10.0	55	48.7%	.292	1.37	3.90	89	0.4	96.6	70.4%	28.3%	51.1%
2021 DC	WAS	MLB	29	2	2	0	54	0	57	48	6	4.7	10.0	63	48.7%	.292	1.37	3.90	89	0.7	96.6	70.4%	28.3%	51.1%

Comparables: Eric Yardley, Brandon Brennan, Phillips Valdez

Do you ever wonder if the A's get mad when they let a player go and watch another team steal their bit of turning trash into treasure? Max Muncy is the best recent example of that; Finnegan might be the latest, going from Oakland to Washington after six years in the minors and emerging as a useful relief arm. He gave out too many walks to climb any higher than "guy you use in the sixth or seventh inning and not with a lead if you can help it," but a 95 mph sinker will play, as will the 50 percent whiff rate on his slider. That makes him a nice candidate to hold down the middle innings going forward—and if he can trim the walks, maybe he can graduate to bigger responsibilities.

Javy Guerra RHP Born: 10/31/85 Age: 35 Bats: R Throws: R Height: 6'1" Weight: 216 Origin: Round 4, 2004 Draft (#118 overall)

YEAR	TEAM	LVL	AGE	W	L	SV	G	GS	IP	H	HR	BB/9	K/9	K	GB%	BABIP	WHIP	ERA	DRA-	WARP	MPH	FA%	Whiff%	CSP
2018	NO	AAA	32	3	0	5	12	0	16²	9	0	1.6	13.0	24	57.6%	.281	0.72	0.00	45	0.6				
2018	MIA	MLB	32	1	1	1	32	0	35²	42	4	3.0	7.6	30	43.6%	.342	1.51	5.55	112	0.0	95.2	52.2%	19.5%	51.5%
2019	BUF	AAA	33	0	1	1	5	0	7¹	4	0	4.9	7.4	6	27.8%	.222	1.09	2.45	101	0.1				
2019	WAS	MLB	33	3	1	1	40	0	53²	55	9	2.0	7.0	42	33.9%	.279	1.25	4.86	96	0.3	95.2	60.0%	19.1%	54.1%
2019	TOR	MLB	33	0	0	1	11	0	14	12	1	3.2	9.6	15	26.3%	.306	1.21	3.86	142	-0.2	95.4	56.1%	17.2%	54.4%
2020	WAS	MLB	34	0	0	0	14	0	15²	19	2	4.0	7.5	13	28.0%	.354	1.66	4.02	121	0.0	93.7	67.0%	25.0%	51.2%
2021 FS	WAS	MLB	35	2	3	0	57	0	50	50	8	3.2	7.7	42	36.1%	.293	1.37	4.57	107	-0.1	94.8	59.9%	20.4%	53.0%

Comparables: Joe Smith, Jared Hughes, John Wyatt

Guerra's name means war, but his presence in a game tends to mean surrender—sometimes on the part of the opposing team, but usually on the part of the Nationals, who used him over the past two seasons as a mop-up man. Guerra's real value has been in an off-the-field role, working as a de facto coach to the refurbished Nationals bullpen. Considering his insights have been said to have helped Tanner Rainey throw strikes more frequently, maybe his name will take on a different meaning heading forward—like, say, "coach" or "instructor."

Ryne Harper RHP Born: 03/27/89 Age: 32 Bats: R Throws: R Height: 6'3" Weight: 215 Origin: Round 37, 2011 Draft (#1136 overall)

YEAR	TEAM	LVL	AGE	W	L	SV	G	GS	IP	H	HR	BB/9	K/9	K	GB%	BABIP	WHIP	ERA	DRA-	WARP	MPH	FA%	Whiff%	CSP
2018	CHA	AA	29	1	2	6	24	0	39	35	0	1.2	11.8	51	39.2%	.365	1.03	2.54	58	1.0				
2018	ROC	AAA	29	0	3	0	14	0	26	26	2	1.7	12.1	35	60.3%	.364	1.19	5.19	57	0.7				
2019	MIN	MLB	30	4	2	1	61	0	54¹	54	7	1.7	8.3	50	38.0%	.301	1.18	3.81	95	0.4	91.0	38.7%	23.9%	52.1%
2020	WAS	MLB	31	1	0	0	23	0	23²	29	5	3.4	9.5	25	34.7%	.343	1.61	7.61	104	0.2	89.9	38.1%	20.4%	52.2%
2021 FS	WAS	MLB	32	2	2	0	57	0	50	46	7	2.4	9.1	50	40.1%	.291	1.20	3.76	90	0.4	90.5	38.5%	22.4%	52.1%
2021 DC	WAS	MLB	32	2	2	0	54	0	57	53	8	2.4	9.1	57	40.1%	.291	1.20	3.76	90	0.6	90.5	38.5%	22.4%	52.1%

Comparables: Josh Fields, Hunter Strickland, Pat Venditte

Harper earned his first Annual comment in last year's book. In said comment, we predicted that hitters might grow wise to his curveball-other-curveball arsenal. That might eventually prove to be the case, but it wasn't true in 2020—the curveballs remained effective, though his fastball grew even less threatening and he finished the season with an ugly ERA. Harper's peripherals suggest he should be given another opportunity to prove he can be a useful middle reliever; at minimum, his surname and jersey number make for an interesting combination in D.C.

Will Harris RHP Born: 08/28/84 Age: 36 Bats: R Throws: R Height: 6'4" Weight: 240 Origin: Round 9, 2006 Draft (#258 overall)

YEAR	TEAM	LVL	AGE	W	L	SV	G	GS	IP	H	HR	BB/9	K/9	K	GB%	BABIP	WHIP	ERA	DRA-	WARP	MPH	FA%	Whiff%	CSP
2018	HOU	MLB	33	5	3	0	61	0	56²	48	3	2.2	10.2	64	52.0%	.308	1.09	3.49	51	1.7	93.5	62.2%	32.4%	42.4%
2019	HOU	MLB	34	4	1	4	68	0	60	42	6	2.1	9.3	62	52.9%	.247	0.93	1.50	70	1.2	92.8	58.0%	29.8%	45.2%
2020	WAS	MLB	35	0	1	1	20	0	17²	21	3	4.6	10.7	21	42.6%	.353	1.70	3.06	85	0.3	92.4	77.7%	28.9%	42.6%
2021 FS	WAS	MLB	36	2	2	4	57	0	50	43	5	3.1	9.5	52	48.7%	.292	1.22	3.34	79	0.7	92.8	64.5%	30.2%	43.8%
2021 DC	WAS	MLB	36	2	2	4	54	0	57	49	6	3.1	9.5	60	48.7%	.292	1.22	3.34	79	1.0	92.8	64.5%	30.2%	43.8%

Comparables: Heath Bell, Trevor Hoffman, Tom Henke

If you can't beat 'em, join 'em. Harris' five years in Houston ended not with a whimper, but a clang—a cutter low and away to Howie Kendrick that ricocheted off the foul pole for the World-Series-winning home-run. Harris once again ran into bad luck with the Nationals, posting a respectable ERA but a career-high walk rate. He issued more free passes in 2020 than he did in 2017, when he threw 28 additional innings. Woof. Harris was particularly beset by lefties, with his curveball generating a swing rate of nearly 60 percent...and a whiff rate of 16. Double woof. Harris has two more years to go as a National, but his legacy with the team might be confined to that one autumn night in Houston.

Cole Henry RHP Born: 07/15/99 Age: 21 Bats: R Throws: R Height: 6'4" Weight: 211 Origin: Round 2, 2020 Draft (#55 overall)

There's a lot to like about Henry, starting with the big strikeout numbers he put up across two seasons (well, one and change) at LSU, his fastball that sits 92–94 mph and his plus curveball. The stuff to worry about is his health and durability after he missed time his freshman year with arm trouble, including right elbow soreness, as well as his high-effort delivery (though he's made some mechanical changes). That risk was likely the main reason he fell to the second round of the 2020 draft, where the Nationals are hoping that it'll be worth the reward. The ceiling is a mid-rotation starter; the floor is Hunter Harvey. Somewhere in the middle—let's call it Matt Barnes Territory—is probably Henry's fate.

Daniel Hudson   RHP   Born: 03/09/87   Age: 34   Bats: R   Throws: R   Height: 6'3"   Weight: 215   Origin: Round 5, 2008 Draft (#150 overall)

YEAR	TEAM	LVL	AGE	W	L	SV	G	GS	IP	H	HR	BB/9	K/9	K	GB%	BABIP	WHIP	ERA	DRA-	WARP	MPH	FA%	Whiff%	CSP
2018	LAD	MLB	31	3	2	0	40	1	46	38	6	3.5	8.6	44	38.2%	.256	1.22	4.11	103	0.2	96.8	54.4%	28.4%	51.3%
2019	TOR	MLB	32	6	3	2	45	1	48	38	5	4.3	9.0	48	41.4%	.260	1.27	3.00	104	0.1	97.2	70.2%	23.2%	47.5%
2019	WAS	MLB	32	3	0	6	24	0	25	18	3	1.4	8.3	23	27.5%	.227	0.88	1.44	77	0.4	97.6	72.4%	22.4%	54.6%
2020	WAS	MLB	33	3	2	10	21	0	20²	15	6	4.8	12.2	28	18.0%	.209	1.26	6.10	124	-0.1	97.9	75.9%	31.2%	51.8%
2021 FS	WAS	MLB	34	2	2	36	57	0	50	44	8	4.1	9.7	54	34.6%	.281	1.34	4.38	101	0.1	97.4	69.5%	26.1%	50.5%
2021 DC	WAS	MLB	34	2	2	36	54	0	57	50	9	4.1	9.7	61	34.6%	.281	1.34	4.38	101	0.3	97.4	69.5%	26.1%	50.5%

Comparables: Wade Davis, David Phelps, Mark Guthrie

A little-known addendum to the MLB rules dictate that the Nationals must overuse a fastball-heavy reliever at some point. In 2019, that reliever was Doolittle, who was asked to carry a leaky bullpen for much of the season; last year, it was Hudson's turn to serve as a fireman. It didn't go nearly as well, with Hudson contributing more fuel than water to the flames. His increasing reliance upon his fastball makes sense—it still tempts hitters to swing—but his slider going from missable to miserable made him ineffectual. Hudson will try to salvage his career for, oh, the fifth or so time in 2021. No matter how it goes, Nationals fans will always have Houston.

Kyle McGowin   RHP   Born: 11/27/91   Age: 29   Bats: R   Throws: R   Height: 6'3"   Weight: 195   Origin: Round 5, 2013 Draft (#157 overall)

YEAR	TEAM	LVL	AGE	W	L	SV	G	GS	IP	H	HR	BB/9	K/9	K	GB%	BABIP	WHIP	ERA	DRA-	WARP	MPH	FA%	Whiff%	CSP
2018	FBG	HI-A	26	1	1	0	2	2	11	8	2	2.5	11.5	14	38.5%	.250	1.00	4.09	96	0.1				
2018	HBG	AA	26	4	3	0	13	13	78	62	7	2.2	10.8	94	47.8%	.284	1.04	3.69	54	2.5				
2018	SYR	AAA	26	3	2	0	8	8	52²	26	3	1.5	7.5	44	43.6%	.177	0.66	1.20	66	1.4				
2018	WAS	MLB	26	0	0	0	5	1	7²	6	2	5.9	9.4	8	33.3%	.211	1.43	5.87	103	0.0	92.4	59.2%	33.3%	38.9%
2019	HBG	AA	27	1	1	0	6	6	32¹	22	2	2.5	10.0	36	38.5%	.263	0.96	2.51	66	0.7				
2019	FRE	AAA	27	7	2	0	11	11	60²	59	8	2.5	10.1	68	46.1%	.323	1.25	3.86	63	2.1				
2019	WAS	MLB	27	0	0	1	7	1	16	22	7	2.2	10.1	18	43.4%	.333	1.62	10.12	74	0.3	92.8	52.7%	30.0%	43.1%
2020	WAS	MLB	28	1	0	1	9	0	11	9	2	4.1	13.1	16	38.5%	.292	1.27	4.91	85	0.2	92.9	28.1%	38.5%	45.5%
2021 FS	WAS	MLB	29	2	2	0	57	0	50	45	7	3.5	9.8	54	40.8%	.292	1.29	4.08	95	0.3	92.8	42.2%	34.2%	43.8%
2021 DC	WAS	MLB	29	2	2	0	48	0	51	46	7	3.5	9.8	55	40.8%	.292	1.29	4.08	95	0.3	92.8	42.2%	34.2%	43.8%

Comparables: Austin Voth, Luis Cessa, Glenn Sparkman

Prior to last season, McGowin's most notable feat as a big-leaguer was a May 24th start in 2019 that marked the turning point of the Nationals season—albeit, obviously, for reasons beyond his own doing. That's still the case.

Tanner Rainey   RHP   Born: 12/25/92   Age: 28   Bats: R   Throws: R   Height: 6'2"   Weight: 235   Origin: Round 2, 2015 Draft (#71 overall)

YEAR	TEAM	LVL	AGE	W	L	SV	G	GS	IP	H	HR	BB/9	K/9	K	GB%	BABIP	WHIP	ERA	DRA-	WARP	MPH	FA%	Whiff%	CSP
2018	LOU	AAA	25	7	2	3	44	0	51	25	2	6.2	11.5	65	35.2%	.225	1.18	2.65	72	0.9				
2018	CIN	MLB	25	0	0	0	8	0	7	13	4	15.4	9.0	7	30.8%	.409	3.57	24.43	201	-0.3	99.7	71.4%	29.9%	38.9%
2019	FRE	AAA	26	2	2	2	16	0	18	16	1	6.0	16.0	32	56.8%	.417	1.56	4.00	54	0.6				
2019	WAS	MLB	26	2	3	0	52	0	48¹	32	6	7.1	13.6	73	51.0%	.286	1.45	3.91	62	1.2	99.4	70.8%	40.7%	43.9%
2020	WAS	MLB	27	1	1	0	20	0	20¹	8	4	3.1	14.2	32	34.3%	.129	0.74	2.66	77	0.4	98.6	60.9%	47.3%	44.7%
2021 FS	WAS	MLB	28	2	2	0	57	0	50	36	6	6.4	13.6	75	43.0%	.296	1.43	4.10	91	0.4	99.2	67.7%	42.0%	43.8%
2021 DC	WAS	MLB	28	2	2	0	54	0	57	41	7	6.4	13.6	86	43.0%	.296	1.43	4.10	91	0.6	99.2	67.7%	42.0%	43.8%

Comparables: John Curtiss, Dan Altavilla, Dovydas Neverauskas

Baseball advice usually boils down to platitudes, whether it's "see the ball, hit the ball" or "just throw strikes." Rainey has probably heard the latter more often than he would like to admit throughout his career, but last season was the first time he took it to heart—to the extent that he threw more than the league-average rate of strikes, something inconceivable as recently as a year ago. Predictably, his walk rate improved: from 17.8 percent in 2019, all the way down to 9.3 percent last season. Rainey's control was about the only thing separating him from consistent high-leverage work; if his gains prove sustainable, don't be surprised if he starts racking up saves sooner than later.

Seth Romero   LHP   Born: 04/19/96   Age: 25   Bats: L   Throws: L   Height: 6'3"   Weight: 240   Origin: Round 1, 2017 Draft (#25 overall)

YEAR	TEAM	LVL	AGE	W	L	SV	G	GS	IP	H	HR	BB/9	K/9	K	GB%	BABIP	WHIP	ERA	DRA-	WARP	MPH	FA%	Whiff%	CSP
2018	HAG	LO-A	22	0	1	0	7	7	25¹	20	3	2.8	12.1	34	42.2%	.279	1.11	3.91	52	0.8				
2020	WAS	MLB	24	0	0	0	3	0	2²	5	1	10.1	16.9	5	40.0%	.444	3.00	13.50	72	0.1	93.0	42.4%	36.4%	42.8%
2021 FS	WAS	MLB	25	2	3	0	57	0	50	44	6	4.5	9.6	53	43.5%	.291	1.40	4.44	101	0.1	93.0	42.4%	36.4%	42.8%
2021 DC	WAS	MLB	25	2	3	0	34	4	51	45	7	4.5	9.6	54	43.5%	.291	1.40	4.44	101	0.4	93.0	42.4%	36.4%	42.8%

Romero went from "Charlie Sheen in *Major League*" to more of an Eddie Harris vibe, as his fastball and slider seem to have lost some of their zip and bite. Despite never pitching above A ball and being just two years removed from Tommy John surgery, he got the big-league call for a trio of relief appearances and even struck out the first batter he faced (though granted, it was Billy Hamilton). Still, Romero gave up a grand slam to Tomás Nido in the same inning, so there are clearly some bugs in the system, starting with a fastball that sat 92 and some wobbly control. There were also a fair number of swings and misses, so this isn't a lost cause. The thing to watch for in 2021 will be whether he can rediscover the upside that made him a first-rounder.

Joe Ross RHP Born: 05/21/93 Age: 28 Bats: R Throws: R Height: 6'4" Weight: 220 Origin: Round 1, 2011 Draft (#25 overall)

YEAR	TEAM	LVL	AGE	W	L	SV	G	GS	IP	H	HR	BB/9	K/9	K	GB%	BABIP	WHIP	ERA	DRA-	WARP	MPH	FA%	Whiff%	CSP
2018	NAT	ROK	25	0	0	0	2	2	6	0	0	4.5	12.0	8	55.6%	.000	0.50	0.00	25	0.3				
2018	SYR	AAA	25	2	0	0	2	2	11²	12	0	3.1	3.1	4	43.2%	.273	1.37	3.09	96	0.1				
2018	WAS	MLB	25	0	2	0	3	3	16	17	3	2.2	3.9	7	36.4%	.269	1.31	5.06	158	-0.3	94.6	56.0%	17.0%	44.7%
2019	FRE	AAA	26	2	3	0	8	8	40	48	2	1.8	7.2	32	45.7%	.380	1.40	4.28	96	0.8				
2019	WAS	MLB	26	4	4	0	27	9	64	74	7	4.6	8.0	57	43.8%	.351	1.67	5.48	130	-0.5	95.8	62.8%	23.6%	45.4%
2021 FS	WAS	MLB	28	8	9	0	26	26	150	152	23	3.5	7.9	130	43.6%	.298	1.41	4.84	108	0.4	95.7	62.2%	22.9%	45.3%
2021 DC	WAS	MLB	28	4	5	0	14	14	72	73	11	3.5	7.9	62	43.6%	.298	1.41	4.84	108	0.4	95.7	62.2%	22.9%	45.3%

Comparables: Zach Davies, Joe Musgrove, Brett Anderson

Sometimes inaction is the best action. The Nationals, in the simpler times of February 2020, entered with a fifth-starter conundrum: Ross, Voth or Fedde. The latter two ended up getting starts throughout the season, while Ross did not—not because he lost the battle or suffered an injury, but because he opted out from the season over COVID-19-related concerns. Ross, who recovered from Tommy John to plug the gap filled by Scherzer's back-related absences in 2019 (most famously during the World Series), figures to return in 2021. Given how Voth and Fedde pitched, the Nationals would be justified to prioritize him in their rotation pecking order.

Jackson Rutledge RHP Born: 04/01/99 Age: 22 Bats: R Throws: R Height: 6'8" Weight: 250 Origin: Round 1, 2019 Draft (#17 overall)

YEAR	TEAM	LVL	AGE	W	L	SV	G	GS	IP	H	HR	BB/9	K/9	K	GB%	BABIP	WHIP	ERA	DRA-	WARP	MPH	FA%	Whiff%	CSP
2019	NAT	ROK	20	0	0	0	1	1	1	4	0	9.0	18.0	2	80.0%	.800	5.00	27.00	194	0.0				
2019	AUB	SS	20	0	0	0	3	3	9	4	2	3.0	6.0	6	41.7%	.091	0.78	3.00	73	0.2				
2019	HAG	LO-A	20	2	0	0	6	6	27¹	14	0	3.6	10.2	31	44.4%	.222	0.91	2.30	70	0.6				
2021 FS	WAS	MLB	22	2	3	0	57	0	50	48	8	5.7	8.1	44	40.5%	.286	1.60	5.48	126	-0.6				

"What if Aaron Judge but a pitcher?" That's what the scientists on the Nationals apparently are trying to answer with Rutledge. A behemoth of a human at 6-foot-8 and 260 pounds, the righty towers over his peers both in size and stuff: He throws 96-100 mph with ease and pairs that with a plus-plus slider, an above-average curveball and a changeup that is still developing but is a viable fourth pitch. It's terrifying to think about what he could do in relief, and that may be his destiny, as his control is very much a work in progress and his durability is an open question. Does that sound like Dellin Betances to anybody else?

Aníbal Sánchez RHP Born: 02/27/84 Age: 37 Bats: R Throws: R Height: 6'0" Weight: 205 Origin: International Free Agent, 2001

YEAR	TEAM	LVL	AGE	W	L	SV	G	GS	IP	H	HR	BB/9	K/9	K	GB%	BABIP	WHIP	ERA	DRA-	WARP	MPH	FA%	Whiff%	CSP
2018	GWN	AAA	34	0	1	0	2	2	6²	9	2	5.4	12.2	9	21.1%	.412	1.95	10.80	55	0.2				
2018	ATL	MLB	34	7	6	0	25	24	136²	106	15	2.8	8.9	135	44.1%	.260	1.08	2.83	61	4.0	92.7	37.6%	25.2%	46.2%
2019	WAS	MLB	35	11	8	0	30	30	166	153	22	3.1	7.3	134	38.0%	.266	1.27	3.85	90	2.5	92.4	35.1%	22.5%	46.2%
2020	WAS	MLB	36	4	5	0	11	11	53	70	11	3.1	7.3	43	39.8%	.347	1.66	6.62	123	-0.2	91.6	32.6%	23.7%	45.1%
2021 FS	WAS	MLB	37	9	9	0	26	26	150	153	24	2.8	7.4	122	40.4%	.291	1.33	4.38	104	0.7	92.3	34.9%	23.4%	45.9%

Comparables: Wandy Rodriguez, Ted Lilly, Kevin Appier

A quirk of butterfly biology: Most monarch butterflies live for a few mere weeks in the summer. But a monarch "super-generation" migrates from their reproduction sites in the northern parts of the United States and Canada to their wintering grounds, only to make the same journey in reverse months later. So too go pitchers. Some emerge with flashes of brilliance in the heat, only to cycle out quickly. Others persist. Sánchez certainly has, first as a star for the Marlins and then again for Detroit in their early-2010s heyday. He then remade himself as a junkballer with seven(ish) pitch types, including the slow, flapping mariposa (butterfly) changeup. Even super-monarchs have to hang 'em up at some point, and Sánchez may be at that point, having watched his ERA and peripherals all transform from solid to marginal last season. Still, if anyone is going to reinvent themselves once more, it's probably the pitcher who is familiar with metamorphosis—as with anything else, the more you do it, the better you know how to.

Max Scherzer RHP Born: 07/27/84 Age: 36 Bats: R Throws: R Height: 6'3" Weight: 215 Origin: Round 1, 2006 Draft (#11 overall)

YEAR	TEAM	LVL	AGE	W	L	SV	G	GS	IP	H	HR	BB/9	K/9	K	GB%	BABIP	WHIP	ERA	DRA-	WARP	MPH	FA%	Whiff%	CSP
2018	WAS	MLB	33	18	7	0	33	33	220²	150	23	2.1	12.2	300	34.2%	.267	0.91	2.53	51	7.7	96.5	50.1%	33.4%	50.0%
2019	WAS	MLB	34	11	7	0	27	27	172¹	144	18	1.7	12.7	243	40.8%	.322	1.03	2.92	50	6.2	96.9	48.3%	34.0%	49.1%
2020	WAS	MLB	35	5	4	0	12	12	67¹	70	10	3.1	12.3	92	33.0%	.355	1.38	3.74	79	1.3	96.8	46.0%	32.6%	48.4%
2021 FS	WAS	MLB	36	10	7	0	26	26	150	122	20	2.2	11.3	187	36.3%	.289	1.06	2.88	71	3.5	96.8	48.1%	33.4%	49.1%
2021 DC	WAS	MLB	36	11	8	0	29	29	174	142	23	2.2	11.3	217	36.3%	.289	1.06	2.88	71	4.5	96.8	48.1%	33.4%	49.1%

Comparables: Jake Peavy, Zack Greinke, Roger Clemens

Pity Odysseus so long at sea; cursed by Poseidon to misadventure and misfortune, his possibility of return 20 years denied. Scherzer's own journey to baseball's Olympus seemed itself snakebit. A 2012 World Series loss. A 2013 ALCS loss. A 2014 ALDS loss. Two more NLDS losses with the Nationals. A brief stint as a cyclops in the legendary "black eye" game. A metaphorical death and resurrection during the 2019 World Series, felled by a neck injury and a delayed start, only to emerge victorious. So pity Scherzer, now home, cursed to sit and think that most troublesome question for heroes long-returned from war: Well...now what?

Stephen Strasburg RHP Born: 07/20/88 Age: 32 Bats: R Throws: R Height: 6'5" Weight: 235 Origin: Round 1, 2009 Draft (#1 overall)

YEAR	TEAM	LVL	AGE	W	L	SV	G	GS	IP	H	HR	BB/9	K/9	K	GB%	BABIP	WHIP	ERA	DRA-	WARP	MPH	FA%	Whiff%	CSP
2018	FBG	HI-A	29	0	1	0	2	2	9	7	1	1.0	12.0	12	50.0%	.261	0.89	1.00	61	0.3				
2018	WAS	MLB	29	10	7	0	22	22	130	118	18	2.6	10.8	156	43.9%	.310	1.20	3.74	66	3.5	97.1	52.0%	28.0%	47.2%
2019	WAS	MLB	30	18	6	0	33	33	209	161	24	2.4	10.8	251	50.4%	.276	1.04	3.32	43	8.3	95.6	48.3%	30.7%	44.7%
2020	WAS	MLB	31	0	1	0	2	2	5	8	1	1.8	3.6	2	35.0%	.368	1.80	10.80	117	0.0	93.2	45.8%	26.3%	42.5%
2021 FS	WAS	MLB	32	9	7	0	26	26	150	134	18	2.6	9.1	151	46.3%	.289	1.19	3.46	83	2.5	95.9	49.1%	29.9%	45.3%
2021 DC	WAS	MLB	32	9	8	0	25	25	145	130	18	2.6	9.1	146	46.3%	.289	1.19	3.46	83	2.8	95.9	49.1%	29.9%	45.3%

Comparables: Jacob deGrom, Clayton Kershaw, Jake Peavy

Strasburg didn't get a real opportunity to follow up on his brilliant postseason efforts from 2019. Instead, injury shortened his truncated season, limiting him to five innings over two appearances before he succumbed to carpal tunnel surgery. He's already retooled once in his career—from fire-thrower to a changeup/curveball artist—and if past performance is a predictor of future performance, past resilience may be a predictor of future adaptability, even as his age increases and velo declines. In other words, the Nationals shouldn't yet fret about the $245 million contract they handed him last winter.

Wander Suero RHP Born: 09/15/91 Age: 29 Bats: R Throws: R Height: 6'4" Weight: 211 Origin: International Free Agent, 2010

YEAR	TEAM	LVL	AGE	W	L	SV	G	GS	IP	H	HR	BB/9	K/9	K	GB%	BABIP	WHIP	ERA	DRA-	WARP	MPH	FA%	Whiff%	CSP
2018	SYR	AAA	26	1	2	1	14	0	17	16	1	2.1	8.5	16	46.0%	.306	1.18	3.71	67	0.3				
2018	WAS	MLB	26	4	1	0	40	0	47²	43	4	2.8	8.9	47	34.3%	.302	1.22	3.59	95	0.3	94.0	79.9%	24.6%	51.1%
2019	WAS	MLB	27	6	9	1	78	0	71¹	64	5	3.3	10.2	81	40.3%	.326	1.26	4.54	74	1.3	95.1	72.1%	29.4%	50.6%
2020	WAS	MLB	28	2	0	0	22	0	23²	20	1	3.8	10.6	28	37.7%	.317	1.27	3.80	86	0.4	93.8	81.1%	32.7%	44.7%
2021 FS	WAS	MLB	29	2	2	0	57	0	50	44	7	3.6	10.3	57	38.6%	.298	1.29	4.07	94	0.3	94.6	75.9%	29.4%	49.2%
2021 DC	WAS	MLB	29	2	2	0	54	0	57	51	8	3.6	10.3	64	38.6%	.298	1.29	4.07	94	0.5	94.6	75.9%	29.4%	49.2%

Comparables: Cam Bedrosian, Dominic Leone, Zach Putnam

If single-pitch relievers are defined as players who throw the same pitch type more than 80 percent of the time, then the 2020 Nationals improbably boasted two such players: Doolittle and Suero. Suero's cutter usage even exceeded Kenley Jansen's—Jansen's cut baseballs at a career-low rate while Suero opted for the other direction, mothballing his curveball in the process. Of particular note, Suero fared much better last year than this against lefties, even though he faced them more frequently in 2020. That's a promising potential development if he wants to remain more than the Nationals' designated rubber arm.

Austin Voth RHP Born: 06/26/92 Age: 29 Bats: R Throws: R Height: 6'2" Weight: 210 Origin: Round 5, 2013 Draft (#166 overall)

YEAR	TEAM	LVL	AGE	W	L	SV	G	GS	IP	H	HR	BB/9	K/9	K	GB%	BABIP	WHIP	ERA	DRA-	WARP	MPH	FA%	Whiff%	CSP
2018	SYR	AAA	26	6	8	0	24	24	125²	119	13	2.9	8.4	117	40.6%	.298	1.27	4.37	92	1.4				
2018	WAS	MLB	26	1	1	0	4	2	12¹	12	3	4.4	8.0	11	42.1%	.265	1.46	6.57	114	0.0	93.0	62.0%	22.0%	51.7%
2019	HBG	AA	27	1	1	0	3	3	11¹	11	1	1.6	8.7	11	36.7%	.345	1.15	4.76	114	-0.1				
2019	FRE	AAA	27	3	5	0	12	12	61¹	68	7	2.2	10.0	68	40.8%	.345	1.35	4.40	75	1.8				
2019	WAS	MLB	27	2	1	0	9	8	43²	33	5	2.7	9.1	44	36.8%	.259	1.05	3.30	83	0.8	94.6	60.5%	28.8%	49.7%
2020	WAS	MLB	28	2	5	0	11	11	49²	57	14	3.3	8.0	44	29.6%	.297	1.51	6.34	159	-1.1	93.6	60.8%	22.2%	49.4%
2021 FS	WAS	MLB	29	8	9	0	26	26	150	149	30	3.2	8.2	137	34.7%	.285	1.35	4.90	111	0.1	93.9	60.8%	24.3%	49.6%
2021 DC	WAS	MLB	29	5	6	0	40	16	93	92	18	3.2	8.2	85	34.7%	.285	1.35	4.90	111	0.3	93.9	60.8%	24.3%	49.6%

Comparables: Alec Mills, Mike Wright, Chris Stratton

Mike Rizzo likes to say that starting pitching wins championships. It certainly worked for the Nationals in 2019, riding four reliable starters (and two bullpen arms) to ascend to baseball's highest peak. It's unclear what Voth's pitching is going to win him or anyone else, other than, perhaps, a ticket back to the minors. His cutter and curve didn't fool hitters, and his ability to find the zone at all wavered. But given the shortened season, dearth of usable arms and the vacancies created by Strasburg and Ross, Voth was nonetheless able to make it through the year without losing his rotation spot. Don't expect that to remain the case heading into 2021.

Austen Williams RHP Born: 12/19/92 Age: 28 Bats: R Throws: R Height: 6'3" Weight: 220 Origin: Round 6, 2014 Draft (#184 overall)

YEAR	TEAM	LVL	AGE	W	L	SV	G	GS	IP	H	HR	BB/9	K/9	K	GB%	BABIP	WHIP	ERA	DRA-	WARP	MPH	FA%	Whiff%	CSP
2018	HBG	AA	25	3	3	1	24	2	51²	34	0	2.3	12.0	69	51.2%	.286	0.91	1.39	52	1.5				
2018	SYR	AAA	25	0	0	1	8	0	16¹	6	0	2.2	11.0	20	58.8%	.176	0.61	0.55	52	0.5				
2018	WAS	MLB	25	0	1	0	10	0	9²	10	5	5.6	7.4	8	20.0%	.208	1.66	5.59	135	-0.1	95.7	53.4%	31.2%	40.6%
2019	HBG	AA	26	0	1	0	5	0	5¹	8	0	5.1	11.8	7	33.3%	.500	2.06	10.12	139	-0.1				
2019	WAS	MLB	26	0	0	0	2	0	0¹	5	2	27.0	27.0	1	40.0%	1.000	18.00	162.00	95	0.0	93.1	37.9%	33.3%	27.2%
2021 FS	WAS	MLB	28	2	2	0	57	0	50	46	7	3.5	8.7	48	40.6%	.287	1.31	4.04	96	0.2	95.1	49.6%	31.8%	37.2%

Comparables: Kevin McGowan, Erick Fedde, Matt Purke

Williams was unseen in 2020 and will remain so in '21 after undergoing Tommy John surgery in the summer. He's got just 12 MLB appearances to his name and probably won't pitch again until he's 29, if he does at all.

BALTIMORE ORIOLES

Essay by Bradford William Davis

Player comments by Jake Mintz and BP staff

Fans of a certain age can probably remember a time where the Orioles were Major League Baseball's model franchise. (That person is not me; not because I'm TikTok young, but because I'm not Methodist-church-bowling-club old.) From 1966 through 1983, they won three titles, six pennants and finished over .500 every single year. They achieved the idyllic, sustained run of contention that has become en vogue for every team, ranging from the Rays to the Hal Steinbrenner-owned Yankees, where not an excess dollar is spent on personnel—and, preferably, considerably less than that.

The more recent editions of the Orioles are the league's model franchise in a different sense—rather than being trendsetters or trailblazers, they're copycatters following the same template every franchise has since Jeff Luhnow launched the Houston Astros into the championship echelon. There's nothing particularly new or original in the Luhnowian blueprint: the first few years entail trading veterans for prospects, losing games, collecting high draft picks—and then, eventually, winning. And, if you don't start winning, your prospects have become veterans, so you can just repeat the cycle.

The five-year plan has become the accepted term for rebuilding, to the point of appearing non-negotiable . What the Orioles have done is just the same thing as the Astros (and other imitators since), only harder—they've stripped down further, cutting closer to the bone than any franchise before them. It's not just the beloved veterans who have been sacrificed for progress; every spot on the roster, down to the arbitration-eligible infield, has been robbed of any hint of copper. Rebuilding has *always* been an ugly business; the Orioles are tearing the veil, right before placing the veil on waivers.

Ⓜ   Ⓜ   Ⓜ

After cratering in the form of an abysmal 47-win season in 2018, the Orioles axed Dan Duquette, the architect of three playoff teams. In his place, Baltimore hired Mike Elias from Houston, where he had witnessed Luhnow stripmining the big-league roster only to do a bang, bang, bang-up job of remaking the Astros into a perennial title contender.

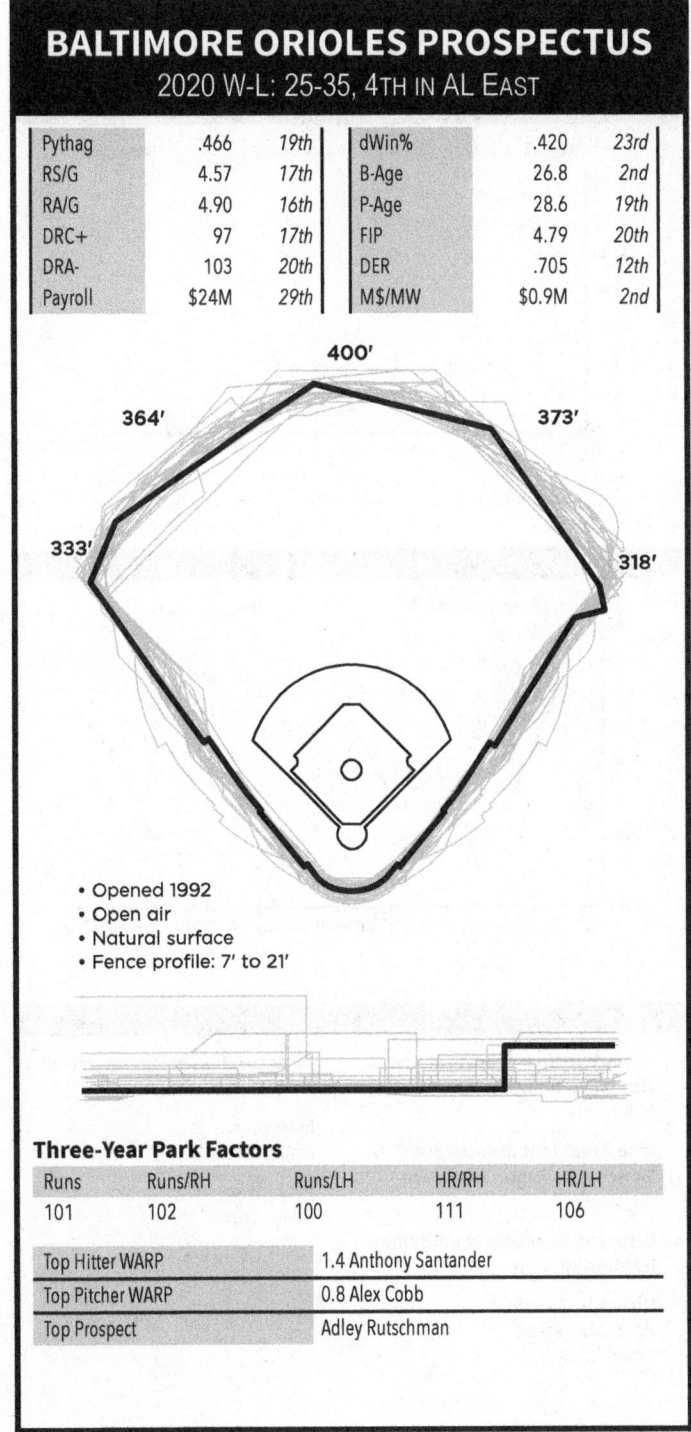

BALTIMORE ORIOLES PROSPECTUS
2020 W-L: 25-35, 4TH IN AL EAST

Pythag	.466	19th	dWin%	.420	23rd
RS/G	4.57	17th	B-Age	26.8	2nd
RA/G	4.90	16th	P-Age	28.6	19th
DRC+	97	17th	FIP	4.79	20th
DRA-	103	20th	DER	.705	12th
Payroll	$24M	29th	M$/MW	$0.9M	2nd

- Opened 1992
- Open air
- Natural surface
- Fence profile: 7' to 21'

Three-Year Park Factors

Runs	Runs/RH	Runs/LH	HR/RH	HR/LH
101	102	100	111	106

Top Hitter WARP	1.4 Anthony Santander
Top Pitcher WARP	0.8 Alex Cobb
Top Prospect	Adley Rutschman

Payroll History (in millions)

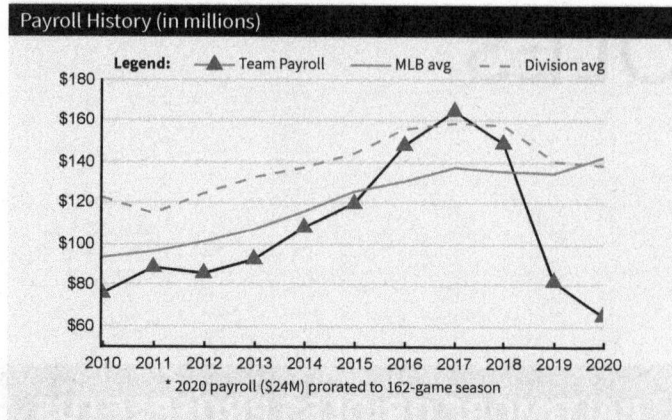

Legend: ▲ Team Payroll — MLB avg - - Division avg

* 2020 payroll ($24M) prorated to 162-game season

Future Commitments (in millions)

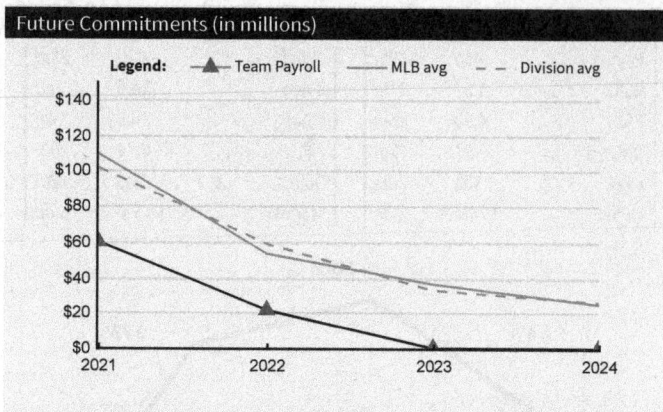

Legend: ▲ Team Payroll — MLB avg - - Division avg

Farm System Ranking

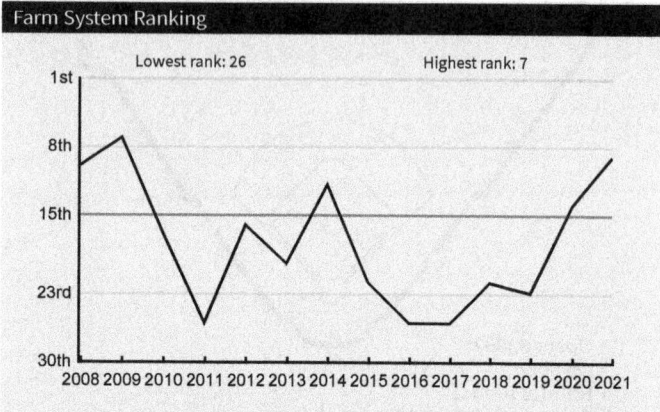

Lowest rank: 26   Highest rank: 7

Personnel

Executive Vice President and General Manager
Mike Elias

Vice President & Assistant General Manager, Analytics
Sig Mejdal

Director, Baseball Development
Eve Rosenbaum

Director, Baseball Administration
Kevin Buck

Director, Player Development
Matt Blood

Manager
Brandon Hyde

BP Alumni
Kevin Carter

By the time Elias took the helm, there wasn't much left to raze. Manny Machado, the best player fielded by the previous regime, had already been traded to the Dodgers. Closer Zack Britton had been shipped to the Yankees. Adam Jones, who had exercised his no-trade clause to remain in town, was a free agent, but Elias showed little interest in retaining the fan favorite as he approached the twilight of his starry career. Too many of the vets who remained, like first baseman Chris Davis and righty Alex Cobb, were ineffective major leaguers making tens of millions more than anyone wanted to pay them.

The Orioles might be further along in their rebuild had they received any surefire big-league pieces in return. Of the eight combined players they added during their 2018 firesale, only Dillon Tate has shown promise at the big-league level. (Outfielder Yusniel Diaz and pitcher Dean Kremer haven't received much of an opportunity yet.) That wasn't Elias' fault. Predictably, he cleared out everything from Duquette's tenure, from competitive payrolls to dozens of front office staff.

All that remains from 2018 was the org's uncanny ability to get finessed by their trade partners, giving up players they failed to evaluate or develop. Though it sounds absurd, Elias entered spring 2019 with two players in the organization who would go on to finish in the top-10 in 2020 Cy Young and Most Valuable Player Award voting, in right-hander Dylan Bundy and outfielder Mike Yastrzemski. He traded each without getting a substantive return.

Bundy became the latest face—displacing Jake Arrieta and Kevin Gausman—of the *Pitchers of Baltimore vs. The Orioles* class action lawsuit by making good on his promise. He turned around his mediocre-to-date career by flourishing with an Angels organization that isn't known for being a pitching factory. Yastrzemski, meanwhile, didn't unlock the recessive gene that made his grandfather a Hall of Famer until he arrived in San Francisco; nü-Yaz has since hit .281/.357/.535 with 31 home runs in 161 games. If only he put up those numbers while wearing the *other* orange and black, the Orioles might have a budding star on their hands. If only they'd given him some playing time to find out what they had.

Most of Elias' problems are ones that he inherited, yes, but he's yet to fix them. Look, he and Sig Mejdal and company were the ones who bought all those Edgertronic cameras and authored all those SQL scripts—getting talented players in the organization to become their best selves is part of their mandate. Their inability to do so goes hand in hand with self-evaluation (or lack thereof) and getting fleeced in trades. There's a feedback loop at play: the players Baltimore trades are bad because they were trained by Baltimore, and the players they receive are bad because they are now subject to the cruel punishment of being trained by Baltimore. If you can't make your own players good, how can you expect to get anything from them? And, further, how can the Astros plan work if the prospects you draft and acquire are never likely to live up to their potential with your organization?

Optimizing the return on players has been an issue for Elias. The last big trade he made in 2019—dumping Jonathan Villar, who they intended to non-tender, on the Marlins for his final year of team control—saw the Orioles recoup a lesser prospect than what the Marlins were able to convert Villar into at the following deadline ... and that was with him having a miserable season at the plate.

What separates these Orioles from other rebuilding teams—even those fully attuned to the guiding force that is The Process—is their indifference to both the literal victories and the symbolic. Most front offices would have touted Villar—or, more recently—José Iglesias, Renato Núñez and Hanser Alberto, a trio that contributed nearly three Wins Above Replacement in 2020 after being added for scraps, as their vision's proof of concept. Not these Orioles, not under Elias.

Iglesias was Baltimore's top hitter, slashing .373/.400/.556 while providing good defense at shortstop. The Orioles waited until the last minute to exercise his affordable club option, however, and then spun him off to the Angels for two prospects who were not considered among the best in a fairly weak system—albeit one that the Orioles seemingly favor more than the consensus. Núñez and Alberto somehow received even less of a gracious sendoff. They were both non-tendered at season's end—that despite Núñez homering 50 times in 263 career games with Baltimore, and the versatile Alberto running his two-year line with the Orioles to .299/.322/.413.

The Orioles could have kept all three players at a reasonable cost: optimistic arbitration projections for Núñez and Alberto had the trio making less than $12 million combined. Yet Elias deemed that to be too much to pay per win. This isn't a bug of The Process so much as it is a feature: you may not win games, but you will keep your job by saving your owner money.

⚾   ⚾   ⚾

The game has changed since the Earl Weaver's glory days. Front offices have Cerebro-level access to data and sophisticated tools with which to synthesize information (in part due to publications like this one). Because there's less mystery about what makes a baseball player good or bad, there's more rational (and supposedly accurate) appraisals of the on-field value said player brings to your team. It's nerdy as hell. But, no shade—math is power. After all, it was math (granted, the back-of-the-napkin kind) that made Weaver's three-run homer and platoon-heavy strategies so effective in their time.

The great paradox of the modern game is that the infusion of science and math has disguised its own dark age, where anticompetiveness has run amok. The undergirding philosophy behind how such data is interpreted and wielded favors keeping as much money as possible in the pocket of team owners, as do the rules (formal or otherwise) for accumulating baseball talent. Such an imbalance provides an acceptable pretext for trading, say, Mookie Betts, of whom there is only one, for a handful of players who cannot hit, field, throw or run as well as Mookie, but, to their credit, are currently exempt from federal wage law. Why not, when the last shall be first in payroll efficiency, and the weak inherit the Earth's best young players in the draft?

Of course, what's less talked about in regards to tanking is that the more socially acceptable it becomes—and it's en vogue at present—the less effective it is as a strategy. That's how the Orioles posted their second-worst record ever and yet they still finished second in the Spencer Torkelson sweepstakes. At least there's always a consolation prize: Even those teams who don't fail hard enough save money.

Without tracing the path from Adam Smith to Charlie Finley to Stuart Sternberg, none of this is new, and it may not even be more nefarious. Just more deft. The language of choice used to convey these strategies is no longer seasoned in jargon picked up on backfields, but in corporate boardrooms. Everything is about probabilistic analysis; optionality; or sustainability, a word whose meaning is in the eyes of whoever reads it last, usually from a sleek Powerpoint slide.

What I'm saying is this: Orioles are not alone, and there are more than enough bird brains to go around.

⚾   ⚾   ⚾

Unless you're Jake Mintz—an O's fan who would gladly elbow Jeffrey Maier in the solar plexus if it meant redeeming the past—you didn't need PECOTA to predict that the 2020 Orioles weren't making the playoffs. The Orioles were projected to go 22-38 over the pandemic-shortened season. Prorated over a normal season, that's a 58- or 59-win pace—abysmal by any standards except their own. But then, a funny thing happened: the Orioles won some games, going 12-8 out of the gate, succeeding against the Red Sox and the Nationals, the last two champions.

Anthony Santander, one of the young guys in their Maybe Talented Enough to Trade in Arbitration bucket, posted a 139 DRC+—a product of cutting down on strikeouts by leaning into his youthful aggression in the strike zone. Alex Cobb regained some of his old luster, and the rest of the pitching staff—a medley of create-a-players to the average fan—were ordinarily mediocre (4.51 ERA) instead of Gleyber Torres' personal batting practice tossers. Chris Davis even joined the party, and drove in a run.

A 12-8 start doesn't have incredible diagnostic merit. But when the season is 60 games long, who cares? That's doubly so when the usual postseason size was boosted from 10 to 16 teams, an attempt to add extra TV revenue to mitigate the loss of gate receipts. Contention is a social construct.

Besides, those 12 wins were in the bank, and not even the Orioles could negatively regress their win total. They tried their best, however, playing themselves down to a 14-19 record entering the August 31 trade deadline. And so, they did what they always do, even if they don't particularly do it well. They threw their stuff on a tarp on the lawn, and they sold.

The odds for maintaining or augmenting weren't in their favor, for understandable reasons. The on-paper talent was bad, and ominously playing to their projections. Though they were in closer position to a playoff seed than expected, they still would have had to leapfrog at least two of the three teams immediately ahead of them: the Tigers, Blue Jays and Twins. It would be all too easy to point at the spreadsheets and shrug helplessly.

However, by the same points or their direct corollary, 2020 was the best opportunity to try something. Consider that the market for decent players who could mitigate an impending regression was in their favor—the low cost the Jays, a team they were in direct competition with (well, you know ... sorta) for a playoff spot rented Taijuan Walker, Robbie Ray and Villar. There was minimal cost to getting better, with little chance in significantly harming their long-term outlook. The Orioles should know this intimately because they were the sellers in a buyer's market, shipping off relievers Mychal Givens and Miguel Castro in separate deals to Colorado and the Mets, and sending Opening Day starter—really; you could look it up—Tommy Milone to the Braves.

Though all three were performing reasonably well for Baltimore, none were world-beaters. The Castro trade was specifically odd all the same, given that, at least from one perspective, he was the kind of young, developing cost-controlled talent the Orioles are and were supposed to be adding to their ranks. Just 25 and blessed with a live arm and a huge jump in strikeout rate, he's the type of player that rebuilding teams generally collect in payment. In return for Castro, they received Kevin Smith, a player believed to be a future number five starter if everything breaks right.

Worse, 2020, in all its chaos, provided case studies of the present reward of a bad team going for it, and the risk of shying away. Look at the Marlins. Miami was not only competing with the Orioles for the top pick in the 2019 draft, they had various factors working against their efforts to be competitive in 2020—namely, being dramatically outscored on the season and serving as MLB's first COVID-19 outbreak. Nonetheless, the Marlins added Starling Marte to their team, qualified for the funky, phony postseason format, and then made the most of it by defeating a much stronger Cubs squad.

Meanwhile, the Orioles were, as they have been so many times, a cautionary tale. They had stripped down their roster so thoroughly that there was little left to trade, and thus, little to get back. Regardless, they tried to rev up their tank. Like all their other endeavors, they failed at their goal, this time via on-field success. By ripping off a hot streak that had them in the waning days of the season in the one position they emphatically did not want: contention.

⚾   ⚾   ⚾

The wretched con of Major League Baseball in 2020—the one the Orioles are three years into clumsily attempting to exploit—is that its competitive structure is increasingly based on moral hazards. This is not exclusive to Baltimore's station within the league. Slide up the win curve and you can watch the reigning pennant winner trade their homegrown ace two months to the date of him pitching them a few outs away of Game 7. Or, a reigning division champ tossing away the Cy Young runner-up in a salary dump. Like every team selling off their good to great players, they will blame it on an unprecedented revenue dip from the pandemic while refusing to discuss how their decades of record profits factor into their decision making. Team social media accounts boast about cost control they received from trading superstars instead of employing them. "IYKYK" (if you know you know), we were told.

Well, WK.

Luck is the residue of design, sure, but what does it say about a franchise that sees good luck as an impairment instead of a chance to accelerate? And what does it say about a league that not only permits such a design fueled by blind, inflexible subservience to projections, but promotes it?

We're seeing this across the league, but especially in Baltimore, where hubris is veiled as humility, costing Baltimore their best chance at being worth anyone's time for the foreseeable future. When your only rubric is probabilistic thinking performed in service of profitability the only possible end is a self-fulfilling prophecy. There's no going for the gold unless one can get it appraised beforehand. Great game we have here. ∎

—Bradford William Davis is a columnist at the New York Daily News.

HITTERS

Hanser Alberto 2B
Born: 10/17/92   Age: 28   Bats: R   Throws: R   Height: 5'11"   Weight: 215   Origin: International Free Agent, 2009

YEAR	TEAM	LVL	AGE	PA	R	2B	3B	HR	RBI	BB	K	SB	CS	Whiff%	AVG/OBP/SLG	DRC+	BABIP	BRR	FRAA	WARP
2018	RR	AAA	25	384	45	17	3	7	58	9	28	0	3		.330/.346/.452	111	.337	-0.8	SS(44): 7.1, 1B(43): -3.5, 2B(9): 1.7	1.5
2018	TEX	MLB	25	30	0	2	0	0	0	2	4	0	1	23.4%	.185/.241/.259	88	.217	-0.4	SS(5): 0.1, 2B(4): -0.1, 3B(3): -0.0	0.0
2019	BAL	MLB	26	550	62	21	2	12	51	16	50	4	4	14.5%	.305/.329/.422	97	.318	1.6	2B(90): -5.0, 3B(66): 5.3, LF(3): -0.1	2.0
2020	BAL	MLB	28	231	35	15	0	3	22	5	30	3	0	17.1%	.283/.306/.393	85	.314	0.2	2B(52): -3.2, 3B(5): 0.6	0.2
2021 FS	BAL	MLB	28	600	64	24	1	14	57	18	88	3	2	15.7%	.265/.294/.389	84	.292	-2.2	2B -2, 3B 3	0.1

Comparables: Jose Lopez, Mel Roach, Jerry Adair

There were more egregious examples of deplorable thriftiness across the league on a depressing non-tender deadline day, but the Birds cutting bait with their leadoff hitter to save a few million still deserves a heavy, exasperated, "MLB's economic system is seriously screwed up" sigh. Alberto is a beautifully flawed player; in 2020 he had the league's fourth-worst average exit velocity and one of its best strikeout rates, and he absolutely crushed lefties. That bizarre offensive profile, plus his average defense at second and third makes him the epitome of a league-average player—something of which the 2021 Orioles could use a few. He was a fan favorite: a distinctive, watchable baseball man and a reason to turn on MASN. Alberto probably wasn't going to be a member of the next good Orioles team, but he still should have been a member of the next bad Orioles team. Chances are he makes it through next season with two strikeouts, no batted balls over 85 mph and a .400 average against lefties. Chapeau, Hanser.

Rylan Bannon 2B Born: 04/22/96   Age: 25   Bats: R   Throws: R   Height: 5'8"   Weight: 180   Origin: Round 8, 2017 Draft (#250 overall)

YEAR	TEAM	LVL	AGE	PA	R	2B	3B	HR	RBI	BB	K	SB	CS	Whiff%	AVG/OBP/SLG	DRC+	BABIP	BRR	FRAA	WARP
2018	RC	HI-A	22	403	58	17	6	20	61	59	103	4	4		.296/.402/.559	160	.367	0.0	3B(54): 2.9, 2B(22): 0.2	2.9
2018	BOW	AA	22	122	16	6	0	2	11	22	24	0	0		.204/.344/.327	99	.243	-1.4	2B(30): -0.9, 3B(2): -0.1	-0.1
2019	BOW	AA	23	444	45	22	4	8	42	47	72	8	4		.255/.345/.394	124	.294	-0.4	3B(69): 1.8, 2B(38): 1.4	2.8
2019	NOR	AAA	23	90	18	10	0	3	17	3	14	0	1		.317/.344/.549	119	.338	-0.3	3B(20): 3.1	0.7
2021 FS	BAL	MLB	25	600	66	26	2	19	65	53	162	1	0		.233/.310/.401	93	.298	0.6	2B 0, 3B 3	1.3
2021 DC	BAL	MLB	25	98	10	4	0	3	10	8	26	0	0		.233/.310/.401	93	.298	0.1	2B 0, 3B 0	0.3

Comparables: Jefry Marte, Taylor Green, James Darnell

As a 5-foot-8 utility infielder who hasn't played any shortstop and isn't dynamic on defense, Bannon has to show he can hit high-level pitching to be more than a bench bat. There've been flashes of raw power and he held his own in Triple-A in 2019, but struggled in the Fall League afterwards. He should see the majors in 2021.

Chris Davis 1B Born: 03/17/86   Age: 35   Bats: L   Throws: R   Height: 6'3"   Weight: 245   Origin: Round 5, 2006 Draft (#148 overall)

YEAR	TEAM	LVL	AGE	PA	R	2B	3B	HR	RBI	BB	K	SB	CS	Whiff%	AVG/OBP/SLG	DRC+	BABIP	BRR	FRAA	WARP
2018	BAL	MLB	32	522	40	12	0	16	49	41	192	2	0	34.4%	.168/.243/.296	56	.237	-4.6	1B(116): -5.4	-3.2
2019	BAL	MLB	33	352	26	9	0	12	36	39	139	0	0	38.0%	.179/.276/.326	64	.270	0.7	1B(97): -4.6, RF(1): -0.6, P(1): -0.0	-1.5
2020	BAL	MLB	34	55	3	3	0	0	1	3	17	0	0	36.8%	.115/.164/.173	65	.171	0.1	1B(15): 1.6	-0.1
2021 FS	BAL	MLB	35	600	60	20	1	20	59	66	226	1	0	36.6%	.188/.288/.349	73	.282	-0.7	1B -6, 3B 0	-1.9
2021 DC	BAL	MLB	35	131	13	4	0	4	13	14	49	0	0	36.6%	.188/.288/.349	73	.282	-0.2	1B -1	-0.4

Comparables: Mike Napoli, Tony Clark, Dave Kingman

Davis' infamous 0-for-54 start to the 2019 season was big news. For the final 20 plate appearances or so of that streak, the whole baseball community was tuned in to every start as the Slugger Formerly Known as Chris Davis flailed his way into the history books. Davis became the sport's biggest meme, its most tragic punchline. Eventually he roped a single into left field off Rick Porcello, and suddenly he was merely the worst hitter in baseball. The baseball world had moved on.

Davis was just as inept in 2020. No one cared. Watching him hit gave off the vibe of living among the ruins of ancient Greece: you know something grand once stood there, something awe-inspiring, but now you're just sleeping on rocks. It must be emphasized that he was once a majestic baseball thing, a mountain with forearms of stone, capable of depositing baseballs into new zip codes. To fall like he's fallen, you've got to reach a certain height in the first place. He was basically phantom IL'ed for the last month-plus of the season, tallying only three at-bats after August 18th. There's been chatter about a buyout, some muttering about how Crush has played his last game, despite the two years left on his contract. Who knows what the future holds, but if this truly is the end, a hefty kudos to a man who reached unimaginable highs and unwatchable lows, but through it all went back out there each day and tried to smack the crap out of the ball.

Yusniel Diaz RF Born: 10/07/96   Age: 24   Bats: R   Throws: R   Height: 6'1"   Weight: 210   Origin: International Free Agent, 2015

YEAR	TEAM	LVL	AGE	PA	R	2B	3B	HR	RBI	BB	K	SB	CS	Whiff%	AVG/OBP/SLG	DRC+	BABIP	BRR	FRAA	WARP
2018	BOW	AA	21	152	23	5	1	5	15	18	28	4	5		.239/.329/.403	96	.267	-0.5	RF(29): 0.3, CF(6): -0.5	-0.1
2018	TUL	AA	21	264	36	10	4	6	30	41	39	8	8		.314/.428/.477	159	.360	1.8	CF(29): -1.7, RF(28): -1.6, LF(2): -0.5	1.5
2019	FRE	HI-A	22	25	0	0	0	0	2	3	7	0	0		.273/.360/.273	88	.400	-0.6	CF(5): -0.4	-0.1
2019	BOW	AA	22	322	45	19	4	11	53	32	67	0	3		.262/.335/.472	150	.303	0.6	RF(53): 1.4, CF(5): 0.3, LF(2): 0.1	2.5
2021 FS	BAL	MLB	24	600	68	26	3	20	68	54	161	6	3		.245/.317/.420	99	.312	-1.9	LF 2, CF 0	1.6
2021 DC	BAL	MLB	24	131	15	5	0	4	15	11	35	1	0		.245/.317/.420	99	.312	-0.4	LF 1	0.3

Comparables: Rene Tosoni, Michael Reed, Domonic Brown

We've reached the point where Díaz's prospect fame almost certainly over-hypes his prospect status. When you smack two dingers in the Futures Game and then become the headliner in a Manny Machado trade days later, your name will hop on the map. And when you're a ripped Cuban dude whose name starts with a Y who got a bunch of money as an amateur ... ooh boy. But in his current state, Díaz has true tweener potential. He's not long for center field (especially in an org with Austin Hays and Cedric Mullins), and evaluators are concerned he won't hit for enough power for the bat to play in a corner. Díaz has a good approach at the plate (check his 14 percent walk rate in LIDOM last year), but the exit velocity numbers are closer to good than great, which just puts a limit on the ceiling and a ton of pressure on the bat. He'll get a a chance in the bigs in 2021 and could be a solid big leaguer, but odds are he's not the super-hyped Machado headliner he once was.

Austin Hays RF   Born: 07/05/95   Age: 26   Bats: R   Throws: R   Height: 6'0"   Weight: 205   Origin: Round 3, 2016 Draft (#91 overall)

YEAR	TEAM	LVL	AGE	PA	R	2B	3B	HR	RBI	BB	K	SB	CS	Whiff%	AVG/OBP/SLG	DRC+	BABIP	BRR	FRAA	WARP
2018	ABD	SS	22	39	6	2	0	0	3	2	7	0	0		.189/.231/.243	92	.233	0.0	RF(5): -0.6	-0.1
2018	BOW	AA	22	288	34	12	2	12	43	12	59	6	3		.242/.271/.432	88	.263	0.9	RF(36): 6.7, LF(16): -0.3, CF(13): -0.1	0.6
2019	FRE	HI-A	23	40	3	0	0	2	6	1	11	0	0		.162/.200/.324	40	.160	0.2	CF(7): -0.7	-0.2
2019	BOW	AA	23	61	9	5	0	3	11	5	11	3	1		.268/.328/.518	142	.286	-1.1	RF(7): 1.2, CF(4): 0.0	0.4
2019	NOR	AAA	23	257	43	16	1	10	27	11	61	6	4		.254/.304/.454	92	.302	4.2	CF(39): 4.8, RF(16): 0.0, LF(1): -0.1	1.3
2019	BAL	MLB	23	75	12	6	0	4	13	7	13	2	0	25.9%	.309/.373/.574	111	.333	0.8	CF(20): 2.3	0.7
2020	BAL	MLB	25	134	20	2	0	4	9	8	25	2	3	20.2%	.279/.328/.393	96	.316	-0.2	CF(23): -0.4, LF(10): 0.4, RF(3): -0.6	0.2
2021 FS	BAL	MLB	25	600	71	25	2	27	74	29	138	5	2	21.7%	.256/.301/.456	101	.295	-0.1	CF 4, LF 0	2.2
2021 DC	BAL	MLB	25	525	62	22	1	24	65	25	120	4	1	21.7%	.256/.301/.456	101	.295	-0.1	CF 3, LF 0	2.0

Comparables: Alex Verdugo, Carl Everett, Dale Murphy

If Derek Jeter is Mr. November and Reggie Jackson is Mr. October, Hays is Mr. September. After a hilariously good final month of 2019 that had Orioles fans doing Mike Trout–related play-index searches, Hays came into 2020 with some real hype. And after leading off in center field against Boston on Opening Day, he had a puncher's chance at becoming The Oriole Your Uncle Has Heard Of™. Alas, it was not to be. A slow start and a fractured rib via HBP caused him to miss a month and lose his job in center to Cedric Mullins. But right when the year seemed lost, Hays returned on September 14 and scorched his way to a .377/.404/.585 slash line with great right field defense over the season's final fortnight. Partially because of the injury and partially due to the pandemic-shortened season, we didn't learn anything new about Hays in 2020. He's still only 25 and can really go get it in the outfield, but there's probably not enough power to play in a corner, which means he'll come into 2021 fighting Mullins for the center field job in a crowded outfield.

Gunnar Henderson SS   Born: 06/29/01   Age: 20   Bats: L   Throws: R   Height: 6'3"   Weight: 195   Origin: Round 2, 2019 Draft (#42 overall)

YEAR	TEAM	LVL	AGE	PA	R	2B	3B	HR	RBI	BB	K	SB	CS	Whiff%	AVG/OBP/SLG	DRC+	BABIP	BRR	FRAA	WARP
2019	ORI	ROK	18	121	21	5	2	1	11	11	28	2	2		.259/.331/.370	64	.338	0.4	SS(21): -1.6	0.0
2021 FS	BAL	MLB	20	600	44	26	3	7	49	31	215	7	3		.206/.252/.304	52	.319	-1.1	SS -1	-2.0

A tall shortstop with big power who will probably slide over to third base sooner rather than later, Henderson is trying to become the first Gunnar in big-league history. Taken with the compensation-round pick after Adley Rutschman went first overall, Henderson went to the Gulf Coast league in 2019 to get his toes into the professional baseball water. Then during the pandemic, the 19-year-old scored a surprising invite to the Orioles' alternate site to face off against baseballers half a decade his elder. Unsurprisingly, he struggled. The BP prospect maestros ranked ol' Gunnar 11th on their team list, but if he shows up in Low-A and rakes, he'll leap up into the top 4 or 5. There's also a chance the swing-and-miss issues manifest themselves further, forcing us to wait even longer for baseball's first Gunnar.

────────────── ★ ★ ★ *2021 Top 101 Prospect* **#66** ★ ★ ★ ──────────────

Heston Kjerstad OF   Born: 02/12/99   Age: 22   Bats: L   Throws: R   Height: 6'3"   Weight: 220   Origin: Round 1, 2020 Draft (#2 overall)

The Orioles surprised prognosticators by taking Kjerstad second overall. But it's not like Elias and Co. snagged a schlub off your local ball field—Kjerstad was on track to be a Golden Spikes finalist. While he lacks the ceiling and premium defensive position you might expect from a no. 2 overall pick, he can really hit. He demolished the best conference in college baseball in his first two seasons and was hitting around .450 with six homers in 16 games before the pandemic happened. His freshman swing was pretty choppy, but he really smoothed things out over his college career without compromising production. He has impressive bat control, with great bat speed and big power. Unless he gets too big and loses speed, he should be able to handle a corner outfield spot. He's a bit overeager at the plate, but who among us wasn't when we were 21? The ideal outcome looks kinda like a taller, harder-to-spell Michael Conforto.

Trey Mancini RF   Born: 03/18/92   Age: 29   Bats: R   Throws: R   Height: 6'4"   Weight: 230   Origin: Round 8, 2013 Draft (#249 overall)

YEAR	TEAM	LVL	AGE	PA	R	2B	3B	HR	RBI	BB	K	SB	CS	Whiff%	AVG/OBP/SLG	DRC+	BABIP	BRR	FRAA	WARP
2018	BAL	MLB	26	636	69	23	3	24	58	44	153	0	1	27.7%	.242/.299/.416	91	.285	0.5	LF(98): 4.5, 1B(47): 2.7	1.5
2019	BAL	MLB	27	679	106	38	2	35	97	63	142	1	0	26.9%	.291/.364/.535	120	.326	-0.9	RF(87): -3.6, 1B(56): 1.7, LF(6): -0.3	2.8
2021 FS	BAL	MLB	29	600	71	23	2	26	76	46	152	0	0	27.2%	.250/.317/.446	102	.301	0.4	1B 0, LF 0	1.6
2021 DC	BAL	MLB	29	459	54	17	1	20	58	35	116	0	0	27.2%	.250/.317/.446	102	.301	0.3	1B 0	1.0

Comparables: Geoff Jenkins, Kevin Reimer, Marcell Ozuna

After a classic "great hitter on bad team" performance in 2019, Mancini missed the entire 2020 season after doctors discovered a tumor in his colon during spring training. Mancini was diagnosed with stage 3 colon cancer and underwent chemotherapy. He finished up treatments in late September, and O's GM Mike Elias indicated that the club expects Mancini to be ready to go next season. One of two remaining members from Baltimore's last postseason team in 2016 (*sigh* Chris Davis is the other), Mancini could be the only guy to bridge the gap between two different eras of good Baltimore teams. Don't forget there was a good reason he was the only Oriole you'd heard of—Mancini can flat-out hit. He had a higher OPS in 2019 than Bryce Harper, DJ LeMahieu and Max Muncy. Whatever 2021 brings for him on the field, the important thing is that Mancini won his showdown with cancer and appears to be on the road back to the diamond.

Richie Martin SS Born: 12/22/94 Age: 26 Bats: R Throws: R Height: 5'11" Weight: 190 Origin: Round 1, 2015 Draft (#20 overall)

YEAR	TEAM	LVL	AGE	PA	R	2B	3B	HR	RBI	BB	K	SB	CS	Whiff%	AVG/OBP/SLG	DRC+	BABIP	BRR	FRAA	WARP
2018	MID	AA	23	509	68	29	8	6	42	44	86	25	10		.300/.368/.439	119	.357	-0.3	SS(96): 9.1, 2B(21): 1.0	3.0
2019	BAL	MLB	24	309	29	8	3	6	23	14	83	10	1	28.5%	.208/.260/.322	50	.272	-0.9	SS(117): -0.8	-0.7
2021 FS	BAL	MLB	26	600	56	19	3	11	52	40	163	12	4	28.5%	.212/.282/.324	67	.282	4.2	SS -3, 2B 0	-0.4
2021 DC	BAL	MLB	26	262	24	8	1	4	23	17	71	5	1	28.5%	.212/.282/.324	67	.282	1.8	SS -1	-0.2

Comparables: Felix Escalona, Tom Matchick, Benji Gil

A stellar glove and speedy shoes have always been stowed safely in Martin's locker. A 2020 spent rehabbing a broken wrist hopefully gave him some time to search for his missing bat.

Ryan McKenna CF Born: 02/14/97 Age: 24 Bats: R Throws: R Height: 5'11" Weight: 185 Origin: Round 4, 2015 Draft (#133 overall)

YEAR	TEAM	LVL	AGE	PA	R	2B	3B	HR	RBI	BB	K	SB	CS	Whiff%	AVG/OBP/SLG	DRC+	BABIP	BRR	FRAA	WARP
2018	FRE	HI-A	21	301	60	18	2	8	37	37	45	5	6		.377/.467/.556	210	.436	2.5	CF(64): -6.2, LF(2): -0.2	3.4
2018	BOW	AA	21	250	35	8	2	3	16	29	56	4	1		.239/.341/.338	90	.312	2.6	CF(55): 3.4, RF(3): 2.1, LF(2): -0.4	0.9
2019	BOW	AA	22	567	78	26	6	9	54	59	121	25	11		.232/.321/.365	111	.287	1.9	CF(98): -4.1, LF(19): 0.6, RF(11): 0.9	2.3
2021 FS	BAL	MLB	24	600	63	25	2	14	59	52	174	10	3		.228/.306/.369	86	.309	0.8	CF -5, LF 0	0.5
2021 DC	BAL	MLB	24	32	3	1	0	0	3	2	9	0	0		.228/.306/.369	86	.309	0.0	CF 0	0.0

Comparables: Rey Fuentes, Michael Bourn, Brian Goodwin

With no minor-league season in 2020, we're forced to read into team decisions to determine what is up with prospects. McKenna, who spent all of 2019 in Double-A, figured to at least get a taste in the majors. Instead, he spent the whole year down at the alternate site. That probably had something to do with service-time tricks, as well as Cedric Mullins and Anthony Santander being way better than expected. The takeaway:even though McKenna remains a promising prospect who can play center and show average power, his bat wasn't electric enough in 2019 or 2020 to force a call-up. He's more physical than you'd expect from a 5-foot-11, 180-pound frame, and all his tools grade out around average. McKenna is almost certainly due for a debut in 2021, but he might find playing time tough to come by depending on how Mullins and Austin Hays (two other center fielders ahead of him on the pecking order) perform.

★ ★ ★ *2021 Top 101 Prospect* **#28** ★ ★ ★

Ryan Mountcastle 1B Born: 02/18/97 Age: 24 Bats: R Throws: R Height: 6'3" Weight: 210 Origin: Round 1, 2015 Draft (#36 overall)

YEAR	TEAM	LVL	AGE	PA	R	2B	3B	HR	RBI	BB	K	SB	CS	Whiff%	AVG/OBP/SLG	DRC+	BABIP	BRR	FRAA	WARP
2018	BOW	AA	21	428	63	19	4	13	59	26	79	2	0		.297/.341/.464	117	.339	-1.5	3B(81): -4.9	0.8
2019	NOR	AAA	22	553	81	35	1	25	83	24	130	2	1		.312/.344/.527	114	.370	-0.9	1B(84): -6.1, LF(26): 2.1, 3B(9): -0.1	1.3
2020	BAL	MLB	23	140	12	5	0	5	23	11	30	0	1	29.2%	.333/.386/.492	104	.398	-0.9	LF(25): -1.7, 1B(10): 0.3	0.0
2021 FS	BAL	MLB	24	600	66	26	2	24	79	28	150	1	0	29.2%	.262/.302/.445	97	.318	-0.3	1B -2, LF -4	0.4
2021 DC	BAL	MLB	24	558	61	24	1	22	74	26	140	1	0	29.2%	.262/.302/.445	97	.318	-0.3	1B -2, LF -4	0.3

Comparables: Dayan Viciedo, Wes Bankston, Brett Wallace

It feels like Mountcastle has been an Orioles prospect since the Ripken days, yet he somehow remains a rookie heading into 2021, despite a 35-game debut campaign. Mountcastle was drafted in the same first round as Alex Bregman and Dansby Swanson, both of whom carry been-around-a-long-while vibes. But after a half-decade in the minors, the Hilltop Fortress finally got his first big-league taste and was superb. You'd bet against him hitting .330 every season, but he's absolutely a Just Knows How To Hit guy who could tickle the .300 mark for the next 10 years. The upside is limited, as he lacks elite exit velocity, swings and misses a tad too much and is underwhelming no matter where he stands in the field. That said, Mountcastle is probably reason no. 1 to actively watch and get excited about the 2021 Orioles.

Cedric Mullins CF Born: 10/01/94 Age: 26 Bats: S Throws: L Height: 5'8" Weight: 175 Origin: Round 13, 2015 Draft (#403 overall)

YEAR	TEAM	LVL	AGE	PA	R	2B	3B	HR	RBI	BB	K	SB	CS	Whiff%	AVG/OBP/SLG	DRC+	BABIP	BRR	FRAA	WARP
2018	BOW	AA	23	218	36	12	5	6	28	15	28	9	1		.313/.362/.512	134	.339	2.4	CF(43): 0.4, LF(2): 0.5	1.5
2018	NOR	AAA	23	269	41	17	3	6	19	22	39	12	0		.269/.333/.438	117	.298	2.2	CF(60): 0.2	1.3
2018	BAL	MLB	23	191	23	9	0	4	11	17	37	2	3	18.2%	.235/.312/.359	82	.279	-0.6	CF(45): -3.8, LF(1): -0.0	-0.2
2019	BOW	AA	24	226	35	11	0	5	18	22	31	20	3		.271/.341/.402	127	.293	2.8	CF(31): 0.9, LF(19): 0.1	1.7
2019	NOR	AAA	24	306	40	8	2	5	24	25	51	13	4		.205/.272/.306	50	.231	1.8	CF(56): 4.1, LF(6): -0.6	-0.3
2019	BAL	MLB	24	74	7	0	2	0	4	4	14	1	0	28.4%	.094/.181/.156	56	.118	0.5	CF(22): 1.4	0.0
2020	BAL	MLB	26	153	16	4	3	3	12	8	37	7	2	22.8%	.271/.315/.407	67	.350	0.5	CF(41): 5.1, LF(4): -0.1, RF(-0.5)	0.4
2021 FS	BAL	MLB	26	600	64	23	4	16	56	41	140	15	4	22.7%	.230/.289/.377	79	.280	6.2	CF 6, LF 0	1.4
2021 DC	BAL	MLB	26	262	28	10	1	7	24	18	61	6	1	22.7%	.230/.289/.377	79	.280	2.7	CF 2, LF 0	0.6

Comparables: Sil Campusano, Milt Cuyler, Cory Sullivan

After a putrid 2019 season in the bigs and bouncing around various Orioles eastern seaboard affiliates, Mullins was a bit of an afterthought heading into 2020. Then, an Austin Hays injury led to a lot of Mullins playing time, and he took advantage. The first thing to know is that he's stupendous in center. Questions about his bat remain. If he can keep his OPS in the .700-plus range and perform on the basepaths, he's César Hernández but with top-tier defense in center. That's a pretty good player. But it's important to keep in mind that the difference between that and Billy Hamilton is a slippery slope.

Renato Núñez 3B Born: 04/04/94 Age: 27 Bats: R Throws: R Height: 6'1" Weight: 220 Origin: International Free Agent, 2010

YEAR	TEAM	LVL	AGE	PA	R	2B	3B	HR	RBI	BB	K	SB	CS	Whiff%	AVG/OBP/SLG	DRC+	BABIP	BRR	FRAA	WARP
2018	NAS	AAA	24	30	3	0	0	0	4	2	6	0	0		.357/.400/.357	104	.455	-0.5	3B(2): -0.2, LF(2): -0.5, 1B(1): 0.3	0.0
2018	NOR	AAA	24	228	25	14	1	5	25	23	49	1	0		.289/.361/.443	129	.356	0.8	3B(38): 0.1, 1B(6): 0.6	1.2
2018	TEX	MLB	24	41	2	1	0	1	2	3	12	0	0	32.0%	.167/.244/.278	94	.208	-0.2	3B(8): 0.9, LF(4): -0.2	0.2
2018	BAL	MLB	24	220	26	13	0	7	20	16	50	0	0	31.2%	.275/.336/.445	95	.333	-0.8	3B(59): -4.0	0.2
2019	BAL	MLB	25	599	72	24	0	31	90	44	142	1	1	27.4%	.244/.311/.460	99	.272	-2.1	1B(24): -1.9, 3B(9): 0.0, LF(1): -0.0	0.6
2020	BAL	MLB	26	216	29	10	0	12	31	17	64	0	0	30.1%	.256/.324/.492	104	.317	-0.8	1B(28): -3.0, 3B(4): 0.3	0.1
2021 FS	BAL	MLB	27	600	70	21	1	30	82	45	170	0	0	28.7%	.236/.305/.446	98	.287	-0.7	3B -3, LF -6	0.1

Comparables: Ryan Shealy, Bob Chance, Mike Jacobs

He eclipsed 1,000 plate appearances in 2020 (becoming the 3,658th MLB player ever to reach that plateau), so we feel confident about the following declaration: Núñez is an average major-league hitter. He's got big-boy power and plasters mistakes in the zone. Since the start of 2019, he has more homers than Paul Goldschmidt, Rhys Hoskins, J.D. Martinez and Carlos Santana, despite trailing all of those guys in plate appearances. This would all be cause for excitement if he could play defense like Evan White or Evan Longoria or even Evan Rachel Wood. Unfortunately, he plays defense like a rock-em-sock-em robot actually made out of rocks. His upper and lower halves refuse to work together. They aren't even on speaking terms. He's got brick-and-mortar hands, firm as granite, with less give than Scrooge. He is as DH as DHes come, and on a 2021 roster trying to dish out at-bats to Trey Mancini, Ryan Mountcastle, Chris Davis and Chance Sisco, things were too tight for Núñez in Baltimore (even if he keeps rockin' and sockin' balls over the wall elsewhere). He was non-tendered.

Rio Ruiz 3B Born: 05/22/94 Age: 27 Bats: L Throws: R Height: 6'1" Weight: 215 Origin: Round 4, 2012 Draft (#129 overall)

YEAR	TEAM	LVL	AGE	PA	R	2B	3B	HR	RBI	BB	K	SB	CS	Whiff%	AVG/OBP/SLG	DRC+	BABIP	BRR	FRAA	WARP
2018	GWN	AAA	24	541	72	25	4	9	72	40	90	2	1		.269/.322/.390	95	.311	1.8	3B(49): 2.3, 1B(35): 1.5, LF(20): 0.1	0.4
2018	ATL	MLB	24	15	1	0	0	0	0	2	5	0	0	37.0%	.083/.267/.083	77	.143	-0.1	3B(1): -0.2	0.0
2019	BAL	MLB	25	413	35	13	2	12	46	40	88	0	1	24.3%	.232/.306/.376	81	.272	-1.4	3B(114): 2.3, 1B(12): 0.3, 2B(1): 0.0	0.6
2020	BAL	MLB	26	204	25	11	0	9	32	17	46	1	2	27.3%	.222/.286/.427	96	.244	0.2	3B(53): -1.2, 2B(1): 0.0, LF(1): -0.0	0.2
2021 FS	BAL	MLB	27	600	62	23	2	19	67	58	145	1	0	25.7%	.222/.301/.384	85	.267	0.6	3B 2, 1B 0	0.3
2021 DC	BAL	MLB	27	525	54	20	2	17	59	51	127	1	0	25.7%	.222/.301/.384	85	.267	0.6	3B 1	0.2

Comparables: Phil Nevin, Greg Norton, Russ Davis

Ok, blind test. Would you rather have Player A or B? Player A: 2.2 WARP, 16 HR, 140 DRC+, .304/.370/.580. Player B: 0.2 WARP, 9 HR, 96 DRC+, .222/.310/398. Same position, but the defensive numbers like Player A a tick more. Who'd you take? Player A? It's not even close? Well, fine then… Player A is Manny Machado and Player B is Ruiz. Knowing what you know now, would you still take Player A? You would. Ok. Well, that's unfortunate because Player A is not on the Orioles anymore. He's on the Padres now doing cool stuff. Ruiz is on the Orioles, though! He's not Manny Machado—as was just proven—but he's fine. The Orioles don't have any third basemen in the minors knocking on the door, so Ruiz probably gets another year as a transitional filler. He's not horrible at anything or spectacular at anything, and he's definitely not Manny Machado.

★ ★ ★ *2021 Top 101 Prospect* **#2** ★ ★ ★

Adley Rutschman C Born: 02/06/98 Age: 23 Bats: S Throws: R Height: 6'2" Weight: 220 Origin: Round 1, 2019 Draft (#1 overall)

YEAR	TEAM	LVL	AGE	PA	R	2B	3B	HR	RBI	BB	K	SB	CS	Whiff%	AVG/OBP/SLG	DRC+	BABIP	BRR	FRAA	WARP
2019	ORI	ROK	21	16	3	0	0	1	3	2	2	1	0		.143/.250/.357	100	.091	0.2	C(2): 0.1	0.1
2019	ABD	SS	21	92	11	7	1	1	15	12	16	0	0		.325/.413/.481	177	.387	-0.1	C(8): -0.2	0.8
2019	DEL	LO-A	21	47	5	1	0	2	8	6	9	0	0		.154/.261/.333	84	.138	0.1	C(6): 0.1	0.1
2021 FS	BAL	MLB	23	600	60	26	2	14	60	42	168	2	0		.235/.294/.371	82	.312	0.4	C 0	1.1
2021 DC	BAL	MLB	23	65	6	2	0	1	6	4	18	0	0		.235/.294/.371	82	.312	0.0	C 0	0.1

YEAR	TEAM	P. COUNT	FRM RUNS	BLK RUNS	THRW RUNS	TOT RUNS
2019	DEL	769			0.1	0.0

If you're going to carry the future of a franchise on your shoulders, they might as well be enormous shoulders. Good thing Rutschman is built like a refrigerator. What's in the fridge? Oh, only the best catching prospect in baseball. He's got a smooth, powerful swing with natural lift from both sides of the plate, he's a well above-average defender who relishes the finer points of handling a pitching staff and he once even scaled a redwood tree in a single bound to save an elderly lady stuck at the top. If it feels like Rutschman is Superman, a thicc prince who was promised, well … yeah. The cancelled minor-league season only extended the honeymoon between Orioles fans and Rutschman. The fans are now past month 20 of emotionally hinging their sports dreams to a baby-faced 22-year-old from Oregon who has only played 37 professional baseball games. It should be noted that for many Orioles fans, a Matt Wieters–shaped cloud hangs over the entire Adley Rutschman Experience. That's unfair to Rutschman (and probably Wieters), but every Orioles fan carries with them the ghosts of Franchise-Altering Catching Prospects Past. That lurking shadow—and the service time tricks that will most likely push back a debut to 2022—are the only worries here. This is what the no. 1 catcher in baseball looks like, and if a few things break right, he might be even better than that.

Yolmer Sánchez 2B   Born: 06/29/92   Age: 29   Bats: S   Throws: R   Height: 5'8"   Weight: 205   Origin: International Free Agent, 2009

YEAR	TEAM	LVL	AGE	PA	R	2B	3B	HR	RBI	BB	K	SB	CS	Whiff%	AVG/OBP/SLG	DRC+	BABIP	BRR	FRAA	WARP
2018	CHW	MLB	26	662	62	34	10	8	55	49	138	14	6	21.6%	.242/.306/.372	80	.300	0.7	3B(141): -1.2, 2B(9): 0.2, SS(4): -0.3	0.7
2019	CHW	MLB	27	555	59	20	4	2	43	44	117	5	4	22.9%	.252/.318/.321	77	.324	0.2	2B(149): 19.0	2.1
2020	CHW	MLB	28	21	7	3	0	1	1	5	5	0	0	26.7%	.312/.476/.688	110	.400	-0.1	3B(5): -0.1, SS(3): 0.1, 2B(1): -0.0	0.1
2021 FS	BAL	MLB	29	600	57	21	4	11	54	43	142	8	4	22.6%	.223/.287/.338	72	.281	-0.8	2B 10, 3B 0	0.6
2021 DC	BAL	MLB	29	525	50	19	3	9	47	38	124	7	4	22.6%	.223/.287/.338	72	.281	-0.7	2B 9, 3B 0	0.8

Comparables: Randy Velarde, Greg Litton, Nick Green

Despite being just 28 years young, Sánchez has been playing professional baseball since 2009, plenty of time to become grizzled. And as a slick-fielding second baseman without power and only average contact ability, he's been around long enough to feel the ground of the game move underneath his feet. Second base defense has been devalued enough that no one was surprised to see Sánchez non-tendered after (deservedly) winning the Gold Glove in 2019, or settle for a minor league deal in the offseason. Veteran players have been devalued that it was further unsurprising that the Giants no longer had at-bats to issue to him when the schedule shrank to 60 games, so he eventually ended 2020 back with the White Sox like he never left. But like most tales when someone is brought back to life unnaturally, it didn't feel right. Sánchez didn't make Mickey Mouse ears to his son after hits, he didn't dunk Gatorade on his head during the pandemic, and even the dyed blonde streaks in his hair seemed tamer. He is only 28, but he has experienced the baseball world now, and while he will survive for a bit longer, his naïveté did not.

Anthony Santander LF   Born: 10/19/94   Age: 26   Bats: S   Throws: R   Height: 6'2"   Weight: 225   Origin: International Free Agent, 2011

YEAR	TEAM	LVL	AGE	PA	R	2B	3B	HR	RBI	BB	K	SB	CS	Whiff%	AVG/OBP/SLG	DRC+	BABIP	BRR	FRAA	WARP
2018	ABD	SS	23	31	6	5	0	1	5	2	5	2	0		.286/.355/.571	130	.318	0.2	RF(5): -0.2	0.0
2018	BOW	AA	23	222	26	9	3	5	22	10	32	4	1		.258/.293/.402	87	.282	0.7	RF(35): -3.6, LF(14): -1.4	-0.7
2018	NOR	AAA	23	47	3	3	0	2	7	2	9	0	0		.182/.213/.386	79	.176	-0.1	RF(8): 1.1, LF(2): -0.3	0.0
2018	BAL	MLB	23	108	8	5	1	1	6	6	21	1	0	25.6%	.198/.250/.297	74	.241	0.0	RF(29): 0.8, LF(1): -0.0	0.0
2019	NOR	AAA	24	209	30	15	0	5	28	13	38	3	2		.259/.311/.415	84	.298	1.1	RF(35): 1.8, LF(8): -0.9	0.2
2019	BAL	MLB	24	405	46	20	1	20	59	19	86	1	2	21.2%	.261/.297/.476	97	.285	-0.5	RF(50): -4.8, LF(40): 8.3, CF(24): 3.8	1.6
2020	BAL	MLB	26	165	24	13	1	11	32	10	25	0	1	25.6%	.261/.315/.575	138	.248	0.7	RF(35): 0.5, LF(2): 0.0	1.4
2021 FS	BAL	MLB	26	600	76	29	1	31	82	33	125	1	0	23.0%	.244/.296/.471	100	.262	-1.3	RF -6, LF 0	0.8
2021 DC	BAL	MLB	26	558	71	27	1	29	77	31	116	1	0	23.0%	.244/.296/.471	100	.262	-1.2	RF -6	0.6

Comparables: Butch Huskey, Jeff Francoeur, Shawn Green

Before an oblique injury ended his season on September 4, Santander was like a ninth-grader before they go on Acutane: the breakout story of the year. Acne jokes aside, "The Bank" was a revelation for the O's, cashing out 11 homers while playing above-average defense in right. Even though he debuted back in 2017, the pride of Margarita Island, Venezuela is only entering his age-26 season. That's sneaky young. Younger than Jake Cronenworth, Shohei Ohtani and Clint Frazier, all of whom had fewer home runs than Santander in 2020. For bad teams to get good, you need a couple waiver claims to break right and develop into real contributors. The smooth-swinging Santander is starting to look like exactly that.

Pedro Severino C   Born: 07/20/93   Age: 27   Bats: R   Throws: R   Height: 6'1"   Weight: 220   Origin: International Free Agent, 2010

YEAR	TEAM	LVL	AGE	PA	R	2B	3B	HR	RBI	BB	K	SB	CS	Whiff%	AVG/OBP/SLG	DRC+	BABIP	BRR	FRAA	WARP
2018	SYR	AAA	24	136	14	5	1	6	13	5	23	0	0		.269/.294/.462	93	.284	-2.1	C(32): 1.1	0.3
2018	WAS	MLB	24	213	14	9	0	2	15	18	47	1	0	22.0%	.168/.254/.247	60	.211	-0.1	C(67): -0.0	0.0
2019	BAL	MLB	25	341	37	13	0	13	44	29	73	3	1	25.0%	.249/.321/.420	90	.285	-2.4	C(89): -13.8	-0.3
2020	BAL	MLB	27	178	17	5	1	5	21	16	40	1	0	28.2%	.250/.322/.388	97	.304	-0.5	C(35): -0.4	0.0
2021 FS	BAL	MLB	27	600	61	21	1	20	70	43	137	2	0	25.8%	.235/.298/.390	85	.279	-0.4	C -6	0.6
2021 DC	BAL	MLB	27	295	30	10	0	9	34	21	67	1	0	25.8%	.235/.298/.390	85	.279	-0.2	C -4	0.2

Comparables: Sal Fasano, Bruce Maxwell, Chris Snyder

YEAR	TEAM	P. COUNT	FRM RUNS	BLK RUNS	THRW RUNS	TOT RUNS
2018	WAS	8442	0.3	0.2	0.1	0.6
2018	SYR	4330	1.4	0.0	0.0	1.4
2019	BAL	12991	-9.6	-4.1	-0.2	-13.9
2020	BAL	4698	-3.2	-0.8	-0.1	-4.0
2021	BAL	9620	-0.5	-2.6	0.6	-2.5

Severino is the most fun second-division starter, first-division backup catcher in baseball. He gestures constantly, and he loves a good point at his pitcher after a well-located heater. No one slaps the dirt harder to emphasize that he wants a curveball down, and if someone hits a bomb, you can count on a heavy head drop or a fierce ripping off of the catcher's mask. Severino is super lovable, incredibly fun to watch and will be a perfect backup to Adley Rutschman whenever the chosen son arrives in Baltimore. There was a moment in 2020 after Severino got off to a really hot start where some folks were like "hmmmmmmm, maybe there's more here," but a slow September doused any hope of a real breakout. Severino is what he is now: a dependable, well-liked presence behind the plate, a slightly above-average hitter for a backstop in the modern game and the best Dominican catcher in the AL East (sorry Gary Sánchez).

Chance Sisco C Born: 02/24/95 Age: 26 Bats: L Throws: R Height: 6'2" Weight: 195 Origin: Round 2, 2013 Draft (#61 overall)

YEAR	TEAM	LVL	AGE	PA	R	2B	3B	HR	RBI	BB	K	SB	CS	Whiff%	AVG/OBP/SLG	DRC+	BABIP	BRR	FRAA	WARP
2018	NOR	AAA	23	151	22	5	0	3	12	16	36	0	0		.242/.344/.352	112	.308	-1.1	C(37): -2.8	0.3
2018	BAL	MLB	23	184	13	8	0	2	16	13	66	1	0	36.0%	.181/.288/.269	57	.293	-1.3	C(55): -2.8	-0.5
2019	NOR	AAA	24	196	31	10	0	10	37	20	44	0	0		.292/.388/.530	131	.339	0.1	C(35): -3.3	1.2
2019	BAL	MLB	24	198	29	7	0	8	20	22	61	0	1	29.6%	.210/.333/.395	91	.276	0.1	C(52): -11.1, 1B(1): -0.0	-0.3
2020	BAL	MLB	25	121	11	4	0	4	10	17	41	0	0	37.5%	.214/.364/.378	100	.321	-1.1	C(26): -0.2	-0.3
2021 FS	BAL	MLB	26	600	67	22	1	21	66	63	190	1	0	33.9%	.230/.335/.401	102	.320	-0.4	C -19, 1B 0	0.6
2021 DC	BAL	MLB	26	295	33	10	0	10	32	31	93	0	0	33.9%	.230/.335/.401	102	.320	-0.2	C -12	-0.1

Comparables: Andrew Knapp, Andrew Susac, John Russell

YEAR	TEAM	P. COUNT	FRM RUNS	BLK RUNS	THRW RUNS	TOT RUNS
2018	BAL	6559	-2.2	0.3	-0.1	-1.9
2018	NOR	5320	-1.3	0.0	-0.8	-2.0
2019	BAL	6734	-9.6	-0.7	-0.5	-10.7
2019	NOR	5154	-1.8	0.3	-0.8	-2.4
2020	BAL	3179	-5.0	-0.9	0.1	-5.8
2021	BAL	9620	-9.2	-1.6	-0.1	-10.8

There are two positive outcomes for Sisco, neither of which really came to the fore in 2020. Either he needs to get more consistent behind the plate, or his bat needs to take another leap forward if he wants to be a 1B/DH type. Ater a hot August, Sisco came down hard in September and finished the year with very similar numbers to his average, yet uninspiring 2019. The one notable feature of his season was that he barrelled balls at a pretty impressive rate (12.3 percent), which would have slotted him in between Christian Yelich and George Springer had Sisco qualified. There's nothing dynamic about Sisco's game. He's as electric as a power outage, but he's probably an average, if unremarkable hitter. That'll play behind the plate if he gets better defensively or if robots take over the strike zone. Otherwise, he'll need to start hitting the ball harder to nail down a long-term role in Baltimore once Adley the Chosen arrives.

DJ Stewart RF Born: 11/30/93 Age: 27 Bats: L Throws: R Height: 6'0" Weight: 230 Origin: Round 1, 2015 Draft (#25 overall)

YEAR	TEAM	LVL	AGE	PA	R	2B	3B	HR	RBI	BB	K	SB	CS	Whiff%	AVG/OBP/SLG	DRC+	BABIP	BRR	FRAA	WARP
2018	NOR	AAA	24	490	59	24	2	12	55	54	103	11	4		.235/.329/.387	105	.278	4.7	RF(88): -14.1, LF(24): 1.9, CF(3): -0.6	-0.2
2018	BAL	MLB	24	47	8	3	0	3	10	4	12	2	1	27.2%	.250/.340/.550	88	.269	0.5	LF(9): 4.4, RF(6): -0.4	0.5
2019	NOR	AAA	25	277	42	19	2	12	47	38	51	5	4		.291/.396/.548	130	.324	-2.1	LF(30): -1.2, RF(22): 1.6	1.4
2019	BAL	MLB	25	142	15	6	0	4	15	14	26	1	2	26.4%	.238/.317/.381	83	.268	-0.3	RF(26): -1.8, LF(11): -0.5	-0.2
2020	BAL	MLB	27	112	13	2	0	7	15	20	38	0	0	36.0%	.193/.355/.455	100	.233	-0.3	RF(21): 3.5, LF(10): 0.1	0.7
2021 FS	BAL	MLB	27	600	69	22	2	23	68	70	174	8	2	31.5%	.219/.323/.408	98	.281	1.5	LF 3, RF -4	1.4
2021 DC	BAL	MLB	27	328	38	12	1	13	37	38	95	4	1	31.5%	.219/.323/.408	98	.281	0.8	LF 2, RF -2	0.8

Comparables: Lyle Mouton, Chris Snelling, Rob Mackowiak

What a weird year. After going hitless in his first 22 trips to the plate, Stewart got sent back to the *OMINOUS DUH DUH DUH DUH* *alternate site*. But upon returning to Baltimore in early September, he looked like a whole new ballplayer, smacking six homers in his first six games back. It was a glorious week, one for the annals of franchise history. But the wind changed one last time as Stewart finished the year with an arctic final two weeks. In conclusion, Stewart is a land of contrasts. Especially considering he made the exact changes we recommended back in 2017, advising him to "find some power and a sustainable on-base percentage." Last year, Stewart was an underwhelming corner outfielder. Now, he has an outside shot to be Outfield Max Muncy. It's not clear if he's actually a good baseball player just yet, but he's added some intrigue to the profile—something we should have mentioned a couple years ago.

Pat Valaika 3B Born: 09/09/92 Age: 28 Bats: R Throws: R Height: 5'11" Weight: 210 Origin: Round 9, 2013 Draft (#259 overall)

YEAR	TEAM	LVL	AGE	PA	R	2B	3B	HR	RBI	BB	K	SB	CS	Whiff%	AVG/OBP/SLG	DRC+	BABIP	BRR	FRAA	WARP
2018	ABQ	AAA	25	147	13	4	1	8	20	7	30	1	1		.216/.252/.432	63	.216	-0.6	2B(9): 0.1, SS(9): 0.4, 1B(8): -0.3	-0.3
2018	COL	MLB	25	133	8	5	0	2	5	9	30	0	0	27.7%	.156/.214/.246	62	.189	0.3	2B(17): -0.6, 1B(15): -0.4, 3B(8): 0.0	-0.3
2019	ABQ	AAA	26	383	60	26	1	22	75	27	90	5	1		.320/.364/.589	118	.370	1.0	2B(36): 1.1, 3B(18): 1.6, SS(18): -1.4	2.3
2019	COL	MLB	26	86	11	5	1	1	4	7	34	0	0	40.1%	.190/.256/.316	60	.318	0.0	2B(13): -0.8, SS(7): 0.1, 3B(3): 0.1	-0.2
2020	BAL	MLB	28	150	24	4	0	8	16	8	34	0	2	29.4%	.277/.315/.475	110	.313	0.6	SS(24): 0.0, 1B(13): -0.4, 2B(13): 1.2	0.7
2021 FS	BAL	MLB	28	600	64	22	1	28	76	33	166	2	1	31.5%	.230/.276/.426	83	.276	-0.1	SS 3, 2B 0	0.7
2021 DC	BAL	MLB	28	361	38	13	1	16	46	19	100	1	0	31.5%	.230/.276/.426	83	.276	-0.1	SS 2, 2B 0	0.6

Comparables: Orlando Miller, Javier Báez, Jonathan Villar

Is Valaika the second coming of DJ LeMahieu? Not hardly, but he *is* another Colorado infielder who left Coors Field only to immediately post significantly better offensive stats. Valaika's playing in 52-of-60 games is a sure sign that some things went wrong in Baltimore, but if he keeps it up with the stick, he'll remain a solid utility option.

Terrin Vavra SS Born: 05/12/97 Age: 24 Bats: L Throws: R Height: 6'1" Weight: 185 Origin: Round 3, 2018 Draft (#96 overall)

YEAR	TEAM	LVL	AGE	PA	R	2B	3B	HR	RBI	BB	K	SB	CS	Whiff%	AVG/OBP/SLG	DRC+	BABIP	BRR	FRAA	WARP
2018	BOI	SS	21	199	22	8	4	4	26	26	40	9	1		.302/.396/.467	142	.373	-0.5	SS(28): 0.8, 2B(16): -2.0	0.7
2019	ASH	LO-A	22	453	79	32	1	10	52	62	62	18	9		.318/.409/.489	151	.350	0.4	SS(53): -1.4, 2B(41): 2.7	4.0
2021 FS	BAL	MLB	24	600	55	27	3	12	59	41	151	11	5		.236/.292/.363	80	.303	-1.5	SS 0, 2B 2	0.7

Comparables: Cole Figueroa, Jurickson Profar, Chase d'Arnaud

Part of the Mychal Givens deal. He's got an outstanding name, the ability to play both middle infield spots and some legit offensive potential. If he proves he can hit for some power outside of Colorado's minor-league launching pads, he'll earn a bigger blurb in next year's book.

PITCHERS

Keegan Akin LHP Born: 04/01/95 Age: 26 Bats: L Throws: L Height: 6'0" Weight: 225 Origin: Round 2, 2016 Draft (#54 overall)

YEAR	TEAM	LVL	AGE	W	L	SV	G	GS	IP	H	HR	BB/9	K/9	K	GB%	BABIP	WHIP	ERA	DRA-	WARP	MPH	FA%	Whiff%	CSP
2018	BOW	AA	23	14	7	0	25	25	137²	114	16	3.8	9.3	142	31.7%	.278	1.25	3.27	87	2.0				
2019	NOR	AAA	24	6	7	0	25	24	112¹	109	10	4.9	10.5	131	32.4%	.333	1.51	4.73	89	2.6				
2020	BAL	MLB	25	1	2	0	8	6	25²	27	3	3.5	12.3	35	34.3%	.358	1.44	4.56	85	0.4	94.2	62.0%	28.5%	52.0%
2021 FS	BAL	MLB	26	8	9	0	26	26	150	140	29	4.4	10.0	166	32.7%	.292	1.43	4.93	106	0.5	94.2	62.0%	28.5%	52.0%
2021 DC	BAL	MLB	26	6	9	0	25	25	114	106	22	4.4	10.0	126	32.7%	.292	1.43	4.93	106	0.8	94.2	62.0%	28.5%	52.0%

Comparables: Conner Menez, Taylor Hearn, Anthony Misiewicz

That a 6-footer with a 92 mph fastball led all Orioles pitchers in strikeouts per nine in 2020 probably says more about the Orioles staff than it does about Akin. While he's certainly not the second coming of Nolan Ryan, the lefty flashed an interesting arsenal in his big-league debut. Built like a clenched fist, Akin uses a high-spin fastball to get more swings up and above the zone than you'd predict from the velocity. For that shtick to work long-term, he must have command of the off-speed stuff arm-side, which he did when he was at his best (a scoreless nine-strikeout performance against Atlanta in September). Think Mark Buehrle with worse command and better stuff—basically a stout lefty who works quickly and relies on nibbling the edges of the zone. He's almost certainly not a frontline guy, but a rotation workhorse who can sponge up innings and get you through the order twice without getting his teeth kicked in? That'll play.

Shawn Armstrong RHP Born: 09/11/90 Age: 30 Bats: R Throws: R Height: 6'2" Weight: 225 Origin: Round 18, 2011 Draft (#548 overall)

YEAR	TEAM	LVL	AGE	W	L	SV	G	GS	IP	H	HR	BB/9	K/9	K	GB%	BABIP	WHIP	ERA	DRA-	WARP	MPH	FA%	Whiff%	CSP
2018	TAC	AAA	27	2	5	15	49	0	56	38	3	4.2	13.2	82	32.8%	.302	1.14	1.77	46	1.9				
2018	SEA	MLB	27	0	1	1	14	0	14²	9	1	1.8	9.2	15	41.7%	.229	0.82	1.23	98	0.1	95.0	78.4%	24.3%	52.2%
2019	BAL	MLB	28	1	0	4	51	0	54¹	58	7	4.3	9.9	60	30.2%	.336	1.55	5.13	111	0.0	94.9	88.2%	26.3%	50.1%
2019	SEA	MLB	28	0	1	0	4	0	3²	8	1	7.4	7.4	3	18.8%	.500	3.00	14.73	154	-0.1	93.9	78.9%	31.2%	54.4%
2020	BAL	MLB	29	2	0	0	14	0	15	9	1	1.8	8.4	14	43.6%	.211	0.80	1.80	89	0.2	95.3	89.0%	26.2%	49.1%
2021 FS	BAL	MLB	30	3	3	0	57	0	50	41	7	3.8	9.8	54	35.9%	.270	1.25	3.77	86	0.5	95.0	87.2%	26.5%	50.2%
2021 DC	BAL	MLB	30	3	3	0	64	0	67	55	10	3.8	9.8	72	35.9%	.270	1.25	3.77	86	0.9	95.0	87.2%	26.5%	50.2%

Comparables: Nick Wittgren, Santiago Casilla, Tommy Kahnle

In the age of advanced metrics, it's easy to get lost in the numbers and lose focus on what they ultimately mean. Armstrong has a high-spin cutter. It has more spin than Kenley Jansen's cutter, which might be impressive if Casey Sadler (who spent 2019 on the Rays and Dodgers—wrong year, Casey—but 2020 on the Cubs and Mariners) didn't have a *higher* spin cutter than Armstrong. Sadler had a 5.12 ERA. Armstrong's strikeout per inning and ERA around 2.00 are promising indicators. Of course, Sadler checked both of those boxes in 2019 before regression hit hard the following year, and Armstrong's hit suppression doesn't look to be any more sustainable. He limits the free passes, though, and as far as waiver pickups go, he looks to be a quality one for Baltimore. The role of fifth most famous American Armstrong is wide open behind Neil, Louis, and Billie Joe. We see no reason Shawn can't claim the spot.

Michael Baumann RHP Born: 09/10/95 Age: 25 Bats: R Throws: R Height: 6'4" Weight: 225 Origin: Round 3, 2017 Draft (#98 overall)

YEAR	TEAM	LVL	AGE	W	L	SV	G	GS	IP	H	HR	BB/9	K/9	K	GB%	BABIP	WHIP	ERA	DRA-	WARP	MPH	FA%	Whiff%	CSP
2018	DEL	LO-A	22	5	0	0	7	7	38	23	0	3.1	11.1	47	50.6%	.284	0.95	1.42	68	0.9				
2018	FRE	HI-A	22	8	5	0	17	17	92²	82	9	3.9	5.7	59	32.9%	.263	1.32	3.88	171	-2.9				
2019	FRE	HI-A	23	1	4	0	11	11	54	40	2	4.0	12.8	77	43.1%	.317	1.19	3.83	77	0.8				
2019	BOW	AA	23	6	2	1	13	11	70	45	2	2.7	8.4	65	41.4%	.242	0.94	2.31	57	1.8				
2021 FS	BAL	MLB	25	8	9	0	26	26	150	135	22	5.0	8.9	148	40.2%	.282	1.46	4.67	108	0.4				
2021 DC	BAL	MLB	25	2	3	0	9	9	40	36	6	5.0	8.9	39	40.2%	.282	1.46	4.67	108	0.3				

Comparables: Ryan Borucki, Patrick Murphy, Matt Hall

An average fastball with a few average secondary offerings, a track record of high-minors success, a decent chance to stick at the back of the rotation and the same name as the dude who writes good stuff for The Ringer. What else do you need to know? He's now on the 40-man roster, so he'll definitely be up and pitching in the coming season. He's in a group of nauseous toddlers (young hurlers) alongside Kyle Bradish, Keegan Akin, Dean Kremer and Kevin Smith who will all get chances to start in 2021 and will all have to impress to remain starters long term. One last irrelevant thing: the Wikipedia page for Baumann's high school, Mahtomedi Senior High in Minnesota, does not have a notable alumni section. If he'd attended an average high school with a few half-famous alumni scattered around, an 18th-century congressman here and a highly respected concert cellist there, he'd probably already be worthy of inclusion. But no, according to the internet masses, neither Baumann nor any of his fellow Mahtomedi Zephyr compatriots are worthy of that title yet. It will be interesting to see just how good Baumann has to be to break that barrier, or whether his impending big-league debut will be enough to rewrite history on its own.

Kyle Bradish RHP Born: 09/12/96 Age: 24 Bats: R Throws: R Height: 6'4" Weight: 190 Origin: Round 4, 2018 Draft (#121 overall)

YEAR	TEAM	LVL	AGE	W	L	SV	G	GS	IP	H	HR	BB/9	K/9	K	GB%	BABIP	WHIP	ERA	DRA-	WARP	MPH	FA%	Whiff%	CSP
2019	IE	HI-A	22	6	7	0	24	18	101	90	9	4.7	10.7	120	43.9%	.314	1.42	4.28	99	0.1				
2021 FS	BAL	MLB	24	2	3	0	57	0	50	46	7	6.0	8.7	48	41.2%	.284	1.60	5.22	122	-0.5				

Comparables: Pierce Johnson, Dietrich Enns, Albert Abreu

Dylan Bundy's leaving Baltimore and immediately fulfilling his potential as a top-10 pitcher in the American League was a tough pill for the Birds to swallow, but Bradish might be the spoonful of sugar that helps the medicine go down. He was the breakout superstar of the Orioles' alternate site in Bowie, sporting a mid-90s heatball and two average secondaries, all from a deceptive motion. He's not as experienced or proven in the high minors as Akin and Kremer and the ceiling isn't as high as Hall or Rodriguez, but if the 24-year-old replicates his 2020 scrimmage performance, he has a shot to break into the major-league rotation in 2021 and turn some heads.

Alex Cobb RHP Born: 10/07/87 Age: 33 Bats: R Throws: R Height: 6'3" Weight: 205 Origin: Round 4, 2006 Draft (#109 overall)

YEAR	TEAM	LVL	AGE	W	L	SV	G	GS	IP	H	HR	BB/9	K/9	K	GB%	BABIP	WHIP	ERA	DRA-	WARP	MPH	FA%	Whiff%	CSP
2018	BAL	MLB	30	5	15	0	28	28	152¹	172	24	2.5	6.0	102	49.6%	.305	1.41	4.90	122	-0.3	93.3	51.5%	17.7%	47.6%
2019	BAL	MLB	31	0	2	0	3	3	12¹	21	9	1.5	5.8	8	48.0%	.293	1.86	10.95	169	-0.3	93.3	47.8%	24.3%	43.6%
2020	BAL	MLB	32	2	5	0	10	10	52¹	52	8	3.1	6.5	38	54.2%	.275	1.34	4.30	100	0.5	93.7	48.1%	23.6%	47.9%
2021 FS	BAL	MLB	33	8	9	0	26	26	150	159	26	3.0	7.0	115	51.5%	.294	1.40	4.98	110	0.2	93.5	49.6%	20.9%	47.4%
2021 DC	BAL	MLB	33	8	11	0	29	29	154	163	26	3.0	7.0	118	51.5%	.294	1.40	4.98	110	0.8	93.5	49.6%	20.9%	47.4%

Comparables: Jeremy Hellickson, Jhoulys Chacín, Matt Garza

Didn't watch a Cobb start this year? That's alright, gather round and we'll fill you in. There were two really good ones, a bunch of average ones and some real Pepé Le Pews. That's life as Alex Cobb, who, when healthy, is about as average a starting pitcher as you'll find. But coming off a three-start, injury-plagued 2019, his impressively forgettable 2020 was actually quite a delight. A man who once upon a time (back in 2013) started and won a Wild Card game for Tampa, Cobb is a different animal now. Tommy John surgery stole his split-change, and Father Time stole his durability. Set to become a free agent after the 2021 season, Cobb floats in this weird, nebulous void of Oriole-dom. He is not a part of Baltimore's future, nor was he a part of its past. He is invisible in plain sight. He's who pitches on nights you don't turn on MASN because you have errands to run, friends to see, a life to lead. And so goes Cobb, who will keep right on pitching, whether you notice him or not.

Thomas Eshelman RHP Born: 06/20/94 Age: 27 Bats: R Throws: R Height: 6'3" Weight: 210 Origin: Round 2, 2015 Draft (#46 overall)

YEAR	TEAM	LVL	AGE	W	L	SV	G	GS	IP	H	HR	BB/9	K/9	K	GB%	BABIP	WHIP	ERA	DRA-	WARP	MPH	FA%	Whiff%	CSP
2018	LHV	AAA	24	2	13	0	27	26	140¹	189	21	2.9	6.7	104	40.6%	.358	1.67	5.84	101	0.9				
2019	REA	AA	25	0	3	0	6	6	28²	43	4	1.9	8.2	26	41.6%	.406	1.71	6.28	144	-0.7				
2019	LHV	AAA	25	1	1	0	4	4	26	23	3	1.7	8.0	23	48.6%	.282	1.08	2.77	103	0.4				
2019	NOR	AAA	25	2	1	0	7	6	38¹	43	6	1.6	6.6	28	40.8%	.301	1.30	4.70	92	0.8				
2019	BAL	MLB	25	1	2	0	10	4	36	47	12	2.8	5.5	22	33.1%	.297	1.61	6.50	179	-1.2	87.6	45.8%	15.4%	51.7%
2020	BAL	MLB	26	3	1	0	12	4	34²	34	7	2.3	4.2	16	35.9%	.245	1.24	3.89	145	-0.5	88.1	43.8%	17.3%	51.5%
2021 FS	BAL	MLB	27	2	3	0	57	0	50	57	12	2.4	6.1	34	37.9%	.290	1.41	5.52	123	-0.5	87.9	44.6%	16.5%	51.6%

Comparables: Walker Lockett, Drew Anderson, Mike Wright

There's something exhilarating about watching Eshelman pitch. The endorphin rush from jumping out of a plane or bungee jumping off a cliff? It's like that, but with loopy curveballs. Only the ever-present proximity to complete and total disaster can truly make you feel alive. Eshelman is Man on Wire, a pitcher living on the edge and occasionally beyond it. His is a kitchen-sink approach. He boasts five distinct pitches, none of which he threw more than 24 percent of the time, all of which are predisposed to be disposed over a fence by a Yankee. A true corner-nibbler with the fourth-lowest average fastball velocity of any starter, Eshelman survived his way to a 3.89 ERA in 2020 by sequencing backward, by hitting his spots, by crossing his fingers. To watch him pitch is to watch him stumble into the darkness, like a blindfolded toddler running toward a hive of wasps; to hold your breath and pray as Luke Voit pops an 85 mph fastball up to second base. Then, like the parent of that toddler, you exhale and await whatever comes next.

Paul Fry LHP Born: 07/26/92 Age: 28 Bats: L Throws: L Height: 6'0" Weight: 205 Origin: Round 17, 2013 Draft (#507 overall)

YEAR	TEAM	LVL	AGE	W	L	SV	G	GS	IP	H	HR	BB/9	K/9	K	GB%	BABIP	WHIP	ERA	DRA-	WARP	MPH	FA%	Whiff%	CSP
2018	BOW	AA	25	3	0	2	15	0	19	10	2	5.2	13.3	28	64.9%	.229	1.11	2.84	56	0.5				
2018	NOR	AAA	25	0	1	0	13	1	23¹	22	2	1.5	11.2	29	51.7%	.351	1.11	3.47	51	0.7				
2018	BAL	MLB	25	1	2	2	35	0	37²	33	1	3.6	8.6	36	57.7%	.311	1.27	3.35	93	0.3	93.2	56.4%	25.4%	44.6%
2019	BAL	MLB	26	1	9	3	66	0	57¹	54	7	4.6	8.6	55	57.0%	.299	1.45	5.34	97	0.4	92.5	52.4%	25.9%	47.2%
2020	BAL	MLB	27	1	0	0	22	0	22	22	3	3.7	11.9	29	57.6%	.339	1.41	2.45	65	0.6	94.1	53.5%	29.2%	46.5%
2021 FS	BAL	MLB	28	3	3	0	57	0	50	43	5	4.4	10.3	57	53.7%	.300	1.36	4.05	90	0.4	93.1	53.3%	26.8%	46.6%
2021 DC	BAL	MLB	28	3	3	0	64	0	67	58	7	4.4	10.3	76	53.7%	.300	1.36	4.05	90	0.8	93.1	53.3%	26.8%	46.6%

Comparables: J.B. Wendelken, Dovydas Neverauskas, Dan Altavilla

With two new ticks on his fastball, Fry took a nice jump forward with a basic but effective fastball-slider combo that gave lefties a tough time. Having the best year of one's life occur in 2020 is a dubious honor, but one Fry can reasonably claim. Every bullpen needs the Second-Best Lefty Reliever™, and he is definitely that. All that to say: he's not a big deal, but more of a Paul Fry.

★　★　★ *2021 Top 101 Prospect* **#53** ★　★　★

DL Hall LHP Born: 09/19/98 Age: 22 Bats: L Throws: L Height: 6'2" Weight: 195 Origin: Round 1, 2017 Draft (#21 overall)

YEAR	TEAM	LVL	AGE	W	L	SV	G	GS	IP	H	HR	BB/9	K/9	K	GB%	BABIP	WHIP	ERA	DRA-	WARP	MPH	FA%	Whiff%	CSP
2018	DEL	LO-A	19	2	7	0	22	20	94¹	68	6	4.0	9.5	100	41.6%	.268	1.17	2.10	78	1.6				
2019	FRE	HI-A	20	4	5	1	19	17	80²	53	3	6.0	12.9	116	34.1%	.301	1.33	3.46	76	1.3				
2021 FS	BAL	MLB	22	2	3	0	57	0	50	45	7	7.2	10.2	56	38.0%	.294	1.70	5.67	127	-0.6				

Comparables: Brailyn Marquez, Dustin May, Alex Reyes

You know what doesn't grow on trees? Pineapples. Oh, also lefty pitching prospects with fastballs in the mid-to-high 90s and two above-average secondary pitches like Hall. His stuff is up there with anyone in the minors, and his strikeout numbers in High-A in 2019 reflected that. He brought that nasty stuff to the alternate site in 2020 and threw pretty well against the stiffest competition that the 22-year-old had ever faced. The other thing you need to know about Hall: He also walks a lot of hitters (check that 2019 line again). There's a world where he figures out the command/control part without sacrificing the zippiness of the arsenal, turning into a strikeout monster atop the Orioles rotation for a half-decade. There's also a world where the walks stick around forever and he's a more fun version of Robbie Ray. There's also a world where we're all just upside down clones of ourselves wearing pink pajamas and baseball doesn't exist, never did and never will. There's endless realities y'all. In most of them, DL Hall spends 2021 in Double-A before debuting in 2022.

Hunter Harvey RHP   Born: 12/09/94   Age: 26   Bats: R   Throws: R   Height: 6'3"   Weight: 210   Origin: Round 1, 2013 Draft (#22 overall)

YEAR	TEAM	LVL	AGE	W	L	SV	G	GS	IP	H	HR	BB/9	K/9	K	GB%	BABIP	WHIP	ERA	DRA-	WARP	MPH	FA%	Whiff%	CSP
2018	BOW	AA	23	1	2	0	9	9	32¹	36	3	2.5	8.4	30	35.1%	.351	1.39	5.57	89	0.4				
2019	BOW	AA	24	2	5	1	14	11	59²	63	14	3.2	9.3	61	37.9%	.316	1.42	5.19	132	-1.1				
2019	NOR	AAA	24	1	1	0	12	0	16²	13	2	2.7	11.9	22	38.1%	.282	1.08	4.32	61	0.5				
2019	BAL	MLB	24	1	0	0	7	0	6¹	3	1	5.7	15.6	11	54.5%	.200	1.11	1.42	75	0.1	99.5	69.6%	25.4%	48.1%
2020	BAL	MLB	25	0	2	0	10	0	8²	8	2	2.1	6.2	6	39.3%	.231	1.15	4.15	113	0.0	98.9	77.2%	23.3%	49.6%
2021 FS	BAL	MLB	26	3	3	14	57	0	50	47	8	3.7	9.0	50	38.4%	.288	1.36	4.65	103	0.0	99.1	74.3%	24.1%	49.0%
2021 DC	BAL	MLB	26	3	3	14	64	0	67	63	11	3.7	9.0	67	38.4%	.288	1.36	4.65	103	0.3	99.1	74.3%	24.1%	49.0%

Comparables: Keury Mella, Jake McGee, Chase De Jong

Pitchers and their injuries. Since joining the Orioles' organization, Harvey has broken his tibula, had Tommy John surgery on his elbow, missed half of 2018 to shoulder soreness and even lost all the skin on the left side of his face in a gasoline accident. Whoops, sorry, sorry ... wrong Harvey. After a healthy 2019 that included a brief big-league stint where he showed off his dynamic high-90s heater and devastating curve, 2020 was back to the injury woes for the long-haired right-hander. A forearm strain kept him on the shelf until early September, and he never got going after he returned. The stuff is still sexy as hell and the ceiling remains a high-leverage, late-inning guy. However, this is the exact type of arm that, in the past, the Orioles never figured out how to develop correctly or keep healthy enough, then ended up as an All-Star on another team (see: Arrieta, Jake). Hopefully, Harvey can stay on the mound in 2021 and fulfill his destiny as Baltimore's flame-throwing closer of the future.

Dean Kremer RHP   Born: 01/07/96   Age: 25   Bats: R   Throws: R   Height: 6'3"   Weight: 185   Origin: Round 14, 2016 Draft (#431 overall)

YEAR	TEAM	LVL	AGE	W	L	SV	G	GS	IP	H	HR	BB/9	K/9	K	GB%	BABIP	WHIP	ERA	DRA-	WARP	MPH	FA%	Whiff%	CSP
2018	RC	HI-A	22	5	3	0	16	16	79	67	7	3.0	13.0	114	39.9%	.353	1.18	3.30	67	1.8				
2018	BOW	AA	22	4	2	0	8	8	45¹	38	3	3.4	10.5	53	37.9%	.315	1.21	2.58	76	0.9				
2018	TUL	AA	22	1	0	0	1	1	7	3	0	3.9	14.1	11	75.0%	.250	0.86	0.00	37	0.3				
2019	FRE	HI-A	23	0	0	0	2	2	9²	6	0	3.7	13.0	14	20.0%	.300	1.03	0.00	73	0.2				
2019	BOW	AA	23	9	4	0	15	15	84²	75	9	3.1	9.2	87	41.1%	.299	1.23	2.98	96	0.3				
2019	NOR	AAA	23	0	2	0	4	4	19¹	30	2	1.9	9.8	21	36.5%	.467	1.76	8.84	156	-0.2				
2020	BAL	MLB	24	1	1	0	4	4	18²	15	0	5.8	10.6	22	30.6%	.306	1.45	4.82	96	0.2	95.2	51.2%	26.4%	50.8%
2021 FS	BAL	MLB	25	9	8	0	26	26	150	135	27	3.3	9.4	156	37.0%	.279	1.26	4.13	93	1.6	95.2	51.2%	26.4%	50.8%
2021 DC	BAL	MLB	25	6	8	0	25	25	116	104	21	3.3	9.4	121	37.0%	.279	1.26	4.13	93	1.6	95.2	51.2%	26.4%	50.8%

Comparables: T.J. Zeuch, Ryan Helsley, Robert Dugger

When he debuted on September 6 (25th anniversary of Ripken's 2,131), Kremer became the first Israeli to pitch in the big leagues. His four-start debut showed glimpses of why he was a key part of the Manny Machado deal. He did enough with his fastball-curve-cutter combo over his first three starts to overcome a lot of hard contact before the gravitational forces of baseball caught up to him in a disastrous final outing against Boston. The curveball is long and loopy; it has good shape but lacks real bite and operates in a slower-than-average 75 mph range. It's not a nasty, gif-able breaking ball, but he commands it and hides it well enough that it's still an effective offering. Kremer should spend most of 2021 in Baltimore's rotation, and while every indicator points towards a reliable back-end starter, he'll get every opportunity to prove he's more dynamic than that.

Travis Lakins Sr. RHP   Born: 06/29/94   Age: 27   Bats: R   Throws: R   Height: 6'1"   Weight: 215   Origin: Round 6, 2015 Draft (#171 overall)

YEAR	TEAM	LVL	AGE	W	L	SV	G	GS	IP	H	HR	BB/9	K/9	K	GB%	BABIP	WHIP	ERA	DRA-	WARP	MPH	FA%	Whiff%	CSP
2018	POR	AA	24	2	2	1	26	6	38	27	3	3.1	9.9	42	47.5%	.250	1.05	2.61	78	0.6				
2018	WOR	AAA	24	1	0	2	10	0	16¹	11	0	2.8	8.3	15	44.4%	.244	0.98	1.65	87	0.2				
2019	WOR	AAA	25	3	4	6	40	1	45	46	4	4.6	8.4	42	39.6%	.328	1.53	4.60	108	0.4				
2019	BOS	MLB	25	0	1	0	16	3	23¹	23	1	3.9	6.9	18	46.6%	.306	1.41	3.86	124	-0.2	95.2	71.0%	25.4%	43.1%
2020	BAL	MLB	26	3	2	1	22	0	25²	25	2	4.6	8.8	25	38.2%	.311	1.48	2.81	94	0.3	94.7	73.6%	22.5%	47.3%
2021 FS	BAL	MLB	27	3	3	0	57	0	50	49	9	4.6	8.3	46	39.7%	.289	1.50	5.29	113	-0.2	94.9	72.7%	23.6%	45.8%
2021 DC	BAL	MLB	27	3	3	0	64	0	67	66	12	4.6	8.3	61	39.7%	.289	1.50	5.29	113	-0.1	94.9	72.7%	23.6%	45.8%

Comparables: Trevor Gott, Victor Alcántara, Michael Lorenzen

The three main characters of the 2019 Orioles bullpen—Miguel Castro, Richard Bleier and Mychal Givens—were all dealt away from Baltimore during the season. The shuffled bullpen chairs of a club that won just shy of 42 percent of its games understandably don't make national headlines, but those empty spots had to go somewhere. That somewhere was Lakins. With Lakins, the Orioles' bullpen strategy of scooping dudes off the waiver wire and seeing what happens worked pretty well. He led the team in innings out of the bullpen to the tune of a sub-three ERA. Now, the advanced metrics aren't too kind—looking at you, 4.89 DRA—but the stuff is playable at the big-league level. Lakins' repertoire includes a high-spin curveball with a hard cutter and a league-average fastball. It's nothing sexy, and he doesn't have the ceiling to throw in high-leverage spots for a good team, but a valuable middle-relief innings sponge seems like an attainable role.

Wade LeBlanc LHP   Born: 08/07/84   Age: 36   Bats: L   Throws: L   Height: 6'3"   Weight: 215   Origin: Round 2, 2006 Draft (#61 overall)

YEAR	TEAM	LVL	AGE	W	L	SV	G	GS	IP	H	HR	BB/9	K/9	K	GB%	BABIP	WHIP	ERA	DRA-	WARP	MPH	FA%	Whiff%	CSP
2018	SEA	MLB	33	9	5	0	32	27	162	151	24	2.2	7.2	130	36.4%	.274	1.18	3.72	113	0.4	87.5	61.1%	21.9%	47.6%
2019	SEA	MLB	34	6	7	0	26	8	121¹	145	28	2.3	6.8	92	40.2%	.309	1.45	5.71	164	-3.4	87.3	58.2%	22.2%	47.4%
2020	BAL	MLB	35	1	0	0	6	6	22¹	27	6	3.2	5.2	13	37.0%	.280	1.57	8.06	158	-0.5	88.2	52.2%	25.0%	49.3%
2021 FS	BAL	MLB	36	2	3	0	57	0	50	55	10	2.6	6.4	35	38.5%	.291	1.39	5.04	114	-0.3	87.5	58.2%	22.5%	47.8%

Comparables: Zach Duke, Edwin Jackson, Ian Kennedy

It was obvious that the Orioles rotation wouldn't be winning any ERA titles the moment they snatched up Tommy Milone and LeBlanc—not one, but two rejects from a 2019 Mariners rotation that finished tied for fourth to last in the league in DRA. LeBlanc made six starts for Baltimore. The first one was alright, the second one was good, the next three were stanky and then he left the final one with a "stress reaction in his throwing elbow." He's a free agent as this book goes to press, and while the market for 36-year-old lefties averaging 87 on the fastball won't be scorching this year, there's no way we've seen the last of LeBlanc. Nine lives on this one.

Zac Lowther LHP   Born: 04/30/96   Age: 25   Bats: L   Throws: L   Height: 6'2"   Weight: 235   Origin: Round 2, 2017 Draft (#74 overall)

YEAR	TEAM	LVL	AGE	W	L	SV	G	GS	IP	H	HR	BB/9	K/9	K	GB%	BABIP	WHIP	ERA	DRA-	WARP	MPH	FA%	Whiff%	CSP
2018	DEL	LO-A	22	3	1	0	6	6	31	12	2	2.6	14.8	51	33.3%	.192	0.68	1.16	49	1.0				
2018	FRE	HI-A	22	5	3	0	17	16	92²	74	6	2.5	9.7	100	36.8%	.292	1.08	2.53	82	1.6				
2019	BOW	AA	23	13	7	0	26	26	148	102	8	3.8	9.4	154	39.4%	.260	1.11	2.55	85	1.4				
2021 FS	BAL	MLB	25	1	2	0	57	0	50	44	7	4.2	9.4	52	38.8%	.286	1.36	4.30	102	0.1				
2021 DC	BAL	MLB	25	1	2	0	6	6	26	23	3	4.2	9.4	27	38.8%	.286	1.36	4.30	102	0.2				

Comparables: David Peterson, Brendan McKay, Tucker Davidson

One of the Orioles' many low-90s-fastball-toting, left-handed, back-end-rotation hopefuls. The stuff isn't particularly sexy, but he has always posted gaudy strikeout numbers, dating back to his days at Xavier.

John Means LHP   Born: 04/24/93   Age: 28   Bats: L   Throws: L   Height: 6'3"   Weight: 230   Origin: Round 11, 2014 Draft (#331 overall)

YEAR	TEAM	LVL	AGE	W	L	SV	G	GS	IP	H	HR	BB/9	K/9	K	GB%	BABIP	WHIP	ERA	DRA-	WARP	MPH	FA%	Whiff%	CSP
2018	BOW	AA	25	1	4	0	8	7	46	43	6	2.5	8.0	41	37.1%	.282	1.22	4.30	80	0.8				
2018	NOR	AAA	25	6	5	0	20	19	111¹	123	9	1.5	7.2	89	33.8%	.326	1.28	3.48	88	1.4				
2018	BAL	MLB	25	0	0	0	1	0	3¹	6	1	0.0	10.8	4	25.0%	.455	1.80	13.50	219	-0.2	91.6	37.9%	22.2%	41.4%
2019	BAL	MLB	26	12	11	0	31	27	155	138	23	2.2	7.0	121	30.7%	.256	1.14	3.60	94	1.9	93.6	50.7%	22.2%	47.1%
2020	BAL	MLB	27	2	4	0	10	10	43²	36	12	1.4	8.7	42	43.9%	.216	0.98	4.53	105	0.3	95.5	52.3%	26.3%	49.7%
2021 FS	BAL	MLB	28	9	8	0	26	26	150	139	26	2.2	8.2	136	36.6%	.273	1.17	3.88	89	2.0	94.1	51.1%	23.4%	47.8%
2021 DC	BAL	MLB	28	8	10	0	29	29	154	143	27	2.2	8.2	139	36.6%	.273	1.17	3.88	89	2.5	94.1	51.1%	23.4%	47.8%

Comparables: Andrew Suárez, Caleb Smith, Erick Fedde

It was a tale of two seasons for the Orioles' 2019 All-Star. He got off to a late start, coming out of Spring Camp 2.0 with some shoulder fatigue, struggled early on and then missed a few starts after his father passed away in mid August. But once he got into the groove of things in the seasons' second month (also its last month, idk if you saw but there was a Pandemic), he was back to 2019 John Means, but even better. The big story here was that his fastball velo jumped 2.1 miles per hour compared to the season before; the fourth biggest velocity leap in the bigs. He didn't throw the fastball any more often, but it generated 11% more swings and misses than 2019 and had an XBA under 2. His fastball went from a necessity to a legit weapon. It's pretty crazy. As an 11th round pick, he's already an astounding developmental success, and if he can piece 2019's cambio with 2020's heater he'll be a solid, postseason startable Big League pitcher for the next few years.

───────── ★ ★ ★ *2021 Top 101 Prospect* **#30** ★ ★ ★ ─────────

Grayson Rodriguez RHP   Born: 11/16/99   Age: 21   Bats: L   Throws: R   Height: 6'5"   Weight: 220   Origin: Round 1, 2018 Draft (#11 overall)

YEAR	TEAM	LVL	AGE	W	L	SV	G	GS	IP	H	HR	BB/9	K/9	K	GB%	BABIP	WHIP	ERA	DRA-	WARP	MPH	FA%	Whiff%	CSP
2018	ORI	ROK	18	0	2	0	9	8	19¹	17	0	3.3	9.3	20	43.4%	.321	1.24	1.40	60	0.7				
2019	DEL	LO-A	19	10	4	0	20	20	94	57	4	3.4	12.4	129	44.2%	.262	0.99	2.68	55	2.8				
2021 FS	BAL	MLB	21	2	3	0	57	0	50	44	7	5.1	9.4	52	39.2%	.282	1.46	4.61	108	-0.1				

Comparables: Hunter Harvey, Tyler Glasnow, Danny Duffy

Over the last decade-plus, Baltimore (or more specifically Bowie, Frederick and Delmarva) has been an abyss where high-pick pitching prospects go to underperform or wallow in obscurity. Even the arms that reached Camden Yards—the Arrietas, the Bundys, the Gausmans—never fully put it together in Baltimore, only to succeed elsewhere. All that is to say: Rodriguez is the first test of the new Orioles regime's ability to develop pitching, because boy oh boy does this dude have the talent to succeed. He's a hulking tree of a man, armed with all the characteristics you want in a future frontline starter: a mid- to high-90s fastball, a plus slider and feel for what could one day be a plus changeup. He's smart, he's pitcher-mean, he knows he's gonna be good and, so far, everything is going to plan. Rodriguez almost certainly won't be up in 2021. However, there's a small but real chance he's the number one pitching prospect in baseball this time next year.

Tanner Scott LHP Born: 07/22/94 Age: 26 Bats: R Throws: L Height: 6'2" Weight: 220 Origin: Round 6, 2014 Draft (#181 overall)

YEAR	TEAM	LVL	AGE	W	L	SV	G	GS	IP	H	HR	BB/9	K/9	K	GB%	BABIP	WHIP	ERA	DRA-	WARP	MPH	FA%	Whiff%	CSP
2018	NOR	AAA	23	0	1	0	10	0	10	12	0	6.8	9.8	13	55.2%	.357	1.58	0.75	74	0.2				
2018	BAL	MLB	23	3	3	0	53	0	53¹	55	6	4.7	12.8	76	46.7%	.383	1.56	5.40	63	1.3	98.8	55.4%	35.2%	43.2%
2019	NOR	AAA	24	3	4	7	30	0	45¹	35	2	3.0	11.3	57	55.9%	.303	1.10	2.98	50	1.7				
2019	BAL	MLB	24	1	1	0	28	0	26¹	28	4	6.5	12.6	37	51.6%	.400	1.78	4.78	92	0.2	97.8	58.7%	34.1%	43.1%
2020	BAL	MLB	25	0	0	1	25	0	20²	12	1	4.4	10.0	23	58.0%	.224	1.06	1.31	73	0.5	98.2	61.5%	35.9%	49.3%
2021 FS	BAL	MLB	26	3	3	3	57	0	50	41	6	5.5	11.2	62	52.0%	.296	1.44	4.32	94	0.3	98.3	58.6%	35.1%	45.3%
2021 DC	BAL	MLB	26	3	3	3	64	0	67	55	8	5.5	11.2	83	52.0%	.296	1.44	4.32	94	0.6	98.3	58.6%	35.1%	45.3%

Comparables: José Alvarado, Keone Kela, Tyler Mahle

After a few years of inconsistent results, the 25-year-old finally put it together, evolving into the overpowering lefty world-crusher that overly optimistic O's fans always thought he could be. It's a pretty simple recipe for success: a bulkier Josh Hader without the hair, Andrew Miller with regular-sized limbs. In other words, it's elite fastball velocity and spin from the left side with one of the best wipeout sliders in the world. Granted, it was only a 20-inning sample, but Scott was actually better against opposite-handed hitters in 2020, thanks mostly to a slider that gained 200 RPM compared to where it was in 2019. The next questions for Scott are: (1) can he maintain this over a full season, and (2) can he do this in multi-inning outings? If 2021 answers yes to both questions, and that's a big if, Scott has a shot to be a top-10 reliever in baseball.

Kevin Smith LHP Born: 05/13/97 Age: 24 Bats: R Throws: L Height: 6'5" Weight: 200 Origin: Round 7, 2018 Draft (#200 overall)

YEAR	TEAM	LVL	AGE	W	L	SV	G	GS	IP	H	HR	BB/9	K/9	K	GB%	BABIP	WHIP	ERA	DRA-	WARP	MPH	FA%	Whiff%	CSP
2018	BRK	SS	21	4	1	0	12	3	23²	12	1	2.3	10.6	28	49.0%	.220	0.76	0.76	130	-0.3				
2019	STL	HI-A	22	5	5	0	17	17	85²	83	5	2.5	10.7	102	44.1%	.359	1.25	3.05	88	0.7				
2019	BNG	AA	22	3	2	0	6	6	31¹	25	1	4.3	8.0	28	39.3%	.289	1.28	3.45	115	-0.2				
2021 FS	BAL	MLB	24	2	3	0	57	0	50	48	8	4.4	8.7	48	39.2%	.291	1.45	4.91	112	-0.2				
2021 DC	BAL	MLB	24	0	0	0	3	3	13	12	2	4.4	8.7	12	39.2%	.291	1.45	4.91	112	0.1				

Comparables: David Peterson, Bernardo Flores Jr., Mitch Keller

See: Lowther, Zac, except he's from Georgia, came to Baltimore in the Miguel Castro trade and has a league-average slider. If you're interested in this type of profile, buckle up because there are two more O's like this.

Cole Sulser RHP Born: 03/12/90 Age: 31 Bats: R Throws: R Height: 6'1" Weight: 190 Origin: Round 25, 2013 Draft (#741 overall)

YEAR	TEAM	LVL	AGE	W	L	SV	G	GS	IP	H	HR	BB/9	K/9	K	GB%	BABIP	WHIP	ERA	DRA-	WARP	MPH	FA%	Whiff%	CSP
2018	AKR	AA	28	3	0	1	6	0	9	3	0	1.0	17.0	17	41.7%	.250	0.44	0.00	50	0.3				
2018	COL	AAA	28	5	4	1	41	0	51²	52	4	2.8	13.6	78	34.7%	.410	1.32	4.53	71	1.0				
2019	DUR	AAA	29	6	3	2	49	4	66	51	4	3.3	12.1	89	31.8%	.309	1.14	3.27	52	2.4				
2019	TB	MLB	29	0	0	0	7	0	7¹	5	0	3.7	11.0	9	35.3%	.294	1.09	0.00	87	0.1	94.5	63.8%	25.8%	42.5%
2020	BAL	MLB	30	1	5	5	19	0	22²	17	2	6.8	7.5	19	37.5%	.250	1.50	5.56	117	0.0	95.1	57.5%	30.2%	43.8%
2021 FS	BAL	MLB	31	2	2	0	57	0	50	43	8	3.8	9.8	54	36.7%	.276	1.29	4.11	93	0.3	95.0	58.6%	29.4%	43.6%
2021 DC	BAL	MLB	31	2	2	0	51	0	54	46	9	3.8	9.8	58	36.7%	.276	1.29	4.11	93	0.5	95.0	58.6%	29.4%	43.6%

Comparables: Jacob Barnes, Andrew Kittredge, Richard Rodríguez

You can't spell C-O-L-E S-U-L-S-E-R without CLOSER. And that was the damn truth on the opening weekend when O's manager Brandon Hyde sent him out for a two-inning save against (what we thought at the time was) a good Boston lineup, and it worked. While there were some bumps along the way—namely the game he blew on July 30 when Aaron Judge hit one to Venus—July and August were going pretty nifty for the short-arming late-bloomer. Sulser was averaging a strikeout per inning and had an ERA under 3.50 on August 22. But back-to-back blown saves against Toronto at the end of August bumped the Proven Sulser out of the ninth inning, and his September was pretty forgettable. He still has above-average velocity, great fastball spin numbers and almost certainly a spot in the 2021 Orioles bullpen, but Baltimore might have to spell out Closer without Cole Sulser going forward.

Dillon Tate RHP Born: 05/01/94 Age: 27 Bats: R Throws: R Height: 6'2" Weight: 195 Origin: Round 1, 2015 Draft (#4 overall)

YEAR	TEAM	LVL	AGE	W	L	SV	G	GS	IP	H	HR	BB/9	K/9	K	GB%	BABIP	WHIP	ERA	DRA-	WARP	MPH	FA%	Whiff%	CSP
2018	BOW	AA	24	2	3	0	7	7	40²	48	3	2.0	4.6	21	61.3%	.328	1.40	5.75	90	0.5				
2018	TRN	AA	24	5	2	0	15	15	82²	67	7	2.7	8.2	75	48.1%	.263	1.11	3.38	66	2.1				
2019	BOW	AA	25	2	3	5	17	2	33²	28	4	2.4	8.0	30	49.0%	.264	1.10	3.48	94	0.0				
2019	NOR	AAA	25	2	0	2	4	0	9	7	1	1.0	7.0	7	65.4%	.240	0.89	2.00	62	0.3				
2019	BAL	MLB	25	0	2	0	16	0	21	18	3	3.9	8.6	20	61.0%	.268	1.29	6.43	95	0.2	95.8	56.6%	21.6%	49.7%
2020	BAL	MLB	26	1	1	0	12	0	16²	9	1	2.7	7.6	14	51.2%	.190	0.84	3.24	87	0.3	96.9	57.9%	25.0%	44.1%
2021 FS	BAL	MLB	27	3	3	0	57	0	50	49	7	3.9	8.0	44	51.2%	.298	1.43	4.88	106	0.0	96.4	57.3%	23.5%	46.6%
2021 DC	BAL	MLB	27	3	3	0	64	0	67	66	9	3.9	8.0	59	51.2%	.298	1.43	4.88	106	0.2	96.4	57.3%	23.5%	46.6%

Comparables: Spencer Turnbull, Rookie Davis, Sam Tuivailala

A former fourth-overall pick, Tate's journey has robbed him of his electric upper-90s fastball and his chance to be a starter. He can still sling it in the mid-90s, though, and he was effective at that velocity, not allowing an extra-base hit on the heater last season. By not dwelling on what he's lost, Tate might have secured himself a career as a middle reliever.

Cesar Valdez RHP Born: 03/17/85   Age: 36   Bats: R   Throws: R   Height: 6'2"   Weight: 200   Origin: International Free Agent, 2005

YEAR	TEAM	LVL	AGE	W	L	SV	G	GS	IP	H	HR	BB/9	K/9	K	GB%	BABIP	WHIP	ERA	DRA-	WARP	MPH	FA%	Whiff%	CSP
2018	YUC	AAA	33	5	0	0	6	6	36¹	39	0	1.2	9.2	37	62.4%	.358	1.21	2.48						
2018	TAB	AAA	33	1	3	0	7	7	30¹	53	3	1.8	6.8	23	42.0%	.435	1.95	5.93						
2019	YUC	AAA	34	15	2	0	23	23	147²	140	6	1.0	7.4	122	56.6%	.311	1.06	2.26						
2020	BAL	MLB	35	1	1	3	9	0	14¹	7	0	1.9	7.5	12	52.6%	.184	0.70	1.26	85	0.2	86.9	15.7%	30.3%	47.3%
2021 FS	BAL	MLB	36	3	3	14	57	0	50	50	8	2.2	7.7	42	48.5%	.293	1.27	4.35	99	0.2	86.9	15.7%	30.3%	47.3%
2021 DC	BAL	MLB	36	3	3	14	64	0	67	68	11	2.2	7.7	57	48.5%	.293	1.27	4.35	99	0.4	86.9	15.7%	30.3%	47.3%

Comparables: Matt Albers, Andrew Miller, Junior Guerra

Coming into the year, the 35-year-old Valdez had not pitched in the majors since 2017 with Toronto, had no track record of success in the bigs and a fastball in the mid-80s. After proving himself at the alternate site, he got the call toward the end of August and spent 14 1/3 innings absolutely carving out of the Orioles bullpen. It was all thanks to his "dead fish" changeup, a mythical offering that Valdez threw a whopping 83 percent of the time, baffling hitters to the tune of a .164 batting average against. He uses it like a knuckleball, floating it all around and below the zone with incredible touch. Scream small sample size all you want, but this is the best trick pitch in baseball right now. Maybe this is a real repeatable gimmick and the longtime journeyman (he's spent time in Taiwan, Mexico, the Dominican Republic, Venezuela and Puerto Rico) has an R.A. Dickey-like five years ahead of him. He pitched well enough to earn a second season making pitches disappear just beneath opposing hitters' bats.

Alexander Wells LHP Born: 02/27/97   Age: 24   Bats: L   Throws: L   Height: 6'1"   Weight: 190   Origin: International Free Agent, 2015

YEAR	TEAM	LVL	AGE	W	L	SV	G	GS	IP	H	HR	BB/9	K/9	K	GB%	BABIP	WHIP	ERA	DRA-	WARP	MPH	FA%	Whiff%	CSP
2018	FRE	HI-A	21	7	8	0	24	24	135	142	19	2.2	6.7	101	35.3%	.302	1.30	3.47	95	1.4				
2019	BOW	AA	22	8	6	0	24	24	137¹	123	10	1.6	6.9	105	40.8%	.276	1.07	2.95	93	0.7				
2021 FS	BAL	MLB	24	2	3	0	57	0	50	53	9	2.3	6.6	36	40.2%	.289	1.32	4.60	110	-0.1				

Comparables: Brock Burke, JoJo Romero, Gabriel Ynoa

See: Lowther, Zac and Smith, Kevin, but Australian, a slower fastball, less impressive strikeout numbers and he wears cool goggles on the mound.

Asher Wojciechowski RHP Born: 12/21/88   Age: 32   Bats: R   Throws: R   Height: 6'4"   Weight: 235   Origin: Round 1, 2010 Draft (#41 overall)

YEAR	TEAM	LVL	AGE	W	L	SV	G	GS	IP	H	HR	BB/9	K/9	K	GB%	BABIP	WHIP	ERA	DRA-	WARP	MPH	FA%	Whiff%	CSP
2018	CHA	AAA	29	0	5	0	6	6	34²	40	12	1.3	9.6	37	26.2%	.308	1.30	7.01	94	0.3				
2018	NOR	AAA	29	5	4	0	19	12	84²	68	14	3.4	9.5	89	29.6%	.256	1.18	3.51	88	1.1				
2019	COL	AAA	30	8	2	0	15	15	84²	67	19	3.3	8.7	82	27.0%	.229	1.16	3.61	88	2.0				
2019	BAL	MLB	30	4	8	0	17	16	82¹	80	17	3.1	8.7	80	29.9%	.279	1.31	4.92	111	0.3	93.4	53.9%	26.1%	45.1%
2020	BAL	MLB	31	1	3	0	10	7	37	45	11	3.6	7.5	31	30.0%	.315	1.62	6.81	157	-0.8	92.6	46.1%	25.6%	47.4%
2021 FS	BAL	MLB	32	2	3	0	57	0	50	51	12	3.5	8.2	45	30.5%	.284	1.42	5.44	119	-0.4	93.0	50.7%	25.9%	46.0%

Comparables: Chris Rusin, Tyler Cloyd, David Huff

Wojciechowski spent this summer challenging ESPN's Adrian Wojnarowski for who could serve up the most bombs. He struggled even in that regard because he didn't stay in the rotation long enough to pose a real threat.

Bruce Zimmermann LHP Born: 02/09/95   Age: 26   Bats: L   Throws: L   Height: 6'2"   Weight: 215   Origin: Round 5, 2017 Draft (#140 overall)

YEAR	TEAM	LVL	AGE	W	L	SV	G	GS	IP	H	HR	BB/9	K/9	K	GB%	BABIP	WHIP	ERA	DRA-	WARP	MPH	FA%	Whiff%	CSP
2018	ROM	LO-A	23	7	3	0	14	14	84²	74	5	1.9	10.5	99	46.6%	.322	1.09	2.76	64	2.1				
2018	MIS	AA	23	2	1	0	6	6	28²	25	3	6.0	8.2	26	37.5%	.293	1.53	3.14	105	0.1				
2018	BOW	AA	23	2	3	0	5	5	21¹	25	2	3.0	6.8	16	27.4%	.329	1.50	5.06	153	-0.5				
2019	BOW	AA	24	5	3	0	18	17	101¹	88	9	3.0	9.0	101	39.6%	.283	1.20	2.58	90	0.7				
2019	NOR	AAA	24	2	3	0	7	7	38²	44	3	4.2	7.7	33	44.7%	.345	1.60	4.89	117	0.4				
2020	BAL	MLB	25	0	0	0	2	1	7	6	2	2.6	9.0	7	50.0%	.222	1.14	7.71	106	0.0	93.7	51.4%	19.2%	52.1%
2021 FS	BAL	MLB	26	8	9	0	26	26	150	155	27	3.7	8.0	133	40.6%	.297	1.44	5.17	112	0.1	93.7	51.4%	19.2%	52.1%
2021 DC	BAL	MLB	26	5	8	0	45	19	110	113	20	3.7	8.0	98	40.6%	.297	1.44	5.17	112	0.3	93.7	51.4%	19.2%	52.1%

Comparables: Anthony Misiewicz, Max Fried, Framber Valdez

See: Lowther, Zac; Smith, Kevin and Wells, Alex, except Zimmermann is actually from Baltimore, so he'll be in the newspaper a bunch and he's probably a smidge less likely to stick in the back of a rotation. Got rocked in a 2020 cup of coffee.

BOSTON RED SOX

Essay by Ben Carsley

Player comments by Ben Carsley and BP staff

On September 1, the Red Sox sent a tweet from their official Twitter account that read "iykyk"—internet shorthand for "if you know, you know"—with an image of a hand about to press a blue "reset" button. The Sox owned a 12-23 record at the time but had achieved their goal for 2020: they had reset the luxury tax, and they wanted the world to know it. Sure, the team was terrible, and yes, they had reduced payroll by jettisoning one of the best players in franchise history. But John Henry—a man with an estimated net worth of nearly $3 billion—was set to save a few million dollars in baseball taxes. The real victory was in hand.

The tweet itself was not the issue, of course. It was merely the baseball equivalent of a Mission Accomplished banner hanging from an aircraft carrier two months into a war without purpose or end, a PR faux pas that perfectly encapsulated the cynicism and self-serving interests required to achieve such "victory" in the first place.

The issue is that the Boston Red Sox proudly announced to the world that they were no longer special.

After long serving as one of the last teams committed to spending their way to championships, the Sox have joined a growing majority of the league in their willingness to abdicate the chief responsibility assigned to a baseball team: to prioritize winning. Instead, Henry and co. now "worship at the altar of financial flexibility," as Jon Tayler so aptly warned would happen in this very space last year. With baseball teams increasingly able to divorce profits from performance, their directives have shifted from "win at all costs" to "win by cutting costs." If Mookie Betts would have to play Iphigenia to Henry's Agamemnon, so be it: the ends justify the means when the ends produce more ROI.

There are many reasons the Betts trade—or, perhaps more aptly, the Betts salary dump—is a baseball tragedy. It deprived the Red Sox of an otherworldly talent on pace to finish as its second-best player ever. It will forever stain the legacy of Henry, once one of baseball's better owners, and pushed new general manager Chaim Bloom into a role of pure villainy. It gutted the foundation of a team that had won 108 games and the World Series just a year earlier. And it turned the Boston Red Sox—a marquee franchise in the midst of their most successful era in franchise history—into

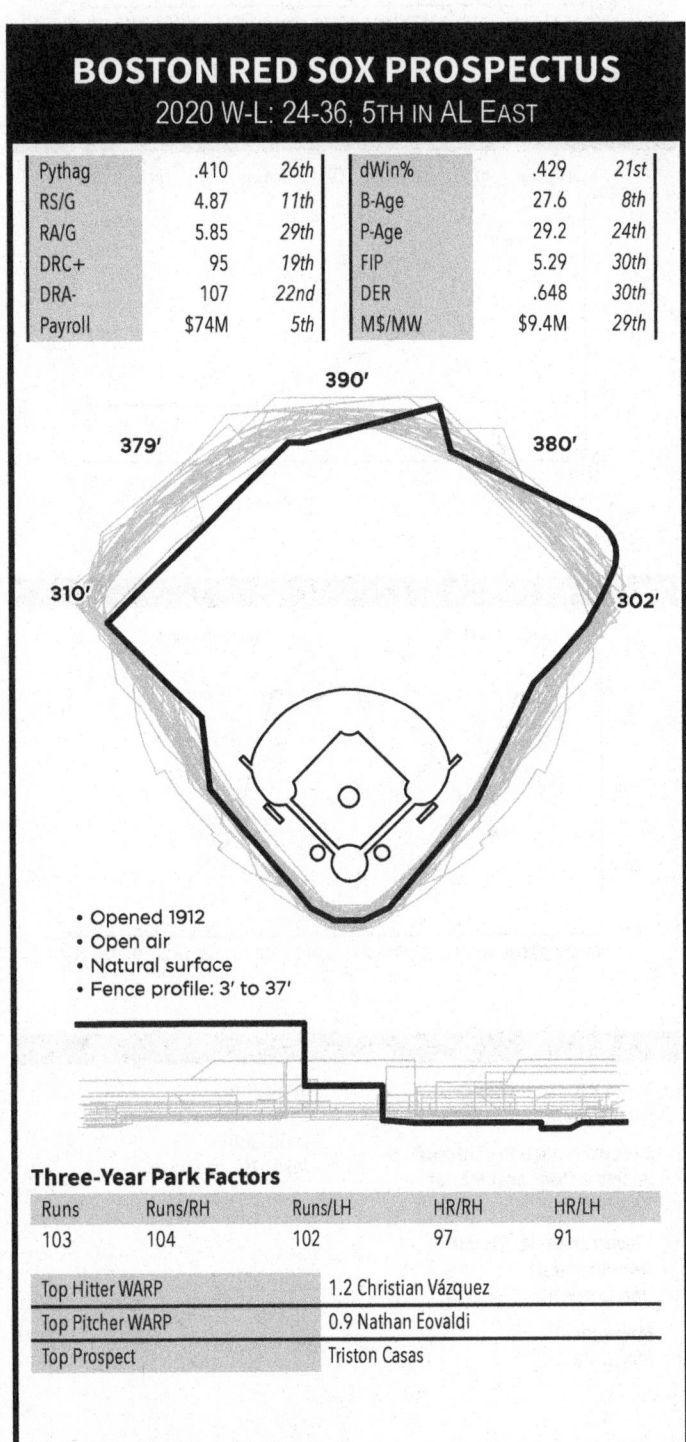

BOSTON RED SOX PROSPECTUS
2020 W-L: 24-36, 5TH IN AL EAST

Pythag	.410	26th	dWin%	.429	21st
RS/G	4.87	11th	B-Age	27.6	8th
RA/G	5.85	29th	P-Age	29.2	24th
DRC+	95	19th	FIP	5.29	30th
DRA-	107	22nd	DER	.648	30th
Payroll	$74M	5th	M$/MW	$9.4M	29th

390'
379'   380'
310'   302'

- Opened 1912
- Open air
- Natural surface
- Fence profile: 3' to 37'

Three-Year Park Factors

Runs	Runs/RH	Runs/LH	HR/RH	HR/LH
103	104	102	97	91

Top Hitter WARP	1.2 Christian Vázquez
Top Pitcher WARP	0.9 Nathan Eovaldi
Top Prospect	Triston Casas

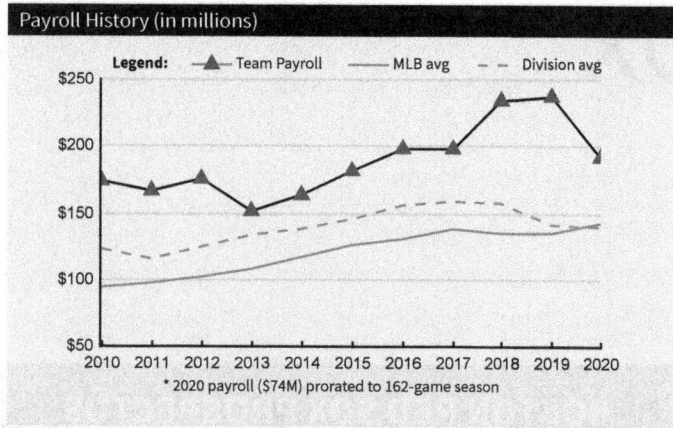

Payroll History (in millions)

* 2020 payroll ($74M) prorated to 162-game season

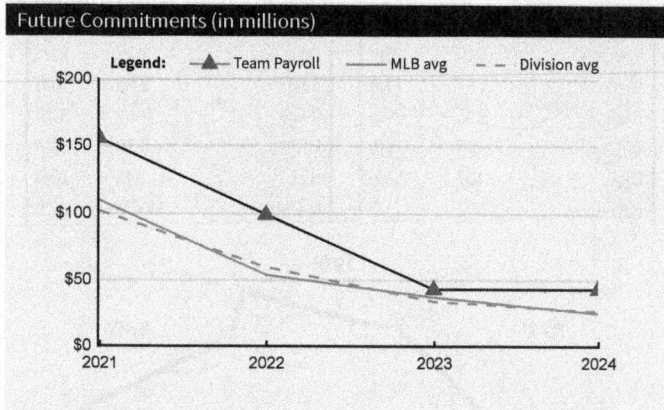

Future Commitments (in millions)

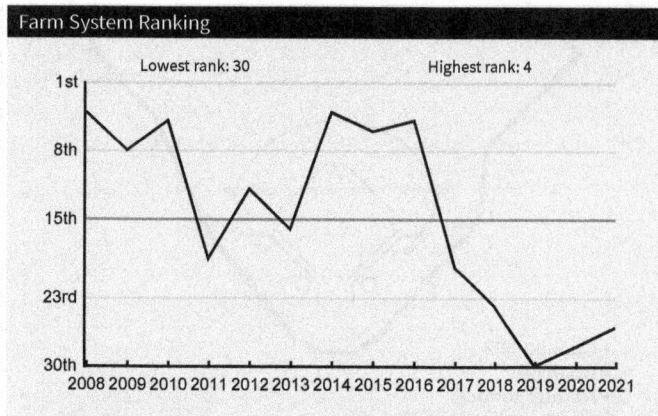

Farm System Ranking

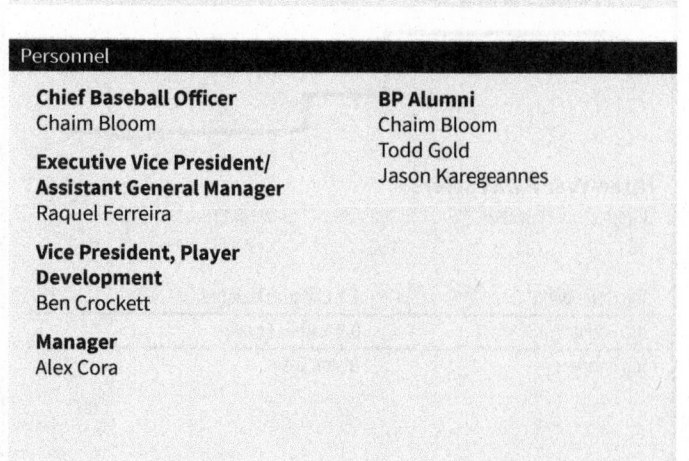

Personnel

Chief Baseball Officer
Chaim Bloom

**Executive Vice President/
Assistant General Manager**
Raquel Ferreira

**Vice President, Player
Development**
Ben Crockett

Manager
Alex Cora

BP Alumni
Chaim Bloom
Todd Gold
Jason Karegeannes

yet another Modern Baseball Corporation: a bloated version of the Tampa Bay Rays or Pittsburgh Pirates with more resources but even less purpose or soul.

Through a Red Sox-colored lens it's tempting to say that there were no winners in the Mookie Betts trade, but in reality, the victors are obvious: the team that acquired him and Betts himself. Betts proved to be the piece the Dodgers needed to get over the World Series hump. His five-tool talents played just as well out west as they did back east, as evidenced by his second-place finish in NL MVP voting. Betts also won by refusing to accept below-market extension offers from the Red Sox. Instead, he inked a 12-year, $365 million deal with the Dodgers that rightly places him behind only Mike Trout in baseball's financial hierarchy. There were victors aplenty in this deal, but none of them are still employed by the Red Sox.

Now that Henry has watched his own team collapse and Betts win another ring, one has to wonder if he fully appreciated the extent to which the Betts trade would undermine his previous efforts. Before committing a baseball high crime, Henry had served as the best owner in Red Sox franchise history. Since he headlined a group that purchased the Red Sox for a then-record $700 million in 2001, Henry's Sox have finished in the top five in payroll all but once, and have placed first or second in spending nine times in 19 tries. He led the renovation of Fenway Park, keeping the Sox in downtown(ish) Boston and preserving a national landmark. It was under Henry that the Sox brought in Theo Epstein, a man who, for better and worse, would become the prototype of the modern baseball executive. He wrote Ben Cherington and Dave Dombrowski blank checks to pursue free agent mega-deals to mixed results. Most importantly, the Sox have won four World Series under Henry's reign after an 86-year drought of infamy.

But while Henry may seem golden compared to his predecessors and his peer set, that's in part because we hold the entire class of baseball owners to far too low a standard. Yes, Henry has spent big bucks on the Red Sox, but the $700 million "investment" he played a major role in securing back in 2001 is now worth an estimated $3.3 *billion*, per Forbes. Henry *should* be spending like crazy—has a mandate too, really—because his ownership of the Red Sox is a license to print money. For those looking to excuse Henry because COVID-19 killed fan attendance, consider that ticket sales make up an ever-shrinking portion of teams' revenue streams. What's more, it *is* actually possible for an ownership group to elect to suffer one season of financial loss amid decades of wild profits instead of transferring those losses down to personnel, players and the fan base. Once upon a time, Henry seemed like the type of owner willing to make such a decision. Now, he seems content to merely follow the crowd.

Though we're living through the death of nuance, Henry's stewardship deserves both praise and scorn. Yes, he's spent more than most owners, and yes, he's played an unquantifiable role in the Red Sox's resurgence of the past two decades. He should also be tried at The Baseball Hague for choosing to draw the financial line at *literally Mookie Betts*. Consider all the ancillary revenue streams he's built up thanks in part to the Red Sox: NESN, *The Boston Globe*, the Fenway Sports Group and, most recently, its real estate subsidiary. Henry could blow past the luxury tax every year without meaningful consequence to his long-term profits. Perhaps you don't want to hold him to that standard, but surely he could've found a way to reduce his tax burden without evicting his franchise's best player.

That leads us to Bloom, Henry's latest choice to serve as architect of a Player Development Machine. Hailed as an innovator who'd deftly led the cash-strapped Rays to perennial relevance, Bloom's early moves in Boston have been as unimaginative as it gets. Trading your best, most expensive players for prospects is not novel or savvy: it is the type of obvious, cop-out "solution" every arm-chair GM deploys in their dynasty leagues. Perhaps Bloom had a mandate from ownership to move Betts, or at least a directive to get under the luxury tax at all costs. If the latter is true, there must have been other ways to do so rather than jettisoning one of the best players in franchise history for a collection of cheap but unproven talent. Is it not better to attach draft capital to Nate Eovaldi to get out from under his contract? To let Jackie Bradley Jr. go for a C-level prospect? To take 40 cents on the dollar for J.D. Martinez if the end result is Betts in Cooperstown with a Red Sox cap? We have no way of knowing if those moves were ever truly on the table, but all are individually *and* collectively preferable to trading Betts.

In large part, Red Sox Nation has recognized the Betts trade for what it is: an unmitigated disaster that benefits no one in New England but Henry. But as always, a smattering of contrarian takes persist. Some Sox fans proved so conditioned to side with ownership they cited the luxury tax as a burden. Some columnists remained so cynically contrarian they argued Betts' contract demands were simply too high. Worse yet was the vocal minority who insisted Betts was never going to sign in Boston long-term, steadfast in the type of reflexive defensiveness often seen from small-market fans who've watched their stars routinely leave for more lucrative pastures.

None of those arguments hold the slightest bit of water. A few million dollars in luxury tax should be a non-issue for a billionaire. To argue that the back-half of Betts' mega-deal may not offer surplus value ignores that the first-half that will—already has, if you recall who just won the World Series—and, if taken to its logical conclusion, suggests teams should never engage with top-flight free agents: another pro-ownership argument. And the only evidence we have that Betts did not want to be in Boston long-term was his unwillingness to accept below-market extension overtures earlier in his career. In fact, Betts himself has said that for a long time, he expected to retire a Red Sox.

There's one more pro-trade argument even more disingenuous than the rest: that it was a good *baseball* move, allowing the Red Sox to get younger and cheaper, to diversify their risk. One needs only contrast Boston's dumpster fire of a 2020 season with the Dodgers' soaring success to put that notion to rest. The haul the Red Sox received for Betts and fellow star David Price included some interesting long-term pieces. Alex Verdugo impressed in his first run as Betts' replacement. The ironically named Jeter Downs is a fine prospect. The Betts trade was not quite so lop-sided as the Ruthian transaction to which it's often compared. But make no mistake about it: it was an abject disaster for the Red Sox on the diamond. It was only a win for Henry's bottom line.

It's tempting for Red Sox fans to drown in a sea of "what-if," but the cold, hard truth is that Betts' departure leaves the Red Sox in an odd state of quasi-contention, "burdened" with too much talent to truly tank over a full season but lacking the pitching needed for a serious run. Xander Bogaerts, Rafael Devers and Verdugo comprise one of the league's better young offensive cores, and the Sox now have some life on the farm thanks to Downs, Triston Casas and others. But this is an organization woefully short on arms even *if* Chris Sale and Eduardo Rodriguez return to health. With a Betts-like talent in tow, perhaps the Sox could've pried their contention cycle open with an otherworldly offense, banking on Bloom's track record of unearthing live arms to patch the holes. Instead, they're purposely entering baseball purgatory, more likely to win 81 games than 65 or 95.

That seems to be the way Henry wants it now. There are legitimate reasons to seek an end to the peaks and valleys the Red Sox have experienced of late: in the past seven seasons, Boston has finished first in the division three times, last three times, and third once. There's an argument to be made in favor of shaving some upside for a higher yearly floor. But it's hard to look at the Betts trade and believe the primary motivator was anything other than saving ownership some cash. Betts represented the single most valuable type of commodity in baseball: a homegrown megastar in his prime without flaws on or off the field. If you really want to compete year-in and year-out, that's the guy you build around, and you figure out the rest. Instead, Sox fans are left only with empty platitudes about "financial flexibility" and "sustainability" as Henry, Tom Werner and co. deploy Bloom and CEO Sam Kennedy as human shields at press conferences, refusing to answer directly for their baseball sins.

Perhaps this all seems a bit dramatic. The Red Sox are hardly the first team to trade a superstar, and they won't be the last. But the Sox haven't just lost Betts; they've lost their identity. Despite a deserved reputation for smearing players on the way out of town, the Sox also had a penchant for taking care of their own. Franchise icons and homegrown heroes such as Jason Varitek, Tim Wakefield, Dustin Pedroia and, of course, David Ortiz, were essentially given lifetime contracts. When others like Jon Lester were shown the door, there were at least credible baseball justifications for their departures. The Sox were an organization that *hoarded* stars: not one that shed them to save a few bucks.

That's no longer the case. Betts will end his career with the Dodgers because Henry has decided he'd rather his team be profitable than good, efficient than special. And if you really need more evidence that baseball is broken than the *Boston Red Sox* trading *Mookie Betts*, just wait a season or two: some other "big-market team" will soon follow suit. The altar of financial flexibility is always hungry for another sacrifice. ▪

—Ben Carsley is an author of Baseball Prospectus.

HITTERS

Jonathan Araúz SS
Born: 08/03/98   Age: 22   Bats: S   Throws: R   Height: 6'0"   Weight: 195   Origin: International Free Agent, 2014

YEAR	TEAM	LVL	AGE	PA	R	2B	3B	HR	RBI	BB	K	SB	CS	Whiff%	AVG/OBP/SLG	DRC+	BABIP	BRR	FRAA	WARP
2018	QC	LO-A	19	237	31	11	6	4	29	30	38	7	6		.299/.392/.471	147	.350	0.4	SS(33): 0.6, 2B(17): 0.4, 3B(3): -0.3	1.9
2018	FAY	HI-A	19	253	25	10	3	4	18	16	36	1	2		.167/.223/.288	38	.180	-2.6	SS(70): -5.5, 2B(1): -0.1	-2.0
2019	FAY	HI-A	20	354	41	19	0	8	42	30	69	5	4		.252/.322/.388	110	.296	-2.5	SS(62): -2.3, 3B(18): 0.8, 2B(6): 0.0	1.3
2019	CC	AA	20	119	12	3	2	3	13	10	19	1	1		.241/.311/.389	118	.267	-0.8	2B(15): -1.7, SS(7): 0.4, 3B(6): 0.2	0.4
2020	BOS	MLB	22	80	8	2	0	1	9	8	21	0	0	22.0%	.250/.325/.319	76	.340	0.3	2B(16): -1.7, 3B(6): -0.3, SS(4): 0.6	-0.1
2021 FS	BOS	MLB	22	600	63	24	3	13	59	49	155	2	1	22.0%	.229/.297/.362	84	.294	-0.7	2B -9, 3B 2	-0.1
2021 DC	BOS	MLB	22	200	21	8	1	4	19	16	51	0	0	22.0%	.229/.297/.362	84	.294	-0.2	2B -3, 3B 1	0.0

Comparables: Domingo Leyba, Gavin Cecchini, Marwin Gonzalez

Look, fielding a competitive roster has its advantages—sometimes it even results in a World Series win—but the downside of competing is that you never get the chance to roster guys like Arauz. Popped with the 17th pick in the 2019 Rule 5 draft, Arauz came to Boston via Houston with a reputation as a glove-first middle infielder with some feel for making contact. He played as advertised, making cameos all across the infield while posting a DRC+ just below league average. That modest combination of skills combined with expanded rosters and Boston's exodus of talent let Arauz hang around on the roster all season, which means the Sox can now stash him in the minors for a few more years. It seems like that's maybe not worth nuking your franchise over, but hey—there's some real potential for surplus value here, and that's what the new Red Sox are all about.

Christian Arroyo 3B
Born: 05/30/95   Age: 26   Bats: R   Throws: R   Height: 6'1"   Weight: 210   Origin: Round 1, 2013 Draft (#25 overall)

YEAR	TEAM	LVL	AGE	PA	R	2B	3B	HR	RBI	BB	K	SB	CS	Whiff%	AVG/OBP/SLG	DRC+	BABIP	BRR	FRAA	WARP
2018	DUR	AAA	23	182	19	12	0	2	20	8	32	2	3		.235/.286/.341	73	.279	1.0	3B(34): -1.2, SS(6): -0.2	-0.2
2018	TB	MLB	23	59	5	2	1	1	6	6	16	0	0	26.0%	.264/.339/.396	85	.361	0.4	2B(8): -0.5, 3B(7): -0.5	0.0
2019	DUR	AAA	24	134	21	9	1	8	29	12	26	1	0		.314/.381/.603	143	.345	1.2	3B(20): 0.3, SS(9): -0.1, 2B(1): 0.1	1.3
2019	TB	MLB	24	57	8	2	0	2	7	5	18	0	0	31.7%	.220/.304/.380	72	.300	0.1	3B(13): -0.4, 2B(1): 0.0	0.0
2020	CLE	MLB	25	0	0	0	0	0	0	0	0	0	0		None/None/None				3B(1): -0.0	0.0
2020	BOS	MLB	25	54	7	1	0	3	8	4	11	0	0	25.7%	.240/.296/.440	94	.250	0.8	2B(13): 3.8, SS(2): -0.2	0.6
2021 FS	BOS	MLB	26	600	63	24	1	16	64	37	145	1	0	27.9%	.229/.286/.370	81	.280	-0.7	2B -5, 3B 0	-0.6
2021 DC	BOS	MLB	26	435	46	17	1	12	46	27	105	1	0	27.9%	.229/.286/.370	81	.280	-0.5	2B -4	0.1

Comparables: Colin Moran, Christian Villanueva, Brian Barden

Get you a man who looks at you the way Chaim Bloom looks at Arroyo. Way back in 2017, Bloom was a senior VP of baseball ops with the Rays when they traded the face of their franchise Evan Longoria to the Giants for a package headlined by Arroyo, who was then a top prospect. It cost Bloom far less to acquire Arroyo the second time around given that Cleveland DFA'd him in August. With the Sox, Arroyo showed just enough defensive versatility and power to prove intriguing without hitting well enough to engender any real excitement. He's still young-ish and he's mashed at Triple-A, but is best viewed as a bench piece with a dash of upside. If nothing else, Red Sox fans are used to rooting for an Arroyo on the periphery of the roster, though hopefully this one refrains from cornrows.

Andrew Benintendi LF
Born: 07/06/94   Age: 27   Bats: L   Throws: L   Height: 5'9"   Weight: 180   Origin: Round 1, 2015 Draft (#7 overall)

YEAR	TEAM	LVL	AGE	PA	R	2B	3B	HR	RBI	BB	K	SB	CS	Whiff%	AVG/OBP/SLG	DRC+	BABIP	BRR	FRAA	WARP
2018	BOS	MLB	23	661	103	41	6	16	87	71	106	21	3	19.3%	.290/.366/.465	117	.328	-1.1	LF(129): 8.2, CF(24): -2.6	3.7
2019	BOS	MLB	24	615	72	40	5	13	68	59	140	10	3	25.2%	.266/.343/.431	94	.333	0.8	LF(131): -5.7, CF(12): 1.5	0.9
2020	BOS	MLB	26	52	4	1	0	0	1	11	17	1	2	33.3%	.103/.314/.128	80	.182	0.2	LF(13): 0.2	0.0
2021 FS	BOS	MLB	26	600	73	27	4	13	54	68	131	13	4	24.0%	.244/.337/.390	100	.302	4.3	LF -7, CF -5	1.0
2021 DC	BOS	MLB	26	501	61	23	3	11	45	56	110	11	3	24.0%	.244/.337/.390	100	.302	3.6	LF -6, CF -4	0.9

Comparables: Dusty Rhodes, Christian Yelich, Nolan Reimold

As Benintendi goes, so go the Red Sox. At his peak, Benny with the Good Hair served as a linchpin of the best team in franchise history. More often, he's underperformed relative to his talent. And in 2020, he may as well not have existed. Benintendi was limited to a handful of games thanks to a rib injury, and with the Sox actively tanking there was no impetus for him to return to action. When he did play he was terrible, and while the sample size is quite small it was concerning to see Benintendi look so lost at the plate following his disappointing 2019. He won't turn 27 until halfway through this season, but we're now two-plus years removed from Benintendi looking like anything special. It's strange to think that a sweet-swinging lefty could need a change of scenery *away* from Boston, but it's sure starting to feel that way.

Xander Bogaerts SS Born: 10/01/92 Age: 28 Bats: R Throws: R Height: 6'2" Weight: 218 Origin: International Free Agent, 2009

YEAR	TEAM	LVL	AGE	PA	R	2B	3B	HR	RBI	BB	K	SB	CS	Whiff%	AVG/OBP/SLG	DRC+	BABIP	BRR	FRAA	WARP
2018	BOS	MLB	25	580	72	45	3	23	103	55	102	8	2	21.0%	.288/.360/.522	130	.317	-0.2	SS(136): 1.5	4.9
2019	BOS	MLB	26	698	110	52	0	33	117	76	122	4	2	20.8%	.309/.384/.555	134	.338	-0.1	SS(153): -20.8	4.3
2020	BOS	MLB	28	225	36	8	0	11	28	21	41	8	0	23.0%	.300/.364/.502	113	.329	1.1	SS(53): -1.4	0.9
2021 FS	BOS	MLB	28	600	78	35	1	21	86	54	116	8	2	21.4%	.286/.356/.476	130	.330	0.3	SS -11	3.2
2021 DC	BOS	MLB	28	568	74	33	1	20	81	51	110	7	2	21.4%	.286/.356/.476	130	.330	0.3	SS -11	3.0

Comparables: Asdrúbal Cabrera, Rico Petrocelli, Khalil Greene

Bogaerts is a bona fide star flirting with a Hall of Fame career path, yet he's often been outshone by otherworldly talents. With Mookie Betts gone, Rafael Devers struggling and Chris Sale hurt, it was finally Bogey's show in 2020, and he looked mighty comfortable in the starring role. In addition to pacing the Sox in DRC+, homers, steals and runs scored, Bogaerts ranked in the top-10 among all shortstops in said categories. For once, FRAA agreed with the eye test and labeled him a fine if unremarkable defender, and he became a more vocal clubhouse leader in Betts' absence. The X-Man is a steadying presence for a franchise in turmoil, and the six-year, $120 million extension he signed in 2019 continues to look like a steal for the only org he's ever known. Bogaerts has an opt out after 2022, though, and while the market doesn't look great for free agents at present, neither do the Red Sox.

Jackie Bradley Jr. CF Born: 04/19/90 Age: 31 Bats: L Throws: R Height: 5'10" Weight: 196 Origin: Round 1, 2011 Draft (#40 overall)

YEAR	TEAM	LVL	AGE	PA	R	2B	3B	HR	RBI	BB	K	SB	CS	Whiff%	AVG/OBP/SLG	DRC+	BABIP	BRR	FRAA	WARP
2018	BOS	MLB	28	535	76	33	4	13	59	46	137	17	1	30.8%	.234/.314/.403	87	.299	2.5	CF(135): 6.1, RF(15): 0.3	1.9
2019	BOS	MLB	29	567	69	28	3	21	62	56	155	8	6	33.0%	.225/.317/.421	86	.281	0.9	CF(144): 0.9, RF(3): 0.4	1.3
2020	BOS	MLB	30	217	32	11	0	7	22	23	48	5	2	26.1%	.283/.364/.450	94	.343	1.5	CF(55): -3.0	0.2
2021 FS	BOS	MLB	31	600	66	28	3	16	67	60	152	10	3	30.5%	.238/.328/.398	101	.304	1.7	CF -7, RF 0	1.4

Comparables: B.J. Upton, Chris Young, Drew Stubbs

Few players embodied the last decade of Red Sox baseball quite like Bradley Jr. and his soaring peaks and low, low valleys. During his time in Boston, Bradley won two World Series rings, an ALCS MVP, made an All-Star team and earned a Gold Glove (and deserved a half-dozen more). He was also a below-average hitter for five of those eight seasons, was benched or platooned a handful of times and played on three last-place teams. A homegrown talent who somehow both under- and over-performed his prospect projections, he spoiled Red Sox fans with his otherworldly defense in center and spoiled appetites with months-long cold streaks at the plate interspersed with inexplicable stretches of dominance. Now entering his age-31 season, Bradley is coming off a strong walk year and makes sense for competitors looking for cost-effective options in center. In theory the Red Sox should fit that description, but it seems likely they'll let Bradley be the latest high-profile departure from a core that won 108 games just two years ago.

────────── ★ ★ ★ *2021 Top 101 Prospect* **#85** ★ ★ ★ ──────────

Triston Casas 3B Born: 01/15/00 Age: 21 Bats: L Throws: R Height: 6'4" Weight: 238 Origin: Round 1, 2018 Draft (#26 overall)

YEAR	TEAM	LVL	AGE	PA	R	2B	3B	HR	RBI	BB	K	SB	CS	Whiff%	AVG/OBP/SLG	DRC+	BABIP	BRR	FRAA	WARP
2018	RSX	ROK	18	5	0	0	0	0	0	1	2	0	0		.000/.200/.000	45	.000		3B(1): -0.0	0.0
2019	GVL	LO-A	19	493	64	25	5	19	78	58	116	3	2		.254/.349/.472	144	.300	-0.9	1B(94): -4.7, 3B(8): -1.2	2.1
2019	SAL	HI-A	19	7	2	1	0	1	3	0	2	0	0		.429/.429/1.000	158	.500	0.1	1B(2): -0.0	0.1
2021 FS	BOS	MLB	21	600	55	27	3	16	64	37	197	0	0		.212/.268/.363	71	.296	1.3	1B -4, 3B 0	-1.7

Comparables: Lars Anderson, Mike Carp, Anthony Rizzo

Good news was hard to come by for the Red Sox last season, but most updates about Casas served as exceptions to that rule. Boston's 2018 first-round pick impressed with his size and power as he continued to grow into a massive 6-foot-5, 250-pound frame. What's even more encouraging is how Casas appeared to gain selectivity at the plate while facing relatively advanced pitching at Boston's alternate camp, perhaps in tribute to his self-proclaimed hero, Joey Votto. Drafting a first base prospect is always a risky proposition, but Casas is emerging as a potential prototypical first-division cold corner power bat. He should start the year as a 21-year-old in Double-A, meaning Green Monsters in the mirror may be closer than they appear.

Rusney Castillo CF Born: 07/09/87 Age: 34 Bats: R Throws: R Height: 5'9" Weight: 207 Origin: International Free Agent, 2014

YEAR	TEAM	LVL	AGE	PA	R	2B	3B	HR	RBI	BB	K	SB	CS	Whiff%	AVG/OBP/SLG	DRC+	BABIP	BRR	FRAA	WARP
2018	WOR	AAA	30	511	56	31	0	5	59	29	80	13	7		.319/.360/.416	132	.372	1.2	CF(97): -4.6, RF(8): -0.4	2.3
2019	WOR	AAA	31	493	63	25	1	17	64	25	63	5	9		.278/.321/.448	101	.291	-1.3	RF(82): 1.9, CF(25): 1.2	1.3
2021 FS	BOS	MLB	33	600	55	26	1	13	61	29	136	1	0		.238/.285/.366	77	.291	-1.1	CF 2, RF 1	0.2

Comparables: Darnell McDonald, Chad Allen, Cory Sullivan

Odds are you and Castillo have more in common than you might think. For starters, you've probably made the same number of major league appearances over the past four seasons. Like Castillo, perhaps you settled down in a strange town you never envisioned yourself living in. And if someone offered you $72.5 million to kill your career and spend a half-decade in Pawtucket, well, just like Castillo, you'd probably grin and bear it. Castillo is finally free of the seven-year pact that long shackled him to Triple-A, but as a 33-year-old outfielder without a defining skill, he might remain mired there for non-contractual reasons. See, there's something else you and Castillo have in common: time doesn't wait for you.

Michael Chavis 2B Born: 08/11/95 Age: 25 Bats: R Throws: R Height: 5'10" Weight: 210 Origin: Round 1, 2014 Draft (#26 overall)

YEAR	TEAM	LVL	AGE	PA	R	2B	3B	HR	RBI	BB	K	SB	CS	Whiff%	AVG/OBP/SLG	DRC+	BABIP	BRR	FRAA	WARP
2018	POR	AA	22	139	23	7	0	6	17	13	35	3	1		.303/.388/.508	144	.383	0.5	3B(18): 1.5, 1B(10): -0.5	1.0
2018	WOR	AAA	22	34	8	3	0	2	7	1	12	0	0		.273/.294/.545	90	.368	0.2	3B(4): -1.2, 1B(1): -0.0	-0.1
2019	WOR	AAA	23	79	11	4	0	7	11	8	21	0	0		.257/.329/.614	142	.256	-0.7	2B(7): 1.6, 3B(7): -0.6, 1B(4): 0.9	0.7
2019	BOS	MLB	23	382	46	10	1	18	58	31	127	2	1	38.3%	.254/.322/.444	93	.347	0.0	1B(49): 2.4, 2B(45): -0.9, 3B(5): -0.2	0.7
2020	BOS	MLB	25	158	16	5	2	5	19	8	50	3	0	38.3%	.212/.259/.377	70	.280	-0.8	1B(24): 1.0, LF(12): -0.5, 2B(8): -0.5	-0.3
2021 FS	BOS	MLB	25	600	66	24	2	23	76	42	199	1	0	38.3%	.225/.290/.407	92	.305	0.4	1B 1, 2B 0	0.8
2021 DC	BOS	MLB	25	468	51	19	1	18	59	33	155	1	0	38.3%	.225/.290/.407	92	.305	0.3	LF -2, 1B 1	0.5

Comparables: Carlos Pena, Tony Clark, Jeff Clement

Chavis had a chance to prove he should be considered a foundational piece of the Next Good Red Sox team. Instead he played a role in Boston's collapse. Despite lucking into as clear a path to playing time as he could have possibly hoped for after an uneven rookie campaign, Chavis was unable to prove he belonged in the lineup every day. His strikeout rate remained sky-high while his walk and homer rates fell, and as the season progressed Chavis lost playing time to the bigger, better version of himself: rookie Bobby Dalbec. Chavis still has plus power and just enough defensive versatility to pique your interest, but it's clear that any team with first-division aspirations can't rely on him as their Plan A in any capacity.

Bobby Dalbec 3B Born: 06/29/95 Age: 26 Bats: R Throws: R Height: 6'4" Weight: 227 Origin: Round 4, 2016 Draft (#118 overall)

YEAR	TEAM	LVL	AGE	PA	R	2B	3B	HR	RBI	BB	K	SB	CS	Whiff%	AVG/OBP/SLG	DRC+	BABIP	BRR	FRAA	WARP
2018	SAL	HI-A	23	419	59	27	2	26	85	60	130	3	1		.256/.372/.573	159	.318	0.9	3B(91): 5.2, SS(1): 0.0	3.8
2018	POR	AA	23	124	14	8	1	6	24	6	46	0	0		.261/.323/.514	96	.377	-0.1	3B(18): -3.9, 1B(2): -0.3	-0.4
2019	POR	AA	24	439	57	15	2	20	57	68	110	6	4		.234/.371/.454	150	.278	-2.2	3B(90): 7.2, 1B(13): 0.9	4.2
2019	WOR	AAA	24	123	12	4	0	7	16	5	29	0	2		.257/.301/.478	83	.278	0.3	3B(17): 2.0, 1B(11): -1.3	0.2
2020	BOS	MLB	25	92	13	3	0	8	16	10	39	0	0	46.2%	.263/.359/.600	92	.394	-0.2	1B(21): 1.8, 3B(2): -0.2	0.2
2021 FS	BOS	MLB	26	600	73	26	1	28	81	55	238	1	0	46.2%	.226/.310/.441	107	.344	-1.0	1B -9, 3B 0	0.8
2021 DC	BOS	MLB	26	568	69	24	1	26	77	52	226	1	0	46.2%	.226/.310/.441	107	.344	-1.0	1B -8	0.5

Comparables: Mat Gamel, Matt Carpenter, Mike Olt

Sometimes prospects can fool you with their early major-league performance. Not so with Dalbec—he showed his true colors from day one. With his broad shoulders and vicious upper-cut swing, Dalbec provides true top-of-the-scale power and the potential to go bridge in every at-bat. But he'll need to dramatically cut back on his strikeouts in order to maximize his pop, and while he improved his approach in the upper minors, his 40-plus percent K rate in the majors is untenable. More often than not, this profile forces a player into a Quad-A or bench bat role. But for every dozen-or-so sluggers who are felled by such an extreme approach, a Joey Gallo emerges and does just enough to make it work. That's the dream for Dalbec, who possesses one more Gallo-ian trait: an absolute firehose of an arm.

Rafael Devers 3B Born: 10/24/96 Age: 24 Bats: L Throws: R Height: 6'0" Weight: 240 Origin: International Free Agent, 2013

YEAR	TEAM	LVL	AGE	PA	R	2B	3B	HR	RBI	BB	K	SB	CS	Whiff%	AVG/OBP/SLG	DRC+	BABIP	BRR	FRAA	WARP
2018	BOS	MLB	21	490	59	24	0	21	66	38	121	5	2	27.6%	.240/.298/.433	94	.281	1.7	3B(116): 11.2	2.8
2019	BOS	MLB	22	702	129	54	4	32	115	48	118	8	8	24.3%	.311/.361/.555	124	.339	0.2	3B(152): 7.2, SS(1): -0.0	5.6
2020	BOS	MLB	24	248	32	16	1	11	43	13	67	0	0	31.8%	.263/.310/.483	95	.325	1.1	3B(57): -8.7	-0.4
2021 FS	BOS	MLB	24	600	77	36	3	22	79	42	152	6	3	27.1%	.260/.318/.458	109	.321	-1.6	3B 10, SS 0	2.8
2021 DC	BOS	MLB	24	568	73	34	2	21	75	40	144	5	2	27.1%	.260/.318/.458	109	.321	-1.5	3B 9	2.6

Comparables: Will Middlebrooks, Hank Blalock, Travis Fryman

If 2019 represented two giant steps forward for Devers, 2020 marked a half-step back. The cherubic slugger hit just .182/.241/.325 through the season's first 20 games while reverting to oft-erratic play at third base. He eventually righted the ship at the plate, hitting .301/.345/.522 over the later two-thirds of Boston's lost season, but still placed just 34th in DRC+ among third baseman—24 spots worse than a year earlier. Devers' talent, age and track record remain points in his favor, but two recurring flaws threaten to stay his ascent to stardom: his troubles against left-handers and his wildness in the field. He hit just .222 against southpaws, albeit in 81 plate appearances, and posted the second-worst FRAA of any third baseman. Both maladies seemed remedied in 2019 but plagued Devers earlier in his career, which makes it tougher to chalk them up to small samples. As such, Devers' upcoming campaign should go a long way toward resolving two outstanding questions about his future: can he stick at third base through his 20s, and is he a merely good hitter or a truly great one? With extension talks and late arbitration years looming, tens of millions of dollars likely hinge on the answers.

Jeter Downs SS   Born: 07/27/98   Age: 22   Bats: R   Throws: R   Height: 5'11"   Weight: 195   Origin: Round 1, 2017 Draft (#32 overall)

YEAR	TEAM	LVL	AGE	PA	R	2B	3B	HR	RBI	BB	K	SB	CS	Whiff%	AVG/OBP/SLG	DRC+	BABIP	BRR	FRAA	WARP
2018	DAY	LO-A	19	524	63	23	2	13	47	52	103	37	10		.257/.351/.402	121	.306	-1.6	2B(73): -2.9, SS(43): -9.3	0.8
2019	RC	HI-A	20	475	76	32	4	19	75	53	96	22	8		.269/.353/.506	126	.302	4.1	SS(91): -4.0, 2B(10): -1.1	2.9
2019	TUL	AA	20	56	14	2	0	5	11	6	10	1	0		.333/.429/.688	166	.333	0.8	SS(11): -0.4, 2B(1): -0.0	0.6
2021 FS	BOS	MLB	22	600	67	27	2	23	77	47	162	16	7		.237/.306/.429	101	.293	-1.3	SS -11, 2B -2	0.6

Comparables: Addison Russell, Daniel Robertson, Lonnie Chisenhall

It's one thing to trade a franchise icon in order to save your billionaire owner a few bucks. It's another to ensure that the return for said icon includes a player named after the most hated rival in your team's history. It will be strange to see a Jeter manning an infield spot for the Red Sox, but we're headed that way in a hurry—Downs continued to impress at Boston's alternate camp, which means a big-league debut is likely right around the corner. He's not the toolsiest prospect in the world, but also lacks much in the way of a weakness. Downs is not a power hitter, but he's got enough pop to keep pitchers honest. He's not a true speedster, but he'll swipe a few bags. He's athletic enough to play a good second base, but should only slide over to short in a pinch. Essentially, Downs is the type of Role 55-ish everyday player Chaim Bloom collected in droves as part of Tampa's front office. He'll provide the Sox with an affordable, acceptable option for several years, though his moniker, involvement in the Mookie Betts trade, and status as the likely heir to Dustin Pedroia mean he'll face plenty of pressure.

Jarren Duran OF   Born: 09/05/96   Age: 24   Bats: L   Throws: R   Height: 6'2"   Weight: 187   Origin: Round 7, 2018 Draft (#220 overall)

YEAR	TEAM	LVL	AGE	PA	R	2B	3B	HR	RBI	BB	K	SB	CS	Whiff%	AVG/OBP/SLG	DRC+	BABIP	BRR	FRAA	WARP
2018	LOW	SS	21	168	28	5	10	2	20	11	26	12	4		.348/.393/.548	168	.406	0.4	2B(20): 4.9, CF(15): 0.1	1.6
2018	GVL	LO-A	21	134	24	9	1	1	15	5	22	12	6		.367/.396/.477	163	.438	1.6	RF(30): -0.0	1.1
2019	SAL	HI-A	22	226	49	13	3	4	19	23	44	18	5		.387/.456/.543	200	.480	3.4	CF(50): 0.2	3.3
2019	POR	AA	22	352	41	11	5	1	19	23	84	28	8		.250/.309/.325	75	.335	5.1	CF(80): -3.3	0.5
2021 FS	BOS	MLB	24	600	60	29	7	8	59	33	163	28	9		.255/.304/.378	84	.348	7.6	CF -5, 2B 0	1.0
2021 DC	BOS	MLB	24	66	6	3	0	0	6	3	17	3	1		.255/.304/.378	84	.348	0.8	CF -1	0.1

Comparables: Engel Beltre, Gorkys Hernández, Noel Cuevas

In a dark and miserable year, a lonely, desperate Red Sox Nation had but one thing to look forward to: #DuranSZN updates on Twitter. Sure, Duran may not be the Red Sox's *best* prospect, but he is arguably their most popular one. He's got a good story as a seventh-rounder now on the periphery of national prospect consciousness. He's got a fun skill set as a speedy outfielder who has reportedly added power to his game. And he's got the distinction of being one of the only prospects with any upside in the org's upper minors. We still don't know if Duran is an everyday player or more of a fourth outfielder, and 2020 deprived us of the chance to watch him face advanced pitching. But nearly every report on Duran from the Sox's alternate site was effusive in its praise. Barring a major influx of outfield talent, Boston figures to have need of his services at some point this year, which means your timeline could be flooded with #DuranSZN updates soon.

Gilberto Jimenez CF   Born: 07/08/00   Age: 20   Bats: S   Throws: R   Height: 5'11"   Weight: 160   Origin: International Free Agent, 2017

YEAR	TEAM	LVL	AGE	PA	R	2B	3B	HR	RBI	BB	K	SB	CS	Whiff%	AVG/OBP/SLG	DRC+	BABIP	BRR	FRAA	WARP
2018	DSL RSB	ROK	17	284	42	10	8	0	22	19	40	16	14		.319/.384/.420	147	.378	-1.0	CF(63): 3.4	2.0
2019	LOW	SS	18	254	35	11	3	3	19	13	38	14	6		.359/.393/.470	190	.413	1.2	CF(57): -9.8, LF(1): -0.1, RF(1): -0.1	1.9
2021 FS	BOS	MLB	20	600	49	26	4	6	53	27	160	19	11		.251/.292/.351	76	.339	-6.5	CF -6, RF 0	-1.2

Comparables: Harold Ramirez, Franklin Barreto, Manuel Margot

For developmental prospects like Jimenez, the lack of a minor league season presented many challenges. Through no fault of his own, Jimenez was unable to hone his approach at the plate and budding switch-hitting abilities against live competition: a disappointment after winning the batting title at short-season Lowell in 2019. We don't know if he's added power or learned to walk more, and we don't know if he's improved his routes in center field. What we do know is that Jimenez took care of the stuff he could control, such as strength training and conditioning, as he reportedly showed up to instructionals looking bigger and stronger. If that translates to more pop for Jimenez he could become a top-100 prospect in short order, but until he gets to face live pitching, we're all in wait-and-see mode.

Blaze Jordan 3B   Born: 12/19/02   Age: 18   Bats: R   Throws: R   Height: 6'2"   Weight: 220   Origin: Round 3, 2020 Draft (#89 overall)

Popped with the 89th pick in the 2020 draft but signed to a massive overslot deal, Jordan has some of the best raw power in the minors and a halfway decent idea how to use it. That his name sounds like a Cody Bellinger-inspired series of Air Force Ones is but an added bonus.

Matthew Lugo SS   Born: 05/09/01   Age: 20   Bats: R   Throws: R   Height: 6'1"   Weight: 185   Origin: Round 2, 2019 Draft (#69 overall)

YEAR	TEAM	LVL	AGE	PA	R	2B	3B	HR	RBI	BB	K	SB	CS	Whiff%	AVG/OBP/SLG	DRC+	BABIP	BRR	FRAA	WARP
2019	RSX	ROK	18	157	19	5	1	1	12	15	36	3	0		.257/.342/.331	124	.340	1.0	SS(30): 1.7	1.2
2019	LOW	SS	18	8	0	0	0	0	1	0	2	0	0		.250/.250/.250	79	.333	-0.1	SS(2): -0.6	-0.1
2021 FS	BOS	MLB	20	600	46	26	2	8	50	31	213	3	1		.209/.257/.310	55	.320	0.6	SS -1	-1.6

Thanks to the lack of a minor league season, we don't know if toolsy shortstop prospect Lugo has started to make good on his potential. Sox fans are used to waiting on production from a Lugo at the six, at least.

J.D. Martinez LF   Born: 08/21/87   Age: 33   Bats: R   Throws: R   Height: 6'3"   Weight: 230   Origin: Round 20, 2009 Draft (#611 overall)

YEAR	TEAM	LVL	AGE	PA	R	2B	3B	HR	RBI	BB	K	SB	CS	Whiff%	AVG/OBP/SLG	DRC+	BABIP	BRR	FRAA	WARP
2018	BOS	MLB	30	649	111	37	2	43	130	69	146	6	1	28.2%	.330/.402/.629	166	.375	-3.9	LF(32): -0.9, RF(25): 2.4	6.3
2019	BOS	MLB	31	657	98	33	2	36	105	72	138	2	0	26.7%	.304/.383/.557	138	.342	-6.2	RF(24): 3.8, LF(15): 0.5	4.2
2020	BOS	MLB	33	237	22	16	0	7	27	22	59	1	0	28.1%	.213/.291/.389	97	.259	-1.5	RF(4): -0.8, LF(3): 0.4	0.2
2021 FS	BOS	MLB	33	600	76	26	1	25	83	59	162	3	1	27.5%	.241/.320/.440	111	.296	-0.6	LF 0, RF 0	2.2
2021 DC	BOS	MLB	33	568	72	24	1	24	78	56	154	2	1	27.5%	.241/.320/.440	111	.296	-0.6	LF 0	1.9

Comparables: Jay Buhner, Nelson Cruz, Ryan Ludwick

There are three main reasons Martinez elected not to opt out of his contract, in essence settling for a two-year, ~$39 million deal to remain with the Red Sox. First, COVID-19 wreaked havoc on baseball's economy, with owners all too eager to ensure players feel the pain of lower profit margins. Second, MLB opted against adopting a universal DH, effectively halving Martinez's market. And third—and perhaps most importantly—Martinez flat-out stunk in 2020. One year after finishing 15th in the majors in DRC+, Martinez hit worse than Ty France and Brandon Crawford, posting his worst offensive output since 2013. It's reasonably safe to assume that Martinez's sudden belly flop stemmed from a small sample on a lifeless team in a weird season. That being said, Martinez is now a 33-year-old DH with declining bat speed who spent more time complaining about the lack of in-game video than he did on base last season. A bounce back is likely, yes, but far from guaranteed.

Yairo Muñoz   OF   Born: 01/23/95   Age: 26   Bats: R   Throws: R   Height: 5'11"   Weight: 200   Origin: International Free Agent, 2012

YEAR	TEAM	LVL	AGE	PA	R	2B	3B	HR	RBI	BB	K	SB	CS	Whiff%	AVG/OBP/SLG	DRC+	BABIP	BRR	FRAA	WARP
2018	MEM	AAA	23	100	11	3	1	3	13	5	18	1	0		.287/.330/.436	104	.329	0.3	SS(13): 0.2, 3B(4): -0.4, LF(4): -0.5	0.2
2018	STL	MLB	23	329	39	16	0	8	42	30	71	5	6	27.2%	.276/.350/.413	101	.338	-2.5	SS(40): -5.4, 2B(26): -0.8, 3B(24): 0.2	0.2
2019	STL	MLB	24	181	20	7	1	2	13	7	37	8	3	27.3%	.267/.298/.355	72	.328	0.8	3B(21): -0.1, SS(17): 0.1, RF(12): -0.5	0.0
2020	BOS	MLB	25	45	6	5	0	1	4	0	11	2	0	35.2%	.333/.333/.511	84	.424	-0.5	LF(7): 0.0, RF(4): 0.4	0.0
2021 FS	BOS	MLB	26	600	62	29	2	14	65	33	140	10	4	28.5%	.248/.296/.388	88	.306	-1.9	SS 0, 3B 0	0.2
2021 DC	BOS	MLB	26	133	13	6	0	3	14	7	31	2	0	28.5%	.248/.296/.388	88	.306	-0.4	SS 0, 3B 0	0.0

Comparables: Bobby Crosby, Addison Russell, Rico Petrocelli

Muñoz started his 2020 season by fulfilling a fantasy that many a baseball fan has had over the years: walking out on the St. Louis Cardinals. After suffering a hamstring injury in late February, Muñoz took an unsanctioned flight back to his native Dominican Republic and refused to return the Cardinals' calls. That prompted a DFA, which allowed the Sox to scoop him up on a minor-league deal a few weeks later. In his limited action in Boston, he was the same guy as in St. Louis: a good hitter with pop but no real defensive home. The Sox have stockpiled such players as of late, so Muñoz figures to face stiff competition for a lasting supersub role. Hopefully he won't walk away from such a chance this time around.

Dustin Pedroia   2B   Born: 08/17/83   Age: 37   Bats: R   Throws: R   Height: 5'9"   Weight: 170   Origin: Round 2, 2004 Draft (#65 overall)

YEAR	TEAM	LVL	AGE	PA	R	2B	3B	HR	RBI	BB	K	SB	CS	Whiff%	AVG/OBP/SLG	DRC+	BABIP	BRR	FRAA	WARP
2018	BOS	MLB	34	13	1	0	0	0	0	2	1	0	0	5.0%	.091/.231/.091	96	.100	-0.1	2B(3): -0.4	0.0
2019	BOS	MLB	35	21	1	0	0	0	1	1	2	0	0	11.8%	.100/.143/.100	86	.111	-0.1	2B(4): -0.2	0.0
2021 FS	BOS	MLB	37	600	63	26	0	9	59	55	96	5	2	10.1%	.262/.333/.366	96	.304	-2.9	2B 0	1.6

Comparables: Jose Vidro, Ian Kinsler, Davey Johnson

One way or another, 2021 will mark the end of Pedroia's career. The 8-year, $110-million extension he signed in June of 2013 once seemed team-friendly, a nod to Pedroia's twin desires to retire in Boston and to help his team at any cost. In reality, it's badly hamstrung the Sox in their self-imposed financial crunch: Pedey's made $44 million to play in just nine games over the past three seasons, and he's about to make $12 million more. We should all be pulling for a baseball lifer like Pedroia, but the cold hard truth is that his left knee has barred him from the majors since April 17, 2019. He may well retire before the season starts, but no one should begrudge him opting for one last shot at appearing under Fenway's bright lights instead.

Kevin Plawecki   C   Born: 02/26/91   Age: 30   Bats: R   Throws: R   Height: 6'2"   Weight: 208   Origin: Round 1, 2012 Draft (#35 overall)

YEAR	TEAM	LVL	AGE	PA	R	2B	3B	HR	RBI	BB	K	SB	CS	Whiff%	AVG/OBP/SLG	DRC+	BABIP	BRR	FRAA	WARP
2018	NYM	MLB	27	277	33	13	2	7	30	28	65	0	1	23.8%	.210/.315/.370	92	.257	-1.2	C(71): -2.0, 1B(3): -0.0	0.8
2019	CLE	MLB	28	174	13	10	0	3	17	12	31	0	1	19.1%	.222/.287/.342	79	.256	-1.3	C(57): 7.8, P(2): -0.0, 1B(1): 0.0	1.1
2020	BOS	MLB	29	89	8	5	1	1	17	5	14	1	0	15.9%	.341/.393/.463	101	.403	-1.4	C(20): -0.4, 1B(2): 0.0, P(1): -0.0	-0.2
2021 FS	BOS	MLB	30	600	62	29	1	14	67	47	126	1	0	19.7%	.246/.322/.384	99	.297	-0.8	C 2, 1B 0	2.5
2021 DC	BOS	MLB	30	167	17	8	0	3	18	13	35	0	0	19.7%	.246/.322/.384	99	.297	-0.2	C 1	0.7

Comparables: Alan Knicely, Terry McGriff, Doug Mirabelli

Relying on BABIP and BABIP alone to assess a player's performance remains the laziest type of "baseball analysis" imaginable, but can you find another way to explain how the lead-footed Plawecki just hit for 100-plus points above his career average?

YEAR	TEAM	P. COUNT	FRM RUNS	BLK RUNS	THRW RUNS	TOT RUNS
2018	NYM	9953	-4.6	2.0	0.0	-2.6
2019	CLE	6790	6.6	2.2	-0.3	8.5
2020	BOS	2969	-3.4	-0.2	0.0	-3.6
2021	BOS	6012	0.0	0.0	0.0	0.1

Hudson Potts 3B Born: 10/28/98 Age: 22 Bats: R Throws: R Height: 6'3" Weight: 218 Origin: Round 1, 2016 Draft (#24 overall)

YEAR	TEAM	LVL	AGE	PA	R	2B	3B	HR	RBI	BB	K	SB	CS	Whiff%	AVG/OBP/SLG	DRC+	BABIP	BRR	FRAA	WARP
2018	LE	HI-A	19	453	66	35	1	17	58	37	112	3	1		.281/.350/.498	144	.348	0.3	3B(99): 0.7, 1B(8): 0.1	2.4
2018	SA	AA	19	89	5	0	0	2	5	10	33	1	0		.154/.258/.231	43	.233	-0.2	3B(21): 0.3	-0.4
2019	AMA	AA	20	448	56	23	1	16	59	32	128	3	1		.227/.290/.406	58	.288	-1.7	3B(86): -6.4, 2B(19): -0.7	-1.2
2021 FS	BOS	MLB	22	600	57	27	2	17	65	37	200	2	1		.217/.274/.369	75	.305	-0.2	3B -6, 2B 0	-1.3

Comparables: Josh Vitters, Jonathan Villar, Matt Dominguez

Acquired for the low price of a few dozen Mitch Moreland games, Potts is a 2016 first-rounder who's perfect for the Red Sox in that he's a corner infielder who strikes out constantly. When it comes to making contact, he makes Bobby Dalbec look like Tony Gwynn.

Hunter Renfroe LF Born: 01/28/92 Age: 29 Bats: R Throws: R Height: 6'1" Weight: 230 Origin: Round 1, 2013 Draft (#13 overall)

YEAR	TEAM	LVL	AGE	PA	R	2B	3B	HR	RBI	BB	K	SB	CS	Whiff%	AVG/OBP/SLG	DRC+	BABIP	BRR	FRAA	WARP
2018	ELP	AAA	26	43	6	1	0	2	4	2	10	0	0		.220/.256/.390	72	.241	-0.1	RF(9): 2.4	0.1
2018	SD	MLB	26	441	53	23	1	26	68	30	109	2	1	30.6%	.248/.302/.504	110	.271	-1.2	LF(58): -1.3, RF(50): 6.6	2.0
2019	SD	MLB	27	494	64	19	1	33	64	46	154	5	0	30.6%	.216/.289/.489	98	.239	-2.2	RF(86): 6.5, LF(67): 0.7, CF(4): -0.0	1.6
2020	TB	MLB	28	139	18	5	0	8	22	14	37	2	0	32.1%	.156/.252/.393	92	.141	-0.6	RF(39): -0.6, 1B(2): 0.1	0.1
2021 FS	BOS	MLB	29	600	72	26	1	31	90	42	173	2	0	30.9%	.219/.281/.446	98	.257	-0.1	RF 1, LF 0	1.5
2021 DC	BOS	MLB	29	435	52	19	1	22	65	31	125	1	0	30.9%	.219/.281/.446	98	.257	-0.1	RF 1	1.0

Comparables: Yasmany Tomás, Brian Buchanan, Jay Bruce

If Renfroe had the season he had for any team other than the Rays—a year in which he actually improved his plate discipline while maintaining his exit velocity and launch angle—he would probably be on Tampa Bay's wishlist. Instead, they designated him for assignment before Thanksgiving because of their crowded infield and his increasing arbitration bill. Former Rays head honcho Chaim Bloom hopes to turn Tampa's trash into Boston's treasure: he inked Renfroe to a one-year, $3.1 million contract to help man Fenway's cavernous right field.

Jeisson Rosario CF Born: 10/22/99 Age: 21 Bats: L Throws: L Height: 6'1" Weight: 191 Origin: International Free Agent, 2016

YEAR	TEAM	LVL	AGE	PA	R	2B	3B	HR	RBI	BB	K	SB	CS	Whiff%	AVG/OBP/SLG	DRC+	BABIP	BRR	FRAA	WARP
2018	FW	LO-A	18	520	79	17	5	3	34	66	107	18	12		.271/.369/.354	97	.347	3.5	CF(113): -1.2, RF(1): -0.2	1.0
2019	LE	HI-A	19	525	67	14	4	3	35	87	114	11	4		.242/.372/.314	117	.322	4.3	CF(111): 0.6, LF(5): 1.7, RF(4): 1.2	3.3
2021 FS	BOS	MLB	21	600	50	25	2	6	50	48	171	6	3		.226/.293/.321	70	.316	-2.0	CF -1, RF 0	-0.7

Comparables: Billy McKinney, Daniel Fields, Anthony Gose

The main piece headed back to Boston in the Mitch Moreland trade, Rosario is a smooth operator in center field who displays plenty of patience at the plate. He's not a burner or a slugger and it's still not entirely clear he can hit, which puts his floor at Juan Lugares and his ceiling at, well, Jackie Bradley Jr.?

Christian Vázquez C Born: 08/21/90 Age: 30 Bats: R Throws: R Height: 5'9" Weight: 205 Origin: Round 9, 2008 Draft (#292 overall)

YEAR	TEAM	LVL	AGE	PA	R	2B	3B	HR	RBI	BB	K	SB	CS	Whiff%	AVG/OBP/SLG	DRC+	BABIP	BRR	FRAA	WARP
2018	BOS	MLB	27	269	24	10	0	3	16	13	41	4	1	14.0%	.207/.257/.283	71	.237	-0.4	C(75): 8.3, 3B(2): -0.0	1.2
2019	BOS	MLB	28	521	66	26	1	23	72	33	101	4	2	20.8%	.276/.320/.477	105	.305	-0.3	C(119): 7.0, 1B(10): 1.0, 3B(4): 0.1	3.5
2020	BOS	MLB	30	189	22	9	0	7	23	16	43	4	3	22.9%	.283/.344/.457	100	.341	0.0	C(42): 1.0, 2B(1): -0.0	1.2
2021 FS	BOS	MLB	30	600	62	27	1	15	70	40	134	5	2	20.5%	.255/.310/.396	94	.310	-1.0	C 12, 1B 0	3.1
2021 DC	BOS	MLB	30	468	49	21	1	12	55	31	105	4	1	20.5%	.255/.310/.396	94	.310	-0.8	C 13	2.9

Comparables: Jesse Gonder, Cal Neeman, Dan Wilson

YEAR	TEAM	P. COUNT	FRM RUNS	BLK RUNS	THRW RUNS	TOT RUNS
2018	BOS	10488	9.0	0.1	0.1	9.2
2019	BOS	16486	12.3	-5.3	0.8	7.8
2020	BOS	6333	4.2	0.0	-0.1	4.1
2021	BOS	16835	15.3	-0.2	0.3	15.4

When the Red Sox signed Vázquez to a three-year extension before the 2018 season, the prevailing question was … why? Little about his 2017 performance looked sustainable, and his deal only bought Boston one more year of potential team control via a 2022 option for $7 million. Vázquez initially rewarded Boston's faith by posting a lower DRC+ than Jesus Sucre, but ever since, he's looked like one of the biggest backstop bargains in the game. He followed up his breakout 2019 by finishing as the fifth-best catcher per WARP and CDA while again hitting for the type of power once thought to be well out of his reach. He's still just 30 years old, and as one of the best overall catchers in the game tied to an uber-reasonable contract, one of its best values as well. The Sox could likely fetch a pretty penny for Vazquez should they opt for a dreaded Full Tank, but doing so would prompt a new prevailing inquiry … isn't Vázquez exactly the type of player you want to build around as you break in new, young pitching?

Alex Verdugo CF Born: 05/15/96 Age: 25 Bats: L Throws: L Height: 6'0" Weight: 192 Origin: Round 2, 2014 Draft (#62 overall)

YEAR	TEAM	LVL	AGE	PA	R	2B	3B	HR	RBI	BB	K	SB	CS	Whiff%	AVG/OBP/SLG	DRC+	BABIP	BRR	FRAA	WARP
2018	OKC	AAA	22	379	44	19	0	10	44	34	47	8	2		.329/.391/.472	129	.359	-0.5	CF(45): 2.0, RF(31): 2.4, LF(13): -0.4	2.2
2018	LAD	MLB	22	86	11	6	0	1	4	8	14	0	0	18.0%	.260/.329/.377	85	.306	1.5	RF(16): -0.1, LF(12): 0.2, CF(8): -1.0	0.1
2019	LAD	MLB	23	377	43	22	2	12	44	26	49	4	1	16.2%	.294/.342/.475	102	.309	1.4	CF(61): -1.2, RF(25): 1.2, LF(22): 2.0	1.7
2020	BOS	MLB	24	221	36	16	0	6	15	17	45	4	0	18.8%	.308/.367/.478	101	.371	1.7	RF(31): -2.2, LF(22): 0.7, CF(1): -0.1	0.9
2021 FS	BOS	MLB	25	600	75	31	2	15	62	50	112	1	0	17.5%	.276/.342/.429	111	.323	-0.8	CF -9, RF 3	2.0
2021 DC	BOS	MLB	25	568	71	29	2	15	58	47	106	1	0	17.5%	.276/.342/.429	111	.323	-0.8	CF -8, RF 3	1.9

Comparables: Austin Hays, Oscar Mercado, Dave Henderson

It's tough to imagine a young player walking into a more daunting situation than the one Verdugo faced last season. In the blink of a salary dump, he went from a part-time player on a juggernaut to the focal point of the dumpster fire that was the 2020 Red Sox. Just 24 years old and with less than a full season of playing time under his belt, Verdugo strolled into Fenway Park to man the same spot—right field—that a franchise icon had been evicted from just months before. Many would've buckled under the weight of the expectations, but Verdugo passed his stress test with flying colors.

Despite the gaze of an irate fanbase and the lingering effects of a back injury that ended his 2019 campaign, Verdugo excelled in Boston from day one. He paced the Sox in batting average, OBP and doubles while placing second in WARP en route to a 12th-place finish in AL MVP voting. He played solid defense across all three outfield spots, seemed fully engaged in all aspects of the game, and brought a high-energy approach to the team. He was as good, if not better, than anyone could've hoped.

The problem, of course, is that while Verdugo was establishing himself in Boston, Mookie Betts was helping the Dodgers win the World Series. It's an unfair comparison, but one that will plague Verdugo throughout his Red Sox career. There's nothing he can do about that, but in year one, Verdugo excelled at everything he could control, showing the talent and health needed to thrive despite the circumstances. He can't make the Betts trade a *good* one for Boston, but he can cement himself as an integral part of the next good Red Sox team. He looks well on his way to doing so.

Connor Wong C Born: 05/19/96 Age: 25 Bats: R Throws: R Height: 6'1" Weight: 178 Origin: Round 3, 2017 Draft (#100 overall)

YEAR	TEAM	LVL	AGE	PA	R	2B	3B	HR	RBI	BB	K	SB	CS	Whiff%	AVG/OBP/SLG	DRC+	BABIP	BRR	FRAA	WARP
2018	RC	HI-A	22	431	64	20	2	19	60	38	138	6	2		.269/.350/.480	113	.372	0.9	C(71): 0.7, 2B(11): -0.5, 3B(1): -0.1	1.2
2019	RC	HI-A	23	302	39	15	6	15	51	21	93	9	2		.245/.306/.507	101	.310	1.3	C(59): 0.7, 2B(10): 1.3, 3B(2): -0.0	1.7
2019	TUL	AA	23	163	17	9	1	9	31	11	50	2	1		.349/.393/.604	162	.467	0.3	C(24): 0.1, 3B(10): -0.8, 2B(4): -0.2	1.5
2021 FS	BOS	MLB	25	600	58	27	3	19	68	37	225	2	0		.218/.277/.382	78	.328	1.0	C -7, 2B 1	0.2

Comparables: Xavier Scruggs, Carlos Moncrief, Mike Gerber

Acquired as part of the Mookie Betts salary dump, Wong offers an extreme power, extreme swing-and-miss profile more commonly seen in corner-infield prospects. If he can make more contact he could be a starting backstop, and if your aunt had wheels she'd be a bus.

YEAR	TEAM	P. COUNT	FRM RUNS	BLK RUNS	THRW RUNS	TOT RUNS
2019	TUL	3381	-0.8	0.0	1.3	0.5
2021	BOS	16650	-4.4	-3.0	0.3	-7.2

Nick Yorke 2B Born: 04/02/02 Age: 19 Bats: R Throws: R Height: 6'0" Weight: 200 Origin: Round 1, 2020 Draft (#17 overall)

The Sox were clearly trying to game the system when they popped Yorke 17th overall in the 2020 draft, as the bat-first infielder signed a deal for nearly $1 million less than slot allowance. It's not that he's a bad prospect—the former Arizona commit has impressive bat-to-ball skills and could move quickly for a prep hitter. But Yorke is a second base prospect without big power or speed and with shoulder surgery on his resume, which is why most in the draftnik community had him as a second- or third-rounder at best. Yorke's below-slot deal did free up the Sox to sign exquisitely named third-rounder Blaze Jordan, but it's fair to wonder if new GM Chaim Bloom got too cute here. We do know this much, at least: between acquiring a Jeter Downs and an N. Yorke, Bloom is very determined to troll his fanbase.

PITCHERS

Matt Andriese RHP Born: 08/28/89 Age: 31 Bats: R Throws: R Height: 6'2" Weight: 215 Origin: Round 3, 2011 Draft (#112 overall)

YEAR	TEAM	LVL	AGE	W	L	SV	G	GS	IP	H	HR	BB/9	K/9	K	GB%	BABIP	WHIP	ERA	DRA-	WARP	MPH	FA%	Whiff%	CSP
2018	ARI	MLB	28	0	3	0	14	1	19	29	8	3.3	9.0	19	42.9%	.382	1.89	9.00	116	0.0	93.8	48.9%	25.9%	48.0%
2018	TB	MLB	28	3	4	0	27	4	59²	55	7	2.7	8.9	59	49.4%	.293	1.22	4.07	109	0.1	93.8	46.1%	25.7%	48.4%
2019	ARI	MLB	29	5	5	1	54	0	70²	72	8	3.4	10.1	79	49.5%	.335	1.40	4.71	74	1.3	94.2	50.5%	25.4%	48.8%
2020	LAA	MLB	30	2	4	2	16	1	32	21	5	3.1	9.3	33	45.7%	.211	1.00	4.50	90	0.5	93.5	43.2%	22.6%	47.8%
2021 FS	BOS	MLB	31	9	8	0	26	26	150	135	19	2.9	9.2	153	46.2%	.289	1.22	3.82	89	2.0	93.9	47.4%	24.7%	48.4%
2021 DC	BOS	MLB	31	5	5	0	45	14	90	81	11	2.9	9.2	91	46.2%	.289	1.22	3.82	89	1.3	93.9	47.4%	24.7%	48.4%

Comparables: Erasmo Ramírez, Alex Colomé, Trevor May

It is not, generally, considered good practice for a front office to acquire a relief pitcher coming off a season head and shoulders beyond their previous best effort. It's basically the Colorado Rockies' entire organizational philosophy, and things aren't going great up there. Predictably, Andriese regressed from his career-best 2019 DRA, and failed to break into an Angels rotation whose only defense against rogue entrants is an ADT security sign so faded it's more baby than blue. Still, a reliable multi-inning reliever is hard to come by, and Andriese, for everything else he lacks, is nothing if not reliable.

Matt Barnes **RHP** Born: 06/17/90 Age: 31 Bats: R Throws: R Height: 6'4" Weight: 208 Origin: Round 1, 2011 Draft (#19 overall)

YEAR	TEAM	LVL	AGE	W	L	SV	G	GS	IP	H	HR	BB/9	K/9	K	GB%	BABIP	WHIP	ERA	DRA-	WARP	MPH	FA%	Whiff%	CSP
2018	BOS	MLB	28	6	4	0	62	0	61²	47	5	4.5	14.0	96	51.5%	.321	1.26	3.65	49	1.9	98.5	54.8%	36.4%	42.8%
2019	BOS	MLB	29	5	4	4	70	0	64¹	51	8	5.3	15.4	110	47.8%	.341	1.38	3.78	56	1.8	98.1	47.1%	36.3%	38.7%
2020	BOS	MLB	30	1	3	9	24	0	23	18	4	5.5	12.1	31	45.5%	.280	1.39	4.30	81	0.4	97.1	54.1%	28.6%	43.2%
2021 FS	*BOS*	*MLB*	*31*	*3*	*2*	*29*	*57*	*0*	*50*	*38*	*5*	*4.7*	*12.2*	*67*	*46.9%*	*.292*	*1.29*	*3.45*	*82*	*0.6*	*97.9*	*50.7%*	*34.2%*	*40.8%*
2021 DC	*BOS*	*MLB*	*31*	*3*	*2*	*29*	*61*	*0*	*64*	*48*	*6*	*4.7*	*12.2*	*86*	*46.9%*	*.292*	*1.29*	*3.45*	*82*	*1.0*	*97.9*	*50.7%*	*34.2%*	*40.8%*

Comparables: Alex Colomé, Neil Ramírez, Tommy Kahnle

Barnes' high-strikeout, high-walk, high-wire act works reasonably well when, as in 2019, he's whiffing among the highest percentage of batters in all of baseball. But one of the biggest problems with such a dangerous approach is how little margin it leaves for error. Barnes still missed a ton of bats in 2020, but an eight percentage point drop in K% is tough to stomach when you're walking every seventh batter you face—even when said drop still leaves your K% in the 30s. Barnes has performed fairly consistently over the past several seasons, and there's no reason to overreact to a 24-game sample. That being said, his recent struggles illustrate that while he may seem capable of breaking into the game's upper echelon of relievers, he's arguably more prone to sliding back into its murky middle tier of firemen.

Ryan Brasier **RHP** Born: 08/26/87 Age: 33 Bats: R Throws: R Height: 6'0" Weight: 227 Origin: Round 6, 2007 Draft (#208 overall)

YEAR	TEAM	LVL	AGE	W	L	SV	G	GS	IP	H	HR	BB/9	K/9	K	GB%	BABIP	WHIP	ERA	DRA-	WARP	MPH	FA%	Whiff%	CSP
2018	WOR	AAA	30	2	5	13	34	0	40¹	29	1	1.8	8.9	40	38.2%	.289	0.92	1.34	65	0.9				
2018	BOS	MLB	30	2	0	0	34	0	33²	19	2	1.9	7.8	29	42.0%	.200	0.77	1.60	79	0.5	98.2	62.6%	31.0%	45.8%
2019	WOR	AAA	31	2	0	0	10	0	9¹	6	1	1.0	12.5	13	45.0%	.263	0.75	0.96	46	0.4				
2019	BOS	MLB	31	2	4	7	62	0	55²	51	9	3.4	9.7	60	32.1%	.284	1.29	4.85	110	0.0	97.5	59.2%	31.2%	44.3%
2020	BOS	MLB	32	1	0	0	25	1	25	24	2	4.0	10.8	30	37.7%	.328	1.40	3.96	83	0.4	97.6	62.0%	34.1%	47.1%
2021 FS	*BOS*	*MLB*	*33*	*3*	*3*	*9*	*57*	*0*	*50*	*43*	*7*	*3.1*	*9.7*	*54*	*37.5%*	*.283*	*1.22*	*3.73*	*91*	*0.4*	*97.6*	*60.7%*	*32.2%*	*45.5%*
2021 DC	*BOS*	*MLB*	*33*	*3*	*3*	*9*	*61*	*0*	*64*	*56*	*9*	*3.1*	*9.7*	*69*	*37.5%*	*.283*	*1.22*	*3.73*	*91*	*0.7*	*97.6*	*60.7%*	*32.2%*	*45.5%*

Comparables: Ryan Tepera, Cory Gearrin, Bryan Shaw

It's never a good sign when one of your most-used relievers finishes a season with more apologies for racially insensitive tweets than saves, but Brasier proved up to that ignominious task. As a pitcher, Brasier found middle ground between his terrific 2018 and his abysmal 2019, settling in as a league-average reliever who misses bats but who also misses the plate too much to truly shine. As a (re)tweeter, he made headlines for Milkshake Duck-ing himself just hours after the Red Sox and Blue Jays agreed to postpone their game in an act of protest against racism and police brutality. It was awfully fun at the time to watch Brasier bark at Gary Sánchez in the 2018 postseason, but now it seems as though the less we hear from Brasier on *or* off the mound, the better.

Colten Brewer **RHP** Born: 10/29/92 Age: 28 Bats: R Throws: R Height: 6'4" Weight: 222 Origin: Round 4, 2011 Draft (#122 overall)

YEAR	TEAM	LVL	AGE	W	L	SV	G	GS	IP	H	HR	BB/9	K/9	K	GB%	BABIP	WHIP	ERA	DRA-	WARP	MPH	FA%	Whiff%	CSP
2018	ELP	AAA	25	3	4	3	37	0	48	40	3	2.8	11.8	63	54.8%	.333	1.15	3.75	52	1.5				
2018	SD	MLB	25	1	0	0	11	0	9²	15	0	6.5	9.3	10	50.0%	.469	2.28	5.59	60	0.2	95.0	68.0%	29.6%	48.7%
2019	WOR	AAA	26	2	3	0	9	0	11	14	2	5.7	8.2	10	54.1%	.353	1.91	4.91	134	0.0				
2019	BOS	MLB	26	1	2	0	58	0	54²	59	6	5.6	8.6	52	52.1%	.335	1.70	4.12	106	0.1	95.4	44.5%	27.3%	43.8%
2020	BOS	MLB	27	0	3	0	11	4	25²	31	6	4.9	8.8	25	51.2%	.329	1.75	5.61	104	0.2	95.3	47.2%	22.6%	43.8%
2021 FS	*BOS*	*MLB*	*28*	*2*	*2*	*0*	*57*	*0*	*50*	*47*	*5*	*5.0*	*8.9*	*49*	*51.1%*	*.302*	*1.51*	*4.80*	*106*	*-0.1*	*95.3*	*46.9%*	*25.5%*	*44.1%*
2021 DC	*BOS*	*MLB*	*28*	*2*	*2*	*0*	*54*	*0*	*58*	*55*	*6*	*5.0*	*8.9*	*57*	*51.1%*	*.302*	*1.51*	*4.80*	*106*	*0.1*	*95.3*	*46.9%*	*25.5%*	*44.1%*

Comparables: Dovydas Neverauskas, Yacksel Ríos, Michael Feliz

The Red Sox have improved the beer selection at Fenway Park in recent years but fell flat when importing Brewer, who gave up nearly a homer per four innings pitched. He does not belong on the 40-man roster of a team that is trying to win games, yet just finished third among Red Sox relievers in innings pitched.

Austin Brice RHP Born: 06/19/92 Age: 29 Bats: R Throws: R Height: 6'4" Weight: 238 Origin: Round 9, 2010 Draft (#287 overall)

YEAR	TEAM	LVL	AGE	W	L	SV	G	GS	IP	H	HR	BB/9	K/9	K	GB%	BABIP	WHIP	ERA	DRA-	WARP	MPH	FA%	Whiff%	CSP
2018	LOU	AAA	26	3	1	1	17	0	23¹	18	2	2.7	9.3	24	35.7%	.296	1.07	2.31	87	0.2				
2018	CIN	MLB	26	2	3	0	33	0	37¹	39	9	3.1	7.7	32	51.8%	.288	1.39	5.79	128	-0.4	95.4	68.4%	21.7%	50.2%
2019	MIA	MLB	27	1	0	0	36	0	44²	37	7	3.6	9.3	46	42.2%	.248	1.23	3.43	92	0.4	94.6	51.0%	26.7%	47.8%
2020	BOS	MLB	28	1	0	0	21	1	19²	17	3	5.9	11.4	25	42.6%	.318	1.53	5.95	89	0.3	94.9	61.8%	34.4%	43.7%
2021 FS	BOS	MLB	29	2	2	0	57	0	50	45	6	3.8	9.9	55	42.0%	.296	1.33	4.28	99	0.2	94.9	57.9%	28.3%	46.9%
2021 DC	BOS	MLB	29	2	2	0	54	0	58	52	7	3.8	9.9	63	42.0%	.296	1.33	4.28	99	0.4	94.9	57.9%	28.3%	46.9%

Comparables: Hansel Robles, Kevin McCarthy, Bobby Parnell

Can you name which of these Brice facts is not true?

A) He is the first player born in Hong Kong to reach the majors

B) He was acquired by the Red Sox for a man named "Angeudis Santos"

C) He just posted the 45th highest BB/9 rate of any pitcher who threw at least 10 IP

D) He was once a part of the Reds' Luis Castillo trade

The answer is C—Brice's walk rate was *43rd* highest.

Nathan Eovaldi RHP Born: 02/13/90 Age: 31 Bats: R Throws: R Height: 6'2" Weight: 217 Origin: Round 11, 2008 Draft (#337 overall)

YEAR	TEAM	LVL	AGE	W	L	SV	G	GS	IP	H	HR	BB/9	K/9	K	GB%	BABIP	WHIP	ERA	DRA-	WARP	MPH	FA%	Whiff%	CSP
2018	CHA	HI-A	28	0	0	0	3	3	6	6	2	0.0	10.5	7	47.1%	.267	1.00	4.50	71	0.1				
2018	BOS	MLB	28	3	3	0	12	11	54	57	3	2.0	8.0	48	45.6%	.327	1.28	3.33	73	1.3	99.8	38.1%	21.3%	51.7%
2018	TB	MLB	28	3	4	0	10	10	57	48	11	1.3	8.4	53	46.9%	.245	0.98	4.26	71	1.4	98.7	41.6%	22.8%	54.6%
2019	BOS	MLB	29	2	1	0	23	12	67²	72	16	4.7	9.3	70	44.3%	.316	1.58	5.99	130	-0.5	99.7	43.6%	26.3%	46.5%
2020	BOS	MLB	30	4	2	0	9	9	48¹	51	8	1.3	9.7	52	49.3%	.339	1.20	3.72	80	1.0	99.5	37.7%	28.1%	49.4%
2021 FS	BOS	MLB	31	9	8	0	26	26	150	138	18	2.7	9.2	153	47.3%	.297	1.22	3.62	87	2.1	99.5	40.6%	25.8%	49.3%
2021 DC	BOS	MLB	31	8	7	0	24	24	133	122	16	2.7	9.2	136	47.3%	.297	1.22	3.62	87	2.3	99.5	40.6%	25.8%	49.3%

Comparables: Jake Odorizzi, Rick Porcello, Anthony DeSclafani

Eovaldi picked a bad time to have a good season. When the quasi-competitive Sox needed Eovaldi most in 2019 he could not answer the bell thanks to his oft-troublesome right elbow and an utter lack of command. Yet when the 2020 Red Sox were in Full Tank Mode, the good Eovaldi showed up once more, posting the best strikeout rate and second-best DRA of his career while pacing the Sox in PWARP. Of course no Eovaldi season is complete without a trip to the IL, and he obliged this time around with a strained calf. All things considered, that counts as good news on the Eovaldi injury front, especially since the Sox still owe their 2018 postseason hero $34 million over the next two seasons.

Durbin Feltman RHP Born: 04/18/97 Age: 24 Bats: R Throws: R Height: 6'0" Weight: 205 Origin: Round 3, 2018 Draft (#100 overall)

YEAR	TEAM	LVL	AGE	W	L	SV	G	GS	IP	H	HR	BB/9	K/9	K	GB%	BABIP	WHIP	ERA	DRA-	WARP	MPH	FA%	Whiff%	CSP
2018	LOW	SS	21	0	0	0	4	0	4	0	0	0.0	15.8	7	83.3%	.000	0.00	0.00	28	0.2				
2018	GVL	LO-A	21	0	1	3	7	0	7	6	0	1.3	18.0	14	28.6%	.429	1.00	2.57	41	0.2				
2018	SAL	HI-A	21	1	0	1	11	0	12¹	12	0	2.9	10.9	15	54.5%	.375	1.30	2.19	55	0.3				
2019	POR	AA	22	2	3	5	43	0	51¹	42	8	5.4	9.5	54	42.6%	.268	1.42	5.26	105	-0.3				
2021 FS	BOS	MLB	24	2	3	0	57	0	50	47	8	5.4	9.3	51	40.4%	.291	1.54	5.16	122	-0.5				

Comparables: Nick Burdi, Evan Phillips, Shawn Armstrong

A once-promising reliever prospect, Feltman said he spent quarantine refining his curveball *and* his command, much like once-promising naval Captain Edward Smith focused on deck chair arrangement *and* iceberg avoidance.

Zack Godley RHP Born: 04/21/90 Age: 31 Bats: R Throws: R Height: 6'3" Weight: 250 Origin: Round 10, 2013 Draft (#288 overall)

YEAR	TEAM	LVL	AGE	W	L	SV	G	GS	IP	H	HR	BB/9	K/9	K	GB%	BABIP	WHIP	ERA	DRA-	WARP	MPH	FA%	Whiff%	CSP
2018	ARI	MLB	28	15	11	0	33	32	178¹	177	16	4.1	9.3	185	47.8%	.329	1.45	4.74	106	1.1	91.5	54.3%	27.8%	43.4%
2019	TOR	MLB	29	1	0	0	6	0	16	15	2	3.9	6.8	12	42.9%	.277	1.38	3.94	107	0.0	91.5	65.3%	28.4%	39.2%
2019	ARI	MLB	29	3	5	2	27	9	76	81	12	4.1	6.9	58	42.9%	.307	1.53	6.39	137	-1.0	91.7	49.0%	23.7%	44.9%
2020	BOS	MLB	30	0	4	0	8	7	28²	42	9	4.4	8.8	28	40.8%	.371	1.95	8.16	127	-0.2	91.1	51.7%	25.6%	43.5%
2021 FS	BOS	MLB	31	2	3	0	57	0	50	51	7	4.2	8.3	46	44.2%	.306	1.48	4.95	113	-0.2	91.5	52.7%	26.0%	43.6%

Comparables: Matt Andriese, Anthony DeSclafani, Jake Odorizzi

A former feel-good story, Godley added injury to insulting performance by ending the year on the IL with a right flexor strain. In total, he gave us the ugliest Godley experience in New England since the Salem Witch Trials.

Jay Groome LHP Born: 08/23/98 Age: 22 Bats: L Throws: L Height: 6'6" Weight: 220 Origin: Round 1, 2016 Draft (#12 overall)

YEAR	TEAM	LVL	AGE	W	L	SV	G	GS	IP	H	HR	BB/9	K/9	K	GB%	BABIP	WHIP	ERA	DRA-	WARP	MPH	FA%	Whiff%	CSP
2019	RSX	ROK	20	0	0	0	2	2	2	2	0	0.0	13.5	3	80.0%	.400	1.00	0.00	65	0.1				
2019	LOW	SS	20	0	0	0	1	1	2	3	0	4.5	13.5	3	28.6%	.429	2.00	4.50	85	0.0				
2021 FS	BOS	MLB	22	2	3	0	57	0	50	45	7	6.2	9.2	51	45.1%	.283	1.59	5.20	122	-0.5				

Comparables: Brusdar Graterol, Carl Edwards Jr., Mat Latos

Not sure if you're an optimist or a pessimist? Ask yourself how you feel about Groome. If you're a glass-half-empty type, you can point to how the 2016 first-rounder has thrown just four official innings since the 2017 season as you notch another win for the TINSTAAPP crowd. If you tend to look on the sunnier side, you'll note that Groom is just 22, fully recovered from Tommy John surgery, and still boasts the type of stuff and workhorse frame that could make him a top-of-the-rotation starter. Young lefties who stand at 6-foot-6 and throw in the mid-90s are among the game's most coveted treasures, which is why Groome is likely to be added to the 40-man roster this offseason despite his history. If he can stay on the mound for a full season, he should skyrocket back up the prospect lists that once held him in such high regard. If not, it's tempting to say we'll all be ready to move on, but at this time next year Groome will *still* only be 23...

Darwinzon Hernandez LHP Born: 12/17/96 Age: 24 Bats: L Throws: L Height: 6'2" Weight: 255 Origin: International Free Agent, 2013

YEAR	TEAM	LVL	AGE	W	L	SV	G	GS	IP	H	HR	BB/9	K/9	K	GB%	BABIP	WHIP	ERA	DRA-	WARP	MPH	FA%	Whiff%	CSP
2018	SAL	HI-A	21	9	5	0	23	23	101	80	1	5.3	11.0	124	43.6%	.331	1.39	3.56	105	0.5				
2018	POR	AA	21	0	0	0	5	0	6	6	0	9.0	15.0	10	35.7%	.429	2.00	3.00	50	0.2				
2019	POR	AA	22	1	4	0	10	9	40¹	33	2	7.1	13.2	59	35.8%	.341	1.61	5.13	103	-0.1				
2019	WOR	AAA	22	1	2	0	7	3	17	10	2	8.5	10.6	20	35.1%	.229	1.53	4.76	96	0.3				
2019	BOS	MLB	22	0	1	0	29	1	30¹	27	1	7.7	16.9	57	42.6%	.441	1.75	4.45	62	0.8	97.7	74.4%	35.5%	47.3%
2020	BOS	MLB	23	1	0	0	7	0	8¹	5	0	8.6	14.0	13	50.0%	.278	1.56	2.16	86	0.1	96.4	72.7%	27.5%	48.5%
2021 FS	BOS	MLB	24	2	2	0	57	0	50	39	5	7.7	11.8	65	40.6%	.299	1.66	5.15	108	-0.1	97.4	73.9%	33.2%	47.6%
2021 DC	BOS	MLB	24	2	2	0	48	0	51	40	5	7.7	11.8	67	40.6%	.299	1.66	5.15	108	0.1	97.4	73.9%	33.2%	47.6%

Comparables: Touki Toussaint, José Castillo, Patrick Sandoval

It was a tough year for Darwinism all around, and that extended to Hernandez. In theory, Boston's decision to punt on the 2020 season should've afforded the fireballing lefty a chance to prove he belonged in a big-league rotation. Instead, Hernandez missed most of the year following a bout with COVID-19, unable to join the active roster until late August. In the few games in which he played, Hernandez looked the same as ever: utterly overpowering and ludicrously wild. His upside is such that he deserves to be a part of Boston's plans moving forward, but at present it's still tough to trust him with much beyond medium-leverage work.

Tanner Houck RHP Born: 06/29/96 Age: 25 Bats: R Throws: R Height: 6'5" Weight: 230 Origin: Round 1, 2017 Draft (#24 overall)

YEAR	TEAM	LVL	AGE	W	L	SV	G	GS	IP	H	HR	BB/9	K/9	K	GB%	BABIP	WHIP	ERA	DRA-	WARP	MPH	FA%	Whiff%	CSP
2018	SAL	HI-A	22	7	11	0	23	23	119	110	11	4.5	8.4	111	49.3%	.299	1.43	4.24	119	-0.4				
2019	POR	AA	23	8	6	0	17	15	82²	86	4	3.5	8.7	80	48.5%	.346	1.43	4.25	112	-0.5				
2019	WOR	AAA	23	0	0	1	16	2	25	19	3	5.0	9.7	27	43.3%	.258	1.32	3.24	72	0.7				
2020	BOS	MLB	24	3	0	0	3	3	17	6	1	4.8	11.1	21	46.9%	.161	0.88	0.53	85	0.3	95.1	62.3%	27.1%	42.8%
2021 FS	BOS	MLB	25	8	9	0	26	26	150	137	19	5.2	9.3	155	45.4%	.294	1.50	4.89	108	0.4	95.1	62.3%	27.1%	42.8%
2021 DC	BOS	MLB	25	7	9	0	25	25	137	125	17	5.2	9.3	141	45.4%	.294	1.50	4.89	108	0.8	95.1	62.3%	27.1%	42.8%

Comparables: Jayson Aquino, Keury Mella, Cal Quantrill

If someone forces you at gunpoint to rewatch part of the 2020 Red Sox season, pick Houck's three starts. Boston's 2017 first-rounder dazzled in his major league cameo, leaning on a wipeout slider, two types of fastball and a funky delivery to pile up the Ks while allowing just one earned run. Houck isn't a finished product, but per the inimitable Alex Speier, it's Houck's athleticism and openness to change that've helped him evolve into a potential rotation piece. The Sox have asked him to tweak his delivery, refine his approach against lefties, bounce between roles and develop a two-seamer he can use up in the zone. The early results haven't always been pretty, but Houck has stuck with it, and he's routinely bounced back from tough starts at various levels. Boston hasn't developed a good, homegrown starter in a long while, which is why Houck's three-game sample led to desperate comps like "Corey Kluber-lite" or "right-handed Chris Sale." In truth, the Sox should be overjoyed if Houck can stick as a No. 3/4 starter with upside. Anything more than that is house money, though given Houck's proven ability to adjust, we can't put it past him.

Robinson Leyer RHP Born: 03/13/93 Age: 28 Bats: R Throws: R Height: 6'2" Weight: 185 Origin: International Free Agent, 2011

YEAR	TEAM	LVL	AGE	W	L	SV	G	GS	IP	H	HR	BB/9	K/9	K	GB%	BABIP	WHIP	ERA	DRA-	WARP	MPH	FA%	Whiff%	CSP
2018	PNS	AA	25	6	3	2	42	0	59	43	4	4.3	9.9	65	39.0%	.277	1.20	2.59	79	0.8				
2019	ARK	AA	26	1	0	1	9	0	10¹	19	0	6.1	9.6	11	38.5%	.487	2.52	8.71	172	-0.5				
2019	POR	AA	26	0	1	0	15	1	23²	13	0	6.5	11.4	30	33.3%	.255	1.27	2.66	87	0.1				
2019	TAC	AAA	26	1	1	0	13	0	19²	20	3	5.0	12.4	27	32.7%	.370	1.58	4.58	94	0.3				
2020	BOS	MLB	27	0	0	0	6	1	4²	12	3	15.4	17.4	9	35.3%	.643	4.29	21.21	112	0.0	97.4	50.0%	36.9%	37.6%
2021 FS	BOS	MLB	28	2	3	0	57	0	50	45	7	5.5	10.1	56	35.4%	.295	1.52	4.82	110	-0.2	97.4	50.0%	36.9%	37.6%

Comparables: Tayler Scott, Josh Ravin, Brandon Brennan

Good luck finding a more absurd stat line than the one just posted by the electric, eclectic Leyer; his strikeout rate could drive, his walk rate should be studying for the PSATs and his ERA could legally drink.

Bryan Mata RHP Born: 05/03/99 Age: 22 Bats: R Throws: R Height: 6'3" Weight: 240 Origin: International Free Agent, 2016

YEAR	TEAM	LVL	AGE	W	L	SV	G	GS	IP	H	HR	BB/9	K/9	K	GB%	BABIP	WHIP	ERA	DRA-	WARP	MPH	FA%	Whiff%	CSP
2018	SAL	HI-A	19	6	3	0	17	17	72	58	1	7.2	7.6	61	56.6%	.297	1.61	3.50	106	0.3				
2019	SAL	HI-A	20	3	1	0	10	10	51¹	38	1	3.2	9.1	52	64.0%	.270	1.09	1.75	75	0.8				
2019	POR	AA	20	4	6	0	11	11	53²	54	6	4.0	9.9	59	50.3%	.350	1.45	5.03	111	-0.3				
2021 FS	BOS	MLB	22	8	10	0	26	26	150	138	19	5.2	8.2	135	46.9%	.282	1.50	5.01	115	-0.2				
2021 DC	BOS	MLB	22	2	4	0	12	12	53	48	6	5.2	8.2	47	46.9%	.282	1.50	5.01	115	0.1				

Comparables: Sixto Sánchez, Lucas Sims, Deolis Guerra

Mata remains one of the Red Sox's best pitching prospects, but it also remains to be seen if he's particularly good. Here's what's new: Mata reportedly added a bit of velocity, hitting 98 mph at the alternate site, and he's continued to prioritize working on his two-seam fastball. Here's what's not new: his pure stuff is still lightyears ahead of his command and control, and it seems increasingly likely that he will have to find major league success out of the 'pen. Mata should get a chance to prove he belongs in the bigs at some point this season, but early results are likely to look a lot like his fastball placement: very hit or miss.

Chris Mazza RHP Born: 10/17/89 Age: 31 Bats: R Throws: R Height: 6'4" Weight: 190 Origin: Round 27, 2011 Draft (#838 overall)

YEAR	TEAM	LVL	AGE	W	L	SV	G	GS	IP	H	HR	BB/9	K/9	K	GB%	BABIP	WHIP	ERA	DRA-	WARP	MPH	FA%	Whiff%	CSP
2018	JAX	AA	28	0	0	0	2	0	6¹	8	2	2.8	2.8	2	39.1%	.286	1.58	4.26	126	-0.1				
2018	ARK	AA	28	1	0	0	4	4	27	15	1	1.3	7.7	23	62.5%	.197	0.70	1.33	78	0.4				
2018	NO	AAA	28	1	1	0	7	0	16	18	4	4.5	7.9	14	58.8%	.298	1.62	3.94	73	0.3				
2019	BNG	AA	29	0	2	0	4	4	23²	26	0	3.0	8.0	21	47.9%	.356	1.44	3.42	119	-0.2				
2019	SYR	AAA	29	3	3	0	14	13	76	65	6	2.1	7.3	62	56.9%	.282	1.09	3.67	57	2.9				
2019	NYM	MLB	29	1	1	0	9	0	16¹	21	0	2.8	6.1	11	40.7%	.389	1.59	5.51	158	-0.4	93.3	78.4%	17.9%	46.4%
2020	BOS	MLB	30	1	2	0	9	6	30	34	3	4.5	8.7	29	34.4%	.356	1.63	4.80	99	0.3	93.8	68.9%	28.9%	47.5%
2021 FS	BOS	MLB	31	8	9	0	26	26	150	151	22	3.3	7.4	123	43.6%	.293	1.38	4.77	110	0.3	93.7	71.4%	26.1%	47.2%
2021 DC	BOS	MLB	31	3	4	0	25	12	64	64	9	3.3	7.4	52	43.6%	.293	1.38	4.77	110	0.3	93.7	71.4%	26.1%	47.2%

Comparables: Murphy Smith, Chad Bettis, Casey Lawrence

Mazza has made it to the majors two years in a row now, and he didn't take the easy way up. A 2011 draftee who had to climb his way back to relevance through stints in the independent Pacific and Atlantic Leagues, he's also been a Rule 5 draft pick (2018, Mets via Mariners) and been DFAd twice. Claimed by the Sox off waivers last winter, Mazza had the honor of giving up 2020's biggest moonshot, a prodigious 495-foot blast to Ronald Acuña Jr. that may not have landed as of printing. He also had the honor of pitching "well" enough to place as the seventh-best Red Sox pitcher by both WARP and DRA, which tells you all you need to know about Boston's historically bad staff.

Collin McHugh RHP Born: 06/19/87 Age: 34 Bats: R Throws: R Height: 6'2" Weight: 191 Origin: Round 18, 2008 Draft (#554 overall)

YEAR	TEAM	LVL	AGE	W	L	SV	G	GS	IP	H	HR	BB/9	K/9	K	GB%	BABIP	WHIP	ERA	DRA-	WARP	MPH	FA%	Whiff%	CSP
2018	HOU	MLB	31	6	2	0	58	0	72¹	45	6	2.6	11.7	94	34.4%	.250	0.91	1.99	60	1.9	93.6	49.6%	31.4%	47.0%
2019	HOU	MLB	32	4	5	0	35	8	74²	62	12	3.6	9.9	82	39.1%	.265	1.23	4.70	101	0.5	92.8	33.4%	28.1%	46.7%
2021 FS	BOS	MLB	34	9	8	0	26	26	150	131	20	3.1	9.6	159	38.5%	.285	1.22	3.55	89	2.0	93.1	38.6%	29.2%	46.8%

Comparables: Carlos Carrasco, Garrett Richards, Jordan Zimmermann

If, like McHugh, you already had a few million dollars in the bank, would you defy public health officials to try and gut it out for the 2020 Boston Red Sox, or would you opt out, take a year off and fully rest your arm? Yeah, that's what we thought.

Joel Payamps RHP Born: 04/07/94 Age: 27 Bats: R Throws: R Height: 6'2" Weight: 225 Origin: International Free Agent, 2010

YEAR	TEAM	LVL	AGE	W	L	SV	G	GS	IP	H	HR	BB/9	K/9	K	GB%	BABIP	WHIP	ERA	DRA-	WARP	MPH	FA%	Whiff%	CSP
2018	JXN	AA	24	9	4	0	25	10	90	70	5	1.7	9.6	96	43.6%	.289	0.97	2.90	68	2.1				
2018	RNO	AAA	24	0	4	0	6	5	26¹	35	5	3.4	8.9	26	31.8%	.366	1.71	7.18	186	-0.9				
2019	JXN	AA	25	3	4	0	7	7	40²	40	2	0.4	8.6	39	47.9%	.325	1.03	2.88	77	0.6				
2019	RNO	AAA	25	2	2	0	8	8	38	41	6	3.8	7.1	30	41.7%	.312	1.50	4.97	91	0.8				
2019	ARI	MLB	25	0	0	0	2	0	4	4	0	6.8	6.8	3	9.1%	.400	1.75	4.50	116	0.0	95.0	59.1%	22.7%	49.5%
2020	ARI	MLB	26	0	0	0	2	0	3	2	0	9.0	6.0	2	12.5%	.250	1.67	3.00	134	0.0	95.6	62.7%	23.5%	44.5%
2021 FS	BOS	MLB	27	2	3	0	57	0	50	50	8	3.9	7.9	44	39.0%	.294	1.44	4.98	113	-0.2	95.4	61.2%	23.2%	46.6%
2021 DC	BOS	MLB	27	1	1	0	18	0	19	19	3	3.9	7.9	16	39.0%	.294	1.44	4.98	113	0.0	95.4	61.2%	23.2%	46.6%

Comparables: Keury Mella, Adrian Houser, Erick Fedde

Payamps got another miniscule audition for the Diamondbacks in 2020. And, just as in the season prior, he didn't do a lot with it. The good news is that his velo jumped as a pure reliever and that just might provide him a lengthier opportunity in 2021.

Martín Pérez LHP   Born: 04/04/91   Age: 30   Bats: L   Throws: L   Height: 6'0"   Weight: 200   Origin: International Free Agent, 2007

YEAR	TEAM	LVL	AGE	W	L	SV	G	GS	IP	H	HR	BB/9	K/9	K	GB%	BABIP	WHIP	ERA	DRA-	WARP	MPH	FA%	Whiff%	CSP
2018	FRI	AA	27	1	0	0	1	1	6	2	0	4.5	6.0	4	58.8%	.118	0.83	0.00	131	-0.1				
2018	RR	AAA	27	1	0	0	1	1	6¹	6	1	0.0	8.5	6	72.2%	.294	0.95	1.42	62	0.2				
2018	TEX	MLB	27	2	7	0	22	15	85¹	116	16	3.8	5.5	52	50.8%	.345	1.78	6.22	163	-2.0	95.2	67.3%	17.9%	48.9%
2019	MIN	MLB	28	10	7	0	32	29	165¹	184	23	3.6	7.3	135	47.9%	.318	1.52	5.12	129	-1.0	95.8	73.2%	21.7%	46.4%
2020	BOS	MLB	29	3	5	0	12	12	62	55	8	4.1	6.7	46	38.4%	.267	1.34	4.50	133	-0.6	94.1	65.1%	22.3%	46.5%
2021 FS	*BOS*	*MLB*	*30*	*8*	*9*	*0*	*26*	*26*	*150*	*155*	*20*	*3.5*	*7.3*	*121*	*44.3%*	*.299*	*1.43*	*4.60*	*109*	*0.3*	*95.2*	*69.8%*	*21.4%*	*46.8%*

Comparables: Jordan Lyles, Kendall Graveman, Tyler Chatwood

Perez perfectly represents the good, bad and ugly of Boston's newfound approach to roster-building. First, the positives: taking low-cost, medium-upside fliers on players is a smart way to round out a team. In Perez, the Sox found a back-of-the-rotation workhorse who paced the team in innings while making just $6 million. Onto the bad: when you're overly reliant on Perez-type fliers, you rob your team of any real upside. It's embarrassing that Perez was Boston's second-best starter by most metrics, yet finished 75th in DRA among pitchers with at least 50 IP, behind stalwarts like Alec Mills and Kris Bubic. And here's the truly ugly part: despite Perez's modestly useful performance (by ERA) and very useful price tag, the Sox still declined his $6.25 million option for 2021, undoubtedly hoping to eke more value out of a cheaper arm. Perez may be little more than an innings-eater, but no matter how much you value "financial flexibility," you've gotta pay *someone* to actually eat said innings.

Nick Pivetta RHP   Born: 02/14/93   Age: 28   Bats: R   Throws: R   Height: 6'5"   Weight: 214   Origin: Round 4, 2013 Draft (#136 overall)

YEAR	TEAM	LVL	AGE	W	L	SV	G	GS	IP	H	HR	BB/9	K/9	K	GB%	BABIP	WHIP	ERA	DRA-	WARP	MPH	FA%	Whiff%	CSP
2018	PHI	MLB	25	7	14	0	33	32	164	163	24	2.8	10.3	188	46.9%	.333	1.30	4.77	75	3.6	96.7	58.9%	28.0%	48.9%
2019	LHV	AAA	26	5	1	0	9	6	41	23	2	4.8	12.7	58	50.6%	.256	1.10	3.07	40	1.9				
2019	PHI	MLB	26	4	6	1	30	13	93²	103	20	3.7	8.6	89	42.6%	.313	1.52	5.38	103	0.6	96.8	51.1%	24.7%	48.7%
2020	BOS	MLB	27	2	0	0	5	2	15²	18	4	3.4	9.8	17	27.7%	.326	1.53	6.89	121	0.0	94.6	49.3%	24.3%	47.3%
2021 FS	*BOS*	*MLB*	*28*	*9*	*8*	*0*	*26*	*26*	*150*	*131*	*19*	*3.7*	*9.9*	*164*	*41.0%*	*.291*	*1.29*	*3.81*	*90*	*1.9*	*96.5*	*54.0%*	*26.0%*	*48.6%*
2021 DC	*BOS*	*MLB*	*28*	*6*	*6*	*0*	*31*	*19*	*108*	*94*	*13*	*3.7*	*9.9*	*118*	*41.0%*	*.291*	*1.29*	*3.81*	*90*	*1.6*	*96.5*	*54.0%*	*26.0%*	*48.6%*

Comparables: Jon Gray, Jakob Junis, Vince Velasquez

In September 2018, the Red Sox were putting the finishing touches on a 108-win season. By September 2020, they were manipulating Pivetta's service time. Oh, how the mighty have fallen. To be fair to Chaim Bloom and co., Pivetta was a decent get for a few dozen innings of Brandon Workman and Heath Hembree. He's big, throws hard, has some track record of major-league success and is just young enough that you can still talk yourself into a pending breakout. But at this point Pivetta's performance speaks for itself, and he continues to prove that velocity alone isn't enough to beat big-league hitters. Perhaps a change of scenery and work with a new staff will unlock Pivetta's potential, but odds are this will go down as yet another example of the Red Sox being lured by the siren song of a pitcher with Great Stuff (TM) and no idea where it's going.

Eduardo Rodriguez LHP   Born: 04/07/93   Age: 28   Bats: L   Throws: L   Height: 6'2"   Weight: 231   Origin: International Free Agent, 2010

YEAR	TEAM	LVL	AGE	W	L	SV	G	GS	IP	H	HR	BB/9	K/9	K	GB%	BABIP	WHIP	ERA	DRA-	WARP	MPH	FA%	Whiff%	CSP
2018	POR	AA	25	0	0	0	2	2	8	3	0	4.5	15.8	14	69.2%	.231	0.88	0.00	96	0.1				
2018	BOS	MLB	25	13	5	0	27	23	129²	119	16	3.1	10.1	146	38.0%	.301	1.26	3.82	84	2.3	95.2	51.6%	26.3%	46.4%
2019	BOS	MLB	26	19	6	0	34	34	203¹	195	24	3.3	9.4	213	48.2%	.318	1.33	3.81	91	2.9	94.9	54.3%	27.6%	44.0%
2021 FS	*BOS*	*MLB*	*28*	*9*	*8*	*0*	*26*	*26*	*150*	*129*	*16*	*3.4*	*9.9*	*164*	*44.1%*	*.291*	*1.24*	*3.46*	*84*	*2.4*	*95.0*	*53.6%*	*27.3%*	*44.6%*
2021 DC	*BOS*	*MLB*	*28*	*7*	*7*	*0*	*22*	*22*	*120*	*103*	*13*	*3.4*	*9.9*	*131*	*44.1%*	*.291*	*1.24*	*3.46*	*84*	*2.3*	*95.0*	*53.6%*	*27.3%*	*44.6%*

Comparables: José Berríos, Zach Eflin, Zach Davies

In a more rational society, Rodriguez would serve as the poster child for why even the healthiest people in the world need to do their part to curb the spread of coronavirus. E-Rod missed the entire season with myocarditis—essentially inflammation of the heart—caused by COVID-19. He was not medically cleared to begin even light exercise such as walking on a treadmill until late September, and while the hope is Rodriguez will be ready to go to start the 2021 season, no one fully understands yet how athletes will or won't recover from the virus. Rodriguez is entering his final year of team control, and a productive, healthy season should leave him poised for a sizable payday. Here's hoping he's well enough to stay on the mound, and here's another plea to wear a mask, no matter how low-risk you believe yourself to be.

Chris Sale LHP   Born: 03/30/89   Age: 32   Bats: L   Throws: L   Height: 6'6"   Weight: 183   Origin: Round 1, 2010 Draft (#13 overall)

YEAR	TEAM	LVL	AGE	W	L	SV	G	GS	IP	H	HR	BB/9	K/9	K	GB%	BABIP	WHIP	ERA	DRA-	WARP	MPH	FA%	Whiff%	CSP
2018	BOS	MLB	29	12	4	0	27	27	158	102	11	1.9	13.5	237	44.0%	.283	0.86	2.11	50	5.6	99.1	50.1%	35.1%	49.4%
2019	BOS	MLB	30	6	11	0	25	25	147¹	123	24	2.3	13.3	218	43.0%	.311	1.09	4.40	60	4.5	96.6	46.3%	32.0%	50.0%
2021 FS	*BOS*	*MLB*	*32*	*10*	*6*	*0*	*26*	*26*	*150*	*115*	*15*	*2.3*	*11.8*	*196*	*41.8%*	*.292*	*1.02*	*2.53*	*65*	*4.0*	*97.4*	*47.6%*	*33.0%*	*49.8%*
2021 DC	*BOS*	*MLB*	*32*	*6*	*4*	*0*	*16*	*16*	*90*	*69*	*9*	*2.3*	*11.8*	*118*	*41.8%*	*.292*	*1.02*	*2.53*	*65*	*2.6*	*97.4*	*47.6%*	*33.0%*	*49.8%*

Comparables: Stephen Strasburg, Johan Santana, Pedro Martinez

For years and years the skeptics told us that Sale's wire-thin frame and unorthodox delivery would cause serious injury, and for years and years the skeptics were wrong. There's no evidence that Sale's slingshot mechanics or slight build directly led to his UCL tear, but tear it did, necessitating Tommy John surgery in late March. In truth, this was a predictable outcome for reasons beyond Sale's body or throwing motion. His average fastball velocity declined by nearly two mph between 2018 and 2019, and several trips to the IL for various arm issues offered clear foreshadowing. The good news is Sale is only set to enter his age-32 season, and many marquee pitchers have returned to form post-TJ in recent years. The suddenly cost-conscious Red Sox must be praying he can follow suit, as he is still owed $135 million over the next five seasons. For reference, you can buy nearly *two* Nate Eovaldi contracts with that much cheddar.

Connor Seabold RHP Born: 01/24/96 Age: 25 Bats: R Throws: R Height: 6'2" Weight: 190 Origin: Round 3, 2017 Draft (#83 overall)

YEAR	TEAM	LVL	AGE	W	L	SV	G	GS	IP	H	HR	BB/9	K/9	K	GB%	BABIP	WHIP	ERA	DRA-	WARP	MPH	FA%	Whiff%	CSP
2018	CLR	HI-A	22	4	4	0	12	12	71²	57	6	1.8	8.5	68	46.5%	.262	0.99	3.77	68	1.7				
2018	REA	AA	22	1	4	0	11	11	58²	55	10	2.9	9.8	64	34.5%	.292	1.26	4.91	74	1.2				
2019	PHE	ROK	23	0	1	0	1	1	2¹	6	0	0.0	7.7	2	54.5%	.545	2.57	11.57	89	0.0				
2019	PHW	ROK	23	0	0	0	2	2	5	1	0	0.0	18.0	10	83.3%	.167	0.20	0.00	85	0.1				
2019	CLR	HI-A	23	1	0	0	2	1	9	4	1	1.0	10.0	10	50.0%	.158	0.56	1.00	58	0.2				
2019	REA	AA	23	3	1	0	7	7	40	35	2	2.2	8.1	36	45.5%	.303	1.12	2.25	84	0.4				
2021 FS	BOS	MLB	25	2	3	0	57	0	50	46	7	3.2	8.5	47	39.5%	.284	1.28	4.09	103	0.0				
2021 DC	BOS	MLB	25	0	0	0	3	3	13	12	1	3.2	8.5	12	39.5%	.284	1.28	4.09	103	0.1				

Comparables: Marco Gonzales, Ryan Helsley, Tyler Wilson

Former Phillies farmhand Connor Seabold has the name of a man destined for Boston and the arsenal of one who's likely to spend some time in Pawtucket. There's no. 4 starter upside here, but a floor that suggests he should start studying South Station train schedules.

Noah Song RHP Born: 05/28/97 Age: 24 Bats: R Throws: R Height: 6'4" Weight: 200 Origin: Round 4, 2019 Draft (#137 overall)

YEAR	TEAM	LVL	AGE	W	L	SV	G	GS	IP	H	HR	BB/9	K/9	K	GB%	BABIP	WHIP	ERA	DRA-	WARP	MPH	FA%	Whiff%	CSP
2019	LOW	SS	22	0	0	0	7	7	17	10	0	2.6	10.1	19	41.5%	.244	0.88	1.06	51	0.5				
2021 FS	BOS	MLB	24	2	3	0	57	0	50	49	8	5.0	8.0	44	37.9%	.291	1.55	5.26	125	-0.6				

The U.S. Navy ruled that Song must put his duty to his nation above his duty to Red Sox Nation; they ordered the Naval Academy grad to report to flight school at Naval Air Station Pensacola last June. He could apply for early release again this spring, but it seems Song is going to spend the next few years focused on an entirely different type of launch angle.

Jeffrey Springs LHP Born: 09/20/92 Age: 28 Bats: L Throws: L Height: 6'3" Weight: 218 Origin: Round 30, 2015 Draft (#888 overall)

YEAR	TEAM	LVL	AGE	W	L	SV	G	GS	IP	H	HR	BB/9	K/9	K	GB%	BABIP	WHIP	ERA	DRA-	WARP	MPH	FA%	Whiff%	CSP
2018	FRI	AA	25	3	2	1	20	0	37¹	39	2	1.7	16.4	68	39.7%	.487	1.23	4.82	40	1.3				
2018	RR	AAA	25	1	2	1	13	0	19¹	12	0	5.6	14.0	30	44.4%	.333	1.24	2.79	42	0.7				
2018	TEX	MLB	25	1	1	0	18	2	32	32	4	3.9	8.7	31	31.6%	.311	1.44	3.38	132	-0.4	93.1	62.7%	27.1%	52.4%
2019	NAS	AAA	26	3	0	0	6	0	7	6	1	0.0	15.4	12	42.9%	.417	0.86	3.86	32	0.3				
2019	TEX	MLB	26	4	1	0	25	0	32¹	38	4	6.4	8.9	32	25.3%	.358	1.89	6.40	163	-0.9	93.6	58.0%	30.2%	50.1%
2020	BOS	MLB	27	0	2	0	16	0	20¹	30	5	3.1	12.4	28	36.5%	.431	1.82	7.08	81	0.4	93.4	46.9%	37.6%	48.7%
2021 FS	BOS	MLB	28	2	2	0	57	0	50	42	7	4.0	10.7	59	34.6%	.291	1.31	3.97	94	0.3	93.4	54.5%	32.5%	50.0%
2021 DC	BOS	MLB	28	2	2	0	42	0	45	38	6	4.0	10.7	53	34.6%	.291	1.31	3.97	94	0.4	93.4	54.5%	32.5%	50.0%

Comparables: Austin Davis, Stephen Tarpley, Dillon Peters

Acquired for Sam Travis back in January 2020, Springs is a tall, lanky left-hander who hasn't pitched well enough to earn spots in the Rangers' or Red Sox's bullpens over the past few years. There's no need to pile on.

Josh Taylor LHP Born: 03/02/93 Age: 28 Bats: L Throws: L Height: 6'5" Weight: 245 Origin: Undrafted Free Agent, 2014

YEAR	TEAM	LVL	AGE	W	L	SV	G	GS	IP	H	HR	BB/9	K/9	K	GB%	BABIP	WHIP	ERA	DRA-	WARP	MPH	FA%	Whiff%	CSP
2018	VIS	HI-A	25	1	2	5	14	0	16	16	1	2.8	11.2	20	42.9%	.366	1.31	2.81	51	0.4				
2018	POR	AA	25	2	5	8	33	0	35²	42	1	4.5	9.3	37	50.9%	.383	1.68	3.79	80	0.5				
2019	WOR	AAA	26	1	1	3	20	0	23¹	18	2	4.2	12.3	32	47.2%	.320	1.24	2.70	60	0.7				
2019	BOS	MLB	26	2	2	0	52	1	47¹	40	5	3.0	11.8	62	44.7%	.321	1.18	3.04	80	0.7	96.2	60.1%	33.7%	42.9%
2020	BOS	MLB	27	1	1	0	8	0	7¹	7	2	6.1	8.6	7	43.5%	.238	1.64	9.82	104	0.1	94.8	52.1%	28.4%	45.9%
2021 FS	BOS	MLB	28	2	2	0	57	0	50	42	5	3.9	9.9	54	46.6%	.288	1.28	3.65	87	0.5	95.9	58.4%	32.5%	43.5%
2021 DC	BOS	MLB	28	2	2	0	42	0	45	38	5	3.9	9.9	49	46.6%	.288	1.28	3.65	87	0.6	95.9	58.4%	32.5%	43.5%

Comparables: Ashton Goudeau, Andrew Suárez, Spencer Turnbull

This was a trying year by anyone's standards, but Taylor had it particularly rough. He was among the bevy of Red Sox southpaws to test positive for COVID-19 in early July, which kept him on the IL until mid-August. When Taylor returned he was ineffectively wild across eight disastrous games before shoulder tendonitis ended his season. Assuming he recovers fully from both ailments, Taylor can still serve as one of Boston's primary lefty relievers, bolstered by his Great Stuff(TM) but hampered by, well, let's be charitable and go with "inconsistent" control. But there are lots of arms in Boston's pen with similar profiles, and it's a shame Taylor was denied a real chance at separating himself from the pack.

Phillips Valdez RHP   Born: 11/16/91   Age: 29   Bats: R   Throws: R   Height: 6'2"   Weight: 160   Origin: International Free Agent, 2008

YEAR	TEAM	LVL	AGE	W	L	SV	G	GS	IP	H	HR	BB/9	K/9	K	GB%	BABIP	WHIP	ERA	DRA-	WARP	MPH	FA%	Whiff%	CSP
2018	HBG	AA	26	0	0	0	5	0	10²	9	0	1.7	6.8	8	43.3%	.300	1.03	2.53	55	0.3				
2018	SYR	AAA	26	6	7	0	26	19	124¹	111	10	3.2	6.9	96	58.0%	.281	1.25	2.75	83	2.0				
2019	NAS	AAA	27	1	7	1	26	14	78²	87	10	4.1	7.4	65	53.3%	.314	1.56	4.92	96	1.4				
2019	TEX	MLB	27	0	0	0	11	0	16	17	3	5.1	10.1	18	52.2%	.326	1.62	3.94	93	0.1	94.1	58.4%	21.8%	50.1%
2020	BOS	MLB	28	1	1	0	24	0	30¹	33	3	4.7	8.9	30	46.6%	.353	1.62	3.26	94	0.4	94.0	45.2%	27.7%	45.2%
2021 FS	BOS	MLB	29	2	2	0	57	0	50	50	5	4.6	8.2	45	49.7%	.308	1.51	5.01	110	-0.1	94.0	48.8%	26.1%	46.5%
2021 DC	BOS	MLB	29	2	2	0	48	0	51	51	5	4.6	8.2	46	49.7%	.308	1.51	5.01	110	0.4	94.0	48.8%	26.1%	46.5%

Comparables: Mike Mayers, Glenn Sparkman, Kevin McCarthy

Valdez should be nicknamed "Exxon" because he paid no real price (3.26 ERA) for courting disaster (33 hits allowed in 30 1/3 innings).

Marcus Walden RHP   Born: 09/13/88   Age: 32   Bats: R   Throws: R   Height: 5'10"   Weight: 198   Origin: Round 9, 2007 Draft (#295 overall)

YEAR	TEAM	LVL	AGE	W	L	SV	G	GS	IP	H	HR	BB/9	K/9	K	GB%	BABIP	WHIP	ERA	DRA-	WARP	MPH	FA%	Whiff%	CSP
2018	WOR	AAA	29	0	4	2	18	5	32²	44	2	4.7	6.6	24	50.4%	.368	1.87	4.96	94	0.2				
2018	BOS	MLB	29	0	0	1	8	0	14²	14	0	1.8	8.6	14	58.5%	.341	1.16	3.68	70	0.3	95.7	45.1%	27.3%	49.0%
2019	BOS	MLB	30	9	2	2	70	0	78	61	6	3.7	8.8	76	55.1%	.266	1.19	3.81	78	1.3	95.7	34.8%	28.9%	43.2%
2020	BOS	MLB	31	0	2	1	15	0	13¹	23	5	6.1	6.8	10	40.4%	.383	2.40	9.45	157	-0.3	93.8	36.5%	18.4%	43.8%
2021 FS	BOS	MLB	32	2	2	0	57	0	50	49	6	4.1	7.7	42	49.1%	.293	1.44	4.69	105	0.0	95.3	35.8%	26.3%	43.7%
2021 DC	BOS	MLB	32	2	2	0	48	0	51	50	6	4.1	7.7	43	49.1%	.293	1.44	4.69	105	0.1	95.3	35.8%	26.3%	43.7%

Comparables: Tommy Layne, Jeff Manship, Justin Grimm

There was stiff competition for the honorific of "most disappointing Red Sox pitcher" last season, but Walden deserves serious consideration. After quietly serving as one of Boston's best relievers in 2019, Walden loudly fell apart. His strikeout rate fell while his walk and homer rates jumped. He threw his four-seam fastball and his slider less in favor of a two-seamer, and the results were disastrous—per Baseball Savant, opponents hit .355 off his cutter and .455 off his sinker. 2020 was a year full of disappointing but small samples, and it'd be short-sighted to write Walden off after just 13 1/3 bad innings. At the same time it's not as if he has a long track record of success, and careers for relievers like Walden can be rather ephemeral.

Thad Ward RHP   Born: 01/16/97   Age: 24   Bats: R   Throws: R   Height: 6'3"   Weight: 182   Origin: Round 5, 2018 Draft (#160 overall)

YEAR	TEAM	LVL	AGE	W	L	SV	G	GS	IP	H	HR	BB/9	K/9	K	GB%	BABIP	WHIP	ERA	DRA-	WARP	MPH	FA%	Whiff%	CSP
2018	LOW	SS	21	0	3	0	11	11	31	33	2	3.5	7.8	27	54.3%	.337	1.45	3.77	159	-0.8				
2019	GVL	LO-A	22	5	2	0	13	13	72¹	51	2	3.1	10.8	87	47.8%	.280	1.05	1.99	66	1.7				
2019	SAL	HI-A	22	3	3	0	12	12	54	38	4	5.3	11.7	70	47.1%	.296	1.30	2.33	89	0.5				
2021 FS	BOS	MLB	24	2	3	0	57	0	50	47	7	5.7	9.0	50	43.7%	.290	1.57	5.30	122	-0.5				

Comparables: Albert Abreu, Justin Grimm, Tyler Thornburg

Ward remains one of Boston's more intriguing pitching prospects, which is why it's notable that he never got the call up from Ft. Myers to join the Sox's alternate site in Pawtucket. Or, put another way, the Sox denied Thad Ward a shot to serve as a ward, which seems more than a thad bit odd.

Ryan Weber RHP   Born: 08/12/90   Age: 30   Bats: R   Throws: R   Height: 6'1"   Weight: 175   Origin: Round 22, 2009 Draft (#658 overall)

YEAR	TEAM	LVL	AGE	W	L	SV	G	GS	IP	H	HR	BB/9	K/9	K	GB%	BABIP	WHIP	ERA	DRA-	WARP	MPH	FA%	Whiff%	CSP
2018	DUR	AAA	27	9	6	1	25	18	115¹	117	9	1.8	6.5	83	53.8%	.305	1.21	2.73	95	1.0				
2018	TB	MLB	27	0	1	0	2	0	5¹	5	0	3.4	1.7	1	52.4%	.238	1.31	5.06	156	-0.1	90.0	74.3%	9.1%	52.7%
2019	WOR	AAA	28	1	5	0	16	16	78	86	9	2.9	7.3	63	53.3%	.328	1.42	4.50	100	1.4				
2019	BOS	MLB	28	2	4	0	18	3	40²	48	5	1.8	6.4	29	48.9%	.319	1.38	5.09	102	0.2	90.8	52.7%	14.6%	50.6%
2020	BOS	MLB	29	1	3	0	17	5	43	44	8	2.9	5.7	27	53.2%	.273	1.35	4.40	110	0.1	90.2	50.9%	15.0%	49.3%
2021 FS	BOS	MLB	30	2	3	0	57	0	50	53	6	2.4	6.4	35	51.5%	.301	1.33	4.50	104	0.0	90.4	52.1%	14.7%	49.9%
2021 DC	BOS	MLB	30	0	0	0	3	3	12	12	1	2.4	6.4	8	51.5%	.301	1.33	4.50	104	0.1	90.4	52.1%	14.7%	49.9%

Comparables: Casey Sadler, Tyler Duffey, Chris Stratton

Weber is a spare tire; useful enough in a pinch, but only designed to get you to the next exit. Since 2015, he's proven to possess the command and craftiness needed to survive for a few dozen innings at a time, but lack the talent required to offer much else. We have over 100 innings telling us Weber is the platonic ideal of a Quad-A pitcher, yet the Sox started the season banking on him to fill a spot in the rotation. You could argue that he disappointed, but that's not really fair—he did what he's always done, and what he's always done just isn't enough. If your plan is to use Weber for spot starts and long relief outings, you've adequately prepared to face some bumps in the road. If you start a long road trip with Weber on one of your rims, well, maybe you shouldn't be the one driving.

Garrett Whitlock RHP Born: 06/11/96 Age: 25 Bats: R Throws: R Height: 6'5" Weight: 190 Origin: Round 18, 2017 Draft (#542 overall)

YEAR	TEAM	LVL	AGE	W	L	SV	G	GS	IP	H	HR	BB/9	K/9	K	GB%	BABIP	WHIP	ERA	DRA-	WARP	MPH	FA%	Whiff%	CSP
2018	CSC	LO-A	22	2	2	0	7	7	40	23	1	1.6	9.9	44	61.1%	.239	0.75	1.12	76	0.7				
2018	TAM	HI-A	22	5	3	0	14	13	70	60	2	3.5	9.5	74	50.8%	.310	1.24	2.44	82	1.1				
2018	TRN	AA	22	1	0	0	2	1	10²	10	0	5.9	3.4	4	55.9%	.294	1.59	0.84	115	0.0				
2019	TRN	AA	23	3	3	0	14	14	70¹	73	4	2.3	7.3	57	55.5%	.322	1.29	3.07	107	-0.2				
2021 FS	BOS	MLB	25	1	1	0	57	0	50	46	6	3.7	7.7	42	50.2%	.281	1.35	4.29	106	0.0				
2021 DC	BOS	MLB	25	1	1	0	36	0	38	35	4	3.7	7.7	32	50.2%	.281	1.35	4.29	106	0.1				

Comparables: Taylor Rogers, Kyle McGowin, Ramón Rosso

Swiped from the Yankees with the fourth pick in the Rule 5 draft, Whitlock is a big right-hander who's still recovering from July 2019 Tommy John surgery. He should be ready for spring training and has a modicum of upside, which arguably already makes him one of the Red Sox's better relievers.

NEW YORK YANKEES

Essay by Randy Wilkins

Player comments by Mike Gianella and BP staff

Closer Aroldis Chapman settled into his stretch position and prepared to deliver another 3-2 pitch to his newfound nemesis, Mike Brosseau. The setting: Petco Park, Game 5 of the American League Divisional Series. Catcher Gary Sánchez implored his closer to throw a back-foot slider to the right-handed Brosseau, but Chapman shook him off. His success had always rested on his otherworldly fastball, and the arrogance that came with overpowering the opposition. That arrogance had delivered a victory to Chapman a month earlier, in his first memorable matchup with Brosseau.

For years, the Yankees and the Rays' relationship had a big brother-little brother dynamic. Dating back to the days of Jonny Gomes and Shelley Duncan, their matchups felt like the small-market Rays were trying to prove themselves to their big market foes. That dynamic changed just a month earlier. With two outs in the ninth inning of that heated contest, Chapman unleashed a ferocious 101 mph fastball that came so close to Brosseau's head that he could hear the seams on the baseball singing. Chapman won the battle that night on another high four-seamer, but he unknowingly kindled a rivalry that came to a head in Game 5 of the ALDS.

As Brosseau dug into the batter's box, preparing for the 10th pitch of his battle with Chapman, it's possible that the embers of his previous confrontation with Chapman floated through his mind. Likewise, he probably knew from experience and scouting reports that the heater was coming. He just needed it to be in the right spot. In a full count, Chapman obliged.

CRACK.

The sound of Brosseau's barrel impacting the inside fastball reverberated off Petco's empty seats so loudly that Yankees fans can still hear the echo. The only things to pierce that heartbreaking sound were the raucous cheers of the little brother winning the sibling rivalry—at least for a year. As Brosseau rounded the bases, floating on a cloud of sweet revenge, a familiar smile of shock spread across Chapman's face. That smile succinctly captures a self-imposed dilemma the Yankees face next season. It is The Smirk of Chapman™.

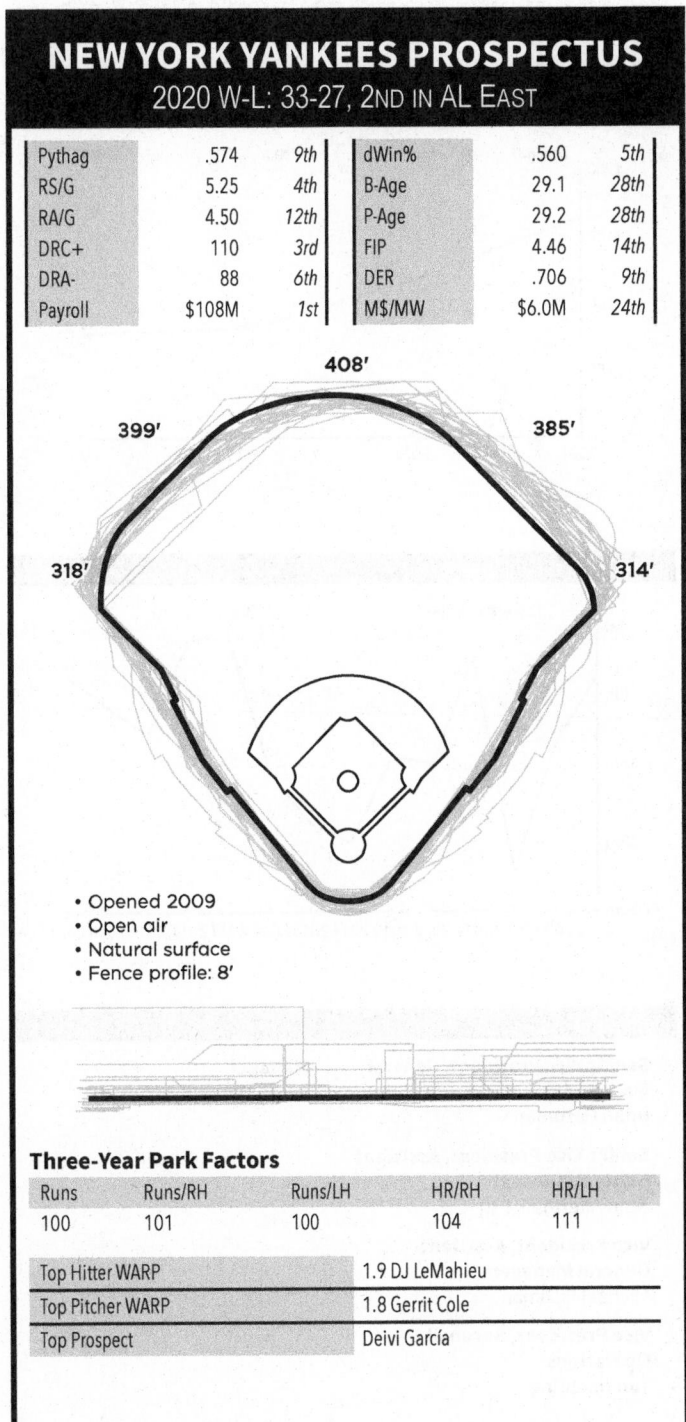

NEW YORK YANKEES PROSPECTUS
2020 W-L: 33-27, 2ND IN AL EAST

Pythag	.574	9th	dWin%	.560	5th
RS/G	5.25	4th	B-Age	29.1	28th
RA/G	4.50	12th	P-Age	29.2	28th
DRC+	110	3rd	FIP	4.46	14th
DRA-	88	6th	DER	.706	9th
Payroll	$108M	1st	M$/MW	$6.0M	24th

408'

399'   385'

318'   314'

- Opened 2009
- Open air
- Natural surface
- Fence profile: 8'

Three-Year Park Factors

Runs	Runs/RH	Runs/LH	HR/RH	HR/LH
100	101	100	104	111

Top Hitter WARP	1.9 DJ LeMahieu
Top Pitcher WARP	1.8 Gerrit Cole
Top Prospect	Deivi García

Payroll History (in millions)

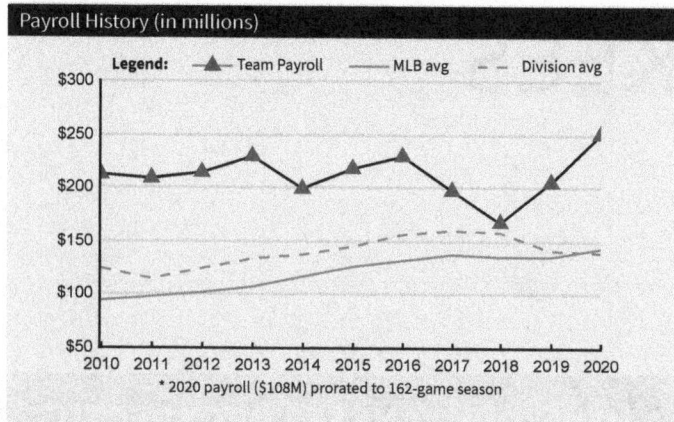

Legend: ▲ Team Payroll — MLB avg -- Division avg

* 2020 payroll ($108M) prorated to 162-game season

Future Commitments (in millions)

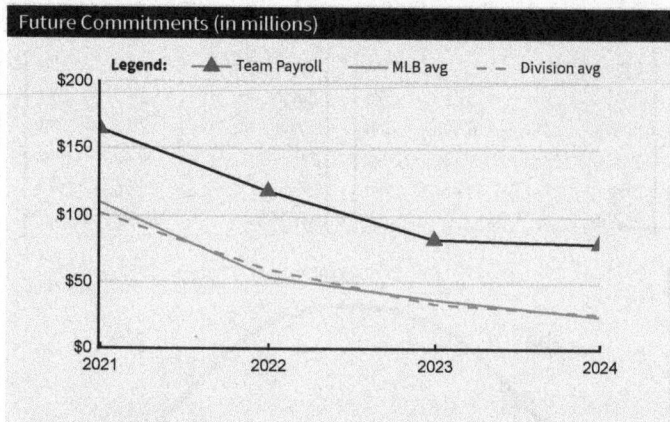

Legend: ▲ Team Payroll — MLB avg -- Division avg

Farm System Ranking

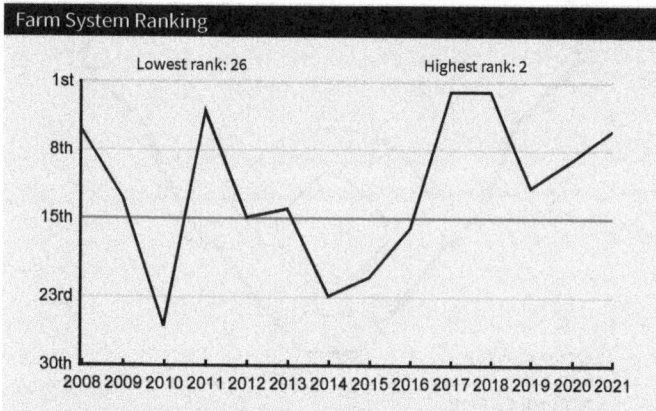

Lowest rank: 26   Highest rank: 2

Personnel

Senior Vice President, General Manager
Brian Cashman

Senior Vice President, Assistant General Manager
Jean Afterman, Esq.

Vice President, Assistant General Manager
Michael Fishman

Vice President, Baseball Operations
Tim Naehring

Manager
Aaron Boone

While the Brosseau home run will live on as *the* Game 5 highlight for years to come, there is a prior at-bat that captures the big-picture predicament of the Yankees. With the score tied at 1-1 in the top of the eighth inning, and Diego Castillo entering the game, Aaron Boone turned to lefty-hitting Mike Ford in place of Kyle Higashioka.

Ford was a member of the 2019 Yankees' "Next Man Up" crew. You remember them. When the Bombers suffered an unusual number of injuries throughout that season, they relied upon their 40-man roster's back-end to pull them through. After spending six years in the minors, Ford made his major-league debut when the Yankees needed him the most. He posted a 125 DRC+ while delivering critical hits along the way, including a memorable walk-off home run against Liam Hendriks that September. Unfortunately for Ford and the team, his 2020 didn't go so well. And that is putting it nicely: He lugged a slash line of .135/.226/.270 with him into the batter's box for one of the most critical at-bats of their 2020 season.

Over the last 20 years, the Yankees had the luxury of turning to their bench and calling upon accomplished veteran sluggers for moments like the one Ford found himself in. A sampling of those names includes Darryl Strawberry, Tim Raines, David Justice, Chilli Davis, Eric Chavez, Andruw Jones, Raul Ibanez, Matt Holliday and even Marcus Thames. It was always a testament to the quality, depth and versatility of the roster, but also its gaudiness; when the organization signed some new star, an older one still under contract slid down to the bench. In 2020, the Yankees' fate was resting on a player whose season should have ended when the alternate site closed shop.

To his credit, Ford battled back from 0-2 to a full count. That's when Castillo delivered a middle-middle hanging slider that Ford could only foul off. Boone had, undoubtedly, brought him into the game to crush *that* mistake. The inches between playoff glory and a missed opportunity reflect an organizational philosophy that continues to limit the full potential of the Yankees' championship-caliber core.

Title windows are a somewhat abstract construct that are nevertheless popular amongst fans and sports media. The idea is that a team's core of players have a finite amount of time together to win a championship. Title windows, then, represent a perceived expiration date that is often rooted in the exploitative nature of pre-free agency contract structures. The further away a talented group of players are from potential big paydays, the larger the window is perceived to be. This is a simplification of the concept, but you get the idea.

Professional sports are one of the few industries with an aversion to both, long-term planning and present-day investing in the product. Baseball franchises willingly think four-to-five years ahead at the most with their major-league roster, usually in an attempt to keep payrolls down and to maintain high profits. It is especially true when a particular team develops multiple prospects into productive major leaguers. Said organization is then thrust onto the clock when that happens. They've entered their title window.

This doesn't have to be the case. If we're sincere, this shouldn't be the case. It especially shouldn't be the case in an uncapped sport like baseball. Franchises should be looking beyond this arbitrary five-year window. It may be conservative to estimate that 25 out of the 30 major-league teams have the resources to extend a productive core's shelf life. This may be a naive and purist view on things, but the point of building a talented core should be to put the team in the best position to win as many titles as possible for as long as possible.

Under George Steinbrenner, the Yankees didn't concern themselves with cycles. They were the Evil Empire, almighty and immutable, a franchise that could afford to reinforce the army with as many mercenaries as necessary. It was sometimes clumsy, and almost always effective. They were the Goliath who stole away Jason Giambi, serving as the antagonists of *Moneyball* and providing the catalyst for the modern age of austerity.

Under Hal Steinbrenner, the Yankees have reimagined how they allocate their immense resources. The organization built a robust analytics department, expanded its research and development team and invested in their minor-league facilities. Brian Cashman believed the franchise was falling behind other teams implementing innovative approaches to close the competitive gap. In Cashman's mind, the team needed an internal makeover more than they required wild expenditures in the free-agent market—though both should have been in reach.

It's difficult to argue with that belief. Beyond the successful development of Aaron Judge, Gary Sánchez, Gleyber Torres and Clint Frazier in recent years (the latter two were originally acquired in trade), the front office discovered diamonds in the rough like Luke Voit and Gio Urshela. The Yankees were not only able to avoid a full teardown a few years back, but they emerged as a real championship contender. Cashman realized his vision.

The concern these days is the team appears satisfied just to have a title window. Now, they are conducting business as if the cost of a championship is greater than the reward of earning one. It is unfair to say the team is complacent: you don't spend over $300 million on Brian Cashman's White Whale, Gerrit Cole, if you're complacent; it *would* be fair to say the Yankees sit in a self-constructed purgatory. It rests between an all-out aggressive approach to maximize everything, and a satisfaction with a good but flawed roster.

Some prefer to see a financial powerhouse flex its muscles at the top end of the free-agent market; that if you're rich, you should be spending lavishly. There's logic to that (hello, Gerrit Cole), but the Yankees should be all about leveraging their immense resources to build the most devastating roster possible, one through 26. The name of the game should be

quality depth. Instead of shopping at Bloomingdale's for nice accessories, the Yankees have been looking through the bargain bins at Kohls for costume jewelry.

Even in an offseason where they acquired one of the best pitchers in the world, the team refused to add at the margins. Instead, they relied on the "Next Man Up" squad from 2019 and suffered the consequences. In 2020, the quintet of Ford, Tyler Wade, Mike Tauchman, Miguel Andújar and Thairo Estrada combined for 0.1 Wins Above Replacement Player. If you compare that with a 2.6 WARP in 2019, the drop-off in production was stark. That lack of productive depth ended up playing a significant role in their inconsistent season.

Of course, no one knew a pandemic was on the horizon. But the Yankees knew more than anyone how important it was to have a deep, quality roster after the injury-marred year of 2019. They chose trust over opportunity, banking on those players repeating their previous performance. That they failed was somewhat predictable: benches over 60-game stretches are like bullpens when it comes to variance. There wasn't enough time for slumps to be worked through, for variance to be overcome. The best route was to acquire as much talent as possible and trust that it'll work out in the end. The Yankees didn't follow that route to roster-building.

After letting incumbent shortstop Didi Gregorius walk in free agency, the position was given to handpicked-successor Gleyber Torres. There's nothing wrong with this choice unto itself, but their refusal to restock the depth from which Torres emerged meant there was no stemming the upcoming ripple effect.

They instead found themselves overly reliant on the likes of Wade, your typical glove-first, bat-second spare infielder (and a lightning rod for some feisty online Yankees fans). Instead of positioning him as a perfectly serviceable "break glass in case of an emergency" option, the Yankees treated him as a necessity.

As was the case in 2019, the injury bug took residence in the Yankees clubhouse and Wade ended up appearing in 87 percent of the squad's games, many of which saw him masquerade as a starter on a team with championship aspirations. Predictably, the Yankees suffered from inconsistency: they were in the midst of at least a five-game winning or losing streak in half their games.

That inconsistency didn't just lie at the feet of shallow position player depth. The pitching suffered from attrition as well. Losing ace reliever Tommy Kahnle early in the season proved to be a major blow to the team, with the Yankees having to turn to the likes of Jonathan Holder, Nick Nelson, Ben Heller, Tyler Lyons and Miguel Yajúre to shoulder the load. One can only wonder how things might have played out in Game 5 if Kahnle had been healthy. Or if more quality depth had been on-hand.

This brings us back to the issue of title windows for the Yankees. The organization willingly chose to rely upon Ford, Wade and the since-non-tendered Holder. Over the last 18 months, the team has made one significant addition: Gerrit Cole. Two trading seasons have passed wherein the Yankees were unable to deliver depth pieces. As of press time, it looks likely that the team will bring most of the old gang back to make another run at a title.

The Yankees' issues extend beyond available resources. Rather, this offseason is the culmination of a philosophy that limits the maximum potential for the team's core. With Aaron Judge, Sánchez and Torres getting closer to bigger paydays, the urgency to win a title in 2021 is greater than ever for this group. That task is much more difficult to achieve when strategy is to make the postseason and then hope for the best.

This hope brings us back to the night The Smirk of Chapman™ reared its ugly head. In a vacuum, the Brosseau home run was a thrilling moment of baseball theater. In a broader context, it signals a transition Yankees fans may struggle to acknowledge: The Yankees are replacing the Dodgers as the exceptional, brand name franchise that struggles to seal the deal.

The irony is Andrew Friedman, the Rays' original architect, was the one delivering a championship to L.A. The difference between the Yankees and Friedman's Dodgers lies in the overall depth manager Dave Roberts was able to wield. Under Friedman, the Dodgers have created a player acquisition philosophy requiring solid contributions across the roster—and even into the reserves. The Dodgers fill their roster with capable players, not just warm bodies. That spot is not a rotating formality based on available player options; on any given day, it can belong to former veteran starters who had been upgraded upon, like Chris Taylor and AJ Pollock, or more inexperienced players who hadn't yet worked themselves into expanded roles, such as Edwin Ríos. The bench isn't an afterthought, a last resort; it's part of the championship formula.

The Smirk of Chapman™, then, is the embodiment of these Yankees. Despite being blessed beyond belief, their fate has been decided and defined by the margins—be it the location of a fastball on the field, or the placement of a comma on a ledger that steers them away from leveraging their greatest strength: their financial might. The difference between a smile and a smirk is a matter of degrees; the difference between the Yankees and Dodgers is, too. ∎

—Randy Wilkins is a filmmaker and co-founder of the New York Yankees blog Views From 314ft.

HITTERS

Kevin Alcantara OF Born: 07/12/02 Age: 18 Bats: R Throws: R Height: 6'6" Weight: 188 Origin: International Free Agent, 2018

YEAR	TEAM	LVL	AGE	PA	R	2B	3B	HR	RBI	BB	K	SB	CS	Whiff%	AVG/OBP/SLG	DRC+	BABIP	BRR	FRAA	WARP
2019	YAE	ROK	16	128	19	5	2	1	13	3	27	3	3		.260/.289/.358	108	.326	0.5	CF(27): -1.3	0.4
2019	DSL NYY	ROK	16	46	7	3	1	0	6	5	9	2	0		.237/.348/.368		.300			
2021 FS	*NYY*	*MLB*	*18*	*600*	*42*	*26*	*3*	*6*	*47*	*23*	*207*	*13*	*6*		*.206/.243/.297*	*45*	*.311*	*-1.8*	*CF -5*	*-3.0*

Alcantara grew up rooting for the Yankees, meaning he can empathize with New York's fan base more than most of his peers. It shouldn't surprise anyone, then, if he's extra motivated to become a starting-caliber outfielder. That way, he can help end the pain and suffering of fans like himself, who have seen the Yankees win only one championship during their lifetimes.

Greg Allen LF Born: 03/15/93 Age: 28 Bats: S Throws: R Height: 6'0" Weight: 185 Origin: Round 6, 2014 Draft (#188 overall)

YEAR	TEAM	LVL	AGE	PA	R	2B	3B	HR	RBI	BB	K	SB	CS	Whiff%	AVG/OBP/SLG	DRC+	BABIP	BRR	FRAA	WARP
2018	COL	AAA	25	205	31	13	0	2	14	19	44	12	6		.298/.395/.409	125	.389	0.3	CF(42): 2.3, LF(5): -0.4, RF(1): 0.5	1.2
2018	CLE	MLB	25	291	36	11	3	2	20	14	58	21	4	20.1%	.257/.310/.343	78	.320	3.4	CF(78): 2.8, RF(16): -0.4, LF(3): -0.1	0.8
2019	COL	AAA	26	226	37	9	3	5	17	20	44	10	5		.268/.358/.419	95	.322	0.6	CF(26): 1.6, LF(15): 1.4, RF(1): 0.0	0.8
2019	CLE	MLB	26	256	30	9	3	4	27	11	53	8	2	24.8%	.229/.290/.346	73	.280	0.8	LF(60): 6.0, CF(18): -1.6, RF(13): 0.1	0.4
2020	SD	MLB	27	4	1	0	0	0	0	2	1	1	1	0	100.0%	.000/.750/.000	88		0.1	LF(1): -0.0, RF(1): -0.0	0.0
2020	CLE	MLB	27	28	3	1	0	1	4	1	9	1	0	37.0%	.160/.214/.320	93	.188	0.0	LF(11): 0.3, CF(4): 0.2	0.1
2021 FS	*NYY*	*MLB*	*28*	*600*	*62*	*23*	*3*	*11*	*57*	*41*	*137*	*21*	*6*	*24.8%*	*.235/.315/.358*	*91*	*.294*	*5.6*	*CF -6, LF 0*	*1.2*
2021 DC	*NYY*	*MLB*	*28*	*67*	*6*	*2*	*0*	*1*	*6*	*4*	*15*	*2*	*0*	*24.8%*	*.235/.315/.358*	*91*	*.294*	*0.6*	*CF -1*	*0.1*

Comparables: Leonys Martin, Cory Sullivan, Jose Gonzalez

Allen is what he is at this point: a speedy center fielder incapable of much offensive production. His defense and baserunning are enough to keep him rosterable, but that could change if and when his athleticism slips.

Miguel Andújar 3B   Born: 03/02/95   Age: 26   Bats: R   Throws: R   Height: 6'0"   Weight: 211   Origin: International Free Agent, 2011

YEAR	TEAM	LVL	AGE	PA	R	2B	3B	HR	RBI	BB	K	SB	CS	Whiff%	AVG/OBP/SLG	DRC+	BABIP	BRR	FRAA	WARP
2018	NYY	MLB	23	606	83	47	2	27	92	25	97	2	1	19.6%	.297/.328/.527	119	.316	-0.1	3B(136): -15.2	2.0
2019	NYY	MLB	24	49	1	0	0	0	1	1	11	0	0	30.9%	.128/.143/.128	62	.162	0.2	3B(4): -0.8	-0.2
2020	NYY	MLB	25	65	5	2	1	1	5	3	9	0	0	22.1%	.242/.277/.355	83	.269	0.5	LF(7): -0.6, 3B(6): -0.5	-0.1
2021 FS	NYY	MLB	26	600	64	30	2	22	75	31	111	1	0	21.4%	.258/.303/.439	101	.286	-0.7	3B -5	0.7
2021 DC	NYY	MLB	26	237	25	12	0	8	29	12	44	0	0	21.4%	.258/.303/.439	101	.286	-0.3	3B -2, LF 0	0.3

Comparables: Danny Valencia, Jorge Cantu, Manny Machado

Andújar nearly won the Rookie of the Year Award in 2018. He's now been an afterthought for the Yankees in the two seasons since. It wasn't because of injury this time; rather, it was because New York needed pitching more than it needed hitting. As a result, the Yankees couldn't find space for him, even on a 28-player roster. On another squad, there would be a place for Andújar's bat, defensive limitations and all; the Yankees, though, already have too many old and injury-susceptible players who need to rotate in at DH. A change of scenery seems inevitable; especially after Andújar's agent complained in September that his client was unfairly and undeservedly demoted.

--- ★ ★ ★ *2021 Top 101 Prospect* **#59** ★ ★ ★ ---

Jasson Dominguez CF   Born: 02/07/03   Age: 18   Bats: S   Throws: R   Height: 5'10"   Weight: 190   Origin: International Free Agent, 2019

If you believe the scouting reports, Dominguez is going to be the next great Yankee outfielder as well as one of the greatest hitters ever to play the game. He should cruise into the Hall of Fame, perhaps even before he retires. That last one is a wee bit hyperbolic, but scouts are crushing on the Dominican youngster. In a normal year, there would be at least some looks against live pitching to offer additional information and context regarding Dominguez's ability. Right now, everyone is playing the same guessing game. What we know for sure is that Dominguez is a year older, albeit still only 18, and that the sight of him taking cuts in batting practice can light up a social media feed. While there are many potential outcomes for Dominguez, and they're not all super rosy, there's also virtually no precedent for a 16-year-old signee with such thunderous tools out of the gate. Put a star by his name: either he'll become one, or we'll learn something in the process.

Ezequiel Duran 2B   Born: 05/22/99   Age: 22   Bats: R   Throws: R   Height: 5'11"   Weight: 185   Origin: International Free Agent, 2017

YEAR	TEAM	LVL	AGE	PA	R	2B	3B	HR	RBI	BB	K	SB	CS	Whiff%	AVG/OBP/SLG	DRC+	BABIP	BRR	FRAA	WARP
2018	PUL	ROK	19	235	34	8	2	4	20	9	65	7	0		.201/.251/.311	17	.265	4.4	2B(51): -1.2, SS(1): -0.2	-1.4
2019	SI	SS	20	277	49	12	4	13	37	25	77	11	4		.256/.329/.496	160	.314	0.6	2B(57): 7.6	3.0
2021 FS	NYY	MLB	22	600	48	26	4	13	58	26	229	13	5		.206/.247/.338	57	.318	2.1	2B 6, SS 0	-0.4

Comparables: Patrick Wisdom, Darrell Ceciliani, Shane Peterson

Duran hopes to finally make his full-season debut in 2021. He has plenty of raw power, but his build and swing-and-miss issues could eventually stop him in his tracks at the higher levels of the minors.

Thairo Estrada 2B   Born: 02/22/96   Age: 25   Bats: R   Throws: R   Height: 5'10"   Weight: 185   Origin: International Free Agent, 2012

YEAR	TEAM	LVL	AGE	PA	R	2B	3B	HR	RBI	BB	K	SB	CS	Whiff%	AVG/OBP/SLG	DRC+	BABIP	BRR	FRAA	WARP
2018	TAM	HI-A	22	47	4	2	0	0	5	0	9	0	0		.222/.234/.267	52	.270	-0.6	SS(8): -0.2	-0.3
2018	SWB	AAA	22	34	1	1	0	0	3	0	8	0	0		.152/.176/.182	27	.200	-0.3	SS(5): 0.0, 2B(3): 0.9	-0.1
2019	SWB	AAA	23	259	39	17	2	8	32	14	50	3	1		.266/.313/.452	86	.304	-1.1	SS(33): 1.7, 2B(24): -0.9, 3B(2): -0.3	0.5
2019	NYY	MLB	23	69	12	3	0	3	12	3	15	4	0	25.5%	.250/.294/.438	87	.283	1.0	2B(17): -1.1, SS(9): 0.3, LF(2): -0.1	0.1
2020	NYY	MLB	24	52	8	0	0	1	3	1	19	1	0	29.4%	.167/.231/.229	61	.250	0.3	2B(20): 0.3, 3B(6): -0.4, SS(3): -0.1	-0.1
2021 FS	NYY	MLB	25	600	58	20	2	15	61	30	145	4	2	27.7%	.234/.283/.359	76	.290	-1.4	2B -12, 3B 0	-1.2
2021 DC	NYY	MLB	25	271	26	9	0	6	27	13	65	2	1	27.7%	.234/.283/.359	76	.290	-0.6	2B -5, 3B 0	-0.5

Comparables: Reid Brignac, Edmundo Sosa, Charlie Culberson

This book is filled with stories of players who could have been helped by a functioning minor-league system, complete with a full slate of games and opportunities to hone their craft and apply the finishing touches in a less-competitive setting. Arguably, there isn't a player who was more screwed by the limitations COVID placed on the game than Estrada. Two years removed from a gunshot wound suffered in a botched robbery attempt, Estrada could have used a healthy consolidation season in the minors as a chance to rediscover his power stroke and cast himself as DJ LeMahieu's heir apparent at the keystone. Instead, 2020 was another lost year for him. He bounced between New York and the alternate site, and he did little with the limited opportunities he received. Estrada isn't old, but the window is narrowing for him to become more than a utility infielder.

Estevan Florial CF   Born: 11/25/97   Age: 23   Bats: L   Throws: R   Height: 6'1"   Weight: 195   Origin: International Free Agent, 2015

YEAR	TEAM	LVL	AGE	PA	R	2B	3B	HR	RBI	BB	K	SB	CS	Whiff%	AVG/OBP/SLG	DRC+	BABIP	BRR	FRAA	WARP
2018	TAM	HI-A	20	339	45	16	3	3	27	44	87	11	10		.255/.354/.361	102	.353	-0.9	CF(59): 1.8, RF(6): -0.2, LF(3): -0.1	0.4
2019	TAM	HI-A	21	301	38	10	3	8	38	24	98	9	5		.237/.297/.383	92	.335	1.0	CF(64): 2.9	1.1
2020	NYY	MLB	23	3	0	0	0	0	0	0	2	0	0	66.7%	.333/.333/.333	90	1.000		CF(1): -0.1	0.0
2021 FS	NYY	MLB	23	600	54	21	3	15	59	45	235	10	5	66.7%	.208/.272/.344	66	.330	-1.9	CF 4, LF 0	-0.5
2021 DC	NYY	MLB	23	33	2	1	0	0	3	2	12	0	0	66.7%	.208/.272/.344	66	.330	-0.1	CF 0	0.0

Comparables: Keon Broxton, Tommy Pham, Daniel Fields

If you're a prospect watcher, it's understandable if you have Florial fatigue. He made his debut on our Top 101 list in 2018 before he was old enough to legally purchase a cocktail, and as tales of his tools and athleticism spread, the blowback was inevitable. Florial has struggled both with making contact and staying healthy, and it's easy to forget that he's just a 23-year-old who did not have an at-bat above A-ball before he made his major-league debut in 2020. It's far too early to put the busted prospect label on him, but he'll need to start developing quickly if he's ever going to make the waiting worth the while.

Mike Ford 1B Born: 07/04/92 Age: 29 Bats: L Throws: R Height: 6'0" Weight: 225 Origin: Undrafted Free Agent, 2013

YEAR	TEAM	LVL	AGE	PA	R	2B	3B	HR	RBI	BB	K	SB	CS	Whiff%	AVG/OBP/SLG	DRC+	BABIP	BRR	FRAA	WARP
2018	SWB	AAA	25	410	48	21	0	15	52	37	70	1	0		.253/.327/.433	114	.275	-0.9	1B(57): -0.2	0.5
2019	SWB	AAA	26	349	59	20	0	23	60	46	55	0	1		.303/.401/.605	141	.300	0.3	1B(44): -3.2, 3B(5): 0.0	1.8
2019	NYY	MLB	26	163	30	7	0	12	25	17	28	0	0	22.1%	.259/.350/.559	125	.243	-0.6	1B(29): -0.2, P(1): -0.0	0.7
2020	NYY	MLB	28	84	5	4	0	2	11	7	16	0	0	26.1%	.135/.226/.270	85	.140	-0.2	1B(13): -1.0	-0.1
2021 FS	NYY	MLB	28	600	73	28	1	28	80	69	124	0	0	23.9%	.243/.338/.462	115	.267	-1.3	1B -4, 3B 0	1.5
2021 DC	NYY	MLB	28	203	24	9	0	9	27	23	42	0	0	23.9%	.243/.338/.462	115	.267	-0.4	1B -1	0.5

Comparables: Jason Giambi, Lyle Overbay, Norm Zauchin

Ford, like the other big-leaguer named Mike who hails from New Jersey, grew up in a suburb that's actually closer to Philadelphia than it is to New York City. Unless Ford is also an Eagles fan (instead of a Giants fan), that's about where the similarities begin and end.

Clint Frazier RF Born: 09/06/94 Age: 26 Bats: R Throws: R Height: 5'11" Weight: 212 Origin: Round 1, 2013 Draft (#5 overall)

YEAR	TEAM	LVL	AGE	PA	R	2B	3B	HR	RBI	BB	K	SB	CS	Whiff%	AVG/OBP/SLG	DRC+	BABIP	BRR	FRAA	WARP
2018	TAM	HI-A	23	26	6	1	0	1	3	4	3	2	0		.250/.385/.450	96	.235	0.3	LF(3): -0.3	0.0
2018	SWB	AAA	23	216	38	14	3	10	21	23	52	4	2		.311/.389/.574	139	.380	0.9	CF(26): -2.9, LF(16): -0.3, RF(4): -0.3	1.0
2018	NYY	MLB	23	41	9	3	0	0	1	5	13	0	0	36.1%	.265/.390/.353	75	.429	0.2	LF(9): -0.7, CF(1): -0.2	-0.1
2019	SWB	AAA	24	269	35	20	1	8	26	17	56	1	2		.247/.305/.433	80	.288	-0.8	LF(52): -0.1, CF(7): -1.3	-0.2
2019	NYY	MLB	24	246	31	14	0	12	38	16	70	1	2	32.6%	.267/.317/.489	99	.329	-0.6	RF(36): -1.7, LF(17): 0.5	0.4
2020	NYY	MLB	26	160	24	6	1	8	26	25	44	3	0	31.8%	.267/.394/.511	117	.338	2.0	RF(28): 1.4, LF(8): -0.2	0.9
2021 FS	NYY	MLB	26	600	71	24	2	25	77	60	176	4	1	32.3%	.237/.323/.439	108	.305	0.5	LF -5, RF -5	1.3
2021 DC	NYY	MLB	26	509	60	21	2	21	65	51	149	3	1	32.3%	.237/.323/.439	108	.305	0.4	LF -4, RF -4	1.1

Comparables: Jay Buhner, Jorge Soler, Wily Mo Pena

Frazier not only emerged as the offensive force that once made scouts drool over his middle-of-the-order potential, he was even a defensive asset, grading out anywhere between above average or better depending on the metric. It turns out that Frazier was trying to play through post-concussion syndrome in 2019, which led to depth-perception issues and, in turn, tentative outfield play due to his fear of running into a wall. Labeled as soft and called malcontent entering the year, Frazier ultimately had a legitimate medical reason for his issues both on and off the field. He even turned things around with the press, drawing praise for his leadership and openness about wearing a mask on the field. Let this be a lesson about how the media needs to do better when assessing the impact of injuries, not only on a player's performance but on his attitude as well.

Brett Gardner CF Born: 08/24/83 Age: 37 Bats: L Throws: L Height: 5'11" Weight: 195 Origin: Round 3, 2005 Draft (#109 overall)

YEAR	TEAM	LVL	AGE	PA	R	2B	3B	HR	RBI	BB	K	SB	CS	Whiff%	AVG/OBP/SLG	DRC+	BABIP	BRR	FRAA	WARP
2018	NYY	MLB	34	609	95	20	7	12	45	65	107	16	2	13.7%	.236/.322/.368	90	.272	4.1	LF(107): 11.8, CF(34): -0.0	2.6
2019	NYY	MLB	35	550	86	26	7	28	74	52	108	10	2	19.7%	.251/.325/.503	109	.265	1.4	CF(98): 1.7, LF(45): -1.9	2.6
2020	NYY	MLB	37	158	20	5	1	5	15	26	35	3	3	24.4%	.223/.354/.392	110	.264	0.7	LF(39): -3.1, CF(10): 1.2	0.5
2021 FS	NYY	MLB	37	600	67	20	2	20	66	68	139	14	3	19.0%	.238/.334/.402	103	.288	5.6	LF 7, CF -1	3.2

Comparables: Gary Redus, Chuck Hinton, Trenidad Hubbard

"But then again, all good things must come to an end."

Q's premature farewell to Captain Jean-Luc Picard in *Star Trek: The Next Generation* will eventually apply to Gardner and his lengthy Yankee career. Even from the beginning, as a rookie in 2008, he was seen as less of a long-term solution and more of a stopgap while the Yankees found a superior option via trade or the free-agent market. Instead, Gardner not only persevered but thrived. His calling card was as one of the best defensive left fielders in baseball, and to that, he added above-average production with his bat and his consistency. He never performed like a superstar but, on a Yankees team filled with great players over the last 13 years, he never needed to. Even if this is it, or mostly it, for him in pinstripes, there's a case to be made for Gardner as the best left fielder in team history.

Aaron Hicks CF Born: 10/02/89 Age: 31 Bats: S Throws: R Height: 6'1" Weight: 205 Origin: Round 1, 2008 Draft (#14 overall)

YEAR	TEAM	LVL	AGE	PA	R	2B	3B	HR	RBI	BB	K	SB	CS	Whiff%	AVG/OBP/SLG	DRC+	BABIP	BRR	FRAA	WARP
2018	NYY	MLB	28	581	90	18	3	27	79	90	111	11	2	23.3%	.248/.366/.467	120	.264	2.3	CF(131): -8.6	2.9
2019	NYY	MLB	29	255	41	10	0	12	36	31	72	1	2	31.7%	.235/.325/.443	99	.286	0.3	CF(58): -6.8	0.3
2020	NYY	MLB	31	211	28	10	2	6	21	41	38	4	1	27.9%	.225/.379/.414	124	.256	0.1	CF(50): -2.4	1.1
2021 FS	NYY	MLB	31	600	73	22	1	22	67	85	128	10	4	27.4%	.229/.343/.412	109	.263	-1.6	CF -13, LF 0	1.1
2021 DC	NYY	MLB	31	543	66	20	1	20	61	77	116	9	3	27.4%	.229/.343/.412	109	.263	-1.4	CF -12	1.0

Comparables: Buddy Bradford, Milton Bradley, Carl Everett

For all we know about Tommy John surgery and its impact on pitchers, significant data gaps remain when it comes to hitters who undergo the procedure. In October 2019, Hicks opted to have the surgery on his throwing elbow. The delayed start of the 2020 season kept Hicks from missing any time, but the version of him who returned looked more like the hitter battling through discomfort in 2019 rather than the four-WARP outfielder he was in the previous seasons. Athletes are often seen as finely tuned machines, but recovery from surgery is mental as well as physical. Hitters coming back from Tommy John can take anywhere from one to three months to mentally adjust to their "new" bodies. Hicks' 2020 should not and can not be evaluated without taking that aspect of his health into consideration.

Kyle Higashioka C   Born: 04/20/90   Age: 31   Bats: R   Throws: R   Height: 6'1"   Weight: 202   Origin: Round 7, 2008 Draft (#230 overall)

YEAR	TEAM	LVL	AGE	PA	R	2B	3B	HR	RBI	BB	K	SB	CS	Whiff%	AVG/OBP/SLG	DRC+	BABIP	BRR	FRAA	WARP
2018	SWB	AAA	28	211	16	10	1	5	22	17	44	2	0		.202/.276/.346	60	.234	-0.7	C(49): 6.6	0.4
2018	NYY	MLB	28	79	6	2	0	3	6	6	16	0	0	28.2%	.167/.241/.319	98	.170	-0.7	C(27): 3.8	0.7
2019	SWB	AAA	29	270	42	13	0	20	56	24	53	0	0		.278/.348/.581	122	.276	-3.2	C(64): 15.2	3.0
2019	NYY	MLB	29	57	8	5	0	3	11	0	26	0	0	28.5%	.214/.211/.464	62	.321	0.6	C(18): 2.1	0.3
2020	NYY	MLB	30	48	7	1	0	4	10	0	11	0	0	23.2%	.250/.250/.521	98	.242	-0.1	C(14): 0.1	0.3
2021 FS	NYY	MLB	31	600	72	22	1	35	84	41	161	0	0	26.2%	.230/.289/.464	97	.259	-1.2	C 20	4.2
2021 DC	NYY	MLB	31	203	24	7	0	11	28	14	54	0	0	26.2%	.230/.289/.464	97	.259	-0.4	C 9	1.7

Comparables: Michael McKenry, Francisco Peña, Brett Nicholas

On September 16, Higashioka became only the third catcher in Yankees history (and the 38th backstop ever) to hit three home runs in a game. Despite the great day, and despite a higher WARP total than starter Gary Sánchez, Higashioka still profiles as a second stringer.

YEAR	TEAM	P. COUNT	FRM RUNS	BLK RUNS	THRW RUNS	TOT RUNS
2018	NYY	3438	3.2	0.8	-0.1	3.9
2018	SWB	6951	7.2	0.6	-0.2	7.6
2019	NYY	2271	1.9	0.1	-0.1	1.9
2019	SWB	9097	15.4	0.0	-0.1	15.4
2020	NYY	1794	1.5	0.1	-0.1	1.6
2021	NYY	7215	8.5	0.4	0.5	9.4

Aaron Judge RF   Born: 04/26/92   Age: 29   Bats: R   Throws: R   Height: 6'7"   Weight: 282   Origin: Round 1, 2013 Draft (#32 overall)

YEAR	TEAM	LVL	AGE	PA	R	2B	3B	HR	RBI	BB	K	SB	CS	Whiff%	AVG/OBP/SLG	DRC+	BABIP	BRR	FRAA	WARP
2018	NYY	MLB	26	498	77	22	0	27	67	76	152	6	3	35.9%	.278/.392/.528	137	.368	1.0	RF(90): 12.6, CF(1): -0.1	4.7
2019	NYY	MLB	27	447	75	18	1	27	55	64	141	3	2	36.8%	.272/.381/.540	131	.360	0.2	RF(92): 8.3	3.6
2020	NYY	MLB	28	114	23	3	0	9	22	10	32	0	1	33.5%	.257/.336/.554	110	.283	0.6	RF(25): 0.8	0.5
2021 FS	NYY	MLB	29	600	93	22	1	39	88	80	193	5	2	35.9%	.257/.366/.535	139	.333	-1.0	RF 2, CF 0	4.6
2021 DC	NYY	MLB	29	543	84	20	1	35	80	73	175	4	1	35.9%	.257/.366/.535	139	.333	-0.9	RF 2	4.1

Comparables: Giancarlo Stanton, Ryan Howard, Adam Dunn

It would be easy when talking about Judge to start off by kvetching about the litany of injuries that have cost him a combined 138 games over the last three seasons. Be it the right calf strain that shelved him last year; the strained oblique in 2019; the chip fracture in his right wrist in 2018; and so on. Heck, this list doesn't even include the right shoulder and rib injuries last spring that would have landed him on the IL if the season had started on time. It is much more fun to focus on what you do get from Judge when he's on the field. Since his rookie season in 2017, he has been the best hitter in baseball not named Mike Trout as judged by DRC+. Even if you're not grading him on a per-at-bat curve, Judge has been one of the top 10 hitters in the game. The only Yankees outfielders with a higher adjusted-OPS in team history (minimum 1,500 PA) are named Ruth, Mantle and DiMaggio. It's best to appreciate what Judge does provide when he is on the field rather than lament what he could be because he sometimes isn't.

Erik Kratz C   Born: 06/15/80   Age: 41   Bats: R   Throws: R   Height: 6'4"   Weight: 250   Origin: Round 29, 2002 Draft (#866 overall)

YEAR	TEAM	LVL	AGE	PA	R	2B	3B	HR	RBI	BB	K	SB	CS	Whiff%	AVG/OBP/SLG	DRC+	BABIP	BRR	FRAA	WARP
2018	SWB	AAA	38	61	10	2	0	4	6	7	10	0	0		.269/.356/.538	127	.263	0.0	C(17): 1.6	0.6
2018	MIL	MLB	38	219	18	6	0	6	23	6	40	1	0	24.6%	.236/.280/.355	90	.264	0.6	C(61): 10.2, P(3): 0.1, 1B(1): -0.0	2.0
2019	SWB	AAA	39	176	27	10	0	7	31	17	21	1	0		.299/.375/.500	122	.305	1.2	C(37): 2.9, 1B(2): -0.2	1.5
2019	TB	MLB	39	17	0	0	0	0	0	0	8	0	0	40.0%	.059/.059/.059	37	.111	-0.1	C(6): -0.7	-0.1
2019	SF	MLB	39	36	1	2	0	1	3	2	6	0	0	20.6%	.125/.222/.281	72	.120	-1.2	C(11): 1.2	0.1
2020	NYY	MLB	40	30	2	2	0	0	4	2	6	0	0	26.7%	.321/.367/.393	89	.409	-0.2	C(12): -0.1, 1B(4): 0.0, P(2): 0.1	0.1
2021 FS	NYY	MLB	41	600	58	24	0	17	61	41	165	1	0	25.8%	.210/.279/.354	72	.267	-1.6	C 8, 1B 0	0.9

Comparables: Henry Blanco, Pat Borders, Benito Santiago

Kratz announced his decision to retire early in the offseason. He drew rave reviews during his time with the Yankees for his mentoring of their minor-league staffs, particularly their Latinx hurlers. It's clear that he offered so much more than what could ever be gleaned from his statistics, and that he should have a future as a coach if he wants it.

YEAR	TEAM	P. COUNT	FRM RUNS	BLK RUNS	THRW RUNS	TOT RUNS
2018	MIL	8285	9.9	1.3	-0.1	11.1
2018	SWB	2267	1.1	0.3	0.0	1.4
2019	TB	666	0.4	-1.0	0.0	-0.7
2019	SF	1470	0.8	0.0	0.0	0.8
2019	SWB	5201	2.5	0.0	0.4	2.8
2020	NYY	1206	0.3	0.1	0.0	0.3
2021	NYY	16650	6.9	0.9	0.2	8.0

DJ LeMahieu 2B Born: 07/13/88 Age: 32 Bats: R Throws: R Height: 6'4" Weight: 220 Origin: Round 2, 2009 Draft (#79 overall)

YEAR	TEAM	LVL	AGE	PA	R	2B	3B	HR	RBI	BB	K	SB	CS	Whiff%	AVG/OBP/SLG	DRC+	BABIP	BRR	FRAA	WARP
2018	COL	MLB	29	580	90	32	2	15	62	37	82	6	5	14.1%	.276/.321/.428	97	.298	4.5	2B(128): 20.1	4.2
2019	NYY	MLB	30	655	109	33	2	26	102	46	90	5	2	15.9%	.327/.375/.518	127	.349	-2.1	2B(75): 4.5, 3B(52): 0.7, 1B(40): 1.5	4.8
2020	NYY	MLB	32	216	41	10	2	10	27	18	21	3	0	11.2%	.364/.421/.590	134	.370	-0.3	2B(37): 4.7, 1B(11): -0.3, 3B(11): -0.5	1.9
2021 FS	NYY	MLB	32	600	84	25	2	19	61	50	89	7	3	14.3%	.306/.368/.466	129	.337	-2.1	2B 19, 3B 0	6.0

Comparables: Brandon Phillips, Adam Kennedy, Omar Infante

Media members and fans alike spent more time in 2020 spilling virtual ink and weeping over the losses of Aaron Judge and Giancarlo Stanton to injuries, but it was LeMahieu's thumb sprain on August 15 that should have had Yankees' rooters holding their collective breath. While LeMahieu missed only two weeks (and nine games) because of the sprain, in a compressed 60-game season, his absence loomed large. Others have bigger names and brighter stars, but make no mistake that he has been the Yankees' best player since he signed a two-year, $24 million pact with the Bombers prior to the '19 season. A free agent as of press time, LeMahieu will be an asset in 2021 wherever he plies his trade at whatever position or positions he is asked to play.

Gary Sánchez C Born: 12/02/92 Age: 28 Bats: R Throws: R Height: 6'2" Weight: 230 Origin: International Free Agent, 2009

YEAR	TEAM	LVL	AGE	PA	R	2B	3B	HR	RBI	BB	K	SB	CS	Whiff%	AVG/OBP/SLG	DRC+	BABIP	BRR	FRAA	WARP
2018	SWB	AAA	25	28	4	0	0	4	4	4	10	0	0		.179/.179/.607	80	.071	0.0	C(5): -0.0	0.0
2018	NYY	MLB	25	374	51	17	0	18	53	46	94	1	0	29.3%	.186/.291/.406	94	.197	-1.4	C(76): -1.4	1.1
2019	NYY	MLB	26	446	62	12	1	34	77	40	125	0	1	32.0%	.232/.316/.525	121	.244	-2.5	C(90): -6.3	2.4
2020	NYY	MLB	28	178	19	4	0	10	24	18	64	0	0	34.0%	.147/.253/.365	84	.159	-0.5	C(41): -0.5	0.0
2021 FS	NYY	MLB	28	600	72	20	1	35	83	55	187	1	0	32.1%	.220/.305/.459	103	.266	-0.7	C -2, 1B 0	2.4
2021 DC	NYY	MLB	28	475	57	16	0	27	66	43	148	1	0	32.1%	.220/.305/.459	103	.266	-0.6	C -1	1.9

Comparables: Josmil Pinto, Geovany Soto, Willson Contreras

YEAR	TEAM	P. COUNT	FRM RUNS	BLK RUNS	THRW RUNS	TOT RUNS
2018	NYY	10936	3.3	-4.3	0.2	-0.8
2019	NYY	12715	-5.1	-0.8	-0.2	-6.1
2020	NYY	5546	0.1	-0.4	-0.1	-0.4
2021	NYY	16835	2.6	-3.2	0.5	0.0

As a standalone season, you can look at nearly any player's truncated, 60-game sample in 2020 and write it off as a ridiculous fluke, no matter how terrific or awful it was. For Sánchez, it is difficult (if not impossible) to not look at what he did last year as part of a trendline that goes back to 2018. Over the last three years, his .200/.294/.455 slash line ranks 10th among catchers with at least 600 plate appearances, but a big chunk of that production stems from a single season. He was the invisible man in the box last year, with his strikeout rate jumping to a whopping 37 percent thanks to his dwindling contact rate on pitches both inside and outside the zone. (To think, the raw numbers are even a little charitable to Sánchez, as his numbers are aided by an extremely hitter-friendly Yankee Stadium.) The lack of offensive output makes the debates about Sánchez's defense irrelevant. It would have been unthinkable three years ago to think he might not be part of New York's long-term core. Now? It's a serious point to consider.

Giancarlo Stanton LF Born: 11/08/89 Age: 31 Bats: R Throws: R Height: 6'6" Weight: 245 Origin: Round 2, 2007 Draft (#76 overall)

YEAR	TEAM	LVL	AGE	PA	R	2B	3B	HR	RBI	BB	K	SB	CS	Whiff%	AVG/OBP/SLG	DRC+	BABIP	BRR	FRAA	WARP
2018	NYY	MLB	28	705	102	34	1	38	100	70	211	5	0	34.5%	.266/.343/.509	116	.333	0.0	RF(37): -1.1, LF(36): -0.0	2.6
2019	NYY	MLB	29	72	8	3	0	3	13	12	24	0	0	34.1%	.288/.403/.492	87	.424	-0.3	LF(10): -1.3, RF(3): -0.4	-0.2
2020	NYY	MLB	31	94	12	7	0	4	11	15	27	1	1	32.7%	.250/.387/.500	98	.333	-0.6		0.1
2021 FS	NYY	MLB	31	600	78	23	1	32	86	72	189	2	0	34.0%	.235/.337/.473	117	.301	-1.2	LF -4, RF 0	2.2
2021 DC	NYY	MLB	31	509	66	19	0	27	73	61	160	2	0	34.0%	.235/.337/.473	117	.301	-1.0	LF -4	1.8

Comparables: Danny Tartabull, Tim Salmon, Reggie Jackson

In the film *Palm Springs*, Nyles is a man who gets trapped reliving the same day repeatedly while attending a destination wedding. Stanton must feel a little bit like Nyles, as he has spent nearly every day of his last two years as a Yankee either injured or answering the same tired questions about his most recent malady. He spent the offseason working diligently to maintain his health through a rigorous strength and conditioning program, but it couldn't prevent him from a strained right calf in late February that would put him on the shelf if the season had opened on time. He was able to take the field for the revised July opener, but it took all of 17 days for him to get hurt again; this time, a strained hamstring cost him a little over a month. Nyles eventually escaped his fourth dimensional prison thanks to his friend's dogged determination to teach herself quantum physics. There is no wormhole or magical portal that can change Stanton's trajectory, unfortunately. Instead, Stanton is relegated to our linear world, where his body will continue to age and his potential for physical breakdowns will increase. Here's hoping he can figure out a way to beat back against that reality sooner than later; lest we be robbed of even more of his prime.

Mike Tauchman CF Born: 12/03/90 Age: 30 Bats: L Throws: L Height: 6'2" Weight: 220 Origin: Round 10, 2013 Draft (#289 overall)

YEAR	TEAM	LVL	AGE	PA	R	2B	3B	HR	RBI	BB	K	SB	CS	Whiff%	AVG/OBP/SLG	DRC+	BABIP	BRR	FRAA	WARP
2018	ABQ	AAA	27	471	84	26	7	20	81	60	70	12	10		.323/.408/.571	146	.345	3.5	CF(65): 4.2, LF(30): 6.1, RF(15): 1.7	4.8
2018	COL	MLB	27	37	5	1	0	0	0	4	15	1	0	37.7%	.094/.194/.125	52	.176	0.1	CF(5): -0.1, LF(3): -0.9, RF(1): -0.0	-0.2
2019	SWB	AAA	28	114	22	10	3	2	16	16	16	4	0		.274/.386/.505	115	.308	1.2	CF(15): 0.4, LF(7): 1.4, RF(6): 0.7	0.8
2019	NYY	MLB	28	296	46	18	1	13	47	34	71	6	0	21.0%	.277/.361/.504	112	.333	2.4	LF(59): 5.3, RF(19): -0.5, CF(14): -0.8	1.9
2020	NYY	MLB	30	111	18	6	0	0	14	14	26	6	0	28.9%	.242/.342/.305	93	.329	0.0	LF(20): 2.0, RF(19): 0.8, CF(5): 0.0	0.4
2021 FS	NYY	MLB	30	600	61	21	3	15	61	59	148	7	3	24.3%	.234/.315/.374	90	.295	1.3	LF 7, RF 1	2.0
2021 DC	NYY	MLB	30	237	24	8	1	6	24	23	58	2	1	24.3%	.234/.315/.374	90	.295	0.5	LF 3, RF 0	0.8

Comparables: Mike Young, Jason Michaels, Geoff Jenkins

One of the most difficult things about baseball, besides the obvious idea that you must see the ball and hit the ball, is getting into and maintaining the rhythm required to perform the feat. Tauchman quickly morphed from the happy-go-lucky story of 2019 into a frustrating player who wasn't able to squeeze enough playing time out of a crowded Yankees outfield to ever get it going. The power that suddenly appeared in 2019 disappeared just as quickly last season, and while the perennial injuries to Aaron Judge and Giancarlo Stanton opened the door for Tauchman, his subpar performance and the emergence of Clint Frazier slammed it shut. One poor season (and a truncated one at that) isn't the death knell for his career, but Tauchman will soon cross into his 30s and will need to rediscover whatever magic he had in '19 if he's going to be anything more than a fourth outfielder.

Gleyber Torres SS Born: 12/13/96 Age: 24 Bats: R Throws: R Height: 6'1" Weight: 205 Origin: International Free Agent, 2013

YEAR	TEAM	LVL	AGE	PA	R	2B	3B	HR	RBI	BB	K	SB	CS	Whiff%	AVG/OBP/SLG	DRC+	BABIP	BRR	FRAA	WARP
2018	SWB	AAA	21	56	6	3	1	1	11	5	10	1	1		.347/.393/.510	117	.400	0.1	3B(8): 0.6, 2B(3): 0.0, SS(3): 0.2	0.3
2018	NYY	MLB	21	484	54	16	1	24	77	42	122	6	2	31.3%	.271/.340/.480	120	.321	0.8	2B(109): 5.4, SS(21): 1.5	3.7
2019	NYY	MLB	22	604	96	26	0	38	90	48	129	5	2	28.0%	.278/.337/.535	124	.296	-1.0	SS(77): -1.4, 2B(65): -1.0	3.9
2020	NYY	MLB	24	160	17	8	0	3	16	22	28	1	0	28.0%	.243/.356/.368	111	.286	0.6	SS(40): -1.1	0.6
2021 FS	NYY	MLB	24	600	70	22	1	25	79	61	135	8	4	28.7%	.247/.330/.439	110	.286	-2.4	SS 3, 2B 0	2.8
2021 DC	NYY	MLB	24	577	68	21	1	24	76	58	130	7	3	28.7%	.247/.330/.439	110	.286	-2.3	SS 3	2.6

Comparables: Evan Longoria, Corey Seager, Hank Blalock

Torres started the season in a prolonged slump, slashing a woeful .231/.341/.295 before landing on the IL on August 21 with left hamstring and quad strains. When he returned on September 5, he looked a lot more like the hitter who had wowed all of New York in his first two seasons. Torres started wearing glasses without lenses–something he did in 2019 on occasion–and seemed more comfortable and relaxed behind the frames. While "Glasses Gleyber" is a fun angle, it's probably nothing more than a framing device. The real change came as Torres adjusted to pitchers throwing him less heat. The key to a lengthy and prosperous big-league career is being able to make those tweaks as the need arises. As such, we see no reason to change our expectations about Torres turning into a star.

Gio Urshela 3B Born: 10/11/91 Age: 29 Bats: R Throws: R Height: 6'0" Weight: 215 Origin: International Free Agent, 2008

YEAR	TEAM	LVL	AGE	PA	R	2B	3B	HR	RBI	BB	K	SB	CS	Whiff%	AVG/OBP/SLG	DRC+	BABIP	BRR	FRAA	WARP
2018	SWB	AAA	26	107	14	7	2	2	12	4	13	0	0		.307/.340/.475	103	.337	0.0	3B(20): 1.1, SS(8): -1.0, 2B(1): -0.0	0.3
2018	BUF	AAA	26	91	7	3	0	0	5	4	9	0	0		.244/.275/.279	104	.269	-0.1	3B(14): -1.4, 1B(7): 0.2, SS(2): 0.2	0.1
2018	COL	AAA	26	42	6	4	0	0	7	5	9	0	0		.324/.405/.432	102	.429	0.3	2B(4): 0.3, 3B(4): 0.3, 1B(2): -0.3	0.1
2018	TOR	MLB	26	46	7	1	0	1	3	2	10	0	0	27.3%	.233/.283/.326	81	.281	-0.2	3B(10): -0.8, SS(8): -0.3	-0.1
2019	NYY	MLB	27	476	73	34	0	21	74	25	87	1	1	22.2%	.314/.355/.534	120	.349	-1.8	3B(123): 5.8, 1B(1): 0.0, LF(1): 0.0	3.4
2020	NYY	MLB	29	174	24	11	0	6	30	18	25	1	0	20.3%	.298/.368/.490	124	.315	-0.5	3B(43): 4.8	1.4
2021 FS	NYY	MLB	29	600	65	28	1	20	76	36	109	1	0	21.7%	.264/.314/.428	101	.296	-1.2	3B 4, 1B 0	1.7
2021 DC	NYY	MLB	29	577	63	27	1	19	73	35	105	1	0	21.7%	.264/.314/.428	101	.296	-1.2	3B 4	1.5

Comparables: Dave Roberts, Brent Morel, Charlie Hayes

No one is more emblematic of the Yankees' new way of doing things than Urshela, a player rejected by Cleveland and Toronto's organizations and who looked to be organizational filler at best when the Yankees purchased his contract in August 2018. Two years later, New York's low-end gamble on Urshela has paid off handsomely, as the club was able to coax more from his bat than anyone expected. A few years ago, the Yankees would have dumped millions on a competent but forgettable veteran (hello, Chase Headley). Now, it seems, they just unearth solid three-WARP players who let New York set it and forget it for years at a time.

Andrew Velazquez 3B Born: 07/14/94 Age: 26 Bats: S Throws: R Height: 5'9" Weight: 170 Origin: Round 7, 2012 Draft (#243 overall)

YEAR	TEAM	LVL	AGE	PA	R	2B	3B	HR	RBI	BB	K	SB	CS	Whiff%	AVG/OBP/SLG	DRC+	BABIP	BRR	FRAA	WARP
2018	MTG	AA	23	36	5	2	1	2	4	1	11	2	0		.229/.250/.514	80	.273	0.8	CF(7): 1.6	0.2
2018	DUR	AAA	23	461	63	16	6	12	41	34	124	29	3		.258/.317/.409	95	.338	5.8	SS(69): -1.8, CF(33): 3.5, 2B(14): -0.7	1.7
2018	TB	MLB	23	12	3	1	0	0	0	1	3	1	0	38.1%	.300/.417/.400	88	.429	0.5	3B(4): -0.0, 2B(2): -0.0, SS(2): 0.1	0.1
2019	DUR	AAA	24	141	20	9	1	4	16	10	30	2	4		.271/.329/.450	75	.326	-1.0	CF(22): 3.5, SS(10): -1.1, 2B(1): 0.0	0.1
2019	COL	AAA	24	46	5	4	1	0	5	0	9	1	1		.244/.261/.378	78	.306	0.3	CF(6): 0.2, SS(5): -0.2, 2B(1): -0.1	-0.3
2019	CLE	MLB	24	12	1	1	0	0	0	1	7	1	0	41.4%	.091/.167/.182	25	.250	0.3	2B(3): 0.0, CF(2): -0.1	-0.1
2019	TB	MLB	24	12	2	1	0	0	0	0	6	0	0	35.5%	.083/.083/.167	67	.167	-0.5	3B(4): -0.6, 2B(2): 0.0, LF(1): -0.0	-0.1
2020	BAL	MLB	26	77	11	1	1	0	3	10	23	4	2	30.6%	.159/.274/.206	74	.250	0.7	SS(30): 1.0, LF(7): -0.1, CF(3): -0.0	0.1
2021 FS	NYY	MLB	26	600	57	24	3	14	56	41	197	13	4	32.3%	.213/.273/.347	66	.303	3.0	SS 2, CF 2	0.1

Comparables: Josh Wilson, Brent Lillibridge, Robert Andino

Perhaps the biggest thing Velazquez brings to the table is "younger brother dragged along to a pick-up game" energy, in that he's a hard-nosed player who is often outclassed on the field. The good news? A recent article at FiveThirtyEight suggests that younger siblings end up the best athletes in the family.

Luke Voit 1B Born: 02/13/91 Age: 30 Bats: R Throws: R Height: 6'3" Weight: 255 Origin: Round 22, 2013 Draft (#665 overall)

YEAR	TEAM	LVL	AGE	PA	R	2B	3B	HR	RBI	BB	K	SB	CS	Whiff%	AVG/OBP/SLG	DRC+	BABIP	BRR	FRAA	WARP
2018	MEM	AAA	27	270	35	16	2	9	36	31	49	0	1		.300/.393/.502	135	.347	-1.3	1B(56): 2.1, LF(1): -0.1	1.2
2018	SWB	AAA	27	32	2	2	0	1	3	3	7	0	0		.310/.375/.483	118	.381	-0.1	1B(3): 0.2	0.1
2018	STL	MLB	27	13	2	0	0	1	3	2	4	0	0	39.1%	.182/.308/.455	158	.167	0.1	1B(3): 0.3	0.2
2018	NYY	MLB	27	148	28	5	0	14	33	15	39	0	0	32.6%	.333/.405/.689	155	.380	1.1	1B(32): -2.7	1.1
2019	NYY	MLB	28	510	72	21	1	21	62	71	142	0	0	35.3%	.263/.378/.464	118	.345	-3.2	1B(83): -3.2	1.3
2020	NYY	MLB	29	234	41	5	0	22	52	17	54	0	0	27.7%	.277/.338/.610	132	.268	0.3	1B(48): -0.7	1.3
2021 FS	NYY	MLB	30	600	87	22	1	38	92	57	154	0	0	32.3%	.270/.351/.532	134	.312	-0.4	1B 1, LF 0	3.6
2021 DC	NYY	MLB	30	577	84	21	1	36	89	54	148	0	0	32.3%	.270/.351/.532	134	.312	-0.4	1B 1	3.5

Comparables: Mike Napoli, Carlos Delgado, Cecil Fielder

So much time has been spent pontificating over whether or not Voit's Production is For Real that you'd think he's Bigfoot, El Chupacabra and The Loch Ness Monster all rolled into one. To be fair to the skeptics, Voit had the non-prospect, late bloomer, dragged-down-by-a second-half-injury in 2019 doubts all rolled into one entering last season. It turns out that when he's healthy, he's not only a productive hitter, but one of the most feared mashers in baseball. Voit sacrificed some selectivity for even more power in 2020, increasing his plate coverage and making additional contact thanks to his smart approach at the dish. The abbreviated season is an endless smorgasbord of "what ifs," and one of the more entertaining of these hypotheticals is wondering if Voit could have broken the Yankees' single-season record of 61 home runs. This only seems silly if you've merely heard the stories without experiencing it for yourself.

Anthony Volpe 2B Born: 04/28/01 Age: 20 Bats: R Throws: R Height: 5'11" Weight: 180 Origin: Round 1, 2019 Draft (#30 overall)

YEAR	TEAM	LVL	AGE	PA	R	2B	3B	HR	RBI	BB	K	SB	CS	Whiff%	AVG/OBP/SLG	DRC+	BABIP	BRR	FRAA	WARP
2019	PUL	ROK+	18	150	19	7	2	2	11	23	38	6	1		.215/.349/.355	99	.289	0.3		0.7
2021 FS	NYY	MLB	20	600	48	26	3	8	51	40	220	11	3		.213/.273/.319	63	.337	4.0		-0.7

Most scouting reports on Volpe refer to him as "steady" and "reliable," rather than spectacular. While there's something to be said for a high floor (perceived or otherwise), that's often just a fancy way of saying he has a low ceiling.

Tyler Wade SS Born: 11/23/94 Age: 26 Bats: L Throws: R Height: 6'1" Weight: 188 Origin: Round 4, 2013 Draft (#134 overall)

YEAR	TEAM	LVL	AGE	PA	R	2B	3B	HR	RBI	BB	K	SB	CS	Whiff%	AVG/OBP/SLG	DRC+	BABIP	BRR	FRAA	WARP
2018	SWB	AAA	23	408	46	18	4	4	27	37	82	11	8		.255/.328/.360	97	.318	-2.1	SS(51): -0.2, LF(12): 2.1, 2B(10): 1.7	1.1
2018	NYY	MLB	23	70	8	4	0	1	5	4	23	1	0	27.8%	.167/.214/.273	55	.238	1.7	2B(26): -0.6, RF(5): -0.1, SS(2): 0.0	-0.1
2019	SWB	AAA	24	335	51	19	4	4	38	23	76	13	5		.296/.352/.425	92	.381	1.6	SS(43): 2.6, 2B(28): 0.7, 3B(4): 0.6	1.4
2019	NYY	MLB	24	108	16	3	1	2	11	11	28	7	0	26.2%	.245/.330/.362	72	.328	0.5	2B(18): 1.8, LF(14): 0.1, 3B(5): -0.5	0.1
2020	NYY	MLB	26	105	19	3	0	3	10	12	22	4	1	19.2%	.170/.288/.307	91	.188	0.0	2B(31): 2.0, SS(22): -3.2	0.1
2021 FS	NYY	MLB	26	600	58	23	3	11	53	52	152	12	3	22.7%	.218/.295/.339	75	.282	4.1	2B 13, SS 0	1.7
2021 DC	NYY	MLB	26	543	53	21	2	10	48	47	138	11	3	22.7%	.218/.295/.339	75	.282	3.7	2B 12, SS 0	1.8

Comparables: Cesar Crespo, Mark Bellhorn, Damian Jackson

It's understandable if you don't want to dive into a comment about Wade, a glove-first, bat-second utility player who, using replacement-level value as a fathometer, has been underwater since joining the Yankees in 2017. He spent the entire year with the big club, but that had more to do with the team's multiple injuries and the absence of a Triple-A team than it did with anything he accomplished. His ability to play any position on the diamond and speed is nice, though he doesn't offer enough with the bat to be more than a reserve. That's fine and all, you just can't say that his major-league tenure has gone swimmingly.

Austin Wells C Born: 07/12/99 Age: 21 Bats: L Throws: R Height: 6'2" Weight: 220 Origin: Round 1, 2020 Draft (#28 overall)

With the exception of Aaron Judge, the first round of the draft has been an exercise in failure and futility for the Yankees over the past decade-plus; the last non-Judge player to sign with the Yanks and make any sort of impact in the majors was Ian Kennedy in 2006. Drafting a catcher probably isn't the best way to break the streak, but the Yankees couldn't pass on Wells and his offensive promise. There's a real chance he's going to have to move out from behind the plate in due time, perhaps before he catches a big-league pitch, yet the hope is that he'll have the stick to stand in left field or possibly first base. Hope hasn't gotten the Yankees far in recent drafts, but what's another penny in the well when you can have a hitter like Wells for pennies?

PITCHERS

Albert Abreu RHP Born: 09/26/95 Age: 25 Bats: R Throws: R Height: 6'2" Weight: 190 Origin: International Free Agent, 2013

YEAR	TEAM	LVL	AGE	W	L	SV	G	GS	IP	H	HR	BB/9	K/9	K	GB%	BABIP	WHIP	ERA	DRA-	WARP	MPH	FA%	Whiff%	CSP
2018	TAM	HI-A	22	4	3	0	13	13	62²	54	9	4.2	9.3	65	43.4%	.278	1.32	4.16	81	1.0				
2019	TRN	AA	23	5	8	0	23	20	96²	103	9	4.9	8.5	91	41.2%	.339	1.61	4.28	139	-2.2				
2020	NYY	MLB	24	0	1	0	2	0	1¹	4	1	13.5	13.5	2	33.3%	.600	4.50	20.25	112	0.0	98.5	51.2%	33.3%	40.1%
2021 FS	NYY	MLB	25	2	2	0	57	0	50	50	9	6.0	8.4	46	39.7%	.296	1.69	6.24	128	-0.7	98.5	51.2%	33.3%	40.1%
2021 DC	NYY	MLB	25	2	2	0	45	0	48	48	8	6.0	8.4	44	39.7%	.296	1.69	6.24	128	-0.4	98.5	51.2%	33.3%	40.1%

Comparables: Hector Perez, Jordan Yamamoto, Keury Mella

If you're a fan of power arms, Abreu is your guy. His fastball–an upper 90s offering with lots of spin and late life–is so electric that the mound should be surrounded with a fence that has one of those "DANGER: HIGH VOLTAGE" signs attached to it during his half-innings. He also sports a quality power curve he can command and mixes in a slider and change when needed. The catch is Abreu can't stay healthy, to the extent that there are legitimate concerns he'll never be able to get a full season of reps as a starting pitcher. He has the stuff to be an elite reliever, but he's running the risk of becoming just another face in a loaded and crowded Yankees bullpen.

Matt Bowman RHP Born: 05/31/91 Age: 30 Bats: R Throws: R Height: 6'0" Weight: 185 Origin: Round 13, 2012 Draft (#410 overall)

YEAR	TEAM	LVL	AGE	W	L	SV	G	GS	IP	H	HR	BB/9	K/9	K	GB%	BABIP	WHIP	ERA	DRA-	WARP	MPH	FA%	Whiff%	CSP
2018	MEM	AAA	27	0	1	1	18	0	23	23	2	3.1	11.7	30	54.8%	.350	1.35	4.30	41	0.8				
2018	STL	MLB	27	0	2	0	22	0	23	29	4	4.3	10.2	26	46.5%	.385	1.74	6.26	123	-0.2	93.8	60.1%	20.5%	47.8%
2019	LOU	AAA	28	1	1	4	29	0	39	28	1	4.2	8.1	35	55.3%	.265	1.18	2.08	77	0.9				
2019	CIN	MLB	28	2	0	0	27	0	32	27	2	3.7	7.0	25	54.5%	.258	1.25	3.66	100	0.2	94.5	72.9%	19.1%	45.7%
2021 FS	NYY	MLB	30	2	2	0	57	0	50	46	5	3.2	8.1	45	52.3%	.290	1.29	3.69	87	0.5	94.3	69.2%	19.5%	46.3%

Comparables: Luis Cessa, Justin Grimm, Ramon E Ramirez

A veteran low-leverage reliever, Bowman hurt his elbow in summer camp and underwent Tommy John surgery in September; he's likely out until the 2022 season, but that didn't stop the Yankees from signing him to a two-year minor-league pact in December.

Zack Britton LHP Born: 12/22/87 Age: 33 Bats: L Throws: L Height: 6'1" Weight: 200 Origin: Round 3, 2006 Draft (#85 overall)

YEAR	TEAM	LVL	AGE	W	L	SV	G	GS	IP	H	HR	BB/9	K/9	K	GB%	BABIP	WHIP	ERA	DRA-	WARP	MPH	FA%	Whiff%	CSP
2018	BAL	MLB	30	1	0	4	16	0	15²	11	1	5.7	7.5	13	64.1%	.263	1.34	3.45	172	-0.5	96.7	94.4%	35.0%	42.3%
2018	NYY	MLB	30	1	0	3	25	0	25	18	2	4.0	7.6	21	77.8%	.229	1.16	2.88	146	-0.5	96.7	93.1%	30.3%	43.0%
2019	NYY	MLB	31	3	1	3	66	0	61¹	38	3	4.7	7.8	53	76.1%	.226	1.14	1.91	71	1.2	96.1	86.1%	27.7%	42.0%
2020	NYY	MLB	32	1	2	8	20	0	19	12	0	3.3	7.6	16	71.7%	.226	1.00	1.89	81	0.4	96.3	80.3%	25.8%	37.4%
2021 FS	NYY	MLB	33	2	2	8	57	0	50	43	3	4.8	8.5	47	70.9%	.285	1.40	3.87	87	0.5	96.2	86.1%	28.1%	40.9%
2021 DC	NYY	MLB	33	2	2	8	56	0	60	52	4	4.8	8.5	56	70.9%	.285	1.40	3.87	87	0.8	96.2	86.1%	28.1%	40.9%

Comparables: Anthony Bass, Tommy Hunter, Jeremy Jeffress

Thrust into the closer's role on Opening Day when Aroldis Chapman was sidelined with COVID, Britton did what he usually does: generate grounders with his mid-90s sinker and keep the ball in the yard. Since joining the Yankees, Britton has a 2.14 ERA, good for third-best all-time among pitchers with at least 100 innings thrown in pinstripes. He's lost a couple of ticks off his fastball since a 2018 injury, but has learned to thrive following an initial adjustment period thanks to increased use of a sharp-breaking curve that gives hitters a different look. The combination of worm burners and weak contact makes Britton a relief ace regardless of his assigned inning of work.

Luis Cessa RHP Born: 04/25/92 Age: 29 Bats: R Throws: R Height: 6'0" Weight: 208 Origin: International Free Agent, 2008

YEAR	TEAM	LVL	AGE	W	L	SV	G	GS	IP	H	HR	BB/9	K/9	K	GB%	BABIP	WHIP	ERA	DRA-	WARP	MPH	FA%	Whiff%	CSP
2018	TRN	AA	26	0	1	0	2	2	10	6	0	0.9	10.8	12	45.8%	.250	0.70	2.70	33	0.4				
2018	SWB	AAA	26	3	0	0	6	5	26¹	19	1	1.4	8.5	25	39.7%	.250	0.87	2.73	53	0.8				
2018	NYY	MLB	26	1	4	2	16	5	44²	51	5	2.6	7.9	39	46.9%	.336	1.43	5.24	72	1.0	96.9	41.8%	27.0%	45.8%
2019	NYY	MLB	27	2	1	1	43	0	81	75	14	3.4	8.3	75	48.3%	.277	1.31	4.11	98	0.5	96.2	41.9%	29.8%	43.5%
2020	NYY	MLB	28	0	0	1	16	0	21²	20	2	2.9	7.1	17	39.7%	.273	1.25	3.32	119	0.0	95.2	31.1%	27.7%	41.0%
2021 FS	NYY	MLB	29	2	2	0	57	0	50	49	9	3.2	8.2	45	43.5%	.290	1.35	4.63	104	0.0	96.1	39.2%	28.8%	43.3%
2021 DC	NYY	MLB	29	2	2	0	56	0	60	59	10	3.2	8.2	54	43.5%	.290	1.35	4.63	104	0.2	96.1	39.2%	28.8%	43.3%

Comparables: Alex Colomé, Tyler Duffey, Trevor Williams

Cessa, who tested positive for COVID-19 on July 4, rattled off a streak of eight consecutive scoreless appearances after settling in upon his return. In a year when innings were at a premium and the schedule was often tempest-tossed, Cessa's rubber arm and yeoman work in middle relief were essential.

Aroldis Chapman LHP Born: 02/28/88 Age: 33 Bats: L Throws: L Height: 6'4" Weight: 218 Origin: International Free Agent, 2010

YEAR	TEAM	LVL	AGE	W	L	SV	G	GS	IP	H	HR	BB/9	K/9	K	GB%	BABIP	WHIP	ERA	DRA-	WARP	MPH	FA%	Whiff%	CSP
2018	NYY	MLB	30	3	0	32	55	0	51¹	24	2	5.3	16.3	93	46.4%	.268	1.05	2.45	47	1.7	102.2	73.8%	37.4%	45.9%
2019	NYY	MLB	31	3	2	37	60	0	57	38	3	3.9	13.4	85	41.5%	.292	1.11	2.21	52	1.7	101.3	68.6%	31.8%	49.4%
2020	NYY	MLB	32	1	1	3	13	0	11²	6	2	3.1	17.0	22	27.8%	.250	0.86	3.09	74	0.3	101.1	76.9%	41.6%	51.1%
2021 FS	NYY	MLB	33	3	2	34	57	0	50	33	5	4.5	13.8	76	40.3%	.285	1.17	2.79	66	1.1	101.5	71.4%	35.0%	48.7%
2021 DC	NYY	MLB	33	3	2	34	56	0	60	40	6	4.5	13.8	91	40.3%	.285	1.17	2.79	66	1.4	101.5	71.4%	35.0%	48.7%

Comparables: Craig Kimbrel, Dellin Betances, Kenley Jansen

After missing nearly a month due to a positive COVID-19 diagnosis, Chapman shook off the rust and concluded the regular season with eight consecutive scoreless outings, allowing only three baserunners and fanning 17 batters. All fans will remember, though, is Chapman allowing the go-ahead and ultimately winning home run in the deciding Game 5 of the ALDS against the Rays, and Mike Brosseau triumphantly rounding the bases in the bottom of the eighth. That memory is inexorably linked to a particularly ugly incident from a month earlier, when Chapman cavalierly threw a 101 mile-per-hour fastball at or towards Brosseau's head, depending on who you believe. MLB was inclined to think it was the latter, as they only issued a three-game suspension for the dangerous pitch. There was a time when fans looked the other way and perhaps even applauded pitchers who engaged in a little chin music. That time has passed, and the near universal negative reaction to the incident is actually a good sign for the future of the sport.

Gerrit Cole RHP   Born: 09/08/90   Age: 30   Bats: R   Throws: R   Height: 6'4"   Weight: 220   Origin: Round 1, 2011 Draft (#1 overall)

YEAR	TEAM	LVL	AGE	W	L	SV	G	GS	IP	H	HR	BB/9	K/9	K	GB%	BABIP	WHIP	ERA	DRA-	WARP	MPH	FA%	Whiff%	CSP
2018	HOU	MLB	27	15	5	0	32	32	200¹	143	19	2.9	12.4	276	36.3%	.288	1.03	2.88	56	6.4	98.7	56.4%	30.9%	49.8%
2019	HOU	MLB	28	20	5	0	33	33	212¹	142	29	2.0	13.8	326	40.0%	.276	0.89	2.50	48	7.9	99.3	54.0%	37.2%	48.7%
2020	NYY	MLB	29	7	3	0	12	12	73	53	14	2.1	11.6	94	37.1%	.242	0.96	2.84	79	1.5	98.6	52.8%	34.2%	47.1%
2021 FS	NYY	MLB	30	10	7	0	26	26	150	117	21	2.5	11.7	194	39.2%	.283	1.06	2.82	68	3.7	99.0	54.2%	34.9%	48.5%
2021 DC	NYY	MLB	30	14	8	0	30	30	193	151	27	2.5	11.7	250	39.2%	.283	1.06	2.82	68	5.3	99.0	54.2%	34.9%	48.5%

Comparables: Cole Hamels, Kyle Hendricks, David Price

There was a great deal of concern over Cole's poor start after he signed a nine-year, $324 million deal that saw him receive the most guaranteed money ever handed to a pitcher (as well as the highest annual average value for any player in major league history). He wasn't bad, but a 3.88 ERA and nine home runs allowed in his first nine starts didn't align with the ace-level production that Yankees fans dreamed about following his introductory press conference.

Okay, take a breath and look carefully at the stat line above. Those marks were actually from Cole's first nine starts of 2019 with the Astros, before he became the apple in New York's eye, not his first nine in 2020 with the Yankees. In both seasons, Cole was fine; he just ran out of road in 2020 because of the shortened season. (Amusingly, he did perform better through his team's first 60 games than he did in 2019, posting an ERA over a full run lower.) It's a long contract, and maybe eight years from now, fans will be calling WFAN to yell about what a bum Cole was. For now, Year One of his Yankee tenure should be considered an unqualified success.

Nestor Cortes LHP   Born: 12/10/94   Age: 26   Bats: R   Throws: L   Height: 5'11"   Weight: 210   Origin: Round 36, 2013 Draft (#1094 overall)

YEAR	TEAM	LVL	AGE	W	L	SV	G	GS	IP	H	HR	BB/9	K/9	K	GB%	BABIP	WHIP	ERA	DRA-	WARP	MPH	FA%	Whiff%	CSP
2018	SWB	AAA	23	6	6	0	23	18	111²	95	13	3.0	7.7	96	33.3%	.264	1.18	3.71	112	-0.1				
2018	BAL	MLB	23	0	0	0	4	0	4²	10	2	7.7	5.8	3	47.4%	.471	3.00	7.71	96	0.0	90.1	62.0%	24.4%	49.2%
2019	SWB	AAA	24	2	2	0	7	6	39²	29	3	2.5	9.5	42	35.0%	.263	1.01	3.86	53	1.6				
2019	NYY	MLB	24	5	1	0	33	1	66²	75	16	3.8	9.3	69	34.5%	.321	1.54	5.67	132	-0.8	91.5	51.8%	25.9%	48.0%
2020	SEA	MLB	25	0	1	0	5	1	7²	12	6	7.0	9.4	8	35.7%	.286	2.35	15.26	172	-0.2	90.3	40.6%	20.3%	46.2%
2021 FS	NYY	MLB	26	2	3	0	57	0	50	46	8	3.4	8.6	47	35.5%	.279	1.31	4.26	101	0.1	91.3	50.3%	24.9%	47.7%

Comparables: Ryan Helsley, Jake Newberry, Alex Reyes

One thing we've discovered over the years is that ERA is a *terrible* metric to measure pitching quality. It's fair to assume Cortes is very grateful we figured that out. Unfortunately, the only number that can help him stay employed is 570,500, his near-minimum salary. It probably won't be enough.

─────────────── ★ ★ ★ *2021 Top 101 Prospect* **#17** ★ ★ ★ ───────────────

Deivi García RHP   Born: 05/19/99   Age: 22   Bats: R   Throws: R   Height: 5'9"   Weight: 163   Origin: International Free Agent, 2015

YEAR	TEAM	LVL	AGE	W	L	SV	G	GS	IP	H	HR	BB/9	K/9	K	GB%	BABIP	WHIP	ERA	DRA-	WARP	MPH	FA%	Whiff%	CSP
2018	CSC	LO-A	19	2	4	0	8	8	40²	31	5	2.2	13.9	63	27.5%	.310	1.01	3.76	50	1.4				
2018	TAM	HI-A	19	2	0	0	5	5	28¹	19	0	2.5	11.1	35	35.4%	.297	0.95	1.27	65	0.7				
2018	TRN	AA	19	1	0	0	1	1	5	0	0	3.6	12.6	7	37.5%	.000	0.40	0.00	71	0.1				
2019	TAM	HI-A	20	0	2	0	4	4	17²	14	0	4.1	16.8	33	50.0%	.438	1.25	3.06	72	0.3				
2019	TRN	AA	20	4	4	0	11	11	53²	43	2	4.4	14.6	87	40.5%	.363	1.29	3.86	88	0.4				
2019	SWB	AAA	20	1	3	0	11	6	40	39	8	4.5	10.1	45	36.7%	.313	1.48	5.40	105	0.6				
2020	NYY	MLB	21	3	2	0	6	6	34¹	35	6	1.6	8.7	33	34.0%	.293	1.19	4.98	105	0.2	94.1	59.6%	22.8%	49.8%
2021 FS	NYY	MLB	22	9	8	0	26	26	150	134	26	3.4	10.2	169	37.3%	.288	1.27	4.28	97	1.3	94.1	59.6%	22.8%	49.8%
2021 DC	NYY	MLB	22	8	7	0	22	22	124	111	21	3.4	10.2	139	37.3%	.288	1.27	4.28	97	1.5	94.1	59.6%	22.8%	49.8%

Comparables: Bryse Wilson, Sixto Sánchez, Luis Severino

García had an outside chance to make the Yankees' Opening Day roster, but it wasn't until late August, when a pair of COVID-induced postponements turned the Subway Series into a frantic marathon of seven-inning doubleheaders, when García was summoned. While his debut against the Metropolitans was stellar, there were more downs than ups during his brief foray against major-league hitters. The numbers weren't great, but the observant eye could pick up on plenty of things to like: his deceptive delivery; the high spin rate on his curve; the vertical drop on his heater; and so on. García is also only 21 years old as of press time, so while 2020 wasn't littered with dominant performances, there is plenty of time for him to put it all together.

Domingo Germán RHP   Born: 08/04/92   Age: 28   Bats: R   Throws: R   Height: 6'2"   Weight: 181   Origin: International Free Agent, 2009

YEAR	TEAM	LVL	AGE	W	L	SV	G	GS	IP	H	HR	BB/9	K/9	K	GB%	BABIP	WHIP	ERA	DRA-	WARP	MPH	FA%	Whiff%	CSP
2018	TAM	HI-A	25	0	0	0	2	2	6	3	0	3.0	12.0	8	15.4%	.231	0.83	0.00	38	0.2				
2018	NYY	MLB	25	2	6	0	21	14	85²	81	15	3.5	10.7	102	39.1%	.300	1.33	5.57	97	0.9	96.3	46.9%	32.6%	46.9%
2019	NYY	MLB	26	18	4	0	27	24	143	125	30	2.5	9.6	153	37.5%	.260	1.15	4.03	87	2.3	95.4	44.9%	28.3%	47.4%
2021 FS	NYY	MLB	28	9	8	0	26	26	150	135	25	3.4	9.8	162	38.8%	.286	1.28	4.12	94	1.6	95.7	45.4%	29.4%	47.2%
2021 DC	NYY	MLB	28	6	5	0	19	19	101	91	16	3.4	9.8	109	38.8%	.286	1.28	4.12	94	1.4	95.7	45.4%	29.4%	47.2%

Comparables: Joe Ross, Joe Musgrove, Nick Pivetta

Germán's year was far more notable for what he didn't do than what he did. In February, he escaped a dune buggy accident in his native Dominican Republic unscathed. In July, he then posted a salty comment on Instagram saying he was "done with baseball" before backtracking almost immediately thereafter. Germán's season was already shortened pre-COVID due to having to serve the remainder of an 81-game suspension under MLB-MLBPA's Joint

Domestic Violence Policy, and when the season was cut to 60 games, any chance of him playing baseball disappeared along with it. The Yankees could have used Germán in the postseason, but announced they wouldn't due to a lack of preparation time. He still has plenty of potential but has a great deal of work to do both on and, perhaps more importantly, off the field if he hopes to make it back to the majors.

Luis Gil   RHP   Born: 06/03/98   Age: 23   Bats: R   Throws: R   Height: 6'2"   Weight: 185   Origin: International Free Agent, 2015

YEAR	TEAM	LVL	AGE	W	L	SV	G	GS	IP	H	HR	BB/9	K/9	K	GB%	BABIP	WHIP	ERA	DRA-	WARP	MPH	FA%	Whiff%	CSP
2018	PUL	ROK	20	2	1	0	10	10	39¹	21	1	5.7	13.3	58	34.2%	.256	1.17	1.37	72	1.1				
2018	SI	SS	20	0	2	0	2	2	6²	11	1	8.1	13.5	10	39.1%	.455	2.55	5.40	300	-0.9				
2019	CSC	LO-A	21	4	5	0	17	17	83	60	1	4.2	12.1	112	47.2%	.311	1.19	2.39	80	1.3				
2019	TAM	HI-A	21	1	0	0	3	3	13	11	0	5.5	7.6	11	40.5%	.297	1.46	4.85	115	-0.1				
2021 FS	NYY	MLB	23	2	3	0	57	0	50	44	8	7.2	9.8	54	38.7%	.282	1.69	5.54	121	-0.5				

Comparables: Domingo Germán, Albert Abreu, Gregory Infante

Appearances can be deceiving. In Gil's case, the ease and effortlessness of his delivery make it seem like he should have plenty of command and control at his disposal. Alas, this isn't the case at all, and his command veers anywhere between "average" and "nonexistent." Gil's upper-90s fastball and slurvy curve are both quality offerings, but a combination of his inconsistent command and his lack of a third pitch make it more likely that he's going to be a future bullpen arm than a rotation mainstay.

Chad Green   RHP   Born: 05/24/91   Age: 30   Bats: L   Throws: R   Height: 6'3"   Weight: 215   Origin: Round 11, 2013 Draft (#336 overall)

YEAR	TEAM	LVL	AGE	W	L	SV	G	GS	IP	H	HR	BB/9	K/9	K	GB%	BABIP	WHIP	ERA	DRA-	WARP	MPH	FA%	Whiff%	CSP
2018	NYY	MLB	27	8	3	0	63	0	75²	64	9	1.8	11.2	94	32.4%	.307	1.04	2.50	75	1.3	97.5	86.6%	28.5%	52.5%
2019	SWB	AAA	28	0	0	0	3	3	7¹	5	0	2.5	17.2	14	23.1%	.385	0.95	2.45	42	0.3				
2019	NYY	MLB	28	4	4	2	54	15	69	66	10	2.5	12.8	98	35.5%	.346	1.23	4.17	76	1.3	98.0	77.1%	30.0%	50.3%
2020	NYY	MLB	29	3	3	1	22	0	25²	13	5	2.8	11.2	32	41.7%	.148	0.82	3.51	85	0.4	96.8	75.1%	31.4%	51.6%
2021 FS	NYY	MLB	30	3	2	0	57	0	50	38	8	2.5	11.7	64	37.6%	.274	1.05	2.92	71	1.0	97.6	78.9%	30.0%	51.2%
2021 DC	NYY	MLB	30	3	2	0	56	0	60	46	9	2.5	11.7	77	37.6%	.274	1.05	2.92	71	1.3	97.6	78.9%	30.0%	51.2%

Comparables: Ken Giles, Raisel Iglesias, Chris Devenski

"Eat your greens" is a tired cliché nearly every kid has heard from their parents at the dinner table as they wanly pushed their vegetables around their plate, hoping a hole would open up and rescue them from their accursed fate. On a loaded Yankees squad, this Green is a bit like those boring vegetables in that he's not going to be the thing that gets you excited about coming to the table; he is, however, a solid part of any nine-inning meal and an integral part of the Yankees' menu. It was Green, after all, who had the highest WARP among Yankees relievers in 2020. There isn't any flash to Green's game, but his "boring" four-seamer gets the job done. And things have changed since you were a kid; they're doing all sorts of wonderful things with vegetable entrees and side dishes these days. You should give them another chance.

J.A. Happ   LHP   Born: 10/19/82   Age: 38   Bats: L   Throws: L   Height: 6'5"   Weight: 205   Origin: Round 3, 2004 Draft (#92 overall)

YEAR	TEAM	LVL	AGE	W	L	SV	G	GS	IP	H	HR	BB/9	K/9	K	GB%	BABIP	WHIP	ERA	DRA-	WARP	MPH	FA%	Whiff%	CSP
2018	TOR	MLB	35	10	6	0	20	20	114	99	17	2.8	10.3	130	44.6%	.286	1.18	4.18	86	1.9	94.5	74.2%	24.9%	48.0%
2018	NYY	MLB	35	7	0	0	11	11	63²	51	10	2.3	8.9	63	32.2%	.252	1.05	2.69	89	1.0	94.0	72.2%	22.7%	48.3%
2019	NYY	MLB	36	12	8	0	31	30	161¹	160	34	2.7	7.8	140	40.5%	.281	1.30	4.91	123	-0.4	93.5	68.3%	23.8%	47.2%
2020	NYY	MLB	37	2	2	0	9	9	49¹	37	8	2.7	7.7	42	43.8%	.227	1.05	3.47	105	0.3	93.1	67.1%	22.7%	47.1%
2021 FS	NYY	MLB	38	9	9	0	26	26	150	144	26	3.3	8.1	135	41.4%	.280	1.33	4.29	100	1.1	93.7	69.5%	23.6%	47.4%

Comparables: Jorge De La Rosa, Kyle Lohse, Todd Stottlemyre

For a guy who was viewed as a bust a few years ago, or as a failure who would never live up to his stellar rookie campaign, it's been an achievement for Happ to grind his way to a serviceable career as a back-end starter well into his late 30s. Did you know that he's one of only 13 pitchers since 2015 with at least 900 innings pitched and an ERA lower than 3.75? That tidbit speaks more to the dwindling role of the starting pitcher in modern baseball than to any greatness on Happ's part, but that kind of reliability makes things easier for any manager, even if it never makes the pitcher in question appointment viewing.

Ben Heller   RHP   Born: 08/05/91   Age: 29   Bats: R   Throws: R   Height: 6'3"   Weight: 210   Origin: Round 22, 2013 Draft (#651 overall)

YEAR	TEAM	LVL	AGE	W	L	SV	G	GS	IP	H	HR	BB/9	K/9	K	GB%	BABIP	WHIP	ERA	DRA-	WARP	MPH	FA%	Whiff%	CSP
2019	SWB	AAA	27	0	0	1	9	4	11	5	0	2.5	10.6	13	54.5%	.227	0.73	0.82	36	0.5				
2019	NYY	MLB	27	0	0	0	6	0	7¹	6	1	3.7	11.0	9	43.8%	.357	1.23	1.23	103	0.0	94.7	49.0%	36.8%	38.3%
2020	NYY	MLB	28	0	0	0	6	0	6	5	2	3.0	9.0	6	29.4%	.200	1.17	3.00	106	0.0	94.9	51.4%	26.5%	44.5%
2021 FS	NYY	MLB	29	2	2	0	57	0	50	43	7	4.5	10.5	58	41.8%	.289	1.36	4.29	96	0.2	94.8	50.5%	30.4%	42.2%
2021 DC	NYY	MLB	29	2	2	0	45	0	48	41	6	4.5	10.5	55	41.8%	.289	1.36	4.29	96	0.4	94.8	50.5%	30.4%	42.2%

Comparables: Shawn Armstrong, Juan Minaya, Santiago Casilla

It took five years and four seasons of sporadic innings for Heller to exhaust his rookie eligibility, a product of both the team's vaunted bullpen depth and an unfortunately-timed UCL tear. As a result, it remains unclear whether he can replicate his minor-league dominance in the majors.

Michael King RHP
Born: 05/25/95   Age: 26   Bats: R   Throws: R   Height: 6'3"   Weight: 210   Origin: Round 12, 2016 Draft (#353 overall)

YEAR	TEAM	LVL	AGE	W	L	SV	G	GS	IP	H	HR	BB/9	K/9	K	GB%	BABIP	WHIP	ERA	DRA-	WARP	MPH	FA%	Whiff%	CSP
2018	TAM	HI-A	23	1	3	0	7	7	40¹	33	1	2.2	10.0	45	58.9%	.305	1.07	1.79	76	0.8				
2018	TRN	AA	23	6	2	0	12	11	82	65	4	1.4	8.3	76	44.7%	.279	0.95	2.09	69	2.0				
2018	SWB	AAA	23	4	0	0	6	6	39	20	3	1.4	7.2	31	54.3%	.167	0.67	1.15	77	0.8				
2019	YAW	ROK	24	0	0	0	3	2	5²	3	0	3.2	12.7	8	75.0%	.250	0.88	4.76	21	0.3				
2019	SI	SS	24	0	0	0	1	1	4	4	0	0.0	0.0	0	46.2%	.308	1.00	0.00	117	0.0				
2019	TRN	AA	24	0	1	0	3	2	12²	20	1	1.4	5.7	8	51.0%	.396	1.74	9.95	142	-0.3				
2019	SWB	AAA	24	3	1	0	4	3	23²	20	3	2.3	10.6	28	47.5%	.293	1.10	4.18	61	0.8				
2019	NYY	MLB	24	0	0	0	1	0	2	2	0	0.0	4.5	1	37.5%	.250	1.00	0.00	106	0.0	92.8	65.9%	5.6%	44.4%
2020	NYY	MLB	25	1	2	0	9	4	26²	30	5	3.7	8.8	26	40.2%	.325	1.54	7.76	106	0.2	94.8	65.7%	21.3%	47.3%
2021 FS	NYY	MLB	26	9	8	0	26	26	150	144	23	2.4	7.8	129	42.7%	.284	1.24	4.06	94	1.5	94.7	65.7%	20.4%	47.2%
2021 DC	NYY	MLB	26	3	3	0	32	9	64	61	9	2.4	7.8	55	42.7%	.284	1.24	4.06	94	0.8	94.7	65.7%	20.4%	47.2%

Comparables: Sterling Sharp, Brandon Workman, Tyler Wilson

King's debut was his crowning achievement, but until he puts the finishing touches on his stuff, he's unlikely to dethrone any of the Yankees' front five. His reign of terrorizing opposing batters will just have to wait.

Brooks Kriske RHP
Born: 02/03/94   Age: 27   Bats: R   Throws: R   Height: 6'3"   Weight: 190   Origin: Round 6, 2016 Draft (#188 overall)

YEAR	TEAM	LVL	AGE	W	L	SV	G	GS	IP	H	HR	BB/9	K/9	K	GB%	BABIP	WHIP	ERA	DRA-	WARP	MPH	FA%	Whiff%	CSP
2018	SI	SS	24	2	2	3	14	0	24²	21	0	2.9	12.0	33	45.5%	.396	1.18	1.09	239	-1.8				
2018	CSC	LO-A	24	0	0	0	2	0	4	4	0	2.2	13.5	6	0.0%	.444	1.25	4.50	65	0.1				
2019	TAM	HI-A	25	1	1	1	7	0	12	4	0	3.8	12.0	16	38.1%	.200	0.75	0.00	53	0.3				
2019	TRN	AA	25	2	2	11	36	0	48²	30	3	4.3	11.8	64	33.3%	.250	1.09	2.59	79	0.4				
2020	NYY	MLB	26	0	0	0	4	0	3²	3	1	17.2	19.6	8	28.6%	.333	2.73	14.73	89	0.1	96.4	68.8%	39.1%	39.1%
2021 FS	NYY	MLB	27	2	2	0	57	0	50	44	9	6.0	11.0	61	33.9%	.293	1.55	5.16	110	-0.2	96.4	68.8%	39.1%	39.1%
2021 DC	NYY	MLB	27	2	2	0	45	0	48	42	8	6.0	11.0	58	33.9%	.293	1.55	5.16	110	0.0	96.4	68.8%	39.1%	39.1%

Comparables: Kyle Keller, Dany Jimenez, Zac Rosscup

An afterthought prior to 2019, Kriske moved up prospect lists after he added a few ticks to his fastball. He'll need to do a better job of commanding his three-pitch arsenal if he's to spare the world from learning if copy editors are willing to run "Kriske Kreme'd" headlines. (They are.)

Jonathan Loaisiga RHP
Born: 11/02/94   Age: 26   Bats: R   Throws: R   Height: 5'11"   Weight: 165   Origin: International Free Agent, 2012

YEAR	TEAM	LVL	AGE	W	L	SV	G	GS	IP	H	HR	BB/9	K/9	K	GB%	BABIP	WHIP	ERA	DRA-	WARP	MPH	FA%	Whiff%	CSP
2018	TAM	HI-A	23	3	0	0	4	4	20	19	0	0.5	11.7	26	51.9%	.365	1.00	1.35	76	0.4				
2018	TRN	AA	23	3	1	0	9	9	34¹	37	6	1.6	10.5	40	38.7%	.356	1.25	3.93	65	0.9				
2018	NYY	MLB	23	2	0	0	9	4	24²	26	3	4.4	12.0	33	52.4%	.383	1.54	5.11	73	0.5	97.5	55.8%	30.6%	46.2%
2019	SWB	AAA	24	0	2	0	5	4	15²	14	3	2.9	10.9	19	46.5%	.275	1.21	6.32	65	0.5				
2019	NYY	MLB	24	2	2	0	15	4	31²	31	6	4.5	10.5	37	40.0%	.316	1.48	4.55	109	0.1	99.0	56.3%	33.2%	44.6%
2020	NYY	MLB	25	3	0	0	12	3	23	21	3	2.7	8.6	22	51.5%	.290	1.22	3.52	84	0.4	98.0	67.3%	23.2%	50.0%
2021 FS	NYY	MLB	26	3	3	0	57	0	50	44	6	3.6	9.7	53	46.1%	.292	1.30	4.05	92	0.4	98.3	60.8%	28.6%	47.1%
2021 DC	NYY	MLB	26	3	3	0	40	6	58	52	7	3.6	9.7	62	46.1%	.292	1.30	4.05	92	0.7	98.3	60.8%	28.6%	47.1%

Comparables: Roberto Osuna, Alex Reyes, Ryan Helsley

Loaisiga has been called "Johnny Lasagna" since his early days as a professional, even though he hails from Nicaragua and his surname is of Spanish origin. The name Loaisiga derives from "Loyzaga", and there is a Loizaga Tower in Spain that stands to this day. The tower is now a museum that houses a collection of Rolls Royce vehicles, with 45 unique models dating back to the 1910 Silver Ghost. All of this is immaterial to Loaisiga's current and future status with the Yankees, but with some cursory research and just a smidgen of imagination, he could have a cool nickname like "Rolls" or "Silver Ghost" instead of a cheesy moniker that sounds like a bad stereotypical mafia name Martin Scorsese would have left on the cutting room floor.

Luis Medina RHP
Born: 05/03/99   Age: 22   Bats: R   Throws: R   Height: 6'1"   Weight: 175   Origin: International Free Agent, 2015

YEAR	TEAM	LVL	AGE	W	L	SV	G	GS	IP	H	HR	BB/9	K/9	K	GB%	BABIP	WHIP	ERA	DRA-	WARP	MPH	FA%	Whiff%	CSP
2018	PUL	ROK	19	1	3	0	12	12	36	32	3	11.5	11.8	47	42.7%	.337	2.17	6.25	108	0.4				
2019	CSC	LO-A	20	1	8	0	20	20	93	86	9	6.5	11.1	115	43.6%	.344	1.65	6.00	145	-2.1				
2019	TAM	HI-A	20	0	0	0	2	2	10²	7	0	2.5	10.1	12	67.9%	.250	0.94	0.84	72	0.2				
2021 FS	NYY	MLB	22	2	3	0	57	0	50	47	9	8.9	9.3	51	43.0%	.286	1.93	6.98	142	-1.1				
2021 DC	NYY	MLB	22	0	0	0	3	3	14	13	2	8.9	9.3	14	43.0%	.286	1.93	6.98	142	-0.2				

Comparables: Huascar Ynoa, Beau Burrows, Jefry Rodriguez

The Yankees seem to pluck pitchers who throw super hard and have a subpar command profile out of thin air. Medina is potentially the most promising of New York's endless cavalcade of arms of this ilk. His secondary pitches quietly improved, pushing him past the limitations of two-pitch bullpen arm while his arm action, athleticism and physicality suggest there is more growth to come. Medina wasn't able to convince the Yankees brass to overlook his lack of experience in the high minors and push him to the majors for a 2020 relief debut, but when and if the minors resume play it's likely that his raw stuff will put him on the fast track to the Bronx.

Jordan Montgomery LHP Born: 12/27/92 Age: 28 Bats: L Throws: L Height: 6'6" Weight: 228 Origin: Round 4, 2014 Draft (#122 overall)

YEAR	TEAM	LVL	AGE	W	L	SV	G	GS	IP	H	HR	BB/9	K/9	K	GB%	BABIP	WHIP	ERA	DRA-	WARP	MPH	FA%	Whiff%	CSP
2018	NYY	MLB	25	2	0	0	6	6	27^1	25	3	4.0	7.6	23	45.7%	.282	1.35	3.62	131	-0.2	91.6	41.1%	23.5%	45.3%
2019	NYY	MLB	26	0	0	0	2	1	4	7	1	0.0	11.2	5	21.4%	.462	1.75	6.75	125	0.0	93.0	50.0%	28.9%	47.9%
2020	NYY	MLB	27	2	3	0	10	10	44	48	7	1.8	9.6	47	43.3%	.323	1.30	5.11	84	0.8	94.2	52.3%	28.2%	47.3%
2021 FS	NYY	MLB	28	9	8	0	26	26	150	139	23	3.2	9.1	151	41.5%	.289	1.29	4.01	92	1.7	93.7	50.4%	27.5%	47.0%
2021 DC	NYY	MLB	28	9	8	0	27	27	140	130	21	3.2	9.1	141	41.5%	.289	1.29	4.01	92	2.0	93.7	50.4%	27.5%	47.0%

Comparables: Nick Pivetta, Daniel Mengden, Jakob Junis

After a long and difficult recovery from Tommy John surgery in 2018, Montgomery was finally able to take the hill and pitch a full season...or, at least, as "full" of a season as the year 2020 could provide. He initially looked shaky, but after shaking off the rust, Montgomery put together a solid string of starts in September that gave the Yankee faithful hope heading into the winter. Provided his command and velocity are back to stay, then there's a present and a future for Montgomery in the Yankees' rotation.

Nick Nelson RHP Born: 12/05/95 Age: 25 Bats: R Throws: R Height: 6'1" Weight: 205 Origin: Round 4, 2016 Draft (#128 overall)

YEAR	TEAM	LVL	AGE	W	L	SV	G	GS	IP	H	HR	BB/9	K/9	K	GB%	BABIP	WHIP	ERA	DRA-	WARP	MPH	FA%	Whiff%	CSP
2018	CSC	LO-A	22	1	1	0	5	5	24^2	18	1	2.6	12.8	35	50.9%	.309	1.01	3.65	74	0.5				
2018	TAM	HI-A	22	7	5	0	18	17	88^1	69	1	4.8	10.1	99	44.9%	.302	1.31	3.36	67	2.1				
2018	TRN	AA	22	0	0	0	3	3	8^2	10	1	9.3	10.4	10	50.0%	.360	2.19	5.19	81	0.1				
2019	TAM	HI-A	23	0	0	0	1	1	3^2	4	0	2.5	17.2	7	57.1%	.571	1.36	0.00	71	0.1				
2019	TRN	AA	23	7	2	0	13	12	65	48	4	4.8	11.5	83	31.1%	.301	1.28	2.35	95	0.3				
2019	SWB	AAA	23	1	1	0	4	4	21	20	2	3.0	10.3	24	44.8%	.321	1.29	4.71	56	0.8				
2020	NYY	MLB	24	1	0	0	11	0	20^2	20	4	4.8	7.8	18	55.7%	.281	1.50	4.79	93	0.3	97.9	57.2%	28.1%	44.4%
2021 FS	NYY	MLB	25	3	3	0	57	0	50	47	7	5.0	9.1	50	43.9%	.296	1.50	5.04	108	-0.1	97.9	57.2%	28.1%	44.4%
2021 DC	NYY	MLB	25	3	3	0	40	6	58	55	8	5.0	9.1	58	43.9%	.296	1.50	5.04	108	0.2	97.9	57.2%	28.1%	44.4%

Comparables: Adonis Rosa, Ryan Helsley, Jenrry Mejia

It was an underwhelming major-league debut for Nelson, but a 20-inning sample isn't enough to write off a pitcher with a hot fastball and three pitches.

Adam Ottavino RHP Born: 11/22/85 Age: 35 Bats: S Throws: R Height: 6'5" Weight: 246 Origin: Round 1, 2006 Draft (#30 overall)

YEAR	TEAM	LVL	AGE	W	L	SV	G	GS	IP	H	HR	BB/9	K/9	K	GB%	BABIP	WHIP	ERA	DRA-	WARP	MPH	FA%	Whiff%	CSP
2018	COL	MLB	32	6	4	6	75	0	77^2	41	5	4.2	13.0	112	42.2%	.243	0.99	2.43	67	1.7	95.7	43.1%	32.9%	48.0%
2019	NYY	MLB	33	6	5	2	73	0	66^1	47	5	5.4	11.9	88	40.1%	.286	1.31	1.90	74	1.2	95.6	41.5%	29.9%	48.4%
2020	NYY	MLB	34	2	3	0	24	0	18^1	20	2	4.4	12.3	25	52.0%	.375	1.58	5.89	72	0.4	95.0	44.8%	26.5%	52.7%
2021 FS	NYY	MLB	35	2	2	0	57	0	50	40	6	5.2	10.8	59	43.8%	.283	1.38	4.01	90	0.4	95.5	42.7%	30.0%	49.3%
2021 DC	NYY	MLB	35	2	2	0	56	0	60	48	7	5.2	10.8	71	43.8%	.283	1.38	4.01	90	0.7	95.5	42.7%	30.0%	49.3%

Comparables: David Hernandez, Wade Davis, Steve Cishek

Analyzing how any player performed in a 60-game sample is challenging work; trying to figure out what it means for a reliever is like trying to figure out the names of those angels dancing on the head of William Sclater's metaphorical pin. In Ottavino's case, it doesn't take an otherworldly magnifying glass and calipers to figure out why his 2020 numbers were terrible. On September 7, Ottavino was hung out to dry in a 12-7 loss against the Blue Jays in a Triple-A bandbox that was hosting games only because Canada had closed its borders to Major League Baseball. Take away that ghastly, zero-inning, six-earned-run outing and Ottavino had a 2.95 ERA. Even with that nightmarish contest on his resume, he posted a 3.35 DRA, or a better rate than he did in his Yankee debut in 2019. He was fine, in other words, and should continue to be a key asset for New York in the final season of his three-year, $27 million pact.

James Paxton LHP Born: 11/06/88 Age: 32 Bats: L Throws: L Height: 6'4" Weight: 227 Origin: Round 4, 2010 Draft (#132 overall)

YEAR	TEAM	LVL	AGE	W	L	SV	G	GS	IP	H	HR	BB/9	K/9	K	GB%	BABIP	WHIP	ERA	DRA-	WARP	MPH	FA%	Whiff%	CSP
2018	SEA	MLB	29	11	6	0	28	28	160^1	134	23	2.4	11.7	208	39.8%	.301	1.10	3.76	59	4.9	97.7	63.6%	30.1%	52.9%
2019	NYY	MLB	30	15	6	0	29	29	150^2	138	23	3.3	11.1	186	39.0%	.315	1.28	3.82	85	2.6	97.6	59.9%	30.7%	47.1%
2020	NYY	MLB	31	1	1	0	5	5	20^1	23	4	3.1	11.5	26	32.1%	.365	1.48	6.64	103	0.2	93.8	56.7%	28.4%	47.1%
2021 FS	NYY	MLB	32	9	8	0	26	26	150	134	25	3.0	10.5	175	38.9%	.294	1.23	3.66	88	2.1	97.2	60.6%	30.3%	48.8%

Comparables: Stephen Strasburg, Matt Harvey, Dallas Keuchel

Paxton's 2020 got off to an inauspicious start even before pitchers and catchers reported, as he required spinal surgery in early February with an estimated recovery time of three-to-four months. Paxton appeared to benefit from the delayed start, but even though he started the newly abbreviated season on time, he looked off his game. His velocity was several miles per hour lower than it had been in 2019, and after five starts, he was shut down for good, this time with a flexor strain. There's no denying that he's an above-average starter when healthy; the question is if he can be relied upon to throw more than 120-140 frames as he heads deeper into his 30s.

★ ★ ★ *2021 Top 101 Prospect* **#96** ★ ★ ★

Clarke Schmidt RHP Born: 02/20/96 Age: 25 Bats: R Throws: R Height: 6'1" Weight: 200 Origin: Round 1, 2017 Draft (#16 overall)

YEAR	TEAM	LVL	AGE	W	L	SV	G	GS	IP	H	HR	BB/9	K/9	K	GB%	BABIP	WHIP	ERA	DRA-	WARP	MPH	FA%	Whiff%	CSP
2018	YAE	ROK	22	0	2	0	3	2	7²	8	1	2.3	14.1	12	50.0%	.412	1.30	7.04	47	0.3				
2018	YAW	ROK	22	0	0	0	3	3	7¹	4	0	2.5	9.8	8	68.8%	.250	0.82	1.23	74	0.2				
2018	SI	SS	22	0	1	0	2	2	8¹	4	0	2.2	10.8	10	36.8%	.211	0.72	1.08	245	-0.6				
2019	YAE	ROK	23	0	0	0	3	3	8¹	6	1	3.2	15.1	14	56.2%	.333	1.08	3.24	38	0.4				
2019	TAM	HI-A	23	4	5	0	13	12	63¹	59	2	3.4	9.8	69	54.6%	.333	1.31	3.84	84	0.7				
2019	TRN	AA	23	2	0	0	3	3	19	14	1	0.5	9.0	19	45.1%	.260	0.79	2.37	79	0.3				
2020	NYY	MLB	24	0	1	0	3	1	6¹	7	0	7.1	9.9	7	42.1%	.368	1.89	7.11	90	0.1	96.4	54.0%	21.8%	48.4%
2021 FS	NYY	MLB	25	8	9	0	26	26	150	147	26	4.1	8.8	146	39.9%	.295	1.44	5.05	111	0.1	96.4	54.0%	21.8%	48.4%
2021 DC	NYY	MLB	25	5	6	0	19	19	93	91	16	4.1	8.8	91	39.9%	.295	1.44	5.05	111	0.4	96.4	54.0%	21.8%	48.4%

Comparables: Dillon Peters, Jonathan Loaisiga, Elieser Hernandez

Schmidt made his debut in 2020, becoming the first person from Acworth, Georgia to reach the majors. Acworth has a rich and storied history but is more recently known as the city where several scenes from the 2011 version of *Footloose* were filmed. Schmidt's dream isn't to break free of a strict minister who won't allow dancing in his small town, but to break into the Yankees' rotation. And he isn't being held back from that dream by a man of the cloth, but rather, by the need for more reps, something he was unable to get last year thanks to shuttering of the minors. We'll see if the Yankees let Schmidt cut loose and kick off his Sunday shoes, or if they'll be Reverend Shaw Moore to his Ren McCormack and keep him burning, yearning and punching his card in the minors for another year.

Luis Severino RHP Born: 02/20/94 Age: 27 Bats: R Throws: R Height: 6'2" Weight: 218 Origin: International Free Agent, 2011

YEAR	TEAM	LVL	AGE	W	L	SV	G	GS	IP	H	HR	BB/9	K/9	K	GB%	BABIP	WHIP	ERA	DRA-	WARP	MPH	FA%	Whiff%	CSP
2018	NYY	MLB	24	19	8	0	32	32	191¹	173	19	2.2	10.3	220	41.5%	.315	1.14	3.39	62	5.6	99.4	50.5%	26.9%	51.2%
2019	NYY	MLB	25	1	1	0	3	3	12	6	0	4.5	12.8	17	37.5%	.250	1.00	1.50	83	0.2	98.0	56.6%	27.5%	47.1%
2021 FS	NYY	MLB	27	10	7	0	26	26	150	130	21	2.7	10.5	175	41.7%	.293	1.17	3.44	81	2.7	99.2	51.2%	26.9%	50.7%
2021 DC	NYY	MLB	27	5	4	0	16	16	82	71	11	2.7	10.5	95	41.7%	.293	1.17	3.44	81	1.7	99.2	51.2%	26.9%	50.7%

Comparables: Germán Márquez, Aaron Nola, Yovani Gallardo

Despite the 1.50 ERA and the absurd 35 percent strikeout rate in three starts to close out 2019, there were warning signs about Severino's health that, in retrospect, made the forearm soreness he suffered from in the postseason and the subsequent Tommy John surgery he underwent in spring more predictable. His velocity was down to its pre-2018 levels, his command looked shaky and perhaps worst of all, he was more tentative about using his devastating slider. Severino's rehab is going well, but he still isn't expected back in pinstripes until June or July of 2021. He has thrown a combined 20 1/3 innings in the regular season and postseason in the last two years, so it's to be determined what he'll have to offer once he returns.

Masahiro Tanaka RHP Born: 11/01/88 Age: 32 Bats: R Throws: R Height: 6'3" Weight: 218 Origin: International Free Agent, 2014

YEAR	TEAM	LVL	AGE	W	L	SV	G	GS	IP	H	HR	BB/9	K/9	K	GB%	BABIP	WHIP	ERA	DRA-	WARP	MPH	FA%	Whiff%	CSP
2018	NYY	MLB	29	12	6	0	27	27	156	141	25	2.0	9.2	159	47.5%	.286	1.13	3.75	88	2.5	93.6	31.5%	29.5%	44.0%
2019	NYY	MLB	30	11	9	0	32	31	182	186	28	2.0	7.4	149	47.5%	.293	1.24	4.45	101	1.6	93.4	32.0%	23.5%	46.7%
2020	NYY	MLB	31	3	3	0	10	10	48	48	9	1.5	8.2	44	42.7%	.291	1.17	3.56	93	0.6	93.9	32.1%	29.7%	44.7%
2021 FS	NYY	MLB	32	9	8	0	26	26	150	143	24	2.1	8.3	138	45.1%	.285	1.19	3.68	89	2.0	93.6	31.9%	26.3%	45.6%

Comparables: Michael Pineda, James Shields, Ricky Nolasco

When the Yankees inked Tanaka to a seven-year, $155 million pact in January of 2014, the expectation was that he would follow in the footsteps of CC Sabathia, Andy Pettitte and Mike Mussina (among others) and be the next great Yankees ace. Instead, Tanaka has been more of a reliable and dependable mainstay than a frontline arm. This isn't a knock on Tanaka. For a pitcher who eschewed Tommy John surgery way back in 2014 in favor of PRP injections, his results have been quite admirable. Tanaka found some of his lost velocity by throwing his fastball less frequently, and while the formula worked for him for years, his recent launch angle and batted ball trends aren't encouraging. Nevertheless, he fits the part as a solid mid-rotation option, and as of press time, he was in line to cash in as a free agent.

Miguel Yajure RHP Born: 05/01/98 Age: 23 Bats: R Throws: R Height: 6'1" Weight: 175 Origin: International Free Agent, 2015

YEAR	TEAM	LVL	AGE	W	L	SV	G	GS	IP	H	HR	BB/9	K/9	K	GB%	BABIP	WHIP	ERA	DRA-	WARP	MPH	FA%	Whiff%	CSP
2018	CSC	LO-A	20	4	3	0	14	14	64²	64	3	2.1	7.8	56	50.3%	.316	1.22	3.90	104	0.2				
2019	TAM	HI-A	21	8	6	0	22	18	127²	110	5	2.0	8.6	122	54.8%	.301	1.08	2.26	78	1.8				
2019	TRN	AA	21	1	0	0	2	2	11	9	0	1.6	9.0	11	35.5%	.290	1.00	0.82	104	0.0				
2020	NYY	MLB	22	0	0	0	3	0	7	3	1	6.4	10.3	8	40.0%	.143	1.14	1.29	93	0.1	93.9	50.0%	22.0%	43.5%
2021 FS	NYY	MLB	23	1	1	0	57	0	50	51	9	3.4	7.9	43	38.2%	.291	1.41	5.07	112	-0.2	93.9	50.0%	22.0%	43.5%
2021 DC	NYY	MLB	23	1	1	0	34	0	36	36	7	3.4	7.9	31	38.2%	.291	1.41	5.07	112	0.0	93.9	50.0%	22.0%	43.5%

Comparables: Jonathan Hernández, Rony García, Zack Littell

Yajure impressed in his major-league debut despite reduced velocity from the year prior. Like many Yankee pitching prospects pressed into service in 2020, he needs more minor-league reps. Should all go well—and it seldom does, in baseball or life—he could become a back-end starter.

TAMPA BAY RAYS

Essay by Elizabeth Strom

Player comments by Tommy Rancel and BP staff

In 1921, a Swiss doctor named Hermann Rorschach published a book called *Psychodiagnostik*. In it, he explained how the images patients perceived in inkblots could offer insight into their personalities. The inkblot test became one of the primary projective personality tests—so-called because test-takers project their feelings onto these images—used by psychologists. When you look at this image do you see a butterfly or a wolf? Your response provides insight into your thought processes and, indeed, your worldview. Sports, and particularly fandom, tend to produce the same effect. The Tampa Bay Rays are baseball's Rorschach test. What you see when you look at them—their small payroll; their shifted fielders; their mix-and-match lineups—tells us something about you and your baseball *Weltanschauung.*

Maybe you see an easy-to-love scrappy melding of young talent, overlooked veterans and lottery-ticket minor-league signees rehabbing from their third Tommy John surgery. Despite the lack of pedigree, these guys somehow manage to be competitive. Over the past 13 seasons, the team has fallen below .500 just four times, two of those just barely under.

Maybe you see an innovative front office. The Rays were early adopters of an analytically driven approach to baseball. They shifted their infield before everyone was doing it—they'll throw a fourth outfielder out there, too, if the data suggest that's where the ball is going. Thanks to the Rays we have a whole new set of pitching roles. The opener. The bulk guy. The as of yet unlabeled lights-out reliever who is not the closer because you use him at the game's highest-leverage point and not exclusively in the ninth inning. They were the first (and perhaps still the only) team to put an analyst in uniform so he could be part of the coaching staff, ensuring that manager Kevin Cash is never more than two steps away from the best research possible.

Do you see a fox head or a jack-o-lantern in this inkblot? Maybe you see a team that is making baseball unwatchable. Their decisions are always data-driven. They aren't going to pay someone to be a good clubhouse guy. They don't care that you like watching name-brand workhorse starters grit their way through nine innings if data suggest that a no-name reliever provides the better eighth-inning matchup. The Rays have been accused of removing the "human

TAMPA BAY RAYS PROSPECTUS
2020 W-L: 40-20, 1ST IN AL EAST

Pythag	.606	3rd	dWin%	.495	13th
RS/G	4.82	12th	B-Age	27.6	7th
RA/G	3.82	4th	P-Age	28.4	17th
DRC+	94	21st	FIP	4.03	7th
DRA-	88	5th	DER	.698	18th
Payroll	$29M	28th	M$/MW	$0.5M	1st

- Opened 1990
- Dome
- Synthetic surface
- Fence profile: 5' to 11'5"

Three-Year Park Factors

Runs	Runs/RH	Runs/LH	HR/RH	HR/LH
95	95	97	97	95

Top Hitter WARP	1.2 Brandon Lowe
Top Pitcher WARP	1.4 Tyler Glasnow
Top Prospect	Wander Franco

Payroll History (in millions)

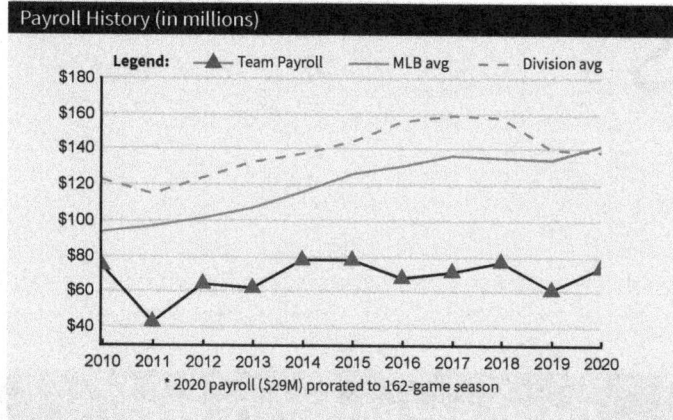

Legend: ▲ Team Payroll — MLB avg - - Division avg

* 2020 payroll ($29M) prorated to 162-game season

Future Commitments (in millions)

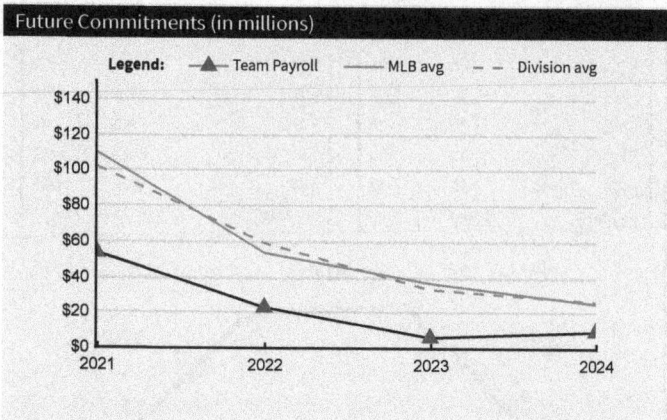

Legend: ▲ Team Payroll — MLB avg - - Division avg

Farm System Ranking

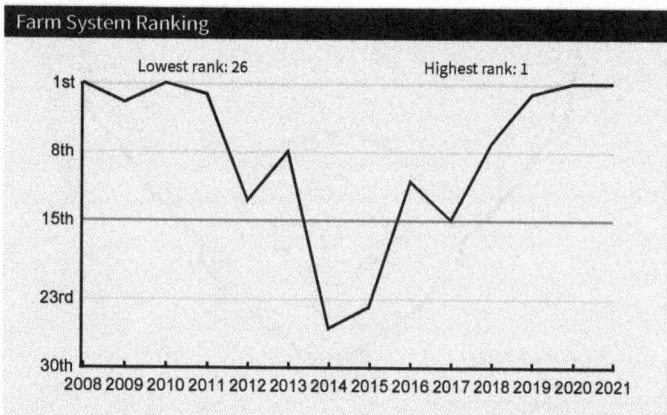

Lowest rank: 26   Highest rank: 1

Personnel

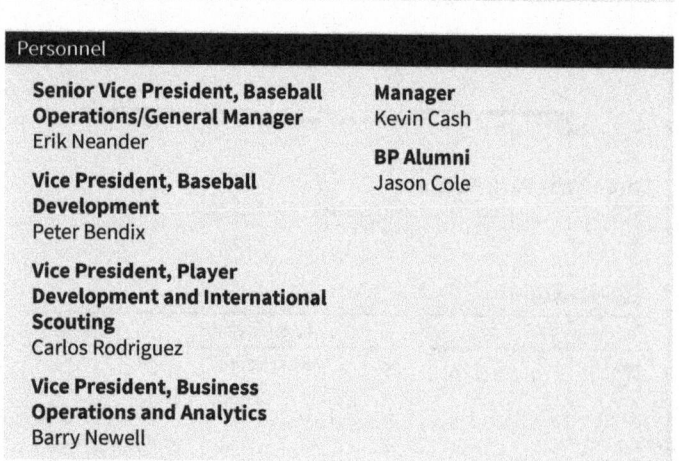

Senior Vice President, Baseball Operations/General Manager
Erik Neander

Vice President, Baseball Development
Peter Bendix

Vice President, Player Development and International Scouting
Carlos Rodriguez

Vice President, Business Operations and Analytics
Barry Newell

Manager
Kevin Cash

BP Alumni
Jason Cole

element" (as though that no-name reliever is not also human!) or of playing an "aesthetically displeasing" brand of baseball.

Perhaps you see stingy owners who lead the perennial push to gain advantage over players who are one bad knee away from career's end. The Rays seldom compete aggressively for top free agents. They dump players as soon as they get the slightest bit expensive in arbitration. Solid major-leaguers like Corey Dickerson or Jake Odorizzi who provide value but not surplus value are disposed of for B-list minor leaguers. The very creativity that has marked the Rays' success also serves to undercut players' financial security. Pitchers, for example, get rewarded for metrics like games started and games saved; dispensing with starters and closers gives you an undifferentiated group of pitchers who will never have the leverage to demand higher salaries. And the Rays ability to succeed by taking advantage of hungry, low-salaried players creates a narrative further damaging to players' collective interests. Maybe you cringe when commentators note that some well-compensated but underperforming veteran "earns more than the entire Rays lineup!" the implication being that the underperforming veteran is the problem in this picture. Do you see a butterfly or a crab?

Or are you haunted by the monstrosity that appears if you try to see both? If those inkblots are ambiguous to disinterested observers, imagine how they look to emotionally invested Rays fans. Do they see a beloved home team giving some sense of belonging to a fragmented and footloose region? Or are the Rays just an asset from which out-of-town billionaires draw profit? This is a team that often plays great baseball, has provided Tampa Bay residents with elite performances and great sports moments. But thanks to the front office's approach to payroll, Rays fans will probably never get to see a star retire or a player go into the Hall of Fame with the "TB" on his cap. Rays fans do, indeed, root for laundry; it's almost a wonder they bother to stitch names on the back. And if the usual indignities of small-market fandom were not enough, the team's ownership announced last year that it intends to pursue a novel "sister city" concept in which the team will split its time between the not-very-good baseball market of Tampa Bay and the not-very-good baseball market of Montreal. Ownership has tried to sell this as a blessing, but fans recognize that it's just another quest for surplus value.

⚾   ⚾   ⚾

What is not up for interpretation is this: the 2020 Rays were a very good team. They won their division; their 40-20 record was second best in the majors. They won their Wild Card series with ease and triumphed in tense elimination games against the Yankees and Astros to reach the World Series. Yet they have no player under consideration for any end-of-season awards. Only manager Kevin Cash was recognized, handily winning the American League Manager of the Year Award.

The Rays' success should not have been a surprise. They finished 2019 with 96 wins. Pre-season, PECOTA projected them for 87 wins and the first AL wild card. They have a core of players who have proven their worth. Blake Snell was just a year off his Cy Young Award; Austin Meadows, Brandon Lowe and Charlie Morton had been 2019 All-Stars; Kevin Kiermaier has been a perennial Gold Glove center fielder whose spectacular catches and outfield assists are frequent highlight-reel features.

But the Rays won games with the help of many players who could not meet even the most generous definition of a "star." They did it, for the most part, with pretty good run prevention, giving up the fourth-fewest runs in the majors. And they did it with just enough hitting: 13th in team ops, 14th in home runs, 12th in runs scored.

As a team, they struck out a lot (highest rate in the majors), and walked a fair amount (fourth highest rate in the majors). Their 80 home runs were average for the league, but they outslugged the competition in the postseason with 34 home runs. Their offense was led by second baseman Brandon Lowe, who built on his strong 2019 rookie performance to show continued power that seems surprising given his slender build. He had a .285 ISO and wRC+ 150 through the regular season although he slumped badly in the postseason. His opposite was Yandy Díaz, known for arms that look like tree trunks, who, in an injury-shortened season, demonstrated a great eye but no power at all. His final offensive line included an impressive .428 OBP, alongside a head-scratching .079 ISO.

And in September they had Randy.

Randy Arozarena was acquired in a somewhat surprising offseason trade with the St. Louis Cardinals. The Rays are known for trading away established stars and getting cost-controlled prospects in return—Austin Meadows, Tyler Glasnow and Willy Adames are among the products of such transactions. But the trade with St. Louis involved Matthew Libertore, a hard-throwing 2018 first-round pick, a rare instance when the Rays traded a high-ceiling prospect for players able to help the team immediately. Arozarena, who had debuted late in 2019, joined the Rays at the end of August and started his assault on major-league pitching. He hit for average and power, and then chewed through pitchers named Cole, McCullers and Greinke to break several postseason records.

The Rays' success, however, was based on preventing runs more than scoring them. They fielded the ball well, although various defensive metrics are split on their team defense (SDI metrics used to assess Gold Glove awards loved their outfield but not the infield; as a team they were league best in UZR/150 but just fifth in DRS). They had some good starting pitching, but their starters did not shine in the regular season. No starting pitcher logged even 60 innings. Yonny Chirinos left for season-ending surgery; both Charlie Morton and Ryan Yarbrough lost weeks to injury. Tyler Glasnow's start was slowed by an early positive COVID-19 test. Blake Snell reported no health issues but seemed thrown off by the interrupted season and needed to be built up very slowly. Of their 60 regular season games, 11 (18 percent) were essentially bullpen days.

The success of the 2020 Rays largely rested on that bullpen, which posted a 3.37 ERA and 3.65 FIP. Their success is all the more impressive because some three-quarters of the projected Opening Day bullpen spent time on the Injured List, a good number of those (Chaz Roe, Colin Poche, Jalen Beeks and Andrew Kittridge) were deemed out for the season. Few of us had Ryan Sherriff, a 30-year-old journeyman who missed all of 2019, pitching meaningful innings in 2020. The bullpen wasn't, however, built entirely with spare parts. Nick Anderson had proven himself in 2019 and he had a strong if injury-shortened regular season with a 0.55 ERA, although his less effective postseason had many unfortunate repercussions. Other high-leverage arms included Diego Castillo, who struggled with control and got a bit lucky to end up with a 1.66 ERA, and Pete Fairbanks, whose 13.6 strikeouts-per-nine rate suggested he'd finally harnessed his swing-and-miss stuff. Despite the reliance on the pen, Cash was able to distribute the workload evenly and avoid overusing anyone; no pitcher was used three days in a row. Expanded rosters helped the Rays ensure that they always had a fresh arm on hand.

⚾   ⚾   ⚾

A team that is more than the sum of its parts needs a manager who melds those parts into an effective collective. As the unassuming manager of a small-market team Kevin Cash may (at least prior to his World Series appearances and Manager of the Year victory) not be known at all but if he's known for anything it's his willingness to pull his starter early. Cash has been the Rays manager for six seasons; in all that time Rays pitchers have pitched two complete games, both coming in the early years of his tenure. To be sure complete games are down across baseball (from 104 in 2015 to 45 in 2019), but Cash is at the cutting edge of this rotation management trend.

Cash has each game mapped out and knows more or less when he will turn it over to his bullpen. He believes strongly in the times through the order penalty, but he also looks at matchups as well as a starter's effectiveness. Game situation is always a factor. If his team is trailing a flailing starter may get more rope. If his team is winning he will maximize matchup advantage without regard to anyone's feelings. It's fair to guess that if we are to see another Rays complete game under Cash it will happen in a Rays loss.

He does not believe that "but he's dealing!" is a reason to change plans. In 2019, he pulled starter Ryan Yarborough one out short of a complete game 1-0 victory. As you might imagine, baseball observers had some feelings about that move, but Cash believed right-handed closer Emilio Pagán had a better shot at getting that last out against Seattle's right-handed hitting Domingo Santana. For a team in the wild card hunt, increasing the chances of winning was more important than the individual accomplishment of a complete game.

Those who have watched Cash, daily, escort grumbling starters from the mound in the fifth or sixth inning were therefore the least shocked by the postseason decisions that left the rest of the baseball world reaching for smelling salts. In must-win Game 7 of the ALDS, with Morton shutting down the Astros in the sixth inning, Cash went to his bullpen. The Rays went on to win that game (although it should be noted that Nick Anderson, who replaced Morton, did give up two runs). In a similar situation in must-win Game 6 of the World Series Cash infamously replaced an even more dominant Snell. This time, when Anderson faltered, it cost them the lead and eventually the game and the series. Cash has been criticized for that move; in an interview he said that even his young daughters are still angry at him. But the poor results in that moment don't discredit the process. When in the lead Cash always prefers to remove his starter before, and not after things start to fall apart. In that instance, one could argue, his mistake was not that he trusted the data that suggested removing Snell. It was that he ignored the data showing that Nick Anderson was not that Unlabeled Lights Out Guy at the moment, having been called on too many times. That game notwithstanding, results suggest his approach works more often than not. The 2020 Rays lost just once in the regular season when ahead after six innings.

⚾   ⚾   ⚾

Looking ahead to 2021, the Rays are well-positioned to contend. Pandemic-induced financial insecurity still hangs over baseball, and could be especially hard on teams with puny revenue streams, already operating on thinner margins. Conversely small-market teams could feel less impact on their bottom line since they earn less from the ticket sales and sponsorships affected by empty stadiums. This could level the financial playing field to where teams like the Rays can compete for free agents.

The Rays will have a core of young players returning in 2021 and may see the promotion of the next wave of budding stars, including top prospect Wander Franco. Their competitive window would seem to be wide open. But when the postseason ended, the Rays announced that they would not pick up the team options on catcher Mike Zunino and, most notably, Charlie Morton, who was scheduled to earn (and projected to deserve) $15 million. (Morton instead signed with the Braves, on a one-year deal worth that exact amount.) For two seasons Morton had been the highly respected and very effective elder statesman of the pitching staff, the man who won elimination games in both 2019 and 2020. A veteran with a World Series ring to his name, if anyone on the pitching staff had the standing to grumble about those Cash early hooks it was Morton, but he accepted Cash's choices with grace. Morton was even photographed sweeping up the clubhouse after his teammates' postseason clinching party left a mess. (Now there's a good clubhouse guy!) But remember, the Rays don't pay for clubhouse guys, or for veteran poise or even, apparently, for a still very good curveball.

Do you see dancing elephants or a tarantula? Charlie Morton, after all, is a 37-year-old who missed part of the shortened 2020 with a sore shoulder. Are the Rays the penny-pinching organization that let him walk, or the keen analysts who are already eyeing the unheralded non-roster invitee who will replace his production in 2021? ■

—Elizabeth Strom is a writer and editor for DRaysBay.

HITTERS

Willy Adames SS   Born: 09/02/95   Age: 25   Bats: R   Throws: R   Height: 6'0"   Weight: 210   Origin: International Free Agent, 2015

YEAR	TEAM	LVL	AGE	PA	R	2B	3B	HR	RBI	BB	K	SB	CS	Whiff%	AVG/OBP/SLG	DRC+	BABIP	BRR	FRAA	WARP
2018	DUR	AAA	22	278	36	9	5	4	34	27	66	3	3		.286/.353/.412	109	.367	1.5	SS(62): 2.4	1.5
2018	TB	MLB	22	323	43	7	0	10	34	31	95	6	5	27.7%	.278/.348/.406	100	.378	2.3	SS(75): -6.7, 2B(10): 1.7	1.2
2019	TB	MLB	23	584	69	25	1	20	52	46	153	4	2	27.2%	.254/.317/.418	93	.320	2.9	SS(152): 12.2	3.8
2020	TB	MLB	25	205	29	15	1	8	23	20	74	2	1	38.7%	.259/.332/.481	88	.388	1.2	SS(53): 2.5	0.5
2021 FS	TB	MLB	25	600	67	24	2	20	72	60	198	4	1	30.7%	.243/.324/.412	100	.348	0.4	SS 6, 2B 0	2.6
2021 DC	TB	MLB	25	574	64	23	2	19	69	58	190	4	1	30.7%	.243/.324/.412	100	.348	0.4	SS 6	2.5

Comparables: Bobby Crosby, Jhonny Peralta, Addison Russell

The last hope for salvaging the David Price trade, Adames is holding up his end of the bargain by becoming a quality everyday shortstop. Always somewhat of a maverick in the field, he is a plus defender at the six who has cut down some of his riskier attempts. At the dish, Adames showed more power at the expense of his strikeout rate. We'll see if that's a legit trend or a byproduct of trying to make up for lost time. Yes, Wander Franco, Xavier Edwards and others are in the system, but don't overlook how good Adames has become.

★ ★ ★ 2021 Top 101 Prospect #20 ★ ★ ★

Randy Arozarena LF   Born: 02/28/95   Age: 26   Bats: R   Throws: R   Height: 5'11"   Weight: 185   Origin: International Free Agent, 2016

YEAR	TEAM	LVL	AGE	PA	R	2B	3B	HR	RBI	BB	K	SB	CS	Whiff%	AVG/OBP/SLG	DRC+	BABIP	BRR	FRAA	WARP
2018	SPR	AA	23	102	22	5	0	7	21	6	25	9	3		.396/.455/.681	193	.492	1.0	RF(12): 1.6, CF(6): -0.4, LF(5): 0.9	1.3
2018	MEM	AAA	23	311	42	16	0	5	28	28	59	17	5		.232/.328/.348	81	.278	0.8	LF(49): -2.7, RF(18): 0.2, CF(10): -0.9	-0.5
2019	SPR	AA	24	116	14	7	2	3	15	13	23	8	5		.309/.422/.515	160	.380	-0.5	CF(13): 0.9, LF(5): 0.0, RF(5): -0.7	0.9
2019	MEM	AAA	24	283	51	18	2	12	38	24	48	9	7		.358/.435/.593	154	.404	-1.2	CF(25): -3.4, RF(20): 4.6, LF(14): 0.5	2.7
2019	STL	MLB	24	23	4	1	0	1	2	2	4	2	1	25.0%	.300/.391/.500	84	.333	-1.7	RF(6): -0.1, CF(5): 0.5, LF(1): -0.1	-0.1
2020	TB	MLB	25	76	15	2	0	7	11	6	22	4	0	36.8%	.281/.382/.641	115	.306	0.5	LF(14): -0.4, RF(3): -0.3, CF(2): 0.1	0.4
2021 FS	TB	MLB	26	600	79	25	2	24	73	49	159	14	5	34.8%	.251/.341/.446	116	.315	0.2	LF -3, CF 0	2.7
2021 DC	TB	MLB	26	574	76	24	2	23	69	47	152	13	5	34.8%	.251/.341/.446	116	.315	0.2	LF -3	2.5

Comparables: Brandon Jones, Dwight Smith, Chris Pettit

In the span of a few months, Arozarena emerged from relative obscurity to author one of the greatest postseasons in the history of the sport. He then followed up that run with something more serious and concerning: an arrest in Mexico after a domestic dispute with his ex-partner concerning their child. She later chose to not press charges.

Mike Brosseau 3B   Born: 03/15/94   Age: 27   Bats: R   Throws: R   Height: 5'10"   Weight: 205   Origin: Undrafted Free Agent, 2016

YEAR	TEAM	LVL	AGE	PA	R	2B	3B	HR	RBI	BB	K	SB	CS	Whiff%	AVG/OBP/SLG	DRC+	BABIP	BRR	FRAA	WARP
2018	MTG	AA	24	417	53	24	3	13	61	29	74	11	4		.262/.327/.449	114	.290	1.4	3B(64): 3.7, 2B(16): 0.0, 1B(10): -0.2	1.6
2019	DUR	AAA	25	315	53	21	1	16	60	34	58	2	3		.304/.394/.567	134	.332	0.9	3B(32): -1.3, 1B(17): -1.1, 2B(7): -0.5	2.0
2019	TB	MLB	25	142	17	7	0	6	16	7	39	1	0	25.5%	.273/.319/.462	92	.345	1.0	2B(26): -0.5, 3B(18): -0.6, RF(6): -0.6	0.3
2020	TB	MLB	26	98	12	5	1	5	12	8	31	2	0	36.1%	.302/.378/.558	105	.412	-0.1	1B(12): 1.1, 3B(11): 2.0, 2B(9): -0.5	0.5
2021 FS	TB	MLB	27	600	72	24	2	22	73	43	167	6	3	30.7%	.250/.323/.429	106	.321	-1.8	2B 0, 3B 1	1.7
2021 DC	TB	MLB	27	202	24	8	0	7	24	14	56	2	1	30.7%	.250/.323/.429	106	.321	-0.6	2B 0, 3B 0	0.6

Comparables: Andy Tracy, Luke Hughes, Danny Espinosa

In 2016, there were 1,216 players drafted. None of them were Brosseau. Proving that you can't keep a lion away from the hunt, he's turned himself into a solid little player with hard work and a little luck. He also provided one of the pivotal moments in the 2020 postseason when he delivered a series-clinching home run off Aroldis Chapman—the same Chapman who had directed a purpose pitch his way earlier in the way. Lions don't bring the cantaloupe, they go and get the antelope. For as long as Brosseau can pair his above-average stick with a versatile glove, he's going to have a spot on someone's roster.

★ ★ ★ 2021 Top 101 Prospect #67 ★ ★ ★

Vidal Bruján 2B   Born: 02/09/98   Age: 23   Bats: S   Throws: R   Height: 5'10"   Weight: 180   Origin: International Free Agent, 2014

YEAR	TEAM	LVL	AGE	PA	R	2B	3B	HR	RBI	BB	K	SB	CS	Whiff%	AVG/OBP/SLG	DRC+	BABIP	BRR	FRAA	WARP
2018	BG	LO-A	20	434	86	18	5	5	41	48	53	43	15		.313/.395/.427	140	.351	8.2	2B(87): 4.4	4.0
2018	CHA	HI-A	20	114	26	7	2	4	12	15	15	12	4		.347/.434/.582	164	.380	1.0	2B(24): 4.5	1.4
2019	CHA	HI-A	21	196	28	8	3	1	15	17	26	24	5		.290/.357/.386	131	.333	5.5	2B(29): 0.7, SS(14): 0.7	2.0
2019	MTG	AA	21	233	28	9	4	3	25	20	35	24	8		.266/.336/.391	95	.304	-2.6	2B(33): 2.7, SS(15): -0.1	0.6
2021 FS	TB	MLB	23	600	61	27	5	10	59	44	110	30	12		.247/.310/.371	86	.293	0.9	2B 15, SS 0	2.7
2021 DC	TB	MLB	23	67	6	3	0	1	6	4	12	3	1		.247/.310/.371	86	.293	0.1	2B 2	0.3

Comparables: Steve Lombardozzi, Corban Joseph, Jose Altuve

Hold with us for a sentence as we make a tenuous reference based on the spelling of two individuals' names. Ready? Here goes. According to the internet, the late author Gore Vidal once said that he died a little whenever a friend succeeded. Rays infield prospects like Mr. Brujan can probably relate. It's not enough that the Rays have Willy Adames and Brandon Lowe entrenched as their big-league double-play combination; they also have Wander Franco, Greg Jones, Xavier Edwards and other top-shelf youngsters jockeying for position on their organizational depth chart. That can make it difficult for anyone else to stand out. Brujan does, however, thanks to a pair of above-average tools (hit and speed). Lest any other Rays infielder feel gutted by our praise of Brujan, we'll end by noting that his defense is such that he could end up on the grass. See? Doesn't that make you feel a little better?

Ji-Man Choi 1B   Born: 05/19/91   Age: 30   Bats: L   Throws: R   Height: 6'1"   Weight: 260   Origin: International Free Agent, 2009

YEAR	TEAM	LVL	AGE	PA	R	2B	3B	HR	RBI	BB	K	SB	CS	Whiff%	AVG/OBP/SLG	DRC+	BABIP	BRR	FRAA	WARP
2018	RMV	AAA	27	163	17	9	0	5	23	32	31	1	0		.302/.436/.488	143	.358	0.2	1B(38): -2.0, LF(1): 0.1	0.6
2018	DUR	AAA	27	86	9	4	0	2	14	11	18	0	0		.270/.360/.405	119	.327	-0.9	1B(18): 0.2, LF(2): -0.0	0.1
2018	TB	MLB	27	189	21	12	1	8	27	24	41	2	0	27.5%	.269/.370/.506	110	.310	1.9	1B(1): -0.0	0.7
2018	MIL	MLB	27	32	4	2	0	2	5	2	14	0	0	40.3%	.233/.281/.500	103	.357	0.3	1B(2): 0.0, LF(1): -0.0	0.1
2019	TB	MLB	28	487	54	20	2	19	63	64	108	2	3	25.5%	.261/.363/.459	116	.303	-2.6	1B(103): -4.4	1.1
2020	TB	MLB	29	145	16	13	0	3	16	20	36	0	0	31.8%	.230/.331/.410	100	.291	-0.2	1B(38): -1.8	0.1
2021 FS	TB	MLB	30	600	73	26	1	20	69	78	155	3	1	27.7%	.230/.338/.410	107	.289	-1.3	1B 0, LF 0	1.2
2021 DC	TB	MLB	30	473	57	21	1	16	54	62	122	3	1	27.7%	.230/.338/.410	107	.289	-1.1	1B 0	1.0

Comparables: Derrek Lee, Tony Clark, Richie Sexson

The most interesting man in the Tampa Bay area (at least for several months of the year), Choi decided to hit right-handed in a big-league game in 2020 just to see what it was like. He went 3 for 11 during his experiment, including a memorable home run—that may not sound like much, but again, he did this on a whim. Choi later became the first Korean-born player to record a hit in the World Series. In between, he made a number of defensive highlight reels thanks to some, uh, aesthetically surprising flexibility that allows him to get into the split position for picks. You can understand, then, why Rays fans are smitten with Choi. The Rays Way often prioritizes efficiency above all else; we'll see if Choi's personality permits him to be the exception.

Yandy Díaz 3B Born: 08/08/91   Age: 29   Bats: R   Throws: R   Height: 6'2"   Weight: 215   Origin: International Free Agent, 2013

YEAR	TEAM	LVL	AGE	PA	R	2B	3B	HR	RBI	BB	K	SB	CS	Whiff%	AVG/OBP/SLG	DRC+	BABIP	BRR	FRAA	WARP
2018	COL	AAA	26	426	53	24	0	3	40	70	75	2	3		.293/.409/.388	144	.360	-2.6	3B(73): -9.6, 1B(12): 0.2	1.5
2018	CLE	MLB	26	120	15	5	2	1	15	11	19	0	0	16.3%	.312/.375/.422	102	.371	-2.0	1B(9): 0.2, 3B(9): 0.2	0.1
2019	TB	MLB	27	347	53	20	1	14	38	35	61	2	2	22.3%	.267/.340/.476	107	.288	-0.5	3B(50): -0.9, 1B(22): -0.1	1.2
2020	TB	MLB	29	138	16	3	0	2	11	23	17	0	0	15.7%	.307/.428/.386	106	.347	-0.4	3B(25): -1.0, 1B(2): -0.1	0.2
2021 FS	TB	MLB	29	600	75	27	2	11	59	81	108	2	1	19.3%	.281/.383/.409	122	.337	-0.1	3B -4, 1B 1	2.6
2021 DC	TB	MLB	29	405	50	18	1	7	40	55	73	1	0	19.3%	.281/.383/.409	122	.337	-0.1	3B -3, 1B 1	1.6

Comparables: Brook Jacoby, Corey Koskie, Bill Sudakis

The Rays acquired Díaz before the 2019 season because of his penchant for hitting the ball hard. The idea was that if they could just get some lift in his swing, Diaz would greatly improve his slugging in part by smoking some pitches over the wall. It was a decent notion, and it worked somewhat in 2019. But in 2020? It did not work at all. Díaz put two-thirds of his batted balls on the ground, resulting in a negative launch angle. His offensive numbers were saved by a good average and a healthy walk rate, but it's a little hard to get juiced for a slow singles hitter without a true defensive home. Having big muscles makes for a cool aesthetic, but so does hitting home runs. The Rays would probably like more of the latter from Díaz in 2021.

★ ★ ★ *2021 Top 101 Prospect* **#93** ★ ★ ★

Xavier Edwards SS Born: 08/09/99   Age: 21   Bats: S   Throws: R   Height: 5'10"   Weight: 175   Origin: Round 1, 2018 Draft (#38 overall)

YEAR	TEAM	LVL	AGE	PA	R	2B	3B	HR	RBI	BB	K	SB	CS	Whiff%	AVG/OBP/SLG	DRC+	BABIP	BRR	FRAA	WARP
2018	SD1	ROK	18	88	19	4	1	0	11	13	10	12	1		.384/.471/.466	193	.438	1.9	SS(15): 3.1	1.2
2018	TRI	SS	18	107	21	4	0	0	5	18	15	10	0		.314/.438/.360	179	.380	-0.3	SS(19): -1.1, 2B(5): -0.0	0.7
2019	FW	LO-A	19	344	44	13	4	1	30	30	35	20	9		.336/.392/.414	141	.371	0.2	2B(51): 4.1, SS(21): 3.1	3.4
2019	LE	HI-A	19	217	32	5	4	0	13	14	19	14	2		.301/.349/.367	101	.331	3.5	2B(36): 0.2, SS(9): -1.2	0.9
2021 FS	TB	MLB	21	600	54	25	3	5	53	44	114	22	7		.273/.330/.366	93	.335	4.3	2B 5, SS 1	2.6

Comparables: José Ramírez, Jorge Polanco, Asdrúbal Cabrera

The dangers of the internet age—and especially the social media age—is that sometimes thoughts that should remain private are expressed publicly. Take, for instance, Blake Snell's raw reaction to the Tommy Pham trade. Snell, who was streaming on Twitch at the time, was dejected that the Rays would move one of their most productive hitters for—among other players—a "slapdick prospect." (Imagine explaining that sentence to Jim Leyland.) It was a funny moment, but it undersells Edwards' ability. He's a potential leadoff hitter, complete with plus bat-to-ball skills and elite speed, who has a chance to remain at shortstop. That's a good player, and one who will have an obvious Players' Weekend nickname once he reaches the Show.

★ ★ ★ *2021 Top 101 Prospect* **#1** ★ ★ ★

Wander Franco SS Born: 03/01/01   Age: 20   Bats: S   Throws: R   Height: 5'10"   Weight: 189   Origin: International Free Agent, 2017

YEAR	TEAM	LVL	AGE	PA	R	2B	3B	HR	RBI	BB	K	SB	CS	Whiff%	AVG/OBP/SLG	DRC+	BABIP	BRR	FRAA	WARP
2018	PRN	ROK	17	273	46	10	7	11	57	27	19	4	3		.351/.418/.587	179	.346	-0.4	SS(53): -5.3	1.6
2019	BG	LO-A	18	272	42	16	5	6	29	30	20	14	9		.318/.390/.506	158	.318	0.1	SS(53): -1.0	2.6
2019	CHA	HI-A	18	223	40	11	2	3	24	26	15	4	5		.339/.408/.464	175	.346	4.3	SS(45): 8.1	3.9
2021 FS	TB	MLB	20	600	63	28	5	11	64	38	88	9	7		.265/.315/.394	95	.298	-6.7	SS 6	1.5
2021 DC	TB	MLB	20	67	7	3	0	1	7	4	9	1	0		.265/.315/.394	95	.298	-0.7	SS 1	0.2

Comparables: Jurickson Profar, Carlos Correa, Ronald Torreyes

Welcome to the 2021 edition of the *Baseball Prospectus Annual*. Wander Franco is still the game's top prospect. Had he played in a regular minor-league season in 2020, he would've likely posted above-average statistics despite being young for his league. He would've made dazzling plays at shortstop thanks to his strong arm and ample range, showed off a plus hit tool from both sides and tapped into his raw power enough to encourage. We would've been noting that, yup, all indications are Franco is a future superstar. Hopefully we'll get to see his talents in the majors once the Rays are done manipulating his service time.

Heriberto Hernandez C Born: 12/16/99   Age: 21   Bats: R   Throws: R   Height: 6'1"   Weight: 180   Origin: International Free Agent, 2017

YEAR	TEAM	LVL	AGE	PA	R	2B	3B	HR	RBI	BB	K	SB	CS	Whiff%	AVG/OBP/SLG	DRC+	BABIP	BRR	FRAA	WARP
2018	DSL RAN2	ROK	18	239	56	15	5	12	49	53	41	5	5		.292/.464/.635	198	.315	0.5	1B(26): -1.5, C(14): 0.8	2.4
2019	RAN	ROK	19	224	42	17	4	11	48	27	57	3	3		.344/.433/.646	176	.440	0.3	RF(18): -1.3, 1B(13): 1.5, C(11): -0.2	1.9
2019	SPO	SS	19	10	4	0	0	0	1	2	3	3	0		.375/.500/.375	163	.600	0.7	RF(1): -0.2	0.1
2021 FS	TB	MLB	21	600	47	27	4	8	50	47	211	7	3		.199/.268/.310	59	.306	-0.4	1B -1, C 0	-1.9

Comparables: Austin Meadows, Oswaldo Arcia, Joc Pederson

It's considered gauche to heap praise on first-base prospects barely out of rookie ball. It's okay in this case, because Hernandez can't really play first base, either; the Rangers moved him around between catcher, left, and first. While ordinarily that might be distracting, Hernandez never stopped hitting, which is probably all he'll be asked to do at the major league level. The Rangers gave him a spot on the alternate site despite his youth, and the limited nature of the practice probably didn't hurt him. To sum up, what you have is a youngster with huge offensive potential who offers very little by way of defense. The Rays will surely put his dynamic bat to use somehow following their acquisition of Hernandez in a deal for Nate Lowe.

Ronaldo Hernández C Born: 11/11/97 Age: 23 Bats: R Throws: R Height: 6'1" Weight: 230 Origin: International Free Agent, 2014

YEAR	TEAM	LVL	AGE	PA	R	2B	3B	HR	RBI	BB	K	SB	CS	Whiff%	AVG/OBP/SLG	DRC+	BABIP	BRR	FRAA	WARP
2018	BG	LO-A	20	449	68	20	1	21	79	31	69	10	4		.284/.339/.494	132	.292	-0.8	C(85): 1.2	2.8
2019	CHA	HI-A	21	427	43	19	3	9	60	17	65	7	0		.265/.299/.397	105	.290	1.8	C(81): 1.9	2.3
2021 FS	TB	MLB	23	600	64	27	2	18	68	32	133	3	1		.243/.292/.395	87	.289	-0.8	C 0	1.4
2021 DC	TB	MLB	23	67	7	3	0	2	7	3	14	0	0		.243/.292/.395	87	.289	-0.1	C 0	0.2

Comparables: Travis d'Arnaud, Jesús Sucre, John Ryan Murphy

Hernandez has a strong arm behind the dish and plus power potential at it. The other aspects of his game need further refinement, which explains why he didn't appear in the majors despite being part of the Rays' 60-player pool and traveling with the taxi squad on a few road trips.

Kevin Kiermaier CF Born: 04/22/90 Age: 31 Bats: L Throws: R Height: 6'1" Weight: 210 Origin: Round 31, 2010 Draft (#941 overall)

YEAR	TEAM	LVL	AGE	PA	R	2B	3B	HR	RBI	BB	K	SB	CS	Whiff%	AVG/OBP/SLG	DRC+	BABIP	BRR	FRAA	WARP
2018	TB	MLB	28	367	44	12	9	7	29	25	91	10	5	30.5%	.217/.282/.370	76	.275	3.1	CF(88): 12.3	1.8
2019	TB	MLB	29	480	60	20	7	14	55	26	104	19	5	25.2%	.228/.278/.398	74	.267	1.9	CF(125): 6.0	1.0
2020	TB	MLB	30	159	16	5	3	3	22	20	42	8	1	30.5%	.217/.321/.362	77	.290	0.1	CF(46): -1.2	0.2
2021 FS	TB	MLB	31	600	60	20	6	15	63	49	151	20	7	27.7%	.220/.294/.366	80	.277	4.3	CF 10	1.9
2021 DC	TB	MLB	31	405	40	13	4	10	42	33	102	13	5	27.7%	.220/.294/.366	80	.277	2.9	CF 7	1.3

Comparables: Peter Bourjos, Austin Jackson, Cito Gaston

There's a case to be made that Kiermaier's 2020 was his best season in years. At minimum, he had his best offensive showing since 2017 thanks to a career-high walk rate. Kiermaier's approach was more disciplined than we're accustomed to seeing from him, and the gains in on-base percentage were enough to offset a similar uptick in strikeout rate. He also avoided the injured list for the first time since 2015. That's probably just a byproduct of the short season, as Kiermaier remains a walking—well, usually a diving or leaping—highlight reel in center field whose tendency to throw caution to the wind is both a blessing and a curse. His altered offensive philosophy suggests that he's capable of greater discernment on one end, though, so perhaps he's learning how to pace himself so that he does not erase himself from the lineup for weeks at a time.

Brandon Lowe 2B Born: 07/06/94 Age: 27 Bats: L Throws: R Height: 5'10" Weight: 185 Origin: Round 3, 2015 Draft (#87 overall)

YEAR	TEAM	LVL	AGE	PA	R	2B	3B	HR	RBI	BB	K	SB	CS	Whiff%	AVG/OBP/SLG	DRC+	BABIP	BRR	FRAA	WARP
2018	MTG	AA	23	240	37	17	1	8	41	35	55	8	2		.291/.400/.508	157	.360	2.1	LF(26): 1.8, 2B(24): -3.2	1.7
2018	DUR	AAA	23	205	36	14	0	14	35	22	47	0	1		.304/.380/.613	171	.339	0.4	2B(31): 1.2, LF(13): 0.9	2.1
2018	TB	MLB	23	148	16	6	2	6	25	16	38	2	1	36.7%	.233/.324/.450	93	.279	0.8	2B(28): -0.6, LF(11): -0.3, RF(5): -0.1	0.3
2019	TB	MLB	24	327	42	17	2	17	51	25	113	5	0	37.8%	.270/.336/.514	107	.377	2.4	2B(69): 3.3, 1B(5): -0.8, RF(5): -0.5	1.7
2020	TB	MLB	26	224	36	9	2	14	37	25	58	3	0	35.8%	.269/.362/.554	127	.309	2.7	2B(44): -5.4, RF(7): 0.8, LF(5): -0.1	1.2
2021 FS	TB	MLB	26	600	81	25	3	29	82	57	169	3	1	36.8%	.247/.327/.473	115	.305	1.3	2B 0, LF 0	3.3
2021 DC	TB	MLB	26	473	64	19	2	23	64	44	133	2	1	36.8%	.247/.327/.473	115	.305	1.0	2B 0, LF 0	2.6

Comparables: Yoán Moncada, Jason Bay, Pete Incaviglia

Lowe was an All-Star during the first half of 2019, and he played like one again during the half-but-actually-whole 2020 campaign. Postseason struggles aside, he was the Rays' best offensive player for most of the year. Indeed, over his last 551 plate appearances, Lowe has put together a line of .270/.347/.530 with 61 extra-base hits (31 of those being home runs)—not bad for someone with the ability to play at second base or in either corner outfield spot. He's locked into a multi-year deal that will pay him $20.5 million over the next four seasons, with a pair of club options after that. Because it's the Rays, there's a strong chance he's traded before those option decisions are due—just don't expect a deal to come anytime soon.

Josh Lowe CF Born: 02/02/98 Age: 23 Bats: L Throws: R Height: 6'4" Weight: 205 Origin: Round 1, 2016 Draft (#13 overall)

YEAR	TEAM	LVL	AGE	PA	R	2B	3B	HR	RBI	BB	K	SB	CS	Whiff%	AVG/OBP/SLG	DRC+	BABIP	BRR	FRAA	WARP
2018	CHA	HI-A	20	455	62	25	3	6	47	47	117	18	6		.238/.322/.361	95	.318	1.1	CF(102): 4.1	0.8
2019	MTG	AA	21	519	70	23	4	18	62	59	132	30	9		.252/.341/.442	128	.316	5.6	CF(110): -7.0, RF(9): 2.2, LF(1): -0.2	3.3
2021 FS	TB	MLB	23	600	60	26	3	16	64	59	212	13	5		.222/.302/.373	86	.333	0.7	CF -1, RF 0	0.8

Comparables: Michael Saunders, Luis Robert, Chris Young

This Lowe, Tampa Bay's top pick in 2016, should make his big-league debut in 2021. There are star-caliber tools here, but there's a good chance he's not going to hit enough against big-league pitching to make the most of them.

Manuel Margot CF Born: 09/28/94 Age: 26 Bats: R Throws: R Height: 5'11" Weight: 180 Origin: International Free Agent, 2011

YEAR	TEAM	LVL	AGE	PA	R	2B	3B	HR	RBI	BB	K	SB	CS	Whiff%	AVG/OBP/SLG	DRC+	BABIP	BRR	FRAA	WARP
2018	SD	MLB	23	519	50	26	8	8	51	32	88	11	10	20.8%	.245/.292/.384	84	.281	0.9	CF(136): -4.9	0.4
2019	SD	MLB	24	441	59	19	3	12	37	38	88	20	4	23.1%	.234/.304/.387	79	.272	4.5	CF(135): -4.6	0.5
2020	TB	MLB	26	159	19	9	0	1	11	13	25	12	4	23.7%	.269/.327/.352	86	.317	-0.4	CF(21): 2.2, LF(18): 1.5, RF(15): 0.2	0.4
2021 FS	TB	MLB	26	600	61	26	5	12	63	44	111	17	6	22.7%	.249/.309/.385	91	.292	2.4	CF -2	1.3
2021 DC	TB	MLB	26	506	51	22	4	10	53	37	94	14	5	22.7%	.249/.309/.385	91	.292	2.1	CF -2, RF -2	0.6

Comparables: Ángel Pagán, Leonys Martin, Cory Sullivan

Margot once seemed destined to become a star in San Diego. He did just that last October—though, unfortunately for the Padres, he did it while playing neutral-site playoff games for the Rays. After homering once during the regular season, he jumped the fence five times in the playoffs, including three times during the AL Championship Series. Of course, the Rays weren't employing Margot because of his power; rather, they were employing him because of his speed and his defense. He delivered in both regards, stealing 12 bases in 16 tries and playing some quality D across the outfield. The Rays always seem to have an excess of outfielders, but Margot fared well enough to earn a second year playing on the turf in St. Pete.

Austin Meadows RF Born: 05/03/95 Age: 26 Bats: L Throws: L Height: 6'3" Weight: 225 Origin: Round 1, 2013 Draft (#9 overall)

YEAR	TEAM	LVL	AGE	PA	R	2B	3B	HR	RBI	BB	K	SB	CS	Whiff%	AVG/OBP/SLG	DRC+	BABIP	BRR	FRAA	WARP
2018	IND	AAA	23	179	27	13	0	2	21	9	24	11	1		.279/.318/.394	150	.314	2.4	CF(22): -1.5, LF(18): 0.1, RF(3): -0.4	1.3
2018	DUR	AAA	23	106	19	11	0	10	22	8	13	1	1		.344/.396/.771	146	.311	-1.6	CF(17): -1.2, RF(4): -0.2, LF(2): -0.0	0.4
2018	TB	MLB	23	26	3	1	0	1	4	2	5	1	0	22.7%	.250/.308/.417	95	.278	-0.1	RF(7): -1.4, LF(1): -0.0	-0.1
2018	PIT	MLB	23	165	16	8	2	5	13	8	35	4	1	19.5%	.292/.327/.468	95	.345	-1.1	CF(15): -0.7, RF(13): -1.1, LF(12): 0.0	0.1
2019	TB	MLB	24	591	83	29	7	33	89	54	131	12	7	23.5%	.291/.364/.558	134	.331	-3.5	RF(57): -3.5, LF(34): 4.6, CF(3): -0.0	3.7
2020	TB	MLB	25	152	19	8	1	4	13	17	50	2	1	31.4%	.205/.296/.371	87	.287	0.3	LF(23): -0.8, RF(4): 0.2	0.0
2021 FS	TB	MLB	26	600	78	25	5	24	68	51	163	12	4	25.1%	.245/.316/.448	105	.306	3.3	RF -10, LF 0	1.4
2021 DC	TB	MLB	26	540	70	22	4	22	61	46	147	10	4	25.1%	.245/.316/.448	105	.306	3.0	RF -9	1.0

Comparables: Yasiel Puig, Bobby Bonds, Danny Tartabull

Meadows tested positive for COVID-19 during the summer, sidelining him for the onset of the season. Perhaps he was still feeling the effects of the virus upon his return, or perhaps he had accumulated too much rust because of the odd circumstances. Whatever the case, he had a miserable season—a far cry from the 2019 performance that earned him MVP consideration. Meadows struck out in nearly a third of his plate appearances while losing nearly 100 points of ISO. We're willing to give him the benefit of the doubt, but another down season and he might find himself fighting for everyday at-bats on an ever-deep Rays roster.

Francisco Mejía C Born: 10/27/95 Age: 25 Bats: S Throws: R Height: 5'8" Weight: 188 Origin: International Free Agent, 2012

YEAR	TEAM	LVL	AGE	PA	R	2B	3B	HR	RBI	BB	K	SB	CS	Whiff%	AVG/OBP/SLG	DRC+	BABIP	BRR	FRAA	WARP
2018	COL	AAA	22	336	32	22	1	7	45	18	58	0	0		.279/.328/.426	101	.321	-1.2	C(41): 4.6, LF(22): -3.2, RF(7): -1.0	0.7
2018	ELP	AAA	22	132	22	8	1	7	23	7	25	0	0		.328/.364/.582	121	.359	0.7	C(26): 1.3	0.9
2018	CLE	MLB	22	4	0	0	0	0	0	2	0	0	0	33.3%	.000/.500/.000	69	.000			0.0
2018	SD	MLB	22	58	6	2	0	3	8	3	19	0	0	28.3%	.185/.241/.389	72	.219	0.2	C(10): -1.7	-0.1
2019	ELP	AAA	23	73	14	8	2	4	12	5	10	0	0		.365/.411/.746	136	.365	-1.0	C(16): 2.6	0.8
2019	SD	MLB	23	244	27	11	2	8	22	13	56	1	1	25.8%	.265/.316/.438	90	.319	2.0	C(60): -0.6, LF(4): 0.3	1.0
2020	SD	MLB	25	42	5	1	0	1	2	1	9	0	0	24.5%	.077/.143/.179	79	.069	0.4	C(16): 0.3	0.1
2021 FS	TB	MLB	25	600	65	21	2	21	72	34	142	1	0	25.8%	.232/.286/.397	87	.272	1.4	C 2, 3B 0	1.7
2021 DC	TB	MLB	25	304	33	10	1	11	36	17	72	0	0	25.8%	.232/.286/.397	87	.272	0.7	C 1	0.9

Comparables: Tony Wolters, Randy Hundley, John Rabb

When the Padres first traded Brad Hand (and Adam Cimber) for Mejía, it looked like highway robbery. Trading a reliever a rebuilding team doesn't need in exchange for a premium catching prospect? That's a no-brainer. Now it looks like the Padres are fortunate it was a low-risk deal, because it appears that Cleveland received the better end of the trade. Hand has continued to excel while Mejía has struggled to gain traction. Even if you dismiss his horrid slash line as an aberration, he's struggled defensively to the extent that a position change would be justifiable. The problem is he hasn't hit well enough to play anywhere else. Mejía will enter 2021 with yet another shot at playing time in Tampa Bay, following the trade that sent Blake Snell to the Padres. He'll battle Mike Zunino for playing time out of the gate.

YEAR	TEAM	P. COUNT	FRM RUNS	BLK RUNS	THRW RUNS	TOT RUNS
2018	SD	1506	-0.7	-0.8	0.0	-1.5
2019	SD	7679	-0.8	0.1	-0.5	-1.2
2019	ELP	2100	1.9	0.0	0.0	1.9
2020	SD	1616	-0.4	-0.1	0.0	-0.5
2021	TB	10822	-1.6	0.3	0.1	-1.2

Brett Phillips RF Born: 05/30/94   Age: 27   Bats: L   Throws: R   Height: 6'0"   Weight: 195   Origin: Round 6, 2012 Draft (#189 overall)

YEAR	TEAM	LVL	AGE	PA	R	2B	3B	HR	RBI	BB	K	SB	CS	Whiff%	AVG/OBP/SLG	DRC+	BABIP	BRR	FRAA	WARP
2018	RMV	AAA	24	299	42	12	7	6	25	36	94	11	0		.240/.331/.411	75	.346	1.1	RF(34): 2.9, CF(20): -1.8, LF(13): -0.2	-0.2
2018	MIL	MLB	24	24	2	0	1	0	4	2	11	0	0	38.9%	.182/.250/.273	42	.364	0.0	RF(7): -0.6, CF(5): 0.5, LF(2): -0.0	-0.1
2018	KC	MLB	24	123	13	4	2	2	7	9	50	1	1	36.0%	.188/.252/.312	45	.311	0.3	CF(23): 4.4, RF(9): 0.3, LF(1): -0.0	0.1
2019	OMA	AAA	25	414	75	8	13	18	54	72	118	22	1		.240/.378/.505	108	.312	3.0	RF(63): 9.4, CF(32): -1.1, LF(3): 0.6	2.5
2019	KC	MLB	25	79	7	2	0	2	6	10	23	3	0	31.2%	.138/.247/.262	76	.167	1.2	CF(23): 1.0, LF(3): 0.5, RF(3): 2.0	0.5
2020	KC	MLB	26	34	8	0	1	1	2	3	8	3	1	31.6%	.226/.294/.387	96	.273	-0.1	CF(11): 0.4, LF(4): 0.2, RF(4): -0.2	0.1
2020	TB	MLB	26	25	2	0	1	1	3	5	7	3	0	41.7%	.150/.320/.400	92	.167	0.4	RF(9): -0.5, CF(4): 0.2, LF(3): 0.0	0.0
2021 FS	*TB*	*MLB*	*27*	*600*	*67*	*22*	*7*	*18*	*64*	*68*	*200*	*8*	*1*	*34.6%*	*.215/.311/.391*	*93*	*.308*	*9.1*	*RF 2, CF 1*	*2.4*
2021 DC	*TB*	*MLB*	*27*	*168*	*18*	*6*	*2*	*5*	*17*	*19*	*56*	*2*	*0*	*34.6%*	*.215/.311/.391*	*93*	*.308*	*2.5*	*RF 1, CF 0*	*0.7*

Comparables: Gary Pettis, Kimera Bartee, Michael Bourn

Before Phillips became the unlikely hero of World Series Game 4, his most memorable moment with the Rays was when he defeated Randy Arozarena in a dance-off outside of Citi Field following Tampa Bay's division-clinching victory. Nearly a month later, the two combined for the Game 4 walk-off victory that left Rays fans doing the electric slide. The whole thing had to be extra special for Phillips, who went to high school just 14 miles away from Tropicana Field, and who had joined Tampa Bay at the deadline to serve as a pinch-runner and defensive sub. If nothing else, it reminded people why baseball is such a great game, even during otherwise trying times: from the unremarkable can come the incredibly fun.

Yoshi Tsutsugo LF Born: 11/26/91   Age: 29   Bats: L   Throws: R   Height: 6'1"   Weight: 225   Origin: International Free Agent, 2019

YEAR	TEAM	LVL	AGE	PA	R	2B	3B	HR	RBI	BB	K	SB	CS	Whiff%	AVG/OBP/SLG	DRC+	BABIP	BRR	FRAA	WARP
2020	TB	MLB	29	185	27	5	1	8	24	26	50	0	0	23.2%	.197/.314/.395	101	.230	0.6	LF(16): -1.3, 3B(14): -1.5	0.1
2021 FS	*TB*	*MLB*	*29*	*600*	*73*	*26*	*1*	*20*	*72*	*68*	*165*			*23.2%*	*.224/.319/.397*	*96*	*.286*			*1.5*
2021 DC	*TB*	*MLB*	*29*	*405*	*49*	*17*	*1*	*13*	*48*	*46*	*111*			*23.2%*	*.224/.319/.397*	*96*	*.286*		*3B 0*	*0.7*

The Rays signed Tsutsugo to a two-year deal with the belief that his ample left-handed power would be great enough to warrant a spot in the lineup regardless of what position he played (and, to be certain, he isn't much of a fielder anywhere). The 29-year-old showed flashes of that plus pop and hit the ball hard with regularity, but it did not translate into enough actual production to cover his lack of defensive value. Additionally, his lack of speed limited the value of his 14 percent walk rate. By the playoffs he was relegated to mostly pinch-hitting duties and the occasional start at DH toward the bottom of the lineup. The Rays must be hoping the positive underlying metrics relative to hitting the ball hard will play out better over the course over a longer season in Tsutsugo's second year stateside.

Joey Wendle 2B Born: 04/26/90   Age: 31   Bats: L   Throws: R   Height: 6'1"   Weight: 195   Origin: Round 6, 2012 Draft (#203 overall)

YEAR	TEAM	LVL	AGE	PA	R	2B	3B	HR	RBI	BB	K	SB	CS	Whiff%	AVG/OBP/SLG	DRC+	BABIP	BRR	FRAA	WARP
2018	TB	MLB	28	545	62	33	6	7	61	37	96	16	4	20.7%	.300/.354/.435	107	.353	3.7	2B(100): 5.8, 3B(20): 1.4, LF(16): -2.4	3.2
2019	TB	MLB	29	263	32	13	2	3	19	14	47	8	3	20.3%	.231/.293/.340	81	.272	-0.2	2B(48): 4.1, 3B(27): -1.1, SS(10): -0.0	0.6
2020	TB	MLB	30	184	24	9	2	4	17	10	35	8	2	18.9%	.286/.342/.435	91	.338	-0.6	3B(28): 2.3, 2B(20): 0.4, SS(10): 1.9	0.7
2021 FS	*TB*	*MLB*	*31*	*600*	*61*	*30*	*4*	*12*	*64*	*31*	*125*	*8*	*2*	*19.9%*	*.258/.312/.394*	*92*	*.314*	*3.2*	*3B 8, 2B 4*	*2.9*
2021 DC	*TB*	*MLB*	*31*	*439*	*44*	*22*	*3*	*8*	*47*	*23*	*91*	*6*	*1*	*19.9%*	*.258/.312/.394*	*92*	*.314*	*2.3*	*3B 6, 2B 3*	*1.9*

Comparables: Robby Thompson, Tadahito Iguchi, Brandon Phillips

Wendle doesn't make much hard contact, but he makes a lot of contact in general and is a capable and versatile defender. His best role remains as a rover who can play three infield positions and some corner outfield while providing more bat-to-ball skills than most of his peers. Wendle is going to continue to draw the superlatives associated with generic-looking white players—gritty, scrappy and so on—yet that shouldn't detract from the value he's provided and should continue to provide to the Rays until they deem his cost to exceed his production. Given that he'll be heading for his second arbitration heading after the 2021 season, that could be, oh, any month now.

Mike Zunino C Born: 03/25/91   Age: 30   Bats: R   Throws: R   Height: 6'2"   Weight: 235   Origin: Round 1, 2012 Draft (#3 overall)

YEAR	TEAM	LVL	AGE	PA	R	2B	3B	HR	RBI	BB	K	SB	CS	Whiff%	AVG/OBP/SLG	DRC+	BABIP	BRR	FRAA	WARP
2018	SEA	MLB	27	405	37	18	0	20	44	24	150	0	0	37.8%	.201/.259/.410	82	.268	-2.2	C(111): 6.4	1.6
2019	TB	MLB	28	289	30	10	1	9	32	20	98	0	0	38.6%	.165/.232/.312	56	.220	-1.5	C(89): 8.3	0.5
2020	TB	MLB	29	84	8	4	0	4	10	6	37	0	0	40.2%	.147/.238/.360	69	.206	-1.3	C(28): 0.8	-0.2
2021 FS	*TB*	*MLB*	*30*	*600*	*70*	*27*	*1*	*27*	*73*	*48*	*234*	*0*	*0*	*38.7%*	*.208/.289/.418*	*89*	*.305*	*-1.1*	*C 3*	*1.9*
2021 DC	*TB*	*MLB*	*30*	*304*	*35*	*13*	*0*	*14*	*37*	*24*	*118*	*0*	*0*	*38.7%*	*.208/.289/.418*	*89*	*.305*	*-0.6*	*C 2*	*1.0*

Comparables: Jarrod Saltalamacchia, Tyler Flowers, John Russell

YEAR	TEAM	P. COUNT	FRM RUNS	BLK RUNS	THRW RUNS	TOT RUNS
2018	SEA	14832	7.5	-1.1	0.4	6.8
2019	TB	11033	7.0	1.7	1.1	9.8
2020	TB	3613	-1.1	-0.6	0.1	-1.7
2021	*TB*	*10822*	*4.6*	*-1.1*	*-0.2*	*3.2*

Sometimes it doesn't pay to go home. The Rays had Zunino return to Florida for a second season with the hope that he would solve their seemingly never-ending quest for a legitimate starting backstop. In the end, they received two years of him hitting .161/.233/.323 with a strikeout rate nearing 40 percent. Despite a batting line that smelled like yesterday, Zunino was still able to make a cool $9 million. Though they declined his $4.5 million team option for 2021, the Rays brought him back into the fold for a less-cool $1.5 million less than that. The lesson here is to forget about having your kid learn to throw lefty; just toss them a catcher's mitt and a copy of Mike Fast's framing articles if you want to set them up for life.

PITCHERS

Nick Anderson RHP Born: 07/05/90 Age: 31 Bats: R Throws: R Height: 6'4" Weight: 205 Origin: Round 32, 2012 Draft (#995 overall)

YEAR	TEAM	LVL	AGE	W	L	SV	G	GS	IP	H	HR	BB/9	K/9	K	GB%	BABIP	WHIP	ERA	DRA-	WARP	MPH	FA%	Whiff%	CSP
2018	ROC	AAA	27	8	2	4	39	4	60	49	8	2.9	13.2	88	28.9%	.323	1.13	3.30	55	1.7				
2019	MIA	MLB	28	2	4	1	45	0	43²	40	5	3.3	14.2	69	28.0%	.368	1.28	3.92	70	0.9	97.3	55.9%	35.3%	47.8%
2019	TB	MLB	28	3	0	0	23	0	21¹	12	3	0.8	17.3	41	32.4%	.290	0.66	2.11	15	1.1	97.8	69.0%	43.1%	53.4%
2020	TB	MLB	29	2	1	6	19	0	16¹	5	1	1.7	14.3	26	20.7%	.143	0.49	0.55	81	0.3	96.4	65.0%	36.9%	45.1%
2021 FS	*TB*	*MLB*	*30*	*3*	*2*	*14*	*57*	*0*	*50*	*35*	*7*	*2.4*	*12.7*	*70*	*30.2%*	*.271*	*0.97*	*2.33*	*59*	*1.3*	*97.2*	*61.1%*	*37.7%*	*48.4%*
2021 DC	*TB*	*MLB*	*30*	*3*	*2*	*14*	*62*	*0*	*66*	*46*	*9*	*2.4*	*12.7*	*92*	*30.2%*	*.271*	*0.97*	*2.33*	*59*	*1.8*	*97.2*	*61.1%*	*37.7%*	*48.4%*

Comparables: Ken Giles, Chad Green, Emilio Pagán

The Rays did not employ a traditional closer in 2020, but it was Anderson who was used most often in the highest-leverage situations. After striking out 42 percent of batters faced in 2019, he struck out a higher percentage last year with fewer walks and home runs allowed. The formula was simple: mix two-thirds fastballs with one-third curveballs and serve hot. That was regular-season Anderson, the one who also battled inflammation in his right arm. The other version, the October one, had a miserable playoff run, becoming the first pitcher to allow a run in seven straight appearances. He walked more batters and surrendered more home runs in the playoffs than he did during the regular season and he later admitted he was fatigued. Despite those circumstances, Anderson is one of the true relief aces in baseball when he's hearty and hale.

★ ★ ★ *2021 Top 101 Prospect* **#24** ★ ★ ★

Shane Baz RHP Born: 06/17/99 Age: 22 Bats: R Throws: R Height: 6'2" Weight: 190 Origin: Round 1, 2017 Draft (#12 overall)

YEAR	TEAM	LVL	AGE	W	L	SV	G	GS	IP	H	HR	BB/9	K/9	K	GB%	BABIP	WHIP	ERA	DRA-	WARP	MPH	FA%	Whiff%	CSP
2018	BRS	ROK	19	4	3	0	10	10	45¹	45	2	4.6	10.7	54	63.0%	.344	1.50	3.97	88	0.9				
2018	PRN	ROK	19	0	2	0	2	2	7	11	1	7.7	6.4	5	48.0%	.417	2.43	7.71	282	-0.5				
2019	BG	LO-A	20	3	2	0	17	17	81¹	63	5	4.1	9.6	87	37.1%	.280	1.23	2.99	79	1.2				
2021 FS	*TB*	*MLB*	*22*	*2*	*3*	*0*	*57*	*0*	*50*	*47*	*7*	*6.2*	*8.2*	*45*	*41.4%*	*.283*	*1.64*	*5.50*	*124*	*-0.5*				

Comparables: Casey Crosby, Daniel Norris, Elvin Ramirez

Baz, the third piece of the Chris Archer return, tends to get overlooked in the deal's accounting because he hasn't yet made his big-league debut. That'll change soon enough. Baz has a high-quality fastball-slider combination that enables him to miss bats and evade barrels (he's yielded 10 homers in 157 professional innings). He's also a good athlete who has exhibited enough knowhow on the mound to like his chances of making future adjustments. Baz still needs to develop his changeup and his command, of course, but there's reason to believe he could make an already bad trade look even worse.

Jalen Beeks LHP Born: 07/10/93 Age: 27 Bats: L Throws: L Height: 5'11" Weight: 215 Origin: Round 12, 2014 Draft (#374 overall)

YEAR	TEAM	LVL	AGE	W	L	SV	G	GS	IP	H	HR	BB/9	K/9	K	GB%	BABIP	WHIP	ERA	DRA-	WARP	MPH	FA%	Whiff%	CSP
2018	WOR	AAA	24	5	5	0	16	16	87¹	70	10	2.6	12.1	117	39.8%	.300	1.09	2.89	79	1.6				
2018	TB	MLB	24	5	0	0	12	0	44¹	41	5	4.1	7.5	37	49.2%	.290	1.38	4.47	115	-0.1	93.6	42.5%	27.0%	45.0%
2018	BOS	MLB	24	0	1	0	2	1	6¹	11	1	5.7	7.1	5	33.3%	.435	2.37	12.79	167	-0.2	93.6	47.4%	20.3%	42.7%
2019	DUR	AAA	25	0	1	0	3	3	10²	8	2	3.4	8.4	10	39.3%	.231	1.12	4.22	81	0.3				
2019	TB	MLB	25	6	3	1	33	3	104¹	115	12	3.5	7.7	89	46.0%	.329	1.49	4.31	141	-1.7	94.2	43.6%	24.2%	46.1%
2020	TB	MLB	26	1	1	1	12	0	19¹	21	1	1.9	12.1	26	41.2%	.408	1.29	3.26	70	0.5	94.7	42.0%	32.9%	50.9%
2021 FS	*TB*	*MLB*	*27*	*2*	*2*	*0*	*57*	*0*	*50*	*46*	*6*	*3.5*	*9.8*	*54*	*43.9%*	*.302*	*1.31*	*3.88*	*92*	*0.4*	*94.2*	*43.3%*	*26.0%*	*46.7%*

Comparables: Anthony Banda, Walker Lockett, Drew Anderson

Beeks looked different last season—and we aren't talking about his mustache. He scrapped his curveball in favor of more cutters and changeups, and he gained a tick on his fastball, allowing him to bump the mid-90s. Correlation does not imply causation, but Beeks' elbow gave way after just 19 innings with his new look. The Rays will cross their fingers that he can make it back before the end of the 2021 campaign. A resurfacing in early 2022 seems more likely.

Nick Bitsko RHP Born: 06/16/02 Age: 19 Bats: R Throws: R Height: 6'4" Weight: 225 Origin: Round 1, 2020 Draft (#24 overall)

The idea that Bitsko was drafted based solely on some videos posted on the internet is a reach: he was *also* drafted because his name sounds like a three-year-old trying to read the branding on a package of Oreos. Either way, he was considered one of the top prospects in the 2021 class before he reclassified to 2020. The pandemic did cost teams valuable in-person looks at Bitsko, but that didn't prevent the Rays from selecting him at No. 24 based on the promise of his prototypical size and stuff. It remains to be seen if offseason shoulder surgery will threaten that promise in the short term.

Diego Castillo RHP Born: 01/18/94 Age: 27 Bats: R Throws: R Height: 6'3" Weight: 250 Origin: International Free Agent, 2014

YEAR	TEAM	LVL	AGE	W	L	SV	G	GS	IP	H	HR	BB/9	K/9	K	GB%	BABIP	WHIP	ERA	DRA-	WARP	MPH	FA%	Whiff%	CSP
2018	DUR	AAA	24	0	1	4	19	0	26¹	15	1	2.4	10.9	32	58.6%	.246	0.84	1.03	38	1.0				
2018	TB	MLB	24	4	2	0	43	11	56²	36	6	2.9	10.3	65	46.0%	.229	0.95	3.18	82	0.9	100.4	54.1%	31.4%	49.0%
2019	TB	MLB	25	5	8	8	65	6	68²	59	8	3.4	10.6	81	55.1%	.302	1.24	3.41	69	1.5	99.8	48.5%	32.7%	47.9%
2020	TB	MLB	26	3	0	4	22	0	21²	12	3	4.6	9.6	23	59.3%	.176	1.06	1.66	83	0.4	98.3	35.3%	38.2%	45.2%
2021 FS	*TB*	*MLB*	*27*	*3*	*3*	*14*	*57*	*0*	*50*	*41*	*5*	*4.2*	*10.4*	*57*	*51.6%*	*.290*	*1.30*	*3.62*	*83*	*0.6*	*99.6*	*46.6%*	*33.7%*	*47.5%*
2021 DC	*TB*	*MLB*	*27*	*3*	*3*	*14*	*62*	*0*	*66*	*54*	*6*	*4.2*	*10.4*	*76*	*51.6%*	*.290*	*1.30*	*3.62*	*83*	*1.0*	*99.6*	*46.6%*	*33.7%*	*47.5%*

Comparables: Keone Kela, Jordan Walden, Dominic Leone

You can make the case that Castillo is the most underrated piece of the Tampa Bay pitching staff. He's now turned in three seasons of 141 ERA+ ball while pitching in high-leverage spots. Because Castillo has seldom been exposed to the ninth inning—he'll enter the year with just 12 career saves—he's unlikely to get expensive until late in the arbitration process. As such, the Rays might not feel the impulse to move him in the next year or two the way they could with some of the more famous members of their relief corps. In that sense, perhaps Castillo's position underneath the radar is a bit of a blessing for the Rays, though we doubt the burly fireballer feels that way himself.

Yonny Chirinos RHP Born: 12/26/93 Age: 27 Bats: R Throws: R Height: 6'2" Weight: 225 Origin: International Free Agent, 2012

YEAR	TEAM	LVL	AGE	W	L	SV	G	GS	IP	H	HR	BB/9	K/9	K	GB%	BABIP	WHIP	ERA	DRA-	WARP	MPH	FA%	Whiff%	CSP
2018	DUR	AAA	24	0	2	0	8	8	30²	35	7	2.1	9.1	31	49.5%	.326	1.37	5.28	97	0.3				
2018	TB	MLB	24	5	5	0	18	7	89²	84	7	2.5	7.5	75	43.4%	.301	1.22	3.51	94	0.9	95.8	63.1%	24.1%	49.8%
2019	TB	MLB	25	9	5	0	26	18	133¹	112	23	1.9	7.6	113	43.4%	.245	1.05	3.85	87	2.0	96.2	56.8%	22.6%	47.8%
2020	TB	MLB	26	0	0	0	3	3	11¹	14	2	3.2	7.9	10	30.6%	.353	1.59	2.38	119	0.0	95.6	60.5%	30.1%	41.1%
2021 FS	TB	MLB	27	2	2	0	57	0	50	48	7	2.5	8.3	45	41.7%	.291	1.24	3.88	95	0.3	96.0	58.6%	23.7%	47.6%

Comparables: Joe Musgrove, Kevin Gausman, Trevor Williams

It looked like Chirinos was, at long last, going to be given a chance to perform as a traditional starter last season—an opportunity that he deserved, if you look at the stats. But Chirinos tried to succeed in the year 2020, so naturally, he landed on the injured list with a triceps issue after two turns through the rotation. He returned and made another start before a more serious ailment—a torn UCL—ended his 2020 and 2021 seasons in one swoop. He'll have celebrated two birthdays before making his next big-league pitch; we can only guess what he wishes for when he blows out those candles.

John Curtiss RHP Born: 04/05/93 Age: 28 Bats: R Throws: R Height: 6'5" Weight: 220 Origin: Round 6, 2014 Draft (#170 overall)

YEAR	TEAM	LVL	AGE	W	L	SV	G	GS	IP	H	HR	BB/9	K/9	K	GB%	BABIP	WHIP	ERA	DRA-	WARP	MPH	FA%	Whiff%	CSP
2018	ROC	AAA	25	2	4	10	38	1	55¹	41	3	5.0	9.9	61	38.1%	.268	1.30	2.77	65	1.2				
2018	MIN	MLB	25	0	1	0	8	0	6¹	8	0	5.7	9.9	7	10.5%	.421	1.89	5.68	118	0.0	95.9	65.2%	26.0%	47.3%
2019	LHV	AAA	26	0	1	0	9	1	12¹	20	5	6.6	10.9	15	35.7%	.405	2.35	10.95	190	-0.4				
2019	SL	AAA	26	2	0	1	13	0	21¹	20	4	5.5	12.2	29	41.5%	.327	1.55	5.91	80	0.5				
2019	LAA	MLB	26	0	0	0	1	0	2¹	2	0	11.6	3.9	1	50.0%	.250	2.14	3.86	143	0.0	93.9	56.2%	26.3%	35.8%
2020	TB	MLB	27	3	0	2	17	3	25	21	3	1.1	9.0	25	42.0%	.273	0.96	1.80	84	0.4	95.9	56.5%	24.4%	51.2%
2021 FS	TB	MLB	28	2	2	4	57	0	50	45	8	3.7	9.8	54	38.9%	.288	1.32	4.31	99	0.2	95.7	57.2%	24.7%	49.8%
2021 DC	TB	MLB	28	2	2	4	56	0	59	53	9	3.7	9.8	63	38.9%	.288	1.32	4.31	99	0.4	95.7	57.2%	24.7%	49.8%

Comparables: Phil Maton, Dan Altavilla, Jonathan Holder

Curtiss spent parts of the last three seasons in the majors with the Twins and Angels before fandangoing his way into the Rays depth chart in 2020. Due to myriad injuries to relievers, Curtiss was pressed into a regular role and served it well. He worked as both an opener and a standard reliever, striking out a batter per inning while keeping the bases relatively clean. Curtiss has a conventional approach, employing a fastball that creeps toward the mid-90s and a slider. Despite the lack of an offspeed item, he was actually more effective against lefties thanks to his control. To wit, Curtiss didn't walk any of the 40 left-handed batters he faced. Reverse splits without obvious explanations tend to be bugs more so than features. We'll see if Curtiss' is the exception.

Oliver Drake RHP Born: 01/13/87 Age: 34 Bats: R Throws: R Height: 6'4" Weight: 220 Origin: Round 43, 2008 Draft (#1286 overall)

YEAR	TEAM	LVL	AGE	W	L	SV	G	GS	IP	H	HR	BB/9	K/9	K	GB%	BABIP	WHIP	ERA	DRA-	WARP	MPH	FA%	Whiff%	CSP
2018	SL	AAA	31	0	0	0	6	0	7²	3	0	1.2	9.4	8	70.6%	.176	0.52	1.17	74	0.1				
2018	LAA	MLB	31	0	1	0	8	0	8²	15	2	1.0	8.3	8	38.7%	.448	1.85	5.19	69	0.2	94.2	47.1%	27.6%	49.2%
2018	TOR	MLB	31	0	0	0	2	0	1²	4	0	0.0	10.8	2	42.9%	.571	2.40	16.20	43	0.1	93.6	58.3%	20.0%	52.2%
2018	CLE	MLB	31	0	0	0	4	0	4¹	7	0	2.1	8.3	4	31.2%	.438	1.85	12.46	57	0.1	93.8	48.1%	29.7%	45.6%
2018	MIN	MLB	31	0	0	0	19	0	20¹	12	2	3.1	9.7	22	49.0%	.204	0.93	2.21	75	0.4	93.7	41.0%	27.3%	45.5%
2018	MIL	MLB	31	1	0	0	11	0	12²	14	0	5.7	10.7	15	54.3%	.412	1.74	6.39	56	0.4	93.8	49.0%	29.7%	50.6%
2019	DUR	AAA	32	1	2	6	19	2	23²	20	2	2.7	15.2	40	46.8%	.400	1.14	4.94	50	0.9				
2019	TB	MLB	32	5	2	2	50	0	56	36	9	3.1	11.2	70	51.2%	.225	0.98	3.21	64	1.4	94.9	40.7%	36.1%	48.0%
2020	TB	MLB	33	0	2	2	11	0	11	7	2	4.9	5.7	7	46.9%	.172	1.18	5.73	106	0.1	92.7	48.0%	28.6%	51.3%
2021 FS	TB	MLB	34	3	2	0	57	0	50	41	5	3.8	10.2	56	47.9%	.286	1.25	3.30	80	0.7	94.3	43.1%	32.9%	48.5%

Comparables: James Hoyt, Fernando Salas, Brad Brach

Sometimes we laugh and sometimes we cry, but we guess you know now. Drake was poised to be one of the Rays' most important relievers before his arm knew when to say when. He experienced bicep tendonitis in August before returning in mid-September, then made the ALDS roster before being removed because of a right flexor strain. The Rays booted him from the roster altogether soon after, paving his path to free agency. At his best, Drake is a reverse-split right-hander that relies heavily on his splitter. If the elbow permits, he should be able to help out another club's bullpen. There is a chance, though, that it may be so far gone that we'll look back and say nothing was the same for Drake again.

Pete Fairbanks RHP Born: 12/16/93 Age: 27 Bats: R Throws: R Height: 6'6" Weight: 225 Origin: Round 9, 2015 Draft (#258 overall)

YEAR	TEAM	LVL	AGE	W	L	SV	G	GS	IP	H	HR	BB/9	K/9	K	GB%	BABIP	WHIP	ERA	DRA-	WARP	MPH	FA%	Whiff%	CSP
2019	DE	HI-A	25	1	0	2	11	0	12¹	10	0	2.9	10.9	15	59.4%	.312	1.14	2.92	74	0.2				
2019	FRI	AA	25	1	0	0	6	0	7¹	2	0	0.0	17.2	14	70.0%	.200	0.27	0.00	35	0.3				
2019	DUR	AAA	25	1	2	0	16	1	17²	15	3	3.1	15.3	30	43.6%	.333	1.19	5.09	51	0.6				
2019	NAS	AAA	25	0	0	0	7	0	6¹	10	1	2.8	15.6	11	27.8%	.562	1.89	11.37	75	0.2				
2019	TEX	MLB	25	0	2	0	8	0	8²	8	4	7.3	15.6	15	42.1%	.267	1.73	9.35	77	0.1	99.2	51.5%	41.0%	44.1%
2019	TB	MLB	25	2	1	2	13	0	12¹	17	1	2.2	9.5	13	42.9%	.390	1.62	5.11	98	0.1	99.3	38.0%	29.1%	50.5%
2020	TB	MLB	26	6	3	0	27	2	26²	23	2	4.7	13.2	39	48.4%	.350	1.39	2.70	66	0.7	99.1	57.6%	37.4%	42.1%
2021 FS	TB	MLB	27	3	3	8	57	0	50	41	6	4.4	11.5	63	44.1%	.299	1.33	3.95	90	0.4	99.1	52.9%	36.3%	44.0%
2021 DC	TB	MLB	27	3	3	8	62	0	66	55	8	4.4	11.5	84	44.1%	.299	1.33	3.95	90	0.7	99.1	52.9%	36.3%	44.0%

Comparables: Michael Feliz, Phil Maton, Dovydas Neverauskas

Remember the scene in *Home Alone* when Macaulay Culkin puts the aftershave on his face? Remember his expression? That's the face Fairbanks makes anytime he's on the mound. Fairbanks throws really hard and is generally effective at getting outs, but his wide-eyed aesthetic is bound to inspire doubts from now until the day he hangs them up. The Rays probably won't mind too much so long as he keeps chucking his fastball in the upper-90s and breaking off nasty sliders. His command still isn't great and probably never will be, but he should continue to get looks in high-leverage situations—even if his eyes suggest he shouldn't.

Josh Fleming LHP Born: 05/18/96 Age: 25 Bats: R Throws: L Height: 6'2" Weight: 220 Origin: Round 5, 2017 Draft (#139 overall)

YEAR	TEAM	LVL	AGE	W	L	SV	G	GS	IP	H	HR	BB/9	K/9	K	GB%	BABIP	WHIP	ERA	DRA-	WARP	MPH	FA%	Whiff%	CSP
2018	BG	LO-A	22	6	1	0	10	10	60	41	1	1.5	6.3	42	56.1%	.234	0.85	1.20	77	1.1				
2018	CHA	HI-A	22	3	3	0	9	7	50¹	51	4	1.6	6.8	38	44.7%	.301	1.19	4.11	70	1.1				
2019	MTG	AA	23	11	4	0	21	17	127²	127	9	1.3	6.5	92	51.6%	.299	1.14	3.31	96	0.3				
2019	DUR	AAA	23	1	3	0	4	3	21	24	6	3.4	6.9	16	65.2%	.286	1.52	5.14	107	0.3				
2020	TB	MLB	24	5	0	0	7	5	32¹	28	5	1.9	7.0	25	63.9%	.250	1.08	2.78	86	0.5	92.2	83.6%	21.1%	45.7%
2021 FS	TB	MLB	25	9	8	0	26	26	150	153	17	2.5	6.7	111	55.2%	.296	1.30	4.06	94	1.6	92.2	83.6%	21.1%	45.7%
2021 DC	TB	MLB	25	5	6	0	19	19	93	95	11	2.5	6.7	69	55.2%	.296	1.30	4.06	94	1.3	92.2	83.6%	21.1%	45.7%

Comparables: Nick Margevicius, David Peterson, Bernardo Flores Jr.

The cavalcade of injuries that disrupted the Rays rotation in 2020 unexpectedly pushed Fleming into big-league action. He proved that he was ready for it despite making just four appearances above Double-A prior to the season. Fleming showed poise and control that outpaced his raw stuff or experience. His low-90s sinker helped him generate a 64 percent grounder rate, and his cutter and changeup kept his platoon split in check. This being the Rays, Fleming figures to be used as a two-times-through-the-order-type moving forward—be it as a starter or as a "bulk guy."

Tyler Glasnow RHP Born: 08/23/93 Age: 27 Bats: L Throws: R Height: 6'8" Weight: 225 Origin: Round 5, 2011 Draft (#152 overall)

YEAR	TEAM	LVL	AGE	W	L	SV	G	GS	IP	H	HR	BB/9	K/9	K	GB%	BABIP	WHIP	ERA	DRA-	WARP	MPH	FA%	Whiff%	CSP
2018	PIT	MLB	24	1	2	0	34	0	56	47	5	5.5	11.6	72	55.9%	.321	1.45	4.34	64	1.4	99.3	72.5%	29.7%	46.3%
2018	TB	MLB	24	1	5	0	11	11	55²	42	10	3.1	10.3	64	43.9%	.248	1.10	4.20	81	0.9	98.9	68.2%	28.1%	48.5%
2019	TB	MLB	25	6	1	0	12	12	60²	40	4	2.1	11.3	76	50.0%	.265	0.89	1.78	56	2.0	99.3	67.3%	28.6%	49.8%
2020	TB	MLB	26	5	1	0	11	11	57¹	43	11	3.5	14.3	91	40.0%	.281	1.13	4.08	71	1.4	99.1	60.6%	32.8%	45.3%
2021 FS	TB	MLB	27	10	7	0	26	26	150	112	17	3.9	12.7	210	43.3%	.293	1.18	2.97	71	3.5	99.2	65.2%	30.5%	47.1%
2021 DC	TB	MLB	27	8	7	0	25	25	132	98	15	3.9	12.7	185	43.3%	.293	1.18	2.97	71	3.4	99.2	65.2%	30.5%	47.1%

Comparables: Lucas Sims, Robert Stephenson, Matt Wisler

There's a lot to like about Glasnow. He has an elite fastball and a Mjölnir curveball that allowed him to strike out nearly 40 percent of the batters he faced despite his predictability. And yet, so much still seems uncertain about his future production. When he's off with his stuff, even slightly, the plot can get away from him quickly. That's because Glasnow is reliant upon chases rather than well-located strikes. This approach works against most teams, but a team that has a few chess players can wait him out. It's easy to think that better control or an improved changeup is right around the bend, but he'll turn 28 before the next edition of this book comes out. As such, he seems more likely to keep up the Jekyll and Hyde thing than develop into the bonafide ace he looks to be when everything is clicking.

Brent Honeywell Jr. RHP Born: 03/31/95 Age: 26 Bats: R Throws: R Height: 6'2" Weight: 195 Origin: Round 2, 2014 Draft (#72 overall)

YEAR	TEAM	LVL	AGE	W	L	SV	G	GS	IP	H	HR	BB/9	K/9	K	GB%	BABIP	WHIP	ERA	DRA-	WARP	MPH	FA%	Whiff%	CSP
2021 FS	TB	MLB	26	9	8	0	26	26	150	134	21	2.9	9.5	157	34.5%	.287	1.22	3.72	94	1.6				
2021 DC	TB	MLB	26	3	4	0	12	12	63	56	9	2.9	9.5	66	34.5%	.287	1.22	3.72	94	0.9				

Honeywell hasn't thrown a pitch in a professional game in over three years. The hope, once again, is that he will resume his career this coming season, though he's coming off his fourth elbow surgery in that time. Give Honeywell this much: he contributed to the Rays' playoff run in his own special way, by which we mean he allowed Randy Arozarena to wear his cowboy boots. "I call them the power boots," Arozarena told MLB.com's Juan Toribio. "My teammates started telling me that those were the boots that were giving me good luck." Now, if only some of that good luck would stick to Honeywell...

Andrew Kittredge RHP Born: 03/17/90 Age: 31 Bats: R Throws: R Height: 6'1" Weight: 230 Origin: Round 45, 2008 Draft (#1360 overall)

YEAR	TEAM	LVL	AGE	W	L	SV	G	GS	IP	H	HR	BB/9	K/9	K	GB%	BABIP	WHIP	ERA	DRA-	WARP	MPH	FA%	Whiff%	CSP
2018	DUR	AAA	28	6	0	2	21	1	46	41	3	2.3	11.3	58	39.0%	.317	1.15	2.74	50	1.4				
2018	TB	MLB	28	3	2	0	33	3	38¹	54	7	4.0	7.0	30	49.6%	.376	1.85	7.75	135	-0.5	94.8	39.9%	22.5%	47.1%
2019	DUR	AAA	29	2	1	6	27	1	37¹	24	3	1.4	13.3	55	49.4%	.280	0.80	1.93	27	1.8				
2019	TB	MLB	29	1	0	0	37	7	49²	51	7	2.2	10.5	58	50.0%	.336	1.27	4.17	76	0.9	96.3	58.1%	31.5%	43.9%
2020	TB	MLB	30	0	0	1	8	1	8	8	0	2.2	3.4	3	57.7%	.308	1.25	2.25	100	0.1	95.9	47.8%	15.0%	58.1%
2021 FS	TB	MLB	31	1	1	0	57	0	50	46	6	2.5	9.3	51	47.1%	.297	1.21	3.57	85	0.6	95.9	52.3%	27.2%	46.5%
2021 DC	TB	MLB	31	1	1	0	25	0	26	24	3	2.5	9.3	26	47.1%	.297	1.21	3.57	85	0.4	95.9	52.3%	27.2%	46.5%

Comparables: Paul Sewald, Evan Marshall, Jacob Barnes

Baseball can be such a cruel game sometimes. Kittredge earned a save on Monday, August 11, and then served as an opener the next night. Five pitches into that "start," he departed with a torn UCL. If he's lucky, and if he heals quickly, his next big-league outing should come late in the 2021 season.

Aaron Loup LHP Born: 12/19/87 Age: 33 Bats: L Throws: L Height: 5'11" Weight: 210 Origin: Round 9, 2009 Draft (#280 overall)

YEAR	TEAM	LVL	AGE	W	L	SV	G	GS	IP	H	HR	BB/9	K/9	K	GB%	BABIP	WHIP	ERA	DRA-	WARP	MPH	FA%	Whiff%	CSP
2018	PHI	MLB	30	0	0	0	9	0	4	4	0	2.2	4.5	2	69.2%	.308	1.25	4.50	155	-0.1	92.3	60.3%	15.2%	51.5%
2018	TOR	MLB	30	0	0	0	50	0	35²	44	4	3.3	10.6	42	48.1%	.385	1.60	4.54	102	0.1	94.0	66.1%	27.4%	49.5%
2019	SD	MLB	31	0	0	0	4	0	3¹	2	0	2.7	13.5	5	57.1%	.286	0.90	0.00	90	0.0	93.2	43.4%	32.0%	48.4%
2020	TB	MLB	32	3	2	0	24	0	25	17	3	1.4	7.9	22	39.4%	.230	0.84	2.52	90	0.4	94.2	49.9%	19.8%	54.7%
2021 FS	TB	MLB	33	2	2	0	57	0	50	45	5	3.0	9.2	51	47.3%	.298	1.25	3.73	89	0.4	94.0	55.5%	22.9%	52.4%

Comparables: Ryan Tepera, Jeremy Jeffress, Anthony Bass

Loup wasn't projected to be anything more than organizational depth when he signed a minor-league deal with the Rays. Then a pandemic happened and half of the bullpen blew out their elbows. Loup ended up throwing more innings in the regular season for Tampa Bay than Diego Castillo, Jalen Beeks, Nick Anderson, Yonny Chirinos, Oliver Drake, Colin Poche, Chaz Roe and Jose Alvarado. Keeping it simple with a low-90s fastball or a cutter nine times out of 10, he worked efficiently and without much traffic. Most importantly, he showed an ability to hang in there against righties—that alone should be enough to net him a big-league deal by the time you pick up this book.

★　★　★ *2021 Top 101 Prospect* **#80** ★　★　★

Shane McClanahan LHP Born: 04/28/97 Age: 24 Bats: L Throws: L Height: 6'1" Weight: 200 Origin: Round 1, 2018 Draft (#31 overall)

YEAR	TEAM	LVL	AGE	W	L	SV	G	GS	IP	H	HR	BB/9	K/9	K	GB%	BABIP	WHIP	ERA	DRA-	WARP	MPH	FA%	Whiff%	CSP
2018	PRN	ROK	21	0	0	0	2	2	4	2	0	2.2	15.8	7	50.0%	.333	0.75	0.00	99	0.1				
2018	RAY	ROK	21	0	0	0	2	2	3	1	0	0.0	18.0	6	50.0%	.250	0.33	0.00	36	0.1				
2019	BG	LO-A	22	4	4	0	11	10	53	38	3	5.3	12.6	74	47.5%	.304	1.30	3.40	78	0.8				
2019	CHA	HI-A	22	6	1	0	9	8	49¹	33	1	1.5	10.8	59	40.7%	.267	0.83	1.46	51	1.5				
2019	MTG	AA	22	1	1	0	4	4	18¹	30	3	2.9	10.3	21	39.7%	.450	1.96	8.35	163	-0.7				
2021 FS	TB	MLB	24	8	9	0	26	26	150	138	23	4.9	9.4	156	40.5%	.291	1.47	4.78	112	0.1				
2021 DC	TB	MLB	24	3	4	0	28	9	63	58	9	4.9	9.4	65	40.5%	.291	1.47	4.78	112	0.2				

Comparables: Julio Urías, Brendan McKay, Austin Voth

McClanahan became the first pitcher in history to make his major-league debut in the postseason. He was used in a low-leverage role, but showed high-leverage stuff: a fastball that touched triple digits, and a slider that sat near 90 mph. His initial introduction to the majors didn't go too hot otherwise—he tossed four innings in the playoffs, surrendering five runs on eight hits and two walks—but he'll likely return to starting in the minors in 2021. Don't be surprised if he ends up pitching meaningful innings for the Rays again this fall, either as a starter or as a late-inning reliever.

Brendan McKay LHP Born: 12/18/95 Age: 25 Bats: L Throws: L Height: 6'2" Weight: 220 Origin: Round 1, 2017 Draft (#4 overall)

YEAR	TEAM	LVL	AGE	W	L	SV	G	GS	IP	H	HR	BB/9	K/9	K	GB%	BABIP	WHIP	ERA	DRA-	WARP	MPH	FA%	Whiff%	CSP
2018	RAY	ROK	22	0	0	0	2	2	6	2	0	1.5	13.5	9	58.3%	.167	0.50	1.50	39	0.3				
2018	BG	LO-A	22	2	0	0	6	6	24²	8	1	0.7	14.6	40	60.5%	.167	0.41	1.09	56	0.8				
2018	CHA	HI-A	22	3	2	0	11	9	47²	45	2	2.1	10.2	54	36.8%	.355	1.17	3.21	62	1.2				
2019	MTG	AA	23	3	0	0	8	7	41²	25	2	1.9	13.4	62	40.5%	.280	0.82	1.30	51	1.2				
2019	DUR	AAA	23	3	0	0	7	6	32	17	1	2.5	11.2	40	45.1%	.232	0.81	0.84	31	1.6				
2019	TB	MLB	23	2	4	0	13	11	49	53	8	2.9	10.3	56	35.4%	.333	1.41	5.14	118	0.0	95.4	70.0%	23.8%	50.1%
2021 FS	TB	MLB	25	9	8	0	26	26	150	130	22	3.0	10.5	175	39.9%	.292	1.20	3.63	86	2.2	95.4	70.0%	23.8%	50.1%
2021 DC	TB	MLB	25	5	5	0	16	16	82	71	12	3.0	10.5	95	39.9%	.292	1.20	3.63	86	1.5	95.4	70.0%	23.8%	50.1%

Comparables: Nick Margevicius, Eric Lauer, Tarik Skubal

McKay entered the spring ranked as one of the consensus 30 or so best prospects in the game: BP had him at 28. It was all downhill from there—and not in the good, easy-breezy sense. McKay had one of the organization's toughest summers, beginning with a positive COVID-19 test. Soon after his return, he was shut down with a sore throwing shoulder, which eventually necessitated surgery. Ruh roh. With all his polish and his theoretical two-way ability (he hasn't really hit in a few years), McKay was supposed to be one of the safer pitching prospects in the game. Let his 2020 be a reminder that there is no such thing.

★ ★ ★ *2021 Top 101 Prospect* **#25** ★ ★ ★

Luis Patiño RHP Born: 10/26/99 Age: 21 Bats: R Throws: R Height: 6'1" Weight: 192 Origin: International Free Agent, 2016

YEAR	TEAM	LVL	AGE	W	L	SV	G	GS	IP	H	HR	BB/9	K/9	K	GB%	BABIP	WHIP	ERA	DRA-	WARP	MPH	FA%	Whiff%	CSP
2018	FW	LO-A	18	6	3	0	17	17	83¹	65	1	2.6	10.6	98	42.1%	.323	1.07	2.16	75	1.7				
2019	LE	HI-A	19	6	8	0	18	17	87	61	4	3.5	11.7	113	40.2%	.278	1.09	2.69	55	2.4				
2019	AMA	AA	19	0	0	0	2	2	7²	8	0	4.7	11.7	10	19.0%	.381	1.57	1.17	92	0.0				
2020	SD	MLB	20	1	0	0	11	1	17¹	18	3	7.3	10.9	21	34.7%	.326	1.85	5.19	110	0.1	98.6	64.8%	26.4%	46.6%
2021 FS	*TB*	*MLB*	*21*	*9*	*9*	*0*	*26*	*26*	*150*	*138*	*25*	*4.3*	*9.5*	*158*	*35.7%*	*.289*	*1.40*	*4.55*	*104*	*0.8*	*98.6*	*64.8%*	*26.4%*	*46.6%*
2021 DC	*TB*	*MLB*	*21*	*4*	*4*	*0*	*40*	*9*	*78*	*71*	*13*	*4.3*	*9.5*	*82*	*35.7%*	*.289*	*1.40*	*4.55*	*104*	*0.5*	*98.6*	*64.8%*	*26.4%*	*46.6%*

Comparables: Jenrry Mejia, Taijuan Walker, Tyler Skaggs

Patiño had an underwhelming first go in the majors. He struggled with his control, seemingly validating the longstanding concerns evaluators had about his crossfire delivery resulting in command woes. In fairness to Patiño, his struggles were understandable (and often clustered, as eight of his 14 walks came during a miserable three-game stretch early on), as he was a 20-year-old who had barely pitched above A-ball entering the season. There's no sense giving up on youngsters this kind of arm talent or work ethic. He'll be back in due time, and he'll be good.

Colin Poche LHP Born: 01/17/94 Age: 27 Bats: L Throws: L Height: 6'3" Weight: 225 Origin: Round 14, 2016 Draft (#419 overall)

YEAR	TEAM	LVL	AGE	W	L	SV	G	GS	IP	H	HR	BB/9	K/9	K	GB%	BABIP	WHIP	ERA	DRA-	WARP	MPH	FA%	Whiff%	CSP
2018	MTG	AA	24	1	0	0	3	0	5	1	0	0.0	16.2	9	28.6%	.143	0.20	0.00	49	0.2				
2018	JXN	AA	24	0	0	1	9	0	11	3	0	1.6	18.8	23	0.0%	.250	0.45	0.00	11	0.6				
2018	DUR	AAA	24	5	0	1	28	2	50	29	2	3.1	14.0	78	25.8%	.300	0.92	1.08	61	1.2				
2019	DUR	AAA	25	2	2	0	20	2	27¹	32	4	3.0	15.8	48	35.4%	.459	1.50	6.26	74	0.7				
2019	TB	MLB	25	5	5	2	51	0	51²	33	9	3.3	12.5	72	18.0%	.238	1.01	4.70	88	0.6	95.0	88.5%	35.1%	50.1%
2021 FS	*TB*	*MLB*	*27*	*3*	*2*	*0*	*57*	*0*	*50*	*35*	*7*	*3.2*	*12.3*	*68*	*27.4%*	*.260*	*1.06*	*2.85*	*71*	*0.9*	*95.0*	*88.5%*	*35.1%*	*50.1%*
2021 DC	*TB*	*MLB*	*27*	*0*	*0*	*0*	*12*	*0*	*13*	*9*	*2*	*3.2*	*12.3*	*17*	*27.4%*	*.260*	*1.06*	*2.85*	*71*	*0.3*	*95.0*	*88.5%*	*35.1%*	*50.1%*

Comparables: Aaron Bummer, A.J. Minter, Phil Maton

Poche is one of the most monomaniacal pitchers in the majors. He threw 769 very nice regular-season fastballs in 2019, as opposed to just 100 non-fastballs. Alas, Poche's elbow popped before he could throw any kind of pitch in 2020, resulting in a year lost to Tommy John surgery.

Cody Reed LHP Born: 04/15/93 Age: 28 Bats: L Throws: L Height: 6'5" Weight: 230 Origin: Round 2, 2013 Draft (#46 overall)

YEAR	TEAM	LVL	AGE	W	L	SV	G	GS	IP	H	HR	BB/9	K/9	K	GB%	BABIP	WHIP	ERA	DRA-	WARP	MPH	FA%	Whiff%	CSP
2018	LOU	AAA	25	4	8	0	18	17	105²	109	13	2.6	8.9	105	45.1%	.329	1.32	3.92	79	1.9				
2018	CIN	MLB	25	1	3	0	17	7	43	45	5	3.1	8.8	42	61.2%	.328	1.40	3.98	97	0.4	94.9	50.2%	24.8%	48.0%
2019	LOU	AAA	26	1	2	0	18	0	20²	13	1	3.5	10.9	25	69.6%	.267	1.02	2.61	57	0.7				
2019	CIN	MLB	26	0	0	0	3	0	6¹	6	0	1.4	9.9	7	76.5%	.353	1.11	1.42	65	0.2	96.2	55.2%	36.0%	55.1%
2020	TB	MLB	27	0	1	0	11	0	12	11	2	6.0	9.0	12	44.1%	.281	1.58	4.50	107	0.1	96.5	50.8%	29.4%	42.4%
2021 FS	*TB*	*MLB*	*28*	*2*	*2*	*0*	*57*	*0*	*50*	*45*	*5*	*4.1*	*9.5*	*52*	*51.5%*	*.298*	*1.36*	*4.08*	*92*	*0.3*	*95.7*	*50.9%*	*27.8%*	*46.0%*
2021 DC	*TB*	*MLB*	*28*	*2*	*2*	*0*	*56*	*0*	*59*	*53*	*6*	*4.1*	*9.5*	*62*	*51.5%*	*.298*	*1.36*	*4.08*	*92*	*0.6*	*95.7*	*50.9%*	*27.8%*	*46.0%*

Comparables: Robert Stephenson, Jeff Hoffman, Aaron Slegers

Reed, a large though rarely in-charge lefty, was one of Tampa Bay's big deadline acquisitions (yes, really). He made just two appearances with the Rays before a pinky injury ended his season and derailed any chance he had of turning into the 2020 version of Nick Anderson. Oh well. It's still easy to envision Reed blossoming into a more effective reliever than he's been thus far in his career. The main reason for that seemingly unearned optimism? A fierce slider that has consistently missed big-league bats, no matter the sample size or his role.

Trevor Richards RHP Born: 05/15/93 Age: 28 Bats: R Throws: R Height: 6'2" Weight: 195 Origin: Undrafted Free Agent, 2016

YEAR	TEAM	LVL	AGE	W	L	SV	G	GS	IP	H	HR	BB/9	K/9	K	GB%	BABIP	WHIP	ERA	DRA-	WARP	MPH	FA%	Whiff%	CSP
2018	NO	AAA	25	3	2	0	6	6	39¹	31	4	0.9	8.5	37	47.2%	.262	0.89	2.06	56	1.3				
2018	MIA	MLB	25	4	9	0	25	25	126¹	121	15	3.8	9.3	130	36.3%	.314	1.39	4.42	79	2.5	92.2	54.8%	25.9%	44.5%
2019	DUR	AAA	26	0	0	0	3	3	5¹	4	0	6.8	13.5	8	33.3%	.333	1.50	1.69	83	0.1				
2019	MIA	MLB	26	3	12	0	23	20	112	104	16	4.1	8.3	103	35.8%	.289	1.38	4.50	116	0.1	92.4	42.3%	27.0%	46.3%
2019	TB	MLB	26	3	0	0	7	2	23¹	23	3	1.9	9.3	24	32.4%	.312	1.20	1.93	97	0.3	91.6	50.0%	24.2%	46.6%
2020	TB	MLB	27	0	0	0	9	4	32	44	6	3.1	7.6	27	33.0%	.362	1.72	5.91	125	-0.1	91.8	50.7%	25.7%	45.2%
2021 FS	*TB*	*MLB*	*28*	*9*	*9*	*0*	*26*	*26*	*150*	*145*	*26*	*3.5*	*8.8*	*146*	*37.3%*	*.291*	*1.37*	*4.68*	*106*	*0.6*	*92.2*	*48.0%*	*26.2%*	*45.6%*
2021 DC	*TB*	*MLB*	*28*	*4*	*5*	*0*	*37*	*12*	*80*	*77*	*14*	*3.5*	*8.8*	*77*	*37.3%*	*.291*	*1.37*	*4.68*	*106*	*0.5*	*92.2*	*48.0%*	*26.2%*	*45.6%*

Comparables: Nick Pivetta, Kevin Gausman, Jon Gray

Richards, who will have to settle for being known as the *other* pitcher the Rays acquired from the Marlins at the 2019 deadline, filled a variety of roles in his first full season with Tampa Bay. His nine appearances included four starts, three bulk outings and a few old-fashioned mop-up assignments. He wasn't particularly great in any of those capacities, but he did start the clincher, which cemented his place in the team yearbook. Richards looks 47 and pitches like he's 37, but he'll be 27 until May—and employed as a utility arm until his changeup loses effectiveness.

Chaz Roe RHP Born: 10/09/86 Age: 34 Bats: R Throws: R Height: 6'5" Weight: 190 Origin: Round 1, 2005 Draft (#32 overall)

YEAR	TEAM	LVL	AGE	W	L	SV	G	GS	IP	H	HR	BB/9	K/9	K	GB%	BABIP	WHIP	ERA	DRA-	WARP	MPH	FA%	Whiff%	CSP
2018	TB	MLB	31	1	3	1	61	0	50¹	35	6	2.9	9.5	53	46.8%	.244	1.01	3.58	82	0.7	93.8	47.4%	26.6%	49.2%
2019	TB	MLB	32	1	3	1	71	0	51	49	3	5.5	11.5	65	43.2%	.359	1.57	4.06	93	0.4	93.3	28.9%	27.8%	48.2%
2020	TB	MLB	33	2	0	1	10	0	9¹	10	0	2.9	8.7	9	26.9%	.385	1.39	2.89	104	0.1	92.7	25.8%	22.1%	49.0%
2021 FS	TB	MLB	34	2	2	0	57	0	50	44	5	3.8	9.7	53	43.5%	.295	1.31	3.80	91	0.4	93.3	33.0%	26.6%	48.6%

Comparables: Steve Cishek, Brad Brach, Tyler Clippard

If you're hungry for Roe's signature slider, you'll have to wait until his kitchen reopens sometime in 2021. He was shut down after 10 appearances because he felt discomfort in his arm that was later discovered to be unrelated to ligament damage. Roe is a season away from reaching free agency, so here's hoping he can make a full recovery and cash in next winter on several years of solid relief work.

Joe Ryan RHP Born: 06/05/96 Age: 25 Bats: R Throws: R Height: 6'2" Weight: 205 Origin: Round 7, 2018 Draft (#210 overall)

YEAR	TEAM	LVL	AGE	W	L	SV	G	GS	IP	H	HR	BB/9	K/9	K	GB%	BABIP	WHIP	ERA	DRA-	WARP	MPH	FA%	Whiff%	CSP
2018	HV	SS	22	2	1	0	12	7	36¹	26	3	3.5	12.6	51	35.4%	.303	1.10	3.72	47	1.3				
2019	BG	LO-A	23	2	2	0	6	6	27²	19	2	3.6	15.3	47	28.6%	.315	1.08	2.93	59	0.7				
2019	CHA	HI-A	23	7	2	0	15	13	82²	47	3	1.3	12.2	112	36.6%	.246	0.71	1.42	41	3.0				
2019	MTG	AA	23	0	0	0	3	3	13¹	11	2	2.7	16.2	24	23.1%	.375	1.12	3.38	85	0.1				
2021 FS	TB	MLB	25	9	8	0	26	26	150	126	22	3.8	10.9	181	35.9%	.288	1.26	3.90	97	1.3				
2021 DC	TB	MLB	25	2	3	0	20	8	50	42	7	3.8	10.9	60	35.9%	.288	1.26	3.90	97	0.5				

Comparables: Alex Reyes, Drew Rasmussen, Brad Mills

Ryan has struck out more than 13 batters per nine so far in his professional career despite relying on his fastball to an unseemly degree. Provided he keeps missing bats like he has, he could end up playing the Josh Fleming role for the Rays in 2021.

Ryan Sherriff LHP Born: 05/25/90 Age: 31 Bats: L Throws: L Height: 6'1" Weight: 190 Origin: Round 28, 2011 Draft (#860 overall)

YEAR	TEAM	LVL	AGE	W	L	SV	G	GS	IP	H	HR	BB/9	K/9	K	GB%	BABIP	WHIP	ERA	DRA-	WARP	MPH	FA%	Whiff%	CSP
2018	STL	MLB	28	0	0	0	5	0	5²	8	1	3.2	4.8	3	57.1%	.350	1.76	6.35	138	-0.1	92.3	72.8%	15.0%	46.4%
2020	TB	MLB	30	1	0	1	10	0	9²	6	0	1.9	1.9	2	56.7%	.200	0.83	0.00	105	0.1	92.7	80.2%	10.0%	51.6%
2021 FS	TB	MLB	31	2	2	0	57	0	50	53	6	2.5	6.3	35	52.3%	.300	1.33	4.31	100	0.1	92.6	78.6%	11.1%	50.5%
2021 DC	TB	MLB	31	2	2	0	56	0	59	62	7	2.5	6.3	41	52.3%	.300	1.33	4.31	100	0.4	92.6	78.6%	11.1%	50.5%

Comparables: Buddy Baumann, Scott Alexander, Andrew Kittredge

Sherriff returned to the majors for the first time since undergoing elbow surgery. Partially because of the three-batter rule, he faced more righties than lefties but was effective all the same, using a fastball nearly 80 percent of the time. He backed up his modest heater with a low-80s slider and he even attempted to toss a changeup for the first time. Sherriff was not scored upon in 10 regular season appearances, and he added two more scoreless frames in the World Series as the capper to his encouraging year. If he keeps that up, he just might earn a badge.

Aaron Slegers RHP Born: 09/04/92 Age: 28 Bats: R Throws: R Height: 6'10" Weight: 260 Origin: Round 5, 2013 Draft (#140 overall)

YEAR	TEAM	LVL	AGE	W	L	SV	G	GS	IP	H	HR	BB/9	K/9	K	GB%	BABIP	WHIP	ERA	DRA-	WARP	MPH	FA%	Whiff%	CSP
2018	ROC	AAA	25	5	7	0	15	15	85¹	85	12	2.0	6.0	57	43.0%	.285	1.22	3.80	112	0.0				
2018	MIN	MLB	25	1	1	0	4	2	13²	17	3	1.3	4.0	6	39.2%	.292	1.39	5.27	133	-0.1	91.9	68.5%	15.0%	48.6%
2019	DUR	AAA	26	6	7	0	26	15	112¹	130	22	2.2	6.4	80	41.0%	.309	1.41	5.05	111	1.2				
2019	TB	MLB	26	0	0	1	1	0	3	3	1	0.0	0.0	0	36.4%	.200	1.00	3.00	138	0.0	91.2	66.7%	8.0%	52.1%
2020	TB	MLB	27	0	0	2	11	1	26	18	1	1.7	6.6	19	56.0%	.233	0.88	3.46	85	0.4	92.5	62.0%	22.4%	48.3%
2021 FS	TB	MLB	28	2	2	0	57	0	50	52	7	2.2	6.7	37	45.8%	.293	1.30	4.52	104	0.0	92.4	63.2%	20.5%	48.5%
2021 DC	TB	MLB	28	2	2	0	56	0	59	62	9	2.2	6.7	43	45.8%	.293	1.30	4.52	104	0.2	92.4	63.2%	20.5%	48.5%

Comparables: Luis Perdomo, Erick Fedde, Jeff Hoffman

Hey, everyone! Thanks for checking back in. Slegers is still tall, of course, but now he looks like he's also an effective pitcher—or, at least, as effective as one can be in a pandemic-shortened season. While throwing slightly fewer fastballs in favor of more sliders, he used his height to his advantage by burying the ball in the zone, which, in turn, resulted in a groundball rate over 50 percent for the first time as a major leaguer. That proved to be beneficial for Slegers in a very obvious and meaningful way, as he allowed one home run in 2020 after permitting seven in his first 32 career innings. He should hold onto a bullpen spot for as long as he can keep the ball in play and throw multiple frames.

Ryan Thompson RHP Born: 06/26/92 Age: 29 Bats: R Throws: R Height: 6'5" Weight: 210 Origin: Round 23, 2014 Draft (#676 overall)

YEAR	TEAM	LVL	AGE	W	L	SV	G	GS	IP	H	HR	BB/9	K/9	K	GB%	BABIP	WHIP	ERA	DRA-	WARP	MPH	FA%	Whiff%	CSP
2019	MTG	AA	27	1	1	0	14	5	20¹	24	1	2.7	8.9	20	44.4%	.371	1.48	3.10	120	-0.3				
2020	TB	MLB	28	1	2	1	25	0	26¹	29	4	2.7	7.9	23	59.0%	.316	1.41	4.44	81	0.5	93.6	60.9%	22.2%	52.8%
2021 FS	TB	MLB	29	3	3	0	57	0	50	49	6	3.2	8.2	45	51.4%	.301	1.34	4.30	99	0.2	93.6	60.9%	22.2%	52.8%
2021 DC	TB	MLB	29	3	3	0	62	0	66	65	8	3.2	8.2	60	51.4%	.301	1.34	4.30	99	0.4	93.6	60.9%	22.2%	52.8%

Comparables: Chris Leroux, Josh Lueke, Eric Yardley

Thompson checks all the buzzword boxes associated with pitching. At 6-foot-5, 200 pounds, he's both "long" and "lanky." His delivery, a violent sidearm motion, makes him "deceptive." And, he's a classic "sinker-slider" right-hander to boot. In the older days, he'd probably be called a "specialist." In this era, he might end up being referred to as an "up-and-down" arm instead.

Michael Wacha RHP Born: 07/01/91   Age: 30   Bats: R   Throws: R   Height: 6'6"   Weight: 215   Origin: Round 1, 2012 Draft (#19 overall)

YEAR	TEAM	LVL	AGE	W	L	SV	G	GS	IP	H	HR	BB/9	K/9	K	GB%	BABIP	WHIP	ERA	DRA-	WARP	MPH	FA%	Whiff%	CSP
2018	STL	MLB	26	8	2	0	15	15	84¹	68	9	3.8	7.6	71	44.7%	.253	1.23	3.20	89	1.3	96.0	43.0%	23.2%	46.2%
2019	STL	MLB	27	6	7	0	29	24	126²	143	26	3.9	7.4	104	48.0%	.318	1.56	4.76	128	-0.7	95.4	50.8%	21.3%	46.1%
2020	NYM	MLB	28	1	4	0	8	7	34	46	9	1.9	9.8	37	36.4%	.366	1.56	6.62	99	0.3	95.9	42.5%	24.6%	48.9%
2021 FS	TB	MLB	29	9	8	0	26	26	150	143	20	3.3	8.5	141	43.8%	.294	1.32	4.12	95	1.5	95.7	47.3%	22.4%	46.8%
2021 DC	TB	MLB	29	7	8	0	35	22	124	118	16	3.3	8.5	116	43.8%	.294	1.32	4.12	95	1.5	95.7	47.3%	22.4%	46.8%

Comparables: Julio Teheran, Mat Latos, Jonathon Niese

No one expected Wacha's first year in Queens to be a replay of his high-water mark in 2017, but he may have dipped beneath even the low expectations that came with his one-year, $3 million contract. The righty was extremely hittable, with almost two-thirds of balls in play taking to the air, and many of them leaving the stadium. When he wasn't getting hit hard, he was suffering from shoulder inflammation that kept him from going deep into games and consigned him to the injured list for part of the season. There were a few encouraging signs in his peripherals—his walk rate was a career low, and his strikeout rate a career high—but hitters slugged .727 and .571 against his four-seamer and cutter, respectively. The Rays saw something they liked, though, and inked him to a repeat of his terms with the Mets.

Cole Wilcox RHP Born: 07/14/99   Age: 21   Bats: R   Throws: R   Height: 6'5"   Weight: 232   Origin: Round 3, 2020 Draft (#80 overall)

The Padres may have drafted Wilcox in the third round, but they paid him like a first-rounder, ponying up more than $3 million so that he'd go pro. Wilcox has the raw stuff and the potential to make the investment look sound, though his command could ultimately force him into relief. He was a part of the four-player package San Diego used to acquire Blake Snell in the offseason.

Ryan Yarbrough LHP Born: 12/31/91   Age: 29   Bats: R   Throws: L   Height: 6'5"   Weight: 205   Origin: Round 4, 2014 Draft (#111 overall)

YEAR	TEAM	LVL	AGE	W	L	SV	G	GS	IP	H	HR	BB/9	K/9	K	GB%	BABIP	WHIP	ERA	DRA-	WARP	MPH	FA%	Whiff%	CSP
2018	TB	MLB	26	16	6	0	38	6	147¹	140	18	3.1	7.8	128	38.2%	.288	1.29	3.91	107	0.3	91.0	63.7%	20.7%	50.6%
2019	DUR	AAA	27	2	1	0	5	4	26	24	2	1.0	12.1	35	42.4%	.344	1.04	3.81	58	1.0				
2019	TB	MLB	27	11	6	0	28	14	141²	121	15	1.3	7.4	117	42.8%	.264	1.00	4.13	81	2.5	89.6	61.0%	22.3%	49.1%
2020	TB	MLB	28	1	4	0	11	9	55²	54	5	1.9	7.1	44	40.9%	.299	1.19	3.56	97	0.6	88.7	59.4%	27.7%	48.1%
2021 FS	TB	MLB	29	9	8	0	26	26	150	142	18	2.2	8.1	135	42.4%	.291	1.20	3.70	87	2.1	89.7	61.2%	23.4%	49.2%
2021 DC	TB	MLB	29	7	7	0	36	24	125	118	15	2.2	8.1	113	42.4%	.291	1.20	3.70	87	2.1	89.7	61.2%	23.4%	49.2%

Comparables: Steven Brault, Sean Manaea, Matt Strahm

The soft-tossing Yarbrough was used as a starter in nine of his 11 appearances, setting a new career-high in start percentage. He rewarded the Rays—we'd like to think they'd consider it a reward, anyway—by working into the sixth inning or later in four of those games, including a seven-inning effort late in the year against the Orioles. Yarbrough isn't going to light up radar guns or contend for a Cy Young Award; what he should have done by the time you read this is offer one of the most interesting arbitration cases in recent memory, as his agent will have to attempt to explain why his client should be compensated as a starter despite more frequently being used as a reliever. Good luck.

TORONTO BLUE JAYS

Essay by Kamila Hinkson

Player comments by Rachael McDaniel and BP staff

The word "unprecedented" was ubiquitous in 2020. At times, it was tiresome to see that word annexed by corporations to serve as a preface to every advertisement, and yet it was a constant reminder of how far we had strayed from the normal we knew. But it is a fitting way to describe what happened August 26, when the members of the Milwaukee Bucks were scheduled to start their playoff game against the Orlando Magic. Instead, they refused to take the court.

The players were demanding justice and accountability for Jacob Blake, a 29-year-Black man who was shot in the back seven times by police in Kenosha, Wisconsin, about 40 miles from Milwaukee. The shooting fanned flames of anger that had been burning for weeks. Months. Years.

The team's collective action had an immediate impact. It made headlines and caught the attention of people outside and inside the sports world, including baseball players. Soon after, the Cincinnati Reds and Milwaukee Brewers announced their game was off too. The Dodgers-Giants and Mariners-Padres contests followed suit. Some Black players on other teams decided to sit out and let their teams play without them. That night's Red Sox-Blue Jays game was played as scheduled, the Bucks' protest coming too late for many teams in the eastern time zone to figure out how to react.

With more teams joining in the protest over the course of the next day, the Blue Jays held a team meeting to decide what to do. There were no African-Americans on the Jays roster that day; Anthony Alford, who had three hits in 16 at-bats (.188) for the season and struggled to find his footing with the team, had been designated for assignment the week before. There are a few Afro-Latino players on the Blue Jays, including Vladimir Guerrero Jr., Teoscar Hernández and Rafael Dolis. Being Afro-Latino comes with views on and experiences with blackness that can be similar to those of African-Americans, but can also be pretty distinct, so it's unclear what their relationship might be to the Black Lives Matter Movement and how they might have been feeling that day.

What we know is that the Blue Jays voted to play the game. Red Sox outfielder Jackie Bradley Jr., the only African-American on that team, told his teammates he didn't want to

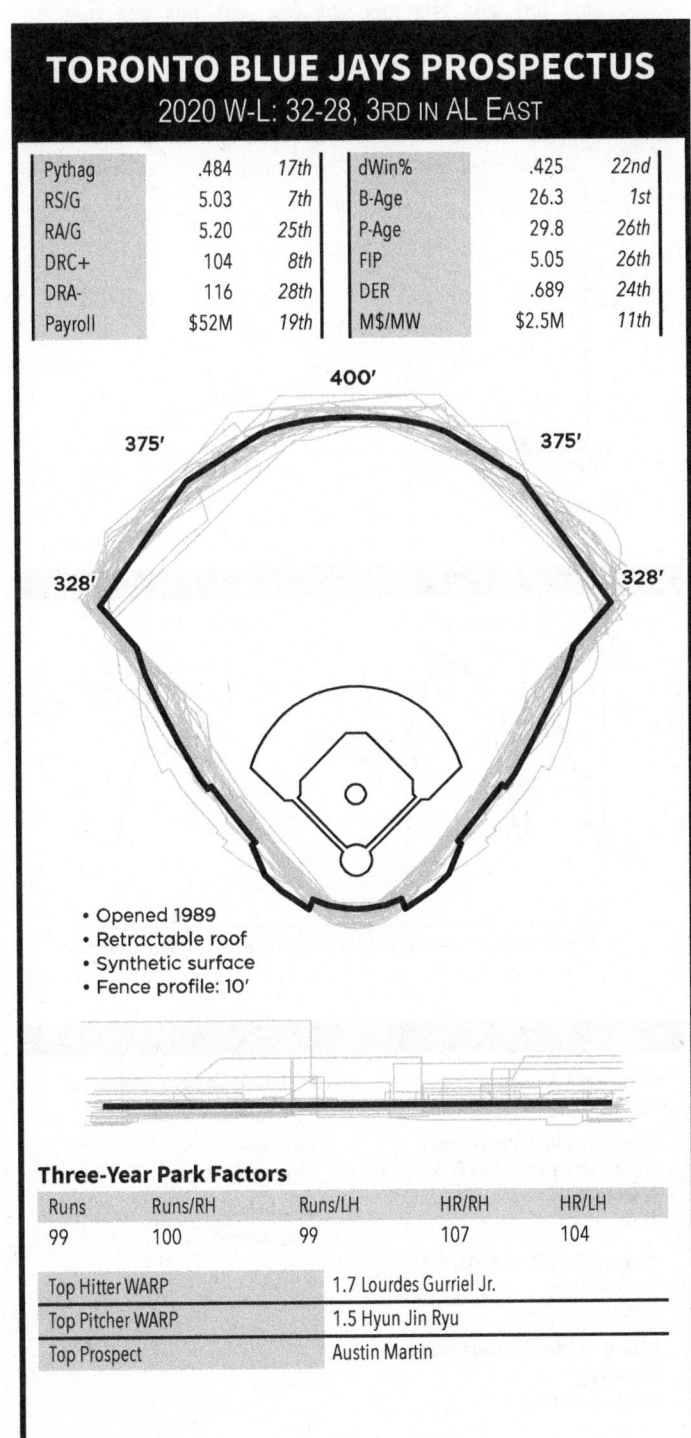

TORONTO BLUE JAYS PROSPECTUS
2020 W-L: 32-28, 3RD IN AL EAST

Pythag	.484	17th	dWin%	.425	22nd
RS/G	5.03	7th	B-Age	26.3	1st
RA/G	5.20	25th	P-Age	29.8	26th
DRC+	104	8th	FIP	5.05	26th
DRA-	116	28th	DER	.689	24th
Payroll	$52M	19th	M$/MW	$2.5M	11th

400'

375'   375'

328'   328'

- Opened 1989
- Retractable roof
- Synthetic surface
- Fence profile: 10'

Three-Year Park Factors

Runs	Runs/RH	Runs/LH	HR/RH	HR/LH
99	100	99	107	104

Top Hitter WARP	1.7 Lourdes Gurriel Jr.
Top Pitcher WARP	1.5 Hyun Jin Ryu
Top Prospect	Austin Martin

Payroll History (in millions)

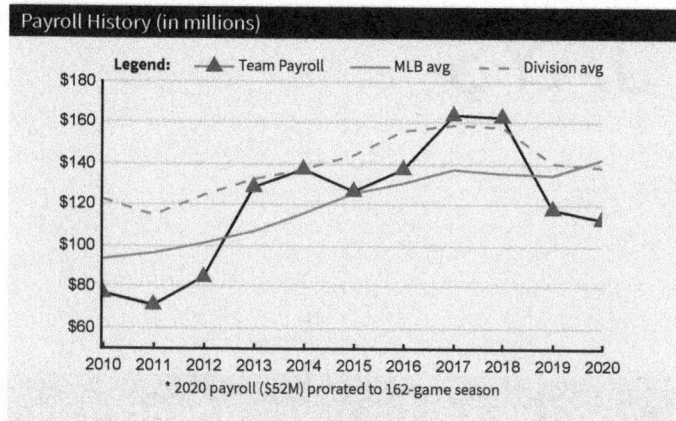

Legend: ▲ Team Payroll — MLB avg - - Division avg

* 2020 payroll ($52M) prorated to 162-game season

Future Commitments (in millions)

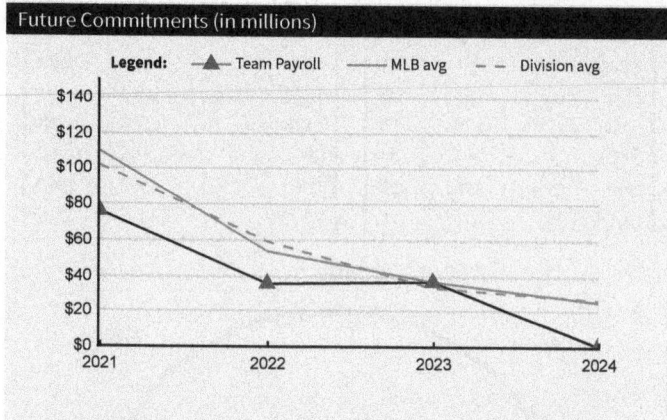

Legend: ▲ Team Payroll — MLB avg - - Division avg

Farm System Ranking

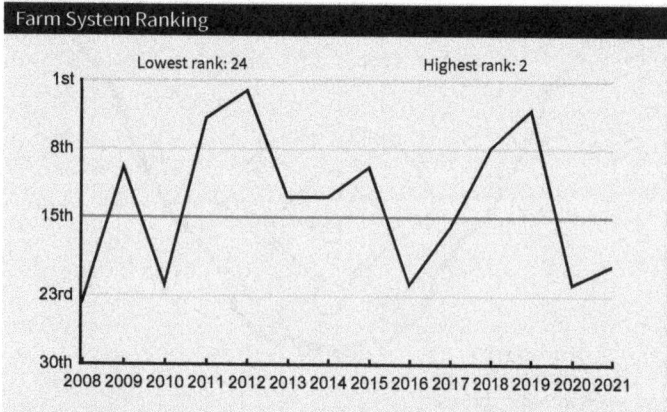

Lowest rank: 24   Highest rank: 2

Personnel

President & CEO
Mark A. Shapiro

Executive Vice President, Baseball Operations & General Manager
Ross Atkins

Senior Vice President, Player Personnel
Tony Lacava

Vice President, International Scouting
Andrew Tinnish

Assistant General Manager
Joe Sheehan

Manager
Charlie Montoyo

BP Alumni
Matt Bishoff

play that night and that he would be sitting out in protest. His decision led to a discussion among his colleagues, and the Red Sox decided to join him. It was only when informed of the Red Sox's decision not to play that the Blue Jays agreed to postpone. At a time when the ground felt like it was shifting in the world of men's professional sports, the Blue Jays chose to stand still.

⚾   ⚾   ⚾

After struggling for a few years in the post-Jose Bautista era, the prospect development team had done their work, and coming into last year, Blue Jays looked like a predictable team. The window was set to open; 2020 would be the first full year that the young stars of the future—Vladimir Guerrero Jr., Bo Bichette, Cavan Biggio, Teoscar Hernández—would play together. The organization did exactly what rising young teams are supposed to do, signing an ace for their rotation in Hyun-jin Ryu, who had been coming off a second-place finish in National League Cy Young Award voting. Maybe they weren't ready to challenge the AL East elite yet, but everything was going according to plan.

The Blue Jays, like many other Grapefruit League teams, were on the field, playing in two split-squad games when Rob Manfred first announced it was shutting down spring training and postponing the start of the season due to the coronavirus pandemic. Dreams of how the season would play out turned to questions of whether it would happen at all, as the league and its players fought bitterly and publicly about how baseball was to be played in 2020, and for how much. And while they were hashing out the details, George Floyd was murdered.

Many have theorized as to why his death, caused by a police officer who knelt on his neck for eight minutes and 46 seconds, became the catalyst that it did. It may have been the brutality of it, the fact it was caught on video, pandemic-induced solitude, a mix of the three or more. What's clear is that it took his death for many people to clue into the violence Black people face and have been facing for centuries. Cities across America boiled over in frustration, pain, and anger.

It was a movement not even Major League Baseball, a league that has never been known for activism, could ignore. Players started to speak out. It took nine days for the league to issue a statement—a statement that didn't include the words Black Lives Matter. "MLB is committed to engaging our communities to invoke change," the statement included, mentioning no specific changes or any indication of what that engagement would entail. The league was on it, probably.

In June, after weeks of negotiations, Major League Baseball finally imposed a 60-game season. As Opening Day approached, the Blue Jays scrambled to find a place to play home games after the Canadian government said "no thanks" to the idea of teams flying in and out of Toronto on a regular basis in a pandemic. They wound up playing at Sahlen Field in Buffalo, the home of the Blue Jays' Triple-A affiliate.

In 2017, Bruce Maxwell knelt during the national anthem, following the lead of NFL quarterback Colin Kaepernick, who sought to protest the unequal treatment of Black people and people of color in the U.S. At the time, the majority of fans equated the protest with disrespect for the nation's armed forces, and Maxwell's act drew heavy criticism. Prior to the 2020 season, he was the only major-league player to kneel. At the time, the majority of fans at the time equated the protest with disrespect of the nation's armed forces. But Floyd's death changed the conversation around kneeling throughout sports.

The public address announcer hadn't even finished announcing the name of the anthem singer when a handful of Blue Jays players—outfielder Anthony Alford, newly converted first baseman Guerrero Jr., shortstop Santiago Espinal and infielder Cavan Biggio—got down on one knee.

No one booed. No one cheered. There was no one to do so, since fans were officially barred due to the coronavirus. The anthem was a recording of Marvin Gaye's performance from the 1983 NBA All-Star Game, and crowd noise from the video made it sound, at least on TV, like the stadium wasn't as empty as it was. Some players wore masks or face coverings, and others didn't; some players stood a little farther apart, but not by much. Some of the Rays knelt as well. For more than two minutes, as Gaye crooned, the players, coaches and managers quietly contemplated the start of a new season, one that would be unlike any other.

A 600-foot black cloth lay on the ground as the anthem played. The cloth was supposed to symbolize unity—the idea came from veteran African-American outfielder Andrew McCutchen—and everyone on the field had been holding it before the anthem started. But both the cloth and the kneeling were league-sanctioned acts of protest. Kneeling when it's rubber-stamped by the league is one thing. Kneeling when Maxwell did, when you don't know if your teammates, let alone your team or the league, will have your back, is something else.

When asked what inspired him to kneel, Biggio, who is white, told reporters he took a knee to support Alford, who was hesitant to kneel due to the fact that he wasn't an everyday player. Alford told reporters he would have knelt regardless but appreciated the support. The action was stripped of its defiance, rendered almost sterile by the league's approval, and yet there was still a player who was worried about the repercussions.

⚾ ⚾ ⚾

The Jays got a taste of the scheduling havoc wrought by the virus pretty early on—a week into the season, a three-game set against the Phillies was postponed after the latter team revealed two staff members tested positive. The plans started to go awry, as they always do. On the field, the team

was dealt a huge blow when closer Ken Giles hurt his elbow and landed on the injured list on opening weekend, effectively wiping out his season.

There were defensive miscues, a slow start by Ryu, an injury to rising star Bo Bichette and some frustratingly close games that all seemed to end in losses. They were the kind of gaffes that could easily be predicted out of a young team, and yet people, in their excitement, rarely do. But there were also bright spots: Teoscar Hernández started hitting and for a (short) time, led the league in home runs. Nate Pearson made his highly anticipated major-league debut. Lourdes Gurriel Jr. showed off in left field, making catches and notching assists as if he'd been an outfielder forever, and hadn't moved there after a cringeworthy case of the yips in 2019.

By August 27, the Blue Jays were a game above .500. The Blue Jays players were idle that day, after agreeing to postpone their game against the Red Sox. But general manager Ross Atkins, trying to bolster a depleted starting rotation, traded for Taijuan Walker.

Walker came to the Jays from the Seattle Mariners, where he was one of 10 African-American players. The Mariners voted not to play August 26, and Walker told reporters in his introductory news conference that it didn't feel right to play that day, and that he would have voiced that opinion if he had been with the Jays, too.

With Walker pitching well, Ryu starting to pick things up too and the bullpen sorting itself out, for the most part, thanks to guys like Anthony Kay, Jordan Romano, Rafael Dolis, AJ Cole and Julian Merryweather, the Jays did indeed eek their way into the playoffs with a 32-28 record, thanks to the expanded playoff format. After the lean years that followed the 2015 and 2016 seasons, it was pleasant and bizarre to watch them celebrate on an empty field in Buffalo, and eavesdrop from our couches on catcher Caleb Joseph delivering a rousing speech to his teammates.

They crashed and burned in the best two-of-three wild card series against the Rays, their season ending where it began, but vowed they would be back in the postseason soon enough. There's no reason to predict otherwise.

⚾ ⚾ ⚾

In many ways, the 2020 season was a triumph for the Blue Jays. No one got COVID-19, first and foremost. They made the playoffs ahead of schedule. The team improved and showed character in a lot of ways. But growth isn't only measured by what happens on the field.

Alford grew up in Mississippi; when he was 12 years old, a police officer drew a gun while searching the car he was in as he returned from a cottage with some friends. Like many Black people in the U.S., Canada, and elsewhere, he used his own experiences to explain the impact of anti-Black racism to the people around him. On Opening Day, Blue Jays infielder Rowdy Tellez, who is Jewish and Mexican, didn't kneel for the anthem, but put his hand on Alford's shoulder and talked about the impact of hearing Alford talk about his experiences. Both Biggio and Guerrero cited Alford's stories as a factor in their decision to kneel. Alford and Bichette also had conversations about race and its impact on opportunity.

In the aftermath of George Floyd's death, Black people around the world shared those kinds of stories more than ever, no doubt hoping that adding their voice to the chorus would help underscore that racism isn't a concept, it is a real thing that real people deal with on a regular basis.

Sitting out for one baseball game, a game they knew would be postponed, seemed like a relatively low-stakes way to signal support for that change. But on August 27, when the Blue Jays had to make a choice, instead of taking a stand, they took the field. In Alford's absence, did anyone step up to give a rousing speech and remind their teammates of the stories they'd heard him tell? If Alford or Walker had been in the room, would that have changed things, transformed an abstract concept into something personal, tangible? If their teammates had been forced to look two Black men in the eye while voting to play, would it have made a difference?

If someone had tried to tell me at the beginning of 2020 that the actions of players in the WNBA and NBA to highlight anti-Black racism would even move the needle in baseball, I would have laughed out loud. What took place was an unquestionable step forward. But for the Blue Jays, after two months of protests and anger and sadness and people baring their souls, there weren't enough people in the room that day who wanted to do a small thing, but a large gesture, to show their support for basic human rights. Where does that leave us?

Some progress is better than none, of course. But wearing a t-shirt is easy. Holding a black cloth during the national anthem is easy. Committing yourself to engaging communities to invoke change is easy, at least easy to say. Creating lasting change is not. The Blue Jays didn't step up when they had the chance. Maybe more than anything else, the team's reticence is a lesson for its fans and a reflection of its burgeoning on-field talent: Things are starting to change, but there's still a ways left to go. ■

—Kamila Hinkson is a journalist for CBC Montreal.

HITTERS

Bo Bichette SS   Born: 03/05/98   Age: 23   Bats: R   Throws: R   Height: 6'0"   Weight: 185   Origin: Round 2, 2016 Draft (#66 overall)

YEAR	TEAM	LVL	AGE	PA	R	2B	3B	HR	RBI	BB	K	SB	CS	Whiff%	AVG/OBP/SLG	DRC+	BABIP	BRR	FRAA	WARP
2018	NH	AA	20	595	95	43	7	11	74	48	101	32	11		.286/.343/.453	124	.331	3.2	SS(116): -4.0, 2B(9): 0.6	3.1
2019	BUF	AAA	21	244	34	16	2	8	32	19	48	15	5		.275/.333/.473	102	.317	-2.0	SS(51): -1.4, 2B(1): -0.0	0.8
2019	TOR	MLB	21	212	32	18	0	11	21	14	50	4	4	24.5%	.311/.358/.571	109	.368	-0.8	SS(42): 4.6	1.5
2020	TOR	MLB	22	128	18	9	1	5	23	5	27	4	1	21.6%	.301/.328/.512	111	.352	-0.9	SS(26): 0.9	0.3
2021 FS	TOR	MLB	23	600	78	33	3	22	73	39	140	15	5	23.2%	.270/.321/.463	112	.323	1.0	SS 2, 2B 0	3.2
2021 DC	TOR	MLB	23	606	79	33	3	22	73	39	141	15	5	23.2%	.270/.321/.463	112	.323	1.0	SS 2	3.2

Comparables: Willy Adames, Alex Rodriguez, Gleyber Torres

Before three innings had been played between the Jays and the Marlins on August 12, the Jays found themselves down 8-0. Bichette was the second batter up in the bottom of the third. He singled with one out, starting a rally that brought in two runs.

It was the beginning of an astonishing comeback, a seven-homer onslaught from the Jays' young bats, and at the center of it all, Bichette was electrifying. He had five hits in six plate appearances, one of them a homer; he stole two bases. The Marlins added three in the fifth, extending their lead even further. But the Jays kept coming, finally tying the game on back-to-back homers from Bichette and Shaw in the eighth. And then they lost—three runs from the Marlins in the top of the 10th. Bichette led off the bottom of the inning with a walk, but no one drove him in. In spite of everything, they sank to 6-9 on the season. A week later, Bichette was gone entirely, the victim of a knee sprain that left him out of the lineup for a month.

Bichette was, at the time of the injury, the Jays' best hitter. More than that, he was an emotional cornerstone of the team, always at the center of everything, always the face the camera focused on when it cut to the dugout. The Jays, before his injury, seemed to be losing in spite of him; when, after he was gone, they won seven in a row and vaulted themselves into postseason contention, they were winning in spite of his absence. He played in fewer than half of their games, but he finished the year as their fourth-best position player. He is still only 22 years old. And when you think of these young Jays, he continues to be the person you think of: rounding the bases after a double, hair flying, or leaping to greet a teammate after a home run, or staring out after a loss, all the expectations of a sparkling future heavy in his face.

Cavan Biggio 2B   Born: 04/11/95   Age: 26   Bats: L   Throws: R   Height: 6'2"   Weight: 200   Origin: Round 5, 2016 Draft (#162 overall)

YEAR	TEAM	LVL	AGE	PA	R	2B	3B	HR	RBI	BB	K	SB	CS	Whiff%	AVG/OBP/SLG	DRC+	BABIP	BRR	FRAA	WARP
2018	NH	AA	23	563	80	23	5	26	99	100	148	20	8		.252/.388/.499	135	.307	3.6	2B(68): 1.5, 2B(34): -1.1, 1B(22): 0.7	3.5
2019	BUF	AAA	24	174	23	8	1	6	27	34	28	5	1		.312/.448/.514	149	.352	0.5	2B(22): 2.0, 1B(7): 0.2, 3B(7): 0.2	1.7
2019	TOR	MLB	24	430	66	17	2	16	48	71	123	14	0	26.0%	.234/.364/.429	112	.309	2.2	2B(85): 0.5, 1B(8): -0.7, RF(9): -0.9	2.1
2020	TOR	MLB	25	265	41	16	0	8	28	41	61	6	0	23.2%	.250/.375/.432	116	.311	0.5	2B(37): -0.3, RF(14): -0.5, 3B(10): 0.1	1.2
2021 FS	TOR	MLB	26	600	81	23	2	19	55	89	157	9	2	24.7%	.233/.354/.409	111	.298	2.4	2B 3, 3B -1	3.2
2021 DC	TOR	MLB	26	573	77	22	2	18	53	85	150	9	2	24.7%	.233/.354/.409	111	.298	2.3	2B 3, 3B -1	2.9

Comparables: Yoán Moncada, Rickie Weeks Jr., Ryan McMahon

Biggio provides hope for the smallest kid on every Little League team: You too can be great. All you have to do is not swing. The patron saint of patience posted the third-lowest swing percentage among qualified major-league hitters, and finished first at refusing to chase, even bettering one Mike Trout. Beyond the walks, Biggio enjoyed the advantages inherent in going 1-0 more often than he went 0-1, employing his limited power to turn fastball counts into line drives over the infielders. The question is whether this unique profile will hold up: He doesn't actually post the phenomenal contact rates you usually see from those who live by singles and walks, and pitchers have yet to challenge him with strikes and try to punish his reticence. Until they do, Biggio's on-base skills and inherited knack for positional versatility—he also acquitted himself well at third—put him among the Jays' best position players, and he adds an interesting dimension to a lineup full of big swings and barrels.

Riley Adams C
Born: 06/26/96 Age: 25 Bats: R Throws: R Height: 6'4" Weight: 235 Origin: Round 3, 2017 Draft (#99 overall)

YEAR	TEAM	LVL	AGE	PA	R	2B	3B	HR	RBI	BB	K	SB	CS	Whiff%	AVG/OBP/SLG	DRC+	BABIP	BRR	FRAA	WARP
2018	DUN	HI-A	22	409	49	26	1	4	43	50	93	3	0		.246/.352/.361	121	.323	-1.3	C(93): 4.3, 1B(1): -0.0	2.2
2019	DUN	HI-A	23	83	12	3	0	3	12	14	18	1	0		.277/.434/.462	168	.341	0.4	C(19): 0.1	1.0
2019	NH	AA	23	332	46	15	2	11	39	32	105	3	1		.258/.349/.439	131	.362	1.0	C(57): -2.5	2.1
2021 FS	TOR	MLB	25	600	62	26	2	15	60	47	200	0	0		.224/.299/.368	84	.323	-0.1	C -1, 1B 0	1.1

Comparables: Adrian Nieto, Dusty Ryan, Jacob Stallings

YEAR	TEAM	P. COUNT	FRM RUNS	BLK RUNS	THRW RUNS	TOT RUNS
2021	TOR	16650	-4.8	2.6	0.0	-2.2

After getting into but a single, ill-fated game in 2019, Diaz entered camp in 2020 competing for the fifth starter spot. He left it quickly, straining a lat in March and spending the summer on the 60-day IL. Since he seems to be destined for a bullpen role without a serviceable, battle-tested changeup, his development was among the most jeopardized by the pandemic-shortened, minor-league-less season.

Santiago Espinal 2B
Born: 11/13/94 Age: 26 Bats: R Throws: R Height: 5'10" Weight: 181 Origin: Round 10, 2016 Draft (#298 overall)

YEAR	TEAM	LVL	AGE	PA	R	2B	3B	HR	RBI	BB	K	SB	CS	Whiff%	AVG/OBP/SLG	DRC+	BABIP	BRR	FRAA	WARP
2018	DUN	HI-A	23	73	9	3	1	2	8	6	10	0	3		.262/.333/.431	106	.283	-0.7	SS(8): 0.7, 2B(6): 0.3, 3B(2): -0.3	0.2
2018	SAL	HI-A	23	281	53	15	3	7	32	18	35	9	1		.312/.363/.477	151	.336	5.2	SS(53): 2.0, 3B(4): -0.3, 2B(2): 0.1	2.8
2018	NH	AA	23	164	17	9	2	1	20	14	22	2	1		.286/.354/.395	108	.328	1.3	2B(16): 0.4, 3B(12): -0.1, SS(12): -1.0	0.5
2019	NH	AA	24	409	46	21	1	5	57	35	50	10	11		.278/.343/.381	125	.310	-2.5	2B(52): 3.3, SS(22): 0.9, CF(12): 3.3	3.0
2019	BUF	AAA	24	112	11	6	0	2	14	7	23	2	2		.317/.360/.433	100	.392	0.9	2B(18): 1.9, SS(11): -0.1	0.6
2020	TOR	MLB	26	66	10	4	0	0	6	4	16	1	0	25.4%	.267/.308/.333	86	.356	0.1	SS(21): 3.6, 3B(2): -0.0, P(2): -0.0	0.4
2021 FS	TOR	MLB	26	600	62	27	2	12	61	41	130	6	3	25.4%	.253/.309/.379	89	.310	-1.5	2B 5, 3B 0	1.6
2021 DC	TOR	MLB	26	404	41	18	1	8	41	28	87	4	2	25.4%	.253/.309/.379	89	.310	-1.0	2B 3, 3B 0	0.9

Comparables: Pablo Reyes, Brock Holt, Josh Rojas

While he showed little aptitude for hitting over his time with the Jays, especially not for any kind of power, Espinal's solid fielding was enough to keep him on the infield through the injury to Bo Bichette. He even got two innings on the mound in one of the Jays' many blowouts. And he was of critical assistance to Vlad Jr. when he needed someone to get his celebration GoPro on. An all-around useful player, indeed.

Derek Fisher RF
Born: 08/21/93 Age: 27 Bats: L Throws: R Height: 6'3" Weight: 215 Origin: Round 1, 2014 Draft (#37 overall)

YEAR	TEAM	LVL	AGE	PA	R	2B	3B	HR	RBI	BB	K	SB	CS	Whiff%	AVG/OBP/SLG	DRC+	BABIP	BRR	FRAA	WARP
2018	FRE	AAA	24	281	44	12	1	10	34	39	85	11	1		.251/.363/.435	113	.347	2.2	CF(33): -2.7, LF(19): -0.7, RF(4): -0.3	0.7
2018	HOU	MLB	24	86	13	2	2	4	11	5	42	2	0	43.4%	.165/.209/.392	48	.257	1.6	LF(26): -1.3, CF(9): -0.4, RF(3): 0.2	-0.3
2019	RR	AAA	25	270	44	9	1	14	36	40	67	8	3		.286/.401/.522	122	.347	-0.5	CF(29): 1.5, RF(21): 1.5, LF(4): -0.1	1.7
2019	TOR	MLB	25	107	14	2	0	6	12	14	43	1	0	43.5%	.161/.271/.376	67	.205	-0.4	LF(27): 0.9, RF(4): -0.3, CF(3): -0.2	-0.1
2019	HOU	MLB	25	60	9	2	1	1	5	7	14	4	1	31.9%	.226/.317/.358	83	.289	1.0	LF(11): -0.0, RF(5): 0.4	0.1
2020	TOR	MLB	27	39	5	2	1	1	7	7	11	0	1	40.3%	.226/.359/.452	98	.300	0.1	RF(10): -0.5, LF(5): -0.9	0.0
2021 FS	TOR	MLB	27	600	71	22	2	25	71	73	209	11	3	40.1%	.223/.324/.424	105	.316	2.9	RF -2, LF 0	2.2
2021 DC	TOR	MLB	27	168	20	6	0	7	20	20	58	3	0	40.1%	.223/.324/.424	105	.316	0.8	RF -1, LF 0	0.5

Comparables: Dave Nicholson, Brandon Boggs, Ben Johnson

Few ballplayers have incurred such universal, unequivocable fan wrath as Fisher did on September 15, when his three miscues (two back-to-back!) precipitated a 20-run deluge from the Yankees. It's unclear when or if he'll have the opportunity to repay the debt; on a healthy roster, Fisher is a fourth outfielder at best, and his corner-only, low-contact profile isn't really a good fit for the position. In the days of actual benches, his ability to work walks and occasionally run into one would have made for a decent lottery ticket pinch hitter, but that's likely all he is now, and that roster spot got outsourced to the sidearming reliever Fisher would strike out against.

Randal Grichuk CF
Born: 08/13/91 Age: 29 Bats: R Throws: R Height: 6'2" Weight: 216 Origin: Round 1, 2009 Draft (#24 overall)

YEAR	TEAM	LVL	AGE	PA	R	2B	3B	HR	RBI	BB	K	SB	CS	Whiff%	AVG/OBP/SLG	DRC+	BABIP	BRR	FRAA	WARP
2018	TOR	MLB	26	462	60	32	1	25	61	27	122	3	2	31.2%	.245/.301/.502	109	.282	2.5	RF(102): 2.4, CF(26): -2.3, LF(1): -0.0	1.9
2019	TOR	MLB	27	628	75	29	5	31	80	35	163	2	1	28.1%	.232/.280/.457	90	.266	-0.2	RF(92): -3.2, CF(62): -4.9	0.1
2020	TOR	MLB	29	231	38	9	0	12	35	13	49	1	1	23.1%	.273/.312/.481	101	.299	1.0	CF(48): -2.4	0.5
2021 FS	TOR	MLB	29	600	72	27	2	30	83	37	160	5	2	27.3%	.236/.290/.455	97	.276	0.0	CF -21, LF 0	-0.8
2021 DC	TOR	MLB	29	573	69	25	2	28	79	35	152	5	2	27.3%	.236/.290/.455	97	.276	0.0	CF -20	-0.4

Comparables: Preston Wilson, Rick Ankiel, Colby Rasmus

For a moment there, it seemed like we might have been witnessing the birth of a new, powerful, fully-realized Grichuk: Over a few weeks in August, he was unstoppable. Then, of course, he stopped, and it became clear that this is what Grichuk has always done. He is the definition of a streaky player, who will have, every so often, hot stretches so hot that they make you believe, followed by long periods of nothingness. But on a team for whom defense has been an ongoing area of concern, Grichuk is still a stabilizing element in the outfield. His catch at the wall to save the clinching game against the Yankees on September 24, at least, endeared him to Jays fans for a few days. (Until he struck out five times in two games in the Wild Card series.)

★ ★ ★ *2021 Top 101 Prospect* **#41** ★ ★ ★

Jordan Groshans SS Born: 11/10/99 Age: 21 Bats: R Throws: R Height: 6'3" Weight: 205 Origin: Round 1, 2018 Draft (#12 overall)

YEAR	TEAM	LVL	AGE	PA	R	2B	3B	HR	RBI	BB	K	SB	CS	Whiff%	AVG/OBP/SLG	DRC+	BABIP	BRR	FRAA	WARP
2018	BLU	ROK	18	48	4	1	0	1	4	2	8	0	0		.182/.229/.273	34	.194	0.1	SS(6): 0.9, 3B(5): -0.0	-0.1
2018	BLU	ROK	18	159	17	12	0	4	39	13	29	0	0		.331/.390/.500	147	.387	-0.8	3B(16): -1.2, SS(15): 0.6	0.6
2019	LAN	LO-A	19	96	12	6	0	2	13	13	21	1	1		.337/.427/.482	169	.433	-0.4	SS(20): -1.8	0.9
2021 FS	TOR	MLB	21	600	51	26	2	10	55	38	181	1	0		.224/.279/.335	69	.313	-0.6	SS 1, 3B 0	-0.7

"Quit making excuses and get better. There's literally nothing to do in this time but to get better. It's not a vacation." If Groshans' Twitter proverbs are any indication, the pandemic and the cancellation of the minor league season haven't slowed him down a bit. The arrival of 2020 draft choice Austin Martin may have completed Groshans' inevitable transition to third, but there's little concern over whether he can handle the position offensively or defensively. The foot injury that cut his breakout 2019 short is fully healed, and the six home runs he hit in spring training 2.0 hinted at a promise to come.

Vladimir Guerrero Jr. 3B Born: 03/16/99 Age: 22 Bats: R Throws: R Height: 6'2" Weight: 250 Origin: International Free Agent, 2015

YEAR	TEAM	LVL	AGE	PA	R	2B	3B	HR	RBI	BB	K	SB	CS	Whiff%	AVG/OBP/SLG	DRC+	BABIP	BRR	FRAA	WARP
2018	NH	AA	19	266	48	19	1	14	60	21	27	3	3		.402/.449/.671	192	.402	-2.9	3B(53): 1.0	2.9
2018	BUF	AAA	19	128	15	7	0	6	16	15	10	0	0		.336/.414/.564	185	.323	-4.8	3B(25): 4.3	1.4
2019	BUF	AAA	20	34	7	1	0	3	8	4	2	1	0		.367/.441/.700	158	.320	-0.2	3B(7): 0.1	0.3
2019	TOR	MLB	20	514	52	26	2	15	69	46	91	0	1	24.5%	.272/.339/.433	100	.308	-3.5	3B(96): -5.1	0.9
2020	TOR	MLB	21	243	34	13	2	9	33	20	38	1	0	24.7%	.262/.329/.462	106	.282	0.4	1B(34): 1.9	0.8
2021 FS	TOR	MLB	22	600	70	30	2	21	80	52	103	4	1	24.6%	.265/.334/.452	114	.291	-0.5	3B 0	2.3
2021 DC	TOR	MLB	22	573	67	29	2	20	76	49	98	3	1	24.6%	.265/.334/.452	114	.291	-0.4	1B 0, 3B 0	2.0

Comparables: Adrián Beltré, Ryan Zimmerman, Eric Chavez

There was little more frustrating to the spirit of the long-suffering Jays fan than watching an early-2020 Vlad plate appearance, the outcome of which always seemed to be the same: a ball absolutely scorched—just demolished—straight into the ground. Guerrero struggled to elevate throughout his rookie campaign, with an average launch angle of just over six degrees. But that total was nothing compared to the early weeks of the 2020 season. In August, though his hard-hit rate on fastballs was over 55 percent, his average launch angle on those pitches was one degree. One degree! When he hit the ball in the air, there was a good chance that you would see it leave the yard—but why couldn't it be hit in the air more often? Combine the frustrated expectations with the growing pains of someone playing a position for the first time without the benefit of a full spring training to adjust, and there was a lot to wring one's hands over.

And yet, as was the case the year prior, Guerrero was still an above-average hitter. He not only maintained his low strikeout rate, but lowered it. And in September, particularly during the season's final weeks, there was a dazzling glimpse of the player that was promised, the player that very well still could be. On September 17, Guerrero struck out on a Masahiro Tanaka slider. Nine games passed until he struck out again. He batted .342/.375/.632 over the 11 games from September 18 to the regular season's end. His average launch angle on fastballs over that time, and for the entire month of September, jumped all the way up to 13.

Since the Jays' early postseason exit, Guerrero has expressed a renewed commitment to focus on conditioning and training. Though it's been said in every assessment of his somewhat underwhelming big-league performance so far, it's worth repeating because it's true: He's still only 21 years old. If these early seasons are just the growing pains, then they've been pretty exceptional.

Lourdes Gurriel Jr. LF Born: 10/10/93 Age: 27 Bats: R Throws: R Height: 6'4" Weight: 215 Origin: International Free Agent, 2016

YEAR	TEAM	LVL	AGE	PA	R	2B	3B	HR	RBI	BB	K	SB	CS	Whiff%	AVG/OBP/SLG	DRC+	BABIP	BRR	FRAA	WARP
2018	NH	AA	24	65	7	3	1	2	14	3	8	1	1		.322/.354/.508	129	.333	0.3	2B(7): -0.1, SS(5): -0.7	0.3
2018	BUF	AAA	24	156	20	8	0	5	30	4	34	3	2		.293/.321/.449	116	.345	-0.9	SS(23): 0.9, 2B(9): 0.2, 1B(1): 0.2	0.7
2018	TOR	MLB	24	263	30	8	0	11	35	9	59	1	2	25.2%	.281/.309/.446	104	.326	-1.7	SS(46): -0.8, 2B(24): -1.1	0.8
2019	BUF	AAA	25	130	18	13	0	4	26	3	23	0	2		.276/.308/.480	104	.309	-3.6	2B(12): -1.1, SS(7): -2.0, LF(7): -1.0	-0.2
2019	TOR	MLB	25	343	52	19	2	20	50	20	86	6	4	32.8%	.277/.327/.541	112	.318	2.0	LF(63): -0.1, 2B(9): -1.3, 1B(3): -0.3	1.5
2020	TOR	MLB	27	224	28	14	0	11	33	14	48	3	1	26.3%	.308/.348/.534	112	.351	0.4	LF(53): 8.2, 1B(1): -0.0	1.7
2021 FS	TOR	MLB	27	600	69	29	1	26	83	29	141	4	2	28.9%	.263/.306/.461	106	.307	-2.6	LF -16, 1B 0	0.5
2021 DC	TOR	MLB	27	573	66	28	1	25	80	28	135	4	2	28.9%	.263/.306/.461	106	.307	-2.5	LF -15	0.1

Comparables: Geoff Jenkins, Alfonso Soriano, Trey Mancini

Gurriel's signing to a seven-year deal in late 2016 was one of the first, defining moves of the Shapiro/Atkins regime—a major international signing, full of potential, with the second son of one of Cuba's premier baseball families coming to Toronto. Four years down the line, that potential only seems more exciting. Gurriel hit the ground running in his rookie season, but with each successive year, he shores up the weaknesses in his game and adds more dazzle to the parts that already had shine. His approach at the plate, with its often wild swings and misses, became more focused; he swung at better pitches, whiffed less often and forced pitchers to throw him strikes. When he hit the ball, as he often did, he hit it with authority. He benefitted, too, from a second season as a permanent outfielder, showing off a powerful arm to lead the league in putouts.

Best of all, he managed to avoid injury. His two major-league seasons before this were nearly as truncated, in terms of games played, as the 2020 season. But those were on account of being hurt: ankles, knees, an errant appendix. This year, he played in all but three games, only seeming to get stronger as the season went on; he nearly hit for the cycle in the final game of the season. Gurriel, along with his outfield-mate Hernandez, has been a delight to watch both on the field and in the dugout.

Teoscar Hernández LF Born: 10/15/92 Age: 28 Bats: R Throws: R Height: 6'2" Weight: 205 Origin: International Free Agent, 2011

YEAR	TEAM	LVL	AGE	PA	R	2B	3B	HR	RBI	BB	K	SB	CS	Whiff%	AVG/OBP/SLG	DRC+	BABIP	BRR	FRAA	WARP
2018	TOR	MLB	25	523	67	29	7	22	57	41	163	5	5	38.5%	.239/.302/.468	103	.313	-0.1	LF(87): -2.0, RF(35): 0.7	1.3
2019	BUF	AAA	26	83	11	0	1	5	11	6	21	3	0		.253/.313/.480	84	.280	0.8	CF(9): -1.5, LF(5): 0.3	0.0
2019	TOR	MLB	26	464	58	19	2	26	65	45	153	6	3	34.8%	.230/.306/.472	100	.293	-0.4	CF(79): -0.8, LF(46): 9.6	2.4
2020	TOR	MLB	28	207	33	7	0	16	34	14	63	6	1	34.9%	.289/.340/.579	123	.348	-1.1	RF(40): -2.6, CF(9): -0.2	1.1
2021 FS	TOR	MLB	28	600	78	25	2	34	91	48	191	11	4	35.8%	.247/.314/.494	115	.313	-1.2	RF 5, CF 0	3.3
2021 DC	TOR	MLB	28	573	74	24	2	33	87	46	183	10	4	35.8%	.247/.314/.494	115	.313	-1.2	RF 5, CF 0	2.9

Comparables: *Pete Incaviglia, Bo Jackson, Geoff Jenkins*

The power has always been there with Hernández; that much is clear. There have been so many tantalizing several-week stretches over the course of his time with the Jays that have hinted at what might be lurking: not just an above-average hitter, as he's been throughout his career so far, but someone beyond even that. Those hot streaks, though, have so often been followed by frigid ones. That began to change in the second half of 2019, and in the two-plus months that constituted the 2020 season, Hernández blossomed. He hit the ball harder than ever before, he cut his (still sky-high) strikeout rate, and, more than anything else, he didn't ever stop hitting. A great first week in July gave way to a scorching August, wherein Hernández alone seemed like he could have generated enough energy to power the team indefinitely. And though an oblique injury slowed his September, his final month, taken as a whole, still fueled optimism. And unlikely as it might have seemed when they acquired him from the Astros in 2017, Hernández, too, has become one of the faces of this team, vibrant and ever-smiling — one of the most important contributors to their success this season, and a vital part of the core group moving forward.

Miguel Hiraldo 3B Born: 09/05/00 Age: 20 Bats: R Throws: R Height: 5'11" Weight: 170 Origin: International Free Agent, 2017

YEAR	TEAM	LVL	AGE	PA	R	2B	3B	HR	RBI	BB	K	SB	CS	Whiff%	AVG/OBP/SLG	DRC+	BABIP	BRR	FRAA	WARP
2018	DSL BLJ	ROK	17	239	41	18	3	2	33	23	30	15	6		.313/.381/.453	170	.355	2.8	SS(46): 2.9, 3B(4): -0.3	2.8
2018	BLU	ROK	17	40	3	4	0	0	3	1	12	3	0		.231/.250/.333	48	.333	-0.3	3B(5): 0.0, SS(4): -0.8	-0.3
2019	BLU	ROK+	18	256	43	20	1	7	37	14	36	11	3		.300/.348/.481	125	.328	1.3		1.7
2019	LAN	LO-A	18	4	0	0	1	0	0	0	0	0	0		.250/.250/.750	79	.250	0.0	2B(1): 0.0	0.0
2021 FS	TOR	MLB	20	600	45	27	2	7	51	27	162	18	6		.218/.258/.319	55	.291	2.5	SS 3, 3B 0	-1.1

Hiraldo used to play the same position as Vladimir Guerrero, Jr.; now he just plays the same position as vaunted prospect Orelvis Martinez. This is the problem with focusing on ordinal prospect lists; in a lesser system, his angry bat and advanced progression would be driving anticipation, but with the Blue Jays he's the fallback for bigger dreams. There's some question defensively about his stocky build, but the good news is that his bat will carry him as far down the defensive spectrum as he needs to go. Hiraldo can hit, and if he continues to do so, that'll be enough, either for Toronto or whichever team takes advantage of their surplus.

Danny Jansen C Born: 04/15/95 Age: 26 Bats: R Throws: R Height: 6'2" Weight: 225 Origin: Round 16, 2013 Draft (#475 overall)

YEAR	TEAM	LVL	AGE	PA	R	2B	3B	HR	RBI	BB	K	SB	CS	Whiff%	AVG/OBP/SLG	DRC+	BABIP	BRR	FRAA	WARP
2018	BUF	AAA	23	360	45	21	1	12	58	44	49	5	1		.275/.390/.473	137	.292	0.2	C(56): -6.0	1.7
2018	TOR	MLB	23	95	12	6	0	3	8	9	17	0	0	16.9%	.247/.347/.432	100	.274	0.9	C(29): 1.0	0.7
2019	TOR	MLB	24	384	41	12	1	13	43	31	79	0	1	20.5%	.207/.279/.360	82	.230	-0.7	C(103): 11.9	2.2
2020	TOR	MLB	25	147	18	7	0	6	20	21	31	0	0	24.9%	.183/.312/.358	108	.190	-1.0	C(43): 0.2	0.7
2021 FS	TOR	MLB	26	600	70	22	1	22	69	64	126	1	0	21.7%	.233/.329/.409	105	.266	-0.4	C 9	3.7
2021 DC	TOR	MLB	26	404	47	14	1	14	46	43	85	1	0	21.7%	.233/.329/.409	105	.266	-0.3	C 9	2.8

Comparables: *Ryan Doumit, Charles Johnson, Mickey Tettleton*

Canadian Zunino took all the things that helped him take a step forward in 2019 and did them a little more. Jansen can't match his division rival's muscle at the plate (his exit velocity ranks near the bottom among even catchers), but he sticks to his approach anyway, which is to swing at pitches he can homer on and let the rest go. It's not pretty baseball—even Mario Mendoza posted a .250 BABIP—but it does the job often enough to provide value. Add to that his excellent defense, and the Blue Jays shouldn't have to worry about their catching position for the rest of this contention cycle.

YEAR	TEAM	P. COUNT	FRM RUNS	BLK RUNS	THRW RUNS	TOT RUNS
2018	TOR	3610	0.6	0.7	-0.2	1.1
2018	BUF	7752	-4.6	0.2	-0.1	-4.8
2019	TOR	14805	10.9	2.1	0.4	13.4
2020	TOR	6284	0.1	0.8	0.0	0.9
2021	TOR	14430	6.0	3.5	0.3	9.9

★ ★ ★ *2021 Top 101 Prospect* **#101** ★ ★ ★

Alejandro Kirk C Born: 11/06/98 Age: 22 Bats: R Throws: R Height: 5'8" Weight: 265 Origin: International Free Agent, 2016

YEAR	TEAM	LVL	AGE	PA	R	2B	3B	HR	RBI	BB	K	SB	CS	Whiff%	AVG/OBP/SLG	DRC+	BABIP	BRR	FRAA	WARP
2018	BLU	ROK	19	244	31	10	1	10	57	33	21	2	0		.354/.443/.558	189	.354	-2.4	C(32): 3.2	2.0
2019	LAN	LO-A	20	96	15	6	1	3	8	18	8	1	0		.299/.427/.519	162	.299	0.9	C(17): 0.1	1.1
2019	DUN	HI-A	20	276	26	25	0	4	36	38	31	2	0		.288/.395/.446	153	.317	-3.4	C(68): 0.8	2.4
2020	TOR	MLB	22	25	4	2	0	1	3	1	4	0	0	21.6%	.375/.400/.583	96	.421	-0.3	C(7): -0.1	0.0
2021 FS	TOR	MLB	22	600	64	30	2	13	65	53	105	0	0	21.6%	.257/.329/.395	100	.297	-0.3	C -4	2.1
2021 DC	TOR	MLB	22	134	14	6	0	3	14	12	23	0	0	21.6%	.257/.329/.395	100	.297	-0.1	C -1	0.3

Comparables: *Luis Campusano, Logan Morrison, Chance Sisco*

Kirk provided the natural evolution of one trend, and the subversion of another. You can't talk about the young catcher/designated hitter without mentioning his size, of course; if his Vogelbachian predecessors were sometimes described as bowling balls, Kirk is a cannonball. That said, his offensive profile is more akin to Willians Astudillo, demonstrating a short swing and excellent bat-to-ball skills, as well as credible blocking and framing skills given his own frame. Where he, and many other prospects, bucked a trend in 2020 is by jumping from A-ball to apply those skills. The Blue Jays, in the thick of a pennant race, wisely decided that if Kirk's lack of athleticism was going to be a problem in the future, they may as well take advantage of the present. A four-hit, triple-shy-of-the-cycle performance on September 21 was his exclamation point, but he only went one start, and that a seven-inning affair, without getting at least one hit. He'll be fun to watch in 2021.

YEAR	TEAM	P. COUNT	FRM RUNS	BLK RUNS	THRW RUNS	TOT RUNS
2020	TOR	1001	-0.6	0.0	0.0	-0.6
2021	TOR	2405	-1.4	0.1	0.0	-1.3

★ ★ ★ *2021 Top 101 Prospect* **#22** ★ ★ ★

Austin Martin   SS   Born: 03/23/99   Age: 22   Bats: R   Throws: R   Height: 6'0"   Weight: 185   Origin: Round 1, 2020 Draft (#5 overall)

Widely considered the best pure hitter in the draft, Toronto was pleasantly surprised to see the former Vanderbilt standout fall to the fifth pick. Despite not being able to jump into a minor-league season, reports from Rochester were glowing on both sides of the ball. Martin did fielding work at infield and outfield positions, and his natural hitting ability and advanced approach are building anticipation for the day when he can actually play in a minor-league game. If there's any cause for caution here, it's the occasional assumption that growth is automatic; Martin could develop power and become one of the league's best hitters, or he could hit a lot of pleasant, sharp line drives over the infielders.

Orelvis Martinez   SS   Born: 11/19/01   Age: 19   Bats: R   Throws: R   Height: 6'1"   Weight: 188   Origin: International Free Agent, 2018

YEAR	TEAM	LVL	AGE	PA	R	2B	3B	HR	RBI	BB	K	SB	CS	Whiff%	AVG/OBP/SLG	DRC+	BABIP	BRR	FRAA	WARP
2019	BLU	ROK	17	163	20	8	5	7	32	14	29	2	0		.275/.352/.549	139	.296	1.1	SS(26): -3.2, 3B(11): -2.0	0.8
2021 FS	TOR	MLB	19	600	43	26	4	7	48	29	187	3	0		.201/.247/.302	49	.287	3.1	SS -3, 3B -1	-2.2

Martinez's 2020 season was one of the most anticipated among Jays prospect-watchers. The teenager with the explosive power was to enter his first full year as a pro—but, of course, that didn't happen. Instead of providing crucial developmental data, Martinez and his fellow Latin American teenagers spent the early stages of quarantine outside a Florida hotel, hitting and throwing balled socks wrapped in tape. Our eager eyes shall have to wait until (hopefully) the spring, when it will become more clear whether he can channel the chaos of his swing into consistent production against higher-level pitching, and non-footwear equipment.

Reese McGuire   C   Born: 03/02/95   Age: 26   Bats: L   Throws: R   Height: 6'0"   Weight: 215   Origin: Round 1, 2013 Draft (#14 overall)

YEAR	TEAM	LVL	AGE	PA	R	2B	3B	HR	RBI	BB	K	SB	CS	Whiff%	AVG/OBP/SLG	DRC+	BABIP	BRR	FRAA	WARP
2018	BUF	AAA	23	369	31	9	2	7	37	33	77	3	2		.233/.312/.339	94	.281	1.6	C(73): 15.0	2.4
2018	TOR	MLB	23	33	5	3	0	2	4	2	9	1	0	30.5%	.290/.333/.581	95	.350	0.3	C(11): 0.7	0.2
2019	BUF	AAA	24	277	30	12	1	5	29	25	44	4	0		.247/.316/.366	77	.276	-3.8	C(71): 4.2	0.7
2019	TOR	MLB	24	105	14	7	0	5	11	7	18	0	0	21.8%	.299/.346/.526	106	.324	0.6	C(30): 5.0	1.2
2020	TOR	MLB	25	45	2	0	0	1	1	0	11	0	0	21.4%	.073/.073/.146	54	.069	-0.5	C(18): 0.0	-0.2
2021 FS	TOR	MLB	26	600	59	25	2	13	58	47	124	2	0	22.5%	.223/.290/.352	77	.264	-0.3	C 12	1.9
2021 DC	TOR	MLB	26	202	20	8	0	4	19	15	41	0	0	22.5%	.223/.290/.352	77	.264	-0.1	C 5	0.8

Comparables: Justin Knoedler, Bryan Holaday, George Kottaras

YEAR	TEAM	P. COUNT	FRM RUNS	BLK RUNS	THRW RUNS	TOT RUNS
2018	TOR	1370	0.4	0.5	-0.1	0.9
2018	BUF	9722	15.4	0.2	0.3	15.8
2019	TOR	4094	5.0	0.4	0.0	5.4
2019	BUF	10274	7.0	0.0	-1.5	5.5
2020	TOR	1815	-0.4	0.1	0.0	-0.2
2021	TOR	7215	4.4	1.5	0.2	6.0

That could certainly have gone better. McGuire opened camp in unique fashion, getting arrested for some extracurricular automotive activity—if you know thyself, you know thyself—and providing ballpark organists around the country with a lifetime of musical ammunition. He proceeded to hand back two seasons' worth of surprising offensive production in one concentrated supply of weapons-grade regression. Those details, combined with the sudden arrival of theoretical catching prospect Alejandro Kirk, dealt a sizable blow to any dreams of working his way into a short-side platoon with starter Danny Jansen. McGuire's defensive acumen, and his lack of options, will keep him in the Blue Jays' plans for a little longer, but only just.

Gabriel Moreno   C   Born: 02/14/00   Age: 21   Bats: R   Throws: R   Height: 5'11"   Weight: 160   Origin: International Free Agent, 2016

YEAR	TEAM	LVL	AGE	PA	R	2B	3B	HR	RBI	BB	K	SB	CS	Whiff%	AVG/OBP/SLG	DRC+	BABIP	BRR	FRAA	WARP
2018	BLU	ROK	18	66	10	5	0	2	14	3	13	1	0		.279/.303/.459	93	.312	-0.8	C(15): 0.0	0.0
2018	BLU	ROK	18	101	14	12	2	2	22	4	7	1	1		.413/.455/.652	211	.429	-2.1	C(17): 0.1	0.9
2019	LAN	LO-A	19	341	47	17	5	12	52	22	38	7	1		.280/.337/.485	130	.282	0.4	C(54): 1.0	2.5
2021 FS	TOR	MLB	21	600	54	26	3	14	63	24	113	7	2		.239/.276/.378	78	.274	1.8	C 0	0.9

Comparables: Chance Sisco, John Ryan Murphy, Manuel Margot

Moreno, an infielder-turned-catcher and the youngest of the Jays' plethora of young backstops, broke onto the scene in 2018, continued to look great at the plate in 2019 as one of the younger players at Low-A Lansing, and was apparently a standout at the Jays' alternate site. After years of failing to deliver on would-be catchers of the future, it's a pleasant change of pace to have so many promising players at the position coming up through the system. With luck, one of them will loose the spectre of Russell Martin from its earthly tether, free to frame the stars in the night sky.

Joe Panik   2B   Born: 10/30/90   Age: 30   Bats: L   Throws: R   Height: 6'1"   Weight: 205   Origin: Round 1, 2011 Draft (#29 overall)

YEAR	TEAM	LVL	AGE	PA	R	2B	3B	HR	RBI	BB	K	SB	CS	Whiff%	AVG/OBP/SLG	DRC+	BABIP	BRR	FRAA	WARP
2018	SF	MLB	27	392	38	14	1	4	24	26	30	4	2	10.7%	.254/.307/.332	86	.265	1.0	2B(94): 4.3, 1B(1): 0.1	1.1
2019	NYM	MLB	28	103	17	4	1	2	12	7	9	0	0	9.4%	.277/.333/.404	91	.289	-0.1	2B(28): -1.4	0.1
2019	SF	MLB	28	388	33	17	1	3	27	36	38	4	2	10.7%	.235/.310/.317	86	.254	-0.5	2B(90): 5.0	1.0
2020	TOR	MLB	30	141	18	6	0	1	7	20	27	0	0	18.3%	.225/.340/.300	94	.283	0.6	2B(18): -2.7, SS(14): 1.1, 3B(12): -1.4	0.0
2021 FS	TOR	MLB	30	600	60	25	2	10	59	58	86	5	2	12.3%	.248/.328/.364	93	.278	0.4	2B -2, 1B 0	1.5

Comparables: Mark Loretta, Frank Bolling, Gene Baker

Now entering his 30s, Panik did not blossom into a slugger in 2020. He did not even return to being a league-average hitter. An extremely slow start at the plate, fueled in part by an uncharacteristic tendency to swing and miss, had Jays fans weeping and gnashing their teeth. But improvements at the plate toward the end of the season—and a fantastic walk rate—netted him more consistent playing time, and saved countless dental visits before year's end.

Travis Shaw   3B   Born: 04/16/90   Age: 31   Bats: L   Throws: R   Height: 6'4"   Weight: 230   Origin: Round 9, 2011 Draft (#292 overall)

YEAR	TEAM	LVL	AGE	PA	R	2B	3B	HR	RBI	BB	K	SB	CS	Whiff%	AVG/OBP/SLG	DRC+	BABIP	BRR	FRAA	WARP
2018	MIL	MLB	28	587	73	23	0	32	86	78	108	5	2	20.5%	.241/.345/.480	120	.242	-0.7	3B(107): 1.8, 2B(39): -0.5, 1B(17): 0.0	3.5
2019	SA	AAA	29	174	27	4	0	12	33	36	37	3	1		.286/.437/.586	160	.299	-2.1	3B(23): 1.0, 1B(10): 0.4, 2B(2): -0.1	1.6
2019	MIL	MLB	29	270	22	5	0	7	16	36	89	0	0	29.8%	.157/.281/.270	70	.216	0.1	3B(71): 2.3, 1B(6): 0.2, 2B(2): -0.0	0.2
2020	TOR	MLB	30	180	17	10	0	6	17	16	50	0	0	29.3%	.239/.306/.411	94	.306	-1.3	3B(37): 1.6, 1B(14): 1.1	0.4
2021 FS	TOR	MLB	31	600	68	23	1	24	73	63	164	5	1	26.4%	.228/.317/.419	98	.282	-0.1	3B 4, 2B -1	1.5

Comparables: Dean Palmer, Wilson Betemit, Phil Nevin

After a disastrous 2019 at the plate, Shaw's 2020 was something of a bounce-back, though it wasn't exactly a great showing. His strikeout rate fell, but remained sky-high, as did his whiff rate; he also walked at a lower rate than he has in four years. He was clearly hitting the ball hard, but it didn't seem to translate into much results-wise. The Blue Jays are left with what will be a common question: Were 60 games just not enough for the exit velocity to find its way into the slugging percentage? Or had it already, hidden by the greater regression of Being Travis Shaw? What he did have to offer was a competent third base, which, in the wake of Vlad Jr.'s move to first, was something the Jays needed. Though no longer: Given the organization's surfeit of minor-league reinforcements, they chose to non-tender Shaw in the autumn.

Kevin Smith   SS   Born: 07/04/96   Age: 25   Bats: R   Throws: R   Height: 6'0"   Weight: 190   Origin: Round 4, 2017 Draft (#129 overall)

YEAR	TEAM	LVL	AGE	PA	R	2B	3B	HR	RBI	BB	K	SB	CS	Whiff%	AVG/OBP/SLG	DRC+	BABIP	BRR	FRAA	WARP
2018	LAN	LO-A	21	204	36	23	4	7	44	17	33	12	1		.355/.407/.639	189	.397	3.1	SS(24): 1.7, 3B(21): 0.7	3.2
2018	DUN	HI-A	21	371	57	8	2	18	49	23	88	17	5		.274/.332/.468	125	.319	4.6	SS(63): 6.9, 2B(13): 1.0, 3B(6): -0.2	3.0
2019	NH	AA	22	468	49	22	2	19	61	29	151	11	6		.209/.263/.402	91	.269	1.4	SS(87): 0.4, 3B(18): -1.1, 2B(5): -0.9	1.5
2021 FS	TOR	MLB	24	600	59	26	2	21	70	33	205	11	3		.214/.263/.386	72	.295	2.3	SS 8, 3B 0	0.8

Comparables: Junior Lake, Orlando Calixte, Brad Harman

The major area of concern for Smith, a solid-but-not-stunning infield defender, is the leap in his strikeout rate—and the attendant decrease in his on-base ability—that he experienced after moving up to Double-A in 2019. Smith is a known swing-changer, having made adjustments in the offseason prior to his 2018 breakout; the next adjustment will have to be made while facing better pitchers.

Rowdy Tellez   1B   Born: 03/16/95   Age: 26   Bats: L   Throws: L   Height: 6'4"   Weight: 255   Origin: Round 30, 2013 Draft (#895 overall)

YEAR	TEAM	LVL	AGE	PA	R	2B	3B	HR	RBI	BB	K	SB	CS	Whiff%	AVG/OBP/SLG	DRC+	BABIP	BRR	FRAA	WARP
2018	BUF	AAA	23	444	43	22	0	13	50	40	74	7	4		.270/.340/.425	122	.298	-0.8	1B(107): -3.0	0.6
2018	TOR	MLB	23	73	10	9	0	4	14	2	21	0	0	29.2%	.314/.329/.614	101	.391	-0.1	1B(17): -0.4	0.1
2019	BUF	AAA	24	109	20	9	0	7	21	14	25	0	0		.366/.450/.688	175	.435	-1.6	1B(26): 1.9	1.1
2019	TOR	MLB	24	409	49	19	0	21	54	29	116	1	1	31.3%	.227/.293/.449	91	.267	-1.1	1B(57): 4.3	0.5
2020	TOR	MLB	25	127	20	5	0	8	23	11	20	0	1	23.5%	.283/.346/.540	118	.276	0.1	1B(19): -0.9	0.3
2021 FS	TOR	MLB	26	600	73	30	1	28	83	53	138	1	0	29.1%	.250/.324/.468	111	.286	-1.1	1B 1	1.8
2021 DC	TOR	MLB	26	539	66	27	1	25	75	48	124	0	0	29.1%	.250/.324/.468	111	.286	-1.0	1B 1	1.6

Comparables: Fernando Seguignol, Tony Clark, Mike Jacobs

After the disappointment of 2019, Tellez thrived in his newfound platoon role in 2020. He started slow, gathered steam through August, then absolutely exploded in September, batting .387/.444/.613 through the nine games he played. Tragically for both Tellez and the Jays, a knee injury knocked him out for the rest of the regular season, though he did make a surprise appearance in the Jays' brief postseason stint, recording a hit and eventually coming around to score in his lone at-bat.

Tellez is a fan favorite, a 30th-round pick who worked his way through the system before a breakout in Triple-A, a survivor of hardship on and off the field. The questions raised by last year's struggles about his long-term viability as a player were especially hard to hear about someone whose journey has been one of the team's most profound stories. All the more satisfying, then, to see his success, even in this shortened season: the mashing of lefties, the vast improvement in his two-strike approach and the attendant drop in his strikeout rate, the same power that he flashed in his 2018 September callup. Tellez has played himself into the Jays' future, at least the not-too-distant one.

Jonathan Villar SS Born: 05/02/91   Age: 30   Bats: S   Throws: R   Height: 6'0"   Weight: 233   Origin: International Free Agent, 2008

YEAR	TEAM	LVL	AGE	PA	R	2B	3B	HR	RBI	BB	K	SB	CS	Whiff%	AVG/OBP/SLG	DRC+	BABIP	BRR	FRAA	WARP
2018	BAL	MLB	27	236	28	4	0	8	24	22	58	21	3	29.7%	.258/.336/.392	84	.319	2.4	2B(36): 1.0, SS(18): 0.5	0.8
2018	MIL	MLB	27	279	26	10	1	6	22	19	80	14	2	29.7%	.261/.315/.377	81	.355	0.5	2B(74): -6.1	-0.3
2019	BAL	MLB	28	714	111	33	5	24	73	61	176	40	9	27.6%	.274/.339/.453	94	.341	5.6	2B(111): 4.0, SS(97): 0.9	3.3
2020	MIA	MLB	29	128	10	4	0	2	9	10	32	9	5	32.3%	.259/.315/.345	63	.337	-1.4	SS(14): -3.5, 2B(12): -0.5, CF(2): -0.2	-0.8
2020	TOR	MLB	29	79	3	1	0	0	6	9	22	7	0	32.1%	.188/.278/.203	62	.271	0.6	2B(13): 1.7, SS(7): 0.1	0.1
2021 FS	TOR	MLB	30	600	67	22	1	14	54	55	168	37	10	29.1%	.242/.316/.371	90	.325	9.4	2B 0, SS 1	2.4

Comparables: Jose Valentin, Alex Gonzalez, Dale Sveum

Acquired at the deadline to shore up the infield and add some baserunning ability, Villar's modest success as a Marlin did not carry over to the Jays. While he did manage to steal seven bases, making him the team leader in that regard, he struggled bitterly at the plate during his month with the team. It wasn't so much a change in his approach as that of his opponents: Pitchers fed him breaking pitches, and he flailed badly at them. His playing time dwindled in the last weeks of the season, and after being pinch-hit for in Game 1 of the Wild Card Series, the camera watched as Villar packed up his stuff and left, disappearing into the darkness of the clubhouse.

PITCHERS

Chase Anderson RHP Born: 11/30/87   Age: 33   Bats: R   Throws: R   Height: 6'1"   Weight: 210   Origin: Round 9, 2009 Draft (#276 overall)

YEAR	TEAM	LVL	AGE	W	L	SV	G	GS	IP	H	HR	BB/9	K/9	K	GB%	BABIP	WHIP	ERA	DRA-	WARP	MPH	FA%	Whiff%	CSP
2018	MIL	MLB	30	9	8	0	30	30	158	131	30	3.2	7.3	128	34.3%	.242	1.19	3.93	123	-0.4	94.3	53.5%	22.1%	46.9%
2019	MIL	MLB	31	8	4	0	32	27	139	126	23	3.2	8.0	124	34.1%	.270	1.27	4.21	99	1.4	95.4	50.8%	23.9%	47.6%
2020	TOR	MLB	32	1	2	0	10	7	33²	45	11	2.7	10.2	38	36.2%	.362	1.63	7.22	115	0.0	93.9	40.3%	28.4%	47.2%
2021 FS	TOR	MLB	33	9	8	0	26	26	150	137	25	3.1	8.6	143	36.1%	.277	1.27	4.04	96	1.4	94.8	49.3%	24.3%	47.4%

Comparables: Jhoulys Chacín, Kyle Gibson, Iván Nova

Anderson had a record-tying performance in 2020. Unfortunately, the record was home runs allowed in an inning, with five. It was a rare burst of notability from the usually anonymous back-end starter, who posted one great start in August, an eight-strikeout, five-inning effort against the Orioles. It was all downhill from there. Some excerpts from headlines describing his outings: "roughed up," "hit hard," "on the wrong side of history." Sounds about right, unfortunately.

Anthony Bass RHP Born: 11/01/87   Age: 33   Bats: R   Throws: R   Height: 6'2"   Weight: 200   Origin: Round 5, 2008 Draft (#165 overall)

YEAR	TEAM	LVL	AGE	W	L	SV	G	GS	IP	H	HR	BB/9	K/9	K	GB%	BABIP	WHIP	ERA	DRA-	WARP	MPH	FA%	Whiff%	CSP
2018	IOW	AAA	30	0	3	3	27	0	32	34	3	1.7	7.0	25	51.0%	.310	1.25	3.38	75	0.6				
2018	CHC	MLB	30	0	0	0	16	0	15¹	18	1	1.8	8.2	14	53.3%	.386	1.37	2.93	106	0.0	95.6	68.4%	20.8%	48.5%
2019	LOU	AAA	31	1	1	9	19	0	20¹	13	1	2.7	8.4	19	52.7%	.222	0.93	2.21	55	0.7				
2019	SEA	MLB	31	2	4	5	44	0	48	30	5	3.2	8.1	43	53.1%	.207	0.98	3.56	70	1.0	97.0	52.7%	27.9%	43.0%
2020	TOR	MLB	32	2	3	7	26	0	25²	17	2	3.2	7.4	21	61.4%	.224	1.01	3.51	84	0.4	96.4	54.2%	28.0%	43.3%
2021 FS	TOR	MLB	33	2	2	0	57	0	50	45	6	3.2	8.1	44	52.6%	.278	1.26	3.51	87	0.5	96.6	54.6%	27.3%	43.6%

Comparables: Jeremy Affeldt, Jeremy Jeffress, Tommy Hunter

Bass appeared in more games than any other Jays pitcher, and for good reason. The journeyman, appearing on the sixth team of his nine-year major league career, threw more sinkers and sliders than ever before, generating whiffs and groundballs at career-high rates. Bass is still not a strikeout artist, and he was certainly not unhittable in 2020. But he was consistent: Game after game, Bass could be relied upon for a solid inning-plus of work, and he made very few appearances that could qualify as meltdowns. Perhaps the symbol of this relief corps, Bass was a pre-season afterthought who ended up playing a critical role in the Jays' postseason run.

Ryan Borucki LHP Born: 03/31/94   Age: 27   Bats: L   Throws: L   Height: 6'4"   Weight: 215   Origin: Round 15, 2012 Draft (#475 overall)

YEAR	TEAM	LVL	AGE	W	L	SV	G	GS	IP	H	HR	BB/9	K/9	K	GB%	BABIP	WHIP	ERA	DRA-	WARP	MPH	FA%	Whiff%	CSP
2018	BUF	AAA	24	6	5	0	13	13	77	62	6	3.3	6.8	58	51.8%	.255	1.17	3.27	84	1.2				
2018	TOR	MLB	24	4	6	0	17	17	97²	96	7	3.0	6.2	67	47.0%	.294	1.32	3.87	101	0.9	93.3	58.7%	19.4%	49.1%
2019	BUF	AAA	25	1	0	0	2	2	11	11	4	2.5	7.4	9	42.4%	.241	1.27	4.91	105	0.2				
2019	TOR	MLB	25	0	1	0	2	2	6²	15	3	8.1	8.1	6	39.3%	.500	3.15	10.80	180	-0.2	93.6	52.3%	23.7%	44.2%
2020	TOR	MLB	26	1	1	0	21	0	16²	12	1	6.5	11.3	21	35.0%	.282	1.44	2.70	94	0.2	96.4	47.8%	32.6%	41.3%
2021 FS	TOR	MLB	27	2	3	0	57	0	50	48	7	3.8	8.9	49	43.3%	.295	1.39	4.62	104	0.0	94.4	54.3%	24.3%	45.9%
2021 DC	TOR	MLB	27	2	3	0	57	0	60	57	9	3.8	8.9	59	43.3%	.295	1.39	4.62	104	0.2	94.4	54.3%	24.3%	45.9%

Comparables: Anthony Banda, Walker Lockett, Daniel Norris

The good news is that Borucki managed to exceed his 2019 total of 6⅓ laborious innings. The better news is that he managed to stay healthy through the 2020 season. And the best news of all is that, in a bullpen role that looks to continue into next season, Borucki thrived. All but three of his 21 appearances were scoreless; all three of his pitches saw upticks in velocity; and increased usage of his new and improved slider-cutter proved incredibly effective, serving as his putaway pitch. He ended the season as one of the Jays' most trusted high-leverage relievers—pretty good for someone who didn't even make the Opening Day roster.

Anthony Castro RHP Born: 04/13/95 Age: 26 Bats: R Throws: R Height: 6'2" Weight: 182 Origin: International Free Agent, 2011

YEAR	TEAM	LVL	AGE	W	L	SV	G	GS	IP	H	HR	BB/9	K/9	K	GB%	BABIP	WHIP	ERA	DRA-	WARP	MPH	FA%	Whiff%	CSP
2018	LAK	HI-A	23	9	4	0	22	20	116²	112	8	3.3	7.8	101	48.7%	.310	1.33	2.93	85	1.6				
2018	ERI	AA	23	0	0	0	3	3	10	8	1	10.8	3.6	4	50.0%	.226	2.00	8.10	100	0.1				
2019	ERI	AA	24	5	3	1	27	18	102¹	75	9	5.7	10.2	116	43.4%	.274	1.37	4.40	98	0.2				
2020	DET	MLB	25	0	0	0	1	0	1	1	1	9.0	9.0	1	0.0%	.000	2.00	18.00	112	0.0	93.1	58.8%	37.5%	40.1%
2021 FS	TOR	MLB	26	1	1	0	57	0	50	48	8	5.2	8.4	46	40.8%	.285	1.54	5.40	117	-0.4	93.1	58.8%	37.5%	40.1%
2021 DC	TOR	MLB	26	1	1	0	22	0	24	23	4	5.2	8.4	22	40.8%	.285	1.54	5.40	117	-0.1	93.1	58.8%	37.5%	40.1%

Comparables: Bruce Billings, Sterling Sharp, Chris Stratton

It took eight years of bush-league buses to get the svelte Castro a single major-league inning last year. He's spent most of his career as a fill-in, moving from rotation to bullpen based on the status of other, more vaunted prospects, but his role has finally stabilized into middle relief. He'll likely begin 2021 in Triple-A after being claimed off waivers by the Blue Jays, but shouldn't have to wait another eight years for his second inning.

A.J. Cole RHP Born: 01/05/92 Age: 29 Bats: R Throws: R Height: 6'5" Weight: 240 Origin: Round 4, 2010 Draft (#116 overall)

YEAR	TEAM	LVL	AGE	W	L	SV	G	GS	IP	H	HR	BB/9	K/9	K	GB%	BABIP	WHIP	ERA	DRA-	WARP	MPH	FA%	Whiff%	CSP
2018	NYY	MLB	26	3	1	0	28	0	38	39	9	3.8	11.6	49	35.9%	.319	1.45	4.26	64	0.9	95.7	30.9%	36.8%	43.3%
2018	WAS	MLB	26	1	1	0	4	2	10¹	16	6	5.2	8.7	10	21.6%	.345	2.13	13.06	174	-0.3	94.2	45.1%	18.3%	49.5%
2019	COL	AAA	27	0	1	2	13	0	17	10	2	2.6	11.1	21	36.1%	.235	0.88	3.18	56	0.6				
2019	CLE	MLB	27	3	1	1	25	0	26	31	4	2.8	10.4	30	30.0%	.360	1.50	3.81	132	-0.3	96.0	45.0%	30.3%	48.1%
2020	TOR	MLB	28	3	0	1	24	0	23¹	19	3	3.5	7.7	20	33.3%	.258	1.20	3.09	112	0.1	95.3	44.1%	27.3%	44.3%
2021 FS	TOR	MLB	29	2	2	0	57	0	50	44	8	3.6	9.2	51	34.9%	.275	1.30	4.11	97	0.2	95.6	41.4%	30.0%	45.6%

Comparables: Mike Foltynewicz, Jon Gray, Kevin Gausman

Cole outperformed his DRA by a significant margin. His slider generated far fewer whiffs than it has in recent seasons. His strikeout rate dropped. How, then, did he manage to be so successful? One could point to the addition of a cutter, or improved performance on his fastball that always seemed to barely avoid the sweet spot of the bat. Either way, he was an unexpectedly valuable contributor to the Jays' August bullpen success.

Rafael Dolis RHP Born: 01/10/88 Age: 33 Bats: R Throws: R Height: 6'4" Weight: 235 Origin: International Free Agent, 2004

YEAR	TEAM	LVL	AGE	W	L	SV	G	GS	IP	H	HR	BB/9	K/9	K	GB%	BABIP	WHIP	ERA	DRA-	WARP	MPH	FA%	Whiff%	CSP
2020	TOR	MLB	32	2	2	5	24	0	24	16	1	5.2	11.6	31	46.3%	.294	1.25	1.50	76	0.5	96.2	61.1%	30.4%	41.3%
2021 FS	TOR	MLB	33	2	2	18	57	0	50	43	5	4.3	9.8	54	49.8%	.290	1.35	3.97	90	0.4	96.2	61.1%	30.4%	41.3%
2021 DC	TOR	MLB	33	2	2	18	57	0	60	52	7	4.3	9.8	65	49.8%	.290	1.35	3.97	90	0.7	96.2	61.1%	30.4%	41.3%

Comparables: Jeremy Jeffress, Ryan Brasier, Anthony Bass

What a long, strange trip it's been for Dolis, who prior to this season hadn't pitched in the majors since 2013. The Jays signed him from NPB's Hanshin Tigers in January, where his numbers were solid, but he was understandably something of an unknown quantity to most fans. As it turned out, Dolis proved a critical part of the Jays' unexpected bullpen success in 2020. Striking out 31 percent of the batters he faced, effectively limiting hard contact and working at a micro-nap-friendly deliberate pace, Dolis and his sinker-slider-splitter mix came second only to Hyun-Jin Ryu in terms of pitcher importance to the Jays. All the more delightful, then, that he came as such a surprise.

Ken Giles RHP Born: 09/20/90 Age: 30 Bats: R Throws: R Height: 6'3" Weight: 210 Origin: Round 7, 2011 Draft (#241 overall)

YEAR	TEAM	LVL	AGE	W	L	SV	G	GS	IP	H	HR	BB/9	K/9	K	GB%	BABIP	WHIP	ERA	DRA-	WARP	MPH	FA%	Whiff%	CSP
2018	FRE	AAA	27	0	0	0	6	0	5¹	9	0	3.4	13.5	8	41.2%	.529	2.06	8.44	26	0.2				
2018	HOU	MLB	27	0	2	12	34	0	30²	36	2	0.9	9.1	31	36.8%	.366	1.27	4.99	76	0.5	98.9	57.8%	30.7%	51.8%
2018	TOR	MLB	27	0	1	14	21	0	19²	18	4	1.8	10.1	22	51.8%	.275	1.12	4.12	71	0.4	98.9	61.3%	30.8%	48.8%
2019	TOR	MLB	28	2	3	23	53	0	53	36	5	2.9	14.1	83	38.9%	.301	1.00	1.87	53	1.6	98.9	50.7%	40.0%	45.0%
2020	TOR	MLB	29	0	0	1	4	0	3²	4	2	9.8	14.7	6	44.4%	.286	2.18	9.82	82	0.1	96.2	38.5%	54.5%	34.3%
2021 FS	TOR	MLB	30	3	2	0	57	0	50	38	6	3.2	11.8	65	40.4%	.283	1.13	2.85	71	0.9	98.7	52.3%	38.4%	45.9%

Comparables: Cody Allen, Chris Devenski, Chad Green

Having Giles anchoring the back end of the Jays bullpen was supposed to be one of their strengths. Losing him for essentially the entire season was a disaster scenario. But that's exactly what happened: Giles made two appearances in July before getting injured. He made two more in September, both of which were so poor as to clearly indicate that something was still wrong. The Jays were able to survive the loss of their best reliever, but with Tommy John surgery and free agency on his horizon, we may have seen the last of him as a Blue Jay.

Thomas Hatch   RHP   Born: 09/29/94   Age: 26   Bats: R   Throws: R   Height: 6'1"   Weight: 205   Origin: Round 3, 2016 Draft (#104 overall)

YEAR	TEAM	LVL	AGE	W	L	SV	G	GS	IP	H	HR	BB/9	K/9	K	GB%	BABIP	WHIP	ERA	DRA-	WARP	MPH	FA%	Whiff%	CSP
2018	TNS	AA	23	8	6	0	26	26	143²	127	16	3.8	7.3	117	42.4%	.285	1.31	3.82	94	1.5				
2019	NH	AA	24	2	3	0	6	6	35¹	25	5	0.5	8.7	34	50.0%	.241	0.76	2.80	76	0.5				
2019	TNS	AA	24	4	10	0	21	21	100	104	13	3.3	8.4	93	35.5%	.329	1.41	4.59	115	-0.8				
2020	TOR	MLB	25	3	1	0	17	1	26¹	18	2	4.4	7.9	23	45.1%	.232	1.18	2.73	105	0.2	96.6	57.4%	31.2%	42.1%
2021 FS	TOR	MLB	26	3	4	0	57	0	50	50	9	3.8	8.1	44	40.3%	.291	1.43	5.14	113	-0.2	96.6	57.4%	31.2%	42.1%
2021 DC	TOR	MLB	26	3	4	0	40	6	66	66	11	3.8	8.1	59	40.3%	.291	1.43	5.14	113	0.1	96.6	57.4%	31.2%	42.1%

Comparables: Keury Mella, Chris Dwyer, Bobby Parnell

Despite his less-than-sparkling DRA, Hatch made an unexpectedly impressive showing in his rookie season, appearing in 17 games and leaving nothing but footprints in most of them. Thanks to being free from the shackles of the academy over the offseason—he finished up his degree in finance in the winter of 2018-19—Hatch had more time to ramp up his throwing program and monitor his health, avoiding the injuries that hampered his performance in 2019. His high-spin fastball, paired with a changeup and a whiff-inducing slider, made him a trusted option in almost any relief situation. If he keeps it up, he'll give himself more personal finances to manage once he hits arbitration.

Anthony Kay   LHP   Born: 03/21/95   Age: 26   Bats: L   Throws: L   Height: 6'0"   Weight: 225   Origin: Round 1, 2016 Draft (#31 overall)

YEAR	TEAM	LVL	AGE	W	L	SV	G	GS	IP	H	HR	BB/9	K/9	K	GB%	BABIP	WHIP	ERA	DRA-	WARP	MPH	FA%	Whiff%	CSP
2018	COL	LO-A	23	4	4	0	13	13	69¹	73	6	2.9	10.1	78	43.3%	.358	1.37	4.54	85	1.0				
2018	STL	HI-A	23	3	7	0	10	10	53¹	51	1	4.6	7.6	45	38.2%	.327	1.46	3.88	87	0.7				
2019	BNG	AA	24	7	3	0	12	12	66¹	38	2	3.1	9.5	70	34.4%	.226	0.92	1.49	54	1.9				
2019	BUF	AAA	24	2	2	0	7	7	36	33	3	5.5	9.8	39	39.6%	.323	1.53	2.50	127	0.2				
2019	SYR	AAA	24	1	3	0	7	7	31¹	40	7	3.2	7.5	26	28.0%	.367	1.63	6.61	120	0.3				
2019	TOR	MLB	24	1	0	0	3	2	14	15	0	3.2	8.4	13	54.5%	.341	1.43	5.79	97	0.1	95.1	61.6%	24.2%	45.0%
2020	TOR	MLB	25	2	0	0	13	0	21	22	3	6.0	9.4	22	37.1%	.322	1.71	5.14	112	0.0	96.1	56.5%	26.1%	46.8%
2021 FS	TOR	MLB	26	8	9	0	26	26	150	148	27	4.3	8.5	141	37.5%	.292	1.47	5.18	113	0.0	95.8	58.0%	25.6%	46.2%
2021 DC	TOR	MLB	26	3	4	0	32	9	70	69	12	4.3	8.5	66	37.5%	.292	1.47	5.18	113	0.1	95.8	58.0%	25.6%	46.2%

Comparables: Gregory Soto, Conner Menez, Alex Reyes

The Blue Jays enrolled Kay in the Earl Weaver Official Starter Certification program, working him into the major leagues by employing him in the middle innings of close games, bridging the gap to the setup men. The traits that qualified him for entry remain, and he still projects as a decent enough starter, but his 2020 performance did raise some concerns. Kay struggled to persuade batters to chase his pitches, especially his curve, which he tended to spike into the clay. This often put him behind in the count, and it often stayed that way. All this bears all the hallmarks of a slow Tommy John recovery; Kay's success will depend on tunneling the fastball and the curve better to put batters on their heels, and reclaiming the initiative.

Alek Manoah   RHP   Born: 01/09/98   Age: 23   Bats: R   Throws: R   Height: 6'6"   Weight: 260   Origin: Round 1, 2019 Draft (#11 overall)

YEAR	TEAM	LVL	AGE	W	L	SV	G	GS	IP	H	HR	BB/9	K/9	K	GB%	BABIP	WHIP	ERA	DRA-	WARP	MPH	FA%	Whiff%	CSP
2019	VAN	SS	21	0	1	0	6	6	17	13	1	2.6	14.3	27	35.3%	.364	1.06	2.65	64	0.4				
2021 FS	TOR	MLB	23	2	3	0	57	0	50	47	8	5.0	9.2	51	34.7%	.294	1.51	5.14	120	-0.4				

It got lost in the news with everything else going on, but this past spring, while excavating near the Devonian Fossil Gorge in Iowa, two undergraduate paleontology students accidentally unearthed a completely unexpected find: the first recorded evidence of a scouting report, etched into stone tablets. It read: "If he develops his changeup, he could be a third starter, but if not, with his fastball and slider, the floor is a late-inning reliever." Historians have long assumed that mankind passed this down from generation to generation by oral tradition since prehistoric times, but this was the first physical evidence confirming the theory. A team is prepared to return to the site next year to seek the ultimate missing link: the fabled 65-grade tool.

Julian Merryweather   RHP   Born: 10/14/91   Age: 29   Bats: R   Throws: R   Height: 6'4"   Weight: 215   Origin: Round 5, 2014 Draft (#158 overall)

YEAR	TEAM	LVL	AGE	W	L	SV	G	GS	IP	H	HR	BB/9	K/9	K	GB%	BABIP	WHIP	ERA	DRA-	WARP	MPH	FA%	Whiff%	CSP
2020	TOR	MLB	28	0	0	0	8	3	13	11	0	4.2	10.4	15	44.1%	.324	1.31	4.15	79	0.3	98.7	57.8%	26.1%	48.4%
2021 FS	TOR	MLB	29	2	2	3	57	0	50	46	7	3.2	9.2	50	42.7%	.291	1.29	4.16	96	0.2	98.7	57.8%	26.1%	48.4%
2021 DC	TOR	MLB	29	2	2	3	57	0	60	56	9	3.2	9.2	61	42.7%	.291	1.29	4.16	96	0.5	98.7	57.8%	26.1%	48.4%

Comparables: Taylor Cole, Artie Lewicki, Jerad Eickhoff

Merryweather pitched 13 effective innings over eight games as a 29-year-old rookie, his velocity, pitch mix and ability to miss bats coming as a pleasant change of pace from Jays bullpens of recent years. But injury, his old enemy, found him once again, with elbow issues felling him before season's end.

Patrick Murphy   RHP   Born: 06/10/95   Age: 26   Bats: R   Throws: R   Height: 6'5"   Weight: 235   Origin: Round 3, 2013 Draft (#83 overall)

YEAR	TEAM	LVL	AGE	W	L	SV	G	GS	IP	H	HR	BB/9	K/9	K	GB%	BABIP	WHIP	ERA	DRA-	WARP	MPH	FA%	Whiff%	CSP
2018	DUN	HI-A	23	10	5	0	26	26	146²	126	5	3.1	8.3	135	57.5%	.299	1.20	2.64	110	0.0				
2018	NH	AA	23	0	0	0	1	1	6	4	0	4.5	9.0	6	50.0%	.267	1.17	3.00	50	0.2				
2019	NH	AA	24.	4	7	0	18	18	84	75	7	2.9	9.2	86	51.6%	.286	1.21	4.71	91	0.5				
2020	TOR	MLB	25	0	0	0	4	0	6	6	0	3.0	7.5	5	50.0%	.333	1.33	1.50	90	0.1	98.1	59.6%	20.8%	49.3%
2021 FS	TOR	MLB	26	1	1	0	57	0	50	46	7	4.2	8.1	45	47.7%	.283	1.41	4.51	102	0.1	98.1	59.6%	20.8%	49.3%
2021 DC	TOR	MLB	26	1	1	0	22	0	24	22	3	4.2	8.1	21	47.7%	.283	1.41	4.51	102	0.1	98.1	59.6%	20.8%	49.3%

Comparables: Jimmy Lambert, Sterling Sharp, Sandy Baez

It's been a long, winding road for Murphy: injuries, a minor-league umpire telling him his delivery was illegal, more injuries after that. In 2020, though, he finally made it to the major leagues, called up from the alternate site in September, and acquitted himself very well over six scant innings. He has all the parts to serve as a bullpen arm, and the experience to appreciate the role.

★ ★ ★ *2021 Top 101 Prospect* **#35** ★ ★ ★

Nate Pearson RHP Born: 08/20/96 Age: 24 Bats: R Throws: R Height: 6'6" Weight: 250 Origin: Round 1, 2017 Draft (#28 overall)

YEAR	TEAM	LVL	AGE	W	L	SV	G	GS	IP	H	HR	BB/9	K/9	K	GB%	BABIP	WHIP	ERA	DRA-	WARP	MPH	FA%	Whiff%	CSP
2018	DUN	HI-A	21	0	1	0	1	1	1²	5	1	0.0	5.4	1	44.4%	.500	3.00	10.80	40	0.1				
2019	DUN	HI-A	22	3	0	0	6	6	21	10	2	1.3	15.0	35	35.1%	.229	0.62	0.86	32	0.9				
2019	NH	AA	22	1	4	0	16	16	62²	41	4	3.0	9.9	69	38.8%	.250	0.99	2.59	65	1.4				
2019	BUF	AAA	22	1	0	0	3	3	18	12	2	1.5	7.5	15	44.0%	.208	0.83	3.00	74	0.5				
2020	TOR	MLB	23	1	0	0	5	4	18	14	5	6.5	8.0	16	38.5%	.191	1.50	6.00	137	-0.2	99.4	50.6%	26.3%	44.9%
2021 FS	TOR	MLB	24	9	9	0	26	26	150	137	25	4.4	9.4	157	38.5%	.287	1.41	4.63	103	0.8	99.4	50.6%	26.3%	44.9%
2021 DC	TOR	MLB	24	7	8	0	24	24	121	111	20	4.4	9.4	126	38.5%	.287	1.41	4.63	103	1.1	99.4	50.6%	26.3%	44.9%

Comparables: Mitch Keller, Marco Gonzales, Tyler Mahle

Pearson's debut was one of the most buzzed-about moments of the season for the Jays, and it didn't take long before it became clear what all the hype was about. The fastball, blazing, perfectly placed on the outside corner. The ridiculously hard slider. The velocity that only increased as the game went on. Unfortunately, the rest of the season wasn't as mind blowing as that debut. It was, in fact, a grind. Pearson seemed to lack the ease and confidence of his minor-league appearances, struggling with command of his pitches and failing to challenge hitters in a way that would play to his strengths. He made only four starts, the final two being very ugly indeed, before hitting the IL with a right flexor strain. But when he returned in relief during the final week of September, when the Jays bullpen was faltering, he was a breath of fresh air, a reminder of the hope that lies in a young team. He pitched two perfect innings during the Jays' last gasp against the Rays, striking out five, all swinging. Spring can't come soon enough.

Robbie Ray LHP Born: 10/01/91 Age: 29 Bats: L Throws: L Height: 6'2" Weight: 215 Origin: Round 12, 2010 Draft (#356 overall)

YEAR	TEAM	LVL	AGE	W	L	SV	G	GS	IP	H	HR	BB/9	K/9	K	GB%	BABIP	WHIP	ERA	DRA-	WARP	MPH	FA%	Whiff%	CSP
2018	ARI	MLB	26	6	2	0	24	24	123²	97	19	5.1	12.0	165	39.9%	.293	1.35	3.93	89	1.9	95.9	54.0%	32.3%	44.9%
2019	ARI	MLB	27	12	8	0	33	33	174¹	150	30	4.3	12.1	235	36.6%	.315	1.34	4.34	83	3.2	94.4	52.8%	33.0%	45.6%
2020	TOR	MLB	28	2	5	0	12	11	51²	53	13	7.8	11.8	68	24.8%	.323	1.90	6.62	183	-1.8	96.1	53.1%	33.0%	42.2%
2021 FS	TOR	MLB	29	9	9	0	26	26	150	130	27	5.3	11.6	193	34.3%	.296	1.46	4.82	105	0.6	95.2	53.1%	32.9%	44.5%
2021 DC	TOR	MLB	29	8	8	0	25	25	134	116	24	5.3	11.6	172	34.3%	.296	1.46	4.82	105	1.0	95.2	53.1%	32.9%	44.5%

Comparables: Jon Gray, A.J. Cole, Mike Foltynewicz

Ray allowed four or more walks in six of his 11 starts in 2020. He also struck out at least six in six of his 11 starts, but at what cost? Even his lone scoreless outing—his final start of the year against the Yankees—featured four walks, which is no way to live. When the Jays acquired him at the deadline from the Diamondbacks, there was some thought that they would be able to fix his free-pass problem. And, indeed, he didn't have any six-walk games with the Jays. (He had three such games with the D'Backs this year.) But he was inconsistent, with solid starts being followed by meltdowns, strikeouts being followed by inexplicable bouts of wildness. As he nears the age of 30, it's becoming clear that Ray's problem is just Ray himself, as with so many Bobby Witts before him. If nothing else, Ray's chaos was fitting for a year as chaotic 2020.

Sean Reid-Foley RHP   Born: 08/30/95   Age: 25   Bats: R   Throws: R   Height: 6'3"   Weight: 230   Origin: Round 2, 2014 Draft (#49 overall)

YEAR	TEAM	LVL	AGE	W	L	SV	G	GS	IP	H	HR	BB/9	K/9	K	GB%	BABIP	WHIP	ERA	DRA-	WARP	MPH	FA%	Whiff%	CSP
2018	NH	AA	22	5	0	0	8	8	44¹	27	3	4.1	10.6	52	51.5%	.240	1.06	2.03	77	0.9				
2018	BUF	AAA	22	7	5	0	16	16	85¹	76	5	3.2	10.3	98	43.0%	.318	1.24	3.90	70	2.0				
2018	TOR	MLB	22	2	4	0	7	7	33¹	31	6	5.7	11.3	42	36.0%	.312	1.56	5.13	110	0.1	95.8	63.2%	29.1%	47.2%
2019	BUF	AAA	23	3	5	0	20	19	89	78	13	6.6	10.6	105	43.0%	.294	1.61	6.47	101	1.5				
2019	TOR	MLB	23	2	4	0	9	6	31²	33	5	6.0	8.0	28	42.4%	.298	1.71	4.26	155	-0.6	94.8	50.2%	23.9%	46.0%
2020	TOR	MLB	24	1	0	0	5	0	6²	3	0	8.1	8.1	6	61.1%	.167	1.35	1.35	89	0.1	96.1	61.7%	30.0%	35.2%
2021 FS	TOR	MLB	25	1	1	0	57	0	50	44	7	5.6	9.7	53	42.8%	.282	1.50	4.93	106	0.0	95.3	55.9%	26.5%	44.4%
2021 DC	TOR	MLB	25	1	1	0	22	0	24	21	3	5.6	9.7	25	42.8%	.282	1.50	4.93	106	0.1	95.3	55.9%	26.5%	44.4%

Comparables: Touki Toussaint, Jake Thompson, Tyler Mahle

Reid-Foley found himself squeezed out of a suddenly overstocked post-deadline Toronto bullpen, and it was probably for the best for all parties, given the reliever's peripherals and past experience. Despite the limited showing, there was reason for encouragement: He simplified his pitch mix, abandoning a feckless curveball and leaning more on the beginning reliever's toolkit, fastball and slider. He also enjoyed the velocity increase that bullpen work sometimes provides, providing a clear path for his future with the organization. The catch? Reid-Foley had a hard enough time throwing straight before he threw harder.

Tanner Roark RHP   Born: 10/05/86   Age: 34   Bats: R   Throws: R   Height: 6'2"   Weight: 238   Origin: Round 25, 2008 Draft (#753 overall)

YEAR	TEAM	LVL	AGE	W	L	SV	G	GS	IP	H	HR	BB/9	K/9	K	GB%	BABIP	WHIP	ERA	DRA-	WARP	MPH	FA%	Whiff%	CSP
2018	WAS	MLB	31	9	15	0	31	30	180¹	181	24	2.5	7.3	146	41.3%	.298	1.28	4.34	109	0.9	93.3	59.2%	20.2%	46.9%
2019	CIN	MLB	32	6	7	0	21	21	110¹	119	14	3.1	8.7	107	36.5%	.332	1.42	4.24	108	0.6	94.1	52.4%	22.0%	45.0%
2019	OAK	MLB	32	4	3	0	10	10	55	61	14	2.1	8.2	50	34.7%	.301	1.35	4.58	137	-0.6	93.6	61.0%	21.0%	48.5%
2020	TOR	MLB	33	2	3	0	11	11	47²	60	14	4.3	7.7	41	35.7%	.329	1.74	6.80	162	-1.2	92.8	53.3%	26.8%	44.1%
2021 FS	TOR	MLB	34	8	9	0	26	26	150	151	26	3.5	7.7	127	37.6%	.289	1.40	4.90	109	0.3	93.4	55.8%	22.5%	45.9%
2021 DC	TOR	MLB	34	8	9	0	27	27	143	144	25	3.5	7.7	121	37.6%	.289	1.40	4.90	109	0.8	93.4	55.8%	22.5%	45.9%

Comparables: Matt Shoemaker, Lance Lynn, Jake Arrieta

Wild, inconsistent, and very often hit hard, Roark starts for the Blue Jays were invariably bumpy rides. He struggled to throw strikes, and, when he did, had a tendency to serve up pitches that opponents could barrel. If there was one thing you could count on from Roark, it was that he wouldn't see the sixth inning; even his best starts were five-and-dives.

Jordan Romano RHP   Born: 04/21/93   Age: 28   Bats: R   Throws: R   Height: 6'5"   Weight: 225   Origin: Round 10, 2014 Draft (#294 overall)

YEAR	TEAM	LVL	AGE	W	L	SV	G	GS	IP	H	HR	BB/9	K/9	K	GB%	BABIP	WHIP	ERA	DRA-	WARP	MPH	FA%	Whiff%	CSP
2018	NH	AA	25	11	8	0	25	25	137¹	122	15	2.7	8.2	125	36.7%	.281	1.19	4.13	104	0.6				
2019	BUF	AAA	26	2	2	5	24	3	37²	37	8	3.3	12.7	53	37.9%	.333	1.35	5.73	87	0.8				
2019	TOR	MLB	26	0	0	0	17	0	15¹	17	4	5.3	12.3	21	48.8%	.351	1.70	7.63	83	0.2	97.0	63.7%	29.5%	45.8%
2020	TOR	MLB	27	2	1	2	15	0	14²	8	2	3.1	12.9	21	58.1%	.207	0.89	1.23	70	0.4	98.3	40.3%	43.8%	45.0%
2021 FS	TOR	MLB	28	2	2	14	57	0	50	42	7	4.7	11.1	61	42.5%	.295	1.38	4.38	98	0.2	97.7	51.2%	37.1%	45.3%
2021 DC	TOR	MLB	28	2	2	14	57	0	60	51	8	4.7	11.1	73	42.5%	.295	1.38	4.38	98	0.4	97.7	51.2%	37.1%	45.3%

Comparables: Michael Feliz, Austin Brice, Keone Kela

There are few indisputable truths in this world, but one of them is that it's better to throw a 90 mph slider than an 85 mph one. Romero abandoned efforts to tinker with a changeup and poured his heart into his two pitches. He leaned on his new hard slider nearly 60 percent of the time, and the result was the third-best whiff rate in the American League (min. 10 IP). The pitch actually gained average velocity as the season went on. A finger injury kept him out of the postseason, but with Ken Giles no longer in the picture, the past future closer is back to being the present future closer, and a near-perfect one at that.

Hyun Jin Ryu LHP   Born: 03/25/87   Age: 34   Bats: R   Throws: L   Height: 6'3"   Weight: 255   Origin: International Free Agent, 2013

YEAR	TEAM	LVL	AGE	W	L	SV	G	GS	IP	H	HR	BB/9	K/9	K	GB%	BABIP	WHIP	ERA	DRA-	WARP	MPH	FA%	Whiff%	CSP
2018	LAD	MLB	31	7	3	0	15	15	82¹	68	9	1.6	9.7	89	45.7%	.282	1.01	1.97	54	2.7	92.1	37.0%	27.5%	49.8%
2019	LAD	MLB	32	14	5	0	29	29	182²	160	17	1.2	8.0	163	49.6%	.282	1.01	2.32	62	5.4	92.6	40.6%	24.9%	47.5%
2020	TOR	MLB	33	5	2	0	12	12	67	60	6	2.3	9.7	72	50.8%	.303	1.15	2.69	74	1.5	91.6	34.7%	26.3%	46.9%
2021 FS	TOR	MLB	34	9	7	0	26	26	150	138	18	2.4	9.0	150	50.1%	.294	1.18	3.42	82	2.6	92.2	38.2%	25.7%	47.6%
2021 DC	TOR	MLB	34	10	8	0	27	27	159	146	19	2.4	9.0	159	50.1%	.294	1.18	3.42	82	3.2	92.2	38.2%	25.7%	47.6%

Comparables: Matt Shoemaker, Johnny Cueto, Felix Hernandez

It was a pleasant surprise when Ryu signed a four-year deal with the Jays last offseason. It was no surprise that he was the Jays' most valuable pitcher by far in 2020. His first couple of starts were shaky, prompting some classic Jays fan sky-is-falling catastrophizing, but proved to be nothing more than rust. After August began, Ryu never failed to complete five innings, despite contending with some shaky defense behind him. Often he worked into the seventh, his turns a consistently welcome reprieve for the many overworked relievers in the Jays bullpen. He managed contact better than pretty much anyone. The story was marred by his lone postseason start, a cacophony of diminished velocity and missed spots, a warrior beaten. But with an actual ace on the team for the first time in years, there's reason to hope that Ryu will be able to make up for that late-September failure in the not-so-distant future.

Where the young position players on his team are known for their ebullience, Ryu brought a quieter, more stabilizing sense of joy to the team. He became an aficionado of the bright, updated powder blues introduced to the Jays' wardrobe this season; along with interpreter Bryan Lee, he was a fixture in the dugout. The key to happiness in life is balance.

Matt Shoemaker RHP   Born: 09/27/86   Age: 34   Bats: R   Throws: R   Height: 6'2"   Weight: 225   Origin: Undrafted Free Agent, 2008

YEAR	TEAM	LVL	AGE	W	L	SV	G	GS	IP	H	HR	BB/9	K/9	K	GB%	BABIP	WHIP	ERA	DRA-	WARP	MPH	FA%	Whiff%	CSP
2018	LAA	MLB	31	2	2	0	7	7	31	29	3	2.9	9.6	33	43.0%	.313	1.26	4.94	125	-0.1	93.8	47.1%	28.8%	46.2%
2019	TOR	MLB	32	3	0	0	5	5	28²	16	3	2.8	7.5	24	51.4%	.183	0.87	1.57	93	0.4	92.7	46.7%	28.5%	41.1%
2020	TOR	MLB	33	0	1	0	6	6	28²	22	8	2.8	8.2	26	50.0%	.197	1.08	4.71	103	0.2	94.1	44.2%	28.5%	50.1%
2021 FS	TOR	MLB	34	2	2	0	57	0	50	48	8	2.8	8.5	47	45.0%	.285	1.27	4.09	98	0.2	93.6	45.5%	28.6%	46.6%

Comparables: Tanner Roark, Ian Kennedy, Homer Bailey

Shoemaker's 2019 season, which started out with a series of dominant outings, was tragically cut short by injury: a freak accident covering a play on the bases, leaving him with a torn ACL. He ended the year having thrown just 28⅔ innings. Hopes were high for a comeback, but Shoemaker ended 2020 having thrown, again, 28⅔ innings. It was injury that slowed him down once more; this time, not a random one, but a persistent shoulder inflammation that hampered his performance when he was on the mound. He was beset by home runs, and most of his appearances were belabored. That wasn't the case for his appearance in the postseason, though, where he pitched a sparkling three innings against the eventual pennant-winning Rays. Before the game, the controversy was that Shoemaker was the one being handed the ball; afterward, the controversy was that it had been taken away from him so early. This is something that Shoemaker has managed to do again and again in his career: come back, prove people wrong. But he's getting older now, and the mid-30s are not a kind age for pitchers with an ever-growing list of injuries behind them.

Ross Stripling   RHP   Born: 11/23/89   Age: 31   Bats: R   Throws: R   Height: 6'3"   Weight: 220   Origin: Round 5, 2012 Draft (#176 overall)

YEAR	TEAM	LVL	AGE	W	L	SV	G	GS	IP	H	HR	BB/9	K/9	K	GB%	BABIP	WHIP	ERA	DRA-	WARP	MPH	FA%	Whiff%	CSP
2018	LAD	MLB	28	8	6	0	33	21	122	123	18	1.6	10.0	136	45.3%	.324	1.19	3.02	65	3.3	93.8	41.1%	26.0%	47.3%
2019	LAD	MLB	29	4	4	0	32	15	90²	84	11	2.0	9.2	93	49.8%	.299	1.15	3.47	71	2.2	92.7	39.0%	24.5%	46.8%
2020	TOR	MLB	30	3	3	1	12	9	49¹	56	13	3.3	7.3	40	40.4%	.295	1.50	5.84	134	-0.4	93.8	43.9%	18.9%	51.2%
2021 FS	TOR	MLB	31	9	8	0	26	26	150	143	22	2.4	8.1	135	44.9%	.286	1.23	3.82	91	1.8	93.3	41.2%	23.0%	48.4%
2021 DC	TOR	MLB	31	8	7	0	24	24	123	117	18	2.4	8.1	111	44.9%	.286	1.23	3.82	91	1.9	93.3	41.2%	23.0%	48.4%

Comparables: Matt Andriese, Raisel Iglesias, Kelvin Herrera

Grizzled coaches used to yell at their struggling starters to "just throw strikes," and now we have proof they were full of it. After struggling with the Dodgers in the first half of the season, the Jays picked up Stripling at the deadline to bolster their rotation, with the hopes that a change of scenery and more playing time might help ease his woes. It didn't. Stripling, in his five September games with the Jays, got hit hard, when he wasn't struggling with walks; this despite the fact that he was actually throwing more pitches in the zone than ever. The problem: His curveball simply didn't generate the whiffs it needs to for Stripling to thrive, and the man clearly knew it, nearly abandoning it for the slider after switching teams. He'll need to find the old magic, because unless he can get batters to chase, strike two will hold no fear over batters.

Trent Thornton   RHP   Born: 09/30/93   Age: 27   Bats: R   Throws: R   Height: 6'0"   Weight: 195   Origin: Round 5, 2015 Draft (#139 overall)

YEAR	TEAM	LVL	AGE	W	L	SV	G	GS	IP	H	HR	BB/9	K/9	K	GB%	BABIP	WHIP	ERA	DRA-	WARP	MPH	FA%	Whiff%	CSP
2018	FRE	AAA	24	9	8	0	24	22	124¹	118	13	2.2	8.8	122	41.6%	.305	1.20	4.42	83	2.3				
2019	TOR	MLB	25	6	9	0	32	29	154¹	156	24	3.6	8.7	149	32.9%	.302	1.41	4.84	124	-0.6	94.6	62.6%	24.5%	43.1%
2020	TOR	MLB	26	0	0	0	3	3	5²	15	0	4.8	9.5	6	29.2%	.625	3.18	11.12	101	0.0	93.6	63.4%	19.1%	46.8%
2021 FS	TOR	MLB	27	1	2	0	57	0	50	49	10	3.4	8.5	47	34.3%	.288	1.37	4.88	110	-0.1	94.5	62.7%	24.2%	43.4%
2021 DC	TOR	MLB	27	1	2	0	26	3	37	36	7	3.4	8.5	34	34.3%	.288	1.37	4.88	110	0.1	94.5	62.7%	24.2%	43.4%

Comparables: Jakob Junis, Walker Lockett, Chase De Jong

Thornton became the unlikely anchor of the woebegone 2019 Jays rotation, accruing the most innings of any pitcher on the team. But any hoped-for development in his sophomore 2020 season was not to be. "Loose bodies" in his elbow hampered his performance in the mere 5⅔ innings, in which he appeared and ended his season in mid-August, with an unclear timeline for return. It was a somber moment indeed in the clubhouse when the right-hander removed his spectacles and handed them to Andrew Kay, completing a ritual that all men must perform, though all dread.

Jacob Waguespack   RHP   Born: 11/05/93   Age: 27   Bats: R   Throws: R   Height: 6'6"   Weight: 235   Origin: Round 37, 2012 Draft (#1126 overall)

YEAR	TEAM	LVL	AGE	W	L	SV	G	GS	IP	H	HR	BB/9	K/9	K	GB%	BABIP	WHIP	ERA	DRA-	WARP	MPH	FA%	Whiff%	CSP
2018	REA	AA	24	1	1	0	7	7	29¹	31	0	4.9	9.5	31	56.8%	.352	1.60	3.99	95	0.3				
2018	LHV	AAA	24	3	5	1	14	8	53¹	54	4	3.4	8.1	48	50.9%	.323	1.39	5.06	89	0.6				
2018	BUF	AAA	24	2	4	0	7	6	39¹	47	3	2.3	7.6	33	51.5%	.349	1.45	5.03	92	0.4				
2019	BUF	AAA	25	2	6	0	12	11	52²	57	9	4.3	8.9	52	47.1%	.327	1.56	5.30	110	0.7				
2019	TOR	MLB	25	5	5	0	16	13	78	75	12	3.3	7.3	63	40.8%	.279	1.33	4.38	116	0.0	94.2	72.8%	21.8%	46.4%
2020	TOR	MLB	26	0	0	0	11	0	17²	27	2	4.6	8.2	16	41.3%	.410	2.04	8.15	100	0.2	94.1	68.2%	24.7%	44.7%
2021 FS	TOR	MLB	27	1	2	0	57	0	50	48	8	3.8	8.2	45	42.7%	.284	1.39	4.72	106	0.0	94.2	71.4%	22.7%	45.9%
2021 DC	TOR	MLB	27	1	2	0	26	3	37	35	6	3.8	8.2	33	42.7%	.284	1.39	4.72	106	0.2	94.2	71.4%	22.7%	45.9%

Comparables: Chase De Jong, Erick Fedde, Brian Matusz

After starting the season with a string of scoreless outings, Waguespack saw his 2020 slide downhill. At first it was a slow trickle: a run allowed here, an error-induced disaster. But in his final three appearances of the season, Waguespack allowed 15 runs (11 earned) in just over six innings, adding up to a very ugly line when everything was accounted for. One of the awkward modern mechanisms of baseball is when a long reliever goes multiple innings and gets rewarded with a drive to Triple-A for the sake of a fresh arm; at least Waguespack made things easier by providing a decent excuse.

Taijuan Walker RHP   Born: 08/13/92   Age: 28   Bats: R   Throws: R   Height: 6'4"   Weight: 235   Origin: Round 1, 2010 Draft (#43 overall)

YEAR	TEAM	LVL	AGE	W	L	SV	G	GS	IP	H	HR	BB/9	K/9	K	GB%	BABIP	WHIP	ERA	DRA-	WARP	MPH	FA%	Whiff%	CSP
2018	ARI	MLB	25	0	0	0	3	3	13	15	1	3.5	6.2	9	40.5%	.341	1.54	3.46	115	0.0	96.0	70.5%	18.8%	53.8%
2019	ARI	MLB	26	0	0	0	1	1	1	1	0	0.0	9.0	1	33.3%	.333	1.00	0.00			94.0	66.7%	20.0%	44.1%
2020	TOR	MLB	27	4	3	0	11	11	53¹	43	8	3.2	8.4	50	38.2%	.243	1.16	2.70	99	0.5	94.8	50.2%	20.5%	48.1%
2021 FS	TOR	MLB	28	9	9	0	26	26	150	143	26	3.3	8.6	143	40.3%	.285	1.33	4.40	104	0.8	94.9	51.9%	20.4%	48.5%

Comparables: Julio Teheran, Shelby Miller, Chad Kuhl

For the first time in years, the Jays were buyers at the trade deadline, and their major area of need was obvious: starting pitching. So they acquired Walker, one of the better options out there, for a single shiny lottery ticket, sending Rookie-level outfielder Alberto Rodríguez to Seattle. Through his five starts in Seattle to open the season, Walker didn't have eye-popping numbers, but he was averaging more than five innings per start, length that the overtaxed bullpen desperately needed. In terms of results, the trade worked out swimmingly for the Jays, with Walker having one of the best September of any starting pitcher in baseball by ERA. Based on his peripherals, Walker will make for a risky acquisition for some ballclub over the winter, though his age, former prospect pedigree and growing distance from Tommy John all provide some reason for optimism.

Simeon Woods Richardson RHP   Born: 09/27/00   Age: 20   Bats: R   Throws: R   Height: 6'3"   Weight: 210   Origin: Round 2, 2018 Draft (#48 overall)

YEAR	TEAM	LVL	AGE	W	L	SV	G	GS	IP	H	HR	BB/9	K/9	K	GB%	BABIP	WHIP	ERA	DRA-	WARP	MPH	FA%	Whiff%	CSP
2018	MTS	ROK	17	1	0	1	5	2	11¹	9	0	3.2	11.9	15	50.0%	.321	1.15	0.00	70	0.3				
2018	KNG	ROK	17	0	0	0	2	2	6	6	1	0.0	16.5	11	38.5%	.417	1.00	4.50	81	0.1				
2019	COL	LO-A	18	3	8	0	20	20	78¹	78	5	2.0	11.1	97	49.5%	.358	1.21	4.25	103	0.1				
2019	DUN	HI-A	18	3	2	0	6	6	28¹	18	1	2.2	9.2	29	33.8%	.246	0.88	2.54	62	0.7				
2021 FS	TOR	MLB	20	2	2	0	57	0	50	44	7	3.4	8.8	48	41.6%	.278	1.27	3.75	96	0.2				

Comparables: Noah Syndergaard, Kolby Allard, Julio Urías

Woods-Richardson, who came over to the Jays in the Marcus Stroman deal, has progressed rapidly through the Jays' system. He's been impressive not only with his ability on the mound—he struck out 29 against walking just seven in 28⅓ innings at high-A Dunedin—but with his maturity, carrying himself in a manner beyond his years even as one of the youngest players at every level he reaches. That bodes well for his ability to wring value out of the lost 2020 season; lacking traditional competition, the Toronto coaching staff at the alternate site focused on mechanical improvements and applying technology. In Woods-Richardson's case, this includes refining a changeup to go with his already excellent fastball and promising curve.

Shun Yamaguchi RHP   Born: 07/11/87   Age: 33   Bats: R   Throws: R   Height: 6'2"   Weight: 225   Origin: International Free Agent, 2019

YEAR	TEAM	LVL	AGE	W	L	SV	G	GS	IP	H	HR	BB/9	K/9	K	GB%	BABIP	WHIP	ERA	DRA-	WARP	MPH	FA%	Whiff%	CSP
2020	TOR	MLB	32	2	4	0	17	0	25²	28	6	6.0	9.1	26	38.7%	.319	1.75	8.06	131	-0.2	93.0	41.0%	28.3%	44.2%
2021 FS	TOR	MLB	33	2	3	0	57	0	50	47	8	4.8	9.3	51	38.4%	.290	1.49	5.15	112	-0.2	93.0	41.0%	28.3%	44.2%
2021 DC	TOR	MLB	33	2	3	0	57	0	60	56	10	4.8	9.3	61	38.4%	.290	1.49	5.15	112	0.0	93.0	41.0%	28.3%	44.2%

In his final outing of the season, Yamaguchi gave up three home runs over the course of a few innings in a Blue Jays blowout—a fitting end to an inconsistent season. The former NPB strikeout leader had an extremely inauspicious start to his MLB career: His first appearances were all in runner-on-second 10th innings, and they were all unmitigated disasters. His subsequent appearances were largely unremarkable, which is exactly what one wants out of middle relief, though even then his pitch maps bear a striking resemblance to a shotgun blast. But it's the memory of his first games, of the flat, slow pitches, the strike-zone nibbling, that still lingers, sometimes as more than a memory. Trust is easy to lose, but so hard to regain.

T.J. Zeuch RHP   Born: 08/01/95   Age: 25   Bats: R   Throws: R   Height: 6'7"   Weight: 245   Origin: Round 1, 2016 Draft (#21 overall)

YEAR	TEAM	LVL	AGE	W	L	SV	G	GS	IP	H	HR	BB/9	K/9	K	GB%	BABIP	WHIP	ERA	DRA-	WARP	MPH	FA%	Whiff%	CSP
2018	DUN	HI-A	22	3	3	0	6	6	36¹	34	4	2.2	5.9	24	61.4%	.275	1.18	3.47	121	-0.2				
2018	NH	AA	22	9	5	0	21	21	120	120	7	2.3	6.1	81	55.2%	.299	1.26	3.08	85	1.9				
2019	DUN	HI-A	23	0	0	0	2	2	8²	7	0	2.1	12.5	12	59.1%	.318	1.04	4.15	44	0.3				
2019	BUF	AAA	23	4	3	0	13	13	78	70	6	3.7	4.5	39	57.8%	.256	1.31	3.69	81	2.1				
2019	TOR	MLB	23	1	2	0	5	3	22²	22	2	4.4	7.9	20	48.5%	.303	1.46	4.76	108	0.1	94.0	52.5%	23.0%	40.8%
2020	TOR	MLB	24	1	0	0	3	1	11¹	9	1	3.2	2.4	3	62.5%	.205	1.15	1.59	100	0.1	93.9	77.3%	15.2%	42.2%
2021 FS	TOR	MLB	25	3	4	0	57	0	50	53	7	3.8	6.2	34	53.1%	.292	1.50	5.34	117	-0.4	94.0	62.6%	19.8%	41.3%
2021 DC	TOR	MLB	25	3	4	0	40	6	66	70	10	3.8	6.2	45	53.1%	.292	1.50	5.34	117	-0.1	94.0	62.6%	19.8%	41.3%

Comparables: Andrew Miller, Elieser Hernandez, Brandon Woodruff

If you think of every baseball season as a jigsaw puzzle, Zeuch's three late-season appearances were blurry pieces of sky and ... leaves? grass? Maybe it's not sky, it's actually water. Still, blurry as they might have been, the puzzle's not complete without them, and it did turn out to be a nice picture when it got finished.

We Need to Do to WAR What We Did to Batting Average

by Russell A. Carleton

It's time to stop yelling at people for quoting batting average. I assume that the reader of *Baseball Prospectus* will know why batting average is a good-but-incomplete measure of a player's (offensive) abilities. (If you aren't, I can sum them up in the question "Isn't it a little weird that we pretend that walks never happened?") But like it or not, batting average still has a place in the historical vocabulary of the game and there are still a lot of fans out there who prefer to speak the old tongue. There's no ground left to be broken on this one. No one inside the game takes batting average seriously anymore, and we have bigger problems to tend to.

Over the last quarter century, the crown jewel of the Sabermetric movement has been Wins Above Replacement. It might not have been the discovery (or set of discoveries pasted together into a number) that changed the game the most, but it was up there, and it has become the most visible "new age" stat, surpassing even on-base percentage in the dialogue among baseball fans. WAR is far superior to what came before it, but complacency breeds all manner of disaster. There are gaps in WAR just like the "why don't we count walks?" gap in batting average. We ignore those gaps at our peril.

WAR was, whether accidentally or purposefully, built to answer a specific question. Its beauty is that unlike the "old school" stats, it does take into account hitting, running, fielding, league context and positional scarcity for position players. For pitchers, it "knows" that some things are a pitcher's fault and some are not. It also intentionally decouples the contributions of an individual player from their team. All of this makes it the ideal tool to answer the question "who should win the MVP?" For those of us still litigating the 2012 Trout-vs-Cabrera MVP vote, it's a wonderful tool to have.

But we need to face up to an uncomfortable truth: WAR is not the answer to every question, even though we treat it like it is. It is very good at generating a leaderboard of players, and that's great, but in the past decade, WAR has been trotted out the framework to analyze just about everything among the *acronymati*. It might still be the *best available* stat to use, but that doesn't always mean that it

is a good stat to use. We need to start asking whether we're using a hammer when a screwdriver is needed. And maybe we need to invent the screwdriver first.

WAR was supposed to model the question "What would have happened if Player X had disappeared before the season started?" The team wouldn't have been completely adrift. There would have been a warm body available to take those plate appearances or throw those innings. Maybe you go to your Triple-A affiliate. Maybe you go to the waiver wire. Maybe you move someone over from another position and plug *that* hole with a replacement-level player.

And there's the first problem in WAR. We know that position matters when determining a player's value. A left fielder who hits like an average left fielder is an average player; a shortstop who hits like an average left fielder is an All-Star. WAR has traditionally used a positional adjustment based on the idea that if a player went from second base to shortstop, there would be something lost along the way. Second sackers usually aren't as gifted defensively, so even if they are good at the keystone, we assume that they would suffer on the other side of the bag. In reverse, we assume that a shortstop who slid over to second would actually show better performance, because second isn't as challenging. These adjustments have traditionally been based on studying the performance of utility players, who have enough of a sample at two positions to make some conclusions. And that seems reasonable until you realize that utility players are a selected sample. They *already* have experience playing in more than one position.

What we've found through research is that when players first make a change from one position to another, it shows that they are rookies. Even if they're going "down" the defensive spectrum, for example moving from short to second, it's a learning curve to really pick up the nuances of the position, even for someone with shortstop skills, and in the meantime, their level of performance is consistent with some of the worst fielders in the league. Eventually, they do figure it out, but the research suggests that it takes a couple of months. So, if a team had to replace a player, would they really be willing to live with that sort of hole in their defense for that long a time? The answer might be yes, and certainly, sometimes teams—especially rebuilding ones—do that, but I'd suggest that the positional spectrum isn't as fluid as WAR makes it out to be. Your center fielder might be a gold glover, but if your catcher gets hurt, you're going to call up another catcher, even if you have a dynamite fourth outfielder who's been begging for playing time. With that in mind, is WAR really modeling reality when it assumes, in effect, that positions are infinitely fungible?

The alternate option to the positional adjustment model is comparing players only to bench players who also played that same position. When you shrink your comparison group—say, only players who actually played second base—you end up with some pretty large variations from year to year in what "replacement level" looks like. A player could put up the same stat line three years in a row and see variations of a win or more because of those changes in "replacement level". The nice thing about batting average is that .300 always means 3-of-10. By using all bench players as a baseline group, it smooths out some of those jumps, and since we can't really predict those jumps before the season, it makes decision-making better. But there's also a psychological benefit to it: even if Smith was, in some cosmic sense, worth 4 wins in one year and 3 wins another, there's still something comforting about WAR smoothing that out to 3.5.

WAR has other problems that we need to cop to as well. On the pitching side, WAR assumes that if a starter had disappeared, someone would have just filled those innings though with much less success. While an ace pitcher might throw 6-7 innings consistently, a replacement starter probably wouldn't go as deep into the game, leaving a greater stress on a team's bullpen. That doesn't get factored into WAR, either. The ability to go deep into games, even if the results are average, is a talent unto itself.

For position players, "replacement level" itself is set to reflect the performance that we see mostly from bench players. They get enough playing time during the course of a season that we can get an idea of what to expect from them, but it's worth remembering that a good bench player and a good long-term replacement are two separate things. A decent hitter with a bad glove is more valuable on a bench because *that's a good pinch hitter*, even if there's an good-glove, no-bat player at Triple-A who projects to be a better player overall. Our idea for "replacement" is based on players who aren't necessarily selected for whether they'd be good long-term replacements.

And then there's how we use WAR to evaluate the moves that teams make. During the hot stove season, it's inevitable that when someone signs a contract, we all pull out the "a win is worth X million" metric and begin opining based on that. It's not the worst approach, but WAR was designed to compare players within the regular season when everyone has a full 26-player roster. In the offseason, each team will likely have a handful of free agents. If one team chose to let them all walk away and signed no one else, there would again be warm bodies to take whatever spots were left, but the best in-house candidate might not be a zero-win player.

Among players who log 100 PA or 50 IP in a year, there's usually enough for about only 22 or 23 players per team who score above replacement level (and that includes the folks who have .01 WAR) in a season. In the offseason, if teams are already five players down from a full roster, the best replacement at the moment might be some marginal prospect in Triple-A who isn't a good idea long-term and who accordingly projects out to half a win below the line. That's probably the first player a GM is thinking about replacing through free agency. Though it might not be unreasonable to sign someone who "only" projects to replacement level for a few million, that "replacement" baseline that is so key to the metric might not be zero in the winter, even if it is during the regular season.

Finally, something that's supposed to be a feature of WAR—the way in which it ignores the context of the team on which a player plays—turns out to be a bit of a bug. In WAR, a run is a run is a run, and if you create that run by hitting a double or stealing a base or making an outstanding catch or striking a batter out, the metric doesn't distinguish between any of those. You did the deed. You get the credit. Again, that's great for sorting out players into a leaderboard. The problem is that general managers aren't putting together a collection of players. They're trying to put together teams, and there actually is context to consider.

Most of the folks reading this far into a *Baseball Prospectus* article will know the one about the "win curve." The point of baseball's regular season is to make the playoffs. Up until the 2020 pandemic messed up everything, that used to take somewhere around 88-90 wins to accomplish. Therefore, a team who projected to win about 86 games and who signed a three-win player was potentially spending their way into a playoff berth. A team who would otherwise have won 76 games may have signed their way to...well, 79 wins. Context matters there.

It matters in other ways, too. If a team is choosing between two players who compile similar WAR totals but in different ways—an all-glove, no-bat player versus their inverse—then WAR treats them as equals. The evidence that we have available tells a different story, and it makes sense when you think of it.

Scoring runs—not vacuum-sealed, theoretical linear-weight runs, but the actual kind that go on the scoreboard—is a collaborative pursuit. A batter can generate a run in isolation by hitting a homer, but the majority of runs are scored when one player gets on base and another drives them in. (There may have been another batter in there who moved things along as well.) What's important to note is that the hitters who are bunched nearby to each other are the most likely to affect each other's chances of scoring runs. The rules of baseball reward lineups that have chains of good hitters. The more good hitters you can cluster together, the more likely they are to be on-base for each other, and, in turn, to drive each other in.

Fielding works, strangely enough, in the opposite direction. There's evidence that a good fielder, say, a skilled shortstop, actually makes the other infielders to either side worse than if a more pedestrian shortstop is playing nearby. Maybe knowing there's a good shortstop next door means that the fielder on third feels a little more at liberty to go a little easier. In a vacuum, the good fielder and the good batter may generate the same value on WAR, but on the field, they might not.

In the same way, WAR doesn't fully appreciate the value that relievers bring to a team. Hitters appear when it's their turn on the card and starters when it's their turn on the calendar. Accordingly, WAR strips away the context of the situation and focuses on what the batter or starter actually did, independent of what was going on around them.

Relievers are the only major group of players where a manager decides at what point in the game to deploy them. When and in what situation a batter appears tells you nothing about the batter's quality; for a reliever, that's the entire point. Good relievers get the situations in which they can have the most impact on the outcome of a game *because they're good at their jobs*. Most of the major formulations of WAR attempt to correct for this, but they still end up with WAR leaderboards for pitchers that include almost exclusively starters; a *win probability added* leaderboard, however, includes a healthy mix of both. A good reliever can add as much actual win potential as a good starter, but WAR doesn't really capture that.

We don't need to go back to Player Evaluation by Archetype Comparison and Emotion. In fact, I hope that WAR sticks around and becomes a more commonly cited part of the baseball statistical conversation. But we need to be a little more circumspect about what we ask WAR to do. We're asking it to do things that it wasn't designed for, and if we're not careful, we might end up with some funky and perhaps damaging results.

—*Russell A. Carleton is an author of Baseball Prospectus.*

CHICAGO CUBS

Essay by Kendra James

Player comments by Collin Whitchurch and BP staff

My husband and I started dating on August 15, 2016. The Cubs were 73-43 at the time, and it was a scheduled off day, which I told him was the only reason that we were able to go out that evening. I joked with friends the next morning, saying that if he made it through not only a Cubs postseason run, but also the 2016 election *and* the debut of *Pitch* (a show about the first woman to pitch in MLB that seemed to have been made specifically for me, and me alone), there was no way we *weren't* getting married. The next day the Cubs won a 4-0 game against the Cardinals and went on to finish August as their best month, with a 22-6 record; we were off to the races.

Being a Cubs fan from 2007-16 was a privilege. I wasn't new, and I had always been proud, but these were the first years as a lifelong in which I was *confident*. Even before Theo Epstein and Joe Maddon came aboard, down in the dugout Lou Pinella brought with him an (often delightfully aggressive) winning energy to the clubhouse. "Sweet" Lou would go to the mats for his players, to the point of ejection and even a four-day suspension. He believed in that team, and through his outbursts early in the 2007 season, we fans could at least tell that Pinella could *see* the same problems we did. What's more, he was willing to make adjustments to fix them, and so, while we ended up swept in the first round of playoffs that year, it felt like there was a hint of promise.

It's possible that I remember those years fondly—even the stretch of iffy seasons from 2010-12—because I remember the world of that era fondly as well. There was a recession, multiple endless wars, a few small-scale pandemics and also the Kardashians, but I was in my early 20s, a fresh college graduate with a job. I had a New York City apartment. Barack Obama was president. *Mad Men* kept getting *better*! The world was my oyster, and when Chicago hired Theo Epstein to be the team's president in 2011, it felt like my team had it made too. Sure, we were both going to have to lose for a little while (Theo made that clear, and so did the paychecks from my job at an education non-profit) but we also both had *plans*, and our timelines aligned. We were going to build our success together.

And the weird thing is … we did. 2016 was one of the best years of my personal and professional life, a culmination of hard work that began in 2011 (mixed with a bit of good luck,

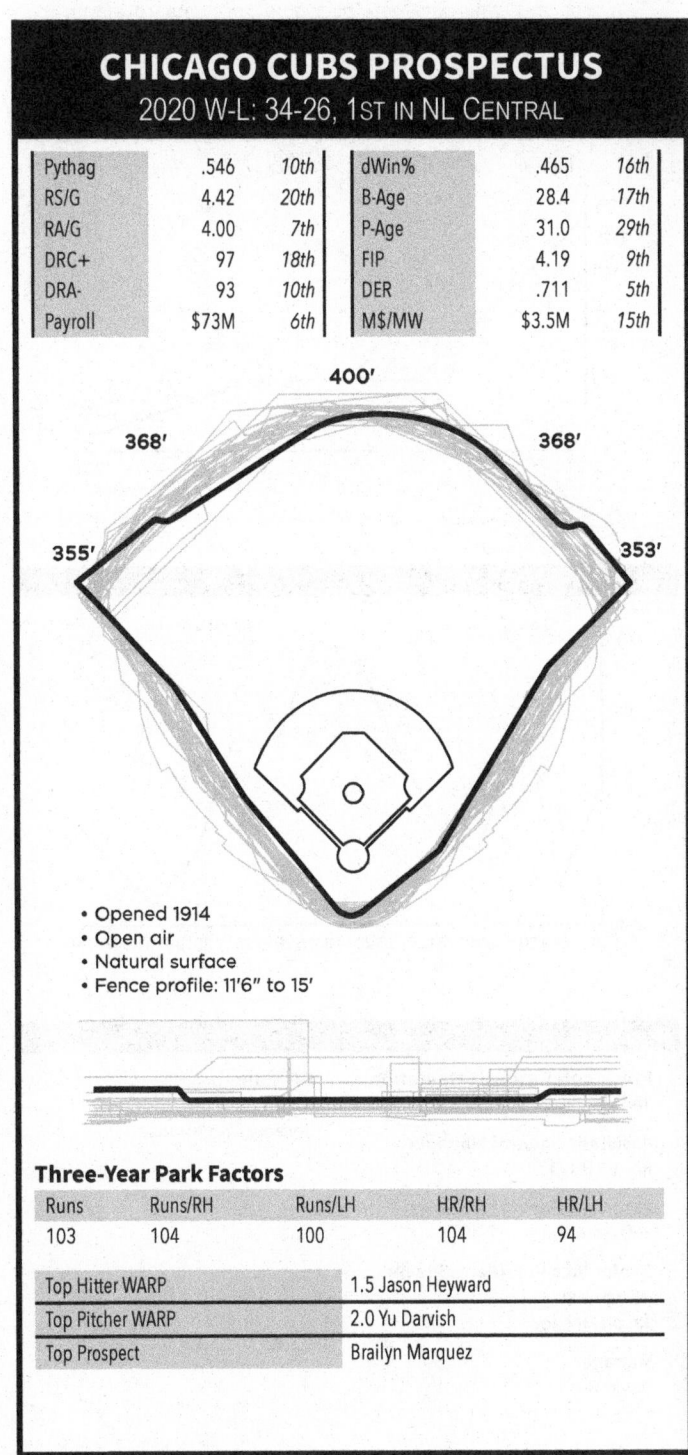

CHICAGO CUBS PROSPECTUS
2020 W-L: 34-26, 1ST IN NL CENTRAL

Pythag	.546	10th	dWin%	.465	16th
RS/G	4.42	20th	B-Age	28.4	17th
RA/G	4.00	7th	P-Age	31.0	29th
DRC+	97	18th	FIP	4.19	9th
DRA-	93	10th	DER	.711	5th
Payroll	$73M	6th	M$/MW	$3.5M	15th

- Opened 1914
- Open air
- Natural surface
- Fence profile: 11'6" to 15'

Three-Year Park Factors

Runs	Runs/RH	Runs/LH	HR/RH	HR/LH
103	104	100	104	94

Top Hitter WARP	1.5 Jason Heyward
Top Pitcher WARP	2.0 Yu Darvish
Top Prospect	Brailyn Marquez

Payroll History (in millions)

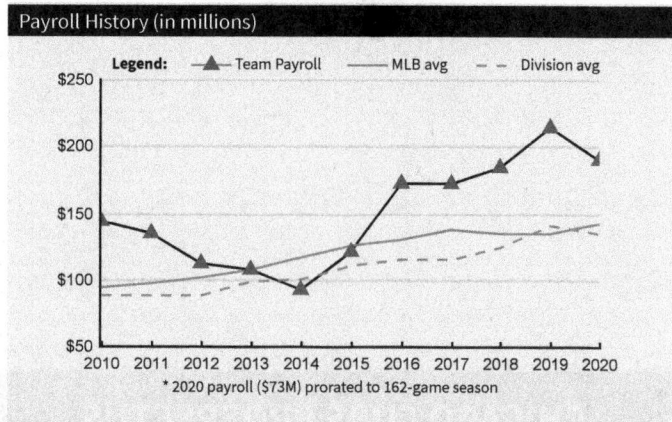

Legend: ▲ Team Payroll — MLB avg -- Division avg

* 2020 payroll ($73M) prorated to 162-game season

Future Commitments (in millions)

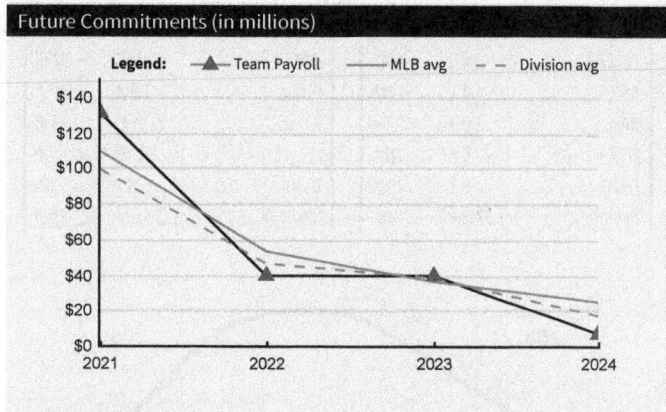

Legend: ▲ Team Payroll — MLB avg -- Division avg

Farm System Ranking

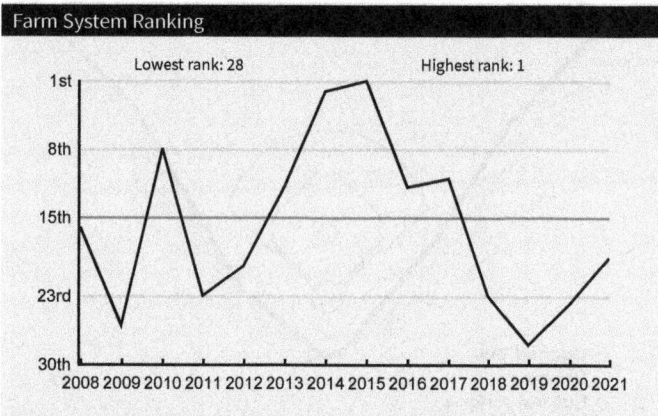

Lowest rank: 28   Highest rank: 1

Personnel

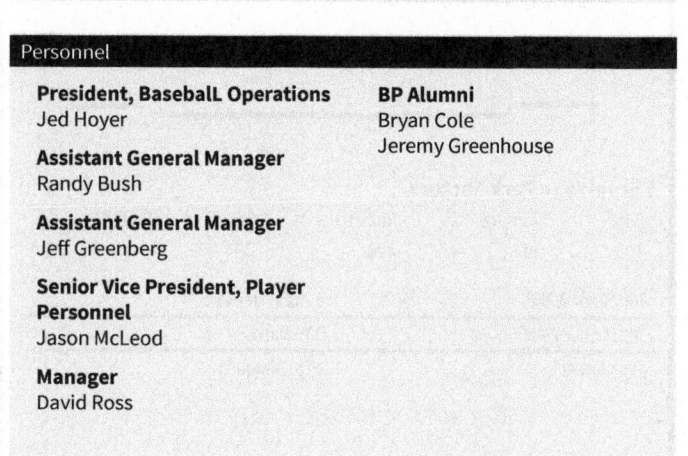

President, Baseball Operations
Jed Hoyer

Assistant General Manager
Randy Bush

Assistant General Manager
Jeff Greenberg

Senior Vice President, Player Personnel
Jason McLeod

Manager
David Ross

BP Alumni
Bryan Cole
Jeremy Greenhouse

just like in any baseball victory) and the giddiness of being in a new relationship. Cynics like to say that your team winning a big game doesn't really affect *you* personally, but after we won the World Series that year, the single, joyous memory of a glass beer stein exploding against a wall just inches above my head at a Cubs bar in New York City erupted after that final out is the sole thing that kept me functioning after the results of the 2016 election came in a week later.

Needless to say that with another contentious election approaching, I—a supremely superstitious baseball fan getting excited for spring training while also watching a pandemic creep across the globe—did not want the Cubs to win the World Series in 2020.

I *did* want to watch at least 100 games, though. Much like in 2016, I was kind of counting on baseball to be the *thing* that got me through another year in a world filled with massive, external challenges that I had no way of controlling. With accomplished, World Series-winning players like Anthony Rizzo, Kris Bryant, Kyle Hendricks and Willson Conteras playing under the management of former teammate David Ross, I expected a lively and promising year, like the ones we'd had in '17 and '18—a season that wouldn't end signaling the need to rebuild, but maybe just to retool. Perhaps we would need to fill out the bench, tighten up our bats or secure a second shortstop so that a Baez injury didn't cause an existential crisis.

Things played out differently, but once again in a year that was shaping up to be yet a professional and personal gem akin to 2016 (maybe *I'm* the problem?), I was determined to make the best of it. A 60-game season starting in July? That was just more time for players to get in shape and better weather to play in. No fans in the stand? Fewer distractions. Weird game start times? I told myself that the sun and shadows at Wrigley wouldn't be able to play their usual tricks with outfielders. Universal Designated Hitter in the National League? Well, I also didn't like Brussels sprouts until age 31, so maybe it was time to give the DH a fresh opportunity to win me over too. Weirder things had already happened in 2020, after all.

The season looked nothing like anything we'd seen in baseball's living memory. The world at large was so off-kilter that judging any player or team on their 2020 performances seems almost unfair. (Sorry, Dodgers fans.) It was a funhouse mirror of a year, where Kyle Schwarber, of all people, ended the year as the worst batter in the National League. The Cubs still managed to piece together wins, opening the season with a Hendricks shutout and paving the way for several near-misses by Jon Lester, Alec Mills and then Hendricks again. Cubs fans saw the first no-hitter (by Mills) since Jake Arrieta's '16 gem. They even made the (modified) playoffs.

In this mirrorverse of a year, Jason Heyward was also having one of his best seasons as Cub—something I've wanted for him since he used part of his initial salary to pay travel, room, and board for David Ross' wife and three kids for away games during his first season in town in 2016. His status as a fundamentally good human being who shows leadership on the field and in the clubhouse (during 17-minute rain delays and otherwise) makes him deeply easy to root for.

Yet that same fundamental goodness was also the final straw in my 2020 season. Heyward, the clear season MVP, pulled double-duty serving as both an offensive and a moral leader for the Cubs. He would've appeared in 51, not 50 games had he (and other players around the league) not made the choice to sit out on August 26 in protest after Jacob Blake was shot and paralyzed by police in Kenosha, Wisconsin. It's said that his teammates didn't want to leave Heyward out on the limb of protest alone, and that they offered to sit out with him. He told them, "No, go play the game. I don't think the game should be canceled. But I think I have to do what I have to do."

This is the part where I tell you that I am a Black woman; that I believe Jason Heyward did the right thing in sitting out; and that as someone who is used to being alone in a room, adrift in opinion, and put on the spot due to my race and gender, I am still in this offseason wrestling with how I feel about the Cubs' decision to play that day instead of rallying behind their Black teammate like six other teams did. A teammate who had been there for them countless times, Heyward literally shepherded them through a king-making season, helped them earn a ring (and a third Gold Glove for himself in the process) and proved his worth again and again. As my feelings about baseball so often do mirror and reflect how I feel about the world and the ways in which I inhabit it, I suspect I will continue to think and look back at that game in the same way I replay personal experiences involving those complicated topics of race, protest and social justice over and over again in my head. I'm not angry at any specific person, or even the team as a whole; the situation just … well, it didn't feel great.

Beyond anything else that happened in 2020, that August 26 game is the main reason I do not anticipate looking back at this season with the fondness or good humor that I occasionally look back at those that fared worse for my Cubs. Watching baseball (or any team sport aside from basketball in the Disney bubble, really) last year was already a moral quandary, and eventually it began to feel actively *bad*. It felt (and, frankly, probably *was*) like something that should not be happening. Like we had not earned it as a country. As my anxiety about the impending election ramped up I became actively worried when we made the playoffs again, and frankly, I was perfectly fine when we were swept, as is our way, this time by the Marlins. (Another strange twist, part of this terrible year that I finally could put to rest.) Baseball was no longer a refuge and I couldn't take the Cubs' struggle on as my own, as I once had, because they had *literally* chosen not to take mine on in return. Like a parent, I wasn't mad, but I was disappointed.

When Theo Epstein announced that he was resigning from his position, I was surprised at my own ambivalence. Then came the offseason and the trade rumors, with names that should have been terrifying, like Anthony Rizzo and Kris Bryant. It became clear that the core of the team Epstein had planned so carefully for in his rebuilding years might no longer exist. In fact, Heyward's name was one of the few that *wasn't* being batted around as a potential trade, likely because he has $65 million coming his way over the next three years. We can be fairly certain that he'll remain a Cub in 2021 and beyond, serving as the Cubs' Alex Gordon.

Plenty of teams are saddled with bad contracts. What makes Heyward's deal easier to stomach is that it comes with a good person—one who played a role in a championship; one who has demonstrated leadership ability; and one who can assist in the transition from this core to the next by imparting his wisdom on his younger teammates.

For all the good Heyward could do in a statesman role, we have to acknowledge that he won't be around forever. His eight-year contract leaves him eligible for free agency approaching in '23 might look far off, but if 2020 has shown us anything it's that April is approximately 76 days long, not 30, and that a year can last anywhere between four and 99 months. Along with newly promoted president Jed Hoyer and whoever will take on Hoyer's former role as GM, Ross and the Cubs need to be looking back at their farm system and (with all the patience and sacrifice necessary) returning it to Epstein-like shape. The focus cannot simply be on 2021, but the next several years, too.

After wanting to see it continue forever in spring, I see a lot of rebuilding in this team's future, and I think that is *good*. Given how deeply superstition and a keen attention to signs (from the catcher, yes, but also the universe) run through baseball, but especially Cubs fandom, 2021 feels like a particularly apt time for this process to commence. America will officially enter its own "rebuilding" period, albeit a bit late. It wasn't leadership that was necessarily my first choice, but it is leadership that I know will set the ship right in order to get us to a point where we can start getting some of those big wins again. It'll be a lot easier to afford playoff tickets after our student loan debt is cancelled, eh? *This* is the sort of mirror I appreciate baseball holding up to my life.

Though 2020 may not have been the season Cubs fans wanted, it wasn't quite the year we wanted either. Whether it's moving back to or from the places we used to call home, finally having the opportunity to reconnect with friends and family in person, picking up the pieces of an major life event lost to the chaos of 2020 or simply reacclimating to living largely outside the confines of our homes, the next 18 to 24 months are going to be a rebuilding time for nearly all of us—on and off the baseball diamond. We're gonna have to lose a little, again, in order to right the ship and eventually win big, but we're gonna be doing it *together*.

—*Kendra James is a freelance pop culture writer and critic.*

HITTERS

Albert Almora Jr. CF Born: 04/16/94 Age: 27 Bats: R Throws: R Height: 6'2" Weight: 190 Origin: Round 1, 2012 Draft (#6 overall)

YEAR	TEAM	LVL	AGE	PA	R	2B	3B	HR	RBI	BB	K	SB	CS	Whiff%	AVG/OBP/SLG	DRC+	BABIP	BRR	FRAA	WARP
2018	CHC	MLB	24	479	62	24	1	5	41	24	83	1	3	24.5%	.286/.323/.378	84	.337	-0.1	CF(137): 2.5, LF(2): -0.1	1.0
2019	IOW	AAA	25	54	6	3	1	0	2	4	7	2	1		.224/.283/.327	56	.262	0.0	CF(12): 2.0	0.1
2019	CHC	MLB	25	363	41	11	1	12	32	16	62	2	1	24.1%	.236/.271/.381	72	.255	-0.4	CF(125): 2.0	0.2
2020	CHC	MLB	26	34	4	1	0	0	1	3	9	0	0	33.3%	.167/.265/.200	72	.238	0.0	CF(28): 1.2	0.0
2021 FS	*CHC*	*MLB*	*27*	*600*	*61*	*26*	*2*	*14*	*66*	*33*	*117*	*3*	*1*	*25.0%*	*.250/.296/.385*	*86*	*.291*	*-0.3*	*CF 2, LF 0*	*1.1*

Comparables: Randy Kutcher, Hiram Bocachica, Ken Gerhart

Once upon a time, way back in 2013, the top of the Cubs' farm system rankings looked like this: 1. Albert Almora, 2. Javier Báez, 3. Jorge Soler. The rest of the list isn't all that important (OK, Dan Vogelbach was fifth), but the next year Almora ranked third behind just Baez and Kris Bryant. He was a top-50 prospect his first three years in organized ball and a top-101 guy five times. This is all to say that Almora once held a lot of promise. Prospects will break your heart, as we all know, and after more than 1,300 career plate appearances we have ample evidence that Almora is a replacement-level outfielder. The contending Cubs finally saw enough in 2020, and he was demoted at the end of August after the acquisition of Cameron Maybin. Almora's glove still provides value, and he's likely to continue to carve out opportunities as a fourth outfielder-type, but the days of waiting on him to live up to his lofty potential are long gone.

★ ★ ★ *2021 Top 101 Prospect* **#89** ★ ★ ★

Miguel Amaya C Born: 03/09/99 Age: 22 Bats: R Throws: R Height: 6'2" Weight: 230 Origin: International Free Agent, 2015

YEAR	TEAM	LVL	AGE	PA	R	2B	3B	HR	RBI	BB	K	SB	CS	Whiff%	AVG/OBP/SLG	DRC+	BABIP	BRR	FRAA	WARP
2018	SB	LO-A	19	479	54	21	2	12	52	50	91	1	0		.256/.349/.403	117	.298	0.6	C(95): 2.5, 1B(9): -0.7	2.5
2019	MB	HI-A	20	410	50	24	0	11	57	54	69	2	0		.235/.351/.402	124	.259	-3.6	C(91): 2.8	2.7
2021 FS	*CHC*	*MLB*	*22*	*600*	*60*	*27*	*1*	*16*	*62*	*37*	*156*	*2*	*0*		*.216/.276/.364*	*74*	*.270*	*-0.1*	*C 1, 1B 0*	*0.5*
2021 DC	*CHC*	*MLB*	*22*	*136*	*13*	*6*	*0*	*3*	*14*	*8*	*35*	*0*	*0*		*.216/.276/.364*	*74*	*.270*	*0.0*	*C 0*	*0.1*

Comparables: Austin Hedges, Alejandro Kirk, Luis Campusano

"A collection of 50s and 55s" was used to describe Amaya in last year's Top 101. That's not super exciting, but it's more than okay when you're talking about a lower-minors catcher with a legitimate shot at sticking behind the plate. During his summer at the Cubs' alternate training site, the team worked on getting Amaya to tap into some of his pull-side power, which he's previously shown in BP but has yet to get into games. If Amaya starts to pair in-game power with his above-average plate discipline, if he continues making good contact and working all fields and if he makes the expected strides defensively…all right, that's a lot of ifs, but the point is that Amaya has a chance to be really good, and his potential seems well within his reach.

Javier Báez SS Born: 12/01/92 Age: 28 Bats: R Throws: R Height: 6'0" Weight: 190 Origin: Round 1, 2011 Draft (#9 overall)

YEAR	TEAM	LVL	AGE	PA	R	2B	3B	HR	RBI	BB	K	SB	CS	Whiff%	AVG/OBP/SLG	DRC+	BABIP	BRR	FRAA	WARP
2018	CHC	MLB	25	645	101	40	9	34	111	29	167	21	9	33.9%	.290/.326/.554	119	.347	3.2	2B(104): -0.6, SS(65): 1.3, 3B(22): 2.1	4.6
2019	CHC	MLB	26	561	89	38	4	29	85	28	156	11	7	35.6%	.281/.316/.531	101	.345	4.3	SS(129): 7.2, 3B(1): 0.1	3.9
2020	CHC	MLB	28	235	27	9	1	8	24	7	75	3	0	38.0%	.203/.238/.360	68	.262	0.5	SS(56): 9.1, LF(1): -0.0	0.9
2021 FS	*CHC*	*MLB*	*28*	*600*	*69*	*27*	*3*	*26*	*82*	*29*	*185*	*13*	*5*	*35.9%*	*.242/.289/.444*	*96*	*.313*	*0.7*	*SS 1, 1B 0*	*1.9*
2021 DC	*CHC*	*MLB*	*28*	*616*	*71*	*28*	*3*	*27*	*85*	*30*	*190*	*13*	*5*	*35.9%*	*.242/.289/.444*	*96*	*.313*	*0.7*	*SS 1*	*1.9*

Comparables: Tim Anderson, Chris Taylor, Jhonny Peralta

Is the most exciting player in baseball still the most exciting player in baseball if no fans are allowed in attendance? In 2020, that answer was in the negative. "I get motivated from my fans," Báez said. "It's really weird, to be honest. It's not an excuse because it's the same for every team. But everybody's different. Some of them like 'em, some of them don't like having fans. We have to deal with it." How much the fan-less experience really affected Báez's play is impossible to judge, but what's not is that the former MVP candidate suffered through the worst season of his career, flailing away at a rate worse than we've ever seen from the already swing-happy shortstop. Báez doesn't need to be patient and in control of the strike zone to be successful, he proved as much the last few years. He does, apparently, need cheering (or booing) fans. If that's the case, 2021 will be as important as ever, as it's the final year before Báez reaches free agency—and, as of press time, it seemed doubtful that fans will be there to start the season.

David Bote 3B Born: 04/07/93 Age: 28 Bats: R Throws: R Height: 6'1" Weight: 205 Origin: Round 18, 2012 Draft (#554 overall)

YEAR	TEAM	LVL	AGE	PA	R	2B	3B	HR	RBI	BB	K	SB	CS	Whiff%	AVG/OBP/SLG	DRC+	BABIP	BRR	FRAA	WARP
2018	IOW	AAA	25	263	34	10	2	13	41	26	63	3	1		.268/.342/.494	129	.312	-0.2	2B(38): -2.9, SS(15): 1.3, 3B(9): 1.3	1.3
2018	CHC	MLB	25	210	23	9	2	6	33	19	60	3	4	33.5%	.239/.319/.408	76	.314	-1.0	3B(56): 2.4, 2B(13): -0.6, 1B(2): 0.0	0.2
2019	CHC	MLB	26	356	47	17	0	11	41	44	93	5	1	32.5%	.257/.362/.422	97	.333	3.7	3B(67): -1.0, 2B(50): 2.0, SS(9): -0.1	1.6
2020	CHC	MLB	27	145	15	3	1	7	29	17	40	2	0	27.8%	.200/.303/.408	87	.228	0.2	3B(33): -3.2, 2B(7): -0.4, 1B(1): 0.0	-0.3
2021 FS	*CHC*	*MLB*	*28*	*600*	*69*	*24*	*2*	*21*	*70*	*59*	*165*	*3*	*1*	*31.1%*	*.235/.323/.415*	*103*	*.300*	*0.6*	*3B 0, 1B 0*	*2.1*
2021 DC	*CHC*	*MLB*	*28*	*581*	*67*	*23*	*2*	*21*	*68*	*57*	*160*	*3*	*1*	*31.1%*	*.235/.323/.415*	*103*	*.300*	*0.6*	*3B 0, 1B 0*	*1.5*

Comparables: Shane Andrews, Andy Tracy, Ian Stewart

Everything about what Bote did for the Cubs in 2020 was pretty much in line with what they saw out of their utility infielder the previous two seasons: plate-discipline numbers, batted-ball data, ball-tracking metrics. If anything, those numbers improved, as Bote started lifting the ball more frequently and hitting the ball harder on average. So, what went wrong? In a word...BABIP. Okay, that's not so much a word as it is a weird acronym, but the point is that Bote got BABIP'd to death in 2020, with that number dropping by more than 100 points from the year prior. That made for a frustrating season, but as Bote sets sail on a new voyage, the prospects of a full, 162-game campaign makes it difficult to worry about him capsizing again.

Kris Bryant 3B   Born: 01/04/92   Age: 29   Bats: R   Throws: R   Height: 6'5"   Weight: 230   Origin: Round 1, 2013 Draft (#2 overall)

YEAR	TEAM	LVL	AGE	PA	R	2B	3B	HR	RBI	BB	K	SB	CS	Whiff%	AVG/OBP/SLG	DRC+	BABIP	BRR	FRAA	WARP
2018	CHC	MLB	26	457	59	28	3	13	52	48	107	2	4	27.4%	.272/.374/.460	109	.342	-2.2	3B(86): 0.8, RF(15): -0.0, LF(14): -0.4	1.9
2019	CHC	MLB	27	634	108	35	1	31	77	74	145	4	0	28.4%	.282/.382/.521	125	.331	2.2	3B(115): -14.3, RF(27): -2.2, LF(23): -1.6	2.7
2020	CHC	MLB	28	147	20	5	1	4	11	12	40	0	0	29.5%	.206/.293/.351	92	.264	1.4	3B(27): -0.6, LF(4): -0.3, 1B(1): 0.0	0.3
2021 FS	CHC	MLB	29	600	86	26	2	24	69	70	161	5	2	28.4%	.254/.362/.461	127	.322	-0.3	3B -2, LF -2	2.9
2021 DC	CHC	MLB	29	581	83	25	2	24	67	68	156	5	2	28.4%	.254/.362/.461	127	.322	-0.3	3B -2, LF -2	2.8

Comparables: Troy Glaus, Scott Rolen, Evan Longoria

Bryant's year began with news that he had lost his grievance against the Cubs alleging they had manipulated his service time in 2015 in order to gain an extra year of team control. The Cubs did manipulate his service time, of course but Bryant lost the case. He then suffered through a lost year. The list of body parts that betrayed the former MVP included, but was not limited to: oblique, wrist, elbow, finger and back. He also missed time with a gastrointestinal issue. If there's a silver lining in Bryant's year, it's that all the injuries can (and probably should) be blamed for his rotten play. A fully healthy Bryant, it can be reasoned, ought to still be viewed as a cornerstone player at either third base or in an outfield corner. Now entering his walk year, Bryant will have to stay healthy and produce if he wants the kind of contract that led the Cubs to suppress his earning potential in the first place.

Willson Contreras C   Born: 05/13/92   Age: 29   Bats: R   Throws: R   Height: 6'1"   Weight: 225   Origin: International Free Agent, 2009

YEAR	TEAM	LVL	AGE	PA	R	2B	3B	HR	RBI	BB	K	SB	CS	Whiff%	AVG/OBP/SLG	DRC+	BABIP	BRR	FRAA	WARP
2018	CHC	MLB	26	544	50	27	5	10	54	53	121	4	1	28.1%	.249/.339/.390	90	.313	0.6	C(133): -14.6, LF(5): -0.8, 1B(1): -0.0	0.5
2019	CHC	MLB	27	409	57	18	2	24	64	38	102	1	2	33.2%	.272/.355/.533	110	.314	-1.9	C(99): -8.7, 1B(2): -0.0, RF(2): 1.1	1.7
2020	CHC	MLB	28	225	37	10	0	7	26	20	57	1	2	33.7%	.243/.356/.407	108	.307	-0.4	C(41): -0.5	1.1
2021 FS	CHC	MLB	29	600	72	24	2	22	76	59	151	4	2	32.0%	.248/.345/.433	115	.307	-0.6	C 2, 1B 0	3.8
2021 DC	CHC	MLB	29	513	62	21	2	19	65	51	129	4	1	32.0%	.248/.345/.433	115	.307	-0.5	C 2	3.1

Comparables: Bobby Estalella, Rick Wilkins, Alex Avila

"But his defense!" was a common retort about Contreras during his three-year ascent into one of the game's best offensive catchers. It wasn't unwarranted, but Contreras—who admitted he hadn't before put much thought into framing—showed marked improvement in his age-28 season. "But his offense!" they'll likely now cry as the commitment to defense coincided with a career-worst batting average and a serious lack of power. Balancing defensive focus with offensive readiness is a challenge for any catcher, but Contreras seems to have found the right equation. Both he and the Cubs should be better for it going forward.

YEAR	TEAM	P. COUNT	FRM RUNS	BLK RUNS	THRW RUNS	TOT RUNS
2018	CHC	18720	-17.8	1.9	0.4	-15.5
2019	CHC	13930	-9.4	0.0	-0.3	-9.7
2020	CHC	5378	2.7	0.4	-0.1	2.9
2021	CHC	15632	-0.8	-0.1	0.5	-0.4

★ ★ ★ *2021 Top 101 Prospect* **#78** ★ ★ ★

Brennen Davis CF   Born: 11/02/99   Age: 21   Bats: R   Throws: R   Height: 6'4"   Weight: 175   Origin: Round 2, 2018 Draft (#62 overall)

YEAR	TEAM	LVL	AGE	PA	R	2B	3B	HR	RBI	BB	K	SB	CS	Whiff%	AVG/OBP/SLG	DRC+	BABIP	BRR	FRAA	WARP
2018	CUBR	ROK	18	72	9	2	0	0	3	10	12	6	1		.298/.431/.333	159	.370	0.0	CF(10): 0.6, RF(4): -0.6	0.3
2019	SB	LO-A	19	204	33	9	3	8	30	18	38	4	1		.305/.381/.525	154	.346	-0.6	LF(23): -1.2, CF(23): -2.1, RF(2): 0.7	1.4
2021 FS	CHC	MLB	21	600	58	26	3	14	63	40	169	8	2		.237/.299/.378	86	.315	1.8	CF 2, LF 0	1.2

Comparables: Jesse Winker, Christian Yelich, Alen Hanson

Davis has spent enough time in South Bend, Indiana to be mistaken for a Notre Dame student. After breaking out there in the Midwest League a year ago, Davis was forced to go back in 2020, working out at the Cubs' alternate site instead of what was expected to be a promotion to Double-A Tennessee. The Cubs valued his development enough to have him in their player pool, and why wouldn't they? At maturation, he could be their starting center fielder while featuring five average or better tools.

Daniel Descalso 2B   Born: 10/19/86   Age: 34   Bats: L   Throws: R   Height: 5'10"   Weight: 190   Origin: Round 3, 2007 Draft (#112 overall)

YEAR	TEAM	LVL	AGE	PA	R	2B	3B	HR	RBI	BB	K	SB	CS	Whiff%	AVG/OBP/SLG	DRC+	BABIP	BRR	FRAA	WARP
2018	ARI	MLB	31	423	54	22	4	13	57	64	110	0	1	28.9%	.238/.353/.436	105	.300	-0.7	2B(52): 3.2, 3B(37): -0.8, 1B(11): -0.0	1.8
2019	IOW	AAA	32	33	5	0	0	2	4	5	8	0	0		.148/.303/.370	74	.118	-0.3	2B(5): -0.0, 3B(4): -0.6	-0.1
2019	CHC	MLB	32	194	20	5	1	2	15	23	57	2	1	29.0%	.173/.271/.250	59	.245	-0.5	2B(45): 2.1, 3B(3): -0.1, 1B(1): -0.0	-0.2
2021 FS	CHC	MLB	34	600	66	24	3	15	60	74	164	4	1	29.0%	.221/.324/.374	93	.292	2.2	2B 6, 3B -4	1.3

Comparables: Tony Graffanino, Dick Green, Damian Jackson

In November 2018, the Cubs traded utility infielder Tommy La Stella to the Angels for a PTBNL. A month later, they replaced him with Descalso. La Stella became an All-Star, Descalso very much did not.

Phillip Ervin RF Born: 07/15/92 Age: 28 Bats: R Throws: R Height: 5'10" Weight: 207 Origin: Round 1, 2013 Draft (#27 overall)

YEAR	TEAM	LVL	AGE	PA	R	2B	3B	HR	RBI	BB	K	SB	CS	Whiff%	AVG/OBP/SLG	DRC+	BABIP	BRR	FRAA	WARP
2018	LOU	AAA	25	202	25	12	4	5	38	20	39	10	7		.289/.373/.491	131	.341	-0.8	LF(37): 5.2, CF(8): -0.5, RF(3): 0.3	1.3
2018	CIN	MLB	25	247	27	10	1	7	31	20	60	6	1	27.3%	.252/.324/.404	96	.310	1.0	LF(39): 0.2, RF(33): -2.7, CF(4): -0.0	0.3
2019	LOU	AAA	26	172	27	8	1	6	26	19	34	6	6		.290/.384/.483	135	.333	2.0	CF(25): 0.9, LF(10): 1.2	1.5
2019	CIN	MLB	26	260	30	11	7	7	23	18	63	4	3	27.7%	.271/.331/.466	94	.339	1.0	LF(61): -5.5, CF(25): 1.1, RF(17): -0.7	0.2
2020	SEA	MLB	28	47	5	3	0	0	4	8	14	0	0	27.7%	.205/.340/.282	88	.320	0.3	RF(18): 0.6	0.1
2020	CIN	MLB	28	42	5	0	0	0	0	6	8	1	0	25.9%	.086/.238/.086	90	.111	0.6	LF(10): -0.8, CF(7): 0.0, RF(1): 0.1	0.0
2021 FS	CHC	MLB	28	600	67	22	3	16	60	62	155	18	6	27.4%	.227/.323/.380	95	.290	4.1	LF 3, RF -2	2.0
2021 DC	CHC	MLB	28	410	45	15	2	11	41	42	106	12	4	27.4%	.227/.323/.380	95	.290	2.8	LF 2, RF -1	1.2

Comparables: Chuck Hinton, Curtis Pride, Al Martin

A former first-round pick, Ervin is now a 28-year-old bat-first corner outfielder coming off a season that saw his limited playing time produce worst-ever offensive results. The tools that led to him being drafted so highly still flash; however, the reason they make movies about late-bloomer comeback miracles is because they're weighed against all the times those miracles don't happen.

Billy Hamilton CF Born: 09/09/90 Age: 30 Bats: S Throws: R Height: 6'0" Weight: 155 Origin: Round 2, 2009 Draft (#57 overall)

YEAR	TEAM	LVL	AGE	PA	R	2B	3B	HR	RBI	BB	K	SB	CS	Whiff%	AVG/OBP/SLG	DRC+	BABIP	BRR	FRAA	WARP
2018	CIN	MLB	27	556	74	16	9	4	29	46	132	34	10	23.9%	.236/.299/.327	70	.309	8.3	CF(150): 4.2	1.2
2019	KC	MLB	28	305	32	12	2	0	12	25	74	18	5	23.5%	.211/.275/.269	55	.286	4.0	CF(90): -2.9	-0.5
2019	ATL	MLB	28	48	9	2	0	0	3	7	13	4	1	21.9%	.268/.375/.317	82	.393	0.5	CF(24): -2.7	-0.2
2020	NYM	MLB	30	25	4	0	0	0	1	1	3	3	1	16.0%	.045/.083/.045	87	.050	0.1	CF(13): -1.0	0.0
2020	CHC	MLB	30	11	6	0	0	1	1	1	4	3	1	33.3%	.300/.364/.600	80	.400	0.7	CF(12): -0.2	0.0
2021 FS	CHC	MLB	30	600	54	17	4	7	48	48	141	44	11	23.4%	.218/.284/.310	63	.280	17.9	CF -9	0.1

Comparables: Cecil Espy, Herm Winningham, Chris Duffy

Since being selected off waivers by Atlanta from Kansas City in August 2019, Hamilton has been employed by four different franchises and has accumulated 120 plate appearances and 16 stolen bases. He sure can fly...and he'll have to continue doing so at his usual rate to avoid changing teams.

Ian Happ CF Born: 08/12/94 Age: 26 Bats: S Throws: R Height: 6'0" Weight: 205 Origin: Round 1, 2015 Draft (#9 overall)

YEAR	TEAM	LVL	AGE	PA	R	2B	3B	HR	RBI	BB	K	SB	CS	Whiff%	AVG/OBP/SLG	DRC+	BABIP	BRR	FRAA	WARP
2018	CHC	MLB	23	462	56	19	2	15	44	70	167	8	4	38.0%	.233/.353/.408	88	.362	2.0	CF(63): -7.9, LF(59): -2.5, RF(24): 0.6	-0.1
2019	IOW	AAA	24	429	66	18	1	16	53	65	113	9	2		.242/.364/.432	99	.307	1.2	CF(79): -4.0, 2B(20): 3.1, LF(2): 0.2	1.5
2019	CHC	MLB	24	156	25	7	1	11	30	15	39	2	0	29.8%	.264/.333/.564	112	.286	1.7	LF(15): -0.4, 2B(13): -0.9, RF(13): 1.2	1.0
2020	CHC	MLB	26	231	27	11	1	12	28	30	63	1	3	35.9%	.258/.361/.505	124	.317	-2.2	CF(51): -8.6, LF(28): -0.3, RF(7): -0.4	0.2
2021 FS	CHC	MLB	26	600	81	25	2	27	68	71	182	6	2	35.3%	.237/.332/.453	115	.306	1.1	CF -8, LF -5	1.8
2021 DC	CHC	MLB	26	581	78	24	2	26	66	69	176	6	2	35.3%	.237/.332/.453	115	.306	1.1	CF -7, LF -5	1.7

Comparables: Preston Wilson, Jose Cruz, Ramón Laureano

Happ has essentially played consecutive two-month seasons, and in each one he's performed a lot like the Cubs probably envisioned when they spent a top-10 pick on him back in 2015. The swing-and-miss in his game isn't going anywhere, but he's made a dent in it while becoming more selective overall. When he makes contact, he hits the crap out of the ball, and even though the sample sizes of the last two years are small, everything about it looks sustainable. A steadying force in a lineup whose stars of yesteryear weren't shining as brightly as we've grown accustomed to, Happ looks primed to take over as the next most integral part of the Cubs' lineup.

Jason Heyward RF Born: 08/09/89 Age: 31 Bats: L Throws: L Height: 6'5" Weight: 240 Origin: Round 1, 2007 Draft (#14 overall)

YEAR	TEAM	LVL	AGE	PA	R	2B	3B	HR	RBI	BB	K	SB	CS	Whiff%	AVG/OBP/SLG	DRC+	BABIP	BRR	FRAA	WARP
2018	CHC	MLB	28	489	67	23	4	8	57	42	60	1	1	16.9%	.270/.335/.395	94	.297	3.0	RF(118): 11.5, CF(25): -2.7	2.0
2019	CHC	MLB	29	589	78	20	4	21	62	68	110	8	3	22.5%	.251/.343/.429	104	.281	-0.4	RF(105): -11.3, CF(84): -1.5	0.8
2020	CHC	MLB	31	181	20	6	2	6	22	30	37	2	0	23.6%	.265/.392/.456	113	.311	2.1	RF(50): 5.8	1.5
2021 FS	CHC	MLB	31	600	63	23	3	16	66	68	116	7	2	21.6%	.251/.342/.404	105	.294	1.7	RF -1, CF 0	2.1
2021 DC	CHC	MLB	31	581	61	23	3	16	64	65	113	7	2	21.6%	.251/.342/.404	105	.294	1.6	RF -1	1.8

Comparables: Jeff DaVanon, Michael Cuddyer, Bobby Kielty

Heyward discourse most often focuses on the $184-million contract he signed before the 2016 season and how he's failed to consistently perform at the level of a player worthy of that salary. Heyward didn't sign himself to that contract, of course, and has by every indication given his all to the Cubs' organization, even if he's failed to live up to the expectations of fans, the people who gave him that contract and, very likely, himself.

On August 26th, Heyward sat out the Cubs' game against the Tigers, joining athletes from across the country in protesting the shooting of Jacob Blake by a police officer earlier that week in Kenosha, Wis. His teammates played without him, and while everyone said the right thing—Heyward indicated that he encouraged them to play—it was a jarring decision. Even if Heyward told them to play—what else was he supposed to say?—his teammates, or even his manager, could have made the simple decision to stand with him in solidarity.

On the field, Heyward was the Cubs' best player by any definition, steadying the offense while Chicago's other top hitters slumped and/or couldn't stay healthy. He showed patience unlike we've ever seen from him before, and he hit the ball harder on average, ripping line drives all over the field while providing his usual sterling defense in right field.

Whether the adjustments Heyward made are sustainable is tough to say given the short season—line-drive rates aren't the most predictive metrics—but even if they're not, the Cubs owe him another $65 million over the final three years of his contract. Heyward, on the other hand, owes the Cubs nothing.

Nico Hoerner SS Born: 05/13/97   Age: 24   Bats: R   Throws: R   Height: 6'1"   Weight: 200   Origin: Round 1, 2018 Draft (#24 overall)

YEAR	TEAM	LVL	AGE	PA	R	2B	3B	HR	RBI	BB	K	SB	CS	Whiff%	AVG/OBP/SLG	DRC+	BABIP	BRR	FRAA	WARP
2018	CUBB	ROK	21	15	3	1	1	0	1	2	0	2	0		.250/.400/.500	120	.250	0.8	SS(3): 0.6	0.2
2018	EUG	SS	21	28	6	0	1	1	2	5	3	4	1		.318/.464/.545	170	.333	-0.5	SS(5): -0.4	0.1
2018	SB	LO-A	21	17	1	1	0	1	3	2	1	0	0		.400/.471/.667	145	.385	0.0	SS(4): -0.4	0.1
2019	CUBR	ROK	22	21	2	1	0	0	0	1	1	0	0		.400/.429/.450	170	.421	0.4	SS(3): -0.3, 2B(1): -0.0	0.2
2019	TNS	AA	22	294	37	16	3	3	22	21	31	8	4		.284/.344/.399	103	.311	1.6	SS(44): -2.6, 2B(16): 0.5, CF(11): 2.8	1.5
2019	CHC	MLB	22	82	13	1	1	3	17	3	11	0	0	18.1%	.282/.305/.436	94	.292	0.3	SS(17): 0.6, 2B(1): 0.1, CF(1): -0.1	0.4
2020	CHC	MLB	23	126	19	4	0	0	13	12	24	3	2	18.3%	.222/.312/.259	81	.279	0.8	2B(37): 3.7, SS(10): 0.5, 3B(6): -0.2	0.5
2021 FS	CHC	MLB	24	600	62	25	3	11	59	43	110	6	2	18.3%	.253/.316/.375	91	.299	2.0	2B 3, CF -2	1.6
2021 DC	CHC	MLB	24	581	60	24	3	10	57	41	106	6	2	18.3%	.253/.316/.375	91	.299	2.0	2B 3, CF -2	1.5

Comparables: Tony Taylor, Glenn Hubbard, Ryne Sandberg

It was a weird season for Hoerner, who was expected to take the mantle at second base for the Cubs. Instead, he bounced around the diamond and struggled to get his bat going. Hoerner's calling card was and continues to be his hit tool, but that has yet to show up against big-league pitching. Given that the rest of his skill set is run-of-the-mill, it's fair to say that any continuation of that theme heading forward would be concerning.

─────────────── ★ ★ ★ *2021 Top 101 Prospect* **#88** ★ ★ ★ ───────────────

Ed Howard SS Born: 08/06/01   Age: 19   Bats: R   Throws: R   Height: 6'2"   Weight: 185   Origin: Round 1, 2020 Draft (#16 overall)

Howard, a product of the White Sox ACE program (which aims to help inner-city Chicago youth develop skills and find opportunities on and off the field), wound up on the other side of town when the Cubs nabbed him 16th overall in last June's draft. As a prep infielder from a cold-weather state, Howard wasn't able to showcase himself much before the pandemic shut down baseball across the globe, but the Cubs obviously believe in his advanced glove and projectable bat. Howard is, almost by default, one of the organization's most important developmental projects as they transition from one era to the next.

Jason Kipnis 2B Born: 04/03/87   Age: 34   Bats: L   Throws: R   Height: 5'11"   Weight: 200   Origin: Round 2, 2009 Draft (#63 overall)

YEAR	TEAM	LVL	AGE	PA	R	2B	3B	HR	RBI	BB	K	SB	CS	Whiff%	AVG/OBP/SLG	DRC+	BABIP	BRR	FRAA	WARP
2018	CLE	MLB	31	601	65	28	1	18	75	60	112	7	1	20.9%	.230/.315/.389	93	.258	-1.2	2B(131): -0.5, CF(14): -2.0	1.1
2019	CLE	MLB	32	511	52	23	1	17	65	40	88	7	2	20.5%	.245/.304/.410	93	.265	0.2	2B(117): -0.0	1.3
2020	CHC	MLB	33	135	13	8	1	3	16	18	41	1	0	26.5%	.237/.341/.404	88	.333	-0.1	2B(36): 0.6, 1B(1): -0.1	0.3
2021 FS	CHC	MLB	34	600	65	28	2	17	64	57	153	9	2	21.9%	.229/.311/.387	90	.288	1.3	2B 0, CF -1	1.4

Comparables: Tadahito Iguchi, Neil Walker, Brian Dozier

Throughout Kipnis' career, announcers have gotten a lot of mileage out of him hailing from Northbrook, Illinois. Kipnis' decision to join the Cubs allowed for that tattered fun fact to be repaired in the form of a "hometown kid" narrative. The more important thing to know here is that, while he finished with an OPS just under the league-average mark, his underlying metrics weren't supportive of his resurgence. Now entering his age-34 season, Kipnis is closer to joining a television booth and picking his own low-hanging biographical fruit than he is to returning to his past All-Star heights.

José Martínez 1B Born: 07/25/88   Age: 32   Bats: R   Throws: R   Height: 6'6"   Weight: 215   Origin: International Free Agent, 2006

YEAR	TEAM	LVL	AGE	PA	R	2B	3B	HR	RBI	BB	K	SB	CS	Whiff%	AVG/OBP/SLG	DRC+	BABIP	BRR	FRAA	WARP
2018	STL	MLB	29	590	64	30	0	17	83	49	104	0	3	21.4%	.305/.364/.457	118	.351	-3.6	1B(84): -10.4, RF(46): 0.2	0.9
2019	STL	MLB	30	373	45	13	2	10	42	35	82	3	0	23.0%	.269/.340/.410	94	.328	0.7	RF(75): -3.5, LF(7): -0.0	0.3
2020	CHC	MLB	32	22	0	0	0	0	0	1	7	0	0	28.3%	.000/.045/.000	73	.000			0.0
2020	TB	MLB	32	76	10	4	0	2	10	9	20	0	0	28.1%	.239/.329/.388	76	.311	0.0	1B(6): 0.0	-0.1
2021 FS	CHC	MLB	32	600	68	27	1	16	69	57	143	2	1	23.4%	.256/.331/.405	103	.320	-1.0	RF -4, 1B -7	0.1

Comparables: Shawn Green, Andre Ethier, Bubba Trammell

The other guy the Rays acquired in the Randy Arozarena trade had a slightly less memorable season. In a month with Tampa, Martínez failed to do what he was acquired to do: hit lefties. He was shipped at the deadline to the Cubs for an actual prospect and he was soon thereafter jettisoned to the alternate site after 22 hitless plate appearances, never to be seen by the Wrigley faithful—er, bleachers—again. Martínez's track record against lefties should net him another big-league job by the time you read this.

Cameron Maybin LF Born: 04/04/87 Age: 34 Bats: R Throws: R Height: 6'3" Weight: 215 Origin: Round 1, 2005 Draft (#10 overall)

YEAR	TEAM	LVL	AGE	PA	R	2B	3B	HR	RBI	BB	K	SB	CS	Whiff%	AVG/OBP/SLG	DRC+	BABIP	BRR	FRAA	WARP
2018	MIA	MLB	31	287	20	12	1	3	20	32	55	8	5	21.0%	.251/.338/.343	88	.308	-2.7	LF(44): 2.1, CF(30): -0.7, RF(24): -0.1	0.3
2018	SEA	MLB	31	97	12	2	1	1	8	6	20	2	0	20.1%	.242/.289/.319	88	.300	-0.2	CF(20): -1.6, LF(12): 0.4	0.0
2019	COL	AAA	32	67	4	3	0	0	5	13	20	1	2		.216/.388/.275	128	.344	-1.9	CF(5): -0.3, LF(4): -0.2, RF(2): -0.1	0.2
2019	NYY	MLB	32	269	48	17	0	11	32	30	72	9	6	28.5%	.285/.364/.494	105	.365	-1.0	LF(46): -0.5, RF(36): 0.7, CF(3): 0.4	0.9
2020	DET	MLB	33	45	5	4	0	1	2	4	13	0	0	30.8%	.244/.311/.415	86	.333	-0.1	RF(12): -0.3	-0.1
2020	CHC	MLB	33	56	3	4	1	0	5	3	12	3	0	31.1%	.250/.304/.365	83	.325	-0.2	RF(7): 0.5, LF(5): 0.2, CF(-5): -0.5	0.0
2021 FS	CHC	MLB	34	600	58	23	2	11	57	59	148	21	8	26.7%	.229/.310/.344	82	.296	-0.7	LF 3, CF -1	0.7

Comparables: Carlos Gómez, Alejandro De Aza, Jerry Martin

Maybin has been acquired by nine teams since the start of 2017. He ended last season with the Cubs, having been traded by the Tigers at the deadline; it was the third time Detroit—and Detroit alone—had dealt him. He probably thought he was done with this nomadic lifestyle nonsense after he did a superb job filling in for an injury-ravaged Yankees team in 2019, but that stability (and his performance in pinstripes) looks to be an outlier. Wherever Maybin ends up, don't get too comfortable with seeing him there; he'll likely be on the move again before long.

Hernán Pérez 2B Born: 03/26/91 Age: 30 Bats: R Throws: R Height: 6'1" Weight: 213 Origin: International Free Agent, 2007

YEAR	TEAM	LVL	AGE	PA	R	2B	3B	HR	RBI	BB	K	SB	CS	Whiff%	AVG/OBP/SLG	DRC+	BABIP	BRR	FRAA	WARP
2018	MIL	MLB	27	334	36	11	2	9	29	17	71	11	3	21.5%	.253/.290/.386	91	.300	0.6	2B(51): -0.9, RF(27): 0.4, 3B(22): 0.4	0.7
2019	SA	AAA	28	121	18	10	0	5	19	14	23	6	0		.290/.372/.523	126	.329	0.8	1B(10): 1.0, 2B(9): -0.3, 3B(5): 0.5	0.8
2019	MIL	MLB	28	246	29	11	0	8	18	11	66	5	1	26.9%	.228/.262/.379	68	.283	-1.7	2B(45): 3.4, SS(21): -1.9, 3B(14): 1.2	0.1
2020	CHC	MLB	29	6	0	0	0	0	0	0	2	0	0	45.5%	.167/.167/.167	72	.250	0.3	1B(2): -0.0, 2B(1): 0.0, LF(1): 0.0	0.0
2021 FS	CHC	MLB	30	600	62	25	2	19	72	30	145	20	5	25.1%	.242/.282/.401	84	.291	5.5	2B 0, LF -1	0.9

Comparables: Pedro Feliz, Charley Smith, Craig Paquette

Pérez's nickname—"Pan Blanco," or, "White Bread"—is appropriate because he's a walking reminder that, like a slice or two of Wonder, some versatile instruments should be left in the pantry when it's time to make a real meal. The Cubs learned that lesson quickly last season, and he appeared in only three games for the big-league team. He'll keep getting jobs until teams realize that just because someone can play everywhere doesn't mean they should play anywhere—except Triple-A, anyway.

Josh Phegley C Born: 02/12/88 Age: 33 Bats: R Throws: R Height: 5'10" Weight: 225 Origin: Round 1, 2009 Draft (#38 overall)

YEAR	TEAM	LVL	AGE	PA	R	2B	3B	HR	RBI	BB	K	SB	CS	Whiff%	AVG/OBP/SLG	DRC+	BABIP	BRR	FRAA	WARP
2018	NAS	AAA	30	139	12	6	3	3	18	15	31	0	0		.235/.331/.412	101	.287	-0.1	C(19): 2.8	0.6
2018	OAK	MLB	30	102	13	7	0	2	15	6	27	0	0	24.6%	.204/.255/.344	75	.258	-0.1	C(39): -1.3	0.1
2019	OAK	MLB	31	342	44	18	0	12	62	15	63	0	1	22.7%	.239/.282/.411	90	.258	-3.0	C(106): -14.3	-0.3
2020	CHC	MLB	32	18	4	0	0	1	2	1	3	0	0	20.0%	.062/.167/.250	93	.000	0.1	C(4): -0.0	0.0
2021 FS	CHC	MLB	33	600	61	28	1	18	68	39	138	2	0	22.7%	.220/.286/.377	82	.261	-0.6	C -11	-0.2

Comparables: Mark Parent, Rod Barajas, Vance Wilson

Phegley made the Cubs' Opening Day roster thanks to the expanded bench, but he was relegated to the alternate site as soon as the rosters were contracted. He's probably best deployed as a third catcher heading forward, though it shouldn't surprise anyone if he gets another run or two as a primary backup.

YEAR	TEAM	P. COUNT	FRM RUNS	BLK RUNS	THRW RUNS	TOT RUNS
2018	OAK	3985	-0.9	-1.5	0.0	-2.3
2018	NAS	2495	2.4	-0.2	0.3	2.5
2019	OAK	13331	-7.1	-5.5	1.0	-11.6
2020	CHC	267	-0.1	0.0	0.0	-0.1
2021	CHC	16650	-8.7	-1.2	-0.5	-10.4

Anthony Rizzo 1B Born: 08/08/89 Age: 31 Bats: L Throws: L Height: 6'3" Weight: 240 Origin: Round 6, 2007 Draft (#204 overall)

YEAR	TEAM	LVL	AGE	PA	R	2B	3B	HR	RBI	BB	K	SB	CS	Whiff%	AVG/OBP/SLG	DRC+	BABIP	BRR	FRAA	WARP
2018	CHC	MLB	28	665	74	29	1	25	101	70	80	6	4	16.9%	.283/.376/.470	128	.287	-5.8	1B(153): 14.4, 2B(1): -0.0, P(1): -0.0	4.1
2019	CHC	MLB	29	613	89	29	3	27	94	71	86	5	2	19.6%	.293/.405/.520	135	.306	-4.9	1B(146): 4.4	3.7
2020	CHC	MLB	31	243	26	6	0	11	24	28	38	3	1	19.5%	.222/.342/.414	123	.218	-1.2	1B(57): -3.2	0.6
2021 FS	CHC	MLB	31	600	88	26	2	26	78	71	101	6	3	18.9%	.268/.384/.489	139	.289	-1.4	1B 10, 2B 0	4.8
2021 DC	CHC	MLB	31	581	85	25	2	25	75	68	98	5	2	18.9%	.268/.384/.489	139	.289	-1.4	1B 10	4.7

Comparables: Boog Powell, Jason Thompson, Willie Aikens

Rizzo accomplished an incredibly rare feat in 2020: He got the Cubs to spend more money than they were required. After all, the $16.5 million team option that was exercised for the last year of his deal didn't have to be spent on baseball—it could have been given to organizations hellbent on denying basic human rights. Maybe it was that Rizzo's performance has been so consistent, and his approval rating so high with the Chicago fans, that even the Ricketts family didn't want to suffer the PR hit that letting him walk for nothing would have inspired. While Rizzo did suffer some decline, it wasn't in the same stratosphere as some of his compatriots; his career-worst DRC+ still rested comfortably above the league-average mark. A gambling man wouldn't wager on the Ricketts continuing to pay Rizzo after 2021—whatever the reason—but even in decline he should remain a reasonably productive first baseman.

Cole Roederer CF   Born: 09/24/99   Age: 21   Bats: L   Throws: L   Height: 6'0"   Weight: 175   Origin: Round 2, 2018 Draft (#77 overall)

YEAR	TEAM	LVL	AGE	PA	R	2B	3B	HR	RBI	BB	K	SB	CS	Whiff%	AVG/OBP/SLG	DRC+	BABIP	BRR	FRAA	WARP
2018	CUBR	ROK	18	161	30	4	4	5	24	18	37	13	4		.275/.354/.465	123	.337	2.1	CF(29): -1.3, RF(4): -1.1, LF(1): -0.5	0.3
2019	SB	LO-A	19	448	45	19	4	9	60	52	112	16	5		.224/.319/.365	91	.285	1.6	CF(95): 3.3, LF(9): -0.7, RF(3): -0.4	1.4
2021 FS	CHC	MLB	21	600	50	26	3	11	56	38	205	14	5		.206/.261/.331	61	.302	1.5	CF 10, LF 0	0.0

Comparables: Trent Grisham, Slade Heathcott, Joe Benson

Roederer was drafted with the compensation pick the Cubs received when Jake Arrieta signed with the Phillies. He struggled in his first full-season assignment in the Midwest League, but he has plenty of time for the bat to come around. In the meantime, he has at least looked like he can stick in center.

Max Schrock 2B   Born: 10/12/94   Age: 26   Bats: L   Throws: R   Height: 5'9"   Weight: 185   Origin: Round 13, 2015 Draft (#404 overall)

YEAR	TEAM	LVL	AGE	PA	R	2B	3B	HR	RBI	BB	K	SB	CS	Whiff%	AVG/OBP/SLG	DRC+	BABIP	BRR	FRAA	WARP
2018	MEM	AAA	23	457	41	22	0	4	42	24	36	10	5		.249/.296/.331	72	.260	-1.7	2B(80): -3.3, 3B(14): -0.2, LF(4): 0.5	-1.1
2019	MEM	AAA	24	303	42	20	1	2	31	37	49	12	2		.275/.366/.381	102	.332	-1.6	3B(56): -4.8, 2B(10): 0.0, LF(7): -0.1	0.6
2020	STL	MLB	26	17	1	0	0	1	1	0	6	0	0	16.2%	.176/.176/.353	81	.200	-0.3	2B(5): 0.2, 3B(2): -0.1, P(1): -0.0	0.0
2021 FS	CHC	MLB	26	600	57	23	2	11	60	39	102	3	1	16.2%	.251/.307/.361	84	.290	0.3	2B -4, 3B -2	0.2
2021 DC	CHC	MLB	26	205	19	7	0	3	20	13	35	1	0	16.2%	.251/.307/.361	84	.290	0.1	2B -1, 3B -1	0.1

Comparables: Yangervis Solarte, Nate Spears, Adrian Cardenas

Schrock has minimal power but he makes contact and gets on base, which is fine since he's a smooth lefty second baseman. The Cubs claimed him off waivers from the Cardinals early in the offseason.

Steven Souza Jr. RF   Born: 04/24/89   Age: 32   Bats: R   Throws: R   Height: 6'4"   Weight: 225   Origin: Round 3, 2007 Draft (#100 overall)

YEAR	TEAM	LVL	AGE	PA	R	2B	3B	HR	RBI	BB	K	SB	CS	Whiff%	AVG/OBP/SLG	DRC+	BABIP	BRR	FRAA	WARP
2018	ARI	MLB	29	272	21	15	3	5	29	28	75	6	1	27.8%	.220/.309/.369	77	.298	0.1	RF(65): -5.9, CF(1): -0.0	-0.8
2020	CHC	MLB	31	31	3	2	0	1	5	4	15	1	0	44.3%	.148/.258/.333	65	.273	0.0	RF(6): -0.3, LF(3): 0.0	-0.1
2021 FS	CHC	MLB	32	600	65	23	2	21	68	66	219	12	4	32.3%	.219/.316/.395	96	.330	-0.2	RF -12, CF 0	-0.1

Comparables: Rob Deer, Dustan Mohr, Jayson Werth

That Souza was able to play at all in 2020 qualifies as a victory, as he missed the preceding season after tearing the ACL, LCL, PCL and posterior lateral capsule in his left knee during spring training. That he was essentially the only major-league addition the Cubs made heading into the year was an indictment on the Ricketts' cheapness. That he was released after just 31 plate appearances—during which he whiffed on nearly half his swings—makes it fair to wonder if he has anything left to offer a major-league team.

Chase Strumpf 2B   Born: 03/08/98   Age: 23   Bats: R   Throws: R   Height: 6'1"   Weight: 191   Origin: Round 2, 2019 Draft (#64 overall)

YEAR	TEAM	LVL	AGE	PA	R	2B	3B	HR	RBI	BB	K	SB	CS	Whiff%	AVG/OBP/SLG	DRC+	BABIP	BRR	FRAA	WARP
2019	CUBR	ROK	21	32	5	3	0	0	1	7	7	0	0		.182/.406/.318	115	.250	0.2	2B(5): 0.4	0.2
2019	EUG	SS	21	111	17	8	0	2	14	15	28	2	0		.292/.405/.449	151	.387	-1.3	2B(24): -3.4	0.3
2019	SB	LO-A	21	28	3	1	0	1	2	1	7	0	0		.125/.214/.292	50	.118	0.0	2B(6): 0.2	-0.1
2021 FS	CHC	MLB	23	600	55	27	2	13	60	41	205	2	0		.217/.285/.352	77	.320	0.1	2B -4	0.0

Strumpf has an advanced approach that will need to carry him since nothing else grades out as above-average, including every part of his surname between the "S" and the "F."

Ildemaro Vargas 2B   Born: 07/16/91   Age: 29   Bats: S   Throws: R   Height: 6'0"   Weight: 180   Origin: International Free Agent, 2008

YEAR	TEAM	LVL	AGE	PA	R	2B	3B	HR	RBI	BB	K	SB	CS	Whiff%	AVG/OBP/SLG	DRC+	BABIP	BRR	FRAA	WARP
2018	RNO	AAA	26	572	78	31	10	7	54	30	46	10	4		.311/.348/.445	99	.329	-3.8	SS(107): -6.0, 2B(17): -0.1	0.7
2018	ARI	MLB	26	20	2	0	0	1	4	1	4	1	0	27.6%	.211/.250/.368	93	.214	0.0	3B(3): 0.3, 2B(2): 0.1, SS(1): -0.0	0.1
2019	RNO	AAA	27	137	20	9	3	2	24	11	5	1	1		.403/.453/.573	144	.407	1.9	SS(13): 0.8, 3B(12): 0.3, 2B(6): 0.4	1.6
2019	ARI	MLB	27	211	25	9	1	6	24	9	24	1	0	12.2%	.269/.299/.413	87	.279	0.4	2B(48): 2.4, 3B(14): -1.1, SS(4): 0.5	0.6
2020	MIN	MLB	29	24	3	1	1	0	2	1	2	0	0	16.7%	.227/.250/.364	82	.238	-0.7	2B(8): 0.8, 3B(1): 0.0	0.0
2020	CHC	MLB	29	9	1	0	0	1	1	0	3	0	0	21.4%	.222/.222/.556	75	.200		2B(5): 0.4, 3B(1): -0.0	0.0
2020	ARI	MLB	29	21	2	0	0	0	0	1	5	0	0	21.1%	.150/.190/.150	79	.200	0.2	1B(5): -0.3, 2B(3): 0.2, 3B(1): -0.1	0.0
2021 FS	CHC	MLB	29	600	58	25	3	11	61	34	85	1	0	14.7%	.251/.299/.367	84	.279	1.7	2B 10, SS -1	2.0
2021 DC	CHC	MLB	29	205	20	8	1	3	20	11	29	0	0	14.7%	.251/.299/.367	84	.279	0.6	2B 4, SS 0	0.7

Comparables: Carlos Garcia, Jerry Adair, Omar Infante

Vargas' home run off Josh Hader in the ninth inning of the Cubs' comeback win over the Brewers on Sept. 12 was one of the least likely of the season. The rest of Vargas' campaign featured zero home runs, nine hits and three different franchises for which he suited up.

PITCHERS

Cory Abbott   RHP   Born: 09/20/95   Age: 25   Bats: R   Throws: R   Height: 6'2"   Weight: 220   Origin: Round 2, 2017 Draft (#67 overall)

YEAR	TEAM	LVL	AGE	W	L	SV	G	GS	IP	H	HR	BB/9	K/9	K	GB%	BABIP	WHIP	ERA	DRA-	WARP	MPH	FA%	Whiff%	CSP
2018	SB	LO-A	22	4	1	0	9	9	47¹	35	5	2.5	10.8	57	38.6%	.275	1.01	2.47	61	1.3				
2018	MB	HI-A	22	4	5	0	13	13	67²	59	3	3.5	9.8	74	44.4%	.316	1.26	2.53	106	0.3				
2019	TNS	AA	23	8	8	0	26	26	146²	112	15	3.2	10.2	166	37.5%	.270	1.12	3.01	86	1.4				
2021 FS	CHC	MLB	25	1	1	0	57	0	50	46	8	4.4	9.2	51	36.9%	.289	1.42	4.75	110	-0.2				
2021 DC	CHC	MLB	25	1	1	0	4	4	19	17	3	4.4	9.2	19	36.9%	.289	1.42	4.75	110	0.1				

Comparables: Ramón Rosso, Matt Hall, Nabil Crismatt

Abbott has moved slowly since being a second-round pick in 2017, but he spent the season at the alternate site and was added to the 40-man roster ahead of the Rule 5 draft. He should be in the mix for a starting shot at some point this year.

Jason Adam   RHP   Born: 08/04/91   Age: 29   Bats: R   Throws: R   Height: 6'3"   Weight: 229   Origin: Round 5, 2010 Draft (#149 overall)

YEAR	TEAM	LVL	AGE	W	L	SV	G	GS	IP	H	HR	BB/9	K/9	K	GB%	BABIP	WHIP	ERA	DRA-	WARP	MPH	FA%	Whiff%	CSP
2018	NWA	AA	26	1	0	0	6	0	11¹	5	0	3.2	13.5	17	36.4%	.227	0.79	1.59	79	0.1				
2018	OMA	AAA	26	2	0	4	11	0	12²	6	0	5.0	10.7	15	31.0%	.214	1.03	1.42	56	0.4				
2018	KC	MLB	26	0	3	0	31	0	32¹	30	9	4.2	10.3	37	28.7%	.269	1.39	6.12	157	-0.8	96.0	61.1%	26.4%	45.6%
2019	BUF	AAA	27	1	3	1	11	0	14	10	2	3.2	12.9	20	16.1%	.276	1.07	2.57	68	0.4				
2019	TOR	MLB	27	3	0	0	23	0	21²	15	1	4.2	7.5	18	26.7%	.237	1.15	2.91	130	-0.2	95.9	61.5%	27.8%	41.6%
2020	CHC	MLB	28	2	1	0	13	0	13²	9	2	5.3	13.8	21	37.9%	.259	1.24	3.29	85	0.2	96.5	53.8%	41.7%	41.3%
2021 FS	CHC	MLB	29	2	2	0	57	0	50	39	8	4.6	11.0	61	31.5%	.268	1.31	4.14	94	0.3	96.1	58.6%	32.5%	42.6%
2021 DC	CHC	MLB	29	2	2	0	51	0	54	42	9	4.6	11.0	66	31.5%	.268	1.31	4.14	94	0.5	96.1	58.6%	32.5%	42.6%

Comparables: Juan Minaya, Austin Brice, Glenn Sparkman

Adam is a walking Johnny Cash song, with Chicago his fourth stop that was featured in "I've Been Everywhere." And with a new slider that induced whiffs nearly a quarter of the time, it could be the last one (Baltimore and its promise of black attire is still out there, after all). A low-leverage arm during his previous major-league chances in Kansas City and Toronto, Adam got more opportunities with the Cubs thanks to some bullpen injuries and inconsistencies, and while his command was sometimes erratic, he missed bats with enough regularity to make one confident his success was more than a small-sample aberration.

Adbert Alzolay   RHP   Born: 03/01/95   Age: 26   Bats: R   Throws: R   Height: 6'1"   Weight: 208   Origin: International Free Agent, 2012

YEAR	TEAM	LVL	AGE	W	L	SV	G	GS	IP	H	HR	BB/9	K/9	K	GB%	BABIP	WHIP	ERA	DRA-	WARP	MPH	FA%	Whiff%	CSP
2018	IOW	AAA	23	2	4	0	8	8	39²	43	4	2.9	6.1	27	35.1%	.310	1.41	4.76	88	0.6				
2019	IOW	AAA	24	2	4	0	15	15	65¹	53	10	4.3	12.5	91	32.1%	.295	1.29	4.41	55	2.5				
2019	CHC	MLB	24	1	1	0	4	2	12¹	13	4	6.6	9.5	13	32.4%	.273	1.78	7.30	113	0.0	95.8	57.3%	26.7%	42.9%
2020	CHC	MLB	25	1	1	0	6	4	21¹	12	1	5.5	12.2	29	43.2%	.256	1.17	2.95	85	0.4	96.5	52.2%	27.5%	46.9%
2021 FS	CHC	MLB	26	9	9	0	26	26	150	132	24	4.5	10.3	171	36.7%	.287	1.37	4.42	99	1.1	96.3	53.6%	27.3%	45.8%
2021 DC	CHC	MLB	26	7	7	0	22	22	113	99	18	4.5	10.3	129	36.7%	.287	1.37	4.42	99	1.2	96.3	53.6%	27.3%	45.8%

Comparables: Alex Reyes, Walker Lockett, Jake Faria

What is Adbert Alzolay? That's not a Jeopardy! answer, but something the Cubs have been asking themselves for many moons now. The 2020 season didn't do a lot to answer that question, as he ping-ponged in and out of the rotation, finding moderate success but failing to prove he can turn a lineup over multiple times. In an age where pitching roles and usages are becoming more blurred, maybe the answer is to use him as a Daily Double—or, at least, someone who works two times through the order regardless of when they enter, a la Ryan Yarbrough. Given that Alzolay is now out of options, the Final Jeopardy phase of a player's career, the Cubs will have to submit their answer (preferably not in the form of a question) soon.

Joe Biagini   RHP   Born: 05/29/90   Age: 31   Bats: R   Throws: R   Height: 6'5"   Weight: 235   Origin: Round 26, 2011 Draft (#807 overall)

YEAR	TEAM	LVL	AGE	W	L	SV	G	GS	IP	H	HR	BB/9	K/9	K	GB%	BABIP	WHIP	ERA	DRA-	WARP	MPH	FA%	Whiff%	CSP
2018	BUF	AAA	28	0	3	0	4	4	21²	19	1	3.3	5.4	13	45.1%	.257	1.25	4.57	88	0.3				
2018	TOR	MLB	28	4	7	0	50	4	72	96	14	3.0	6.6	53	47.3%	.355	1.67	6.00	127	-0.6	96.6	60.8%	20.6%	45.7%
2019	HOU	MLB	29	0	1	0	13	0	14²	21	6	5.5	6.1	10	50.0%	.341	2.05	7.36	241	-1.0	94.8	57.8%	21.6%	42.9%
2019	TOR	MLB	29	3	1	1	50	0	50	50	8	3.1	9.0	50	44.4%	.311	1.34	3.78	97	0.3	95.2	48.5%	30.5%	43.3%
2020	HOU	MLB	30	0	0	0	4	0	4¹	10	1	8.3	8.3	4	47.4%	.500	3.23	20.77	92	0.1	94.8	63.6%	28.3%	41.3%
2021 FS	CHC	MLB	31	2	3	0	57	0	50	51	7	3.5	7.8	43	46.5%	.299	1.42	4.71	104	0.0	95.5	55.2%	25.9%	43.8%

Comparables: Erasmo Ramírez, Jacob Barnes, Felix Peña

Here's one mystery the Astros couldn't solve. The brief clues available on what attempts were made to rejuvenate Biagini's career hinted at an against-the-grain emphasis on the sinker, with a curveball-cutter secondary mix and the four-seam fastball exterminated altogether. It did nothing to arrest the decline Biagini suffered after arriving in Houston. He was bumped off the roster after the season ended, and picked up by the Cubs.

Rex Brothers LHP   Born: 12/18/87   Age: 33   Bats: L   Throws: L   Height: 6'0"   Weight: 205   Origin: Round 1, 2009 Draft (#34 overall)

YEAR	TEAM	LVL	AGE	W	L	SV	G	GS	IP	H	HR	BB/9	K/9	K	GB%	BABIP	WHIP	ERA	DRA-	WARP	MPH	FA%	Whiff%	CSP
2018	MIS	AA	30	3	1	0	11	0	13¹	7	1	7.4	12.8	19	46.7%	.207	1.35	4.05	64	0.3				
2018	GWN	AAA	30	2	4	1	32	0	27¹	26	1	10.9	12.2	37	43.5%	.391	2.16	7.24	96	0.1				
2018	ATL	MLB	30	0	0	0	1	0	0	0	0			0							98.0	91.7%	0.0%	34.5%
2019	SWB	AAA	31	0	3	0	34	0	45²	37	6	7.1	16.0	81	38.2%	.378	1.60	4.93	82	1.0				
2020	CHC	MLB	32	0	0	0	3	0	3¹	2	2	8.1	21.6	8	25.0%	.000	1.50	8.10	80	0.1	97.2	53.3%	48.5%	33.1%
2021 FS	CHC	MLB	33	2	3	0	57	0	50	37	6	7.3	13.1	72	41.0%	.299	1.57	4.54	100	0.1	97.2	55.3%	46.0%	33.1%

Comparables: Anthony Bass, Brad Boxberger, Brandon Morrow

The Brothers Grimm is an underrated adventure fantasy film released in 2005 by Terry Gillam of *Monty Python* and *Brazil* fame. Rex Brothers is an up-and-down reliever whose major-league story seems likely to end soon, if not happily.

Burl Carraway LHP   Born: 05/27/99   Age: 22   Bats: L   Throws: L   Height: 6'0"   Weight: 173   Origin: Round 2, 2020 Draft (#51 overall)

With a name that sounds like someone cast in a John Huston film, Carraway features a rising fastball with elite velo and a 12-6 curveball that figures to induce its share of whiffs. Whether or not his other pitches develop like the Cubs hoped when they drafted him in the second round will determine whether he's an A-list celebrity or some forgettable face relegated to the background.

Andrew Chafin LHP   Born: 06/17/90   Age: 31   Bats: R   Throws: L   Height: 6'2"   Weight: 235   Origin: Round 1, 2011 Draft (#43 overall)

YEAR	TEAM	LVL	AGE	W	L	SV	G	GS	IP	H	HR	BB/9	K/9	K	GB%	BABIP	WHIP	ERA	DRA-	WARP	MPH	FA%	Whiff%	CSP
2018	ARI	MLB	28	1	6	0	77	0	49¹	41	0	4.6	9.7	53	50.4%	.313	1.34	3.10	94	0.4	95.2	56.6%	32.3%	42.7%
2019	ARI	MLB	29	2	2	0	77	0	52²	52	6	3.1	11.6	68	41.6%	.359	1.33	3.76	79	0.8	95.5	61.1%	34.2%	45.6%
2020	CHC	MLB	30	1	2	1	15	0	9²	11	2	4.7	12.1	13	40.7%	.360	1.66	6.52	87	0.2	95.1	73.4%	26.0%	45.7%
2021 FS	CHC	MLB	31	2	2	0	57	0	50	42	6	4.3	10.6	58	46.7%	.294	1.33	3.73	90	0.4	95.3	62.0%	32.3%	44.8%

Comparables: Alex Colomé, Jeff Manship, Luis Avilán

Chafin was limited by a sprained finger to too few appearances to get a read on if the lefty could be relied upon to get right-handed hitters out on a regular basis in the three-batter-minimum era. The small sample wasn't promising, however, as the Sheriff allowed a .937 OPS to righties in 21 plate appearances.

Tyler Chatwood RHP   Born: 12/16/89   Age: 31   Bats: R   Throws: R   Height: 5'11"   Weight: 200   Origin: Round 2, 2008 Draft (#74 overall)

YEAR	TEAM	LVL	AGE	W	L	SV	G	GS	IP	H	HR	BB/9	K/9	K	GB%	BABIP	WHIP	ERA	DRA-	WARP	MPH	FA%	Whiff%	CSP
2018	IOW	AAA	28	0	1	0	2	2	6²	5	0	13.5	5.4	4	61.1%	.278	2.25	9.45	126	0.0				
2018	CHC	MLB	28	4	6	0	24	20	103²	92	9	8.2	7.4	85	51.5%	.291	1.80	5.30	162	-2.4	95.1	58.9%	22.3%	43.4%
2019	CHC	MLB	29	5	3	2	38	5	76²	65	8	4.3	8.7	74	52.9%	.286	1.33	3.76	79	1.3	97.7	71.0%	25.2%	44.7%
2020	CHC	MLB	30	2	2	0	5	5	18²	22	2	4.3	12.1	25	38.5%	.400	1.66	5.30	88	0.3	96.2	51.7%	29.3%	45.3%
2021 FS	CHC	MLB	31	2	3	0	57	0	50	45	6	5.8	9.4	52	49.2%	.295	1.56	4.84	107	-0.1	96.5	63.3%	24.9%	44.3%

Comparables: Chris Tillman, Wily Peralta, Erasmo Ramírez

On July 1, 2020, Netflix released a rebooted version of *Unsolved Mysteries*, the popular documentary TV show that originally aired on NBC in the late-'80s. Among the phenomena investigated were ghosts in Japan, UFO sightings in Berkshire County, Mass. and a prison escape in Ohio. If the series gets another season, they should explore what would've happened if Chatwood had been able to play a full season in 2020. Much maligned after signing a three-year, $38 million deal with the Cubs ahead of the 2018 campaign, Chatwood went back to the rotation for the start of this season and struck out 19 and allowed just one earned run in his first 12 ⅔ innings. He got lit up in his third start, so maybe there isn't much intrigue, but a forearm strain limited him to only 3 ⅔ innings the rest of the way. The arsenal adjustments he made—decreased usage of the four-seamer, an improved cutter and more cutter usage—were enough to make you wonder if he has staying power in the rotation once again. Maybe we'll find out next season, either on Netflix or on the field.

Zach Davies RHP   Born: 02/07/93   Age: 28   Bats: R   Throws: R   Height: 6'0"   Weight: 180   Origin: Round 26, 2011 Draft (#785 overall)

YEAR	TEAM	LVL	AGE	W	L	SV	G	GS	IP	H	HR	BB/9	K/9	K	GB%	BABIP	WHIP	ERA	DRA-	WARP	MPH	FA%	Whiff%	CSP
2018	WIS	LO-A	25	1	0	0	4	4	19	19	2	0.0	9.0	19	62.7%	.347	1.00	2.84	60	0.5				
2018	BLX	AA	25	1	1	0	2	2	11	7	1	3.3	9.8	12	50.0%	.250	1.00	4.09	42	0.4				
2018	RMV	AAA	25	0	3	0	5	5	17	18	0	6.4	6.9	13	40.7%	.340	1.76	6.35	100	0.2				
2018	MIL	MLB	25	2	7	0	13	13	66	67	8	2.9	6.7	49	47.1%	.299	1.33	4.77	104	0.5	91.8	56.4%	20.3%	43.6%
2019	MIL	MLB	26	10	7	0	31	31	159²	155	20	2.9	5.7	102	39.1%	.276	1.29	3.55	108	0.8	90.2	52.4%	17.2%	41.4%
2020	SD	MLB	27	7	4	0	12	12	69¹	55	9	2.5	8.2	63	40.7%	.250	1.07	2.73	94	0.9	90.3	39.1%	25.6%	41.5%
2021 FS	CHC	MLB	28	9	9	0	26	26	150	144	23	3.3	8.0	133	42.8%	.286	1.33	4.25	99	1.1	90.4	48.4%	20.4%	41.7%
2021 DC	CHC	MLB	28	9	9	0	27	27	151	145	23	3.3	8.0	134	42.8%	.286	1.33	4.25	99	1.6	90.4	48.4%	20.4%	41.7%

Comparables: Jair Jurrjens, Jonathon Niese, John Danks

Davies enjoyed a career year in San Diego after coming over from Milwaukee as part of the Luis Urías trade, and it might not be a fluke. He started throwing his changeup more while significantly decreasing the use of his sinker. (He threw his cutter a little more, too.) Shocker: Davies throwing his best pitch more worked out pretty well, with opposing batters whiffing on it about 35 percent of the time. Speaking of whiffs, Davies' once paltry strikeout rate shot up to about 23 percent, which was still below average but closer to respectable. The improved bat-missing ability allowed him to give the Padres some much-needed quality innings. It's worth pointing out that he did benefit from some BABIP luck, so his 2.73 ERA is a bit deceptive. Davies, now entering his walk year, can only hope that continues.

Kyle Hendricks RHP   Born: 12/07/89   Age: 31   Bats: R   Throws: R   Height: 6'3"   Weight: 190   Origin: Round 8, 2011 Draft (#264 overall)

YEAR	TEAM	LVL	AGE	W	L	SV	G	GS	IP	H	HR	BB/9	K/9	K	GB%	BABIP	WHIP	ERA	DRA-	WARP	MPH	FA%	Whiff%	CSP
2018	CHC	MLB	28	14	11	0	33	33	199	184	22	2.0	7.3	161	46.3%	.285	1.15	3.44	69	5.0	88.4	61.8%	22.0%	50.4%
2019	CHC	MLB	29	11	10	0	30	30	177	168	19	1.6	7.6	150	41.1%	.292	1.13	3.46	79	3.6	88.6	62.2%	22.1%	50.2%
2020	CHC	MLB	30	6	5	0	12	12	81¹	73	10	0.9	7.1	64	47.1%	.272	1.00	2.88	88	1.3	89.1	55.0%	24.7%	50.7%
2021 FS	CHC	MLB	31	9	8	0	26	26	150	146	21	1.8	7.7	128	45.5%	.288	1.17	3.65	87	2.2	88.7	60.0%	22.8%	50.4%
2021 DC	CHC	MLB	31	11	9	0	29	29	177	172	25	1.8	7.7	151	45.5%	.288	1.17	3.65	87	3.1	88.7	60.0%	22.8%	50.4%

Comparables: David Price, Tom Seaver, James Shields

In 2014, a program named Eugene Goostman, which simulates a 13-year-old Ukrainian boy, reportedly passed the Turing test at an event organized by the University of Reading, although many disputed the results. Similarly, in 2018, a Google Duplex reservation system made a phone call to a hair salon to schedule an appointment for a haircut. Whether or not the Turing test has truly been passed is unknown, but that's mostly because it hasn't been given to Hendricks, who you might well suspect is a robot; not in some crazy, Westworld-esque way, just in the dull, reliable manner that you'd find on an assembly line. All Hendricks does is go to work, start after start, year after year and puts up consistent numbers without much drama or exception. We'd say it's boring, but it's a pretty exciting proposition if you're his engineer—er, we mean his manager.

Jonathan Holder RHP   Born: 06/09/93   Age: 28   Bats: R   Throws: R   Height: 6'2"   Weight: 232   Origin: Round 6, 2014 Draft (#182 overall)

YEAR	TEAM	LVL	AGE	W	L	SV	G	GS	IP	H	HR	BB/9	K/9	K	GB%	BABIP	WHIP	ERA	DRA-	WARP	MPH	FA%	Whiff%	CSP
2018	SWB	AAA	25	1	0	0	4	1	6	5	1	1.5	12.0	8	53.3%	.286	1.00	3.00	55	0.2				
2018	NYY	MLB	25	1	3	0	60	1	66	53	4	2.6	8.2	60	29.2%	.263	1.09	3.14	96	0.5	94.2	55.4%	24.1%	47.5%
2019	SWB	AAA	26	1	1	2	9	0	12¹	13	1	1.5	10.9	15	45.7%	.364	1.22	2.92	66	0.4				
2019	NYY	MLB	26	5	2	0	34	1	41¹	43	8	2.4	10.0	46	38.5%	.307	1.31	6.31	96	0.3	93.8	54.5%	25.7%	49.4%
2020	NYY	MLB	27	3	0	0	18	0	21²	25	3	4.6	5.8	14	50.0%	.301	1.66	4.98	104	0.1	93.4	52.4%	24.1%	45.2%
2021 FS	CHC	MLB	28	1	1	0	57	0	50	45	6	2.7	8.7	48	41.5%	.285	1.22	3.69	87	0.5	93.8	54.0%	24.7%	47.5%
2021 DC	CHC	MLB	28	1	1	0	28	0	30	27	4	2.7	8.7	29	41.5%	.285	1.22	3.69	87	0.4	93.8	54.0%	24.7%	47.5%

Comparables: Phil Maton, Dominic Leone, Dan Altavilla

Holder continues to occupy a spot on a team's 40-man roster despite a plummeting strikeout rate, a spike in walks, loss of control and an ERA north of 5.00 for the second consecutive season. All of which tells us a lot more about teams' needs to fill innings than anything else. You might just say that utility is in the eye of Holder's employer. That employer as of press time was the Cubs, who signed him to a non-guaranteed deal after he fell out of favor with the Yankees.

Jeremy Jeffress RHP   Born: 09/21/87   Age: 33   Bats: R   Throws: R   Height: 6'0"   Weight: 205   Origin: Round 1, 2006 Draft (#16 overall)

YEAR	TEAM	LVL	AGE	W	L	SV	G	GS	IP	H	HR	BB/9	K/9	K	GB%	BABIP	WHIP	ERA	DRA-	WARP	MPH	FA%	Whiff%	CSP
2018	MIL	MLB	30	8	1	15	73	0	76²	49	5	3.2	10.4	89	57.7%	.250	0.99	1.29	58	2.0	97.4	53.2%	31.0%	47.5%
2019	MIL	MLB	31	3	4	1	48	0	52	54	5	2.9	8.0	46	47.8%	.327	1.37	5.02	98	0.3	95.8	64.3%	20.8%	47.0%
2020	CHC	MLB	32	4	1	8	22	0	23¹	10	1	4.6	6.6	17	54.4%	.161	0.94	1.54	101	0.2	94.7	41.3%	24.6%	44.6%
2021 FS	CHC	MLB	33	2	2	0	57	0	50	47	5	4.3	8.3	46	51.1%	.292	1.42	4.24	99	0.2	96.0	55.0%	24.9%	46.6%

Comparables: Chuck McElroy, Ryan Tepera, Bryan Shaw

Notable predictions made by inventor Ray Kurzweil included the demise of the Soviet Union because of new technologies; that computers could beat the best human chess players by the year 2000; and the invention of text-to-speech devices for the blind. Big deal; we'd like to see Kurzweil predict what's to come from Jeffress during any given season. The veteran right-hander went from All-Star and dependable late-inning arm to being released by the Brewers in the span of a year, so naturally he became the Cubs' best reliever in 2020, supplanting Craig Kimbrel as closer and hocus-pocusing his way through the shortened season with just four earned runs crossing the plate. That success came despite an arsenal change (more splitters, fewer fastballs) that saw his whiff rate sink to unthinkable depths while his walk rate skyrocketed. Relievers are weird, and relievers in a 60-game season are even weirder, so even Kurzweil would struggle to figure out what Jeffress is likeliest to do in 2021.

Ryan Jensen RHP   Born: 11/23/97   Age: 23   Bats: R   Throws: R   Height: 6'0"   Weight: 180   Origin: Round 1, 2019 Draft (#27 overall)

YEAR	TEAM	LVL	AGE	W	L	SV	G	GS	IP	H	HR	BB/9	K/9	K	GB%	BABIP	WHIP	ERA	DRA-	WARP	MPH	FA%	Whiff%	CSP
2019	EUG	SS	21	0	0	0	6	6	12	7	0	10.5	14.2	19	68.2%	.318	1.75	2.25	141	-0.2				
2021 FS	CHC	MLB	23	2	3	0	57	0	50	48	8	8.6	9.2	51	44.9%	.292	1.92	6.82	146	-1.2				

The Cubs' first-round pick in 2019, Jensen started for only one year in college and, as a result, carries significant risk. That he wasn't included at the team's alternate site means we won't know exactly what the Cubs have here for a while longer.

Craig Kimbrel RHP   Born: 05/28/88   Age: 33   Bats: R   Throws: R   Height: 6'0"   Weight: 215   Origin: Round 3, 2008 Draft (#96 overall)

YEAR	TEAM	LVL	AGE	W	L	SV	G	GS	IP	H	HR	BB/9	K/9	K	GB%	BABIP	WHIP	ERA	DRA-	WARP	MPH	FA%	Whiff%	CSP
2018	BOS	MLB	30	5	1	42	63	0	62¹	31	7	4.5	13.9	96	28.8%	.218	0.99	2.74	57	1.7	98.9	64.6%	40.0%	40.7%
2019	CHC	MLB	31	0	4	13	23	0	20²	21	9	5.2	13.1	30	28.8%	.279	1.60	6.53	124	-0.2	97.8	66.6%	32.8%	41.1%
2020	CHC	MLB	32	0	1	2	18	0	15¹	10	2	7.0	16.4	28	33.3%	.320	1.43	5.28	80	0.3	98.5	62.3%	35.4%	43.0%
2021 FS	CHC	MLB	33	2	2	27	57	0	50	35	7	4.6	13.4	74	33.6%	.277	1.21	3.41	79	0.7	98.5	64.4%	36.5%	41.6%
2021 DC	CHC	MLB	33	2	2	27	45	0	48	33	6	4.6	13.4	71	33.6%	.277	1.21	3.41	79	0.8	98.5	64.4%	36.5%	41.6%

Comparables: Kenley Jansen, Dellin Betances, Billy Wagner

In Kimbrel's first appearance of the season, he faced six batters, walked four and got one out. In his second appearance, he faced five batters and allowed two home runs. In his third appearance, he faced three batters and two of them reached base. In his fourth appearance, he pitched an inning and allowed a run. Kimbrel was actually quite good after that, posting a 1.54 ERA after being removed from the closer's role, and he went the entire month of September without issuing a walk. Kimbrel is unlikely to return to his dominant peak as he enters his mid-30s, but there's still a talented reliever in there. After two uneven, abbreviated seasons in Chicago, maybe a normal one will finally allow us to see it.

Jon Lester LHP   Born: 01/07/84   Age: 37   Bats: L   Throws: L   Height: 6'4"   Weight: 240   Origin: Round 2, 2002 Draft (#57 overall)

YEAR	TEAM	LVL	AGE	W	L	SV	G	GS	IP	H	HR	BB/9	K/9	K	GB%	BABIP	WHIP	ERA	DRA-	WARP	MPH	FA%	Whiff%	CSP
2018	CHC	MLB	34	18	6	0	32	32	181²	174	24	3.2	7.4	149	38.0%	.294	1.31	3.32	99	1.8	92.7	50.3%	20.5%	47.0%
2019	CHC	MLB	35	13	10	0	31	31	171²	205	26	2.7	8.7	165	42.3%	.350	1.50	4.46	114	0.3	92.2	38.8%	21.3%	45.3%
2020	CHC	MLB	36	3	3	0	12	12	61	64	11	2.5	6.2	42	47.8%	.277	1.33	5.16	133	-0.5	90.9	41.2%	18.2%	45.3%
2021 FS	CHC	MLB	37	8	9	0	26	26	150	157	24	3.3	7.3	122	45.0%	.297	1.41	4.71	109	0.3	92.0	42.3%	20.3%	45.7%

Comparables: Aníbal Sánchez, Zack Greinke, Justin Verlander

Cinematic history is littered with stories of once-great virtuosos clinging desperately to greatness, or going back for one last run at glory: *Sunset Boulevard, Birdman, Incredibles, A Mighty Wind* (sort of), basically every Sylvester Stallone movie ever made. Lester entered the season as one of the most accomplished starting pitchers of his generation. He doesn't have the hardware of a Verlander or Kershaw, but he's been consistently excellent for a decade and a half and he has the eighth most innings pitched in major-league history as well as the distinct honor of having pitched for three World Series winners. So, that there was a legitimate case for the Cubs to *avoid* using him in the postseason says a lot. It never came to that, as the Cubs lost to the Marlins in two games, but Lester's slow, age-related decline seemed to speed up last season: He stopped missing bats, gave up a whole lot of hard contact and essentially turned every opposite-handed batter who came to the plate into the AL Rookie of the Year. This is clearly Lester's swan song, and even if it doesn't turn out quite like *Uncle Drew*, it would probably make for a better movie.

Dillon Maples RHP   Born: 05/09/92   Age: 29   Bats: R   Throws: R   Height: 6'2"   Weight: 230   Origin: Round 14, 2011 Draft (#429 overall)

YEAR	TEAM	LVL	AGE	W	L	SV	G	GS	IP	H	HR	BB/9	K/9	K	GB%	BABIP	WHIP	ERA	DRA-	WARP	MPH	FA%	Whiff%	CSP
2018	IOW	AAA	26	2	3	10	41	0	38²	22	1	9.1	17.5	75	57.4%	.350	1.58	2.79	10	2.2				
2018	CHC	MLB	26	1	0	0	9	0	5¹	7	2	8.4	15.2	9	30.8%	.455	2.25	11.81	108	0.0	98.5	23.9%	20.5%	47.4%
2019	IOW	AAA	27	4	4	7	38	0	43	21	1	7.5	16.5	79	62.7%	.303	1.33	3.77	27	2.0				
2019	CHC	MLB	27	1	0	0	14	0	11²	6	2	7.7	13.9	18	68.2%	.200	1.37	5.40	82	0.2	98.3	33.3%	44.2%	45.4%
2020	CHC	MLB	28	0	0	0	2	0	1	1	0	36.0	9.0	1	25.0%	.250	5.00	18.00	119	0.0	98.1	37.5%	60.0%	31.9%
2021 FS	CHC	MLB	29	1	1	0	57	0	50	36	4	7.7	13.1	72	52.4%	.300	1.59	4.73	99	0.2	98.3	32.2%	42.2%	43.6%
2021 DC	CHC	MLB	29	1	1	0	22	0	24	17	2	7.7	13.1	35	52.4%	.300	1.59	4.73	99	0.2	98.3	32.2%	42.2%	43.6%

Comparables: Giovanny Gallegos, Carl Edwards Jr., Dominic Leone

The abbreviated Dillon Maples Experience was much the same as the full-season version: a clean inning with a strikeout on a trademark slider, followed by a four-walk outing in which he failed to retire a batter. Only Maples could raise a career walk rate already approaching 20 percent.

★ ★ ★ *2021 Top 101 Prospect* **#63** ★ ★ ★

Brailyn Marquez LHP   Born: 01/30/99   Age: 22   Bats: L   Throws: L   Height: 6'4"   Weight: 185   Origin: International Free Agent, 2015

YEAR	TEAM	LVL	AGE	W	L	SV	G	GS	IP	H	HR	BB/9	K/9	K	GB%	BABIP	WHIP	ERA	DRA-	WARP	MPH	FA%	Whiff%	CSP
2018	EUG	SS	19	1	4	0	10	10	47²	46	5	2.6	9.8	52	50.8%	.333	1.26	3.21	272	-4.3				
2018	SB	LO-A	19	0	0	0	2	2	7	7	0	2.6	9.0	7	33.3%	.333	1.29	2.57	75	0.1				
2019	SB	LO-A	20	5	4	0	17	17	77¹	64	4	5.0	11.9	102	50.8%	.337	1.38	3.61	108	-0.1				
2019	MB	HI-A	20	4	1	0	5	5	26¹	21	1	2.4	8.9	26	44.4%	.282	1.06	1.71	81	0.3				
2020	CHC	MLB	21	0	0	0	1	0	0²	2	0	40.5	13.5	1	33.3%	.667	7.50	67.50	133	0.0	99.5	48.5%	36.4%	36.8%
2021 FS	CHC	MLB	22	8	9	0	26	26	150	143	22	5.0	8.9	148	44.0%	.294	1.51	5.08	111	0.2	99.5	48.5%	36.4%	36.8%
2021 DC	CHC	MLB	22	3	4	0	32	9	68	64	10	5.0	8.9	67	44.0%	.294	1.51	5.08	111	0.2	99.5	48.5%	36.4%	36.8%

Comparables: Huascar Ynoa, Julio Teheran, Luis Severino

Walk, walk, wild pitch, RBI groundout, strikeout, walk, wild pitch, double. The Cubs promoted Marquez ahead of their season finale, giving the young left-hander what amounted to a playoff audition. He entered in the eighth inning against the White Sox in a game the Cubs were leading 10-1, and that was the sequence of events that followed. Suffice it to say it didn't work, and he instead wound up watching the Cubs' two playoff games from the comfort of the taxi squad. That Marquez was even considered for such a role is evidence of the promise the lefty showed while spending the season working at the team's alternate training site. He remains one of the most talented near-ready arms in the minor leagues, even if his career 67.50 ERA might hurt to look at until that next opportunity comes around.

Alec Mills RHP   Born: 11/30/91   Age: 29   Bats: R   Throws: R   Height: 6'4"   Weight: 205   Origin: Round 22, 2012 Draft (#673 overall)

YEAR	TEAM	LVL	AGE	W	L	SV	G	GS	IP	H	HR	BB/9	K/9	K	GB%	BABIP	WHIP	ERA	DRA-	WARP	MPH	FA%	Whiff%	CSP
2018	IOW	AAA	26	5	12	0	23	23	124²	121	10	3.0	7.8	108	39.1%	.307	1.30	4.84	80	2.5				
2018	CHC	MLB	26	0	1	0	7	2	18	11	1	3.5	11.5	23	51.2%	.250	1.00	4.00	54	0.6	92.2	58.9%	27.6%	46.9%
2019	IOW	AAA	27	6	4	0	19	18	104	116	17	2.6	8.3	96	38.6%	.332	1.40	5.11	90	2.3				
2019	CHC	MLB	27	1	0	1	9	4	36	31	5	2.8	10.5	42	48.9%	.299	1.17	2.75	75	0.7	91.4	54.2%	28.1%	43.7%
2020	CHC	MLB	28	5	5	0	11	11	62¹	53	13	2.7	6.6	46	47.6%	.233	1.16	4.48	117	0.0	91.6	58.9%	18.0%	46.9%
2021 FS	CHC	MLB	29	9	8	0	26	26	150	143	21	3.1	8.0	133	44.7%	.288	1.30	4.11	95	1.5	91.6	57.7%	21.3%	46.1%
2021 DC	CHC	MLB	29	9	8	0	25	25	139	132	19	3.1	8.0	124	44.7%	.288	1.30	4.11	95	1.8	91.6	57.7%	21.3%	46.1%

Comparables: Chris Stratton, Luke Farrell, Austin Voth

In the annals of unlikely no-hitters, Mills' feat—accomplished September 13th against the Brewers—doesn't quite rank with the likes of Philip Humber or Bud Smith. He's certainly no Bobo Holloman, either, and there is no evidence that he was on LSD. But Mills' feat was, undeniably, unlikely. The soft-tossing right-hander did it with a fastball that ticks in four miles per hour slower than the league-average heater. He did it after being a college walk-on. He did it as a former 22nd-round pick. And he did it after three years spent as Quad-A roster filler. Unexpected no-hitters don't always launch grand careers—see some of the names above—but the most important part of Mills' year is that he established himself as a legitimate back-of-the-rotation starter who can get out big-league hitters with his deception and his contact-management skills. Perhaps, given everything else we knew about Mills entering the year, that's the most unlikely part of his season. (Nah, it's still the no-no.)

José Quintana LHP   Born: 01/24/89   Age: 32   Bats: R   Throws: L   Height: 6'1"   Weight: 220   Origin: International Free Agent, 2006

YEAR	TEAM	LVL	AGE	W	L	SV	G	GS	IP	H	HR	BB/9	K/9	K	GB%	BABIP	WHIP	ERA	DRA-	WARP	MPH	FA%	Whiff%	CSP
2018	CHC	MLB	29	14	11	0	33	33	179²	170	27	3.5	8.3	165	42.0%	.291	1.33	4.11	110	0.8	93.3	68.3%	20.7%	49.0%
2019	CHC	MLB	30	13	9	0	32	31	171	191	20	2.4	8.0	152	43.6%	.329	1.39	4.68	92	2.3	92.9	61.8%	20.9%	47.1%
2020	CHC	MLB	31	0	0	0	4	1	10	10	1	2.7	10.8	12	42.3%	.360	1.30	4.50	92	0.1	93.5	60.1%	27.6%	42.5%
2021 FS	CHC	MLB	32	9	8	0	26	26	150	146	23	2.5	8.6	143	43.3%	.296	1.26	3.93	95	1.4	93.1	63.8%	21.3%	47.4%

Comparables: Rick Porcello, Masahiro Tanaka, Matt Harvey

Even by 2020 standards, Quintana had an abbreviated season brought about by an unfortunate dishwashing accident. After a slippery knife caused the once reliable southpaw to go under one, he returned for a nondescript 10 innings of league-average work. After nearly a decade as a steady mid-rotation arm, Quintana will likely have to settle for a back-end gig.

Colin Rea RHP   Born: 07/01/90   Age: 31   Bats: R   Throws: R   Height: 6'5"   Weight: 235   Origin: Round 12, 2011 Draft (#383 overall)

YEAR	TEAM	LVL	AGE	W	L	SV	G	GS	IP	H	HR	BB/9	K/9	K	GB%	BABIP	WHIP	ERA	DRA-	WARP	MPH	FA%	Whiff%	CSP
2018	SA	AA	27	0	3	0	6	6	24	32	3	4.9	7.9	21	39.0%	.367	1.88	7.12	81	0.4				
2018	ELP	AAA	27	3	2	0	12	9	51¹	58	11	4.0	8.6	49	43.4%	.336	1.58	5.08	103	0.4				
2019	IOW	AAA	28	14	4	0	26	26	148	142	17	3.6	7.3	120	44.8%	.294	1.36	3.95	83	3.8				
2020	CHC	MLB	29	1	1	0	9	2	14	15	3	1.3	6.4	10	44.0%	.255	1.21	5.79	111	0.0	95.0	51.4%	17.4%	51.7%
2021 FS	CHC	MLB	30	2	3	0	57	0	50	52	9	3.7	7.5	41	42.4%	.294	1.46	5.10	117	-0.3	95.0	51.4%	17.4%	51.7%

Comparables: Jordan Lyles, Kendall Graveman, Chris Stratton

Rea saw his fair share of mop-up work in the final month of the season. He's still going to be known as the person whose injury situation forced the Padres to trade Luis Castillo back to the Marlins just three days after acquiring him.

Kyle Ryan LHP   Born: 09/25/91   Age: 29   Bats: L   Throws: L   Height: 6'5"   Weight: 215   Origin: Round 12, 2010 Draft (#373 overall)

YEAR	TEAM	LVL	AGE	W	L	SV	G	GS	IP	H	HR	BB/9	K/9	K	GB%	BABIP	WHIP	ERA	DRA-	WARP	MPH	FA%	Whiff%	CSP
2018	IOW	AAA	26	1	2	0	22	8	66	48	9	2.5	8.3	61	58.9%	.236	1.00	2.86	71	1.5				
2019	CHC	MLB	27	4	2	0	73	0	61	55	5	4.3	8.6	58	56.7%	.301	1.38	3.54	82	0.9	91.1	46.7%	23.6%	47.8%
2020	CHC	MLB	28	1	0	1	18	0	15²	16	5	3.4	6.3	11	49.0%	.250	1.40	5.17	126	-0.1	90.5	51.9%	16.7%	44.5%
2021 FS	CHC	MLB	29	2	2	0	57	0	50	47	6	3.7	7.9	44	52.0%	.291	1.37	4.23	97	0.2	90.9	48.1%	21.7%	46.9%
2021 DC	CHC	MLB	29	2	2	0	51	0	54	51	6	3.7	7.9	47	52.0%	.291	1.37	4.23	97	0.4	90.9	48.1%	21.7%	46.9%

Comparables: Luke Jackson, Drew VerHagen, A.J. Cole

There have been 21 players in major-league history with the surname Ryan. Nolan, of course, leads them all with 157.9 career WARP. More recently, there was Brendan and B.J. Before that, there was a John, a Johnny, three Mikes and three Jacks, none of whom inspired the Amazon original series. In the 1800s, there was even a Cyclone Ryan, who was from Capperwhite, Ireland, and who played in 12 total games for the New York Metropolitans and Boston Beaneaters. This Ryan, Kyle, is the first of his name to ever grace a major-league field. While he'll never reach the stature of the all-timer Nolan, nor finish with the career wealth of Brendan or B.J., he should continue to find work as a low-leverage sinkerballer capable of overcoming the platoon advantage.

Justin Steele LHP Born: 07/11/95 Age: 25 Bats: L Throws: L Height: 6'2" Weight: 205 Origin: Round 5, 2014 Draft (#139 overall)

YEAR	TEAM	LVL	AGE	W	L	SV	G	GS	IP	H	HR	BB/9	K/9	K	GB%	BABIP	WHIP	ERA	DRA-	WARP	MPH	FA%	Whiff%	CSP
2018	CUBB	ROK	22	0	0	0	5	5	18¹	9	1	2.0	13.3	27	40.5%	.229	0.71	1.47	23	0.9				
2018	MB	HI-A	22	2	1	0	4	4	18¹	12	0	2.9	9.3	19	41.3%	.261	0.98	2.45	85	0.3				
2018	TNS	AA	22	0	1	0	2	2	10	8	1	2.7	6.3	7	22.6%	.241	1.10	3.60	79	0.2				
2019	TNS	AA	23	0	6	0	11	11	38²	45	3	4.7	9.8	42	39.3%	.412	1.68	5.59	137	-0.8				
2021 FS	CHC	MLB	25	8	10	0	26	26	150	143	22	5.0	8.7	144	40.0%	.292	1.51	5.12	116	-0.3				
2021 DC	CHC	MLB	25	4	5	0	30	12	76	72	11	5.0	8.7	73	40.0%	.292	1.51	5.12	116	0.1				

Comparables: Albert Abreu, Bernardo Flores Jr., Hector Perez

Steele spent three days on the Cubs' active roster without making an appearance. He's got a long way to go before his name starts showing up in Google search results over the director of such cinematic masterpieces as *Death and Cremation*, *Gutshot Straight* and, of course, *Sergeant X*.

Ryan Tepera RHP Born: 11/03/87 Age: 33 Bats: R Throws: R Height: 6'1" Weight: 195 Origin: Round 19, 2009 Draft (#580 overall)

YEAR	TEAM	LVL	AGE	W	L	SV	G	GS	IP	H	HR	BB/9	K/9	K	GB%	BABIP	WHIP	ERA	DRA-	WARP	MPH	FA%	Whiff%	CSP
2018	TOR	MLB	30	5	5	7	68	0	64²	55	9	3.3	9.5	68	43.7%	.291	1.22	3.62	109	0.0	96.7	61.3%	30.6%	43.2%
2019	TOR	MLB	31	0	2	0	23	1	21²	20	5	3.3	5.8	14	42.0%	.238	1.29	4.98	122	-0.1	95.0	57.1%	26.3%	41.2%
2020	CHC	MLB	32	0	1	0	21	0	20²	17	2	5.2	13.5	31	40.0%	.349	1.40	3.92	80	0.4	95.4	46.1%	44.0%	36.0%
2021 FS	CHC	MLB	33	2	2	0	57	0	50	42	7	4.2	10.3	57	41.8%	.284	1.31	3.96	93	0.3	95.8	54.3%	34.8%	39.9%

Comparables: Ryan Brasier, Jeremy Jeffress, Luis García

Matthew Lewis, Dev Patel, Ryan Tepera. What are memorable glow-ups, Alex? Tepera spent five years in Toronto as a mostly anonymous middle reliever who was pretty solid in the run-prevention department, but lacking the type of stuff that would allow you to trust him in high-leverage spots. In his first year in Chicago, he upped his strikeout rate, not just incrementally, but to more than four strikeouts per nine more than any other season in his career. His whiff rate was in the 99th percentile in the majors, generating swinging strikes on nearly half of his pitches. The reason? An uptick in the usage of his cutter, which looks like his fastball coming out but features a serious late dip and about a six-mph difference. The walk rate went up along with the strikeouts, which prevented Tepera from truly entering "elite reliever" territory, but like Neville Longbottom or the Slumdog Millionaire, he went from "oh yeah, that guy" to someone who earned a MVP vote (accidentally or not, it still counts).

Duane Underwood Jr. RHP Born: 07/20/94 Age: 26 Bats: R Throws: R Height: 6'2" Weight: 210 Origin: Round 2, 2012 Draft (#67 overall)

YEAR	TEAM	LVL	AGE	W	L	SV	G	GS	IP	H	HR	BB/9	K/9	K	GB%	BABIP	WHIP	ERA	DRA-	WARP	MPH	FA%	Whiff%	CSP
2018	IOW	AAA	23	4	10	0	27	20	119¹	127	8	2.8	7.9	105	41.2%	.337	1.37	4.53	78	2.5				
2018	CHC	MLB	23	0	1	0	1	1	4	2	1	6.8	6.8	3	50.0%	.111	1.25	2.25	178	-0.1	94.5	53.2%	12.1%	46.1%
2019	IOW	AAA	24	3	7	0	33	10	81²	84	8	4.5	10.5	95	45.7%	.349	1.53	5.07	79	2.1				
2019	CHC	MLB	24	0	0	0	12	0	11²	13	2	2.3	10.0	13	50.0%	.344	1.37	5.40	75	0.2	96.7	59.5%	27.3%	46.5%
2020	CHC	MLB	25	1	0	0	17	0	20²	25	5	2.6	11.8	27	38.9%	.408	1.50	5.66	89	0.3	96.6	46.3%	36.4%	42.8%
2021 FS	CHC	MLB	26	2	2	0	57	0	50	45	7	4.1	9.7	54	42.5%	.291	1.36	4.35	98	0.2	96.5	50.3%	32.6%	44.0%
2021 DC	CHC	MLB	26	2	2	0	51	0	54	48	7	4.1	9.7	58	42.5%	.291	1.36	4.35	98	0.4	96.5	50.3%	32.6%	44.0%

Comparables: Alex Reyes, Lucas Sims, Ricardo Pinto

The Cubs have been waiting for Underwood to become a quality part of their bullpen for so long that it's easy to forget that they were once waiting for him to become a quality part of their rotation. He finally saw regular major-league action in 2020, and while he was limited to low-leverage work, he showed signs of having some staying power despite his unsightly ERA. Underwood began relying more on his changeup than ever before and saw a career-best whiff rate with it. A lot of strikeouts and few walks is a recipe for success for any pitcher, but Underwood allowed too much contact to be counted on for high-leverage work. Still, there's something to be said for becoming a legitimate big-league relief option—like that it's more than we'd seen from him in the past, and it's reason to keep an eye on him in 2021.

Rowan Wick RHP Born: 11/09/92 Age: 28 Bats: L Throws: R Height: 6'3" Weight: 234 Origin: Round 9, 2012 Draft (#300 overall)

YEAR	TEAM	LVL	AGE	W	L	SV	G	GS	IP	H	HR	BB/9	K/9	K	GB%	BABIP	WHIP	ERA	DRA-	WARP	MPH	FA%	Whiff%	CSP
2018	SA	AA	25	2	4	5	29	0	31¹	22	0	6.0	12.1	42	56.3%	.314	1.37	3.16	62	0.7				
2018	ELP	AAA	25	2	0	9	20	0	22²	16	3	4.0	8.7	22	45.9%	.224	1.15	1.99	103	0.1				
2018	SD	MLB	25	0	1	0	10	0	8¹	13	1	1.1	7.6	7	36.7%	.414	1.68	6.48	91	0.1	96.2	87.2%	20.3%	56.0%
2019	IOW	AAA	26	1	0	6	27	0	35	25	3	2.3	11.3	44	48.8%	.272	0.97	1.80	37	1.5				
2019	CHC	MLB	26	2	0	2	31	0	33¹	22	0	4.3	9.4	35	53.5%	.259	1.14	2.43	78	0.5	97.3	68.0%	26.1%	49.3%
2020	CHC	MLB	27	0	1	4	19	0	17¹	18	1	3.1	10.4	20	39.6%	.362	1.38	3.12	87	0.3	96.3	65.2%	25.9%	47.6%
2021 FS	CHC	MLB	28	2	2	11	57	0	50	41	6	3.8	10.0	55	44.8%	.283	1.26	3.59	83	0.6	96.9	68.0%	25.7%	49.0%
2021 DC	CHC	MLB	28	2	2	11	51	0	54	45	6	3.8	10.0	59	44.8%	.283	1.26	3.59	83	0.8	96.9	68.0%	25.7%	49.0%

Comparables: Dan Altavilla, Phil Maton, Jonathan Holder

On August 22, Wick entered the Cubs' game against the White Sox in the seventh inning with his team trailing 3-2. He walked Yasmani Grandal on five pitches, and then got ahead 0-2 on José Abreu. On the fourth pitch of that plate appearance, Abreu deposited a hanging curve into the left-field bleachers. That the home run came amid a stretch of six homers in three days by Abreu made it, perhaps, inevitable. But it was notable for Wick in that it was his first allowed in 45 ⅔ innings, a stretch that included 47 games dating back to Sept. 7, 2019, when, as a San Diego Padre, he allowed a home run to the Reds' Scott Schebler. Sure, Abreu lit up Wick, but the righty has helped turn out the lights on opponents ever since the Cubs acquired him at a small cost.

Brad Wieck LHP Born: 10/14/91 Age: 29 Bats: L Throws: L Height: 6'8" Weight: 257 Origin: Round 7, 2014 Draft (#205 overall)

YEAR	TEAM	LVL	AGE	W	L	SV	G	GS	IP	H	HR	BB/9	K/9	K	GB%	BABIP	WHIP	ERA	DRA-	WARP	MPH	FA%	Whiff%	CSP
2018	SA	AA	26	1	2	10	27	0	28	20	1	2.6	11.6	36	29.0%	.279	1.00	1.93	53	0.8				
2018	ELP	AAA	26	3	0	2	17	0	18¹	16	2	4.4	16.7	34	42.1%	.400	1.36	3.44	40	0.7				
2018	SD	MLB	26	0	0	0	5	0	7	3	1	0.0	12.9	10	28.6%	.154	0.43	1.29	59	0.2	93.4	64.5%	30.0%	55.3%
2019	ELP	AAA	27	1	1	2	14	0	17²	16	5	3.1	17.3	34	29.4%	.379	1.25	6.11	58	0.6				
2019	IOW	AAA	27	1	0	0	6	0	5²	4	0	4.8	17.5	11	22.2%	.444	1.24	1.59	115	0.0				
2019	SD	MLB	27	0	1	0	30	0	24²	26	7	3.3	11.3	31	33.3%	.306	1.42	6.57	113	-0.1	95.3	79.9%	24.3%	47.2%
2019	CHC	MLB	27	2	1	0	14	0	10	2	1	3.6	16.2	18	21.4%	.077	0.60	3.60	15	0.5	95.0	71.1%	37.8%	49.1%
2020	CHC	MLB	28	0	0	0	1	0	1	1	1	9.0	18.0	2	0.0%	.000	2.00	18.00	85	0.0	92.0	70.0%	33.3%	38.8%
2021 FS	CHC	MLB	29	1	1	0	57	0	50	37	7	3.9	12.5	69	35.1%	.280	1.18	3.35	79	0.7	95.0	76.2%	28.1%	47.9%
2021 DC	CHC	MLB	29	1	1	0	34	0	36	26	5	3.9	12.5	49	35.1%	.280	1.18	3.35	79	0.6	95.0	76.2%	28.1%	47.9%

Comparables: Kyle Finnegan, Phillips Valdez, Daniel Stumpf

Wieck pitched in the Cubs' season opener against the Brewers, and then was shut down with a hamstring strain and leg injury that eventually cost him the rest of the season. The tall lefty will now have to generate anew the momentum he had this time last year.

Dan Winkler RHP Born: 02/02/90 Age: 31 Bats: R Throws: R Height: 6'3" Weight: 205 Origin: Round 20, 2011 Draft (#618 overall)

YEAR	TEAM	LVL	AGE	W	L	SV	G	GS	IP	H	HR	BB/9	K/9	K	GB%	BABIP	WHIP	ERA	DRA-	WARP	MPH	FA%	Whiff%	CSP
2018	ATL	MLB	28	4	0	2	69	0	60¹	52	3	3.0	10.3	69	39.8%	.312	1.19	3.43	78	1.0	94.8	33.9%	28.5%	43.5%
2019	SAC	AAA	29	0	1	0	12	0	14	6	1	3.2	5.8	9	56.8%	.139	0.79	0.64	45	0.5				
2019	GWN	AAA	29	0	1	2	18	0	16²	16	1	9.7	10.8	20	41.3%	.333	2.04	4.86	118	0.1				
2019	ATL	MLB	29	3	1	0	27	0	21²	18	5	4.6	9.1	22	30.5%	.241	1.34	4.98	127	-0.2	94.1	33.9%	33.5%	41.9%
2020	CHC	MLB	30	0	0	0	18	0	18¹	11	3	5.4	8.8	18	41.3%	.190	1.20	2.95	110	0.1	94.7	32.4%	27.6%	40.8%
2021 FS	CHC	MLB	31	2	2	0	57	0	50	43	7	4.9	9.2	51	40.1%	.274	1.41	4.52	102	0.1	94.6	33.4%	29.5%	42.2%
2021 DC	CHC	MLB	31	2	2	0	51	0	54	46	8	4.9	9.2	55	40.1%	.274	1.41	4.52	102	0.3	94.6	33.4%	29.5%	42.2%

Comparables: Mychal Givens, Raisel Iglesias, Pedro Báez

Winkler entered the ninth inning of Game 1 of the Cubs' Wild Card Series against the Marlins, faced three batters, retired them all and struck out two. That was a fairly standard appearance for him in 2020—not so much the result, but the fact that he came into a game in which the result was all but decided. Ah, right, we forgot to mention that the Marlins were leading 5-1 when Winkler entered. Those are the kinds of situations he found himself pitching in all year long. To wit: of the 76 batters Winkler faced last season, 42 were classified as "low-leverage" plate appearances. Good enough for a spot in the bullpen, just not good enough to trust with the game on the line. It's not a glamorous job, but hey, it pays the bills.

CINCINNATI REDS

Essay by Sridhar Pappu

Player comments by Ken Funck and BP staff

There's a moment early in Joe Morgan's career with the Reds, in many ways a forgotten one, that I turned to when learning of the Hall of Fame second baseman's death, at age 77, last fall. It is 1972 and he is in Oakland—his hometown—part of a Cincinnati team that had reached the World Series for the second time in three seasons. Morgan was meant as the last piece for a team desperate to win and win now. And yet he is still hitless going into the last of the ninth in Game Five.

But now, none of that matters. Facing elimination, the Reds have rallied and hold a one-run lead in the ninth with one out and Blue Moon Odom on third base. When Bert Campaneris hits a pop-up into foul territory, Morgan waves off first baseman Tony Perez to make the catch.

Within seconds, chaos. Stumbling after the catch, Morgan's become aware of Odom's decision to come home. He either regains his composure or has composure enough to throw to an upright Johnny Bench, who turns towards third base, tagging Odom before falling on top of him for the final out.

This is the definitive Morgan: The awareness of Odom. The ability to place the ball in the precise spot needed even after he's slipped. An understanding of where the game's greatest catcher needed it in order to make the play. A display of on-field intelligence that, even now, has few peers.

This is also Morgan's true star-turning moment. Only a year before most had never heard of him, and those within baseball viewed him as angry and underachieving, an undersized and overall pedestrian second baseman, destined to languish with the Astros. But he had been spectacular in his 1972 regular season with the Reds, and with this play he's shown that he not only belongs on this great team, but that he's determined to make it better.

"You guys didn't win anything until I got here," Morgan would say later of his time with the Reds. "You didn't save me. I saved you."

For a man who in retirement openly loathed modern metrics, there is little doubt of how well these numbers serve his legacy now. In four of his first five seasons with the Reds, his lowest WARP total was 7.7. In winning his first National League MVP Award in 1975, he had 9.5 WARP, a number Mike Trout has eclipsed only once. The following year, in earning

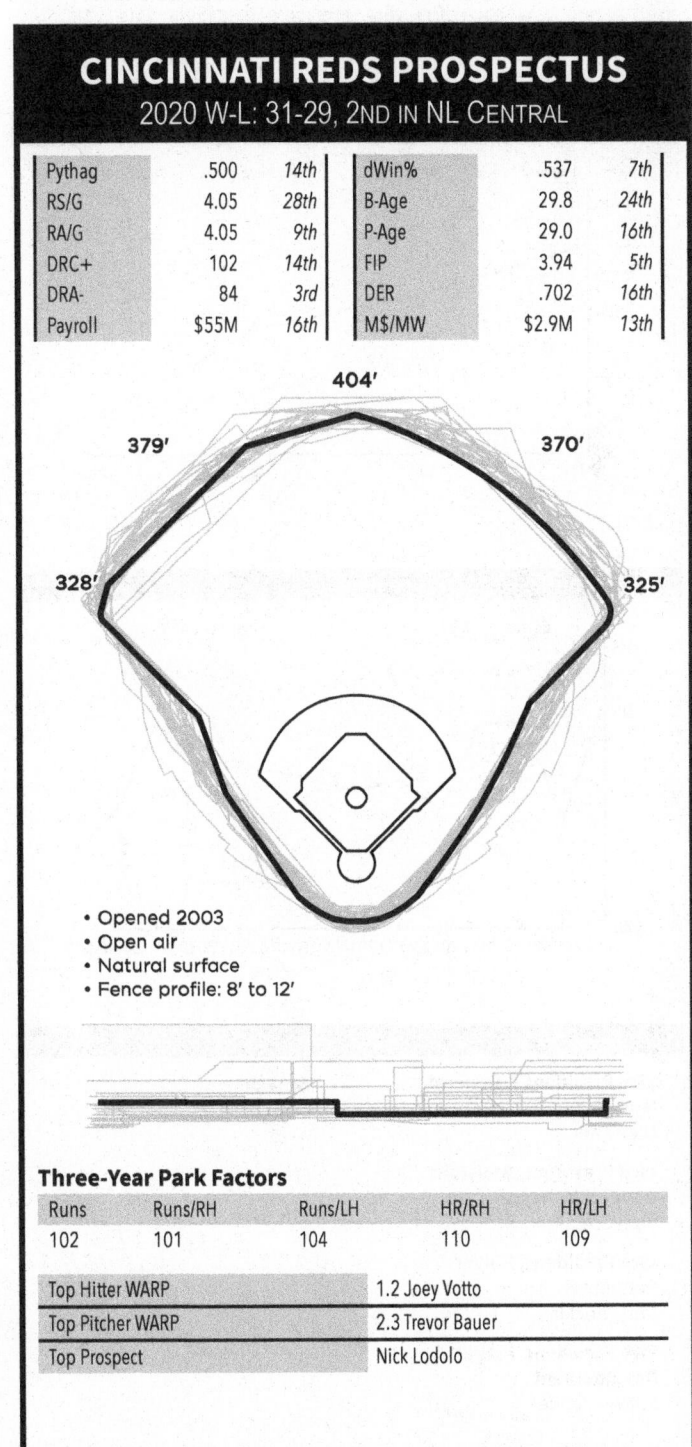

CINCINNATI REDS PROSPECTUS
2020 W-L: 31-29, 2ND IN NL CENTRAL

Pythag	.500	14th	dWin%	.537	7th
RS/G	4.05	28th	B-Age	29.8	24th
RA/G	4.05	9th	P-Age	29.0	16th
DRC+	102	14th	FIP	3.94	5th
DRA-	84	3rd	DER	.702	16th
Payroll	$55M	16th	M$/MW	$2.9M	13th

404'
379'
370'
328'
325'

- Opened 2003
- Open air
- Natural surface
- Fence profile: 8' to 12'

Three-Year Park Factors

Runs	Runs/RH	Runs/LH	HR/RH	HR/LH
102	101	104	110	109

Top Hitter WARP	1.2 Joey Votto
Top Pitcher WARP	2.3 Trevor Bauer
Top Prospect	Nick Lodolo

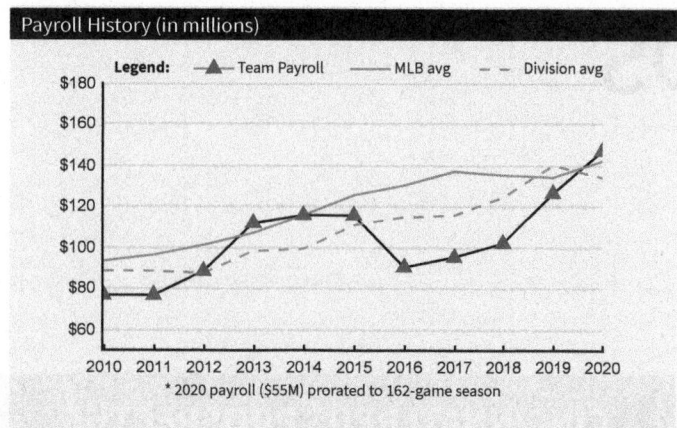

Payroll History (in millions)

Legend: Team Payroll — MLB avg - - Division avg

* 2020 payroll ($55M) prorated to 162-game season

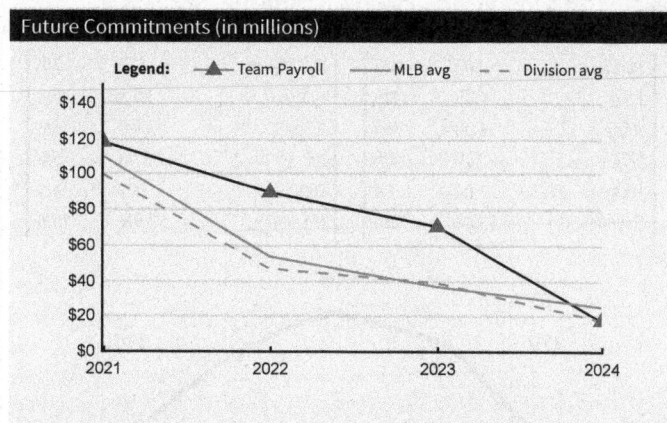

Future Commitments (in millions)

Legend: Team Payroll — MLB avg - - Division avg

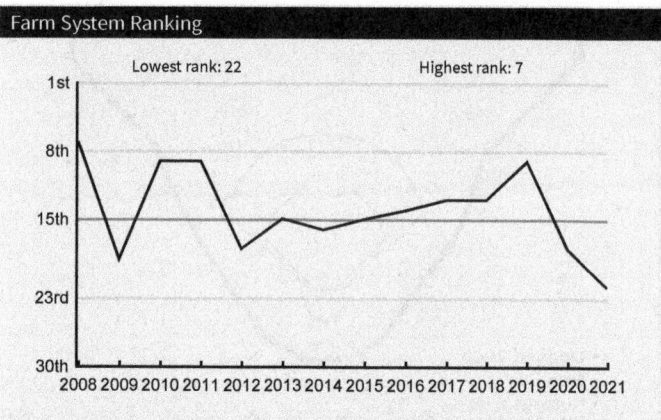

Farm System Ranking

Lowest rank: 22   Highest rank: 7

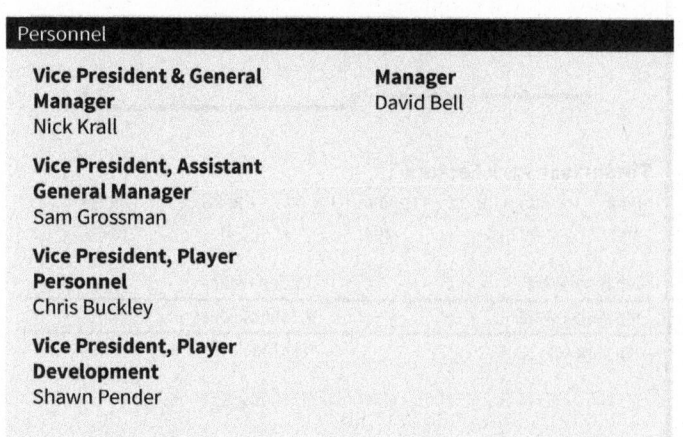

Personnel

Vice President & General Manager
Nick Krall

Vice President, Assistant General Manager
Sam Grossman

Vice President, Player Personnel
Chris Buckley

Vice President, Player Development
Shawn Pender

Manager
David Bell

his second MVP, he led the league not only in OBP, OPS and OPS+, but slugging as well. Even at 5-foot-7, surrounded by some of the great power hitters of their generation, Morgan showed there was nothing "little" about him.

There are those still in Cincinnati who will admit to how upset and even angry they were upon hearing about Morgan's arrival in a multi-player trade in the winter of 1971. It wasn't about him. Nor was it about the others the Reds would receive from Houston— including future Gold Glove center fielder César Gerónimo and pitcher Jack Billingham, who proved himself an invaluable member of the team's starting staff.

This was about the players that the Reds had sent off in return. They had handed the Astros the affable, power hitting first baseman Lee May, who, along with Perez, Johnny Bench and Pete Rose, had come through the Cincinnati system. Gone too was the former NL Rookie of the Year Tommy Helms, himself a Gold Glove second baseman. *Cincinnati Enquirer* columnist Bob Hertz equated trading these two to the United States sending "Dwight Eisenhower to the Germans during World War II." In the immediate aftermath, there were few fans who disagreed.

"We made the deal to get the balance we think we need to make us a contender," general manager Bob Howsam explained, citing Morgan's speed. "We feel we have enough power to win. May had his greatest year last year and we still finished fourth."

It all feels familiar. Howsam had seen a team that he felt that lacked diversity in its offense and felt bold, desperate measures were needed in order to make sure it returned to championship form. Now, nearly four decades later, Cincinnati finds itself in much the same place—looking back at the previous season in disbelief, trying to determine what kind of team they want to be.

"The way we built our team this year, we knew we were...probably going to be more of a power team, more station-to-station," former president of baseball operations Dick Williams told *The Athletic* after the season's disheartening end. "We don't have a lot of sprinters on this team. There's not a lot of base stealing, hit-and-run type action you're going to see. But we definitely will have the coaching staff looking, re-evaluating their messaging to the players, their approach to the players."

Williams manages to somehow temper an undeniable frustration. There is no doubt that he must have felt what so many fans did on those tortured summer afternoons and evenings for most of the "60-game sprint." By my own estimate, I watched 50 of these—what else was on?— during which I had resigned myself from the first inning on to the idea that the offense would not support the brilliant starting pitching. I was ready to watch nine innings of batters struggling to put the ball in play.

Seldom can you quantify a lack of joy. But one can here. The Reds' .212 batting average was last in the league in 2020. It also was the worst in this team's history. They ranked 28th in both doubles and runs per game. In 21 games of the abbreviated season, Cincinnati failed to score more than two runs. In his own season post-mortem, the *Enquirer's* Bobby Nightengale pointed out that the Reds' league-worst .245 BIBP was "the lowest by any team since the 1968 New York Yankees (.241) and the second-lowest number by a team since the end of the Deadball era in 1920."

The fact they even managed to post a winning, playoff-worthy record in 2020 should have meant something. But for most of the year it did not. The team's dependence on home runs began to wear on those who waited patiently for the season, almost from the start. In theory, scoring this way should be fun. But I cannot count how times I received a message from one of the friends with whom I've shared a daily game text chain for close to a decade that proclaimed in one way or another: "A double!" Or, "A hit! An actual base hit!"

I suppose that's why the two-game collapse, a historic one, to the Braves in the Wild Card round, did not induce the same kind of anguish one might expect. You knew this, or something like this, might happen. When the Reds failed to score in the first inning of Game One when it all seemed set up for them, one felt they had returned to their August form. At that moment, going scoreless for 22 innings didn't seem implausible.

In the weeks that followed, no one I know asked "What might have been?" By this time, some were in fact ready to see the season end, move on from the very thing they felt might deliver some happiness, even when that feeling has been at a premium. The Reds simply weren't fun—even when they did win. That too feels strange to say, but only one team had a higher three-true-outcome (TTO) percentage than Cincinnati's .407, and their inability to put multiple hits together proved maddening. (Though it must be said that the only team who bested that average was the American League Champion Tampa Bay Rays, and they correctly believe that, save falling in six games in the World Series, it worked out pretty well.)

"We hit home runs, we took walks, those were great," said Reds general manager Nick Krall in one interview after being tapped to run the Baseball Operations Department following Williams' departure in the offseason. "But at the end of the day, we need to figure out how to get more singles and more runs in from the bases.

"I know that we struggled with batting average of balls in play," he went on. "We struggled with batting average in general. We've got to figure out ways to put guys in a better position to succeed or be able to have guys use the whole field and take advantage of when a shift is out there."

This struggle seemed inexplicable given the moves the team made in winter. Even with the shortened season, the Reds knew what they had in Luis Castillo, Sonny Gray and Trevor Bauer—three pitchers each of whom in any given year might be the ace on anyone's staff. They knew where to devote the large chunk of the $164 million in their free-agent money: To established hitters like Mike Moustakas and Nick

Castellanos, and the slight, slashing outfielder Shogo Akiyama, the Reds' first Japanese-born player. They gave this team, in the eyes of many, an actual chance to win the National League pennant.

But it didn't work, or maybe there was no way it could. The truncated season meant there was little room for error for players to work themselves out of this. Moreover, the Reds are not alone in their winter of self-reflection which, more and more, feels like an all-consuming angst. Across baseball there is an inward search going on, one that goes well beyond TTO. No less than the one-time boy prince, Theo Epstein, expressed his own concerns about what he saw, even as he made his own, hopefully temporary, exit from the game. A truncated season that so many people had waited for gave us a glimpse into baseball's troubling present. I don't think Reds fans were alone in their exasperation watching something we looked forward to, thought we needed, only to come away asking, "Did we really need *this*?"

Since the abrupt end to the campaign, few have taken solace in good things they did see: the return to winning baseball and the postseason after a seven-year absence. The late-season run in which the Reds, once left for dead, won 11 of their last 14 games to earn a spot and have a chance in October. Trevor Bauer doing what Tom Seaver and Mario Soto and Jim Maloney could not: win the National League Cy Young Award, the very first for the Reds. Akiyama's outfield play earning him consideration for a Gold Glove, and catcher Tucker Barnhart actually winning one.

Morgan, clearly sick, said nothing of the Reds troubles this summer. But, given his past comments, we know what he must have felt. In the hours of his death, after looking back at that play and thinking of what his time in Cincinnati meant to the Reds and to baseball, I realized that Morgan meant something else for many. There are those who knew him as only the sound of Sunday Night Baseball, broadcasting alongside Jon Miller on ESPN for 21 seasons.

It is not an entirely pleasant association. His commentary, especially during his last decade on the air, made Morgan the avatar of the baseball establishment, one unable to accept innovation, gripping to the past in a sport whose great failings had been an inability to act and accept change, even when it was clear that change was desperately needed.

In spite of this, there is something to gain from this part of Morgan's life. The very thing he feared has taken place in baseball and certainly with his Reds. Within his imperfect reasoning about strategy and his general on-air crankiness, one can see that certain concerns are now widespread: the precipitous decline of African-American players, predominance of the base-to-base play whose dullness threatens to keep fans away and a general disdain for creating runs through the hit-and-run and the stolen base. TTO might guarantee outcomes, but it often ensures unwatchable baseball.

There are those that have felt that with Morgan's death, it might be time to let go of the "Machine." For so long, its dominance has unfairly overshadowed every Reds team since. I've often joked that growing up in Southwest Ohio, you learn the names of the "Great Eight," the starting lineup for the team's 1975 and 1976 teams, before you're able to spell. We are reminded of them through statues around the stadium, and through the great mural that dominates the entrance to Great American Ballpark. There is a strong, smart case for finally moving on.

But they still have lessons to give. Once, Bob Howsam defied orthodoxy in making the trade with Houston, knowing that the Reds desperately needed to find a new way to win. To do this now would require a far harder reinvention, one that goes against the new precepts of baseball, one that attempts to reconcile the game's past and present.

Perhaps it's impossible. But you truly cannot honor that team, or Joe Morgan, by pining for something that you may never find again. To try, however, is perhaps the only actual path for the Reds to return to the World Series after 30 years. And to do so will require Reds ownership to demonstrate the kind of awareness that Joe Morgan displayed when he found that ball in foul territory and cocked his arm to throw, knowing a runner was breaking for home. ■

—Sridhar Pappu is the author of The Year of The Pitcher: Bob Gibson, Denny McLain and the End of Baseball's Golden Age.

HITTERS

Shogo Akiyama CF   Born: 04/16/88   Age: 33   Bats: L   Throws: R   Height: 6'0"   Weight: 190   Origin: International Free Agent, 2019

YEAR	TEAM	LVL	AGE	PA	R	2B	3B	HR	RBI	BB	K	SB	CS	Whiff%	AVG/OBP/SLG	DRC+	BABIP	BRR	FRAA	WARP
2020	CIN	MLB	32	183	16	6	1	0	9	25	34	7	3	19.1%	.245/.357/.297	84	.314	0.6	LF(36): 1.2, CF(21): 1.4	0.5
2021 FS	CIN	MLB	33	600	75	25	2	10	54	67	124			19.1%	.253/.346/.371	98	.315			1.6
2021 DC	CIN	MLB	33	479	60	20	1	8	43	53	99			19.1%	.253/.346/.371	98	.315		LF -2, CF -2	1.0

The Akiyama that Reds fans were treated to last September is the version they hope to see going forward. You know, the lefty spark plug at the top of the order with the .317/.456/.365 batting line and five stolen bases, not the guy who slapped .196/.282/.250 up to that point. Akiyama impressed everyone out of the gate with his speed, baseball IQ and Gold Glove-caliber outfield defense, but it took a while for his offensive game to click. His power missed its flight from Japan and he struggled in limited exposure to same-side pitching, but Akiyama's tremendous contact skills and patient, all-fields approach give him a good chance to reach base at a steady clip. Even if he remains little more than a slap hitter, his combination of speed, defense and table-setting skills should make him a solid outfield contributor this year.

Aristides Aquino RF   Born: 04/22/94   Age: 27   Bats: R   Throws: R   Height: 6'4"   Weight: 220   Origin: International Free Agent, 2011

YEAR	TEAM	LVL	AGE	PA	R	2B	3B	HR	RBI	BB	K	SB	CS	Whiff%	AVG/OBP/SLG	DRC+	BABIP	BRR	FRAA	WARP
2018	PNS	AA	24	445	49	20	2	20	55	35	112	4	5		.240/.306/.448	103	.282	-1.3	RF(108): 7.7	0.8
2018	CIN	MLB	24	1	0	0	0	0	0	0	1	0	0	100.0%	.000/.000/.000	87		-0.7	RF(1): -0.1	-0.1
2019	LOU	AAA	25	323	56	13	1	28	53	23	81	5	1		.299/.356/.636	148	.321	0.2	RF(64): 3.4, CF(5): 1.8	2.9
2019	CIN	MLB	25	225	31	8	0	19	47	16	60	7	0	35.1%	.259/.316/.576	114	.266	0.3	RF(54): 0.9	1.0
2020	CIN	MLB	26	56	7	1	0	2	8	6	18	1	0	38.5%	.170/.304/.319	76	.222	0.3	LF(13): 0.5, RF(4): -0.0, CF(1): -0.1	0.0
2021 FS	CIN	MLB	27	600	72	21	3	36	82	41	186	4	1	36.1%	.229/.292/.477	98	.274	1.7	RF 0, CF 0	1.4
2021 DC	CIN	MLB	27	273	33	9	1	16	37	18	84	1	0	36.1%	.229/.292/.477	98	.274	0.8	LF 0, RF 0	0.6

Comparables: Bubba Trammell, Lyle Mouton, Jay Buhner

Despite his power-packed 2019 debut, Aquino was a victim of Cincinnati's "win now" approach last year when the signings of Nick Castellanos and Shogo Akiyama left him without a clear path to big league playing time. The recipe had called for Aquino to simmer a bit in Triple-A, but COVID-19 changed everything and he never found his power groove while shuttling in and out of the Cincinnati clubhouse. Aquino is older than you think and is a liability with the glove, but the thunder in his bat is real. Of course, so is his penchant to swing from the heels and make too little contact and too many outs, making it likely his career will take an alpine path with a few high peaks surrounding long, sustained valleys.

Tucker Barnhart C   Born: 01/07/91   Age: 30   Bats: L   Throws: R   Height: 5'11"   Weight: 192   Origin: Round 10, 2009 Draft (#299 overall)

YEAR	TEAM	LVL	AGE	PA	R	2B	3B	HR	RBI	BB	K	SB	CS	Whiff%	AVG/OBP/SLG	DRC+	BABIP	BRR	FRAA	WARP
2018	CIN	MLB	27	522	50	21	3	10	46	54	96	0	4	20.3%	.248/.328/.372	85	.291	-3.3	C(118): -9.6, 1B(11): -0.7	0.2
2019	CIN	MLB	28	364	32	14	0	11	40	44	83	1	0	23.9%	.231/.328/.380	89	.278	-3.7	C(102): 15.3, 1B(3): 0.0	2.5
2020	CIN	MLB	29	110	10	3	0	5	13	12	28	0	0	24.6%	.204/.291/.388	91	.231	-0.5	C(36): -0.2, 1B(2): 0.0	0.5
2021 FS	CIN	MLB	30	600	67	23	1	19	63	64	133	2	1	22.9%	.240/.327/.399	95	.287	-0.7	C 6, 1B 0	2.6
2021 DC	CIN	MLB	30	376	42	14	1	12	39	40	83	1	0	22.9%	.240/.327/.399	95	.287	-0.4	C 5	1.7

Comparables: Vic Correll, Mike Fitzgerald, Keith Osik

Metallic-hued hand coverings are once again the hottest item in the Tucker Barnhart catalog, as the veteran receiver earned his second Gold Glove award and the first ever to be determined entirely by defensive metrics. (Ed. note: We've come a long way, baby.) Barnhart's framing has improved over the years and he did an excellent job controlling the running game last summer, which combined with his always-solid blocking and receiving skills to make him a worthy recipient. At the plate, Barnhart gave up switch-hitting and batted exclusively from the left side yet still produced his usual slightly-below-average offensive numbers. That precipitated a virtual job-share with the slightly more potent bat of Curt Casali, as the Reds continued to try anything to shake their lineup out of the doldrums. Barnhart has one guaranteed year left on his current deal, and it will be interesting to see if his defense is valued enough for his $7.5 million option to be picked up.

YEAR	TEAM	P. COUNT	FRM RUNS	BLK RUNS	THRW RUNS	TOT RUNS
2018	CIN	17031	-11.5	3.6	-0.3	-8.1
2019	CIN	13047	10.1	4.9	-0.3	14.8
2020	CIN	4801	2.4	0.8	-0.4	2.8
2021	CIN	13228	-0.2	2.4	1.3	3.5

Alex Blandino 2B Born: 11/06/92 Age: 28 Bats: R Throws: R Height: 6'0" Weight: 190 Origin: Round 1, 2014 Draft (#29 overall)

YEAR	TEAM	LVL	AGE	PA	R	2B	3B	HR	RBI	BB	K	SB	CS	Whiff%	AVG/OBP/SLG	DRC+	BABIP	BRR	FRAA	WARP
2018	CIN	MLB	25	147	14	4	0	1	8	13	41	0	0	18.4%	.234/.324/.289	79	.337	2.3	2B(21): -1.4, 3B(15): -1.2, SS(11): -0.8	0.0
2019	LOU	AAA	26	293	36	13	1	5	24	40	73	1	3		.247/.386/.372	108	.335	-3.2	2B(35): -1.6, SS(18): -1.1, 3B(15): 0.8	0.8
2019	CIN	MLB	26	50	6	1	0	1	3	10	14	0	0	18.2%	.250/.420/.361	90	.348	-0.3	2B(10): 0.1, 3B(4): -0.0, 1B(3): -0.0	0.1
2021 FS	CIN	MLB	28	600	67	21	1	16	58	68	172	3	1	18.3%	.226/.336/.369	97	.307	-1.0	SS 1, 2B -3	1.3
2021 DC	CIN	MLB	28	136	15	4	0	3	13	15	39	0	0	18.3%	.226/.336/.369	97	.307	-0.2	SS 0, 2B -1	0.3

Comparables: Drew Sutton, Colin Walsh, Max Moroff

Blandino is a product of Silicon Valley and was once a well-regarded start-up. Yet seven years after being drafted in the first round out of Stanford he has yet to become a permanent feature of the MLB platform. Blandino has a solid batting eye, draws walks and slaps singles, but lacks the range, arm and athleticism for shortstop and the power to be a real asset anywhere else. His is a hard skill set to monetize, though he may be able to eventually eke out his pension in a utility role.

Tyler Callihan 2B Born: 06/22/00 Age: 21 Bats: L Throws: R Height: 6'1" Weight: 205 Origin: Round 3, 2019 Draft (#85 overall)

YEAR	TEAM	LVL	AGE	PA	R	2B	3B	HR	RBI	BB	K	SB	CS	Whiff%	AVG/OBP/SLG	DRC+	BABIP	BRR	FRAA	WARP
2019	BIL	ROK+	19	21	3	0	1	1	7	1	4	2	0		.400/.429/.650	156	.467	0.1		0.2
2019	GRN	ROK+	19	217	27	10	5	5	26	9	46	9	3		.260/.297/.439	85	.313	-0.4		0.3
2021 FS	CIN	MLB	21	600	45	26	4	8	51	28	195	18	5		.209/.250/.316	54	.303	5.6		-1.2

Losing a developmental year is hard on every minor leaguer but especially an older prep prospect like Callihan, who already has less time than most to determine which infield position his iffy glove can handle and prove his power bat can play there.

Nick Castellanos RF Born: 03/04/92 Age: 29 Bats: R Throws: R Height: 6'4" Weight: 203 Origin: Round 1, 2010 Draft (#44 overall)

YEAR	TEAM	LVL	AGE	PA	R	2B	3B	HR	RBI	BB	K	SB	CS	Whiff%	AVG/OBP/SLG	DRC+	BABIP	BRR	FRAA	WARP
2018	DET	MLB	26	678	88	46	5	23	89	49	151	2	1	30.2%	.298/.354/.500	124	.361	3.4	RF(142): -2.8	3.5
2019	DET	MLB	27	439	57	37	3	11	37	31	96	2	1	25.1%	.273/.328/.462	104	.332	-1.7	RF(89): 0.9	1.1
2019	CHC	MLB	27	225	43	21	0	16	36	10	47	0	1	30.7%	.321/.356/.646	141	.347	0.1	RF(48): 0.9, LF(11): -0.6	1.8
2020	CIN	MLB	28	242	37	11	2	14	34	19	69	0	2	34.2%	.225/.298/.486	108	.257	-1.7	RF(57): -3.0	0.2
2021 FS	CIN	MLB	29	600	81	32	3	30	83	43	164	3	1	29.8%	.259/.320/.496	114	.317	-0.1	RF -7, 3B 0	1.7
2021 DC	CIN	MLB	29	582	78	31	3	29	81	42	159	2	1	29.8%	.259/.320/.496	114	.317	-0.1	RF -7	1.7

Comparables: Matt Williams, Todd Frazier, Travis Fryman

Most big-dollar baseball contracts are chock-full of various potential award bonuses, and some of them are fun to ponder. One example: Castellanos will take home a cool hundred large for each and every Gold Glove award he earns. Makes you wonder if he's been playing the long game as he butchers his way down the defensive spectrum, secretly taking grounders in darkened ballparks while his agent yells "Pickin' Machine!" to prepare for his shocking reveal as a premiere first sacker. Probably not; by all accounts Castellanos has worked hard to improve as an outfielder, to little avail. Luckily he can still hit the snot out of the ball, at least when he makes contact. His whiff rate spiked last year, which caused his batting average and on-base percentage to plummet. The Reds had best hope that was an anomaly rather than a trend or Castellanos is in danger of turning into an expensive out-maker instead of a middle-of-the-order force.

Matt Davidson 1B Born: 03/26/91 Age: 30 Bats: R Throws: R Height: 6'3" Weight: 230 Origin: Round 1, 2009 Draft (#35 overall)

YEAR	TEAM	LVL	AGE	PA	R	2B	3B	HR	RBI	BB	K	SB	CS	Whiff%	AVG/OBP/SLG	DRC+	BABIP	BRR	FRAA	WARP
2018	CHW	MLB	27	496	51	23	0	20	62	52	165	0	0	33.7%	.228/.319/.419	101	.313	-3.9	1B(45): -3.1, 3B(14): 0.9, P(3): 0.1	0.3
2019	NAS	AAA	28	528	74	24	0	33	101	42	151	1	0		.264/.339/.527	111	.315	-2.6	1B(70): -5.1, 3B(27): -0.2, P(1): 0.1	1.0
2020	CIN	MLB	29	47	3	1	0	3	11	4	13	0	0	27.8%	.163/.234/.395	96	.148	-0.2	P(3): -0.0, 1B(2): 0.1	0.1
2021 FS	CIN	MLB	30	600	64	22	1	26	72	50	212	0	0	32.4%	.212/.291/.406	84	.294	-1.0	1B -8, 3B -1	-1.3

Comparables: Dave Kingman, Jeff Liefer, Craig Wilson

Davidson parlayed the 33 minor league dingers he blasted in 2019 into a spring training non-roster invite, and when COVID-19 changed the rules of the game, guess who became the first home designated hitter in Reds history? Davidson popped out weakly, then bounced into a 6-4-3, and things went downhill from there—consider that he only managed one more hit against right-handed pitching than you did last year. On the plus side, the would-be two-way player was able to toss three more blowout innings and showcase his glorious, looping, time-bending curveball, even freezing Mike Freeman with it for a backwards K. Previous talk of Davidson getting a real shot at a bullpen job never seemed to go anywhere, which from an aesthetic standpoint is a real shame. What does anyone have to lose?

Kyle Farmer   2B   Born: 08/17/90   Age: 30   Bats: R   Throws: R   Height: 6'0"   Weight: 205   Origin: Round 8, 2013 Draft (#244 overall)

YEAR	TEAM	LVL	AGE	PA	R	2B	3B	HR	RBI	BB	K	SB	CS	Whiff%	AVG/OBP/SLG	DRC+	BABIP	BRR	FRAA	WARP
2018	OKC	AAA	27	312	37	24	1	7	36	17	50	1	1		.288/.333/.451	105	.325	-2.2	3B(31): 3.2, C(29): -6.9, SS(8): -0.9	0.3
2018	LAD	MLB	27	77	1	4	1	0	9	5	15	0	0	21.0%	.235/.312/.324	80	.296	-0.4	3B(22): 1.2, C(1): 0.0, 1B(1): -0.0	0.2
2019	CIN	MLB	28	197	22	6	0	9	27	10	59	4	1	29.5%	.230/.279/.410	76	.284	-1.5	2B(41): -1.0, 1B(18): -0.1, C(15): 0.2	-0.2
2020	CIN	MLB	30	70	4	3	0	0	4	5	13	1	0	25.0%	.266/.329/.312	94	.333	-0.4	SS(15): -0.2, 2B(13): 0.1, 3B(2): -0.1	0.1
2021 FS	CIN	MLB	30	600	63	24	1	17	65	37	141	2	0	27.3%	.242/.300/.390	87	.294	-0.4	SS -1, 2B -6	0.1
2021 DC	CIN	MLB	30	376	39	15	1	11	41	23	88	1	0	27.3%	.242/.300/.390	87	.294	-0.3	SS -1, 2B -4	0.2

Comparables: Steve Scarsone, Danny Espinosa, Jason Maxwell

The more challenging the defensive position a backup can credibly play, the less pressure there is on his bat to earn his paycheck. By proving last year that he can handle shortstop in addition to being an actual by-gosh catcher, Farmer may have earned himself a lifetime pass to the training table even if his lumber continues to slumber. Managers will love Farmer because his peerless flexibility backstops any managerial move they can imagine making; regulars will gain comfort from the fact he's already fulfilled his career ambitions and isn't gunning for their job, unlike some 22-year-old middle infielder with invisibly quick hands and a penchant for loud contact. Farmer has enough skill with the bat to someday post a .700 OPS, but that's now become a bonus, not a requirement.

Freddy Galvis   SS   Born: 11/14/89   Age: 31   Bats: S   Throws: R   Height: 5'10"   Weight: 195   Origin: International Free Agent, 2006

YEAR	TEAM	LVL	AGE	PA	R	2B	3B	HR	RBI	BB	K	SB	CS	Whiff%	AVG/OBP/SLG	DRC+	BABIP	BRR	FRAA	WARP
2018	SD	MLB	28	656	62	31	5	13	67	45	147	8	6	26.7%	.248/.299/.380	81	.304	-1.2	SS(160): -8.9, 2B(5): -0.5	0.4
2019	CIN	MLB	29	116	12	4	0	5	16	7	33	0	1	27.0%	.234/.284/.411	87	.286	-0.6	2B(27): -1.4, SS(7): -0.5	0.0
2019	TOR	MLB	29	473	55	24	1	18	54	21	112	4	1	28.9%	.267/.299/.444	92	.318	-1.8	SS(103): -2.0, 2B(5): -0.2	1.3
2020	CIN	MLB	31	159	18	5	0	7	16	13	30	1	1	26.6%	.220/.308/.404	98	.231	-0.9	SS(33): -0.2, 2B(16): 0.2	0.4
2021 FS	CIN	MLB	31	600	62	24	2	21	70	37	133	9	4	27.6%	.239/.292/.404	85	.278	-0.8	SS -4, 2B 0	0.4

Comparables: Greg Gagne, Chris Woodward, Shawon Dunston

Galvis always plays with infectious energy, dreadlocks flying as he pirouettes through the infield dirt to register another improbable assist or bounds from the dugout to congratulate a teammate. His enthusiasm and plus glove in the middle infield will always find him work, but his anemic bat keeps him from being anyone's long-term solution. Galvis continues to launch the occasional home run but rarely walks and doesn't make enough hard contact to make him an asset at the plate. As long as he can flash the leather he's ideally cast as a veteran infield stabilizer who can boost the spirits of a rebuilding club's young pitching staff, which is good work if you can get it.

Jose Garcia   SS   Born: 04/05/98   Age: 23   Bats: R   Throws: R   Height: 6'2"   Weight: 175   Origin: International Free Agent, 2017

YEAR	TEAM	LVL	AGE	PA	R	2B	3B	HR	RBI	BB	K	SB	CS	Whiff%	AVG/OBP/SLG	DRC+	BABIP	BRR	FRAA	WARP
2018	DAY	LO-A	20	517	61	22	4	6	53	19	112	13	9		.245/.290/.344	84	.307	1.8	SS(93): -0.7, 2B(29): -1.8	0.3
2019	DAY	HI-A	21	452	58	37	1	8	55	25	83	15	2		.280/.343/.436	143	.329	-0.8	SS(100): 0.7	3.8
2020	CIN	MLB	22	68	4	0	0	0	2	1	26	1	1	40.3%	.194/.206/.194	45	.317	-0.8	SS(21): 1.3	-0.2
2021 FS	CIN	MLB	23	600	54	22	2	12	56	31	191	7	3	40.3%	.217/.271/.332	64	.306	-0.8	SS 1, 2B 0	-0.7
2021 DC	CIN	MLB	23	410	37	15	1	8	38	21	130	5	2	40.3%	.217/.271/.332	64	.306	-0.6	SS 1	-0.5

Comparables: Chris Nelson, Marcus Semien, Gleyber Torres

Don't make too much out of Garcia's struggles at the plate last year, as the young Cuban had never before faced Double-A pitching, let alone the ungodly breaking stuff they throw in The Show. Tall and lean, Garcia's speed and natural athleticism stands out even in the lofty company of a major-league clubhouse and he impressed the brass during spring training with his high baseball IQ. At the plate he's a work in progress, with fringy power but notable bat-to-ball skills and a mature approach that give him a chance to avoid the bottom of the order. Garcia displayed a flair for the dramatic in his big-league debut and has the range and arm to be a plus shortstop. He would obviously benefit from a more normal development path, but it's easy to picture Garcia growing into a solid first-division player.

Brian Goodwin   LF   Born: 11/02/90   Age: 30   Bats: L   Throws: R   Height: 6'0"   Weight: 200   Origin: Round 1, 2011 Draft (#34 overall)

YEAR	TEAM	LVL	AGE	PA	R	2B	3B	HR	RBI	BB	K	SB	CS	Whiff%	AVG/OBP/SLG	DRC+	BABIP	BRR	FRAA	WARP
2018	OMA	AAA	27	44	6	4	0	2	9	4	11	0	0		.225/.295/.475	88	.259	0.1	CF(3): -0.5, LF(2): 0.9, RF(2): -0.4	0.0
2018	WAS	MLB	27	79	9	1	0	3	12	10	26	3	1	30.2%	.200/.321/.354	80	.270	-1.8	LF(11): -0.2, RF(10): -0.7, CF(7): 0.1	-0.2
2018	KC	MLB	27	101	11	5	0	3	13	6	31	1	1	26.0%	.266/.317/.415	83	.367	0.2	CF(25): -0.7, LF(1): -0.1	0.1
2019	LAA	MLB	28	458	65	29	3	17	47	38	129	7	3	27.6%	.262/.326/.470	99	.337	-1.3	LF(68): -4.0, CF(39): -3.7, RF(17): 4.1	0.9
2020	CIN	MLB	30	55	5	2	0	2	5	5	19	4	0	33.7%	.163/.236/.327	86	.207	0.5	CF(16): -2.4, LF(2): -0.0, RF(1): -0.0	-0.1
2020	LAA	MLB	30	109	12	7	1	4	17	12	35	1	0	33.9%	.242/.330/.463	92	.333	0.6	LF(14): -1.2, RF(11): 2.3, CF(4): 0.1	0.2
2021 FS	CIN	MLB	30	600	64	28	1	22	68	53	190	6	2	29.5%	.230/.305/.414	88	.312	-0.1	CF -9, LF -2	-0.2

Comparables: Pete Incaviglia, Geoff Jenkins, Marcus Thames

In the baseball equivalent the "it's not you, it's me" break-up, the Angels rewarded Goodwin's season-and-a-half of good work in their employ by shipping him off to Cincinnati at the deadline last summer for pitcher/Biggles character Packy Naughton in order to make more room for high-ceiling prospects Jo Adell and, eventually, Brandon Marsh. Predictably, Goodwin fell apart, scuffling along at the sub-replacement rate that has defined most of his career. A former Nats first rounder, Goodwin has a little power, a little speed, a little patience and a lot of track record painting him as a fourth outfielder with a poor hit tool who can't quite cover center field.

Scott Heineman RF Born: 12/04/92 Age: 28 Bats: R Throws: R Height: 6'1" Weight: 205 Origin: Round 11, 2015 Draft (#318 overall)

YEAR	TEAM	LVL	AGE	PA	R	2B	3B	HR	RBI	BB	K	SB	CS	Whiff%	AVG/OBP/SLG	DRC+	BABIP	BRR	FRAA	WARP
2018	FRI	AA	25	31	6	2	0	1	10	7	5	2	1		.522/.613/.739	260	.611	-0.9	CF(5): -0.9, LF(2): 0.0	0.4
2018	RR	AAA	25	469	68	20	2	11	57	32	93	16	8		.295/.355/.429	111	.353	4.0	RF(48): 1.7, CF(44): -3.3, LF(13): -0.7	1.4
2019	NAS	AAA	26	182	34	6	2	8	25	17	45	4	3		.340/.412/.553	139	.426	-1.1	RF(13): 0.8, LF(11): 1.6, 1B(9): -1.0	1.3
2019	TEX	MLB	26	85	8	6	0	2	7	9	20	1	2	28.9%	.213/.306/.373	87	.264	-0.5	CF(9): -0.5, RF(8): -0.5, LF(6): 0.1	-0.1
2020	TEX	MLB	28	54	6	3	0	1	7	2	11	3	0	24.5%	.154/.185/.269	81	.175	0.1	CF(17): 2.0, LF(3): -0.2, 1B(1): 0.1	0.2
2021 FS	*CIN*	*MLB*	*28*	*600*	*64*	*26*	*2*	*19*	*67*	*44*	*158*	*8*	*4*	*26.9%*	*.238/.308/.406*	*92*	*.299*	*-2.0*	*LF -5, 1B -2*	*0.0*
2021 DC	*CIN*	*MLB*	*28*	*136*	*14*	*5*	*0*	*4*	*15*	*10*	*35*	*1*	*0*	*26.9%*	*.238/.308/.406*	*92*	*.299*	*-0.5*	*LF -1, 1B 0*	*-0.1*

Comparables: Alfredo Marte, Jeff Baker, Brandon Moss

Heineman barely missed out on the family batting title this season, falling just short of his brother Tyler, a backup catcher with the Giants who hit .190. He did homer, though, whereas Tyler failed to leave the yard. One can imagine a good-natured but spirited Thanksgiving conflict over this, followed by an hour-long scoreless game of cornhole.

Austin Hendrick CF Born: 06/15/01 Age: 20 Bats: L Throws: L Height: 6'0" Weight: 195 Origin: Round 1, 2020 Draft (#12 overall)

The Reds nabbed Hendrick with their first pack in last summer's draft and are now impatiently awaiting the day they can unleash his lefty swing on professional pitching in game situations. The Pennsylvania prep product has plus raw power and electrifying bat speed, whipping through the zone to attack pitches and launch towering shots to the right field alley. There will probably be a lot of swing-and-miss in his game, but when he makes contact it has That Sound. There's plenty of work to do, but Hendrick has the arm, athleticism and thunder of a prototypical right fielder and potential home run champ.

Rece Hinds SS Born: 09/05/00 Age: 20 Bats: R Throws: R Height: 6'4" Weight: 215 Origin: Round 2, 2019 Draft (#49 overall)

YEAR	TEAM	LVL	AGE	PA	R	2B	3B	HR	RBI	BB	K	SB	CS	Whiff%	AVG/OBP/SLG	DRC+	BABIP	BRR	FRAA	WARP
2019	GRN	ROK+	18	10	1	0	0	0	1	2	3	0	0		.000/.286/.000	30	.000	0.2		0.0
2021 FS	*CIN*	*MLB*	*20*	*600*	*45*	*26*	*2*	*7*	*49*	*35*	*228*				*.200/.253/.298*	*53*	*.322*			*-1.9*

Hinds has only played three professional games since the Reds chose him in the second round of the 2019 draft, but was able to show off his immense raw power and plus makeup as the youngest player at the club's alternate training site; he may not stick at the hot corner, but the juice in his bat just might be an asset anywhere.

Jonathan India 3B Born: 12/15/96 Age: 24 Bats: R Throws: R Height: 6'0" Weight: 200 Origin: Round 1, 2018 Draft (#5 overall)

YEAR	TEAM	LVL	AGE	PA	R	2B	3B	HR	RBI	BB	K	SB	CS	Whiff%	AVG/OBP/SLG	DRC+	BABIP	BRR	FRAA	WARP
2018	GRN	ROK	21	62	11	2	1	3	12	15	12	1	0		.261/.452/.543	160	.290	0.6	3B(12): -0.6, SS(2): -0.2	0.4
2018	BIL	ROK	21	10	1	0	0	0	0	0	4	0	1		.250/.400/.250	55	.500	-0.2	SS(3): -0.3	-0.1
2018	DAY	LO-A	21	112	17	7	0	3	11	13	28	5	0		.229/.339/.396	103	.292	1.5	3B(21): 2.4, SS(4): -0.1	0.6
2019	DAY	HI-A	22	367	50	15	5	8	30	37	84	7	5		.256/.346/.410	129	.319	-1.8	3B(74): -9.2, 2B(5): 0.0	1.0
2019	CHA	AA	22	145	24	3	0	3	14	22	26	4	0		.270/.414/.378	141	.314	0.2	3B(33): -0.4	1.1
2021 FS	*CIN*	*MLB*	*24*	*600*	*67*	*24*	*2*	*17*	*61*	*62*	*182*	*3*	*1*		*.225/.322/.384*	*96*	*.309*	*0.9*	*3B -7, 2B 0*	*0.3*
2021 DC	*CIN*	*MLB*	*24*	*68*	*7*	*2*	*0*	*2*	*6*	*7*	*20*	*0*	*0*		*.225/.322/.384*	*96*	*.309*	*0.1*	*3B -1*	*0.0*

Comparables: Kyle Kubitza, Kelvin Gutierrez, Ty France

Instead of doom-scrolling, raiding the fridge and posting self-righteous jeremiads on social media like the rest of us, India used his COVID summer productively. A good defensive third baseman, the former top draft pick spent his time at Cincinnati's alternate camp working out at second base, increasing his versatility and earning a shot to play a position where his solid-if-uninspiring bat could shine rather than merely survive. India has a disciplined approach and makes hard contact, but hasn't shown the power you would ideally want to see from a third sacker. If he can hack the keystone every day it would raise his ceiling considerably; if not he is unlikely to be more than a fringe-average starter at the hot corner.

Travis Jankowski RF Born: 06/15/91 Age: 30 Bats: L Throws: R Height: 6'2" Weight: 190 Origin: Round 1, 2012 Draft (#44 overall)

YEAR	TEAM	LVL	AGE	PA	R	2B	3B	HR	RBI	BB	K	SB	CS	Whiff%	AVG/OBP/SLG	DRC+	BABIP	BRR	FRAA	WARP
2018	ELP	AAA	27	94	17	4	0	1	11	11	21	4	3		.362/.452/.450	113	.483	1.5	CF(20): 2.5	0.7
2018	SD	MLB	27	387	45	12	3	4	17	37	73	24	7	17.8%	.259/.332/.346	78	.319	4.5	RF(58): 3.3, CF(34): -1.7, LF(32): -2.2	0.4
2019	ELP	AAA	28	183	27	6	0	0	12	21	32	7	2		.312/.393/.350	91	.388	0.8	CF(19): -2.2, RF(10): -0.5, LF(8): 0.6	0.2
2019	SD	MLB	28	24	4	0	0	0	0	2	4	2	2	17.6%	.182/.250/.182	77	.222	0.7	CF(5): 0.5, RF(5): -0.1, LF(2): -0.1	0.1
2020	CIN	MLB	29	17	3	0	0	0	0	2	7	2	1	33.3%	.067/.176/.067	71	.125	0.2	CF(9): 0.2, RF(3): -0.0, LF(1): -0.0	0.0
2021 FS	*CIN*	*MLB*	*30*	*600*	*57*	*19*	*1*	*7*	*47*	*62*	*159*	*25*	*8*	*19.6%*	*.232/.318/.319*	*76*	*.319*	*2.3*	*CF -1, LF -3*	*0.3*

Comparables: Carroll Hardy, Cameron Maybin, Ryan Christenson

A fleet outfielder, Jankowski has by far the most stolen bases (64) of any Jankowski in major league history, needing just nine more to edge out Travis Fryman for the all-time Travis lead. We'll say he's second on the list for players with the middle name Paul because we bet you can't look that up.

Mike Moustakas 2B   Born: 09/11/88   Age: 32   Bats: L   Throws: R   Height: 6'0"   Weight: 225   Origin: Round 1, 2007 Draft (#2 overall)

YEAR	TEAM	LVL	AGE	PA	R	2B	3B	HR	RBI	BB	K	SB	CS	Whiff%	AVG/OBP/SLG	DRC+	BABIP	BRR	FRAA	WARP
2018	KC	MLB	29	417	46	21	1	20	62	30	63	3	0	20.8%	.249/.309/.468	108	.247	-2.6	3B(76): 11.3, 1B(4): -0.2	2.7
2018	MIL	MLB	29	218	20	12	0	8	33	19	40	1	1	24.2%	.256/.326/.441	106	.282	-2.6	3B(52): 0.5	0.8
2019	MIL	MLB	30	584	80	30	1	35	87	53	98	3	0	24.8%	.254/.329/.516	118	.250	-2.8	3B(105): -0.7, 2B(47): -1.9	2.9
2020	CIN	MLB	32	163	13	9	0	8	27	18	36	1	0	24.4%	.230/.331/.468	115	.247	-0.9	2B(32): -3.3, 1B(10): -0.3, 3B(2): 0.2	0.3
2021 FS	CIN	MLB	32	600	73	29	1	33	90	49	120	2	0	24.0%	.251/.326/.491	111	.269	-1.1	2B -8, 1B 0	1.3
2021 DC	CIN	MLB	32	582	71	28	1	32	87	48	117	2	0	24.0%	.251/.326/.491	111	.269	-1.0	2B -8, 1B 0	2.0

Comparables: Joe Crede, Scott Brosius, Ty Wigginton

Speaking of third basemen who learned how to hack the keystone, for the first time in his career Moustakas played the majority of his innings at second base. His sure hands and solid fundamentals overcame subpar range to grade out as average defensively, though as Moose is approaching the age where we all lose a few steps, he likely won't be able to keep that up. At the plate Moustakas set a career high in both walk and strikeout rates, which meant he just took a slightly different route to his usual meh-OBP, mmm-SLG offensive destination. He also missed some time with illness and a quad strain, and given the poor health record of second baseman in their 30s Reds fans had best get used to hearing that sort of thing. Moose was worth his multi-million dollar salary last year, but the next few years still look plenty risky.

Mark Payton LF   Born: 12/07/91   Age: 29   Bats: L   Throws: L   Height: 5'8"   Weight: 180   Origin: Round 7, 2014 Draft (#212 overall)

YEAR	TEAM	LVL	AGE	PA	R	2B	3B	HR	RBI	BB	K	SB	CS	Whiff%	AVG/OBP/SLG	DRC+	BABIP	BRR	FRAA	WARP
2018	SWB	AAA	26	237	29	6	2	6	25	34	49	2	6		.259/.368/.401	121	.312	-0.1	LF(40): -0.1, CF(12): -0.1, RF(3): 0.1	0.8
2019	LV	AAA	27	447	80	30	3	30	97	45	76	7	4		.334/.400/.653	138	.348	0.6	LF(64): 6.1, RF(43): -0.2, CF(5): 0.7	3.7
2020	CIN	MLB	29	20	0	1	0	0	0	2	5	1	0	31.8%	.167/.250/.222	88	.231		LF(6): -0.1	0.0
2021 FS	CIN	MLB	29	600	66	24	3	23	72	51	150	1	0	31.8%	.244/.316/.431	98	.297	0.9	LF 3, RF 1	1.9
2021 DC	CIN	MLB	29	273	30	10	1	10	33	23	68	0	0	31.8%	.244/.316/.431	98	.297	0.4	LF 1, RF 0	0.9

Comparables: Gabe Gross, Alejandro De Aza, Chris Aguila

Via the Rule 5 draft and an eventual trade, Payton parlayed the 30 bombs he hit in 2019—nearly matching his five-year minor league career total—into a big-league roster spot. That power surge happened in Vegas and will stay in Vegas, but Payton has the lefty bat, wheels and glove of a potential reserve outfielder.

Leonardo Rivas SS   Born: 10/10/97   Age: 23   Bats: S   Throws: R   Height: 5'10"   Weight: 150   Origin: International Free Agent, 2014

YEAR	TEAM	LVL	AGE	PA	R	2B	3B	HR	RBI	BB	K	SB	CS	Whiff%	AVG/OBP/SLG	DRC+	BABIP	BRR	FRAA	WARP
2018	BUR	LO-A	20	547	62	16	7	4	34	84	138	16	10		.233/.355/.326	106	.325	-0.3	SS(92): 4.6, 2B(26): 1.1	2.4
2019	ANG	ROK	21	25	6	0	0	0	0	8	4	1	0		.062/.375/.062	108	.083	0.9	SS(6): -0.2	0.2
2019	IE	HI-A	21	338	44	14	5	6	26	39	90	4	2		.236/.328/.377	100	.318	0.3	SS(46): 1.0, 2B(9): -0.7, CF(9): 0.4	1.3
2021 FS	CIN	MLB	23	600	57	26	4	10	56	65	188	13	5		.225/.318/.349	86	.329	0.5	SS 4, 2B -1	1.4

Comparables: Jorge Mateo, Junior Lake, Manny Machado

Ever noticed that whenever someone says a player is "listed at" a certain height, it carries the implication the height in question is ... in question? Anyway, Rivas is "listed at" five-foot-ten. Sure, he hits with all the force of a ping pong ball in place of a cue ball, but if he can crouch his way to double-digit walks in the upper levels, it could boost him to a major-league utility role. There no one would have impetus to doubt the listed height—as long as he stays away from Aaron Judge in view of photographers.

Nick Senzel CF   Born: 06/29/95   Age: 26   Bats: R   Throws: R   Height: 6'1"   Weight: 205   Origin: Round 1, 2016 Draft (#2 overall)

YEAR	TEAM	LVL	AGE	PA	R	2B	3B	HR	RBI	BB	K	SB	CS	Whiff%	AVG/OBP/SLG	DRC+	BABIP	BRR	FRAA	WARP
2018	LOU	AAA	23	192	23	12	2	6	25	19	39	8	2		.312/.380/.512	150	.370	1.9	2B(28): -0.8, 3B(14): 0.8, SS(1): -0.0	1.6
2019	LOU	AAA	24	38	7	1	0	1	2	3	13	0	0		.257/.316/.371	66	.381	0.4	CF(8): -1.2	-0.1
2019	CIN	MLB	24	414	55	20	4	12	42	30	101	14	5	23.7%	.256/.315/.427	87	.319	-0.1	CF(96): -4.6, 2B(1): 0.0	0.4
2020	CIN	MLB	25	78	8	6	0	2	8	6	15	2	1	23.2%	.186/.247/.357	99	.204	-1.4	CF(23): 0.1	0.0
2021 FS	CIN	MLB	26	600	64	26	3	22	70	51	146	11	4	23.6%	.241/.311/.423	97	.290	-0.2	CF -15, 2B 0	-0.2
2021 DC	CIN	MLB	26	479	51	21	2	17	56	41	116	9	3	23.6%	.241/.311/.423	97	.290	-0.2	CF -12	0.2

Comparables: Chris Young, Colby Rasmus, Ryan Thompson

Senzel reported to camp nominally healthy, having recovered from fall shoulder surgery, but as is the norm for his injury-plagued career he didn't remain that way. He hyperextended his elbow in summer camp, sprained a finger, pulled his groin and missed time due to illness on two separate occasions. Along the way he also made a full transition to center field, where his wheels will make him an asset, but struggled mightily at the dish. Senzel makes plenty of contact but has yet to show much power and lofted far too many lazy fly balls last year. The broad set of tools that once made him the second-overall pick can still be seen, but it's hard to say how much of his struggles have been due to his physical ailments and how much is due to him just not being as talented a hitter as we expected. This absolutely could be the year Senzel finally puts it all together and starts earning All-Star votes in the center pasture, but we wouldn't bet on it.

Michael Siani CF Born: 07/16/99   Age: 21   Bats: L   Throws: L   Height: 6'1"   Weight: 188   Origin: Round 4, 2018 Draft (#109 overall)

YEAR	TEAM	LVL	AGE	PA	R	2B	3B	HR	RBI	BB	K	SB	CS	Whiff%	AVG/OBP/SLG	DRC+	BABIP	BRR	FRAA	WARP
2018	GRN	ROK	18	205	24	6	3	2	13	16	35	6	4		.288/.351/.386	117	.342	-0.1	CF(45): 6.5	1.0
2019	DAY	LO-A	19	531	75	10	6	6	39	46	108	45	15		.253/.333/.339	95	.317	7.4	CF(112): 24.7, RF(5): -0.7, LF(1): 0.0	4.8
2021 FS	CIN	MLB	21	600	50	25	3	8	53	34	169	29	12		.235/.286/.338	71	.323	-1.9	CF 14, RF 0	1.0

Comparables: Derek Hill, Carlos Gómez, Joe Benson

Siani is a true center fielder whose speed and cannon arm will play at the highest level, but has yet to show enough power or consistency at the plate to profile as anything more than a fourth outfielder.

Dwight Smith LF Born: 10/26/92   Age: 28   Bats: L   Throws: R   Height: 6'0"   Weight: 210   Origin: Round 1, 2011 Draft (#53 overall)

YEAR	TEAM	LVL	AGE	PA	R	2B	3B	HR	RBI	BB	K	SB	CS	Whiff%	AVG/OBP/SLG	DRC+	BABIP	BRR	FRAA	WARP
2018	BUF	AAA	25	361	39	25	1	6	42	44	53	9	3		.268/.358/.413	127	.302	-0.3	LF(62): 1.2, RF(14): -0.1	1.5
2018	TOR	MLB	25	75	9	8	0	2	8	7	13	0	0	22.8%	.262/.347/.477	99	.294	-0.4	LF(19): -1.5, RF(6): 0.7	0.1
2019	NOR	AAA	26	49	9	2	0	3	12	3	8	0	0		.311/.367/.556	117	.324	-0.1	LF(5): -0.3, RF(2): 0.1	0.2
2019	BAL	MLB	26	392	46	16	3	13	53	26	82	5	1	28.2%	.241/.297/.412	81	.274	-0.1	LF(86): -0.7	0.0
2020	BAL	MLB	28	72	9	3	0	2	6	7	19	1	0	26.5%	.222/.306/.365	85	.279	0.0	LF(16): 0.4	-0.1
2021 FS	CIN	MLB	28	600	60	24	2	17	66	53	142	3	1	27.4%	.232/.307/.387	88	.283	0.2	LF -4, RF -3	0.0

Comparables: Todd Hollandsworth, Chad Allen, Eric Valent

Smith has added muscle and mass over the last few years, causing him to lose speed (his 25.6 ft/sec sprint speed places him behind a few catchers) and get worse on defense, and it didn't help him add any power to the profile. Other than that, Mrs. Lincoln, how was the play?

Tyler Stephenson C Born: 08/16/96   Age: 24   Bats: R   Throws: R   Height: 6'4"   Weight: 225   Origin: Round 1, 2015 Draft (#11 overall)

YEAR	TEAM	LVL	AGE	PA	R	2B	3B	HR	RBI	BB	K	SB	CS	Whiff%	AVG/OBP/SLG	DRC+	BABIP	BRR	FRAA	WARP
2018	DAY	HI-A	21	450	60	20	1	11	59	45	98	1	0		.250/.338/.392	116	.301	0.2	C(97): -3.3	1.5
2019	CHA	AA	22	363	47	19	1	6	44	37	60	0	0		.285/.372/.410	128	.331	-2.1	C(87): -11.8	1.3
2020	CIN	MLB	24	20	4	0	0	2	6	2	9	0	0	26.7%	.294/.400/.647	80	.500	0.0	C(4): -0.0	0.0
2021 FS	CIN	MLB	24	600	60	23	1	18	62	49	184	0	0	26.7%	.229/.302/.378	85	.312	-0.4	C 1	1.4
2021 DC	CIN	MLB	24	273	27	10	0	8	28	22	83	0	0	26.7%	.229/.302/.378	85	.312	-0.2	C 1, 1B 0	0.5

Comparables: Jason Castro, Alex Avila, Christian Vázquez

YEAR	TEAM	P. COUNT	FRM RUNS	BLK RUNS	THRW RUNS	TOT RUNS
2020	CIN	396	0.0	0.0	0.0	0.0
2021	CIN	7215	0.6	0.5	0.2	1.3

A former first-rounder out of a Georgia high school back in what feels like the cretaceous period, Stephenson has overcome more misfortune than a Coen Brothers protagonist to finally make a splash in Cincinnati. His debut couldn't have gone much better, as Stephenson went deep in his first at bat and showed great promise down the stretch. Tall for a catcher, Stephenson nevertheless blocks and receives well enough to succeed and if he can improve his throwing he could become an above-average defender. At the plate he has both patience and power but his hit tool is nothing to write home about, all of which adds up to a potential plus bat behind the dish. Although he's entering his age-24 season, Stephenson has put in only one half-season in the high minors and would benefit from some time in Triple-A. If he can stay healthy he has the skills to be a frontline big-league catcher.

Eugenio Suárez 3B Born: 07/18/91   Age: 29   Bats: R   Throws: R   Height: 5'11"   Weight: 213   Origin: International Free Agent, 2008

YEAR	TEAM	LVL	AGE	PA	R	2B	3B	HR	RBI	BB	K	SB	CS	Whiff%	AVG/OBP/SLG	DRC+	BABIP	BRR	FRAA	WARP
2018	CIN	MLB	26	606	79	22	2	34	104	64	142	1	1	25.7%	.283/.366/.526	136	.322	-3.5	3B(143): -7.6, SS(3): 0.0	3.8
2019	CIN	MLB	27	662	87	22	2	49	103	70	189	3	2	29.1%	.271/.358/.572	131	.312	-7.9	3B(158): 0.1	4.4
2020	CIN	MLB	29	231	29	8	0	15	38	30	67	2	0	31.7%	.202/.312/.470	112	.214	0.5	3B(57): -4.3	0.5
2021 FS	CIN	MLB	29	600	83	21	1	39	95	66	171	4	2	29.1%	.255/.350/.526	129	.304	-1.6	3B -3, SS 0	3.0
2021 DC	CIN	MLB	29	582	80	21	1	37	92	64	166	4	2	29.1%	.255/.350/.526	129	.304	-1.5	3B -3	2.9

Comparables: Dean Palmer, Wilson Betemit, Jung Ho Kang

Suárez overcame a horrendous start with a torrid stretch in August and September to put up numbers that would be a good match for his power-packed 2019 breakout, except for that .100 point drop in batting average on balls in play and a small reduction in home runs per fly ball. Back in the buggy-whip days of sabermetrics we may have just described that as bad luck, but now that every ballpark is stuffed with more surveillance devices than Boris Badenov's suitcase, there are oceans of batted ball data to sort through. They show Suárez had pretty much the same profile last year but got under just a few more fly balls, resulting in the small power reduction. He also faced a shift almost 70 percent of the time, way more than in 2019, and struggled against it. Both of those things tend to even out over time, so maybe the lazy, low-tech analysis was just as accurate. With a little luck, Suárez should be back to bombing away as usual this year.

Joey Votto 1B Born: 09/10/83 Age: 37 Bats: L Throws: R Height: 6'2" Weight: 220 Origin: Round 2, 2002 Draft (#44 overall)

YEAR	TEAM	LVL	AGE	PA	R	2B	3B	HR	RBI	BB	K	SB	CS	Whiff%	AVG/OBP/SLG	DRC+	BABIP	BRR	FRAA	WARP
2018	CIN	MLB	34	623	67	28	2	12	67	108	101	2	0	17.9%	.284/.417/.419	124	.333	-2.6	1B(139): 11.6	3.7
2019	CIN	MLB	35	608	79	32	1	15	47	76	123	5	0	19.2%	.261/.357/.411	108	.313	-4.3	1B(133): 4.6	1.6
2020	CIN	MLB	37	223	32	8	0	11	22	37	43	0	0	22.5%	.226/.354/.446	123	.235	1.1	1B(50): 3.7	1.2
2021 FS	CIN	MLB	37	600	83	25	1	21	63	99	127	4	1	19.8%	.264/.394/.447	129	.318	-0.2	1B 13	4.5
2021 DC	CIN	MLB	37	582	81	25	1	20	61	96	123	4	1	19.8%	.264/.394/.447	129	.318	-0.2	1B 13	4.3

Comparables: Lance Berkman, Harmon Killebrew, Jeff Bagwell

In mid-August the Reds were struggling to get production from the leadoff spot, eyed up Votto's .378 on-base percentage, and asked the future Hall of Famer to take over at the top of the order. Three weeks, one benching and a .203/.289/.365 line later, Votto was mercifully moved back into the three hole and slashed .250/.409/.596 the rest of the way. "He really doesn't care where he hits," Reds manager David Bell said, but someone should ask Votto's bat what it thinks because a similar experiment in 2019 ended just as tragically. Perhaps it's a subconscious Canadian thing where you don't want to make the pitcher feel bad about himself right off the bat, but whatever the reason, it's probably best to ship that idea off to the Territories for good. Votto is not the legendary lumberman he once was but his batting eye and contact skills are still evident. There's no reason he can't bounce back and post a few more solidly productive years.

Nick Williams LF Born: 09/08/93 Age: 27 Bats: L Throws: L Height: 6'3" Weight: 208 Origin: Round 2, 2012 Draft (#93 overall)

YEAR	TEAM	LVL	AGE	PA	R	2B	3B	HR	RBI	BB	K	SB	CS	Whiff%	AVG/OBP/SLG	DRC+	BABIP	BRR	FRAA	WARP
2018	PHI	MLB	24	448	53	12	3	17	50	32	111	3	2	27.3%	.256/.324/.425	98	.312	-1.4	RF(95): -9.8, LF(19): -1.5	-0.4
2019	LHV	AAA	25	210	33	15	2	10	25	14	52	1	0		.316/.381/.574	130	.391	1.4	LF(20): 1.2, CF(16): 1.0, RF(11): 1.8	1.7
2019	PHI	MLB	25	112	9	4	0	2	5	4	43	0	0	28.7%	.151/.196/.245	45	.230	0.4	LF(23): 0.0, RF(5): -0.3	-0.4
2021 FS	CIN	MLB	27	600	65	23	3	21	69	35	180	2	1	27.8%	.232/.290/.401	84	.305	1.0	RF -7, LF -2	-0.8

Comparables: Doug Frobel, Jayson Werth, Byron Browne

Williams is a poor corner outfielder who strikes out a ton, but he's only 27, has some skill with the bat, was once a top prospect and has put up perfectly acceptable numbers whenever he's received consistent playing time; there might still be something here.

Jesse Winker LF Born: 08/17/93 Age: 27 Bats: L Throws: L Height: 6'3" Weight: 215 Origin: Round 1, 2012 Draft (#49 overall)

YEAR	TEAM	LVL	AGE	PA	R	2B	3B	HR	RBI	BB	K	SB	CS	Whiff%	AVG/OBP/SLG	DRC+	BABIP	BRR	FRAA	WARP
2018	CIN	MLB	24	334	38	16	0	7	43	49	46	0	0	15.4%	.299/.405/.431	117	.336	-2.6	RF(47): -1.0, LF(34): -3.5	0.8
2019	CIN	MLB	25	384	51	17	2	16	38	38	60	0	2	18.0%	.269/.357/.473	114	.286	0.6	LF(72): 1.4, CF(21): 0.0, RF(18): 1.6	2.2
2020	CIN	MLB	27	183	27	7	0	12	23	28	46	1	0	29.0%	.255/.388/.544	125	.283	-0.2	LF(15): 1.0, RF(1): -0.2	1.1
2021 FS	CIN	MLB	27	600	77	25	1	25	76	79	129	1	0	21.4%	.272/.381/.476	129	.322	-1.5	LF -1, CF 0	3.5
2021 DC	CIN	MLB	27	479	61	20	1	20	60	63	103	1	0	21.4%	.272/.381/.476	129	.322	-1.2	LF -1	2.6

Comparables: Rusty Greer, Carmelo Martinez, Gary Roenicke

Yeah, we know, correlation is not causation, but it's interesting to note that the first time Winker was able to stay healthy for a full season was also the only season he could spend considerable time as the designated hitter. It was also a short season, so there's no knowing whether Winker would have stayed upright through a full slate of games, but in any case it all came together last year for the lanky lefty. Winker managed to display both patience and power at the same time and finally did some damage against portside pitching, albeit in a very small sample. He even seemed more comfortable in the outfield when he did don his glove. This is the Winker we had only seen glimpses of before but knew existed, and if he can avoid injury during his prime expect him to be a lineup force for years to come.

PITCHERS

Tejay Antone RHP Born: 12/05/93 Age: 27 Bats: R Throws: R Height: 6'4" Weight: 230 Origin: Round 5, 2014 Draft (#155 overall)

YEAR	TEAM	LVL	AGE	W	L	SV	G	GS	IP	H	HR	BB/9	K/9	K	GB%	BABIP	WHIP	ERA	DRA-	WARP	MPH	FA%	Whiff%	CSP
2018	DAY	HI-A	24	6	3	0	17	17	96	95	6	2.7	7.7	82	47.1%	.308	1.29	4.03	98	0.6				
2019	CHA	AA	25	7	4	0	13	13	74²	63	4	2.7	7.6	63	56.8%	.277	1.14	3.38	86	0.7				
2019	LOU	AAA	25	4	8	0	14	13	71²	93	7	3.9	8.8	70	51.1%	.402	1.73	4.65	134	0.1				
2020	CIN	MLB	26	0	3	0	13	4	35¹	20	4	4.1	11.5	45	48.7%	.216	1.02	2.80	80	0.7	97.6	40.5%	34.4%	44.2%
2021 FS	CIN	MLB	27	9	8	0	26	26	150	134	20	4.1	9.2	152	50.3%	.286	1.35	4.20	92	1.7	97.6	40.5%	34.4%	44.2%
2021 DC	CIN	MLB	27	8	7	0	44	21	130	116	17	4.1	9.2	132	50.3%	.286	1.35	4.20	92	1.8	97.6	40.5%	34.4%	44.2%

Comparables: Scott Barlow, Jake Esch, Chase De Jong

Antone possesses Jake Arrieta's frame and beard but never really resembled a true power pitcher until training at the APEC facility in Texas during the 2019-20 offseason. The work he put in transformed his mundane two-seamer into a high-spin demon that can reach the high-90s, and his curveball and slider improved into plus offerings. Antone impressed in the spring, dominated in the Reds bullpen last summer and even made four starts. His strikeout rate was elite, though a few extra walks shoulder-surfed their way in and caused his numbers to be far better when he worked in relief. The Reds hope Antone can gain a little more command of his newfound arsenal and make another go at cracking the rotation, but at a minimum they've found a late-blooming and versatile weapon.

Brandon Bailey RHP
Born: 10/19/94　Age: 26　Bats: R　Throws: R　Height: 5'10"　Weight: 195　Origin: Round 6, 2016 Draft (#172 overall)

YEAR	TEAM	LVL	AGE	W	L	SV	G	GS	IP	H	HR	BB/9	K/9	K	GB%	BABIP	WHIP	ERA	DRA-	WARP	MPH	FA%	Whiff%	CSP
2018	FAY	HI-A	23	5	8	0	20	16	97²	69	6	4.0	10.4	113	37.9%	.270	1.15	2.49	52	3.2				
2018	CC	AA	23	1	0	1	5	1	24²	21	5	3.3	8.4	23	37.5%	.239	1.22	4.01	50	0.7				
2019	CC	AA	24	4	5	0	22	17	92²	72	12	4.0	10.0	103	36.4%	.268	1.22	3.30	86	0.8				
2020	HOU	MLB	25	0	0	0	5	0	7¹	6	1	3.7	4.9	4	31.8%	.238	1.23	2.45	127	0.0	93.5	61.9%	23.4%	48.2%
2021 FS	CIN	MLB	26	1	2	0	57	0	50	49	9	4.5	9.1	50	35.5%	.295	1.49	5.33	112	-0.2	93.5	61.9%	23.4%	48.2%
2021 DC	CIN	MLB	26	1	2	0	32	3	31	30	6	4.5	9.1	31	35.5%	.295	1.49	5.33	112	0.0	93.5	61.9%	23.4%	48.2%

Comparables: Tyler Wilson, Dane Dunning, Jonathan Holder

Nobody will be shocked to learn that Bailey's low-90s fastball plays up because of a high spin rate—an apparent prerequisite for Houston pitching prospects. What sets Bailey apart from most of the other bullpen debutants is the depth of his arsenal. He threw five distinct offerings in his brief glimpse of the majors, a relic from spending the majority of his pro career as a starter. He lacks the durability and efficiency to do so at the highest level, but he should go on bailing out other starters in multi-inning outings with his diverse range of looks.

Trevor Bauer RHP
Born: 01/17/91　Age: 30　Bats: R　Throws: R　Height: 6'1"　Weight: 205　Origin: Round 1, 2011 Draft (#3 overall)

YEAR	TEAM	LVL	AGE	W	L	SV	G	GS	IP	H	HR	BB/9	K/9	K	GB%	BABIP	WHIP	ERA	DRA-	WARP	MPH	FA%	Whiff%	CSP
2018	CLE	MLB	27	12	6	1	28	27	175¹	134	9	2.9	11.3	221	43.7%	.299	1.09	2.21	55	5.7	96.5	42.2%	31.5%	44.3%
2019	CLE	MLB	28	9	8	0	24	24	156²	127	22	3.6	10.6	185	39.3%	.278	1.21	3.79	96	1.9	96.7	41.2%	29.5%	44.0%
2019	CIN	MLB	28	2	5	0	10	10	56¹	57	12	3.0	10.9	68	33.5%	.321	1.35	6.39	112	0.1	96.2	45.3%	29.2%	44.2%
2020	CIN	MLB	29	5	4	0	11	11	73	41	9	2.1	12.3	100	35.4%	.215	0.79	1.73	81	1.4	96.2	47.8%	30.4%	43.6%
2021 FS	CIN	MLB	30	10	7	0	26	26	150	122	24	3.3	11.6	193	38.2%	.286	1.18	3.42	80	2.8	96.5	43.7%	30.1%	44.0%

Comparables: Jake Odorizzi, Julio Teheran, Kevin Gausman

Love him or hate him—and there are probably good reasons for both—Bauer is the most interesting player in today's game. His iconoclasm, his embrace and application of science and technology, his arrogance and his ceaseless trolling fit well in a world where nerd culture and social self-promotion are celebrated, and poorly in a game where old school stoicism has long been the example. Seeing Bauer ride the perhaps-not-that-mysterious increase in his spin rate to a Cy Young award made some feel like a lab-assisted Ivan Drago had unfairly knocked out Rocky Balboa, while others marveled that someone as human-scaled as Bauer could even compete in the ring, let alone dominate. But dominate he did, in a way that looks nothing like a fluke. Whatever your thoughts about his method or his madness, Bauer has constructed and mastered a devastating five-pitch arsenal and enters his 30s having been mostly healthy for seven straight years. That's an ace.

Jesse Biddle LHP
Born: 10/22/91　Age: 29　Bats: L　Throws: L　Height: 6'5"　Weight: 220　Origin: Round 1, 2010 Draft (#27 overall)

YEAR	TEAM	LVL	AGE	W	L	SV	G	GS	IP	H	HR	BB/9	K/9	K	GB%	BABIP	WHIP	ERA	DRA-	WARP	MPH	FA%	Whiff%	CSP
2018	GWN	AAA	26	0	0	1	4	0	6¹	3	0	1.4	11.4	8	23.1%	.231	0.63	0.00	48	0.2				
2018	ATL	MLB	26	6	1	1	60	0	63²	50	6	4.4	9.5	67	55.2%	.280	1.27	3.11	91	0.6	96.2	55.2%	25.9%	51.1%
2019	GWN	AAA	27	1	0	0	4	0	5¹	6	1	1.7	10.1	6	40.0%	.385	1.31	3.38	74	0.1				
2019	TEX	MLB	27	0	0	0	4	0	5¹	4	2	8.4	11.8	7	69.2%	.182	1.69	11.81	164	-0.2	94.4	41.7%	27.9%	49.3%
2019	ATL	MLB	27	0	1	0	15	0	11²	18	1	7.7	8.5	11	39.5%	.405	2.40	5.40	109	0.0	95.4	52.5%	23.5%	45.8%
2019	SEA	MLB	27	0	0	0	11	0	11	20	2	5.7	6.5	8	40.9%	.429	2.45	9.82	173	-0.4	95.3	64.6%	17.0%	47.3%
2020	CIN	MLB	28	0	0	0	1	0	0²	1	0	13.5	13.5	1	100.0%	.500	3.00	0.00	80	0.0	97.2	45.0%	11.1%	54.1%
2021 FS	CIN	MLB	29	2	3	0	57	0	50	48	7	5.1	8.9	49	47.3%	.303	1.54	4.97	108	-0.1	95.7	54.8%	23.4%	49.0%

Comparables: Jason Adam, Austin Brice, Caleb Smith

Biddle only made one appearance for the Reds before shoulder woes once again shelved him, the latest in a series of unfortunate events—including a hailstorm-induced concussion—that have derailed the former top prospect during a career most notable for its dogged perseverance. Having turned down a minor-league assignment, he'll have to persevere elsewhere.

Archie Bradley RHP
Born: 08/10/92　Age: 28　Bats: R　Throws: R　Height: 6'4"　Weight: 215　Origin: Round 1, 2011 Draft (#7 overall)

YEAR	TEAM	LVL	AGE	W	L	SV	G	GS	IP	H	HR	BB/9	K/9	K	GB%	BABIP	WHIP	ERA	DRA-	WARP	MPH	FA%	Whiff%	CSP
2018	ARI	MLB	25	4	5	3	76	0	71²	62	9	2.5	9.4	75	49.2%	.283	1.14	3.64	100	0.4	97.3	81.6%	20.4%	51.3%
2019	ARI	MLB	26	4	5	18	66	1	71²	67	5	4.5	10.9	87	45.5%	.341	1.44	3.52	94	0.6	97.3	69.6%	23.9%	46.8%
2020	CIN	MLB	27	2	0	6	16	0	18¹	17	1	1.5	8.8	18	39.2%	.320	1.09	2.95	88	0.3	95.6	65.9%	23.0%	48.8%
2021 FS	CIN	MLB	28	2	2	0	57	0	50	45	7	3.5	10.0	55	43.9%	.298	1.31	4.07	93	0.3	97.0	72.1%	22.8%	48.3%

Comparables: Randall Delgado, Matt Wisler, Brad Hand

Bradley was shipped from Arizona to Cincinnati at last year's trade deadline to help shore up the Reds bullpen and provided his new employers with exactly the sort of near-stellar production we've grown to expect from him. Bradley's mid-90s heater and low-spin curveball don't excite when judged against other late-inning relievers, but he sequences well, keeps the ball in the yard, deploys his changeup effectively against lefties and last year posted the lowest walk rate of his career. The former top prospect hasn't grown into a front-line starter or All-Star closer, but Bradley should continue to provide the sort of long-term, consistent late-inning competence every team craves. The Reds' decision to non-tender him speaks more of penury than performance.

Luis Castillo RHP Born: 12/12/92 Age: 28 Bats: R Throws: R Height: 6'2" Weight: 200 Origin: International Free Agent, 2012

YEAR	TEAM	LVL	AGE	W	L	SV	G	GS	IP	H	HR	BB/9	K/9	K	GB%	BABIP	WHIP	ERA	DRA-	WARP	MPH	FA%	Whiff%	CSP
2018	CIN	MLB	25	10	12	0	32	32	173²	164	28	2.6	8.8	169	46.4%	.288	1.23	4.40	106	1.1	97.8	57.2%	28.8%	49.0%
2019	CIN	MLB	26	15	8	0	32	32	190²	139	22	3.7	10.7	226	54.6%	.265	1.14	3.40	61	5.7	98.1	50.6%	35.9%	39.9%
2020	CIN	MLB	27	4	6	0	12	12	70	62	5	3.1	11.4	89	58.4%	.329	1.23	3.21	59	2.2	98.8	52.3%	32.8%	48.4%
2021 FS	CIN	MLB	28	10	7	0	26	26	150	120	16	3.6	10.6	176	54.2%	.285	1.20	3.20	73	3.3	98.2	52.5%	33.4%	44.3%
2021 DC	CIN	MLB	28	12	7	0	29	29	172	138	18	3.6	10.6	202	54.2%	.285	1.20	3.20	73	4.2	98.2	52.5%	33.4%	44.3%

Comparables: Aaron Nola, Danny Salazar, Nick Pivetta

There's no question that Castillo has top-shelf stuff that rivals any starter in the game. His fastball sits comfortably in the high 90s, his slider generates plenty of empty swings and his legendary changeup is effective against both righties and lefties. Yet Castillo has not yet put together an award-worthy effort to match the Coles, deGroms and Biebers that surround him on the swinging-strike leaderboard. Perhaps it's pitch selection, perhaps it's experience, perhaps it's just luck. Last spring our own Matthew Trueblood suggested a liberal application of the slider to help address his platoon issues and Castillo actually did break it out a little more often, but lefties slugged .583 against it. However that plays out in the long run, Castillo seems to be just one tweak away from making his whole at least equal to the sum of his parts. Once that happens the hardware will follow.

José De León RHP Born: 08/07/92 Age: 28 Bats: R Throws: R Height: 6'2" Weight: 215 Origin: Round 24, 2013 Draft (#724 overall)

YEAR	TEAM	LVL	AGE	W	L	SV	G	GS	IP	H	HR	BB/9	K/9	K	GB%	BABIP	WHIP	ERA	DRA-	WARP	MPH	FA%	Whiff%	CSP
2019	DUR	AAA	26	2	1	1	17	13	51¹	41	4	4.7	12.8	73	30.2%	.330	1.32	3.51	78	1.4				
2019	TB	MLB	26	1	0	0	3	0	4	3	0	6.8	15.8	7	44.4%	.333	1.50	2.25	63	0.1	94.8	57.5%	45.0%	49.5%
2020	CIN	MLB	27	0	0	0	5	0	6	6	1	16.5	15.0	10	42.9%	.385	2.83	18.00	95	0.1	96.9	69.3%	37.7%	43.4%
2021 FS	CIN	MLB	28	3	3	0	57	0	50	44	8	4.8	10.5	58	35.1%	.292	1.43	4.85	104	0.0	96.3	66.0%	39.7%	45.1%
2021 DC	CIN	MLB	28	3	3	0	41	6	63	56	11	4.8	10.5	73	35.1%	.292	1.43	4.85	104	0.3	96.3	66.0%	39.7%	45.1%

Comparables: Ben Lively, Daniel Mengden, Dinelson Lamet

De León survived his Tommy John surgery in a literal sense, but his career remains in critical condition after walking almost a third of the batters he faced last year; he still can crank out mid-90s fastballs and Bugs Bunny changeups, but until he regains some sense of where they're going he's not going anywhere.

Edgar Ernesto Garcia RHP Born: 10/04/96 Age: 24 Bats: R Throws: R Height: 6'1" Weight: 205 Origin: International Free Agent, 2014

YEAR	TEAM	LVL	AGE	W	L	SV	G	GS	IP	H	HR	BB/9	K/9	K	GB%	BABIP	WHIP	ERA	DRA-	WARP	MPH	FA%	Whiff%	CSP
2018	REA	AA	21	7	2	8	47	0	59²	45	6	3.8	10.3	68	38.7%	.264	1.17	3.32	56	1.6				
2019	LHV	AAA	22	2	1	8	25	0	29	15	4	2.5	11.8	38	29.5%	.193	0.79	2.48	41	1.2				
2019	PHI	MLB	22	2	0	0	37	0	39	38	11	6.0	10.2	44	32.7%	.300	1.64	5.77	119	-0.2	95.5	49.7%	32.1%	38.5%
2020	TB	MLB	23	0	0	1	4	0	3¹	3	2	10.8	2.7	1	27.3%	.111	2.10	10.80	148	-0.1	94.0	52.4%	16.7%	42.2%
2021 FS	CIN	MLB	24	1	1	0	57	0	50	47	9	5.3	9.6	53	34.8%	.290	1.54	5.19	113	-0.2	95.3	50.0%	30.3%	38.9%
2021 DC	CIN	MLB	24	1	1	0	29	0	31 ·	29	6	5.3	9.6	33	34.8%	.290	1.54	5.19	113	0.0	95.3	50.0%	30.3%	38.9%

Comparables: Joe Jiménez, Carter Capps, Chris Perez

Garcia is a young, hard-hurling reliever who has multiple option years remaining. It was perplexing, then, that the Phillies decided he was an expandable piece of their 40-player roster without so much as giving him an audition in the traveling house-of-horrors that was their 2020 bullpen. We'd joke that Garcia paid homage to his old teammates by giving up four runs in three innings with the Rays, but by the time you read this he'll probably have bumped his command grade enough to become a legitimate big-league reliever.

Amir Garrett LHP Born: 05/03/92 Age: 29 Bats: R Throws: L Height: 6'5" Weight: 239 Origin: Round 22, 2011 Draft (#685 overall)

YEAR	TEAM	LVL	AGE	W	L	SV	G	GS	IP	H	HR	BB/9	K/9	K	GB%	BABIP	WHIP	ERA	DRA-	WARP	MPH	FA%	Whiff%	CSP
2018	CIN	MLB	26	1	2	0	66	0	63	56	8	3.6	10.1	71	38.2%	.308	1.29	4.29	98	0.4	97.2	63.2%	32.0%	47.5%
2019	CIN	MLB	27	5	3	0	69	0	56	44	7	5.6	12.5	78	54.3%	.303	1.41	3.21	68	1.2	97.3	42.0%	39.0%	41.7%
2020	CIN	MLB	28	1	0	1	21	0	18¹	10	4	3.4	12.8	26	44.4%	.188	0.93	2.45	81	0.4	97.0	44.5%	43.7%	40.3%
2021 FS	CIN	MLB	29	2	2	23	57	0	50	41	6	4.6	11.5	64	45.1%	.293	1.33	3.94	87	0.5	97.2	48.2%	38.2%	42.9%
2021 DC	CIN	MLB	29	2	2	23	53	0	56	45	7	4.6	11.5	71	45.1%	.293	1.33	3.94	87	0.7	97.2	48.2%	38.2%	42.9%

Comparables: Dylan Covey, Adam Plutko, Steven Brault

Garrett uses a pitching mound the same way Clark Kent uses a phone booth. In goes the mild-mannered Amir and out comes AG, who pitches with intensity, passion and the best strikeout scream in baseball. AG can dominate same-side hitters with his lethal fastball/slider combo, allowing them just one single in 28 at-bats last year, but patient righty bats can feast on the occasional mistake, rendering him better suited to a set-up role than the ninth inning. AG's boisterous energy can be infectious between the lines, but Amir helped his teammates just as much in the clubhouse last summer by quietly sharing his experiences growing up Black in the United States. It's sometimes easy to forget that ballparks are ultimately a workplace, and both Amir and AG have important roles to play there.

Sonny Gray RHP   Born: 11/07/89   Age: 31   Bats: R   Throws: R   Height: 5'10"   Weight: 195   Origin: Round 1, 2011 Draft (#18 overall)

YEAR	TEAM	LVL	AGE	W	L	SV	G	GS	IP	H	HR	BB/9	K/9	K	GB%	BABIP	WHIP	ERA	DRA-	WARP	MPH	FA%	Whiff%	CSP
2018	NYY	MLB	28	11	9	0	30	23	130¹	138	14	3.9	8.5	123	50.5%	.327	1.50	4.90	111	0.4	95.2	57.2%	25.2%	45.1%
2019	CIN	MLB	29	11	8	0	31	31	175¹	122	17	3.5	10.5	204	50.5%	.259	1.08	2.87	61	5.3	94.9	50.5%	28.2%	42.7%
2020	CIN	MLB	30	5	3	0	11	11	56	42	4	4.2	11.6	72	51.9%	.290	1.21	3.70	75	1.3	94.5	55.4%	29.6%	42.6%
2021 FS	CIN	MLB	31	9	8	0	26	26	150	131	20	4.0	10.5	174	50.5%	.297	1.32	4.01	89	2.0	94.8	53.2%	28.0%	43.2%
2021 DC	CIN	MLB	31	11	8	0	29	29	166	145	22	4.0	10.5	193	50.5%	.297	1.32	4.01	89	2.7	94.8	53.2%	28.0%	43.2%

Comparables: Chris Archer, Jake Odorizzi, Zack Wheeler

New York is a notoriously tough place for men named Sonny, whether real or fictional. Sonny Corleone was ambushed at a tollbooth and brought down in a hail of gunfire. Sonny Red was jumped and murdered in his own basement by a crew led by Sonny Black, who was in turn betrayed by undercover FBI agent Joe Pistone. Sonny Gray's unfortunate Bronx sojourn didn't end quite so dramatically, but putting Yankee Stadium in his rear-view mirror has placed his career back in the fast lane. Since arriving in Cincinnati two seasons ago, Gray is once again pitching like the frontline starter he had been in Oakland. He uses five pitches to keep hitters off-balance, spotting sinkers and four-seamers in on the hands before getting righties to chase his slider low-and-away or fooling lefties with his hammer curve or the occasional *cambio*. Of course, the same pitches with a similar approach face-planted in pinstripes, so should the Reds be concerned Gray might suddenly turn back into a pumpkin? Fuhgeddaboudit.

Hunter Greene RHP   Born: 08/06/99   Age: 21   Bats: R   Throws: R   Height: 6'4"   Weight: 215   Origin: Round 1, 2017 Draft (#2 overall)

YEAR	TEAM	LVL	AGE	W	L	SV	G	GS	IP	H	HR	BB/9	K/9	K	GB%	BABIP	WHIP	ERA	DRA-	WARP	MPH	FA%	Whiff%	CSP
2018	DAY	LO-A	18	3	7	0	18	18	68¹	66	6	3.0	11.7	89	42.6%	.355	1.30	4.48	79	1.2				
2021													No projection											

Comparables: Kolby Allard, Roberto Osuna, Jordan Lyles

When Baseball Prospectus co-founder Gary Huckabay coined the term TINSTAAPP (There Is No Such Thing As A Pitching Prospect), he specifically had talented but untested high school pitchers like Greene in mind. Of course Greene absolutely exists, and absolutely is a pitching prospect, but the concern Huckabay was expressing about the high risks associated with drafting prep arms still apply. Since the Reds tabbed him with the second pick of the 2017 draft and decided his future lay on the mound rather than at shortstop, Greene has only thrown 73 professional innings before the combination of Tommy John surgery and Donny John plague sidelined him for more than two full seasons. The fireballing Californian should be lighting up radar guns again this summer, but there's still the matter of sorting out his secondaries, gaining command, mastering the art of pitch sequencing, conquering the upper minors and maintaining arm health before we'll know whether Greene's estimable stuff can ever shine in a big-league rotation.

Ryan Hendrix RHP   Born: 12/16/94   Age: 26   Bats: R   Throws: R   Height: 6'3"   Weight: 215   Origin: Round 5, 2016 Draft (#138 overall)

YEAR	TEAM	LVL	AGE	W	L	SV	G	GS	IP	H	HR	BB/9	K/9	K	GB%	BABIP	WHIP	ERA	DRA-	WARP	MPH	FA%	Whiff%	CSP
2018	DAY	HI-A	23	4	4	12	44	0	51	38	2	4.6	13.9	79	49.5%	.340	1.25	1.76	56	1.3				
2019	RED	ROK	24	1	0	0	4	2	5	1	0	0.0	14.4	8	44.4%	.111	0.20	0.00	10	0.3				
2019	CHA	AA	24	3	0	2	16	0	19¹	14	0	3.7	10.7	23	43.8%	.292	1.14	2.33	82	0.1				
2021 FS	CIN	MLB	26	1	1	0	57	0	50	43	8	5.1	10.5	58	41.6%	.289	1.44	4.72	105	0.0				
2021 DC	CIN	MLB	26	1	1	0	35	0	37	32	6	5.1	10.5	43	41.6%	.289	1.44	4.72	105	0.1				

Comparables: David Bednar, Stephen Nogosek, JD Hammer

Aggie alumnus Hendrix deploys mid-90s heat and a power curve in aid of the killer strikeout rates that portend success in a big league bullpen and the medium-bad walk rates that point to the middle innings.

Jeff Hoffman RHP   Born: 01/08/93   Age: 28   Bats: R   Throws: R   Height: 6'5"   Weight: 215   Origin: Round 1, 2014 Draft (#9 overall)

YEAR	TEAM	LVL	AGE	W	L	SV	G	GS	IP	H	HR	BB/9	K/9	K	GB%	BABIP	WHIP	ERA	DRA-	WARP	MPH	FA%	Whiff%	CSP
2018	ABQ	AAA	25	6	8	0	21	21	105²	105	9	4.0	8.7	102	44.1%	.334	1.44	4.94	89	1.6				
2018	COL	MLB	25	0	0	0	6	1	8²	15	0	7.3	5.2	5	53.1%	.469	2.54	9.35	161	-0.2	94.7	53.9%	18.5%	42.8%
2019	ABQ	AAA	26	6	8	0	17	16	85¹	105	19	3.2	10.3	98	42.4%	.363	1.58	7.70	113	1.0				
2019	COL	MLB	26	2	6	0	15	15	70	77	21	4.4	8.7	68	34.9%	.303	1.59	6.56	142	-0.9	95.6	58.8%	21.7%	47.7%
2020	COL	MLB	27	2	1	1	16	0	21¹	32	3	3.8	8.4	20	35.6%	.414	1.92	9.28	113	0.0	96.5	54.6%	22.2%	46.4%
2021 FS	CIN	MLB	28	2	2	0	57	0	50	51	10	3.9	8.5	47	38.5%	.297	1.46	5.44	115	-0.3	95.8	57.3%	21.7%	47.1%
2021 DC	CIN	MLB	28	2	2	0	47	0	50	51	10	3.9	8.5	47	38.5%	.297	1.46	5.44	115	-0.1	95.8	57.3%	21.7%	47.1%

Comparables: Daniel Mengden, Robert Stephenson, Erick Fedde

His combination of prolific prospect status and poor results may lead one to believe that Hoffman is a left-handed pitcher, and you would have good reason to think that—right-handers have eaten him alive like an elementary school tour of a Goldfish cracker factory. He's faced over 500 right-handed batters in the majors and they have a 1.000 OPS against him; nobody's ever been that bad against righties for that long as a fellow northpaw. The Rockies shifted him to mid-inning duties and it didn't help, because he throws the same fastball in those innings for batters to hammer all over the metropolitan area. Maybe he really is left-handed and forgot. He'll try to recall his handedness and one-time dominance in Cincinnati.

Nate Jones   RHP   Born: 01/28/86   Age: 35   Bats: R   Throws: R   Height: 6'5"   Weight: 230   Origin: Round 5, 2007 Draft (#179 overall)

YEAR	TEAM	LVL	AGE	W	L	SV	G	GS	IP	H	HR	BB/9	K/9	K	GB%	BABIP	WHIP	ERA	DRA-	WARP	MPH	FA%	Whiff%	CSP
2018	CHW	MLB	32	2	2	5	33	0	30	28	4	4.5	9.6	32	40.2%	.293	1.43	3.00	101	0.1	98.6	64.7%	30.7%	47.1%
2019	CHW	MLB	33	0	1	1	13	0	10¹	10	2	6.1	8.7	10	51.7%	.296	1.65	3.48	110	0.0	96.1	58.3%	25.9%	46.0%
2020	CIN	MLB	34	0	1	0	21	0	18²	25	5	2.9	11.1	23	40.0%	.400	1.66	6.27	97	0.2	97.4	53.5%	33.0%	46.3%
2021 FS	CIN	MLB	35	2	2	0	57	0	50	46	8	3.5	9.4	52	42.5%	.290	1.31	4.18	95	0.3	97.5	57.3%	30.9%	46.4%

Comparables: Brad Brach, Steve Cishek, Tyler Clippard

"Make 'em hit ya. Trust your stuff. Challenge 'em. Throw it over the plate." Sometimes listening to trusty pitching coach chestnuts like those can lead to pitchers posting greatly improved walk and strikeout rates, like Jones did last year. The downside is that letting your fastball sublet a studio in the heart of the zone can also lead to lots of hard contact, and the location heat map of Jones' mid-90s sinker last year looks like three eggs frying in the middle of an oversized skillet. Hitters laid off his slider and tattooed his two-seamer, spraying line drives all over the yard and over the fence. Jones still has stuff that can survive in a big-league bullpen, but only if he can remember how to work the edges.

Joel Kuhnel   RHP   Born: 02/19/95   Age: 26   Bats: R   Throws: R   Height: 6'4"   Weight: 280   Origin: Round 11, 2016 Draft (#318 overall)

YEAR	TEAM	LVL	AGE	W	L	SV	G	GS	IP	H	HR	BB/9	K/9	K	GB%	BABIP	WHIP	ERA	DRA-	WARP	MPH	FA%	Whiff%	CSP
2018	DAY	HI-A	23	1	4	17	44	0	53¹	54	2	1.9	9.4	56	51.0%	.347	1.22	3.04	73	0.8				
2019	CHA	AA	24	3	2	10	25	0	35²	26	5	2.0	7.6	30	39.4%	.212	0.95	2.27	66	0.6				
2019	LOU	AAA	24	2	1	4	16	0	18	13	1	4.0	10.0	20	37.8%	.273	1.17	2.00	70	0.5				
2019	CIN	MLB	24	1	0	0	11	0	9²	8	1	4.7	8.4	9	53.6%	.259	1.34	4.66	89	0.1	98.3	61.4%	29.4%	42.7%
2020	CIN	MLB	25	1	0	0	3	0	3	4	2	0.0	9.0	3	30.0%	.250	1.33	6.00	102	0.0	98.0	57.9%	15.8%	47.9%
2021 FS	CIN	MLB	26	2	3	0	57	0	50	49	8	3.0	7.9	43	39.8%	.291	1.33	4.38	100	0.1	98.2	60.2%	24.8%	44.4%

Comparables: Sam Tuivailala, Jensen Lewis, Bruce Rondón

Kuhnel is a Texas-sized Longhorn alum who strives to bait 'em with his mid-90s heat and hook 'em with his plus slider, but he'll need to improve his fastball command if he wants to target the big fish.

————————————— ★ ★ ★ *2021 Top 101 Prospect* **#57** ★ ★ ★ —————————————

Nick Lodolo   LHP   Born: 02/05/98   Age: 23   Bats: L   Throws: L   Height: 6'6"   Weight: 205   Origin: Round 1, 2019 Draft (#7 overall)

YEAR	TEAM	LVL	AGE	W	L	SV	G	GS	IP	H	HR	BB/9	K/9	K	GB%	BABIP	WHIP	ERA	DRA-	WARP	MPH	FA%	Whiff%	CSP
2019	BIL	ROK+	21	0	1	0	6	6	11¹	12	1	0.0	16.7	21	32.0%	.458	1.06	2.38	49	0.5				
2019	DAY	LO-A	21	0	0	0	2	2	7	6	0	0.0	11.6	9	50.0%	.333	0.86	2.57	69	0.1				
2021 FS	CIN	MLB	23	2	3	0	57	0	50	50	8	4.3	7.9	43	38.2%	.296	1.49	5.13	121	-0.5				

The lack of a minor league season was clearly an impediment to the development of young pitchers like Lodolo. On the bright side, it also means that Lodolo's 2019 debut numbers remain his only numbers, so his impeccable 30:0 career professional strikeout-to-walk ratio remains intact. Drafted out of TCU with the seventh-overall pick in 2019, Lodolo is a tall lefty with mid-90s heat, a sharp slider, a plus change and a proven ability to throw strikes. His combination of stuff and polish give him a high floor, and after spending a year with pitching coordinator Kyle Boddy and his Driveline techniques who knows what his ceiling might become.

Michael Lorenzen   RHP   Born: 01/04/92   Age: 29   Bats: R   Throws: R   Height: 6'3"   Weight: 220   Origin: Round 1, 2013 Draft (#38 overall)

YEAR	TEAM	LVL	AGE	W	L	SV	G	GS	IP	H	HR	BB/9	K/9	K	GB%	BABIP	WHIP	ERA	DRA-	WARP	MPH	FA%	Whiff%	CSP
2018	CIN	MLB	26	4	2	1	45	3	81	78	6	3.8	6.0	54	49.4%	.294	1.38	3.11	131	-0.8	97.2	51.5%	16.6%	48.6%
2019	CIN	MLB	27	1	4	7	73	0	83¹	68	9	3.0	9.2	85	44.3%	.274	1.15	2.92	77	1.4	98.4	35.8%	31.0%	44.2%
2020	CIN	MLB	28	3	1	0	18	2	33²	30	3	4.5	9.4	35	50.0%	.300	1.40	4.28	85	0.6	98.9	40.5%	35.5%	39.7%
2021 FS	CIN	MLB	29	9	8	0	26	26	150	136	19	4.0	9.1	151	47.8%	.291	1.35	4.10	91	1.9	98.3	40.9%	29.2%	43.8%
2021 DC	CIN	MLB	29	4	4	0	65	6	88	79	11	4.0	9.1	88	47.8%	.291	1.35	4.10	91	1.1	98.3	40.9%	29.2%	43.8%

Comparables: Drew VerHagen, Kevin McCarthy, Austin Brice

Lorenzen has spent six seasons in Cincinnati, but like a high school football player whose recruitment portfolio lists his position as "Athlete" the Reds are still working through how best to deploy him. He can play a credible center field and knows how to hit but the idea of Mikey Biceps becoming a true two-way player seems to have reached its expiration date. Instead Lorenzen has found success as a multi-inning reliever and spot starter, where his high-octane fastball and three secondaries miss just enough bats to overcome the occasional flurry of walks. Two successful starts down the stretch last year gave Lorenzen hope he can move back into the rotation, but the strapping Californian is best cast as a rubber-armed bullpen security blanket.

Tyler Mahle RHP Born: 09/29/94 Age: 26 Bats: R Throws: R Height: 6'3" Weight: 210 Origin: Round 7, 2013 Draft (#225 overall)

YEAR	TEAM	LVL	AGE	W	L	SV	G	GS	IP	H	HR	BB/9	K/9	K	GB%	BABIP	WHIP	ERA	DRA-	WARP	MPH	FA%	Whiff%	CSP
2018	LOU	AAA	23	2	1	0	5	5	29²	22	4	3.3	6.1	20	37.8%	.212	1.11	2.73	157	-0.7				
2018	CIN	MLB	23	7	9	0	23	23	112	125	22	4.3	8.8	110	37.6%	.329	1.59	4.98	140	-1.3	95.5	67.7%	24.1%	49.5%
2019	LOU	AAA	24	1	2	0	3	3	9	8	0	3.0	13.0	13	60.0%	.400	1.22	4.00	69	0.3				
2019	CIN	MLB	24	3	12	0	25	25	129²	136	25	2.4	9.0	129	47.0%	.308	1.31	5.14	98	1.3	95.8	56.7%	23.1%	49.1%
2020	CIN	MLB	25	2	2	0	10	9	47²	34	6	4.0	11.3	60	30.2%	.255	1.15	3.59	97	0.5	96.2	55.9%	33.8%	43.7%
2021 FS	CIN	MLB	26	9	8	0	26	26	150	139	25	3.0	9.9	165	39.1%	.295	1.26	4.18	93	1.7	95.9	59.0%	26.4%	47.6%
2021 DC	CIN	MLB	26	9	8	0	27	27	137	127	23	3.0	9.9	150	39.1%	.295	1.26	4.18	93	2.0	95.9	59.0%	26.4%	47.6%

Comparables: Reynaldo López, Jake Faria, Antonio Senzatela

Since arriving in Cincinnati four seasons ago Mahle has continually tinkered with his pitches and his process, and last year something seemed to click. In a series of adjustments best imagined as an up-tempo 80s training montage, Mahle rose before dawn, drank six raw eggs for breakfast, ditched his curve ball and cutter in favor of a new, sharp-breaking slider-cutter hybrid, somehow added significantly more spin to all his pitches and shocked the world. He was suddenly striking out more than a batter per inning, and his new breaker paired so well with the splitter Mahle deploys against lefty bats that he was able to erase his often ghastly platoon splits. Mahle also reverted to his extreme fly-ball tendencies yet managed to keep most of them in the yard, a combination that seems unlikely to continue in Cincinnati's bandbox. Taken together, even with a few more gopher balls thrown in, this latest version of Mahle should thrive in the middle of the rotation.

Wade Miley LHP Born: 11/13/86 Age: 34 Bats: L Throws: L Height: 6'2" Weight: 220 Origin: Round 1, 2008 Draft (#43 overall)

YEAR	TEAM	LVL	AGE	W	L	SV	G	GS	IP	H	HR	BB/9	K/9	K	GB%	BABIP	WHIP	ERA	DRA-	WARP	MPH	FA%	Whiff%	CSP
2018	BLX	AA	31	1	2	0	7	7	25¹	27	3	1.4	9.9	28	59.4%	.393	1.22	3.55	77	0.5				
2018	MIL	MLB	31	5	2	0	16	16	80²	71	3	3.0	5.6	50	50.4%	.274	1.21	2.57	92	1.1	93.4	20.0%	22.4%	42.3%
2019	HOU	MLB	32	14	6	0	33	33	167¹	164	23	3.3	7.5	140	49.1%	.289	1.34	3.98	111	0.6	92.8	21.9%	23.2%	42.6%
2020	CIN	MLB	33	0	3	0	6	4	14¹	15	1	5.7	7.5	12	52.3%	.326	1.67	5.65	109	0.1	92.7	14.0%	30.8%	39.6%
2021 FS	CIN	MLB	34	8	9	0	26	26	150	155	23	4.2	7.5	125	49.1%	.299	1.50	5.11	109	0.3	92.9	20.7%	23.9%	42.3%
2021 DC	CIN	MLB	34	7	8	0	24	24	121	125	18	4.2	7.5	101	49.1%	.299	1.50	5.11	109	0.7	92.9	20.7%	23.9%	42.3%

Comparables: Homer Bailey, Iván Nova, Tommy Milone

After the Cubs ambushed him for six runs in under two innings during his first Redlegs start, Miley limped off with a groin injury (insert joke here), returned to make three more starts before a bum wing cost him another month and limited him to two mop-up appearances down the stretch. That's not exactly the production Cincinnati hoped for when they signed the low-velo junkballer to solidify the end of their rotation. We all know what Miley is and what he isn't, and it's a coin flip whether his moxie and pitchability can induce enough ground balls to walk the razor's edge one more time.

Josh Osich LHP Born: 09/03/88 Age: 32 Bats: L Throws: L Height: 6'2" Weight: 235 Origin: Round 6, 2011 Draft (#207 overall)

YEAR	TEAM	LVL	AGE	W	L	SV	G	GS	IP	H	HR	BB/9	K/9	K	GB%	BABIP	WHIP	ERA	DRA-	WARP	MPH	FA%	Whiff%	CSP
2018	SAC	AAA	29	0	0	0	37	2	45¹	56	2	3.6	8.3	42	44.0%	.370	1.63	4.96	87	0.6				
2018	SF	MLB	29	0	0	0	12	0	12	20	2	5.2	7.5	10	45.2%	.450	2.25	8.25	148	-0.2	96.9	48.5%	27.4%	49.7%
2019	CHW	MLB	30	4	0	0	57	0	67²	62	15	2.0	8.1	61	41.3%	.260	1.14	4.66	92	0.6	96.3	16.9%	27.6%	48.7%
2020	CIN	MLB	31	1	1	0	17	1	18¹	21	6	2.5	11.8	24	54.5%	.306	1.42	6.38	81	0.4	94.2	37.5%	26.5%	48.7%
2021 FS	CIN	MLB	32	2	2	0	57	0	50	47	7	3.5	9.0	49	46.2%	.295	1.33	4.10	97	0.2	95.7	24.9%	27.3%	48.8%

Comparables: Hunter Strickland, Heath Hembree, Sam Freeman

Osich was a "trade-deadline addition" in only the strictest definition of the phrase. That the Cubs felt the need to surrender an asset for him served as an indictment of boh the market and the state of Chicago's bullpen. To his credit, he started missing bats at an above-average rate for the first time in his career. His DRA suggested he was better than his ERA, too. Even so, the Cubs mostly stashed him at the alternate site in lieu of giving him serious big-league burn, suggesting even they weren't sold on him being more than a depth piece. Then they designated him for assignment, suggesting it even more strongly.

Noé Ramirez RHP Born: 12/22/89 Age: 31 Bats: R Throws: R Height: 6'3" Weight: 205 Origin: Round 4, 2011 Draft (#142 overall)

YEAR	TEAM	LVL	AGE	W	L	SV	G	GS	IP	H	HR	BB/9	K/9	K	GB%	BABIP	WHIP	ERA	DRA-	WARP	MPH	FA%	Whiff%	CSP
2018	LAA	MLB	28	7	5	1	69	1	83¹	75	15	3.2	10.3	95	43.7%	.290	1.26	4.54	75	1.5	91.6	42.0%	27.9%	46.4%
2019	LAA	MLB	29	5	4	0	51	7	67²	59	9	2.7	10.5	79	38.1%	.299	1.17	3.99	79	1.1	90.6	28.4%	31.0%	47.0%
2020	LAA	MLB	30	1	0	0	21	0	21	15	2	3.9	6.0	14	39.3%	.220	1.14	3.00	113	0.0	90.1	36.0%	25.3%	44.2%
2021 FS	CIN	MLB	31	2	2	3	57	0	50	48	9	3.7	8.9	49	39.5%	.292	1.37	4.79	104	0.0	90.8	34.1%	28.8%	46.2%
2021 DC	CIN	MLB	31	2	2	3	47	0	50	48	9	3.7	8.9	49	39.5%	.292	1.37	4.79	104	0.2	90.8	34.1%	28.8%	46.2%

Comparables: Heath Hembree, Tommy Kahnle, Paul Sewald

In a September postgame appearance answering questions via Zoom, Anthony Rendon had his session crashed by Ramirez, who introduced himself as "your Mexican teammate here" and grilled Rendon on his choice of taco. Rendon gave a quintessentially Texan answer, answering with Steak Fajita (a Californian would say Carne Asada) and quipping, "Y'all put avocado on everything." By that description Ramirez has been the avocado of the Angels bullpen in recent seasons, popping up everywhere (151 innings between 2018-19) and adding a little something despite the continued protests of overuse by detractors. His barely 90 mph velocity is starting to tilt toward almost 90 mph, and the righty last season ceased outpacing his ERA by DRA after his strikeout rate plummeted. Falling out of favor with manager Joe Maddon despite ultimately good traditional stats, Ramirez twice went at least nine days between appearances. Every avocado goes brown a little faster than you think it's going to be.

Tony Santillan RHP   Born: 04/15/97   Age: 24   Bats: R   Throws: R   Height: 6'3"   Weight: 240   Origin: Round 2, 2015 Draft (#49 overall)

YEAR	TEAM	LVL	AGE	W	L	SV	G	GS	IP	H	HR	BB/9	K/9	K	GB%	BABIP	WHIP	ERA	DRA-	WARP	MPH	FA%	Whiff%	CSP
2018	DAY	HI-A	21	6	4	0	15	15	86²	81	5	2.3	7.6	73	42.3%	.302	1.19	2.70	105	0.2				
2018	PNS	AA	21	4	3	0	11	11	62¹	65	8	2.3	8.8	61	43.9%	.318	1.30	3.61	88	0.8				
2019	CHA	AA	22	2	8	0	21	21	102¹	110	8	4.7	8.1	92	32.8%	.342	1.60	4.84	118	-1.0				
2021 FS	CIN	MLB	24	2	3	0	57	0	50	50	9	5.2	7.8	43	37.3%	.286	1.58	5.72	121	-0.5				
2021 DC	CIN	MLB	24	2	3	0	40	4	56	56	10	5.2	7.8	48	37.3%	.286	1.58	5.72	121	-0.2				

Comparables: Touki Toussaint, Miguel Almonte, Jonathan Hernández

Let's hope the industrial-sized Santillan gets another opportunity to finally post a solid season in a Double-A rotation this summer; his fastball/slider combo can flash plus, but his iffy changeup will determine whether he's destined for the bullpen.

Lucas Sims RHP   Born: 05/10/94   Age: 27   Bats: R   Throws: R   Height: 6'2"   Weight: 225   Origin: Round 1, 2012 Draft (#21 overall)

YEAR	TEAM	LVL	AGE	W	L	SV	G	GS	IP	H	HR	BB/9	K/9	K	GB%	BABIP	WHIP	ERA	DRA-	WARP	MPH	FA%	Whiff%	CSP
2018	LOU	AAA	24	0	2	0	5	5	28¹	20	5	1.6	10.2	32	29.2%	.224	0.88	3.81	84	0.4				
2018	GWN	AAA	24	4	3	0	15	14	73	66	6	4.2	10.2	83	42.6%	.333	1.37	2.84	88	1.0				
2018	ATL	MLB	24	0	0	0	6	0	10¹	12	2	7.0	8.7	10	42.4%	.323	1.94	7.84	142	-0.2	94.8	55.7%	24.1%	37.4%
2018	CIN	MLB	24	0	0	0	3	0	5¹	3	1	8.4	10.1	6	23.1%	.167	1.50	6.75	80	0.1	94.0	55.0%	34.0%	49.3%
2019	LOU	AAA	25	5	0	0	16	16	79	69	9	4.1	11.6	102	31.0%	.324	1.33	4.56	71	2.5				
2019	CIN	MLB	25	2	1	0	24	4	43	31	8	4.0	11.9	57	25.3%	.256	1.16	4.60	88	0.6	95.3	50.6%	34.1%	40.7%
2020	CIN	MLB	26	3	0	0	20	0	25²	13	3	3.9	11.9	34	41.8%	.192	0.94	2.45	84	0.4	95.6	48.1%	35.2%	41.8%
2021 FS	CIN	MLB	27	2	2	11	57	0	50	41	8	4.4	11.3	62	35.5%	.289	1.32	4.29	93	0.3	95.4	50.0%	34.0%	41.3%
2021 DC	CIN	MLB	27	2	2	11	53	0	56	46	9	4.4	11.3	70	35.5%	.289	1.32	4.29	93	0.5	95.4	50.0%	34.0%	41.3%

Comparables: Robert Stephenson, Drew Anderson, Matt Wisler

"Be great at what you're good at" is Cincinnati's new pitching motto, and Sims has taken that to heart and found success in the Reds bullpen. The former Brave ditched his changeup and focused on increasing the spin on his already gyroscopic fastball and breakers, resulting in the debut of his unholy terror of a slurve. It darts under the hands of baffled lefties, plays peek-a-boo with righties and allows Sims to change eye levels by working his four-seamer up in the zone. His command is still fringy and gopher balls will always be a risk, but Sims has developed an arsenal that can work in the late innings.

Tyler Thornburg RHP   Born: 09/29/88   Age: 32   Bats: R   Throws: R   Height: 5'11"   Weight: 190   Origin: Round 3, 2010 Draft (#96 overall)

YEAR	TEAM	LVL	AGE	W	L	SV	G	GS	IP	H	HR	BB/9	K/9	K	GB%	BABIP	WHIP	ERA	DRA-	WARP	MPH	FA%	Whiff%	CSP
2018	WOR	AAA	29	0	1	0	15	1	12²	11	3	4.3	7.8	11	20.0%	.216	1.34	4.26	120	-0.1				
2018	BOS	MLB	29	2	0	0	25	0	24	28	6	3.8	7.9	21	37.3%	.319	1.58	5.62	111	0.0	94.4	55.6%	20.9%	46.2%
2019	OKC	AAA	30	0	0	0	12	0	12	11	3	6.8	11.2	15	22.6%	.286	1.67	6.00	81	0.3				
2019	WOR	AAA	30	0	2	0	11	1	10²	17	5	7.6	11.0	13	23.7%	.364	2.44	12.66	175	-0.2				
2019	BOS	MLB	30	0	0	0	16	0	18²	21	4	4.8	10.6	22	30.2%	.347	1.66	7.71	133	-0.2	95.1	55.0%	20.9%	43.6%
2020	CIN	MLB	31	0	0	0	7	0	7	6	0	6.4	12.9	10	23.5%	.353	1.57	3.86	91	0.1	94.8	57.2%	32.2%	46.2%
2021 FS	CIN	MLB	32	2	3	0	57	0	50	47	10	4.7	9.4	52	31.7%	.283	1.48	5.24	113	-0.2	94.8	55.7%	23.9%	45.0%

Comparables: Alex Colomé, Anthony Bass, Justin Grimm

Thornburg worked his way back from thoracic outlet surgery to post seven promising innings in the Cincinnati bullpen before breaking down again; he'll spend all of 2021 getting acquainted with the new ligament in his elbow.

MILWAUKEE BREWERS

Essay by Matt Trueblood

Player comments by Matt Trueblood and BP staff

Officially, the Milwaukee Brewers did not cease play on September 14; they continued on into the playoffs, until they were sent home by the eventual champion Los Angeles Dodgers in quick order. You can still forgive any Brewers fan who watched that day's action—a doubleheader against the St. Louis Cardinals—and walked away without optimism for the weeks ahead. That void of hope wasn't the team's results (they split the pair), but the play of Christian Yelich, Milwaukee's bellwether. Yelich went 1 for 8 with six strikeouts on the day. Both games ranked among his four worst of the season, as judged by Baseball Reference's Win Probability Added.

Seeing Yelich swing through Daniel Ponce de Leon fastballs was disheartening, but the day's enduring image was when he swung over a Genesis Cabrera breaking ball, his eyes drawn back to the catcher's mitt with his bat still pointed skyward. Yelich, as he started toward the dugout, signaled his own disappointment with a universal sign of frustration: he rotated his shoulders quickly—the way one might if they missed out on the lottery by a single digit, or if they forgot to tape their favorite show. He held the pose for several strides, until he was nearly out of view (and, in 2020 terms, off the stage).

It was that kind of year for both Yelich and the Brewers. Milwaukee reached the playoffs for a third year in a row but they did so on a technicality; through the generosity of the expanded postseason bracket, and a losing record. What's worse is they did it with the realization that baseball—and, indeed, life—can change quickly, and not always for the better. There are few better examples of that reality than Milwaukee's relationship with Yelich.

⚾   ⚾   ⚾

Too often these days, it feels as though big-league teams are forcing themselves to choose between being in the money-making business or being in the winning business. No one but billionaires thinks those two things are actually in conflict, but the distinction has defined seasons for a number of teams recently, and at times it can seem to define the league as a whole. The Brewers, as the smallest-market team (depending on how you count these things), ostensibly face

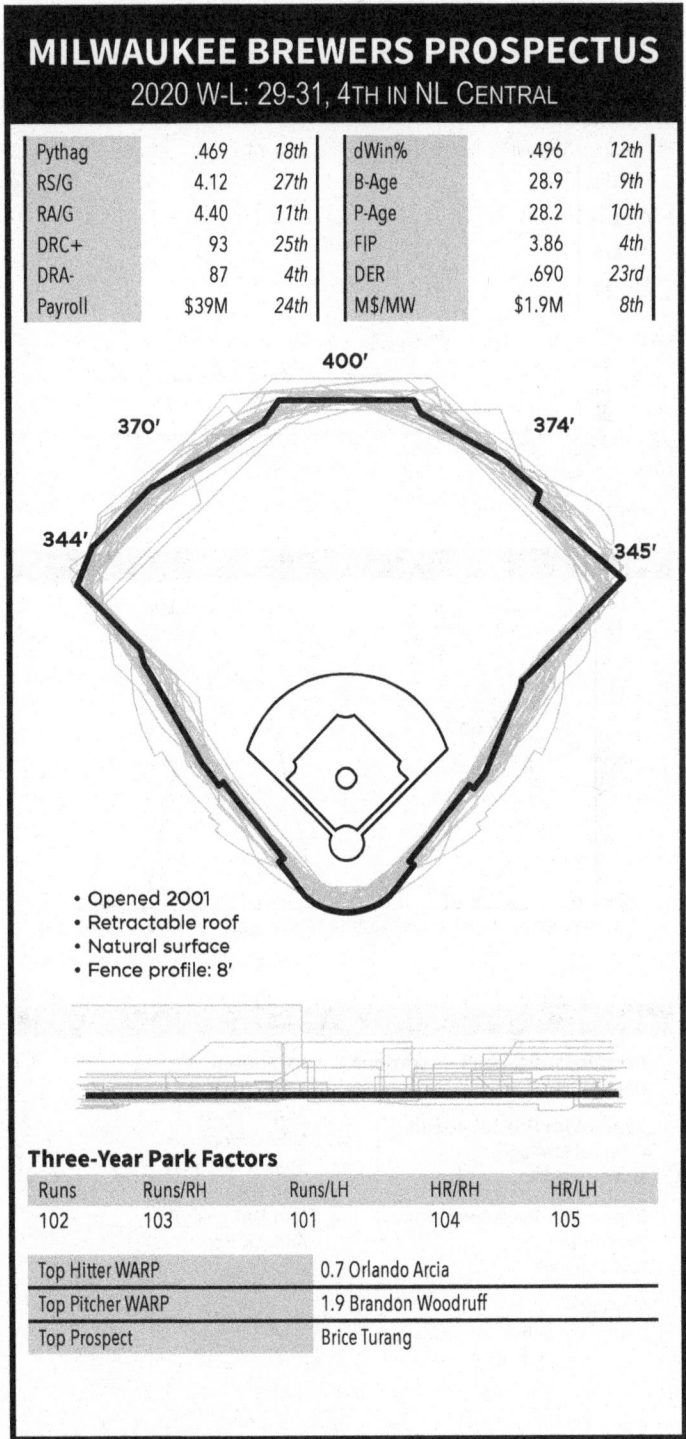

MILWAUKEE BREWERS PROSPECTUS
2020 W-L: 29-31, 4TH IN NL CENTRAL

Pythag	.469	18th	dWin%	.496	12th
RS/G	4.12	27th	B-Age	28.9	9th
RA/G	4.40	11th	P-Age	28.2	10th
DRC+	93	25th	FIP	3.86	4th
DRA-	87	4th	DER	.690	23rd
Payroll	$39M	24th	M$/MW	$1.9M	8th

400'
370'   374'
344'   345'

- Opened 2001
- Retractable roof
- Natural surface
- Fence profile: 8'

Three-Year Park Factors

Runs	Runs/RH	Runs/LH	HR/RH	HR/LH
102	103	101	104	105

Top Hitter WARP	0.7 Orlando Arcia
Top Pitcher WARP	1.9 Brandon Woodruff
Top Prospect	Brice Turang

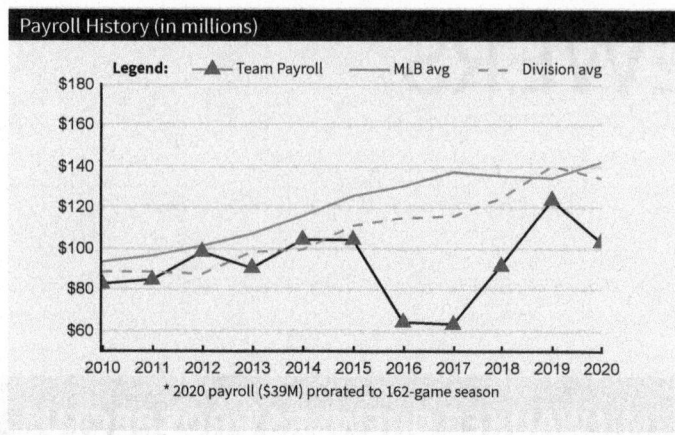

Payroll History (in millions)

Legend: ▲ Team Payroll — MLB avg - - Division avg

*2020 payroll ($39M) prorated to 162-game season

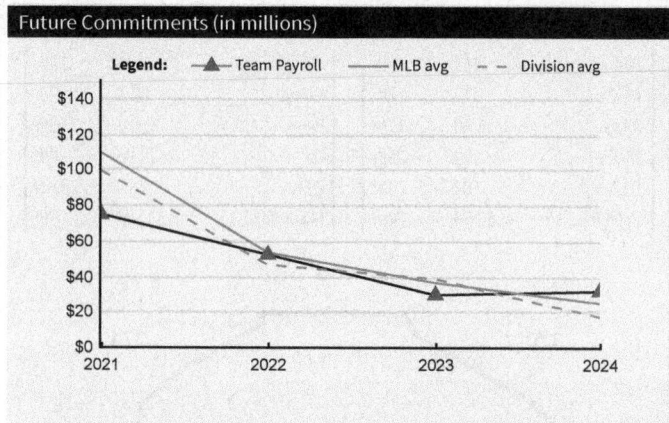

Future Commitments (in millions)

Legend: ▲ Team Payroll — MLB avg - - Division avg

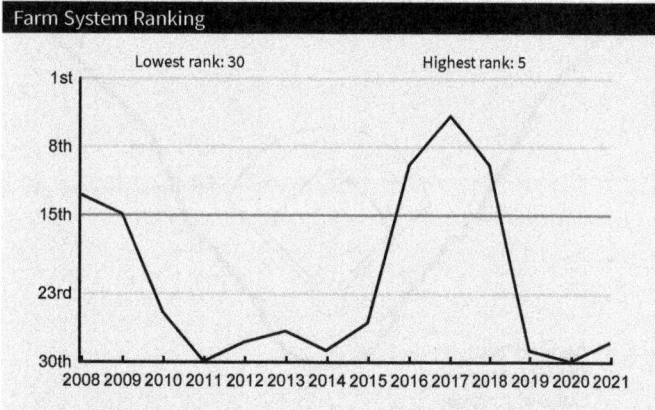

Farm System Ranking

Lowest rank: 30   Highest rank: 5

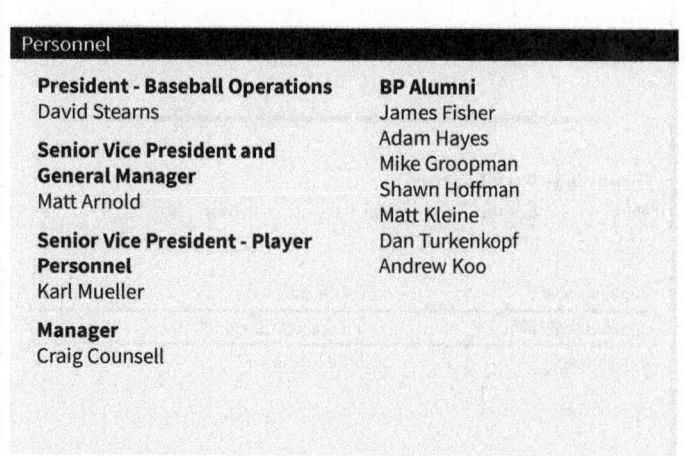

Personnel

President - Baseball Operations
David Stearns

Senior Vice President and General Manager
Matt Arnold

Senior Vice President - Player Personnel
Karl Mueller

Manager
Craig Counsell

BP Alumni
James Fisher
Adam Hayes
Mike Groopman
Shawn Hoffman
Matt Kleine
Dan Turkenkopf
Andrew Koo

as much pressure as anyone to choose one of those paradigms. Instead, since last March, they've staked out their own path by going all-in on the Christian Yelich business.

When president of baseball operations David Stearns acquired Yelich in January 2018, he and his front office paid a handsome price. Even at the time, it was clear that Yelich had untapped potential, but that wasn't the primary reason his price tag was so high. More than his relative youth or his athleticism or his impressive hard-hit rate, Yelich's contract made him the Marlins outfielder in the greatest demand. When the Brewers obtained the rights to his services, they did so for up to five seasons, at a total cost of no more than $58.25 million. Yelich's then-teammates, Giancarlo Stanton and Marcell Ozuna, were coming off MVP and career seasons—the kind of years teams could only hope for from Yelich. Yet Yelich had the highest trade value of the three, and brought the most back, because of finances.

One year later, Yelich had more than made good on his upside, with a historic second half that vaulted him to a well-deserved MVP award of his own. Another year on, he'd come within a fluke September injury of repeating, and yet the Brewers still had him under their control for three seasons at less than $42 million. This is why teams adore early-career extensions like the one to which the Marlins inked Yelich in March 2015: they create massive upside for the team, lend them cost certainty, and hardly ever lose value, except in the final year or two before an especially disappointing player hits free agency.

As great as Yelich had proved himself to be, he turned 28 prior to the 2020 season, meaning that he'd be 30 in 2022 and would effectively hit free agency at 31, after making $15 million that year. Even superstars are often in noticeable decline by the time they reach 31, and Yelich is a corner outfielder who (for all the other dazzling things about his prior two seasons) has already lost a step or two defensively. For a team operating on a purely cost- and flexibility-conscious model, letting Yelich play out the string on that deal would have been the obvious move.

Instead, the Brewers behaved in a proactive manner with Yelich, signing him to a new long-term contract roughly a week before the coronavirus pandemic shut the sport down. The new deal extended the Brewers' control of Yelich through 2029. It preserved his salaries for 2020 and 2021, but beginning in 2022 (when the Brewers had that $15-million option on him), it gave him a raise to $26 million per year. Yelich will make that much all the way through 2028, with a mutual option at the end of the deal worth another $20 million.

The contract hasn't kicked in yet, but the Brewers might already have some concerns.

Yelich's 2020 was its own kind of pain for a team so invested in a particular player. There's little reason to be overly concerned, but he struggled in a real way amid the bizarre circumstances of the season, and in his first action since suffering a fractured kneecap. He fanned nearly 31 percent of the time, so while he did hit into bad luck (his .259

batting average on balls in play was the lowest of his career by nearly 70 points despite a career-high exit velocity), one can't chalk his struggles up to that alone. The graceful, lethal swing he'd honed so perfectly over the previous two years, with its exquisitely-controlled violence, only showed up in flashes and he wasn't confident enough in it to trigger it with the necessary frequency. Too many deep counts inevitably led to strikeouts, and even though he hit the ball as hard as ever, there were too many counts in which that hard contact was impossible or easily defended.

Last season showed that, like other teams who have double-downed with a player whose first team-friendly contract turned out especially well (the Rays, with Evan Longoria; the Brewers themselves, with Ryan Braun; the Tigers, with Miguel Cabrera; the Nationals with Ryan Zimmerman; and others), the Brewers are especially exposed if Yelich turns downhill more quickly than expected. With the deferrals to which Yelich agreed, the Brewers will be making seven-figure payments to him at least into the early 2040s.

Last season also highlighted the conflict that will define the Brewers' next decade: Can they build a winner around Yelich, and, if so, how can they pull that off when neither their budget nor their farm system figures to offer relief?

⚾   ⚾   ⚾

The Brewers have made a habit out of flouting their abnormal tolerance for risk to maximize their chances: they've traded their last two competitive-balance draft picks for affordable big-league role players; they've dealt role players for unusually far-off players, clearing the low-dollar contracts attached to vets like Adam Lind and David Phelps, plus adding entry-level minor-leaguers (again) without paying their signing bonuses. Milwaukee will save a buck wherever they can, especially if it doesn't wholly short-circuit their competitive aspirations.

The trades they use to thread the needle of acquiring young players might be a bit offensive to our sensibilities, but the opportunity costs involved are minimal, and they've proved to be able to get real value out of those moves. They have operated, especially over the last two years, like a team deeply concerned with having good, young talent at hand, but far less so with boasting a top-ranked farm system. Their pipeline has some players, even now, who will sneak up on teams. They just don't have the prospect capital to pull off another Yelich-type deal. For most franchises, and certainly for this one, that's a once-in-a-generation trade. (Keeping that in mind helps one understand the team's decision to double down on their MVP in the first place.)

The Brewers, as a result, have to suffer risk in ways that other teams might take for granted. Keeping both Brandon Woodruff and Corbin Burnes in the starting rotation, given their profiles and the adversity each had encountered, looked like a bit of a stretch. The Brewers did it anyway and now they have two front-end starters with exceptional stuff.

In the bullpen, where they continue to tolerate and even foster certain things other teams would never permit, the team keeps finding gems. In 2020, that was Rookie of the Year winner Devin Williams, a frustrating, injury-hampered first-round pick who more than made good after learning a screwball. (He calls it a changeup.) Josh Hader continues apace at the back end, not quite at the levels of durability or brilliance he achieved when he first entered the majors, but still very much a dominating closer. The team still asks relievers to get more than three outs at an unusual rate (they ranked 11th in the majors in that regard); still embraces strange arm angles and deliveries and still seems to get more out of their pen than most of their rivals do, either in spite of or because of their risk tolerance.

One problem with Milwaukee's approach is that risks are deemed risks for a reason. We know from research (and from experience) that even the savviest risk taker fails—a lot. The Brewers sure did, so far as it pertained to their 2020 lineup. Hence Justin Smoak and Brock Holt being handed their walking papers before the season ended; hence Omar Narváez and Eric Sogard falling flat; hence waiver-claim Daniel Vogelbach being given a late-season opportunity. (The Brewers *did* hit on Jedd Gyorko, but they surprisingly declined his option to begin the winter.)

Another problem is that the Brewers' risks were almost certain to be low-yield. The exception was handing Avisaíl García a two-year pact worth $20 million (plus a club option) in exchange for the opportunity to see if Milwaukee could unlock his long-rumored upside. García's first season in town went poorly—he had his worst offensive showing in years—but at least there was a ceiling on the transaction. Too many of the Brewers' other gambles lacked one.

Moving forward, the need is obvious. The mandate is even more so. The question is: With few prospects to trade, will the Brewers have the guts to wade into free agency and make some expensive additions to their core? From a divisional perspective, this might be the ideal time for Milwaukee to push its chips to the middle: the Cardinals are aging; the Cubs and the Reds are bailing on competing; the Pirates are the Pirates. The Brewers are, not to be literal, the wild card.

Being in the Yelich business means making the most of his prime, which is happening right now. This team was aggressive in consecutive winters not so long ago, signing Cain to that five-year, $85-million deal the same year they traded for Yelich, then inking Yasmani Grandal and Mike Moustakas to bargain deals after 2018. That was during two historically frigid offseasons. The next few winters figure to be chilly as well, as the league adjusts to the impact the COVID-19 pandemic has had (and will have) on revenues while keeping a little in the coffers in case of a work stoppage in 2022.

Undeniably, the pandemic hurt every big-league team, and it hurt the Brewers even more than most. The team's local TV rights are not the bonanza others' are, making the team highly reliant on game-day revenues. The culture the club has created within its community has generally made that perfectly viable, but in a season without fans, they felt an especially acute pain.

Still, the uncertainty that waits around the bend presents the Brewers with an opportunity—the team that loves to take chances should embrace what other teams might consider to be the loftiest risk: spending money. Milwaukee has seemed to satisfy itself with taking a large number of small gambles, instead of being opportunistic and aiming high. That strategy is incompatible with the broader, Yelich-focused business model. The Brewers, then, would be wise to go back to the playbook that netted them Cain, Grandal, Moustakas and even Yelich himself.

The extraordinarily high floor for revenue set by national TV-rights deals; the promise of multiple effective, safe COVID-19 vaccines; and Yelich's new deal make the team's best way forward clear: spend some money, build a thunderous lineup around a player who might wear the ball-and-glove logo on a plaque in Cooperstown someday and take advantage of a soft NL Central over the next half-decade. Milwaukee shouldn't be in the business of doing anything less. ∎

—Matthew Trueblood is an author of Baseball Prospectus.

HITTERS

Orlando Arcia SS   Born: 08/04/94   Age: 26   Bats: R   Throws: R   Height: 6'0"   Weight: 187   Origin: International Free Agent, 2010

YEAR	TEAM	LVL	AGE	PA	R	2B	3B	HR	RBI	BB	K	SB	CS	Whiff%	AVG/OBP/SLG	DRC+	BABIP	BRR	FRAA	WARP
2018	RMV	AAA	23	96	16	5	1	2	8	10	15	2	1		.341/.417/.494	130	.397	2.3	SS(22): 3.9	1.3
2018	MIL	MLB	23	366	32	16	0	3	30	15	87	7	4	28.9%	.236/.268/.307	58	.305	2.0	SS(116): 3.8	0.4
2019	MIL	MLB	24	546	51	16	1	15	59	43	109	8	5	24.6%	.223/.283/.350	74	.253	-0.7	SS(150): -2.3	0.5
2020	MIL	MLB	26	189	22	10	1	5	20	14	32	2	0	23.2%	.260/.317/.416	96	.292	-0.4	SS(57): 3.2, P(2): -0.0, CF(1): -0.1	0.7
2021 FS	MIL	MLB	26	600	61	23	2	16	65	41	122	11	4	25.0%	.240/.295/.382	86	.279	-0.5	SS 7	1.5
2021 DC	MIL	MLB	26	576	58	22	2	15	63	39	117	11	4	25.0%	.240/.295/.382	86	.279	-0.5	SS 6	1.5

Comparables: Jason Donald, JT Riddle, Leo Cardenas

"Insofar as the clutch hitter is not a sportswriter's myth, he is a vulgarity, like a writer who writes only for money," John Updike wrote in his only published work about baseball. What Arcia's career supposes is, maybe it isn't. Updike, after all, was writing about Ted Williams; the only way for Williams to elevate his game in clutch moments would have been to focus less than he might have in other, lesser moments since pitchers always gave Williams their best when the game was on the line. For Arcia, it's different. If he's giving his usual focus to a big moment, he might gain an edge over pitchers, because their minds are often on the better hitters on the other side of the lineup card. That, perhaps, is how Arcia so often seems to ambush hurlers in high-leverage situations, and how he has (for instance) slugged .568 for his postseason career. (Or, maybe it's blind luck. Either way, he made huge strides at bat in 2020, counterbalancing his defensive decline.)

Ryan Braun LF   Born: 11/17/83   Age: 37   Bats: R   Throws: R   Height: 6'2"   Weight: 205   Origin: Round 1, 2005 Draft (#5 overall)

YEAR	TEAM	LVL	AGE	PA	R	2B	3B	HR	RBI	BB	K	SB	CS	Whiff%	AVG/OBP/SLG	DRC+	BABIP	BRR	FRAA	WARP
2018	MIL	MLB	34	447	59	25	1	20	64	34	85	11	5	22.8%	.254/.313/.469	107	.274	-0.8	LF(93): -4.9, 1B(18): -0.4, RF(1): -0.2	0.8
2019	MIL	MLB	35	508	70	31	2	22	75	34	105	11	1	24.5%	.285/.343/.505	110	.325	0.7	LF(110): -7.1, RF(2): -0.2	1.4
2020	MIL	MLB	37	141	14	7	1	8	26	7	27	1	0	29.1%	.233/.281/.488	106	.232	-1.2	RF(20): 0.6, 1B(1): -0.0	0.3
2021 FS	MIL	MLB	37	600	72	29	1	26	80	46	136	13	4	25.1%	.249/.314/.452	106	.286	1.0	LF -10, 1B 0	1.2

Comparables: George Foster, Matt Holliday, Ryan Klesko

This is, in all likelihood, the valedictory comment for Ryan Braun. He'll remain a controversial figure, but he could absolutely rake, and he is the enduring symbol of an era in which the Brewers returned to regular contender status.

Lorenzo Cain CF   Born: 04/13/86   Age: 35   Bats: R   Throws: R   Height: 6'2"   Weight: 214   Origin: Round 17, 2004 Draft (#496 overall)

YEAR	TEAM	LVL	AGE	PA	R	2B	3B	HR	RBI	BB	K	SB	CS	Whiff%	AVG/OBP/SLG	DRC+	BABIP	BRR	FRAA	WARP
2018	MIL	MLB	32	620	90	25	2	10	38	71	94	30	7	17.8%	.308/.395/.417	121	.357	4.3	CF(138): 2.1	4.5
2019	MIL	MLB	33	623	75	30	0	11	48	50	106	18	8	19.1%	.260/.325/.372	87	.301	1.0	CF(143): -1.6	1.2
2020	MIL	MLB	34	21	4	1	0	0	2	3	2	0	0	22.2%	.333/.429/.389	104	.375	0.2	CF(5): 0.2	0.1
2021 FS	MIL	MLB	35	600	70	24	1	12	57	51	117	20	5	18.8%	.268/.340/.392	104	.322	3.8	CF 4	3.1
2021 DC	MIL	MLB	35	576	67	23	1	12	55	49	112	19	5	18.8%	.268/.340/.392	104	.322	3.7	CF 4	3.0

Comparables: Roberto Kelly, Torii Hunter, Dave Henderson

Cain said that when he opted out of the balance of the season on August 1, it was not only out of fear of COVID-19 but also with a desire to re-establish his faith. It's not a bad idea for the aging center fielder to give a little faith just now; going forward, he'll need to get some from teams. Since 2007, the only center fielders to qualify for the batting title at age 35 or older are Brett Gardner and Mike Cameron. Cain had a season in 2019 that demonstrated why it's so rare for an aging player to stick in center, and now he's set to turn 35 without having had a chance to redeem himself.

Mario Feliciano C   Born: 11/20/98   Age: 22   Bats: R   Throws: R   Height: 6'1"   Weight: 200   Origin: Round 2, 2016 Draft (#75 overall)

YEAR	TEAM	LVL	AGE	PA	R	2B	3B	HR	RBI	BB	K	SB	CS	Whiff%	AVG/OBP/SLG	DRC+	BABIP	BRR	FRAA	WARP
2018	CAR	HI-A	19	165	20	7	1	3	12	13	59	2	0		.205/.282/.329	53	.318	0.5	C(25): -0.6	-0.5
2019	CAR	HI-A	20	482	62	25	4	19	81	29	139	2	1		.273/.324/.477	118	.351	-5.1	C(61): -0.4	1.7
2021 FS	MIL	MLB	22	600	58	25	3	14	59	35	188	2	0		.214/.268/.351	70	.295	1.5	C -1	0.2
2021 DC	MIL	MLB	22	67	6	2	0	1	6	3	21	0	0		.214/.268/.351	70	.295	0.2	C 0	0.0

Comparables: Wilin Rosario, Wilson Ramos, Nick Williams

Without full, competitive games against other teams' affiliates, minor-league catchers didn't get the chance to work on managing the flow of a game, situational pitch-calling or other nuances. On the other hand, they did get extra time with a select set of pitchers, and the opportunity to develop a rapport and familiarity with them that might otherwise take years to establish. Feliciano took advantage of the latter in 2020, drawing rave reviews from several hurlers while showing off his very good, power-centric offensive game. Most young prospects saw their roads to the majors elongated by the lost minor-league season; Feliciano might have shortened his.

Ben Gamel LF   Born: 05/17/92   Age: 29   Bats: L   Throws: L   Height: 5'11"   Weight: 177   Origin: Round 10, 2010 Draft (#325 overall)

YEAR	TEAM	LVL	AGE	PA	R	2B	3B	HR	RBI	BB	K	SB	CS	Whiff%	AVG/OBP/SLG	DRC+	BABIP	BRR	FRAA	WARP
2018	TAC	AAA	26	94	19	8	3	1	16	10	12	4	0		.349/.415/.554	135	.394	2.5	LF(8): -0.7, CF(6): -0.1, RF(1): -0.3	0.6
2018	SEA	MLB	26	293	37	14	4	1	19	31	60	7	3	21.0%	.272/.358/.370	98	.350	3.3	LF(48): -1.4, RF(40): -1.9, CF(4): 0.5	0.7
2019	MIL	MLB	27	356	47	18	0	7	33	40	104	2	2	22.6%	.248/.337/.373	81	.347	0.5	LF(70): -1.6, RF(23): 0.0, CF(22): -0.3	0.1
2020	MIL	MLB	28	127	13	8	1	3	10	13	39	0	2	28.6%	.237/.315/.404	82	.333	-1.9	RF(27): -2.0, CF(11): -0.9, LF(1): 0.1	-0.3
2021 FS	MIL	MLB	29	600	62	24	3	13	57	57	168	5	2	23.9%	.239/.317/.372	88	.325	2.0	LF -5, RF -2	0.2

Comparables: Jason Grabowski, Eric Valent, Danny Walton

Gamel was one of the great line-drive machines in baseball in 2020, with a league-leading 60 percent of his batted balls carrying a launch angle between 0 and 30 degrees. Unfortunately, he managed that in conjunction with the sudden, disastrous spike in strikeout rate he'd begun in 2019. A patient hitter, he got slightly more aggressive, but he guessed wrong too often and his swing became grooved. Pitchers predictably found the holes. He also dealt with a balky quadriceps muscle all year, resulting in an alarming loss of speed that further limited him. In 2021, his challenges will be to avail himself of good health by continuing to square up the ball—and to make more contact on the edges of the zone.

Avisaíl García RF   Born: 06/12/91   Age: 30   Bats: R   Throws: R   Height: 6'4"   Weight: 250   Origin: International Free Agent, 2007

YEAR	TEAM	LVL	AGE	PA	R	2B	3B	HR	RBI	BB	K	SB	CS	Whiff%	AVG/OBP/SLG	DRC+	BABIP	BRR	FRAA	WARP
2018	CHA	AAA	27	28	5	3	0	3	9	3	9	0	0		.360/.429/.840	130	.462	-0.3	RF(5): -0.2	0.0
2018	CHW	MLB	27	385	47	11	2	19	49	20	102	3	1	33.9%	.236/.281/.438	98	.271	-1.4	RF(87): 6.3	1.2
2019	TB	MLB	28	530	61	25	2	20	72	31	125	10	4	32.1%	.282/.332/.464	103	.340	-3.5	RF(92): -3.7, CF(12): 2.1	0.9
2020	MIL	MLB	29	207	20	10	0	2	15	20	49	1	3	34.7%	.238/.333/.326	93	.315	-0.7	CF(44): -8.9, RF(5): -0.2	-0.5
2021 FS	MIL	MLB	30	600	70	26	2	17	63	43	153	7	2	33.2%	.250/.317/.406	99	.316	-0.3	RF -1, CF 0	1.2
2021 DC	MIL	MLB	30	576	67	25	2	17	60	41	147	6	2	33.2%	.250/.317/.406	99	.316	-0.3	RF -1, CF 0	1.2

Comparables: Glenallen Hill, Sammy Sosa, Brennan Boesch

Baseball is most fun to watch when it froths with hustle. García keeps every game in which he plays agitated in just that way. His best physical comp might be mid-career Dave Winfield; it's hard to think of many others who were athletic enough to play the outfield well despite being built like a tight end. He accepted the job of replacing Cain after the veteran center fielder opted out of the season, and he was stretched as an everyday guy in center. Nevertheless, García absolutely barrels after balls, throws well and busts his ass out of the batter's box any time he smells an infield hit. He had a major power outage in 2020, and without the pop he'd finally found over the preceding seasons, he's back to being a second-division starter.

Eduardo Garcia SS   Born: 07/10/02   Age: 18   Bats: R   Throws: R   Height: 6'2"   Weight: 160   Origin: International Free Agent, 2019

YEAR	TEAM	LVL	AGE	PA	R	2B	3B	HR	RBI	BB	K	SB	CS	Whiff%	AVG/OBP/SLG	DRC+	BABIP	BRR	FRAA	WARP
2019	DSL BRW	ROK	16	40	6	2	0	1	3	6	9	1	1		.312/.450/.469		.409			
2021												No projection								

Garcia, a lanky and toolsy shortstop, held his own at the Brewers' alternate site—an impressive feat for a player born just after Milwaukee hosted the 2002 All-Star Game.

Jedd Gyorko 3B Born: 09/23/88 Age: 32 Bats: R Throws: R Height: 5'10" Weight: 205 Origin: Round 2, 2010 Draft (#59 overall)

YEAR	TEAM	LVL	AGE	PA	R	2B	3B	HR	RBI	BB	K	SB	CS	Whiff%	AVG/OBP/SLG	DRC+	BABIP	BRR	FRAA	WARP
2018	STL	MLB	29	402	49	19	1	11	47	44	77	2	0	25.2%	.262/.346/.416	109	.303	-1.2	3B(96): -4.8, 2B(17): 0.1, 1B(5): 0.1	1.3
2019	OKC	AAA	30	26	5	1	0	1	5	3	5	0	0		.273/.385/.455	89	.312	-0.8	1B(4): -0.2, 3B(2): -0.1	-0.1
2019	STL	MLB	30	62	5	0	0	2	7	6	14	2	0	28.5%	.196/.274/.304	78	.225	-0.1	3B(12): 0.5, 2B(2): 0.1, 1B(1): -0.0	0.1
2019	LAD	MLB	30	39	1	1	0	0	2	3	10	0	0	24.6%	.139/.205/.167	53	.192	-0.3	3B(9): 0.3, 1B(7): -0.8, 2B(1): 0.6	-0.1
2020	MIL	MLB	32	135	19	3	0	9	17	15	38	0	0	31.8%	.248/.333/.504	108	.278	0.2	1B(30): -1.7, 2B(11): 0.4, P(1): -0.0	0.4
2021 FS	MIL	MLB	32	600	69	20	1	27	79	57	160	3	1	28.3%	.238/.316/.432	103	.288	0.0	3B 5, 2B 1	2.1

Comparables: Jeff Kent, Neil Walker, Brian Dozier

In the majors, the margins in which a player's season is defined are so thin they can sometimes seem vanishing. That goes almost triple in a 60-game season. Gyorko hit batted balls at 100 or more miles per hour, with a launch angle between 0 and 35 degrees, in about 12 percent of his plate appearances in 2020. For the half-decade prior thereto, he fluctuated between 8 and 11 percent. The difference seems impossibly small because it is, but it led to the best OPS of Gyorko's career thanks in no small part to the small sample in question. (It doesn't hurt, though, that he also showed a bit better plate discipline and continued a recent streak of being well-liked in the clubhouse.) So much of Milwaukee's last offseason went wrong; inking Gyorko to a one-year deal with an option, however, qualified as a win, which is why their decision to decline said option was all the more puzzling.

Payton Henry C Born: 06/24/97 Age: 24 Bats: R Throws: R Height: 6'2" Weight: 215 Origin: Round 6, 2016 Draft (#171 overall)

YEAR	TEAM	LVL	AGE	PA	R	2B	3B	HR	RBI	BB	K	SB	CS	Whiff%	AVG/OBP/SLG	DRC+	BABIP	BRR	FRAA	WARP
2018	WIS	LO-A	21	389	44	15	2	10	41	38	124	1	3		.234/.327/.380	100	.335	-2.5	C(93): 1.4	1.1
2019	CAR	HI-A	22	482	49	22	1	14	75	26	142	1	1		.242/.315/.395	98	.324	-2.5	C(67): 2.4	1.4
2021 FS	MIL	MLB	24	600	54	26	2	15	60	38	229	0	0		.199/.266/.338	65	.309	-0.4	C -2, 1B 0	-0.5

Comparables: Eric Haase, Zach Green, Jose Lobaton

There's something pleasingly blue-collar about Henry's name. It fits a middle-tier catching prospect like a custom-made chest protector. Henry has made a name for himself, too, by making steady progress as both a powerful hitter and a sturdy, strong-armed receiver. Most middle-tier catching prospects end up being pulled off the shelves and dumped into the backup backstop bargain bin, though. Barring a swing and approach change focused on a quicker load and earlier, better swing decisions, Henry's profile (and his name) will both fit well there, too.

Keston Hiura 2B Born: 08/02/96 Age: 24 Bats: R Throws: R Height: 6'0" Weight: 202 Origin: Round 1, 2017 Draft (#9 overall)

YEAR	TEAM	LVL	AGE	PA	R	2B	3B	HR	RBI	BB	K	SB	CS	Whiff%	AVG/OBP/SLG	DRC+	BABIP	BRR	FRAA	WARP
2018	CAR	HI-A	21	228	38	16	3	7	23	14	47	4	6		.320/.382/.529	158	.386	0.6	2B(15): 0.6	1.5
2018	BLX	AA	21	307	36	18	2	6	20	22	56	11	5		.272/.339/.416	116	.323	0.6	2B(64): -3.5	0.5
2019	SA	AAA	22	243	44	16	1	19	46	23	64	7	2		.329/.407/.681	154	.389	0.0	2B(46): -1.6	2.1
2019	MIL	MLB	22	348	51	23	2	19	49	25	107	9	3	36.2%	.303/.368/.570	114	.402	-0.5	2B(81): -4.9	1.3
2020	MIL	MLB	24	246	30	4	0	13	32	16	85	3	2	42.6%	.212/.297/.410	97	.273	-0.2	2B(49): -5.6	0.0
2021 FS	MIL	MLB	24	600	73	24	3	24	75	40	197	8	3	39.6%	.242/.313/.437	104	.332	1.6	2B -6	2.0
2021 DC	MIL	MLB	24	576	70	23	3	23	72	38	189	7	3	39.6%	.242/.313/.437	104	.332	1.5	2B -6	1.7

Comparables: Mark Reynolds, Paul DeJong, Pedro Álvarez

It seemed reasonable, given Hiura's amateur and minor-league track record, to hope that his high rookie strikeout rate would be resolved by simple adjustments. A (shortened) season later, it's clear that more than tweaks and a moment to catch his breath will be required. Beaten consistently by high fastballs, Hiura has shown no facility for a shortened or secondary swing. Pitchers are able to exploit him as a result. He's clearly not going to add value as a defender, so going forward, his utility will depend on finding a more flexible approach and a more fluid set of mechanics in the box.

Cooper Hummel OF Born: 11/28/94 Age: 26 Bats: S Throws: R Height: 5'10" Weight: 198 Origin: Round 18, 2016 Draft (#531 overall)

YEAR	TEAM	LVL	AGE	PA	R	2B	3B	HR	RBI	BB	K	SB	CS	Whiff%	AVG/OBP/SLG	DRC+	BABIP	BRR	FRAA	WARP
2018	CAR	HI-A	23	404	51	25	0	8	50	63	93	3	1		.260/.397/.410	136	.339	-1.5	LF(28): -1.8, RF(23): -0.5, C(8): -0.4	1.0
2019	BLX	AA	24	419	62	8	5	17	56	62	100	4	7		.249/.384/.450	138	.301	-1.1	LF(75): 6.3, RF(4): 0.5	3.2
2021 FS	MIL	MLB	26	600	67	25	2	18	68	71	178	1	0		.224/.330/.392	100	.303	0.3	LF 5, C 0	2.4

Comparables: Fernando Perez, Steven Souza Jr., John Raynor

Looking for a developmental reset button, converted outfielder Cooper Hummel tried to slide back behind the plate in 2020. He might stick there this time, but only because teams will let almost anyone soak up innings at catcher in the minor leagues.

Tim Lopes 2B   Born: 06/24/94   Age: 27   Bats: R   Throws: R   Height: 5'11"   Weight: 180   Origin: Round 6, 2012 Draft (#191 overall)

YEAR	TEAM	LVL	AGE	PA	R	2B	3B	HR	RBI	BB	K	SB	CS	Whiff%	AVG/OBP/SLG	DRC+	BABIP	BRR	FRAA	WARP
2018	BUF	AAA	24	385	41	19	3	2	29	26	58	18	8		.277/.325/.364	107	.322	6.9	2B(69): 4.4, 3B(18): -1.0, LF(1): -0.1	1.9
2019	TAC	AAA	25	420	59	31	2	10	60	36	72	26	9		.302/.362/.476	98	.344	2.8	2B(63): -7.6, 3B(21): 0.8	0.9
2019	SEA	MLB	25	128	11	7	0	1	12	15	29	6	3	28.2%	.270/.359/.360	90	.354	0.2	LF(33): -0.2, 2B(3): 0.0, RF(3): -0.4	0.2
2020	SEA	MLB	26	151	16	12	0	2	15	6	34	5	0	29.5%	.238/.278/.364	81	.299	0.4	LF(17): -1.8, RF(12): 0.5, 3B(1): 0.0	-0.1
2021 FS	MIL	MLB	27	600	57	27	2	9	57	44	140	13	3	29.0%	.235/.298/.349	80	.298	3.0	3B 1, RF -4	0.2
2021 DC	MIL	MLB	27	237	22	10	1	3	22	17	55	5	1	29.0%	.235/.298/.349	80	.298	1.2	3B 0, RF -2	-0.1

Comparables: Mark Smith, Larry Bigbie, Tony Longmire

In a Mariners organization bursting with players who are just very, very excited for the opportunity, Lopes is perhaps their patron saint. He demonstrates no skills one would consider above-average for a major leaguer, and it's perfectly in keeping with his profile that his 2020 DRA (93) was better than his 2020 DRC+. Nonetheless, Lopes is one of those players bound to stick around the big leagues far longer than his skillset warrants, the Henry Cotto of our wearying times. Expect him to bounce around the outer rims of the MLB galaxy before inexplicably hitting a home run in an ALCS game and achieving folk hero status. Best guess here says it's for the Yankees. For now, he'll have to settle for playing for the Brewers following a December waiver claim.

Tristen Lutz OF   Born: 08/22/98   Age: 22   Bats: R   Throws: R   Height: 6'2"   Weight: 210   Origin: Round 1, 2017 Draft (#34 overall)

YEAR	TEAM	LVL	AGE	PA	R	2B	3B	HR	RBI	BB	K	SB	CS	Whiff%	AVG/OBP/SLG	DRC+	BABIP	BRR	FRAA	WARP
2018	WIS	LO-A	19	503	63	33	3	13	63	46	139	9	3		.245/.321/.421	114	.322	-0.9	RF(68): -11.4, LF(29): 1.9, CF(14): -2.9	-0.2
2019	CAR	HI-A	20	477	62	24	3	13	54	46	137	3	2		.255/.335/.419	108	.343	-1.5	CF(71): -3.0, RF(39): -2.4	0.9
2021 FS	MIL	MLB	22	600	55	27	3	16	63	36	214	2	1		.211/.268/.361	71	.309	0.3	CF -2, RF -6	-1.5

Comparables: Michael Saunders, Yorman Rodriguez, Jordan Schafer

A 2020 minor-league season likely would have seen Lutz reach Double-A, and thus face the superior arms who might fully exploit his strikeout-prone profile. Then again, it might also have seen him finally tap fully into his power, especially after offseason surgery to repair a sports hernia gave way to a strong spring training. Instead, Lutz languished at the alternate site, still swinging and missing too much but showing plenty of athletic ability and potential pop. His big test has been pushed back to 2021.

Luke Maile C   Born: 02/06/91   Age: 30   Bats: R   Throws: R   Height: 6'3"   Weight: 225   Origin: Round 8, 2012 Draft (#272 overall)

YEAR	TEAM	LVL	AGE	PA	R	2B	3B	HR	RBI	BB	K	SB	CS	Whiff%	AVG/OBP/SLG	DRC+	BABIP	BRR	FRAA	WARP
2018	TOR	MLB	27	231	22	13	1	3	27	25	67	2	0	30.6%	.248/.333/.366	84	.351	0.2	C(66): 9.5	1.7
2019	TOR	MLB	28	129	9	2	1	2	9	8	33	1	0	23.3%	.151/.205/.235	54	.190	-0.2	C(44): 7.2, P(2): -0.0	0.6
2021 FS	MIL	MLB	30	600	55	21	1	12	53	45	166	2	1	26.9%	.200/.269/.314	61	.263	0.1	C 15, 1B 0	1.0
2021 DC	MIL	MLB	30	67	6	2	0	1	5	5	18	0	0	26.9%	.200/.269/.314	61	.263	0.0	C 2	0.2

Comparables: Joel Skinner, Mike DiFelice, Paul Bako

The Brewers are the latest team seeking to score and allow fewer runs by employing Maile as their backup catcher. Has anybody ever seen Maile and Jeff Mathis in the same room? If not, can someone please check on Mathis?

YEAR	TEAM	P. COUNT	FRM RUNS	BLK RUNS	THRW RUNS	TOT RUNS
2018	TOR	9173	8.1	0.1	0.1	8.3
2019	TOR	6007	5.2	0.8	0.3	6.3
2021	MIL	2405	1.9	0.1	0.1	2.0

Mark Mathias 2B   Born: 08/02/94   Age: 26   Bats: R   Throws: R   Height: 6'0"   Weight: 200   Origin: Round 3, 2015 Draft (#93 overall)

YEAR	TEAM	LVL	AGE	PA	R	2B	3B	HR	RBI	BB	K	SB	CS	Whiff%	AVG/OBP/SLG	DRC+	BABIP	BRR	FRAA	WARP
2018	AKR	AA	23	476	65	25	3	8	45	59	94	11	2		.232/.338/.370	103	.277	-1.0	2B(105): 6.5, 1B(1): 0.0	1.3
2019	COL	AAA	24	478	62	31	2	12	59	51	91	13	2		.269/.355/.442	104	.314	1.7	2B(52): 1.7, 3B(47): -1.8, SS(3): -0.7	1.8
2020	MIL	MLB	26	36	2	3	0	0	4	0	7	1	0	24.6%	.278/.278/.361	83	.345	-0.4	RF(8): 0.6, LF(4): 0.1, 1B(1): 0.1	0.0
2021 FS	MIL	MLB	26	600	60	26	2	14	60	51	149	1	0	24.6%	.222/.302/.362	85	.279	0.4	2B 4, 3B -1	1.2
2021 DC	MIL	MLB	26	373	37	16	1	9	37	32	93	0	0	24.6%	.222/.302/.362	85	.279	0.2	2B 3, 3B -1	0.6

Comparables: Tug Hulett, Nick Franklin, Ian Kinsler

Middling. Mediocre. Milquetoast. Maybe Mathias deserves better than the connotations that go with those words, but they fit, both alliteratively and factually.

Garrett Mitchell OF   Born: 09/04/98   Age: 22   Bats: L   Throws: R   Height: 6'3"   Weight: 215   Origin: Round 1, 2020 Draft (#20 overall)

Milwaukee's extremely value-focused draft strategy paid off when Mitchell, inexplicably, slid all the way to the 20th pick. Though a collegiate position player faces pressure to demonstrate immediate polish and produce quickly, Mitchell has shown that capacity. He lacks power right now but has a swing that could eventually actualize it. He runs more than well enough to play center field for most of the next decade. A good approach and solid contact skills set a high floor for his offensive output. Particularly in the changing world of player development and Minor League Baseball, Mitchell should be a rapid riser.

Omar Narváez C Born: 02/10/92 Age: 29 Bats: L Throws: R Height: 5'11" Weight: 220 Origin: International Free Agent, 2008

YEAR	TEAM	LVL	AGE	PA	R	2B	3B	HR	RBI	BB	K	SB	CS	Whiff%	AVG/OBP/SLG	DRC+	BABIP	BRR	FRAA	WARP
2018	CHW	MLB	26	322	30	14	1	9	30	38	65	0	2	18.2%	.275/.366/.429	109	.330	0.0	C(85): -17.6	0.0
2019	SEA	MLB	27	482	63	12	0	22	55	47	92	0	0	22.6%	.278/.353/.460	123	.306	-1.5	C(98): -12.3, 2B(1): -0.0	2.3
2020	MIL	MLB	28	126	8	4	0	2	10	16	39	0	0	29.6%	.176/.294/.269	77	.254	-0.1	C(39): -0.4	0.3
2021 FS	MIL	MLB	29	600	64	21	1	17	64	67	139	1	0	23.5%	.249/.339/.393	101	.308	-0.4	C -8, 1B 0	1.6
2021 DC	MIL	MLB	29	271	29	9	0	7	29	30	62	0	0	23.5%	.249/.339/.393	101	.308	-0.2	C -5	0.6

Comparables: Jim Pagliaroni, Tim Hosley, Russell Martin

YEAR	TEAM	P. COUNT	FRM RUNS	BLK RUNS	THRW RUNS	TOT RUNS
2018	CHW	11337	-10.8	-4.6	-0.1	-15.6
2019	SEA	13812	-8.2	-4.3	-1.0	-13.5
2020	MIL	4886	4.2	0.1	0.1	4.4
2021	MIL	9620	-2.4	-1.1	-0.3	-3.7

In 2019, Narváez finished 31st (out of 33) in our holistic Catcher Defensive Adjustment. In 2020, this time out of 31, he finished first. First! What a happy turn of events, and exactly what he needed in order to go from disposable second-division starter (albeit one who hit .277/.362/.419 from 2017-19) to plausible All-Star Game participant. In a cruel twist of fate, Narváez's stick is what failed him last season. His bat speed stayed in quarantine, and he started striking out at an alarming rate, as well as generating much less authoritative contact when he did meet the ball. The good news: if you had to guess that only one of these transformations will stick in 2021, the better bet would be the defensive one. The bad news: it's still a gamble.

Jacob Nottingham C Born: 04/03/95 Age: 26 Bats: R Throws: R Height: 6'2" Weight: 220 Origin: Round 6, 2013 Draft (#167 overall)

YEAR	TEAM	LVL	AGE	PA	R	2B	3B	HR	RBI	BB	K	SB	CS	Whiff%	AVG/OBP/SLG	DRC+	BABIP	BRR	FRAA	WARP
2018	RMV	AAA	23	196	33	10	2	10	36	14	59	2	1		.281/.347/.528	95	.367	-0.6	C(32): -0.3, 1B(9): -0.0	0.3
2018	MIL	MLB	23	24	2	1	0	0	0	4	8	0	0	34.1%	.200/.333/.250	71	.333	-0.1	C(8): -0.5	0.0
2019	SA	AAA	24	332	40	21	0	5	40	28	95	6	1		.231/.313/.355	73	.318	-1.4	C(66): 11.7, 1B(8): 0.2	1.4
2019	MIL	MLB	24	7	1	0	0	1	4	0	2	0	0	30.8%	.333/.429/.833	96	.333		C(6): -0.3, 1B(1): -0.0	0.0
2020	MIL	MLB	25	54	8	1	0	4	13	5	20	0	0	38.3%	.188/.278/.458	82	.208	0.0	C(19): 0.7	0.4
2021 FS	MIL	MLB	26	600	63	24	1	19	62	44	203	1	0	37.1%	.208/.285/.370	79	.292	0.2	C 2, 1B 2	1.1
2021 DC	MIL	MLB	26	271	28	11	0	8	28	19	92	0	0	37.1%	.208/.285/.370	79	.292	0.1	C 1, 1B 1	0.3

Comparables: Max Ramirez, Josh Donaldson, Tyler Flowers

YEAR	TEAM	P. COUNT	FRM RUNS	BLK RUNS	THRW RUNS	TOT RUNS
2018	MIL	955	-0.7	0.2	0.0	-0.5
2018	RMV	4222	1.5	-1.1	-0.2	0.2
2019	MIL	163	0.0	-0.1		-0.1
2019	SA	9444	12.0	0.0	-0.9	11.1
2020	MIL	2326	1.6	0.0	0.0	1.6
2021	MIL	4810	0.6	0.9	0.2	1.7

Even the meanest foul tip to the mask won't leave one as reliably whiplashed or confused as trying to pin down Nottingham's ever-moving reputation as a prospect. Initially, he was a bat-first catcher, unlikely even to stick at that spot. Then, he and Brewers field coordinator and catching instructor Charlie Greene worked tirelessly together until he emerged as a solid defender—but suddenly, one without adequate punch. Now, there's some evidence that he's finding the (modestly) happy medium, He still has swing-and-miss issues at the plate and occasional lapses behind it, but he projects as a solid backup with positive tactical value.

Hedbert Perez OF Born: 04/04/03 Age: 18 Bats: L Throws: L Height: 5'10" Weight: 160 Origin: International Free Agent, 2019

Perez, a teenage toolshed, has big-league bloodlines and a ton of upside, which gave the Brewers both the confidence and the incentive needed to carry a very green prospect at their alternate site last summer.

Jace Peterson 3B Born: 05/09/90 Age: 31 Bats: L Throws: R Height: 6'0" Weight: 215 Origin: Round 1, 2011 Draft (#58 overall)

YEAR	TEAM	LVL	AGE	PA	R	2B	3B	HR	RBI	BB	K	SB	CS	Whiff%	AVG/OBP/SLG	DRC+	BABIP	BRR	FRAA	WARP
2018	BAL	MLB	28	235	21	13	2	3	28	30	55	13	2	24.2%	.195/.308/.325	76	.252	1.3	3B(35): 1.9, LF(21): -0.4, 2B(18): -0.5	0.2
2018	NYY	MLB	28	11	0	0	0	0	0	1	3	0	1	28.6%	.300/.364/.300	73	.429	-0.3	LF(2): -0.2, RF(1): -0.0	-0.1
2019	NOR	AAA	29	377	58	25	5	10	46	46	56	13	3		.313/.398/.512	130	.350	-0.9	3B(38): 1.2, 1B(26): 1.8, 2B(9): 2.6	2.7
2019	BAL	MLB	29	108	14	3	1	2	11	6	24	4	1	30.2%	.220/.269/.330	79	.267	0.7	LF(18): 3.3, 3B(9): -0.0, 2B(5): 0.7	0.5
2020	MIL	MLB	30	61	6	1	0	2	5	15	20	1	0	34.6%	.200/.393/.356	97	.292	-0.3	RF(13): -0.9, 1B(4): -0.0, 3B(4): 0.3	0.0
2021 FS	MIL	MLB	31	600	61	23	3	12	56	77	152	10	3	29.3%	.221/.327/.353	88	.288	1.5	3B 2, LF 3	1.4

Comparables: Damian Jackson, Daniel Descalso, Tony Graffanino

Long-ago first rounder Jace Peterson seems to have stalled out as a utility man playing on minor-league deals, but he did tweak his swing (more torque, better lift to the pull field) and approach (extreme patience) successfully.

Manny Piña C Born: 06/05/87 Age: 34 Bats: R Throws: R Height: 6'0" Weight: 222 Origin: International Free Agent, 2004

YEAR	TEAM	LVL	AGE	PA	R	2B	3B	HR	RBI	BB	K	SB	CS	Whiff%	AVG/OBP/SLG	DRC+	BABIP	BRR	FRAA	WARP
2018	MIL	MLB	31	337	39	13	2	9	28	21	62	2	0	18.3%	.252/.307/.395	90	.285	-3.6	C(92): 7.0, 1B(1): -0.0	1.6
2019	MIL	MLB	32	179	10	8	0	7	25	16	50	0	0	27.2%	.228/.313/.411	89	.284	-0.5	C(53): 8.3, 3B(1): -0.0	1.4
2020	MIL	MLB	33	45	4	1	0	2	5	3	11	0	0	27.6%	.231/.333/.410	100	.269	-0.2	C(13): 0.4	0.3
2021 FS	MIL	MLB	34	600	63	21	1	20	69	43	146	2	1	23.7%	.240/.310/.401	95	.290	-0.3	C 4, 1B 0	2.4
2021 DC	MIL	MLB	34	101	10	3	0	3	11	7	24	0	0	23.7%	.240/.310/.401	95	.290	-0.1	C 1	0.4

Comparables: Adam Melhuse, Damian Miller, John Buck

It seems lazy to compare Piña to a pineapple itself. He's stout, is tough and (in certain situations, given certain vulnerabilities) can deliver a jolt of unexpected pain in a couple of ways. He adds a bit of levity and passion to a clubhouse, does the dirty work required of a backup catcher with aplomb and has a balanced skill set on the field. He has to be used wisely to be valuable (keep pineapple off your pizzas, people!), but he's nice to have around. Plus, he too appeared in the background of every episode of *Psych*. (He didn't, but be honest: you wouldn't have known either way.)

YEAR	TEAM	P. COUNT	FRM RUNS	BLK RUNS	THRW RUNS	TOT RUNS
2018	MIL	12539	4.8	1.3	0.5	6.7
2019	MIL	6204	6.4	2.0	-0.1	8.3
2020	MIL	1750	1.0	0.1	-0.1	1.0
2021	MIL	3608	0.0	0.3	0.4	0.7

Corey Ray CF Born: 09/22/94 Age: 26 Bats: L Throws: L Height: 6'0" Weight: 196 Origin: Round 1, 2016 Draft (#5 overall)

YEAR	TEAM	LVL	AGE	PA	R	2B	3B	HR	RBI	BB	K	SB	CS	Whiff%	AVG/OBP/SLG	DRC+	BABIP	BRR	FRAA	WARP
2018	BLX	AA	23	600	86	32	7	27	74	60	176	37	7		.239/.323/.477	117	.303	0.5	CF(125): 1.8, LF(6): 1.4, RF(3): 0.5	2.4
2019	BLX	AA	24	46	5	3	0	0	0	6	14	3	2		.250/.348/.325	115	.385	0.1	CF(10): 1.6, LF(1): -0.2	0.4
2019	SA	AAA	24	230	23	8	0	7	21	20	89	3	1		.188/.261/.329	44	.283	-0.4	CF(41): -5.0, RF(8): -1.3, LF(2): -0.3	-1.2
2021 FS	MIL	MLB	26	600	57	26	3	14	55	48	226	15	5		.195/.265/.337	61	.300	1.9	CF 1, RF 1	-0.7
2021 DC	MIL	MLB	26	135	12	6	0	3	12	10	50	3	1		.195/.265/.337	61	.300	0.4	CF 0, RF 0	-0.2

Comparables: Melky Mesa, Tommy Pham, Keon Broxton

The Brewers were more secretive than most clubs about what happened at their alternate site, electing not to share data or video with other teams for scouting purposes and limiting what they shared via social media. Ray is one of the players who doesn't mind that. Now 26, the former top-five pick still has more first names than solid seasons in the minors, and his major flaws (an overly long swing and deficient pitch recognition) were in evidence even against his team's less-than-elite minor-league arms. He doesn't have another year of too many strikeouts and too few hits hanging on his résumé, but he's still a year closer to officially becoming a bust.

Eric Sogard 2B Born: 05/22/86 Age: 35 Bats: L Throws: R Height: 5'10" Weight: 180 Origin: Round 2, 2007 Draft (#81 overall)

YEAR	TEAM	LVL	AGE	PA	R	2B	3B	HR	RBI	BB	K	SB	CS	Whiff%	AVG/OBP/SLG	DRC+	BABIP	BRR	FRAA	WARP
2018	RMV	AAA	32	101	10	4	0	0	11	10	16	0	1		.225/.297/.270	62	.267	1.6	2B(18): 1.2, SS(5): 1.2	0.2
2018	MIL	MLB	32	113	7	3	0	0	2	12	23	3	0	12.6%	.134/.241/.165	72	.173	0.3	SS(24): 0.0, 2B(22): 0.1, LF(1): -0.2	0.1
2019	BUF	AAA	33	38	7	2	0	1	6	7	4	0	0		.267/.395/.433	118	.269	0.7	3B(5): 0.6, 2B(2): 0.4	0.3
2019	TB	MLB	33	119	14	6	0	3	10	9	16	2	0	12.1%	.266/.328/.404	104	.289	-0.1	2B(31): 0.7	0.5
2019	TOR	MLB	33	323	45	17	2	10	30	29	47	6	0	10.9%	.300/.362/.477	112	.326	3.0	2B(43): -1.4, 3B(6): 1.7, RF(6): 0.3	1.7
2020	MIL	MLB	34	128	10	5	0	1	10	11	20	0	0	9.1%	.209/.281/.278	92	.242	-0.1	3B(30): 4.3, 2B(9): 0.1, SS(7): -0.1	0.6
2021 FS	MIL	MLB	35	600	66	27	1	12	57	57	106	7	2	10.7%	.252/.329/.381	95	.293	-0.5	2B 3, SS 1	2.1

Comparables: Mike Gallego, Jerry Hairston, Bernie Allen

While the temptation to ascribe all of Sogard's power surge in 2019 to the aeroball is understandable, it was probably something closer to being within his control, yet further from being sustainable: good luck. He specializes in lowish but lofted line drives, balls that often fall in front of outfielders when hit softly but can split gaps or clear fences when he happens to really rip into a pitch. A pitcher must make a bad mistake in a bad count for Sogard to find that power. His 2020 line reflects some of the other kind of luck, though, and he's better than those numbers suggest. Alas, he's about to turn 35 and has dealt with nagging lower-leg injuries. There's a fair chance he might never again get to put his skills on full display.

Tyrone Taylor CF Born: 01/22/94 Age: 27 Bats: R Throws: R Height: 6'0" Weight: 194 Origin: Round 2, 2012 Draft (#92 overall)

YEAR	TEAM	LVL	AGE	PA	R	2B	3B	HR	RBI	BB	K	SB	CS	Whiff%	AVG/OBP/SLG	DRC+	BABIP	BRR	FRAA	WARP
2018	RMV	AAA	24	481	73	23	9	20	80	27	74	13	4		.278/.321/.504	98	.292	2.3	CF(56): 0.5, LF(39): 7.2, RF(26): 1.0	1.8
2019	SA	AAA	25	375	44	20	1	14	59	28	85	5	0		.269/.334/.461	92	.317	0.3	RF(47): 1.6, CF(43): 8.5, LF(5): 0.2	1.7
2019	MIL	MLB	25	12	1	2	0	0	1	1	1	0	0	12.5%	.400/.500/.600	88	.444	-0.4	RF(8): -0.1, CF(3): -0.3	0.0
2020	MIL	MLB	26	41	6	4	0	2	6	2	8	0	0	26.0%	.237/.293/.500	103	.250	-0.5	RF(10): -0.3, CF(9): -0.3, LF(2): -0.0	0.0
2021 FS	MIL	MLB	27	600	65	25	2	21	70	37	129	2	0	23.9%	.235/.293/.409	88	.269	0.9	RF 1, LF 0	1.0
2021 DC	MIL	MLB	27	203	22	8	0	7	23	12	43	0	0	23.9%	.235/.293/.409	88	.269	0.3	RF 0, LF 0	0.2

Comparables: Scott Cousins, Cole Garner, Carlos Moncrief

Taylor has great speed, and his compact frame and torque-heavy swing imply real power potential. He's also a solid if unspectacular defensive outfielder. Unfortunately, he still hasn't found consistent success at the upper levels, or in the big leagues. His swing is the thing: he has a complicated load, in which his hands come way down and his barrel tips a bit, and he doesn't seem able to get loft on his swing and deliver the barrel to the hitting zone on time as consistently as he might. Unless that changes, he'll be confined to a fourth-outfielder role. There are worse fates.

Brice Turang SS Born: 11/21/99 Age: 21 Bats: L Throws: R Height: 6'0" Weight: 173 Origin: Round 1, 2018 Draft (#21 overall)

YEAR	TEAM	LVL	AGE	PA	R	2B	3B	HR	RBI	BB	K	SB	CS	Whiff%	AVG/OBP/SLG	DRC+	BABIP	BRR	FRAA	WARP
2018	BRG	ROK	18	57	11	2	0	0	7	9	6	8	1		.319/.421/.362	156	.357	0.0	SS(12): 2.0	0.5
2019	WIS	LO-A	19	357	57	13	4	2	31	49	54	21	4		.287/.384/.376	141	.339	3.2	SS(43): 0.6, 2B(28): 0.9	3.2
2019	CAR	HI-A	19	207	25	6	2	1	6	34	47	9	1		.200/.338/.276	99	.268	1.6	SS(35): -2.6, 2B(5): -0.8	0.6
2021 FS	MIL	MLB	21	600	52	26	3	7	52	52	161	15	4		.234/.304/.336	78	.319	5.2	SS -2, 2B -2	0.4

Comparables: José Peraza, Asdrúbal Cabrera, Jorge Polanco

It's hard to be projected to become a regular, in this day and age, with power that could play at least a grade below average. That's the needle Turang is trying to thread, but he's unusually well-equipped for the task. He's small by 21st-century standards, but he has some explosiveness in all of his actions. He's likely to stick at shortstop for a while; he runs really well, and it's not showcase speed; he wreaks real havoc with his aggressiveness and savvy on the bases; and he also boasts a solid hit tool, including an advanced approach. Losing a full season of competitive reps might have a disproportionate effect on him, but Turang's feel for the game should help him overcome it.

Luis Urías 2B   Born: 06/03/97   Age: 24   Bats: R   Throws: R   Height: 5'9"   Weight: 186   Origin: International Free Agent, 2013

YEAR	TEAM	LVL	AGE	PA	R	2B	3B	HR	RBI	BB	K	SB	CS	Whiff%	AVG/OBP/SLG	DRC+	BABIP	BRR	FRAA	WARP
2018	ELP	AAA	21	533	83	30	7	8	45	67	109	2	1		.296/.398/.447	116	.373	1.4	2B(90): 10.2, SS(20): 3.4, 3B(11): 1.1	3.7
2018	SD	MLB	21	53	5	1	0	2	5	3	10	1	0	22.0%	.208/.264/.354	84	.216	0.3	2B(12): -0.2	0.1
2019	ELP	AAA	22	339	62	19	4	19	50	36	62	7	2		.315/.398/.600	124	.343	2.5	SS(53): 8.5, 2B(21): 4.1	3.8
2019	SD	MLB	22	249	27	8	1	4	24	25	56	0	1	23.6%	.223/.329/.326	83	.284	0.0	SS(41): -5.4, 2B(26): -1.7, 3B(1): -0.2	-0.2
2020	MIL	MLB	23	120	11	4	1	0	11	10	32	2	2	22.8%	.239/.308/.294	64	.338	-0.6	3B(30): 2.0, 2B(10): 1.7, SS(8): 0.4	0.0
2021 FS	MIL	MLB	24	600	66	21	3	12	59	62	132	1	0	23.2%	.252/.345/.378	103	.314	1.8	3B 1, 2B 1	2.8
2021 DC	MIL	MLB	24	576	63	20	3	11	56	59	126	1	0	23.2%	.252/.345/.378	103	.314	1.7	3B 1, 2B 1	2.1

Comparables: Dansby Swanson, Billy Consolo, Gene Alley

Calling 2020 a lost season for Urías might be too charitable. His athleticism and his feel to hit continued a two-year downward trend. No unexpected power showed up, and although some tweaks to his swing suggest he's searching for some, there's no real evidence that it's coming. Acquired as potentially a long-term, dynamic shortstop, he needs to fix mechanical and approach problems just to make his way back to being a solid everyday player. Even then, it might not be at short, after all.

Daniel Vogelbach 1B   Born: 12/17/92   Age: 28   Bats: L   Throws: R   Height: 6'0"   Weight: 270   Origin: Round 2, 2011 Draft (#68 overall)

YEAR	TEAM	LVL	AGE	PA	R	2B	3B	HR	RBI	BB	K	SB	CS	Whiff%	AVG/OBP/SLG	DRC+	BABIP	BRR	FRAA	WARP
2018	TAC	AAA	25	378	54	16	0	20	60	77	59	0	1		.290/.434/.545	165	.299	-6.0	1B(53): -2.9	1.8
2018	SEA	MLB	25	102	9	2	0	4	13	13	26	0	0	23.6%	.207/.324/.368	91	.246	0.6	1B(20): -1.1	0.0
2019	SEA	MLB	26	558	73	17	0	30	76	92	149	0	0	26.9%	.208/.341/.439	117	.232	-1.7	1B(57): -3.2	1.6
2020	MIL	MLB	28	67	13	2	0	4	12	8	18	0	0	22.5%	.328/.418/.569	102	.417	0.4	1B(2): 0.5	0.2
2020	SEA	MLB	28	64	3	1	0	2	4	11	13	0	0	22.1%	.094/.250/.226	104	.079	-0.3		0.1
2020	TOR	MLB	28	5	0	0	0	0	0	1	2	0	0	20.0%	.000/.200/.000	102	.000			0.0
2021 FS	MIL	MLB	28	600	75	22	1	26	77	95	158	0	0	25.5%	.242/.368/.450	123	.301	-0.6	1B -8	1.7
2021 DC	MIL	MLB	28	509	64	19	1	22	65	81	134	0	0	25.5%	.242/.368/.450	123	.301	-0.5	1B -7	1.5

Comparables: Tony Solaita, Carlos Delgado, Mike Napoli

The Internet has tried to adopt Vogelbach as an unapologetic beefy slugger, refusing to do anything but swing for the fences. His charisma and his all-over thickness make him seem a bit happy-go-lucky, but in reality, he's a 28-year-old hunk of waiver bait fighting like mad to become something more. In 2020, he implemented a secondary swing geared to take fastballs away to left field. It didn't generate a ton of hits, but it did bring down his whiff rate considerably. Vogelbach's patience, eagerness to use the whole field and big-time power makes him more promising than he should be at this stage of this career.

Christian Yelich RF   Born: 12/05/91   Age: 29   Bats: L   Throws: R   Height: 6'3"   Weight: 195   Origin: Round 1, 2010 Draft (#23 overall)

YEAR	TEAM	LVL	AGE	PA	R	2B	3B	HR	RBI	BB	K	SB	CS	Whiff%	AVG/OBP/SLG	DRC+	BABIP	BRR	FRAA	WARP
2018	MIL	MLB	26	651	118	34	7	36	110	68	135	22	4	23.0%	.326/.402/.598	143	.373	2.4	LF(90): -7.3, RF(75): 2.1, CF(20): 0.4	4.8
2019	MIL	MLB	27	580	100	29	3	44	97	80	118	30	2	28.3%	.329/.429/.671	166	.355	3.7	RF(124): -1.6, LF(6): 0.5, CF(1): -0.0	6.5
2020	MIL	MLB	29	247	39	7	1	12	22	46	76	4	2	33.6%	.205/.356/.430	107	.259	0.2	LF(51): -7.4	-0.1
2021 FS	MIL	MLB	29	600	87	24	3	29	80	83	162	15	3	28.7%	.267/.375/.497	134	.337	6.1	LF -9, CF 0	4.0
2021 DC	MIL	MLB	29	576	83	23	2	27	77	79	156	15	3	28.7%	.267/.375/.497	134	.337	5.9	LF -9	3.8

Comparables: Nolan Reimold, Greg Vaughn, Mike Young

If there's any player whose 2020 demands to be ignored, it would seem to be Yelich. He still hit the ball harder on average than almost anyone in baseball, and he still drew tons of walks. Most of his numbers can be explained away as bad luck in a shortened season, and for a prime-aged, MVP-caliber player with a broad skill set, that sort of dismissal seems to be in order. And yet...Yelich's swing was never quite right: he lost the ability to consistently generate loft; he whiffed on high, inside fastballs and low, outside breaking balls not only more often than he has in the past but at a truly disastrous rate; and he was slower on the bases and lousy in left field. It's easy to call it a lost season after a bifurcated spring training and with endless externalities dividing everyone's attention; it just doesn't quite explain this. Since Yelich will turn 30 in December, an explanation would be a big comfort.

Freddy Zamora SS   Born: 11/01/98   Age: 22   Bats: R   Throws: R   Height: 6'1"   Weight: 190   Origin: Round 2, 2020 Draft (#53 overall)

The Brewers rarely miss a chance to take a well-rounded position player with a high draft pick. It wasn't too surprising to see them jump on Zamora in the second round. He was available only because he missed the short-lived season due to a suspension and ACL injury. If you want to dream on him as an everyday shortstop, you have to do so by hoping his compact swing translates to healthy contact rates and a quick ascension through pro ball, because he's a bit undertooled in terms of both power and speed. His sure hands, good actions and above-average arm will outweigh those issues for only a few years, after which he's a second baseman or maybe a utility player. Still, that package suits what Milwaukee looks for pretty nicely.

PITCHERS

Brett Anderson LHP
Born: 02/01/88   Age: 33   Bats: L   Throws: L   Height: 6'4"   Weight: 230   Origin: Round 2, 2006 Draft (#55 overall)

YEAR	TEAM	LVL	AGE	W	L	SV	G	GS	IP	H	HR	BB/9	K/9	K	GB%	BABIP	WHIP	ERA	DRA-	WARP	MPH	FA%	Whiff%	CSP
2018	NAS	AAA	30	2	1	0	7	7	32¹	32	0	1.7	10.0	36	57.3%	.340	1.18	2.78	70	0.8				
2018	OAK	MLB	30	4	5	0	17	17	80¹	90	10	1.5	5.3	47	55.4%	.309	1.28	4.48	88	1.2	92.6	49.6%	17.1%	49.3%
2019	OAK	MLB	31	13	9	0	31	31	176	181	20	2.5	4.6	90	54.0%	.280	1.31	3.89	115	0.2	93.2	62.2%	17.1%	51.3%
2020	MIL	MLB	32	4	4	0	10	10	47	50	6	1.9	6.1	32	59.6%	.293	1.28	4.21	99	0.4	92.0	54.3%	19.7%	45.9%
2021 FS	MIL	MLB	33	8	9	0	26	26	150	163	20	2.7	6.1	102	56.2%	.299	1.39	4.54	107	0.5	92.8	58.4%	17.8%	49.7%

Comparables: Trevor Cahill, Jhoulys Chacín, Homer Bailey

Whenever Anderson pitches, you kind of wish you could just call it off and spare everyone the aggravation. He needs a good-sized zone, so if he's not getting calls early, tensions rise quickly between his team and the umpires. Hitters, meanwhile, spike a lot of helmets in regret just beyond first base as they try to tee off on a five-pitch assortment of borderline strikes that dive past their sweet spot, leading to weak groundouts. Then, finally, the lack of strikeouts catches up to Anderson, as a ball trickles through or finds a gap with runners aboard, and the southpaw stomps to the showers, muttering about the shift or modern pitcher usage or his crummy luck. It's no fun, but it keeps working just well enough that no one wants to say "uncle."

Aaron Ashby LHP
Born: 05/24/98   Age: 23   Bats: R   Throws: L   Height: 6'2"   Weight: 181   Origin: Round 4, 2018 Draft (#125 overall)

YEAR	TEAM	LVL	AGE	W	L	SV	G	GS	IP	H	HR	BB/9	K/9	K	GB%	BABIP	WHIP	ERA	DRA-	WARP	MPH	FA%	Whiff%	CSP
2018	HEL	ROK	20	1	2	1	6	3	20¹	18	3	3.5	8.4	19	48.3%	.273	1.28	6.20						
2018	WIS	LO-A	20	1	1	0	7	7	37¹	40	1	2.2	11.3	47	50.5%	.398	1.31	2.17	59	1.1				
2019	WIS	LO-A	21	3	4	0	11	10	61	47	4	4.1	11.8	80	48.9%	.319	1.23	3.54	91	0.5				
2019	CAR	HI-A	21	2	6	0	13	13	65	54	1	4.4	7.6	55	47.3%	.286	1.32	3.46	98	0.2				
2021 FS	MIL	MLB	23	2	3	0	57	0	50	47	7	5.3	8.5	47	44.9%	.287	1.54	5.06	118	-0.4				

Comparables: Patrick Sandoval, Cristian Javier, Brock Burke

Only halfway through the season did Ashby even get an invite to Milwaukee's alternate site, and he wasn't there to audition for a late-season cameo. Rather, the team brought him back (technically to an affiliate where he'd had success in 2019) to continue working with him on a four-pitch mix that packs real promise. He doesn't have front-of-the-rotation projection, but Ashby throws hard enough and repeats an easy delivery well enough to hope that he'll hone his command, get comfortable using all of his stuff and become an innings-eating southpaw. His slider is the pitch to watch; if or when it turns a corner, so will he.

Alec Bettinger RHP
Born: 07/13/95   Age: 25   Bats: R   Throws: R   Height: 6'2"   Weight: 210   Origin: Round 10, 2017 Draft (#294 overall)

YEAR	TEAM	LVL	AGE	W	L	SV	G	GS	IP	H	HR	BB/9	K/9	K	GB%	BABIP	WHIP	ERA	DRA-	WARP	MPH	FA%	Whiff%	CSP
2018	WIS	LO-A	22	5	4	0	12	11	62²	59	6	2.4	7.2	50	34.0%	.291	1.21	3.73	82	1.0				
2018	CAR	HI-A	22	1	6	0	13	12	54²	70	10	2.8	9.2	56	31.4%	.377	1.59	6.91	118	-0.1				
2019	BLX	AA	23	5	7	0	26	26	146¹	121	13	2.2	9.7	157	40.4%	.286	1.07	3.44	84	1.5				
2021 FS	MIL	MLB	25	2	3	0	57	0	50	49	8	3.8	8.2	45	39.2%	.289	1.41	4.85	111	-0.2				
2021 DC	MIL	MLB	25	2	3	0	24	6	46	45	8	3.8	8.2	41	39.2%	.289	1.41	4.85	111	0.1				

Comparables: Nabil Crismatt, Adam Conley, Cy Sneed

The Brewers probably didn't expect much from Bettinger when they selected him as a University of Virginia senior in the 10th round of the 2017 draft. He's since increased his velocity and proved he can command four pitches, suggesting he should have a big-league future.

Zack Brown RHP
Born: 12/15/94   Age: 26   Bats: R   Throws: R   Height: 6'1"   Weight: 199   Origin: Round 5, 2016 Draft (#141 overall)

YEAR	TEAM	LVL	AGE	W	L	SV	G	GS	IP	H	HR	BB/9	K/9	K	GB%	BABIP	WHIP	ERA	DRA-	WARP	MPH	FA%	Whiff%	CSP
2018	BRG	ROK	23	0	0	0	1	1	2	3	0	4.5	13.5	3	16.7%	.500	2.00	0.00	10	0.1				
2018	BLX	AA	23	9	1	0	22	21	125²	95	8	2.6	8.3	116	55.5%	.258	1.04	2.44	72	2.8				
2019	SA	AAA	24	3	7	0	25	23	116²	138	16	4.9	7.6	98	52.3%	.349	1.73	5.79	134	0.2				
2021 FS	MIL	MLB	26	2	3	0	57	0	50	48	8	4.2	7.6	42	50.5%	.280	1.43	4.74	113	-0.3				

Comparables: Erik Johnson, Ryan Helsley, Nabil Crismatt

Few pitchers make any kind of lasting mark in the majors after twice being left unprotected in the Rule 5 Draft. That said, Brown is better than almost anyone who meets that criterion. The Brewers' organizational philosophy about such decisions is one of the most aggressive in the majors, and since Brown had no opportunity to bounce back from a poor 2019 in competitive 2020 contests, the team rolled the dice to keep an extra spot on their 40-man roster. He did, by most accounts, have a productive summer at the club's alternate site, but that didn't answer the questions about his confidence or ability to throw strikes that cropped up in 2019. With a delivery long on effort and short on early stability, Brown doesn't project to develop starter-caliber control, and his stuff might tick up if he moves to the bullpen.

Corbin Burnes RHP Born: 10/22/94 Age: 26 Bats: R Throws: R Height: 6'3" Weight: 225 Origin: Round 4, 2016 Draft (#111 overall)

YEAR	TEAM	LVL	AGE	W	L	SV	G	GS	IP	H	HR	BB/9	K/9	K	GB%	BABIP	WHIP	ERA	DRA-	WARP	MPH	FA%	Whiff%	CSP
2018	RMV	AAA	23	3	4	0	19	13	78²	83	7	3.5	9.3	81	46.9%	.347	1.45	5.15	75	1.8				
2018	MIL	MLB	23	7	0	0	30	0	38	27	4	2.6	8.3	35	48.5%	.235	1.00	2.61	75	0.7	97.0	58.8%	32.0%	50.5%
2019	SA	AAA	24	0	1	0	8	7	22¹	29	2	3.6	10.1	25	48.5%	.409	1.70	8.46	76	0.6				
2019	MIL	MLB	24	1	5	1	32	4	49	70	17	3.7	12.9	70	44.1%	.424	1.84	8.82	102	0.3	97.7	56.8%	36.7%	45.6%
2020	MIL	MLB	25	4	1	0	12	9	59²	37	2	3.6	13.3	88	47.2%	.285	1.02	2.11	60	1.8	97.5	67.7%	34.8%	40.8%
2021 FS	MIL	MLB	26	10	7	0	26	26	150	120	18	4.0	11.6	193	45.7%	.293	1.25	3.50	81	2.7	97.5	63.2%	35.1%	43.4%
2021 DC	MIL	MLB	26	9	8	0	27	27	137	110	16	4.0	11.6	176	45.7%	.293	1.25	3.50	81	2.8	97.5	63.2%	35.1%	43.4%

Comparables: Michael Feliz, John Gant, Ryan Helsley

Home-run rates tend to even out from one season to the next, but if you even begin to read Burnes' breakout campaign as merely the good kind of regression, you'll miss out on a much richer, better and truer story. Blessed with a live arm that allows him to generate both velocity and spin, Burnes saw too many of his pitches flatten out and fly straight down the middle in 2019. He and the Brewers went to work before the season even ended, with bullpen coach Steve Karsay encouraging him as he took his first steps toward fixing his issues. Together, Burnes and the organization got him back to throwing a sinker, rather than a four-seamer, and he developed a truly filthy cutter. His 2020 was even more truncated than most, but he's found a pair of pitches with which he can miss bats, manage contact and throw enough strikes to keep hitters hacking.

J.P. Feyereisen RHP Born: 02/07/93 Age: 28 Bats: R Throws: R Height: 6'2" Weight: 215 Origin: Round 16, 2014 Draft (#488 overall)

YEAR	TEAM	LVL	AGE	W	L	SV	G	GS	IP	H	HR	BB/9	K/9	K	GB%	BABIP	WHIP	ERA	DRA-	WARP	MPH	FA%	Whiff%	CSP
2018	SWB	AAA	25	6	6	1	37	0	60	56	5	3.8	8.8	59	33.1%	.321	1.35	3.45	103	0.0				
2019	SWB	AAA	26	10	2	7	40	0	61¹	37	6	4.5	13.8	94	35.2%	.270	1.11	2.49	42	2.5				
2020	MIL	MLB	27	0	0	0	6	0	9¹	4	3	4.8	6.8	7	33.3%	.048	0.96	5.79	132	-0.1	94.6	54.0%	34.7%	39.3%
2021 FS	MIL	MLB	28	2	2	0	57	0	50	43	8	4.4	10.4	57	36.7%	.285	1.36	4.37	98	0.2	94.6	54.0%	34.7%	39.3%
2021 DC	MIL	MLB	28	2	2	0	42	0	45	39	7	4.4	10.4	52	36.7%	.285	1.36	4.37	98	0.3	94.6	54.0%	34.7%	39.3%

Comparables: Rowan Wick, Jake Barrett, Justin Shafer

With mid-90s rising heat and a pair of pitches that play off it well, Feyereisen just has to throw strikes to be an excellent reliever. (Alas.)

Dylan File RHP Born: 06/04/96 Age: 25 Bats: R Throws: R Height: 6'1" Weight: 205 Origin: Round 21, 2017 Draft (#624 overall)

YEAR	TEAM	LVL	AGE	W	L	SV	G	GS	IP	H	HR	BB/9	K/9	K	GB%	BABIP	WHIP	ERA	DRA-	WARP	MPH	FA%	Whiff%	CSP
2018	WIS	LO-A	22	8	10	0	25	25	136¹	152	15	1.8	7.5	114	39.1%	.336	1.32	3.96	89	1.7				
2019	CAR	HI-A	23	6	4	0	12	12	66¹	71	4	0.9	8.5	63	42.4%	.347	1.18	3.80	97	0.2				
2019	BLX	AA	23	9	2	0	14	14	80²	74	5	1.7	8.1	73	44.4%	.303	1.10	2.79	95	0.3				
2021 FS	MIL	MLB	25	2	2	0	57	0	50	51	8	2.7	7.2	40	42.7%	.288	1.32	4.58	109	-0.1				
2021 DC	MIL	MLB	25	2	2	0	18	6	38	38	6	2.7	7.2	30	42.7%	.288	1.32	4.58	109	0.2				

Comparables: Tyler Wilson, Tobi Stoner, Matt Bowman

He'll never rank as an elite prospect, but File is more than an anonymous face in a pitching crowd thanks to great control of a four-pitch mix.

Josh Hader LHP Born: 04/07/94 Age: 27 Bats: L Throws: L Height: 6'3" Weight: 180 Origin: Round 19, 2012 Draft (#582 overall)

YEAR	TEAM	LVL	AGE	W	L	SV	G	GS	IP	H	HR	BB/9	K/9	K	GB%	BABIP	WHIP	ERA	DRA-	WARP	MPH	FA%	Whiff%	CSP
2018	MIL	MLB	24	6	1	12	55	0	81¹	36	9	3.3	15.8	143	28.0%	.221	0.81	2.43	44	2.7	96.9	79.1%	39.4%	51.7%
2019	MIL	MLB	25	3	5	37	61	0	75²	41	15	2.4	16.4	138	22.0%	.232	0.81	2.62	45	2.6	97.6	84.1%	41.7%	50.7%
2020	MIL	MLB	26	1	2	13	21	0	19	8	3	4.7	14.7	31	26.5%	.161	0.95	3.79	89	0.3	96.4	67.8%	38.7%	44.8%
2021 FS	MIL	MLB	27	3	2	34	57	0	50	31	6	4.1	14.3	79	30.0%	.266	1.08	2.61	63	1.2	97.1	78.9%	40.4%	49.6%
2021 DC	MIL	MLB	27	3	2	34	55	0	58	36	7	4.1	14.3	92	30.0%	.266	1.08	2.61	63	1.5	97.1	78.9%	40.4%	49.6%

Comparables: Edwin Díaz, Tyler Glasnow, José Leclerc

Maybe it's impossible to sustain the level of dominance and utility Hader achieved in 2018. What we can say for sure is that it's impossible to sustain without a third reliable pitch or plus command. Hader remains a strikeout monster, but after two years fanning nearly half his opposing batters, his K rate slipped under 40 percent. Believing his troublesome vulnerability to homers in 2019 stemmed from throwing too many fastballs, he upped his slider usage. That just made the plate elusive, so he developed a walk problem. To make matters worse, his velocity and whiff rate also dipped. Hader's average plate appearance lasted 4.8 pitches, which accelerated his move into a traditional closer role. He got at least four outs 72 times in the first two-and-a-half seasons of his career; in 2020, he did that once. He's firmly among the ranks of the one-inning relievers now, even if he's better than most of them.

Adrian Houser RHP Born: 02/02/93 Age: 28 Bats: R Throws: R Height: 6'3" Weight: 222 Origin: Round 2, 2011 Draft (#69 overall)

YEAR	TEAM	LVL	AGE	W	L	SV	G	GS	IP	H	HR	BB/9	K/9	K	GB%	BABIP	WHIP	ERA	DRA-	WARP	MPH	FA%	Whiff%	CSP
2018	BLX	AA	25	0	1	0	8	8	26²	30	3	2.4	10.1	30	48.1%	.370	1.39	4.72	94	0.3				
2018	RMV	AAA	25	2	3	0	13	13	52	66	6	3.1	6.4	37	53.4%	.359	1.62	5.19	97	0.6				
2018	MIL	MLB	25	0	0	0	7	0	13²	13	0	4.6	5.3	8	39.5%	.302	1.46	3.29	112	0.0	96.1	66.4%	23.8%	44.7%
2019	SA	AAA	26	2	0	0	4	4	21¹	13	2	1.7	9.7	23	51.9%	.212	0.80	1.27	28	1.1				
2019	MIL	MLB	26	6	7	0	35	18	111¹	101	14	3.0	9.5	117	53.8%	.304	1.24	3.72	74	2.5	96.2	67.3%	24.3%	47.2%
2020	MIL	MLB	27	1	6	0	12	11	56	63	8	3.4	7.1	44	59.3%	.325	1.50	5.30	94	0.7	95.4	64.0%	22.5%	44.9%
2021 FS	MIL	MLB	28	9	8	0	26	26	150	143	17	3.6	8.4	140	55.1%	.296	1.35	4.23	96	1.4	95.9	65.9%	23.5%	46.1%
2021 DC	MIL	MLB	28	8	9	0	27	27	145	138	17	3.6	8.4	135	55.1%	.296	1.35	4.23	96	1.8	95.9	65.9%	23.5%	46.1%

Comparables: Aaron Slegers, Austin Voth, John Gant

Unfortunately famous for repeatedly vomiting behind the mound when called upon in relief, Houser held down his lunch (or disposed of it in proper receptacles) as a full-time starter in 2020. On balance, he might be better off as a puking penman. His sinker is a good pitch, but not such an overwhelming one as to let him turn the lineup card over or pitch effectively to lefties with it, and his secondary stuff is pedestrian. His lousy ERA was no fluke. As a reliever, though, the stuff works, so maybe he just needs a manager willing to bring a bucket with them to the mound when they bring him in with runners on base.

Antoine Kelly LHP Born: 12/05/99 Age: 21 Bats: L Throws: L Height: 6'6" Weight: 205 Origin: Round 2, 2019 Draft (#65 overall)

YEAR	TEAM	LVL	AGE	W	L	SV	G	GS	IP	H	HR	BB/9	K/9	K	GB%	BABIP	WHIP	ERA	DRA-	WARP	MPH	FA%	Whiff%	CSP
2019	BRB	ROK	19	0	0	0	9	9	28²	21	0	1.6	12.9	41	43.5%	.339	0.91	1.26	32	1.4				
2019	WIS	LO-A	19	0	1	0	1	1	3	5	2	12.0	12.0	4	44.4%	.500	3.00	18.00	153	-0.1				
2021 FS	MIL	MLB	21	2	3	0	57	0	50	46	8	4.9	9.3	51	40.0%	.292	1.48	4.89	116	-0.3				

It's easy to make bets on pitchers like Kelly with a second-round pick. If it doesn't pan out, you never look bad; if it does, you look awfully good. Right now, the Brewers look awfully good. Kelly continued to flash triple-digit heat, and he made plenty of the hoped-for strides in developing his slider and changeup at the club's alternate site in 2020. He's not going to knock on the door of the majors right away, but only because there's still time to dream on him as a flamethrowing three-pitch starter. If he does end up in a relief role, he'll be a terror—and soon.

Eric Lauer LHP Born: 06/03/95 Age: 26 Bats: R Throws: L Height: 6'3" Weight: 228 Origin: Round 1, 2016 Draft (#25 overall)

YEAR	TEAM	LVL	AGE	W	L	SV	G	GS	IP	H	HR	BB/9	K/9	K	GB%	BABIP	WHIP	ERA	DRA-	WARP	MPH	FA%	Whiff%	CSP
2018	LE	HI-A	23	0	0	0	1	1	3	3	0	3.0	12.0	4	50.0%	.500	1.33	0.00	83	0.0				
2018	ELP	AAA	23	2	1	0	4	4	21¹	13	1	3.8	9.3	22	46.3%	.231	1.03	2.53	135	-0.2				
2018	SD	MLB	23	6	7	0	23	23	112	127	15	3.7	8.0	100	35.8%	.336	1.54	4.34	117	0.1	93.7	57.8%	20.6%	51.5%
2019	SD	MLB	24	8	10	0	30	29	149²	158	20	3.1	8.3	138	40.5%	.318	1.40	4.45	99	1.5	94.1	53.0%	20.1%	51.6%
2020	MIL	MLB	25	0	2	0	4	2	11	17	2	7.4	9.8	12	21.1%	.417	2.36	13.09	162	-0.3	93.6	52.5%	29.1%	44.7%
2021 FS	MIL	MLB	26	9	9	0	26	26	150	149	25	3.4	8.4	140	37.1%	.294	1.37	4.68	105	0.6	93.9	54.1%	21.1%	50.9%
2021 DC	MIL	MLB	26	3	3	0	11	11	53	52	9	3.4	8.4	49	37.1%	.294	1.37	4.68	105	0.4	93.9	54.1%	21.1%	50.9%

Comparables: Ryan Borucki, Conner Menez, Andrew Suárez

Things just didn't click for Lauer in the early stages of the shortened season, and the Brewers seized an opportunity to look beyond 2020. Lauer's release point was a bit down in his four appearances. His cutter flattened out, his slider bled into his cutter and his changeup was lifeless. Still, it was four total appearances, and Lauer has a track record to suggest he'd have recovered. Before he could, the team sent him to their alternate site and never brought him back, even as they got desperate for starting pitching down the stretch. Lauer will have to attempt a total reset in 2021, which figures to be difficult, but the Brewers seem to prefer having avoided allowing him to become Super Two-eligible to having given him a longer look.

Max Lazar RHP Born: 06/03/99 Age: 22 Bats: R Throws: R Height: 6'3" Weight: 185 Origin: Round 11, 2017 Draft (#324 overall)

YEAR	TEAM	LVL	AGE	W	L	SV	G	GS	IP	H	HR	BB/9	K/9	K	GB%	BABIP	WHIP	ERA	DRA-	WARP	MPH	FA%	Whiff%	CSP
2018	HEL	ROK	19	3	3	0	14	14	68	74	7	2.0	7.3	55	43.2%	.313	1.31	4.37						
2019	BRG	ROK	20	0	1	0	3	3	6	4	0	0.0	15.0	10	27.3%	.364	0.67	1.50	18	0.3				
2019	WIS	LO-A	20	7	3	1	19	10	79	67	5	1.7	12.4	109	37.0%	.337	1.04	2.39	74	1.3				
2021 FS	MIL	MLB	22	2	3	0	57	0	50	46	7	3.0	8.6	47	35.9%	.283	1.26	3.94	100	0.1				

Comparables: Luis Perdomo, Demarcus Evans, Joe Musgrove

Projectable righty Lazar doesn't yet have a plus pitch or even average velocity or spin, but he's shown feel and could take off if the heat ticks up.

Josh Lindblom RHP Born: 06/15/87 Age: 34 Bats: R Throws: R Height: 6'4" Weight: 240 Origin: Round 2, 2008 Draft (#61 overall)

YEAR	TEAM	LVL	AGE	W	L	SV	G	GS	IP	H	HR	BB/9	K/9	K	GB%	BABIP	WHIP	ERA	DRA-	WARP	MPH	FA%	Whiff%	CSP
2020	MIL	MLB	33	2	4	0	12	10	45¹	42	6	3.2	10.3	52	27.5%	.316	1.28	5.16	111	0.1	91.5	35.1%	29.8%	42.9%
2021 FS	MIL	MLB	34	9	9	0	26	26	150	144	29	2.8	8.9	147	31.1%	.286	1.28	4.46	101	1.0	91.5	35.1%	29.8%	42.9%
2021 DC	MIL	MLB	34	8	9	0	27	27	137	132	26	2.8	8.9	135	31.1%	.286	1.28	4.46	101	1.3	91.5	35.1%	29.8%	42.9%

Comparables: Anthony Swarzak, Jared Hughes, Andrew Miller

There's danger in reading too much into any performance in 2020, because of everything from the length of the season to the circumstances under which it was played. Lindblom struggled in his reentry into Stateside baseball, but all of the reasons why he was attractive remained in evidence. His high-spin four-seamer opens up the top of the zone, though his mechanics make it a bit tough for him to consistently spot it there. He has a good cutter and two variants on his changeup, including a splitter that was instrumental to his KBO revival. His slider is a bit slurvy, but it works. He just needs better luck.

Freddy Peralta RHP Born: 06/04/96 Age: 25 Bats: R Throws: R Height: 5'11" Weight: 199 Origin: International Free Agent, 2013

YEAR	TEAM	LVL	AGE	W	L	SV	G	GS	IP	H	HR	BB/9	K/9	K	GB%	BABIP	WHIP	ERA	DRA-	WARP	MPH	FA%	Whiff%	CSP
2018	RMV	AAA	22	6	2	0	13	13	61	49	1	4.1	12.8	87	44.7%	.350	1.26	3.10	62	1.8				
2018	MIL	MLB	22	6	4	0	16	14	78¹	49	8	4.6	11.0	96	30.4%	.238	1.14	4.25	116	0.1	93.9	77.6%	26.9%	49.2%
2019	SA	AAA	23	0	0	0	4	0	7	4	0	3.9	21.9	17	25.0%	.500	1.00	1.29	11	0.4				
2019	MIL	MLB	23	7	3	1	39	8	85	87	15	3.9	12.2	115	31.6%	.343	1.46	5.29	101	0.6	97.1	78.4%	29.5%	49.7%
2020	MIL	MLB	24	3	1	0	15	1	29¹	22	2	3.7	14.4	47	33.3%	.333	1.16	3.99	67	0.8	95.4	65.8%	39.8%	40.9%
2021 FS	MIL	MLB	25	10	7	0	26	26	150	111	21	4.0	12.5	207	36.0%	.280	1.19	3.33	77	3.0	95.9	74.9%	31.6%	47.2%
2021 DC	MIL	MLB	25	5	4	0	58	9	95	70	13	4.0	12.5	131	36.0%	.280	1.19	3.33	77	1.9	95.9	74.9%	31.6%	47.2%

Comparables: Phil Hughes, Daniel Norris, Lance McCullers Jr.

Peralta's wild, low-slot crossfire delivery makes his fastball appear not so much a prototypical modern riser as it does an old-fashioned hop ball. The arm action says sinker, but it's never a true sinker, and sometimes it positively jumps up to the hitter's neck or so. That makes him a tough at-bat and enables him to induce plenty of weak contact. He became impossible to handle when he added a slider, a great fit for that delivery, with its cutback and the hip swing to get his back leg over an imaginary picket fence at the end. Peralta is best suited to the bullpen, but he's valuable there as a multi-inning, multi-pitch weapon.

Angel Perdomo LHP Born: 05/07/94 Age: 27 Bats: L Throws: L Height: 6'8" Weight: 265 Origin: International Free Agent, 2011

YEAR	TEAM	LVL	AGE	W	L	SV	G	GS	IP	H	HR	BB/9	K/9	K	GB%	BABIP	WHIP	ERA	DRA-	WARP	MPH	FA%	Whiff%	CSP
2018	DUN	HI-A	24	1	5	1	26	12	79¹	68	5	4.0	11.3	100	44.2%	.328	1.30	3.63	69	1.7				
2019	BLX	AA	25	2	0	0	7	0	15¹	6	0	4.7	12.3	21	42.9%	.222	0.91	1.17	53	0.4				
2019	SA	AAA	25	3	2	1	40	0	54	47	8	6.3	14.3	86	32.2%	.358	1.57	5.17	85	1.1				
2020	MIL	MLB	26	0	0	0	3	0	2²	3	0	23.6	16.9	5	66.7%	.500	3.75	20.25	87	0.0	96.3	68.2%	36.4%	38.7%
2021 FS	MIL	MLB	27	2	2	0	57	0	50	44	7	6.4	11.0	61	39.2%	.298	1.60	5.37	113	-0.2	96.3	68.2%	36.4%	38.7%
2021 DC	MIL	MLB	27	2	2	0	49	0	52	46	8	6.4	11.0	63	39.2%	.298	1.60	5.37	113	-0.1	96.3	68.2%	36.4%	38.7%

Comparables: Stephen Tarpley, Austen Williams, Justin Shafer

Perdomo, a gigantic lefty, has enormous stuff; either the strike zones he throws to are very small, or he has what you might charitably describe as "strike-throwing problems."

Luis Perdomo RHP Born: 05/09/93 Age: 28 Bats: R Throws: R Height: 6'2" Weight: 201 Origin: International Free Agent, 2003

YEAR	TEAM	LVL	AGE	W	L	SV	G	GS	IP	H	HR	BB/9	K/9	K	GB%	BABIP	WHIP	ERA	DRA-	WARP	MPH	FA%	Whiff%	CSP
2018	ELP	AAA	25	6	3	0	13	13	75	72	12	2.5	7.3	61	56.5%	.284	1.24	3.72	88	1.2				
2018	SD	MLB	25	1	6	0	12	10	44²	62	4	4.4	7.9	39	43.1%	.392	1.88	7.05	145	-0.6	95.0	63.1%	19.4%	47.4%
2019	ELP	AAA	26	2	1	1	11	0	15	21	3	2.4	10.2	17	51.1%	.419	1.67	3.60	103	0.2				
2019	SD	MLB	26	2	4	0	47	1	72	69	6	2.2	6.9	55	52.0%	.296	1.21	4.00	88	0.8	95.6	54.5%	19.9%	49.4%
2020	SD	MLB	27	0	0	0	10	1	17¹	13	3	5.2	8.3	16	60.4%	.222	1.33	5.71	91	0.2	95.5	42.8%	26.4%	45.9%
2021 FS	MIL	MLB	28	2	2	0	57	0	50	49	6	3.2	8.6	47	53.0%	.301	1.33	4.09	99	0.2	95.5	53.8%	21.2%	48.2%

Comparables: Daniel Mengden, Jakob Junis, Jorge López

Perdomo will miss the season after undergoing Tommy John surgery. Even before he was released in November, he was unnervingly close to qualifying for free agency despite not accomplishing a whole lot in his five years in the majors.

Drew Rasmussen RHP Born: 07/27/95 Age: 25 Bats: R Throws: R Height: 6'1" Weight: 211 Origin: Round 6, 2018 Draft (#185 overall)

YEAR	TEAM	LVL	AGE	W	L	SV	G	GS	IP	H	HR	BB/9	K/9	K	GB%	BABIP	WHIP	ERA	DRA-	WARP	MPH	FA%	Whiff%	CSP
2019	WIS	LO-A	23	0	0	0	1	1	2	1	0	0.0	13.5	3	66.7%	.333	0.50	0.00	49	0.1				
2019	CAR	HI-A	23	0	0	0	4	4	11¹	7	0	1.6	12.7	16	40.0%	.304	0.79	1.59	52	0.3				
2019	BLX	AA	23	1	3	0	22	18	61	49	4	4.3	11.4	77	46.9%	.321	1.28	3.54	88	0.5				
2020	MIL	MLB	24	1	0	0	12	0	15¹	17	3	5.3	12.3	21	53.7%	.368	1.70	5.87	81	0.3	99.2	68.2%	32.0%	45.1%
2021 FS	MIL	MLB	25	3	3	0	57	0	50	42	5	4.1	10.5	58	47.2%	.295	1.31	3.76	86	0.5	99.2	68.2%	32.0%	45.1%
2021 DC	MIL	MLB	25	3	3	0	53	4	66	56	7	4.1	10.5	77	47.2%	.295	1.31	3.76	86	0.9	99.2	68.2%	32.0%	45.1%

Comparables: Alex Reyes, Cliff Bartosh, Carter Capps

Having already needed two Tommy John surgeries, Rasmussen is wildly unlikely to suddenly turn over a new leaf as a starting pitcher. Oh no, he's a power reliever, all the way, baby. That's why it was odd to see him use two fairly distinct breaking balls and bust out a changeup during his rookie campaign. If that works, great; but in a more realistic scenario, he could take the fastball (which touches triple digits), the slider and an occasionally choked-off change against lefties and blossom into a solid setup man. Not getting lost in the weeds with the twin breaking pitches seems vital.

Ethan Small LHP Born: 02/14/97 Age: 24 Bats: L Throws: L Height: 6'4" Weight: 215 Origin: Round 1, 2019 Draft (#28 overall)

YEAR	TEAM	LVL	AGE	W	L	SV	G	GS	IP	H	HR	BB/9	K/9	K	GB%	BABIP	WHIP	ERA	DRA-	WARP	MPH	FA%	Whiff%	CSP
2019	BRG	ROK	22	0	0	0	2	2	3	0	0	0.0	15.0	5	50.0%	.000	0.00	0.00	27	0.2				
2019	WIS	LO-A	22	0	2	0	5	5	18	11	0	2.0	15.5	31	30.3%	.333	0.83	1.00	51	0.6				
2021 FS	MIL	MLB	24	2	3	0	57	0	50	45	7	4.4	10.2	56	36.7%	.295	1.40	4.47	110	-0.2				

If this works, it's going to be really fun to watch Small pitch. He's gambled on himself over and over, from trading in a full ride to a small school to walk on at Mississippi State (ignoring pre-draft offers in the low to mid-six figures) to going back for his senior year there after being a 28th-round pick as a junior, despite having had Tommy John surgery in the interim. The bets all paid, though, as Small put up video-game numbers in 2019, was a first-round pick as a result and now looks like a fast mover through the minors. He lacks top-end velocity, but he varies his delivery, hides the ball and uses his long frame to create great extension from a high arm slot. At the alternate site in 2020, he added and worked to polish a slider, which sounds ambitious for a pitcher with his profile. Betting against him has proven to be unwise.

Brent Suter LHP Born: 08/29/89 Age: 31 Bats: L Throws: L Height: 6'4" Weight: 213 Origin: Round 31, 2012 Draft (#965 overall)

YEAR	TEAM	LVL	AGE	W	L	SV	G	GS	IP	H	HR	BB/9	K/9	K	GB%	BABIP	WHIP	ERA	DRA-	WARP	MPH	FA%	Whiff%	CSP
2018	MIL	MLB	28	8	7	0	20	18	101¹	102	18	1.7	7.5	84	32.2%	.286	1.19	4.44	112	0.3	88.6	68.9%	23.2%	50.1%
2019	SA	AAA	29	0	0	0	4	2	11²	4	0	1.5	13.9	18	40.9%	.190	0.51	0.00	10	0.7				
2019	MIL	MLB	29	4	0	0	9	0	18¹	10	1	0.5	7.4	15	51.0%	.188	0.60	0.49	84	0.2	89.3	78.1%	26.8%	52.8%
2020	MIL	MLB	30	2	0	0	16	4	31²	30	4	1.4	10.8	38	52.9%	.321	1.11	3.13	73	0.7	87.9	79.1%	31.1%	46.6%
2021 FS	MIL	MLB	31	10	7	0	26	26	150	129	16	1.9	9.2	154	46.0%	.285	1.08	2.79	69	3.6	88.4	74.4%	27.0%	49.0%
2021 DC	MIL	MLB	31	5	4	0	49	12	90	77	10	1.9	9.2	92	46.0%	.285	1.08	2.79	69	2.2	88.4	74.4%	27.0%	49.0%

Comparables: Sam Gaviglio, Jacob Barnes, Matt Andriese

Literally leaning into his natural funk, Suter developed a new semi-windup in 2020. He started from a side-saddle set position, then performed a deep drop step, with his right heel getting a couple of feet off toward third base as he bent forward at the waist, his face and glove pointing toward first base. Then came the change of direction, with that right leg swinging up into a high kick, then leading him well toward first base in a crossfire delivery. It's never easy to bully hitters with a fastball that sits in the mid-80s, but Suter managed it, not only with his distracting gesticulations but by tailoring his heat to each batter and each sequence he deployed. Fellow lefties got more sinkers than in the past. Righties got a version of his four-seamer from that wild, angled delivery that might be better classified as a cutter. His changeup firmed up and worked off the heat better. Suter is as smart as he is quirky, and his excellent control forces batters to find a way to barrel something if they want to reach base. Lately, they're not having much luck.

Justin Topa RHP Born: 03/07/91 Age: 30 Bats: R Throws: R Height: 6'4" Weight: 200 Origin: Round 17, 2013 Draft (#509 overall)

YEAR	TEAM	LVL	AGE	W	L	SV	G	GS	IP	H	HR	BB/9	K/9	K	GB%	BABIP	WHIP	ERA	DRA-	WARP	MPH	FA%	Whiff%	CSP
2018	FRI	AA	27	2	3	0	9	6	41	53	4	2.9	7.5	34	48.1%	.383	1.61	5.71	118	-0.3				
2019	CAR	HI-A	28	0	3	3	15	0	16	14	1	1.1	10.7	19	43.2%	.310	1.00	4.50	70	0.2				
2019	BLX	AA	28	0	3	0	18	0	24	22	0	3.0	8.2	22	47.2%	.314	1.25	2.62	97	0.0				
2020	MIL	MLB	29	0	1	0	6	0	7²	7	1	0.0	14.1	12	55.6%	.353	0.91	2.35	72	0.2	99.5	70.3%	26.6%	53.6%
2021 FS	MIL	MLB	30	2	2	0	57	0	50	46	7	2.9	8.8	48	45.6%	.287	1.25	3.94	93	0.3	99.5	70.3%	26.6%	53.6%
2021 DC	MIL	MLB	30	2	2	0	49	0	52	48	7	2.9	8.8	50	45.6%	.287	1.25	3.94	93	0.5	99.5	70.3%	26.6%	53.6%

Comparables: Robert Stock, Matt Dermody, Ryan Mattheus

Stories as winding as Topa's don't usually end in the big leagues. He was undrafted out of high school; a 17th-rounder even as a senior out of Long Island University in 2013; released by the Pirates, then left unprotected by the Rangers and deemed a minor-league free agent after 2018. He didn't even land with a club until Opening Day of 2019. when the Brewers scooped him up. Since then, he's pitched 48 solid innings for them, including eight in the majors in 2020. He strides wide open, throws from a low three-quarters slot and generates excellent separation with a power sinker at 98 mph and a slider that sweeps all the way across the plate. He's a true, late-innings relief weapon, even if it's taken three organizations and seven years to get there.

Devin Williams RHP Born: 09/21/94 Age: 26 Bats: R Throws: R Height: 6'2" Weight: 200 Origin: Round 2, 2013 Draft (#54 overall)

YEAR	TEAM	LVL	AGE	W	L	SV	G	GS	IP	H	HR	BB/9	K/9	K	GB%	BABIP	WHIP	ERA	DRA-	WARP	MPH	FA%	Whiff%	CSP
2018	CAR	HI-A	23	0	3	0	14	14	34	40	2	5.8	9.3	35	37.3%	.384	1.82	5.82	97	0.3				
2019	BLX	AA	24	7	2	4	31	0	53¹	34	3	4.9	12.8	76	47.4%	.282	1.18	2.36	79	0.5				
2019	MIL	MLB	24	0	0	0	13	0	13²	18	2	4.0	9.2	14	40.0%	.381	1.76	3.95	105	0.0	98.2	61.0%	25.0%	45.2%
2020	MIL	MLB	25	4	1	0	22	0	27	8	1	3.0	17.7	53	61.1%	.200	0.63	0.33	42	1.1	98.3	43.9%	51.8%	41.4%
2021 FS	MIL	MLB	26	2	2	8	57	0	50	36	5	4.0	12.8	71	46.6%	.290	1.18	3.05	71	0.9	98.2	48.7%	44.3%	42.5%
2021 DC	MIL	MLB	26	2	2	8	55	0	58	42	6	4.0	12.8	82	46.6%	.290	1.18	3.05	71	1.2	98.2	48.7%	44.3%	42.5%

Comparables: Elieser Hernandez, Domingo Germán, Yacksel Ríos

There are some ... dare we say "rules" about changeups. They often steer four and a half inches more to the arm side than a pitcher's fastball; they very rarely have a foot of vertical movement relative to the fastball; they almost never have that much movement in both dimensions; and they never, ever do so with a 12-MPH velocity differential. Oh, and they seldom have higher spin rates than the pitcher's heat, and they certainly aren't supposed to have 500 more RPM. Williams' thingamajig defies all the rules. Call it the Airbender. Call it unhittable. Call it a 53-percent strikeout rate wrapped up in a single pitch, the best weapon anyone in the majors has in their arsenal. Just don't call Williams's screwball a changeup.

Brandon Woodruff RHP   Born: 02/10/93   Age: 28   Bats: L   Throws: R   Height: 6'4"   Weight: 243   Origin: Round 11, 2014 Draft (#326 overall)

YEAR	TEAM	LVL	AGE	W	L	SV	G	GS	IP	H	HR	BB/9	K/9	K	GB%	BABIP	WHIP	ERA	DRA-	WARP	MPH	FA%	Whiff%	CSP
2018	RMV	AAA	25	3	2	0	17	17	71¹	67	8	4.0	8.6	68	49.3%	.296	1.39	4.04	95	0.9				
2018	MIL	MLB	25	3	0	1	19	4	42¹	36	4	3.0	10.0	47	54.0%	.294	1.18	3.61	70	0.9	97.5	64.1%	25.3%	50.0%
2019	MIL	MLB	26	11	3	0	22	22	121²	109	12	2.2	10.6	143	45.1%	.322	1.14	3.62	66	3.4	98.1	64.1%	25.5%	49.6%
2020	MIL	MLB	27	3	5	0	13	13	73²	55	9	2.2	11.1	91	50.0%	.269	0.99	3.05	70	1.9	98.3	65.1%	29.0%	49.8%
2021 FS	MIL	MLB	28	10	7	0	26	26	150	120	15	2.9	10.6	177	47.7%	.287	1.13	2.85	69	3.7	98.1	64.5%	27.0%	49.7%
2021 DC	MIL	MLB	28	10	7	0	27	27	151	121	15	2.9	10.6	178	47.7%	.287	1.13	2.85	69	4.1	98.1	64.5%	27.0%	49.7%

Comparables: Daniel Mengden, Joe Musgrove, Zach Davies

We no longer have to wonder what role Woodruff will fill. He's a starter, and he slots comfortably into the upper half of even a very good rotation. His control has never been bad, but his command has come a long way recently. That said, he achieved his modest gains in 2020 by becoming a two-fastball pitcher and leaning more heavily on the changeup. It's not hard to see how he's locating more efficiently, given that he's throwing his breaking stuff less often. The tweak he made to his four-seamer to create separation from the sinker made that pitch a bit easier to square up, and the sinker itself misses bats only the way most sinkers do (which is to say infrequently). In 2021, he'll have to find the feel to get back to trusting his breaking balls so he can evade lumber when it proves necessary.

Eric Yardley RHP   Born: 08/18/90   Age: 30   Bats: R   Throws: R   Height: 6'0"   Weight: 170   Origin: Undrafted Free Agent, 2013

YEAR	TEAM	LVL	AGE	W	L	SV	G	GS	IP	H	HR	BB/9	K/9	K	GB%	BABIP	WHIP	ERA	DRA-	WARP	MPH	FA%	Whiff%	CSP
2018	SA	AA	27	2	4	0	34	0	39¹	40	2	2.7	6.2	27	62.8%	.325	1.32	3.43	83	0.4				
2018	ELP	AAA	27	3	0	1	14	0	21²	25	2	2.9	4.2	10	58.4%	.311	1.48	5.40	91	0.2				
2019	ELP	AAA	28	0	2	7	43	0	63²	60	3	2.0	7.4	52	62.3%	.303	1.16	2.83	41	2.6				
2019	SD	MLB	28	0	1	0	10	0	11²	12	1	2.3	5.4	7	61.0%	.289	1.29	2.31	89	0.1	87.6	67.4%	22.7%	44.4%
2020	MIL	MLB	29	2	0	0	24	0	23¹	19	2	3.9	7.3	19	62.7%	.262	1.24	1.54	89	0.3	89.5	65.1%	19.0%	46.9%
2021 FS	MIL	MLB	30	2	2	0	57	0	50	49	5	2.9	7.3	40	59.3%	.295	1.31	4.13	94	0.3	89.0	65.6%	19.9%	46.3%
2021 DC	MIL	MLB	30	2	2	0	55	0	58	57	6	2.9	7.3	46	59.3%	.295	1.31	4.13	94	0.5	89.0	65.6%	19.9%	46.3%

Comparables: Mike Morin, Tyler Rogers, Emilio Pagán

Yardley does everything a hurler can do to create deception and force hitters into defensive postures. Namely, he hides the ball for a long time as he begins his delivery and then lets the arm out in a long arc before sweeping it around to his thigh-high, below-sidearm release. Hitters can sometimes hit his sinker hard, and they can sometimes get his slider up in the air; doing both at once, meaning a hard-hit ball in the air, is almost out of the question. If he had any command of the slider, he'd be truly devastating, but it might cost him too much of that funk to get there. As it stands, he's a solid middle reliever and a future standout on one of those nightmare-fuel Arm Clock graphics.

PITTSBURGH PIRATES

Essay by Alex Kirshner

Player comments by Kate Preusser and BP staff

Cueeeeeeetoooooo. Cueeeeeeetoooooo.

The Pirates will not win a World Series in my lifetime, for reasons that are already apparent or will become apparent. But that doesn't bother me much, because 2013 gave me a better night than any championship ever could. Unintentionally, the Pittsburgh Baseball Club created that moment with two decades of consistent ineptitude.

It was the 2013 National League Wild Card Game. Bottom of the second. One out, two balls, one strike. Johnny Cueto was shaky for the Reds and about to unravel in front of a mob of yinzers serenading him with a drawn-out call of his name. An inning after he'd let the Pirates open the scoring on a Marlon Byrd homer to left. Cueto paced around the rubber, dropped the ball as the crowd chanted, picked it back up and then left a belt-high fastball over the plate.

The roar when Russell Martin took Cueto way deep was the kind every fan should hear once in-person. Everyone in the park sensed it was gone off the bat, but the yells were tempered at first—these *were* the Pirates, and this was a big night and we *had* been burned enough times. When Ryan Ludwick ran out of space in left-center and the ball landed in a sea of black, *that's* when it became primal. That was the sound of the release when 39,000 people realize something is about to happen that hasn't happened in a long time. It was the sound of the longest streak of losing in major North American pro sports (*20 years*) becoming undone.

That night was a triumph. It was also the moment the Pirates stopped going up and started going down. Before the 2020 season, the Pirates cleaned house, finally getting rid of the last of the people who played meaningful roles in building them up to that night in 2013. In the last years of the last decade, the Pirates made a show of striving for mediocrity with a chance at lucking into something greater. But they didn't even make a cursory effort in perhaps the most variance-friendly season ever: a 60-game sprint before an expanded playoff.

The Pirates are the worst team in baseball entering 2021. They've been here before. This time, though, they've made sure their fanbase has no reason to believe in the rebuild to come.

PITTSBURGH PIRATES PROSPECTUS
2020 W-L: 19-41, 5TH IN NL CENTRAL

Pythag	.361	29th	dWin%	.344	28th
RS/G	3.65	30th	B-Age	27.8	4th
RA/G	4.97	19th	P-Age	28.2	13th
DRC+	85	29th	FIP	4.86	21st
DRA-	108	23rd	DER	.706	10th
Payroll	$24M	30th	M$/MW	$6.3M	25th

- Opened 2001
- Open air
- Natural surface
- Fence profile: 6' to 21'

Three-Year Park Factors

Runs	Runs/RH	Runs/LH	HR/RH	HR/LH
96	96	96	89	98

Top Hitter WARP	1.0 Adam Frazier
Top Pitcher WARP	0.9 Joe Musgrove
Top Prospect	Ke'Bryan Hayes

Payroll History (in millions)

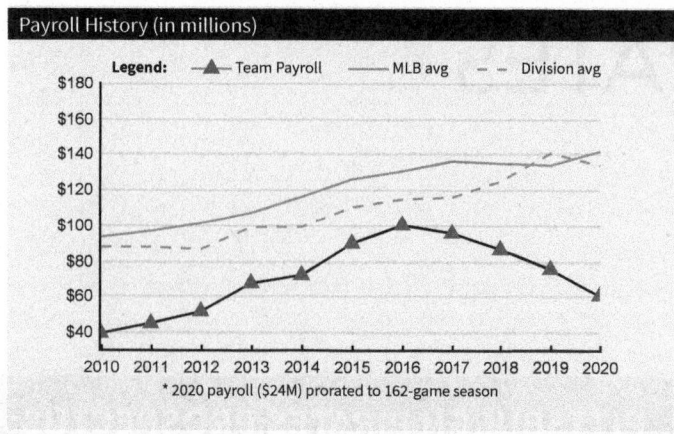

Legend: Team Payroll — MLB avg — — Division avg

* 2020 payroll ($24M) prorated to 162-game season

Future Commitments (in millions)

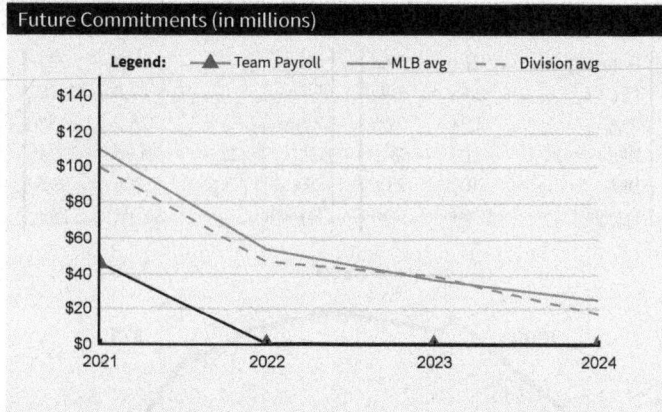

Legend: Team Payroll — MLB avg — — Division avg

Farm System Ranking

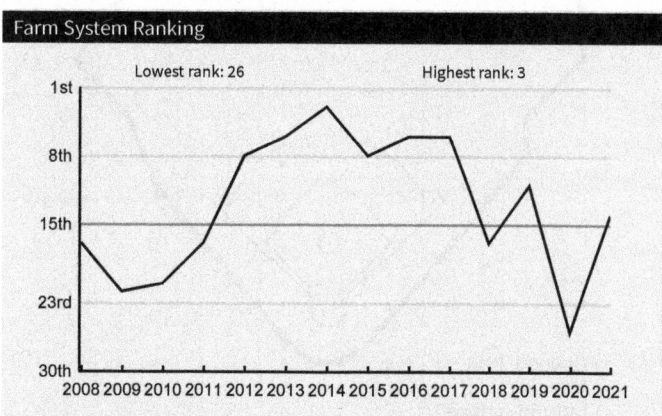

Lowest rank: 26   Highest rank: 3

Personnel

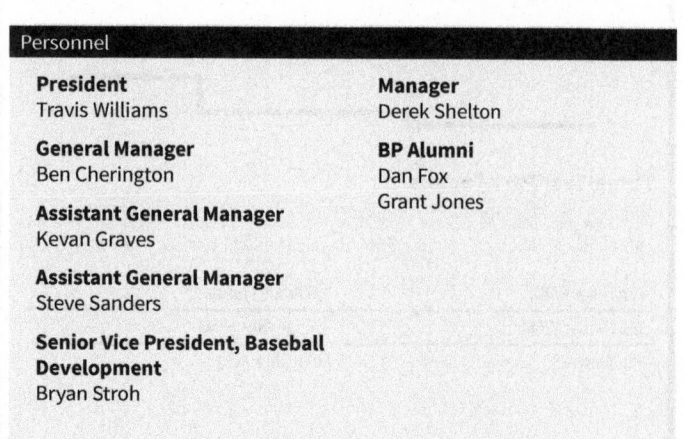

President
Travis Williams

General Manager
Ben Cherington

Assistant General Manager
Kevan Graves

Assistant General Manager
Steve Sanders

Senior Vice President, Baseball Development
Bryan Stroh

Manager
Derek Shelton

BP Alumni
Dan Fox
Grant Jones

The neat thing about being bad is that you are most likely on the way up; you're at least not on the way *down*. Being on the way up is exciting for a fan—albeit less so if you don't have a credible belief that you will then *stay* up. The Pirates stayed up for a spell after 2013, the year the Cardinals beat them in five games in the Division Series. They were elite in both 2014 and 2015, when the misfortune of sharing a division with the Cardinals forced them into two more Wild Card Games. You know the story by now: they lost those games to peak Madison Bumgarner and peak Jake Arrieta. If they'd made another Wild Card Game, they probably would have faced a time-traveling Fernando Valenzuela. Sometimes things do not work out.

The Pirates had a young talent core after 2013. They stayed good the next two years despite not straying from newspaper magnate and team owner's Bob Nutting's established practice of avoiding aggressive major-league expenditures who would help the team stay relevant.

Nutting had authorized a few moves over the prior two years that qualified as lavish by the Pirates' standards: two years and $17 million for Martin, two years and $14 million for Franciso Liriano and picking up $13 million of the $31 million left on A.J. Burnett's Yankees deal. These commitments drew praise at the time, but more than that, they created more optimism than what would wind up being fulfilled.

The Pirates were a low-budget operation generations before Nutting's arrival. In 1950, Branch Rickey told Ralph Kiner he'd need to take a pay cut to stay with Pittsburgh, and when Kiner balked at the idea, Rickey told him, "We finished last with you. We can finish last without you." Then he traded him. Being cheap (or thrifty, depending on how you view labor-management dynamics) has long been a feature of the Pirates, and Nutting is only noteworthy because his net worth is measured in billions.

A loud camp of fans and local media couldn't stand Nutting's continual choice not to spend big, but some of us were okay with it—and even chastised *the non-believers* for not going along. After all, the Pirates could've spent $120 million on Matt Holliday in 2010 and been terrible anyway; better to conserve resources and get ready to spend to supplement a team that might be good once Nutting's underlings had built the farm system into something sustainable. Nutting and his team frequently alluded to a future in which the Pirates might invest more.

"A lot has been made of our payroll," then-GM Neal Huntington said that year, during a 105-loss campaign. "The easiest way to describe our payroll is that it's a result, not a goal—the result of trading players on the downside of their prime who were making a lot of money." Nutting, too, suggested the Pirates would pay up if the time were ever right: "Payroll is driven by the age and experience of those players. As those players mature, those dollars are going to need to mature with them. I think the payroll continues to be a distraction from the process of building the team."

It barely happened, outside of an eventual bargain extension for Andrew McCutchen and those big-for-the-Pirates value adds. The team went from 30th in Opening Day payroll in 2012 to 26th in 2013, then 28th in 2014, then 24th in 2015. They finished two games behind the Cardinals the latter two years and ran into pitching freight trains in the Wild Card Game both times. They jumped to 20th in 2016, but by that point they'd missed The Window, that period where low-spending teams have a chance to compete with their developed talent before it starts to cost a lot of money.

The realization the Pirates weren't going to supplement their elite teams of the early to mid-2010s with expensive outside acquisitions came gradually. It set in with each in a series of moves that could've made sense individually but added up to a clear betrayal of a fanbase that had been patient and expected some financial effort when the time was right. It was a slowly escalating deconstruction of a special team, with no serious effort at reinforcing it.

Ahead of 2016, they traded a productive second baseman (Neil Walker) for a bad starter (Jonathon Niese) because Walker was due to make at least $10 million in his last year arbitration. They saved less than $2 million to get 110 innings of sub-replacement-level mound work. Niese was supposed to help replace J.A. Happ, who'd provided a sub-2.00 ERA in 63 innings as a deadline pickup the year before, but he left for the Blue Jays when the Pirates wouldn't offer him more than two years. (Toronto offered three years and $36 million, which turned out to be a bargain). The Pirates' plan included spending $2 million on a 38-year-old Ryan Vogelsong, which went as you'd expect. They also made a poor attempt at Moneyballing by signing John Jaso (two years, $8 million) to play first base, a deal that returned less than one win in two seasons of regular starts. Jaso was, predictably, among the position's weakest hitters.

In 2017, cheapness blended with poor evaluation. The Pirates gave intermediate-sized deals to Francisco Cervelli, Iván Nova and David Freese, all contracts they'd later ship off. They also dumped the remainder of Liriano's contract on the Blue Jays, giving up two future major leaguers, Reese McGuire and Harold Ramirez, to do it. And as the season drew to a close, they let their second-best reliever, Juan Nicaso, go on an irrevocable waiver claim *to a division rival*, the Cardinals, without getting anything in return. At least it saved Nutting $600,000.

In 2018, with a surprisingly decent team, the Pirates made one of their versions of a "go for it" move—the kind of aggressive risk they liked to take to get a player who might be great and was on a good contract, so they wouldn't have to shell out for one in free agency. It wound up being one of the worst trades in recent baseball history: Chris Archer in, Tyler Glasnow and Austin Meadows (and more) out. You can't be stingy *and* bad at evaluating your own and others' talent.

Archer was supposed to replace Gerrit Cole, whom the Pirates misused and then traded with two years of club control remaining. Again, you can't be bad in too many ways all at once.

Ordinarily, there'd be room for some optimism now that Nutting has fired Huntington, the man chiefly responsible for all of those moves and non-moves. The Pirates were bad enough in 2020 to pick first in 2021's draft, in an era when it's not easy to botch the top pick as badly as, say, Dave Littlefield did when he took Bryan Bullington in 2002.

But every calamity Huntington inflicted on the Pirates was underpinned by Nutting's lack of interest in making the financial effort required to field a winner. And the Pirates replaced Huntington with Ben Cherington, as close to a Huntington clone as they could've found: in addition to nearly identical biographies that trace from New Hampshire upbringings to Amherst College to UMass to the Cleveland front office, Huntington helped Cherington get his start.

In swapping GMs, the Pirates have redecorated a shaky house without touching the foundation. Cherington may prove wiser than Huntington on his own terms—not trading Mitch Keller and Travis Swaggerty for a declining starter would be ideal—but he'll be constrained in similar ways. Even if he steers the ship wisely and gets the Pirates to contention by 2023, will he have any margin for error to keep them there beyond 2025? It's impossible to believe, and the slow bleed of the last great Pirates core has made it too painful to be worth investing hope.

Having a Scrooge of an owner is not unique. But Nutting exemplifies something unique about team-owner capitalism: the way it can take an opening and turn it into a peak. The way it can take a team on the rise, one a city falls deeply in love with, and then let it die on the vine. The way it can take the most joyful thing about sports, the journey, and make anyone on the ride live in constant fear of an elephant stepping out into the road.

The fun of the 2013-15 Pirates wasn't just that they'd been bad and were suddenly good. It was that they could *stay* good if the franchise thought it worthwhile. Sure, Bumgarner declares your pennant dreams dead on arrival one year. Sure, Arrieta does the same thing the next. There's no reason one of the best teams in baseball has to fall apart—unless the person signing the checks doesn't care to hold it together. It became exceedingly clear that Nutting did not care.

In this way, the Pirates' stinginess is a renewable poison. It has left a fanbase seething with anger over what could've been for those great McCutchen-era teams, of course, but it has also made it functionally impossible to believe in the long-range hopes of future good Pirates teams.

The Pirates also embark on this long rebuild with almost nothing of interest at the major-league level. The last Pirates team to be the worst in baseball was 2010's, but that team rolled out six starting position players who at least figured to have a chance of being significant players on their next contender. (It turns out three were, plus one starting pitcher.) The 2021 Pirates will start the year with *maybe* two or three useful pieces of the franchise's next good team on the roster, along with a number of veterans Cherington should've traded in his first months on the job. In addition to everything else, it isn't easy to watch these Pirates and feel inspiration.

The last time the team was this bad, years of mismanagement and not spending big had the bizarre effect of making the Pirates even more fun when the good times finally rolled. Part of it was the newness: the first time experiencing a packed ballpark on the shore of the Allegheny River every night, the first time seeing a whole caravan of Pirates in the All-Star Game, the first time seeing McCutchen on the cover of *Sports Illustrated*, the first time *Sunday Night Baseball* establishes a regular presence at your team's stadium. That feeling can never be felt again.

But part of the joy was the belief that success didn't have to be fleeting, because once a team builds something worth maintaining, maybe the guy in charge will do the work to sustain it. That feeling can also never be felt again. Nutting has lost any credibility that he will hold up his end of the bargain he made with Pirates fans who didn't quit long before that night in 2013, when Cueto dropped the ball. The owner has spent the rest of the decade dropping it himself. ▪

—Alex Kirshner's work has appeared at The Ringer, Slate, SB Nation, and elsewhere.

HITTERS

Anthony Alford CF Born: 07/20/94 Age: 26 Bats: R Throws: R Height: 6'1" Weight: 210 Origin: Round 3, 2012 Draft (#112 overall)

YEAR	TEAM	LVL	AGE	PA	R	2B	3B	HR	RBI	BB	K	SB	CS	Whiff%	AVG/OBP/SLG	DRC+	BABIP	BRR	FRAA	WARP
2018	DUN	HI-A	23	25	2	1	0	0	2	3	8	0	1		.200/.360/.250	72	.333	0.2	CF(2): -0.3, RF(2): -0.4, SS(1): 0.0	-0.1
2018	BUF	AAA	23	416	52	22	1	5	34	30	112	17	7		.240/.310/.344	95	.327	4.5	CF(43): 2.9, LF(31): -1.7, RF(28): -1.0	0.8
2018	TOR	MLB	23	21	3	0	0	0	1	2	9	1	0	37.1%	.105/.190/.105	74	.200	0.7	LF(7): 0.2, RF(3): -0.1, CF(1): -0.0	0.1
2019	BUF	AAA	24	319	46	16	3	7	37	31	94	22	8		.259/.343/.411	94	.365	1.4	RF(26): 3.8, CF(24): -4.4, LF(12): 1.4	0.8
2019	TOR	MLB	24	30	3	0	0	1	1	1	11	2	0	41.1%	.179/.233/.286	66	.250	0.3	LF(6): -0.3, RF(5): -0.0, CF(2): -0.1	0.0
2020	PIT	MLB	26	13	2	0	1	1	4	1	1	0	0	38.9%	.250/.308/.667	84	.200		CF(4): -0.5, LF(1): -0.2	-0.1
2020	TOR	MLB	26	16	3	0	0	1	3	0	7	3	0	47.4%	.188/.188/.375	91	.250	0.4	LF(5): 0.0, CF(2): -0.4, RF(1): -0.0	0.0
2021 FS	*PIT*	*MLB*	*26*	*600*	*59*	*24*	*2*	*14*	*58*	*48*	*195*	*12*	*5*	*42.3%*	*.213/.288/.348*	*74*	*.304*	*0.2*	*LF 1, RF 2*	*0.1*
2021 DC	*PIT*	*MLB*	*26*	*431*	*42*	*17*	*1*	*10*	*41*	*34*	*140*	*9*	*3*	*42.3%*	*.213/.288/.348*	*74*	*.304*	*0.1*	*LF 1, RF 2*	*-0.1*

Comparables: Clete Thomas, Drew Stubbs, Tyler Naquin

After being designated by Toronto, Alford's fresh start in Pittsburgh came to an abrupt halt in early September after an unfortunate tête-à-tête with the center-field wall in PNC Park. The good news is that he has history with both GM Ben Cherington and manager Derek Shelton, and the Pirates like his speed/defense combo as well as the potential pop in his bat. Alford runs the bases like a Rolls-Royce on a silk track, and when healthy will help a team with the second-fewest stolen bases in the NL in 2020.

Socrates Brito RF Born: 09/06/92 Age: 28 Bats: L Throws: L Height: 6'2" Weight: 205 Origin: International Free Agent, 2010

YEAR	TEAM	LVL	AGE	PA	R	2B	3B	HR	RBI	BB	K	SB	CS	Whiff%	AVG/OBP/SLG	DRC+	BABIP	BRR	FRAA	WARP
2018	RNO	AAA	25	478	85	34	5	17	69	44	104	15	4		.318/.383/.540	136	.384	2.1	RF(66): 5.3, CF(27): 0.3, LF(23): 3.5	3.6
2018	ARI	MLB	25	44	3	0	0	1	3	3	9	0	1	25.6%	.175/.227/.250	82	.194	0.1	RF(11): -0.1, LF(3): -0.1, CF(1): -0.0	0.0
2019	BUF	AAA	26	428	66	28	7	16	67	29	97	11	7		.282/.328/.510	106	.333	-1.4	LF(44): 1.8, RF(35): 4.8, CF(6): -0.8	1.6
2019	TOR	MLB	26	43	5	0	1	0	2	4	17	0	0	41.0%	.077/.163/.128	52	.136	0.0	RF(12): -0.8, CF(4): -0.2, LF(1): -0.1	-0.2
2021 FS	*PIT*	*MLB*	*28*	*600*	*61*	*25*	*6*	*18*	*66*	*37*	*164*	*3*	*1*	*35.7%*	*.227/.279/.393*	*76*	*.290*	*4.5*	*RF 1, LF 0*	*0.5*

Comparables: Matt Carson, Alexis Gomez, Cole Garner

If the Platonic ideal prides the purity of an idea over its physical reality, the Socratic Brito ideal prides the promise of tools over their in-game manifestation. An intriguing collection of tools has not yet coalesced into everyday, playable skills, and he's running out of time for that to happen. A rebound project with Toronto, he dropped a rung on the organizational talent ladder in 2019 and left as a free agent, signing with the Pirates. However, he missed summer camp with a positive COVID test, and finally opted out of the season after tragically losing his brother to the virus. He could return to the Pirates, who certainly aren't going anywhere this season, or find another team to take a chance on translating the thought-experiment into reality.

Will Craig   1B   Born: 11/16/94   Age: 26   Bats: R   Throws: R   Height: 6'3"   Weight: 220   Origin: Round 1, 2016 Draft (#22 overall)

YEAR	TEAM	LVL	AGE	PA	R	2B	3B	HR	RBI	BB	K	SB	CS	Whiff%	AVG/OBP/SLG	DRC+	BABIP	BRR	FRAA	WARP
2018	ALT	AA	23	549	73	30	3	20	102	42	128	6	3		.248/.321/.448	109	.288	0.6	1B(122): 8.8	1.3
2019	IND	AAA	24	556	69	23	0	23	78	44	146	2	3		.249/.326/.435	94	.304	-0.4	1B(111): 0.7, RF(13): -1.1	0.2
2020	PIT	MLB	26	4	0	0	0	0	0	0	1	0	0	30.8%	.000/.000/.000	85	.000		1B(2): -0.1	0.0
2021 FS	*PIT*	*MLB*	*26*	*600*	*66*	*31*	*1*	*18*	*67*	*41*	*171*	*0*	*0*	*30.8%*	*.233/.304/.399*	*90*	*.306*	*-0.9*	*1B 4, RF 0*	*0.4*
2021 DC	*PIT*	*MLB*	*26*	*165*	*18*	*8*	*0*	*5*	*18*	*11*	*47*	*0*	*0*	*30.8%*	*.233/.304/.399*	*90*	*.306*	*-0.3*	*1B 1*	*0.2*

Comparables: Chad Santos, Brad Nelson, Bryan LaHair

When the Pirates called Craig up this year, he joined the great tradition of Pete Rose, Ernie Banks, and Stephen Drew, as players whose names are also sentences. Unlike those boldly declarative fellows, this Craig requires some interrogation: Will Craig hit? The 2016 first-rounder has shown an ability to hit for average and for power in pro ball, although never both at the same time. With Pittsburgh limited by the lack of the DH and both Bell and Moran blocking him at first, the more pressing question is not Will Craig, but Where Craig, and the answer seems to be a power-hungry AL team that won't mind his all-or-nothing approach in the box.

Oneil Cruz   SS   Born: 10/04/98   Age: 22   Bats: L   Throws: R   Height: 6'7"   Weight: 215   Origin: International Free Agent, 2015

YEAR	TEAM	LVL	AGE	PA	R	2B	3B	HR	RBI	BB	K	SB	CS	Whiff%	AVG/OBP/SLG	DRC+	BABIP	BRR	FRAA	WARP
2018	WV	LO-A	19	443	66	25	7	14	59	34	100	11	5		.286/.343/.488	128	.346	2.5	SS(102): -5.9	2.1
2019	PIR	ROK	20	11	0	1	0	0	1	1	1	1	0		.600/.636/.700	208	.667	0.3	SS(3): -0.2	0.2
2019	BRD	HI-A	20	145	21	6	1	7	16	8	38	7	3		.301/.345/.515	152	.374	0.1	SS(35): 2.2	1.6
2019	ALT	AA	20	136	14	8	3	1	17	15	35	3	1		.269/.346/.412	121	.365	1.1	SS(35): 2.9	1.3
2021 FS	*PIT*	*MLB*	*22*	*600*	*61*	*31*	*5*	*15*	*62*	*41*	*208*	*8*	*4*		*.233/.290/.390*	*78*	*.346*	*-0.3*	*SS 5, 3B 0*	*0.5*
2021 DC	*PIT*	*MLB*	*22*	*66*	*6*	*3*	*0*	*1*	*6*	*4*	*22*	*0*	*0*		*.233/.290/.390*	*78*	*.346*	*0.0*	*SS 1*	*0.1*

Comparables: Nick Franklin, Jonathan Villar, Yu Chang

Nicknamed "la girafa" by his teammates, "la tarantula" might be more appropriate for a 6-foot-7 shortstop who seems to be all legs and arms. Scouts are divided on whether or not the lanky, limb-a-riffic Cruz will stick in the dirt or eventually move to the outfield, where his strong arm and easy plus power should play well in a corner. Cruz compensates for his XL levers by keeping his hands back and close to his body throughout his load before unleashing his bat in the zone like an abyssal tentacle. But the swing can get long at times and he's vulnerable to a pitcher attacking him inside. When he makes contact, however, the ball goes fast, and it goes far. An off-season auto accident in the Dominican Republic, where Cruz had returned to care for his pregnant girlfriend, clouds his future in baseball; prosecutors allege Cruz had alcohol in his system when his jeep struck a motorbike traveling without its lights, killing the driver and both passengers. If convicted, he could face anywhere from three to five years in prison. Even if he is acquitted of criminal negligence, he could face consequences for breaking the DR's strict curfew implemented to contain the spread of COVID-19 on the island.

Phillip Evans   3B   Born: 09/10/92   Age: 28   Bats: R   Throws: R   Height: 5'10"   Weight: 215   Origin: Round 15, 2011 Draft (#462 overall)

YEAR	TEAM	LVL	AGE	PA	R	2B	3B	HR	RBI	BB	K	SB	CS	Whiff%	AVG/OBP/SLG	DRC+	BABIP	BRR	FRAA	WARP
2018	LV	AAA	25	245	34	8	1	14	39	21	42	4	3		.256/.327/.493	85	.255	-1.0	3B(22): -0.6, SS(19): -1.0, 2B(18): -3.4	-0.3
2018	NYM	MLB	25	23	1	0	0	0	1	2	8	1	0	32.5%	.143/.217/.143	73	.231	0.1	3B(3): -0.1, 2B(2): -0.0, 1B(1): 0.0	0.0
2019	IOW	AAA	26	539	79	30	3	17	61	57	74	1	4		.283/.371/.470	110	.303	0.9	3B(95): -4.2, 1B(15): -0.2, 2B(15): 1.7	2.2
2020	PIT	MLB	28	45	6	2	0	1	9	5	7	0	1	35.1%	.359/.444/.487	104	.419	-0.1	3B(8): -0.8, 1B(1): -0.0, LF(1): -0.0	0.0
2021 FS	*PIT*	*MLB*	*28*	*600*	*64*	*24*	*2*	*17*	*67*	*46*	*131*	*0*	*0*	*34.7%*	*.248/.315/.397*	*95*	*.296*	*-0.2*	*3B -1, 1B 0*	*0.8*
2021 DC	*PIT*	*MLB*	*28*	*530*	*56*	*21*	*1*	*15*	*59*	*41*	*115*	*0*	*0*	*34.7%*	*.248/.315/.397*	*95*	*.296*	*-0.1*	*3B -1, 1B 0*	*0.5*

Comparables: Brian Barden, Cristhian Adames, Matt Duffy

It took six long years for Evans to climb up the ladder of the Mets' minor league system before he met hitting coach Kevin Long, who helped him unlock his bat. That burgeoning power, combined with the same solid plate discipline he's shown throughout the minors, caught Pittsburgh's eye. The fact that the team was shy on utility players also helped, and he made the club out of spring training 2.0. Evans was off to his best start ever as a pro when he collided with outfielder Gregory Polanco while chasing a foul ball, breaking his jaw and ending his season. It's a shame, because Evans is the kind of feel-good success story Pirates fans could have used last year, but the next chapter will have to wait until this spring. (Un)luckily for Pirates fans, they'll probably still need to feel good then, too.

Adam Frazier **2B**   Born: 12/14/91   Age: 29   Bats: L   Throws: R   Height: 5'10"   Weight: 180   Origin: Round 6, 2013 Draft (#179 overall)

YEAR	TEAM	LVL	AGE	PA	R	2B	3B	HR	RBI	BB	K	SB	CS	Whiff%	AVG/OBP/SLG	DRC+	BABIP	BRR	FRAA	WARP
2018	IND	AAA	26	137	10	5	2	0	18	11	20	1	3		.223/.289/.298	72	.262	-0.9	2B(17): 0.0, RF(7): -0.6, LF(5): 0.4	-0.4
2018	PIT	MLB	26	352	52	23	2	10	35	29	53	1	3	14.0%	.277/.342/.456	103	.305	1.7	2B(55): 2.5, LF(14): 0.7, RF(13): -0.6	1.6
2019	PIT	MLB	27	608	80	33	7	10	50	40	75	5	5	15.7%	.278/.336/.417	94	.306	1.0	2B(142): -6.4	1.1
2020	PIT	MLB	29	230	22	7	0	7	23	17	35	1	3	16.5%	.230/.297/.364	96	.246	0.9	2B(41): 0.5, LF(14): 1.9	1.0
2021 FS	PIT	MLB	29	600	70	32	4	12	57	47	97	8	5	15.7%	.264/.333/.407	98	.304	-3.2	2B -3, LF 1	1.4
2021 DC	PIT	MLB	29	564	66	30	4	11	53	44	91	8	5	15.7%	.264/.333/.407	98	.304	-3.0	2B -2, LF 1	1.4

Comparables: Ray Durham, Mark Ellis, D'Angelo Jimenez

Lefties who elevate do well at PNC Park with the short porch and Clemente Wall, and Frazier has parlayed that into 10-home run seasons over each of the past two years to go along with elite defense at second. The Pirates even gave him some outfield reps to gussy him up as a superutility for the trade deadline, but apparently the market was cold, likely due to him hitting the ball this season with all the impact of a Sternly Worded Email. With two more years of team control, he's one of Pittsburgh's better off-season trade chips, but his defensive chops could also help out a young pitching staff that's slightly above league average in groundball rate.

──────────────── ★ ★ ★ *2021 Top 101 Prospect* **#39** ★ ★ ★ ────────────────

Nick Gonzales **SS**   Born: 05/27/99   Age: 22   Bats: R   Throws: R   Height: 5'10"   Weight: 190   Origin: Round 1, 2020 Draft (#7 overall)

A smaller stature and a lack of prospect pedigree held up some teams on Gonzales, so the Pirates were able to pounce on one of the draft's best pure hitters with the seventh pick. Shortly after signing, Pittsburgh sent him to the alternate training site, where he reportedly made hard contact against more advanced pitchers and earned praise from coaches for his mature approach on and off the field. A walk-on in college, Gonzales' work ethic compares favorably to legendary workhorse Alex Bregman, as does his short, powerful swing and lightning-quick hands. If not for the pandemic, he'd likely have shared Bregman's fast track to the majors; Gonzales swings an "angry bat," as one Pirates coach described it.

Erik González **SS**   Born: 08/31/91   Age: 29   Bats: R   Throws: R   Height: 6'3"   Weight: 205   Origin: International Free Agent, 2008

YEAR	TEAM	LVL	AGE	PA	R	2B	3B	HR	RBI	BB	K	SB	CS	Whiff%	AVG/OBP/SLG	DRC+	BABIP	BRR	FRAA	WARP
2018	CLE	MLB	26	143	17	10	1	1	16	5	34	3	0	26.9%	.265/.301/.375	73	.347	1.9	2B(30): 2.0, 3B(20): 0.9, SS(16): 0.2	0.5
2019	IND	AAA	27	81	6	3	1	1	10	3	29	1	1		.192/.222/.295	33	.292	-2.0	SS(9): -0.7, 2B(8): 0.8	-0.5
2019	PIT	MLB	27	156	15	4	1	1	6	9	37	4	1	29.4%	.254/.301/.317	65	.333	-0.1	SS(26): 1.4, 3B(16): 0.5, LF(4): -0.5	0.1
2020	PIT	MLB	29	193	14	13	1	3	20	8	51	2	3	32.1%	.227/.255/.359	74	.292	-1.0	SS(38): -2.2, 3B(13): 1.6	-0.2
2021 FS	PIT	MLB	29	600	57	29	2	11	53	26	168	6	3	30.6%	.222/.262/.345	62	.296	-2.0	SS 0, 3B 2	-1.2
2021 DC	PIT	MLB	29	431	41	20	2	8	38	19	120	4	2	30.6%	.222/.262/.345	62	.296	-1.4	SS 0, 3B 1	-0.8

Comparables: Alex Gonzalez, Orlando Miller, Benji Gil

A hot start from the beginning of the season until mid-August plus solid defense at a premium position put some spice on his name at the trade deadline. But apparently the market was lukewarm, and rightfully so, as his performance over the remainder of the season proved. Defensive flexibility + speed + not a black hole at the plate = not a terrible utility-player profile. But given Pittsburgh's healthy supply of infielders and low relative demand for expertise, the 30-year-old González seems ticketed to be here for a moderately-okay time, not a long time.

──────────────── ★ ★ ★ *2021 Top 101 Prospect* **#7** ★ ★ ★ ────────────────

Ke'Bryan Hayes **3B**   Born: 01/28/97   Age: 24   Bats: R   Throws: R   Height: 5'10"   Weight: 205   Origin: Round 1, 2015 Draft (#32 overall)

YEAR	TEAM	LVL	AGE	PA	R	2B	3B	HR	RBI	BB	K	SB	CS	Whiff%	AVG/OBP/SLG	DRC+	BABIP	BRR	FRAA	WARP
2018	ALT	AA	21	508	64	31	7	7	47	57	84	12	5		.293/.375/.444	128	.344	-0.8	3B(116): 9.0	3.5
2019	IND	AAA	22	480	64	30	2	10	53	43	90	12	1		.265/.336/.415	96	.311	2.3	3B(104): 8.2	2.3
2020	PIT	MLB	23	95	17	7	2	5	11	9	20	1	0	18.1%	.376/.442/.682	115	.450	0.6	3B(24): 3.0	0.7
2021 FS	PIT	MLB	24	600	68	28	4	14	64	51	139	7	2	18.1%	.254/.327/.403	99	.319	4.0	3B 14	3.0
2021 DC	PIT	MLB	24	564	64	26	4	13	60	48	131	7	2	18.1%	.254/.327/.403	99	.319	3.8	3B 13	2.8

Comparables: Andy Marte, Ian Stewart, Willy Aybar

"You are always new," wrote poet John Keats to Fanny Brawne in 1820, and 200 years later, the sentiment is echoed among Pirates fans marveling over their exciting young rookie. A positive COVID-19 test kept him from making his debut until September, but the son of former Pirate Charlie Hayes was electric, unveiling a new aspect to his game each night: dazzling snags at third; a mature approach in the box, especially with two strikes; smart and speedy baserunning; an ability to hit to all fields; and tantalizing flashes of power in the bat. With a tooled-up skillset and a billboard-ready smile, Hayes the Younger is the kind of player long-suffering Pirates fans can dream on, and deserve to love as a "joy forever."

Mason Martin **1B**   Born: 06/02/99   Age: 22   Bats: L   Throws: R   Height: 6'0"   Weight: 201   Origin: Round 17, 2017 Draft (#508 overall)

YEAR	TEAM	LVL	AGE	PA	R	2B	3B	HR	RBI	BB	K	SB	CS	Whiff%	AVG/OBP/SLG	DRC+	BABIP	BRR	FRAA	WARP
2018	BRS	ROK	19	269	42	10	1	10	40	42	87	2	2		.233/.357/.422	110	.328	1.4	1B(52): -1.7	-0.3
2018	WV	LO-A	19	173	16	8	0	4	18	18	62	1	1		.200/.302/.333	82	.310	0.0	1B(43): -3.0	-0.8
2019	GBO	LO-A	20	355	58	19	3	23	83	46	103	8	2		.262/.361/.575	163	.311	-1.5	1B(77): 4.1	2.9
2019	BRD	HI-A	20	201	32	13	1	12	46	22	65	0	1		.239/.333/.528	129	.303	-0.8	1B(47): 3.4	1.1
2021 FS	PIT	MLB	22	600	55	27	2	15	60	55	241	2	1		.188/.270/.333	65	.304	-0.6	1B 6, RF 0	-1.2

Comparables: Bobby Bradley, Chris Carter, Tyler O'Neill

A 17th-rounder who has never cracked a Top 100 list, the Pirates are nonetheless high on Martin, who earned their Minor League Player of the Year Award in 2019. With his bodybuilder father, Martin spent lockdown building strength, trimming his body fat towards the single digits, and gaining more flexibility to increase his swing speed. There is significant concern over the strikeout rate, especially as he enters the upper minors, but Martin knows how to take his walks, and the power is of the true light-tower variety, even if they have to widen the doors at Pirate City in order to admit his enormous biceps.

Colin Moran 3B Born: 10/01/92 Age: 28 Bats: L Throws: R Height: 6'4" Weight: 220 Origin: Round 1, 2013 Draft (#6 overall)

YEAR	TEAM	LVL	AGE	PA	R	2B	3B	HR	RBI	BB	K	SB	CS	Whiff%	AVG/OBP/SLG	DRC+	BABIP	BRR	FRAA	WARP
2018	PIT	MLB	25	465	49	19	1	11	58	39	82	0	2	19.7%	.277/.340/.407	99	.316	-1.5	3B(116): -2.7	1.2
2019	PIT	MLB	26	503	46	30	1	13	80	30	117	0	1	24.6%	.277/.322/.429	84	.341	-0.7	3B(121): -18.7, 2B(11): 0.1, 1B(8): -0.4	-1.1
2020	PIT	MLB	28	200	28	10	0	10	23	19	52	0	0	28.1%	.247/.325/.472	103	.291	-0.6	1B(22): 0.7, 3B(4): -0.3	0.3
2021 FS	PIT	MLB	28	600	68	33	2	18	75	52	153	1	0	24.6%	.259/.331/.432	103	.331	-0.8	1B -10, LF -1	0.3
2021 DC	PIT	MLB	28	630	72	35	2	19	79	54	160	1	0	24.6%	.259/.331/.432	103	.331	-0.9	1B -11, LF -1	0.1

Comparables: David Freese, Kevin Kouzmanoff, Eric Munson

Like a frozen french bread pizza heated up by the drunkest person at the party, he was hot at the ends and ice-cold in the middle of the truncated season. Moran walks up to "Start Me Up," by the Stones, an appropriate throwback for a player who looks like he belongs on a three-color baseball card. And perhaps that fueled his hot start, as he was the first player to five homers, reaching that mark on the first of August. He'd then wait another two weeks before hitting another, and only tally four more over the remainder of the season, two in the last four games. To be fair, those weeks were marked with many stops and starts for the Pirates due to the pandemic, making it hard for Moran to hit his stride. He'd end the season strong, with the kind of Three-True-Outcomes line that makes his full-time move to first a palatable one, value-wise.

John Ryan Murphy C Born: 05/13/91 Age: 30 Bats: R Throws: R Height: 5'11" Weight: 200 Origin: Round 2, 2009 Draft (#76 overall)

YEAR	TEAM	LVL	AGE	PA	R	2B	3B	HR	RBI	BB	K	SB	CS	Whiff%	AVG/OBP/SLG	DRC+	BABIP	BRR	FRAA	WARP
2018	ARI	MLB	27	223	19	9	0	9	24	11	71	0	0	30.2%	.202/.244/.375	69	.256	-1.0	C(68): 10.2	1.2
2019	RNO	AAA	28	136	26	7	0	9	26	12	34	0	0		.250/.316/.524	91	.272	1.4	C(31): -1.7	0.5
2019	GWN	AAA	28	50	5	0	0	1	3	2	13	0	0		.170/.220/.234	30	.212	0.1	C(14): 0.2	-0.1
2019	ARI	MLB	28	69	9	3	0	4	7	6	28	0	0	39.4%	.177/.250/.419	67	.233	0.3	C(18): 1.4, P(2): 0.0	0.2
2019	ATL	MLB	28	1	0	0	0	0	0	0	0	0	0	0.0%	.000/.000/.000	142	.000		C(1): -0.0	0.0
2020	PIT	MLB	29	63	6	2	0	0	2	4	28	0	0	45.8%	.172/.226/.207	42	.333	-0.1	C(23): -0.0, P(1): -0.0	-0.3
2021 FS	PIT	MLB	30	600	59	24	1	17	60	44	199	1	0	37.6%	.205/.268/.352	66	.286	-0.8	C 11, 1B 0	0.9
2021 DC	PIT	MLB	30	66	6	2	0	1	6	4	21	0	0	37.6%	.205/.268/.352	66	.286	-0.1	C 2	0.1

Comparables: Orlando McFarlane, Ron Karkovice, Austin Romine

YEAR	TEAM	P. COUNT	FRM RUNS	BLK RUNS	THRW RUNS	TOT RUNS
2018	ARI	7638	9.3	0.3	-0.1	9.6
2019	ATL	31	0.0	0.0	0.0	0.0
2019	ARI	2433	0.0	1.3	0.0	1.3
2020	PIT	2713	0.7	-0.2	-0.1	0.4
2021	PIT	2405	1.2	0.0	0.1	1.3

Like that SNL skit about all moms having The Cut, all backup catchers have The Shag. JRM's fate was sealed when he showed up to summer camp with a thick crop of Gosewisch coming out of the back of his cap. The Pirates already have a somewhat light-hitting but Gold Glove-caliber defensive catcher in Stallings, so Murphy's presence on the roster is redundant. Fortunately for him, the Pirates' catching corps depth consists of a bag of shin guards, Michael Perez and a dartboard tied to an office chair.

Kevin Newman SS Born: 08/04/93 Age: 27 Bats: R Throws: R Height: 6'0" Weight: 185 Origin: Round 1, 2015 Draft (#19 overall)

YEAR	TEAM	LVL	AGE	PA	R	2B	3B	HR	RBI	BB	K	SB	CS	Whiff%	AVG/OBP/SLG	DRC+	BABIP	BRR	FRAA	WARP
2018	IND	AAA	24	477	74	30	2	4	35	31	50	28	11		.302/.350/.407	122	.333	3.2	SS(83): 2.9, 2B(21): -0.6	3.0
2018	PIT	MLB	24	97	7	2	0	0	6	4	23	0	1	21.7%	.209/.247/.231	61	.275	-0.6	SS(24): -1.4, 2B(8): -0.7	-0.3
2019	IND	AAA	25	35	5	2	0	0	1	5	7	0	1		.233/.343/.300	84	.304	0.7	SS(4): -0.4, LF(2): -0.3, CF(2): 0.0	0.1
2019	PIT	MLB	25	531	61	20	6	12	64	28	62	16	8	13.8%	.308/.353/.446	106	.333	0.9	SS(104): -1.3, 2B(23): -0.0, 3B(6): 0.5	2.8
2020	PIT	MLB	27	172	12	5	0	1	10	12	21	0	1	14.6%	.224/.281/.276	86	.250	-0.5	SS(23): -0.9, 2B(20): 0.5	0.1
2021 FS	PIT	MLB	27	600	64	27	3	9	59	37	90	9	3	14.5%	.261/.315/.374	90	.297	0.9	2B -1, SS -1	1.1
2021 DC	PIT	MLB	27	199	21	9	1	3	19	12	29	3	1	14.5%	.261/.315/.374	90	.297	0.3	2B 0, SS 0	0.4

Comparables: Jimmy Rollins, Angel Berroa, Zoilo Versalles

The good: Newman once again proved allergic to striking out, carrying that part of his 2019 breakthrough forward. The bad: literally everything else, as the regression monster came to collect on an inflated slash line belied by weak batted-ball data. The ugly: continued defensive struggles up the middle, and a pre-pitch routine slightly less rhythmic than the dinner party scene in *Beetlejuice*. Newman claims an abdominal injury suffered in late August didn't affect his play, but he lost over a hundred points on his slash line across the board after being lifted from the game with discomfort. He wasn't hitting the ball hard before, but after, he might as well have been swinging a soggy Pixy Stix at the plate. That's bad news for a player whose value is tied to his bat, so hopefully the injury was actually the culprit, and Newman can take the off-season to heal, sort out his twitchy pre-pitch routine, and live to fight another Day-O.

Jared Oliva CF Born: 11/27/95 Age: 25 Bats: R Throws: R Height: 6'2" Weight: 205 Origin: Round 7, 2017 Draft (#208 overall)

YEAR	TEAM	LVL	AGE	PA	R	2B	3B	HR	RBI	BB	K	SB	CS	Whiff%	AVG/OBP/SLG	DRC+	BABIP	BRR	FRAA	WARP
2018	BRD	HI-A	22	454	75	24	4	9	47	40	91	33	8		.275/.354/.424	126	.332	4.3	CF(101): -7.6	1.4
2019	ALT	AA	23	507	70	24	6	6	42	42	104	36	10		.277/.352/.398	128	.347	4.2	CF(113): -1.2, LF(1): -0.1	3.4
2020	PIT	MLB	25	16	0	0	0	0	0	0	6	1	0	37.0%	.188/.188/.188	68	.300	0.0	LF(4): -0.7, CF(1): 0.1	-0.1
2021 FS	PIT	MLB	25	600	59	27	5	11	59	40	179	23	6	37.0%	.232/.295/.364	80	.323	7.9	CF -1, LF -1	1.0
2021 DC	PIT	MLB	25	298	29	13	2	5	29	20	89	11	3	37.0%	.232/.295/.364	80	.323	3.9	CF 0, LF 0	0.4

Comparables: Daniel Fields, Tyler Naquin, Bryan Reynolds

It's hard not to root for Oliva, an overshadowed backup on his powerhouse prep team (Keston Hiura was among his teammates) and a walk-on at Arizona who blossomed after a stance change in his draft year. Oliva might not have the raw physical tools of a super-prospect, but he has the sixth tool of a high baseball IQ, constantly recording ideas and impressions in a notebook he carries into the dugout every game. Thanks to that feedback loop, Oliva is quick to make targeted adjustments when he struggles, without flailing around and losing the bedrock of his overall process. That ability to analyze, reflect and quickly correct course has propelled the 2017 seventh-rounder through Pittsburgh's system, leading to a debut at PNC Park in 2020. He likely profiles at worst as a speed-and-defense fourth outfielder, but one with enough on-base ability to compensate for below-average power.

Liover Peguero SS Born: 12/31/00 Age: 20 Bats: R Throws: R Height: 6'1" Weight: 160 Origin: International Free Agent, 2017

YEAR	TEAM	LVL	AGE	PA	R	2B	3B	HR	RBI	BB	K	SB	CS	Whiff%	AVG/OBP/SLG	DRC+	BABIP	BRR	FRAA	WARP
2018	DSL DB1	ROK	17	90	14	3	3	1	16	6	12	4	1		.309/.356/.457	129	.343	-0.3	SS(21): 0.9	0.6
2018	DIA	ROK	17	71	8	0	0	0	5	5	17	3	2		.197/.254/.197	73	.265	-0.9	SS(19): 2.2	0.1
2019	MIS	ROK+	18	156	34	7	3	5	27	12	34	8	1		.364/.410/.559	153	.448	1.7		1.6
2019	HIL	SS	18	93	13	4	2	0	11	8	17	3	1		.262/.333/.357	103	.328	0.1	SS(18): -0.1	0.4
2021 FS	PIT	MLB	20	600	46	26	4	7	51	29	188	13	4		.227/.268/.329	62	.327	4.1	SS 4	-0.2

Nailing (or failing) that first big trade is a crucial tone-setter for the duration of a new GM's tenure. It's too early to grade out the trade of Starling Marte for a pair of 19-year-olds in Peguero and hard-throwing righty Brennan Malone, but it certainly feels like the arrow is pointing in Pittsburgh's direction, even without the evidence of a minor-league season. Lean and long-legged, Peguero has a clean, balanced swing approach from the right side with plus bat speed and a good feel for the hitting zone. He should also continue to add power as he grows into his frame. On the dirt, he's a smooth and capable defender who projects to stick at short. Humble, enthusiastic, and deeply committed to his craft, the genial "Peggy" is a force in the clubhouse—he was a team leader on his NWL Championship Hillsboro Hops team—and likely a fan favorite in Pittsburgh for years to come, putting an early shine on that trade return.

Michael Perez C Born: 08/07/92 Age: 28 Bats: L Throws: R Height: 5'10" Weight: 195 Origin: Round 5, 2011 Draft (#154 overall)

YEAR	TEAM	LVL	AGE	PA	R	2B	3B	HR	RBI	BB	K	SB	CS	Whiff%	AVG/OBP/SLG	DRC+	BABIP	BRR	FRAA	WARP
2018	RNO	AAA	25	240	30	9	1	6	29	20	40	0	1		.284/.342/.417	97	.322	-1.3	C(57): 8.7	1.6
2018	TB	MLB	25	80	9	5	0	1	11	3	19	0	0	26.0%	.284/.304/.392	87	.357	-1.8	C(24): -3.6	-0.3
2019	DUR	AAA	26	216	23	7	0	13	42	28	51	0	2		.245/.338/.495	116	.258	0.9	C(44): 1.2	1.5
2019	TB	MLB	26	55	6	5	0	0	2	8	19	0	0	40.9%	.217/.345/.326	73	.370	-1.2	C(20): 0.9, 1B(2): 0.0	0.1
2020	TB	MLB	28	93	7	3	0	1	13	7	27	0	0	30.0%	.167/.237/.238	76	.228	-0.8	C(38): 0.8, 1B(1): 0.1	0.0
2021 FS	PIT	MLB	28	600	63	29	2	17	62	50	174	0	0	32.0%	.231/.301/.387	82	.309	0.1	C -5, 1B 0	0.6
2021 DC	PIT	MLB	28	298	31	14	1	8	31	24	86	0	0	32.0%	.231/.301/.387	82	.309	0.0	C -4	0.1

Comparables: Tim Laudner, Ron Karkovice, Ben Davis

The Pirates claimed Perez off waivers from the Rays shortly after the World Series. He's just a backup catcher, albeit one freshly christened with Postseason Success.

YEAR	TEAM	P. COUNT	FRM RUNS	BLK RUNS	THRW RUNS	TOT RUNS
2018	TB	3023	-3.5	0.5	0.0	-2.9
2019	TB	2100	0.1	0.9	-0.2	0.7
2020	TB	3701	-1.3	-0.2	-0.1	-1.6
2021	PIT	10822	-5.8	-0.7	0.4	-6.1

Gregory Polanco RF   Born: 09/14/91   Age: 29   Bats: L   Throws: L   Height: 6'5"   Weight: 235   Origin: International Free Agent, 2009

YEAR	TEAM	LVL	AGE	PA	R	2B	3B	HR	RBI	BB	K	SB	CS	Whiff%	AVG/OBP/SLG	DRC+	BABIP	BRR	FRAA	WARP
2018	PIT	MLB	26	535	75	32	6	23	81	61	117	12	2	24.0%	.254/.340/.499	106	.287	0.7	RF(124): 1.3	1.8
2019	IND	AAA	27	54	5	4	0	1	11	9	16	2	0		.267/.389/.422	111	.393	1.0	RF(8): -1.1	0.2
2019	PIT	MLB	27	167	23	8	1	6	17	12	49	3	1	32.3%	.242/.301/.425	79	.316	0.5	RF(36): 0.4	0.0
2020	PIT	MLB	29	174	12	6	0	7	22	13	65	3	1	43.0%	.153/.214/.325	73	.193	-0.8	RF(39): 2.0	-0.1
2021 FS	PIT	MLB	29	600	62	30	3	21	71	55	176	12	3	33.4%	.225/.302/.409	87	.295	2.8	RF -3, LF 0	0.4
2021 DC	PIT	MLB	29	530	55	26	2	18	63	49	155	10	3	33.4%	.225/.302/.409	87	.295	2.5	RF -3	0.3

Comparables: Brennan Boesch, Derek Bell, Dave Clark

He's always late on fastballs, but his penitence is real
He can't make solid contact, you can't count on him to steal
We hate to have to say it, but we very firmly feel
Polanco's not an asset to the Pirates

(We'd like to say a word on his behalf:
You can't blame him ... for the pitching staff)

How do you solve a problem like Polanco
Eleven million owed, to be quite blunt
How do you solve a problem like Polanco?
A swing change? A PED? More bunts?

Oh, how do you trade a player like Polanco? [MUSIC SWELLS]
Pray the Yankees fall back in the hunt

Bryan Reynolds LF   Born: 01/27/95   Age: 26   Bats: S   Throws: R   Height: 6'3"   Weight: 205   Origin: Round 2, 2016 Draft (#59 overall)

YEAR	TEAM	LVL	AGE	PA	R	2B	3B	HR	RBI	BB	K	SB	CS	Whiff%	AVG/OBP/SLG	DRC+	BABIP	BRR	FRAA	WARP
2018	ALT	AA	23	383	56	18	3	7	46	43	73	4	4		.302/.381/.438	133	.362	-0.2	CF(43): -3.2, LF(42): -3.6, RF(3): 1.3	1.3
2019	IND	AAA	24	57	10	1	1	5	11	7	11	3	2		.367/.446/.735	178	.394	-0.7	CF(13): -1.3	0.5
2019	PIT	MLB	24	546	83	37	4	16	68	46	121	3	2	26.2%	.314/.377/.503	110	.387	1.5	LF(79): -0.4, RF(31): 0.1, CF(25): -1.9	2.2
2020	PIT	MLB	25	208	24	6	2	7	19	21	57	1	1	27.8%	.189/.275/.357	86	.231	-2.2	LF(37): 1.2, CF(17): 0.9	0.5
2021 FS	PIT	MLB	26	600	68	26	4	18	71	53	164	1	0	26.8%	.248/.323/.418	100	.324	1.9	CF -6, LF -3	1.1
2021 DC	PIT	MLB	26	530	60	23	4	16	63	47	145	1	0	26.8%	.248/.323/.418	100	.324	1.7	CF -5, LF -2	1.0

Comparables: Justin Upton, Marty Cordova, Chris Heisey

"Sophomore slump" doesn't begin to cover the tumble Reynolds' bat took between his standout rookie year and 2020, but there are still things to like in this profile. He's still barreling up the ball and hitting line drives to all fields, even if he's not hitting it quite as hard as last season; his low BABIP suggests a certain amount of bad luck, given the exit velo and line drive rate; and he's shown himself to be a solid defender in center. Not a burner on the bases, Reynolds is nonetheless a smart runner who can take the extra base and does all the little things well. The profile has all the sex appeal of a sloth in a Speedo, but it's a perfectly serviceable one. It'll likely look even better next season, once his strikeout percentage settles back down to career levels after a feverish spike caused by an acute case of Trying To Do Too Much for the offensively punchless Pirates.

Jacob Stallings C   Born: 12/22/89   Age: 31   Bats: R   Throws: R   Height: 6'5"   Weight: 215   Origin: Round 7, 2012 Draft (#226 overall)

YEAR	TEAM	LVL	AGE	PA	R	2B	3B	HR	RBI	BB	K	SB	CS	Whiff%	AVG/OBP/SLG	DRC+	BABIP	BRR	FRAA	WARP
2018	IND	AAA	28	278	37	22	1	3	40	15	51	1	2		.285/.335/.414	116	.343	-1.4	C(63): -4.7	0.8
2018	PIT	MLB	28	41	2	0	0	0	5	3	9	0	0	22.8%	.216/.268/.216	74	.276	0.5	C(13): 0.1	0.1
2019	IND	AAA	29	61	11	9	0	2	7	4	9	0	0		.275/.361/.569	115	.286	-3.2	C(15): 0.6	0.2
2019	PIT	MLB	29	210	26	5	0	6	13	16	40	0	0	24.7%	.262/.325/.382	95	.303	0.6	C(61): 13.6, P(1): -0.0	2.3
2020	PIT	MLB	31	143	13	7	0	3	18	15	40	0	0	26.1%	.248/.326/.376	96	.337	-1.0	C(42): 1.3	0.8
2021 FS	PIT	MLB	31	600	59	27	1	14	61	39	160	1	0	25.3%	.234/.294/.366	79	.304	-0.9	C 7, 1B 0	1.5
2021 DC	PIT	MLB	31	298	29	13	0	7	30	19	79	0	0	25.3%	.234/.294/.366	79	.304	-0.5	C 4	0.8

Comparables: Dave Duncan, Ramon Castro, Cal Neeman

YEAR	TEAM	P. COUNT	FRM RUNS	BLK RUNS	THRW RUNS	TOT RUNS
2018	PIT	1479	-0.7	0.5	0.0	-0.2
2018	IND	8836	-6.1	0.3	-0.1	-6.0
2019	PIT	7741	8.7	3.6	0.3	12.6
2019	IND	2150	0.9	0.0	0.1	1.0
2020	PIT	6186	2.7	1.1	-0.1	3.7
2021	PIT	10822	1.0	1.7	0.3	3.0

Behold the field in which the Pirates grow their catchers, and see that it is barren. A career backup who was a senior sign in 2012, Stallings ascended to the starting job after free agent signee Luke Maile went down with a broken finger during summer camp. Proving that 6'4" is not too tall for a catcher, he was again one of the best behind the dish this season, tying for the lead in the NL in runners caught stealing along with exceptional framing abilities and softer hands than a Victorian debutante. He wasn't a black hole at the plate, either, and would have led the Pirates in WARP if not for the emergence of Ke'Bryan Hayes. By the end of the season he was the team's Roberto Clemente Award nominee and a Gold Glove candidate, which is quite the glow-up for a player twice waived and cleared. He works well with this developing pitching staff and will likely continue to do so until the Pirates invest in a legitimate starting catching option, either in the draft or free agency or by propping a lululemon bag with a string tied to it over a Chipotle burrito.

Travis Swaggerty OF   Born: 08/19/97   Age: 23   Bats: L   Throws: L   Height: 5'11"   Weight: 180   Origin: Round 1, 2018 Draft (#10 overall)

YEAR	TEAM	LVL	AGE	PA	R	2B	3B	HR	RBI	BB	K	SB	CS	Whiff%	AVG/OBP/SLG	DRC+	BABIP	BRR	FRAA	WARP
2018	WV	SS	20	158	22	9	1	4	15	15	40	9	3		.288/.365/.453	146	.379	0.9	CF(36): -0.6	0.7
2018	WV	LO-A	20	71	6	1	1	1	5	7	18	0	0		.129/.225/.226	43	.159	-0.6	CF(16): 0.7	-0.3
2019	BRD	HI-A	21	524	79	20	3	9	40	57	116	23	8		.265/.347/.381	123	.334	-0.2	CF(121): 7.4	3.7
2021 FS	PIT	MLB	23	600	54	26	2	13	60	42	191	9	4		.221/.281/.353	75	.311	-0.9	CF 6	0.5

Comparables: Aaron Hicks, Jake Cave, Anthony Alford

The Pirates weren't put off by Swaggerty's poor performance after an aggressive promotion to full-season ball in his draft year. Instead they moved him up the ladder again to High-A, where he initially got off to a slow start but finished strong, with a .306/.375/.430 line in the second half. Swaggerty was ready to show that he's cleaned up the swing mechanics that led to many of his contact issues, but his coming-out party, and hopeful ascent to Top-100 lists, will have to wait. Even if he never taps into his raw over-the-fence power in games, there's an everyday centerfielder profile here, with good speed on the bases, a strong arm and solid defensive instincts, and an ability to take walks and get on base, provided the long layoff doesn't cost him the mechanical gains he made in 2019.

Cole Tucker SS   Born: 07/03/96   Age: 25   Bats: S   Throws: R   Height: 6'3"   Weight: 205   Origin: Round 1, 2014 Draft (#24 overall)

YEAR	TEAM	LVL	AGE	PA	R	2B	3B	HR	RBI	BB	K	SB	CS	Whiff%	AVG/OBP/SLG	DRC+	BABIP	BRR	FRAA	WARP
2018	ALT	AA	21	589	77	21	7	5	44	55	104	35	12		.259/.333/.356	90	.310	3.4	SS(131): -0.6	1.3
2019	IND	AAA	22	353	51	15	4	8	28	38	73	11	3		.261/.346/.413	102	.319	1.2	SS(70): -4.7, 2B(6): 0.8	1.3
2019	PIT	MLB	22	159	16	10	3	2	13	10	40	0	0	25.9%	.211/.266/.361	62	.276	1.3	SS(45): -1.1	0.0
2020	PIT	MLB	24	116	17	3	0	1	8	5	31	1	0	30.5%	.220/.252/.275	60	.295	0.1	CF(20): -1.5, RF(16): -0.9, 2B(1): -0.0	-0.6
2021 FS	PIT	MLB	24	600	60	30	5	10	55	45	157	14	5	28.2%	.234/.297/.365	78	.311	2.2	2B 1, SS 0	0.6
2021 DC	PIT	MLB	24	364	36	18	3	6	33	27	95	8	3	28.2%	.234/.297/.365	78	.311	1.3	CF -2, RF -1	0.0

Comparables: Alex Gonzalez, Felipe Lopez, Darrel Chaney

If one were to pen a cliché pop-country song about Tucker, it'd probably mention something about "long legs and bad decisions." On the surface, these both seem undeniable: the teeny-tiny walk rate compared to the much larger strikeout rate, and the fact that whoever designed his lower half had a heavy hand on the knee-to-hip ratio dial, or just had extra left over after making Nick Madrigal. But Tucker's swing decisions are mostly average to good. The problem is he struggles to make contact, and when he does, the quality of that contact has been poor. It's too early to worry about a player with fewer than 400 career PAs, especially since the Pirates tossed him into the outfield, where he fared well in both right and center despite being a dirt-dweller his whole career. Long legs are cliché for a reason: they get things done, but we'd like to see those legs used better in Tucker's top-heavy swing. Tucker did spend the 2020 off-season working on creating more loft in his swing path and moving his hands to keep his bat on plane in the zone longer, but those adjustments hadn't yet shown up at the plate before his season ended prematurely due to concussion.

PITCHERS

Chris Archer RHP   Born: 09/26/88   Age: 32   Bats: R   Throws: R   Height: 6'2"   Weight: 195   Origin: Round 5, 2006 Draft (#161 overall)

YEAR	TEAM	LVL	AGE	W	L	SV	G	GS	IP	H	HR	BB/9	K/9	K	GB%	BABIP	WHIP	ERA	DRA-	WARP	MPH	FA%	Whiff%	CSP
2018	TB	MLB	29	3	5	0	17	17	96	102	11	2.9	9.6	102	45.3%	.343	1.39	4.31	92	1.3	96.5	45.6%	29.1%	48.6%
2018	PIT	MLB	29	3	3	0	10	10	52¹	53	8	3.1	10.3	60	45.5%	.331	1.36	4.30	96	0.6	96.7	49.3%	28.1%	45.6%
2019	PIT	MLB	30	3	9	0	23	23	119²	114	25	4.1	10.8	143	35.2%	.304	1.41	5.19	90	1.8	96.0	50.5%	29.7%	45.4%
2021 FS	PIT	MLB	32	9	8	0	26	26	150	137	24	3.5	10.1	168	40.2%	.298	1.31	4.13	96	1.4	96.2	49.1%	29.4%	46.2%

Comparables: Sonny Gray, Zack Wheeler, Gio González

Proof that life does not give us what we deserve, the affable Archer's tenure in Pittsburgh took another disastrous turn when he was diagnosed with Thoracic Outlet Syndrome in June, ruling him out for the season. TOS isn't as predictable a recovery process as Tommy John, but promising data is emerging as the procedure becomes more common and therefore more studied. As a pitcher who relies more on mixing his secondaries and his swing-and-miss slider rather than overpowering velocity, which can be affected by TOS surgery, he's a good candidate to bounce back from this condition. However, while it's likely Archer will return to the mound, it's almost certain he'll do it wearing a different cap, as the always unstinting Bob Nutting made the agonizing choice of paying him $250,000 rather than $11 million for his option.

Tyler Bashlor RHP   Born: 04/16/93   Age: 28   Bats: R   Throws: R   Height: 6'0"   Weight: 195   Origin: Round 11, 2013 Draft (#326 overall)

YEAR	TEAM	LVL	AGE	W	L	SV	G	GS	IP	H	HR	BB/9	K/9	K	GB%	BABIP	WHIP	ERA	DRA-	WARP	MPH	FA%	Whiff%	CSP
2018	BNG	AA	25	0	3	7	20	0	24	14	2	4.5	11.2	30	26.4%	.245	1.08	2.62	67	0.5				
2018	NYM	MLB	25	0	3	0	24	0	32	26	6	3.4	7.0	25	28.4%	.227	1.19	4.22	126	-0.3	98.4	68.8%	24.4%	45.7%
2019	SYR	AAA	26	3	2	8	33	0	37	29	3	3.6	9.0	37	34.0%	.277	1.19	3.41	69	1.0				
2019	NYM	MLB	26	0	3	0	24	0	22	21	6	7.0	8.2	20	31.8%	.254	1.73	6.95	162	-0.6	97.9	62.2%	25.9%	49.2%
2020	PIT	MLB	27	0	0	0	8	0	8¹	9	2	4.3	6.5	6	46.2%	.292	1.56	8.64	108	0.0	97.5	48.9%	22.4%	49.4%
2021 FS	PIT	MLB	28	1	1	0	57	0	50	46	8	4.0	9.0	50	35.0%	.287	1.38	4.79	106	0.0	98.0	61.3%	24.6%	48.1%
2021 DC	PIT	MLB	28	1	1	0	25	0	27	25	4	4.0	9.0	27	35.0%	.287	1.38	4.79	106	0.1	98.0	61.3%	24.6%	48.1%

Comparables: Michael Mariot, Yacksel Ríos, J.B. Wendelken

At the risk of invoking unfortunate comps, Bashlor does occasionally remind us that he has Great Stuff. The Joe Kelly parallels extend to his wavering control, but Kelly's pout game and even his moderately successful seasons remain as elusive to Bashlor as a well-located fastball.

Steven Brault LHP Born: 04/29/92 Age: 29 Bats: L Throws: L Height: 6'0" Weight: 195 Origin: Round 11, 2013 Draft (#339 overall)

YEAR	TEAM	LVL	AGE	W	L	SV	G	GS	IP	H	HR	BB/9	K/9	K	GB%	BABIP	WHIP	ERA	DRA-	WARP	MPH	FA%	Whiff%	CSP
2018	IND	AAA	26	0	1	0	5	0	5¹	6	0	6.8	11.8	7	40.0%	.400	1.88	3.38	79	0.1				
2018	PIT	MLB	26	6	3	0	45	5	91²	84	10	5.6	8.1	82	47.0%	.292	1.54	4.61	126	-0.7	94.7	65.0%	24.5%	46.8%
2019	PIT	MLB	27	4	6	0	25	19	113¹	117	15	4.2	7.9	100	42.7%	.313	1.50	5.16	90	1.6	93.8	64.3%	23.3%	46.8%
2020	PIT	MLB	28	1	3	0	11	10	42²	29	2	4.6	8.0	38	49.6%	.243	1.20	3.38	109	0.2	94.2	50.7%	23.9%	44.4%
2021 FS	PIT	MLB	29	8	9	0	26	26	150	148	21	4.8	8.6	142	46.4%	.301	1.52	5.22	112	0.1	94.1	60.6%	23.7%	46.1%
2021 DC	PIT	MLB	29	5	9	0	24	24	109	107	15	4.8	8.6	103	46.4%	.301	1.52	5.22	112	0.4	94.1	60.6%	23.7%	46.1%

Comparables: Chris Stratton, Alec Mills, Adam Plutko

The Final Boss of the Pirates' Pitchers With Personality rotation, the heavily-tattooed Brault is not content to show off by himself, but likes to get his teammates in on the act. He hosts a podcast with Trevor Williams, and Josh Bell appears on the album of Broadway covers he released last spring. However, the results on the mound have been middling until recently, when new pitching coach Oscar Marin adjusted Brault's pitch mix to feature less of his toothsome four-seamer, which he used to throw about half the time, and instead lean more heavily on his secondaries, especially a grounder-inducing changeup. But the biggest change Marin made was encouraging Brault to stop poring over scouting reports and instead trust his catcher to call the game while he focused solely on executing pitches. It may be antithetical to an actor, but giving focus away seems to have worked for Brault, whose last two starts of the season were the best of his Pirates career. As with everything else in 2020, it's small sample size theater, but then again, the the-ah-tre is where Brault is the most comfortable.

JT Brubaker RHP Born: 11/17/93 Age: 27 Bats: R Throws: R Height: 6'3" Weight: 185 Origin: Round 6, 2015 Draft (#187 overall)

YEAR	TEAM	LVL	AGE	W	L	SV	G	GS	IP	H	HR	BB/9	K/9	K	GB%	BABIP	WHIP	ERA	DRA-	WARP	MPH	FA%	Whiff%	CSP
2018	ALT	AA	24	2	2	0	6	6	35	29	1	2.1	9.0	35	61.2%	.289	1.06	1.80	60	1.0				
2018	IND	AAA	24	8	4	0	22	22	119	121	7	2.7	7.3	96	49.0%	.323	1.32	3.10	89	1.5				
2019	WV	SS	25	0	0	0	2	2	6²	5	0	5.4	5.4	4	42.1%	.263	1.35	1.35	112	0.0				
2019	IND	AAA	25	2	1	0	4	4	21	19	2	1.7	8.6	20	52.5%	.298	1.10	2.57	58	0.8				
2020	PIT	MLB	26	1	3	0	11	9	47¹	48	6	3.2	9.1	48	47.4%	.321	1.37	4.94	85	0.8	95.7	49.8%	27.6%	45.2%
2021 FS	PIT	MLB	27	9	9	0	26	26	150	146	20	3.3	8.5	141	48.4%	.300	1.34	4.48	100	1.1	95.7	49.8%	27.6%	45.2%
2021 DC	PIT	MLB	27	2	3	0	11	11	48	46	6	3.3	8.5	45	48.4%	.300	1.34	4.48	100	0.5	95.7	49.8%	27.6%	45.2%

Comparables: Keury Mella, Chris Stratton, Walker Lockett

The 26-year-old rookie Brubaker has a rainforest-lush beard and deeply haunted eyes, eyes that have Seen Things, those Things apparently being the David Lynch joint known as the 2020 Pirates. Between a lack of prospect pedigree and missing most of 2019 with a forearm strain, he's about as under-the-radar as it gets, but there's late-inning potential here as a reliever who can touch 98 paired with a hard slider-cutter hybrid. As a starter, the fastball velocity drops slightly, but only into the 94-95 range, with above-average spin dotted at the top and bottom of the zone with late movement; alongside the scythe-like slider he adds a high-spin curveball that's been graded as average-plus but attracted significant whiffs in a limited MLB sample size. On the mound he comes right at hitters, working at a pace that suggests the game interrupted him mid-Netflix binge. Fantasy players should snatch him up on the cheap; the Eyes are not what they seem.

Blake Cederlind RHP Born: 01/04/96 Age: 25 Bats: R Throws: R Height: 6'4" Weight: 205 Origin: Round 5, 2016 Draft (#165 overall)

YEAR	TEAM	LVL	AGE	W	L	SV	G	GS	IP	H	HR	BB/9	K/9	K	GB%	BABIP	WHIP	ERA	DRA-	WARP	MPH	FA%	Whiff%	CSP
2018	WV	LO-A	22	3	2	1	19	1	28¹	21	1	2.9	11.4	36	50.0%	.312	1.06	2.86	62	0.6				
2018	BRD	HI-A	22	1	2	3	17	0	21¹	26	2	8.0	7.6	18	58.0%	.358	2.11	7.59	135	-0.4				
2019	BRD	HI-A	23	0	0	2	7	0	7²	4	0	7.0	9.4	8	50.0%	.200	1.30	1.17	77	0.1				
2019	ALT	AA	23	5	1	2	31	0	45²	31	1	3.2	8.3	42	48.8%	.252	1.03	1.77	81	0.4				
2019	IND	AAA	23	0	1	0	3	0	6	11	1	3.0	7.5	5	52.0%	.435	2.17	7.50	166	-0.1				
2020	PIT	MLB	24	0	0	0	5	0	4	3	0	2.2	9.0	4	54.5%	.273	1.00	4.50	87	0.1	100.0	100.0%	32.1%	53.3%
2021 FS	PIT	MLB	25	1	1	0	57	0	50	49	7	5.6	8.2	45	45.9%	.297	1.61	5.65	118	-0.4	100.0	100.0%	32.1%	53.3%
2021 DC	PIT	MLB	25	1	1	0	25	0	27	26	3	5.6	8.2	24	45.9%	.297	1.61	5.65	118	-0.1	100.0	100.0%	32.1%	53.3%

Comparables: Stephen Nogosek, José Ruiz, James Norwood

This past spring training Cederlind sported a glorious golden mane, which, combined with his tendency to stick out his tongue and widen his eyes mid-delivery, made it seem like a War Boy had slipped loose of Immortan Joe and was throwing triple-digit heat. (He also has a legit strikeout strut that would make Foghorn Leghorn envious.) He cut the hair before making his MLB debut, and more's the pity, but the stuff was plenty loud on its own; the first pitch he threw in MLB came in at 98 mph, and he'll regularly work 98-100, complemented with a slider at 90-92 that ties up hitters. As with any reliever with big big stuff, there's volatility present, but when he's on he shows flashes of being a top-tier closer, able to dot high-octane stuff around the zone like a War Boy wielding silver spray paint. Witness him!

Kyle Crick RHP Born: 11/30/92 Age: 28 Bats: L Throws: R Height: 6'4" Weight: 225 Origin: Round 1, 2011 Draft (#49 overall)

YEAR	TEAM	LVL	AGE	W	L	SV	G	GS	IP	H	HR	BB/9	K/9	K	GB%	BABIP	WHIP	ERA	DRA-	WARP	MPH	FA%	Whiff%	CSP
2018	PIT	MLB	25	3	2	2	64	0	60¹	45	3	3.4	9.7	65	41.2%	.269	1.13	2.39	98	0.4	97.4	72.8%	27.4%	48.0%
2019	PIT	MLB	26	3	7	0	52	0	49	41	10	6.4	11.2	61	41.5%	.274	1.55	4.96	114	-0.1	96.5	62.3%	29.6%	46.8%
2020	PIT	MLB	27	0	1	0	7	0	5²	7	0	6.4	11.1	7	33.3%	.389	1.94	1.59	97	0.1	92.5	45.2%	31.8%	39.3%
2021 FS	PIT	MLB	28	2	2	3	57	0	50	41	5	5.5	10.2	56	39.8%	.287	1.44	4.37	95	0.3	96.4	63.9%	29.1%	46.4%
2021 DC	PIT	MLB	28	2	2	3	57	0	60	49	6	5.5	10.2	67	39.8%	.287	1.44	4.37	95	0.5	96.4	63.9%	29.1%	46.4%

Comparables: Phil Maton, Archie Bradley, John Curtiss

Crick's fastball velocity was down significantly, his slider lost about 250 RPM, and he had two different stints on the IL for a lat strain. But also, he enters arbitration for the first time this year making the minimum with only five innings pitched in 2020. "This wine is awful," declares Moira Rose/Ben Cherington. "Get me another glass."

Wil Crowe RHP Born: 09/09/94   Age: 26   Bats: R   Throws: R   Height: 6'2"   Weight: 228   Origin: Round 2, 2017 Draft (#65 overall)

YEAR	TEAM	LVL	AGE	W	L	SV	G	GS	IP	H	HR	BB/9	K/9	K	GB%	BABIP	WHIP	ERA	DRA-	WARP	MPH	FA%	Whiff%	CSP
2018	AUB	SS	23	0	0	0	1	1	3	2	0	6.0	3.0	1	62.5%	.250	1.33	0.00	106	0.0				
2018	FBG	HI-A	23	11	0	0	16	15	87	71	6	3.1	8.1	78	45.8%	.270	1.16	2.69	71	2.0				
2018	HBG	AA	23	0	5	0	5	5	26¹	31	4	5.5	5.1	15	42.5%	.325	1.78	6.15	100	0.2				
2019	HBG	AA	24	7	6	0	16	16	95¹	85	8	2.1	8.4	89	48.1%	.297	1.12	3.87	92	0.5				
2019	FRE	AAA	24	0	4	0	10	10	54	66	7	4.3	6.8	41	41.2%	.337	1.70	6.17	126	0.3				
2020	WAS	MLB	25	0	2	0	3	3	8¹	14	5	8.6	8.6	8	27.6%	.375	2.64	11.88	180	-0.3	93.2	57.2%	19.4%	40.9%
2021 FS	PIT	MLB	26	8	10	0	26	26	150	154	27	4.7	7.3	122	38.6%	.291	1.55	5.53	121	-0.7	93.2	57.2%	19.4%	40.9%
2021 DC	PIT	MLB	26	3	4	0	12	12	59	60	10	4.7	7.3	48	38.6%	.291	1.55	5.53	121	0.0	93.2	57.2%	19.4%	40.9%

Comparables: Mitch White, Brady Lail, Joel Payamps

MLB debuts are supposed to be happy moments, but Crowe will probably want to forget every inning of his brief stay at the top in 2020. The former second-round pick got a shot as a fill-in starter for a trio of doubleheaders late in the season and was bombed from orbit in all three, failing to make it past the fourth inning each time. Crowe, a mid-rotation prospect thanks to a hard fastball and a mix of average or better secondary offerings, was moved to the Pirates in the Josh Bell trade, meaning he'll get a fresh start to help him forget the misery that was his first go at the big leagues.

Michael Feliz RHP Born: 06/28/93   Age: 28   Bats: R   Throws: R   Height: 6'4"   Weight: 240   Origin: International Free Agent, 2010

YEAR	TEAM	LVL	AGE	W	L	SV	G	GS	IP	H	HR	BB/9	K/9	K	GB%	BABIP	WHIP	ERA	DRA-	WARP	MPH	FA%	Whiff%	CSP
2018	IND	AAA	25	2	1	2	9	0	10	13	2	0.9	10.8	12	40.0%	.393	1.40	7.20	50	0.3				
2018	PIT	MLB	25	1	2	0	47	0	47²	49	6	4.3	10.4	55	33.1%	.331	1.51	5.66	116	-0.1	97.0	73.6%	24.3%	46.1%
2019	IND	AAA	26	0	0	2	10	0	15	13	4	4.2	13.2	22	34.3%	.364	1.33	1.20	63	0.5				
2019	PIT	MLB	26	4	4	0	58	1	56¹	44	11	4.3	11.7	73	35.8%	.264	1.26	3.99	69	1.2	97.5	73.4%	29.0%	46.7%
2020	PIT	MLB	27	0	0	0	3	0	1²	4	1	10.8	10.8	2	28.6%	.500	3.60	32.40	91	0.0	96.2	55.0%	27.8%	35.6%
2021 FS	PIT	MLB	28	2	2	1	57	0	50	40	7	4.4	10.8	60	35.7%	.279	1.29	3.89	89	0.4	97.3	72.4%	27.5%	45.9%
2021 DC	PIT	MLB	28	2	2	1	57	0	60	48	8	4.4	10.8	72	35.7%	.279	1.29	3.89	89	0.7	97.3	72.4%	27.5%	45.9%

Comparables: Keone Kela, Phil Maton, Dan Altavilla

Early 2000s Canadian indie rock band Hot Hot Heat had one driving mandate: to create abnormally catchy post-punk pop songs. With a similarly fixed mindset, Astros pitching development (Deliz arrived from Houston in the Gerrit Cole trade) prides the almighty strikeout and Hot Hot Heat, without worrying so much about limiting walks. Elite velocity can prop up that approach, but Feliz's fastball is more mid-90s than high-90s, and poor command means he falls behind in counts and cannot effectively access his putaway weapon in the slider, resulting in walks or poorly-located fastballs that get punished. A forearm strain wiped out most of his 2020 season, and might have been the reason he'd lost a full tick off his fastball. As it turns out, relying entirely on frenetically-paced earworms with no clear direction isn't a sustainable way to build an enduring musical career, nor a late-innings reliever.

Carson Fulmer RHP Born: 12/13/93   Age: 27   Bats: R   Throws: R   Height: 6'0"   Weight: 215   Origin: Round 1, 2015 Draft (#8 overall)

YEAR	TEAM	LVL	AGE	W	L	SV	G	GS	IP	H	HR	BB/9	K/9	K	GB%	BABIP	WHIP	ERA	DRA-	WARP	MPH	FA%	Whiff%	CSP
2018	CHA	AAA	24	5	6	0	25	9	67²	70	10	5.5	8.2	62	38.5%	.321	1.64	5.32	150	-1.5				
2018	CHW	MLB	24	2	4	0	9	8	32¹	37	8	6.7	8.1	29	33.0%	.299	1.89	8.07	180	-1.0	94.4	55.3%	18.3%	44.9%
2019	CHA	AAA	25	1	2	1	24	0	34	31	2	5.6	13.5	51	32.5%	.372	1.53	4.76	70	0.9				
2019	CHW	MLB	25	1	2	0	20	2	27¹	26	5	6.6	8.2	25	45.9%	.263	1.68	6.26	135	-0.4	95.3	43.9%	24.3%	45.5%
2020	PIT	MLB	26	0	0	0	10	0	10¹	8	1	4.4	9.6	11	53.6%	.259	1.26	4.35	73	0.2	93.7	54.3%	32.5%	42.9%
2021 FS	PIT	MLB	27	1	1	0	57	0	50	44	7	5.4	9.5	52	40.2%	.285	1.50	5.06	108	-0.1	94.7	49.6%	24.6%	44.7%
2021 DC	PIT	MLB	27	1	1	0	31	0	33	29	5	5.4	9.5	34	40.2%	.285	1.50	5.06	108	0.0	94.7	49.6%	24.6%	44.7%

Comparables: Chase De Jong, Lucas Sims, Robert Stephenson

After thunking around the waiver wire like a plinko chip, Fulmer landed in Pittsburgh for a second time, which is good, as it has potential to benefit both sides. As a high-profile former top draft pick widely considered a bust, molding Fulmer into an effective major-league reliever would be a feather in the cap of the Pirates' new analytics-friendly regime and a sign that the don't-call-it-a-rebuild might plod along at a slightly less ponderous pace. For Fulmer, the literal poster child for why excessive head whack is considered undesirable in pitching prospects, he gets not only a fresh start, but also a Dorothy-in-Oz experience of what experiences are available outside the world of black-and-white.

Geoff Hartlieb RHP Born: 12/09/93   Age: 27   Bats: R   Throws: R   Height: 6'5"   Weight: 240   Origin: Round 29, 2016 Draft (#885 overall)

YEAR	TEAM	LVL	AGE	W	L	SV	G	GS	IP	H	HR	BB/9	K/9	K	GB%	BABIP	WHIP	ERA	DRA-	WARP	MPH	FA%	Whiff%	CSP
2018	ALT	AA	24	8	2	10	47	0	58¹	56	3	3.7	8.6	56	61.7%	.325	1.37	3.24	78	0.8				
2019	IND	AAA	25	4	1	3	26	0	39²	31	0	3.4	11.3	50	63.3%	.316	1.16	2.50	53	1.4				
2019	PIT	MLB	25	0	1	0	29	0	35	52	8	4.6	9.8	38	45.2%	.415	2.00	9.00	104	0.1	98.1	70.4%	23.3%	49.2%
2020	PIT	MLB	26	1	0	0	21	0	22¹	16	1	7.7	7.7	19	60.0%	.254	1.57	3.63	98	0.2	95.9	53.5%	24.9%	45.6%
2021 FS	PIT	MLB	27	2	2	0	57	0	50	47	5	5.3	9.0	50	54.0%	.304	1.54	4.93	105	0.0	97.0	62.3%	24.1%	47.5%
2021 DC	PIT	MLB	27	2	2	0	44	0	47	44	5	5.3	9.0	47	54.0%	.304	1.54	4.93	105	0.1	97.0	62.3%	24.1%	47.5%

Comparables: John Curtiss, Phil Maton, Yacksel Ríos

Born with an extra bone in his foot, Hartlieb spent his first year in the bigs pitching in constant pain. He had offseason surgery prior to 2020 to address it, but then had to readjust his mechanics accordingly. Hartlieb's Instagram bio describes him as a "seasonal employee of the Pittsburgh Pirates," but the Pirates seem poised to count on him full-time next year.

Derek Holland LHP Born: 10/09/86 Age: 34 Bats: S Throws: L Height: 6'2" Weight: 213 Origin: Round 25, 2006 Draft (#748 overall)

YEAR	TEAM	LVL	AGE	W	L	SV	G	GS	IP	H	HR	BB/9	K/9	K	GB%	BABIP	WHIP	ERA	DRA-	WARP	MPH	FA%	Whiff%	CSP
2018	SF	MLB	31	7	9	0	36	30	171¹	154	19	3.5	8.9	169	39.6%	.294	1.29	3.57	84	2.9	93.3	56.9%	24.0%	49.5%
2019	CHC	MLB	32	0	1	0	20	1	15²	14	3	5.7	6.3	11	36.2%	.256	1.53	6.89	48	0.5	95.3	67.4%	22.5%	46.8%
2019	SF	MLB	32	2	4	0	31	7	68²	68	17	4.6	9.3	71	41.4%	.291	1.50	5.90	143	-1.1	94.5	60.9%	27.5%	47.9%
2020	PIT	MLB	33	1	3	0	12	5	40²	42	12	3.3	10.0	45	37.1%	.288	1.40	6.86	147	-0.7	93.8	46.7%	26.5%	46.9%
2021 FS	PIT	MLB	34	2	3	0	57	0	50	49	9	3.5	8.7	48	39.5%	.295	1.38	4.73	108	-0.1	94.0	56.1%	25.7%	48.1%

Comparables: Iván Nova, Homer Bailey, Matt Shoemaker

Wanting to improve on a lousy 2019, when he lost control of his slider and had to rely heavily on his sinker, Holland did all the right things. He hooked up with old friend pitching coach Oscar Marin, whom he knew from the Rangers organization, signed a minor-league deal with the Pirates, showed up to camp and assumed the role of Veteran Leader. Marin, well-versed in the art of retreads from two years as the Mariners' MiLB pitching coordinator in 2017-18, had Holland increase his changeup usage, pairing it with an uptick in throwing his four-seamer at the top of the zone as well as at the bottom, and added some more horizontal movement to his 12-6 slider. It didn't work, thanks partly to an outrageously high HR/FB%, which will happen when you throw a bunch of mediocre four-seamers up in the zone. Still, you have to admire the 33-year-old for trying, as well as for being the first active MLB player ejected from the stands during his team's game. Suck it, Strasburg.

Sam Howard LHP Born: 03/05/93 Age: 28 Bats: R Throws: L Height: 6'4" Weight: 190 Origin: Round 3, 2014 Draft (#82 overall)

YEAR	TEAM	LVL	AGE	W	L	SV	G	GS	IP	H	HR	BB/9	K/9	K	GB%	BABIP	WHIP	ERA	DRA-	WARP	MPH	FA%	Whiff%	CSP
2018	ABQ	AAA	25	3	8	0	21	21	96	106	13	3.2	7.5	80	36.7%	.332	1.46	5.06	104	0.7				
2018	COL	MLB	25	0	0	0	4	0	4	5	0	6.8	2.2	1	53.3%	.333	2.00	2.25	189	-0.2	92.3	48.8%	17.0%	50.5%
2019	ABQ	AAA	26	4	1	1	42	0	50²	50	5	4.1	11.0	62	44.2%	.363	1.44	3.91	61	1.6				
2019	COL	MLB	26	2	0	0	20	0	19	21	5	4.7	10.9	23	38.2%	.333	1.63	6.63	80	0.3	94.2	44.1%	32.8%	43.0%
2020	PIT	MLB	27	2	3	0	22	0	21	17	4	3.9	11.6	27	29.4%	.277	1.24	3.86	105	0.1	93.6	37.4%	35.8%	38.2%
2021 FS	PIT	MLB	28	2	2	0	57	0	50	45	7	3.6	9.7	54	37.4%	.294	1.32	4.30	96	0.2	93.8	40.6%	33.8%	40.6%
2021 DC	PIT	MLB	28	2	2	0	44	0	47	42	7	3.6	9.7	50	37.4%	.294	1.32	4.30	96	0.4	93.8	40.6%	33.8%	40.6%

Comparables: Steven Brault, Erick Fedde, Cody Reed

Howard is a long-limbed crossfire lefty with a fastball-slider combo who pitches like an atomic-age starburst clock that wished to be a real baseball player, but got monkey-pawed into the 2020 Pirates bullpen instead. That still might be preferable to pitching in Colorado, which is where the Pirates claimed him from, and his numbers did trend in a moderately more positive direction in Pittsburgh, netting a few more whiffs overall. What's most interesting about Howard isn't him as a player but as a bellwether of the current player development in Pittsburgh, indicating the Pirates are able to pick up waiver wire dross and magic it up into gold, or at least in this case, polished brass.

Jared Jones RHP Born: 08/06/01 Age: 19 Bats: L Throws: R Height: 6'1" Weight: 180 Origin: Round 2, 2020 Draft (#44 overall)

Jones tantalized scouts as a prep talent with a right arm capable of launching balls at warp speeds from the outfield, but most scouts believe the two-way prospect's future is on the mound, where his exceptional arm speed manifests in a tailing fastball that kisses triple digits. A high-effort, short-armed overhand delivery and bulldog mentality on the mound seem to telegraph a future bullpen role as a high-leverage reliever, especially as his second-best pitch currently is a swing-and-miss slider that mostly just lacks consistency. The Pirates have him working on a changeup and a curve and will give their second-rounder every opportunity to start, but a fast track to The Show as a power reliever feels like the likelier outcome.

Keone Kela RHP Born: 04/16/93 Age: 28 Bats: R Throws: R Height: 6'1" Weight: 220 Origin: Round 12, 2012 Draft (#396 overall)

YEAR	TEAM	LVL	AGE	W	L	SV	G	GS	IP	H	HR	BB/9	K/9	K	GB%	BABIP	WHIP	ERA	DRA-	WARP	MPH	FA%	Whiff%	CSP
2018	PIT	MLB	25	0	1	0	16	0	15¹	10	2	2.9	12.9	22	27.3%	.258	0.98	2.93	53	0.5	98.3	58.7%	35.2%	50.4%
2018	TEX	MLB	25	3	3	24	38	0	36²	28	3	3.4	10.8	44	39.4%	.278	1.15	3.44	78	0.6	98.5	64.3%	29.4%	49.6%
2019	PIT	MLB	26	2	0	1	32	0	29²	19	3	3.3	10.0	33	36.5%	.225	1.01	2.12	78	0.5	98.2	53.5%	27.1%	46.9%
2020	PIT	MLB	27	0	0	0	3	0	2	3	1	4.5	13.5	3	50.0%	.400	2.00	4.50	86	0.0	97.7	48.1%	26.9%	40.9%
2021 FS	PIT	MLB	28	2	2	0	57	0	50	39	6	4.4	11.4	63	38.5%	.282	1.27	3.52	83	0.6	98.3	57.0%	28.7%	47.6%

Comparables: Dominic Leone, Dan Altavilla, Phil Maton

Part of Pittsburgh's failure to add to their farm system at the trade deadline wasn't their fault, as their main piece of trade bait wound up bitten by the injury bug. A positive COVID test kept Kela out until August, and when he did return, a forearm strain polished off what remained of his Pirates career. Given his talent, a contending team seeking back-end bullpen help should snatch the hard-throwing righty up; given his health, temperament, and the state of the market, they might not.

Mitch Keller RHP   Born: 04/04/96   Age: 25   Bats: R   Throws: R   Height: 6'2"   Weight: 210   Origin: Round 2, 2014 Draft (#64 overall)

YEAR	TEAM	LVL	AGE	W	L	SV	G	GS	IP	H	HR	BB/9	K/9	K	GB%	BABIP	WHIP	ERA	DRA-	WARP	MPH	FA%	Whiff%	CSP
2018	ALT	AA	22	9	2	0	14	14	86	64	7	3.3	8.0	76	53.8%	.252	1.12	2.72	80	1.6				
2018	IND	AAA	22	3	2	0	10	10	52¹	59	3	3.8	9.8	57	32.7%	.368	1.55	4.82	81	0.9				
2019	IND	AAA	23	7	5	0	19	19	103²	94	9	3.0	10.7	123	43.2%	.331	1.24	3.56	69	3.3				
2019	PIT	MLB	23	1	5	0	11	11	48	72	6	3.0	12.2	65	39.3%	.478	1.83	7.12	85	0.8	97.3	59.5%	26.6%	48.2%
2020	PIT	MLB	24	1	1	0	5	5	21²	9	4	7.5	6.6	16	42.3%	.104	1.25	2.91	135	-0.2	96.6	55.9%	21.2%	42.3%
2021 FS	PIT	MLB	25	9	9	0	26	26	150	140	21	4.4	9.1	151	41.5%	.297	1.43	4.68	102	0.9	97.0	57.9%	24.2%	45.6%
2021 DC	PIT	MLB	25	6	8	0	24	24	121	113	17	4.4	9.1	122	41.5%	.297	1.43	4.68	102	1.1	97.0	57.9%	24.2%	45.6%

Comparables: Jake Faria, Zac Gallen, Griffin Canning

IL stints were up across MLB in 2020, but the luckless Pirates seemed to fall out of the Injury Tree and hit all the branches on the way down. The worst sting for future-focused Pirates fans was the loss of their top pitching prospect to an oblique injury after just two starts. For Keller, he lost precious development time as he continued to adjust to the more-discerning eyes of MLB batters. After his fastball got hit around in his debut year, Keller worked more on spinning it up in the zone in 2020, but more often than not wound up sailing lower-velocity fastballs up towards the cardboard cutout fans. It also affected his best secondary in his 12-6 curve, which lost a good deal of its plus drop and wasn't as effective a weapon. Keller looked much better in his return from the IL, with his fastball zooming up to 96-98, but consistency will be required for him to earn the money and fame accorded a frontline starter. Avoiding injuries and global pandemics is a good place to start.

Chad Kuhl RHP   Born: 09/10/92   Age: 28   Bats: R   Throws: R   Height: 6'3"   Weight: 210   Origin: Round 9, 2013 Draft (#269 overall)

YEAR	TEAM	LVL	AGE	W	L	SV	G	GS	IP	H	HR	BB/9	K/9	K	GB%	BABIP	WHIP	ERA	DRA-	WARP	MPH	FA%	Whiff%	CSP
2018	PIT	MLB	25	5	5	0	16	16	85	89	14	3.5	8.6	81	36.5%	.319	1.44	4.55	94	1.0	97.2	59.0%	23.6%	49.4%
2020	PIT	MLB	27	2	3	0	11	9	46¹	35	8	5.4	8.5	44	41.8%	.239	1.36	4.27	115	0.0	95.9	43.9%	27.0%	44.3%
2021 FS	PIT	MLB	28	8	9	0	26	26	150	147	24	4.2	8.7	144	44.1%	.297	1.45	4.98	108	0.4	96.4	49.6%	25.7%	46.2%
2021 DC	PIT	MLB	28	6	9	0	25	25	129	126	20	4.2	8.7	124	44.1%	.297	1.45	4.98	108	0.8	96.4	49.6%	25.7%	46.2%

Comparables: Taijuan Walker, Michael Fulmer, Zach Davies

In his much-anticipated return from TJ surgery, Kuhl displayed the consistency of an oatmeal sandwich for much of the season. The challenge of returning from a major injury and the attendant downtick in stuff as he built innings, combined with a shortened, start-and-stop season and a nagging torn fingernail on his pitching hand, added up to a performance that can be wiped away in favor of a fresh start in '21. New pitching coach Oscar Marin has shown he's not afraid to toy with pitchers' arsenals, but that hasn't yet borne out in Kuhl's offerings. He's still throwing his sinking fastball 42 percent of the time, and it got hit hard (6 HR, .667 SLG), though he was much improved after a midseason IL stint. Kuhl Hand believers will note his best start of the year was his last one, when he blanked the Cubs over seven innings.

Brennan Malone RHP   Born: 09/08/00   Age: 20   Bats: R   Throws: R   Height: 6'4"   Weight: 205   Origin: Round 1, 2019 Draft (#33 overall)

YEAR	TEAM	LVL	AGE	W	L	SV	G	GS	IP	H	HR	BB/9	K/9	K	GB%	BABIP	WHIP	ERA	DRA-	WARP	MPH	FA%	Whiff%	CSP
2019	DIA	ROK	18	1	2	0	6	3	7	4	0	6.4	9.0	7	33.3%	.222	1.29	5.14	68	0.2				
2019	HIL	SS	18	0	0	0	1	0	1	0	0	0.0	9.0	1	50.0%	.000	1.00	0.00	68	0.0				
2021 FS	PIT	MLB	20	2	3	0	57	0	50	52	8	6.6	7.9	44	35.9%	.300	1.77	6.37	143	-1.1				

It's hard to overlook a 6'4" chunk of rock face like Malone's. But through a combination of factors—he threw only eight innings as a pro before being shipped to the no-frills Steel City, lifting weights in his North Carolina driveway through most of the COVID-shortened season—even die-hard yinzers might not know the gem-in-waiting they have in Malone, who is built to factory specs for a frontline starter. A thrower more than a pitcher in high school, Malone is learning to harness his elite velocity while working on sharpening his occasionally-loopy curveball and changeup. A late-breaking slider with tight spin remains his best out pitch and can give righties fits. If the Pirates go chalk and select Vanderbilt's Kumar Rocker first overall in the 2021 draft, the potential one-two punch of Rocker and Malone could drive twin road graders over NL Central lineups for years to come, years from now.

Carmen Mlodzinski RHP   Born: 02/19/99   Age: 22   Bats: R   Throws: R   Height: 6'2"   Weight: 232   Origin: Round 1, 2020 Draft (#31 overall)

Pronounced "Ma-jin-ski," the former Gamecock was snatched up by the Pirates with the 31st-overall pick in the 2020 draft despite limited looks, thanks largely to a strong performance on the Cape where he showcased swing-and-miss stuff on a mid-90s fastball and a hard slider/curveball. That alone gives him a safe floor in the bullpen, but he also throws a cutter and a solid changeup, all with plus command, that give him solid middle-of-the-rotation potential. With an abbreviated college track record and absolutely no social media where fans can follow his journey, Mlodzinski will continue working, building a mlodzystery, and choosing his pitches carefully.

Joe Musgrove RHP   Born: 12/04/92   Age: 28   Bats: R   Throws: R   Height: 6'5"   Weight: 230   Origin: Round 1, 2011 Draft (#46 overall)

YEAR	TEAM	LVL	AGE	W	L	SV	G	GS	IP	H	HR	BB/9	K/9	K	GB%	BABIP	WHIP	ERA	DRA-	WARP	MPH	FA%	Whiff%	CSP
2018	IND	AAA	25	1	1	0	2	2	10²	10	0	1.7	9.3	11	37.5%	.312	1.12	5.06	67	0.3				
2018	PIT	MLB	25	6	9	0	19	19	115¹	113	12	1.8	7.8	100	45.9%	.297	1.18	4.06	76	2.5	95.2	50.3%	23.7%	53.6%
2019	PIT	MLB	26	11	12	0	32	31	170¹	168	21	2.1	8.3	157	44.1%	.300	1.22	4.44	73	4.0	94.8	49.5%	24.7%	49.1%
2020	PIT	MLB	27	1	5	0	8	8	39²	33	5	3.6	12.5	55	47.3%	.318	1.24	3.86	73	0.9	94.5	39.1%	33.0%	45.6%
2021 FS	PIT	MLB	28	9	8	0	26	26	150	137	20	2.4	9.9	164	44.5%	.303	1.18	3.62	84	2.4	94.8	47.3%	26.4%	49.1%
2021 DC	PIT	MLB	28	8	8	0	27	27	140	128	18	2.4	9.9	153	44.5%	.303	1.18	3.62	84	2.7	94.8	47.3%	26.4%	49.1%

Comparables: Kevin Gausman, Jameson Taillon, Zach Davies

The one they call "Big Joe" wears a cornicello necklace, a pointy, twisted gold horn meant to protect one from the evil eye or anyone who wants to talk about the Gerrit Cole trade. Maybe Musgrove should take it in to get serviced, though, as he missed a third of this shortened season with triceps inflammation, perhaps caused by pointing to the sky at the four homers he served up in under 15 innings before the injury. Musgrove improved significantly upon his return from the IL, giving up a single long ball and setting a career-best mark for strikeout percentage. He's an excellent sleeper fantasy target in 2021, but approach with caution, as even his cornicello can't protect him from the trade winds in Pittsburgh.

Cody Ponce RHP Born: 04/25/94 Age: 27 Bats: R Throws: R Height: 6'6" Weight: 255 Origin: Round 2, 2015 Draft (#55 overall)

YEAR	TEAM	LVL	AGE	W	L	SV	G	GS	IP	H	HR	BB/9	K/9	K	GB%	BABIP	WHIP	ERA	DRA-	WARP	MPH	FA%	Whiff%	CSP
2018	BLX	AA	24	7	6	0	29	11	95	88	10	3.2	8.3	88	43.6%	.294	1.28	4.36	85	1.3				
2019	BLX	AA	25	1	3	1	27	0	38¹	33	1	2.8	10.3	44	54.5%	.330	1.17	3.29	90	0.1				
2019	ALT	AA	25	0	0	1	3	1	6	3	1	1.5	9.0	6	40.0%	.143	0.67	6.00	63	0.1				
2019	IND	AAA	25	1	3	0	4	4	18²	18	4	3.4	9.6	20	52.7%	.275	1.34	5.30	81	0.5				
2020	PIT	MLB	26	1	1	0	5	3	17	12	5	3.2	6.4	12	35.4%	.163	1.06	3.18	144	-0.2	94.7	68.3%	19.1%	48.8%
2021 FS	PIT	MLB	27	1	2	0	57	0	50	46	8	3.3	7.8	43	41.6%	.275	1.30	4.43	101	0.1	94.7	68.3%	19.1%	48.8%
2021 DC	PIT	MLB	27	1	2	0	22	3	33	30	5	3.3	7.8	28	41.6%	.275	1.30	4.43	101	0.2	94.7	68.3%	19.1%	48.8%

Comparables: Asher Wojciechowski, Wes Parsons, Erick Fedde

If you're looking at your favorite team's rotation and wondering why they all boast the personality of a wafer cookie, it's because the Pirates are hogging all of the fun pitchers. Mustachioed, merry and a little mischievous, Ponce's persona is more colorful than his stuff, although some dream of moving "The Big Fella" to the 'pen where his fastball could play into the upper 90s paired with a hard, slider-ish cutter that wipes out lefties. But Ponce impressed in a rotation audition, showcasing an ability to spot both the fastball and the cutter all over the zone, along with an average curve that has swing-and-miss potential and a changeup he spent quarantine improving. He might have the prototypical wacky reliever sense of humor, but everything else about this profile feels back-end starter-like, at least until proven otherwise.

Quinn Priester RHP Born: 09/15/00 Age: 20 Bats: R Throws: R Height: 6'3" Weight: 195 Origin: Round 1, 2019 Draft (#18 overall)

YEAR	TEAM	LVL	AGE	W	L	SV	G	GS	IP	H	HR	BB/9	K/9	K	GB%	BABIP	WHIP	ERA	DRA-	WARP	MPH	FA%	Whiff%	CSP
2019	PIR	ROK	18	1	1	0	8	7	32²	29	1	2.8	10.2	37	57.3%	.322	1.19	3.03	116	0.1				
2019	WV	SS	18	0	0	0	1	1	4	3	0	9.0	9.0	4	90.0%	.300	1.75	4.50	100	0.0				
2021 FS	PIT	MLB	20	2	3	0	57	0	50	50	8	5.4	8.1	44	47.9%	.297	1.61	5.68	131	-0.7				

Priester was the last first-rounder selected by the previous regime and surprise, surprise, he throws a sinker. But he also throws a gorgeous 12-6 curveball that was among the best in his draft class and commands his pitches well, with clean mechanics and more polish than is typical for a cold-weather prep prospect. The 19-year-old was summoned to join the player pool at Altoona when Ke'Bryan Hayes was called up, and was reportedly sitting 96-97, touching 98, with his fastball this summer. He's also working on a changeup that was undeveloped, probably because unlike other top pitching prospects he didn't have a pitching coach until joining the Pirates organization. Prior to being called to the player pool, Priester made an impression with Pirates fans this summer when the Cary, IL native and erstwhile Cubs fan joined his mother to cheer on his new team from a Wrigleyville rooftop—a place he visited often with his grandfather, whom he had lost to COVID-19 just months earlier. It is an undeniable tragedy John Foley will never be able to watch his grandson pitch from those same bleachers, but what a special moment it will be when Priester makes his debut at Wrigley Field. Book your rooftop seat now.

Richard Rodríguez RHP Born: 03/04/90 Age: 31 Bats: R Throws: R Height: 6'4" Weight: 220 Origin: International Free Agent, 2010

YEAR	TEAM	LVL	AGE	W	L	SV	G	GS	IP	H	HR	BB/9	K/9	K	GB%	BABIP	WHIP	ERA	DRA-	WARP	MPH	FA%	Whiff%	CSP
2018	IND	AAA	28	0	0	0	2	0	5	1	0	3.6	16.2	9	14.3%	.143	0.60	0.00	16	0.2				
2018	PIT	MLB	28	4	3	0	63	0	69¹	55	5	2.5	11.4	88	35.9%	.311	1.07	2.47	63	1.7	94.5	75.1%	30.9%	50.6%
2019	PIT	MLB	29	4	5	1	72	0	65¹	65	14	3.2	8.7	63	43.7%	.280	1.35	3.72	96	0.5	94.8	85.2%	23.9%	48.2%
2020	PIT	MLB	30	3	2	4	24	0	23¹	15	3	1.9	13.1	34	38.5%	.250	0.86	2.70	76	0.5	94.5	72.4%	36.0%	46.1%
2021 FS	PIT	MLB	31	2	2	23	57	0	50	42	7	2.7	10.5	58	38.1%	.286	1.15	3.50	82	0.6	94.7	79.5%	28.7%	48.2%
2021 DC	PIT	MLB	31	2	2	23	57	0	60	51	9	2.7	10.5	69	38.1%	.286	1.15	3.50	82	0.9	94.7	79.5%	28.7%	48.2%

Comparables: Paul Sewald, Andrew Kittredge, Jacob Barnes

Pittsburgh had two of the top 50 relievers in a year where bullpens were inventing new ways to shave years off fans' lives, so it's weird that both of them finished the year as Pirates, especially as both are 30-year-olds just now entering their first year of arbitration. Of the two, Rodríguez has more of the late-inning profile, with a high-spin fastball/slider combo. He doubled said slider usage in 2020 and saw an attendant rise in whiffs, ranking in the top five percent of all pitchers in strikeout percentage, but also dabbled dangerously with hard-hit balls when the breaking pitches didn't break. It's possible some poor outings right at the deadline colored league perception, or maybe Ben Cherington set the price too high, but dealing neither pitcher at the deadline feels like a missed opportunity both for the team and for fans around the league who white-knuckled their way through late innings in the playoffs.

José Soriano RHP Born: 10/20/98 Age: 22 Bats: R Throws: R Height: 6'3" Weight: 220 Origin: International Free Agent, 2016

YEAR	TEAM	LVL	AGE	W	L	SV	G	GS	IP	H	HR	BB/9	K/9	K	GB%	BABIP	WHIP	ERA	DRA-	WARP	MPH	FA%	Whiff%	CSP
2018	BUR	LO-A	19	1	6	0	14	14	46¹	34	1	6.8	8.2	42	45.3%	.284	1.49	4.47	89	0.6				
2019	ANG	ROK	20	0	1	0	3	3	4²	5	0	5.8	15.4	8	25.0%	.417	1.71	1.93	34	0.2				
2019	BUR	LO-A	20	5	6	0	17	15	77²	53	5	5.6	9.7	84	54.0%	.262	1.30	2.55	90	0.7				
2021 FS	PIT	MLB	22	1	2	0	57	0	50	49	8	6.5	8.3	46	44.2%	.295	1.71	6.05	130	-0.7				
2021 DC	PIT	MLB	22	1	2	0	22	3	33	32	5	6.5	8.3	30	44.2%	.295	1.71	6.05	130	-0.3				

Comparables: Chris Flexen, Alex Reyes, Huascar Ynoa

Going under the knife is rarely fortuitous, especially in the case of Tommy John surgery. Still, getting TJ a month before the world ended and took the minor-league season with it—as Soriano did in February—counts as pretty solid timing. The Pirates still took him with the top pick in the Rule 5 Draft, and while he's likely to be sidelined into 2021, his mid-90s velocity gives him a chance to stick in a relief role once he heals.

Chris Stratton RHP   Born: 08/22/90   Age: 30   Bats: R   Throws: R   Height: 6'2"   Weight: 205   Origin: Round 1, 2012 Draft (#20 overall)

YEAR	TEAM	LVL	AGE	W	L	SV	G	GS	IP	H	HR	BB/9	K/9	K	GB%	BABIP	WHIP	ERA	DRA-	WARP	MPH	FA%	Whiff%	CSP
2018	SAC	AAA	27	3	0	0	4	4	24	25	3	3.0	9.0	24	43.7%	.324	1.38	3.00	80	0.5				
2018	SF	MLB	27	10	10	0	28	26	145	153	19	3.4	7.0	112	42.9%	.308	1.43	5.09	111	0.5	92.6	62.2%	21.0%	49.9%
2019	PIT	MLB	28	1	1	0	28	0	46²	50	7	2.9	9.1	47	38.4%	.328	1.39	3.66	87	0.5	94.9	63.7%	25.6%	48.3%
2019	LAA	MLB	28	0	2	0	7	5	29¹	43	6	5.5	6.8	22	42.3%	.378	2.08	8.59	185	-1.0	92.3	46.7%	22.7%	44.2%
2020	PIT	MLB	29	2	1	0	27	0	30	26	3	3.9	11.7	39	48.1%	.303	1.30	3.90	77	0.6	94.9	46.6%	35.3%	43.2%
2021 FS	PIT	MLB	30	2	2	5	57	0	50	47	7	3.4	9.1	50	43.0%	.297	1.33	4.24	96	0.2	93.9	56.3%	25.9%	47.0%
2021 DC	PIT	MLB	30	2	2	5	57	0	60	56	8	3.4	9.1	60	43.0%	.297	1.33	4.24	96	0.5	93.9	56.3%	25.9%	47.0%

Comparables: Sam Gaviglio, Kendall Graveman, Joe Kelly

In case you forgot from the comment above, the duo of Stratton-Rodríguez were worth more wins than the rest of the Pirates bullpen combined, so it's odd neither were moved at the trade deadline. Rodríguez has the more prototypical swing-and-miss stuff, but Stratton has a starter's complement of pitches with better underlying metrics, including elite spin on both his fastball and curve and an ability to generate lots of whiffs. In a perfect world, Stratton acts as a long reliever and Rodríguez is the setup man to Cederlind, but in another, more perfect world, both of them have been turned into prospects to further boost Pittsburgh's farm system.

Jameson Taillon RHP   Born: 11/18/91   Age: 29   Bats: R   Throws: R   Height: 6'5"   Weight: 230   Origin: Round 1, 2010 Draft (#2 overall)

YEAR	TEAM	LVL	AGE	W	L	SV	G	GS	IP	H	HR	BB/9	K/9	K	GB%	BABIP	WHIP	ERA	DRA-	WARP	MPH	FA%	Whiff%	CSP
2018	PIT	MLB	26	14	11	0	33	33	198	186	20	2.1	8.4	184	46.0%	.301	1.18	3.18	76	4.2	96.7	57.3%	24.1%	48.5%
2019	PIT	MLB	27	2	3	0	7	7	37¹	34	4	1.9	7.2	30	48.3%	.263	1.12	4.10	76	0.8	96.4	47.2%	24.2%	48.3%
2021 FS	PIT	MLB	29	9	8	0	26	26	150	143	17	2.5	8.5	141	47.0%	.299	1.23	3.73	86	2.2	96.6	54.5%	24.2%	48.5%
2021 DC	PIT	MLB	29	4	5	0	16	16	81	77	9	2.5	8.5	76	47.0%	.299	1.23	3.73	86	1.4	96.6	54.5%	24.2%	48.5%

Comparables: Gerrit Cole, Joe Musgrove, Michael Wacha

Now a two-time Tommy John veteran as well as a cancer survivor, Taillon's so tough, anchors have tattoos of him. The former second-overall pick knows the odds of pitchers returning successfully from a second TJ surgery are against him, but he's buoyed by a positive attitude and survivor's mindset, fueled by the extensive time he's spent giving back in charitable endeavors around Pittsburgh. He's also optimistic about significant changes he's made in his mechanics (shortening his arm path) and delivery (using his legs more) which he says have his elbow feeling better than ever, and has also adjusted his training and recovery schedule to focus on long-term arm health. The odds might not be favorable, but Taillon makes it very hard to bet against him. Who would want to, anyway?

Nik Turley LHP   Born: 09/11/89   Age: 31   Bats: L   Throws: L   Height: 6'4"   Weight: 230   Origin: Round 50, 2008 Draft (#1502 overall)

YEAR	TEAM	LVL	AGE	W	L	SV	G	GS	IP	H	HR	BB/9	K/9	K	GB%	BABIP	WHIP	ERA	DRA-	WARP	MPH	FA%	Whiff%	CSP
2020	PIT	MLB	30	0	3	1	25	0	21²	13	1	4.6	8.3	20	32.8%	.211	1.11	4.98	111	0.1	96.1	55.5%	25.8%	47.1%
2021 FS	PIT	MLB	31	2	3	0	57	0	50	48	8	4.3	9.6	53	36.0%	.301	1.45	5.06	110	-0.2	96.1	55.5%	25.8%	47.1%
2021 DC	PIT	MLB	31	2	3	0	57	0	60	58	10	4.3	9.6	64	36.0%	.301	1.45	5.06	110	0.0	96.1	55.5%	25.8%	47.1%

Comparables: Neil Ramírez, Matt Magill, T.J. McFarland

A former 50th-round pick who's spent time with six different organizations plus stints in indy ball and LIDOM; significant time missed due to a PED suspension followed by TJ surgery; a three-year gap, longer than some MLB careers, between appearances in a big-league game. Turley took a circuitous journey to his first Opening Day at 30 years old, but he's more than just a feel-good story. The surface numbers don't look great but the stuff is legit: a fastball he'll spin in the top of the zone for swinging strikes and a big curve with significant two-plane break that isn't a Twitter-famous pitch yet, but should be, both for its wild movement path and the utterly hideous swings it can induce. His mound demeanor is best described as "mid-transformation werewolf doing an oral report on the Necronomicon," so proceed accordingly, gif-makers.

Trevor Williams RHP   Born: 04/25/92   Age: 29   Bats: R   Throws: R   Height: 6'3"   Weight: 235   Origin: Round 2, 2013 Draft (#44 overall)

YEAR	TEAM	LVL	AGE	W	L	SV	G	GS	IP	H	HR	BB/9	K/9	K	GB%	BABIP	WHIP	ERA	DRA-	WARP	MPH	FA%	Whiff%	CSP
2018	PIT	MLB	26	14	10	0	31	31	170²	146	15	2.9	6.6	126	40.5%	.265	1.18	3.11	95	2.0	93.2	69.4%	18.9%	46.0%
2019	PIT	MLB	27	7	9	0	26	26	145²	162	27	2.7	7.0	113	36.9%	.308	1.41	5.38	117	0.1	93.6	66.7%	22.4%	46.4%
2020	PIT	MLB	28	2	8	0	11	11	55¹	66	15	3.4	8.0	49	43.3%	.315	1.57	6.18	130	-0.4	93.3	51.1%	24.3%	42.3%
2021 FS	PIT	MLB	29	1	2	0	57	0	50	50	7	3.1	7.7	42	42.1%	.295	1.35	4.57	102	0.1	93.4	62.8%	22.1%	45.1%
2021 DC	PIT	MLB	29	1	2	0	6	6	32	32	4	3.1	7.7	27	42.1%	.295	1.35	4.57	102	0.3	93.4	62.8%	22.1%	45.1%

Comparables: José Ureña, Kevin Gausman, Mike Foltynewicz

After drastically altering his pitch mix early in the season, almost halving his use of the fastball, by late September his usage had crept back up, and with it a league-leading number of homers surrendered. A peek at his xBA/xSLG indicates he's been unlucky with his breaking pitches, but it's been an undeniably bumpy road for Williams in the Steel City. Always open and unflinchingly honest, Williams is the first to admit the 2020 season wore at him on and off the mound; unfortunately for him, the pitching-rich Pirates didn't need to keep him around to figure things out. Instead, they thanked him for the memes and designated him for assignment.

ST. LOUIS CARDINALS

Essay by Jasmyn Wimbish

Player comments by Ken Funck and BP staff

To quote one-half of the legendary rap group OutKast:

"Baby boy, you only funky as your last cut
You focus on the past, your ass'll be a 'has-what'"

If that isn't a perfect verse to describe the St. Louis Cardinals, then I don't know what is.

St. Louis loves talking about the generations of tradition and success that have littered its organizational record books. There's even a book passed around to players in the franchise called "The Cardinal Way." It serves as one part instruction manual to detail what is expected of you based on the illustrious history of past players, and one part guide book to point players in the right direction with game-related questions.

For the past seven years, the Cardinals have ranked in the top three in attendance because of that tradition. Hell, that tradition is part of what sucked me into becoming a fan of the team in the first place. The first time I visited Busch Stadium it was like that moment when Harry Potter first lays his eyes on Hogwarts, in all its enormity and magic. Everything about the ballpark feels steeped in tradition and history. From the statues of all-time greats Stan Musial, Lou Brock and Bob Gibson on the corner of Clark Ave. and 8th Street, to the 11 World Series banners and 23 National League pennants displayed around the ballpark that signify that this isn't just any old ball club.

You can tell St. Louis is a city serious about baseball and its support of the Cardinals from the moment you immerse yourself in the atmosphere. But that history can only carry them so far, and while the Cardinals have benefited from it in the form of ticket sales, fan-generated revenue and championships in the past, it has also made them susceptible to making more mistakes of late when it comes to the product on the field.

It's easy to take your eye off the ball when you're among the most valuable baseball franchises in the league. But like OutKast said, the Cardinals are only as funky as their last cut, and the fact of the matter is, since winning 100 games in 2016, which resulted in a disappointing divisional round

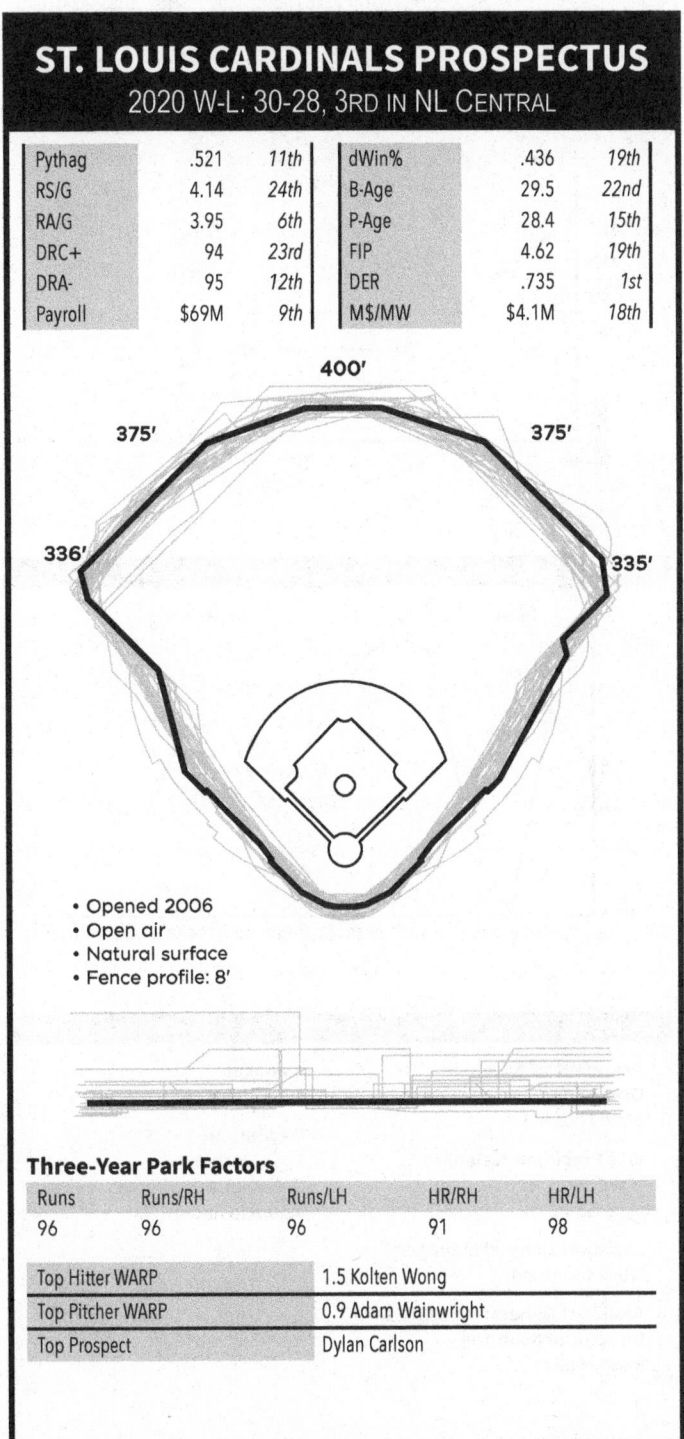

ST. LOUIS CARDINALS PROSPECTUS
2020 W-L: 30-28, 3RD IN NL CENTRAL

Pythag	.521	11th	dWin%	.436	19th
RS/G	4.14	24th	B-Age	29.5	22nd
RA/G	3.95	6th	P-Age	28.4	15th
DRC+	94	23rd	FIP	4.62	19th
DRA-	95	12th	DER	.735	1st
Payroll	$69M	9th	M$/MW	$4.1M	18th

- Opened 2006
- Open air
- Natural surface
- Fence profile: 8'

Three-Year Park Factors

Runs	Runs/RH	Runs/LH	HR/RH	HR/LH
96	96	96	91	98

Top Hitter WARP	1.5 Kolten Wong
Top Pitcher WARP	0.9 Adam Wainwright
Top Prospect	Dylan Carlson

Payroll History (in millions)

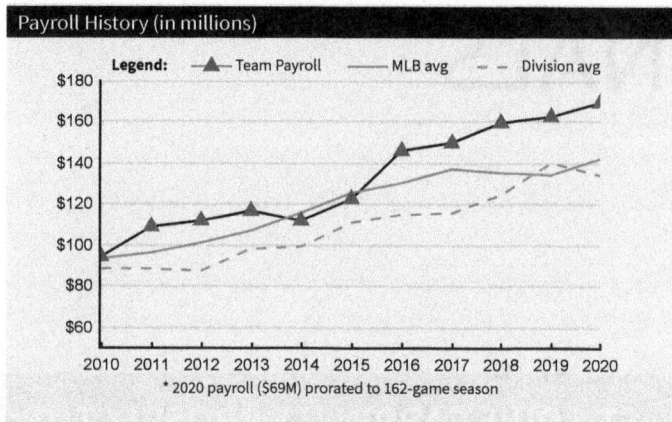

Legend: ▲ Team Payroll — MLB avg -- Division avg

2020 payroll ($69M) prorated to 162-game season

Future Commitments (in millions)

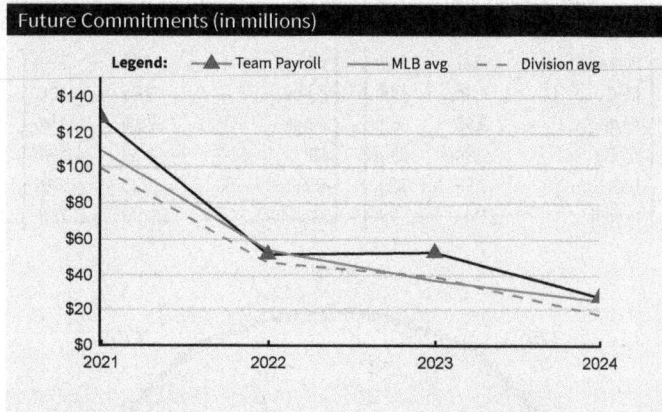

Legend: ▲ Team Payroll — MLB avg -- Division avg

Farm System Ranking

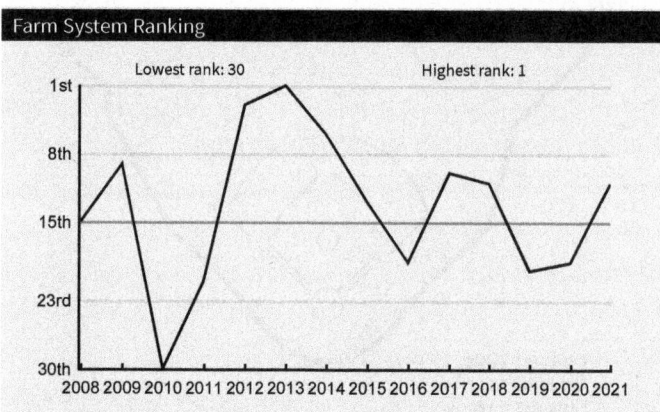

Lowest rank: 30   Highest rank: 1

Personnel

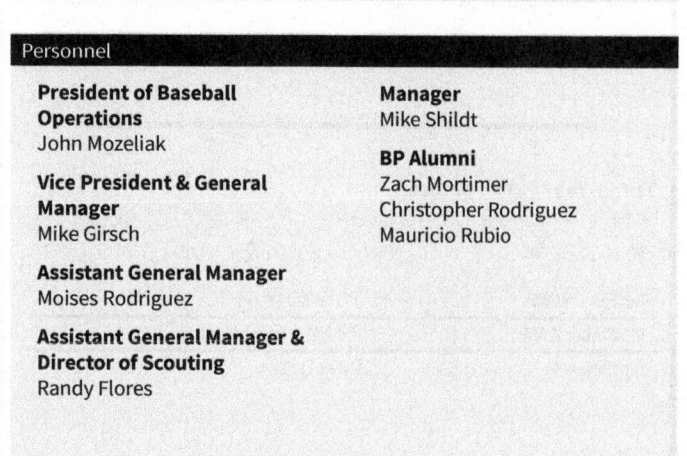

President of Baseball Operations
John Mozeliak

Vice President & General Manager
Mike Girsch

Assistant General Manager
Moises Rodriguez

Assistant General Manager & Director of Scouting
Randy Flores

Manager
Mike Shildt

BP Alumni
Zach Mortimer
Christopher Rodriguez
Mauricio Rubio

playoff loss, St. Louis has been an average ball club that is still resting on the achievements of past teams, rather than focusing on the future.

Take, for instance, when St. Louis tried to pitch itself to Giancarlo Stanton in 2017. The angle the front office reportedly used was focusing on tradition and the past championships the Cardinals have won. But Stanton wanted to hear about the future and what this team can do going forward. In the end, harping on what was wasn't enough to convince Stanton to waive his no-trade clause, and the two-time Silver Slugger ended up on a Yankees team with an incredibly bright future.

It's evidence that the history and strong branding the Cardinals have built going back decades isn't enough to sell the biggest-named players in the league on their team. The team responded by acquiring Paul Goldschmidt via trade, a move that, after a worrying first season, deserves praise. But the very fact that the Cardinals were forced to expend resources to obtain a star, rather than sign one through free agency, is telling. The product on the field needs to match the messaging of the franchise, and right now that's not happening.

In regard to the players the Cardinals have brought in recently, either through trade or free agency, there've been quite a few who haven't lived up to expectation. Marcell Ozuna is the most recent example. Ozuna was traded to the Cardinals when the Miami Marlins were holding their latest fire sale. After posting back-to-back All-Star seasons in Miami, complete with a Gold Glove and Silver Slugger award, St. Louis thought he would solve its lack of a big bat in the lineup. After all, Ozuna was just coming off a season in which he smacked 37 home runs.

Instead, in the two seasons he had in St. Louis, his production took a dip. He wasn't as dominant as he was in Miami, and it showed across almost every major statistical category at the plate. His slugging percentage dropped, his on-base percentage fell from .350 the prior two seasons with Miami, to .327 with St. Louis. His DRC+ fell accordingly, as his 109 and 111 figures, while still above average, paled in comparison to the 134 he had just recorded with the Marlins. His defense, whether truly deserving of a Gold Glove or not when with Miami, deteriorated significantly over his tenure in St. Louis.

What is interesting about Ozuna, though, is after the Cards decided not to bring him back as a free agent before the start of the 2020 season, he joined the Atlanta Braves, where he went on to have one of the best seasons of his career. He led the league in home runs and RBI, and had an eye-popping on-base percentage of .431 to go along with a .338 batting average, resulting in a 151 DRC+, good for fourth in the majors and tied with Mike Trout.

And that's not the first time a Cardinals player left the organization after suboptimal production, and found significant success with another team. Tommy Pham certainly comes to mind, as does Dexter Fowler. Watching the Fowler experience unfold is especially resonant of Ozuna.

After five straight seasons of above-league average offensive production, Fowler had a strong initial season with St. Louis before watching his offense all but disappear. He's rebounded a bit the last two seasons, but not anywhere approaching his previous highs. It's fair to say he's underwhelmed both at the plate and in the field while battling through injuries that have repeatedly cost him time.

There's also Mike Leake, who the Cardinals paid big money to be an anchor in the rotation, though he never lived up to the contract. St. Louis signed the veteran pitcher to a five-year, $80 million deal, and after posting ERAs of 4.69 in 2016, and 4.29 in the first half of 2017, St. Louis traded him (and some of his salary) to the Mariners with little to show for it.

The Cardinals are far from the only team that has whiffed on signings and trades, but for a franchise that has historically seen more success than failure in that arena, the moves made in the last five years are especially jarring.

It's also not the only area where the Cardinals have struggled recently. St. Louis used to be a franchise that were kings of the process in developing players and finding the diamonds in the rough. It was evident enough that they inspired the hashtag #CardinalsDevilMagic, suggesting they were so good at turning nothing into something, there must be some dark arts involved. For years, the Cardinals farm system ranked among the best in the league despite their winning records, but recently, they've turned into a farm system for other teams, who continue to steal promising prospects in exchange for minimal success.

It's still early, but the name Randy Arozarena might haunt the Cardinals for years to come. The 25-year-old outfielder made a name for himself during the playoffs when he broke the record for most home runs by a rookie in a single postseason (seven), and followed that up by setting a new big-league record for most homers in one postseason (10). To top it off, he also set single-postseason records for hits (29) and total bases (64). By the time the World Series was over, it almost felt like Arozarena was the Rays' offense.

But before he became a household name with Tampa Bay, Arozarena was buried on the Cardinals bench or playing Triple-A ball, where he hit .396 in 2018 and .358 in 2019. Meanwhile, St. Louis was scratching its head trying to figure out how to make a dollar out of 15 cents with outfielders like Harrison Bader, who was hitting .200 at the time.

Context is key: The Cardinals traded Arozarena for coveted pitching prospect Matthew Liberatore (who could end up being phenomenal in a few years), but president of baseball operations John Mozeliak did admit fault in trading Arozarena after seeing him burst out in the postseason, saying "we will revisit how we rank our own players and make sure that we don't have something like this happen again."

That may be true, but it still doesn't take the sting away from that trade. Especially when you consider that he got just 23 plate appearances in 2019, while Bader (84 DRC+), José Martínez (94), and Yairo Muñoz (73)—all of whom came up

through St. Louis' farm system as well—were underwhelming for long stretches of time on offense. That's a clear oversight by a franchise that typically prides itself on being the best at identifying talent.

St. Louis failed to give Arozarena a big enough opportunity in the majors to show what he could do, and instead hoped to get production out of guys who hadn't been consistent.

It's also not the first time the Cardinals have misevaluated their own talent, whether that's trading Tommy Pham, whose OPS would've been a ray of sunshine in St. Louis' lineup prior to 2020, underestimating Luke Voit's abilities, or sticking too long with Matt Carpenter at third base when Tommy Edman was clearly better defensively, running the bases and at the plate in most statistical categories.

The Pham situation, though, is the perfect example of the Cardinals not having a great handle on its own talent. Pham was traded essentially to make room for the excess in outfielding talent that existed within the Cardinals farm system, along with some rumblings of discord between the player and the front office. But it's been two years since that trade happened and St. Louis is still hurting for quality outfielders.

Munoz was cut after he ghosted the franchise over frustrations with how he was being used, Martinez was traded with Arozarena to the Rays for Liberatore, and while Bader and Tyler O'Neill may be great defenders, their performances at the dish raise doubts about their usefulness, especially in a lineup already devoid of a ton of hitting power.

How does a franchise that was once dominant at identifying great talent within its own farm system fail to see that their in-house replacements suddenly compound problems by bringing in talent that doesn't peak while trading away talent that does?? It's a problem that St. Louis needs to solve in a hurry.

It would be remiss not to mention the fact that the Cardinals did make a trip to the NLCS in 2019 against the eventual champion Washington Nationals. St. Louis also still managed to make the postseason last year after having to postpone a good portion of its schedule due to a COVID-19 outbreak within the locker room, and pushed the San Diego Padres to three games in the Wild Card round.

But the Cardinals have never been known to be a franchise satisfied with just making the postseason, or just making it out of the Wild Card round. This is not the Pittsburgh Pirates essay. Past success keeps fans coming out in droves to Busch Stadium, but it won't keep them there if the Cardinals continue to rest on their laurels of being a once dominant ball club. Otherwise, more players like Arozarena will slip through the cracks, and guys like Stanton will be unimpressed with their sales pitches because instead of being focused on the future, they'll still be talking about the past. Fortunately, flags fly forever, even the sepia-toned ones.

—Jasmyn Wimbish is an author for CBS Sports.

HITTERS

Harrison Bader CF Born: 06/03/94   Age: 27   Bats: R   Throws: R   Height: 6'0"   Weight: 210   Origin: Round 3, 2015 Draft (#100 overall)

YEAR	TEAM	LVL	AGE	PA	R	2B	3B	HR	RBI	BB	K	SB	CS	Whiff%	AVG/OBP/SLG	DRC+	BABIP	BRR	FRAA	WARP
2018	STL	MLB	24	427	61	20	2	12	37	31	125	15	3	28.4%	.264/.334/.422	90	.358	2.8	CF(74): 9.1, RF(38): 1.6, LF(6): 0.1	2.2
2019	MEM	AAA	25	75	23	3	0	7	15	8	16	3	0		.317/.427/.698	157	.325	1.4	CF(16): 1.7	1.0
2019	STL	MLB	25	406	54	14	3	12	39	46	117	11	3	26.6%	.205/.314/.366	83	.268	4.5	CF(122): 14.4	2.5
2020	STL	MLB	26	125	21	7	2	4	11	13	40	3	1	28.3%	.226/.336/.443	85	.317	-0.7	CF(49): -3.6	-0.4
2021 FS	STL	MLB	27	600	70	22	2	20	68	50	187	11	4	27.5%	.227/.311/.396	100	.306	0.4	CF 13, LF 0	3.3
2021 DC	STL	MLB	27	334	39	12	1	11	38	27	104	6	2	27.5%	.227/.311/.396	100	.306	0.2	CF 7	1.9

Comparables: Ruben Rivera, Larry Hisle, Drew Stubbs

Bader is a good boy, yes he is, who plays with the energy, enthusiasm and natural athleticism of a golden retriever. He bounds around the bases with reckless abandon and lives to chase down balls in the gap and finish innings with a dive, a catch, an impish grin and a contented trot back to the dugout. However, breaking stuff can leave him nosing through the azaleas in a confused and futile search for that tennis ball you only pretended to throw. Bader isn't a hacker so much as a guy who works deeps counts and gets fooled too often, leading to strikeouts in almost a third of his plate appearances last year. Everything else in his game is trending in the right direction, and Bader's combination of superlative defense, speed, walks and occasional power should make him a solid regular even if his two-strike approach never improves—and, as a result, he should be the recipient of plenty of boops on the nose, with the occasional belly rub mixed in.

★ ★ ★ *2021 Top 101 Prospect* **#16** ★ ★ ★

Dylan Carlson RF Born: 10/23/98   Age: 22   Bats: S   Throws: L   Height: 6'2"   Weight: 205   Origin: Round 1, 2016 Draft (#33 overall)

YEAR	TEAM	LVL	AGE	PA	R	2B	3B	HR	RBI	BB	K	SB	CS	Whiff%	AVG/OBP/SLG	DRC+	BABIP	BRR	FRAA	WARP
2018	PEO	LO-A	19	57	5	3	0	2	9	10	10	2	0		.234/.368/.426	134	.257	-0.7	RF(10): 2.3, CF(4): -0.3	0.4
2018	PMB	HI-A	19	441	63	19	3	9	53	52	78	6	3		.247/.345/.386	113	.286	1.7	RF(50): 4.7, LF(37): -0.1, CF(1): -0.1	1.2
2019	SPR	AA	20	483	81	24	6	21	59	52	98	18	7		.281/.364/.518	150	.315	3.1	CF(87): -10.2, RF(9): -0.3, LF(5): -0.5	2.7
2019	MEM	AAA	20	79	14	4	2	5	9	6	18	2	1		.361/.418/.681	141	.429	0.1	CF(8): -0.5, LF(7): 0.0, RF(3): -0.2	0.6
2020	STL	MLB	22	119	11	7	1	3	16	8	35	1	1	30.3%	.200/.252/.364	80	.260	-0.4	RF(18): 1.8, CF(17): -0.8, LF(10): -0.3	0.2
2021 FS	STL	MLB	22	600	65	23	3	19	68	49	180	4	2	30.3%	.216/.287/.381	87	.282	1.0	CF -8, LF 1	-0.1
2021 DC	STL	MLB	22	534	58	20	3	17	60	44	160	4	1	30.3%	.216/.287/.381	87	.282	0.9	CF -7, LF 1	0.0

Comparables: Colby Rasmus, Nomar Mazara, Lastings Milledge

When St. Louis nabbed Carlson in the 2016 draft, he became the 10th outfielder or corner man they've chosen in the first round this century. None of the previous nine have posted a 2-win year in Redbird laundry, and only a handful of Piscotty and Rasmus joints earned even a single win, which proves that Cardinals Devil Magic can't always overcome the perpetual drag of drafting late. As for Carlson, look past the ugly numbers he put up as a 21-year-old rookie, trust your eyes and bet on him breaking the pattern. After an early September demotion to clear his head, the young switch-hitter showcased the approach, power and bat-to-ball skills of a future middle-of-the-order force. Carlson has good wheels and can handle center field but is a plus defender in a corner, where he'll be a value-priced building block for the next half-decade.

Matt Carpenter 3B Born: 11/26/85   Age: 35   Bats: L   Throws: R   Height: 6'4"   Weight: 210   Origin: Round 13, 2009 Draft (#399 overall)

YEAR	TEAM	LVL	AGE	PA	R	2B	3B	HR	RBI	BB	K	SB	CS	Whiff%	AVG/OBP/SLG	DRC+	BABIP	BRR	FRAA	WARP
2018	STL	MLB	32	677	111	42	0	36	81	102	158	4	1	24.4%	.257/.374/.523	135	.291	-1.5	1B(95): -3.6, 3B(76): 4.8, 2B(11): -0.6	4.6
2019	STL	MLB	33	492	59	20	2	15	46	63	129	6	1	25.9%	.226/.334/.392	95	.285	-1.9	3B(107): -6.5, 1B(4): -0.2	0.7
2020	STL	MLB	35	169	22	6	0	4	24	23	48	0	0	33.7%	.186/.325/.314	98	.250	0.0	3B(30): 4.2, 1B(6): -0.3	0.6
2021 FS	STL	MLB	35	600	70	26	1	19	70	85	167	3	1	27.3%	.224/.346/.400	108	.293	-0.4	3B 0, 1B 0	1.8
2021 DC	STL	MLB	35	534	62	23	1	17	62	75	148	3	1	27.3%	.224/.346/.400	108	.293	-0.3	3B 0, 1B 0	1.7

Comparables: Howard Johnson, Scott Rolen, Eric Chavez

"I'm a dog chasing cars. I wouldn't know what to do with one if I caught it!" Heath Ledger's Joker (still the best) said that, but it could just as well have been the current incarnation of Carpenter. The former 13th-round pick has built an impressive career out of grinding through at-bats, waiting for a pitch he can handle and putting a hurt on it. Carpenter's plate discipline and batting eye remain top shelf, and he still earns his free passes and sorts through buckets of pitches looking for the one with his name on it. But these days Carpenter doesn't know what to do with the meatballs he does catch, bouncing them harmlessly into the shift or swinging through them en route to a career-worst strikeout rate. His glove has become a millstone, and while the designated hitter came to the Senior Circuit last year the limited demand for a designated walker is unlikely to extend Carpenter's career as an everyday player. His peak was a joy to behold, but as he enters the back half of his 30s he's best cast as a professional pinch-hitter and veteran clubhouse presence.

Austin Dean   LF   Born: 10/14/93   Age: 27   Bats: R   Throws: R   Height: 6'0"   Weight: 215   Origin: Round 4, 2012 Draft (#137 overall)

YEAR	TEAM	LVL	AGE	PA	R	2B	3B	HR	RBI	BB	K	SB	CS	Whiff%	AVG/OBP/SLG	DRC+	BABIP	BRR	FRAA	WARP
2018	JAX	AA	24	88	13	8	1	3	14	6	7	0	0		.420/.466/.654	196	.437	-2.0	LF(21): 0.5	0.8
2018	NO	AAA	24	358	58	12	4	9	54	33	49	2	2		.326/.397/.475	134	.360	0.5	LF(45): -2.2, RF(37): -0.8	1.5
2018	MIA	MLB	24	122	16	4	0	4	14	7	22	1	0	17.1%	.221/.279/.363	92	.241	1.1	LF(31): 0.5	0.4
2019	NO	AAA	25	282	48	19	1	18	57	28	52	4	3		.337/.401/.635	147	.364	2.2	1B(26): 0.7, LF(22): 2.0, RF(11): 1.3	2.6
2019	MIA	MLB	25	189	17	14	0	6	21	9	47	0	2	21.9%	.225/.261/.404	77	.270	1.0	LF(44): -2.8, 1B(5): -0.1, RF(5): 0.3	-0.2
2020	STL	MLB	27	7	1	1	0	0	0	3	2	0	0	35.7%	.250/.571/.500	85	.500		LF(2): 0.0, 1B(1): -0.0, RF(1): -0.0	0.0
2021 FS	*STL*	*MLB*	*27*	*600*	*67*	*24*	*2*	*21*	*77*	*45*	*143*	*1*	*0*	*21.5%*	*.243/.303/.415*	*101*	*.288*	*0.7*	*LF -2, RF -1*	*1.4*
2021 DC	*STL*	*MLB*	*27*	*200*	*22*	*8*	*0*	*7*	*25*	*15*	*47*	*0*	*0*	*21.5%*	*.243/.303/.415*	*101*	*.288*	*0.2*	*LF -1, RF 0*	*0.4*

Comparables: Henry Rodriguez, Mark Smith, Craig Monroe

Dean has spent the last few years alternately raking in the high minors and face-planting in the National League, and, at age 27, fits one of the game's most unfortunate labels: Quad-A tweener.

Paul DeJong   SS   Born: 08/02/93   Age: 27   Bats: R   Throws: R   Height: 6'0"   Weight: 205   Origin: Round 4, 2015 Draft (#131 overall)

YEAR	TEAM	LVL	AGE	PA	R	2B	3B	HR	RBI	BB	K	SB	CS	Whiff%	AVG/OBP/SLG	DRC+	BABIP	BRR	FRAA	WARP
2018	STL	MLB	24	490	68	25	1	19	68	36	123	1	1	25.3%	.241/.313/.433	101	.288	3.1	SS(114): 0.3	2.7
2019	STL	MLB	25	664	97	31	1	30	78	62	149	9	5	24.4%	.233/.318/.444	103	.259	0.5	SS(157): 7.1	4.2
2020	STL	MLB	27	174	17	6	0	3	25	17	50	1	0	32.3%	.250/.322/.349	87	.340	0.4	SS(45): -3.2	-0.1
2021 FS	*STL*	*MLB*	*27*	*600*	*69*	*23*	*1*	*22*	*78*	*46*	*170*	*3*	*1*	*26.4%*	*.233/.304/.409*	*98*	*.295*	*-1.1*	*SS 2, 2B 0*	*1.9*
2021 DC	*STL*	*MLB*	*27*	*567*	*65*	*22*	*1*	*21*	*74*	*44*	*161*	*3*	*1*	*26.4%*	*.233/.304/.409*	*98*	*.295*	*-1.0*	*SS 2*	*1.8*

Comparables: Jhonny Peralta, Corey Seager, Bobby Crosby

A plus defensive shortstop with serious juice in his bat, DeJong has already blasted more home runs than all other Normal residents combined, which makes the Illinois State alum's power outage last year a bit of a mystery. His swings were even whiffier than usual, but when he did make contact DeJong lofted as many flyballs and smacked them just as hard as he has in the past. So, why did almost all of them settle into outfielders' gloves? Because he got a little underneath most of them, causing his rate of home runs per flyball to crater. Unless you're a Giancarlo-class Natural Born Slugger, that's a metric prone to great variation over time. With a few small adjustments and a little luck DeJong should be back launching bombs with aplomb next year; like most of us, then, he'd be wise to toss 2020 in the memory hole and work toward a more normal future.

Tommy Edman   SS   Born: 05/09/95   Age: 26   Bats: S   Throws: R   Height: 5'10"   Weight: 180   Origin: Round 6, 2016 Draft (#196 overall)

YEAR	TEAM	LVL	AGE	PA	R	2B	3B	HR	RBI	BB	K	SB	CS	Whiff%	AVG/OBP/SLG	DRC+	BABIP	BRR	FRAA	WARP
2018	SPR	AA	23	498	71	23	3	6	36	35	76	27	5		.299/.350/.403	114	.345	3.4	SS(65): -1.4, 2B(22): 1.1, 3B(22): 0.7	1.9
2018	MEM	AAA	23	76	13	0	1	1	5	8	11	3	0		.318/.382/.394	119	.357	1.0	2B(14): 1.4, SS(3): -0.1	0.6
2019	MEM	AAA	24	218	39	12	4	7	29	15	33	9	0		.305/.356/.513	102	.333	3.7	2B(25): 0.0, SS(10): -1.5, 3B(9): -0.5	1.1
2019	STL	MLB	24	349	59	17	7	11	36	16	61	15	1	18.7%	.304/.350/.500	109	.346	4.7	3B(55): 0.3, 2B(29): 0.7, RF(12): 1.0	2.3
2020	STL	MLB	25	227	29	7	1	5	26	16	48	2	4	19.1%	.250/.317/.368	84	.301	1.5	3B(31): 0.3, SS(13): -1.1, RF(13): -1.5	0.0
2021 FS	*STL*	*MLB*	*26*	*600*	*71*	*25*	*5*	*13*	*62*	*38*	*126*	*13*	*2*	*18.9%*	*.255/.310/.392*	*97*	*.307*	*8.9*	*2B 6, 3B 1*	*3.2*
2021 DC	*STL*	*MLB*	*26*	*567*	*67*	*23*	*4*	*12*	*58*	*36*	*119*	*13*	*2*	*18.9%*	*.255/.310/.392*	*97*	*.307*	*8.4*	*2B 6, 3B 1*	*3.0*

Comparables: Max Alvis, Wes Helms, Dave Hollins

Last summer's limited release of *The Edman Who Fell To Earth* may have been somewhat predictable and disappointing, but there was enough talent on display to expect a successful run. Smashing double-digit home runs and slugging an ultra-cool .500 during his 2019 debut was a totally alien experience for Edman, so no one should have been surprised when the fleet switch-hitter went back to his offensive roots by slapping singles, drawing the occasional walk and posting mundane numbers in line with what you should expect from him going forward. Overexposed as a headline player, Edman's speed and capable defense all around the diamond buoys his chances to carve out a long and versatile career.

Dexter Fowler   RF   Born: 03/22/86   Age: 35   Bats: S   Throws: R   Height: 6'5"   Weight: 205   Origin: Round 14, 2004 Draft (#410 overall)

YEAR	TEAM	LVL	AGE	PA	R	2B	3B	HR	RBI	BB	K	SB	CS	Whiff%	AVG/OBP/SLG	DRC+	BABIP	BRR	FRAA	WARP
2018	STL	MLB	32	334	40	10	0	8	31	38	75	5	2	26.3%	.180/.278/.298	77	.210	2.0	RF(75): -4.3	-0.4
2019	STL	MLB	33	574	69	24	1	19	67	74	141	8	5	27.3%	.238/.346/.409	100	.293	-0.5	RF(118): -0.3, CF(58): -3.4	1.2
2020	STL	MLB	34	101	14	2	0	4	15	10	28	1	1	31.9%	.233/.317/.389	95	.293	-0.1	RF(27): -2.3	-0.2
2021 FS	*STL*	*MLB*	*35*	*600*	*67*	*20*	*2*	*17*	*67*	*75*	*163*	*9*	*4*	*27.9%*	*.228/.334/.382*	*105*	*.296*	*0.4*	*RF -4, CF 0*	*1.7*
2021 DC	*STL*	*MLB*	*35*	*467*	*52*	*16*	*2*	*13*	*52*	*58*	*127*	*7*	*3*	*27.9%*	*.228/.334/.382*	*105*	*.296*	*0.3*	*RF -3*	*1.1*

Comparables: Rick Monday, Mike Cameron, Andy Van Slyke

Fowler built on his solid, if unspectacular, 2019 bounceback by posting a .279/.347/.485 line through August before being sidelined for treatment of his ulcerative colitis. When the lanky outfielder returned three weeks later he cratered, finishing off another replacement-level summer. Fowler's walk and strikeout rates were the worst of his career, he's a double-in-waiting when he stands in right field, and blah blah miserable blah. Let's also not forget his intelligence and openness, his megawatt smile, the way he quietly lives his faith, and his generosity to fans, teammates and needy strangers. There's one season left on Fowler's deal with the Cardinals, during which both sides expected and perhaps deserved a little more from each other. Those five years won't be what he's remembered for.

Paul Goldschmidt 1B Born: 09/10/87 Age: 33 Bats: R Throws: R Height: 6'3" Weight: 220 Origin: Round 8, 2009 Draft (#246 overall)

YEAR	TEAM	LVL	AGE	PA	R	2B	3B	HR	RBI	BB	K	SB	CS	Whiff%	AVG/OBP/SLG	DRC+	BABIP	BRR	FRAA	WARP
2018	ARI	MLB	30	690	95	35	5	33	83	90	173	7	4	26.5%	.290/.389/.533	136	.359	-1.3	1B(155): 1.7	4.1
2019	STL	MLB	31	682	97	25	1	34	97	78	166	3	1	26.3%	.260/.346/.476	119	.302	-0.8	1B(159): -7.3	1.9
2020	STL	MLB	33	231	31	13	0	6	21	37	43	1	0	23.7%	.304/.417/.466	126	.364	-0.7	1B(52): 2.7	1.3
2021 FS	STL	MLB	33	600	83	24	1	21	77	90	140	12	4	25.7%	.269/.383/.454	138	.330	1.5	1B 1	4.1
2021 DC	STL	MLB	33	567	78	22	1	20	73	85	133	12	3	25.7%	.269/.383/.454	138	.330	1.4	1B 1	3.9

Comparables: Fred McGriff, Harmon Killebrew, Carlos Delgado

The Cardinals signed Goldschmidt to get on base and provide power in the middle of their lineup, and he's done exactly that—just not quite both at the same time. Goldschmidt's 2019 season featured the power and run production we've grown to expect from him, but his batting average and on-base percentage were those of a mere mortal. Last year he once again reached base at an elite rate but posted by far the lowest isolated power mark of his career, sacrificing some pull-side pop in order to avoid strikeouts and stroke a few more line drives to right field. Whether he chooses the Slugger or Hitter avatar going forward he'll still be worth the $22 million he's due each of the next four seasons, but America's First Baseman is no longer tied to the .300/.400/.500 Goldy standard.

★ ★ ★ 2021 Top 101 Prospect #23 ★ ★ ★

Nolan Gorman 3B Born: 05/10/00 Age: 21 Bats: L Throws: R Height: 6'1" Weight: 210 Origin: Round 1, 2018 Draft (#19 overall)

YEAR	TEAM	LVL	AGE	PA	R	2B	3B	HR	RBI	BB	K	SB	CS	Whiff%	AVG/OBP/SLG	DRC+	BABIP	BRR	FRAA	WARP
2018	JC	ROK	18	167	41	10	1	11	28	24	37	1	3		.350/.443/.664	209	.411	-0.7	3B(33): 7.6	2.2
2018	PEO	LO-A	18	107	8	3	0	6	16	10	39	0	2		.202/.280/.426	77	.255	-0.5	3B(25): 3.9	0.3
2019	PEO	LO-A	19	282	41	14	3	10	41	32	79	2	0		.241/.344/.448	128	.312	0.4	3B(51): 8.4	2.6
2019	PMB	HI-A	19	230	24	16	3	5	21	13	73	0	1		.256/.304/.428	107	.365	-2.1	3B(49): -5.9	0.0
2021 FS	STL	MLB	21	600	55	27	3	15	62	43	224	1	0		.209/.272/.354	70	.320	0.9	3B 3	-0.7

Comparables: Ryan McMahon, Austin Riley, Tyler Goeddel

Last year in this space, after noting that Gorman would predictably start at one minor-league level, dominate, gain a promotion and then see both his strikeouts and power spike, we asked the universe to "get more creative writers." If that plea in any way caused the universe to shake things up by inviting, y'know, 2020 upon us, please accept our apologies. Gorman spent last summer at the club's alternate training site working to reduce his worrisome strikeout rate while retaining his light-tower power—a story archetype writers call "Overcoming the Monster." Here's hoping the next chapter is revealed later this year.

Ivan Herrera C Born: 06/01/00 Age: 21 Bats: R Throws: R Height: 5'11" Weight: 220 Origin: International Free Agent, 2016

YEAR	TEAM	LVL	AGE	PA	R	2B	3B	HR	RBI	BB	K	SB	CS	Whiff%	AVG/OBP/SLG	DRC+	BABIP	BRR	FRAA	WARP
2018	CAR	ROK	18	130	23	6	4	1	25	11	20	1	1		.348/.423/.500	154	.409	-1.9	C(20): 0.6	0.6
2019	PEO	LO-A	19	291	41	10	0	8	42	35	56	1	1		.286/.381/.423	138	.337	-0.1	C(64): -1.0	2.4
2019	PMB	HI-A	19	65	7	0	0	1	5	5	16	0	0		.276/.338/.328	116	.357	-1.1	C(18): -0.1	0.3
2021 FS	STL	MLB	21	600	60	24	2	10	58	34	178	1	0		.241/.294/.352	82	.333	0.5	C -2	1.0
2021 DC	STL	MLB	21	66	6	2	0	1	6	3	19	0	0		.241/.294/.352	82	.333	0.1	C 0	0.1

Comparables: Chance Sisco, Wil Myers, Hank Conger

Herrera vaulted up prospect lists after a standout 2019 season where he showcased a well-rounded set of tools and a surprisingly mature approach for a teenager in full-season leagues. The young Panamanian continued to impress during spring training, where he was an eager participant in Yadi's kaffeeklatsch, and at the team's summer complex, where he worked hard to implement the master's lessons on defense and leadership. Herrera has the tools and the makeup to grow into a solid receiver, a swing that can generate average power and a birth certificate indicating he could be the first St. Louis catching prospect in a generation to be ready for the big-league job at the precise moment the big-league job is ready for him.

Andrew Knizner C Born: 02/03/95 Age: 26 Bats: R Throws: R Height: 6'1" Weight: 225 Origin: Round 7, 2016 Draft (#226 overall)

YEAR	TEAM	LVL	AGE	PA	R	2B	3B	HR	RBI	BB	K	SB	CS	Whiff%	AVG/OBP/SLG	DRC+	BABIP	BRR	FRAA	WARP
2018	SPR	AA	23	313	39	13	0	7	41	23	40	0	1		.313/.365/.434	133	.339	-1.4	C(74): -7.3	1.0
2018	MEM	AAA	23	61	3	5	0	0	4	4	8	0	0		.315/.383/.407	116	.370	-0.1	C(16): 1.8	0.5
2019	MEM	AAA	24	280	41	10	0	12	34	24	37	2	0		.276/.357/.463	111	.281	-0.8	C(61): -17.2	0.2
2019	STL	MLB	24	58	7	2	0	2	7	4	14	2	0	29.5%	.226/.293/.377	82	.270	0.5	C(16): -4.4, 1B(1): -0.0	-0.2
2020	STL	MLB	25	17	1	1	0	0	4	0	5	0	0	28.9%	.250/.235/.312	71	.333		C(7): -0.1	-0.1
2021 FS	STL	MLB	26	600	67	26	1	16	71	39	124	1	0	29.3%	.251/.313/.397	100	.294	-0.7	C -14, 1B 0	0.9
2021 DC	STL	MLB	26	434	48	19	1	12	52	28	90	1	0	29.3%	.251/.313/.397	100	.294	-0.5	C -13	0.3

Comparables: Hank Conger, Elias Díaz, Curtis Thigpen

YEAR	TEAM	P. COUNT	FRM RUNS	BLK RUNS	THRW RUNS	TOT RUNS
2019	STL	2098	-4.0	-0.4	0.1	-4.3
2020	STL	679	-0.3	0.0	0.0	-0.3
2021	STL	15632	-15.4	2.5	0.8	-12.2

André-François Raffray, age 47, once signed a contract that required him to pay Jeanne Calment, age 90, a generous monthly stipend until she died, after which Raffray would inherit her apartment. For 30 years the French lawyer waited and watched as Calment continued to dance, cycle, smoke and cash his checks until Raffray passed away, his patience unfulfilled. You know where we're going with this. Knizner has been the latest Raffray to haunt the Cardinals clubhouse, fated to spend his mid-20s watching Yadier Molina stare down Father Time. He's a bat-first backstop with a career

.303/.369/.461 minor league line and a compact swing that can make enough noise to drown out his often sketchy receiving skills. Knizner has struggled mightily at the plate during his first few trips to The Lou, however, and if he doesn't figure out big league pitching soon he won't be around long enough to inherit anyone's starting gig behind the dish.

Brad Miller 2B Born: 10/18/89 Age: 31 Bats: L Throws: R Height: 6'2" Weight: 195 Origin: Round 2, 2011 Draft (#62 overall)

YEAR	TEAM	LVL	AGE	PA	R	2B	3B	HR	RBI	BB	K	SB	CS	Whiff%	AVG/OBP/SLG	DRC+	BABIP	BRR	FRAA	WARP
2018	RMV	AAA	28	31	4	0	0	1	2	3	9	1	0		.185/.258/.296	46	.222	-0.7	SS(6): 0.2, 2B(1): 0.1	-0.1
2018	TB	MLB	28	174	16	10	1	5	21	16	51	0	0	31.6%	.256/.322/.429	81	.343	-0.6	1B(35): -2.1, 2B(6): 0.2	-0.4
2018	MIL	MLB	28	80	5	3	1	2	8	6	31	0	0	35.0%	.230/.287/.378	83	.366	-0.7	2B(15): 0.1, SS(6): -0.4, 1B(1): 0.0	0.0
2019	SWB	AAA	29	163	31	9	1	10	29	24	40	1	3		.294/.399/.596	132	.341	-0.7	2B(13): -0.9, LF(11): 0.6, 3B(10): -1.3	0.8
2019	CLE	MLB	29	40	4	3	0	1	4	4	10	1	0	29.7%	.250/.325/.417	81	.320	0.7	2B(13): 0.4	0.1
2019	PHI	MLB	29	130	22	3	1	12	21	11	35	1	0	31.1%	.263/.331/.610	128	.268	0.3	3B(19): 0.4, LF(16): 1.3, SS(1): 0.0	1.1
2020	STL	MLB	31	171	21	8	1	7	25	25	46	1	0	35.7%	.232/.357/.451	104	.289	-0.5	3B(15): -0.0, SS(2): -0.1, 2B(1): 0.1	0.3
2021 FS	STL	MLB	31	600	70	24	3	22	77	69	171	5	2	33.6%	.224/.319/.413	103	.287	0.5	2B -2, 1B -1	1.9

Comparables: Woodie Held, Stephen Drew, Jose Valentin

The fact that Miller, a man who over the previous season-and-a-half had been traded by the Rays and released or sold by the Brewers, Dodgers, Cleveland, Yankees and Phillies, wound up co-leading St. Louis with seven home runs last year speaks well of his resilience and poorly of the Cardinals offense. The vagabond lefty came out hot, slashing .317/.450/.619 through September 1, before struggling mightily the rest of the way. It's that streakiness, alongside his inability to play in the middle of the diamond, which has left Miller riding the rails so frequently despite his obvious offensive talent. At least he can now say he's the greatest DH in Cardinals history, which ought to count for something in this crazy mixed-up world.

Yadier Molina C Born: 07/13/82 Age: 38 Bats: R Throws: R Height: 5'11" Weight: 225 Origin: Round 4, 2000 Draft (#113 overall)

YEAR	TEAM	LVL	AGE	PA	R	2B	3B	HR	RBI	BB	K	SB	CS	Whiff%	AVG/OBP/SLG	DRC+	BABIP	BRR	FRAA	WARP
2018	STL	MLB	35	503	55	20	0	20	74	29	66	4	3	17.3%	.261/.314/.436	110	.264	-2.3	C(121): 1.4, 1B(5): 0.0	3.1
2019	STL	MLB	36	452	45	24	0	10	57	23	58	6	0	19.1%	.270/.312/.399	91	.289	-2.4	C(111): 0.6, 1B(4): 0.0, 3B(1): -0.0	1.7
2020	STL	MLB	38	156	12	2	0	4	16	6	21	0	0	23.9%	.262/.303/.359	91	.281	-1.0	C(42): -0.2, 1B(2): -0.0	0.5
2021 FS	STL	MLB	38	600	57	23	0	13	67	32	98	6	2	19.8%	.252/.300/.372	86	.282	-1.9	C 3, 1B 0	1.5

Comparables: Ramon Hernandez, Mike Redmond, Carlos Ruiz

It's clear that Molina, who crossed the 2,000-hit plateau last year, is no longer quite the offensive or defensive force he once was. It's also clear that doesn't really matter at this point, that his career has soared well past any need to apply objective analysis. There's no way we can quantify how much value his game-calling skills, leadership and confidence-building influence provides to his organization, so we have to take the word of every teammate, coach, manager and opponent when they say it's immense. And that, too, no

YEAR	TEAM	P. COUNT	FRM RUNS	BLK RUNS	THRW RUNS	TOT RUNS
2018	STL	17406	2.3	1.2	0.1	3.7
2019	STL	15645	0.3	1.5	-0.1	1.8
2020	STL	5637	2.2	0.0	-0.2	2.1
2021	STL	16650	1.8	2.3	1.4	5.5

longer really matters. Willie Nelson claims that Trigger, his beat up old Martin, has the greatest tone of any guitar in the world. There's no way that's objectively true, but as long as Trigger's worn and battle-scarred body holds up and is able to produce sound, who in their right mind would argue Willie Nelson would be better playing something else?

Elehuris Montero 3B Born: 08/17/98 Age: 22 Bats: R Throws: R Height: 6'3" Weight: 235 Origin: International Free Agent, 2014

YEAR	TEAM	LVL	AGE	PA	R	2B	3B	HR	RBI	BB	K	SB	CS	Whiff%	AVG/OBP/SLG	DRC+	BABIP	BRR	FRAA	WARP
2018	PEO	LO-A	19	425	68	28	3	15	69	33	81	2	0		.322/.381/.529	163	.372	0.3	3B(77): 2.7	4.0
2018	PMB	HI-A	19	106	13	9	0	1	13	5	22	1	0		.286/.330/.408	116	.355	0.6	3B(20): 0.8	0.4
2019	SPR	AA	20	238	23	8	0	7	18	14	74	0	1		.188/.235/.317	33	.245	-0.4	3B(52): -6.2	-1.4
2021 FS	STL	MLB	22	600	61	24	2	18	66	35	193	1	0		.215/.267/.365	76	.292	0.2	3B -3	-0.9
2021 DC	STL	MLB	22	334	34	13	1	10	36	19	107	0	0		.215/.267/.365	76	.292	0.1	2B 0, 3B -2	-0.2

Comparables: Josh Vitters, Nick Castellanos, Dilson Herrera

Fate kept Montero from getting another crack at Double-A to prove his punchless 2019 was a mere injury-marred blip; time and plus raw power are in his corner, but contact issues and a lack of athleticism that might force him across the diamond are threatening to knock his prospect status cold.

John Nogowski 1B Born: 01/05/93 Age: 28 Bats: R Throws: L Height: 6'0" Weight: 245 Origin: Round 34, 2014 Draft (#1032 overall)

YEAR	TEAM	LVL	AGE	PA	R	2B	3B	HR	RBI	BB	K	SB	CS	Whiff%	AVG/OBP/SLG	DRC+	BABIP	BRR	FRAA	WARP
2018	CAR	ROK	25	34	5	0	0	0	3	3	4	1	0		.345/.412/.345	141	.385	1.4	1B(7): 0.4	0.2
2018	SPR	AA	25	347	41	10	0	12	61	41	21	0	2		.309/.392/.463	148	.296	-2.0	1B(78): 15.0, LF(2): -0.1	2.7
2019	MEM	AAA	26	463	77	22	1	15	75	69	54	1	2		.295/.413/.476	128	.308	-6.2	1B(107): 12.1, P(3): -0.1	2.8
2020	STL	MLB	27	4	0	0	0	0	0	0	1	0	0	25.0%	.250/.250/.250	66	.333	-0.4	1B(1): 0.0	-0.1
2021 FS	STL	MLB	28	600	73	27	1	16	68	59	102	0	0	25.0%	.265/.347/.414	117	.299	-1.2	1B 10, LF 0	3.1
2021 DC	STL	MLB	28	233	28	10	0	6	26	23	39	0	0	25.0%	.265/.347/.414	117	.299	-0.5	1B 4	1.3

Comparables: Daric Barton, David Cooper, Dan Johnson

A former 34th-round pick, Nogowski made it all the way to the Show last summer. He's walked more than he's whiffed in his minor-league career, but his lack of a first baseman's power makes him more of a no-go-ski going forward.

Tyler O'Neill LF Born: 06/22/95 Age: 26 Bats: R Throws: R Height: 5'11" Weight: 200 Origin: Round 3, 2013 Draft (#85 overall)

YEAR	TEAM	LVL	AGE	PA	R	2B	3B	HR	RBI	BB	K	SB	CS	Whiff%	AVG/OBP/SLG	DRC+	BABIP	BRR	FRAA	WARP
2018	MEM	AAA	23	273	61	9	2	26	63	29	68	3	1		.311/.385/.693	162	.324	1.0	LF(33): -1.3, RF(21): 7.8, CF(6): -1.0	2.9
2018	STL	MLB	23	142	29	5	0	9	23	7	57	2	0	46.1%	.254/.303/.500	89	.364	2.2	RF(24): 0.7, LF(16): 1.1, CF(3): -0.4	0.5
2019	MEM	AAA	24	166	26	5	0	11	26	14	51	3	0		.265/.325/.517	104	.322	0.7	LF(25): 0.2, RF(11): 1.0	0.6
2019	STL	MLB	24	151	18	6	0	5	16	10	53	1	0	41.4%	.262/.311/.411	75	.386	-0.9	LF(33): -3.3, RF(8): -0.2, CF(3): 0.3	-0.4
2020	STL	MLB	25	157	20	5	0	7	19	15	43	3	1	33.9%	.173/.261/.360	95	.189	-0.6	LF(48): 8.4	0.9
2021 FS	STL	MLB	26	600	70	22	2	26	80	53	195	1	0	38.3%	.218/.295/.417	98	.285	0.9	LF -13, CF 0	0.2
2021 DC	STL	MLB	26	367	43	14	1	16	49	32	119	1	0	38.3%	.218/.295/.417	98	.285	0.6	LF -8	0.2

Comparables: Billy Ashley, Bo Jackson, Pete Incaviglia

First, the good news: O'Neill walked more, struck out less and began to take advantage of his blazing speed and natural athleticism to play a tremendous, Gold Glove-winning left field last year. His swinging strike rate was no longer among the worst in the league, and it wasn't even extraordinarily awful. However, more frequent contact came at the expense of his calling card: power. O'Neill simply stopped hitting the ball hard, posting a .187 isolated power score that barely exceeds sluggers like Freddy Galvis and José Iglesias and a league-low batting average on balls in play. His exit velocity last year was in the 36th percentile. Now that O'Neill has worked to regain some mastery of the strike zone it's possible he can add some thunder back into his swing, but that's easier said than done. Any fool can solve one side of a Rubik's Cube; solving all six at once is the real trick.

Rangel Ravelo 1B Born: 04/24/92 Age: 29 Bats: R Throws: R Height: 6'1" Weight: 235 Origin: Round 6, 2010 Draft (#188 overall)

YEAR	TEAM	LVL	AGE	PA	R	2B	3B	HR	RBI	BB	K	SB	CS	Whiff%	AVG/OBP/SLG	DRC+	BABIP	BRR	FRAA	WARP
2018	MEM	AAA	26	399	57	19	2	13	67	42	49	0	1		.308/.392/.487	136	.328	0.6	1B(54): 3.6, LF(36): -1.7, RF(1): 0.1	2.1
2019	MEM	AAA	27	381	50	20	1	12	56	37	61	0	1		.299/.383/.473	118	.336	-0.3	1B(43): 1.4, LF(36): 2.9, 3B(5): -0.1	1.9
2019	STL	MLB	27	43	4	2	0	2	7	3	12	0	0	24.1%	.205/.256/.410	76	.231	-0.1	1B(9): -0.5	-0.1
2020	STL	MLB	28	41	5	1	0	1	6	4	6	0	0	28.7%	.171/.244/.286	91	.167	0.3	RF(4): -0.6, 1B(3): -0.1, LF(1): 0.1	0.1
2021 FS	STL	MLB	29	600	66	27	1	18	73	52	128	0	0	26.8%	.245/.322/.405	105	.288	-0.7	1B 4, LF -1	1.8

Comparables: Steve Pearce, Chris Marrero, Chris Carter

Ravelo has minimal power but makes contact and gets on base, which would be fine if he were a smooth left-handed second baseman instead of either a stiff right-handed first baseman or the short side of a DH platoon.

Edmundo Sosa SS Born: 03/06/96 Age: 25 Bats: R Throws: R Height: 6'0" Weight: 210 Origin: International Free Agent, 2012

YEAR	TEAM	LVL	AGE	PA	R	2B	3B	HR	RBI	BB	K	SB	CS	Whiff%	AVG/OBP/SLG	DRC+	BABIP	BRR	FRAA	WARP
2018	SPR	AA	22	279	34	17	1	7	32	9	52	1	2		.276/.308/.429	92	.319	1.4	SS(43): -4.8, 3B(11): 1.6, 2B(10): -2.0	-0.2
2018	MEM	AAA	22	209	31	13	0	5	27	13	42	5	2		.262/.321/.408	88	.310	0.7	SS(28): 1.1, 2B(12): -0.3, 3B(10): -0.3	0.4
2018	STL	MLB	22	3	1	0	0	0	0	0	1	0	0	28.6%	.000/.333/.000	83	.000		2B(1): 0.0	0.0
2019	MEM	AAA	23	496	70	18	5	17	62	17	96	2	3		.291/.335/.466	94	.332	0.7	SS(84): 4.0, 2B(17): 0.9, 3B(15): -1.3	2.2
2019	STL	MLB	23	10	2	0	0	0	0	1	2	1	0	21.4%	.250/.400/.250	84	.333	-0.1	2B(4): -0.1	0.0
2021 FS	STL	MLB	25	600	60	23	2	15	65	25	154	1	0	22.7%	.231/.275/.363	78	.290	0.7	2B -3, 3B 0	-0.1
2021 DC	STL	MLB	25	367	37	14	1	9	39	15	94	0	0	22.7%	.231/.275/.363	78	.290	0.4	2B -2, 3B 0	0.0

Comparables: Reid Brignac, Brent Lillibridge, Thairo Estrada

This is the point in the Cardinals chapter where we generally anoint our pick for the next second-tier prospect to take a big swig of Devil Magic brand hard seltzer; we're never right, of course, but...just watch hacktastic, vacuum-gloved middle infielder Sosa duplicate his uncharacteristically solid Memphis numbers at the keystone in Busch next year.

Lane Thomas CF Born: 08/23/95 Age: 25 Bats: R Throws: R Height: 6'0" Weight: 185 Origin: Round 5, 2014 Draft (#144 overall)

YEAR	TEAM	LVL	AGE	PA	R	2B	3B	HR	RBI	BB	K	SB	CS	Whiff%	AVG/OBP/SLG	DRC+	BABIP	BRR	FRAA	WARP
2018	SPR	AA	22	435	63	16	4	21	67	43	101	13	9		.260/.337/.487	107	.298	-0.5	CF(83): 4.0, RF(10): -0.5	1.0
2018	MEM	AAA	22	140	21	7	2	6	21	7	33	4	1		.275/.321/.496	100	.326	1.0	CF(32): 1.5	0.6
2019	MEM	AAA	23	304	42	17	2	10	44	32	80	11	6		.268/.352/.460	97	.343	0.6	CF(37): 5.0, LF(32): -2.4, RF(3): -0.2	1.1
2019	STL	MLB	23	44	6	0	1	4	12	4	8	1	1	21.1%	.316/.409/.684	110	.308	0.3	CF(19): 2.1, RF(5): 0.4, LF(2): -0.1	0.5
2020	STL	MLB	25	40	5	2	0	1	2	4	13	0	0	28.1%	.111/.200/.250	79	.136	-0.1	RF(14): -0.0, CF(7): -0.3	-0.1
2021 FS	STL	MLB	25	600	66	23	3	21	70	47	195	9	4	25.3%	.218/.286/.392	89	.295	-0.8	CF 0, RF -1	0.9
2021 DC	STL	MLB	25	200	22	7	1	7	23	15	65	3	1	25.3%	.218/.286/.392	89	.295	-0.3	CF 0, RF 0	0.2

Comparables: Brian Anderson, Harrison Bader, Jai Miller

The Cardinals have yet to really find out what they have in "Fast Lane" Thomas. He flashes a tantalizing speed-defense-power combo that can surely make you lose your mind but he hasn't stayed between the lines long enough to prove it's not a mirage, losing time to a broken wrist in 2019 and COVID-19 last summer. Thomas can dazzle in center field and is a blur on the basepaths, though he has yet to swipe bases with a high success rate. His bat is a work in progress with power that might only be fringe average, but he has a good approach, takes his walks and makes enough contact to keep his head above water. A healthy Thomas should make a fine fourth outfielder, and has an outside chance of growing into something more.

Jhon Torres **RF** Born: 03/29/00 Age: 21 Bats: R Throws: R Height: 6'4" Weight: 199 Origin: International Free Agent, 2016

YEAR	TEAM	LVL	AGE	PA	R	2B	3B	HR	RBI	BB	K	SB	CS	Whiff%	AVG/OBP/SLG	DRC+	BABIP	BRR	FRAA	WARP
2018	CAR	ROK	18	75	11	6	0	4	14	8	13	1	1		.397/.493/.683	207	.457	0.2	RF(15): 5.2	1.1
2018	INDB	ROK	18	111	16	3	0	4	16	11	24	3	0		.273/.351/.424	125	.324	-0.3	RF(24): 5.6, CF(1): -0.1	0.6
2019	JC	ROK+	19	133	24	9	0	6	17	19	36	0	2		.286/.391/.527	150	.366	0.8		1.1
2019	PEO	LO-A	19	75	4	3	0	0	8	7	29	0	1		.167/.240/.212	49	.282	-0.6	RF(20): 3.8	0.1
2021 FS	STL	MLB	21	600	48	26	2	8	51	41	215	4	2		.205/.267/.310	59	.317	-1.8	RF 13, CF -1	-0.6

Comparables: Teoscar Hernández, José Martínez, Gabriel Guerrero

Torres has the build, arm and raw power of a prototypical right fielder, and he has enough of an idea at the plate to turn his tools into consistent production. He's yet to conquer full-season ball, let alone the high minors, but there's plenty to like here.

───────────────── ★ ★ ★ *2021 Top 101 Prospect* **#92** ★ ★ ★ ─────────────────

Jordan Walker **3B** Born: 05/22/02 Age: 19 Bats: R Throws: R Height: 6'5" Weight: 220 Origin: Round 1, 2020 Draft (#21 overall)

The Cardinals' top pick last summer, Walker is a high ceiling prospect straight out of Central Casting. You want physicality? Tall and strong with an ideal frame that presages top shelf power. Athleticism? Soft hands and smooth movements that make him a good bet to stay in the infield. Intelligence and makeup? A Duke scholarship and parents who went to Harvard and MIT. Personal tie to St. Louis? Walker's mom got her Master's at Wash U. Myth-making, if apocryphal, story? Kid broke his grandmother's windshield hitting a home run in tee-ball. The road from draftee to star is long and arduous and nothing is guaranteed, but this is the clay from which legends can be sculpted.

Matt Wieters **C** Born: 05/21/86 Age: 35 Bats: S Throws: R Height: 6'5" Weight: 235 Origin: Round 1, 2007 Draft (#5 overall)

YEAR	TEAM	LVL	AGE	PA	R	2B	3B	HR	RBI	BB	K	SB	CS	Whiff%	AVG/OBP/SLG	DRC+	BABIP	BRR	FRAA	WARP
2018	WAS	MLB	32	271	24	8	0	8	30	30	45	0	1	17.3%	.238/.330/.374	100	.261	-0.8	C(73): -4.0	0.9
2019	STL	MLB	33	183	15	4	0	11	27	12	47	1	1	24.0%	.214/.268/.435	96	.223	-0.8	C(54): -7.4	0.0
2020	STL	MLB	34	41	3	1	0	0	4	3	10	0	0	19.3%	.200/.300/.229	78	.280	0.0	C(18): -0.1	-0.1
2021 FS	STL	MLB	35	600	64	22	1	18	67	49	147	2	0	20.9%	.224/.294/.370	86	.273	-0.9	C -14	-0.2

Comparables: Erik Kratz, Miguel Montero, Jason Varitek

YEAR	TEAM	P. COUNT	FRM RUNS	BLK RUNS	THRW RUNS	TOT RUNS
2018	WAS	9180	-3.7	1.1	0.3	-2.2
2019	STL	6279	-8.7	1.2	0.3	-7.2
2020	STL	1742	-0.8	0.0	0.0	-0.8
2021	STL	16650	-14.0	1.6	-0.8	-13.2

Wieters remains a perfectly acceptable backup receiver and a long-term MLB survivor of the sort we would celebrate if he weren't Matt Wieters. The unfairness of that is understood by every bright middle schooler who received conflicting "A" and "Needs Improvement" marks for the same class. (Full disclosure: that describes many of us here at Baseball Prospectus). Wieters has overcome injuries, inconsistency and outlandish expectations to earn four All-Star nods and two Gold Gloves. He's among the top-50 catchers in career home runs, the top 100 in WARP and in Jay Jaffe's JAWS metric. Over his 12 seasons he's only signed one multi-year deal: a two-year pact with the Nats who still owe him for half of the deferred second year. Unlike so many players who the popular imagination labels as disappointments, Wieters isn't still playing because teams owe him money, but because teams still want to pay him money. Good on you, mate.

Justin Williams **LF** Born: 08/20/95 Age: 25 Bats: L Throws: R Height: 6'1" Weight: 235 Origin: Round 2, 2013 Draft (#52 overall)

YEAR	TEAM	LVL	AGE	PA	R	2B	3B	HR	RBI	BB	K	SB	CS	Whiff%	AVG/OBP/SLG	DRC+	BABIP	BRR	FRAA	WARP
2018	MEM	AAA	22	76	8	3	0	3	11	5	17	0	1		.217/.276/.391	85	.240	-1.1	LF(10): 4.2, RF(7): 0.9	0.4
2018	DUR	AAA	22	386	41	18	0	8	46	25	81	4	3		.258/.312/.376	97	.315	-2.7	RF(80): 13.7, LF(2): 1.0	1.3
2018	TB	MLB	22	1	0	0	0	0	0	0	0	0	0	0.0%	.000/.000/.000	82	.000		RF(1): -0.0	0.0
2019	SPR	AA	23	61	7	1	0	1	3	4	17	1	0		.193/.246/.263	56	.256	-0.1	LF(12): -0.7, RF(2): -0.1	-0.2
2019	MEM	AAA	23	119	20	5	0	7	26	16	30	0	0		.353/.437/.608	145	.439	-0.5	RF(25): 3.9	1.2
2020	STL	MLB	25	6	0	0	0	0	0	1	2	0	0	40.0%	.200/.333/.200	71	.333		RF(2): -0.1	0.0
2021 FS	STL	MLB	25	600	61	27	2	17	69	40	158	0	0	37.5%	.239/.295/.389	86	.305	-0.2	LF 5, RF 1	1.0
2021 DC	STL	MLB	25	66	6	3	0	1	7	4	17	0	0	37.5%	.239/.295/.389	86	.305	0.0	LF 1, RF 0	0.1

Comparables: Fernando Martinez, Brandon Moss, Josh Kroeger

Williams, a slow-burn outfield prospect, has a solid corner-outfield glove and hits the ball hard but has yet to take consistent advantage of his tools. Last year we damned him with the faint praise of not being quite as good as Randy Arozarena; the Cardinals would be thrilled if that were true this year.

Masyn Winn **SS** Born: 03/21/02 Age: 19 Bats: R Throws: R Height: 5'11" Weight: 180 Origin: Round 2, 2020 Draft (#54 overall)

A second-round pick, Winn is a high-energy two-way player with speed, power potential, soft hands and athleticism at shortstop, as well as high-90s velocity on the mound. There's lots of work to do, but the Cardinals have started developing him as both a pitcher and a position player, hoping for a win-win.

Kolten Wong 2B Born: 10/10/90 Age: 30 Bats: L Throws: R Height: 5'7" Weight: 185 Origin: Round 1, 2011 Draft (#22 overall)

YEAR	TEAM	LVL	AGE	PA	R	2B	3B	HR	RBI	BB	K	SB	CS	Whiff%	AVG/OBP/SLG	DRC+	BABIP	BRR	FRAA	WARP
2018	STL	MLB	27	407	41	18	2	9	38	31	60	6	5	18.2%	.249/.332/.388	90	.275	-2.0	2B(119): 6.0	1.2
2019	STL	MLB	28	549	61	25	4	11	59	47	83	24	4	18.4%	.285/.361/.423	102	.321	3.2	2B(147): 18.6	4.1
2020	STL	MLB	30	208	26	4	2	1	16	20	30	5	2	16.2%	.265/.350/.326	86	.311	1.3	2B(53): 10.7	1.5
2021 FS	STL	MLB	30	600	76	28	4	10	50	53	101	14	3	17.7%	.267/.352/.396	109	.313	5.1	2B 10	4.5

Comparables: Ray Durham, D'Angelo Jimenez, Mark Ellis

Does it make sense to describe a player as both steady and volatile? You can make book on Wong providing speed, Gold Glove-caliber fielding, plenty of contact and enough walks to keep him from ever being a true lineup sink, but the quality of that contact careens wildly from year to year. In his good years Wong produces just enough pop to be an above-average bat at the keystone, but more frequently he's the Midwest's premiere supplier of routine grounders. Last year Wong put up one of the league's lowest barrel percentages and posted the worst isolated power mark in Missouri, a state where Nicky Lopez is also employed. His ever-present glove, wheels and on-base skills make him a nice complementary piece in the seven hole, but he'll usually break your heart if you cast Wong as a top-of-the-order spark plug. The Cardinals, who declined his affordable club option to begin the offseason, reinforced as much.

PITCHERS

Génesis Cabrera LHP Born: 10/10/96 Age: 24 Bats: L Throws: L Height: 6'2" Weight: 180 Origin: International Free Agent, 2013

YEAR	TEAM	LVL	AGE	W	L	SV	G	GS	IP	H	HR	BB/9	K/9	K	GB%	BABIP	WHIP	ERA	DRA-	WARP	MPH	FA%	Whiff%	CSP
2018	SPR	AA	21	1	3	0	5	5	24²	24	3	4.7	7.7	21	34.2%	.300	1.50	4.74	104	0.0				
2018	MTG	AA	21	7	6	0	21	20	113²	90	11	4.5	9.8	124	34.7%	.282	1.29	4.12	109	0.2				
2019	MEM	AAA	22	5	6	0	20	18	99	107	20	3.5	9.6	106	39.8%	.333	1.47	5.91	105	1.5				
2019	STL	MLB	22	0	2	1	13	2	20¹	23	2	4.9	8.4	19	37.3%	.328	1.67	4.87	113	0.0	98.3	61.0%	18.1%	48.3%
2020	STL	MLB	23	4	1	1	19	0	22¹	10	3	6.4	12.9	32	34.1%	.171	1.16	2.42	90	0.3	98.2	56.4%	40.3%	46.8%
2021 FS	STL	MLB	24	2	2	0	57	0	50	43	7	5.2	10.2	56	36.3%	.285	1.44	4.57	105	0.0	98.3	58.2%	31.7%	47.4%
2021 DC	STL	MLB	24	2	2	0	50	0	53	45	7	5.2	10.2	60	36.3%	.285	1.44	4.57	105	0.2	98.3	58.2%	31.7%	47.4%

Comparables: Beau Burrows, Justus Sheffield, Caleb Ferguson

There was a time not so long ago, a time when phones plugged into walls, maps lived in glove compartments and fictional TV presidents disarmed opponents with logic, during which Cabrera's crackling lefty heat would have made him a unicorn. In today's game his velo isn't even in the top 10 percent, but, when you combine it with two effective secondaries and a flailing, Carlos Marmol-like delivery, you can see why he generates swinging strikes at an elite rate. Like Marmol, fewer than half of the batters Cabrera faced last year managed to put the ball in play; and, also like Marmol, Cabrera's lack of command and control can produce flurries of walks, plunks, wild pitches, gopher balls and self-inflicted rallies. Few mid-20s fireballers ever fully cure their wildness, so Cabrera's future likely lies in high-leverage relief (though, once more like Marmol, he'll be a leading cause of managerial hypertension if allowed to work the ninth).

Seth Elledge RHP Born: 05/20/96 Age: 25 Bats: R Throws: R Height: 6'3" Weight: 240 Origin: Round 4, 2017 Draft (#123 overall)

YEAR	TEAM	LVL	AGE	W	L	SV	G	GS	IP	H	HR	BB/9	K/9	K	GB%	BABIP	WHIP	ERA	DRA-	WARP	MPH	FA%	Whiff%	CSP
2018	MOD	HI-A	22	5	1	9	31	0	38¹	18	1	3.5	12.7	54	46.2%	.224	0.86	1.17	63	0.8				
2018	SPR	AA	22	3	1	4	13	0	16²	13	3	3.2	10.8	20	37.2%	.270	1.14	4.32	47	0.5				
2019	SPR	AA	23	3	3	3	26	0	33¹	34	3	3.5	11.6	43	42.9%	.388	1.41	3.78	107	-0.3				
2019	MEM	AAA	23	3	1	0	21	3	34¹	28	3	5.0	8.4	32	38.0%	.284	1.37	4.72	98	0.5				
2020	STL	MLB	24	1	0	0	12	0	11²	11	2	6.2	10.8	14	39.3%	.346	1.63	4.63	95	0.1	94.9	64.9%	27.9%	43.5%
2021 FS	STL	MLB	25	1	1	0	57	0	50	43	6	4.6	9.7	53	41.1%	.285	1.39	4.28	100	0.1	94.9	64.9%	27.9%	43.5%
2021 DC	STL	MLB	25	1	1	0	28	0	29	25	3	4.6	9.7	31	41.1%	.285	1.39	4.28	100	0.2	94.9	64.9%	27.9%	43.5%

Comparables: Sammy Gervacio, Steven Okert, Jacob Rhame

When you take the already small sample of a single reliever season, apply the COVID-19 reduction, apply the rookie factor and carve off a platoon split, there's good reason not to make too much of Elledge's struggles against lefties last year. On the other hand, a 1.300 OPS draws the eye and is exactly the concern that always exists for a two-pitch reliever like Elledge. The young Texan doesn't have eye-popping stuff but he misses bats and his inflated walk rate last season doesn't align with his solid minor-league numbers. Elledge should be able to scratch out a career in middle relief, but he'll need to be spotted carefully unless he can find some voodoo to tame portside hitters.

Junior Fernández RHP Born: 03/02/97 Age: 24 Bats: R Throws: R Height: 6'3" Weight: 215 Origin: International Free Agent, 2014

YEAR	TEAM	LVL	AGE	W	L	SV	G	GS	IP	H	HR	BB/9	K/9	K	GB%	BABIP	WHIP	ERA	DRA-	WARP	MPH	FA%	Whiff%	CSP
2018	PMB	HI-A	21	1	0	3	8	0	9²	9	0	1.9	6.5	7	42.9%	.321	1.14	0.00	68	0.2				
2018	SPR	AA	21	0	0	0	16	0	21	19	1	6.9	7.3	17	35.5%	.295	1.67	5.14	93	0.1				
2019	PMB	HI-A	22	0	0	4	9	0	11²	8	0	6.2	8.5	11	45.2%	.258	1.37	1.54	93	0.0				
2019	SPR	AA	22	1	1	5	18	0	29	18	0	3.4	13.0	42	44.3%	.295	1.00	1.55	62	0.6				
2019	MEM	AAA	22	2	1	2	18	0	24¹	17	0	4.1	10.0	27	62.9%	.274	1.15	1.48	48	0.9				
2019	STL	MLB	22	0	1	0	13	0	11²	9	2	4.6	12.3	16	50.0%	.269	1.29	5.40	68	0.3	98.7	41.7%	43.4%	39.1%
2020	STL	MLB	23	0	0	0	3	0	3	6	1	6.0	6.0	2	33.3%	.455	2.67	18.00	101	0.0	96.3	55.7%	20.0%	46.2%
2021 FS	STL	MLB	24	1	1	0	57	0	50	46	6	6.4	9.1	50	44.2%	.291	1.64	5.49	118	-0.4	98.0	45.9%	36.5%	41.2%
2021 DC	STL	MLB	24	1	1	0	28	0	29	26	4	6.4	9.1	29	44.2%	.291	1.64	5.49	118	-0.1	98.0	45.9%	36.5%	41.2%

Comparables: Víctor Arano, Jonathan Hernández, Julio Urías

The government will stipulate that Fernández has a triple-digit fastball suited for high-leverage innings if the defense will concede there is not yet enough evidence to convict his slider or changeup of aiding and abetting.

Jack Flaherty RHP Born: 10/15/95 Age: 25 Bats: R Throws: R Height: 6'4" Weight: 225 Origin: Round 1, 2014 Draft (#34 overall)

YEAR	TEAM	LVL	AGE	W	L	SV	G	GS	IP	H	HR	BB/9	K/9	K	GB%	BABIP	WHIP	ERA	DRA-	WARP	MPH	FA%	Whiff%	CSP
2018	MEM	AAA	22	4	1	0	5	5	31²	22	2	2.0	11.7	41	44.0%	.274	0.92	2.27	35	1.4				
2018	STL	MLB	22	8	9	0	29	29	158	109	21	3.5	11.1	195	42.1%	.252	1.08	3.25	68	3.9	95.6	55.3%	31.6%	46.0%
2019	STL	MLB	23	11	8	0	33	33	196¹	135	25	2.5	10.6	231	39.7%	.244	0.97	2.75	50	7.1	96.5	57.7%	30.9%	46.4%
2020	STL	MLB	24	4	3	0	9	9	40¹	33	6	3.6	10.9	49	44.1%	.284	1.21	4.91	85	0.7	96.2	55.6%	34.5%	44.8%
2021 FS	STL	MLB	25	10	7	0	26	26	150	119	18	3.4	10.7	177	41.4%	.278	1.17	3.19	80	2.8	96.2	56.7%	31.7%	46.0%
2021 DC	STL	MLB	25	10	9	0	29	29	172	136	21	3.4	10.7	204	41.4%	.278	1.17	3.19	80	3.6	96.2	56.7%	31.7%	46.0%

Comparables: Luis Severino, Lance McCullers Jr., Yovani Gallardo

First, some perspective.

Over 9 starts during April and May of 2019, with no designated hitter, Jacob deGrom posted a 4.68 ERA, allowing a .744 OPS. Over the full season, deGrom posted a 2.43 ERA and allowed a .565 OPS. He won the Cy Young Award.

Over eight of his nine starts last season, with the designated hitter, Flaherty pitched to a 3.13 ERA and allowed a .582 OPS. In his other start, the Brewers lit into him for nine runs over three innings. Over the full season, Flaherty posted a 4.91 ERA and allowed a .677 OPS. Some considered him a disappointment.

That Milwaukee faceplant happened, but the limitations of short-season plague ball didn't allow Flaherty enough innings to wash it clean. He allowed a few more walks and home runs than normal, but his strikeout rate remained elite. He has estimable command and his wide repertoire, especially that disappearing slider, can be fearsome. Flaherty is 25 years old, healthy, and under team control for 3 more seasons.

He is who you thought he was.

Giovanny Gallegos RHP Born: 08/14/91 Age: 29 Bats: R Throws: R Height: 6'2" Weight: 215 Origin: International Free Agent, 2011

YEAR	TEAM	LVL	AGE	W	L	SV	G	GS	IP	H	HR	BB/9	K/9	K	GB%	BABIP	WHIP	ERA	DRA-	WARP	MPH	FA%	Whiff%	CSP
2018	MEM	AAA	26	0	0	1	13	0	16²	7	0	1.6	8.6	16	42.5%	.179	0.60	0.54	54	0.5				
2018	SWB	AAA	26	2	1	2	17	0	27²	24	1	2.3	13.3	41	36.4%	.365	1.12	3.90	46	0.9				
2018	NYY	MLB	26	0	0	1	4	0	10	10	2	2.7	9.0	10	37.0%	.333	1.30	4.50	120	-0.1	95.3	58.6%	18.2%	50.5%
2018	STL	MLB	26	0	0	0	2	0	1¹	1	0	0.0	13.5	2	0.0%	.333	0.75	0.00	152	0.0	95.9	64.0%	16.7%	46.4%
2019	STL	MLB	27	3	2	1	66	0	74	44	9	1.9	11.3	93	33.5%	.222	0.81	2.31	57	2.0	94.9	55.2%	34.7%	46.4%
2020	STL	MLB	28	2	2	4	16	0	15	9	1	2.4	12.6	21	40.6%	.258	0.87	3.60	76	0.3	95.7	48.9%	38.1%	47.2%
2021 FS	STL	MLB	29	2	2	24	57	0	50	37	6	2.4	11.2	62	35.8%	.267	1.02	2.54	68	1.0	95.1	54.1%	34.4%	46.8%
2021 DC	STL	MLB	29	2	2	24	50	0	53	39	7	2.4	11.2	66	35.8%	.267	1.02	2.54	68	1.2	95.1	54.1%	34.4%	46.8%

Comparables: Dominic Leone, Nick Wittgren, Ryan Dull

Gallegos worked with his usual grit and determination last year, overcoming an undisclosed euphemism in July and a groin pull in September to post another solid season in the Cardinals bullpen. His high-spin fastball isn't explosive but Gallegos commands it well and his breaker is pure kryptonite. He calls it a slider even though it has 12-6 break like a curve and can fall off the table in a manner that would make Bruce Sutter smile with fond remembrance. Gallegos is no spring chicken, having kicked around the Yankees organization for years before finally getting a chance in St Louis to unleash his slide-piece on an unready world, but he's a good bet to spend his 30s troubling the sleep of big-league hitters.

John Gant RHP Born: 08/06/92 Age: 28 Bats: R Throws: R Height: 6'4" Weight: 200 Origin: Round 21, 2011 Draft (#642 overall)

YEAR	TEAM	LVL	AGE	W	L	SV	G	GS	IP	H	HR	BB/9	K/9	K	GB%	BABIP	WHIP	ERA	DRA-	WARP	MPH	FA%	Whiff%	CSP
2018	MEM	AAA	25	5	1	0	8	8	49	45	5	2.9	7.7	42	47.9%	.290	1.24	1.65	66	1.3				
2018	STL	MLB	25	7	6	0	26	19	114	91	9	4.5	7.5	95	44.4%	.255	1.30	3.47	90	1.6	95.4	55.4%	26.4%	48.5%
2019	STL	MLB	26	11	1	3	64	0	66¹	51	4	4.6	8.1	60	46.3%	.275	1.28	3.66	88	0.7	97.9	55.7%	27.4%	48.5%
2020	STL	MLB	27	0	3	0	17	0	15	9	0	4.2	10.8	18	63.9%	.250	1.07	2.40	73	0.3	95.8	52.3%	32.7%	49.0%
2021 FS	STL	MLB	28	2	2	0	57	0	50	43	5	3.8	9.3	51	48.3%	.285	1.29	3.66	89	0.4	96.6	55.0%	27.8%	48.6%
2021 DC	STL	MLB	28	2	2	0	50	0	53	46	5	3.8	9.3	54	48.3%	.285	1.29	3.66	89	0.6	96.6	55.0%	27.8%	48.6%

Comparables: Robert Stephenson, Joe Musgrove, Matt Wisler

As the 2020 season wore on you could hear the phrase more and more, muttered by despondent batters as they shuffled aimlessly towards the dugout: "Who is John Gant?" He is a shadowy figure with impressively high walk and strikeout rates, the Two True Outcomes most expressive of his individualism; home runs were completely avoided, as they would unjustly reward spectators with souvenirs they have not themselves produced. As for those copious groundball outs, they are most assuredly not a form of collectivism; Gant creates them, his infielders merely cogs in a machine to collect and dispose as per his implicit design. Fluent in five pitches, objectively productive and occasionally dominant, Gant does more than merely earn his keep in a big-league bullpen; he thrives.

Austin Gomber LHP   Born: 11/23/93   Age: 27   Bats: L   Throws: L   Height: 6'5"   Weight: 220   Origin: Round 4, 2014 Draft (#135 overall)

YEAR	TEAM	LVL	AGE	W	L	SV	G	GS	IP	H	HR	BB/9	K/9	K	GB%	BABIP	WHIP	ERA	DRA-	WARP	MPH	FA%	Whiff%	CSP
2018	MEM	AAA	24	7	3	0	12	11	68¹	65	9	2.6	10.0	76	38.1%	.315	1.24	3.42	58	2.2				
2018	STL	MLB	24	6	2	0	30	12	81¹	83	8	3.8	8.1	73	38.1%	.322	1.44	4.32	110	0.2	95.0	50.4%	21.9%	49.8%
2019	MEM	AAA	25	4	0	0	8	8	45¹	42	5	3.2	10.3	52	37.6%	.333	1.28	2.98	57	1.7				
2020	STL	MLB	26	1	1	0	14	4	29	19	1	4.7	8.4	27	48.0%	.243	1.17	1.86	95	0.3	94.0	52.5%	26.6%	48.7%
2021 FS	STL	MLB	27	9	8	0	26	26	150	133	18	3.9	9.6	160	42.8%	.290	1.32	3.93	94	1.6	94.4	51.6%	24.5%	49.2%
2021 DC	STL	MLB	27	5	6	0	48	14	108	95	13	3.9	9.6	115	42.8%	.290	1.32	3.93	94	1.3	94.4	51.6%	24.5%	49.2%

Comparables: Jalen Beeks, Rookie Davis, Eric Skoglund

Gomber bounced back from an injury-plagued 2019 to post a breakthrough season in a swingman role. He's a tall drink of water who lives in the low-90s with his fastball and who relies on his knuckle-curve (along with an improving slider and the occasional changeup) to keep batters off-balance and induce weak contact. Gomber uncharacteristically struggled a bit with his control last year but that shouldn't be a long-term concern. He's not likely to post another sub-2 ERA and there's nothing exciting about his profile, but Gomber has shown the steady competence necessary to survive at the back end of the rotation or in long relief.

Ryan Helsley RHP   Born: 07/18/94   Age: 26   Bats: R   Throws: R   Height: 6'2"   Weight: 230   Origin: Round 5, 2015 Draft (#161 overall)

YEAR	TEAM	LVL	AGE	W	L	SV	G	GS	IP	H	HR	BB/9	K/9	K	GB%	BABIP	WHIP	ERA	DRA-	WARP	MPH	FA%	Whiff%	CSP
2018	SPR	AA	23	3	2	0	7	7	41	30	5	4.4	9.7	44	45.4%	.253	1.22	4.39	67	1.0				
2018	MEM	AAA	23	2	1	0	5	5	26²	18	2	3.0	11.5	34	36.5%	.267	1.01	3.71	51	0.9				
2019	MEM	AAA	24	2	3	1	17	7	37¹	29	3	4.8	9.9	41	41.5%	.289	1.31	4.58	63	1.2				
2019	STL	MLB	24	2	0	0	24	0	36²	34	5	2.9	7.9	32	33.0%	.282	1.25	2.95	103	0.1	100.1	56.6%	22.3%	51.5%
2020	STL	MLB	25	1	1	1	12	0	12	8	3	6.0	7.5	10	33.3%	.167	1.33	5.25	139	-0.1	99.2	43.3%	31.9%	48.3%
2021 FS	STL	MLB	26	2	2	0	57	0	50	45	8	4.4	8.8	48	37.8%	.277	1.39	4.48	106	0.0	99.8	52.1%	25.5%	50.4%
2021 DC	STL	MLB	26	2	2	0	50	0	53	48	8	4.4	8.8	51	37.8%	.277	1.39	4.48	106	0.2	99.8	52.1%	25.5%	50.4%

Comparables: Drew Anderson, Alex Reyes, Antonio Bastardo

Jordan Hicks' absence and Carlos Martínez's intended return to the rotation provided Helsley a chance last summer to move up the bullpen pecking order and perhaps audition for the closer role. Unfortunately the young Oklahoman contracted COVID-19, missed the whole of August and never seemed to find his control or his rhythm when he returned. At his best Helsley can command his rising high-90s heat and produce plenty of empty swings with his sharp cutter and power curve, a broad enough repertoire for a starting role but with a few too many walks sprinkled in. Helsley has the stuff, makeup and moxie to thrive in the late innings, and if normal ever returns he has a shot to someday make the ninth his workplace.

Tink Hence RHP   Born: 08/06/02   Age: 18   Bats: R   Throws: R   Height: 6'1"   Weight: 175   Origin: Round 2, 2020 Draft (#63 overall)

One of St. Louis' second-round picks, Hence displayed a lightning-fast arm, potential mid-90s heat and three usable secondaries despite being young for his Arkansas prep class; it should go without saying his is a name to remember.

Jordan Hicks RHP   Born: 09/06/96   Age: 24   Bats: R   Throws: R   Height: 6'2"   Weight: 220   Origin: Round SUP, 2015 Draft (#105 overall)

YEAR	TEAM	LVL	AGE	W	L	SV	G	GS	IP	H	HR	BB/9	K/9	K	GB%	BABIP	WHIP	ERA	DRA-	WARP	MPH	FA%	Whiff%	CSP
2018	STL	MLB	21	3	4	6	73	0	77²	59	2	5.2	8.1	70	60.6%	.266	1.34	3.59	134	-1.0	103.0	78.0%	24.4%	47.1%
2019	STL	MLB	22	2	2	14	29	0	28²	16	2	3.5	9.7	31	67.2%	.215	0.94	3.14	66	0.7	103.5	60.3%	30.8%	45.9%
2021 FS	STL	MLB	24	1	1	1	57	0	50	45	4	5.9	9.1	50	56.8%	.297	1.56	4.80	105	0.0	103.2	70.8%	27.0%	46.6%
2021 DC	STL	MLB	24	1	1	1	28	0	29	26	2	5.9	9.1	29	56.8%	.297	1.56	4.80	105	0.1	103.2	70.8%	27.0%	46.6%

Comparables: Daniel Norris, Sandy Alcantara, Miguel Castro

Hicks was already slated to miss most of last year recovering from Tommy John surgery before COVID-19 hit. Given the young flamethrower's diabetes, he wisely decided to reduce the potential of adding serious illness to injury by opting out of the 2020 season. Hicks is best known for lobbing triple-digit thunderbolts, but when we last saw him on a big-league mound he was flashing an improved slider and better control. Big-league hitters sitting dead-red can turn around anyone's fastball with a quickness, so Hicks' ability to fool them with spin will determine whether or not he can grow into a truly dominant closer. He's only 24, so time and raw talent are on his side.

Dakota Hudson RHP   Born: 09/15/94   Age: 26   Bats: R   Throws: R   Height: 6'5"   Weight: 215   Origin: Round 1, 2016 Draft (#34 overall)

YEAR	TEAM	LVL	AGE	W	L	SV	G	GS	IP	H	HR	BB/9	K/9	K	GB%	BABIP	WHIP	ERA	DRA-	WARP	MPH	FA%	Whiff%	CSP
2018	MEM	AAA	23	13	3	0	19	19	111²	107	1	3.1	7.0	87	57.6%	.315	1.30	2.50	75	2.6				
2018	STL	MLB	23	4	1	0	26	0	27¹	19	0	5.9	6.3	19	62.5%	.237	1.35	2.63	143	-0.5	97.4	60.7%	22.9%	47.2%
2019	STL	MLB	24	16	7	1	33	32	174²	160	22	4.4	7.0	136	56.3%	.275	1.41	3.35	92	2.4	95.4	61.7%	23.8%	46.2%
2020	STL	MLB	25	3	2	0	8	8	39	24	5	3.5	7.2	31	57.7%	.192	1.00	2.77	88	0.6	94.8	58.6%	21.9%	44.1%
2021 FS	STL	MLB	26	2	3	0	57	0	50	46	5	4.3	7.8	43	55.5%	.285	1.41	4.26	103	0.1	95.4	61.0%	23.3%	45.8%

Comparables: Antonio Senzatela, Dana Eveland, Brad Hand

Hudson was sidelined after eight starts last summer and underwent Tommy John surgery, which is unfortunate in a lot of ways. It deprives Hudson of the chance to compete at the game he loves and build towards a higher salary; it deprives the Cardinals of a potential mid-rotation cog; and it deprives analysts of the opportunity to see if Hudson can continue to out-pitch his peripherals. It's not a mystery how he's keeping runs off the board despite sub-par walk and strikeout rates and plenty of hard contact: lots of groundballs coupled with a low batting average on balls in play and a high strand rate. But ground balls tend to lead to more hits, not fewer, so you'd expect a lot more of those hard-hit grounders to turn into singles over time. Hasn't happened yet, though, and with Hudson likely missing most of the coming year we'll have to wait a while to see if he can keep thumbing his nose at expectations.

Rob Kaminsky LHP   Born: 09/02/94   Age: 26   Bats: R   Throws: L   Height: 6'0"   Weight: 195   Origin: Round 1, 2013 Draft (#28 overall)

YEAR	TEAM	LVL	AGE	W	L	SV	G	GS	IP	H	HR	BB/9	K/9	K	GB%	BABIP	WHIP	ERA	DRA-	WARP	MPH	FA%	Whiff%	CSP
2018	AKR	AA	23	1	1	4	23	0	26^1	22	2	6.2	7.5	22	70.7%	.274	1.52	3.08	110	-0.1				
2019	AKR	AA	24	2	1	1	19	0	31^1	22	2	2.3	8.6	30	57.1%	.244	0.96	2.30	79	0.3				
2019	COL	AAA	24	1	0	1	23	0	24^2	26	3	5.1	11.3	31	56.7%	.359	1.62	5.11	98	0.3				
2020	STL	MLB	25	0	0	0	5	0	4^2	3	0	3.9	5.8	3	60.0%	.200	1.07	1.93	94	0.1	93.0	42.9%	17.6%	44.2%
2021 FS	STL	MLB	26	2	3	0	57	0	50	45	5	4.7	8.1	45	53.8%	.282	1.43	4.19	101	0.1	93.0	42.9%	17.6%	44.2%

Comparables: Brady Lail, Alex Reyes, Chase De Jong

After eight years, ligament replacement surgery and a round trip to Cleveland, it took a global pandemic to bring Kaminsky to the St. Louis bullpen. His brief but solid debut may give him a chance to stick around a while.

Kwang Hyun Kim LHP   Born: 07/22/88   Age: 32   Bats: L   Throws: L   Height: 6'2"   Weight: 195   Origin: International Free Agent, 2019

YEAR	TEAM	LVL	AGE	W	L	SV	G	GS	IP	H	HR	BB/9	K/9	K	GB%	BABIP	WHIP	ERA	DRA-	WARP	MPH	FA%	Whiff%	CSP
2020	STL	MLB	31	3	0	1	8	7	39	28	3	2.8	5.5	24	50.0%	.217	1.03	1.62	116	0.0	92.2	48.3%	18.3%	48.6%
2021 FS	STL	MLB	32	9	9	0	26	26	150	147	19	3.2	7.2	120	46.0%	.286	1.34	4.17	100	1.0	92.2	48.3%	18.3%	48.6%
2021 DC	STL	MLB	32	7	9	0	25	25	139	136	18	3.2	7.2	111	46.0%	.286	1.34	4.17	100	1.4	92.2	48.3%	18.3%	48.6%

After 11 successful seasons in the KBO with the SK Wyverns, Kim negotiated a global pandemic, unexpected isolation from his family, a kidney ailment and an organization committed to using him in the bullpen to eventually succeed in a big-league rotation. Wyverns are mythical creatures that look like dragons, but walk on two legs and don't breathe fire. Similarly, Kim doesn't breathe fire but succeeds by working the bottom of the zone with his low-velo fastball and a wide assortment of offspeed junk that keeps hitters from timing him up. There's very little swing-and-miss but lots of routine ground balls and since Kim doesn't walk anyone that's been enough so far to keep runs off the board. It's hard to consistently succeed in today's game while allowing that much contact, so Kim's novelty is likely to fade and big-league hitters will figure him out soon enough.

★ ★ ★ 2021 Top 101 Prospect #43 ★ ★ ★

Matthew Liberatore LHP   Born: 11/06/99   Age: 21   Bats: L   Throws: L   Height: 6'4"   Weight: 200   Origin: Round 1, 2018 Draft (#16 overall)

YEAR	TEAM	LVL	AGE	W	L	SV	G	GS	IP	H	HR	BB/9	K/9	K	GB%	BABIP	WHIP	ERA	DRA-	WARP	MPH	FA%	Whiff%	CSP
2018	RAY	ROK	18	1	2	0	8	8	27^2	16	0	3.6	10.4	32	45.2%	.258	0.98	0.98	92	0.4				
2018	PRN	ROK	18	1	0	0	1	1	5	5	0	3.6	9.0	5	41.7%	.417	1.40	3.60	184	-0.1				
2019	BG	LO-A	19	6	2	0	16	15	78^1	70	2	3.6	8.7	76	55.7%	.312	1.29	3.10	98	0.4				
2021 FS	STL	MLB	21	2	3	0	57	0	50	48	7	5.4	7.9	44	47.4%	.287	1.56	5.16	120	-0.4				

Comparables: Brailyn Marquez, Randall Delgado, Tyler Chatwood

Randy Arozarena's rocket ride to postseason glory last year has put unfair pressure on both Liberatore (the man he was traded for) to grow into an ace and on the Cardinals (the team who made the trade) to help Liberatore do so as soon as possible. Luckily for everyone involved, Liberatore might just have the goods. A surprisingly polished prep lefty, Liberatore has a tall frame and a clean delivery, and he can hit the mid-90s with his fastball before uncorking knee-buckling benders that could eventually rank among the league's best. Without a new minor-league season to overwrite them, Liberatore's mundane strikeout numbers as a teenager in the Midwest League are still a gnawing concern to some but team officials (surprise!) raved about his development at their Springfield complex over the summer. Liberatore has a high floor, and, if Uncle Charlie grows into a true wipeout offering, he could one day front a rotation.

Carlos Martínez RHP   Born: 09/21/91   Age: 29   Bats: R   Throws: R   Height: 6'0"   Weight: 200   Origin: International Free Agent, 2009

YEAR	TEAM	LVL	AGE	W	L	SV	G	GS	IP	H	HR	BB/9	K/9	K	GB%	BABIP	WHIP	ERA	DRA-	WARP	MPH	FA%	Whiff%	CSP
2018	SPR	AA	26	0	0	0	3	1	7	6	3	0.0	7.7	6	28.6%	.167	0.86	3.86	74	0.1				
2018	STL	MLB	26	8	6	5	33	18	118^2	100	5	4.6	8.9	117	48.6%	.296	1.35	3.11	103	0.9	97.2	44.2%	25.1%	48.9%
2019	STL	MLB	27	4	2	24	48	0	48^1	39	2	3.4	9.9	53	57.1%	.301	1.18	3.17	67	1.1	98.3	51.0%	28.5%	47.2%
2020	STL	MLB	28	0	3	0	5	5	20	32	6	4.5	7.7	17	51.3%	.371	2.10	9.90	117	0.0	95.6	50.2%	19.7%	43.9%
2021 FS	STL	MLB	29	9	8	0	26	26	150	138	15	3.8	8.7	144	51.6%	.294	1.35	4.02	95	1.5	97.2	48.0%	24.8%	47.1%
2021 DC	STL	MLB	29	6	7	0	21	21	111	102	11	3.8	8.7	106	51.6%	.294	1.35	4.02	95	1.5	97.2	48.0%	24.8%	47.1%

Comparables: Michael Wacha, Tom Gordon, Mike Foltynewicz

It was a lost season for Martínez, who entered the season with high hopes of reclaiming a spot in the Cardinals rotation but was shelled in his first start before COVID-19 laid him low. One of the few players to cop to being hospitalized by the virus, when Martínez returned his fastball had lost three clicks and he couldn't get anyone out. He has a deep and effective arsenal, a history of success as both a starter and a closer and the only blemishes on his track record are from when he was injured or ill. On the other hand, Martinez's diminished velocity is concerning and he hasn't been truly healthy since 2017. The best choice heading forward may be to stick him back in the 'pen and see if he can sit in the mid-90s in short stints without breaking down.

Miles Mikolas RHP   Born: 08/23/88   Age: 32   Bats: R   Throws: R   Height: 6'4"   Weight: 230   Origin: Round 7, 2009 Draft (#204 overall)

YEAR	TEAM	LVL	AGE	W	L	SV	G	GS	IP	H	HR	BB/9	K/9	K	GB%	BABIP	WHIP	ERA	DRA-	WARP	MPH	FA%	Whiff%	CSP
2018	STL	MLB	29	18	4	0	32	32	200²	186	16	1.3	6.5	146	48.1%	.282	1.07	2.83	75	4.5	96.1	48.6%	20.3%	51.8%
2019	STL	MLB	30	9	14	0	32	32	184	193	27	1.6	7.0	144	47.4%	.304	1.22	4.16	84	3.3	95.6	51.4%	21.8%	48.5%
2021 FS	STL	MLB	32	9	8	0	26	26	150	148	18	1.7	7.2	120	47.4%	.290	1.17	3.57	89	2.0	95.8	50.4%	21.3%	49.7%
2021 DC	STL	MLB	32	6	6	0	19	19	104	102	12	1.7	7.2	83	47.4%	.290	1.17	3.57	89	1.7	95.8	50.4%	21.3%	49.7%

Comparables: Dan Straily, Kyle Hendricks, Heath Hembree

Doctors often ask overweight middle-aged men to address their high blood pressure through diet and exercise in order to avoid medication; this rarely works, since there's a reason they are overweight middle-aged men in the first place. Similarly, attempts to treat a pitcher's sore elbow with platelet rich plasma injections often seem to merely delay the inevitable date with the knife. Mikolas went the PRP route after reporting to spring training with a forearm strain, hoping he could be ready for the season's delayed July start. He wasn't, and subsequent surgery on his flexor tendon caused him to miss all of 2020. He should be ready for spring training, assuming spring training is ready for him, and if he's healthy there's no reason Mikolas shouldn't be able to settle back into the middle of the Cardinals rotation.

Andrew Miller LHP   Born: 05/21/85   Age: 36   Bats: L   Throws: L   Height: 6'7"   Weight: 200   Origin: Round 1, 2006 Draft (#6 overall)

YEAR	TEAM	LVL	AGE	W	L	SV	G	GS	IP	H	HR	BB/9	K/9	K	GB%	BABIP	WHIP	ERA	DRA-	WARP	MPH	FA%	Whiff%	CSP
2018	CLE	MLB	33	2	4	2	37	0	34	31	3	4.2	11.9	45	47.7%	.329	1.38	4.24	68	0.7	95.6	43.3%	31.0%	50.2%
2019	STL	MLB	34	5	6	6	73	0	54²	45	11	4.4	11.5	70	36.6%	.283	1.32	4.45	76	1.0	95.2	38.6%	30.8%	48.4%
2020	STL	MLB	35	1	1	4	16	0	13	9	0	3.5	11.1	16	61.3%	.290	1.08	2.77	75	0.3	93.3	40.0%	31.4%	47.8%
2021 FS	STL	MLB	36	2	2	3	57	0	50	40	5	3.6	10.9	60	46.1%	.290	1.22	3.45	84	0.6	94.9	39.7%	31.0%	48.6%
2021 DC	STL	MLB	36	2	2	3	50	0	53	43	5	3.6	10.9	64	46.1%	.290	1.22	3.45	84	0.8	94.9	39.7%	31.0%	48.6%

Comparables: Tyler Clippard, Pedro Strop, Ian Kennedy

Miller lost two more ticks of velocity last season but his slider was still hell on wheels, especially against his fellow Leftorium patrons who went 3-for-29 facing him, all singles. The old dog even added a new trick, unveiling a sinker that helped him post the highest groundball rate of his career with nary a gopher ball to be seen. Miller's option year vested down the stretch, and while he's no longer Andrew Friggin' Miller he remains an above-average reliever who misses enough bats to be worth his final eight-figure paycheck.

Johan Oviedo RHP   Born: 03/02/98   Age: 23   Bats: R   Throws: R   Height: 6'5"   Weight: 245   Origin: International Free Agent, 2016

YEAR	TEAM	LVL	AGE	W	L	SV	G	GS	IP	H	HR	BB/9	K/9	K	GB%	BABIP	WHIP	ERA	DRA-	WARP	MPH	FA%	Whiff%	CSP
2018	PEO	LO-A	20	10	10	1	25	23	121²	108	6	5.8	8.7	118	36.5%	.304	1.54	4.22	92	1.3				
2019	PMB	HI-A	21	5	0	0	6	5	33²	29	1	3.2	9.4	35	46.7%	.308	1.22	1.60	87	0.3				
2019	SPR	AA	21	7	8	0	23	23	113	120	9	5.1	10.2	128	42.0%	.368	1.63	5.65	130	-1.9				
2020	STL	MLB	22	0	3	0	5	5	24²	24	3	3.6	5.8	16	40.7%	.269	1.38	5.47	134	-0.2	97.0	56.1%	21.5%	47.2%
2021 FS	STL	MLB	23	8	10	0	26	26	150	153	27	4.8	7.7	127	38.7%	.289	1.56	5.74	127	-1.2	97.0	56.1%	21.5%	47.2%
2021 DC	STL	MLB	23	4	8	0	22	22	99	101	17	4.8	7.7	84	38.7%	.289	1.56	5.74	127	-0.4	97.0	56.1%	21.5%	47.2%

Comparables: Rony García, Touki Toussaint, Huascar Ynoa

The Cardinals' COVID nightmare last summer forced them to toss a few talented but unprepared young arms to the wolves, and Oviedo was among them. He's a Bunyanesque figure on the mound who can unleash mid-90s fastballs all day that overpower the kids in the bus leagues, but a lack of command, control or consistency in his breaking stuff left him helpless against major-league bats. Oviedo has four pitches, a bulldog mentality and an ideal starter's frame but if the development staff can't sand away all those rough edges he's destined for middle relief.

Daniel Ponce de Leon RHP   Born: 01/16/92   Age: 29   Bats: R   Throws: R   Height: 6'3"   Weight: 200   Origin: Round 9, 2014 Draft (#285 overall)

YEAR	TEAM	LVL	AGE	W	L	SV	G	GS	IP	H	HR	BB/9	K/9	K	GB%	BABIP	WHIP	ERA	DRA-	WARP	MPH	FA%	Whiff%	CSP
2018	MEM	AAA	26	9	4	0	19	18	96¹	69	4	4.7	10.3	110	28.8%	.275	1.24	2.24	82	1.9				
2018	STL	MLB	26	0	2	1	11	4	33	24	2	3.5	8.5	31	35.6%	.259	1.12	2.73	78	0.6	95.5	61.8%	28.0%	49.8%
2019	MEM	AAA	27	8	4	0	16	16	84¹	62	7	4.6	9.2	86	35.9%	.256	1.25	2.88	50	3.4				
2019	STL	MLB	27	1	2	0	13	8	48²	36	6	4.8	9.6	52	45.5%	.256	1.27	3.70	72	1.1	95.6	70.6%	27.0%	44.8%
2020	STL	MLB	28	1	3	0	9	8	32²	23	8	5.5	12.4	45	28.9%	.221	1.32	4.96	110	0.1	95.2	61.1%	31.4%	43.9%
2021 FS	STL	MLB	29	9	8	0	26	26	150	115	19	4.8	10.6	176	35.1%	.265	1.30	3.77	90	1.9	95.4	65.1%	29.1%	45.1%
2021 DC	STL	MLB	29	6	7	0	22	22	113	86	15	4.8	10.6	132	35.1%	.265	1.30	3.77	90	1.8	95.4	65.1%	29.1%	45.1%

Comparables: Carlos Martínez, Alec Mills, Chris Stratton

Last summer the world was awash in messages telling us to "avoid contact," and clearly Ponce de Leon took that to heart. Like his teammate Genesis Cabrera, less than half of the batters facing Ponce de Leon put the ball in play—not counting the big pile of dingers he allowed, a natural by-product of his league-leading fly-ball rate. His four-seamer sits in the low 90s with good rise and movement and can be an elite pitch when he commands it, especially high in the zone. But too often he misses his spot, leading to walks and gopher balls and crooked numbers on the scoreboard. Ponce de Leon has a decent hook and a cutter that took two steps forward last year, giving him a starter's arsenal that probably works best in relief.

Roel Ramirez RHP Born: 05/26/95 Age: 26 Bats: R Throws: R Height: 6'0" Weight: 235 Origin: Round 8, 2013 Draft (#248 overall)

YEAR	TEAM	LVL	AGE	W	L	SV	G	GS	IP	H	HR	BB/9	K/9	K	GB%	BABIP	WHIP	ERA	DRA-	WARP	MPH	FA%	Whiff%	CSP
2018	CHA	HI-A	23	0	0	1	8	0	12²	4	0	0.0	9.9	14	53.6%	.143	0.32	0.00	77	0.2				
2018	SPR	AA	23	0	0	0	10	0	10²	8	1	4.2	8.4	10	35.7%	.259	1.22	5.06	53	0.3				
2018	MTG	AA	23	3	1	0	26	1	40²	37	4	3.8	10.2	46	35.5%	.320	1.33	3.32	77	0.6				
2019	SPR	AA	24	5	3	1	41	5	72¹	76	6	3.6	10.0	80	40.0%	.363	1.45	4.98	105	-0.4				
2020	STL	MLB	25	0	0	0	1	0	0²	6	4	13.5	13.5	1	33.3%	1.000	10.50	81.00	122	0.0	94.4	63.3%	21.4%	44.8%
2021 FS	STL	MLB	26	2	3	0	57	0	50	49	8	3.7	8.8	48	38.2%	.298	1.40	4.73	112	-0.2	94.4	63.3%	21.4%	44.8%

Comparables: James Norwood, Madison Younginer, Dovydas Neverauskas

Ramirez made one appearance last season and is now the only player in major league history to allow four or more home runs while retiring one or fewer batters in his career. If the Cardinals never give him another chance to wash away that regret, they should at least give him a Burt Lancaster mustache, pay for medical school and set him up in a small-town practice outside Laredo.

Alex Reyes RHP Born: 08/29/94 Age: 26 Bats: R Throws: R Height: 6'4" Weight: 220 Origin: International Free Agent, 2012

YEAR	TEAM	LVL	AGE	W	L	SV	G	GS	IP	H	HR	BB/9	K/9	K	GB%	BABIP	WHIP	ERA	DRA-	WARP	MPH	FA%	Whiff%	CSP
2018	SPR	AA	23	1	0	0	1	1	7²	1	0	3.5	15.3	13	20.0%	.111	0.52	0.00	10	0.5				
2018	MEM	AAA	23	1	0	0	1	1	7	1	0	1.3	16.7	13	22.2%	.125	0.29	0.00	17	0.4				
2018	STL	MLB	23	0	0	0	1	1	4	3	0	4.5	4.5	2	40.0%	.300	1.25	0.00	182	-0.1	96.9	57.5%	10.3%	43.0%
2019	PMB	HI-A	24	0	1	0	2	2	9¹	9	0	2.9	10.6	11	53.8%	.346	1.29	1.93	75	0.2				
2019	MEM	AAA	24	1	3	0	10	7	28	27	5	7.7	12.2	38	37.7%	.355	1.82	7.39	106	0.4				
2019	STL	MLB	24	0	1	0	4	0	3	2	1	18.0	3.0	1	30.0%	.111	2.67	15.00	136	0.0	98.8	59.4%	16.7%	42.1%
2020	STL	MLB	25	2	1	1	15	1	19²	14	1	6.4	12.4	27	35.6%	.302	1.42	3.20	83	0.4	99.3	60.4%	34.6%	43.0%
2021 FS	STL	MLB	26	2	2	7	57	0	50	37	5	6.0	12.0	66	37.5%	.282	1.42	4.00	92	0.4	99.1	60.2%	31.4%	42.9%
2021 DC	STL	MLB	26	2	2	7	45	0	47	35	5	6.0	12.0	62	37.5%	.282	1.42	4.00	92	0.5	99.1	60.2%	31.4%	42.9%

Comparables: Lucas Sims, Jake Faria, Antonio Senzatela

After all the struggles, it turned out to be as easy as one-two-three.

Game One. One former top prospect on the bump, one at the dish.

Two on. Two out. Two runs ahead. Two innings left in a playoff game. Tatis digs in. Reyes takes two deep breaths, rocks back and fires.

Three pitches. Three fastballs, all triple-digit. The third runs inside and Tatis fists it to short. Out number three. Then three more, and a postseason save. Three lost seasons, gone but not forgotten.

After years of injuries and setbacks—all of them unfortunate, some of them self-inflicted—it was both a joy and a relief to watch Reyes at long last earn his moment in the sun. The explosive fastball, hammer curve and diving slider, the strikeouts and the awkward swings, are all still there. So are the free passes and the questions about his role. Four years ago in this space we wrote that it's nearly impossible to thrive in a starting role while walking 12 percent of the batters you face; Reyes has now walked nearly 15 percent in his staccato big league career. His future should be in the late innings, but with Reyes it's almost never that easy.

Ricardo Sánchez LHP Born: 04/11/97 Age: 24 Bats: L Throws: L Height: 5'10" Weight: 220 Origin: International Free Agent, 2013

YEAR	TEAM	LVL	AGE	W	L	SV	G	GS	IP	H	HR	BB/9	K/9	K	GB%	BABIP	WHIP	ERA	DRA-	WARP	MPH	FA%	Whiff%	CSP
2018	DAN	ROK	21	1	0	0	2	2	11²	11	1	2.3	6.9	9	54.1%	.278	1.20	3.09	70	0.3				
2018	MIS	AA	21	2	5	0	13	13	57²	65	3	3.7	6.9	44	40.7%	.333	1.54	4.06	134	-0.7				
2019	ARK	AA	22	8	12	0	27	27	146	157	10	2.3	8.3	135	48.5%	.349	1.34	4.44	116	-1.2				
2020	STL	MLB	23	0	0	0	3	0	5¹	5	1	8.4	6.8	4	35.3%	.250	1.88	6.75	123	0.0	92.9	49.6%	23.5%	41.0%
2021 FS	STL	MLB	24	2	3	0	57	0	50	50	7	4.9	7.7	42	42.9%	.291	1.55	5.15	119	-0.4	92.9	49.6%	23.5%	41.0%

Comparables: Justus Sheffield, Génesis Cabrera, Beau Burrows

Let's hope well-traveled lefty Sánchez can smile when he remembers the high heat he blew past Ian Happ for his first career punchout last August; he'll need all the positive vibes he can muster while he rehabs from offseason elbow surgery.

Zack Thompson LHP Born: 10/28/97 Age: 23 Bats: L Throws: L Height: 6'2" Weight: 215 Origin: Round 1, 2019 Draft (#19 overall)

YEAR	TEAM	LVL	AGE	W	L	SV	G	GS	IP	H	HR	BB/9	K/9	K	GB%	BABIP	WHIP	ERA	DRA-	WARP	MPH	FA%	Whiff%	CSP
2019	CAR	ROK	21	0	0	0	2	2	2	3	0	0.0	18.0	4	66.7%	.500	1.50	0.00	32	0.1				
2019	PMB	HI-A	21	0	0	0	11	0	13¹	16	0	2.7	12.8	19	48.6%	.471	1.50	4.05	137	-0.3				
2021 FS	STL	MLB	23	2	3	0	57	0	50	48	8	4.3	8.6	47	42.4%	.293	1.46	4.97	120	-0.4				

With no minor-league season last year, pitching prospects lost the irreplaceable opportunity to hone their craft in game situations against hundreds of different batters. Of course, spending the summer in the controlled environment of a team's alternate site allowed them avoid the wear and tear of travel and lessened the chance of incidental injury. On balance, that might have been a good thing for Thompson, a high-floor, low-ceiling lefty with four quality pitches but none that scream plus-plus. He suffered through arm problems in both high school and college and he wasn't exactly babied in his years at the University of Kentucky, so leaving a little more tread on the tires last year may make it more likely the development staff will eventually deliver him to the middle of the Cardinals rotation safe and sound.

Adam Wainwright RHP Born: 08/30/81 Age: 39 Bats: R Throws: R Height: 6'7" Weight: 230 Origin: Round 1, 2000 Draft (#29 overall)

YEAR	TEAM	LVL	AGE	W	L	SV	G	GS	IP	H	HR	BB/9	K/9	K	GB%	BABIP	WHIP	ERA	DRA-	WARP	MPH	FA%	Whiff%	CSP
2018	SPR	AA	36	1	0	0	3	3	10	5	0	0.0	8.1	9	42.3%	.192	0.50	0.00	92	0.1				
2018	MEM	AAA	36	1	0	0	2	2	9	8	0	4.0	11.0	11	38.1%	.381	1.33	0.00	64	0.3				
2018	STL	MLB	36	2	4	0	8	8	40¹	41	5	4.0	8.9	40	47.9%	.319	1.46	4.46	84	0.7	91.9	37.9%	23.7%	45.5%
2019	STL	MLB	37	14	10	0	31	31	171²	181	22	3.4	8.0	153	48.1%	.323	1.43	4.19	93	2.2	91.9	38.4%	19.6%	48.5%
2020	STL	MLB	38	5	3	0	10	10	65²	54	9	2.1	7.4	54	42.9%	.247	1.05	3.15	97	0.7	91.4	36.7%	24.2%	46.5%
2021 FS	STL	MLB	39	9	9	0	26	26	150	148	20	3.1	8.2	136	45.3%	.296	1.33	4.13	102	0.9	91.8	37.9%	21.3%	47.7%

Comparables: *Jim Bunning, Gaylord Perry, Fergie Jenkins*

It's been years since Wainwright led the league in anything but affability, yet last year Uncle Charlie was back in black ink after pacing the league in complete games. Sure, there were only two, and one was of the shortened COVID doubleheader variety, but the other was a bona fide 120-pitch gem on his 39th birthday. Wainwright remained both durable and productive last year, silently dissecting lineups while long-time bridge partner Yadier Molina sent out signals only the two of them understand. Waino and Yadi have started 289 games together, fourth on the all-time battery list and only 35 behind leaders Mickey Lolich and Bill Freehan. Health, money or roster decisions might get in the way, but they might just have enough gas left in the tank to get there.

Tyler Webb LHP Born: 07/20/90 Age: 30 Bats: L Throws: L Height: 6'5" Weight: 240 Origin: Round 10, 2013 Draft (#314 overall)

YEAR	TEAM	LVL	AGE	W	L	SV	G	GS	IP	H	HR	BB/9	K/9	K	GB%	BABIP	WHIP	ERA	DRA-	WARP	MPH	FA%	Whiff%	CSP
2018	ELP	AAA	27	1	1	0	19	0	22	20	1	3.3	11.5	28	37.5%	.345	1.27	2.05	64	0.5				
2018	MEM	AAA	27	0	0	0	11	1	19²	9	1	1.8	9.6	21	38.6%	.190	0.66	2.29	68	0.4				
2018	SD	MLB	27	0	1	0	4	0	5	6	2	5.4	7.2	4	41.2%	.267	1.80	12.60	184	-0.2	90.3	60.4%	23.7%	45.7%
2018	STL	MLB	27	0	0	0	18	0	15¹	16	1	3.5	6.5	11	29.2%	.326	1.43	1.76	150	-0.3	91.8	59.7%	22.9%	51.1%
2019	MEM	AAA	28	0	1	0	5	0	6²	7	0	2.7	6.8	5	45.0%	.350	1.35	2.70	88	0.1				
2019	STL	MLB	28	2	1	1	65	0	55	33	7	3.8	7.9	48	41.2%	.187	1.02	3.76	81	0.8	91.5	65.3%	22.9%	48.6%
2020	STL	MLB	29	1	1	1	21	0	21²	17	2	2.9	7.9	19	39.3%	.259	1.11	2.08	96	0.2	91.4	59.8%	25.3%	52.3%
2021 FS	STL	MLB	30	2	2	0	57	0	50	45	7	3.2	8.4	46	41.3%	.274	1.25	3.84	95	0.3	91.5	62.9%	23.7%	49.9%
2021 DC	STL	MLB	30	2	2	0	50	0	53	47	7	3.2	8.4	49	41.3%	.274	1.25	3.84	95	0.5	91.5	62.9%	23.7%	49.9%

Comparables: *Shawn Armstrong, Mike Morin, Nick Wittgren*

The new "three-batter minimum" rule forced lefty specialist Webb to face more right-handed bats last year. A career-killer? Maybe not. He still put up his usual decent numbers, proving true the old adage "you can take the LOOGY out of the game, eventually, but you can't take the game out of the LOOGY."

Kodi Whitley RHP Born: 02/21/95 Age: 26 Bats: R Throws: R Height: 6'3" Weight: 220 Origin: Round 27, 2017 Draft (#814 overall)

YEAR	TEAM	LVL	AGE	W	L	SV	G	GS	IP	H	HR	BB/9	K/9	K	GB%	BABIP	WHIP	ERA	DRA-	WARP	MPH	FA%	Whiff%	CSP
2018	PEO	LO-A	23	4	2	9	41	2	71²	67	2	3.3	8.5	68	45.4%	.322	1.30	2.51	72	1.3				
2019	PMB	HI-A	24	0	0	0	3	0	4¹	1	0	4.2	10.4	5	37.5%	.125	0.69	0.00	63	0.1				
2019	SPR	AA	24	1	4	7	31	0	39¹	31	3	3.0	10.5	46	40.0%	.277	1.12	1.83	57	0.9				
2019	MEM	AAA	24	2	0	2	16	0	23²	21	0	1.5	10.3	27	27.7%	.323	1.06	1.52	45	0.9				
2020	STL	MLB	25	0	0	0	4	0	4²	2	1	1.9	9.6	5	36.4%	.100	0.64	1.93	95	0.1	95.1	53.2%	33.3%	45.7%
2021 FS	STL	MLB	26	1	2	0	57	0	50	46	8	2.5	8.8	49	35.6%	.285	1.22	3.88	95	0.3	95.1	53.2%	33.3%	45.7%
2021 DC	STL	MLB	26	1	2	0	39	0	41	38	6	2.5	8.8	40	35.6%	.285	1.22	3.88	95	0.3	95.1	53.2%	33.3%	45.7%

Comparables: *Cody Ege, Wei-Chieh Huang, Colton Murray*

Time spent successfully recovering from COVID-19 and a sore elbow limited Whitley to four appearances in his Cardinals debut, but the strapping young right-hander showed enough to earn a spot on the team's playoff roster and future plans. His four-seamer sat in the mid-90s but he can reach back for more when he needs it, his changeup and slider both miss bats and unlike so many other live-armed relief prospects he avoids ball four. Gopher balls will be an intermittent problem for him but Whitley has the stuff to headline a major-league bullpen; if that doesn't pan out, he has the name to headline a major pop tour.

Jake Woodford RHP Born: 10/28/96 Age: 24 Bats: R Throws: R Height: 6'4" Weight: 215 Origin: Round 1, 2015 Draft (#39 overall)

YEAR	TEAM	LVL	AGE	W	L	SV	G	GS	IP	H	HR	BB/9	K/9	K	GB%	BABIP	WHIP	ERA	DRA-	WARP	MPH	FA%	Whiff%	CSP
2018	SPR	AA	21	3	8	0	16	16	81	94	13	3.9	6.2	56	46.9%	.313	1.59	5.22	96	0.5				
2018	MEM	AAA	21	5	5	0	12	12	64	64	5	3.8	6.3	45	36.2%	.295	1.42	4.50	108	0.4				
2019	MEM	AAA	22	9	8	0	26	26	151²	124	22	4.5	7.8	131	37.0%	.249	1.31	4.15	69	4.9				
2020	STL	MLB	23	1	0	0	12	1	21	20	7	2.1	6.9	16	45.3%	.228	1.19	5.57	113	0.0	94.3	77.8%	20.4%	48.8%
2021 FS	STL	MLB	24	2	3	0	57	0	50	51	7	4.5	7.4	41	41.2%	.295	1.54	5.38	120	-0.4	94.3	77.8%	20.4%	48.8%
2021 DC	STL	MLB	24	2	3	0	37	3	49	50	7	4.5	7.4	40	41.2%	.295	1.54	5.38	120	-0.2	94.3	77.8%	20.4%	48.8%

Comparables: *Jonathan Hernández, Brad Hand, Enyel De Los Santos*

Woodford may someday make it as a swingman but big-league hitters took him to the woodshed during his big league debut, homering once every three innings and posting slash stats reminiscent of a good Eddie Rosario season; it's not easy to register both a FIP nearing 7 and a WHIP nearing 1.

CHICAGO WHITE SOX

Essay by Adrian Burgos Jr.

Player comments by James Fegan and BP staff

Emotions overcame José Abreu on November 12, when informed that he had been voted the American League Most Valuable Player. Abreu was at a loss of words at first. It was a major accomplishment for "Pito," the Cuban native's family nickname. He composed himself after about a minute. Then he shared why he pointed to a photo of his grandmother, who had been one of Abreu's lifelong supporters but had recently died. Joy mixed with grief. It was a combination that would become familiar to many in 2020.

In winning the 2020 AL MVP Award Abreu became the first Cuban baseball defector to earn the title in the majors. His story is quite different than the other two Cuban-born MVP winners. Fellow AL MVPs Zoilo Versalles (1965) and José Canseco (1988) were both born in Cuba, but they were not defectors in the same sense as Abreu. The Sox first baseman left his native land after becoming a standout in Cuba's National Series.

Abreu's award-winning season was a major part of the 2020 White Sox success. Just as notable, he was his part of the distinct Latino flavor of the Southside squad. The team featured Latinos from across the Americas all around the diamond, from the infield to the outfield, the starting rotation and bullpen, and at the managerial helm.

Managing the Southsiders

The Southsiders made the playoffs with Mexican-American manager Rick Renteria. It was the first time the White Sox qualified for the postseason since 2008, when another Latino manager, Ozzie Guillen, led the team to the playoffs.

Renteria's connection with Latino players had been part of the organization's plan for success for several years. His ability to communicate effectively, whether in English or Spanish, and also his familiarity with American and Latino cultures were components that the Sox hoped would enable Renteria to build clubhouse chemistry and success on the field. In a 2018 interview Renteria shared with me his approach to working with players.

"You have people coming from every walk of life. I don't try to target so much on where they're from. I look for baseball players. I look for guys that play the game ... It's not in and of itself that you speak the language, Spanish or English or

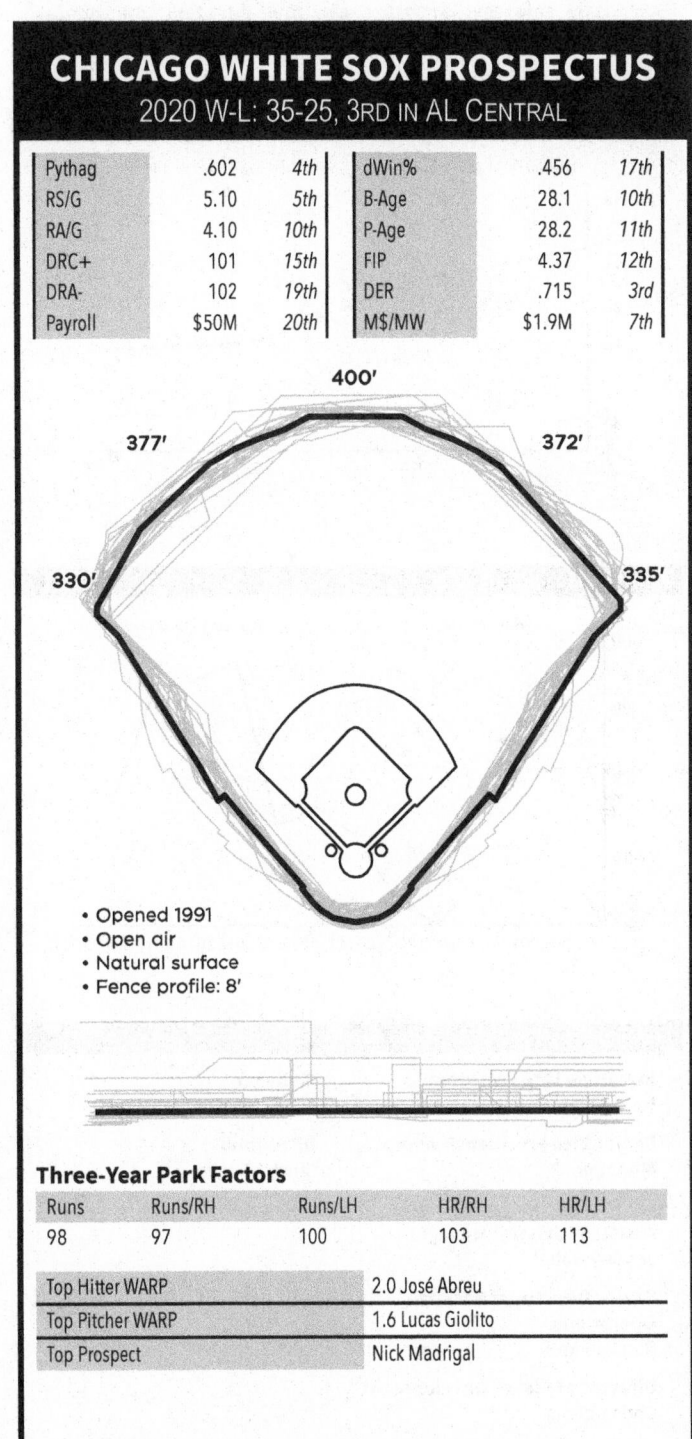

CHICAGO WHITE SOX PROSPECTUS
2020 W-L: 35-25, 3RD IN AL CENTRAL

Pythag	.602	4th	dWin%	.456	17th
RS/G	5.10	5th	B-Age	28.1	10th
RA/G	4.10	10th	P-Age	28.2	11th
DRC+	101	15th	FIP	4.37	12th
DRA-	102	19th	DER	.715	3rd
Payroll	$50M	20th	M$/MW	$1.9M	7th

400'
377'
372'
330'
335'

- Opened 1991
- Open air
- Natural surface
- Fence profile: 8'

Three-Year Park Factors

Runs	Runs/RH	Runs/LH	HR/RH	HR/LH
98	97	100	103	113

Top Hitter WARP	2.0 José Abreu
Top Pitcher WARP	1.6 Lucas Giolito
Top Prospect	Nick Madrigal

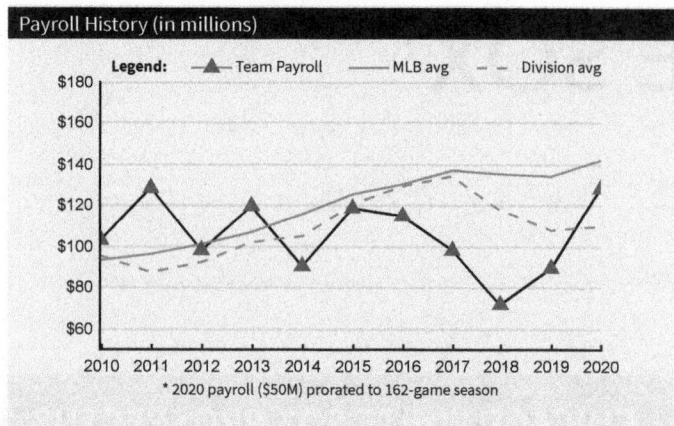

Payroll History (in millions)

Legend: ▲ Team Payroll — MLB avg - - Division avg

* 2020 payroll ($50M) prorated to 162-game season

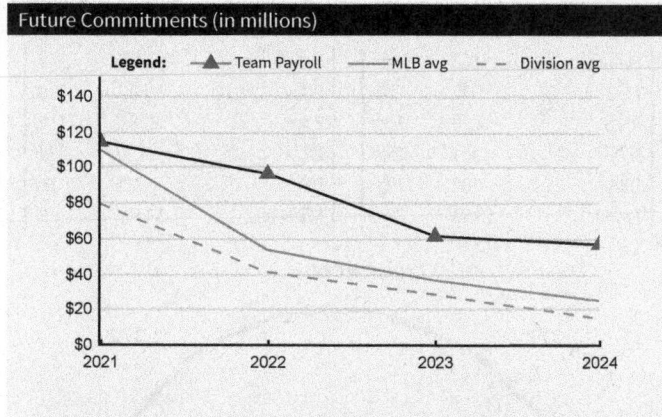

Future Commitments (in millions)

Legend: ▲ Team Payroll — MLB avg - - Division avg

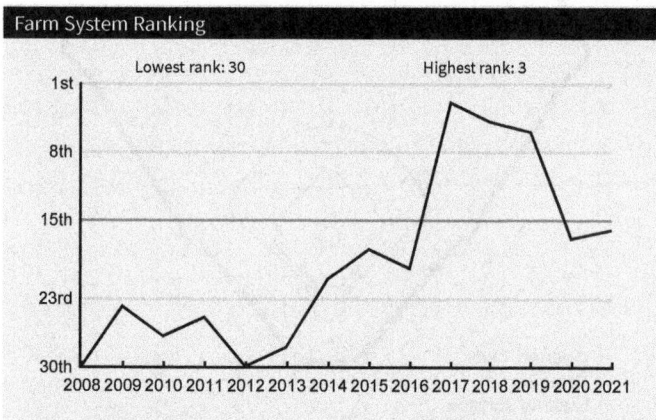

Farm System Ranking

Lowest rank: 30   Highest rank: 3

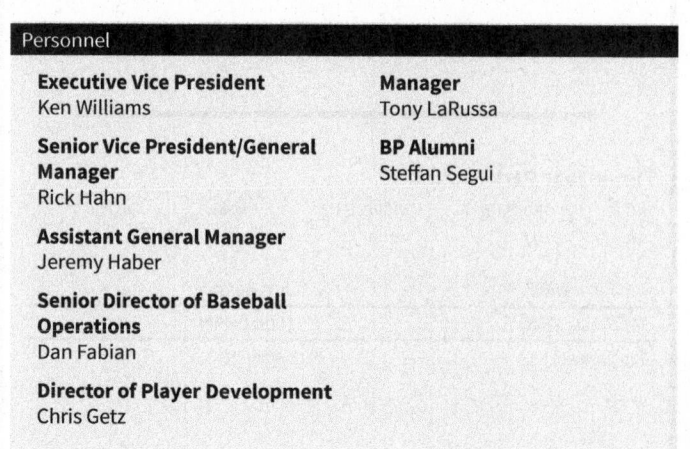

Personnel

Executive Vice President
Ken Williams

Senior Vice President/General Manager
Rick Hahn

Assistant General Manager
Jeremy Haber

Senior Director of Baseball Operations
Dan Fabian

Director of Player Development
Chris Getz

Manager
Tony LaRussa

BP Alumni
Steffan Segui

whatever language you speak … it has more to do with how you create a message, how you can present it. Make guys understand the concept that you're trying to impart to them. And if it works, they get it. And if it doesn't, you keep trying to find a new way."

Renteria kept trying to find a way. In 2020 he enjoyed his most successful season as a big league manager. He guided the White Sox to a 35-25 record and a second place finish in the AL Central.

Chicago's Latino Flavor is a Negro League Throwback

The Latino flavor of the White Sox 2020 squad was hard to miss. In no game was this more obvious than the August 1 contest versus the Royals. Cubans Luis Robert, Yoán Moncada, Abreu and Yasmani Grandal were penciled into the top of Chicago's batting order. It was the first time in MLB history Cuban-born players batted in the first four slots in a team's lineup. Ironically this historical moment occurred in Kansas City, where a hundred years earlier the Negro National League was founded by Rube Foster, an African-American ballplayer-turned-team owner who called Chicago home.

The 2020 White Sox provided powerful reminders of the history that Chicago shared with Black baseball. The Southsiders' former home ballpark, the original Comiskey Park, hosted Black baseball's showcase East-West Classic from the 1930s through the 1950s. The lineup Renteria put together throughout the 2020 campaign evoked memories of Negro League baseball. Even more, the Sox starting nine often resembled the lineups that the New York Cubans would have in the Negro Leagues.

Before he became "Minnie" and a star with the White Sox, Orestes Miñoso got his professional start in the U.S. with the NY Cubans club in 1946. The Negro League's Cubans team included Latino talent from the Dominican Republic, Puerto Rico, and Venezuela in addition to players from Cuba.

The 2020 Sox likewise featured its own regular cast of Latino players. Cuban native Grandal started most games behind the plate. Fellow Cuban Abreu anchored the infield at first. Nick Madrigal, a Mexican-American player from California, took regular turns at second base after his in-season promotion. The Sox lone African-American starter Tim Anderson continued to flourish at shortstop. A third Cuban, Moncada, fielded the hot corner.

Three Latinos composed the Sox starting outfield most games. Rookie Luis Robert patrolled center field. The manner Robert roamed the outfield at times seemed a modern version of Philadelphia Phillies center fielder Gary Maddox—of whom announcer Ralph Kiner once described "two-thirds of the earth is covered by water. The other third is covered by Gary Maddox." On occasion it verged on the comical. That much was clear when Robert called off Eloy Jiménez on a fly ball hit almost directly to the Sox left fielder. Jiménez struck a pose in faux anger and then laughed with his outfield partner. For Jiménez, 2020 saw his development into an offensive threat and not a sophomore slump. The same could not be said for fellow Venezuelan Nomar Mazara who took regular turns starting in right field although not quite getting on track at the plate.

The Sox moundsmen also featured a Latino contingent. The Latino relief corps enjoyed more success than their Latino counterpart in the starting rotation as Cuban-American Carlos Rodón was lost for much of 2020 due to injury and Dominican Reynaldo López started on the mound while battling his own injury woes and ineffectiveness. Alex Colomé and Jimmy Cordero were among the more called upon members of the Sox bullpen by Renteria, with Colomé often dominating in the closer role.

A Return to Postseason in Abnormal Times

As the White Sox positioned themselves to ascend the AL Central with their young nucleus of stars, the signing of Dallas Keuchel and Grandal as free agents proved important additions in 2020. Keuchel stabilized the Sox starting rotation, providing a veteran presence and an experienced postseason arm among Chicago's young starters. Grandal gave the team a catcher who could both command the game from behind the plate and pose a serious threat when he stepped into the batter's box.

Given the effects of the pandemic, the work of Renteria and other managers was more difficult than ever. Managing motivation, rule changes and the simple routine-building that goes into the marathon, or in this case the 5K, was a monumental task amidst postponements and positive test results. The feel at the ballpark was quite different. No fans were permitted to attend games until the World Series in October. The sounds of the game were amplified. No longer was the crack of the bat the sole sound that regularly reverberated throughout the ballparks. It was much easier to hear players bench jockeying, protesting umpires' calls, or encouraging one another. One could also hear Spanish more easily, whether it was the sounds of Bad Bunny or J Balvin as the walk-up music as batters strode to the plate or Latino players chatting each other up. This was particularly true of White Sox games.

In these abnormal times the White Sox qualified for an expanded postseason. For a while the Southsiders seemed they might even claim the AL Central title. Abreu stayed hot for almost the entire 60-game schedule, averaging an RBI a game and leading the AL in home runs and RBI while coming in fourth in batting average. Anderson expressed his joy of playing baseball while also speaking powerfully on racial issues inside and outside of baseball in the ongoing Black Lives Matter protests.

The Sox stumbled in late September, winning just two of their last ten games. The spiral allowed the Minnesota Twins to pass them in the Central standings and the home field advantage that would have come in the early rounds. The formula for success still seemed to be working as the Sox headed into Game 3 of the ALDS. Chicago hit Oakland starter Mike Fiers hard, though Robert's 487-foot home run ended up providing the lone run. Renteria gave the starting nod to rookie Dane Dunning but turned to the bullpen after just four batters. The relief corps fared poorly; they walked nine batters and ultimately lost the game. In the fallout, the front office sent Dunning and a prospect to the Texas Rangers for veteran Lance Lynn, hopeful they had landed someone to fill the role of a Game 3 postseason starter, and confident that, as the roster matures, they'll need another one.

Looking Back to Move Ahead

Renteria and the Sox parted ways after the Los Angeles Dodgers claimed their first World Series since 1988. The dismissal, described as a mutual decision, acknowledged that his "fingerprints will be all over that club and a big part of that success will be due to him" but that the choice was made "to take that next step ... putting us in a place to succeed." What elements Reneteria lacked for this next step went unstated. The Sox's managerial hire was itself a harkening back to the 1980s. The return of Tony LaRussa to the Southside surprised many. After all, LaRussa had been fired as White Sox manager 35 years ago—only three members of the 2020 squad were even alive then.

Hiring LaRussa is an abrupt departure from the plan that had paired Renteria with a young, Latino-centric squad. The move raised its own set of serious questions. How will the Latino players respond to LaRussa's managerial approach, communication style and ideas of managing personalities? Will Jimenéz and Robert flourish or flounder under LaRussa? The two budding Latino stars weren't even teenagers when LaRussa last managed.

It's a very real concern given his 2016 statements (which he doubled down on in early 2020) about players dishonoring the flag and his questioning the sincerity of Colin Kaepernick and other athletes engaging in peaceful protests, ideas that are out of step with the modern sports world with Black athletes and others openly expressing views in support of Black Lives Matter. His new shortstop, Tim Anderson, is at the forefront of these conversations. LaRussa took time during his first press conference to address his 2016 statements, which were made when he was in charge of the Arizona Diamondbacks' front office and responsible for setting an organizational tone. He said he was educated by what transpired in 2020. Yet, it is worth noting how interactions with players are quite different as a manager compared to the front office head. They are more personal, intimate and occur every day. White Sox success next season may well depend on how much their players trust LaRussa's evolution and the degree to which they feel he has their back in the game and that this support extends to their engagement with the public on social issues and on how their lives matter. ■

-Adrian Burgos, Jr. is a Professor of History at the University of Illinois.

HITTERS

José Abreu 1B Born: 01/29/87   Age: 34   Bats: R   Throws: R   Height: 6'3"   Weight: 250   Origin: International Free Agent, 2013

YEAR	TEAM	LVL	AGE	PA	R	2B	3B	HR	RBI	BB	K	SB	CS	Whiff%	AVG/OBP/SLG	DRC+	BABIP	BRR	FRAA	WARP
2018	CHW	MLB	31	553	68	36	1	22	78	37	109	2	0	24.6%	.265/.325/.473	114	.294	0.0	1B(114): 4.9	2.3
2019	CHW	MLB	32	693	85	38	1	33	123	36	151	2	2	25.3%	.284/.330/.503	108	.320	-5.1	1B(125): -10.5	0.2
2020	CHW	MLB	33	262	43	15	0	19	60	18	59	0	0	30.1%	.317/.370/.617	140	.350	-0.4	1B(54): 2.7	2.0
2021 FS	CHW	MLB	34	600	80	30	1	31	93	37	141	2	0	26.6%	.278/.339/.508	128	.323	-1.5	1B 0	2.8
2021 DC	CHW	MLB	34	607	81	30	1	31	94	38	142	2	0	26.6%	.278/.339/.508	128	.323	-1.5	1B 0	2.9

Comparables: Cecil Fielder, Adrián González, Lee May

It's time to face facts that are borne out by the statistical record. After every veteran player with any latent trade value was dealt away from the White Sox over the course of the 2017 season, Abreu pulled a book from a bookshelf (let's say it was "Sense and Sensibility") in the White Sox clubhouse, opening up the hatch to a secret lair below Guaranteed Rate Field. After descending a staircase into the lair, Abreu entered a hyperbaric chamber. Within the chamber, he entered a sensory deprivation tank. Within the deprivation tank, he was encased in mylar so that he was preserved in mint condition, but with slits cut for ventilation so he did not die. Within the mylar, he was paired with a big ol' fuzzy grizzly bear who was also hibernating at the same time and served as his snuggle buddy for the duration of the 2018 and 2019 seasons. When he emerged in the middle of 2020 as play resumed, the 33-year-old Abreu was physically ready to mash like the days of old. As a parting gift for the doppelgänger who played in his stead for two seasons, Abreu offered him a lovely 1983 Bordeaux, as the secret lair doubles as a wine cellar. The doppelgänger was an above-average hitter in his own right and deserves a big league contract, though maybe he'll just come back and play for the White Sox next season.

Micker Adolfo OF Born: 09/11/96   Age: 24   Bats: R   Throws: R   Height: 6'4"   Weight: 240   Origin: International Free Agent, 2013

YEAR	TEAM	LVL	AGE	PA	R	2B	3B	HR	RBI	BB	K	SB	CS	Whiff%	AVG/OBP/SLG	DRC+	BABIP	BRR	FRAA	WARP
2018	WS	HI-A	21	336	48	18	1	11	50	34	92	2	1		.282/.369/.464	136	.372	-1.5		0.8
2019	WSX	ROK	22	58	8	5	0	2	3	7	21	0	0		.260/.362/.480	86	.407	-3.1		-0.3
2019	BIR	AA	22	95	5	7	0	0	9	14	36	0	3		.205/.337/.295	95	.372	-3.3		-0.3
2021 FS	CHW	MLB	24	600	59	26	1	15	56	45	245	1	0		.201/.274/.341	69	.331	-0.6	RF-7	-1.8
2021 DC	CHW	MLB	24	67	6	2	0	1	6	5	27	0	0		.201/.274/.341	69	.331	-0.1	RF-1	-0.2

Comparables: Chris Parmelee, Alex Jackson, Scott Moore

The pandemic changed much about the fundamental nature of American life, but it left a writeup of Adolfo fundamentally unaltered. A big man who possesses top-of-the-scale raw power, he urgently needs a matured approach to wield it during games due to an unremarkable hit tool, and he cannot seem to consistently get into games to undergo that refinement.

Tim Anderson SS Born: 06/23/93   Age: 28   Bats: R   Throws: R   Height: 6'1"   Weight: 185   Origin: Round 1, 2013 Draft (#17 overall)

YEAR	TEAM	LVL	AGE	PA	R	2B	3B	HR	RBI	BB	K	SB	CS	Whiff%	AVG/OBP/SLG	DRC+	BABIP	BRR	FRAA	WARP
2018	CHW	MLB	25	606	77	28	3	20	64	30	149	26	8	27.8%	.240/.281/.406	91	.289	6.5	SS(151): 9.1	3.8
2019	CHW	MLB	26	518	81	32	0	18	56	15	109	17	5	24.5%	.335/.357/.508	112	.399	4.3	SS(122): 1.7	3.9
2020	CHW	MLB	27	221	45	11	1	10	21	10	50	5	2	30.9%	.322/.357/.529	104	.383	1.7	SS(49): -1.3	0.8
2021 FS	CHW	MLB	28	600	74	27	2	19	59	23	152	16	4	27.3%	.267/.301/.428	97	.332	3.3	SS 0	2.0
2021 DC	CHW	MLB	28	574	71	25	2	19	56	22	145	15	4	27.3%	.267/.301/.428	97	.332	3.2	SS 0	2.0

Comparables: Dale Sveum, Ian Desmond, Kurt Abbott

It's of the deepest irony that the bat-flipping iconoclast who declares the game of baseball boring, outwardly expresses his lack of reverence for the sport's outmoded customs, and surely has inspired a legion of detractors, is perhaps the most old-school hitter in the league. Anderson has enough bat speed to turn and burn 20 home runs per season, and has in the past. But his breakout into a productive hitter largely lies in his predilection for so-called "good pieces of hitting." Every old crank who wishes they never had to hear about exit velocity, launch angle, or watch games determined by a couple of solo shots interspersed between dozens of strikeouts has the strangest bedfellow in Anderson, who has dedicated himself to flipping as many singles to right field as humanly possible. He lets everything on the outer half get deep and sprays it. He's impossible to jam because he can tuck his hands in quickly and rarely looks to pull. If you actually do get him to roll over a ball to the left side, he's a threat to sprint out an infield single. His exit velocity is unremarkable. His BABIP is unsustainably sky high. He also has a .331 batting average over his last 706 at-bats. Which leads to one last bit of irony: For those who cling to the value of batting average, posting .331 is the way to make it valuable.

Zack Collins C Born: 02/06/95   Age: 26   Bats: L   Throws: R   Height: 6'3"   Weight: 230   Origin: Round 1, 2016 Draft (#10 overall)

YEAR	TEAM	LVL	AGE	PA	R	2B	3B	HR	RBI	BB	K	SB	CS	Whiff%	AVG/OBP/SLG	DRC+	BABIP	BRR	FRAA	WARP
2018	BIR	AA	23	531	58	24	1	15	68	101	158	5	0		.234/.382/.404	124	.329	-3.2	C(74): -14.4	0.3
2019	CHA	AAA	24	367	56	19	1	19	74	62	98	0	0		.282/.403/.548	133	.346	0.8	C(50): -4.6, 1B(20): -1.6	2.1
2019	CHW	MLB	24	102	10	3	1	3	12	14	39	0	0	37.3%	.186/.307/.349	78	.295	0.0	C(10): -3.0, 1B(1): -0.1	-0.3
2020	CHW	MLB	25	18	1	1	0	0	0	2	5	0	0	42.4%	.062/.167/.125	96	.091	0.2	C(2): -0.0, 1B(1): -0.0	0.0
2021 FS	CHW	MLB	26	600	67	23	1	20	64	85	214	0	0	38.4%	.203/.320/.376	95	.301	0.0	C -17, 1B 0	0.2
2021 DC	CHW	MLB	26	236	26	9	0	8	25	33	84	0	0	38.4%	.203/.320/.376	95	.301	0.0	C -9	-0.2

Comparables: Chris Carter, Dusty Ryan, Yasmani Grandal

The $3.4 million signing bonus that Collins received as the 10th-overall pick in 2016 probably keeps him from cracking any list of the top-10,000 people affected by the reduced major league season or the canceled minor league season. But save for 18 plate appearances and a three-pitch strikeout in the playoffs, one of the best catching situations in the league did not involve him, and he couldn't even crush Triple-A pitching again for old times' sake. No questions about his future were firmly answered in Schaumburg sim games, and all that the playoffs run provided were celebration videos that indicated his dancing is driven by makeup and want, rather than hip swivel.

YEAR	TEAM	P. COUNT	FRM RUNS	BLK RUNS	THRW RUNS	TOT RUNS
2018	BIR	10822	-12.2	-0.9	-0.7	-13.8
2019	CHW	1653	-1.8	-1.1	0.0	-2.9
2019	CHA	7026	-3.9	-0.1	-0.3	-4.3
2020	CHW	143	0.0	0.0		0.0
2021	CHW	6012	-5.0	-3.2	0.2	-8.0

Jarrod Dyson CF Born: 08/15/84 Age: 36 Bats: L Throws: R Height: 5'9" Weight: 165 Origin: Round 50, 2006 Draft (#1475 overall)

YEAR	TEAM	LVL	AGE	PA	R	2B	3B	HR	RBI	BB	K	SB	CS	Whiff%	AVG/OBP/SLG	DRC+	BABIP	BRR	FRAA	WARP
2018	ARI	MLB	33	237	29	4	2	2	12	27	34	16	3	16.9%	.189/.282/.257	70	.216	2.6	CF(41): 3.3, RF(18): 0.0, LF(6): 1.1	0.6
2019	ARI	MLB	34	452	65	11	2	7	27	47	85	30	4	21.5%	.230/.313/.320	77	.274	6.3	CF(103): -3.7, RF(21): 4.0, LF(16): 0.0	0.8
2020	CHW	MLB	36	11	3	0	0	0	0	0	1	2	0	5.0%	.300/.300/.300	75	.333	0.1	LF(6): -0.1, CF(2): -0.2, RF(1): 0.1	-0.1
2020	PIT	MLB	36	55	6	0	0	0	5	4	10	4	0	23.4%	.157/.218/.157	79	.195	0.4	CF(21): 0.0	0.1
2021 FS	CHW	MLB	36	600	56	19	2	8	53	50	113	38	8	20.5%	.229/.304/.323	76	.276	14.3	CF -3, RF 0	1.0

Comparables: Bill Bruton, Tom Goodwin, Cesar Geronimo

There is some element of Dyson's game that has steadily grown with his accumulation of knowledge. The sheer volume of pitcher deliveries he has watched, the catalogue of pick-off moves he has collected in his mind have built a compendium of information on how to run the bases that outpaces what his feet can deliver. His top speed at this point in life is slower than that of Eloy Jiménez, Nicky Delmonico, or simply the average major league player, and yet he's stolen 36 bases in 40 attempts over the last two seasons. At 36 years of age, he is physically slipping in a myriad of easily noticeable ways, and yet some part of him is rapidly getting better, almost keeping pace with the mounting limitations. It's a marvel worth celebrating, studying and commemorating. But since his bat is just fully cooked beyond belief as part of this, it's probably not worth rostering.

Adam Eaton RF Born: 12/06/88 Age: 32 Bats: L Throws: L Height: 5'9" Weight: 176 Origin: Round 19, 2010 Draft (#571 overall)

YEAR	TEAM	LVL	AGE	PA	R	2B	3B	HR	RBI	BB	K	SB	CS	Whiff%	AVG/OBP/SLG	DRC+	BABIP	BRR	FRAA	WARP
2018	WAS	MLB	29	370	55	18	1	5	33	38	64	9	1	18.1%	.301/.394/.411	106	.364	0.4	RF(67): 5.7, LF(10): -0.5	1.7
2019	WAS	MLB	30	656	103	25	7	15	49	65	106	15	3	17.7%	.279/.365/.428	101	.319	3.6	RF(139): 4.3, LF(7): -0.0	2.5
2020	WAS	MLB	32	176	22	11	1	4	17	12	32	3	0	16.7%	.226/.285/.384	90	.260	1.1	RF(41): 0.2	0.2
2021 FS	CHW	MLB	32	600	70	25	3	12	57	55	120	11	3	17.5%	.249/.334/.377	99	.301	2.3	RF 6, LF 0	2.2
2021 DC	CHW	MLB	32	540	63	22	2	10	51	50	108	9	3	17.5%	.249/.334/.377	99	.301	2.1	RF 5	2.0

Comparables: Lloyd Moseby, Tony Gonzalez, Mitch Webster

A mortgage is something that you're initially excited about—a house! A new and shiny house! Then the first major renovation hits, then you're like—a house! A terrible and costly house! Then it mostly settles into being something that will never be as valuable as it used to be, even though you have to keep paying for it for longer than you'd like. The whole experience makes you really pine for that old apartment you had before signing the mortgage, especially when that old apartment is Lucas Giolito and that house is post-prime Adam Eaton, who the Nationals elected against keeping around despite a track record of being an above-average hitter. Eaton rejoined the White Sox on a one-year deal, suggesting they did indeed pine for that old apartment.

Edwin Encarnación 1B Born: 01/07/83 Age: 38 Bats: R Throws: R Height: 6'1" Weight: 230 Origin: Round 9, 2000 Draft (#274 overall)

YEAR	TEAM	LVL	AGE	PA	R	2B	3B	HR	RBI	BB	K	SB	CS	Whiff%	AVG/OBP/SLG	DRC+	BABIP	BRR	FRAA	WARP
2018	CLE	MLB	35	579	74	16	1	32	107	63	132	3	0	26.2%	.246/.336/.474	124	.265	-5.1	1B(23): 0.8	2.1
2019	SEA	MLB	36	289	48	7	0	21	49	41	55	0	1	26.2%	.241/.356/.531	134	.220	0.6	1B(45): -0.6, 2B(1): -0.0	1.7
2019	NYY	MLB	36	197	33	11	0	13	37	17	48	0	0	24.1%	.249/.325/.531	127	.267	-1.7	1B(12): -0.4	0.8
2020	CHW	MLB	37	181	19	5	0	10	19	16	54	0	0	32.6%	.157/.250/.377	92	.156	-0.7		0.1
2021 FS	CHW	MLB	38	600	73	21	0	31	83	69	165	1	0	27.5%	.224/.324/.447	109	.263	-1.2	1B -5, 2B 0	1.0

Comparables: Paul Konerko, Kevin Millar, Tino Martinez

While there are some enormous cockatoos that can live up to 80 years, the sort of smaller parrot you might let perch on your forearm as you circle the bases typically has a shelf life of 15-20 trips around the sun. Signs that your parrot might be nearing the end of its impressive run would be an exploding infield pop-up rate, pronounced troubles turning around velocity, and of course, "parrot fever." Encarnación didn't experience that last one in 2020, but there have been noises under the hood of his batted ball profile for a few years now, and even in a 60-game season, the engine just began to spurt smoke by the time the White Sox limped into the playoffs. And unlike how this metaphor became horribly mixed, Encarnación's production has become frustratingly one-dimensional at the end of a great career.

Adam Engel CF Born: 12/09/91 Age: 29 Bats: R Throws: R Height: 6'2" Weight: 220 Origin: Round 19, 2013 Draft (#573 overall)

YEAR	TEAM	LVL	AGE	PA	R	2B	3B	HR	RBI	BB	K	SB	CS	Whiff%	AVG/OBP/SLG	DRC+	BABIP	BRR	FRAA	WARP
2018	CHW	MLB	26	463	49	17	4	6	29	18	129	16	8	31.2%	.235/.279/.336	68	.322	1.5	CF(140): 10.0	1.0
2019	CHA	AAA	27	277	43	13	4	9	29	22	62	13	3		.270/.347/.464	92	.328	4.0	CF(58): 7.4, LF(5): -0.4, RF(1): -0.1	1.6
2019	CHW	MLB	27	248	26	10	2	6	26	14	78	3	3	32.6%	.242/.304/.383	64	.343	0.6	CF(86): 0.8	-0.1
2020	CHW	MLB	29	93	11	5	1	3	12	3	19	1	0	26.5%	.295/.333/.477	85	.348	0.2	RF(25): -0.6, LF(9): -0.6, CF(3): -0.6	-0.1
2021 FS	CHW	MLB	29	600	60	22	3	15	60	38	175	18	6	30.7%	.219/.284/.358	76	.291	3.5	CF 3, RF -2	0.5
2021 DC	CHW	MLB	29	270	27	10	1	7	27	17	78	8	2	30.7%	.219/.284/.358	76	.291	1.6	CF 1, RF -1	0.1

Comparables: Reggie Taylor, Kimera Bartee, Jordan Schafer

Years of howling "Adam Engel is a backup at best" from the bleachers and into the swirling winds of Guaranteed Rate Field was finally intoned in 2020, after three years of muscular outfield defense and very musclebound swings-and-misses at the plate. After years of struggles, it can be forgiven that the message was garbled into "Adam Engel is a backup, the best." Sure, this turn of phrase is as corny as buying into Engel's 93 plate appearances in 2020 as proof that he's awesome now. But his effectiveness against left-handed pitching has proven fairly sticky, and combines with his typically sterling and fleet-footed defense. That's usually a starter set for, yes, a decent backup outfielder. First called up in 2017 as the White Sox were selling off every major league asset of consequence, Engel was thrust into a bunch of playing time he would have otherwise never received, thanks to a rebuild. But a stable role and production might finally come from playing less.

Leury García CF   Born: 03/18/91   Age: 30   Bats: S   Throws: R   Height: 5'8"   Weight: 185   Origin: International Free Agent, 2007

YEAR	TEAM	LVL	AGE	PA	R	2B	3B	HR	RBI	BB	K	SB	CS	Whiff%	AVG/OBP/SLG	DRC+	BABIP	BRR	FRAA	WARP
2018	CHW	MLB	27	275	23	7	4	4	32	9	69	12	1	28.8%	.271/.303/.376	74	.355	1.8	LF(40): 1.4, CF(26): -0.8, RF(16): 0.7	0.3
2019	CHW	MLB	28	618	93	27	3	8	40	21	139	15	5	24.7%	.279/.310/.378	78	.353	7.9	CF(80): -5.4, RF(45): -2.7, LF(24): -0.3	0.3
2020	CHW	MLB	29	63	6	1	0	3	8	4	9	0	0	21.3%	.271/.317/.441	107	.277	0.2	SS(10): 0.3, 2B(5): 0.0, RF(3): -0.0	0.3
2021 FS	CHW	MLB	30	600	60	24	2	12	61	29	139	14	5	24.9%	.253/.300/.374	84	.316	-0.3	2B 2, SS 1	0.7
2021 DC	CHW	MLB	30	202	20	8	0	4	20	9	47	4	1	24.9%	.253/.300/.374	84	.316	-0.1	2B 1, SS 0	0.3

Comparables: Randy Kutcher, John Shelby, Juan Lagares

If there's some level of utilitymanitude that is too perfect for this world, surely García has found it. How else does someone banjax two separate seasons with injuries related to sliding head first into first base? The White Sox have lauded García's ability to "roll out of bed and play," but such boasts were undermined by his actual attempt to do just that in the 2020 Wild Card Series, fresh off a seven-week absence for a torn left thumb ligament.

Luis González CF   Born: 09/10/95   Age: 25   Bats: L   Throws: L   Height: 6'1"   Weight: 180   Origin: Round 3, 2017 Draft (#87 overall)

YEAR	TEAM	LVL	AGE	PA	R	2B	3B	HR	RBI	BB	K	SB	CS	Whiff%	AVG/OBP/SLG	DRC+	BABIP	BRR	FRAA	WARP
2018	KAN	LO-A	22	255	35	16	2	8	26	21	57	7	2		.300/.358/.491	144	.365	-0.6	CF(39): -1.0, RF(13): -1.9	1.1
2018	WS	HI-A	22	288	50	24	3	6	45	27	46	3	5		.313/.376/.504	145	.354	5.8	CF(31): 3.9, LF(14): 0.2, RF(12): -0.6	2.5
2019	BIR	AA	23	535	63	18	4	9	59	47	89	17	9		.247/.316/.359	103	.281	1.0	CF(60): 0.7, RF(29): 1.1, LF(20): 2.0	2.1
2020	CHW	MLB	25	2	1	0	0	0	0	0	1	0	0	100.0%	.000/.500/.000	81		0.1	LF(1): -0.0, CF(1): -0.0	0.0
2021 FS	CHW	MLB	25	600	61	26	3	15	68	45	154	5	2	100.0%	.234/.298/.383	88	.296	-0.2	CF 2, RF 2	1.5

Comparables: Braxton Lee, Roger Bernadina, Rey Fuentes

The first ball hit to González in the outfield as a major leaguer struck the heel of his glove and dropped to the grass. His only time on base on record came on a hit by pitch. But even working his way up to emergency reserve represents an upgrade over the way González's 2019 ended in Double-A Birmingham.

Yasmani Grandal C   Born: 11/08/88   Age: 32   Bats: S   Throws: R   Height: 6'2"   Weight: 230   Origin: Round 1, 2010 Draft (#12 overall)

YEAR	TEAM	LVL	AGE	PA	R	2B	3B	HR	RBI	BB	K	SB	CS	Whiff%	AVG/OBP/SLG	DRC+	BABIP	BRR	FRAA	WARP
2018	LAD	MLB	29	518	65	23	2	24	68	72	124	2	1	27.3%	.241/.349/.466	112	.278	-4.4	C(135): 17.7, 1B(2): -0.0	4.7
2019	MIL	MLB	30	632	79	26	2	28	77	109	139	5	1	25.5%	.246/.380/.468	123	.279	-7.5	C(137): 19.9, 1B(20): 0.2	6.1
2020	CHW	MLB	32	194	27	7	0	8	27	30	58	0	0	30.7%	.230/.351/.422	108	.299	0.1	C(32): 1.0, 1B(6): -0.1	1.2
2021 FS	CHW	MLB	32	600	78	24	1	25	74	87	174	3	1	27.2%	.234/.350/.437	116	.303	-1.1	C 15, 1B 0	5.1
2021 DC	CHW	MLB	32	540	70	22	1	22	67	78	156	3	1	27.2%	.234/.350/.437	116	.303	-1.0	C 18, 1B 0	4.8

Comparables: Jorge Posada, Mickey Tettleton, Geovany Soto

Not allowed to review in-game video of his swings due to a combination of COVID-19 and anti-Astros restrictions, Grandal's mistake-speed power bat racked up a career-high strikeout rate in 2020. Rightly assessing that pitch-framing is valued above all, Grandal also racked up his normally large number of wild pitches and strangely dropped tags. On an Instagram post dedicated to his wedding anniversary with his wife, a commenter asked him why his speed rating was a 6 on MLB The Show. It seems like the answer should be

YEAR	TEAM	P. COUNT	FRM RUNS	BLK RUNS	THRW RUNS	TOT RUNS
2018	LAD	16816	15.7	0.8	0.1	16.5
2019	MIL	18740	19.4	1.8	-0.1	21.1
2020	CHW	4830	3.7	0.3	-0.2	3.8
2021	CHW	14430	16.7	0.4	1.0	18.0

obvious: He is very slow. But while you may not like it, this is what peak catcher performance looks like. Grandal batflips his many walks, has cool bat drops when he uppercuts the mistakes he runs into and games the goofy system baseball has for calling strikes to help out his pitcher. Aesthetically, it's not the best. But Grandal knows how the game is being played, and for now, is still thriving at it.

Eloy Jiménez LF   Born: 11/27/96   Age: 24   Bats: R   Throws: R   Height: 6'4"   Weight: 235   Origin: International Free Agent, 2013

YEAR	TEAM	LVL	AGE	PA	R	2B	3B	HR	RBI	BB	K	SB	CS	Whiff%	AVG/OBP/SLG	DRC+	BABIP	BRR	FRAA	WARP
2018	BIR	AA	21	228	36	15	2	10	42	18	39	0	0		.317/.368/.556	158	.344	-1.3	LF(30): -3.6, RF(13): -1.8	0.7
2018	CHA	AAA	21	228	28	13	1	12	33	14	30	0	1		.355/.399/.597	169	.371	-1.8	LF(41): -0.2, RF(6): 0.0	1.8
2019	CHW	MLB	22	504	69	18	2	31	79	30	134	0	0	32.8%	.267/.315/.513	105	.308	1.0	LF(114): -0.7	1.7
2020	CHW	MLB	24	226	26	14	0	14	41	12	56	0	0	29.2%	.296/.332/.559	113	.340	-0.4	LF(54): -7.9	0.1
2021 FS	CHW	MLB	24	600	78	27	2	34	97	36	155	1	0	31.4%	.271/.320/.513	121	.317	-0.4	LF -4, RF 0	2.8
2021 DC	CHW	MLB	24	574	75	26	1	33	93	35	148	1	0	31.4%	.271/.320/.513	121	.317	-0.4	LF -4	2.7

Comparables: Pete Incaviglia, Justin Upton, Greg Luzinski

Humanity is capable of containing multitudes, reconciling contradictions within itself, and living as a dichotomy. As such, Jiménez is a pure, almost poetic savant at the plate. He's almost too good at hitting to care about pitch selection. His ceaseless aggression is counterbalanced by the larger discipline of his overall goals; a steadfast refusal to give in to the trap of pulling, knowing he's too strong to concede to a search for power. He swings at anything, yet tightens up in key situations. He is not as good as he will be yet. He is also, almost self-referentially, a galoot. He injured himself banging his head against the fence on defense in the opening weekend, and effectively ended his season by stepping on a base wrong while running. He flopped into the protective netting along the left field foul line as a galling defensive lowlight in August, and then repeated the performance later on the year seemingly as a bit. He is both self-aware about his fielding shortcomings, good humored about it, and burning with discontent about it. He can do it all, as we all can.

★ ★ ★ *2021 Top 101 Prospect* **#12** ★ ★ ★

Nick Madrigal 2B Born: 03/05/97 Age: 24 Bats: R Throws: R Height: 5'8" Weight: 175 Origin: Round 1, 2018 Draft (#4 overall)

YEAR	TEAM	LVL	AGE	PA	R	2B	3B	HR	RBI	BB	K	SB	CS	Whiff%	AVG/OBP/SLG	DRC+	BABIP	BRR	FRAA	WARP
2018	WSX	ROK	21	17	2	0	0	0	1	1	0	0	1		.154/.353/.154	106	.154	-0.4	2B(2): -0.1, SS(1): -0.1	-0.1
2018	KAN	LO-A	21	49	9	3	0	0	6	1	0	2	2		.341/.347/.409	143	.319	1.1	2B(12): 0.9	0.5
2018	WS	HI-A	21	107	14	4	0	0	9	5	5	6	3		.306/.355/.347	120	.319	0.0	2B(25): -1.8	0.1
2019	WS	HI-A	22	218	20	10	2	2	27	17	6	17	4		.272/.346/.377	114	.269	3.6	2B(41): 3.4	1.6
2019	BIR	AA	22	180	30	11	2	1	16	14	5	14	6		.341/.400/.451	154	.348	0.3	2B(39): 0.1	1.6
2019	CHA	AAA	22	134	26	6	1	1	12	13	5	4	3		.331/.398/.424	102	.336	0.5	2B(28): 1.5	0.6
2020	CHW	MLB	23	109	8	3	0	0	11	4	7	2	1	10.8%	.340/.376/.369	101	.365	-1.5	2B(29): 1.7	0.4
2021 FS	*CHW*	*MLB*	*24*	*600*	*66*	*26*	*2*	*7*	*60*	*34*	*50*	*19*	*8*	*10.8%*	*.301/.352/.399*	*111*	*.320*	*-2.2*	*2B 3, SS 0*	*3.2*
2021 DC	*CHW*	*MLB*	*24*	*540*	*59*	*24*	*2*	*6*	*54*	*31*	*45*	*17*	*7*	*10.8%*	*.301/.352/.399*	*111*	*.320*	*-2.0*	*2B 3*	*2.9*

Comparables: Breyvic Valera, Jarrett Hoffpauir, Eric Sogard

Madrigal's bold and ceaseless pursuit of on-brand activities has reached the point where it's necessary to arrange them in a hierarchy. His 3.3 percent swinging strike rate is low, but two players with 100 plate appearances posted lower figures, and they both chased out of the zone less often than Madrigal. He'll need to clean that up. Similarly, his 6.4 percent strikeout rate was second-lowest, but ceding the crown to Tommy La Stella will probably stick with him all winter. Instead, the most on-brand Madrigal accomplishment of 2020 was trying so hard to go from first-to-third on a fairly firm single to center field that he popped his left shoulder out of its socket, limiting his debut season to just 109 plate appearances. (He also posted a higher on-base rate than slugging percentage, but that's a basic-level Madrigal feat). In future years, Chicago's preordained spark plug will look to substitute increased defensive precision and heady baserunning, rather than just merely hyper-aggressive baserunning, to his collection of on-brand activities. Until that comes together, we'll have to settle for Madrigal trying so hard his body breaks apart as proof that he's the genuine article.

Nomar Mazara RF Born: 04/26/95 Age: 26 Bats: L Throws: L Height: 6'4" Weight: 215 Origin: International Free Agent, 2011

YEAR	TEAM	LVL	AGE	PA	R	2B	3B	HR	RBI	BB	K	SB	CS	Whiff%	AVG/OBP/SLG	DRC+	BABIP	BRR	FRAA	WARP
2018	TEX	MLB	23	536	61	25	1	20	77	40	116	1	0	25.4%	.258/.317/.436	97	.298	-1.2	RF(113): -10.2, LF(2): -0.2	-0.2
2019	TEX	MLB	24	469	69	27	1	19	66	28	108	4	1	27.4%	.268/.318/.469	94	.312	-1.4	RF(101): -5.1	0.1
2020	CHW	MLB	25	149	13	6	0	1	15	10	44	0	1	28.5%	.228/.295/.294	70	.330	-1.4	RF(42): 1.0	-0.3
2021 FS	*CHW*	*MLB*	*26*	*600*	*64*	*23*	*1*	*18*	*69*	*48*	*153*	*2*	*1*	*27.1%*	*.245/.314/.398*	*95*	*.307*	*-0.5*	*RF -15, LF 0*	*-0.5*

Comparables: Brennan Boesch, Jeremy Hermida, George Thomas

Man, that one home run Mazara hit in 2020 was cooked. Turned-and-burned on a high fastball with plus velocity and carry—from Trevor Bauer, no less—with that pristine left-handed uppercut stroke and flung a no-doubter around the right field foul pole and deep into an Ohio night as if he were Jim Thome himself. Ignore the numbers for a second and dream on the tools and skills present, or ignore them for a year or five. Like every great, alluring dream, there are questions that pick at the reality until it falls apart and dissolves. That there was only one home run all year to dream on is only an exaggeration of a career-long trend, where the numbers have never been there and only flashes have emerged that hinted there should be so much more. There probably should be more than there was in 2020 when an already chaotic season was shortened by his own illness, but poor production amid cool highlights has already been ignored too many times with Mazara.

Danny Mendick SS Born: 09/28/93 Age: 27 Bats: R Throws: R Height: 5'10" Weight: 195 Origin: Round 22, 2015 Draft (#652 overall)

YEAR	TEAM	LVL	AGE	PA	R	2B	3B	HR	RBI	BB	K	SB	CS	Whiff%	AVG/OBP/SLG	DRC+	BABIP	BRR	FRAA	WARP
2018	BIR	AA	24	529	62	25	0	14	59	57	90	20	10		.247/.340/.395	109	.275	1.4	SS(131): -4.2	1.6
2019	CHA	AAA	25	558	75	26	1	17	64	66	96	19	8		.279/.368/.444	102	.313	0.3	2B(48): 4.2, SS(42): 2.4, 3B(38): -0.9	2.8
2019	CHW	MLB	25	40	6	0	0	2	4	1	11	0	0	28.8%	.308/.325/.462	88	.385	0.0	SS(5): 0.0, 2B(3): -0.4, 3B(3): 0.7	0.1
2020	CHW	MLB	27	114	11	4	1	3	6	6	25	0	1	25.4%	.243/.281/.383	81	.287	0.2	2B(28): 2.9, SS(4): 0.0, 3B(3): 0.1	0.4
2021 FS	*CHW*	*MLB*	*27*	*600*	*64*	*25*	*1*	*16*	*65*	*49*	*143*	*6*	*2*	*26.0%*	*.238/.309/.384*	*90*	*.294*	*-1.0*	*3B 3, 2B 4*	*1.9*
2021 DC	*CHW*	*MLB*	*27*	*202*	*21*	*8*	*0*	*5*	*21*	*16*	*48*	*2*	*0*	*26.0%*	*.238/.309/.384*	*90*	*.294*	*-0.3*	*3B 1, 2B 1*	*0.5*

Comparables: Ramón Urías, Ian Kinsler, Corban Joseph

The truly great backup second basemen constantly escalate the tension of whether they should be a starting second baseman. An idealized representative would have to somehow perform as well as possible in their role, while never actually challenging the appropriateness of said role. To this end, Mendick hit .303/.338/.515 in a rollicking three-week period while White Sox starting second baseman Nick Madrigal was on the injured list. With Mendick's multi-positional utility, it gave birth to calls that he should be a starter of some kind. As an idealized backup, Mendick defused this hysteria by hitting .146/.186/.171 during all the points of the season where Madrigal was not on the injured list. He even committed his lone error of the season while Madrigal was healthy. For his next trick, Mendick will need to defuse the tension surrounding the question that he is not a major leaguer, since the White Sox optioned him to the alternate site by the end of the season.

Yermín Mercedes C Born: 02/14/93 Age: 28 Bats: R Throws: R Height: 5'11" Weight: 235 Origin: International Free Agent, 2011

YEAR	TEAM	LVL	AGE	PA	R	2B	3B	HR	RBI	BB	K	SB	CS	Whiff%	AVG/OBP/SLG	DRC+	BABIP	BRR	FRAA	WARP
2018	WS	HI-A	25	410	58	24	1	14	64	40	67	4	0		.289/.362/.478	146	.317	0.1	C(78): 1.4, 1B(14): -0.6	2.9
2019	BIR	AA	26	167	19	7	0	6	18	17	25	2	0		.327/.389/.497	166	.353	-0.8	C(34): 6.7	2.5
2019	CHA	AAA	26	220	35	12	0	17	62	24	42	0	0		.310/.386/.647	142	.306	-2.4	C(24): 3.2, 1B(4): -0.6, 3B(2): -0.3	1.6
2020	CHW	MLB	27	1	0	0	0	0	0	0	0	0	0	0.0%	.000/.000/.000	82	.000			0.0
2021 FS	CHW	MLB	28	600	74	27	1	30	93	46	144	0	0	0.0%	.263/.326/.485	120	.305	-0.8	C 7, 1B 0	4.4
2021 DC	CHW	MLB	28	33	4	1	0	1	5	2	7	0	0	0.0%	.263/.326/.485	120	.305	0.0	C 0	0.3

Comparables: Ryan Doumit, Travis d'Arnaud, Tim Federowicz

As a power-hitting, big leg-kicking, rollie pollie of a baseball player, Mercedes has always come across as better suited to legend than a projectable member of a major league roster. Apparently the White Sox agreed, marooning Mercedes to either the alternate site in Schaumburg, or as a particularly ebullient member of the traveling taxi squad. As such, Mercedes lives on in memory as the guy who hit the crap out of everything during intrasquad games and sputtered around the bases joyfully. Never was he submitted to questions like "Oh boy, we're not really sure if this guy can catch, are we?" or "He really not very fast, is he?" or "Jeez, why did he do that?" and everyone is the better for it. Well, except for Mercedes, perhaps, who likely can hit at a major league proficiency and, at 28 years of age, would like to get paid for it at some point. To that end, well, who knows? Being interesting and cool does not always equate to a team allotting hundreds of plate appearances to a catcher/DH/first base/third base/left field hybrid, and even all the Willians Astudillo hype never materialized into steady work. Legends live forever, though.

Yoán Moncada 3B Born: 05/27/95 Age: 26 Bats: S Throws: R Height: 6'2" Weight: 225 Origin: International Free Agent, 2015

YEAR	TEAM	LVL	AGE	PA	R	2B	3B	HR	RBI	BB	K	SB	CS	Whiff%	AVG/OBP/SLG	DRC+	BABIP	BRR	FRAA	WARP
2018	CHW	MLB	23	650	73	32	6	17	61	67	217	12	6	31.1%	.235/.315/.400	89	.344	-0.4	2B(149): -12.7	-0.2
2019	CHW	MLB	24	559	83	34	5	25	79	40	154	10	3	31.1%	.315/.367/.548	123	.406	3.5	3B(129): 10.3	5.1
2020	CHW	MLB	25	231	28	8	3	6	24	28	72	0	0	30.7%	.225/.320/.385	87	.315	0.8	3B(52): 1.5	0.3
2021 FS	CHW	MLB	26	600	76	25	3	20	68	66	193	14	5	31.0%	.243/.333/.424	108	.342	0.2	3B 5, 2B 0	3.1
2021 DC	CHW	MLB	26	574	72	24	3	19	65	63	185	13	5	31.0%	.243/.333/.424	108	.342	0.2	3B 5	2.3

Comparables: Brandon Lowe, Danny Espinosa, Ryan McMahon

If the hundreds of thousands of deaths, millions of cases and more or less the shutdown of the global economy weren't enough to convince you that COVID-19 is a serious issue, perhaps the trials of a healthy 25-year-old Moncada will resonate. Statistically, he simply went back to normal after simple variance saw him cosplay as a top-50 position player in the sport for all of 2019. Physically, Moncada was a ghost after testing positive for the virus in July. After every burst of speed, reserved for only when the moment truly demanded it from him, his hands were planted squarely on his hips as he strained to regain his breath. When he squeezed the handle of his bat, the strength he always felt had eroded and his average exit velocity plummeted. He is young, he is in fabulous shape and is an incredible athlete, and no one knows what comes next.

Luis Robert CF Born: 08/03/97 Age: 23 Bats: R Throws: R Height: 6'2" Weight: 210 Origin: International Free Agent, 2017

YEAR	TEAM	LVL	AGE	PA	R	2B	3B	HR	RBI	BB	K	SB	CS	Whiff%	AVG/OBP/SLG	DRC+	BABIP	BRR	FRAA	WARP
2018	WSX	ROK	20	18	5	2	1	0	2	0	3	3	0		.389/.389/.611	142	.467	1.3	CF(2): 0.4	0.2
2018	KAN	LO-A	20	50	5	3	1	0	4	4	12	4	2		.289/.360/.400	104	.394	-0.2	CF(10): 0.0	0.0
2018	WS	HI-A	20	140	21	6	1	0	11	8	37	8	2		.244/.317/.309	84	.341	0.5	CF(27): 3.1, RF(4): -0.4, LF(1): -0.1	0.2
2019	WS	HI-A	21	84	21	5	3	8	24	4	20	8	2		.453/.512/.920	273	.553	-1.2	CF(13): 1.9	1.6
2019	BIR	AA	21	244	43	16	3	8	29	13	54	21	6		.314/.362/.518	127	.384	2.5	CF(36): 1.9, RF(7): -0.8, LF(2): 0.0	1.8
2019	CHA	AAA	21	223	44	10	5	16	39	11	55	7	3		.297/.341/.634	114	.324	1.2	CF(47): 6.5	1.7
2020	CHW	MLB	23	227	33	8	0	11	31	20	73	9	2	41.8%	.233/.302/.436	86	.300	0.1	CF(56): 11.2	1.4
2021 FS	CHW	MLB	23	600	67	22	3	26	75	39	195	21	6	41.8%	.235/.298/.432	97	.314	5.5	CF 10, LF 0	3.4
2021 DC	CHW	MLB	23	574	64	21	3	24	72	38	187	20	6	41.8%	.235/.298/.432	97	.314	5.3	CF 10	3.2

Comparables: Victor Robles, Larry Hisle, Wily Mo Pena

In spring training of 2018, Yoán Moncada went to the movies. He saw the late Chadwick Boseman portray King T'Challa on screen, or mostly a CGI facsimile of him hopping onto speeding cars, and glowing purple at select intervals and whatever the hell else happened in that movie. In that profound moment, Moncada was struck with a thought: Luis Robert...or so the story goes. Out of the theater, Moncada came armed with a nickname for Robert—La Pantera—and effectively a comp. After a year, or one bizarrely shortened season, in the majors, Robert's dizzying toolset is no longer an international scouting tall tale or even a minor league legend. He really does turn every bouncer into a potential infield single, scoot around center field as if he were riding a moped, and swat massive home runs with apparent ease. But in this gritty, realistic workup of the premise of a superhero trying to play major league baseball, Robert's 2020 included the month where he just has his timing thrown off by pitchers changing their approaches toward him, or that none of the science in Wakanda nor even straight injections of vibranium itself can instill plate discipline. That can only come with time.

Blake Rutherford   RF   Born: 05/02/97   Age: 24   Bats: L   Throws: R   Height: 6'3"   Weight: 210   Origin: Round 1, 2016 Draft (#18 overall)

YEAR	TEAM	LVL	AGE	PA	R	2B	3B	HR	RBI	BB	K	SB	CS	Whiff%	AVG/OBP/SLG	DRC+	BABIP	BRR	FRAA	WARP
2018	WS	HI-A	21	487	67	25	9	7	78	34	90	15	8		.293/.345/.436	120	.351	1.1	RF(73): -2.5, LF(15): -2.7, CF(13): -1.4	0.4
2019	BIR	AA	22	480	50	17	3	7	49	37	117	9	2		.265/.319/.365	95	.342	2.4	RF(68): 1.7, LF(29): -1.7, CF(1): -0.1	1.0
2021 FS	CHW	MLB	24	600	58	24	3	11	57	41	172	4	1		.228/.284/.348	74	.309	1.4	LF -16, CF 0	-1.9
2021 DC	CHW	MLB	24	33	3	1	0	0	3	2	9	0	0		.228/.284/.348	74	.309	0.1	LF -1	-0.1

Comparables: Jorge Bonifacio, Daniel Johnson, Bronson Sardinha

People in the White Sox organization say Rutherford tapped into his power at long last during his unrecorded, unbroadcasted alternate site simulated games. It seems convenient that the fundamental question hanging over Rutherford's increasingly platoon-corner-outfield profile was answered by a method that no one could independently verify, but from the perspective of assessing his trade value or immediate major-league viability, it's not very convenient at all.

Gavin Sheets   1B   Born: 04/23/96   Age: 25   Bats: L   Throws: L   Height: 6'5"   Weight: 245   Origin: Round 2, 2017 Draft (#49 overall)

YEAR	TEAM	LVL	AGE	PA	R	2B	3B	HR	RBI	BB	K	SB	CS	Whiff%	AVG/OBP/SLG	DRC+	BABIP	BRR	FRAA	WARP
2018	WS	HI-A	22	497	58	28	2	6	61	52	81	1	0		.293/.368/.407	131	.344	-3.9	1B(107): -4.3	0.3
2019	BIR	AA	23	527	56	18	1	16	83	54	99	3	1		.267/.345/.414	128	.305	-6.3	1B(110): 3.8	1.9
2021 FS	CHW	MLB	25	600	65	24	1	16	65	49	143	0	0		.242/.311/.386	93	.299	-0.3	1B 1	0.4
2021 DC	CHW	MLB	25	33	3	1	0	0	3	2	7	0	0		.242/.311/.386	93	.299	0.0	1B 0	0.0

Comparables: Andy Wilkins, Chris Parmelee, Will Craig

If one look at Sheets' hulking, muscled frame doesn't give away what role he is seeking to fill at the major league level, a five-minute look at his best left-handed power strokes in a batting practice session should settle the matter. But at this point, the professional resumé consists of a few months at Double-A Birmingham in 2019 where he looked the part, buried amid power outages and an Arizona Fall League showing that nibble away at the viability of such a bat-first profile.

─────── ★　★　★ *2021 Top 101 Prospect* **#14** ★　★　★ ───────

Andrew Vaughn   1B   Born: 04/03/98   Age: 23   Bats: R   Throws: R   Height: 6'0"   Weight: 215   Origin: Round 1, 2019 Draft (#3 overall)

YEAR	TEAM	LVL	AGE	PA	R	2B	3B	HR	RBI	BB	K	SB	CS	Whiff%	AVG/OBP/SLG	DRC+	BABIP	BRR	FRAA	WARP
2019	WSX	ROK	21	16	3	2	0	1	4	0	3	0	0		.600/.625/.933	221	.727	-0.2	1B(2): -0.3	0.1
2019	KAN	LO-A	21	103	14	7	0	2	11	14	18	0	0		.253/.388/.410	137	.297	1.2	1B(19): -0.5	0.6
2019	WS	HI-A	21	126	16	8	0	3	21	16	17	0	1		.252/.349/.411	139	.270	-0.3	1B(16): -0.3	0.5
2021 FS	CHW	MLB	23	600	60	26	1	13	58	44	149	0	0		.228/.295/.355	82	.289	-0.4	1B -2	-0.8
2021 DC	CHW	MLB	23	405	40	18	1	8	39	29	100	0	0		.228/.295/.355	82	.289	-0.3	1B -1	-0.3

The baseball viewing public's interest in Vaughn, an ivory-colored bowling ball of a man, fails to stretch far beyond his predilection for studiously drilling fastballs to right field and dragging his barrel to flick off speed to left field, all with the requisite strength of a highly sentient bowling ball. From anecdotal observations of a summer of simulated games and multiple stretches in big league training camp, Vaughn continued to play his part with the consistency of a bowling ball rolling down a smoothened ramp. To spice things up, the White Sox had Vaughn get some work at third base and right field, which do not seem like ideal roles for a bowling ball. But a bowling ball with an expanded skill set seems fascinating.

Seby Zavala   C   Born: 08/28/93   Age: 27   Bats: R   Throws: R   Height: 5'11"   Weight: 210   Origin: Round 12, 2015 Draft (#352 overall)

YEAR	TEAM	LVL	AGE	PA	R	2B	3B	HR	RBI	BB	K	SB	CS	Whiff%	AVG/OBP/SLG	DRC+	BABIP	BRR	FRAA	WARP
2018	BIR	AA	24	232	32	7	0	11	31	27	65	0	0		.271/.358/.472	132	.339	0.0	C(31): 4.0	1.5
2018	CHA	AAA	24	191	18	15	0	2	20	6	44	0	2		.243/.267/.359	81	.304	-1.2	C(35): -3.0	-0.4
2019	CHA	AAA	25	331	49	14	0	20	45	26	116	1	1		.222/.296/.471	77	.282	-1.7	C(52): 6.8, 1B(18): -0.3	0.7
2019	CHW	MLB	25	12	1	0	0	0	0	0	9	0	0	62.5%	.083/.083/.083	51	.333	0.0	C(3): 0.2	0.0
2021 FS	CHW	MLB	27	600	57	20	1	16	57	41	219	0	0	62.5%	.198/.263/.332	62	.292	-0.6	C -21, 1B 0	-2.8
2021 DC	CHW	MLB	27	67	6	2	0	1	6	4	24	0	0	62.5%	.198/.263/.332	62	.292	-0.1	C -3	-0.4

Comparables: Cameron Rupp, Kyle Skipworth, Chad Santos

YEAR	TEAM	P. COUNT	FRM RUNS	BLK RUNS	THRW RUNS	TOT RUNS
2018	CHA	4736	-2.6	0.0	-0.1	-2.8
2018	BIR	4315	3.3	0.1	0.4	3.8
2019	CHW	345	0.1	0.1	0.0	0.2
2019	CHA	7394	5.4	-0.1	0.4	5.8
2021	CHW	2405	0.9	-4.1	-0.2	-3.4

Optimism that Zavala's raw pop would wriggle its way into big league games has been in short supply since he hit Triple-A. But a team that had two All-Stars, a former 10th-overall pick, and a guy who posted 1.047 OPS in their catching depth still insisted on carrying Zavala as the *fifth* catcher on their 40-man roster for an entire calendar year, so perhaps the savvy game-caller has qualities that can't be easily appreciated from the outside.

PITCHERS

Aaron Bummer LHP   Born: 09/21/93   Age: 27   Bats: L   Throws: L   Height: 6'3"   Weight: 215   Origin: Round 19, 2014 Draft (#558 overall)

YEAR	TEAM	LVL	AGE	W	L	SV	G	GS	IP	H	HR	BB/9	K/9	K	GB%	BABIP	WHIP	ERA	DRA-	WARP	MPH	FA%	Whiff%	CSP
2018	CHA	AAA	24	2	3	0	31	0	30²	27	0	3.2	8.8	30	63.2%	.314	1.24	2.64	71	0.6				
2018	CHW	MLB	24	0	1	0	37	0	31²	40	1	2.8	9.9	35	62.2%	.402	1.58	4.26	82	0.4	95.0	65.8%	24.0%	48.5%
2019	CHA	AAA	25	0	0	0	5	0	7²	7	0	2.3	7.0	6	87.0%	.333	1.17	2.35	71	0.2				
2019	CHW	MLB	25	0	0	1	58	0	67²	43	4	3.2	8.0	60	69.7%	.229	0.99	2.13	61	1.7	97.3	76.1%	24.4%	51.3%
2020	CHW	MLB	26	1	0	0	9	0	9¹	5	0	4.8	13.5	14	68.4%	.263	1.07	0.96	74	0.2	97.2	85.1%	35.0%	45.1%
2021 FS	CHW	MLB	27	2	2	29	57	0	50	42	4	4.6	10.0	55	63.1%	.292	1.36	3.74	85	0.5	96.8	75.5%	25.9%	49.9%
2021 DC	CHW	MLB	27	2	2	29	52	0	55	46	5	4.6	10.0	61	63.1%	.292	1.36	3.74	85	0.8	96.8	75.5%	25.9%	49.9%

Comparables: Keynan Middleton, A.J. Minter, Jonathan Holder

After his breakout 2019 campaign, Bummer was placed in an unexpected position: Kids were contacting him on social media trying to replicate his wonky mechanics. He quite simply had always thought his mechanics were a mess, and possibly a hindrance. Bummer's low three-quarters delivery conjures the word "sling" to mind as clearly as any major league throwing motion. His professional career had previously been defined by struggles, injury and command issues. Even stranger, he found himself spending the first part of the year weighing a long-term extension offer, after assuming he would spend his relief career navigating injury and performance flare-ups. In his first season on a deal that could make him a member of the White Sox through 2026, he indeed dealt with injury, missed most of the year with a bicep nerve issue and only made a tepid return by the end of the season in time for a brief playoff run. In between all this, when on the mound, he wielded that sling like David, which is where all the attention comes from.

Zack Burdi RHP   Born: 03/09/95   Age: 26   Bats: R   Throws: R   Height: 6'3"   Weight: 210   Origin: Round 1, 2016 Draft (#26 overall)

YEAR	TEAM	LVL	AGE	W	L	SV	G	GS	IP	H	HR	BB/9	K/9	K	GB%	BABIP	WHIP	ERA	DRA-	WARP	MPH	FA%	Whiff%	CSP
2018	WSX	ROK	23	0	1	0	7	1	6¹	5	0	5.7	9.9	7	62.5%	.312	1.42	2.84	112	0.0				
2019	KAN	LO-A	24	1	1	0	3	0	3	4	0	3.0	18.0	6	28.6%	.571	1.67	9.00	58	0.1				
2019	BIR	AA	24	0	3	3	17	0	19²	24	5	5.9	11.0	24	30.0%	.345	1.88	6.41	135	-0.5				
2020	CHW	MLB	25	0	1	0	8	0	7¹	11	4	3.7	13.5	11	39.1%	.368	1.91	11.05	89	0.1	99.1	50.0%	40.5%	43.4%
2021 FS	CHW	MLB	26	1	1	0	57	0	50	43	7	4.7	10.0	55	39.9%	.285	1.40	4.41	100	0.1	99.1	50.0%	40.5%	43.4%
2021 DC	CHW	MLB	26	1	1	0	31	0	33	28	5	4.7	10.0	36	39.9%	.285	1.40	4.41	100	0.2	99.1	50.0%	40.5%	43.4%

Comparables: Joe Jiménez, Sam Tuivailala, Trevor Gott

Four years after he was drafted—which is a little later than you envision for a decorated, first-round college closer—Burdi made his major league debut. Three years after his UCL put in for a sabbatical for recovery and self-discovery—which is longer than you envision for the grueling Tommy John surgery rehab, but not unprecedented—something resembling his old top shelf velocity returned, as he hit 99 mph frequently in major league games. And maybe it would be ideal for the White Sox pitching development if Burdi's return to top velocity and fluid delivery came purely through coaching and not Burdi saying he saw a video on Twitter and mimicked it. Even with all those qualifiers, Burdi made it back to the majors, he threw hard, he looked good, he flashed all three of his pitches and all was right in the world besides the fact that he got absolutely, relentlessly tattooed by major league hitting in his first turn.

Dylan Cease RHP   Born: 12/28/95   Age: 25   Bats: R   Throws: R   Height: 6'2"   Weight: 200   Origin: Round 6, 2014 Draft (#169 overall)

YEAR	TEAM	LVL	AGE	W	L	SV	G	GS	IP	H	HR	BB/9	K/9	K	GB%	BABIP	WHIP	ERA	DRA-	WARP	MPH	FA%	Whiff%	CSP
2018	WS	HI-A	22	9	2	0	13	13	71²	52	5	3.5	10.3	82	46.9%	.278	1.12	2.89	61	2.1				
2018	BIR	AA	22	3	0	0	10	10	52¹	30	3	3.8	13.4	78	50.0%	.273	0.99	1.72	58	1.6				
2019	CHA	AAA	23	5	2	0	15	15	68¹	75	4	4.2	9.5	72	53.1%	.372	1.57	4.48	92	1.5				
2019	CHW	MLB	23	4	7	0	14	14	73	78	15	4.3	10.0	81	45.7%	.326	1.55	5.79	108	0.4	98.2	51.5%	26.1%	42.5%
2020	CHW	MLB	24	5	4	0	12	12	58¹	50	12	5.2	6.8	44	39.8%	.239	1.44	4.01	157	-1.3	99.2	47.8%	25.3%	41.9%
2021 FS	CHW	MLB	25	8	9	0	26	26	150	137	22	5.0	8.8	146	42.9%	.282	1.47	4.78	106	0.5	98.7	49.5%	25.7%	42.2%
2021 DC	CHW	MLB	25	7	8	0	24	24	126	115	19	5.0	8.8	123	42.9%	.282	1.47	4.78	106	0.9	98.7	49.5%	25.7%	42.2%

Comparables: Reynaldo López, Mitch Keller, Tyler Mahle

The difference in attitudes toward major league-ready top pitching prospect and post-hype, below-average starting pitcher is stark, and yet Cease has made the journey in a mere 26 big league starts. Even finishing off an objectively poor debut season in 2019, he punctuated the year by overpowering a poor Tigers lineup, and looked dominant for stretches of spring training and summer workouts. So to alter the conception of his career from an immense talent primed for an imminent ascent took some doing, like issuing more walks than anyone else in the sport, or failing to record an out in the sixth inning in the month of September. Mostly, Cease never looked like who he was promised to be at any point. His velocity is overwhelming, his slider darts toward the earth like a meteor, but neither played like it against big league hitters, suggesting spin issues that need not just simple development to mature, but fundamental change.

Steve Cishek RHP   Born: 06/18/86   Age: 35   Bats: R   Throws: R   Height: 6'6"   Weight: 215   Origin: Round 5, 2007 Draft (#166 overall)

YEAR	TEAM	LVL	AGE	W	L	SV	G	GS	IP	H	HR	BB/9	K/9	K	GB%	BABIP	WHIP	ERA	DRA-	WARP	MPH	FA%	Whiff%	CSP
2018	CHC	MLB	32	4	3	4	80	0	70¹	45	5	3.6	10.0	78	46.8%	.241	1.04	2.18	104	0.2	92.3	62.3%	29.4%	46.7%
2019	CHC	MLB	33	4	6	7	70	0	64	48	7	4.1	8.0	57	49.4%	.246	1.20	2.95	83	0.9	92.5	59.2%	22.5%	44.4%
2020	CHW	MLB	34	0	0	0	22	0	20	21	4	4.0	9.4	21	32.2%	.309	1.50	5.40	121	0.0	92.5	47.6%	27.2%	46.0%
2021 FS	CHW	MLB	35	2	2	0	57	0	50	45	6	3.8	8.5	47	42.3%	.283	1.34	4.19	99	0.2	92.4	57.1%	25.5%	45.4%

Comparables: Brad Brach, Tyler Clippard, Pedro Strop

Society is crumbling, the oceans are boiling, the West Coast is burning, and by the time this book is published, everything will be unfathomably worse than when this was written. And as we fall to our knees in torment, searching for answers on how it all got this bad and how many warning signs were missed, know that by July of 2020, an unflinching indicator that humanity was irreparably broken had already appeared. For that is when Steve Cishek, side-arming, slider-slinging right-hander of 11 major league seasons, lost the ability to get right-handers out. Dingers fly, and chaos reigns.

Alex Colomé RHP Born: 12/31/88 Age: 32 Bats: R Throws: R Height: 6'1" Weight: 225 Origin: International Free Agent, 2007

YEAR	TEAM	LVL	AGE	W	L	SV	G	GS	IP	H	HR	BB/9	K/9	K	GB%	BABIP	WHIP	ERA	DRA-	WARP	MPH	FA%	Whiff%	CSP
2018	TB	MLB	29	2	5	11	23	0	21²	24	1	3.3	9.6	23	54.5%	.354	1.48	4.15	87	0.3	95.9	36.8%	30.4%	48.9%
2018	SEA	MLB	29	5	0	1	47	0	46¹	35	6	2.5	9.5	49	42.5%	.254	1.04	2.53	88	0.5	96.7	49.3%	30.0%	45.5%
2019	CHW	MLB	30	4	5	30	62	0	61	42	7	3.4	8.1	55	44.1%	.217	1.07	2.80	81	0.9	95.8	29.0%	29.1%	45.7%
2020	CHW	MLB	31	2	0	12	21	0	22¹	13	0	3.2	6.4	16	51.6%	.203	0.94	0.81	91	0.3	95.9	28.4%	30.9%	41.1%
2021 FS	CHW	MLB	32	2	2	0	57	0	50	46	7	3.4	8.3	46	46.0%	.282	1.31	4.07	98	0.2	96.1	33.0%	29.9%	44.7%

Comparables: Adam Warren, Sean Marshall, Sam LeCure

The man who took a PED suspension for a horse steroid and flipped it into making "The Horse" his Players Weekend nickname naturally applied his flair for absurd literalism to his job the past two years. The White Sox traded for Colomé with the expectation that he would get outs and convert saves. He has converted 42 out of 46 saves since 2019, and he's gotten about 74 percent of opposing hitters out. They did not acquire him to get outs in a traditionally sustainable way, so he eschewed that element of his performance. They did not acquire him to come in and blow everyone away, and lend a bunch of confidence to the idea that he can do that every time, or that every save he records isn't reliant on a light sprinkling of defensive heroics, so he didn't do it. Maybe, in private pre-series meetings, they told him to flip in his 89-90 mph cutter over and over again that every hitter tries to swat to the moon but rolls over to third base instead, because that is like, *all* he does.

Jimmy Cordero RHP Born: 10/19/91 Age: 29 Bats: R Throws: R Height: 6'4" Weight: 235 Origin: International Free Agent, 2012

YEAR	TEAM	LVL	AGE	W	L	SV	G	GS	IP	H	HR	BB/9	K/9	K	GB%	BABIP	WHIP	ERA	DRA-	WARP	MPH	FA%	Whiff%	CSP
2018	SYR	AAA	26	4	1	6	41	0	46	43	0	4.3	10.4	53	51.9%	.341	1.41	1.96	67	0.9				
2018	WAS	MLB	26	1	2	0	22	0	19	23	2	5.7	5.7	12	57.4%	.318	1.84	5.68	143	-0.3	100.2	61.7%	24.6%	43.8%
2019	FRE	AAA	27	0	1	3	12	0	15	17	3	5.4	10.2	17	53.3%	.333	1.73	6.00	87	0.3				
2019	CHA	AAA	27	3	1	4	13	0	17²	14	0	1.0	7.1	14	72.5%	.275	0.91	0.51	44	0.7				
2019	CHW	MLB	27	1	0	0	30	0	36	24	3	2.8	7.8	31	61.5%	.226	0.97	2.75	71	0.7	99.8	68.6%	29.7%	49.6%
2019	TOR	MLB	27	0	1	0	1	0	1¹	2	1	0.0	0.0	0	40.0%	.250	1.50	6.75	127	0.0	98.1	53.3%	14.3%	55.8%
2020	CHW	MLB	28	1	2	0	30	0	26²	33	2	3.0	7.4	22	51.1%	.356	1.57	6.08	94	0.3	98.6	68.9%	21.4%	47.4%
2021 FS	CHW	MLB	29	2	2	0	57	0	50	47	5	4.1	8.0	44	53.1%	.292	1.42	4.43	100	0.1	99.3	67.7%	25.0%	47.9%
2021 DC	CHW	MLB	29	2	2	0	52	0	55	52	6	4.1	8.0	48	53.1%	.292	1.42	4.43	100	0.3	99.3	67.7%	25.0%	47.9%

Comparables: Kevin McCarthy, Juan Minaya, Wander Suero

Once per year, a certain man is challenged to single-handedly demonstrate that if you throw an effective reliever over and over again, he gradually grows less effective. If we cheat and include the brief presence of the White Sox in the playoffs, Cordero managed to set a career-high with 32 appearances in 2020, in a season that lasted about two months. If that sounds like a lot on paper, it felt like he pitched in every single one. It's worth debating if a hot 30-game performance at the tail end of a year that included getting waived three times (Cordero's 2019), is as useful as being the manager's designated guy to provide increasingly mediocre innings when all other plans for the night have hit the rocks (his 2020). The latter endures the contempt of most onlookers in exchange for the appreciation of his most immediate supervisor. Then again, maybe he'll just stop getting cooked by left-handers if he figures out how to throw his changeup correctly again. Who can say?

─────────── ★ ★ ★ *2021 Top 101 Prospect* #36 ★ ★ ★ ───────────

Garrett Crochet LHP Born: 06/21/99 Age: 22 Bats: L Throws: L Height: 6'6" Weight: 218 Origin: Round 1, 2020 Draft (#11 overall)

YEAR	TEAM	LVL	AGE	W	L	SV	G	GS	IP	H	HR	BB/9	K/9	K	GB%	BABIP	WHIP	ERA	DRA-	WARP	MPH	FA%	Whiff%	CSP
2020	CHW	MLB	21	0	0	0	5	0	6	3	0	0.0	12.0	8	61.5%	.231	0.50	0.00	81	0.1	101.6	84.7%	40.5%	48.9%
2021 FS	CHW	MLB	22	9	9	0	26	26	150	145	23	3.7	8.3	137	44.9%	.290	1.38	4.61	106	0.5	101.6	84.7%	40.5%	48.9%
2021 DC	CHW	MLB	22	2	3	0	9	9	44	42	6	3.7	8.3	40	44.9%	.290	1.38	4.61	106	0.3	101.6	84.7%	40.5%	48.9%

For someone who threw 10 innings on record in between two separate injuries, Crochet had a rollicking good time of a season. He got drafted 11th overall in June, he got millions of dollars, he got called up to the majors in September, he got to 100 mph with the fastball regularly, and got to taste postseason baseball. That triple-digit heater with ride hisses like a menacing snake. It's impressive, even jarring on sight. And as a result, so is Crochet. He coils his left forearm close to his shoulder, unfurls and hisses, and it's stunning to imagine what he could be. It's also just a flash, since between his shoulder aching and COVID-19 he had one outing for his junior season at Tennessee and left Game 3 of the Wild Card Series with a forearm strain. At a certain point, injuries become part of the story, not just what keeps it shrouded in mystery. Crochet has shown that in equal portion with his pyrotechnics, but the hissing lingers longer in memory.

Andrew Dalquist RHP Born: 11/13/00 Age: 20 Bats: R Throws: R Height: 6'1" Weight: 175 Origin: Round 3, 2019 Draft (#81 overall)

YEAR	TEAM	LVL	AGE	W	L	SV	G	GS	IP	H	HR	BB/9	K/9	K	GB%	BABIP	WHIP	ERA	DRA-	WARP	MPH	FA%	Whiff%	CSP
2019	WSX	ROK	18	0	0	0	3	3	3	2	0	6.0	6.0	2	33.3%	.222	1.33	0.00	104	0.0				
2021 FS	CHW	MLB	20	2	3	0	57	0	50	53	8	5.7	7.3	40	37.5%	.302	1.72	6.24	140	-1.0				

There are many younger players in professional baseball, but few are younger-looking than Dalquist. The six-foot-one, 20-year-old wood sprite commands three pitches and has the athleticism and projection to imagine him working in a major league rotation in three years, at which time he could accrue enough facial hair to look 15 years of age.

Bernardo Flores Jr. LHP   Born: 08/23/95   Age: 25   Bats: L   Throws: L   Height: 6'4"   Weight: 190   Origin: Round 7, 2016 Draft (#206 overall)

YEAR	TEAM	LVL	AGE	W	L	SV	G	GS	IP	H	HR	BB/9	K/9	K	GB%	BABIP	WHIP	ERA	DRA-	WARP	MPH	FA%	Whiff%	CSP
2018	WS	HI-A	22	5	4	0	12	12	77²	75	5	2.0	6.7	58	52.7%	.298	1.18	2.55	72	1.8				
2018	BIR	AA	22	3	5	0	13	13	78¹	79	5	1.6	5.4	47	47.8%	.306	1.19	2.76	85	1.2				
2019	WSX	ROK	23	0	0	0	4	4	12	17	2	0.8	9.8	13	54.3%	.455	1.50	3.75	118	0.0				
2019	KAN	LO-A	23	0	0	0	1	1	3	6	0	3.0	0.0	0	69.2%	.462	2.33	9.00	174	-0.1				
2019	BIR	AA	23	3	8	0	15	15	78¹	74	10	1.7	7.9	69	53.6%	.284	1.14	3.33	90	0.5				
2020	CHW	MLB	24	0	0	0	2	0	2	4	0	0.0	9.0	2	62.5%	.500	2.00	9.00	85	0.0	93.5	59.3%	20.0%	58.8%
2021 FS	CHW	MLB	25	1	1	0	57	0	50	51	7	2.7	6.9	38	49.2%	.292	1.33	4.42	103	0.0	93.5	59.3%	20.0%	58.8%
2021 DC	CHW	MLB	25	1	1	0	31	0	33	34	4	2.7	6.9	25	49.2%	.292	1.33	4.42	103	0.1	93.5	59.3%	20.0%	58.8%

Comparables: Ryan Helsley, Robert Dugger, Jorge Alcala

In both High-A and Double-A, Flores' predilection for racking up groundball outs with yeoman-like repetition earned him the nickname Mr. Quality Start. In the wacky world of projecting pitchers, this most likely ends in him never getting them, instead scrapping his way toward pitching one or two innings of mid-leverage relief. Flores relieved in college, so officially nothing about this path makes sense other than to say that this is baseball.

Matt Foster   RHP   Born: 01/27/95   Age: 26   Bats: R   Throws: R   Height: 6'0"   Weight: 210   Origin: Round 20, 2016 Draft (#596 overall)

YEAR	TEAM	LVL	AGE	W	L	SV	G	GS	IP	H	HR	BB/9	K/9	K	GB%	BABIP	WHIP	ERA	DRA-	WARP	MPH	FA%	Whiff%	CSP
2018	WS	HI-A	23	2	1	7	21	0	28	25	1	2.2	12.9	40	42.9%	.400	1.14	2.57	66	0.6				
2018	BIR	AA	23	0	4	1	24	0	32	33	3	3.7	8.4	30	42.1%	.326	1.44	3.94	83	0.4				
2019	BIR	AA	24	0	0	1	6	0	9²	3	0	1.9	11.2	12	31.6%	.158	0.52	0.00	46	0.3				
2019	CHA	AAA	24	4	1	4	37	0	55	46	9	3.1	10.1	62	35.9%	.280	1.18	3.76	60	1.8				
2020	CHW	MLB	25	6	1	0	23	2	28²	16	2	2.8	9.7	31	34.8%	.212	0.87	2.20	90	0.4	95.2	57.2%	30.3%	47.5%
2021 FS	CHW	MLB	26	2	2	0	57	0	50	42	8	3.4	10.1	55	37.8%	.277	1.24	3.79	89	0.4	95.2	57.2%	30.3%	47.5%
2021 DC	CHW	MLB	26	2	2	0	52	0	55	47	9	3.4	10.1	61	37.8%	.277	1.24	3.79	89	0.6	95.2	57.2%	30.3%	47.5%

Comparables: Trevor Kelley, Keith Butler, David Bednar

Foster is six feet tall, and no one would argue he's secretly six foot one, which is fairly short for a pitcher. He can rev it up to 94 mph out of the 'pen, which if watching the World Series is any indication, is hideously and embarrassingly slow. He was a 20th-round draft pick out of Alabama after two years in junior college, and in his single season at Tuscaloosa, he started zero games. He retired briefly at the start of the 2017 season, which would have been his first professional season, only to return and anonymously earn his way to Triple-A. He was a shocking addition to the White Sox 40-man roster in November of 2019, regarded as organizational filler by rival scouts and an afterthought for all of spring training and summer camp. Then he got called up and got people out, and kept doing it, unabated, all the way until the playoffs. He wiped out top-level hitters with a changeup he claims was taught to him full cloth by minor league pitching coach Matt Zaleski. Foster's story is one of incredible work ethic, perseverance, and Zaleski himself would point that his average velocity is countered by exceptional fastball carry, and that more raw ingredients of his changeup were present early in his career than he lets on. Still, many people are of the mind that plus relievers are indeed popping up out of literally nowhere, and Foster's emergence will only encourage them.

Jace Fry   LHP   Born: 07/09/93   Age: 27   Bats: L   Throws: L   Height: 6'1"   Weight: 220   Origin: Round 3, 2014 Draft (#77 overall)

YEAR	TEAM	LVL	AGE	W	L	SV	G	GS	IP	H	HR	BB/9	K/9	K	GB%	BABIP	WHIP	ERA	DRA-	WARP	MPH	FA%	Whiff%	CSP
2018	CHA	AAA	24	0	0	0	5	0	6²	3	1	0.0	14.8	11	53.8%	.167	0.45	1.35	36	0.3				
2018	CHW	MLB	24	2	3	4	59	1	51¹	37	4	3.5	12.3	70	43.9%	.282	1.11	4.38	66	1.2	95.2	34.3%	34.6%	43.7%
2019	CHW	MLB	25	3	4	0	68	0	55	44	7	7.0	11.1	68	56.9%	.289	1.58	4.75	83	0.8	94.4	25.1%	36.6%	40.7%
2020	CHW	MLB	26	0	1	0	18	0	19²	16	3	5.5	11.0	24	48.9%	.295	1.42	3.66	88	0.3	92.0	38.9%	34.3%	39.3%
2021 FS	CHW	MLB	27	2	2	0	57	0	50	40	5	5.4	11.2	62	50.5%	.289	1.40	3.90	89	0.4	93.9	30.7%	35.6%	41.0%
2021 DC	CHW	MLB	27	2	2	0	42	0	44	35	4	5.4	11.2	54	50.5%	.289	1.40	3.90	89	0.5	93.9	30.7%	35.6%	41.0%

Comparables: Aaron Bummer, A.J. Minter, Anthony Banda

In the collection of White Sox food last names, Fry is obviously primarily a side dish who cannot make the whole meal work on his own. Jake Burger being delayed for two seasons by Achilles tears and tendinitis is primarily responsible for keeping the Sox away from true transcendence on the diamond. It's certainly a factor in why the left-hander feels compelled to throw so many sliders. But a failure to take Seth Beer in the 2018 draft showed an inability or unwillingness to commit fully to the true ceiling of an entire brewpub menu in place on a single infield. There has to be full organizational commitment for something like this to work. And half-hearted efforts like selecting Adisyn Coffey in the third round of the 2020 draft will not make things right. What kind of life involves eating fries while drinking coffee? Still, thanks to some mild improvements in some truly awful 2019 control numbers, Fry will continue his wait in a major league bullpen, to be the finishing piece in a baseball-food last name pairing that will set Twitter ablaze for approximately 37 minutes during a single nationally televised White Sox game.

Lucas Giolito   RHP   Born: 07/14/94   Age: 26   Bats: R   Throws: R   Height: 6'6"   Weight: 245   Origin: Round 1, 2012 Draft (#16 overall)

YEAR	TEAM	LVL	AGE	W	L	SV	G	GS	IP	H	HR	BB/9	K/9	K	GB%	BABIP	WHIP	ERA	DRA-	WARP	MPH	FA%	Whiff%	CSP
2018	CHW	MLB	23	10	13	0	32	32	173¹	166	27	4.7	6.5	125	44.4%	.269	1.48	6.13	147	-2.5	94.8	59.5%	21.6%	46.9%
2019	CHW	MLB	24	14	9	0	29	29	176²	131	24	2.9	11.6	228	35.6%	.274	1.06	3.41	57	5.7	96.4	55.0%	32.5%	50.1%
2020	CHW	MLB	25	4	3	0	12	12	72¹	47	8	3.5	12.1	97	43.5%	.255	1.04	3.48	76	1.6	96.1	50.6%	36.6%	45.6%
2021 FS	CHW	MLB	26	9	7	0	26	26	150	119	21	3.8	11.2	187	41.0%	.279	1.22	3.54	83	2.5	95.9	54.8%	31.1%	47.9%
2021 DC	CHW	MLB	26	11	9	0	29	29	174	138	25	3.8	11.2	217	41.0%	.279	1.22	3.54	83	3.4	95.9	54.8%	31.1%	47.9%

Comparables: José Berríos, Tyler Mahle, Taijuan Walker

In 2019, Giolito completed one of the most stunning personal reinventions ever seen play out on the major league level. The way he remade his delivery, his arsenal, and his mental approach is a story to return to whenever anyone is weighing whether to give up on a talented, dedicated player, no matter how deep the struggles to get. The funny thing, though, is that lives aren't stories; at least not crisp, concise one with clear endings and morals. Giolito went home after his cathartic season and sought a way to follow it up. In most concrete respects, he failed to up the drama, producing a predictable sequel that hit the same notes as the original. His slight increase in strikeout rate was also accompanied by more walks, as he dared hitters to chase a little more often. At his core he still rides a fastball paired with a devastating changeup coming from an abnormally tall man, and his efforts to incorporate spin are mostly subplots. That he threw 2020's first no-hitter and took a perfect game into the seventh inning of his first playoff start doesn't mean a ton in terms of what kind of pitcher he is, but the highlights will get played over the credits of his still-incredible story.

Gio González LHP Born: 09/19/85 Age: 35 Bats: R Throws: L Height: 6'0" Weight: 205 Origin: Round 1, 2004 Draft (#38 overall)

YEAR	TEAM	LVL	AGE	W	L	SV	G	GS	IP	H	HR	BB/9	K/9	K	GB%	BABIP	WHIP	ERA	DRA-	WARP	MPH	FA%	Whiff%	CSP
2018	MIL	MLB	32	3	0	0	5	5	25¹	14	2	3.6	7.8	22	42.6%	.182	0.95	2.13	73	0.6	91.8	58.2%	29.1%	41.2%
2018	WAS	MLB	32	7	11	0	27	27	145²	153	15	4.3	7.8	126	45.5%	.321	1.53	4.57	96	1.7	91.7	56.5%	23.1%	45.8%
2019	SWB	AAA	33	2	1	0	3	3	15	19	1	3.6	11.4	19	45.2%	.439	1.67	6.00	111	0.2				
2019	MIL	MLB	33	3	2	0	19	17	87¹	76	9	3.8	8.0	78	44.6%	.282	1.29	3.50	90	1.3	90.8	51.9%	26.0%	37.5%
2020	CHW	MLB	34	1	2	0	12	4	31²	40	6	5.4	9.7	34	43.3%	.374	1.86	4.83	122	-0.1	91.6	47.0%	32.4%	38.8%
2021 FS	CHW	MLB	35	9	9	0	26	26	150	143	21	4.5	8.3	138	45.2%	.291	1.46	4.51	104	0.7	91.3	52.6%	26.8%	40.8%

Comparables: *Johnny Cueto, Clay Buchholz, Jordan Zimmermann*

When the White Sox drafted a teenaged Gio González out of Hialeah High School in 2004, they did so with the expectation that he would one day be able to help their starting rotation. At the end of the 2005 season, they got a little impatient with waiting for him to be ready to do that and dealt him away. Jim Thome was involved. It made sense. A year later, while acquiring Gavin Floyd to help their starting rotation, they got González again. It seemed worthwhile. They figured he might help the rotation one day. A brisk 13 months later, they got impatient again and traded him in January of 2008. Life is fickle. Floyd's entire career has grown and eroded before our eyes, Thome is in the Hall of Fame, and the Sox added González for the 2020 season, figuring he could help their starting rotation. Somewhere between the 16 years, the over 1,900 big league innings, and the league shutting down for four months, the team underwent some reflection. González's shoulder aches frequently now, he cracks 90 mph infrequently, and his walk numbers resemble his prospect days in a bad way. Put on the spot, the Sox weren't convinced he could help their rotation, limiting him to a swingman role across 12 appearances.

Codi Heuer RHP Born: 07/03/96 Age: 25 Bats: R Throws: R Height: 6'5" Weight: 190 Origin: Round 6, 2018 Draft (#168 overall)

YEAR	TEAM	LVL	AGE	W	L	SV	G	GS	IP	H	HR	BB/9	K/9	K	GB%	BABIP	WHIP	ERA	DRA-	WARP	MPH	FA%	Whiff%	CSP
2018	GTF	ROK	21	0	1	0	14	14	38	49	4	3.3	8.3	35	56.3%	.369	1.66	4.74	95	0.5				
2019	WS	HI-A	22	4	1	2	20	0	38¹	34	0	1.9	10.1	43	61.9%	.327	1.10	2.82	73	0.5				
2019	BIR	AA	22	2	3	9	22	0	29¹	25	0	2.1	6.8	22	59.8%	.298	1.09	1.84	77	0.3				
2020	CHW	MLB	23	3	0	1	21	0	23²	12	1	3.4	9.5	25	50.0%	.193	0.89	1.52	84	0.4	98.9	65.8%	33.9%	45.6%
2021 FS	CHW	MLB	24	2	2	4	57	0	50	46	6	4.0	8.3	46	51.4%	.285	1.37	4.22	98	0.2	98.9	65.8%	33.9%	45.6%
2021 DC	CHW	MLB	24	2	2	4	52	0	55	50	7	4.0	8.3	51	51.4%	.285	1.37	4.22	98	0.4	98.9	65.8%	33.9%	45.6%

Comparables: *Alex Claudio, Michael Tonkin, Keynan Middleton*

There's a whole host of minor leaguers who were squeezed out of any real opportunity to demonstrate improvement in their craft enough to merit major league playing time in 2020. And then there was a host of guys who showed up for summer camp and, despite not having much experience, showed that it would be in everyone's best interest to just get the hell out of their way and let them play. Out of some broad coincidence, the latter group was largely populated by relievers who threw in the upper-90s with wild movement like Heuer touts. The pandemic canceled the 20 innings Heuer would have spent immolating Triple-A hitters for the sake of drawing his bosses' attention, but kept intact the part where he ascended up the chain of leverage in the White Sox relief corps, pitched into the eighth as his team locked up its first playoff berth in a dozen years, and factored heavily into their playoff series. In 2018, Heuer was a pretty bad starting pitcher in rookie ball. Some guys need years of minor league development, and some guys need a move to the 'pen, and a cut to the chase.

Jared Kelley RHP Born: 10/03/01 Age: 19 Bats: R Throws: R Height: 6'3" Weight: 215 Origin: Round 2, 2020 Draft (#47 overall)

The comparisons to large animals known for dragging heavy payloads come fast and furious when Kelley's name comes up. For the horse and/or ox-like 19-year-old, the only thing about him that looks its age is his lack of a statistical record, as he transitioned after the draft from cooking overmatched Houston-area high schoolers for all of 12 innings in his senior year, to being overmatched against Quad-A hitters in uncounted sim games in Schaumburg.

Dallas Keuchel LHP Born: 01/01/88 Age: 33 Bats: L Throws: L Height: 6'2" Weight: 220 Origin: Round 7, 2009 Draft (#221 overall)

YEAR	TEAM	LVL	AGE	W	L	SV	G	GS	IP	H	HR	BB/9	K/9	K	GB%	BABIP	WHIP	ERA	DRA-	WARP	MPH	FA%	Whiff%	CSP
2018	HOU	MLB	30	13	11	0	35	35	211²	216	18	2.5	6.8	160	54.3%	.300	1.30	3.70	86	3.4	91.0	69.0%	19.8%	45.0%
2019	ROM	LO-A	31	0	0	0	1	1	7	1	0	1.3	11.6	9	76.9%	.077	0.29	0.00						
2019	MIS	AA	31	0	0	0	1	1	7	11	0	1.3	5.1	4	42.3%	.440	1.71	3.86	144	-0.2				
2019	ATL	MLB	31	8	8	0	19	19	112²	115	16	3.1	7.3	91	58.3%	.303	1.37	3.75	87	1.9	89.9	74.0%	21.2%	41.2%
2020	CHW	MLB	32	6	2	0	11	11	63¹	52	2	2.4	6.0	42	52.0%	.258	1.09	1.99	99	0.6	88.9	65.5%	23.8%	43.3%
2021 FS	*CHW*	*MLB*	*33*	*9*	*8*	*0*	*26*	*26*	*150*	*150*	*19*	*3.2*	*7.2*	*119*	*54.4%*	*.291*	*1.36*	*4.27*	*98*	*1.2*	*90.0*	*69.9%*	*21.5%*	*43.1%*
2021 DC	*CHW*	*MLB*	*33*	*10*	*10*	*0*	*29*	*29*	*172*	*172*	*22*	*3.2*	*7.2*	*136*	*54.4%*	*.291*	*1.36*	*4.27*	*98*	*1.9*	*90.0*	*69.9%*	*21.5%*	*43.1%*

Comparables: Garrett Richards, Wade Miley, Homer Bailey

In the typical major league delivery of 2020, there's a point of explosion: a moment when the pitcher's body bursts forward through the path their front leg has already stalked out, and everything moves too fast to track in real time. Keuchel never gets blurry on the TV screen when he's pitching. Every inch of how far he strides toward home plate plays out smoothly visible in real time. Possibly as a result, he does not throw very hard and his velocity figures to continue its retreat until it has yielded every inch of major league-caliber territory over time. Possibly also as a result of never having that moment of explosion, where everything is moving too overwhelmingly fast in his delivery to possibly control, Keuchel places the ball where he wants. If that sounds like one notch above phrenology as analysis, it's this sort of belief in the ineffable that is required to see Keuchel's defiance of run estimators and the necessity of missing bats as something eternal and sustainable, rather than a brief marvel that should be celebrated for how long it has already managed to last.

★ ★ ★ *2021 Top 101 Prospect* **#37** ★ ★ ★

Michael Kopech RHP Born: 04/30/96 Age: 25 Bats: R Throws: R Height: 6'3" Weight: 225 Origin: Round 1, 2014 Draft (#33 overall)

YEAR	TEAM	LVL	AGE	W	L	SV	G	GS	IP	H	HR	BB/9	K/9	K	GB%	BABIP	WHIP	ERA	DRA-	WARP	MPH	FA%	Whiff%	CSP
2018	CHA	AAA	22	7	7	0	24	24	126¹	101	9	4.3	12.1	170	38.7%	.319	1.27	3.70	105	0.5				
2018	CHW	MLB	22	1	1	0	4	4	14¹	20	4	1.3	9.4	15	28.3%	.381	1.53	5.02	152	-0.3	97.6	62.5%	21.5%	51.0%
2021 FS	*CHW*	*MLB*	*25*	*9*	*8*	*0*	*26*	*26*	*150*	*131*	*21*	*5.2*	*10.3*	*171*	*37.2%*	*.291*	*1.46*	*4.66*	*96*	*1.4*	*97.6*	*62.5%*	*21.5%*	*51.0%*
2021 DC	*CHW*	*MLB*	*25*	*5*	*5*	*0*	*102*	*19*	*89*	*78*	*12*	*5.2*	*10.3*	*101*	*37.2%*	*.291*	*1.46*	*4.66*	*96*	*0.9*	*97.6*	*62.5%*	*21.5%*	*51.0%*

Comparables: Trevor Bauer, Henry Owens, Matt Wisler

Contrary to popular belief, Michael Kopech did actually pitch in 2020. It came in March, in the absolute last spring training game the White Sox played before COVID-19 shut down the American sports world for months on end. Pulsing with adrenaline in something closer to his actual "real" return to the mound from Tommy John surgery than a few outings in 2019 instructional league, Kopech hit 100 mph with his first fastball, then hit 101 mph, and within 11 pitches, his perfect single inning of work was over. He was still buzzing a half hour later when he spoke to reports; outdoors, with all of them standing six feet away. He was too jacked up to remember when he was scheduled to pitch next.

"I assume it's in five days," he said.

In fairness, Kopech's assumption performed about as well as everyone else's in the post-pandemic world. When the White Sox next contacted Kopech about pitching in 2020, it came with the weight of uncertainty about virus testing, safety, proper ramp-up time for a season, sacrificing contact with family, and a host of other uncertainties, and Kopech decided not to take part. That judgment, equally of its time, figures to age better.

Jimmy Lambert RHP Born: 11/18/94 Age: 26 Bats: R Throws: R Height: 6'2" Weight: 190 Origin: Round 5, 2016 Draft (#146 overall)

YEAR	TEAM	LVL	AGE	W	L	SV	G	GS	IP	H	HR	BB/9	K/9	K	GB%	BABIP	WHIP	ERA	DRA-	WARP	MPH	FA%	Whiff%	CSP
2018	WS	HI-A	23	5	7	0	13	13	70²	57	5	2.7	10.2	80	39.9%	.301	1.10	3.95	67	1.8				
2018	BIR	AA	23	3	1	0	5	5	25	20	2	2.2	10.8	30	40.0%	.286	1.04	2.88	56	0.8				
2019	BIR	AA	24	3	4	0	11	11	59¹	62	11	4.1	10.6	70	37.0%	.338	1.50	4.55	114	-0.4				
2020	CHW	MLB	25	0	0	0	2	0	2	2	0	0.0	9.0	2	33.3%	.333	1.00	0.00	100	0.0	96.3	48.5%	28.6%	53.3%
2021 FS	*CHW*	*MLB*	*26*	*1*	*1*	*0*	*57*	*0*	*50*	*48*	*8*	*3.6*	*8.8*	*48*	*36.7%*	*.289*	*1.37*	*4.63*	*106*	*0.0*	*96.3*	*48.5%*	*28.6%*	*53.3%*
2021 DC	*CHW*	*MLB*	*26*	*1*	*1*	*0*	*13*	*3*	*25*	*24*	*4*	*3.6*	*8.8*	*24*	*36.7%*	*.289*	*1.37*	*4.63*	*106*	*0.1*	*96.3*	*48.5%*	*28.6%*	*53.3%*

Comparables: Sterling Sharp, Patrick Murphy, Brandon Woodruff

In another world, it's Lambert, not Dane Dunning, who is nominally starting Chicago's decidedly cursed Game 3 playoff loss in Oakland. The White Sox tabbed Lambert for their Opening Day roster because they felt he was ahead of the former first rounder at the time. Despite sitting at similar lower-90s velocities, Lambert is more at home throwing like a power pitcher. He gets convincing ride at the top of the zone with his four-seamer and has a curveball and changeup that work off of it well. The rub is that Lambert might have only been sitting at Dunning-like velocities because his surgically repaired elbow was already barking. Now instead of the seemingly standard issue rite of passage of Tommy John surgery, his path appears more like two full years of arm troubles with fits of activity sprinkled in. Lambert has the arsenal to start, but two relief appearances mixed amid injury present a worst-case scenario for his future.

Reynaldo López RHP   Born: 01/04/94   Age: 27   Bats: R   Throws: R   Height: 6'1"   Weight: 220   Origin: International Free Agent, 2012

YEAR	TEAM	LVL	AGE	W	L	SV	G	GS	IP	H	HR	BB/9	K/9	K	GB%	BABIP	WHIP	ERA	DRA-	WARP	MPH	FA%	Whiff%	CSP
2018	CHW	MLB	24	7	10	0	32	32	188²	165	25	3.6	7.2	151	33.0%	.260	1.27	3.91	126	-0.7	98.0	60.9%	21.2%	49.2%
2019	CHW	MLB	25	10	15	0	33	33	184	203	35	3.2	8.3	169	34.6%	.317	1.46	5.38	144	-2.6	98.0	58.6%	24.7%	51.3%
2020	CHW	MLB	26	1	3	0	8	8	26¹	28	9	5.1	8.2	24	33.3%	.268	1.63	6.49	152	-0.5	96.0	51.4%	22.2%	48.3%
2021 FS	CHW	MLB	27	8	9	0	26	26	150	143	28	3.9	8.6	142	34.9%	.281	1.39	4.80	108	0.4	97.7	58.2%	23.4%	50.3%
2021 DC	CHW	MLB	27	3	4	0	48	6	70	67	13	3.9	8.6	66	34.9%	.281	1.39	4.80	108	0.2	97.7	58.2%	23.4%	50.3%

Comparables: José Berríos, Zach Eflin, Daniel Mengden

From his first pitch of 2020, thrown in late July of this bizarre, accursed season, López never found the top-of-the-scale velocity that always served as the bedrock of his young career. He received a visit from the team's trainer before the end of his first inning, and soon after, an accompanying IL stint. Eventually, López would claim that the pain in his shoulder subsided, but the damage was done. What remained in its wake was an unflattering portrayal of what López has developed over the last few years alongside the velocity that always staved off the disaster. The mistakes he made while flagging into the low-90s by the end of outings were even more noticeable than they were at 96 mph. His changeup and slider had always had their moments, but the consistency necessary to pitch backward never surfaced. Maybe in a normal year, or simply with the benefit of an offseason, López's shoulder will heal, and the easy upper-90s will return. But even so, the same shortcomings will define his future.

Lance Lynn RHP   Born: 05/12/87   Age: 34   Bats: S   Throws: R   Height: 6'5"   Weight: 250   Origin: Round 1, 2008 Draft (#39 overall)

YEAR	TEAM	LVL	AGE	W	L	SV	G	GS	IP	H	HR	BB/9	K/9	K	GB%	BABIP	WHIP	ERA	DRA-	WARP	MPH	FA%	Whiff%	CSP
2018	NYY	MLB	31	3	2	0	11	9	54¹	58	2	2.3	10.1	61	47.4%	.364	1.33	4.14	96	0.6	95.5	78.3%	23.5%	46.8%
2018	MIN	MLB	31	7	8	0	20	20	102¹	105	12	5.5	8.8	100	51.2%	.322	1.63	5.10	123	-0.3	95.7	77.0%	23.7%	42.5%
2019	TEX	MLB	32	16	11	0	33	33	208¹	195	21	2.5	10.6	246	39.9%	.322	1.22	3.67	64	5.9	96.5	71.4%	28.6%	49.2%
2020	TEX	MLB	33	6	3	0	13	13	84	64	13	2.7	9.5	89	36.2%	.243	1.06	3.32	96	0.9	96.1	67.5%	25.4%	49.5%
2021 FS	CHW	MLB	34	9	8	0	26	26	150	134	23	3.4	9.7	161	39.2%	.285	1.28	4.02	94	1.6	96.2	71.5%	26.6%	48.2%
2021 DC	CHW	MLB	34	11	10	0	30	30	190	169	29	3.4	9.7	204	39.2%	.285	1.28	4.02	94	2.6	96.2	71.5%	26.6%	48.2%

Comparables: Francisco Liriano, Jake Arrieta, Ian Kennedy

A couple notable things about Lynn's 2020 campaign: First, he threw a shutout with his razor, growing a majestic monstrosity of a beard that combined the woodsy-ness of Grizzly Adams with the unkempt-itude of Captain Lou Albano. It was truly a sight to behold. Second, and perhaps most importantly, Lynn cemented his status as one of the very best starters in the American League, giving up more than three runs just once in his first 12 starts, with an ERA a shade below 2.60, before the wheels completely came off in his final outing of the season. Lynn has always predominantly relied on his high-spin heater, and this season was no exception. The righty chucked fastballs over half the time, and only five starters threw a higher percentage of four seamers this year. The White Sox struck quickly in the offseason, acquiring the coveted starter to fortify their rotation for a potential playoff run.

Evan Marshall RHP   Born: 04/18/90   Age: 31   Bats: R   Throws: R   Height: 6'2"   Weight: 235   Origin: Round 4, 2011 Draft (#124 overall)

YEAR	TEAM	LVL	AGE	W	L	SV	G	GS	IP	H	HR	BB/9	K/9	K	GB%	BABIP	WHIP	ERA	DRA-	WARP	MPH	FA%	Whiff%	CSP
2018	COL	AAA	28	1	1	4	20	0	24	18	1	1.1	7.9	21	66.2%	.258	0.88	1.12	79	0.3				
2018	CLE	MLB	28	0	0	0	10	0	7	12	0	5.1	11.6	9	56.5%	.522	2.29	7.71	81	0.1	94.9	54.7%	33.8%	43.0%
2019	CHA	AAA	29	3	0	2	9	0	10	8	0	0.9	11.7	13	43.5%	.364	0.90	0.00	46	0.4				
2019	CHW	MLB	29	4	2	0	55	0	50²	42	5	4.3	7.3	41	50.7%	.266	1.30	2.49	104	0.2	95.0	43.9%	24.6%	40.4%
2020	CHW	MLB	30	2	1	0	23	0	22²	17	1	2.8	11.9	30	53.6%	.291	1.06	2.38	63	0.6	94.4	29.2%	34.7%	42.6%
2021 FS	CHW	MLB	31	2	2	8	57	0	50	44	5	3.7	9.6	53	50.6%	.290	1.29	3.74	88	0.5	94.7	38.8%	29.0%	41.4%
2021 DC	CHW	MLB	31	2	2	8	52	0	55	48	6	3.7	9.6	58	50.6%	.290	1.29	3.74	88	0.7	94.7	38.8%	29.0%	41.4%

Comparables: Javy Guerra, Ryan Webb, JC Ramírez

Evan Marshall has a theory he has shared a few times: He could always do this. He believes he always had the talent to be the shutdown reliever he was in 2020, and always had the physical ability. Despite velocity that he would describe as just fast enough to set up the rest of his arsenal, he could always post elite strikeout rates. The difference now is that he's smarter, more thoughtful and deliberate in his sequencing. The impacts and lessons of all of his previous outings and failures have materialized into a useful tool he could carry with him. The other difference Marshall cited was no longer being consumed with "flying objects," referencing the 105 mph line drive that struck him in the face and nearly killed him during a Triple-A game in 2015. He asserts that time has allowed him to pitch without being consumed by concern of a repeat. What a radical notion that our failures and traumas are not only recoverable, but just stepping stones on the path to our best selves. Only in baseball.

Carlos Rodón LHP Born: 12/10/92 Age: 28 Bats: L Throws: L Height: 6'3" Weight: 250 Origin: Round 1, 2014 Draft (#3 overall)

YEAR	TEAM	LVL	AGE	W	L	SV	G	GS	IP	H	HR	BB/9	K/9	K	GB%	BABIP	WHIP	ERA	DRA-	WARP	MPH	FA%	Whiff%	CSP
2018	CHA	AAA	25	1	0	0	3	3	12²	10	0	3.6	15.6	22	56.5%	.435	1.18	1.42	67	0.3				
2018	CHW	MLB	25	6	8	0	20	20	120²	97	15	4.1	6.7	90	41.6%	.243	1.26	4.18	146	-1.8	95.8	59.8%	21.3%	47.6%
2019	CHW	MLB	26	3	2	0	7	7	34²	33	4	4.4	11.9	46	41.5%	.322	1.44	5.19	83	0.6	94.1	51.9%	28.5%	46.8%
2020	CHW	MLB	27	0	2	0	4	2	7²	9	1	3.5	7.0	6	28.0%	.333	1.57	8.22	151	-0.1	96.7	51.1%	23.3%	48.7%
2021 FS	CHW	MLB	28	8	9	0	26	26	150	136	24	4.8	9.7	161	40.0%	.289	1.44	4.64	107	0.5	95.3	55.9%	24.2%	47.4%

Comparables: Daniel Mengden, Daniel Norris, Zach Davies

There's a crowd, a seemingly growing one, that has responded to the waves of pitching injuries and resulting surgeries with a mixture of patience and resignation. "Just get the surgery!" they howl, annoyed with how all the efforts to rehab and forestall such a leap seemingly stall the end date where injuries can be forgotten about forever. But there is no surgery that can deliver that final erasure of physical trauma. It all adds up and compiles, and even the found footholds are known to be temporary. Four years removed from a promising sophomore campaign that served as portent for his best years in the majors, Rodón is still looking for a spot to rest his feet where the ground will not give way beneath. There have been incisions made to his incisions made into his shoulder and elbow over the past three years. At times, in 2020, the mid-90s velocity flickered into being, just long enough to cast a shadow. But the residue of it all still hangs over him. There is no surgery that can recreate the Rodón of 2016, just an exploratory one to discover what remains of him in 2021.

Jonathan Stiever RHP Born: 05/12/97 Age: 24 Bats: R Throws: R Height: 6'2" Weight: 215 Origin: Round 5, 2018 Draft (#138 overall)

YEAR	TEAM	LVL	AGE	W	L	SV	G	GS	IP	H	HR	BB/9	K/9	K	GB%	BABIP	WHIP	ERA	DRA-	WARP	MPH	FA%	Whiff%	CSP
2018	GTF	ROK	21	0	1	0	13	13	28	23	3	2.9	12.5	39	47.7%	.323	1.14	4.18	76	0.8				
2019	KAN	LO-A	22	4	6	0	14	14	74	88	10	1.7	9.4	77	43.8%	.363	1.38	4.74	123	-0.7				
2019	WS	HI-A	22	6	4	0	12	12	71	56	7	1.6	9.8	77	40.4%	.278	0.97	2.15	64	1.7				
2020	CHW	MLB	23	0	1	0	2	2	6¹	7	4	5.7	4.3	3	40.9%	.167	1.74	9.95	148	-0.1	94.2	53.3%	14.5%	48.4%
2021 FS	CHW	MLB	24	2	2	0	57	0	50	50	8	3.4	7.8	43	40.4%	.287	1.37	4.74	108	-0.1	94.2	53.3%	14.5%	48.4%
2021 DC	CHW	MLB	24	2	2	0	25	4	43	43	7	3.4	7.8	37	40.4%	.287	1.37	4.74	108	0.2	94.2	53.3%	14.5%	48.4%

Comparables: Beau Burrows, Felix Jorge, Andrew Heaney

As of March 2020, Stiever found himself in the Carolina League, sidelined by forearm soreness; that he ended the season with major league experience makes it hard to spin his year as a negative. Stopping short of that, it's fairer to be confused about where he stands. The results—one suitable outing against a moribund offense, one night of getting absolutely tattooed—fit alongside his place on the developmental track. But since he achieved them lacking the power stuff, velocity and swing-and-miss results that defined his ascent to prospect status, it was a dispiriting coda to a year that began with an injury scare. Stiever is an exceptional athlete with the ability to spin it. He seemed to gain some feel for a changeup even as his mid-90s heat took a break, and those raw ingredients will spur optimism going forward. But if the takeaway from 2020 for most prospects is confusion over how to assess how much they progressed without minor league action, Stiever's major league turn did not pump more certainty into the information gap.

Matthew Thompson RHP Born: 08/11/00 Age: 20 Bats: R Throws: R Height: 6'3" Weight: 195 Origin: Round 2, 2019 Draft (#45 overall)

YEAR	TEAM	LVL	AGE	W	L	SV	G	GS	IP	H	HR	BB/9	K/9	K	GB%	BABIP	WHIP	ERA	DRA-	WARP	MPH	FA%	Whiff%	CSP
2019	WSX	ROK	18	0	0	0	2	2	2	2	0	0.0	9.0	2	33.3%	.333	1.00	0.00	64	0.1				
2021 FS	CHW	MLB	20	2	3	0	57	0	50	53	8	5.5	7.5	41	38.2%	.304	1.68	6.10	140	-1.0				

The best photos of Thompson in action still find him in a Cypress Ranch High School uniform. Updates about his progress on backfields and alternate sites are light on descriptions of actual innings pitched, and center around if he's figured out how to throw a changeup. Yet his build, athleticism and burgeoning command all point to someone who could grow into a rotation role, assuming minor league baseball ever comes back and he actually gets to pitch.

Emilio Vargas RHP Born: 08/12/96 Age: 24 Bats: R Throws: R Height: 6'3" Weight: 230 Origin: International Free Agent, 2013

YEAR	TEAM	LVL	AGE	W	L	SV	G	GS	IP	H	HR	BB/9	K/9	K	GB%	BABIP	WHIP	ERA	DRA-	WARP	MPH	FA%	Whiff%	CSP
2018	VIS	HI-A	21	8	5	0	20	19	108	92	7	3.4	11.7	140	39.3%	.335	1.23	2.50	80	1.7				
2018	JXN	AA	21	1	3	0	6	6	35²	31	6	2.0	7.6	30	42.2%	.245	1.09	4.04	80	0.6				
2019	DIA	ROK	22	0	2	0	3	3	10¹	9	1	1.7	10.5	12	32.0%	.333	1.06	4.35	48	0.4				
2019	JXN	AA	22	5	3	0	17	17	85²	74	10	2.4	7.4	70	43.1%	.261	1.13	3.78	92	0.5				
2021 FS	CHW	MLB	24	1	2	0	57	0	50	49	9	4.1	8.1	45	40.9%	.284	1.44	5.09	121	-0.5				
2021 DC	CHW	MLB	24	1	2	0	15	4	32	31	5	4.1	8.1	28	40.9%	.284	1.44	5.09	121	-0.1				

Comparables: Pedro Avila, Anthony Swarzak, Brady Lail

The Diamondbacks have a thing for guys with vertical arm slots and Emilio Vargas fits that mold. Maybe the White Sox do too, since they claimed him off waivers in November. He seems likely to see some big-league time if he can survive the winter on the 40-man roster.

CLEVELAND

Essay by Stephanie Springer

Player comments by Darius Austin and BP staff

While the shortened 2020 MLB season will forever be linked with a pandemic, the underlying story is one of exceptionalism granted by baseball's status as America's pastime. Baseball has long enjoyed exemptions from the rules and social mores to which the vast majority of us must comply, and we can turn to a single week for Cleveland by way of illustration.

First, let's set the season's context. Although negotiations between MLB and MLBPA regarding financial obligations were contentious, all parties agreed that measures must be taken to protect the health of the players before pre-season activities resumed. It was generally understood that MLB would cooperate with epidemiologists and federal, state, and local public health authorities to provide evidence-based guidance to teams and players. Public health experts widely agreed that wearing a mask over our mouths and noses would reduce transmission of SARS-CoV-2. We also knew that maintaining physical distance from others—in particular, avoiding indoor spaces—would slow the spread of the virus. Accordingly, stadium facilities were reconfigured so as to allow for adequate ventilation and space between players. Facial coverings were strongly encouraged, while interactions with people outside of family, teammates, and MLB personnel were forbidden. These measures were deemed all the more critical given the risk of asymptomatic transmission.

Epidemiologists and virologists agreed that frequent testing was a critical tool for mitigating spread of the virus; however, across the United States, there was a lack of adequate diagnostic testing, with a constant shortage of laboratory reagents and long turnaround times. Major League Baseball equipped their partner Sports Medicine Research and Testing Laboratory with the equipment and consumables needed for PCR testing of thousands of league personnel each week. Anticipating public criticism, MLB pledged to offer free diagnostic and antibody testing to healthcare workers and first responders in team cities. This gesture of goodwill, coupled with the country's desire for a distraction during challenging times, contributed to the sentiment that MLB was doing its part to support communities.

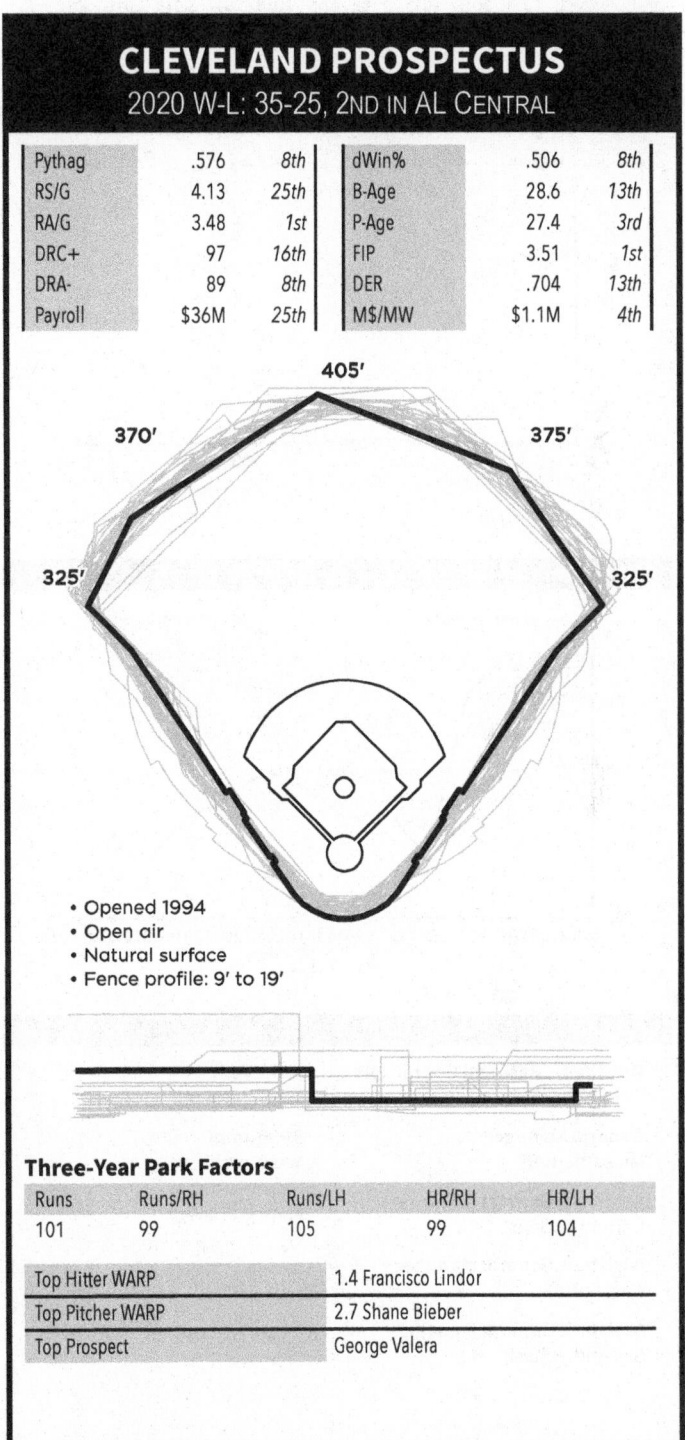

CLEVELAND PROSPECTUS
2020 W-L: 35-25, 2ND IN AL CENTRAL

Pythag	.576	8th	dWin%	.506	8th
RS/G	4.13	25th	B-Age	28.6	13th
RA/G	3.48	1st	P-Age	27.4	3rd
DRC+	97	16th	FIP	3.51	1st
DRA-	89	8th	DER	.704	13th
Payroll	$36M	25th	M$/MW	$1.1M	4th

405'
370'   375'
325'   325'

- Opened 1994
- Open air
- Natural surface
- Fence profile: 9' to 19'

Three-Year Park Factors

Runs	Runs/RH	Runs/LH	HR/RH	HR/LH
101	99	105	99	104

Top Hitter WARP	1.4 Francisco Lindor
Top Pitcher WARP	2.7 Shane Bieber
Top Prospect	George Valera

Payroll History (in millions)

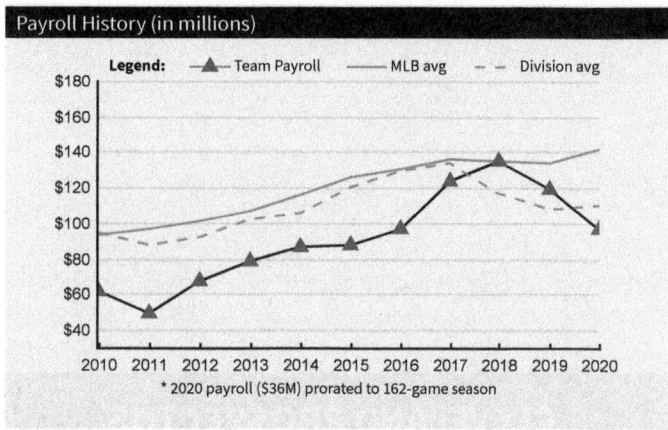

Legend: — Team Payroll — MLB avg - - Division avg

* 2020 payroll ($36M) prorated to 162-game season

Future Commitments (in millions)

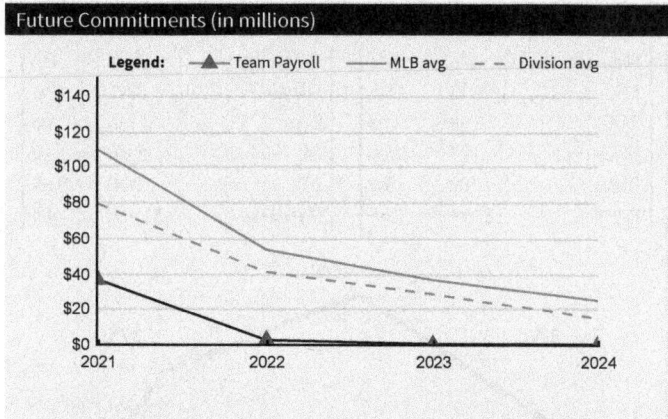

Legend: — Team Payroll — MLB avg - - Division avg

Farm System Ranking

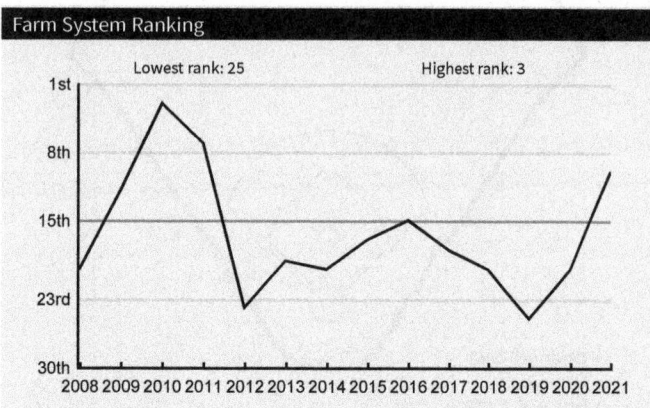

Lowest rank: 25   Highest rank: 3

Personnel

President, Baseball Operations
Chris Antonetti

General Manager
Mike Chernoff

Assistant General Manager
Carter Hawkins

Assistant General Manager
Matt Forman

Assistant General Manager
Sky Andrecheck

Manager
Terry Francona

BP Alumni
Max Marchi
Ethan Purser
Keith Woolner

Although there was a general consensus on how to slow the spread of the virus, little was known about the disease itself, and the prognosis and outcomes of COVID-19 were still not well understood. The long term ramifications of COVID-19 had yet to be ascertained. This point was made abundantly clear to MLB when the Red Sox' Eduardo Rodriguez became the exemplar of what could happen to a young, healthy athlete who developed COVID-19. Rodriguez tested positive for COVID-19 and was diagnosed with cardiac myocarditis, an inflammation of the heart muscle. It was rapidly determined that he would not play the 2020 season, but reports were hopeful that Rodriguez would recover quickly. However, it is not clear if the severity of his condition was widely known; follow up reports months later celebrated that Rodriguez was again able to walk unassisted, indicating that his condition was much more severe than previously reported.

One might think that seeing COVID-19 affect a contemporary in this way would have served as a warning to other baseball players who may have been concerned about their or their teammates' health. If fear did not suffice as motivation, surely the mandates in the MLB health and safety protocols would ensure compliance? Or perhaps embarrassment and shaming on social media would deter violators. Indeed, it was just such derision and backlash that resulted after Cleveland's first violation of MLB protocols: Just after the beginning of summer camp, outfielder Franmil Reyes posted photos of himself on social media where he wasn't wearing a mask. Reyes issued an apology for ignoring MLB protocols, and endangering both his teammates' health and the season.

As tenuous as it was, summer camp continued and the season began; less than two weeks later, starting pitchers Mike Clevinger and Zach Plesac chose to violate MLB health and safety protocols by visiting friends during an away series in Chicago.

On Saturday, August 8th, Plesac took the mound against the White Sox for his third start of the season. That same night, he opted to visit friends while in Chicago. The following day, his indiscretion was revealed, and he was sent home by car service to isolate him from his teammates. Initial comments from teammates expressed their disappointment but confidence that this would be handled internally.

As more details emerged, the story only grew worse: fellow starting pitcher Mike Clevinger had been out and about on Saturday as well. Not only did he lie, he did not confess when his teammate's night out was revealed. Clevinger defended Plesac, allowing him to bear the brunt of the judgement of a night out, letting Plesac stand alone and take the punishment for violating protocol. To top it all off, Clevenger flew home on the team plane on Sunday evening, potentially jeopardizing his teammates' health. Plesac's subsequent video confession, flaunting his decision to socialize and hide the truth upon returning to the team, threw salt in the wound.

Team chemistry is a nebulous concept, warmly embraced by some while harshly denied by others. When we speak of team chemistry, we usually speak of it as an additive, positive effect. But in the grand balance of the universe, it stands to reason that the positive cannot exist without the negative, and we should also consider that team chemistry can have a detrimental effect. When trust is breached and the bonds between teammates are fractured, it can have a deleterious effect.

Thus, it was no surprise when Cleveland players had harsh comments for their teammates. Francisco Lindor did not mince words: "At the end of the day, we have to sit and look ourselves in the mirror. And it's not about the person you see in the mirror—it's about who's behind you, the other people. It's not about that one person in general. It's about everybody around him and the family members that are behind us...We're in a time right now with COVID-19, with racism, everything. This is a time to be selfless. This is when we have to sit back and understand this is not about one person specifically. It's about everybody. You have to go out there and understand that it's about your neighbor and your neighbor's neighbors. It's not just you specifically."

Lindor's comments highlight the egregious violation that Plesac and Clevinger committed. The problem wasn't just that Clevinger and Plesac broke MLB COVID-19 protocols or ignored public health guidance; they had failed to consider the impact of their behavior on others—behavior that ultimately got Clevinger sent packing for 80 cents on the dollar. And it wasn't just their teammates on the field—Plesac and Clevinger violated the trust of their community. Their selfishness placed their team at heightened risk of catching a highly contagious virus—whether that team is Cleveland or the general public. By skirting the rules, Clevinger and Plesac sent an unambiguous message: they were above the rules which MLB had put into place, the same protocols that everyone else was expected to follow.

Plesac and Clevinger's behavior is emblematic of a larger issue, as this exceptionalistic attitude pervades MLB and its affiliated organizations. For most of the 2020 season, denizens of many states were subject to travel restrictions and quarantine mandates, but MLB was granted exemptions to bypass these local travel and quarantine requirements. The rest of the country waited in long lines for COVID-19 testing, only to wait up to a week for test results; meanwhile, professional athletes could skip the line and the wait. Further, MLB actively contributed to the strain of the testing infrastructure by using laboratory reagents for their own tests, and not testing community members who indirectly supported the return of the baseball season. Although they had initially promised to provide diagnostic and antibody testing to healthcare workers and first responders, investigative reporting revealed that the league neglected to follow through on its offers.

Major League Baseball's lackadaisical adherence to public health guidelines was not the only breach of community goodwill in 2020 or in years prior. Cleveland is as good an example of any in baseball, how a team that has benefitted from primacy granted to sports and business, and especially sports businesses acts more as a parasite than in a mutualistic manner. Baseball teams trade on cultural value, capitalizing on a built-in fan (consumer) base by trading in cultural value only to shirk their obligation to reinvest into that culture. Cleveland's payroll of late peaked in 2018, but was on the decline for a second consecutive season in 2020 despite notable holes in their outfield. Instead of making news by bringing in players to address those weaknesses, the team was instead making waves for all but announcing that their star shortstop wouldn't be with the team long term, as owner Larry Dolan stated "enjoy him while you can."

Dolan bought the team in 1999 for $323 million. As of April 2020, the franchise was valued by Forbes at $1.15 billion. Whether Lindor will live up to the contract he seeks and may ultimately receive is to be determined, but there's no doubt of his value to the fans in Cleveland, except perhaps in the minds of Dolan and his front office.

Further still, the league has disrupted the symbiosis between professional baseball and local communities by dismantling the minor league system and withdrawing from small town America. This isn't just a matter of a warm sentimental feeling; we may never know the entirety of the economic benefits the minor league system brought to these small towns, and the vacuum left behind as short season teams consolidate will inevitably lead to a loss of jobs in baseball and in the local hospitality industry.

Being a member of a community confers benefits, but in exchange, there is also a tacit understanding that we must be responsible members of the community. We rely upon the collective efforts of our neighbors to protect us, but we also take it upon ourselves to ensure that our individual actions do no harm. As members of a community, we wishfully believe that having a professional sporting organization unites us with shared experiences and hometown pride. By rooting for a team, we're not just supporting the team, but demonstrating our support for the city as well. But as much as the community may support its hometown teams, the reverse is simply not true. We offer MLB financial incentives and exemptions to laws in order to enjoin professional baseball to join our communities, but MLB seeks to reap these benefits without honoring the unspoken commitment to take accountability for their actions.

This one week in Cleveland's season is representative of the selfish desire to take advantage of the benefits provided by a community without also being mindful of how our actions impact said community. It's a form of exceptionalism exhibited by MLB as a whole, the same exceptionalism that characterized the American response to the pandemic. Clevinger and Plesac did not hold themselves accountable for their actions and their betrayal of their teammates, just as MLB has not held itself accountable for violating the goodwill generously provided by the communities in which it operates. We should not be surprised when we see that same exceptionalism in our sports teams, who somehow think that calls for racial equality and social justice, and yes, infectious disease prevention does not apply to them.

During the pandemic, we vigilantly maintain at least six feet of space between ourselves and others, but this physical distance heightens our awareness of the emotional distance we are creating. We worry that being too close together promotes the spread of the virus, and we also worry that not seeing our family, friends, and colleagues in person slowly wears away our humanity and connections. But our communities are based not on physical proximity, but out of our shared concern for our neighbors and our neighbor's neighbors well being, health, and safety. Community is its own chemistry, a sense of shared obligation and pride, a foxhole miles wide. It requires not just an obedience, but a sense of willingness, a declaration of playing for a team instead of for one's self.

Long after the novel coronavirus becomes a treatable condition, after vaccines are widely distributed, will we remember who thought they were the exception to the rules? Will we remember who in our community took action to protect others, or who failed to fulfil their promises and obligations to the community? ▨

—Stephanie Springer's writing has appeared in The Hardball Times and Baseball Prospectus.

Katherine Acquavella, Mike Axisa, and R.J. Anderson, "Cleveland places Mike Clevinger and Zach Plesac on restricted list for breaking COVID-19 protocols", CBS Sports, August 11, 2020. https://www.cbssports.com/mlb/news/cleveland-places-mike-clevinger-and-zach-plesac-on-restricted-list-for-breaking-covid-19-protocols//p>

Paul Hoynes, "Cleveland Indians place right-handers Zach Plesac, Mike Clevinger on restricted list", Cleveland.com, August 11, 2020. https://www.cleveland.com/tribe/2020/08/cleveland-indians-place-right-handers-zach-plesac-mike-clevinger-on-restricted-list.html

Ricky O'Donnell, "The Cleveland Indians were right to blast their teammates for breaking Covid protocol", SB Nation, August 12, 2020. https://www.sbnation.com/mlb/2020/8/12/21365118/cleveland-indians-covid-protocol-partying-chicago-coronavirus

Zack Meisel, "Terry Francona, Chris Antonetti and Francisco Lindor on the state of the Indians", The Athletic, August 11, 2020. https://theathletic.com/1989753/2020/08/11/terry-francona-chris-antonetti-and-francisco-lindor-on-the-state-of-the-indians/

Bradford William Davis, "MLB promised free COVID-19 testing for essential workers. We're still waiting", New York Daily News, September 24, 2020. https://www.nydailynews.com/sports/baseball/ny-mlb-covid-testing-health-workers-20200924-lgrlvj4qjfh3pnudvixpgzqwbe-story.html

HITTERS

★ ★ ★ *2021 Top 101 Prospect* **#87** ★ ★ ★

Gabriel Arias SS
Born: 02/27/00   Age: 21   Bats: R   Throws: R   Height: 6'1"   Weight: 201   Origin: International Free Agent, 2016

YEAR	TEAM	LVL	AGE	PA	R	2B	3B	HR	RBI	BB	K	SB	CS	Whiff%	AVG/OBP/SLG	DRC+	BABIP	BRR	FRAA	WARP
2018	FW	LO-A	18	504	54	27	3	6	55	41	149	3	3		.240/.302/.352	84	.340	-0.5	SS(111): 6.2, 3B(6): 0.2	1.2
2019	LE	HI-A	19	506	62	21	4	17	75	24	126	8	4		.304/.341/.474	121	.380	1.5	SS(104): -11.4, 3B(10): 1.4, 2B(2): -0.4	2.1
2021 FS	CLE	MLB	21	600	51	26	3	13	59	28	220	1	0		.220/.261/.348	64	.333	0.6	SS -2, 3B 0	-1.0

Comparables: Franklin Barreto, Gleyber Torres, Xander Bogaerts

Arias is so tooled-up he could co-host with Tim Taylor. Someone shouted "MORE POWER!" on the set before the 2019 season, and he obliged by hitting 17 of his 23 career home runs. In true "Tool Time" fashion, there's no guarantee that the rest of Arias' tools—specifically his hit—will be used correctly, but he has a chance for four average or better offerings when all is said and done. Perhaps that's why the Padres felt comfortable shipping him off as part of the Mike Clevinger payout. Oh well. Arias can take solace in knowing he no longer has to sculpt ice using a chainsaw to garner attention, the way he did in San Diego's loaded system.

Jake Bauers LF
Born: 10/06/95   Age: 25   Bats: L   Throws: L   Height: 6'1"   Weight: 195   Origin: Round 7, 2013 Draft (#208 overall)

YEAR	TEAM	LVL	AGE	PA	R	2B	3B	HR	RBI	BB	K	SB	CS	Whiff%	AVG/OBP/SLG	DRC+	BABIP	BRR	FRAA	WARP
2018	DUR	AAA	22	222	31	14	0	5	24	23	47	10	6		.279/.357/.426	124	.345	0.9	1B(46): -0.4, LF(4): 0.3, RF(2): -0.2	0.6
2018	TB	MLB	22	388	48	22	2	11	48	54	104	6	6	28.4%	.201/.316/.384	86	.252	2.5	1B(76): -2.4, LF(16): 0.5, RF(4): 0.0	0.0
2019	COL	AAA	23	103	13	7	0	3	15	14	26	8	2		.247/.350/.427	95	.317	0.1	LF(15): 2.1, 1B(6): 0.1, CF(1): 0.0	0.3
2019	CLE	MLB	23	423	46	16	1	12	43	45	115	3	3	24.0%	.226/.312/.371	85	.290	0.7	LF(53): 0.1, 1B(31): -2.2	-0.1
2021 FS	CLE	MLB	25	600	66	25	1	17	62	70	154	6	2	25.4%	.222/.320/.378	93	.280	-0.9	1B -2, LF 1	0.5
2021 DC	CLE	MLB	25	399	44	16	1	11	41	47	102	4	1	25.4%	.222/.320/.378	93	.280	-0.6	1B -1, LF 1	0.2

Comparables: Mike Carp, Carlos Delgado, Derrek Lee

We apologize for going back to the well with the Jack Bauer references, but it's apparent that Bauers is…well, the anti-Bauer. Whereas Bauer gets the call in the most desperate of situations—assassination attempts, nuclear threats and poor primetime ad rates—Bauers went unsummoned despite Cleveland's outfield emergency. They employed 11 players as starting outfielders in 2020, yet he remained stored away at the Alternate Site like an unneeded bit character. Bauers *is* entering his age-24 season—ahem—so maybe there's some reason to hope that he can avert disaster. If he fails to make good on it, that ticking clock you'll hear will be counting down the hours until he's designated for assignment.

Bobby Bradley 1B Born: 05/29/96 Age: 25 Bats: L Throws: R Height: 6'1" Weight: 225 Origin: Round 3, 2014 Draft (#97 overall)

YEAR	TEAM	LVL	AGE	PA	R	2B	3B	HR	RBI	BB	K	SB	CS	Whiff%	AVG/OBP/SLG	DRC+	BABIP	BRR	FRAA	WARP
2018	AKR	AA	22	421	49	19	3	24	64	45	105	1	0		.214/.304/.477	106	.226	-2.3	1B(97): 1.4	0.0
2018	COL	AAA	22	128	11	7	2	3	19	11	43	0	0		.254/.323/.430	99	.377	0.3	1B(29): 1.5	0.2
2019	COL	AAA	23	453	65	23	0	33	74	46	153	0	0		.264/.344/.567	124	.336	-2.5	1B(98): 1.9	1.7
2019	CLE	MLB	23	49	4	5	0	1	4	4	20	0	0	38.9%	.178/.245/.356	53	.292	-0.1	1B(5): -0.2	-0.2
2021 FS	CLE	MLB	25	600	65	27	1	22	67	52	222	0	0	38.9%	.202/.280/.387	78	.293	-0.3	1B -1	-1.0
2021 DC	CLE	MLB	25	399	43	18	1	15	44	35	148	0	0	38.9%	.202/.280/.387	78	.293	-0.2	1B -1	-0.6

Comparables: Pete Alonso, Ryan O'Hearn, Jerry Sands

If your only positions are first base and designated hitter, and the big club employs Carlos Santana and Franmil Reyes, opportunities are going to be few and far between. Bradley received zero during the shortened season, so we're no closer to knowing whether his power can offset his swing-and-miss issues. Or, viewed from another perspective, maybe we are—he's likelier to hit the waiver-wire by the time you read this than lock down a spot.

Yu Chang SS Born: 08/18/95 Age: 25 Bats: R Throws: R Height: 6'1" Weight: 180 Origin: International Free Agent, 2013

YEAR	TEAM	LVL	AGE	PA	R	2B	3B	HR	RBI	BB	K	SB	CS	Whiff%	AVG/OBP/SLG	DRC+	BABIP	BRR	FRAA	WARP
2018	COL	AAA	22	518	56	28	2	13	62	44	144	4	3		.256/.330/.411	102	.341	-3.3	SS(94): -7.3, 3B(23): -0.7, 2B(9): -0.9	0.3
2019	COL	AAA	23	283	45	15	1	9	39	26	67	4	1		.253/.322/.427	92	.306	0.9	2B(23): 0.4, SS(22): 0.2, 3B(17): -0.7	0.8
2019	CLE	MLB	23	84	8	2	1	1	6	11	22	0	0	25.6%	.178/.286/.274	76	.240	-0.9	3B(25): -0.3, SS(8): -0.1	-0.1
2020	CLE	MLB	25	13	1	0	0	0	1	2	4	0	0	19.2%	.182/.308/.182	85	.286	-0.2	SS(4): 0.2, 3B(3): -0.1, 2B(2): 0.3	0.1
2021 FS	CLE	MLB	25	600	62	23	3	20	64	51	190	2	0	24.4%	.207/.286/.373	80	.279	1.5	2B -6, 3B -3	-0.4
2021 DC	CLE	MLB	25	199	20	7	1	6	21	17	63	0	0	24.4%	.207/.286/.373	80	.279	0.5	2B -2, 3B -1	-0.1

Comparables: Brandon Wood, Edmundo Sosa, Matt Reynolds

Chang is caught in an awkward position. He's old enough to hold down a big-league roster spot on a permanent basis, but he can't seem to break through. Of the 240 available starts on Cleveland's dirt in 2020, 232 went to the same quartet that started on Opening Day. Just three of those starts found their way to Chang, who hasn't done much in his various cameos to warrant more. The problem with being old enough but seemingly not good enough for a major-league role is that, before long, you find yourself too old to be considered a prospect, then you find yourself out of chances. Calendar page by calendar page, Chang is inching closer to that fate.

Delino DeShields CF Born: 08/16/92 Age: 28 Bats: R Throws: R Height: 5'9" Weight: 190 Origin: Round 1, 2010 Draft (#8 overall)

YEAR	TEAM	LVL	AGE	PA	R	2B	3B	HR	RBI	BB	K	SB	CS	Whiff%	AVG/OBP/SLG	DRC+	BABIP	BRR	FRAA	WARP
2018	FRI	AA	25	26	2	0	0	0	0	8	2	2	2		.278/.500/.278	171	.312	-0.9	CF(5): -0.5	0.1
2018	TEX	MLB	25	393	52	14	1	2	22	43	83	20	4	20.7%	.216/.310/.281	72	.280	3.4	CF(102): 10.3	1.5
2019	NAS	AAA	26	75	10	3	0	3	11	8	17	8	0		.258/.338/.439	92	.304	1.6	CF(13): 1.1, LF(1): 0.8	0.5
2019	TEX	MLB	26	408	42	15	4	4	32	38	100	24	6	22.7%	.249/.325/.347	76	.333	4.9	CF(112): 6.9	1.4
2020	CLE	MLB	28	120	10	3	2	0	7	9	29	3	2	29.1%	.252/.310/.318	66	.346	-0.8	CF(35): 4.6	0.2
2021 FS	CLE	MLB	28	600	59	22	2	8	49	63	154	30	8	23.6%	.230/.316/.325	80	.308	6.6	CF 7, LF 0	1.8

Comparables: Jermaine Allensworth, Carroll Hardy, Ryan Christenson

What could say more about the 2020 Cleveland outfield than the light-hitting DeShields *raising* the unit's collective OPS? How about this: at .575, the Cleveland outfield had the worst OPS in MLB history. There's an element of small-sample variance to that tidbit, best evidenced by the 2020 Pirates ranking second-worst. Nonetheless, playing on the grass for Cleveland meant hitting like a player from the Dead Ball Era. We would say 'hitting like a Cleveland Spider', except the infamous 1899 Spiders actually put up a better offensive performance. DeShields himself maintained his career offensive level, by the way, and is a perfectly fine fourth outfielder with speed and good defense.

Mike Freeman 2B Born: 08/04/87 Age: 33 Bats: L Throws: R Height: 6'0" Weight: 195 Origin: Round 11, 2010 Draft (#331 overall)

YEAR	TEAM	LVL	AGE	PA	R	2B	3B	HR	RBI	BB	K	SB	CS	Whiff%	AVG/OBP/SLG	DRC+	BABIP	BRR	FRAA	WARP
2018	IOW	AAA	30	330	51	15	2	6	38	25	66	6	6		.272/.328/.394	100	.329	1.8	SS(55): 2.7, 2B(16): -0.1, CF(4): -0.4	1.4
2018	CHC	MLB	30	1	0	0	0	0	0	0	0	0	0	50.0%	None/None/None	91			2B(1): -0.0	0.0
2019	COL	AAA	31	33	6	0	0	3	3	9	7	1	0		.208/.424/.583	146	.143	0.0	SS(4): 0.2, 2B(2): 0.1, 3B(2): 0.2	0.3
2019	CLE	MLB	31	213	27	8	0	4	24	22	61	1	2	25.1%	.277/.362/.390	78	.388	1.3	2B(33): 2.1, 3B(18): -0.1, SS(9): -0.4	0.4
2020	CLE	MLB	33	43	5	3	0	0	3	3	11	0	0	31.6%	.237/.302/.316	89	.321	-0.1	3B(6): -0.2, 2B(4): -0.2, LF(4): 0.4	0.0
2021 FS	CLE	MLB	33	600	58	19	1	12	55	52	168	1	0	26.4%	.220/.295/.333	74	.296	0.4	SS 4, 2B 1	0.4

Comparables: Mark Bellhorn, Mike Fontenot, Michael Martinez

The highlight of Freeman's 2020 was a tweet. You know the one, where he suggested that José Ramírez should have a higher WAR, an assessment he was uniquely qualified to make as the replacement in question. Give Freeman this much: he's self-aware. Give him this, too: he has outstanding taste in walk-up music, as his every plate appearance summons some premium Chris Stapleton. You know the one: *Say the word and he'll be there for you/J-Ram, Freeman will be your WAR's parachute.*

Tyler Freeman SS Born: 05/21/99 Age: 22 Bats: R Throws: R Height: 6'0" Weight: 170 Origin: Round 2, 2017 Draft (#71 overall)

YEAR	TEAM	LVL	AGE	PA	R	2B	3B	HR	RBI	BB	K	SB	CS	Whiff%	AVG/OBP/SLG	DRC+	BABIP	BRR	FRAA	WARP
2018	MV	SS	19	301	49	29	4	2	38	8	22	14	3		.352/.405/.511	180	.372	3.5	SS(52): -0.1, 2B(10): -0.2	2.7
2019	LC	LO-A	20	272	51	16	3	3	24	18	28	11	4		.292/.382/.424	141	.320	2.6	SS(57): 0.5, 2B(3): -0.2	2.6
2019	LYN	HI-A	20	275	38	16	2	0	20	8	25	8	1		.319/.354/.397	129	.350	1.2	SS(57): -1.0, 2B(3): 0.1	1.9
2021 FS	CLE	MLB	22	600	60	28	3	7	57	30	97	10	3		.259/.318/.366	90	.303	1.5	2B -4, SS 2	1.2
2021 DC	CLE	MLB	22	66	6	3	0	0	6	3	10	1	0		.259/.318/.366	90	.303	0.2	2B 0, SS 0	0.1

Comparables: José Rondón, Wilmer Flores, Luis Sardiñas

For most prospects, the loss of the 2020 season meant an almost total absence of information. It only grew the legend of Freeman, who seemed to generate more buzz from the alternate site than anyone else. Sporadic Twitter reports—including from a family member—indicated that he was hitting for more power, producing at least eight home runs in game action. What any of that means when we don't know any of the other context, from number of plate appearances to most of the opposing pitchers, is much harder to say. What we *can* say—with confidence—is a vacancy will be opening up in Cleveland's infield soon, probably by the time you read this. Freeman is a prime candidate to claim it as his own before long.

Andrés Giménez SS Born: 09/04/98 Age: 22 Bats: L Throws: R Height: 5'11" Weight: 161 Origin: International Free Agent, 2015

YEAR	TEAM	LVL	AGE	PA	R	2B	3B	HR	RBI	BB	K	SB	CS	Whiff%	AVG/OBP/SLG	DRC+	BABIP	BRR	FRAA	WARP
2018	STL	HI-A	19	351	43	20	4	6	30	22	70	28	11		.282/.348/.432	112	.343	3.4	SS(83): 14.2, 2B(2): -0.1	3.1
2018	BNG	AA	19	153	19	9	1	0	16	9	22	10	3		.277/.344/.358	100	.330	1.2	SS(36): -1.3, 2B(1): 0.2	0.4
2019	BNG	AA	20	479	54	22	5	9	37	24	102	28	16		.250/.309/.387	91	.306	-2.9	SS(112): -0.7	1.3
2020	NYM	MLB	22	132	22	3	2	3	12	7	28	8	1	25.7%	.263/.333/.398	94	.318	0.6	SS(23): -2.5, 2B(19): 0.1, 3B(10): 0.2	0.1
2021 FS	CLE	MLB	22	600	62	28	4	14	64	33	137	20	9	25.7%	.248/.310/.390	89	.308	-2.6	SS 6, 2B 0	1.5
2021 DC	CLE	MLB	22	533	55	24	3	12	57	30	122	17	8	25.7%	.248/.310/.390	89	.308	-2.3	SS 5	1.3

Comparables: Carter Kieboom, Franklin Barreto, José Iglesias

Giménez lost a bit of his luster when selling out for power in 2019, seeing an overall decrease in offensive production. So it was something of a surprise when he opened up the 2020 season as a member of the gameday roster, initially serving as a speed-and-defense complement to Robinson Canó, who possessed neither. By the end of the season, it quickly became clear that he had surpassed incumbent shortstop Amed Rosario in virtually every facet of shortstop play, and getting more comfortable with his swing has at least partially rectified the mistakes of his down season in Binghamton. No longer a rookie, Giménez's profile is back to where it was at the peak of his prospect powers: a do-it-all shortstop without a key carrying tool, but with above-average skills across the board. A useful player that is more than the sum of his parts, now all he needs is everyday playing time at the highest level to tease out if his ultimate role will be second-division starter, or perhaps something more dynamic. He'll get that time in Cleveland as the centerpiece of the trade that saw Francisco Lindor and Carlos Carrasco head to Flushing.

Austin Hedges C Born: 08/18/92 Age: 28 Bats: R Throws: R Height: 6'1" Weight: 223 Origin: Round 2, 2011 Draft (#82 overall)

YEAR	TEAM	LVL	AGE	PA	R	2B	3B	HR	RBI	BB	K	SB	CS	Whiff%	AVG/OBP/SLG	DRC+	BABIP	BRR	FRAA	WARP
2018	ELP	AAA	25	31	7	3	0	3	11	3	9	0	0		.407/.452/.852	151	.500	0.0	C(6): 0.5	0.3
2018	SD	MLB	25	326	29	14	2	14	37	21	90	3	0	28.0%	.231/.282/.429	88	.280	-2.1	C(83): 11.8	2.1
2019	SD	MLB	26	347	28	9	0	11	36	27	109	1	0	33.7%	.176/.252/.311	61	.228	0.9	C(95): 28.2, 3B(2): -0.0	2.9
2020	SD	MLB	28	71	7	1	0	3	6	6	18	1	1	20.9%	.158/.258/.333	75	.162	0.0	C(28): 0.5	0.3
2020	CLE	MLB	28	12	0	0	0	0	0	0	5	0	0	40.9%	.083/.083/.083	73	.143		C(6): -0.0	0.0
2021 FS	CLE	MLB	28	600	61	23	1	22	66	39	174	3	1	30.4%	.206/.267/.374	70	.257	-0.9	C 20, 3B 0	2.2
2021 DC	CLE	MLB	28	266	27	10	0	9	29	17	77	1	0	30.4%	.206/.267/.374	70	.257	-0.4	C 12	1.3

Comparables: Humberto Cota, Ron Karkovice, Jesus Flores

Hedges' work with leather confronts the viewer with their own perceptions, forcing them to consider the very nature of the strike zone and the intersection between catcher and umpire. He blurs the distinction between ball and strike, often turning the former into the latter with skillful and wilful manipulation of space. It's a nice contrast from his lackluster work with the lumber, which makes it hard to go all Aldous Huxley with things. But behind the plate? Oh, behind the plate the artist embeds us in the constant conflict between command and chaos and the imagined and the real, leaving the observer to wonder what other dualities can exist.

YEAR	TEAM	P. COUNT	FRM RUNS	BLK RUNS	THRW RUNS	TOT RUNS
2018	SD	12042	13.0	0.1	-0.4	12.7
2019	SD	13488	26.0	1.5	0.3	27.8
2020	SD	2971	1.7	0.4	0.0	2.1
2020	CLE	585	0.4	0.2	0.0	0.5
2021	CLE	9620	10.4	0.8	0.2	11.3

Cesar Hernandez 2B Born: 05/23/90 Age: 31 Bats: S Throws: R Height: 5'10" Weight: 195 Origin: International Free Agent, 2006

YEAR	TEAM	LVL	AGE	PA	R	2B	3B	HR	RBI	BB	K	SB	CS	Whiff%	AVG/OBP/SLG	DRC+	BABIP	BRR	FRAA	WARP
2018	PHI	MLB	28	708	91	15	3	15	60	95	155	19	6	20.3%	.253/.356/.362	101	.315	2.0	2B(154): 3.7	2.9
2019	PHI	MLB	29	667	77	31	3	14	71	45	100	9	2	17.2%	.279/.333/.408	90	.313	-1.2	2B(157): -4.7	0.8
2020	CLE	MLB	30	261	35	20	0	3	20	24	57	0	0	20.1%	.283/.355/.408	92	.364	-0.3	2B(58): 5.3	1.1
2021 FS	CLE	MLB	31	600	76	28	2	11	51	62	132	13	5	18.9%	.270/.351/.396	107	.341	-0.2	2B -2, SS 0	2.6

Comparables: Robby Thompson, Tony Graffanino, Akinori Iwamura

The Department of Statistical Quirks had such fun with the Khris Davis .247 streak that we figure it's time to find out just how esoteric a fact can be and remain entertaining.

Warning: it's about fielding percentage. Are you ready? Hernández repeated his .981 fielding percentage at second base for the *fifth* consecutive year, a feat never before accomplished by any qualified position player. Should we make a t-shirt to celebrate the occasion? All right, fine, .981 24/7 doesn't quite have the same ring to it.

Still, is the consistency more fun because it belongs to Hernández, a player frequently called out for his miscues? Do the ongoing baserunning errors (Hernández led the league in outs on the bases) make it even more implausible that he owns a record of this nature? Is it fun because it's actually surprising that in thousands upon thousands of position player seasons, this has never happened before?

The true test of whether this fact is fun will come next fall, when we either feel the impulse to check Hernández's fielding percentage, or we don't. Then, and only then, we'll have our answer.

Daniel Johnson RF Born: 07/11/95 Age: 25 Bats: L Throws: L Height: 5'10" Weight: 200 Origin: Round 5, 2016 Draft (#154 overall)

YEAR	TEAM	LVL	AGE	PA	R	2B	3B	HR	RBI	BB	K	SB	CS	Whiff%	AVG/OBP/SLG	DRC+	BABIP	BRR	FRAA	WARP
2018	HBG	AA	22	391	48	19	7	6	31	23	90	21	4		.267/.321/.410	95	.338	-2.3	RF(54): 6.3, CF(33): -2.9, LF(4): -0.7	0.2
2019	AKR	AA	23	167	25	7	2	10	33	16	39	6	3		.253/.337/.534	121	.276	-2.3	CF(24): -2.3, RF(10): -0.3, LF(4): -0.6	0.2
2019	COL	AAA	23	380	51	27	5	9	44	34	79	6	7		.306/.371/.496	122	.370	-1.5	RF(48): 6.4, CF(21): 1.2, LF(9): 0.0	2.4
2020	CLE	MLB	25	13	0	0	0	0	0	1	5	0	0	42.9%	.083/.154/.083	77	.143		RF(4): -0.6, LF(1): -0.1	-0.1
2021 FS	CLE	MLB	25	600	59	24	3	18	65	39	168	11	4	42.9%	.231/.293/.389	86	.298	0.7	RF 4, LF 0	1.1
2021 DC	CLE	MLB	25	266	26	10	1	8	28	17	74	5	2	42.9%	.231/.293/.389	86	.298	0.3	RF 2	0.4

Comparables: Wladimir Balentien, Ben Francisco, Corey Hart

For as bad as Cleveland's outfield was, it's disappointing that the toolsy, oft-injured Johnson was provided only 13 plate appearances to provide a jolt. Considering the brevity of the sample, we'll err on the optimistic side and say Cleveland just wanted to get a look at their older options rather than it being an indictment on Johnson and his long-term prospects.

────────── ★ ★ ★ *2021 Top 101 Prospect* **#52** ★ ★ ★ ──────────

Nolan Jones 3B Born: 05/07/98 Age: 23 Bats: L Throws: R Height: 6'2" Weight: 185 Origin: Round 2, 2016 Draft (#55 overall)

YEAR	TEAM	LVL	AGE	PA	R	2B	3B	HR	RBI	BB	K	SB	CS	Whiff%	AVG/OBP/SLG	DRC+	BABIP	BRR	FRAA	WARP
2018	LC	LO-A	20	389	46	12	0	16	49	63	97	2	1		.279/.393/.464	150	.347	-0.9	3B(76): -4.1	2.3
2018	LYN	HI-A	20	130	23	9	0	3	17	26	34	0	0		.298/.438/.471	154	.418	0.1	3B(28): -0.3	0.9
2019	LYN	HI-A	21	324	48	12	1	7	41	65	84	5	3		.286/.435/.425	172	.396	-1.4	3B(72): -3.4	2.8
2019	AKR	AA	21	211	33	10	2	8	22	31	63	2	0		.253/.370/.466	149	.346	0.8	3B(44): 0.0	1.8
2021 FS	CLE	MLB	23	600	68	27	2	17	62	68	217	1	0		.235/.326/.393	99	.364	0.0	3B -1	1.0
2021 DC	CLE	MLB	23	199	22	9	0	5	20	22	72	0	0		.235/.326/.393	99	.364	0.0	3B 0, RF 0	0.4

Comparables: Austin Riley, Matt Davidson, Tyler O'Neill

Jones' defense at third base is not why the team is excited about adding him to the lineup. Rather, he's been projected to slide away from the hot corner for most of his pro career. That might happen before he takes a grounder in the big leagues, with Cleveland giving him some reps in the outfield at fall instructs. Lord knows they could use Jones' bat in the lineup as soon as possible.

Sandy León C Born: 03/13/89 Age: 32 Bats: S Throws: R Height: 5'10" Weight: 235 Origin: International Free Agent, 2007

YEAR	TEAM	LVL	AGE	PA	R	2B	3B	HR	RBI	BB	K	SB	CS	Whiff%	AVG/OBP/SLG	DRC+	BABIP	BRR	FRAA	WARP
2018	BOS	MLB	29	288	30	12	0	5	22	15	75	1	0	22.7%	.177/.232/.279	57	.226	-0.7	C(87): 11.7	1.1
2019	WOR	AAA	30	26	2	0	0	0	0	1	6	0	1		.120/.154/.120	30	.158	-0.5	C(7): 0.8	-0.1
2019	BOS	MLB	30	191	14	3	0	5	19	13	47	0	0	20.4%	.192/.251/.297	65	.231	-0.2	C(65): 2.9, 1B(1): -0.0	0.4
2020	CLE	MLB	31	81	4	1	0	2	4	14	21	0	0	30.6%	.136/.296/.242	90	.163	-0.4	C(24): 0.7	0.3
2021 FS	CLE	MLB	32	600	58	22	1	14	58	51	164	1	0	24.0%	.211/.287/.336	71	.276	-0.6	C 2, 1B 0	0.4

Comparables: Martín Maldonado, Todd Pratt, Bob Geren

YEAR	TEAM	P. COUNT	FRM RUNS	BLK RUNS	THRW RUNS	TOT RUNS
2018	BOS	11245	11.6	0.1	0.1	11.8
2019	BOS	8122	4.8	-1.0	-0.2	3.6
2020	CLE	3027	1.1	-0.1	0.0	1.0
2021	CLE	16650	6.6	-1.6	-0.2	4.8

Terry Francona is prone to describing León as a future manager. He, along with the rest of Cleveland's catchers, sure hit like skippers in 2020. Cleveland's catchers collectively hit .135/.251/.197, the all-time worst performance of any position relative to the league OPS. There's no doubt that León's luck on balls in play was rotten. He also had a terribly inconsistent routine, going from Yadi-esque usage with six consecutive starts in mid-August, to dealing with more important matters on the family medical emergency list, then receiving only sporadic appearances in September after Cleveland acquired Hedges. Despite all that, León should take solace in knowing he was Cleveland's best producer behind the plate—and that if and when he's done playing, he'll probably prove Francona's assertion about his future correct.

Jordan Luplow RF   Born: 09/26/93   Age: 27   Bats: R   Throws: R   Height: 6'1"   Weight: 195   Origin: Round 3, 2014 Draft (#100 overall)

YEAR	TEAM	LVL	AGE	PA	R	2B	3B	HR	RBI	BB	K	SB	CS	Whiff%	AVG/OBP/SLG	DRC+	BABIP	BRR	FRAA	WARP
2018	IND	AAA	24	357	41	25	3	8	49	39	64	7	2		.287/.367/.462	140	.336	-1.7	LF(41): 4.3, RF(38): 1.4	2.3
2018	PIT	MLB	24	103	16	1	3	3	7	10	18	2	2	22.9%	.185/.272/.359	84	.197	-0.4	LF(16): 5.4, RF(11): -0.3, CF(3): 0.1	0.6
2019	COL	AAA	25	57	12	3	0	2	7	10	14	2	1		.311/.456/.511	125	.414	-0.5	LF(10): 1.5, RF(2): -0.2	0.4
2019	CLE	MLB	25	261	42	15	1	15	38	33	61	3	2	26.4%	.276/.372/.551	125	.313	0.3	RF(42): 3.4, LF(34): 0.3, CF(4): -0.0	1.9
2020	CLE	MLB	27	92	8	5	1	2	8	12	19	0	1	19.9%	.192/.304/.359	97	.224	0.5	LF(21): -1.8, RF(9): 0.3	0.1
2021 FS	CLE	MLB	27	600	67	24	2	24	73	64	140	2	1	24.0%	.230/.322/.426	104	.268	0.2	RF -8, LF 3	1.4
2021 DC	CLE	MLB	27	333	37	13	1	13	40	35	78	1	0	24.0%	.230/.322/.426	104	.268	0.1	RF -5, LF 2	0.7

Comparables: Justin Upton, Dan Thomas, Brad Wilkerson

They say you can't predict baseball, but they probably weren't thinking about Luplow's platoon numbers when they said it, as he remains resolutely reliable in that facet of the game. Another year of solid performance against southpaws was undermined by his even more dependable inability to hit same-handed pitching. Luplow now owns the largest platoon split for a right-handed batter in major league history, with 393 points separating his damage against lefties from his failure against righties. (Pertinent fact: he is yet to record a hit against an offspeed pitch thrown by a righty in his major league career.) Despite that, Luplow defied probability and almost extended Cleveland's playoff run with a game-tying pinch-hit double against right-hander Jonathan Loaisiga. Maybe they were right after all.

Oscar Mercado RF   Born: 12/16/94   Age: 26   Bats: R   Throws: R   Height: 6'2"   Weight: 197   Origin: Round 2, 2013 Draft (#57 overall)

YEAR	TEAM	LVL	AGE	PA	R	2B	3B	HR	RBI	BB	K	SB	CS	Whiff%	AVG/OBP/SLG	DRC+	BABIP	BRR	FRAA	WARP
2018	COL	AAA	23	119	12	5	1	0	5	13	23	6	4		.252/.342/.320	94	.325	-2.2	CF(24): -0.8, RF(7): 0.3, LF(1): 0.1	-0.1
2018	MEM	AAA	23	427	73	21	1	8	42	36	64	31	8		.285/.351/.408	108	.323	8.1	CF(89): -2.6, LF(5): -0.5, RF(2): -0.1	1.8
2019	COL	AAA	24	140	24	10	1	4	15	16	32	14	3		.294/.396/.496	129	.373	1.1	CF(19): 5.4, LF(5): 1.1, RF(4): 0.2	1.5
2019	CLE	MLB	24	482	70	25	3	15	54	28	84	15	4	23.4%	.269/.318/.443	97	.300	2.3	CF(82): 8.3, LF(24): -1.6, RF(9): -1.1	2.2
2020	CLE	MLB	26	93	6	1	0	1	6	5	27	3	0	29.8%	.128/.174/.174	61	.169	0.9	CF(21): 3.8, LF(12): 0.3	0.2
2021 FS	CLE	MLB	26	600	60	28	2	15	63	40	141	22	8	24.9%	.234/.295/.376	82	.288	-0.9	CF 2, LF -1	0.5
2021 DC	CLE	MLB	26	399	40	18	1	10	41	27	94	15	5	24.9%	.234/.295/.376	82	.288	-0.6	CF 1, LF -1	0.4

Comparables: Devon White, Billy Conigliaro, Luis Matos

As sequels go, Mercado's sophomore effort was the worst since *Speed 2: Cruise Control*. It made about an equal amount of sense. Mercado's performance was so lifeless that even Jason Patric could emulate it. The action sequences he orchestrated on the basepaths and in the field that made him a hit in the first place were still present, but they were fewer in number and harder to get amped up about with the sheer dross he offered at the plate. Cleveland banished him from the limelight by mid-August, yet he seemed no better when he returned for September. There's enough here to greenlight a third installment. After that, we'll see.

Owen Miller SS   Born: 11/15/96   Age: 24   Bats: R   Throws: R   Height: 5'11"   Weight: 197   Origin: Round 3, 2018 Draft (#84 overall)

YEAR	TEAM	LVL	AGE	PA	R	2B	3B	HR	RBI	BB	K	SB	CS	Whiff%	AVG/OBP/SLG	DRC+	BABIP	BRR	FRAA	WARP
2018	TRI	SS	21	216	22	8	3	2	20	15	24	4	4		.335/.395/.440	158	.369	-2.5	SS(43): 3.3	1.4
2018	FW	LO-A	21	114	18	11	0	2	13	4	17	0	0		.336/.368/.495	134	.382	0.9	3B(13): -2.8, SS(7): -0.4	0.4
2019	AMA	AA	22	560	76	28	2	13	68	46	86	5	5		.290/.355/.430	112	.328	1.3	SS(71): 5.1, 2B(48): 0.5, 3B(6): -0.3	3.4
2021 FS	CLE	MLB	24	600	63	28	2	13	63	37	129	1	0		.258/.313/.390	93	.315	-0.3	2B 3, 3B 0	1.7
2021 DC	CLE	MLB	24	33	3	1	0	0	3	2	7	0	0		.258/.313/.390	93	.315	0.0	2B 0	0.1

Comparables: Gregorio Petit, Chris Valaika, Eugenio Suárez

Both Cleveland shortstop prospect archetypes came over in the Clevinger deal. Along with a raw, projectable high-ceiling type in Arias, they received Miller, a polished hitter with advanced bat-to-ball skills who's likely to be contributing in the majors sometime in 2021.

Tyler Naquin RF   Born: 04/24/91   Age: 30   Bats: L   Throws: R   Height: 6'2"   Weight: 195   Origin: Round 1, 2012 Draft (#15 overall)

YEAR	TEAM	LVL	AGE	PA	R	2B	3B	HR	RBI	BB	K	SB	CS	Whiff%	AVG/OBP/SLG	DRC+	BABIP	BRR	FRAA	WARP
2018	CLE	MLB	27	183	22	7	0	3	23	6	42	1	1	20.1%	.264/.295/.356	78	.331	1.0	RF(39): 5.2, CF(19): 0.2, LF(5): -0.4	0.6
2019	CLE	MLB	28	294	34	19	0	10	34	14	66	4	2	25.1%	.288/.325/.467	93	.345	-0.3	RF(68): 12.2, LF(15): 4.1	2.0
2020	CLE	MLB	29	141	15	8	1	4	20	5	40	0	1	30.9%	.218/.248/.383	75	.275	-0.3	RF(39): 1.9	0.2
2021 FS	CLE	MLB	30	600	61	31	2	18	68	43	170	5	2	26.4%	.249/.310/.415	95	.328	-0.9	RF 11, CF 4	2.9

Comparables: Cory Snyder, Jay Bruce, Clete Thomas

The 60-game season left us onlookers more desperate than usual for indicators of surprise breakouts. A combination of small-sample theater and the dire state of the Cleveland offense conspired to cast Naquin in the shockingly premature role of offensive savior. He recovered from a toe fracture to quickly become an everyday player by producing the second-best OPS in a lineup that could hardly be bothered to field more than a few capable sticks at a time. That was 20 games in; by the time that sample doubled, it was obvious that he was not an emerging offensive juggernaut, or even a reliable above-average bat. He was simply the same Tyler Naquin who seems incapable of producing at a tolerable level for long.

Bo Naylor C   Born: 02/21/00   Age: 21   Bats: L   Throws: R   Height: 6'0"   Weight: 195   Origin: Round 1, 2018 Draft (#29 overall)

YEAR	TEAM	LVL	AGE	PA	R	2B	3B	HR	RBI	BB	K	SB	CS	Whiff%	AVG/OBP/SLG	DRC+	BABIP	BRR	FRAA	WARP
2018	INDB	ROK	18	139	17	3	3	2	17	21	28	5	1		.274/.381/.402	126	.341	0.3	C(19): -0.4, 3B(5): -0.7	0.3
2019	LC	LO-A	19	453	60	18	10	11	65	43	104	7	5		.243/.313/.421	97	.296	0.9	C(85): 3.4	2.2
2021 FS	CLE	MLB	21	600	52	26	5	12	58	41	191	5	2		.221/.277/.355	72	.314	1.8	C 1, 3B 0	0.6

Comparables: Jorge Alfaro, Joe Benson, Greg Golson

The unconventional season might have accelerated Naylor's development in at least one regard: it afforded him the opportunity to work with more advanced pitchers than he'd have encountered in A-ball. He doesn't need to rush to ensure a family reunion, either, as recently-acquired brother Josh is set to be in the organization for the next half-decade.

Josh Naylor RF   Born: 06/22/97   Age: 24   Bats: L   Throws: L   Height: 5'11"   Weight: 250   Origin: Round 1, 2015 Draft (#12 overall)

YEAR	TEAM	LVL	AGE	PA	R	2B	3B	HR	RBI	BB	K	SB	CS	Whiff%	AVG/OBP/SLG	DRC+	BABIP	BRR	FRAA	WARP
2018	SA	AA	21	574	72	22	1	17	74	64	69	5	5		.297/.383/.447	138	.317	-5.1	LF(89): -20.4, 1B(29): 0.6	-0.4
2019	ELP	AAA	22	252	51	20	1	10	42	28	30	1	0		.314/.389/.547	117	.326	0.0	RF(29): -2.2, LF(22): 1.0	1.0
2019	SD	MLB	22	279	29	15	0	8	32	25	64	1	1	22.2%	.249/.315/.403	81	.302	-0.2	LF(33): 0.7, RF(31): -4.1	-0.3
2020	SD	MLB	23	38	4	0	1	1	4	1	4	1	0	18.6%	.278/.316/.417	84	.290	0.4	RF(4): -0.4, 1B(3): 0.2, LF(3): -0.0	0.0
2020	CLE	MLB	23	66	9	3	0	0	2	4	8	0	0	13.9%	.230/.277/.279	82	.264	1.6	LF(19): -0.6, 1B(2): -0.0	0.1
2021 FS	CLE	MLB	24	600	62	24	1	17	69	47	113	3	1	20.1%	.246/.311/.394	92	.282	-0.4	LF -16, 1B 0	-1.1
2021 DC	CLE	MLB	24	433	45	18	1	12	49	34	82	2	0	20.1%	.246/.311/.394	92	.282	-0.3	LF -12, 1B 0	-0.6

Comparables: Domonic Brown, Geoff Jenkins, Alex Gordon

If Tyler Naquin's rise and fall was exaggerated because of the 60-game campaign, Naylor took the effect to another level by erasing a season of poor production with a single game. He did nothing to spark life into the moribund Cleveland outfield upon arriving from San Diego, failing to hit a homer in a Cleveland uniform—until the playoffs, that is. Naylor marked his postseason debut with four hits in Game 1 of the American League Wild Card Series, with three of those coming against Gerrit Cole. He later became the first player in history to record a hit in his first five postseason plate appearances when he doubled in Game 2. The decision to pinch-hit for him during the final frames of that contest sparked so much ire that one might have thought his season-long line resembled that of Ted Williams and not...well, himself. To be clear, Naylor is young and talented enough for this to represent a turning point. The challenge for him is to have his monster raw power and his impressive contact skills align more frequently. He should get the chance as Cleveland's regular first baseman.

Roberto Pérez C   Born: 12/23/88   Age: 32   Bats: R   Throws: R   Height: 5'11"   Weight: 220   Origin: Round 33, 2008 Draft (#1011 overall)

YEAR	TEAM	LVL	AGE	PA	R	2B	3B	HR	RBI	BB	K	SB	CS	Whiff%	AVG/OBP/SLG	DRC+	BABIP	BRR	FRAA	WARP
2018	CLE	MLB	29	210	16	9	1	2	19	21	70	1	0	32.5%	.168/.256/.263	52	.257	-0.2	C(58): 11.1	0.9
2019	CLE	MLB	30	449	46	9	1	24	63	45	127	0	0	30.4%	.239/.321/.452	100	.285	-1.1	C(118): 25.7	4.7
2020	CLE	MLB	32	110	6	2	0	1	5	11	38	0	0	30.1%	.165/.264/.216	57	.259	-0.7	C(32): -0.3	-0.1
2021 FS	CLE	MLB	32	600	61	21	1	16	59	68	197	1	0	30.6%	.204/.302/.347	80	.291	-0.5	C 19	2.8
2021 DC	CLE	MLB	32	333	34	12	0	9	32	38	109	0	0	30.6%	.204/.302/.347	80	.291	-0.3	C 14	2.0

Comparables: Todd Pratt, Kelly Stinnett, Jason Castro

YEAR	TEAM	P. COUNT	FRM RUNS	BLK RUNS	THRW RUNS	TOT RUNS
2018	CLE	7976	10.9	1.6	-0.2	12.2
2019	CLE	16305	15.5	8.8	1.5	25.8
2020	CLE	4053	1.3	0.5	-0.3	1.4
2021	CLE	12025	11.9	1.4	1.5	14.8

There was little opportunity for Pérez to prove that his unexpected offensive breakout was more than a one-year fluke. He suffered a strained shoulder in his first game, necessitating an IL stint, and he never recovered at the plate thereafter. The distinct similarity to Pérez's pre-breakout line (minus a home run or two) further confounds the matter. Fortunately, offensive production is not what he's paid for. Management validated as much by picking up his $5.5 million option on the strength of his defensive prowess, which earned him a second Gold Glove Award in a row. It would be a useful bonus for Cleveland if Pérez returned to slugging 20-plus homers, but they seem likely to remain devoted to him based on what he does behind the plate rather than at it.

Yasiel Puig RF   Born: 12/07/90   Age: 30   Bats: R   Throws: R   Height: 6'2"   Weight: 240   Origin: International Free Agent, 2012

YEAR	TEAM	LVL	AGE	PA	R	2B	3B	HR	RBI	BB	K	SB	CS	Whiff%	AVG/OBP/SLG	DRC+	BABIP	BRR	FRAA	WARP
2018	LAD	MLB	27	444	60	21	1	23	63	36	87	15	5	24.2%	.267/.327/.494	120	.286	2.4	RF(118): -4.5	1.9
2019	CLE	MLB	28	207	25	15	1	2	23	21	44	5	2	26.4%	.297/.377/.423	101	.380	-1.5	RF(48): 2.7	0.6
2019	CIN	MLB	28	404	51	15	1	22	61	23	89	14	5	29.4%	.252/.302/.475	101	.272	-2.8	RF(98): 2.1	0.9
2021 FS	CLE	MLB	30	600	72	25	1	22	75	53	135	14	5	27.2%	.250/.324/.429	108	.294	-1.4	RF -3	1.6

Comparables: Larry Walker, Matt Joyce, Jason Lane

Since his debut with the Dodgers in 2013, Cuban émigré Puig has been one of the most polarizing players. His talent is undeniable—when healthy and on his game, he's one the few genuine five-tool players in the majors. Off the field, his eccentricities have rubbed some clubhouses, writers and fans the wrong way, though much of this opprobrium reads as thinly-veiled racism toward a player, and personality, that refuses to fall in line with the normative expectations of "traditional" (read: white) baseball culture. Unfortunately, there was no on-field Puig in 2020 to remind us of the good times, and Puig only made the news in more troubling ways. A COVID-19 infection nullified a contract agreement with Atlanta, and even more disturbing, in October Puig was sued by a woman claiming that the then-Dodger sexually assaulted her at a Lakers game in 2018. Puig's future has never been less certain, but the skills should be intact, presuming he can find a team willing to show them off to the best effect.

José Ramírez 3B Born: 09/17/92 Age: 28 Bats: S Throws: R Height: 5'9" Weight: 190 Origin: International Free Agent, 2009

YEAR	TEAM	LVL	AGE	PA	R	2B	3B	HR	RBI	BB	K	SB	CS	Whiff%	AVG/OBP/SLG	DRC+	BABIP	BRR	FRAA	WARP
2018	CLE	MLB	25	698	110	38	4	39	105	106	80	34	6	13.8%	.270/.387/.552	146	.252	5.2	3B(137): -3.5, 2B(16): -0.7	6.6
2019	CLE	MLB	26	542	68	33	3	23	83	52	74	24	4	14.3%	.255/.327/.479	115	.256	2.6	3B(126): 2.4	3.6
2020	CLE	MLB	28	254	45	16	1	17	46	31	43	10	3	16.6%	.292/.386/.607	146	.294	0.8	3B(57): -10.8	1.1
2021 FS	CLE	MLB	28	600	88	34	2	30	88	65	92	21	5	14.9%	.278/.363/.523	137	.289	5.0	3B -2, 2B -1	4.5
2021 DC	CLE	MLB	28	599	88	34	2	29	88	65	92	21	5	14.9%	.278/.363/.523	137	.289	5.0	3B -2, 2B -1	4.4

Comparables: Edgardo Alfonzo, Morgan Ensberg, Chipper Jones

You ought to know by now that Ramírez is an obsessed Mario Kart player. It's perhaps fair to write, then, that he succeeded in avoiding the banana peel that caused him to spin off course early in 2019. Instead, he followed up his second-half comeback by racing out of the blocks with a turbo-charged first week. Although Ramírez later fell back to the pack during the middle portion of the season, he shelled opposition pitchers at every turn down the stretch and bolted back to the top of the leaderboard to assert himself in the MVP race once more. Defensive metrics were divided over whether or not he bombed in the field, but he remains a star in the box.

Franmil Reyes RF Born: 07/07/95 Age: 26 Bats: R Throws: R Height: 6'5" Weight: 265 Origin: International Free Agent, 2012

YEAR	TEAM	LVL	AGE	PA	R	2B	3B	HR	RBI	BB	K	SB	CS	Whiff%	AVG/OBP/SLG	DRC+	BABIP	BRR	FRAA	WARP
2018	ELP	AAA	22	250	50	11	1	16	52	37	59	0	0		.324/.428/.614	165	.382	1.9	RF(46): -2.2	2.0
2018	SD	MLB	22	285	36	9	0	16	31	24	80	0	0	31.6%	.280/.340/.498	111	.345	0.3	RF(75): -7.1	0.3
2019	CLE	MLB	23	194	26	10	0	10	35	18	63	0	0	39.7%	.237/.304/.468	105	.301	-0.8	RF(3): 0.6	0.4
2019	SD	MLB	23	354	43	9	0	27	46	29	93	0	0	34.7%	.255/.314/.536	114	.268	0.4	RF(83): 1.4	1.6
2020	CLE	MLB	25	241	27	10	0	9	34	24	69	0	0	38.5%	.275/.344/.450	97	.355	0.0	LF(1): -0.1	0.4
2021 FS	CLE	MLB	25	600	73	24	1	29	88	55	174	0	0	36.5%	.251/.324/.465	112	.316	-0.9	RF 0	2.2
2021 DC	CLE	MLB	25	566	69	23	1	27	83	52	164	0	0	36.5%	.251/.324/.465	112	.316	-0.8		2.0

Comparables: Wily Mo Pena, Jay Buhner, Victor Diaz

Reyes atoned for a slow start with a beastly August. When he started September by collecting eight hits in two games, his seasonal OPS stood at .962. That was as good as it got. Reyes did not hit another home run until the season's final day, at which point his numbers were almost identical to the year prior. The most consistent elements of his game at this point are the absurdity of his home runs, often mammoth in nature, and of his defense—remember, he's a full-time DH for a reason. If or until Reyes can overcome his streakiness, he's going to remain a frustrating talent who seems capable of much more than what shows up under his WAR column.

Brayan Rocchio SS Born: 01/13/01 Age: 20 Bats: S Throws: R Height: 5'10" Weight: 150 Origin: International Free Agent, 2017

YEAR	TEAM	LVL	AGE	PA	R	2B	3B	HR	RBI	BB	K	SB	CS	Whiff%	AVG/OBP/SLG	DRC+	BABIP	BRR	FRAA	WARP
2018	INDB	ROK	17	158	21	10	1	1	17	10	17	14	8		.343/.389/.448	165	.378	1.2	SS(26): 5.2, 3B(8): -1.1, 2B(1): -0.1	1.5
2018	DSL IND1	ROK	17	111	19	2	3	1	12	5	14	8	5		.323/.391/.434	137	.369	-1.0	SS(14): -0.2, 2B(8): 0.6, 3B(1): 0.5	0.6
2019	MV	SS	18	295	33	12	3	5	27	20	40	14	8		.250/.310/.373	106	.276	-1.8	SS(62): 5.5, 2B(7): 0.6	1.8
2021 FS	CLE	MLB	20	600	50	26	3	9	55	26	139	24	13		.237/.277/.347	70	.299	-8.1	SS 5, 2B 0	-0.8

Comparables: Sergio Alcántara, Willi Castro, Amed Rosario

If you were wondering where Cleveland's next compact, switch-hitting middle infielder with good contact skills was going to come from, Rocchio is a leading contender. He's not the *only* contender, but Cleveland is hardly likely to object if they end up with two in the lineup again.

Amed Rosario SS Born: 11/20/95 Age: 25 Bats: R Throws: R Height: 6'2" Weight: 190 Origin: International Free Agent, 2012

YEAR	TEAM	LVL	AGE	PA	R	2B	3B	HR	RBI	BB	K	SB	CS	Whiff%	AVG/OBP/SLG	DRC+	BABIP	BRR	FRAA	WARP
2018	NYM	MLB	22	592	76	26	8	9	51	29	119	24	11	26.1%	.256/.295/.381	82	.310	2.8	SS(146): -6.6	1.0
2019	NYM	MLB	23	655	75	30	7	15	72	31	124	19	10	24.2%	.287/.323/.432	95	.338	1.5	SS(152): -6.0, LF(1): -0.1	2.3
2020	NYM	MLB	25	147	20	3	1	4	15	4	34	0	1	24.3%	.252/.272/.371	68	.305	0.1	SS(44): -5.8	-0.8
2021 FS	CLE	MLB	25	600	63	25	5	13	62	30	141	14	6	24.7%	.261/.303/.398	89	.327	1.9	SS -1, 3B 0	1.2
2021 DC	CLE	MLB	25	499	52	21	4	11	51	25	117	12	5	24.7%	.261/.303/.398	89	.327	1.6	2B 0, SS -1	1.2

Comparables: Josh Rutledge, Ian Desmond, Michael Young

With Andrés Giménez looming on the horizon, the abridged 2020 season may have been Rosario's last chance to establish himself as a first-division starting shortstop. Despite a promising 2019 campaign as a 23-year-old, Rosario's 2020 accentuated his flaws and masked his strengths over a disappointing two months. His overaggressiveness at the plate was even more pronounced, as no player in the National League took a free pass less frequently. Oft credited for his athleticism, Rosario only attempted to steal a single base all season (he was thrown out) and his defense at shortstop continued to leave much to be desired. For years, a move to center field has been bandied about, and with this performance behind him, it might not be a bad idea to pick up a few more positions: a super-utility profile might be the new ceiling for this former top-10 prospect. Whethere he takes the field on the dirt or in the grass will be up to new management after Rosario was included in the four-player package that saw Francisco Lindor and Carlos Carrasco head to New York.

Carson Tucker SS   Born: 01/24/02   Age: 19   Bats: R   Throws: R   Height: 6'2"   Weight: 180   Origin: Round 1, 2020 Draft (#23 overall)

As if graduating from high school during a pandemic wasn't stressful enough, Tucker has a whole lot else on his plate to manage. He was selected one pick earlier than his brother, Cole, but it's hard to brag about that sort of thing given that Cole is the one on a big-league roster. (Okay, so it's just the Pirates; still!) Tucker also has to hear about how he's the first shortstop Cleveland has taken in round one since 2011, when they snagged some youngster from Puerto Rico—Francisco something or another. Anyway, provided Tucker can block out all the noise around his selection, he should be able to develop into a well-rounded player who can win the sibling rivalry. As for topping the other guy? Well, there's no need to get greedy.

★ ★ ★ *2021 Top 101 Prospect* **#48** ★ ★ ★

George Valera CF   Born: 11/13/00   Age: 20   Bats: L   Throws: L   Height: 5'11"   Weight: 185   Origin: International Free Agent, 2017

YEAR	TEAM	LVL	AGE	PA	R	2B	3B	HR	RBI	BB	K	SB	CS	Whiff%	AVG/OBP/SLG	DRC+	BABIP	BRR	FRAA	WARP
2018	INDB	ROK	17	22	4	1	0	1	6	3	3	1	1		.333/.409/.556	144	.333	-0.5	CF(3): 0.4, LF(1): -0.3, RF(1): 1.6	0.2
2019	MV	SS	18	188	22	7	1	8	29	29	52	6	2		.236/.356/.446	132	.296	-0.3	CF(25): 0.7, RF(11): -3.5, LF(5): 4.4	1.1
2019	LC	LO-A	18	26	1	0	1	0	3	2	9	0	2		.087/.192/.174	34	.143	-1.0	RF(3): 1.2, LF(2): 1.6	0.0
2021 FS	*CLE*	*MLB*	*20*	*600*	*50*	*26*	*2*	*13*	*57*	*39*	*217*	*10*	*8*		*.199/.257/.329*	*60*	*.299*	*-9.7*	*CF -1, RF -2*	*-2.7*

Valera may have signed in 2017, but he's been limited to fewer than 100 games played by injuries, careful management and now the pandemic. He has an All-Star ceiling and he just turned 20 in November, yet it's fair to wonder if all the starting and stopping will impact his long-term development.

Bradley Zimmer CF   Born: 11/27/92   Age: 28   Bats: L   Throws: R   Height: 6'5"   Weight: 220   Origin: Round 1, 2014 Draft (#21 overall)

YEAR	TEAM	LVL	AGE	PA	R	2B	3B	HR	RBI	BB	K	SB	CS	Whiff%	AVG/OBP/SLG	DRC+	BABIP	BRR	FRAA	WARP
2018	COL	AAA	25	28	1	0	0	1	1	1	11	1	0		.148/.179/.259	15	.200	0.1	CF(5): -0.2	-0.2
2018	CLE	MLB	25	114	14	5	0	2	9	7	44	4	1	35.6%	.226/.281/.330	48	.367	1.4	CF(34): 5.4	0.4
2019	COL	AAA	26	26	5	1	1	1	2	3	6	2	0		.364/.440/.636	112	.467	0.6	CF(6): -0.1	0.2
2019	CLE	MLB	26	14	1	0	0	0	0	1	7	0	0	44.4%	.000/.071/.000	71	.000	0.3	RF(4): -0.4, CF(2): 0.2	0.0
2020	CLE	MLB	28	50	3	0	0	1	3	7	14	2	1	36.6%	.162/.360/.243	103	.217	-0.6	LF(8): -0.2, CF(7): -0.0, RF(7): -0.4	-0.1
2021 FS	*CLE*	*MLB*	*28*	*600*	*60*	*21*	*2*	*16*	*58*	*60*	*206*	*24*	*5*	*37.0%*	*.208/.307/.351*	*83*	*.307*	*9.3*	*CF 11, RF -1*	*2.6*
2021 DC	*CLE*	*MLB*	*28*	*399*	*39*	*14*	*1*	*10*	*38*	*39*	*137*	*16*	*3*	*37.0%*	*.208/.307/.351*	*83*	*.307*	*6.2*	*CF 7, RF -1*	*1.7*

Comparables: Chad Hermansen, Kirk Nieuwenhuis, Ryan Thompson

No one would tempt fate as to suggest Zimmer was in the best shape of his life when the 2020 season began. He was, however, in the kind of shape that allowed him to play baseball, which has seldom been the case for much of his recent career. Zimmer's body didn't betray him, either, even if the season did. As a player sorely in need of reps (he's taken fewer than 300 trips to the plate across the past three years), the cancellation of the minor-league season was a huge blow. He was, in turn, thrown back in at the big-league side of things in order to get his hacks—and yes, that's the operative word for what he did, as he recorded more strikeouts than hits-plus-walks. The most disappointing part of these seemingly interminable career interruptions might be that if Zimmer ever does put together another full season, it'll be without the full power of the physical gifts that used to tantalize us, evaluators and fans alike.

PITCHERS

Logan Allen LHP   Born: 05/23/97   Age: 24   Bats: R   Throws: L   Height: 6'3"   Weight: 220   Origin: Round 8, 2015 Draft (#231 overall)

YEAR	TEAM	LVL	AGE	W	L	SV	G	GS	IP	H	HR	BB/9	K/9	K	GB%	BABIP	WHIP	ERA	DRA-	WARP	MPH	FA%	Whiff%	CSP
2018	SA	AA	21	10	6	0	20	19	121	89	7	2.8	9.3	125	42.6%	.270	1.05	2.75	67	2.8				
2018	ELP	AAA	21	4	0	0	5	5	27²	21	4	4.2	8.5	26	36.8%	.236	1.23	1.63	132	-0.2				
2019	COL	AAA	22	1	1	0	5	5	22¹	31	6	4.8	7.3	18	21.3%	.368	1.93	7.66	174	-0.4				
2019	ELP	AAA	22	4	3	0	13	13	57²	61	8	3.4	9.8	63	45.5%	.340	1.44	5.15	78	1.6				
2019	SD	MLB	22	2	3	0	8	4	25¹	33	4	4.6	5.0	14	51.7%	.349	1.82	6.75	137	-0.3	95.1	48.7%	21.7%	46.7%
2019	CLE	MLB	22	0	0	0	1	0	2¹	3	0	0.0	11.6	3	16.7%	.500	1.29	0.00	168	-0.1	95.8	42.5%	21.7%	50.6%
2020	CLE	MLB	23	0	0	0	3	0	10²	12	1	5.9	5.9	7	47.1%	.333	1.78	3.38	134	-0.1	95.4	45.7%	24.3%	47.8%
2021 FS	*CLE*	*MLB*	*24*	*8*	*10*	*0*	*26*	*26*	*150*	*163*	*26*	*4.5*	*7.8*	*130*	*42.3%*	*.310*	*1.59*	*5.87*	*125*	*-1.0*	*95.3*	*47.2%*	*22.7%*	*47.3%*
2021 DC	*CLE*	*MLB*	*24*	*5*	*9*	*0*	*33*	*22*	*115*	*125*	*20*	*4.5*	*7.8*	*99*	*42.3%*	*.310*	*1.59*	*5.87*	*125*	*-0.4*	*95.3*	*47.2%*	*22.7%*	*47.3%*

Comparables: Génesis Cabrera, JoJo Romero, Caleb Ferguson

Allen's time with Cleveland can be summed up in a word: anonymity. He wasn't the biggest name moved in the three-way trade that landed him with the Fightin' Franconas, nor has he been the most omnipresent in the year and a half since. His 2020 season comprised three low-leverage, mop-up relief appearances, making him four-for-four in that regard for his Cleveland career. To make matters worse, Cleveland used its second-round pick on a left-handed pitcher named...Logan Allen. Given the Younger Allen's polish, and the Older Allen's invisibility, it's possible he isn't even the best Logan Allen in the organization anymore.

Shane Bieber RHP   Born: 05/31/95   Age: 26   Bats: R   Throws: R   Height: 6'3"   Weight: 200   Origin: Round 4, 2016 Draft (#122 overall)

YEAR	TEAM	LVL	AGE	W	L	SV	G	GS	IP	H	HR	BB/9	K/9	K	GB%	BABIP	WHIP	ERA	DRA-	WARP	MPH	FA%	Whiff%	CSP
2018	AKR	AA	23	3	0	0	5	5	31	26	1	0.3	8.7	30	47.3%	.278	0.87	1.16	61	0.9				
2018	COL	AAA	23	3	1	0	8	8	48²	30	3	1.1	8.7	47	52.0%	.227	0.74	1.66	69	1.2				
2018	CLE	MLB	23	11	5	0	20	19	114²	130	13	1.8	9.3	118	46.2%	.356	1.33	4.55	74	2.6	94.7	57.4%	26.2%	51.3%
2019	CLE	MLB	24	15	8	0	34	33	214¹	186	31	1.7	10.9	259	44.4%	.298	1.05	3.28	75	4.9	94.4	45.8%	30.8%	44.9%
2020	CLE	MLB	25	8	1	0	12	12	77¹	46	7	2.4	14.2	122	48.4%	.267	0.87	1.63	53	2.6	95.3	53.6%	40.7%	39.6%
2021 FS	CLE	MLB	26	10	6	0	26	26	150	120	18	2.1	11.9	197	45.5%	.296	1.04	2.66	65	4.0	94.7	50.0%	33.2%	44.2%
2021 DC	CLE	MLB	26	13	9	0	30	30	196	157	24	2.1	11.9	258	45.5%	.296	1.04	2.66	65	5.7	94.7	50.0%	33.2%	44.2%

Comparables: Luis Severino, Danny Salazar, Joe Musgrove

The pitching Triple Crown; first in just about every other pitching category you can think of, and a few more besides; the third-best ERA+ of all time, and the best since Pedro Martinez's transcendent 2000 season; and so on. Bieber's accomplishments last year were diminished but not invalidated by the shortened season—only the very best hurlers can have 12-start runs this dominant. Bieber added a cutter to his already high-grade repertoire and ripped through every lineup he faced, striking out at least eight in each game and hitting double-digits in two-thirds of those starts. The one blemish on his record was a playoff stumble against the Yankees, a cruel end to an otherwise flawless season.

Tanner Burns RHP   Born: 12/28/98   Age: 22   Bats: R   Throws: R   Height: 6'0"   Weight: 215   Origin: Round 1, 2020 Draft (#36 overall)

Burns is the kind of polished, low-frills pitcher Cleveland seems to extract more from than other organizations. He slid in the draft because of injury concerns, but if he can stay healthy then don't be surprised if he's quick to rise—and long to stay—in a big-league rotation.

Joey Cantillo LHP   Born: 12/18/99   Age: 21   Bats: L   Throws: L   Height: 6'4"   Weight: 220   Origin: Round 16, 2017 Draft (#468 overall)

YEAR	TEAM	LVL	AGE	W	L	SV	G	GS	IP	H	HR	BB/9	K/9	K	GB%	BABIP	WHIP	ERA	DRA-	WARP	MPH	FA%	Whiff%	CSP
2018	SD2	ROK	18	2	2	0	11	9	45¹	33	0	2.4	11.5	58	57.3%	.303	0.99	2.18	29	2.1				
2018	FW	LO-A	18	0	1	0	1	1	3²	4	0	7.4	12.3	5	70.0%	.400	1.91	9.82	89	0.0				
2019	FW	LO-A	19	9	3	0	19	19	98	58	3	2.5	11.7	127	42.7%	.264	0.87	1.93	44	3.5				
2019	LE	HI-A	19	1	1	0	3	3	13²	12	2	4.6	10.5	16	38.5%	.270	1.39	4.61	77	0.2				
2021 FS	CLE	MLB	21	2	3	0	57	0	50	43	7	4.7	9.7	54	42.8%	.283	1.39	4.22	103	0.0				

Comparables: Tyler Danish, Miguel Castro, José Fernández

Underwhelming fastball? Check. Minimal prospect hype? Check? Gets by on deception and pitchability? Check. Cantillo's upside is probably back-end starter, but that tag comes with significant subtext now that he's relocated from San Diego to Cleveland.

Aaron Civale RHP   Born: 06/12/95   Age: 26   Bats: R   Throws: R   Height: 6'2"   Weight: 215   Origin: Round 3, 2016 Draft (#92 overall)

YEAR	TEAM	LVL	AGE	W	L	SV	G	GS	IP	H	HR	BB/9	K/9	K	GB%	BABIP	WHIP	ERA	DRA-	WARP	MPH	FA%	Whiff%	CSP
2018	AKR	AA	23	5	7	0	21	21	106¹	115	12	1.8	6.6	78	46.5%	.310	1.28	3.89	79	2.0				
2019	AKR	AA	24	4	0	0	5	5	30¹	26	3	1.8	7.1	24	42.2%	.264	1.05	2.67	100	0.0				
2019	COL	AAA	24	3	1	0	8	8	42¹	38	4	1.9	9.8	46	37.8%	.298	1.11	2.13	61	1.5				
2019	CLE	MLB	24	3	4	0	10	10	57²	44	4	2.5	7.2	46	40.9%	.252	1.04	2.34	105	0.4	94.1	67.3%	21.4%	41.4%
2020	CLE	MLB	25	4	6	0	12	12	74	82	11	1.9	8.4	69	45.1%	.333	1.32	4.74	95	0.9	93.0	60.0%	25.0%	45.4%
2021 FS	CLE	MLB	26	9	8	0	26	26	150	146	22	2.7	8.1	134	42.9%	.292	1.28	4.13	96	1.4	93.4	62.4%	23.9%	44.1%
2021 DC	CLE	MLB	26	9	9	0	27	27	159	155	23	2.7	8.1	142	42.9%	.292	1.28	4.13	96	2.0	93.4	62.4%	23.9%	44.1%

Comparables: Tyler Duffey, Jakob Junis, Scott Lewis

A largely successful sophomore campaign unraveled for Civale in his last start of the season, and against the Pirates of all teams. A disastrous outing raised his ERA by almost a full run, washing away much of his progress. Civale increased his whiffs from his rookie season, and that could be credited to an increased reliance on his curveball. Alas, even with six pitches to choose from, he doesn't have a killer putaway offering. Cleveland has worked its magic with Shane Bieber and Zach Plesac, so it would be simultaneously remarkable and unsurprising if Civale became the latest in this rotation to vastly exceed expectations.

Emmanuel Clase RHP   Born: 03/18/98   Age: 23   Bats: R   Throws: R   Height: 6'2"   Weight: 206   Origin: International Free Agent, 2015

YEAR	TEAM	LVL	AGE	W	L	SV	G	GS	IP	H	HR	BB/9	K/9	K	GB%	BABIP	WHIP	ERA	DRA-	WARP	MPH	FA%	Whiff%	CSP
2018	SPO	SS	20	1	1	12	22	0	28¹	16	0	1.9	8.6	27	61.1%	.225	0.78	0.64	241	-2.2				
2019	DE	HI-A	21	2	0	1	6	0	7	4	0	1.3	14.1	11	76.9%	.308	0.71	0.00	61	0.1				
2019	FRI	AA	21	1	2	11	33	1	37²	34	1	1.9	9.3	39	61.3%	.317	1.12	3.35	76	0.4				
2019	TEX	MLB	21	2	3	1	21	1	23¹	20	2	2.3	8.1	21	59.1%	.281	1.11	2.31	80	0.4	101.0	78.8%	25.6%	49.4%
2021 FS	CLE	MLB	23	2	2	3	57	0	50	47	6	4.0	8.7	48	52.8%	.298	1.40	4.36	98	0.2	101.0	78.8%	25.6%	49.4%
2021 DC	CLE	MLB	23	2	2	2	53	0	57	54	6	4.0	8.7	55	52.8%	.298	1.40	4.36	98	0.4	101.0	78.8%	25.6%	49.4%

Comparables: Yennsy Diaz, Carlos Sanabria, Germán Márquez

Whatever expectations were created by Clase headlining the Corey Kluber trade, it's safe to say that missing the entire season wasn't among them. The former Ranger looked to be among those who benefited from the late start to the schedule, giving him extra time to recover from the teres major strain that would have cost him a month or two of the season. His subsequent suspension for a positive boldenone test not only negated that advantage, but ultimately ensured he wouldn't make a big-league appearance in 2020. Cleveland will still have plenty of time to see if Clase and his triple-digit velocity and nasty cutter can make someone in the trade a winner.

★ ★ ★ *2021 Top 101 Prospect* **#100** ★ ★ ★

Daniel Espino RHP Born: 01/05/01   Age: 20   Bats: R   Throws: R   Height: 6'2"   Weight: 205   Origin: Round 1, 2019 Draft (#24 overall)

YEAR	TEAM	LVL	AGE	W	L	SV	G	GS	IP	H	HR	BB/9	K/9	K	GB%	BABIP	WHIP	ERA	DRA-	WARP	MPH	FA%	Whiff%	CSP
2019	INDR	ROK	18	0	1	0	6	6	13²	7	1	3.3	10.5	16	48.4%	.207	0.88	1.98	33	0.6				
2019	MV	SS	18	0	2	0	3	3	10	9	1	4.5	16.2	18	31.8%	.381	1.40	6.30	60	0.3				
2021 FS	*CLE*	*MLB*	*20*	*2*	*3*	*0*	*57*	*0*	*50*	*48*	*8*	*6.5*	*9.8*	*54*	*37.3%*	*.301*	*1.68*	*5.86*	*134*	*-0.8*				

Espino was brought along slowly after being drafted and 2020, unsurprisingly, did little to change that. The 20-year-old flamethrower will have less than 25 pro innings to his name at the time of publication, so this is a key year for determining whether he can translate his exciting arsenal into at least a mid-rotation ceiling.

Brad Hand LHP Born: 03/20/90   Age: 31   Bats: L   Throws: L   Height: 6'3"   Weight: 215   Origin: Round 2, 2008 Draft (#52 overall)

YEAR	TEAM	LVL	AGE	W	L	SV	G	GS	IP	H	HR	BB/9	K/9	K	GB%	BABIP	WHIP	ERA	DRA-	WARP	MPH	FA%	Whiff%	CSP
2018	CLE	MLB	28	0	1	8	28	0	27²	19	3	4.2	13.3	41	40.7%	.291	1.16	2.28	77	0.5	95.6	48.1%	31.4%	52.7%
2018	SD	MLB	28	2	4	24	41	0	44¹	33	5	3.0	13.2	65	46.5%	.301	1.08	3.05	70	0.9	96.0	44.3%	33.0%	49.9%
2019	CLE	MLB	29	6	4	34	60	0	57¹	53	6	2.8	13.2	84	27.2%	.364	1.24	3.30	86	0.7	94.7	45.8%	30.7%	49.7%
2020	CLE	MLB	30	2	1	16	23	0	22	13	0	1.6	11.9	29	26.5%	.265	0.77	2.05	91	0.3	93.4	48.1%	24.8%	51.1%
2021 FS	*CLE*	*MLB*	*31*	*3*	*2*	*0*	*57*	*0*	*50*	*40*	*7*	*3.2*	*12.0*	*66*	*35.5%*	*.295*	*1.16*	*3.27*	*80*	*0.7*	*94.7*	*46.4%*	*29.7%*	*50.4%*

Comparables: Jeurys Familia, Erasmo Ramírez, Liam Hendriks

Hand's struggles over the second half of 2019 initially looked as though they would continue into 2020 and cast a long shadow over the short season. When the White Sox did damage in consecutive bouts in late July, his ERA was a perilous 15.43. Hand fought back and never lost control, allowing a single earned run across August and September to finish with a perfect save record. The Yankees then smashed his streak and launched Cleveland off the postseason stage in what turned out to be his final appearance with the franchise, as his once-reasonable club option was declined. Cleveland might end up looking more smart than cheap in a year's time: Hand's velocity plummeted and his whiff rate went with it, suggesting his shiny ERA and save percentage could well dip next.

Ethan Hankins RHP Born: 05/23/00   Age: 21   Bats: R   Throws: R   Height: 6'6"   Weight: 200   Origin: Round 1, 2018 Draft (#35 overall)

YEAR	TEAM	LVL	AGE	W	L	SV	G	GS	IP	H	HR	BB/9	K/9	K	GB%	BABIP	WHIP	ERA	DRA-	WARP	MPH	FA%	Whiff%	CSP
2018	INDB	ROK	18	0	0	0	2	2	3	4	0	0.0	18.0	6	28.6%	.571	1.33	6.00	18	0.2				
2019	MV	SS	19	0	0	0	9	8	38²	23	1	4.2	10.0	43	55.1%	.253	1.06	1.40	68	0.8				
2019	LC	LO-A	19	0	3	0	5	5	21¹	20	3	5.1	11.8	28	47.2%	.340	1.50	4.64	113	-0.1				
2021 FS	*CLE*	*MLB*	*21*	*2*	*3*	*0*	*57*	*0*	*50*	*46*	*8*	*6.0*	*8.9*	*49*	*46.0%*	*.283*	*1.60*	*5.43*	*123*	*-0.5*				

The past year gave very little indication of whether Hankins can harness his crossfire delivery sufficiently for a rotation spot. Instead, the lasting image of his year will be the disbelieving laugh he uttered after being taken deep by Reds first-round outfielder Austin Hendrick in instructs.

Sam Hentges LHP Born: 07/18/96   Age: 24   Bats: L   Throws: L   Height: 6'6"   Weight: 245   Origin: Round 4, 2014 Draft (#128 overall)

YEAR	TEAM	LVL	AGE	W	L	SV	G	GS	IP	H	HR	BB/9	K/9	K	GB%	BABIP	WHIP	ERA	DRA-	WARP	MPH	FA%	Whiff%	CSP
2018	LYN	HI-A	21	6	6	0	23	23	118¹	114	4	4.0	9.3	122	37.8%	.348	1.41	3.27	84	1.9				
2019	AKR	AA	22	2	13	0	26	26	128²	148	11	4.5	8.7	125	34.0%	.358	1.65	5.11	146	-3.4				
2021 FS	*CLE*	*MLB*	*24*	*2*	*3*	*0*	*57*	*0*	*50*	*49*	*8*	*5.6*	*8.4*	*46*	*35.1%*	*.293*	*1.61*	*5.59*	*123*	*-0.5*				
2021 DC	*CLE*	*MLB*	*24*	*2*	*3*	*0*	*26*	*4*	*43*	*42*	*7*	*5.6*	*8.4*	*40*	*35.1%*	*.293*	*1.61*	*5.59*	*123*	*-0.2*				

Comparables: Chris Flexen, Pedro Avila, Michael Fulmer

Hentges consistently bumped the upper-90s during spring training, raising eyebrows about what he could do in a relief role. That feels like a lifetime ago, we know. In due time, Hentges' attempts at starting will probably feel the same way—especially if he keeps pumping that gas as a seventh-inning type.

Cam Hill RHP Born: 05/24/94   Age: 27   Bats: R   Throws: R   Height: 6'1"   Weight: 200   Origin: Round 17, 2014 Draft (#518 overall)

YEAR	TEAM	LVL	AGE	W	L	SV	G	GS	IP	H	HR	BB/9	K/9	K	GB%	BABIP	WHIP	ERA	DRA-	WARP	MPH	FA%	Whiff%	CSP
2018	COL	AAA	24	0	0	3	16	0	13²	15	5	5.3	8.6	13	36.6%	.278	1.68	6.59	105	0.0				
2019	LC	LO-A	25	0	0	0	5	0	6	3	0	1.5	12.0	8	35.7%	.214	0.67	0.00	50	0.2				
2019	COL	AAA	25	4	2	1	21	0	24²	23	5	4.4	13.1	36	50.0%	.353	1.42	4.74	79	0.6				
2020	CLE	MLB	26	2	0	1	18	0	18¹	11	4	2.5	7.9	16	38.8%	.156	0.87	4.91	114	0.0	93.5	48.5%	29.8%	45.4%
2021 FS	*CLE*	*MLB*	*27*	*2*	*2*	*0*	*57*	*0*	*50*	*45*	*8*	*3.6*	*9.6*	*53*	*40.1%*	*.288*	*1.31*	*4.24*	*97*	*0.2*	*93.5*	*48.5%*	*29.8%*	*45.4%*
2021 DC	*CLE*	*MLB*	*27*	*2*	*2*	*0*	*53*	*0*	*57*	*51*	*9*	*3.6*	*9.6*	*60*	*40.1%*	*.288*	*1.31*	*4.24*	*97*	*0.4*	*93.5*	*48.5%*	*29.8%*	*45.4%*

Comparables: Jake Barrett, Trevor Gott, Dan Jennings

After a difficult six-year journey to the majors that included Tommy John surgery, Hill wasted no time in his debut by making a run at a major league record. His first five appearances were not only scoreless, Hill did not allow a walk or a hit, the second-longest such streak to start a career in major league history. He even notched his first career save in the process. Sadly, he fell one game short of tying Seranthony Domínguez when Yoán Moncada took him deep to start his sixth appearance. The numbers the rest of the way were far more pedestrian. Recapturing his pre-surgery velocity and developing better command will be key to finding more sustainable success. Regardless of what happens next, Hill had a debut to remember in a season no one will ever forget.

James Karinchak RHP
Born: 09/22/95   Age: 25   Bats: R   Throws: R   Height: 6'3"   Weight: 215   Origin: Round 9, 2017 Draft (#282 overall)

YEAR	TEAM	LVL	AGE	W	L	SV	G	GS	IP	H	HR	BB/9	K/9	K	GB%	BABIP	WHIP	ERA	DRA-	WARP	MPH	FA%	Whiff%	CSP
2018	LC	LO-A	22	3	0	1	7	0	11¹	8	0	5.6	15.9	20	55.0%	.400	1.32	0.79	64	0.3				
2018	LYN	HI-A	22	1	1	13	25	0	27	14	1	5.7	15.0	45	35.6%	.310	1.15	1.00	60	0.7				
2018	AKR	AA	22	0	1	0	10	0	10¹	7	1	10.5	13.9	16	28.6%	.300	1.84	2.61	117	-0.1				
2019	INDB	ROK	23	0	0	0	3	0	3	0	0	6.0	24.0	8	0.0%	.000	0.67	0.00	25	0.1				
2019	AKR	AA	23	0	0	6	10	0	10	2	0	1.8	21.6	24	55.6%	.222	0.40	0.00	37	0.3				
2019	COL	AAA	23	1	1	2	17	0	17¹	14	2	6.8	21.8	42	47.8%	.571	1.56	4.67	43	0.7				
2019	CLE	MLB	23	0	0	0	5	0	5¹	3	0	1.7	13.5	8	38.5%	.231	0.75	1.69	79	0.1	97.6	56.4%	34.7%	47.2%
2020	CLE	MLB	24	1	2	1	27	0	27	14	4	5.3	17.7	53	22.5%	.342	1.11	2.67	62	0.8	96.8	50.2%	45.5%	41.8%
2021 FS	CLE	MLB	25	2	2	29	57	0	50	32	6	5.2	15.5	86	35.2%	.301	1.23	3.07	72	0.9	96.9	50.9%	44.2%	42.5%
2021 DC	CLE	MLB	25	2	2	29	53	0	57	37	7	5.2	15.5	98	35.2%	.301	1.23	3.07	72	1.2	96.9	50.9%	44.2%	42.5%

Comparables: Roberto Osuna, Cody Allen, Trey Wingenter

Karinchak bristles with barely contained energy. His left foot taps the mound as though he's revving up for his leg kick. When he's particularly amped, his whole body rocks from side to side pre-pitch. He sprints off the field at the end of an inning, suggesting the act of pitching has rejuvenated rather than tired him. In some ways, it's reminiscent of Hunter Pence at the plate. Whereas Pence is quirky, however, Karinchak is altogether more threatening. Perhaps it's the way the ball explodes out of his hand, or the endless attempts his shoulders make to burst out of his jersey. Whatever the reason, it's working on hitters: almost half of whom fell to strikes.

Phil Maton RHP
Born: 03/25/93   Age: 28   Bats: R   Throws: R   Height: 6'2"   Weight: 206   Origin: Round 20, 2015 Draft (#597 overall)

YEAR	TEAM	LVL	AGE	W	L	SV	G	GS	IP	H	HR	BB/9	K/9	K	GB%	BABIP	WHIP	ERA	DRA-	WARP	MPH	FA%	Whiff%	CSP
2018	SA	AA	25	0	0	0	5	0	5²	5	1	1.6	11.1	7	33.3%	.286	1.06	1.59	28	0.2				
2018	ELP	AAA	25	0	0	2	6	0	6¹	5	0	1.4	14.2	10	40.0%	.333	0.95	2.84	56	0.2				
2018	SD	MLB	25	0	2	0	45	0	47¹	50	3	4.4	10.5	55	35.1%	.364	1.54	4.37	98	0.3	92.8	63.5%	32.7%	43.5%
2019	COL	AAA	26	0	1	3	9	0	10²	5	1	3.4	14.3	17	44.4%	.235	0.84	2.53	39	0.4				
2019	ELP	AAA	26	2	1	2	13	0	18²	17	2	2.9	14.5	30	57.5%	.405	1.23	2.89	37	0.8				
2019	CLE	MLB	26	0	0	0	9	0	12¹	4	1	4.4	9.5	13	46.4%	.111	0.81	2.92	55	0.4	92.5	70.4%	24.7%	49.5%
2019	SD	MLB	26	0	0	0	21	0	24¹	34	6	2.2	7.4	20	44.3%	.350	1.64	7.77	116	-0.1	93.3	77.1%	24.8%	48.8%
2020	CLE	MLB	27	3	3	0	23	0	21²	23	1	2.5	13.3	32	44.4%	.415	1.34	4.57	70	0.5	95.1	79.7%	37.3%	47.8%
2021 FS	CLE	MLB	28	2	2	0	57	0	50	40	5	3.0	11.2	61	42.9%	.291	1.14	3.08	73	0.9	93.7	73.7%	31.3%	47.2%
2021 DC	CLE	MLB	28	2	2	0	53	0	57	46	6	3.0	11.2	70	42.9%	.291	1.14	3.08	73	1.1	93.7	73.7%	31.3%	47.2%

Comparables: Jonathan Holder, Fernando Cabrera, Dan Altavilla

Maton was a revelation for much of the season. His ultra high-spin four-seamer gained an edge with a velocity bump. While throwing 94 is unremarkable in the modern game, it proved lethal once combined with the fastball at the top of the zone, trademark knee-buckling curveball and further incorporation of a mid-80s cutter that also revolves at an incredible rate. Maton was thus one of the best relievers in the game by almost all measures, except for the one that counts: run prevention. Much of Maton's misfortune on balls in play came when he had runners on base, allowing almost 40 percent of those runners to score in a few bad outings and leaving his ERA looking much like his career mark. Sustaining this level of performance over a full season will produce results more representative of his dizzying stuff.

———————————— ★ ★ ★ *2021 Top 101 Prospect* **#73** ★ ★ ★ ————————————

Triston McKenzie RHP
Born: 08/02/97   Age: 23   Bats: R   Throws: R   Height: 6'5"   Weight: 165   Origin: Round 1, 2015 Draft (#42 overall)

YEAR	TEAM	LVL	AGE	W	L	SV	G	GS	IP	H	HR	BB/9	K/9	K	GB%	BABIP	WHIP	ERA	DRA-	WARP	MPH	FA%	Whiff%	CSP
2018	AKR	AA	20	7	4	0	16	16	90²	63	8	2.8	8.6	87	33.3%	.234	1.00	2.68	86	1.4				
2020	CLE	MLB	22	2	1	0	8	6	33¹	21	6	2.4	11.3	42	40.0%	.217	0.90	3.24	85	0.6	95.3	53.3%	29.2%	45.6%
2021 FS	CLE	MLB	23	9	8	0	26	26	150	133	25	2.9	10.2	170	36.2%	.287	1.21	3.81	90	1.9	95.3	53.3%	29.2%	45.6%
2021 DC	CLE	MLB	23	6	7	0	22	22	111	98	18	2.9	10.2	125	36.2%	.287	1.21	3.81	90	1.8	95.3	53.3%	29.2%	45.6%

Comparables: Noah Syndergaard, Tyler Skaggs, Jenrry Mejia

McKenzie overwhelmed hitters at times during his rookie season. He punched out 10 in his debut, and he limited opponents to three hits or fewer in each of his first five turns. The durability concerns that have plagued his career resurfaced alarmingly quickly: he went from sitting at 95 mph in his first start to 91 in his sixth, at which point he was moved to the bullpen in preparation for the playoffs. McKenzie still looks like a strong gust of wind could topple him from the mound and, while he has a starter's arsenal, his failure to maintain velocity over even half of a shortened season renews the doubts about his ability to do so over 30-plus starts.

Oliver Pérez LHP
Born: 08/15/81   Age: 39   Bats: L   Throws: L   Height: 6'3"   Weight: 225   Origin: International Free Agent, 1999

YEAR	TEAM	LVL	AGE	W	L	SV	G	GS	IP	H	HR	BB/9	K/9	K	GB%	BABIP	WHIP	ERA	DRA-	WARP	MPH	FA%	Whiff%	CSP
2018	SWB	AAA	36	1	0	0	16	0	14	17	1	1.9	9.6	15	33.3%	.421	1.43	2.57	71	0.3				
2018	CLE	MLB	36	1	1	0	51	0	32¹	17	1	1.9	12.0	43	45.6%	.239	0.74	1.39	58	0.9	93.9	51.0%	35.2%	52.1%
2019	CLE	MLB	37	2	4	1	67	0	40²	38	5	2.7	10.6	48	43.6%	.314	1.23	3.98	87	0.5	94.0	51.0%	28.3%	51.4%
2020	CLE	MLB	38	1	1	1	21	0	18	13	0	3.0	7.0	14	44.9%	.265	1.06	2.00	99	0.2	92.5	56.9%	19.4%	53.7%
2021 FS	CLE	MLB	39	2	2	0	57	0	50	44	6	3.0	9.4	52	41.4%	.288	1.22	3.69	88	0.5	93.5	52.9%	26.6%	52.3%

Comparables: Arthur Rhodes, Tom Gordon, Rich Hill

Pérez led the American League in 2019 with 33 appearances facing two or fewer batters, which made him one of the obvious potential casualties of the three-batter minimum rule. It might have cost him his typical platoon advantage and a few strikeouts, but it had as little effect on his topline run prevention as it did on the length of games. He was called upon more sparingly than he would have been in the days of the LOOGY, and his peripherals suggest that a longer season might have eventually had a negative effect on those results. Then again, they would also have suggested that his career was unlikely to last much longer a decade ago, and he's now the longest-tenured pitcher in the Show, so there's no sense counting him out just yet.

Zach Plesac RHP Born: 01/21/95 Age: 26 Bats: R Throws: R Height: 6'3" Weight: 220 Origin: Round 12, 2016 Draft (#362 overall)

YEAR	TEAM	LVL	AGE	W	L	SV	G	GS	IP	H	HR	BB/9	K/9	K	GB%	BABIP	WHIP	ERA	DRA-	WARP	MPH	FA%	Whiff%	CSP
2018	LYN	HI-A	23	8	5	0	22	22	122²	124	8	2.4	8.1	111	42.7%	.330	1.28	4.04	81	2.2				
2018	AKR	AA	23	3	1	0	4	4	22	19	1	1.6	8.6	21	27.9%	.305	1.05	2.45	85	0.3				
2019	AKR	AA	24	1	1	0	6	6	37¹	23	0	1.4	8.2	34	48.5%	.237	0.78	0.96	53	1.1				
2019	COL	AAA	24	3	1	0	4	4	26¹	19	2	1.0	10.6	31	27.7%	.270	0.84	2.73	47	1.1				
2019	CLE	MLB	24	8	6	0	21	21	115²	102	19	3.1	6.8	88	39.2%	.257	1.23	3.81	128	-0.6	95.4	50.6%	21.7%	49.5%
2020	CLE	MLB	25	4	2	0	8	8	55¹	38	8	1.0	9.3	57	38.0%	.224	0.80	2.28	89	0.8	94.4	37.6%	29.8%	50.1%
2021 FS	CLE	MLB	26	9	8	0	26	26	150	139	25	2.6	8.9	148	38.4%	.284	1.21	3.93	92	1.8	95.0	45.7%	24.8%	49.7%
2021 DC	CLE	MLB	26	9	9	0	27	27	154	142	25	2.6	8.9	152	38.4%	.284	1.21	3.93	92	2.3	95.0	45.7%	24.8%	49.7%

Comparables: Zach Eflin, Erick Fedde, Daniel Mengden

The story of Plesac's season was his violation of the COVID-19 protocols, an error that was compounded by a non-apology video that he filmed while driving without a seatbelt. (Clearly he has an abnormally and uncomfortably high tolerance for risk.) In said video, he defended his acts and blamed the fallout on negative media coverage—as opposed to, say, one of his teammates threatening to retire if he remained on the active roster. Predictably, the team demoted him and left him out of the rotation for more than three weeks, which is a long time when the season lasts two months. There are a lot of sad elements to Plesac's 2020; one of the saddest is that, if he had sacrificed his individual desires for the sake of the collective benefit, then this space would've been devoted to singing his praises after a seeming breakout.

Adam Plutko RHP Born: 10/03/91 Age: 29 Bats: R Throws: R Height: 6'3" Weight: 215 Origin: Round 11, 2013 Draft (#321 overall)

YEAR	TEAM	LVL	AGE	W	L	SV	G	GS	IP	H	HR	BB/9	K/9	K	GB%	BABIP	WHIP	ERA	DRA-	WARP	MPH	FA%	Whiff%	CSP
2018	COL	AAA	26	7	3	0	14	14	84²	47	5	1.7	8.6	81	27.2%	.199	0.74	1.70	81	1.4				
2018	CLE	MLB	26	4	5	1	17	12	76²	78	21	2.7	7.0	60	27.3%	.259	1.32	5.28	161	-1.7	92.8	59.8%	19.0%	46.1%
2019	COL	AAA	27	1	3	0	4	4	15²	21	1	2.3	9.2	16	22.0%	.408	1.60	7.47	135	0.0				
2019	CLE	MLB	27	7	5	0	21	20	109¹	115	22	2.1	6.4	78	31.6%	.280	1.29	4.86	159	-2.4	92.5	54.0%	18.9%	46.4%
2020	CLE	MLB	28	2	2	1	10	4	27²	30	5	2.3	4.9	15	26.9%	.287	1.34	4.88	168	-0.8	92.3	78.3%	23.3%	46.6%
2021 FS	CLE	MLB	29	8	9	0	26	26	150	154	34	2.6	7.0	115	29.3%	.274	1.31	4.95	113	0.0	92.5	60.5%	19.9%	46.4%
2021 DC	CLE	MLB	29	4	6	0	39	12	95	97	21	2.6	7.0	73	29.3%	.274	1.31	4.95	113	0.2	92.5	60.5%	19.9%	46.4%

Comparables: Dylan Covey, Alec Mills, Austin Voth

Autocorrect insists on changing Plutko to Pluto, which serves as an unintentionally cutting yet apt evaluation of his place within Cleveland's pitching galaxy. He's always the last name on the leaderboards, orbiting a different plane than the one occupied by the Civales, let alone the Biebers and the Plesacs. Because he's out of options, and because he's never finished above the replacement-level line, it's possible that he loses his planetary status sooner than later, perhaps leaving him drifting into the deep space that is the waiver wire right around the season's launch date.

Cal Quantrill RHP Born: 02/10/95 Age: 26 Bats: L Throws: R Height: 6'3" Weight: 195 Origin: Round 1, 2016 Draft (#8 overall)

YEAR	TEAM	LVL	AGE	W	L	SV	G	GS	IP	H	HR	BB/9	K/9	K	GB%	BABIP	WHIP	ERA	DRA-	WARP	MPH	FA%	Whiff%	CSP
2018	SA	AA	23	6	5	0	22	22	117	135	12	2.9	7.8	101	44.2%	.339	1.48	5.15	84	1.6				
2018	ELP	AAA	23	3	1	0	6	6	31	39	4	1.5	6.4	22	48.6%	.337	1.42	3.48	85	0.5				
2019	ELP	AAA	24	4	2	0	7	7	35²	38	3	3.0	8.3	33	50.5%	.324	1.40	4.54	77	1.0				
2019	SD	MLB	24	6	8	0	23	18	103	106	15	2.4	7.8	89	43.3%	.297	1.30	5.16	89	1.5	95.9	56.7%	22.4%	45.0%
2020	CLE	MLB	25	2	0	1	18	3	32	31	4	2.2	8.7	31	44.6%	.310	1.22	2.25	93	0.4	96.0	54.0%	25.0%	46.9%
2021 FS	CLE	MLB	26	9	8	0	26	26	150	145	21	3.0	8.2	135	44.2%	.292	1.31	4.22	97	1.3	95.9	55.9%	23.1%	45.6%
2021 DC	CLE	MLB	26	4	5	0	34	12	76	73	10	3.0	8.2	68	44.2%	.292	1.31	4.22	97	0.8	95.9	55.9%	23.1%	45.6%

Comparables: Trevor Williams, Kevin Gausman, Yonny Chirinos

Sometimes it pays to zig when everyone else is zagging. Quantrill doubled-down on a contrarian strategy in the modern game, betting on his sinker while fading his four-seam fastball. It appeared to pay off in the short term, bringing success more befitting of his original draft and prospect status, even as the Padres opted to swap him for a more well-established pitcher. Quantrill's sinker more closely resembles his changeup and slider at release, a similarity that depressed the quality of contact and enabled the right-hander to keep his four-seamer in reserve as a putaway option. There's no sense reading too much into a small sample, but we're interested to learn whether a winter under Cleveland's watch can help Quantrill take the next step forward, the way Bieber and Plesac have the past few years.

Jefry Rodriguez RHP Born: 07/26/93 Age: 27 Bats: R Throws: R Height: 6'6" Weight: 232 Origin: International Free Agent, 2012

YEAR	TEAM	LVL	AGE	W	L	SV	G	GS	IP	H	HR	BB/9	K/9	K	GB%	BABIP	WHIP	ERA	DRA-	WARP	MPH	FA%	Whiff%	CSP
2018	HBG	AA	24	5	3	0	13	13	68	55	6	3.7	9.5	72	51.9%	.282	1.22	3.31	71	1.6				
2018	SYR	AAA	24	2	2	0	6	6	32²	32	0	4.1	8.3	30	44.8%	.340	1.44	3.58	95	0.3				
2018	WAS	MLB	24	3	3	0	14	8	52	43	8	6.4	6.8	39	42.9%	.245	1.54	5.71	164	-1.3	97.5	65.0%	21.0%	46.1%
2019	COL	AAA	25	1	0	0	5	3	21²	16	1	4.6	6.6	16	52.5%	.250	1.25	4.15	86	0.5				
2019	CLE	MLB	25	1	5	0	10	8	46²	48	5	4.0	6.4	33	48.3%	.301	1.48	4.63	143	-0.6	96.3	70.0%	18.8%	47.0%
2021 FS	CLE	MLB	27	2	3	0	57	0	50	48	7	5.1	8.0	44	46.5%	.289	1.53	5.01	112	-0.2	96.8	68.1%	19.6%	46.6%

Comparables: Scott Barlow, Spencer Turnbull, Keury Mella

Last season was a case of déjà vu for Rodríguez, as well as a case of ne l'a pas vu for everyone else. He was *hors de combat* for the Opening Day roster with a back injury before the same shoulder trouble that interrupted his '19 campaign provided the *dénouement* of a frustrating season. May his third season prove to be le charme.

Nick Wittgren RHP Born: 05/29/91 Age: 30 Bats: R Throws: R Height: 6'2" Weight: 216 Origin: Round 9, 2012 Draft (#287 overall)

YEAR	TEAM	LVL	AGE	W	L	SV	G	GS	IP	H	HR	BB/9	K/9	K	GB%	BABIP	WHIP	ERA	DRA-	WARP	MPH	FA%	Whiff%	CSP
2018	NO	AAA	27	0	5	2	25	0	29¹	34	4	2.5	10.4	34	44.3%	.357	1.43	5.22	61	0.8				
2018	MIA	MLB	27	2	1	0	32	0	33²	29	1	4.0	8.3	31	45.5%	.283	1.31	2.94	85	0.4	93.9	70.1%	22.5%	48.9%
2019	CLE	MLB	28	5	1	4	55	0	57²	47	10	2.3	9.4	60	39.1%	.253	1.08	2.81	100	0.3	93.9	66.4%	23.2%	48.6%
2020	CLE	MLB	29	2	0	0	25	0	23²	18	4	2.3	10.6	28	32.2%	.259	1.01	3.42	101	0.2	94.5	60.7%	29.0%	47.8%
2021 FS	CLE	MLB	30	2	2	5	57	0	50	44	8	2.7	9.7	53	37.5%	.285	1.20	3.84	91	0.4	94.1	65.3%	24.9%	48.4%
2021 DC	CLE	MLB	30	2	2	5	53	0	57	51	9	2.7	9.7	61	37.5%	.285	1.20	3.84	91	0.6	94.1	65.3%	24.9%	48.4%

Comparables: Shawn Armstrong, Addison Reed, Emilio Pagán

There was a nasty surprise lurking beneath the shiny surface of Wittgren's ERA in his first season in Cleveland: he allowed the highest average exit velocity of any pitcher with at least 100 batted balls. That might have been the impetus behind a curious tweak to his pitch mix, one that saw him torn more to the pitch that allowed the hardest contact, his changeup. He didn't misread the printout; what he did was he found a little extra movement on the offering and generated a career-high whiff rate. Alas, that didn't cure Wittgren's problem with quality contact so much as it moved it to a different pitch: hitters teed off on the curve instead, albeit without it harming his ERA. Without more explosive stuff, he may always be a pitcher who gives up loud contact; of course, it may not matter if he can continue to evolve and continue to keep runs off the board.

DETROIT TIGERS

Essay by Craig Calcaterra

Player comments by Matt Sussman and BP staff

There's a trope that exists in fiction in which a once successful and respected figure, having fallen on hard times or having suffered disgrace, is forced to take on a job of last resort.

Maybe they're a military figure who, after suffering ignominious defeat, has been exiled to a remote, backwater post. Maybe they're a hot-shot politician or businessman who got caught up in scandal and now find themselves as a fish-out-of-water, volunteering for some lost cause or opening up a small shop in a small town. Maybe they're an entertainer who squandered opportunities or committed acts of self-sabotage and find themselves doing dinner theater or pitching reverse mortgages on cable TV. It can be anything, really.

The idea, though, is not that the station they've been reduced to in life is the end point of their character arc. Rather, it's the starting point. The starting point for their redemption quest.

The redemption quest begins with our character in a bad place but one in which they are granted a final chance to do better. Usually, that chance involves a seemingly impossible task. Usually it involves rallying a ragtag band of misfits to do something great. Something no one believed they ever had in them. To take down a formidable enemy. To put on a show. To win the big game. Whatever it is, getting there won't be easy, but our disgraced hero—after experiencing some early bumps in the road—finds a way to transform the ragtag band of misfits from a dysfunctional group of losers into a well-oiled machine. This may or may not involve a training montage. In the end, though, the misfits stand victorious and our disgraced hero stands redeemed.

This, of course, is where A.J. Hinch and the 2021 Detroit Tigers find themselves. They're the Bad News Bears the day Morris Buttermaker shows up, except instead of being a washed up alcoholic, Hinch was a manager who failed to manage his players in a responsible way. They're the Mighty Ducks right after Gordon Bombay is placed in charge of them except, instead of a DUI, Hinch was asleep at the wheel during baseball's biggest cheating scandal in a century. If not for that he'd still be in Houston. If not for the Tigers' run of ineptitude, the gig wouldn't have come available. It's

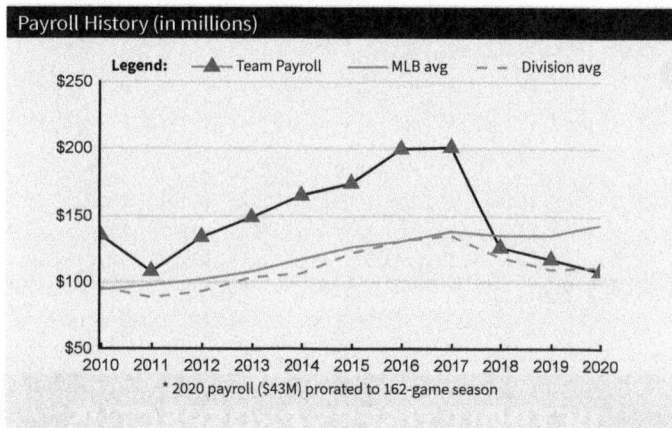

Payroll History (in millions)

* 2020 payroll ($43M) prorated to 162-game season

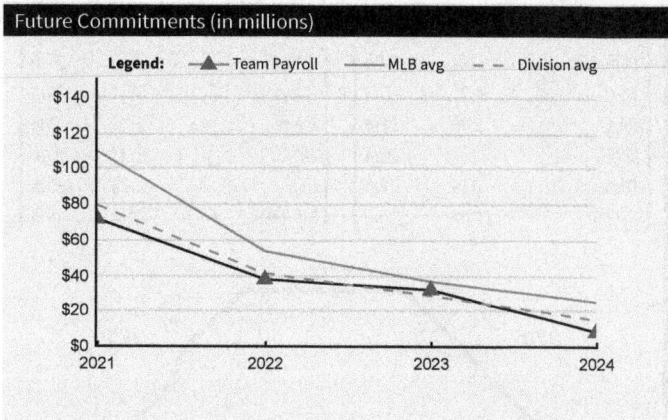

Future Commitments (in millions)

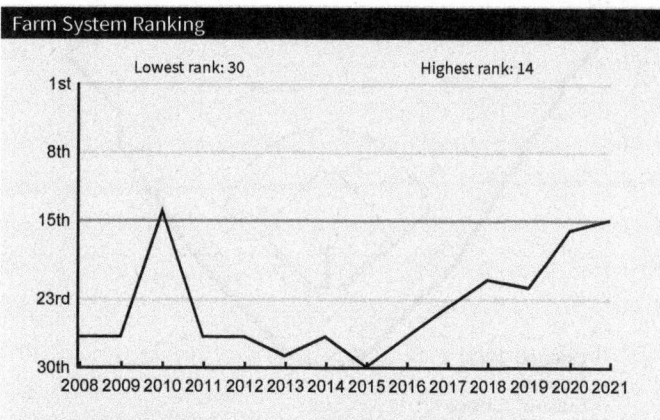

Farm System Ranking

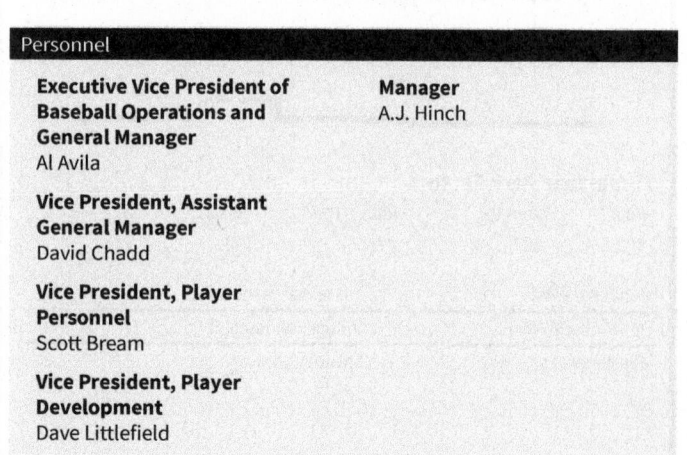

Personnel

Executive Vice President of Baseball Operations and General Manager
Al Avila

Vice President, Assistant General Manager
David Chadd

Vice President, Player Personnel
Scott Bream

Vice President, Player Development
Dave Littlefield

Manager
A.J. Hinch

all the more appropriate—and cinematic—that, like so many disgraced heroes in fiction, Hinch's rock bottom features him going home again and starting over, as it were. No, that one season he played for the Tigers in 2003 is not quite as resonant as Gordon Bombay going back to the same peewee hockey league where he starred as a kid, but it's close enough as far as life imitating art goes.

The bunch that is likely to take the field for the 2021 Detroit Tigers is definitely ragtag. And many of them match up to stock characters in the Hollywood versions of this story.

Shortstop Willi Castro and third baseman Jeimer Candelario are what pass for the talented guys who could actually be someplace better but aren't due to circumstance. Hinch will have to teach them how to be engaged in the present rather than looking to the future and teach them how to be leaders. Matthew Boyd, Spencer Turnbull and Michael Fulmer—the embodiment of what has made these sacks so sad over the past few years—will have to be taught to find something more inside of themselves than they thought was there. Youngsters Casey Mize, Tarik Skubal, Spencer Torkelson, Isaac Paredes and Daz Cameron are the green ones who've been brought into a losing culture and need to be shown a different way lest any of that old stuff stick to them in their formative stage. Miguel Cabrera is the past-his-prime graybeard Hinch will ask to give his all and hope for a miracle. Add in some hired guns to work behind the plate and to cover the gaps before the kids establish themselves, and you have a nearly straight-from-central-casting assemblage of misfits.

One can imagine a scenario in which Hinch takes these players—and whatever other players the Tigers acquire over the course of the next couple of years—and molds them into winners. That they take a big step forward, out of the cellar, in 2021 not unlike how the White Sox and the Padres did in 2020. That, in due time, the Tigers are not only good, but are approaching great, and even surpass the level those Justin Verlander and Cabrera-led teams of the Jim Leyland years achieved and win a World Series. If and when that happens, Hinch's redemption quest will be considered complete by most observers. The former champion, knocked off his pedestal and having hit rock bottom, will have completed his climb back to the top. And then the credits will roll.

There's only one problem with that. Setting aside the fact that Hinch is a real person and not a fictional character, his mere athletic success—be it in reality or in fiction—would not be indicia of actual redemption. Of moral redemption. And it is moral redemption Hinch's story requires here, because his failures were moral failures, not athletic ones. A proper story of moral redemption requires that those be addressed and learned from. It requires so much more.

The first thing any student of fiction learns about a moral redemption story is that it requires some shock or disruption in the hero's life. The thing that sends him into a crisis from which he must be redeemed. We'll give Hinch that. He was disgraced with the Astros, got fired and suspended, and now he's managing a last place Tigers team. It's a good start.

The next thing required of a redemption story is the requirement of a seemingly impossible challenge. Given where the Tigers have been for the past few years and where they look to be now, I'd say that beating out the White Sox, Twins and Cleveland as currently constructed qualifies as a challenge. If Hinch plays out the arc as described above, again, he's done it. Two-for-two. Not bad! But now it gets tougher.

In any proper redemption story the hero must, from his low point, and in the face of the big challenge, either discover or rediscover his inner moral code or choose to face it employing his past immoral or amoral path. That's the big turning point, really. Because it's important to note here that Hinch could very well win a World Series with the Tigers having learned nothing from the ignominy he earned in Houston. He could simply do what he always did, benefit from an infusion of talent, and come out on top in the end. If that happens—if Hinch is hoisted upon the shoulders of his players after the final out of a World Series—has he simply found success or has he truly been redeemed?

I figure not many people care about any of those things. In sports, we tend to consider redemption in only the most shallow of ways. We see Michael Vick come back and run for some touchdowns and somehow claim that means something. We see Tiger Woods win a major in his 40s and see it as an appropriate final scene in his redemption story as well. No matter what the scandal or failing of a given sports figure faces or experiences, we're quick to brush aside once they show that they're still able to bring it once the whistle blows or the umpire yells "play ball!" At the same time, if the scandal-bound sports figure does not come back on the field or perform to his old standards, we assume he is not redeemed no matter how deep and healing his actual redemption quest happened to be.

Tigers fans, for sure, aren't going to examine A.J. Hinch's character arc to determine whether his rallying of the ragtag band of misfits satisfied all of the conditions of a proper moral redemption story. To most of them the results will be all that matters. Which, it should be pointed out, is the ethos that got Hinch and the Astros in trouble in the first place. There will be many, however, particularly in the media, who will judge Hinch's redemption arc on a 1-to-1 basis with his won-loss record in Detroit. Who will be the first to consider the success of Willi Castro, Jeimer Candelario, Matthew

Boyd, Spencer Turnbull, Michael Fulmer, Casey Mize, Tarik Skubal, Spencer Torkelson, Isaac Paredes, Daz Cameron and, yes, even Miguel Cabrera, to be a direct comment on what lessons Hinch did or did not learn during his year in the wilderness following his dismissal and suspension.

I'd like to think, though, that he'd be held to at least a slightly higher standard. I'd hope that, like Gordon Bombay, Morris Buttermaker and all of the other fallen characters put on the path to redemption, Hinch will learn things about himself and teach things to others while on that path. Things that he would not have known had it not been for his earlier downfall. Things that might make that redemption complete and fulfilling as opposed to the superficial redemption we tend to ascribe to anyone who finds mere success after failure.

I'd like that. I'd like to believe something satisfying like that would happen. But being realistic, I know that's not in the cards. At the very least it's not anything outsiders will ever see, because life isn't the movies, A.J. Hinch isn't a character, real people's lives tend not to follow neat narratives, and redemption is hardly ever a truly public process.

Hinch may learn lessons from his mistakes in Houston. He may become a better person because of those lessons. He may, however, lose 102 games a year with the Tigers before being fired and never give the public any sign that he's grown since January 2020. In contrast he may, notwithstanding his relatively contrite and reflective words since the Astros fired him, learn nothing much at all from his experience apart from the importance of not getting caught doing something wrong, and win 102 games a year and three pennants, all while giving lip service to the sign stealing scandal being a blessing in disguise or a turning point or some such.

No matter what the outcome—one of those two extremes or something in between—we'll never truly know what's in his heart. We're not going to be privy to his actual growth or lack thereof, even if he says so or if the press ascribes those things to him. Unlike the movies, sports do not provide us with that kind of clear view into a character's heart. In light of that, perhaps we shouldn't try to make narratives out of sports figures. A.J. Hinch included. ▪

—Craig Calcaterra is the writer and editor of the Cup Of Coffee newsletter.

HITTERS

Sergio Alcántara SS Born: 07/10/96 Age: 24 Bats: S Throws: R Height: 5'9" Weight: 151 Origin: International Free Agent, 2012

YEAR	TEAM	LVL	AGE	PA	R	2B	3B	HR	RBI	BB	K	SB	CS	Whiff%	AVG/OBP/SLG	DRC+	BABIP	BRR	FRAA	WARP
2018	ERI	AA	21	494	53	18	3	1	37	42	95	8	5		.271/.335/.333	88	.342	-2.5	SS(93): -0.6, 2B(20): -0.3	0.3
2019	ERI	AA	22	378	46	10	0	2	26	48	71	7	6		.247/.346/.296	100	.308	0.1	SS(73): 4.4, 2B(29): 1.8	2.2
2020	DET	MLB	24	23	2	0	1	1	1	2	4	0	0	10.7%	.143/.217/.381	88	.125	0.0	2B(6): -0.9, 3B(6): -0.4	-0.1
2021 FS	DET	MLB	24	600	59	26	3	7	53	50	140	4	2	10.7%	.241/.307/.346	81	.311	-0.9	2B -1, SS 0	0.4
2021 DC	DET	MLB	24	198	19	8	1	2	17	16	46	1	0	10.7%	.241/.307/.346	81	.311	-0.3	2B 0, 3B 0	0.1

Comparables: Jack Reinheimer, Tony Giarratano, Cristhian Adames

The scrawny Alcántara seared the major leagues last year, as he started off with a home run in his debut game, a triple in his second, and probably should have halted the season there. The corrugated cardboard lumber he swings will keep him from earning anything more than a smattering of playing time: The thing about having the bat knocked out of your hands is that it at least insinuates the ability to make contact. He and teammate Harold Castro are the two lightest players in baseball in the last 10 years (151 pounds). Stack one on the other's shoulders and you've got quite the second baseman.

Akil Baddoo CF Born: 08/16/98 Age: 22 Bats: L Throws: L Height: 6'1" Weight: 210 Origin: Round 2, 2016 Draft (#74 overall)

YEAR	TEAM	LVL	AGE	PA	R	2B	3B	HR	RBI	BB	K	SB	CS	Whiff%	AVG/OBP/SLG	DRC+	BABIP	BRR	FRAA	WARP
2018	CR	LO-A	19	517	83	22	11	11	40	74	124	24	5		.243/.351/.419	116	.311	4.7	CF(97): -12.1, LF(3): 0.1	1.0
2019	FTM	HI-A	20	131	15	3	3	4	9	12	39	6	2		.214/.290/.393	89	.280	1.6	CF(21): -2.7, LF(6): -0.2	0.1
2021 FS	DET	MLB	22	600	54	26	8	12	60	52	194	13	4		.212/.287/.364	76	.307	6.8	CF -13, LF 0	-0.5
2021 DC	DET	MLB	22	66	6	2	0	1	6	5	21	1	0		.212/.287/.364	76	.307	0.7	CF -1	-0.1

Comparables: Joe Benson, Clint Frazier, Aaron Hicks

The third-overall pick in the Rule 5 draft, Baddoo struggled mightily in High-A to close out the 2019 season, and there's little to suggest he'll survive a full season in the majors. Of course, the Tigers' entire outfield is populated by players who probably don't belong in the big leagues, so at least Baddoo is their type.

Jorge Bonifacio OF Born: 06/04/93 Age: 28 Bats: R Throws: R Height: 6'1" Weight: 220 Origin: International Free Agent, 2009

YEAR	TEAM	LVL	AGE	PA	R	2B	3B	HR	RBI	BB	K	SB	CS	Whiff%	AVG/OBP/SLG	DRC+	BABIP	BRR	FRAA	WARP
2018	OMA	AAA	25	58	11	5	1	0	9	7	12	0	0		.392/.466/.529	157	.513	-0.2	RF(13): -1.2	0.3
2018	KC	MLB	25	270	31	16	2	4	23	29	71	0	1	29.1%	.225/.312/.360	84	.301	0.0	RF(55): -0.8, LF(7): -1.0	-0.1
2019	OMA	AAA	26	500	67	18	5	20	62	38	121	6	4		.222/.284/.417	73	.252	0.4	LF(56): 9.6, RF(42): 3.7	0.8
2019	KC	MLB	26	21	3	3	0	0	3	1	7	0	0	29.3%	.350/.381/.500	67	.538	-0.3	RF(4): -0.3, LF(1): 0.0	-0.1
2020	DET	MLB	27	94	8	3	0	2	17	5	26	0	0	32.7%	.221/.277/.326	76	.288	0.3	LF(19): 0.9, RF(10): 0.2	0.0
2021 FS	DET	MLB	28	600	60	23	4	17	68	49	177	1	0	30.8%	.226/.297/.380	86	.301	2.5	RF -11, LF 0	-0.4

Comparables: Kevin Roberson, Dustan Mohr, Brian Buchanan

Remember the golden age of clutch hitting, which started around when baseball was invented and ended around the mid-2000s? Bonifacio had a season for that age: a 1.301 OPS with runners in scoring position, and .337 otherwise. Data has shown this isn't a projectable skill unless he starts believing in ghosts and then pictures them on base. The one-time Top 101 prospect has struggled to manifest his raw power into actual power and demonstrates the vestiges of athleticism in right field, but has yet to find the one ballpark that is truly haunted. We're not telling you which one it is, either.

Miguel Cabrera 1B Born: 04/18/83 Age: 38 Bats: R Throws: R Height: 6'4" Weight: 249 Origin: International Free Agent, 1999

YEAR	TEAM	LVL	AGE	PA	R	2B	3B	HR	RBI	BB	K	SB	CS	Whiff%	AVG/OBP/SLG	DRC+	BABIP	BRR	FRAA	WARP
2018	DET	MLB	35	157	17	11	0	3	22	22	27	0	0	22.7%	.299/.395/.448	108	.352	0.5	1B(32): -0.0	0.4
2019	DET	MLB	36	549	41	21	0	12	59	48	108	0	0	24.5%	.282/.346/.398	100	.336	-4.4	1B(26): -1.5	0.3
2020	DET	MLB	37	231	28	4	0	10	35	24	51	1	0	31.6%	.250/.329/.417	102	.283	-0.5		0.5
2021 FS	DET	MLB	38	600	71	25	1	16	69	65	139	0	0	27.0%	.258/.344/.402	110	.321	-1.0	1B 0	1.6
2021 DC	DET	MLB	38	562	67	23	1	15	65	61	130	0	0	27.0%	.258/.344/.402	110	.321	-1.0		1.8

Comparables: Fred McGriff, Lance Berkman, Jason Giambi

No one would have faulted him for climbing stiffly onto that retirement pony and riding it into the sunset, or even getting a fresh start with a playoff team by taking the Verlander's way out. But Cabrera seemed content with cementing his status as the lone recognizable face in an abysmal rebuild. He's holding his own as well, passing icon after icon on the leaderboard while adjusting to hit for power with whatever joints in his limbs still rotate. He ought to pass Ruth in hits, Gehrig in home runs, Ortiz in RBI and possibly Bonds in doubles. In all, a fine season will make him the seventh card-carrying member of the Society of 3,000-500 Gentlemen.

Daz Cameron CF Born: 01/15/97 Age: 24 Bats: R Throws: R Height: 6'2" Weight: 185 Origin: Round 1, 2015 Draft (#37 overall)

YEAR	TEAM	LVL	AGE	PA	R	2B	3B	HR	RBI	BB	K	SB	CS	Whiff%	AVG/OBP/SLG	DRC+	BABIP	BRR	FRAA	WARP
2018	LAK	HI-A	21	246	35	9	3	3	20	25	69	10	4		.259/.346/.370	117	.366	2.5	CF(38): 1.9, RF(18): 0.9	1.2
2018	ERI	AA	21	226	32	12	5	5	35	25	53	12	5		.285/.367/.470	123	.366	3.4	CF(34): -7.0, RF(16): 1.5	0.7
2018	TOL	AAA	21	62	8	4	1	0	6	2	15	2	2		.211/.246/.316	55	.279	0.7	CF(14): 0.3, RF(1): 0.0	-0.1
2019	TOL	AAA	22	528	68	22	6	13	43	62	152	17	8		.214/.330/.377	86	.291	2.4	CF(93): -1.0, RF(19): 5.4	1.3
2020	DET	MLB	23	59	4	2	1	0	3	2	19	1	0	26.5%	.193/.220/.263	68	.289	0.1	RF(16): 0.5	-0.1
2021 FS	DET	MLB	24	600	59	23	7	12	58	50	204	16	7	26.5%	.216/.293/.355	77	.322	2.8	RF 19, LF 0	2.3
2021 DC	DET	MLB	24	198	19	7	2	4	19	16	67	5	2	26.5%	.216/.293/.355	77	.322	0.9	RF 6	0.6

Comparables: Anthony Gose, Michael Saunders, Dalton Pompey

Father-son comparisons tend to evaporate when the progeny eclipses the progenitor. Cody Bellinger outdid Clay's career in about two months. Bobby Bonds was memory-holed by Barry. The Junior is the peak-performance Griffey. But the other way around? Tony Gwynn, Jr. was always chasing dad. Terry Francona didn't have the playing career of his father, and as penance, people call him Tito. Now that Cameron has debuted, it's important to note Mike beat him to the majors according to age by exactly 53 weeks. It's hard to envision the younger Cameron finishing with 1,700 career hits and nearly 300 home runs like Pops, especially since the plate skills remain a yellow flag, but it's easy to see him patrol center field and time warp back to the early 2000s Mariners.

Jeimer Candelario 3B   Born: 11/24/93   Age: 27   Bats: S   Throws: R   Height: 6'1"   Weight: 221   Origin: International Free Agent, 2010

YEAR	TEAM	LVL	AGE	PA	R	2B	3B	HR	RBI	BB	K	SB	CS	Whiff%	AVG/OBP/SLG	DRC+	BABIP	BRR	FRAA	WARP
2018	DET	MLB	24	619	78	28	3	19	54	66	160	3	2	25.6%	.224/.317/.393	91	.279	-2.4	3B(140): -4.1	0.9
2019	TOL	AAA	25	178	30	10	2	9	33	22	35	0	0		.320/.416/.588	153	.367	-1.4	3B(30): 0.1, 1B(7): -0.4	1.5
2019	DET	MLB	25	386	33	17	2	8	32	43	99	3	1	25.8%	.203/.306/.337	78	.262	-1.0	3B(69): -1.0, 1B(20): -0.2	0.0
2020	DET	MLB	27	206	30	11	3	7	29	20	49	1	1	27.8%	.297/.369/.503	113	.372	0.7	1B(43): 1.6, 3B(10): 1.5	1.0
2021 FS	DET	MLB	27	600	68	26	4	16	71	64	153	2	0	26.3%	.238/.328/.399	102	.303	2.3	1B -5, 3B 0	1.0
2021 DC	DET	MLB	27	562	63	24	4	15	67	60	143	2	0	26.3%	.238/.328/.399	102	.303	2.1	1B -5	0.7

Comparables: Phil Nevin, Russ Davis, Wilson Betemit

Candelario may be the dramatic type. Not the sports talk radio controversy type, or the Shakespeare in the Park type, but the erratic production from season to season type. It's the worst category of drama for someone trying to stay in the lineup, but after a forgettable 2019 that resulted in a Triple-A demotion, Candelario roared back with conviction, slapping the label off the ball, improving his batting and slugging averages against both fastballs and offspeed pitches equally. His line drive attitude will keep his homer total in the low 20s at best, and his move to first base was more out of roster-based necessity than defensive inferiority. PECOTA doesn't project levels of drama for the 2021 season, but it's unofficially in the "TNT Original Series" range.

Harold Castro 3B   Born: 11/30/93   Age: 27   Bats: L   Throws: R   Height: 5'10"   Weight: 151   Origin: International Free Agent, 2011

YEAR	TEAM	LVL	AGE	PA	R	2B	3B	HR	RBI	BB	K	SB	CS	Whiff%	AVG/OBP/SLG	DRC+	BABIP	BRR	FRAA	WARP
2018	ERI	AA	24	116	10	5	0	0	10	4	21	2	1		.282/.310/.327	78	.344	0.1	2B(14): -1.6, 3B(8): 0.9, LF(3): 0.0	-0.3
2018	TOL	AAA	24	251	24	8	0	2	19	5	47	3	3		.257/.270/.315	67	.309	1.0	3B(30): -0.1, SS(22): -1.7, 2B(12): -2.1	-0.7
2018	DET	MLB	24	10	2	0	0	0	0	0	2	1	0	33.3%	.300/.300/.300	79	.375	-0.1	SS(4): 0.1, 2B(2): 0.0	0.0
2019	TOL	AAA	25	134	20	5	1	4	25	9	26	1	3		.328/.371/.484	123	.387	1.6	2B(23): -1.0, 1B(2): 0.1, 3B(2): 0.1	0.9
2019	DET	MLB	25	369	30	10	4	5	38	9	86	4	2	24.5%	.291/.305/.384	77	.367	-2.8	2B(34): -2.1, CF(30): -0.0, 3B(10): -0.9	-0.4
2020	DET	MLB	27	54	6	4	0	0	3	5	11	0	0	24.3%	.347/.407/.429	97	.447	0.1	LF(6): 0.0, 3B(4): 0.1, RF(4): 0.3	0.1
2021 FS	DET	MLB	27	600	57	26	4	8	60	22	137	7	3	24.5%	.264/.295/.371	78	.334	0.7	2B -3, 3B 2	0.0
2021 DC	DET	MLB	27	297	28	13	2	4	29	10	68	3	1	24.5%	.264/.295/.371	78	.334	0.4	2B -2, 3B 1	-0.1

Comparables: Bo Hart, Jerry Buchek, Fred Manrique

If Castro were the main protagonist in *Where's Waldo* books, kids would stop reading them in sheer frustration; he starts everywhere and is impossible to find. He missed a month with a lame hammy in an already teensy season, and still managed to start a game at every position except second base. It's entirely possible he's writing himself into the lineup with the purple crayon. He lacks the requisite power or speed to secure substantial lineup card placement, but Hittin' Harold's batting average hasn't lied to him yet.

Willi Castro SS   Born: 04/24/97   Age: 24   Bats: S   Throws: R   Height: 6'1"   Weight: 170   Origin: International Free Agent, 2013

YEAR	TEAM	LVL	AGE	PA	R	2B	3B	HR	RBI	BB	K	SB	CS	Whiff%	AVG/OBP/SLG	DRC+	BABIP	BRR	FRAA	WARP
2018	ERI	AA	21	114	12	9	2	4	13	6	25	4	1		.324/.366/.562	95	.395	-0.8	SS(10): 0.7, 2B(9): -0.2	0.1
2018	AKR	AA	21	410	55	20	2	5	39	28	84	13	4		.245/.303/.350	95	.304	1.3	SS(96): 7.5	1.9
2019	TOL	AAA	22	525	75	28	8	11	62	37	110	17	4		.301/.366/.467	110	.369	0.3	SS(111): -15.3, 2B(7): 0.2, 3B(1): -0.0	1.6
2019	DET	MLB	22	110	10	6	1	1	8	6	34	0	1	30.7%	.230/.284/.340	68	.333	0.9	SS(29): 1.1	0.3
2020	DET	MLB	23	140	21	4	2	6	24	7	38	0	1	30.8%	.349/.381/.550	102	.448	-1.4	SS(27): -2.3, 3B(8): -0.6, 2B(1): -0.0	0.0
2021 FS	DET	MLB	24	600	65	23	6	13	67	33	159	9	3	30.8%	.255/.306/.394	90	.335	3.4	SS -1, 2B 0	1.5
2021 DC	DET	MLB	24	562	61	21	5	12	63	31	149	8	3	30.8%	.255/.306/.394	90	.335	3.2	SS -1	1.3

Comparables: Tim Anderson, Marcus Semien, Stephen Drew

Say this about the Tigers: They have a middle infielder type. While all the other contenders are cranking taters, Detroit has a metric pantload of tryhards up the middle who rely on speed, defense, line drive power and absolutely no name recognition or patience. Castro is in the thick of the bunch. His slash line resembled Trea Turner's rookie season, as he slapped every ball between short and third and beat out half the throws. Batting average may be going out of style, but hitting 100 points above the league average never will. He may be more of a second baseman due to the defense, but the bat-on-ball skills will keep him on the lineup card somewhere ahead of the 53 identical players behind him on the depth chart.

Kody Clemens 2B   Born: 05/15/96   Age: 25   Bats: L   Throws: R   Height: 6'1"   Weight: 170   Origin: Round 3, 2018 Draft (#79 overall)

YEAR	TEAM	LVL	AGE	PA	R	2B	3B	HR	RBI	BB	K	SB	CS	Whiff%	AVG/OBP/SLG	DRC+	BABIP	BRR	FRAA	WARP
2018	WM	LO-A	22	174	18	10	2	4	17	21	27	3	1		.302/.387/.477	140	.342	-0.9	2B(39): -1.6	0.8
2018	LAK	HI-A	22	46	6	2	0	1	3	2	12	1	0		.238/.283/.357	66	.300	0.3	2B(11): 0.2	-0.1
2019	LAK	HI-A	23	469	43	24	7	11	59	45	101	11	3		.238/.314/.411	112	.283	-2.3	2B(99): -0.7	1.4
2019	ERI	AA	23	54	5	2	0	1	4	6	18	0	0		.170/.278/.277	54	.250	-0.6	2B(13): 1.6	0.0
2021 FS	DET	MLB	25	600	58	27	3	17	66	43	173	3	1		.225/.286/.382	83	.295	1.7	2B 1	1.1

Comparables: Ryan Schimpf, Taylor Featherston, Sam Haggerty

Famous-named second baseman Clemens spent last summer on a makeshift independent league team managed by his dad and oldest brother. He is the youngest of Roger's four large adult sons and has the best chance of any of them to become a big leaguer. One of the Constellation Energy League's ballclubs, the Sugar Land Skeeters, got promoted to Triple-A as the Astros' affiliate; Clemens can only hope to follow suit.

C.J. Cron 1B   Born: 01/05/90   Age: 31   Bats: R   Throws: R   Height: 6'4"   Weight: 235   Origin: Round 1, 2011 Draft (#17 overall)

YEAR	TEAM	LVL	AGE	PA	R	2B	3B	HR	RBI	BB	K	SB	CS	Whiff%	AVG/OBP/SLG	DRC+	BABIP	BRR	FRAA	WARP
2018	TB	MLB	28	560	68	28	1	30	74	37	145	1	2	29.0%	.253/.323/.493	117	.293	-3.5	1B(61): 2.6	1.9
2019	MIN	MLB	29	499	51	24	0	25	78	29	107	0	0	25.3%	.253/.311/.469	100	.277	-2.6	1B(117): 8.0	1.3
2020	DET	MLB	30	52	9	3	0	4	8	9	16	0	0	31.3%	.190/.346/.548	99	.182	-0.3	1B(13): 1.1	0.2
2021 FS	DET	MLB	31	600	73	24	2	27	89	40	156	3	1	27.1%	.234/.301/.437	105	.276	-0.8	1B 10	2.2

Comparables: Matt Adams, Mark Trumbo, Andres Galarraga

Seven of Cron's eight hits went for extra bases and half cleared the wall. A walking obelisk of ISO, said walking turned into a severe limp that required knee surgery, limiting his 2020 to two weeks of bopping and a pocketful of what-ifs. He was already on a trajectory of nothing but one-year deals for the rest of his career, plugging into lineup sinkholes wherever they may arise, because when you're a right-handed first baseman, it's a little-known rule that you can only sign one-year or 10-year deals.

Travis Demeritte LF   Born: 09/30/94   Age: 26   Bats: R   Throws: R   Height: 6'0"   Weight: 180   Origin: Round 1, 2013 Draft (#30 overall)

YEAR	TEAM	LVL	AGE	PA	R	2B	3B	HR	RBI	BB	K	SB	CS	Whiff%	AVG/OBP/SLG	DRC+	BABIP	BRR	FRAA	WARP
2018	MIS	AA	23	494	69	22	5	17	63	57	140	6	2		.222/.316/.416	102	.284	-2.2	LF(119): -5.9, 3B(1): 0.1, CF(1): -0.2	-0.5
2019	GWN	AAA	24	399	68	28	2	20	73	51	106	4	3		.286/.387/.558	136	.358	0.0	LF(38): 0.1, RF(36): -2.0	2.3
2019	DET	MLB	24	186	24	7	2	3	10	14	63	3	0	35.2%	.225/.286/.343	61	.337	1.7	RF(47): 3.8	0.0
2020	DET	MLB	26	33	5	1	0	0	4	3	14	0	0	49.1%	.172/.273/.207	63	.333	0.2	RF(12): 0.6, LF(2): 0.5, P(1): -0.0	0.0
2021 FS	DET	MLB	26	600	58	24	5	15	62	55	232	3	1	38.3%	.204/.284/.359	78	.323	3.6	RF 0, 2B 0	0.4
2021 DC	DET	MLB	26	66	6	2	0	1	6	6	25	0	0	38.3%	.204/.284/.359	78	.323	0.4	RF 0	0.0

Comparables: Joe Borchard, Doug Frobel, Jason Repko

Best-case scenario for Demeritte: He finally realizes his power potential and sticks around as a fourth outfielder, pinch hitting in the eighth inning of three-run deficits and leaving them untouched. Worst case: He keeps going down to Triple-A, falling victim to the easiest surname play on words in transaction history.

Dillon Dingler C   Born: 09/17/98   Age: 22   Bats: R   Throws: R   Height: 6'3"   Weight: 210   Origin: Round 2, 2020 Draft (#38 overall)

Dingler's truncated junior season had 10 extra-base hits in 13 games (half of 'em homers) with legitimate catching defense that put the scouts on notice, giving him sudden first-round potential, but second-round reality. Still, he John Hancocked a record signing bonus for an Ohio State Buckeye, surpassing Nick Swisher 18 years prior, though he likely won't get his own chapter in a Michael Lewis book about it. He spent some time in the Tigers' 60-man pool, but being relatively new at catching (he was a center fielder two years ago), we likely won't see him swishing or dingling in the majors for at least a few years.

Niko Goodrum SS   Born: 02/28/92   Age: 29   Bats: S   Throws: R   Height: 6'3"   Weight: 198   Origin: Round 2, 2010 Draft (#71 overall)

YEAR	TEAM	LVL	AGE	PA	R	2B	3B	HR	RBI	BB	K	SB	CS	Whiff%	AVG/OBP/SLG	DRC+	BABIP	BRR	FRAA	WARP
2018	DET	MLB	26	492	55	29	3	16	53	42	132	12	4	29.9%	.245/.315/.432	97	.312	-1.3	2B(64): 1.0, 1B(37): -0.8, SS(12): -1.4	0.9
2019	DET	MLB	27	472	61	27	5	12	45	46	137	12	3	31.9%	.248/.322/.421	86	.337	3.4	SS(38): 3.6, 2B(22): -1.9, LF(20): -0.2	1.6
2020	DET	MLB	28	179	15	7	1	5	20	18	69	7	1	38.4%	.184/.263/.335	74	.276	-1.2	SS(31): 3.6, 2B(11): 0.5	0.2
2021 FS	DET	MLB	29	600	65	24	4	15	59	54	210	9	3	33.3%	.213/.288/.364	80	.315	4.2	2B -4, SS 3	0.6
2021 DC	DET	MLB	29	562	60	22	4	14	55	50	196	9	3	33.3%	.213/.288/.364	80	.315	3.9	2B -4, SS 3	0.8

Comparables: Jeff Baker, Geronimo Pena, Danny Espinosa

Goodrum became the first player in history with two doubles, three strikeouts, five RBI and a walk in a game. This bizarre sampler of outcomes wouldn't have been noteworthy without the three whiffs, which were the story of his 2020, and his entire career, for that matter. Strikeouts aren't awful if you're raking. Goodrum does not rake, although has been known to comb on occasion. Having him on your roster means you have defensive versatility down the lineup, a position type that is getting increasingly common. But only one of them is named Niko.

★ ★ ★ *2021 Top 101 Prospect* **#19** ★ ★ ★

Riley Greene RF   Born: 09/28/00   Age: 20   Bats: L   Throws: L   Height: 6'3"   Weight: 200   Origin: Round 1, 2019 Draft (#5 overall)

YEAR	TEAM	LVL	AGE	PA	R	2B	3B	HR	RBI	BB	K	SB	CS	Whiff%	AVG/OBP/SLG	DRC+	BABIP	BRR	FRAA	WARP
2019	TIW	ROK	18	43	9	3	0	2	8	5	12	0	0		.351/.442/.595	164	.478	-1.6	CF(9): -1.9	0.1
2019	NOR	SS	18	100	12	3	1	1	7	11	25	1	0		.295/.380/.386	127	.403	-1.5	CF(21): 3.5	0.7
2019	WM	LO-A	18	108	13	2	2	2	13	6	26	4	0		.219/.278/.344	62	.268	0.8	CF(20): 1.9, RF(4): -0.0	0.2
2021 FS	DET	MLB	20	600	48	26	3	9	53	33	209	6	2		.214/.265/.323	61	.323	1.5	CF 8, RF 0	-0.1

It's July in Comerica Park, and Greene just robbed someone of a home run by reaching over the left field wall. This may be a lucid dream about the future of the team but it was literally last year's training camp, and a reminder that there's a very exciting outfielder waiting in the wings. The 20-year-old with baseball-smacking potential probably would have completed his High-A season in The Normal Times, so this year's league will presumably contain multiple vowels.

Grayson Greiner C Born: 10/11/92 Age: 28 Bats: R Throws: R Height: 6'6" Weight: 239 Origin: Round 3, 2014 Draft (#99 overall)

YEAR	TEAM	LVL	AGE	PA	R	2B	3B	HR	RBI	BB	K	SB	CS	Whiff%	AVG/OBP/SLG	DRC+	BABIP	BRR	FRAA	WARP
2018	TOL	AAA	25	180	12	8	1	4	23	21	42	0	0		.266/.350/.405	115	.336	0.3	C(44): 11.2	2.1
2018	DET	MLB	25	116	9	6	0	0	12	17	32	0	1	26.6%	.219/.328/.281	78	.313	0.3	C(30): -0.5	0.3
2019	TOL	AAA	26	53	8	1	0	2	4	4	16	0	0		.250/.321/.396	89	.333	0.5	C(9): 1.1	0.3
2019	DET	MLB	26	224	18	5	1	5	19	13	70	0	0	32.3%	.202/.251/.308	55	.276	-0.9	C(58): -2.9	-0.5
2020	DET	MLB	28	55	8	2	0	3	8	3	20	0	0	31.7%	.118/.182/.333	78	.107	-0.3	C(18): -0.3	-0.1
2021 FS	*DET*	*MLB*	*28*	*600*	*61*	*22*	*2*	*16*	*64*	*48*	*196*	*1*	*0*	*31.3%*	*.209/.278/.353*	*75*	*.291*	*1.3*	*C -5*	*0.2*
2021 DC	*DET*	*MLB*	*28*	*397*	*40*	*14*	*1*	*11*	*42*	*31*	*130*	*0*	*0*	*31.3%*	*.209/.278/.353*	*75*	*.291*	*0.9*	*C -4*	*0.0*

Comparables: Ron Karkovice, Paul Bako, Jeff Mathis

"Missing: tall catcher." Greiner's whereabouts are completely known, but this poster is a complete scouting summary of his hitting, size and primary position.

YEAR	TEAM	P. COUNT	FRM RUNS	BLK RUNS	THRW RUNS	TOT RUNS
2018	DET	4496	-0.6	-0.2	0.0	-0.9
2018	TOL	6038	9.5	0.5	0.3	10.3
2019	DET	8636	-2.4	0.3	0.2	-2.0
2019	TOL	1168	1.2	0.0	0.0	1.2
2020	DET	2451	-0.3	0.0	0.0	-0.3
2021	*DET*	*14430*	*-2.5*	*-1.3*	*-0.1*	*-3.9*

Robbie Grossman LF Born: 09/16/89 Age: 31 Bats: S Throws: L Height: 6'0" Weight: 216 Origin: Round 6, 2008 Draft (#174 overall)

YEAR	TEAM	LVL	AGE	PA	R	2B	3B	HR	RBI	BB	K	SB	CS	Whiff%	AVG/OBP/SLG	DRC+	BABIP	BRR	FRAA	WARP
2018	MIN	MLB	28	465	50	27	1	5	48	60	83	0	1	16.0%	.273/.367/.384	105	.329	-4.9	RF(52): -2.6, LF(34): 1.2	0.6
2019	OAK	MLB	29	482	57	21	3	6	38	59	86	9	4	15.4%	.240/.334/.348	96	.288	-4.3	LF(112): 3.2, RF(20): -1.3, CF(1): 0.1	0.9
2020	OAK	MLB	31	192	23	12	2	8	23	21	38	8	1	18.4%	.241/.344/.482	119	.267	0.9	LF(46): 2.7, CF(2): 0.0, RF(1): -0.1	1.1
2021 FS	*DET*	*MLB*	*31*	*600*	*63*	*23*	*1*	*13*	*59*	*77*	*134*	*4*	*2*	*16.4%*	*.229/.333/.361*	*97*	*.282*	*-0.7*	*LF 7, RF -2*	*1.8*
2021 DC	*DET*	*MLB*	*31*	*496*	*52*	*19*	*1*	*11*	*49*	*63*	*110*	*4*	*1*	*16.4%*	*.229/.333/.361*	*97*	*.282*	*-0.6*	*LF 6, RF -2*	*1.6*

Comparables: Jack Voigt, Daniel Nava, Jason Michaels

Mathematically, a gross refers to a dozen dozen, 144, of something. It's etymologically distinct from the other definitions of gross, and the term's use is encouraged by the Dozenal Society of America (which advocates for a base-12 numerical system). By that metric, Grossman's 2020 season was as unsuccessful as each of his major league seasons, and all campaigns since his 144 DRC+ in Triple-A in 2014. By most other metrics, it was a career year for the 31-year-old, who was above average at the plate, in the field, *and* on the basepaths for a three-win pace thanks to a new pull-heavy, fly ball approach. The DRC+ likely won't ever reach gross heights, though his 119 mark was just short of a great gross (120) and looks to be repeatable.

Derek Hill CF Born: 12/30/95 Age: 25 Bats: R Throws: R Height: 6'2" Weight: 190 Origin: Round 1, 2014 Draft (#23 overall)

YEAR	TEAM	LVL	AGE	PA	R	2B	3B	HR	RBI	BB	K	SB	CS	Whiff%	AVG/OBP/SLG	DRC+	BABIP	BRR	FRAA	WARP
2018	LAK	HI-A	22	383	45	9	3	4	33	33	109	35	12		.239/.307/.318	82	.338	3.7	CF(55): -2.5, LF(27): -2.1, RF(21): 0.4	-0.5
2019	ERI	AA	23	526	78	19	5	14	45	38	147	21	13		.243/.311/.394	92	.321	0.7	CF(80): 1.4, RF(37): 7.8, LF(2): -0.2	2.2
2020	DET	MLB	25	12	3	0	0	0	1	0	6	0	0	40.9%	.091/.167/.091	67	.200	0.0	CF(10): -0.2	-0.1
2021 FS	*DET*	*MLB*	*25*	*600*	*60*	*24*	*6*	*11*	*53*	*42*	*213*	*25*	*9*	*40.9%*	*.219/.280/.349*	*73*	*.333*	*4.5*	*CF -1, RF 4*	*0.5*

Comparables: Matthew den Dekker, Xavier Avery, Daniel Fields

Once a highly regarded prospect, Hill's development was interrupted by nagging injuries, but thanks to someone else's fractured hand, he finally hit the big leagues six years after his first-round christening. He can run, field and throw, and he's got a real knack for highlight-reel diving catches. Assuming this is the complete list of skills one needs as a position player, he's good as gold.

JaCoby Jones CF Born: 05/10/92 Age: 29 Bats: R Throws: R Height: 6'2" Weight: 201 Origin: Round 3, 2013 Draft (#87 overall)

YEAR	TEAM	LVL	AGE	PA	R	2B	3B	HR	RBI	BB	K	SB	CS	Whiff%	AVG/OBP/SLG	DRC+	BABIP	BRR	FRAA	WARP
2018	DET	MLB	26	467	54	22	6	11	34	24	142	13	5	30.9%	.207/.266/.364	67	.281	4.3	CF(67): 4.0, LF(55): 2.7	0.7
2019	DET	MLB	27	333	39	19	3	11	26	27	94	7	2	26.2%	.235/.310/.430	87	.304	1.2	CF(85): -7.8	0.0
2020	DET	MLB	28	108	19	9	0	5	14	7	34	1	1	33.7%	.268/.333/.515	90	.356	0.3	CF(28): -1.9	0.0
2021 FS	*DET*	*MLB*	*29*	*600*	*60*	*25*	*5*	*15*	*60*	*44*	*204*	*10*	*3*	*29.4%*	*.211/.283/.362*	*77*	*.306*	*3.4*	*CF 3, LF 0*	*0.8*
2021 DC	*DET*	*MLB*	*29*	*463*	*46*	*20*	*4*	*11*	*46*	*34*	*157*	*8*	*2*	*29.4%*	*.211/.283/.362*	*77*	*.306*	*2.6*	*CF 3*	*0.7*

Comparables: Ruben Rivera, Reggie Taylor, Michael A. Taylor

Progression is almost never linear. There are setbacks, slumps and inopportune spells of bad luck that seem inexplicable to us when someone follows a breakout year with mediocrity. We trust in regression to the mean. It's those wretched do-gooders who make four straight years of improvements that throw us into convulsions. Jones' OPS improved by a total 100 points in each of the last four seasons, starting from the lowest of bars. The improvements turned him from hanger-on to capable starter. His whiffs and walks still lag behind the major league median, but with his speed and instincts Jones will remain a useful starting center fielder, and everybody likes those, especially if they don't regress.

Parker Meadows CF   Born: 11/02/99   Age: 21   Bats: L   Throws: R   Height: 6'5"   Weight: 205   Origin: Round 2, 2018 Draft (#44 overall)

YEAR	TEAM	LVL	AGE	PA	R	2B	3B	HR	RBI	BB	K	SB	CS	Whiff%	AVG/OBP/SLG	DRC+	BABIP	BRR	FRAA	WARP
2018	TIW	ROK	18	85	16	2	1	4	8	8	25	3	1		.284/.376/.500	125	.378	0.0	CF(20): -3.1	-0.1
2018	NOR	SS	18	21	4	1	0	0	2	2	6	0	0		.316/.381/.368	97	.462	0.1	CF(6): 0.0	0.0
2019	WM	LO-A	19	504	52	15	2	7	40	47	113	14	8		.221/.296/.312	78	.277	-1.1	CF(101): -2.3, RF(16): 0.8	0.0
2021 FS	DET	MLB	21	600	49	25	2	10	53	35	205	8	4		.213/.265/.323	60	.317	-3.0	CF 1, RF 0	-1.4

Comparables: Derrick Robinson, Mickey Moniak, Carlos Tocci

Meadows spent the summer at the Tigers' alternate site, with the aim of making mechanical adjustments to a long swing that contributed to his struggles in his first stint in full-season ball. Until he makes some movement in the minors, he'll henceforth be known as Austin's little brother, not to be confused with the other Austin's little brother: Round Rock.

Isaac Paredes 3B   Born: 02/18/99   Age: 22   Bats: R   Throws: R   Height: 5'11"   Weight: 213   Origin: International Free Agent, 2015

YEAR	TEAM	LVL	AGE	PA	R	2B	3B	HR	RBI	BB	K	SB	CS	Whiff%	AVG/OBP/SLG	DRC+	BABIP	BRR	FRAA	WARP
2018	LAK	HI-A	19	347	50	19	2	12	48	32	54	1	0		.259/.338/.455	126	.274	0.3	SS(59): 3.2, 2B(22): 0.5, 3B(3): -0.1	2.0
2018	ERI	AA	19	155	20	9	0	3	22	19	22	1	0		.321/.406/.458	141	.358	0.3	3B(18): 0.6, SS(15): 0.9, 2B(2): 0.1	1.2
2019	ERI	AA	20	552	63	23	1	13	66	57	61	5	3		.282/.368/.416	137	.298	-2.3	3B(81): -3.4, SS(32): 0.1	3.4
2020	DET	MLB	21	108	7	4	0	1	6	8	24	0	0	17.6%	.220/.278/.290	81	.280	-0.4	3B(33): -2.4	-0.3
2021 FS	DET	MLB	22	600	67	27	2	15	66	48	125	1	0	17.6%	.244/.315/.390	97	.291	0.5	3B 0, 2B 0	1.5
2021 DC	DET	MLB	22	463	51	21	2	11	51	37	97	0	0	17.6%	.244/.315/.390	97	.291	0.4	3B 0	0.8

Comparables: Wilmer Flores, Francisco Lindor, J.P. Crawford

Paredes arrived in Detroit last summer as part of the Great Call-Up, and in jumping straight from Double-A, found himself overmatched for the first time in his career. There are three other players in the last century who primarily manned third base at 21 years old with Paredes' body type, by height and weight. One was Dayán Viciedo, a reasonable projection in terms of offense productivity. Another is Edgardo Alfonzo, who had far more middle infield prowess. The last is Adrián Beltré, which is a wildly unfair comp so we'll stop right there. Of the three, Alfonzo may be the shrewdest parallel and best-case scenario: modest power, some mobility and a prescient eye for strikes.

Victor Reyes LF   Born: 10/05/94   Age: 26   Bats: S   Throws: R   Height: 6'5"   Weight: 194   Origin: International Free Agent, 2011

YEAR	TEAM	LVL	AGE	PA	R	2B	3B	HR	RBI	BB	K	SB	CS	Whiff%	AVG/OBP/SLG	DRC+	BABIP	BRR	FRAA	WARP
2018	DET	MLB	23	219	35	5	3	1	12	5	46	9	1	22.1%	.222/.239/.288	63	.277	0.1	LF(34): -3.2, CF(21): 2.2, RF(9): -0.7	-0.6
2019	TOL	AAA	24	308	50	19	1	10	58	14	50	10	6		.304/.334/.481	105	.335	0.4	RF(36): 0.8, CF(31): -0.4	1.0
2019	DET	MLB	24	292	29	16	5	3	25	14	64	9	3	21.1%	.304/.336/.431	88	.384	-0.4	CF(37): -0.1, LF(21): 2.0, RF(9): -0.2	0.6
2020	DET	MLB	26	213	30	7	2	4	14	9	45	8	2	26.5%	.277/.315/.391	92	.340	0.7	CF(30): 2.1, LF(22): 0.3, RF(18): -0.0	0.5
2021 FS	DET	MLB	26	600	65	25	7	10	55	27	133	11	4	23.6%	.266/.302/.392	87	.331	4.1	RF 2, CF 1	1.3
2021 DC	DET	MLB	26	529	58	22	6	9	49	23	117	10	4	23.6%	.266/.302/.392	87	.331	3.6	RF 2, CF 1	1.1

Comparables: Cecil Espy, Billy Cowan, Greg Allen

A line drive swing isn't always a compliment. For Reyes, it's all he has, and the skill is coming along nicely. Unable to consistently whack the ball 400 feet, he has worked on striving for good contact while using the uncoachable skill of speed to convert the hard-hit singles into extra bases. The plate aggression makes ball four a scarcity, but line drives will play in any league, as hitting enough of those is bound to turn some into long balls. Seasons of 20 doubles and 20 steals—feats that happen about 20 times a season across the majors—are entirely within reach for this former Rule 5 pick.

Jake Rogers C   Born: 04/18/95   Age: 26   Bats: R   Throws: R   Height: 6'1"   Weight: 192   Origin: Round 3, 2016 Draft (#97 overall)

YEAR	TEAM	LVL	AGE	PA	R	2B	3B	HR	RBI	BB	K	SB	CS	Whiff%	AVG/OBP/SLG	DRC+	BABIP	BRR	FRAA	WARP
2018	ERI	AA	23	408	57	15	1	17	56	41	112	7	1		.219/.305/.412	88	.261	2.7	C(98): 29.4, 1B(1): 0.0	4.2
2019	ERI	AA	24	112	17	3	1	5	21	19	26	0	0		.302/.429/.535	164	.356	-1.7	C(21): 2.3	1.2
2019	TOL	AAA	24	191	29	10	1	9	31	18	53	0	0		.223/.321/.458	88	.269	-2.7	C(48): 9.5	1.3
2019	DET	MLB	24	128	11	3	0	4	8	13	51	0	0	31.5%	.125/.222/.259	52	.175	-0.4	C(34): -4.0	-0.6
2021 FS	DET	MLB	26	600	64	20	3	19	65	53	204	3	1	31.5%	.200/.283/.363	80	.279	2.1	C -6, 1B 0	0.6
2021 DC	DET	MLB	26	231	25	7	1	7	25	20	78	1	0	31.5%	.200/.283/.363	80	.279	0.8	C -3	0.1

Comparables: Lucas May, Luke Montz, Tom Murphy

The defensively pragmatic Rogers took a year off from collecting major league stats against his will, though putting a year's worth of natural calamity between himself and his 2019 production couldn't hurt his standing. Whether or not he remains the Tigers' catcher of the future, and whether or not this is levied as a criticism toward said future, Rogers should be able to bang just enough bombs to justify a catcher's batting average equal to your average league bowling score.

YEAR	TEAM	P. COUNT	FRM RUNS	BLK RUNS	THRW RUNS	TOT RUNS
2019	DET	5389	-1.4	-2.2	0.2	-3.3
2019	TOL	6997	7.3	0.0	1.2	8.4
2021	DET	8418	0.0	-3.6	-0.2	-3.8

Austin Romine C Born: 11/22/88 Age: 32 Bats: R Throws: R Height: 6'1" Weight: 216 Origin: Round 2, 2007 Draft (#94 overall)

YEAR	TEAM	LVL	AGE	PA	R	2B	3B	HR	RBI	BB	K	SB	CS	Whiff%	AVG/OBP/SLG	DRC+	BABIP	BRR	FRAA	WARP
2018	NYY	MLB	29	265	30	12	0	10	42	17	67	1	0	26.4%	.244/.295/.417	85	.292	-3.1	C(76): 6.8	1.2
2019	NYY	MLB	30	240	29	12	0	8	35	10	50	1	1	22.7%	.281/.310/.439	89	.327	-1.0	C(70): -2.5, P(1): -0.0	0.6
2020	DET	MLB	32	135	12	5	0	2	17	4	47	0	0	29.9%	.238/.259/.323	51	.354	-0.9	C(37): -0.6, 1B(1): 0.2	-0.5
2021 FS	DET	MLB	32	600	58	25	1	13	64	32	172	2	1	26.2%	.232/.279/.358	75	.310	-0.3	C -3, 1B 0	0.2

Comparables: Humberto Quintero, Robert Machado, Damon Berryhill

YEAR	TEAM	P. COUNT	FRM RUNS	BLK RUNS	THRW RUNS	TOT RUNS
2018	NYY	10494	4.2	2.2	0.0	6.3
2019	NYY	9536	-2.2	0.9	0.1	-1.1
2020	DET	5408	-0.7	0.2	0.3	-0.2
2021	DET	16650	-1.5	0.1	-1.7	-3.1

There's something wildly psychotic about growing huge swaths of facial hair during hot summers in a job that requires extra headgear, but it probably stems from overcompensating for years of Yankees paychecks. So the verdict is in: Romine, a reliable backup catcher, is now a certified Beard Guy as well. He also has a history with Miguel Cabrera, getting into a shoving match during a 2017 game as opponents, then voluntarily spending a year as teammates. This also shows he's able to bury the hatchet, and in needing a location for it, could explain the heavy beard.

Jonathan Schoop 2B Born: 10/16/91 Age: 29 Bats: R Throws: R Height: 6'1" Weight: 225 Origin: International Free Agent, 2008

YEAR	TEAM	LVL	AGE	PA	R	2B	3B	HR	RBI	BB	K	SB	CS	Whiff%	AVG/OBP/SLG	DRC+	BABIP	BRR	FRAA	WARP
2018	MIL	MLB	26	134	16	4	0	4	21	7	41	1	0	33.2%	.202/.246/.331	82	.259	1.0	2B(31): 1.4, SS(15): 1.1	0.5
2018	BAL	MLB	26	367	45	18	1	17	40	12	74	0	1	26.5%	.244/.273/.447	83	.262	-0.6	2B(85): 7.9, SS(2): -0.0	1.1
2019	MIN	MLB	27	464	61	23	1	23	59	20	115	1	1	32.2%	.256/.304/.473	93	.297	-1.8	2B(113): -5.8	0.3
2020	DET	MLB	29	177	26	4	2	8	23	8	39	0	0	27.8%	.278/.324/.475	91	.316	1.2	2B(44): 0.6	0.6
2021 FS	DET	MLB	29	600	72	26	2	22	78	26	147	1	0	30.0%	.245/.291/.420	95	.293	-0.2	2B 4, SS 0	2.2

Comparables: Jedd Gyorko, Howie Kendrick, Scooter Gennett

Schoop is today's version of Jay Bell, in that he's a second baseman who can crush and you're not sure how old he is or what team he's on anymore. If you bought this book to find out what team Schoop played for in 2020, then money well spent. But for as much as he elevates, he's had trouble leading his team in home runs. In 2016, Schoop hit 25 for the Orioles—and was 22 short of the team lead. The next year he upgraded to 32—and missed Manny Machado's mark by one. Two years ago he belted 23, a paltry eighth on the Bomba Squad. And just when eight seemed like enough before landing on the IL, Miguel Cabrera came out of nowhere with a hot finish to beat him by two. Bell didn't lead his team until his 14th season, so draft Schoop for your fantasy team in 2026 and not a moment sooner.

Christin Stewart LF Born: 12/10/93 Age: 27 Bats: L Throws: R Height: 6'0" Weight: 220 Origin: Round 1, 2015 Draft (#34 overall)

YEAR	TEAM	LVL	AGE	PA	R	2B	3B	HR	RBI	BB	K	SB	CS	Whiff%	AVG/OBP/SLG	DRC+	BABIP	BRR	FRAA	WARP
2018	TOL	AAA	24	522	69	21	3	23	77	67	108	0	0		.264/.364/.480	136	.296	0.8	LF(97): 9.8, RF(12): -0.7	3.5
2018	DET	MLB	24	72	7	1	1	2	10	10	13	0	0	24.1%	.267/.375/.417	106	.304	-0.3	LF(15): -0.9	0.1
2019	LAK	HI-A	25	25	2	1	0	1	5	3	3	0	0		.350/.400/.550	144	.333	0.2	LF(3): -0.4	0.1
2019	TOL	AAA	25	102	14	2	0	4	14	18	25	1	0		.289/.422/.458	139	.370	-0.1	LF(16): -3.4	0.4
2019	DET	MLB	25	416	32	25	1	10	40	34	103	0	1	28.2%	.233/.305/.388	85	.290	-4.1	LF(89): -12.5	-1.3
2020	DET	MLB	27	99	6	3	0	3	9	5	30	0	0	32.2%	.167/.224/.300	75	.207	-0.1	LF(32): -1.0	-0.3
2021 FS	DET	MLB	27	600	65	24	3	21	74	56	176	0	0	28.9%	.219/.306/.400	94	.284	1.3	LF -4, RF 0	0.9
2021 DC	DET	MLB	27	198	21	8	1	7	24	18	58	0	0	28.9%	.219/.306/.400	94	.284	0.4	LF -1	0.3

Comparables: Larry Bigbie, Alex Gordon, Ryan Langerhans

One way to define potential energy is to picture a rock at the top of a hill. It has the potential to roll down and collide into something. The higher the hill, the more potential energy the rock possesses. Stewart is that rock on a hill and has yet to budge. This is because he's having trouble hitting anything other than a fastball, which certainly won't play well in a highly televised professional league. He has a long track record of beltin' from the left side in the minors, but with lumbering instincts in the outfield, he'll need to start hitting like a DH (designated hitter) or else become DH (dormant on a hill).

─────────────── ★ ★ ★ *2021 Top 101 Prospect* **#13** ★ ★ ★ ───────────────

Spencer Torkelson 3B Born: 08/26/99 Age: 21 Bats: R Throws: R Height: 6'1" Weight: 220 Origin: Round 1, 2020 Draft (#1 overall)

A 70-grade name if you're a mechanical engineer, Torkelson and his power bat should've replaced Adrián González at the turn of the century as the most recent first baseman to be yoinked first by a bunch of performative dorks in the MLB Draft. But Detroit has a premonition of trying him out at third base (since that worked out so well for Miguel Cabrera for about three minutes), instead making this factoid about Phil Nevin in 1992. The young man spent last year splashing around in the 60-man player pool, working with Hall of Fame luminaries such as Alan Trammell, a man whom Torkelson sheepishly admitted he had not heard of until being drafted. He broke a Barry Bonds home run school record at Arizona State as a freshman, and once he gets to the major leagues, he almost certainly will not do that again.

PITCHERS

Tyler Alexander LHP
Born: 07/14/94　Age: 26　Bats: R　Throws: L　Height: 6'2"　Weight: 200　Origin: Round 2, 2015 Draft (#65 overall)

YEAR	TEAM	LVL	AGE	W	L	SV	G	GS	IP	H	HR	BB/9	K/9	K	GB%	BABIP	WHIP	ERA	DRA-	WARP	MPH	FA%	Whiff%	CSP
2018	ERI	AA	23	3	2	0	9	9	48	64	7	1.7	6.6	35	42.2%	.361	1.52	3.75	83	0.8				
2018	TOL	AAA	23	3	6	0	17	15	92	120	9	1.3	5.9	60	45.5%	.355	1.45	4.79	93	1.0				
2019	TOL	AAA	24	5	10	0	20	16	98¹	112	18	2.1	9.9	108	39.9%	.346	1.37	5.13	111	1.2				
2019	DET	MLB	24	1	4	0	13	8	53²	68	9	1.2	7.9	47	36.9%	.347	1.40	4.86	122	-0.2	92.3	54.6%	18.3%	51.7%
2020	DET	MLB	25	2	3	0	14	2	36¹	39	8	2.2	8.4	34	45.7%	.320	1.32	3.96	106	0.2	92.0	43.7%	21.9%	46.0%
2021 FS	DET	MLB	26	3	5	0	57	0	50	52	8	2.1	8.2	45	41.8%	.306	1.29	4.53	108	-0.1	92.1	49.2%	20.1%	48.9%
2021 DC	DET	MLB	26	3	5	0	67	4	84	88	13	2.1	8.2	76	41.8%	.306	1.29	4.53	108	0.2	92.1	49.2%	20.1%	48.9%

Comparables: Anthony Misiewicz, Nestor Cortes, Jalen Beeks

Look at a chart of Alexander's pitch usage from game to game or month to month, and you'll find it resembles a plate of spaghetti. He has five different pitches (or six, depending on where you look), and will throw any of them in any count. He can bounce between starts and long relief. He wears number 70 and barely throws 90. He had a mustache in the minor leagues. He's the archetypal crafty lefty (but not Krafty, because if this junkballer had anything that resembled cheese they'd call him Utz).

Matthew Boyd LHP
Born: 02/02/91　Age: 30　Bats: L　Throws: L　Height: 6'3"　Weight: 234　Origin: Round 6, 2013 Draft (#175 overall)

YEAR	TEAM	LVL	AGE	W	L	SV	G	GS	IP	H	HR	BB/9	K/9	K	GB%	BABIP	WHIP	ERA	DRA-	WARP	MPH	FA%	Whiff%	CSP
2018	DET	MLB	27	9	13	0	31	31	170¹	146	27	2.7	8.4	159	29.7%	.259	1.16	4.39	116	0.2	93.5	48.8%	23.7%	49.0%
2019	DET	MLB	28	9	12	0	32	32	185¹	178	39	2.4	11.6	238	34.6%	.310	1.23	4.56	80	3.7	94.2	53.9%	31.4%	49.8%
2020	DET	MLB	29	3	7	0	12	12	60¹	67	15	3.3	9.0	60	37.5%	.310	1.48	6.71	140	-0.7	93.3	52.7%	27.9%	46.0%
2021 FS	DET	MLB	30	9	8	0	26	26	150	134	22	3.0	9.4	156	35.8%	.285	1.23	3.83	93	1.7	93.8	52.4%	28.7%	48.6%
2021 DC	DET	MLB	30	7	10	0	27	27	143	128	21	3.0	9.4	149	35.8%	.285	1.23	3.83	93	2.0	93.8	52.4%	28.7%	48.6%

Comparables: Steven Matz, Chris Stratton, Andrew Heaney

You've heard of the Mendoza Line; now feast your pupils on the Boyd Beginning: on August 12, Tim Anderson and Eloy Jiménez kickstarted the game with back-to-back home runs off him. In Boyd's very next start, Anderson and Yoán Moncada did it again. Three starts later, you guessed it, more back-to-back leadoff taters thanks to Jorge Polanco and Josh Donaldson. It was the first time any pitcher had a Boyd Beginning three times in a season. And according to Elias Sports, it was the first time any pitcher did that three times in a whole *career*, and it was Boyd's fourth such Beginning. This homer-prone lefty now joins elite company with Hall of Famer Greg Maddux as pitchers with namesake unofficial starting pitcher statistics.

Beau Burrows RHP
Born: 09/18/96　Age: 24　Bats: R　Throws: R　Height: 6'2"　Weight: 210　Origin: Round 1, 2015 Draft (#22 overall)

YEAR	TEAM	LVL	AGE	W	L	SV	G	GS	IP	H	HR	BB/9	K/9	K	GB%	BABIP	WHIP	ERA	DRA-	WARP	MPH	FA%	Whiff%	CSP
2018	ERI	AA	21	10	9	0	26	26	134	126	12	3.8	8.5	127	30.3%	.311	1.36	4.10	148	-2.6				
2019	TOL	AAA	22	2	6	0	15	15	65¹	68	12	4.4	8.4	61	34.5%	.303	1.53	5.51	117	0.6				
2020	DET	MLB	23	0	0	0	5	0	6²	8	3	1.4	4.0	3	40.0%	.227	1.35	5.40	122	0.0	95.1	54.5%	19.6%	47.1%
2021 FS	DET	MLB	24	1	2	0	57	0	50	51	9	4.2	7.7	42	33.6%	.293	1.51	5.46	122	-0.5	95.1	54.5%	19.6%	47.1%
2021 DC	DET	MLB	24	1	2	0	28	3	40	41	7	4.2	7.7	34	33.6%	.293	1.51	5.46	122	-0.2	95.1	54.5%	19.6%	47.1%

Comparables: Nick Neidert, Luis Ortiz, Ariel Jurado

Last summer, Bo Bichette was often the target of a cascade of puns, because he's already a productive player in the major leagues and Bo rhymes with many words. And thanks to breakthrough advancements in homophone technology, Burrows could encounter the same fate now that he has finally tasted the major leagues. His fastball is low-to-mid 90s, his emerging changeup bailed him out and he's going to be well suited to round out the rotation this year. Threau Burrows.

José Cisnero RHP
Born: 04/11/89　Age: 32　Bats: R　Throws: R　Height: 6'3"　Weight: 245　Origin: International Free Agent, 2007

YEAR	TEAM	LVL	AGE	W	L	SV	G	GS	IP	H	HR	BB/9	K/9	K	GB%	BABIP	WHIP	ERA	DRA-	WARP	MPH	FA%	Whiff%	CSP
2019	TOL	AAA	30	1	2	7	32	2	40	36	3	4.7	11.0	49	41.9%	.327	1.43	2.70	88	0.8				
2019	DET	MLB	30	0	4	0	35	0	35¹	35	5	4.8	10.2	40	37.0%	.323	1.53	4.33	109	0.0	98.5	60.8%	26.9%	48.7%
2020	DET	MLB	31	3	3	0	29	0	29²	23	1	3.0	10.3	34	36.8%	.293	1.11	3.03	85	0.5	97.9	63.0%	32.4%	44.4%
2021 FS	DET	MLB	32	3	3	0	57	0	50	43	7	3.8	9.8	54	36.5%	.285	1.30	4.01	95	0.3	98.1	62.0%	29.9%	46.4%
2021 DC	DET	MLB	32	3	3	0	62	0	66	57	9	3.8	9.8	72	36.5%	.285	1.30	4.01	95	0.5	98.1	62.0%	29.9%	46.4%

Comparables: Tyler Thornburg, Anthony Bass, Jake Petricka

Cisnero has some odd characteristics that quite don't add up. He's an extreme flyball pitcher who was shelled on contact, yet miraculously avoided the home run. He led the league in innings among relievers who didn't allow multiple dingers. That he's able to get strike three with his heat or his hook is handy; that it adds up to a middle-inning option who keeps it in the ballpark is a wild find. Yes, he had Comerica Park to help, but he also avoided moonshots when he pitched in Minute Maid many moons ago. Swing-and-miss stuff will always play, so we'll have plenty of time to unwrap this riddle.

Alex Faedo RHP Born: 11/12/95 Age: 25 Bats: R Throws: R Height: 6'5" Weight: 225 Origin: Round 1, 2017 Draft (#18 overall)

YEAR	TEAM	LVL	AGE	W	L	SV	G	GS	IP	H	HR	BB/9	K/9	K	GB%	BABIP	WHIP	ERA	DRA-	WARP	MPH	FA%	Whiff%	CSP
2018	LAK	HI-A	22	2	4	0	12	12	61	49	3	1.9	7.5	51	32.0%	.263	1.02	3.10	66	1.5				
2018	ERI	AA	22	3	6	0	12	12	60	54	15	3.3	8.8	59	26.3%	.250	1.27	4.95	94	0.6				
2019	ERI	AA	23	6	7	0	22	22	115¹	104	17	2.0	10.5	134	32.5%	.299	1.12	3.90	77	1.7				
2021 FS	DET	MLB	25	2	3	0	57	0	50	49	8	3.3	8.8	48	31.5%	.295	1.35	4.54	114	-0.3				

Comparables: Jordan Yamamoto, Ryan Helsley, Robert Dugger

Injuries and COVID-19 quarantine caused Faedo to miss time throwing in nebulous stat-free environments. The former first-rounder and College World Series hero will be in the majors soon, however, ready to disappoint the fans in attendance who thought they might get to see Mize or Manning. Not that there's anything wrong with Faedo; he's developed into a perfectly adequate back-end starter, with a fastball that technically reaches the plate and a slider that can miss enough bats to get him out of the inning after five or so batters. There are worse things, and folks in Detroit have been watching them for a few years, so fan expectations will find a suitable baseline in Faedo, in all his high-floor, low-ceiling glory.

Buck Farmer RHP Born: 02/20/91 Age: 30 Bats: L Throws: R Height: 6'4" Weight: 232 Origin: Round 5, 2013 Draft (#156 overall)

YEAR	TEAM	LVL	AGE	W	L	SV	G	GS	IP	H	HR	BB/9	K/9	K	GB%	BABIP	WHIP	ERA	DRA-	WARP	MPH	FA%	Whiff%	CSP
2018	DET	MLB	27	3	4	0	66	1	69¹	67	6	5.3	7.4	57	40.7%	.302	1.56	4.15	122	-0.4	96.0	57.6%	26.7%	45.3%
2019	DET	MLB	28	6	6	0	73	1	67²	62	8	3.2	9.7	73	46.8%	.310	1.27	3.72	80	1.1	96.4	49.0%	29.6%	44.4%
2020	DET	MLB	29	1	0	0	23	0	21¹	20	3	2.1	5.9	14	51.4%	.258	1.17	3.80	93	0.3	94.5	52.8%	19.9%	47.3%
2021 FS	DET	MLB	30	3	3	3	57	0	50	47	6	3.4	8.1	45	45.1%	.290	1.34	4.26	100	0.1	95.8	52.2%	26.7%	45.3%
2021 DC	DET	MLB	30	3	3	3	62	0	66	63	8	3.4	8.1	59	45.1%	.290	1.34	4.26	100	0.4	95.8	52.2%	26.7%	45.3%

Comparables: Casey Sadler, Chris Stratton, Jordan Lyles

It's tough for a relief pitcher to stand out when they come and go like fruit flies. Farmer stands out by being the only active MLB pitcher with the given name George. He blends in by being the Tigers' setup man. He traded some velo on his fastball for some much-needed command, and it paid off with his career-best walk rate; however, away went the strikeouts as well as the utility of his changeup. It may have been an adjustment of the microseason, but becoming a pitch-to-contact strategist is the wrong trend as we head into the '20s. It's as anachronistic as being called Buck.

Michael Fulmer RHP Born: 03/15/93 Age: 28 Bats: R Throws: R Height: 6'3" Weight: 246 Origin: Round 1, 2011 Draft (#44 overall)

YEAR	TEAM	LVL	AGE	W	L	SV	G	GS	IP	H	HR	BB/9	K/9	K	GB%	BABIP	WHIP	ERA	DRA-	WARP	MPH	FA%	Whiff%	CSP
2018	LAK	HI-A	25	0	0	0	2	2	6	1	0	0.0	16.5	11	37.5%	.125	0.17	0.00	38	0.2				
2018	DET	MLB	25	3	12	0	24	24	132¹	128	19	3.1	7.5	110	44.8%	.289	1.31	4.69	104	1.0	97.9	61.0%	23.4%	48.5%
2020	DET	MLB	27	0	2	0	10	10	27²	45	8	3.9	6.5	20	35.9%	.394	2.06	8.78	151	-0.5	94.8	70.5%	19.3%	43.3%
2021 FS	DET	MLB	28	9	9	0	26	26	150	149	19	3.4	7.9	131	42.5%	.297	1.37	4.41	103	0.8	96.5	65.0%	21.7%	46.3%
2021 DC	DET	MLB	28	4	7	0	21	21	88	87	11	3.4	7.9	76	42.5%	.297	1.37	4.41	103	0.8	96.5	65.0%	21.7%	46.3%

Comparables: Chad Kuhl, Zach Davies, Brett Anderson

Having your elbow tendons ripped out and replaced by completely different tendons is more painful than it sounds, and the long road back to a professional baseball mound is more treacherous than you may imagine. First things first, Fulmer made it back in one piece. And compared to Lance McCullers Jr., whose surgery and recovery times pretty much overlapped, it went much worse. Fulmer's velocity hasn't returned yet, but his dangerous slider did. He'll continue his recovery in 2021 and work on stretching out and returning to Rookie of the Year form, now wearing the scars of time.

Kyle Funkhouser RHP Born: 03/16/94 Age: 27 Bats: R Throws: R Height: 6'3" Weight: 225 Origin: Round 4, 2016 Draft (#115 overall)

YEAR	TEAM	LVL	AGE	W	L	SV	G	GS	IP	H	HR	BB/9	K/9	K	GB%	BABIP	WHIP	ERA	DRA-	WARP	MPH	FA%	Whiff%	CSP
2018	ERI	AA	24	4	5	0	17	17	89	88	10	3.9	9.0	89	42.2%	.329	1.43	3.74	85	1.3				
2018	TOL	AAA	24	0	2	0	2	2	8²	8	0	10.4	7.3	7	50.0%	.333	2.08	6.23	78	0.2				
2019	ERI	AA	25	3	1	0	4	4	23²	16	2	1.1	11.0	29	45.3%	.275	0.80	1.90	57	0.6				
2019	TOL	AAA	25	3	7	0	18	18	63¹	79	3	7.7	9.2	65	53.8%	.396	2.10	8.53	160	-0.7				
2020	DET	MLB	26	1	1	0	13	0	17¹	22	3	5.7	6.2	12	48.3%	.345	1.90	7.27	120	0.0	97.0	61.8%	23.2%	46.0%
2021 FS	DET	MLB	27	1	2	0	57	0	50	47	6	6.0	8.5	47	46.1%	.291	1.61	5.25	114	-0.3	97.0	61.8%	23.2%	46.0%
2021 DC	DET	MLB	27	1	2	0	37	0	39	36	5	6.0	8.5	36	46.1%	.291	1.61	5.25	114	-0.1	97.0	61.8%	23.2%	46.0%

Comparables: Dillon Tate, Spencer Turnbull, Rookie Davis

Da Funk wasn't quite ready to bring Da Noize, but that didn't stop the Tigers from corralling him into the bullpen. He's yet to look effective in three seasons above Double-A, which means it's time to reevaluate the starter profile. He found some strike three success with his slider, and that may be enough. Fastball-slider combos never go out of style, not in this house.

Bryan Garcia   RHP   Born: 04/19/95   Age: 26   Bats: R   Throws: R   Height: 6'1"   Weight: 215   Origin: Round 6, 2016 Draft (#175 overall)

YEAR	TEAM	LVL	AGE	W	L	SV	G	GS	IP	H	HR	BB/9	K/9	K	GB%	BABIP	WHIP	ERA	DRA-	WARP	MPH	FA%	Whiff%	CSP
2019	LAK	HI-A	24	0	0	1	4	0	4	3	1	4.5	13.5	6	33.3%	.286	1.25	4.50	75	0.0				
2019	ERI	AA	24	0	0	1	3	0	4	1	1	0.0	18.0	8	20.0%	.000	0.25	2.25	44	0.1				
2019	TOL	AAA	24	3	0	0	31	0	33¹	26	4	3.8	8.9	33	46.2%	.253	1.20	2.97	78	0.8				
2019	DET	MLB	24	0	0	0	7	0	6²	9	1	6.8	9.4	7	61.9%	.400	2.10	12.15	99	0.0	95.6	51.9%	29.2%	45.8%
2020	DET	MLB	25	2	1	4	26	0	21²	18	0	4.2	5.0	12	42.9%	.257	1.29	1.66	111	0.1	95.7	64.2%	20.1%	47.1%
2021 FS	DET	MLB	26	3	3	15	57	0	50	48	6	3.5	8.2	45	43.1%	.293	1.36	4.35	102	0.1	95.7	61.6%	22.0%	46.9%
2021 DC	DET	MLB	26	3	3	15	62	0	66	63	9	3.5	8.2	60	43.1%	.293	1.36	4.35	102	0.3	95.7	61.6%	22.0%	46.9%

Comparables: Jake Newberry, Ben Heller, Thyago Vieira

Garcia quickly learned what happens when outs occur under your purview in the Tigers bullpen: You get higher leverage work. After averting crooked numbers by entering bases loaded situations and leaving them clean in back-to-back nights, Garcia was thrust into the closer's role as the clock ran down on the season. He converted four of five, all with some pretty nasty strikeout-to-walk numbers, and not the good kind. The former college closer buzzed down bats in the minor leagues, so his track record of strike threes should diverge from the Todd Jones career arc (though Detroit may be the only team that could stomach it) and into some semblance of late-inning legerdemain.

Rony García   RHP   Born: 12/19/97   Age: 23   Bats: R   Throws: R   Height: 6'3"   Weight: 200   Origin: International Free Agent, 2015

YEAR	TEAM	LVL	AGE	W	L	SV	G	GS	IP	H	HR	BB/9	K/9	K	GB%	BABIP	WHIP	ERA	DRA-	WARP	MPH	FA%	Whiff%	CSP
2018	CSC	LO-A	20	3	4	0	14	14	71	73	5	1.6	7.9	62	32.7%	.312	1.21	4.18	90	0.7				
2018	TAM	HI-A	20	1	5	0	9	9	48	47	2	2.8	8.4	45	40.8%	.326	1.29	4.50	129	-0.6				
2019	TAM	HI-A	21	0	2	0	5	4	25	21	2	2.5	9.0	25	32.4%	.288	1.12	2.16	82	0.3				
2019	TRN	AA	21	4	11	0	20	20	105¹	94	14	3.2	8.9	104	33.8%	.282	1.25	4.44	113	-0.7				
2020	DET	MLB	22	1	0	0	15	2	21	25	7	3.9	6.0	14	34.2%	.273	1.62	8.14	160	-0.5	94.5	84.7%	20.0%	46.7%
2021 FS	DET	MLB	23	1	1	0	57	0	50	52	9	3.9	7.3	40	34.8%	.292	1.47	5.39	122	-0.5	94.5	84.7%	20.0%	46.7%
2021 DC	DET	MLB	23	1	1	0	24	0	26	27	4	3.9	7.3	21	34.8%	.292	1.47	5.39	122	-0.1	94.5	84.7%	20.0%	46.7%

Comparables: Jonathan Hernández, Tyler Mahle, Pedro Avila

Garcia picked a swell time to be a Rule 5 pick. There's nothing particularly plus about any of his pitches, but he throws them all for strikes, giving him a low but wide ceiling—the bungalow of relievers.

Joe Jiménez   RHP   Born: 01/17/95   Age: 26   Bats: R   Throws: R   Height: 6'3"   Weight: 272   Origin: Undrafted Free Agent, 2013

YEAR	TEAM	LVL	AGE	W	L	SV	G	GS	IP	H	HR	BB/9	K/9	K	GB%	BABIP	WHIP	ERA	DRA-	WARP	MPH	FA%	Whiff%	CSP
2018	DET	MLB	23	5	4	3	68	0	62²	53	5	3.2	11.2	78	36.2%	.304	1.20	4.31	68	1.4	97.6	67.2%	30.6%	47.3%
2019	DET	MLB	24	4	7	9	66	0	59²	56	13	3.5	12.4	82	29.1%	.319	1.32	4.37	82	0.9	97.0	68.3%	31.6%	51.7%
2020	DET	MLB	25	1	3	5	25	0	22²	25	7	2.4	8.7	22	30.9%	.295	1.37	7.15	141	-0.3	96.2	62.2%	26.4%	48.8%
2021 FS	DET	MLB	26	3	3	0	57	0	50	43	8	3.4	9.9	55	31.4%	.278	1.24	4.01	96	0.2	96.9	66.4%	29.9%	49.8%
2021 DC	DET	MLB	26	3	3	0	62	0	66	57	10	3.4	9.9	72	31.4%	.278	1.24	4.01	96	0.5	96.9	66.4%	29.9%	49.8%

Comparables: Sam Tuivailala, Keone Kela, Keynan Middleton

The one-time All-Star is starting to pitch like he'd rather have the four-day break in July. Jiménez's lively fastball lost just enough zip and break to turn it into the most depressing of pitches, a Tigers reliever fastball, and he was demoted from the ninth-inning role late in the season. While he's still in his mid-20s, the sample is becoming large enough to expect flashes of untold brilliance followed by devastating sugar crashes. This makes him the archetypal bad-team closer and good-team relief role player, and understanding his streakiness may be the key to a long career.

─── ★　★　★ *2021 Top 101 Prospect* **#46** ★　★　★ ───

Matt Manning   RHP   Born: 01/28/98   Age: 23   Bats: R   Throws: R   Height: 6'6"   Weight: 195   Origin: Round 1, 2016 Draft (#9 overall)

YEAR	TEAM	LVL	AGE	W	L	SV	G	GS	IP	H	HR	BB/9	K/9	K	GB%	BABIP	WHIP	ERA	DRA-	WARP	MPH	FA%	Whiff%	CSP
2018	WM	LO-A	20	3	3	0	11	11	55²	47	3	4.5	12.3	76	40.5%	.346	1.35	3.40	69	1.3				
2018	LAK	HI-A	20	4	4	0	9	9	51¹	32	4	3.3	11.4	65	45.8%	.243	0.99	2.98	76	1.0				
2018	ERI	AA	20	0	1	0	2	2	10²	11	0	3.4	11.0	13	39.3%	.423	1.41	4.22	65	0.3				
2019	ERI	AA	21	11	5	0	24	24	133²	93	7	2.6	10.0	148	47.2%	.259	0.98	2.56	56	3.6				
2021 FS	DET	MLB	23	9	8	0	26	26	150	125	18	4.4	9.4	156	43.5%	.274	1.33	3.87	97	1.3				
2021 DC	DET	MLB	23	3	4	0	12	12	63	52	7	4.4	9.4	65	43.5%	.274	1.33	3.87	97	0.8				

Comparables: Luis Severino, Ian Anderson, Stephen Gonsalves

Six Tigers prospects made their major league debuts in 2020. Manning wasn't one of them, having suffered the same type of forearm strain that befell Alex Faedo. Things looked grim, especially under the cloaking device that is the alternate training site, but the fears seem to be unfounded; he declared that in a normal season, the injury would have shut him down for a few weeks at most. That puts him in line to be ready for 2021, if 2021 itself is, and to co-chair a rotation with Casey Mize that will prove one of the most exciting of the young decade. A two-sport prep talent who remodeled his delivery in the minors, Manning's arsenal is still a little less refined than his collegiate colleagues, but his ceiling is as high as anyone's, and it'll be fun to watch him reach for it.

★ ★ ★ *2021 Top 101 Prospect* **#27** ★ ★ ★

Casey Mize **RHP** Born: 05/01/97 Age: 24 Bats: R Throws: R Height: 6'3" Weight: 220 Origin: Round 1, 2018 Draft (#1 overall)

YEAR	TEAM	LVL	AGE	W	L	SV	G	GS	IP	H	HR	BB/9	K/9	K	GB%	BABIP	WHIP	ERA	DRA-	WARP	MPH	FA%	Whiff%	CSP
2018	TIW	ROK	21	0	0	0	1	1	2	0	0	4.5	18.0	4	100.0%	.000	0.50	0.00	10	0.1				
2018	LAK	HI-A	21	0	1	0	4	4	11²	13	2	1.5	7.7	10	44.1%	.344	1.29	4.63	91	0.1				
2019	LAK	HI-A	22	2	0	0	6	6	30²	11	0	1.5	8.8	30	45.1%	.157	0.52	0.88	37	1.2				
2019	ERI	AA	22	6	3	0	15	15	78²	69	5	2.1	8.7	76	41.7%	.295	1.11	3.20	85	0.8				
2020	DET	MLB	23	0	3	0	7	7	28¹	29	7	4.1	8.3	26	38.2%	.268	1.48	6.99	129	-0.2	95.6	72.0%	23.7%	44.7%
2021 FS	DET	MLB	24	8	9	0	26	26	150	151	24	3.0	8.1	134	39.2%	.297	1.35	4.78	111	0.1	95.6	72.0%	23.7%	44.7%
2021 DC	DET	MLB	24	6	10	0	24	24	126	127	20	3.0	8.1	113	39.2%	.297	1.35	4.78	111	0.6	95.6	72.0%	23.7%	44.7%

Comparables: Shawn Chacon, Tyler Mahle, Archie Bradley

Two years from draft to debut is a short window, though less so for a pitcher with Mize's ability and pedigree. The Tigers made the surprise decision to promote their top prospect early in the season, after a 9-12 start gave them a one-in-six chance of attending 2020's general-admission playoffs. A week earlier (when they were 9-5) or a year later (when they'll be 0-0) might have made more sense. You don't expect rawness from a 1-1 selection, but in seven starts he offered nothing but crudités; at times it appeared as though he was still trying to shake the lingering effects of a nagging shoulder problem from 2019. The fastball darted, the two-seamer ran and the splitter, a powerful, late-biting pitch, hid. But he missed spots and couldn't get ahead, looking masterful one inning and losing his mechanics the next. In an era when teams are overly cautious with their prospects for dubious (economic) reasons, the Tigers really ought to be careful with Mize, who still can be a top-flight candidate. He may not break camp in the rotation, but the minor development sorely needed for a pitcher of this station will help this burgeoning ace start cooking.

Daniel Norris **LHP** Born: 04/25/93 Age: 28 Bats: L Throws: L Height: 6'2" Weight: 185 Origin: Round 2, 2011 Draft (#74 overall)

YEAR	TEAM	LVL	AGE	W	L	SV	G	GS	IP	H	HR	BB/9	K/9	K	GB%	BABIP	WHIP	ERA	DRA-	WARP	MPH	FA%	Whiff%	CSP
2018	DET	MLB	25	0	5	0	11	8	44¹	46	8	3.9	10.4	51	31.2%	.319	1.47	5.68	114	0.1	92.1	52.7%	24.2%	49.3%
2019	DET	MLB	26	3	13	0	32	29	144¹	154	25	2.4	7.8	125	42.2%	.312	1.33	4.49	106	0.9	92.9	51.5%	23.1%	49.8%
2020	DET	MLB	27	3	1	0	14	1	27²	25	2	2.3	9.1	28	56.2%	.295	1.16	3.25	78	0.6	94.6	47.6%	27.6%	47.8%
2021 FS	DET	MLB	28	3	3	0	57	0	50	47	7	3.4	9.0	49	44.4%	.295	1.33	4.26	101	0.1	93.1	50.8%	24.2%	49.3%
2021 DC	DET	MLB	28	3	3	0	62	0	66	62	9	3.4	9.0	65	44.4%	.295	1.33	4.26	101	0.3	93.1	50.8%	24.2%	49.3%

Comparables: Matt Wisler, Robert Stephenson, Carlos Rodón

If you're a team building a pitching staff by rejecting the orthodoxy of five good starters and five good relievers in lieu of 13 amorphous, useful arms, Norris is going to make your list. He was never able to get quite stretched out following an unfortunate cacophony of maladies, but he had a clean bill of health going out there in multi-inning spurts. In particular, he found increased success when he trusted his changeup and became an extreme groundball pitcher, a stark departure from his previous work. If you're looking for someone who can last five innings every five days, he has the merchandise for it, but he seems to be in a groove going fewer innings with fewer rest days. For someone who's battled every year to stay healthy, you take what you can get.

Iván Nova **RHP** Born: 01/12/87 Age: 34 Bats: R Throws: R Height: 6'5" Weight: 250 Origin: International Free Agent, 2004

YEAR	TEAM	LVL	AGE	W	L	SV	G	GS	IP	H	HR	BB/9	K/9	K	GB%	BABIP	WHIP	ERA	DRA-	WARP	MPH	FA%	Whiff%	CSP
2018	PIT	MLB	31	9	9	0	29	29	161	171	26	2.0	6.4	114	44.5%	.290	1.28	4.19	102	1.3	94.8	66.9%	19.9%	46.6%
2019	CHW	MLB	32	11	12	0	34	34	187	225	30	2.3	5.5	114	45.4%	.323	1.45	4.72	154	-3.6	94.4	54.2%	18.5%	47.2%
2020	DET	MLB	33	1	1	0	4	4	19	22	4	4.3	4.3	9	54.3%	.273	1.63	8.53	111	0.1	94.1	59.2%	19.7%	48.0%
2021 FS	DET	MLB	34	2	3	0	57	0	50	56	8	2.8	6.1	33	48.0%	.302	1.44	5.08	120	-0.4	94.5	58.1%	19.0%	47.1%

Comparables: Jeff Francis, Homer Bailey, Joe Saunders

Nova's curveball still made batters redden with rage. The problem is that baseball is not Angry Birds, and one cannot simply heave really impressive parabolas into a hodgepodge of twigs and pigs and expect success. You need the fastball. Or, if you have Nova's fastball, you need to never walk batters. Nova suffered and re-suffered a triceps injury, leading to a one-third of one-third of a season, one in which he did in fact walk batters. Spending half a decade in the Yankees' rotation will always give him an extra look (known as the Chien-Ming Wang Doctrine), so watch for Nova in a spring training comeback narrative where he tries to clear levels with three-star outings.

Franklin Pérez **RHP** Born: 12/06/97 Age: 23 Bats: R Throws: R Height: 6'3" Weight: 197 Origin: International Free Agent, 2014

YEAR	TEAM	LVL	AGE	W	L	SV	G	GS	IP	H	HR	BB/9	K/9	K	GB%	BABIP	WHIP	ERA	DRA-	WARP	MPH	FA%	Whiff%	CSP
2018	TIG	ROK	20	0	1	0	3	3	8	3	0	0.0	5.6	5	27.3%	.136	0.38	4.50	84	0.1				
2018	LAK	HI-A	20	0	1	0	4	4	11¹	15	2	6.4	7.1	9	43.2%	.371	2.03	7.94	111	0.0				
2019	LAK	HI-A	21	0	0	0	2	2	7²	7	1	5.9	7.0	6	45.5%	.286	1.57	2.35	126	-0.1				
2021 FS	DET	MLB	23	2	3	0	57	0	50	47	7	4.1	7.5	41	33.9%	.282	1.41	4.42	108	-0.1				

Comparables: Michael Fulmer, Junior Fernández, Duane Underwood Jr.

It's no small irony that Pérez was finally healthy the season there was no season. It's hard to even conceptualize a full year from the young righty, who has pitched just 27 professional innings since being the marquee prospect in the Justin Verlander trade; the future Hall-of-Famer matched that workload in the 2017 postseason alone. Pérez is still just 22 but has a mountain of memories to make up. It's another irony that because of the injuries, and his spot on the 40-man roster dictated by his (inactive) service time, he wasn't able to attend some much-needed instructional league work with the other prospects his age. Instead, the Tigers will hope their time with him at the alternate site did some good, and that he'll start next season at Double-A.

John Schreiber RHP   Born: 03/05/94   Age: 27   Bats: R   Throws: R   Height: 6'2"   Weight: 210   Origin: Round 15, 2016 Draft (#445 overall)

YEAR	TEAM	LVL	AGE	W	L	SV	G	GS	IP	H	HR	BB/9	K/9	K	GB%	BABIP	WHIP	ERA	DRA-	WARP	MPH	FA%	Whiff%	CSP
2018	ERI	AA	24	3	7	18	49	0	58	47	2	2.9	9.2	59	41.0%	.296	1.14	2.48	57	1.5				
2019	ERI	AA	25	0	0	0	5	0	7	4	1	3.9	15.4	12	57.1%	.231	1.00	2.57	60	0.1				
2019	TOL	AAA	25	6	4	4	48	0	59¹	39	4	3.2	10.6	70	41.0%	.250	1.01	2.28	49	2.2				
2019	DET	MLB	25	2	0	0	13	0	13	16	3	2.8	13.2	19	37.1%	.406	1.54	6.23	103	0.0	93.8	61.8%	28.6%	47.5%
2020	DET	MLB	26	0	1	0	15	0	15²	19	2	2.3	8.0	14	33.3%	.347	1.47	6.32	102	0.1	91.7	52.0%	18.2%	45.0%
2021 FS	DET	MLB	27	2	2	0	57	0	50	44	6	3.4	9.6	53	38.7%	.289	1.27	3.95	94	0.3	92.5	55.6%	22.0%	45.9%
2021 DC	DET	MLB	27	2	2	0	49	0	52	46	7	3.4	9.6	55	38.7%	.289	1.27	3.95	94	0.5	92.5	55.6%	22.0%	45.9%

Comparables: Phil Maton, Colton Murray, Ryan Dull

The slopball-lovin' Schreiber has Zack Greinke-type stuff from a sidearm angle, but unfortunately has to throw it with John Schreiber's arm. His main contribution to date is a follow-through that makes him look like he's being pulled offstage by an invisible, vaudeville cane. Everyone makes their mark in their own way.

───────── ★ ★ ★ *2021 Top 101 Prospect* **#99** ★ ★ ★ ─────────

Tarik Skubal LHP   Born: 11/20/96   Age: 24   Bats: L   Throws: L   Height: 6'3"   Weight: 215   Origin: Round 9, 2018 Draft (#255 overall)

YEAR	TEAM	LVL	AGE	W	L	SV	G	GS	IP	H	HR	BB/9	K/9	K	GB%	BABIP	WHIP	ERA	DRA-	WARP	MPH	FA%	Whiff%	CSP
2018	TIW	ROK	21	1	0	0	2	1	3	2	0	3.0	15.0	5	85.7%	.286	1.00	0.00	25	0.2				
2018	NOR	SS	21	0	0	1	4	0	12	8	0	1.5	12.8	17	45.8%	.333	0.83	0.75	61	0.3				
2018	WM	LO-A	21	2	0	1	3	0	7¹	5	0	1.2	13.5	11	21.4%	.357	0.82	0.00	40	0.3				
2019	LAK	HI-A	22	4	5	0	15	15	80¹	62	5	2.1	10.9	97	39.0%	.294	1.01	2.58	68	1.7				
2019	ERI	AA	22	2	3	0	9	9	42¹	25	2	3.8	17.4	82	39.1%	.343	1.02	2.13	49	1.3				
2020	DET	MLB	23	1	4	0	8	7	32	28	9	3.1	10.4	37	27.4%	.253	1.22	5.62	137	-0.3	96.9	60.1%	29.5%	46.5%
2021 FS	DET	MLB	24	9	8	0	26	26	150	129	24	3.3	10.7	177	32.4%	.287	1.23	3.84	94	1.5	96.9	60.1%	29.5%	46.5%
2021 DC	DET	MLB	24	4	6	0	21	21	86	74	13	3.3	10.7	101	32.4%	.287	1.23	3.84	94	1.2	96.9	60.1%	29.5%	46.5%

Comparables: Brendan McKay, Eric Lauer, Nick Margevicius

There's not much good news for the minor leagues these days, but one uplifting story is they no longer have to get struck out by Skubal and his massive leg kick on a regular basis. Of all the next-gen Tigers pitchers, his stuff might be as good as or better than Casey Mize's, which explains why they were called up in tandem. The raw left-hander did slightly better than the no. 1 pick, maintaining a double-digit K/9 but getting dogged by far too many orbital white spheres. Still, he improved as the season ripened, and the minor league strikeout artist's debut showed more than enough to put him on the inside track for a rotation spot. You're welcome, minor leaguers.

Gregory Soto LHP   Born: 02/11/95   Age: 26   Bats: L   Throws: L   Height: 6'1"   Weight: 236   Origin: International Free Agent, 2012

YEAR	TEAM	LVL	AGE	W	L	SV	G	GS	IP	H	HR	BB/9	K/9	K	GB%	BABIP	WHIP	ERA	DRA-	WARP	MPH	FA%	Whiff%	CSP
2018	LAK	HI-A	23	8	8	0	25	23	113¹	101	4	5.6	9.1	115	45.8%	.306	1.51	4.45	83	1.7				
2019	ERI	AA	24	0	1	0	3	3	13¹	10	2	2.7	8.1	12	54.1%	.229	1.05	2.02	76	0.2				
2019	TOL	AAA	24	0	3	0	6	5	23¹	25	2	5.0	11.6	30	46.9%	.371	1.63	6.94	106	0.3				
2019	DET	MLB	24	0	5	0	33	7	57²	74	9	5.2	7.0	45	48.5%	.344	1.86	5.77	156	-1.3	97.9	70.7%	20.0%	51.2%
2020	DET	MLB	25	0	1	2	27	0	23	16	2	5.1	11.3	29	53.7%	.269	1.26	4.30	79	0.5	99.0	79.7%	28.8%	48.7%
2021 FS	DET	MLB	26	2	3	12	57	0	50	46	6	5.6	9.2	50	47.4%	.296	1.55	4.97	110	-0.2	98.3	73.8%	23.1%	50.3%
2021 DC	DET	MLB	26	2	3	12	62	0	66	61	8	5.6	9.2	67	47.4%	.296	1.55	4.97	110	0.0	98.3	73.8%	23.1%	50.3%

Comparables: Thomas Pannone, Conner Menez, Matt Hall

After opening some games in 2019 in cringeworthy fashion, Soto pared down his options, cleaned up his delivery and stuck with two pitches in late innings. Moving to a slide-step delivery helped add some racing stripes to his sinker, and he now slings it harder than any left-hander, scraping triple digits. The slider is the simple baguette to the sinker's entrée. He tosses a few too many balls four to make him comfortable as a ninth-inning hurler, but having this Soto around certainly adds a dynamic alternative as the game reaches its final courses.

Spencer Turnbull RHP   Born: 09/18/92   Age: 28   Bats: R   Throws: R   Height: 6'3"   Weight: 211   Origin: Round 2, 2014 Draft (#63 overall)

YEAR	TEAM	LVL	AGE	W	L	SV	G	GS	IP	H	HR	BB/9	K/9	K	GB%	BABIP	WHIP	ERA	DRA-	WARP	MPH	FA%	Whiff%	CSP
2018	TIW	ROK	25	0	0	0	1	1	2²	1	0	10.1	10.1	3	50.0%	.167	1.50	0.00	19	0.1				
2018	LAK	HI-A	25	0	0	0	1	1	4²	2	0	11.6	11.6	6	40.0%	.200	0.43	0.00	59	0.1				
2018	ERI	AA	25	4	7	0	19	19	98²	92	4	3.6	9.6	105	54.3%	.332	1.34	4.47	79	1.8				
2018	TOL	AAA	25	1	1	0	2	2	13¹	8	0	2.0	12.8	19	40.0%	.296	0.82	2.02	56	0.4				
2018	DET	MLB	25	0	2	0	4	3	16¹	17	1	2.2	8.3	15	48.0%	.327	1.29	6.06	111	0.1	96.0	63.5%	21.2%	48.7%
2019	TOL	AAA	26	0	0	0	1	1	3²	1	0	0.0	17.2	7	60.0%	.200	0.27	0.00	30	0.2				
2019	DET	MLB	26	3	17	0	30	30	148¹	154	14	3.6	8.9	146	48.0%	.333	1.44	4.61	106	0.9	95.9	64.8%	24.7%	45.6%
2020	DET	MLB	27	4	4	0	11	11	56²	47	2	4.6	8.1	51	48.8%	.288	1.34	3.97	87	0.9	96.4	66.0%	28.3%	46.5%
2021 FS	DET	MLB	28	9	9	0	26	26	150	140	18	4.2	9.0	150	49.0%	.298	1.41	4.54	104	0.7	96.1	65.2%	25.8%	46.0%
2021 DC	DET	MLB	28	7	11	0	27	27	145	136	18	4.2	9.0	145	49.0%	.298	1.41	4.54	104	1.2	96.1	65.2%	25.8%	46.0%

Comparables: Kevin Gausman, Erick Fedde, Zach Davies

Can't give up home runs if you keep walking batters, says the meme of the smiling man pointing to his head. With some outrageously bendy pitches, Turnbull is turning into an effectively wild type, hold the effectively. His 14:1 walk-to-home run ratio isn't unprecedented, as a list of such pitchers is extensive, but the entire list is pretty much relievers. You have to go back to Brandon Duckworth in 2001 to find a starter who gave up 14 times as many free passes as long balls in a season. Maybe it's just that the batters know to lay off the pitches. Maybe it's as simple as having an animal in the last name. The science is inconclusive.

José Ureña RHP Born: 09/12/91 Age: 29 Bats: R Throws: R Height: 6'2" Weight: 208 Origin: International Free Agent, 2008

YEAR	TEAM	LVL	AGE	W	L	SV	G	GS	IP	H	HR	BB/9	K/9	K	GB%	BABIP	WHIP	ERA	DRA-	WARP	MPH	FA%	Whiff%	CSP
2018	MIA	MLB	26	9	12	0	31	31	174	155	19	2.6	6.7	130	49.3%	.275	1.18	3.98	89	2.6	97.6	58.8%	20.4%	46.1%
2019	MIA	MLB	27	4	10	3	24	13	84²	99	13	2.8	6.6	62	48.7%	.325	1.48	5.21	117	0.0	97.7	63.1%	21.3%	45.2%
2020	MIA	MLB	28	0	3	0	5	5	23¹	22	4	5.0	5.8	15	45.9%	.257	1.50	5.40	128	-0.1	96.9	60.9%	27.1%	47.4%
2021 FS	DET	MLB	29	8	9	0	26	26	150	153	20	3.6	7.0	116	47.0%	.295	1.43	4.91	110	0.2	97.5	60.9%	22.0%	46.0%
2021 DC	DET	MLB	29	5	7	0	41	16	104	106	14	3.6	7.0	81	47.0%	.295	1.43	4.91	110	0.4	97.5	60.9%	22.0%	46.0%

Comparables: Trevor Williams, Mike Foltynewicz, Matt Harrison

Ureña was a late scratch from his planned first start due to a positive COVID test, in one of the earliest signs of the burgeoning outbreak in the Marlins clubhouse. Despite early media reports that he was asymptomatic, he was not ready to come back when the Marlins resumed play and ultimately missed nearly six weeks with the virus. The bad luck didn't end there, either; he got drilled by a comebacker on the very last day of the regular season and broke his pitching arm, taking him out of the playoffs. When able to take the mound, Ureña was the same pitcher he's always been: a flamethrower who just doesn't have enough else going for him to be more than a back-end starter. The capper on a terrible, horrible, no good, very bad year? The Marlins designated him for assignment upon acquiring Adam Cimber and he latched on with the Tigers.

Joey Wentz LHP Born: 10/06/97 Age: 23 Bats: L Throws: L Height: 6'5" Weight: 220 Origin: Round 1, 2016 Draft (#40 overall)

YEAR	TEAM	LVL	AGE	W	L	SV	G	GS	IP	H	HR	BB/9	K/9	K	GB%	BABIP	WHIP	ERA	DRA-	WARP	MPH	FA%	Whiff%	CSP
2018	FLO	HI-A	20	3	4	0	16	16	67	49	3	3.2	7.1	53	44.4%	.251	1.09	2.28	86	0.9				
2018	DAY	HI-A	20	0	0	0	1	1	4	1	0	2.2	4.5	2		.091	0.50	0.00						
2019	ERI	AA	21	2	0	0	5	5	25²	20	3	1.4	13.0	37	19.3%	.315	0.94	2.10	67	0.5				
2019	MIS	AA	21	5	8	0	20	20	103	90	13	3.9	8.7	100	32.6%	.283	1.31	4.72	113	-0.7				
2021 FS	DET	MLB	23	2	3	0	57	0	50	47	8	5.0	8.6	47	32.4%	.288	1.50	4.93	117	-0.3				

Comparables: Trevor Rogers, Génesis Cabrera, Lucas Giolito

Wentz, the next-in-line Tigers pitching prospect, took the Tommy John pledge last March; he should be ready to heave the ol' pellet in the general direction of uniformed athletes by midsummer. He lacks the pure stuff of the Mizes and Mannings who went before him, and is more likely to prove a fourth starter than a second, but he does wield a nasty, fading changeup that serves as an out pitch. The goal will be for him to see the majors by September.

Jordan Zimmermann RHP Born: 05/23/86 Age: 35 Bats: R Throws: R Height: 6'2" Weight: 225 Origin: Round 2, 2007 Draft (#67 overall)

YEAR	TEAM	LVL	AGE	W	L	SV	G	GS	IP	H	HR	BB/9	K/9	K	GB%	BABIP	WHIP	ERA	DRA-	WARP	MPH	FA%	Whiff%	CSP
2018	DET	MLB	32	7	8	0	25	25	131¹	140	28	1.8	7.6	111	36.2%	.289	1.26	4.52	106	0.8	92.5	45.3%	20.7%	48.2%
2019	DET	MLB	33	1	13	0	23	23	112	145	19	2.0	6.6	82	41.4%	.341	1.52	6.91	138	-1.2	91.5	46.9%	20.4%	46.7%
2020	DET	MLB	34	0	0	0	3	2	5²	11	0	3.2	9.5	6	45.0%	.550	2.29	7.94	83	0.1	90.7	53.7%	18.9%	47.5%
2021 FS	DET	MLB	35	2	3	0	57	0	50	55	8	2.1	7.0	39	39.9%	.305	1.35	4.76	114	-0.3	91.8	46.7%	20.4%	47.3%

Comparables: Johnny Cueto, Ricky Nolasco, Homer Bailey

Five years and $110 million ago, Zimmermann entered Detroit as the seemingly final piece of a team with one last chance to contend. He began the 2016 season with an 0.55 ERA in April, a practically since-unmatched page of a calendar. The next half-decade of service was a thorough garroting of the soul, be it by injury or early exit. He limped to the finish line with a one-inning, zero-run start—a thank you for trying, if you will. We'll always have 2014, a simpler time when managers got flak for pulling pitchers in the *ninth* inning of a critical postseason game. Anyway, what we're saying is Kevin Cash will never be Zimmermann's manager.

KANSAS CITY ROYALS

Essay by Justin Klugh

Player comments by Craig Brown and BP staff

Pssst!

You there, in the Mahomes jersey! Come join me over here, by the fountain!

You know, I've been called a lot of things in my time: A scoundrel. A wastrel. A Kansas City flimflam man. The "Harold Hill" of committing crimes without a marching band. But when the summertime comes, I'm just a baseball fan like the rest of you.

Speaking of which, what would you do if I told you there's a ball team—right here in town, in fact—that's got the guts to recreate itself, but the fortitude not to surrender? That's got a skipper who earned his playing time with a mouthful of blood? That has a general manager ready to shield his boys from the sweet embrace of adult films?

Would you say, "Golly, that's a club I'd give my eyeballs for an afternoon!"

Well, get ready to soothe those sockets, friend—the 2021 Royals are playing at home tonight! And I've got a pair of tickets, just for you.

For a fair price, of course.

You're "too busy?" For *baseball*? The sport our forefathers played with broomsticks and wads of rubber bands in the street, using open manholes for bases? The sport that brought America together one magical summer with only a couple dozen dingers and a handful of pills? The game that Rob Manfred fell so head-over-Florsheims in love with, he can't even talk about it without his mouth crinkling into that thing he calls a smile? The pastime that was so important to this country that after two major in-season viral outbreaks, the league decided the only cure was to *keep playing baseball*??

Nobody's "too busy" for baseball around here. You could be lazing in a sun-drenched Kauffman Stadium seat this very night, taking in this game of kings and knaves. The Royals play a style of ball that's swift, pure and American; which may explain why they lose so often. Heh, heh.

Lighten up, pal. You're blind as an umpire if you don't see our great nation taking some L's. The trick is to not take too many in a row.

KANSAS CITY ROYALS PROSPECTUS
2020 W-L: 26-34, 4TH IN AL CENTRAL

Pythag	.457	22nd	dWin%	.403	24th
RS/G	4.13	26th	B-Age	28.4	15th
RA/G	4.53	13th	P-Age	27.7	6th
DRC+	91	27th	FIP	4.57	18th
DRA-	101	18th	DER	.690	22nd
Payroll	$34M	27th	M$/MW	$2.0M	9th

410'
387' 387'
330' 330'

- Opened 1973
- Open air
- Natural surface
- Fence profile: 9' to 11'

Three-Year Park Factors

Runs	Runs/RH	Runs/LH	HR/RH	HR/LH
100	100	101	90	92

Top Hitter WARP	1.2 Whit Merrifield
Top Pitcher WARP	1.3 Brady Singer
Top Prospect	Bobby Witt Jr.

Payroll History (in millions)

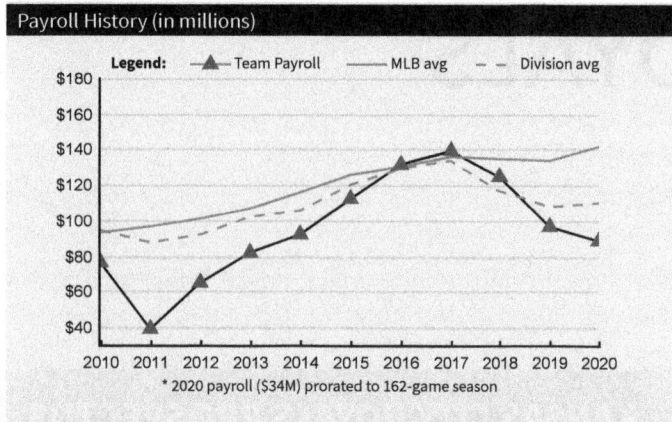

Legend: Team Payroll — MLB avg — Division avg

* 2020 payroll ($34M) prorated to 162-game season

Future Commitments (in millions)

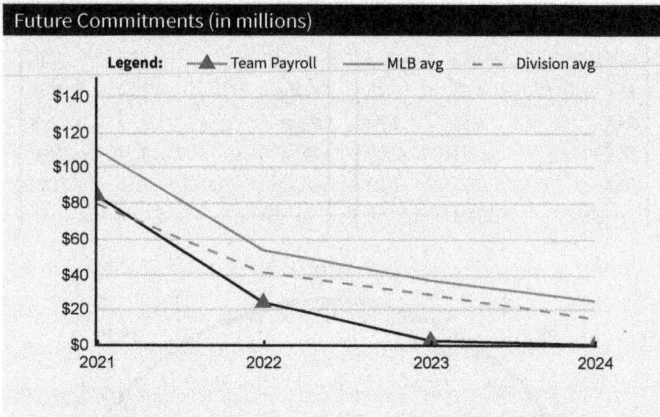

Legend: Team Payroll — MLB avg — Division avg

Farm System Ranking

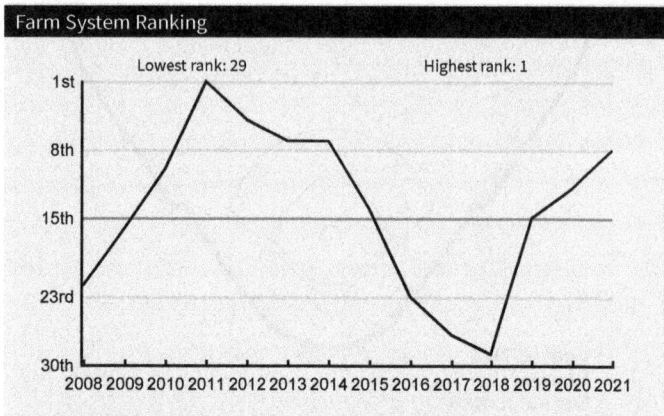

Lowest rank: 29   Highest rank: 1

Personnel

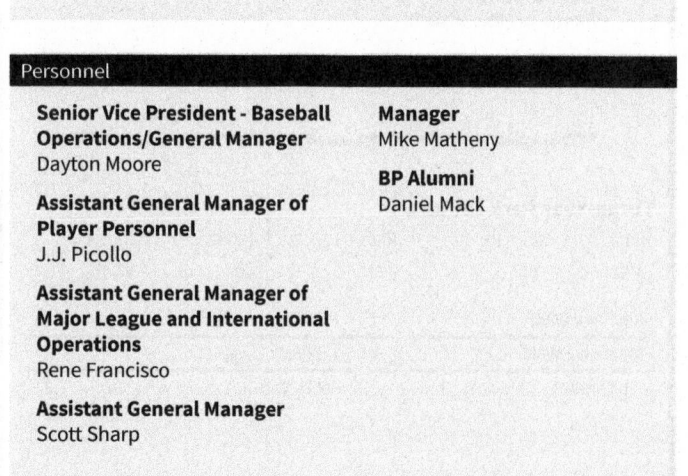

Senior Vice President - Baseball Operations/General Manager
Dayton Moore

Assistant General Manager of Player Personnel
J.J. Picollo

Assistant General Manager of Major League and International Operations
Rene Francisco

Assistant General Manager
Scott Sharp

Manager
Mike Matheny

BP Alumni
Daniel Mack

In fact, I know what you're thinking: "Didn't these Royals just lose over a hundred games? That sounds like a lot!" Well, check the papers, friend. They've lost over *two* hundred in the past three seasons. But *this* Royals team is different. This team is going to *win*. Why? Because they *deserve* to. And when's the last time America didn't get what it deserved?

It's coming back to you now, isn't it? "Wasn't this team in the World Series just five short years ago?" They sure were, pal. Won the whole thing, too. That was a fast bunch. Didn't homer a ton. Knew how to flip the leather. Pinch ran like they had a track team on the bench. But time is mean for no reason, and those days are long behind us now.

Those boys are gone, is my point. Salvador Perez is still here, at least; sure, his tendons have been moved around a bit, but the old man can still thrill a cardboard cutout or two. But even Alex Gordon has packed it up and headed back to the flatlands to sip tea and watch the sunset over the plains. Sure, he deserves it, but it's difficult to watch him go.

You know what happens when teams break apart in baseball, don't you? Well, what happens in *any* business when the numbers are down? Any sensible businessman would be giving the place a gasoline shower and having a smoke. Then, it's time to collect on the insurance and start a new life. In baseball, we call that "rebuilding."

The Royals may seem like they're doing that, but according to them at the beginning of the 2020 season—they're not! I heard Dayton Moore and Mike Matheny will throw a chair if they hear the word "rebuild" so much as whispered by the breeze. In fact, I'm not sure if we should even be talking about this. Anybody asks, we're just a couple of fellas standing here, having a good old fashioned how's-your-mother.

Anyway, what was I saying? Oh, right—Moore went off like a dog at the moon when somebody brought up his Royals rebuilding; all *"We are done with that,"* and *"We have an obligation to win as many games as possible,"* and even, *"There is an expectation for these players to perform and to win. That's what we're here for."* I think that last one's straight from the good book itself. The Bible Belt isn't just a place, y'know; it's what's holding up Dayton Moore's pants.

The point is, these Royals weren't some bunch of torpid layabouts in 2020, preening in the sun like Missouri street lizards. These were fully charged batsmen with steam coming out of their ears for nine innings. Did they win a lot of games? They did not. Did they score a lot of runs? They did not. But as they pushed onward, future champions emerged and the vision of glory in the days ahead began to form like an honest-to-God Rockefeller painting for all those still watching.

Just take this Adalberto Mondesi, why don't you. Kid's got a head full of snakes. He led the league in swiping bases that didn't belong to him, and you better believe the other teams hated it. Brady Singer didn't allow a run for 14 straight innings. Kris Bubic was among the rookie strikeout leaders. Word is, somewhere in Nebraska they've got a warehouse packed with fresh-armed studs, flourishing like the miles and miles of government corn surrounding them. I hadn't ever seen more intimidating youths in one place since that gang of street urchins surrounded me in a boxcar.

Change is inevitable, pal. You know it, same as I did the day I woke up with a bunch of preteens hoisting me in the air, about to throw me from a moving train. During a time like this for a team, the clubhouse becomes a junction of swiftly forgotten substitutes, auditioners, prospects, hangers-on, blackguards and ragamuffins. Old favorites depart, new faces arrive, players are packaged up and shipped out of town. The manager is one of the only constants, overseeing every step forward and backward: a stoic presence, nodding sagely from the doorway of his office as the team takes shape.

Friend, meet Mike Matheny. In 2012 he was on the other side of the Show-Me with the Cardinals, where he was a first-time manager, a former lousy hitter and a defensive catcher who was once hit in the face with a fastball. This was a battle-hardened, punch-taking, star-spangled roughneck; the kind of fellow who gets handed the key to his hometown. I had a front row seat to that show for a while, hanging around outside the players entrance—Joe Kelly used to pay me to find "cool rocks" for him throw at trains—and let me tell you: Matheny was a man who made up for his lack of leadership skills with a strong desire to have better leadership skills.

After being hired by the Royals, Matheny was celebrated for looking at the flaws in his managerial style and trying to improve between his first job and his second one, going so far as to enroll in a ten-week online baseball analytics course. Did you know they can fit college inside a computer now? Incredible stuff.

He's got something few other managers do: A published manifesto. Thomas Paine! Edmund Burke! Karl Marx! Mike Matheny! They all had ideas too powerful to live exclusively in their brains; ideas to recalibrate society, to rebel against tyrants, and in Matheny's case, to suggest not screaming at children while coaching youth sports.

Matheny was definitely in it to win it in 2020, very nearly almost half the time, making more moves per game than any other manager in baseball. That meant more steal attempts, more bunts, more pinch hitters, more relief pitchers, more action. Matheny was a manager who was trying to *manage*. Was it successful? Friend, what's more exciting, the runner taking off for second or getting tagged out at the end? Life is all about anticipation. What's important is that the Royals are *not* rebuilding. They are re-expecting to win. Just like they always have. And they've got the perfect manager to do that.

Did you know that the first game in Kansas City Royals history was a thrilling, 4-3 walk-off win? Once it was finally over, it was a great relief to those watching. They'd feared, as the absurd game entered its twelfth inning and fourth hour, that this whole baseball thing meant a lifetime sentence.

And how about that last game in Kansas City Royals history? A victorious, 3-1 season finale, twice-delayed; the first time for three months due to the pandemic, and the

second time for 95 minutes due to rain. Once it was finally over, it was a great relief to those watching, as earlier in the year, fans had wondered when they'd ever see a baseball season completed again.

So you see? Baseball—watching it, playing it, deciding whether or not it should continue during a pandemic—is all about finding that narrow margin between too much and too little into which you can wedge yourself. Me? I wedge myself into a crawl space every night, because it's the only way I feel safe in the dark. Plus, if any gangs of children are looking for me, they can't reach that high with their scrawny, emaciated arms.

Forgive me for getting philosophical, but I guess that's kind of like life now: Cramming our slovenly existences into smaller and smaller spaces. It's made it easier to forget what we used to recognize. Baseball dropped 102 games off its schedule in 2020 in the name of public health and safety and became a manic 60-game carnival with basically no rules. That's not the always-thrilling, well-managed, competently-overseen baseball I know! So for the Royals, for the league, for everybody; 2020 was all about the potential to get things right. Eventually. And now 2021 is here, to continue that potential.

So you see: Baseball's not just about knowing who you are! It's knowing who you *could* be!

Tell me, chum; when you get up in the morning, your hair askew, lips parched, eyes shot with blood from another sleepless night in plague times, do you see yourself in that mirror and think, "Yep, that's me all right!"

No! You give yourself a few slaps, scream into a pillow, put on your best suit and tie and strap in for another industrious day in the living room.

That's our Royals, friend—not some deluded bunch of powder blue porn-haters! Well, not entirely. They're fully aware of how they woke up this morning; only instead of tossing fitfully between nightmares last night, they lost 241 baseball games. And they're still getting up for work, just like you.

So when they say they're not rebuilding, when they say they're here to win, you believe them! I sure do! In this league, you don't keep signing guys named "Mike" because you're trying to lose.

Now, whether or not they succeed is entirely different. But believing is half the battle! The other half is evaluating and developing talent up the middle; stockpiling several generations' worth of pitchers; fortifying franchise infrastructure; properly timing the promotions of top prospects; acquiring the right free agents to fill in the gaps; and getting the nod from ownership to spend like your hair's on fire, if need be.

Yes, you're right. That's a lot of things to jam into one half. But "believing" deserves to be its own half of the process, because it's hard! Just ask anyone who has ever given up on anything—a job, a project, a person. They're everywhere!

So, go ahead. Take the tickets for tonight's game. We can work out a fair price for them, I'm sure. What's the going rate for a train ticket out of town? I'd settle for that. I'm looking forward to stepping onboard, rather than running alongside with the sheriff on my tail.

Excellent. Friend, you won't regret this. Baseball is all about believing in the potential of the seemingly impossible. It's a lot like life in that way, don't you think? And when life gets bad, we all need those nine innings to believe in something on occasion, don't we? Things like, *what if that run comes into score even those there's two outs, or maybe we'll someday live in a world where attending a baseball game doesn't require you to sign a document clearing MLB of liability if you get sick and die.*

Before we part, friend, let me level with you. I've learned a few lessons walking these streets in my sharp tie and brimmed cap. One is: Never wager with a man who is ready to die.

But the biggest lesson I've learned is that when the world starts taking things from you, what you manage to hang onto matters so much more. While billionaires the world over scrambled to protect themselves after COVID, Royals bigwigs did the unthinkable and instituted pay cuts at the executive level only, preventing them from having to make layoffs or furloughs to team employees. That move told anybody watching that while the world had changed, the Royals had maintained what was important to them: Keeping their people employed.

Isn't that beautiful? Sorry. I need a moment.

Come, let's stare into the churning flow of this fountain together and think about how nice that is. Maybe we can toss in a penny or a quarter or a fifty dollar bill and make a wish. I'm fresh out of cash, though, so why don't you just go ahead and toss your largest bill in there. I'll stay behind and make sure no one fishes it out.

Say, was that a train whistle? I better catch it. Take care, friend, and remember: You can't win 'em all; but you can try to. And that's a lot like winning itself. Except for the score. And the outcome. And the standings.

Farewell! ▣

—Justin Klugh is an author of Baseball Prospectus.

HITTERS

Franchy Cordero CF   Born: 09/02/94 Age: 26 Bats: L Throws: R Height: 6'3" Weight: 226 Origin: International Free Agent, 2011

YEAR	TEAM	LVL	AGE	PA	R	2B	3B	HR	RBI	BB	K	SB	CS	Whiff%	AVG/OBP/SLG	DRC+	BABIP	BRR	FRAA	WARP
2018	ELP	AAA	23	31	3	1	0	1	1	4	10	3	0		.259/.355/.407	66	.375	0.6	LF(3): -0.4, CF(3): -0.8	-0.1
2018	SD	MLB	23	154	19	5	1	7	19	14	55	5	2	34.7%	.237/.307/.439	72	.338	0.6	LF(22): 0.4, CF(11): -1.3, RF(4): -0.8	-0.2
2019	ELP	AAA	24	51	7	2	1	3	8	4	19	0	0		.217/.294/.500	60	.292	0.5	CF(9): 0.6	0.0
2019	SD	MLB	24	20	2	1	0	0	1	4	7	1	0	38.6%	.333/.450/.400	74	.556	0.6	CF(5): -0.4, RF(4): -0.3	0.0
2020	KC	MLB	26	42	7	3	0	2	7	4	4	1	0	20.2%	.211/.286/.447	96	.188	0.3	RF(8): -0.5, CF(5): -0.5, LF(1): 0.2	0.0
2021 FS	KC	MLB	26	600	62	26	8	14	65	44	192	11	4	29.5%	.223/.287/.382	80	.316	6.3	CF -8, LF 3	0.3
2021 DC	KC	MLB	26	531	55	23	7	12	58	38	169	9	3	29.5%	.223/.287/.382	80	.316	5.6	CF -7, LF 2	0.2

Comparables: Ruben Rivera, Alex Escobar, Ryan Thompson

When we meet Officer Nordberg in the opening minutes of The Naked Gun, he's shot several times, bangs his head on a pipe, burns his hand on a stove, falls against some wet paint, crushes his fingers under a window, stumbles headfirst into a wedding cake and steps into a bear trap before mercifully falling overboard. Cordero's injuries are nowhere near as comical, but they're almost as plentiful as poor, pitiful Nordberg's. Last year saw the third consecutive season he landed on the 60-day IL; this time around it was a sprained right wrist that put him on the shelf, but at least he made it back on the field. Small victories. As the Royals assemble their 2021 outfield, he will get every chance to contribute. All he has to do is … you know … stay healthy.

Hunter Dozier 3B   Born: 08/22/91 Age: 29 Bats: R Throws: R Height: 6'4" Weight: 220 Origin: Round 1, 2013 Draft (#8 overall)

YEAR	TEAM	LVL	AGE	PA	R	2B	3B	HR	RBI	BB	K	SB	CS	Whiff%	AVG/OBP/SLG	DRC+	BABIP	BRR	FRAA	WARP
2018	OMA	AAA	26	143	18	7	0	1	11	24	43	2	1		.254/.385/.339	115	.392	-0.2	3B(19): 0.6, RF(13): 1.2, 1B(4): -0.0	0.6
2018	KC	MLB	26	388	36	19	4	11	34	24	109	2	3	28.4%	.229/.278/.395	80	.296	-0.3	1B(51): -7.5, 3B(37): -5.9, RF(2): -0.0	-1.5
2019	KC	MLB	27	586	75	29	10	26	84	55	148	2	2	27.0%	.279/.348/.522	118	.339	-1.8	3B(100): -0.3, RF(20): 0.4, 1B(7): -0.8	3.0
2020	KC	MLB	29	186	29	4	2	6	12	27	48	4	0	30.9%	.228/.344/.392	103	.288	0.9	1B(28): -0.8, RF(18): -0.5, LF(2): 0.1	0.3
2021 FS	KC	MLB	29	600	70	25	5	17	71	61	175	3	1	28.3%	.233/.316/.401	100	.312	2.4	3B -3, LF 2	1.3
2021 DC	KC	MLB	29	531	62	22	4	15	63	54	155	2	1	28.3%	.233/.316/.401	100	.312	2.1	3B -3, LF 2	1.3

Comparables: Butch Hobson, Bill Hall, Nick Castellanos

A COVID-19 casualty at the end of summer camp, Dozier struggled offensively once he returned to the lineup. His exit velocity was down and his hard-hit rate tumbled to 10 points below his career average. He was disciplined at the plate, chasing just a quarter of pitches out of the strikezone, but his whiff rate was elevated, especially against breaking pitches. Always a bit of a defensive nomad, wandering between the corners in the infield and the outfield, he found a home at first base. And as the Royals collected options for their outfield like a penny-pincher clipping coupons, the cold corner looks to be his most likely future home.

Lucius Fox SS Born: 07/02/97 Age: 24 Bats: S Throws: R Height: 6'1" Weight: 185 Origin: International Free Agent, 2015

YEAR	TEAM	LVL	AGE	PA	R	2B	3B	HR	RBI	BB	K	SB	CS	Whiff%	AVG/OBP/SLG	DRC+	BABIP	BRR	FRAA	WARP
2018	CHA	HI-A	20	404	54	17	1	2	30	42	79	23	7		.282/.371/.353	124	.358	2.1	SS(79): -1.5	1.8
2018	MTG	AA	20	120	14	3	1	1	9	8	20	6	2		.221/.284/.298	70	.259	0.6	SS(26): -0.7	-0.1
2019	MTG	AA	21	431	60	16	8	3	33	53	89	37	11		.230/.340/.342	106	.293	0.6	SS(79): -3.9, 2B(12): 1.4, 3B(9): 1.4	2.0
2019	DUR	AAA	21	49	6	0	1	0	1	6	15	2	0		.143/.250/.190	47	.222	0.6	SS(12): 0.4, 2B(1): -0.1	0.0
2021 FS	KC	MLB	23	600	58	26	4	6	51	52	176	22	8		.224/.302/.329	76	.320	3.6	3B 1, SS -1	0.5
2021 DC	KC	MLB	23	166	16	7	1	1	14	14	48	6	2		.224/.302/.329	76	.320	1.0	3B 0, SS 0	0.0

Comparables: Tyler Wade, Hanley Ramirez, Eugenio Suárez

If the Royals had a profile on Tinder, they would swipe right on speedy athletes who struggle to get on base consistently and lack a power projection. They matched with Fox in a midseason trade with Tampa in exchange for Brett Phillips.

Maikel Franco 3B Born: 08/26/92 Age: 28 Bats: R Throws: R Height: 6'1" Weight: 225 Origin: International Free Agent, 2010

YEAR	TEAM	LVL	AGE	PA	R	2B	3B	HR	RBI	BB	K	SB	CS	Whiff%	AVG/OBP/SLG	DRC+	BABIP	BRR	FRAA	WARP
2018	PHI	MLB	25	465	48	17	1	22	68	29	62	1	0	21.1%	.270/.314/.467	109	.270	1.5	3B(117): -2.7	2.1
2019	LHV	AAA	26	46	5	2	1	2	6	5	7	0	0		.175/.283/.425	83	.161	-0.3	3B(11): 0.9	0.1
2019	PHI	MLB	26	428	48	17	0	17	56	36	61	0	0	22.0%	.234/.297/.409	88	.236	-1.0	3B(110): 2.5, 1B(2): -0.0	1.1
2020	KC	MLB	28	243	23	16	0	8	38	16	38	1	0	24.6%	.278/.321/.457	104	.298	-0.2	3B(51): -1.8, 1B(2): -0.0	0.3
2021 FS	KC	MLB	28	600	66	28	1	19	79	43	103	1	0	22.8%	.244/.301/.408	97	.267	-0.6	3B -4, 1B 0	0.5

Comparables: Joe Crede, Aramis Ramirez, Mike Moustakas

Freed from the yoke of expectations that accompanied him in Philadelphia, Franco settled into the Royals lineup—and clubhouse—and enjoyed his best overall offensive season since 2015. It wasn't happenstance. After signing with Kansas City, he made his way to Miami for some offseason hitting work with Royals hitting coaches Pedro Grifol and Mike Tosar. The result: His average exit velocity on batted balls was down, but he made more regular—and solid—contact, increasing his line drive rate by a third. A resulting bump in his BABIP followed and he was a mainstay for the Royals in the heart of their order. He also made hay against lefties, something he hasn't done consistently over his career.

Cam Gallagher C Born: 12/06/92 Age: 28 Bats: R Throws: R Height: 6'3" Weight: 230 Origin: Round 2, 2011 Draft (#65 overall)

YEAR	TEAM	LVL	AGE	PA	R	2B	3B	HR	RBI	BB	K	SB	CS	Whiff%	AVG/OBP/SLG	DRC+	BABIP	BRR	FRAA	WARP
2018	OMA	AAA	25	303	28	13	0	4	42	26	38	1	0		.265/.334/.358	84	.294	-2.0	C(72): 11.9	1.5
2018	KC	MLB	25	69	5	3	0	1	7	3	15	0	0	20.0%	.206/.250/.302	84	.250	-1.6	C(20): 2.4	0.3
2019	KC	MLB	26	142	14	7	0	3	12	11	28	0	1	17.5%	.238/.312/.365	91	.281	-0.6	C(44): 3.8	0.9
2020	KC	MLB	28	60	10	5	0	1	3	6	11	0	0	21.2%	.283/.356/.434	91	.341	1.0	C(25): -0.4	0.2
2021 FS	KC	MLB	28	600	63	27	1	12	61	49	121	1	0	19.1%	.241/.310/.366	89	.289	-0.7	C 0	1.6
2021 DC	KC	MLB	28	132	14	6	0	2	13	10	26	0	0	19.1%	.241/.310/.366	89	.289	-0.1	C 0	0.4

Comparables: Bruce Bochy, Sal Fasano, Larry Howard

Being a backup catcher on the Royals when Salvador Perez is healthy is a bit like being a weatherman in San Diego: Nobody cares. But when an eye ailment sent the first-stringer to the sidelines, the understudy was ready. Gallagher enjoyed the finest offensive season of his oft-interrupted major-league career, posting career highs in rate stats across the board. As a reward, he is preparing his lines for 2021, just in case he's called upon again.

YEAR	TEAM	P. COUNT	FRM RUNS	BLK RUNS	THRW RUNS	TOT RUNS
2018	KC	2414	1.5	1.0	0.0	2.6
2018	OMA	9980	11.3	0.3	0.1	11.7
2019	KC	5506	3.7	0.9	-0.3	4.3
2020	KC	2736	-0.1	-0.1	0.0	-0.1
2021	KC	4810	1.3	-0.4	-0.1	0.9

Alex Gordon LF Born: 02/10/84 Age: 37 Bats: L Throws: R Height: 6'1" Weight: 220 Origin: Round 1, 2005 Draft (#2 overall)

YEAR	TEAM	LVL	AGE	PA	R	2B	3B	HR	RBI	BB	K	SB	CS	Whiff%	AVG/OBP/SLG	DRC+	BABIP	BRR	FRAA	WARP
2018	KC	MLB	34	568	56	24	0	13	54	50	124	12	2	24.0%	.245/.324/.370	89	.299	-1.9	LF(125): 3.3, CF(11): -0.9, RF(1): 0.1	0.8
2019	KC	MLB	35	633	77	31	1	13	76	51	100	5	3	22.0%	.266/.345/.396	96	.301	0.6	LF(146): -2.7, P(2): -0.0	1.2
2020	KC	MLB	36	184	15	4	0	4	11	18	37	0	0	22.6%	.209/.299/.307	83	.246	0.1	LF(49): 1.5	0.5
2021 FS	KC	MLB	37	600	59	26	1	11	60	57	147	7	3	22.6%	.231/.323/.354	90	.298	-1.8	LF -3, CF 0	0.4

Comparables: Cliff Floyd, Greg Vaughn, Gus Zernial

In many ways, Gordon's career mirrored the fortunes of the Royals. Drafted as a third baseman, he scuffled, struggled and underachieved through his first several seasons in Kansas City. A brief exile to Triple-A, a position shift and a relationship with Rusty Kuntz transformed him into one of the top outfielders in the league during his prime. As the Royals shot up the American League ranks and reached the pinnacle, he was the steady veteran presence; the leader by example. The ninth-inning dinger to tie Game One of the 2015 World Series against closer Jeurys Familia will forever be an iconic moment of that championship season. The last five years haven't been as kind, as injury and age once again conspired against a top athlete; retirement beckoned. Someday, his number will be enshrined alongside other Royal icons George Brett, Frank White and Dick Howser. Enjoy retirement—and the pizza—Gordo.

BASEBALL PROSPECTUS 2021

Kyle Isbel OF   Born: 03/03/97   Age: 24   Bats: L   Throws: R   Height: 5'11"   Weight: 183   Origin: Round 3, 2018 Draft (#94 overall)

YEAR	TEAM	LVL	AGE	PA	R	2B	3B	HR	RBI	BB	K	SB	CS	Whiff%	AVG/OBP/SLG	DRC+	BABIP	BRR	FRAA	WARP
2018	IDF	ROK	21	119	27	10	1	4	18	14	17	12	3		.381/.454/.610	195	.429	-0.8	CF(19): 4.5, RF(2): 1.1, LF(1): 0.3	1.6
2018	LEX	LO-A	21	174	30	12	1	3	14	12	43	12	3		.289/.345/.434	110	.377	2.8	CF(27): 0.8, LF(11): -0.5	0.7
2019	ROY	ROK	22	27	9	2	0	2	7	2	5	3	1		.360/.407/.680	154	.389	1.0	CF(6): 1.6	0.5
2019	WIL	HI-A	22	214	26	7	3	5	23	15	44	8	3		.216/.282/.361	85	.253	1.8	CF(32): -2.3, RF(12): 0.5	0.2
2021 FS	KC	MLB	24	600	55	26	3	13	60	39	173	17	7		.228/.285/.361	78	.307	-0.6	CF 1, RF 1	0.2

Comparables: Paulo Orlando, Abraham Almonte, Rosell Herrera

There aren't a lot of hitting prospects in the Royals' system, especially compared to the young arms that are on the edge of a breakthrough. With good pitch recognition and decent enough bat speed, Isbel represents one of the batters with the most potential. He was scorching hot to open 2019 until a hamate injury sidelined him for a couple of months and ultimately sabotaged his second half. He got back on track in the AFL and then COVID-19 meant he lost an entire minor-league season—although he did spend August and September at the club's alternate training site. Like just about every other prospect toiling in the mid-minors, he'll do well to get back on the field with a full season of competition. And if this baseball thing doesn't work out, he could always hit the lanes. It's likely he's the second-best bowler in baseball next to Mookie Betts, but that's an argument for the 2021 edition of Bowling Prospectus.

Khalil Lee CF   Born: 06/26/98   Age: 23   Bats: L   Throws: L   Height: 5'10"   Weight: 170   Origin: Round 3, 2016 Draft (#103 overall)

YEAR	TEAM	LVL	AGE	PA	R	2B	3B	HR	RBI	BB	K	SB	CS	Whiff%	AVG/OBP/SLG	DRC+	BABIP	BRR	FRAA	WARP
2018	WIL	HI-A	20	301	42	13	4	4	41	48	75	14	3		.270/.402/.406	140	.371	2.2	CF(57): 3.8, RF(9): 0.3	2.2
2018	NWA	AA	20	118	15	5	0	2	10	11	28	2	2		.245/.330/.353	82	.319	0.6	CF(17): 0.3, LF(9): 0.7	0.0
2019	NWA	AA	21	546	74	21	3	8	51	65	154	53	12		.264/.363/.372	117	.374	3.7	RF(55): -6.0, CF(45): -5.7, LF(8): -0.1	1.2
2021 FS	KC	MLB	23	600	61	28	4	11	56	56	218	18	7		.217/.303/.350	81	.345	1.0	RF -9, LF 0	-0.5
2021 DC	KC	MLB	23	66	6	3	0	1	6	6	24	2	0		.217/.303/.350	81	.345	0.1	RF -1	-0.1

Comparables: Clint Frazier, Austin Jackson, Luis Alexander Basabe

Is Lee a future everyday player or just a speedy fourth outfielder who'll leave you wanting more? In a kinder parallel universe, Lee may have been given the opportunity to start to answer that question via a full season of at-bats against high-minors pitching. Instead, he spent all of 2020 at the Royals' alternate site, and while reports there were encouraging, they didn't do enough to move the needle. Lee remains an enigma: too talented to fall out of the Royals' top-10 prospects list, but too inconsistent at the plate to enter the true National Prospect Consciousness™. Kansas City liked him enough to add him to the 40-man this winter, but not so much that they refrained from signing Michael A. Taylor to fill the speedy fourth outfielder role.

Nicky Lopez 2B   Born: 03/13/95   Age: 26   Bats: L   Throws: R   Height: 5'11"   Weight: 175   Origin: Round 5, 2016 Draft (#163 overall)

YEAR	TEAM	LVL	AGE	PA	R	2B	3B	HR	RBI	BB	K	SB	CS	Whiff%	AVG/OBP/SLG	DRC+	BABIP	BRR	FRAA	WARP
2018	NWA	AA	23	325	42	8	5	2	27	33	23	9	4		.331/.397/.416	123	.351	2.8	SS(58): -4.8, 2B(14): 0.4	1.2
2018	OMA	AAA	23	256	33	6	2	7	26	27	29	6	2		.278/.364/.417	120	.294	0.0	SS(36): -1.0, 2B(18): 1.7	1.3
2019	OMA	AAA	24	138	27	6	1	3	13	20	5	9	3		.353/.457/.500	139	.352	-1.3	SS(17): 3.5, 2B(14): 1.0	1.5
2019	KC	MLB	24	402	44	22	2	2	30	18	51	1	1	15.0%	.240/.276/.325	61	.273	2.5	2B(76): 1.3, SS(33): 1.2	0.0
2020	KC	MLB	25	192	15	8	0	1	13	18	41	0	5	21.1%	.201/.286/.266	73	.260	-0.6	2B(53): 6.3, SS(4): 0.1, 3B(2): -0.0	0.6
2021 FS	KC	MLB	26	600	60	29	4	7	55	48	110	8	3	17.7%	.246/.314/.354	83	.298	1.7	2B 11, SS 0	2.1
2021 DC	KC	MLB	26	531	53	26	3	6	49	42	97	7	2	17.7%	.246/.314/.354	83	.298	1.5	2B 10	2.0

Comparables: Brad Wellman, Mark Grudzielanek, Tilson Brito

Let's go for the positive and start with the defense. Lopez excelled at the keystone, exhibiting excellent range and a killer double play pivot. The glovework was worth eight Defensive Runs Saved, tops in the AL at his position, and garnered a nomination for a Gold Glove. That's the good. Now for the … less positive. Coming up through the minors, Lopez was a grinder at the plate, battling every plate appearance, drawing walks at an above-average clip while keeping strikeouts at bay. But that approach hasn't materialized in the majors. With a depressed on-base percentage, another issue is he just doesn't make hard contact. His average exit velocity ranked 189 out of 194 batters who put more than 100 balls in play in 2020 and he ranked in the 96th percentile in outs above average. In other words, he's an out machine on both offense and defense.

Ryan McBroom 1B   Born: 04/09/92   Age: 29   Bats: R   Throws: L   Height: 6'3"   Weight: 225   Origin: Round 15, 2014 Draft (#444 overall)

YEAR	TEAM	LVL	AGE	PA	R	2B	3B	HR	RBI	BB	K	SB	CS	Whiff%	AVG/OBP/SLG	DRC+	BABIP	BRR	FRAA	WARP
2018	TRN	AA	26	111	13	5	1	4	14	7	27	0	3		.324/.378/.510	133	.408	-0.4	1B(20): 0.9, RF(2): -0.1	0.4
2018	SWB	AAA	26	393	49	18	1	11	46	25	106	1	4		.295/.339/.443	106	.383	-1.2	1B(45): -1.5, RF(34): 2.8, LF(9): -0.7	0.3
2019	SWB	AAA	27	482	87	29	0	26	66	58	100	2	2		.315/.402/.574	141	.356	-3.8	1B(62): -1.2, RF(37): -0.3, LF(5): 0.5	2.6
2019	KC	MLB	27	83	8	5	0	0	6	7	25	0	0	25.5%	.293/.361/.360	72	.440	0.1	RF(12): -1.5, 1B(6): -0.5, LF(3): -0.1	-0.3
2020	KC	MLB	28	85	8	3	0	6	10	4	30	0	0	37.8%	.247/.282/.506	91	.311	-0.2	1B(10): -0.6, LF(3): -0.2, RF(1): 0.0	0.0
2021 FS	KC	MLB	29	600	67	23	1	22	78	42	192	0	0	33.1%	.237/.301/.408	98	.320	-0.7	1B -2, LF 0	0.7
2021 DC	KC	MLB	29	33	3	1	0	1	4	2	10	0	0	33.1%	.237/.301/.408	98	.320	0.0	1B 0	0.0

Comparables: Eric Munson, Bryan LaHair, Matt Clark

After opening the season as the right-handed hitting portion of a self-described "soft platoon" by the Royals, McBroom found himself spending the second half either on the bench or at the alternate site. He generally can hold his own against same-siders—hence the platoon being "soft"—but his offensive production was way down across the board.

308 - Kansas City Royals

Whit Merrifield RF Born: 01/24/89 Age: 32 Bats: R Throws: R Height: 6'1" Weight: 195 Origin: Round 9, 2010 Draft (#269 overall)

YEAR	TEAM	LVL	AGE	PA	R	2B	3B	HR	RBI	BB	K	SB	CS	Whiff%	AVG/OBP/SLG	DRC+	BABIP	BRR	FRAA	WARP
2018	KC	MLB	29	707	88	43	3	12	60	61	114	45	10	19.1%	.304/.367/.438	119	.352	3.5	2B(108): 2.3, CF(30): 1.4, RF(8): -0.1	4.4
2019	KC	MLB	30	735	105	41	10	16	74	45	126	20	10	20.0%	.302/.348/.463	109	.350	-1.9	2B(82): 6.2, RF(61): -6.4, CF(17): 1.5	3.0
2020	KC	MLB	31	265	38	12	0	9	30	12	33	12	3	16.2%	.282/.325/.440	113	.295	0.2	RF(34): 0.7, CF(23): 0.1, 2B(15): 1.5	1.2
2021 FS	KC	MLB	32	600	75	29	3	13	56	36	100	23	7	18.8%	.271/.323/.410	102	.310	5.0	RF -11, 2B 1	1.8
2021 DC	KC	MLB	32	597	75	29	3	13	55	36	99	23	7	18.8%	.271/.323/.410	102	.310	5.0	RF -11, 2B 1	1.4

Comparables: Howie Kendrick, Brandon Phillips, Jeff Kent

Merrifield goes by the moniker "Two-Hit Whit" and with good reason. No hitter has had as many games with two hits or more over the last three seasons than his 133. Last year, he became a much more disciplined hitter, cutting down on his chase rate on pitches out of the zone while he upped his contact rate on pitches in the zone. Still, he must have done something to anger the BABIP gods as he endured a brutal 4-for-41 stretch in the middle of the year. Penance paid, he got back to that two-hit thing to close out the season on a high note. He's also something of a Swiss Army knife in the field, having logged time at five different positions in each of those last three years. And his sprint speed ranks in the 89th percentile. Is there anything he can't do? He is probably working on a cure for COVID-19 as you read this; that is if Dolly Parton hasn't already cracked it.

Adalberto Mondesi SS Born: 07/27/95 Age: 25 Bats: S Throws: R Height: 6'1" Weight: 200 Origin: International Free Agent, 2011

YEAR	TEAM	LVL	AGE	PA	R	2B	3B	HR	RBI	BB	K	SB	CS	Whiff%	AVG/OBP/SLG	DRC+	BABIP	BRR	FRAA	WARP
2018	OMA	AAA	22	133	19	8	3	5	21	8	30	10	0		.250/.295/.492	74	.291	1.2	SS(18): 0.6, 2B(6): 0.8	0.2
2018	KC	MLB	22	291	47	13	3	14	37	11	77	32	7	34.1%	.276/.306/.498	104	.335	0.3	SS(61): 1.2, 2B(12): 0.9	1.6
2019	OMA	AAA	23	37	5	1	1	1	3	4	13	2	1		.242/.324/.424	67	.368	0.5	SS(6): 0.1	0.0
2019	KC	MLB	23	443	58	20	10	9	62	19	132	43	7	38.2%	.263/.291/.424	75	.357	3.1	SS(100): 6.3	1.6
2020	KC	MLB	25	233	33	11	3	6	22	11	70	24	8	40.4%	.256/.294/.416	60	.350	-0.3	SS(59): 2.9	-0.3
2021 FS	KC	MLB	25	600	62	23	9	15	67	30	186	39	7	38.3%	.229/.271/.383	76	.313	23.7	SS 9, 2B 0	3.5
2021 DC	KC	MLB	25	597	61	23	8	15	67	30	185	38	7	38.3%	.229/.271/.383	76	.313	23.6	SS 8	3.4

Comparables: Tim Anderson, Chris Owings, Michael Young

You have eggs, butter and flour, the essential ingredients for a soufflé. But if you don't use them correctly, the soufflé falls and you set off smoke alarms as it chars in the oven. With power, speed and off-the-charts athleticism, Mondesi has the ingredients to be a superstar in this league. Injuries have held him back in the past, but he was finally healthy in an abbreviated 2020. It was supposed to be the year where everything came together … but the season was one fallen soufflé after another. He whiffed in 30 percent of his plate appearances, made contact on just over 73 percent of his swings on pitches in the zone and led the league in caught stealing. What's the baking equivalent of seeing a ton of breaking balls off the plate?

Ryan O'Hearn 1B Born: 07/26/93 Age: 27 Bats: L Throws: L Height: 6'3" Weight: 220 Origin: Round 8, 2014 Draft (#243 overall)

YEAR	TEAM	LVL	AGE	PA	R	2B	3B	HR	RBI	BB	K	SB	CS	Whiff%	AVG/OBP/SLG	DRC+	BABIP	BRR	FRAA	WARP
2018	OMA	AAA	24	406	47	21	1	11	52	45	97	2	0		.232/.322/.391	90	.286	3.9	1B(69): -6.3, LF(13): -2.1	-0.8
2018	KC	MLB	24	170	23	10	2	12	30	20	45	0	0	31.2%	.262/.353/.597	129	.293	-3.6	1B(31): 0.4, LF(1): -0.1	0.5
2019	OMA	AAA	25	149	20	10	1	9	28	17	31	0	0		.295/.383/.597	129	.322	0.5	1B(25): 0.0	0.8
2019	KC	MLB	25	370	32	13	1	14	38	39	99	0	1	26.2%	.195/.281/.369	79	.230	-1.0	1B(94): -5.0, LF(2): -0.1	-1.0
2020	KC	MLB	27	132	7	6	0	2	18	18	37	0	0	29.9%	.195/.303/.301	83	.267	-0.7	1B(27): -0.3	-0.1
2021 FS	KC	MLB	27	600	66	26	2	19	72	65	182	0	0	28.0%	.214/.303/.382	90	.286	0.3	1B -2, LF 0	0.0
2021 DC	KC	MLB	27	99	10	4	0	3	11	10	30	0	0	28.0%	.214/.303/.382	90	.286	0.0	1B 0	0.0

Comparables: Nick Esasky, Tommy Medica, Derrek Lee

O'Hearn was limited to just 12 plate appearances against left-handed pitching as part of a "soft" platoon at first base. (That sounds like a real platoon to us.) He actually held his own against same siders in 2020, small sample be damned. It was with the alleged platoon advantage where things fell apart. He upped his line drive rate which should have helped his offensive fortunes, but he continues to struggle mightily against off-speed stuff and can't hit a curve. His power took another hit for the second consecutive season. Relegated to both pinch and designated hitting in September, he closed out a forgettable season with three hits over his final 46 plate appearances. (Which has us wondering how we can remove the word "hitter" from pinch hitter and designated hitter and have it make sense.) Those successful 44 games from 2018 are looking like an outlier and are further and further in the rearview mirror.

Edward Olivares OF Born: 03/06/96 Age: 25 Bats: R Throws: R Height: 6'2" Weight: 188 Origin: International Free Agent, 2014

YEAR	TEAM	LVL	AGE	PA	R	2B	3B	HR	RBI	BB	K	SB	CS	Whiff%	AVG/OBP/SLG	DRC+	BABIP	BRR	FRAA	WARP
2018	LE	HI-A	22	575	79	25	10	12	62	29	102	21	8		.277/.321/.429	103	.319	2.8	CF(115): 0.6, RF(7): 0.5, LF(4): 1.9	1.1
2019	AMA	AA	23	551	85	25	2	18	77	43	98	35	10		.283/.349/.453	113	.317	3.7	RF(105): 5.5, CF(19): -0.1	2.9
2020	SD	MLB	24	36	4	1	0	1	3	2	14	0	1	25.0%	.176/.222/.294	67	.263	-0.3	LF(7): 0.1, RF(6): -0.1, CF(1): 0.0	-0.1
2020	KC	MLB	24	65	5	1	1	2	7	2	11	0	1	24.5%	.274/.292/.419	69	.300	-0.2	CF(10): -0.2, LF(7): 0.2, RF(5): 0.3	-0.1
2021 FS	KC	MLB	25	600	63	21	5	17	70	37	156	14	5	24.6%	.237/.297/.391	91	.300	4.5	LF -1, RF 1	1.5
2021 DC	KC	MLB	25	431	45	15	4	12	50	26	112	10	4	24.6%	.237/.297/.391	91	.300	3.2	LF -1, RF 1	1.0

Comparables: Nomar Mazara, Johnny Field, Billy McKinney

When the Royals acquired Franchy Cordero in July, conventional wisdom at the time believed the Padres made the move in part to create an opportunity for Olivares in their outfield. Then Olivares was dealt to Kansas City at the trade deadline in August. Baseball is weird that way. Still, following the retirement of Alex Gordon and a perpetual revolving door in center, the Royals are on the hunt for outfielders. Olivares brings a developing power profile, plus speed and can certainly hold his own in the expansive Kauffman Stadium outfield. There are some fourth outfielder rumblings around him, but the Royals can afford to provide him with an opportunity to see if he can exceed those expectations.

── ★ ★ ★ *2021 Top 101 Prospect* **#97** ★ ★ ★ ──

Erick Pena CF Born: 02/20/03 Age: 18 Bats: L Throws: R Height: 6'3" Weight: 180 Origin: International Free Agent, 2019

Do you dig tools? Peña may just be the prospect for you. The Royals splashed the cash in the 2019 IFA period, awarding the center fielder with a $3.8 million bonus and it didn't take long for the Carlos Beltran comps to surface. The youngster already has balance and bat speed in the toolkit with plenty of room to grow. The Royals had enough faith to keep him in Kansas City after the regular season ended so he could take part in instructional league games where the competition level was somewhere between Double and Triple-A. The reports were glowing. The Yankees' Jasson Dominguez will be the name dominating headlines from this J2 class for a good while yet, but don't sleep on Peña's significant upside.

Salvador Perez C Born: 05/10/90 Age: 31 Bats: R Throws: R Height: 6'3" Weight: 250 Origin: International Free Agent, 2006

YEAR	TEAM	LVL	AGE	PA	R	2B	3B	HR	RBI	BB	K	SB	CS	Whiff%	AVG/OBP/SLG	DRC+	BABIP	BRR	FRAA	WARP
2018	KC	MLB	28	544	52	23	0	27	80	17	108	1	1	23.6%	.235/.274/.439	103	.245	-3.7	C(96): -8.1, 1B(3): 0.0	1.3
2020	KC	MLB	30	156	22	12	0	11	32	3	36	1	0	26.9%	.333/.353/.633	135	.375	-1.2	C(34): -0.7, 1B(3): -0.3	1.1
2021 FS	KC	MLB	31	600	74	28	1	27	93	21	137	1	0	25.2%	.252/.289/.458	105	.283	-0.6	C -6, 1B 0	2.2
2021 DC	KC	MLB	31	531	66	25	1	24	82	19	121	1	0	25.2%	.252/.289/.458	105	.283	-0.5	C -7	1.7

Comparables: *Wilson Ramos, Javy Lopez, Ivan Rodriguez*

YEAR	TEAM	P. COUNT	FRM RUNS	BLK RUNS	THRW RUNS	TOT RUNS
2018	KC	14217	-9.9	-0.6	0.8	-9.7
2020	KC	4651	1.6	-0.1	-0.1	1.5
2021	KC	18038	-7.7	-0.4	0.6	-7.6

DRC+ has been kinder to Perez than almost any other offensive metric, but even then he's hovered around league-average for many of the last several seasons. Maybe the fact that he caught over 5,300 innings from 2014 to 2018—second to Yadier Molina, but over 300 more than third-place Jon Lucroy) had something to do with that. A year away from catching while rehabbing from Tommy John surgery, along with a rigorous offseason hitting program with Royals' special assignment hitting coach Mike Tosar resulted in his best offensive performance of his career. Between a bout of COVID-19 and blurred vision that sidelined him in the middle of the season, he ripped the ball consistently, with a hard-hit rate of 47 percent. Defensively, he even improved his framing, posting a positive CSAA for the first time since 2013. And the surgically repaired arm? Good as new it would appear. He gunned down 27 percent of would-be thieves. You never want to miss a year due to injury, but he's a testament to the benefits of what a year away can do when you put in the work to get back to where you belong.

Carlos Santana 1B Born: 04/08/86 Age: 35 Bats: S Throws: R Height: 5'11" Weight: 210 Origin: International Free Agent, 2004

YEAR	TEAM	LVL	AGE	PA	R	2B	3B	HR	RBI	BB	K	SB	CS	Whiff%	AVG/OBP/SLG	DRC+	BABIP	BRR	FRAA	WARP
2018	PHI	MLB	32	679	82	28	2	24	86	110	93	2	1	19.3%	.229/.352/.414	108	.231	0.2	1B(149): -0.7, 3B(19): 0.6	1.8
2019	CLE	MLB	33	686	110	30	1	34	93	108	108	4	0	20.3%	.281/.397/.515	137	.293	1.1	1B(135): 3.9	4.8
2020	CLE	MLB	34	255	34	7	0	8	30	47	43	0	0	20.7%	.199/.349/.350	108	.212	1.4	1B(60): -4.2	0.2
2021 FS	KC	MLB	35	600	77	26	1	19	78	98	111	3	1	20.2%	.242/.369/.424	126	.273	0.2	1B 2, 3B 0	3.1
2021 DC	KC	MLB	35	597	77	26	1	19	78	97	111	3	1	20.2%	.242/.369/.424	126	.273	0.2	1B 2	3.1

Comparables: *Kevin Youkilis, Boog Powell, Don Mincher*

Santana's offensive potency and consistency are often taken for granted. To wit, did you know that last season was the first time in his career he finished with an OPS+ below 100? It's true. In Santana's first 10 seasons, he was reliably average or better in every single one of them. The good news is that he retained his impeccable eye at the plate and made a lot of hard outs, suggesting there's still some magic left in his stick. The bad news is that his timing couldn't have been worse: not only did Cleveland turn down his $17.5 million option, but they did so just months away from his 35th birthday. Santana will attempt to get back to being old steady before he's deemed too old to receive steady burn.

Jorge Soler RF Born: 02/25/92 Age: 29 Bats: R Throws: R Height: 6'4" Weight: 235 Origin: International Free Agent, 2012

YEAR	TEAM	LVL	AGE	PA	R	2B	3B	HR	RBI	BB	K	SB	CS	Whiff%	AVG/OBP/SLG	DRC+	BABIP	BRR	FRAA	WARP
2018	KC	MLB	26	257	27	18	0	9	28	28	69	3	1	36.4%	.265/.354/.466	100	.340	-0.5	RF(52): -1.0	0.4
2019	KC	MLB	27	679	95	33	1	48	117	73	178	3	1	32.4%	.265/.354/.569	141	.294	-4.3	RF(56): 0.4	4.5
2020	KC	MLB	28	174	17	8	0	8	24	19	60	0	0	37.2%	.228/.326/.443	91	.317	-0.5	RF(8): -0.7	0.0
2021 FS	KC	MLB	29	600	82	26	1	27	84	70	195	2	0	34.1%	.232/.331/.449	119	.311	-0.7	RF 0, LF 0	2.8
2021 DC	KC	MLB	29	597	82	26	1	27	83	70	194	2	0	34.1%	.232/.331/.449	119	.311	-0.7	RF 0	2.6

Comparables: *Jay Buhner, Jeremy Hermida, Jay Bruce*

Baseball can be cruel. Once you think you have this game licked, it can turn on you in an instant. One year removed from playing in every game and setting the Royals' single-season home run record, Soler was once again bitten by the injury bug and saw his power output decline precipitously. The nadir of his season came not when he landed on the IL for an oblique strain, but rather in a five-game stretch in mid-August where he struck out 15 times in 19 plate appearances. The Soler Power may have dimmed in 2020, but with an average exit velocity and hard-hit rate both in the 93rd percentile of all hitters, it's still glimmering. He just needs to rediscover how to tap into that power to get the same kind of results he saw in the prior year. Perhaps another offseason of work with Mike Tosar, the hitting guru who turned his career around with sessions in 2017 and 2018 can flip the switch. Shine on.

Bubba Starling CF Born: 08/03/92 Age: 28 Bats: R Throws: R Height: 6'4" Weight: 215 Origin: Round 1, 2011 Draft (#5 overall)

YEAR	TEAM	LVL	AGE	PA	R	2B	3B	HR	RBI	BB	K	SB	CS	Whiff%	AVG/OBP/SLG	DRC+	BABIP	BRR	FRAA	WARP
2018	OMA	AAA	25	41	5	2	0	0	2	5	6	1	0		.257/.350/.314	87	.310	-0.2	CF(10): -0.7, RF(1): -0.1	-0.1
2019	OMA	AAA	26	285	34	11	2	7	38	21	59	9	3		.310/.358/.448	100	.374	0.0	CF(51): 3.1, RF(18): 2.2	1.4
2019	KC	MLB	26	197	26	7	0	4	12	9	56	2	0	30.0%	.215/.255/.317	63	.286	3.8	CF(36): 5.8, RF(23): -0.4, LF(6): -0.6	0.5
2020	KC	MLB	28	64	5	1	0	1	5	4	27	0	0	37.8%	.169/.219/.237	49	.281	0.4	CF(29): -2.5, LF(1): -0.0, RF(1): -0.0	-0.5
2021 FS	KC	MLB	28	600	54	20	2	13	56	39	214	4	1	32.8%	.198/.256/.314	58	.294	1.4	CF -1, RF 2	-1.3

Comparables: Stevie Wilkerson, Hiram Bocachica, Billy Beane

The former fifth-overall pick from suburban Kansas City just wrapped his 10th year in the organization. The pitch recognition issues that plagued Starling in his early years haven't been resolved and his defense in center— once a calling card due to his athleticism and speed—has been spotty at best. Sadly, the local kid didn't make good.

Michael A. Taylor CF Born: 03/26/91 Age: 30 Bats: R Throws: R Height: 6'4" Weight: 215 Origin: Round 6, 2009 Draft (#172 overall)

YEAR	TEAM	LVL	AGE	PA	R	2B	3B	HR	RBI	BB	K	SB	CS	Whiff%	AVG/OBP/SLG	DRC+	BABIP	BRR	FRAA	WARP
2018	WAS	MLB	27	385	46	22	3	6	28	29	116	24	6	32.0%	.227/.287/.357	66	.320	1.3	CF(113): 8.9, 1B(1): -0.0	0.8
2019	HBG	AA	28	247	36	16	2	9	35	25	69	10	6		.248/.324/.463	121	.315	3.9	CF(43): -1.2, RF(6): -0.1	1.5
2019	WAS	MLB	28	97	10	7	0	1	3	7	34	6	0	34.6%	.250/.305/.364	57	.396	-0.6	CF(25): -0.0, RF(7): -0.8	-0.3
2020	WAS	MLB	29	99	11	6	0	5	16	6	27	0	0	28.7%	.196/.253/.424	88	.217	-0.5	LF(14): 2.3, CF(11): 0.0, RF(11): 0.2	0.2
2021 FS	KC	MLB	30	600	62	26	3	16	64	45	194	24	7	31.5%	.210/.273/.361	75	.290	5.4	CF 8, 1B 0	1.5
2021 DC	KC	MLB	30	265	27	11	1	7	28	20	85	10	3	31.5%	.210/.273/.361	75	.290	2.4	CF 4	0.6

Comparables: Kirk Nieuwenhuis, Laynce Nix, Drew Stubbs

The Royals, seemingly more than any other team in baseball, have a thing for speedy, no-hit outfielders. Taylor, who joined Kansas City after being released by the Nationals, is the latest in a long line (though he probably won't be the last). The upside here is that he's moved in a small deadline deal and ends up part of a classic World Series moment. Shy of that, he's going to be changing teams frequently as he enters his final year before qualifying for free agency.

Meibrys Viloria C Born: 02/15/97 Age: 24 Bats: L Throws: R Height: 5'11" Weight: 225 Origin: International Free Agent, 2013

YEAR	TEAM	LVL	AGE	PA	R	2B	3B	HR	RBI	BB	K	SB	CS	Whiff%	AVG/OBP/SLG	DRC+	BABIP	BRR	FRAA	WARP
2018	WIL	HI-A	21	407	34	16	1	6	44	40	75	2	1		.260/.342/.360	107	.313	-2.8	C(88): 2.8	1.3
2018	KC	MLB	21	29	4	2	0	0	4	1	9	0	0	33.3%	.259/.286/.333	73	.389	0.1	C(10): -1.0	0.0
2019	NWA	AA	22	248	21	12	0	1	24	24	60	2	0		.264/.344/.332	97	.358	0.9	C(58): -6.3	0.5
2019	KC	MLB	22	148	7	7	0	1	15	10	44	0	1	28.7%	.211/.259/.286	59	.293	-0.5	C(41): -3.6	-0.4
2020	KC	MLB	23	24	1	1	0	0	0	2	9	0	0	37.8%	.190/.292/.238	68	.333	-0.2	C(15): 0.4	-0.1
2021 FS	KC	MLB	24	600	55	24	2	8	50	44	172	1	0	30.6%	.216/.283/.316	64	.300	-0.1	C -11	-1.5
2021 DC	KC	MLB	24	33	3	1	0	0	2	2	9	0	0	30.6%	.216/.283/.316	64	.300	0.0	C -1	-0.1

Comparables: Dave Duncan, Ben Davis, Ron Karkovice

YEAR	TEAM	P. COUNT	FRM RUNS	BLK RUNS	THRW RUNS	TOT RUNS
2018	KC	1178	0.0	-0.8	0.0	-0.9
2019	KC	5921	-4.0	0.0	0.3	-3.7
2019	NWA	8588	-7.7	0.0	0.3	-7.5
2020	KC	1408	-0.6	-0.2	0.0	-0.8
2021	KC	1202	-0.5	-0.3	0.0	-0.8

The pandemic meant that for the second consecutive year, Viloria missed out on what should have been competitive developmental time in the minor leagues. Although he spent most of his summer at the Royals' alternate site, he did manage a call-up when Salvador Perez landed on the IL with blurred vision. The tools remain the same—raw. He has a strong arm behind the dish but could improve his framing. On the flip side he hasn't shown much in his cups of coffee, but what should we expect from a 23-year-old who has a half-season of Double-A ball under his belt. Out of options heading into 2021, the Royals will have to get creative—and lucky—if they are to get him the additional developmental time he so desperately needs.

────────── ★ ★ ★ *2021 Top 101 Prospect* #9 ★ ★ ★ ──────────

Bobby Witt Jr. SS Born: 06/14/00 Age: 21 Bats: R Throws: R Height: 6'1" Weight: 190 Origin: Round 1, 2019 Draft (#2 overall)

YEAR	TEAM	LVL	AGE	PA	R	2B	3B	HR	RBI	BB	K	SB	CS	Whiff%	AVG/OBP/SLG	DRC+	BABIP	BRR	FRAA	WARP
2019	ROY	ROK	19	180	30	2	5	1	27	13	35	9	1		.262/.317/.354	94	.323	-0.1	SS(26): 3.3	0.8
2021 FS	KC	MLB	21	600	43	25	4	6	48	29	193	13	3		.211/.253/.305	52	.308	7.4	SS 3	-0.7

There's a certain amount of hype that accompanies the second-overall selection in the draft. The hype accelerated for Witt following a successful—if shortened—spring training, a robust summer camp and a productive turn in the Royals' alternate site in August and September. At just 20 years old and a year and a half removed from high school, dammit if the kid didn't carry himself like a pro. Sure, he's been around the game his entire life, thanks to his dad who enjoyed a 16-year major league career, but still, this was something else. At the plate, you could see the quick hands, the bat speed, the feel for the barrel. In the field you could see the range, the glove action and the strong arm. And to round it off, you could see the plus-plus athleticism. We're talking about a potential five-tool talent. And as they say in Dollar Sign On The Muscle, the kid has the good face.

PITCHERS

Scott Barlow RHP Born: 12/18/92 Age: 28 Bats: R Throws: R Height: 6'3" Weight: 215 Origin: Round 6, 2011 Draft (#194 overall)

YEAR	TEAM	LVL	AGE	W	L	SV	G	GS	IP	H	HR	BB/9	K/9	K	GB%	BABIP	WHIP	ERA	DRA-	WARP	MPH	FA%	Whiff%	CSP
2018	OMA	AAA	25	1	4	1	13	10	45²	54	9	4.1	9.9	50	36.3%	.360	1.64	6.11	77	1.0				
2018	KC	MLB	25	1	1	0	6	0	15	16	2	1.8	9.0	15	40.4%	.311	1.27	3.60	82	0.2	92.9	53.0%	24.1%	50.8%
2019	OMA	AAA	26	0	0	1	3	0	6	3	0	4.5	7.5	5	21.4%	.214	1.00	0.00	82	0.1				
2019	KC	MLB	26	3	3	1	61	0	70¹	64	6	4.7	11.8	92	39.3%	.341	1.44	4.22	86	0.9	96.3	43.0%	33.8%	44.2%
2020	KC	MLB	27	2	1	2	32	0	30	27	4	2.7	11.7	39	45.3%	.324	1.20	4.20	75	0.7	96.6	37.3%	37.6%	42.4%
2021 FS	KC	MLB	28	2	2	1	57	0	50	41	5	4.1	10.6	59	41.2%	.291	1.29	3.70	89	0.4	96.3	41.5%	34.6%	44.0%
2021 DC	KC	MLB	28	2	2	1	57	0	61	50	6	4.1	10.6	72	41.2%	.291	1.29	3.70	89	0.7	96.3	41.5%	34.6%	44.0%

Comparables: Michael Feliz, Clay Holmes, Erick Fedde

Barlow entered manager Mike Matheny's Circle of Bullpen Trust and never left, racking up a major league-leading 32 appearances. Using the tired-but-true reliever formula of heaters up and breakers down, his slider remained his knockout pitch, garnering a breezy 42 percent whiff rate and a .217 batting average against. A minor-league free agent from the Dodgers organization whom the Royals penned to a split contract and awarded a spot on the 40-man roster before he ever tossed a big-league inning, he represents exactly the type of player the small-market Royals need to grab when assembling a bullpen.

Ronald Bolaños RHP Born: 08/23/96 Age: 24 Bats: R Throws: R Height: 6'2" Weight: 230 Origin: International Free Agent, 2016

YEAR	TEAM	LVL	AGE	W	L	SV	G	GS	IP	H	HR	BB/9	K/9	K	GB%	BABIP	WHIP	ERA	DRA-	WARP	MPH	FA%	Whiff%	CSP
2018	LE	HI-A	21	6	9	0	25	23	125	138	13	3.6	8.5	118	42.6%	.342	1.50	5.11	97	0.7				
2019	LE	HI-A	22	5	2	0	10	10	53²	37	4	3.9	9.1	54	48.2%	.246	1.12	2.85	69	1.1				
2019	AMA	AA	22	8	5	0	15	13	76²	71	7	3.5	10.3	88	46.5%	.335	1.32	4.23	100	0.0				
2019	SD	MLB	22	0	2	0	5	3	19²	17	3	5.5	8.7	19	39.3%	.264	1.47	5.95	123	-0.1	97.8	62.7%	24.1%	45.1%
2020	KC	MLB	23	0	2	0	2	2	3²	8	2	7.4	4.9	2	53.3%	.462	3.00	12.27	109	0.0	98.3	58.9%	15.6%	50.2%
2021 FS	KC	MLB	24	2	3	0	57	0	50	48	6	5.1	8.1	45	43.9%	.292	1.53	5.18	116	-0.3	97.9	61.8%	22.1%	46.3%
2021 DC	KC	MLB	24	2	3	0	29	6	50	48	6	5.1	8.1	45	43.9%	.292	1.53	5.18	116	0.0	97.9	61.8%	22.1%	46.3%

Comparables: Chris Flexen, Touki Toussaint, Blake Snell

A dearth of starters to open the season pressed Bolaños—acquired in a summer camp deal from San Diego for reliever Tim Hill—into the rotation, but the prospect struggled to keep runners off the bases in a pair of abbreviated starts. The Cuban, a member of the Padres' heralded J2 class of 2016, possesses an electric arm but is still searching for command. Even in his short stint in the bigs, it was obvious he was catching far too much of the plate, especially with the heater coming in around 95 mph. Unfortunately, the slider was living a bit too down the middle, as well. Exiled to the alternate site after the second week of the season, he'll remain in the Royals' plans in some shape going forward. But electricity isn't much use if you can't harness the current.

Kris Bubic LHP Born: 08/19/97 Age: 23 Bats: L Throws: L Height: 6'3" Weight: 220 Origin: Round 1, 2018 Draft (#40 overall)

YEAR	TEAM	LVL	AGE	W	L	SV	G	GS	IP	H	HR	BB/9	K/9	K	GB%	BABIP	WHIP	ERA	DRA-	WARP	MPH	FA%	Whiff%	CSP
2018	IDF	ROK	20	2	3	0	10	10	38	38	2	4.5	12.6	53	41.2%	.379	1.50	4.03	29	1.8				
2019	LEX	LO-A	21	4	1	0	9	9	47²	27	3	2.8	14.2	75	44.6%	.273	0.88	2.08	49	1.6				
2019	WIL	HI-A	21	7	4	0	17	17	101²	76	3	2.4	9.7	110	41.4%	.299	1.01	2.30	72	1.9				
2020	KC	MLB	22	1	6	0	10	10	50	52	8	4.0	8.8	49	45.0%	.312	1.48	4.32	110	0.2	94.1	54.2%	24.9%	48.3%
2021 FS	KC	MLB	23	9	9	0	26	26	150	138	18	4.4	9.4	157	44.6%	.298	1.42	4.41	102	0.9	94.1	54.2%	24.9%	48.3%
2021 DC	KC	MLB	23	6	8	0	24	24	121	111	14	4.4	9.4	126	44.6%	.298	1.42	4.41	102	1.1	94.1	54.2%	24.9%	48.3%

Comparables: Trevor Rogers, Patrick Sandoval, Brock Burke

Given his repeatable mechanics and a consistent arm slot, it wasn't a surprise that Bubic, the youngest of the baby Royals starting pitching prospect quartet, made his way to the majors in 2020. That arm slot repetition comes in handy because Bubic sports a 12 mph separation between his heater and his change, inducing awkward swings from many a batter. It was the development of a wipeout curve, though, that truly accelerated his timeline to The Show. He threw the yakker over 15 percent of the time and surrendered only four base hits—all singles—with the majority of the curveballs put in play finding their way to webbing of his infielder's mitts. That's a tidy .174 BAA on the pitch, in case you were wondering. He's the first pitcher in franchise history to make the jump from A-ball to the majors and with that successful third pitch, it stands to reason he'll be making his home in the Kansas City rotation for years to come.

Austin Cox LHP Born: 03/28/97 Age: 24 Bats: L Throws: L Height: 6'4" Weight: 185 Origin: Round 5, 2018 Draft (#152 overall)

YEAR	TEAM	LVL	AGE	W	L	SV	G	GS	IP	H	HR	BB/9	K/9	K	GB%	BABIP	WHIP	ERA	DRA-	WARP	MPH	FA%	Whiff%	CSP
2018	BUR	ROK	21	1	1	0	9	9	33¹	29	1	4.0	13.8	51	42.1%	.373	1.32	3.78	95	0.6				
2019	LEX	LO-A	22	5	3	0	13	13	75¹	59	5	2.6	9.2	77	39.8%	.262	1.08	2.75	79	1.2				
2019	WIL	HI-A	22	3	3	0	11	10	55¹	53	6	2.6	8.5	52	32.5%	.322	1.25	2.77	107	-0.2				
2021 FS	KC	MLB	24	2	3	0	57	0	50	48	7	4.6	8.2	45	35.3%	.290	1.48	4.83	116	-0.3				

Comparables: Nick Margevicius, David Peterson, Julio Urías

Cox doesn't have the prospect juice of his starting pitching peers in the Royals organization, but he does pique some interest. His breaking pitches—a pair of curveballs with different breaks along with a hard slider—allow him to get by in the low 90s with his fastball. He lacks the pedigree and draft status of the Fab Four from the Royals' 2018 draft, but his command of those pitches—along with a stellar work ethic—has him knocking on the door to The Show.

Danny Duffy LHP Born: 12/21/88 Age: 32 Bats: L Throws: L Height: 6'3" Weight: 185 Origin: Round 3, 2007 Draft (#96 overall)

YEAR	TEAM	LVL	AGE	W	L	SV	G	GS	IP	H	HR	BB/9	K/9	K	GB%	BABIP	WHIP	ERA	DRA-	WARP	MPH	FA%	Whiff%	CSP
2018	KC	MLB	29	8	12	0	28	28	155	161	23	4.1	8.2	141	35.2%	.305	1.49	4.88	123	-0.4	95.5	55.8%	23.4%	49.6%
2019	NWA	AA	30	1	0	0	2	2	10¹	8	1	0.0	9.6	11	46.2%	.280	0.77	0.87	66	0.2				
2019	KC	MLB	30	7	6	0	23	23	130²	125	21	3.2	7.9	115	35.0%	.285	1.31	4.34	109	0.6	94.5	53.0%	24.2%	51.0%
2020	KC	MLB	31	4	4	0	12	11	56¹	53	10	3.5	9.1	57	31.7%	.287	1.33	4.95	129	-0.4	94.4	53.4%	25.6%	48.3%
2021 FS	KC	MLB	32	8	9	0	26	26	150	144	25	3.5	9.0	149	33.7%	.293	1.35	4.54	108	0.4	94.8	53.9%	24.4%	49.8%
2021 DC	KC	MLB	32	7	10	0	25	25	139	134	23	3.5	9.0	138	33.7%	.293	1.35	4.54	108	0.9	94.8	53.9%	24.4%	49.8%

Comparables: Jhoulys Chacín, Trevor Cahill, Brett Anderson

With a rotation of prospects on the horizon, Duffy, a pitching staff mainstay since 2011, has unlocked grizzled veteran status. He's been an averageish starter the last three seasons while navigating sundry injuries. The Royals handled him with care in 2020, rarely letting him pass 90 pitches; he averaged just 14 outs per start. He's been a rumored trade candidate in the past, but with one year remaining on an extension signed prior to the 2017 season, his trade value is well past its peak. Perhaps manager Mike Matheny tipped his hand for 2021 when he used the lefty out of the bullpen for his final appearance of 2020. He's experienced success there in the past, and with all those young arms lining up for rotation innings, that may be the best location for the Duffman to finish out his Royals career.

Foster Griffin LHP Born: 07/27/95 Age: 25 Bats: R Throws: L Height: 6'3" Weight: 225 Origin: Round 1, 2014 Draft (#28 overall)

YEAR	TEAM	LVL	AGE	W	L	SV	G	GS	IP	H	HR	BB/9	K/9	K	GB%	BABIP	WHIP	ERA	DRA-	WARP	MPH	FA%	Whiff%	CSP
2018	NWA	AA	22	10	12	0	28	26	152²	197	20	2.4	6.9	117	37.4%	.360	1.55	5.13	103	0.4				
2019	OMA	AAA	23	8	6	0	25	25	130²	134	20	4.4	7.6	111	48.9%	.295	1.52	5.23	90	3.0				
2020	KC	MLB	24	1	0	0	1	0	1²	0	0	0.0	5.4	1	80.0%	.000	0.00	0.00	103	0.0	93.8	30.4%	30.8%	38.2%
2021 FS	KC	MLB	25	2	3	0	57	0	50	50	6	4.5	7.3	40	44.2%	.293	1.51	4.89	115	-0.3	93.8	30.4%	30.8%	38.2%

Comparables: Zack Littell, Sal Romano, Justus Sheffield

At a crossroads after the 2019 season, Griffin found a pitching consultant, embraced Rapsodo technology and threw 23 innings for Tigres Del Licey in the Dominican Winter League. In an age of power pitchers, the fastball isn't going to impress. But with an improved cutter, he was rewarded with a spot on the 40-man, and ultimately, a spot on the Opening Day roster. He made his major-league debut on his 25th birthday, recorded five outs ... and left the game with what was ultimately diagnosed as a torn UCL. Pitching can be such a cruel art. He will spend 2021 rehabbing from Tommy John, and with the young arms on the Royals' horizon, will face an uphill battle to get big-league innings down the road. But dammit, this story needs a better ending.

Jesse Hahn RHP Born: 07/30/89 Age: 31 Bats: R Throws: R Height: 6'5" Weight: 210 Origin: Round 6, 2010 Draft (#191 overall)

YEAR	TEAM	LVL	AGE	W	L	SV	G	GS	IP	H	HR	BB/9	K/9	K	GB%	BABIP	WHIP	ERA	DRA-	WARP	MPH	FA%	Whiff%	CSP
2019	KC	MLB	29	0	1	0	6	0	4²	7	1	11.6	13.5	7	42.9%	.462	2.79	13.50	115	0.0	96.5	62.6%	30.4%	50.2%
2020	KC	MLB	30	1	0	3	18	0	17¹	4	0	4.2	9.9	19	45.9%	.108	0.69	0.52	85	0.3	96.6	56.5%	24.2%	46.8%
2021 FS	KC	MLB	31	2	3	0	57	0	50	47	6	3.9	8.7	48	45.2%	.297	1.39	4.39	103	0.0	96.6	57.7%	25.4%	47.4%
2021 DC	KC	MLB	31	2	3	0	57	0	61	58	7	3.9	8.7	59	45.2%	.297	1.39	4.39	103	0.3	96.6	57.7%	25.4%	47.4%

Comparables: Trevor Cahill, Jhoulys Chacín, Dan Straily

You never want to hear the words "a second Tommy John surgery" from the doctor examining your MRI. After undergoing a TJ operation in 2010, and after injuring his elbow after just a handful of Cactus League innings, Hahn wasn't looking forward to another arduous rehab process. Instead, he underwent a repair procedure similar to the one Seth Maness had a couple of years prior, where the torn tendon was reinforced with strong sutures. It worked. At full health and pitching in relief, Hahn went mostly with a sinker/curve combo and it was lethal. Opponents hit just .088 against a two-seamer that averaged 95 mph. And of the 20 plate appearances that ended on his curve, not a single ball dropped for a base hit. By the last week of the season, he was closing games. As the Royals continue their quest to build a better bullpen, he's in the mix to remain in the ninth-inning role.

Matt Harvey RHP Born: 03/27/89 Age: 32 Bats: R Throws: R Height: 6'4" Weight: 220 Origin: Round 1, 2010 Draft (#7 overall)

YEAR	TEAM	LVL	AGE	W	L	SV	G	GS	IP	H	HR	BB/9	K/9	K	GB%	BABIP	WHIP	ERA	DRA-	WARP	MPH	FA%	Whiff%	CSP
2018	CIN	MLB	29	7	7	0	24	24	128	132	21	2.0	7.8	111	43.4%	.299	1.25	4.50	107	0.7	96.3	58.7%	21.1%	53.1%
2018	NYM	MLB	29	0	2	0	8	4	27	33	6	3.0	6.7	20	39.8%	.318	1.56	7.00	93	0.3	94.3	61.2%	18.2%	49.7%
2019	LAA	MLB	30	3	5	0	12	12	59²	63	13	4.4	5.9	39	43.1%	.276	1.54	7.09	156	-1.2	95.0	47.6%	22.1%	47.7%
2020	KC	MLB	31	0	3	0	7	4	11²	27	6	3.9	7.7	10	42.0%	.477	2.74	11.57	128	-0.1	96.1	53.5%	17.5%	48.4%
2021 FS	KC	MLB	32	2	3	0	57	0	50	52	7	3.1	7.5	41	40.6%	.300	1.39	4.59	111	-0.2	95.8	54.1%	20.7%	50.2%

Comparables: Yovani Gallardo, Masahiro Tanaka, David Price

Given their situation as one of the smaller of the small market clubs, the Royals often have to take a stroll in the discount pitching aisle, looking for bargains as they shop for innings. Recent past purchases have included Clay Buchholz, Homer Bailey and now Harvey. The pitcher formerly known as the Dark Knight is still finding his way after injuries have diminished his heater and, more worryingly, robbed him of his command. Purchases in the discount pitching aisle come as-is, without the option of a refund. Sometimes it just doesn't work. But that won't stop the Royals from keeping their frequent shopper card up to date.

Carlos Hernández RHP   Born: 03/11/97   Age: 24   Bats: R   Throws: R   Height: 6'4"   Weight: 250   Origin: International Free Agent, 2016

YEAR	TEAM	LVL	AGE	W	L	SV	G	GS	IP	H	HR	BB/9	K/9	K	GB%	BABIP	WHIP	ERA	DRA-	WARP	MPH	FA%	Whiff%	CSP
2018	LEX	LO-A	21	6	5	0	15	15	79¹	71	7	2.6	9.3	82	41.4%	.299	1.18	3.29	130	-0.9				
2019	ROY	ROK	22	0	2	0	5	5	11	14	1	2.5	9.8	12	41.2%	.394	1.55	7.36	59	0.4				
2019	BUR	ROK+	22	0	0	0	3	3	10²	11	1	10.1	11.0	13	33.3%	.345	2.16	9.28	125	0.0				
2019	LEX	LO-A	22	3	3	0	7	7	36	34	5	2.2	10.8	43	37.2%	.326	1.19	3.50	86	0.4				
2020	KC	MLB	23	0	1	0	5	3	14²	19	4	3.7	8.0	13	42.6%	.349	1.70	4.91	111	0.0	98.9	51.4%	25.4%	48.2%
2021 FS	KC	MLB	24	8	10	0	26	26	150	146	21	5.0	8.2	137	41.2%	.293	1.53	5.14	116	-0.3	98.9	51.4%	25.4%	48.2%
2021 DC	KC	MLB	24	3	6	0	16	16	71	69	10	5.0	8.2	65	41.2%	.293	1.53	5.14	116	0.1	98.9	51.4%	25.4%	48.2%

Comparables: Luis Perdomo, Nick Neidert, Seranthony Domínguez

Every season, in every organization, there's a player who massively exceeds expectations. That player was Hernandez for Kansas City. Invited to the major-league camp in spring training, he was ultimately left out of the 60-man mix when teams reconvened for summer camp. But when the Royals had an opening, they called and the right-hander was ready. He made his big-league debut just a couple of weeks later. He features a mid-90s heater and an above-average curve to pair with a decent change. Signed as a 19-year-old out of Venezuela, he's shown adaptability at every stop on his journey, striking out over a batter per inning along the way. Even with the plethora of pitching prospects in the org, the Royals see him as a starter.

Greg Holland RHP   Born: 11/20/85   Age: 35   Bats: R   Throws: R   Height: 5'10"   Weight: 205   Origin: Round 10, 2007 Draft (#306 overall)

YEAR	TEAM	LVL	AGE	W	L	SV	G	GS	IP	H	HR	BB/9	K/9	K	GB%	BABIP	WHIP	ERA	DRA-	WARP	MPH	FA%	Whiff%	CSP
2018	STL	MLB	32	0	2	0	32	0	25	34	1	7.9	7.9	22	37.5%	.384	2.24	7.92	151	-0.5	94.6	42.9%	27.2%	43.6%
2018	WAS	MLB	32	2	0	3	24	0	21¹	9	1	4.2	10.5	25	47.7%	.186	0.89	0.84	84	0.3	94.3	44.2%	37.1%	40.9%
2019	HBG	AA	33	1	0	0	8	0	9	4	0	3.0	9.0	9	36.4%	.182	0.78	0.00	70	0.1				
2019	ARI	MLB	33	1	2	17	40	0	35²	25	5	6.1	10.3	41	44.8%	.244	1.37	4.54	91	0.3	93.7	47.3%	29.9%	42.5%
2020	KC	MLB	34	3	0	6	28	0	28¹	20	1	2.2	9.8	31	50.7%	.275	0.95	1.91	77	0.6	94.7	37.4%	30.0%	46.8%
2021 FS	KC	MLB	35	2	2	23	57	0	50	44	6	4.8	9.5	52	44.5%	.289	1.42	4.25	99	0.2	94.3	42.4%	30.2%	44.2%
2021 DC	KC	MLB	35	2	2	23	57	0	61	53	7	4.8	9.5	64	44.5%	.289	1.42	4.25	99	0.4	94.3	42.4%	30.2%	44.2%

Comparables: David Robertson, Francisco Rodríguez, Mark Melancon

"Clapton is god," read the graffiti in London just before the guitarist joined Cream, the trio that ultimately launched the supergroup era of rock. As closer, Holland filled a similar, leading role for the Royals' own super bullpen trio known as HDH while they hammered batters in 2014 & '15. Pitching on a shredded UCL for most of his final season for the Royals, The Dirty South went as long as he could before it finally gave out in the September stretch run. Since returning from that injury, he's pitched well in short bursts, so it wasn't exactly a surprise the 60-game season suited him well, and once again, with a heart full of soul, he found himself closing games for the Royals. No supergroups last forever, his bullpenmates have moved on and he's unplugged now, but still getting the job done.

Jakob Junis RHP   Born: 09/16/92   Age: 28   Bats: R   Throws: R   Height: 6'3"   Weight: 220   Origin: Round 29, 2011 Draft (#876 overall)

YEAR	TEAM	LVL	AGE	W	L	SV	G	GS	IP	H	HR	BB/9	K/9	K	GB%	BABIP	WHIP	ERA	DRA-	WARP	MPH	FA%	Whiff%	CSP
2018	KC	MLB	25	9	12	0	30	30	177	182	32	2.2	8.3	164	41.8%	.300	1.27	4.37	123	-0.4	93.0	53.3%	22.2%	49.2%
2019	KC	MLB	26	9	14	0	31	31	175¹	192	31	3.0	8.4	164	43.0%	.318	1.43	5.24	121	-0.3	93.3	50.8%	22.6%	47.7%
2020	KC	MLB	27	0	2	0	8	6	25¹	35	7	2.1	6.8	19	46.0%	.350	1.62	6.39	118	0.0	93.4	49.2%	20.5%	50.9%
2021 FS	KC	MLB	28	2	2	0	57	0	50	51	7	2.8	8.1	45	42.4%	.303	1.34	4.67	111	-0.2	93.3	51.3%	22.3%	48.5%
2021 DC	KC	MLB	28	2	2	0	51	0	55	56	8	2.8	8.1	49	42.4%	.303	1.34	4.67	111	0.0	93.3	51.3%	22.3%	48.5%

Comparables: Daniel Mengden, Nick Pivetta, Dylan Bundy

It's a simple pitching philosophy: Hard stuff up, breaking stuff down. The Royals started preaching this in 2020 and Junis is one of the pitchers who embraced the evolution of organizational philosophy. But pitching, no matter the philosophy, is an unforgiving art. Miss the location by millimeters and punishment will follow. The right-hander lives on a slider/fastball combo and struggled to locate the former with consistency and got lit up on the latter when he wasn't able to elevate it enough. The sum of the parts were far too many tasty pitches in the fat part of the zone which led to some well-fed hitters. He finished the season in the bullpen and that figures to be his home long-term. Given his pitch combo it wouldn't be surprising to see him thrive in a relief role.

Brad Keller RHP   Born: 07/27/95   Age: 25   Bats: R   Throws: R   Height: 6'5"   Weight: 250   Origin: Round 8, 2013 Draft (#240 overall)

YEAR	TEAM	LVL	AGE	W	L	SV	G	GS	IP	H	HR	BB/9	K/9	K	GB%	BABIP	WHIP	ERA	DRA-	WARP	MPH	FA%	Whiff%	CSP
2018	KC	MLB	22	9	6	0	41	20	140¹	133	7	3.2	6.2	96	54.5%	.294	1.30	3.08	108	0.6	96.2	69.8%	21.3%	46.5%
2019	KC	MLB	23	7	14	0	28	28	165¹	154	15	3.8	6.6	122	50.4%	.283	1.35	4.19	102	1.4	95.9	66.7%	19.9%	45.7%
2020	KC	MLB	24	5	3	0	9	9	54²	39	2	2.8	5.8	35	51.6%	.233	1.02	2.47	91	0.7	94.8	59.2%	19.5%	49.1%
2021 FS	KC	MLB	25	9	9	0	26	26	150	148	17	3.8	7.0	117	50.5%	.291	1.41	4.43	104	0.7	95.7	65.5%	20.1%	46.7%
2021 DC	KC	MLB	25	7	10	0	25	25	147	145	16	3.8	7.0	115	50.5%	.291	1.41	4.43	104	1.2	95.7	65.5%	20.1%	46.7%

Comparables: Lucas Giolito, Antonio Senzatela, Eduardo Rodriguez

Does Keller sell real estate on the side? He should consider it, if not, because the story of his season was location, location, location. Improved command of both his fastball and slider allowed him to live on the edges of the zone rather than the middle of it, leading to the best season of his career. Location! The slider has above-average downward break, and he was consistently able to keep it down and in the zone. Location! Down enough that if the hitter made contact, the result was generally a ground ball—nearly 53 percent of all balls in play for the right-hander were worm-burners. And … results! There's not a lot of flash there—among the 81 pitchers who threw at least 50 innings he ranked 76th in strikeout rate—but you can't argue with the outcome.

Ian Kennedy RHP Born: 12/19/84 Age: 36 Bats: R Throws: R Height: 6'0" Weight: 210 Origin: Round 1, 2006 Draft (#21 overall)

YEAR	TEAM	LVL	AGE	W	L	SV	G	GS	IP	H	HR	BB/9	K/9	K	GB%	BABIP	WHIP	ERA	DRA-	WARP	MPH	FA%	Whiff%	CSP
2018	KC	MLB	33	3	9	0	22	22	119²	125	20	3.0	7.9	105	29.6%	.302	1.38	4.66	118	0.0	93.7	58.6%	19.3%	49.2%
2019	KC	MLB	34	3	2	30	63	0	63¹	64	6	2.4	10.4	73	43.4%	.349	1.28	3.41	72	1.3	96.1	67.5%	24.3%	51.6%
2020	KC	MLB	35	0	2	0	15	1	14	20	7	3.2	9.6	15	37.5%	.325	1.79	9.00	131	-0.1	95.0	49.8%	21.5%	51.0%
2021 FS	KC	MLB	36	2	3	0	57	0	50	46	7	3.1	8.5	47	37.9%	.282	1.28	4.00	101	0.1	94.9	61.1%	21.8%	50.6%

Comparables: Aníbal Sánchez, Ervin Santana, Mike Fiers

On Royals radio broadcasts, longtime announcer Denny Mathews is known for his understated home run call: "Annnnnd ... gone!" he gruffly intones no matter if it's celebratory for a home team batsman or a call of despair for a local hurler. No Royals reliever was on the receiving end of such calls more than Kennedy, who, just a year after a revelatory move to the bullpen, lost velocity and a whole lotta baseballs over the fence. Playing out the final year of a five-year pact signed after the 2015 season, he hits the free agent market as a 36-year-old pitcher coming off the worst season of his career. Some club looking to add a reclamation project to their bullpen will take a flier.

★ ★ ★ *2021 Top 101 Prospect* **#95** ★ ★ ★

Jackson Kowar RHP Born: 10/04/96 Age: 24 Bats: R Throws: R Height: 6'5" Weight: 180 Origin: Round 1, 2018 Draft (#33 overall)

YEAR	TEAM	LVL	AGE	W	L	SV	G	GS	IP	H	HR	BB/9	K/9	K	GB%	BABIP	WHIP	ERA	DRA-	WARP	MPH	FA%	Whiff%	CSP
2018	LEX	LO-A	21	0	1	0	9	9	26¹	19	2	4.1	7.5	22	53.4%	.239	1.18	3.42	80	0.4				
2019	WIL	HI-A	22	5	3	0	13	13	74	68	4	2.7	8.0	66	44.9%	.305	1.22	3.53	97	0.3				
2019	NWA	AA	22	2	7	0	13	13	74¹	73	8	2.5	9.4	78	45.5%	.323	1.26	3.51	96	0.3				
2021 FS	KC	MLB	24	2	3	0	57	0	50	48	6	4.2	7.8	43	42.5%	.289	1.44	4.76	113	-0.2				
2021 DC	KC	MLB	24	0	0	0	3	3	14	13	1	4.2	7.8	12	42.5%	.289	1.44	4.76	113	0.0				

Comparables: Robert Dugger, Jorge Alcala, Anthony Misiewicz

Who doesn't love a list? When the Royals popped five collegiate pitchers with their first five picks of the 2018 draft, it was irresistible to rank them in some sort of category. Upside? Closest to majors? Floor? Set 'em up and rank 'em! With a fastball/change combo, Kowar was probably the least sexy of the five and would generally rank toward the bottom of such lists after the draft. (That's not a criticism ... the Royals selected some exciting, electric arms.) But since then he's added some velocity to the heater, bringing it up to the mid-90s while maintaining a change that can fade and dive. All he's missing is a quality breaking pitch to make the upside really jump. Still, he projects to the rotation, which might be why the Royals ranked him second among the five.

★ ★ ★ *2021 Top 101 Prospect* **#21** ★ ★ ★

Asa Lacy LHP Born: 06/02/99 Age: 22 Bats: L Throws: L Height: 6'4" Weight: 215 Origin: Round 1, 2020 Draft (#4 overall)

Perhaps it's true and there's no such thing as a pitching prospect. But damn if the Royals aren't trying to figure it out. Lacy, the fourth-overall selection in the 2020 draft out of Texas A&M, joins the stable of collegiate arms the club has drafted the last couple of years. Since arriving on campus three years prior, he added muscle to an athletic frame and started hitting the mid-90s with the heat. While that's tantalizing to be sure, it's the slider, with nasty horizontal break coming out of the same slot as the fastball, that makes scouts swoon. Ever see an actual scout swoon? Strikeout 46 batters in 24 innings with a four-pitch mix and you need to order a round of smelling salts. Kansas City has been aggressive with their young college arms, moving them quickly through the system, so it will be interesting to see where they start the right-hander after an abbreviated collegiate season and a summer of inter-squad matchups.

Richard Lovelady LHP Born: 07/07/95 Age: 26 Bats: L Throws: L Height: 6'0" Weight: 185 Origin: Round 10, 2016 Draft (#313 overall)

YEAR	TEAM	LVL	AGE	W	L	SV	G	GS	IP	H	HR	BB/9	K/9	K	GB%	BABIP	WHIP	ERA	DRA-	WARP	MPH	FA%	Whiff%	CSP
2018	OMA	AAA	22	3	3	9	46	0	73	53	3	2.6	8.8	71	49.5%	.266	1.01	2.47	55	2.1				
2019	OMA	AAA	23	1	2	4	24	0	26¹	26	1	2.4	9.9	29	52.7%	.357	1.25	3.08	38	1.1				
2019	KC	MLB	23	0	3	0	25	0	20	30	2	3.6	7.7	17	50.0%	.418	1.90	7.65	115	-0.1	95.6	60.8%	17.7%	52.6%
2020	KC	MLB	24	0	0	0	1	0	1	1	1	9.0	0.0	0	33.3%	.000	2.00	9.00	153	0.0	93.0	53.8%	0.0%	37.7%
2021 FS	KC	MLB	25	2	2	0	57	0	50	46	5	3.1	8.5	47	48.2%	.294	1.29	3.85	93	0.3	95.5	60.5%	16.8%	51.9%
2021 DC	KC	MLB	25	2	2	0	57	0	61	57	6	3.1	8.5	57	48.2%	.294	1.29	3.85	93	0.6	95.5	60.5%	16.8%	51.9%

Comparables: José Quijada, Tanner Scott, Nestor Cortes

When your name is literally "Dick Lovelady," your options for future employment are fairly limited. You *could* be the inspiration for a series of romance novels best read quickly and discreetly and on the beach. You could become the Used Car Sales director of the fourth-most prosperous Chevy dealership in your Tri-State area. Or you could emerge as a major-league reliever who conspicuously leads the league in shirsey sales. Our protagonist doesn't miss enough bats or retire enough righties to walk through door no. 3, but there's huge demand for used cars right now.

★ ★ ★ *2021 Top 101 Prospect* **#70** ★ ★ ★

Daniel Lynch **LHP** Born: 11/17/96 Age: 24 Bats: L Throws: L Height: 6'6" Weight: 190 Origin: Round 1, 2018 Draft (#34 overall)

YEAR	TEAM	LVL	AGE	W	L	SV	G	GS	IP	H	HR	BB/9	K/9	K	GB%	BABIP	WHIP	ERA	DRA-	WARP	MPH	FA%	Whiff%	CSP
2018	BUR	ROK	21	0	0	0	3	3	11¹	9	0	1.6	11.1	14	55.2%	.310	0.97	1.59	68	0.3				
2018	LEX	LO-A	21	5	1	0	9	9	40	35	1	1.4	10.6	47	48.0%	.351	1.02	1.57	83	0.6				
2019	ROY	ROK	22	0	0	0	3	3	9	6	0	3.0	12.0	12	55.6%	.333	1.00	1.00	42	0.4				
2019	BUR	ROK+	22	1	0	0	2	2	9	13	1	3.0	7.0	7	55.2%	.429	1.78	4.00	170	-0.2				
2019	WIL	HI-A	22	5	2	0	15	15	78¹	76	4	2.6	8.8	77	46.9%	.324	1.26	3.10	91	0.5				
2021 FS	KC	MLB	24	2	2	0	57	0	50	46	6	3.5	8.3	45	45.8%	.285	1.32	3.96	99	0.1				

Comparables: Julio Urías, Albert Abreu, Tarik Skubal

It's about *The Stuff*. And Lynch has it in spades. A fastball that tickles 99 mph with life, a slider that has plus-potential and an above-average change … Yeah, that's *The Stuff* alright. The next step was to harness that into a repeatable, smooth delivery that maintains a center of balance and sync. He reported to the alternate camp site in the summer and remained in Kansas City for an extended camp following the end of the season in hopes of making up for lost minor-league innings. There he continued to refine those mechanics while toying with an improved changeup. Even though a couple of his comrades in arms accelerated their timetable and debuted in the majors in 2020, he remains the starting pitching prospect with the highest upside.

Mike Minor **LHP** Born: 12/26/87 Age: 33 Bats: R Throws: L Height: 6'4" Weight: 210 Origin: Round 1, 2009 Draft (#7 overall)

YEAR	TEAM	LVL	AGE	W	L	SV	G	GS	IP	H	HR	BB/9	K/9	K	GB%	BABIP	WHIP	ERA	DRA-	WARP	MPH	FA%	Whiff%	CSP
2018	TEX	MLB	30	12	8	0	28	28	157	138	25	2.2	7.6	132	34.4%	.259	1.12	4.18	129	-0.9	94.9	49.5%	22.4%	50.5%
2019	TEX	MLB	31	14	10	0	32	32	208¹	190	30	2.9	8.6	200	40.5%	.288	1.24	3.59	82	3.9	94.3	44.7%	26.3%	50.0%
2020	KC	MLB	32	1	6	0	12	11	56²	50	11	3.2	9.8	62	35.3%	.269	1.24	5.56	107	0.3	92.8	50.7%	27.3%	50.0%
2021 FS	KC	MLB	33	9	8	0	26	26	150	134	20	3.1	9.3	154	37.6%	.286	1.24	3.71	92	1.8	94.1	47.1%	25.7%	50.1%
2021 DC	KC	MLB	33	8	9	0	27	27	140	125	19	3.1	9.3	144	37.6%	.286	1.24	3.71	92	2.1	94.1	47.1%	25.7%	50.1%

Comparables: Trevor Cahill, Alex Cobb, Jhoulys Chacín

After calling for a pop-up to be dropped to notch his 200th strikeout in 2019, Minor learned baseball is 90 percent people imagining an unwritten rule, tricking themselves into believing that rule exists, and then getting mad about it. In 2020 he learned the other 10 percent is velocity, as his fastball lost another tick, for a total loss of 3.5 mph since 2017. This time the performance dipped with it and Minor struggled to prevent runs in both Texas, where he signed a three-year deal after the 2017 season, and Oakland, where he was traded mid-season. With below-average performance preventing him from getting deep into games, Minor probably wouldn't have hit 200 strikeouts across a full season, either, so maybe next time just catch the pop-up. He'll head to Kansas City on a two-year deal, where he rekindled his career once already.

Mike Montgomery **LHP** Born: 07/01/89 Age: 32 Bats: L Throws: L Height: 6'5" Weight: 220 Origin: Round 1, 2008 Draft (#36 overall)

YEAR	TEAM	LVL	AGE	W	L	SV	G	GS	IP	H	HR	BB/9	K/9	K	GB%	BABIP	WHIP	ERA	DRA-	WARP	MPH	FA%	Whiff%	CSP
2018	CHC	MLB	28	5	6	0	38	19	124	131	10	2.8	6.2	86	50.5%	.311	1.37	3.99	102	0.9	93.4	49.6%	21.6%	49.7%
2019	IOW	AAA	29	1	1	0	2	2	10	3	0	3.6	7.2	8	55.6%	.111	0.70	2.70	34	0.5				
2019	KC	MLB	29	2	7	0	13	13	64	78	12	3.0	7.2	51	50.7%	.349	1.55	4.64	146	-1.0	93.3	39.9%	22.3%	41.9%
2019	CHC	MLB	29	1	2	0	20	0	27	35	6	4.3	6.0	18	42.4%	.345	1.78	5.67	181	-0.9	94.5	47.4%	21.0%	45.0%
2020	KC	MLB	30	0	0	0	3	1	5¹	6	1	1.7	6.8	4	55.6%	.294	1.31	5.06	105	0.0	91.3	37.1%	19.0%	39.7%
2021 FS	KC	MLB	31	2	3	0	57	0	50	52	6	3.6	7.6	42	50.2%	.305	1.44	4.67	112	-0.2	93.6	44.6%	21.6%	45.1%

Comparables: Erasmo Ramírez, Drew Pomeranz, Neil Ramírez

When Montgomery was acquired from the Cubs in July of 2019, one couldn't help but think he was a placeholder. Under club control until after the 2021 season, he could use his five-pitch arsenal to shore up the rotation and eat a modest amount of innings. However one man's injury is another man's opportunity and when Montgomery was sidelined with a lat strain after his first appearance in 2020, it opened the door for Kris Bubic to step forward in the rotation. Outrighted to the minors following the season, he refused the assignment and elected free agency. It looks like the Royals didn't need a placeholder after all.

Jake Newberry **RHP** Born: 11/20/94 Age: 26 Bats: R Throws: R Height: 6'2" Weight: 205 Origin: Round 37, 2012 Draft (#1123 overall)

YEAR	TEAM	LVL	AGE	W	L	SV	G	GS	IP	H	HR	BB/9	K/9	K	GB%	BABIP	WHIP	ERA	DRA-	WARP	MPH	FA%	Whiff%	CSP
2018	NWA	AA	23	2	0	12	25	0	29²	29	2	2.4	11.2	37	32.5%	.360	1.25	2.12	56	0.7				
2018	OMA	AAA	23	3	0	3	16	0	20	13	1	2.7	7.2	16	49.1%	.231	0.95	0.90	69	0.4				
2018	KC	MLB	23	2	0	0	14	0	13¹	13	3	6.1	7.4	11	32.5%	.270	1.65	4.72	125	-0.1	95.3	54.8%	26.5%	47.1%
2019	OMA	AAA	24	2	2	0	22	0	28	29	3	4.5	9.6	30	37.0%	.342	1.54	3.86	79	0.6				
2019	KC	MLB	24	1	0	0	27	0	31	29	7	4.6	8.4	29	34.1%	.262	1.45	3.77	152	-0.7	95.5	52.5%	27.5%	42.7%
2020	KC	MLB	25	1	0	1	20	0	22	20	3	4.9	9.8	24	37.5%	.321	1.45	4.09	114	0.0	95.0	45.2%	36.2%	41.9%
2021 FS	KC	MLB	26	2	3	0	57	0	50	46	7	4.4	9.2	50	36.1%	.286	1.41	4.62	108	-0.1	95.2	49.3%	31.5%	42.8%
2021 DC	KC	MLB	26	2	3	0	57	0	61	56	9	4.4	9.2	62	36.1%	.286	1.41	4.62	108	0.1	95.2	49.3%	31.5%	42.8%

Comparables: Michael Tonkin, Trevor Gott, Evan Phillips

As rosters and bullpens expand, there will always be room for guys like Newberry. Of his 20 appearances in 2020, only two came while the Royals held a lead. But aside from a couple of poor outings, he did his job and kept his team within shouting distance. For the first time in his major-league career, he featured the slider more than his fastball. Smart move. The slider features more drop than break and comes with plenty of swing and miss—opponents whiffed on 48 percent of their swings against the pitch. When contact is made on the slider, it's generally weak. He's not going to be called on to secure the lead in the seventh or to bridge to the closer in the eighth. He's not a fireman, nor one who will rack up the saves. But he's a steady presence in the back of a bullpen. That's worth something.

Brady Singer RHP Born: 08/04/96 Age: 24 Bats: R Throws: R Height: 6'5" Weight: 210 Origin: Round 1, 2018 Draft (#18 overall)

YEAR	TEAM	LVL	AGE	W	L	SV	G	GS	IP	H	HR	BB/9	K/9	K	GB%	BABIP	WHIP	ERA	DRA-	WARP	MPH	FA%	Whiff%	CSP
2019	WIL	HI-A	22	5	2	0	10	10	57²	51	1	2.0	8.3	53	54.8%	.327	1.11	1.87	105	-0.1				
2019	NWA	AA	22	7	3	0	16	16	90²	86	8	2.6	8.4	85	49.3%	.304	1.24	3.47	81	1.1				
2020	KC	MLB	23	4	5	0	12	12	64¹	52	8	3.2	8.5	61	53.7%	.260	1.17	4.06	87	1.0	95.2	57.9%	24.3%	47.8%
2021 FS	KC	MLB	24	9	9	0	26	26	150	142	17	3.8	8.3	137	50.1%	.295	1.37	4.31	101	1.0	95.2	57.9%	24.3%	47.8%
2021 DC	KC	MLB	24	7	9	0	25	25	139	132	15	3.8	8.3	127	50.1%	.295	1.37	4.31	101	1.4	95.2	57.9%	24.3%	47.8%

Comparables: Jered Weaver, T.J. Zeuch, Michael Fulmer

Singer was the first of five college arms drafted in the first two rounds of the 2018 draft by the Royals, and he continued to lead the way in 2020. He was the first of his class to reach the majors, where he ultimately led all rookies in innings pitched and strikeouts. Singer relies on a sinker/slider combo that induced the fourth-highest ground ball rate among qualified starters. The focus heading into this year was the third pitch in his arsenal—a newly refined change. After throwing it only five percent of the time, he's still figuring out how to trust the pitch as it continues to be a work in progress. The Royals were happy with how he was able to command the *cambio* though, and it will again be the focus of his offseason. He may not bring the highest upside of the Royals' young guns, but he's at the head of the class.

Josh Staumont RHP Born: 12/21/93 Age: 27 Bats: R Throws: R Height: 6'3" Weight: 205 Origin: Round 2, 2015 Draft (#64 overall)

YEAR	TEAM	LVL	AGE	W	L	SV	G	GS	IP	H	HR	BB/9	K/9	K	GB%	BABIP	WHIP	ERA	DRA-	WARP	MPH	FA%	Whiff%	CSP
2018	OMA	AAA	24	2	5	1	41	5	74¹	59	4	6.3	12.5	103	41.3%	.331	1.49	3.51	76	1.4				
2019	OMA	AAA	25	1	5	2	32	12	51¹	31	4	6.5	13.0	74	48.6%	.262	1.32	3.16	43	2.1				
2019	KC	MLB	25	0	0	0	16	0	19¹	21	4	4.7	7.0	15	32.3%	.293	1.60	3.72	163	-0.5	98.2	69.6%	22.7%	46.7%
2020	KC	MLB	26	2	1	0	26	0	25²	20	2	5.6	13.0	37	28.6%	.333	1.40	2.45	91	0.4	101.2	72.5%	36.7%	45.8%
2021 FS	KC	MLB	27	2	3	8	57	0	50	41	7	6.7	12.2	67	36.1%	.298	1.57	5.09	112	-0.2	100.3	71.6%	32.3%	46.1%
2021 DC	KC	MLB	27	2	3	8	57	0	61	50	9	6.7	12.2	82	36.1%	.298	1.57	5.09	112	0.0	100.3	71.6%	32.3%	46.1%

Comparables: Lucas Sims, Drew Anderson, Robert Stephenson

Heater. Smoke. Gas. Cheddar. Pick your slang. Staumont threw 28 pitches over 100 mph last year, third-most in the majors. He maxed out at a blistering 102.2 mph. Then there's the hook. Yakker. Hammer. Uncle Charlie. Now go ahead and pick your curveball slang. He also features a knee-buckling 12-to-6 breaking ball that comes in 20 mph slower than the fastball. We know that hitting is incredibly difficult ... against a pitcher like this, how is any kind of contact ever possible? A repertoire this lethal gets you some Twitter time from @PitchingNinja, with good reason. If there's a knock here, it's that the control isn't always there. That will probably keep him from closing out wins, but when he brings a flamethrower and an axis-altering hook to the mound, who really cares what inning he pitches? If you buy a ticket, this is the guy you want to see. When he's on, it's tons of fun. If manager Mike Matheny is summoning him from the bullpen, we're calling the neighbors and waking the kids.

Kyle Zimmer RHP Born: 09/13/91 Age: 29 Bats: R Throws: R Height: 6'3" Weight: 225 Origin: Round 1, 2012 Draft (#5 overall)

YEAR	TEAM	LVL	AGE	W	L	SV	G	GS	IP	H	HR	BB/9	K/9	K	GB%	BABIP	WHIP	ERA	DRA-	WARP	MPH	FA%	Whiff%	CSP
2019	OMA	AAA	27	2	4	1	37	12	54	46	6	5.5	8.7	52	44.4%	.276	1.46	4.33	72	1.5				
2019	KC	MLB	27	0	1	0	15	0	18¹	28	2	9.3	8.8	18	41.5%	.413	2.56	10.80	174	-0.6	98.1	60.9%	26.6%	46.7%
2020	KC	MLB	28	1	0	0	16	1	23	14	0	3.9	10.2	26	51.9%	.259	1.04	1.57	77	0.5	95.6	48.1%	30.0%	46.3%
2021 FS	KC	MLB	29	2	2	0	57	0	50	43	5	5.2	9.4	52	42.8%	.285	1.44	4.30	99	0.2	96.7	53.7%	28.5%	46.5%
2021 DC	KC	MLB	29	2	2	0	51	0	55	47	6	5.2	9.4	57	42.8%	.285	1.44	4.30	99	0.4	96.7	53.7%	28.5%	46.5%

Comparables: Brooks Pounders, Juan Minaya, Luke Farrell

Zimmer's long and winding road saw myriad injuries and setbacks, *recoveries* and *rehabs*, culminating in *rediscovered* velocity, a 2019 major-league debut, and a lack of command. *Rebuilt* mechanics courtesy of an encounter with Tom House led to *resounding* success last year. It should be noted the Royals handled him with care, pitching him on *repeat* days only once, although they did let him go multiple innings in six of his outings. While a starter's profile still lurks, the Royals remain committed to him as a *reliever*.

Tyler Zuber RHP Born: 06/16/95 Age: 26 Bats: R Throws: R Height: 5'11" Weight: 175 Origin: Round 6, 2017 Draft (#180 overall)

YEAR	TEAM	LVL	AGE	W	L	SV	G	GS	IP	H	HR	BB/9	K/9	K	GB%	BABIP	WHIP	ERA	DRA-	WARP	MPH	FA%	Whiff%	CSP
2018	LEX	LO-A	23	2	2	9	23	0	29	26	4	1.2	14.9	48	31.1%	.386	1.03	3.10	48	0.9				
2018	WIL	HI-A	23	1	4	9	20	0	22	22	1	3.7	9.0	22	41.5%	.333	1.41	4.91	80	0.3				
2019	WIL	HI-A	24	3	2	11	21	0	29¹	16	0	3.4	11.7	38	34.4%	.254	0.92	1.23	55	0.7				
2019	NWA	AA	24	1	2	10	22	0	26	18	2	1.7	10.4	30	27.0%	.276	0.88	2.42	60	0.5				
2020	KC	MLB	25	1	2	0	23	0	22	15	4	8.2	12.3	30	37.5%	.256	1.59	4.09	102	0.2	96.1	44.4%	25.6%	44.8%
2021 FS	KC	MLB	26	2	3	0	57	0	50	43	7	4.4	10.6	58	37.0%	.294	1.36	4.26	101	0.1	96.1	44.4%	25.6%	44.8%
2021 DC	KC	MLB	26	2	3	0	57	0	61	53	8	4.4	10.6	71	37.0%	.294	1.36	4.26	101	0.3	96.1	44.4%	25.6%	44.8%

Comparables: Tony Gonsolin, Zac Reininger, Jacob Webb

Of the 22 innings Zuber pitched, he retired the side in order only five times, issuing 20 free passes over those frames. Zuber should leave the highwire acts to the Flying Wallendas if he wants to stick around.

MINNESOTA TWINS

Essay by Nathalie Alonso

Player comments by Brendan Gawlowski and BP staff

Curses are part of the mystique of baseball. The 2004 season saw the end of one of the most infamous of those alleged maledictions: The Curse of the Bambino. Its victims, the Boston Red Sox, exorcised their demons the night of October 27, when they swept the St. Louis Cardinals to win their first World Series title in 86 years.

One could argue that the curse ended a week earlier, in Game 7 of the American League Championship Series, when Boston completed a historic comeback from a 3-0 deficit in the best-of-seven series, something no other team in professional sports has accomplished before or since. That the comeback happened in the Bronx, against the Yankees, the team at the opposite end of the Bambino's curse, was poetic.

Those who dabble in the occult, and even those who don't, might fancy the idea that a new curse saw its genesis in the Bronx during that same postseason.

A few weeks before the Red Sox completed their historic comeback, a left-hander with a wipeout changeup by the name of Johan Santana took the mound for the Minnesota Twins for Game 1 of the American League Division Series. Santana, who would claim his first AL Cy Young Award the following month, shut out the Yankees while striking out five to help the Twins kick off the playoffs with a 2-0 win.

Unless you've been living under a rock (and given the way 2020 unfolded, no one would blame you for it), you are likely aware that something extraordinary has happened in the 16 years since Santana's gem: The Twins have played 18 postseason games in that span, including three more against the Yankees in that 2004 ALDS, and somehow, inexplicably and maddeningly, they have managed to lose every single one of them.

With their loss in Game 1 of the 2020 American League Wild Card Series against the Astros, the Twins' postseason losing streak stretched to 17 games, which made it not just the longest active streak across all North American professional sports, but the longest in the *history* of North American pro sports. The Twins extended their run of misery to 18 losses a day later, and were summarily swept out of the playoffs.

Here's what that list looks like at the moment:

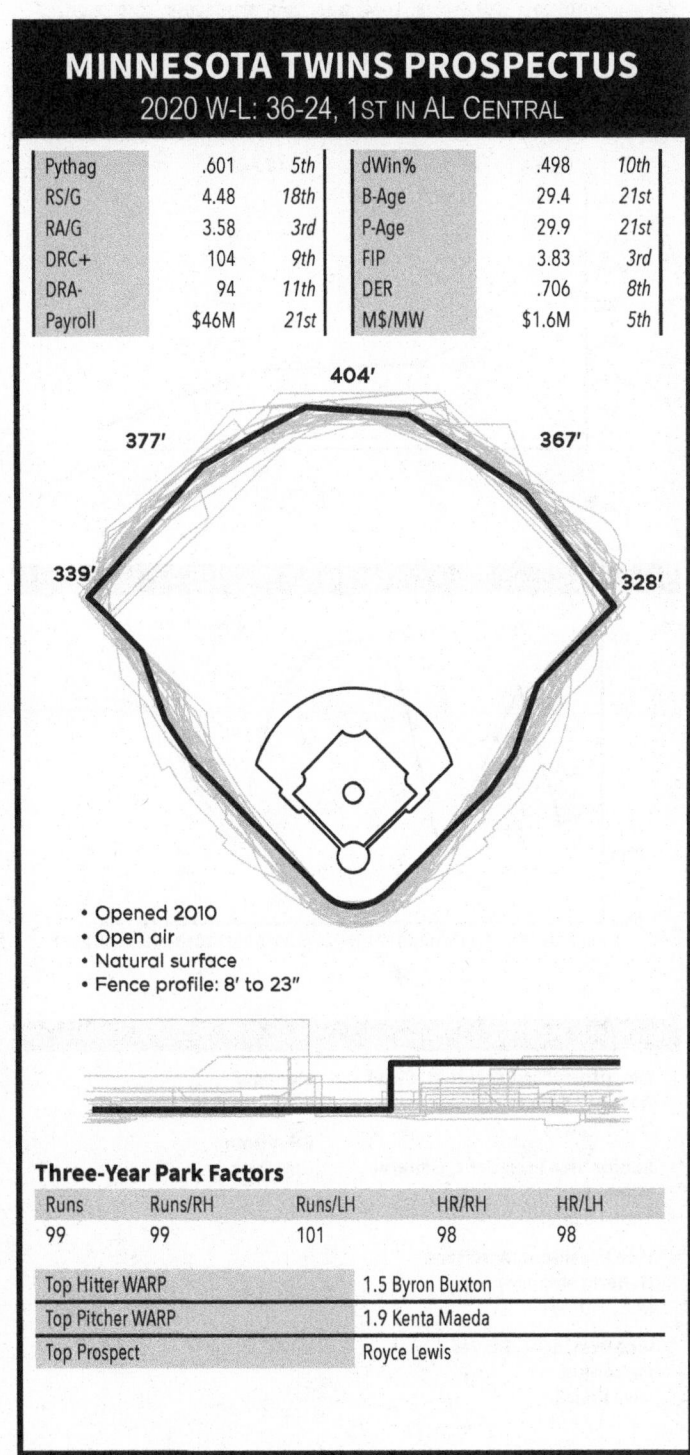

MINNESOTA TWINS PROSPECTUS
2020 W-L: 36-24, 1ST IN AL CENTRAL

Pythag	.601	5th	dWin%	.498	10th
RS/G	4.48	18th	B-Age	29.4	21st
RA/G	3.58	3rd	P-Age	29.9	21st
DRC+	104	9th	FIP	3.83	3rd
DRA-	94	11th	DER	.706	8th
Payroll	$46M	21st	M$/MW	$1.6M	5th

404'
377' 367'
339' 328'

- Opened 2010
- Open air
- Natural surface
- Fence profile: 8' to 23"

Three-Year Park Factors

Runs	Runs/RH	Runs/LH	HR/RH	HR/LH
99	99	101	98	98

Top Hitter WARP	1.5 Byron Buxton
Top Pitcher WARP	1.9 Kenta Maeda
Top Prospect	Royce Lewis

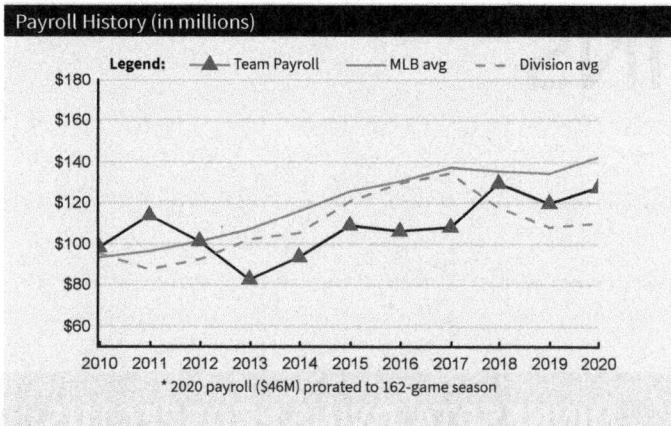

Payroll History (in millions)

Legend: ▲ Team Payroll — MLB avg - - Division avg

* 2020 payroll ($46M) prorated to 162-game season

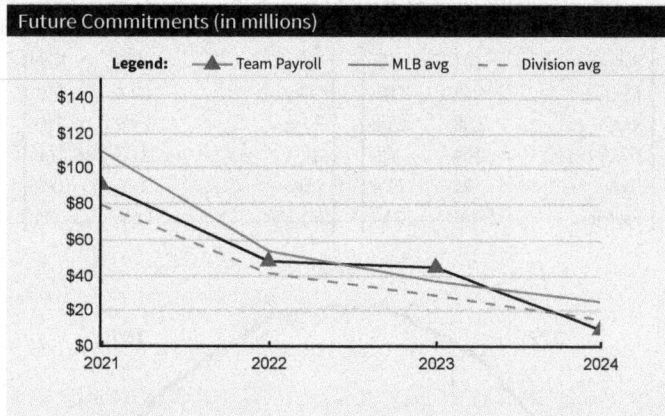

Future Commitments (in millions)

Legend: ▲ Team Payroll — MLB avg - - Division avg

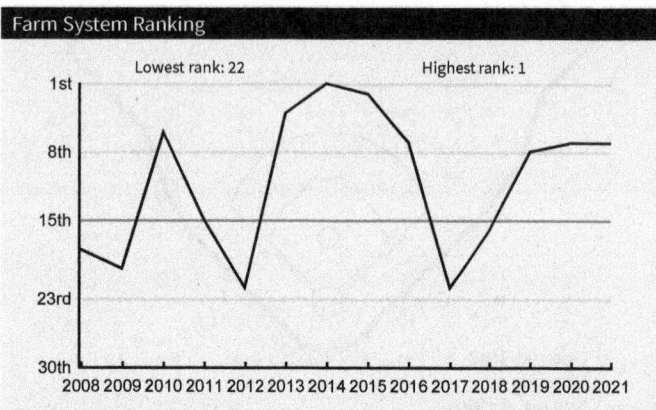

Farm System Ranking

Lowest rank: 22   Highest rank: 1

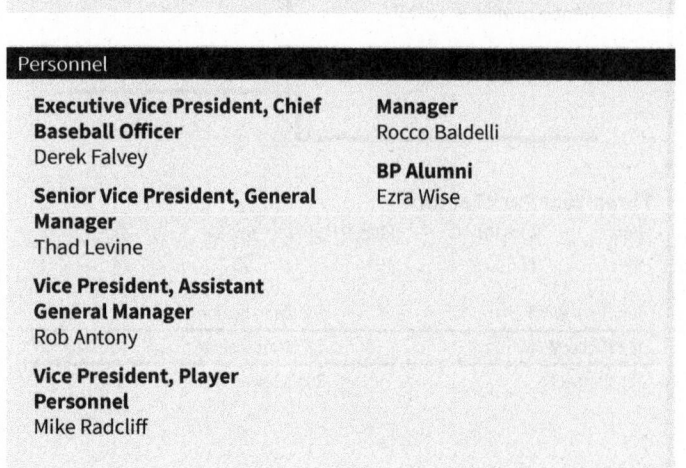

Personnel

Executive Vice President, Chief Baseball Officer
Derek Falvey

Senior Vice President, General Manager
Thad Levine

Vice President, Assistant General Manager
Rob Antony

Vice President, Player Personnel
Mike Radcliff

Manager
Rocco Baldelli

BP Alumni
Ezra Wise

- **Minnesota Twins:** 18 games (2004- present)
- **Chicago Blackhawks:** 16 games (1975-79)
- **Detroit Pistons:** 14 games (2008- present)
- **Los Angeles Kings:** 14 games (1993-2001)
- **Boston Red Sox:** 13 games (1986-1995)
- **New York Knicks:** 13 games (2001-2012)

To put the streak in perspective, when it began Twins legend Joe Mauer was still a rookie. Rocco Baldelli, the club's current manager, was 22 years old and coming off his second full season in the majors. Second baseman Luis Arráez was seven years old. And perhaps most mind-blowing: Ageless wonder Nelson Cruz, the nap-loving 40-year-old slugger who paced the 2020 Twins with 16 home runs and a .992 OPS, *had not yet made his Major League debut.*

The historic dimensions of Minnesota's playoffs woes are stunning enough that we should go ahead and say it: The Twins are cursed.

You might point to the Curse of the Bambino and argue that 16 years is a drop in the bucket when it comes to baseball droughts. The Chicago Cubs, who went 108 years between their most recent titles as a result of a curse that's been pinned on a goat, would agree. And Cleveland has not won a Fall Classic since 1948, the longest active drought in the majors, and we don't go around saying they are cursed. (Though maybe we should?)

Still, it's much easier to wrap one's mind around extended playoff and championship droughts than around 18 consecutive postseason losses. Winning a World Series requires an alchemical blend of talent, depth, health and luck. Winning a single game? That is a simpler endeavor. Sometimes, a hit that falls unexpectedly or an errant throw will suffice. Even while mired in their respective curses, the Red Sox and Cubs won postseason games and series. The math supports that observation: Using FiveThirty Eight's Elo ratings, folks at the Harvard Sports Analysis Collective calculated that Minnesota's odds of losing 18 consecutive games were 0.002 percent, or about 1 in 54,000.

Of the Twins 18 straight postseason losses, 13 (!) have come at the hands of the Yankees. Then there's the fact that the Twins held the lead at some point in 11 of those 18 losses while also being outscored 107-48 during the streak. Consider also that 28 of the other 29 Major League Baseball teams (the Seattle Mariners are the other exception) have won at least one postseason game since Santana stifled the Yankees on October 5, 2004.

Some of those 18 losses have been more frustrating than others. If you are looking for evidence of a curse, your best fodder might be Game 2 of the 2009 ALDS against—who else—the Yankees. In that contest, what might have been a leadoff double by Mauer down the left field line in the top of the 11th inning, with the score tied at 3-3, was instead ruled a foul ball by umpire Phil Cuzzi. Mauer wound up on base with a single, and Minnesota followed with a couple more singles after that, but they ultimately did not score, and the Yankees walked off in the bottom of the frame.

It's worth nothing that much has changed for the Twins in the last 16 years, and not just as far the roster is concerned. In 2010, they abandoned the aging Hubert H. Humphrey Metrodome for Target Field. And once perceived as lagging behind in the analytics revolution that has redefined many aspects of the game, in recent years they have become one of the most forward-thinking in that regard, from the front office to the dugout. Yet none of those changes has translated into even a solitary postseason win.

The Twins' historic postseason misery is a sobering reminder that, even with all the number crunching in the world, baseball—and October baseball in particular—remains defiant in its ability to humble you. Said Cruz after the Twins were eliminated by the Astros, "Like life, baseball is also tough. It's unpredictable."

⚾   ⚾   ⚾

Curses are meant to be broken, and entering 2020, the Twins appeared poised to do just that. After pacing the American League with 307 in home runs in 2019, a season that was defined by record-setting power across the majors, and winning a franchise-record 101 games, the self-proclaimed "Bomba Squad" added more thump by signing slugging third baseman Josh Donaldson to the largest contract in franchise history. Pitching also became a strength for the Twins thanks largely to the acquisition of Kenta Maeda, who went 6-1 with a 2.70 ERA in 11 starts in 2020 and finished second in the voting for the AL Cy Young Award.

And for once, a playoff matchup seemed to favor Minnesota, which came into the AL Wild Card Series as the favorites over the maligned Astros, who, less than a year removed from their sign-stealing scandal, made the postseason despite posting a losing record. Houston did so without its ace, Justin Verlander, and after having lost Gerrit Cole to free agency over the winter.

But in the end, Bomba Squad 2.0 could not capitalize on the circumstances. Injuries were partly to blame: Because of a calf issue that limited him to 28 regular season games, Donaldson didn't even make the roster for the Wild Card

Series. Center fielder Byron Buxton, who was hit in the helmet by a pitch during the last week of the regular season, did not start Game 2.

So, after fending off Cleveland and White Sox to claim their second consecutive American League Central title during a shortened 60-game season due to the COVID-19 pandemic, Minnesota's hitters posted a .119 average and .399 OPS in the AL Wild Card Series on their way to being swept by Houston. In the process, they forfeited what might have been their best shot at making a deep October run with its current core.

But curses aren't broken by the merely obvious or great. They're broken by the resilient. By the people and teams who dare to ask "why not?" We need only look back to 2019, when the Nationals, unable to get out of the NLDS in every instance prior, managed to unseat the powerhouse Dodgers on their way to the first title in franchise history. Was it the best Nationals squad in recent memory? No. Did that stop them? You know the answer.

If the Twins make it back to the playoffs this year, full seasons from a healthy Donaldson and Buxton could be a big reason why. The Twins have their ace in Maeda, who still has three years left on his contract. José Berríos will also be back, with another chance to blossom into the ace-caliber he has long appeared on the brink of becoming.

The 2021 Minnesota Twins will be brimming with young talent, too. Some of those fresh faces arrived in 2020, notably outfielder Alex Kirilloff, who made his big-league debut in Game 2 of the AL Wild Card Series, and became the first position player in Major League Baseball history to record his first career hit in the postseason. Catching prospect Ryan Jeffers, who had a solid debut last year, should be a factor for Minnesota in 2021, as could top pitching prospects Jhoan Duran and Jordan Balazovic. All these young players haven't been around long enough to learn not to ask "why not?"

Of course, to break an 18-game postseason game losing streak, you have to get to the postseason first. And Minnesota's path to October now looks more complicated with the rise of the White Sox as legitimate contenders in the AL Central. The task may have gotten harder, but nothing about breaking curses is supposed to be easy.

—Nathalie Alonso is an editorial producer & reporter @LasMayores, the Spanish-language website for @MLB.

HITTERS

Ehire Adrianza   3B   Born: 08/21/89   Age: 31   Bats: S   Throws: R   Height: 6'1"   Weight: 195   Origin: International Free Agent, 2006

YEAR	TEAM	LVL	AGE	PA	R	2B	3B	HR	RBI	BB	K	SB	CS	Whiff%	AVG/OBP/SLG	DRC+	BABIP	BRR	FRAA	WARP
2018	MIN	MLB	28	366	42	23	1	6	39	24	82	5	1	19.0%	.251/.301/.379	82	.313	0.7	SS(64): -6.1, 3B(28): 0.6, 1B(10): -0.9	0.0
2019	MIN	MLB	29	236	34	8	3	5	22	20	40	0	2	18.2%	.272/.349/.416	100	.311	-1.2	3B(24): -0.0, SS(24): 1.4, 1B(20): -1.1	0.8
2020	MIN	MLB	31	101	10	7	0	0	3	11	23	1	0	18.1%	.191/.287/.270	89	.258	0.4	3B(23): -1.0, SS(9): 0.1, 2B(5): -0.4	0.0
2021 FS	MIN	MLB	31	600	61	28	2	11	60	50	132	9	3	18.4%	.235/.309/.361	87	.291	-0.4	SS 3, 3B 2	1.1

Comparables: Chris Gomez, Eric Bruntlett, Dale Berra

"The Twins were so unstoppable in 2019 that even Adrianza hit!" may be a terrible one-liner, but it's an adequate snapshot of his recent production.

Luis Arraez 2B Born: 04/09/97 Age: 24 Bats: L Throws: R Height: 5'10" Weight: 175 Origin: International Free Agent, 2013

YEAR	TEAM	LVL	AGE	PA	R	2B	3B	HR	RBI	BB	K	SB	CS	Whiff%	AVG/OBP/SLG	DRC+	BABIP	BRR	FRAA	WARP
2018	FTM	HI-A	21	258	27	14	3	1	20	19	28	2	3		.320/.373/.421	130	.356	-2.4	2B(40): 1.7, 3B(6): 0.3, SS(5): 0.3	1.0
2018	CHA	AA	21	195	25	6	0	2	16	13	16	2	0		.298/.345/.365	110	.315	0.0	2B(27): -1.0, 3B(10): 0.3, SS(9): 1.4	0.5
2019	PNS	AA	22	164	18	6	1	0	14	18	13	3	3		.342/.415/.397	176	.376	-0.9	2B(15): -0.1, 3B(15): 4.2, SS(5): 0.5	2.2
2019	ROC	AAA	22	73	8	4	0	0	8	6	2	1	0		.348/.397/.409	129	.354	-0.9	SS(8): 0.4, 2B(4): 1.5, 3B(3): -0.1	0.6
2019	MIN	MLB	22	366	54	20	1	4	28	36	29	2	2	8.1%	.334/.399/.439	121	.355	2.9	2B(49): -2.8, LF(21): 1.5, 3B(17): -0.2	2.3
2020	MIN	MLB	23	121	16	9	0	0	13	8	11	0	0	10.1%	.321/.364/.402	114	.353	0.3	2B(31): 1.2	0.7
2021 FS	MIN	MLB	24	600	63	29	2	7	61	45	70	1	0	8.8%	.297/.353/.397	109	.330	-0.6	2B -2, 3B 1	2.5
2021 DC	MIN	MLB	24	539	56	26	2	6	55	41	63	1	0	8.8%	.297/.353/.397	109	.330	-0.6	2B -2, 3B 1	2.3

Comparables: Dustin Pedroia, Ron Hunt, Gil McDougald

Last season, Arraez became the first player since 2008 to record 100 plate appearances and slug over .400 without hitting a homer (Joaquin Arias was the last to do it). The key to his success is that he's the best contact hitter in the world. Over the past two seasons, nobody has missed less often when they've swung (he has a three percent whiff rate), and he's far and away the best in the game at making contact with balls off the plate (89 percent; next closest is Nick Markakis at 82 percent). It all works because Arraez is more of a spray hitter than a slap hitter, adept at hitting to all fields with just enough doubles power to make outfielders think twice before they creep in. As the only 80-bat, 20-power player in baseball, Arraez is a throwback and a refreshing reminder of the sport's capacity for variance. For however homogeneous this game has gotten in recent years, there will always be a few unicorns in baseball.

Willians Astudillo C Born: 10/14/91 Age: 29 Bats: R Throws: R Height: 5'9" Weight: 225 Origin: International Free Agent, 2008

YEAR	TEAM	LVL	AGE	PA	R	2B	3B	HR	RBI	BB	K	SB	CS	Whiff%	AVG/OBP/SLG	DRC+	BABIP	BRR	FRAA	WARP
2018	ROC	AAA	26	307	30	17	1	12	38	10	14	7	4		.276/.314/.469	109	.255	-1.4	C(39): 2.5, 3B(28): 0.6, LF(6): 0.8	1.3
2018	MIN	MLB	26	97	9	4	1	3	21	2	3	0	0	9.1%	.355/.371/.516	128	.341	0.4	C(16): 2.1, 3B(6): -0.0, 2B(2): 0.0	1.0
2019	ROC	AAA	27	83	18	1	0	5	19	2	2	1	1		.423/.446/.628	168	.389	0.6	C(8): 1.3, 3B(5): 0.4, RF(5): -0.6	1.1
2019	MIN	MLB	27	204	28	9	0	4	21	5	8	0	0	9.1%	.268/.299/.379	94	.258	-2.1	C(21): -0.4, 1B(15): -0.3, 3B(13): -0.5	0.4
2020	MIN	MLB	29	16	4	1	0	1	3	0	2	0	0	17.2%	.250/.250/.500	95	.231	0.1	C(6): -0.0	0.1
2021 FS	MIN	MLB	29	600	70	26	1	20	77	19	45	1	0	9.7%	.274/.313/.433	108	.268	-0.8	C 3, 3B -2	2.5
2021 DC	MIN	MLB	29	202	23	9	0	6	26	6	15	0	0	9.7%	.274/.313/.433	108	.268	-0.3	C 1, 3B -1	0.9

Comparables: Ken Retzer, Mackey Sasser, Del Rice

It's now been two years since Astudillo emerged from minor-league obscurity. His rectangular frame, bizarre positional flexibility and retrograde knack for contact endeared him to a larger audience than most 26-year-old afterthoughts generally garner. But right when he seemed poised to become a cult hero, a funny thing happened: the Twins suddenly got good. A 90-loss team has the luxury of giving a vaguely promising misfit several hundred at-bats to see if they've unearthed a hidden gem. Contenders don't, and after a cold streak in 2019 and a cup of coffee last season, it's clear that Astudillo is no longer in Minnesota's plans. The indy-ball vibes here are strong, but perhaps a cellar-dweller can find use for him before he fades into the hinterlands.

YEAR	TEAM	P. COUNT	FRM RUNS	BLK RUNS	THRW RUNS	TOT RUNS
2018	MIN	2271	1.1	0.5	0.0	1.6
2018	ROC	5323	1.4	0.3	0.3	1.9
2019	MIN	2577	-0.3	0.0	-0.1	-0.4
2019	ROC	1130	1.5	0.0	0.0	1.4
2020	MIN	595	0.2	0.0	0.0	0.2
2021	MIN	4810	1.2	-0.2	0.3	1.4

Alex Avila C Born: 01/29/87 Age: 34 Bats: L Throws: R Height: 5'11" Weight: 210 Origin: Round 5, 2008 Draft (#163 overall)

YEAR	TEAM	LVL	AGE	PA	R	2B	3B	HR	RBI	BB	K	SB	CS	Whiff%	AVG/OBP/SLG	DRC+	BABIP	BRR	FRAA	WARP
2018	ARI	MLB	31	234	13	6	0	7	20	37	90	0	0	36.2%	.165/.299/.304	61	.253	-1.4	C(61): 3.2, 1B(3): 0.0, P(1): -0.0	0.2
2019	ARI	MLB	32	201	22	8	0	9	24	36	68	1	0	37.4%	.207/.353/.421	95	.287	-1.1	C(54): 2.1, P(2): -0.0	1.0
2020	MIN	MLB	33	62	6	2	0	1	2	11	22	0	0	35.1%	.184/.355/.286	86	.308	0.0	C(22): 0.2	0.0
2021 FS	MIN	MLB	34	600	74	22	1	18	62	101	224	1	0	36.5%	.218/.356/.382	110	.355	-1.0	C -11, 1B -1	1.9

Comparables: Jason Castro, David Ross, Rick Wilkins

Casual fans who spot Avila's name in the lineup may still harbor a vague impression of him as some kind of All-Star. After a third consecutive dalliance with the Mendoza Line, though, it's clear that the 34-year-old is in the twilight of his career. A good eye, competent glove and solid reputation in the clubhouse should keep him in the league for a couple more years. Wherever he winds up this offseason, he can expect to play most Sunday afternoons and loiter in shin guards the rest of the week. Hey, there are worse gigs.

YEAR	TEAM	P. COUNT	FRM RUNS	BLK RUNS	THRW RUNS	TOT RUNS
2018	ARI	8064	3.7	0.3	0.0	4.0
2019	ARI	7141	-0.1	2.3	0.7	2.9
2020	MIN	2454	-0.8	0.0	0.0	-0.8
2021	MIN	16650	-10.2	0.9	0.6	-8.8

Travis Blankenhorn 2B Born: 08/03/96 Age: 24 Bats: L Throws: R Height: 6'2" Weight: 235 Origin: Round 3, 2015 Draft (#80 overall)

YEAR	TEAM	LVL	AGE	PA	R	2B	3B	HR	RBI	BB	K	SB	CS	Whiff%	AVG/OBP/SLG	DRC+	BABIP	BRR	FRAA	WARP
2018	FTM	HI-A	21	493	52	24	6	11	57	34	127	6	4		.231/.299/.387	89	.297	1.2	2B(58): -12.9, 3B(41): -0.8, LF(4): 0.3	-1.5
2019	FTM	HI-A	22	61	6	4	0	1	3	9	12	0	0		.269/.377/.404	133	.333	-0.3	LF(6): -1.1, 2B(5): -0.3, 3B(2): -0.1	0.2
2019	PNS	AA	22	410	50	18	2	18	51	18	93	11	0		.278/.312/.474	119	.323	2.7	2B(67): 3.2, LF(18): 0.1	2.5
2020	MIN	MLB	24	4	0	1	0	0	0	0	0	0	0	11.1%	.333/.500/.667	89	.333	0.0	2B(1): -0.2	0.0
2021 FS	MIN	MLB	24	600	63	31	4	20	76	33	188	3	1	11.1%	.230/.284/.411	90	.309	1.3	2B -7, 3B 0	0.5
2021 DC	MIN	MLB	24	202	21	10	1	6	25	11	63	1	0	11.1%	.230/.284/.411	90	.309	0.4	2B -2	0.2

Comparables: Tyler Ladendorf, Cavan Biggio, Chad Pinder

While you can accuse Blankenhorn of plenty of defensive shortcomings, his bat is worth its weight in gold. If the Twins can't find a spot for him, rebuilding clubs will be lurking.

Byron Buxton CF   Born: 12/18/93   Age: 27   Bats: R   Throws: R   Height: 6'2"   Weight: 190   Origin: Round 1, 2012 Draft (#2 overall)

YEAR	TEAM	LVL	AGE	PA	R	2B	3B	HR	RBI	BB	K	SB	CS	Whiff%	AVG/OBP/SLG	DRC+	BABIP	BRR	FRAA	WARP
2018	ROC	AAA	24	148	22	11	1	4	14	9	42	4	1		.272/.331/.456	103	.367	1.4	CF(28): 9.0	1.3
2018	MIN	MLB	24	94	8	4	0	0	4	3	28	5	0	28.9%	.156/.183/.200	57	.226	0.3	CF(27): 1.4	0.0
2019	MIN	MLB	25	295	48	30	4	10	46	19	68	14	3	28.8%	.262/.314/.513	98	.314	4.4	CF(86): 14.2	2.9
2020	MIN	MLB	27	135	19	3	0	13	27	2	36	2	1	28.9%	.254/.267/.577	114	.241	0.5	CF(39): 8.6	1.5
2021 FS	MIN	MLB	27	600	69	24	4	24	77	38	179	17	5	28.9%	.226/.282/.421	93	.285	6.0	CF 27	4.8
2021 DC	MIN	MLB	27	505	58	20	3	21	65	32	150	14	4	28.9%	.226/.282/.421	93	.285	5.1	CF 22	4.1

Comparables: Reggie Taylor, Ryan Thompson, Corey Patterson

Each year, MLB's Playing Rules Committee evaluates how they can make the game a better viewing experience. This year, perhaps they can start by asking themselves "How do we get more Byron Buxtons on the field?"

Buxton is not an efficient ballplayer. The Pete Reiser of his day, Buxton's incredible motor and belligerence toward the outfield wall will simply not allow him to stay in the lineup with any regularity. Between that, his propensity to strike out and allergy to the free pass, he's an incredibly flawed player. And yet, this author doesn't give a damn about any of that. As the three-true-outcome events threaten to suffocate the sport, Buxton's game offers an appealing alternative. More than anyone in this era, Buxton and his elite athleticism break the mold of what we imagine a star to look and play like. With jaw-dropping speed, sterling defense in center and a newfound power stroke, he's a human highlight reel and an avatar for what the game desperately needs more of—and, ideally, more from.

Keoni Cavaco SS   Born: 06/02/01   Age: 20   Bats: R   Throws: R   Height: 6'2"   Weight: 195   Origin: Round 1, 2019 Draft (#13 overall)

YEAR	TEAM	LVL	AGE	PA	R	2B	3B	HR	RBI	BB	K	SB	CS	Whiff%	AVG/OBP/SLG	DRC+	BABIP	BRR	FRAA	WARP
2019	TWI	ROK	18	92	9	4	0	1	6	4	35	1	1		.172/.217/.253	28	.275	-0.6	SS(20): 0.5	-0.3
2021 FS	MIN	MLB	20	600	41	26	2	7	47	25	276	6	2		.196/.236/.289	42	.365	-0.8	SS 1	-2.5

A late growth spurt helped Cavaco blossom plus power and speed as an upperclassman and propelled him into the first round of the 2019 draft. He doesn't have a particularly long track record of elite performance, and while he's now everything you'd want in an athlete, he's also a somewhat volatile prospect and a guy that evaluators wanted to see more of in 2020. So much for that. Time will tell, but Cavaco may be the kind of player most affected by a lost season, a toolsy youngster still growing into his frame who could have really benefited from additional reps against age-appropriate competition.

Jake Cave CF   Born: 12/04/92   Age: 28   Bats: L   Throws: L   Height: 6'0"   Weight: 200   Origin: Round 6, 2011 Draft (#209 overall)

YEAR	TEAM	LVL	AGE	PA	R	2B	3B	HR	RBI	BB	K	SB	CS	Whiff%	AVG/OBP/SLG	DRC+	BABIP	BRR	FRAA	WARP
2018	ROC	AAA	25	250	26	9	1	6	28	26	55	4	2		.269/.352/.403	114	.327	-0.1	RF(36): 5.4, CF(17): -0.6, LF(6): 1.6	1.3
2018	MIN	MLB	25	309	54	16	2	13	45	18	102	2	1	30.6%	.265/.313/.473	93	.363	3.1	CF(70): -7.5, RF(11): 0.3, LF(4): -0.5	0.3
2019	ROC	AAA	26	214	37	18	4	7	39	15	50	5	0		.352/.393/.592	140	.437	1.1	CF(37): -3.5, RF(7): -0.8	1.3
2019	MIN	MLB	26	228	28	11	2	8	25	21	71	0	0	31.8%	.258/.351/.455	89	.358	1.3	RF(45): -1.7, CF(23): 0.2, LF(10): 0.4	0.3
2020	MIN	MLB	28	123	17	3	2	4	15	5	44	0	2	39.7%	.221/.285/.389	69	.323	-0.3	CF(22): -3.1, RF(12): 0.6, LF(7): 0.0	-0.4
2021 FS	MIN	MLB	28	600	62	23	4	17	69	41	203	1	0	34.1%	.230/.295/.387	89	.329	2.1	LF 1, CF -5	0.6
2021 DC	MIN	MLB	28	370	38	14	2	11	42	25	125	1	0	34.1%	.230/.295/.387	89	.329	1.3	LF 0, CF -3	0.4

Comparables: Preston Wilson, Ruben Rivera, Tyler Naquin

Much like this author's work in the kitchen, the holes in Cave's game got exposed in more regular action last year. He slumped early, started pressing, got a little swing happy and ultimately pitchers were able to coax more chases on balls out of the strike zone than in years past. Lefties in particular ate his lunch, striking him out 15 times in 32 at-bats. It would be premature to use these struggles as evidence to suggest that one of baseball's best fourth outfielders can't hack it in everyday duty; we're only talking about 40 games, and 2020 is not the best year to draw big conclusions from. For now though, the Twins will be happy to return him to his usual post as a weapon off the bench and an insurance policy for Byron Buxton's inevitable bouts with the center field wall.

Gilberto Celestino CF   Born: 02/13/99   Age: 22   Bats: R   Throws: L   Height: 6'0"   Weight: 170   Origin: International Free Agent, 2015

YEAR	TEAM	LVL	AGE	PA	R	2B	3B	HR	RBI	BB	K	SB	CS	Whiff%	AVG/OBP/SLG	DRC+	BABIP	BRR	FRAA	WARP
2018	ELZ	ROK	19	117	13	4	1	1	13	6	16	8	2		.266/.308/.349	87	.301	1.1	CF(23): -1.0	-0.1
2018	TRI	SS	19	142	18	8	0	4	21	10	25	14	0		.323/.387/.480	167	.374	1.6	CF(16): 0.9, RF(12): 2.6, LF(3): -0.8	1.2
2019	CR	LO-A	20	503	52	24	3	10	51	48	81	14	8		.276/.350/.409	137	.317	-3.6	CF(83): 3.7, RF(25): -3.6	3.0
2019	FTM	HI-A	20	33	6	4	0	0	3	2	4	0	0		.300/.333/.433	124	.333	0.2	CF(4): -0.8, RF(3): -0.3	0.0
2021 FS	MIN	MLB	22	600	58	27	2	11	59	36	170	13	3		.228/.280/.348	74	.307	2.9	CF 2, RF 0	0.3

Comparables: Jake Cave, Domonic Brown, Dalton Pompey

In 2019 Celestino had an encouraging, if not quite jaw-dropping campaign in the Midwest League, which normally would have punched his ticket for High-A the following spring. Instead, with minor league action cancelled, Celestino was deemed sufficiently promising to warrant an assignment to the alternate training site. There, he spent his evenings getting on a first-name basis with St. Paul's DoorDash drivers, and his days facing pitchers who were all some combination of older, better and more experienced than himself. We don't know how he performed. Only Twins personnel can tell us that and they don't really have any incentive to do that for us. As MLB teams scrap their minor-league affiliates, we can bet that we'll see more of this kind of thing: more prospects sent to sink or swim against better and older players. It'll be an interesting experiment: perhaps Celestino's performance going forward will give us some indication of its merits.

Nelson Cruz DH Born: 07/01/80 Age: 41 Bats: R Throws: R Height: 6'2" Weight: 230 Origin: International Free Agent, 1998

YEAR	TEAM	LVL	AGE	PA	R	2B	3B	HR	RBI	BB	K	SB	CS	Whiff%	AVG/OBP/SLG	DRC+	BABIP	BRR	FRAA	WARP
2018	SEA	MLB	37	591	70	18	1	37	97	55	122	1	0	30.4%	.256/.342/.509	131	.264	-1.2	RF(4): 0.1	3.1
2019	MIN	MLB	38	521	81	26	0	41	108	56	131	0	1	32.4%	.311/.392/.639	151	.351	-1.0		4.1
2020	MIN	MLB	40	214	33	6	0	16	33	25	58	0	0	34.2%	.303/.397/.595	141	.360	-0.7		1.4
2021 FS	MIN	MLB	40	600	84	23	0	32	94	59	173	1	0	32.4%	.262/.346/.494	133	.326	-1.4	RF -6	3.3

Comparables: Reggie Jackson, Matt Stairs, Reggie Sanders

Cruz may not be the greatest old player in recent memory—Barry Bonds springs to mind—but at a time when 33 passes for old, he is the game's premier elder statesman. Turning 40 didn't slow him down a bit, as he slugged above .500 for the eighth year running and was on pace for yet another 40-homer season. Despite the monster year, you can squint and see the faintest signs of decline. His average exit velocity dropped, and using Statcast metrics, both his batting average and slugging percentage were higher than expected based on the quality of his contact. Still, even if Cruz is finally on the back half of the mountain, there are quite a few switchbacks between him and sea level. He should earn his keep for another year or two.

Josh Donaldson 3B Born: 12/08/85 Age: 35 Bats: R Throws: R Height: 6'1" Weight: 210 Origin: Round 1, 2007 Draft (#48 overall)

YEAR	TEAM	LVL	AGE	PA	R	2B	3B	HR	RBI	BB	K	SB	CS	Whiff%	AVG/OBP/SLG	DRC+	BABIP	BRR	FRAA	WARP
2018	TOR	MLB	32	159	22	11	0	5	16	21	44	2	0	34.2%	.234/.333/.423	106	.303	-0.4	3B(26): -0.9, 1B(1): 0.1	0.5
2018	CLE	MLB	32	60	8	3	0	3	7	10	10	0	0	23.9%	.280/.400/.520	106	.297	-0.8	3B(12): -0.9	0.1
2019	ATL	MLB	33	659	96	33	0	37	94	100	154	4	2	29.9%	.259/.379/.521	130	.292	-1.0	3B(148): 1.2	5.1
2020	MIN	MLB	35	102	14	2	0	6	11	18	24	0	0	34.5%	.222/.373/.469	111	.231	0.3	3B(26): -0.4	0.4
2021 FS	MIN	MLB	35	600	86	25	1	25	76	87	149	4	1	30.9%	.239/.358/.448	126	.286	-0.6	3B -4, 1B 0	2.8
2021 DC	MIN	MLB	35	539	77	22	1	23	68	79	134	4	1	30.9%	.239/.358/.448	126	.286	-0.5	3B -4	2.5

Comparables: Scott Rolen, Matt Carpenter, Howard Johnson

Does Donaldson still have a shot at a Hall-of-Fame career? By traditional standards, the answer is no. Entering his age-35 season, he has barely 1,000 hits to his name. His 225 career homers are nothing to sneeze at, but hardly special for his time. His .272/.369/.508 batting line is impressive but irreparably dampened by the run environment when he first broke out. He has no postseason heroics to fall back upon. He won an MVP, but so did Justin Morneau. Even the sabermetrically savvy will be inclined to glance at his 35 WARP, note that he has a lower JAWS score (top seven seasons of WAR added together) than Evan Longoria, and scroll on to other things. Maybe that's the right approach.

Get a little creative though, and you can make a case.

First, Donaldson may not have the seven elite seasons, but he clearly has five. In that time, playing in the best era for third basemen the game has ever seen, Donaldson reigned. You have to imagine that at least one of Nolan Arenado, Kris Bryant, Manny Machado, Anthony Rendon and Longoria will be inducted someday, and Donaldson was better with the bat than most of them in their primes. He also didn't get a real shot in the big leagues until he was 26. There may have been good reasons for that, but in an era where players generally create most of their value in their early 20s, it's remarkable how good Donaldson has been without getting to play in that time. Moreover, players don't have 20-year careers anymore, and as that trend accelerates, the electorate should strive to induct the players who burned brightest even if they were great for a shorter period of time than stars of previous generations.

Certainly this is all up for debate, and it's reasonable to be intrigued by Donaldson's case and still think he has more work to do to merit the honor. Fortunately for him, he's 35 and still has time to pad his totals. If he ages gracefully, he'll be a tough one for the BBWAA.

Mitch Garver C Born: 01/15/91 Age: 30 Bats: R Throws: R Height: 6'1" Weight: 220 Origin: Round 9, 2013 Draft (#260 overall)

YEAR	TEAM	LVL	AGE	PA	R	2B	3B	HR	RBI	BB	K	SB	CS	Whiff%	AVG/OBP/SLG	DRC+	BABIP	BRR	FRAA	WARP
2018	MIN	MLB	27	335	38	19	2	7	45	29	72	0	0	23.2%	.268/.335/.414	99	.330	-1.3	C(86): -8.5, 1B(5): -0.1, P(1): -0.0	0.5
2019	MIN	MLB	28	359	70	16	1	31	67	41	87	0	0	24.0%	.273/.365/.630	148	.277	-0.7	C(82): 4.7, 1B(1): -0.0	4.4
2020	MIN	MLB	29	81	8	1	0	2	5	7	37	0	0	39.6%	.167/.247/.264	56	.294	-0.3	C(22): 0.6, 1B(1): -0.0	-0.3
2021 FS	MIN	MLB	30	600	76	24	2	25	76	61	192	0	0	27.1%	.239/.324/.440	113	.321	0.0	C -5, 1B 0	2.8
2021 DC	MIN	MLB	30	269	34	11	0	11	34	27	86	0	0	27.1%	.239/.324/.440	113	.321	0.0	C -4	1.2

Comparables: Jorge Posada, Todd Hundley, Rick Wilkins

YEAR	TEAM	P. COUNT	FRM RUNS	BLK RUNS	THRW RUNS	TOT RUNS
2018	MIN	11863	-8.2	0.2	-0.4	-8.4
2019	MIN	11037	4.2	-0.3	-0.4	3.5
2020	MIN	2772	-0.6	-0.1	0.0	-0.8
2021	MIN	9620	-4.1	-0.2	0.0	-4.3

Garver must have gotten drunk on power in 2019 because last year he looked like he had a bad hangover. There are many reasons his production fell so dramatically, but one that stands out is his performance on fastballs. In 2019, he hit over .300, slugged .800 and smacked 25 dingers against the heater. His whiff rate against the pitch was a bit high, but not notably so. In 2020 though, he went from missing 15 percent of fastballs to whiffing more than a third of the time. He also missed offspeed pitches more often, but he already struggled with those, and it's the performance against heaters that is most concerning going forward. You can survive in the big leagues while flailing at curveballs, but you won't if you can't catch up to the cheese. Whether last year's crash stemmed from an intercostal strain, a launch angle that might have tipped a bit too high for a swing that starts so flat or just the worst run of 80 at-bats in his life, Garver needs to forget this nightmare ever happened.

Marwin Gonzalez 3B   Born: 03/14/89   Age: 32   Bats: S   Throws: R   Height: 6'1"   Weight: 205   Origin: International Free Agent, 2005

YEAR	TEAM	LVL	AGE	PA	R	2B	3B	HR	RBI	BB	K	SB	CS	Whiff%	AVG/OBP/SLG	DRC+	BABIP	BRR	FRAA	WARP
2018	HOU	MLB	29	552	61	25	3	16	68	53	126	2	3	24.8%	.247/.324/.409	100	.301	1.5	LF(73): 0.7, SS(39): -2.7, 2B(32): -0.2	1.6
2019	MIN	MLB	30	463	52	19	0	15	55	31	98	1	0	23.8%	.264/.322/.414	91	.310	-1.2	RF(44): -4.8, 3B(40): 5.0, 1B(21): 0.7	1.1
2020	MIN	MLB	31	199	15	4	0	5	22	17	41	0	0	23.8%	.211/.286/.320	90	.241	-1.2	3B(23): -1.0, 2B(21): -1.1, 1B(14): -0.3	-0.3
2021 FS	MIN	MLB	32	600	64	28	1	16	70	45	139	6	2	24.1%	.244/.309/.394	94	.297	-1.7	LF -3, SS -1	0.2

Comparables: Jhonny Peralta, Ian Desmond, Asdrúbal Cabrera

Not only did Gonzalez apologize and express remorse for his part in Houston's Banging Scheme, but he actually seemed to mean it (which gave him a leg up on some of his former teammates and two legs up on the rest). It's hard to let him off the hook entirely though, because it seems increasingly likely that he benefited substantially from the con. After a down 2019, Gonzalez cratered in 2020. He's a .248/.311/.387 hitter since leaving the Astros, and the discipline he displayed while laying off wayward breaking balls and changeups back in 2017-18 evaporated the second he bid adieu to Harris County's most lopsided garbage can. He's still rosterable given his positional flexibility, but any remaining plaudits of his late-blooming batting acumen should probably be thrown in the trash.

Nick Gordon SS   Born: 10/24/95   Age: 25   Bats: L   Throws: R   Height: 6'0"   Weight: 160   Origin: Round 1, 2014 Draft (#5 overall)

YEAR	TEAM	LVL	AGE	PA	R	2B	3B	HR	RBI	BB	K	SB	CS	Whiff%	AVG/OBP/SLG	DRC+	BABIP	BRR	FRAA	WARP
2018	CHA	AA	22	181	22	10	3	5	20	11	27	7	2		.333/.381/.525	139	.366	-1.4	SS(34): 2.4, 2B(6): -0.3	1.2
2018	ROC	AAA	22	410	40	13	4	2	29	23	82	13	3		.212/.262/.283	53	.264	2.8	SS(69): 2.6, 2B(30): 4.1	-0.1
2019	ROC	AAA	23	319	49	29	3	4	40	18	65	14	4		.298/.342/.459	107	.364	-0.1	SS(40): 1.6, 2B(30): -1.4	1.5
2021 FS	MIN	MLB	25	600	58	28	4	9	56	37	158	7	3		.230/.286/.345	75	.305	1.1	2B 3, SS 1	0.6
2021 DC	MIN	MLB	25	67	6	3	0	1	6	4	17	0	0		.230/.286/.345	75	.305	0.1	2B 0, SS 0	0.1

Comparables: Orlando Arcia, Darwin Barney, Reid Brignac

At his prospect apex you could dream on Gordon as an everyday middle infielder who could approximate the value, if not quite the shape, of his older brother Dee's career. That ship has sailed.

Wander Javier SS   Born: 12/29/98   Age: 22   Bats: R   Throws: R   Height: 6'1"   Weight: 165   Origin: International Free Agent, 2015

YEAR	TEAM	LVL	AGE	PA	R	2B	3B	HR	RBI	BB	K	SB	CS	Whiff%	AVG/OBP/SLG	DRC+	BABIP	BRR	FRAA	WARP
2019	CR	LO-A	20	342	43	9	1	11	37	35	116	2	0		.177/.278/.323	69	.243	-0.9	SS(66): 2.0	0.3
2021 FS	MIN	MLB	22	600	49	25	2	12	54	41	238	3	1		.188/.253/.309	54	.304	0.2	SS 1	-1.5

Comparables: Yadiel Rivera, Jai Miller, Michael Chavis

Our lead prospect writer, Jeffrey Paternostro, has made a parlor game out of telling readers he has no idea what to expect from Wander Javier. For those reading this space for more insight, we must regrettably refer you back to Jeffrey.

Ryan Jeffers C   Born: 06/03/97   Age: 24   Bats: R   Throws: R   Height: 6'4"   Weight: 235   Origin: Round 2, 2018 Draft (#59 overall)

YEAR	TEAM	LVL	AGE	PA	R	2B	3B	HR	RBI	BB	K	SB	CS	Whiff%	AVG/OBP/SLG	DRC+	BABIP	BRR	FRAA	WARP
2018	ELZ	ROK	21	129	29	7	0	3	16	20	16	0	1		.422/.543/.578	243	.482	-1.0	C(10): 0.7	1.5
2018	CR	LO-A	21	155	19	10	0	4	17	14	30	0	0		.288/.361/.446	144	.343	0.4	C(22): 0.2	1.2
2019	FTM	HI-A	22	315	35	11	0	10	40	28	64	0	0		.256/.330/.402	121	.297	-2.7	C(57): 0.7	1.6
2019	PNS	AA	22	99	13	5	0	4	9	9	19	0	0		.287/.374/.483	142	.328	1.4	C(17): -0.9	0.8
2020	MIN	MLB	23	62	5	0	0	3	7	5	19	0	0	33.3%	.273/.355/.436	92	.364	-0.5	C(25): -0.1	0.1
2021 FS	MIN	MLB	24	600	71	25	1	19	71	48	168	1	0	33.3%	.256/.327/.417	108	.336	-0.5	C 0	3.1
2021 DC	MIN	MLB	24	269	32	11	0	8	32	21	75	0	0	33.3%	.256/.327/.417	108	.336	-0.2	C 0	1.3

Comparables: Devin Mesoraco, Danny Jansen, Jake Fox

YEAR	TEAM	P. COUNT	FRM RUNS	BLK RUNS	THRW RUNS	TOT RUNS
2019	PNS	2243	-0.3	0.0	-0.4	-0.7
2020	MIN	2804	0.3	-0.1	0.1	0.3
2021	MIN	9620	0.6	-1.1	-0.7	-1.2

It took just two seasons for Jeffers to vault from the second round of the draft to starting catcher on a playoff team. Part of that was a function of timing: Mitch Garver and Alex Aliva forgot how to hit and a virus of modest renown hamstrung Minnesota's efforts to find a proven replacement. The Twins rolled the dice on Jeffers and did he ever rise to the occasion. It was only 23 games but he hit well down the stretch, bringing his power into games enough to offset the swing-and-miss issues that prospect analysts accurately prognosticated. Perhaps more importantly, he demonstrated that his receiving skills have grown considerably since college, and all but put to bed any lingering concerns that he'll have to move to first base soon. He doesn't have the world's highest ceiling and he'll need to prove he can maintain the power as the league acclimates to him, but it's starting to look like Minnesota's catcher of the future has arrived ahead of schedule.

Max Kepler RF   Born: 02/10/93   Age: 28   Bats: L   Throws: L   Height: 6'4"   Weight: 225   Origin: International Free Agent, 2009

YEAR	TEAM	LVL	AGE	PA	R	2B	3B	HR	RBI	BB	K	SB	CS	Whiff%	AVG/OBP/SLG	DRC+	BABIP	BRR	FRAA	WARP
2018	MIN	MLB	25	611	80	30	4	20	58	71	96	4	5	17.8%	.224/.319/.408	102	.236	2.7	RF(117): 10.2, CF(55): -1.3	2.9
2019	MIN	MLB	26	596	98	32	0	36	90	60	99	1	5	20.2%	.252/.336/.519	125	.244	-3.7	RF(84): 6.0, CF(60): -3.6	3.5
2020	MIN	MLB	27	196	27	9	0	9	23	22	36	3	0	21.2%	.228/.321/.439	114	.236	-0.3	RF(44): -2.7, CF(2): -0.4	0.3
2021 FS	MIN	MLB	28	600	83	29	2	25	69	66	119	5	2	19.9%	.242/.333/.451	115	.267	-2.1	RF 4, CF 0	3.0
2021 DC	MIN	MLB	28	573	79	28	2	24	66	63	113	5	2	19.9%	.242/.333/.451	115	.267	-2.0	RF 4, CF 0	2.7

Comparables: Jeremy Hermida, Michael Cuddyer, Brennan Boesch

If you're looking for a player who embodies the "first-division regular" descriptor, Kepler fits the bill perfectly. Arguably the league's most graceful player, he posted another productive campaign at the plate with his trademark good defense in right field. The one knock on his game? BABIP, of all things. Among players with 2,000 PA's over the last five years, only Todd Frazier and Albert Pujols are under Kepler's .252 mark. Given his relatively high launch angle and pedestrian exit velocity, a low BABIP isn't totally surprising. Nevertheless, as a speedy lefty who has reached base less often than his batted-tracking metrics suggest he should've throughout his career, he's due for a BABIP spike one of these years. When it comes, he'll deserve a spot on the All-Star team.

★ ★ ★ *2021 Top 101 Prospect* **#71** ★ ★ ★

Alex Kirilloff RF Born: 11/09/97 Age: 23 Bats: L Throws: L Height: 6'2" Weight: 195 Origin: Round 1, 2016 Draft (#15 overall)

YEAR	TEAM	LVL	AGE	PA	R	2B	3B	HR	RBI	BB	K	SB	CS	Whiff%	AVG/OBP/SLG	DRC+	BABIP	BRR	FRAA	WARP
2018	CR	LO-A	20	281	36	20	5	13	56	24	47	1	1		.333/.391/.607	162	.364	-0.8	RF(53): -4.0, CF(0): -0.0	1.5
2018	FTM	HI-A	20	280	39	24	2	7	45	14	39	3	2		.362/.393/.550	162	.399	-0.8	RF(51): 0.4, CF(3): 0.3	1.7
2019	PNS	AA	21	411	47	18	2	9	43	29	76	7	6		.283/.343/.413	120	.333	-3.3	RF(41): -4.0, 1B(35): 0.3, LF(8): -1.0	0.6
2021 FS	MIN	MLB	23	600	65	26	3	16	69	35	143	1	0		.252/.301/.401	92	.311	0.4	1B 1, LF -1	0.8
2021 DC	MIN	MLB	23	505	55	22	2	14	58	29	120	1	0		.252/.301/.401	92	.311	0.3	1B 1, LF -1	0.6

Comparables: Brandon Moss, Carlos González, Tyler Austin

Kirilloff became the third player to make his MLB debut in the postseason and the first to record a base hit when he singled against Jose Urquidy. The fact that the Twins felt comfortable thrusting the 22-year-old into the lineup in an elimination game speaks volumes about how they regard Kirilloff. Wrist injuries dampened his numbers in 2019, but when healthy, he has impressive pop and projects to have two plus tools at full maturity. The jury's still out on whether he'll be able to fake it in a corner-outfield spot or have to shift to first base, but his bat is going to carry him regardless of where he ends up.

★ ★ ★ *2021 Top 101 Prospect* **#83** ★ ★ ★

Trevor Larnach RF Born: 02/26/97 Age: 24 Bats: L Throws: R Height: 6'4" Weight: 223 Origin: Round 1, 2018 Draft (#20 overall)

YEAR	TEAM	LVL	AGE	PA	R	2B	3B	HR	RBI	BB	K	SB	CS	Whiff%	AVG/OBP/SLG	DRC+	BABIP	BRR	FRAA	WARP
2018	ELZ	ROK	21	75	10	5	0	2	16	10	11	2	0		.311/.413/.492	168	.340	-1.5	RF(14): 3.8	0.6
2018	CR	LO-A	21	102	17	8	1	3	10	11	17	1	0		.297/.373/.505	149	.338	0.7	RF(17): -1.5	0.5
2019	FTM	HI-A	22	361	33	26	1	6	44	35	74	4	1		.316/.382/.459	165	.389	-1.4	RF(59): -8.1, LF(9): -0.4	1.9
2019	PNS	AA	22	181	26	4	0	7	22	22	50	0	0		.295/.387/.455	146	.390	-0.3	RF(29): -2.2, LF(5): -0.1	0.8
2021 FS	MIN	MLB	24	600	65	27	2	15	64	51	170	0	0		.237/.307/.378	91	.318	-0.2	LF 0, RF -2	0.5
2021 DC	MIN	MLB	24	337	36	15	1	8	35	28	96	0	0		.237/.307/.378	91	.318	-0.1	LF 0, RF -1	0.3

Comparables: Mac Williamson, Preston Tucker, Marcell Ozuna

Larnach's prospect pedigree perhaps deserves more attention, but this one is actually pretty simple: He's a mediocre right fielder but a potential 60/60 bat thanks to a smooth swing, good approach and booming natural power. Whether in 2021 or 2022, Larnach should crack the lineup sooner rather than later.

★ ★ ★ *2021 Top 101 Prospect* **#31** ★ ★ ★

Royce Lewis SS Born: 06/05/99 Age: 22 Bats: R Throws: R Height: 6'2" Weight: 200 Origin: Round 1, 2017 Draft (#1 overall)

YEAR	TEAM	LVL	AGE	PA	R	2B	3B	HR	RBI	BB	K	SB	CS	Whiff%	AVG/OBP/SLG	DRC+	BABIP	BRR	FRAA	WARP
2018	CR	LO-A	19	327	50	23	0	9	53	24	49	22	4		.315/.368/.485	151	.349	3.7	SS(67): 0.8	3.2
2018	FTM	HI-A	19	208	33	6	3	5	21	19	35	6	4		.255/.327/.399	106	.291	1.7	SS(45): -4.8	0.3
2019	FTM	HI-A	20	418	55	17	3	10	35	27	90	16	8		.238/.289/.376	96	.281	-1.5	SS(84): 4.0	1.8
2019	PNS	AA	20	148	18	9	1	2	14	11	33	6	2		.231/.291/.358	66	.287	2.0	SS(29): -2.6, 2B(1): 0.0, 3B(1): -0.0	0.3
2021 FS	MIN	MLB	22	600	62	27	3	14	63	40	151	14	5		.230/.288/.369	82	.290	0.1	SS 0, CF 1	0.6
2021 DC	MIN	MLB	22	101	10	4	0	2	10	6	25	2	0		.230/.288/.369	82	.290	0.0	SS 0, CF 0	0.1

Comparables: José Rondón, Amed Rosario, Tony Wolters

Lewis is perhaps the most volatile top-tier prospect in baseball. The tools and intangibles that made him the first pick of the draft back in 2017 are mostly intact. He still projects to play a premium position, still looks like he could develop plus game power, still runs really well, still has baseball people raving about his elite makeup. For a kid who reached Double-A as a 20-year-old, everything seems to be pointing in the right direction. And yet, it's hard to shake the impression that Lewis has been trending downward for the better part of the last two years. It started with a disappointing statistical season in 2019. Facing tough competition in a pitcher's league, Lewis endured growing pains in High-A ball, where his approach backed up and he lost some of his feel to hit. Minnesota promoted him to Double-A anyway, and he again struggled, finishing the year with a .290 OBP across both levels. Perhaps more troublingly, the scouting reports matched the numbers. Lewis' swing and hitting mechanics looked uncharacteristically messy, which screwed up his timing and left him off balance against good breaking stuff. And while it still looks like he'll play an important position defensively, it increasingly looks like it won't be short, at least not in the long run. All of this could have been chalked up to a down year if he'd been able to shrug off his slump in 2020 but, of course, there was no 2020 for minor leaguers. Where does that leave us? Lewis is an uber-talented kid, and the kind of guy you'd love to see succeed. He's also two years removed from his last productive season, and while evaluators still like him plenty, there are more whispers about a long developmental path than there were 18 months ago. He wouldn't be the first star to take a step back before bursting forward, and he may be just a mechanical tweak from a reset. Twins fans should hope so, because while Lewis is still a very promising player, he's no longer a "can't-miss" prospect.

Tzu-Wei Lin 2B Born: 02/15/94 Age: 27 Bats: L Throws: R Height: 5'9" Weight: 180 Origin: International Free Agent, 2012

YEAR	TEAM	LVL	AGE	PA	R	2B	3B	HR	RBI	BB	K	SB	CS	Whiff%	AVG/OBP/SLG	DRC+	BABIP	BRR	FRAA	WARP
2018	WOR	AAA	24	302	33	20	2	5	25	23	64	3	4		.307/.362/.448	129	.385	-0.4	SS(51): 1.6, CF(9): 0.9, 2B(6): 0.1	2.1
2018	BOS	MLB	24	73	15	6	1	1	6	8	17	0	1	27.3%	.246/.329/.415	79	.319	0.2	SS(23): -0.3, CF(6): -0.6, 2B(4): 0.0	0.1
2019	WOR	AAA	25	250	30	11	1	4	22	21	58	6	2		.246/.308/.357	84	.311	1.5	SS(27): 4.6, 2B(15): 1.7, LF(6): 1.7	1.2
2019	BOS	MLB	25	22	3	2	0	0	1	2	6	1	1	26.8%	.200/.273/.300	70	.286	0.0	2B(8): -0.3, SS(2): -0.0, CF(1): -0.0	0.0
2020	BOS	MLB	26	57	2	1	0	0	3	2	17	0	0	28.4%	.154/.182/.173	61	.222	0.0	SS(12): 0.0, 2B(6): 0.0, LF(4): 0.1	-0.1
2021 FS	MIN	MLB	27	600	57	25	4	10	55	47	152	5	2	27.9%	.225/.289/.342	72	.295	0.5	SS 8, CF 1	0.8

Comparables: Reid Brignac, Ray Olmedo, Ryan Goins

There's no sadder or more succinct way to break down Lin's horrendous 2020 than to point out that he allowed as many runs in his one inning on the mound (three) as he drove in during his 26 games as a hitter.

Jorge Polanco SS Born: 07/05/93 Age: 28 Bats: S Throws: R Height: 5'11" Weight: 208 Origin: International Free Agent, 2009

YEAR	TEAM	LVL	AGE	PA	R	2B	3B	HR	RBI	BB	K	SB	CS	Whiff%	AVG/OBP/SLG	DRC+	BABIP	BRR	FRAA	WARP
2018	MIN	MLB	24	333	38	18	3	6	42	25	62	7	7	15.7%	.288/.345/.427	97	.345	-3.0	SS(76): -9.7	0.1
2019	MIN	MLB	25	704	107	40	7	22	79	60	116	4	3	17.4%	.295/.356/.485	119	.328	4.9	SS(142): -0.7	5.3
2020	MIN	MLB	27	226	22	8	0	4	19	13	35	4	2	16.8%	.258/.304/.354	102	.292	-0.6	SS(53): 1.7	0.8
2021 FS	MIN	MLB	27	600	61	29	3	14	66	45	106	8	4	17.0%	.267/.326/.413	104	.308	-0.7	SS -6	1.5
2021 DC	MIN	MLB	27	573	58	28	3	13	63	43	101	8	3	17.0%	.267/.326/.413	104	.308	-0.7	SS -6	1.5

Comparables: Angel Berroa, Jeff Blauser, Khalil Greene

Polanco moving off shortstop has always seemed a matter of when, not if, given his sub-par glove at the six. A career-worst slash line appears disastrous in that context, except DRC+ was far more generous and Polanco turned in an almost error-free performance to convince the majority of the defensive metrics that he was average—if not better—with the glove. Whether we can believe that over a sample of barely 50 games is another matter. Talk about him moving to a super-utility role suggests the team is inclined to disregard it. Minnesota would prefer that he go back to the five-win level of performance that made his current contract look like a stroke of genius. As long as he's an average regular in some regard, they won't complain too much about how he gets there.

Brent Rooker OF Born: 11/01/94 Age: 26 Bats: R Throws: R Height: 6'3" Weight: 225 Origin: Round 1, 2017 Draft (#35 overall)

YEAR	TEAM	LVL	AGE	PA	R	2B	3B	HR	RBI	BB	K	SB	CS	Whiff%	AVG/OBP/SLG	DRC+	BABIP	BRR	FRAA	WARP
2018	CHA	AA	23	568	72	32	4	22	79	56	150	6	1		.254/.333/.465	115	.316	-4.7	1B(47): -5.7, LF(44): -8.2	-1.2
2019	TWI	ROK	24	7	2	0	0	0	0	1	0	0	0		.333/.429/.333	131	.333	-0.1	LF(1): 0.1	0.0
2019	ROC	AAA	24	274	41	16	0	14	47	35	95	2	0		.281/.398/.535	122	.417	2.6	LF(56): -0.6	1.5
2020	MIN	MLB	26	21	4	2	0	1	5	0	5	0	0	27.3%	.316/.381/.579	102	.385		RF(4): -0.1, LF(1): -0.1	0.0
2021 FS	MIN	MLB	26	600	61	25	2	17	67	50	207	1	0	27.3%	.209/.288/.364	83	.301	0.1	LF -9, 1B 0	-0.8
2021 DC	MIN	MLB	26	269	27	11	0	8	30	22	92	0	0	27.3%	.209/.288/.364	83	.301	0.0	LF -4	-0.3

Comparables: Travis Demeritte, Matt Clark, Will Craig

Wrist and groin injuries kept Rooker from the majors in 2019 and a global pandemic nearly did the same in 2020. If that wasn't enough, after his belated late-summer debut, he soon succumbed to a broken forearm after getting drilled by a wayward changeup. Upon his return, he'll soon find that the only thing harder than reaching the big city is staying there. The former first-rounder has formidable pop and a promising track record, but he struggles with spin and plays for a team already flush in corner bats. As a 26-year-old right-right type with little defensive value, he won't get many chances and has very little margin for error when they come.

Eddie Rosario LF Born: 09/28/91 Age: 29 Bats: L Throws: R Height: 6'1" Weight: 180 Origin: Round 4, 2010 Draft (#135 overall)

YEAR	TEAM	LVL	AGE	PA	R	2B	3B	HR	RBI	BB	K	SB	CS	Whiff%	AVG/OBP/SLG	DRC+	BABIP	BRR	FRAA	WARP
2018	MIN	MLB	26	592	87	31	2	24	77	30	104	8	2	23.4%	.288/.323/.479	112	.316	6.8	LF(125): 5.9, RF(5): -0.2, CF(4): 0.1	3.6
2019	MIN	MLB	27	590	91	28	1	32	109	22	86	3	1	21.4%	.276/.300/.500	109	.273	0.9	LF(124): -8.8, RF(11): -0.5, CF(3): 0.0	1.5
2020	MIN	MLB	29	231	31	7	0	13	42	19	34	3	1	22.7%	.257/.316/.476	126	.248	0.9	LF(51): 0.1	1.4
2021 FS	MIN	MLB	29	600	71	27	1	26	91	32	115	7	3	22.2%	.261/.302/.458	105	.285	-1.7	LF -10, RF -1	0.8

Comparables: Alfonso Soriano, Joe Carter, Mark Quinn

For those inclined to gin up a narrative based on two months of shaky data, Rosario's 2020 campaign provides sufficient fodder. Squint, and you'll note that his average exit velocity is squarely in line with career norms. From there, you can point to the best walk and strikeout numbers of his career and say that the only thing masking a mini-breakout was horrible luck on balls in play. Dig a little deeper though, and it's less clear whether he's actually changed anything about his approach. For one, he hasn't stopped offering at pitches off the plate: The uptick in his walk rate was actually the product of swinging far less often at pitches in the strike zone, which subsequently led to longer at-bats and more free passes. He also made more contact on every type of pitch, which is good when the ball is in the strike zone and generally lousy when it's not. If forced to choose whether Rosario is now a better hitter because he's become more selective, or simply coming off a strong two months against relatively weak pitching, the latter seems the likelier explanation.

Aaron Sabato 1B   Born: 06/04/99   Age: 22   Bats: R   Throws: R   Height: 6'2"   Weight: 230   Origin: Round 1, 2020 Draft (#27 overall)

There aren't a lot of right-right first basemen who hear their name called in the first round of the draft, particularly bad-bodied guys with fewer than 400 college at-bats under their belt. In Sabato, the Twins are getting a draft-eligible sophomore who mashed in the ACC. He smacked 25 dingers in 80 games at North Carolina, slugged .700 and posted very encouraging walk and strikeout numbers in his truncated season. That performance in one of college baseball's power conferences made him an interesting target for any front office incorporating college metrics into their evaluation, as Minnesota does. Twins fans will have to hope that those models are on to something, because Sabato is a risky and somewhat divisive prospect. Everyone loves the bat, particularly the power, but first basemen really have to hit to have value, particularly if they're like Sabato and don't offer anything special at the cold corner. This seems like the kind of pick we'll be able to judge relatively quickly: Three years from now, he'll either be in the middle of the order, or Minnesota will want a mulligan.

Miguel Sanó 3B   Born: 05/11/93   Age: 28   Bats: R   Throws: R   Height: 6'4"   Weight: 272   Origin: International Free Agent, 2009

YEAR	TEAM	LVL	AGE	PA	R	2B	3B	HR	RBI	BB	K	SB	CS	Whiff%	AVG/OBP/SLG	DRC+	BABIP	BRR	FRAA	WARP
2018	FTM	HI-A	25	77	11	2	0	2	12	13	21	0	0		.328/.442/.453	162	.463	0.2	3B(10): 0.4	0.6
2018	ROC	AAA	25	36	2	1	0	2	5	6	8	0	0		.267/.389/.500	129	.300	0.2	3B(4): 1.5, 1B(1): -0.0	0.3
2018	MIN	MLB	25	299	32	14	0	13	41	31	115	0	0	36.8%	.199/.281/.398	82	.286	-1.0	3B(56): 0.1, 1B(11): 0.1	0.2
2019	MIN	MLB	26	439	76	19	2	34	79	55	159	0	1	37.7%	.247/.346/.576	127	.319	-2.5	3B(91): -3.2, 1B(9): -0.6	2.5
2020	MIN	MLB	27	205	31	12	0	13	25	18	90	0	0	42.6%	.204/.278/.478	91	.301	1.7	1B(52): -3.5	-0.2
2021 FS	MIN	MLB	28	600	80	26	1	33	91	70	246	1	0	39.2%	.230/.324/.481	122	.353	-0.5	1B 12, 3B 0	4.1
2021 DC	MIN	MLB	28	573	76	25	1	32	87	67	235	1	0	39.2%	.230/.324/.481	122	.353	-0.5	1B 11	3.6

Comparables: Mark Reynolds, Russell Branyan, Chris Carter

Sanó continued his Hosmerian pattern of following a promising season with a clunker, headlined by a strikeout rate that would embarrass Mark Reynolds. Is it too early to call Sanó's career a dissapointment? It sounds premature, and to be fair, the "bust" label would clearly be a step too far: He's made an All-Star team, compiled eight career WARP and deserves his place in the middle of a pretty good lineup. Still, there's a significant gap between the 70-grade star scouts projected and the useful but flawed player he's become. With each passing year, it appears increasingly likely that this is the real Sanó: A good, not great, hitter who will mash for stretches and then slump horribly for weeks at a time. He has too much power to write off his potential entirely, but as a bad-bodied 27-year-old with no speed and less defensive value, there's a chance Sanó's best baseball is already behind him.

Alerick Soularie OF   Born: 07/05/99   Age: 22   Bats: R   Throws: R   Height: 6'0"   Weight: 175   Origin: Round 2, 2020 Draft (#59 overall)

Soularie was Minnesota's second-round pick, a center fielder out of Tennessee who signed for $900,000. A good hitter with an excellent eye and feel for hard contact to all fields, he is a skills-over-tools kind of prospect. He's not especially physical nor particularly fast. He also has kind of an awkward swing and few evaluators expect him to stay in center. Most scouts see him as a tweener with a chance to start if he grows into more power, and the consensus is that the Twins reached here. Still, guys who can get the fat part of the bat on the ball like this don't grow on trees, and Soularie did put up good numbers in a very tough college league. It's a bat you can dream on, even if the pick seems a tad underwhelming.

LaMonte Wade Jr LF   Born: 01/01/94   Age: 27   Bats: L   Throws: L   Height: 6'1"   Weight: 205   Origin: Round 9, 2015 Draft (#260 overall)

YEAR	TEAM	LVL	AGE	PA	R	2B	3B	HR	RBI	BB	K	SB	CS	Whiff%	AVG/OBP/SLG	DRC+	BABIP	BRR	FRAA	WARP
2018	CHA	AA	24	201	30	2	1	7	27	26	20	5	2		.298/.393/.444	141	.301	1.5	LF(25): 1.1, CF(10): 1.1, RF(8): -0.2	1.3
2018	ROC	AAA	24	294	24	9	3	4	21	38	54	5	1		.229/.337/.336	97	.277	0.2	LF(58): 2.8, RF(16): 0.5	0.5
2019	ROC	AAA	25	334	47	12	1	5	24	56	48	7	2		.246/.392/.356	106	.280	0.8	RF(34): -6.5, LF(28): -1.4, CF(11): -1.0	0.3
2019	MIN	MLB	25	69	10	2	1	2	5	11	9	0	1	17.4%	.196/.348/.375	104	.200	0.0	CF(14): 0.9, LF(8): -0.6, RF(6): -0.7	0.2
2020	MIN	MLB	26	44	3	3	0	0	1	4	9	1	1	15.4%	.231/.318/.308	88	.300	0.1	1B(4): -0.1, CF(4): -0.2, LF(3): -0.3	-0.1
2021 FS	MIN	MLB	27	600	68	26	2	12	60	71	121	1	0	16.3%	.246/.347/.383	104	.299	0.7	LF 3, 1B 0	2.4
2021 DC	MIN	MLB	27	168	19	7	0	3	16	20	34	0	0	16.3%	.246/.347/.383	104	.299	0.2	LF 1, 1B 0	0.6

Comparables: César Puello, Shin-Soo Choo, Gabe Gross

You might say that LaMonte wade-d into the Twins lineup after a mid-August injury to Byron Buxton. He found the waters deep and choppy though, and will likely spend 2021 bobbing between Rochester and Minneapolis.

PITCHERS

Jorge Alcala RHP Born: 07/28/95 Age: 25 Bats: R Throws: R Height: 6'3" Weight: 205 Origin: International Free Agent, 2014

YEAR	TEAM	LVL	AGE	W	L	SV	G	GS	IP	H	HR	BB/9	K/9	K	GB%	BABIP	WHIP	ERA	DRA-	WARP	MPH	FA%	Whiff%	CSP
2018	FAY	HI-A	22	1	4	2	10	7	38²	25	2	4.2	10.5	45	45.7%	.256	1.11	3.03	70	0.9				
2018	CC	AA	22	2	3	1	9	5	40²	36	1	3.8	8.2	37	40.9%	.310	1.30	3.54	83	0.5				
2018	CHA	AA	22	0	4	0	5	4	20	23	4	6.3	9.9	22	31.7%	.339	1.85	5.85	107	0.0				
2019	PNS	AA	23	5	7	0	26	16	102²	114	12	3.2	9.2	105	37.6%	.355	1.47	5.87	129	-1.8				
2019	ROC	AAA	23	1	0	0	5	0	7²	4	0	2.3	12.9	11	53.3%	.267	0.78	0.00	38	0.3				
2019	MIN	MLB	23	0	0	0	2	0	1²	1	0	5.4	5.4	1	0.0%	.200	1.20	0.00	118	0.0	97.1	65.5%	35.7%	37.1%
2020	MIN	MLB	24	2	1	0	16	0	24	21	3	3.0	10.1	27	39.0%	.321	1.21	2.62	87	0.4	99.4	46.4%	32.2%	46.6%
2021 FS	MIN	MLB	25	2	2	0	57	0	50	44	6	4.6	9.4	52	39.0%	.288	1.41	4.36	101	0.1	99.3	47.3%	32.4%	46.2%
2021 DC	MIN	MLB	25	2	2	0	55	0	59	52	7	4.6	9.4	61	39.0%	.288	1.41	4.36	101	0.3	99.3	47.3%	32.4%	46.2%

Comparables: Hector Perez, Robert Dugger, Hunter Wood

The planet, country and sport of baseball are all barely recognizable vestiges of what we all took for granted five years ago. In this strange and less hospitable environment, it's nice to depend on certain things, no matter how trifling. This brings us to Alcala. At a time when even obscure prospects are seemingly six months of weighted-ball work from stardom, it's good that we can still count on some wild but promising righties to get a modest velocity bump in the bullpen after the whole five-walks-per-nine thing got them kicked out of a Triple-A rotation. It's even better when that in turn leads to a big-league promotion and a career of solid (if rarely spectacular) relief work.

Homer Bailey RHP Born: 05/03/86 Age: 35 Bats: R Throws: R Height: 6'4" Weight: 223 Origin: Round 1, 2004 Draft (#7 overall)

YEAR	TEAM	LVL	AGE	W	L	SV	G	GS	IP	H	HR	BB/9	K/9	K	GB%	BABIP	WHIP	ERA	DRA-	WARP	MPH	FA%	Whiff%	CSP
2018	LOU	AAA	32	2	2	0	7	6	37²	41	4	2.4	6.7	28	35.8%	.314	1.35	4.78	95	0.3				
2018	CIN	MLB	32	1	14	0	20	20	106¹	141	23	2.8	6.3	75	41.9%	.331	1.64	6.09	134	-0.9	95.3	56.0%	19.5%	49.6%
2019	OAK	MLB	33	6	3	0	13	13	73¹	73	9	1.8	8.3	68	42.8%	.302	1.20	4.30	75	1.6	95.1	52.5%	24.8%	50.2%
2019	KC	MLB	33	7	6	0	18	18	90	89	12	3.8	8.1	81	45.9%	.302	1.41	4.80	111	0.3	95.1	49.3%	23.5%	46.6%
2020	MIN	MLB	34	1	0	0	2	2	8	6	1	3.4	7.9	7	36.4%	.238	1.12	3.38	110	0.0	94.2	47.4%	23.4%	47.5%
2021 FS	MIN	MLB	35	8	9	0	26	26	150	157	24	3.1	7.6	126	43.0%	.299	1.39	4.67	112	0.0	95.1	51.8%	23.0%	48.5%

Comparables: Clay Buchholz, Ian Kennedy, Johnny Cueto

As much as anything, baseball in 2020 was an exercise in creative human resourcing. Thus, you could pay someone like Bailey $7 million to join your rotation, start him in the home opener, stick him onto the injured list for six weeks, recall him to make a critical start down the stretch and DFA him a few days later without really alienating anyone. Back in 2019, Bailey became the latest starter to enjoy newfound success after spamming his best offspeed pitch—a vanishing splitter—while curtailing his fastball usage. After such an abbreviated season, there's a chance he gets lost in the free-agent shuffle, but Bailey ought to retain the promising sheen he had 12 months ago.

Jordan Balazovic RHP Born: 09/17/98 Age: 22 Bats: R Throws: R Height: 6'5" Weight: 215 Origin: Round 5, 2016 Draft (#153 overall)

YEAR	TEAM	LVL	AGE	W	L	SV	G	GS	IP	H	HR	BB/9	K/9	K	GB%	BABIP	WHIP	ERA	DRA-	WARP	MPH	FA%	Whiff%	CSP
2018	CR	LO-A	19	7	3	0	12	11	61²	54	5	2.6	11.4	78	46.5%	.327	1.17	3.94	65	1.6				
2019	CR	LO-A	20	2	1	0	4	4	20²	15	1	1.7	14.4	33	42.2%	.318	0.92	2.18	40	0.8				
2019	FTM	HI-A	20	6	4	0	15	14	73	52	3	2.6	11.8	96	44.3%	.283	1.00	2.84	66	1.6				
2021 FS	MIN	MLB	22	1	2	0	57	0	50	47	7	3.8	9.6	53	38.2%	.299	1.38	4.69	115	-0.3				
2021 DC	MIN	MLB	22	1	2	0	6	6	29	27	4	3.8	9.6	30	38.2%	.299	1.38	4.69	115	0.1				

Comparables: Stephen Gonsalves, Lucas Giolito, Dustin May

Balazovic has never carried a starter's workload and he just lost a year to build arm strength. On paper, he has most of the ingredients we like in a back-end starter; but, between the lack of reps and a somewhat violent delivery, a future in the bullpen looks more likely than it did 12 months ago.

José Berríos RHP   Born: 05/27/94   Age: 27   Bats: R   Throws: R   Height: 6'0"   Weight: 205   Origin: Round 1, 2012 Draft (#32 overall)

YEAR	TEAM	LVL	AGE	W	L	SV	G	GS	IP	H	HR	BB/9	K/9	K	GB%	BABIP	WHIP	ERA	DRA-	WARP	MPH	FA%	Whiff%	CSP
2018	MIN	MLB	24	12	11	0	32	32	192¹	159	25	2.9	9.5	202	40.7%	.271	1.14	3.84	94	2.4	95.2	60.4%	26.0%	46.7%
2019	MIN	MLB	25	14	8	0	32	32	200¹	194	26	2.3	8.8	195	41.9%	.301	1.22	3.68	91	2.9	94.8	55.2%	23.3%	48.5%
2020	MIN	MLB	26	5	4	0	12	12	63	57	8	3.7	9.7	68	40.2%	.295	1.32	4.00	90	0.9	96.2	51.5%	27.4%	47.4%
2021 FS	MIN	MLB	27	9	8	0	26	26	150	134	20	3.2	9.6	159	41.1%	.290	1.25	3.78	91	1.8	95.3	55.5%	25.0%	47.8%
2021 DC	MIN	MLB	27	10	10	0	29	29	174	155	23	3.2	9.6	185	41.1%	.290	1.25	3.78	91	2.6	95.3	55.5%	25.0%	47.8%

Comparables: Jake Odorizzi, Zach Davies, Luke Weaver

Is Berríos an ace? The answer depends on how you define the term. While DRA isn't quite as enamored with his production as other third-order metrics, four consecutive durable years of sub-100 DRA- baseball comfortably makes him one of the 30 best starters in the game. On the scouting side of things, the definition tightens up considerably. To earn the "ace" label by the strictest criteria, you have to be one of the 10ish best pitchers and for that, Berríos would need to take another step forward. Catch him on the right day, when he's dotting his fastball and flummoxing hitters with the comically sweeping curve, and it looks possible. In the long run, we think he'll settle below that. He's a wee-bit too hittable to be a true No. 1, particularly given that the ungodly movement on his pitches leads to a fair amount of walks and traffic on the bases. None of this should be interpreted as a knock: No. 2 starters don't grow on trees and Berríos is fun as hell to watch. The Twins have a great one here, and fans should hope Derek Falvey and company are able to keep him in town for years to come.

Dakota Chalmers RHP   Born: 10/08/96   Age: 24   Bats: R   Throws: R   Height: 6'3"   Weight: 175   Origin: Round 3, 2015 Draft (#97 overall)

YEAR	TEAM	LVL	AGE	W	L	SV	G	GS	IP	H	HR	BB/9	K/9	K	GB%	BABIP	WHIP	ERA	DRA-	WARP	MPH	FA%	Whiff%	CSP
2019	TWI	ROK	22	1	0	0	4	4	13¹	8	0	5.4	12.8	19	64.0%	.320	1.20	4.05	48	0.5				
2019	FTM	HI-A	22	1	1	0	5	5	21¹	12	0	6.3	12.2	29	54.5%	.273	1.27	3.38	71	0.4				
2021 FS	MIN	MLB	24	1	1	0	57	0	50	44	8	9.1	10.8	60	41.3%	.293	1.90	6.59	137	-0.9				
2021 DC	MIN	MLB	24	1	1	0	33	0	35	30	5	9.1	10.8	42	41.3%	.293	1.90	6.59	137	-0.5				

Comparables: Albert Abreu, Nick Neidert, Demarcus Evans

Chalmers has three plus pitches and zero clue where any of them are going. The modern game's tolerance for "throw hard first, beg for forgiveness later" hurlers helped him land a spot on Minnesota's 40-man roster last season; perhaps he'll throw more strikes after the inevitable shift to the bullpen.

Tyler Clippard RHP   Born: 02/14/85   Age: 36   Bats: R   Throws: R   Height: 6'3"   Weight: 200   Origin: Round 9, 2003 Draft (#274 overall)

YEAR	TEAM	LVL	AGE	W	L	SV	G	GS	IP	H	HR	BB/9	K/9	K	GB%	BABIP	WHIP	ERA	DRA-	WARP	MPH	FA%	Whiff%	CSP
2018	TOR	MLB	33	4	3	7	73	1	68²	57	13	3.0	11.1	85	20.0%	.275	1.17	3.67	79	1.1	92.5	42.6%	31.7%	45.5%
2019	CLE	MLB	34	1	0	0	53	3	62	38	8	2.2	9.3	64	31.0%	.207	0.85	2.90	84	0.8	91.2	40.8%	28.2%	46.3%
2020	MIN	MLB	35	2	1	0	26	2	26	19	2	1.4	9.0	26	29.4%	.258	0.88	2.77	97	0.3	90.5	38.0%	28.3%	46.7%
2021 FS	MIN	MLB	36	2	2	0	57	0	50	40	7	3.1	9.3	51	29.7%	.259	1.16	3.32	86	0.5	91.4	40.5%	29.2%	46.2%

Comparables: Pedro Strop, Michael Gonzalez, Brian Fuentes

There were 35 pitchers who suited up for the 2011 All-Star Game. One of them is no longer with us. Two are in the Hall of Fame. Twenty-five were out of baseball in 2020. Only four are anywhere near as good now as they were nine years ago: Michael Pineda, Clayton Kershaw, Justin Verlander and Tyler Clippard. Intuitively, we all understand that it's hard to maintain such a high level of performance for a decade, but in the context of his All-Star peers, Clippard's run looks downright remarkable. There aren't many signs that he's slowing down, either. He just notched his third consecutive season with a WHIP below one and 11th straight year with an above average DRA-. He's maybe not the sexiest pitcher around (glasses notwithstanding) but history will remember him as one of the more under-appreciated players of the 2010s.

Randy Dobnak RHP   Born: 01/17/95   Age: 26   Bats: R   Throws: R   Height: 6'1"   Weight: 230   Origin: Undrafted Free Agent, 2017

YEAR	TEAM	LVL	AGE	W	L	SV	G	GS	IP	H	HR	BB/9	K/9	K	GB%	BABIP	WHIP	ERA	DRA-	WARP	MPH	FA%	Whiff%	CSP
2018	CR	LO-A	23	10	5	0	24	20	129	138	6	1.7	5.9	84	46.0%	.318	1.26	3.14	109	0.1				
2019	FTM	HI-A	24	3	0	0	4	4	22¹	18	0	1.6	5.6	14	57.6%	.273	0.99	0.40	77	0.3				
2019	PNS	AA	24	4	2	0	11	10	66²	58	6	0.8	8.2	61	59.1%	.281	0.96	2.56	75	1.0				
2019	ROC	AAA	24	5	2	0	9	7	46	28	0	3.5	6.7	34	60.2%	.220	1.00	2.15	50	1.8				
2019	MIN	MLB	24	2	1	1	9	5	28¹	27	1	1.6	7.3	23	54.0%	.302	1.13	1.59	94	0.3	94.5	59.0%	27.0%	46.5%
2020	MIN	MLB	25	6	4	0	10	10	46²	50	3	2.5	5.2	27	61.0%	.311	1.35	4.05	91	0.6	93.5	48.5%	20.6%	46.0%
2021 FS	MIN	MLB	26	9	9	0	26	26	150	158	16	3.3	6.6	110	57.1%	.302	1.42	4.60	105	0.6	93.7	51.4%	22.4%	46.1%
2021 DC	MIN	MLB	26	7	8	0	35	24	128	134	13	3.3	6.6	94	57.1%	.302	1.42	4.60	105	0.9	93.7	51.4%	22.4%	46.1%

Comparables: Kevin Gausman, Aaron Sanchez, Jhoulys Chacín

Dobnak's time in the spotlight came in 2019, and given that he went from substitute teacher to Marty Bystrom in the course of six months, it's hard to argue he didn't deserve it. While he actually pitched somewhat worse in 2020—inevitably, really, given the surface-level stats he racked up in 2019—10 average starts in his second spin through the league carries a lot more credibility than four miraculous ones out of nowhere. The low strikeout rate gives us some concern, but we're still pretty confident that he'll slot into the back-end of a rotation for at least a few seasons. He's what passes for a pitch-to-contact hurler these days, and while it seems a little off-key for a guy with Dobnak's background to wind up as a generic no. 4 starter, it sure beats the hell out of teaching algebra.

Tyler Duffey RHP Born: 12/27/90 Age: 30 Bats: R Throws: R Height: 6'3" Weight: 220 Origin: Round 5, 2012 Draft (#160 overall)

YEAR	TEAM	LVL	AGE	W	L	SV	G	GS	IP	H	HR	BB/9	K/9	K	GB%	BABIP	WHIP	ERA	DRA-	WARP	MPH	FA%	Whiff%	CSP
2018	ROC	AAA	27	4	4	3	31	0	59	48	5	3.1	9.6	63	42.5%	.283	1.15	2.90	88	0.5				
2018	MIN	MLB	27	2	2	0	19	1	25	26	6	1.4	6.8	19	34.9%	.260	1.20	7.20	120	-0.1	95.2	61.7%	22.5%	48.8%
2019	ROC	AAA	28	0	0	1	7	0	13²	8	0	3.3	14.5	22	44.0%	.333	0.95	1.32	48	0.5				
2019	MIN	MLB	28	5	1	0	58	0	57²	44	8	2.2	12.6	81	36.2%	.275	1.01	2.50	62	1.4	95.8	54.0%	33.2%	47.0%
2020	MIN	MLB	29	1	1	0	22	0	24	13	2	2.2	11.6	31	55.6%	.212	0.79	1.88	71	0.6	94.2	43.8%	36.4%	42.9%
2021 FS	MIN	MLB	30	2	2	12	57	0	50	42	6	2.7	10.8	60	44.7%	.293	1.15	3.28	82	0.6	95.2	51.7%	32.9%	45.9%
2021 DC	MIN	MLB	30	2	2	12	55	0	59	50	7	2.7	10.8	70	44.7%	.293	1.15	3.28	82	0.9	95.2	51.7%	32.9%	45.9%

Comparables: Chris Stratton, Erasmo Ramírez, Jordan Lyles

It was hard for a player to "prove" anything in 2020's condensed campaign, so let's just say that The Doof gave "strong indications" that his 2019 breakout was legitimate. If anything, he might be even a little better now, as Duffey managed to continue missing bats while suddenly turning into a ground ball machine. It's no coincidence that his numbers improved once he mothballed his change and started throwing curves every other pitch. Nobody has ever figured out how to hit his deuce, and by spamming it more often in 2020, hitters were in turn less prepared for the heat—which, in turn, helped it perform better than in years past even as he lost a tick of velocity. While it seems that he's been around forever now, he actually won't be a free agent until after 2023, so Twins fans can expect to see Duffey working in high-leverage situations for years to come.

Jhoan Duran RHP Born: 01/08/98 Age: 23 Bats: R Throws: R Height: 6'5" Weight: 230 Origin: International Free Agent, 2014

YEAR	TEAM	LVL	AGE	W	L	SV	G	GS	IP	H	HR	BB/9	K/9	K	GB%	BABIP	WHIP	ERA	DRA-	WARP	MPH	FA%	Whiff%	CSP
2018	CR	LO-A	20	2	1	0	6	6	36	19	2	2.5	11.0	44	66.2%	.218	0.81	2.00	55	1.1				
2018	KC	LO-A	20	5	4	0	15	15	64²	69	6	3.9	9.9	71	51.1%	.348	1.50	4.73	75	1.3				
2019	FTM	HI-A	21	2	9	0	16	15	78	63	5	3.6	11.0	95	51.6%	.317	1.21	3.23	90	0.6				
2019	PNS	AA	21	3	3	0	7	7	37	34	2	2.2	10.0	41	63.0%	.330	1.16	4.86	128	-0.6				
2021 FS	MIN	MLB	23	8	9	0	26	26	150	137	23	4.2	8.7	145	51.6%	.280	1.39	4.55	109	0.3				
2021 DC	MIN	MLB	23	2	2	0	8	8	34	31	5	4.2	8.7	32	51.6%	.280	1.39	4.55	109	0.2				

Comparables: Adonis Medina, Johan Oviedo, Huascar Ynoa

Duran was a consensus top-100 prospect entering 2020, an ascending arm blessed with 100-mph heat and two secondaries that should miss bats. After holding his own in Double-A the previous year, it was a bit surprising that the 23-year-old never got out of the alternate training site in '20, particularly given the trouble Minnesota had finding a stable fifth starter. Assuming nothing is amiss, he should be tracking for whatever constitutes a high-minors assignment this spring, and could debut as soon as this summer.

Rich Hill LHP Born: 03/11/80 Age: 41 Bats: L Throws: L Height: 6'5" Weight: 221 Origin: Round 4, 2002 Draft (#112 overall)

YEAR	TEAM	LVL	AGE	W	L	SV	G	GS	IP	H	HR	BB/9	K/9	K	GB%	BABIP	WHIP	ERA	DRA-	WARP	MPH	FA%	Whiff%	CSP
2018	LAD	MLB	38	11	5	0	25	24	132²	108	20	2.8	10.2	150	37.9%	.272	1.12	3.66	87	2.1	91.2	58.8%	24.8%	54.5%
2019	LAD	MLB	39	4	1	0	13	13	58²	48	10	2.8	11.0	72	47.3%	.284	1.12	2.45	69	1.5	92.2	52.6%	26.0%	56.1%
2020	MIN	MLB	40	2	2	0	8	8	38²	28	3	4.0	7.2	31	41.1%	.240	1.16	3.03	119	0.0	89.7	46.8%	16.0%	50.3%
2021 FS	MIN	MLB	41	9	8	0	26	26	150	131	18	3.3	9.6	159	43.0%	.288	1.24	3.52	88	2.1	91.1	53.0%	22.4%	53.7%

Comparables: Tom Gordon, LaTroy Hawkins, Dennis Eckersley

History has not been kind to those predicting Hill's demise. He's had Steve Blass disease and Tommy John surgery, suffered the indignity of a demotion from the Trembley-era Orioles, battled approximately a thousand blisters and yet here he is, still getting outs at the age of 40. So, with no small amount of trepidation: Hill looks like he's really slowing down. His sparkly ERA and FIP figures from last season are undercut by an alarming dip in strikeouts and uptick in walks. Under the hood, things look no better. He lost two ticks on his fastball, and his famously invincible curve wasn't quite so devastating. Traditionally, it's a pitch that steals strikes, induces grounders and draws a fair amount of whiffs to boot. Last year, hitters swung and missed far less and started hitting it in the air more often. A suspiciously low homer rate kept everything glued together, but that won't hold unless his velocity comes back. All told, he's the old man of the league, his stuff is in decline and he hasn't managed to average even five innings per start since 2018. He'll deservedly get another chance in 2021, but at long last, the end appears nigh.

Zack Littell RHP Born: 10/05/95 Age: 25 Bats: R Throws: R Height: 6'4" Weight: 220 Origin: Round 11, 2013 Draft (#327 overall)

YEAR	TEAM	LVL	AGE	W	L	SV	G	GS	IP	H	HR	BB/9	K/9	K	GB%	BABIP	WHIP	ERA	DRA-	WARP	MPH	FA%	Whiff%	CSP
2018	CHA	AA	22	0	3	0	5	5	23	28	3	2.7	12.5	32	34.4%	.446	1.52	5.87	78	0.4				
2018	ROC	AAA	22	6	6	0	19	15	106	100	5	3.4	8.3	98	39.5%	.310	1.32	3.57	86	1.4				
2018	MIN	MLB	22	0	2	0	8	2	20¹	25	3	4.9	6.2	14	43.1%	.324	1.77	6.20	149	-0.4	94.6	58.5%	17.9%	49.2%
2019	ROC	AAA	23	3	3	1	20	7	63	55	11	3.6	9.7	68	47.9%	.278	1.27	3.71	68	2.0				
2019	MIN	MLB	23	6	0	0	29	0	37	34	4	2.2	7.8	32	38.1%	.300	1.16	2.68	111	0.0	96.1	49.1%	27.3%	50.6%
2020	MIN	MLB	24	0	0	0	6	0	6¹	12	5	4.3	4.3	3	33.3%	.368	2.37	9.95	163	-0.2	95.8	54.7%	13.3%	53.5%
2021 FS	MIN	MLB	25	2	3	0	57	0	50	48	8	3.4	8.3	46	41.1%	.287	1.35	4.43	107	-0.1	95.7	52.3%	22.6%	50.8%

Comparables: Touki Toussaint, Kyle Ryan, Robert Gsellman

We're not sure whether Littell will spend most of his time hopping back and forth between the majors and Triple-A or the majors and an alternate training site; we're considerably more sure that he'll be hopping in either case.

Kenta Maeda RHP   Born: 04/11/88   Age: 33   Bats: R   Throws: R   Height: 6'1"   Weight: 185   Origin: International Free Agent, 2016

YEAR	TEAM	LVL	AGE	W	L	SV	G	GS	IP	H	HR	BB/9	K/9	K	GB%	BABIP	WHIP	ERA	DRA-	WARP	MPH	FA%	Whiff%	CSP
2018	LAD	MLB	30	8	10	2	39	20	125¹	115	13	3.1	11.0	153	39.9%	.323	1.26	3.81	62	3.6	93.5	44.4%	31.8%	46.1%
2019	LAD	MLB	31	10	8	3	37	26	153²	114	22	3.0	9.9	169	39.5%	.245	1.07	4.04	67	4.1	93.9	37.3%	32.6%	45.4%
2020	MIN	MLB	32	6	1	0	11	11	66²	40	9	1.4	10.8	80	47.5%	.208	0.75	2.70	74	1.5	93.5	25.9%	34.8%	43.9%
2021 FS	MIN	MLB	33	10	6	0	26	26	150	115	16	2.5	10.3	172	43.8%	.272	1.06	2.53	66	4.0	93.7	35.3%	33.1%	45.1%
2021 DC	MIN	MLB	33	10	7	0	27	27	156	120	16	2.5	10.3	179	43.8%	.272	1.06	2.53	66	4.5	93.7	35.3%	33.1%	45.1%

Comparables: Carlos Carrasco, Jacob deGrom, Corey Kluber

The idea that a player can be "underrated" is a fraught and tired concept, but Maeda never really received his due as one of the better pitchers in baseball during his Dodgers days. For all their success and competence, Los Angeles never quite seemed to appreciate what they had here. Despite averaging about four WARP per season, the Dodgers shuttled Maeda between the rotation and bullpen throughout his time in town, and they dealt him and his absurdly affordable contract to Minnesota for bullpen help last winter. Brusdar Graterol was a fine pick-up, of course, but even the best of relievers look a little underwhelming compared to a guy who finished second in the Cy Young balloting. Given a permanent spot in the rotation, Maeda thrived in the Twin Cities. He led the league in WHIP, struck out nearly a third of the hitters he faced and finally saw his ERA catch up to his peripherals. He may not be the second best pitcher in the AL going forward, but it should come as no surprise if he's in the top 10 or 15. It's familiar turf for him, after all.

Jake Odorizzi RHP   Born: 03/27/90   Age: 31   Bats: R   Throws: R   Height: 6'2"   Weight: 190   Origin: Round 1, 2008 Draft (#32 overall)

YEAR	TEAM	LVL	AGE	W	L	SV	G	GS	IP	H	HR	BB/9	K/9	K	GB%	BABIP	WHIP	ERA	DRA-	WARP	MPH	FA%	Whiff%	CSP
2018	MIN	MLB	28	7	10	0	32	32	164¹	151	20	3.8	8.9	162	28.2%	.293	1.34	4.49	125	-0.6	92.9	54.3%	24.8%	42.2%
2019	MIN	MLB	29	15	7	0	30	30	159	139	16	3.0	10.1	178	34.3%	.305	1.21	3.51	86	2.7	94.3	57.8%	27.9%	45.4%
2020	MIN	MLB	30	0	1	0	4	4	13²	16	4	2.0	7.9	12	34.9%	.308	1.39	6.59	117	0.0	94.1	41.8%	19.9%	45.0%
2021 FS	MIN	MLB	31	9	8	0	26	26	150	131	24	3.7	9.2	153	35.0%	.272	1.28	3.91	98	1.3	93.9	55.2%	26.2%	44.3%

Comparables: Ervin Santana, Nathan Eovaldi, Anthony DeSclafani

Odorizzi took a qualifying offer in lieu of hitting free agency last winter. That choice seemed reasonable back then but aged like an investment in downtown real estate. The long-dormant hot stove sparked to life days after the right-hander pledged to stay with the Twins, so instead of cashing in on a career year, he'll now have to test the waters in a market that will almost certainly be far less player-friendly. To make matters worse, his All-Star 2019 feels like a distant memory. In 2020, he was only healthy enough to make four forgettable starts, playing a bit role on Minnesota's division-winning club. Whoever ultimately wins the Odorizzi stands to pick up a pretty good pitcher at a very affordable price.

Michael Pineda RHP   Born: 01/18/89   Age: 32   Bats: R   Throws: R   Height: 6'7"   Weight: 280   Origin: International Free Agent, 2005

YEAR	TEAM	LVL	AGE	W	L	SV	G	GS	IP	H	HR	BB/9	K/9	K	GB%	BABIP	WHIP	ERA	DRA-	WARP	MPH	FA%	Whiff%	CSP
2018	FTM	HI-A	29	0	0	0	2	2	6	7	0	0.0	6.0	4	35.0%	.350	1.17	1.50	83	0.1				
2019	MIN	MLB	30	11	5	0	26	26	146	141	23	1.7	8.6	140	35.1%	.294	1.16	4.01	97	1.6	94.8	55.5%	25.7%	49.2%
2020	MIN	MLB	31	2	0	0	5	5	26²	25	0	2.4	8.4	25	37.2%	.321	1.20	3.38	86	0.4	94.1	50.1%	29.3%	48.2%
2021 FS	MIN	MLB	32	9	8	0	26	26	150	146	22	2.3	8.6	143	39.3%	.296	1.23	3.94	97	1.3	94.7	54.3%	26.5%	49.0%
2021 DC	MIN	MLB	32	8	8	0	24	24	131	127	19	2.3	8.6	125	39.3%	.296	1.23	3.94	97	1.6	94.7	54.3%	26.5%	49.0%

Comparables: Masahiro Tanaka, Stephen Strasburg, Ricky Nolasco

Pineda has lived a full baseball life. A top prospect, he burst onto the scene as a rookie flamethrower, earning an All-Star nod in his first season. He was then dealt to the sport's most historic franchise in a blockbuster deal, only to miss two seasons with shoulder problems. Since then, he hasn't always been great, but he sure has been notable: Rotation savior, pine-tar user, strikeout rate leader, booed out of the Bronx, missed another year on the shelf and, finally, emerged on the other side as a dependable starter in Minnesota. Last season, he channeled the home-run suppressing form of the earliest days of his career, as he was the only pitcher in 2020 to start multiple games and not allow a home run. He no longer resembles the flamethrower he was in his youth, but as he's matured, he's learned how to work off of his slider and change. Pineda's a better pitcher for it, and a reminder that, for starters especially, velocity isn't everything.

Hansel Robles RHP   Born: 08/13/90   Age: 30   Bats: R   Throws: R   Height: 6'0"   Weight: 220   Origin: International Free Agent, 2008

YEAR	TEAM	LVL	AGE	W	L	SV	G	GS	IP	H	HR	BB/9	K/9	K	GB%	BABIP	WHIP	ERA	DRA-	WARP	MPH	FA%	Whiff%	CSP
2018	LV	AAA	27	0	0	2	8	0	7²	7	1	5.9	8.2	7	60.9%	.273	1.57	3.52	104	0.0				
2018	LAA	MLB	27	0	1	2	37	0	36¹	32	2	3.7	8.9	36	39.2%	.303	1.29	2.97	109	0.0	98.7	67.5%	27.3%	49.6%
2018	NYM	MLB	27	2	2	0	16	0	19²	21	7	4.6	10.5	23	25.9%	.304	1.58	5.03	83	0.3	97.3	69.0%	25.5%	50.7%
2019	LAA	MLB	28	5	1	23	71	1	72²	58	6	2.0	9.3	75	38.0%	.283	1.02	2.48	75	1.3	99.0	56.3%	26.9%	49.6%
2020	LAA	MLB	29	0	2	1	18	0	16²	19	4	5.4	10.8	20	32.7%	.341	1.74	10.26	108	0.1	97.6	52.1%	30.7%	48.1%
2021 FS	MIN	MLB	30	2	2	0	57	0	50	43	7	3.9	9.6	53	35.9%	.280	1.30	4.25	96	0.2	98.6	58.0%	27.7%	49.3%
2021 DC	MIN	MLB	30	2	2	0	55	0	59	51	8	3.9	9.6	63	35.9%	.280	1.30	4.25	96	0.5	98.6	58.0%	27.7%	49.3%

Comparables: Shawn Armstrong, Evan Marshall, Nick Wittgren

Robles took a big step back after being one of the league's best relievers in 2019, as his walk and home run rates overcorrected from his career year. But frankly, if you weren't expecting this, the "fool me twice" rule comes into effect. Not that Robles had been that good before, but his control vacillates more than a Mariah Carey vocal range showcase. In terms of lyrics, the newly minted 30-year-old is more Vampire Weekend: "Nobody knows what the future holds / It's bad enough just getting old." On the wrong side of the age hill, the Twins, who inked him over the winter, will tolerate Robles' inconsistency less and less moving forward even if the velocity recovers.

Taylor Rogers LHP Born: 12/17/90 Age: 30 Bats: L Throws: L Height: 6'3" Weight: 190 Origin: Round 11, 2012 Draft (#340 overall)

YEAR	TEAM	LVL	AGE	W	L	SV	G	GS	IP	H	HR	BB/9	K/9	K	GB%	BABIP	WHIP	ERA	DRA-	WARP	MPH	FA%	Whiff%	CSP
2018	MIN	MLB	27	1	2	2	72	0	68¹	49	3	2.1	9.9	75	43.7%	.282	0.95	2.63	74	1.3	95.2	53.0%	27.1%	51.5%
2019	MIN	MLB	28	2	4	30	60	0	69	58	8	1.4	11.7	90	49.7%	.312	1.00	2.61	57	1.9	96.2	50.1%	26.2%	53.8%
2020	MIN	MLB	29	2	4	9	21	0	20	26	2	1.8	10.8	24	43.5%	.400	1.50	4.05	81	0.4	95.8	54.5%	23.6%	55.7%
2021 FS	MIN	MLB	30	2	2	28	57	0	50	45	6	2.3	10.0	55	46.4%	.301	1.16	3.34	83	0.6	95.9	51.9%	25.7%	53.7%
2021 DC	MIN	MLB	30	2	2	28	55	0	59	53	7	2.3	10.0	65	46.4%	.301	1.16	3.34	83	0.9	95.9	51.9%	25.7%	53.7%

Comparables: Dylan Floro, Andrew Chafin, Tyler Duffey

As a general principle, you shouldn't place too much emphasis on 2020 numbers, for obvious reasons. With Rogers though, there are some underlying indicators that suggest he's taken a step backward. First, his velocity dropped. His average fastball velocity didn't dip much, but he lost more than a tick and a half off his slider from 2019, and not surprisingly batters fared much better against it in 2020. He's also now a two-pitch pitcher. The curve had long been one of his best offerings, but he's felt less comfortable throwing it in recent seasons and all but shelved it last year. More predictability and lower velocity is a bad combination, and if it's the new normal, Minnesota probably shouldn't count on him as their relief ace anymore.

Sergio Romo RHP Born: 03/04/83 Age: 38 Bats: R Throws: R Height: 5'11" Weight: 185 Origin: Round 28, 2005 Draft (#852 overall)

YEAR	TEAM	LVL	AGE	W	L	SV	G	GS	IP	H	HR	BB/9	K/9	K	GB%	BABIP	WHIP	ERA	DRA-	WARP	MPH	FA%	Whiff%	CSP
2018	TB	MLB	35	3	4	25	73	5	67¹	65	11	2.7	10.0	75	36.6%	.312	1.26	4.14	62	1.7	87.7	30.1%	31.9%	44.0%
2019	MIA	MLB	36	2	0	17	38	0	37²	33	4	3.1	7.9	33	36.4%	.274	1.22	3.58	118	-0.2	87.4	26.2%	30.1%	43.0%
2019	MIN	MLB	36	0	1	3	27	0	22²	17	3	1.6	10.7	27	35.0%	.246	0.93	3.18	55	0.6	87.3	22.0%	30.6%	41.3%
2020	MIN	MLB	37	1	2	5	24	0	20	16	3	3.1	10.3	23	31.5%	.255	1.15	4.05	109	0.1	86.7	25.8%	28.6%	41.1%
2021 FS	MIN	MLB	38	2	2	0	57	0	50	44	6	2.7	9.0	50	36.4%	.281	1.19	3.41	87	0.5	87.3	26.3%	30.3%	42.5%

Comparables: Trevor Hoffman, Tom Henke, Rafael Betancourt

Like an ultimate frisbee player vainly chasing a disc, batters are still reaching for Romo's slider and catching nothing but air. You would think the best players in the world would have cracked this particular case by now: Romo's only weapon is a long but relatively slow sweeping breaking ball. Odds are, if it starts on one side of the plate, it's going to end up on the other. If you're a lefty and it looks like it'll fly over the adjacent batter's box, dust off your "slap this one foul" swing, because it's probably coming in the back door. And if he tries to catch you flat-footed with a fastball...well, it's only 85 mph these days and, as all the Twitter experts have decided, eighty-poo is nothing to sweat. The veteran keeps ticking along though, and while you could speculate that a slight velo downtick is cause for concern, we're not ready to do so. Father Time comes for 'em all eventually, but Romo struck out more than 10 per nine, suggesting he still has another year or two in the tank.

Devin Smeltzer LHP Born: 09/07/95 Age: 25 Bats: R Throws: L Height: 6'3" Weight: 195 Origin: Round 5, 2016 Draft (#161 overall)

YEAR	TEAM	LVL	AGE	W	L	SV	G	GS	IP	H	HR	BB/9	K/9	K	GB%	BABIP	WHIP	ERA	DRA-	WARP	MPH	FA%	Whiff%	CSP
2018	CHA	AA	22	0	0	4	10	0	12	14	0	1.5	12.0	16	30.6%	.400	1.33	3.00	63	0.3				
2018	TUL	AA	22	5	5	0	23	14	83²	94	9	2.0	7.2	67	37.2%	.323	1.35	4.73	85	1.0				
2019	PNS	AA	23	3	1	0	5	5	30	19	0	0.9	9.9	33	42.3%	.268	0.73	0.60	54	0.8				
2019	ROC	AAA	23	1	4	0	15	14	74¹	68	14	2.3	8.6	71	37.6%	.274	1.17	3.63	80	2.0				
2019	MIN	MLB	23	2	2	1	11	6	49	50	8	2.2	7.0	38	37.7%	.294	1.27	3.86	114	0.0	90.8	45.8%	20.7%	49.3%
2020	MIN	MLB	24	2	0	0	7	1	16	19	2	2.8	8.4	15	35.3%	.354	1.50	6.75	118	0.0	89.1	33.2%	25.0%	48.0%
2021 FS	MIN	MLB	25	8	9	0	26	26	150	151	26	2.7	8.3	139	37.7%	.294	1.31	4.57	109	0.3	90.2	41.3%	22.2%	48.9%
2021 DC	MIN	MLB	25	6	8	0	22	22	113	114	20	2.7	8.3	104	37.7%	.294	1.31	4.57	109	0.6	90.2	41.3%	22.2%	48.9%

Comparables: Ranger Suárez, Nestor Cortes, Lewis Thorpe

Aesthetically, Smeltzer brings the funk. He starts his delivery by gyrating toward second base and then sharply merry-go-rounding his way to the plate, which has the effect of a man trying to dislocate his pitching shoulder and stab his catcher at the same time. Everything's a bit less interesting once the ball leaves his hand. The southpaw lacks a plus secondary to buttress mediocre velocity and if he's to have a long career, he'll need to survive on guile and deception.

Cody Stashak RHP Born: 06/04/94 Age: 27 Bats: R Throws: R Height: 6'2" Weight: 180 Origin: Round 13, 2015 Draft (#380 overall)

YEAR	TEAM	LVL	AGE	W	L	SV	G	GS	IP	H	HR	BB/9	K/9	K	GB%	BABIP	WHIP	ERA	DRA-	WARP	MPH	FA%	Whiff%	CSP
2018	CHA	AA	24	1	1	4	35	2	55²	47	4	2.1	11.2	69	31.2%	.321	1.08	2.75	68	1.2				
2019	PNS	AA	25	2	3	4	19	0	28¹	28	4	1.6	12.7	40	27.4%	.353	1.16	4.76	107	-0.2				
2019	ROC	AAA	25	5	0	0	14	2	25	17	1	1.4	12.2	34	40.7%	.276	0.84	1.44	47	1.0				
2019	MIN	MLB	25	0	1	0	18	1	25	29	3	0.4	9.0	25	24.7%	.351	1.20	3.24	119	-0.1	93.0	54.0%	31.1%	54.7%
2020	MIN	MLB	26	1	0	0	11	0	15	11	2	1.8	10.2	17	37.8%	.257	0.93	3.00	89	0.2	93.1	55.1%	29.9%	42.7%
2021 FS	MIN	MLB	27	2	2	0	57	0	50	44	8	2.7	10.2	56	32.1%	.286	1.19	3.79	94	0.3	93.1	54.5%	30.5%	48.9%
2021 DC	MIN	MLB	27	2	2	0	55	0	59	52	10	2.7	10.2	66	32.1%	.286	1.19	3.79	94	0.5	93.1	54.5%	30.5%	48.9%

Comparables: Jonathan Holder, Erick Fedde, Wes Parsons

A scoop of mint chip in a sugar cone. A 2004 Honda Accord. An empty parking space two aisles from the door. Blue Moon. A Lyft ride with a driver who sprayed only one bottle of Axe in their Prius. The Arizona State Sun Devils football team. Junior Mints. The Cars. Sixty-one degrees with the sun just poking through. Ticket to Ride. Movie theaters. Kauffman Stadium. A 25-minute bike ride. Cody Stashak.

Caleb Thielbar LHP Born: 01/31/87 Age: 34 Bats: R Throws: L Height: 6'0" Weight: 205 Origin: Round 18, 2009 Draft (#556 overall)

YEAR	TEAM	LVL	AGE	W	L	SV	G	GS	IP	H	HR	BB/9	K/9	K	GB%	BABIP	WHIP	ERA	DRA-	WARP	MPH	FA%	Whiff%	CSP
2018	ERI	AA	31	3	0	0	27	0	38	28	1	0.7	9.5	40	35.6%	.273	0.82	1.42	70	0.7				
2018	TOL	AAA	31	4	1	0	12	0	19	20	2	0.9	5.2	11	38.1%	.295	1.16	3.32	73	0.3				
2019	TOL	AAA	32	2	1	4	50	0	76¹	74	7	1.9	10.8	92	38.1%	.345	1.18	3.30	72	2.0				
2020	MIN	MLB	33	2	1	0	17	0	20	14	0	4.0	9.9	22	27.5%	.275	1.15	2.25	97	0.2	92.1	54.4%	29.4%	50.7%
2021 FS	MIN	MLB	34	2	2	0	57	0	50	45	7	2.9	9.0	49	36.6%	.285	1.23	3.75	92	0.3	92.1	54.4%	29.4%	50.7%
2021 DC	MIN	MLB	34	2	2	0	55	0	59	53	8	2.9	9.0	58	36.6%	.285	1.23	3.75	92	0.6	92.1	54.4%	29.4%	50.7%

Comparables: Sam Freeman, Javy Guerra, Ryan Buchter

While it's not quite as improbable as Daniel Bard's comeback in Colorado, Thielbar's return from the wilderness is a great story in its own right. After years of injuries and bus rides and Triple-A hotels, the lefty finally called it quits after 2019 and took a job as Augustana University's pitching coach. It proved to be a quick stint on campus. Minnesota coaxed him to Fort Myers to give the mound one more shot, which proved an excellent decision for all parties, as Thielbar recaptured his 2013-14 form and emerged as a solid contributor in the Twins bullpen. He's not quite a late-inning guy— his lone hold came in the sixth inning— but regardless of his ultimate role, his ascension from D-II coach to major league reliever is one of the better things to come out of 2020—unless you pitch for the Vikings, perhaps.

Lewis Thorpe LHP Born: 11/23/95 Age: 25 Bats: R Throws: L Height: 6'1" Weight: 218 Origin: International Free Agent, 2012

YEAR	TEAM	LVL	AGE	W	L	SV	G	GS	IP	H	HR	BB/9	K/9	K	GB%	BABIP	WHIP	ERA	DRA-	WARP	MPH	FA%	Whiff%	CSP
2018	CHA	AA	22	8	4	0	22	21	108	105	13	2.5	10.9	131	37.1%	.329	1.25	3.58	82	1.8				
2018	ROC	AAA	22	0	3	0	4	4	21²	20	3	2.5	10.8	26	42.9%	.321	1.20	3.32	78	0.4				
2019	ROC	AAA	23	5	4	0	20	19	96¹	91	13	2.3	11.1	119	39.9%	.322	1.20	4.58	72	2.9				
2019	MIN	MLB	23	3	2	0	12	2	27²	38	3	3.3	10.1	31	34.9%	.438	1.73	6.18	109	0.0	93.3	50.0%	27.9%	48.7%
2020	MIN	MLB	24	0	1	0	7	1	16¹	24	4	5.5	5.5	10	35.1%	.377	2.08	6.06	180	-0.6	92.3	47.4%	20.7%	50.7%
2021 FS	MIN	MLB	25	9	9	0	26	26	150	142	23	3.8	8.8	147	37.6%	.290	1.37	4.41	105	0.7	92.9	48.8%	24.6%	49.6%
2021 DC	MIN	MLB	25	5	6	0	46	12	96	91	14	3.8	8.8	94	37.6%	.290	1.37	4.41	105	0.6	92.9	48.8%	24.6%	49.6%

Comparables: Justus Sheffield, Cionel Pérez, Ranger Suárez

In 2019, Thorpe was a feel-good story, a perennially injured prospect who finally put his arm troubles behind him and made his big-league debut. In 2020? Well, at least there weren't any fans around to see it.

Not With an Eruption, But With a Tweet

by Eric Nusbaum

In the late 1980s, two pals decided that what they wanted more than anything in the world was to own a minor-league baseball team. Jerry Walker and Bill Tucker loved baseball in the kind of way that inspires monologues in Kevin Costner movies. Walker lived in Oregon and Tucker in New York. They met in Florida, at a fantasy camp hosted by Mickey Mantle and Whitey Ford. And in 1989, they became the proud owners of the Bellingham Mariners.

In 1997, after the Mariners had swapped their Northwest League affiliation for Everett, Wash., Walker and Tucker took up with the Giants and moved down the freeway to Keizer, Oregon, a newly incorporated city bordering the state capital of Salem. Keizer provided the land and the public works necessary to build a ballpark, and the newly christened Volcanoes paid for the construction privately.

It was a beautiful thing: a successful public-private partnership. It was baseball as an organic, local family business. On opening night, the mayor of Keizer was lowered onto the field via helicopter to throw out the first pitch. A sellout crowd of 5,000 filled Volcanoes Stadium. The game was rained out, but the future was bright. The region had a long tradition of minor-league ball dating back to the Oregon State League in 1904. But with the Volcanoes, it felt like a community was being born.

⚾　　⚾　　⚾

The Salem-Keizer Volcanoes were 26 years old when they were fatally tweeted into something like oblivion by the social media department of the major league franchise they had once called partners.

That was in December. The Giants' tweet went like this:

OFFICIAL: The following 4 teams have been invited to join our player development system as part of the new affiliates agreement with @MLB

- *Sacramento River Cats (AAA)*
- *Richmond Flying Squirrels (AA)*
- *Eugene Emeralds (Class A Advanced)*
- *San Jose Giants (Class A)*

Suddenly, where Major League Baseball and the Giants were concerned, it was as if the Salem-Keizer Volcanoes no longer existed—as if they never had.

The Volcanoes were a Low-A club in a relatively sparsely populated part of the country. Unless you lived in Oregon's Willamette Valley or had a deep vested interest in the success of the youngest and rawest of Giants prospects, the Volcanoes would have been just another team—a small thread in the fabric of minor-league baseball in America, which is itself just one small thread in the fabric of a great big country.

The Volcanoes are one of 42 minor-league franchises that were deemed superfluous as Major League Baseball reorganized its player-development system into a pattern that would fit more neatly onto a PowerPoint slide than the sprawling ecosystem that preceded it.

The changes—in Salem-Keizer and in baseball at large—did not come as a complete surprise. Word got out in December of 2019 that some clubs might be losing their affiliation. Volcanoes management spent the entirety of the COVID-19 pandemic struggling to survive as a business while seeking out some sense from MLB and their parent Giants of what their future might look like. For months, they were put off and put off. "We don't know anything. We don't know what the future looks like. We don't know what's going to happen." Finally, they learned of their fate—not one of the minor-league clubs "invited" to affiliate with the Giants for the 2021 season—via tweet.

In the weeks afterwards, members of the Giants front office still didn't return phone calls, emails or texts from Salem-Keizer.

To MLB and its 30 clubs, the consolidation of the minor leagues from a freeform mass of semi-independent outposts into an efficient, orderly extension of the league itself was merely a business decision. Help the bottom line, etc. But the thing is, baseball is not merely a business. And even if it were—MLB is not the only business *in* baseball.

The remaking of the minors will forever alter the balance of power in the relationships between parent clubs and affiliates across the country—a balance that was always precarious, even in the best of times. It will consolidate more of the "brand" of pro baseball in the hands of a company that for all the fan surveys and consultant-driven moves has proven to be blithely unaware of what fans actually like about the sport. And it will devastate individual clubs like the Volcanoes, communities like Salem-Keizer and families across the country—and perhaps, in the long run, devastate the sport of baseball itself. All for the sake of short-term profits and efficiency.

⚾   ⚾   ⚾

The Volcanoes have always been a family operation to their core. In the beginning, Jerry Walker and his wife Lisa operated the team while Tucker lived most of the year in New York. Their son Mickey was born just after their inaugural season ended. Now Mickey is 23 years old, and the Volcanoes CEO.

"I always say I've done every single job there is to do in a minor-league ballpark, starting at six years old shagging home run balls during batting practice to concessions to cleanup crew to the front office to mascots to bat boy—I've done it all. I've been involved in basically every aspect since I was old enough to use the restroom by myself."

Mickey Walker literally grew up with the franchise. He watched the Volcanoes mature into an institution and the city of Keizer fill out around the ballpark. "When we came in '97 there was farmland surrounding the stadium," he said. "It almost felt like a field of dreams kind of thing. You had to drive through a wheat field just to get to the stadium."

Now there's a giant shopping center down the street—constructed only after the ballpark established the area as a commercial destination. There's even an In-N-Out Burger, and when it first opened, the waiting cars queued up in the stadium parking lot.

Mickey saw future Giants stars like Sergio Romo and Pablo Sandoval come through when he was just a boy—plus cameo appearances from the likes of Buster Posey and Tim Lincecum. The Volcanoes of the mid-aughts were dominant, predicting the good things to come in San Francisco. Of course winning at the minor-league level doesn't necessarily mean anything when it comes to future big-league results. But the Giants and Volcanoes had a good relationship. There was open communication and a sense that both sides were helping one another.

To run a minor-league franchise is to make one compromise after another. On one hand, you want to win for your fans—but, on the other, you realize that you are not in control of the players on the roster. On one hand, you are charged with the well-being and development of players with millions of dollars invested into them; on the other hand, you are a small business with narrow margins and you don't necessarily have the resources to treat them as a major-league club might hope.

The most successful minor-league clubs create a positive culture. They create a community that players want to be a part of; that they feel they can succeed in. This is what the Volcanoes established as the first stop for many Giants prospects. The first place where they'd put on a pro baseball uniform and the first place where they'd play with wooden bats in front of pro baseball fans.

"It really was a great entry for our minor-league players into the Giants organization to go somewhere that they could compete year in and year out," said Bobby Evans, former longtime Giants executive.

When the Giants were at the peak of their powers, Evans even invited Mickey Walker down to San Francisco to work as a bat boy for a series. Walker was a gangly teenager by then. When he showed up in the clubhouse, he was immediately recognized by Sandoval and Romo who started reminiscing about the good old days in Salem-Keizer.

⚾   ⚾   ⚾

In many ways, the Salem-Keizer Volcanoes have been exactly what a minor-league team is supposed to be: creative and corny and a perfect fit for their community. In 2017, the team started a game at 9:30 AM, then distributed glasses to fans so that they could hold baseball's first-ever solar eclipse delay. They're involved in local charities. You can rent out Volcanoes Stadium on AirBnB. When wildfires ravaged Oregon last summer, the team volunteered the stadium as a shelter for evacuees.

In other words, the Volcanoes are not just a baseball team and their stadium is not just a building. It acts as a second home, a gathering place for a city. Baseball isn't even the point. Community is the point. Bill Post is an original Volcanoes season-ticket holder and a former radio DJ in Salem-Keizer, and he spent more than a decade as the team's PA announcer. Now he represents the town of Keizer in the Oregon state house.

"You didn't go to Volcanoes stadium to watch baseball," he said. "You went to hang out with Bob and Sue and Joe and Fred, have a beer and a hot dog. And the baseball is kind of a side thing."

Which brings us to the present moment in which we are reminded that the Volcanoes may not just be a baseball team, but they are definitely that. For as long as they have been in Salem-Keizer, they have been a part of the official pro baseball ecosystem: their roster filled out by the Giants, their opponents' rosters filled out by other big-league clubs. And as such, their fate has been determined by the forces that are guiding the entire sport. Now, they are left on their own: with no parent club to help cover costs and few fellow franchises with which they could theoretically band together to start over. The Northwest League is moving on without them.

The Volcanoes were born of baseball's joyful innocence: they are the product of a friendship that spanned the entire continental U.S. and was built on a mutual love of the sport. Their demise—at least as a part of affiliated ball—comes steeped in baseball's truly American cynicism.

Last year Pat O'Conner, the president of Minor League Baseball, appeared at the Northwest League's annual meetings. This was before the COVID-19 pandemic gave baseball a pretense for what was to come. O'Connor shared with the Northwest League owners that MLB was considering eliminating short season A-ball altogether; considering cutting 42 minor-league franchises.

"It was one of the most shocking days of my life personally—and probably a lot of other people's," said Walker. "He kind of said it and everyone looked at each other like, 'Is this a joke? Are you serious?'"

But he was serious. Volcanoes management began their year-long search for clarity, even as the pandemic shut down their season. All those "we don't know yets" began to add up. Even Post, the PA-announcer-turned-state-rep tried to step in on their behalf, firing off missives on his official Oregon State House letterhead.

Nothing worked. In the end, there was not even an explanation. The reasons remained unspoken. None of it was a secret. Major League Baseball believes it can cut costs; its franchises believe they can take advantage of analytics to evaluate from a smaller pool of talent; the sport can reach audiences and develop young fans in markets like Salem-Keizer through social media and online broadcasting. All of it leaves more control in the commissioner's office. All of it leaves more control with the parent franchises. None of it helps the people of Salem-Keizer.

"I don't think their goal going into this was 'we're going to screw over 42 communities'," said Mickey Walker. "I don't think that's what they thought. I think they knew that was going to be the byproduct. They saw an opportunity to save money, they saw a way to do it and they were able to pull it off."

As the holidays passed by and the calendar flipped to 2021, the Walker family began to plot out what an independent baseball future might look like in Salem-Keizer. The Giants still had not called back. MLB was not offering any meaningful help. But Volcanoes Stadium would not sit empty.

The Volcanoes were born because two baseball-loving buddies desperately wanted to own a ballclub. And it was baseball that Jerry Walker and Bill Tucker loved—not one particular vision of the sport, or one particular business plan. The club has succeeded for a quarter century with ingenuity, with sincerity and with community. And those are the forces that will propel baseball in Salem-Keizer forward without MLB, without the Giants, without the Northwest League. The plan, according to Mickey Walker, is to build something bigger. Instead of being a franchise without a home, the Volcanoes will simply become the home. They're starting their own league. ■

—Eric Nusbaum is the author of Stealing Home: Los Angeles, the Dodgers, and the Lives Caught in Between.

ARIZONA DIAMONDBACKS

Essay by Grant Brisbee

Player comments by Jeff Wiser and BP staff

The name of the game show is "Hiccup ... or the New Normal?", or at least that's what it reads on the two-foot-high neon letters behind you. You're standing behind a podium, not sure how you got there. The lighting is calibrated wrong and oriented directly into your eyeballs. As you grimace and shield your eyes, you look around and realize that you're being watched. The host, the contestants next to you, the studio audience ... they're all staring at you, half-annoyed, half-amused and expecting you to say something.

"The Arizona Diamondbacks...", the host says, trying to prompt you. You stare back, trying to reconstruct the last few hours.

You have regrets about eating the packet of powdered gravy you found in the parking lot.

"The Arizona..." he says again, this time followed by a pause, as if it's the very idea of the state of Arizona that's confusing you, which is understandable.

"...Diamondbacks," he finishes.

Oh. You get it. You're supposed to answer the question. Hiccup? Or the new normal? The studio audience shouts along with the second sentence when the host says it. It's a nice touch.

On August 18th, the Arizona Diamondbacks beat the Oakland Athletics, 10-1. They stood two games over .500, with a 13-11 record, firmly in postseason position. It's where most observers expected them to be all along. They were contenders.

On September 9th, they lost to the Dodgers in extra innings. They were 15-29. You don't have to be a mathemagician to realize exactly how horribly they had screwed up over those 22 days. They had won two games and lost a billionty. Even by the standards of 2020, those must have been three looooooooooooooooooooong weeks.

Hiccup? Or the new normal? The applause sign lights up. The studio audience goes wild.

Start with the basic concept that we all understand: You get to ignore 2020 entirely, in every facet of life, in every context, for the rest of eternity. It never existed. If you were born in 2000, you will celebrate your 21st birthday in 2022,

ARIZONA DIAMONDBACKS PROSPECTUS

2020 W-L: 25-35, 5TH IN NL WEST

Pythag	.456	23rd	dWin%	.386	25th
RS/G	4.48	19th	B-Age	29.7	27th
RA/G	4.92	17th	P-Age	28.0	18th
DRC+	95	20th	FIP	4.99	23rd
DRA-	111	26th	DER	.697	19th
Payroll	$57M	15th	M$/MW	$5.6M	23rd

407'

376'   376'

330'   335'

- Opened 1998
- Retractable roof
- Synthetic surface
- Fence profile: 7'6" to 25'

Three-Year Park Factors

Runs	Runs/RH	Runs/LH	HR/RH	HR/LH
103	102	107	100	101

Top Hitter WARP	1.6 Kole Calhoun
Top Pitcher WARP	1.6 Zac Gallen
Top Prospect	Kristian Robinson

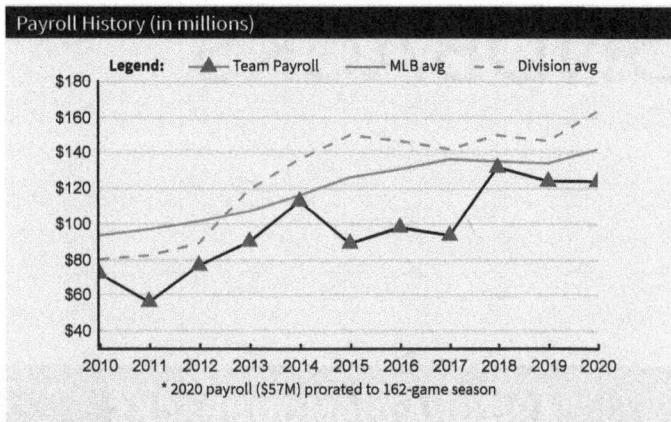

Payroll History (in millions)

Legend: Team Payroll — MLB avg — — Division avg

* 2020 payroll ($57M) prorated to 162-game season

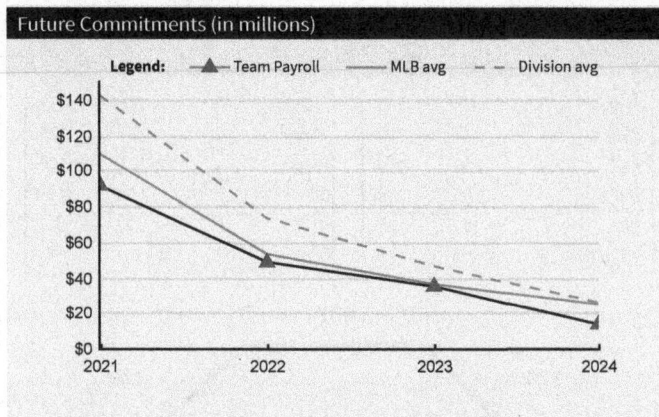

Future Commitments (in millions)

Legend: Team Payroll — MLB avg — — Division avg

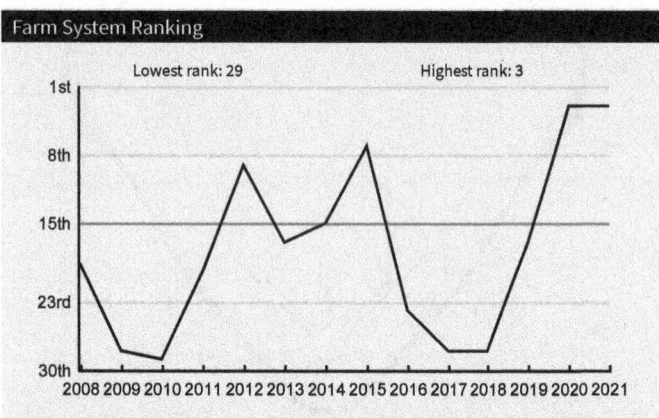

Farm System Ranking

Lowest rank: 29   Highest rank: 3

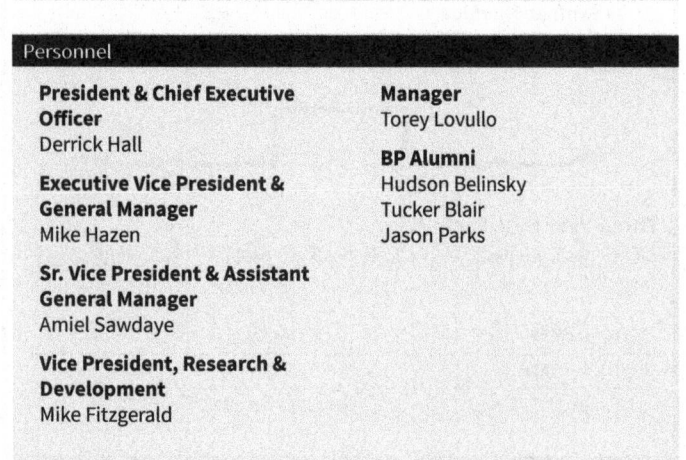

Personnel

President & Chief Executive Officer
Derrick Hall

Executive Vice President & General Manager
Mike Hazen

Sr. Vice President & Assistant General Manager
Amiel Sawdaye

Vice President, Research & Development
Mike Fitzgerald

Manager
Torey Lovullo

BP Alumni
Hudson Belinsky
Tucker Blair
Jason Parks

and you'll understand completely. Any baby born in the year 2020 will suffer from a *Pirates of Penzance*-like fate because their birth didn't exist in the first place.

But that doesn't mean there weren't enormous, bright, fluttering red flags draped over the Diamondbacks in 2020. The highest on-base percentage from a returning player in next season's lineup was David Peralta's .339, and he had to hit .300 to get there. A dip in a 33-year-old's batting average is all that stands between him feebly leading the team in OBP and being an offensive liability, and he's the best they've got.

The team's misery was compounded by the disastrous season from Madison Bumgarner, who might be one of the team's only significant financial splurges for a while. The front office sized the team up, figured they were a reliable starter short of being a World Series contender, plugged their nose, said a few prayers on behalf of the soft market and took a chance on an over-30 pitcher with a heckuva Wikipedia page and declining velocity. He struck out two batters in his first inning as a Diamondback, and allowed 31 runs in the 40 innings after that. He was the only starter in 2020 with more earned runs than strikeouts, which seems bad.

The lineup was miserable. The pitching acquisitions were dreadful. What's supposed to change?

The new normal. That's your answer. This is the new normal, and it's what the Diamondbacks can expect for the next several years. They bought the wrong pitcher, they have a surprisingly old lineup, an impressive-but-distant farm system and a mid-market payroll chained to their ankle. It's not likely to improve soon.

Except ... hold on a second. This was a team that was built by a front office that correctly identified the state of the franchise, one in need of a reload instead of a rebuild. They traded Paul Goldschmidt with a plan, and it looked successful in its first trial run. Christian Walker was an effective, low-budget replacement for the power. Carson Kelly made up for whatever he was lacking. Luke Weaver was going to be a rotation monster for years to come. This was a team that was pointed in the right direction *just a few months ago*. The third-to-last sentence of the Diamondbacks essay in the 2020 Baseball Prospectus Annual was "But if the current indicators are to be trusted at all, it appears that brighter days are ahead."

What changed since then? What reversed the fortunes of the Diamondbacks so drastically? A 60-game season? A three-week stretch that never had time to even out? We've already established that 2020 doesn't count for anything. There were metaphorical mosquitoes the size of basset hounds flying around the entire year, and they sucked us all dry, but they're gone now.

Probably.

Maybe.

This is the still the organization that was confident enough to trade a top-100 prospect like Jazz Chisholm away to get a less-heralded pitcher and have it work out *brilliantly*. Zac Gallen's historic start to his career is proof that the

Diamondbacks aren't just smart, they're creative and wily. It takes equal parts moxie and guile to zero in on a pitcher like that, on a rebuilding team that desperately wanted to develop starting pitching, and figure out how to pry him away. That's some nifty sleight of hand.

They correctly scouted Merrill Kelly, local gadfly and KBO veteran, as someone who could get more outs for less money than the typical pitcher, and they committed several million dollars on that belief. It's a move that made them look smart. Let the other teams fight over the expensive starting pitchers like Trevor Bauer and Max Scherzer. The Diamondbacks will find their own pitchers, and they'll be better at it than almost anyone else.

It's a hiccup. Hold your breath, drink a glass of water, eat a spoonful of sugar, stand on your head, do whatever it takes. But this is a hiccup. You open your mouth to announce your answer, and every member of the studio audience leans toward the stage.

But, wait wait wait wait waaaaait a second. Have you noticed how sneaky-old the Diamondbacks' lineup is for a team that's in a reload/rebuild? Kole Calhoun, one of their leading power sources, is 33. Christian Walker will turn 30 by the time the season starts. Peralta turns 34 in August. Eduardo Escobar—one of the most disappointing players in a season filled with disappointment on all sides—will be 32, and it's not like this was his only bad year out of the last 10. He's a relatively recent discovery, only transcending the super-utility label a couple of years ago. The offensive emergence of Nick Ahmed turned him into a ridiculously valuable two-way player, but he'll be 31, and this doesn't have to last forever.

Now look for the next wave. Daulton Varsho might be here to stay, Pavin Smith made his debut and Geraldo Perdomo looks like he could make the 2021 roster at some point. But this is still a young farm system, at least on the offensive side, and a collection that missed out on a year's worth of development in live ball. Kristian Robinson is only 20. Corbin Carroll and Alek Thomas are both under 21, and they've never played in the upper minors. They certainly could constitute the next wave of magical snakes. But they could also be a latter-day Conor Jackson/Carlos Quentin/Stephen Drew, who accumulate a few wins over their careers, but far away from Phoenix. Don't count your prospects before they debut.

It might be two years before the farm system bears fruit. Maybe three. Maybe never.

This is the new normal. The entire franchise is going to sink into a boggy pit, employing all their tricks and talent to keep their head above the surface, and the Dodgers will do a little goat dance around them for the next 30 years or so. They're old and cheap, and they haven't proven that they can spin prospect straw into major-league gold, so there's no reason to assume they can. It wouldn't be surprising, but it isn't something to place a large cash wager on. It never is without evidence.

And when the Dodgers are dancing around them, the already-rich Giants might be reborn. The Padres have already made the transition from perennial laughingstock to powerhouse, apparently, and though they've behaved like a small market in the past, they're now the only professional sports team in a metropolitan area of three million souls. The Rockies might … look, every single mother of everyone involved with the Rockies is very, very proud of everything they've accomplished.

As you start to announce your answer, you realize it's the dumbest thing you've ever heard. A top-third farm system isn't enough to have hope, especially when it's coupled with a new, forward-thinking front office that's already demonstrated a knack for finding hidden or unheralded talent? Poppycock.

The Diamondbacks don't need to ape the Dodgers. They don't need to spend as much as the Giants might in the future. They just need to spit out a bunch of prospects, like the Padres did, to get good. And make the same kind of prudent, creative trades that the new regime has already made. That's it. That's the secret sauce. The reason the Rays were capable of winning a pennant, and why the A's were contenders to do the same, is that baseball is still set up to screw young players. The under-30 players are usually the best players, and they're paid the least, by design. Get the good players, keep them for a few years while watering the good-player plants in the garden, then trade the good players for more good-player plants. It's not a novel idea, but it sure does work.

If the Diamondbacks are really run by smart people, from the front office to the coaching staff, they'll elbow their way into the conversation, just like they've done in the past. This is the franchise that lost 97 games in their first season and won 100 games in the next. They lost 97 games in 2010 and won the division in 2011. They lost 93 games in 2016, then won 93 games in 2017.

Why, they keep rising from the ashes like some sort of … mythical … ash-rising creature. If you believe in the front office, you believe in their ability to be better than expected, sooner than expected. The question isn't "Hiccup … or the New Normal?" It's *do you believe in this front office's ability to find and secure baseball talent*? They have a surprisingly impressive resume so far. And if you believe in that ability, then, yeah, it's a hiccup.

Just know that the margin of error for the Arizona Diamondbacks is freakishly thin. They're chasing the richest, smartest, most successful team in the land. They're pitted against the Giants, another financial powerhouse with a front office that sprung from the Dodgers' thigh, like Dionysus from Zeus. They have to overcome another franchise, the Padres, that has to do the same prospect-to-production trick that the Diamondbacks have to pull off, except they've already done it. And they also have to match up against the Rockies, who play in a city that "was named the best place to live in the United States by U.S. News & World Report[22]," according to Wikipedia.

You refuse to answer the question. There are no hiccups. There is no new normal. There is only baseball, and the Diamondbacks might have an idea of how to play baseball better than other teams. Just give them time.

The host scowls at your announcement. No one has ever refused to answer the question before. But he shakes it off and turns over the next index card, after docking you 20 points.

The year … 2020? Hiccup? Or the new normal?

You look at the studio audience. Everyone is smiling, but they're gross, malevolent smiles, with arched eyebrows and sunken eyes. They flash mouths filled with sharp teeth, as if they'd all been filed into a point.

The host turns to you expectantly after the other contestant said something that you didn't hear. Now it's your turn. Hiccup? Or the new normal? Your brain sinks into your stomach. You'd like to go home now. ▪

—*Grant Brisbee writes about the San Francisco Giants for The Athletic.*

HITTERS

Nick Ahmed SS Born: 03/15/90 Age: 31 Bats: R Throws: R Height: 6'2" Weight: 200 Origin: Round 2, 2011 Draft (#85 overall)

YEAR	TEAM	LVL	AGE	PA	R	2B	3B	HR	RBI	BB	K	SB	CS	Whiff%	AVG/OBP/SLG	DRC+	BABIP	BRR	FRAA	WARP
2018	ARI	MLB	28	564	61	33	5	16	70	40	109	5	4	25.3%	.234/.290/.411	89	.265	-0.4	SS(148): 15.1	3.3
2019	ARI	MLB	29	625	79	33	6	19	82	52	113	8	2	21.3%	.254/.316/.437	92	.280	2.4	SS(158): 6.0	3.2
2020	ARI	MLB	30	217	29	10	1	5	29	18	46	4	0	27.6%	.266/.327/.402	85	.324	0.3	SS(57): -6.1	-0.5
2021 FS	ARI	MLB	31	600	61	27	3	14	65	45	132	8	3	23.9%	.238/.299/.380	88	.288	1.0	SS 11	2.3
2021 DC	ARI	MLB	31	571	58	25	3	13	62	42	126	8	3	23.9%	.238/.299/.380	88	.288	0.9	SS 11	2.2

Comparables: Royce Clayton, Greg Gagne, Angel Berroa

The Diamondbacks have had a lot of choices present themselves at shortstop over the years. Would they go with Chris Owings or Didi Gregorius? They chose Owings who then slid quickly to second to make more permanent space for Ahmed. Faced with another future fork in the road, the team wasted no time in moving first-overall pick Dansby Swanson. Arizona even dealt the rising Jazz Chisholm before he could face off with Ahmed for duties at the six. It can seem as if Ahmed has been the incumbent about as often as Dianne Feinstein and, after signing an extension in the offseason, should retain his seat for the foreseeable future. Will Geraldo Perdomo eventually take the torch? History, at the very least, remains on Ahmed's side.

Seth Beer 1B Born: 09/18/96 Age: 24 Bats: L Throws: R Height: 6'3" Weight: 225 Origin: Round 1, 2018 Draft (#28 overall)

YEAR	TEAM	LVL	AGE	PA	R	2B	3B	HR	RBI	BB	K	SB	CS	Whiff%	AVG/OBP/SLG	DRC+	BABIP	BRR	FRAA	WARP
2018	TRI	SS	21	51	9	3	0	4	7	6	10	0	0		.293/.431/.659	177	.296	-0.8	LF(7): -1.0, 1B(4): -0.1	0.1
2018	QC	LO-A	21	132	15	7	0	3	16	15	17	1	0		.348/.443/.491	160	.391	-1.2	RF(10): -0.9, LF(9): -1.1, 1B(7): -0.5	0.6
2018	FAY	HI-A	21	114	15	4	0	5	19	4	22	0	1		.262/.307/.439	106	.287	-2.2	LF(13): -1.4, 1B(6): -0.2	-0.4
2019	FAY	HI-A	22	152	24	8	0	9	34	14	30	0	3		.328/.414/.602	188	.359	-1.6	1B(16): 0.0, LF(15): -0.7	1.3
2019	JXN	AA	22	101	8	7	0	1	17	8	25	0	1		.205/.297/.318	74	.270	0.0	1B(14): -0.7, LF(10): -0.4	-0.2
2019	CC	AA	22	280	40	9	0	16	52	24	58	0	0		.299/.407/.543	176	.333	-3.1	1B(46): 0.8, LF(8): -0.1	2.1
2021 FS	ARI	MLB	24	600	77	27	2	25	81	44	159	0	0		.259/.338/.461	121	.323	-0.1	1B -1, LF 0	2.7

Comparables: Anthony Santander, Michael Taylor, Greg Bird

Chase Field has some issues. First and foremost, it lacks some charm even for those who frequent the stadium. The air conditioning runs at high capacity for much of the baseball season. The need to keep the roof closed for large swaths of the calendar makes it so difficult to grow grass that the team opts for artificial turf. Then there are matters of ownership and upkeep which result in legal battles aplenty. But Chase Field has one thing surely going for it: The beer prices are perennially amongst the lowest in the league. That counts for something, right? The Beer in question here has to be encouraged about the strong prospects of a DH in the National League because that's where he's best suited. He won't hit cheapies, either. If all goes according to plan, Beer may just raise the price of admission at Chase Field before long.

Kole Calhoun RF Born: 10/14/87 Age: 33 Bats: L Throws: L Height: 5'10" Weight: 210 Origin: Round 8, 2010 Draft (#264 overall)

YEAR	TEAM	LVL	AGE	PA	R	2B	3B	HR	RBI	BB	K	SB	CS	Whiff%	AVG/OBP/SLG	DRC+	BABIP	BRR	FRAA	WARP
2018	LAA	MLB	30	552	71	18	2	19	57	53	133	6	2	28.5%	.208/.283/.369	85	.241	-0.2	RF(136): -3.7, CF(4): -0.2	-0.2
2019	LAA	MLB	31	632	92	29	1	33	74	70	162	4	1	32.3%	.232/.325/.467	110	.265	0.6	RF(150): 7.2, CF(2): -0.1	3.1
2020	ARI	MLB	33	228	35	9	0	16	40	28	50	1	1	32.7%	.226/.338/.526	126	.211	0.1	RF(48): 2.9	1.6
2021 FS	ARI	MLB	33	600	77	23	2	26	76	62	147	4	1	31.5%	.230/.319/.436	107	.266	0.9	RF -3, CF 0	1.8
2021 DC	ARI	MLB	33	571	74	21	2	25	73	59	140	3	1	31.5%	.230/.319/.436	107	.266	0.8	RF -2	1.7

Comparables: Michael Cuddyer, Jeffrey Hammonds, Cody Ross

Human civilization has been strolling the face of the earth for quite a long time. The strolling takes place simply because we're all quite literally stuck to earth's crust. We don't float, we can't fly, and most of us get a rude reminder of this when we recognize we don't jump as high as we once did. But until the 17th century no one entirely knew why. It was Newton's work, of course, that settled it all. He determined that gravity was a real thing and that what went up must certainly come down. Calhoun was happy in 2020 to showcase that the inverse can also be true as he soared to unfamiliar heights in his first season in the desert, posting career highs in DRC+ (127), slugging percentage (.526), and walk rate (12.3 percent)

★ ★ ★ *2021 Top 101 Prospect* **#34** ★ ★ ★

Corbin Carroll OF   Born: 08/21/00   Age: 20   Bats: L   Throws: L   Height: 5'10"   Weight: 165   Origin: Round 1, 2019 Draft (#16 overall)

YEAR	TEAM	LVL	AGE	PA	R	2B	3B	HR	RBI	BB	K	SB	CS	Whiff%	AVG/OBP/SLG	DRC+	BABIP	BRR	FRAA	WARP
2019	DIA	ROK	18	137	23	6	3	2	14	24	29	16	1		.288/.409/.450	160	.366	2.7	CF(23): -0.1, LF(5): -0.6, RF(3): -0.4	1.3
2019	HIL	SS	18	49	13	3	4	0	6	5	12	2	0		.326/.408/.581	116	.452	0.8	CF(11): 0.0	0.3
2021 FS	*ARI*	*MLB*	*20*	*600*	*48*	*26*	*5*	*6*	*51*	*43*	*203*	*24*	*3*		*.220/.281/.327*	*69*	*.335*	*16.9*	*CF -3, LF -1*	*0.9*

One doesn't have to look far ahead to see what's coming in the very near future. Carroll will be given every moniker, every descriptor, every platitude that Diamondbacks fans have heard applied to countless others over the years. He will run the bases like a man possessed, just like Eric Byrnes did. He will do the little things well, just like Chris Owings did. He will play with absolute grit and determination, just like Willie Bloomquist did. He will excel defensively just like Cliff Pennington did. These narratives have been alive and well in Arizona for some time and Carroll is going to have to get used to them. But there's one other thing—Carroll has talent more reminiscent of Justin Upton. Here's to hoping the Diamondbacks can work that into their spiel, too.

Eduardo Escobar 3B   Born: 01/05/89   Age: 32   Bats: S   Throws: R   Height: 5'10"   Weight: 210   Origin: International Free Agent, 2006

YEAR	TEAM	LVL	AGE	PA	R	2B	3B	HR	RBI	BB	K	SB	CS	Whiff%	AVG/OBP/SLG	DRC+	BABIP	BRR	FRAA	WARP
2018	ARI	MLB	29	223	30	11	0	8	21	18	35	1	1	20.5%	.268/.327/.444	113	.281	0.5	3B(54): -4.9	0.8
2018	MIN	MLB	29	408	45	37	3	15	63	34	91	1	1	25.9%	.274/.338/.514	115	.325	-0.1	3B(77): -2.1, SS(21): -0.0, 2B(1): 0.1	2.1
2019	ARI	MLB	30	699	94	29	10	35	118	50	130	5	1	24.8%	.269/.320/.511	116	.283	-0.6	3B(144): -8.4, 2B(33): 1.1	3.3
2020	ARI	MLB	31	222	22	7	3	4	20	15	41	1	0	21.6%	.212/.270/.335	84	.244	1.7	3B(47): 1.7, 2B(3): -0.1	0.2
2021 FS	*ARI*	*MLB*	*32*	*600*	*63*	*25*	*4*	*18*	*75*	*42*	*127*	*4*	*1*	*23.9%*	*.236/.295/.399*	*90*	*.274*	*2.3*	*3B -7, 2B 0*	*0.2*
2021 DC	*ARI*	*MLB*	*32*	*538*	*56*	*22*	*4*	*16*	*67*	*38*	*114*	*3*	*1*	*23.9%*	*.236/.295/.399*	*90*	*.274*	*2.1*	*3B -6, 2B 0*	*0.1*

Comparables: Greg Dobbs, Larry Parrish, Max Alvis

A 60-game season is tough. We are so used to drawing conclusions on a bigger sample that having confidence in such a tightly framed snapshot is difficult. Then there are guys like Escobar where, after watching him play, you thought to yourself, "Thank goodness it's over," when the season came to a close. An absolute bargain in the first year of his new contract, Escobar's struggles in year two were both easy and hard to divine. The easy part: He just stopped hitting. The hard part: There's not a clear reason why. His average and max exit velos were similar to prior years, there wasn't a massive change in batted-ball profile, his walk and strikeout rates were comparable, heck even his hard-hit rate was almost exactly the same. The best tonic for both viewer and player was that the year came to a close. Next year brings a clean slate and plenty of motivation; Escobar will have much to prove in his walk year.

Jon Jay OF   Born: 03/15/85   Age: 36   Bats: L   Throws: L   Height: 5'11"   Weight: 200   Origin: Round 2, 2006 Draft (#74 overall)

YEAR	TEAM	LVL	AGE	PA	R	2B	3B	HR	RBI	BB	K	SB	CS	Whiff%	AVG/OBP/SLG	DRC+	BABIP	BRR	FRAA	WARP
2018	ARI	MLB	33	320	46	10	5	2	22	14	56	1	1	22.0%	.235/.304/.325	80	.284	-0.1	RF(45): 1.9, LF(14): -1.9, CF(10): -0.5	-0.1
2018	KC	MLB	33	266	28	9	2	1	18	19	39	3	2	17.2%	.307/.363/.374	79	.360	-0.5	LF(27): 1.2, CF(15): 1.8, RF(9): 0.2	0.3
2019	CHA	AAA	34	55	8	2	0	0	6	2	10	1	0		.358/.382/.396	93	.442	0.0	RF(11): -1.4	-0.1
2019	CHW	MLB	34	182	12	8	0	0	9	8	30	0	0	15.5%	.267/.311/.315	77	.324	0.3	RF(33): -4.6, LF(13): -1.6	-0.7
2020	ARI	MLB	35	57	5	1	0	1	4	3	12	0	0	21.6%	.160/.211/.240	87	.175	0.0	RF(9): 0.4, CF(5): 0.1, LF(4): -0.1	0.0
2021 FS	*ARI*	*MLB*	*36*	*600*	*58*	*23*	*3*	*5*	*52*	*38*	*129*	*4*	*1*	*18.7%*	*.249/.318/.337*	*82*	*.318*	*1.8*	*RF -6, LF -5*	*-0.8*

Comparables: Marquis Grissom, Coco Crisp, Mike Devereaux

Jay's second tour of duty with the Diamondbacks was a brief one. The shortened season cut into his opportunities, but not as much as his poor performance did.

Carson Kelly C   Born: 07/14/94   Age: 26   Bats: R   Throws: R   Height: 6'2"   Weight: 210   Origin: Round 2, 2012 Draft (#86 overall)

YEAR	TEAM	LVL	AGE	PA	R	2B	3B	HR	RBI	BB	K	SB	CS	Whiff%	AVG/OBP/SLG	DRC+	BABIP	BRR	FRAA	WARP
2018	MEM	AAA	23	349	38	14	1	7	41	48	48	0	0		.269/.378/.395	113	.299	-0.6	C(83): 10.1, 1B(1): 0.0	2.8
2018	STL	MLB	23	42	1	0	0	0	3	3	7	0	0	20.0%	.114/.205/.114	74	.143	-0.2	C(16): -0.9	0.0
2019	ARI	MLB	24	365	46	19	0	18	47	48	79	0	0	23.2%	.245/.348/.478	115	.271	-1.2	C(101): -0.1, 3B(1): -0.0	2.5
2020	ARI	MLB	26	129	11	5	0	5	19	6	29	0	0	26.3%	.221/.264/.385	87	.250	-0.7	C(38): 0.5, P(1): -0.0	0.5
2021 FS	*ARI*	*MLB*	*26*	*600*	*68*	*26*	*1*	*19*	*71*	*56*	*133*	*0*	*0*	*24.1%*	*.240/.318/.404*	*101*	*.283*	*-0.7*	*C 3, 1B 0*	*2.8*
2021 DC	*ARI*	*MLB*	*26*	*437*	*49*	*19*	*1*	*14*	*52*	*41*	*97*	*0*	*0*	*24.1%*	*.240/.318/.404*	*101*	*.283*	*-0.5*	*C 3*	*2.0*

Comparables: Alex Avila, Josmil Pinto, Jim Pagliaroni

Phoenix is one of the driest metro areas in the United States, though Las Vegas actually holds the title. Kelly took to the starting catcher role in 2019 like a duck to water, hitting more like a corner bat than a backstop. Fast forward a year, and his offensive production all but evaporated in the desert air. It's not just on the surface, either, as digging into his peripheral stats only supports the arid topline numbers. He'll spend the offseason looking for a more productive watering hole in the lineup, but if he can't find one in 2021, well, it's going to burn.

YEAR	TEAM	P. COUNT	FRM RUNS	BLK RUNS	THRW RUNS	TOT RUNS
2018	STL	1735	-0.8	-0.3	0.0	-1.1
2019	ARI	13169	-0.9	2.6	0.3	2.0
2020	ARI	4964	3.1	0.0	0.1	3.3
2021	*ARI*	*13228*	*5.7*	*-0.5*	*-0.8*	*4.3*

Domingo Leyba 2B Born: 09/11/95 Age: 25 Bats: S Throws: R Height: 5'11" Weight: 200 Origin: International Free Agent, 2006

YEAR	TEAM	LVL	AGE	PA	R	2B	3B	HR	RBI	BB	K	SB	CS	Whiff%	AVG/OBP/SLG	DRC+	BABIP	BRR	FRAA	WARP
2018	JXN	AA	22	358	43	17	2	5	30	35	46	5	2		.269/.344/.381	113	.300	-1.7	2B(72): -2.9, SS(8): 0.5	0.5
2019	RNO	AAA	23	498	85	37	3	19	77	32	78	0	2		.300/.351/.519	92	.325	2.9	SS(67): -4.0, 2B(42): 2.9, 3B(2): 0.0	1.7
2019	ARI	MLB	23	30	6	2	1	0	5	4	9	0	0	29.7%	.280/.367/.440	84	.412	0.0	2B(8): 0.4, SS(2): 0.1, 3B(1): -0.0	0.1
2021 FS	ARI	MLB	25	600	62	22	2	14	63	43	130	1	0	29.7%	.233/.294/.363	83	.280	1.3	2B 2, SS -3	0.7

Comparables: Brent Lillibridge, Stephen Drew, Matt Reynolds

Domingo Leyba didn't see any action in 2020 due to a preseason suspension for performance-enhancing drug Boldenone. Beyond that, injuries have robbed Leyba of critical development time over three of the past four seasons.

Tim Locastro LF Born: 07/14/92 Age: 28 Bats: R Throws: R Height: 6'1" Weight: 195 Origin: Round 13, 2013 Draft (#385 overall)

YEAR	TEAM	LVL	AGE	PA	R	2B	3B	HR	RBI	BB	K	SB	CS	Whiff%	AVG/OBP/SLG	DRC+	BABIP	BRR	FRAA	WARP
2018	OKC	AAA	25	356	61	23	2	4	25	28	52	18	2		.279/.389/.409	120	.327	4.2	CF(46): -3.7, 2B(30): -1.8, 1B(11): 0.6	1.5
2018	LAD	MLB	25	14	6	1	0	0	0	2	5	4	0	23.5%	.182/.357/.273	77	.333	0.4	CF(4): -0.1, LF(1): -0.0	0.0
2019	RNO	AAA	26	143	35	11	2	8	21	10	24	9	1		.301/.394/.618	116	.319	1.9	CF(20): -1.4, RF(7): -0.2, LF(4): -0.4	0.7
2019	ARI	MLB	26	250	38	12	2	1	17	14	44	17	0	21.2%	.250/.357/.340	85	.310	0.3	LF(34): 1.6, RF(25): -0.0, CF(20): -1.9	0.2
2020	ARI	MLB	28	82	15	4	1	2	7	8	14	4	0	14.1%	.290/.395/.464	114	.340	-0.7	CF(13): 3.2, LF(7): -0.3, RF(6): -0.3	0.5
2021 FS	ARI	MLB	28	600	73	21	3	12	52	37	115	18	3	18.9%	.245/.336/.374	102	.292	11.5	CF -8, LF 4	3.1
2021 DC	ARI	MLB	28	403	49	14	2	8	35	24	77	12	2	18.9%	.245/.336/.374	102	.292	7.7	CF -5, LF 3	2.0

Comparables: Mike Huff, Felipe Crespo, Gene Stephens

Gimmicks are an age-old tradition in America. Buy this supplement and you'll lose 15 pounds! Put this in your gas tank and you'll get 10 percent more horsepower! If you call now, we'll include a second worthless piece of garbage for FREE! When it comes to Locastro, the gimmick is an obvious one. He was hit in nearly 10 percent of his plate appearances in 2019— practically a human bullseye. But that's a disservice to the sneaky skills that Locastro has developed. He's always been a threat on the bases, a capable outfielder at all three positions and has shown real growth at the plate. Locastro isn't a gimmick and neither is his game—he's a strong role player pushing for more.

Ketel Marte 2B Born: 10/12/93 Age: 27 Bats: S Throws: R Height: 6'1" Weight: 210 Origin: International Free Agent, 2010

YEAR	TEAM	LVL	AGE	PA	R	2B	3B	HR	RBI	BB	K	SB	CS	Whiff%	AVG/OBP/SLG	DRC+	BABIP	BRR	FRAA	WARP
2018	ARI	MLB	24	580	68	26	12	14	59	54	79	6	1	16.2%	.260/.332/.437	102	.282	0.6	2B(131): 4.5, SS(28): 1.8	2.9
2019	ARI	MLB	25	628	97	36	9	32	92	53	86	10	2	17.7%	.329/.389/.592	140	.342	1.9	CF(96): -8.3, 2B(83): -2.9, SS(11): -0.9	4.5
2020	ARI	MLB	27	195	19	14	1	2	17	7	21	1	0	14.1%	.287/.323/.409	101	.311	0.3	2B(41): 1.1, CF(3): -0.0, SS(2): -0.0	0.8
2021 FS	ARI	MLB	27	600	77	29	5	15	66	45	90	7	2	16.5%	.273/.332/.432	112	.303	4.3	2B 1, CF -3	3.2
2021 DC	ARI	MLB	27	571	73	27	5	14	63	42	86	7	2	16.5%	.273/.332/.432	112	.303	4.1	2B 1, CF -3	3.1

Comparables: Jay Bell, Angel Berroa, Didi Gregorius

For three of the last four seasons, Marte has been a league-average hitter. It's just that the one outlier was, well, otherworldly. It'd be easy to call that outlying season just that—a blip on the radar. Marte notched fewer hard-hit balls in 2020, pulled the ball less often, hit it on the ground more, and registered his lowest power output since his rookie debut in 2015. The eye test, however, suggested that nothing much had changed from a season ago. Marte still swung like a tempest possessed his soul and the baseball was the sole object of his deepest aggressions. He still has an ability to do things that few others can, yet his produced outcomes changed in a way that surely cast uncertainty on the forecast.

Wyatt Mathisen 3B Born: 12/30/93 Age: 27 Bats: R Throws: R Height: 6'0" Weight: 210 Origin: Round 2, 2012 Draft (#69 overall)

YEAR	TEAM	LVL	AGE	PA	R	2B	3B	HR	RBI	BB	K	SB	CS	Whiff%	AVG/OBP/SLG	DRC+	BABIP	BRR	FRAA	WARP
2018	ALT	AA	24	41	9	3	1	1	3	11	7	1	1		.385/.585/.692	193	.474	-0.2	1B(5): -0.3, 2B(5): 0.7, 3B(1): 0.1	0.5
2018	IND	AAA	24	282	34	13	0	9	45	23	59	2	2		.248/.330/.413	115	.285	1.2	1B(57): -0.0, 3B(15): -2.1, 2B(1): -0.1	0.5
2019	DIA	ROK	25	31	4	3	0	0	3	6	3	1	0		.348/.516/.478	201	.400	0.3	3B(4): 0.2, 2B(1): 0.2	0.4
2019	RNO	AAA	25	345	72	19	1	23	61	39	84	1	0		.283/.403/.601	122	.318	0.1	3B(59): 0.2, 2B(20): 0.6, 1B(9): 0.1	2.2
2020	ARI	MLB	26	33	5	0	0	2	5	5	12	0	0	33.9%	.222/.364/.444	97	.308	0.1	3B(7): 0.2	0.1
2021 FS	ARI	MLB	27	600	70	22	2	22	74	56	167	1	0	33.9%	.238/.328/.415	108	.304	0.4	3B -6, 1B 0	1.3
2021 DC	ARI	MLB	27	100	11	3	0	3	12	9	27	0	0	33.9%	.238/.328/.415	108	.304	0.1	3B -1	0.2

Comparables: Jefry Marte, Mike Brosseau, Matthew Brown

The 69th-overall pick in the 2012 draft, Mathisen slid nicely into his big-league debut in 2020. He's the kind of Quad-A player that teams covet as he can handle a few infield spots, though he's best at the corners, and has finally figured out how to tap into his power more regularly.

David Peralta LF Born: 08/14/87 Age: 33 Bats: L Throws: L Height: 6'1" Weight: 220 Origin: International Free Agent, 2005

YEAR	TEAM	LVL	AGE	PA	R	2B	3B	HR	RBI	BB	K	SB	CS	Whiff%	AVG/OBP/SLG	DRC+	BABIP	BRR	FRAA	WARP
2018	ARI	MLB	30	614	75	25	5	30	87	48	124	4	0	23.8%	.293/.352/.516	121	.328	1.2	LF(138): -11.0, RF(5): -0.5	2.1
2019	ARI	MLB	31	423	48	29	3	12	57	35	87	0	0	24.3%	.275/.343/.461	96	.327	-2.8	LF(93): 13.4	2.0
2020	ARI	MLB	33	218	19	10	1	5	34	13	45	1	0	21.1%	.300/.339/.433	88	.361	-0.2	LF(45): 4.2	0.7
2021 FS	ARI	MLB	33	600	67	30	4	16	74	45	136	4	1	23.2%	.273/.336/.434	109	.338	2.4	LF 1, RF 0	2.7
2021 DC	ARI	MLB	33	571	64	28	4	15	71	43	129	4	1	23.2%	.273/.336/.434	109	.338	2.3	LF 1	2.6

Comparables: Gary Ward, Matt Diaz, Kirk Gibson

What did the worms ever do to Peralta? They didn't ruin his pitching shoulder all those years ago. They didn't make the Cardinals cut him loose and they didn't relegate him to indy ball. All that toiling in obscurity, then the arduous journey to where he belonged in the first place ... what did the worms ever do to Peralta? They didn't keep him from running the bases like a locomotive. They didn't keep him from winning a Gold Glove, being named the defensive player of the year, or nabbing a Silver Slugger. What did the worms ever do to Peralta? They didn't keep him from developing a simple, powerful stroke from the left side, one that's wildly efficient. They didn't demand that he keep from launching that hard contact into the Arizona night sky. They didn't mandate the ground balls that hold back his game. What did the worms ever do to Peralta?

★ ★ ★ *2021 Top 101 Prospect* **#90** ★ ★ ★

Geraldo Perdomo SS Born: 10/22/99 Age: 21 Bats: S Throws: R Height: 6'2" Weight: 185 Origin: International Free Agent, 2016

YEAR	TEAM	LVL	AGE	PA	R	2B	3B	HR	RBI	BB	K	SB	CS	Whiff%	AVG/OBP/SLG	DRC+	BABIP	BRR	FRAA	WARP
2018	MIS	ROK	18	29	3	0	1	0	2	7	4	1	1		.455/.586/.545	247	.556	0.4	SS(5): 0.3, 2B(1): -0.2	0.5
2018	DIA	ROK	18	101	20	4	2	1	8	14	17	14	1		.314/.416/.442	172	.382	2.6	SS(14): 2.6, 2B(8): 0.5	1.3
2018	HIL	SS	18	127	20	3	2	3	14	18	23	9	4		.301/.421/.456	148	.359	1.4	SS(30): 3.9	1.3
2019	KC	LO-A	19	385	48	16	3	2	36	56	56	20	8		.268/.394/.357	126	.318	-2.2	SS(80): 2.1, 2B(11): -0.1	2.7
2019	VIS	HI-A	19	114	15	5	0	1	11	14	11	6	5		.301/.407/.387	128	.325	-0.2	SS(26): -1.0	0.6
2021 FS	ARI	MLB	21	600	61	25	3	7	54	56	148	17	9		.240/.320/.345	87	.317	-4.6	SS 6, 2B 0	1.1
2021 DC	ARI	MLB	21	33	3	1	0	0	2	3	8	0	0		.240/.320/.345	87	.317	-0.3	SS 0	0.1

Comparables: J.P. Crawford, Asdrúbal Cabrera, Hanser Alberto

Choose your own adventure books were all the rage in the '90s. Perdomo wouldn't know much about them, having been born in October of '99. That hasn't stopped him from striking out on his own path, though he isn't much for striking out otherwise. The lanky shortstop has supreme control of the strike zone for someone so young, and the big question with his bat is whether he'll fill out his frame enough to develop game power. His slick up-the-middle glove paired with a precocious approach should propel him to the majors, so whatever adventure he chooses, it'll have a major-league backdrop.

★ ★ ★ *2021 Top 101 Prospect* **#15** ★ ★ ★

Kristian Robinson CF Born: 12/11/00 Age: 20 Bats: R Throws: R Height: 6'3" Weight: 190 Origin: International Free Agent, 2017

YEAR	TEAM	LVL	AGE	PA	R	2B	3B	HR	RBI	BB	K	SB	CS	Whiff%	AVG/OBP/SLG	DRC+	BABIP	BRR	FRAA	WARP
2018	MIS	ROK	17	74	13	1	0	3	10	11	21	5	3		.300/.419/.467	119	.405	0.5	CF(10): -2.3, LF(7): 0.4	0.0
2018	DIA	ROK	17	182	35	11	0	4	31	16	46	7	5		.272/.341/.414	127	.351	1.3	CF(26): -5.3, LF(6): -0.9, RF(4): 2.2	0.1
2019	HIL	SS	18	189	29	10	1	9	35	23	47	14	3		.319/.407/.558	208	.398	-0.1	CF(22): 1.6, RF(18): 3.8	2.8
2019	KC	LO-A	18	102	14	3	1	5	16	8	29	3	2		.217/.294/.435	90	.259	-0.3	CF(18): 0.6, RF(5): 0.2, LF(2): -0.3	0.2
2021 FS	ARI	MLB	20	600	53	26	2	12	58	40	222	15	7		.216/.275/.342	68	.335	-3.6	CF 3, RF 3	-0.5

Is it too early to dub Robinson the Bahamian Beast? Okay, maybe the moniker is a scoche premature, but the writing is on the wall. Players of his size with his level of athleticism don't grow on trees and there are simply things that Robinson can do that others can't. He turned heads at the Diamondbacks' alternate site all summer long and, according to reports, really grew as a ballplayer. His acumen for the game developed rapidly as he saw much more advanced pitching than ever before. In short, he's figuring it out and doing so quickly. For all he can do that others can't, though, he's going to have to prove he can consistently make contact before he truly makes the leap.

Josh Rojas 3B Born: 06/30/94 Age: 27 Bats: L Throws: R Height: 6'1" Weight: 200 Origin: Round 26, 2017 Draft (#781 overall)

YEAR	TEAM	LVL	AGE	PA	R	2B	3B	HR	RBI	BB	K	SB	CS	Whiff%	AVG/OBP/SLG	DRC+	BABIP	BRR	FRAA	WARP
2018	FAY	HI-A	24	105	20	11	2	1	10	15	13	12	0		.311/.410/.511	154	.355	0.1	2B(10): 1.0, 1B(7): -0.0, LF(3): -0.5	0.7
2018	CC	AA	24	451	64	23	4	7	45	53	76	26	14		.251/.338/.385	106	.291	1.0	LF(36): 2.2, 3B(16): 2.3, 1B(13): 1.4	1.1
2019	CC	AA	25	195	29	13	2	8	30	22	28	13	6		.322/.405/.561	179	.348	0.0	2B(30): 0.6, 1B(12): 0.8, 3B(2): -0.2	2.1
2019	RR	AAA	25	244	49	16	3	12	39	30	36	19	4		.310/.402/.586	149	.325	2.1	2B(15): -1.5, SS(15): 0.9, LF(13): 1.4	2.8
2019	RNO	AAA	25	40	11	4	1	3	14	5	6	1	0		.514/.575/.943	152	.577	-0.3	SS(2): -0.4, LF(2): -0.0, RF(2): 0.1	1.9
2019	ARI	MLB	25	157	17	7	0	2	16	18	41	4	2	28.8%	.217/.312/.312	76	.295	-1.7	LF(33): 2.7, RF(6): 0.0, 2B(1): 0.0	0.0
2020	ARI	MLB	26	70	9	0	0	0	2	7	16	1	1	25.6%	.180/.257/.180	73	.234	0.3	2B(8): -0.0, SS(2): -0.4, LF(1): -0.1	-0.1
2021 FS	ARI	MLB	27	600	70	23	5	16	61	60	147	19	6	27.4%	.240/.322/.400	99	.302	7.2	2B -3, SS 0	2.1
2021 DC	ARI	MLB	27	269	31	10	2	7	27	27	66	8	2	27.4%	.240/.322/.400	99	.302	3.2	2B -1, SS 0	1.0

Comparables: Duane Walker, Charlie Manuel, James Mouton

When the Diamondbacks dealt Zack Greinke to the Astros, it wasn't Rojas who headlined the deal. He felt very much like a throw-in—he was a senior sign utility player who'd done some nice work in the minors, but nothing flashy. But when Rojas came to Phoenix he made an unexpected splash, thanks to some injuries that hit the big-league club. He hit .291/.350/.455 over his first 60 plate appearances and looked the part of a mostly outfielding utility man. The problem is, of course, that he hasn't hit a lick since. He's a fair defender in the outfield and can handle the infield, too, but that first impression certainly hasn't held up. Without more offense, it's hard to see how he weaves his way into regular playing time.

Pavin Smith 1B Born: 02/06/96 Age: 25 Bats: L Throws: L Height: 6'2" Weight: 210 Origin: Round 1, 2017 Draft (#7 overall)

YEAR	TEAM	LVL	AGE	PA	R	2B	3B	HR	RBI	BB	K	SB	CS	Whiff%	AVG/OBP/SLG	DRC+	BABIP	BRR	FRAA	WARP
2018	VIS	HI-A	22	504	63	25	1	11	54	57	65	3	2		.255/.343/.392	112	.275	-1.1	1B(109): 9.0, RF(1): -0.1	0.6
2019	JXN	AA	23	507	62	29	6	12	67	59	61	2	1		.291/.370/.466	142	.310	-5.9	1B(79): 2.5, RF(28): -2.6, LF(13): 1.0	2.5
2020	ARI	MLB	24	44	7	0	1	1	4	5	8	1	0	23.8%	.270/.341/.405	90	.300	-0.2	1B(5): 0.2, LF(3): 0.1, RF(2): -0.3	-0.1
2021 FS	ARI	MLB	25	600	67	27	5	14	67	56	114	0	0	23.8%	.255/.328/.406	100	.300	2.7	1B 4, RF -2	1.5
2021 DC	ARI	MLB	25	437	48	19	3	10	49	40	83	0	0	23.8%	.255/.328/.406	100	.300	2.0	1B 3, RF -1	1.2

Comparables: Rangel Ravelo, Jordan Brown, Chris Parmelee

There's no denying that the lumbering slugger has really faded in popularity across baseball. The optimization of swings has resulted in smaller, slighter players being able to hit the ball hard enough— and far enough—to warrant regular playing time while their teams accumulate the benefits associated with greater athleticism. Smith certainly has the latter—he's quite athletic for a first baseman and can even play left field in a pinch. But the former prerequisite—that whole optimized swing thing—still seems to evade him dating back to his days at the University of Virginia. His 2020 big-league debut was fine aside from the continued absence of power production. If he can find his way to in-game power, he'll be one of the more well-rounded cold cornermen in the game.

★ ★ ★ *2021 Top 101 Prospect* **#47** ★ ★ ★

Alek Thomas CF Born: 04/28/00 Age: 21 Bats: L Throws: L Height: 5'11" Weight: 175 Origin: Round 2, 2018 Draft (#63 overall)

YEAR	TEAM	LVL	AGE	PA	R	2B	3B	HR	RBI	BB	K	SB	CS	Whiff%	AVG/OBP/SLG	DRC+	BABIP	BRR	FRAA	WARP
2018	MIS	ROK	18	134	26	11	1	2	17	11	19	4	3		.341/.396/.496	160	.392	-1.0	CF(20): 0.1, LF(7): 0.5	0.8
2018	DIA	ROK	18	138	24	3	5	0	10	13	18	8	2		.325/.394/.431	166	.381	1.6	CF(13): -2.1, LF(11): -2.4, RF(2): -0.2	0.4
2019	KC	LO-A	19	402	63	21	7	8	48	43	72	11	6		.312/.393/.479	153	.372	0.4	CF(76): -10.1, LF(7): 0.2, RF(7): 0.8	2.5
2019	VIS	HI-A	19	104	13	2	0	2	7	9	33	4	5		.255/.327/.340	89	.373	0.4	CF(23): 2.6	0.6
2021 FS	ARI	MLB	21	600	52	26	4	10	57	36	163	7	6		.238/.288/.359	76	.318	-4.5	CF -6, LF 0	-1.0

Comparables: Kyle Tucker, Albert Almora Jr., Manuel Margot

Let's take you back to your SAT days, but the ones before they added a writing section. We had it so easy, we just didn't know it.

Thomas : hitting :: DJ Khaled : winning.

We'll give you the answer: It's all either does, no matter what. It's as easy to overlook Thomas in the Diamondbacks center field picture as it is to ignore Khaled in a song that features Ludacris, Rick Ross, T-Pain, and Snoop Dogg, but do so at your own peril. Kristian Robinson and Corbin Carroll might garner most of the attention, but keep your eye on Thomas. He owns a gorgeous left-handed swing and plus raw power, and is advanced on both sides of the ball. Like Khaled, Thomas is also a grinder, and he receives rave reviews for his makeup and dedication to the game. One area they differ? Thomas is substance over flash, while the same can't be said for Khaled, though both will remind you of the value of putting in that work.

Josh VanMeter LF Born: 03/10/95 Age: 26 Bats: L Throws: R Height: 5'11" Weight: 190 Origin: Round 5, 2013 Draft (#148 overall)

YEAR	TEAM	LVL	AGE	PA	R	2B	3B	HR	RBI	BB	K	SB	CS	Whiff%	AVG/OBP/SLG	DRC+	BABIP	BRR	FRAA	WARP
2018	PNS	AA	23	121	13	10	0	1	14	23	19	5	2		.284/.420/.421	145	.342	-0.4	LF(15): -0.9, 2B(9): -0.4, SS(5): -0.5	0.4
2018	LOU	AAA	23	362	40	25	6	11	45	28	73	5	3		.253/.309/.464	109	.292	-2.7	2B(47): -3.8, LF(23): -1.3, 3B(10): 1.1	0.2
2019	LOU	AAA	24	211	43	14	1	14	43	24	37	8	3		.348/.429/.669	159	.371	0.2	2B(22): 0.1, 1B(13): 0.4, 3B(10): -0.4	2.0
2019	CIN	MLB	24	260	33	13	1	8	23	29	56	9	3	22.3%	.237/.327/.408	99	.279	-1.2	LF(47): 2.3, 2B(18): 0.2, 1B(17): 0.4	0.8
2020	CIN	MLB	25	38	3	1	0	1	1	3	16	1	0	34.3%	.059/.158/.176	70	.059	0.3	2B(7): -0.2, 1B(3): -0.0	-0.1
2020	ARI	MLB	25	41	6	2	0	1	5	4	8	0	0	26.2%	.194/.293/.333	70	.222	-0.1	2B(10): -1.2, 3B(2): -0.0	-0.1
2021 FS	ARI	MLB	26	600	65	26	3	18	67	55	154	6	1	24.9%	.222/.298/.386	86	.276	2.4	2B -5, 1B 0	0.4
2021 DC	ARI	MLB	26	100	10	4	0	3	11	9	25	1	0	24.9%	.222/.298/.386	86	.276	0.4	2B -1	0.1

Comparables: Alex Gordon, Larry Bigbie, Ryan Langerhans

Every coin has two sides. Take, for example, 1870's French five-franc piece. On the first side is the goddess Ceres, a representative of agriculture, crops, and fertility. Ceres was a motherly figure above all else, and being a mother to the Third Republic is something you can hang your hat on. The reverse side denotes the coin's date and displays lush wreaths, a sign of freedom and prosperity. If VanMeter were a coin he'd have two distinct sides, too. One would be of a useful, athletic utility man in the Kiké Hernández mold. The other would be of a guy who just can't quite do enough with the stick to, well, stick. The Diamondbacks appear willing to flip that coin in 2021.

Daulton Varsho C Born: 07/02/96 Age: 25 Bats: L Throws: R Height: 5'10" Weight: 205 Origin: Round 2, 2017 Draft (#68 overall)

YEAR	TEAM	LVL	AGE	PA	R	2B	3B	HR	RBI	BB	K	SB	CS	Whiff%	AVG/OBP/SLG	DRC+	BABIP	BRR	FRAA	WARP
2018	DIA	ROK	21	12	4	2	1	1	1	0	1	0	0		.500/.500/1.083	187	.500	0.1	C(2): -0.0	0.1
2018	VIS	HI-A	21	342	44	11	3	11	44	30	71	19	3		.286/.363/.451	132	.341	2.5	C(55): 1.4	1.8
2019	JXN	AA	22	452	85	25	4	18	58	42	63	21	5		.301/.378/.520	155	.317	5.9	C(76): -5.7, CF(4): -1.2	4.3
2020	ARI	MLB	24	115	16	5	2	3	9	12	33	3	1	30.0%	.188/.287/.366	87	.246	0.1	CF(14): 2.0, C(10): -0.1, LF(5): -0.1	0.3
2021 FS	ARI	MLB	24	600	71	24	7	21	72	47	157	12	3	30.0%	.243/.313/.434	102	.303	8.6	CF -5, C 1	3.1
2021 DC	ARI	MLB	24	470	56	19	6	16	56	37	123	9	2	30.0%	.243/.313/.434	102	.303	6.7	CF -4, C 0	2.0

Comparables: Blake Swihart, Alex Avila, Tyler Stephenson

The Diamondbacks' highest-rated homegrown position player prospect to debut since Justin Upton didn't exactly put on a primetime show in the majors. His line was reminiscent of a backup catcher rather than that of a leading man. Billed as more than a catcher, he didn't disappoint in that regard. Varsho piled up more work in center field than he did behind the dish by a wide margin, highlighting his versatility while mostly looking the part in the field. One small hook on which to hang your hat? He did begin to look slightly more comfortable in his at-bats as the season progressed. Season One of The VarShow might not have met expectations, but don't sleep on Season Two.

Stephen Vogt C Born: 11/01/84 Age: 36 Bats: L Throws: R Height: 6'0" Weight: 211 Origin: Round 12, 2007 Draft (#365 overall)

YEAR	TEAM	LVL	AGE	PA	R	2B	3B	HR	RBI	BB	K	SB	CS	Whiff%	AVG/OBP/SLG	DRC+	BABIP	BRR	FRAA	WARP
2019	SAC	AAA	34	72	9	3	0	4	7	14	11	0	0		.241/.389/.500	121	.233	-0.7	C(9): -0.3, 1B(6): -0.4, LF(1): -0.1	0.3
2019	SF	MLB	34	280	30	24	2	10	40	20	66	3	1	26.9%	.263/.314/.490	105	.311	-0.2	C(60): -1.0, LF(7): -0.2, 1B(1): 0.0	1.4
2020	ARI	MLB	36	81	6	5	0	1	7	8	18	0	0	19.6%	.167/.247/.278	88	.204	-0.5	C(23): -0.4, 1B(1): 0.1	0.2
2021 FS	ARI	MLB	36	600	62	28	2	17	67	52	140	2	0	24.7%	.222/.294/.377	84	.268	0.2	C 1, 1B 0	1.2
2021 DC	ARI	MLB	36	235	24	11	0	6	26	20	54	0	0	24.7%	.222/.294/.377	84	.268	0.1	C 0	0.5

Comparables: Lance Parrish, Mike Macfarlane, Javy Lopez

YEAR	TEAM	P. COUNT	FRM RUNS	BLK RUNS	THRW RUNS	TOT RUNS
2019	SF	7706	-1.6	-0.6	-0.5	-2.7
2020	ARI	2961	1.3	0.1	0.0	1.3
2021	ARI	8418	-1.6	1.0	0.2	-0.4

There's no real way to skirt around the fact that Vogt was quite bad last year. Yeah, it was a weird season, and yeah, Vogt was donning a new jersey, but nothing seemed to go right for the veteran. Brought in to serve as a sort of limited platoon partner with Carson Kelly, the lefty didn't hit righties well. The sample was tiny and perhaps that should limit any conclusions, but Vogt did a few things in particular that dragged down his BABIP and the rest of his line. He hit more ground balls, he hit them weakly, and he pulled them a bunch. That makes for some easy groundouts considering his (in)ability to run. Reversing course is paramount in 2021 considering his age and proximity to retirement.

Christian Walker 1B Born: 03/28/91 Age: 30 Bats: R Throws: R Height: 6'0" Weight: 210 Origin: Round 4, 2012 Draft (#132 overall)

YEAR	TEAM	LVL	AGE	PA	R	2B	3B	HR	RBI	BB	K	SB	CS	Whiff%	AVG/OBP/SLG	DRC+	BABIP	BRR	FRAA	WARP
2018	RNO	AAA	27	359	68	25	4	18	71	26	86	1	0		.299/.354/.568	117	.351	-1.3	1B(64): 3.4, LF(18): -0.9	0.9
2018	ARI	MLB	27	53	6	2	0	3	6	3	22	1	0	33.8%	.163/.226/.388	58	.208	0.2	1B(7): 0.2, LF(1): -0.1	-0.1
2019	ARI	MLB	28	603	86	26	1	29	73	67	155	8	1	28.7%	.259/.348/.476	112	.312	1.7	1B(142): 10.8	3.1
2020	ARI	MLB	29	243	35	18	1	7	34	19	50	1	1	27.1%	.271/.333/.459	107	.317	0.1	1B(43): 3.1	0.9
2021 FS	ARI	MLB	30	600	70	25	2	22	80	52	151	2	0	28.3%	.237/.312/.421	102	.286	0.9	1B 4, 3B 0	1.6
2021 DC	ARI	MLB	30	605	71	25	2	23	81	52	153	2	0	28.3%	.237/.312/.421	102	.286	0.9	1B 4	1.6

Comparables: Tony Clark, Brian Daubach, Adam LaRoche

No one feels like cooking on Friday night. At the end of a long week the quickest route to relief and gratification is letting someone else cook for you. After this principle is embraced, the immediate question is whether one should dress up and go out, or order in from the comfort of their own sofa. Going out has its perks—virtually every option is available and one can get that fancy, special meal from that exclusive restaurant that'll make the friend group jealous. If Freddie Freeman is that fancy restaurant, Walker is more like In-N-Out (and not just because he's a Christian). Some think he's wildly overrated, others love what he brings to the table. Mostly, he gets the job done at a minimal cost.

Andy Young 2B Born: 05/10/94 Age: 27 Bats: R Throws: R Height: 6'0" Weight: 200 Origin: Round 37, 2016 Draft (#1126 overall)

YEAR	TEAM	LVL	AGE	PA	R	2B	3B	HR	RBI	BB	K	SB	CS	Whiff%	AVG/OBP/SLG	DRC+	BABIP	BRR	FRAA	WARP
2018	PMB	HI-A	24	351	43	10	2	12	34	31	59	4	0		.276/.372/.444	137	.304	-0.1	2B(73): -4.5, 3B(7): -0.5, SS(1): -0.0	1.1
2018	SPR	AA	24	152	18	3	1	9	24	7	26	0	2		.319/.395/.556	146	.340	-0.9	2B(30): -2.8, 3B(7): -0.7	0.4
2019	JXN	AA	25	263	36	15	2	8	28	18	53	1	1		.260/.363/.453	128	.305	-0.3	2B(47): -2.5, SS(8): -1.1, 3B(6): 0.2	1.2
2019	RNO	AAA	25	277	53	10	3	21	53	24	68	2	2		.280/.373/.611	109	.305	0.9	SS(25): 1.3, 3B(23): -1.0, 2B(22): 0.1	1.5
2020	ARI	MLB	26	34	3	2	0	1	4	5	10	0	0	50.8%	.192/.382/.385	96	.267	0.0	2B(4): -0.1, 3B(3): -0.5, LF(1): -0.0	0.0
2021 FS	ARI	MLB	27	600	75	21	4	25	79	40	174	1	0	50.8%	.240/.324/.443	114	.305	2.5	SS 0, 3B -3	3.1
2021 DC	ARI	MLB	27	100	12	3	0	4	13	6	29	0	0	50.8%	.240/.324/.443	114	.305	0.4	SS 0, 3B 0	0.4

Comparables: Josh Satin, Michael Hollimon, Drew Sutton

There's been plenty of dialogue over the last half decade regarding the trouble that modern baseball has caused for certain types of players. No longer can teams effectively hide terrible defenders in left field to make way for their bats. Most teams have chosen defensive value at catcher over an ability to hit. Starting pitchers just aren't used like workhorses anymore (with a few obvious exceptions). But some players benefit from the construction of the modern baseball roster and Young may be one of them. He doesn't have a true defensive home to speak of, but he can man a few spots serviceably, and the bat, well, that's the ticket. He can hit, has some pop, and can afford manager Torey Lovullo some luxuries in how he's deployed. He's unlikely to be an everyday guy, but instead a bench piece that gets steady action—a valuable player by today's standards.

PITCHERS

Rogelio Armenteros RHP   Born: 06/30/94   Age: 27   Bats: R   Throws: R   Height: 6'1"   Weight: 243   Origin: International Free Agent, 2014

YEAR	TEAM	LVL	AGE	W	L	SV	G	GS	IP	H	HR	BB/9	K/9	K	GB%	BABIP	WHIP	ERA	DRA-	WARP	MPH	FA%	Whiff%	CSP
2018	FRE	AAA	24	8	1	1	22	21	118	106	15	3.7	10.2	134	37.2%	.302	1.31	3.74	79	2.5				
2019	RR	AAA	25	6	7	0	19	18	84¹	90	14	3.3	9.1	85	31.9%	.328	1.43	4.80	94	1.7				
2019	HOU	MLB	25	1	1	1	5	2	18	17	1	2.5	9.0	18	36.5%	.314	1.22	4.00	107	0.1	94.0	48.3%	25.2%	43.3%
2021 FS	ARI	MLB	27	9	9	0	26	26	150	134	24	4.1	9.2	153	36.1%	.280	1.35	4.34	100	1.1	94.0	48.3%	25.2%	43.3%
2021 DC	ARI	MLB	27	3	3	0	26	8	55	49	8	4.1	9.2	56	36.1%	.280	1.35	4.34	100	0.5	94.0	48.3%	25.2%	43.3%

Comparables: Daniel Mengden, Walker Lockett, Drew Anderson

After waiting so long for a spot in Houston's rotation, Armenteros would have been at the front of the queue when holes started to appear, if not for elbow surgery to remove a bone spur. Others jumped the line while he recovered, leaving him waiting once more for an opportunity, one that may now arrive sooner with a change of scenery.

Jeremy Beasley RHP   Born: 11/20/95   Age: 25   Bats: R   Throws: R   Height: 6'3"   Weight: 245   Origin: Round 30, 2017 Draft (#895 overall)

YEAR	TEAM	LVL	AGE	W	L	SV	G	GS	IP	H	HR	BB/9	K/9	K	GB%	BABIP	WHIP	ERA	DRA-	WARP	MPH	FA%	Whiff%	CSP
2018	BUR	LO-A	22	0	2	0	6	5	23	16	0	2.7	7.4	19	39.7%	.254	1.00	2.35	79	0.4				
2018	IE	HI-A	22	3	2	1	9	6	44¹	48	4	2.2	9.7	48	40.9%	.364	1.33	3.05	93	0.3				
2018	MOB	AA	22	3	3	0	10	7	44¹	32	3	2.8	7.5	37	41.7%	.248	1.04	2.44	97	0.3				
2019	MOB	AA	23	6	7	0	23	22	108²	110	13	3.5	8.4	102	46.2%	.312	1.40	4.06	106	-0.3				
2019	SL	AAA	23	1	0	0	3	3	13²	19	1	4.0	8.6	13	37.0%	.400	1.83	7.90	121	0.1				
2020	ARI	MLB	24	0	0	0	1	0	0¹	2	0	0.0	27.0	1	0.0%	1.000	6.00	0.00	78	0.0	92.4	37.5%	28.6%	41.9%
2021 FS	ARI	MLB	25	2	3	0	57	0	50	48	7	4.2	8.1	44	41.8%	.290	1.44	4.73	110	-0.2	92.4	37.5%	28.6%	41.9%
2021 DC	ARI	MLB	25	0	0	0	3	3	12	11	1	4.2	8.1	10	41.8%	.290	1.44	4.73	110	0.1	92.4	37.5%	28.6%	41.9%

Comparables: Robert Dugger, Jorge Alcala, P.J. Walters

If timing is everything then Beasley should ask for his money back. The righty acquired for Matt Andriese made one appearance, faced three batters, got one out, and suffered a shoulder injury that ended his season in 2020. He's either a back-end starter or a middle/long reliever long term, just like Andriese was.

Travis Bergen LHP   Born: 10/08/93   Age: 27   Bats: L   Throws: L   Height: 6'1"   Weight: 215   Origin: Round 7, 2015 Draft (#212 overall)

YEAR	TEAM	LVL	AGE	W	L	SV	G	GS	IP	H	HR	BB/9	K/9	K	GB%	BABIP	WHIP	ERA	DRA-	WARP	MPH	FA%	Whiff%	CSP
2018	DUN	HI-A	24	0	1	1	16	0	21	16	0	2.6	13.3	31	43.5%	.348	1.05	1.71	73	0.3				
2018	NH	AA	24	4	1	7	27	0	35²	26	2	2.3	10.9	43	37.0%	.270	0.98	0.50	62	0.8				
2019	SAC	AAA	25	0	0	1	15	0	16²	13	2	5.4	8.1	15	45.8%	.239	1.38	3.78	87	0.3				
2019	SF	MLB	25	2	0	0	21	0	19²	18	4	4.1	8.2	18	38.6%	.264	1.37	5.49	108	0.0	92.1	68.9%	17.8%	47.9%
2020	ARI	MLB	26	1	0	1	8	0	8¹	5	1	9.7	11.9	11	43.8%	.267	1.68	3.24	96	0.1	94.1	64.2%	26.7%	39.4%
2021 FS	ARI	MLB	27	2	2	1	57	0	50	43	7	4.0	9.8	54	40.8%	.282	1.31	4.03	95	0.3	92.9	67.0%	21.5%	44.3%
2021 DC	ARI	MLB	27	2	2	1	51	0	54	46	7	4.0	9.8	58	40.8%	.282	1.31	4.03	95	0.5	92.9	67.0%	21.5%	44.3%

Comparables: Aaron Bummer, Randy Rosario, Austin Davis

Out with the old and in with the new(er). The Diamondbacks traded Andrew Chafin and filled his lefty specialist role with Bergen, for whom they traded Robbie Ray, at the 2020 trade deadline. The lefty can touch 95 mph but throwing strikes remains a challenge. He should get plenty of opportunities to rein it in this coming season..

J.B. Bukauskas RHP   Born: 10/11/96   Age: 24   Bats: R   Throws: R   Height: 6'0"   Weight: 210   Origin: Round 1, 2017 Draft (#15 overall)

YEAR	TEAM	LVL	AGE	W	L	SV	G	GS	IP	H	HR	BB/9	K/9	K	GB%	BABIP	WHIP	ERA	DRA-	WARP	MPH	FA%	Whiff%	CSP
2018	AST	ROK	21	0	0	0	1	1	1²	5	0	0.0	10.8	2	12.5%	.625	3.00	10.80	39	0.1				
2018	TRI	SS	21	0	0	0	3	3	8¹	8	0	2.2	9.7	9	45.5%	.364	1.20	0.00	235	-0.5				
2018	QC	LO-A	21	1	2	0	4	4	15	15	0	4.2	12.6	21	50.0%	.405	1.47	4.20	33	0.6				
2018	FAY	HI-A	21	3	0	0	5	5	28	13	1	4.2	10.0	31	58.7%	.194	0.93	1.61	67	0.7				
2018	CC	AA	21	0	0	0	1	1	6	1	0	3.0	12.0	8	60.0%	.100	0.50	0.00	64	0.1				
2019	JXN	AA	22	0	1	0	2	2	7	10	0	6.4	14.1	11	38.9%	.556	2.14	7.71	150	-0.2				
2019	CC	AA	22	2	4	1	20	14	85²	81	8	5.7	10.3	98	46.1%	.332	1.58	5.25	125	-1.3				
2021 FS	ARI	MLB	24	1	1	0	57	0	50	44	6	6.1	9.4	52	43.4%	.286	1.57	4.98	115	-0.3				
2021 DC	ARI	MLB	24	1	1	0	31	0	33	29	4	6.1	9.4	34	43.4%	.286	1.57	4.98	115	-0.1				

Comparables: Carson Fulmer, Duane Underwood Jr., Jorge Alcala

Bukauskas continues to soldier on with an undefined role. The longer the decision takes, the more inevitable it seems that he'll become a reliever. That's okay because he has the tools to be a good one quite soon. Excellent relievers can be more valuable than fringy starters these days anyway.

Madison Bumgarner LHP Born: 08/01/89 Age: 31 Bats: R Throws: L Height: 6'4" Weight: 255 Origin: Round 1, 2007 Draft (#10 overall)

YEAR	TEAM	LVL	AGE	W	L	SV	G	GS	IP	H	HR	BB/9	K/9	K	GB%	BABIP	WHIP	ERA	DRA-	WARP	MPH	FA%	Whiff%	CSP
2018	SF	MLB	28	6	7	0	21	21	129²	118	14	3.0	7.6	109	42.1%	.277	1.24	3.26	99	1.3	92.2	34.4%	21.6%	49.0%
2019	SF	MLB	29	9	9	0	34	34	207²	191	30	1.9	8.8	203	35.2%	.292	1.13	3.90	91	2.9	93.1	43.1%	24.7%	48.6%
2020	ARI	MLB	30	1	4	0	9	9	41²	47	13	2.8	6.5	30	33.3%	.266	1.44	6.48	189	-1.6	89.8	39.9%	17.4%	48.3%
2021 FS	ARI	MLB	31	8	9	0	26	26	150	152	26	2.3	7.9	131	36.0%	.292	1.28	4.48	107	0.4	92.2	40.8%	22.7%	48.6%
2021 DC	ARI	MLB	31	8	9	0	25	25	142	144	24	2.3	7.9	124	36.0%	.292	1.28	4.48	107	0.9	92.2	40.8%	22.7%	48.6%

Comparables: Stephen Strasburg, Nathan Eovaldi, Kyle Hendricks

Yelp reviews are a dicey proposition. Sure, all people have bad opinions some of the time but, in the aggregate, there's often a shred of truth with enough accumulated perspectives. There's no denying the wisdom of the crowds, but it can be hard to tell if the majority has established a greater truth, or if it's just a bunch of nitpicky jerks. Finding signal amidst the noise on Bumgarner's season one, however, likely would take precious few submissions (be they novice reviewers or seasoned evaluators). The altered and delayed start of the 2020 season reportedly set him back as the veteran struggled with velocity, location and the health of his back, all of which kept him from repeating his familiar success. His hypothetical Yelp reviews would be sure to contain complaints about quality, quantity and cost. That's enough to put your local restaurant out of business instantly. The Diamondbacks, however, have four more years of Bumgarner on the menu. They might need to let customers know the dish comes pre-cooked.

Slade Cecconi RHP Born: 06/24/99 Age: 22 Bats: R Throws: R Height: 6'4" Weight: 219 Origin: Round 1, 2020 Draft (#33 overall)

Cecconi is short on track record but big on stuff. The 33rd-overall pick in June was a draft-eligible sophomore who can pump the gas. With a legit four-pitch mix and an ability to throw strikes, Cecconi has as much upside as any pitching prospect in the Diamondbacks' system, though he's yet to throw a professional pitch.

Taylor Clarke RHP Born: 05/13/93 Age: 28 Bats: R Throws: R Height: 6'4" Weight: 220 Origin: Round 3, 2015 Draft (#76 overall)

YEAR	TEAM	LVL	AGE	W	L	SV	G	GS	IP	H	HR	BB/9	K/9	K	GB%	BABIP	WHIP	ERA	DRA-	WARP	MPH	FA%	Whiff%	CSP
2018	RNO	AAA	25	13	8	0	27	27	152	149	12	2.6	7.4	125	38.0%	.304	1.27	4.03	92	2.2				
2019	VIS	HI-A	26	1	0	0	1	1	6	3	0	0.0	4.5	3	64.7%	.176	0.50	0.00	59	0.2				
2019	RNO	AAA	26	3	1	0	8	8	36²	41	6	4.2	6.9	28	33.9%	.318	1.58	6.63	101	0.6				
2019	ARI	MLB	26	5	5	1	23	15	84²	86	23	3.2	7.1	67	39.2%	.260	1.37	5.31	132	-0.7	95.3	53.2%	23.1%	45.7%
2020	ARI	MLB	27	3	0	0	12	5	43¹	35	8	4.4	8.3	40	44.3%	.237	1.29	4.36	105	0.3	95.3	45.5%	22.3%	45.5%
2021 FS	ARI	MLB	28	8	9	0	26	26	150	147	26	3.6	8.1	135	39.3%	.286	1.39	4.80	111	0.1	95.3	50.0%	22.8%	45.6%
2021 DC	ARI	MLB	28	4	5	0	47	9	84	82	14	3.6	8.1	75	39.3%	.286	1.39	4.80	111	0.2	95.3	50.0%	22.8%	45.6%

Comparables: Buck Farmer, Robert Stephenson, Jeff Hoffman

The importance of hydration isn't lost on baseball players and critical liquids aren't just reserved for starters. Out in the bullpen, bottles of water, jugs of Gatorade and a carafe of coffee are standard fare. But Clarke was drinking something else in 2020. Some strange serum turned a lackluster Dr. Jekyll into a much more potent Mr. Hyde. Clarke was dubious again as a starting pitcher but batters managed just a .169/.272/.366 line off of him as a reliever. His ERA was a run and half better in relief and, while he didn't necessarily light the world on fire, he may have cemented his role going forward. The Diamondbacks have struggled to find consistency in the bullpen and Clarke looks to be part of the solution.

Stefan Crichton RHP Born: 02/29/92 Age: 29 Bats: R Throws: R Height: 6'3" Weight: 205 Origin: Round 23, 2013 Draft (#699 overall)

YEAR	TEAM	LVL	AGE	W	L	SV	G	GS	IP	H	HR	BB/9	K/9	K	GB%	BABIP	WHIP	ERA	DRA-	WARP	MPH	FA%	Whiff%	CSP
2018	RNO	AAA	26	0	2	0	14	0	16	19	4	5.6	9.6	17	55.1%	.341	1.81	10.12	78	0.3				
2019	RNO	AAA	27	4	3	1	36	0	57¹	52	4	2.4	8.2	52	57.9%	.300	1.17	3.61	50	2.1				
2019	ARI	MLB	27	1	0	0	28	0	30¹	23	3	2.4	9.8	33	52.5%	.260	1.02	3.56	76	0.5	94.5	63.6%	24.3%	49.9%
2020	ARI	MLB	28	2	2	5	26	0	26	22	1	3.1	8.0	23	47.9%	.292	1.19	2.42	89	0.4	93.7	61.4%	22.2%	48.3%
2021 FS	ARI	MLB	29	2	2	26	57	0	50	48	6	2.8	8.4	46	48.8%	.298	1.28	4.11	97	0.2	94.0	62.4%	23.1%	49.0%
2021 DC	ARI	MLB	29	2	2	26	57	0	60	58	7	2.8	8.4	56	48.8%	.298	1.28	4.11	97	0.4	94.0	62.4%	23.1%	49.0%

Comparables: Kevin McCarthy, Juan Minaya, Shawn Armstrong

While a lost season for a franchise is a downer for just about everyone, it does present an opportunity for those at the fringes. Crichton is one of those guys. He entered the year firmly entrenched in the bullpen and navigated his way to the closer's role following Archie Bradley's move to Cincinnati. While his peripherals are fairly mundane, Crichton has shown a feel for avoiding opponents' barrels—in fact, he's only allowed four "barrels" per Statcast across 56 1/3 innings over the past two seasons. He'll need to keep that up because he doesn't miss the number of bats normally required of a bullpen anchor.

Jon Duplantier RHP
Born: 07/11/94   Age: 26   Bats: L   Throws: R   Height: 6'4"   Weight: 240   Origin: Round 3, 2016 Draft (#89 overall)

YEAR	TEAM	LVL	AGE	W	L	SV	G	GS	IP	H	HR	BB/9	K/9	K	GB%	BABIP	WHIP	ERA	DRA-	WARP	MPH	FA%	Whiff%	CSP
2018	DIA	ROK	23	0	0	0	2	2	7	5	0	2.6	11.6	9	43.8%	.312	1.00	1.29	37	0.3				
2018	JXN	AA	23	5	1	0	14	14	67	52	4	3.8	9.1	68	54.0%	.284	1.19	2.69	99	0.5				
2019	DIA	ROK	24	0	0	0	2	2	2	5	1	13.5	13.5	3	50.0%	.571	4.00	18.00	194	-0.1				
2019	VIS	HI-A	24	0	0	0	1	1	3	2	0	0.0	9.0	3	50.0%	.333	0.67	0.00	103	0.0				
2019	RNO	AAA	24	1	2	0	13	11	38	31	1	6.6	10.4	44	44.7%	.330	1.55	5.21	60	1.4				
2019	ARI	MLB	24	1	1	1	15	3	36²	39	2	4.4	8.3	34	42.5%	.359	1.55	4.42	117	-0.1	94.1	59.0%	20.6%	47.9%
2021 FS	ARI	MLB	26	1	1	0	57	0	50	46	6	4.8	9.3	51	45.4%	.297	1.47	4.75	107	-0.1	94.1	59.0%	20.6%	47.9%
2021 DC	ARI	MLB	26	1	1	0	28	3	27	25	3	4.8	9.3	27	45.4%	.297	1.47	4.75	107	0.1	94.1	59.0%	20.6%	47.9%

Comparables: Ryan Helsley, Yonny Chirinos, Jordan Montgomery

Another year, another round of injuries for Duplantier. The former third-rounder was seen as a potential steal back in 2016, but the injury concerns that pushed him to the 89th overall pick have been a steady presence. It was elbow trouble in 2020 that kept the 26-year-old from contributing and he now seems destined for relief.

Zac Gallen RHP
Born: 08/03/95   Age: 25   Bats: R   Throws: R   Height: 6'2"   Weight: 198   Origin: Round 3, 2016 Draft (#106 overall)

YEAR	TEAM	LVL	AGE	W	L	SV	G	GS	IP	H	HR	BB/9	K/9	K	GB%	BABIP	WHIP	ERA	DRA-	WARP	MPH	FA%	Whiff%	CSP
2018	NO	AAA	22	8	9	0	25	25	133¹	148	14	3.2	9.2	136	38.6%	.354	1.47	3.65	79	2.8				
2019	NO	AAA	23	9	1	0	14	14	91¹	48	10	1.7	11.0	112	46.3%	.198	0.71	1.77	16	5.2				
2019	ARI	MLB	23	2	3	0	8	8	43²	37	5	3.7	10.9	53	44.5%	.305	1.26	2.89	70	1.1	95.6	50.7%	30.2%	45.2%
2019	MIA	MLB	23	1	3	0	7	7	36¹	25	3	4.5	10.7	43	34.1%	.259	1.18	2.72	89	0.6	94.4	48.3%	28.5%	45.2%
2020	ARI	MLB	24	3	2	0	12	12	72	55	9	3.1	10.2	82	46.4%	.269	1.11	2.75	78	1.5	95.2	39.2%	30.4%	42.4%
2021 FS	ARI	MLB	25	10	7	0	26	26	150	127	18	3.1	10.2	170	43.3%	.290	1.20	3.38	81	2.6	95.3	43.9%	30.0%	43.7%
2021 DC	ARI	MLB	25	10	8	0	27	27	159	135	19	3.1	10.2	181	43.3%	.290	1.20	3.38	81	3.2	95.3	43.9%	30.0%	43.7%

Comparables: José Berríos, Jack Flaherty, Jake Odorizzi

Biz Markie's career as a musician got off to an inauspicious start. His debut album dropped in 1988 and hardly anyone paid attention to "Goin' Off." The leading song on that album was titled, "Pickin' Boogers," and it should come as no surprise that few took notice. But a year later, things transformed for Markie. An odd, piano-laden rap dubbed, "Just a Friend" took the Billboard charts by storm. The song was everywhere. It holds two unique spots as both one of the greatest songs of hip-hop and also one of the most remarkable one-hit wonders ever. Gallen was born six years after "Just a Friend" hit the airwaves, and following a nifty bit of Bizness that sent Jazz Chisholm to the Marlins, he appears poised to be anything but a one-hit wonder—and could well end up the Markie acquisition of the Mike Hazen era. His sophomore effort proved that he's got staying power and won't be plummeting off the charts anytime soon.

Kevin Ginkel RHP
Born: 03/24/94   Age: 27   Bats: L   Throws: R   Height: 6'4"   Weight: 235   Origin: Round 22, 2016 Draft (#659 overall)

YEAR	TEAM	LVL	AGE	W	L	SV	G	GS	IP	H	HR	BB/9	K/9	K	GB%	BABIP	WHIP	ERA	DRA-	WARP	MPH	FA%	Whiff%	CSP
2018	VIS	HI-A	24	1	1	4	20	0	27¹	20	2	1.0	13.2	40	36.1%	.310	0.84	0.99	48	0.8				
2018	JXN	AA	24	5	0	5	34	0	42²	26	3	1.9	12.7	60	35.9%	.264	0.82	1.69	54	1.2				
2019	DIA	ROK	25	0	0	0	2	0	2	0	0	4.5	4.5	1	50.0%	.000	0.50	0.00	79	0.0				
2019	JXN	AA	25	1	2	5	14	0	16²	9	2	2.7	14.0	26	42.4%	.241	0.84	2.16	49	0.4				
2019	RNO	AAA	25	1	0	6	15	0	16²	10	2	4.3	19.4	36	39.1%	.381	1.08	1.62	31	0.8				
2019	ARI	MLB	25	3	0	2	25	0	24¹	15	2	3.3	10.4	28	34.5%	.232	0.99	1.48	78	0.4	95.3	54.0%	32.4%	42.5%
2020	ARI	MLB	26	0	2	1	19	0	16	21	3	7.3	10.1	18	29.2%	.400	2.12	6.75	119	0.0	97.0	59.7%	32.9%	42.2%
2021 FS	ARI	MLB	27	2	2	7	57	0	50	39	6	4.0	11.1	61	35.9%	.281	1.24	3.52	85	0.6	96.3	57.2%	32.7%	42.4%
2021 DC	ARI	MLB	27	2	2	7	57	0	60	47	8	4.0	11.1	74	35.9%	.281	1.24	3.52	85	0.8	96.3	57.2%	32.7%	42.4%

Comparables: Kyle Crick, Phil Maton, Keone Kela

The old saw is that it's better to be lucky than good. It's a tautology, of course—true in any given moment that it's said, but with no regard for the instances surrounding it. It's stupid, is what we're trying to say. Being good is a repeatable skill. Being lucky … less so. A year ago, Ginkel was probably more the former than the latter. His 2019 batting average on balls in play was leaner than a dinner on the Atkins diet. Last season, he went full Keto without reading the fine print. Turns out that being lucky or good is being spoiled for choice because Ginkel was neither. His ERA didn't dip below double-digits until his 12th appearance of the season in late August, and reached a season-low of 6.32 only briefly before he was optioned to the alternate site in mid-September. He'll have to try another diet in 2021.

Junior Guerra RHP
Born: 01/16/85   Age: 36   Bats: R   Throws: R   Height: 6'0"   Weight: 235   Origin: International Free Agent, 2001

YEAR	TEAM	LVL	AGE	W	L	SV	G	GS	IP	H	HR	BB/9	K/9	K	GB%	BABIP	WHIP	ERA	DRA-	WARP	MPH	FA%	Whiff%	CSP
2018	MIL	MLB	33	7	9	0	32	27	147	151	21	3.4	8.7	142	42.7%	.318	1.41	4.16	100	1.3	95.1	69.0%	24.8%	46.5%
2019	MIL	MLB	34	9	5	3	72	0	83²	58	11	3.9	8.3	77	43.2%	.221	1.12	3.55	82	1.2	96.1	60.2%	25.9%	45.0%
2020	ARI	MLB	35	1	2	0	25	0	23²	17	1	5.7	8.0	21	46.2%	.258	1.35	3.04	96	0.3	95.3	60.6%	26.9%	44.5%
2021 FS	ARI	MLB	36	2	3	0	57	0	50	46	6	4.4	8.1	44	44.7%	.283	1.42	4.30	102	0.1	95.6	63.6%	25.7%	45.5%

Comparables: Ian Kennedy, Jeff Samardzija, Mike Fiers

If you like wine and you don't like paying a ton for it, it's likely you spend an inordinate amount of time browsing the aisles at Trader Joe's. The selection is massive and every label showcases tasting notes that don't seem to match the price point. Blackberry, overripe plum, vanilla and tobacco for just six bucks? What a steal! Then, upon consumption, yeah, this tastes like a $6 bottle of wine. For 10 times as much money you could score something actually remarkable. Considering that dinner tonight consists of Trader Joe's lasagna, however, a $6 wine may actually be the right call. There's something to be said for a proper pairing, after all.

Bryce Jarvis RHP   Born: 12/26/97   Age: 23   Bats: L   Throws: R   Height: 6'2"   Weight: 195   Origin: Round 1, 2020 Draft (#18 overall)

Not many people know that Duke University has a flux capacitor on campus. Fewer are aware that it is property of the baseball team. Jarvis was clearly the university's trial case because, as an underclassman, he was a total throwback. Upper-80s heater, good changeup, breaking balls that didn't vary in velo much from the fastball. After time traveling, Jarvis emerged his junior year as a guy who'd broken into the modern realm with a fastball approaching the mid 90s at times, and helping the rest of his arsenal play up. Strong, albeit abbreviated, results immediately followed, and Jarvis found himself selected in the middle of the first round of the 2020 draft. He could move quickly and is arguably the Diamondbacks' best pitching prospect.

Levi Kelly RHP   Born: 05/14/99   Age: 22   Bats: R   Throws: R   Height: 6'4"   Weight: 205   Origin: Round 8, 2018 Draft (#249 overall)

YEAR	TEAM	LVL	AGE	W	L	SV	G	GS	IP	H	HR	BB/9	K/9	K	GB%	BABIP	WHIP	ERA	DRA-	WARP	MPH	FA%	Whiff%	CSP
2018	DIA	ROK	19	0	0	0	4	4	6	3	0	3.0	9.0	6	46.7%	.200	0.83	0.00	57	0.2				
2019	KC	LO-A	20	5	1	0	22	22	100¹	72	4	3.5	11.3	126	46.0%	.293	1.11	2.15	65	2.4				
2021 FS	ARI	MLB	22	2	3	0	57	0	50	46	7	5.3	9.0	49	42.2%	.287	1.52	4.97	116	-0.3				

Comparables: Neftalí Feliz, Casey Crosby, Robert Stephenson

Adjusted expectations became the norm last year, and while all of the uncertainty threw some players off their game, Kelly took full advantage of the opportunity. The youngster made the Diamondbacks' 60-man roster, then proceeded to throw a handful of highly impressive relief innings in July against big-league regulars in summer camp, often making them look overmatched. In hindsight, striking out Eduardo Escobar looks less impressive now but Kelly flashed real, quality stuff. His mid-90s gas and deadly slider play right now, and his changeup flashes enough to give hope that he could have three quality offerings. The effort in his delivery still suggests a relief role, but look for the Diamondbacks to keep him as a starter a bit longer in hopes of turning the former eighth-round pick into a rotation piece.

Merrill Kelly RHP   Born: 10/14/88   Age: 32   Bats: R   Throws: R   Height: 6'2"   Weight: 210   Origin: Round 8, 2010 Draft (#251 overall)

YEAR	TEAM	LVL	AGE	W	L	SV	G	GS	IP	H	HR	BB/9	K/9	K	GB%	BABIP	WHIP	ERA	DRA-	WARP	MPH	FA%	Whiff%	CSP
2019	ARI	MLB	30	13	14	0	32	32	183¹	184	29	2.8	7.8	158	41.9%	.294	1.31	4.42	101	1.6	94.1	65.4%	22.4%	49.0%
2020	ARI	MLB	31	3	2	0	5	5	31¹	26	5	1.4	8.3	29	45.6%	.247	0.99	2.59	87	0.5	93.9	65.5%	23.5%	51.0%
2021 FS	ARI	MLB	32	9	9	0	26	26	150	146	23	3.0	8.2	136	42.9%	.290	1.31	4.28	101	1.0	94.0	65.5%	22.6%	49.4%
2021 DC	ARI	MLB	32	7	8	0	22	22	120	117	18	3.0	8.2	109	42.9%	.290	1.31	4.28	101	1.2	94.0	65.5%	22.6%	49.4%

Comparables: Rick Porcello, Ian Kennedy, Ervin Santana

It took Kelly nine years from the time he was drafted to make the majors. That includes five years in the minors and four in Korea, where he was good enough to earn a two-year major-league pact from the Diamondbacks. He soaked up innings at the back of the rotation in 2019, and when more was asked of him heading into 2020, he was up to the task ... through five starts. Baseball is cruel, and what took nine years (and then some) to achieve has been imperiled in the flash of an eye: Kelly required surgery to address thoracic outlet syndrome. The recovery from that surgery is fraught, and the results for those who do come back haven't been inspiring. According to research by FanGraphs' Jay Jaffe, only five pitchers since 2001 have returned to produce better ERA- totals post-surgery than prior to going under the knife. It's a tough blow for a player whose performance laid the groundwork for others like Josh Lindblom and Chris Flexen to reimagine their big-league careers after stints in Korea.

Mike Leake RHP   Born: 11/12/87   Age: 33   Bats: R   Throws: R   Height: 5'10"   Weight: 165   Origin: Round 1, 2009 Draft (#8 overall)

YEAR	TEAM	LVL	AGE	W	L	SV	G	GS	IP	H	HR	BB/9	K/9	K	GB%	BABIP	WHIP	ERA	DRA-	WARP	MPH	FA%	Whiff%	CSP
2018	SEA	MLB	30	10	10	0	31	31	185²	207	23	1.6	5.8	119	49.4%	.307	1.30	4.36	99	1.8	90.5	59.4%	16.8%	50.7%
2019	ARI	MLB	31	3	3	0	10	10	60	74	15	1.2	4.0	27	45.0%	.292	1.37	4.35	184	-2.1	90.5	57.5%	17.1%	50.4%
2019	SEA	MLB	31	9	8	0	22	22	137	153	26	1.2	6.6	100	47.7%	.298	1.26	4.27	120	-0.2	90.1	58.9%	18.6%	51.3%
2021 FS	ARI	MLB	33	8	9	0	26	26	150	169	25	1.9	6.5	109	46.8%	.305	1.34	4.71	113	-0.1	90.4	58.8%	17.7%	50.9%

Comparables: Jeremy Hellickson, Rick Porcello, Brad Radke

Leake was the first big-league player to opt out of the 2020 season. Now 33 years old, it remains to be seen if he can continue his durable, innings-eating, back-end starter ways.

Yoan López RHP   Born: 01/02/93   Age: 28   Bats: R   Throws: R   Height: 6'3"   Weight: 205   Origin: International Free Agent, 2015

YEAR	TEAM	LVL	AGE	W	L	SV	G	GS	IP	H	HR	BB/9	K/9	K	GB%	BABIP	WHIP	ERA	DRA-	WARP	MPH	FA%	Whiff%	CSP
2018	JXN	AA	25	2	6	12	45	0	61²	38	4	3.8	12.7	87	35.3%	.260	1.04	2.92	58	1.6				
2018	ARI	MLB	25	0	0	0	10	0	9	7	2	1.0	11.0	11	52.2%	.250	0.89	3.00	85	0.1	98.5	67.2%	28.8%	54.4%
2019	ARI	MLB	26	2	7	1	70	0	60²	52	11	2.5	6.2	42	43.3%	.234	1.14	3.41	106	0.1	98.1	57.1%	21.3%	47.9%
2020	ARI	MLB	27	0	1	0	20	0	19²	21	4	4.1	7.3	16	54.8%	.293	1.53	5.95	102	0.2	96.9	54.7%	25.2%	48.3%
2021 FS	ARI	MLB	28	2	3	0	57	0	50	48	7	3.6	8.6	47	44.2%	.293	1.37	4.49	104	0.0	97.7	56.8%	22.8%	48.3%
2021 DC	ARI	MLB	28	2	3	0	57	0	60	57	9	3.6	8.6	57	44.2%	.293	1.37	4.49	104	0.2	97.7	56.8%	22.8%	48.3%

Comparables: Mike Mayers, John Curtiss, Archie Bradley

You could see it coming, couldn't you? In 2019, López got damn lucky. He outperformed his ERA by almost two full runs according to DRA and, night after night, got away with fat fastballs and hanging sliders that managed, somehow, to repeatedly go unpunished. That's not to say his stuff was so filthy that it couldn't be hit. It often was hit, and hit hard, but hit right at a defender again and again. Regression is a you-know-what and it caught up with him in 2020 in a very predictable, debilitating way. The once-prized Cuban has a flat fastball that he can't throw carefully enough for strikes to get to his decent slider. He's running out of leash and, without some improvement, 2021 could be his swan song in the desert.

Corbin Martin RHP Born: 12/28/95 Age: 25 Bats: R Throws: R Height: 6'2" Weight: 228 Origin: Round 2, 2017 Draft (#56 overall)

YEAR	TEAM	LVL	AGE	W	L	SV	G	GS	IP	H	HR	BB/9	K/9	K	GB%	BABIP	WHIP	ERA	DRA-	WARP	MPH	FA%	Whiff%	CSP
2018	FAY	HI-A	22	2	0	1	4	3	19	4	0	3.3	12.3	26	63.9%	.111	0.58	0.00	65	0.5				
2018	CC	AA	22	7	2	0	21	18	103	84	7	2.4	8.4	96	47.7%	.277	1.09	2.97	69	2.3				
2019	RR	AAA	23	2	1	0	9	8	37¹	33	2	4.3	10.8	45	38.7%	.348	1.37	3.13	61	1.3				
2019	HOU	MLB	23	1	1	0	5	5	19¹	23	8	5.6	8.8	19	42.6%	.283	1.81	5.59	147	-0.3	97.2	62.6%	23.8%	44.3%
2021 FS	ARI	MLB	25	9	8	0	26	26	150	133	21	4.2	9.3	154	42.1%	.284	1.35	4.18	98	1.2	97.2	62.6%	23.8%	44.3%
2021 DC	ARI	MLB	25	1	2	0	8	8	32	28	4	4.2	9.3	32	42.1%	.284	1.35	4.18	98	0.4	97.2	62.6%	23.8%	44.3%

Comparables: Brandon Bielak, Mitch Keller, Wade LeBlanc

Delayed gratification isn't something Americans are much accustomed to. Jeff Bezos and company have made acquiring tangible benefits easier than ever no matter where you live or what you seek. But there's something to be said for the buildup, for anticipation. When it comes to Martin, well, that's all the Diamondbacks can lean on. His recovery from Tommy John hasn't hit any publicly reported snags and it feels as if the best prospect acquired in the team's trade of Zack Greinke will finally see the field in Sedona Red come 2021. Considering Seth Beer's defensive issues and J.B. Bukauskas' strike-throwing troubles, a lot hinges on when, and more importantly, how Martin reacquaints himself with the majors.

Humberto Mejía RHP Born: 03/03/97 Age: 24 Bats: R Throws: R Height: 6'4" Weight: 235 Origin: International Free Agent, 2013

YEAR	TEAM	LVL	AGE	W	L	SV	G	GS	IP	H	HR	BB/9	K/9	K	GB%	BABIP	WHIP	ERA	DRA-	WARP	MPH	FA%	Whiff%	CSP
2018	BAT	SS	21	1	6	0	15	12	62²	55	8	2.0	8.5	59	36.9%	.275	1.10	3.30	113	0.0				
2019	CLI	LO-A	22	5	1	1	13	10	66²	42	4	2.6	9.2	68	32.7%	.229	0.92	2.02	55	1.9				
2019	JUP	HI-A	22	0	1	0	5	4	23²	15	2	1.9	8.0	21	43.8%	.210	0.85	2.28	63	0.5				
2020	MIA	MLB	23	0	2	0	3	3	10	13	3	5.4	9.9	11	29.0%	.357	1.90	5.40	115	0.0	94.0	52.2%	22.0%	46.6%
2021 FS	ARI	MLB	24	2	3	0	57	0	50	50	8	3.4	8.0	44	36.1%	.291	1.38	4.75	111	-0.2	94.0	52.2%	22.0%	46.6%
2021 DC	ARI	MLB	24	0	0	0	3	3	12	12	2	3.4	8.0	10	36.1%	.291	1.38	4.75	111	0.1	94.0	52.2%	22.0%	46.6%

Comparables: Joe Musgrove, David Paulino, Beau Burrows

Part of the Starling Marté return, Mejía made his big-league debut in 2020 out of pure necessity. A virus-ravaged Miami squad turned to him in a pinch, then dealt him to the Diamondbacks where his arsenal likely fits best in a relief role.

Keury Mella RHP Born: 08/02/93 Age: 27 Bats: R Throws: R Height: 6'2" Weight: 230 Origin: International Free Agent, 2012

YEAR	TEAM	LVL	AGE	W	L	SV	G	GS	IP	H	HR	BB/9	K/9	K	GB%	BABIP	WHIP	ERA	DRA-	WARP	MPH	FA%	Whiff%	CSP
2018	PNS	AA	24	7	3	0	16	16	85	70	8	3.3	9.2	87	47.6%	.279	1.19	3.07	88	1.1				
2018	LOU	AAA	24	2	1	0	5	5	23	20	1	2.3	5.5	14	39.4%	.275	1.13	2.74	117	-0.1				
2018	CIN	MLB	24	0	0	0	4	0	9¹	13	4	7.7	7.7	8	29.0%	.360	2.25	8.68	201	-0.4	96.7	70.8%	24.1%	51.0%
2019	LOU	AAA	25	8	14	0	27	27	142²	160	22	3.5	6.4	102	52.0%	.308	1.51	5.05	110	1.8				
2019	CIN	MLB	25	0	0	0	2	0	3²	5	0	4.9	9.8	4	33.3%	.417	1.91	7.36	99	0.0	96.9	77.4%	27.8%	41.1%
2020	ARI	MLB	26	2	0	0	11	0	10	10	1	2.7	9.0	10	44.8%	.321	1.30	1.80	92	0.1	96.8	67.3%	24.3%	45.5%
2021 FS	ARI	MLB	27	2	3	0	57	0	50	49	7	4.0	7.7	42	45.9%	.290	1.43	4.85	110	-0.2	96.8	69.1%	24.5%	46.6%
2021 DC	ARI	MLB	27	2	3	0	57	0	60	59	8	4.0	7.7	51	45.9%	.290	1.43	4.85	110	0.0	96.8	69.1%	24.5%	46.6%

Comparables: Chase De Jong, Drew Anderson, Lucas Sims

Early aughts alternative band Sum 41 had a hit on their hands with their album *All Killer, No Filler*. Mella fits that theme so long as one flips the title around. Don't let the ERA fool you—with his merely okay stuff and command, he can get in too deep and leave with a fat lip.

Hector Rondón RHP Born: 02/26/88 Age: 33 Bats: R Throws: R Height: 6'3" Weight: 225 Origin: International Free Agent, 2004

YEAR	TEAM	LVL	AGE	W	L	SV	G	GS	IP	H	HR	BB/9	K/9	K	GB%	BABIP	WHIP	ERA	DRA-	WARP	MPH	FA%	Whiff%	CSP
2018	HOU	MLB	30	2	5	15	63	0	59	58	4	3.1	10.2	67	47.2%	.340	1.32	3.20	62	1.4	98.8	61.7%	30.4%	49.0%
2019	HOU	MLB	31	3	2	0	62	1	60²	56	10	3.0	7.1	48	50.3%	.264	1.25	3.71	117	-0.2	98.3	60.1%	22.7%	47.0%
2020	ARI	MLB	32	1	0	0	23	0	20	25	6	5.0	10.3	23	35.5%	.339	1.80	7.65	119	0.0	97.2	59.2%	19.4%	48.7%
2021 FS	ARI	MLB	33	2	2	0	57	0	50	46	6	3.1	8.8	48	44.2%	.291	1.27	3.69	92	0.4	98.1	60.2%	23.6%	48.0%

Comparables: Pedro Báez, Bryan Shaw, Rafael Soriano

Rondón still throws about as hard as he used to—he might have lost a tick or so from his absolute peak in 2018—but he hasn't been nearly as effective of late. In 2019, he couldn't miss bats anymore, following an eight percentage point drop in strikeout rate. Last year saw a rebound in his ability to induce swings and misses but a 3.5 percentage point uptick in walk rate *and* he gave up double-digit hits per nine. He was getting battered in the zone when he could actually manage to find it. At 33 years old, Rondón is going to have to rediscover himself—and maybe ease up on his sinker usage—if he wants to find a big-league deal.

Caleb Smith LHP Born: 07/28/91 Age: 29 Bats: R Throws: L Height: 6'0" Weight: 206 Origin: Round 14, 2013 Draft (#434 overall)

YEAR	TEAM	LVL	AGE	W	L	SV	G	GS	IP	H	HR	BB/9	K/9	K	GB%	BABIP	WHIP	ERA	DRA-	WARP	MPH	FA%	Whiff%	CSP
2018	MIA	MLB	26	5	6	0	16	16	77¹	63	10	3.8	10.2	88	28.2%	.279	1.24	4.19	90	1.1	94.3	59.1%	27.4%	48.7%
2019	JAX	AA	27	0	0	0	2	2	9¹	7	4	1.9	18.3	19	25.0%	.250	0.96	5.79	58	0.2				
2019	MIA	MLB	27	10	11	0	28	28	153¹	128	33	3.5	9.9	168	26.0%	.252	1.23	4.52	93	2.0	93.5	53.7%	28.0%	47.1%
2020	ARI	MLB	28	0	0	0	5	4	14	6	3	7.7	9.6	15	27.3%	.100	1.29	2.57	134	-0.1	93.4	51.3%	35.4%	45.0%
2021 FS	ARI	MLB	29	9	8	0	26	26	150	123	25	4.1	10.2	170	30.0%	.268	1.28	3.99	95	1.5	93.7	54.5%	28.6%	47.2%
2021 DC	ARI	MLB	29	5	6	0	25	25	77	63	12	4.1	10.2	87	30.0%	.268	1.28	3.99	95	1.0	93.7	54.5%	28.6%	47.2%

Comparables: Steven Brault, Austin Brice, Marco Gonzales

There's a dirty little secret that's rarely whispered and almost certainly never spoken aloud: Some of Dave Stewart's trades were alright. Take, for example, the one that netted the Diamondbacks left-hander Robbie Ray. For a few years there, Ray was quite valuable and, often, a dominant-if-flawed starting pitcher. When he wasn't on, he was still able to rack up strikeouts but walked too many and was prone to the long ball. Smith isn't wholly dissimilar in that the free passes and dingers can pile up on him without the elite strikeout numbers. Will a return to full health and a change of scenery do him well? That's the gamble Hazen is making. If he's right, the Marlins might have to stop picking up his calls, because between Zac Gallen and Smith they'll have given up 40 percent of a starting rotation.

Riley Smith RHP Born: 01/15/95 Age: 26 Bats: R Throws: R Height: 6'1" Weight: 175 Origin: Round 24, 2016 Draft (#719 overall)

YEAR	TEAM	LVL	AGE	W	L	SV	G	GS	IP	H	HR	BB/9	K/9	K	GB%	BABIP	WHIP	ERA	DRA-	WARP	MPH	FA%	Whiff%	CSP
2018	VIS	HI-A	23	8	6	0	26	25	151¹	141	15	2.9	8.8	148	48.2%	.310	1.25	3.57	80	2.4				
2019	JXN	AA	24	4	4	0	13	13	71¹	65	4	2.0	7.8	62	48.6%	.298	1.14	2.27	80	0.9				
2019	RNO	AAA	24	2	2	0	12	12	62²	85	15	2.9	6.9	48	41.7%	.352	1.68	6.89	141	-0.1				
2020	ARI	MLB	25	2	0	0	6	0	18¹	15	1	2.5	8.8	18	46.8%	.311	1.09	1.47	85	0.3	95.3	62.8%	13.9%	53.5%
2021 FS	ARI	MLB	26	2	2	1	57	0	50	50	6	2.7	7.7	42	45.0%	.297	1.31	4.24	100	0.1	95.3	62.8%	13.9%	53.5%
2021 DC	ARI	MLB	26	2	2	1	57	0	60	60	8	2.7	7.7	51	45.0%	.297	1.31	4.24	100	0.4	95.3	62.8%	13.9%	53.5%

Comparables: Tyler Wilson, Dillon Tate, Michael King

The latter portion of the 2020 season provided few cheering opportunities for Diamondbacks fans, but Smith provided some moments to smile about. Long relief suited the contact-oriented, strike-throwing righty. A similar role may await him in 2021.

Blake Walston LHP Born: 06/28/01 Age: 20 Bats: L Throws: L Height: 6'5" Weight: 175 Origin: Round 1, 2019 Draft (#26 overall)

YEAR	TEAM	LVL	AGE	W	L	SV	G	GS	IP	H	HR	BB/9	K/9	K	GB%	BABIP	WHIP	ERA	DRA-	WARP	MPH	FA%	Whiff%	CSP
2019	DIA	ROK	18	0	0	0	3	2	5	2	0	0.0	19.8	11	83.3%	.333	0.40	1.80	20	0.3				
2019	HIL	SS	18	0	0	0	3	3	6	6	0	3.0	9.0	6	41.2%	.353	1.33	3.00	122	-0.1				
2021 FS	ARI	MLB	20	2	3	0	57	0	50	49	8	5.3	9.1	50	41.1%	.304	1.58	5.43	127	-0.6				

The saying is to never judge a book by its cover because it doesn't adequately relay to the reader what is going to happen in the book. The same can be true for pitching prospects, but sometimes what's on the surface is a good reflection of the whole package. So it is with Walston, who is the definition of "projectable" at a lean 6-foot-5. He'll sit in the low-to-mid 90s with his fastball, but the hope is he starts to see some velocity creep as he focuses on baseball (he was a quarterback in high school) and pack good weight onto his lanky frame. The curveball is a potential plus offering, but both his changeup and a recently developed slider lag behind. Add it all up and you get a mid-rotation outcome should everything come together, and more in the tank if there's a velocity bump. As with any book or prospect, though, you've got to read all the way to the end to know how it turns out.

Luke Weaver RHP Born: 08/21/93 Age: 27 Bats: R Throws: R Height: 6'2" Weight: 185 Origin: Round 1, 2014 Draft (#27 overall)

YEAR	TEAM	LVL	AGE	W	L	SV	G	GS	IP	H	HR	BB/9	K/9	K	GB%	BABIP	WHIP	ERA	DRA-	WARP	MPH	FA%	Whiff%	CSP
2018	STL	MLB	24	7	11	0	30	25	136¹	150	19	3.6	8.0	121	41.8%	.325	1.50	4.95	103	1.1	95.8	57.7%	22.4%	48.9%
2019	ARI	MLB	25	4	3	0	12	12	64¹	55	6	2.0	9.7	69	40.8%	.292	1.07	2.94	73	1.5	96.2	52.1%	26.0%	47.4%
2020	ARI	MLB	26	1	9	0	12	12	52	63	10	3.1	9.5	55	32.7%	.349	1.56	6.58	110	0.2	96.1	54.0%	24.9%	47.3%
2021 FS	ARI	MLB	27	9	8	0	26	26	150	138	21	3.0	9.5	157	37.4%	.294	1.26	3.87	93	1.7	96.0	54.7%	24.4%	47.9%
2021 DC	ARI	MLB	27	7	7	0	24	24	121	111	17	3.0	9.5	127	37.4%	.294	1.26	3.87	93	1.7	96.0	54.7%	24.4%	47.9%

Comparables: Kevin Gausman, José Berríos, Jake Odorizzi

You've had a long week. A long several weeks, really. But it's Friday and it's time to shine, cut loose, change things up, and bring the heat. Only one problem—your wardrobe isn't complying and insists on throwing you a curveball. Nothing you want to wear is clean but instead soiled and tarnished ever so slightly. So you go digging through your closet and find that designer shirt you never wear. It's not that old and it was purchased with the promise of making you look both smart and cool. But every time you slip it on there's just something that doesn't work. No good with denim, no good with khaki. It's too soon to throw it out, so back on the hanger it goes to be deployed at a later date with hopefully, somehow, better results.

Taylor Widener RHP Born: 10/24/94   Age: 26   Bats: L   Throws: R   Height: 6'0"   Weight: 230   Origin: Round 12, 2016 Draft (#368 overall)

YEAR	TEAM	LVL	AGE	W	L	SV	G	GS	IP	H	HR	BB/9	K/9	K	GB%	BABIP	WHIP	ERA	DRA-	WARP	MPH	FA%	Whiff%	CSP
2018	JXN	AA	23	5	8	0	26	25	137¹	99	12	2.8	11.5	176	34.8%	.276	1.03	2.75	64	3.6				
2019	RNO	AAA	24	6	7	0	23	23	100	133	23	3.7	9.8	109	30.8%	.383	1.74	8.10	138	0.0				
2020	ARI	MLB	25	0	1	0	12	0	20	14	5	5.4	9.9	22	37.3%	.196	1.30	4.50	123	-0.1	96.2	65.1%	29.6%	48.1%
2021 FS	ARI	MLB	26	2	2	0	57	0	50	45	8	4.2	9.6	53	34.2%	.288	1.38	4.51	104	0.0	96.2	65.1%	29.6%	48.1%
2021 DC	ARI	MLB	26	2	2	0	51	0	54	49	8	4.2	9.6	57	34.2%	.288	1.38	4.51	104	0.2	96.2	65.1%	29.6%	48.1%

Comparables: Nabil Crismatt, Tyler Thornburg, Ryan Helsley

Widener's debut season didn't exactly go as he'd hoped. His relative lack of height, mixed with a flat fastball and iffy command, made for some ugly outings. Once thought of as a rotation option, he'll need to turn things around in 2021 just to prove he belongs in the bullpen.

Alex Young LHP Born: 09/09/93   Age: 27   Bats: L   Throws: L   Height: 6'3"   Weight: 220   Origin: Round 2, 2015 Draft (#43 overall)

YEAR	TEAM	LVL	AGE	W	L	SV	G	GS	IP	H	HR	BB/9	K/9	K	GB%	BABIP	WHIP	ERA	DRA-	WARP	MPH	FA%	Whiff%	CSP
2018	JXN	AA	24	5	1	0	9	9	50²	49	3	2.8	8.5	48	37.4%	.324	1.28	3.91	75	1.0				
2018	RNO	AAA	24	5	4	0	20	12	80	99	12	2.6	6.9	61	42.4%	.341	1.52	5.96	95	1.0				
2019	RNO	AAA	25	4	3	0	20	8	54²	66	6	4.3	10.5	64	48.8%	.380	1.68	6.09	89	1.1				
2019	ARI	MLB	25	7	5	0	17	15	83¹	72	14	2.9	7.7	71	48.6%	.252	1.19	3.56	88	1.3	90.6	59.4%	27.4%	44.9%
2020	ARI	MLB	26	2	4	0	15	7	46¹	51	11	2.7	7.6	39	36.7%	.288	1.40	5.44	137	-0.5	92.2	54.6%	24.5%	46.5%
2021 FS	ARI	MLB	27	9	9	0	26	26	150	146	21	3.3	8.1	134	41.7%	.292	1.35	4.39	103	0.8	91.4	57.1%	26.0%	45.6%
2021 DC	ARI	MLB	27	4	5	0	52	8	86	84	12	3.3	8.1	77	41.7%	.292	1.35	4.39	103	0.5	91.4	57.1%	26.0%	45.6%

Comparables: Matt Hall, Ryan Borucki, Max Fried

They say money isn't everything but it makes life a lot easier. It seems like one would need a pretty large sum to test that hypothesis, but the logic checks out. If velocity is currency for pitchers, Young got richer by adding a tick to his fastball and its sinking and cutting variants last year. That's no small deal for Young, a guy who was pushing toward the mid-90s at times in college but registered an average fastball velo below 90 mph in 2019 as a first-time big-leaguer. The problem is that he didn't get much for his money. His meager strikeout rate held as did his ability to limit walks, but what made him vulnerable is what happened when batters made contact. In that regard, he fared terribly and there's no simple remedy.

COLORADO ROCKIES

Essay by Tom Ley

Player comments by Matt Sussman and BP staff

There's a moment from my life as a Colorado Rockies fan that I don't like to dwell on too often, due to embarrassment. It was an hour or so before the start of Game 1 of the 2007 World Series, which the Rockies had ridden into on the back of an improbable, delirious run of games in which they were essentially unbeatable. I was 19 and preparing to watch the game with my family in a Denver bar packed with sweaty, exuberant baseball fans. My brother and I started talking about the team and decided, while quite literally high off having watched our favorite baseball team put together one of the more shocking World Series runs in history, that this was just the beginning.

We giddily reminded each other that the Rockies had Troy Tulowitzki, Matt Holliday, Garrett Atkins, Todd Helton and Brad Hawpe on the team. We had Jeff Francis and Ubaldo Jiménez and Franklin Morales, too. What we had was *a core*, a group of players that a good team could be—had been!—built around. One of us, totally giving ourselves over to the euphoria of the moment, may have even invoked the '96 Yankees as a point of comparison.

We were dumb! Extremely dumb. The Rockies would go on to get swept and humiliated by the Red Sox in that series, and the core of stud players that my brother and I had goofily marveled at was soon smashed and scattered. I bring this memory up here not because I wish to embarrass myself in front of the esteemed readers of the Baseball Prospectus Annual, but because it is an illustrative example of what it's felt like to watch the Rockies try and mostly fail to build winning baseball teams over the course of their 28-year existence.

The Rockies have always had good players. For as deranged as my brother and I may have been on that night in 2007, there is no denying the fact that Holliday, who had a 1.012 OPS in 2007 and produced 6 WAR, was a deserved NL MVP runner-up. Nor is there any denying the greatness of Tulowitzki, who had just finished his first full season as a big-leaguer by producing 6.8 WAR and establishing himself as one of the best young players in the game. You must even admit that Jeff Francis—no, sorry, nevermind, we are not talking about Jeff Francis. We are moving on!

COLORADO ROCKIES PROSPECTUS
2020 W-L: 26-34, 4TH IN NL WEST

Pythag	.380	28th	dWin%	.375	26th
RS/G	4.58	15th	B-Age	29.2	23rd
RA/G	5.88	30th	P-Age	27.3	4th
DRC+	93	26th	FIP	5.11	28th
DRA-	109	24th	DER	.685	26th
Payroll	$54M	17th	M$/MW	$4.5M	20th

- Opened 1995
- Open air
- Natural surface
- Fence profile: 8' to 16'6"

Three-Year Park Factors

Runs	Runs/RH	Runs/LH	HR/RH	HR/LH
112	112	112	109	111

Top Hitter WARP	1.5 Nolan Arenado
Top Pitcher WARP	1.8 Germán Márquez
Top Prospect	Zac Veen

Payroll History (in millions)

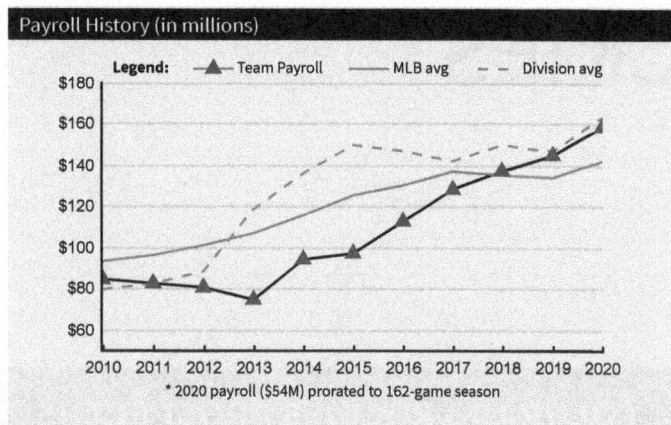

Legend: — Team Payroll — MLB avg - - - Division avg

* 2020 payroll ($54M) prorated to 162-game season

Future Commitments (in millions)

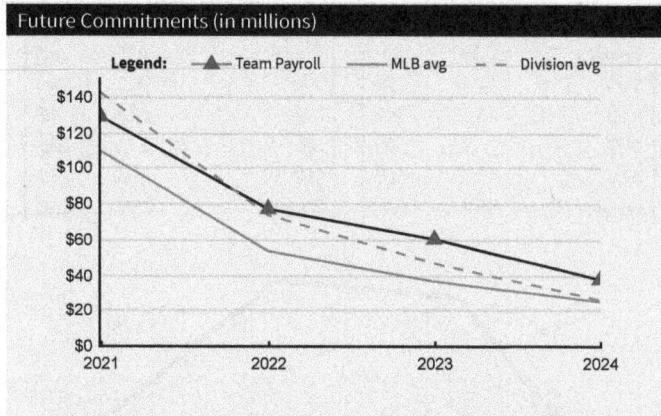

Legend: — Team Payroll — MLB avg - - - Division avg

Farm System Ranking

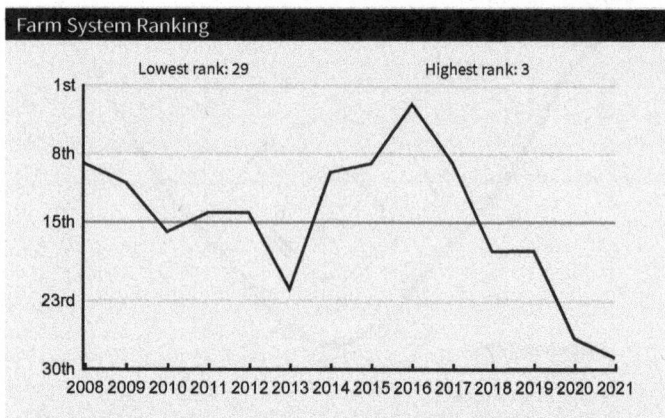

Lowest rank: 29   Highest rank: 3

Personnel

General Manager
Jeff Bridich

Manager
Bud Black

**Assistant General Manager -
Baseball Operations**
Zach Rosenthal

**Assistant General Manager -
Player Development**
Zach Wilson

**Assistant General Manager -
Player Personnel**
Jon Weil

Before that 2007 crew there was Todd Helton flirting with .400; there was Larry Walker winning the MVP on his way to the Hall of Fame; there was Andres Galarraga, Vinny Castilla and Dante Bichette being good enough to earn their nickname as The Blake Street Bombers. Pick out any Rockies roster from years past, even the ones in which the team's record was especially miserable, and more often than not you'll find yourself looking at a list that includes some legitimately good players. The Rockies have always managed to find and develop real, meaningful talent to put on the programs. They've just never been very good at completing the second step to creating a winning baseball team: actually filling out the rest of the roster with useful baseball players.

This inability to actually turn building blocks into a building has perhaps never been more obvious than it is right now. Take a look at the rosters that have been assembled by Jeff Bridich since he took over the general manager role in 2015. Over that period of time the Rockies have finished above .500 in just two seasons, both of which culminated in uninspiring playoff appearances. They have managed to do this all while having the roster anchored by a frankly excellent core of hitters.

I'm serious! This is not 19-year-old me shouting beer-soaked proclamations from a bar booth. Since 2015, Nolan Arenado, Trevor Story and Charlie Blackmon have combined to amass 69.8 WAR while wearing Rockies uniforms. Now pick basically any successful team from that same period of time, and see how their top three hitters by WAR stack up against the Rockies' crew. Kris Bryant, Javy Baez and Anthony Rizzo? 67.5 WAR. Justin Turner, Corey Seager and Cody Bellinger? 61.5 WAR. Jose Altuve, George Springer and Alex Bregman? 76.7 WAR.

Are you ready for the horrifying twist? Here it is: All of the hitters who made at least one plate appearance for the Rockies from 2015-2020 and are not named Trevor Story, Nolan Arenado or Charlie Blackmon combined to earn an additional *six wins above replacement*. Six! Apply the same criteria to the Cubs, Dodgers, and Astros and you end up with, respectively, 69.3, 103.1, and 100 additional WAR provided by hitters outside of the team's Top 3.

It seems as if this should not be possible. It is fair to acknowledge the payroll discrepancies that naturally make it harder for Rockies to fill out a productive lineup than it is for the Dodgers, but it also feels fair to say that if you gave any half-decent GM a few million dollars to spend in the free-agent market every year for the last five years, they would be able to cobble together a collection of dudes who could provide more than 6 WAR over the course of a half decade. Bridich has had a lot more than just a few million dollars to spend.

There was the $70 million he splurged on Ian Desmond, the $27.5 million spent on Gerardo Parra and the $24 million that went to Daniel Murphy. Then there was the $24 million not spent on DJ LeMahieu, who fetched that much money from the Yankees in the 2018 offseason and immediately started playing like an MVP candidate.

It gets worse! We must unfortunately revisit Bridich's attempt to imitate the champion 2015 Royals by assembling a super bullpen, which amounted to spending a combined $135 million on Jason Motte, Mike Dunn, Wade Davis, Jake McGee and Bryan Shaw. Add these fellas' contributions to those of the aforementioned crew of free-agent hitters and what do you get? Negative 3.7 WAR. Drew Butera was a better pitcher than they were collectively, even on a rate basis. Like I said, being a Rockies fan is very frustrating.

Some of these missteps could have been corrected with the rise of home-grown talent. The best way to fill a giant hole in your payroll is to develop some studs from the farm system and get a bunch of wins out of them while paying them peanuts. This is another one of those things that good baseball teams tend to be good at, and which the Rockies have been horrifyingly bad at. Unless you are a close observer of the Rockies, it's entirely possible that you have never even heard of Ryan McMahon, Jeff Hoffman, Brendan Rodgers, Jon Gray, Garrett Hampson or Raimel Tapia. That's because none of these players are very good at baseball, despite all having been tabbed at one point or another as potential stars.

Would you like to hear a particularly grim story about just how bad the Rockies are at developing their own talent? Do you remember Tyler Matzek? The Rockies drafted him 11th overall in the 2009 draft, and he came into their system with the stuff and pedigree of a potential ace. During his years with the Rockies, he developed a debilitating case of the yips that robbed him of his ability to throw the ball in anything resembling much of a straight line, and washed out of the sport in 2016. Bad luck for the Rockies, right? Can't do much about a guy getting the yips.

Matzek spent the 2020 season as an anchor in the Atlanta Braves' bullpen, posting a 2.79 ERA in 21 appearances, and striking out 43 batters in 29 innings.

What's to be made of this kind of abject failure at building a baseball team? The impulse is to throw mud, to call Bridich and the rest of the Rockies front office morons for having spent money on players they thought would be good but were actually bad, to sneer and invoke teams like the Oakland A's and Tampa Bay Rays as examples of small-market clubs that actually understand how to find wins on the margins and build contending teams on the fly. And honestly, how can you not laugh at the Rockies spending $135 million on a bullpen full of duds while those other teams were busy figuring out how to get to the World Series by signing all the Jake Diekmans and Aaron Loups of the world for a few bags of pennies? (Even McGee got his ring after being revived by the Dodgers.)

I'd like to offer a different way of looking at the Rockies' most recent failures at roster construction, and to do so by, perversely, borrowing a phrase from the sort of analytics-minded person who would most eagerly scoff at Colorado's efforts: Sometimes the process is more important than the results. Which is to say, it's good when a team with the Rockies' market size and ambition decides to spend money.

Yes, the money Bridich has spent over the last five years has unequivocally been wasted, but the intentions behind those signings were good. Bridich wasn't wrong to identify the bullpen as a thing worth investing in, he was just wrong to think building a good one actually had to cost money. He wasn't wrong to spend money on hitters to pad the lineup around his three stars, he just picked the wrong hitters, guessing the money was better spent on Ian Desmond and Daniel Murphy rather than LeMahieu—who was already a key member of the Rockies' lineup!—and, say, Marcell Ozuna.

Perhaps it seems like I am setting an exceptionally low bar here—after all, it has historically been a GM's job to figure out which players are worth spending money on and which are not—but given recent trends in baseball, it's something of a virtue to be willing to spend any money at all. We're several years into an era in which the free-agent market just gets colder every winter, and what can be charitably described as soft collusion has made it extremely difficult for even the league's best free agents to receive competitive offers for their services.

It feels like we are headed towards a grim future in which every team in the league agrees that there are only two ways to play for a championship: be like the Dodgers or be like the Rays. The few teams that can afford to spend like the Dodgers will go on offering themselves up as landing spots for the very best players in the league; the many teams who will see following Rays' blueprint as a more sensible course of action will continue to squeeze and squeeze and squeeze their payrolls while trying to game their way into a Wild Card spot. This may seem like an alarmist vision of the future, but it's hard to watch teams like Chicago and Cleveland go from being World Series contestants to belt-tighteners within four seasons and not hear sirens. The Reds tried for one year and they're already exhausted.

Now is a time in which the league needs *more* teams like the Rockies, not fewer. If baseball is going to continue to be a sport in which competition matters, in which players can be expected to have their efforts rewarded in an equitable market, then there simply have to be some teams in the league that are willing to slap $70 million on the table for players of Ian Desmond's (apparent) caliber. Or even $7 million, to outbid the smart teams on their non-tendered free agents and dumpster dives.

It's possible to imagine a future in which the Rockies continue to spend like they have over the last half decade *and* actually manage to win some baseball games. There is currently a lot of ground for the taking in baseball's marketplace, just begging to be staked out by a mid-market team that's willing to spend good money in pursuit of wins. The Rockies could be that team, if they were just smarter about how their money gets spent.

The trouble is that being that kind of smart, the kind of smart that isn't synonymous with frugality and arbitrage, is a hard thing to be. If Jeff Bridich knew better than to spend $52 million on Wade Davis, he wouldn't be Jeff Bridich. And if he weren't Jeff Bridich, he'd probably be one of the scores of

GMs who have accepted that spending real money on roster construction is a virtue that no longer needs to be bothered with. Which leads us to the worst possible outcome, and the most likely one: A future in which Bridich accepts that the days of free-spending are over, but in which he is just as dense about where money needs to be saved as he has been about where it should be spent.

The first big move the Rockies made this offseason was non-tendering David Dahl instead of paying him $3 million. The 26-year-old outfielder was an All-Star in 2019, and the only player from the team's latest batch of prospects who ever looked, even for a moment, like a potential star. If the Rockies are going to be as unskilled at austerity as they have been at scouting, spending, and development, then things are about to get much, much worse. ■

—Tom Ley is a co-owner of Defector.

HITTERS

Nolan Arenado 3B Born: 04/16/91 Age: 30 Bats: R Throws: R Height: 6'2" Weight: 215 Origin: Round 2, 2009 Draft (#59 overall)

YEAR	TEAM	LVL	AGE	PA	R	2B	3B	HR	RBI	BB	K	SB	CS	Whiff%	AVG/OBP/SLG	DRC+	BABIP	BRR	FRAA	WARP
2018	COL	MLB	27	673	104	38	2	38	110	73	122	2	2	24.7%	.297/.374/.561	137	.314	-2.9	3B(152): 9.1	6.2
2019	COL	MLB	28	662	102	31	2	41	118	62	93	3	2	20.9%	.315/.379/.583	135	.312	2.0	3B(154): 14.2	7.1
2020	COL	MLB	29	201	23	9	0	8	26	15	20	0	0	17.9%	.253/.303/.434	114	.241	0.4	3B(48): 5.3	1.5
2021 FS	COL	MLB	30	600	79	28	3	30	93	54	93	2	1	21.3%	.277/.347/.512	128	.287	0.5	3B 8	4.2
2021 DC	COL	MLB	30	571	76	27	3	29	89	51	88	2	1	21.3%	.277/.347/.512	128	.287	0.4	3B 7	4.0

Comparables: Ryan Zimmerman, Eric Chavez, Aramis Ramirez

This may have been the only case of a superstar whose swing opted out of the season without telling his body. After five straight years of the type of small-market MVP baseball that would make George Brett blush, Arenado had the power but not the groove. His DRC+ fell off a cliff—and in Denver it'll be impossible to narrow down which one it was—before a bum shoulder put an exclamation mark of dung onto his 2020. It's best not to read much into 200 plate appearances when the previous 3000 told a much different story, such as being the active leader among third basemen in slugging percentage. He still made his highlight plays. His batting discipline numbers all stayed the same. Maybe he was just put off by all the lifeless cardboard cutouts, like the rest of us.

Charlie Blackmon RF Born: 07/01/86 Age: 35 Bats: L Throws: L Height: 6'3" Weight: 221 Origin: Round 2, 2008 Draft (#72 overall)

YEAR	TEAM	LVL	AGE	PA	R	2B	3B	HR	RBI	BB	K	SB	CS	Whiff%	AVG/OBP/SLG	DRC+	BABIP	BRR	FRAA	WARP
2018	COL	MLB	31	696	119	31	7	29	70	59	134	12	4	20.2%	.291/.358/.502	122	.329	-0.6	CF(151): -21.7	2.1
2019	COL	MLB	32	634	112	42	7	32	86	40	104	2	5	19.6%	.314/.364/.576	129	.334	0.4	RF(135): -8.8	3.0
2020	COL	MLB	34	247	31	12	1	6	42	19	44	2	1	23.5%	.303/.356/.448	115	.347	1.0	RF(50): -0.2	1.2
2021 FS	COL	MLB	34	600	76	28	5	22	82	45	121	11	4	20.8%	.292/.359/.490	123	.344	1.7	RF -9, CF 0	2.9
2021 DC	COL	MLB	34	604	77	29	5	22	83	46	122	11	4	20.8%	.292/.359/.490	123	.344	1.7	RF -9	2.5

Comparables: Ellis Burks, Carlos Beltrán, Larry Hisle

Could someone hit .400 in the short season? Blackmon gave it the college try, registering .406 at nearly the halfway mark (and even hitting .500 through 17 games) before parachuting with a line around .200 the rest of the way to finish 19th overall. It wasn't as prodigious a quest as Todd Helton's two decades prior (though both were in great position in mid-August, a tremendous feat when freed of any other context). Batting race aside, age snuck up on Blackmon and his densely-hedged chin; at this point, most of his productivity is the result of making good but not monstrous contact. So in a way, he's forever locked in a batting average race.

Drew Butera C Born: 08/09/83 Age: 37 Bats: R Throws: R Height: 6'1" Weight: 212 Origin: Round 5, 2005 Draft (#149 overall)

YEAR	TEAM	LVL	AGE	PA	R	2B	3B	HR	RBI	BB	K	SB	CS	Whiff%	AVG/OBP/SLG	DRC+	BABIP	BRR	FRAA	WARP
2018	COL	MLB	34	16	2	0	0	1	3	2	2	0	0	9.7%	.214/.312/.429	78	.182	0.1	C(6): -0.9, 1B(4): 0.0	-0.1
2018	KC	MLB	34	166	11	9	0	2	18	13	37	0	0	22.6%	.188/.259/.289	79	.232	1.2	C(48): -6.9, 1B(2): 0.9, P(1): -0.0	-0.1
2019	ABQ	AAA	35	262	38	16	2	9	40	33	55	2	0		.300/.389/.511	108	.356	0.3	C(65): -5.7	1.1
2019	COL	MLB	35	49	6	3	0	0	3	4	14	0	0	27.7%	.163/.229/.233	62	.233	0.5	C(14): 0.2, 1B(3): 0.0	0.1
2020	COL	MLB	37	43	4	2	0	0	4	2	11	0	0	27.2%	.154/.190/.205	75	.207	-0.3	C(25): -0.2, 1B(5): -0.1, P(1): 0.2	0.0
2021 FS	COL	MLB	37	600	58	25	2	14	55	45	169	1	0	24.7%	.213/.280/.344	69	.283	0.3	C -6, 1B 0	-0.6

Comparables: Mike DiFelice, Ron Tingley, Jamie Quirk

You know when you have a tube of toothpaste and you squeeze it really hard to get those last dabs out, delaying the need to acquire a completely new tube of toothpaste? Anyway, Butera was in the majors last year.

YEAR	TEAM	P. COUNT	FRM RUNS	BLK RUNS	THRW RUNS	TOT RUNS
2018	COL	751	-0.7	-0.1	0.0	-0.9
2018	KC	6603	-6.4	0.0	-0.2	-6.7
2019	COL	1969	-1.3	1.2	0.0	-0.1
2020	COL	1958	0.0	0.1	0.0	0.1
2021	COL	16650	-9.9	3.5	0.4	-6.0

Yonathan Daza LF Born: 02/28/94 Age: 27 Bats: R Throws: R Height: 6'2" Weight: 207 Origin: International Free Agent, 2010

YEAR	TEAM	LVL	AGE	PA	R	2B	3B	HR	RBI	BB	K	SB	CS	Whiff%	AVG/OBP/SLG	DRC+	BABIP	BRR	FRAA	WARP
2018	HFD	AA	24	228	27	18	2	4	29	7	24	4	5		.306/.330/.461	117	.330	-0.6	CF(30): 1.3, RF(16): 4.2, LF(4): -1.0	1.1
2019	ABQ	AAA	25	418	67	30	4	11	48	25	52	12	9		.364/.404/.548	122	.399	-1.2	CF(87): 4.1, LF(2): 0.0	2.8
2019	COL	MLB	25	105	7	1	1	0	3	7	21	1	0	23.4%	.206/.257/.237	59	.260	1.2	CF(24): -0.5, LF(3): 1.0, RF(3): 0.1	0.0
2021 FS	COL	MLB	27	600	59	25	5	10	60	29	127	6	3	23.4%	.254/.297/.376	80	.312	0.0	CF 1, LF -1	0.3
2021 DC	COL	MLB	27	268	26	11	2	4	26	13	56	2	1	23.4%	.254/.297/.376	80	.312	0.0	CF 1, LF 0	0.1

Comparables: Xavier Paul, Jason Bourgeois, Charlie Blackmon

Prospect development is not linear; in fact, sometimes, it's a mobius strip. To put it in perspective, Daza's been in the Rockies' system for longer than Airbnb has been in existence. There's no question about his ability to patrol center field, but the other half of the inning only looks good if the suddenly 27-year-old is in the PCL.

Niko Decolati RF Born: 08/12/97 Age: 23 Bats: R Throws: R Height: 6'1" Weight: 215 Origin: Round 6, 2018 Draft (#186 overall)

YEAR	TEAM	LVL	AGE	PA	R	2B	3B	HR	RBI	BB	K	SB	CS	Whiff%	AVG/OBP/SLG	DRC+	BABIP	BRR	FRAA	WARP
2018	GJ	ROK	20	304	55	15	3	11	56	34	56	17	5		.327/.414/.532	157	.381	2.6	RF(58): 5.2, LF(1): 0.1, CF(1): -0.5	2.1
2019	ASH	LO-A	21	331	42	13	4	6	38	13	80	15	6		.265/.334/.399	89	.341	0.4	CF(57): -1.7, RF(17): 2.2	0.7
2021 FS	COL	MLB	23	600	50	26	3	8	52	38	187	13	6		.216/.283/.325	69	.311	-1.7	RF 5, CF -2	-0.5

Comparables: Whit Merrifield, Aaron Altherr, Alex Presley

A Boulder native, Decolati is hoping his athleticism will turn him into a major league outfielder, because right now he just sounds like the largest boulder in northern Italy.

Ian Desmond CF Born: 09/20/85 Age: 35 Bats: R Throws: R Height: 6'3" Weight: 217 Origin: Round 3, 2004 Draft (#84 overall)

YEAR	TEAM	LVL	AGE	PA	R	2B	3B	HR	RBI	BB	K	SB	CS	Whiff%	AVG/OBP/SLG	DRC+	BABIP	BRR	FRAA	WARP
2018	COL	MLB	32	619	82	21	8	22	88	53	146	20	6	28.9%	.236/.307/.422	89	.279	0.8	1B(138): -2.6, LF(18): 0.8, SS(3): -0.1	0.2
2019	COL	MLB	33	482	64	31	4	20	65	34	119	3	3	26.4%	.255/.310/.479	85	.304	0.4	CF(74): -12.8, LF(44): -2.9, P(1): -0.0	-0.8
2021 FS	COL	MLB	35	600	62	21	3	17	62	44	174	14	5	27.4%	.232/.296/.378	80	.310	2.8	CF -4, LF -2	-0.4
2021 DC	COL	MLB	35	537	55	19	3	15	56	39	156	13	4	27.4%	.232/.296/.378	80	.310	2.5	CF -4, LF -1	-0.3

Comparables: Jhonny Peralta, Dale Sveum, Chris Woodward

Desmond had a pretty good season in 2020. Sure, by opting out of the year for COVID-19 concerns, he fell 0.1 WARP shy of his PECOTA projections. But the oft-maligned shortstop-turned-first baseman-turned-center fielder made an impassioned post on Instagram, explaining how the Black Lives Matter protest had cemented his own feelings about the issues of race facing baseball. He was particularly concerned about the accessibility issues facing poorer children in the era of expensive travel ball. He spent the summer helping his family, while also working to re-establish the Sarasota Youth Baseball Program where he himself had started down his path. It was a small victory, and it'll create more small victories and start kids walking down their own paths, long after the 2020 season is just a memory.

Elias Díaz C Born: 11/17/90 Age: 30 Bats: R Throws: R Height: 6'1" Weight: 223 Origin: International Free Agent, 2008

YEAR	TEAM	LVL	AGE	PA	R	2B	3B	HR	RBI	BB	K	SB	CS	Whiff%	AVG/OBP/SLG	DRC+	BABIP	BRR	FRAA	WARP
2018	PIT	MLB	27	277	33	12	0	10	34	21	40	0	1	21.7%	.286/.339/.452	112	.302	0.5	C(70): 0.6	1.9
2019	IND	AAA	28	30	5	3	0	0	4	1	5	0	0		.414/.433/.517	117	.500	0.0	C(6): 0.7	0.2
2019	PIT	MLB	28	332	31	14	0	2	28	23	55	0	0	23.3%	.241/.296/.307	72	.285	1.3	C(96): -11.0	-0.4
2020	COL	MLB	30	73	4	2	0	2	9	5	15	0	0	27.9%	.235/.288/.353	87	.275	0.2	C(24): -0.0	0.1
2021 FS	COL	MLB	30	600	58	25	1	12	59	40	120	1	0	23.8%	.244/.300/.362	80	.293	-0.3	C 1	1.0
2021 DC	COL	MLB	30	436	42	18	1	8	43	29	87	1	0	23.8%	.244/.300/.362	80	.293	-0.2	C -1	0.5

Comparables: Vance Wilson, Dick Billings, Brook Fordyce

A year after being identified as the poorest framer in the entire league, Díaz figured, shoot, if he can't steal strike three, he might as well go to the pitching staff that allows the most balls in play. Clever transaction. As a backup he carried the Rockies catching crew from a power perspective, being the only one of the lot who cleared the outfield wall at least once. He can "run into one", as they like to say, about as often as he can frame into one.

YEAR	TEAM	P. COUNT	FRM RUNS	BLK RUNS	THRW RUNS	TOT RUNS
2018	PIT	9208	-1.2	-2.0	0.1	-3.1
2019	PIT	12603	-14.4	0.1	-0.1	-14.4
2020	COL	2173	0.3	-0.2	0.0	0.1
2021	COL	15632	-5.7	-1.5	-0.5	-7.7

Josh Fuentes 3B Born: 02/19/93 Age: 28 Bats: R Throws: R Height: 6'2" Weight: 209 Origin: Undrafted Free Agent, 2014

YEAR	TEAM	LVL	AGE	PA	R	2B	3B	HR	RBI	BB	K	SB	CS	Whiff%	AVG/OBP/SLG	DRC+	BABIP	BRR	FRAA	WARP
2018	ABQ	AAA	25	586	93	39	12	14	95	21	103	3	5		.327/.354/.517	109	.376	2.5	3B(110): 6.2, 1B(21): 0.6, 2B(1): 0.3	2.7
2019	ABQ	AAA	26	437	66	23	2	17	64	25	118	1	1		.254/.298/.448	66	.314	0.2	3B(96): 10.3, 1B(1): -0.1, 2B(1): -0.0	0.8
2019	COL	MLB	26	56	8	1	0	3	7	1	20	1	0	38.6%	.218/.232/.400	72	.281	0.1	1B(11): -0.3, 3B(2): -0.0	-0.1
2020	COL	MLB	27	103	14	7	0	2	17	2	29	1	0	24.3%	.306/.320/.439	79	.406	0.2	1B(26): 4.4, 3B(6): -0.5, LF(2): -0.0	0.3
2021 FS	COL	MLB	28	600	59	22	5	18	70	24	170	1	1	28.2%	.244/.288/.402	82	.319	3.3	1B -2, 2B 0	0.0
2021 DC	COL	MLB	28	436	43	16	4	13	51	18	123	1	0	28.2%	.244/.288/.402	82	.319	2.4	1B -1	-0.2

Comparables: Will Middlebrooks, Chris Johnson, Matt Macri

WalkScore.com recently rated Denver as America's 16th walkable city, making it "somewhat walkable. Some errands can be accomplished on foot." It would have ranked higher but Fuentes got a chunk of playing time, and both of his walks were on four straight pitches. For all the cuts, he comes out with a modest average and immodest strikeout rate. He'll need more than that to see more action, either at first base or backing up his cousin Nolan Arenado at third. Otherwise he's not long for the roster, and knowing him, he'll take the train.

Garrett Hampson 2B
Born: 10/10/94   Age: 26   Bats: R   Throws: R   Height: 5'11"   Weight: 196   Origin: Round 3, 2016 Draft (#81 overall)

YEAR	TEAM	LVL	AGE	PA	R	2B	3B	HR	RBI	BB	K	SB	CS	Whiff%	AVG/OBP/SLG	DRC+	BABIP	BRR	FRAA	WARP
2018	HFD	AA	23	172	28	8	2	4	15	21	17	19	1		.304/.391/.466	135	.323	3.5	SS(18): 0.4, 2B(17): 1.7, CF(3): -0.1	1.6
2018	ABQ	AAA	23	332	53	17	4	6	25	30	58	17	4		.314/.377/.459	109	.372	0.9	2B(44): -0.1, SS(23): -2.3, CF(6): 1.4	1.1
2018	COL	MLB	23	48	3	3	1	0	4	7	12	2	0	23.2%	.275/.396/.400	81	.393	1.1	SS(8): 0.2, 2B(7): 0.6, CF(1): -0.1	0.2
2019	ABQ	AAA	24	117	15	9	1	2	9	5	25	7	2		.266/.310/.422	63	.329	1.0	2B(15): 0.3, SS(10): -1.5	-0.1
2019	COL	MLB	24	327	40	9	4	8	27	24	88	15	3	23.5%	.247/.302/.385	70	.322	3.5	2B(50): -1.1, CF(31): -0.8, SS(15): -0.1	0.1
2020	COL	MLB	26	184	25	4	3	5	11	13	60	6	1	29.6%	.234/.287/.383	72	.330	2.0	2B(26): -1.8, CF(20): -2.2, LF(7): 0.0	-0.4
2021 FS	COL	MLB	26	600	64	19	9	14	58	47	173	25	6	26.2%	.248/.312/.393	87	.340	15.5	2B 0, CF 0	2.7
2021 DC	COL	MLB	26	470	50	15	7	11	45	37	136	20	5	26.2%	.248/.312/.393	87	.340	12.1	2B 0, CF 0	2.1

Comparables: Jerry Buchek, Roberto Mejia, Bobby Hill

Speed is somewhat of a cursed tool with baseball players; it defines you more than the other four, perhaps because it's the one that cannot be learned. When development is a priority, a slow slugger will always get more playing time than a speedy slapper. By sprint speed, Hampson is one of the 10 fastest runners in the league. It helps that he can play infield and outfield, but the lagging bat makes him a perfect pinch runner/fourth outfielder. Having said that about his swinging struggles, he *is* the first guy to homer twice in a 23-5 loss.

Sam Hilliard RF
Born: 02/21/94   Age: 27   Bats: L   Throws: L   Height: 6'5"   Weight: 236   Origin: Round 15, 2015 Draft (#437 overall)

YEAR	TEAM	LVL	AGE	PA	R	2B	3B	HR	RBI	BB	K	SB	CS	Whiff%	AVG/OBP/SLG	DRC+	BABIP	BRR	FRAA	WARP
2018	HFD	AA	24	484	58	22	3	9	40	41	151	23	14		.262/.327/.389	97	.379	0.3	RF(70): 3.5, LF(29): -1.8, CF(12): -0.5	0.3
2019	ABQ	AAA	25	559	109	29	7	35	101	54	164	22	5		.262/.335/.558	98	.316	0.5	RF(83): -0.2, CF(34): 5.2, LF(10): -0.6	1.8
2019	COL	MLB	25	87	13	4	2	7	13	9	23	2	0	26.9%	.273/.356/.649	108	.298	0.7	CF(17): 0.6, RF(6): 1.7, LF(5): -1.2	0.5
2020	COL	MLB	26	114	13	2	2	6	10	9	42	3	0	38.9%	.210/.272/.438	70	.281	1.0	LF(14): 3.2, RF(13): 0.2, CF(10): -0.4	0.3
2021 FS	COL	MLB	27	600	63	25	6	20	67	48	215	16	7	34.8%	.225/.292/.405	81	.332	2.5	CF 5, LF 0	0.8
2021 DC	COL	MLB	27	537	56	22	5	18	60	43	193	14	6	34.8%	.225/.292/.405	81	.332	2.2	CF 5, LF 0	0.8

Comparables: Carlos Peguero, Curtis Granderson, Daniel Palka

There's a theory going around that all Rockies outfielders are nothing more than mild derivatives of Larry Walker, the ur-Rockies outfielder. Hilliard has the speed and the power but lacks the swing to leverage either. The breakout year in Albuquerque was almost certainly inflated, as more mature pitching kept him fishing for big game and winding up with nothing but boot after flavorless boot. Despite that—and admittedly it was a lean year for dingers in Colorado—he had the team's finest ratio of HR/PA. With that in mind, conking baseballs into bleachers forgives most other on-field transgressions, so the potential for home runs will tempt Bud Black into giving him playing time over the rest of the Walkerlings.

Matt Kemp LF
Born: 09/23/84   Age: 36   Bats: R   Throws: R   Height: 6'4"   Weight: 225   Origin: Round 6, 2003 Draft (#181 overall)

YEAR	TEAM	LVL	AGE	PA	R	2B	3B	HR	RBI	BB	K	SB	CS	Whiff%	AVG/OBP/SLG	DRC+	BABIP	BRR	FRAA	WARP
2018	LAD	MLB	33	506	62	25	0	21	85	36	115	0	0	29.7%	.290/.338/.481	115	.339	-2.1	LF(75): -1.5, RF(51): -2.2	1.6
2019	SYR	AAA	34	36	3	0	0	1	3	2	7	0	0		.235/.278/.324	71	.269	-0.5	LF(3): -0.7	-0.2
2019	CIN	MLB	34	62	4	2	0	1	5	1	19	0	0	41.5%	.200/.210/.283	72	.268	0.0	LF(17): -1.6	-0.2
2020	COL	MLB	36	132	18	3	0	6	21	15	41	1	0	36.2%	.239/.326/.419	91	.314	0.3	LF(1): 0.1	0.2
2021 FS	COL	MLB	36	600	60	20	1	23	71	40	176	1	0	33.9%	.233/.288/.401	82	.300	-0.4	LF -17, RF -4	-1.9

Comparables: Andruw Jones, Dale Murphy, Carl Everett

Most National League fans love themselves some hittin' pitchers. There's a smaller share who don't mind if the DH permeates both leagues, and within that, a niche who absolutely want it, and a subset within that niche that is just Kemp himself, desparately depending on it. The former star center fielder has diminished bat speed and is primarily a platoon bench player, at this point which means his playing time goes up if all 30 teams ban their pitcher from wearing a helmet. Kemp and his degenerative hip managed to stay productive for a very long time, if less so over the last two years, spanning four organizations. He seems content living the organized sporting life and the teams seem content handing him a uniform with his name on it; maybe he'll hang around just long enough to DH his way to 300 career home runs.

Grant Lavigne 1B
Born: 08/27/99   Age: 21   Bats: L   Throws: R   Height: 6'4"   Weight: 220   Origin: Round 1, 2018 Draft (#42 overall)

YEAR	TEAM	LVL	AGE	PA	R	2B	3B	HR	RBI	BB	K	SB	CS	Whiff%	AVG/OBP/SLG	DRC+	BABIP	BRR	FRAA	WARP
2018	GJ	ROK	18	258	45	13	2	6	38	45	40	12	7		.350/.477/.519	189	.410	-0.6	1B(53): -6.8	1.1
2019	ASH	LO-A	19	526	52	19	0	7	64	68	129	8	9		.236/.347/.327	87	.314	-4.4	1B(112): 0.9	-0.5
2021 FS	COL	MLB	21	600	51	26	2	8	51	48	180	3	3		.219/.290/.319	69	.312	-4.6	1B -3	-2.3

Comparables: Ronald Guzmán, Eric Hosmer, Dominic Smith

After laying waste to rookie ball in 2018, Lavigne took on the challenge of Low-A in 2019 and fell flat. That, combined with the forced sabbatical of 2020, might cause one to think there are unanswered questions here, but no. It's pretty straightforward: If he hits home runs, he's going to be a good first baseman. If he doesn't, he won't. He's the first Lavigne to not be associated with being complicated.

Ryan McMahon 2B
Born: 12/14/94   Age: 26   Bats: L   Throws: R   Height: 6'2"   Weight: 219   Origin: Round 2, 2013 Draft (#42 overall)

YEAR	TEAM	LVL	AGE	PA	R	2B	3B	HR	RBI	BB	K	SB	CS	Whiff%	AVG/OBP/SLG	DRC+	BABIP	BRR	FRAA	WARP
2018	ABQ	AAA	23	242	40	15	3	11	48	15	61	3	2		.290/.339/.531	106	.353	1.9	1B(43): -1.9, 2B(10): -1.0, 3B(2): -0.3	0.2
2018	COL	MLB	23	202	17	9	1	5	19	18	64	1	0	33.3%	.232/.307/.376	74	.327	0.9	1B(31): -1.1, 3B(17): 0.1, 2B(10): 0.9	-0.1
2019	COL	MLB	24	539	70	22	1	24	83	56	160	5	1	32.5%	.250/.329/.450	92	.323	-0.1	2B(113): 6.9, 3B(22): -0.5, 1B(19): -0.6	1.7
2020	COL	MLB	26	193	23	6	1	9	26	18	66	0	1	31.6%	.215/.295/.419	85	.286	0.2	2B(33): -0.5, 3B(14): 2.7, 1B(12): 0.8	0.5
2021 FS	COL	MLB	26	600	66	23	3	26	75	53	196	3	1	32.3%	.240/.315/.440	98	.329	2.4	2B 5, 1B -3	1.8
2021 DC	COL	MLB	26	470	52	18	2	20	58	41	154	2	0	32.3%	.240/.315/.440	98	.329	1.9	2B 4, 1B -2	1.4

Comparables: Danny Espinosa, Mark Bellhorn, Jared Sandberg

There is something endearing about a baseballer with incredible power, but without the ability to wield it. Sure, A-Rod, Pujols and Cabrera were able to bop seemingly at will. The McMahons of the league can "make that sound" when they strike the bad pitch correctly, and they do that nearly enough, but when the dust settles on the season, we're left with a collection of homers and a larger collection of nothing. It's part and parcel of the player's allure and humanity: They do one thing extremely well, but only sometimes, and that's completely relatable. We're all rooting for that random season where he scrapes a .220 average and belts 40 beyond the walls.

Daniel Murphy 1B
Born: 04/01/85   Age: 36   Bats: L   Throws: R   Height: 6'1"   Weight: 223   Origin: Round 13, 2006 Draft (#394 overall)

YEAR	TEAM	LVL	AGE	PA	R	2B	3B	HR	RBI	BB	K	SB	CS	Whiff%	AVG/OBP/SLG	DRC+	BABIP	BRR	FRAA	WARP
2018	HBG	AA	33	44	8	2	0	2	7	6	4	0	0		.243/.364/.459	120	.226	0.5	2B(8): -0.6, 1B(2): 0.3	0.2
2018	CHC	MLB	33	146	23	6	0	6	13	7	23	2	0	17.0%	.297/.329/.471	111	.318	0.7	2B(33): -1.1	0.6
2018	WAS	MLB	33	205	17	9	0	6	29	13	17	1	0	9.9%	.300/.341/.442	114	.302	-1.0	2B(38): -2.9, 1B(14): -0.6	0.4
2019	COL	MLB	34	478	56	35	1	13	78	32	74	1	1	15.0%	.279/.328/.452	97	.307	0.0	1B(110): 5.9, 2B(3): 0.4	1.2
2020	COL	MLB	35	132	10	3	0	3	16	7	21	0	0	14.3%	.236/.275/.333	90	.260	-1.7	1B(29): 0.1	0.0
2021 FS	COL	MLB	36	600	64	30	2	17	76	40	93	3	1	14.5%	.275/.332/.434	102	.307	0.0	2B 0, 1B 3	2.2

Comparables: Aaron Hill, Carlos Baerga, Brandon Phillips

A career dud year at age 35 made it a fairly simple decision for the Rockies to say no to another year of *that* for $12 million. He clearly succumbed to Chronic Second Baseman Dystrophy, better known outside the medical world as Dan Uggla Syndrome. This usually happens to folk in their mid 30s, and there's no known cure. He tried to hide it by playing a lot of first base, but you can't fool anyone. It follows you. Plenty have tried. Having an NLCS MVP in his trophy case could give him another year or so to hang around a team and pinch hit if he chooses, because avoiding strikeouts is his only party trick left.

Chris Owings SS
Born: 08/12/91   Age: 29   Bats: R   Throws: R   Height: 5'10"   Weight: 185   Origin: Round 1, 2009 Draft (#41 overall)

YEAR	TEAM	LVL	AGE	PA	R	2B	3B	HR	RBI	BB	K	SB	CS	Whiff%	AVG/OBP/SLG	DRC+	BABIP	BRR	FRAA	WARP
2018	RNO	AAA	26	92	15	4	2	1	11	1	17	1	2		.286/.293/.407	64	.342	1.4	2B(10): -0.2, 3B(6): 0.3, CF(3): -0.4	0.0
2018	ARI	MLB	26	309	34	15	0	4	22	24	75	11	4	24.7%	.206/.272/.302	69	.265	0.8	RF(43): -1.1, CF(16): 1.2, 3B(15): -0.8	-0.4
2019	WOR	AAA	27	183	26	11	0	11	34	15	50	6	4		.325/.385/.595	140	.404	-1.0	SS(18): 0.3, 2B(10): 1.5, 3B(6): -0.3	1.4
2019	KC	MLB	27	145	9	4	1	2	9	8	55	4	1	32.8%	.133/.193/.222	34	.205	0.9	2B(13): -1.8, 3B(12): 1.4, CF(7): -0.2	-0.7
2019	BOS	MLB	27	51	4	2	0	1	5	6	23	1	1	38.9%	.156/.255/.267	29	.286	-1.0	2B(12): 0.2, SS(7): 0.7, 3B(1): -0.0	-0.3
2020	COL	MLB	29	44	9	1	0	2	5	3	11	1	0	34.5%	.268/.318/.439	100	.321	0.4	2B(8): -0.3, 3B(2): -0.2, LF(2): -0.1	0.1
2021 FS	COL	MLB	29	600	57	22	4	16	62	36	165	16	4	30.9%	.223/.276/.367	70	.289	6.1	SS 3, 2B 0	0.1

Comparables: Alex Gonzalez, Josh Rutledge, Greg Gagne

Having already endured two nadirs before his 28th birthday, there was nowhere for Owings but to go up. Even retiring from baseball would be somewhat of a relief. No more getting roasted by the fellas at the batter's box. No more two-week road trips. No more "talk about" reporter questions. Perhaps plenty of fresh air on a farm, or maybe by the ocean? Mess around with watercolors? Check out the farmers' market? But with him being relatively young, Owings opted for more baseball and held his own. It was technically a career high by OPS, but it was also technically a month in Colorado. He's a utility player with chaotic production, what's not to love?

Kevin Pillar CF
Born: 01/04/89   Age: 32   Bats: R   Throws: R   Height: 6'0"   Weight: 200   Origin: Round 32, 2011 Draft (#979 overall)

YEAR	TEAM	LVL	AGE	PA	R	2B	3B	HR	RBI	BB	K	SB	CS	Whiff%	AVG/OBP/SLG	DRC+	BABIP	BRR	FRAA	WARP
2018	TOR	MLB	29	542	65	40	2	15	59	18	98	14	3	22.4%	.252/.282/.426	93	.281	3.3	CF(142): 9.0	2.8
2019	TOR	MLB	30	17	1	0	0	0	1	0	3	0	0	12.9%	.062/.059/.062	26	.071	0.0	CF(4): 0.1	-0.1
2019	SF	MLB	30	628	82	37	3	21	87	18	86	14	5	17.9%	.264/.293/.442	86	.275	4.1	CF(129): -10.8, RF(27): 0.2	0.4
2020	COL	MLB	31	97	14	5	1	2	13	5	18	4	1	24.9%	.308/.351/.451	105	.366	1.0	CF(21): -3.1, RF(1): -0.1	0.2
2020	BOS	MLB	31	126	20	7	2	4	13	8	23	1	1	25.7%	.274/.325/.470	108	.311	1.3	RF(24): -1.5, CF(6): 0.7, LF(2): 0.3	0.6
2021 FS	COL	MLB	32	600	65	29	3	17	69	27	113	14	5	21.0%	.254/.298/.413	89	.291	1.0	CF -9, RF 0	0.3

Comparables: Henry Cotto, Tsuyoshi Shinjo, Gerald Williams

Corinthian to the core, Pillar is going to get his share of home runs because he's contact-prone and swings upward. In 2019 he became the fourth San Francisco center fielder to sock at least 20 in a season (Marquis Grissom, Chili Davis and someone named Mays are the others). That consistency made him ideal trade deadline fodder for the sinking Red Sox, assuming you can call what Colorado did a playoff push. The existence of power and presence of batting average, coupled with extra-base speed and range, gives Pillar the bare minimum of everything you want in a center fielder. Aging into his 30s doesn't give the team much more than the low-ceiling skill set, but you can't hold up a ceiling without a pillar.

Brendan Rodgers 2B Born: 08/09/96 Age: 24 Bats: R Throws: R Height: 6'0" Weight: 204 Origin: Round 1, 2015 Draft (#3 overall)

YEAR	TEAM	LVL	AGE	PA	R	2B	3B	HR	RBI	BB	K	SB	CS	Whiff%	AVG/OBP/SLG	DRC+	BABIP	BRR	FRAA	WARP
2018	HFD	AA	21	402	49	23	2	17	62	30	76	12	3		.275/.342/.493	113	.301	0.6	SS(58): -6.7, 2B(21): -2.1, 3B(17): 1.7	0.9
2018	ABQ	AAA	21	72	5	4	0	0	5	1	16	0	0		.232/.264/.290	48	.302	-0.3	SS(11): -1.8, 3B(4): -0.2, 2B(3): -0.5	-0.5
2019	ABQ	AAA	22	160	34	10	1	9	21	14	27	0	0		.350/.412/.622	130	.380	2.0	2B(27): -1.9, SS(6): -0.1, 3B(3): 0.3	1.2
2019	COL	MLB	22	81	8	2	0	0	7	4	27	0	0	31.1%	.224/.272/.250	46	.347	1.5	2B(16): 1.1, SS(9): -1.1	-0.1
2020	COL	MLB	24	21	1	1	0	0	2	0	6	0	0	30.6%	.095/.095/.143	83	.133	0.0	2B(5): -0.9, SS(1): -0.0	-0.1
2021 FS	COL	MLB	24	600	62	21	3	23	74	35	171	2	1	30.9%	.234/.291/.409	86	.297	1.1	2B -2, SS -3	0.5
2021 DC	COL	MLB	24	201	21	7	1	7	24	11	57	0	0	30.9%	.234/.291/.409	86	.297	0.4	2B -1, SS -1	0.2

Comparables: Josh Barfield, Reid Brignac, Luis Urías

After years of hype and promise, including four years in the top 20 of our prospect lists, Rodgers hasn't quite located that sweet swing that propelled him through the bush-league ranks. The 2020 numbers encompassed an 11-day stretch, which is exactly one Scaramucci, so hold it against him if you must, but the track record before that still stands. The loud contact should eventually make its way into the bat he routinely holds; however if he struggles in yet another year he may need to hire Kayleigh McEnany to write this paragraph next time.

Drew Romo C Born: 08/29/01 Age: 19 Bats: S Throws: R Height: 6'1" Weight: 205 Origin: Round 1, 2020 Draft (#35 overall)

Romo is the first high school catcher taken in the first round since Joe Mauer who played on consecutive under-18 Team USA teams. Any lingering correlation, however, will fail to include the former Twins MVP's sideburns. His foremost skills reside in squatting and sticking a glove in front of his face, and having the sort of body shape that led someone to suggest catching in the first place. And as with all highly-ranked catching prospects, he comes with the usual assortment of praise for intangibles pre-installed. Still, it's the burgeoning promise in standing upright and holding manufactured timber products that tempted the Rockies into using their first-round competitive balance pick on him.

Aaron Schunk 3B Born: 07/24/97 Age: 23 Bats: R Throws: R Height: 6'2" Weight: 205 Origin: Round 2, 2019 Draft (#62 overall)

YEAR	TEAM	LVL	AGE	PA	R	2B	3B	HR	RBI	BB	K	SB	CS	Whiff%	AVG/OBP/SLG	DRC+	BABIP	BRR	FRAA	WARP
2019	BOI	SS	21	192	31	12	2	6	23	14	25	4	1		.306/.370/.503	138	.329	1.8	3B(37): 7.4	2.2
2021 FS	COL	MLB	23	600	55	27	3	13	61	36	144	6	2		.232/.287/.367	80	.290	1.3	3B 7	0.6

Schunk, a second or possibly third baseman, is constantly turning heads in the minor leagues. Possibly because of the bat, but mostly because his last name is being said and people are wondering what that sound is.

Trevor Story SS Born: 11/15/92 Age: 28 Bats: R Throws: R Height: 6'2" Weight: 213 Origin: Round 1, 2011 Draft (#45 overall)

YEAR	TEAM	LVL	AGE	PA	R	2B	3B	HR	RBI	BB	K	SB	CS	Whiff%	AVG/OBP/SLG	DRC+	BABIP	BRR	FRAA	WARP
2018	COL	MLB	25	656	88	42	6	37	108	47	168	27	6	24.8%	.291/.348/.567	127	.345	-0.8	SS(156): -2.0	5.0
2019	COL	MLB	26	656	111	38	5	35	85	58	174	23	8	26.5%	.294/.363/.554	117	.361	3.5	SS(144): -0.3	4.9
2020	COL	MLB	28	259	41	13	4	11	28	24	63	15	3	25.7%	.289/.355/.519	125	.354	0.6	SS(57): 0.5	1.5
2021 FS	COL	MLB	28	600	83	27	5	29	83	53	169	16	5	25.9%	.263/.337/.498	120	.332	4.5	SS -3	3.7
2021 DC	COL	MLB	28	571	79	26	5	28	79	50	161	15	5	25.9%	.263/.337/.498	120	.332	4.3	SS -3	3.5

Comparables: Mark Reynolds, Javier Báez, Matt Chapman

It wouldn't be rude to look back and declare that Colorado held the most coveted left side of any infield of the last half-decade, a tandem easy to overlook when their team has won a total of one postseason match. Story, who replaced Troy Tulowitzki more seamlessly than anyone imagined, is basically Francisco Lindor minus the glove. That's not to say he can't field; he can, it's just that he's young and athletic enough to spearhead shortstop for now. Among this generation's shortstops he's at the top of the class in home runs and stolen bases, though he's one of the worst at swingin' and missin'. He's a top-tier shortstop, perhaps the most prized of baseball archetypes, and while his team's (lack of) success isn't his fault, that type of player only means good things for your fantasy team.

Raimel Tapia LF Born: 02/04/94 Age: 27 Bats: L Throws: L Height: 6'3" Weight: 175 Origin: International Free Agent, 2010

YEAR	TEAM	LVL	AGE	PA	R	2B	3B	HR	RBI	BB	K	SB	CS	Whiff%	AVG/OBP/SLG	DRC+	BABIP	BRR	FRAA	WARP
2018	ABQ	AAA	24	473	81	33	9	11	62	32	85	21	3		.302/.352/.495	99	.354	1.4	CF(65): -5.2, RF(24): -0.0, LF(15): -2.2	0.2
2018	COL	MLB	24	27	6	2	1	1	6	2	7	0	0	28.1%	.200/.259/.480	87	.235	0.7	CF(6): -0.4, LF(1): -0.0, RF(1): -0.0	0.1
2019	COL	MLB	25	447	54	23	5	9	44	21	100	9	3	26.7%	.275/.309/.415	79	.341	-0.4	LF(91): 1.7, CF(13): -0.4, RF(6): -0.6	0.1
2020	COL	MLB	26	206	26	8	2	1	17	14	38	8	2	18.9%	.321/.369/.402	83	.392	1.8	LF(36): -2.0, RF(3): -0.4	-0.1
2021 FS	COL	MLB	27	600	68	29	8	10	54	34	131	13	4	23.5%	.282/.330/.421	97	.356	5.2	LF -5, CF 0	1.6
2021 DC	COL	MLB	27	537	61	26	7	9	48	30	117	11	4	23.5%	.282/.330/.421	97	.356	4.7	LF -4	1.3

Comparables: Brian Lesher, Mark Brouhard, Todd Hollandsworth

He smacks the ball on the ground and runs for average, making Tapia a perfect leadoff hitter if the year is 1989. His breakout average in the short season still didn't help him in DRC's eyes, because the lion's share of those hits were singles. You'd expect a fast leadoff dude to bring in a few more doubles, or even cover more ground in left field. We knew Harold Reynolds, we watched Harold Reynolds, and you, sir, are no Harold Reynolds.

Michael Toglia 1B Born: 08/16/98 Age: 22 Bats: S Throws: L Height: 6'5" Weight: 226 Origin: Round 1, 2019 Draft (#23 overall)

YEAR	TEAM	LVL	AGE	PA	R	2B	3B	HR	RBI	BB	K	SB	CS	Whiff%	AVG/OBP/SLG	DRC+	BABIP	BRR	FRAA	WARP
2019	BOI	SS	20	176	25	7	0	9	26	28	45	1	1		.248/.369/.483	131	.290	0.3	1B(38): -0.2	0.6
2021 FS	COL	MLB	22	600	50	26	2	12	56	40	209	1	0		.198/.256/.321	58	.292	-0.2	1B 0	-2.4

Despite registering nary a stat, Toglia got some reps at the fabled alternate site last summer to prepare for an exciting career in professional first base management. He remains an athletic defender by first-base standards and an extremely promising hitter except by first-base standards.

──────────────── ★ ★ ★ *2021 Top 101 Prospect* **#49** ★ ★ ★ ────────────────

Zac Veen OF   Born: 12/12/01   Age: 19   Bats: L   Throws: R   Height: 6'4"   Weight: 190   Origin: Round 1, 2020 Draft (#9 overall)

While everybody in 2020 was waiting for a vaccine, the Colorado Rockies waited until the ninth-overall pick in the amateur draft for a Zac Veen. As a high school outfielder, he may take just as much time to go through clinical phases before he's completely inoculated from the horrors of major league curveballs and pinpoint command. His 6'4" frame should help him develop decent power, but may in turn scooch him into a corner outfield spot. Veen is the first outfielder taken by Colorado in the first round since David Dahl, and both were out of high school and bat left-handed. Veen is more well-rounded than the offense-leaning Dahl, and should he start developing similar power, we can only hope that Veen home runs will be called "flew shots."

Ryan Vilade SS   Born: 02/18/99   Age: 22   Bats: R   Throws: R   Height: 6'2"   Weight: 226   Origin: Round 2, 2017 Draft (#48 overall)

YEAR	TEAM	LVL	AGE	PA	R	2B	3B	HR	RBI	BB	K	SB	CS	Whiff%	AVG/OBP/SLG	DRC+	BABIP	BRR	FRAA	WARP
2018	ASH	LO-A	19	533	77	20	4	5	44	49	96	17	13		.274/.353/.368	112	.333	-1.9	SS(116): -6.3	1.1
2019	LAN	HI-A	20	587	92	27	10	12	71	56	94	24	7		.303/.367/.466	118	.341	2.5	SS(83): -4.0, 3B(46): -4.3	2.6
2021 FS	COL	MLB	22	600	55	26	4	10	57	49	157	10	6		.242/.310/.362	87	.322	-2.7	SS -5, 3B -1	-0.1

Comparables: Tyler Wade, Amed Rosario, Yolmer Sánchez

Vilade went from a promising offensive-leaning shortstop to a promising offensive-leaning third baseman last spring. If he leans any more he'll be in foul territory, so he should knock it off.

Colton Welker 3B   Born: 10/09/97   Age: 23   Bats: R   Throws: R   Height: 6'1"   Weight: 235   Origin: Round 4, 2016 Draft (#110 overall)

YEAR	TEAM	LVL	AGE	PA	R	2B	3B	HR	RBI	BB	K	SB	CS	Whiff%	AVG/OBP/SLG	DRC+	BABIP	BRR	FRAA	WARP
2018	LAN	HI-A	20	509	74	32	0	13	82	42	103	5	1		.333/.383/.489	139	.395	1.1	3B(92): -9.3, 1B(6): -0.7	1.2
2019	HFD	AA	21	394	37	23	1	10	53	32	68	2	1		.252/.313/.408	112	.281	-2.8	3B(63): -1.5, 1B(27): 2.2	1.3
2021 FS	COL	MLB	23	600	64	26	2	17	67	38	146	3	1		.252/.306/.403	89	.314	-0.2	1B 5, 3B -5	0.3
2021 DC	COL	MLB	23	100	10	4	0	2	11	6	24	0	0		.252/.306/.403	89	.314	0.0	1B 1, 3B -1	0.0

Comparables: Matt Dominguez, Lonnie Chisenhall, Andy LaRoche

The great sieve known as "pitchers with better stuff" has diminished corner infielder **Colton Welker**'s power profile. Despite the holes in the swing, he's pretty good at the other two true outcomes. Fortunately, when a prospect is blocked by someone like Nolan Arenado, they have all the time they need—maybe if Welker waits long enough, the game will change enough to outlaw balls in play entirely.

Tony Wolters C   Born: 06/09/92   Age: 29   Bats: L   Throws: R   Height: 5'10"   Weight: 207   Origin: Round 3, 2010 Draft (#87 overall)

YEAR	TEAM	LVL	AGE	PA	R	2B	3B	HR	RBI	BB	K	SB	CS	Whiff%	AVG/OBP/SLG	DRC+	BABIP	BRR	FRAA	WARP
2018	COL	MLB	26	216	19	4	4	3	27	26	32	2	0	17.8%	.170/.292/.286	75	.188	2.5	C(64): 10.7, 2B(2): 0.0, LF(2): -0.0	1.8
2019	COL	MLB	27	411	42	17	2	1	42	36	68	0	1	20.0%	.262/.337/.329	84	.314	3.4	C(112): -4.5, 2B(8): -0.0, 3B(1): -0.0	1.2
2020	COL	MLB	28	109	10	4	0	0	8	6	30	0	0	27.4%	.230/.280/.270	63	.329	0.0	C(39): -0.7, 2B(4): -0.0	-0.5
2021 FS	COL	MLB	29	600	59	26	4	7	50	54	146	3	1	21.4%	.238/.322/.348	82	.316	1.5	C 2, 2B 0	1.4

Comparables: Duffy Dyer, Raul Casanova, John Rabb

Wolters hits like the ninth person in a lineup, which obviously wasn't commonplace in the Before Times version of the National League. But he was the last hitter in each of his 35 starts. It's not fair to say he hits like a pitcher, since 2019 NL hurlers OPSed .329 and he comfortably coasted past that. But given that he's one of the league's weakest batters, and with his framing in decline, a more accurate (and brutal) way of putting it is that he hits and catches like a Wolters.

YEAR	TEAM	P. COUNT	FRM RUNS	BLK RUNS	THRW RUNS	TOT RUNS
2018	COL	8013	10.2	-0.6	0.2	9.7
2019	COL	15067	-8.8	1.4	1.1	-6.4
2020	COL	4715	-2.3	-0.5	0.1	-2.8
2021	COL	16650	4.7	-3.3	-0.7	0.6

PITCHERS

Yency Almonte RHP   Born: 06/04/94   Age: 27   Bats: S   Throws: R   Height: 6'5"   Weight: 223   Origin: Round 17, 2012 Draft (#537 overall)

YEAR	TEAM	LVL	AGE	W	L	SV	G	GS	IP	H	HR	BB/9	K/9	K	GB%	BABIP	WHIP	ERA	DRA-	WARP	MPH	FA%	Whiff%	CSP
2018	ABQ	AAA	24	3	5	1	18	10	43²	44	8	2.9	7.0	34	42.2%	.293	1.33	5.56	97	0.5				
2018	COL	MLB	24	0	0	0	14	0	14²	15	1	2.5	8.6	14	45.2%	.341	1.30	1.84	97	0.1	97.0	62.9%	26.0%	45.8%
2019	ABQ	AAA	25	2	3	5	30	0	30	29	2	7.8	9.6	32	49.4%	.318	1.83	4.20	100	0.4				
2019	COL	MLB	25	0	1	0	28	0	34	39	7	3.7	7.7	29	32.7%	.305	1.56	5.56	131	-0.4	97.5	56.8%	24.7%	44.6%
2020	COL	MLB	26	3	0	1	24	0	27²	25	2	2.0	7.5	23	55.6%	.291	1.12	2.93	82	0.5	96.8	42.8%	28.1%	44.1%
2021 FS	COL	MLB	27	2	2	0	57	0	50	49	7	4.3	8.2	45	45.0%	.293	1.46	5.10	109	-0.1	97.1	50.7%	26.4%	44.5%
2021 DC	COL	MLB	27	2	2	0	49	0	52	51	8	4.3	8.2	47	45.0%	.293	1.46	5.10	109	0.0	97.1	50.7%	26.4%	44.5%

Comparables: Chase De Jong, Drew Anderson, Jorge López

Trying to make the Rockies' staff out of groundball pitchers is the equivalent of making the entire plane out of the black box. And yet, Almonte was the rare reliever to avert mayday in the Colorado bullpen, thanks to a four-seamer that wound up on the ground and a slider that wound up in the catcher's mitt. Two-pitch dandies are everywhere in the league, but Almonte started tossing in a changeup with the hopes of moving into the rotation someday. The opportunity hasn't come yet, but controlling air traffic late in games isn't a bad gig either.

Daniel Bard RHP   Born: 06/25/85   Age: 36   Bats: R   Throws: R   Height: 6'4"   Weight: 197   Origin: Round 1, 2006 Draft (#28 overall)

YEAR	TEAM	LVL	AGE	W	L	SV	G	GS	IP	H	HR	BB/9	K/9	K	GB%	BABIP	WHIP	ERA	DRA-	WARP	MPH	FA%	Whiff%	CSP
2020	COL	MLB	35	4	2	6	23	0	24²	22	2	3.6	9.9	27	48.5%	.312	1.30	3.65	79	0.5	98.8	56.3%	28.7%	52.6%
2021 FS	COL	MLB	36	2	2	23	57	0	50	50	7	5.6	8.2	45	47.9%	.301	1.63	5.85	119	-0.4	98.8	56.3%	28.7%	52.6%
2021 DC	COL	MLB	36	2	2	23	49	0	52	52	7	5.6	8.2	47	47.9%	.301	1.63	5.85	119	-0.2	98.8	56.3%	28.7%	52.6%

Comparables: Pedro Strop, Tyler Clippard, Joe Smith

It was a crisp Boston spring evening. Bard was facing the Houston Astros of the National League. PITCHf/x was all the rage, and Statcast was but a glimmer in its eye. The Boston Marathon bombing had happened a couple weeks prior. "Blurred Lines" just hit the airwaves. Bard looked in and threw ball four to Carlos Corporán. Nine pitches, eight balls. It was April 28, 2013, his last major league appearance and one day before Nolan Arenado's first.

Fast forward seven years, through multiple last-ditch, angst-ridden minor league comebacks, past three years completely free from the merciless grip of organized baseball. Bard entered a dirty inning in a stadium that didn't even have surveyor's marks back then. Now teammates with Arenado, he made four outs without allowing a run (or a walk). In fact, his walk rate, strikeout rate, velocity—all of it—returned to dominance, and all that was required to overcome what the elders call the "yips" was waiting long enough to forget they happened.

Now that we have the technology, we also know he spins fastballs with the fourth-highest rpm in the majors. He even closed out games, more than doubling his career save total. Suddenly it's 2021 and you're glad Daniel Bard is your closer, but can't shake the feeling that Jonathan Papelbon still has the next inning.

Ben Bowden LHP   Born: 10/21/94   Age: 26   Bats: L   Throws: L   Height: 6'4"   Weight: 249   Origin: Round 2, 2016 Draft (#45 overall)

YEAR	TEAM	LVL	AGE	W	L	SV	G	GS	IP	H	HR	BB/9	K/9	K	GB%	BABIP	WHIP	ERA	DRA-	WARP	MPH	FA%	Whiff%	CSP
2018	ASH	LO-A	23	3	0	0	15	0	15¹	17	2	2.9	14.7	25	43.2%	.429	1.43	3.52	67	0.3				
2018	LAN	HI-A	23	4	2	0	34	0	36²	35	6	3.7	13.0	53	31.5%	.341	1.36	4.17	93	0.1				
2019	HFD	AA	24	0	0	20	26	0	25²	8	1	2.5	14.7	42	33.3%	.175	0.58	1.05	39	0.8				
2019	ABQ	AAA	24	1	3	1	22	0	26	29	4	5.9	12.8	37	34.3%	.379	1.77	5.88	92	0.4				
2021 FS	COL	MLB	26	1	1	0	57	0	50	43	8	5.0	11.4	63	36.6%	.298	1.42	4.59	104	0.0				
2021 DC	COL	MLB	26	1	1	0	32	0	34	29	5	5.0	11.4	42	36.6%	.298	1.42	4.59	104	0.1				

Comparables: Ryan Burr, Yohan Ramirez, Caleb Frare

Throwing ridiculously hard as a lefty out of college with command is a surefire way to scoot through the minors, but Bowden, a 2016 draftee, has been dinged by injuries here and there. Maybe this year, though. Most assessors agree on what he is: a guy who can challenge hitters with his fastball, and when that's not working, challenge them with a fastball. The disparity is more about how much to care about lefty relievers. Get as excited as you deem fit.

Ryan Castellani RHP   Born: 04/01/96   Age: 25   Bats: R   Throws: R   Height: 6'4"   Weight: 218   Origin: Round 2, 2014 Draft (#48 overall)

YEAR	TEAM	LVL	AGE	W	L	SV	G	GS	IP	H	HR	BB/9	K/9	K	GB%	BABIP	WHIP	ERA	DRA-	WARP	MPH	FA%	Whiff%	CSP
2018	HFD	AA	22	7	9	0	26	26	134¹	135	15	4.7	6.1	91	37.4%	.293	1.53	5.49	113	0.0				
2019	ABQ	AAA	23	2	5	0	10	10	43¹	54	14	6.2	9.8	47	44.8%	.336	1.94	8.31	164	-0.5				
2020	COL	MLB	24	1	4	0	10	9	43¹	37	12	5.4	5.2	25	37.6%	.207	1.45	5.82	179	-1.4	94.8	49.4%	25.0%	43.8%
2021 FS	COL	MLB	25	8	11	0	26	26	150	161	29	5.0	6.9	115	38.8%	.294	1.64	6.28	128	-1.3	94.8	49.4%	25.0%	43.8%
2021 DC	COL	MLB	25	5	9	0	22	22	108	116	21	5.0	6.9	82	38.8%	.294	1.64	6.28	128	-0.5	94.8	49.4%	25.0%	43.8%

Comparables: Ariel Jurado, Sean Reid-Foley, Duane Underwood Jr.

Rookie seasons can be unforgiving, but Castellani—thrust into starts out of necessity rather than on merit—had one for the confessional. Returning from a positive COVID-19 test in June, he averaged more than one home run per appearance, threw ball four more often than strike three, had a FIP above 7, and did it all with a BABIP right around .200. Other than that last one, nary a metric cast him in a positive light, and while he was even worse in the PCL the year before that, starting there may be the divine path to statistical forgiveness.

Wade Davis RHP   Born: 09/07/85   Age: 35   Bats: R   Throws: R   Height: 6'5"   Weight: 225   Origin: Round 3, 2004 Draft (#75 overall)

YEAR	TEAM	LVL	AGE	W	L	SV	G	GS	IP	H	HR	BB/9	K/9	K	GB%	BABIP	WHIP	ERA	DRA-	WARP	MPH	FA%	Whiff%	CSP
2018	COL	MLB	32	3	6	43	69	0	65¹	43	8	3.6	10.7	78	41.3%	.238	1.06	4.13	87	0.8	95.6	49.1%	29.7%	40.1%
2019	COL	MLB	33	1	6	15	50	0	42²	51	7	6.1	8.9	42	39.8%	.349	1.88	8.65	129	-0.4	95.1	46.2%	25.1%	41.1%
2020	COL	MLB	34	0	1	2	5	0	4¹	9	3	6.2	6.2	3	42.1%	.375	2.77	20.77	136	0.0	93.4	40.3%	19.6%	40.9%
2021 FS	COL	MLB	35	2	3	0	57	0	50	47	7	5.3	8.7	48	40.0%	.289	1.53	4.99	108	-0.1	95.1	46.6%	26.1%	40.7%

Comparables: Arthur Rhodes, Steve Cishek, Jim Gott

That might be all they wrote for Davis' multifaceted career. A ballooned ERA and evaporating velo, coupled with a shoulder injury, led to an abrupt adieu with Colorado, who knocked him off the roster in the final week of this silly season. We may see a return in some capacity—he was replaced as closer by Daniel Bard, after all—but if that was the final chapter, let us remember Davis as a middling Rays starter who turned into the Trojan workhorse in Now That's What I Call A Wil Myers Trade Vol. 1. Or as the lockdown setup man for baseball's unlikely Brigadoon, the World Series-bound Royals, allowing one run in 25 of their postseason innings. And possibly, we can remember him for that one moderately neato Cubs season. But as they have written about Mike Hampton, let us forget he ever pitched for the Rockies.

Jairo Díaz RHP   Born: 05/27/91   Age: 30   Bats: R   Throws: R   Height: 6'0"   Weight: 254   Origin: International Free Agent, 2007

YEAR	TEAM	LVL	AGE	W	L	SV	G	GS	IP	H	HR	BB/9	K/9	K	GB%	BABIP	WHIP	ERA	DRA-	WARP	MPH	FA%	Whiff%	CSP
2019	ABQ	AAA	28	1	0	6	16	0	20	12	0	2.7	9.9	22	64.6%	.250	0.90	0.45	31	0.9				
2019	COL	MLB	28	6	4	5	56	0	57²	56	7	3.0	9.8	63	49.1%	.318	1.30	4.53	71	1.2	98.8	56.0%	29.5%	47.6%
2020	COL	MLB	29	1	2	4	24	0	20	31	4	6.3	7.7	17	40.3%	.409	2.25	7.65	131	-0.2	97.1	57.7%	23.5%	43.5%
2021 FS	COL	MLB	30	2	2	0	57	0	50	49	7	4.1	8.6	47	48.2%	.305	1.46	4.90	106	0.0	98.2	56.7%	27.2%	46.0%
2021 DC	COL	MLB	30	2	2	0	43	0	46	45	6	4.1	8.6	43	48.2%	.305	1.46	4.90	106	0.1	98.2	56.7%	27.2%	46.0%

Comparables: Hansel Robles, Shawn Armstrong, Mike Morin

Relievers shouldn't aspire to be starters. They should aspire to be commissioners. If Díaz were to run the league, the first thing he'd (presumably) do is allow each reliever to wipe one bad appearance off their stats, because it usually messes up their ERA. In fact, take away one two-out, seven-run nightmare and his 2020 ERA sheds three runs. He would naturally become corrupted with this absolute power, as Lord Acton would suggest. It would turn into scrubbing the stats for all games against one team; suddenly he's removed all the Giants games, now it's down to 3.44. Not satisfied, it would turn into nullifying the numbers for any appearance in which it was raining, or it looked like it was going to rain, or when it was raining somewhere. Suddenly he's accidentally deleted his entire statistical year, we're devoid of data, and we'd say his 2019 looked pretty great, I wonder what he was up to last season, can't wait to see him this year.

Phillip Diehl LHP   Born: 07/16/94   Age: 26   Bats: L   Throws: L   Height: 6'2"   Weight: 169   Origin: Round 27, 2016 Draft (#818 overall)

YEAR	TEAM	LVL	AGE	W	L	SV	G	GS	IP	H	HR	BB/9	K/9	K	GB%	BABIP	WHIP	ERA	DRA-	WARP	MPH	FA%	Whiff%	CSP
2018	TAM	HI-A	23	2	2	3	25	0	48²	37	2	2.2	14.6	79	42.0%	.357	1.01	3.14	48	1.5				
2018	TRN	AA	23	0	1	1	14	0	26²	18	2	3.7	9.8	29	33.8%	.254	1.09	1.35	53	0.8				
2019	HFD	AA	24	0	0	0	11	0	13¹	5	0	2.0	8.1	12	58.1%	.161	0.60	0.00	59	0.3				
2019	ABQ	AAA	24	2	1	0	39	0	45¹	54	16	3.0	10.3	52	36.2%	.333	1.52	6.75	127	0.0				
2019	COL	MLB	24	0	0	0	10	0	7¹	10	1	2.5	9.8	8	20.8%	.391	1.64	7.36	128	-0.1	91.7	44.9%	37.9%	41.6%
2020	COL	MLB	25	0	0	0	6	0	6	7	2	1.5	6.0	4	45.0%	.278	1.33	10.50	95	0.1	91.2	55.2%	16.3%	43.9%
2021 FS	COL	MLB	26	1	1	0	57	0	50	47	8	3.6	9.3	51	37.6%	.293	1.35	4.59	101	0.1	91.4	50.6%	25.9%	42.9%
2021 DC	COL	MLB	26	1	1	0	32	0	34	32	6	3.6	9.3	35	37.6%	.293	1.35	4.59	101	0.2	91.4	50.6%	25.9%	42.9%

Comparables: Travis Bergen, Trevor Kelley, James Pazos

Our advanced pitching numbers noticeably temper the small sample shellacking that put control artist Diehl's 2020 ERA into double digits. This is why DRA stands for Denver Redemption Algorithms.

Carlos Estévez RHP   Born: 12/28/92   Age: 28   Bats: R   Throws: R   Height: 6'6"   Weight: 277   Origin: International Free Agent, 2011

YEAR	TEAM	LVL	AGE	W	L	SV	G	GS	IP	H	HR	BB/9	K/9	K	GB%	BABIP	WHIP	ERA	DRA-	WARP	MPH	FA%	Whiff%	CSP
2018	ABQ	AAA	25	0	1	1	28	0	28¹	37	6	3.5	11.1	35	38.1%	.397	1.69	6.35	73	0.5				
2019	COL	MLB	26	2	2	0	71	0	72	70	12	2.9	10.1	81	38.4%	.305	1.29	3.75	84	1.0	99.7	69.3%	30.7%	52.5%
2020	COL	MLB	27	1	3	1	26	0	24	33	6	3.4	10.1	27	29.9%	.380	1.75	7.50	123	-0.1	98.7	61.5%	25.1%	49.4%
2021 FS	COL	MLB	28	2	2	0	57	0	50	45	8	3.4	9.5	52	36.8%	.289	1.30	4.28	95	0.3	99.3	66.6%	28.8%	51.4%
2021 DC	COL	MLB	28	2	2	0	43	0	46	42	7	3.4	9.5	48	36.8%	.289	1.30	4.28	95	0.4	99.3	66.6%	28.8%	51.4%

Comparables: Michael Tonkin, Phil Maton, Nick Goody

Having Charlie Sheen's birth name has to grate on a relief pitcher with a big fastball. The two Estévezes have previously met in person but clearly the real pitcher didn't heed the fictional pitcher's cautionary tale of avoiding substandard sequels to breakout performances. He struggled with command throughout the season, becoming a historical footnote when Albert Pujols tied Willie Mays on the home run list thanks to one of his throws. (It is unknown what milestones Clu Haywood touched thanks to The Wild Thing, but we will canonically assume it was several.) The third installment of *Major League* was titled "Back To The Minors." No reason we're mentioning this. Just thought it was neat information.

Kyle Freeland LHP   Born: 05/14/93   Age: 28   Bats: L   Throws: L   Height: 6'4"   Weight: 204   Origin: Round 1, 2014 Draft (#8 overall)

YEAR	TEAM	LVL	AGE	W	L	SV	G	GS	IP	H	HR	BB/9	K/9	K	GB%	BABIP	WHIP	ERA	DRA-	WARP	MPH	FA%	Whiff%	CSP
2018	COL	MLB	25	17	7	0	33	33	202¹	182	17	3.1	7.7	173	45.5%	.288	1.25	2.85	86	3.3	93.8	52.5%	21.9%	48.0%
2019	ABQ	AAA	26	0	4	0	6	6	29²	40	4	4.9	8.5	28	53.5%	.396	1.89	8.80	132	0.1				
2019	COL	MLB	26	3	11	0	22	22	104¹	126	25	3.4	6.8	79	46.2%	.310	1.58	6.73	129	-0.6	94.0	52.1%	21.4%	47.0%
2020	COL	MLB	27	2	3	0	13	13	70²	77	9	2.9	5.9	46	50.0%	.305	1.42	4.33	109	0.3	93.9	33.3%	20.6%	45.7%
2021 FS	COL	MLB	28	9	9	0	26	26	150	157	21	3.4	7.1	118	49.8%	.301	1.43	4.78	104	0.7	93.9	46.0%	21.3%	46.9%
2021 DC	COL	MLB	28	9	10	0	27	27	156	163	22	3.4	7.1	122	49.8%	.301	1.43	4.78	104	1.3	93.9	46.0%	21.3%	46.9%

Comparables: Jordan Montgomery, Daniel Mengden, Cody Reed

Philosophical question: If you throw a changeup more often than a fastball, is the fastball really the changeup? Freeland blew everyone's augmented minds (it's legal in Colorado, after all) by leaning on the slower option way more than the faster one, especially when behind in the count. The four-seam usage was cut nearly in half, perhaps an adjustment due to a forgettable 2019. Beyond a decent slider he doesn't often get the swing and miss, so his game is getting people off balance and having them stay on the ground. (Because, again, it's legal there.) An admirable philosophy in a stadium built for pitcher nihilism.

Mychal Givens RHP
Born: 05/13/90   Age: 31   Bats: R   Throws: R   Height: 6'0"   Weight: 230   Origin: Round 2, 2009 Draft (#54 overall)

YEAR	TEAM	LVL	AGE	W	L	SV	G	GS	IP	H	HR	BB/9	K/9	K	GB%	BABIP	WHIP	ERA	DRA-	WARP	MPH	FA%	Whiff%	CSP
2018	BAL	MLB	28	0	7	9	9	0	76²	61	4	3.5	9.3	79	37.6%	.285	1.19	3.99	108	0.1	97.4	76.9%	25.0%	53.2%
2019	BAL	MLB	29	2	6	11	58	0	63	49	13	3.7	12.3	86	38.4%	.271	1.19	4.57	63	1.6	97.5	70.3%	34.2%	50.1%
2020	COL	MLB	30	1	1	1	22	0	22¹	16	5	4.0	10.1	25	23.2%	.216	1.16	3.63	113	0.0	96.9	65.1%	27.7%	48.8%
2021 FS	COL	MLB	31	2	2	3	57	0	50	39	6	3.8	10.7	59	34.7%	.276	1.21	3.50	79	0.7	97.3	70.7%	30.0%	50.6%
2021 DC	COL	MLB	31	2	2	3	49	0	52	41	7	3.8	10.7	61	34.7%	.276	1.21	3.50	79	0.9	97.3	70.7%	30.0%	50.6%

Comparables: Vinnie Pestano, Antonio Bastardo, Jeurys Familia

There are no givens in life, especially when it comes to Rockies pitching, so Jeff Bridich decided to be cute and literally change that by acquiring the longtime Orioles setup man for some infield futures. Prior to the trade, the sidearm slinger began the season with 10 consecutive scoreless innings, thanks to Givens' successful gambit of having batters weakly deposit his pitches into the crab-infused atmosphere on the eastern seaboard. So you don't need much of an imagination to know how that played in the mountains.

Chi Chi González RHP
Born: 01/15/92   Age: 29   Bats: R   Throws: R   Height: 6'3"   Weight: 210   Origin: Round 1, 2013 Draft (#23 overall)

YEAR	TEAM	LVL	AGE	W	L	SV	G	GS	IP	H	HR	BB/9	K/9	K	GB%	BABIP	WHIP	ERA	DRA-	WARP	MPH	FA%	Whiff%	CSP
2019	ABQ	AAA	27	4	5	0	16	15	87	105	15	3.7	7.9	76	50.4%	.345	1.62	6.10	99	1.6				
2019	COL	MLB	27	2	6	0	14	12	63	59	11	4.7	6.6	46	42.9%	.261	1.46	5.29	126	-0.3	94.0	54.8%	20.5%	46.5%
2020	COL	MLB	28	0	2	0	6	4	19²	22	3	4.6	7.3	16	35.5%	.328	1.63	6.86	119	0.0	94.2	59.9%	18.7%	45.8%
2021 FS	COL	MLB	29	2	3	0	57	0	50	53	8	4.1	7.3	40	44.1%	.302	1.52	5.35	115	-0.3	94.1	56.4%	19.9%	46.3%

Comparables: P.J. Walters, José Ureña, Tyler Chatwood

The best thing that can be said about González's season is he swapped out his slider for a curveball. Perhaps the second-best thing that can be said for someone whose offerings were bludgeoned about the ballpark was that at least there weren't more home runs.

Jon Gray RHP
Born: 11/05/91   Age: 29   Bats: R   Throws: R   Height: 6'4"   Weight: 225   Origin: Round 1, 2013 Draft (#3 overall)

YEAR	TEAM	LVL	AGE	W	L	SV	G	GS	IP	H	HR	BB/9	K/9	K	GB%	BABIP	WHIP	ERA	DRA-	WARP	MPH	FA%	Whiff%	CSP
2018	ABQ	AAA	26	1	0	0	2	2	10²	7	1	3.4	11.0	13	63.0%	.231	1.03	3.38	70	0.3				
2018	COL	MLB	26	12	9	0	31	31	172¹	180	27	2.7	9.6	183	47.5%	.326	1.35	5.12	99	1.7	96.9	49.7%	29.2%	48.8%
2019	COL	MLB	27	11	8	0	26	25	150	147	19	3.4	8.9	149	49.9%	.318	1.35	3.84	81	2.9	97.8	52.7%	26.3%	48.6%
2020	COL	MLB	28	2	4	0	8	8	39	45	6	2.5	5.1	22	36.7%	.293	1.44	6.69	136	-0.4	95.4	49.4%	22.1%	46.8%
2021 FS	COL	MLB	29	9	9	0	26	26	150	154	24	3.2	7.9	132	43.3%	.301	1.39	4.75	104	0.8	97.0	51.1%	26.3%	48.3%
2021 DC	COL	MLB	29	8	9	0	25	25	142	145	22	3.2	7.9	124	43.3%	.301	1.39	4.75	104	1.2	97.0	51.1%	26.3%	48.3%

Comparables: Kevin Gausman, Vince Velasquez, Jake Odorizzi

It's a love story you've heard many times: Boy finds baseball. Boy loves baseball. Boy throws baseball hard. Boy finds major league team. Major league team is the Rockies. Boy's ERA swells up to the size of a genetically-modified grapefruit. By "love story" it would have been more appropriate to say "horror story," and Elisabeth Kübler-Ross did once say there are only two real human emotions, love and fear. So there is nothing more human than spending six seasons as a Rockies pitcher, and Gray is one of the few who has truly lived.

Tyler Kinley RHP
Born: 01/31/91   Age: 30   Bats: R   Throws: R   Height: 6'4"   Weight: 220   Origin: Round 16, 2013 Draft (#472 overall)

YEAR	TEAM	LVL	AGE	W	L	SV	G	GS	IP	H	HR	BB/9	K/9	K	GB%	BABIP	WHIP	ERA	DRA-	WARP	MPH	FA%	Whiff%	CSP
2018	NO	AAA	27	2	2	8	40	0	40	32	6	5.0	12.6	56	38.3%	.326	1.35	2.92	50	1.3				
2018	MIA	MLB	27	0	0	0	9	0	7²	6	0	4.7	10.6	9	55.0%	.300	1.30	7.04	51	0.2	98.7	55.4%	29.4%	45.7%
2018	MIN	MLB	27	0	0	0	4	0	3¹	9	2	10.8	10.8	4	60.0%	.538	3.90	24.30	58	0.1	97.5	67.9%	33.3%	39.0%
2019	NO	AAA	28	0	1	2	14	0	15²	4	1	4.0	10.9	19	35.5%	.100	0.70	1.72	36	0.7				
2019	MIA	MLB	28	3	1	1	52	0	49¹	43	5	6.6	8.4	46	38.4%	.288	1.60	3.65	119	-0.3	96.3	42.3%	29.5%	42.7%
2020	COL	MLB	29	0	2	0	24	0	23²	13	2	4.6	9.9	26	45.5%	.212	1.06	5.32	86	0.4	97.3	33.6%	36.2%	43.5%
2021 FS	COL	MLB	30	2	2	0	57	0	50	43	7	5.3	10.3	57	41.3%	.293	1.46	4.59	98	0.2	96.8	40.3%	32.1%	43.0%
2021 DC	COL	MLB	30	2	2	0	49	0	52	45	7	5.3	10.3	59	41.3%	.293	1.46	4.59	98	0.4	96.8	40.3%	32.1%	43.0%

Comparables: Emilio Pagán, Jacob Barnes, Ryan Dull

Kinley is a one-card reliever, but it's a dominant-suit face card: "try and hit my slider." It's one of the league's best, but as is the case with singular sensations, this has led to a chorus line of walks. The fastball is serviceable, but even for sitting at 96 mph, it's surprisingly hittable. Kinley's job when he gets into the game is making everybody looking on—batter, catcher, umpire, fielders, manager, himself—a little more uncomfortable than normal, which is the entire point of baseball, admittedly.

Peter Lambert RHP Born: 04/18/97 Age: 24 Bats: R Throws: R Height: 6'2" Weight: 208 Origin: Round 2, 2015 Draft (#44 overall)

YEAR	TEAM	LVL	AGE	W	L	SV	G	GS	IP	H	HR	BB/9	K/9	K	GB%	BABIP	WHIP	ERA	DRA-	WARP	MPH	FA%	Whiff%	CSP
2018	HFD	AA	21	8	2	0	15	15	92²	80	6	1.2	7.3	75	48.9%	.285	0.99	2.23	96	0.9				
2018	ABQ	AAA	21	2	5	0	11	11	55¹	72	5	2.4	5.0	31	50.3%	.349	1.57	5.04	100	0.5				
2019	ABQ	AAA	22	2	2	0	11	11	60¹	63	10	2.4	7.6	51	52.6%	.294	1.31	5.07	65	2.1				
2019	COL	MLB	22	3	7	0	19	19	89¹	119	18	3.6	5.7	57	46.1%	.338	1.74	7.25	152	-1.6	94.3	53.0%	16.8%	47.0%
2021 FS	COL	MLB	24	8	10	0	26	26	150	167	25	3.3	6.7	111	46.8%	.307	1.48	5.42	116	-0.3	94.3	53.0%	16.8%	47.0%
2021 DC	COL	MLB	24	2	3	0	9	9	38	42	6	3.3	6.7	28	46.8%	.307	1.48	5.42	116	0.1	94.3	53.0%	16.8%	47.0%

Comparables: Jake Thompson, Zach Eflin, Jaime Barria

A lambert is a unit of measurement used to convey the luminance of light. A Peter Lambert is a unit that underwent Tommy John surgery last summer and won't burn brightly until 2022.

Germán Márquez RHP Born: 02/22/95 Age: 26 Bats: R Throws: R Height: 6'1" Weight: 230 Origin: International Free Agent, 2011

YEAR	TEAM	LVL	AGE	W	L	SV	G	GS	IP	H	HR	BB/9	K/9	K	GB%	BABIP	WHIP	ERA	DRA-	WARP	MPH	FA%	Whiff%	CSP
2018	COL	MLB	23	14	11	0	33	33	196	179	24	2.6	10.6	230	47.3%	.314	1.20	3.77	72	4.7	97.5	55.0%	28.4%	49.9%
2019	COL	MLB	24	12	5	0	28	28	174	174	29	1.8	9.1	175	48.2%	.308	1.20	4.76	66	4.7	97.7	52.1%	26.8%	50.6%
2020	COL	MLB	25	4	6	0	13	13	81²	78	6	2.8	8.0	73	50.4%	.300	1.26	3.75	79	1.7	97.9	52.4%	26.3%	49.6%
2021 FS	COL	MLB	26	9	8	0	26	26	150	144	21	2.7	8.8	147	48.8%	.301	1.26	3.98	90	1.9	97.7	52.9%	27.1%	50.1%
2021 DC	COL	MLB	26	10	9	0	27	27	170	164	23	2.7	8.8	166	48.8%	.301	1.26	3.98	90	2.7	97.7	52.9%	27.1%	50.1%

Comparables: Luis Severino, Lucas Giolito, José Berríos

We've spent several paragraphs over the years discussing the merits of Márquez's ace status using the advanced numbers. If you're sick of the long division, then let's stare at the raw ones for a second: In each of his starts, he always made it five innings and once made it into the eighth. He allowed at least one run in each of his starts. He was second in the league in innings and tied for the lead in batters faced. Liván Hernández may weep at the state of innings eaters these days, but Márquez is the modern day gourmand. Now back to the calculus: While his DRA isn't even in the top 50, his workload multiplies that into a top 20 pitcher, or a second-tier ace. You may not like it, but this is what peak performance looks like.

Scott Oberg RHP Born: 03/13/90 Age: 31 Bats: R Throws: R Height: 6'2" Weight: 207 Origin: Round 15, 2012 Draft (#468 overall)

YEAR	TEAM	LVL	AGE	W	L	SV	G	GS	IP	H	HR	BB/9	K/9	K	GB%	BABIP	WHIP	ERA	DRA-	WARP	MPH	FA%	Whiff%	CSP
2018	ABQ	AAA	28	1	0	3	13	0	15¹	14	1	1.2	8.2	14	60.0%	.342	1.04	1.76	86	0.2				
2018	COL	MLB	28	8	1	0	56	0	58²	45	4	1.8	8.7	57	57.7%	.270	0.97	2.45	77	1.0	97.0	55.1%	27.9%	48.0%
2019	COL	MLB	29	6	1	5	49	0	56	39	5	3.7	9.2	57	49.3%	.246	1.11	2.25	67	1.2	96.0	52.2%	27.9%	47.4%
2021 FS	COL	MLB	31	1	1	6	57	0	50	45	5	3.0	9.4	52	51.3%	.297	1.24	3.59	82	0.6	96.3	53.2%	27.9%	47.6%
2021 DC	COL	MLB	31	1	1	6	38	0	40	36	4	3.0	9.4	41	51.3%	.297	1.24	3.59	82	0.6	96.3	53.2%	27.9%	47.6%

Comparables: Shawn Armstrong, Nick Wittgren, Emilio Pagán

You may be surprised to learn Oberg is fourth all-time in Rockies history in pitching win probability added, but then again you may not be, because it's a list of Rockies pitchers and things always get weird after the first couple names. The injury-addled setup man built up a reputation out of reliability, so his absence was felt last year when blood clots ravaged his body for the third time, wiping out his entire 2020. He's under contract through '22, a reward for his understated dominance; given that there are so many more weird Rockies lists for him to ascend, this could just be the tip of the Oberg.

AJ Ramos RHP Born: 09/20/86 Age: 34 Bats: R Throws: R Height: 5'10" Weight: 200 Origin: Round 21, 2009 Draft (#638 overall)

YEAR	TEAM	LVL	AGE	W	L	SV	G	GS	IP	H	HR	BB/9	K/9	K	GB%	BABIP	WHIP	ERA	DRA-	WARP	MPH	FA%	Whiff%	CSP
2018	NYM	MLB	31	2	2	0	28	0	19²	17	3	6.9	10.1	22	27.5%	.292	1.63	6.41	87	0.2	94.1	36.7%	29.1%	44.7%
2020	COL	MLB	33	0	0	0	3	0	2²	4	1	10.1	3.4	1	18.2%	.300	2.62	3.38	150	0.0	93.4	33.3%	16.1%	44.5%
2021 FS	COL	MLB	34	2	3	0	57	0	50	47	8	5.6	8.8	49	34.9%	.289	1.58	5.37	114	-0.3	93.9	35.5%	24.5%	44.7%

Comparables: Michael Gonzalez, Pedro Strop, Brad Brach

Ramos would have been the biggest comeback story in the Rockies bullpen, if Daniel Bard hadn't landed his 99.99th-percentile outcome. An All-Star five years ago, the former electric Marlins and incandescent Mets closer recovered from torn labrum surgery, missing over two calendar years of organized baseball. Announcing a comeback in the summer was a bold gambit, given that MLB was trying to do the same thing. After coming up lame on deals with the Dodgers and Cubs, the Rockies ultimately gave him a few innings in the final week. His stuff was never blow-away, but rather move-enough to create missed swings, but in the teensy 2020 sample he most certainly did not do that. It's always nice to have someone that has a 40-save season in your ranks, though you'd prefer those saves didn't predate the Trump Administration.

Ryan Rolison LHP Born: 07/11/97 Age: 23 Bats: R Throws: L Height: 6'2" Weight: 213 Origin: Round 1, 2018 Draft (#22 overall)

YEAR	TEAM	LVL	AGE	W	L	SV	G	GS	IP	H	HR	BB/9	K/9	K	GB%	BABIP	WHIP	ERA	DRA-	WARP	MPH	FA%	Whiff%	CSP
2018	GJ	ROK	20	0	1	0	9	9	29	15	2	2.5	10.6	34	65.7%	.200	0.79	1.86	72	0.8				
2019	ASH	LO-A	21	2	1	0	3	3	14²	8	0	1.2	8.6	14	37.8%	.216	0.68	0.61	49	0.5				
2019	LAN	HI-A	21	6	7	0	22	22	116¹	129	22	2.9	9.1	118	43.6%	.327	1.44	4.87	94	0.6				
2021 FS	COL	MLB	23	1	1	0	57	0	50	50	8	4.0	7.9	44	43.1%	.296	1.46	5.06	115	-0.3				
2021 DC	COL	MLB	23	1	1	0	4	4	21	21	3	4.0	7.9	18	43.1%	.296	1.46	5.06	115	0.0				

Comparables: Braxton Garrett, Kris Bubic, Patrick Sandoval

There are fewer cursed accolades than "top Rockies pitching prospect," but at least Rolison isn't being considered for Spinal Tap's next drummer. The team actually considered promoting him for the stretch run, given that they lacked a lefty reliever and Rolison sports the quality fastball-slider combo for the gig. Instead, he'll begin the season in Double-A trying not to think about how his curveball will behave in Coors. Then again, he might still be better off in Colorado than, say, Tampa Bay, where he wouldn't make their Top-10 list unless it went to 11.

Antonio Santos RHP   Born: 10/06/96   Age: 24   Bats: R   Throws: R   Height: 6'3"   Weight: 223   Origin: International Free Agent, 2015

YEAR	TEAM	LVL	AGE	W	L	SV	G	GS	IP	H	HR	BB/9	K/9	K	GB%	BABIP	WHIP	ERA	DRA-	WARP	MPH	FA%	Whiff%	CSP
2018	ASH	LO-A	21	1	10	0	15	15	86¹	100	8	1.3	9.0	86	50.7%	.355	1.30	4.48	80	1.4				
2018	LAN	HI-A	21	4	3	0	12	12	65²	74	15	2.9	7.7	56	37.0%	.303	1.45	5.21	158	-1.9				
2019	LAN	HI-A	22	3	6	0	18	18	99¹	116	11	1.6	8.7	96	39.3%	.349	1.35	4.35	106	-0.2				
2019	HFD	AA	22	3	3	0	8	8	45²	47	3	2.0	8.7	44	38.2%	.338	1.25	4.93	104	-0.1				
2020	COL	MLB	23	0	1	0	3	1	6	14	1	6.0	6.0	4	36.0%	.542	3.00	16.50	140	-0.1	95.7	59.4%	11.7%	45.7%
2021 FS	COL	MLB	24	1	1	0	57	0	50	55	9	2.8	6.9	38	38.0%	.304	1.42	5.44	116	-0.3	95.7	59.4%	11.7%	45.7%
2021 DC	COL	MLB	24	1	1	0	21	0	23	25	4	2.8	6.9	17	38.0%	.304	1.42	5.44	116	-0.1	95.7	59.4%	11.7%	45.7%

Comparables: Chase De Jong, Randy Rosario, Blake Snell

Santos was rinsed in his first few outings, but he has an out pitch, he's got it around here somewhere, just give him a minute or so, we are going to love it when we see it, please hold, thank you for your patience.

Antonio Senzatela RHP   Born: 01/21/95   Age: 26   Bats: R   Throws: R   Height: 6'1"   Weight: 236   Origin: International Free Agent, 2011

YEAR	TEAM	LVL	AGE	W	L	SV	G	GS	IP	H	HR	BB/9	K/9	K	GB%	BABIP	WHIP	ERA	DRA-	WARP	MPH	FA%	Whiff%	CSP
2018	ABQ	AAA	23	3	1	0	8	8	37²	29	1	2.9	10.0	42	47.4%	.301	1.09	2.15	92	0.5				
2018	COL	MLB	23	6	6	0	23	13	90¹	94	10	3.0	6.9	69	46.5%	.303	1.37	4.38	114	0.1	96.0	64.1%	20.9%	47.6%
2019	ABQ	AAA	24	1	1	0	7	7	34¹	45	7	2.6	3.1	12	48.4%	.317	1.60	5.77	115	0.4				
2019	COL	MLB	24	11	11	0	25	25	124²	161	19	4.1	5.5	76	53.5%	.336	1.75	6.71	146	-1.9	95.9	63.7%	17.9%	47.9%
2020	COL	MLB	25	5	3	0	12	12	73¹	71	9	2.2	5.0	41	50.8%	.268	1.21	3.44	101	0.6	96.5	56.0%	18.5%	49.3%
2021 FS	COL	MLB	26	8	10	0	26	26	150	172	25	3.4	6.1	102	50.0%	.308	1.52	5.61	119	-0.5	96.1	61.0%	18.6%	48.4%
2021 DC	COL	MLB	26	8	11	0	27	27	154	176	25	3.4	6.1	104	50.0%	.308	1.52	5.61	119	0.1	96.1	61.0%	18.6%	48.4%

Comparables: Zach Eflin, Erasmo Ramírez, Tyler Mahle

Look, they're all underrated pitchers. They can't all be Kershaws and Scherzers. Bury the u-word when discussing Senzatela, and discuss him often because that name comfortably rolls off the tongue. The Rockies righty finished in the NL's top 10 in home runs per nine and walks per nine. That he accomplished this as a Coorsman with the league's absolute worst strikeout rate meant the fielders, they were busy. Since he can pitch deep into games and avoid the two bad true outcomes with the ground game, he'll be rated just fine.

Robert Stephenson RHP   Born: 02/24/93   Age: 28   Bats: R   Throws: R   Height: 6'3"   Weight: 205   Origin: Round 1, 2011 Draft (#27 overall)

YEAR	TEAM	LVL	AGE	W	L	SV	G	GS	IP	H	HR	BB/9	K/9	K	GB%	BABIP	WHIP	ERA	DRA-	WARP	MPH	FA%	Whiff%	CSP
2018	LOU	AAA	25	11	6	0	20	20	113	74	12	4.5	10.8	135	38.0%	.240	1.16	2.87	75	2.3				
2018	CIN	MLB	25	0	2	0	4	3	11²	17	2	9.3	8.5	11	32.5%	.395	2.49	9.26	145	-0.2	94.7	36.4%	25.5%	47.1%
2019	CIN	MLB	26	3	2	0	57	0	64²	43	9	3.3	11.3	81	31.4%	.231	1.04	3.76	77	1.1	96.6	36.2%	39.0%	43.7%
2020	CIN	MLB	27	0	0	0	10	0	10	11	8	2.7	11.7	13	23.1%	.167	1.40	9.90	140	-0.1	96.1	30.1%	39.5%	44.9%
2021 FS	COL	MLB	28	2	2	0	57	0	50	43	9	4.8	11.1	61	33.6%	.292	1.41	4.74	103	0.1	96.3	35.0%	37.9%	44.3%
2021 DC	COL	MLB	28	2	2	0	43	0	46	40	8	4.8	11.1	56	33.6%	.292	1.41	4.74	103	0.2	96.3	35.0%	37.9%	44.3%

Comparables: Jeff Hoffman, Matt Wisler, John Gant

You know how we so often write that a reliever with iffy command and fly-ball tendencies always runs the risk of a sudden, random bout of gopheritis crushing their season? That was Stephenson last year, who followed up his long-anticipated 2019 bullpen breakout by allowing eight home runs in 10 innings, with fully half of the fly balls he allowed landing in the bleachers. He also missed most of August with a sore back, so like all the other disappointing Stephenson years it's best to just let the river wash this one away and move on. The swing-and-miss stuff remains undeniable, but time is no longer on Stephenson's side.

Jesus Tinoco RHP   Born: 04/30/95   Age: 26   Bats: R   Throws: R   Height: 6'4"   Weight: 258   Origin: International Free Agent, 2011

YEAR	TEAM	LVL	AGE	W	L	SV	G	GS	IP	H	HR	BB/9	K/9	K	GB%	BABIP	WHIP	ERA	DRA-	WARP	MPH	FA%	Whiff%	CSP
2018	HFD	AA	23	9	12	0	26	26	141	149	23	2.4	8.4	132	37.6%	.315	1.33	4.79	89	1.8				
2019	ABQ	AAA	24	3	1	1	29	0	34	33	4	4.8	6.1	23	56.2%	.287	1.50	3.97	85	0.7				
2019	COL	MLB	24	0	3	1	24	0	36	36	12	5.5	7.0	28	43.6%	.245	1.61	4.75	140	-0.6	96.0	62.3%	22.4%	43.8%
2020	COL	MLB	25	0	0	0	6	0	8²	3	0	7.3	6.2	6	78.9%	.158	1.15	1.04	83	0.2	95.7	68.1%	24.6%	36.7%
2021 FS	COL	MLB	26	2	3	0	57	0	50	50	7	4.9	7.5	41	46.6%	.296	1.56	5.13	111	-0.2	95.9	63.8%	23.0%	42.0%

Comparables: Chase De Jong, Corey Oswalt, Keury Mella

Tinoco has a lively fastball and a decent curve but has trouble finding the strike zone. Then again, Colorado traded him to Miami only to claim him back a month later, so his own team has trouble locating *him*.

LOS ANGELES DODGERS

Essay by Robert O'Connell

Player comments by Matt Trueblood and BP staff

In the sixth inning of Game 5 of last October's National League Championship Series, Max Muncy came to the plate to face Braves reliever Will Smith. The Dodgers trailed in the game, 2-1, and in the series, 3-1. Muncy had been an important and emblematic figure in the team's run of success throughout the late 2010s—a former Quad-A anonym who, washing ashore on the paradise island of the Dodger lineup, had transformed himself into one of baseball's canniest observers of the strike zone—but L.A. fans would likely have preferred to see someone else up in that spot, with a man on second and two outs. Mookie Betts, maybe, with his ability to steer the game to himself in the biggest moments. Or Corey Seager, who had spent the postseason to that point dispensing homers to every section of empty bleachers. Or even Cody Bellinger, the 2019 NL MVP who had tailed off in 2020 but whose spiraling swing suggested the sort of theatrics the moment called for.

But, no: it was Muncy's turn, so he set up in the box and went to work, assuming a squatty, dorkily prepared left-handed stance. Smith threw five straight sliders, three balls and two strikes, and Muncy let them all pass by. Then Smith went with a fastball, 96 miles per hour, wire-straight and inches from the outside corner, a nearly perfect pitch. Muncy didn't budge at it.

The walk wasn't much—it might easily have ended up one of the many morsels of misplaced hope that amounted to the team's recent playoff history—until it was. Six pitches later, L.A.'s Will Smith, a young catcher with the accelerated readiness common to Dodger youngsters, cracked a home run (on another full count) to left, putting his team up, 4-2. The homer felt different that it would have minutes before, had it not followed Muncy's plate appearance. Taking the lead then would have been just a sample of the semi-random good fortune baseball metes out in games stocked with star players. Doing it this way, via a slow then sudden accumulation of patient baseball, felt something like a parable.

⚾   ⚾   ⚾

LOS ANGELES DODGERS PROSPECTUS
2020 W-L: 43-17, 1st in NL West

Pythag	.719	1st	dWin%	.624	1st
RS/G	5.82	1st	B-Age	28.6	18th
RA/G	3.55	2nd	P-Age	27.6	8th
DRC+	118	1st	FIP	3.59	2nd
DRA-	82	1st	DER	.733	2nd
Payroll	$95M	2nd	M$/MW	$3.1M	14th

- Opened 1962
- Open air
- Natural surface
- Fence profile: 4' to 8'

Three-Year Park Factors

Runs	Runs/RH	Runs/LH	HR/RH	HR/LH
96	95	100	104	107

Top Hitter WARP	2.9 Mookie Betts
Top Pitcher WARP	1.5 Clayton Kershaw
Top Prospect	Josiah Gray

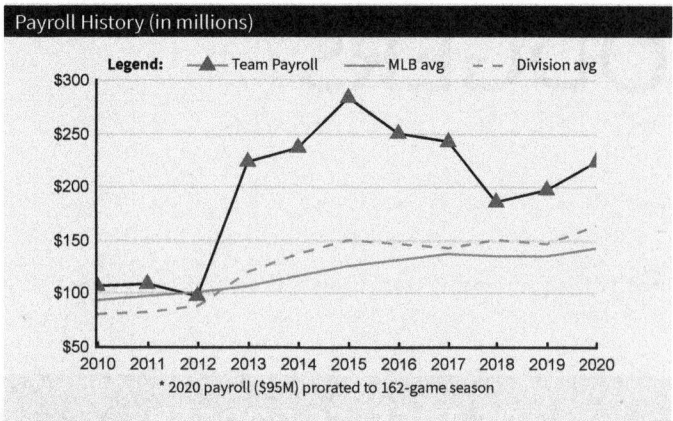

Payroll History (in millions)

Legend: ▲ Team Payroll — MLB avg – – Division avg

* 2020 payroll ($95M) prorated to 162-game season

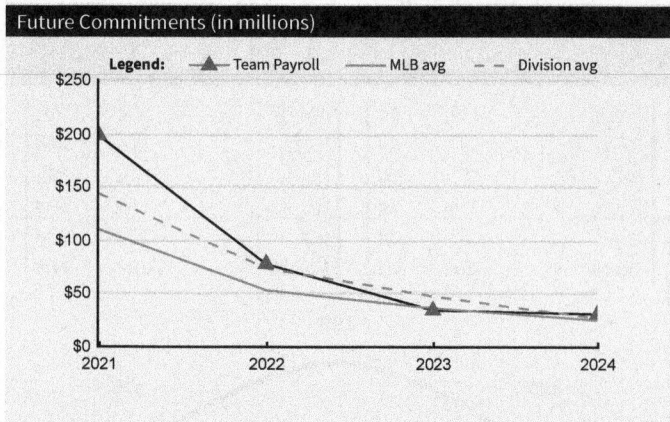

Future Commitments (in millions)

Legend: ▲ Team Payroll — MLB avg – – Division avg

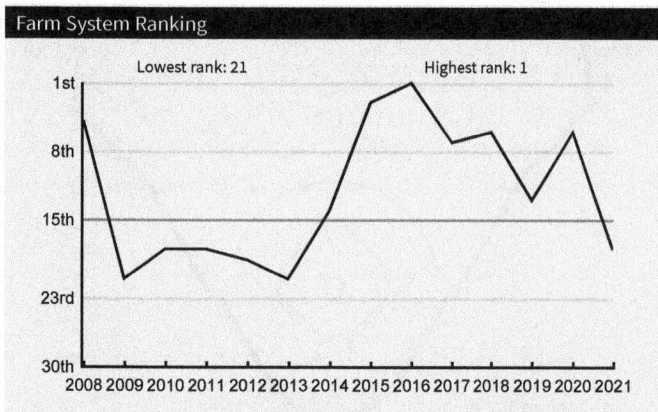

Farm System Ranking

Lowest rank: 21   Highest rank: 1

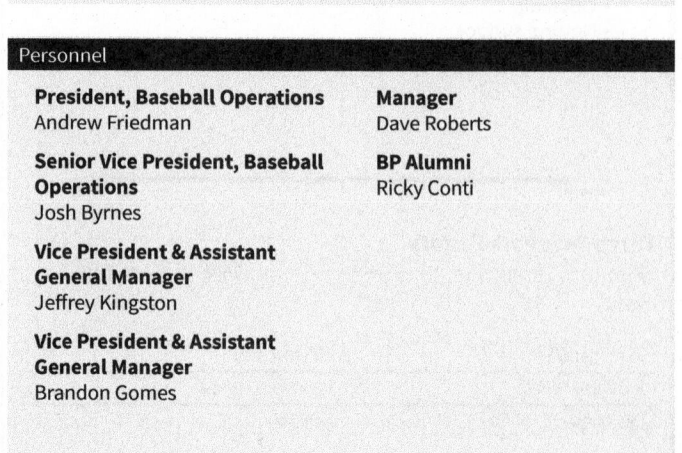

Personnel

President, Baseball Operations
Andrew Friedman

Manager
Dave Roberts

Senior Vice President, Baseball Operations
Josh Byrnes

BP Alumni
Ricky Conti

Vice President & Assistant General Manager
Jeffrey Kingston

Vice President & Assistant General Manager
Brandon Gomes

Just over a week later, the Dodgers won the World Series. They'd polished off the comeback against Atlanta, with Bellinger getting his moment in Game 7, thwacking the go-ahead homer to center-right and yanking his shoulder out of its socket in the celebration that followed. They took the Series in 6; their pitching matched Tampa Bay's, and their lineup outslugged the Rays'.

A few minutes after the final out, L.A. manager Dave Roberts stepped to a microphone on a podium, plump with pride. "I told you," he said to some semblance of a Dodger crowd, spread at some semblance of proper distance across the ballpark in Arlington, Texas, "this was our year!"

It was the kind of thing managers say at times like those, but it was a little odd to hear nonetheless, and not only because the notion of 2020 being *anybody's* year, even a champion's, didn't quite resolve. Teams with the Dodgers' trajectory—that mercifully break through after a long period of falling short—tend to possess some identifiable difference, a knack or vibe or approach (real or projected) that distinguishes them from their past disappointed selves. But L.A.'s title run was noteworthy for how closely it hewed to the patterns of their failures. They had the same sort of stacked roster and the same measured-to-the-atom approach. They faced the same October turbulence. To frame the championship as an exception was to do the team that won it a disservice. Anyone can catch a run of luck. It's harder for a group to develop itself as best it can, to devise and believe in its principles, and then to wait.

⚾   ⚾   ⚾

Betts, of course, was new, and crucial. He was the Dodgers' best player during the abbreviated regular season and spent the postseason treating games as playgrounds of pure possibility. He draped himself over outfield walls to bring back home runs; he dashed to whichever base he liked. His hitting numbers tumbled at times—these things happen, in October, in Dodger blue—but it hardly mattered. He played in montage, hands-first-sliding into second and lining a homer and smiling at the pitcher whom he'd just saved two earned runs, one sequence bleeding into the next.

The ethos that brought Betts to L.A., though, wasn't new at all. Where other teams hold to certain patterns of team-building, the Dodgers under Andrew Friedman improve any way they can. Some years, this means spotting a figure like Muncy, with a deep-packed seed of a skill. Some years, it's as simple as seeing that a team is willing to part with one of the best players in baseball, and nabbing him up.

The rest of the cast was familiar. Seager, the stolid and sweet-swinging shortstop. Bellinger, a colt of a player, all limbs and joints and jangling speed. Walker Buehler, matching fastballs with anyone, and the scuffed-up sometimes-virtuosos of the L.A. bullpen. And Clayton Kershaw, the fated embodiment of the whole damn stunning mess.

The temptation is to point to what broke differently. Seager put together the best stretch of his career: 22 hits, 11 walks, and eight homers over 18 playoff games. Kershaw reached a truce with the specters that had haunted his postseason career, winning four of his five starts and parceling 37 strikeouts across 30 clenched-teeth innings. Roberts broke his habit of using his bullpen to maximize narrative tension; it was Julio Urías, not Kershaw or Kenley Jansen, who ran the season's last pitch over the inside corner.

Still, a lot stayed the same. Against Atlanta, the reason L.A. trailed in the first place was a familiar mélange of puzzling baseball: loud bats quieting, relievers flinching at big moments, Kershaw offering up a clunker, apparently requisite even in this redemptive year. That they fought back and won seemed more like time-released logic—this is how this team is supposed to play, right?—than freshly discovered verve.

In the World Series, the Dodgers *really* biffed it, turning the last moments of Game 4 into a case against their own title bona fides. Had they lost the series, the sequence—Jansen throwing a toothless cutter, Chris Taylor juggling a routine single in center, Smith bobbling an on-target throw to the plate and gifting the Rays a win—would have become shorthand for the era.

The crucial difference, then, didn't have to do with basic makeup or ineffable championship quality but with something slipperier. You could call this luck, or timing, or just time. Big plays fell into the innings that needed them, from the same players who'd failed in similar spots. It isn't that the Dodgers couldn't win before and now could. It's that they didn't win before, and now did.

⚾   ⚾   ⚾

It's impossible, or at least pointless, to talk or think or write about the Dodgers without talking or thinking or writing about Kershaw. The question of what a World Series means to L.A. is really, What does it mean to him? Many baseball fans felt no small amount of vicarious joy when the last strike was called and he charged the infield, a look of near-hyperventilation on his face. Some surely harbored a little frustration, that Kershaw's very good playoff run hadn't notched up to a level of blazing all-timer excellence. (Wouldn't have been lovely to see him as Series MVP?) But mostly there was relief—visible from Kershaw and his teammates, palpable from more or less everyone else in the baseball universe. "You want to talk about a narrative?" Roberts said in that echoey postgame speech. "How about being a champion? He's a champion forever."

But in his four postseason wins, set opposite a blowout defeat in his lone appearance against Atlanta, Kershaw didn't so much vindicate as clarify himself. His pre-2020 playoff struggles—the shorthand of the doubled ERA never having quite captured the assortment of big asks, bad breaks, and outlier nights that produced it—have widely been taken as

a kind of enduring exception, something that didn't square with the evidence of his regular-season excellence. It may be closer to the truth to consider the two records as opposite sides of a coin. Kershaw has been dominant in outcome but never in approach; he's never made the sport look easy. To watch him work, especially with his present-day low-90s fastball and increasingly balky curve, is to be awed by commitment, not virtuosity. He's a distinctly effortful superstar, and the playoffs have had a way of illustrating just how close to failure his usual success lies.

This October presented its usual challenges. Kershaw breezed past the barely qualified Brewers in the Wild Card round—eight innings, 13 strikeouts, a general air of preamble—but the rest was a struggle. In the divisional round, Manny Machado and Eric Hosmer belted back-to-back sixth-inning homers; he left shortly thereafter, clinging to a one-run lead. In the Series opener, which Kershaw started due not to ace's honors but to the quirks of the rotation schedule, he struggled through a 21-pitch first inning before finding his footing. In Game 5 against the Rays, with Kershaw having given up a pair of runs and encountered a few more nervy moments, Roberts pulled him after five and two-thirds. The slider—the pitch that has become, over the back half of his career, his most trustworthy—had seen him through. It came out of his hand as if barbed, biting heavily into the undersides of bats which then chunked ground balls to the L.A. infielders. It was effective but inelegant; each time, it seemed as if it cost something to throw it.

Looking at Kershaw on the mound, you might not have been able to spot much difference between 2020 and the postseasons prior. He had the same sweatlogged hair and wrenching delivery, wore the same expression: one of intense conviction when he let go of a pitch and deep disappointment when it ended up somewhere he didn't intend. He nodded and yelled and set his jaw in familiar patterns. But after Roberts pulled him for what would end up being the last time of his first championship season, cameras found Kershaw and his manager in the dugout, sharing a smile and a hug.

Before, Kershaw's most famous postseason exits followed the template of disappointment building to defeat. Now: tenuous hope, then victory. Those inclined to look for reasons for the shift could find them. Regular-season slippage, from otherworldly to merely excellent, might have unburdened Kershaw of some measure of imposed expectation. Possibly it persuaded Roberts to give him earlier and more compassionate hooks.

But that he remained foundationally the same player, while achieving a different result, reinforced what may be the central lesson of baseball—one more substantial, anyway, than anything to do with managerial decision-making. Do what you can, again and again, let fate fiddle at the margins, and you'll have something new. Two days after Kershaw's last start, the Dodgers had their title, one that seemed to have been owed to them, individually and as a collective, for a good while. Did they deserve it more, in October 2020, than they had in all those well-credentialed and ultimately disheartening Octobers prior? Only in that they'd waited longer to receive it, and remained themselves in the meantime. ▪

—Robert O'Connell's work has appeared in The Atlantic, the New York Times, the Guardian, Deadspin, Sports Illustrated, and elsewhere.

HITTERS

Jacob Amaya SS
Born: 09/03/98   Age: 22   Bats: R   Throws: R   Height: 6'0"   Weight: 180   Origin: Round 11, 2017 Draft (#340 overall)

YEAR	TEAM	LVL	AGE	PA	R	2B	3B	HR	RBI	BB	K	SB	CS	Whiff%	AVG/OBP/SLG	DRC+	BABIP	BRR	FRAA	WARP
2018	OGD	ROK	19	155	41	9	3	3	24	27	29	11	4		.346/.465/.535	181	.432	3.2	SS(25): -0.7, 2B(8): -2.0	1.5
2018	GL	LO-A	19	119	13	1	0	1	5	20	18	3	3		.265/.390/.306	130	.316	-1.8	SS(21): 2.2, 2B(5): -0.2	0.7
2019	GL	LO-A	20	470	68	25	4	6	58	74	83	4	4		.262/.381/.394	145	.314	-0.5	SS(51): -3.8, 2B(49): 1.9, 3B(4): 0.1	3.6
2019	RC	HI-A	20	89	14	3	2	1	13	7	15	1	3		.250/.307/.375	98	.292	0.3	SS(14): -2.1, 2B(4): 1.0, 3B(1): -0.0	0.2
2021 FS	LAD	MLB	22	600	55	27	3	9	55	57	161	3	2		.237/.314/.351	86	.321	-1.8	SS -1, 2B 3	1.0

Comparables: Eugenio Suárez, Pete Kozma, Sean Rodríguez

He's underpowered, but infielder Jacob Amaya has good contact skills, doesn't expand his strike zone, and keeps his motor revved at higher RPM than a Trevor Bauer fastball.

Austin Barnes C
Born: 12/28/89   Age: 31   Bats: R   Throws: R   Height: 5'10"   Weight: 187   Origin: Round 9, 2011 Draft (#283 overall)

YEAR	TEAM	LVL	AGE	PA	R	2B	3B	HR	RBI	BB	K	SB	CS	Whiff%	AVG/OBP/SLG	DRC+	BABIP	BRR	FRAA	WARP
2018	LAD	MLB	28	238	32	5	0	4	14	31	67	4	3	19.3%	.205/.329/.290	74	.287	1.1	C(61): 10.0, 2B(19): 0.2	1.5
2019	OKC	AAA	29	104	19	6	0	6	17	14	20	1	1		.264/.375/.540	104	.274	-0.1	C(13): 2.1, 2B(6): -0.3	0.6
2019	LAD	MLB	29	242	28	12	1	5	25	23	56	3	0	22.5%	.203/.293/.340	78	.248	2.4	C(64): 8.4, 2B(1): 0.1	1.6
2020	LAD	MLB	31	104	14	3	0	1	9	13	24	3	0	25.0%	.244/.353/.314	92	.323	0.0	C(28): 0.1	0.6
2021 FS	LAD	MLB	31	600	67	20	2	14	57	71	143	7	2	22.4%	.232/.337/.365	99	.292	0.2	C 15, 2B 0	4.0
2021 DC	LAD	MLB	31	207	23	7	0	5	19	24	49	2	1	22.4%	.232/.337/.365	99	.292	0.1	C 7	1.6

Comparables: Doug Mirabelli, Hal King, Jerry Goff

It takes an ugly mistake by an opposing pitcher for Barnes to generate much pop. He tried getting more aggressive early in counts in 2020, but it didn't pay dividends. Happily, though, he need not hit much in order to be a valuable part of a club because he's one of the best pitch-framers in baseball. At the plate, he makes up for lousy bat speed by forcing pitchers to throw him strikes (and thereby drawing a fair number of walks). Behind it, he not only keeps the edges of the strike zone open, but makes up for a below-average arm with quick feet and hands.

YEAR	TEAM	P. COUNT	FRM RUNS	BLK RUNS	THRW RUNS	TOT RUNS
2018	LAD	7110	8.3	1.0	-0.1	9.2
2019	LAD	8092	8.5	0.7	-0.2	8.9
2020	LAD	3848	3.1	0.0	0.2	3.2
2021	LAD	7215	8.1	-0.4	-0.3	7.4

Matt Beaty 1B
Born: 04/28/93   Age: 28   Bats: L   Throws: R   Height: 6'0"   Weight: 215   Origin: Round 12, 2015 Draft (#372 overall)

YEAR	TEAM	LVL	AGE	PA	R	2B	3B	HR	RBI	BB	K	SB	CS	Whiff%	AVG/OBP/SLG	DRC+	BABIP	BRR	FRAA	WARP
2018	OKC	AAA	25	120	13	10	0	1	12	12	17	0	0		.277/.378/.406	109	.321	-0.3	1B(16): -0.3, LF(5): 1.0, 2B(4): -0.1	0.3
2019	OKC	AAA	26	135	17	7	1	3	18	10	12	0	0		.306/.378/.455	92	.321	-0.4	1B(11): -0.9, 3B(11): 1.4, LF(8): 1.0	0.3
2019	LAD	MLB	26	268	36	19	1	9	46	17	33	5	0	18.0%	.265/.317/.458	93	.275	1.1	1B(35): -0.7, LF(34): 0.6, 3B(9): -0.5	0.5
2020	LAD	MLB	27	54	8	1	0	2	5	2	14	0	0	25.8%	.220/.278/.360	81	.265	-0.3	1B(13): -0.8, LF(2): 0.2	-0.1
2021 FS	LAD	MLB	28	600	65	31	1	19	71	39	115	1	0	19.7%	.258/.317/.426	99	.296	-1.2	3B -1, LF 3	1.2
2021 DC	LAD	MLB	28	380	41	19	0	12	45	24	73	1	0	19.7%	.258/.317/.426	99	.296	-0.8	3B -1, LF 2	0.8

Comparables: John Mabry, Greg Colbrunn, Robb Quinlan

There's a bunch of theoretical power upside here because Beaty has demonstrated the ability to generate high-end exit velocity, and he's just 28 in April. The gap between theory and practice can be considerable, though, and in Beaty's case, there are at least two reasons to be skeptical. One is the classic modern quandary: he mostly hits ground balls and low line drives. Launch angles are easy enough to fix, though, especially if you play for the Dodgers. That introduces the other problem: Beaty has a massive hole in his swing. Get it anywhere on the inner third or off the plate inside and he's tied in knots.

Cody Bellinger CF
Born: 07/13/95   Age: 25   Bats: L   Throws: L   Height: 6'4"   Weight: 203   Origin: Round 4, 2013 Draft (#124 overall)

YEAR	TEAM	LVL	AGE	PA	R	2B	3B	HR	RBI	BB	K	SB	CS	Whiff%	AVG/OBP/SLG	DRC+	BABIP	BRR	FRAA	WARP
2018	LAD	MLB	22	632	84	28	7	25	76	69	151	14	1	29.3%	.260/.343/.470	112	.312	3.3	1B(110): -0.9, CF(78): 2.0, RF(5): -0.2	2.8
2019	LAD	MLB	23	661	121	34	3	47	115	95	108	15	5	23.6%	.305/.406/.629	157	.302	0.4	RF(115): 13.3, 1B(36): 1.9, CF(25): 0.1	8.0
2020	LAD	MLB	25	243	33	10	0	12	30	30	42	6	1	23.3%	.239/.333/.455	117	.245	0.1	CF(39): 4.8, 1B(19): 0.2, RF(1): -0.0	1.5
2021 FS	LAD	MLB	25	600	83	26	2	36	94	74	130	9	2	24.9%	.263/.360/.531	134	.285	2.3	CF 4, 1B 0	4.6
2021 DC	LAD	MLB	25	587	81	25	2	35	92	73	127	9	2	24.9%	.263/.360/.531	134	.285	2.3	CF 4, 1B 0	4.8

Comparables: Bob Robertson, Mark McGwire, Fred McGriff

If Tolstoy were alive in 2020, he'd say that good seasons are all alike, but every down year is down in its own way. In 2019, Bellinger and Christian Yelich raced neck-and-neck for the NL MVP award. They were shockingly alike: lanky, powerful, gawkily handsome, graceful, faster than their frames suggest, with swings that appear long but that never seem to miss their targets. Then, in 2020, they both had ugly, frustrating seasons. Their derailments could hardly have been more unequal though. Bellinger mostly hit into bad luck. He had some small swing issues, mishit the ball, and expanded his zone slightly more often, but he continued to draw plenty of walks, rarely struck out, and looked like himself whenever he did get off his 'A' swing. Yelich's troubles are serious. Bellinger's feel like a blip and PECOTA is inclined to agree.

Mookie Betts RF Born: 10/07/92 Age: 28 Bats: R Throws: R Height: 5'9" Weight: 180 Origin: Round 5, 2011 Draft (#172 overall)

YEAR	TEAM	LVL	AGE	PA	R	2B	3B	HR	RBI	BB	K	SB	CS	Whiff%	AVG/OBP/SLG	DRC+	BABIP	BRR	FRAA	WARP
2018	BOS	MLB	25	614	129	47	5	32	80	81	91	30	6	15.6%	.346/.438/.640	178	.368	3.8	RF(120): 10.7, CF(14): 0.4, 2B(1): 0.0	8.9
2019	BOS	MLB	26	706	135	40	5	29	80	97	101	16	3	14.6%	.295/.391/.524	137	.309	5.7	RF(132): 11.9, CF(17): 1.6	6.9
2020	LAD	MLB	28	246	47	9	1	16	39	24	38	10	2	13.8%	.292/.366/.562	150	.289	5.2	RF(52): 4.7, 2B(1): -0.1, CF(1): -0.1	2.9
2021 FS	LAD	MLB	28	600	92	29	2	29	74	63	94	19	4	14.7%	.288/.368/.522	141	.301	7.4	RF 13, 2B 0	6.8
2021 DC	LAD	MLB	28	622	95	30	2	31	77	66	97	20	4	14.7%	.288/.368/.522	141	.301	7.6	RF 14	7.0

Comparables: Jack Clark, Rocky Colavito, Ron Jones

Betts continues to carve his way into the record books and the ongoing dialogue that is baseball history. When the Red Sox traded him to the Dodgers in February, we had occasion to wonder whether Betts would match the almost vengeful greatness of Frank Robinson after the Reds traded him to Baltimore in 1965. (He basically did.) When Al Kaline died in April, we had a chance to ponder the comparisons thoughtful observers draw between the crisp, intelligent, all-around, all-out game Betts plays, and the way Kaline played at his best. When Betts led the Dodgers' wildcat strike of a game in late August in solidarity with ongoing protests against systemic racism, we were afforded an opportunity to slot him in alongside the other great Black ballplayers who demanded that an unjust world become a bit less so. And throughout this bizarre season, we watched Betts sustain his greatness in a way not even the other players who had been in the conversation with him as the best in the game could match. By all indications, he will remain an extraordinarily well-rounded superstar (on and off the diamond) for another decade.

★ ★ ★ *2021 Top 101 Prospect* **#91** ★ ★ ★

Michael Busch 2B Born: 11/09/97 Age: 23 Bats: L Throws: R Height: 6'0" Weight: 207 Origin: Round 1, 2019 Draft (#31 overall)

YEAR	TEAM	LVL	AGE	PA	R	2B	3B	HR	RBI	BB	K	SB	CS	Whiff%	AVG/OBP/SLG	DRC+	BABIP	BRR	FRAA	WARP
2019	DOD1	ROK	21	16	1	0	0	0	0	1	2	0	0		.077/.250/.077	70	.091	-0.1	2B(4): -0.2	0.0
2019	GL	LO-A	21	19	4	0	0	0	2	6	3	0	0		.182/.474/.182	132	.222	0.6	2B(4): 0.2	0.2
2021 FS	LAD	MLB	23	600	53	26	2	12	56	46	173	3	1		.211/.284/.335	74	.286	0.5	2B 1	0.4

You don't have to squint that hard to see a Max Muncy future for Busch. In fact, that might undersell him if he continues on this trajectory. A first-round pick in 2019, Busch has hit (and hit good pitching) at absolutely every level at which he's been evaluated. His swing has easy lift and plenty of explosion. He spent the downtime (due to COVID-19) focusing on his quickness and athleticism, which figure to increase his chances of sticking at second base. Slide a slugging, disciplined college first baseman with a compact swing just that little bit up the defensive spectrum, and he becomes a stud prospect.

Diego Cartaya C Born: 09/07/01 Age: 19 Bats: R Throws: R Height: 6'2" Weight: 199 Origin: International Free Agent, 2018

YEAR	TEAM	LVL	AGE	PA	R	2B	3B	HR	RBI	BB	K	SB	CS	Whiff%	AVG/OBP/SLG	DRC+	BABIP	BRR	FRAA	WARP
2019	DSL BAU	ROK	17	57	11	2	2	1	9	5	11	0	0		.240/.316/.420		.282			
2019	DOD2	ROK	17	150	25	10	0	3	13	11	31	1	0		.296/.353/.437	126	.359	1.9	C(28): -0.2	1.1
2021 FS	LAD	MLB	19	600	45	27	2	7	50	28	202	1	0		.214/.257/.312	55	.319	0.2	C 0	-1.0

Demonstrating considerable trust in his touted makeup and dedication to catching, the Dodgers brought Cartaya to their alternate site to help handle a valuable, veteran pitching corps. It was the natural choice, not only because the team invested heavily in him as a top-billed Venezuelan signee in 2018, but because he's physically and mentally beyond his years. With a tall and powerful frame as well as a surprisingly controlled swing, Cartaya looks likely to knock on the door of the majors at a younger age than most catchers do.

Enrique Hernández 2B Born: 08/24/91 Age: 29 Bats: R Throws: R Height: 5'11" Weight: 190 Origin: Round 6, 2009 Draft (#191 overall)

YEAR	TEAM	LVL	AGE	PA	R	2B	3B	HR	RBI	BB	K	SB	CS	Whiff%	AVG/OBP/SLG	DRC+	BABIP	BRR	FRAA	WARP
2018	LAD	MLB	26	462	67	17	3	21	52	50	78	2	0	21.4%	.256/.336/.470	112	.266	1.9	CF(63): -0.8, 2B(41): -0.3, SS(22): -1.3	2.2
2019	LAD	MLB	27	460	57	19	1	17	64	36	97	4	0	26.8%	.237/.304/.411	91	.266	1.3	2B(85): 1.1, CF(20): -1.4, RF(17): 0.3	1.1
2020	LAD	MLB	29	148	20	8	1	5	20	6	31	0	1	24.5%	.230/.270/.410	93	.260	0.2	2B(30): 3.9, RF(9): -0.6, LF(5): 0.7	0.7
2021 FS	LAD	MLB	29	600	67	26	2	23	72	53	139	3	1	24.9%	.229/.302/.416	94	.265	0.2	2B 0, CF -3	1.2

Comparables: Geronimo Pena, Jason Kipnis, Jeff Kent

If you catch yourself saying that many players are worth substantially more or less to their team than WARP shows, you're probably letting subjectivity govern your evaluations too much. If you can't identify the occasional case in which that's true, though, you err in the other direction, and you risk misunderstanding baseball as a mere game of digital tallies. Hernández excels in every area which we still can't objectively measure well. He not only plays all over the diamond, but is above-average in just about every spot. He brings levity to the clubhouse, moves freely between what might otherwise become cliques, and still puts in the work required to be a consistent player on the field. He also comes up big in big moments, with a career .827 OPS when the game is within a run of being tied. In Game 7 of the NLCS, the Dodgers were within a run when Hernández pinch-hit to lead off the bottom of the sixth inning. When he was done, they were tied.

Kody Hoese 3B   Born: 07/13/97   Age: 23   Bats: R   Throws: R   Height: 6'4"   Weight: 200   Origin: Round 1, 2019 Draft (#25 overall)

YEAR	TEAM	LVL	AGE	PA	R	2B	3B	HR	RBI	BB	K	SB	CS	Whiff%	AVG/OBP/SLG	DRC+	BABIP	BRR	FRAA	WARP
2019	DOD2	ROK	21	68	14	5	1	3	13	10	11	1	0		.357/.456/.643	185	.395	1.9	3B(6): -0.5	0.8
2019	GL	LO-A	21	103	15	3	1	2	16	8	14	0	0		.264/.330/.385	102	.286	-0.2	3B(12): 0.7	0.3
2021 FS	LAD	MLB	23	600	53	26	3	9	56	40	156	1	0		.240/.298/.353	80	.317	1.0	3B 0	-0.2

When a pandemic hits and opportunities start drying up, it pays to be someone in whom your organization has already made a heavy investment. A 2019 first-round pick, Hoese was a priority assignee to the alternate site, and when that closed down, he moved right on to the fall instructional league in Arizona. No Dodgers swing path magic is needed here; Hoese already has leverage and lift, to go along with plenty of strength and fluid athleticism in his swing. They're always looking for a developmental twist to wring a little extra value out of a player though, which is how Hoese came to split his time between third base and shortstop. (Put nothing past this organization; they are the original and quintessential coconut snatchers.) He impressed on every level and against all the competition he could find in 2020.

Gavin Lux 2B   Born: 11/23/97   Age: 23   Bats: L   Throws: R   Height: 6'2"   Weight: 190   Origin: Round 1, 2016 Draft (#20 overall)

YEAR	TEAM	LVL	AGE	PA	R	2B	3B	HR	RBI	BB	K	SB	CS	Whiff%	AVG/OBP/SLG	DRC+	BABIP	BRR	FRAA	WARP
2018	RC	HI-A	20	404	64	23	7	11	48	43	68	11	7		.324/.396/.520	145	.374	-1.8	SS(66): -0.6, 2B(17): 0.8	2.2
2018	TUL	AA	20	120	21	4	1	4	9	14	20	2	2		.324/.408/.495	149	.370	1.3	SS(26): -0.6	0.9
2019	TUL	AA	21	291	45	7	4	13	37	28	60	7	3		.313/.375/.521	166	.358	-2.6	SS(55): -3.0, 2B(7): 0.5	2.4
2019	OKC	AAA	21	232	54	18	4	13	39	33	42	3	3		.392/.478/.719	176	.451	-1.2	SS(36): -2.8, 2B(12): -0.3	2.7
2019	LAD	MLB	21	82	12	4	1	2	9	7	24	2	0	29.9%	.240/.305/.400	74	.327	0.1	2B(22): -0.9	-0.1
2020	LAD	MLB	23	69	8	2	0	3	8	6	19	1	0	26.1%	.175/.246/.349	87	.195	0.2	2B(18): 2.2	0.3
2021 FS	LAD	MLB	23	600	71	24	4	23	72	54	163	7	3	27.8%	.252/.323/.443	105	.320	1.6	2B 0, SS 0	2.6
2021 DC	LAD	MLB	23	553	65	22	4	21	67	50	151	6	2	27.8%	.252/.323/.443	105	.320	1.5	2B 0	2.5

Comparables: Yu Chang, Daniel Robertson, Franchy Cordero

Don't read too much into Lux's struggles in extremely limited action across two fragmented seasons of big-league action. He has to make some adjustments—a second swing for when he can anticipate being attacked at the top of the zone, more balance in his swing and a cleaner transfer of energy from back to front side, things players only add to their games once the competition forces them to do so—but the pieces of a superstar all remain. He's excellent at second base and will be more than adequate if he's needed at shortstop again. He runs well. Once he cleans up his minor approach issues, he'll have consistently average-plus power. His circumstances have made his development seem rockier than it really is.

Zach McKinstry 2B   Born: 04/29/95   Age: 26   Bats: L   Throws: R   Height: 6'0"   Weight: 180   Origin: Round 33, 2016 Draft (#1001 overall)

YEAR	TEAM	LVL	AGE	PA	R	2B	3B	HR	RBI	BB	K	SB	CS	Whiff%	AVG/OBP/SLG	DRC+	BABIP	BRR	FRAA	WARP
2018	GL	LO-A	23	72	12	2	2	3	8	16	16	2	1		.377/.542/.660	191	.500	-0.7	SS(11): -1.2, 2B(5): 0.1, LF(1): -0.1	0.7
2018	RC	HI-A	23	114	20	7	1	2	8	17	22	0	0		.308/.447/.473	124	.388	0.3	2B(17): -0.5, 3B(5): 1.7, SS(5): -0.1	0.5
2018	TUL	AA	23	87	7	2	1	2	8	4	21	0	0		.193/.230/.313	54	.233	-0.2	3B(14): 0.8, 2B(9): 0.5, SS(2): -0.2	-0.2
2019	TUL	AA	24	384	53	16	4	12	52	37	74	8	8		.279/.352/.455	146	.323	-0.5	2B(49): -2.7, SS(29): 1.8, 3B(10): -0.1	2.7
2019	OKC	AAA	24	95	17	8	2	7	26	6	18	0	1		.382/.421/.753	152	.422	-0.4	SS(17): -0.1, 2B(3): 0.4, 3B(2): 0.2	1.0
2020	LAD	MLB	25	7	1	1	0	0	0	0	3	0	0	37.5%	.286/.286/.429	69	.500		2B(1): -0.0, RF(1): 0.1	0.0
2021 FS	LAD	MLB	26	600	66	23	3	20	67	55	173	3	1	37.5%	.242/.321/.412	98	.319	1.0	2B 1, SS 3	2.3
2021 DC	LAD	MLB	26	276	30	10	1	9	30	25	79	1	0	37.5%	.242/.321/.412	98	.319	0.5	2B 1, SS 2	1.1

Comparables: Rougned Odor, German Duran, Cesar Hernandez

If the season had lasted 162 games, with the vagaries and attrition inherent to a schedule of that length, McKinstry would have gotten a more meaningful look in 2020. He's precisely the kind of player whom the Dodgers are adept at developing: a versatile, sure-handed infielder with a sneakily sound left-handed bat. He doesn't have Max Muncy-like power, nor the prospect sheen of a Gavin Lux or Corey Seager, but McKinstry has already added both bat speed and loft since joining the Los Angeles system, and he seems primed to take on a bigger role as a utility man in 2021.

Max Muncy 1B   Born: 08/25/90   Age: 30   Bats: L   Throws: R   Height: 6'0"   Weight: 215   Origin: Round 5, 2012 Draft (#169 overall)

YEAR	TEAM	LVL	AGE	PA	R	2B	3B	HR	RBI	BB	K	SB	CS	Whiff%	AVG/OBP/SLG	DRC+	BABIP	BRR	FRAA	WARP
2018	OKC	AAA	27	38	7	2	0	2	4	6	5	0	0		.312/.421/.562	131	.320	0.7	1B(7): 0.1, 3B(3): 0.2	0.3
2018	LAD	MLB	27	481	75	17	2	35	79	79	131	3	0	29.0%	.263/.391/.582	145	.299	2.3	1B(84): -0.5, 3B(38): 0.3, 2B(13): -0.9	3.9
2019	LAD	MLB	28	589	101	22	1	35	98	90	149	4	1	28.9%	.251/.374/.515	131	.283	4.1	2B(70): -0.1, 1B(65): 4.2, 3B(35): 3.2	5.1
2020	LAD	MLB	30	248	36	4	0	12	27	39	60	1	0	26.8%	.192/.331/.389	108	.203	0.6	1B(35): -2.6, 3B(16): 1.0, 2B(12): -0.1	0.6
2021 FS	LAD	MLB	30	600	82	23	1	32	81	88	159	2	0	28.3%	.244/.366/.486	127	.293	-0.9	3B 6, 1B 1	4.1
2021 DC	LAD	MLB	30	553	75	21	1	29	74	81	147	2	0	28.3%	.244/.366/.486	127	.293	-0.8	3B 6, 1B 1	3.5

Comparables: Ji-Man Choi, Steve Bilko, Tony Solaita

No one is slump-proof in a 60-game sample. Muncy's 2020 line proves that. Looking past the raw numbers, though, he had another very solid season, generating tons of hard contact, lifting the ball to the pull field, and torturing pitchers with his patience. Had it not been for a pre-season broken finger that remained sore, his results might have better matched those he posted over the two prior campaigns. In the playoffs, he walked 20 times and fanned only 21. Mostly a liability in the field, he nonetheless helped save the season by alerting Clayton Kershaw to an attempted steal of home in the World Series. He's a relentlessly dangerous hitter and a fine baserunner. That makes him a championship-caliber first baseman.

Joc Pederson LF Born: 04/21/92 Age: 29 Bats: L Throws: L Height: 6'1" Weight: 220 Origin: Round 11, 2010 Draft (#352 overall)

YEAR	TEAM	LVL	AGE	PA	R	2B	3B	HR	RBI	BB	K	SB	CS	Whiff%	AVG/OBP/SLG	DRC+	BABIP	BRR	FRAA	WARP
2018	LAD	MLB	26	443	65	27	3	25	56	40	85	1	5	25.4%	.248/.321/.522	117	.253	0.9	LF(116): -1.3, CF(32): -2.4, RF(2): -0.1	1.9
2019	LAD	MLB	27	514	83	16	3	36	74	50	111	1	1	24.3%	.249/.339/.538	122	.249	2.6	LF(84): 0.5, RF(39): -0.0, 1B(20): -1.0	3.0
2020	LAD	MLB	28	138	21	4	0	7	16	11	34	1	0	31.0%	.190/.285/.397	91	.200	-0.6	LF(23): -0.5, RF(8): 0.9	0.2
2021 FS	LAD	MLB	29	600	80	26	1	35	83	72	156	5	2	26.0%	.240/.348/.500	123	.275	-2.0	LF -2, CF -8	2.2

Comparables: Rick Ankiel, Don Lock, Preston Wilson

A hole opened up in Pederson's swing in 2020, across the top of the strike zone, and the shortened season prevented him from closing it. The swings and misses on elevated pitches reflected issues that also led to more pulled ground balls, allowing shifts to devour much of his usual production. In the postseason though, he got hot, reminding everyone how much upside there is in a patient lefty slugger with good power. He's strictly a corner outfielder at this point, and not a terrific one, but when he works the count and gets his pitch, he can drive it consistently enough to be a solid regular. His pop is ballpark-proof, too; he hits the kind of homers that no deep right field can turn into flyouts.

DJ Peters CF Born: 12/12/95 Age: 25 Bats: R Throws: R Height: 6'6" Weight: 225 Origin: Round 4, 2016 Draft (#131 overall)

YEAR	TEAM	LVL	AGE	PA	R	2B	3B	HR	RBI	BB	K	SB	CS	Whiff%	AVG/OBP/SLG	DRC+	BABIP	BRR	FRAA	WARP
2018	TUL	AA	22	559	79	23	3	29	60	45	192	1	2		.236/.320/.473	95	.316	-3.6	CF(96): -3.1, RF(29): 1.4, LF(4): 0.1	-0.4
2019	TUL	AA	23	288	31	10	1	11	42	27	93	1	0		.241/.329/.422	104	.331	-0.6	CF(48): -1.2, RF(20): 1.1	0.9
2019	OKC	AAA	23	255	40	10	1	12	39	33	74	1	1		.260/.388/.490	120	.339	0.0	CF(56): -0.9	1.4
2021 FS	LAD	MLB	25	600	62	24	2	17	58	48	229	1	0		.204/.286/.355	77	.317	0.3	CF -6, LF 0	-0.5
2021 DC	LAD	MLB	25	103	10	4	0	2	10	8	39	0	0		.204/.286/.355	77	.317	0.1	CF -1	-0.1

Comparables: Corey Brown, Matthew den Dekker, Wil Myers

He's a gym rat. He's a cage rat. He's coachable, he's personable, and he's downright Brobdingnagian. It's just not clear that Peters is going to make enough contact for all of that to matter.

AJ Pollock CF Born: 12/05/87 Age: 33 Bats: R Throws: R Height: 6'1" Weight: 210 Origin: Round 1, 2009 Draft (#17 overall)

YEAR	TEAM	LVL	AGE	PA	R	2B	3B	HR	RBI	BB	K	SB	CS	Whiff%	AVG/OBP/SLG	DRC+	BABIP	BRR	FRAA	WARP
2018	ARI	MLB	30	460	61	21	5	21	65	31	100	13	2	24.0%	.257/.316/.484	106	.284	1.1	CF(109): -7.6	1.3
2019	LAD	MLB	31	342	49	15	1	15	47	23	74	5	1	26.8%	.266/.327/.468	97	.300	-0.3	CF(62): -8.6, LF(18): -0.1	0.2
2020	LAD	MLB	33	210	30	9	0	16	34	12	45	2	2	24.5%	.276/.314/.566	121	.277	-0.4	LF(27): -3.1, CF(16): -1.4	0.3
2021 FS	LAD	MLB	33	600	75	26	2	31	87	44	129	16	5	25.3%	.258/.320/.488	116	.284	2.8	LF -2, CF -3	3.0
2021 DC	LAD	MLB	33	483	60	21	2	25	70	35	104	13	4	25.3%	.258/.320/.488	116	.284	2.3	LF -2, CF -2	2.1

Comparables: Ellis Burks, Carlos Beltrán, Torii Hunter

Without anything material actually changing, Pollock cracked homers at a pace that could have pushed him past 40 had the league played a full 162 games. He's typically an almost frustratingly consistent hitter (that is to say, immune to hot streaks if not injuries), has real power, is still plenty athletic enough to be a plus in left field and seems comfortable in slightly less than a full-time role in which he can stay fresh.

Zach Reks LF Born: 11/12/93 Age: 27 Bats: L Throws: R Height: 6'2" Weight: 190 Origin: Round 10, 2017 Draft (#310 overall)

YEAR	TEAM	LVL	AGE	PA	R	2B	3B	HR	RBI	BB	K	SB	CS	Whiff%	AVG/OBP/SLG	DRC+	BABIP	BRR	FRAA	WARP
2018	RC	HI-A	24	38	8	3	1	2	7	1	5	1	0		.405/.421/.703	177	.433	0.7	1B(4): -0.5, LF(1): -0.2	0.3
2018	TUL	AA	24	296	37	14	1	3	33	34	73	5	3		.288/.368/.385	107	.387	-2.4	LF(22): 0.0, RF(11): 0.3, 1B(6): -0.7	-0.2
2019	TUL	AA	25	133	29	2	1	9	22	15	27	1	1		.310/.394/.584	189	.329	1.3	LF(19): -0.8, 1B(6): -0.8	1.3
2019	OKC	AAA	25	385	57	19	1	19	71	48	104	2	0		.284/.382/.520	113	.359	0.9	LF(77): -3.8	1.3
2021 FS	LAD	MLB	27	600	68	27	1	18	66	55	178	1	0		.257/.333/.415	102	.352	-0.7	LF -3, 1B 0	1.3
2021 DC	LAD	MLB	27	69	7	3	0	2	7	6	20	0	0		.257/.333/.415	102	.352	-0.1	LF 0	0.1

Comparables: Jason Botts, John-Ford Griffin, Andrew Lambo

He's already 27 and just now clawed his way onto a 40-man roster, but Zach Reks is a lefty batter who can generate power and won't get himself out, so he's got a chance to hang around a bit.

Edwin Ríos 3B Born: 04/21/94 Age: 27 Bats: L Throws: R Height: 6'3" Weight: 220 Origin: Round 6, 2015 Draft (#192 overall)

YEAR	TEAM	LVL	AGE	PA	R	2B	3B	HR	RBI	BB	K	SB	CS	Whiff%	AVG/OBP/SLG	DRC+	BABIP	BRR	FRAA	WARP
2018	OKC	AAA	24	341	45	25	0	10	55	23	110	0	1		.304/.355/.482	116	.433	-2.4	3B(38): -4.2, 1B(28): -1.3, LF(17): -1.6	0.1
2019	OKC	AAA	25	444	72	23	2	31	91	37	153	2	2		.270/.340/.575	106	.349	-2.6	3B(67): 1.7, 1B(25): 0.6, LF(8): 1.9	1.8
2019	LAD	MLB	25	56	10	2	1	4	8	9	21	0	0	33.3%	.277/.393/.617	87	.409	-0.2	1B(12): -0.4, 3B(5): -0.5, LF(1): -0.0	-0.1
2020	LAD	MLB	26	83	13	6	0	8	17	4	18	0	0	36.1%	.250/.301/.645	124	.216	-0.3	3B(21): -1.4, 1B(6): -0.1	0.2
2021 FS	LAD	MLB	27	600	68	30	1	27	77	39	188	0	0	35.0%	.232/.293/.442	92	.300	-1.0	3B -6, 1B 1	-0.2
2021 DC	LAD	MLB	27	483	55	24	1	22	62	31	151	0	0	35.0%	.232/.293/.442	92	.300	-0.8	3B -5, 1B 0	-0.1

Comparables: Zach Green, Zach Lutz, Josh Fields

The flourish of Ríos' high finish after a long, tremendously powerful swing—the way he obviously relishes it, especially when he gets into one and knows it's gone—is a thing of left-handed beauty. The thing is, that's a bit of a left-handed compliment. That swing is never going to generate high contact rates. To sustain the slugging success he's had in the upper minors and limited big-league action, he's going to have to stay aggressive, which means he'll never walk much. He's fringy at third base and likely to be confined to first and/or DH soon. That makes him a risky proposition as a regular, but as a bench bat, he's dangerous in all the right ways.

★ ★ ★ *2021 Top 101 Prospect* **#74** ★ ★ ★

Keibert Ruiz C   Born: 07/20/98   Age: 22   Bats: S   Throws: R   Height: 6'0"   Weight: 225   Origin: International Free Agent, 2015

YEAR	TEAM	LVL	AGE	PA	R	2B	3B	HR	RBI	BB	K	SB	CS	Whiff%	AVG/OBP/SLG	DRC+	BABIP	BRR	FRAA	WARP
2018	TUL	AA	19	415	44	14	0	12	47	26	33	0	1		.268/.328/.401	92	.266	-3.8	C(86): 3.5	0.5
2019	TUL	AA	20	310	33	9	0	4	25	28	21	0	0		.254/.329/.330	104	.261	-3.5	C(61): 0.5	1.1
2019	OKC	AAA	20	40	6	0	0	2	9	2	1	0	0		.316/.350/.474	87	.286	0.9	C(9): -0.5	0.2
2020	LAD	MLB	22	8	1	0	0	1	1	0	3	0	0	21.4%	.250/.250/.625	91	.250		C(2): -0.0	0.0
2021 FS	*LAD*	*MLB*	*22*	*600*	*67*	*25*	*2*	*18*	*69*	*35*	*106*	*0*	*0*	*21.4%*	*.262/.311/.416*	*97*	*.293*	*-0.2*	*C -4*	*1.8*
2021 DC	*LAD*	*MLB*	*22*	*69*	*7*	*2*	*0*	*2*	*7*	*4*	*12*	*0*	*0*	*21.4%*	*.262/.311/.416*	*97*	*.293*	*0.0*	*C -1*	*0.2*

Comparables: Ryan Sweeney, Jake Bauers, Michael Brantley

YEAR	TEAM	P. COUNT	FRM RUNS	BLK RUNS	THRW RUNS	TOT RUNS
2018	TUL	12404	5.3	-0.6	-0.4	4.2
2019	TUL	8965	3.3	0.0	-2.2	1.2
2020	LAD	315	-0.1	0.0	0.0	-0.1
2021	*LAD*	*2405*	*-0.5*	*0.1*	*-0.1*	*-0.5*

Ruiz was sidelined by COVID-19 just before the resumption of spring training. His symptoms were (relatively) mild and he bounced back well, but the time in isolation as well as the lost weight and conditioning were unfriendly, even to a player whom some scouts had wished would slim down a bit. Once he reached the alternate site, Ruiz continued work he'd been doing before the interregnum, as he and three Dodgers coaches worked to unlock the power in his lower half. His setup in the box is unorthodox, but his swing has become steadily more smooth and modern over the last few years and the tumblers seemed to fall into place as 2020 progressed. He briefly reached the majors—homering in his first at-bat—and should be back sometime in 2021, as a sturdy, well-rounded catcher.

Corey Seager SS   Born: 04/27/94   Age: 27   Bats: L   Throws: R   Height: 6'4"   Weight: 215   Origin: Round 1, 2012 Draft (#18 overall)

YEAR	TEAM	LVL	AGE	PA	R	2B	3B	HR	RBI	BB	K	SB	CS	Whiff%	AVG/OBP/SLG	DRC+	BABIP	BRR	FRAA	WARP
2018	LAD	MLB	24	115	13	5	1	2	13	11	17	0	0	21.0%	.267/.348/.396	103	.301	0.8	SS(25): 0.3	0.7
2019	LAD	MLB	25	541	82	44	1	19	87	44	98	1	0	25.8%	.272/.335/.483	105	.303	0.7	SS(132): 1.2	3.1
2020	LAD	MLB	26	232	38	12	1	15	41	17	37	1	0	25.8%	.307/.358/.585	138	.309	0.2	SS(43): 4.8	2.1
2021 FS	*LAD*	*MLB*	*27*	*600*	*82*	*32*	*1*	*28*	*82*	*53*	*113*	*3*	*1*	*25.5%*	*.280/.351/.502*	*126*	*.311*	*-1.3*	*SS -1*	*3.7*
2021 DC	*LAD*	*MLB*	*27*	*587*	*80*	*31*	*1*	*27*	*81*	*51*	*111*	*3*	*1*	*25.5%*	*.280/.351/.502*	*126*	*.311*	*-1.2*	*SS -1*	*3.6*

Comparables: Troy Tulowitzki, Hanley Ramirez, Francisco Lindor

Any list of the most improved hitters of 2020 has to include Seager, and he wasn't bad even before 2020. Extremely aggressive within the zone, but with a swing that generates high contact rates and power to all fields, Seager was the only player in the majors to produce a hard-hit ball (>95 mph) at a launch angle between 0 and 35 degrees in 30 percent of his plate appearances. He's fully healthy for the first time in years, and the serious and studious approach he takes to his craft is beginning to shine through. All of that only became more obvious during the postseason, which he capped off with the World Series MVP award.

Will Smith C   Born: 03/28/95   Age: 26   Bats: R   Throws: R   Height: 5'10"   Weight: 195   Origin: Round 1, 2016 Draft (#32 overall)

YEAR	TEAM	LVL	AGE	PA	R	2B	3B	HR	RBI	BB	K	SB	CS	Whiff%	AVG/OBP/SLG	DRC+	BABIP	BRR	FRAA	WARP
2018	TUL	AA	23	307	48	14	0	19	53	36	75	4	0		.264/.358/.532	131	.295	-1.8	C(33): 7.4, 3B(33): -1.3	2.0
2018	OKC	AAA	23	98	9	4	0	1	6	7	37	1	0		.138/.206/.218	7	.216	1.4	C(16): 1.4, 3B(10): 0.3	-0.4
2019	OKC	AAA	24	270	48	11	2	20	54	40	49	1	0		.268/.381/.603	137	.253	0.9	C(52): -0.1, 3B(1): -0.1	2.5
2019	LAD	MLB	24	196	30	9	0	15	42	18	52	2	0	25.0%	.253/.337/.571	122	.264	-0.6	C(46): 4.5	1.9
2020	LAD	MLB	25	137	23	9	0	8	25	20	22	0	0	15.5%	.289/.401/.579	151	.294	-1.3	C(34): 0.3	1.0
2021 FS	*LAD*	*MLB*	*26*	*600*	*81*	*24*	*1*	*36*	*90*	*66*	*144*	*2*	*0*	*20.0%*	*.250/.348/.513*	*131*	*.277*	*0.1*	*C 3, 2B 0*	*5.0*
2021 DC	*LAD*	*MLB*	*26*	*518*	*70*	*21*	*1*	*31*	*78*	*57*	*125*	*2*	*0*	*20.0%*	*.250/.348/.513*	*131*	*.277*	*0.1*	*C 3*	*4.3*

Comparables: Geovany Soto, Lance Berkman, Tom Haller

YEAR	TEAM	P. COUNT	FRM RUNS	BLK RUNS	THRW RUNS	TOT RUNS
2018	TUL	4379	7.0	0.1	0.6	7.7
2019	LAD	6644	2.1	1.2	-0.1	3.2
2020	LAD	4351	-1.4	-0.6	0.0	-2.0
2021	*LAD*	*14430*	*1.6*	*-0.5*	*0.3*	*1.3*

Somehow, Smith keeps getting better. It's equal parts easy and impossible to explain: He's just an extremely athletic backstop who has always had solid contact skills and a sound approach, plus good makeup, and once the Dodgers folded him into their state-of-the-art player development machine, he launched—literally. Of the 350-odd hitters who had at least 50 batted balls last year, Smith had the seventh-highest average launch angle. Yet he didn't have the attendant problem with popping the ball up that plagues practically every such hitter. He also did so while making more contact because his plate discipline went from quite good to exceptional. The only bad news was behind the plate, where Smith no longer looks like the difference-maker he once projected to be. Still, there's a word for a fringe-average defensive catcher who carries Justin Turner's batted-ball profile, controls the zone like Carlos Santana, and runs like Bo Bichette: superstar.

Chris Taylor LF   Born: 08/29/90   Age: 30   Bats: R   Throws: R   Height: 6'1"   Weight: 196   Origin: Round 5, 2012 Draft (#161 overall)

YEAR	TEAM	LVL	AGE	PA	R	2B	3B	HR	RBI	BB	K	SB	CS	Whiff%	AVG/OBP/SLG	DRC+	BABIP	BRR	FRAA	WARP
2018	LAD	MLB	27	604	85	35	8	17	63	55	178	9	6	31.6%	.254/.331/.444	102	.345	0.9	SS(81): 3.7, CF(50): -4.5, LF(24): 1.5	2.7
2019	LAD	MLB	28	414	52	29	4	12	52	37	115	8	0	31.7%	.262/.333/.462	91	.344	3.0	LF(56): 0.8, SS(39): -4.6, 2B(20): -1.9	0.8
2020	LAD	MLB	30	214	30	10	2	8	32	26	55	3	2	32.9%	.270/.366/.476	107	.344	0.3	SS(20): -0.0, LF(19): 0.5, 2B(13): 1.2	1.0
2021 FS	LAD	MLB	30	600	66	25	4	19	70	61	168	11	4	32.1%	.244/.328/.419	105	.319	1.9	LF 6, CF -2	2.9
2021 DC	LAD	MLB	30	483	53	20	3	15	57	49	135	9	3	32.1%	.244/.328/.419	105	.319	1.5	LF 5, CF -1	2.3

Comparables: Brad Miller, Woodie Held, Jose Valentin

You won't hear most youth coaches recommend wrestling as a companion sport for an aspiring baseball player, save perhaps a catcher, but there's something to it. Wrestlers develop the special relationship with the ground that any elite athlete needs, but which can be especially relevant to baseball. They quickly develop a fine understanding of the application of leverage. Taylor, who comes from a wrestling family, is proof of these things. He's an expert in his own swing, having sought the help of the best swing technicians in the country and used their advice to find improbable power. Generating that pop required some movements that led to a lot of whiffs, so in 2020, he quieted a few things and made more consistent contact. Speaking of leverage, he remains an impressively sterling performer (in the field and in the batter's box) in big moments—both during the regular season and the postseason, even if that's not the first thing you recall about Taylor this year.

Justin Turner 3B   Born: 11/23/84   Age: 36   Bats: R   Throws: R   Height: 5'11"   Weight: 202   Origin: Round 7, 2006 Draft (#204 overall)

YEAR	TEAM	LVL	AGE	PA	R	2B	3B	HR	RBI	BB	K	SB	CS	Whiff%	AVG/OBP/SLG	DRC+	BABIP	BRR	FRAA	WARP
2018	LAD	MLB	33	426	62	31	1	14	52	47	54	2	1	13.2%	.312/.406/.518	146	.334	0.3	3B(96): 11.1	5.1
2019	LAD	MLB	34	549	80	24	0	27	67	51	88	2	0	17.1%	.290/.372/.509	133	.304	-1.3	3B(124): 2.2, 2B(1): -0.0	4.5
2020	LAD	MLB	36	175	26	9	1	4	23	18	26	1	0	20.5%	.307/.400/.460	133	.347	-1.4	3B(32): 2.6	1.1
2021 FS	LAD	MLB	36	600	79	27	1	23	80	56	106	4	1	17.1%	.280/.370/.472	131	.312	-0.9	3B 6, 2B 0	4.2

Comparables: Mike Lowell, Douglas DeCinces, Aramis Ramirez

Winter is coming for one of the great early adopters of the fly-ball revolution. He's still exceptionally disciplined at the plate, but more of Turner's swings are coming up empty when he does expand the zone (as is inevitable). He's still a solid third baseman, but the stocky athleticism that once made him a great defender is fading. A hamstring strain shortened his short season. Yet through a thousand changes to his stance, setup and body, Turner has remained impressively constant in terms of profile and production. He'll keep a high floor, even as his decline continues.

★ ★ ★ *2021 Top 101 Prospect* **#77** ★ ★ ★

Miguel Vargas 3B   Born: 11/17/99   Age: 21   Bats: R   Throws: R   Height: 6'3"   Weight: 205   Origin: International Free Agent, 2017

YEAR	TEAM	LVL	AGE	PA	R	2B	3B	HR	RBI	BB	K	SB	CS	Whiff%	AVG/OBP/SLG	DRC+	BABIP	BRR	FRAA	WARP
2018	OGD	ROK	18	103	25	11	1	2	22	8	13	6	1		.394/.447/.596	202	.443	1.2	3B(13): 0.5, 1B(6): -0.4, 2B(2): 0.4	1.2
2018	DOD2	ROK	18	37	6	3	1	0	2	5	3	1	0		.419/.514/.581	203	.464	-0.7	1B(5): 0.8, 3B(4): 1.1	0.4
2018	GL	LO-A	18	89	4	1	1	0	6	10	20	0	0		.213/.307/.253	68	.281	-0.5	3B(19): 3.1	0.1
2019	GL	LO-A	19	323	53	20	2	5	45	35	43	9	1		.325/.399/.464	162	.363	-2.5	3B(59): 2.2, 1B(2): 0.4, 2B(2): 0.4	3.1
2019	RC	HI-A	19	236	23	18	1	2	32	20	40	4	3		.284/.353/.408	127	.341	-2.3	3B(43): -1.9, 1B(6): 0.4	0.8
2021 FS	LAD	MLB	21	600	55	28	3	10	58	42	142	3	1		.245/.304/.365	84	.312	0.4	3B 0, 1B 1	0.1

Comparables: Matt Dominguez, Mike Moustakas, Rafael Devers

With a father who became a legend in Cuban baseball, great pure hitting skills, and a dearth of non-batting value, Vargas is shaping up to be Yuli Gurriel redux.

Jake Vogel OF   Born: 10/12/01   Age: 19   Bats: R   Throws: R   Height: 5'11"   Weight: 165   Origin: Round 3, 2020 Draft (#100 overall)

An overslot high-school draftee, Vogel has excellent speed, a swing that already flashes good power and an advanced eye at the plate, which he showed off against advanced competition at the Dodgers' alternate site.

PITCHERS

Scott Alexander LHP   Born: 07/10/89   Age: 31   Bats: L   Throws: L   Height: 6'2"   Weight: 195   Origin: Round 6, 2010 Draft (#179 overall)

YEAR	TEAM	LVL	AGE	W	L	SV	G	GS	IP	H	HR	BB/9	K/9	K	GB%	BABIP	WHIP	ERA	DRA-	WARP	MPH	FA%	Whiff%	CSP
2018	LAD	MLB	28	2	1	3	73	1	66	57	4	3.7	7.6	56	71.0%	.298	1.27	3.68	119	-0.3	95.1	85.6%	27.4%	46.4%
2019	LAD	MLB	29	3	2	0	28	0	17¹	17	2	3.6	4.7	9	61.0%	.263	1.38	3.63	113	0.0	94.1	88.8%	21.4%	44.2%
2020	LAD	MLB	30	2	0	0	13	0	12¹	9	2	6.6	6.6	9	67.6%	.226	1.46	2.92	97	0.1	94.5	83.2%	23.2%	45.1%
2021 FS	LAD	MLB	31	1	1	0	57	0	50	48	5	4.0	7.5	41	63.9%	.295	1.43	4.38	99	0.2	94.7	85.8%	24.6%	45.5%
2021 DC	LAD	MLB	31	1	1	0	33	0	35	34	3	4.0	7.5	29	63.9%	.295	1.43	4.38	99	0.2	94.7	85.8%	24.6%	45.5%

Comparables: Dan Jennings, Andrew Kittredge, Heath Hembree

His sinker still burns worms, but Alexander's inability to throw his slider for strikes threatens to leave him snakebitten.

Pedro Báez RHP   Born: 03/11/88   Age: 33   Bats: R   Throws: R   Height: 6'0"   Weight: 232   Origin: International Free Agent, 2007

YEAR	TEAM	LVL	AGE	W	L	SV	G	GS	IP	H	HR	BB/9	K/9	K	GB%	BABIP	WHIP	ERA	DRA-	WARP	MPH	FA%	Whiff%	CSP
2018	LAD	MLB	30	4	3	0	55	0	56¹	46	4	3.7	9.9	62	35.1%	.290	1.22	2.88	74	1.0	97.6	62.8%	31.3%	44.0%
2019	LAD	MLB	31	7	2	1	71	0	69²	43	6	3.0	8.9	69	35.6%	.215	0.95	3.10	75	1.3	97.4	50.7%	31.8%	42.1%
2020	LAD	MLB	32	0	0	2	18	0	17	10	2	3.7	6.9	13	36.0%	.167	1.00	3.18	112	0.0	95.6	42.2%	28.8%	42.4%
2021 FS	LAD	MLB	33	2	2	0	57	0	50	41	7	3.7	8.9	49	36.9%	.262	1.24	3.55	85	0.5	97.0	51.6%	31.0%	42.6%

Comparables: Hector Rondón, Bryan Shaw, Shawn Kelley

For years, Báez has been infamous for working slowly. Quietly though, he's done us all the favor of keeping at-bats relatively short, which kept his appearances from being as soporific as they might have been. The proof of that came in 2020, when he lost 1.5 mph on his fastball, used his slider and changeup more to try to cover for it, threw 4.37 pitches per plate appearance and became fully unwatchable. (Also, despite a fine ERA, he was quite a bit worse.)

Clayton Beeter RHP   Born: 10/09/98   Age: 22   Bats: R   Throws: R   Height: 6'2"   Weight: 220   Origin: Round 2, 2020 Draft (#66 overall)

A second-round pick, Beeter has three plus offerings and a name that would make him the Dodgers' best starter ever, but he's already wearing two surgical scars.

Walker Buehler RHP   Born: 07/28/94   Age: 26   Bats: R   Throws: R   Height: 6'2"   Weight: 185   Origin: Round 1, 2015 Draft (#24 overall)

YEAR	TEAM	LVL	AGE	W	L	SV	G	GS	IP	H	HR	BB/9	K/9	K	GB%	BABIP	WHIP	ERA	DRA-	WARP	MPH	FA%	Whiff%	CSP
2018	RC	HI-A	23	0	0	0	1	1	3	2	0	3.0	15.0	5	83.3%	.333	1.00	3.00	135	0.0				
2018	OKC	AAA	23	1	0	0	3	3	13	10	0	2.8	11.1	16	60.6%	.303	1.08	2.08	69	0.3				
2018	LAD	MLB	23	8	5	0	24	23	137¹	95	12	2.4	9.9	151	49.6%	.249	0.96	2.62	71	3.3	98.3	59.6%	25.7%	49.5%
2019	LAD	MLB	24	14	4	0	30	30	182¹	153	20	1.8	10.6	215	42.1%	.292	1.04	3.26	59	5.7	98.4	60.2%	26.8%	49.6%
2020	LAD	MLB	25	1	0	0	8	8	36²	24	7	2.7	10.3	42	36.6%	.198	0.95	3.44	87	0.6	99.0	62.3%	28.4%	47.0%
2021 FS	LAD	MLB	26	10	7	0	26	26	150	124	20	2.6	10.5	175	41.8%	.282	1.12	3.14	75	3.2	98.5	60.4%	26.9%	49.1%
2021 DC	LAD	MLB	26	11	6	0	27	27	156	129	21	2.6	10.5	182	41.8%	.282	1.12	3.14	75	3.7	98.5	60.4%	26.9%	49.1%

Comparables: Luke Weaver, Luis Severino, Roberto Osuna

Blisters are a stupid part of baseball. No sour grapes here; that's just a fact. It's nice, in a sense, to know that creating extraordinary spin and speed when throwing a ball has a physical cost, but when that cost takes the form of a friction burn on a fingertip, and when that tiny injury can sideline and constrain a pitcher for weeks, it really exposes the folly and caprice of the baseball universe. Buehler has been trying to assert himself as one of the most exciting young pitchers in the majors for three years now, with a five-pitch power arsenal few can match. In 2020, though, the weakness of the skin on his index finger was enough to keep his tremendous talent from fully manifesting.

Gerardo Carrillo RHP   Born: 09/13/98   Age: 22   Bats: R   Throws: R   Height: 5'10"   Weight: 154   Origin: International Free Agent, 2016

YEAR	TEAM	LVL	AGE	W	L	SV	G	GS	IP	H	HR	BB/9	K/9	K	GB%	BABIP	WHIP	ERA	DRA-	WARP	MPH	FA%	Whiff%	CSP
2018	DOD2	ROK	19	2	0	1	4	1	11	6	0	1.6	10.6	13	57.7%	.231	0.73	0.82	48	0.4				
2018	GL	LO-A	19	2	1	0	9	9	49	35	3	2.8	6.8	37	49.6%	.235	1.02	1.65	80	0.9				
2019	RC	HI-A	20	5	9	0	23	21	86	87	3	5.3	9.0	86	54.2%	.339	1.60	5.44	107	-0.2				
2021 FS	LAD	MLB	22	2	3	0	57	0	50	49	7	4.9	7.5	41	46.9%	.289	1.54	5.37	123	-0.5				

Comparables: Rony García, Rob Kaminsky, Junior Fernández

Carrillo could be a good reliever, but if he cleans up his mechanics in the way other young Dodgers recently have, he might even stick as a solid starter.

Caleb Ferguson LHP   Born: 07/02/96   Age: 25   Bats: R   Throws: L   Height: 6'3"   Weight: 226   Origin: Round 38, 2014 Draft (#1149 overall)

YEAR	TEAM	LVL	AGE	W	L	SV	G	GS	IP	H	HR	BB/9	K/9	K	GB%	BABIP	WHIP	ERA	DRA-	WARP	MPH	FA%	Whiff%	CSP
2018	TUL	AA	21	3	0	0	8	8	39	31	2	2.3	9.2	40	39.8%	.284	1.05	1.38	82	0.6				
2018	OKC	AAA	21	0	0	0	2	2	8	6	0	7.9	13.5	12	21.1%	.316	1.62	2.25	92	0.1				
2018	LAD	MLB	21	7	2	2	29	3	49	43	8	2.2	10.8	59	45.3%	.292	1.12	3.49	70	1.0	96.0	71.9%	26.3%	54.6%
2019	OKC	AAA	22	0	0	1	13	1	15¹	9	1	2.9	15.8	27	46.2%	.320	0.91	1.76	26	0.7				
2019	LAD	MLB	22	1	2	0	46	2	44²	39	7	5.4	10.9	54	38.5%	.294	1.48	4.84	100	0.2	96.3	78.0%	23.4%	49.2%
2020	LAD	MLB	23	2	1	0	21	1	18²	16	4	1.4	13.0	27	51.1%	.293	1.02	2.89	69	0.5	96.7	79.6%	29.1%	51.4%
2021 FS	LAD	MLB	24	3	2	0	57	0	50	40	6	3.6	11.0	61	43.0%	.285	1.21	3.19	77	0.8	96.3	76.9%	25.6%	51.1%

Comparables: Julio Urías, Nick Neidert, Génesis Cabrera

Substituting a slider (he calls it a cutter, reinforcing the need to throw it hard) for his big-breaking curveball turned Ferguson into an elite reliever; Tommy John surgery turned him into a non-factor for 2021.

Dylan Floro RHP Born: 12/27/90 Age: 30 Bats: L Throws: R Height: 6'2" Weight: 203 Origin: Round 13, 2012 Draft (#422 overall)

YEAR	TEAM	LVL	AGE	W	L	SV	G	GS	IP	H	HR	BB/9	K/9	K	GB%	BABIP	WHIP	ERA	DRA-	WARP	MPH	FA%	Whiff%	CSP
2018	CIN	MLB	27	3	2	0	25	0	36¹	39	2	3.0	6.7	27	55.8%	.319	1.40	2.72	117	-0.1	94.9	62.4%	20.9%	48.3%
2018	LAD	MLB	27	3	1	0	29	0	27²	18	1	3.6	10.1	31	52.2%	.254	1.05	1.63	70	0.6	95.4	64.8%	31.5%	45.0%
2019	LAD	MLB	28	5	3	0	50	0	46²	46	4	2.7	8.1	42	48.3%	.307	1.29	4.24	93	0.4	95.4	67.5%	26.3%	51.1%
2020	LAD	MLB	29	3	0	0	25	0	24¹	23	1	1.5	7.0	19	57.3%	.297	1.11	2.59	83	0.4	95.0	46.9%	23.3%	45.2%
2021 FS	LAD	MLB	30	1	1	0	57	0	50	49	6	2.4	7.6	42	52.7%	.295	1.26	3.86	91	0.4	95.2	59.9%	25.1%	48.1%
2021 DC	LAD	MLB	30	1	1	0	38	0	41	40	5	2.4	7.6	34	52.7%	.295	1.26	3.86	91	0.4	95.2	59.9%	25.1%	48.1%

Comparables: Hansel Robles, Tyler Duffey, Mike Morin

The three-batter-minimum rule inspired Floro to work hard on his changeup during the offseason, and in 2020, he became a three-pitch pitcher with two offerings dominating against each type of hitter: sinker-slider to righties and sinker-changeup to lefties. With better feel, he trusted the grip on his changeup more, didn't overthrow it and threw more strikes. The overall effect was a lower strikeout rate, but an exceptionally low opponent exit velocity and another solid season for an above-average middle reliever. Ironically, though, the changeup's real moment in the spotlight came against a righty—when Floro, tasked with stemming the tide in Game 6 of the World Series, retired red-hot Randy Arozarena on three straight cambios.

Tony Gonsolin RHP Born: 05/14/94 Age: 27 Bats: R Throws: R Height: 6'3" Weight: 205 Origin: Round 9, 2016 Draft (#281 overall)

YEAR	TEAM	LVL	AGE	W	L	SV	G	GS	IP	H	HR	BB/9	K/9	K	GB%	BABIP	WHIP	ERA	DRA-	WARP	MPH	FA%	Whiff%	CSP
2018	RC	HI-A	24	4	2	0	17	17	83²	72	5	2.8	11.4	106	37.2%	.321	1.17	2.69	80	1.3				
2018	TUL	AA	24	6	0	0	9	9	44¹	32	3	3.2	9.9	49	36.0%	.269	1.08	2.44	70	1.0				
2019	OKC	AAA	25	2	4	0	13	13	41¹	41	4	4.6	10.9	50	35.0%	.327	1.50	4.35	61	1.5				
2019	LAD	MLB	25	4	2	1	11	6	40	26	4	3.4	8.3	37	40.9%	.208	1.02	2.92	86	0.6	95.5	48.3%	26.9%	43.1%
2020	LAD	MLB	26	2	2	0	9	8	46²	32	2	1.4	8.9	46	33.6%	.252	0.84	2.31	83	0.8	96.6	47.5%	29.8%	46.3%
2021 FS	LAD	MLB	27	9	8	0	26	26	150	131	25	3.2	9.4	156	36.8%	.275	1.23	3.82	88	2.1	96.1	47.8%	28.6%	45.0%
2021 DC	LAD	MLB	27	9	6	0	43	21	130	113	21	3.2	9.4	135	36.8%	.275	1.23	3.82	88	2.1	96.1	47.8%	28.6%	45.0%

Comparables: Joe Musgrove, Kevin Gausman, Ricky Nolasco

Pairing command with control has, perhaps, led us to think of the skill too much as a matter of location. Gonsolin poses an argument in favor of shifting that paradigm. Scouts' hesitations about him centered on his iffy command (and control), but in 2020, he shook off that criticism. A slight quieting-down of what is still a deceptive delivery, featuring a high front side and high arm slot, led to a walk rate of four percent but, more importantly, he executed consistently and missed more bats. He was first untrusted, then untrustworthy in October, but Gonsolin has all the makings of a solid three-pitch starter with good command—even if not in the traditional sense.

Victor González LHP Born: 11/16/95 Age: 25 Bats: L Throws: L Height: 6'0" Weight: 180 Origin: International Free Agent, 2012

YEAR	TEAM	LVL	AGE	W	L	SV	G	GS	IP	H	HR	BB/9	K/9	K	GB%	BABIP	WHIP	ERA	DRA-	WARP	MPH	FA%	Whiff%	CSP
2018	OGD	ROK	22	1	2	0	4	2	8	18	1	4.5	7.9	7	54.3%	.500	2.75	13.50	76	0.2				
2018	GL	LO-A	22	0	3	0	6	6	25²	33	3	1.8	6.3	18	33.0%	.353	1.48	5.61	77	0.5				
2019	RC	HI-A	23	2	1	0	8	5	27¹	17	0	4.6	11.9	36	47.7%	.274	1.13	1.65	60	0.6				
2019	TUL	AA	23	3	1	2	15	8	48¹	48	4	2.6	8.2	44	52.1%	.319	1.28	2.23	94	0.2				
2019	OKC	AAA	23	0	0	0	15	0	14	16	3	2.6	8.4	13	54.5%	.317	1.43	3.86	99	0.2				
2020	LAD	MLB	24	3	0	0	15	1	20¹	13	0	0.9	10.2	23	69.2%	.250	0.74	1.33	64	0.6	96.4	62.8%	33.6%	44.6%
2021 FS	LAD	MLB	25	2	2	0	57	0	50	46	6	3.6	8.7	48	54.5%	.290	1.32	4.06	93	0.3	96.4	62.8%	33.6%	44.6%
2021 DC	LAD	MLB	25	2	2	0	44	0	46	42	5	3.6	8.7	44	54.5%	.290	1.32	4.06	93	0.4	96.4	62.8%	33.6%	44.6%

Comparables: Max Fried, Drew Anderson, Randy Rosario

For most of his pro career, González lacked the command required of a quality big-leaguer. He had the funky, low arm slot, the wiggle on the sinker, and a decent slider, but his delivery left him spinning off toward the third-base dugout, causing insufficient precision. During the coronal interregnum, though, he made a significant mechanical change and the Dodgers found a dominant southpaw for their bullpen. By getting much deeper into his legs, González was able to maintain better posture, a more direct line to the plate and more consistent timing. The result was a run of 107 batters faced (including some key postseason appearances) with six walks, no homers allowed and all the makings of a star reliever being born.

Brusdar Graterol RHP Born: 08/26/98 Age: 22 Bats: R Throws: R Height: 6'1" Weight: 265 Origin: International Free Agent, 2014

YEAR	TEAM	LVL	AGE	W	L	SV	G	GS	IP	H	HR	BB/9	K/9	K	GB%	BABIP	WHIP	ERA	DRA-	WARP	MPH	FA%	Whiff%	CSP
2018	CR	LO-A	19	3	2	0	8	8	41¹	30	3	2.0	11.1	51	64.1%	.270	0.94	2.18	76	0.8				
2018	FTM	HI-A	19	5	2	0	11	11	60²	59	0	2.8	8.3	56	48.3%	.343	1.29	3.12	88	0.7				
2019	TWI	ROK	20	0	0	0	2	2	3	1	0	0.0	12.0	4	60.0%	.200	0.33	0.00	51	0.1				
2019	PNS	AA	20	6	0	1	12	9	52²	32	2	3.6	8.5	50	55.0%	.234	1.01	1.71	60	1.3				
2019	ROC	AAA	20	1	0	0	4	0	5¹	4	1	3.4	11.8	7	50.0%	.273	1.12	5.06	66	0.2				
2019	MIN	MLB	20	1	1	0	10	0	9²	10	1	1.9	9.3	10	51.9%	.346	1.24	4.66	70	0.2	100.3	67.4%	18.7%	52.8%
2020	LAD	MLB	21	1	2	0	23	2	23¹	18	1	1.2	5.0	13	63.8%	.250	0.90	3.09	87	0.4	100.7	70.8%	15.2%	54.8%
2021 FS	LAD	MLB	22	2	2	4	57	0	50	48	6	3.4	7.9	44	53.8%	.292	1.35	4.36	98	0.2	100.6	69.9%	16.0%	54.3%
2021 DC	LAD	MLB	22	2	2	4	49	0	52	50	6	3.4	7.9	45	53.8%	.292	1.35	4.36	98	0.4	100.6	69.9%	16.0%	54.3%

Comparables: Bryse Wilson, Alex Reyes, Deivi García

When Graterol suffered a minor knee injury on September 10, Dave Roberts dismissed the problem by saying, "[Graterol] is a big, strong guy. He loves mangoes. I'll get him a mango and he'll be fine." That's a very common form of baseball joke. Clubhouses can be as awkward as any other workplace. People find out one thing you like or dislike, immediately stop learning about you and assume that single preference reliably defines your entire personality. As Graterol proved in the postseason, his gregariousness and competitiveness run deeper than his willingness to pitch through pain in exchange for tropical fruit. His 100 mph sinker does seem as heavy as a mango, though, and his slider is good enough to keep hitters honest. In order to make the leap to relief ace status, he'll need to develop more depth on his breaking ball.

★　　★　　★　*2021 Top 101 Prospect* **#55**　★　　★　　★

Josiah Gray RHP Born: 12/21/97 Age: 23 Bats: R Throws: R Height: 6'1" Weight: 190 Origin: Round 2, 2018 Draft (#72 overall)

YEAR	TEAM	LVL	AGE	W	L	SV	G	GS	IP	H	HR	BB/9	K/9	K	GB%	BABIP	WHIP	ERA	DRA-	WARP	MPH	FA%	Whiff%	CSP
2018	GRN	ROK	20	2	2	0	12	12	52¹	29	1	2.9	10.1	59	36.4%	.219	0.88	2.58	76	1.3				
2019	GL	LO-A	21	1	0	0	5	5	23¹	13	0	2.7	10.0	26	37.0%	.241	0.86	1.93	46	0.8				
2019	RC	HI-A	21	7	0	0	12	12	67¹	52	3	1.7	10.7	80	36.3%	.293	0.97	2.14	47	2.2				
2019	TUL	AA	21	3	2	0	9	8	39¹	33	0	2.5	9.4	41	34.3%	.317	1.12	2.75	67	0.8				
2021 FS	LAD	MLB	23	1	1	0	57	0	50	44	6	3.7	8.8	48	35.8%	.279	1.30	4.03	97	0.2				
2021 DC	LAD	MLB	23	1	1	0	27	0	29	25	4	3.7	8.8	28	35.8%	.279	1.30	4.03	97	0.2				

Comparables: Yohander Méndez, Brett Cecil, Carl Edwards Jr.

The Dodgers insist that the controlled, collaborative (more than competitive) setting of the alternate site actually helped Gray, whose rising fastball is just too effective (and too much fun) to stop throwing when he has the chance (need) to win a ballgame. Reports say Gray's plus slider grew more consistent and his feel for his changeup improved as he threw both pitches (plus a curveball) more often than he might have otherwise. All that said, the lost season means we still need some answers. Gray's fastball velocity fluctuates a lot. Game settings at the upper levels will help show how he holds his velo as starts progress, where he's going to sit with the heat and whether the added confidence in his secondary stuff can make everything play up.

Andre Jackson RHP Born: 05/01/96 Age: 25 Bats: R Throws: R Height: 6'3" Weight: 210 Origin: Round 12, 2017 Draft (#370 overall)

YEAR	TEAM	LVL	AGE	W	L	SV	G	GS	IP	H	HR	BB/9	K/9	K	GB%	BABIP	WHIP	ERA	DRA-	WARP	MPH	FA%	Whiff%	CSP
2018	DOD2	ROK	22	2	0	0	4	3	18¹	18	0	2.0	15.2	31	40.0%	.450	1.20	3.44	112	0.1				
2018	GL	LO-A	22	1	5	0	14	14	49²	48	3	7.4	8.2	45	46.2%	.319	1.79	4.35	153	-1.1				
2019	GL	LO-A	23	4	1	0	10	10	48¹	29	1	3.5	9.3	50	46.7%	.237	0.99	2.23	66	1.1				
2019	RC	HI-A	23	3	1	0	15	15	66¹	61	5	5.2	12.3	91	45.9%	.368	1.49	3.66	96	0.3				
2021 FS	LAD	MLB	25	2	3	0	57	0	50	45	7	6.6	9.2	51	41.9%	.287	1.65	5.36	119	-0.4				

Comparables: Mike Montgomery, T.J. Zeuch, Alex Reyes

The sturdy, right-handed Jackson throws hard and registers good spin on his heat, but his changeup remains ahead of his breaking stuff.

Kenley Jansen RHP Born: 09/30/87 Age: 33 Bats: S Throws: R Height: 6'5" Weight: 265 Origin: International Free Agent, 2004

YEAR	TEAM	LVL	AGE	W	L	SV	G	GS	IP	H	HR	BB/9	K/9	K	GB%	BABIP	WHIP	ERA	DRA-	WARP	MPH	FA%	Whiff%	CSP
2018	LAD	MLB	30	1	5	38	69	0	71²	54	13	2.1	10.3	82	35.6%	.234	0.99	3.01	57	2.0	94.7	94.2%	28.2%	48.9%
2019	LAD	MLB	31	5	3	33	62	0	63	51	9	2.3	11.4	80	32.5%	.273	1.06	3.71	72	1.3	94.3	87.7%	32.2%	47.3%
2020	LAD	MLB	32	3	1	11	27	0	24¹	19	2	3.3	12.2	33	24.6%	.309	1.15	3.33	82	0.4	93.7	90.4%	30.8%	46.1%
2021 FS	LAD	MLB	33	2	1	36	57	0	50	37	6	2.0	11.0	61	33.6%	.268	0.98	2.39	59	1.3	94.2	90.1%	30.8%	47.4%
2021 DC	LAD	MLB	33	2	1	36	44	0	46	34	5	2.0	11.0	56	33.6%	.268	0.98	2.39	59	1.3	94.2	90.1%	30.8%	47.4%

Comparables: Craig Kimbrel, Dellin Betances, Francisco Rodríguez

Dave Roberts has a special relationship with his future Hall of Fame closer. He treats Jansen like a beloved son, giving him countless opportunities to be the hero and trusting him more than anyone else might. Because of that foundation of love and respect, he also earned the right to challenge Jansen and he did so in 2020. Roberts noted that Jansen's velocity would sometimes lag in a given appearance, unless or until he got into trouble. He instructed the aging relief ace, in so many words, not to keep any of his best stuff in the tank. When Jansen's movement and command failed him late in the season, Roberts (tactfully, but decisively) let Julio Urías seal the club's pennant and World Series title. To Jansen's credit, he was much more glad to have won than indignant at being passed over. He's likely finished as an elite closer, but far from finished as a solid reliever and teammate.

Tommy Kahnle RHP Born: 08/07/89 Age: 31 Bats: R Throws: R Height: 6'1" Weight: 230 Origin: Round 5, 2010 Draft (#175 overall)

YEAR	TEAM	LVL	AGE	W	L	SV	G	GS	IP	H	HR	BB/9	K/9	K	GB%	BABIP	WHIP	ERA	DRA-	WARP	MPH	FA%	Whiff%	CSP
2018	SWB	AAA	28	2	2	1	25	0	24²	23	2	4.0	13.5	37	37.9%	.375	1.38	4.01	40	0.9				
2018	NYY	MLB	28	2	0	1	24	0	23¹	23	3	5.8	11.6	30	38.7%	.339	1.63	6.56	90	0.2	97.1	54.3%	34.9%	45.9%
2019	NYY	MLB	29	3	2	0	72	0	61¹	45	9	2.9	12.9	88	50.0%	.279	1.06	3.67	49	2.0	98.3	43.7%	36.6%	47.1%
2020	NYY	MLB	30	0	0	0	1	0	1	1	0	9.0	27.0	3	100.0%	.500	2.00	0.00	64	0.0	98.0	35.0%	66.7%	59.5%
2021 FS	LAD	MLB	31	3	2	0	57	0	50	38	5	4.2	11.9	65	45.2%	.291	1.25	3.16	77	0.8	98.1	45.6%	37.0%	47.2%

Comparables: Jacob Barnes, Mychal Givens, Brad Boxberger

Middle relievers are essential components of a well-oiled modern baseball machine, but their absence is noticed more often than their presence. Kahnle made it into only one game in 2020 before being sidelined by forearm tightness that then led to the obligatory Tommy John surgery. His absence made the Yankees bullpen leaner, and in a year where starting pitchers weren't pushed nearly as hard because of an abbreviated ramp-up to a shortened season, that thinness impacted the team even more than it would have in a normal season. Kahnle could return in 2021 for the Dodgers, who inked him to a two-year pact over the winter, but that's only if he hits his most optimistic rehab targets.

Joe Kelly RHP Born: 06/09/88 Age: 33 Bats: R Throws: R Height: 6'1" Weight: 174 Origin: Round 3, 2009 Draft (#98 overall)

YEAR	TEAM	LVL	AGE	W	L	SV	G	GS	IP	H	HR	BB/9	K/9	K	GB%	BABIP	WHIP	ERA	DRA-	WARP	MPH	FA%	Whiff%	CSP
2018	BOS	MLB	30	4	2	2	73	0	65²	57	4	4.4	9.3	68	48.3%	.301	1.36	4.39	101	0.3	100.2	55.4%	25.7%	45.8%
2019	LAD	MLB	31	5	4	1	55	0	51¹	49	6	3.9	10.9	62	62.6%	.323	1.38	4.56	67	1.2	99.6	50.9%	26.4%	48.7%
2020	LAD	MLB	32	0	0	0	12	1	10	8	0	6.3	8.1	9	57.7%	.308	1.50	1.80	86	0.2	98.2	36.8%	27.5%	44.0%
2021 FS	LAD	MLB	33	1	1	0	57	0	50	45	7	4.3	9.5	52	51.7%	.290	1.39	4.39	97	0.2	99.6	50.3%	26.3%	47.0%
2021 DC	LAD	MLB	33	1	1	0	38	0	41	37	5	4.3	9.5	43	51.7%	.290	1.39	4.39	97	0.3	99.6	50.3%	26.3%	47.0%

Comparables: Trevor Cahill, Diego Segui, Jhoulys Chacín

When life throws you curveballs, throw them back. Or at some Astros. Kelly certainly did. After (ahem) unsuccessful attempts to improve his control during quarantine, he simply showed up and started spinning his vicious power curve—the one that sometimes eclipses 90 miles per hour, with genuine curveball depth. No pitcher in the PITCHf/x Era has thrown curves as often as Kelly did in 2020. It didn't turn him into an unstoppable force because he still struggles to stay healthy and to throw strikes, but it makes him a bit more interesting and (as Kelly does so well) it keeps one wondering: what if his simplified arsenal and breaking-ball primacy finally allow him to tap into his full potential?

Clayton Kershaw LHP Born: 03/19/88 Age: 33 Bats: L Throws: L Height: 6'4" Weight: 225 Origin: Round 1, 2006 Draft (#7 overall)

YEAR	TEAM	LVL	AGE	W	L	SV	G	GS	IP	H	HR	BB/9	K/9	K	GB%	BABIP	WHIP	ERA	DRA-	WARP	MPH	FA%	Whiff%	CSP
2018	LAD	MLB	30	9	5	0	26	26	161¹	139	17	1.6	8.6	155	47.7%	.276	1.04	2.73	69	4.1	92.5	41.2%	23.0%	50.6%
2019	LAD	MLB	31	16	5	0	29	28	178¹	145	28	2.1	9.5	189	46.3%	.267	1.04	3.03	68	4.7	91.7	43.9%	28.1%	46.4%
2020	LAD	MLB	32	6	2	0	10	10	58¹	41	8	1.2	9.6	62	52.7%	.232	0.84	2.16	75	1.3	93.0	40.8%	27.7%	50.6%
2021 FS	LAD	MLB	33	10	6	0	26	26	150	125	17	1.8	9.6	160	49.6%	.280	1.03	2.55	64	4.1	92.2	42.5%	26.8%	48.5%
2021 DC	LAD	MLB	33	13	6	0	27	27	167	139	19	1.8	9.6	178	49.6%	.280	1.03	2.55	64	4.9	92.2	42.5%	26.8%	48.5%

Comparables: Felix Hernandez, Jacob deGrom, Carlos Carrasco

When the Dodgers developed an official (non-exclusive) partnership with Driveline Baseball, they surely envisioned something like Kershaw's 2020. Folding the resources that organization offers into the structure of the team's instruction and development makes it safer and easier for a future Hall of Famer to make what might otherwise feel like a desperate move. Besides, when attaching the term 'Driveline' to pitching, it's just Kershaw's style of hitch-and-fire, over-the-top, straight-ahead mechanics that spring to mind. Through his work at Driveline and elsewhere, the best southpaw of his generation added back some lost velocity, rediscovered the vertical separation he wanted on his slider and reclaimed his ace status in the Dodgers rotation—if only for one more year.

Corey Knebel RHP Born: 11/26/91 Age: 29 Bats: R Throws: R Height: 6'3" Weight: 224 Origin: Round 1, 2013 Draft (#39 overall)

YEAR	TEAM	LVL	AGE	W	L	SV	G	GS	IP	H	HR	BB/9	K/9	K	GB%	BABIP	WHIP	ERA	DRA-	WARP	MPH	FA%	Whiff%	CSP
2018	MIL	MLB	26	4	3	16	57	0	55¹	38	7	3.6	14.3	88	49.5%	.304	1.08	3.58	56	1.5	98.5	70.9%	32.3%	49.2%
2020	MIL	MLB	28	0	0	0	15	0	13¹	15	4	5.4	10.1	15	33.3%	.314	1.73	6.08	121	0.0	96.4	62.7%	21.8%	44.4%
2021 FS	LAD	MLB	29	1	1	0	57	0	50	39	6	4.6	11.6	64	41.0%	.282	1.29	3.70	84	0.6	97.6	67.3%	27.6%	47.1%
2021 DC	LAD	MLB	29	1	1	0	38	0	41	32	5	4.6	11.6	52	41.0%	.282	1.29	3.70	84	0.6	97.6	67.3%	27.6%	47.1%

Comparables: Dominic Leone, Cam Bedrosian, Carl Edwards Jr.

He still spins his fastball and knuckle-curve well, but Knebel didn't bring his full velocity back from Tommy John surgery, and hitters noticed.

Adam Kolarek LHP Born: 01/14/89 Age: 32 Bats: L Throws: L Height: 6'3" Weight: 215 Origin: Round 11, 2010 Draft (#332 overall)

YEAR	TEAM	LVL	AGE	W	L	SV	G	GS	IP	H	HR	BB/9	K/9	K	GB%	BABIP	WHIP	ERA	DRA-	WARP	MPH	FA%	Whiff%	CSP
2018	DUR	AAA	29	5	1	4	31	1	44²	35	1	2.4	10.5	52	60.7%	.309	1.05	1.61	71	0.8				
2018	TB	MLB	29	1	0	2	31	0	34¹	38	0	1.3	5.0	19	57.8%	.328	1.25	3.93	95	0.3	92.9	63.8%	20.4%	53.6%
2019	TB	MLB	30	4	3	1	54	0	43¹	39	6	2.9	7.5	36	63.4%	.264	1.22	3.95	77	0.7	92.4	82.8%	22.3%	46.2%
2019	LAD	MLB	30	2	0	0	26	0	11²	9	1	1.5	6.9	9	73.5%	.242	0.94	0.77	77	0.2	91.5	83.2%	32.2%	46.4%
2020	LAD	MLB	31	3	0	1	20	0	19	11	1	1.9	6.2	13	61.8%	.185	0.79	0.95	83	0.3	91.1	83.7%	17.8%	46.0%
2021 FS	LAD	MLB	32	1	1	0	57	0	50	47	5	3.0	7.8	43	60.6%	.292	1.29	3.92	91	0.4	92.0	79.7%	22.0%	47.5%
2021 DC	LAD	MLB	32	1	1	0	38	0	41	39	4	3.0	7.8	35	60.6%	.292	1.29	3.92	91	0.4	92.0	79.7%	22.0%	47.5%

Comparables: Josh Osich, Matt Grace, Brandon Workman

Side-arm sinkerballers aren't supposed to be this strapping. That's the most peculiar thing about Kolarek. Nearly everyone who throws anything like the way he does is either short or wiry. Kolarek is built like a starter, but pitches like he was born for the (dying) role of matchup bullpen lefty. In 2020, he proved he can more than withstand the implementation of the three-batter-minimum rule, and only partially because that rule has turned out to be toothless. His sinker has both elite sink and elite run, and he's getting better at spotting it with each passing year. Hitters are still trying to figure out why he's not more normal—as he saws them off.

Dustin May RHP Born: 09/06/97 Age: 23 Bats: R Throws: R Height: 6'6" Weight: 180 Origin: Round 3, 2016 Draft (#101 overall)

YEAR	TEAM	LVL	AGE	W	L	SV	G	GS	IP	H	HR	BB/9	K/9	K	GB%	BABIP	WHIP	ERA	DRA-	WARP	MPH	FA%	Whiff%	CSP
2018	RC	HI-A	20	7	3	0	17	17	98¹	91	9	1.6	8.6	94	55.9%	.296	1.10	3.29	88	1.1				
2018	TUL	AA	20	2	2	0	6	6	34¹	27	0	3.1	7.3	28	53.5%	.267	1.14	3.67	88	0.4				
2019	TUL	AA	21	3	5	0	15	15	79¹	71	5	2.3	9.8	86	50.5%	.311	1.15	3.74	78	1.1				
2019	OKC	AAA	21	3	0	0	5	5	27¹	21	0	3.0	7.9	24	59.2%	.280	1.10	2.30	39	1.3				
2019	LAD	MLB	21	2	3	0	14	4	34²	33	2	1.3	8.3	32	45.0%	.316	1.10	3.63	93	0.4	98.0	88.2%	20.6%	52.0%
2020	LAD	MLB	22	3	1	0	12	10	56	45	9	2.6	7.1	44	53.4%	.235	1.09	2.57	91	0.8	99.5	81.5%	19.2%	53.2%
2021 FS	LAD	MLB	23	9	8	0	26	26	150	148	21	2.9	7.9	132	50.8%	.294	1.31	4.36	98	1.2	99.0	83.5%	19.6%	52.8%
2021 DC	LAD	MLB	23	8	7	0	43	21	128	126	18	2.9	7.9	112	50.8%	.294	1.31	4.36	98	1.4	99.0	83.5%	19.6%	52.8%

Comparables: Luis Severino, Lucas Giolito, Bryse Wilson

Did you know May is from Justin, TX? That's an awfully good setup, for either a Dr. Seuss riff or an Abbott and Costello homage. This is the guy who, by loading up on protein between workouts each winter, has steadily packed good weight onto his Seussian frame, and whose competitiveness and work ethic have helped him become one of the league's hardest throwers. Despite the distinctly modern velocity, he's as much of a throwback as a Vaudeville partner act, having not only junked his four-seamer in favor of a zone-pounding, grounder-inducing sinker, but electing a slurve he feels confident throwing for strikes over the bat-missing yakker that gave him such strikeout upside. If he can make a tweak or two to get those whiffs back, oh, the places he'll go.

Jake McGee LHP Born: 08/06/86 Age: 34 Bats: L Throws: L Height: 6'4" Weight: 229 Origin: Round 5, 2004 Draft (#135 overall)

YEAR	TEAM	LVL	AGE	W	L	SV	G	GS	IP	H	HR	BB/9	K/9	K	GB%	BABIP	WHIP	ERA	DRA-	WARP	MPH	FA%	Whiff%	CSP
2018	COL	MLB	31	2	4	1	61	0	51¹	59	10	2.8	8.2	47	40.7%	.327	1.46	6.49	137	-0.7	96.2	86.3%	22.4%	53.2%
2019	COL	MLB	32	0	2	0	45	0	41¹	47	11	2.4	7.6	35	35.1%	.300	1.40	4.35	129	-0.4	95.6	80.4%	19.5%	51.3%
2020	LAD	MLB	33	3	1	0	24	0	20¹	14	2	1.3	14.6	33	37.2%	.300	0.84	2.66	65	0.6	96.5	96.9%	33.3%	59.5%
2021 FS	LAD	MLB	34	2	2	0	57	0	50	45	9	2.6	9.6	53	38.3%	.281	1.19	3.77	91	0.4	96.0	87.1%	24.6%	54.4%

Comparables: Nick Vincent, Chaz Roe, Oliver Drake

Small mechanical changes can sometimes beget big differences in the quality of a pitcher's stuff. In McGee's case, a slight alteration to his arm path let him reclaim the 1.5 mph he'd lost over the previous two years. As the most fastball-heavy hurler in the majors, McGee needs that extra juice more than anyone, thus it made a huge difference when he rediscovered it. He still requires limited, intelligent usage, but his utility in the right role is considerable.

Bobby Miller RHP Born: 04/05/99 Age: 22 Bats: L Throws: R Height: 6'5" Weight: 220 Origin: Round 1, 2020 Draft (#29 overall)

Is "a gigantic Walker Buehler" a fair comp to throw on anyone? Have you ever heard of Betteridge's Law of headlines? It also applies to first sentences of BP Annual player comments. Still, Miller is exciting. He's big and thickly built, but with the bouncy explosion and fiery demeanor Buehler brings to the mound. His fastball sits in the upper 90s and can show either heavy action at the bottom of the zone or rise at the top of it. He's worked to flesh out two distinct sliders (one more cutter than true slider) and two changeups (one a split-change). Best of all, though, the Dodgers were able to make him their first-round pick with confidence—despite the limited looks afforded by the COVID spring—thanks to the trust they have in scout Marty Lamb, who's been in their organization for over 20 years and whose Midwest coverage area has netted the team a fistful of recent top draftees. Holding onto and valuing veteran scouts pays off for the teams wise enough to do so.

David Price LHP Born: 08/26/85 Age: 35 Bats: L Throws: L Height: 6'5" Weight: 215 Origin: Round 1, 2007 Draft (#1 overall)

YEAR	TEAM	LVL	AGE	W	L	SV	G	GS	IP	H	HR	BB/9	K/9	K	GB%	BABIP	WHIP	ERA	DRA-	WARP	MPH	FA%	Whiff%	CSP
2018	BOS	MLB	32	16	7	0	30	30	176	151	25	2.6	9.1	177	40.2%	.275	1.14	3.58	83	3.2	94.5	46.6%	22.8%	49.9%
2019	BOS	MLB	33	7	5	0	22	22	107¹	109	15	2.7	10.7	128	41.0%	.336	1.31	4.28	96	1.3	94.1	52.0%	26.0%	49.7%
2021 FS	LAD	MLB	35	9	8	0	26	26	150	143	25	2.6	9.0	149	40.2%	.290	1.24	4.06	94	1.6	94.3	49.7%	24.7%	49.8%
2021 DC	LAD	MLB	35	9	7	0	25	25	137	130	23	2.6	9.0	136	40.2%	.290	1.24	4.06	94	1.9	94.3	49.7%	24.7%	49.8%

Comparables: Carlos Carrasco, Felix Hernandez, Johnny Cueto

As it turned out, relatively few big-league players got seriously sick due to the global pandemic that defined 2020. Nevertheless, there were several points at which it looked not only as though the season might be thwarted, but that a full-fledged breakout might steer the sport into crisis and worsen the national disaster that is COVID-19. There remains an argument that playing the season did the latter. Price, who will put well over $200 million in the bank during his career even after accounting for the choice to surrender his 2020 paycheck, made the best choice for his family by opting out of the campaign. He's likely to pitch for the Dodgers for the first time in 2021, probably with a fresher arm, one fewer fastball, and (still) plenty of ways to get outs.

Dennis Santana RHP   Born: 04/12/96   Age: 25   Bats: R   Throws: R   Height: 6'2"   Weight: 190   Origin: International Free Agent, 2013

YEAR	TEAM	LVL	AGE	W	L	SV	G	GS	IP	H	HR	BB/9	K/9	K	GB%	BABIP	WHIP	ERA	DRA-	WARP	MPH	FA%	Whiff%	CSP
2018	TUL	AA	22	0	2	0	8	8	38²	26	3	3.3	11.9	51	53.3%	.261	1.03	2.56	55	1.2				
2018	OKC	AAA	22	1	1	0	2	2	11	10	0	1.6	11.5	14	41.4%	.357	1.09	2.45	57	0.4				
2018	LAD	MLB	22	1	0	0	1	0	3²	6	0	2.5	9.8	4	23.1%	.500	1.91	12.27	84	0.0	95.5	53.6%	31.2%	44.0%
2019	OKC	AAA	23	5	9	0	27	17	93¹	111	16	5.1	10.1	105	42.2%	.365	1.76	6.94	133	0.1				
2019	LAD	MLB	23	0	0	0	3	0	5	6	1	7.2	10.8	6	46.7%	.357	2.00	7.20	107	0.0	94.5	56.7%	30.4%	39.8%
2020	LAD	MLB	24	1	2	0	12	0	17	15	4	3.7	9.5	18	32.6%	.262	1.29	5.29	111	0.1	96.3	38.7%	28.3%	50.7%
2021 FS	LAD	MLB	25	2	2	0	57	0	50	45	8	4.7	9.4	52	41.2%	.285	1.44	4.96	107	-0.1	95.9	43.0%	28.9%	48.3%
2021 DC	LAD	MLB	25	2	2	0	32	4	48	43	8	4.7	9.4	50	41.2%	.285	1.44	4.96	107	0.2	95.9	43.0%	28.9%	48.3%

Comparables: Touki Toussaint, Zack Littell, Tyler Mahle

The highlight of Santana's season came in a late-July outing against Houston that felt like a late-September affair, as he struck out four over 2 1/3 innings—all in extras—spurring the Dodgers to a 4-2 win.

Blake Treinen RHP   Born: 06/30/88   Age: 33   Bats: R   Throws: R   Height: 6'5"   Weight: 225   Origin: Round 7, 2011 Draft (#226 overall)

YEAR	TEAM	LVL	AGE	W	L	SV	G	GS	IP	H	HR	BB/9	K/9	K	GB%	BABIP	WHIP	ERA	DRA-	WARP	MPH	FA%	Whiff%	CSP
2018	OAK	MLB	30	9	2	38	68	0	80¹	46	2	2.4	11.2	100	51.0%	.233	0.83	0.78	49	2.5	99.3	67.1%	35.8%	47.8%
2019	OAK	MLB	31	6	5	16	57	0	58²	58	9	5.7	9.1	59	43.2%	.308	1.62	4.91	115	-0.2	98.5	67.1%	26.1%	43.6%
2020	LAD	MLB	32	3	3	1	27	0	25²	23	1	2.8	7.7	22	65.3%	.297	1.21	3.86	76	0.6	98.3	64.9%	22.9%	46.0%
2021 FS	LAD	MLB	33	2	2	7	57	0	50	45	5	3.9	8.9	49	54.4%	.292	1.34	3.90	89	0.4	98.6	66.5%	27.8%	45.4%
2021 DC	LAD	MLB	33	2	2	7	44	0	46	41	5	3.9	8.9	45	54.4%	.292	1.34	3.90	89	0.5	98.6	66.5%	27.8%	45.4%

Comparables: Pedro Báez, Steve Cishek, Hector Rondón

The 2018 version of Treinen, with the extraordinary ability to both limit hard contact and miss bats at elite rates, was a two-fastball guy. He also added a cutter that year, as a variant on his slider. With four pitches, he was able to neutralize left-handed batters for the first time, elevating him to relief ace status. Alas, that proved too hard a balance to sustain—at least at that level. After he crashed back to Earth, he landed with the Dodgers, a one-fastball organization who had him put the four-seamer and cutter on the shelf against righties and minimized his exposure to lefties. Now he's a fireballing sinker-slider monster against righties, with the consistent execution and confidence to use his weaker offerings to keep southpaws off balance. The 2018 version of him is gone for good, but so is the 2018 version of you, dear reader.

Julio Urías LHP   Born: 08/12/96   Age: 24   Bats: L   Throws: L   Height: 6'0"   Weight: 225   Origin: International Free Agent, 2012

YEAR	TEAM	LVL	AGE	W	L	SV	G	GS	IP	H	HR	BB/9	K/9	K	GB%	BABIP	WHIP	ERA	DRA-	WARP	MPH	FA%	Whiff%	CSP
2018	RC	HI-A	21	0	0	0	4	4	7¹	6	3	4.9	16.0	13	46.2%	.300	1.36	4.91	67	0.2				
2018	LAD	MLB	21	0	0	0	3	0	4	1	0	0.0	15.8	7	50.0%	.167	0.25	0.00	42	0.1	95.2	69.0%	39.4%	58.5%
2019	LAD	MLB	22	4	3	4	37	8	79²	59	7	3.1	9.6	85	38.8%	.257	1.08	2.49	69	1.8	97.1	60.3%	29.9%	45.5%
2020	LAD	MLB	23	3	0	0	11	10	55	45	5	2.9	7.4	45	32.3%	.256	1.15	3.27	107	0.3	95.6	56.3%	26.0%	52.1%
2021 FS	LAD	MLB	24	9	8	0	26	26	150	133	21	3.7	8.8	146	36.5%	.278	1.30	3.94	91	1.8	96.3	58.5%	28.1%	48.9%
2021 DC	LAD	MLB	24	9	6	0	39	22	130	115	18	3.7	8.8	127	36.5%	.278	1.30	3.94	91	1.9	96.3	58.5%	28.1%	48.9%

Comparables: Taijuan Walker, Junior Fernández, Sandy Alcantara

One can tell the story of Urías' 2020 in many ways. There's a sonorous historical echo here, as one lightly scouted left-hander from western Mexico stepped forward to take on a dominant role for the Dodgers in October. Even his delivery occasionally evoked Fernando Valenzuela. The former phenom also made huge, profoundly modern developmental strides, adding depth to his changeup, lateral movement to both of his breaking balls and (at long last, at the urging of Dave Roberts and Mark Prior) the consistent zone-pounding approach that had been missing in the past. Still, it feels important to sum things up this way, too: After four years of trepidation over whether Aroldis Chapman or Roberto Osuna would record the final out of a World Series, a known perpetrator of domestic violence actually did so. By most accounts, Urías has shown both contrition and thoughtful dedication to improving his behavior going forward, but he still shoved his girlfriend to the ground in a parking lot. His heroism in October doesn't erase those actions or the pain they caused—not only to his family but to victims everywhere.

Mitch White RHP   Born: 12/28/94   Age: 26   Bats: R   Throws: R   Height: 6'3"   Weight: 210   Origin: Round 2, 2016 Draft (#65 overall)

YEAR	TEAM	LVL	AGE	W	L	SV	G	GS	IP	H	HR	BB/9	K/9	K	GB%	BABIP	WHIP	ERA	DRA-	WARP	MPH	FA%	Whiff%	CSP
2018	TUL	AA	23	6	7	0	22	22	105¹	114	12	2.9	7.5	88	47.6%	.319	1.41	4.53	108	0.0				
2019	TUL	AA	24	1	0	0	7	7	30	18	3	2.1	11.1	37	43.1%	.217	0.83	2.10	61	0.7				
2019	OKC	AAA	24	3	6	0	16	13	63²	73	13	3.4	9.6	68	41.6%	.351	1.52	6.50	101	1.0				
2020	LAD	MLB	25	1	0	0	2	0	3	1	0	3.0	6.0	2	12.5%	.125	0.67	0.00	110	0.0	94.6	50.0%	22.7%	42.3%
2021 FS	LAD	MLB	26	9	9	0	26	26	150	142	25	4.1	9.0	150	40.8%	.290	1.40	4.71	105	0.7	94.6	50.0%	22.7%	42.3%
2021 DC	LAD	MLB	26	3	3	0	24	8	49	46	8	4.1	9.0	49	40.8%	.290	1.40	4.71	105	0.3	94.6	50.0%	22.7%	42.3%

Comparables: Chase De Jong, Andrew Moore, Nabil Crismatt

It's nearly time to find out whether White's mid-90s heat will play up in relief. Maybe the Dodgers could give him a sinker, since they've become the leaders of a movement back to that recently-abandoned pitch. That would help establish some lateral separation between White's heat and his pair of breaking balls because, right now, there's not enough of it. Without that separation, he's heavily reliant on changing eye levels and commanding all three pitches. For a guy with a spotty health history and a track record of control outstripping command, that might be too heavy a lift.

Alex Wood LHP Born: 01/12/91 Age: 30 Bats: R Throws: L Height: 6'4" Weight: 215 Origin: Round 2, 2012 Draft (#85 overall)

YEAR	TEAM	LVL	AGE	W	L	SV	G	GS	IP	H	HR	BB/9	K/9	K	GB%	BABIP	WHIP	ERA	DRA-	WARP	MPH	FA%	Whiff%	CSP
2018	LAD	MLB	27	9	7	0	33	27	151²	143	14	2.4	8.0	135	48.5%	.295	1.21	3.68	76	3.3	91.5	43.0%	23.8%	47.2%
2019	CIN	MLB	28	1	3	0	7	7	35²	41	11	2.3	7.6	30	36.3%	.300	1.40	5.80	129	-0.2	91.1	50.3%	24.9%	45.9%
2020	LAD	MLB	29	0	1	0	9	2	12²	17	2	4.3	10.7	15	39.0%	.385	1.82	6.39	99	0.1	92.3	48.2%	28.7%	45.0%
2021 FS	LAD	MLB	30	2	2	0	57	0	50	48	7	2.5	8.6	47	43.9%	.292	1.24	3.86	93	0.3	91.6	45.9%	25.0%	46.4%

Comparables: Kevin Gausman, Mike Clevinger, Rafael Montero

His exquisite combination of herk and jerk has afforded Wood a relatively long career, but thanks to his fading stuff and the cinch the league has tightened around situational relievers, he's running out of ways to be valuable.

SAN DIEGO PADRES

Essay by Zach Crizer

Player comments by Luis Torres and BP staff

Eric Hosmer has a look on his face. You know the one. Scott Boras is sitting next to him on the dais and, in the course of discussing what the freshly signed first baseman could mean to the San Diego Padres, has launched into a metaphoric foretelling of a volcanic eruption. Hosmer, understandably, appears to be knocked off his mental balance—the way you might be when an uncle makes the pivot from frozen waffles to the impending arrival of Judgment Day.

"I think the organization is a volcano of hot talent lava," Boras says. "To turn that lava into major league rock, that's a hard thing to do. It's a very, very difficult thing to do," the agent continues. "What Eric Hosmer brings is he went through all that in Kansas City. He along with many people were all prospects. They were, too, that major league lava, and they turned into championship rocks. When you can have a young veteran champion, I think your chances of guiding lava into rocks are pretty good, and I think that's the destiny and the plan."

That word: *plan*. The Padres always seem to have plans. One of the most salient lessons of semi-recent psychological research—and extremely recent universal human experience—dictates that we are terrible at predicting the future. The Padres are proof that teams often are, too. Bad at assessing the risks we face and bad at gauging the chances of our dreams coming true. It's a testament to the power of human adaptability that we survive putting ourselves in so many positions to escape.

As baseball fans, we suffer from unrealistic optimism: Our rebuild isn't in danger of stalling out and drifting perilously back toward the launch pad (that only happens to the Phillies). Every prospect will land. Every trade will pay dividends tomorrow. Our core will coalesce into not just a moment of glory, but an era of unmatched prosperity. The modern analytical movement has moved to counter this blindness, throwing open the shutters on baseball's dreamers. But then there are the Padres, who court the peril of grandiose expectations. From an initial abject failure sprung a prophecy brought to a sort of fruition, and from that an even bigger dream that suddenly involves Blake Snell and Yu Darvish, a new spectacular unseen promise.

SAN DIEGO PADRES PROSPECTUS
2020 W-L: 37-23, 2ND IN NL WEST

Pythag	.639	2nd	dWin%	.567	3rd
RS/G	5.42	3rd	B-Age	27.3	5th
RA/G	4.02	8th	P-Age	28.2	14th
DRC+	110	4th	FIP	4.01	6th
DRA-	89	7th	DER	.703	14th
Payroll	$67M	10th	M$/MW	$2.6M	12th

- Opened 2004
- Open air
- Natural surface
- Fence profile: 5' to 12'

Three-Year Park Factors

Runs	Runs/RH	Runs/LH	HR/RH	HR/LH
96	97	94	96	91

Top Hitter WARP	2.1 Manny Machado
Top Pitcher WARP	2.1 Dinelson Lamet
Top Prospect	CJ Abrams

Payroll History (in millions)

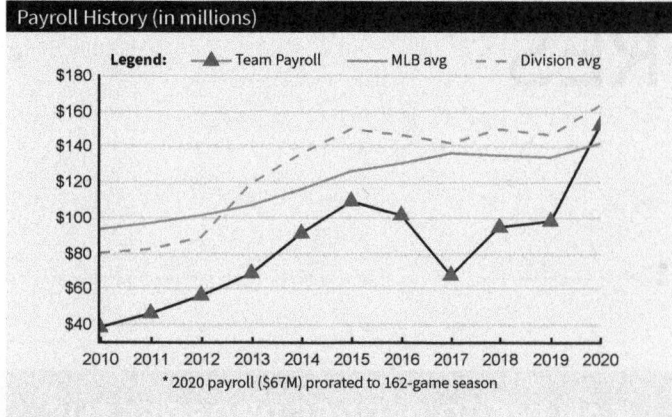

Legend: Team Payroll — MLB avg — Division avg

* 2020 payroll ($67M) prorated to 162-game season

Future Commitments (in millions)

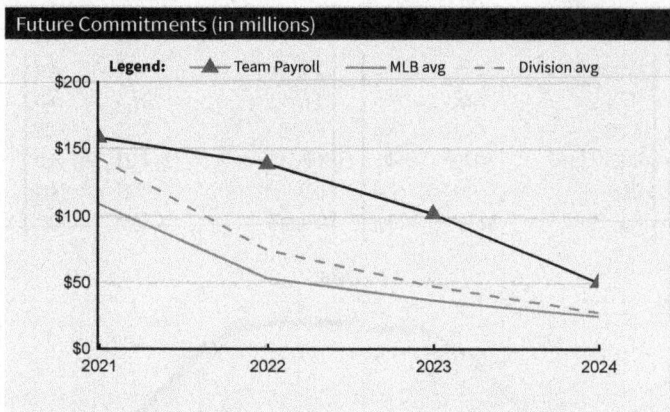

Legend: Team Payroll — MLB avg — Division avg

Farm System Ranking

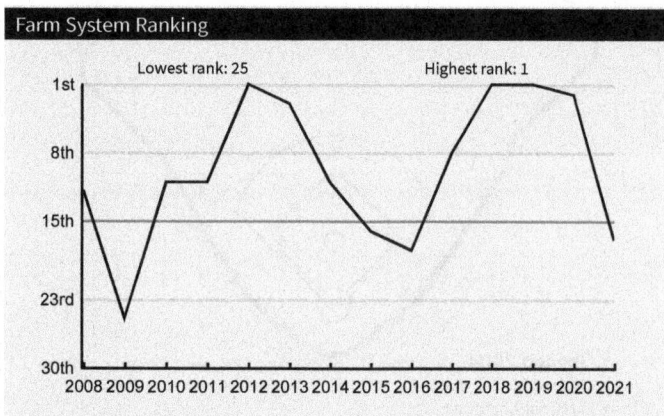

Lowest rank: 25   Highest rank: 1

Personnel

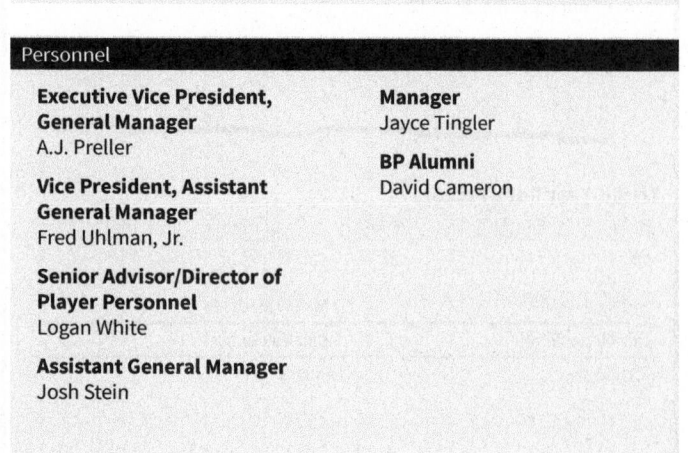

Executive Vice President, General Manager
A.J. Preller

Vice President, Assistant General Manager
Fred Uhlman, Jr.

Senior Advisor/Director of Player Personnel
Logan White

Assistant General Manager
Josh Stein

Manager
Jayce Tingler

BP Alumni
David Cameron

On the day the club inked Hosmer, the gathering heat emanated chiefly from Fernando Tatis Jr., who was already a top-10 prospect in baseball. Lean, lanky and impossibly springy, the shortstop is the self-evident icon of the Padres in a microcosmic way almost too apt to be possible. Tatis is kinetic and potential energy in one. He was brought to the organization in the dismantling of A.J. Preller's first swing at contention—a fruit of the fire—and his rapid ascent from James Shields trade deep cut to San Diego Baseball Frodo heralded that this plan might be the one to rule them all.

These heightened hopes were built on something sturdier, or at least something resembling the game's modern model. Build a system, promote cheap young stars, smooth out the roster through free agency. But as the Los Angeles Dodgers' dominance of the NL West marched on, Hosmer didn't turn out to be the immediate spark San Diego might have hoped. The new plan was beginning to look suspiciously similar to the old plan, the one that brought Matt Kemp's infectious smile and arthritic hip, a brief and costly glimmer of hope. By the time the Boston Red Sox thwarted the Dodgers and defensive savant Yasmani Grandal in the 2018 World Series, the franchises were reaching feverish levels of anxious yearning—the Dodgers for rings, the Padres for relevance.

Needing to feel some shift, or perhaps to provide a boost while they waited, the Padres leapt at the chance to add Manny Machado in free agency. Meanwhile, the farm system blossomed. When Tatis and Machado made their San Diego debuts simultaneously on Opening Day 2019, side by side, it was hard not to think the team had definitely, absolutely entered a new phase.

Seven months and 85 losses later, the Padres fired manager Andy Green. A few days after that, then-chairman Ron Fowler called the decisive late-season slump his "worst 2 ½ months of ownership." In a conversation with players, then a chat with fans, and then in an interview with the San Diego Union-Tribune, he was surprisingly frank (refreshingly so, in the contemporary world of ownership margin-measuring).

"I said if we don't win in 2020, heads will roll," Fowler told the paper.

The Padres won.

In the hushed, faraway world of 2020, they were the team that did the most to dissolve the screen between viewer and action. Tatis rocketed out to the best start of any player in the league, drawing the attention of more and more wandering eyes. When he pounced on an innocuous 3-0 pitch against the lowly Texas Rangers, it sparked and absorbed all the oxygen in the baseball ecosystem for days on end. With takes burning around them, the Padres reacted with a delirious run of grand slams that cemented their status as the best circus in town for a socially distanced populace. The Padres, their fanbase perennially hemmed into the corner of the country by Dodger blue, was rapidly becoming every city's second-favorite team.

Machado turned the page on his middling 2019 season so thoroughly that it was eventually he, not Tatis, who figured most prominently in MVP discussions. But it wasn't just the new wave that led this charge; the punchlines of old forgotten plans re-emerged. Hosmer hit like a star as well as a leader. The enigmatic Wil Myers posted a career (third of a) year. Jurickson Profar played well, and often.

The schedule provided no shortage of chances to measure progress. Sequestered to regional play for 2020, the Padres were sentenced to contest one-sixth of their games against the Dodgers. From the first meeting, on Aug. 3, the games were rapid-fire exercises in building and shaking confidence. Trent Grisham homered against Walker Buehler as part of a torrid start. Little-discussed trade acquisition Jake Cronenworth appeared as a replacement for an injured Eric Hosmer and started making leaping grabs at first base. Dinelson Lamet faced off with Dustin May. The Padres lost the series, 2-1, but felt credible.

A week later they again hurled themselves up against that overstuffed behemoth of talent, this time splitting a four-game set. It appeared, as the two teams stampeded toward and into the playoffs, that their only NL rivals were each other. Still, the Padres almost stumbled on the way to their October trial.

And it was in the NL wild-card series against St. Louis that the Padres put the stench of the contenders that weren't behind them. Backed into a corner in the three-game series, the grave, metallic taste of a fluke crept in. What if the late season fade was a sign of things to come for Tatis? What if it was just a hot 60 games? What if they don't do it in a full season? What if they never do this in front of actual corporeal fans?

Mid-2010s despair was burbling to the surface when Tatis and Machado finally struck in the sixth inning of Game 2, erasing a four-run deficit with back-to-back home runs, darts into the seats beyond left field. The coup de grâce arrived an inning later, as Tatis belted a backbreaking second homer and propelled his bat into the sky. The camera trembled in a hollowed out park, an eruption. As they left home for the last time in 2020, after vanquishing their foes in Game 3, fans assembled in person outside the gates of Petco Park. They waited for the players who had lifted their expectations and they cheered them on—reveling in the glow, fanning the flames.

San Diego's breakout season eventually ended at the hands of those Dodgers, the juggernauts they hope to replace. But there were mitigating circumstances behind the Division Series sweep. Injuries rendered ascendant ace Lamet and trade deadline acquisition Mike Clevinger moot, kneecapping the starting rotation and eventually the whole staff. The pitching wore so thin that prospect Ryan Weathers was summoned to make his major-league debut in the least friendly of circumstances. In the end, it gave Padres fans a wide berth to keep chasing the comparison, and Preller an obvious area for upgrades. By the time 2020 actually ended, Padres fans could view their weakness as fortified, their Dodgers problem as addressed. They could say "Wait til next year" not with resignation, but with an edge.

⚾   ⚾   ⚾

"Affective forecasting" is the practice of predicting how you will feel in the future. Daniel Gilbert and Timothy Wilson coined the term in the 1990s, giving a name to the undercurrent that sways so many decisions. While they were at it, they documented just how bad we are at this sort of prediction too.

We overestimate how far the pendulum will swing in either direction, traumatic or triumphant. The good news, as Gilbert explained in an interview with Smithsonian Magazine, is that people tend to recover from tragedy much more quickly and completely than they would ever expect. He continues: "The bad news is that the good things that happen to us don't feel as good or last as long as we think they will. So all that wonderful stuff we're aiming for—winning the lottery, getting promoted, whatever we think will change our lives—probably won't do it after all. We're resilient in both directions. We rebound from distress but we also rebound from joy."

"Wait til next year" is the universal baseball fan signal for this subconscious rebound, and also for a particular sort of unquenchable dissatisfaction. The long-smoldering Los Angeles core no longer needs to utter that rite of the fall. They proceeded to win it all in 2020, finally, ending a drought that lasted 30 years and intensified into a pox upon a mighty team's house over the past half decade. Like if the Cubs or Red Sox sagas were adapted to a one-act play.

Sports are arranged to unravel the hedonic treadmill problem by dropping an actual destination on the map once annually and firing the starting gun. It's an appealingly condensed, low-stakes plaything version of the pursuit of happiness where a discrete goal is either achieved or missed. It's hard to say it works any better than our real life attempts at setting satisfying goals, though.

Relevance and rings. Fans crave one until the moment they have it. Then they crave the other.

If there was a single moment that the city of San Diego crossed that line, it was on December 28, when the organization made its own priorities transparent. In the span of 12 hours the Padres rotation was remade via the thunderous dual trades for Darvish and Snell. While both men are under contract for three years, there can be no confusion: The volcano is ready.

⚾   ⚾   ⚾

There isn't much evidence the two forms of desire can coexist within the same collective psyche. But if there's ever been a team with the conditions to forge a fusion, it might be these Padres.

Birthed in 1969, the franchise has still never won a World Series, but it doesn't need that phrase either. The marketing department has to talk of trophies now, but fans should resist the urge to pin this group's hopes to a title. Yes, championships are the salvation we are promised—and few have ever unleashed more joy into the world than Chicago's triumph in 2016. They're also exactly the sort of carrots that dart beyond one's grasp. When thirst for a ring rules all, the quest to quench it can turn into a depressing rush to nowhere. The day when this team and the memories it created get parted out for Single-A arms will come soon enough.

In the realm of stimuli-seeking fandom, the choice between relief and revelation should be an obvious one. How sad it would be to fixate on the future, after all, when the Padres are so damn fun in the present? But as with rapturous doomsday predictions or, say, volcanic eruptions, calamity and creation are sometimes hard to separate.

The modern game of baseball makes its money in the future tense: the projection, the prospect list, the promises. Blake Snell and Yu Darvish trying on their new jerseys for the first time. Ownership reinforcing their beliefs. *We're going to win.* And yet the moments where we can live most vicariously and most vividly through a baseball team dance on the tightrope between that calamity and creation. Like Hosmer's mad dash home in the clinching game of the 2015 World Series—dynamic, breathtaking and emblematic of those Royals teams—the peak of fan experience is in heated moments of fluidity. It's the swing of a Tatis Jr. home run, existing in all tenses at once.

This team's temperature is still rising. It could be that this Padres core wins a title, or several titles. It could be they win no titles at all. Yes, the prediction Boras made for the Padres was of championships. It envisioned lava turning to rock, a denouement; cooling, solidifying. But the part that spoke to the energy of the moment, that made it on the T-shirt, was the lava. ■

—Zach Crizer is the baseball editor at Yahoo Sports.

HITTERS

★ ★ ★ *2021 Top 101 Prospect* **#10** ★ ★ ★

CJ Abrams SS Born: 10/03/00 Age: 20 Bats: L Throws: R Height: 6'2" Weight: 185 Origin: Round 1, 2019 Draft (#6 overall)

YEAR	TEAM	LVL	AGE	PA	R	2B	3B	HR	RBI	BB	K	SB	CS	Whiff%	AVG/OBP/SLG	DRC+	BABIP	BRR	FRAA	WARP
2019	SD1	ROK	18	156	40	12	8	3	22	10	14	14	6		.401/.442/.662	198	.425	-0.7	SS(28): 6.9	2.5
2019	FW	LO-A	18	9	1	1	0	0	0	1	0	1	0		.250/.333/.375	121	.250	0.1	SS(1): -0.1	0.0
2021 FS	SD	MLB	20	600	47	27	5	8	53	31	132	30	10		.225/.270/.337	66	.280	6.1	SS 5	0.5

Abrams, the sixth pick in the 2019 draft, is one of the top shortstop prospects in baseball thanks to his above-average power-speed potential. If there's one thing the Padres need, it's another dynamic young shortstop.

★ ★ ★ *2021 Top 101 Prospect* **#61** ★ ★ ★

Luis Campusano C Born: 09/29/98 Age: 22 Bats: R Throws: R Height: 5'11" Weight: 232 Origin: Round 2, 2017 Draft (#39 overall)

YEAR	TEAM	LVL	AGE	PA	R	2B	3B	HR	RBI	BB	K	SB	CS	Whiff%	AVG/OBP/SLG	DRC+	BABIP	BRR	FRAA	WARP
2018	FW	LO-A	19	284	26	11	0	3	40	19	43	0	1		.288/.345/.365	116	.335	-1.1	C(38): -0.8, 1B(4): 0.2	0.8
2019	LE	HI-A	20	482	63	31	1	15	80	52	57	0	0		.321/.394/.508	167	.336	-4.4	C(76): -2.6, 1B(2): 0.0	3.9
2020	SD	MLB	22	4	2	0	0	1	1	0	2	0	0	37.5%	.333/.500/1.333	81				0.0
2021 FS	SD	MLB	22	600	61	26	1	17	72	40	138	0	0	37.5%	.248/.304/.398	94	.299	-0.6	C -1, 1B 0	1.8
2021 DC	SD	MLB	22	130	13	5	0	3	15	8	29	0	0	37.5%	.248/.304/.398	94	.299	-0.1	C 0	0.4

Comparables: Alejandro Kirk, Jarrod Saltalamacchia, Chance Sisco

In the span of two months, Campusano experienced the high of hitting a home run in his big-league debut, and the low of being arrested in Georgia for felony marijuana possession. Per the *San Diego Union-Tribune*, Campusano had 79 grams of weed in his possession when he was pulled over. State law stipulates that having more than 28.35 grams (or an ounce) is a felony that is punishable by up to 10 years in jail. If Campusano's arrest is a blemish on anything, it's on a society that stomachs such harsh penalties for harmless acts.

Victor Caratini C Born: 08/17/93 Age: 27 Bats: S Throws: R Height: 6'1" Weight: 215 Origin: Round 2, 2013 Draft (#65 overall)

YEAR	TEAM	LVL	AGE	PA	R	2B	3B	HR	RBI	BB	K	SB	CS	Whiff%	AVG/OBP/SLG	DRC+	BABIP	BRR	FRAA	WARP
2018	IOW	AAA	24	137	13	7	0	4	22	18	25	0	0		.313/.409/.478	138	.364	-0.6	C(18): -2.2, 1B(12): 1.6, 3B(1): -0.0	0.8
2018	CHC	MLB	24	200	21	7	0	2	21	12	42	0	0	22.1%	.232/.293/.304	69	.290	-0.6	C(37): -0.8, 1B(20): 0.5, 3B(3): -0.0	0.0
2019	CHC	MLB	25	279	31	11	0	11	34	29	59	1	0	22.4%	.266/.348/.447	102	.305	-1.4	C(59): 3.7, 1B(23): -0.5, 3B(2): -0.1	1.5
2020	CHC	MLB	27	132	10	7	0	1	16	12	31	0	1	23.6%	.241/.333/.328	85	.321	-1.5	C(22): -0.4, 1B(3): 0.0	0.0
2021 FS	SD	MLB	27	600	62	21	1	15	63	55	141	1	0	22.8%	.241/.323/.373	93	.300	0.1	C -1, 1B 0	1.4
2021 DC	SD	MLB	27	195	20	7	0	4	20	18	45	0	0	22.8%	.241/.323/.373	93	.300	0.0	C 0	0.4

Comparables: Sal Fasano, Chris Snyder, Ben Davis

The advent of the universal DH seemed like a prime opportunity for the Cubs to move Kyle Schwarber out of left field. Instead, they prioritized finding additional playing time for Caratini, who hit like a starter in 2019 but remained blocked by Willson Contreras at catcher. Caratini received more starts at DH than any other Cub, but his offensive breakout didn't carry over—he struck out more frequently, walked less and his power evaporated entirely. Once thought to be undercast as a backup, Caratini's step backward qualifies as a disappointment. Oh well; he remains a solid defender who should continue to find work spelling starters behind the dish. He'll try to find room to work in a crowded Padres backstop rotation following a December trade, though his relationship with Yu Darvish should give him a leg up.

YEAR	TEAM	P. COUNT	FRM RUNS	BLK RUNS	THRW RUNS	TOT RUNS
2018	CHC	4981	-1.0	0.3	0.1	-0.6
2018	IOW	2846	-1.9	0.0	-0.1	-2.0
2019	CHC	6899	3.4	0.9	-0.1	4.2
2020	CHC	2834	0.9	-0.1	0.0	0.8
2021	SD	3608	0.2	-0.3	0.1	0.0

Jason Castro C Born: 06/18/87 Age: 34 Bats: L Throws: R Height: 6'3" Weight: 215 Origin: Round 1, 2008 Draft (#10 overall)

YEAR	TEAM	LVL	AGE	PA	R	2B	3B	HR	RBI	BB	K	SB	CS	Whiff%	AVG/OBP/SLG	DRC+	BABIP	BRR	FRAA	WARP
2018	MIN	MLB	31	74	4	3	0	1	3	9	26	0	0	29.8%	.143/.257/.238	57	.216	-0.7	C(19): 2.5	0.2
2019	MIN	MLB	32	275	39	9	0	13	30	33	88	0	0	37.1%	.232/.332/.435	100	.307	1.0	C(78): 3.5	1.9
2020	SD	MLB	33	30	3	5	0	0	3	2	10	0	0	30.4%	.179/.233/.357	86	.278	-0.4	C(9): 0.2	0.0
2020	LAA	MLB	33	62	5	4	0	2	6	10	23	0	0	36.5%	.192/.323/.385	87	.296	-0.3	C(17): -0.3	0.1
2021 FS	SD	MLB	34	600	63	25	1	18	62	68	211	1	0	35.8%	.204/.302/.363	81	.300	-0.5	C 4	1.4

Comparables: Jason LaRue, David Ross, Tom Wilson

YEAR	TEAM	P. COUNT	FRM RUNS	BLK RUNS	THRW RUNS	TOT RUNS
2018	MIN	3157	1.4	0.9	0.1	2.3
2019	MIN	10695	6.1	-1.9	-0.3	3.9
2020	SD	1135	0.4	-0.2	0.0	0.1
2020	LAA	2172	0.8	-0.3	0.0	0.5
2021	SD	16650	5.9	-1.6	0.3	4.6

Castro was part of the Padres' overhaul of their dismal catching situation at the trade deadline. He departs as he arrived, a serviceable though aging catcher. Unsurprisingly, his defense and framing skills are eroding, and he has struck out in over a third of his plate appearances since 2018. At his age, that isn't going to get any better. On the bright side, plate discipline ages well, and Castro's is still quite good. A team with a need at catcher could do a lot worse than taking a chance on him for 2021.

Jake Cronenworth SS Born: 01/21/94 Age: 27 Bats: L Throws: R Height: 6'0" Weight: 187 Origin: Round 7, 2015 Draft (#208 overall)

YEAR	TEAM	LVL	AGE	PA	R	2B	3B	HR	RBI	BB	K	SB	CS	Whiff%	AVG/OBP/SLG	DRC+	BABIP	BRR	FRAA	WARP
2018	MTG	AA	24	470	75	18	4	4	50	43	69	21	3		.254/.323/.344	106	.291	5.6	SS(59): -4.6, 3B(28): 5.4, 2B(18): -2.5	1.6
2018	DUR	AAA	24	26	4	3	0	0	2	1	5	1	0		.240/.269/.360	93	.300	1.1	3B(5): -0.5, 2B(1): 0.0, SS(1): -0.2	0.1
2019	DUR	AAA	25	406	75	26	4	10	45	49	62	12	5		.334/.429/.520	137	.382	0.7	SS(64): -1.7, 2B(11): 1.3, P(7): 0.1	3.4
2020	SD	MLB	26	192	26	15	3	4	20	18	30	3	1	16.4%	.285/.354/.477	115	.324	-0.1	2B(38): -1.1, SS(11): -1.3, 1B(10): 1.2	0.8
2021 FS	SD	MLB	27	600	61	31	4	11	64	53	122	5	2	16.4%	.254/.330/.395	99	.311	1.7	SS -1, 2B 0	1.9
2021 DC	SD	MLB	27	554	56	29	4	10	59	49	113	4	1	16.4%	.254/.330/.395	99	.311	1.6	LF 0, SS -1	1.7

Comparables: Josh Rutledge, Justin Sellers, Luis Valbuena

The word "cronen" is derived from a Middle Dutch word that means "to crown." That seems fitting, as Cronenworth demonstrated his worth for the NL Rookie of the Year Award. You usually don't see players get traded away from the Rays and get better. Cronenworth proved to be an exception. Though he was excellent in Triple-A in 2019, the Rays seemingly decided they had enough middle-infield depth to include him in the Tommy Pham trade. Given that Cronenworth seemed more likely to be a bench piece (and, perhaps, also a bullpen piece), it was a worthwhile gamble. Credit to the Padres for seeing something more, and credit to Cronenworth for making the most of his shot, but beware the small samples of 2020: Cronenworth cooled down the stretch and we won't know what's signal and what's noise for a while.

Greg Garcia 2B Born: 08/08/89 Age: 31 Bats: L Throws: R Height: 6'0" Weight: 200 Origin: Round 7, 2010 Draft (#229 overall)

YEAR	TEAM	LVL	AGE	PA	R	2B	3B	HR	RBI	BB	K	SB	CS	Whiff%	AVG/OBP/SLG	DRC+	BABIP	BRR	FRAA	WARP
2018	STL	MLB	28	208	15	6	0	3	15	20	37	3	1	17.5%	.221/.309/.304	80	.259	0.2	2B(31): -0.4, SS(17): 1.9, 3B(15): -0.5	0.4
2019	SD	MLB	29	372	52	13	4	4	31	53	83	0	2	16.1%	.248/.364/.354	87	.323	2.4	2B(74): 2.1, 3B(13): -0.6, SS(9): 0.2	1.1
2020	SD	MLB	31	71	6	3	0	0	11	7	18	1	0	18.3%	.200/.279/.250	73	.279	1.0	2B(11): 0.4, 3B(10): 0.6	0.2
2021 FS	SD	MLB	31	600	61	20	2	8	52	73	143	3	2	16.7%	.236/.342/.336	92	.311	-0.2	2B -2, 3B -1	1.1

Comparables: Dave Berg, Damian Jackson, Frank Menechino

When your only offensive skill is being able to take a walk...well, sooner or later you're going to be told to take a walk. Garcia, who barely hit last year and is on the wrong side of 30, is nearing that point.

Trent Grisham CF Born: 11/01/96 Age: 24 Bats: L Throws: L Height: 5'11" Weight: 224 Origin: Round 1, 2015 Draft (#15 overall)

YEAR	TEAM	LVL	AGE	PA	R	2B	3B	HR	RBI	BB	K	SB	CS	Whiff%	AVG/OBP/SLG	DRC+	BABIP	BRR	FRAA	WARP
2018	BLX	AA	21	405	45	10	2	7	31	63	87	11	3		.233/.356/.337	108	.292	-1.8	RF(85): 3.5, LF(15): 1.1, CF(6): 2.3	1.0
2019	BLX	AA	22	283	34	14	3	13	41	44	50	6	4		.254/.371/.504	161	.269	-0.4	CF(59): 3.3	3.1
2019	SA	AAA	22	158	37	8	3	13	30	23	22	6	1		.381/.471/.776	192	.384	0.3	CF(31): 3.3, LF(3): -0.1	2.6
2019	MIL	MLB	22	183	24	6	2	6	24	20	47	1	0	23.7%	.231/.328/.410	89	.283	2.2	CF(21): -1.1, LF(17): -1.8, RF(16): 0.3	0.3
2020	SD	MLB	24	252	42	8	3	10	26	31	64	10	1	24.4%	.251/.352/.456	94	.310	-2.7	CF(59): 2.1	0.7
2021 FS	SD	MLB	24	600	78	23	4	21	62	73	166	9	3	24.2%	.236/.336/.422	105	.304	4.0	CF -2, LF 0	2.3
2021 DC	SD	MLB	24	554	72	21	4	19	57	68	153	9	3	24.2%	.236/.336/.422	105	.304	3.7	CF -2	2.4

Comparables: Rick Monday, Larry Hisle, Mack Jones

Grisham was always a frustrating prospect coming up through the Brewers' system. The former 15th-overall pick never quite lived up to expectations, especially for someone who was considered to be a "safe" hitting prospect. After an underwhelming major-league debut in 2019, the Brewers seemingly gave up on him and traded him to San Diego as part of the Luis Urías deal. Now that looks like a mistake. A notoriously passive hitter, Grisham started swinging at pitches in the zone more frequently while still drawing plenty of walks. Even if his true-talent level is that of a below-average hitter, the fact that he can stick in center field should make him a starter for years to come.

★ ★ ★ *2021 Top 101 Prospect* **#64** ★ ★ ★

Robert Hassell III **CF**   Born: 08/15/01   Age: 19   Bats: L   Throws: L   Height: 6'2"   Weight: 195   Origin: Round 1, 2020 Draft (#8 overall)

Leading up to the draft, there were persistent rumors that the Padres just absolutely loved Hassell and his beautiful swing. They panned out when the team popped him a pick ahead of Zac Veen, a more touted prep outfielder, and quickly signed him away from his Vanderbilt commitment to bring him to the alternate site. As befitting the aesthetic adjectives attached by all to his smooth left-handed stroke, Hassell has an extremely advanced hit tool for a high school bat, along with projectable power for down the road. He was a legitimate prospect on the mound as well, enough so that there were ideas that he might be a two-way player as a pro, though the Padres aren't planning on using him as such. If he can achieve success in pro ball, he'll be one of the best outfield prospects around—maybe even one of the best prospects, period—in short order.

Hudson Head **CF**   Born: 04/08/01   Age: 20   Bats: L   Throws: L   Height: 6'1"   Weight: 180   Origin: Round 3, 2019 Draft (#84 overall)

YEAR	TEAM	LVL	AGE	PA	R	2B	3B	HR	RBI	BB	K	SB	CS	Whiff%	AVG/OBP/SLG	DRC+	BABIP	BRR	FRAA	WARP
2019	SD1	ROK	18	141	19	7	3	1	12	15	29	3	3		.283/.383/.417	124	.363	-0.3	CF(26): -5.9	0.1
2021 FS	SD	MLB	20	600	45	26	3	7	49	32	203	7	4		.205/.257/.304	53	.307	-1.6	CF -11	-2.9

Head, a center-field quality athlete with a promising stick, has a chance to be the third big-league player to hail from Winston Churchill High School in Texas, joining Scott Dunn and Randy Choate.

Eric Hosmer **1B**   Born: 10/24/89   Age: 31   Bats: L   Throws: L   Height: 6'4"   Weight: 226   Origin: Round 1, 2008 Draft (#3 overall)

YEAR	TEAM	LVL	AGE	PA	R	2B	3B	HR	RBI	BB	K	SB	CS	Whiff%	AVG/OBP/SLG	DRC+	BABIP	BRR	FRAA	WARP
2018	SD	MLB	28	677	72	31	2	18	69	62	142	7	4	27.6%	.253/.322/.398	83	.302	-2.6	1B(157): 7.8	0.1
2019	SD	MLB	29	667	72	29	2	22	99	40	163	0	3	29.0%	.265/.310/.425	86	.323	-0.2	1B(157): -3.9	-0.6
2020	SD	MLB	31	156	23	6	0	9	36	9	28	4	0	20.4%	.287/.333/.517	110	.296	0.6	1B(32): -0.1	0.3
2021 FS	SD	MLB	31	600	70	26	1	21	81	50	127	4	2	27.0%	.266/.332/.440	109	.312	-1.7	1B 0	1.3
2021 DC	SD	MLB	31	554	65	24	1	20	74	46	117	4	1	27.0%	.266/.332/.440	109	.312	-1.5	1B 0	1.2

Comparables: Eric Karros, Greg Walker, Jesus Guzman

Hosmer has benefited from the inverse of the perception issues that Manny Machado has suffered from. He is so well regarded among his peers and outsiders that people tend to believe that he is a better player than he is. Nowadays, front offices are generally smart enough not to put excess value on soft factors, but Hosmer bucked that trend to earn an eight-year, $144 million deal that looked like it was going south just two seasons in. Thankfully, he started hitting like 2017 Hosmer again before breaking his finger on September 7 on—of all things, a bunt attempt. (Say a little prayer for Dave Cameron, folks.) The biggest change for Hosmer in 2020 was putting the ball in the air a lot more frequently than in the past (34.2 percent versus 23.1 percent), which is something he had been urged to do for his entire career. If he keeps that up, who knows? Maybe reality will align with perception after all.

Ha-seong Kim **SS**   Born: 10/17/95   Age: 25   Bats: R   Throws: R   Height: 5'9"   Weight: 168   Origin: International Free Agent, 2020

Late in the season, Kiwoom announced that they would be posting their shortstop over the winter, allowing Kim to pursue a lifelong dream of playing in the major leagues. While there's some debate over how well, and how quickly, Kim's promising bat will acclimate to MLB arms, there's little doubt that he's the best hitter to ever arrive from the KBO. Easily a top-100 prospect in baseball, the 25-year-old Kim was the best athlete in the KBO last year and he's pretty clearly outgrown his native league. Offensively, he's a complete player, demonstrating his abilities to make contact, hit with power, gauge the strike zone and even steal bases. Defensively, reviews are mixed. He's a plus runner with a good first step, and he has more than enough range to play short in the big leagues. His arm is good enough as well, though not plus, and given his accuracy issues (particularly on the run) it's fair to round down and grade it as average. While he gets to plenty of balls, his hands aren't the cleanest, and when you add it all up, there's a chance that he ultimately fits better at second or third. Regardless, Kim should be at least a good regular, and if his bat translates he could be the biggest transpacific sensation since Ichiro.

Manny Machado **3B**   Born: 07/06/92   Age: 29   Bats: R   Throws: R   Height: 6'3"   Weight: 218   Origin: Round 1, 2010 Draft (#3 overall)

YEAR	TEAM	LVL	AGE	PA	R	2B	3B	HR	RBI	BB	K	SB	CS	Whiff%	AVG/OBP/SLG	DRC+	BABIP	BRR	FRAA	WARP
2018	BAL	MLB	25	413	48	21	1	24	65	45	51	8	1	20.5%	.315/.387/.575	141	.311	-0.5	SS(96): -4.5	3.5
2018	LAD	MLB	25	296	36	14	2	13	42	25	53	6	1	24.7%	.273/.338/.487	141	.296	1.4	SS(51): -4.5, 3B(16): 3.1	2.8
2019	SD	MLB	26	661	81	21	2	32	85	65	128	5	3	24.3%	.256/.334/.462	106	.274	-1.3	3B(119): -10.4, SS(37): -5.2	1.5
2020	SD	MLB	28	254	44	12	1	16	47	26	37	6	3	21.7%	.304/.370/.580	140	.297	-0.2	3B(56): 4.8	2.1
2021 FS	SD	MLB	28	600	83	24	1	31	91	57	105	6	2	23.1%	.271/.344/.500	130	.283	-1.5	3B -6, SS 0	3.1
2021 DC	SD	MLB	28	586	81	23	1	30	89	56	102	6	2	23.1%	.271/.344/.500	130	.283	-1.4	3B -6	2.7

Comparables: Casey McGehee, Ryan Zimmerman, Hank Blalock

One would have a hard time finding a player as talented and as unpopular as Machado is who lives outside of Houston (just imagine if he were an Astro) In his first full year in San Diego, those hoping for Machado to go bust got some hope. His offense was a far cry from what it was in 2018, and he didn't take well to a return to shortstop. Thankfully, the rise of Fernando Tatís Jr. allowed Machado to return to third. Not only did Machado become a defensive asset again, but he also started hitting like it was 2018. He pulled the ball more frequently and improved his plate discipline and contact rates, the latter of which was the difference between a 19.4 and 14.6 strikeout rate. His performance over a full season extrapolates to over six WARP, which would more than justify his contract and placement alongside the game's top players—even if he'll probably never receive the flowers he deserves from a fair chunk of the baseball world.

Jorge Mateo SS Born: 06/23/95 Age: 26 Bats: R Throws: R Height: 6'0" Weight: 182 Origin: International Free Agent, 2012

YEAR	TEAM	LVL	AGE	PA	R	2B	3B	HR	RBI	BB	K	SB	CS	Whiff%	AVG/OBP/SLG	DRC+	BABIP	BRR	FRAA	WARP
2018	NAS	AAA	23	510	50	17	16	3	45	29	139	25	10		.230/.280/.353	57	.316	1.1	SS(123): -0.8, 2B(4): -0.5	-0.8
2019	LV	AAA	24	566	95	29	14	19	78	29	145	24	11		.289/.330/.504	81	.366	3.2	SS(100): 16.6, 2B(14): -0.2	2.9
2020	SD	MLB	25	28	4	3	0	0	2	1	11	1	0	35.1%	.154/.185/.269	66	.267	-0.7	2B(5): 0.6, LF(3): -0.0, RF(3): -0.1	-0.1
2021 FS	SD	MLB	26	600	59	23	8	15	61	33	193	20	8	35.1%	.217/.265/.369	73	.300	5.0	2B -1, CF -1	0.2
2021 DC	SD	MLB	26	195	19	7	2	4	20	10	62	6	2	35.1%	.217/.265/.369	73	.300	1.6	3B 0, 2B 0	0.0

Comparables: Erick Mejia, Robert Andino, Jonathan Villar

It's fair to write that Mateo's only real skill is running fast. It's also fair to write that we're as surprised as you are that his comment doesn't appear in the Royals chapter.

Mitch Moreland 1B Born: 09/06/85 Age: 35 Bats: L Throws: L Height: 6'3" Weight: 245 Origin: Round 17, 2007 Draft (#530 overall)

YEAR	TEAM	LVL	AGE	PA	R	2B	3B	HR	RBI	BB	K	SB	CS	Whiff%	AVG/OBP/SLG	DRC+	BABIP	BRR	FRAA	WARP
2018	BOS	MLB	32	459	57	23	4	15	68	50	102	2	0	28.0%	.245/.325/.433	102	.288	-2.5	1B(116): 2.4	0.8
2019	BOS	MLB	33	335	48	17	1	19	58	34	74	1	0	28.1%	.252/.328/.507	111	.271	-2.6	1B(85): 4.3	1.2
2020	SD	MLB	35	73	8	5	0	2	8	4	14	0	0	29.2%	.203/.247/.362	116	.226	-0.4	1B(16): -2.0	0.0
2020	BOS	MLB	35	79	14	4	0	8	21	11	18	0	0	33.6%	.328/.430/.746	120	.341	0.1	1B(22): -0.1	0.3
2021 FS	SD	MLB	35	600	69	25	1	26	81	54	149	1	0	29.0%	.230/.308/.431	99	.268	-0.7	1B 7	1.4

Comparables: Dae-Ho Lee, Garrett Jones, Andres Galarraga

Moreland was one of the top hitters available at the deadline, a statement that says as much about the marketplace as it does about him and his hot first half. Unfortunately, he couldn't maintain his pace after shipping out west. Moreland's plate discipline took a dive after the trade and he started pressing more at the plate. The Padres were unimpressed, to the extent that they declined the same club option that appeared to be a gimme at the midway point. Moreland should, nevertheless, find work elsewhere as a platoon first baseman.

Wil Myers LF Born: 12/10/90 Age: 30 Bats: R Throws: R Height: 6'3" Weight: 207 Origin: Round 3, 2009 Draft (#91 overall)

YEAR	TEAM	LVL	AGE	PA	R	2B	3B	HR	RBI	BB	K	SB	CS	Whiff%	AVG/OBP/SLG	DRC+	BABIP	BRR	FRAA	WARP
2018	SD	MLB	27	343	39	25	1	11	39	30	94	13	1	24.9%	.253/.318/.446	90	.327	1.3	3B(36): -4.3, LF(31): 0.8, RF(10): 1.4	0.6
2019	SD	MLB	28	490	58	22	1	18	53	51	168	16	7	32.5%	.239/.321/.418	84	.344	-1.6	LF(98): -2.8, CF(66): -1.1, 1B(7): -0.3	0.0
2020	SD	MLB	30	218	34	14	2	15	40	18	56	2	1	26.4%	.288/.353/.606	138	.331	1.9	RF(52): 1.0, 1B(2): -0.1	1.8
2021 FS	SD	MLB	30	600	71	24	2	27	82	59	170	18	6	29.2%	.240/.319/.451	112	.296	2.4	RF 11, 1B -2	3.4
2021 DC	SD	MLB	30	554	65	22	2	25	75	54	157	17	5	29.2%	.240/.319/.451	112	.296	2.2	RF 10, 1B -2	3.2

Comparables: Mike Jacobs, Adam LaRoche, Ike Davis

Myers' career has been marred by inconsistency in performance, in position, in reputation. It's jarring to realize he's only entering his age-30 season—it seems that time flies when you (and everyone else) can't decide if you're a replacement-level albatross or something a little more valuable. Myers was the latter in 2020. He posted the best DRC+ of his career, and did so without being forced to play a position that was beyond his reach, like center or third base. Indeed, he had the kind of year that everyone envisioned he would have when he was a young buck. The Padres, who owe him another $45 million, hope he can have a few more of those now that he's an older buck.

Austin Nola C Born: 12/28/89 Age: 31 Bats: R Throws: R Height: 6'0" Weight: 197 Origin: Round 5, 2012 Draft (#167 overall)

YEAR	TEAM	LVL	AGE	PA	R	2B	3B	HR	RBI	BB	K	SB	CS	Whiff%	AVG/OBP/SLG	DRC+	BABIP	BRR	FRAA	WARP
2018	NO	AAA	28	262	26	16	0	2	32	27	43	2	0		.279/.370/.376	111	.333	-2.2	C(68): 6.2	1.7
2019	TAC	AAA	29	229	36	15	1	7	37	29	40	4	1		.327/.415/.520	119	.377	-3.4	C(28): 2.8, 1B(24): -0.8, 3B(3): 0.3	1.2
2019	SEA	MLB	29	267	37	12	1	10	31	23	63	1	0	23.1%	.269/.342/.454	101	.325	-0.5	1B(59): 2.4, 2B(15): 1.0, C(7): 0.4	0.9
2020	SD	MLB	31	74	9	4	0	2	9	9	17	0	0	22.4%	.222/.324/.381	119	.267	0.7	C(17): 0.3	0.6
2020	SEA	MLB	31	110	15	5	1	5	19	9	17	0	0	18.5%	.306/.373/.531	118	.325	-0.6	C(27): -0.1, 1B(2): 0.2, 3B(1): 0.0	0.8
2021 FS	SD	MLB	31	600	63	23	1	15	68	53	131	1	0	21.6%	.239/.316/.378	95	.287	-0.2	C 9, 1B 0	2.5
2021 DC	SD	MLB	31	456	48	17	1	12	52	40	99	0	0	21.6%	.239/.316/.378	95	.287	-0.2	C 8	2.3

Comparables: Brian Daubach, Adam LaRoche, Paul Sorrento

Nola, part of the Padres' haul from the Mariners at the trade deadline, took the spot vacated by Austin Hedges, who was sent to Cleveland in a separate deal. Aaron's older brother is a late bloomer, having converted to catcher when he was 27 years old. Perhaps predictably, Nola is the inverse of Hedges: he's a bat-first backstop whose mitt is tolerable, but not exceptional. Baseball analysis is built on precedent, and there's precious little of that for this kind of career arc. As such, it's hard to have confidence that Nola will continue to be one of the game's best-hitting catchers heading into his age-31 season. The Padres don't have much to lose, though, and Nola deserves the opportunity to keep going for as long as he can.

Brian O'Grady OF Born: 05/17/92 Age: 29 Bats: L Throws: R Height: 6'2" Weight: 215 Origin: Round 8, 2014 Draft (#245 overall)

YEAR	TEAM	LVL	AGE	PA	R	2B	3B	HR	RBI	BB	K	SB	CS	Whiff%	AVG/OBP/SLG	DRC+	BABIP	BRR	FRAA	WARP
2018	PNS	AA	26	214	27	12	4	6	30	27	41	4	1		.258/.354/.472	123	.294	-1.5	LF(23): -2.8, 1B(12): -0.1, RF(12): 0.5	0.1
2018	LOU	AAA	26	162	27	9	2	8	29	12	39	5	4		.306/.365/.562	135	.367	0.4	LF(29): -0.6, 1B(12): 0.6, CF(2): 0.0	0.8
2019	LOU	AAA	27	489	71	30	1	28	77	51	136	20	4		.280/.359/.550	111	.342	2.0	1B(64): -1.5, CF(33): 1.6, LF(15): 1.6	1.8
2019	CIN	MLB	27	48	4	2	1	2	3	4	17	0	0	43.6%	.190/.292/.429	75	.261	-0.5	CF(11): -0.2, LF(6): 0.1, 1B(2): -0.2	-0.1
2020	TB	MLB	28	5	2	1	0	0	0	0	1	1	0	17.6%	.400/.400/.600	83	.500	0.2	1B(1): -0.0, LF(1): -0.0, CF(1): -0.1	0.0
2021 FS	SD	MLB	29	600	60	25	4	20	65	58	190	6	2	38.9%	.213/.298/.391	86	.289	2.3	CF 5, LF 1	0.9
2021 DC	SD	MLB	29	162	16	6	1	5	17	15	51	1	0	38.9%	.213/.298/.391	86	.289	0.6	CF 1, LF 0	0.3

Comparables: Mitch Jones, Travis Ishikawa, Matt Clark

O'Grady saw action at three positions in two games last season with the Rays. His three-corners versatility and left-handed pop (he homered 30 times in 2019) should enable him to have some kind of big-league career as a bench player. The more important matter, if you ask us, is whether he'll be christened as the Notorious B.O.G. or Beef O'Grady. Can't go wrong either way, we s'pose.

Jorge Oña OF Born: 12/31/96 Age: 24 Bats: R Throws: R Height: 6'0" Weight: 235 Origin: International Free Agent, 2016

YEAR	TEAM	LVL	AGE	PA	R	2B	3B	HR	RBI	BB	K	SB	CS	Whiff%	AVG/OBP/SLG	DRC+	BABIP	BRR	FRAA	WARP
2018	LE	HI-A	21	410	44	24	2	8	44	33	110	0	2		.239/.312/.380	88	.317	-2.1	RF(59): -1.3	-1.3
2019	AMA	AA	22	103	11	2	0	5	18	11	26	2	1		.348/.417/.539	170	.433	0.7	LF(15): -2.3	0.6
2020	SD	MLB	23	15	3	1	0	1	2	2	7	0	0	54.8%	.250/.400/.583	78	.500	0.1	RF(1): -0.0	0.0
2021 FS	SD	MLB	24	600	60	20	2	18	65	47	211	1	0	54.8%	.218/.290/.364	82	.319	0.4	RF -6, LF -4	-0.9
2021 DC	SD	MLB	24	293	29	9	0	8	32	23	103	0	0	54.8%	.218/.290/.364	82	.319	0.2	RF -3, LF -2	-0.4

Comparables: Rymer Liriano, Zoilo Almonte, Marcell Ozuna

Oña's strikeout and fielding woes have always been concerning, but the universal DH could well give him a chance at a career that entails more than being a designated pinch-hitter—well, sort of, anyway.

Tommy Pham LF Born: 03/08/88 Age: 33 Bats: R Throws: R Height: 6'1" Weight: 223 Origin: Round 16, 2006 Draft (#496 overall)

YEAR	TEAM	LVL	AGE	PA	R	2B	3B	HR	RBI	BB	K	SB	CS	Whiff%	AVG/OBP/SLG	DRC+	BABIP	BRR	FRAA	WARP
2018	TB	MLB	30	174	35	7	6	7	22	25	43	5	1	28.4%	.343/.448/.622	121	.442	0.9	LF(37): -0.5, CF(3): -0.2	0.9
2018	STL	MLB	30	396	67	11	0	14	41	42	97	10	6	24.1%	.248/.331/.399	121	.303	3.8	CF(91): -5.1	2.3
2019	TB	MLB	31	654	77	33	2	21	68	81	123	25	4	20.2%	.273/.369/.450	115	.316	-0.2	LF(123): -9.6	2.0
2020	SD	MLB	32	125	13	2	0	3	12	15	27	6	0	27.0%	.211/.312/.312	91	.253	0.1	LF(18): -0.6	0.1
2021 FS	SD	MLB	33	600	70	21	2	18	71	73	153	18	5	22.6%	.248/.347/.406	112	.316	3.0	LF -5, CF 0	2.5
2021 DC	SD	MLB	33	554	65	19	1	17	65	67	141	17	5	22.6%	.248/.347/.406	112	.316	2.7	LF -5	2.0

Comparables: Jason Bay, Kirk Gibson, Justin Upton

The phamtastic Pham was the headliner in the trade that also brought Cronenworth to town, though you wouldn't get that impression by looking at their statlines. Indeed, they more or less swapped the offensive performances that projections and analysts alike expected them to have. Pham's rough season can be blamed on his health. He tested positive for COVID-19 in July, then missed a month of the season because of a broken bone in his left hand. This offseason he was stabbed—one of those cases, evidently, of being at the wrong strip club at the wrong time. Given his track record, he should be a bounce-back candidate in 2021—right in time for his walk year.

Jurickson Profar OF Born: 02/20/93 Age: 28 Bats: S Throws: R Height: 6'0" Weight: 184 Origin: International Free Agent, 2009

YEAR	TEAM	LVL	AGE	PA	R	2B	3B	HR	RBI	BB	K	SB	CS	Whiff%	AVG/OBP/SLG	DRC+	BABIP	BRR	FRAA	WARP
2018	TEX	MLB	25	594	82	35	6	20	77	54	88	10	0	18.7%	.254/.335/.458	109	.269	2.2	SS(68): -8.6, 3B(51): -3.7, 1B(24): 0.3	1.8
2019	OAK	MLB	26	518	65	24	2	20	67	48	75	9	1	20.2%	.218/.301/.410	96	.218	0.4	2B(124): -12.5, LF(7): 0.0, 1B(1): -0.0	0.2
2020	SD	MLB	27	202	28	6	0	7	25	15	28	7	1	20.2%	.278/.343/.428	104	.293	2.0	LF(36): -2.4, 2B(17): -3.5, RF(2): 0.2	0.3
2021 FS	SD	MLB	28	600	70	25	2	19	72	55	101	6	1	19.8%	.251/.333/.418	110	.276	1.5	SS -5, 2B -6	1.6

Comparables: D'Angelo Jimenez, Ted Lepcio, Ray Durham

After a disappointing year in Oakland, Profar found salvation in San Diego in the company of two longtime admirers, Preller and Tingler. Not only did he have one of his best offensive seasons, he expanded his (at-times shaky) defensive role by splitting time between left field and second base. Profar is never going to live up to the star potential he was believed to have as a prospect, but he's hitting the free-agent market after having played in nearly 90 percent of his teams' games over the last three seasons and he should find a starting role for his age-28 season.

Fernando Tatis Jr. SS Born: 01/02/99 Age: 22 Bats: R Throws: R Height: 6'3" Weight: 217 Origin: International Free Agent, 2015

YEAR	TEAM	LVL	AGE	PA	R	2B	3B	HR	RBI	BB	K	SB	CS	Whiff%	AVG/OBP/SLG	DRC+	BABIP	BRR	FRAA	WARP
2018	SA	AA	19	394	77	22	4	16	43	33	109	16	5		.286/.355/.507	136	.370	3.0	SS(83): -1.9	2.4
2019	SD	MLB	20	372	61	13	6	22	53	30	110	16	6	35.3%	.317/.379/.590	118	.410	7.1	SS(83): 0.9	3.4
2020	SD	MLB	21	257	50	11	2	17	45	27	61	11	3	28.2%	.277/.366/.571	126	.306	0.7	SS(57): -5.5	0.9
2021 FS	SD	MLB	22	600	85	22	4	31	79	50	165	20	8	31.6%	.254/.323/.487	121	.306	1.7	SS 0, 2B 0	3.7
2021 DC	SD	MLB	22	554	79	21	4	28	73	46	153	18	7	31.6%	.254/.323/.487	121	.306	1.5	SS 0	3.4

Comparables: Darryl Strawberry, Bo Bichette, Ronald Acuña Jr.

Hey, did you know Tatís' father once hit two grand slams in an—we're kidding, we're kidding. Tatís has more than earned the right to stop sharing the stage with his old man, even if that fun fact will never die—broadcasters were still harping on Mike Piazza's being a 62nd-round draft pick when he was pushing 40. In 2020, Tatis continued his metamorphosis from top prospect to top player. He was never going to sustain his .410 BABIP of 2019, but he altered his game to adjust for that, making significant improvements to his strikeout and walk rates. He hit the ball harder, too—much, much harder. According to Statcast, Tatis had a league-leading 96.1 mph exit velocity in 2020, as compared to 90.4 mph in 2019. As for defense, the only way Tatís is going to win a Gold Glove is with his bat, but he did a better job of syncing his internal clock and there's no reason to think he's sliding off the six spot anytime soon. At just 21 years old, he seems certain to be a perennial MVP candidate.

PITCHERS

Austin Adams RHP Born: 05/05/91 Age: 30 Bats: R Throws: R Height: 6'3" Weight: 220 Origin: Round 8, 2012 Draft (#267 overall)

YEAR	TEAM	LVL	AGE	W	L	SV	G	GS	IP	H	HR	BB/9	K/9	K	GB%	BABIP	WHIP	ERA	DRA-	WARP	MPH	FA%	Whiff%	CSP
2018	SYR	AAA	27	1	4	9	41	0	46¹	47	1	3.9	15.2	78	40.2%	.447	1.45	3.50	28	1.9				
2018	WAS	MLB	27	0	0	0	2	0	1	1	0	27.0	0.0	0	50.0%	.250	4.00	0.00	223	-0.1	96.2	58.3%	20.0%	44.0%
2019	FRE	AAA	28	0	1	1	8	0	10	7	0	2.7	18.0	20	47.1%	.412	1.00	2.70	33	0.4				
2019	SEA	MLB	28	2	2	0	29	2	31	20	4	4.1	14.8	51	49.2%	.291	1.10	3.77	54	0.9	96.6	35.2%	41.1%	45.6%
2019	WAS	MLB	28	0	0	0	1	0	1	0	0	18.0	18.0	2	100.0%	.000	2.00	9.00	50	0.0	95.7	51.5%	22.2%	35.2%
2020	SD	MLB	29	0	0	0	3	0	4	3	1	4.5	15.8	7	50.0%	.286	1.25	4.50	85	0.1	94.6	16.2%	48.0%	40.9%
2021 FS	SD	MLB	30	1	1	0	57	0	50	35	5	5.5	14.0	77	44.5%	.300	1.32	3.57	82	0.6	96.2	33.2%	41.3%	44.3%
2021 DC	SD	MLB	30	1	1	0	33	0	35	24	3	5.5	14.0	54	44.5%	.300	1.32	3.57	82	0.5	96.2	33.2%	41.3%	44.3%

Comparables: Shawn Armstrong, Richard Rodríguez, Emilio Pagán

Adams didn't make his season debut until late in the season because of a torn ACL suffered in 2019. When he took the mound, he was more reliant on his wipeout slider than ever, throwing it nearly 90 percent of the time. His high walk rate will make Padres fans and coaches nervous, but his excellent ability to miss bats should help limit the damage.

Dan Altavilla RHP Born: 09/08/92 Age: 28 Bats: R Throws: R Height: 5'11" Weight: 226 Origin: Round 5, 2014 Draft (#141 overall)

YEAR	TEAM	LVL	AGE	W	L	SV	G	GS	IP	H	HR	BB/9	K/9	K	GB%	BABIP	WHIP	ERA	DRA-	WARP	MPH	FA%	Whiff%	CSP
2018	TAC	AAA	25	0	2	0	9	1	6²	9	2	5.4	9.4	7	34.8%	.333	1.95	9.45	56	0.2				
2018	SEA	MLB	25	3	2	0	22	0	20²	11	2	6.5	10.0	23	37.8%	.209	1.26	2.61	77	0.4	98.3	53.1%	32.0%	43.9%
2019	ARK	AA	26	3	0	4	14	0	16¹	7	1	1.7	13.8	25	41.9%	.200	0.61	1.10	37	0.6				
2019	TAC	AAA	26	2	1	0	14	0	14	11	0	7.1	16.1	25	48.1%	.407	1.57	8.36	57	0.5				
2019	SEA	MLB	26	2	1	0	17	0	14²	9	1	7.4	11.0	18	44.1%	.250	1.43	5.52	93	0.1	98.6	59.3%	26.6%	45.8%
2020	SD	MLB	27	2	3	1	22	0	20¹	18	3	5.3	10.6	24	34.0%	.300	1.48	5.75	110	0.1	99.2	46.8%	31.6%	47.0%
2021 FS	SD	MLB	28	2	2	0	57	0	50	39	7	5.2	11.2	62	38.5%	.278	1.37	4.09	93	0.3	98.9	51.4%	30.3%	46.1%
2021 DC	SD	MLB	28	2	2	0	50	0	53	41	7	5.2	11.2	65	38.5%	.278	1.37	4.09	93	0.5	98.9	51.4%	30.3%	46.1%

Comparables: Dominic Leone, Phil Maton, Keone Kela

After Altavilla arrived in San Diego as part of the Austin Nola trade, he had himself a nice little September. It's hard to draw a greater conclusion than this: He's the same pitcher he has been for years. He still has trouble finding the strike zone, like Luis Perdomo, but, unlike Perdomo, he doesn't strike out enough hitters to make him anything more than a back-end reliever.

Michel Baez RHP Born: 01/21/96 Age: 25 Bats: R Throws: R Height: 6'8" Weight: 220 Origin: International Free Agent, 2016

YEAR	TEAM	LVL	AGE	W	L	SV	G	GS	IP	H	HR	BB/9	K/9	K	GB%	BABIP	WHIP	ERA	DRA-	WARP	MPH	FA%	Whiff%	CSP
2018	LE	HI-A	22	4	7	0	17	17	86²	73	5	3.4	9.6	92	34.6%	.304	1.22	2.91	79	1.4				
2018	SA	AA	22	0	3	0	4	4	18¹	22	4	5.9	10.3	21	30.8%	.375	1.85	7.36	65	0.4				
2019	AMA	AA	23	3	2	1	15	0	27	22	1	3.7	12.7	38	37.5%	.333	1.22	2.00	70	0.4				
2019	SD	MLB	23	1	1	0	24	1	29²	25	3	4.2	8.5	28	38.4%	.268	1.31	3.03	117	-0.1	97.4	58.7%	24.0%	41.7%
2020	SD	MLB	24	0	0	0	3	1	4²	7	0	3.9	13.5	7	35.7%	.500	1.93	7.71	81	0.1	96.4	55.6%	26.1%	38.6%
2021 FS	SD	MLB	25	1	2	0	57	0	50	45	8	4.0	9.7	53	36.6%	.285	1.34	4.44	102	0.1	97.2	58.0%	24.5%	41.1%
2021 DC	SD	MLB	25	1	2	0	25	3	36	32	6	4.0	9.7	38	36.6%	.285	1.34	4.44	102	0.2	97.2	58.0%	24.5%	41.1%

Comparables: Ryan Perry, Miguel Castro, Kevin Siegrist

Báez hasn't thrown at least six innings in an appearance since August 2018. He's spent the past two years pitching almost exclusively out of the bullpens. His arsenal includes two good pitches in his mid-90s fastball and changeup, as well as a few other below-average offerings. Any which way you slice it, Báez is probably a reliever. Given the opportunity, he could be a pretty good one.

David Bednar RHP Born: 10/10/94 Age: 26 Bats: L Throws: R Height: 6'1" Weight: 249 Origin: Round 35, 2016 Draft (#1044 overall)

YEAR	TEAM	LVL	AGE	W	L	SV	G	GS	IP	H	HR	BB/9	K/9	K	GB%	BABIP	WHIP	ERA	DRA-	WARP	MPH	FA%	Whiff%	CSP
2018	LE	HI-A	23	2	4	10	47	0	69¹	65	4	3.8	12.5	96	40.1%	.365	1.36	2.73	75	1.0				
2019	AMA	AA	24	2	5	14	44	0	58	49	4	2.8	13.3	86	46.6%	.354	1.16	2.95	69	0.9				
2019	SD	MLB	24	0	2	0	13	0	11	10	3	4.1	11.5	14	27.6%	.292	1.36	6.55	92	0.1	96.5	43.4%	32.6%	50.0%
2020	SD	MLB	25	0	0	0	4	0	6¹	11	1	2.8	7.1	5	36.0%	.417	2.05	7.11	106	0.0	97.7	59.3%	27.7%	52.1%
2021 FS	SD	MLB	26	2	2	0	57	0	50	45	7	3.4	9.9	55	40.9%	.292	1.28	4.06	95	0.3	97.0	50.9%	30.3%	51.0%
2021 DC	SD	MLB	26	0	1	0	16	0	17	15	2	3.4	9.9	18	40.9%	.292	1.28	4.06	95	0.1	97.0	50.9%	30.3%	51.0%

Comparables: Pedro Araujo, Matt Foster, Zac Reininger

Bednar relied more heavily on his fastball at the expense of his curve and splitter in 2020, but the only thing that improved was his walk rate. If he wants to be an effective middle reliever, he's going to need to miss more bats.

Nick Burdi RHP Born: 01/19/93 Age: 28 Bats: R Throws: R Height: 6'3" Weight: 225 Origin: Round 2, 2014 Draft (#46 overall)

YEAR	TEAM	LVL	AGE	W	L	SV	G	GS	IP	H	HR	BB/9	K/9	K	GB%	BABIP	WHIP	ERA	DRA-	WARP	MPH	FA%	Whiff%	CSP
2018	IND	AAA	25	0	2	0	5	0	5	9	0	7.2	9.0	5	31.6%	.474	2.60	5.40	64	0.1				
2018	PIT	MLB	25	0	0	0	2	0	1¹	3	1	13.5	13.5	2	33.3%	.400	3.75	20.25	40	0.0	98.5	71.4%	35.7%	46.9%
2019	PIT	MLB	26	2	1	0	11	0	8²	11	1	3.1	17.7	17	20.0%	.526	1.62	9.35	54	0.3	98.2	45.3%	36.6%	50.4%
2020	PIT	MLB	27	0	1	1	3	0	2¹	2	0	7.7	15.4	4	25.0%	.500	1.71	3.86	97	0.0	99.6	54.3%	35.0%	44.5%
2021 FS	SD	MLB	28	2	2	0	57	0	50	40	7	4.3	11.2	62	37.9%	.285	1.28	3.66	86	0.5	98.6	49.7%	36.1%	48.5%

Comparables: Jimmie Sherfy, Rowan Wick, Sam Freeman

What ancient ill lies heavy over the house Burdi? Like brother Zack, Nick has struggled with injuries over his career, but seemed poised to open 2020 as the Pirates' closer, armed with his triple-digit fastball and wipeout slider. Instead he pitched all of 2.1 innings before going on the IL, and wound up having a second Tommy John surgery in October, with a lengthy timetable (16-18 months) to return. Pittsburgh designated Burdi in November, paving the way for the Padres to add him over the winter. Given that closers are worth millions and interns are cheap, it's probably still worth poking around in the woods outside Casa Burdi for a cursed amulet buried beneath a lightning-blasted tree, just in case.

José Castillo LHP Born: 01/10/96 Age: 25 Bats: L Throws: L Height: 6'6" Weight: 252 Origin: International Free Agent, 2012

YEAR	TEAM	LVL	AGE	W	L	SV	G	GS	IP	H	HR	BB/9	K/9	K	GB%	BABIP	WHIP	ERA	DRA-	WARP	MPH	FA%	Whiff%	CSP
2018	SA	AA	22	2	1	5	12	0	15	14	0	4.8	15.6	26	34.4%	.452	1.47	3.00	44	0.5				
2018	ELP	AAA	22	1	0	3	10	0	11¹	6	1	1.6	10.3	13	39.3%	.192	0.71	0.79	70	0.2				
2018	SD	MLB	22	3	3	0	37	0	38¹	23	3	2.8	12.2	52	37.3%	.250	0.91	3.29	67	0.8	97.0	55.2%	33.9%	48.7%
2019	SD	MLB	23	0	0	0	1	0	0²	0	0	13.5	27.0	2			1.50	0.00	106	0.0	96.7	64.7%	40.0%	37.4%
2021 FS	SD	MLB	25	1	1	0	57	0	50	40	6	4.5	11.4	63	37.2%	.285	1.30	3.85	90	0.4	97.0	55.7%	34.2%	48.2%
2021 DC	SD	MLB	25	1	1	0	33	0	35	28	4	4.5	11.4	44	37.2%	.285	1.30	3.85	90	0.4	97.0	55.7%	34.2%	48.2%

Comparables: Mauricio Cabrera, Cionel Pérez, Jacob Nix

Castillo missed all of 2020 because of shoulder trouble, bringing his two-year total to 10 appearances between the majors and the minors. He turned 25 in January, so he still has time to get healthy and have a legitimate career as a setup pitcher.

Mike Clevinger RHP Born: 12/21/90 Age: 30 Bats: R Throws: R Height: 6'4" Weight: 215 Origin: Round 4, 2011 Draft (#135 overall)

YEAR	TEAM	LVL	AGE	W	L	SV	G	GS	IP	H	HR	BB/9	K/9	K	GB%	BABIP	WHIP	ERA	DRA-	WARP	MPH	FA%	Whiff%	CSP
2018	CLE	MLB	27	13	8	0	32	32	200	164	21	3.0	9.3	207	40.3%	.280	1.16	3.02	78	4.1	96.0	52.9%	27.9%	48.8%
2019	CLE	MLB	28	13	4	0	21	21	126	96	10	2.6	12.1	169	40.5%	.306	1.06	2.71	68	3.3	97.5	51.1%	35.3%	46.0%
2020	SD	MLB	29	3	2	0	8	8	41²	34	6	3.0	8.6	40	33.6%	.277	1.15	3.02	105	0.3	97.0	46.8%	30.4%	47.6%
2021 FS	SD	MLB	30	2	2	0	57	0	50	42	7	3.4	10.3	57	37.6%	.285	1.23	3.50	86	0.5	96.9	50.9%	31.7%	47.3%

Comparables: Kevin Gausman, Anthony DeSclafani, Zack Wheeler

Clevinger arrived in San Diego from Cleveland as part of a nine-player swap that crowned the team's busy deadline. He was excellent in his four starts after the trade, but it's been downhill since, and not in the good, easy-breezy way. A strained elbow limited Clevinger to a single inning in the postseason, and he underwent Tommy John surgery early in the offseason, wiping out his 2021. Both the Padres and Clevinger will have a lot riding on his 2022 season—the former hoping he justifies the trade, the latter needing a good performance to ensure a quality free-agent contract after that year.

Nabil Crismatt RHP Born: 12/25/94 Age: 26 Bats: R Throws: R Height: 6'1" Weight: 220 Origin: International Free Agent, 2011

YEAR	TEAM	LVL	AGE	W	L	SV	G	GS	IP	H	HR	BB/9	K/9	K	GB%	BABIP	WHIP	ERA	DRA-	WARP	MPH	FA%	Whiff%	CSP
2018	BNG	AA	23	8	6	0	18	18	105¹	95	8	3.2	9.0	105	44.6%	.309	1.25	3.59	78	2.0				
2018	LV	AAA	23	3	4	0	9	9	38²	61	8	4.4	8.1	35	44.6%	.421	2.07	8.84	99	0.4				
2019	ARK	AA	24	4	5	0	14	13	83²	57	6	1.2	9.6	89	43.3%	.242	0.81	1.94	55	2.3				
2019	TAC	AAA	24	0	5	0	13	8	46²	67	15	4.0	13.1	68	33.8%	.419	1.89	9.06	150	-0.3				
2020	STL	MLB	25	0	0	0	6	0	8¹	6	2	1.1	8.6	8	50.0%	.200	0.84	3.24	93	0.1	90.7	41.2%	27.4%	46.2%
2021 FS	SD	MLB	26	1	2	0	57	0	50	46	7	3.4	9.3	51	41.4%	.291	1.30	4.23	99	0.1	90.7	41.2%	27.4%	46.2%
2021 DC	SD	MLB	26	1	2	0	25	3	36	33	5	3.4	9.3	37	41.4%	.291	1.30	4.23	99	0.3	90.7	41.2%	27.4%	46.2%

Comparables: Chase De Jong, Ryan Helsley, Andrew Moore

A few up-and-down innings in St. Louis last year did little to tell us whether Crismatt can make his low-velo mix work in a big-league bullpen, nor whether it's appropriate to call the pitch you most frequently throw a "changeup." Maybe Crismatt can provide more answers now that he's part of the Padres.

Yu Darvish RHP Born: 08/16/86 Age: 34 Bats: R Throws: R Height: 6'5" Weight: 220 Origin: International Free Agent, 2012

YEAR	TEAM	LVL	AGE	W	L	SV	G	GS	IP	H	HR	BB/9	K/9	K	GB%	BABIP	WHIP	ERA	DRA-	WARP	MPH	FA%	Whiff%	CSP
2018	SB	LO-A	31	0	0	0	2	2	6	4	1	1.5	9.0	6	37.5%	.200	0.83	1.50	92	0.1				
2018	CHC	MLB	31	1	3	0	8	8	40	36	7	4.7	11.0	49	36.8%	.296	1.43	4.95	105	0.3	96.2	69.1%	25.5%	50.4%
2019	CHC	MLB	32	6	8	0	31	31	178²	140	33	2.8	11.5	229	45.1%	.268	1.10	3.98	55	6.0	96.7	39.8%	30.3%	47.5%
2020	CHC	MLB	33	8	3	0	12	12	76	59	5	1.7	11.0	93	42.8%	.297	0.96	2.01	67	2.0	97.6	30.1%	32.2%	52.4%
2021 FS	SD	MLB	34	10	7	0	26	26	150	122	18	2.9	10.6	175	43.0%	.283	1.14	3.20	76	3.1	97.0	38.6%	30.6%	49.4%
2021 DC	SD	MLB	34	11	8	0	29	29	169	138	21	2.9	10.6	198	43.0%	.283	1.14	3.20	76	3.9	97.0	38.6%	30.6%	49.4%

Comparables: Max Scherzer, Corey Kluber, Carlos Carrasco

What is the difference between an overpaid disappointment and a Cy Young finalist? By DRA, Darvish was actually a better pitcher in 2019 than he was in the season in which he finished third in Cy Young voting. The biggest difference? That pesky gopherball. With the baseballs less juiced in 2020, Darvish's home run rate plummeted; everything else stayed as good as it ever was, and not in some lame, Toby Keith-ass way. Some of it even got better. Darvish cut his walk rate, starting throwing his breaking stuff far more often and reduced his fastball usage to a career-low 16.6 percent. Even more impressive, despite playing all of his games against the Central divisions, he didn't exactly do what he did against the dregs of the league: His final eight starts came against teams who finished with a winning record. All of that adds up to a pitcher who is exactly the type of ace many long believed he was, and who the Padres hope he will continue to be.

★ ★ ★ *2021 Top 101 Prospect* **#11** ★ ★ ★

MacKenzie Gore LHP Born: 02/24/99 Age: 22 Bats: L Throws: L Height: 6'2" Weight: 197 Origin: Round 1, 2017 Draft (#3 overall)

YEAR	TEAM	LVL	AGE	W	L	SV	G	GS	IP	H	HR	BB/9	K/9	K	GB%	BABIP	WHIP	ERA	DRA-	WARP	MPH	FA%	Whiff%	CSP
2018	FW	LO-A	19	2	5	0	16	16	60²	61	5	2.7	11.0	74	40.5%	.354	1.30	4.45	59	1.8				
2019	LE	HI-A	20	7	1	0	15	15	79¹	36	4	2.3	12.5	110	36.5%	.212	0.71	1.02	34	3.2				
2019	AMA	AA	20	2	1	0	5	5	21²	20	3	3.3	10.4	25	44.6%	.321	1.29	4.15	86	0.2				
2021 FS	SD	MLB	22	9	8	0	26	26	150	126	22	4.0	10.3	171	39.8%	.278	1.29	3.95	98	1.3				
2021 DC	SD	MLB	22	4	4	0	12	12	64	53	9	4.0	10.3	73	39.8%	.278	1.29	3.95	98	0.8				

Comparables: Brailyn Marquez, Deivi García, José Suarez

The shortened season and lack of a minor-league campaign robbed everyone of the debut of one of the game's best young pitchers. He's drawn Clayton Kershaw comparisons in the past because of his left-handedness, his fierce breaking ball and a high leg kick. Gore is unlikely to become Kershaw, mind you, but the upside is such that you can understand why the Padres resisted rushing him to the Show. If he ends up making his major league debut in 2021—and he ought to—he'll still be only 22 years old. What was once a weak Padres' rotation is coming along, but a fully realized Gore, meaning the version of him that can safely be described as a no. 2 starter, would go a long way towards helping San Diego stand toe-to-toe (and arm-to-arm) with the actual Kershaw, his Dodgers and the rest of the league's elite teams.

Javy Guerra RHP Born: 09/25/95 Age: 25 Bats: L Throws: R Height: 6'0" Weight: 185 Origin: International Free Agent, 2012

YEAR	TEAM	LVL	AGE	W	L	SV	G	GS	IP	H	HR	BB/9	K/9	K	GB%	BABIP	WHIP	ERA	DRA-	WARP	MPH	FA%	Whiff%	CSP
2019	LE	HI-A	23	0	0	1	17	0	17	13	2	2.6	12.2	23	34.2%	.306	1.06	3.71	75	0.2				
2019	SD	MLB	23	0	0	0	8	0	8²	7	3	3.1	6.2	6	48.1%	.167	1.15	5.19	125	-0.1	99.9	76.9%	17.2%	52.8%
2020	SD	MLB	24	1	0	0	14	0	13¹	25	1	3.4	8.1	12	51.0%	.500	2.25	10.12	86	0.2	100.3	68.1%	21.2%	49.6%
2021 FS	SD	MLB	25	1	1	0	57	0	50	47	7	3.3	8.3	46	45.3%	.290	1.32	4.22	99	0.2	100.2	70.5%	20.1%	50.5%
2021 DC	SD	MLB	25	1	1	0	33	0	35	33	5	3.3	8.3	32	45.3%	.290	1.32	4.22	99	0.2	100.2	70.5%	20.1%	50.5%

Once a promising shortstop prospect, Guerra's inability to hit and strong arm led to him hopping on the mound before the 2019 season. He was shockingly effective for a newcomer, though his upper-90s sinker-slider combo with the occasional changeup mixed in hasn't yet led to success in the majors. Guerra's backstory is unusual, but his profile is ubiquitous. Given that essential fungibility the Padres will likely keep him on a short leash.

Tim Hill LHP Born: 02/10/90 Age: 31 Bats: R Throws: L Height: 6'4" Weight: 200 Origin: Round 32, 2014 Draft (#963 overall)

YEAR	TEAM	LVL	AGE	W	L	SV	G	GS	IP	H	HR	BB/9	K/9	K	GB%	BABIP	WHIP	ERA	DRA-	WARP	MPH	FA%	Whiff%	CSP
2018	KC	MLB	28	1	4	2	70	0	45²	46	4	2.8	8.3	42	60.7%	.313	1.31	4.53	111	0.0	93.1	76.4%	19.7%	55.6%
2019	OMA	AAA	29	1	1	3	27	0	29²	26	2	1.8	9.1	30	55.0%	.308	1.08	2.12	44	1.2				
2019	KC	MLB	29	2	0	1	46	0	39²	31	4	2.9	8.8	39	56.2%	.270	1.11	3.63	74	0.7	92.0	75.5%	20.7%	54.1%
2020	SD	MLB	30	3	0	0	23	0	18	17	3	3.0	10.0	20	52.9%	.292	1.28	4.50	81	0.3	92.8	89.9%	22.8%	47.9%
2021 FS	SD	MLB	31	2	2	0	57	0	50	45	5	2.6	8.9	49	53.7%	.294	1.20	3.42	83	0.6	92.6	80.6%	21.2%	52.4%
2021 DC	SD	MLB	31	2	2	0	50	0	53	48	5	2.6	8.9	52	53.7%	.294	1.20	3.42	83	0.8	92.6	80.6%	21.2%	52.4%

Comparables: Adam Kolarek, Josh Osich, Nick Ramirez

The Royals traded Hill to the Padres before the season, perhaps because they suspected he would be unable to repeat his 2019 with the three-batter-minimum in place. The Royals were right, but Hill remains an effective left-on-left reliever who can provide value with some careful micromanagement.

Pierce Johnson RHP Born: 05/10/91 Age: 30 Bats: R Throws: R Height: 6'2" Weight: 202 Origin: Round 1, 2012 Draft (#43 overall)

YEAR	TEAM	LVL	AGE	W	L	SV	G	GS	IP	H	HR	BB/9	K/9	K	GB%	BABIP	WHIP	ERA	DRA-	WARP	MPH	FA%	Whiff%	CSP
2018	SAC	AAA	27	0	0	0	4	17	0	22²	15	1	4.0	11.9	30	32.7%	.275	1.10	3.57	67	0.5				
2018	SF	MLB	27	3	2	0	37	0	43²	38	5	4.5	7.4	36	39.1%	.270	1.37	5.56	112	-0.1	95.3	50.2%	24.5%	46.2%
2020	SD	MLB	29	3	1	0	24	0	20	15	2	4.0	12.2	27	31.8%	.310	1.20	2.70	87	0.3	97.6	45.8%	40.0%	46.5%
2021 FS	SD	MLB	30	2	2	0	57	0	50	39	7	3.8	11.5	64	37.0%	.281	1.21	3.38	81	0.6	96.5	47.9%	32.7%	46.3%
2021 DC	SD	MLB	30	2	2	0	50	0	53	41	7	3.8	11.5	67	37.0%	.281	1.21	3.38	81	0.8	96.5	47.9%	32.7%	46.3%

Comparables: Hansel Robles, Dylan Floro, Mike Morin

Johnson had forgettable big-league stints with the Cubs and Giants before heading overseas for a season with the Hanshin Tigers. That turned out to be a worthwhile detour for him, as he posted a 1.38 ERA and a 7.00 strikeout-to-walk ratio in 58 appearances, a performance which, in turn, persuaded the Padres to hand over a multi-year deal worth $5 million. Johnson delivered in year one, working around walks to strike out over a third of the batters he faced. Another season like that and the Padres will assuredly exercise their $3 million club option for 2022.

Dinelson Lamet RHP Born: 07/18/92 Age: 28 Bats: R Throws: R Height: 6'3" Weight: 228 Origin: International Free Agent, 2014

YEAR	TEAM	LVL	AGE	W	L	SV	G	GS	IP	H	HR	BB/9	K/9	K	GB%	BABIP	WHIP	ERA	DRA-	WARP	MPH	FA%	Whiff%	CSP
2019	LE	HI-A	26	0	2	0	3	3	9	11	1	5.0	14.0	14	27.3%	.476	1.78	8.00	127	-0.1				
2019	ELP	AAA	26	1	0	0	3	3	15	10	3	2.4	11.4	19	51.4%	.219	0.93	4.80	41	0.7				
2019	SD	MLB	26	3	5	0	14	14	73	62	12	3.7	12.9	105	35.3%	.314	1.26	4.07	65	2.0	97.8	54.8%	31.8%	46.2%
2020	SD	MLB	27	3	1	0	12	12	69	39	5	2.6	12.1	93	38.0%	.234	0.86	2.09	68	1.8	99.0	46.5%	32.6%	46.7%
2021 FS	SD	MLB	28	10	7	0	26	26	150	114	19	3.7	11.8	196	38.9%	.280	1.18	3.26	78	2.9	98.5	50.1%	32.2%	46.4%
2021 DC	SD	MLB	28	9	7	0	25	25	142	108	18	3.7	11.8	186	38.9%	.280	1.18	3.26	78	3.1	98.5	50.1%	32.2%	46.4%

Comparables: Nick Pivetta, Luis Castillo, Jon Gray

Lamet's season might have eliminated any fear that he'd end up in the bullpen. He cut his run average roughly in half, continued to strike out over a third of the batters he faced and lowered his walk rate by two percentage points, thus achieving a better-than-average rate for the first time in his major-league career. One significant change Lamet made was to use his sinker—a pitch that has fallen more and more out of favor league-wide during the launch-angle revolution era—less than ever. In its place, he relied more on his four-seamer and slider. Regression is likely in 2021, but that doesn't mean he can't be an impactful member of the starting rotation.

Justin Lange RHP Born: 09/11/01 Age: 19 Bats: R Throws: R Height: 6'4" Weight: 220 Origin: Round 1, 2020 Draft (#34 overall)

The Padres picked up hard-throwing Texas prep Lange with a competitive balance pick after the first round. After a major winter and spring velocity spike, he was suddenly sitting mid-90s and touching triple-digits leading up to the draft, making him one of the few late pop-ups in an amateur season that barely happened. Lange continued to impress at the alternate site and instructs, holding his gains and flashing a hard slider with significant promise. All caveats about high school pitchers aside—and Lange certainly does need a lot of work on command and secondary offerings—there's a lot of projection and hope here.

Joey Lucchesi LHP Born: 06/06/93 Age: 28 Bats: L Throws: L Height: 6'5" Weight: 225 Origin: Round 4, 2016 Draft (#114 overall)

YEAR	TEAM	LVL	AGE	W	L	SV	G	GS	IP	H	HR	BB/9	K/9	K	GB%	BABIP	WHIP	ERA	DRA-	WARP	MPH	FA%	Whiff%	CSP
2018	LE	HI-A	25	0	0	0	1	1	4	0	0	0.0	13.5	6	66.7%	.000	0.00	0.00	48	0.1				
2018	ELP	AAA	25	0	1	0	1	1	2²	7	1	13.5	6.8	2	27.3%	.600	4.12	23.62	108	0.0				
2018	SD	MLB	25	8	9	0	26	26	130	125	23	3.0	10.0	145	44.7%	.310	1.29	4.08	84	2.3	92.3	64.2%	26.0%	50.0%
2019	SD	MLB	26	10	10	0	30	30	163²	144	23	3.1	8.7	158	46.6%	.274	1.22	4.18	85	2.9	92.2	64.9%	25.6%	47.1%
2020	SD	MLB	27	0	1	0	3	2	5²	13	0	3.2	7.9	5	37.5%	.542	2.65	7.94	100	0.0	91.4	65.0%	31.6%	47.9%
2021 FS	SD	MLB	28	9	8	0	26	26	150	138	21	3.4	9.1	151	45.2%	.291	1.30	4.01	95	1.5	92.2	64.7%	26.0%	47.9%
2021 DC	SD	MLB	28	2	2	0	9	9	43	39	6	3.4	9.1	43	45.2%	.291	1.30	4.01	95	0.6	92.2	64.7%	26.0%	47.9%

Comparables: Andrew Suárez, Daniel Norris, Marco Gonzales

Lucchesi had an abysmal 2020. He appeared three times, allowed a run per inning and otherwise spent his summer at the alternate site—not what you would've expected from someone who made 56 starts the preceding two years. Lucchesi has shown enough promise in the past (he entered the year with a career 97 ERA+ and a 3.06 strikeout-to-walk ratio) to think he'll earn a rotation spot with some team, even if it seems increasingly likely that said team will reside somewhere other than San Diego.

Adrian Morejon LHP Born: 02/27/99 Age: 22 Bats: L Throws: L Height: 5'11" Weight: 224 Origin: International Free Agent, 2016

YEAR	TEAM	LVL	AGE	W	L	SV	G	GS	IP	H	HR	BB/9	K/9	K	GB%	BABIP	WHIP	ERA	DRA-	WARP	MPH	FA%	Whiff%	CSP
2018	SD1	ROK	19	0	1	0	1	1	2²	5	0	0.0	13.5	4	44.4%	.556	1.88	6.75	56	0.1				
2018	LE	HI-A	19	4	4	0	13	13	62²	54	6	3.4	10.1	70	51.5%	.306	1.24	3.30	75	1.1				
2019	AMA	AA	20	0	4	0	16	16	36	29	3	3.8	11.0	44	48.9%	.292	1.22	4.25	56	1.0				
2019	SD	MLB	20	0	0	0	5	2	8	15	1	3.4	10.1	9	36.7%	.483	2.25	10.12	104	0.0	97.8	53.9%	19.7%	50.5%
2020	SD	MLB	21	2	2	0	9	4	19¹	20	7	1.9	11.6	25	46.0%	.302	1.24	4.66	88	0.3	98.2	56.2%	28.5%	46.3%
2021 FS	SD	MLB	22	9	9	0	26	26	150	138	22	3.9	9.5	157	43.8%	.292	1.36	4.36	100	1.0	98.1	55.7%	26.4%	47.3%
2021 DC	SD	MLB	22	5	6	0	33	16	95	87	14	3.9	9.5	99	43.8%	.292	1.36	4.36	100	0.9	98.1	55.7%	26.4%	47.3%

Comparables: Luiz Gohara, Jesús Luzardo, Kolby Allard

Morejón recovered from a rough introduction to the majors in 2019, posting excellent strikeout and walk rates over a 19-inning sample. The wildest part of his year was his proclivity to give up the long ball. For context: Pitchers as a whole yielded home runs to 3.5 percent of the batters they faced; Morejón gave up a gopherball to 8.9 percent of the batters he faced. Obviously there's no reason to believe that will remain the case heading forward—pitchers with this kind of stuff don't yield more than three homers per nine on a true-talent basis. The more interesting subplot is whether the Padres return Morejón to a rotation or keep him in the bullpen because of his size and injury history.

Chris Paddack RHP   Born: 01/08/96   Age: 25   Bats: R   Throws: R   Height: 6'5"   Weight: 217   Origin: Round 8, 2015 Draft (#236 overall)

YEAR	TEAM	LVL	AGE	W	L	SV	G	GS	IP	H	HR	BB/9	K/9	K	GB%	BABIP	WHIP	ERA	DRA-	WARP	MPH	FA%	Whiff%	CSP
2018	LE	HI-A	22	4	1	0	10	10	52¹	43	3	0.7	14.3	83	43.2%	.374	0.90	2.24	45	1.9				
2018	SA	AA	22	3	2	0	7	7	37²	23	1	1.0	8.8	37	43.6%	.239	0.72	1.91	58	1.1				
2019	SD	MLB	23	9	7	0	26	26	140²	107	23	2.0	9.8	153	39.2%	.239	0.98	3.33	65	4.0	96.0	61.0%	24.8%	50.7%
2020	SD	MLB	24	4	5	0	12	12	59	60	14	1.8	8.8	58	46.8%	.289	1.22	4.73	97	0.6	96.1	61.6%	26.0%	48.9%
2021 FS	SD	MLB	25	10	7	0	26	26	150	127	19	2.1	9.3	155	44.2%	.277	1.08	2.99	75	3.2	96.0	61.2%	25.3%	50.0%
2021 DC	SD	MLB	25	9	7	0	25	25	137	116	17	2.1	9.3	142	44.2%	.277	1.08	2.99	75	3.3	96.0	61.2%	25.3%	50.0%

Comparables: Luis Severino, Shane Bieber, Aaron Nola

Paddack took a step back following a promising rookie season. He still excelled at limiting free passes, but his strikeout percentage dipped and he allowed more home runs on a rate basis. Paddack has been a two-pitch pitcher for the most part, leaning on his fastball-changeup combination. That approach didn't work so well last season, as opponents hit .308 against the heater. He did introduce a cutter during the season, and while the results weren't great, the development of that pitch could go a long way in helping him get back to good.

Emilio Pagán RHP   Born: 05/07/91   Age: 30   Bats: L   Throws: R   Height: 6'2"   Weight: 208   Origin: Round 10, 2013 Draft (#297 overall)

YEAR	TEAM	LVL	AGE	W	L	SV	G	GS	IP	H	HR	BB/9	K/9	K	GB%	BABIP	WHIP	ERA	DRA-	WARP	MPH	FA%	Whiff%	CSP
2018	NAS	AAA	27	1	0	0	5	0	6	5	2	0.0	16.5	11	38.5%	.273	0.83	3.00	30	0.3				
2018	OAK	MLB	27	3	1	0	55	0	62	55	13	2.8	9.1	63	25.4%	.256	1.19	4.35	97	0.4	95.7	66.4%	29.6%	51.0%
2019	DUR	AAA	28	0	0	2	4	1	6	2	0	6.0	15.0	10	45.5%	.182	1.00	0.00	35	0.3				
2019	TB	MLB	28	4	2	20	66	0	70	45	12	1.7	12.3	96	35.0%	.228	0.83	2.31	59	1.9	97.2	61.5%	35.1%	49.9%
2020	SD	MLB	29	0	1	2	22	0	22	14	4	3.7	9.4	23	30.9%	.196	1.05	4.50	111	0.1	96.1	62.4%	26.7%	46.1%
2021 FS	SD	MLB	30	2	2	9	57	0	50	37	7	2.7	10.7	59	30.8%	.254	1.05	2.84	72	0.9	96.6	62.9%	31.6%	49.2%
2021 DC	SD	MLB	30	2	2	9	50	0	53	39	8	2.7	10.7	62	30.8%	.254	1.05	2.84	72	1.1	96.6	62.9%	31.6%	49.2%

Comparables: Nick Wittgren, Paul Sewald, Ryan Dull

Pagán played on his fourth different team in as many years when the Rays traded him as part of the Manuel Margot deal. He was supposed to give the Padres yet another high-grade reliever. Alas, that isn't how things played out. His control faltered, leading to a walk rate that was nearly double his career rate going into the season, and he once again proved home-run prone. Pagán seems to have a Saberhagen-like tendency to alternate between good and bad years, so expect a rebound effort in 2021.

Drew Pomeranz LHP   Born: 11/22/88   Age: 32   Bats: R   Throws: L   Height: 6'5"   Weight: 246   Origin: Round 1, 2010 Draft (#5 overall)

YEAR	TEAM	LVL	AGE	W	L	SV	G	GS	IP	H	HR	BB/9	K/9	K	GB%	BABIP	WHIP	ERA	DRA-	WARP	MPH	FA%	Whiff%	CSP
2018	WOR	AAA	29	0	2	0	5	5	19²	16	7	5.9	5.5	12	55.9%	.173	1.47	5.49	97	0.2				
2018	BOS	MLB	29	2	6	0	26	11	74	87	12	5.4	8.0	66	37.8%	.344	1.77	6.08	176	-2.3	91.6	58.9%	17.9%	43.6%
2019	MIL	MLB	30	0	1	2	25	1	26¹	16	4	2.7	15.4	45	46.8%	.279	0.91	2.39	10	1.6	96.1	76.5%	38.0%	48.6%
2019	SF	MLB	30	2	9	0	21	17	77²	89	17	4.2	10.7	92	36.3%	.353	1.61	5.68	121	-0.2	94.2	63.8%	23.6%	48.7%
2020	SD	MLB	31	1	0	4	20	0	18²	9	1	4.8	14.0	29	47.1%	.242	1.02	1.45	77	0.4	96.2	79.6%	34.7%	48.1%
2021 FS	SD	MLB	32	2	2	31	57	0	50	40	6	4.4	10.9	60	41.7%	.286	1.31	3.71	87	0.5	94.8	66.8%	26.1%	47.4%
2021 DC	SD	MLB	32	2	2	31	50	0	53	43	6	4.4	10.9	64	41.7%	.286	1.31	3.71	87	0.7	94.8	66.8%	26.1%	47.4%

Comparables: Liam Hendriks, Tyler Thornburg, Alex Colomé

It's generally held as a bad idea to give a four-year contract to any reliever, even if they have a proven track record. Thus, the Padres were gambling when they handed a four-year pact to Pomeranz after he made 24 appearances in relief to close out the 2019 season. He was awesome for the Brewers, to be clear, but the rule of thumb is to pay for neither past production nor small-sample sizes. A year in, Pomeranz looks like the exception to all kinds of evaluative principles. He struck out nearly 40 percent of the batters he faced on the season, all but eliminated contact that wasn't of the groundball or pop-up variety, and didn't allow a run until his final appearance of the season. Pomeranz's elevated walk rate was the one blemish on his record, but, reread the previous sentence and try to feign concern.

Nick Ramirez LHP   Born: 08/01/89   Age: 31   Bats: L   Throws: L   Height: 6'4"   Weight: 232   Origin: Round 4, 2011 Draft (#131 overall)

YEAR	TEAM	LVL	AGE	W	L	SV	G	GS	IP	H	HR	BB/9	K/9	K	GB%	BABIP	WHIP	ERA	DRA-	WARP	MPH	FA%	Whiff%	CSP
2018	BLX	AA	28	8	0	1	19	0	30²	17	2	3.8	9.7	33	53.3%	.205	0.98	1.76	66	0.6				
2018	RMV	AAA	28	3	3	0	20	2	37²	44	3	5.0	4.3	18	47.8%	.318	1.73	5.73	105	0.1				
2019	ERI	AA	29	1	0	0	3	3	14¹	11	1	1.3	12.6	20	45.5%	.323	0.91	2.51	61	0.3				
2019	TOL	AAA	29	0	1	0	2	2	9	12	1	3.0	10.0	10	44.8%	.393	1.67	2.00	106	0.1				
2019	DET	MLB	29	5	4	0	46	0	79²	76	11	4.0	8.4	74	45.4%	.288	1.39	4.07	92	0.7	91.5	58.4%	28.2%	41.2%
2020	DET	MLB	30	0	0	0	5	0	10²	8	3	3.4	9.3	11	50.0%	.185	1.12	5.91	102	0.1	91.3	60.8%	23.5%	41.7%
2021 FS	SD	MLB	31	2	2	0	57	0	50	45	5	4.3	8.5	47	46.1%	.288	1.39	4.10	98	0.2	91.5	58.8%	27.4%	41.3%

Comparables: Ryne Harper, Matt Grace, Brian Moran

It's always fun to go back and look at what players were when they were drafted: Jim Thome was a shortstop. Eddie Murray started off as a catcher. But conversions don't get more rare than Ramirez, who began as a first baseman before climbing onto the mound. A changeup artist by trade, he doesn't have the stamina to start or the velo to close, but he avoids hard contact consistently enough to labor multiple innings through during the soft, chewy, nougaty center of the game.

Garrett Richards RHP Born: 05/27/88 Age: 33 Bats: R Throws: R Height: 6'2" Weight: 210 Origin: Round 1, 2009 Draft (#42 overall)

YEAR	TEAM	LVL	AGE	W	L	SV	G	GS	IP	H	HR	BB/9	K/9	K	GB%	BABIP	WHIP	ERA	DRA-	WARP	MPH	FA%	Whiff%	CSP
2018	LAA	MLB	30	5	4	0	16	16	76¹	64	11	4.0	10.3	87	50.0%	.279	1.28	3.66	83	1.4	97.5	50.4%	28.5%	47.5%
2019	LE	HI-A	31	0	1	0	3	3	6²	8	1	10.8	10.8	8	47.4%	.389	2.40	8.10	184	-0.3				
2019	SD	MLB	31	0	1	0	3	3	8²	10	2	6.2	11.4	11	41.7%	.381	1.85	8.31	77	0.2	96.2	58.0%	30.5%	46.0%
2020	SD	MLB	32	2	2	0	14	10	51¹	47	7	3.0	8.1	46	40.5%	.284	1.25	4.03	99	0.5	96.5	54.8%	25.9%	46.9%
2021 FS	SD	MLB	33	9	9	0	26	26	150	141	21	4.1	8.7	144	44.2%	.290	1.40	4.32	101	1.0	96.8	53.6%	27.1%	47.0%

Comparables: Tyson Ross, Luis Tiant, Chris Short

Richards' name doesn't come up as frequently in those "what-if he had stayed healthy" conversations as, say, Troy Tulowitzki's or Grady Sizemore's, but it's still a shame that injuries had limited him to just 31 starts over four seasons following his high-quality performances in 2014-15. For that reason it was heartening to see him stay more or less healthy in 2020, and to do so while being reasonably productive. Richards' home-run rate remained on the high side, and it's worth wondering if we were getting a glimpse of his future when the Padres shifted him to the bullpen late in the year. Pitching relief beats wondering about the career you might have had.

Trevor Rosenthal RHP Born: 05/29/90 Age: 31 Bats: R Throws: R Height: 6'2" Weight: 230 Origin: Round 21, 2009 Draft (#639 overall)

YEAR	TEAM	LVL	AGE	W	L	SV	G	GS	IP	H	HR	BB/9	K/9	K	GB%	BABIP	WHIP	ERA	DRA-	WARP	MPH	FA%	Whiff%	CSP
2019	HBG	AA	29	0	1	0	10	0	9¹	9	2	6.8	10.6	11	46.2%	.292	1.71	5.79	124	-0.2				
2019	TOL	AAA	29	0	0	0	6	0	5¹	8	2	10.1	15.2	9	53.3%	.462	2.62	10.12	163	-0.1				
2019	DET	MLB	29	0	0	0	10	0	9	3	0	11.0	12.0	12	17.6%	.176	1.56	7.00	125	-0.1	99.8	68.8%	33.3%	42.0%
2019	WAS	MLB	29	0	1	0	12	0	6¹	8	0	21.3	7.1	5	35.0%	.400	3.63	22.74	155	-0.2	99.9	75.5%	25.7%	43.5%
2020	SD	MLB	30	1	0	11	23	0	23²	12	2	3.0	14.5	38	38.6%	.238	0.85	1.90	61	0.7	100.0	71.1%	37.7%	48.4%
2021 FS	SD	MLB	31	2	2	0	57	0	50	37	5	5.4	12.1	67	42.8%	.286	1.35	3.66	86	0.5	99.9	71.5%	34.3%	46.0%

Comparables: Mychal Givens, Jeurys Familia, Kelvin Herrera

Rosenthal is a great example of reliever variance. It would've been justifiable to think his big-league career was nearing its end after he allowed seven runs and recorded zero outs over his first four appearances in 2019. Instead, Rosenthal reestablished himself in 2020. Following a deadline deal that sent him out west, he permitted just one run and one walk while fanning 17 of the 35 batters he faced. Rosenthal did throw an uneasy amount of pitches down the middle, but he got away with it more often than not. Much like the failson of an oil tycoon, he should keep getting jobs so long as he can pump gas and avoid fires.

Blake Snell LHP Born: 12/04/92 Age: 28 Bats: L Throws: L Height: 6'4" Weight: 225 Origin: Round 1, 2011 Draft (#52 overall)

YEAR	TEAM	LVL	AGE	W	L	SV	G	GS	IP	H	HR	BB/9	K/9	K	GB%	BABIP	WHIP	ERA	DRA-	WARP	MPH	FA%	Whiff%	CSP
2018	TB	MLB	25	21	5	0	31	31	180²	112	16	3.2	11.0	220	44.7%	.242	0.97	1.89	54	6.0	97.8	51.4%	34.7%	44.6%
2019	TB	MLB	26	6	8	0	23	23	107	96	14	3.4	12.4	147	37.9%	.343	1.27	4.29	73	2.5	97.2	48.4%	38.2%	42.9%
2020	TB	MLB	27	4	2	0	11	11	50	42	10	3.2	11.3	63	48.4%	.288	1.20	3.24	82	0.9	96.8	50.6%	34.0%	41.4%
2021 FS	SD	MLB	28	10	7	0	26	26	150	115	16	3.9	11.5	192	43.8%	.284	1.20	3.09	74	3.3	97.3	49.9%	35.9%	43.0%
2021 DC	SD	MLB	28	9	7	0	27	27	148	113	16	3.9	11.5	189	43.8%	.284	1.20	3.09	74	3.6	97.3	49.9%	35.9%	43.0%

Comparables: Joe Musgrove, Nick Pivetta, Jakob Junis

You know the story by now, but, for posterity's sake: Snell was rolling in Game 6 of the World Series. He got into a little bit of trouble and Kevin Cash pulled him. It didn't work out—Nick Anderson continued his woeful October—and the Rays lost. Cash's decision to yank Snell has been debated to death—somehow, the likelihood that the Rays' plan works if they just insert one of their non-gassed relievers gets ignored—so we're not going to relegislate it here. What we will do is note that Snell popped up in trade rumors over the winter, and his eventual exit from Tampa Bay will go a long way in answering whether he's fancier Ryan Yarbrough or a legitimate front-of-the-rotation stud who should be left in during the most important game of the—wait, here comes Cash to make an author change. The Rays gave Snell another quick hook over the winter, moving him to the Padres despite three years of team control remaining on his below-market deal.

Craig Stammen RHP Born: 03/09/84 Age: 37 Bats: R Throws: R Height: 6'2" Weight: 228 Origin: Round 12, 2005 Draft (#354 overall)

YEAR	TEAM	LVL	AGE	W	L	SV	G	GS	IP	H	HR	BB/9	K/9	K	GB%	BABIP	WHIP	ERA	DRA-	WARP	MPH	FA%	Whiff%	CSP
2018	SD	MLB	34	8	3	0	73	0	79	65	3	1.9	10.0	88	48.8%	.304	1.04	2.73	63	1.9	93.5	67.6%	29.8%	47.1%
2019	SD	MLB	35	8	7	4	76	0	82	80	13	1.6	8.0	73	50.6%	.284	1.16	3.29	87	1.0	94.5	72.2%	21.6%	45.8%
2020	SD	MLB	36	4	2	0	24	0	24	27	2	1.5	7.5	20	57.0%	.333	1.29	5.62	78	0.5	93.8	82.5%	24.1%	48.9%
2021 FS	SD	MLB	37	2	2	0	57	0	50	47	5	2.1	7.9	44	52.9%	.292	1.20	3.53	86	0.5	94.1	73.6%	24.1%	46.9%
2021 DC	SD	MLB	37	2	2	0	50	0	53	50	6	2.1	7.9	46	52.9%	.292	1.20	3.53	86	0.7	94.1	73.6%	24.1%	46.9%

Comparables: Jesse Chavez, Matt Belisle, Mark Guthrie

A lot of care needs to be exercised in drawing conclusions from the pandemic-shortened season, and Stammen is a prime example of that. If you only look at his runs allowed, it seems as if he had a brutal year. Au contraire! Stammen actually improved his DRA from year-to-year by making gains with his strikeout, walk and home-run rates. He gave up a few more hits, but otherwise appeared to be just as good (or perhaps better) than he was the year before.

Matt Strahm LHP Born: 11/12/91 Age: 29 Bats: R Throws: L Height: 6'2" Weight: 190 Origin: Round 21, 2012 Draft (#643 overall)

YEAR	TEAM	LVL	AGE	W	L	SV	G	GS	IP	H	HR	BB/9	K/9	K	GB%	BABIP	WHIP	ERA	DRA-	WARP	MPH	FA%	Whiff%	CSP
2018	SA	AA	26	1	0	0	9	2	14¹	14	1	2.5	13.8	22	42.4%	.406	1.26	2.51	71	0.3				
2018	SD	MLB	26	3	4	0	41	5	61¹	39	6	3.1	10.1	69	35.5%	.228	0.98	2.05	88	0.7	95.5	58.0%	27.9%	53.0%
2019	SD	MLB	27	6	11	0	46	16	114²	121	22	1.7	9.3	118	35.6%	.315	1.25	4.71	88	1.7	94.0	38.1%	23.5%	54.0%
2020	SD	MLB	28	0	1	0	19	0	20²	14	3	1.7	6.5	15	44.1%	.196	0.87	2.61	100	0.2	94.3	55.8%	22.1%	52.9%
2021 FS	SD	MLB	29	2	2	4	57	0	50	45	7	2.5	9.0	50	38.8%	.284	1.19	3.84	92	0.4	94.3	44.8%	24.1%	53.6%
2021 DC	SD	MLB	29	2	2	4	50	0	53	48	8	2.5	9.0	53	38.8%	.284	1.19	3.84	92	0.5	94.3	44.8%	24.1%	53.6%

Comparables: Michael Lorenzen, Carlos Martínez, Austin Brice

Clevinger's long lost left-handed brother was used exclusively out of the bullpen for the first time in his career, and not solely against lefties, either. Considering Strahm's starter/reliever splits, it's probably the best route for him going forward. He has done a tremendous job at limiting walks, especially compared to the beginning of his career, when he'd hand out free passes every other inning. That growth has made it easier to buy into him as a solid enough middle-relief option for now and for years to come. Strahm required knee surgery after the season, though he is expected to be ready for game action by the time you flip this page.

Ryan Weathers LHP Born: 12/17/99 Age: 21 Bats: R Throws: L Height: 6'1" Weight: 230 Origin: Round 1, 2018 Draft (#7 overall)

YEAR	TEAM	LVL	AGE	W	L	SV	G	GS	IP	H	HR	BB/9	K/9	K	GB%	BABIP	WHIP	ERA	DRA-	WARP	MPH	FA%	Whiff%	CSP
2018	SD2	ROK	18	0	2	0	4	4	9¹	8	2	2.9	8.7	9	69.0%	.222	1.18	3.86	98	0.2				
2018	FW	LO-A	18	0	1	0	3	3	9	11	0	1.0	9.0	9	54.8%	.367	1.33	3.00	82	0.1				
2019	FW	LO-A	19	3	7	0	22	22	96	101	6	1.7	8.4	90	44.6%	.348	1.24	3.84	112	-0.3				
2021 FS	SD	MLB	21	1	1	0	57	0	50	50	7	3.3	7.1	39	43.1%	.285	1.37	4.70	114	-0.3				
2021 DC	SD	MLB	21	1	1	0	4	4	20	20	3	3.3	7.1	15	43.1%	.285	1.37	4.70	114	0.1				

Comparables: Brailyn Marquez, Noah Syndergaard, Luis Severino

Weathers barely missed out on becoming the first pitcher to ever make his major-league debut during the playoffs, having been edged by Rays lefty Shane McClanahan. Though he pitched in relief, the way his father David used to, he's expected to have a career as a mid-to-back end starter thanks to a well-rounded arsenal and above-average command.

Taylor Williams RHP Born: 07/21/91 Age: 29 Bats: S Throws: R Height: 5'11" Weight: 185 Origin: Round 4, 2013 Draft (#122 overall)

YEAR	TEAM	LVL	AGE	W	L	SV	G	GS	IP	H	HR	BB/9	K/9	K	GB%	BABIP	WHIP	ERA	DRA-	WARP	MPH	FA%	Whiff%	CSP
2018	MIL	MLB	26	1	3	0	56	0	53	53	6	4.2	9.7	57	35.9%	.329	1.47	4.25	96	0.4	97.1	64.9%	32.5%	44.6%
2019	SA	AAA	27	3	3	6	46	0	54	40	8	3.5	9.5	57	53.1%	.242	1.13	2.83	53	1.9				
2019	MIL	MLB	27	1	1	0	10	0	14²	22	1	4.3	9.2	15	59.2%	.438	1.98	9.82	101	0.1	96.7	63.3%	26.4%	44.4%
2020	SD	MLB	28	1	1	6	15	0	14²	14	1	4.3	12.3	20	40.5%	.361	1.43	6.14	81	0.3	96.2	45.2%	31.9%	43.7%
2021 FS	SD	MLB	29	2	2	0	57	0	50	45	6	4.1	9.9	54	45.6%	.295	1.36	4.25	97	0.2	96.7	57.5%	30.8%	44.2%
2021 DC	SD	MLB	29	0	1	0	16	0	17	15	2	4.1	9.9	18	45.6%	.295	1.36	4.25	97	0.1	96.7	57.5%	30.8%	44.2%

Comparables: Dominic Leone, Cam Bedrosian, Shawn Armstrong

Williams landed in San Diego at the 2020 trade deadline, but he made only one appearance after the deal, an outing in which he faced five batters and gave up a run. His underlying measures suggest he's much better than his unsightly career run average.

Trey Wingenter RHP Born: 04/15/94 Age: 27 Bats: R Throws: R Height: 6'7" Weight: 237 Origin: Round 17, 2015 Draft (#507 overall)

YEAR	TEAM	LVL	AGE	W	L	SV	G	GS	IP	H	HR	BB/9	K/9	K	GB%	BABIP	WHIP	ERA	DRA-	WARP	MPH	FA%	Whiff%	CSP
2018	ELP	AAA	24	3	3	4	40	0	44¹	29	4	4.9	10.8	53	48.1%	.250	1.20	3.45	75	0.8				
2018	SD	MLB	24	0	0	0	22	0	19	13	3	5.2	12.8	27	40.5%	.256	1.26	3.79	63	0.5	99.1	68.5%	36.6%	49.2%
2019	AMA	AA	25	0	1	0	1	0	0²	2	1	13.5	13.5	1	33.3%	.500	4.50	54.00	159	0.0				
2019	ELP	AAA	25	0	0	1	3	0	3¹	1	0	0.0	18.9	7	75.0%	.250	0.30	0.00	24	0.2				
2019	SD	MLB	25	1	3	1	51	1	51	34	5	4.9	12.5	71	36.3%	.269	1.22	5.65	72	1.0	97.8	55.1%	36.4%	45.4%
2021 FS	SD	MLB	27	2	2	0	57	0	50	39	6	5.4	11.8	65	41.0%	.285	1.39	4.23	96	0.2	98.0	57.2%	36.4%	46.0%
2021 DC	SD	MLB	27	0	0	0	11	0	11	8	1	5.4	11.8	14	41.0%	.285	1.39	4.23	96	0.1	98.0	57.2%	36.4%	46.0%

Comparables: Keynan Middleton, J.P. Feyereisen, Ian Gibaut

Wingenter's strikeout and whiff rates continue to be elite, but he's going to have trouble sticking around for long if his walk and strand rates remain elite as well, just not in the normal sense of the word. We feel safe suggesting better days are ahead—his hard-hit rate is in line with the league-average, suggesting there isn't some underlying contact-management flaw here—but we reserve the right to change our mind if he keeps having these problems through another season.

Kirby Yates RHP Born: 03/25/87 Age: 34 Bats: L Throws: R Height: 5'10" Weight: 205 Origin: Round 26, 2005 Draft (#798 overall)

YEAR	TEAM	LVL	AGE	W	L	SV	G	GS	IP	H	HR	BB/9	K/9	K	GB%	BABIP	WHIP	ERA	DRA-	WARP	MPH	FA%	Whiff%	CSP
2018	SD	MLB	31	5	3	12	65	0	63	41	6	2.4	12.9	90	43.2%	.263	0.92	2.14	42	2.2	95.3	58.3%	34.8%	43.2%
2019	SD	MLB	32	0	5	41	60	0	60²	41	2	1.9	15.0	101	47.5%	.328	0.89	1.19	41	2.2	94.7	57.1%	34.6%	44.5%
2020	SD	MLB	33	0	1	2	6	0	4¹	7	1	8.3	16.6	8	38.5%	.500	2.54	12.46	81	0.1	94.5	64.4%	41.3%	45.1%
2021 FS	SD	MLB	34	3	2	0	57	0	50	36	5	3.1	12.4	68	40.7%	.282	1.07	2.56	67	1.0	94.8	58.1%	35.3%	44.2%

Comparables: Brad Brach, Blake Parker, Oliver Drake

After two stellar seasons as one of the best relievers in baseball, Yates had a walk year to forget. He threw four disastrous innings before having to undergo season-ending surgery to remove bone chips from his pitching elbow. The good news is that he should be ready for the spring. The bad news is that a reliever going into his age-34 season and coming off elbow surgery is probably not going to get the big free-agent contract he seemed slated to receive. That's a rough break for someone who has had to grind his way to this point.

SAN FRANCISCO GIANTS

Essay by Russell A. Carlton

Player comments by Jon Hegglund and BP staff

Ten years ago, when my age started with "30-something", rather than "40-something", the San Francisco Giants were basking in the glow of what was their first World Series title since moving to California. We know what happened next. The Giants missed the playoffs in 2011, but won the 2012 World Series, missed the playoffs in 2013, and then won the 2014 World Series. Having once again missed the playoffs the year prior, the 2016 Giants struggled back in Game 3 of the NLDS against the Cubs, managing to win in 13 innings, then lead Game 4 by three in the ninth, allowing, for a brief moment, the even-year magic potion to seem strangely real. But as the Cubs scored four runs in the top of the inning and eventually became the first non-Giants even-year champs since the 2008 Phillies, everyone preemptively declared them to be a dynasty.

Chances are that the person reading this essay is a Giants fan—we know that you flip to your favorite team first—and so when I say the word "dynasty", you might be a little more willing to apply it to those teams of a decade or so ago. But there are some of you who are just "fans of the game" reading this one who might be looking back and find yourself saying, "Oh yeah, I guess that was a dynasty" In fact, you're more likely to apply the "D word" to the Cubs and their good-but-never-quite-fulfilled run in the second half of the 2010s.

But then since 2017, the Giants seemed to have left their hearts somewhere else. The 2020 season marked their fourth consecutive losing campaign, meaning that a Giants fan in Merced just went through the entirety of high school without seeing a winning team. It's not like 2021 promises to be all that much better. There is talent coming up on the farm, but this is the year of transition to the new generation and most of the old guard will be departing. Madison Bumgarner has already decamped for Arizona. Hunter Pence finally learned to parallel park and retired. Brian Wilson is back to singing Beach Boys songs. And this will be the final ride for the Brandons, Belt and Crawford, and perhaps even Buster Posey, who has a $22 million team option for 2022.

Posey's place in Giants lore is secure and the bat is still there so that even if he becomes a serviceable first baseman for a few years, that'll be good enough to pick up a few more career WARP and get into the Hall of Fame on the Joe Mauer path—particularly if those last years are all with the Giants.

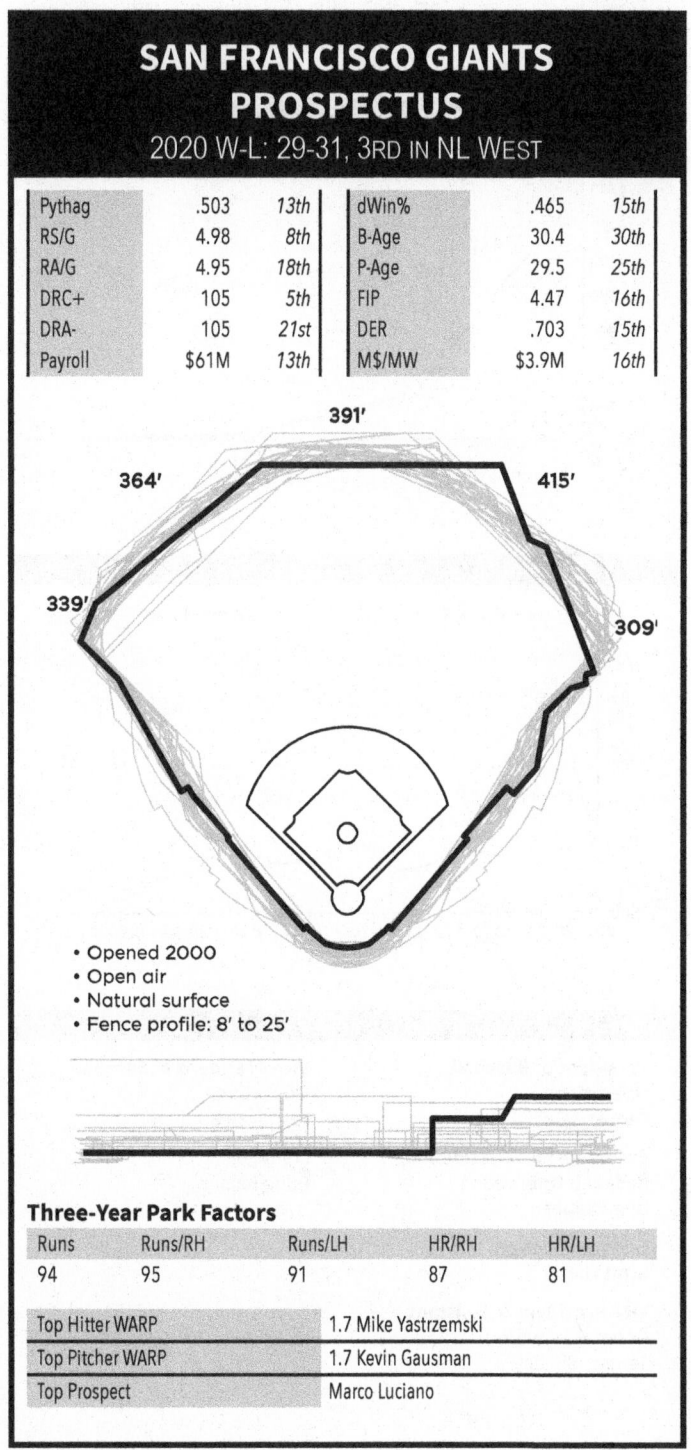

SAN FRANCISCO GIANTS PROSPECTUS
2020 W-L: 29-31, 3RD IN NL WEST

Pythag	.503	13th	dWin%	.465	15th
RS/G	4.98	8th	B-Age	30.4	30th
RA/G	4.95	18th	P-Age	29.5	25th
DRC+	105	5th	FIP	4.47	16th
DRA-	105	21st	DER	.703	15th
Payroll	$61M	13th	M$/MW	$3.9M	16th

391'

364'

415'

339'

309'

- Opened 2000
- Open air
- Natural surface
- Fence profile: 8' to 25'

Three-Year Park Factors

Runs	Runs/RH	Runs/LH	HR/RH	HR/LH
94	95	91	87	81

Top Hitter WARP	1.7 Mike Yastrzemski
Top Pitcher WARP	1.7 Kevin Gausman
Top Prospect	Marco Luciano

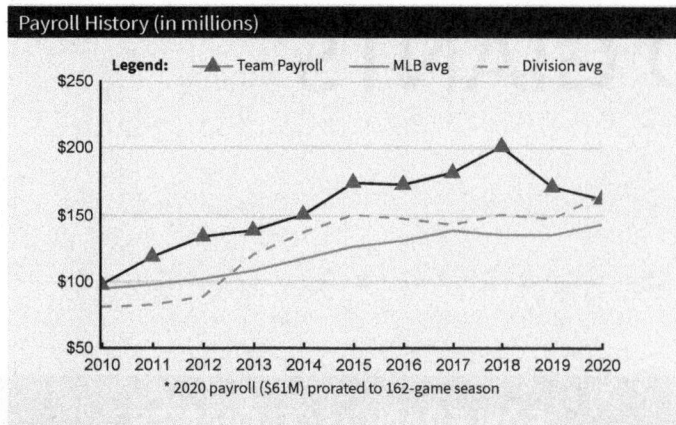

Payroll History (in millions)

Legend: ▲ Team Payroll — MLB avg - - Division avg

* 2020 payroll ($61M) prorated to 162-game season

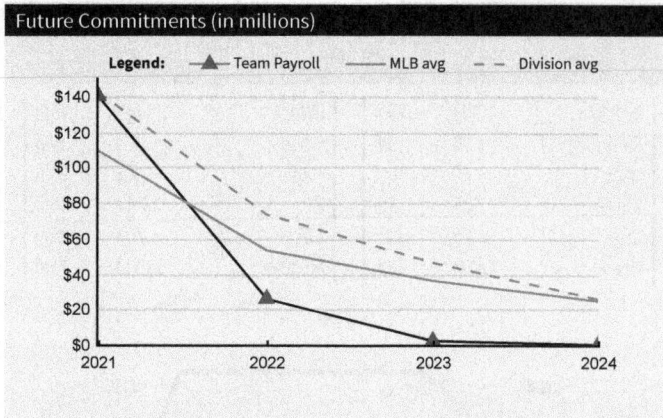

Future Commitments (in millions)

Legend: ▲ Team Payroll — MLB avg - - Division avg

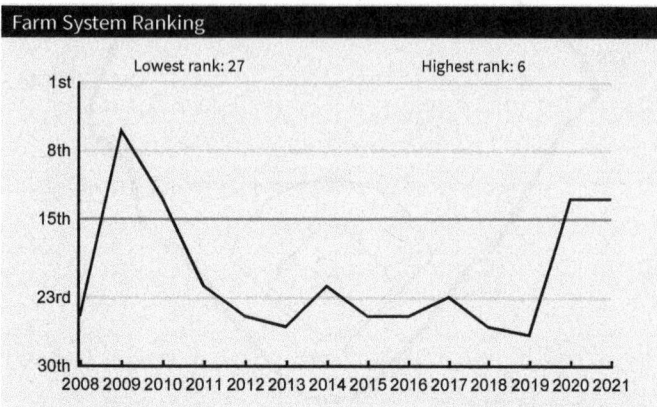

Farm System Ranking

Lowest rank: 27   Highest rank: 6

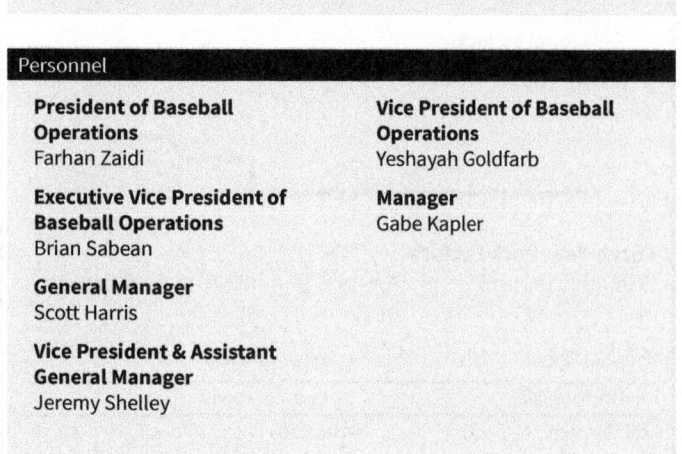

Personnel

President of Baseball Operations
Farhan Zaidi

Executive Vice President of Baseball Operations
Brian Sabean

General Manager
Scott Harris

Vice President & Assistant General Manager
Jeremy Shelley

Vice President of Baseball Operations
Yeshayah Goldfarb

Manager
Gabe Kapler

But the Brandons have both been mainstays of the team for most of a decade. And like the Giants overall, I don't think they've ever gotten their due as to how important and valuable they have been over the years.

Belt, in particular, always seemed to never quite connect. A decade ago in our *Baseball Prospectus* annual, he was described as "flat-out Ruthian" in the minor leagues. Now that the flower has bloomed, we find that Belt has had an above-average OBP and excellent defense at first and some "doubles power," but to date has never had a 20-home run season. It translates into a good, though not overwhelming first base profile. Had Belt been an unheralded prospect who showed up and produced seasons of 0.8, 3.0, 1.3, 2.7, 1.8, 2.1, 1.9, and (in a shortened 2020 season) 1.3 WARP, over the course of eight seasons, that would be seen as a player development marvel. It always seems so much less interesting when it's someone who was supposed to be that 6 WARP per year cornerstone. Crawford didn't have the same hype coming up as a prospect, and has made a career of being a just-below-average hitter, relative to the league, but one who could play a very good version of shortstop. Those who know a little bit about WARP know that's a recipe for a decent player.

Part of the problem is that they are both making in excess of $15 million per year. Had they been young enough to be arb-eligible, that sort of (projected) salary would have probably made them a non-tender candidate. Fifteen million dollars is the sort of salary that, even though we all know the whole "a win has been worth $8 to $10 million in the free agent market over the past few years" thing, feels like it should be attached to someone who provides more value. And I get it. No one will ever make the case that Belt or Crawford are hidden superstars, but it's worth pointing out how valuable a consistently average player is in Major League Baseball.

Warning! Gory Mathematical Details Ahead!

In 2019—I'm going to ignore 2020 because the shortened season makes a mess of these comparisons—there were 127 hitters who posted a WARP of at least 2.0 wins. If you take it down to the level of 1.5 wins, you get 166 hitters. On an average team, players like Belt and Crawford, who have consistently put up WARP scores in that range, settle into the "fourth- or fifth-best overall" range of the eight regular position player starters on the team. They may or may not be the fourth- or fifth-best hitter, because WARP includes defense and baserunning. Belt and Crawford are gloriously average regulars in any given season. Not bad. Not great. Average. Before you consider that too great a curse, read on.

I looked at all position players who logged at least 100 PA in a given season and who debuted after 1996. I looked at all player seasons between 1996 and 2019, again excluding 2020 because of the shortened schedule. Between those years, there were 1,680 unique individuals who logged at least one season of 100 PA, two of whom were Crawford and Belt. During that span, Crawford and Belt both notched six seasons above 1.5 WARP. Not bad. Forty-four other players can make that claim. Where does that place the Brandons in the grand scheme of things?

Number of 1.5 win seasons	Percent of Sample	Cumulative Percentage
0	54.9%	54.9%
1	14.3%	69.3%
2	7.3%	76.5%
3	6.1%	82.7%
4	3.5%	86.2%
5	3.5%	89.7%
6	2.7%	92.4%
7	1.8%	94.3%
8+	5.9%	100.0%

(note: due to rounding, some of the percentages might look a tiny bit off)

If we look at the Brandons from this perspective, looking over their *full body of work* (to date), they are part of the elite 10 percent of their contemporaries who were consistently able to produce boringly average outcomes year after year, even if they never had anything close to an MVP campaign. (If you want to give Belt credit for his 1.3 WARP performance in 2020 over 60 games, he reaches the top six percent.) It doesn't look all that impressive when viewed as a single season, but longevity is its own skill, and one that never gets its proper due when we talk about major leaguers. We love our supernovae, who explode for a season or two, but forget our North Stars quietly sitting there night after night guiding the way.

There will be a few more players—in this sample, the ones who perhaps debuted in 2018 and will eventually cross the line of six seasons of 1.5 WARP or more, but haven't had the chance to do that yet—that will join them in that club, but it won't change the overall conclusion. Brandons Crawford and Belt have played a different role than perhaps Giants' fans had hoped for, but one that was important all along and certainly not one to be sad about.

This coming season might be the last time that fans get to see either one in San Francisco. They're on the wrong side of 30-something, along with a lot of the rest of the team, and that core hasn't been very good lately. Some of you have seen this movie before. The teardown is coming, if it isn't already here. The guard will change. Brian Sabean is already gone, and the Giants got one of those newfangled "analytics" GMs to run the show. This team will probably be built differently than the old one was. Maybe there will eventually be a new dynasty in (Northern) California, but for a little while, those memories of Bumgarner's five innings of relief in 2014 will be the only thing that will keep Giants fans warm at Mega Interwebs Stadium. But as you look back, maybe it's time to appreciate how important the Brandons were to that time period. They've done something that not a lot of players can say that they have. They stuck around.

And I hope that fans will stick around too. There's a talent to sticking through the tough times. Eventually, there will be a resurgence by the Bay, and there's a 50/50 shot that it will happen in an even year. Some new generation of players will start hitting balls into McCovey Cove and eventually they'll have their magic moments. Maybe even one of the Brandons will be around to see them, still chugging along and putting up solid-if-not-spectacular performances. And that will still be valuable. ■

—*Russell A. Carleton is an author of Baseball Prospectus.*

HITTERS

Patrick Bailey C Born: 05/29/99 Age: 22 Bats: S Throws: R Height: 6'2" Weight: 207 Origin: Round 1, 2020 Draft (#13 overall)

Spending a first-round pick on Bailey, a bat-first catcher who is only two years behind a franchise building block at the position, may seem like an inefficiency, until you think for a minute about all the things that can go wrong with catching prospects. Besides, even if Bart pans out as hoped, Bailey's switch-hitting power bat should play somewhere, be it at a different position or with another team.

★ ★ ★ *2021 Top 101 Prospect* **#29** ★ ★ ★

Joey Bart C Born: 12/15/96 Age: 24 Bats: R Throws: R Height: 6'2" Weight: 238 Origin: Round 1, 2018 Draft (#2 overall)

YEAR	TEAM	LVL	AGE	PA	R	2B	3B	HR	RBI	BB	K	SB	CS	Whiff%	AVG/OBP/SLG	DRC+	BABIP	BRR	FRAA	WARP
2018	GIO	ROK	21	25	3	1	1	0	1	1	7	0	0		.261/.320/.391	83	.375	-0.1	C(4): -0.1	0.0
2018	SK	SS	21	203	35	14	2	13	39	12	40	2	1		.298/.369/.613	146	.318	1.2	C(32): -1.0	1.0
2019	SJ	HI-A	22	251	37	10	2	12	37	14	50	5	2		.265/.315/.479	112	.291	1.0	C(50): -1.9	1.2
2019	RIC	AA	22	87	9	4	1	4	11	7	21	0	2		.316/.368/.544	163	.382	-1.2	C(15): 0.2	0.8
2020	SF	MLB	24	111	15	5	2	0	7	3	41	0	0	34.5%	.233/.288/.320	48	.387	-0.5	C(32): 0.1	-0.4
2021 FS	SF	MLB	24	600	66	24	5	19	73	30	200	2	1	34.5%	.236/.289/.406	93	.330	2.3	C 0	2.2
2021 DC	SF	MLB	24	302	33	12	2	10	37	15	101	1	0	34.5%	.236/.289/.406	93	.330	1.2	C 0	1.0

Comparables: Luis Exposito, John Hicks, Jose Lobaton

YEAR	TEAM	P. COUNT	FRM RUNS	BLK RUNS	THRW RUNS	TOT RUNS
2019	RIC	2187	0.4	0.0	0.1	0.5
2020	SF	4088	0.3	0.0	0.2	0.5
2021	*SF*	*8418*	*1.8*	*0.1*	*-0.3*	*1.6*

Bart, a former first-round pick out of Georgia Tech, made his major-league debut in August, an outcome that was likely even if the season had not been derailed by a global pandemic. The wrinkle in this plan, of course, was the lack of early-season reps at Triple-A, which meant throwing Bart into the middle of the strangest of seasons and the unlikeliest of playoff runs. The Giants were probably not surprised by a rocky debut that featured little power and far too many strikeouts at the plate, and a steep defensive learning curve behind it. There's plenty of college and minor-league data suggesting Bart is still the heir apparent to Posey, but the questions raised by his performance were likely enough to confirm that a longer pass through Triple-A may be the best outcome for all concerned.

Brandon Belt 1B Born: 04/20/88 Age: 33 Bats: L Throws: L Height: 6'3" Weight: 231 Origin: Round 5, 2009 Draft (#147 overall)

YEAR	TEAM	LVL	AGE	PA	R	2B	3B	HR	RBI	BB	K	SB	CS	Whiff%	AVG/OBP/SLG	DRC+	BABIP	BRR	FRAA	WARP
2018	SF	MLB	30	456	50	18	2	14	46	49	107	4	0	25.9%	.253/.342/.414	107	.311	-0.6	1B(104): 9.9, LF(8): 0.3	2.1
2019	SF	MLB	31	616	76	32	3	17	57	83	127	4	3	22.8%	.234/.339/.403	105	.275	-2.2	1B(144): 7.2, LF(14): -0.5, RF(1): -0.0	1.9
2020	SF	MLB	32	179	25	13	1	9	30	30	36	0	0	23.6%	.309/.425/.591	146	.356	-0.8	1B(47): 0.4	1.4
2021 FS	SF	MLB	33	600	74	26	3	19	75	85	146	3	2	23.6%	.241/.355/.423	117	.301	0.1	1B 15, LF 0	3.8
2021 DC	SF	MLB	33	504	62	22	3	16	63	71	123	3	1	23.6%	.241/.355/.423	117	.301	0.1	1B 13	3.2

Comparables: Derrek Lee, Brian Daubach, Jeff Conine

There was considerable speculation about whether or not the short season would be a net benefit or detriment to the health of pitchers. Would the short stretch help preserve arms that had been habitually overworked? Or would the inconsistent off-season and quick ramp-up lead to more injuries? What we *should* have focused on was whether or not the 60-game season could fall outside of the inevitable, bad-luck injury to Belt, or whether his curse was so strong that he could play a six-game season and still take an unfortunate ball to an unfortunate place, or twist, tear or break something while performing a harmless everyday action. Well, the results are in, and: the 60-game Belt was the best Belt, with him setting career-bests in nearly every rate-based category. It probably didn't hurt that fences were moved to limit the massive right- and center-field acreage in Oracle Park, and (perhaps more significantly) that the closure of the right field archway portholes cut down on winds blowing in from the bay. Nonetheless, Belt was magnificent, and more importantly, injury-free...albeit not by much, as he had surgery to remove a bone spur from his heel two weeks after the conclusion of the season. Perhaps even one additional playoff game would have been a bridge too far. We won't even speculate on adding another hundred games to that total for future seasons, but he'll always have those two beautiful months in 2020.

★ ★ ★ *2021 Top 101 Prospect* **#75** ★ ★ ★

Hunter Bishop OF Born: 06/25/98 Age: 23 Bats: L Throws: R Height: 6'5" Weight: 210 Origin: Round 1, 2019 Draft (#10 overall)

YEAR	TEAM	LVL	AGE	PA	R	2B	3B	HR	RBI	BB	K	SB	CS	Whiff%	AVG/OBP/SLG	DRC+	BABIP	BRR	FRAA	WARP
2019	GIO	ROK	21	29	4	3	0	1	3	9	11	2	0		.250/.483/.550	113	.500	0.4	CF(4): -1.0	0.0
2019	SK	SS	21	117	21	1	1	4	9	29	28	4	2		.224/.427/.400	176	.278	-0.3	CF(22): -2.2	0.7
2021 FS	SF	MLB	23	600	54	26	2	12	57	56	217	10	4		.204/.286/.335	74	.315	0.1	CF -8	-0.9

Looking at Bishop's game is like binge-watching *Diners, Drive-Ins, and Dives*. It all looks so tempting, even in its aggressive lack of subtlety. Power from the left side: OFF THE HOOK. Upper-cut swing: MMM-HMMM. Speed: RIGHTEOUS. Lanky, athletic frame: SHUT THE FRONT DOOR. Ability to take a walk: FUNKALICIOUS. Your mouth is already watering, even if your gut tells you that the strikeouts might cause some sharp pains and center field will likely disappear from the menu. Still, for an organization whose outfield is a bit bland yet, Bishop is one prospect who could take the Giants on the express bus to Flavortown.

Alexander Canario CF Born: 05/07/00 Age: 21 Bats: R Throws: R Height: 6'1" Weight: 165 Origin: International Free Agent, 2016

YEAR	TEAM	LVL	AGE	PA	R	2B	3B	HR	RBI	BB	K	SB	CS	Whiff%	AVG/OBP/SLG	DRC+	BABIP	BRR	FRAA	WARP
2018	GIB	ROK	18	208	36	5	2	6	19	27	51	8	5		.250/.357/.403	114	.317	-0.5	CF(44): 1.0	0.4
2019	GIO	ROK	19	46	13	3	1	7	14	2	9	1	0		.395/.435/1.000	285	.370	-0.3	CF(8): -0.7	0.8
2019	SK	SS	19	219	38	17	1	9	40	18	71	3	1		.301/.365/.539	158	.419	-1.0	CF(26): -8.1, RF(16): -1.1	0.5
2021 FS	SF	MLB	21	600	46	27	3	9	51	36	211	13	6		.199/.253/.310	53	.302	-1.5	CF -7, RF 2	-2.6

Comparables: Greg Halman, Victor Robles, Austin Meadows

A dislocated shoulder during fall instructs, and a subsequent labrum surgery, has pressed the pause button on Canario's development. Power has been the 20-year-old's calling card, so one can only wish him a full recovery before speculating about his future role with the club.

Curt Casali C Born: 11/09/88 Age: 32 Bats: R Throws: R Height: 6'2" Weight: 220 Origin: Round 10, 2011 Draft (#317 overall)

YEAR	TEAM	LVL	AGE	PA	R	2B	3B	HR	RBI	BB	K	SB	CS	Whiff%	AVG/OBP/SLG	DRC+	BABIP	BRR	FRAA	WARP
2018	DUR	AAA	29	104	13	5	0	4	20	7	19	0	0		.274/.327/.453	110	.301	-0.1	C(26): 1.0	0.6
2018	CIN	MLB	29	156	15	10	0	4	16	12	32	0	2	23.7%	.293/.355/.450	101	.352	0.1	C(38): -4.1, 1B(6): 0.1, 2B(1): -0.0	0.3
2019	CIN	MLB	30	236	24	9	0	8	32	25	59	0	0	22.4%	.251/.331/.411	102	.308	0.1	C(67): 6.0, 1B(4): 0.0	1.8
2020	CIN	MLB	32	93	10	3	0	6	8	14	29	2	0	28.2%	.224/.366/.500	112	.268	-0.8	C(29): -0.1	0.5
2021 FS	SF	MLB	32	600	71	25	1	23	70	64	182	1	0	24.6%	.239/.333/.427	105	.319	-1.3	C 3, 1B 0	3.0
2021 DC	SF	MLB	32	134	15	5	0	5	15	14	40	0	0	24.6%	.239/.333/.427	105	.319	-0.3	C 1	0.7

Comparables: Tom Wilson, Rich Rowland, Jason LaRue

Casali once again held up his end as the righty/good-hit/decent-frame/poor-block half of Cincinnati's backstop platoon. Among National League catchers only Will Smith and Austin Nola posted a higher DRC+, fueled by Casali's .290/.389/.613 line against southpaws. His worst two offensive seasons occurred when he came to the plate more than 200 times so concerns that the veteran receiver would be overexposed if used in an expanded role, and

YEAR	TEAM	P. COUNT	FRM RUNS	BLK RUNS	THRW RUNS	TOT RUNS
2018	CIN	4858	-2.1	-1.3	-0.2	-3.5
2019	CIN	8395	4.5	1.8	-0.3	6.0
2020	CIN	3610	1.0	-0.3	0.0	0.7
2021	SF	4810	1.8	-0.6	-0.1	1.1

saw more same-side pitching, are warranted. Good catchers are hard to find and even harder to develop, so Casali's consistent competence and noted game-calling skills should keep him challenging teammates to off-season games of CupCheck for years to come. The Giants snagged him in free agency after the Reds non-tendered Casali in the offseason.

Zack Cozart 3B   Born: 08/12/85   Age: 35   Bats: R   Throws: R   Height: 6'0"   Weight: 205   Origin: Round 2, 2007 Draft (#79 overall)

YEAR	TEAM	LVL	AGE	PA	R	2B	3B	HR	RBI	BB	K	SB	CS	Whiff%	AVG/OBP/SLG	DRC+	BABIP	BRR	FRAA	WARP
2018	LAA	MLB	32	253	29	13	2	5	18	19	42	0	0	18.0%	.219/.296/.362	90	.244	-0.2	3B(35): -0.7, 2B(16): -0.2, SS(15): 0.3	0.5
2019	LAA	MLB	33	107	4	2	0	0	7	5	16	0	0	18.3%	.124/.178/.144	66	.143	0.4	3B(31): 0.5, SS(5): -1.0, 2B(1): -0.1	-0.1
2021 FS	SF	MLB	35	600	64	24	3	15	64	51	118	3	1	18.1%	.226/.301/.367	88	.262	1.8	SS -2, 3B 0	0.7

Comparables: Clint Barmes, Royce Clayton, Shane Halter

Behold baseball's New Economics: in December of 2019, the Giants traded for Cozart and first-rounder Will Wilson in exchange for extremely minor minor-leaguer Garrett Williams. The Angels were able to clear Cozart's contract in their efforts to free up money for a possible Gerrit Cole signing (which: womp womp). The Giants were happy to take on Cozart's contract, along with his injured shoulder, to acquire Wilson and immediately add a top-five prospect to the system. The pretense of a Cozart comeback was given up in January, when the shortstop-turned-third-baseman was released almost one month to the day after his trade to San Francisco. Farhan Zaidi's effective purchase of a prospect for the cost of a big contract may have laid a blueprint that other clubs will follow. Will this gambit work on anyone but the Angels? We'll find out soon enough.

Brandon Crawford SS   Born: 01/21/87   Age: 34   Bats: L   Throws: R   Height: 6'1"   Weight: 223   Origin: Round 4, 2008 Draft (#117 overall)

YEAR	TEAM	LVL	AGE	PA	R	2B	3B	HR	RBI	BB	K	SB	CS	Whiff%	AVG/OBP/SLG	DRC+	BABIP	BRR	FRAA	WARP
2018	SF	MLB	31	594	63	28	2	14	54	50	122	4	5	29.2%	.254/.325/.394	95	.302	0.5	SS(146): 15.3	4.0
2019	SF	MLB	32	560	58	24	2	11	59	53	117	3	2	28.3%	.228/.304/.350	79	.274	-3.4	SS(142): 0.9	0.9
2020	SF	MLB	33	193	26	12	0	8	28	15	47	1	2	31.6%	.256/.326/.465	98	.303	-1.7	SS(53): 3.4	0.6
2021 FS	SF	MLB	34	600	62	28	3	15	67	50	147	5	2	29.4%	.236/.309/.384	91	.297	0.7	SS 2	1.5
2021 DC	SF	MLB	34	572	59	27	3	14	64	47	140	5	1	29.4%	.236/.309/.384	91	.297	0.7	SS 2	1.4

Comparables: Chris Woodward, Cliff Pennington, Jay Bell

The long tail of Crawford's career is aging about as well as his flowing, wavy, intentionally unkempt, unfailingly moist hair. Depending on your tastes, this could be either insult or compliment. On the plus side, there has scarcely been a more reliable position player in the major leagues over the last decade than Crawford. Since assuming the full-time job during 2012, the second of the Giants' three World Series-winning years, Crawford has played in at least 143 games from 2013 through 2019 (appearing in 54 games in the shortened 2020). Yet, recognizing that the bat has been roughly league-average for several seasons and the defense has declined to merely "good" feels like finding a few more strands in the shower drain each year. There's not enough in the negative column to jeopardize his role for 2021, but after that, Crawford's six-year deal will be at an end, and he might be overdue for a cut.

Jaylin Davis RF   Born: 07/01/94   Age: 27   Bats: R   Throws: R   Height: 5'11"   Weight: 205   Origin: Round 24, 2015 Draft (#710 overall)

YEAR	TEAM	LVL	AGE	PA	R	2B	3B	HR	RBI	BB	K	SB	CS	Whiff%	AVG/OBP/SLG	DRC+	BABIP	BRR	FRAA	WARP
2018	FTM	HI-A	23	227	23	10	0	5	19	23	57	3	2		.271/.354/.397	123	.355	4.1	RF(50): -6.2, LF(2): -0.2	0.3
2018	CHA	AA	23	267	30	14	2	6	34	21	69	5	2		.275/.341/.425	110	.359	-0.2	RF(50): 2.5, CF(1): -0.1	0.5
2019	PNS	AA	24	251	34	9	0	10	25	36	64	7	3		.274/.382/.458	155	.345	-0.2	RF(42): -2.0, LF(8): 0.8, CF(4): 0.4	1.8
2019	SAC	AAA	24	117	21	6	0	10	27	14	28	1	1		.333/.419/.686	138	.375	0.9	RF(16): 3.1, CF(7): 0.6, LF(4): -0.0	1.2
2019	ROC	AAA	24	173	39	11	1	15	42	15	46	2	0		.331/.405/.708	159	.387	0.3	RF(32): 2.8, CF(6): 0.5	1.8
2019	SF	MLB	24	47	2	0	0	1	3	3	11	1	2	43.5%	.167/.255/.238	68	.200	-0.7	RF(15): -0.5	-0.2
2020	SF	MLB	26	12	2	0	0	1	1	0	6	0	0	44.4%	.167/.167/.417	81	.200	-0.1	RF(4): -0.0	0.0
2021 FS	SF	MLB	26	600	69	25	2	24	80	47	218	3	1	43.8%	.230/.300/.423	103	.332	0.5	RF -9, LF 0	0.9
2021 DC	SF	MLB	26	33	3	1	0	1	4	2	12	0	0	43.8%	.230/.300/.423	103	.332	0.0	RF 0	0.0

Comparables: Jason Perry, Adolis Garcia, Michael Reed

The ridiculous excess of 2019 Triple-A batting lines has generated enough disinformation that it's surprising Rachel Maddow hasn't led a week of nightly shows with this issue. We may be sorting through the inflated averages and Ruthian power numbers for a while still, trying to separate good intel from fake news. Davis' case may be one of the easier ones to crack, however: a 2019 that saw him bang 35 homers and maintain a nearly .400 on-base percentage might have been the stuff of momentary headlines, but his limited run in the majors has suggested his story is just another dead-end. With some encouraging indications that Davis has adjusted his swing plane, it may be a little early to consign him to yesterday's news; he will need to show that he can make more regular contact, though, if his major-league career is ever going to make it above the fold.

Alex Dickerson LF   Born: 05/26/90   Age: 31   Bats: L   Throws: L   Height: 6'2"   Weight: 226   Origin: Round 3, 2011 Draft (#91 overall)

YEAR	TEAM	LVL	AGE	PA	R	2B	3B	HR	RBI	BB	K	SB	CS	Whiff%	AVG/OBP/SLG	DRC+	BABIP	BRR	FRAA	WARP
2019	ELP	AAA	29	113	17	5	1	5	20	14	18	0	0		.372/.469/.606	125	.417	0.6	1B(6): -0.5, LF(6): 0.3, RF(3): 0.1	0.7
2019	SF	MLB	29	171	28	13	3	6	26	13	35	1	1	22.2%	.290/.351/.529	103	.339	0.5	LF(44): -4.5, RF(1): -0.2	0.1
2019	SD	MLB	29	19	1	0	0	0	2	0	7	0	0	40.5%	.158/.158/.158	67	.250	0.2	LF(6): -0.1	0.0
2020	SF	MLB	30	170	28	10	1	10	27	16	30	0	0	23.4%	.298/.371/.576	128	.312	-0.1	LF(41): -0.3, RF(5): 0.7	0.8
2021 FS	SF	MLB	31	600	80	31	4	21	78	51	123	4	1	23.7%	.266/.341/.462	122	.308	1.6	LF -6, 1B 0	2.8
2021 DC	SF	MLB	31	403	54	20	2	14	52	34	83	3	1	23.7%	.266/.341/.462	122	.308	1.1	LF -4	2.0

Comparables: Rondell White, Jason Kubel, Marty Cordova

After a mostly-uneventful career that alternated between bench player and injured player, A-Dick managed to pack enough drama into the past September to make up for lost time. On the first day of the month, he took full advantage of Coors Field, blasting three homers and notching six RBI in a five-hit outing (all career highs, of course). Almost two weeks later, he returned a false positive on a COVID-19 test, causing a cancelled game, fears for the team's schedule and concerns for his pregnant wife Jennifer. All's well that ends well, and September concluded with a healthy and hitting Dickerson and a new member of the family, as Jennifer delivered Levi on the 24th. Dickerson showed enough on the field to earn a look for a strong-side, corner outfield platoon spot in 2021. He'll hope to provide plenty of power and on-base ability—this time with none of the past September's drama.

Mauricio Dubón SS
Born: 07/19/94   Age: 26   Bats: R   Throws: R   Height: 6'0"   Weight: 173   Origin: Round 26, 2013 Draft (#773 overall)

YEAR	TEAM	LVL	AGE	PA	R	2B	3B	HR	RBI	BB	K	SB	CS	Whiff%	AVG/OBP/SLG	DRC+	BABIP	BRR	FRAA	WARP
2018	RMV	AAA	23	114	18	9	2	4	18	2	19	6	3		.343/.348/.574	106	.379	1.5	SS(23): 0.3, 2B(4): 0.6	0.7
2019	SAC	AAA	24	112	23	4	0	4	9	10	9	1	2		.323/.391/.485	102	.326	0.6	SS(17): -0.1, 2B(7): 0.3	0.9
2019	SA	AAA	24	427	59	22	1	16	47	18	59	9	6		.297/.333/.475	102	.316	-0.9	SS(83): 4.1, 2B(12): 0.7, 3B(1): -0.0	2.4
2019	SF	MLB	24	109	12	5	0	4	9	5	19	3	1	21.2%	.279/.312/.442	88	.309	1.1	2B(22): 3.8, SS(9): -0.4	0.7
2019	MIL	MLB	24	2	0	0	0	0	0	0	1	0	0	10.0%	.000/.000/.000	84	.000		SS(1): -0.0	0.0
2020	SF	MLB	26	177	21	4	1	4	19	15	36	2	3	24.3%	.274/.337/.389	96	.328	-0.5	CF(44): 1.3, 2B(8): 0.6, SS(8): -0.1	0.6
2021 FS	SF	MLB	26	600	63	21	3	15	67	34	123	13	5	23.2%	.254/.301/.384	90	.300	1.8	SS 1, 2B 0	1.5
2021 DC	SF	MLB	26	572	60	20	3	14	64	33	117	12	4	23.2%	.254/.301/.384	90	.300	1.7	CF -4, SS 1	0.9

Comparables: Devon White, Billy Conigliaro, Roberto Kelly

The awkward masonry of the Giants' roster only works with the right type of mortar. Fitting the worn brick of aging players on legacy contracts (Longoria, Belt, Posey) with pieces repurposed from the post-prospect junkyard (Yaz, Slater, Dickerson) demands some multipositional spackle, something flexible and springy enough to survive the inevitable stresses of a rebuilding team. Dubón is the adhesive substance of this slapdash edifice. Bouncing around from second, to shortstop and ultimately finding his best use in center field, Dubón gave the Giants credible defense, passable on-base ability and all the speed you can handle. Even if he'll never be a load-bearing keystone, he can help a team in transition avoid catastrophic structural failure.

Steven Duggar RF
Born: 11/04/93   Age: 27   Bats: L   Throws: R   Height: 6'1"   Weight: 187   Origin: Round 6, 2015 Draft (#186 overall)

YEAR	TEAM	LVL	AGE	PA	R	2B	3B	HR	RBI	BB	K	SB	CS	Whiff%	AVG/OBP/SLG	DRC+	BABIP	BRR	FRAA	WARP
2018	SAC	AAA	24	356	52	27	4	4	21	39	103	11	4		.272/.354/.421	103	.392	-0.1	CF(74): 9.6	1.9
2018	SF	MLB	24	152	20	11	1	2	17	10	44	5	1	27.3%	.255/.303/.390	70	.354	3.6	CF(40): -3.4	0.0
2019	SAC	AAA	25	102	24	6	1	3	13	18	21	2	3		.337/.461/.542	138	.424	0.2	CF(19): 0.4	0.9
2019	SF	MLB	25	281	26	12	2	4	28	16	78	1	4	27.0%	.234/.278/.341	61	.313	-1.4	CF(39): 2.1, RF(34): -0.8	-0.6
2020	SF	MLB	27	36	3	2	0	0	3	1	11	1	0	20.4%	.176/.222/.235	68	.261	-0.8	LF(11): 0.4, RF(7): -0.3, CF(4): -0.3	-0.2
2021 FS	SF	MLB	27	600	61	25	4	11	55	54	183	7	4	26.3%	.226/.300/.351	79	.320	-0.8	CF 2, RF -4	0.0
2021 DC	SF	MLB	27	134	13	5	0	2	12	12	40	1	0	26.3%	.226/.300/.351	79	.320	-0.2	LF 0, CF 1	-0.1

Comparables: Chad Hermansen, Laynce Nix, Luis Terrero

Not to be confused with the Diggers, a far-left Haight-Ashbury commune from the '60s, Duggar's Summer of Love was really only a couple of months as the starting center fielder in 2019. Since then, it's been too many bad trips to the plate, and he may be far out of the Giants' plans now.

Wilmer Flores 2B
Born: 08/06/91   Age: 29   Bats: R   Throws: R   Height: 6'2"   Weight: 213   Origin: International Free Agent, 2007

YEAR	TEAM	LVL	AGE	PA	R	2B	3B	HR	RBI	BB	K	SB	CS	Whiff%	AVG/OBP/SLG	DRC+	BABIP	BRR	FRAA	WARP
2018	NYM	MLB	26	429	43	25	0	11	51	29	42	0	0	13.7%	.267/.319/.417	105	.269	-3.2	1B(83): -2.6, 2B(13): 0.1, 3B(10): -1.1	0.4
2019	ARI	MLB	27	285	31	18	0	9	37	15	31	0	0	10.8%	.317/.361/.487	117	.332	-0.2	2B(64): -5.4, 1B(16): 0.1	1.0
2020	SF	MLB	29	213	30	11	1	12	32	13	36	1	0	17.8%	.268/.315/.515	117	.272	-1.5	1B(14): 0.6, 2B(14): 1.2, 3B(3): -0.4	0.9
2021 FS	SF	MLB	29	600	72	26	1	23	85	35	98	1	0	14.4%	.259/.309/.438	109	.276	-0.5	2B -3, 3B -1	1.6
2021 DC	SF	MLB	29	302	36	13	0	11	42	17	49	0	0	14.4%	.259/.309/.438	109	.276	-0.3	2B -2, SS 0	0.9

Comparables: Aaron Hill, Robinson Canó, Carlos Baerga

Before the five-year fever dream that saw the Giants win three championships, the history of the team in San Francisco had been one of the sadder stories in the majors: three Series appearances, three losses, each uniquely painful (Bobby Richardson, Scott Spiezio/Troy Glaus) and/or bizarre (the 1989 Loma Prieta earthquake). There was also that cursed 1993 season that saw the team win 103 games, only to miss out on the playoffs because "Western" Division rival Atlanta Braves won 104. We digress. Flores made his case to be a spiritual OG (Original Giant) during the season's final weekend, after his three-run, possible-playoff-clinching homer was swept into the dustbin of history by Trent Grisham's walk-off shot. Ah well. The Giants will be happy to have Flores back, for the second season of a two-year deal, to create happier memories in 2021.

Evan Longoria 3B
Born: 10/07/85   Age: 35   Bats: R   Throws: R   Height: 6'1"   Weight: 213   Origin: Round 1, 2006 Draft (#3 overall)

YEAR	TEAM	LVL	AGE	PA	R	2B	3B	HR	RBI	BB	K	SB	CS	Whiff%	AVG/OBP/SLG	DRC+	BABIP	BRR	FRAA	WARP
2018	SF	MLB	32	512	51	25	4	16	54	22	101	3	1	20.5%	.244/.281/.412	89	.274	-5.2	3B(123): -10.5	-0.5
2019	SF	MLB	33	508	59	19	2	20	69	43	112	3	1	25.6%	.254/.325/.437	99	.291	0.1	3B(119): 6.6	2.6
2020	SF	MLB	35	209	26	10	1	7	28	11	39	0	1	21.0%	.254/.297/.425	96	.280	-0.8	3B(52): -2.0	0.0
2021 FS	SF	MLB	35	600	63	26	2	18	74	39	132	3	1	23.1%	.236/.293/.391	90	.278	-0.1	3B 0	0.4
2021 DC	SF	MLB	35	538	57	23	2	16	67	35	119	3	1	23.1%	.236/.293/.391	90	.278	-0.1	3B 0	0.4

Comparables: Ryan Zimmerman, Eric Chavez, Scott Rolen

If it seems like Longoria has been in San Francisco a lot longer than three years, it may be because he's been part of a narrative that the Giants have had to live with since the final days of the Sabean/Evans era: too many older, expensive players locked up for the long term. In addition to Longo, there's Belt, Crawford, Cueto and (even though it be blasphemy) Posey. When you press on that plotline, you see that Longoria has not been a complete disaster, and in fact has been roughly the same offensive player since his final year in Tampa Bay. But the other side of "not a complete disaster" is "slightly below league-average corner infielder, with declining defensive skills." It's not a profile that's much in demand these days. Batted-ball metrics from 2020 suggest that Longoria had a late-career uptick in power; it would be immensely helpful if he could pair this thump with a modicum of patience, lest Zaidi, Kapler and company begin to run short on theirs.

★ ★ ★ *2021 Top 101 Prospect* **#8** ★ ★ ★

Marco Luciano SS   Born: 09/10/01   Age: 19   Bats: R   Throws: R   Height: 6'2"   Weight: 178   Origin: International Free Agent, 2018

YEAR	TEAM	LVL	AGE	PA	R	2B	3B	HR	RBI	BB	K	SB	CS	Whiff%	AVG/OBP/SLG	DRC+	BABIP	BRR	FRAA	WARP
2019	GIO	ROK	17	178	46	9	2	10	38	27	39	8	6		.322/.438/.616	194	.378	1.2	SS(31): 1.6	2.4
2019	SK	SS	17	38	6	4	0	0	4	5	6	1	0		.212/.316/.333	96	.259	-0.2	SS(9): -0.8	0.0
2021 FS	SF	MLB	19	600	46	27	2	7	50	39	198	13	7		.205/.263/.306	58	.303	-4.0	SS 2	-1.5

Whether it's responsible or not to base a player's comment off of a video from a fall instructional league game will be a matter for historians. But, absent a trove of 2020 data on the Giants' top prospect, we were left with one scene from early November: a static, centerfield video of Luciano absolutely cranking a fastball from Rockies lefty Ryan Rolison with a 119 mph EV bomb to the pull side. Among major-league hitters in 2020, the only player to top this exit velocity was Giancarlo Stanton. Though we only have a center-field view, Giants coach Matt Daniels tweeted that it was "quite possibly the furthest [sic] home run I've ever witnessed in person." For good measure, Luciano executed an exasperated hurl of a bat flip, as if disgusted that pitcher and ball had the hubris to even hope for success. Luciano still has a bit of a journey to Oracle Park, but his legend has already landed at SFO, taken BART into the city, grabbed a Tesora from Philz Coffee and now waits expectantly at 24 Willie Mays Plaza for his owner to claim him.

Luis Matos OF   Born: 01/28/02   Age: 19   Bats: R   Throws: R   Height: 5'11"   Weight: 160   Origin: International Free Agent, 2018

YEAR	TEAM	LVL	AGE	PA	R	2B	3B	HR	RBI	BB	K	SB	CS	Whiff%	AVG/OBP/SLG	DRC+	BABIP	BRR	FRAA	WARP
2019	DSL GIA	ROK	17	270	60	24	2	7	47	19	30	20	2		.362/.430/.570		.386			
2019	GIO	ROK	17	20	5	1	0	0	1	1	1	1	1		.438/.550/.500	182	.467	-0.2	CF(5): -0.7	0.1
2021 FS	SF	MLB	19	600	45	26	2	7	49	28	188	41	8		.211/.259/.306	55	.304	17.4	CF -7	-0.4

A 2019 July 2nd signing from Venezuela, Matos is still in that blessed dreamland where the tools could become anything: elite batting average, plate discipline, surprising power upside, lightning speed, the defense to stick in center field. Anything seldom becomes everything, but there should be at least a couple of somethings in Matos' future.

Hunter Pence RF   Born: 04/13/83   Age: 38   Bats: R   Throws: R   Height: 6'4"   Weight: 216   Origin: Round 2, 2004 Draft (#64 overall)

YEAR	TEAM	LVL	AGE	PA	R	2B	3B	HR	RBI	BB	K	SB	CS	Whiff%	AVG/OBP/SLG	DRC+	BABIP	BRR	FRAA	WARP
2018	SAC	AAA	35	111	11	4	0	1	13	6	24	0	0		.301/.342/.369	94	.380	-0.1	RF(12): 0.1, LF(11): 0.2	0.1
2018	SF	MLB	35	248	19	11	1	4	24	11	59	5	1	31.2%	.226/.258/.332	66	.282	0.4	LF(44): -3.1, RF(12): -1.2	-0.8
2019	TEX	MLB	36	316	53	17	1	18	59	26	69	6	1	31.1%	.297/.358/.552	121	.333	0.9	LF(16): 1.1, RF(8): 0.1	1.7
2020	SF	MLB	37	56	4	0	1	2	6	3	15	0	0	32.1%	.096/.161/.250	68	.086	0.1	LF(5): 0.2, RF(5): -0.0	-0.1
2021 FS	SF	MLB	38	600	59	23	2	15	67	43	159	4	1	31.3%	.228/.287/.362	82	.292	0.4	RF 1, LF 2	0.4

Comparables: Jason Lane, Brian Jordan, Ruben Sierra

Of the four stops on Pence's résumé, San Francisco saw his most successful run and became his spiritual home. Arriving in 2012, just in time for the second of the Giants' three titles, Pence instantly became a middle-of-the-order bat, reliable everyday right fielder and a scooter-riding, coffee-loving, fan-engaging free spirit beloved of the Bay's aging hippies and tech bros alike. After an improbable 2019 fountain-of-youth rejuvenation in Arlington, Pence returned to play his swan song in Oracle Park—but, sadly, only the cardboard fans were there to hear it. While it would have been nice for Pence to receive a proper send-off, Giants fans will remember the giddy, buzzing, glory years of the early teens, not the feeble valediction that ended, in August, the career of one of the most distinctive and likable players of the current century.

Buster Posey C   Born: 03/27/87   Age: 34   Bats: R   Throws: R   Height: 6'1"   Weight: 213   Origin: Round 1, 2008 Draft (#5 overall)

YEAR	TEAM	LVL	AGE	PA	R	2B	3B	HR	RBI	BB	K	SB	CS	Whiff%	AVG/OBP/SLG	DRC+	BABIP	BRR	FRAA	WARP
2018	SF	MLB	31	448	47	22	1	5	41	45	53	3	2	13.5%	.284/.359/.382	106	.316	-1.3	C(88): 0.1, 1B(13): 1.5	2.4
2019	SF	MLB	32	445	43	24	0	7	38	34	71	0	0	18.6%	.257/.320/.368	85	.296	-1.4	C(101): 14.9, 1B(4): -0.1	2.7
2021 FS	SF	MLB	34	600	68	27	1	11	63	59	89	4	1	16.9%	.267/.346/.387	106	.301	-0.4	C 5, 1B 5	3.7
2021 DC	SF	MLB	34	504	57	23	1	9	53	50	75	3	1	16.9%	.267/.346/.387	106	.301	-0.4	C 5, 1B 4	2.9

Comparables: Johnny Bench, Gary Carter, Brian McCann

YEAR	TEAM	P. COUNT	FRM RUNS	BLK RUNS	THRW RUNS	TOT RUNS
2018	SF	12351	0.9	0.7	0.1	1.7
2019	SF	13868	10.1	2.2	1.6	13.8
2021	SF	8418	3.2	1.5	0.7	5.4

As a likely Hall-of-Famer and most significant remaining link to the Giants' championship era, Posey has earned the privilege of directing the last act of his playing career as he sees fit. Fortunately for Farhan Zaidi, whatever the franchise cornerstone wants is likely to dovetail with current organizational aspirations. Posey should be fully healthy after opting out of 2020 (so he could visit his newly adopted twin daughters, who had to spend time in the neonatal intensive care unit), returning in 2021 to his age-34 season and the final guaranteed year on his contract (with a team option in 2022). While it's difficult to tell whether the decline in his bat (just look at the DRC+ plummet since 2017) is due to persistent injury or the inevitability of skills erosion after a decade of full-time catching in the majors, Posey's defense has remained solidly above average. With Bart now ready to try his hand against major-league competition, Posey has a chance to share the load at backstop, possibly cycling to first base a time or two a week (though an NL designated hitter would obviously benefit Posey more than most). One of two paths seems likely for Posey in the coming season: a healthy callback to his previous, younger excellence—thereby letting Bart gain reps in Triple-A—or an on-the-job mentorship of his eventual successor at the big-league level. Either of these outcomes would suit the rebuilding Giants just fine.

★ ★ ★ *2021 Top 101 Prospect* **#32** ★ ★ ★

Heliot Ramos **CF** Born: 09/07/99   Age: 21   Bats: R   Throws: R   Height: 6'0"   Weight: 188   Origin: Round 1, 2017 Draft (#19 overall)

YEAR	TEAM	LVL	AGE	PA	R	2B	3B	HR	RBI	BB	K	SB	CS	Whiff%	AVG/OBP/SLG	DRC+	BABIP	BRR	FRAA	WARP
2018	AUG	LO-A	18	535	61	24	8	11	52	35	136	8	7		.245/.313/.396	106	.319	1.8	CF(113): -4.5	0.7
2019	SJ	HI-A	19	338	51	18	0	13	40	32	85	6	7		.306/.385/.500	142	.385	0.1	CF(71): -5.1	1.7
2019	RIC	AA	19	106	13	6	1	3	15	10	33	2	3		.242/.321/.421	120	.339	-1.6	CF(19): -1.5	0.2
2021 FS	SF	MLB	21	600	63	25	5	15	65	37	217	6	4		.226/.284/.377	84	.339	-1.2	CF 0	0.6
2021 DC	SF	MLB	21	33	3	1	0	0	3	2	11	0	0		.226/.284/.377	84	.339	-0.1	RF 0	0.0

Comparables: Jo Adell, Anthony Gose, Cristian Pache

A rough 2019 introduction to Double-A and the rapid ascendancy of Marco Luciano pushed Ramos into the shadows a bit. He's still there, the bat is still great, but the profile is now more corner-outfield than center. Trimming the swing-and-miss should be the last challenge for Ramos to clear before leveling up to the majors.

Darin Ruf **1B** Born: 07/28/86   Age: 34   Bats: R   Throws: R   Height: 6'2"   Weight: 232   Origin: Round 20, 2009 Draft (#617 overall)

YEAR	TEAM	LVL	AGE	PA	R	2B	3B	HR	RBI	BB	K	SB	CS	Whiff%	AVG/OBP/SLG	DRC+	BABIP	BRR	FRAA	WARP
2020	SF	MLB	34	100	11	6	0	5	18	13	23	1	0	26.3%	.276/.370/.517	115	.322	-0.4	LF(22): 1.2, 1B(4): 0.1, RF(3): -0.4	0.4
2021 FS	SF	MLB	34	600	75	26	1	22	83	48	162	1	0	26.3%	.240/.312/.422	105	.299	-0.4		2.1
2021 DC	SF	MLB	34	336	42	15	1	12	46	27	90	0	0	26.3%	.240/.312/.422	105	.299	-0.2	LF -1	0.9

Comparables: Brian Daubach, Tony Clark, Wil Myers

You better believe the 2020 Vogelsong Award winner gets the full-comment treatment here. After three years as a Samsung Lion, Ruf returned to American shores looking much more like the middle-of-the-order producer he showed in the KBO than the one-dimensional power bat who washed out with the Phillies. While in Korea, he added patience and worked on hitting to all fields, elevating him above a short-side platoon slot for the time being. To be fair, his role was greatly enhanced by the NL use of the DH in 2020, but the bat seemed to argue a case that, even at 34 and likely ticketed for a bench role, Ruf may have a surprisingly smooth second MLB act.

Casey Schmitt **3B** Born: 03/01/99   Age: 22   Bats: R   Throws: R   Height: 6'2"   Weight: 200   Origin: Round 2, 2020 Draft (#49 overall)

Despite having both pitching and hitting success as a two-way player at San Diego State, the Giants' third-round pick Schmitt is more Jared Walsh than Shohei Ohtani. Oh, you didn't know Walsh tried his hand at pitching for a while? Exactly.

Austin Slater **LF** Born: 12/13/92   Age: 28   Bats: R   Throws: R   Height: 6'1"   Weight: 204   Origin: Round 8, 2014 Draft (#238 overall)

YEAR	TEAM	LVL	AGE	PA	R	2B	3B	HR	RBI	BB	K	SB	CS	Whiff%	AVG/OBP/SLG	DRC+	BABIP	BRR	FRAA	WARP
2018	SAC	AAA	25	223	32	24	2	5	32	21	39	8	2		.344/.417/.564	163	.405	1.4	RF(29): 0.6, 1B(13): -0.1, LF(6): -0.9	1.8
2018	SF	MLB	25	225	21	6	1	1	23	20	69	7	0	28.6%	.251/.333/.307	63	.377	1.3	LF(25): 1.8, 1B(21): 0.1, RF(14): -0.3	-0.2
2019	SAC	AAA	26	296	47	17	0	12	45	46	69	6	2		.308/.436/.529	139	.388	0.6	1B(38): 2.5, 3B(11): -1.4, LF(8): -0.6	2.1
2019	SF	MLB	26	192	20	9	3	5	21	22	59	1	0	32.9%	.238/.333/.417	73	.337	-0.7	RF(46): -0.2, 1B(8): -0.8, LF(2): -0.1	-0.4
2020	SF	MLB	28	104	18	2	1	5	7	16	22	8	1	25.3%	.282/.408/.506	117	.328	0.4	RF(9): 1.5, LF(3): 0.4	0.6
2021 FS	SF	MLB	28	600	77	19	3	17	58	63	160	3	1	29.3%	.248/.338/.396	109	.323	2.2	RF -2, LF 0	2.1
2021 DC	SF	MLB	28	269	34	8	1	7	26	28	72	1	0	29.3%	.248/.338/.396	109	.323	1.0	RF -1, LF 0	0.9

Comparables: Jason Repko, Michael Restovich, Byron Browne

Last year's 60-game season already created an artificially small statistical snapshot; capturing the essence of Slater's impressive 2020 requires us to pare down the sample even smaller, to the season's first month. After August, Slater went from being sidelined with a right elbow flexor strain to being used only as a DH—a predicament that left him far less effective. But gosh, what a month August was, with Slater teeing off on the (mostly southpaw) arms of the Western, uh…Conference. He got there by upping both launch angle and walk rate, suggesting there's more a Quad-A ceiling to his bat. Unlike a previous generation's namesake, this Slater will likely be saved not by the bell but, rather, by playing the platoon wingman to a strong-sided Zack Morris type. So long as he keeps feasting on southpaws like they're a heaping of french fries at The Max, he should be able to avoid having his career screech to a halt.

Donovan Solano **SS** Born: 12/17/87   Age: 33   Bats: R   Throws: R   Height: 5'8"   Weight: 210   Origin: International Free Agent, 2005

YEAR	TEAM	LVL	AGE	PA	R	2B	3B	HR	RBI	BB	K	SB	CS	Whiff%	AVG/OBP/SLG	DRC+	BABIP	BRR	FRAA	WARP
2018	DOD2	ROK	30	27	3	1	0	0	3	0	1	0	0		.440/.444/.480	195	.440	-0.1	SS(5): 1.6, 2B(1): 0.0	0.4
2018	OKC	AAA	30	340	38	21	1	4	43	16	40	4	1		.318/.353/.430	107	.348	-1.2	SS(65): -1.9, 2B(10): 0.7, 3B(4): 0.5	1.1
2019	SAC	AAA	31	97	12	4	0	2	16	9	11	0	0		.322/.392/.437	111	.351	-0.9	2B(14): 0.4, 3B(10): 0.3, SS(1): -0.0	0.5
2019	SF	MLB	31	228	27	13	1	4	23	10	49	0	1	19.0%	.330/.360/.456	100	.409	1.7	2B(36): -2.6, SS(19): 0.5, 3B(2): 0.0	0.9
2020	SF	MLB	33	203	22	15	1	3	29	10	39	0	0	22.0%	.326/.365/.463	109	.396	-1.6	2B(45): -4.3, 3B(5): -0.9, SS(2): -0.3	0.0
2021 FS	SF	MLB	33	600	62	26	1	10	64	28	128	0	0	20.7%	.269/.310/.379	91	.331	-0.2	2B -1, 1B 0	1.1
2021 DC	SF	MLB	33	572	60	25	1	9	61	27	122	0	0	20.7%	.269/.310/.379	91	.331	-0.2	2B -1	1.3

Comparables: Terry Shumpert, Dick Green, Randy Velarde

There's no shortage of killjoys out there who will "well, actually" you when you refer to Solano by his newly-minted "Donnie Barrels" nickname. The fact that his barrel percentage is *only* in the 21st percentile shouldn't dampen the rest of Solano's two-season breakout as a legitimately good hitter after what seemed like a short (and pretty much finished) career as a utility infielder. While the smart money is on regression to something less than the sixth-best batting average in the majors, Solano 2.0 seems plenty capable of spraying line drives around the park, whatever Statcast pedants may call them. Heading into his final arb year at the advanced age of 33, the current Giants front office approaches personnel decisions with a Raysian unsentimentality, so even a catchy nickname is no guarantee of an everyday role in 2021.

Luis Toribio 3B   Born: 09/28/00   Age: 20   Bats: L   Throws: R   Height: 6'1"   Weight: 165   Origin: International Free Agent, 2017

YEAR	TEAM	LVL	AGE	PA	R	2B	3B	HR	RBI	BB	K	SB	CS	Whiff%	AVG/OBP/SLG	DRC+	BABIP	BRR	FRAA	WARP
2018	DSL GIA	ROK	17	274	44	13	1	10	39	51	62	4	1		.270/.423/.479	157	.333	-1.8	3B(47): -5.6	1.2
2019	GIO	ROK	18	234	45	15	3	3	33	45	54	4	5		.297/.436/.459	166	.400	-0.3	3B(41): -6.4	1.4
2019	SK	SS	18	13	2	1	0	0	0	2	5	0	0		.273/.385/.364	105	.500	-1.4	3B(3): -0.6	-0.2
2021 FS	*SF*	*MLB*	*20*	*600*	*48*	*27*	*2*	*7*	*49*	*48*	*224*	*4*	*1*		*.199/.270/.303*	*58*	*.322*	*0.7*	*3B -10*	*-3.1*

Comparables: Austin Riley, Ryan McMahon, Sherten Apostel

Evan Longoria's seemingly interminable contract (remember how mad people got about that?) finally ends after 2022, and the Giants hope Toribio can step in around then to take over the hot corner and be the middle-of-the-order power bat that Longoria stopped being even before he made his way from one Bay to the other.

Chadwick Tromp C   Born: 03/21/95   Age: 26   Bats: R   Throws: R   Height: 5'8"   Weight: 221   Origin: International Free Agent, 2013

YEAR	TEAM	LVL	AGE	PA	R	2B	3B	HR	RBI	BB	K	SB	CS	Whiff%	AVG/OBP/SLG	DRC+	BABIP	BRR	FRAA	WARP
2018	PNS	AA	23	98	9	5	0	0	10	12	18	0	1		.247/.340/.306	102	.313	-0.4	C(25): 3.7	0.7
2018	LOU	AAA	23	195	20	8	1	2	14	15	24	2	2		.264/.333/.356	102	.293	-2.2	C(51): 1.8	0.7
2019	RED	ROK	24	61	10	5	0	2	16	11	10	0			.271/.410/.500	148	.297	0.8	C(10): -0.2	0.5
2019	LOU	AAA	24	90	15	2	1	7	21	11	25	0	1		.286/.389/.610	125	.333	0.5	C(22): -2.2	0.5
2020	SF	MLB	25	64	11	1	0	4	10	1	20	0	0	34.4%	.213/.219/.426	81	.231	0.2	C(23): -0.1	0.4
2021 FS	*SF*	*MLB*	*26*	*600*	*60*	*23*	*2*	*14*	*61*	*44*	*161*	*1*	*0*	*34.4%*	*.216/.282/.343*	*76*	*.278*	*0.0*	*C 12*	*1.9*
2021 DC	*SF*	*MLB*	*26*	*67*	*6*	*2*	*0*	*1*	*6*	*5*	*17*	*0*	*0*	*34.4%*	*.216/.282/.343*	*76*	*.278*	*0.0*	*C 2*	*0.3*

Comparables: J.R. Towles, Rob Bowen, Jason Jaramillo

While Tromp possesses an 80-grade name (with a similarly excellent spoonerism), his baseball-related skill set is considerably less exceptional. Still, a power bat and capable defense is the minimum requirement for a backup job in the bigs, and a memeable name is an added benefit for a team's social media coordinator, if not the team itself.

YEAR	TEAM	P. COUNT	FRM RUNS	BLK RUNS	THRW RUNS	TOT RUNS
2018	LOU	6895	1.8	0.1	1.1	3.0
2018	PNS	3305	3.4	0.3	-0.1	3.5
2019	LOU	3028	-1.8	0.0	-0.4	-2.3
2020	SF	2756	2.0	-0.1	0.0	1.9
2021	*SF*	*2405*	*1.9*	*0.2*	*0.1*	*2.1*

Will Wilson SS   Born: 07/21/98   Age: 22   Bats: R   Throws: R   Height: 6'0"   Weight: 184   Origin: Round 1, 2019 Draft (#15 overall)

YEAR	TEAM	LVL	AGE	PA	R	2B	3B	HR	RBI	BB	K	SB	CS	Whiff%	AVG/OBP/SLG	DRC+	BABIP	BRR	FRAA	WARP
2019	ORM	ROK+	20	200	23	10	3	5	18	14	47	0	0		.281/.335/.449	94	.353	-0.8		0.6
2021 FS	*SF*	*MLB*	*22*	*600*	*44*	*26*	*3*	*7*	*48*	*32*	*204*	*1*	*0*		*.202/.250/.300*	*51*	*.303*	*1.3*		*-1.9*

In a trade that was entirely emblematic of both Farhan Zaidi's approach to talent acquisition and the financial landscape of 2020 baseball at large, Wilson, an Angels first-round pick from 2019, was essentially purchased by the Giants for the cost of Zack Cozart's contract. It was unlikely the injured Cozart would ever play for the Giants, and he in fact did not, as he was released well before spring training even began. Wilson's hopes remain higher: he is a polished college bat, albeit one with strikeout and groundball proclivities. After some seasoning in the upper-minors, he could slot into second or third base, even if he may not have the glove to be Brandon Crawford's heir apparent at shortstop. Will he be worth it? Chances are, we'll see Wilson soon enough to know. Say that three times fast.

Mike Yastrzemski LF   Born: 08/23/90   Age: 30   Bats: L   Throws: L   Height: 5'10"   Weight: 178   Origin: Round 14, 2013 Draft (#429 overall)

YEAR	TEAM	LVL	AGE	PA	R	2B	3B	HR	RBI	BB	K	SB	CS	Whiff%	AVG/OBP/SLG	DRC+	BABIP	BRR	FRAA	WARP
2018	BOW	AA	27	117	13	10	0	1	11	10	30	2	1		.202/.276/.327	76	.270	1.5	LF(14): 0.9, RF(7): 1.5, CF(4): -0.1	0.2
2018	NOR	AAA	27	374	48	18	6	9	49	44	75	6	4		.265/.359/.441	129	.320	4.3	LF(50): 8.7, CF(36): 2.2, RF(8): 2.3	3.5
2019	SAC	AAA	28	163	38	11	1	12	25	22	36	2	2		.316/.414/.676	145	.344	2.2	CF(21): -0.2, LF(8): -0.3, RF(7): 0.4	1.6
2019	SF	MLB	28	411	64	22	3	21	55	32	107	2	4	27.6%	.272/.334/.518	111	.325	0.5	LF(61): -0.5, RF(56): 0.3, CF(7): -0.3	1.7
2020	SF	MLB	30	225	39	14	4	10	35	30	55	2	1	24.9%	.297/.400/.568	123	.370	-0.2	RF(31): 3.4, CF(24): 1.4, LF(8): 0.2	1.7
2021 FS	*SF*	*MLB*	*30*	*600*	*82*	*27*	*5*	*23*	*68*	*61*	*161*	*2*	*1*	*26.3%*	*.246/.332/.448*	*115*	*.310*	*2.4*	*RF 11, CF 0*	*4.2*
2021 DC	*SF*	*MLB*	*30*	*572*	*78*	*26*	*5*	*22*	*65*	*58*	*154*	*2*	*1*	*26.3%*	*.246/.332/.448*	*115*	*.310*	*2.3*	*RF 10, CF 0*	*3.8*

Comparables: Reggie Sanders, Brad Hawpe, Jesse Barfield

It was a great story in 2019—Hall of Famer's grandson who worked hard through the minors, made it to the bigs with a rebuilding team and even hit a home run in Fenway Park of all places!—and here we were, ready for the closing credits of the inspirational baseball film. But then Yaz produced a sequel that few expected: improved plate discipline, excellent quality of contact, defense good enough to play a passable center field, all the while inspiring sputtering mea culpas from writers and analysts all-too-ready to dismiss the late bloomer. We walked into the theater thinking we were getting a warmed-over *Rudy* knockoff, and Yaz gave us *The Thirty-Year-Old MVP Candidate*. Even if the next episode is more of the same, it'll be the kind of fan service that will disappoint absolutely no one.

PITCHERS

Melvin Adon RHP Born: 06/09/94 Age: 27 Bats: L Throws: R Height: 6'3" Weight: 246 Origin: International Free Agent, 2015

YEAR	TEAM	LVL	AGE	W	L	SV	G	GS	IP	H	HR	BB/9	K/9	K	GB%	BABIP	WHIP	ERA	DRA-	WARP	MPH	FA%	Whiff%	CSP
2018	SJ	HI-A	24	2	5	0	16	15	77²	82	6	3.9	8.2	71	53.7%	.342	1.49	4.87	116	-0.4				
2019	RIC	AA	25	2	6	14	36	0	45	38	2	5.2	11.8	59	50.5%	.360	1.42	2.60	103	-0.2				
2019	SAC	AAA	25	0	1	0	12	0	10¹	16	1	7.0	15.7	18	50.0%	.517	2.32	13.94	106	0.1				
2021 FS	SF	MLB	27	2	3	0	57	0	50	45	6	5.1	9.2	51	45.7%	.290	1.48	4.63	113	-0.2				

Comparables: Vicente Campos, Gonzalez Germen, James Marvel

If you have triple-digit heat but no idea where it's going, you might be less a pitcher than a threat to public safety. Unfortunately for Melvin Adon (but perhaps not for batters, catchers, umpires and proximate bystanders), an unspecified arm injury in the Dominican Winter League may silence the sirens for the time being.

Shaun Anderson RHP Born: 10/29/94 Age: 26 Bats: R Throws: R Height: 6'4" Weight: 228 Origin: Round 3, 2016 Draft (#88 overall)

YEAR	TEAM	LVL	AGE	W	L	SV	G	GS	IP	H	HR	BB/9	K/9	K	GB%	BABIP	WHIP	ERA	DRA-	WARP	MPH	FA%	Whiff%	CSP
2018	RIC	AA	23	6	5	0	17	16	94	93	9	2.1	8.9	93	46.9%	.318	1.22	3.45	60	2.7				
2018	SAC	AAA	23	2	2	0	8	8	47¹	48	5	2.1	6.5	34	43.2%	.295	1.25	4.18	89	0.7				
2019	SAC	AAA	24	2	1	0	8	8	38¹	36	3	3.1	9.6	41	53.3%	.320	1.28	3.76	60	1.4				
2019	SF	MLB	24	3	5	2	28	16	96	111	13	3.6	6.6	70	39.7%	.327	1.55	5.44	133	-0.8	95.1	58.5%	20.8%	46.3%
2020	SF	MLB	25	0	0	0	18	0	15¹	10	3	7.0	10.6	18	37.8%	.206	1.43	3.52	108	0.1	96.6	39.7%	33.6%	41.3%
2021 FS	SF	MLB	26	9	9	0	26	26	150	146	22	3.6	8.5	141	42.6%	.292	1.37	4.49	106	0.5	95.4	54.6%	23.5%	45.2%
2021 DC	SF	MLB	26	4	5	0	38	12	79	76	11	3.6	8.5	74	42.6%	.292	1.37	4.49	106	0.4	95.4	54.6%	23.5%	45.2%

Comparables: Walker Lockett, Drew Anderson, Justin Grimm

Sometimes the obvious story is the accurate one. Absent a viable third pitch, Anderson was moved from the rotation to the 'pen in late 2019, and he pitched exclusively in relief during a shortened season which was made even shorter by an excursion to the Alternate Site. Out of the bullpen, Anderson adopted a slider-dominant approach that was offset with a credible mid-90s four-seamer. The slider gets the whiffs, but the heater gets bashed a little too hard and frequently for him to slot into the ninth inning. The upshot: he's not a starter and he's not a closer; he's a just-fine bullpen piece until he's not.

Tyler Anderson LHP Born: 12/30/89 Age: 31 Bats: L Throws: L Height: 6'2" Weight: 213 Origin: Round 1, 2011 Draft (#20 overall)

YEAR	TEAM	LVL	AGE	W	L	SV	G	GS	IP	H	HR	BB/9	K/9	K	GB%	BABIP	WHIP	ERA	DRA-	WARP	MPH	FA%	Whiff%	CSP
2018	COL	MLB	28	7	9	0	32	32	176	165	30	3.0	8.4	164	36.8%	.282	1.27	4.55	107	1.0	93.9	44.5%	25.3%	50.0%
2019	COL	MLB	29	0	3	0	5	5	20²	33	8	4.8	10.0	23	38.9%	.403	2.13	11.76	116	0.0	93.5	47.6%	24.2%	50.4%
2020	SF	MLB	30	4	3	0	13	11	59²	58	5	3.8	6.2	41	28.9%	.288	1.39	4.37	144	-0.9	92.2	47.0%	24.6%	47.1%
2021 FS	SF	MLB	31	9	9	0	26	26	150	149	22	3.2	7.6	126	34.7%	.290	1.35	4.29	106	0.6	93.1	46.0%	24.9%	48.8%

Comparables: Anthony DeSclafani, Sam Gaviglio, Brent Suter

Anderson is yet another beneficiary of Farhan Zaidi's Emma Lazarus approach to player acquisition, through which he ardently collects the league's tired, poor, discarded, misdeveloped and/or post-injury players yearning to breathe free on a major-league roster. Among these huddled masses, Anderson in particular found the air much more comfortable at sea level than a mile above it. As a starter for the Rockies, the lefty showed just enough to make us feel bad that he was stuck in Colorado. After being picked up on waivers by the Giants, Anderson used the season's delayed commencement to fully work his way back from surgery on his left knee, and he emerged in 2020 as a starter more useful than consistently good. Under team control for another year, it remains to be seen if Anderson can assimilate into a Giants rotation that is certain to include a varied cast of characters.

Caleb Baragar LHP Born: 04/09/94 Age: 27 Bats: R Throws: L Height: 6'3" Weight: 215 Origin: Round 9, 2016 Draft (#275 overall)

YEAR	TEAM	LVL	AGE	W	L	SV	G	GS	IP	H	HR	BB/9	K/9	K	GB%	BABIP	WHIP	ERA	DRA-	WARP	MPH	FA%	Whiff%	CSP
2018	AUG	LO-A	24	2	2	0	16	11	67	62	9	1.7	9.8	73	23.6%	.321	1.12	4.03	80	1.0				
2018	SJ	HI-A	24	1	2	0	8	1	11¹	13	0	4.8	9.5	12	47.4%	.342	1.68	4.76	66	0.2				
2018	SAC	AAA	24	0	0	0	2	0	3²	3	1	0.0	0.0	0	14.3%	.154	0.82	2.45	104	0.0				
2019	SJ	HI-A	25	0	1	0	5	4	16²	15	2	4.3	11.9	22	35.7%	.333	1.38	2.70	71	0.3				
2019	RIC	AA	25	5	5	0	22	21	120	83	12	3.2	8.0	107	28.4%	.225	1.05	3.45	76	1.8				
2019	SAC	AAA	25	0	0	0	1	1	4¹	6	1	4.2	12.5	6	33.3%	.455	1.85	10.38	77	0.1				
2020	SF	MLB	26	5	1	0	24	0	22¹	17	3	2.0	7.7	19	20.6%	.233	0.99	4.03	126	-0.1	95.4	75.1%	19.1%	53.8%
2021 FS	SF	MLB	27	2	2	0	57	0	50	50	10	3.7	8.3	46	28.8%	.284	1.41	5.16	121	-0.5	95.4	75.1%	19.1%	53.8%
2021 DC	SF	MLB	27	2	2	0	51	0	54	54	11	3.7	8.3	49	28.8%	.284	1.41	5.16	121	-0.3	95.4	75.1%	19.1%	53.8%

Comparables: Ben Braymer, Aaron Sanchez, Joe Ross

Kill the win? Baragar would like to adopt the win, give it its own en suite bedroom, swaddle it in sheets of obscenely high thread count, buy it a pony and start up a college fund for it. Although only logging 22 ⅓ innings, Baragar's five W's equaled the total of some hurlers you'll probably recognize: Aaron Nola, Max Scherzer, Trevor Bauer, Tyler Glasnow and José Berríos, for starters. The bad news for Baragar (and any potential win-based arbitration case he might make in a few years) is that his profile—a high-spin, mid-90s four-seamer, and little else—sets him up for a short relief role. He's more likely to have a season with five saves than five wins (with either outcome an extreme longshot), but he'll always have 2020 on the back of his baseball card.

Tyler Beede RHP Born: 05/23/93 Age: 28 Bats: R Throws: R Height: 6'2" Weight: 216 Origin: Round 1, 2014 Draft (#14 overall)

YEAR	TEAM	LVL	AGE	W	L	SV	G	GS	IP	H	HR	BB/9	K/9	K	GB%	BABIP	WHIP	ERA	DRA-	WARP	MPH	FA%	Whiff%	CSP
2018	SAC	AAA	25	4	9	0	33	10	74	82	10	6.8	9.1	75	39.0%	.353	1.86	7.05	108	0.3				
2018	SF	MLB	25	0	1	0	2	2	7²	9	0	9.4	10.6	9	45.5%	.409	2.22	8.22	94	0.1	94.3	51.8%	30.6%	41.3%
2019	SAC	AAA	26	2	2	0	7	7	34²	24	3	3.6	12.7	49	33.8%	.300	1.10	2.34	49	1.4				
2019	SF	MLB	26	5	10	0	24	22	117	127	22	3.5	8.7	113	44.0%	.312	1.48	5.08	107	0.7	96.0	56.2%	26.2%	45.3%
2021 FS	SF	MLB	28	8	9	0	26	26	150	140	21	4.3	9.5	158	43.1%	.296	1.42	4.61	107	0.5	95.9	56.0%	26.4%	45.2%
2021 DC	SF	MLB	28	4	5	0	38	12	85	79	12	4.3	9.5	89	43.1%	.296	1.42	4.61	107	0.5	95.9	56.0%	26.4%	45.2%

Comparables: Joe Ross, Clay Holmes, Rookie Davis

When we last saw Beede on a mound, he was perhaps the most consistent starter in the tail-end of the Giants' 2019 season. Following a 2020 lost to Tommy John rehab, the Giants are counting on a healthy Beede to pick up where he left off—as a mid-rotation starter with upside for more. How might he achieve that ever-elusive "more"? He might consider going away from his bread-and-butter four-seamer, as it didn't fool major-league hitters during his up-and-down 2019. Add "refining pitch mix" to the to-do list, too, along with the inevitable rehab steps that will keep Beede from a major-league mound until sometime in the middle of the 2021 season.

John Brebbia RHP Born: 05/30/90 Age: 31 Bats: L Throws: R Height: 6'1" Weight: 200 Origin: Round 30, 2011 Draft (#929 overall)

YEAR	TEAM	LVL	AGE	W	L	SV	G	GS	IP	H	HR	BB/9	K/9	K	GB%	BABIP	WHIP	ERA	DRA-	WARP	MPH	FA%	Whiff%	CSP
2018	MEM	AAA	28	2	0	2	11	0	13²	16	3	2.6	15.8	24	6.1%	.433	1.46	4.61	29	0.6				
2018	STL	MLB	28	3	3	2	45	0	50²	43	5	2.8	10.7	60	32.3%	.299	1.16	3.20	65	1.2	96.7	53.2%	29.6%	49.7%
2019	STL	MLB	29	3	4	0	66	0	72²	59	6	3.3	10.8	87	27.8%	.293	1.18	3.59	83	1.0	95.5	56.6%	29.0%	49.5%
2021 FS	SF	MLB	31	2	2	0	57	0	50	41	8	2.4	10.0	55	30.1%	.270	1.10	3.35	87	0.5	95.8	55.7%	29.2%	49.5%
2021 DC	SF	MLB	31	1	1	0	19	0	20	16	3	2.4	10.0	22	30.1%	.270	1.10	3.35	87	0.3	95.8	55.7%	29.2%	49.5%

Comparables: Hansel Robles, Nick Wittgren, Emilio Pagán

Brebbia has already overcome a 30th-round draft slot, release from the Yankees, two years in independent ball and a serious case of chia beard to carve out a bullpen career, so Tommy John surgery should just be a speed bump for him. The Giants signed him over the winter, banking on him making a full recovery.

Trevor Cahill RHP Born: 03/01/88 Age: 33 Bats: R Throws: R Height: 6'4" Weight: 223 Origin: Round 2, 2006 Draft (#66 overall)

YEAR	TEAM	LVL	AGE	W	L	SV	G	GS	IP	H	HR	BB/9	K/9	K	GB%	BABIP	WHIP	ERA	DRA-	WARP	MPH	FA%	Whiff%	CSP
2018	NAS	AAA	30	0	1	0	3	3	13²	7	0	5.3	11.2	17	80.6%	.226	1.10	2.63	37	0.6				
2018	OAK	MLB	30	7	4	0	21	20	110	90	8	3.4	8.2	100	51.5%	.281	1.19	3.76	77	2.3	93.8	41.1%	27.9%	44.4%
2019	LAA	MLB	31	4	9	0	37	11	102¹	111	25	3.4	7.1	81	45.9%	.283	1.47	5.98	122	-0.4	93.5	36.5%	24.2%	47.7%
2020	SF	MLB	32	1	2	0	11	6	25	16	3	5.0	11.2	31	32.2%	.236	1.20	3.24	89	0.4	92.3	35.5%	28.7%	42.2%
2021 FS	SF	MLB	33	2	3	0	57	0	50	45	6	4.3	9.5	52	45.6%	.291	1.38	4.13	100	0.1	93.3	37.5%	26.1%	45.7%

Comparables: Jhoulys Chacín, Tom Gorzelanny, Ryan Dempster

If Cahill can somehow make the necessary sacrifices to keep the Injury Gods from his door, there may be a useful final act of his up-and-down career. He has steadily moved away from his sinker, an excellent turf-pounder that managed to outrun the launch angle episteme. He now features that pitch in a more balanced mix with a changeup and curve, a recipe for success during the good times, and for mere survival otherwise. Cahill's days as a rotation fixture are likely behind him, but there may be some life left in a relief arm, provided it, and the rest of him, can stay one step ahead of the bones, muscles, joints and ligaments that seem to have been fated, throughout his career, to let him down.

Sam Coonrod RHP Born: 09/22/92 Age: 28 Bats: R Throws: R Height: 6'1" Weight: 225 Origin: Round 5, 2014 Draft (#148 overall)

YEAR	TEAM	LVL	AGE	W	L	SV	G	GS	IP	H	HR	BB/9	K/9	K	GB%	BABIP	WHIP	ERA	DRA-	WARP	MPH	FA%	Whiff%	CSP
2018	SJ	HI-A	25	0	0	0	6	0	6¹	5	0	2.8	18.5	13	33.3%	.417	1.11	5.68	23	0.3				
2019	SAC	AAA	26	2	4	3	33	1	32¹	41	4	5.0	12.0	43	45.2%	.420	1.82	6.96	119	0.1				
2019	SF	MLB	26	5	1	0	33	0	27²	19	3	4.9	6.5	20	49.3%	.225	1.23	3.58	96	0.2	98.4	65.3%	22.7%	47.2%
2020	SF	MLB	27	0	2	3	18	0	14²	17	2	4.3	9.2	15	45.7%	.341	1.64	9.82	89	0.2	100.0	58.9%	29.1%	48.9%
2021 FS	SF	MLB	28	2	3	22	57	0	50	46	6	4.5	9.1	50	43.4%	.293	1.42	4.60	106	0.0	99.2	62.1%	25.9%	48.0%
2021 DC	SF	MLB	28	2	3	22	57	0	61	56	7	4.5	9.1	61	43.4%	.293	1.42	4.60	106	0.2	99.2	62.1%	25.9%	48.0%

Comparables: Austin Brice, Ryne Stanek, Pierce Johnson

Despite serving as a nominal closer for a short stretch, Coonrod's season would have been eminently forgettable were it not for two bookending events that tied his own, small story to much larger ones. The first: In late July, after many MLB players agreed to kneel in protest of the police shooting of Jacob Blake and in support of the Black Lives Matter movement, Coonrod remained standing, citing his inability to reconcile his Christian beliefs with support for racial justice. The second: On September 25, he came into a crucial late-inning game to protect a slim lead that would have likely ensured an improbable playoff appearance for the Giants. Unable to command his fastball, he grooved an 88-mph changeup, which Trent Grisham deposited in the empty right field bleachers for a walkoff in Petc...er, Oracle Park (don't ask, it was 2020). For all of the juice on his fastball, Coonrod's season can be summed up by a failure to figure out the world's change, or his own.

Seth Corry LHP   Born: 11/03/98   Age: 22   Bats: L   Throws: L   Height: 6'2"   Weight: 195   Origin: Round 3, 2017 Draft (#96 overall)

YEAR	TEAM	LVL	AGE	W	L	SV	G	GS	IP	H	HR	BB/9	K/9	K	GB%	BABIP	WHIP	ERA	DRA-	WARP	MPH	FA%	Whiff%	CSP
2018	GIO	ROK	19	3	1	0	9	9	38	38	1	4.0	9.9	42	42.6%	.352	1.45	2.61	105	0.4				
2018	SK	SS	19	1	2	0	5	5	19²	14	1	6.9	7.8	17	51.9%	.245	1.47	5.49	300	-2.2				
2019	AUG	LO-A	20	9	3	0	27	26	122²	73	4	4.3	12.6	172	43.2%	.272	1.07	1.76	68	2.7				
2021 FS	SF	MLB	22	2	3	0	57	0	50	46	7	7.1	9.6	53	40.7%	.297	1.72	5.88	128	-0.7				

Comparables: Brailyn Marquez, Huascar Ynoa, Johan Oviedo

Corry is precisely the type of pop-up prospect it would have been particularly informative to see in 2020. The Utah high school draftee was barely a whisper on prospect lists until he ran roughshod over the Sally League in 2019, though his strikeout dominance and batted-ball luck covered for some spotty control. The velocity foundation is there for a mid-rotation lefty; it would have been nice to spend 2020 tracking the progression of his secondaries and the refinement of his mechanics. Alas. we'll have to wait a little longer to see if his breakout was a sustainable developmental leap or something else.

Johnny Cueto RHP   Born: 02/15/86   Age: 35   Bats: R   Throws: R   Height: 5'11"   Weight: 229   Origin: International Free Agent, 2004

YEAR	TEAM	LVL	AGE	W	L	SV	G	GS	IP	H	HR	BB/9	K/9	K	GB%	BABIP	WHIP	ERA	DRA-	WARP	MPH	FA%	Whiff%	CSP
2018	SAC	AAA	32	0	0	0	2	2	7²	5	0	1.2	11.7	10	38.9%	.278	0.78	0.00	77	0.2				
2018	SF	MLB	32	3	2	0	9	9	53	46	8	2.2	6.5	38	42.4%	.259	1.11	3.23	101	0.5	92.0	46.8%	21.8%	46.3%
2019	SJ	HI-A	33	0	1	0	2	2	7	8	1	1.3	6.4	5	52.2%	.333	1.29	6.43	117	-0.1				
2019	SAC	AAA	33	0	1	0	2	2	10¹	10	2	0.0	7.8	9	51.6%	.286	0.97	2.61	75	0.3				
2019	SF	MLB	33	1	2	0	4	4	16	11	3	5.1	7.3	13	51.1%	.200	1.25	5.06	90	0.2	93.0	51.3%	19.6%	42.9%
2020	SF	MLB	34	2	3	0	12	12	63¹	61	9	3.7	8.0	56	42.2%	.284	1.37	5.40	108	0.3	93.2	43.6%	19.9%	43.8%
2021 FS	SF	MLB	35	9	9	0	26	26	150	146	21	3.0	7.7	128	43.2%	.287	1.31	4.29	103	0.8	93.0	45.0%	20.2%	44.1%
2021 DC	SF	MLB	35	8	9	0	27	27	143	140	20	3.0	7.7	122	43.2%	.287	1.31	4.29	103	1.3	93.0	45.0%	20.2%	44.1%

Comparables: Aníbal Sánchez, Jordan Zimmermann, Freddy Garcia

In an age of Driveline-inspired pitch design, PhD-powered biomechanical studies and the ruthless efficiencies applied to workouts, diet and sleep, Cueto is a throwback. His Instagram is a dizzying pendulum swing between absurdly decadent feasts and intensely penitent workouts, the latter reflecting an impressive strength and flexibility at odds with his highly relatable thiccness. On the mound, his motion is less a refined, repeatable mechanism for pitch delivery than a stylized performance resembling some minor form of modern dance, as he varies occasional quick pitches with comically baroque moves, at times freezing into statuesque poses for what feels like several seconds. There was a time when all of Cueto's flair was supported by skills and stamina that garnered him a couple of six-WARP seasons in the mid-2010s. Sadly, but inevitably, the skills have eroded, a demise perhaps accelerated by a Tommy John surgery that cost him nearly all of his 2019. Cueto remains a viable back-end starter—for now—but regardless of the declining career arc, he will stop, start, twist, turn, shimmy, herk and jerk against the dying of the light.

Anthony DeSclafani RHP   Born: 04/18/90   Age: 31   Bats: R   Throws: R   Height: 6'2"   Weight: 195   Origin: Round 6, 2011 Draft (#199 overall)

YEAR	TEAM	LVL	AGE	W	L	SV	G	GS	IP	H	HR	BB/9	K/9	K	GB%	BABIP	WHIP	ERA	DRA-	WARP	MPH	FA%	Whiff%	CSP
2018	PNS	AA	28	0	1	0	2	2	8	5	0	1.1	13.5	12	58.8%	.294	0.75	2.25	93	0.1				
2018	LOU	AAA	28	0	2	0	2	2	11¹	15	5	1.6	7.9	10	43.2%	.312	1.50	6.35	124	-0.1				
2018	CIN	MLB	28	7	8	0	21	21	115	118	24	2.3	8.5	108	40.7%	.298	1.29	4.93	115	0.2	95.5	57.9%	23.0%	49.8%
2019	CIN	MLB	29	9	9	0	31	31	166²	151	29	2.6	9.0	167	42.0%	.276	1.20	3.89	80	3.3	96.2	55.4%	23.5%	46.1%
2020	CIN	MLB	30	1	2	0	9	7	33²	41	7	4.3	6.7	25	39.5%	.318	1.69	7.22	137	-0.4	96.6	51.3%	23.2%	41.8%
2021 FS	SF	MLB	31	9	9	0	26	26	150	144	21	2.9	8.2	136	41.1%	.288	1.28	4.08	99	1.1	96.2	55.0%	23.3%	46.0%
2021 DC	SF	MLB	31	7	8	0	25	25	124	119	18	2.9	8.2	112	41.1%	.288	1.28	4.08	99	1.3	96.2	55.0%	23.3%	46.0%

Comparables: Jake Odorizzi, Nathan Eovaldi, Shaun Marcum

The 2020 highlights for DeSclafani were the August birth of his first child, a son named Cru, and the 11 scoreless innings the dad-to-be twirled to start the season. The lowlights were every outing after that, as Disco Demolition Night broke out whenever the New Jersey native took the mound. DeSclafani pitched his way out of the rotation and off the post-season roster, a bad result for his walk year. The sore shoulder that plagued him at the beginning of the year may have been a contributing factor, but the most likely culprit is also the simplest: poor fastball command. His velocity and the shape of his breaking pitches were normal, but he repeatedly missed his spots, walked the yard and served up more meatballs than a deli counter at lunch rush. DeSclafani has always been prone to the long ball and his stuff is never overpowering enough to play on its own, but when he's healthy and precise he can survive at the back end of the rotation. He'll try to be both of those things with San Francisco, inking a one-year, $6 million pact over the winter.

Jarlin García LHP   Born: 01/18/93   Age: 28   Bats: L   Throws: L   Height: 6'3"   Weight: 215   Origin: International Free Agent, 2010

YEAR	TEAM	LVL	AGE	W	L	SV	G	GS	IP	H	HR	BB/9	K/9	K	GB%	BABIP	WHIP	ERA	DRA-	WARP	MPH	FA%	Whiff%	CSP
2018	NO	AAA	25	2	2	0	10	9	48²	57	5	2.6	6.1	33	38.0%	.323	1.46	4.81	86	0.8				
2018	MIA	MLB	25	3	3	0	29	7	66	59	16	3.8	5.5	40	43.3%	.223	1.32	4.91	123	-0.3	93.9	52.1%	19.3%	49.2%
2019	NO	AAA	26	2	0	0	7	0	9¹	6	1	3.9	10.6	11	38.1%	.250	1.07	1.93	68	0.3				
2019	MIA	MLB	26	4	2	0	53	0	50²	40	4	2.8	6.9	39	46.3%	.250	1.11	3.02	80	0.8	94.8	39.8%	20.9%	52.1%
2020	SF	MLB	27	2	1	0	19	0	18¹	11	0	3.4	6.9	14	46.0%	.220	0.98	0.49	94	0.2	95.2	48.6%	15.8%	56.0%
2021 FS	SF	MLB	28	3	3	0	57	0	50	48	6	3.9	8.1	44	43.9%	.289	1.39	4.48	106	0.0	94.6	45.7%	19.1%	52.2%
2021 DC	SF	MLB	28	3	3	0	49	4	62	59	8	3.9	8.1	55	43.9%	.289	1.39	4.48	106	0.2	94.6	45.7%	19.1%	52.2%

Comparables: John Gant, Michael Feliz, Austin Brice

Formerly known as Jarlin the Marlin, García the Giant took well to the other coast, allowing only one earned run over the course of the season. His contact-heavy profile suggests that his ERA will inevitably float upriver, at which point he might be forced downstream to Anaheim, where he could leverage his middle name to become Emmanuel the Angel.

Rico Garcia RHP Born: 01/10/94 Age: 27 Bats: R Throws: R Height: 5'9" Weight: 201 Origin: Round 30, 2016 Draft (#890 overall)

YEAR	TEAM	LVL	AGE	W	L	SV	G	GS	IP	H	HR	BB/9	K/9	K	GB%	BABIP	WHIP	ERA	DRA-	WARP	MPH	FA%	Whiff%	CSP
2018	LAN	HI-A	24	7	7	0	16	15	100	99	12	2.0	9.1	101	45.1%	.316	1.21	3.42	85	1.2				
2018	HFD	AA	24	6	2	0	11	11	67	54	8	2.7	8.2	61	43.4%	.266	1.10	2.28	89	0.9				
2019	HFD	AA	25	8	2	0	13	13	68	41	4	3.0	11.5	87	47.3%	.261	0.94	1.85	60	1.7				
2019	ABQ	AAA	25	2	4	0	13	13	61¹	77	14	4.1	7.5	51	35.6%	.335	1.71	6.90	122	0.5				
2019	COL	MLB	25	0	1	0	2	1	6	9	3	7.5	3.0	2	39.1%	.300	2.33	10.50	149	-0.1	93.3	61.6%	16.2%	45.8%
2020	SF	MLB	26	1	1	0	12	0	10	13	1	3.6	6.3	7	45.5%	.375	1.70	5.40	104	0.1	97.3	56.5%	22.4%	44.2%
2021 FS	*SF*	*MLB*	*27*	*2*	*3*	*0*	*57*	*0*	*50*	*48*	*7*	*4.2*	*8.2*	*45*	*41.6%*	*.289*	*1.43*	*4.51*	*108*	*-0.1*	*96.2*	*57.9%*	*20.7%*	*44.6%*

Comparables: Chase De Jong, Keury Mella, Sean Poppen

"It's not an excuse; it's an explanation" is a good way for a pitcher to justify bad Coors Field performances. After a move to Oracle Park, Garcia found that his former home wasn't done with him: half his earned-run output for the season came during a three-run September blowup in Denver. Rocky Mountain high, indeed.

Kevin Gausman RHP Born: 01/06/91 Age: 30 Bats: L Throws: R Height: 6'2" Weight: 190 Origin: Round 1, 2012 Draft (#4 overall)

YEAR	TEAM	LVL	AGE	W	L	SV	G	GS	IP	H	HR	BB/9	K/9	K	GB%	BABIP	WHIP	ERA	DRA-	WARP	MPH	FA%	Whiff%	CSP
2018	BAL	MLB	27	5	8	0	21	21	124	139	21	2.3	7.5	104	47.8%	.317	1.38	4.43	98	1.3	96.8	58.8%	24.7%	47.2%
2018	ATL	MLB	27	5	3	0	10	10	59²	50	5	2.7	6.6	44	42.7%	.260	1.14	2.87	69	1.5	96.2	57.0%	24.9%	45.9%
2019	GWN	AAA	28	0	1	0	1	1	7	6	1	1.3	12.9	10	62.5%	.357	1.00	2.57	53	0.3				
2019	ATL	MLB	28	3	7	0	16	16	80	92	12	3.0	9.6	85	36.1%	.354	1.49	6.19	106	0.4	96.6	56.6%	28.3%	46.3%
2019	CIN	MLB	28	0	2	0	15	1	22¹	21	3	2.0	11.7	29	41.1%	.346	1.16	4.03	57	0.7	96.6	56.4%	36.9%	43.2%
2020	SF	MLB	29	3	3	0	12	10	59²	50	8	2.4	11.9	79	40.7%	.298	1.11	3.62	73	1.4	97.5	51.1%	33.1%	48.2%
2021 FS	*SF*	*MLB*	*30*	*9*	*8*	*0*	*26*	*26*	*150*	*130*	*19*	*3.1*	*10.3*	*171*	*42.3%*	*.291*	*1.22*	*3.52*	*88*	*2.1*	*96.9*	*55.4%*	*29.4%*	*46.8%*
2021 DC	*SF*	*MLB*	*30*	*9*	*9*	*0*	*27*	*27*	*148*	*128*	*19*	*3.1*	*10.3*	*168*	*42.3%*	*.291*	*1.22*	*3.52*	*88*	*2.5*	*96.9*	*55.4%*	*29.4%*	*46.8%*

Comparables: Anthony DeSclafani, Jake Odorizzi, Julio Teheran

If a Gaussian curve is a symmetrical, bell-shaped distribution, the Gausman curve—or any third pitch, for that matter—is still a nearly null set. Gausman continues to survive as he always has, on a competent fastball and a devastating splitter. You might think this sounds like a profile ideal for a high-leverage reliever, perhaps even a closer. In fact, he was the closest thing the Giants had to a rotation anchor, where his two-pitch act enjoyed the spacious coordinates of Oracle Park (and a number of pitcher's parks in the West) enough to make him the de facto ace of a beleaguered staff. Gausman's acceptance of a qualifying offer for 2021 suggests that the current formula solves a problem for both sides.

Trevor Gott RHP Born: 08/26/92 Age: 28 Bats: R Throws: R Height: 5'10" Weight: 182 Origin: Round 6, 2013 Draft (#178 overall)

YEAR	TEAM	LVL	AGE	W	L	SV	G	GS	IP	H	HR	BB/9	K/9	K	GB%	BABIP	WHIP	ERA	DRA-	WARP	MPH	FA%	Whiff%	CSP
2018	SYR	AAA	25	1	1	3	28	0	29¹	23	1	2.5	11.7	38	55.7%	.319	1.06	3.68	67	0.6				
2018	WAS	MLB	25	0	2	0	20	0	19	19	4	4.7	7.1	15	56.1%	.283	1.53	5.68	136	-0.3	96.3	74.8%	16.9%	52.6%
2019	SF	MLB	26	7	0	1	50	0	52²	41	4	2.9	9.7	57	42.8%	.278	1.10	4.44	79	0.9	96.1	77.2%	23.6%	49.2%
2020	SF	MLB	27	1	2	4	15	0	11²	13	7	6.2	6.2	8	20.0%	.182	1.80	10.03	231	-0.7	97.2	64.1%	24.7%	43.2%
2021 FS	*SF*	*MLB*	*28*	*2*	*2*	*0*	*57*	*0*	*50*	*46*	*6*	*3.8*	*8.6*	*47*	*42.2%*	*.285*	*1.34*	*4.25*	*101*	*0.1*	*96.4*	*73.8%*	*23.1%*	*48.2%*
2021 DC	*SF*	*MLB*	*28*	*2*	*2*	*0*	*51*	*0*	*54*	*49*	*7*	*3.8*	*8.6*	*51*	*42.2%*	*.285*	*1.34*	*4.25*	*101*	*0.3*	*96.4*	*73.8%*	*23.1%*	*48.2%*

Comparables: Yacksel Ríos, Dovydas Neverauskas, Ian Krol

If some small price could wipe the period of August 14- 17 from Gott's memory, he would gladly pay it. In an inning and a third, stretched across three outings—two on consecutive days at home to the A's, and one two days later in Anaheim—he had himself a properly dystopian stretch, giving up 11 earned runs, including five homers. Outside of that cursed half-week, Gott was great, surrendering only two runs in his remaining innings, and even serving an early-season stint as closer. Perhaps there's an object lesson about what happens when you mainly rely on one pitch, even if it's a perfectly good 96 mph four-seamer. It's a small-sample pity, because the back of his baseball card would look awfully pretty on the 2020 line but for a four-day stretch in which Gott got got.

Sean Hjelle RHP Born: 05/07/97 Age: 24 Bats: R Throws: R Height: 6'11" Weight: 228 Origin: Round 2, 2018 Draft (#45 overall)

YEAR	TEAM	LVL	AGE	W	L	SV	G	GS	IP	H	HR	BB/9	K/9	K	GB%	BABIP	WHIP	ERA	DRA-	WARP	MPH	FA%	Whiff%	CSP
2018	SK	SS	21	0	0	0	12	12	21¹	24	4	1.7	9.3	22	49.3%	.317	1.31	5.06	212	-1.2				
2019	AUG	LO-A	22	1	2	0	9	9	40²	41	3	2.0	9.7	44	62.4%	.336	1.23	2.66	109	-0.1				
2019	SJ	HI-A	22	5	5	0	14	14	77²	73	2	2.2	8.5	73	65.5%	.329	1.18	2.78	84	0.9				
2019	RIC	AA	22	1	2	0	5	5	25¹	38	1	3.2	7.5	21	47.1%	.430	1.86	6.04	153	-0.8				
2021 FS	*SF*	*MLB*	*24*	*2*	*3*	*0*	*57*	*0*	*50*	*49*	*7*	*3.4*	*7.4*	*40*	*43.0%*	*.288*	*1.38*	*4.60*	*113*	*-0.2*				

Comparables: Beau Burrows, Jeremy Bleich, Braden Shipley

Two things about Hjelle: he's 6-foot-11 and his last name is pronounced like the preserved fruit spread, or the colloquialism of "jealous." You'd be *jelly* of his height on a basketball court, but you'd probably trade a few inches for a few ticks on the heater if you were building the next Giant ace.

Dominic Leone RHP   Born: 10/26/91   Age: 29   Bats: R   Throws: R   Height: 5'10"   Weight: 215   Origin: Round 16, 2012 Draft (#491 overall)

YEAR	TEAM	LVL	AGE	W	L	SV	G	GS	IP	H	HR	BB/9	K/9	K	GB%	BABIP	WHIP	ERA	DRA-	WARP	MPH	FA%	Whiff%	CSP
2018	MEM	AAA	26	1	1	0	10	0	10	14	3	5.4	6.3	7	37.1%	.344	2.00	7.20	67	0.2				
2018	STL	MLB	26	1	2	0	29	0	24	27	3	3.0	9.8	26	30.6%	.353	1.46	4.50	90	0.2	95.8	95.4%	29.8%	45.8%
2019	MEM	AAA	27	1	0	0	23	0	31²	20	3	4.0	11.9	42	33.3%	.246	1.07	2.84	46	1.2				
2019	STL	MLB	27	1	0	1	40	0	40²	39	9	4.9	10.2	46	38.4%	.294	1.50	5.53	116	-0.1	95.7	83.7%	30.3%	40.1%
2020	CLE	MLB	28	0	0	0	12	0	9²	14	3	4.7	14.9	16	30.8%	.478	1.97	8.38	93	0.1	96.2	64.4%	36.8%	37.2%
2021 FS	SF	MLB	29	2	2	0	57	0	50	43	8	4.2	10.5	58	36.7%	.289	1.34	4.13	96	0.2	95.8	80.8%	31.9%	40.4%

Comparables: Shawn Armstrong, Cam Bedrosian, Taylor Williams

Leone elevated his slider to primary pitch status for the first time and with good reason: he drew whiffs on two-thirds of swings, struck out 14 and allowed only two singles. The results from his collective fastballs raise the question: can he be a slider-*only* pitcher?

Conner Menez LHP   Born: 05/29/95   Age: 26   Bats: L   Throws: L   Height: 6'2"   Weight: 206   Origin: Round 14, 2016 Draft (#425 overall)

YEAR	TEAM	LVL	AGE	W	L	SV	G	GS	IP	H	HR	BB/9	K/9	K	GB%	BABIP	WHIP	ERA	DRA-	WARP	MPH	FA%	Whiff%	CSP
2018	SJ	HI-A	23	2	5	0	11	11	50¹	48	2	3.8	12.5	70	44.1%	.374	1.37	4.83	67	1.1				
2018	RIC	AA	23	6	4	0	15	15	74	73	1	4.1	11.2	92	37.3%	.381	1.45	4.38	84	1.2				
2018	SAC	AAA	23	1	1	0	2	2	11	6	0	4.1	7.4	9	50.0%	.214	1.00	3.27	82	0.2				
2019	RIC	AA	24	3	3	0	11	11	59²	37	5	3.0	10.6	70	35.7%	.237	0.96	2.72	71	1.1				
2019	SAC	AAA	24	3	1	0	12	11	61¹	60	12	4.4	12.3	84	32.0%	.345	1.47	4.84	78	1.7				
2019	SF	MLB	24	0	1	0	8	3	17	13	4	6.4	11.6	22	28.2%	.265	1.47	5.29	83	0.3	92.7	61.2%	27.9%	48.0%
2020	SF	MLB	25	1	0	0	7	0	11¹	6	2	4.0	6.4	8	29.0%	.143	0.97	2.38	128	-0.1	93.1	54.4%	20.3%	43.7%
2021 FS	SF	MLB	26	9	8	0	26	26	150	124	20	4.5	9.6	160	35.0%	.270	1.33	4.11	98	1.2	92.9	58.2%	24.5%	46.1%
2021 DC	SF	MLB	26	5	6	0	21	21	84	69	11	4.5	9.6	89	35.0%	.270	1.33	4.11	98	0.9	92.9	58.2%	24.5%	46.1%

Comparables: Matt Hall, Gregory Soto, Anthony Misiewicz

Menez did little to separate himself from the glut of lefties in the Giants bullpen in 2020. The ERA was pretty, but a 92 mph four-seamer isn't going to get it done as his primary pitch. Mixing in more of his breaking pitches is the likely way forward for him to find leg room.

Reyes Moronta RHP   Born: 01/06/93   Age: 28   Bats: R   Throws: R   Height: 5'10"   Weight: 265   Origin: International Free Agent, 2011

YEAR	TEAM	LVL	AGE	W	L	SV	G	GS	IP	H	HR	BB/9	K/9	K	GB%	BABIP	WHIP	ERA	DRA-	WARP	MPH	FA%	Whiff%	CSP
2018	SF	MLB	25	5	2	1	69	0	65	34	4	5.1	10.9	79	42.5%	.213	1.09	2.49	69	1.4	98.4	51.0%	35.3%	47.2%
2019	SF	MLB	26	3	7	0	56	0	56²	41	4	5.2	11.1	70	37.9%	.274	1.31	2.86	84	0.8	98.7	58.3%	29.4%	45.5%
2021 FS	SF	MLB	28	2	2	0	57	0	50	38	5	5.0	11.2	62	39.1%	.277	1.33	3.61	86	0.5	98.6	55.8%	31.4%	46.1%
2021 DC	SF	MLB	28	2	2	0	57	0	61	46	7	5.0	11.2	75	39.1%	.277	1.33	3.61	86	0.8	98.6	55.8%	31.4%	46.1%

Comparables: José Leclerc, Keone Kela, Dan Altavilla

Given the carousel of failed closers that cycled through Gabe Kapler's bullpen in 2020, the job could very well be Moronta's to lose. The case for Moronta: high-90s heat combined with a diving slider. The challenge for Moronta: recovering from a Tommy John surgery, and perhaps picking up a little more command along the way.

Wandy Peralta LHP   Born: 07/27/91   Age: 29   Bats: L   Throws: L   Height: 6'0"   Weight: 217   Origin: International Free Agent, 2009

YEAR	TEAM	LVL	AGE	W	L	SV	G	GS	IP	H	HR	BB/9	K/9	K	GB%	BABIP	WHIP	ERA	DRA-	WARP	MPH	FA%	Whiff%	CSP
2018	LOU	AAA	26	1	0	0	13	0	14¹	13	1	4.4	6.3	10	54.8%	.300	1.40	3.14	80	0.2				
2018	CIN	MLB	26	2	2	0	59	0	45¹	58	2	6.2	6.2	31	47.2%	.350	1.96	5.36	168	-1.4	97.2	48.8%	23.0%	48.3%
2019	LOU	AAA	27	0	0	0	12	0	11	11	0	0.8	5.7	7	48.6%	.314	1.09	3.27	80	0.2				
2019	SF	MLB	27	0	0	0	8	0	5²	4	1	1.6	7.9	5	73.3%	.214	0.88	3.18	59	0.2	97.2	48.8%	36.1%	41.5%
2019	CIN	MLB	27	1	1	0	39	0	34	36	10	4.0	7.1	27	45.8%	.268	1.50	6.09	138	-0.5	96.8	34.6%	32.3%	42.0%
2020	SF	MLB	28	1	1	0	25	0	27¹	22	3	3.6	8.2	25	44.7%	.260	1.21	3.29	90	0.4	96.0	35.4%	29.0%	44.8%
2021 FS	SF	MLB	29	2	3	0	57	0	50	47	5	4.5	8.2	45	47.7%	.293	1.45	4.47	103	0.0	96.6	39.0%	28.9%	44.6%
2021 DC	SF	MLB	29	2	3	0	57	0	61	57	6	4.5	8.2	55	47.7%	.293	1.45	4.47	103	0.3	96.6	39.0%	28.9%	44.6%

Comparables: Austin Brice, Kevin McCarthy, Mike Mayers

While Wandy was something less than magic, he was something more than a LOOGY for the Giants in 2020—a good thing, since the three-batter rule has forced many specialists to adapt to the more demanding LTOGY role. In addition to a mid-90s heater, Peralta has an out pitch for each side of the plate: the slider to lefties, and the changeup to right-handed hitters. The former is still a better pitch than the latter, which keeps up a visible, if not extreme, platoon split. Peralta may not be able to cast strong spells on opposing hitters, but he has enough skill to conjure at least one more year in a major-league bullpen.

Tyler Rogers RHP

Born: 12/17/90   Age: 30   Bats: R   Throws: R   Height: 6'3"   Weight: 181   Origin: Round 10, 2013 Draft (#312 overall)

YEAR	TEAM	LVL	AGE	W	L	SV	G	GS	IP	H	HR	BB/9	K/9	K	GB%	BABIP	WHIP	ERA	DRA-	WARP	MPH	FA%	Whiff%	CSP
2018	SAC	AAA	27	3	2	3	51	0	67²	50	4	3.1	8.0	60	60.5%	.257	1.08	2.13	76	1.2				
2019	SAC	AAA	28	4	2	5	49	1	62	59	6	4.1	8.0	55	61.5%	.303	1.40	4.21	82	1.4				
2019	SF	MLB	28	2	0	0	17	0	17²	12	0	1.5	8.2	16	68.0%	.245	0.85	1.02	81	0.3	83.8	67.1%	16.5%	55.1%
2020	SF	MLB	29	3	3	3	29	0	28	31	2	1.9	8.7	27	53.5%	.349	1.32	4.50	79	0.6	84.1	64.2%	24.2%	52.6%
2021 FS	SF	MLB	30	2	2	14	57	0	50	47	4	2.9	8.1	44	57.5%	.298	1.27	3.79	91	0.4	84.0	65.0%	22.1%	53.3%
2021 DC	SF	MLB	30	2	2	14	57	0	61	58	5	2.9	8.1	54	57.5%	.298	1.27	3.79	91	0.6	84.0	65.0%	22.1%	53.3%

Comparables: Eric Yardley, Emilio Pagán, Mike Morin

It's de rigueur for any mention of Rogers to mention his older twin, Taylor, who slings filth from the left side for the Twins. These stories often comment on how different the brothers are, and isn't that just *weird*? Rarely do journalists seek an explanation for this radical disparity. Even though the twins were born just a minute apart, Tyler suffers acutely from *younger twin syndrome*, an affliction that manifests in acts of rebellion that are so mild and so inoffensive that they can scarcely be read as such. This helps explain the little-seen back piece that features a full portrait of Brad Ziegler in mid-submarine delivery, emblazoned with "LIVIN' FREE AT 83" in Old English script. Some rebels are without a cause, but Rogers has made his fight very clear: swim against the current of extreme velocity long enough to carve out a successful role in a big-league bullpen with his funky delivery and excellent control. There's no indication that Rogers is close to burning out; we'll have to see whether or not he fades away.

Jeff Samardzija RHP

Born: 01/23/85   Age: 36   Bats: R   Throws: R   Height: 6'4"   Weight: 233   Origin: Round 5, 2006 Draft (#149 overall)

YEAR	TEAM	LVL	AGE	W	L	SV	G	GS	IP	H	HR	BB/9	K/9	K	GB%	BABIP	WHIP	ERA	DRA-	WARP	MPH	FA%	Whiff%	CSP
2018	SAC	AAA	33	0	2	0	4	4	17	17	5	1.6	10.6	20	40.4%	.286	1.18	5.29	86	0.3				
2018	SF	MLB	33	1	5	0	10	10	44²	47	6	5.2	6.0	30	28.9%	.289	1.63	6.25	160	-1.0	95.1	63.2%	20.8%	46.3%
2019	SF	MLB	34	11	12	0	32	32	181¹	152	28	2.4	6.9	140	36.1%	.242	1.11	3.52	90	2.7	93.8	69.0%	20.0%	48.1%
2020	SF	MLB	35	0	2	0	4	4	16²	21	7	2.2	3.2	6	20.0%	.241	1.50	9.72	219	-0.9	92.5	54.0%	13.4%	49.2%
2021 FS	SF	MLB	36	8	10	0	26	26	150	164	30	2.7	6.3	104	32.8%	.288	1.40	5.15	124	-0.9	93.8	66.6%	19.3%	48.0%

Comparables: Ian Kennedy, Mike Fiers, Aníbal Sánchez

For several years, Shark has been more tail than teeth—as the fastball has lost bite, the long, last phase of his career has suffered from injury setbacks, home-run troubles and sinker-smashing hitters, all of these woes intermittently obscured by his ability to log innings while swimming just above the ERA waterline. When sharks are near the end, do they disappear into the depths or hunt for easier prey closer to shore? Released by the Giants into free-agent waters at the end of the season, Samardzija will no longer be the apex predator; instead he'll be fighting for his food in a crowded and inhospitable ecosystem.

Sam Selman LHP

Born: 11/14/90   Age: 30   Bats: R   Throws: L   Height: 6'2"   Weight: 198   Origin: Round 2, 2012 Draft (#66 overall)

YEAR	TEAM	LVL	AGE	W	L	SV	G	GS	IP	H	HR	BB/9	K/9	K	GB%	BABIP	WHIP	ERA	DRA-	WARP	MPH	FA%	Whiff%	CSP
2018	NWA	AA	27	1	2	0	12	0	12¹	12	0	8.0	15.3	21	33.3%	.444	1.86	6.57	84	0.1				
2018	OMA	AAA	27	0	2	0	23	0	28¹	22	0	6.0	11.8	37	43.3%	.328	1.45	4.13	62	0.7				
2019	RIC	AA	28	0	0	0	4	0	7	3	0	1.3	16.7	13	50.0%	.273	0.57	0.00	45	0.2				
2019	SAC	AAA	28	3	2	0	39	1	48	25	4	3.0	15.2	81	41.4%	.253	0.85	2.06	14	2.6				
2019	SF	MLB	28	0	0	0	10	0	10¹	6	2	5.2	8.7	10	30.8%	.174	1.16	4.35	111	0.0	92.0	42.5%	31.1%	43.0%
2020	SF	MLB	29	1	1	1	24	0	19¹	13	2	4.2	10.7	23	31.2%	.244	1.14	3.72	92	0.3	92.8	41.0%	29.9%	47.7%
2021 FS	SF	MLB	30	2	2	0	57	0	50	38	6	4.9	11.7	64	38.4%	.282	1.32	3.91	93	0.3	92.6	41.4%	30.2%	46.5%
2021 DC	SF	MLB	30	2	2	0	51	0	54	41	6	4.9	11.7	70	38.4%	.282	1.32	3.91	93	0.5	92.6	41.4%	30.2%	46.5%

Comparables: Hoby Milner, Eric Yardley, Dakota Bacus

Like scores of other pitchers, Selman should be a LOOGY but woke to find himself in a three-batter-minimum world. Even though he was pretty hittable by righty bats, and he still struggles with walks, his slider is good enough that the Giants should probably hold rather than sell, man.

Nick Swiney LHP

Born: 02/12/99   Age: 22   Bats: R   Throws: L   Height: 6'3"   Weight: 187   Origin: Round 2, 2020 Draft (#67 overall)

Do three wolves make a pack? Swiney joined fellow NC State products Will Wilson and Patrick Bailey in the Giants organization. He's a three-pitch lefty who will race his former teammates to see which canis lupus is the hungriest to get to the majors.

Tony Watson LHP

Born: 05/30/85   Age: 36   Bats: L   Throws: L   Height: 6'3"   Weight: 224   Origin: Round 9, 2007 Draft (#278 overall)

YEAR	TEAM	LVL	AGE	W	L	SV	G	GS	IP	H	HR	BB/9	K/9	K	GB%	BABIP	WHIP	ERA	DRA-	WARP	MPH	FA%	Whiff%	CSP
2018	SF	MLB	33	4	6	0	72	0	66	54	4	1.9	9.8	72	43.7%	.299	1.03	2.59	74	1.2	94.2	51.1%	27.0%	54.3%
2019	SF	MLB	34	2	2	0	60	0	54	56	9	2.0	6.8	41	45.1%	.290	1.26	4.17	114	-0.1	94.5	51.5%	25.9%	49.0%
2020	SF	MLB	35	1	0	2	21	0	18	13	3	1.5	7.5	15	50.0%	.196	0.89	2.50	99	0.2	91.4	37.9%	27.2%	44.6%
2021 FS	SF	MLB	36	2	2	0	57	0	50	47	5	2.1	7.6	42	46.6%	.286	1.18	3.25	86	0.5	93.6	48.0%	26.5%	49.4%

Comparables: Brandon Kintzler, Pedro Strop, Joe Smith

It's easy for statheads to scoff at the save: it's a statistic more dependent on circumstance than skill. Everyone knows this. But Watson may have entered 2020 thinking, after two partial seasons as a closer in Pittsburgh a few years ago, that he may never again get that catcher's handshake after a close game. A lefty who, like so many others, has backgrounded the sinker, Watson now survives on a diet that mixes his former bread-and-butter with a changeup that stymies righties. It's a profile that makes him more than a LOOGY but less than a ninth-inning arm. Thanks to a combination of fluid bullpen roles and no obvious shutdown guy, Watson logged not one, but two saves for the Giants. While these unlikely, stochastic saves may well be the last of his career, there should be no shortage of teams needing a skilled, seasoned lefty for innings other than the ninth.

Logan Webb RHP Born: 11/18/96 Age: 24 Bats: R Throws: R Height: 6'1" Weight: 220 Origin: Round 4, 2014 Draft (#118 overall)

YEAR	TEAM	LVL	AGE	W	L	SV	G	GS	IP	H	HR	BB/9	K/9	K	GB%	BABIP	WHIP	ERA	DRA-	WARP	MPH	FA%	Whiff%	CSP
2018	SJ	HI-A	21	1	3	0	21	20	74	54	2	4.4	9.0	74	46.9%	.275	1.22	1.82	123	-0.7				
2018	RIC	AA	21	1	2	0	6	6	30²	30	4	3.2	7.6	26	50.0%	.292	1.34	3.82	80	0.6				
2019	AUG	LO-A	22	1	0	0	2	1	10	4	0	2.7	8.1	9	58.3%	.167	0.70	0.90	62	0.2				
2019	RIC	AA	22	1	4	0	8	7	41¹	41	2	2.6	10.2	47	65.0%	.331	1.28	2.18	89	0.3				
2019	SAC	AAA	22	0	0	0	1	1	7	7	0	0.0	9.0	7	63.2%	.368	1.00	1.29	64	0.2				
2019	SF	MLB	22	2	3	0	8	8	39²	44	5	3.2	8.4	37	47.5%	.333	1.46	5.22	85	0.7	94.6	56.4%	22.8%	45.6%
2020	SF	MLB	23	3	4	0	13	11	54¹	61	4	4.0	7.6	46	52.1%	.350	1.56	5.47	97	0.6	94.8	48.6%	22.9%	47.1%
2021 FS	SF	MLB	24	9	9	0	26	26	150	146	18	4.0	8.3	137	50.9%	.298	1.42	4.53	105	0.6	94.7	51.0%	22.9%	46.6%
2021 DC	SF	MLB	24	6	9	0	25	25	121	118	14	4.0	8.3	110	50.9%	.298	1.42	4.53	105	0.9	94.7	51.0%	22.9%	46.6%

Comparables: Scott Olsen, Patrick Corbin, Joe Ross

Sometimes the narrative doesn't always go to plan; sometimes it just ends up being a little more circuitous, requiring patience and faith. We're very clearly in the "patience and faith" phase of Webb's story. His trip through the Giants system has been far from a fairy tale: He was derailed by Tommy John surgery, then nabbed for an 80-game PED suspension. Upon arrival in the majors in 2019, he found that mid-90s heat with spotty command wasn't enough to sustain success, and in 2020 he dialed down the four-seamer usage to feature his changeup more prominently. Going into his age-24 season, Webb may not quite be ready for a full-time rotation gig, but he should still have plenty of chances to bend his narrative arc toward happier outcomes.

Matt Wisler RHP Born: 09/12/92 Age: 28 Bats: R Throws: R Height: 6'3" Weight: 215 Origin: Round 7, 2011 Draft (#233 overall)

YEAR	TEAM	LVL	AGE	W	L	SV	G	GS	IP	H	HR	BB/9	K/9	K	GB%	BABIP	WHIP	ERA	DRA-	WARP	MPH	FA%	Whiff%	CSP
2018	GWN	AAA	25	4	4	0	13	13	70	79	6	1.8	8.4	65	45.8%	.354	1.33	4.37	66	1.8				
2018	LOU	AAA	25	1	1	0	8	2	19²	19	0	1.4	9.6	21	35.7%	.339	1.12	1.83	74	0.4				
2018	ATL	MLB	25	1	1	0	7	3	26²	30	6	1.7	7.1	21	27.9%	.300	1.31	5.40	89	0.3	94.4	53.4%	22.2%	49.5%
2018	CIN	MLB	25	0	0	0	11	0	13¹	11	2	1.4	7.4	11	39.0%	.237	0.97	2.02	95	0.1	93.5	42.1%	23.2%	51.2%
2019	SD	MLB	26	2	2	0	21	0	29	34	5	3.1	10.6	34	43.5%	.367	1.52	5.28	79	0.5	94.5	28.6%	32.3%	47.8%
2019	SEA	MLB	26	1	2	0	23	8	22¹	22	5	2.4	11.7	29	26.7%	.309	1.25	6.04	92	0.2	94.1	29.8%	31.7%	44.4%
2020	MIN	MLB	27	0	1	1	18	4	25¹	15	2	5.0	12.4	35	23.2%	.241	1.14	1.07	98	0.2	93.5	16.6%	36.1%	48.8%
2021 FS	SF	MLB	28	2	2	0	57	0	50	43	8	3.2	10.2	56	32.6%	.282	1.23	3.83	95	0.3	94.1	27.9%	32.0%	47.8%
2021 DC	SF	MLB	28	2	2	0	57	0	61	53	10	3.2	10.2	69	32.6%	.282	1.23	3.83	95	0.5	94.1	27.9%	32.0%	47.8%

Comparables: Robert Stephenson, Archie Bradley, Brett Cecil

Wisler is your friend who breaks board games by finding a dominant strategy and then steadfastly refusing to do anything different. In 2020, he took pitch spamming to its logical conclusion by firing his slider on 84 percent of his tosses. To put that in context, nobody else throws one even two-thirds of the time, and only Jake McGee throws any pitch (fastball in this case) as often as Wisler uses the slide piece. The plan worked, as the right-hander produced the best numbers of his career and emerged as a valuable multi-inning weapon in a very strong bullpen. Still, it's worth emphasizing just how weird Wisler's transition from generic four-pitch righty to one-trick pony has been. He's very predictable, doesn't have an unusual spin profile, gives up a ton of fly balls and needs to generate a bunch of called strikes and weak contact to make everything work. We're going to need to see this twice before buying in completely but at the very least, Wisler is far more interesting now than he was this time last year. Sometimes the fifth time (or team) is the charm.

HOUSTON ASTROS

Essay by Rob Arthur

Player comments by Darius Austin and BP staff

The root of the Houston Astros' success over the last five seasons can be traced to a few of the worst teams ever—or, specifically, to the draft picks they resulted in. Houston built its dynasty through one of the most severe and desolate tank jobs in the sport's history. After three consecutive 100-loss seasons, from 2011-13, the Astros emerged with an overhauled front office, a loaded farm system and the core of a roster that would win 100-plus three years in a row. That bunch would eventually claim a World Series title as well as a pair of pennants.

The goal of then-GM Jeff Luhnow's strategy wasn't to ping-pong between championships and no. 1 picks, of course: it was to build a sustainably competitive franchise, one that could replace core after core and stay strong indefinitely. To make this vision a reality, the Astros constructed one of the greatest player-development machines baseball has seen, amending the league's blueprint along the way, as competitors tried to copy how Houston identified and trained players.

Though Luhnow is now more than a year removed from running the show, following his dismissal stemming from the sign-stealing scandal, the stage is nearly set to test his process—to see if the Astros can transcend the success cycle, even as their core graduates into free agency and/or enters the decline phase of their careers.

The thinking behind the success cycle concept goes like this: success is a blessing, but it's also a curse from a front-office perspective. With each year that a team sits at the top of the league, it subtracts from its draft haul, a drain that is felt most acutely at the top of the first round. Without a supply of top-tier picks, the Astros—and other teams like them—have to do more with less. Whereas, at the beginning of their rebuild, the Astros could passively absorb the best talents in the draft, since becoming a good team they've had to work harder to uncover gems.

This negative feedback loop tends to propel teams toward cycles of contention, establishing windows of three to five years' worth of excellence before a rebuild becomes necessary. And yet, every front office dreams (or ought to dream) of escaping that loop. The notion of a player-development machine so efficient and effective that it can

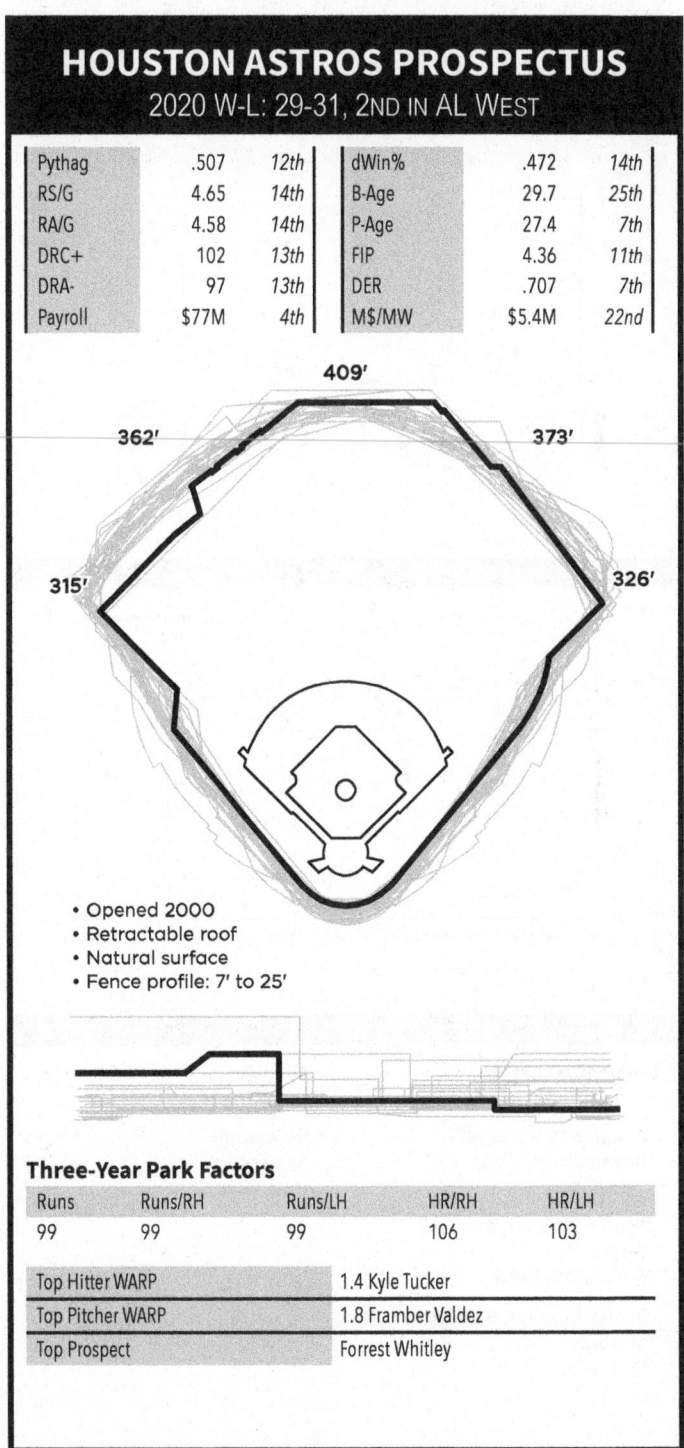

HOUSTON ASTROS PROSPECTUS
2020 W-L: 29-31, 2ND IN AL WEST

Pythag	.507	12th	dWin%	.472	14th
RS/G	4.65	14th	B-Age	29.7	25th
RA/G	4.58	14th	P-Age	27.4	7th
DRC+	102	13th	FIP	4.36	11th
DRA-	97	13th	DER	.707	7th
Payroll	$77M	4th	M$/MW	$5.4M	22nd

409'

362'   373'

315'   326'

- Opened 2000
- Retractable roof
- Natural surface
- Fence profile: 7' to 25'

Three-Year Park Factors

Runs	Runs/RH	Runs/LH	HR/RH	HR/LH
99	99	99	106	103

Top Hitter WARP	1.4 Kyle Tucker
Top Pitcher WARP	1.8 Framber Valdez
Top Prospect	Forrest Whitley

Payroll History (in millions)

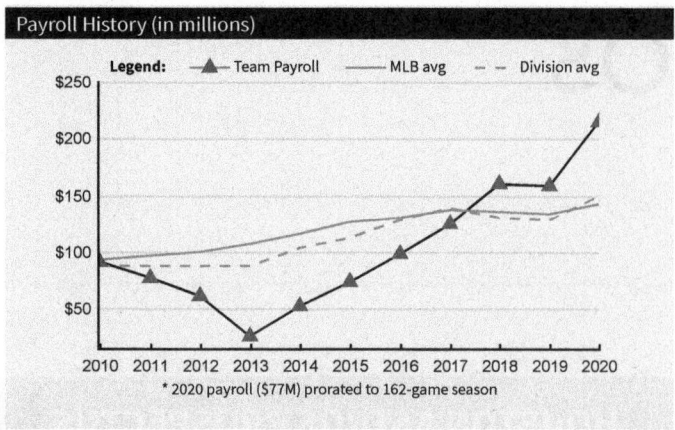

Legend: Team Payroll — MLB avg --- Division avg

* 2020 payroll ($77M) prorated to 162-game season

Future Commitments (in millions)

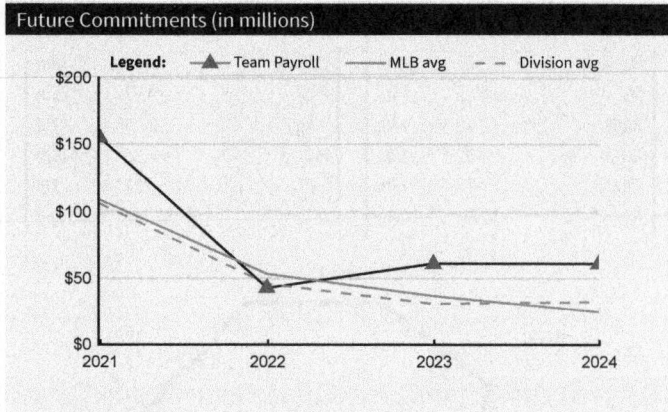

Legend: Team Payroll — MLB avg --- Division avg

Farm System Ranking

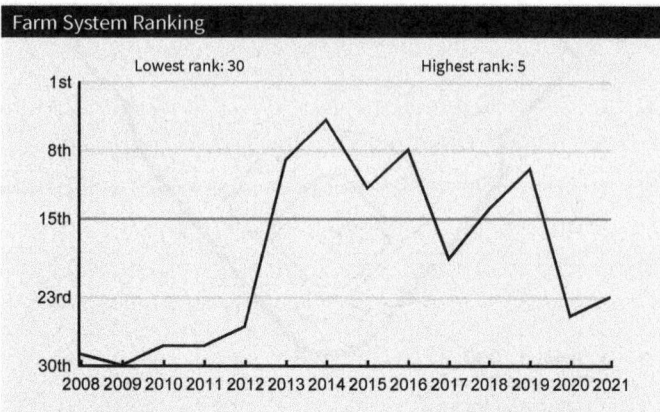

Lowest rank: 30   Highest rank: 5

Personnel

General Manager
James Click

Assistant GM, Player Development
Pete Putila

Senior Director, Baseball Operations
Armando Velasco

Senior Director, Baseball Strategy
Bill Firkus

Manager
Dusty Baker

BP Alumni
James Click
Ryan Lind

continuously churn out a full roster's worth of high-level major-league talent without requiring sky-high payrolls is the baseball equivalent of a nuclear fusion reactor: It's possible, but nobody has ever managed to make it work.

Sure, the Dodgers and Yankees can contend year after year, and do so partially by continuously graduating talented prospects, but they also supplement their rosters with exorbitant spending. Astros owner Jim Crane plainly doesn't want to match that level of financial investment, meaning Houston has to operate more like the Rays and the Cardinals, two teams who, despite apparent player-development chops, have had to take a down year every once in a while to restock their cupboard (for the Rays, 2016; for the Cardinals, 2017-18).

The Astros arguably made more progress toward baseball's fusion reactor than any team in recent memory. Luhnow and his since-departed lieutenant Sig Mejdal revolutionized the science of player development. As chronicled in Ben Lindbergh and Travis Sawchik's book, *The MVP Machine*, Mejdal and Luhnow brought new data-gathering instruments to the minors, rewired (and sometimes fired) coaching and scouting staffs and helped bridge the divide between the nerds in the front office and the players on the field. Their tactics ranged from the obvious (telling pitchers to throw their best pitches more frequently) to the arcane (installing high-speed cameras in minor-league parks). Most importantly, they worked—and we have the numbers to prove it.

Measuring development is hard, not least because it's not a linear process. Prospects don't just improve in a steplike fashion, becoming better each year until they're ready for the bigs. It's messy and complicated: they take steps forward and back, adjust to a new league and then get injured, take a successful cup of coffee in the major leagues and then can't hack it in Triple-A. So, we can't rely on the normal measures of progress. The average change in hitting or pitching ability from year to year, for example, means almost nothing when systems thrive or wilt on whether two or three prospects make it. It doesn't matter if a team's Double-A prospects consistently get 2 to 3 percent better each year if that makes them only into better Triple-A roster fillers. Good systems produce major leaguers, not just better minor leaguers.

Instead of concerning ourselves with the average change in skill each year, I used the number of players who break out as the most important metric. This criterion better matches the idea that it's not about the typical grind of development so much as the players taking big steps forward; those are the prospects who show up on rankings, who may make it to the majors and who may even become impact players.

I quantified the idea of a "breakout" by using a threshold of 10 percent better performance from year to year. If a player was league-average in Year One but 110 percent of league-average in Year Two, then that qualifies. A surprisingly small number of prospects meet this criteria: only about 10 percent of all the player-seasons (minimum 200 plate appearances) in the last five years qualify as "breakouts" as I've defined the term. This stability is thanks in part to Baseball Prospectus' Deserved Run Average and Deserved Runs Created statistics, which subtract a lot of the noise and variation that come from small-sample size, players switching leagues or home parks and other factors that make it look like a player has become a hitting god when really they just moved to the PCL.

By this metric, lots of teams are good at hitting development or good at pitching development, but few are great at both. The Cardinals, for example, excel at drawing breakouts out of their batters, as attested to by José Martinez, Paul DeJong and others. The Athletics are not normally known for their pitcher talents, but in recent years they have brought up breakout hurlers like Sonny Gray, Sean Manaea and Jharel Cotton. Houston is the rare example of a team who excels at turning out players both on the mound and in the batter's box.

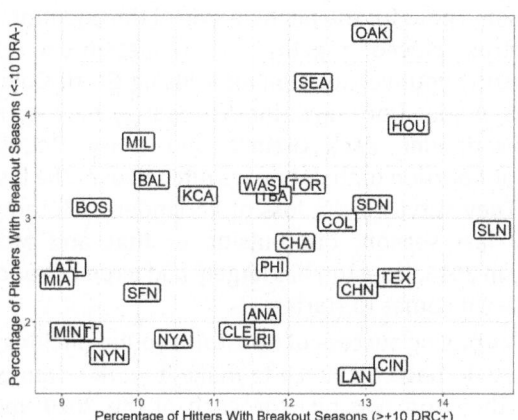

Name	Year	Change in DRA-
Trent Thornton	2016	-29.75
Evan Grills	2016	-28.58
Trent Thornton	2017	-8.86
Brandon Bailey	2018	-7.19
Cy Sneed	2017	-3.03
Trent Thornton	2018	-2.81
Jose Urquidy	2016	-2.07
Keegan Yuhl	2016	-1.88

Houston pitchers with large improvements in DRA- relative to the prior year (>500 batters faced). Players with bolded names have accrued playing time in MLB.

Name	Year	Percent Improvement (DRC+)	PA
Ramón Laureano	2016	58.27%	555
Daz Cameron	2017	56.56%	522
Taylor Jones	2018	54.06%	530
Osvaldo Duarte	2018	46.07%	535
Corey Julks	2018	37.05%	521
Jason Martin	2017	25.18%	518
Ronnie Dawson	2017	12.21%	518
Derek Fisher	2016	11.55%	566
Josh Rojas	2018	10.41%	556
Kyle Tucker	2017	6.56%	619

Houston players with large improvements in DRC+ relative to the prior year (>500 PA). Players with bolded names have accrued playing time in MLB.

Indeed, no team surpasses their skill in both aspects of development. The Cardinals are in a virtual tie, although due much more to their batsmen than their arms; everyone else is far behind these two teams, which share a common player development DNA by way of Mejdal and Luhnow. Even the vaunted Dodgers, whose core has proven to be every bit as good or better than the Astros since 2015, have leaned less on their homegrown talent. (In some cases, harvesting other teams' talents, like the Dodgers did with Mookie Betts, was the better move than trying to build an outfielder as good in-house.)

All this player-development success has translated into one of the strongest cores of the current era. The Baseball Gauge calculates a "homegrown WAR" metric that measures how many wins above replacement come from players developed by a team. Four of Houston's five squads ranked in the top 20 of all teams since 2015 by this measurement, putting the team far in the lead over the full five-season span. The gap between Houston and second-place Boston in homegrown WAR was roughly the same as the gap between Boston and sixth-place Cleveland, both front offices with their own notable player-development success.

But Houston's recent dominance in this measure doesn't guarantee that they will continue to stay so strong—the coming years appear certain to test their processes in that regard.

The average age of Houston's hitters, according to Baseball Reference, has increased by almost four years since 2015—a byproduct of fielding largely the same group of regulars. The core that powered them to a championship and more than 500 wins in the last six seasons is getting older and starting to show signs of being worse for it, from Josh Reddick's dramatic dropoff (and subsequent departure) to Yuli Gurriel and Jose Altuve's anemic batting in 2020. The Astros are also experiencing the other realities that come with players amassing service time and gaining earning power: Houston lost George Springer to free agency over the winter, and Carlos Correa may follow suit after the 2021 season. The ascents of Kyle Tucker and, before him, Yordan Alvarez should help offset some of those losses, albeit likely not all of them.

The same goes for the pitching side of the equation, where the Astros pieced together a competent-enough and significantly younger rotation after losing Gerrit Cole to the Yankees. A year from now, the Astros may have to replace Justin Verlander, Zack Greinke and Lance McCullers, a significant portion of their innings pitched over the last three years. They survived the loss of Verlander to Tommy John surgery last season, but outside of that and McCullers surgery in 2018, Houston has largely had a run of good injury luck when it comes to starters.

The surprising success of Houston's young pitching shows that they do have a chance to make it work—even without having their top two picks in each of the 2020 and 2021 drafts. The Astros will have to lean on alternate means of talent acquisition. That means producing players like Framber Valdez, the 26-year-old Dominican starter signed as an amateur international free-agent, will take on greater importance. Other promising hurlers have followed similar paths through their system, from Jose Urquidy to Cristian Javier. With any luck, the Astros will hit on another Collin McHugh—a waiver-wire find—or help another Dallas Keuchel—originally a seventh-round pick—reach and prosper at the big-league level with their careful instruction.

As clear as Houston's success in helping improve their hitters and pitchers has been, it's harder to place 2020 in the arc of their story. With little explanation, the Astros went from one of the most dominant teams in history in 2019 to an also-ran that fortuitously made the postseason. But, coming as it did on the heels of morale-crushing revelations about Houston's sign-stealing scheme, perhaps their performance ought to be graded on a curve. After all, Dusty Baker led the team to within a few runs of another World Series appearance. Their playoff run may augur well for their ability to replace lost talent and continue to push deep into future postseasons.

The Astros sure hope so, anyway. Though they've managed to produce some historically great rosters, the coming years will offer their steepest player-development challenge yet. As the current core begins to age out of its productive years, will the Astros be able to replace them? The real crucible for Luhnow's vision was whether they could continuously turn over that level of talent after their tanking ended.

In 2021, and over the next few seasons, we'll start to see whether Houston is able, under James Click's watch, to realize the modern front office dream of a perpetual contention machine. Or, if like most teams before them, they'll have to start all over again. ▪

—Rob Arthur is an author of Baseball Prospectus.

HITTERS

Jose Altuve 2B   Born: 05/06/90   Age: 31   Bats: R   Throws: R   Height: 5'6"   Weight: 166   Origin: International Free Agent, 2007

YEAR	TEAM	LVL	AGE	PA	R	2B	3B	HR	RBI	BB	K	SB	CS	Whiff%	AVG/OBP/SLG	DRC+	BABIP	BRR	FRAA	WARP
2018	HOU	MLB	28	599	84	29	2	13	61	55	79	17	4	17.8%	.316/.386/.451	126	.352	2.4	2B(130): -7.9	3.2
2019	HOU	MLB	29	548	89	27	3	31	74	41	82	6	5	20.9%	.298/.353/.550	118	.303	-0.5	2B(121): -0.6, SS(1): -0.0	3.0
2020	HOU	MLB	30	210	32	9	0	5	18	17	39	2	3	20.4%	.219/.286/.344	78	.250	2.4	2B(48): 2.5	0.4
2021 FS	HOU	MLB	31	600	80	27	2	23	74	48	100	17	5	20.0%	.283/.351/.474	120	.312	2.2	2B -5, SS 0	3.4
2021 DC	HOU	MLB	31	551	73	25	2	21	68	44	92	15	5	20.0%	.283/.351/.474	120	.312	2.0	2B -5	3.1

Comparables: Ian Kinsler, Robinson Canó, Keith Lockhart

Altuve was one player for whom sign-stealing decline couldn't be offered as a lazy explanation for a poor 2020; the trash can was not banged for him, nor did he see the same improvements in his plate discipline that many colleagues enjoyed. The abbreviated campaign was his worst since his rookie season. While we've seen the power suffer along with his ailing knee before, for the first time ever, he didn't hit for average. That failing can only partly be attributed to BABIP misfortune as Altuve also posted a career-worst strikeout rate. A declining contact trend can be seen all the way back to 2014. The keystone of this team had a lot of leeway beneath him then. Now he's run out of room.

Yordan Alvarez OF   Born: 06/27/97   Age: 24   Bats: L   Throws: R   Height: 6'5"   Weight: 225   Origin: International Free Agent, 2016

YEAR	TEAM	LVL	AGE	PA	R	2B	3B	HR	RBI	BB	K	SB	CS	Whiff%	AVG/OBP/SLG	DRC+	BABIP	BRR	FRAA	WARP
2018	CC	AA	21	190	39	13	0	12	46	19	45	5	2		.325/.389/.615	164	.377	0.2	LF(31): 3.6, 1B(5): -0.1	1.6
2018	FRE	AAA	21	189	24	8	0	8	28	23	47	1	0		.259/.349/.452	109	.315	-2.0	LF(34): -6.3	-0.5
2019	RR	AAA	22	253	50	16	0	23	71	38	50	2	1		.343/.443/.742	176	.355	-2.3	LF(27): 0.3, 1B(9): -1.1, RF(2): -0.2	2.4
2019	HOU	MLB	22	369	58	26	0	27	78	52	94	0	0	25.0%	.313/.412/.655	148	.366	-0.5	LF(10): -0.5	2.8
2020	HOU	MLB	23	9	2	0	0	1	4	0	1	0	0	14.3%	.250/.333/.625	88	.167	-0.2		0.0
2021 FS	HOU	MLB	24	600	87	35	1	39	103	70	162	2	0	24.6%	.295/.385/.592	153	.362	-0.7	1B 0, LF 0	5.6
2021 DC	HOU	MLB	24	551	80	32	1	36	95	64	148	2	0	24.6%	.295/.385/.592	153	.362	-0.6		4.9

Comparables: Mark McGwire, Fred McGriff, Giancarlo Stanton

In hindsight, Alvarez's knee trouble was the early warning that the 2020 Astros would not live up to the lofty standards they set over the past three seasons. The 2019 Rookie of the Year's absence robbed them of one of their most potent weapons. His recovery wasn't helped by a COVID-19 diagnosis but that may have just delayed the inevitable surgery he underwent on both knees. This declining offense desperately needs him back at full strength in 2021 if they're to have any hope of becoming feared once again.

Michael Brantley   LF   Born: 05/15/87   Age: 34   Bats: L   Throws: L   Height: 6'2"   Weight: 209   Origin: Round 7, 2005 Draft (#205 overall)

YEAR	TEAM	LVL	AGE	PA	R	2B	3B	HR	RBI	BB	K	SB	CS	Whiff%	AVG/OBP/SLG	DRC+	BABIP	BRR	FRAA	WARP
2018	CLE	MLB	31	631	89	36	2	17	76	48	60	12	3	11.2%	.309/.364/.468	118	.319	1.4	LF(134): -3.4	2.8
2019	HOU	MLB	32	637	88	40	2	22	90	51	66	3	2	10.9%	.311/.372/.503	121	.320	0.0	LF(120): -7.4, RF(9): -0.8	2.5
2020	HOU	MLB	33	187	24	15	0	5	22	17	28	2	0	16.4%	.300/.364/.476	117	.336	-1.1	LF(19): 1.9	0.9
2021 FS	HOU	MLB	34	600	71	31	1	18	75	52	87	8	2	12.3%	.286/.355/.454	117	.314	-0.2	LF -8, RF 0	2.2

Comparables: Dusty Baker, Shannon Stewart, Kevin McReynolds

Dr. Smooth rolled out his collection of highly successful numbers once again, further distancing himself from a tumultuous mid-career blip with reassuring daily consistency. There are signs of age: for the first time in his career, Brantley occupied a new slot at DH more often than his regular outfield berth, while he came up empty with his hacks a little more often than we're used to. Brantley's still at the top of the game when it comes to playing those hits, which is as good a sign as any that he'll make a slick segue into his role with another station.

Alex Bregman   3B   Born: 03/30/94   Age: 27   Bats: R   Throws: R   Height: 6'0"   Weight: 192   Origin: Round 1, 2015 Draft (#2 overall)

YEAR	TEAM	LVL	AGE	PA	R	2B	3B	HR	RBI	BB	K	SB	CS	Whiff%	AVG/OBP/SLG	DRC+	BABIP	BRR	FRAA	WARP
2018	HOU	MLB	24	705	105	51	1	31	103	96	85	10	4	12.9%	.286/.394/.532	149	.289	-1.6	3B(136): 5.4, SS(28): -0.4, 2B(2): -0.1	7.4
2019	HOU	MLB	25	690	122	37	2	41	112	119	83	5	1	14.5%	.296/.423/.592	157	.281	-3.8	3B(99): 6.6, SS(65): 4.7	8.6
2020	HOU	MLB	26	180	19	12	1	6	22	24	26	0	0	14.7%	.242/.350/.451	125	.254	0.3	3B(42): 0.3	0.9
2021 FS	HOU	MLB	27	600	84	32	2	30	86	78	96	8	2	14.1%	.276/.381/.527	139	.289	0.6	3B 8, 2B 0	5.3
2021 DC	HOU	MLB	27	619	87	33	2	31	89	80	99	8	2	14.1%	.276/.381/.527	139	.289	0.7	3B 8	5.3

Comparables: Chipper Jones, Eric Chavez, David Wright

The sign-stealing scandal would have been the perfect opportunity for a Bregman heel turn. What we got instead was a series of deflections, followed by a press conference apology as poorly scripted as the clunkiest wrestling promo. The third baseman followed that up with a good, albeit muted season that, like the WWE itself, lacked any intensity without antagonistic fans in attendance. Bregman was something of a tweener to begin with, so perhaps the Astros simply didn't know where to take this storyline. In the absence of a proper apology, let's be honest: it would have been far more entertaining if Bregman had opened that presser by declaring "IT'S ME, MANFRED! IT WAS ME ALL ALONG!"

Carlos Correa   SS   Born: 09/22/94   Age: 26   Bats: R   Throws: R   Height: 6'4"   Weight: 220   Origin: Round 1, 2012 Draft (#1 overall)

YEAR	TEAM	LVL	AGE	PA	R	2B	3B	HR	RBI	BB	K	SB	CS	Whiff%	AVG/OBP/SLG	DRC+	BABIP	BRR	FRAA	WARP
2018	HOU	MLB	23	468	60	20	1	15	65	53	111	3	0	24.1%	.239/.323/.405	98	.282	0.8	SS(109): 7.2	2.8
2019	HOU	MLB	24	321	42	16	1	21	59	35	75	1	0	23.6%	.279/.358/.568	125	.303	-0.6	SS(75): -2.3	2.3
2020	HOU	MLB	26	221	22	9	0	5	25	16	49	0	0	24.3%	.264/.326/.383	84	.324	0.1	SS(57): -2.4	-0.1
2021 FS	HOU	MLB	26	600	68	24	1	24	74	63	137	5	1	24.0%	.261/.346/.451	114	.312	0.1	SS 2	3.3
2021 DC	HOU	MLB	26	585	66	24	1	23	72	61	133	5	1	24.0%	.261/.346/.451	114	.312	0.1	SS 2	3.2

Comparables: Corey Seager, Alex Rodriguez, Hanley Ramirez

To paraphrase Correa himself after the Astros dumped the luckless Twins out of the playoffs: what *are* we going to say now? With a standard 10-team postseason format, this comment would have been exploring the disappointment of his offensive performance in a rare season of good health. The expanded bracket instead afforded a sub-.500 team the opportunity to sneak into October and truly infuriate the fans who had already been denied the opportunity to express their disgust at the sign-stealing scheme in person. Correa jumped on that opportunity like a forewarned hitter on a fastball, combining a scorching run at the plate with quotes that cast the Astros as the victims and placed himself firmly at the center of the storm.

It wasn't the first time Correa drew the ongoing vitriol from this saga. He clashed with Cody Bellinger when the Dodgers star suggested Jose Altuve's 2017 MVP award was stolen, and was the target of Joe Kelly's infamous pout that precipitated one of the few bench-clearing incidents of the year. The lightning rod role energized him in a way that it hadn't during the regular season, as his six homers and 1.221 OPS brought Houston to the brink of another World Series. To answer his question: many people are going to say exactly the same thing as they were saying before, responding as vehemently as Correa's personal intensity warrants. No matter what he does, Correa is going to have to deal with the repercussions of the scandal for the rest of his career. If this postseason is the way he responds going forwards, opposing fans are going to have to deal with him being extremely good indeed.

Ronnie Dawson   CF   Born: 05/19/95   Age: 26   Bats: L   Throws: R   Height: 6'2"   Weight: 217   Origin: Round 2, 2016 Draft (#61 overall)

YEAR	TEAM	LVL	AGE	PA	R	2B	3B	HR	RBI	BB	K	SB	CS	Whiff%	AVG/OBP/SLG	DRC+	BABIP	BRR	FRAA	WARP
2018	FAY	HI-A	23	376	51	18	1	10	49	39	96	29	11		.247/.331/.398	116	.317	-2.3	CF(88): 4.8	1.3
2018	CC	AA	23	123	18	6	1	6	14	6	34	6	3		.289/.341/.518	113	.365	1.9	CF(24): 0.1, RF(5): -0.4	0.4
2019	CC	AA	24	459	71	20	2	17	50	47	141	13	10		.212/.320/.403	97	.281	1.1	CF(78): -2.6, RF(10): -0.7, LF(2): 2.6	1.3
2019	RR	AAA	24	39	1	1	0	0	3	3	11	1	0		.147/.231/.176	25	.208	0.1	CF(6): -0.5, RF(4): -0.0	-0.2
2021 FS	HOU	MLB	26	600	62	26	2	20	63	45	198	13	7		.218/.291/.387	77	.303	-4.7	CF 5, LF 1	0.1
2021 DC	HOU	MLB	26	275	28	12	1	9	29	21	90	6	3		.218/.291/.387	77	.303	-2.1	CF 2, LF 0	0.1

Comparables: Joe Benson, Matthew den Dekker, Tommy Pham

As Houston dealt with an outfield exodus, the athletic Dawson was one of the few obvious upper-minors names available for depth. In that light, their decision to not add him to the 40-man ahead of the Rule 5 draft—for the second consecutive year—offers little encouragement for his chances of finding even a part-time role.

Aledmys Díaz 2B Born: 08/01/90 Age: 30 Bats: R Throws: R Height: 6'1" Weight: 195 Origin: International Free Agent, 2014

YEAR	TEAM	LVL	AGE	PA	R	2B	3B	HR	RBI	BB	K	SB	CS	Whiff%	AVG/OBP/SLG	DRC+	BABIP	BRR	FRAA	WARP
2018	TOR	MLB	27	452	55	26	0	18	55	23	62	3	4	22.6%	.263/.303/.453	107	.269	-1.8	SS(95): -5.8, 3B(38): -0.5	1.5
2019	HOU	MLB	28	247	36	12	1	9	40	26	28	2	0	19.6%	.271/.356/.467	108	.268	1.9	1B(26): -0.8, 2B(25): 0.6, 3B(19): -0.8	1.1
2020	HOU	MLB	30	59	8	5	0	3	6	1	12	0	0	26.5%	.241/.254/.483	98	.256	0.0	2B(10): -0.1, 3B(3): -0.2, 1B(2): 0.2	0.1
2021 FS	HOU	MLB	30	600	66	27	1	23	73	41	106	5	2	21.9%	.247/.309/.429	96	.269	-0.9	2B 3, 1B -2	1.3
2021 DC	HOU	MLB	30	275	30	12	0	10	33	19	48	2	1	21.9%	.247/.309/.429	96	.269	-0.4	2B 1, 1B -1	0.6

Comparables: Miguel Tejada, J.J. Hardy, Alexei Ramirez

Good utility players need to be able to bide their time and be ready whenever called upon. Houston appeared to have coaxed a higher level of plate discipline out of Díaz, a development that promised a productive season ahead. A groin strain sorely tested that patience as the utilityman was forced to miss a month after appearing in just one game. Upon his return, Díaz slipped back into his free-swinging ways, chasing in areas he shouldn't as though he was trying to cram a season's worth of production into a fraction of the time. His approach still resulted in some powerful moments, but success was rare when it came to reaching base. He didn't even swing any more often; he just picked the wrong pitches to go after. Díaz will need to recapture his 2019 composure at the plate if he's to be a dependable utility bat and not an all-or-nothing wildcard.

Dustin Garneau C Born: 08/13/87 Age: 33 Bats: R Throws: R Height: 6'2" Weight: 205 Origin: Round 19, 2009 Draft (#571 overall)

YEAR	TEAM	LVL	AGE	PA	R	2B	3B	HR	RBI	BB	K	SB	CS	Whiff%	AVG/OBP/SLG	DRC+	BABIP	BRR	FRAA	WARP
2018	CHA	AAA	30	160	19	9	0	7	22	16	38	0	2		.252/.340/.468	113	.295	-0.3	C(39): -0.9, 1B(1): -0.3, LF(1): -0.2	0.5
2018	NAS	AAA	30	80	8	3	0	2	9	5	10	0	0		.208/.263/.333	67	.210	-1.3	C(18): -2.2	-0.4
2018	CHW	MLB	30	3	0	0	0	0	1	1	0	0	0	37.5%	.500/.667/.500	98	.500	-0.3	C(1): -0.3	0.0
2019	SL	AAA	31	98	16	8	0	6	13	11	28	0	0		.229/.347/.542	91	.265	-0.6	C(26): 8.7	1.1
2019	LV	AAA	31	32	2	2	1	1	3	3	9	0	0		.308/.387/.577	99	.412	-1.0	C(7): -0.1, 1B(1): 0.0	0.1
2019	LAA	MLB	31	82	11	3	0	2	7	8	17	0	0	20.8%	.232/.346/.362	87	.280	-0.5	C(27): -0.0, 1B(1): -0.0	0.2
2019	OAK	MLB	31	19	3	2	0	1	7	2	4	0	0	17.9%	.294/.368/.588	108	.333	-0.2	C(7): -0.0	0.1
2020	HOU	MLB	33	46	4	0	1	1	4	6	15	0	0	38.2%	.158/.273/.289	70	.227	0.0	C(17): -0.2	-0.1
2021 FS	HOU	MLB	33	600	65	21	1	24	65	52	173	1	0	27.5%	.209/.292/.392	83	.260	-0.1	C -13, 1B 0	-0.2

Comparables: Jose Lobaton, Josh Phegley, Dusty Wathan

The out-of-options Garneau discovered that being the primary backup has its disadvantages compared to the third catcher role. He has never started more than 33 big-league games in a season or caught over 300 innings at the level. Garneau would get his reps by catching several hundred more innings at Triple-A, a level where he'd also been excellent with the stick. Playing behind Martín Maldonado provided little more work than backing up Yadier Molina: Garneau was lucky if he saw more than a handful of plate appearances a week and caught barely 20 percent of the team's innings, going as many as nine games between starts. Extra rest did not seem to help his performance. His final start for the team took that to a new extreme, coming in ALCS Game 3, 16 days after his final regular season start. He struck out in both plate appearances. If Garneau just wants to play, the Astros waiving him might not be the worst thing in the world.

YEAR	TEAM	P. COUNT	FRM RUNS	BLK RUNS	THRW RUNS	TOT RUNS
2018	CHW	154	0.0	0.1	0.0	0.1
2018	NAS	2512	-2.1	-0.2	0.7	-1.6
2019	OAK	703	0.1	-0.2	0.0	-0.1
2019	LAA	3375	0.4	0.0	0.0	0.4
2019	SL	3857	7.2	0.1	0.6	7.9
2020	HOU	1966	-0.1	-0.3	0.1	-0.3
2021	HOU	16650	-9.4	-1.5	-0.4	-11.3

Yuli Gurriel 1B Born: 06/09/84 Age: 37 Bats: R Throws: R Height: 6'0" Weight: 215 Origin: International Free Agent, 2016

YEAR	TEAM	LVL	AGE	PA	R	2B	3B	HR	RBI	BB	K	SB	CS	Whiff%	AVG/OBP/SLG	DRC+	BABIP	BRR	FRAA	WARP
2018	HOU	MLB	34	573	70	33	1	13	85	23	63	5	1	15.7%	.291/.323/.428	109	.306	1.1	1B(109): 1.5, 3B(21): 1.2, 2B(15): -1.0	2.0
2019	HOU	MLB	35	612	85	40	2	31	104	37	65	5	3	14.9%	.298/.343/.541	119	.289	-1.5	1B(110): 7.3, 3B(42): 0.4, 2B(4): -0.2	3.4
2020	HOU	MLB	36	230	27	12	1	6	22	12	27	0	1	15.6%	.232/.274/.384	107	.235	-0.8	1B(55): 4.6	0.8
2021 FS	HOU	MLB	37	600	64	32	1	22	79	28	85	4	1	15.2%	.261/.304/.439	96	.275	-1.8	1B 11, 2B 0	1.6
2021 DC	HOU	MLB	37	585	62	31	1	21	77	27	83	4	1	15.2%	.261/.304/.439	96	.275	-1.8	1B 11	1.5

Comparables: Steve Garvey, Eric Karros, Cecil Cooper

In notorious sabermetric masterpiece Bull Durham, Crash Davis foresaw our future fixation on BABIP when highlighting the difference between hitting .250 and .300: one hit a week. Crash would have approved of Gurriel's democratic approach to strikeouts but, for all his sage advice, he had little to say on the topic of how to turn a season around when there's a mere 10 weeks to work with. Gurriel squeezed every ounce of juice out of the 2019 ball and then suffered a drastic reversal of fortunes, an object lesson in how a 60-game sample can affect even the most dependable hitter. Almost everything was identical to his career numbers: the strikeout, walk, and swing rates; exit velocity and launch angle; DRC+. Almost. The one thing that didn't hold up was the production itself. Few of Gurriel's flares, gorks, or dying quails seemed to materialize in hits, condemning him to career worsts in all three slash line components. Baseball's shortest season only proved the inescapable truth of Crash's words: one more dying quail per week would have seen Gurriel hit .280.

Taylor Jones 1B Born: 12/06/93 Age: 27 Bats: R Throws: R Height: 6'7" Weight: 230 Origin: Round 19, 2016 Draft (#577 overall)

YEAR	TEAM	LVL	AGE	PA	R	2B	3B	HR	RBI	BB	K	SB	CS	Whiff%	AVG/OBP/SLG	DRC+	BABIP	BRR	FRAA	WARP
2018	CC	AA	24	367	45	25	1	13	63	45	78	2	0		.314/.409/.528	160	.377	-3.2	1B(70): 4.1, LF(7): -0.8	1.9
2018	FRE	AAA	24	163	16	7	1	5	17	16	46	0	0		.210/.294/.378	82	.266	-1.3	1B(29): -1.6, LF(1): -0.3	-0.6
2019	RR	AAA	25	531	86	28	0	22	84	68	112	0	1		.291/.388/.501	122	.336	-1.7	1B(68): 6.3, LF(27): 0.5, 3B(15): 1.0	2.9
2020	HOU	MLB	27	22	3	1	0	1	3	1	7	0	0	30.2%	.190/.227/.381	86	.231	-0.3	1B(3): -0.4	-0.1
2021 FS	HOU	MLB	27	600	67	24	1	25	71	57	184	0	0	30.2%	.232/.318/.424	96	.306	-0.7	LF -3, 1B 1	0.2
2021 DC	HOU	MLB	27	275	30	11	0	11	32	26	84	0	0	30.2%	.232/.318/.424	96	.306	-0.3	LF -1, 1B 0	0.3

Comparables: Chris Duncan, Matt Olson, Matt Clark

Jones has been late to a lot of things. He transitioned to hitting late, spending his initial college years predominantly on the mound. He started trying out positions other than first base even later, playing both third and left field for the first time in 2019. He was late to debut in the majors, doing so at the age of 26 after this complicated path through pro ball. It's impressive that he made it at all, in a lot of ways, but merely turning up at some point isn't going to cut it now. Jones needs to be on time at the plate, or he'll never get enough of his raw pop into games to be anything but an occasional party-crasher.

Martín Maldonado C Born: 08/16/86 Age: 34 Bats: R Throws: R Height: 6'0" Weight: 230 Origin: Round 27, 2004 Draft (#803 overall)

YEAR	TEAM	LVL	AGE	PA	R	2B	3B	HR	RBI	BB	K	SB	CS	Whiff%	AVG/OBP/SLG	DRC+	BABIP	BRR	FRAA	WARP
2018	HOU	MLB	31	114	15	4	1	4	12	3	25	0	0	24.6%	.231/.257/.398	75	.263	-0.6	C(40): 2.0	0.4
2018	LAA	MLB	31	290	24	14	0	5	32	13	73	0	1	27.8%	.223/.284/.332	74	.287	-0.1	C(77): 1.1	0.6
2019	CHC	MLB	32	13	0	0	0	0	0	2	5	0	0	36.8%	.000/.154/.000	-25	.000	-0.1	C(4): -0.2	-0.2
2019	KC	MLB	32	263	26	15	0	6	17	17	55	0	0	22.2%	.227/.291/.366	76	.270	-4.6	C(73): 1.8	0.3
2019	HOU	MLB	32	98	20	4	0	6	10	13	26	0	0	29.3%	.202/.316/.464	96	.212	0.0	C(26): 0.1, 1B(1): -0.0	0.5
2020	HOU	MLB	34	165	19	4	0	6	24	27	51	1	0	29.2%	.215/.350/.378	97	.295	-1.6	C(47): -0.4	0.2
2021 FS	HOU	MLB	34	600	63	22	1	20	61	53	178	1	0	26.6%	.215/.303/.375	81	.283	-1.2	C 5, 1B 0	1.4
2021 DC	HOU	MLB	34	447	47	16	0	15	45	40	132	1	0	26.6%	.215/.303/.375	81	.283	-0.9	C 5	1.2

Comparables: Ron Karkovice, Todd Pratt, Chris Gimenez

Ahead of Game 7 of the ALCS, Lance McCullers praised Maldonado's "will to win" and "grit." That might sound like Hawk Harrelson excusing a poor offensive performance with intangibles, but Maldonado three-true-outcomed his way to an average offensive season while also carrying out an impressive feat of pitcher management that is somewhat unquantifiable. Let's try anyway. Fifteen rookies pitched for the Astros in 2020, a number only matched by the COVID-depleted Marlins. Those rookies ended up pitching more than half of Houston's innings, leading the league. Maldonado guided the newcomers through the vast majority, handling almost three-quarters of the time behind the plate. He then started all but one of the team's playoff games—entering the other for the final four

YEAR	TEAM	P. COUNT	FRM RUNS	BLK RUNS	THRW RUNS	TOT RUNS
2018	HOU	4771	1.7	-0.3	0.2	1.6
2018	LAA	11404	4.1	-0.8	0.3	3.7
2019	KC	10492	-1.4	3.3	0.3	2.1
2019	CHC	571	-0.1	-0.3	0.0	-0.3
2019	HOU	3403	-0.5	0.9	-0.3	0.1
2020	HOU	6449	-1.4	0.3	-0.2	-1.4
2021	HOU	15632	1.8	2.1	1.3	5.2

innings—to shepherd this rookie-reliant pitching staff within one game of the World Series. The Astros believed in Maldonado enough to not only bring him back to the team for the third time in three years but also to entrust him with almost all of their catching work. While his statistical résumé as a framer appears to be getting less impressive as he ages, his colleagues will tell you he excels at practically everything else.

Chas McCormick RF Born: 04/19/95 Age: 26 Bats: R Throws: L Height: 6'0" Weight: 208 Origin: Round 21, 2017 Draft (#631 overall)

YEAR	TEAM	LVL	AGE	PA	R	2B	3B	HR	RBI	BB	K	SB	CS	Whiff%	AVG/OBP/SLG	DRC+	BABIP	BRR	FRAA	WARP
2018	FAY	HI-A	23	209	26	13	3	2	27	19	34	7	0		.264/.332/.401	109	.305	0.9	RF(44): 1.9, LF(7): 0.0	0.5
2018	CC	AA	23	282	33	10	1	2	28	24	32	12	4		.280/.344/.352	108	.308	-0.2	RF(24): 1.9, LF(23): -1.8, CF(22): 1.0	0.4
2019	CC	AA	24	223	26	3	3	4	22	39	28	9	3		.277/.426/.395	151	.310	0.7	LF(40): 5.2, CF(6): -0.3, RF(3): -0.9	2.1
2019	RR	AAA	24	225	39	3	3	10	44	28	34	7	1		.262/.347/.466	101	.261	0.0	RF(22): 0.2, CF(16): 0.6, LF(12): 1.2	0.8
2021 FS	HOU	MLB	26	600	65	24	3	15	62	54	119	7	2		.248/.324/.392	96	.293	3.1	RF 3, LF 4	2.4
2021 DC	HOU	MLB	26	378	41	15	2	9	39	34	75	4	1		.248/.324/.392	96	.293	1.9	RF 2, LF 3	1.5

Comparables: Jerry Owens, Mike Tauchman, JB Shuck

While several organizations named high-end prospects with no major-league experience to their postseason rosters, Houston's addition of McCormick prompted one prevailing response: "Who?" Lack of respect for the Pennsylvania State Athletic Conference aside, McCormick has excellent minor-league plate discipline numbers with burgeoning power, but there's doubt it'll play in the bigs, a concern the Astros are poised to test.

Freudis Nova SS Born: 01/12/00 Age: 21 Bats: R Throws: R Height: 6'1" Weight: 180 Origin: International Free Agent, 2016

YEAR	TEAM	LVL	AGE	PA	R	2B	3B	HR	RBI	BB	K	SB	CS	Whiff%	AVG/OBP/SLG	DRC+	BABIP	BRR	FRAA	WARP
2018	AST	ROK	18	157	21	3	1	6	28	6	21	9	5		.308/.331/.466	126	.317	0.4	SS(24): -0.8, 2B(9): 0.0	0.4
2019	QC	LO-A	19	299	35	20	1	3	29	15	67	10	7		.259/.301/.369	104	.330	-0.4	SS(32): -3.0, 2B(23): -0.0, 3B(18): -0.6	0.8
2021 FS	HOU	MLB	21	600	47	27	2	9	53	28	172	14	7		.219/.260/.326	59	.298	-4.1	SS -6, 2B 0	-2.5

Comparables: Tim Beckham, Ryan Mountcastle, Javy Guerra

When it comes to prospects, it's not nature or nurture so much as nature and nurture. Nova's standing to date has largely been driven by the former, thanks to his projectable frame, defensive athleticism and bat speed. Missing a full season of pro ball-related activities will offer some insight into how much of the latter he needs to become a big-league regular.

★ ★ ★ *2021 Top 101 Prospect* **#82** ★ ★ ★

Jeremy Peña SS Born: 09/22/97   Age: 23   Bats: R   Throws: R   Height: 6'0"   Weight: 202   Origin: Round 3, 2018 Draft (#102 overall)

YEAR	TEAM	LVL	AGE	PA	R	2B	3B	HR	RBI	BB	K	SB	CS	Whiff%	AVG/OBP/SLG	DRC+	BABIP	BRR	FRAA	WARP
2018	TRI	SS	20	156	22	5	0	1	10	18	19	3	0		.250/.340/.309	133	.282	-1.0	SS(32): -0.5, 2B(4): 0.0	0.5
2019	QC	LO-A	21	289	44	8	4	5	41	35	57	17	6		.293/.389/.421	153	.357	3.3	SS(60): -2.1, 2B(2): -0.3	2.9
2019	FAY	HI-A	21	185	28	13	3	2	13	12	33	3	4		.317/.378/.467	144	.383	1.8	SS(29): -0.2, 2B(11): 0.1, 3B(1): -0.0	1.7
2021 FS	HOU	MLB	23	600	60	26	3	12	58	42	150	8	4		.239/.301/.370	83	.306	-1.2	SS -9, 2B 0	-0.4
2021 DC	HOU	MLB	23	68	6	2	0	1	6	4	17	0	0		.239/.301/.370	83	.306	-0.1	SS -1	0.0

Comparables: Darnell Sweeney, Zach Walters, Andy Burns

The Astros were so focused on stocking their 60-man roster with players who would help in 2020 that for much of the season, they had none of their top prospects at Corpus Christi. Peña was one of the few who joined the group in September, speaking to Houston's high opinion of the middle infielder. Given his broad range of skills, there's already a strong base for a major-league contributor of some sort. The team expects greater things, with the belief there's more power in the bat than he's shown to date. It's an exciting thought for a player who was already riding significant buzz from 2019: a version of Peña with home run pop would be one of the most well-rounded prospects in the game.

Josh Reddick RF Born: 02/19/87   Age: 34   Bats: L   Throws: R   Height: 6'2"   Weight: 197   Origin: Round 17, 2006 Draft (#523 overall)

YEAR	TEAM	LVL	AGE	PA	R	2B	3B	HR	RBI	BB	K	SB	CS	Whiff%	AVG/OBP/SLG	DRC+	BABIP	BRR	FRAA	WARP
2018	HOU	MLB	31	487	63	13	2	17	47	49	77	7	2	17.4%	.242/.318/.400	105	.258	-1.0	RF(111): -2.0, LF(43): 0.4	1.2
2019	HOU	MLB	32	550	57	19	3	14	56	36	66	5	2	14.8%	.275/.319/.409	97	.288	-2.2	RF(119): 5.2, LF(29): -1.1, CF(9): -0.4	1.3
2020	HOU	MLB	33	210	22	11	1	4	23	20	42	1	0	22.7%	.245/.316/.378	94	.294	-0.9	RF(50): 0.7	0.2
2021 FS	HOU	MLB	34	600	65	25	2	18	68	52	111	7	2	17.8%	.260/.326/.414	98	.298	-0.2	RF -2, LF -1	1.0

Comparables: Dan Ford, Alex Rios, Michael Cuddyer

Faithfully adhering to the aging curve brought Reddick great success. There were the tremendously productive years in Oakland from his mid-to-late 20s, and an extension of the peak with his excellent debut in Houston, followed by two more perfectly solid early-30s efforts. That slope proved more hazardous in 2020 as he tumbled down to replacement level, now below-average in all facets of the game. It's time for Reddick to buck the trend if he wants to continue his career, as the next point on this graph puts him beneath the threshold for a major-league roster spot.

George Springer RF Born: 09/19/89   Age: 31   Bats: R   Throws: R   Height: 6'3"   Weight: 221   Origin: Round 1, 2011 Draft (#11 overall)

YEAR	TEAM	LVL	AGE	PA	R	2B	3B	HR	RBI	BB	K	SB	CS	Whiff%	AVG/OBP/SLG	DRC+	BABIP	BRR	FRAA	WARP
2018	HOU	MLB	28	620	102	26	0	22	71	64	122	6	4	24.5%	.265/.346/.434	114	.303	1.5	CF(80): -2.8, RF(77): 2.6, LF(1): -0.0	2.9
2019	HOU	MLB	29	556	96	20	3	39	96	67	113	6	2	26.8%	.292/.383/.591	140	.305	2.5	CF(75): 2.4, RF(59): 4.1	5.4
2020	HOU	MLB	31	222	37	6	2	14	32	24	38	1	2	25.3%	.265/.359/.540	141	.259	0.0	CF(42): -2.0, RF(9): -1.5	1.3
2021 FS	HOU	MLB	31	600	94	25	1	37	74	68	129	7	4	25.8%	.277/.373/.546	141	.305	-3.9	CF -2, RF 2	4.5

Comparables: Jay Buhner, Danny Tartabull, Reggie Jackson

Springer was born less than two hours from Gillette Stadium and grew up a Patriots fan. He appears to have learned something from his boyhood team about responding to accusations of cheating: he resumed his consistent excellence without missing a beat. Where other Astros seemed deflated offensively by the scandal, Springer proved that spying on opponents is entirely unnecessary for him to dominate. He followed up regular season career bests in strikeout rate and DRC+ by maintaining a postseason record that's so successful it might as well have been orchestrated by Bill Belichick.

Myles Straw CF Born: 10/17/94   Age: 26   Bats: R   Throws: R   Height: 5'10"   Weight: 178   Origin: Round 12, 2015 Draft (#349 overall)

YEAR	TEAM	LVL	AGE	PA	R	2B	3B	HR	RBI	BB	K	SB	CS	Whiff%	AVG/OBP/SLG	DRC+	BABIP	BRR	FRAA	WARP
2018	CC	AA	23	294	47	7	3	1	17	35	42	35	6		.327/.414/.390	141	.386	4.4	CF(58): 6.0, RF(6): 2.0	2.8
2018	FRE	AAA	23	304	48	10	3	0	14	38	60	35	3		.257/.349/.317	94	.330	3.8	CF(43): 4.9, RF(25): 1.4, SS(1): -0.0	1.4
2018	HOU	MLB	23	10	4	0	0	1	1	1	0	2	0	0.0%	.333/.400/.667	108	.250	0.7	RF(5): -0.1, CF(3): -0.0, LF(1): 0.1	0.1
2019	RR	AAA	24	313	46	11	3	1	33	32	50	19	4		.321/.391/.394	105	.386	2.5	CF(31): 4.9, SS(30): -1.1, 2B(5): -0.4	1.9
2019	HOU	MLB	24	128	27	4	2	0	7	19	24	8	1	12.4%	.269/.378/.343	91	.345	3.5	SS(26): 1.4, CF(11): -0.8, LF(8): 0.3	0.8
2020	HOU	MLB	26	86	8	4	0	0	8	4	22	6	2	19.7%	.207/.244/.256	78	.283	-0.3	CF(27): -1.6, SS(1): -0.0	-0.3
2021 FS	HOU	MLB	26	600	65	26	4	6	51	57	146	22	6	15.6%	.265/.338/.365	95	.353	7.0	CF 8, 2B 0	3.1
2021 DC	HOU	MLB	26	482	52	21	3	5	41	46	117	18	5	15.6%	.265/.338/.365	95	.353	5.6	CF 7	2.6

Comparables: Tony Scott, Aaron Hicks, Jim Nettles

Straw hit the ball in the air more often in 2020. For a man who has more pro seasons under his belt than home runs, that's the equivalent of taking a Formula One car off-road. As if that wasn't enough of a penalty to his offensive performance, he stalled in the box with alarming regularity, striking out in more than a quarter of plate appearances. He did get to spend more time in the outfield, where his wheels can be put to better use. As far as Straw's chances of being more than a backup go, the plate is where the rubber meets the road. The majors are probably just a class above where he should be competing in that regard.

Garrett Stubbs C Born: 05/26/93 Age: 28 Bats: L Throws: R Height: 5'10" Weight: 170 Origin: Round 8, 2015 Draft (#229 overall)

YEAR	TEAM	LVL	AGE	PA	R	2B	3B	HR	RBI	BB	K	SB	CS	Whiff%	AVG/OBP/SLG	DRC+	BABIP	BRR	FRAA	WARP
2018	FRE	AAA	25	340	60	19	6	4	38	35	53	6	0		.310/.382/.455	117	.361	3.0	C(75): 10.5, RF(2): -0.2, 1B(1): -0.0	3.2
2019	RR	AAA	26	235	33	11	0	7	23	24	38	12	2		.240/.332/.397	85	.261	0.7	C(54): 8.8, 2B(5): -0.8, LF(1): -0.1	1.5
2019	HOU	MLB	26	39	8	3	0	0	2	4	7	1	0	22.4%	.200/.282/.286	79	.250	0.2	C(11): -1.5, LF(7): -0.1, RF(1): -0.0	-0.1
2020	HOU	MLB	27	10	1	0	0	0	1	0	0	0	1	26.7%	.125/.111/.125	93	.111	-0.1	C(8): -0.0, LF(3): 0.1	0.0
2021 FS	HOU	MLB	28	600	64	25	2	16	58	56	112	5	1	23.3%	.235/.317/.382	89	.269	2.2	C -1, 1B 0	1.8
2021 DC	HOU	MLB	28	241	25	10	0	6	23	22	45	2	0	23.3%	.235/.317/.382	89	.269	0.9	C -1	0.7

While we argue about the three-true-outcomes problem in modern baseball, Stubbs was busy doing something about it: all of his plate appearances ended in a ball in play. It might turn out to be more of an argument in TTO's favor, but let's see him do it over a few hundred plate appearances before we rush to judgement.

Comparables: Raffy Lopez, Carlos Ruiz, Vinny Rottino

YEAR	TEAM	P. COUNT	FRM RUNS	BLK RUNS	THRW RUNS	TOT RUNS
2018	FRE	11107	7.8	0.2	1.5	9.1
2019	HOU	1145	-0.5	-0.9	0.0	-1.4
2020	HOU	400	0.1	0.0	0.0	0.1
2021	HOU	8418	0.0	-1.8	0.1	-1.7

Abraham Toro 3B Born: 12/20/96 Age: 24 Bats: S Throws: R Height: 6'0" Weight: 206 Origin: Round 5, 2016 Draft (#157 overall)

YEAR	TEAM	LVL	AGE	PA	R	2B	3B	HR	RBI	BB	K	SB	CS	Whiff%	AVG/OBP/SLG	DRC+	BABIP	BRR	FRAA	WARP
2018	FAY	HI-A	21	349	54	20	1	14	56	45	62	5	1		.257/.361/.473	151	.278	1.7	3B(81): 3.4	2.9
2018	CC	AA	21	202	16	15	2	2	22	17	46	3	3		.230/.317/.371	87	.298	-2.6	3B(43): -0.7	-0.5
2019	CC	AA	22	435	65	22	4	16	70	48	77	4	1		.306/.393/.513	161	.346	-0.6	3B(85): 6.3, 2B(11): 0.2, 1B(6): 0.1	4.6
2019	RR	AAA	22	79	17	9	0	1	10	10	5	0	1		.424/.506/.606	174	.443	1.9	3B(8): -0.7, 2B(4): -0.2, 1B(1): -0.0	1.0
2019	HOU	MLB	22	89	13	3	2	2	9	9	19	1	1	18.3%	.218/.303/.385	79	.259	-0.1	3B(24): -0.8, 1B(1): 0.0	0.0
2020	HOU	MLB	24	97	13	2	0	3	9	3	23	1	1	23.8%	.149/.237/.276	79	.164	-0.9	3B(14): -0.0, 1B(4): 0.3, 2B(1): -0.1	-0.1
2021 FS	HOU	MLB	24	600	65	22	3	23	70	45	148	2	0	21.7%	.226/.302/.412	89	.268	1.4	3B 2, C 0	0.8
2021 DC	HOU	MLB	24	275	29	10	1	10	32	21	68	1	0	21.7%	.226/.302/.412	89	.268	0.6	LF 0, 3B 1	0.4

Comparables: Josh Bell, Cody Asche, Mat Gamel

Blocked at both infield corners, Toro looked set to spend the season as a rarely-used bench bat. Injuries at both third base and DH offered him an early opportunity to show he could be more. Instead he reinforced the case for the bench role. Yuli Gurriel's extension and the lack of impact at the plate will likely condemn Toro to another backup campaign, unless he makes a transition to an outfield corner and develops the bat to go with it.

Kyle Tucker RF Born: 01/17/97 Age: 24 Bats: L Throws: R Height: 6'4" Weight: 199 Origin: Round 1, 2015 Draft (#5 overall)

YEAR	TEAM	LVL	AGE	PA	R	2B	3B	HR	RBI	BB	K	SB	CS	Whiff%	AVG/OBP/SLG	DRC+	BABIP	BRR	FRAA	WARP
2018	FRE	AAA	21	465	86	27	3	24	93	48	84	20	4		.332/.400/.590	160	.364	1.7	RF(54): 0.3, LF(32): -0.4, CF(4): -0.4	3.6
2018	HOU	MLB	21	72	10	2	1	0	4	6	13	1	1	23.4%	.141/.236/.203	72	.176	-0.4	LF(20): -2.1, RF(3): 0.2, CF(2): -0.0	-0.3
2019	RR	AAA	22	536	92	26	3	34	97	60	116	30	5		.266/.354/.555	114	.280	1.3	RF(60): 3.2, LF(40): -0.3, 1B(11): 0.3	2.4
2019	HOU	MLB	22	72	15	6	0	4	11	4	20	5	0	30.1%	.269/.319/.537	87	.326	0.6	LF(11): -0.4, RF(11): 0.9, 1B(4): 0.0	0.2
2020	HOU	MLB	23	228	33	12	6	9	42	18	46	8	1	22.5%	.268/.325/.512	116	.303	0.2	LF(41): 3.1, RF(7): 0.5	1.4
2021 FS	HOU	MLB	24	600	75	30	5	32	89	48	135	14	4	23.8%	.259/.327/.512	117	.291	4.7	RF -1, LF -4	2.7
2021 DC	HOU	MLB	24	585	73	29	5	31	87	47	132	14	4	23.8%	.259/.327/.512	117	.291	4.6	RF -1, LF -3	2.6

Comparables: Luis Gonzalez, Alex Johnson, Mel Hall

Tucker's prospect standing long appeared at odds with Houston's reticence to hand him a starting role. The team continued to insist that Josh Reddick would start over Tucker right up until the much-delayed Opening Day, when Yordan Alvarez's absence left a void in the lineup. Tucker showed he could hold his own and laced a league-leading triple total, but he fell a little short of the truly explosive offensive performance that he produced in the minors. He was still one of the biggest offensive threats on a disappointing Houston offense, and his starting role is not under threat regardless. Free agency severely depleted the established outfield, leaving Tucker, at just 24, as the presumptive cornerstone for the next half-decade.

PITCHERS

Bryan Abreu RHP Born: 04/22/97 Age: 24 Bats: R Throws: R Height: 6'1" Weight: 225 Origin: International Free Agent, 2013

YEAR	TEAM	LVL	AGE	W	L	SV	G	GS	IP	H	HR	BB/9	K/9	K	GB%	BABIP	WHIP	ERA	DRA-	WARP	MPH	FA%	Whiff%	CSP
2018	TRI	SS	21	2	0	0	4	2	16	11	2	3.4	12.4	22	29.4%	.281	1.06	1.12	273	-1.4				
2018	QC	LO-A	21	4	1	3	10	5	38¹	22	2	4.0	16.0	68	47.0%	.317	1.02	1.64	55	1.1				
2019	FAY	HI-A	22	1	0	0	3	3	14²	9	2	3.7	15.3	25	38.5%	.292	1.02	3.68	63	0.3				
2019	CC	AA	22	6	2	2	20	13	76²	60	6	5.6	11.9	101	42.5%	.310	1.41	5.05	87	0.6				
2019	HOU	MLB	22	0	0	0	7	0	8²	4	0	3.1	13.5	13	50.0%	.250	0.81	1.04	95	0.1	96.6	32.2%	46.8%	42.3%
2020	HOU	MLB	23	0	0	0	4	0	3¹	1	0	18.9	8.1	3	37.5%	.125	2.40	2.70	121	0.0	94.8	35.5%	23.5%	36.7%
2021 FS	HOU	MLB	24	2	3	0	57	0	50	43	8	5.9	10.8	59	40.7%	.290	1.52	5.08	106	0.0	95.8	33.7%	36.6%	39.8%
2021 DC	HOU	MLB	24	0	0	0	10	0	11	9	1	5.9	10.8	13	40.7%	.290	1.52	5.08	106	0.0	95.8	33.7%	36.6%	39.8%

Comparables: Jorge Alcala, Cristian Javier, Demarcus Evans

Dreams of an elite bullpen piece remain just that as far as Abreu is concerned. With a lively fastball and slider/curve combo and with potential yet to be realized, the hope was that Abreu could harness some command to become a late-inning weapon. Instead he showed up lacking not only the command but also the velocity. The 95-plus heat evaporated, as his brief follow-up saw him struggle to average 93 with little idea of where anything was going. The Astros cited poor conditioning and overthinking as the causes of Abreu's struggles, demoting him after he walked seven of the 20 batters he faced.

Brandon Bielak RHP Born: 04/02/96   Age: 25   Bats: L   Throws: R   Height: 6'2"   Weight: 208   Origin: Round 11, 2017 Draft (#331 overall)

YEAR	TEAM	LVL	AGE	W	L	SV	G	GS	IP	H	HR	BB/9	K/9	K	GB%	BABIP	WHIP	ERA	DRA-	WARP	MPH	FA%	Whiff%	CSP
2018	FAY	HI-A	22	5	3	2	14	7	55²	44	2	2.7	12.0	74	41.9%	.331	1.10	2.10	52	1.8				
2018	CC	AA	22	2	5	0	11	10	61¹	52	4	3.2	8.4	57	50.3%	.296	1.21	2.35	83	0.9				
2019	CC	AA	23	3	0	0	8	6	36	29	3	3.5	8.2	33	53.0%	.268	1.19	3.75	82	0.4				
2019	RR	AAA	23	8	4	0	15	14	85²	69	10	3.8	9.0	86	42.8%	.271	1.23	4.41	56	3.3				
2020	HOU	MLB	24	3	3	0	12	6	32	39	9	4.8	7.3	26	35.9%	.323	1.75	6.75	161	-0.8	94.5	63.8%	27.5%	44.6%
2021 FS	HOU	MLB	25	2	2	0	57	0	50	49	9	4.5	8.3	46	41.1%	.291	1.49	5.21	110	-0.1	94.5	63.8%	27.5%	44.6%
2021 DC	HOU	MLB	25	2	2	0	17	6	39	38	7	4.5	8.3	36	41.1%	.291	1.49	5.21	110	0.2	94.5	63.8%	27.5%	44.6%

Comparables: Ryan Helsley, Carlos Rosa, Kyle Wright

A strike-thrower all the way through the minors, Bielak couldn't find the balance against baseball's best. His fastball was crushed when he threw it in the zone, and he couldn't spot it effectively enough to make his secondaries play up. Nibbling around the edges only led to more walks. Bielak has to walk a tightrope if he's to stick as a fifth starter. Wobbles like this will quickly consign him to a role as a safety net.

Humberto Castellanos RHP Born: 04/03/98   Age: 23   Bats: R   Throws: R   Height: 5'11"   Weight: 218   Origin: International Free Agent, 2015

YEAR	TEAM	LVL	AGE	W	L	SV	G	GS	IP	H	HR	BB/9	K/9	K	GB%	BABIP	WHIP	ERA	DRA-	WARP	MPH	FA%	Whiff%	CSP
2018	TRI	SS	20	0	0	1	2	0	2	1	0	0.0	9.0	2	100.0%	.200	0.50	0.00	184	-0.1				
2018	QC	LO-A	20	3	2	4	21	0	43	40	0	2.3	10.0	48	48.0%	.320	1.19	2.09	60	1.0				
2019	QC	LO-A	21	3	0	4	14	0	36¹	29	4	1.5	11.4	46	43.6%	.281	0.96	3.22	69	0.6				
2019	FAY	HI-A	21	1	1	3	15	0	25²	30	1	2.1	9.5	27	62.5%	.377	1.40	3.16	121	-0.4				
2019	RR	AAA	21	0	1	0	5	0	12²	4	1	2.1	7.1	10	53.3%	.103	0.55	1.42	51	0.5				
2020	HOU	MLB	22	0	1	0	8	0	10²	12	2	4.2	10.1	12	46.9%	.333	1.59	6.75	92	0.1	91.9	50.2%	21.9%	51.3%
2021 FS	HOU	MLB	23	1	1	0	57	0	50	48	8	3.3	8.4	46	47.3%	.290	1.33	4.51	97	0.2	91.9	50.2%	21.9%	51.3%
2021 DC	HOU	MLB	23	1	1	0	31	0	33	31	5	3.3	8.4	30	47.3%	.290	1.33	4.51	97	0.2	91.9	50.2%	21.9%	51.3%

Comparables: Keone Kela, Trevor Gott, Patrick Sandoval

Castellanos brought the heat in one sense: by plunking Ramón Laureano, precipitating an extensive fracas and suspensions for Laureano and Astros coach Alex Cintrón. His low-90s fastball was considerably less fiery, but it surprisingly drew more whiffs than his other offerings, a sign that it's going to be hard for this arsenal to succeed long-term.

Chris Devenski RHP Born: 11/13/90   Age: 30   Bats: R   Throws: R   Height: 6'3"   Weight: 219   Origin: Round 25, 2011 Draft (#771 overall)

YEAR	TEAM	LVL	AGE	W	L	SV	G	GS	IP	H	HR	BB/9	K/9	K	GB%	BABIP	WHIP	ERA	DRA-	WARP	MPH	FA%	Whiff%	CSP
2018	HOU	MLB	27	2	3	2	50	1	47¹	42	9	2.5	9.7	51	33.3%	.277	1.16	4.18	80	0.7	95.9	41.6%	31.6%	46.6%
2019	HOU	MLB	28	2	3	0	61	1	69	69	13	2.7	9.4	72	33.2%	.298	1.30	4.83	112	-0.1	96.6	44.1%	28.2%	46.2%
2020	HOU	MLB	29	0	1	0	4	0	3²	7	1	7.4	12.3	5	46.2%	.500	2.73	14.73	81	0.1	94.1	38.5%	30.0%	43.2%
2021 FS	HOU	MLB	30	2	2	0	57	0	50	43	8	2.9	9.5	52	35.4%	.278	1.20	3.63	85	0.6	96.3	43.0%	29.1%	46.1%

Comparables: Ken Giles, Emilio Pagán, Hansel Robles

Devenski symbolized not only Houston's bullpen woes, but their struggles overall. A unit that was very recently one of the best in baseball fell apart, ravaged by injury and poor performance. His Astros tenure concluded with four appearances, two trips to the IL and season-ending surgery to remove a bone spur in his troublesome elbow.

Luis Garcia RHP Born: 12/13/96   Age: 24   Bats: R   Throws: R   Height: 6'1"   Weight: 244   Origin: International Free Agent, 2017

YEAR	TEAM	LVL	AGE	W	L	SV	G	GS	IP	H	HR	BB/9	K/9	K	GB%	BABIP	WHIP	ERA	DRA-	WARP	MPH	FA%	Whiff%	CSP
2018	TRI	SS	21	0	0	0	5	3	16¹	7	0	4.4	15.4	28	43.3%	.233	0.92	0.00	237	-1.1				
2018	QC	LO-A	21	7	2	0	19	10	69	58	4	4.3	9.1	70	37.3%	.300	1.32	2.48	74	1.3				
2019	QC	LO-A	22	4	0	1	9	6	43	23	4	3.3	12.6	60	41.1%	.221	0.91	2.93	55	1.2				
2019	FAY	HI-A	22	6	4	0	15	12	65²	43	5	4.7	14.8	108	45.3%	.311	1.17	3.02	66	1.4				
2020	HOU	MLB	23	0	1	0	5	1	12¹	7	1	3.6	6.6	9	41.2%	.182	0.97	2.92	110	0.0	96.0	59.1%	26.1%	45.2%
2021 FS	HOU	MLB	24	2	3	0	57	0	50	43	8	5.3	10.1	56	40.6%	.283	1.46	4.74	101	0.1	96.0	59.1%	26.1%	45.2%
2021 DC	HOU	MLB	24	0	0	0	3	3	13	11	2	5.3	10.1	14	40.6%	.283	1.46	4.74	101	0.1	96.0	59.1%	26.1%	45.2%

Comparables: Vince Velasquez, Jorge Alcala, Cristian Javier

This Luis Garcia might be the worst-ranked and least-known of the current batch of prospects with the same name, but he made the jump from High-A to the majors without looking overmatched. His five-pitch mix includes a changeup and slider that both drew whiffs from big-league hitters. If his command can come around enough to earn a spot in the rotation, Garcia might yet be able to climb the Luis Garcia Power Rankings, although he'll have a hard time topping the version starting on the dirt for the Nationals at the age of 20.

Zack Greinke   **RHP**   Born: 10/21/83   Age: 37   Bats: R   Throws: R   Height: 6'2"   Weight: 200   Origin: Round 1, 2002 Draft (#6 overall)

YEAR	TEAM	LVL	AGE	W	L	SV	G	GS	IP	H	HR	BB/9	K/9	K	GB%	BABIP	WHIP	ERA	DRA-	WARP	MPH	FA%	Whiff%	CSP
2018	ARI	MLB	34	15	11	0	33	33	207²	181	28	1.9	8.6	199	44.8%	.273	1.08	3.21	68	5.3	91.4	48.7%	25.9%	45.1%
2019	HOU	MLB	35	8	1	0	10	10	62²	58	6	1.3	7.5	52	51.1%	.291	1.07	3.02	71	1.5	92.1	43.1%	26.0%	46.8%
2019	ARI	MLB	35	10	4	0	23	23	146	117	15	1.3	8.3	135	41.9%	.266	0.95	2.90	62	4.3	91.7	47.7%	23.4%	47.7%
2020	HOU	MLB	36	3	3	0	12	12	67	67	6	1.2	9.0	67	41.8%	.321	1.13	4.03	81	1.3	90.0	42.4%	27.8%	45.4%
2021 FS	HOU	MLB	37	9	8	0	26	26	150	143	25	1.8	8.5	142	42.6%	.289	1.16	3.69	84	2.4	91.3	45.9%	25.5%	46.3%
2021 DC	HOU	MLB	37	13	8	0	30	30	184	176	30	1.8	8.5	174	42.6%	.289	1.16	3.69	84	3.5	91.3	45.9%	25.5%	46.3%

Comparables: Mike Mussina, Justin Verlander, Fergie Jenkins

Greinke produced a striking portfolio of moments that defined both his incomparable career and the entire 2020 season. There was his decision to take his seat with a group of cardboard cutouts on August 7, an effort at more effective social distancing given the limitations of dugouts. That was followed by a duo of iconic Greinke incidents on August 23. An inning after he had thrown a 54 mph eephus for a strike—a pitchout attempt gone awry in a manner only he could conjure—the 17-year veteran was unhappy with the condition of the mound. Upon calling out the groundskeepers to fix it, Greinke sat down on the grass, a cross-legged Zen-like figure waiting for the issue to be resolved. There's more: a whole essay could be devoted to the topic of if or when he was calling his own pitches from the mound. Amidst all the chaos, there was something calming about Greinke going about his business in a typically unconventional manner. The most comforting aspect of all was his reaction to our fascination with his antics, treating them as if they were disappointingly mundane rather than moments that could only come from one man.

Josh James   **RHP**   Born: 03/08/93   Age: 28   Bats: R   Throws: R   Height: 6'3"   Weight: 234   Origin: Round 34, 2014 Draft (#1006 overall)

YEAR	TEAM	LVL	AGE	W	L	SV	G	GS	IP	H	HR	BB/9	K/9	K	GB%	BABIP	WHIP	ERA	DRA-	WARP	MPH	FA%	Whiff%	CSP
2018	CC	AA	25	0	0	1	6	4	21²	17	1	4.2	15.8	38	57.8%	.364	1.25	2.49	35	0.9				
2018	FRE	AAA	25	6	4	0	17	17	92²	62	8	3.8	12.9	133	39.6%	.280	1.09	3.40	50	3.3				
2018	HOU	MLB	25	2	0	0	6	3	23	15	3	2.7	11.3	29	41.5%	.240	0.96	2.35	71	0.5	99.9	59.9%	31.1%	46.7%
2019	HOU	MLB	26	5	1	1	49	1	61¹	46	10	5.1	14.7	100	35.4%	.308	1.32	4.70	68	1.3	99.3	63.3%	36.7%	46.6%
2020	HOU	MLB	27	1	0	0	13	2	17¹	15	4	8.8	10.9	21	32.6%	.282	1.85	7.27	137	-0.2	98.5	57.8%	30.6%	43.1%
2021 FS	HOU	MLB	28	2	2	0	57	0	50	39	8	5.2	11.7	65	38.1%	.282	1.37	4.33	92	0.3	99.2	61.5%	34.5%	45.6%
2021 DC	HOU	MLB	28	2	2	0	17	6	37	29	5	5.2	11.7	48	38.1%	.282	1.37	4.33	92	0.5	99.2	61.5%	34.5%	45.6%

Comparables: Erick Fedde, Scott Barlow, Ryne Stanek

A major-league baseball field: one of the most hostile places on Earth. This young right-handed pitcher fights to survive in a system that can sustain only a limited amount of his kind. His arm is his weapon, capable of launching projectiles at 100 miles per hour. It's an exceptional physical feat. His prey can be struck down before they have time to react—if he gets it right.

This is not only a case of raw strength. Extraordinary coordination is required too. Not all learn it. This youngster is not at full health, and is wild. Too wild, and he misses the target. Now the hunter becomes the hunted, foe primed to counterattack. The pitcher flees, hoping to fight again another day. He might have escaped this time, but he's still in peril. There will be others waiting to take his place if he does not learn how to thrive.

Cristian Javier   **RHP**   Born: 03/26/97   Age: 24   Bats: R   Throws: R   Height: 6'1"   Weight: 213   Origin: International Free Agent, 2015

YEAR	TEAM	LVL	AGE	W	L	SV	G	GS	IP	H	HR	BB/9	K/9	K	GB%	BABIP	WHIP	ERA	DRA-	WARP	MPH	FA%	Whiff%	CSP
2018	QC	LO-A	21	2	2	1	11	7	49¹	28	3	4.2	14.6	80	30.4%	.281	1.03	1.82	42	1.8				
2018	FAY	HI-A	21	5	4	0	14	11	60²	44	6	4.0	9.8	66	31.8%	.257	1.17	3.41	69	1.4				
2019	FAY	HI-A	22	2	0	1	7	5	28²	15	1	5.0	12.6	40	33.3%	.226	1.08	0.94	59	0.7				
2019	CC	AA	22	6	3	3	17	11	74	31	5	4.7	13.9	114	29.2%	.198	0.95	2.07	43	2.5				
2019	RR	AAA	22	0	0	0	2	2	11	5	1	3.3	13.1	16	17.4%	.182	0.82	1.64	54	0.4				
2020	HOU	MLB	23	5	2	0	12	10	54¹	36	11	3.0	8.9	54	29.3%	.194	0.99	3.48	128	-0.3	94.2	63.1%	22.5%	48.1%
2021 FS	HOU	MLB	24	9	9	0	26	26	150	128	30	4.7	10.7	178	30.2%	.276	1.38	4.67	100	1.1	94.2	63.1%	22.5%	48.1%
2021 DC	HOU	MLB	24	7	6	0	22	22	113	96	22	4.7	10.7	134	30.2%	.276	1.38	4.67	100	1.2	94.2	63.1%	22.5%	48.1%

Comparables: Jorge Alcala, Mitch Keller, Carlos Rodón

Javier bailed out an Astros staff that desperately needed pitching help, weaving the latest strand of a relentlessly successful pro career. His four-seamer might have below-average velocity, but it tied most hitters down with pop-ups and weak fly balls. While a few too many of those flies escaped the field of play, Javier kept the numbers on base under wraps via a sweeping slider that generated whiffs on 57 percent of swings. A more reliable third pitch would secure his spot in the rotation. There's already enough here to leave hitters' heads spinning in shorter stints.

Lance McCullers Jr.   **RHP**   Born: 10/02/93   Age: 27   Bats: L   Throws: R   Height: 6'1"   Weight: 202   Origin: Round 1, 2012 Draft (#41 overall)

YEAR	TEAM	LVL	AGE	W	L	SV	G	GS	IP	H	HR	BB/9	K/9	K	GB%	BABIP	WHIP	ERA	DRA-	WARP	MPH	FA%	Whiff%	CSP
2018	HOU	MLB	24	10	6	0	25	22	128¹	100	12	3.5	10.0	142	54.9%	.279	1.17	3.86	73	3.0	96.3	37.3%	31.6%	43.9%
2020	HOU	MLB	26	3	3	0	11	11	55	44	5	3.3	9.2	56	58.9%	.279	1.16	3.93	78	1.1	96.0	44.1%	29.7%	43.8%
2021 FS	HOU	MLB	27	9	8	0	26	26	150	129	17	4.2	10.2	169	55.4%	.294	1.33	3.98	88	2.1	96.1	41.1%	30.5%	43.9%
2021 DC	HOU	MLB	27	9	7	0	25	25	137	118	16	4.2	10.2	154	55.4%	.294	1.33	3.98	88	2.3	96.1	41.1%	30.5%	43.9%

Comparables: Yovani Gallardo, Luis Castillo, Scott Kazmir

McCullers made a largely successful return from Tommy John surgery, albeit with some diminished velocity. It wasn't his high heat that was affected so much as his curveball, however. Its descent into the low-80s band added a little more drop, but also some extra-base hits. Opposing hitters slugged .481 against the pitch and appeared to adopt an all-or-nothing approach once the playoffs rolled around. McCullers served up seven dingers in total across three postseason starts, including three off the curve, while also punching out 23 in 14 2/3 frames. The results on the breaker, both in reality and expected, have been slowly but steadily getting worse since 2016. McCullers can get by just fine if he halts the decline here, but it's no longer a pitch that would get thrown 24 times in a row or feature on the cover of *Sports Illustrated*.

Roberto Osuna RHP Born: 02/07/95 Age: 26 Bats: R Throws: R Height: 6'2" Weight: 217 Origin: International Free Agent, 2011

YEAR	TEAM	LVL	AGE	W	L	SV	G	GS	IP	H	HR	BB/9	K/9	K	GB%	BABIP	WHIP	ERA	DRA-	WARP	MPH	FA%	Whiff%	CSP
2018	HOU	MLB	23	2	2	12	23	0	22²	17	1	1.2	7.5	19	44.4%	.258	0.88	1.99	79	0.4	96.8	47.4%	29.1%	48.3%
2018	TOR	MLB	23	0	0	9	15	0	15¹	16	0	0.6	7.6	13	38.3%	.340	1.11	2.93	88	0.2	97.5	67.4%	23.8%	50.3%
2019	HOU	MLB	24	4	3	38	66	0	65	45	8	1.7	10.1	73	39.2%	.236	0.88	2.63	72	1.3	98.6	49.3%	34.2%	46.4%
2020	HOU	MLB	25	0	0	1	4	0	4¹	3	0	0.0	6.2	3	61.5%	.231	0.69	2.08	89	0.1	96.0	46.3%	28.6%	55.5%
2021 FS	*HOU*	*MLB*	*26*	*3*	*2*	*0*	*57*	*0*	*50*	*42*	*7*	*2.2*	*9.6*	*53*	*40.2%*	*.277*	*1.10*	*3.06*	*73*	*0.9*	*98.1*	*50.4%*	*32.3%*	*47.5%*

Comparables: Huston Street, Keone Kela, Yimi García

A year after Brandon Taubman's Osuna-defending outburst that led to the assistant GM's termination, Houston removed Osuna himself from the organization rather more quietly. The decision seemed obvious when elbow trouble ended his season after four appearances and the initial recommendation was Tommy John surgery. It was slightly less obvious when a second opinion suggested Osuna could rehab the injury without surgery, with the closer playing catch before the season was over. The kicker was the $10 million or so that he was likely to earn in arbitration, leading the Astros to put him on waivers at the first available opportunity. That it took money and health to bring about the end of Osuna's tenure in Houston should surprise no one. In reality, the obvious decision was the one they should have taken two and a half years earlier, when considering whether to trade for a player who was arrested and suspended for domestic abuse.

Enoli Paredes RHP Born: 09/28/95 Age: 25 Bats: R Throws: R Height: 5'11" Weight: 171 Origin: International Free Agent, 2015

YEAR	TEAM	LVL	AGE	W	L	SV	G	GS	IP	H	HR	BB/9	K/9	K	GB%	BABIP	WHIP	ERA	DRA-	WARP	MPH	FA%	Whiff%	CSP
2018	QC	LO-A	22	2	3	2	16	5	55²	28	0	4.2	11.5	71	44.9%	.220	0.97	1.46	68	1.2				
2018	FAY	HI-A	22	4	1	0	8	0	13¹	6	1	2.0	12.8	19	32.1%	.200	0.68	1.35	54	0.4				
2019	FAY	HI-A	23	3	1	0	10	6	44	21	3	4.3	12.1	59	44.0%	.205	0.95	1.64	53	1.2				
2019	CC	AA	23	2	3	1	12	6	50	29	1	3.8	12.4	69	35.8%	.269	1.00	3.78	58	1.2				
2020	HOU	MLB	24	3	3	0	22	0	20²	18	1	4.8	8.7	20	43.1%	.304	1.40	3.05	96	0.2	97.9	68.2%	32.3%	49.6%
2021 FS	*HOU*	*MLB*	*25*	*2*	*2*	*4*	*57*	*0*	*50*	*45*	*8*	*5.3*	*10.3*	*57*	*39.9%*	*.295*	*1.50*	*5.08*	*107*	*-0.1*	*97.9*	*68.2%*	*32.3%*	*49.6%*
2021 DC	*HOU*	*MLB*	*25*	*2*	*2*	*4*	*53*	*0*	*56*	*50*	*9*	*5.3*	*10.3*	*64*	*39.9%*	*.295*	*1.50*	*5.08*	*107*	*0.2*	*97.9*	*68.2%*	*32.3%*	*49.6%*

Comparables: Freddy Peralta, Adonis Rosa, David Bednar

Paredes rapidly flattens his body out and then explodes back to his full height during his delivery, a process that often finishes with a jaunty hop as the pitch crosses the plate. It's the product of a huge stride that helps to propel his high-90s fastball from a relatively compact frame and puts his release point about as low as it's possible to get without being labeled a side-armer. When Paredes locates the heater up in the zone, the plane is consequently so flat that hitters have real trouble getting the barrel to the ball. In the lower regions, it's not so effective. His command needs some work if he's going to hit those more favorable spots consistently. No matter where the pitch is located, having the pitcher pop up off the mound like a jack-in-a-box is going to remain distracting for hitters.

Brad Peacock RHP Born: 02/02/88 Age: 33 Bats: R Throws: R Height: 6'1" Weight: 207 Origin: Round 41, 2006 Draft (#1231 overall)

YEAR	TEAM	LVL	AGE	W	L	SV	G	GS	IP	H	HR	BB/9	K/9	K	GB%	BABIP	WHIP	ERA	DRA-	WARP	MPH	FA%	Whiff%	CSP
2018	HOU	MLB	30	3	5	3	61	1	65	56	11	2.8	13.3	96	37.3%	.317	1.17	3.46	56	1.8	94.6	54.6%	31.6%	45.5%
2019	HOU	MLB	31	7	6	0	23	15	91²	78	15	3.0	9.4	96	37.8%	.267	1.19	4.12	104	0.6	93.8	58.5%	21.7%	47.5%
2020	HOU	MLB	32	0	0	0	3	0	2¹	3	0	3.9	11.6	3	28.6%	.429	1.71	7.71	91	0.0	91.8	50.8%	22.7%	40.4%
2021 FS	*HOU*	*MLB*	*33*	*2*	*2*	*0*	*57*	*0*	*50*	*45*	*9*	*3.4*	*9.9*	*54*	*38.0%*	*.288*	*1.29*	*4.26*	*96*	*0.2*	*94.0*	*57.2%*	*24.4%*	*46.7%*

Comparables: Trevor Cahill, Jhoulys Chacín, Joe Kelly

Millions tuned in to Peacock in 2020—the streaming service, that is. The days of appointment viewing for the Astros righty appear to be long gone. Two full ticks came off the fastball, with none of the swing-and-miss stuff that generated his peak ratings. A nerve issue in his neck was followed by shoulder discomfort, and it was the shoulder that got him taken off the air after three episodes. He's unlikely to be renewed for another season in Houston. Finally a free agent at the age of 33, Peacock's timing couldn't be worse for entering the market. Comcast's turned out to be excellent, though.

Cionel Pérez LHP Born: 04/21/96 Age: 25 Bats: L Throws: L Height: 5'11" Weight: 162 Origin: International Free Agent, 2016

YEAR	TEAM	LVL	AGE	W	L	SV	G	GS	IP	H	HR	BB/9	K/9	K	GB%	BABIP	WHIP	ERA	DRA-	WARP	MPH	FA%	Whiff%	CSP
2018	CC	AA	22	6	1	1	16	11	68¹	54	3	2.9	10.9	83	46.8%	.304	1.11	1.98	62	1.7				
2018	FRE	AAA	22	1	0	0	4	0	5¹	5	0	10.1	10.1	6	50.0%	.357	2.06	3.38	63	0.1				
2018	HOU	MLB	22	0	0	0	8	0	11¹	6	3	5.6	9.5	12	57.7%	.130	1.15	3.97	102	0.0	96.9	63.2%	26.3%	41.6%
2019	AST	ROK	23	0	0	0	3	3	5²	6	0	4.8	22.2	14	37.5%	.857	1.59	3.18	10	0.3				
2019	FAY	HI-A	23	1	0	0	1	0	2	2	0	0.0	4.5	1	71.4%	.286	1.00	0.00	88	0.1				
2019	RR	AAA	23	2	1	0	13	10	47	53	6	4.6	8.2	43	52.4%	.346	1.64	5.36	100	0.8				
2019	HOU	MLB	23	1	1	0	5	0	9	11	3	2.0	7.0	7	48.4%	.286	1.44	10.00	139	-0.1	97.2	61.5%	23.6%	42.0%
2020	HOU	MLB	24	0	0	0	7	0	6¹	7	0	8.5	11.4	8	61.1%	.389	2.05	2.84	80	0.1	96.5	62.5%	31.5%	40.3%
2021 FS	*HOU*	*MLB*	*25*	*2*	*2*	*0*	*57*	*0*	*50*	*46*	*6*	*5.4*	*9.1*	*50*	*48.4%*	*.294*	*1.53*	*4.93*	*104*	*0.0*	*96.8*	*62.3%*	*27.5%*	*41.2%*
2021 DC	*HOU*	*MLB*	*25*	*2*	*2*	*0*	*53*	*0*	*56*	*52*	*7*	*5.4*	*9.1*	*56*	*48.4%*	*.294*	*1.53*	*4.93*	*104*	*0.2*	*96.8*	*62.3%*	*27.5%*	*41.2%*

Comparables: Yohander Méndez, Justus Sheffield, Ranger Suárez

The decision to leave Pérez off the ALCS roster in favor of Chase De Jong and his 14.73 ERA speaks volumes about how much trust the team is willing to place in the former teenage star. A delayed start to the season didn't help, nor did walking almost a batter per inning in his limited work. Length and command were plainly stated as the reasons for the choice, which is a neat encapsulation of where we're at with Pérez. The stuff still plays on the sporadic occasions he does locate but his innings total keeps dropping every season and there's little evidence he can handle being a multi-inning reliever, let alone start. We have never seen Pérez face even 50 batters in a single major-league season, his options exhausted for little return. Nevertheless, Houston has to make a decision: either place their trust in Pérez as a regular member of their staff or designate him for assignment.

Ryan Pressly RHP Born: 12/15/88 Age: 32 Bats: R Throws: R Height: 6'2" Weight: 206 Origin: Round 11, 2007 Draft (#354 overall)

YEAR	TEAM	LVL	AGE	W	L	SV	G	GS	IP	H	HR	BB/9	K/9	K	GB%	BABIP	WHIP	ERA	DRA-	WARP	MPH	FA%	Whiff%	CSP
2018	HOU	MLB	29	1	0	2	26	0	23¹	11	1	1.2	12.3	32	62.5%	.213	0.60	0.77	38	0.9	97.4	34.7%	37.6%	47.6%
2018	MIN	MLB	29	1	1	0	51	0	47²	46	5	3.6	13.0	69	48.3%	.366	1.36	3.40	44	1.6	97.8	48.7%	38.0%	47.3%
2019	HOU	MLB	30	2	3	3	55	0	54¹	37	6	2.0	11.9	72	52.4%	.258	0.90	2.32	53	1.6	97.2	35.7%	36.0%	47.0%
2020	HOU	MLB	31	1	3	12	23	0	21	21	2	3.0	12.4	29	48.1%	.365	1.33	3.43	74	0.5	96.3	37.1%	36.5%	44.6%
2021 FS	HOU	MLB	32	2	2	35	57	0	50	40	6	3.1	11.5	63	47.4%	.290	1.15	3.13	72	0.9	97.1	38.7%	36.7%	46.4%
2021 DC	HOU	MLB	32	2	2	35	53	0	56	45	7	3.1	11.5	71	47.4%	.290	1.15	3.13	72	1.2	97.1	38.7%	36.7%	46.4%

Comparables: Alex Colomé, Bryan Shaw, Hunter Strickland

Pressly has cruised almost effortlessly through innings since Houston acquired him, so naturally his opportunity to take the helm in the ninth arrived when the situation turned stormy. Roberto Osuna's season was wrecked by UCL trouble, tossing Pressly into the closer role almost immediately upon his return from elbow discomfort of his own. The 31-year-old's velocity took a dive, and he proceeded to give up runs in back-to-back appearances for the first time since joining the team. As most of Houston's staff sank around him and a swath of rookies scrambled to plug the holes, Pressly steadied the ship and pitched to a 2.21 ERA the rest of the way, tripling his career save total in the process. As if to underline the point that he was the safest pair of hands around, he sailed through four postseason save opportunities with scoreless innings.

Austin Pruitt RHP Born: 08/31/89 Age: 31 Bats: R Throws: R Height: 5'10" Weight: 185 Origin: Round 9, 2013 Draft (#278 overall)

YEAR	TEAM	LVL	AGE	W	L	SV	G	GS	IP	H	HR	BB/9	K/9	K	GB%	BABIP	WHIP	ERA	DRA-	WARP	MPH	FA%	Whiff%	CSP
2018	DUR	AAA	28	3	0	1	14	4	39²	26	2	1.6	11.1	49	48.9%	.261	0.83	2.95	41	1.5				
2018	TB	MLB	28	2	3	4	23	0	69²	72	7	2.1	5.4	42	49.1%	.290	1.26	4.65	81	1.0	93.2	43.9%	20.3%	50.7%
2019	DUR	AAA	29	3	3	0	18	6	48¹	61	9	2.2	9.5	51	48.7%	.364	1.51	5.40	104	0.6				
2019	TB	MLB	29	3	0	0	14	2	47	47	7	2.3	7.5	39	52.1%	.301	1.26	4.40	97	0.3	93.2	44.0%	24.9%	46.7%
2021 FS	HOU	MLB	31	2	2	0	57	0	50	49	7	2.1	8.0	44	47.5%	.293	1.22	3.94	88	0.4	93.2	44.0%	23.0%	48.4%
2021 DC	HOU	MLB	31	2	2	0	53	0	56	55	8	2.1	8.0	50	47.5%	.293	1.22	3.94	88	0.7	93.2	44.0%	23.0%	48.4%

Comparables: Erasmo Ramírez, Joe Biagini, Chris Stratton

A hairline fracture that cost Pruitt the entire season came as something of a surprise, as the former Ray appeared confident in July that his elbow discomfort was not that serious. His acquisition was the last move made by Jeff Luhnow, who apparently felt the same way about his players making a racket in the dugout.

Brooks Raley LHP Born: 06/29/88 Age: 33 Bats: L Throws: L Height: 6'3" Weight: 200 Origin: Round 6, 2009 Draft (#200 overall)

YEAR	TEAM	LVL	AGE	W	L	SV	G	GS	IP	H	HR	BB/9	K/9	K	GB%	BABIP	WHIP	ERA	DRA-	WARP	MPH	FA%	Whiff%	CSP
2020	HOU	MLB	32	0	1	1	21	0	20	13	3	2.7	12.2	27	38.3%	.233	0.95	4.95	79	0.4	91.4	68.8%	31.7%	48.6%
2021 FS	HOU	MLB	33	2	2	0	57	0	50	48	8	3.9	8.5	47	40.7%	.292	1.41	4.95	106	0.0	91.4	68.8%	31.7%	48.6%
2021 DC	HOU	MLB	33	2	2	0	53	0	56	54	9	3.9	8.5	52	40.7%	.292	1.41	4.95	106	0.2	91.4	68.8%	31.7%	48.6%

Comparables: Chris Rusin, Héctor Noesi, Zack Britton

It may come as a surprise that Raley made more starts than all but eight major-league players from 2015-2019, not least because he hadn't been seen in the majors since 2013. The erstwhile Cubs depth option became one of the most dependable arms in the KBO for the Lotte Giants, making at least 30 starts every year with a combined 4.13 ERA over more than 900 innings. Raley could still only garner a non-roster invite to spring training and eventually got assigned to the bullpen by the Reds, who deemed him expendable after a mere four appearances. The grateful Astros saw past the ERA and velocity to the spin numbers and snapped him up. Raley immediately began to lean on his slider along with his cutter, whiffing more than a third of batters while holding those who did make contact to the lowest average exit velocity in baseball. The veteran lefty might have another five-year run left in him if these improvements hold up over a longer campaign.

Nivaldo Rodriguez RHP Born: 04/16/97 Age: 24 Bats: R Throws: R Height: 6'1" Weight: 214 Origin: International Free Agent, 2016

YEAR	TEAM	LVL	AGE	W	L	SV	G	GS	IP	H	HR	BB/9	K/9	K	GB%	BABIP	WHIP	ERA	DRA-	WARP	MPH	FA%	Whiff%	CSP
2018	TRI	SS	21	4	1	1	14	7	55²	45	3	2.1	8.1	50	42.8%	.271	1.04	2.91	260	-4.5				
2019	QC	LO-A	22	3	1	0	6	6	31	23	2	1.2	11.3	39	31.6%	.284	0.87	1.16	54	0.9				
2019	FAY	HI-A	22	3	5	2	18	9	74	46	5	3.8	9.1	75	49.5%	.223	1.04	2.92	59	1.8				
2020	HOU	MLB	23	0	1	0	5	0	8²	15	3	6.2	8.3	8	43.8%	.414	2.42	6.23	118	0.0	94.8	49.2%	22.6%	44.6%
2021 FS	HOU	MLB	24	1	1	0	57	0	50	50	9	4.1	8.2	45	42.7%	.295	1.46	5.19	110	-0.2	94.8	49.2%	22.6%	44.6%
2021 DC	HOU	MLB	24	1	1	0	21	0	22	22	3	4.1	8.2	19	42.7%	.295	1.46	5.19	110	0.0	94.8	49.2%	22.6%	44.6%

Comparables: Bryan Abreu, Jorge Alcala, Darrell Osteen

Rodriguez was at the forefront of a glut of aggressive promotions. Events far beyond his control conspired to thrust him into the limelight almost immediately, with no minors work available and a big club that needed live arms. The challenging debut may at least make the upper minors feel more manageable when he gets an opportunity to tackle them.

Alex Santos II RHP Born: 02/10/02 Age: 19 Bats: R Throws: R Height: 6'3" Weight: 185 Origin: Round 2, 2020 Draft (#72 overall)

Stripped of their first- and second-round picks as a punishment for the sign-stealing scandal, Houston would have been without a top-100 choice entirely were it not for the compensation pick at 72nd overall from Gerrit Cole signing with New York. There was some symmetry to the selection, although Santos himself may not be delighted: he's a lifelong Yankees fan from the Bronx. He possesses an impressively deep arsenal for a high-school pitcher with a fastball already sitting in the mid-90s. Perhaps most important given the team that drafted him, he spent much of the pre-draft period at his father's baseball academy with a Rapsodo machine tracking his sessions for scouts. Santos might have preferred to join Cole in New York, but he may have landed in the best place to maximize his development as a pitcher.

Andre Scrubb RHP Born: 01/13/95 Age: 26 Bats: R Throws: R Height: 6'4" Weight: 270 Origin: Round 8, 2016 Draft (#251 overall)

YEAR	TEAM	LVL	AGE	W	L	SV	G	GS	IP	H	HR	BB/9	K/9	K	GB%	BABIP	WHIP	ERA	DRA-	WARP	MPH	FA%	Whiff%	CSP
2018	GL	LO-A	23	3	2	2	19	0	30	33	3	4.8	10.2	34	37.6%	.366	1.63	5.10	82	0.4				
2018	RC	HI-A	23	4	0	3	14	0	23²	8	0	4.2	10.6	28	35.2%	.148	0.80	0.38	47	0.7				
2018	TUL	AA	23	0	0	0	5	0	9¹	6	0	4.8	9.6	10	54.2%	.250	1.18	1.93	104	0.0				
2019	CC	AA	24	0	0	3	12	0	17	21	0	5.3	10.6	20	42.3%	.404	1.82	3.71	127	-0.3				
2019	TUL	AA	24	6	1	0	29	2	47²	35	3	4.3	10.6	56	53.7%	.276	1.22	2.45	109	-0.4				
2020	HOU	MLB	25	1	0	1	20	0	23²	15	1	7.6	9.1	24	46.6%	.250	1.48	1.90	98	0.2	95.1	53.1%	24.8%	41.6%
2021 FS	HOU	MLB	26	2	2	0	57	0	50	44	6	6.6	9.5	52	46.6%	.291	1.63	5.25	108	-0.1	95.1	53.1%	24.8%	41.6%
2021 DC	HOU	MLB	26	2	2	0	42	0	45	40	6	6.6	9.5	47	46.6%	.291	1.63	5.25	108	0.1	95.1	53.1%	24.8%	41.6%

Comparables: Ryan Burr, Andrew McKirahan, Scott Alexander

Circumstances conspired to send almost the entire Astros bullpen to the IL, and Scrubb was not only called into action but thrust into some high-leverage innings. His mid-90s fastball appears to be genuinely difficult to square up, helping him to overcome a walk rate that threatened to eclipse his strikeout rate. The free passes led to a few nervy innings, but ultimately Scrubb was welcome relief for a bullpen urgently in need of some TLC.

Joe Smith RHP Born: 03/22/84 Age: 37 Bats: R Throws: R Height: 6'2" Weight: 211 Origin: Round 3, 2006 Draft (#94 overall)

YEAR	TEAM	LVL	AGE	W	L	SV	G	GS	IP	H	HR	BB/9	K/9	K	GB%	BABIP	WHIP	ERA	DRA-	WARP	MPH	FA%	Whiff%	CSP
2018	HOU	MLB	34	5	1	0	56	0	45²	34	7	2.4	9.1	46	43.3%	.239	1.01	3.74	100	0.2	89.4	65.1%	22.4%	50.5%
2019	HOU	MLB	35	1	0	0	28	0	25	19	2	1.8	7.9	22	49.3%	.254	0.96	1.80	87	0.3	90.0	57.6%	21.2%	56.5%
2021 FS	HOU	MLB	37	2	2	2	57	0	50	47	7	2.3	8.8	48	45.5%	.292	1.20	3.79	86	0.5	89.7	61.3%	21.8%	53.5%
2021 DC	HOU	MLB	37	2	2	2	53	0	56	53	8	2.3	8.8	54	45.5%	.292	1.20	3.79	86	0.7	89.7	61.3%	21.8%	53.5%

Comparables: Jeremy Affeldt, Matt Albers, Justin Speier

Smith's statistics aren't going to tell the story of 2020. There is an absence of information rather than an explanation for his missing numbers. When enough time has passed, readers will be left guessing whether a torn UCL or a global pandemic was responsible for an absent season. We should do our best to remember those, like Smith, who opted out of the season to preserve the health of their loved ones.

Ryne Stanek RHP Born: 07/26/91 Age: 29 Bats: R Throws: R Height: 6'4" Weight: 226 Origin: Round 1, 2013 Draft (#29 overall)

YEAR	TEAM	LVL	AGE	W	L	SV	G	GS	IP	H	HR	BB/9	K/9	K	GB%	BABIP	WHIP	ERA	DRA-	WARP	MPH	FA%	Whiff%	CSP
2018	DUR	AAA	26	0	1	2	10	0	9²	5	1	5.6	15.8	17	58.8%	.250	1.14	1.86	24	0.4				
2018	TB	MLB	26	2	3	0	59	29	66¹	45	8	3.7	11.0	81	32.5%	.253	1.09	2.98	74	1.4	99.4	60.1%	34.2%	44.1%
2019	MIA	MLB	27	0	2	1	22	0	21¹	17	4	8.0	11.8	28	30.8%	.271	1.69	5.48	85	0.3	98.6	52.0%	36.9%	38.9%
2019	TB	MLB	27	0	2	0	41	27	55²	44	7	3.2	9.9	61	30.6%	.264	1.15	3.40	101	0.4	98.9	57.4%	33.7%	42.2%
2020	MIA	MLB	28	0	0	0	9	0	10	11	3	7.2	9.9	11	34.5%	.308	1.90	7.20	119	0.0	97.2	43.9%	33.7%	42.9%
2021 FS	HOU	MLB	29	2	2	0	57	0	50	41	8	5.1	10.6	58	35.7%	.274	1.39	4.18	97	0.2	98.8	55.2%	34.4%	42.1%

Comparables: Dominic Leone, Austin Brice, Giovanny Gallegos

Henry Wadsworth Longfellow once wrote a famous poem about ships that pass in the night. Stanek was dealt to Miami in the Nick Anderson deal only a year and a half ago, and at the time he was a more accomplished major-league pitcher than Anderson despite being slightly younger. Since the trade, Anderson has been just about the best reliever in baseball—at least in the regular season—and Stanek has been close to the worst. His career is at risk of disappearing into darkness if he doesn't turn this ship around.

Blake Taylor LHP Born: 08/17/95 Age: 25 Bats: L Throws: L Height: 6'3" Weight: 220 Origin: Round 2, 2013 Draft (#51 overall)

YEAR	TEAM	LVL	AGE	W	L	SV	G	GS	IP	H	HR	BB/9	K/9	K	GB%	BABIP	WHIP	ERA	DRA-	WARP	MPH	FA%	Whiff%	CSP
2018	STL	HI-A	22	1	8	0	17	16	75²	72	4	5.4	8.6	72	49.1%	.318	1.55	5.59	87	1.0				
2018	LV	AAA	22	2	0	0	2	2	11	11	0	7.4	9.0	11	62.1%	.393	1.82	4.09	86	0.2				
2019	STL	HI-A	23	2	2	7	21	0	27¹	24	1	4.0	9.5	29	64.5%	.315	1.32	2.63	101	-0.1				
2019	BNG	AA	23	0	1	3	18	0	39	25	1	2.8	10.4	45	50.0%	.245	0.95	1.85	68	0.6				
2020	HOU	MLB	24	2	1	1	22	0	20²	13	2	5.2	7.4	17	50.0%	.196	1.21	2.18	97	0.2	95.7	76.5%	19.9%	50.6%
2021 FS	HOU	MLB	25	2	2	0	57	0	50	46	6	5.5	8.4	46	50.1%	.290	1.54	4.99	104	0.0	95.7	76.5%	19.9%	50.6%
2021 DC	HOU	MLB	25	2	2	0	42	0	45	42	5	5.5	8.4	42	50.1%	.290	1.54	4.99	104	0.2	95.7	76.5%	19.9%	50.6%

Comparables: Nestor Cortes, Randy Rosario, Dovydas Neverauskas

Like your friend who frustrates you by using the same move over and over again on *Tekken*, Taylor spammed opponents with his four-seam fastball. Hitters did no better than your attempts to defend the repetitive onslaught, proving unable to cope. Taylor's heater restricted foes to a .120 average in the regular season, with a solitary extra-base hit. It was all the more remarkable for his usage, as he threw the fifth-highest percentage of four-seamers in the league, and his whiff rate, which was unimpressive. The pitch instead draws poor contact or catches hitters looking. It cuts in an unconventional, deceptive manner, breaking away from lefties and jamming righties inside. He did mix in a slider occasionally with far less success. Major-league hitters might eventually figure out the counter that negates this strategy. For now, if it ain't broke, don't fix it.

Jose Urquidy RHP   Born: 05/01/95   Age: 26   Bats: R   Throws: R   Height: 6'0"   Weight: 217   Origin: International Free Agent, 2015

YEAR	TEAM	LVL	AGE	W	L	SV	G	GS	IP	H	HR	BB/9	K/9	K	GB%	BABIP	WHIP	ERA	DRA	WARP	MPH	FA%	Whiff%	CSP
2018	TRI	SS	23	0	0	0	4	4	11¹	15	0	1.6	7.9	10	39.5%	.395	1.50	2.38	297	-1.1				
2018	FAY	HI-A	23	2	2	0	9	7	46	40	2	1.6	7.4	38	48.9%	.284	1.04	2.35	78	0.9				
2019	CC	AA	24	2	2	0	7	6	33	28	2	1.4	10.9	40	42.0%	.302	1.00	4.09	63	0.7				
2019	RR	AAA	24	5	3	0	13	12	70	67	15	2.1	12.1	94	31.9%	.313	1.19	4.63	59	2.6				
2019	HOU	MLB	24	2	1	0	9	7	41	38	6	1.5	8.8	40	35.0%	.286	1.10	3.95	88	0.6	95.3	47.3%	28.3%	49.8%
2020	HOU	MLB	25	1	1	0	5	5	29²	22	4	2.4	5.2	17	35.6%	.209	1.01	2.73	138	-0.3	94.9	54.5%	20.9%	52.0%
2021 FS	HOU	MLB	26	9	9	0	26	26	150	149	30	2.8	8.2	136	36.7%	.287	1.31	4.63	102	0.9	95.1	50.8%	24.7%	50.9%
2021 DC	HOU	MLB	26	9	8	0	25	25	147	146	29	2.8	8.2	133	36.7%	.287	1.31	4.63	102	1.4	95.1	50.8%	24.7%	50.9%

Comparables: Kevin Gausman, Luke Weaver, Rafael Montero

If all you knew about Urquidy's season was his ERA, his WHIP and that he was back on the mound for three playoff starts, plus an appearance in a decisive Game 7 of the ALCS, you might assume that he'd spent six months successfully building upon the stellar World Series start he delivered for Houston a year prior. All you would have missed from the narrative was a scandal that rocked baseball, a global pandemic and Urquidy's own positive COVID-19 test that limited him to a handful of regular season turns. The stuff didn't play nearly as well when it came to missing bats, and as a result the underlying numbers were much less encouraging than those from his debut. The Astros were either unconcerned by such a small sample or decided their decimated staff was not in a position to do without Urquidy in the postseason rotation. For everyone's sake, let's hope that 2021 is less turbulent.

Framber Valdez LHP   Born: 11/19/93   Age: 27   Bats: L   Throws: L   Height: 5'11"   Weight: 239   Origin: International Free Agent, 2015

YEAR	TEAM	LVL	AGE	W	L	SV	G	GS	IP	H	HR	BB/9	K/9	K	GB%	BABIP	WHIP	ERA	DRA-	WARP	MPH	FA%	Whiff%	CSP
2018	CC	AA	24	4	5	1	20	13	94¹	92	7	2.8	11.4	120	56.8%	.365	1.28	4.10	72	1.8				
2018	FRE	AAA	24	2	0	0	2	1	8²	8	0	3.1	9.3	9	47.8%	.348	1.27	4.15	100	0.1				
2018	HOU	MLB	24	4	1	0	8	5	37	22	3	5.8	8.3	34	69.6%	.213	1.24	2.19	136	-0.4	94.4	69.0%	22.9%	43.9%
2019	RR	AAA	25	5	2	1	10	7	44¹	29	3	3.5	13.8	68	72.2%	.302	1.04	3.25	27	2.3				
2019	HOU	MLB	25	4	7	0	26	8	70²	74	9	5.6	8.7	68	62.0%	.319	1.67	5.86	116	-0.1	95.5	61.4%	26.1%	48.6%
2020	HOU	MLB	26	5	3	0	11	10	70²	63	5	2.0	9.7	76	59.7%	.314	1.12	3.57	68	1.8	95.4	58.6%	24.4%	51.0%
2021 FS	HOU	MLB	27	9	8	0	26	26	150	131	15	4.3	10.4	173	59.4%	.306	1.36	3.96	87	2.2	95.3	60.8%	24.9%	49.4%
2021 DC	HOU	MLB	27	11	7	0	27	27	159	139	15	4.3	10.4	184	59.4%	.306	1.36	3.96	87	2.8	95.3	60.8%	24.9%	49.4%

Comparables: Max Fried, Ryan Borucki, Matt Hall

Two identical samples in back-to-back seasons. The first cast doubts over Valdez's chances to stick in the majors; the second left observers wondering how Houston could possibly have done without him. What changed? Given the year, the team and the repertoire, the obvious answer is that Valdez turned to his elite curveball far more often. What actually happened was as much of a mindset adjustment as a technical change, as the southpaw worked with the team's mental skills coaches to find the focus and composure that so often eluded him in blow-ups throughout 2019. There was a pitch mix tweak too, as the four-seam was largely shelved in favor of more sinkers, and the composure extended to his control, with his walk rate more than halved. The curve was utilized at the same rate and remained exceptional, providing the majority of Valdez's strikeouts and helping him finish with the third-best DRA among AL starters. By the end of the playoffs, the team appeared to trust him more than any other starter. A much larger sample should be forthcoming.

Justin Verlander RHP   Born: 02/20/83   Age: 38   Bats: R   Throws: R   Height: 6'5"   Weight: 235   Origin: Round 1, 2004 Draft (#2 overall)

YEAR	TEAM	LVL	AGE	W	L	SV	G	GS	IP	H	HR	BB/9	K/9	K	GB%	BABIP	WHIP	ERA	DRA-	WARP	MPH	FA%	Whiff%	CSP
2018	HOU	MLB	35	16	9	0	34	34	214	156	28	1.6	12.2	290	29.3%	.274	0.90	2.52	52	7.3	97.1	61.2%	31.9%	51.6%
2019	HOU	MLB	36	21	6	0	34	34	223	137	36	1.7	12.1	299	36.1%	.218	0.80	2.58	51	7.9	96.6	49.9%	33.7%	48.1%
2020	HOU	MLB	37	1	0	0	1	1	6	3	2	1.5	10.5	7	61.5%	.091	0.67	3.00	88	0.1	96.6	54.8%	25.7%	50.5%
2021 FS	HOU	MLB	38	3	2	0	57	0	50	39	7	2.3	10.8	60	35.7%	.267	1.03	2.73	66	1.1	96.8	53.8%	32.9%	49.3%

Comparables: A.J. Burnett, John Lackey, Steve Carlton

Pitching until the age of 45 is an ambitious goal for anyone. Verlander seemed a more likely candidate than most to achieve his stated aim. After all, he overcame the injuries and poor performance that accompany many typical mid-30s decline phases and dragged himself back to the pinnacle of the game. Shattering the aging curve is one thing, but doing so with a torn UCL is quite another. That's not to say that pitchers don't come back from Tommy John in their late 30s or beyond; just ask Jamie Moyer. Even Moyer didn't go on to pitch for another half-dozen years afterwards, which is what Verlander will have to do if we're to see him on a major league mound at 45.

★ ★ ★ *2021 Top 101 Prospect* **#69** ★ ★ ★

Forrest Whitley **RHP** Born: 09/15/97 Age: 23 Bats: R Throws: R Height: 6'7" Weight: 238 Origin: Round 1, 2016 Draft (#17 overall)

YEAR	TEAM	LVL	AGE	W	L	SV	G	GS	IP	H	HR	BB/9	K/9	K	GB%	BABIP	WHIP	ERA	DRA-	WARP	MPH	FA%	Whiff%	CSP
2018	CC	AA	20	0	2	0	8	8	26¹	15	2	3.8	11.6	34	37.7%	.220	0.99	3.76	70	0.6				
2019	AST	ROK	21	0	2	0	2	2	4¹	2	0	18.7	20.8	10	50.0%	.333	2.54	8.31	70	0.1				
2019	FAY	HI-A	21	1	0	0	2	2	8¹	4	0	1.1	11.9	11	44.4%	.222	0.60	2.16	46	0.3				
2019	CC	AA	21	2	2	0	6	6	22²	18	2	7.5	14.3	36	46.7%	.372	1.63	5.56	112	-0.1				
2019	RR	AAA	21	0	3	0	8	5	24¹	35	9	5.5	10.7	29	30.7%	.400	2.05	12.21	157	-0.2				
2021 FS	HOU	MLB	23	8	9	0	26	26	150	132	28	5.3	10.7	177	37.3%	.288	1.48	5.09	110	0.2				
2021 DC	HOU	MLB	23	4	4	0	12	12	64	56	12	5.3	10.7	75	37.3%	.288	1.48	5.09	110	0.3				

Comparables: Julio Urías, Lucas Sims, Jonathan Hernández

Whitley's absence from the majors in 2020 will extend his spell at number one on the Astros prospect list to four consecutive years. It's a run that highlights his top-tier potential and simultaneously veers into prospect fatigue territory, if not sheer exhaustion. The twists and turns of Whitley's journey to the majors didn't stop in the absence of a minor-league campaign. When he arrived at spring training with some considerable extra offseason weight, designed to improve his durability, the team declared he wasn't physically ready to compete for a job. They tinkered with his delivery, resulting in further mechanical changes, some of which Whitley then ditched by the time summer camp rolled around. That wasn't the only thing he lost, as an unconventional diet plan left him rail-thin. After all that, the team seemed positive about his progress and a debut looked imminent—until forearm soreness in early August forced a shutdown. Nothing more serious appears to have come of the issue, and Whitley is still a youthful 23, but with every additional complication one can't help but feel that we might not see the Forrest for the injuries.

LOS ANGELES ANGELS

Essay by David Roth

Player comments by Ginny Searle and BP staff

In this moment of crudity and avarice and shameless unrepentant bad faith, in the unnerving context of society's most powerful concerns no longer even bothering to act as if they're bound by norms or rules or laws, while being spun through innumerable concurrent crises, it is natural and understandable to wish that your favorite baseball team might be run like a humble family business. If you want to be a jerk about it, it is true that the Gambinos and the Sacklers and the Falwells are also family businesses, but not every family enterprise is quite as gnarled or brutal as the big ones everywhere squeezing and bilking and immiserating the rest of humanity. There are other such businesses that really do resemble the revered American ideal, and which exist as literal brick-and-mortar manifestations of the human drive to provide and succeed and create.

That last bit is the family business dream as it is sold, mostly, although the gilded goblins squatting atop everything cast a cold and ironic shadow over that sentimental concept. But fans who have felt that wish—those on the wrong end of sudden executive austerity, or lost in some ill-defined and quite possibly endless rebuild—know what it's about, which is finally nothing more or less than sensing a human face and some identifiable human motivations behind the behavior of the team to which they have committed some objectively unwise chunk of emotional wellbeing. It's a bad idea to put the happiness of some (or really any) months of your life in the hands of a damn baseball team, but no one who cares about the Angels, or any other baseball team, got into it because it seemed like the savvy thing to do. The salient question, where the uniquely blessed and persistently cursed Angels are concerned, is why and how all that caring came to feel like such a waste.

There are many worse teams and let's say several more dysfunctional organizations than the Angels. Some of the former are quite clearly not trying to be anything at all beyond Recipients Of Profit-Sharing Distributions and the monies owed them in television deals; others are actively trying to be bad, so that they might someday maybe be good; still others are engaged in data-driven arbitrage campaigns so intricate and sophisticated that the actual baseball

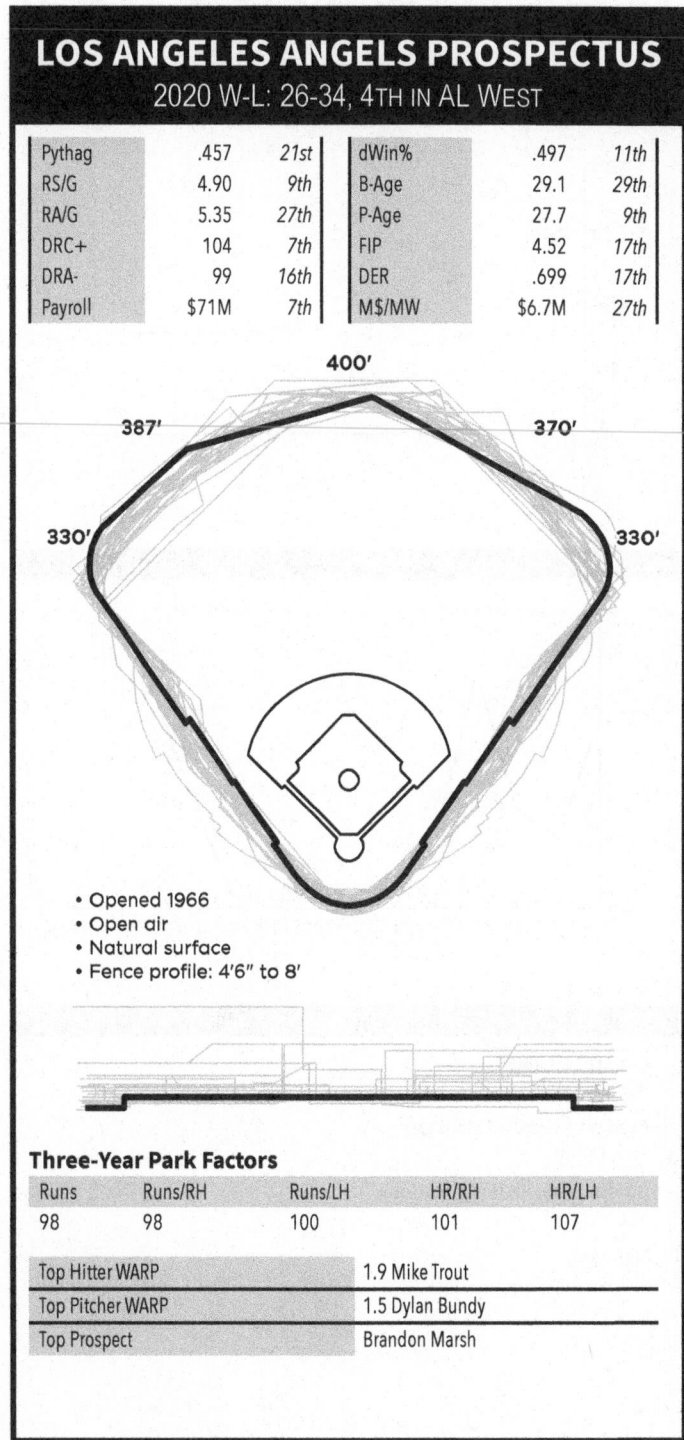

LOS ANGELES ANGELS PROSPECTUS
2020 W-L: 26-34, 4TH IN AL WEST

Pythag	.457	21st	dWin%	.497	11th
RS/G	4.90	9th	B-Age	29.1	29th
RA/G	5.35	27th	P-Age	27.7	9th
DRC+	104	7th	FIP	4.52	17th
DRA-	99	16th	DER	.699	17th
Payroll	$71M	7th	M$/MW	$6.7M	27th

400'
387'   370'
330'   330'

- Opened 1966
- Open air
- Natural surface
- Fence profile: 4'6" to 8'

Three-Year Park Factors

Runs	Runs/RH	Runs/LH	HR/RH	HR/LH
98	98	100	101	107

Top Hitter WARP	1.9 Mike Trout
Top Pitcher WARP	1.5 Dylan Bundy
Top Prospect	Brandon Marsh

Payroll History (in millions)

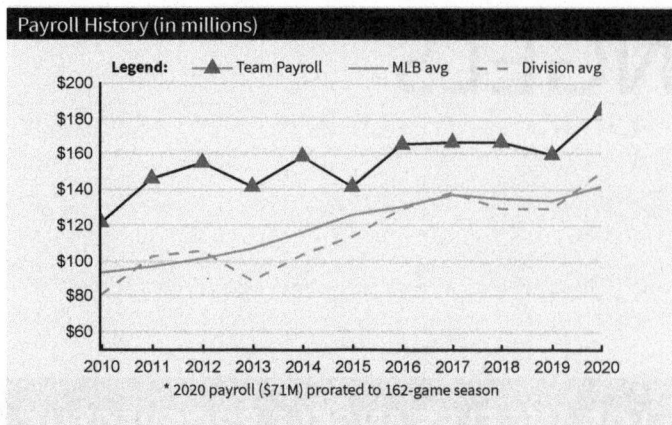

Legend: Team Payroll — MLB avg - - Division avg

* 2020 payroll ($71M) prorated to 162-game season

Future Commitments (in millions)

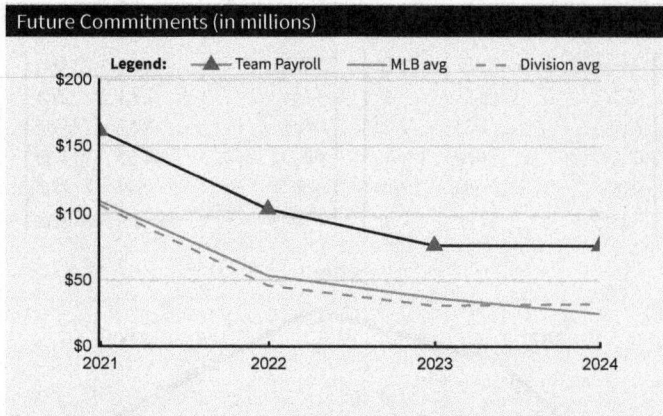

Legend: Team Payroll — MLB avg - - Division avg

Farm System Ranking

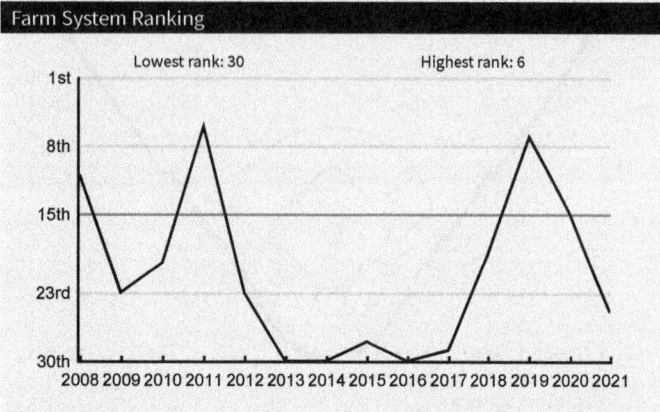

Lowest rank: 30   Highest rank: 6

Personnel

General Manager
Perry Minasian

Assistant General Manager
Alex Tamin

Director, Baseball Operations
Andrew Ball

Manager
Joe Maddon

product seems rather beside the point. This is just how Major League Baseball works at this moment, and while it objectively sucks on its merits, the Angels are at least not one of those teams. They really are trying to win, and over the last five seasons they have mostly lost.

A club that is run according to a proprietary algorithm or opaque AI protocols or just an overtly cynical financial mandate is at bottom not factoring the interest of its fans into the equation at all. It's a financial gambit, and as such hard to love even when it is also competent enough to be admired. But a team that is run according to the whims of actual humans—one run as a family business, and so uniquely dysfunctional in the ways that only unhappy families can be—can be self-thwarting and repellent in the ways that only humans are. Systems focused on efficiency tend towards degradation; the pressures of the marketplace push the people trapped underneath those rational and merciless structures inexorably down and out. But nothing on earth fucks up quite as consistently or stubbornly as people do. This is what social scientists call "the funny part."

Any family business, if permitted to atrophy over a sufficiently long period of time without any meaningful consequence, will eventually collapse into the dead-star density of the Wilpon-era Mets or the circa-now Trumps—a feudal and floundering enterprise ruled by soggy and unappeasable patriarchs and scrapped over among cruel, lazy, utterly unremarkable heirs from which only certain sour noises can escape. Make *values* the central tenet of an organization and that organization will ultimately be a prisoner of the powerful people whose idiosyncratic ad-hoc values those are. If the owners are sufficiently weird, you wind up with selectively pious and broadly inexplicable organizational philosophies like those seen in Colorado and Kansas City in the last decades. If the owners are just replacement-level rich people, the team will in time come to reflect their bulletproof mediocrity. And if a team is run by a highly leveraged investment group that purchased the team with copious amounts of debt—as the Marlins are, for instance, and as other teams will be as franchise values continue to outrun the prices that even unconscionably rich people can pay—then that team will look and function and feel precisely like what it is, which is a way for investors to claim the annualized return on investment they believe is their right.

Given the realities of that last option, a team and its fans being beholden to one rich man's pride starts to seem comparatively appealing. This has traditionally been a popular model, and not just because the grandiosity of vain rich men has occasionally inspired them to create—or, at least, sufficiently compelled them to allow others to construct—great baseball organizations. But, again, all this is dependent on those men. It's dependent upon the readiness and depth of their wealth, of course, but also and more saliently the scope of their vanity. It is one thing for an owner to view his team as a legacy, a towering accomplishment that he will bequeath to his family and community and The

Ages when he's gone; it is another for the owner to consent to let other people, who are not as rich but much more knowledgeable, run the thing.

When and where this works, it works. When it doesn't, you have the Los Angeles Angels of Anaheim, the baseball team owned and controlled by a very rich man named Arte Moreno. In some important ways, the Angels are decently positioned for future success. They have literally the best baseball player on earth and the coolest erstwhile two-way talent in a damn century, a rejuvenated farm system, a hotshot new GM, a new manager with a World Series pedigree, and an owner willing to spend on talent. That all sounds pretty good, and on paper even looks pretty good provided you skim the pitching-related part of the prospectus. But the Angels are still Arte Moreno's team, and so still both very much a family business and an object lesson in being careful what you wish for.

Ⓟ Ⓟ Ⓟ

"That's not the job it should be," an MLB GM told the *Los Angeles Times'* Bill Shaikin in September, as the Angels prepared to move on from GM Billy Eppler after five years. "It should be a great job. It should be one of the easiest recruitment jobs in the game. Who doesn't want to live there? To me, it's one of the best locations in the world. But something is going on there that is cannibalizing what they're doing."

As a general rule, it is wise to be skeptical about people talking shit anonymously, and doubly so when those people work in baseball. But when Anonymous Shit-Talking GM Guy is right, he's right—if not necessarily about Orange County, which is fine except when and where it's the worst place on earth, then definitely about the tremendous latent potential in the team that plays there. The perception among the MLB execs that spoke to Shaikin was that Moreno's overbearing and overwhelmingly unhelpful ownership was the team's biggest and stickiest problem, and that can be true even if a bunch of anonymous MLB types claim as much. But Moreno's is a very specific type of bad ownership.

The issue is not that Moreno doesn't care about winning, or is unwilling to commit his vast personal fortune to that end; he does, and he has been. The problem is that Moreno wants to win *his way*, with his guys and his hunches and his antique rich guy's conception of what winning baseball is all about. This is something like the single shared value of America's Extremely Rich People; Moreno can see that his team is losing, and hate that, but he is unwilling or unable to adjust any of his curdled priors or loosen his grip even when it has been proven that His Way does not work. If you're rich enough, you can just go on like this indefinitely; baseball, with its clearly delineated and highly public results, tends to make that failure easier to hide.

Moreno has spent the last decade and change sticking defiantly to his guns, nudging and dealing and trying again in the expectation that this time he will turn out to be right. The

Angels won the AL West five times during the first six years of Moreno's ownership, although they won just one postseason series during that stretch. Since 2009, the year in which Mike Trout led one of the great June Draft hauls in history, the Angels have made the postseason just once. Trout, who has been the best player in the sport since 2012, still has just 12 postseason at-bats. Whatever Moreno is trying to do here has clearly failed, and yet improbably and obstinately it goes on more or less as it has.

Nothing collapsed, exactly, during those years of atrophy and drift. That was the thing: nothing much changed at all. Everything just declined, even as Trout announced himself as the greatest player of his era. To the extent that Eppler succeeded during his tenure as GM, it was in finally forcing some upgrades and updates to an organization that had become expensively and rather proudly dated as it rotely ran it back year after year. Eppler won a power struggle with long-tenured manager Mike Scioscia and replaced him first with Brad Ausmus and then, after just one year, Joe Maddon; Eppler scouted and spent and successfully turned one of the sport's most barren farm systems into one that is if nothing else currently flush in promising outfield prospects. It helped, albeit in ways that are unlikely to benefit the 2021 model.

The team somehow never managed to finish above .500 under Eppler, but the organization that Perry Minasian inherited from him late in 2020 was both more contemporary than it had been and nothing like state-of-the-art. Shaikin noted that the Angels had just 43 baseball operations staffers at the start of the 2020 season, whereas the Dodgers had 62; Moreno furloughed a massive percentage of the club's player development staff and swathes of minor league coaches in June, although the organization brought some cross-checkers back before the draft. In terms of decision-making, no executive has more say than Moreno himself, who obsesses over hiring managers, vetoes his front office's moves when the spirit moves him—he personally shot down a February trade that Eppler worked out with the Dodgers that would have brought in Joc Pederson and Ross Stripling—plays favorites, and is generally always a whim away from reacquiring Vernon Wells. The man's favorite team is the Los Angeles Angels, and he wants them to win the World Series *this year*. The whole organization is pegged to that blank and goofy urge. Of course it doesn't work.

Ⓟ Ⓟ Ⓟ

Ownership's lack of interest and investment in player development has kept the team stuck in an endless and vexing present in which Trout shines, blameless and brilliant, from the center of a grim maelstrom of imported patches and limping leftovers and readily available non-answers. Every half decade or so, the farm system produces a useful everyday player—David Fletcher really is pretty good, and while Jo Adell was decidedly not in his 2020 debut it would be foolish to stop believing before he's even played in front of fans—and those players slot in wherever there is space. And then it just happens roughly the same way the next year, and the year after that.

It all has managed to remain reliably purgatorial despite Trout's persistent excellence and the tantalizing presence of Shohei Ohtani and Moreno's willingness to buy talent where available. Minasian quickly went to work in the offseason, replacing Andrelton Simmons—there is no greater testament to the void in which this team exists than the fact that it instantly made *Andrelton Simmons* forgettable—with José Iglesias and adding closer Raisel Iglesias and lefty Alex Claudio to the bullpen at a notably minimal cumulative outlay. But it is striking that a team with both Anthony Rendon and Mike Trout still feels so urgently in need of refurbishment. The 2020 season was too short and flukish and grim to mean much, but Adell and Ohtani could hardly have been worse, Justin Upton wasn't much better, and the best pitcher on the roster was either Dylan Bundy or reliever Mike Mayers. That is still true as I write this.

It will surely change, although as always the question is how much. Minasian is not under the same austerity orders as many other big league GM's—Moreno didn't commit to raising the payroll in 2021, but did say "let's put it this way, it's not going down"—and that is an advantage in itself. "One of things that makes this job so intriguing is this is not a 100-loss team," Minasian said in November. "This is not a five-to-seven year rebuild. This is going to be a competitive club." Minasian has displayed a knack in his previous gigs for identifying undervalued talent, but the Angels will need to both pull some gems off the curb and pay MSRP for top-of-the-market talent if they're going to dramatically change their outlook for 2021. This is a heavy lift on its own, but when ESPN's Buster Olney polled former Angels employees in November about how Minasian might make things work in Anaheim, every answer resolved to managing Moreno. It's his team, after all.

Managing Moreno means that longer-term decisions will necessarily take a backseat to near-term ones, which is nothing new. The broader work of building out this organization into something more sustainable, which amounts to making a headstrong and proudly out-of-touch old grouch with a lot of money yield some authority over something he knows nothing about for the first time in his life, is the more difficult bit. That is more or less the challenge facing a great many other American institutions at this moment, as it happens. In sclerotic family businesses as in any other crumbling institution, accountability is the first and most devastating casualty. When the only rule in effect is "the rich guys are going to do whatever they want, without any conceivable consequence" it is not difficult to see how things will unfold, or how they become so difficult to fix.

And yet it would be foolish, here or elsewhere, to say that things can't get better for this team, even if by accident. The Angels have Mike Trout, and Anthony Rendon, and as much Shohei Ohtani as heaven allows, and however much Justin Upton there is left. Even the pitching, which I have politely avoided talking about until this point, has some promise—Dylan Bundy shouldn't be the team's ace, but a rotation that features him and young starters Griffin Canning and Patrick Sandoval could become workable if sufficiently good pitchers are slotted in above them all. This is not a division-winning roster at present, but such a team could be built upon it given the necessary resources and room to move. That's a load-bearing "could," but you know that by now.

Given the broader retrenchment in the league and the subsequent shock of this last and mostly lost pandemic season, a sufficiently creative and sufficiently empowered Angels front office *could* flip this gilded dud of a roster into a contender with relative ease. The Angels could be any number of things, up to and including a contender, but what sets them apart, as one of the league's truest family businesses, is that they'll only become what their owner will let them be. They are Arte Moreno's team, no more and no less. They could be something more, but also this is what they are. That's what makes them infuriating, and keeps their circumstances so infuriatingly familiar.

—*David Roth is a co-owner at Defector.*

HITTERS

★ ★ ★ 2021 Top 101 Prospect #76 ★ ★ ★

Jordyn Adams CF Born: 10/18/99 Age: 21 Bats: R Throws: R Height: 6'2" Weight: 180 Origin: Round 1, 2018 Draft (#17 overall)

YEAR	TEAM	LVL	AGE	PA	R	2B	3B	HR	RBI	BB	K	SB	CS	Whiff%	AVG/OBP/SLG	DRC+	BABIP	BRR	FRAA	WARP
2018	ANG	ROK	18	82	8	2	2	0	5	10	23	5	2		.243/.354/.329	83	.362	0.9	CF(14): -4.2, RF(1): 0.0	-0.5
2018	ORM	ROK	18	40	5	4	1	0	8	4	7	0	1		.314/.375/.486	113	.379	-0.8	CF(8): 3.1	0.3
2019	ANG	ROK	19	14	4	1	0	0	4	1	3	4	0		.538/.571/.615	160	.700	0.6	CF(3): 2.0	0.4
2019	BUR	LO-A	19	428	52	15	2	7	31	50	94	12	5		.250/.346/.358	122	.316	2.4	CF(73): -1.2, LF(9): 2.5, RF(8): -0.4	2.6
2019	IE	HI-A	19	40	7	1	1	1	1	5	14	0	1		.229/.325/.400	94	.350	0.2	CF(4): 0.4, LF(2): -0.3, RF(2): -0.3	0.1
2021 FS	LAA	MLB	21	600	50	26	3	9	54	41	200	5	2		.218/.278/.332	68	.323	-0.5	CF 0, LF 1	-0.5

Comparables: Aaron Hicks, Kyle Tucker, Slade Heathcott

Speaking about Adams' approach to games, fellow high-upside, eye-catching tools prospect Brandon Marsh described him as "like a caged bird that just got released, like a gazelle or something that can fly." This raises several questions—about the non-avian taxonomy of gazelles, about whether Marsh could name a species of bird if asked, about what kinds of birds Marsh has seen in what sorts of cages—but in any case the simile illustrates the explosive, immediate potential Adams evidences to scouts and casual watchers alike. It seems eminently possible in a year or so Marsh hands off the top prospect reins to ~~something that can fly~~ Adams, provided the high school two-sport star is able to continue advancing his bat in a more normal season of reps.

Jo Adell RF Born: 04/08/99 Age: 22 Bats: R Throws: R Height: 6'3" Weight: 215 Origin: Round 1, 2017 Draft (#10 overall)

YEAR	TEAM	LVL	AGE	PA	R	2B	3B	HR	RBI	BB	K	SB	CS	Whiff%	AVG/OBP/SLG	DRC+	BABIP	BRR	FRAA	WARP
2018	BUR	LO-A	19	108	23	7	1	6	29	11	26	4	1		.326/.398/.611	160	.391	1.2	CF(16): -0.4, RF(3): -0.9, LF(1): -0.3	0.9
2018	IE	HI-A	19	262	46	19	3	12	42	15	63	9	2		.290/.345/.546	141	.345	2.0	CF(36): -5.6, RF(8): -1.1, LF(7): 0.5	0.7
2018	MOB	AA	19	71	14	6	0	2	6	6	22	2	0		.238/.324/.429	98	.333	-0.3	CF(17): -1.9	-0.1
2019	IE	HI-A	20	27	4	1	0	2	5	1	10	0	0		.280/.333/.560	114	.385	0.3	CF(3): 0.5, RF(2): -0.1, LF(1): -0.1	0.2
2019	MOB	AA	20	182	28	15	0	8	23	19	41	6	0		.308/.390/.553	167	.369	0.5	RF(19): -1.2, CF(17): -3.5, LF(5): 1.9	1.5
2019	SL	AAA	20	132	22	11	0	0	8	10	43	1	0		.264/.321/.355	66	.410	2.5	RF(13): -0.5, LF(9): 0.6, CF(4): -0.7	0.0
2020	LAA	MLB	21	132	9	4	0	3	7	7	55	0	1	42.1%	.161/.212/.266	46	.258	0.2	RF(34): 0.3, CF(4): 0.5	-0.4
2021 FS	LAA	MLB	22	600	57	24	3	18	65	38	226	6	2	42.1%	.214/.272/.372	74	.322	2.3	RF -19, CF -1	-2.1
2021 DC	LAA	MLB	22	512	49	21	2	15	55	32	193	5	1	42.1%	.214/.272/.372	74	.322	1.9	RF -16, CF -1	-2.1

Comparables: Matt Kemp, Jay Bruce, Colby Rasmus

You needn't be a fanatical Annual reader to know of BP's institutional affinity for Adell. He's an easy player to believe in, with his tools and upside evident even before his age allowed him to fully sketch his potential. He did that and more ahead of his debut season, which counterveiled his immense promise as a pithy reminder of the pitfalls of a prospect of his sort. Contact skills often round out later when a prospect has prodigious power, but rarely does a successful major-league hitter carry a 66.5 percent contact rate on pitches in the zone. That was almost 20 percent lower than the 2020 league average, and was also the seventh-lowest single-season rate (minimum 100 PA) since tracking began in 2002. The six players who had a year worse than Adell's 2020 don't inspire confidence outside of Joey Gallo, and the Adam Dunn profile is a perilous path to trod. A sample too small to exempt rookie eligibility provides ample reason to dream on a better second campaign, but this is Anaheim, where Mike Trout goes right and nothing else. As many times as Angels fans were reminded of Trout's 2011 struggles another, more disquieting, name came to mind: Brandon Wood. Adell's DRC+ was actually an order of magnitude worse than Wood's disastrous rookie showing, though there's little reason to expect his career arc to be at all similar. The skillset seems too undeniable, plus the scouting industry misses less than it used to. Considering how his noun-named forebears diverged in their first complete seasons, this comment will likely seem ridiculous or foreboding before long.

Franklin Barreto 2B Born: 02/27/96 Age: 25 Bats: R Throws: R Height: 5'10" Weight: 208 Origin: International Free Agent, 2012

YEAR	TEAM	LVL	AGE	PA	R	2B	3B	HR	RBI	BB	K	SB	CS	Whiff%	AVG/OBP/SLG	DRC+	BABIP	BRR	FRAA	WARP
2018	NAS	AAA	22	333	54	16	1	18	46	39	106	5	2		.259/.357/.514	128	.337	3.5	2B(60): -2.2, SS(11): 0.4	1.9
2018	OAK	MLB	22	75	10	4	0	5	16	1	29	0	0	38.6%	.233/.253/.493	76	.308	-1.1	2B(26): -1.7, SS(2): -0.0	-0.3
2019	LV	AAA	23	424	88	29	5	19	65	42	113	15	1		.295/.374/.552	108	.374	2.2	2B(47): -5.1, SS(30): 0.1, 3B(9): 0.8	1.8
2019	OAK	MLB	23	58	6	2	0	2	5	1	23	1	0	41.4%	.123/.138/.263	50	.156	0.5	2B(17): -0.2, SS(5): -0.2	-0.1
2020	OAK	MLB	24	10	5	0	0	0	0	0	7	0	0	65.0%	.000/.000/.000	40	.000	0.0	2B(4): 0.2, SS(3): -0.0	0.0
2020	LAA	MLB	24	18	0	0	0	0	2	0	8	1	0	50.0%	.118/.167/.118	49	.222	-0.1	2B(2): 0.2, 3B(2): 0.1, SS(1): -0.1	0.0
2021 FS	LAA	MLB	25	600	62	23	3	21	66	41	219	9	2	44.6%	.221/.286/.391	83	.324	2.7	2B -8, 3B 0	0.2
2021 DC	LAA	MLB	25	136	14	5	0	4	15	9	49	2	0	44.6%	.221/.286/.391	83	.324	0.6	2B -2	0.1

Comparables: Isan Díaz, Josh VanMeter, Scott Kingery

Barreto's trade deadline acquisition meant the book officially closed on the Josh Donaldson trade, with the A's having received a penultimate season of Brett Lawrie, 219 plate appearances from Barreto over four seasons, and Tommy La Stella for September and seven October games. The apparently inequitable swap smarts even more given the strange usage the A's elected for Barreto, who has played between 21 and 32 major-league games in each of the past four seasons. The .549 OPS makes that choice hard to dispute, but it's nevertheless about as suboptimal a path one could design for getting a player comfortable at the major league level. It's a six-month soft launch, with no grand opening in sight—not a venture being set up for success. With Barreto having appeared at four defensive positions in the majors and the Angels lacking much in the way of versatility, they have little reason not to give the still-somehow-young infielder an extended look.

David Fletcher SS Born: 05/31/94 Age: 27 Bats: R Throws: R Height: 5'9" Weight: 185 Origin: Round 6, 2015 Draft (#195 overall)

YEAR	TEAM	LVL	AGE	PA	R	2B	3B	HR	RBI	BB	K	SB	CS	Whiff%	AVG/OBP/SLG	DRC+	BABIP	BRR	FRAA	WARP
2018	SL	AAA	24	275	55	25	5	6	37	16	21	7	2		.350/.394/.559	137	.364	3.4	SS(31): 3.4, 2B(18): -1.6, 3B(8): 1.6	2.6
2018	LAA	MLB	24	307	35	18	2	1	25	15	34	3	0	10.2%	.275/.316/.363	91	.307	3.5	2B(43): 1.8, 3B(33): 4.7, SS(7): -0.6	1.6
2019	LAA	MLB	25	653	83	30	4	6	49	55	64	8	3	9.8%	.290/.350/.384	100	.317	-4.5	3B(90): 1.5, 2B(42): 1.5, SS(39): -0.5	2.5
2020	LAA	MLB	26	230	31	13	0	3	18	20	25	2	1	8.6%	.319/.376/.425	105	.348	0.2	SS(27): -0.1, 2B(15): 1.3, 3B(8): -0.3	0.9
2021 FS	LAA	MLB	27	600	71	28	2	8	48	42	78	7	2	9.5%	.278/.333/.383	99	.311	1.3	2B 0, SS 1	2.3
2021 DC	LAA	MLB	27	580	69	27	2	8	46	41	75	7	2	9.5%	.278/.333/.383	99	.311	1.3	2B 0, SS 1	2.4

Comparables: Rich McKinney, Chris Sabo, Ray Knight

The David and Goliath comparison is almost too easy—he's listed at a probably generous 5'9", has a contact-oriented, power-averse profile out of line with the modern game, and the man's last name is Fletcher, for god's sake. Fine, a slingshot doesn't quite propel arrows, but still, Fletcher is doing things his own way, and making it work. His .095 isolated slugging is third-worst among batters with at least 1,000 plate appearances since 2018, while his 10.3 percent strikeout rate third-best. The hardest-to-strike out batter in that frame, Andrelton Simmons, recalls the tenuous line walked by the contact-reliant:

A little slippage compounds into a lot, and Fletcher is a merely good (rather than all-world) defender, though Simmons' impending free agency might give Fletcher a longer look at short. If double-digit homers aren't coming, the doubles can never dry up without the production doing the same. Still, much like the biblical David, Fletcher is inspiring faith.

José Iglesias SS   Born: 01/05/90   Age: 31   Bats: R   Throws: R   Height: 5'11"   Weight: 195   Origin: International Free Agent, 2009

YEAR	TEAM	LVL	AGE	PA	R	2B	3B	HR	RBI	BB	K	SB	CS	Whiff%	AVG/OBP/SLG	DRC+	BABIP	BRR	FRAA	WARP
2018	DET	MLB	28	464	43	31	3	5	48	19	47	15	6	13.1%	.269/.310/.389	92	.291	1.6	SS(122): 4.7	2.3
2019	CIN	MLB	29	530	62	21	3	11	59	20	70	6	6	15.6%	.288/.318/.407	86	.315	3.0	SS(144): 6.5	2.5
2020	BAL	MLB	30	150	16	17	0	3	24	3	17	0	0	14.5%	.373/.400/.556	111	.407	-0.6	SS(24): -1.4	0.4
2021 FS	LAA	MLB	31	600	64	31	1	11	65	28	81	10	5	14.8%	.269/.313/.393	93	.296	-3.5	SS 3	1.3
2021 DC	LAA	MLB	31	546	59	28	1	10	59	25	74	9	4	14.8%	.269/.313/.393	93	.296	-3.2	SS 2	1.2

Comparables: Dale Berra, Kevin Elster, Marco Scutaro

Iglesias on the 2020 Orioles was like a high school senior being forced to play a few games on JV. Despite struggling through multiple leg injuries that limited him to only 22 starts in the field, he had the best offensive year of his career, posting an OPS over .950 and the best expected batting average in baseball. There were moments last year when the O's treated him like a shortstop version of 1988 Kirk Gibson, where Iglesias would enter the game to pinch hit in the late innings, slap a single through the hole and limp his way down to first. It was a weird sight, the slight, slap-hitting shortstop with a career 84 OPS+ before the season, acting like Terrell Owens on one leg in the Super Bowl. Was his sudden sluggage a blip or a breakthrough? That's the Angels' concern now, after they imported Iglesias to backfill a hole left by Andrelton Simmons' free agency. No one can consistently rival Simmons' skill with the leather, but Iglesias should be a solid stand-in, whether he brings his bat or not.

Jeremiah Jackson SS   Born: 03/26/00   Age: 21   Bats: R   Throws: R   Height: 6'0"   Weight: 165   Origin: Round 2, 2018 Draft (#57 overall)

YEAR	TEAM	LVL	AGE	PA	R	2B	3B	HR	RBI	BB	K	SB	CS	Whiff%	AVG/OBP/SLG	DRC+	BABIP	BRR	FRAA	WARP
2018	ANG	ROK	18	91	13	4	2	5	14	7	25	6	1		.317/.374/.598	150	.396	1.3	SS(21): -1.3	0.5
2018	ORM	ROK	18	100	13	6	3	2	9	8	34	4	1		.198/.260/.396	26	.286	-0.3	SS(21): -1.7, 2B(1): -0.0	-0.7
2019	ORM	ROK+	19	287	47	14	2	23	60	23	96	5	1		.265/.331/.609	110	.314	1.0		1.3
2021 FS	LAA	MLB	21	600	42	26	3	9	49	32	256	5	1		.176/.226/.286	36	.302	2.7	SS -3, 2B 0	-3.0

Another player whose future is clouded by the lack of 2020 data, there's a lot we don't know about Jackson: Can he stick at shortstop as his frame fills out? Is striking out a third of the time to be expected, moving forward? Most importantly, how much of the Pioneer League-record tying home run power is real? He can move well and has a strong arm, so sliding over to second or third wouldn't be a huge long-term concern to his viability given the showcase he put on in Rookie ball. Really, the biggest red flag for Jackson given the system in which he's developing is that he's not an outfielder, the only position which the Angels seem interested in developing.

Jahmai Jones 2B   Born: 08/04/97   Age: 23   Bats: R   Throws: R   Height: 6'0"   Weight: 204   Origin: Round 2, 2015 Draft (#70 overall)

YEAR	TEAM	LVL	AGE	PA	R	2B	3B	HR	RBI	BB	K	SB	CS	Whiff%	AVG/OBP/SLG	DRC+	BABIP	BRR	FRAA	WARP
2018	IE	HI-A	20	347	47	10	5	8	35	43	63	13	3		.235/.338/.383	111	.272	1.5	2B(70): -6.9	-0.1
2018	MOB	AA	20	212	33	10	4	2	20	24	51	11	1		.245/.335/.375	103	.323	-1.5	2B(45): -1.7	-0.1
2019	MOB	AA	21	544	66	22	3	5	50	50	109	9	11		.234/.308/.324	79	.288	2.3	2B(110): 14.4, CF(7): 0.3, LF(4): -0.6	2.3
2020	LAA	MLB	23	7	2	0	0	0	1	0	2	0	0	28.6%	.429/.429/.429	89	.600	-0.1	2B(2): -0.0	0.0
2021 FS	LAA	MLB	23	600	61	25	3	12	59	46	160	11	4	28.6%	.227/.295/.357	81	.297	0.6	2B 6, LF 0	1.3
2021 DC	LAA	MLB	23	34	3	1	0	0	3	2	9	0	0	28.6%	.227/.295/.357	81	.297	0.0	2B 0	0.1

Comparables: Luis Valbuena, Eddie Rosario, Abraham Toro

Forget keeping up with the Joneses. A number of Angels prospects have leapfrogged the infielder in recent years, while he changed positions and never really brought everything together in the batter's box. Jones debuted in the majors last year, but it wasn't enough to obfuscate the feeling of his prospect potential having stalled. Now he's got to figure out how to keep up with everyone else.

D'Shawn Knowles OF   Born: 01/16/01   Age: 20   Bats: S   Throws: R   Height: 6'0"   Weight: 165   Origin: International Free Agent, 2017

YEAR	TEAM	LVL	AGE	PA	R	2B	3B	HR	RBI	BB	K	SB	CS	Whiff%	AVG/OBP/SLG	DRC+	BABIP	BRR	FRAA	WARP
2018	ANG	ROK	17	130	19	4	1	1	14	15	27	7	4		.301/.385/.381	134	.384	1.1	LF(13): -3.1, CF(9): -0.5, RF(6): -0.3	0.0
2018	ORM	ROK	17	123	27	9	2	4	15	13	38	2	3		.321/.398/.550	123	.463	0.3	CF(17): -1.2, RF(9): 1.8, LF(1): -0.1	0.4
2019	ORM	ROK+	18	286	38	11	4	6	28	25	76	5	4		.244/.311/.392	70	.312	-0.3		0.0
2021 FS	LAA	MLB	20	600	45	26	3	7	49	37	221	7	3		.199/.254/.300	50	.315	-1.3	CF 0, RF 0	-2.5

The year Beyoncé Knowles was 19, her group Destiny's Child released *Survivor*, one of the seminal albums of the 2000s, and Beyoncé went solo, launching perhaps the most successful pop career of all time. As with so many other players, the outfielder Knowles found himself on the sidelines in 2020, missing a chance to make his own age-19 year something great. Much like Beyoncé, though, Knowles began to untether himself from another act with whom he's often been associated (fellow Angels 2017 Bahamian glove-and-speed outfielder Trent Deveaux), a higher offensive ceiling drawing more attention his way. It's a crowded Angels outfield, both at the majors and below, but entering a crowded space didn't ever slow down Beyoncé.

Kevin Maitan 3B Born: 02/12/00 Age: 21 Bats: S Throws: R Height: 6'2" Weight: 190 Origin: International Free Agent, 2016

YEAR	TEAM	LVL	AGE	PA	R	2B	3B	HR	RBI	BB	K	SB	CS	Whiff%	AVG/OBP/SLG	DRC+	BABIP	BRR	FRAA	WARP
2018	ORM	ROK	18	284	42	13	1	8	26	19	66	1	2		.248/.306/.397	64	.303	1.1	3B(40): 3.3, SS(20): -3.1	-0.4
2019	BUR	LO-A	19	532	56	11	3	12	46	39	164	7	4		.214/.278/.323	68	.295	-1.9	3B(92): -6.9, 2B(21): -2.8	-1.4
2021 FS	LAA	MLB	21	600	45	25	2	10	52	30	225	2	1		.194/.239/.303	45	.301	0.0	3B -2, SS -2	-3.2

Comparables: Dustin Peterson, Alex Liddi, Michael Chavis

Still 20 at the time of this book's publication, it'd be beyond premature to say it's too late for Maitan. You'd be forgiven the mistake, however, given how thoroughly he's been forgotten amidst a middling farm system. Just two years after he was declared a free agent and the Angels gave him a $2.2 million bonus (itself two years after an original $4.25 million bonus), Maitan was left exposed to the Rule 5 draft. There's still time for a major leaguer to emerge, but chances of Maitan regaining his prospect luster are about as strong as of him moving back to shortstop.

──────────── ★ ★ ★ *2021 Top 101 Prospect* #44 ★ ★ ★ ────────────

Brandon Marsh CF Born: 12/18/97 Age: 23 Bats: L Throws: R Height: 6'4" Weight: 215 Origin: Round 2, 2016 Draft (#60 overall)

YEAR	TEAM	LVL	AGE	PA	R	2B	3B	HR	RBI	BB	K	SB	CS	Whiff%	AVG/OBP/SLG	DRC+	BABIP	BRR	FRAA	WARP
2018	BUR	LO-A	20	154	26	12	1	3	24	21	40	4	0		.295/.390/.470	136	.400	2.9	CF(14): 1.2, RF(13): -1.3, LF(6): 0.7	1.2
2018	IE	HI-A	20	426	59	15	6	7	46	52	118	10	4		.256/.348/.385	107	.356	4.3	CF(50): -0.8, RF(33): 3.0, LF(7): 0.5	1.1
2019	MOB	AA	21	412	48	21	2	7	43	47	92	18	5		.300/.383/.428	141	.384	2.6	CF(55): -0.7, RF(19): 1.8, LF(13): -3.0	2.9
2021 FS	LAA	MLB	23	600	62	26	4	13	60	46	194	7	2		.240/.303/.377	85	.345	3.1	CF 0, LF 0	0.9
2021 DC	LAA	MLB	23	68	7	3	0	1	6	5	22	0	0		.240/.303/.377	85	.345	0.4	CF 0	0.1

Comparables: Michael Saunders, Jordan Schafer, Chris Young

For all the accusations of organizational rudderlessness that have dogged the Angels for a decade, the organization's preferences in the draft have remained consistent—shoot for high-upside hitters, especially outfielders, who can contribute positively with all five tools. When you have a Mike Trout hammer, all you see are fish nails, apparently. Marsh hasn't quite gotten there with the power yet, and the lost year of development smarts here especially. Without the morass of 2020, he might have had a chance to work out his issues in the big leagues; it's not the common prospect who ascends to the top spot in an organization without ever breaking double-digit homers at a minor-league stop. The defensive reputation is that good; even if the Angels outfield is bogged down already, Marsh's glove makes room for itself. The demands of the major-league roster meant that by the end of 2020, he was taking reps at first base at the Angels alternate site in Long Beach—an unexpected turn for the player who might one day push Mike Trout to an outfield corner.

Orlando Martinez RF Born: 02/17/98 Age: 23 Bats: L Throws: L Height: 6'0" Weight: 185 Origin: International Free Agent, 2017

YEAR	TEAM	LVL	AGE	PA	R	2B	3B	HR	RBI	BB	K	SB	CS	Whiff%	AVG/OBP/SLG	DRC+	BABIP	BRR	FRAA	WARP
2018	ORM	ROK	20	53	11	5	0	2	10	4	9	3	2		.375/.415/.604	143	.421	1.0	LF(8): -1.0, RF(1): -0.1	0.2
2018	BUR	LO-A	20	238	27	12	1	3	25	17	56	6	5		.289/.340/.394	106	.373	-1.2	RF(20): 1.9, LF(18): -1.0, CF(13): 0.3	0.4
2019	IE	HI-A	21	422	55	21	4	12	49	36	79	5	4		.263/.325/.434	110	.299	1.4	CF(41): 3.4, RF(21): -2.2, LF(20): 1.6	1.9
2021 FS	LAA	MLB	23	600	57	27	2	15	64	36	172	3	2		.236/.285/.379	80	.313	-1.5	CF 6, LF 1	0.8

Comparables: César Puello, Kirk Nieuwenhuis, Jake Cave

With an organizational outfield depth chart littered with athletic players worth keeping an eye or two on, Martinez is the underdog of the brood. Lacking a marketable skill but capable of contributing a little bit of everything, his best bet is probably to pray to David DeJesus, the patron saint of the 50 OFP, and hope that he can get enough time as a fourth outfielder to prove himself worthy of being a third.

Shohei Ohtani RHP/DH Born: 07/05/94 Age: 27 Bats: L Throws: R Height: 6'4" Weight: 210 Origin: International Free Agent, 2017

YEAR	TEAM	LVL	AGE	PA	R	2B	3B	HR	RBI	BB	K	SB	CS	Whiff%	AVG/OBP/SLG	DRC+	BABIP	BRR	FRAA	WARP
2018	LAA	MLB	23	367	59	21	2	22	61	37	102	10	4	30.8%	.285/.361/.564	128	.350	-2.3	P(10): 0.7	1.7
2019	LAA	MLB	24	425	51	20	5	18	62	33	110	12	3	27.3%	.286/.343/.505	105	.354	-1.5		0.8
2020	LAA	MLB	26	175	23	6	0	7	24	22	50	7	1	32.2%	.190/.291/.366	87	.229	0.4	P(2): -0.0	0.1
2021 FS	LAA	MLB	26	600	72	25	3	26	80	59	172	14	4	29.6%	.241/.322/.447	106	.306	2.5	1B 0	1.6
2021 DC	LAA	MLB	26	375	45	15	1	16	50	37	107	9	3	29.6%	.241/.322/.447	106	.306	1.6		1.3

Comparables: Craig Wilson, Dave Kingman, Richie Sexson

In Ohtani's first Annual comment three years ago, he was likened to Halley's Comet—a once-in-a-lifetime occurrence people will remember watching for the rest of their lives. That remains true even as it becomes questionable whether the comet has passed us by, leaving us only with the memories. Ohtani's 2020 was a total loss, not only ruining a season but also threatening his viability as a major-league pitcher. Two abortive, disastrous starts featuring sharply diminished velocity—it was even worse than the three mph topline loss, given his 2018 figure was bogged down in his last few starts before shutdown—were all the NPB import got in his third season stateside. Worse than even that, he looked lost, both at the plate and in general. He's running it back for another attempt at a two-way season, but if 2021 goes poorly, it would be unsurprising if we're back to waiting another lifetime for a player of Ohtani's ilk.

Kyren Paris SS Born: 11/11/01 Age: 19 Bats: R Throws: R Height: 6'0" Weight: 165 Origin: Round 2, 2019 Draft (#55 overall)

YEAR	TEAM	LVL	AGE	PA	R	2B	3B	HR	RBI	BB	K	SB	CS	Whiff%	AVG/OBP/SLG	DRC+	BABIP	BRR	FRAA	WARP
2019	ANG	ROK	17	13	4	1	0	0	2	3	4	0	0		.300/.462/.400	110	.500	0.3	SS(3): -0.5	0.0
2021 FS	LAA	MLB	19	600	44	26	2	6	47	35	238	4	1		.204/.255/.296	52	.341	0.7	SS -1	-1.9

Late in 2020, the Netflix Twitter account, promoting the platform's hit series *Emily in Paris,* took to Twitter to clarify that Kyren Paris is actually meant to be pronounced with a French accent—Kyren Pah-ree (so it rhymes). The research shows all sorts of benefits to taking players who are young for their draft class—like Paris, 17 at the time of his selection—but it's less clear how those benefits manifest when they hardly play the following two seasons due to a broken hamate bone and an international pandemic. Paris still carries plenty of promise, thanks to ha versatile defensive skillset that could allow the Angels to spread him across the field like a creamy brie. The only question is how much the baguette-like crunch of lost development time will cost the not-quite-as-young prospect.

Albert Pujols 1B Born: 01/16/80 Age: 41 Bats: R Throws: R Height: 6'3" Weight: 235 Origin: Round 13, 1999 Draft (#402 overall)

YEAR	TEAM	LVL	AGE	PA	R	2B	3B	HR	RBI	BB	K	SB	CS	Whiff%	AVG/OBP/SLG	DRC+	BABIP	BRR	FRAA	WARP
2018	LAA	MLB	38	498	50	20	0	19	64	28	65	1	0	17.6%	.245/.289/.411	101	.247	-1.9	1B(70): 3.8	1.0
2019	LAA	MLB	39	545	55	22	0	23	93	43	68	3	0	18.1%	.244/.305/.430	98	.238	-5.0	1B(98): -0.4, 3B(1): -0.0	0.2
2020	LAA	MLB	40	163	15	8	0	6	25	9	25	0	0	22.2%	.224/.270/.395	93	.230	-1.1	1B(26): 2.3	0.1
2021 FS	LAA	MLB	41	600	61	23	0	22	74	39	103	2	0	19.0%	.237/.291/.403	86	.253	-1.0	1B 0, 3B 0	-0.4
2021 DC	LAA	MLB	41	409	42	16	0	15	51	26	70	1	0	19.0%	.237/.291/.403	86	.253	-0.7	1B 0	-0.1

Comparables: Eddie Murray, Jason Giambi, Rafael Palmeiro

Asked in May whether he planned to return to play past the final season of his ten-year contract in 2021, Pujols demurred that he hadn't "closed that door." Judging by the Coleridge-ian reputation of that contract, you might assume that door had already closed ahead of the 40-year-old, with no window jarring open. It's possible that'll be the case, a decision as much out of his hands as the 312 times he's been intentionally walked (second most all-time). And to say the legendary first baseman wasn't that bad is the loudest damnation, with the faintest of praise. They can't all be Nelson Cruz, loosing the majors' best pure power well into his thirties, and that a 40-year-old who has been in the big leagues for half of his life is still here, almost justifiably, is something. If Pujols can be almost justifiable for 2022, someone will probably justify it. In the meantime, get into the room while you can.

Anthony Rendon 3B Born: 06/06/90 Age: 31 Bats: R Throws: R Height: 6'1" Weight: 200 Origin: Round 1, 2011 Draft (#6 overall)

YEAR	TEAM	LVL	AGE	PA	R	2B	3B	HR	RBI	BB	K	SB	CS	Whiff%	AVG/OBP/SLG	DRC+	BABIP	BRR	FRAA	WARP
2018	WAS	MLB	28	597	88	44	2	24	92	55	82	2	1	14.0%	.308/.374/.535	133	.323	2.9	3B(136): -5.7	4.4
2019	WAS	MLB	29	646	117	44	3	34	126	80	86	5	1	12.9%	.319/.412/.598	150	.323	1.0	3B(146): -4.5, 2B(1): -0.0	6.3
2020	LAA	MLB	30	232	29	11	1	9	31	38	31	0	0	14.7%	.286/.418/.497	143	.302	0.6	3B(52): -8.4	0.9
2021 FS	LAA	MLB	31	600	83	31	1	26	87	78	99	6	2	13.6%	.284/.388/.507	143	.309	-0.7	3B -3, 2B 0	4.2
2021 DC	LAA	MLB	31	614	85	32	1	26	89	79	102	7	2	13.6%	.284/.388/.507	143	.309	-0.7	3B -3	4.3

Comparables: Bill Melton, Howard Johnson, Eric Chavez

If you're looking for reasons to fret, Rendon's never-laudable defense at the hot corner appeared to regress further in 2020, his FRAA the sixth worst in MLB. If you're seizing on that, though, here is some genuine advice for you: Find better things to worry about; there are innumerable contenders. Truly, the former National maintained his forward momentum with the bat from his walk year, hitting nearly as well as the guy who plays center field. Fans can lament the loss of seeing Rendon in person and in pristine form, but there's little reason beyond typical aging concerns to expect a cliff in the next few sixths of his massive contract. And if the defensive slippage portends a shift to first base in the latter half of the six-year deal, well, it's not like the Angels won't have an opening there in the near future.

Luis Rengifo 2B Born: 02/26/97 Age: 24 Bats: S Throws: R Height: 5'10" Weight: 195 Origin: International Free Agent, 2013

YEAR	TEAM	LVL	AGE	PA	R	2B	3B	HR	RBI	BB	K	SB	CS	Whiff%	AVG/OBP/SLG	DRC+	BABIP	BRR	FRAA	WARP
2018	IE	HI-A	21	190	36	11	3	2	16	27	22	22	8		.323/.426/.466	174	.365	2.5	SS(36): 3.9, 2B(2): -0.0	2.3
2018	MOB	AA	21	180	37	10	5	2	21	23	22	13	2		.305/.417/.477	143	.346	-1.0	SS(30): -3.4, 2B(9): -0.8	0.7
2018	SL	AAA	21	219	36	9	5	3	27	25	31	6	6		.274/.358/.421	111	.310	3.3	2B(31): -1.5, SS(16): 0.1	1.0
2019	SL	AAA	22	122	16	4	1	5	14	11	24	3	3		.273/.336/.464	76	.305	-0.4	2B(12): 3.6, SS(12): 0.9, LF(3): 0.5	0.5
2019	LAA	MLB	22	406	44	18	3	7	33	40	93	2	5	24.3%	.238/.321/.364	84	.300	-0.4	2B(104): -1.6, SS(12): 1.2	0.5
2020	LAA	MLB	23	106	12	1	0	1	3	14	26	3	1	24.5%	.156/.269/.200	77	.206	1.0	2B(32): -1.0, 3B(1): 0.0, SS(1): -0.0	0.1
2021 FS	LAA	MLB	24	600	62	22	4	11	54	59	145	17	9	24.4%	.221/.305/.346	82	.280	-4.7	2B 1, SS 0	0.3
2021 DC	LAA	MLB	24	136	14	5	0	2	12	13	32	4	2	24.4%	.221/.305/.346	82	.280	-1.1	2B 0, SS 0	0.1

Comparables: Jurickson Profar, Mark Bellhorn, Tony Bernazard

Despite a career batting line more befitting a catcher, Rengifo impressed in his rookie 2019 with his play at second and surprising pop (18 doubles in just over 400 plate appearances). Playable at short, the overall package was enticing enough the Dodgers made Rengifo the only named Angel in an ultimately scrapped six-player trade that would have returned Joc Pederson, Ross Stripling, and Andy Pages. That would have marked the infielder's third time being traded in as many years, but it's because Rengifo is valued—teams see enticing potential futures, or did, before 2020 dimmed that hope. Without a turnaround next season, expectations will collapse as quickly as the trade that almost moved Rengifo from Los Angeles to Los Angeles.

Andrelton Simmons SS Born: 09/04/89 Age: 31 Bats: R Throws: R Height: 6'2" Weight: 195 Origin: Round 2, 2010 Draft (#70 overall)

YEAR	TEAM	LVL	AGE	PA	R	2B	3B	HR	RBI	BB	K	SB	CS	Whiff%	AVG/OBP/SLG	DRC+	BABIP	BRR	FRAA	WARP
2018	LAA	MLB	28	600	68	26	5	11	75	35	44	10	2	13.7%	.292/.337/.417	106	.300	3.8	SS(145): -6.8	2.9
2019	LAA	MLB	29	424	47	19	0	7	40	24	37	10	2	14.2%	.264/.309/.364	80	.277	-0.1	SS(102): 10.5	2.0
2020	LAA	MLB	31	127	19	7	0	0	10	8	16	2	0	16.3%	.297/.346/.356	84	.343	0.6	SS(30): 1.4	0.3
2021 FS	LAA	MLB	31	600	65	26	1	10	57	39	72	12	4	14.5%	.269/.323/.381	95	.293	0.5	SS 7	2.4

Comparables: Orlando Cabrera, Julio Franco, Ramon Martinez

The phrase "thirtysomething shortstop" is almost an oxymoron at this point. In 2020, two of the top 19 shortstops in baseball, according to WARP, were 30 years of age or older. In 2019, none cracked the top 20. Simmons' defense has been and remains his calling card, despite increasing noise about his efficacy where once the metrics sang in harmonious acclaim. In his first taste of free agency after a blueprint-making team-friendly contract, it's Simmons' offensive abilities that will give prospective suitors pause. After a few seasons in which it appeared he'd turned a corner from his slap-hitting youth, "Simba" has regressed at the plate, if not quite to the bug-eating extremity of his movie counterpart. Still excellent at making contact, Simmons will have to stop showing that talent off, especially on pitches out of the zone, if he wants to match his animated equivalent's triumphant third act.

Max Stassi C   Born: 03/15/91   Age: 30   Bats: R   Throws: R   Height: 5'10"   Weight: 200   Origin: Round 4, 2009 Draft (#123 overall)

YEAR	TEAM	LVL	AGE	PA	R	2B	3B	HR	RBI	BB	K	SB	CS	Whiff%	AVG/OBP/SLG	DRC+	BABIP	BRR	FRAA	WARP
2018	HOU	MLB	27	250	28	13	0	8	27	23	74	0	0	33.4%	.226/.316/.394	85	.302	-0.1	C(82): 14.5	2.3
2019	LAA	MLB	28	49	3	0	0	0	2	5	15	0	0	37.0%	.071/.163/.071	24	.103	0.0	C(20): 3.4	0.1
2019	HOU	MLB	28	98	4	1	0	1	3	7	34	0	0	32.9%	.167/.235/.211	60	.255	-1.3	C(26): 6.1, 1B(3): -0.0, P(1): -0.0	0.5
2020	LAA	MLB	29	105	12	2	0	7	20	11	21	0	0	26.5%	.278/.352/.533	117	.277	-0.5	C(31): 0.8	0.9
2021 FS	LAA	MLB	30	600	67	22	1	24	72	57	169	1	0	31.3%	.222/.309/.408	95	.276	-0.8	C 12, 1B 0	3.2
2021 DC	LAA	MLB	30	375	42	14	0	15	45	36	106	0	0	31.3%	.222/.309/.408	95	.276	-0.5	C 10	2.2

Comparables: Jason LaRue, Tim Laudner, John Russell

YEAR	TEAM	P. COUNT	FRM RUNS	BLK RUNS	THRW RUNS	TOT RUNS
2018	HOU	9684	13.9	0.1	-0.1	14.0
2019	HOU	3717	6.6	-0.2	-0.1	6.3
2019	LAA	2392	3.9	-0.5	-0.1	3.3
2020	LAA	4049	1.5	0.3	0.2	2.1
2021	LAA	13228	8.7	1.6	-0.6	9.7

Sometimes a headline tells you everything you need to know, like "Celebrity Chef's 'Paleo for Babies' Book on Hold Over Infant-Death Fears." In Stassi's case, the headline was "Historically Futile Batter More Than Doubled DRC+ Year-Over-Year." Sure, the prior figure was a 49, but an above-average batting line is a win for any catcher, especially one with Stassi's defensive prowess. There are reasons to expect the breakout at the plate was genuine: He posted marks well beyond career averages in strikeout rate, exit velocity, walk rate, and isolated slugging, plus all the traditional stats. It seems foolish to expect a recurrence, especially once pitchers realize that the jig is up; only six hitters with 100 plate appearances saw more pitches in the zone than Stassi. Not that he's terrible at easing off bad pitches, but more nibbling will require an adjustment. Still, the handling abilities make Stassi a capable backstop even if he regresses to average (for a catcher) at the plate.

Matt Thaiss 1B   Born: 05/06/95   Age: 26   Bats: L   Throws: R   Height: 6'0"   Weight: 215   Origin: Round 1, 2016 Draft (#16 overall)

YEAR	TEAM	LVL	AGE	PA	R	2B	3B	HR	RBI	BB	K	SB	CS	Whiff%	AVG/OBP/SLG	DRC+	BABIP	BRR	FRAA	WARP
2018	MOB	AA	23	176	24	10	2	6	25	16	35	2	1		.287/.352/.490	123	.331	-1.1	1B(36): 2.6	0.5
2018	SL	AAA	23	400	54	24	6	10	51	28	68	6	3		.277/.328/.457	94	.314	0.2	1B(77): 5.4	0.3
2019	SL	AAA	24	372	63	17	2	14	49	59	64	1	0		.274/.390/.477	108	.303	1.3	3B(47): -2.5, 1B(23): -1.4	1.2
2019	LAA	MLB	24	164	17	7	0	8	23	17	52	0	0	33.3%	.211/.293/.422	91	.264	-1.6	3B(43): -3.5, 1B(13): 0.5	-0.1
2020	LAA	MLB	25	25	3	0	0	1	1	4	8	0	0	32.1%	.143/.280/.286	87	.167	-0.3	1B(2): -0.2, 2B(1): 0.2, 3B(1): -0.0	0.0
2021 FS	LAA	MLB	26	600	71	24	3	20	65	61	158	0	0	33.1%	.235/.320/.407	98	.296	1.3	1B 3, 3B 0	1.3
2021 DC	LAA	MLB	26	68	8	2	0	2	7	7	17	0	0	33.1%	.235/.320/.407	98	.296	0.1	LF 0, 1B 0	0.2

Comparables: Ronald Guzmán, Ryan Garko, Chris Duncan

In eight 2020 games, Thaiss appeared twice at first base, twice at DH, once at second, once at third, once in left field, and once as a pinch runner. You could call it versatility, in the same sense that you could use Spam to make a hundred different meals, but you probably wouldn't want to. Like canned meat, Thaiss isn't particularly essential at any position or meal; but also like canned meat, he'll be around just about forever, in the back of the pantry, just in case.

Mike Trout CF   Born: 08/07/91   Age: 29   Bats: R   Throws: R   Height: 6'2"   Weight: 235   Origin: Round 1, 2009 Draft (#25 overall)

YEAR	TEAM	LVL	AGE	PA	R	2B	3B	HR	RBI	BB	K	SB	CS	Whiff%	AVG/OBP/SLG	DRC+	BABIP	BRR	FRAA	WARP
2018	LAA	MLB	26	608	101	24	4	39	79	122	124	24	2	18.7%	.312/.460/.628	183	.346	1.5	CF(125): -2.5	8.2
2019	LAA	MLB	27	600	110	27	2	45	104	110	120	11	2	19.1%	.291/.438/.645	176	.298	3.4	CF(122): 6.5	8.9
2020	LAA	MLB	29	241	41	9	2	17	46	35	56	1	1	19.5%	.281/.390/.603	150	.300	0.4	CF(52): -1.8	1.9
2021 FS	LAA	MLB	29	600	101	24	2	40	97	102	141	18	4	19.1%	.292/.427/.601	175	.336	6.1	CF -8	7.6
2021 DC	LAA	MLB	29	614	104	25	2	40	99	105	144	19	4	19.1%	.292/.427/.601	175	.336	6.2	CF -8	7.8

Comparables: Mickey Mantle, Eric Davis, Ken Griffey Jr.

Trout is supposed to be a protagonist. Someone of his talents, his evident greatness, has to be bored, uncomfortable with languishing. "How dull it is to pause," and all that. What's a six-year playoff drought but a lacuna, no invitation to the playoff ball a relegation to the sideline. Trout is Ulysses but Trout is Achilles, the most powerful and yet swift-footed, in particular the iteration from Shakespeare's *Troilus and Cressida*. There is no need for introduction, no proof of prowess necessary; he is his own archetype. He is sidelined from the narrative, if not nearly so loudly as *any* Shakespeare character, and though he'd never speak it the team's failure must chafe; Trout can scarce do more to propel the Angels forward but still, "No man is beaten voluntary." Friends with fortune he might be, but soon we will be talking about Trout outrunning time, whether absence from the playoff are enough to make his "deeds forgot." Like all players, Trout's heel is time, and it's well past for the Angels to stop wasting his.

Justin Upton LF Born: 08/25/87 Age: 33 Bats: R Throws: R Height: 6'1" Weight: 215 Origin: Round 1, 2005 Draft (#1 overall)

YEAR	TEAM	LVL	AGE	PA	R	2B	3B	HR	RBI	BB	K	SB	CS	Whiff%	AVG/OBP/SLG	DRC+	BABIP	BRR	FRAA	WARP
2018	LAA	MLB	30	613	80	18	1	30	85	64	176	8	2	31.4%	.257/.344/.463	116	.321	-1.6	LF(140): 17.0	4.4
2019	LAA	MLB	31	256	34	8	0	12	40	32	78	1	1	32.6%	.215/.309/.416	91	.261	0.5	LF(56): -3.1	0.1
2020	LAA	MLB	33	166	20	5	0	9	22	11	43	0	2	29.9%	.204/.289/.422	100	.219	-1.4	LF(39): 0.5	0.2
2021 FS	LAA	MLB	33	600	71	23	1	29	79	60	180	8	3	31.4%	.229/.317/.445	105	.286	-0.9	LF 12	3.2
2021 DC	LAA	MLB	33	546	65	21	1	27	72	54	163	7	2	31.4%	.229/.317/.445	105	.286	-0.8	LF 11	2.9

Comparables: Jonny Gomes, Dan Pasqua, Geoff Jenkins

It's hard to remember, with the perspective of the last two seasons, just how rosy things were looking for Upton after 2018. A season into a five-year extension, he had matched his usual All-Star-level output. The next year brought the most significant injury of Upton's career, a turf toe that cost him the majority of the season and never saw him work up to full strength. A consecutive curtailed season mired in mediocrity makes it hard to see more from the former phenom going forward, though the backloaded final two years of his contract will ensure he'll have numerous opportunities to rebound. The drop in walk rate is a concern, but it doesn't correlate with a major shift in his plate discipline profile, so it doesn't appear as if he's caught Pujolsitis. If you're looking for a reason to get invested in that bounceback, consider that Upton's 1,841 strikeouts already have him 17th all-time; the longer he receives full-time play the better the chances Upton can close the 756 strikeout cushion separating him from Mr. October.

Jared Walsh 1B Born: 07/30/93 Age: 27 Bats: L Throws: L Height: 6'0" Weight: 210 Origin: Round 39, 2015 Draft (#1185 overall)

YEAR	TEAM	LVL	AGE	PA	R	2B	3B	HR	RBI	BB	K	SB	CS	Whiff%	AVG/OBP/SLG	DRC+	BABIP	BRR	FRAA	WARP
2018	IE	HI-A	24	178	28	8	1	13	36	24	50	0	1		.275/.365/.604	167	.308	-0.6	1B(26): 0.3, RF(5): 0.7, P(2): -0.0	1.0
2018	MOB	AA	24	173	26	13	0	8	26	21	48	1	0		.289/.382/.537	128	.372	-0.8	1B(37): 2.0, P(2): -0.0	0.5
2018	SL	AAA	24	198	32	13	0	8	37	16	56	0	0		.270/.333/.478	114	.345	1.8	RF(27): -5.7, LF(14): -1.7, 1B(6): -0.2	-0.1
2019	SL	AAA	25	454	90	30	0	36	86	59	115	0	0		.325/.423/.686	145	.374	0.7	1B(58): 4.6, P(13): 0.5, RF(3): -0.0	3.6
2019	LAA	MLB	25	87	6	5	1	1	5	6	35	0	0	32.4%	.203/.276/.329	58	.349	-0.2	1B(24): 0.6, P(5): -0.0	-0.3
2020	LAA	MLB	27	108	19	4	2	9	26	5	15	0	0	22.8%	.293/.324/.646	121	.256	0.4	1B(29): -0.9, RF(2): -0.0	0.3
2021 FS	LAA	MLB	27	600	77	24	2	31	82	47	157	0	0	26.5%	.244/.312/.468	106	.286	0.1	1B 6, LF 0	2.1
2021 DC	LAA	MLB	27	512	65	21	1	26	70	40	134	0	0	26.5%	.244/.312/.468	106	.286	0.0	1B 5	1.7

Comparables: Mark Hamilton, Rhyne Hughes, Chris Carter

A nominal two-way player, Walsh's more arresting doubling in 2020 was that of his DRC+, raising the possibility that he will be the player to finally unseat Albert Pujols from a starting role. It's unclear whether the Angels still view the otherwise-1B-only slugger, who drew attention by homering six times (and tripling!) in a seven-game stretch in September, as a modern-day Brooks Kieschnick. After being called up at the tail end of August (and totaling 13 plate appearances to that point), Walsh batted 95 times in September, suggesting he'll have plenty of runway next year to continue to prove his offensive worth. Just don't expect a similar breakout pending on the mound—he still barely scrapes 90 with his four-seamer.

Taylor Ward OF Born: 12/14/93 Age: 27 Bats: R Throws: R Height: 6'1" Weight: 200 Origin: Round 1, 2015 Draft (#26 overall)

YEAR	TEAM	LVL	AGE	PA	R	2B	3B	HR	RBI	BB	K	SB	CS	Whiff%	AVG/OBP/SLG	DRC+	BABIP	BRR	FRAA	WARP
2018	MOB	AA	24	179	26	8	0	6	25	29	33	8	1		.345/.453/.520	186	.409	-1.6	3B(33): -2.8	1.4
2018	SL	AAA	24	267	42	18	0	8	35	36	61	10	2		.352/.442/.537	150	.450	-4.4	3B(53): -10.4	0.6
2018	LAA	MLB	24	147	14	3	0	6	15	9	45	2	0	23.6%	.178/.245/.333	76	.214	-2.4	3B(40): -2.3	-0.4
2019	SL	AAA	25	512	102	34	1	27	71	80	101	11	5		.306/.427/.584	139	.347	3.0	LF(74): 8.9, 3B(17): -0.6, 1B(6): -0.8	4.6
2019	LAA	MLB	25	48	4	3	0	1	2	6	23	0	0	41.5%	.190/.292/.333	59	.389	-0.2	LF(9): -0.4, 3B(4): -0.6	-0.2
2020	LAA	MLB	27	102	16	6	2	0	5	8	28	2	0	23.6%	.277/.333/.383	90	.394	0.8	RF(19): 0.1, LF(17): 0.5, 1B(2): 0.0	0.2
2021 FS	LAA	MLB	27	600	66	24	1	19	68	67	164	1	0	26.9%	.246/.337/.407	105	.321	-0.3	RF 1, LF 2	2.3
2021 DC	LAA	MLB	27	307	34	12	0	9	34	34	84	0	0	26.9%	.246/.337/.407	105	.321	-0.2	RF 0, LF 1	1.1

Comparables: Bobby Smith, Russ Davis, Freddy Garcia

Originally drafted as a catcher, Ward saw his bat blossom along with his switch to third base in 2018, and was major-league ready just in time to be blocked by the Angels' signing of Anthony Rendon. A ward without a home, the measure of versatility so many prospects have these days allowed him to nevertheless crack the team's Opening Day roster as a fourth outfielder. While the plate discipline was markedly improved over previous major-league stints, a 27.5 percent strikeout rate is only ever impressive in a relative sense, compared to 2019's mark of 47.9 percent. Without another step, the whispers of a Quad-A profile will linger, especially with Ward having failed to homer in 2020 after 27 in Triple-A the prior season. He should be allowed time at DH next year if nothing else, but as always, our lives balance on the whims of other people.

PITCHERS

Justin Anderson RHP Born: 09/28/92 Age: 28 Bats: L Throws: R Height: 6'3" Weight: 230 Origin: Round 14, 2014 Draft (#419 overall)

YEAR	TEAM	LVL	AGE	W	L	SV	G	GS	IP	H	HR	BB/9	K/9	K	GB%	BABIP	WHIP	ERA	DRA-	WARP	MPH	FA%	Whiff%	CSP
2018	SL	AAA	25	0	0	0	3	0	5	0	0	1.8	10.8	6	77.8%	.000	0.20	0.00	78	0.1				
2018	LAA	MLB	25	3	3	4	57	0	55¹	42	3	6.5	10.9	67	52.7%	.310	1.48	4.07	101	0.3	99.1	44.9%	37.2%	42.2%
2019	LAA	MLB	26	3	0	1	54	0	47	42	6	6.1	11.5	60	34.7%	.308	1.57	5.55	99	0.3	96.0	47.1%	28.0%	42.2%
2021 FS	LAA	MLB	28	2	3	0	57	0	50	42	7	5.5	10.2	56	42.3%	.281	1.45	4.42	100	0.1	97.1	46.3%	31.4%	42.2%

Comparables: Kyle Crick, Sam Tuivailala, Dovydas Neverauskas

Speaking about his feelings about undergoing Tommy John surgery—after an injury on his first pitch in an intrasquad game—Anderson said, "It's an issue you think won't ever happen." He must have been watching a different Angels squad the past half-decade. Having surgery in July means it's tenuous to expect Anderson to appear in 2021.

Luke Bard RHP Born: 11/13/90 Age: 30 Bats: R Throws: R Height: 6'3" Weight: 200 Origin: Round 1, 2012 Draft (#42 overall)

YEAR	TEAM	LVL	AGE	W	L	SV	G	GS	IP	H	HR	BB/9	K/9	K	GB%	BABIP	WHIP	ERA	DRA-	WARP	MPH	FA%	Whiff%	CSP
2018	ROC	AAA	27	3	3	1	32	0	48¹	54	6	3.4	9.7	52	34.8%	.358	1.49	4.66	87	0.4				
2018	LAA	MLB	27	0	0	0	8	0	11²	10	4	3.9	10.0	13	31.2%	.214	1.29	5.40	152	-0.3	93.9	55.4%	20.6%	46.1%
2019	SL	AAA	28	2	4	1	16	1	19	28	4	4.7	12.3	26	31.6%	.453	2.00	7.11	139	-0.1				
2019	LAA	MLB	28	3	3	0	32	3	49	41	8	2.4	7.3	40	36.9%	.248	1.10	4.78	98	0.3	96.0	44.1%	28.7%	47.0%
2020	LAA	MLB	29	0	0	0	6	0	5¹	7	2	0.0	11.8	7	18.8%	.357	1.31	6.75	100	0.0	95.8	45.6%	33.3%	47.9%
2021 FS	LAA	MLB	30	2	2	0	57	0	50	47	9	3.2	9.3	51	34.3%	.289	1.31	4.57	103	0.0	95.8	45.5%	28.4%	47.0%
2021 DC	LAA	MLB	30	2	2	0	46	0	48	45	9	3.2	9.3	49	34.3%	.289	1.31	4.57	103	0.2	95.8	45.5%	28.4%	47.0%

Comparables: Nick Wittgren, Shawn Armstrong, Mike Morin

If this Bard is Shakespeare, he's one of the lesser-known works—nothing objectionable, or tragic, certainly, just nothing you'd be likely to see at the theater (when that was still a thing). It feels cruel, in this context, to choose *Comedy of Errors*, but few managers have likely felt, with Bard on the mound, *All's Well That Ends Well*.

Jaime Barria RHP Born: 07/18/96 Age: 24 Bats: R Throws: R Height: 6'1" Weight: 210 Origin: International Free Agent, 2013

YEAR	TEAM	LVL	AGE	W	L	SV	G	GS	IP	H	HR	BB/9	K/9	K	GB%	BABIP	WHIP	ERA	DRA-	WARP	MPH	FA%	Whiff%	CSP
2018	SL	AAA	21	0	0	0	5	5	18	20	2	2.5	9.5	19	28.3%	.353	1.39	3.50	98	0.2				
2018	LAA	MLB	21	10	9	0	27	27	134¹	121	17	3.3	6.8	101	37.0%	.272	1.27	3.35	126	-0.5	92.8	49.6%	24.5%	45.0%
2019	SL	AAA	22	3	3	0	10	10	48¹	73	16	1.9	8.2	44	26.3%	.368	1.72	9.68	149	-0.3				
2019	LAA	MLB	22	4	10	0	19	13	82²	92	24	2.9	8.2	75	35.2%	.287	1.44	6.42	158	-1.9	93.2	36.9%	22.2%	47.3%
2020	LAA	MLB	23	1	0	0	7	5	32¹	27	3	2.5	7.5	27	33.7%	.261	1.11	3.62	100	0.3	93.8	43.1%	23.1%	50.1%
2021 FS	LAA	MLB	24	8	9	0	26	26	150	150	31	3.3	7.8	130	33.7%	.282	1.37	4.97	110	0.2	93.2	42.4%	23.2%	47.2%
2021 DC	LAA	MLB	24	6	7	0	36	19	111	111	22	3.3	7.8	96	33.7%	.282	1.37	4.97	110	0.5	93.2	42.4%	23.2%	47.2%

Comparables: Jordan Lyles, Lucas Giolito, José Berríos

Barria's 2020 presents a solid argument for those who favor K% to K/9 as an indicator of a pitcher's out-getting prowess. While his K/9 dropped precipitously, Barria's strikeout rate remained level at 20.5 percent; mediocre, but not a reason for concern. If Barria gets to that place in general, it'll be a win after his first two big-league seasons implied he might not be cut out for MLB. His slider is the key; his primary pitch, he managed to avoid throwing it down the middle in 2020, and it showed. The strikeouts per nine vanished simply because Barria wasn't consistently getting into and then working out of jams. He walked fewer batters and allowed fewer baserunners generally, and while we're looking at percentages, he cut his home run rate, season-over-season, a hilarious 65 percent. It amounted to a profile only slightly better than league average, but both pitcher and team will accept that with grace.

Cam Bedrosian RHP Born: 10/02/91 Age: 29 Bats: R Throws: R Height: 6'1" Weight: 225 Origin: Round 1, 2010 Draft (#29 overall)

YEAR	TEAM	LVL	AGE	W	L	SV	G	GS	IP	H	HR	BB/9	K/9	K	GB%	BABIP	WHIP	ERA	DRA-	WARP	MPH	FA%	Whiff%	CSP
2018	LAA	MLB	26	5	4	1	71	0	64	63	7	3.7	8.0	57	48.1%	.316	1.39	3.80	93	0.5	95.1	55.5%	22.0%	48.0%
2019	LAA	MLB	27	3	3	1	59	7	61¹	48	7	3.2	9.4	64	48.5%	.253	1.14	3.23	71	1.3	94.5	47.8%	30.3%	45.8%
2020	LAA	MLB	28	0	0	0	11	0	14²	10	0	3.7	6.8	11	31.7%	.244	1.09	2.45	112	0.0	93.9	52.7%	22.9%	47.8%
2021 FS	LAA	MLB	29	2	2	0	57	0	50	46	8	3.7	9.2	51	42.8%	.285	1.33	4.19	98	0.2	94.5	50.9%	26.6%	46.8%

Comparables: Arodys Vizcaíno, Dominic Leone, Jorge Julio

Much as a first-round flamethrower ending up in the bullpen will always spell disappointment to some, "Bedrock" nevertheless lived up to the sobriquet in his seven-year career with the Angels—apparently at an end after the team outrighted him in October. Though never consistent enough to decisively move to the *above-* half of average, even as he bled velocity, the major league scion was an integral, steadying presence to an Angels bullpen getting repackaged more often than the Nintendo 3DS. The penny-pinching financial landscape magnified what might be either short-season strangeness or declining stuff—MLB has room yet for relievers striking out 6.8 batters per nine, but maybe not of Bedrosian's ilk. If there's any comfort to be had, it's that his head start out the door of the Angels' bullpen was a short one, given that the rest got non-tendered in a fit of planned obsolescence less than two months later.

Dylan Bundy RHP Born: 11/15/92 Age: 28 Bats: S Throws: R Height: 6'1" Weight: 225 Origin: Round 1, 2011 Draft (#4 overall)

YEAR	TEAM	LVL	AGE	W	L	SV	G	GS	IP	H	HR	BB/9	K/9	K	GB%	BABIP	WHIP	ERA	DRA-	WARP	MPH	FA%	Whiff%	CSP
2018	BAL	MLB	25	8	16	0	31	31	171²	188	41	2.8	9.6	184	33.6%	.318	1.41	5.45	119	-0.1	93.5	55.8%	26.9%	50.1%
2019	BAL	MLB	26	7	14	0	30	30	161²	161	29	3.2	9.0	162	41.1%	.297	1.35	4.79	100	1.6	93.0	50.0%	28.2%	46.8%
2020	LAA	MLB	27	6	3	0	11	11	65²	51	5	2.3	9.9	72	41.0%	.274	1.04	3.29	78	1.4	92.2	41.9%	29.5%	50.2%
2021 FS	LAA	MLB	28	9	8	0	26	26	150	130	23	3.0	9.6	159	39.9%	.278	1.21	3.71	86	2.2	92.9	49.3%	28.2%	48.5%
2021 DC	LAA	MLB	28	11	8	0	29	29	172	149	26	3.0	9.6	182	39.9%	.278	1.21	3.71	86	3.0	92.9	49.3%	28.2%	48.5%

Comparables: Jakob Junis, Vince Velasquez, Jon Gray

A new piece of conventional wisdom has taken root in the last few years: If a pitch is bad, the pitcher should stop using it. No, really, that's what has taken teams, pitchers, and the epherma of coaches, trainers, and advisors guiding players more than a century to nail down. Bundy has seen his four-seam fastball velocity dip nearly five ticks since its 2016 peak (not that Bundy was especially effective with heat). So, between 2018 and 2020, Bundy cut his four-seam usage from 48 to 34 percent, remaking himself a junkballer—just one who still strikes batter out. Completing the transformation meant

Bundy finally delivered on that fourth-overall pick promise, nearly posting his best season by value in a third of a season. No one can keep ahead of declining velocity forever, unless Bundy is going to be the first pitcher of the 21st century to improve when their fastball velocity dips into the 80s. Which is not to say it's impossible; the man already survived the Orioles pitching development system.

Ty Buttrey RHP Born: 03/31/93 Age: 28 Bats: L Throws: R Height: 6'6" Weight: 240 Origin: Round 4, 2012 Draft (#151 overall)

YEAR	TEAM	LVL	AGE	W	L	SV	G	GS	IP	H	HR	BB/9	K/9	K	GB%	BABIP	WHIP	ERA	DRA-	WARP	MPH	FA%	Whiff%	CSP
2018	WOR	AAA	25	1	1	1	32	0	44	36	4	2.9	13.1	64	45.2%	.320	1.14	2.25	58	1.1				
2018	LAA	MLB	25	0	1	4	16	0	16¹	15	0	2.8	11.0	20	55.6%	.341	1.22	3.31	64	0.4	98.3	58.0%	30.1%	47.3%
2019	LAA	MLB	26	6	7	2	72	0	72¹	69	8	2.9	10.5	84	44.7%	.323	1.27	3.98	72	1.4	98.8	57.2%	27.2%	49.9%
2020	LAA	MLB	27	2	3	5	27	0	26¹	28	4	3.1	6.2	18	47.6%	.304	1.41	5.81	102	0.2	97.9	58.2%	20.0%	45.6%
2021 FS	LAA	MLB	28	2	2	4	57	0	50	45	6	3.8	9.3	51	45.8%	.290	1.33	4.10	93	0.3	98.5	57.5%	25.1%	48.3%
2021 DC	LAA	MLB	28	2	2	4	57	0	61	55	8	3.8	9.3	62	45.8%	.290	1.33	4.10	93	0.6	98.5	57.5%	25.1%	48.3%

Comparables: Jordan Walden, Dovydas Neverauskas, Michael Feliz

By the 2019 All-Star Break, Buttrey seemed to have cemented himself in the Angels' bullpen: Through his first 58 1/3 career innings, he posted a 2.78 ERA with 70 strikeouts. In 56 2/3 innings since, with a 5.78 ERA and 52 punchouts, Buttrey has torched his reputation worse than the final episode of *Dexter*. The reliever's malady is hard to diagnose; you don't double your ERA going from 98-and-a-slider to 97-and-a-slider. His fastball lost some of its drop, and hitters squared up on it, driving up his contact rate nearly 10 percent across the board. It wouldn't be the first time something got predictable in later seasons. Like Showtime's first hit show, though, the promise of a legitimate star reliever will keep the Angels trusting Buttrey as long as they can justify, maybe beyond. Some allusion to a return to form, though, will swiftly become necessary if the Angels ever start needing relievers for games that matter. No one wants to be remembered only for an irredeemable finale.

Griffin Canning RHP Born: 05/11/96 Age: 25 Bats: R Throws: R Height: 6'2" Weight: 180 Origin: Round 2, 2017 Draft (#47 overall)

YEAR	TEAM	LVL	AGE	W	L	SV	G	GS	IP	H	HR	BB/9	K/9	K	GB%	BABIP	WHIP	ERA	DRA-	WARP	MPH	FA%	Whiff%	CSP
2018	IE	HI-A	22	0	0	0	2	2	8²	4	0	3.1	12.5	12	50.0%	.222	0.81	0.00	16	0.5				
2018	MOB	AA	22	1	0	0	10	10	45²	27	2	3.7	9.7	49	45.9%	.229	1.01	1.97	81	0.8				
2018	SL	AAA	22	3	3	0	13	13	59	68	6	3.4	9.8	64	40.9%	.378	1.53	5.49	83	1.1				
2019	SL	AAA	23	1	0	0	3	3	16	13	0	1.1	9.6	17	39.0%	.317	0.94	0.56	42	0.7				
2019	LAA	MLB	23	5	6	0	18	17	90¹	80	14	3.0	9.6	96	36.8%	.281	1.22	4.58	92	1.2	95.5	42.1%	32.3%	45.0%
2020	LAA	MLB	24	2	3	0	11	11	56¹	54	8	3.7	8.9	56	36.1%	.307	1.37	3.99	102	0.4	94.2	40.5%	27.3%	42.9%
2021 FS	LAA	MLB	25	9	9	0	26	26	150	136	24	3.9	9.3	155	37.8%	.284	1.35	4.40	99	1.1	94.9	41.3%	29.9%	44.0%
2021 DC	LAA	MLB	25	8	8	0	25	25	132	119	21	3.9	9.3	136	37.8%	.284	1.35	4.40	99	1.4	94.9	41.3%	29.9%	44.0%

Comparables: Zac Gallen, Mitch Keller, Zack Wheeler

Canning can't claim canny command, can't uncan 98 mph heaters like seemingly most of the league these days, saw his UCL cankered by damage that ultimately didn't derail his canter of a season. He probably won't be canonized into the brief set of Angels aces anytime soon, instead settling in his second season into more of an average, end-rotation arm. He caught enough can-of-corns to win his first Gold Glove, at least. Canvassing for a pitcher to use their fastball less isn't exactly revolutionary these days, but Canning has a decent cantrip in his curveball and could stand to cannibalize his fastball usage further. Canceling the Tommy John surgery might mean this year's step back is the new normal, but candidly, the Angels would be perfectly canty with their farm system producing any reliable starter.

Alex Claudio LHP Born: 01/31/92 Age: 29 Bats: L Throws: L Height: 6'3" Weight: 188 Origin: Round 27, 2010 Draft (#826 overall)

YEAR	TEAM	LVL	AGE	W	L	SV	G	GS	IP	H	HR	BB/9	K/9	K	GB%	BABIP	WHIP	ERA	DRA-	WARP	MPH	FA%	Whiff%	CSP
2018	TEX	MLB	26	4	2	1	66	1	68¹	91	4	1.7	5.4	41	62.0%	.370	1.52	4.48	104	0.2	87.6	52.0%	24.7%	45.1%
2019	MIL	MLB	27	2	2	0	83	0	62	57	8	3.5	6.4	44	56.0%	.268	1.31	4.06	101	0.3	87.4	46.2%	24.7%	41.2%
2020	MIL	MLB	28	0	0	1	20	0	19	18	2	2.8	7.1	15	45.8%	.281	1.26	4.26	98	0.2	87.2	39.3%	26.0%	41.6%
2021 FS	LAA	MLB	29	2	2	0	57	0	50	49	5	2.6	7.3	40	54.9%	.295	1.28	3.92	91	0.4	87.4	46.0%	25.0%	42.3%
2021 DC	LAA	MLB	29	2	2	0	57	0	61	60	6	2.6	7.3	49	54.9%	.295	1.28	3.92	91	0.6	87.4	46.0%	25.0%	42.3%

Comparables: Cam Bedrosian, Dominic Leone, Michael Lorenzen

Alex Claudio wouldn't have gotten this far if he couldn't surprisingly invent stuff that works from time to time, but it's hard to see how he survives for long in a three-batter-minimum league.

───────── ★ ★ ★ *2021 Top 101 Prospect* **#86** ★ ★ ★ ─────────

Reid Detmers LHP Born: 07/08/99 Age: 21 Bats: L Throws: L Height: 6'2" Weight: 210 Origin: Round 1, 2020 Draft (#10 overall)

The Angels' first pitcher selected in the first round since 2014, Detmers immediately moved into their top echelon of prospects and fills in the "name like a senator from a Southern state who you always forget" hole in the system. He's also a dearly-needed arm, and a lefty at that. With "polish" atop every scouting report, a strong performance at the alternate site created some buzz that Detmers was ready for his debut last year. While the velocity merely spans the low 90s, a relatively complete four-pitch mix never had trouble eliciting punchouts at Louisville, especially as he tinkered with a new grip on an old slider that gave the pitch some healthy bite. It's the oversized curveball that marks the arsenal, however, a pitch that demands attention from the batter and speeds up his harder pitches. An aggressive assignment is likely given the Angels' perennial need of starters, so that role, like his slider, is just a matter of the quality of his grip.

Andrew Heaney LHP   Born: 06/05/91   Age: 30   Bats: L   Throws: L   Height: 6'2"   Weight: 200   Origin: Round 1, 2012 Draft (#9 overall)

YEAR	TEAM	LVL	AGE	W	L	SV	G	GS	IP	H	HR	BB/9	K/9	K	GB%	BABIP	WHIP	ERA	DRA-	WARP	MPH	FA%	Whiff%	CSP
2018	IE	HI-A	27	1	0	0	1	1	6¹	2	0	1.4	8.5	6	73.3%	.133	0.47	1.42	70	0.1				
2018	LAA	MLB	27	9	10	0	31	31	185	179	29	2.2	9.0	184	41.9%	.299	1.22	4.14	81	3.5	94.3	58.1%	26.5%	50.8%
2019	LAA	MLB	28	4	6	0	18	18	95¹	93	20	2.8	11.1	118	32.7%	.312	1.29	4.91	108	0.5	94.3	58.0%	31.3%	49.6%
2020	LAA	MLB	29	4	3	0	12	12	66²	63	9	2.6	9.4	70	38.3%	.302	1.23	4.46	89	1.0	93.4	58.0%	28.0%	50.9%
2021 FS	LAA	MLB	30	9	8	0	26	26	150	139	27	2.7	10.1	167	37.8%	.293	1.23	4.11	95	1.5	94.0	58.0%	28.7%	50.4%
2021 DC	LAA	MLB	30	9	8	0	25	25	145	135	26	2.7	10.1	162	37.8%	.293	1.23	4.11	95	1.9	94.0	58.0%	28.7%	50.4%

Comparables: Nick Tropeano, Kevin Gausman, Alex Wood

Heaney has a career like a sine wave: He's always up and down, never stretching the amplitude quite so far. He reached an upper bound not so far back, and if down was the only way to go from there, it's not his fault. It's just how the equation, written into the DNA of his arm, was written. His velocity waned, even as his groundball rate pulled out of its own nadir; his contact rate spiked, even while he got ahead in the count at new levels of success. It might not add up to the most interesting problem, but then math has always bored some. Still, coming up on his walk year, Heaney continues to intrigue for the same reason math's ability to predict intoxicates: If you know the function, you can predict where the curve is going next. Crucially, though, you have to get the math right, because Heaney's next step, free agency, will check your work.

Aaron Hernandez RHP   Born: 12/02/96   Age: 24   Bats: R   Throws: R   Height: 6'1"   Weight: 170   Origin: Round 3, 2018 Draft (#93 overall)

YEAR	TEAM	LVL	AGE	W	L	SV	G	GS	IP	H	HR	BB/9	K/9	K	GB%	BABIP	WHIP	ERA	DRA-	WARP	MPH	FA%	Whiff%	CSP
2019	IE	HI-A	22	1	4	0	20	15	72²	75	6	5.7	10.0	81	38.6%	.354	1.67	4.46	124	-1.0				
2021 FS	LAA	MLB	24	2	3	0	57	0	50	49	8	6.7	8.4	46	37.0%	.294	1.73	6.02	134	-0.8				

Comparables: Randy Rosario, Daniel Moskos, Justin Dunn

One of those starting pitching prospects widely expected to eventually transition to relief—inconsistent, sometimes marginal velocity; spotty track record of turns through a rotation; lots of walks—Hernandez's 2020 might have been offered a ruling had he been able to take the mound. Now, the lack of clarity on his future remains, with the added complication of a path that will be chosen for him *in absentia*.

Raisel Iglesias RHP   Born: 01/04/90   Age: 31   Bats: R   Throws: R   Height: 6'2"   Weight: 190   Origin: International Free Agent, 2014

YEAR	TEAM	LVL	AGE	W	L	SV	G	GS	IP	H	HR	BB/9	K/9	K	GB%	BABIP	WHIP	ERA	DRA-	WARP	MPH	FA%	Whiff%	CSP
2018	CIN	MLB	28	2	5	30	66	0	72	52	12	3.1	10.0	80	38.6%	.234	1.07	2.38	77	1.2	97.8	50.1%	34.0%	47.9%
2019	CIN	MLB	29	3	12	34	68	0	67	61	12	2.8	12.0	89	29.9%	.318	1.22	4.16	78	1.1	97.7	47.8%	33.8%	45.8%
2020	CIN	MLB	30	4	3	8	22	0	23	16	1	2.0	12.1	31	38.9%	.288	0.91	2.74	75	0.5	98.1	46.3%	39.0%	48.9%
2021 FS	LAA	MLB	31	3	2	32	57	0	50	40	6	3.2	11.1	61	37.9%	.282	1.15	3.18	75	0.8	97.8	48.0%	35.1%	47.1%
2021 DC	LAA	MLB	31	3	2	32	57	0	61	48	8	3.2	11.1	75	37.9%	.282	1.15	3.18	75	1.1	97.8	48.0%	35.1%	47.1%

Comparables: Mychal Givens, Kelvin Herrera, Jacob Barnes

Some restaurants have a signature dish that is widely known, and when you eat there you're certain it will be the best thing on the menu. At other places there are dishes you know are very, very good and rarely disappoint, but you can't help wondering if you should order something else to see if it's better. Pasta Raisel at GAB has often felt more like the latter than the former. Since moving to the bullpen during the 2016 season the lightning-armed Cuban has often been very good, but has never been quite the consistently dominant force his stuff portends. Iglesias bounced back from a subpar 2019 to post the best walk and whiff rates of his career and was only taken deep once after allowing 12 dingers in each of the previous two seasons. That last part isn't sustainable while pitching in the Cincinnati launching pad, so it's less likely Iglesias found another gear last year than there were just fewer games for his inevitable clunkers to find him. Maybe he won't need it in Anaheim.

Mike Mayers RHP   Born: 12/06/91   Age: 29   Bats: R   Throws: R   Height: 6'2"   Weight: 220   Origin: Round 3, 2013 Draft (#93 overall)

YEAR	TEAM	LVL	AGE	W	L	SV	G	GS	IP	H	HR	BB/9	K/9	K	GB%	BABIP	WHIP	ERA	DRA-	WARP	MPH	FA%	Whiff%	CSP
2018	MEM	AAA	26	0	0	3	5	0	7²	5	0	4.7	9.4	8	47.6%	.263	1.17	0.00	73	0.1				
2018	STL	MLB	26	2	1	1	50	0	51²	59	7	2.6	8.5	49	41.6%	.344	1.43	4.70	90	0.5	98.4	60.4%	23.2%	48.4%
2019	MEM	AAA	27	0	1	6	20	1	20	21	4	3.1	10.3	23	52.7%	.327	1.40	3.15	86	0.4				
2019	STL	MLB	27	0	1	0	16	0	19	21	3	5.2	7.6	16	21.7%	.316	1.68	6.63	164	-0.5	96.9	53.2%	29.1%	44.1%
2020	LAA	MLB	28	2	0	2	29	0	30	18	2	2.7	12.9	43	32.4%	.242	0.90	2.10	74	0.7	95.9	57.8%	35.7%	45.1%
2021 FS	LAA	MLB	29	2	2	4	57	0	50	43	7	3.1	10.0	55	37.2%	.281	1.21	3.76	88	0.5	96.8	57.6%	30.6%	45.8%
2021 DC	LAA	MLB	29	2	2	4	57	0	61	52	9	3.1	10.0	68	37.2%	.281	1.21	3.76	88	0.8	96.8	57.6%	30.6%	45.8%

Comparables: Drew VerHagen, Austin Brice, Casey Sadler

Following a 2019 so dreadful it got him booted out of St. Louis, Mayers bucked the trend and made 2020 his year. He added a new cutter, cribbed from an Instagram post of Mariano Rivera tracing his grip on a baseball for Roy Halladay, and by the end of the season was basically the only reliever Joe Maddon could rely upon. There was a second change, presumably spurred by a MySpace message we didn't hear about: Mayers made his slider his most-used pitch, making both of his fastballs less predictable. The reinvention elicited the best strikeout rate of Mayers' career that, unrealistically low ERA or not, cements him as the Angels' most trusted in-house relief option. Only four other pitchers reached 30 innings last year without a single start.

Hoby Milner LHP Born: 01/13/91 Age: 30 Bats: L Throws: L Height: 6'3" Weight: 175 Origin: Round 7, 2012 Draft (#248 overall)

YEAR	TEAM	LVL	AGE	W	L	SV	G	GS	IP	H	HR	BB/9	K/9	K	GB%	BABIP	WHIP	ERA	DRA-	WARP	MPH	FA%	Whiff%	CSP
2018	LHV	AAA	27	0	0	0	25	0	26¹	21	2	4.8	9.6	28	44.1%	.288	1.33	2.39	84	0.3				
2018	DUR	AAA	27	1	0	2	15	1	14¹	14	1	1.9	13.2	21	40.0%	.394	1.19	3.77	73	0.2				
2018	PHI	MLB	27	0	0	0	10	0	4²	6	1	5.8	7.7	4	41.2%	.312	1.93	7.71	187	-0.2	91.3	69.8%	10.8%	45.3%
2018	TB	MLB	27	0	0	0	4	0	2²	3	2	6.8	13.5	4	14.3%	.200	1.88	6.75	214	-0.1	90.4	62.5%	26.9%	49.3%
2019	DUR	AAA	28	3	3	12	50	0	61²	47	7	1.9	13.0	89	43.2%	.305	0.97	3.06	38	2.6				
2019	TB	MLB	28	0	0	0	4	0	3²	4	0	2.5	7.4	3	25.0%	.333	1.36	7.36	109	0.0	89.1	68.6%	14.3%	52.7%
2020	LAA	MLB	29	0	0	0	19	0	13¹	13	5	4.0	8.8	13	38.5%	.235	1.43	8.10	106	0.1	89.2	53.8%	19.8%	49.4%
2021 FS	LAA	MLB	30	2	2	0	57	0	50	43	7	2.9	9.8	54	39.4%	.286	1.19	3.52	86	0.5	89.4	57.7%	18.7%	49.5%

Comparables: Nick Wittgren, Tyler Webb, Ryan Weber

A nominal LOOGy, you'd hope Milner was better against sinistral batters than a .678 career OPS allowed. Sure, that's .067 points better than the league average since Milner's 2017 debut, but also smaller than the margin between league average and Milner's OPS against all batters. Much like his initials, it's enough to make you go hm.

Packy Naughton LHP Born: 04/16/96 Age: 25 Bats: R Throws: L Height: 6'2" Weight: 195 Origin: Round 9, 2017 Draft (#257 overall)

YEAR	TEAM	LVL	AGE	W	L	SV	G	GS	IP	H	HR	BB/9	K/9	K	GB%	BABIP	WHIP	ERA	DRA-	WARP	MPH	FA%	Whiff%	CSP
2018	DAY	LO-A	22	5	10	0	28	28	154	168	12	2.0	8.0	137	38.3%	.344	1.31	4.03	99	1.1				
2019	DAY	HI-A	23	5	2	0	9	9	51¹	49	2	1.6	8.8	50	43.6%	.320	1.13	2.63	86	0.5				
2019	CHA	AA	23	6	10	0	19	19	105²	109	8	2.2	6.9	81	39.1%	.309	1.28	3.66	100	0.1				
2021 FS	LAA	MLB	25	1	2	0	57	0	50	50	8	3.2	7.2	39	37.8%	.289	1.38	4.63	110	-0.2				
2021 DC	LAA	MLB	25	1	2	0	6	6	28	28	4	3.2	7.2	22	37.8%	.289	1.38	4.63	110	0.1				

Comparables: Nick Margevicius, Josh Fleming, Yohander Méndez

With a name like a Flannery O'Connor character and a fifth-starter ceiling, Naughton came to town along with PTBNL Jose Salvador in the deadline deal that sent Brian Goodwin to the Reds. The outfielder was non-tendered by Cincinnati just months later and Naughton was left unprotected ahead of the Rule 5 deadline, reminding everyone that, much like an O'Connor story, sometimes nobody wins.

Oliver Ortega RHP Born: 10/02/96 Age: 24 Bats: R Throws: R Height: 6'0" Weight: 165 Origin: International Free Agent, 2015

YEAR	TEAM	LVL	AGE	W	L	SV	G	GS	IP	H	HR	BB/9	K/9	K	GB%	BABIP	WHIP	ERA	DRA-	WARP	MPH	FA%	Whiff%	CSP
2018	BUR	LO-A	21	4	5	0	19	18	82	64	6	4.5	9.4	86	32.7%	.276	1.28	3.51	98	0.6				
2019	IE	HI-A	22	4	5	2	21	16	94¹	67	8	4.7	11.5	121	43.9%	.277	1.23	3.34	70	1.7				
2019	MOB	AA	22	0	3	0	5	5	16²	23	0	4.3	7.6	14	50.8%	.390	1.86	8.64	138	-0.4				
2021 FS	LAA	MLB	24	2	3	0	57	0	50	46	8	5.7	8.8	48	43.7%	.283	1.57	5.23	116	-0.3				
2021 DC	LAA	MLB	24	0	0	0	11	0	12	11	1	5.7	8.8	11	43.7%	.283	1.57	5.23	116	0.0				

Comparables: Beau Burrows, Albert Abreu, Jarlin García

Mid-90s velocity that can get up to 99; a 12-to-6 curveball that combines with the heat to get healthy strikeout totals; an inconsistent delivery that results in equally healthy walk rates; a third pitch that isn't really, yet—if you're reading all that and mentally slotting Ortega into the Angels bullpen of 2022, the only rebuttal would be that the Angels *really* need to develop a starting pitcher with some upside. Perhaps a wandering hermit will happen by Salt Lake and pass on, via oral tradition, the ancient lost secrets of the changeup.

Felix Peña RHP Born: 02/25/90 Age: 31 Bats: R Throws: R Height: 6'2" Weight: 220 Origin: International Free Agent, 2009

YEAR	TEAM	LVL	AGE	W	L	SV	G	GS	IP	H	HR	BB/9	K/9	K	GB%	BABIP	WHIP	ERA	DRA-	WARP	MPH	FA%	Whiff%	CSP
2018	SL	AAA	28	1	2	0	10	9	33¹	30	2	4.3	10.3	38	38.6%	.346	1.38	3.51	85	0.6				
2018	LAA	MLB	28	3	5	0	19	17	92²	87	12	2.7	8.3	85	43.0%	.290	1.24	4.18	92	1.2	94.2	57.9%	26.0%	46.1%
2019	LAA	MLB	29	8	3	0	22	7	96¹	80	16	3.2	9.4	101	44.0%	.256	1.18	4.58	84	1.4	93.6	49.2%	29.4%	46.3%
2020	LAA	MLB	30	3	0	2	25	0	26²	27	2	2.7	9.8	29	50.6%	.333	1.31	4.05	72	0.6	96.0	48.5%	27.8%	47.7%
2021 FS	LAA	MLB	31	2	2	0	57	0	50	45	7	3.8	9.6	53	43.5%	.289	1.33	4.31	97	0.2	94.3	51.1%	28.2%	46.6%
2021 DC	LAA	MLB	31	2	2	0	57	0	61	55	9	3.8	9.6	65	43.5%	.289	1.33	4.31	97	0.4	94.3	51.1%	28.2%	46.6%

Comparables: Jacob Barnes, Joe Biagini, Paul Sewald

Even allowing for the "combined" qualifier, the list of starting pitchers involved in a no-hitter is a short one. The list of starting pitchers unceremoniously kicked to the bullpen the next season can't go too far beyond finger counting. In Peña's case, there was the extenuating circumstance of a torn ACL ending his 2019, with the ultimate result that he was never quite able to complete the build-up to the attenuated season. Having fallen behind, he's likely entrenched in the bullpen now barring numerous injuries in the Angels' rotation, but the culprit is less underperformance than how much the onetime marginal starter/swingman thrived in a traditional relief role. The velocity was back after a drop (preceding the injury), but the most encouraging note was a home run rate half of his major-league average. It's unlikely there's another turn towards the rotation in Peña's future, but much as combined no-hitter is sweet regardless of the modifier, a dominant relief pitcher (provided he can continue to control fly balls) is a great outcome regardless of how many times it comes via the "converted starter" route.

José Quijada   LHP   Born: 11/09/95   Age: 25   Bats: L   Throws: L   Height: 5'11"   Weight: 215   Origin: International Free Agent, 2013

YEAR	TEAM	LVL	AGE	W	L	SV	G	GS	IP	H	HR	BB/9	K/9	K	GB%	BABIP	WHIP	ERA	DRA-	WARP	MPH	FA%	Whiff%	CSP
2018	JAX	AA	22	0	2	4	17	0	22¹	13	1	2.8	11.7	29	31.2%	.255	0.90	2.42	72	0.4				
2018	NO	AAA	22	2	4	3	27	0	40²	24	2	4.9	11.5	52	32.3%	.250	1.13	3.32	67	0.9				
2019	NO	AAA	23	1	0	4	22	0	29¹	27	5	3.7	10.7	35	33.8%	.293	1.33	4.30	83	0.6				
2019	MIA	MLB	23	2	3	1	34	0	29²	27	10	7.9	13.3	44	32.9%	.288	1.79	5.76	104	0.1	95.6	71.7%	34.3%	45.0%
2020	LAA	MLB	24	0	1	0	6	0	3²	6	1	4.9	14.7	6	36.4%	.500	2.18	7.36	71	0.1	94.7	68.5%	33.3%	49.2%
2021 FS	LAA	MLB	25	2	2	0	57	0	50	42	8	4.8	10.6	59	34.2%	.279	1.38	4.51	98	0.2	95.4	71.2%	34.1%	45.7%
2021 DC	LAA	MLB	25	2	2	0	46	0	48	40	8	4.8	10.6	56	34.2%	.279	1.38	4.51	98	0.3	95.4	71.2%	34.1%	45.7%

Comparables: Tanner Scott, Richard Lovelady, Jake Newberry

Picked up on waivers in February, Quijada managed to spend the entire season on the 40-man while only pitching 3⅓ innings, in which he looked roughly the same as in his debut season (not a compliment). The Angels clearly see something worth keeping around, but "not good enough to crack the 2020 Angels bullpen" is the headliner and the punchline, all in one.

Chris Rodriguez   RHP   Born: 07/20/98   Age: 22   Bats: R   Throws: R   Height: 6'2"   Weight: 185

YEAR	TEAM	LVL	AGE	W	L	SV	G	GS	IP	H	HR	BB/9	K/9	K	GB%	BABIP	WHIP	ERA	DRA-	WARP	MPH	FA%	Whiff%	CSP
2019	IE	HI-A	20	0	0	0	3	3	9¹	6	0	3.9	12.5	13	68.4%	.316	1.07	0.00	64	0.2				
2021 FS	LAA	MLB	22	2	3	0	57	0	50	45	7	4.0	8.7	48	43.1%	.283	1.35	4.26	105	0.0				

Comparables: Ian Anderson, Danny Duffy, Beau Burrows

Once again healthy after a back injury and related issues limited him to three starts at High-A ball between 2018 and 2019, the exigency that was 2020 prevented Rodriguez from getting fully back on track. He still impressed enough at the Angels' alternate site, with his upper-90s velocity, to be added to the 40-man roster for Rule 5 protection. The track to the majors, especially for pitchers, has always provided plenty of puddles to jump in the best of times.

Patrick Sandoval   LHP   Born: 10/18/96   Age: 24   Bats: L   Throws: L   Height: 6'3"   Weight: 190   Origin: Round 11, 2015 Draft (#319 overall)

YEAR	TEAM	LVL	AGE	W	L	SV	G	GS	IP	H	HR	BB/9	K/9	K	GB%	BABIP	WHIP	ERA	DRA-	WARP	MPH	FA%	Whiff%	CSP
2018	QC	LO-A	21	7	1	1	14	10	65	58	4	1.5	9.8	71	45.9%	.305	1.06	2.49	70	1.5				
2018	FAY	HI-A	21	2	0	1	5	3	23	12	1	1.6	10.2	26	46.2%	.216	0.70	2.74	59	0.7				
2018	IE	HI-A	21	1	0	0	3	3	14²	6	0	3.7	12.9	21	46.7%	.200	0.82	0.00	51	0.5				
2018	MOB	AA	21	1	0	0	4	4	19²	12	0	3.7	12.4	27	35.7%	.286	1.02	1.37	52	0.7				
2019	MOB	AA	22	0	3	0	5	4	20	14	1	3.1	14.4	32	50.0%	.310	1.05	3.60	52	0.6				
2019	SL	AAA	22	4	4	0	15	15	60¹	84	7	5.2	9.8	66	42.7%	.403	1.97	6.41	141	-0.1				
2019	LAA	MLB	22	0	4	0	10	9	39¹	35	6	4.3	9.6	42	45.8%	.293	1.37	5.03	89	0.6	94.8	46.5%	32.8%	44.9%
2020	LAA	MLB	23	1	5	0	9	6	36²	37	10	2.9	8.1	33	55.3%	.260	1.34	5.65	101	0.3	94.5	44.6%	27.6%	47.9%
2021 FS	LAA	MLB	24	9	8	0	26	26	150	135	19	4.4	9.1	152	48.9%	.288	1.40	4.27	96	1.4	94.7	45.5%	29.9%	46.6%
2021 DC	LAA	MLB	24	6	6	0	22	22	104	93	13	4.4	9.1	105	48.9%	.288	1.40	4.27	96	1.3	94.7	45.5%	29.9%	46.6%

Comparables: Cristian Javier, Ranger Suárez, Logan Allen

We all tell ourselves little lies in the interest of self-care. "It won't affect me tomorrow if I watch this next episode before bed." "I'll start eating healthier when I finish this bag of chips." "No one noticed me trip over my own feet just now." For pitchers underperforming without their stuff ghosting them, the lie is pretty uniform: "I was tipping my pitches." In some cases, it's probably true, but you never hear the story, "I was tipping my pitches and it turned out fine." More likely, it's an explanation seeking a reason, a pitcher stricken by the vagaries of a short stint putting a reason to what might be better explained as random. In any case, it was a step-back sophomore season for a starting pitcher for whom the Angels have high hopes.

José Suarez   LHP   Born: 01/03/98   Age: 23   Bats: L   Throws: L   Height: 5'10"   Weight: 225   Origin: International Free Agent, 2014

YEAR	TEAM	LVL	AGE	W	L	SV	G	GS	IP	H	HR	BB/9	K/9	K	GB%	BABIP	WHIP	ERA	DRA-	WARP	MPH	FA%	Whiff%	CSP
2018	IE	HI-A	20	0	1	0	2	2	9	6	0	1.0	18.0	18	66.7%	.400	0.78	2.00	17	0.5				
2018	MOB	AA	20	2	1	0	7	7	29²	34	0	2.4	15.5	51	36.8%	.500	1.42	3.03	54	0.9				
2018	SL	AAA	20	1	4	0	17	17	78¹	81	5	4.0	8.4	73	47.6%	.336	1.48	4.48	95	1.0				
2019	SL	AAA	21	2	1	0	7	6	32¹	24	3	4.7	8.6	31	44.3%	.247	1.27	3.62	53	1.3				
2019	LAA	MLB	21	2	6	0	19	15	81	100	23	3.7	8.0	72	36.2%	.326	1.64	7.11	184	-2.9	93.3	47.2%	25.3%	46.8%
2020	LAA	MLB	22	0	2	0	2	2	2¹	10	1	19.3	7.7	2	46.7%	.643	6.43	38.57	152	0.0	94.7	45.5%	32.4%	39.6%
2021 FS	LAA	MLB	23	8	10	0	26	26	150	153	27	4.9	8.5	142	39.8%	.301	1.58	5.70	121	-0.7	93.4	47.0%	25.9%	46.2%
2021 DC	LAA	MLB	23	4	6	0	27	16	83	85	14	4.9	8.5	78	39.8%	.301	1.58	5.70	121	-0.1	93.4	47.0%	25.9%	46.2%

Comparables: Kolby Allard, Jaime Barria, Luis Severino

It was easy to dismiss Suarez's rookie 2019, when circumstance pressed him into major-league service well ahead of schedule, and predictable results ensured. The follow-up campaign might be just as easy to hand-wave as a mere two starts; how much can we learn from two starts? Two gory statlines, though, compound, even before getting into the *fun fact** (*not for Angels fans) portion of this comment: Another Angels pitcher, Shohei Ohtani, made a dismal statement with two 2020 starts, and his near-40 ERA would be the fourth-worst pitcher season in Angels history (no minimum innings) if Suarez's own astounding ERA didn't edge him out. As with Ohtani, should Suarez' 2021 not provide answers, the questions will threaten to drown out all else in depressing noise.

Julio Teheran   RHP   Born: 01/27/91   Age: 30   Bats: R   Throws: R   Height: 6'2"   Weight: 205   Origin: International Free Agent, 2007

YEAR	TEAM	LVL	AGE	W	L	SV	G	GS	IP	H	HR	BB/9	K/9	K	GB%	BABIP	WHIP	ERA	DRA-	WARP	MPH	FA%	Whiff%	CSP
2018	ATL	MLB	27	9	9	0	31	31	175²	122	26	4.3	8.3	162	38.0%	.218	1.17	3.94	90	2.5	92.4	61.9%	28.5%	44.0%
2019	ATL	MLB	28	10	11	0	33	33	174²	148	22	4.3	8.3	162	38.7%	.270	1.32	3.81	94	2.2	91.8	63.8%	22.2%	45.4%
2020	LAA	MLB	29	0	4	0	10	9	31¹	39	12	4.6	5.7	20	36.0%	.273	1.76	10.05	191	-1.2	91.3	60.3%	14.6%	45.7%
2021 FS	LAA	MLB	30	8	9	0	26	26	150	147	29	4.1	7.8	129	38.2%	.278	1.44	5.05	113	0.0	91.9	62.7%	22.6%	45.1%

Comparables: Jonathon Niese, Jake Odorizzi, Kevin Gausman

An adaption of Henry James' novella *The Turn of the Screw* caught everyone's attention in the latter half of 2020, giving everyone the Halloween scares the rest of the world had just been in too-scant supply of. What's *The Haunting of Bly Manor*? We were referring to Teheran's 2020, the real haunted house story. The velocity has been in decline for a while, and that trend continued, but no one could have prepared for the newly-made Angel to accumulate a number of home runs equal to sixty percent of his strikeout total. The DRA doubling makes a bit more sense in that light. Beyond tamping down homers, Teheran will need to regain his old control if he's to make his abysmal season a memory. Even if he can, he's as likely to remember the season as *The Turn of the Screw*'s storyteller: "'Nothing but the impression. I took that *here'*—he tapped his heart. 'I've never lost it.'"

OAKLAND ATHLETICS

Essay by Noah Frank

Player comments by Ginny Searle and BP staff

Stay.

In the baseball world, where each fan base has layers of its own inside jokes printed on T-shirts, from season-long slogans to sly references long forgotten from a 14-inning June affair some number of years back, it's hard to imagine any as personal, as desperate, as meaningful as this one. A green background with gold letters, all stock caps except that distinctive A, differentiated from the blocky, red varieties in Arizona and Orange County, and even the other cursive one from Atlanta, it is unmistakable to any baseball fan.

The word is part demand, part plea. It's not about winning today, or in October. It's not some cute play on words. It's as simple and intrinsic as any aspect of A's fandom—the understanding of and constant, low-grade anxiety driven by the possibility that the team might be snatched away and relocated to some other city with shinier things to offer. That someday, there may not be games to win, or even to show up and enjoy a few beers and brats while losing. It's Joel Barish pleading with Clementine Kruczynski in a darkened hallway at the end of "Eternal Sunshine of the Spotless Mind," knowing there's no storybook ending, that this will always be imperfect, that things may well be destined to fail. OK. Just stay.

Because as bad as things ever looked, as the prospect of a new ballpark was dangled, then snatched away time after time, as star after star found greener pastures elsewhere, at least the A's had Billy Beane.

After never achieving his perceived potential on the field, Beane hung up his spikes in 1990 and took a role in the front office with the Athletics as an advance scout. In the 23 years since Beane ascended to general manager, the A's have made the playoffs 11 times, winning seven AL West titles. They have won 230 games more than they have lost. The only teams with more regular season wins in that span: the Braves, Cardinals, Dodgers, Red Sox and Yankees.

In all, Beane spent has more than 30 years with the A's, building a consistent winner, driving the game's statistical and player analysis revolution, and inspiring a best-selling and oft-misunderstood book and film still referenced and riffed off of in broadcasts today, nearly two decades after it was written.

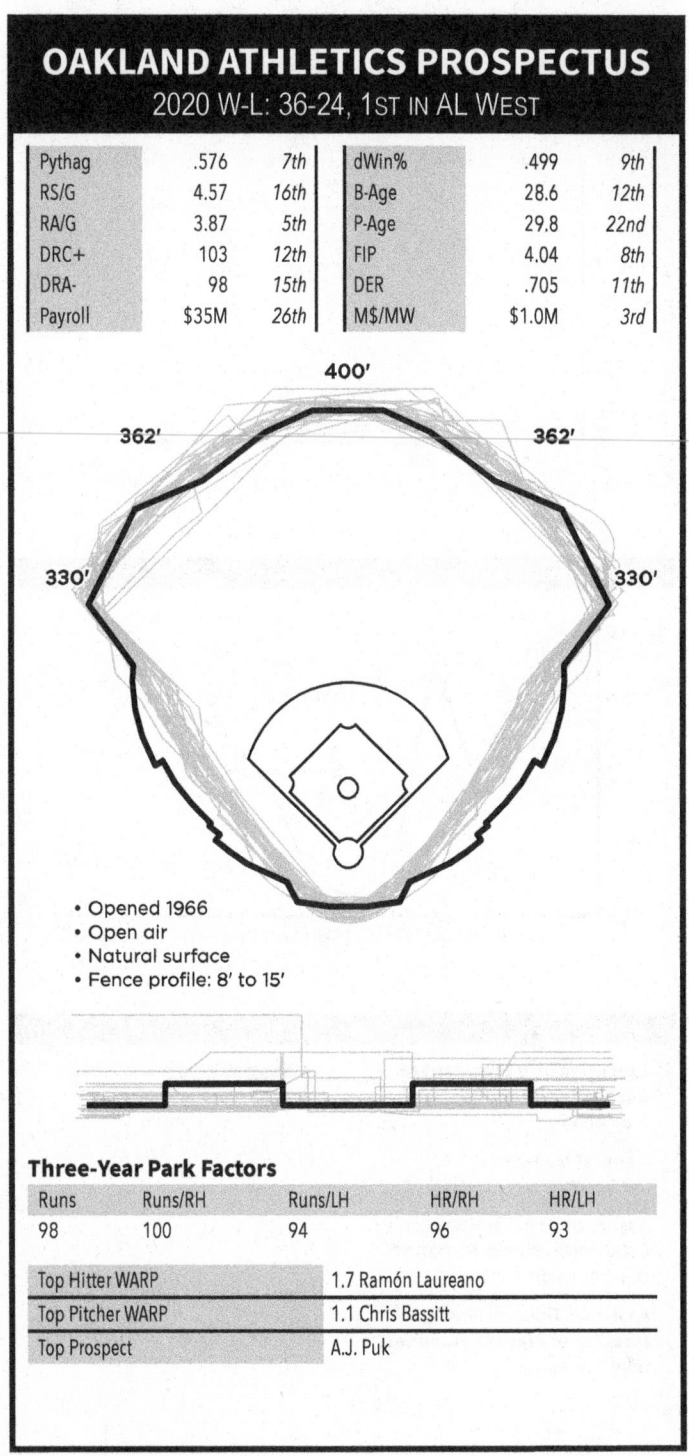

OAKLAND ATHLETICS PROSPECTUS
2020 W-L: 36-24, 1ST IN AL WEST

Pythag	.576	7th	dWin%	.499	9th
RS/G	4.57	16th	B-Age	28.6	12th
RA/G	3.87	5th	P-Age	29.8	22nd
DRC+	103	12th	FIP	4.04	8th
DRA-	98	15th	DER	.705	11th
Payroll	$35M	26th	M$/MW	$1.0M	3rd

400'
362'   362'
330'   330'

- Opened 1966
- Open air
- Natural surface
- Fence profile: 8' to 15'

Three-Year Park Factors

Runs	Runs/RH	Runs/LH	HR/RH	HR/LH
98	100	94	96	93

Top Hitter WARP	1.7 Ramón Laureano
Top Pitcher WARP	1.1 Chris Bassitt
Top Prospect	A.J. Puk

Payroll History (in millions)

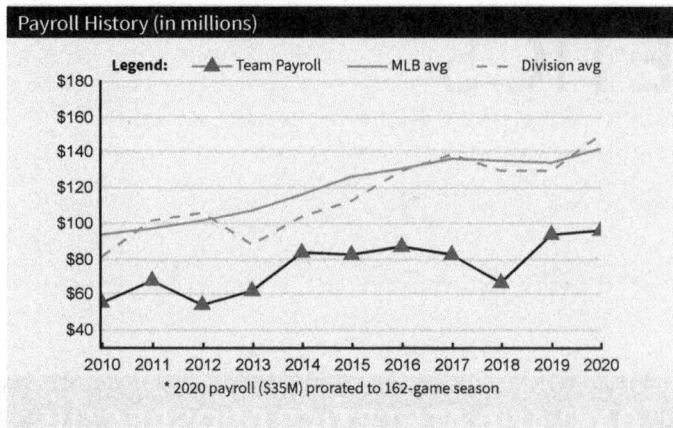

* 2020 payroll ($35M) prorated to 162-game season

Future Commitments (in millions)

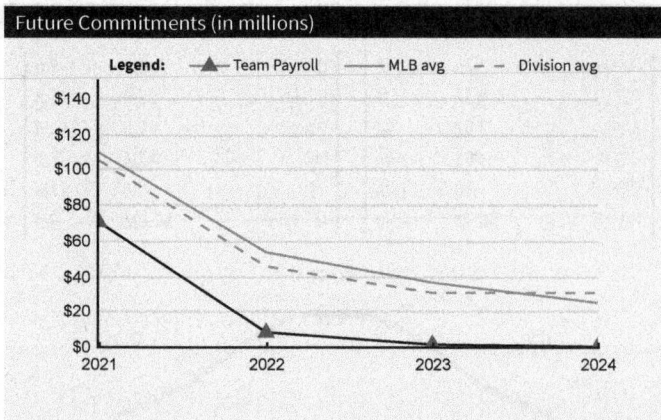

Farm System Ranking

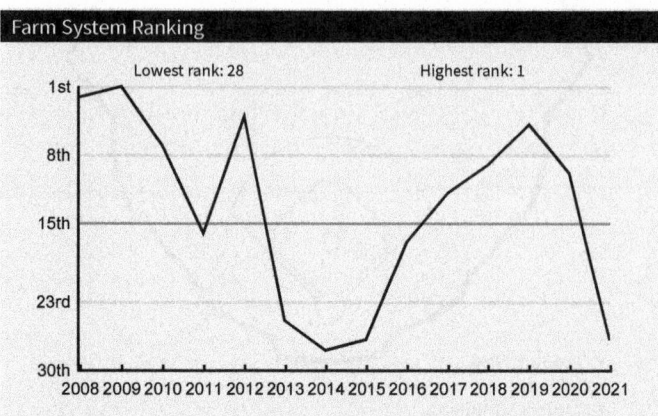

Personnel

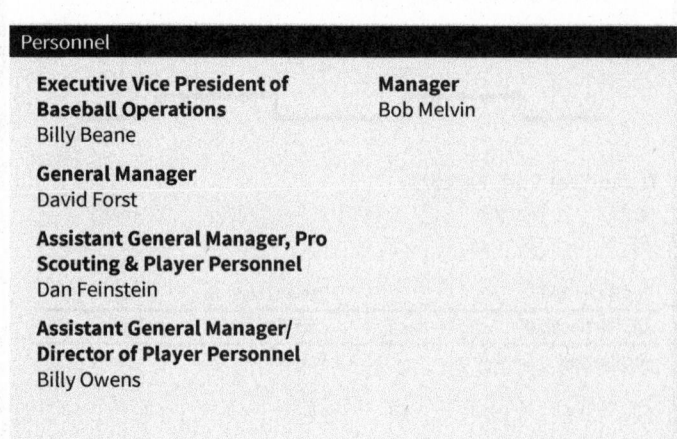

Executive Vice President of Baseball Operations
Billy Beane

General Manager
David Forst

Assistant General Manager, Pro Scouting & Player Personnel
Dan Feinstein

Assistant General Manager/ Director of Player Personnel
Billy Owens

Manager
Bob Melvin

Thirty years. Thirty years is far more than a generation in baseball. It's a lifetime. Thirty years ago, fresh off three straight runs to the Fall Classic, the now-notoriously-frugal Oakland Athletics had the highest payroll in baseball. Thirty years before that, they were in Kansas City. Thirty years before that, in Philadelphia. Thirty years before that, they were playing their inaugural season as a charter member of the American League.

For an executive with so much upheaval built into the ethos of his roster management, Beane's own stability has been no small achievement. He knew his shit didn't work in the playoffs, yet still he soldiered on. He came back, year after year, to try again. As other teams cycled through GMs and rebuilds, he found a way to compete, more often than not.

His was a philosophy built around patience. Sure, in a practical sense it was about working long counts, drawing walks, forcing a pitcher to beat you multiple times in the same at-bat, grinding agonizing at-bats and stacking high pitch counts at all times, pushing opposing hurlers out of their comfort zones and toward fatigue and error. It was about wringing out the guy the opponent wanted on the mound to get to the guys they least wanted out there, as early as possible; knives out for the fifth or sixth inning, ready to filet the soft underbelly of the bullpen; to build a lead into the late frames, as the heavy, wet marine layer crept into the East Bay night to suck the life out of any would-be late game heroics from the visitors.

So, too, was patience the philosophy of A's fandom. Patience was their virtue, within seasons and without. Patience through slow starts would be rewarded with scalding summer streaks, including the Miguel Tejada-fueled fever dream of 2002, punctuated by Scott Hatteberg's indelible blast. Patience waiting for prospects to mature and matriculate to the big leagues. Patience for the next window to open. Patience, watching the stars of that window walk away in free agency, watching the front office trade the others to get enough of a return of minor league talent to flip the hourglass over again, to watch and wait once more.

Oakland has waited for another title since the year Beane left the playing field for the front office. Amid all that chaos, the constant turnover and heartbreak, the Godot of a new ballpark, he was the constant. In Billy we trusted.

The original screenplay for "Moneyball" involved an animated Bill James explaining sabermetric principles to the audience and we can thank the baseball gods that never came to fruition. But the chronological frame of story—from the 2001 postseason through the 2002 postseason—failed to provide the redemptive arc from failure to success that we usually demand of our sports movies. The A's lost in the division series, in five games, both times (as well as both the year prior, and the year after this span; truly Sisyphusian). So the Hollywood framing settled on Beane's decision, both for baseball and his family, to turn down the money, and the Red Sox, and to stay.

But A's fans are now facing the prospect of the alternate ending, Beane himself leaving, and for Boston no less. In October, it was reported that Beane's new venture capital group, Redball Acquisition Corp., was pursuing a 20-25 percent stake in Fenway Sports Group. Yes, Fenway, as in the Red Sox and other professional sports holdings, owned by the same John Henry who nearly lured Beane away 18 years prior. If the deal goes through, with Beane attached, it will mean the end of his time in Oakland, as he'll be forced to sell his ownership stake with the A's.

Of course, the Beane era was always going to come to an end eventually. But the fact that he stayed despite Henry's offer in 2002 to make him the highest-paid GM in baseball, despite the multiple rebuilds and reloads in the years since, despite the trauma of four straight Game 5 eliminations and the singular horror of the 2014 AL Wild Card Game, it felt like he might just stay forever. Or until the A's won a title. Or, at least, until they secured a new stadium.

Never mind that Beane's been in more of an executive role the last few years. His presence has defined the club's existence for as long as anyone in the game. But if Beane's done with all this, if he's given up without ever achieving a title, or even a formal plan for that elusive ballpark, what are A's fans left with?

Whatever the A's have been—have meant—to baseball, begins with Beane. Their methods have been copied and improved upon and combined with more money to more success all over the league. First Theo and the Red Sox, then countless other copycats, leading to Moneyball's final form, the McKinsey-steeped Astros. They reflect back every bit of optimization the A's initially brought to the sport, but in grander and more grotesque ways, like the soulless, alien mimics produced in The Shimmer of "Annihilation."

Nietzche told us to beware of fighting with monsters, lest we become monsters ourselves. Maybe the fun of trying to outsmart and outmaneuver everyone else, to succeed in spite of the limitations placed upon him, has been extinguished for Beane. Maybe it has for all of us.

After all, even Theo—who spent less than a decade each in his championship runs with both the Red Sox and the Cubs—has unexpectedly left his post and the sport as a whole, to walk the earth or hide out in the Jundland Wastes of Tatooine. Beane alone stepping away is momentous enough; add Theo's self-exile to the mix, and you're looking at a seismic shift among the power players who have shifted the way we think about the sport.

Michael Lewis' "Moneyball" hit the shelves in bookstores on June 17, 2003, 25 days after an unknown Tennessean everyman with a beer belly, a goatee and a name that would be laughed out of any Hollywood pitch meeting upended the poker world. Chris Moneymaker's stunning success, turning a $40 online qualifier entry into the grandest prize in the game, changed Texas Hold 'Em and poker in America forever. Where once there was easy money for the seasoned pros to pick off, suddenly a wave of sharp young minds, the same kinds of

Ivy League quants that would begin to populate front offices around MLB, were plying their skills to swipe the shirts and annual vacation budgets from unsuspecting Vegas tourists and novices online all over the world.

The same human evaluation that scouting departments rely upon was present in poker as well, the eye-test still able to find tells a computer would never see. But it quickly became apparent that the math was more important, and those able to sort the data and apply its lessons most efficiently would win in the long run. Poker, like the baseball season, is a marathon. And the same way that the market inefficiency targeting principles of "Moneyball" soon commanded front office decision-making around the league, so did Game Theory Optimal among poker players. Now, even if you're armed with the best knowledge and tactics, so is nearly everyone else.

One thing has differentiated Beane's approach from that of his acolytes: Even as the Marlins popularized the complete, years-long teardowns that dictate team behavior, and Cleveland proved themselves trendsetters by backing off spending to get just worse enough to remain competitive, Beane has tried to find ways to win every year where it was possible, never enduring more than three straight losing campaigns, cycling through the ideas of rebuilds within seasons and offseasons. The A's have made efforts to compete, to try their best, if they have had any chance of making the postseason, but they've also happily sold the farm without a second thought once those chances were reasonably gone to accelerate their next competitive window. They've done things as cheaply as they could, but there has been no reason to believe they haven't tried to squeeze as many wins as possible out of the rosters they've assembled.

Maybe Beane's approach was always soulless arbitrage, but at least it seemed to be in the service of putting the best possible team on the field within the constraints placed upon him. Whether or not ownership was being honest about the limits of those constraints, the baseball operations themselves always felt transparent. It always felt like they were trying, that they were always upholding the social contract between a major league baseball team and its fans. There was never any shame in wearing green and gold, a not insignificant qualifier in today's game.

In many ways, it's easy for A's fans to be hopeful about the future, because that's all they've ever had. There are transcendent young stars at the corner infield spots and fireballing southpaws on the brink of maturing into front-line starters. But it's simultaneously impossible not to be nervous about that same future—as uncertain as ever, with slashes to payroll both on the field and in the front office, with stadium plans still in limbo, with the sport still accounting for the losses from the pandemic—whether Beane chooses to leave or decides, once more, to stay. ▪

—*Noah Frank is a writer and editor in Washington, D.C.*

HITTERS

Austin Allen C Born: 01/16/94 Age: 27 Bats: L Throws: R Height: 6'2" Weight: 219 Origin: Round 4, 2015 Draft (#117 overall)

YEAR	TEAM	LVL	AGE	PA	R	2B	3B	HR	RBI	BB	K	SB	CS	Whiff%	AVG/OBP/SLG	DRC+	BABIP	BRR	FRAA	WARP
2018	SA	AA	24	498	59	31	0	22	56	37	97	0	3		.290/.351/.506	137	.325	-2.1	C(91): 14.6, 1B(19): -1.5	4.0
2019	ELP	AAA	25	298	52	27	0	21	67	22	56	0	0		.330/.379/.663	128	.345	-2.5	C(61): 7.2, 1B(12): -0.1	2.8
2019	SD	MLB	25	71	4	4	0	0	3	6	21	0	0	30.2%	.215/.282/.277	61	.318	0.0	C(19): -0.2, 1B(2): 0.1	0.0
2020	OAK	MLB	26	32	1	1	0	1	3	1	14	0	0	36.9%	.194/.219/.323	68	.312	-0.3	C(14): 0.0	-0.1
2021 FS	OAK	MLB	27	600	68	23	1	24	74	38	178	0	0	33.1%	.238/.293/.415	93	.304	-0.8	C 3, 1B 0	2.0
2021 DC	OAK	MLB	27	100	11	3	0	4	12	6	29	0	0	33.1%	.238/.293/.415	93	.304	-0.1	C 1	0.4

Comparables: Yan Gomes, Ryan Doumit, Travis d'Arnaud

YEAR	TEAM	P. COUNT	FRM RUNS	BLK RUNS	THRW RUNS	TOT RUNS
2018	SA	12636	8.3	1.0	3.0	12.4
2019	SD	2293	-0.1	-0.4	0.0	-0.5
2019	ELP	9133	6.9	0.0	-1.2	5.7
2020	OAK	1309	0.1	0.1	0.0	0.2
2021	OAK	3608	0.4	0.0	-0.1	0.3

Allen's efficacy with the tools of ignorance has long been considered the stumbling block that might limit a plus power bat from a major-league role: After breaking 20 home runs at all of High-A, Double-A, and Triple-A (the latter in fewer than 300 plate appearances), Allen remained bogged down by both poorly regarded defense and an ostentatious Padres system. Thus he found himself traded to Oakland for Jurickson Profar, whom Oakland appeared prepared to non-tender in lieu of a trade partner. After winning the backup role out of summer camp, Allen posted another sub-.600 OPS and struggled enough that he was demoted a month into the season. Behind the plate, however, Allen looked acceptable, ensuring he'll get another chance to prove his bat can translate to the bigs and serving as a reminder that just because you show someone another side of yourself, they don't have to like *that* side either.

Nick Allen SS Born: 10/08/98 Age: 22 Bats: R Throws: R Height: 5'8" Weight: 166 Origin: Round 3, 2017 Draft (#81 overall)

YEAR	TEAM	LVL	AGE	PA	R	2B	3B	HR	RBI	BB	K	SB	CS	Whiff%	AVG/OBP/SLG	DRC+	BABIP	BRR	FRAA	WARP
2018	BEL	LO-A	19	512	51	17	6	0	34	34	85	24	8		.239/.301/.302	75	.289	3.7	SS(121): 5.2	1.1
2019	STK	HI-A	20	328	45	22	5	3	25	28	52	13	5		.292/.362/.434	134	.348	-4.4	SS(45): 4.7, 2B(24): -1.6	2.1
2021 FS	OAK	MLB	22	600	55	26	4	7	52	36	152	13	5		.226/.279/.327	68	.297	-0.2	SS 10, 2B 0	0.5
2021 DC	OAK	MLB	22	67	6	3	0	0	5	4	17	1	0		.226/.279/.327	68	.297	0.0	SS 1	0.1

Comparables: José Rondón, Amed Rosario, Sergio Alcántara

Though you might not know it from looking at Oakland's system, teams are allowed to have position player prospects who impress on both offense and defense. In fairness to Allen, he tantalized with the bat in High-A during the 2019 season, but make no mistake: the glove is the carrying tool. A season of reps might have clarified if a league-average offensive baseline is a feasible expectation for the 21-year-old, might even have allowed him to step in as Marcus Semien's replacement when he inevitably leaves for less-green greener pastures, but even if the bat renders the profile more (pre-2020) José Iglesias than Andrelton Simmons, Oakland will find a way to utilize Allen and solve one of their longest-running inefficiencies: no lineup options that feature two players with the same last name (so as to confuse opposing managers).

Austin Beck OF Born: 11/21/98 Age: 22 Bats: R Throws: R Height: 6'1" Weight: 200 Origin: Round 1, 2017 Draft (#6 overall)

YEAR	TEAM	LVL	AGE	PA	R	2B	3B	HR	RBI	BB	K	SB	CS	Whiff%	AVG/OBP/SLG	DRC+	BABIP	BRR	FRAA	WARP
2018	BEL	LO-A	19	534	58	29	4	2	60	30	117	8	6		.296/.335/.383	105	.377	-4.8	CF(113): 2.0	0.9
2019	STK	HI-A	20	367	40	22	4	8	49	24	126	2	2		.251/.302/.411	92	.372	-0.1	CF(69): -0.3, RF(10): 2.7	1.1
2021 FS	OAK	MLB	22	600	48	27	3	8	52	37	224	3	1		.214/.267/.324	61	.339	0.2	CF -7, RF 0	-1.7

Comparables: Yorman Rodriguez, Mickey Moniak, Willy García

Selected sixth-overall in 2017, Beck has yet to pass the *Morning Phase* of his career; being left off Oakland's 60-man player pool deprived him of much-needed time to improve at the plate and highlighted just how far the team perceives the outfielder to be from contributing at the major-league level.

Skye Bolt RF Born: 01/15/94 Age: 27 Bats: S Throws: R Height: 6'2" Weight: 180 Origin: Round 4, 2015 Draft (#128 overall)

YEAR	TEAM	LVL	AGE	PA	R	2B	3B	HR	RBI	BB	K	SB	CS	Whiff%	AVG/OBP/SLG	DRC+	BABIP	BRR	FRAA	WARP
2018	STK	HI-A	24	209	28	8	4	9	32	31	47	9	3		.266/.382/.521	137	.308	2.1	CF(45): -8.1, LF(4): -0.6	0.2
2018	MID	AA	24	315	41	18	3	10	37	27	75	10	1		.256/.325/.446	104	.315	1.7	CF(50): -3.1, RF(19): 0.8	0.2
2019	LV	AAA	25	347	57	19	3	11	61	37	94	7	5		.269/.350/.459	81	.351	-0.3	RF(40): 8.5, CF(37): 1.1, LF(7): 0.8	1.1
2019	OAK	MLB	25	11	1	1	0	0	0	1	3	0	0	29.4%	.100/.182/.200	76	.143	-0.1	CF(3): 0.0, RF(1): 0.0	0.0
2021 FS	OAK	MLB	27	600	63	22	3	19	65	49	195	5	2	29.4%	.208/.279/.370	78	.284	1.2	CF -6, LF 5	0.2
2021 DC	OAK	MLB	27	67	7	2	0	2	7	5	21	0	0	29.4%	.208/.279/.370	78	.284	0.1	CF -1, LF 1	0.0

Comparables: Jai Miller, Brad Snyder, Brent Clevlen

The 2008 film *Bolt* features an eponymous dog who stars in a television show in which he has superpowers; the narrative of the film concerns the dog becoming lost and learning he does not actually have superpowers. Drafted for big tools that have never quite come together as hoped, perhaps Bolt would be bolstered by the film's conclusion, when the dog learns the power of leaning into the strengths one does possess.

Seth Brown **OF**   Born: 07/13/92   Age: 28   Bats: L   Throws: L   Height: 6'1"   Weight: 223   Origin: Round 19, 2015 Draft (#578 overall)

YEAR	TEAM	LVL	AGE	PA	R	2B	3B	HR	RBI	BB	K	SB	CS	Whiff%	AVG/OBP/SLG	DRC+	BABIP	BRR	FRAA	WARP
2018	MID	AA	25	555	66	38	3	14	90	47	142	5	0		.283/.342/.454	110	.365	1.3	1B(115): -3.7, RF(8): 4.7, LF(4): -0.2	0.2
2019	LV	AAA	26	500	101	29	6	37	104	38	127	8	1		.297/.352/.634	112	.330	-0.2	1B(64): 0.6, LF(17): 1.0, RF(9): -0.8	1.6
2019	OAK	MLB	26	83	11	8	2	0	13	7	23	1	0	31.8%	.293/.361/.453	82	.423	1.0	LF(23): 0.3, 1B(4): -0.7	0.1
2020	OAK	MLB	28	5	0	0	0	0	0	0	2	0	0	55.6%	.000/.000/.000	74	.000		1B(3): 0.0	0.0
2021 FS	OAK	MLB	28	600	66	25	3	23	75	42	192	1	0	33.8%	.227/.285/.415	89	.302	2.0	LF -3, 1B 0	0.1
2021 DC	OAK	MLB	28	369	41	15	2	14	46	25	118	0	0	33.8%	.227/.285/.415	89	.302	1.2	LF -2, 1B 0	0.3

Comparables: Ben Paulsen, Joe Koshansky, Rhyne Hughes

Progressing steadily through Oakland's system after being selected in the 19th round, and hitting solidly at every stop, Brown will be feeling more like Charlie if he doesn't get a sustained shot at the majors this year.

Mark Canha **OF**   Born: 02/15/89   Age: 32   Bats: R   Throws: R   Height: 6'2"   Weight: 209   Origin: Round 7, 2010 Draft (#227 overall)

YEAR	TEAM	LVL	AGE	PA	R	2B	3B	HR	RBI	BB	K	SB	CS	Whiff%	AVG/OBP/SLG	DRC+	BABIP	BRR	FRAA	WARP
2018	OAK	MLB	29	411	60	22	0	17	52	34	87	1	2	21.3%	.249/.328/.449	115	.281	-0.3	CF(62): -5.9, LF(51): 1.4, 1B(15): -0.8	1.5
2019	OAK	MLB	30	497	80	16	3	26	58	67	107	3	2	23.0%	.273/.396/.517	134	.308	1.3	CF(56): -3.8, RF(27): 1.9, 1B(15): -1.3	3.5
2020	OAK	MLB	31	243	32	12	2	5	33	37	54	4	0	24.1%	.246/.387/.408	127	.307	0.0	RF(17): 1.7, LF(15): 1.3, CF(9): 0.5	1.6
2021 FS	OAK	MLB	32	600	72	24	2	22	77	64	149	3	1	23.1%	.234/.340/.422	113	.284	0.5	LF 4, RF 1	3.0
2021 DC	OAK	MLB	32	570	68	23	2	21	73	61	141	3	1	23.1%	.234/.340/.422	113	.284	0.5	LF 4, RF 1	2.7

Comparables: Alex Gordon, Jason Kubel, Greg Vaughn

One unsung casualty of the pandemic upending reality was that of content for Canha's Instagram account, @bigleaguefoodie. Before the pandemic ended in-restaurant dining, Canha uploaded meal pics from stops all over the country to his 20,000-plus followers. Apart from some frankly cruel pictures of ballpark food, the feed largely went dark throughout 2020. Canha's bat, though, didn't, despite what might be suggested by the 118-point OPS dropoff. The dingers largely didn't recur, but he improved on a career-high walk rate and saw a negligible drop-off per DRC+. The glove remained versatile and per FRAA, was the most productive of Canha's career. It wasn't a step forward from 2019's breakout, but neither was it a step back—and any foodie knows if you like a dish enough the first time, you don't mind ordering it again.

Matt Chapman **3B**   Born: 04/28/93   Age: 28   Bats: R   Throws: R   Height: 6'0"   Weight: 215   Origin: Round 1, 2014 Draft (#25 overall)

YEAR	TEAM	LVL	AGE	PA	R	2B	3B	HR	RBI	BB	K	SB	CS	Whiff%	AVG/OBP/SLG	DRC+	BABIP	BRR	FRAA	WARP
2018	OAK	MLB	25	616	100	42	6	24	68	58	146	1	2	23.6%	.278/.356/.508	125	.338	3.8	3B(145): 15.6	6.2
2019	OAK	MLB	26	670	102	36	3	36	91	73	146	1	1	23.9%	.249/.342/.506	120	.270	-3.2	3B(156): 12.9	5.2
2020	OAK	MLB	27	152	22	9	2	10	25	8	54	0	0	36.2%	.232/.276/.535	92	.291	0.3	3B(36): -5.6, SS(1): 0.0	-0.3
2021 FS	OAK	MLB	28	600	80	27	3	32	91	57	188	2	1	26.2%	.235/.316/.483	117	.294	0.9	3B 21	4.8
2021 DC	OAK	MLB	28	570	76	26	3	30	87	55	179	2	0	26.2%	.235/.316/.483	117	.294	0.9	3B 20	4.5

Comparables: Dean Palmer, J.D. Davis, Pedro Álvarez

The Hunger Games: Mockingjay; *The Godfather: Part III*; Chapman's 2020 season. We're sorry, the category was "disappointing third trilogy entries." Bothered all season by a hip injury, Chapman noted that he never felt like he had his legs under him even before a torn hip labrum in mid-September necessitated surgery and ended his worst of four campaigns. It showed at the plate, where a 35.5 percent strikeout and 5.3 percent walk rate (both career-worsts) resulted in the lowest DRC+ of his career. More worrisome, the toll was evident on the defense that had just won consecutive platinum gloves: Chapman struggled to make some basic plays and the trademark, awesome (in the original sense, heavy on "awe") arm sometimes faltered. No matter how evident it is an injury was the culprit, the seriousness of the malady ensures concern over the latent superstar will linger until he's back to gunning out runners from unfathomable distances across the diamond.

Logan Davidson **SS**   Born: 12/26/97   Age: 23   Bats: S   Throws: R   Height: 6'3"   Weight: 185   Origin: Round 1, 2019 Draft (#29 overall)

YEAR	TEAM	LVL	AGE	PA	R	2B	3B	HR	RBI	BB	K	SB	CS	Whiff%	AVG/OBP/SLG	DRC+	BABIP	BRR	FRAA	WARP
2019	VER	SS	21	238	42	7	0	4	12	31	55	5	0		.239/.345/.332	132	.308	1.5	SS(50): 11.8	3.0
2021 FS	OAK	MLB	23	600	51	26	2	11	56	38	198	4	0		.214/.270/.332	67	.310	1.5	SS 11	0.7

Comparables: Yamaico Navarro, Andy Parrino, David Adams

The A's have more shortstop prospects than their stadium has problems, but Davidson could become the best of the bunch, if the 2019 first-rounder's hit tool ultimately translates as well as the arm, glove, speed, and raw power have so far.

Khris Davis **LF**   Born: 12/21/87   Age: 33   Bats: R   Throws: R   Height: 5'11"   Weight: 205   Origin: Round 7, 2009 Draft (#226 overall)

YEAR	TEAM	LVL	AGE	PA	R	2B	3B	HR	RBI	BB	K	SB	CS	Whiff%	AVG/OBP/SLG	DRC+	BABIP	BRR	FRAA	WARP
2018	OAK	MLB	30	654	98	28	1	48	123	59	175	0	0	33.7%	.247/.326/.549	138	.261	-4.6	LF(11): -1.9	3.4
2019	OAK	MLB	31	533	61	11	0	23	73	47	146	0	0	35.4%	.220/.293/.387	91	.264	-1.6	LF(4): -0.3	0.1
2020	OAK	MLB	33	99	9	5	0	2	10	10	26	0	0	33.0%	.200/.303/.329	89	.259	-0.2		0.0
2021 FS	OAK	MLB	33	600	66	21	1	25	75	57	181	1	0	34.5%	.212/.297/.403	92	.265	-0.8	LF 0	1.0
2021 DC	OAK	MLB	33	369	40	13	0	15	46	35	111	1	0	34.5%	.212/.297/.403	92	.265	-0.5		0.4

Comparables: Justin Upton, Geoff Jenkins, Marcus Thames

No one was ever quite sure what to make of Davis, even when he was hitting .247 annually and averaging 40 home runs between 2015 and 2018. Come 2019, right on the heels of an extension with the highest average annual value in A's history, the Khrush era suddenly appeared over. On the surface 2020 was only a confirmation Davis had gone off a steep cliff, with another sub-.700 OPS losing him playing time down the stretch. He did rebound to a .894 OPS in 32 September plate appearances, but the sample size speaks for itself: If you're going to believe in Davis in his age-33 season you're doing so on sentiment. Hoping for sentiment to pay off for the A's is a fool's errand, but Davis is the player who stayed, who bought the whole team Nintendo Switches upon signing his extension (to play Mario Kart on road trips), who got starts in six of seven playoff games after two torpid regular seasons; if anyone on the A's gets the benefit of sentiment, it's him.

Greg Deichmann RF Born: 05/31/95 Age: 26 Bats: L Throws: R Height: 6'2" Weight: 205 Origin: Round 2, 2017 Draft (#43 overall)

YEAR	TEAM	LVL	AGE	PA	R	2B	3B	HR	RBI	BB	K	SB	CS	Whiff%	AVG/OBP/SLG	DRC+	BABIP	BRR	FRAA	WARP
2018	ASGR	ROK	23	43	9	2	2	1	7	5	8	0	0		.289/.372/.526	125	.345	-0.1	RF(11): -0.4	0.0
2018	STK	HI-A	23	185	18	14	0	6	21	17	63	0	1		.199/.276/.392	65	.276	-0.1	RF(28): 0.7, LF(8): -0.8, 1B(5): -0.1	-0.8
2019	MID	AA	24	340	42	10	2	11	36	34	103	19	5		.219/.300/.375	91	.289	2.7	RF(69): -0.0, CF(3): 0.2	0.7
2021 FS	OAK	MLB	26	600	62	25	3	18	64	47	216	10	2		.206/.274/.368	77	.300	3.9	RF 1, LF -1	0.0

Comparables: Sam Hilliard, Roger Kieschnick, Aristides Aquino

Deichmann sort of needed the 2020 season to be the one in which he pulled it all together, being a 25-year-old corner outfielder who had never posted a .700 OPS above Low-A ball. A lot of people didn't get what they wanted in 2020, though, and the A's clearly see something in the LSU product, being that they put him on the 40-man over the winter.

Dustin Fowler CF Born: 12/29/94 Age: 26 Bats: L Throws: L Height: 6'0" Weight: 198 Origin: Round 18, 2013 Draft (#554 overall)

YEAR	TEAM	LVL	AGE	PA	R	2B	3B	HR	RBI	BB	K	SB	CS	Whiff%	AVG/OBP/SLG	DRC+	BABIP	BRR	FRAA	WARP
2018	NAS	AAA	23	238	37	17	6	4	27	9	40	13	2		.342/.366/.522	121	.400	0.2	CF(51): -12.9, LF(2): 0.6	-0.1
2018	OAK	MLB	23	203	19	3	2	6	23	8	47	6	4	23.0%	.224/.256/.354	84	.262	-1.0	CF(57): -3.8, LF(3): -0.2, RF(3): -0.1	-0.2
2019	LV	AAA	24	606	98	22	7	25	89	42	145	12	4		.277/.333/.477	81	.332	0.8	CF(89): -3.5, RF(30): 1.3, LF(6): -0.5	0.5
2021 FS	OAK	MLB	26	600	65	25	6	19	72	29	153	10	3	23.0%	.240/.281/.410	86	.296	5.5	LF -5, RF -1	0.8
2021 DC	OAK	MLB	26	100	10	4	1	3	12	4	25	1	0	23.0%	.240/.281/.410	86	.296	0.9	LF -1, RF 0	0.1

Comparables: Jason Pridie, Curtis Granderson, Jake Cave

Fowler hasn't appeared in the majors since 2018, when he appeared much diminished after knee surgery the previous year. That he remains on Oakland's roster at all indicates plans for future usage, or at least an unwillingness to give up on the top prospect netted in the Sonny Gray trade, though it's unclear where Fowler will find time in a crowded outfield.

Jonah Heim C Born: 06/27/95 Age: 26 Bats: S Throws: R Height: 6'4" Weight: 220 Origin: Round 4, 2013 Draft (#129 overall)

YEAR	TEAM	LVL	AGE	PA	R	2B	3B	HR	RBI	BB	K	SB	CS	Whiff%	AVG/OBP/SLG	DRC+	BABIP	BRR	FRAA	WARP
2018	STK	HI-A	23	348	41	21	1	7	49	29	60	3	1		.292/.353/.433	117	.337	-0.9	C(55): -0.1	0.8
2018	MID	AA	23	154	16	4	0	1	11	10	22	0	0		.182/.238/.234	22	.205	-0.9	C(38): 1.6	-0.8
2019	MID	AA	24	208	20	12	0	5	34	24	27	0	1		.282/.370/.431	137	.307	-1.6	C(43): 7.7	2.3
2019	LV	AAA	24	119	22	9	0	4	19	11	18	0	0		.358/.412/.557	124	.395	-0.5	C(28): 2.2	1.0
2020	OAK	MLB	25	41	5	0	0	0	5	3	3	0	0	10.9%	.211/.268/.211	94	.229	-0.1	C(12): 0.3	0.2
2021 FS	OAK	MLB	26	600	60	26	1	13	61	44	124	0	0	10.9%	.226/.287/.356	77	.267	-0.7	C 2	0.8
2021 DC	OAK	MLB	26	134	13	5	0	3	13	9	27	0	0	10.9%	.226/.287/.356	77	.267	-0.2	C 1	0.2

Comparables: Sandy León, Jose Reyes, Steven Lerud

YEAR	TEAM	P. COUNT	FRM RUNS	BLK RUNS	THRW RUNS	TOT RUNS
2019	LV	3229	1.1	0.0	0.2	1.3
2020	OAK	1456	0.0	0.0	0.0	-0.1
2021	OAK	4810	0.2	0.4	0.1	0.7

The Battle of Helm's Deep, the climax of Peter Jackson's adaptation of *The Two Towers*, is one of the most revered and complex battle scenes ever put to film—it was shot over four months (mostly during the night) and utilized a 1:4 scale miniature that still spanned 50 feet long. The battle for Heim, depth, was less epic in scale—midway through the season, the seven-year minors veteran (on his third organization) got the call to replace Austin Allen as the A's backup. The defense is better-regarded in Heim's case than Allen's, but backup has long appeared the top of the scale—even if you forgive the disastrous first shot at Double-A in 2018, a solid eye in the box is the only notable offensive tool. The battle for a backup role nevertheless ended in a decisive win for Heim—he got rostered for the playoffs, though he didn't appear.

Tony Kemp 2B Born: 10/31/91 Age: 29 Bats: L Throws: R Height: 5'6" Weight: 160 Origin: Round 5, 2013 Draft (#137 overall)

YEAR	TEAM	LVL	AGE	PA	R	2B	3B	HR	RBI	BB	K	SB	CS	Whiff%	AVG/OBP/SLG	DRC+	BABIP	BRR	FRAA	WARP
2018	FRE	AAA	26	183	33	6	5	0	19	19	15	13	2		.335/.407/.435	110	.367	3.5	2B(25): -0.5, CF(14): -1.4	0.7
2018	HOU	MLB	26	295	37	15	0	6	30	32	44	9	3	18.3%	.263/.351/.392	105	.296	-0.5	LF(61): -2.8, CF(32): 0.3, 2B(7): 0.0	0.7
2019	CHC	MLB	27	93	8	3	2	1	12	7	18	0	1	23.1%	.183/.258/.305	66	.215	0.8	2B(14): 0.0, LF(6): 0.5, RF(3): 0.1	0.0
2019	HOU	MLB	27	186	23	6	2	7	17	16	29	4	3	16.9%	.227/.308/.417	99	.233	-1.1	2B(29): -0.9, LF(14): 0.7, CF(11): 0.1	0.4
2020	OAK	MLB	29	114	15	5	0	0	4	15	14	3	1	13.6%	.247/.363/.301	106	.284	0.4	2B(43): -2.1, LF(3): -0.1	0.3
2021 FS	OAK	MLB	29	600	66	26	4	10	59	59	99	10	4	17.3%	.248/.331/.374	97	.286	1.9	2B -9, LF 0	1.1
2021 DC	OAK	MLB	29	436	48	19	3	7	43	42	72	7	2	17.3%	.248/.331/.374	97	.286	1.4	2B -6, LF 0	0.9

Comparables: Tommy Harper, Mike Huff, Mike Lum

The first in a cadre of A's second basemen that never netted Oakland their second baseman of the future, Kemp moved back to the AL West in an offseason trade from Chicago and failed to thrive in the first starting role he's had in his career. Even if you're amenable to DRC+'s suggestion he was better than his dire slugging percentage suggests, the defense was also rough, and the combination disappointing enough that Oakland went with an outside hire in Tommy La Stella's trade deadline acquisition. If your employer brought in someone with your same skills and started handing them your responsibilities, you'd probably read the tea leaves. It wasn't a disastrous enough season for Kemp to be non-tendered, but you get the sense there's little hope on the team's end for a breakout or a starting role.

Tommy La Stella 2B Born: 01/31/89 Age: 32 Bats: L Throws: R Height: 5'11" Weight: 180 Origin: Round 8, 2011 Draft (#266 overall)

YEAR	TEAM	LVL	AGE	PA	R	2B	3B	HR	RBI	BB	K	SB	CS	Whiff%	AVG/OBP/SLG	DRC+	BABIP	BRR	FRAA	WARP
2018	CHC	MLB	29	192	23	8	0	1	19	17	27	0	1	17.1%	.266/.340/.331	84	.312	0.7	3B(26): -1.8, 2B(15): 0.3, P(1): -0.0	0.2
2019	LAA	MLB	30	321	49	8	0	16	44	20	28	0	0	11.8%	.295/.346/.486	119	.282	-1.0	2B(46): -1.8, 3B(30): -1.1, 1B(3): -0.0	1.5
2020	OAK	MLB	31	111	16	6	2	1	11	12	5	0	0	10.9%	.289/.369/.423	124	.293	0.5	2B(18): 0.9, 3B(6): -0.2	0.7
2020	LAA	MLB	31	117	15	8	0	4	14	15	7	1	0	11.5%	.273/.371/.475	124	.258	-1.5	2B(15): -3.2, 1B(10): 0.0	0.1
2021 FS	OAK	MLB	32	600	75	25	1	17	65	57	69	1	0	12.1%	.263/.341/.414	110	.274	-0.4	2B -6, 3B -6	1.3

Comparables: Davey Johnson, Mark Loretta, Glenn Hubbard

Last winter, people were saying it in whispers: "Tommy La Stella is ... come closer ... *good*." It seemed like a prank, a joke as cruel as La Stella being selected to his first All-Star team in the midst of a storybook 2019 season and almost immediately fracturing his right tibia via foul ball. When this season finally arrived, though, La Stella was just as good as in his first season with the Angels, and continued producing after being traded upstate to Oakland. The 30-home run pace didn't recur (frankly, if you expected it to, that's on you), but La Stella was actually the better hitter in 2020, proving the only joke was on the Cubs for never getting him the starting role he found in the AL West and rode into free agency.

Jake Lamb 3B Born: 10/09/90 Age: 30 Bats: L Throws: R Height: 6'3" Weight: 215 Origin: Round 6, 2012 Draft (#213 overall)

YEAR	TEAM	LVL	AGE	PA	R	2B	3B	HR	RBI	BB	K	SB	CS	Whiff%	AVG/OBP/SLG	DRC+	BABIP	BRR	FRAA	WARP
2018	ARI	MLB	27	238	34	8	0	6	31	26	65	1	2	28.6%	.222/.307/.348	79	.286	1.6	3B(52): -3.7	0.0
2019	RNO	AAA	28	46	5	2	0	1	7	7	12	0	0		.179/.304/.308	70	.231	0.0	3B(6): -0.8, 1B(5): -0.0	-0.1
2019	ARI	MLB	28	226	26	8	2	6	30	32	55	1	0	25.8%	.193/.323/.353	94	.234	2.3	3B(36): -1.6, 1B(24): -1.3	0.4
2020	OAK	MLB	30	49	5	4	0	3	9	2	8	0	0	21.6%	.267/.327/.556	75	.265	0.0	3B(11): -1.9	-0.2
2020	ARI	MLB	30	50	2	1	0	0	1	6	17	0	1	31.0%	.116/.240/.140	78	.192	-0.2	1B(12): 0.2, 3B(3): 0.0	-0.1
2021 FS	OAK	MLB	30	600	65	24	3	19	66	70	166	5	2	26.7%	.212/.313/.381	94	.270	1.0	3B -11, 1B -1	-0.4

Comparables: Jack Howell, Ian Stewart, Mike Pagliarulo

There are no extant masks that were actually worn in Greek theater, given that they tended to be made from perishable materials such as wood or linen. Examples you might be familiar with, like the comedy and tragedy masks, are taken from paintings or terracotta simulacrums. It's theorized, though, that the comedy and tragedy masks were fashioned in the likeness of different points in Lamb's 2020 season: The first, when he was designated for assignment by the flailing D'Backs in early September with a .380 OPS; the second when he posted a mark 500 points higher as the fill-in for Matt Chapman and made the A's playoff roster. It was an almost self-parodic addition by the Oakland front office, made only more so by the fact it worked.

Ramón Laureano CF Born: 07/15/94 Age: 26 Bats: R Throws: R Height: 5'11" Weight: 203 Origin: Round 16, 2014 Draft (#466 overall)

YEAR	TEAM	LVL	AGE	PA	R	2B	3B	HR	RBI	BB	K	SB	CS	Whiff%	AVG/OBP/SLG	DRC+	BABIP	BRR	FRAA	WARP
2018	NAS	AAA	23	284	44	12	1	14	35	31	70	11	2		.297/.380/.524	144	.358	1.7	RF(45): 6.2, CF(19): -0.5, LF(1): -0.0	2.5
2018	OAK	MLB	23	176	27	12	1	5	19	16	50	7	1	29.1%	.288/.358/.474	92	.388	1.4	CF(47): 3.0	0.9
2019	OAK	MLB	24	481	79	29	0	24	67	27	123	13	2	27.9%	.288/.340/.521	115	.342	2.2	CF(110): 9.0, RF(13): 5.1	4.2
2020	OAK	MLB	26	222	27	8	1	6	25	24	58	2	1	25.0%	.213/.338/.366	107	.270	0.8	CF(53): 8.3	1.7
2021 FS	OAK	MLB	26	600	76	26	2	21	71	52	169	18	4	27.0%	.241/.327/.424	108	.312	6.0	CF -6, LF 0	2.4
2021 DC	OAK	MLB	26	570	72	25	2	20	68	50	161	17	4	27.0%	.241/.327/.424	108	.312	5.7	CF -5	2.5

Comparables: Preston Wilson, Jose Cruz, Joc Pederson

Sometimes, a person comes to represent something beyond themselves. Laureano charged the Astros dugout on August 11, instigating the first bench-clearing of the 2020 season and ensuring a suspension, for the most personal of reasons: He heard Astros hitting coach Alex Cintrón say something about his mother. (Cintrón denies the maternal insult, but was suspended 20 games for saying *something* to provoke Laureano, compared to an eventual four games for the outfielder.) In a season without fans to needle the Houston players, though, Laureano's rush toward the dugout went beyond the personal for all those still feeling aggrieved by a squad that saw little reprisal. He's also established himself as one of the best defensive center fielders in baseball, adding baserunning skills to a package that's star-level even if he never takes the next step as a batter. This version of Laureano, even with a four-game suspension, was by WARP the 13th best position player in baseball.

Vimael Machín 2B Born: 09/25/93 Age: 27 Bats: L Throws: R Height: 5'11" Weight: 185 Origin: Round 10, 2015 Draft (#293 overall)

YEAR	TEAM	LVL	AGE	PA	R	2B	3B	HR	RBI	BB	K	SB	CS	Whiff%	AVG/OBP/SLG	DRC+	BABIP	BRR	FRAA	WARP
2018	MB	HI-A	24	141	20	6	0	2	14	28	23	1	0		.209/.369/.318	124	.241	0.0	2B(17): 0.1, 3B(10): -0.1	0.4
2018	TNS	AA	24	296	30	10	1	5	28	39	54	2	1		.220/.330/.328	88	.259	-2.2	2B(35): -4.5, 1B(12): -1.3, 3B(12): -0.5	-1.1
2019	TNS	AA	25	498	47	26	1	6	61	63	57	8	2		.294/.386/.403	145	.322	-1.5	SS(47): -3.9, 2B(44): 2.8, 3B(26): -0.4	3.7
2019	IOW	AAA	25	31	7	1	1	1	4	6	5	0	0		.320/.452/.560	119	.368	-0.9	1B(5): -0.9, 2B(3): -0.1, 3B(3): -0.1	0.0
2020	OAK	MLB	27	71	11	2	0	0	0	8	10	0	0	20.8%	.206/.296/.238	92	.245	1.0	3B(10): -0.4, SS(6): 1.1, 2B(3): -0.3	0.2
2021 FS	OAK	MLB	27	600	64	28	1	11	60	63	122	0	0	20.8%	.246/.330/.370	97	.300	-0.8	SS -11, 2B -2	-0.2
2021 DC	OAK	MLB	27	167	18	7	0	3	16	17	34	0	0	20.8%	.246/.330/.370	97	.300	-0.2	SS -3, 2B 0	0.1

Comparables: Eric Young Jr., Nate Spears, Sherman Johnson

The Rays might have copped the A's reputation as the most ruthless, astute pursuants of the temptress Efficiency, but the Rule 5 Draft is perhaps MLB's foremost arena where a front office can make something out of nothing, and Machin's pick-up from the Cubs was a savvy move. At 27, it's probably unrealistic to expect much further development from Machin, and in that way the pick goes against the recent grain of young, highly unpolished Rule 5 draftees. Appearing at all four infield positions and demonstrating solid pitch selection—he struck out just two times more than he walked with Oakland, and twice in the minors posted a better walk than strikeout rate—Machin figures to have set himself up to fill a utility role in the immediate future.

Sean Murphy C Born: 10/04/94 Age: 26 Bats: R Throws: R Height: 6'3" Weight: 228 Origin: Round 3, 2016 Draft (#83 overall)

YEAR	TEAM	LVL	AGE	PA	R	2B	3B	HR	RBI	BB	K	SB	CS	Whiff%	AVG/OBP/SLG	DRC+	BABIP	BRR	FRAA	WARP
2018	MID	AA	23	289	51	26	2	8	43	23	47	3	0		.288/.358/.498	133	.324	2.1	C(65): 14.5	3.4
2019	ASGO	ROK	24	32	8	2	0	1	1	4	4	0	0		.214/.312/.393	122	.217	0.2	C(8): -0.1	0.2
2019	LV	AAA	24	140	25	6	1	10	30	15	31	0	1		.308/.386/.625	122	.329	-1.3	C(27): 1.5	1.0
2019	OAK	MLB	24	60	14	5	0	4	8	6	16	0	0	29.8%	.245/.333/.566	97	.273	1.1	C(18): -1.6	0.2
2020	OAK	MLB	26	140	21	5	0	7	14	24	37	0	0	25.0%	.233/.364/.457	112	.278	-0.5	C(43): -0.2	0.7
2021 FS	OAK	MLB	26	600	73	24	1	24	75	61	157	1	0	26.1%	.236/.320/.430	108	.285	-0.3	C -3	2.8
2021 DC	OAK	MLB	26	436	53	18	1	18	54	44	114	0	0	26.1%	.236/.320/.430	108	.285	-0.2	C -3	1.9

Comparables: Josmil Pinto, Geovany Soto, Bobby Estalella

YEAR	TEAM	P. COUNT	FRM RUNS	BLK RUNS	THRW RUNS	TOT RUNS
2018	NAS	422	0.0	0.0	0.0	0.0
2019	OAK	2060	-0.2	-1.2	0.0	-1.4
2019	LV	4014	1.1	0.2	-0.5	0.8
2020	OAK	5458	-1.2	0.0	-0.1	-1.3
2021	OAK	15632	-1.2	-2.4	0.3	-3.4

It sounds like a backhanded compliment to say something or someone is good, but not in the way you'd expect. It suggests an inviting quality, but also something off-putting: It's what one might say about a tenuous, slightly opaque new technology, or hyperpop music, or Sean Murphy's rookie season. A top-five catcher in terms of DRC+ and bases on balls, Murphy impressed enough to place just off the podium in AL Rookie of the Year voting. All of which is impressive enough, considering Murphy was perceived more as a glove-first prospect with potential for some pop. There was little expectation he'd bring to the majors a judicious eye that placed him third among all catchers in on-base percentage (minimum 100 plate appearances). The glove looked more tenuous, but given hardiness that allowed him to appear in 43 games and catch every playoff inning—another reversal, given an injury-fraught path to the majors—there's enough here to profile Murphy as an average or better starter.

Matt Olson 1B Born: 03/29/94 Age: 27 Bats: L Throws: R Height: 6'5" Weight: 225 Origin: Round 1, 2012 Draft (#47 overall)

YEAR	TEAM	LVL	AGE	PA	R	2B	3B	HR	RBI	BB	K	SB	CS	Whiff%	AVG/OBP/SLG	DRC+	BABIP	BRR	FRAA	WARP
2018	OAK	MLB	24	660	85	33	0	29	84	70	163	2	1	27.7%	.247/.335/.453	114	.292	-2.6	1B(162): 3.8	2.2
2019	OAK	MLB	25	547	73	26	0	36	91	51	138	0	0	28.5%	.267/.351/.545	133	.300	-1.9	1B(127): 11.7	4.1
2020	OAK	MLB	26	245	28	4	1	14	42	34	77	1	0	35.0%	.195/.310/.424	101	.227	0.3	1B(60): 4.7	1.1
2021 FS	OAK	MLB	27	600	81	22	1	32	90	78	180	1	0	30.1%	.235/.343/.476	125	.292	-0.6	1B 6, 3B 0	3.4
2021 DC	OAK	MLB	27	604	81	22	1	32	91	78	181	1	0	30.1%	.235/.343/.476	125	.292	-0.6	1B 6	3.4

Comparables: Paul Goldschmidt, Mike Napoli, Chris Carter

Defense is rarely incidental for a first baseman; what is already the least valuable position on the defensive spectrum becomes something of a self-fulfilling prophecy as players who are already slow, lack range, or have other defensive limitations are shifted down the spectrum to an eventual home at first. This to say that exemplary defense at first base is a rarity more because of incidental factors than an inherent reality of the position. Olson is the majors' preeminent example of this, following up a star-making 2019 where his 11.7 FRAA was best among primary first basemen and 21st in the majors, he was just as resplendent in the field in 2020's short season. The offense was average, a big step back, but not enough of a counterweight from the defense to drop Olson out of the top 50 position players by WARP.

Chad Pinder 2B Born: 03/29/92 Age: 29 Bats: R Throws: R Height: 6'2" Weight: 210 Origin: Round 2, 2013 Draft (#71 overall)

YEAR	TEAM	LVL	AGE	PA	R	2B	3B	HR	RBI	BB	K	SB	CS	Whiff%	AVG/OBP/SLG	DRC+	BABIP	BRR	FRAA	WARP
2018	OAK	MLB	26	333	43	12	1	13	27	27	88	0	2	28.4%	.258/.332/.436	109	.325	0.8	LF(64): 4.8, 2B(21): -1.3, 3B(16): 0.2	1.8
2019	OAK	MLB	27	370	45	21	0	13	47	20	88	0	1	25.9%	.240/.290/.416	81	.284	0.9	LF(46): 2.4, RF(34): 4.2, 2B(21): -2.1	0.7
2020	OAK	MLB	28	61	8	3	0	2	8	5	13	0	0	21.7%	.232/.295/.393	94	.268	-0.3	2B(13): -1.8, 3B(7): 0.4, LF(2): -0.0	0.0
2021 FS	OAK	MLB	29	600	64	24	1	21	70	38	163	2	0	25.9%	.225/.287/.392	86	.279	-0.5	SS 3, 2B -6	0.3
2021 DC	OAK	MLB	29	503	54	20	1	17	59	32	137	1	0	25.9%	.225/.287/.392	86	.279	-0.4	SS 2, 2B -5	0.5

Comparables: Marcus Thames, Matt Luke, Pete Incaviglia

Pinder has two definitions: the first is a word for peanut, chiefly used in the South; the second is a word for a person who impounds animals, chiefly used in the U.K. You might notice the A's Pinder doesn't get a definition, because he continued to staunchly refuse one. Appearing at "only" four positions (in contrast to seven, all but pitcher and catcher, in the previous two seasons), Pinder was right in line with his career offensive baseline, but he saw no play at shortstop and center fielder and also posted the worst FRAA of his five seasons, calling into question whether he's still a "super"-utility going forward. A bench player who can fill in at multiple positions, you want; a bench player who can be slotted in anywhere on the field, you need. Divergent definitions.

Stephen Piscotty RF Born: 01/14/91 Age: 30 Bats: R Throws: R Height: 6'4" Weight: 211 Origin: Round 1, 2012 Draft (#36 overall)

YEAR	TEAM	LVL	AGE	PA	R	2B	3B	HR	RBI	BB	K	SB	CS	Whiff%	AVG/OBP/SLG	DRC+	BABIP	BRR	FRAA	WARP
2018	OAK	MLB	27	605	78	41	0	27	88	42	114	2	0	25.4%	.267/.331/.491	120	.290	-1.4	RF(151): -9.3	1.7
2019	OAK	MLB	28	393	46	17	1	13	44	29	84	2	0	29.0%	.249/.309/.412	94	.289	1.1	RF(90): -3.7	0.4
2020	OAK	MLB	29	171	17	6	0	5	29	9	53	4	0	33.6%	.226/.271/.358	79	.304	0.2	RF(44): -6.9	-0.8
2021 FS	OAK	MLB	30	600	65	25	1	20	72	51	160	5	2	29.0%	.237/.312/.401	98	.298	-1.1	RF -7	0.4
2021 DC	OAK	MLB	30	503	55	21	1	16	60	43	134	4	1	29.0%	.237/.312/.401	98	.298	-0.9	RF -6	0.3

Comparables: Michael Cuddyer, Mike Marshall, Ryan Church

Sometimes, everything points in the wrong direction—phone battery dwindling, frustration mounting, mental list of tasks to complete before heading home never-ending. In Piscotty's case those markers were concrete, as he posted the highest strikeout (31 percent) and lowest walk (5.3 percent) rates of his six-year career along with his worst marks in all of batting average, on-base, slugging, and isolated slugging percentages, plus DRC+. The defense has always been shaky and passable baserunning is hardly useful when you can't get on base—by WARP, Piscotty was the worst Athletic by more than half a win. Only the remaining two years of a six-year deal signed early in his career ensure Piscotty's starting role into 2021.

Robert Puason SS Born: 09/11/02 Age: 18 Bats: S Throws: R Height: 6'3" Weight: 165 Origin: International Free Agent, 2019

The Dominican-born Puason keeps a list of the people who helped him—and those who declined to do so. Given how quickly the shortstop, ultimately signed by the A's for $5.1 million in 2019 following a failed verbal agreement with Atlanta, has jumped up prospect lists, you wouldn't want to be on his bad list.

Marcus Semien SS Born: 09/17/90 Age: 30 Bats: R Throws: R Height: 6'0" Weight: 195 Origin: Round 6, 2011 Draft (#201 overall)

YEAR	TEAM	LVL	AGE	PA	R	2B	3B	HR	RBI	BB	K	SB	CS	Whiff%	AVG/OBP/SLG	DRC+	BABIP	BRR	FRAA	WARP
2018	OAK	MLB	27	703	89	35	2	15	70	61	131	14	6	20.4%	.255/.318/.388	98	.296	5.4	SS(159): 16.2	5.4
2019	OAK	MLB	28	747	123	43	7	33	92	87	102	10	8	18.5%	.285/.369/.522	134	.294	1.8	SS(161): 4.2	7.5
2020	OAK	MLB	30	236	28	9	1	7	23	25	50	4	0	23.3%	.223/.305/.374	101	.260	1.4	SS(53): 7.4	1.6
2021 FS	OAK	MLB	30	600	78	27	2	21	62	58	133	10	4	20.2%	.244/.319/.420	104	.285	-1.4	SS 7	2.9

Comparables: Woodie Held, Jhonny Peralta, Khalil Greene

It's rare to have a star position player for whom excellence in hitting is a secondary quality, but for a fleeting few seasons the A's had two such players in Ramón Laureano and Semien. In the latter case, that's dependent on agreement with FRAA's stellar evaluation as opposed to some conflicting metrics, but suffice it to say Semien is an especially well-rounded player when that trait is becoming something of a given league-wide. Semien's walk year was a step back from a 2019 that saw him as the best hitter on the A's, amounting to a WARP among the 10 best in the majors. A reversion to the league-average hitting of past seasons left it unclear if Oakland declining to tender a qualifying offer was typical A's stinginess or characteristic of a cold reception looming on the open market.

Tyler Soderstrom C Born: 11/24/01 Age: 19 Bats: L Throws: R Height: 6'2" Weight: 200 Origin: Round 1, 2020 Draft (#26 overall)

Expected to go well before the 26th pick in the first round, the A's went well over-slot to coax Soderstrom from his commitment to UCLA and wasted no time in kickstarting his development, adding him to their 60-player pool. Oakland is continuing to develop him at catcher, but the pure hitting talent and raw power are what made their executives so gleeful he fell to them. (Presumably also happy for the bragging rights is father Steve, picked 20 spots ahead of his scion in 1993.) Soderstrom earned rave reviews for the hitting ability he displayed in his professional debut, though he needs time behind the plate in games before anyone will anoint him as the A's catcher of the future.

PITCHERS

Chris Bassitt RHP Born: 02/22/89 Age: 32 Bats: R Throws: R Height: 6'5" Weight: 217 Origin: Round 16, 2011 Draft (#501 overall)

YEAR	TEAM	LVL	AGE	W	L	SV	G	GS	IP	H	HR	BB/9	K/9	K	GB%	BABIP	WHIP	ERA	DRA-	WARP	MPH	FA%	Whiff%	CSP
2018	NAS	AAA	29	5	5	0	18	14	81²	86	6	2.8	9.1	83	42.8%	.349	1.36	4.30	80	1.6				
2018	OAK	MLB	29	2	3	0	11	7	47²	40	4	3.6	7.7	41	43.6%	.265	1.24	3.02	116	0.0	94.0	82.3%	17.4%	51.9%
2019	LV	AAA	30	0	0	0	2	2	8	8	2	2.2	10.1	9	58.3%	.273	1.25	4.50	53	0.3				
2019	OAK	MLB	30	10	5	0	28	25	144	125	21	2.9	8.8	141	40.6%	.268	1.19	3.81	91	2.0	95.5	78.7%	21.0%	51.9%
2020	OAK	MLB	31	5	2	0	11	11	63	56	6	2.4	7.9	55	43.9%	.278	1.16	2.29	86	1.0	94.6	77.5%	23.0%	52.3%
2021 FS	OAK	MLB	32	9	8	0	26	26	150	139	21	3.2	8.7	144	43.0%	.286	1.28	4.07	96	1.4	95.1	78.6%	21.3%	52.0%
2021 DC	OAK	MLB	32	8	8	0	25	25	142	131	19	3.2	8.7	136	43.0%	.286	1.28	4.07	96	1.8	95.1	78.6%	21.3%	52.0%

Comparables: Trevor Cahill, Jhoulys Chacín, Kyle Gibson

It was a career year for Bassitt, who didn't flounder, and ended up as the team's best starter by both ERA and WARP. It's a less lofty perch per the advanced metrics, which saw Bassitt as slightly improved from the prior season but largely still a mid-rotation starter. Never having surpassed a 23 percent strikeout rate and lacking pinpoint command, it's unclear if Bassitt has a much higher ceiling than what he showed in a small-sample-size-boosted 2020. It was still enough to drum up an eighth-place Cy Young finish, though, and two seasons of this version of Bassitt has enough tang that, come 2021, people will take more than a flier.

Paul Blackburn RHP Born: 12/04/93 Age: 27 Bats: R Throws: R Height: 6'1" Weight: 196 Origin: Round 1, 2012 Draft (#56 overall)

YEAR	TEAM	LVL	AGE	W	L	SV	G	GS	IP	H	HR	BB/9	K/9	K	GB%	BABIP	WHIP	ERA	DRA-	WARP	MPH	FA%	Whiff%	CSP
2018	OAK	MLB	24	2	3	0	6	6	27²	33	2	2.0	6.2	19	47.8%	.344	1.41	7.16	86	0.5	91.3	40.4%	18.8%	42.8%
2019	LV	AAA	25	11	3	0	24	22	132²	133	18	2.3	6.2	92	53.7%	.293	1.26	4.34	66	4.4				
2019	OAK	MLB	25	0	2	0	4	1	11	19	3	3.3	6.5	8	50.0%	.400	2.09	10.64	114	0.0	92.4	61.2%	24.5%	42.4%
2020	OAK	MLB	26	0	1	0	1	1	2¹	5	0	7.7	7.7	2	50.0%	.500	3.00	27.00	96	0.0	91.0	50.0%	10.5%	42.3%
2021 FS	*OAK*	*MLB*	*27*	*3*	*4*	*0*	*57*	*0*	*50*	*52*	*6*	*3.9*	*6.8*	*37*	*50.1%*	*.294*	*1.48*	*4.94*	*112*	*-0.2*	*91.7*	*50.7%*	*20.1%*	*42.6%*
2021 DC	*OAK*	*MLB*	*27*	*3*	*4*	*0*	*51*	*4*	*68*	*70*	*9*	*3.9*	*6.8*	*51*	*50.1%*	*.294*	*1.48*	*4.94*	*112*	*0.0*	*91.7*	*50.7%*	*20.1%*	*42.6%*

Comparables: Zach Davies, Daniel Mengden, Joe Ross

Judging by his facial hair, Blackburn is a fan of symmetry. It must be some small comfort as he approaches his age-27 season, then, that he does so with a matching ERA from the previous season. "Small" being the operative word there.

Wandisson Charles RHP Born: 09/07/96 Age: 24 Bats: R Throws: R Height: 6'4" Weight: 263 Origin: International Free Agent, 2015

YEAR	TEAM	LVL	AGE	W	L	SV	G	GS	IP	H	HR	BB/9	K/9	K	GB%	BABIP	WHIP	ERA	DRA-	WARP	MPH	FA%	Whiff%	CSP
2018	BEL	LO-A	21	0	0	0	11	0	11	6	1	13.9	15.5	19	52.6%	.278	2.09	4.09	80	0.1				
2019	BEL	LO-A	22	1	0	0	13	0	22¹	12	1	8.1	14.9	37	48.8%	.275	1.43	3.22	76	0.3				
2019	STK	HI-A	22	2	0	2	18	0	25²	14	1	6.3	13.7	39	32.7%	.277	1.25	3.16	68	0.4				
2019	MID	AA	22	1	0	0	9	0	14¹	9	1	3.1	10.7	17	31.4%	.235	0.98	1.88	68	0.2				
2021 FS	*OAK*	*MLB*	*24*	*2*	*3*	*0*	*57*	*0*	*50*	*40*	*7*	*10.6*	*13.1*	*72*	*36.4%*	*.305*	*1.99*	*6.56*	*135*	*-0.9*				

Comparables: Cristian Javier, Steven Okert, Seth Elledge

Protected from the Rule 5 Draft in 2020 but not 2019, Charles must have impressed at the Athletics' alternate site, or at least given reason for the organization to expect the 100-and-a-slider righty would hew more to the 226 strikeouts in 170 1/3 minors innings than the 150 walks.

Jeff Criswell RHP Born: 03/10/99 Age: 22 Bats: R Throws: R Height: 6'4" Weight: 225 Origin: Round 2, 2020 Draft (#58 overall)

The A's 2020 second-round pick, a college junior out of Michigan, Criswell signed with the same organization for which his father played minor-league ball in the 80s. Featuring a relatively advanced four-seam fastball-slider-changeup mix, Criswell could stick in the rotation or have a shot to be a dominant reliever, given he touched 100 in relief during the tail end of the 2019 season. Professing equanimity regarding his eventual role and having led a faux-graduation ceremony for his Michigan teammates who were denied an actual chance to walk, the makeup appears as advanced as the stuff.

Jake Diekman LHP Born: 01/21/87 Age: 34 Bats: L Throws: L Height: 6'4" Weight: 195 Origin: Round 30, 2007 Draft (#923 overall)

YEAR	TEAM	LVL	AGE	W	L	SV	G	GS	IP	H	HR	BB/9	K/9	K	GB%	BABIP	WHIP	ERA	DRA-	WARP	MPH	FA%	Whiff%	CSP
2018	ARI	MLB	31	0	1	0	24	0	14¹	18	2	5.0	11.3	18	52.4%	.400	1.81	7.53	139	-0.2	97.2	67.9%	31.1%	46.8%
2018	TEX	MLB	31	1	1	2	47	0	39	31	2	5.3	11.1	48	48.0%	.302	1.38	3.69	141	-0.6	96.8	62.4%	27.5%	45.4%
2019	KC	MLB	32	0	6	0	48	0	41²	33	3	5.0	13.6	63	47.9%	.330	1.34	4.75	55	1.2	97.5	51.0%	38.3%	47.5%
2019	OAK	MLB	32	1	1	0	28	0	20¹	16	0	7.1	9.3	21	44.4%	.302	1.57	4.43	98	0.1	97.3	59.1%	29.2%	46.8%
2020	OAK	MLB	33	2	0	0	21	0	21¹	8	1	5.1	13.1	31	60.0%	.184	0.94	0.42	66	0.6	97.0	59.3%	40.8%	50.1%
2021 FS	*OAK*	*MLB*	*34*	*3*	*2*	*20*	*57*	*0*	*50*	*38*	*4*	*5.1*	*11.8*	*65*	*50.0%*	*.291*	*1.33*	*3.67*	*85*	*0.6*	*97.2*	*57.4%*	*35.1%*	*47.6%*
2021 DC	*OAK*	*MLB*	*34*	*3*	*2*	*20*	*58*	*0*	*62*	*47*	*5*	*5.1*	*11.8*	*81*	*50.0%*	*.291*	*1.33*	*3.67*	*85*	*0.9*	*97.2*	*57.4%*	*35.1%*	*47.6%*

Comparables: Chaz Roe, Sam Freeman, Cory Gearrin

The A's bullpen led the majors with a 2.72 ERA, which is the sort of thing that happens when a pitcher like Diekman allows just one earned run in 21 1/3 innings. The presumptive closer—and on an affordable contract, natch—showed signs of a breakout in 2019, but nothing could have predicted a 2020 in which he was nigh-unhittable. To be fair, it's hard to predict someone deciding to cop Chaz Roe's slider after seeing it on Twitter a day into the season and putting up a 19.6 percent whiff rate with it. This century, just two pitchers, 2020 Devin Williams and 2006 Matt Smith, allowed fewer than his 3.38 hits per nine innings (minimum 20 innings pitched). It's basically an impossible feat across a full season, as evidenced by none of the pitchers surpassing 30 innings. When you strike out 37 percent of batters, though, you get to break the rules a little bit. The walk rate is a ~~little~~ lot higher than you want, but again, Diekman gets to break the rules as long as he's this untouchable.

Mike Fiers RHP Born: 06/15/85 Age: 36 Bats: R Throws: R Height: 6'2" Weight: 211 Origin: Round 22, 2009 Draft (#676 overall)

YEAR	TEAM	LVL	AGE	W	L	SV	G	GS	IP	H	HR	BB/9	K/9	K	GB%	BABIP	WHIP	ERA	DRA-	WARP	MPH	FA%	Whiff%	CSP
2018	OAK	MLB	33	5	2	0	10	9	53	45	12	1.9	8.8	52	42.5%	.246	1.06	3.74	89	0.8	92.0	51.2%	21.1%	51.0%
2018	DET	MLB	33	7	6	0	21	21	119	121	20	2.0	6.6	87	38.0%	.278	1.24	3.48	108	0.6	91.5	46.7%	19.2%	49.1%
2019	OAK	MLB	34	15	4	0	33	33	184²	166	30	2.6	6.1	126	38.9%	.256	1.19	3.90	103	1.4	92.4	51.7%	18.3%	49.7%
2020	OAK	MLB	35	6	3	0	11	11	59	65	9	2.4	5.6	37	34.5%	.293	1.37	4.58	131	-0.5	89.8	44.9%	15.7%	49.4%
2021 FS	*OAK*	*MLB*	*36*	*8*	*10*	*0*	*26*	*26*	*150*	*167*	*30*	*2.8*	*6.4*	*107*	*37.6%*	*.294*	*1.43*	*5.31*	*124*	*-1.0*	*91.6*	*49.2%*	*18.0%*	*49.6%*

Comparables: Aníbal Sánchez, Ian Kennedy, Ted Lilly

It's hard to fathom how, exactly, Fiers might have captured the public's interest more in 2020 than in the preceding year, when he tossed the second no-hitter of his career and then, after the season, went on the record about the Astros cheating scheme, pushing the first of a series of dominoes that cost the Astros their GM and both Houston and Boston their manager (and also the Mets, because the Mets). Despite his offseason notoriety, Fiers was mostly anonymous on the field, losing two ticks off his fastball and going below replacement level, with the worst DRA on the A's, for only the second time in a 10-year career.

Liam Hendriks RHP   Born: 02/10/89   Age: 32   Bats: R   Throws: R   Height: 6'0"   Weight: 230   Origin: International Free Agent, 2007

YEAR	TEAM	LVL	AGE	W	L	SV	G	GS	IP	H	HR	BB/9	K/9	K	GB%	BABIP	WHIP	ERA	DRA-	WARP	MPH	FA%	Whiff%	CSP
2018	NAS	AAA	29	4	1	6	23	1	25¹	21	1	1.4	15.3	43	35.7%	.377	0.99	2.84	48	0.8				
2018	OAK	MLB	29	0	1	0	25	8	24	25	3	3.8	8.2	22	39.4%	.324	1.46	4.12	104	0.1	97.2	70.1%	25.8%	47.0%
2019	OAK	MLB	30	4	4	25	75	2	85	61	5	2.2	13.1	124	30.3%	.315	0.96	1.80	56	2.4	98.6	70.6%	36.1%	48.4%
2020	OAK	MLB	31	3	1	14	24	0	25¹	14	1	1.1	13.1	37	28.8%	.260	0.67	1.78	66	0.7	97.8	70.5%	36.2%	49.4%
2021 FS	OAK	MLB	32	3	2	0	57	0	50	38	6	2.2	12.1	67	35.2%	.282	1.01	2.41	65	1.1	98.3	70.6%	35.0%	48.5%

Comparables: Tommy Hunter, Brett Cecil, Jeanmar Gómez

As fickle as relievers tend to be, Hendriks was eerily consistent between 2019 and 2020; his most notable change was dropping an already excellent WHIP by one-third, to an unfathomable 0.67. That and a 40-save pace earned Hendriks first-team All-MLB honors, a cool achievement even if it's not necessarily one a reader is likely to have heard of before this comment. Another sterling season also all-but ensured the pending free agent would be out of Oakland's price range, meaning you can make a little game out of the relievers surrounding Hendriks here: Who will be next season's out-of-nowhere relief ace on a highly affordable salary, whose simultaneous improvements in strikeout, walk, and hit rates confound hitters as much as evaluators? Wait for the buzzer to guess—*ding*

Grant Holmes RHP   Born: 03/22/96   Age: 25   Bats: L   Throws: R   Height: 6'0"   Weight: 226   Origin: Round 1, 2014 Draft (#22 overall)

YEAR	TEAM	LVL	AGE	W	L	SV	G	GS	IP	H	HR	BB/9	K/9	K	GB%	BABIP	WHIP	ERA	DRA-	WARP	MPH	FA%	Whiff%	CSP
2018	STK	HI-A	22	0	0	0	2	2	6	4	1	3.0	12.0	8	46.7%	.214	1.00	4.50	78	0.1				
2019	MID	AA	23	6	5	0	22	16	81²	71	9	3.0	8.4	76	50.4%	.282	1.20	3.31	98	0.1				
2021 FS	OAK	MLB	25	3	4	0	57	0	50	46	7	4.7	8.4	46	45.3%	.280	1.46	4.85	114	-0.3				
2021 DC	OAK	MLB	25	3	4	0	41	6	65	60	10	4.7	8.4	61	45.3%	.280	1.46	4.85	114	0.0				

Comparables: Robert Dugger, Jesse Biddle, Nabil Crismatt

Speaking of his progression through the minors, Holmes said, "It's pretty crazy how slo-mo it is." Oh, sorry, correction here—he was speaking about an Edgertronic camera. Well, confusion is understandable at the close of a seventh professional season, though he might have broken into the majors if afforded a complete slate of games.

Daulton Jefferies RHP   Born: 08/02/95   Age: 25   Bats: L   Throws: R   Height: 6'0"   Weight: 182   Origin: Round 1, 2016 Draft (#37 overall)

YEAR	TEAM	LVL	AGE	W	L	SV	G	GS	IP	H	HR	BB/9	K/9	K	GB%	BABIP	WHIP	ERA	DRA-	WARP	MPH	FA%	Whiff%	CSP
2018	ASGR	ROK	22	0	0	0	1	1	2	1	0	0.0	22.5	5	0.0%	.500	0.50	0.00	10	0.1				
2019	STK	HI-A	23	1	0	0	5	3	15	10	1	1.2	12.6	21	44.1%	.273	0.80	2.40	52	0.4				
2019	MID	AA	23	1	2	0	21	12	64	63	7	1.0	10.1	72	41.0%	.329	1.09	3.66	69	1.1				
2020	OAK	MLB	24	0	1	0	1	1	2	5	2	9.0	4.5	1	30.0%	.375	3.50	22.50	116	0.0	95.5	81.1%	23.1%	52.0%
2021 FS	OAK	MLB	25	9	8	0	26	26	150	139	23	2.4	8.9	148	39.6%	.286	1.20	3.79	94	1.6	95.5	81.1%	23.1%	52.0%
2021 DC	OAK	MLB	25	4	5	0	16	16	77	71	11	2.4	8.9	76	39.6%	.286	1.20	3.79	94	1.1	95.5	81.1%	23.1%	52.0%

Comparables: Dean Kremer, Jharel Cotton, Jose Urquidy

You might've heard of the Darwin Awards, but what about the Daulton Awards? They're awarded annually for excellence in Daultons, and our man Jefferies is taking one home. You might not think two innings, five earned runs and a loss in one's major-league debut qualifies one for an award, but Daulton isn't a popular name. For Jefferies, who only really came back from a 2017 Tommy John surgery in 2019, it was impressive to see a mostly on-track debut, no matter how curtailed. The A's were likely more interested in the mid-90s heat from a starter, in any case. Jefferies holding onto the award next year depends on if he can keep to the rotation in a full season.

James Kaprielian RHP   Born: 03/02/94   Age: 27   Bats: R   Throws: R   Height: 6'3"   Weight: 225   Origin: Round 1, 2015 Draft (#16 overall)

YEAR	TEAM	LVL	AGE	W	L	SV	G	GS	IP	H	HR	BB/9	K/9	K	GB%	BABIP	WHIP	ERA	DRA-	WARP	MPH	FA%	Whiff%	CSP
2019	STK	HI-A	25	2	2	0	11	10	36¹	35	6	2.0	10.7	43	32.0%	.319	1.18	4.46	92	0.2				
2019	MID	AA	25	2	1	0	7	5	27²	18	2	2.6	8.5	26	40.8%	.232	0.94	1.63	61	0.6				
2019	LV	AAA	25	0	0	0	1	1	4	6	0	0.0	13.5	6	16.7%	.500	1.50	2.25	70	0.1				
2020	OAK	MLB	26	0	0	0	2	0	3²	4	2	4.9	9.8	4	36.4%	.222	1.64	7.36	112	0.0	96.5	69.0%	37.5%	39.2%
2021 FS	OAK	MLB	27	2	3	0	57	0	50	46	8	3.3	9.1	50	38.2%	.287	1.30	4.25	101	0.1	96.5	69.0%	37.5%	39.2%
2021 DC	OAK	MLB	27	2	3	0	58	0	62	57	9	3.3	9.1	62	38.2%	.287	1.30	4.25	101	0.3	96.5	69.0%	37.5%	39.2%

Comparables: Joe Musgrove, Walker Lockett, Dillon Tate

Since being drafted 16th overall in 2015, Kaprielian has pitched in just 29 games. After 2020 it can at least be said two of those appearances were in the major leagues. The velocity looked to be more or less back after dipping in his return campaign from Tommy John, sowing hope the dream of a top-of-the-rotation starter isn't wholly dead—though the better money's on waiting for a season where he doesn't pitch the majority of his frames at High-A.

Jesús Luzardo LHP Born: 09/30/97 Age: 23 Bats: L Throws: L Height: 6'0" Weight: 218 Origin: Round 3, 2016 Draft (#94 overall)

YEAR	TEAM	LVL	AGE	W	L	SV	G	GS	IP	H	HR	BB/9	K/9	K	GB%	BABIP	WHIP	ERA	DRA-	WARP	MPH	FA%	Whiff%	CSP
2018	STK	HI-A	20	2	1	0	3	3	14²	6	0	3.1	15.3	25	56.0%	.240	0.75	1.23	34	0.6				
2018	MID	AA	20	7	3	0	16	16	78²	58	5	2.1	9.8	86	44.3%	.270	0.97	2.29	69	1.8				
2018	NAS	AAA	20	1	1	0	4	4	16	25	2	3.9	10.1	18	51.0%	.469	2.00	7.31	61	0.5				
2019	ASGR	ROK	21	0	0	0	1	1	2	1	0	0.0	22.5	5	100.0%	.500	0.50	0.00	18	0.1				
2019	STK	HI-A	21	1	0	0	3	1	10	6	1	0.0	16.2	18	44.4%	.312	0.60	0.90	44	0.3				
2019	LV	AAA	21	1	1	0	7	7	31	29	3	2.3	9.9	34	55.1%	.306	1.19	3.19	52	1.2				
2019	OAK	MLB	21	0	0	2	6	0	12	5	1	2.2	12.0	16	42.3%	.160	0.67	1.50	68	0.3	98.2	48.5%	37.7%	44.5%
2020	OAK	MLB	22	3	2	0	12	9	59	58	9	2.6	9.0	59	46.2%	.308	1.27	4.12	93	0.8	97.6	53.3%	29.7%	46.2%
2021 FS	OAK	MLB	23	9	8	0	26	26	150	131	19	3.6	10.0	165	45.7%	.289	1.28	3.82	91	1.8	97.7	52.8%	30.6%	46.0%
2021 DC	OAK	MLB	23	8	8	0	25	25	134	117	17	3.6	10.0	148	45.7%	.289	1.28	3.82	91	2.1	97.7	52.8%	30.6%	46.0%

Comparables: Julio Urías, José Suarez, Patrick Sandoval

With a Tommy John surgery, lat strain and shoulder strain—that's pretty much every part of the arm a pitcher might injure—all presenting roadblocks between being drafted in 2016 and his major-league debut in 2019, it's a minor victory Luzardo was simply able to hang in the rotation throughout 2020. That's the sort of thing that only gets said, though, when the results disappoint—after dominating in a short relief stint in 2019, he was merely average as he transitioned to the rotation. While he did well to avoid the injury bug, he couldn't avoid being snakebitten, racking up a 17.6 percent HR/FB ratio despite a stingy 30 percent flyball rate overall. No good comeback story ends with the hero doing just sorta okay; audiences want to see dominance, and Luzardo won't get back on the road to domination unless he can control his mechanics (and thus his exit velocities) better.

Sean Manaea LHP Born: 02/01/92 Age: 29 Bats: R Throws: L Height: 6'5" Weight: 245 Origin: Round 1, 2013 Draft (#34 overall)

YEAR	TEAM	LVL	AGE	W	L	SV	G	GS	IP	H	HR	BB/9	K/9	K	GB%	BABIP	WHIP	ERA	DRA-	WARP	MPH	FA%	Whiff%	CSP
2018	OAK	MLB	26	12	9	0	27	27	160²	141	21	1.8	6.0	108	43.3%	.249	1.08	3.59	90	2.4	92.5	56.2%	20.2%	53.4%
2019	STK	HI-A	27	0	2	0	3	3	8¹	14	1	4.3	10.8	10	42.9%	.481	2.16	9.72	192	-0.4				
2019	LV	AAA	27	3	1	0	5	5	28	16	5	1.9	13.8	43	47.3%	.224	0.79	3.21	25	1.5				
2019	OAK	MLB	27	4	0	0	5	5	29²	16	3	2.1	9.1	30	40.0%	.194	0.78	1.21	82	0.6	92.5	63.5%	28.3%	45.7%
2020	OAK	MLB	28	4	3	0	11	11	54	57	7	1.3	7.5	45	50.0%	.311	1.20	4.50	86	0.9	92.9	54.3%	22.1%	50.9%
2021 FS	OAK	MLB	29	9	8	0	26	26	150	140	21	2.4	8.8	146	46.1%	.288	1.21	3.77	92	1.7	92.7	56.5%	22.3%	51.1%
2021 DC	OAK	MLB	29	8	8	0	25	25	137	128	19	2.4	8.8	133	46.1%	.288	1.21	3.77	92	2.0	92.7	56.5%	22.3%	51.1%

Comparables: Trevor Williams, Jerad Eickhoff, José Ureña

Pokémon Black and White, the fifth generation in the highest-grossing media franchise of all time, earned some of the loftiest praise of the series for an anti-hero who asked a seemingly obvious question: "Do these pets want to fight?" Manaea, in 2020, also learned the value of asking obvious questions, when he took a 10-day layoff between August and September to ask "what if I pitched harder?" While he's still a solid three ticks below the velocity he brought to the majors, it's notable the southpaw reversed a trend of diminished velocity that had held for every season between 2015 and 2019, gaining 2.5 mph between August and October, and mixed that with an improved changeup. His results improved substantially as the season went on, and he cut his final ERA in half after it had peaked at 9.00 mid-season.

T.J. McFarland LHP Born: 06/08/89 Age: 32 Bats: L Throws: L Height: 6'3" Weight: 200 Origin: Round 4, 2007 Draft (#137 overall)

YEAR	TEAM	LVL	AGE	W	L	SV	G	GS	IP	H	HR	BB/9	K/9	K	GB%	BABIP	WHIP	ERA	DRA-	WARP	MPH	FA%	Whiff%	CSP
2018	ARI	MLB	29	2	2	1	47	0	72	64	4	2.8	5.2	42	66.7%	.269	1.19	2.00	105	0.2	91.8	72.7%	20.0%	41.6%
2019	ARI	MLB	30	0	0	0	51	0	56	71	6	3.2	5.6	35	59.8%	.349	1.62	4.82	134	-0.7	90.6	68.6%	22.0%	42.5%
2020	OAK	MLB	31	2	0	0	23	0	20²	26	5	2.2	3.9	9	59.7%	.292	1.50	4.35	107	0.1	90.2	59.8%	16.3%	40.5%
2021 FS	OAK	MLB	32	2	3	0	57	0	50	53	5	3.4	5.9	32	60.0%	.295	1.44	4.48	107	-0.1	90.8	67.4%	20.0%	41.8%

Comparables: Jeff Manship, Justin Grimm, Anthony Bass

Everyone's trying to recapture something. For some, it's something as simple as the feeling of youth they had in high school. Others just want the thrill of another entire conversation without saying "um" once. For T.J. McFarland, the green light is the 2018 season he finished with a 2.00 ERA and a 14 percent strikeout rate. He returned the strikeout rate in 2019 but saw the ERA more than double. Picked up by Oakland off waivers from Arizona, McFarland's 2020 was more of the same except this season featured a sub-10 percent strikeout rate, the second-worst in the majors (minimum 20 innings). You can't capture lightning in a bottle, but also McFarland might never have been lightning.

Frankie Montas RHP   Born: 03/21/93   Age: 28   Bats: R   Throws: R   Height: 6'2"   Weight: 255   Origin: International Free Agent, 2009

YEAR	TEAM	LVL	AGE	W	L	SV	G	GS	IP	H	HR	BB/9	K/9	K	GB%	BABIP	WHIP	ERA	DRA-	WARP	MPH	FA%	Whiff%	CSP
2018	NAS	AAA	25	4	5	0	15	15	71²	69	7	3.3	7.7	61	46.7%	.302	1.33	4.65	86	1.2				
2018	OAK	MLB	25	5	4	0	13	11	65	74	5	2.9	6.0	43	41.9%	.329	1.46	3.88	124	-0.2	97.7	72.5%	19.3%	51.3%
2019	OAK	MLB	26	9	2	0	16	16	96	84	8	2.2	9.7	103	49.6%	.297	1.11	2.62	64	2.7	98.4	56.8%	26.0%	49.1%
2020	OAK	MLB	27	3	5	0	11	11	53	57	10	3.9	10.2	60	36.6%	.329	1.51	5.60	107	0.3	97.7	62.0%	28.9%	50.9%
2021 FS	OAK	MLB	28	9	8	0	26	26	150	139	22	3.6	9.6	160	41.1%	.295	1.32	4.16	97	1.3	98.0	61.3%	26.2%	50.2%
2021 DC	OAK	MLB	28	8	9	0	27	27	145	134	21	3.6	9.6	154	41.1%	.295	1.32	4.16	97	1.7	98.0	61.3%	26.2%	50.2%

Comparables: Joe Musgrove, Jorge López, John Gant

In 2019, not having Frankie Montas was a big storyline for the A's in their Wild Card Game. In 2020, Montas took the win in the decisive game in the Wild Card Series—only he did it in relief. A year removed from a dominant half-season halted by a suspension for PED use, there's still lack of clarity about what sort of pitcher, exactly, Montas is. He was unilaterally worse in 2020—the K/9 went up, but that's because Montas got outs less often and highlights more a limitation of the metric than anything else; his K% slightly decreased. He walked the same number of batters as he did the previous season in 43 fewer innings. The steady decrease in velocity over the past two seasons is concerning. but even should that stabilize it'll be unclear what to make of Montas; at a certain point there's a sort of consistency in inconsistency.

Yusmeiro Petit RHP   Born: 11/22/84   Age: 36   Bats: R   Throws: R   Height: 6'1"   Weight: 252   Origin: International Free Agent, 2001

YEAR	TEAM	LVL	AGE	W	L	SV	G	GS	IP	H	HR	BB/9	K/9	K	GB%	BABIP	WHIP	ERA	DRA-	WARP	MPH	FA%	Whiff%	CSP
2018	OAK	MLB	33	7	3	0	74	0	93	76	13	1.7	7.4	76	35.0%	.242	1.01	3.00	83	1.3	91.0	47.5%	20.0%	51.1%
2019	OAK	MLB	34	5	3	0	80	0	83	57	11	1.1	7.7	71	30.0%	.214	0.81	2.71	80	1.3	90.6	45.8%	25.1%	48.9%
2020	OAK	MLB	35	2	1	0	26	0	21²	19	3	2.1	7.1	17	31.8%	.254	1.11	1.66	111	0.1	89.8	42.4%	26.2%	49.8%
2021 FS	OAK	MLB	36	2	2	0	57	0	50	47	9	2.0	7.9	43	33.7%	.272	1.17	3.71	95	0.3	90.5	45.6%	23.9%	49.7%

Comparables: Matt Belisle, Mark Melancon, Turk Farrell

Since transitioning to relief full-time in 2015, here are Petit's cFIPs: 101, 102, 86 102, 101, 105. Apart from a 2017 season in Anaheim that earned him a two-year contract with an option, even as his DRA- marks have bounced around below 100, Petit has largely been the same pitcher: someone whose stuff indicates average performance but consistently manages to turn in better results. The run prevention skill still played in 2020, but inflated walk and home run rates paired with the worst fastball velocity of his relief career portend a looming cliff. "Time's a goon, right?"

A.J. Puk LHP   Born: 04/25/95   Age: 26   Bats: L   Throws: L   Height: 6'7"   Weight: 248   Origin: Round 1, 2016 Draft (#6 overall)

YEAR	TEAM	LVL	AGE	W	L	SV	G	GS	IP	H	HR	BB/9	K/9	K	GB%	BABIP	WHIP	ERA	DRA-	WARP	MPH	FA%	Whiff%	CSP
2019	STK	HI-A	24	0	0	0	3	3	6	5	2	6.0	13.5	9	33.3%	.300	1.50	6.00	109	0.0				
2019	MID	AA	24	0	0	0	6	1	8¹	9	2	3.2	14.0	13	57.9%	.412	1.44	4.32	121	-0.1				
2019	LV	AAA	24	4	1	0	9	0	11	7	3	2.5	13.1	16	41.7%	.190	0.91	4.91	46	0.4				
2019	OAK	MLB	24	2	0	0	10	0	11¹	10	1	4.0	10.3	13	44.8%	.321	1.32	3.18	70	0.2	98.9	63.9%	30.9%	51.5%
2021 FS	OAK	MLB	26	9	7	0	26	26	150	124	18	3.5	10.6	176	43.8%	.286	1.21	3.39	82	2.6	98.9	63.9%	30.9%	51.5%
2021 DC	OAK	MLB	26	6	5	0	39	16	97	80	11	3.5	10.6	114	43.8%	.286	1.21	3.39	82	1.8	98.9	63.9%	30.9%	51.5%

Comparables: Thomas Pannone, Bryan Garcia, Gregory Soto

Stagnation isn't really a thing when it comes to prospect evaluation; opinions are constantly shifting as new data comes in. When no data is coming in? Well, it shifts anyway, though you might not know it from Puk. For four straight years coming into the 2020 season he'd been among the top trio of A's prospects, even as injuries took most of the prior two campaigns. When a shoulder injury delayed his debut in the shortened season, then aborted it entirely, it was easy to feel the industry tea leaves shift from "someone who's going to impress when we see him" to "someone we're never going to get to see impress." It's an understandable assumption given 36 2/3 innings pitched across three years, and one that won't go away until Puk has an injury-free season, maybe a couple at this point. He'll have that chance, though—roommate Jesús Luzardo's middling but healthy 2020 would be a worthy blueprint. Besides, the A's don't mind waiting for a career to start in earnest, provided the player in question is still cost-controlled when the self-discovery is complete.

Miguel Romero RHP   Born: 04/23/94   Age: 27   Bats: R   Throws: R   Height: 6'0"   Weight: 202   Origin: International Free Agent, 2017

YEAR	TEAM	LVL	AGE	W	L	SV	G	GS	IP	H	HR	BB/9	K/9	K	GB%	BABIP	WHIP	ERA	DRA-	WARP	MPH	FA%	Whiff%	CSP
2018	STK	HI-A	24	1	2	13	22	0	29¹	21	3	1.5	10.1	33	54.8%	.265	0.89	1.84	65	0.6				
2018	MID	AA	24	1	1	1	22	0	30	35	4	3.6	9.9	33	41.6%	.378	1.57	6.00	70	0.5				
2019	LV	AAA	25	4	1	3	45	1	72²	65	11	4.5	10.0	81	47.8%	.286	1.39	3.96	68	2.1				
2021 FS	OAK	MLB	27	1	2	0	57	0	50	46	8	4.2	9.2	51	44.3%	.289	1.40	4.77	111	-0.2				
2021 DC	OAK	MLB	27	1	2	0	41	0	43	40	6	4.2	9.2	44	44.3%	.289	1.40	4.77	111	0.0				

Comparables: Zac Reininger, Wei-Chieh Huang, Chad Sobotka

In 1666, Isaac Newton presented his theory of universal gravitation to the Royal Society in London when he was just 23 years old, foreshadowing the rough age at which people would start giving up on prospects in 2021. Consistently reaching the upper-90s boundary of his velocity range in the last few years, Romero has a chance to become a useful bullpen piece even in the comparatively superannuated years of his late 20s.

Burch Smith RHP   Born: 04/12/90   Age: 31   Bats: R   Throws: R   Height: 6'4"   Weight: 225   Origin: Round 14, 2011 Draft (#443 overall)

YEAR	TEAM	LVL	AGE	W	L	SV	G	GS	IP	H	HR	BB/9	K/9	K	GB%	BABIP	WHIP	ERA	DRA-	WARP	MPH	FA%	Whiff%	CSP
2018	KC	MLB	28	1	6	0	38	6	78	90	15	4.6	8.9	77	39.7%	.341	1.67	6.92	140	-1.1	96.1	61.8%	24.2%	48.9%
2019	SAC	AAA	29	1	1	0	3	2	15	16	1	5.4	10.8	18	51.2%	.385	1.67	4.20	111	0.2				
2019	SA	AAA	29	6	3	0	15	15	77¹	49	6	4.3	9.9	85	39.2%	.239	1.11	2.33	56	2.9				
2019	MIL	MLB	29	0	1	0	7	0	12²	16	3	7.1	9.9	14	32.5%	.351	2.05	7.82	139	-0.2	95.1	61.7%	27.7%	47.7%
2019	SF	MLB	29	0	0	0	10	0	8²	10	0	4.2	6.2	6	29.0%	.333	1.62	2.08	170	-0.3	95.6	67.1%	17.6%	49.0%
2020	OAK	MLB	30	2	0	1	6	0	12	7	1	0.8	9.8	13	30.0%	.207	0.67	2.25	91	0.2	96.6	72.5%	29.1%	50.9%
2021 FS	OAK	MLB	31	2	2	8	57	0	50	44	7	4.2	9.4	52	38.1%	.283	1.36	4.39	101	0.1	95.9	64.2%	25.0%	49.0%
2021 DC	OAK	MLB	31	2	2	8	47	0	49	44	7	4.2	9.4	51	38.1%	.283	1.36	4.39	101	0.3	95.9	64.2%	25.0%	49.0%

Comparables: Erasmo Ramírez, Liam Hendriks, Matt Magill

In 2018, Smith was a feel-good story, re-emerging in the majors after a five-year lacuna to pitch in 38 games for Kansas City. The results were awful, leading to his ouster. In 2019 with Milwaukee, the results were again awful, leading again to his mid-season ouster. He latched on with San Francisco later that year and has since posted strong ERAs for both Bay Area squads. In 2020, he earned (per DRA) the strong results and the contract he was tendered.

Joakim Soria RHP   Born: 05/18/84   Age: 37   Bats: R   Throws: R   Height: 6'3"   Weight: 208   Origin: International Free Agent, 2001

YEAR	TEAM	LVL	AGE	W	L	SV	G	GS	IP	H	HR	BB/9	K/9	K	GB%	BABIP	WHIP	ERA	DRA-	WARP	MPH	FA%	Whiff%	CSP
2018	MIL	MLB	34	3	1	0	26	0	22	18	2	2.5	10.6	26	43.1%	.286	1.09	4.09	65	0.5	94.4	71.2%	26.2%	50.1%
2018	CHW	MLB	34	0	3	16	40	0	38²	35	2	2.3	11.4	49	32.7%	.327	1.16	2.56	52	1.1	94.3	63.0%	30.8%	45.8%
2019	OAK	MLB	35	2	4	1	71	1	69	51	9	2.6	10.3	79	37.5%	.253	1.03	4.30	71	1.4	94.6	68.2%	28.9%	51.2%
2020	OAK	MLB	36	2	2	2	22	0	22¹	18	4	4.0	9.7	24	29.0%	.279	1.25	2.82	96	0.3	94.4	65.5%	23.5%	47.8%
2021 FS	OAK	MLB	37	2	2	0	57	0	50	43	6	3.2	9.3	51	37.5%	.279	1.23	3.43	86	0.5	94.5	66.9%	27.5%	49.4%

Comparables: Tom Henke, Sergio Romo, Lee Smith

Everything trended in the wrong direction for Soria in 2020—strikeout, walk and hit rates; exit velocity; and DRA, by which he had the second-worst season of his career. At 35, the age has been trending in the wrong direction for some time. The ERA was right, though, coming in below the mark Soria's established across 15 seasons. When someone's been around this long, oftentimes you have all the signs you need. Regardless of advanced metrics, the Soria of 2020 looked the same as in previous seasons by velocity and by results. With the journeyman hitting the open market again, teams will gravitate toward the results Soria has a career-long track record of providing.

Lou Trivino RHP   Born: 10/01/91   Age: 29   Bats: R   Throws: R   Height: 6'5"   Weight: 235   Origin: Round 11, 2013 Draft (#341 overall)

YEAR	TEAM	LVL	AGE	W	L	SV	G	GS	IP	H	HR	BB/9	K/9	K	GB%	BABIP	WHIP	ERA	DRA-	WARP	MPH	FA%	Whiff%	CSP
2018	NAS	AAA	26	0	0	1	4	0	5¹	2	0	1.7	16.9	10	37.5%	.250	0.56	1.69	27	0.2				
2018	OAK	MLB	26	8	3	4	69	1	74	53	8	3.8	10.0	82	46.2%	.257	1.14	2.92	69	1.6	99.2	53.7%	29.8%	47.9%
2019	OAK	MLB	27	4	6	0	61	0	60	61	7	4.7	8.6	57	43.8%	.320	1.53	5.25	95	0.4	98.8	50.8%	27.7%	46.5%
2020	OAK	MLB	28	0	0	0	20	0	23¹	16	3	3.9	10.0	26	40.4%	.241	1.11	3.86	91	0.3	96.8	58.8%	28.5%	45.1%
2021 FS	OAK	MLB	29	3	2	0	57	0	50	41	5	4.2	9.7	54	44.0%	.279	1.30	3.64	86	0.5	98.4	53.7%	28.5%	46.5%
2021 DC	OAK	MLB	29	3	2	0	58	0	62	51	7	4.2	9.7	67	44.0%	.279	1.30	3.64	86	0.8	98.4	53.7%	28.5%	46.5%

Comparables: Cam Bedrosian, Dominic Leone, Arodys Vizcaíno

It's not uncommon for a band's first album to be its best—The Strokes, Arcade Fire, The Velvet Underground. Sometimes, a revelatory introduction is followed up with more excellence, a declaration that this is the standard. Sometimes, you get *Room on Fire*. At that point, you have to wonder: which one was the outlier? Trivino rested on that precipice coming into 2020, following a rookie 2018 season that had him appearing as one of the league's best relievers and a 2019 that was only slightly better than indicated by the 5.25 ERA. The short season provided glimpses of how Trivino got to the peak of 2018, his K/9 again breaking double digits, but the diminished velocity and average results give little reason to expect him to again match the heights of his debut.

J.B. Wendelken RHP   Born: 03/24/93   Age: 28   Bats: R   Throws: R   Height: 6'1"   Weight: 242   Origin: Round 13, 2012 Draft (#421 overall)

YEAR	TEAM	LVL	AGE	W	L	SV	G	GS	IP	H	HR	BB/9	K/9	K	GB%	BABIP	WHIP	ERA	DRA-	WARP	MPH	FA%	Whiff%	CSP
2018	MID	AA	25	0	1	3	11	0	13¹	11	3	6.8	15.5	23	39.3%	.333	1.57	3.38	56	0.3				
2018	NAS	AAA	25	1	1	3	22	1	35¹	29	2	2.5	13.2	52	45.7%	.351	1.10	2.80	37	1.4				
2018	OAK	MLB	25	0	0	0	13	0	16²	8	1	2.7	7.6	14	39.5%	.167	0.78	0.54	92	0.1	97.0	60.9%	26.8%	51.7%
2019	LV	AAA	26	6	3	3	30	1	38²	47	8	4.4	10.0	43	46.1%	.364	1.71	5.59	115	0.2				
2019	OAK	MLB	26	3	1	0	27	0	32²	21	2	2.5	9.4	34	36.0%	.229	0.92	3.58	84	0.4	96.4	60.6%	27.0%	49.8%
2020	OAK	MLB	27	1	1	0	21	0	25	17	2	4.0	11.2	31	46.0%	.246	1.12	1.80	77	0.5	96.2	58.1%	26.8%	47.2%
2021 FS	OAK	MLB	28	3	2	12	57	0	50	39	6	3.4	10.5	58	40.7%	.272	1.18	3.27	80	0.7	96.4	59.3%	26.9%	48.7%
2021 DC	OAK	MLB	28	3	2	12	58	0	62	49	6	3.4	10.5	72	40.7%	.272	1.18	3.27	80	1.0	96.4	59.3%	26.9%	48.7%

Comparables: Jonathan Holder, Dovydas Neverauskas, Dan Altavilla

1 new email Subject: Try Dr. J.B. Wendelken's Intoxicating Skin Potions! Body: Re-liven your skin, with the new traditional stylings of Dr. Wendelken. Featuring new-age ingredients like 11.2 K/9 and 4.0 BB/9, you can still depend on Dr. Wendelken's for a proven combination of 95-and-a-slider and a strong ERA. It's more than just the old-timeyest name on the market; Dr. Wendelken's will emerge as a central piece of your bullpen (of skincare) when you least expect it, when your old standbys just aren't cutting it anymore. We know we're new to the market and our supply chain has been limited in past years (62 career major-league innings before 2020), but we plan to stick around. Stock up today!

SEATTLE MARINERS

Essay by Emily Nemens

Player comments by Nathan Bishop and BP staff

The 20th anniversary of the Kingdome's implosion—March 26, 2000—shouldn't have been a news item in 2020. It was Opening Day of Major League Baseball! But then, on March 9, Rudy Gobert caressed some microphones, and North American professional sports fell like so many dominos, with MLB spring training pressing pause on the ominous date of Friday the 13th. On that day, Commissioner Manfred said the regular season would be postponed for at least two weeks—but everyone knew it would be much longer than that.

Sports stations were suddenly desperate for content. On TV, they replayed entire postseasons, while websites featured athletes' at-home workout regimens (remember the dog squats, those patient retrievers and black labs?) and deep-fried turkey tips (care of the Mariners' own Marco Gonzales). After talking through possible rosters upwards and down, hosts reached out to every sort of adjacent content (including debut novelists who reimagined the 2011 spring training to include a fictional team called the LA Lions, ahem). There were a lot of highlight reels.

March 26 arrived: Opening Day, except not. Cue the dynamite. Watching that gray henge crumble in 2020 felt one part nostalgic, one part portent for the season ahead—a dramatic explosion, expectations (and edifices) go poof, and then we're left with nothing but this lurking cloud of particulate. The detonation of 2020 was unplanned, of course, but in 2000 the implosion was very much engineered—a feat, even. In a span shorter than the time it takes to sing "Take me Out to the Ball Game," over 20 miles of detonation cord, wicked along the ribs of the dome and around its concrete body, went off in a coordinated ignition that looked downright orchestral. As one newscaster said at the time, it was an "unbelievable sight to see a completely functional building turned to dust in fifteen seconds." Well, mostly functional. It did have a bad habit of dropping ceiling tiles, and architecture critic Paul Goldberger wrote that the multi-purpose concrete dome was cursed with "a deadly heavy-handedness."

That March 2000 day in Seattle was a memorable one. Elliott Bay was full of bobbing sailboats—the Kingdome sat just a few blocks away from the water—and Seattlites perched on hills and overpasses around the city. The

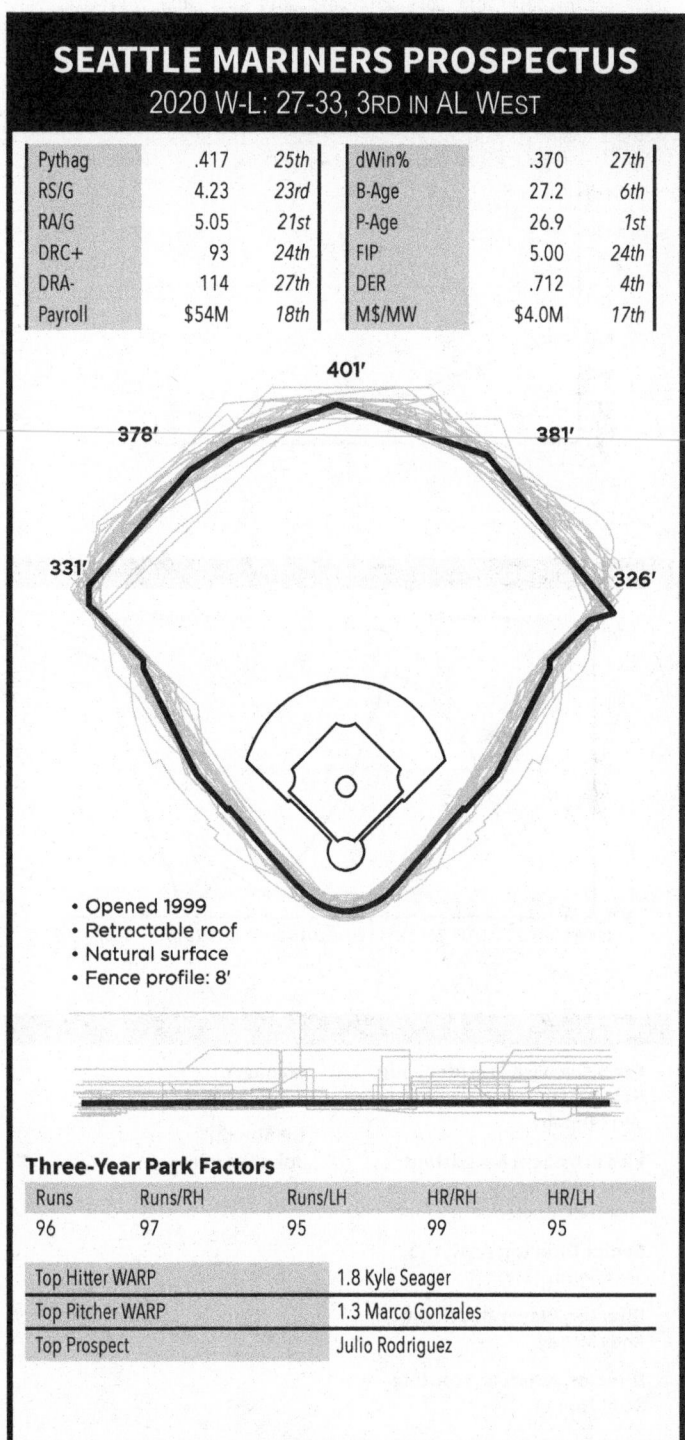

SEATTLE MARINERS PROSPECTUS
2020 W-L: 27-33, 3RD IN AL WEST

Pythag	.417	25th	dWin%	.370	27th
RS/G	4.23	23rd	B-Age	27.2	6th
RA/G	5.05	21st	P-Age	26.9	1st
DRC+	93	24th	FIP	5.00	24th
DRA-	114	27th	DER	.712	4th
Payroll	$54M	18th	M$/MW	$4.0M	17th

401'
378'   381'
331'   326'

- Opened 1999
- Retractable roof
- Natural surface
- Fence profile: 8'

Three-Year Park Factors

Runs	Runs/RH	Runs/LH	HR/RH	HR/LH
96	97	95	99	95

Top Hitter WARP	1.8 Kyle Seager
Top Pitcher WARP	1.3 Marco Gonzales
Top Prospect	Julio Rodriguez

Payroll History (in millions)

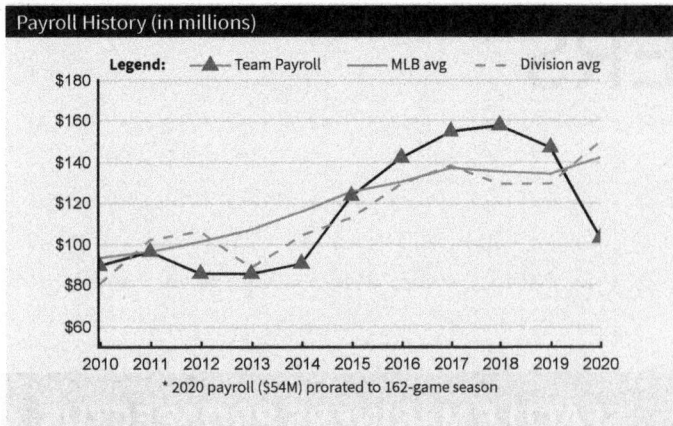

Legend: ▲ Team Payroll — MLB avg - - Division avg

* 2020 payroll ($54M) prorated to 162-game season

Future Commitments (in millions)

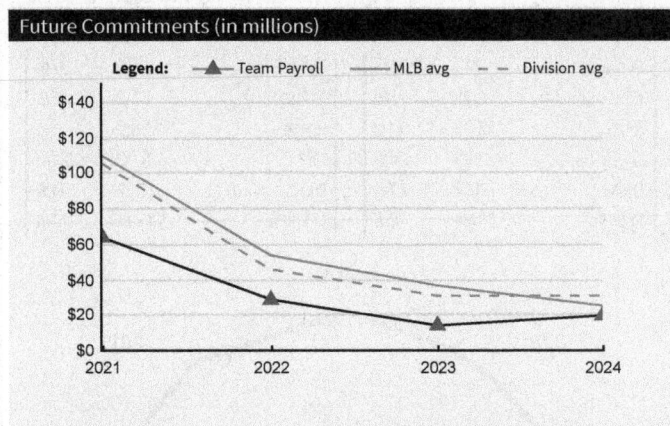

Legend: ▲ Team Payroll — MLB avg - - Division avg

Farm System Ranking

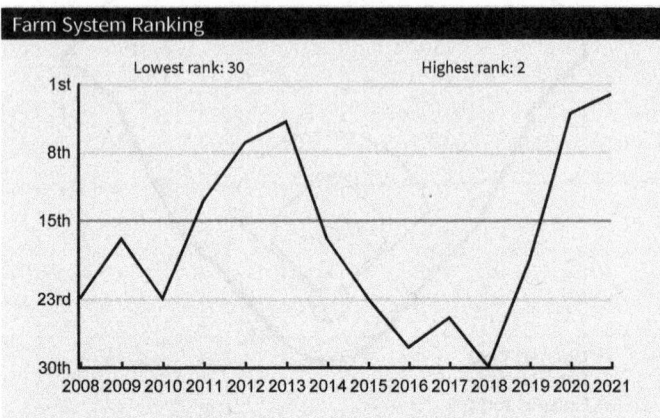

Lowest rank: 30   Highest rank: 2

Personnel

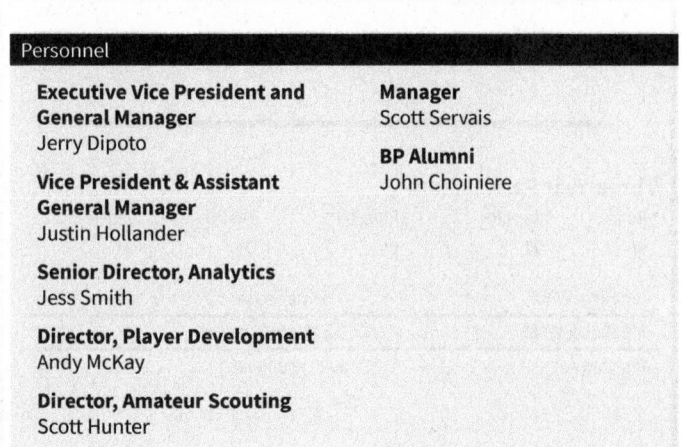

Executive Vice President and General Manager
Jerry Dipoto

Vice President & Assistant General Manager
Justin Hollander

Senior Director, Analytics
Jess Smith

Director, Player Development
Andy McKay

Director, Amateur Scouting
Scott Hunter

Manager
Scott Servais

BP Alumni
John Choiniere

explosions started, the building went down, cheers went up on hills. Seattle had already fallen in love with its new Safeco Field; to the Kingdome they said good riddance.

It's worth focusing on those hills for a second: Lore is that Seattle has seven hills, just like Rome, but the fact well known to any biker or driver of a manual transmission is that the city has plenty more than that. It's just that this town, younger than baseball, in a state itself established a dozen years after the National League, still has a chip on its shoulder about its relative youth, and august associations could only help with credibility. Right?

While Seattle may be one of the league's younger teams (it and the Blue Jays joined the majors in 1977), they are the only active team left to not have appeared in the World Series. If postseason performance is a sign of a club's maturity, if reaching the Fall Classic some sort of arrival into adulthood and legitimacy, then the team's lack of arrival is keeping it what—eternally young? That the Mariners hold another ignoble title again as they enter into the 2021 season—the longest current drought of postseason appearances among the four major American sports—signals either immaturity or obsolescence. To look at the Mariners' lineup (with Dee Gordon's departure, at the time of this writing, only one player on the 40-man roster, third baseman Kyle Seager, was born before 1990), it is certainly the former. In 2020 the Mariners had the youngest team in the league, and while it'll be a few months until we can determine if they'll hold that distinction again in 2021, even the addition of a few veterans can't bring their average up by much.

Youth can be a hindrance to success, a handicap or inferiority complex, but it is important to Seattle's identity, too. The Mariners have made a franchise of catching athletes at the start of their careers. On his first pitch, April 10, 1989, Ken Griffey Jr. hit a home run. He was still (barely) a teenager at the time of the blast, but he earned the moniker "The Kid" and kept it well into his 20s and along his course to becoming a generational player. Alex Rodriguez was drafted by the Mariners at 17, had his own set of teenage plate appearances, and spent his less-complicated early 20s with the Mariners, four of those years as an All-Star. Randy Johnson may have gone into the Hall of Fame as a Diamondback (a decision that still stings to many Seattleites), but first, he struck out over 2,000 batters as a Mariner.

Off the field, a few generations of youth culture (Jimi Hendrix, Nirvana) helped keep Seattle young in the eyes of the nation's cultural zeitgeist. Lest you forget, Nirvana's "Smells like Teen Spirit," that anthem of disaffected adolescence, came out of Seattle, and for a reason. That Seattle was new but not so new, self-aware but not self-empowered, could describe the city and its baseball team. When you reach the kind of wall a surly adolescence presents, there are two options: slouch against it or climb over it. More seasons than not, Seattle's tried for number two, couldn't gain purchase, and settled for option one.

Along with that slouching posture, Seattle has a habit of helping itself along in the chutes-and-ladders game of starting back at zero, of forever preserving its youth (even when it doesn't intend to). The Great Seattle Fire, for one: that wiped out its oldest neighborhood. That implosion was unintended, while other destructions felt more mindful: in the early twentieth century Seattle made a practice of cutting into those vista-ful hills and regrading them so their slopes could become viable real estate. A byproduct was that the tidal flats just south of downtown got a lot of new dirt. That dirt became a neighborhood (Sodo) and its warehouse and industrial uses slowly got pushed aside to make way for Seattle's sports franchises and their parking lots (enter the Kingdome).

The Mariners have had their own series of implosive moments, some intentional demolitions, some less so. Griffey's busted wrist, incurred in a collision with the centerfield wall: unintentional. Lou Pinella's tirades: intentional. Loyal fans will remember the 2008 Mariners being the first team to reach the shameful milestone of 100-losses with a $100-million payroll. Cue the dynamite in the front office. The implosion of the next GM, Jack Zduriencik, was more of a slow-motion collapse, also not intended. Jerry Dipoto followed, and the current GM managed to implode his first plan (which involved decimating the farm system in search of the wild-card berth) and still keep his job. On to plan two, which involves building up the youngest team in baseball so it becomes a viable contender in the early part of the 2020s.

Dipoto predicted the 2019 season would not be objectively good (and, at 68-94, it was not); the 2020 season was one he thought held promise. As discussed in last year's Baseball Prospectus, he predicted by 2020 or 2021, the Mariners would be "a threat to win the World Series." That obviously didn't happen in 2020. The Mariners, in their shortened season, landed with a respectably bad 27-33—better than many in the majors, but still not within reach of the expanded playoff bracket. Many an M's fan felt a little flutter of hope in Marco Gonzales complete game against the Angels, wherein he struck out Mike Trout three times. Trout's bad game might not have been a proper implosion, but it was a pretty satisfying wipeout.

Dipoto was bullish on 2020, but Seager—arguably the only success of Zduriencik's recruitment strategy—was a bit more clear-eyed about the goals of the 2020 season: "There's going to be a lot of guys in the clubhouse that don't know things. You have to ask questions and have someone that can answer them." Who has two thumbs, has spent his whole career with Seattle, and looked like he was holding the short end of the answering bat? That guy, the oldest on the team at the ripe old age of 33. "My role is to help all the guys kind of continue to grow and help them along. That benefits me, too...If we improve a lot and we get better quickly, that's great for me."

If 2020 was a season for questions and answers, what better backdrop than a season that is all question marks, where every team is unsettled by COVID risks and safety protocols? It didn't make up for the experience of games played, of course, but maybe guys who didn't know what a cheering stadium sounds like didn't miss it as much. And while sixty games was a disappointment for many athletes at their peaks (such as Trout) who hoped for career-besting performances this year, the scrawny 2020 season may have been a blessing in disguise for a bench full of rookies and otherwise young players who just needed to learn the ropes, stay healthy, and gain experience on the way to better, brighter seasons. For the Mariners, perhaps the worst thing lost was the opportunity for Kyle Lewis to go from hot to cold to hot again—his first month was breathlessly exciting to watch, his second a bit wobbly. If he'd played through three months, four, five, would he have evened out, or would he have run aground? After his early-career knee injuries, the prudent route would be not to wait around to see. And it hardly mattered—despite his slower September, he was still the unanimous pick for Rookie of the Year.

Even if Lewis hadn't redeemed himself in the eyes of the BBWAA, the good thing is that next spring he will be a year older, a year wiser and a year stronger. Same with Evan White, the other rookie of the Mariners' year—the 2017 first-round draft pick, with his impossible wingspan, nabbed a Gold Glove at first base. J.P. Crawford, the shortstop, caught one, too. Both men have work to do at the plate—White was second in the league in strikeouts—but presumably the young infielders were teaching their veteran mentor at third a few things, too.

Seattle riffs off of Rome's seven hills, but the Italian capital's other maxim on city planning is perhaps even more helpful to the Emerald City: "Rome wasn't built in a day." The same could be said for Seattle's wayward, well-meaning baseball franchise—building a team takes time. But it also takes concerted effort, as indicated by the 2020 Tampa Bay Rays. Watching that even younger franchise reach the World Series felt, to Mariners fans, like getting lapped and then lapped again. The Mariners have always wanted to win, but haven't quite acted on it, not in a concerted, coordinated effort. To return to the wall metaphor, the Mariners get stuck about four feet up the climb and can't find another handhold. There are no pegs, no chalk marks for a safe route. No wonder Dipoto dropped off the wall and assumed the slouch of GMs before.

But after so many years—and several front office administrations—of that defeatist posture, of hoping the raw talent, the short game, and some supernatural leaps would get them to October (but knowing it likely wouldn't), maybe the Mariners have finally come to realize there is another way to deal with the wall. Cue the dynamite.

Here's what we learned on March 26, 2000. The great thing about intentional implosion, about dynamite as an element of construction, is that after the dust has settled and the rubble has been cleared, you have a great big empty canvas on which to make your mark. A new stadium gets erected. A new farm system is built—this time, more determinedly so (I'm looking at Jarred Kelenic, Julio Rodríguez, Emerson Hancock and company). Most franchises figure out the up-and-over route to maturity, but Seattleites have gone their own slow, weird way through most things, adolescence included. The Mariners are perhaps, at last, both self-aware and self-empowered, and with that kismet they'll know how to make something out of the clearing.

It feels appropriate to hum Nirvana as we wait. No, not the disaffected anthem of "Teen Spirit"—I'd point surly Seattle fans to Nirvana's third and final album, *In Utero*. The Mariners' has been a long gestation, but if we are to believe Dipoto, it should be coming to a close this season. The anthem of that album? "All Apologies," which opens with the question, "What else should I be?" Maybe the M's finally have an answer to that mournful, frustrated query. That answer: a team that plays in October. ∎

—Emily Nemens is the author of The Cactus League.

HITTERS

Braden Bishop CF Born: 08/22/93 Age: 27 Bats: R Throws: R Height: 6'1" Weight: 178 Origin: Round 3, 2015 Draft (#94 overall)

YEAR	TEAM	LVL	AGE	PA	R	2B	3B	HR	RBI	BB	K	SB	CS	Whiff%	AVG/OBP/SLG	DRC+	BABIP	BRR	FRAA	WARP
2018	ARK	AA	24	394	70	20	0	8	33	37	68	5	2		.284/.361/.412	139	.331	-1.9	CF(81): -0.9, RF(2): -0.1, LF(1): -0.1	1.7
2019	MOD	HI-A	25	29	7	1	1	0	3	2	9	0	0		.240/.345/.360	55	.375	1.4	CF(3): 0.6	0.2
2019	TAC	AAA	25	211	29	15	0	8	31	23	44	2	2		.276/.360/.486	92	.321	-0.2	CF(34): 0.7, RF(6): 1.0, LF(1): 0.0	0.6
2019	SEA	MLB	25	60	3	0	0	0	4	3	21	0	0	30.7%	.107/.153/.107	44	.171	0.2	CF(20): -0.6, LF(4): 0.2, RF(1): -0.1	-0.2
2020	SEA	MLB	27	34	2	2	0	0	4	2	10	1	0	32.2%	.167/.242/.233	84	.250	-0.4	RF(8): 0.6, CF(3): -0.3, LF(2): -0.2	0.0
2021 FS	SEA	MLB	27	600	58	22	1	11	55	46	160	2	0	31.3%	.223/.295/.335	77	.294	0.3	LF 4, RF -4	0.2
2021 DC	SEA	MLB	27	166	16	6	0	3	15	12	44	0	0	31.3%	.223/.295/.335	77	.294	0.1	LF 1, RF -1	0.0

Comparables: Harrison Bader, Xavier Paul, Kirk Nieuwenhuis

As a professional athlete, Bishop has the charisma, thoughtfulness, and drive to make a lasting positive impact in the world and potentially evoke real social change. Unfortunately, he can't hit, and performance is ultimately, tragically what determines the limits of one's signal strength.

J.P. Crawford SS Born: 01/11/95 Age: 26 Bats: L Throws: R Height: 6'2" Weight: 199 Origin: Round 1, 2013 Draft (#16 overall)

YEAR	TEAM	LVL	AGE	PA	R	2B	3B	HR	RBI	BB	K	SB	CS	Whiff%	AVG/OBP/SLG	DRC+	BABIP	BRR	FRAA	WARP
2018	CLR	HI-A	23	49	8	1	0	1	4	7	14	0	0		.143/.265/.238	51	.185	0.0	SS(8): -0.6, 3B(3): 0.5	-0.2
2018	LHV	AAA	23	68	6	2	1	1	7	5	17	1	0		.259/.358/.379	83	.350	-1.7	SS(16): 0.2	-0.1
2018	PHI	MLB	23	138	17	6	3	3	12	13	37	2	0	27.7%	.214/.319/.393	78	.286	0.2	SS(30): 0.6, 3B(13): -0.6	0.2
2019	TAC	AAA	24	138	20	7	0	3	15	19	25	3	0		.319/.420/.457	108	.382	2.6	SS(31): 0.1	1.0
2019	SEA	MLB	24	396	43	21	4	7	46	43	83	5	3	21.2%	.226/.313/.371	83	.275	-1.9	SS(93): 4.6	1.3
2020	SEA	MLB	25	232	33	7	2	2	24	23	39	6	3	18.3%	.255/.336/.338	93	.303	2.0	SS(53): 5.0	1.2
2021 FS	SEA	MLB	26	600	73	23	3	12	48	71	121	3	1	20.6%	.237/.334/.371	96	.286	1.6	SS 5, 2B 0	2.3
2021 DC	SEA	MLB	26	565	69	22	3	12	45	67	114	3	1	20.6%	.237/.334/.371	96	.286	1.5	SS 5	2.3

Comparables: Andre Rodgers, Julio Lugo, Ricky Gutierrez

Top prospects face a tough grading curve. A 25-year-old shortstop hitting a hair below league average while playing Gold Glove-winning defense should be considered a wild success story. But when you're in your seventh professional season, most of which has been spent well within Top 10 MLB prospect lists, anything less than true stardom can feel like missed potential. At this point it's probably unfair to grade Crawford as a potential Lindorian infield keystone, especially given his Spike Owen-level power. Whether that's what Seattle expected when they acquired him two years ago for Jean Segura is unclear, and also irrelevant. He'll be 26 this year and appears poised to be a highly-capable major league shortstop for years to come. Despite the sport's brutal ecosystem, that's a success for anyone, regardless of hype.

Jake Fraley CF Born: 05/25/95 Age: 26 Bats: L Throws: L Height: 6'0" Weight: 195 Origin: Round 2, 2016 Draft (#77 overall)

YEAR	TEAM	LVL	AGE	PA	R	2B	3B	HR	RBI	BB	K	SB	CS	Whiff%	AVG/OBP/SLG	DRC+	BABIP	BRR	FRAA	WARP
2018	CHA	HI-A	23	260	39	19	7	4	41	26	44	11	8		.347/.415/.547	162	.407	-2.2	LF(31): 2.6, CF(21): 2.1, RF(12): 0.1	2.1
2019	ARK	AA	24	259	40	15	2	11	47	23	55	16	5		.313/.386/.539	190	.370	-0.3	RF(21): -1.3, LF(12): -1.1, CF(12): -2.5	2.1
2019	TAC	AAA	24	168	28	12	3	8	33	11	34	6	2		.276/.333/.553	102	.304	-1.3	CF(22): 0.9, RF(9): -0.7, LF(6): 0.5	0.5
2019	SEA	MLB	24	41	3	2	0	0	1	0	14	0	0	27.1%	.150/.171/.200	63	.231	-0.7	CF(11): -1.5, RF(1): 0.0	-0.3
2020	SEA	MLB	25	29	3	1	1	0	0	2	11	2	1	31.4%	.154/.241/.269	68	.267	0.0	RF(6): -0.1, LF(1): 0.6	0.0
2021 FS	SEA	MLB	26	600	63	24	5	20	71	40	172	20	9	29.3%	.232/.295/.408	90	.301	-1.1	LF -2, RF 1	0.7
2021 DC	SEA	MLB	26	265	28	10	2	8	31	17	76	8	4	29.3%	.232/.295/.408	90	.301	-0.5	LF -1, RF 0	0.2

Comparables: Josh Kroeger, Randy Arozarena, Tyler O'Neill

The Mariners touted Fraley as a "five-tool" prospect, but never really elaborated on what those were. The mystery deepened as the team turned to seemingly every other outfielder, infielder, and sports radio host in the organization while he languished at the alternate site. Given his recent baseball performance, we assume those five tools will prove to be financial planning, cooking, personal magenetism, guitar, and Mario speed runs.

Ty France 3B   Born: 07/13/94   Age: 26   Bats: R   Throws: R   Height: 5'11"   Weight: 217   Origin: Round 34, 2015 Draft (#1017 overall)

YEAR	TEAM	LVL	AGE	PA	R	2B	3B	HR	RBI	BB	K	SB	CS	Whiff%	AVG/OBP/SLG	DRC+	BABIP	BRR	FRAA	WARP
2018	SA	AA	23	479	66	22	2	17	77	33	70	3	4		.263/.349/.448	121	.276	1.3	3B(101): -7.7, 1B(1): -0.0	0.9
2018	ELP	AAA	23	110	18	8	0	5	19	13	19	0	0		.287/.382/.532	131	.310	0.6	3B(19): 2.8, 1B(9): 0.1	0.9
2019	ELP	AAA	24	348	83	27	1	27	89	30	51	1	0		.399/.477/.770	183	.410	1.0	3B(32): -1.8, 1B(29): -2.3, 2B(15): -2.5	3.7
2019	SD	MLB	24	201	20	8	1	7	24	9	49	0	2	24.0%	.234/.294/.402	77	.279	0.4	3B(36): -0.6, 2B(21): 2.2, P(2): 0.1	0.3
2020	SD	MLB	26	61	9	4	0	2	10	5	15	0	0	27.7%	.309/.377/.491	101	.395	0.6	1B(5): 0.4, 3B(2): 0.3	0.2
2020	SEA	MLB	26	94	10	5	1	2	13	6	22	0	0	24.2%	.302/.362/.453	97	.387	-0.2	2B(10): -0.5, 3B(4): 0.2	0.1
2021 FS	SEA	MLB	26	600	71	23	1	23	79	38	147	1	0	24.7%	.255/.329/.438	110	.309	-0.6	2B -1, 3B -1	1.7
2021 DC	SEA	MLB	26	432	51	16	1	17	57	27	106	0	0	24.7%	.255/.329/.438	110	.309	-0.4	2B -1, 3B -1	1.4

Comparables: Freddy Garcia, Phil Nevin, Travis Metcalf

Any serious discussion on France should at least mention how tragically close his name comes to giving us the 80-grade spoonerism "Fry Trance". That his wide carriage and non-angular frame would have made this nickname even more apt just drives the knife deeper. Nonetheless, there's plenty to love about the thumping DH/3B. While the 183 DRC+ he posted in Triple-A in 2018 looks like a comical outlier, his above-average offensive profile makes him the first potential Kyle Seager successor Seattle has had in years. At worst, France should provide an acceptable few years at DH until the Mariners sign a 45-year-old Nelson Cruz to push for the 2025 World Series.

Sam Haggerty 2B   Born: 05/26/94   Age: 27   Bats: S   Throws: R   Height: 5'11"   Weight: 175   Origin: Round 24, 2015 Draft (#724 overall)

YEAR	TEAM	LVL	AGE	PA	R	2B	3B	HR	RBI	BB	K	SB	CS	Whiff%	AVG/OBP/SLG	DRC+	BABIP	BRR	FRAA	WARP
2018	AKR	AA	24	351	44	21	5	4	37	57	77	24	7		.243/.373/.396	115	.314	1.2	3B(41): -5.0, SS(19): -0.3, LF(11): 0.4	0.8
2019	BRK	SS	25	25	5	3	0	0	4	4	8	0	0		.333/.440/.476	117	.538	0.8	3B(2): 0.1, 2B(1): -0.3, SS(1): 0.1	0.2
2019	BNG	AA	25	292	39	8	5	2	13	40	78	19	4		.259/.370/.356	118	.369	4.2	CF(25): 0.2, 2B(23): -1.2, 3B(4): -0.2	1.7
2019	SYR	AAA	25	49	9	4	1	1	9	4	10	4	0		.310/.383/.524	106	.387	-0.6	2B(7): -0.4, LF(5): -0.5, SS(2): -0.0	0.0
2019	NYM	MLB	25	4	2	0	0	0	0	0	3	0	0	37.5%	.000/.000/.000	57	.000	0.5	2B(1): -0.0, RF(1): 0.0	0.0
2020	SEA	MLB	26	54	7	4	0	1	6	4	16	4	0	36.2%	.260/.315/.400	95	.364	0.9	LF(10): 2.0, 3B(1): 0.1, RF(1): -0.1	0.3
2021 FS	SEA	MLB	27	600	63	22	4	10	49	64	191	21	6	36.3%	.206/.297/.323	75	.300	5.9	2B -9, LF -2	-0.5
2021 DC	SEA	MLB	27	199	21	7	1	3	16	21	63	7	2	36.3%	.206/.297/.323	75	.300	2.0	2B -3, LF -1	-0.1

Comparables: Ryan Schimpf, Michael Reed, Tyler Goeddel

Haggerty not only profiles as a fringe 25th man on a major league roster, he's theoretically a 26th, 27th, or even a 28th as well. Clearly, he's a man of many talents. One of his legitimate skills is discerning bad pitches, leading to strong walk rates; sadly, one of them is not hitting good pitches, thus poor strikeout rates. Given his sketchy, stopgap defense and doubles-at-best power, Haggerty (whose middle name, we feel compelled to mention, is Onofrio) is probably trending toward 29th or 30th man as his age moves toward 27 and 28.

Mitch Haniger RF   Born: 12/23/90   Age: 30   Bats: R   Throws: R   Height: 6'2"   Weight: 199   Origin: Round 1, 2012 Draft (#38 overall)

YEAR	TEAM	LVL	AGE	PA	R	2B	3B	HR	RBI	BB	K	SB	CS	Whiff%	AVG/OBP/SLG	DRC+	BABIP	BRR	FRAA	WARP
2018	SEA	MLB	27	683	90	38	4	26	93	70	148	8	2	23.4%	.285/.366/.493	128	.336	-3.5	RF(144): 5.0, CF(35): -2.8, LF(2): -0.2	3.9
2019	SEA	MLB	28	283	46	13	1	15	32	30	81	4	0	26.1%	.220/.314/.463	101	.257	2.0	RF(43): 3.2, CF(24): 0.4	1.4
2021 FS	SEA	MLB	30	600	77	26	2	26	77	61	157	5	1	24.6%	.251/.341/.458	119	.308	0.4	RF 3, LF 0	3.4
2021 DC	SEA	MLB	30	398	51	17	1	17	51	40	104	3	1	24.6%	.251/.341/.458	119	.308	0.3	RF 2	2.2

Comparables: Jay Buhner, Jesse Barfield, Jay Bruce

Haniger was well on his way to becoming an established star in 2019 when a foul ball launched itself directly into his gentleman area, rupturing a testicle. What unfolded was a series of frustrating setbacks: His rehab led to a torn adductor muscle in his core, which led to a herniated disc in his back, which led to re-injuring his core, which led to re-injuring his back. Eventually they just stopped adding details.

If the skills Haniger showed from 2017-2019 remain intact—and at 30 there's a fair enough chance they are—he could return to form and be one of the American League's best right fielders. His ability to grind out at-bats, hit for power, and play quality-if-unspectacular defense forms a broad level of above-average skills, and one Seattle would be very grateful to have in its lineup. Otherwise, Mariners fans will recall another Seattle outfielder whose potential-laden career was sidelined by flukey bad luck: Franklin Gutierrez.

★ ★ ★ *2021 Top 101 Prospect* **#6** ★ ★ ★

Jarred Kelenic OF   Born: 07/16/99   Age: 21   Bats: L   Throws: L   Height: 6'1"   Weight: 190   Origin: Round 1, 2018 Draft (#6 overall)

YEAR	TEAM	LVL	AGE	PA	R	2B	3B	HR	RBI	BB	K	SB	CS	Whiff%	AVG/OBP/SLG	DRC+	BABIP	BRR	FRAA	WARP
2018	KNG	ROK	18	200	33	8	4	5	33	22	39	11	1		.253/.350/.431	124	.300	2.5	CF(43): 5.8	1.3
2018	MTS	ROK	18	51	9	2	2	1	9	4	11	4	0		.413/.451/.609	183	.514	-0.1	CF(9): 2.0	0.5
2019	WV	LO-A	19	218	33	14	3	11	29	25	45	7	4		.309/.394/.586	180	.356	-0.5	CF(33): -1.8, RF(8): -0.1, LF(3): 2.3	2.3
2019	MOD	HI-A	19	190	36	13	1	6	22	17	49	10	3		.290/.353/.485	137	.368	1.4	CF(32): 1.1, RF(8): -1.2, LF(2): -0.1	1.3
2019	ARK	AA	19	92	11	4	1	6	17	8	17	3	0		.253/.315/.542	134	.246	0.6	CF(12): 0.6, RF(5): 0.6, LF(3): -0.2	0.7
2021 FS	SEA	MLB	21	600	67	27	4	22	73	39	181	11	4		.237/.292/.423	93	.310	1.7	CF -5, LF 0	1.1
2021 DC	SEA	MLB	21	99	11	4	0	3	12	6	29	1	0		.237/.292/.423	93	.310	0.3	CF -1	0.2

Comparables: Oscar Taveras, Byron Buxton, Travis Snider

The Mariners franchise hasn't made the postseason since the sitcom *Friends* was at the height of its ratings power. Yes, Seattle and playoff baseball have been on quite a break. If Dipoto's rebuild is finally going to bring the two together again it's going to be because the Mets hired Robinson Canó's former agent as general manager at just the right time to be party to a potential all-time swindle.

When talking about prospects, the term "well-rounded" sometimes connotes a low-ceiling. That would be a mistake in Kelenic's case. He is indeed well-rounded, but rather than lacking any plus skills, his game simply lacks any glaring weaknesses. This is a top-10 prospect who can handle center field (at worst, capably) and put up a 134 DRC+ in Double-A at 19. That he is only *arguably* Seattle's best prospect says much more about the system's recent rise (and fellow outfield prospect Julio Rodríguez) than it does about any limits on Kelenic's future. He'll almost certainly be ready for the majors in 2021, almost just as certainly well before he makes his debut. When he does arrive, even with 2020 Rookie of the Year Kyle Lewis in the fold, there's a good chance he'll rank as Seattle's best outfielder by the time we write the 2022 Annual.

Kyle Lewis CF Born: 07/13/95 Age: 25 Bats: R Throws: R Height: 6'4" Weight: 205 Origin: Round 1, 2016 Draft (#11 overall)

YEAR	TEAM	LVL	AGE	PA	R	2B	3B	HR	RBI	BB	K	SB	CS	Whiff%	AVG/OBP/SLG	DRC+	BABIP	BRR	FRAA	WARP
2018	MOD	HI-A	22	211	21	18	0	5	32	11	55	0	0		.260/.303/.429	103	.333	0.3	CF(23): -3.1, RF(11): -0.7, LF(2): 0.1	-0.3
2018	ARK	AA	22	152	18	8	0	4	20	17	32	1	0		.220/.309/.371	90	.255	-2.0	CF(29): -2.6, RF(1): -0.0	-0.6
2019	ARK	AA	23	517	61	25	2	11	62	56	152	3	2		.263/.342/.398	111	.367	-3.3	LF(49): 0.1, CF(36): -4.0, RF(15): -1.2	0.8
2019	SEA	MLB	23	75	10	5	0	6	13	3	29	0	0	39.0%	.268/.293/.592	84	.351	0.8	RF(17): 0.0, CF(2): 0.1	0.1
2020	SEA	MLB	25	242	37	3	0	11	28	34	71	5	1	36.3%	.262/.364/.437	108	.341	1.4	CF(57): 0.2	1.0
2021 FS	SEA	MLB	25	600	72	23	2	22	73	60	188	1	0	36.8%	.240/.321/.421	103	.326	0.3	CF -10, LF 0	1.0
2021 DC	SEA	MLB	25	565	68	22	2	21	69	57	177	1	0	36.8%	.240/.321/.421	103	.326	0.3	CF -9	1.1

Comparables: Ramón Laureano, Joc Pederson, Adolfo Phillips

After a catastrophic knee injury suffered when a catcher (in Single-A) blocked the plate, the former Golden Spikes Award winner spent years slowly regaining his timing and athleticism. The pace of that recovery led to many assuming a big league career wasn't in the cards. Lewis persevered, however, and after a flashy, home run-filed cup of coffee, he was handed the everyday center field job for 2020. He ran with it like Usain Bolt in London, improving his plate discipline, hitting for power, and moving on that surgically-repaired knee well enough to play a perfectly acceptable center field. The year resulted in both a unanimous Rookie of the Year award selection and some pretty significant questions about this future, given a severe second-half slump (.545 OPS). Pitchers acclimated to his fast start, and he responded by hitting the ball harder than ever, upwards, converting line drives to fly balls. The short season probably interrupted the usual rhythm of adjustment and readjustment for every young hitter. It also probably demonstrated what Lewis is: streaky as hell, and a quality player when it's all given time to average out.

Shed Long Jr. 2B Born: 08/22/95 Age: 25 Bats: L Throws: R Height: 5'8" Weight: 184 Origin: Round 12, 2013 Draft (#375 overall)

YEAR	TEAM	LVL	AGE	PA	R	2B	3B	HR	RBI	BB	K	SB	CS	Whiff%	AVG/OBP/SLG	DRC+	BABIP	BRR	FRAA	WARP
2018	PNS	AA	22	522	75	22	5	12	56	57	123	19	6		.261/.353/.412	113	.333	3.7	2B(123): -1.9	1.4
2019	TAC	AAA	23	250	38	7	4	9	36	20	65	1	3		.274/.335/.460	75	.346	0.5	2B(21): 0.2, 3B(21): -0.9, LF(12): 0.9	0.2
2019	SEA	MLB	23	168	21	12	1	5	15	16	40	3	3	27.2%	.263/.333/.454	90	.327	0.8	2B(24): 1.0, LF(16): -0.4, 3B(1): -0.1	0.4
2020	SEA	MLB	25	128	10	5	0	3	9	11	37	4	0	34.5%	.171/.242/.291	59	.221	1.2	2B(32): -5.3, LF(1): 0.1	-0.7
2021 FS	SEA	MLB	25	600	63	24	3	18	62	52	174	6	2	31.2%	.220/.295/.378	82	.289	1.3	2B 0, LF -1	0.8
2021 DC	SEA	MLB	25	332	35	13	1	10	34	29	96	3	1	31.2%	.220/.295/.378	82	.289	0.7	2B 0, LF 0	0.5

Comparables: Jordany Valdespin, Bret Boone, Jeff Kent

The M's Opening Day second baseman, Long was given the opportunity to be an everyday player for the first time. Injury and performance both conspired to make it an opportunity largely missed. There's no doubt that if Long is going to bounce back it will be on the strength of the power he flashed in 2019. In his encore, that power was only really used to jump on the occasional mistake, and even then he swung through many of them as his contact rates tumbled. Combine that with below-average plate discipline and questionable defense, and it's hard to visualize a scenario (barring injury) where he reclaims the starting position in Seattle. With Dylan Moore's breakout and organizational depth ever-improving, Long's road to success is now, well, not short.

José Marmolejos 1B Born: 01/02/93 Age: 28 Bats: L Throws: L Height: 6'2" Weight: 239 Origin: International Free Agent, 2011

YEAR	TEAM	LVL	AGE	PA	R	2B	3B	HR	RBI	BB	K	SB	CS	Whiff%	AVG/OBP/SLG	DRC+	BABIP	BRR	FRAA	WARP
2018	SYR	AAA	25	539	52	25	1	8	57	39	97	0	0		.266/.319/.369	105	.313	-2.1	1B(73): -1.3, RF(30): -1.6, LF(21): -2.5	-0.4
2019	HBG	AA	26	43	8	2	0	2	10	4	6	0	0		.308/.372/.513	134	.323	0.3	LF(7): -0.2	0.3
2019	FRE	AAA	26	382	53	29	2	16	63	28	80	1	0		.315/.366/.545	112	.370	-3.9	1B(48): 0.7, LF(23): 1.4, RF(14): -0.8	1.0
2020	SEA	MLB	27	115	12	4	0	6	18	7	32	0	1	33.0%	.206/.261/.411	85	.232	-0.2	LF(18): 0.6, 1B(5): -0.3, RF(2): 0.1	0.0
2021 FS	SEA	MLB	28	600	60	24	2	21	70	40	163	0	0	33.0%	.230/.288/.398	84	.288	0.2	LF -1, 1B 0	0.0
2021 DC	SEA	MLB	28	531	53	22	2	18	62	35	144	0	0	33.0%	.230/.288/.398	84	.288	0.2	LF -1, 1B 0	0.1

Comparables: Scott Thorman, Garrett Jones, Dayan Viciedo

There's a noticeable dissonance between the abnormality of the 2020 season and the traditional abnormality that was the Seattle Mariners roster; the twin phenomena conspired to make a lot of major league dreams true. One of those was Marmolejos, a thumping first baseman who finally made it to the show in this 10th season in professional baseball ... starting Opening Day in left field. After a brutal 3-for-29 start, the longtime farmhand made way for other die rolls, though he did return in the second half with an .801 OPS. Given the impending arrival of real outfield prospects and the fact that he really shouldn't be playing the field anyway, Marmolejos will probably remain bound to 2020, a sliver of a year's fever dream. But one of the less horrific parts, perhaps?

Noelvi Marte SS Born: 10/16/01   Age: 19   Bats: R   Throws: R   Height: 6'1"   Weight: 181   Origin: International Free Agent, 2018

YEAR	TEAM	LVL	AGE	PA	R	2B	3B	HR	RBI	BB	K	SB	CS	Whiff%	AVG/OBP/SLG	DRC+	BABIP	BRR	FRAA	WARP
2019	DSL SEA	ROK	17	299	56	18	4	9	54	29	55	17	7		.309/.371/.511		.351			
2021															No projection					

It's rare for a team to hit it big on the international market in back-to-back seasons, but after Seattle scored with Julio Rodríguez they may have done it again with Marte. A big, powerful shortstop, the teenaged Dominican may end up outgrowing the position. While that would be a loss for Seattle, it's not a huge one, because the early returns on his bat are very exciting. Without a traditional stat line to scout, we're left with 300 plate appearances in 2019 in the Dominican rookie league, and close to 300 scouting reports and news stories gushing over Marte's offensive ceiling. We did finally receive one new data point by which to triangulate, as the enigmatic prospect appeared in the Arizona Fall League and acquitted himself well before positive COVID-19 tests shut it down.

Dylan Moore OF Born: 08/02/92   Age: 28   Bats: R   Throws: R   Height: 6'0"   Weight: 185   Origin: Round 7, 2015 Draft (#198 overall)

YEAR	TEAM	LVL	AGE	PA	R	2B	3B	HR	RBI	BB	K	SB	CS	Whiff%	AVG/OBP/SLG	DRC+	BABIP	BRR	FRAA	WARP
2018	BLX	AA	25	91	12	7	3	3	18	7	16	6	1		.373/.429/.639	157	.438	-0.4	2B(9): -0.6, 1B(7): -0.8, SS(3): -0.3	0.3
2018	RMV	AAA	25	363	58	24	6	11	40	28	52	17	6		.280/.346/.492	110	.303	3.3	3B(54): 0.2, 2B(25): -2.3, 1B(9): 0.3	1.3
2019	TAC	AAA	26	35	3	0	0	0	7	3	3	2	1		.172/.294/.172	49	.192	0.3	SS(3): -0.1, 2B(2): 0.2, 3B(1): -0.0	-0.1
2019	SEA	MLB	26	282	31	14	2	9	28	25	92	11	9	28.3%	.206/.302/.389	79	.288	-1.1	SS(31): 0.1, LF(31): 2.1, 2B(18): 1.5	0.4
2020	SEA	MLB	28	159	26	9	0	8	17	14	43	12	5	27.2%	.255/.358/.496	117	.314	0.4	LF(13): -1.0, RF(13): 1.4, 2B(10): 0.6	0.9
2021 FS	SEA	MLB	28	600	74	25	2	21	66	48	173	17	7	27.8%	.227/.312/.406	98	.293	-2.3	LF 5, 2B -1	1.5
2021 DC	SEA	MLB	28	598	73	25	2	21	66	48	172	17	7	27.8%	.227/.312/.406	98	.293	-2.3	LF 5, 2B -1	1.4

Comparables: Billy Ashley, Danny Walton, Pete Incaviglia

The Jerry Dipoto Mariners have earned a bit of a reputation for doing what the kids used to call "galaxy braining." For those of you fortunate enough to not have your brains disordered by social media, you'll recognize it by its ancestral term: out-thinking the room. This is to say that in 2018, when Seattle gave a major league contract to a lifetime minor leaguer entering his age-27 season, there were some chuckles at the team's expense. After a 2019 that justified a lot of those chuckles Moore showed up to the abbreviated 2020 campaign with more muscle and a heart filled with ill-intent towards baseballs. Moore used them to add more than two miles to his average exit velocity, 100 points to his slugging percentage, and 40 points to his DRC+. Add in some defensive utility (he played seven positions in 2020), and Moore is either a fun story in a weird season or another in a moderate but steadily growing series of developmental success stories for Seattle.

Tom Murphy C Born: 04/03/91   Age: 30   Bats: R   Throws: R   Height: 6'1"   Weight: 218   Origin: Round 3, 2012 Draft (#105 overall)

YEAR	TEAM	LVL	AGE	PA	R	2B	3B	HR	RBI	BB	K	SB	CS	Whiff%	AVG/OBP/SLG	DRC+	BABIP	BRR	FRAA	WARP
2018	ABQ	AAA	27	264	40	16	3	17	49	22	76	4	2		.258/.333/.568	109	.306	-0.9	C(52): 6.9	1.7
2018	COL	MLB	27	96	5	7	1	2	11	3	44	0	1	43.2%	.226/.250/.387	45	.404	-0.7	C(22): -0.3	-0.3
2019	SEA	MLB	28	281	32	12	1	18	40	19	87	2	0	30.7%	.273/.324/.535	105	.340	-0.9	C(67): 4.7, P(3): -0.0, LF(1): -0.0	2.0
2021 FS	SEA	MLB	30	600	68	23	2	27	75	39	220	2	0	32.3%	.218/.278/.419	86	.304	1.2	C 7, 1B 0	2.2
2021 DC	SEA	MLB	30	232	26	8	1	10	29	15	85	0	0	32.3%	.218/.278/.419	86	.304	0.5	C 3	0.9

Comparables: Kevin Brown, J.P. Arencibia, Russell Branyan

YEAR	TEAM	P. COUNT	FRM RUNS	BLK RUNS	THRW RUNS	TOT RUNS
2018	COL	2826	-0.3	0.0	0.0	-0.3
2019	SEA	9506	3.5	0.8	0.7	5.0
2021	SEA	8418	0.4	1.2	0.0	1.6

Murphy's stoic face and catching duties bely a combination of athleticism and strength rivaling any player on Seattle's major league roster. In 2019 he broke out and put those skills on display, improving his defense and unleashing massive dingers into the Pacific Northwest gloaming. In 2020 he broke down, as a foot injury sidelined him for the entire season. While the Mariners are very high on Cal Raleigh as the catcher of the future, there's every reason to treat Murphy as the backstop of the present, at least for 2021. If his defensive improvements from two years ago hold, he should be able to easily withstand some offensive regression. If the regression doesn't come, The Murph will be the second late-blooming catcher in as many years (after now-Padre Austin Nola) to find in Seattle the birthplace of his major league success.

Cal Raleigh C Born: 11/26/96   Age: 24   Bats: S   Throws: R   Height: 6'3"   Weight: 215   Origin: Round 3, 2018 Draft (#90 overall)

YEAR	TEAM	LVL	AGE	PA	R	2B	3B	HR	RBI	BB	K	SB	CS	Whiff%	AVG/OBP/SLG	DRC+	BABIP	BRR	FRAA	WARP
2018	EVE	SS	21	167	25	10	1	8	29	18	29	1	1		.288/.367/.534	140	.309	0.3	C(25): -0.2	0.7
2019	MOD	HI-A	22	348	48	19	0	22	66	33	69	4	0		.261/.336/.535	150	.267	0.8	C(55): 0.9	3.1
2019	ARK	AA	22	159	16	6	0	7	16	14	47	0	0		.228/.296/.414	108	.286	-0.6	C(26): -0.0	0.6
2021 FS	SEA	MLB	24	600	72	26	1	30	86	43	174	1	0		.238/.298/.459	103	.290	-0.4	C 2	2.9

Comparables: Jason Castro, Yasmani Grandal, Max Ramirez

YEAR	TEAM	P. COUNT	FRM RUNS	BLK RUNS	THRW RUNS	TOT RUNS
2019	ARK	3371	1.0	0.0	-1.4	-0.4
2021	SEA	16650	0.9	-0.8	-0.2	-0.1

Big-bodied catchers call to mind Dr. Tobais Funke's thoughts on open marriages: "Everyone deludes themselves into thinking it will work, but it never does. But...it might for us." Raleigh's future behind the dish will continue to be closely tied to how well he hits, which thus far in his career he has done very well. His defense, at least for now, seems unlikely to embarrass; his glove work is solid and footwork generally acceptable. If he hits well for a catcher, which, granted, requires maybe two extra-base hits a week these days, his path to Seattle seems clear. If he hits *really* well for a catcher, Seattle is going to have to figure out a way to limit his wear and tear behind the dish to protect his bat. If he hits just okay for a catcher, well, the calculus becomes a lot simpler, but in a way neither Raleigh or Seattle would prefer.

Joe Rizzo 3B Born: 03/31/98 Age: 23 Bats: L Throws: R Height: 5'10" Weight: 194 Origin: Round 2, 2016 Draft (#50 overall)

YEAR	TEAM	LVL	AGE	PA	R	2B	3B	HR	RBI	BB	K	SB	CS	Whiff%	AVG/OBP/SLG	DRC+	BABIP	BRR	FRAA	WARP
2018	MOD	HI-A	20	508	46	21	2	4	55	40	108	6	1		.241/.303/.321	77	.303	-0.9	3B(99): 0.5, 2B(6): -0.1, 1B(5): -0.3	-1.0
2019	MOD	HI-A	21	570	77	30	3	10	63	45	94	0	3		.295/.354/.423	131	.343	4.0	3B(85): -2.3, 1B(31): -2.1, 2B(8): -0.5	3.0
2021 FS	SEA	MLB	23	600	53	27	2	11	58	42	175	0	0		.230/.287/.350	74	.315	-0.3	3B 0, 1B -1	-0.9

Comparables: Ryan Wheeler, Jeimer Candelario, Brandon Laird

Rizzo managed to get his slugging a tick over .400 after repeating the Cal league. He'll need to buff his bat-to-ball skills to a Lyle Overbay-level sheen and/or find a magic lamp and wish for Evan White-grade defensive skills in order to progress into the upper minors in 2021. The M's felt comfortable enough in his lamplessness to leave him unprotected in the Rule 5 draft.

★ ★ ★ *2021 Top 101 Prospect* **#3** ★ ★ ★

Julio Y. Rodríguez OF Born: 12/29/00 Age: 20 Bats: R Throws: R Height: 6'3" Weight: 180 Origin: International Free Agent, 2017

YEAR	TEAM	LVL	AGE	PA	R	2B	3B	HR	RBI	BB	K	SB	CS	Whiff%	AVG/OBP/SLG	DRC+	BABIP	BRR	FRAA	WARP
2018	DSL SEA	ROK	17	255	50	13	9	5	36	30	40	10	0		.315/.404/.525	165	.364	0.6	RF(44): 8.1, CF(6): -0.1	2.5
2019	WV	LO-A	18	295	50	20	1	10	50	20	65	1	3		.293/.359/.490	159	.351	0.0	RF(40): 4.7, CF(22): -0.2	2.8
2019	MOD	HI-A	18	72	13	6	3	2	19	5	10	0	0		.462/.514/.738	254	.528	0.5	CF(13): -3.4, RF(3): -0.5	0.9
2021 FS	SEA	MLB	20	600	55	27	5	13	62	35	177	4	1		.231/.285/.375	81	.314	3.7	RF 4, CF -4	0.5

Comparables: Bryce Harper, Jason Heyward, Chris Marrero

Every big idea needs a wow factor, and for Seattle's rebuild, it's Rodriguez. Featuring one of the elite hit tools in the minor leagues, he has never failed to destroy the pitching at every level he has faced. The big right-hander's bat control, plate discipline, and above-average athleticism give his offense arguably as high a ceiling as any prospect in the game. While nagging injuries have cost him some development time, and his large frame may see him moved off his current corner outfield spot sooner rather than later, he's still going to be just 20 years old for all of 2021. Even a median outcome for his offensive development should produce a quality young bat, and if he reaches his full potential Seattle will have one of the great offensive forces in the sport for years to come. With an exuberant, outgoing personality Rodriguez has become the defacto poster child for Dipoto's Great AL West Conquest (departure date: TBD) for a team desparate to make the playoffs for just the second time since Rodriguez has been alive.

Kyle Seager 3B Born: 11/03/87 Age: 33 Bats: L Throws: R Height: 6'0" Weight: 216 Origin: Round 3, 2009 Draft (#82 overall)

YEAR	TEAM	LVL	AGE	PA	R	2B	3B	HR	RBI	BB	K	SB	CS	Whiff%	AVG/OBP/SLG	DRC+	BABIP	BRR	FRAA	WARP
2018	SEA	MLB	30	630	62	36	1	22	78	38	138	2	2	22.4%	.221/.273/.400	90	.251	-1.6	3B(154): 11.2, 2B(1): -0.0	2.5
2019	TAC	AAA	31	42	5	2	0	0	7	3	7	0	0		.256/.310/.308	70	.312	-0.7	3B(5): 0.0	-0.1
2019	SEA	MLB	31	443	55	19	1	23	63	44	86	2	2	21.2%	.239/.321/.468	113	.248	-2.4	3B(104): -0.2	2.2
2020	SEA	MLB	33	248	35	12	0	9	40	32	33	5	0	20.4%	.241/.355/.433	130	.240	1.9	3B(53): 2.4	1.8
2021 FS	SEA	MLB	33	600	71	28	1	24	80	58	109	3	1	21.3%	.238/.323/.431	104	.256	-1.3	3B 7, 2B 0	2.1
2021 DC	SEA	MLB	33	565	67	26	1	22	75	55	102	2	1	21.3%	.238/.323/.431	104	.256	-1.2	3B 6	1.9

Comparables: Ryan Zimmerman, Adrián Beltré, Sean Berry

Kyle Seager is a player defined by competence and its disparate narrative spins. From 2011-2013, he was Dustin Ackley's College Teammate, an afterthought with little pop and utility player upside. From 2014-2016, he was a quiet star on a contending team, thriving behind the supernova talents and personalities of Félix Hernández, Robinson Canó, and Nelson Cruz. From 2017-2020, he has been "overpaid," an aging anchor with a contract and clubhouse personality the team would happily rid itself of, if only there were a market for him.

After suffering a wrist injury in spring training and a slow first half in 2019, Seager re-shaped his offense, posting a second-half wRC+ of 129. That success at the plate continued into 2020, when this reminder of its past was arguably Seattle's best offensive player. In fact, over his past 162 games (stretching back to the doom-filled 2018) Kyle Seager has posted a line of .250/.329/.470, eerily similar to his career numbers of .257/.325/.445. He's Kyle Seager again, same as he ever was: a 3-to-5 win player to set your watch to, and despite his many narratives, the best third baseman in franchise history.

Dee Strange-Gordon 2B Born: 04/22/88 Age: 33 Bats: L Throws: R Height: 5'11" Weight: 166 Origin: Round 4, 2008 Draft (#127 overall)

YEAR	TEAM	LVL	AGE	PA	R	2B	3B	HR	RBI	BB	K	SB	CS	Whiff%	AVG/OBP/SLG	DRC+	BABIP	BRR	FRAA	WARP
2018	SEA	MLB	30	588	62	17	8	4	36	9	80	30	12	15.6%	.268/.288/.349	75	.304	4.2	2B(81): 2.5, CF(53): 0.7, SS(8): -0.4	0.9
2019	SEA	MLB	31	421	36	12	6	3	34	18	61	22	5	15.9%	.275/.304/.359	78	.313	2.2	2B(111): 0.5, SS(2): 0.2	0.5
2020	SEA	MLB	32	82	12	1	0	0	3	5	13	3	2	18.4%	.200/.268/.213	75	.242	0.1	2B(13): -1.7, LF(13): 0.7, SS(3): -0.4	-0.2
2021 FS	SEA	MLB	33	600	54	20	4	6	55	24	104	35	10	16.2%	.257/.294/.342	74	.304	9.7	2B 2, CF 1	1.4

Comparables: Tony Womack, Julian Javier, Joe Inglett

For many, the love of baseball is rooted in the analysis of numbers. For them, Dee Strange-Gordon's time in Seattle is an easy bust. He was brought to Seattle as an experiment: Could a highly athletic, established major league middle-infielder be converted into an outfielder on the fly? Due to Robinson Canó's suspension in 2018, we never really found out, although early returns pointed to "probably not." Strange-Gordon arrived in Seattle along with international slot money the Mariners had ear-marked for their failed pursuit of Shohei Othani. He arrived to help the team end the longest playoff absence in major American sports find the postseason. They did not. So many failures—small and large, personal and organizational—ripple from Strange-Gordon's time in the Emerald City.

So it's up to you if that's how you would like to think of him. That's how we normally do it as baseball fans. The name on the back of the jersey failed the name on the front, and in so doing hollowed out the man in between the two. Before we participate in that same old exercise here, however, we should acknowledge that amidst all that failure Strange-Gordon was a far, far, better teammate and humanitarian than he was a baseball player in Seattle. His advocacy for local charities, his willingness to mentor, advise, and assist younger teammates (even those brought in to replace him), and his willingness to speak out on domestic violence, mental health, and other issues haunting American life stand, at minimum, alongside what he did between the foul lines.

That Strange-Gordon spent his time in Seattle struggling to do his job well is the reality we usually talk about here. Often we'd use it as a cudgel to grind some axe against an executive, cite something about inefficiencies, and maybe make a bad pun. We'll still do that plenty, but that the quality of the player never once affected the quality of the man is something worthy of praise, and well overdue praise at that.

Luis Torrens C   Born: 05/02/96   Age: 25   Bats: R   Throws: R   Height: 6'0"   Weight: 208   Origin: International Free Agent, 2013

YEAR	TEAM	LVL	AGE	PA	R	2B	3B	HR	RBI	BB	K	SB	CS	Whiff%	AVG/OBP/SLG	DRC+	BABIP	BRR	FRAA	WARP
2018	LE	HI-A	22	515	62	36	3	6	73	26	77	1	1		.280/.320/.406	100	.318	1.8	C(85): 1.0, 1B(3): 0.0	0.8
2019	AMA	AA	23	397	50	23	1	15	62	42	67	1	2		.300/.373/.500	134	.331	-2.6	C(85): 3.0, 1B(1): 0.2	3.1
2019	SD	MLB	23	16	2	1	0	0	0	2	6	0	0	34.6%	.214/.312/.286	74	.375	0.4	C(4): 0.4	0.1
2020	SD	MLB	24	13	0	1	0	0	0	1	2	0	0	27.8%	.273/.333/.364	94	.333	-0.3	C(7): -0.0	0.0
2020	SEA	MLB	24	65	5	4	0	1	6	6	13	0	0	19.8%	.254/.323/.373	91	.311	-0.3	C(17): 0.0	-0.2
2021 FS	SEA	MLB	25	600	60	24	1	16	64	51	134	0	0	22.7%	.232/.303/.372	86	.279	-0.2	C -15, 1B 0	-0.2
2021 DC	SEA	MLB	25	332	33	13	1	8	35	28	74	0	0	22.7%	.232/.303/.372	86	.279	-0.1	C -11	-0.4

Comparables: Nick Hundley, Ryan Lavarnway, Blake Swihart

A recurring theme of the 2020 Mariners was "not bad given what was expected, which was nothing." Torrens certainly fits the mold. A midseason acquisition in the trade that sent Austin Nola to San Diego, the Venezuelan backstop showed significant offensive improvement in 2020, posting nearly a league average offensive line, which coupled nicely with his nearly average defensive line. With Tom Murphy coming off injury and Cal Raleigh pegged the future by the organization, Torrens most likely looks to spend 2021 shuffling up and down the I-5 corridor between Tacoma and Seattle. That sounds bleak but recent infrastructure improvements have made the freeway interchange much more convenient, and the nearby casino has a new gaming and conference center. Also, food is cheaper in Tacoma.

YEAR	TEAM	P. COUNT	FRM RUNS	BLK RUNS	THRW RUNS	TOT RUNS
2019	SD	495	-0.1	0.4		0.3
2019	AMA	12535	-2.8	0.0	5.2	2.5
2020	SD	597	-0.5	-0.1	0.0	-0.6
2020	SEA	2281	-1.9	-0.3	0.0	-2.2
2021	SEA	12025	-10.0	-1.8	0.0	-11.8

★ ★ ★ *2021 Top 101 Prospect* **#72** ★ ★ ★

Taylor Trammell CF   Born: 09/13/97   Age: 23   Bats: L   Throws: L   Height: 6'2"   Weight: 213   Origin: Round 1, 2016 Draft (#35 overall)

YEAR	TEAM	LVL	AGE	PA	R	2B	3B	HR	RBI	BB	K	SB	CS	Whiff%	AVG/OBP/SLG	DRC+	BABIP	BRR	FRAA	WARP
2018	DAY	HI-A	20	461	71	19	4	8	41	58	105	25	10		.277/.375/.406	125	.358	-0.8	CF(60): -1.7, LF(29): 4.5, RF(14): -0.7	1.7
2019	AMA	AA	21	133	14	4	1	4	10	13	36	3	4		.229/.316/.381	89	.295	-0.6	CF(31): -1.4	0.1
2019	CHA	AA	21	381	47	8	3	6	33	54	86	17	4		.236/.349/.336	110	.299	2.1	LF(91): -0.7, CF(1): 0.1	1.5
2021 FS	SEA	MLB	23	600	63	25	4	14	59	57	185	19	7		.229/.307/.372	89	.321	2.4	LF 3, CF 0	1.5

Comparables: Ryan Kalish, Michael Saunders, Brandon Nimmo

If there were ever a prospect to make you sigh in relief that the old scouts vs. stats wars are over, it's Trammell. In the Ancient Times, a.k.a. 2012, stat guys would sit you down and Clockwork Orange your eyes open while they harangued you about how Trammell's route efficiency makes him a suspect center fielder. Scouts would cue up Futures Games highlights, show you hand-clocked home-to-first times, and ask you if you'd seen *Trouble With the Curve*. It's good that both sides have learned to appreciate what the other has to offer. Rather than argue over what Trammell is or isn't we can be brief: He's a fabulously athletic player with 70-grade speed, enough power to hit 30 home runs in a season, and enough contact and route-running issues to worry if either will ever translate to the major leagues. If it all pans out Trammell will be one of the best and most exciting outfielders in the league, but he'll have to show he can hit consistently in a way that, up until now, he simply has not.

Donovan Walton 2B   Born: 05/25/94   Age: 27   Bats: L   Throws: R   Height: 5'10"   Weight: 175   Origin: Round 5, 2016 Draft (#147 overall)

YEAR	TEAM	LVL	AGE	PA	R	2B	3B	HR	RBI	BB	K	SB	CS	Whiff%	AVG/OBP/SLG	DRC+	BABIP	BRR	FRAA	WARP
2018	MOD	HI-A	24	256	35	12	3	3	19	30	37	8	3		.309/.402/.433	148	.358	-0.3	2B(36): -4.2, SS(19): 1.0	1.1
2018	ARK	AA	24	238	22	14	1	1	22	21	34	3	1		.236/.325/.327	83	.276	-1.4	2B(62): 6.2	0.2
2019	ARK	AA	25	558	72	22	3	11	50	63	72	10	13		.300/.390/.427	159	.333	-2.0	SS(103): 12.4, 2B(19): 1.6	6.6
2019	SEA	MLB	25	19	2	0	0	0	2	3	5	0	1	34.8%	.188/.316/.188	82	.273	-0.2	SS(5): -0.7, 2B(2): -0.5	-0.1
2020	SEA	MLB	26	14	0	1	0	0	3	1	5	0	1	42.9%	.154/.214/.231	85	.250		SS(4): 0.0, 2B(1): -0.0	0.0
2021 FS	SEA	MLB	27	600	61	23	2	13	62	50	136	4	2	38.6%	.233/.307/.362	87	.287	-1.3	SS 14, 1B 0	2.3
2021 DC	SEA	MLB	27	33	3	1	0	0	3	2	7	0	0	38.6%	.233/.307/.362	87	.287	-0.1	SS 1	0.1

Comparables: Gavin Cecchini, Vimael Machín, Steve Tolleson

A Bloomquist by any other name, Walton will spend 2021 as he spends all years: fulfilling the words of the Good Book. "Wherever two or more are in need of grit, Donovan is with thee."

Evan White 1B Born: 04/26/96 Age: 25 Bats: R Throws: L Height: 6'3" Weight: 220 Origin: Round 1, 2017 Draft (#17 overall)

YEAR	TEAM	LVL	AGE	PA	R	2B	3B	HR	RBI	BB	K	SB	CS	Whiff%	AVG/OBP/SLG	DRC+	BABIP	BRR	FRAA	WARP
2018	MOD	HI-A	22	538	72	27	7	11	66	52	103	4	3		.303/.375/.458	144	.363	-0.5	1B(106): 5.5	2.1
2019	ARK	AA	23	400	61	13	2	18	55	29	92	2	0		.293/.350/.488	153	.346	1.1	1B(88): -5.3	1.9
2020	SEA	MLB	24	202	19	7	0	8	26	18	84	1	2	38.1%	.176/.252/.346	65	.264	-0.4	1B(54): -1.3	-0.8
2021 FS	SEA	MLB	25	600	65	24	2	24	75	43	217	0	0	38.1%	.233/.293/.420	93	.335	1.0	1B -2	0.2
2021 DC	SEA	MLB	25	565	61	23	2	22	71	40	205	0	0	38.1%	.233/.293/.420	93	.335	0.9	1B -2	0.2

Comparables: Brad Eldred, Billy Ashley, Nick Evans

Long ballyhooed as the best defensive first base prospect in memory, White delivered on that side of the ball, winning the first of likely many Gold Glove awards and displaying a level of athleticism rarely seen around a position typically manned by your Lukes Voit and Pauls Konerko. Unfortunately for White and the Mariners, the other parts of his scouting profile also proved accurate. Those "other parts" expressed concern about his ability to hit major league pitching, and a 65 DRC+ and 42% K-rate isn't going to work for a strong-defensive catcher, let alone a first baseman.

White's aforementioned athleticism fuels above average raw power at the plate, and it's very much worth noting he rebounded from "disastrous" at the start of the season to merely "below league average" the rest of the way. The tools that made him a first-round pick flash all the time, and there's always that sweet, sweet defense, even if it feels a bit wasted at baseball's most fungible defensive position. The Mariners will give him every opportunity in 2021 to prove the value of the latter, and continue to progress with the former. It's clear they believe this kid is one in a million.

PITCHERS

Brandon Brennan RHP Born: 07/26/91 Age: 29 Bats: R Throws: R Height: 6'4" Weight: 207 Origin: Round 4, 2012 Draft (#141 overall)

YEAR	TEAM	LVL	AGE	W	L	SV	G	GS	IP	H	HR	BB/9	K/9	K	GB%	BABIP	WHIP	ERA	DRA-	WARP	MPH	FA%	Whiff%	CSP
2018	BIR	AA	26	4	3	1	40	1	69²	54	4	2.7	9.0	70	52.1%	.267	1.08	3.10	53	2.0				
2018	CHA	AAA	26	1	1	0	4	0	5	3	0	5.4	16.2	9	75.0%	.375	1.20	5.40	25	0.2				
2019	TAC	AAA	27	1	0	0	9	0	8²	5	1	4.2	10.4	10	82.4%	.250	1.04	1.04	55	0.3				
2019	SEA	MLB	27	3	6	0	44	0	47¹	34	6	4.6	8.9	47	54.4%	.235	1.23	4.56	73	0.9	96.3	51.5%	34.4%	44.1%
2020	SEA	MLB	28	0	0	0	5	0	7¹	7	2	6.1	8.6	7	38.1%	.263	1.64	3.68	109	0.0	94.8	51.3%	32.7%	40.5%
2021 FS	SEA	MLB	29	2	2	0	57	0	50	44	6	4.9	9.2	50	49.8%	.284	1.43	4.33	98	0.2	96.0	51.5%	34.1%	43.4%
2021 DC	SEA	MLB	29	2	2	0	46	0	49	43	6	4.9	9.2	49	49.8%	.284	1.43	4.33	98	0.3	96.0	51.5%	34.1%	43.4%

Comparables: Hansel Robles, Dominic Leone, Kyle Finnegan

You've already been warned to take 2020 stats with a grain of salt, but in Brennan's case, what work you see was marred by the recovery of a strained oblique that erased most of his short season. Of course, you also have perfectly good 2019 numbers that say the same thing: The former Rule 5 pick can't throw his breaking pitches for strikes, and shouldn't throw his four-seam at all. This is not an ideal combination for a pitcher.

Sam Carlson RHP Born: 12/03/98 Age: 22 Bats: R Throws: R Height: 6'4" Weight: 195 Origin: Round 2, 2017 Draft (#55 overall)

Despite throwing only three professional innings since being drafted in 2017, the once highly touted Carlson is still just 22. People that age aren't supposed to have it all figured out anyway, so he's right on schedule.

Sam Delaplane RHP Born: 03/27/95 Age: 26 Bats: R Throws: R Height: 5'11" Weight: 175 Origin: Round 23, 2017 Draft (#693 overall)

YEAR	TEAM	LVL	AGE	W	L	SV	G	GS	IP	H	HR	BB/9	K/9	K	GB%	BABIP	WHIP	ERA	DRA-	WARP	MPH	FA%	Whiff%	CSP
2018	CLI	LO-A	23	4	2	10	39	0	59²	54	5	3.3	15.1	100	49.3%	.386	1.27	1.96	39	2.1				
2019	MOD	HI-A	24	3	2	2	21	0	31²	22	2	4.0	17.6	62	36.0%	.417	1.14	4.26	62	0.6				
2019	ARK	AA	24	3	1	5	25	0	37	13	2	2.2	14.1	58	35.9%	.180	0.59	0.49	32	1.4				
2021 FS	SEA	MLB	26	1	1	0	57	0	50	39	7	4.0	12.5	69	39.3%	.289	1.23	3.66	90	0.4				
2021 DC	SEA	MLB	26	1	1	0	29	0	30	23	4	4.0	12.5	41	39.3%	.289	1.23	3.66	90	0.3				

Comparables: Bryan Garcia, Kodi Whitley, Tyler Rogers

A 23rd-round pick in 2017, Delaplane is easily Seattle's best relief prospect. His motion is a tight coil, leg half raised, torquing his body from the right edge of the rubber toward the center of the mound. It's a very satisfying delivery, especially, as in an act of foreshadowing, he punches the ball into his glove in the windup, a precursor to a slider evading the bat and striking the catcher's mitt. That slider is a major weapon: Gripped like a curveball and thrown with the twist of a doorknob, it 's heavier than the average breaking ball, which accounts for the impressive strikeout totals. He belongs in the M's bullpen on Opening Day.

Robert Dugger RHP Born: 07/03/95 Age: 26 Bats: R Throws: R Height: 6'0" Weight: 198 Origin: Round 18, 2016 Draft (#537 overall)

YEAR	TEAM	LVL	AGE	W	L	SV	G	GS	IP	H	HR	BB/9	K/9	K	GB%	BABIP	WHIP	ERA	DRA-	WARP	MPH	FA%	Whiff%	CSP
2018	JUP	HI-A	22	3	1	0	7	7	41¹	40	2	1.5	7.4	34	56.3%	.309	1.14	2.40	77	0.8				
2018	JAX	AA	22	7	6	0	18	18	109¹	100	13	3.0	8.8	107	34.9%	.299	1.24	3.79	113	0.0				
2019	JAX	AA	23	6	6	0	13	13	70²	57	6	2.7	9.3	73	45.0%	.282	1.10	3.31	80	0.9				
2019	NO	AAA	23	2	4	0	10	10	53¹	74	12	2.9	8.3	49	36.7%	.376	1.71	7.59	174	-0.9				
2019	MIA	MLB	23	0	4	0	7	7	34¹	33	6	4.5	6.6	25	38.5%	.265	1.46	5.77	130	-0.2	91.7	59.2%	22.3%	43.4%
2020	MIA	MLB	24	0	0	0	4	1	10²	21	5	2.5	3.4	4	30.6%	.364	2.25	12.66	180	-0.4	93.9	53.8%	11.3%	49.9%
2021 FS	SEA	MLB	25	2	2	0	57	0	50	52	10	3.5	6.9	38	36.0%	.286	1.45	5.46	121	-0.5	92.5	57.2%	18.4%	45.7%
2021 DC	SEA	MLB	25	2	2	0	46	0	49	51	10	3.5	6.9	37	36.0%	.286	1.45	5.46	121	-0.3	92.5	57.2%	18.4%	45.7%

Comparables: Jorge Alcala, Justin Dunn, Bobby Parnell

A somewhat promising back-end pitching prospect in the before times, Dugger's 2020 claim to fame was as the spot starter for José Ureña in the fateful July 26 game that Miami inexplicably played as their COVID outbreak was starting to spiral. Dugger was claimed off waivers by the Mariners (his original team) in December.

Justin Dunn RHP Born: 09/22/95 Age: 25 Bats: R Throws: R Height: 6'2" Weight: 185 Origin: Round 1, 2016 Draft (#19 overall)

YEAR	TEAM	LVL	AGE	W	L	SV	G	GS	IP	H	HR	BB/9	K/9	K	GB%	BABIP	WHIP	ERA	DRA-	WARP	MPH	FA%	Whiff%	CSP
2018	STL	HI-A	22	2	3	0	9	9	45²	43	2	3.0	10.1	51	39.8%	.331	1.27	2.36	71	1.0				
2018	BNG	AA	22	6	5	0	15	15	89²	85	7	3.7	10.5	105	43.8%	.353	1.36	4.22	73	1.9				
2019	ARK	AA	23	9	5	0	25	25	131²	118	13	2.7	10.8	158	37.5%	.314	1.19	3.55	94	0.6				
2019	SEA	MLB	23	0	0	0	4	4	6²	2	0	12.2	6.8	5	43.8%	.125	1.65	2.70	109	0.0	94.1	58.8%	22.2%	42.6%
2020	SEA	MLB	24	4	1	0	10	10	45²	31	10	6.1	7.5	38	32.3%	.179	1.36	4.34	161	-1.1	93.0	54.8%	22.2%	45.4%
2021 FS	SEA	MLB	25	8	9	0	26	26	150	138	25	4.7	8.5	141	36.0%	.276	1.45	4.96	110	0.2	93.1	55.2%	22.2%	45.1%
2021 DC	SEA	MLB	25	6	9	0	24	24	116	107	20	4.7	8.5	109	36.0%	.276	1.45	4.96	110	0.6	93.1	55.2%	22.2%	45.1%

Comparables: Robert Dugger, Jordan Yamamoto, T.J. Zeuch

Some hurlers make pitching look easy, a simple, metronomic, back-and-forth activity with the occasional slow pirouette to watch a teammate field a grounder or drift under a lazy fly ball, but mostly just a calisthenics-heavy game of catch with a man dressed like a ninja turtle. Others make pitching look like Roger Murtaugh in *Lethal Weapon 2*; sitting on a toilet, sweating, desperate to be anywhere else, and hoping not to die. Dunn is one of the latter. The inconsistency of his command and velocity lead to high pitch counts and low-inning starts, without the fun eight-pitch strikeouts that usually come with those. Coming into Dunn's age-26 season the bullpen looks more and more likely, though the raw stuff still provides hope of a late-blooming back-end starter hiding in there somewhere.

Carl Edwards Jr. RHP Born: 09/03/91 Age: 29 Bats: R Throws: R Height: 6'3" Weight: 170 Origin: Round 48, 2011 Draft (#1464 overall)

YEAR	TEAM	LVL	AGE	W	L	SV	G	GS	IP	H	HR	BB/9	K/9	K	GB%	BABIP	WHIP	ERA	DRA-	WARP	MPH	FA%	Whiff%	CSP
2018	CHC	MLB	26	3	2	0	58	0	52	36	2	5.5	11.6	67	30.9%	.283	1.31	2.60	98	0.3	96.3	75.8%	33.5%	42.6%
2019	IOW	AAA	27	2	0	0	14	0	14²	12	2	3.7	8.6	14	54.8%	.250	1.23	3.07	69	0.4				
2019	CHC	MLB	27	1	1	0	20	0	15¹	8	3	5.3	10.0	17	24.3%	.147	1.11	5.87	112	0.0	95.8	76.2%	21.6%	47.0%
2019	SD	MLB	27	0	0	0	2	0	1²	4	0	21.6	10.8	2	37.5%	.500	4.80	32.40	76	0.0	95.5	66.7%	30.4%	43.2%
2020	SEA	MLB	28	0	0	1	5	0	4²	2	0	1.9	11.6	6	60.0%	.200	0.64	1.93	86	0.1	94.6	66.1%	41.7%	47.4%
2021 FS	SEA	MLB	29	2	2	0	57	0	50	36	5	5.6	10.8	59	40.2%	.264	1.35	3.48	83	0.6	95.9	74.5%	30.2%	44.5%

Comparables: Dominic Leone, Ken Giles, Arodys Vizcaíno

Edwards came into 2020 needing to prove he could command his quality, high-velocity fastball well enough to put some of the shine back on what was once a promising relief career. Despite an encouraging handful of appearances before a forearm strain cut the short season shorter, it's hard to think much of that changed. For now, Edwards will have to add "staying healthy" to an already long list of things he needs to prove to recapture his career's momentum. The stuff is willing, but the circumstances have been finicky.

Aaron Fletcher LHP Born: 02/25/96   Age: 25   Bats: L   Throws: L   Height: 6'0"   Weight: 220   Origin: Round 14, 2018 Draft (#431 overall)

YEAR	TEAM	LVL	AGE	W	L	SV	G	GS	IP	H	HR	BB/9	K/9	K	GB%	BABIP	WHIP	ERA	DRA-	WARP	MPH	FA%	Whiff%	CSP
2018	NAT	ROK	22	0	0	0	1	0	2	4	0	4.5	9.0	2	50.0%	.667	2.50	9.00	54	0.1				
2018	AUB	SS	22	2	1	0	12	7	29	30	0	0.9	9.9	32	61.0%	.366	1.14	2.48	237	-2.0				
2019	HAG	LO-A	23	2	3	1	15	0	28	14	0	1.6	9.0	28	41.7%	.200	0.68	1.61	50	0.8				
2019	FBG	HI-A	23	3	1	0	12	0	26	15	1	2.8	11.1	32	54.2%	.241	0.88	1.38	58	0.6				
2019	HBG	AA	23	0	0	0	5	0	6¹	7	0	2.8	12.8	9	62.5%	.438	1.42	4.26	96	0.0				
2019	ARK	AA	23	0	0	0	9	0	13	14	0	2.1	10.4	15	55.6%	.389	1.31	3.46	114	-0.2				
2020	SEA	MLB	24	0	0	0	6	0	4¹	7	1	14.5	14.5	7	46.2%	.500	3.23	12.46	96	0.0	94.5	65.3%	26.3%	40.0%
2021 FS	SEA	MLB	25	2	3	0	57	0	50	48	7	4.1	8.8	48	45.8%	.295	1.42	4.77	107	-0.1	94.5	65.3%	26.3%	40.0%
2021 DC	SEA	MLB	25	0	0	0	11	0	12	11	1	4.1	8.8	11	45.8%	.295	1.42	4.77	107	0.0	94.5	65.3%	26.3%	40.0%

Comparables: Alex Vesia, Phillip Diehl, Alex Reyes

Fletcher made his major league debut in 2020 against all odds and a good amount of reason. In celebration, we offer a glint of optimism: All the Fletchers in baseball history, dating all the way back to Sam "Bats Unknown" Fletcher in 1909, have combined for a 6.45 ERA on a mere 47 2/3 innings. In terms of the latter, Aaron is already nearly a tenth of the way there. In fact, he's already surpassed the median Fletcher in career strikeouts. So don't think of his 2020 line as a failure; think of it as taking part in a proud tradition.

Chris Flexen RHP Born: 07/01/94   Age: 27   Bats: R   Throws: R   Height: 6'3"   Weight: 250   Origin: Round 14, 2012 Draft (#440 overall)

YEAR	TEAM	LVL	AGE	W	L	SV	G	GS	IP	H	HR	BB/9	K/9	K	GB%	BABIP	WHIP	ERA	DRA-	WARP	MPH	FA%	Whiff%	CSP
2018	LV	AAA	23	6	7	0	18	17	92	109	11	3.0	7.6	78	41.3%	.356	1.52	4.40	109	0.5				
2018	NYM	MLB	23	0	2	0	4	1	6¹	14	2	8.5	4.3	3	40.0%	.429	3.16	12.79	166	-0.2	94.3	62.3%	14.1%	45.0%
2019	SYR	AAA	24	5	3	0	26	14	78²	94	11	2.4	10.5	92	43.9%	.382	1.46	4.46	109	1.0				
2019	NYM	MLB	24	0	3	0	9	1	13²	15	1	8.6	6.6	10	34.0%	.304	2.05	6.59	123	-0.1	96.8	61.7%	20.4%	47.1%
2021 FS	SEA	MLB	26	8	9	0	26	26	150	144	25	3.8	8.2	137	41.1%	.284	1.39	4.68	107	0.5	96.2	61.8%	19.0%	46.7%
2021 DC	SEA	MLB	26	5	7	0	19	19	97	93	16	3.8	8.2	88	41.1%	.284	1.39	4.68	107	0.7	96.2	61.8%	19.0%	46.7%

Comparables: Keury Mella, Lucas Sims, Jayson Aquino

Flexen's dominant finish to the season—three runs and 42 strikeouts in 31 October innings, followed by 38 punchouts and a 1.91 ERA in 28 postseason frames—underscored what we knew all along: On talent, he had little reason to spend his age-25 season in South Korea. A million dollars and a chance to escape the Wilpons' domain would tempt any young fellow, though, and so off he went to Doosan. Flexen's gamble paid off handsomely, as a strong season in the KBO undoubtedly aided his long-term MLB prospects more than anything else he could have done in 2020. His gas was a good five ticks faster than the average KBO heater, and when he located his slider effectively, he was practically unhittable; his highlight reel features some of the season's most embarrassing and half-hearted swings-and-misses. The only flaw in his game at this point is injuries: Even after missing 10 starts, 140 innings was a career high, a total that provided an advantage against the limited workloads of other free agents. He signed a two-year contract with the Seattle Mariners, and will compete for a spot in their six-man rotation in 2021.

Joey Gerber RHP Born: 05/03/97   Age: 24   Bats: R   Throws: R   Height: 6'4"   Weight: 215   Origin: Round 8, 2018 Draft (#238 overall)

YEAR	TEAM	LVL	AGE	W	L	SV	G	GS	IP	H	HR	BB/9	K/9	K	GB%	BABIP	WHIP	ERA	DRA-	WARP	MPH	FA%	Whiff%	CSP
2018	EVE	SS	21	1	0	6	13	0	14	9	0	3.9	13.5	21	59.3%	.333	1.07	1.93	156	-0.4				
2018	CLI	LO-A	21	0	0	2	9	0	11²	9	0	3.9	17.0	22	35.0%	.450	1.20	2.31	45	0.4				
2019	MOD	HI-A	22	0	2	8	25	0	26	17	0	4.2	13.5	39	37.5%	.309	1.12	3.46	49	0.7				
2019	ARK	AA	22	1	2	0	19	0	22²	21	2	2.8	11.9	30	37.9%	.345	1.24	1.59	88	0.1				
2020	SEA	MLB	23	1	1	0	17	0	15²	13	1	2.9	3.4	6	42.0%	.245	1.15	4.02	125	-0.1	95.7	65.2%	20.2%	51.0%
2021 FS	SEA	MLB	24	1	1	0	57	0	50	47	8	4.0	8.8	48	41.0%	.286	1.39	4.63	105	0.0	95.7	65.2%	20.2%	51.0%
2021 DC	SEA	MLB	24	1	1	0	34	0	36	33	5	4.0	8.8	35	41.0%	.286	1.39	4.63	105	0.1	95.7	65.2%	20.2%	51.0%

Comparables: Jose Santiago, Randy Moffitt, Miles Mikolas

Owner of a mid-90's fastball and a moderately amusing Twitter account (@gerb_nation), Gerber has one publicly-distinguishing feature. It is not the fastball.

★ ★ ★ *2021 Top 101 Prospect* **#38** ★ ★ ★

Logan Gilbert RHP Born: 05/05/97   Age: 24   Bats: R   Throws: R   Height: 6'6"   Weight: 225   Origin: Round 1, 2018 Draft (#14 overall)

YEAR	TEAM	LVL	AGE	W	L	SV	G	GS	IP	H	HR	BB/9	K/9	K	GB%	BABIP	WHIP	ERA	DRA-	WARP	MPH	FA%	Whiff%	CSP
2019	WV	LO-A	22	1	0	0	5	5	22²	9	2	2.4	14.3	36	22.5%	.184	0.66	1.59	31	1.0				
2019	MOD	HI-A	22	5	3	0	12	12	62¹	52	3	1.7	10.5	73	45.5%	.322	1.03	1.73	65	1.4				
2019	ARK	AA	22	4	2	0	9	9	50	34	2	2.7	10.1	56	32.5%	.274	0.98	2.88	73	0.8				
2021 FS	SEA	MLB	24	1	2	0	57	0	50	44	7	3.7	9.6	53	34.5%	.285	1.30	4.10	100	0.1				
2021 DC	SEA	MLB	24	1	2	0	6	6	30	26	4	3.7	9.6	32	34.5%	.285	1.30	4.10	100	0.3				

Comparables: Jordan Yamamoto, David Price, Sean Nolin

A first-round pick in 2018, Gilbert was an advanced college arm drafted to ascend rapidly and reinforce a Seattle rotation in desperate need of power pitching. Perhaps fortunately for the young right-hander, the 2019 season happened, and suddenly the organization was a lot less desperate. His classic four-pitch arsenal maxes out with a plus curveball with big, sharp, one-to-seven movement, complemented by an above average fastball and slider. The changeup still needs work, but even with it as a show-me offering Gilbert profiles as the best drafted/developed arm of the Dipoto Regime. He should be ready for major-league action as soon as, the "timing" works out in 2021.

Marco Gonzales LHP Born: 02/16/92 Age: 29 Bats: L Throws: L Height: 6'1" Weight: 197 Origin: Round 1, 2013 Draft (#19 overall)

YEAR	TEAM	LVL	AGE	W	L	SV	G	GS	IP	H	HR	BB/9	K/9	K	GB%	BABIP	WHIP	ERA	DRA-	WARP	MPH	FA%	Whiff%	CSP
2018	SEA	MLB	26	13	9	0	29	29	166²	172	17	1.7	7.8	145	44.7%	.320	1.22	4.00	79	3.3	91.6	32.5%	21.1%	49.4%
2019	SEA	MLB	27	16	13	0	34	34	203	210	23	2.5	6.5	147	41.2%	.295	1.31	3.99	118	0.0	90.2	39.6%	18.0%	50.9%
2020	SEA	MLB	28	7	2	0	11	11	69²	59	8	0.9	8.3	64	37.6%	.263	0.95	3.10	89	1.0	89.8	45.2%	19.7%	53.2%
2021 FS	SEA	MLB	29	9	8	0	26	26	150	150	25	2.1	8.1	134	39.7%	.292	1.23	4.04	98	1.2	90.4	39.6%	19.1%	51.2%
2021 DC	SEA	MLB	29	9	10	0	201	29	174	174	29	2.1	8.1	155	39.7%	.292	1.23	4.04	98	1.4	90.4	39.6%	19.1%	51.2%

Comparables: Kevin Gausman, Jon Gray, Sean Manaea

If there's one thing Jerry Dipoto loves more than trading, it's talking. The man has his own podcast, and he uses it to offer rose-tinted projections on anyone and anything graced by Mariner teal. The experience can be simultaneously a thrilling look behind the scenes of a major league baseball front office, and a tiresome exercise in PR. Dipoto's relentless hype, combined with a fastball that red-lines at 90 mph and a DRA that has long insisted, "This is all going to fall apart any minute now," have contributed to the delayed acknowledgment of Gonzales as a quality major league starting pitcher. The former first-round pick increased his usage of cutter and fastball in 2020 to set a career high strikeout rate (23.5 percent) and a career low walk rate (2.9 percent). When a player's K/BB ratio starts getting into prime Cliff Lee territory, it's time to start revising those back-end starter ceiling projections. That said, unless Gonzales enrolls in the James Paxton School of Magical Velocity Acquisition, it's hard to imagine him getting much better than he was in 2020. Even with some mild regression in 2021, though, he has proven himself the wheat in Jerry Dipoto's mountains of verbal chaff.

Kendall Graveman RHP Born: 12/21/90 Age: 30 Bats: R Throws: R Height: 6'2" Weight: 200 Origin: Round 8, 2013 Draft (#235 overall)

YEAR	TEAM	LVL	AGE	W	L	SV	G	GS	IP	H	HR	BB/9	K/9	K	GB%	BABIP	WHIP	ERA	DRA-	WARP	MPH	FA%	Whiff%	CSP
2018	NAS	AAA	27	2	1	0	4	4	24	35	3	2.6	6.0	16	54.9%	.405	1.75	4.50	96	0.3				
2018	OAK	MLB	27	1	5	0	7	7	34¹	44	9	3.4	7.1	27	56.4%	.324	1.66	7.60	120	0.0	95.7	57.1%	19.6%	44.5%
2020	SEA	MLB	29	1	3	0	11	2	18²	15	2	3.9	7.2	15	48.1%	.250	1.23	5.79	106	0.1	97.7	68.1%	18.6%	46.4%
2021 FS	SEA	MLB	30	2	3	7	57	0	50	51	8	3.4	7.6	42	48.6%	.296	1.41	4.89	111	-0.2	96.9	63.8%	19.0%	45.7%
2021 DC	SEA	MLB	30	2	3	7	58	0	61	63	10	3.4	7.6	51	48.6%	.296	1.41	4.89	111	0.0	96.9	63.8%	19.0%	45.7%

Comparables: Chris Stratton, Jordan Lyles, Luke Hochevar

After a first act you could call "Charlie Morton: The Early Years," Graveman appeared in Peoria after more than a year missed from Tommy John surgery, and spent spring training looking like "Charlie Morton: The Later Years". Gone was middling velocity, low-strikeout pitcher from Oakland. In his place: a vengeful demon, flinging 97 mph two-seamers at the corners. Unfortunately, after just two starts, he landed on the IL with what was originally called neck spasms, later revealed to be complications from a benign bone tumor in the spine, an issue that will eventually demand surgery. Graveman was able to return for the season's final month, but fatigue and pain limited him to relief. Baseball fans will be rooting hard for him to get fully healthy for 2021, both for humanitarian reasons, and because that two-seamer burning the crisp desert air was really something to see.

★　★　★　*2021 Top 101 Prospect* **#50** ★　★　★

Emerson Hancock RHP Born: 05/31/99 Age: 22 Bats: R Throws: R Height: 6'4" Weight: 213 Origin: Round 1, 2020 Draft (#6 overall)

Everyone has a type, and Jerry Dipoto's is college pitchers. As the sixth-overall pick of the 2020 draft, Hancock joins George Kirby, Logan Gilbert, Isaiah Campbell, and other recent draftees in Seattle. The Georgia product features a classic power arsenal, with a fastball touching 99, and a hard, mid-80s slider. He'll need to improve his comfort with his changeup, largely because hitters in the SEC didn't really need to see a changeup to struggle with a 99 mph fastball. If Hancock reaches his potential, he's an upper-rotation arm for the 2023 Mariners. Regardless, he's another arrow in a Seattle quiver that is now bristling with talented young arms, increasing the odds a few of them hit the target.

Yoshihisa Hirano RHP Born: 03/08/84 Age: 37 Bats: R Throws: R Height: 6'1" Weight: 185 Origin: International Free Agent, 2017

YEAR	TEAM	LVL	AGE	W	L	SV	G	GS	IP	H	HR	BB/9	K/9	K	GB%	BABIP	WHIP	ERA	DRA-	WARP	MPH	FA%	Whiff%	CSP
2018	ARI	MLB	34	4	3	3	75	0	66¹	49	6	3.1	8.0	59	50.6%	.251	1.09	2.44	99	0.3	93.3	53.6%	28.2%	42.4%
2019	ARI	MLB	35	5	5	1	62	0	53	51	7	3.7	10.4	61	44.2%	.317	1.38	4.75	93	0.4	92.7	47.9%	31.8%	41.1%
2020	SEA	MLB	36	0	1	4	13	0	12¹	18	2	5.8	8.0	11	48.8%	.390	2.11	5.84	94	0.1	91.7	45.2%	26.7%	39.9%
2021 FS	SEA	MLB	37	2	2	0	57	0	50	46	6	3.9	8.3	46	47.4%	.285	1.36	4.06	96	0.2	92.7	49.1%	29.7%	41.3%

Comparables: Jesse Chavez, Carlos Torres, Ricardo Rincon

The 2020 baseball season left us with a data set even a chaste Puritan would term "meager." That goes doubly so for relief pitchers, and triply for relief pitchers who missed the first half of the already-shortened season due to contracting a mysterious, new disease whose health ramifications are still largely unknown. Given these chaotic factors, it's impressive that once he was finally able to join the Mariners for the season's final month, Hirano's performance was very nearly identical to his career major-league norms. An uptick in walks and a downtick on his fastball could be a sign of age-induced decline for the soon-to-be 37-year-old, or it could be just 12 innings in the weirdest baseball season in history.

Yusei Kikuchi LHP Born: 06/17/91 Age: 30 Bats: L Throws: L Height: 6'0" Weight: 200 Origin: International Free Agent, 2019

YEAR	TEAM	LVL	AGE	W	L	SV	G	GS	IP	H	HR	BB/9	K/9	K	GB%	BABIP	WHIP	ERA	DRA-	WARP	MPH	FA%	Whiff%	CSP
2019	SEA	MLB	28	6	11	0	32	32	161²	195	36	2.8	6.5	116	43.9%	.310	1.52	5.46	160	-3.6	94.9	49.1%	20.0%	50.9%
2020	SEA	MLB	29	2	4	0	9	9	47	41	3	3.8	9.0	47	52.8%	.306	1.30	5.17	83	0.8	96.6	77.4%	30.2%	49.7%
2021 FS	SEA	MLB	30	9	9	0	26	26	150	148	21	3.5	8.2	136	46.5%	.296	1.38	4.46	101	0.9	95.4	57.8%	23.2%	50.5%
2021 DC	SEA	MLB	30	7	8	0	24	24	126	124	18	3.5	8.2	114	46.5%	.296	1.38	4.46	101	1.2	95.4	57.8%	23.2%	50.5%

Comparables: Martín Pérez, Matthew Boyd, Tyler Anderson

We fed Kikuchi's 2020 pitching line into the MLB Player Narrative-O-Matic 3000, but it immediately began grinding horribly and spitting out acrid smoke. It shouldn't have been a surprise: The left-hander underperformed his FIP by two runs, and he did just about everything he failed to do in a disastrous 2019: limited home runs, evoked groundballs, posted above-average chase and whiff rates. By all accounts Kikuchi should have had a triumphant bounceback season, having shelved his slow curveball and replaced it with a hard, tight slider that paired well with the fastball. So where did it go wrong?

At the beginning, mostly. Despite a lackluster (but not egregious) walk rate, Kikuchi too often put himself in a hole, posting a first strike rate that was third-worst among qualified pitchers. Command, and particularly fastball command, was never his calling card, and on 0-0 he got the pitch over the plate less often than the breaking pitch made to look like a fastball. It meant that for all his improvements, Kikuchi was routinely putting himself at a disadvantage. The silver lining to all this is that it's an easier fix than some other problems. If Kikuchi vary his tactics and reacquaint himself with strike one, we may finally see the pitcher we've long been waiting for.

--- ★ ★ ★ *2021 Top 101 Prospect* **#68** ★ ★ ★ ---

George Kirby RHP Born: 02/04/98 Age: 23 Bats: R Throws: R Height: 6'4" Weight: 215 Origin: Round 1, 2019 Draft (#20 overall)

YEAR	TEAM	LVL	AGE	W	L	SV	G	GS	IP	H	HR	BB/9	K/9	K	GB%	BABIP	WHIP	ERA	DRA-	WARP	MPH	FA%	Whiff%	CSP
2019	EVE	SS	21	0	0	0	9	8	23	24	1	0.0	9.8	25	45.3%	.365	1.04	2.35	72	0.5				
2021 FS	SEA	MLB	23	2	3	0	57	0	50	50	7	3.4	7.3	40	40.2%	.290	1.38	4.58	112	-0.2				

Another iteration of the Jerry Dipoto Advanced Right-Handed College Draft Pick-O-Matic, the Kirby Model features the same upper 90's fastball as is now standard with the line. It also features a customized Carlos Silva-Walk Reduction Valve (patent pending), which has kept Kirby from issuing a walk as a professional (albeit in only 23 official innings). Kirby's secondary stuff is a bit same-y and will probably never be better than average. His ability to stick in a major league rotation is going to come down to his ability to command that blazing heater, and not just in a way that "challenges" rookie league hitters with pure velocity down the pipe. If he does, he's got center-of-rotation upside. If he doesn't, well, bullpens need pitchers too.

Brady Lail RHP Born: 08/09/93 Age: 27 Bats: R Throws: R Height: 6'2" Weight: 200 Origin: Round 18, 2012 Draft (#577 overall)

YEAR	TEAM	LVL	AGE	W	L	SV	G	GS	IP	H	HR	BB/9	K/9	K	GB%	BABIP	WHIP	ERA	DRA-	WARP	MPH	FA%	Whiff%	CSP
2018	TRN	AA	24	1	0	0	10	0	19¹	22	2	3.7	9.3	20	34.5%	.370	1.55	5.59	66	0.4				
2018	SWB	AAA	24	4	6	0	27	0	43²	43	6	5.8	9.5	46	43.0%	.322	1.63	5.36	73	0.7				
2019	TRN	AA	25	3	1	1	14	1	31	18	1	3.5	13.6	47	43.5%	.283	0.97	1.74	56	0.7				
2019	SWB	AAA	25	1	1	0	11	0	15²	19	3	1.7	9.8	17	37.5%	.356	1.40	7.47	100	0.2				
2019	NYY	MLB	25	0	0	0	1	0	2²	2	1	3.4	6.8	2	57.1%	.167	1.12	10.12	123	0.0	92.9	56.5%	26.1%	35.1%
2020	SEA	MLB	26	0	0	0	8	0	16¹	14	5	3.9	6.6	12	32.0%	.200	1.29	4.41	183	-0.6	92.4	64.3%	17.1%	46.8%
2021 FS	SEA	MLB	27	2	3	0	57	0	50	47	9	3.6	8.3	45	36.9%	.279	1.36	4.54	106	0.0	92.4	63.6%	17.9%	45.7%

Comparables: Chase De Jong, Joe Ross, Daniel Norris

Lail finally mastered Triple-A on his fifth try—his first came during the Obama administration—and it earned him eight 2020 relief appearances. In seven, the team was already behind; in the eighth, he coughed up the lead.

Nick Margevicius LHP Born: 06/18/96 Age: 25 Bats: L Throws: L Height: 6'5" Weight: 220 Origin: Round 7, 2017 Draft (#198 overall)

YEAR	TEAM	LVL	AGE	W	L	SV	G	GS	IP	H	HR	BB/9	K/9	K	GB%	BABIP	WHIP	ERA	DRA-	WARP	MPH	FA%	Whiff%	CSP
2018	FW	LO-A	22	5	5	0	13	13	76¹	79	5	1.1	10.3	87	37.0%	.349	1.15	3.07	76	1.5				
2018	LE	HI-A	22	5	3	0	10	9	58²	69	5	1.2	9.1	59	36.0%	.379	1.31	4.30	99	0.2				
2019	AMA	AA	23	4	4	0	12	12	69	75	14	1.7	6.9	53	42.7%	.296	1.28	4.30	109	-0.3				
2019	SD	MLB	23	2	6	0	17	12	57	73	12	3.0	6.6	42	42.7%	.332	1.61	6.79	142	-0.8	90.3	54.1%	22.9%	49.6%
2020	SEA	MLB	24	2	3	0	10	7	41¹	38	6	3.0	7.8	36	36.7%	.281	1.26	4.57	117	0.0	92.2	64.2%	19.9%	48.2%
2021 FS	SEA	MLB	25	9	9	0	26	26	150	152	25	3.1	7.6	126	40.8%	.290	1.36	4.64	106	0.5	91.3	59.3%	21.4%	48.9%
2021 DC	SEA	MLB	25	3	5	0	14	14	71	72	12	3.1	7.6	59	40.8%	.290	1.36	4.64	106	0.5	91.3	59.3%	21.4%	48.9%

Comparables: David Peterson, Eric Lauer, Josh Fleming

If you are a soft-tossing left-handed pitcher whose success largely hinges upon an ability to keep your fly balls from sailing over the fence, chances are Dipoto's Fabulous Fringe Factory has, at minimum, touched your career. Forced out of San Diego by actual prospects, Margevicius was a waiver wire pickup by Seattle and immediately filled the back end of the rotation with exactly the level of production you would expect for someone with an upper 80's fastball and no true out pitch. There's always the chance the secondary stuff can be refined to make him something more than a swing guy/back end starter—Marco Gonzales is proof of concept—but absent anything unexpected this is a pitcher whose 5.68 DRA represented a substantial improvement from the previous season. For now, we'll give him four out of 10 Buehrles and hope there's another 1-2 mph in the fastball to be found somewhere.

Keynan Middleton RHP Born: 09/12/93 Age: 27 Bats: R Throws: R Height: 6'3" Weight: 215 Origin: Round 3, 2013 Draft (#95 overall)

YEAR	TEAM	LVL	AGE	W	L	SV	G	GS	IP	H	HR	BB/9	K/9	K	GB%	BABIP	WHIP	ERA	DRA-	WARP	MPH	FA%	Whiff%	CSP
2018	LAA	MLB	24	0	0	6	16	0	17²	14	1	4.6	8.2	16	33.3%	.295	1.30	2.04	123	-0.1	98.5	64.4%	24.5%	44.7%
2019	LAA	MLB	25	0	0	0	11	0	7²	4	0	8.2	7.0	6	35.0%	.200	1.43	1.17	107	0.0	96.4	57.3%	23.1%	43.2%
2020	LAA	MLB	26	0	1	0	13	0	12	12	2	4.5	8.2	11	22.2%	.294	1.50	5.25	125	-0.1	99.0	59.0%	25.0%	49.8%
2021 FS	SEA	MLB	27	2	3	0	57	0	50	44	8	4.8	9.8	54	33.3%	.278	1.42	4.67	105	0.0	98.3	60.0%	24.4%	47.0%
2021 DC	SEA	MLB	27	2	3	0	58	0	61	54	10	4.8	9.8	66	33.3%	.278	1.42	4.67	105	0.2	98.3	60.0%	24.4%	47.0%

Comparables: Phil Maton, Sam Tuivailala, Edubray Ramos

2017 seems so long ago. Remember when the US was in the Paris Climate Agreement, *The Leftovers* was still shattering hearts on HBO, and Middleton was the the Angels' closer apparent? If he watches HBO, Middleton might sympathize with *The Leftovers'* portrayal of Earth after two percent of the population disappears without a trace. Since his return, Middleton has been something like 98 percent of himself, and the difference yawns. While he regained his pre-Tommy John velocity in 2020, Middleton struggled so badly to locate his pitches that he was demoted to the Angels' alternate site in August. Still, while Middleton understands acutely what it's like to experience three years in which everything gets worse, there's reason (in his case, at least) to hope for things to improve. Pitchers whose stuff doesn't come back all the way from Tommy John surgery are common, but so are pitchers whose stuff comes back but whose precision takes longer. A surprise non-tender, the Mariners scooped him up; he'll either be the closer or in the PCL by the time the US rejoins the PCA.

Wyatt Mills RHP Born: 01/25/95 Age: 26 Bats: R Throws: R Height: 6'4" Weight: 190 Origin: Round 3, 2017 Draft (#93 overall)

YEAR	TEAM	LVL	AGE	W	L	SV	G	GS	IP	H	HR	BB/9	K/9	K	GB%	BABIP	WHIP	ERA	DRA-	WARP	MPH	FA%	Whiff%	CSP
2018	MOD	HI-A	23	6	0	11	35	0	42¹	29	1	1.9	10.4	49	52.9%	.280	0.90	1.91	71	0.7				
2018	ARK	AA	23	0	2	0	9	0	10²	18	0	3.4	8.4	10	42.5%	.450	2.06	10.12	80	0.1				
2019	ARK	AA	24	4	2	8	41	0	52²	43	2	2.9	11.3	66	52.7%	.320	1.14	4.27	88	0.2				
2021 FS	SEA	MLB	26	2	2	0	57	0	50	43	6	3.9	9.5	52	46.1%	.280	1.30	4.04	96	0.2				
2021 DC	SEA	MLB	26	1	1	0	17	0	18	15	2	3.9	9.5	18	46.1%	.280	1.30	4.04	96	0.1				

Comparables: Matt Foster, JD Hammer, Cody Ege

Some pitchers have changeups; some relievers, just by entering the game with a different look, basically *are* changeups. With a name like a secondary character from *Tombstone*, it's appropriate that Mills fires the ball from the hip. Look for him and his blazing sidearm to bring some justice to the AL West in 2021.

Anthony Misiewicz LHP Born: 11/01/94 Age: 26 Bats: R Throws: L Height: 6'1" Weight: 200 Origin: Round 18, 2015 Draft (#545 overall)

YEAR	TEAM	LVL	AGE	W	L	SV	G	GS	IP	H	HR	BB/9	K/9	K	GB%	BABIP	WHIP	ERA	DRA-	WARP	MPH	FA%	Whiff%	CSP
2018	ARK	AA	23	3	12	0	21	21	98	133	14	2.7	8.4	91	41.9%	.375	1.65	5.51	86	1.3				
2019	ARK	AA	24	1	2	0	7	7	35²	36	0	1.8	9.1	36	48.0%	.367	1.21	2.52	91	0.2				
2019	TAC	AAA	24	8	6	0	19	17	95²	95	17	2.6	8.4	89	42.8%	.292	1.29	5.36	78	2.6				
2020	SEA	MLB	25	0	2	0	21	0	20	20	2	2.7	11.2	25	31.4%	.367	1.30	4.05	80	0.4	94.9	76.8%	31.6%	44.6%
2021 FS	SEA	MLB	26	2	2	3	57	0	50	47	8	3.5	8.9	49	39.7%	.290	1.35	4.42	101	0.1	94.9	76.8%	31.6%	44.6%
2021 DC	SEA	MLB	26	2	2	3	46	0	49	46	8	3.5	8.9	48	39.7%	.290	1.35	4.42	101	0.3	94.9	76.8%	31.6%	44.6%

Comparables: Keury Mella, Chase De Jong, Andrew Moore

After bouncing along the Mallex Smith Seattle-to-Tampa Bay-to-Seattle developmental circuit, Misiewicz spent the entirety of 2020 wearing navy (and teal). For a team that featured one of the very worst bullpens in the sport, the left-hander was one of the few bright spots, setting a career-best strikeout rate by mixing a cutter and slurvy curveball with a mid-90's heater. Those questionable secondaries are why Misiewicz was never a particularly heralded prospect, and when he gets hit, he tends to get hit hard. But he's made it work so far, primarily by putting those enticing hittable pitches just out of reach. Unlike practically every other reliever that made an appearance for the Mariners last year, he figures to be back.

Rafael Montero RHP Born: 10/17/90 Age: 30 Bats: R Throws: R Height: 6'0" Weight: 190 Origin: International Free Agent, 2011

YEAR	TEAM	LVL	AGE	W	L	SV	G	GS	IP	H	HR	BB/9	K/9	K	GB%	BABIP	WHIP	ERA	DRA-	WARP	MPH	FA%	Whiff%	CSP
2019	RAN	ROK	28	0	0	0	5	3	7	2	0	0.0	15.4	12	45.5%	.182	0.29	0.00	15	0.4				
2019	FRI	AA	28	0	0	0	5	2	9	15	0	2.0	15.0	15	25.9%	.556	1.89	7.00	128	-0.2				
2019	TEX	MLB	28	2	0	0	22	0	29	23	5	1.6	10.6	34	40.3%	.269	0.97	2.48	86	0.4	97.5	46.8%	29.8%	45.1%
2020	TEX	MLB	29	0	1	8	17	0	17²	12	2	3.1	9.7	19	26.7%	.238	1.02	4.08	110	0.1	97.3	72.0%	25.0%	47.0%
2021 FS	SEA	MLB	30	2	2	26	57	0	50	43	6	3.5	10.3	57	38.3%	.290	1.26	3.71	88	0.5	97.4	59.0%	27.5%	46.0%
2021 DC	SEA	MLB	30	2	2	26	58	0	61	52	8	3.5	10.3	69	38.3%	.290	1.26	3.71	88	0.8	97.4	59.0%	27.5%	46.0%

Comparables: Kevin Gausman, Erasmo Ramírez, Chris Stratton

Don Rafael Montero jailed Anthony Hopkins and pretended Catherine Zeta-Jones was his daughter before trying to buy California with stolen gold in *The Mask of Zorro*. He saved four of his eight games in 2020 with the Rangers against teams from the Golden State, making him a much more successful Rafael Montero than his silver screen counterpart. Since coming back from Tommy John surgery in 2019, Montero has tossed 46⅔ innings, all from the bullpen, striking out almost 30 percent of opposing hitters. He has all but scrapped his slider in favor of more high-90s heaters, which in turn has helped his changeup play up, holding offenses to a .267 slugging percentage against the offspeed offering. It's fair to say the former top prospect has found his calling, and although it's not as a starter, he has certainly carved out a role for himself moving forward. He should pitch meaningful innings with the Mariners following an offseason trade.

Andres Muñoz   RHP   Born: 01/16/99   Age: 22   Bats: R   Throws: R   Height: 6'2"   Weight: 243   Origin: International Free Agent, 2015

YEAR	TEAM	LVL	AGE	W	L	SV	G	GS	IP	H	HR	BB/9	K/9	K	GB%	BABIP	WHIP	ERA	DRA-	WARP	MPH	FA%	Whiff%	CSP
2018	TRI	SS	19	0	0	0	5	0	5²	0	0	3.2	14.3	9	42.9%	.000	0.35	0.00	187	-0.3				
2018	SA	AA	19	2	1	7	20	0	19	11	0	5.2	9.0	19	54.5%	.250	1.16	0.95	68	0.4				
2019	AMA	AA	20	0	2	4	16	0	16²	9	1	5.9	18.4	34	40.7%	.320	1.20	2.16	42	0.5				
2019	ELP	AAA	20	3	2	2	19	0	19	16	3	3.3	11.4	24	51.1%	.317	1.21	3.79	59	0.6				
2019	SD	MLB	20	1	1	1	22	0	23	16	2	4.3	11.7	30	39.3%	.264	1.17	3.91	81	0.3	101.9	68.0%	31.8%	45.9%
2021 FS	SEA	MLB	22	2	2	0	57	0	50	41	6	4.3	10.6	58	43.8%	.286	1.31	3.96	91	0.4	101.9	68.0%	31.8%	45.9%
2021 DC	SEA	MLB	22	0	0	0	11	0	12	10	1	4.3	10.6	14	43.8%	.286	1.31	3.96	91	0.1	101.9	68.0%	31.8%	45.9%

Comparables: Ryan Wagner, Miguel Castro, Luiz Gohara

Before he was sidelined with Tommy John surgery in spring, Muñoz had an 80-grade fastball and a future as a top-tier closer. The degree to which he recovers this heat correlates directly to the chances that history will refer not to the "Austin Nola trade" but to the "Andrés Muñoz trade."

Ljay Newsome   RHP   Born: 11/08/96   Age: 24   Bats: R   Throws: R   Height: 5'11"   Weight: 210   Origin: Round 26, 2015 Draft (#785 overall)

YEAR	TEAM	LVL	AGE	W	L	SV	G	GS	IP	H	HR	BB/9	K/9	K	GB%	BABIP	WHIP	ERA	DRA-	WARP	MPH	FA%	Whiff%	CSP
2018	MOD	HI-A	21	6	10	0	26	26	138²	169	24	0.8	8.0	123	31.3%	.339	1.31	4.87	90	1.4				
2019	MOD	HI-A	22	6	6	0	18	18	100²	105	11	0.8	11.1	124	25.5%	.357	1.13	3.75	87	0.9				
2019	ARK	AA	22	3	4	0	9	9	48²	41	4	1.3	6.5	35	34.9%	.262	0.99	2.77	83	0.5				
2020	SEA	MLB	23	0	1	0	5	4	15²	20	4	0.6	5.2	9	42.1%	.302	1.34	5.17	118	0.0	93.3	49.4%	21.8%	53.5%
2021 FS	SEA	MLB	24	9	9	0	26	26	150	156	28	1.7	7.2	120	37.6%	.289	1.24	4.39	104	0.8	93.3	49.4%	21.8%	53.5%
2021 DC	SEA	MLB	24	3	4	0	14	14	61	63	11	1.7	7.2	49	37.6%	.289	1.24	4.39	104	0.5	93.3	49.4%	21.8%	53.5%

Comparables: Tyler Mahle, Chih-Wei Hu, José Ureña

Every infomercial has that series of soundbites with overjoyed past customers swearing that PRODUCT changed their lives for the better. When the Mariners cut the infomercial for their Gas Camp, an offseason pitching summit designed to increase velocity, maximize pitch mix efficiency, and otherwise make you the best pitcher you can be, Newsome will be one of the breathless apostles. A relatively anonymous 26th-round draft pick in 2015, Newsome used increased velocity and command to skyrocket through three levels in 2019, enjoying a cup of big league coffee in 2020. While his ceiling is unlikely any higher than long reliever, his success stands as the proof of concept the Mariners will point to moving forward when evangelizing their future young pitching prospects.

Yohan Ramirez   RHP   Born: 05/06/95   Age: 26   Bats: R   Throws: R   Height: 6'4"   Weight: 190   Origin: International Free Agent, 2016

YEAR	TEAM	LVL	AGE	W	L	SV	G	GS	IP	H	HR	BB/9	K/9	K	GB%	BABIP	WHIP	ERA	DRA-	WARP	MPH	FA%	Whiff%	CSP
2018	QC	LO-A	23	5	7	1	15	10	58	40	6	4.3	9.6	62	52.7%	.243	1.17	2.95	85	0.8				
2018	FAY	HI-A	23	1	1	2	14	0	20	16	0	6.3	9.0	20	67.3%	.308	1.50	3.15	71	0.4				
2019	FAY	HI-A	24	1	2	0	10	7	43²	22	0	4.5	14.2	69	53.6%	.262	1.01	2.89	56	1.2				
2019	CC	AA	24	3	5	1	17	8	62¹	42	5	7.5	12.9	89	43.4%	.285	1.51	4.76	97	0.0				
2020	SEA	MLB	25	0	0	3	16	0	20²	9	3	8.7	11.3	26	13.6%	.146	1.40	2.61	151	-0.4	97.1	59.8%	30.1%	42.6%
2021 FS	SEA	MLB	26	1	2	0	57	0	50	43	9	7.3	10.8	60	33.2%	.283	1.67	6.09	124	-0.6	97.1	59.8%	30.1%	42.6%
2021 DC	SEA	MLB	26	1	2	0	26	3	35	30	6	7.3	10.8	42	33.2%	.283	1.67	6.09	124	-0.2	97.1	59.8%	30.1%	42.6%

Comparables: Chad Sobotka, Wei-Chieh Huang, Tony Gonsolin

Pete Rose once said he would walk through hell in a gasoline suit to play baseball. Presumably both the gasoline and the match would be provided by Ramirez, who walked nearly as many batters as he struck out in 2020; only 48 percent of batters he faced put the ball in play. While this summary conjures the vision of another dystopian data point in nu-baseball's quest for pure three-outcomes play, the actual aesthetic experience of watching Ramirez pitch is gleefully, almost rapturously chaotic. If you ever wondered what it would be like to drive a car with a 700 horsepower engine not only lacking any safety or comfort features, but evan an ackknowledgement that safety and comfort exist as abstract concepts, this is the relief pitcher for you. He could flame out in a year or make a mechanical adjustment, harness his upper-90s fastball and wipeout slider, and become a shutdown closer. Either way, don't break glass in case of emergency, because you will quickly run out of glass.

Casey Sadler   RHP   Born: 07/13/90   Age: 30   Bats: R   Throws: R   Height: 6'3"   Weight: 205   Origin: Round 25, 2010 Draft (#747 overall)

YEAR	TEAM	LVL	AGE	W	L	SV	G	GS	IP	H	HR	BB/9	K/9	K	GB%	BABIP	WHIP	ERA	DRA-	WARP	MPH	FA%	Whiff%	CSP
2018	IND	AAA	27	6	5	1	27	8	77	79	7	3.0	7.1	61	43.8%	.310	1.36	3.39	82	1.1				
2018	PIT	MLB	27	0	0	0	2	0	4¹	9	0	6.2	6.2	3	57.9%	.474	2.77	8.31	112	0.0	93.9	59.3%	17.1%	48.2%
2019	DUR	AAA	28	1	1	1	11	3	32²	30	5	1.4	12.1	44	38.8%	.312	1.07	2.76	60	1.1				
2019	OKC	AAA	28	0	0	1	2	1	6	8	1	1.5	13.5	9	56.2%	.467	1.50	6.00	41	0.3				
2019	LAD	MLB	28	4	0	1	24	1	27	25	3	2.7	6.7	20	47.6%	.278	1.22	2.33	101	0.1	95.3	34.4%	22.7%	44.0%
2019	TB	MLB	28	0	0	0	9	0	19¹	16	2	2.3	5.1	11	54.8%	.233	1.09	1.86	110	0.0	94.9	44.3%	22.8%	44.3%
2020	SEA	MLB	29	1	2	0	17	0	19¹	15	3	5.6	9.8	21	41.5%	.245	1.40	5.12	84	0.3	94.2	35.6%	30.0%	43.3%
2021 FS	SEA	MLB	30	2	2	0	57	0	50	47	7	3.2	8.8	48	46.8%	.292	1.31	4.14	96	0.2	94.7	37.9%	25.5%	43.9%
2021 DC	SEA	MLB	30	2	2	0	58	0	61	57	8	3.2	8.8	59	46.8%	.292	1.31	4.14	96	0.5	94.7	37.9%	25.5%	43.9%

Comparables: Chris Stratton, Matt Albers, Ryan Weber

Look at those numbers above, and consider that Sadler beat his 99th-percentile PECOTA projections from last year to reach them. He did it with the same stock-standard hint-of-salt 3.5-pitch mix he's always had, except leaning more heavily on his best pitch, the curve (37 percent usage) and throwing it just all over the place. Hitters couldn't restrain themselves, leading to a career-high whiff rate. Could it happen again? Sure, but if it does, at some point he's going to graduate to a leverage index above "facing Casey Sadler in the fourth inning of a game" and he may need another trick.

Justus Sheffield LHP   Born: 05/13/96   Age: 25   Bats: L   Throws: L   Height: 5'10"   Weight: 195   Origin: Round 1, 2014 Draft (#31 overall)

YEAR	TEAM	LVL	AGE	W	L	SV	G	GS	IP	H	HR	BB/9	K/9	K	GB%	BABIP	WHIP	ERA	DRA-	WARP	MPH	FA%	Whiff%	CSP
2018	TRN	AA	22	1	2	0	5	5	28	16	1	4.5	12.5	39	40.7%	.259	1.07	2.25	73	0.6				
2018	SWB	AAA	22	6	4	0	20	15	88	66	3	3.7	8.6	84	45.9%	.264	1.16	2.56	83	1.4				
2018	NYY	MLB	22	0	0	0	3	0	2²	4	1	10.1	0.0	0	54.5%	.300	2.62	10.12	146	-0.1	95.7	54.4%	5.3%	39.4%
2019	ARK	AA	23	5	3	0	12	12	78	62	4	2.1	9.8	85	42.6%	.294	1.03	2.19	77	1.1				
2019	TAC	AAA	23	2	6	0	13	12	55	59	12	6.7	7.9	48	53.2%	.292	1.82	6.87	102	0.9				
2019	SEA	MLB	23	0	1	0	8	7	36	44	5	4.5	9.2	37	52.7%	.379	1.72	5.50	119	0.0	94.6	47.8%	30.1%	46.5%
2020	SEA	MLB	24	4	3	0	10	10	55¹	52	2	3.3	7.8	48	49.7%	.314	1.30	3.58	89	0.8	93.5	48.0%	19.8%	48.0%
2021 FS	SEA	MLB	25	9	9	0	26	26	150	146	21	4.2	8.5	142	47.9%	.298	1.44	4.65	104	0.7	93.9	48.0%	23.0%	47.4%
2021 DC	SEA	MLB	25	7	9	0	25	25	134	131	19	4.2	8.5	127	47.9%	.298	1.44	4.65	104	1.1	93.9	48.0%	23.0%	47.4%

Comparables: Yohander Méndez, Kohl Stewart, Sean Reid-Foley

Cursed with both the "twice-traded prospect" and "low spin rate" stigmas, Sheffield's largely disappointing 2019 knocked him off most prospect lists. He responded by knocking 25 percent off his walk rate, nearly that much off his DRA, and putting together a strong enough season to justify down-ballot Rookie of the Year votes. Another feather in the cap of a development system rapidly changing its industry-wide reputation, Sheffield used a varied pitch mix, a tough, biting slider, and hilariously low home run-rate to largely silence whispers that he was destined for the bullpen. While the atrophying of his once-elite stuff will most likely keep him from being anything more than a third or fourth starter in a playoff-caliber rotation, the concerns that Seattle was hilariously swindled in the James Paxton are largely allayed, at least for now.

Drew Steckenrider RHP   Born: 01/10/91   Age: 30   Bats: R   Throws: R   Height: 6'4"   Weight: 217   Origin: Round 8, 2012 Draft (#257 overall)

YEAR	TEAM	LVL	AGE	W	L	SV	G	GS	IP	H	HR	BB/9	K/9	K	GB%	BABIP	WHIP	ERA	DRA-	WARP	MPH	FA%	Whiff%	CSP
2018	MIA	MLB	27	4	4	5	71	0	64²	55	7	3.8	10.3	74	33.7%	.296	1.27	3.90	99	0.4	96.5	76.4%	25.3%	50.7%
2019	MIA	MLB	28	0	2	0	15	0	14¹	9	6	3.1	8.8	14	31.6%	.094	0.98	6.28	121	-0.1	96.2	62.0%	21.4%	48.7%
2021 FS	SEA	MLB	30	2	2	0	57	0	50	40	7	3.6	10.0	55	37.0%	.270	1.22	3.40	84	0.6	96.4	72.2%	24.1%	50.1%

Comparables: Dominic Leone, Shawn Armstrong, Hansel Robles

Just two years ago, Steckenrider looked like a dominant late-inning reliever, or perhaps even a future closer. He missed most of 2019 and all of 2020 with elbow problems, and was outrighted and declared free agency after the season.

Erik Swanson RHP   Born: 09/04/93   Age: 27   Bats: R   Throws: R   Height: 6'3"   Weight: 220   Origin: Round 8, 2014 Draft (#246 overall)

YEAR	TEAM	LVL	AGE	W	L	SV	G	GS	IP	H	HR	BB/9	K/9	K	GB%	BABIP	WHIP	ERA	DRA-	WARP	MPH	FA%	Whiff%	CSP
2018	SI	SS	24	0	0	0	2	2	6²	8	0	0.0	8.1	6	47.6%	.381	1.20	4.05	102	0.0				
2018	TRN	AA	24	5	0	0	8	7	42²	22	0	3.2	11.6	55	34.5%	.253	0.87	0.42	75	0.9				
2018	SWB	AAA	24	3	2	0	14	13	72¹	63	10	1.7	9.7	78	35.5%	.283	1.06	3.86	75	1.5				
2019	TAC	AAA	25	0	1	0	10	6	24¹	28	5	4.4	10.4	28	35.2%	.348	1.64	5.55	114	0.2				
2019	SEA	MLB	25	1	5	2	27	8	58	56	17	1.9	8.1	52	37.4%	.241	1.17	5.74	121	-0.2	94.9	67.9%	22.7%	49.1%
2020	SEA	MLB	26	0	2	0	9	0	7²	11	3	2.3	10.6	9	33.3%	.381	1.70	12.91	114	0.0	97.9	74.5%	29.6%	49.7%
2021 FS	SEA	MLB	27	1	1	0	57	0	50	47	9	2.7	8.8	48	36.0%	.280	1.25	4.24	99	0.1	95.5	69.1%	24.0%	49.2%
2021 DC	SEA	MLB	27	1	1	0	23	0	24	22	4	2.7	8.8	23	36.0%	.280	1.25	4.24	99	0.2	95.5	69.1%	24.0%	49.2%

Comparables: Erick Fedde, Michael Lorenzen, Drew Anderson

If ever, for some strange reason, you wanted to make a case against the value of velocity, just present Swanson's 2020 as Exhibit A. The big right-hander converted full-time to relief in the shortened-season and added nearly three miles per hour to his fastball in the process. Even with only a tiny increase in walk rate, the extra spice did almost nothing good, as his DRA soared from "very bad" to "Stop! He's already dead!" As always with relievers and their miniscule sample sizes, one year could simply be noise, and that goes double for any reliever in whatever the 2020 season was. Swanson's velocity *should* give him the ability to succeed in a major league bullpen, but first he's going to have to figure out how not only to get batter to chase, but also to get them to miss: Batters actually made contact nine percent more often on his pitches *outside* the zone than the ones *in* it.

Juan Then RHP   Born: 02/07/00   Age: 21   Bats: R   Throws: R   Height: 6'1"   Weight: 175   Origin: International Free Agent, 2016

YEAR	TEAM	LVL	AGE	W	L	SV	G	GS	IP	H	HR	BB/9	K/9	K	GB%	BABIP	WHIP	ERA	DRA-	WARP	MPH	FA%	Whiff%	CSP
2018	YAE	ROK	18	0	3	0	11	11	50	38	2	2.0	7.6	42	45.4%	.259	0.98	2.70	100	0.5				
2019	MAR	ROK	19	0	0	0	1	0	2	2	0	0.0	9.0	2	20.0%	.400	1.00	0.00	83	0.0				
2019	EVE	SS	19	0	3	0	7	6	30¹	24	1	2.7	9.5	32	34.6%	.299	1.09	3.56	65	0.7				
2019	WV	LO-A	19	1	2	0	3	3	16	7	1	2.2	7.9	14	29.3%	.150	0.69	2.25	59	0.4				
2021 FS	SEA	MLB	21	2	3	0	57	0	50	49	7	3.6	7.8	43	38.0%	.293	1.40	4.60	112	-0.2				

Comparables: Rony García, Luis Severino, Antonio Santos

One of the many members of the "Dipoto Takesy Backsies Program," Then was shipped off to New York, only to be re-acquired by Seattle. Unlike most of the players in this fraternity, the slightly-built right-hander may have been well worth the effort, or at least he just made good use of his time during the exchange program. Stll only 21, Then will look to push his power arsenal to the mid-minors in 2021. Should he build off the success he showed in 2019, his place in Seattle's Top 10 prospects list (no small feat these days) will be secure.

Will Vest RHP Born: 06/06/95   Age: 26   Bats: R   Throws: R   Height: 6'0"   Weight: 180   Origin: Round 12, 2017 Draft (#365 overall)

YEAR	TEAM	LVL	AGE	W	L	SV	G	GS	IP	H	HR	BB/9	K/9	K	GB%	BABIP	WHIP	ERA	DRA-	WARP	MPH	FA%	Whiff%	CSP
2018	WM	LO-A	23	3	4	5	20	0	35^1	43	0	3.1	11.2	44	53.9%	.422	1.56	4.84	72	0.6				
2018	LAK	HI-A	23	1	0	0	10	0	13^1	16	1	1.4	8.1	12	53.3%	.349	1.35	6.08	94	0.1				
2019	LAK	HI-A	24	1	1	3	14	0	21^1	9	1	3.0	12.7	30	46.3%	.205	0.75	0.84	56	0.5				
2019	ERI	AA	24	2	4	4	20	0	27	31	4	3.0	8.3	25	43.4%	.342	1.48	5.33	121	-0.4				
2019	TOL	AAA	24	0	0	1	3	0	6^2	9	1	2.7	4.0	3	63.6%	.381	1.65	2.70	155	-0.1				
2021 FS	SEA	MLB	26	1	2	0	57	0	50	47	7	4.0	8.4	46	43.7%	.284	1.39	4.64	110	-0.2				
2021 DC	SEA	MLB	26	1	2	0	40	0	43	40	6	4.0	8.4	40	43.7%	.284	1.39	4.64	110	0.0				

Comparables: Steve Hathaway, Tyler Rogers, Chad Girodo

Vest (who does not go by William but will be treated as such by this comment for the pure sake of pun avoidance) allegedly built up his fastball velocity in 2020 to form a combination with an already-decent breaking ball, providing the upside of a seventh-inning guy. The problem with using a Rule 5 pick on a middle reliever is that one of their principle virtues is their fungibility; teams have to rotate fresh arms to Triple-A and back. Vest can probably justify his lack of flexibility, however, given the rest of the Mariners' bullpen.

TEXAS RANGERS

Essay by Bailey Freeman

Player comments by Mark Barry and BP staff

"Yeah, they did me dirty with the picture here."
Rangers slugger Joey Gallo is unhappy with his photos in *MLB The Show*, the popular baseball video game series. "Let's look at it again," he says to his live stream audience on Twitch. Gallo flips through flattering headshots and action variants of his teammates Mike Minor and Elvis Andrus. The selected images ooze competence and charisma. When Gallo finds himself in the game, competence turns to comedy. The first photo shows Gallo at the end of his swing, but his face tells a different story. With his head tilted towards the sky, eyes closed, and mouth agape, he appears to be belting a Mariah Carey high note. "Why in the hell did they think that THIS would be a good picture to put for me?" The second photo, a close-up, shows the slugger staring down the camera with a deranged expression. The face of the franchise has become an embarrassing mugshot.

The video clip of Gallo's flabbergasted reaction has been viewed 138,000 times. The act of live streaming a video game to viewers may seem foreign to some, but in the weeks after spring training was shut down, it became a form of fan outreach. Representatives from all 30 teams flocked to the live streaming platform Twitch.TV and put together the *MLB The Show* Players League, a tournament in which ballplayers faced off against each other as their digital counterparts. Some of baseball's brightest stars, like Fernando Tatís Jr. and Juan Soto, were participants. The competition drummed up plenty of goodwill for Gallo, who led Texas to the playoffs with a 23-6 record. Sadly, the Rangers' success on PlayStation did not translate to real life.

In many ways, Gallo's experience with *The Show* mirrored the feelings of many Rangers fans in 2020. Their new stadium sat empty, and the promise of a franchise to supply a team worthy of its energy fell through. But it's not uncommon for either video games or baseball teams to fail to deliver the experience described on the back of the box.

⚾ ⚾ ⚾

It's a little jarring to revisit the early concept art detailing Globe Life Field, the theoretical new home of the Rangers. The sun bleached pastels of 2019 feel downright Rockwellian a year later, and the concourses and pavilions are teeming

TEXAS RANGERS PROSPECTUS
2020 W-L: 22-38, 5TH IN AL WEST

Pythag	.350	30th	dWin%	.304	30th
RS/G	3.73	29th	B-Age	27.9	3rd
RA/G	5.20	26th	P-Age	29.3	20th
DRC+	83	30th	FIP	4.92	22nd
DRA-	111	25th	DER	.708	6th
Payroll	$65M	12th	M$/MW	$11.8M	30th

407'
372'   374'
329'   326'

- Opened 2020
- Retractable roof
- Synthetic surface
- Fence profile: 8'

Three-Year Park Factors

Runs	Runs/RH	Runs/LH	HR/RH	HR/LH
109	108	111	103	106

Top Hitter WARP	0.8 Joey Gallo
Top Pitcher WARP	1.2 Lance Lynn
Top Prospect	Leody Taveras

Payroll History (in millions)

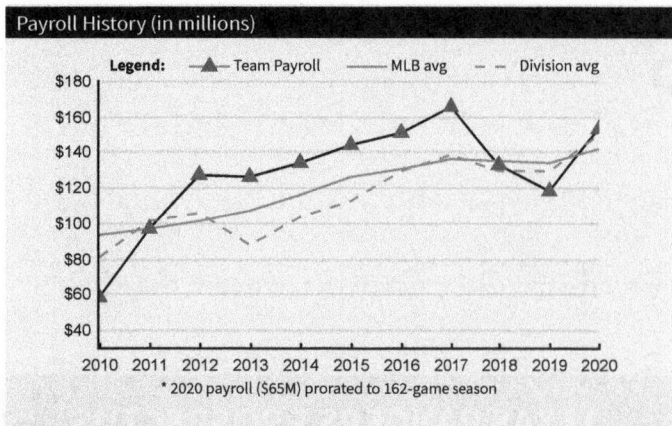

Legend: ▲ Team Payroll — MLB avg - - Division avg

* 2020 payroll ($65M) prorated to 162-game season

Future Commitments (in millions)

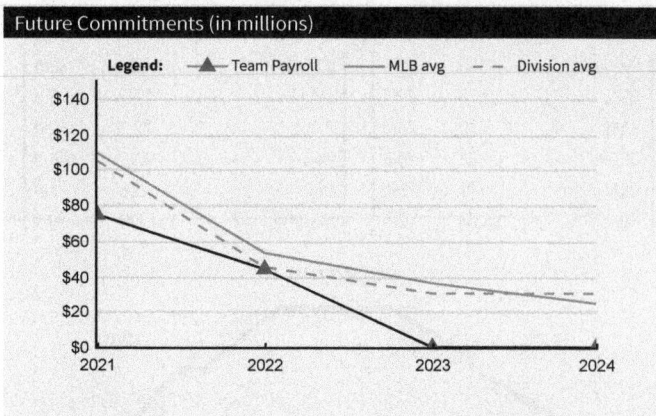

Legend: ▲ Team Payroll — MLB avg - - Division avg

Farm System Ranking

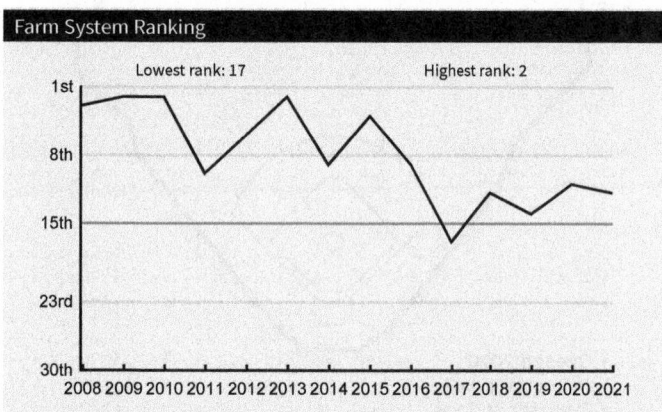

Lowest rank: 17   Highest rank: 2

Personnel

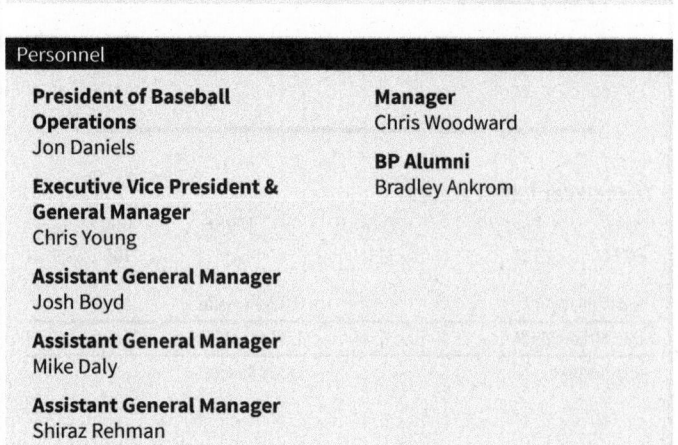

President of Baseball Operations
Jon Daniels

Executive Vice President & General Manager
Chris Young

Assistant General Manager
Josh Boyd

Assistant General Manager
Mike Daly

Assistant General Manager
Shiraz Rehman

Manager
Chris Woodward

BP Alumni
Bradley Ankrom

with (photoshopped) life, crowds and activities. It's designed to look like an open-air playground, a permanent summer day; it's also designed to deserve the millions in public money devoted to the city's third stadium in half a century.

The new ballpark lacks the grandeur of its neighbor, AT&T Stadium, home of the Dallas Cowboys. AT&T, better known colloquially as "Jerry World" after Cowboys owner Jerry Jones, is the stadium equivalent of a gaudy McMansion. And if Jerry World is a mansion, the newly constructed Globe Life Field is the metal shed in the backyard. It's a *very* nice shed, but it's still a shed. When construction was complete, fans found it to be quite understated compared to the initial renderings. One common complaint was that the stadium's interior was dimmer and gloomier than expected. The effect was in part due to a foreign concept, and one that necessitated the building altogether: a retractable metal roof, a belated solution to the common 100-plus degree three-plus hour games of August.

When Globe Life Park was approved in 2016, the Rangers had tremendous aspirations, envisioning themselves as a franchise immune to the ebbs and flows of competitive cycles. The team was en route to its fifth playoff appearance in seven tries, and 90-win seasons were becoming an expectation. Meanwhile, the farm system looked strong, in part because the team relied more on international signings than draft choices. Joey Gallo, Nomar Mazara, Dillon Tate and Lewis Brinson led a prospect class ready to reinforce the existing nucleus of Elvis Andrus, Rougned Odor, and the healthy-any-day-now former number-one prospect Jurickson Profar. They headlined a generation that was expected to continue the Rangers' winning ways, effortlessly replacing the production of players like Adrián Beltré, Josh Hamilton and Ian Kinsler.

That second prospect wave never materialized. Brinson was traded to Milwaukee before his big-league debut, while Profar and Mazara were eventually shipped off after failing to reach stardom. Gallo remains with the Rangers, where a .253/.389/.598 slash line in his injury-shortened 2019 campaign made him into a dark horse MVP candidate. In 2020, Gallo's DRC+ fell from 128 to 84, as his exit velocity dipped and his line drives started hanging in the air. Leody Taveras, the last surviving member of that 2016 class, finally made his debut (at the age of 21) and hit like a 21-year-old. The offense-oriented prospects the team acquired in trade, Nick Solak and Willie Calhoun, failed to provide any offense. Ronald Guzmán was the lone regular to post a league-average OPS, and then only barely; he subsequently lost his job when the team acquired Nate Lowe in the offseason. Only a final-series sweep prevented them from earning next year's first-overall draft pick.

While the prospects haven't panned out as expected, they've also struggled to attract big name free agents. As the opening of the new ballpark grew closer, Texas kept tabs on the likes of Bryce Harper, Manny Machado and Gerrit Cole, but wasn't hyper-competitive for their services. The Rangers front office came closest to making a splash signing with

Anthony Rendon, a Texas native. A free agent's market is typically dictated by how many years teams are willing to offer. The Los Angeles Angels offered Rendon a fully guaranteed seven-year deal worth $245 million. The Rangers' offer? Six years plus an option. In a moment of candor, Rangers GM Jon Daniels simply stated "I'm not going to sugar coat it: It sucks," in response to barely missing out on Rendon.

The long-tenured Daniels has now been promoted to Director of Baseball Operations, with former pitcher Chris Young taking over as the club's general manager. The task ahead of them is a difficult one: How to market a team without a star, or a core. Daniels has made some shrewd mid-level signings, perhaps none better than Lance Lynn for three years and $30 million, but despite the brand new $1.2 billion stadium and the fifth-largest media market in the country, austerity has defined the Rangers' approach to free agency and player salaries. The organization can split the cost of a new ballpark with Arlington's taxpayers, but the cost of an elite third baseman like Rendon falls squarely on the shoulders of ownership.

The 2020 season was an unmitigated disaster on the field, but it also may have been a blessing for the franchise, a jolt heavy enough to dislodge the team from its doldrums. Daniels and Young appear to have finally committed to a full rebuild. The team held on to Lynn at last year's deadline, but with a year remaining on his contract, the Rangers sent him to the White Sox for a promising arm in Dane Dunning. Andrus, whose bat and glove have both slipped, was formally demoted, and Gold Glover Isiah Kiner-Falefa has been anointed the team's starting shortstop.

From here the marketing gets easier; after all, major-league teams have been selling the hard rebuild as a philosophy for a decade now. It starts with the kids. Even if the future isn't ready in 2021, a future is ready: Sam Huff, Sherten Apostel and Anderson Tejeda all made the jump from High-A to the majors last year; along with the post-hype prospects of 2020, they'll combine to form one of the youngest offenses in the league. The kids won't have to play well, at least not all the time; they just have to play, and

do something amazing once in a while to stitch into the television commercials. On the off days, there's always an opportunity to hint at the exit velocity of Bayron Lora or hype up top prospect Josh Jung. It's easy to sell the future, especially when everyone would like to forget the present.

It may not even be all false advertising. Taveras could lock down center field, making adjustments in his second tour of the majors. Solak could finally be the man to displace Odor as Kiner-Falefa did to Andrus. Free agent leftovers Kyle Gibson and Jordan Lyles could provide the team value by pitching well enough to pitch elsewhere, and Kolby Allard and Kyle Cody could continue making progress. It's probably a pipe dream, but people like pipe dreams. The Rangers are the concept art of baseball teams.

Reclaiming their new ballpark in front of their home fans will be a welcome start. Globe Life Field was the reluctant star of the 2020 postseason, as the home of the Rangers became the guest house of the World Series champion Dodgers. It's telling that the current Globe Life Field home run leader isn't a Texas Ranger, but rather Corey Seager. The Dodgers didn't just make themselves at home. They kept their boots on and tracked mud all over the carpets. Texas fans were left to squint at the blue jerseys on their televisions and imagine what it would be like for their own players to make those home run-saving grabs.

⚾　　⚾　　⚾

A few days after his viral outburst, Joey Gallo logs into *MLB The Show* on his PlayStation. Per his request, the game's developers have updated his in-game photos. He now appears as a competent athlete capable of striking fear in his opponents. Optimistic Rangers fans will wait for their beloved franchise to receive its own patch, so that they can be portrayed in a more flattering light in the years to come. The pessimists will note that they've been making these games since Ian Kinsler was a rookie, and they never quite get out all the bugs. ▪

—Bailey Freeman is the creator of the Youtube channel Foolish Baseball.

HITTERS

Maximo Acosta SS Born: 10/29/02 Age: 18 Bats: R Throws: R Height: 6'1" Weight: 170 Origin: International Free Agent, 2019

Among the many reasons to be bummed out by the cancellation of minor-league baseball for 2020 is the lost development time for promising players. Acosta was set for his first year stateside after signing the second-largest bonus the Rangers shelled out during the 2019 J2 period, his $1.65 million trailing only Bayron Lora among the international free agent class. Heading into this season, it was arguably Acosta who had more buzz, blending a decent conceptualization of the zone with power and speed, and drawing early Gleyber Torres comps. There's definitely a nonzero chance that, had he played in 2020, we'd be talking about Acosta as one of the "Next Dudes", rapidly progressing through organizational levels and soaring up prospect lists alike. Acosta will enter 2021 at a different point in his career than previously projected, but the raw talent the Rangers saw is still there.

Luisangel Acuna SS Born: 03/12/02 Age: 19 Bats: R Throws: R Height: 5'10" Weight: 155 Origin: International Free Agent, 2018

YEAR	TEAM	LVL	AGE	PA	R	2B	3B	HR	RBI	BB	K	SB	CS	Whiff%	AVG/OBP/SLG	DRC+	BABIP	BRR	FRAA	WARP
2019	DSL RGR1	ROK	17	240	61	11	3	2	29	34	26	17	6		.342/.438/.455		.381			
2021											No projection									

Throughout history, brothers have cut their individual paths to fame in the same field: John Wilkes and Edwin Booth, Richard and David Attenborough, Noah and Liam Gallagher. It's not exactly commonplace, but also not exceedingly rare, although the quality of the combinations do vary greatly. Baseball provides its fair share of familial duos running the gamut of effectiveness and acclaim. At one, more evenly successful end, you have Sandy and Roberto Alomar, or the more modern Corey and Kyle Seager. But for every evenly matched set, there's also a Cal and Billy Ripken or Jose and Ozzie Canseco-type mismatch of production. When the Rangers signed Acuna out of Venezuela in July 2018 for a little over $400,000 (more than quadrupling the bonus of his brother, Ronald Jr., from 2014), they added a new sibling rivalry to the ranks. Only time will tell whether the Acuñas will be the Uptons or Giambis, but if Luisangel's hot start, including a near-.900 OPS as a 17-year-old in the Dominican Summer League, is any indication, the Acuñas could be a balanced familial force the likes of which baseball hasn't yet seen.

Elvis Andrus SS   Born: 08/26/88   Age: 32   Bats: R   Throws: R   Height: 6'0"   Weight: 210   Origin: International Free Agent, 2005

YEAR	TEAM	LVL	AGE	PA	R	2B	3B	HR	RBI	BB	K	SB	CS	Whiff%	AVG/OBP/SLG	DRC+	BABIP	BRR	FRAA	WARP
2018	TEX	MLB	29	428	53	20	3	6	33	28	66	5	3	20.3%	.256/.308/.367	90	.292	0.5	SS(97): -6.4	0.8
2019	TEX	MLB	30	648	81	27	4	12	72	34	96	31	8	19.5%	.275/.313/.393	88	.305	2.0	SS(146): 1.0	2.4
2020	TEX	MLB	32	111	11	5	0	3	7	8	15	3	1	19.5%	.194/.252/.330	86	.200	-0.1	SS(29): -0.2	0.1
2021 FS	TEX	MLB	32	600	63	27	2	12	61	41	98	19	6	19.6%	.248/.305/.378	88	.282	1.9	SS 3	1.6
2021 DC	TEX	MLB	32	462	48	21	2	9	47	31	75	14	5	19.6%	.248/.305/.378	88	.282	1.4	SS 3	1.2

Comparables: Jason Bartlett, Tom Foley, Kurt Stillwell

If you google Andrus, the People Also Ask section provides "What happened to Elvis Andrus?" as the number one response. It's a fair question. Were they querying the fate of a late-career power surge that helped him maintain his grip on shortstop, despite eroding efensive skills? Perhaps the question was referring to the balky back that kept Andrus sidelined for most of the season. Or maybe it was an attempt to find another clip of dugout shenanigans featuring former teammate Adrian Beltre. There was a time when a Texas youth movement centered on him, but now he's the aging veteran with two years and $28.5 million unpaid, and a team at least that many years away from contention. Manager Chris Woodward already assigned the starting shortstop job to Isiah Kiner-Falefa, signaling the end of an era in which Andrus has served as a fixture for the last dozen Opening Days. Maybe a more appropriate question is, "What happened to the last 12 years?"

Sherten Apostel 3B   Born: 03/11/99   Age: 22   Bats: R   Throws: R   Height: 6'4"   Weight: 235   Origin: International Free Agent, 2018

YEAR	TEAM	LVL	AGE	PA	R	2B	3B	HR	RBI	BB	K	SB	CS	Whiff%	AVG/OBP/SLG	DRC+	BABIP	BRR	FRAA	WARP
2018	BRS	ROK	19	175	28	7	0	7	26	32	42	3	1		.259/.406/.460	157	.319	-0.9	3B(35): 3.6	1.2
2018	SPO	SS	19	49	7	1	0	1	10	9	8	0	1		.351/.469/.459	201	.400	0.0	3B(8): -0.6	0.4
2019	HIC	LO-A	20	319	38	13	1	15	43	28	71	2	1		.258/.332/.470	119	.290	-3.0	3B(70): 1.6, 1B(12): 0.0	1.4
2019	DE	HI-A	20	159	18	5	1	4	16	23	49	0	0		.237/.352/.378	116	.341	1.6	3B(41): 1.4	1.1
2020	TEX	MLB	21	21	1	1	0	0	0	1	9	0	0	50.0%	.100/.143/.150	63	.182	-0.1	1B(5): 0.3, 3B(2): -0.2	-0.1
2021 FS	TEX	MLB	22	600	60	24	2	16	61	55	222	2	1	50.0%	.209/.287/.358	77	.318	-0.2	1B 0, 3B 2	-0.4
2021 DC	TEX	MLB	22	198	19	8	0	5	20	18	73	0	0	50.0%	.209/.287/.358	77	.318	-0.1	1B 0, 3B 1	-0.2

Comparables: Josh Bell, Will Middlebrooks, Jeimer Candelario

While call-up stories aren't one-size-fits-all, they typically sound something like this: Prospect gets call, prospect calls loved ones, prospect meets team in appointed location, prospect prepares with team before his debut. Easy, right? Thanks to 2020, Apostel's call up was a bit different. After a typical practice day at the team's alternate site, the 21-year-old went home, made some lunch, and scrolled through Netflix before finally drifting off for a nap. He awoke to the buzzing of his phone and several missed calls from the Rangers' director of minor league operations, whereupon Apostel learned he needed to be at the stadium, ready to play, in 20 minutes for the second half of a doubleheader. Despite hitting every red light on the way, Apostel debuted at the hot corner, making his first appearance as a big leaguer after not spending any time at a level more advanced than High-A. He even got a hit in the seventh inning. It's probably unlikely that Apostel will start the 2021 season in Arlington, but his patient approach at the dish combined with some budding pop should put him in position to be a fixture for the Rangers at third base in the not-too-distant future, depending on traffic.

Willie Calhoun LF   Born: 11/04/94   Age: 26   Bats: L   Throws: R   Height: 5'8"   Weight: 200   Origin: Round 4, 2015 Draft (#132 overall)

YEAR	TEAM	LVL	AGE	PA	R	2B	3B	HR	RBI	BB	K	SB	CS	Whiff%	AVG/OBP/SLG	DRC+	BABIP	BRR	FRAA	WARP
2018	RR	AAA	23	469	66	32	0	9	47	32	47	4	0		.295/.352/.432	119	.315	-3.2	LF(91): -11.9	0.0
2018	TEX	MLB	23	108	8	5	0	2	11	6	24	0	0	20.5%	.222/.269/.333	86	.267	-0.7	LF(27): -2.8	-0.3
2019	NAS	AAA	24	172	23	8	0	8	28	32	24	1	1		.297/.433/.529	141	.311	-0.8	LF(33): -6.5, 2B(3): 0.2	0.6
2019	TEX	MLB	24	337	51	14	1	21	48	23	53	0	0	15.9%	.269/.323/.524	118	.262	1.1	LF(71): -7.1	1.1
2020	TEX	MLB	26	108	3	2	1	1	13	5	17	0	0	14.7%	.190/.231/.260	76	.214	-1.2	LF(8): -0.0	-0.2
2021 FS	TEX	MLB	26	600	70	27	2	22	74	45	108	0	0	15.9%	.248/.311/.429	100	.272	-0.1	LF -3, 2B 0	1.4
2021 DC	TEX	MLB	26	561	65	25	2	21	70	42	101	0	0	15.9%	.248/.311/.429	100	.272	-0.1	LF -3	0.9

Comparables: Ozzie Timmons, Kevin Mitchell, Kevin Mench

When thinking about Calhoun's early big-league career, the word snakebit jumps out. How else to describe a year's worth of plate appearances, spread over four years of tumult? In the words of the Rolling Stones (and lots of car commercials), you can't always get what you want. After a first couple of seasons filled with more starts and stops than a traffic jam on I-20, it looked like Calhoun finally locked down an everyday role, breaking through with a 2019 campaign where he launched 14 dingers in his last 52 games. That all came to a screeching halt with an errant 95-mph fastball to the jaw from Julio Urías in spring training. While the fractured jaw was obviously bad, the psychological impact remained long after the bones had knitted. Calhoun himself admitted to skittishness when facing left-handed pitching. The Rangers brought him along slowly against lefties, and after that kind of trauma, it might take awhile for Calhoun to regain his comfort. It's another speed bump in his ascension, but let's hope time is on his side.

Shin-Soo Choo LF Born: 07/13/82 Age: 38 Bats: L Throws: L Height: 5'11" Weight: 205 Origin: International Free Agent, 2000

YEAR	TEAM	LVL	AGE	PA	R	2B	3B	HR	RBI	BB	K	SB	CS	Whiff%	AVG/OBP/SLG	DRC+	BABIP	BRR	FRAA	WARP
2018	TEX	MLB	35	665	83	30	1	21	62	92	156	6	1	26.9%	.264/.377/.434	116	.330	-0.9	RF(34): -2.0, LF(26): -0.6	2.2
2019	TEX	MLB	36	660	93	31	2	24	61	78	165	15	1	29.3%	.265/.371/.455	112	.333	-0.2	RF(42): -4.1, LF(40): -0.4	2.0
2020	TEX	MLB	38	127	13	3	0	5	15	13	33	6	2	32.9%	.236/.323/.400	89	.284	0.8	LF(16): 1.1, RF(3): 0.7	0.2
2021 FS	TEX	MLB	38	600	78	23	1	18	55	69	166	9	2	29.2%	.243/.348/.401	109	.323	1.3	RF -7, LF 0	1.6

Comparables: Jeromy Burnitz, Jayson Werth, Matt Stairs

When the Rangers dished out $130 million to Choo seven years ago, they probably envisioned something different than what they received. They likely pictured elite plate discipline, with a rare combination of power and speed, not to mention a cannon arm from right field, all of which he delievered, at least in spurts. Injuries slowed Choo down on the bases, but he still worked a bunch of walks, and was even named an All-Star for the first time in 2018, in his age-35 season. It's possible to frame his tenure in Texas as a disappointment, but doing so would severely diminish the rest of what Choo brings to the table. There are plenty of guys within the Rangers organization that look up to Choo. Realizing he was losing a step, and that Leody Taveras was the lead-off hitter of the future, Choo volunteered to slide down the order and provide mentorship to the rookie. When a global pandemic rocked baseball (and pretty much everything else), Choo gave $1,000 to each of the organization's 190 minor leaguers struggling to make ends meet. The Rangers' nominee for the 2020 Roberto Clemente Award, Choo has meant a lot to the team in more than just on-field contribution. He wraps up that mega deal as South Korea's all-time leader in MLB homers, his 218 home runs more than the field combined. With questions swirling about Choo's next step, it's important to consider the totality of his contributions, and to celebrate a career spent serving the game.

David Dahl LF Born: 04/01/94 Age: 27 Bats: L Throws: R Height: 6'2" Weight: 197 Origin: Round 1, 2012 Draft (#10 overall)

YEAR	TEAM	LVL	AGE	PA	R	2B	3B	HR	RBI	BB	K	SB	CS	Whiff%	AVG/OBP/SLG	DRC+	BABIP	BRR	FRAA	WARP
2018	ABQ	AAA	24	78	7	7	0	2	9	1	19	1	0		.286/.295/.455	85	.357	-0.6	CF(6): 0.4, RF(6): 0.2, LF(5): 1.7	0.1
2018	COL	MLB	24	271	31	11	3	16	48	19	68	5	3	30.5%	.273/.325/.534	112	.311	-1.3	LF(34): 2.9, RF(30): -1.4, CF(8): -0.4	1.1
2019	COL	MLB	25	413	67	28	5	15	61	28	110	4	4	30.8%	.302/.353/.524	103	.386	2.1	CF(40): 1.3, LF(39): 0.2, RF(24): -4.7	1.3
2020	COL	MLB	26	99	9	2	2	0	9	4	28	1	0	31.2%	.183/.222/.247	67	.258	0.7	CF(17): 0.5, LF(4): -0.7, RF(2): 0.1	-0.2
2021 FS	TEX	MLB	27	600	67	24	5	19	64	35	170	8	3	30.8%	.241/.290/.409	86	.312	4.3	LF 6, CF 0	1.5
2021 DC	TEX	MLB	27	462	51	18	4	14	49	27	131	6	2	30.8%	.241/.290/.409	86	.312	3.3	LF 4, CF 0	1.2

Comparables: Al Martin, Trey Mancini, Corey Dickerson

This is the first time a Dahl followed up a breakthrough performance with such a disappointment since *Charlie and the Great Glass Elevator*. Soreness wiped out all instances of his power, and his 2020 ranks among the most deficient seasons in Rockies history. (By OPS, minimum 50 PAs, it was sixth-worst). Despite that, it was a minor surprise that the Rockies non-tendered him; the Rangers quickly snatched him up hoping for a rebound. The more you ascribe the slump to the bad back, and the more likely you are to think back injuries go away, the more hopeful you become that he'll be way more effective than the other Dahl's third installment, *Charlie and the White House*, which was abandoned after one chapter.

Derek Dietrich 2B Born: 07/18/89 Age: 31 Bats: L Throws: R Height: 6'2" Weight: 205 Origin: Round 2, 2010 Draft (#79 overall)

YEAR	TEAM	LVL	AGE	PA	R	2B	3B	HR	RBI	BB	K	SB	CS	Whiff%	AVG/OBP/SLG	DRC+	BABIP	BRR	FRAA	WARP
2018	MIA	MLB	28	551	72	26	2	16	45	29	140	2	0	25.5%	.265/.330/.421	100	.336	1.7	LF(97): -8.4, 1B(33): -1.9, 2B(4): -0.1	0.4
2019	CIN	MLB	29	306	41	8	2	19	43	28	74	1	1	30.8%	.187/.328/.462	112	.176	1.5	2B(58): -3.1, 1B(21): -0.7, 1B(16): -1.1	1.1
2020	TEX	MLB	31	75	9	1	0	5	8	9	21	1	1	33.1%	.197/.347/.459	99	.200	-0.1	1B(6): -0.5, 2B(3): -0.5, 3B(3): 0.1	0.0
2021 FS	TEX	MLB	31	600	74	22	3	26	78	48	160	2	0	29.0%	.245/.351/.454	122	.304	1.5	3B -4, LF -4	2.4

Comparables: Kelly Johnson, Rickie Weeks Jr., Junior Spivey

Dietrich looks like a man who practices transcendental meditation in an igloo formed out of old Axe Spray cans. He's also the model of a modern pinch hitter, and the antonym of the Dave Hansens and Lenny Harrises of yesteryear. It seems strange to think, but he could hang around for years doing this; few can make their inconsistency so consistently productive.

Justin Foscue 2B Born: 03/02/99 Age: 22 Bats: R Throws: R Height: 6'0" Weight: 203 Origin: Round 1, 2020 Draft (#14 overall)

It was a bit of a surprise when the Rangers nabbed Justin Foscue out of Mississippi State with the 14th pick in the 2020 MLB Draft, but the infielder offers a fairly high floor at the plate, blending a solid hit tool with above-average plate discipline. The Rangers have made it clear that longtime second baseman Rougned Odor won't stand as an obstacle, so Foscue is slated to man the keystone for now, with third base also a possibility. His big-league upside will depend on how much the power he demonstrated in college will translate.

Joey Gallo CF Born: 11/19/93 Age: 27 Bats: L Throws: R Height: 6'5" Weight: 250 Origin: Round 1, 2012 Draft (#39 overall)

YEAR	TEAM	LVL	AGE	PA	R	2B	3B	HR	RBI	BB	K	SB	CS	Whiff%	AVG/OBP/SLG	DRC+	BABIP	BRR	FRAA	WARP
2018	TEX	MLB	24	577	82	24	1	40	92	74	207	3	4	40.9%	.206/.312/.498	115	.249	1.9	LF(85): -6.3, 1B(35): 3.1, RF(16): 3.4	2.7
2019	TEX	MLB	25	297	54	15	1	22	49	52	114	4	2	41.4%	.253/.389/.598	128	.368	1.7	CF(38): 0.8, LF(34): 4.1	2.6
2020	TEX	MLB	27	226	23	8	0	10	26	29	79	2	0	37.5%	.181/.301/.378	84	.240	1.6	RF(53): 5.3, CF(1): -0.0	0.8
2021 FS	TEX	MLB	27	600	78	24	2	33	85	86	229	5	2	39.8%	.206/.328/.460	112	.290	0.3	RF 3, 1B 0	2.6
2021 DC	TEX	MLB	27	561	73	22	2	31	80	80	214	5	2	39.8%	.206/.328/.460	112	.290	0.3	RF 2	2.5

Comparables: Adam Dunn, Kyle Schwarber, Rob Deer

Can you name the dude with 80 power,
Hits 'em a hundred miles an hour
Joey Gallo! Joey Gallo! (whip crack)

Well, he swings real hard, puts the hammer down
He's the only true outcome endorsed by a clown
Joey Gallo! Joey Gallo!

[ANNOUNCER VOICE] Globe Life Field has ruled it unsafe to sit in the bleachers during Joey Gallo BP.

Cannon for an arm and a stealthy quick stride,
Patrols the outfield with a long-legged glide.
Joey Gallo! Joey Gallo! (Yah!)
Oblique, hamate, wrist—he gets injured each year,
It's the only thing stopping a successful career.
He's Joey Gallo, woah! Joey Gallo!

Ronald Guzmán 1B Born: 10/20/94 Age: 26 Bats: L Throws: L Height: 6'5" Weight: 235 Origin: International Free Agent, 2011

YEAR	TEAM	LVL	AGE	PA	R	2B	3B	HR	RBI	BB	K	SB	CS	Whiff%	AVG/OBP/SLG	DRC+	BABIP	BRR	FRAA	WARP
2018	TEX	MLB	23	428	46	18	2	16	58	33	121	1	0	30.0%	.235/.306/.416	91	.299	1.9	1B(117): 1.9	0.6
2019	NAS	AAA	24	135	22	8	0	5	16	17	31	0	0		.308/.400/.504	113	.383	-1.3	1B(23): 0.5	0.3
2019	TEX	MLB	24	295	34	20	0	10	36	32	87	1	2	33.0%	.219/.308/.414	85	.282	-2.5	1B(81): 6.2	0.3
2020	TEX	MLB	26	86	10	1	1	4	9	7	24	1	0	31.6%	.244/.314/.436	89	.300	0.0	1B(24): 2.0	0.2
2021 FS	TEX	MLB	26	600	65	24	2	21	72	50	171	1	0	31.7%	.235/.307/.411	94	.302	0.8	1B 4	0.9
2021 DC	TEX	MLB	26	231	25	9	1	8	28	19	65	0	0	31.7%	.235/.307/.411	94	.302	0.3	1B 1	0.4

Comparables: Derrek Lee, Bob Chance, Ron Jackson

It's awfully tough to be a 1B-only prospect, especially when you're a 1B-only prospect who doesn't hit for a lot of power. There was a time when Guzman was considered an interesting, if not exciting, prospect, as he doubled his way up the ladder. Upon being thrust into big-league action, Guzman didn't hit much, but he did flash the leather, wowing with uncanny stretches at the cold corner. The novelty and newness was exciting. Fast forward to 2020 and the offense remains as middling as ever and the defense is slipping, calling into question Guzman's usefulness. In fact, perhaps the most intriguing part of Guzman's early career has been his allegiance to animal welfare, with him adopting a condor, his nickname-sake, and naming the bird "Guzzy". While The Condor adopting a condor is a heartwarming story, Guzman will have to soar at the plate in the very near future if he doesn't want to meet the same fate as his feathery friend, flirting with the endangered species list.

★ ★ ★ *2021 Top 101 Prospect* **#98** ★ ★ ★

Sam Huff C Born: 01/14/98 Age: 23 Bats: R Throws: R Height: 6'5" Weight: 240 Origin: Round 7, 2016 Draft (#219 overall)

YEAR	TEAM	LVL	AGE	PA	R	2B	3B	HR	RBI	BB	K	SB	CS	Whiff%	AVG/OBP/SLG	DRC+	BABIP	BRR	FRAA	WARP
2018	HIC	LO-A	20	448	53	22	3	18	55	23	140	9	1		.241/.292/.439	96	.317	-0.1	C(56): 1.9, 1B(11): -0.4	0.4
2019	HIC	LO-A	21	114	22	5	0	15	29	6	37	4	1		.333/.368/.796	216	.375	0.8	C(14): 0.9	1.8
2019	DE	HI-A	21	405	49	17	2	13	43	27	117	2	5		.262/.326/.425	110	.347	-2.7	C(51): 1.9, 1B(4): 0.1	1.5
2020	TEX	MLB	22	33	5	3	0	3	4	2	11	0	0	40.7%	.355/.394/.742	103	.471	-0.8	C(10): 0.1	0.0
2021 FS	TEX	MLB	23	600	60	25	2	20	67	39	228	3	1	40.7%	.217/.276/.383	78	.326	-0.5	C -3, 1B 0	0.2
2021 DC	TEX	MLB	23	231	23	9	0	7	25	15	87	1	0	40.7%	.217/.276/.383	78	.326	-0.2	C -2	0.1

Comparables: Jorge Alfaro, Eric Haase, Tommy Joseph

YEAR	TEAM	P. COUNT	FRM RUNS	BLK RUNS	THRW RUNS	TOT RUNS
2020	TEX	1459	-0.6	0.0	0.0	-0.6
2021	TEX	8418	-3.6	0.4	0.1	-3.1

In the history of Major League Baseball, just four catchers (Joe Mauer, Matt Wieters, Sandy Alomar, Jr., and Larry McLean) have eclipsed Huff's 6'4" frame. He also hits the ball in keeping with his stature: Had Huff qualified, only Fernando Tatis, Jr. would have posted a higher percentage of hard hit balls, which is decent company to keep. The 2020 success at the plate will likely regress some, as can be expected from a guy that jumped to the big leagues without experience above High-A. Still, three dingers in his first 10 games as a big leaguer is a decent start, and the bar on offense behind the plate is so low these days that, even with regression, Huff has the chance to be an excellent offensive catcher. How about the defense, you ask? Well, he's not a disaster or a liability, which isn't exactly a ringing endorsement, but it'll allow him to start most days of the week.

★ ★ ★ *2021 Top 101 Prospect* **#56** ★ ★ ★

Josh Jung 3B Born: 02/12/98 Age: 23 Bats: R Throws: R Height: 6'2" Weight: 215 Origin: Round 1, 2019 Draft (#8 overall)

YEAR	TEAM	LVL	AGE	PA	R	2B	3B	HR	RBI	BB	K	SB	CS	Whiff%	AVG/OBP/SLG	DRC+	BABIP	BRR	FRAA	WARP
2019	RAN	ROK	21	19	5	1	1	1	5	2	3	0	0		.588/.632/.941	227	.692	-0.2	3B(3): -0.7	0.2
2019	HIC	LO-A	21	179	18	13	0	1	23	16	29	4	1		.287/.363/.389	136	.341	0.6	3B(35): 2.5	1.5
2021 FS	TEX	MLB	23	600	55	27	2	9	54	36	157	3	1		.227/.281/.334	71	.300	0.5	3B 13	0.3
2021 DC	TEX	MLB	23	99	9	4	0	1	8	6	25	0	0		.227/.281/.334	71	.300	0.1	3B 2	0.1

Jung was born in San Antonio, TX, where he'd later go to high school. He went to Texas Tech for college, and was drafted in the first round by the Texas Rangers. As the great American poet, Tim Riggins, once said: "Texas, forever". Despite being a clear fish out of water in High-A Hickory (in North Carolina, can you *imagine*?), Jung still displayed his personal blend of high-contact offense with above-average defense. He should be more comfortable back in Texas at Double-A Frisco, where he's likely to start next season, and manager Chris Woodward has already hinted at the likelihood of Jung manning the hot corner in Arlington at some point during the 2021 campaign. His long-term power output will likely depend on whether some of his all-field approach turns into pull-side dingers, but there's definitely pop in Jung's bat, and there's plenty of time for him to figure out what kind of player he'll be. If everything's bigger in Texas, Jung's prospect hype train should shortly follow suit.

Isiah Kiner-Falefa 3B   Born: 03/23/95   Age: 26   Bats: R   Throws: R   Height: 5'11"   Weight: 190   Origin: Round 4, 2013 Draft (#130 overall)

YEAR	TEAM	LVL	AGE	PA	R	2B	3B	HR	RBI	BB	K	SB	CS	Whiff%	AVG/OBP/SLG	DRC+	BABIP	BRR	FRAA	WARP
2018	TEX	MLB	23	396	43	18	2	4	34	28	62	7	5	14.8%	.261/.325/.357	85	.306	-0.6	3B(46): 3.4, C(35): -10.1, 2B(20): -0.2	0.1
2019	FRI	AA	24	71	7	4	0	2	11	8	9	1	0		.283/.380/.450	152	.300	-0.1	C(9): -0.7, 3B(4): 1.5, SS(1): -0.1	0.7
2019	NAS	AAA	24	37	3	3	0	0	2	1	6	1	0		.147/.216/.235	33	.179	-0.7	SS(4): 0.2, C(2): 0.0	-0.2
2019	TEX	MLB	24	222	23	12	1	1	21	14	49	3	0	18.7%	.238/.299/.322	71	.307	1.8	C(38): -11.0, 3B(25): 1.7	-0.5
2020	TEX	MLB	25	228	28	4	3	3	10	14	32	8	5	15.8%	.280/.329/.370	82	.316	1.2	3B(46): -0.2, SS(15): 0.7	0.2
2021 FS	TEX	MLB	26	600	63	25	3	8	57	42	103	5	2	16.4%	.263/.328/.365	94	.312	1.0	3B 17, SS 0	3.1
2021 DC	TEX	MLB	26	561	59	24	2	7	53	39	96	5	2	16.4%	.263/.328/.365	94	.312	0.9	3B 16, SS 0	2.6

Comparables: Tim Hulett, Aaron Boone, Frank Kostro

The Rangers moved into a new stadium this year. The concept art was undoubtedly beautiful, but the finished product somewhat less so, unless you're hoping for a ballpark more reminiscent of a Home Depot. One Ranger that did enjoy his new digs, however, was Kiner-Falefa, who led the team in hitting at home, coming up just shy of .300 in 28 games. Over the last couple of seasons, the team tried to fit him into a jack-of-all-trades, master of none role, including a spell as the backup backstop. This year Kiner-Falefa shed the tools of ignorance, making appearances exclusively splitting time at third base and shortstop, showing good hands at both spots. The problem is that the offensive threshold at third is much higher than it is behind the dish, and Kiner-Falefa hits like a shortstop at best. Jon Daniels considered this, and made him their starting shortstop for 2021.

Bayron Lora RF   Born: 09/29/02   Age: 18   Bats: R   Throws: R   Height: 6'3"   Weight: 190   Origin: International Free Agent, 2019

You might not know a lot about Lora, the enormous teenager that signed for a cool $4 million in the 2019 J2 signing period, and that's okay. For serious baseball card collectors, though, Lora has been a hot name in 2020, with his Bowman Chrome autograph card fetching upwards of $4,000 at online retailers. Gone are the days of putting cards in your bicycle spokes, apparently. While that lofty price tag seems a little premature, Lora is an awfully exciting prospect, possessing light-tower power and displaying decent athleticism for his advanced size at a non-advanced age. You could say that card collectors are taking the same risk that the Rangers took—putting a down payment on a dude that has the ability to out-earn the initial investment.

Nate Lowe 1B   Born: 07/07/95   Age: 26   Bats: L   Throws: R   Height: 6'4"   Weight: 220   Origin: Round 13, 2016 Draft (#390 overall)

YEAR	TEAM	LVL	AGE	PA	R	2B	3B	HR	RBI	BB	K	SB	CS	Whiff%	AVG/OBP/SLG	DRC+	BABIP	BRR	FRAA	WARP
2018	CHA	HI-A	22	220	39	15	0	10	44	25	33	0	0		.356/.432/.588	207	.391	-2.4	1B(35): -2.9	1.7
2018	MTG	AA	22	225	36	11	0	13	42	35	30	1	1		.340/.444/.606	211	.349	1.9	1B(39): -0.4	2.7
2018	DUR	AAA	22	110	18	6	1	4	16	8	27	0	0		.260/.327/.460	116	.319	-1.2	1B(25): -0.1	0.0
2019	DUR	AAA	23	406	63	24	0	16	63	72	82	1	0		.289/.421/.508	142	.341	-0.6	1B(72): -1.0, 3B(5): 0.3	2.3
2019	TB	MLB	23	169	24	8	0	7	19	13	50	0	0	27.2%	.263/.325/.454	88	.340	1.0	1B(21): 0.1, 3B(4): -0.2	0.1
2020	TB	MLB	25	76	10	2	0	4	11	9	28	1	0	29.4%	.224/.316/.433	85	.314	-0.3	1B(15): -0.6, 3B(2): -0.1	-0.1
2021 FS	TEX	MLB	25	600	71	25	1	22	75	68	181	0	0	28.1%	.254/.345/.438	114	.344	-0.5	1B -1, 3B -1	1.7
2021 DC	TEX	MLB	25	396	47	16	1	15	50	45	119	0	0	28.1%	.254/.345/.438	114	.344	-0.3	1B -1, 3B 0	1.2

Comparables: Tony Clark, Brad Eldred, Carlos Delgado

The Rangers, who had been chasing Lowe for a while, caught him last winter as part of the winter's most boring six-player trade. He's been a slightly above-average hitter in 245 big-league plate appearances, but the Rays never seem compelled to give him an extended look. The rebuilding Rangers, on the other hand, have every reason to see if Lowe can walk-and-bop enough to serve as their first baseman of the present and the future.

Jeff Mathis C   Born: 03/31/83   Age: 38   Bats: R   Throws: R   Height: 6'0"   Weight: 205   Origin: Round 1, 2001 Draft (#33 overall)

YEAR	TEAM	LVL	AGE	PA	R	2B	3B	HR	RBI	BB	K	SB	CS	Whiff%	AVG/OBP/SLG	DRC+	BABIP	BRR	FRAA	WARP
2018	ARI	MLB	35	218	15	9	1	1	20	20	66	0	0	32.5%	.200/.272/.272	63	.292	-0.4	C(63): 18.5, 2B(1): -0.1, P(1): -0.0	2.0
2019	TEX	MLB	36	244	17	9	0	2	12	15	87	1	0	36.7%	.158/.209/.224	40	.243	0.7	C(86): -2.8, P(2): -0.0	-0.8
2020	TEX	MLB	37	68	6	1	1	3	9	5	24	1	0	36.6%	.161/.221/.355	71	.194	0.1	C(24): 0.4	0.0
2021 FS	TEX	MLB	38	600	51	22	1	11	48	40	212	2	0	35.6%	.185/.245/.293	46	.276	0.3	C 19, 2B 0	0.3

Comparables: Paul Bako, José Molina, Mike DiFelice

There are so few certainties in life. Death, sure. Taxes, almost definitely. Mathis behind the dish for a big-league club? Now we're talking. Much has been made of his bat, or lack thereof, over the years, and there's no sugar coating it. It's very, very bad, especially in a year when the pitchers aren't providing a floor. Having said that, it's pretty remarkable that a guy with a career .194 batting average has still been worth 9.0 WARP, and despite never being within 10 percentage points of a league average DRC+, has lasted 17 seasons at a

YEAR	TEAM	P. COUNT	FRM RUNS	BLK RUNS	THRW RUNS	TOT RUNS
2018	ARI	8692	11.8	2.3	0.0	14.1
2019	TEX	11131	-1.8	0.8	-1.0	-2.0
2020	TEX	3081	0.8	0.0	-0.1	0.7
2021	TEX	16650	11.3	2.3	0.7	14.3

position not necessarily known for durable superstars. It shouldn't surprise anyone that Mathis has hinted at the idea of following up his playing career with one in a managerial role, as it's basically a job that he's been doing on-field training for over the better part of the last decade. If another backup job doesn't unearth itself, it's very easy to envision Mathis filling out the lineup card and having a ton of success while doing so. After all, in that job he won't be tasked with, you know, hitting.

Rougned Odor 2B   Born: 02/03/94   Age: 27   Bats: L   Throws: R   Height: 5'11"   Weight: 200   Origin: International Free Agent, 2011

YEAR	TEAM	LVL	AGE	PA	R	2B	3B	HR	RBI	BB	K	SB	CS	Whiff%	AVG/OBP/SLG	DRC+	BABIP	BRR	FRAA	WARP
2018	TEX	MLB	24	535	76	23	2	18	63	43	127	12	12	23.3%	.253/.326/.424	97	.305	1.0	2B(127): 7.5	2.4
2019	TEX	MLB	25	581	77	30	1	30	93	52	178	11	9	29.4%	.205/.283/.439	87	.244	-2.8	2B(137): -12.8	-0.6
2020	TEX	MLB	26	148	15	4	0	10	30	7	47	0	1	26.0%	.167/.209/.413	69	.157	0.3	2B(37): 1.0	0.0
2021 FS	TEX	MLB	27	600	65	22	2	28	79	38	166	13	6	27.3%	.215/.278/.419	86	.253	-2.1	2B 0	0.9
2021 DC	TEX	MLB	27	198	21	7	0	9	26	12	54	4	2	27.3%	.215/.278/.419	86	.253	-0.7	2B 0	0.3

Comparables: Danny Espinosa, Derek Dietrich, Scooter Gennett

In 2017, Odor played in a major league-leading 162 games. In 2018, he led the American League in times caught stealing. In 2019, he struck out 178 times, which, you guess it, paced the AL. In 2020, Odor was the only guy in the league to take off his skate and try to stab a guy. Ok, fine, one of those is made up. It has been a strange career for Odor, who has run the gamut of contact-oriented prospect, emerging power hitter, and a dude that pretty much can't hit at all—all before the age of 27. After breaking through in 2016, the Rangers provided Odor with a nice contract extension, complete with two horses (seriously). He rewarded the club with a line of .215/.279/.416 over the next four seasons. In actuality, the team should have held its horses. Sunk costs aren't recognized often enough in sports, and it makes sense. In a landscape where egos and emotions run high, nobody wants to admit to a costly mistake. Could Odor hit 30 homers again? Sure! Could he steal double-digit bases while also getting thrown out a bunch? Almost definitely! Would those be mostly empty numbers that likely impede the development of the next guy up in the organization? Therein lies the rub.

Danny Santana OF   Born: 11/07/90   Age: 30   Bats: S   Throws: R   Height: 5'11"   Weight: 195   Origin: International Free Agent, 2007

YEAR	TEAM	LVL	AGE	PA	R	2B	3B	HR	RBI	BB	K	SB	CS	Whiff%	AVG/OBP/SLG	DRC+	BABIP	BRR	FRAA	WARP
2018	GWN	AAA	27	342	57	21	3	16	40	15	80	12	5		.264/.294/.497	103	.301	1.5	CF(45): 1.1, 2B(14): 1.3, LF(9): 3.0	1.3
2018	ATL	MLB	27	32	4	3	0	0	2	3	11	1	1	28.4%	.179/.281/.286	70	.294	-0.7	LF(6): 0.1, CF(3): -0.1, RF(1): -0.1	-0.1
2019	NAS	AAA	28	40	4	4	1	0	6	4	10	1	1		.343/.425/.514	117	.480	1.1	SS(3): 0.8, RF(3): -0.2, 2B(1): 0.1	0.3
2019	TEX	MLB	28	511	81	23	6	28	81	25	151	21	6	32.2%	.283/.324/.534	106	.353	3.6	1B(44): 0.9, CF(27): 0.6, 2B(17): 0.8	2.1
2020	TEX	MLB	30	63	6	4	0	1	7	7	24	2	0	40.8%	.145/.238/.273	69	.226	0.3	1B(9): -0.6, CF(4): 0.9, LF(1): -0.0	-0.1
2021 FS	TEX	MLB	30	600	63	25	3	19	66	31	184	18	6	33.5%	.216/.264/.378	70	.285	1.7	CF -2, LF 2	-0.2

Comparables: Randy Kutcher, Corey Patterson, Carlos Gómez

Who built Stonehenge? What happened to Amelia Earhart? Why did someone think Rocky V would be a good idea? History is chock full of great mysteries, but perhaps none greater than this: What in the hell was up with Danny Santana in 2019? After bouncing around in a few MLB organizations, Santana signed a minor-league deal with the Rangers and proceeded to post career-high offensive numbers, including 28 homers—more than double his cumulative career total to that point. Then came the Great Regression. Santana got just one hit in his first 17 trips to the plate to kick off the season, battling injuries and flat-out poor performance until a balky elbow ended his season for good. In September, he underwent a modified Tommy John surgery, where an internal brace was used to repair and connect ligaments as opposed to human tendons. In theory, the switch-hitter could be back in Arlington in March 2021, but whether or not he'll 1) recover from the innovative procedure or 2) reclaim his form and spot in the lineup lies hidden in the shroud of the future.

Nick Solak OF   Born: 01/11/95   Age: 26   Bats: R   Throws: R   Height: 5'11"   Weight: 185   Origin: Round 2, 2016 Draft (#62 overall)

YEAR	TEAM	LVL	AGE	PA	R	2B	3B	HR	RBI	BB	K	SB	CS	Whiff%	AVG/OBP/SLG	DRC+	BABIP	BRR	FRAA	WARP
2018	MTG	AA	23	565	91	17	3	19	76	68	112	21	6		.282/.384/.450	138	.330	-0.5	2B(60): -6.9, LF(40): -3.3, CF(18): 0.8	1.7
2019	DUR	AAA	24	349	56	13	1	17	47	39	80	3	2		.266/.353/.485	107	.303	-3.6	2B(61): -7.5, LF(17): 0.4, CF(2): -0.2	0.3
2019	NAS	AAA	24	128	23	6	0	10	27	6	25	2	0		.347/.386/.653	134	.369	0.7	2B(22): 0.4, RF(4): 0.3, LF(3): 0.1	1.0
2019	TEX	MLB	24	135	19	6	1	5	17	15	29	2	0	22.4%	.293/.393/.491	109	.354	1.3	3B(11): -0.1, 2B(5): -0.7	0.6
2020	TEX	MLB	25	233	27	10	0	2	23	18	42	7	1	19.1%	.268/.326/.344	88	.320	2.5	LF(29): -0.6, 2B(17): -1.7, CF(13): 0.0	0.3
2021 FS	TEX	MLB	26	600	74	29	2	19	73	51	129	4	1	20.1%	.273/.346/.441	116	.328	0.8	2B -5, LF -2	2.7
2021 DC	TEX	MLB	26	561	69	27	2	17	68	48	121	4	1	20.1%	.273/.346/.441	116	.328	0.8	2B -5, LF -2	2.4

Comparables: Ozzie Timmons, Kevin Mench, Alex Gordon

We could talk about Solak's college team, the Louisville Cardinals, chock full of future big leaguers (and big-league hopefuls) like Will Smith, Brendan McKay, and Corey Ray. However, that team was bounced prematurely in the postseason, thanks to a date with UC Santa Barbara and future-Cy Young award winner Shane Bieber. We could check in with Solak's other alma mater, Naperville North High School, and maybe tie in some cute references to fellow alum Bob Odenkirk, maybe a Better Call Saul nod, hoping Solak can transform from Jimmy McGill to Saul Goodman. Without any standout options, that pretty much just leaves us with a discussion of Solak's slightly underwhelming rookie campaign. For a guy that has been considered "bat-only" for most of his pro career, you're probably looking for more than 12 extra base hits in over 200 trips to the plate. Still, Solak can hit, he can run, and he can fake defense in a couple of spots. He'll be useful for the Rangers moving forward (with the possibility for more), no matter how you want to contextualize it.

★　★　★ *2021 Top 101 Prospect* **#26** ★　★　★

Leody Taveras CF   Born: 09/08/98   Age: 22   Bats: S   Throws: R   Height: 6'2"   Weight: 195   Origin: International Free Agent, 2015

YEAR	TEAM	LVL	AGE	PA	R	2B	3B	HR	RBI	BB	K	SB	CS	Whiff%	AVG/OBP/SLG	DRC+	BABIP	BRR	FRAA	WARP
2018	DE	HI-A	19	580	65	16	7	5	48	51	96	19	11		.246/.312/.332	90	.292	0.3	CF(123): 7.0, RF(3): 0.0	0.8
2019	DE	HI-A	20	290	44	7	4	2	25	31	62	21	5		.294/.368/.376	123	.378	-0.4	CF(34): -0.6, RF(23): 4.0, LF(7): -0.7	1.7
2019	FRI	AA	20	293	32	12	4	3	31	23	60	11	8		.265/.320/.375	97	.327	0.5	CF(65): 8.1	1.8
2020	TEX	MLB	22	134	20	6	1	4	6	14	43	8	0	30.4%	.227/.308/.395	84	.319	1.1	CF(33): 0.9	0.4
2021 FS	*TEX*	*MLB*	*22*	*600*	*64*	*23*	*4*	*11*	*47*	*45*	*172*	*13*	*6*	*30.4%*	*.228/.288/.351*	*74*	*.311*	*0.1*	*CF 2, LF 0*	*0.1*
2021 DC	*TEX*	*MLB*	*22*	*528*	*56*	*21*	*4*	*9*	*42*	*40*	*151*	*11*	*5*	*30.4%*	*.228/.288/.351*	*74*	*.311*	*0.1*	*CF 2*	*0.1*

Comparables: Derrick Robinson, Luis Alexander Basabe, Xavier Avery

Former MacArthur Fellow and Pulitzer Prize winning poet Mark Strand once wrote that "the future is always beginning now." It's an idea that is profound enough in its simplicity, and five years after signing with the Rangers as a 16-year-old out of the Dominican Republic, it's an idea that can finally apply to Taveras. After spending years tabbed as the center fielder of the future in Arlington, while lingering amid top-100 lists, Taveras made his big-league debut in 2020. Although his offensive prowess didn't set the world ablaze, he did strike out less frequently as the season progressed, flashing newly minted plate discipline skills while acclimating to battling major-league hurlers from the lead-off spot. As with many rookies, it will be a process for Taveras to develop into a weapon at the plate, and it would appear as though it will be on-the-job training for him moving forward, because, well, the future is now for the center fielder of the future. As another great American poet and two-time iHeartRadio Music Award winner, Pitbull, once said, "If you continue to work hard, let that be the fuel to your fire."

Anderson Tejeda SS   Born: 05/01/98   Age: 23   Bats: S   Throws: R   Height: 6'0"   Weight: 200   Origin: International Free Agent, 2014

YEAR	TEAM	LVL	AGE	PA	R	2B	3B	HR	RBI	BB	K	SB	CS	Whiff%	AVG/OBP/SLG	DRC+	BABIP	BRR	FRAA	WARP
2018	DE	HI-A	20	522	76	17	5	19	74	49	142	11	4		.259/.331/.439	119	.330	3.0	SS(105): 2.9, 2B(12): 1.6	2.9
2019	DE	HI-A	21	181	22	10	1	4	24	17	58	9	4		.234/.315/.386	83	.333	1.3	SS(39): 2.4	0.8
2020	TEX	MLB	22	77	7	4	1	3	8	2	30	4	1	39.4%	.253/.273/.453	76	.381	0.1	SS(18): -0.2, 2B(4): -0.1	0.0
2021 FS	*TEX*	*MLB*	*23*	*600*	*59*	*25*	*5*	*19*	*67*	*33*	*229*	*5*	*2*	*39.4%*	*.218/.265/.390*	*75*	*.327*	*2.7*	*2B 7, SS 0*	*1.1*
2021 DC	*TEX*	*MLB*	*23*	*165*	*16*	*7*	*1*	*5*	*18*	*9*	*63*	*1*	*0*	*39.4%*	*.218/.265/.390*	*75*	*.327*	*0.7*	*2B 2, SS 0*	*0.3*

Comparables: Junior Lake, Gleyber Torres, Marcus Semien

Hitting is really hard. In most cases it combines the mental acuity and strategy of a master-level chess match with the physical prowess necessary to use a piece of lumber to smack a cork wound in yarn and cowhide, all with a reaction time of less than half a second. Take Tejeda, for instance. The 22-year-old was one of many rookies to debut without experience above High-A this season, and his first bout with big-league pitching went about as expected. Initially, Tejeda saw a bunch of fastballs, and he was ready, socking a pair of dingers in his first 11 games with the big club. Pitchers adjusted, chucking more breaking balls Tejeda's way as the season progressed, and the rookie struggled, shedding light on Tejada's biggest issue—his propensity for succumbing to the strikeout, no matter what pitch was coming. But there's one nice thing about hitting, especially for the inexperienced: You get so many tries. Tejeda will get his chance at a rebuttal, at some point.

Bubba Thompson OF   Born: 06/09/98   Age: 23   Bats: R   Throws: R   Height: 6'1"   Weight: 180   Origin: Round 1, 2017 Draft (#26 overall)

YEAR	TEAM	LVL	AGE	PA	R	2B	3B	HR	RBI	BB	K	SB	CS	Whiff%	AVG/OBP/SLG	DRC+	BABIP	BRR	FRAA	WARP
2018	HIC	LO-A	20	363	52	18	5	8	42	23	104	32	7		.289/.344/.446	117	.396	6.1	CF(67): 1.1, LF(17): 0.7	1.9
2019	DE	HI-A	21	228	24	8	2	5	21	21	72	12	3		.178/.261/.312	54	.246	2.6	LF(34): 1.5, LF(20): -1.8, RF(2): -0.3	-0.2
2021 FS	*TEX*	*MLB*	*23*	*600*	*50*	*26*	*3*	*12*	*57*	*33*	*224*	*22*	*8*		*.204/.256/.332*	*58*	*.314*	*1.3*	*CF -3, LF 5*	*-1.0*

Comparables: Bubba Starling, Daz Cameron, Tommy Pham

If you bet that a dude named Bubba Thompson was someone SEC schools would be falling all over themselves to recruit, well, you'd be right. Tennessee and Mississippi both wanted him to play quarterback. Auburn thought they had secured Thompson's talents only for him to commit to Alabama, a reverse Kick Six, in a sense. Of course, it all was moot in the end, as Thompson signed with the Rangers before enrolling in classes. In the time since, the outfielder has surged up Texas' organizational rankings, blending the type of athleticism that made offensive coordinators salivate and the speed and ability to make hard contact that got him drafted in the first round. Thompson has definitely missed his fair share of time since the start of the 2019 campaign, so there will likely be plenty of rust to shake off. Having said that, it wasn't long ago when he was considered one of the better prospects in the game, and potentially the long-term future in center field.

Jose Trevino C   Born: 11/28/92   Age: 28   Bats: R   Throws: R   Height: 5'11"   Weight: 210   Origin: Round 6, 2014 Draft (#186 overall)

YEAR	TEAM	LVL	AGE	PA	R	2B	3B	HR	RBI	BB	K	SB	CS	Whiff%	AVG/OBP/SLG	DRC+	BABIP	BRR	FRAA	WARP
2018	FRI	AA	25	201	18	7	1	3	16	13	27	0	1		.234/.284/.332	76	.255	-0.8	C(38): 8.0	0.6
2018	TEX	MLB	25	8	0	0	0	0	3	0	1	0	0	6.7%	.250/.250/.250	82	.286		C(3): -0.5	0.0
2019	RAN	ROK	26	38	3	1	0	1	6	2	2	0	0		.167/.211/.278	68	.152	-0.3	C(8): -0.0	0.0
2019	NAS	AAA	26	156	16	10	0	2	22	8	28	2	0		.226/.263/.336	45	.263	0.7	C(40): 6.4	0.5
2019	TEX	MLB	26	126	18	9	0	2	13	3	27	0	0	22.7%	.258/.272/.383	77	.312	-0.7	C(40): 0.5	0.3
2020	TEX	MLB	28	83	10	8	0	2	9	3	15	0	0	20.2%	.250/.280/.434	95	.279	0.7	C(21): -0.1, 1B(1): -0.0	0.4
2021 FS	*TEX*	*MLB*	*28*	*600*	*55*	*28*	*1*	*13*	*63*	*27*	*116*	*0*	*0*	*21.2%*	*.228/.266/.355*	*68*	*.265*	*-1.2*	*C 5*	*0.4*
2021 DC	*TEX*	*MLB*	*28*	*363*	*33*	*17*	*0*	*8*	*38*	*16*	*70*	*0*	*0*	*21.2%*	*.228/.266/.355*	*68*	*.265*	*-0.7*	*C 4*	*0.4*

Comparables: Josh Phegley, Todd Greene, Mark Parent

On offense, going from Jeff Mathis to pretty much anyone is akin to jumping from roller skates to a Tesla. While that might be too high of praise to heap on Trevino, the rookie took to major-league pitching with aplomb, hitting .291/.333/.473 in his first 60 trips to the plate before an errant swing injured his wrist and ended his season. Perhaps more importantly for the Rangers' plans, he acquitted himself just as nicely behind the plate, posting better defensive metrics than all but 13 other backstops, allowing zero passed balls and significantly improving his framing. With top prospect Sam Huff breathing down his neck, it's progress that Trevino will need to continue if he wants to keep getting first-team reps donning the catcher's mask. Even still, his high-contact approach–in addition to steadily improving defense–should help Trevino to keep getting chances for the foreseeable future, in the Rangers' organization or elsewhere.

YEAR	TEAM	P. COUNT	FRM RUNS	BLK RUNS	THRW RUNS	TOT RUNS
2018	TEX	281	-0.2	-0.2		-0.4
2018	FRI	5465	6.0	0.5	0.6	7.1
2019	TEX	5134	0.8	0.0	0.0	0.8
2019	NAS	5718	7.3	0.2	0.0	7.4
2020	TEX	2650	1.8	0.0	0.1	1.8
2021	TEX	13228	5.7	-1.3	-0.5	3.9

Steele Walker OF Born: 07/30/96 Age: 24 Bats: L Throws: L Height: 5'11" Weight: 190 Origin: Round 2, 2018 Draft (#46 overall)

YEAR	TEAM	LVL	AGE	PA	R	2B	3B	HR	RBI	BB	K	SB	CS	Whiff%	AVG/OBP/SLG	DRC+	BABIP	BRR	FRAA	WARP
2018	WSX	ROK	21	13	0	0	0	0	0	1	1	0	0		.455/.538/.455	179	.500	-0.1	CF(1): -0.0, RF(1): -0.3	0.0
2018	GTF	ROK	21	38	4	1	0	2	4	1	7	1	1		.206/.263/.412	73	.192	0.4	CF(8): -2.0	-0.2
2018	KAN	LO-A	21	126	13	5	0	3	17	8	29	5	1		.186/.246/.310	57	.214	0.3	CF(21): 1.2	-0.3
2019	KAN	LO-A	22	87	6	10	3	0	11	8	15	4	2		.365/.437/.581	179	.443	-0.4	CF(16): -1.7, RF(4): -0.1	0.6
2019	WS	HI-A	22	441	59	26	2	10	51	42	63	9	5		.269/.346/.426	126	.294	-1.0	CF(81): -2.5	2.0
2021 FS	TEX	MLB	24	600	60	28	2	14	62	34	151	5	3		.228/.283/.369	76	.287	-1.9	CF -5, RF 0	-0.6

Comparables: Lastings Milledge, Charlie Blackmon, Matt Szczur

Though 2020 was mostly a lost development year for Walker, the joy his trade to the Rangers brought to Twitter users dying to make puns about 90s syndicated television justified the cost. Less obvious, but equally vital information: His name doubles as something you should never do when visiting a nursing home.

Eli White 2B Born: 06/26/94 Age: 27 Bats: R Throws: R Height: 6'3" Weight: 195 Origin: Round 11, 2016 Draft (#322 overall)

YEAR	TEAM	LVL	AGE	PA	R	2B	3B	HR	RBI	BB	K	SB	CS	Whiff%	AVG/OBP/SLG	DRC+	BABIP	BRR	FRAA	WARP
2018	MID	AA	24	578	81	30	8	9	55	62	116	18	9		.306/.388/.450	132	.379	3.2	2B(66): 2.8, SS(42): 2.6, 3B(19): -1.4	3.3
2019	NAS	AAA	25	499	63	20	5	14	43	43	136	14	5		.253/.337/.418	79	.333	1.7	SS(92): -6.8, CF(22): -0.5, 2B(2): 0.0	0.6
2020	TEX	MLB	26	52	5	2	0	0	3	3	16	1	1	26.2%	.188/.231/.229	73	.273	-0.6	LF(13): -1.5, RF(3): -0.1, CF(1): -0.2	-0.2
2021 FS	TEX	MLB	27	600	60	23	3	13	57	46	190	6	2	26.2%	.226/.297/.355	78	.322	1.9	RF -3, CF -3	-0.2
2021 DC	TEX	MLB	27	165	16	6	1	3	15	12	52	1	0	26.2%	.226/.297/.355	78	.322	0.5	RF -1, CF -1	-0.2

Comparables: Brandon Hicks, José Rondón, Tim Beckham

In *The Book of Eli*, a blind Denzel Washington treks across a post-apocalyptic United States on foot, in an attempt to preserve culture by delivering the last remaining copy of the Bible to Alcatraz. Eli White trekked from Oakland to Arlington, after being swapped for Jurickson Profar, in an attempt to preserve the organization's positional flexibility. Though he made his big-league debut in the outfield, White played up the middle on the dirt as a minor leaguer, providing serviceable, if not better, defense to blend with his "little bit of power/little bit of speed" profile at the plate. The book *on* Eli is breaking balls. Lots and lots of breaking balls. Breaking balls early and breaking balls often.

PITCHERS

Kolby Allard LHP Born: 08/13/97 Age: 23 Bats: L Throws: L Height: 6'1" Weight: 195 Origin: Round 1, 2015 Draft (#14 overall)

YEAR	TEAM	LVL	AGE	W	L	SV	G	GS	IP	H	HR	BB/9	K/9	K	GB%	BABIP	WHIP	ERA	DRA-	WARP	MPH	FA%	Whiff%	CSP
2018	GWN	AAA	20	6	4	0	19	19	112¹	102	6	2.7	7.1	89	37.3%	.301	1.21	2.72	94	1.1				
2018	ATL	MLB	20	1	1	0	3	1	8	19	3	4.5	3.4	3	33.3%	.457	2.88	12.38	188	-0.3	90.9	62.7%	12.3%	46.5%
2019	GWN	AAA	21	7	5	0	20	20	110	119	15	2.9	8.0	98	49.2%	.334	1.41	4.17	93	2.3				
2019	NAS	AAA	21	0	0	0	1	1	5	4	0	3.6	14.4	8	44.4%	.444	1.20	0.00	47	0.2				
2019	TEX	MLB	21	4	2	0	9	9	45¹	52	3	3.8	6.6	33	45.1%	.327	1.57	4.96	123	-0.1	93.5	79.6%	19.0%	52.3%
2020	TEX	MLB	22	0	6	0	11	8	33²	31	4	5.3	8.6	32	34.3%	.284	1.51	7.75	129	-0.2	92.8	77.2%	23.2%	53.1%
2021 FS	TEX	MLB	23	8	10	0	26	26	150	161	27	3.7	7.7	128	40.5%	.304	1.49	5.32	117	-0.3	93.0	77.6%	20.9%	52.5%
2021 DC	TEX	MLB	23	5	8	0	22	22	106	114	19	3.7	7.7	90	40.5%	.304	1.49	5.32	117	0.2	93.0	77.6%	20.9%	52.5%

Comparables: José Suarez, Julio Teheran, Taijuan Walker

Allard's statline reflected the woes of the year at large. The lefty spent his sophomore season in Texas serving up a litany of free passes, posting one of the highest walk rates in baseball before ultimately finding his way to the bullpen for his final three appearances. Even so, if you peel off a Coors Field start that yielded six earned in three innings, followed up by another four in 2/3 of an inning in Seattle, you're looking at a much better bottom line. And why stop there? By eliminating two more back-to-back September starts against the A's and those pesky Mariners where Allard gave up 14 runs in 4 2/3 frames, well, now you're looking at a Cy Young candidate. Unfortunately, neither Allard nor the rest of us have those time-travel capabilities, so we're stuck with what we've got. For the southpaw, there's still time to turn things around. His changeup has slowly morphed into his best pitch, and with a usage rate under 13 percent, untapped efficiency is available. In addition, more than half of the baserunners allowed by Allard came around to score, a shocking number that should regress favorably. If it doesn't, though, it's very possible that Allard's presence in the Rangers' plans could be erased from existence.

Kohei Arihara RHP Born: 08/11/92 Age: 28 Bats: R Throws: R Height: 6'3" Weight: 222 Origin: International Free Agent, 2020

Waseda University, whose storied baseball program predates the Yomiuri Giants, the oldest professional club in Japan, has produced three major leaguers: Satoru Komiya, Nori Aoki, and Tsuyoshi Wada. In 2021, Arihara is set to become the fourth. Unlike his rubber-toeing predecessors, the right-hander gets to test himself before he turns 30, with health and prime stuff, including a low-90s fastball and a low-80s changeup, seemingly intact. While Arihara doesn't possess the upside of the last two hurlers posted by Nippon Ham—Yu Darvish and Shohei Ohtani—he is capable of serving as an adequate mid-rotation starter in the major leagues.

Wes Benjamin LHP Born: 07/26/93 Age: 27 Bats: R Throws: L Height: 6'2" Weight: 210 Origin: Round 5, 2014 Draft (#156 overall)

YEAR	TEAM	LVL	AGE	W	L	SV	G	GS	IP	H	HR	BB/9	K/9	K	GB%	BABIP	WHIP	ERA	DRA-	WARP	MPH	FA%	Whiff%	CSP
2018	RAN	ROK	24	0	0	0	3	3	7	3	0	1.3	11.6	9	61.5%	.231	0.57	0.00	59	0.2				
2018	FRI	AA	24	5	6	0	15	15	79²	76	9	2.6	8.1	72	37.4%	.296	1.24	3.62	91	0.8				
2019	NAS	AAA	25	7	6	1	27	25	135¹	154	24	3.5	7.6	114	35.1%	.316	1.53	5.52	104	2.1				
2020	TEX	MLB	26	2	1	0	8	1	22¹	24	4	2.8	8.5	21	34.3%	.303	1.39	4.84	114	0.0	92.9	50.1%	26.7%	47.9%
2021 FS	TEX	MLB	27	2	2	0	57	0	50	51	9	3.3	8.0	44	35.1%	.294	1.40	5.02	113	-0.2	92.9	50.1%	26.7%	47.9%
2021 DC	TEX	MLB	27	2	2	0	53	0	56	58	11	3.3	8.0	49	35.1%	.294	1.40	5.02	113	-0.1	92.9	50.1%	26.7%	47.9%

Comparables: Ryan Borucki, Matt Hall, Dillon Peters

Back-end starter. It's a designation that gets tossed around a lot, typically reserved for someone that logs innings, posts an ERA in the high fours, and always seems to find a job. Depending on your era, think Milt Wilcox or Kevin Gross or Miguel Batista. It's awfully early, but Benjamin could be headed to enter those hallowed grounds. He's a lefty (which certainly helps) with a super-spinny fastball that hitters have yet to figure out, slugging just .256 against the 91-94 mph offering this season. There's also room to improve his mediocre strikeout totals, with Benjamin getting more swinging strikes than league average. It didn't hurt when he phased out his changeup in favor of the four-seamer as the season progressed, a classic "trade your worst pitch for your best pitch" swap. Benjamin's career as a big leaguer is obviously in its infancy, but it's also clear that there's a path for him to bounce around, soaking up instantly-forgotten innings for years to come. Pete Smith and Frank Castillo will greet him into the club with open arms.

Brock Burke LHP Born: 08/04/96 Age: 24 Bats: L Throws: L Height: 6'4" Weight: 210 Origin: Round 3, 2014 Draft (#96 overall)

YEAR	TEAM	LVL	AGE	W	L	SV	G	GS	IP	H	HR	BB/9	K/9	K	GB%	BABIP	WHIP	ERA	DRA-	WARP	MPH	FA%	Whiff%	CSP
2018	CHA	HI-A	21	3	5	0	16	13	82	85	4	3.3	9.5	87	45.4%	.349	1.40	3.84	82	1.2				
2018	MTG	AA	21	6	1	0	9	9	55¹	39	2	2.3	11.5	71	35.3%	.285	0.96	1.95	68	1.3				
2019	FRI	AA	22	3	5	0	9	9	45¹	34	2	2.4	9.7	49	47.5%	.271	1.01	3.18	56	1.2				
2019	NAS	AAA	22	0	0	0	2	2	8	12	1	6.8	12.4	11	50.0%	.478	2.25	7.88	138	0.0				
2019	TEX	MLB	22	0	2	0	6	6	26²	30	6	3.7	4.7	14	48.4%	.279	1.54	7.42	139	-0.3	94.2	61.3%	13.1%	50.5%
2021 FS	TEX	MLB	24	1	1	0	57	0	50	49	7	3.7	7.8	43	44.2%	.294	1.41	4.62	104	0.0	94.2	61.3%	13.1%	50.5%
2021 DC	TEX	MLB	24	1	1	0	23	0	25	24	3	3.7	7.8	21	44.2%	.294	1.41	4.62	104	0.1	94.2	61.3%	13.1%	50.5%

Comparables: Pedro Avila, Logan Allen, Patrick Sandoval

In Greek mythology, Sisyphus was tasked with forever rolling a giant boulder up a hill, only for it to roll back down whenever he got close to the top. Burke debuted in the big leagues in 2019, logging three consecutive quality starts in his first three outings. From there, well, the boulder got a little creaky. In his next three starts, Burke made it through a combined 8⅔ innings, giving up 19 earned runs, and serving up six dingers before a shoulder impingement shuttered the rest of his season. The injury wasn't thought to be serious, but it did delay the southpaw's start to the 2020 campaign. Then, while ramping up, Burke was diagnosed with a torn labrum, succumbing to surgery and requiring 12 months of rehab. And just like that, the boulder had returned to its original resting place. He'll start pushing it back up the hill starting in March 2021, hopefully with different results.

Jesse Chavez RHP Born: 08/21/83 Age: 37 Bats: R Throws: R Height: 6'1" Weight: 175 Origin: Round 42, 2002 Draft (#1252 overall)

YEAR	TEAM	LVL	AGE	W	L	SV	G	GS	IP	H	HR	BB/9	K/9	K	GB%	BABIP	WHIP	ERA	DRA-	WARP	MPH	FA%	Whiff%	CSP
2018	CHC	MLB	34	2	1	4	32	0	39	26	3	1.2	9.7	42	41.7%	.247	0.79	1.15	65	0.9	94.2	92.9%	21.7%	53.0%
2018	TEX	MLB	34	3	1	1	30	0	56¹	58	10	1.9	8.0	50	45.3%	.296	1.24	3.51	71	1.1	94.3	69.6%	25.1%	53.6%
2019	TEX	MLB	35	3	5	1	48	9	78	82	12	2.5	8.3	72	41.6%	.311	1.33	4.85	104	0.4	92.4	70.8%	18.4%	47.8%
2020	TEX	MLB	36	0	0	0	18	0	17	20	6	3.7	6.9	13	39.3%	.280	1.59	6.88	137	-0.2	92.3	78.7%	15.4%	49.6%
2021 FS	TEX	MLB	37	2	3	0	57	0	50	49	8	2.9	7.7	42	41.1%	.287	1.31	4.29	102	0.1	92.9	74.7%	19.4%	49.8%

Comparables: Craig Stammen, Matt Belisle, Jim Brewer

There's an old school of thought that the optimist interpretation of being traded is that at least there's one team that actively wants the player. It's meant to be comforting. Chavez has played for nine teams and he's been traded eight times. Running through the returns is both an exercise in "remembering some guys" and a reminder that sometimes the biggest names don't always yield the most productive return. In 2006, the Rangers traded Chavez to Pittsburgh for Kip Wells. Three years later, the Pirates shipped him to the Rays for Akinori Iwamura. Chavez's time in Tampa was short lived, because later that offseason, the team sent him to Atlanta for Rafael Soriano. As a deadline deal in 2010, the Braves traded Chavez with Gregor Blanco and Tim Collins to the Royals, recouping Rick Ankiel and Kyle Farnsworth. Kansas City waived him, and Chavez was picked up by the A's. In 2015, Oakland and Toronto flipped arms, with the A's shipping Chavez north of the border in exchange for Liam Hendriks. The next trade deadline saw Chavez move to Hollywood, joining the Dodgers for Mike Bolsinger. After signing with the Angels the following offseason, and the Rangers a year later, Chavez was traded to the Cubs for Tyler Thomas. He re-signed in Arlington the following offseason. Over the course of those dealings, Chavez amassed 9.5 WARP. After the trades, the guys that he was traded for accumulated 9.1 WARP combined. The lesson: Always trade for Jesse Chavez.

Kyle Cody RHP Born: 08/09/94 Age: 26 Bats: R Throws: R Height: 6'7" Weight: 225 Origin: Round 6, 2016 Draft (#189 overall)

YEAR	TEAM	LVL	AGE	W	L	SV	G	GS	IP	H	HR	BB/9	K/9	K	GB%	BABIP	WHIP	ERA	DRA-	WARP	MPH	FA%	Whiff%	CSP
2018	RAN	ROK	23	0	0	0	2	2	5	2	0	1.8	16.2	9	50.0%	.250	0.60	0.00	22	0.3				
2020	TEX	MLB	25	1	1	0	8	5	22²	15	1	5.2	7.1	18	47.5%	.233	1.24	1.59	98	0.2	96.1	50.3%	21.3%	47.3%
2021 FS	TEX	MLB	26	8	9	0	26	26	150	143	22	4.5	8.7	145	44.1%	.292	1.45	4.80	106	0.5	96.1	50.3%	21.3%	47.3%
2021 DC	TEX	MLB	26	3	5	0	14	14	62	59	9	4.5	8.7	60	44.1%	.292	1.45	4.80	106	0.4	96.1	50.3%	21.3%	47.3%

Comparables: Aaron Blair, Alex Meyer, Jordan Montgomery

The fact that Cody tossed a big-league pitch this season was only slightly more impressive than him throwing a competitive pitch at all, as the tall righty last took the mound in July 2018 thanks to Tommy John surgery. His mid-rotation upside is still there, even if his sparkly 2020 ERA is likely to sink faster than fellow Chippewa Falls native Jack Dawson.

Hans Crouse RHP Born: 09/15/98 Age: 22 Bats: L Throws: R Height: 6'4" Weight: 180 Origin: Round 2, 2017 Draft (#66 overall)

YEAR	TEAM	LVL	AGE	W	L	SV	G	GS	IP	H	HR	BB/9	K/9	K	GB%	BABIP	WHIP	ERA	DRA-	WARP	MPH	FA%	Whiff%	CSP
2018	SPO	SS	19	5	1	0	8	8	38	25	2	2.6	11.1	47	35.5%	.253	0.95	2.37	91	0.4				
2018	HIC	LO-A	19	0	2	0	5	5	16²	18	1	4.3	8.1	15	38.5%	.340	1.56	2.70	135	-0.2				
2019	HIC	LO-A	20	6	1	0	19	19	87²	86	12	2.0	7.7	75	31.3%	.295	1.20	4.41	105	0.1				
2021 FS	TEX	MLB	22	2	3	0	57	0	50	50	8	4.1	8.0	44	32.6%	.292	1.46	5.05	118	-0.4				

Comparables: Joe Ross, Robert Gsellman, Felix Doubront

A fun way to spend the winter months is to compile a thorough, definitive list of the greatest Hanses of history. It's a time-honored tradition. Hans Gruber, the greatest movie villain of all time, is number one. Apologies to fans of Hans Geiger, the inventor of the Geiger counter, as his measurement of radiation brings him just short (ranked number six). Hans Christian Anderson ranks highly for his beloved fairy tales, but perhaps not as high as you'd think (number nine), and while Hans, of the famed comedy duo Hans and Franz, is good for a chuckle, his schtick gets old quickly (number 54). Hans Zimmer is responsible for some of the greatest modern movie scores and that's good enough to get him just outside the top-10 (number 11). Hans-Ulrich Rudel is last. Where Crouse slots in is still to be decided. He's got the size and two plus pitches, which bodes well for his tenure in the rotation, but unfortunately he also has the spotty command and violent delivery of a relief risk. A third pitch and improved precision will go a long way to determining whether Crouse is closer to Hans Holzer, Austrian-American author, parapsychologist, and host of the television show Ghost Hunters (number 13) or Hans, the late skate-shop owner from Mighty Ducks (number 35).

★ ★ ★ *2021 Top 101 Prospect* **#60** ★ ★ ★

Dane Dunning RHP Born: 12/20/94 Age: 26 Bats: R Throws: R Height: 6'4" Weight: 225 Origin: Round 1, 2016 Draft (#29 overall)

YEAR	TEAM	LVL	AGE	W	L	SV	G	GS	IP	H	HR	BB/9	K/9	K	GB%	BABIP	WHIP	ERA	DRA-	WARP	MPH	FA%	Whiff%	CSP
2018	WS	HI-A	23	1	1	0	4	4	24¹	20	2	1.1	11.5	31	61.3%	.300	0.95	2.59	74	0.5				
2018	BIR	AA	23	5	2	0	11	11	62	57	0	3.3	10.0	69	48.8%	.343	1.29	2.76	76	1.3				
2020	CHW	MLB	25	2	0	0	7	7	34	25	4	3.4	9.3	35	44.6%	.239	1.12	3.97	91	0.5	93.6	60.6%	27.6%	43.0%
2021 FS	TEX	MLB	26	9	8	0	26	26	150	137	21	3.5	9.4	156	43.9%	.291	1.30	4.13	95	1.5	93.6	60.6%	27.6%	43.0%
2021 DC	TEX	MLB	26	6	8	0	22	22	115	105	16	3.5	9.4	120	43.9%	.291	1.30	4.13	95	1.5	93.6	60.6%	27.6%	43.0%

Comparables: Tyler Wilson, Sean Manaea, Jordan Montgomery

A lot of wondrous and remarkable work goes into being as reliably boring as Dunning manages to be. There's a lot of command and a mastery of a wide arsenal that goes into surviving while sitting 91-92 mph with a fastball in 2020. It demands practice and repetition of cutting and riding the heater to every quadrant of the zone to simply earn the status of being "not overpowering" as opposed to simply being dead meat. Most of Dunning's primary weapons aren't much use against left-handers and that's a real shortcoming he will have to manage, but developing a whole second release point and style of pitching, just to be pedestrian against them, is all a remarkable work-around just to get by. And of course, emerging back on the mound, two years after his first elbow sprain, Tommy John surgery, rehab, skipping Triple-A and getting called up in the middle of a pandemic, all just to bore tens of thousands with eating innings the way he was presaged four years ago, is all very remarkable. He'll be boring people in Texas after he was the centerpiece of the Rangers return in a trade for Lance Lynn.

Demarcus Evans RHP Born: 10/22/96 Age: 24 Bats: R Throws: R Height: 6'5" Weight: 265 Origin: Round 25, 2015 Draft (#738 overall)

YEAR	TEAM	LVL	AGE	W	L	SV	G	GS	IP	H	HR	BB/9	K/9	K	GB%	BABIP	WHIP	ERA	DRA-	WARP	MPH	FA%	Whiff%	CSP
2018	HIC	LO-A	21	4	1	9	35	0	56	28	1	4.3	16.6	103	34.8%	.314	0.98	1.77	56	1.4				
2019	DE	HI-A	22	4	0	6	17	0	22¹	9	0	6.9	16.1	40	45.5%	.290	1.16	0.81	62	0.4				
2019	FRI	AA	22	2	0	6	30	0	37²	14	2	5.3	14.3	60	34.9%	.197	0.96	0.96	48	1.0				
2020	TEX	MLB	23	0	0	0	4	0	4	3	1	0.0	9.0	4	33.3%	.250	0.75	2.25	100	0.0	95.5	66.7%	29.6%	40.6%
2021 FS	TEX	MLB	24	2	2	0	57	0	50	38	7	6.8	12.9	71	37.0%	.297	1.53	4.65	100	0.1	95.5	66.7%	29.6%	40.6%
2021 DC	TEX	MLB	24	2	2	0	53	0	56	43	7	6.8	12.9	80	37.0%	.297	1.53	4.65	100	0.3	95.5	66.7%	29.6%	40.6%

Comparables: Cristian Javier, Carlos Sanabria, Carlos Estévez

The first batter Evans faced in his big-league career was Albert Pujols, who promptly welcomed the righty to The Show with a homer. The rest of the league welcomed him much more politely, thanks to his heavy 95 mph heater and wipeout curve that induces a ton of whiffs.

Kyle Gibson RHP Born: 10/23/87 Age: 33 Bats: R Throws: R Height: 6'6" Weight: 215 Origin: Round 1, 2009 Draft (#22 overall)

YEAR	TEAM	LVL	AGE	W	L	SV	G	GS	IP	H	HR	BB/9	K/9	K	GB%	BABIP	WHIP	ERA	DRA-	WARP	MPH	FA%	Whiff%	CSP
2018	MIN	MLB	30	10	13	0	32	32	196²	177	23	3.6	8.2	179	49.6%	.286	1.30	3.62	94	2.5	95.2	57.7%	26.9%	40.3%
2019	MIN	MLB	31	13	7	0	34	29	160	175	23	3.1	9.0	160	51.1%	.333	1.44	4.84	114	0.3	95.1	50.3%	29.4%	38.8%
2020	TEX	MLB	32	2	6	0	12	12	67¹	73	12	4.0	7.8	58	51.2%	.313	1.53	5.35	119	-0.1	93.9	49.4%	23.4%	41.1%
2021 FS	TEX	MLB	33	9	9	0	26	26	150	147	20	3.8	8.2	136	50.4%	.295	1.40	4.56	103	0.8	94.8	52.0%	27.1%	39.8%
2021 DC	TEX	MLB	33	8	10	0	27	27	151	148	21	3.8	8.2	137	50.4%	.295	1.40	4.56	103	1.3	94.8	52.0%	27.1%	39.8%

Comparables: Jhoulys Chacín, Iván Nova, Chase Anderson

To say Gibson's first year away from Minnesota was a little bumpy would be akin to saying that Rowan was slightly in over his head with his Worcestershire Pear Tree in the Season 11 bread episode of The Great British Bake Off (read: an understatement). Gibson struggled with his sinker (which, incidentally, so did Rowan), and especially had trouble when getting behind in the count. While that's normally pretty typical for most hurlers, opponents slashed .318/.496/.557 against Gibson in hitters' counts, posting an OPS over 200 points higher than the league average. Sometimes an entire season starts to feel like a 2-0 count. There weren't many positives to take from the campaign; given the chaos of 2020, perhaps the tick he lost on his pitches will show back up with a normal spring? Gibson might be better off dumping this bake of a season in the bin and starting from scratch in 2021, his second of a three-year deal in Texas.

Taylor Hearn LHP Born: 08/30/94 Age: 26 Bats: L Throws: L Height: 6'6" Weight: 230 Origin: Round 5, 2015 Draft (#164 overall)

YEAR	TEAM	LVL	AGE	W	L	SV	G	GS	IP	H	HR	BB/9	K/9	K	GB%	BABIP	WHIP	ERA	DRA-	WARP	MPH	FA%	Whiff%	CSP
2018	FRI	AA	23	1	2	0	5	5	25	29	5	3.2	11.9	33	36.2%	.375	1.52	5.04	87	0.3				
2018	ALT	AA	23	3	6	0	19	19	104	75	6	3.3	9.3	107	37.7%	.258	1.09	3.12	76	2.1				
2019	NAS	AAA	24	1	3	0	4	4	20	14	3	4.5	11.7	26	26.7%	.262	1.20	4.05	59	0.7				
2019	TEX	MLB	24	0	1	0	1	1	0¹	3	0	108.0	0.0	0	50.0%	.750	21.00	108.00	38	0.0	92.8	69.2%	8.3%	45.1%
2020	TEX	MLB	25	0	0	0	14	0	17¹	13	2	5.7	11.9	23	26.8%	.282	1.38	3.63	102	0.1	97.2	60.5%	24.5%	49.4%
2021 FS	TEX	MLB	26	2	3	0	57	0	50	44	8	4.8	10.6	59	35.1%	.293	1.43	4.74	105	0.0	96.9	61.1%	23.4%	49.1%
2021 DC	TEX	MLB	26	2	3	0	59	0	63	56	11	4.8	10.6	74	35.1%	.293	1.43	4.74	105	0.2	96.9	61.1%	23.4%	49.1%

Comparables: Conner Menez, Keegan Akin, Joe Palumbo

Under different circumstances, Hearn's professional debut in Arlington might have come across the street in Cowboy Stadium. Not for the Dallas Cowboys, mind you, but as the latest in a long line of cowboy champions. At the age of 17 Hearn, a native Texan, opted for a new challenge with the hardball rather than following in the footsteps of his grandfather, father, and three uncles in rodeo. In both universes, Hearn was due for a rough ride. After a balky elbow ejected what was to be his rookie 2019 campaign, he returned to the mound in early August, squaring off against the Mariners—the team that roughed him up in his first big-league action. While he certainly triumphed in the quest to return from injury, the next obstacle in his way might just be those Mariners, a team responsible for 10 of the 12 earned runs Hearn has surrendered thus far in his career. Though he's definitely been dealt a rough stock, signs point to Hearn not only being up for the task, but also able to rope success like a, well, you get it.

Jimmy Herget RHP Born: 09/09/93 Age: 27 Bats: R Throws: R Height: 6'3" Weight: 170 Origin: Round 6, 2015 Draft (#175 overall)

YEAR	TEAM	LVL	AGE	W	L	SV	G	GS	IP	H	HR	BB/9	K/9	K	GB%	BABIP	WHIP	ERA	DRA-	WARP	MPH	FA%	Whiff%	CSP
2018	LOU	AAA	24	1	3	0	50	0	59²	59	5	3.2	9.8	65	35.3%	.329	1.34	3.47	80	0.8				
2019	LOU	AAA	25	3	4	2	48	0	58²	41	7	5.5	10.4	68	34.5%	.246	1.31	2.91	64	1.8				
2019	CIN	MLB	25	0	0	0	5	0	6¹	8	2	4.3	0.0	0	21.7%	.286	1.74	4.26	174	-0.2	94.7	50.7%	18.8%	42.4%
2020	TEX	MLB	26	1	0	0	20	1	19²	13	2	6.4	7.8	17	35.2%	.216	1.37	3.20	117	0.0	95.2	54.3%	25.7%	49.7%
2021 FS	TEX	MLB	27	2	2	0	57	0	50	47	9	4.3	9.0	49	34.5%	.283	1.42	4.91	109	-0.1	95.1	53.9%	24.8%	48.8%
2021 DC	TEX	MLB	27	2	2	0	47	0	50	47	9	4.3	9.0	49	34.5%	.283	1.42	4.91	109	0.1	95.1	53.9%	24.8%	48.8%

Comparables: Jacob Rhame, Nick Rumbelow, Trevor Gott

After being scooped up off of waivers from Cincinnati, Herget made 20 appearances for the Rangers, threading the needle, walking the tightrope, and tiptoeing through a minefield of excess walks. Pretty impressive to do them all at the same time; more so to do it and escape with such a tidy ERA.

Jonathan Hernández RHP Born: 07/06/96 Age: 25 Bats: R Throws: R Height: 6'3" Weight: 190 Origin: International Free Agent, 2013

YEAR	TEAM	LVL	AGE	W	L	SV	G	GS	IP	H	HR	BB/9	K/9	K	GB%	BABIP	WHIP	ERA	DRA-	WARP	MPH	FA%	Whiff%	CSP
2018	DE	HI-A	21	4	2	0	10	10	57¹	37	6	2.7	12.1	77	50.8%	.263	0.94	2.20	50	2.0				
2018	FRI	AA	21	4	4	0	12	12	64	58	6	5.1	8.0	57	50.6%	.299	1.47	4.92	90	0.6				
2019	FRI	AA	22	5	9	0	22	16	96	100	11	3.6	8.9	95	47.1%	.331	1.44	5.16	117	-1.0				
2019	TEX	MLB	22	2	1	0	9	2	16²	14	3	7.0	10.3	19	52.2%	.256	1.62	4.32	103	0.1	98.7	48.5%	32.6%	37.4%
2020	TEX	MLB	23	5	1	0	27	0	31	24	2	2.3	9.0	31	45.1%	.278	1.03	2.90	84	0.5	99.4	47.5%	33.8%	43.3%
2021 FS	TEX	MLB	24	2	3	25	57	0	50	45	6	5.0	9.1	50	45.5%	.292	1.47	4.62	102	0.1	99.2	47.8%	33.4%	41.5%
2021 DC	TEX	MLB	24	2	3	25	59	0	63	57	8	5.0	9.1	63	45.5%	.292	1.47	4.62	102	0.3	99.2	47.8%	33.4%	41.5%

Comparables: Touki Toussaint, Zack Littell, Tyrell Jenkins

Devin Williams, James Karinchak, Tejay Antone, and...Hernández? Through the first month of the season, it certainly looked as though the latter was planting his flag as one of the most dominant young relievers in the game. As for the second month of the season, well, let's just say he's not quite there yet. There are plenty of months still to come.

John King LHP Born: 09/14/94 Age: 26 Bats: L Throws: L Height: 6'2" Weight: 215 Origin: Round 10, 2017 Draft (#314 overall)

YEAR	TEAM	LVL	AGE	W	L	SV	G	GS	IP	H	HR	BB/9	K/9	K	GB%	BABIP	WHIP	ERA	DRA-	WARP	MPH	FA%	Whiff%	CSP
2018	RAN	ROK	23	0	0	0	1	1	1²	3	0	5.4	5.4	1	71.4%	.429	2.40	5.40	264	-0.1				
2018	SPO	SS	23	0	0	0	1	1	3	5	0	0.0	6.0	2	25.0%	.417	1.67	6.00	300	-0.4				
2019	HIC	LO-A	24	1	2	0	5	5	26¹	31	1	0.7	9.9	29	63.3%	.385	1.25	3.42	117	-0.2				
2019	DE	HI-A	24	2	4	0	14	14	71	59	4	1.4	7.7	61	54.8%	.282	0.99	2.03	79	1.0				
2020	TEX	MLB	25	1	0	0	6	0	10¹	13	2	3.5	7.8	9	55.6%	.324	1.65	6.10	91	0.1	94.7	63.4%	19.5%	49.5%
2021 FS	TEX	MLB	26	1	2	0	57	0	50	51	7	3.4	7.3	40	47.1%	.297	1.41	4.77	107	-0.1	94.7	63.4%	19.5%	49.5%
2021 DC	TEX	MLB	26	1	2	0	6	6	25	25	3	3.4	7.3	20	47.1%	.297	1.41	4.77	107	0.0	94.7	63.4%	19.5%	49.5%

Comparables: Randy Rosario, Anthony Kay, Gregory Soto

Another result of the suddenly popular A-ball-to-majors pipeline, the hard-throwing lefty King earned all nine of his strikeouts swinging. Should this trend continue throughout his career, a 100 percent swinging-strikeout rate would likely be a major-league record.

Corey Kluber RHP Born: 04/10/86 Age: 35 Bats: R Throws: R Height: 6'4" Weight: 215 Origin: Round 4, 2007 Draft (#134 overall)

YEAR	TEAM	LVL	AGE	W	L	SV	G	GS	IP	H	HR	BB/9	K/9	K	GB%	BABIP	WHIP	ERA	DRA-	WARP	MPH	FA%	Whiff%	CSP
2018	CLE	MLB	32	20	7	0	33	33	215	179	25	1.4	9.3	222	44.5%	.277	0.99	2.89	63	6.1	93.8	41.6%	27.1%	46.4%
2019	CLE	MLB	33	2	3	0	7	7	35²	44	4	3.8	9.6	38	39.3%	.374	1.65	5.80	127	-0.2	93.5	39.8%	28.5%	43.6%
2020	TEX	MLB	34	0	0	0	1	1	1	0	0	9.0	9.0	1	0.0%	.000	1.00	0.00	107	0.0	93.0	50.0%	12.5%	36.3%
2021 FS	TEX	MLB	35	9	8	0	26	26	150	137	21	2.7	9.0	150	42.3%	.288	1.22	3.58	88	2.0	93.7	41.2%	27.3%	45.5%

Comparables: Max Scherzer, Zack Greinke, Johnny Cueto

The Texas Rangers were founded in 1823. Not the baseball team, but the law enforcement unit. For more than a century the organization was responsible for apprehending outlaws across the nation, achieving national notoriety and public adoration alike, blending a no-nonsense attitude with unquestionable results. Kluber was a natural fit for the brand. When the two-time Cy Young winner joined the Rangers (the baseball team this time) last December, there were some injury concerns. Kluber pitched one competitive inning in 2020, and the team declined his $18 million option, making him a free agent. All told, he burned bright and reached the pinnacle of his profession twice, even starting three of the seven World Series games in 2016. There's something poetic about the aging gunslinger reaching deep down for one last ride, one last pitch. Whether or not it's that time for Kluber, like his Ranger namesakes, his Texas-sized presence is certainly receding.

José Leclerc RHP Born: 12/19/93 Age: 27 Bats: R Throws: R Height: 6'0" Weight: 195 Origin: International Free Agent, 2010

YEAR	TEAM	LVL	AGE	W	L	SV	G	GS	IP	H	HR	BB/9	K/9	K	GB%	BABIP	WHIP	ERA	DRA-	WARP	MPH	FA%	Whiff%	CSP
2018	TEX	MLB	24	2	3	12	59	0	57²	24	1	3.9	13.1	84	30.9%	.217	0.85	1.56	64	1.4	97.4	47.7%	41.1%	44.2%
2019	TEX	MLB	25	2	4	14	70	3	68²	52	7	5.1	13.1	100	34.4%	.312	1.33	4.33	61	1.8	98.5	50.2%	33.0%	43.5%
2020	TEX	MLB	26	0	0	1	2	0	2	2	0	9.0	13.5	3	0.0%	.400	2.00	4.50	99	0.0	95.9	57.4%	43.8%	35.0%
2021 FS	TEX	MLB	27	3	2	10	57	0	50	35	6	6.1	12.6	70	34.3%	.273	1.38	3.91	87	0.5	98.1	49.8%	35.5%	43.4%
2021 DC	TEX	MLB	27	3	2	10	59	0	63	44	8	6.1	12.6	88	34.3%	.273	1.38	3.91	87	0.8	98.1	49.8%	35.5%	43.4%

Comparables: Reyes Moronta, Edwin Díaz, Corey Knebel

Going into the season, there was some question whether Leclerc would remain the team's closer after a rocky 2019. Afterwards, there was no question. He saved one game in his usual shotgun-pellet fashion, and then felt shoulder discomfort warming up for save two, which never came. Rafael Montero seized the role in Texas, so there was little left for the sporadically great Leclerc to do except heal, demonstrate value, and wait for another opportunity. With Montero shipped to Seattle, it may be here already.

Jordan Lyles RHP Born: 10/19/90 Age: 30 Bats: R Throws: R Height: 6'5" Weight: 230 Origin: Round 1, 2008 Draft (#38 overall)

YEAR	TEAM	LVL	AGE	W	L	SV	G	GS	IP	H	HR	BB/9	K/9	K	GB%	BABIP	WHIP	ERA	DRA-	WARP	MPH	FA%	Whiff%	CSP
2018	SD	MLB	27	2	4	0	24	8	71¹	71	12	2.4	7.8	62	45.7%	.291	1.26	4.29	131	-0.6	95.7	48.8%	21.5%	50.2%
2018	MIL	MLB	27	1	0	0	11	0	16¹	12	0	5.0	12.1	22	42.1%	.316	1.29	3.31	57	0.5	96.2	47.6%	31.2%	46.6%
2019	PIT	MLB	28	5	7	0	17	17	82¹	88	16	3.6	9.8	90	41.4%	.327	1.47	5.36	92	1.1	94.4	52.9%	24.6%	46.0%
2019	MIL	MLB	28	7	1	0	11	11	58²	43	9	3.4	8.6	56	38.8%	.227	1.11	2.45	78	1.2	94.1	50.6%	21.5%	44.4%
2020	TEX	MLB	29	1	6	0	12	9	57²	67	12	3.6	5.6	36	40.5%	.286	1.56	7.02	155	-1.2	94.1	48.1%	16.9%	48.2%
2021 FS	TEX	MLB	30	8	9	0	26	26	150	153	25	3.6	7.4	123	41.9%	.292	1.42	4.90	110	0.2	94.5	50.2%	21.3%	46.9%
2021 DC	TEX	MLB	30	6	10	0	25	25	129	132	21	3.6	7.4	106	41.9%	.292	1.42	4.90	110	0.7	94.5	50.2%	21.3%	46.9%

Comparables: Chris Stratton, Vin Mazzaro, Kendall Graveman

They should really make the whole plane out of the black box, and Lyles should make his whole career out of being a Brewer. In two separate stints, Lyles went 8-1 with Milwaukee, with a 2.64 ERA and 78 strikeouts in 75 innings. Everywhere else, well, made the heart grow fonder. Perhaps he just really loved a fresh, icy cold Miller Lite after each game, or maybe he couldn't get enough of the jumbo burgers at Kopp's Frozen Custard. As a dual-sport star in high school, it's possible that Lyles dreamed of jumping in a Lyft to Lambeau Field and catching passes from Aaron Rodgers, or as an avid golfer, he liked the proximity to the majestic greens of Whistling Straits or Erin Hills. Whatever the reason, Lyles had a disappointing first year with the Rangers, having difficulty finding consistent velocity and shying away from the primarily two-pitch arsenal that found so much success in 2019. The good news is that his curveball was still pretty good, inducing a decent number of whiffs and holding opposing offenses to putrid slugging numbers. The bad news is that his fastball got tattooed, leading to questions as to whether its previous success was dreamed in a PBR and bratwurst-induced stupor.

Brett Martin   **LHP**   Born: 04/28/95   Age: 26   Bats: L   Throws: L   Height: 6'4"   Weight: 200   Origin: Round 4, 2014 Draft (#126 overall)

YEAR	TEAM	LVL	AGE	W	L	SV	G	GS	IP	H	HR	BB/9	K/9	K	GB%	BABIP	WHIP	ERA	DRA-	WARP	MPH	FA%	Whiff%	CSP
2018	FRI	AA	23	2	10	0	29	15	89	138	7	2.9	9.7	96	48.2%	.449	1.88	7.28	95	0.5				
2019	NAS	AAA	24	0	0	1	10	0	12²	10	0	2.8	13.5	19	57.1%	.357	1.11	0.71	37	0.5				
2019	TEX	MLB	24	2	3	0	51	2	62¹	72	7	2.6	9.0	62	53.0%	.340	1.44	4.76	91	0.6	95.6	52.2%	27.8%	49.3%
2020	TEX	MLB	25	1	1	0	15	0	14²	8	2	5.5	4.9	8	50.0%	.143	1.16	1.84	122	0.0	95.7	53.2%	17.3%	43.6%
2021 FS	TEX	MLB	26	2	3	0	57	0	50	48	7	3.4	8.2	45	49.5%	.291	1.34	4.23	98	0.2	95.6	52.4%	25.2%	47.9%
2021 DC	TEX	MLB	26	2	3	0	59	0	63	60	8	3.4	8.2	57	49.5%	.291	1.34	4.23	98	0.4	95.6	52.4%	25.2%	47.9%

Comparables: Randy Rosario, Jesus Tinoco, Conner Menez

You know the part of the horror movie where the killer is sneaking up behind an oblivious teenage victim, ready to attack, when said victim somehow slips away unscathed? That's kind of like Martin's 2020 campaign, where the lefty walked more guys than he struck out, stranded runners at an unsustainable clip, and held opponents beneath the Mendoza Line on balls in play only to escape with a sub-2.00 ERA.

Juan Nicasio   **RHP**   Born: 08/31/86   Age: 34   Bats: R   Throws: R   Height: 6'4"   Weight: 250   Origin: International Free Agent, 2006

YEAR	TEAM	LVL	AGE	W	L	SV	G	GS	IP	H	HR	BB/9	K/9	K	GB%	BABIP	WHIP	ERA	DRA-	WARP	MPH	FA%	Whiff%	CSP
2018	SEA	MLB	31	1	6	1	46	0	42	53	6	1.1	11.4	53	35.8%	.402	1.38	6.00	60	1.1	96.0	70.7%	23.5%	51.0%
2019	PHI	MLB	32	2	3	1	47	0	47¹	57	4	4.0	8.6	45	45.6%	.368	1.65	4.75	110	0.0	95.9	54.5%	21.1%	48.4%
2020	TEX	MLB	33	0	0	0	2	0	1¹	5	1	13.5	6.8	1	25.0%	.571	5.25	40.50	119	0.0	95.5	67.4%	17.6%	43.9%
2021 FS	TEX	MLB	34	2	2	0	57	0	50	46	6	2.9	8.3	45	42.0%	.284	1.25	3.73	90	0.4	95.9	60.0%	21.7%	48.9%

Comparables: Tommy Hunter, Wade Davis, Daniel Hudson

It was a brief season for Nicasio even by 2020 standards; it took two weeks for the Rangers to call him up from their alternate site, and two days for him to take personal leave to be with his family in the Dominican Republic. That gave him just long enough to leave a mark, even if it wasn't technically his mark: Nicasio's final batter faced was Fernando Tatis, Jr., who hit a rather newsworthy 3-0 grand slam and sparked the 2,432,935th debate on unwritten rules in baseball.

Joe Palumbo   **LHP**   Born: 10/26/94   Age: 26   Bats: L   Throws: L   Height: 6'0"   Weight: 195   Origin: Round 30, 2013 Draft (#910 overall)

YEAR	TEAM	LVL	AGE	W	L	SV	G	GS	IP	H	HR	BB/9	K/9	K	GB%	BABIP	WHIP	ERA	DRA-	WARP	MPH	FA%	Whiff%	CSP
2018	RAN	ROK	23	0	0	0	3	3	9	5	1	1.0	15.0	15	56.2%	.267	0.67	4.00	23	0.5				
2018	DE	HI-A	23	1	4	0	6	6	27	24	3	2.0	11.3	34	41.7%	.304	1.11	2.67	63	0.7				
2018	FRI	AA	23	1	0	0	2	2	9¹	6	0	2.9	9.6	10	39.1%	.261	0.96	1.93	74	0.2				
2019	FRI	AA	24	0	0	0	11	10	53²	43	5	4.2	11.6	69	39.1%	.311	1.27	3.19	74	0.9				
2019	NAS	AAA	24	3	0	0	6	6	27	13	4	3.3	13.0	39	40.4%	.188	0.85	2.67	36	1.3				
2019	TEX	MLB	24	0	3	0	7	4	16²	21	7	4.3	11.3	21	34.0%	.333	1.74	9.18	116	0.0	95.5	56.7%	22.8%	49.7%
2020	TEX	MLB	25	0	1	0	2	0	2¹	3	1	11.6	19.3	5	33.3%	.400	2.57	11.57	86	0.0	94.1	57.6%	42.9%	46.9%
2021 FS	TEX	MLB	26	9	8	0	26	26	150	132	23	3.8	10.8	180	38.0%	.296	1.31	4.17	95	1.5	95.2	56.9%	27.0%	49.1%
2021 DC	TEX	MLB	26	2	3	0	9	9	44	38	7	3.8	10.8	52	38.0%	.296	1.31	4.17	95	0.6	95.2	56.9%	27.0%	49.1%

Comparables: Thomas Pannone, Yacksel Ríos, Jarlin García

After transferring following his sophomore year in high school, Palumbo had to reclassify as a sophomore thanks to obscure age limitations established by his new private school in West Islip, New York. The reclassification cost him a year of eligibility, making his junior season his final one. In order to get reps as an 18-year-old, Palumbo joined the Long Island Black Sox, a local men's league team, where he was discovered by a Rangers area scout. He was drafted in the 30th round in 2013, and from there he undertook the usual development process. Well, aside from the Tommy John surgery in 2018 and the bouts with ulcerative colitis in 2020. Other than that, Palumbo is just your regular, run-of-the-mill lefty with huge fastball spin and a solid three-pitch mix. Wait, did that say run-of-the-mill? It meant to read "potential mid-rotation starter."

Tyler Phillips   **RHP**   Born: 10/27/97   Age: 23   Bats: R   Throws: R   Height: 6'5"   Weight: 225   Origin: Round 16, 2015 Draft (#468 overall)

YEAR	TEAM	LVL	AGE	W	L	SV	G	GS	IP	H	HR	BB/9	K/9	K	GB%	BABIP	WHIP	ERA	DRA-	WARP	MPH	FA%	Whiff%	CSP
2018	HIC	LO-A	20	11	5	0	22	22	128	117	4	1.0	8.7	124	52.8%	.308	1.02	2.67	64	3.2				
2019	DE	HI-A	21	2	2	0	6	6	37²	28	1	1.4	6.7	28	54.3%	.262	0.90	1.19	71	0.7				
2019	FRI	AA	21	7	9	0	18	16	93¹	95	15	1.9	7.1	74	50.9%	.292	1.23	4.72	108	-0.4				
2021 FS	TEX	MLB	23	2	3	0	57	0	50	49	7	2.6	6.9	38	46.3%	.282	1.28	4.24	102	0.1				
2021 DC	TEX	MLB	23	2	3	0	30	6	54	53	8	2.6	6.9	41	46.3%	.282	1.28	4.24	102	0.4				

Comparables: Rony García, Gabriel Ynoa, Joe Ross

The Rangers protected Phillips from the Rule 5 draft heading into 2020, despite the righty struggling in his first taste of advanced competition at Double-A. His pitch mix says starter, and his stats say he has good control, but his command within the zone might not be able to protect him from a role in middle relief.

Joely Rodríguez LHP Born: 11/14/91   Age: 29   Bats: L   Throws: L   Height: 6'1"   Weight: 200   Origin: International Free Agent, 2009

YEAR	TEAM	LVL	AGE	W	L	SV	G	GS	IP	H	HR	BB/9	K/9	K	GB%	BABIP	WHIP	ERA	DRA-	WARP	MPH	FA%	Whiff%	CSP
2018	NOR	AAA	26	5	3	2	33	1	49¹	49	1	3.3	9.5	52	56.2%	.333	1.36	4.56	69	1.0				
2020	TEX	MLB	28	0	0	0	12	0	12²	8	0	3.6	12.1	17	50.0%	.276	1.03	2.13	74	0.3	96.4	67.2%	26.3%	47.1%
2021 FS	TEX	MLB	29	3	3	0	57	0	50	44	5	4.3	10.2	56	51.5%	.298	1.36	4.05	92	0.3	96.4	67.2%	26.3%	47.1%
2021 DC	TEX	MLB	29	3	3	0	59	0	63	55	7	4.3	10.2	71	51.5%	.298	1.36	4.05	92	0.6	96.4	67.2%	26.3%	47.1%

Comparables: Kyle Ryan, Luke Jackson, Mike Mayers

It took a two-year excursion to Japan (and a shiny new changeup) to revitalize Rodríguez, who transformed from afterthought to legit lefty arm out of the pen in 2020. It was one of the biggest reclamation projects in Tokyo since the unveiling of Tokyo Waterfront City way back in, uh, also 2020. It was a long year.

Cole Winn RHP Born: 11/25/99   Age: 21   Bats: R   Throws: R   Height: 6'2"   Weight: 190   Origin: Round 1, 2018 Draft (#15 overall)

YEAR	TEAM	LVL	AGE	W	L	SV	G	GS	IP	H	HR	BB/9	K/9	K	GB%	BABIP	WHIP	ERA	DRA-	WARP	MPH	FA%	Whiff%	CSP
2019	HIC	LO-A	19	4	4	0	18	18	68²	59	5	5.1	8.5	65	46.6%	.292	1.43	4.46	112	-0.2				
2021 FS	TEX	MLB	21	2	3	0	57	0	50	49	8	6.8	7.6	42	41.9%	.285	1.74	6.03	135	-0.8				

Comparables: Max Fried, Tyler Chatwood, Luke Jackson

It must be strange dominating as a prep arm, chucking mid-90s heat with excellent command, being selected in the first round of the MLB Draft and not even be the most successful right-handed pitcher from your own high school. Such is the case for Winn, who donned the same red, gold, and white of the Lutheran Lancers in Orange County as Gerrit Cole. He did show improvement over the course of his first season as a pro, posting a 2.56 ERA while nearly striking out a batter per inning in his last seven starts of 2019. Of course, it's difficult to gauge how any young hurler will handle a season spent in noncompetitive action at his team's alternate site, but less wear and tear on a young arm is probably not a bad thing, and if the extra development and coaching could help Winn trim a few free passes from his walk rate, he could remain on track to fulfill his destiny as a mid-to-backend starter in Arlington sometime soon.

Baseball Privilege in the Year of Our Dying 2020

by Steven Goldman

It was a shattering year, but baseball fans were granted a small but significant escape from the pervasiveness of death by the back of the baseball card. Unlike the scores of human beings lost to zoonosis and infection (unfortunate but natural processes), arrogance and neglect (matters of choice, not inevitability) as well as our inherent transience, our memories of the baseball dead are immutable, set in permanent type. We will no longer have Tom Seaver, but we will have the notion of 311 wins. We will not have Al Kaline, but we will have an impression of 3,007 hits. These numbers lack the corporeality of the people they belonged to, but they have an emotional solidity in the mind. This is our privilege, though only a flimsy and dangerously misleading one.

When the former Emma Gifford, estranged wife of the English novelist and poet Thomas Hardy, died in 1912, he found himself dwelling not on their long years of co-antagonism, but the romantic early days of their relationship. Hindsight and years of hatred could do nothing to erode the reality of the days when they were young and in love, a period forever frozen and inaccessible. Despite knowing the pain that would come of their courtship, Hardy very much wanted to experience that version of his wife again:

> Woman much missed, how you call to me, call to me,
> Saying that now you are not as you were
> When you had changed from the one who was all to me,
> But as at first, when our day was fair.
>
> Can it be you that I hear? Let me view you, then,
> Standing as when I drew near to the town
> Where you would wait for me: yes, as I knew you then,
> Even to the original air-blue gown!

—from "The Voice," Thomas Hardy, 1912

Hardy gave up hopes of literally revisiting the past, accepting that Emma was "ever consigned to existlessness," the fate of all living things in this universe. The facts are simple: Eternal matter takes momentary shape in the form of a tree, a dog, a poet, Babe Ruth, tells itself a story of its own permanent consciousness, and then is slowly robbed of that illusion by time, blight, the axe, the combination of an unmindful driver and a slipped leash, senescence, heart disease, cancer, COVID-19. The matter gives itself back to the universe and reemerges in some other form. So it goes with the 365,000 American victims of COVID-19 and the 1.9 million dead worldwide. The world, which we believe to be solid, is always falling away from us. Yet, a Glenn Beckert (1940-2020) or Bill Pocoroba (1953-2020) card or Baseball Prospectus player-page partially fulfills Hardy's wish: Bring up Lou Brock's (1939-2020) statistics and it is always October 4, 1964, when was 25 and had just finished pulling St. Louis to a pennant with a .348 average and 33 stolen bases. He is, for us, "as at first, when our day was fair."

Baseball statistics like Brock's or Dick Allen's (1942-2020) tell more of a story than they at first appear to; the pandemic statistics, reflecting our half-hearted attempts at mitigation, say less with the powerful exception that they reveal our true disregard for human life. The former particularizes its subjects and the latter erases them. Unlike our beloved ballplayers, the fate of the vast majority of the 1.9 million will be universal oblivion, just like the mostly anonymous victims of all our other holocausts, accidental and intentional. This too is part of the inevitability of existlessness, which extends not only to our physical forms, but the very memory of our existence, fight it though we may.

This headstone passes the lonely decades in the woods of Louisiana:

Courtesy Sarah Goldman

WILLIAM SHARP.
BORN. OCT. 1796
DIED. OCT. 1882.
THIS IS OLD GRAN.
FATHER SHARP. HO
GIVE THIS CEMETA
RY TO HIS GRAN.CHI
LDREN. FOR.BURRYING
GROUND. MAY.HE.
REST. IN.
GLORY. REMEMB
ER.
ME. *(sic)*

The plaintive cry of "Remember me" echoes down the years but the painful irony is that the sound has been severed from the person who issued it. Baseball is different. Tony Fernandez (1962-2020) and Johnny Antonelli (1930-2020) are exempted. Whitey Ford (1928-2020) and Mike McCormick (1938-2020) need not have shouted into the void to ward off their erasure. The candles for Bob Watson (1946-2020), Claudell Washington (1954-2020) and Jim Wynn (1942-2020) will remain lit. Horace Clarke (1939-2020) and Damaso Garcia (1957-2020) will cling to the fringes of consciousness without quite tumbling over the edge. Tom Seaver (1944-2020), Jay Johnstone (1945-2020) and Steve Dalkowski (1939-2020), each of whose passing was due at least in part to the illimitable dominion of the coronavirus, will not be subsumed among the millions of corpses, lost amidst funerals indefinitely postponed until a safer time—at least for a while. We have their statistics and baseball cards, films and videos, autographs on old baseballs, and we will venerate these relics of the horsehide saints until they too go to dust.

In the midst of death we are changed; as Drew Gilpin Faust wrote in *The Republic of Suffering: Death and the American Civil War*, her book about the nation's reaction to the deaths of something like three-quarters of a million or more Americans from 1860-1865 (many more killed by communicable diseases burning through the closely-packed cantonments than by bullets), "Human beings are rarely simply passive victims of death ... If they are survivors, they must assume new identities established by their persistence in face of others' annihilation." Sometimes those new identities result in great activity: People in mourning have often been galvanized into heroic acts of memory like building statues or organizing cemeteries. A paltry few dedicate themselves to averting repetitions of the tragedy, while others don black and never take it off again, withdrawing into their sadness.

We in baseball are with the memorializers. We dedicate plaques to raise the dead and deny the mortality of individual people; by extension we can overlook the transience of entire peoples, civilizations, and species. It's a pleasant illusion that requires constant reaffirmation, for out of the corners of our eyes we can always see the skeleton of an aurochs wandering amidst the fallen ziggurats of Babylon.

We'll each be disillusioned in the end. For now, though, we're granted a mitigation of grief that does not apply to those who actually knew and loved Bob Gibson (1935-2020) and Joe Morgan (1943-2020) firsthand. Al Kaline (1934-2020) and Tony Taylor's (1935-2020) grandchildren will rend their garments, but we who cherish them more abstractly will get to go on pretending that in some way that matters they're still here and will be here forever.

Silly word, "forever." If we have learned anything this year it's that forever has an unpredictable terminus, a sudden stop without a handrail to grab on to, though a respirator may be offered as we go tumbling off into negation. In 2020, the very notion of human progress suffered a severe rebuke; when extinction comes, far too many of our fellow troglodytes-in-trousers will be found not seeking appropriate remedies but berating their local Starbucks barista because they were asked to put on a mask before being served. No doubt there were also 1940 Londoners who insisted on having their tea made just so before descending into the Underground when the air-raid siren blew, a decision which tacitly prioritized momentary comfort ahead of their short-term survival and the long-term perpetuation of their genetic line. Unfortunately, their present-day equivalents will spread a million or so germs if they blow the foam off of their hard-won cappuccino, thus taking a few of us with them—perhaps including a cherished ballplayer or two. And yet we baseball fans will still have those ballplayers as well, so long as their achievements continue to be regarded.

Achievement too is momentary; there are great plays of the past unperformed, great books unread, and great songs unsung, not to mention great players uncelebrated. As Mel Brooks wrote in his song, "Hope for the Best, Expect the Worst," "You could be Tolstoy or Fannie Hurst." In her day, Fannie Hurst undoubtedly sold many more books than did Tolstoy and had more films adapted from her work, but now it's as if she never existed. The 138-foot high Babe Ruth "bat" that used to stand outside of Gate 4 at old Yankee Stadium will someday be as quaint an artefact as the Serpent Column or Cleopatra's Needle. Few will know the meaning behind 714 or 60 or .847. Human notions that seem permanent run their course and vanish: Gods, systems of government, national pastimes.

In 2020 we continued to deny, through our shifting rebellions against and negotiations with a virus and our meaningless Hall of Fame arguments, that we are one cough or sneeze away from being forgotten ephemera. It is the irony of our avoidance that animates Shelley's "Ozymandias." As his 1818 poem suggests, this is not a new idea, but an old one forever in need of rediscovery, particularly at moments like ours. During the years of the Black Death in Europe, Irish monk John Clyn wrote an up-to-the-minute history of the experience, simultaneously justifying and ending the effort by writing, "So that notable deeds should not perish with time, and be lost from the memory of future generations, I, seeing these many ills, and that the whole world encompassed by evil, waiting among the dead for death to come, have committed to writing what I have truly heard and examined; and so that the writing does not perish with the writer, or the work fail with the workman, I leave parchment for continuing the work, in case anyone should still be alive in the future and any son of Adam can escape this pestilence and continue the work thus begun."

Our still-ongoing pandemic is not what Clyn witnessed and was most likely killed by, a communicable disease so unfathomable by then-current medical understanding that it murdered something like 25 percent of the global population. COVID-19 isn't that because the virus is less aggressive than the plague bacillus, because in the intervening years medical science has given us a greater understanding of viruses and more tools with which to fight them, because most of us live in ways less conducive to the spread of microorganisms overall and lastly because our incomplete efforts at containment have slowed its spread. For that reason, we need not worry that the sons or daughters of Adam won't be around to think from time to time of Don Larsen (1929-2020), Bob Oliver (1943-2020) and Ron Perranoski (1936-2020), at least not in the near term. As a species we were very lucky that COVID-19 is a less efficient killer than it might have been. Simultaneously, over a million individuals, fathers and mothers and Tom Seaver were very unlucky given that it was a highly efficient killer of *them*
.

We cherish Seaver's numbers, but it is only when we cherish *all* the numbers—his 311, the 1.4 million of which he is a part *and* the 7.6 billion remaining—that we'll be worthy of the privilege those numbers grant us. The alternative is too horrifying to accept. Consider a variation on a very old story: The last man on Earth sat alone in a room looking at his baseball cards. No one knocked. ▨

—*Steven Goldman is an author of Baseball Prospectus.*

Take Me Out to the Ballstudio

by Adam Sobsey

The pivotal moment of the 2020 World Series came in Game 5. The series was tied at two games apiece. The Dodgers led by a run going into the bottom of the fourth inning, but the Rays' Manny Margot drew a leadoff walk from Dodgers pitcher Clayton Kershaw, stole second base and advanced to third on an error, all with no outs. That sequence tipped the series' Win Expectancy into Tampa Bay's favor for the first time since Game Three, barely: 51 percent. The highest stakes, the biggest moment, the thinnest margin.

Kershaw got the next two outs without letting the run score from third. Margot, perhaps recognizing the importance of the moment—or perhaps acting on sheer creative instinct—took a walking lead, walked some more and then broke into a shocking straight steal of home. Kershaw, his back to the runner, was alerted by shouts from his first baseman, Max Muncy, and the Dodgers' dugout. Had the game been played at Tampa Bay's Tropicana Field, as it ordinarily would have been, he'd have been facing the Rays' dugout, but safety measures taken under the COVID-19 pandemic moved the entire 2020 postseason to neutral sites; in Arlington's Globe Life Field the visitors—that night, nominally, the Dodgers—occupied the first-base side.

Kershaw stepped off the rubber and snapped a throw home to nab Margot by a fraction of an inch. Inning over. In the top of the next inning, Muncy hit a solo homer to add an insurance run, and the Dodgers went on to win the game. They won the next one as well, and with it their first championship since the year Clayton Kershaw was born.

Three nights later, Kershaw appeared, via the safety of a video screen, on the talk show *Jimmy Kimmel Live!* The host asked him a hypothetical question: Had the stadium been full of fans instead of only a quarter full (also per MLB's COVID-19 protocols), when Margot broke for home, would Kershaw have heard Muncy yelling?

Kershaw said: "I don't know, probably not!"

The whole 2020 season raised hypothetical questions like Kimmel's. If the pandemic hadn't shortened the season from 162 games to 60, how much would have been different? For example, how much less tired or less injured (or more injured) would players on postseason rosters have been? During the truncated regular season, what was the effect of players contracting the coronavirus and missing some games (or, in a few cases, avoiding contracting coronavirus by sitting out the entire season and missing all the games)?

What about the related postponements when players tested positive? Also postponements due to western wildfires and political protests? How did the year's enormous upheavals off the field affect players' moods, and thus their performances on it?

If MLB hadn't responded to the pandemic by canceling the minor-league season altogether, which prospects might have played their way into the major leagues during the regular season—and perhaps made playoff rosters as well? (And what about three minor leaguers who made their major-league debuts during the playoffs, more than in the entire history of MLB combined)? How did the expanded, 16-team postseason, a compensation for the shortened regular season, alter the outcome of the tournament? What about playing it at neutral sites, where no more than 11,500 fans were allowed in the stands? And the larger, unspoken, hypothetical questions arcing over all these others: How much was the 2020 season like real baseball? Should its results and statistics come with an asterisk—or even count? Would it have been better off not played at all?

A month and a day before Game 5, Sam Miller published an ESPN article, "How empty ballparks would have changed MLB history—and could alter games this October." One of the examples he cited was in Game 1 of the 1983 World Series. A lengthy fan-related game delay caused Baltimore Orioles starter Scott McGregor to lose his focus and give up a tie-breaking home run to Philadelphia's Garry Maddox in the top of the eighth inning, instantly turning a 50-50 Win Expectancy tossup into a 75-25 advantage for the Phillies, who went on to win the game. The delay, Miller noted, was caused by an unscheduled live television interview with a fan who was leaving the game early, President Ronald Reagan.

After the Orioles lost, McGregor complained to reporters, "There is a certain flow to the game."

⚾   ⚾   ⚾

One of the more eccentric and obscure titles in the baseball library is an illustrated novel for young-adult readers, written in 1978, called *Noonan: A Novel About Baseball, ESP, and Time Warps*. Perhaps the reason for its lack of impact in its own time is that it was published before its time had come, which is appropriate to the time-warp story Noonan tells. Its events open in the year 1896, when the title character, Johnny Noonan, an up-and-coming young phenom pitcher—only 15 years old—is hit in the head by a foul liner and knocked out cold. When he wakes up, it's 100 years later, 1996, and Johnny finds that he has an extraordinary new superpower: He is psychokinetic. He can will an object to move just by thinking at it. Quite a tool for a pitcher to have. It will make him unhittable, literally.

In real life, 1996 was the year when, in the eighth inning of Game 1 of the American League Championship Series, Baltimore outfielder Tony Tarasco was interfered with on an attempted catch at Yankee Stadium's right-field wall by teenage Yankees fan Jeffrey Maier. The umpire later admitted that he misjudged the play when he called it a home run instead of an out, tying the game and tilting the odds sharply in favor of the Yankees, who went on not only to beat Baltimore but also to win the World Series: a legendary postseason incident that wouldn't have occurred if there'd been no fans (or no fallible human umpires) in attendance.

Nor could *Noonan's* author and illustrator, Leonard Everett Fisher, have known about another Baltimore Orioles game, in 2015, that was played in Camden Yards with no fans in attendance, also for safety reasons, although very different ones. Protests, riots and looting had broken out around Baltimore after Freddie Gray, a Black American, died in the custody of police officers who were later charged with homicide (none were convicted). Fisher's novel was not inspired by real examples of games played before empty stands because in 1978 there had never been any. He knew about fan-less baseball only because he imagined it. He imagined quite a lot about baseball, and Johnny's psychokinesis is only a small part of it. It isn't even the most imaginative.

Johnny wakes up in 1996 to an America deep in a crisis, which has arisen from a previous crisis 13 years earlier: The world ran out of oil. "Within one searing week, civilization […] stopped working." The week was in October of 1983, the year and month Scott McGregor complained, in real life, "There is a certain flow to the game."

The end of oil unites the nations of the world in the harnessing of nuclear power, but by 1996, this "oil-less world, sweet and reliable, bright with eternal promise […] had become a humming bore," Fisher laments. Machines run everything and "people no longer had a clear idea what they were supposed to be or do." As a consequence, Americans have succumbed to "a numbing, sleep-inducing effect that exhausted the country's great creative instincts." The triumph of efficiency is the death of creativity.

And the national pastime has become "the tedious symbol of the new malaise." Idle managers send electronic messages from the dugout to players outfitted with "a microscopic transistor receiver." Umpires have been replaced with "scanning devices […] that determined the outcome of every play." A "status panel" tracks and records all data and statistics. During telecasts, a 10-second ad is shown after every single pitch.

And everyone has to watch it. In *Noonan's* 1996, baseball can only be seen on television. No fans are allowed to attend ballgames anymore. There isn't even anywhere for them to sit. Ballparks have been "stripped of their seats, walled in, and roofed over," and converted into "ballstudios" resembling soundstages set up for TV production crews. Left out of the picture in every part of the new dispensation, by 1996 Americans "were beginning to lose interest in the national pastime."

Until Johnny Noonan comes along. Signed in secret by the New York Mets, he makes his big-league debut in the World Series and throws a perfect game—an immaculate game, in fact: 81 pitches, 27 strikeouts. In the clincher a few days later, he throws another one. The country is electrified, and electrified again by a one-off Old-timers' game in which Pete Rose (manager of the Yankees in *Noonan's* 1996) slams one of Nolan Ryan's soft-toss pitches into an electronic scanner, setting it on fire and igniting a brawl.

"The fans liked what they saw," Fisher writes: "real umps, rhubarbs, excitement—humanity." After Johnny Noonan wins the World Series for the Mets, the franchise announces plans to demolish its ballstudio and build an old-fashioned, 90,000-seat ballpark in Brooklyn. The conflict is over, and the soul of the game—and, possibly, the country—is saved.

But not for long.

During the offseason, rumors circulate that Johnny is a hoax. (His psychokinesis could have been a TV studio trick, after all.) The World Series loser—the Cubs, of course—demands a replay without Johnny on the Mets' roster. Players around the league threaten to strike if he is permitted to keep pitching the following year. Meanwhile, Russia tries to find its own psychokinetic wunderkind, incited to keep up in an unexpected new arms race. The peaceful new world order achieved after the end of oil is suddenly in jeopardy.

Far from solving baseball's problem, Johnny is actually its apotheosis: the inhuman game taken to its logical and efficient extreme by a player with robotic ability. The outcome of his every pitch is presumed, and there aren't even interfering fans present to heckle him into a mental lapse, which would be the only way he could ever fail. Just as one global crisis has led, after a brief concord, to another via the perils of perfection and the evils of efficiency, so Johnny, the embodiment of that same pattern, has plunged baseball into a new crisis of its own—which threatens to embroil the whole world. Johnny isn't baseball's savior; he's the next launch angle epidemic. Whatever our malaise, baseball is always the symbol. In *Noonan*, at least, the symbol can feed back on the malaise.

⚾   ⚾   ⚾

After the 2020 season, baseball discourse grew thick with questions and worry over "aesthetics." Fans have long complained about it—reactionary calls for a return to "small-ball" and jeers at the "three true outcomes"—but now some of the very parties who had led the sport's progress toward greater efficiency were casting doubt on the consequences of that efficiency. Sabermetricians, including some employed by Baseball Prospectus, fretted over baseball's watchability and even defended the dying art of bunting. Departing Chicago Cubs' president Theo Epstein, on his way out the door, took a parting shot—at himself and his cohort: He blamed "executives like me, who have spent a lot of time using analytics to try to optimize individual and team performance," for "unwittingly [having] a negative impact on the aesthetic value of the game."

Even broadcasters, whose job it is to narrate, color and animate the events on the field—especially in a year of no fans, who depended more than ever on our representative media witnesses—participated in the critique. During the World Series, ESPN's Jess Mendoza, waiting out another of the countless pitching changes that have helped sabotage Scott McGregor's "certain flow to the game," acknowledged the intelligence behind bringing in another reliever but confessed: "It's still hard to watch."

Mendoza was calling the World Series on the radio. Baseball is alive there. You don't have to watch the pitching changes. You can mute out the humming bore of ads during those changes, go and pour yourself a drink or take the laundry out of the dryer and fold it while you listen. These diversions don't distract you. They become part of your experience of the game. It's fan interference in the best sense, increasing the action and enlarging the field where it takes place, which isn't in any ballstudio—where, in the 2020 regular season, there were no fans present except cardboard cutouts sitting in for fans. On the radio, the game is played in your mind. And that is, ultimately, where every game takes place. Even when watched, baseball is the most notional, the most cerebral of sports. A hypothetical question accompanies each pitch toward the plate, and it doesn't require Johnny Noonan to make it veer, plunge, turn somersaults, or stop in midair.

Baseball is the national pastime because America is a hypothetical question, too. A nation on paper. In 2020, both baseball executives and national executives chose profit over people. They would seem to prefer, if it were possible, to do business with few producers and passive consumers, with streamlined farm systems or none at all, and with fans kept far from the field. Most do not have Theo Epstein's self-awareness and sense of responsibility, and if we let them, they will keep increasing our distance from their machinery, subjecting us to their terms for what it produces and how we experience it, until we can no longer ask for what we want from it, or even interfere with it at all. The virus itself was far less important than what we did and didn't do in response to it. The games postponed by the league meant less than the ones the players refused to play and the ones we refused to watch. The fraction of a major-league season that was salvaged meant less than the minor-league season that was canceled. Efficiency is a crisis. Aesthetics are a walking lead away from it. It doesn't matter that Manny Margot was thrown out at the plate. It doesn't matter if he knew that when he broke for home, it was more than an effort to steal a run and tie a game. It was an act of imagination and protest. ■

—*Adam Sobsey is the lead author of Bull City Summer.*

NIPPON PROFESSIONAL BASEBALL

Essay by Kaz Yamazaki

Player comments by Kaz Yamazaki and BP staff

Heading into the 2020 season, PECOTA projected Adam Jones to hit .251/.297/.408 and to strike out in 19.5 percent of his plate appearances against big-league pitching. By the time that forecast was published last spring, it appeared to serve no purpose. Jones, a five-time All-Star, had long since signed with the Orix Buffaloes of Nippon Professional Baseball, Japan's top league. One look at Jones's actual performance with the Buffaloes—he batted .258/.331/.417 and he punched out in 19.5 percent of his plate appearances—and it's clear that PECOTA's forecast served a purpose after all, just not the one American fans would've expected.

Countless hours observing baseball on both sides of the Pacific Ocean will lead one to the conclusion that the better half of regulars in NPB are capable of holding a role on a major-league team. If the relationship between MLB and NPB resembled that of MLB and the minor leagues in the early parts of the 20th century, meaning that any big-league club could purchase a player from Japan at their will, there would be no fewer than 150 players from the Far East inhabiting the majors and upper minors.

Jones may be just a single data point, but PECOTA offers additional evidence that the gap between the majors and NPB has shrunk. Below is a list of hitters who were new to NPB in 2020 who had at least a year of MLB service time. Accompanying them is their 50th percentile PECOTA projections (excluding Jerry Sands, who spent the previous two seasons in the KBO):

Player	AVG	OBP	SLG	K%	BB%
Adam Jones	.251	.297	.408	19.5	4.8
Justin Bour	.245	.335	.483	27.1	11.6
Gerardo Parra	.244	.293	.385	19.5	5.6
Alcides Escobar	.239	.280	.351	17.1	4.4
Jose Pirela	.252	.301	.431	24.3	6.0
Tyler Austin	.216	.295	.430	35.9	9.6
Cory Spangenberg	.242	.298	.380	32.3	6.8

And here are the actual numbers they put up in their first go-around in the Far East:

Player	AVG	OBP	SLG	K%	BB%
Adam Jones	.258	.331	.417	19.5	9.5
Justin Bour	.243	.338	.422	23.2	11.9
Gerardo Parra	.267	.305	.384	22.7	5.2
Alcides Escobar	.273	.312	.329	12.9	3.2
Jose Pirela	.266	.312	.411	15.7	5.6
Tyler Austin	.286	.364	.605	25.7	10.8
Cory Spangenberg	.268	.326	.482	33.7	7.2

Bour was roughly a league-average hitter in his first campaign with Hanshin, although it wasn't enough to meet Tigers fans' exorbitant expectations. Bour's 2020 Central League brethren Parra, Escobar, and Pirela more or less landed within the realm of their respective projected numbers as well (aside from Pirela's strikeout rate). In addition, Escobar ranked dead last in WAR among NPB position players at a whopping -2.4, according to DeltaGraphs. There is little doubt why all four of them were let go by their respective clubs after just one season.

Obviously, this a limited number of cases, and there were players—Austin and Spangenberg—who outperformed what PECOTA had them doing against MLB pitching. And there's some room to factor in the difficulty in facing an entire league of fresh faces, especially one where pitching is done with a very different style. Still, it seems reasonable to conclude that Japan, and specifically the NPB, is no longer a safe haven where MLB castoffs and dimming stars are promised immediate success and rejuvenation.

Matt Clark would know. He had two stints in the NPB and appeared in 16 games in the majors. "Yuki Yanagita and Seiya Suzuki would be (big-league) All-Stars, I think," he said. "Tetsuto Yamada would be interesting to see for sure. The talent level has gone significantly up recently."

In November 2019, the Japan National Team dominated an international tournament, winning eight of their nine games during the Premier 12 en route to their second-consecutive title in the international contest. One of the eight wins came against a Team Mexico featuring Clark, who went hitless in three trips to the plate as Mexico's starting DH. He reported that the Japanese hurlers on the roster—a group that didn't include some of the country's best arms—"could compete day in and day out [in the majors]."

The National Team isn't the only Japanese squad capable of holding their own these days, either. The Fukuoka SoftBank Hawks offered some sense of normality amid the sheer chaos of 2020. They clinched the Pacific League pennant by 14 games over the second-place Chiba Lotte Marines before steamrolling the Yomiuri Giants with a four-game sweep in the Japan Series for a second consecutive year. It was the Hawks' fourth championship in as many years, and their seventh in their last 10 tries. They've authored one of the most dominant runs in professional baseball history, a legitimate dynasty.

"The Hawks could beat some of the bottom major-league teams," said one talent evaluator. The cornerstone of the lineup is Yanagita, the clear-cut best player in the league who seems capable of tearing up even top-end major-league pitching. The supporting cast, most notably shortstop Kenta Imamiya (who lost the better part of 2020 to injury) and backstop Takuya Kai show both, superb glove work and sufficient ability at the plate, making them potential regulars at the game's highest levels.

The Hawks' rotation is led by bonafide ace Kodai Senga, who many believe to have frontline starter potential if and when he departs for the United States. Nao Higashihama has been a Senga's reliable sidekick over the years behind a solid four-pitch mix and command. He could be the ace on half of other NPB pitching staffs, and is capable of holding a rotation

spot in the big leagues. The third spot occupants have varied from year to year, and have included some with MLB service time, including Tsuyoshi Wada and former All-Star Matt Moore. In a sense, Softbank plays major-league quality baseball on both sides of the ball every other night.

For as far as NPB—and Japanese baseball as a whole—has come, there is one difference that must be acknowledged. Senga's major-league caliber stuff notwithstanding, the rest of the aforementioned names lag behind in stuff: Higashihama and Moore averaged just under 92 mph with their fastballs; Wada checked in at a measly 87 mph. In 2020, NPB hurlers as a whole averaged around 90 mph, a couple of ticks slower than their stateside counterparts.

Of course, that doesn't necessarily preclude big-league success—one of the MLB season's enduring highlights was Alec Mills' no hitter, and his arsenal would fit right in as part of an NPB game—and it doesn't mean that they're without means of retiring batters. The results of Jones and his colleagues are pretty good evidence that the softer Japanese pitching isn't inferior, just different. It's a good way to start treating the NPB as a whole.

—Kaz Yamazaki is an author of Baseball Prospectus.

HITTERS

Aoki Norichika 青木 宣親 OF Born: 01/05/82 Age: 39 Bats: L Throws: R Height: 5'9" Weight: 180

YEAR	TEAM	LVL	AGE	PA	R	2B	3B	HR	RBI	BB	K	SB	CS	Whiff%	AVG/OBP/SLG	DRC+	BABIP	BRR	FRAA	WARP
2018	YKL	NPB	36	567	85	37	3	10	67	51	48	3	4		.327/.409/.475					
2019	YKL	NPB	37	565	84	19	2	16	58	61	72	1	2		.297/.385/.442					
2020	YKL	NPB	38	425	64	30	1	18	51	62	51	2	1		.317/.424/.557					

If Aoki were a fictional player in a baseball manga, 2020 would be the grand finale; a veteran, after a lengthy tenure in the big leagues, returning to his struggling first professional team and putting up some of the best offensive numbers in the league, including career-highs in OPS and ISO at the age of 38. Well, aside from the part where instead of winning the pennant on the final day, the Swallows finish 25 games back. While the inevitable decline awaits on the horizon, Aoki, who was been an above-average-to-plus regular in each of the last three seasons upon his return to Yakult, seems to have some gas left in the tank and should bridge the gap between now and the next great Swallows team.

Asamura Hideto 浅村 栄斗 2B Born: 11/12/90 Age: 30 Bats: R Throws: R Height: 5'11" Weight: 172

YEAR	TEAM	LVL	AGE	PA	R	2B	3B	HR	RBI	BB	K	SB	CS	Whiff%	AVG/OBP/SLG	DRC+	BABIP	BRR	FRAA	WARP
2018	SEI	NPB	27	640	104	27	0	32	127	68	105	4	2		.310/.383/.527					
2019	RAK	NPB	28	635	93	26	2	33	92	93	162	1	1		.263/.372/.507					
2020	RAK	NPB	29	529	72	25	0	32	104	91	111	1	1		.280/.408/.560					

In his second year as a Golden Eagle, Asamura flirted with career highs in walks and long balls, leading the entire NPB in the latter. His new heights in patience led to the highest walk rate of his career, his OBP exceeding .400 for the first time in a full season. Asamura, who turned 30 at the end of the regular season, has established himself as one of the most prominent, bonafide superstars of this generation and perhaps the best player coming out of Osaka Toin HS, one of the powerhouse schools in the amateur scene, in the last 20 years.

Tyler Austin 1B Born: 09/06/91 Age: 29 Bats: R Throws: R Height: 6'2" Weight: 220 Origin: Round 13, 2010 Draft (#415 overall)

YEAR	TEAM	LVL	AGE	PA	R	2B	3B	HR	RBI	BB	K	SB	CS	Whiff%	AVG/OBP/SLG	DRC+	BABIP	BRR	FRAA	WARP
2018	ROC	AAA	26	40	6	2	1	3	8	1	10	0	0		.263/.300/.605	118	.280	-0.1	1B(7): -0.5	0.0
2018	SWB	AAA	26	108	14	9	0	6	14	8	32	0	0		.253/.315/.525	111	.311	0.0	1B(17): -0.6, RF(2): -0.5, LF(1): 0.1	0.0
2018	MIN	MLB	26	136	18	4	0	9	24	11	42	0	1	37.4%	.236/.294/.488	100	.270	-0.3	1B(15): 0.1	0.2
2018	NYY	MLB	26	132	16	6	0	8	23	8	53	1	1	40.1%	.223/.280/.471	95	.311	-0.1	1B(27): -1.3	0.0
2019	SA	AAA	27	63	15	3	0	4	10	8	17	3	1		.333/.413/.611	129	.412	0.1	1B(13): 0.5, LF(1): -0.0	0.3
2019	MIN	MLB	27	5	1	1	0	0	0	1	3	0	0	55.6%	.250/.400/.500	83	1.000		1B(2): -0.1	0.0
2019	SF	MLB	27	147	24	2	1	8	20	17	57	1	0	39.6%	.185/.279/.400	81	.246	1.4	LF(22): 2.0, 1B(12): -0.5, RF(3): -0.0	0.3
2019	MIL	MLB	27	27	5	2	0	1	4	6	7	1	0	35.6%	.200/.370/.450	111	.231	0.4	1B(9): -0.1	0.1

Comparables: Joe Koshansky, Mitch Jones, Christian Walker

In his second bayside franchise and country in as many years, the former Yankees prospect clobbered the second-most dingers on the team, despite missing nearly half the season. He did even better on a rate basis, as he led all NPB hitters with at least 200 plate appearances in ISO and was in the 75th percentile in OBP. However, this likely overperformance of his true talent in an abbreviated campaign means he is doomed to fail to meet the unreasonably high expectations from the fans and media alike. He may want to have a talk with another former Yankee acquainted with the perils of the small sample, Kevin Maas.

Wladimir Balentien LF Born: 07/02/84   Age: 37   Bats: R   Throws: R   Height: 6'2"   Weight: 220

YEAR	TEAM	LVL	AGE	PA	R	2B	3B	HR	RBI	BB	K	SB	CS	Whiff%	AVG/OBP/SLG	DRC+	BABIP	BRR	FRAA	WARP
2018	YKL	NPB	33	602	72	22	0	38	131	85	121	1	1		.268/.370/.533					
2019	YKL	NPB	34	468	65	13	0	33	93	54	117	0	1		.280/.363/.554					
2020	FKU	NPB	35	218	16	7	0	9	22	25	59	0	1		.167/.261/.346					

Presumably, more than a fair share of scouting reports on Balentien from the early-to-mid 2000s mentioned his enormous raw power. The particularly prescient among them even insisted he would go on to have a lengthy career in Asia if things didn't click for him stateside. It's hard to imagine, however, anyone envisioning him unleashing 60 dingers to break Sadaharu Oh's sacred single-season NPB home run record in 2013, which happened a year after having his own AZL seasonal home run record broken. As of the end of the 2020 campaign, the Curaçao naitive ranks 43rd on the NPB all-time leaderboard with 297 long balls, despite playing roughly half the games of his closest peers. He has been in Japan for so long that in one sense, he has become Japanese; he can be on the roster without occupying one of his team's foreign player spots. On the flip side of the coin, time has crept up on him. It's been quite a run, but there's a good chance Balentien won't play beyond 2021 after his current two-year contract expires.

Kevin Cron 1B Born: 02/17/93   Age: 28   Bats: R   Throws: R   Height: 6'5"   Weight: 255   Origin: Round 14, 2014 Draft (#420 overall)

YEAR	TEAM	LVL	AGE	PA	R	2B	3B	HR	RBI	BB	K	SB	CS	Whiff%	AVG/OBP/SLG	DRC+	BABIP	BRR	FRAA	WARP
2018	RNO	AAA	25	438	57	28	1	22	97	36	100	1	0		.309/.368/.554	125	.359	0.0	3B(57): -3.7, 1B(46): 6.6	2.2
2019	RNO	AAA	26	377	81	20	1	38	105	61	77	1	2		.331/.449/.777	178	.328	-2.3	1B(69): 8.2, 3B(15): -0.3	4.5
2019	ARI	MLB	26	78	12	4	0	6	16	4	28	0	1	42.0%	.211/.269/.521	83	.237	-0.1	1B(12): -0.4, 3B(1): -0.0	0.0
2020	ARI	MLB	27	20	0	0	0	0	0	1	7	0	0	38.1%	.000/.150/.000	75	.000		1B(1): -0.0	0.0

Comparables: Josh Whitesell, Tyler Moore, Mark Hamilton

While it may come as a surprise, there's a budding market for collectible VHS tapes. No kidding—those clunky tapes we all watched, complete with their poor sound quality and worse picture, have some market value these days. Nostalgia can get the best of us sometimes, and that's where Cron comes in. His big self has a big swing that can lead to big power when he squares up the baseball, but that doesn't happen very often. Cron is not a dynamic player and even with the DH in the National League this season he would look out of position. He would have been your prototypical masher a decade or two ago. But these days? Well, he's an outdated archetype in an evolved game that frankly requires more refinement than Cron has ever shown. He's about to find out if VHS tapes work any better in the NPB.

Genda Sosuke 源田 壮亮 IF Born: 02/16/93   Age: 28   Bats: L   Throws: R   Height: 5'9"   Weight: 160

YEAR	TEAM	LVL	AGE	PA	R	2B	3B	HR	RBI	BB	K	SB	CS	Whiff%	AVG/OBP/SLG	DRC+	BABIP	BRR	FRAA	WARP
2018	SEI	NPB	25	666	92	27	9	4	57	48	101	34	8		.278/.333/.374					
2019	SEI	NPB	26	609	90	23	6	2	41	40	67	30	9		.274/.324/.350					
2020	SEI	NPB	27	518	67	14	5	1	21	38	80	18	8		.270/.327/.330					

Even though he's never eclipsed even average production with the bat, Genda has established himself as a human highlight reel with his slick glove at the six. As for the only flaw in his game—a severe lack of in-game power—well, to borrow some advice from his wife Misa Etō, a former member of the idol group Nogizaka46, "Happy! Happy! Everybody be happy!" The Lions seem perfectly happy with Genda, as they have penciled him into the starting lineup in every game since they drafted him in the third round of the 2016 draft, aside from a nine-game stretch in April 2019 in which he suffered a bruised wrist after he was plunked by a pitch.

Adam Jones RF Born: 08/01/85   Age: 35   Bats: R   Throws: R   Height: 6'2"   Weight: 215   Origin: Round 1, 2003 Draft (#37 overall)

YEAR	TEAM	LVL	AGE	PA	R	2B	3B	HR	RBI	BB	K	SB	CS	Whiff%	AVG/OBP/SLG	DRC+	BABIP	BRR	FRAA	WARP
2018	BAL	MLB	32	613	54	35	0	15	63	24	93	7	1	24.0%	.281/.313/.419	99	.311	1.0	CF(106): -11.8, RF(33): 2.0, LF(2): 0.1	1.0
2019	ARI	MLB	33	528	66	25	1	16	67	31	101	2	1	27.0%	.260/.313/.414	90	.296	1.0	RF(130): -6.2, CF(1): -0.0	0.1
2020	ORX	NPB	34	338	29	12	0	12	43	32	66	1	0		.258/.331/.417					

Comparables: Torii Hunter, Dave Henderson, Roberto Kelly

Jones's first foray in the NPB might have seemed disappointing to Buffaloes fans who expected more from the five-time MLB All-Star. In the meantime, he was dealing with everything, from a new country and culture to a language barrier and, most notably, an unusual schedule. While nagging minor injuries forced him to miss 37 games, he did show flashes of his talent when in the lineup, launching moonshots to the fifth deck at Osaka Dome in addition to notching the 2,000th base hit of his career between MLB and NPB on September 10. Considering his age, he might just be a league-average hitter in the NPB at this point, which would still be a major upgrade over what Orix could otherwise offer in 2021. That may be a bit of a letdown for those nostalgic for the days of yore, when stars like Reggie Smith and Bob Horner cast their limelight on the league, but it's pretty easily one of the lesser letdowns of the year.

Kai Takuya 甲斐 拓也 C Born: 11/05/92   Age: 28   Bats: R   Throws: R   Height: 5'5"   Weight: 176

YEAR	TEAM	LVL	AGE	PA	R	2B	3B	HR	RBI	BB	K	SB	CS	Whiff%	AVG/OBP/SLG	DRC+	BABIP	BRR	FRAA	WARP
2018	FKU	NPB	25	363	27	13	1	7	37	26	79	2	1		.213/.274/.328					
2019	FKU	NPB	26	454	42	15	0	11	43	50	114	9	4		.260/.346/.387					
2020	FKU	NPB	27	360	44	15	0	11	33	43	80	4	4		.211/.317/.377					

Disappointingly, the Hawks have yet to bestow the nickname "Cobra" upon their starting catcher. Instead, he's widely known as "Kai Cannon"—a nickname derived from his top-shelf arm, which he used to gun down six would-be base thieves in the 2018 Japan Series against Hiroshima en route to the Series MVP honor, despite going 2-for-14. Obviously, the arm is his calling card, but it's not the only tool in the shed, a la Morty Smith in a post-apocalypse dimension fighting tournament. Kai has been roughly a league-average hitter over the last two years and has gotten on base at better than a .300 clip, while adding some pop from the ninth spot of the loaded Hawks lineup. Not a bad career so far for the fourth-to-last pick in the 2011 draft.

Kondoh Kensuke 近藤 健介 OF Born: 08/09/93 Age: 27 Bats: L Throws: R Height: 5'8" Weight: 190

YEAR	TEAM	LVL	AGE	PA	R	2B	3B	HR	RBI	BB	K	SB	CS	Whiff%	AVG/OBP/SLG	DRC+	BABIP	BRR	FRAA	WARP
2018	NHF	NPB	24	555	59	29	3	9	69	87	90	5	0		.323/.427/.457					
2019	NHF	NPB	25	600	74	32	5	2	59	103	81	1	4		.302/.422/.400					
2020	NHF	NPB	26	467	56	31	1	5	60	89	72	4	0		.340/.465/.469					

Batting above .300 and getting on base at a .400 or better clip in five of the last six seasons, including a .413/.567/.557 slash line in his injury-shortened 2017 campaign, Kondoh has established himself as one of the best pure hitters of this generation. Nothing gets by him; he posted the lowest swinging-strike rate of any qualified hitter in 2020, in part because he never swings at anything outside the zone (16.5 percent). Unlike many hitters, however, he doesn't sell out for contact at the expense of power, as more than 40 percent of his balls were hard-hit, easily in the top quadrant of the NPB. His bat-to-ball skills are so good that Netflix might consider creating a variety show called "Squaring Up with Kensuke Kondoh."

Leonys Martin CF Born: 03/06/88 Age: 33 Bats: L Throws: R Height: 6'2" Weight: 200 Origin: International Free Agent, 2011

YEAR	TEAM	LVL	AGE	PA	R	2B	3B	HR	RBI	BB	K	SB	CS	Whiff%	AVG/OBP/SLG	DRC+	BABIP	BRR	FRAA	WARP
2018	CLE	MLB	30	17	3	0	0	2	4	1	2	0	1	36.4%	.333/.353/.733	98	.250	0.4	CF(5): 0.1, RF(1): -0.0	0.1
2018	DET	MLB	30	336	45	15	3	9	29	29	75	7	3	25.3%	.251/.321/.409	100	.305	0.7	CF(74): 18.5	3.2
2019	CHB	NPB	31	228	32	9	0	14	39	26	57	3	3		.232/.342/.495					
2019	CLE	MLB	31	264	32	7	0	9	19	21	78	4	5	33.5%	.199/.276/.343	70	.255	0.7	CF(65): 2.7	0.3
2020	CHB	NPB	32	448	72	15	0	25	65	70	100	7	2		.234/.382/.485					

Comparables: Pete Whisenant, Cameron Maybin, Devon White

In his first full season with Lotte, the cannon-armed Cuban led the team in home runs, runs scored, and ISO. Martín's 25 long balls marked the second-highest total by a Marine in the last 15 years, trailing only Brandon Laird in 2019, and the most by a left-handed Lotte hitter since Seung-Yuop Lee, who hit 30 taters all the way back in 2005. That story tells you two things; a) the Marines have traditionally been power-deprived since they moved across the Tokyo Bay, from Kawasaki to Makuhari, in 1992; and b) Martín has enjoyed a power surge in his 1.5 years in Japan. In fact, Martín ranked fifth on the team in homers in 2019 despite playing his first game with them in late July. He has now walloped two-thirds of his MLB career home run total, and in under a quarter of the plate appearances. It puts him on track to hit the other third by the end of August 2021, having inked an extension that will keep him in Chiba for two more years.

Mogi Eigoro 茂木 栄五郎 SS/3B Born: 02/14/94 Age: 27 Bats: L Throws: R Height: 5'7" Weight: 165

YEAR	TEAM	LVL	AGE	PA	R	2B	3B	HR	RBI	BB	K	SB	CS	Whiff%	AVG/OBP/SLG	DRC+	BABIP	BRR	FRAA	WARP
2018	RAK	NPB	24	413	42	12	2	7	24	42	83	12	4		.247/.328/.349					
2019	RAK	NPB	25	648	86	28	6	13	55	66	121	7	5		.282/.358/.421					
2020	RAK	NPB	26	321	43	14	4	7	33	39	52	8	3		.301/.396/.457					

Even though he missed 47 games with nagging injuries, Mogi showed top-shelf offensive production on a rate basis in his first season as the captain of the Golden Eagles. Health has been the sole blemish of his otherwise flawless career, as minor injuries have sidelined him in four of his five professional campaigns to date. Watching his prowess on the field only makes it easier to miss him when he's gone. He shows controlled aggression at the dish and on the basepaths, often taking demonstrative hacks early in the count, but exhibiting the patience to draw free passes in nearly 10 percent of his career plate appearances. Even taking some missed time into account, Mogi is still a building block of the Rakuten teams contending for the postseason year in and year out.

Mori Tomoya 森 友哉 C Born: 08/08/95 Age: 25 Bats: L Throws: R Height: 5'6" Weight: 176

YEAR	TEAM	LVL	AGE	PA	R	2B	3B	HR	RBI	BB	K	SB	CS	Whiff%	AVG/OBP/SLG	DRC+	BABIP	BRR	FRAA	WARP
2018	SEI	NPB	22	552	67	34	2	16	80	70	105	7	2		.275/.366/.457					
2019	SEI	NPB	23	573	96	34	2	23	105	72	89	3	2		.329/.413/.547					
2020	SEI	NPB	24	405	46	15	2	9	38	38	67	4	2		.251/.325/.380					

It seemed as if everything finally came to fruition for the Lions' 2013 first-round pick, one of the most praised high school backstops in recent memory, as he ran away with the 2019 Pacific League MVP award. However, contrary to Seibu fans' optimism, Mori took a huge step backward with the bat in 2020, recording career lows in all three slash line stats. His OPS was the lowest in any professional stint consisting of more than 10 plate appearances, including a 15-game stint with the Melbourne Aces three winters ago. Still, even with the reduced offensive numbers, thanks to his durability, he was one of the most productive catchers in the NPB. It's hard to detect a sign indicating a significant decline in his true talent level, though, and it looked like he was dealing with timing issues throughout the season. Assuming 2021 resembles a traditional schedule, it's more likely than not that Mori will return to being a top-shelf force at and behind the plate.

Murakami Munetaka 村上 宗隆 1B/3B Born: 02/02/00 Age: 21 Bats: L Throws: R Height: 6'2" Weight: 213

YEAR	TEAM	LVL	AGE	PA	R	2B	3B	HR	RBI	BB	K	SB	CS	Whiff%	AVG/OBP/SLG	DRC+	BABIP	BRR	FRAA	WARP
2019	YKL	NPB	19	593	76	20	0	36	96	74	184	5	4		.231/.332/.481					
2020	YKL	NPB	20	515	70	30	2	28	86	87	115	11	5		.307/.427/.585					

In his second full season, the wunderkind took the Central League by storm as a 20-year-old, a meteoric ascent resembling that of Beth Harmon in the chess scene in the 1960s. Unlike Harmon, Murakami won't be a world champion at the age of 22, as Yakult is likely to hold on to his services into his mid-20s. In 2020, he showed an improved approach at the plate, cutting down on whiffs both inside and outside the strike zone while more than maintaining his walk rate and slugging numbers, en route to being a top-10 hitter in the country. Additionally, he's no sloth on the bases, swiping 11 bases, three of which came during the same trip around the diamond in a November game. A catcher in high school, Murakami is still adapting to both infield corners, but even if his glove fails to improve beyond below-average, the bat can absolutely carry him to stardom.

Nishikawa Haruki 西川 遥輝 OF Born: 04/16/92 Age: 29 Bats: L Throws: R Height: 5'11" Weight: 176

YEAR	TEAM	LVL	AGE	PA	R	2B	3B	HR	RBI	BB	K	SB	CS	Whiff%	AVG/OBP/SLG	DRC+	BABIP	BRR	FRAA	WARP
2018	NHF	NPB	26	636	90	25	6	10	48	96	103	44	3		.278/.391/.405					
2019	NHF	NPB	27	651	88	26	6	5	41	93	111	19	5		.288/.393/.385					
2020	NHF	NPB	28	523	82	17	3	5	39	92	84	42	7		.306/.430/.396					

One of the most efficient base thieves in recent memory, Nishikawa has swiped 287 bags while getting caught just 45 times over the course of his 10-year professional career. The speed—consistently sub-four seconds to first from the left side of the plate—enables him to fit in all three outfield positions, although he may not have the instincts to be a plus major-league defender in center field, which he has manned exclusively for the last three seasons. At the plate, Nishikawa combines an advanced approach with top-notch bat-to-ball skills, as he recorded the lowest chase rate and ranked in the 80th percentile in contact rate among all NPB batsmen (min. 200 PA). The biggest stench in the profile is his power, or lack thereof, but the second-round pick in the 2010 draft is a perfectly adequate fourth outfielder at least, and perhaps even more when he adjusts to major-league game speed.

Okamoto Kazuma 岡本 和真 3B Born: 06/30/96 Age: 25 Bats: R Throws: R Height: 6'0" Weight: 212

YEAR	TEAM	LVL	AGE	PA	R	2B	3B	HR	RBI	BB	K	SB	CS	Whiff%	AVG/OBP/SLG	DRC+	BABIP	BRR	FRAA	WARP
2018	YOM	NPB	22	616	82	26	0	33	100	72	120	2	1		.309/.394/.541					
2019	YOM	NPB	23	628	84	29	0	31	94	62	132	3	0		.265/.343/.485					
2020	YOM	NPB	24	500	79	26	0	31	97	55	85	2	0		.275/.362/.545					

Ever since he secured a starting role, Yomiuri's first-round pick in the 2014 draft has been a consistent presence in their lineup, missing a total of just two games while being one of the most prominent dinger mashers in the country. In 2020, Okamoto led the Central League in home runs and RBIs (hey, triple crown stats are still a huge deal in Japan). It's safe to say the Giants have found their lineup cornerstone of the 2020s in the 24-year-old, as the guy who plays next to him in the infield heads further into his 30s.

José Osuna 3B Born: 12/12/92 Age: 28 Bats: R Throws: R Height: 6'2" Weight: 235 Origin: International Free Agent, 2009

YEAR	TEAM	LVL	AGE	PA	R	2B	3B	HR	RBI	BB	K	SB	CS	Whiff%	AVG/OBP/SLG	DRC+	BABIP	BRR	FRAA	WARP
2018	IND	AAA	25	342	45	26	0	9	59	31	51	5	3		.321/.378/.497	156	.353	1.4	3B(47): 4.6, 1B(24): -0.7, RF(9): 2.7	3.4
2018	PIT	MLB	25	111	14	9	0	3	11	3	22	0	0	24.3%	.226/.252/.396	79	.256	0.8	1B(12): 1.9, 3B(7): -0.2, RF(7): 0.1	0.3
2019	IND	AAA	26	83	13	7	1	2	13	9	22	2	0		.268/.361/.479	113	.354	0.2	RF(12): -2.6, LF(3): -0.2, 1B(1): -0.0	0.1
2019	PIT	MLB	26	285	41	20	0	10	36	18	48	0	0	22.6%	.264/.310/.456	93	.285	-1.1	1B(31): 1.2, RF(23): -0.5, 3B(19): 1.0	0.6
2020	PIT	MLB	28	82	6	3	0	4	11	4	16	0	1	28.1%	.205/.244/.397	93	.207	-0.7	1B(9): -0.3, RF(7): 0.4, 3B(5): 0.3	0.1

Comparables: Lance Niekro, Ken Harvey, Brian R. Hunter

Osuna is your friend who shows up to the barbecue with two bags of ice right when you've run out; he's good in a pinch. He's also your friend who is only good in a pinch—you didn't assign them more than two bags of ice for a reason, and the party would go on without him. Osuna can't tolerate more exposure to quality pitching without his flaws in the field and at the plate becoming readily apparent. He's a reliable guy, but not one you want to rely on too much, unless your team, like his new one, makes its home in Tokyo.

Mel Rojas Jr. CF Born: 05/24/90 Age: 31 Bats: S Throws: R Height: 6'2" Weight: 225 Origin: Round 3, 2010 Draft (#84 overall)

YEAR	TEAM	LVL	AGE	PA	R	2B	3B	HR	RBI	BB	K	SB	CS	Whiff%	AVG/OBP/SLG	DRC+	BABIP	BRR	FRAA	WARP
2018	KT	KBO	28	645	114	30	1	43	114	71	142	18	13		.305/.388/.590					
2019	KT	KBO	29	578	68	30	3	24	104	49	120	4	4		.322/.381/.530					
2020	KT	KBO	30	628	116	39	1	47	135	65	132	0	1		.349/.417/.680					

While all international players in the KBO must constantly decide whether to remain large fish in a small pond, the choice Rojas faced must have felt particularly agonizing. On the one hand, he's done just about all he can do in the KBO. Rojas came within a whisker of the Triple Crown in 2020 and easily won the league's MVP. In Suwon, he's a club legend and the franchise's best ever player. He's 30 now, and as one of the only foreign players in the league without MLB experience, one imagines that he was sorely tempted by the chance to play in the majors. Major league clubs were poking around, and there's no reason to think he couldn't have parlayed his big numbers into a one-year deal and perhaps a seven-figure salary.

At the same time, Rojas's game is not likely to translate all that well. The logical comparison is Eric Thames, and while Thames has enjoyed some success since returning stateside, he also has more raw power and a significantly better eye than Rojas. Perhaps Mel Jr. would be content to be the lite version of Eric Thames and take a job as someone's fourth or fifth outfielder. Then again, maybe not. To watch Rojas last year was to watch a man on top of the world. On the field and in the dugout he radiates joy, and he takes an obvious pride in being KT's talisman. It seems like an awful lot to give up just to become another cog in MLB's machine. And yet he opted for a third path, splitting the difference, signing a two-year, $5 million contract to join the Hanshin Tigers of the NPB.

Sakamoto Hayato 坂本 勇人 2B Born: 12/14/88 Age: 32 Bats: R Throws: R Height: 6'1" Weight: 176

YEAR	TEAM	LVL	AGE	PA	R	2B	3B	HR	RBI	BB	K	SB	CS	Whiff%	AVG/OBP/SLG	DRC+	BABIP	BRR	FRAA	WARP
2018	YOM	NPB	29	502	87	27	2	18	67	61	83	9	5		.345/.424/.537					
2019	YOM	NPB	30	639	103	26	0	40	94	77	123	5	3		.312/.396/.575					
2020	YOM	NPB	31	479	64	28	1	19	65	62	85	4	1		.289/.379/.500					

As was the case for many of us, 2020 was a down year for the captain of the most popular club in the country. However, the number of memorable moments he produced was on par with previous years. On September 9, he posted the first three-homer game in his career. On November 8, two weeks after Yomiuri drafted a second Hayato Sakamoto (this one a high school catcher), the original version notched his 2,000th career hit, becoming the second-youngest NPB player to reach the milestone. At 32, he is likely to be in the gradual decline phase of his career, but his odds of accumulating another 1,000 base knocks—a tier reached only by Isao Harimoto in NPB history—are quite high.

Sano Keita 佐野 恵太 OF Born: 11/28/94 Age: 26 Bats: L Throws: R Height: 5'10" Weight: 185

YEAR	TEAM	LVL	AGE	PA	R	2B	3B	HR	RBI	BB	K	SB	CS	Whiff%	AVG/OBP/SLG	DRC+	BABIP	BRR	FRAA	WARP
2018	YKO	NPB	23	130	6	4	0	5	14	3	26	1	0		.230/.246/.381					
2019	YKO	NPB	24	215	23	10	0	5	33	13	39	0	0		.295/.344/.420					
2020	YKO	NPB	25	415	48	48	1	20	69	42	58	0	0		.328/.395/.532					

The biggest question the Baystars faced coming into the 2020 season was whether they would be capable of filling the Yoshi Tsutsugo-sized hole in the lineup. Sano, Tsutsugo's replacement in both the cleanup spot and team captain role, did more than merely pick up where the current Rays slugger left off. Having accrued just 369 plate appearances in his first three seasons as a pro, the ninth-round pick in the 2016 draft finished in the top 10 among all qualified NPB hitters in OBP and took home the Central League batting crown. While his BABIP seems inflated at first glance, at a lofty .343 (and .346 in 215 trips to the plate in 2019), his elite ability to annihilate baseballs indicates that these marks might be sustainable.

Domingo Santana LF Born: 08/05/92 Age: 28 Bats: R Throws: R Height: 6'5" Weight: 232 Origin: International Free Agent, 2009

YEAR	TEAM	LVL	AGE	PA	R	2B	3B	HR	RBI	BB	K	SB	CS	Whiff%	AVG/OBP/SLG	DRC+	BABIP	BRR	FRAA	WARP
2018	RMV	AAA	25	227	30	10	2	8	35	36	75	2	0		.283/.401/.487	123	.425	-2.6	RF(50): -10.4	-0.5
2018	MIL	MLB	25	235	21	14	1	5	20	20	77	1	1	36.3%	.265/.328/.412	82	.386	-0.2	RF(55): -2.0	-0.2
2019	SEA	MLB	26	507	63	20	1	21	69	50	164	8	3	32.0%	.253/.329/.441	101	.347	0.1	LF(59): -4.2, RF(42): -3.0	0.6
2020	CLE	MLB	28	84	6	3	0	2	12	13	25	0	0	27.6%	.157/.298/.286	80	.209	0.0	RF(16): 0.7, LF(9): 0.3	0.0

Comparables: Jay Buhner, Rob Deer, Jorge Soler

There's always something to cling on to with players like Santana, who need only a single moment to remind us what they're capable of doing. His time to shine came on August 8, when he obliterated a Steve Cishek sinker so thoroughly that it looked as though the ball might clear all of the seats in left-center. The problem with Santana is those awe-inspiring moments are happening less and less frequently. He slumped his way to an August DFA and will try to pick up the pieces with his fourth team in four years, this time the Yakult Swallows.

Shuto Ukyo 周東 佑京 **OF** Born: 02/10/96 Age: 25 Bats: R Throws: R Height: 6'0" Weight: 165

YEAR	TEAM	LVL	AGE	PA	R	2B	3B	HR	RBI	BB	K	SB	CS	Whiff%	AVG/OBP/SLG	DRC+	BABIP	BRR	FRAA	WARP
2019	FKU	NPB	23	114	39	3	2	1	6	2	27	25	5		.196/.212/.294					
2020	FKU	NPB	24	346	48	8	7	1	27	24	79	50	6		.270/.325/.352					

Perhaps there's a tree in rural Japan on which 80-grade speedsters like Shuto grow. At least three players capable of beating 3.9 seconds from home to first man every NPB club's roster. With blazing speed combined with base-running instincts, Shuto topped them all, and led the entire NPB in stolen bases by a fair margin despite not qualifying for the batting title. Fifteen of his 50 stolen bases came in 13 consecutive games in October, topping Yutaka Fukumoto's NPB record and Bert Campaneris' MLB record simultaneously. Defensively he split time mostly between the two middle infield positions (as well as cameo appearances in the outfield and at third base), where he struggled with body control and committed a league-leading 12 errors, but his blazing speed helped him cover tons of ground and made him an above-average fielder overall. While it's unlikely he'll ever hit for over-the-fence power, his skill set should keep him on the top of the loaded Hawks lineup for at least the first half of the decade.

Justin Smoak **1B** Born: 12/05/86 Age: 34 Bats: S Throws: L Height: 6'4" Weight: 220 Origin: Round 1, 2008 Draft (#11 overall)

YEAR	TEAM	LVL	AGE	PA	R	2B	3B	HR	RBI	BB	K	SB	CS	Whiff%	AVG/OBP/SLG	DRC+	BABIP	BRR	FRAA	WARP
2018	TOR	MLB	31	594	67	34	0	25	77	83	155	0	1	25.5%	.242/.350/.457	117	.296	-5.1	1B(134): -7.2	0.8
2019	TOR	MLB	32	500	54	16	0	22	61	79	106	0	0	23.7%	.208/.342/.406	110	.223	-2.0	1B(89): -5.5	0.7
2020	MIL	MLB	34	126	14	7	0	5	15	10	40	0	0	31.3%	.186/.262/.381	78	.232	-1.1	1B(31): -4.0	-0.8
2020	SF	MLB	34	6	0	0	0	0	0	0	2	0	0	33.3%	.000/.000/.000	76	.000			0.0

Comparables: Paul Sorrento, Mark Johnson, John Jaha

By any measure, the top of the first round in the 2008 amateur draft was thick with high-impact college bats: Pedro Alvarez, Gordon Beckham, Yonder Alonso and of course, Buster Posey. Smoak was well in the conversation to be the best of these, and yet for all of his career longevity, the switch-hitter out of South Carolina has eked out a decade-long career that hasn't even tallied four wins—what we'd call a "meh" year for a healthy Posey. It all never really gelled for more than short stretches: the patience was there but the contact wasn't; the power showed but the patience couldn't hold; all the while, offspeed pitches remained the stuff of nightmares. A dismal start to 2020 with the Brewers, and then a perfunctory three-game spell with the Giants before his release, leaves his comment here, for a team you may not even know he'd joined. If this comment sounds elegiac, take heart from the fact that Smoak is not too old to ignite a comeback, if he can convince a team that there's still some glow in the embers. He'll seek to rekindle the flame with a new set of Giants, those of Yomiuri, in 2021.

Suzuki Seiya 鈴木 誠也 **OF** Born: 08/18/94 Age: 26 Bats: R Throws: R Height: 5'11" Weight: 182

YEAR	TEAM	LVL	AGE	PA	R	2B	3B	HR	RBI	BB	K	SB	CS	Whiff%	AVG/OBP/SLG	DRC+	BABIP	BRR	FRAA	WARP
2018	HRO	NPB	23	520	86	32	2	30	94	88	116	4	4		.320/.438/.618					
2019	HRO	NPB	24	612	112	31	0	28	87	103	81	25	16		.335/.453/.565					
2020	HRO	NPB	25	514	85	26	2	25	75	72	73	6	4		.300/.409/.544					

Since he became a full-time regular in 2016 at the age of 21, Suzuki has been a fixture in the Carp lineup. His numbers have been so consistent that we could just copy and paste the comment from this space three years ago. Barring a major injury (frankly, unthinkable) that significantly alters his skill set or free agency timetable, we should expect him to arrive stateside in a couple of years. One of the destinations could be Minnesota, who could send him to their Triple-A affiliate for a rehab assignment, making him a literal Saint Seiya.

Eric Thames **1B** Born: 11/10/86 Age: 34 Bats: L Throws: R Height: 5'11" Weight: 235 Origin: Round 7, 2008 Draft (#219 overall)

YEAR	TEAM	LVL	AGE	PA	R	2B	3B	HR	RBI	BB	K	SB	CS	Whiff%	AVG/OBP/SLG	DRC+	BABIP	BRR	FRAA	WARP
2018	MIL	MLB	31	278	41	10	3	16	37	29	97	7	0	34.0%	.219/.306/.478	96	.284	2.3	RF(31): -0.3, 1B(29): -0.9, LF(10): 0.7	0.6
2019	MIL	MLB	32	459	67	23	2	25	61	51	140	3	2	32.6%	.247/.346/.505	111	.313	1.8	1B(105): -1.4, RF(12): -0.1	1.5
2020	WAS	MLB	34	140	10	5	0	3	12	14	42	1	0	29.2%	.203/.300/.317	80	.282	-0.6	1B(27): 0.1	-0.1

Comparables: Brandon Moss, Dave Kingman, Carlos Pena

The Nationals signed Thames to mash against righties—he had slugged better than .500 against them in 2019—as part of a first-base platoon with Ryan Zimmerman. By the time the season started, Zimmerman had opted out over COVID-related concerns. Thames' bat did the same, leaving the Nationals with a colder-than-usual cold corner. He'll spend 2021 in Tokyo as a member of the Yomiuri Giants, hoping that another tour of Asia can defibrillate his career a second time.

Tonosaki Shuta 外崎 修汰 **IF** Born: 12/20/92 Age: 28 Bats: R Throws: R Height: 5'8" Weight: 171

YEAR	TEAM	LVL	AGE	PA	R	2B	3B	HR	RBI	BB	K	SB	CS	Whiff%	AVG/OBP/SLG	DRC+	BABIP	BRR	FRAA	WARP
2018	SEI	NPB	25	510	70	24	3	18	67	47	101	25	9		.287/.357/.472					
2019	SEI	NPB	26	621	96	27	6	26	90	63	132	22	6		.274/.353/.493					
2020	SEI	NPB	27	500	62	18	2	8	43	54	87	21	7		.247/.335/.353					

With the speed to swipe 20 bases in any given season, above-average pop, the versatility to handle both middle infield positions in addition to some outfield (although he has predominantly played second base since Hideto Asamura's departure from Seibu) and a below-average yet playable contact rate, one could say Tonosaki's skill set is similar to that of Jonathan Villar. While you can't compare apples to oranges (Tonosaki's family runs an apple farm; Villar wore orange with the Orioles), the Lions' keystone defender is capable of being a more-than-adequate MLB utility guy who plays more roles than Tatiana Maslany in Orphan Black if he ever wishes to test himself at the highest level of the game.

Yamada Tetsuto 山田 哲人 **IF** Born: 07/16/92 Age: 28 Bats: R Throws: R Height: 5'10" Weight: 163

YEAR	TEAM	LVL	AGE	PA	R	2B	3B	HR	RBI	BB	K	SB	CS	Whiff%	AVG/OBP/SLG	DRC+	BABIP	BRR	FRAA	WARP
2018	YKL	NPB	25	637	130	30	4	34	89	106	119	33	4		.315/.432/.582					
2019	YKL	NPB	26	641	102	35	5	35	98	110	121	33	3		.271/.401/.560					
2020	YKL	NPB	27	384	52	17	1	12	52	48	83	8	4		.254/.346/.419					

After single-handedly carrying the Swallows on his back for the better part of the 2010s, Yamada's numbers plummeted in the first year of a new decade. He recorded career-worsts in various offensive stats since he became a full-time regular in 2013. Some of his slump can be attributed to the nagging injuries he dealt throughout the season, which forced him to miss 26 games and barely qualify for the batting title. He also seemed to want to hack his way out of his slump, chasing more pitches out of the zone. Yamada, who is still just 28, can be back to his perennial All-Star self should he return to full strength. At least Yakult believes so, signing him to a seven-year extension to keep him in a (occasionally hideous neon green) Swallows uniform through his mid-30s.

Yanagita Yuki 柳田 悠岐 **OF** Born: 10/09/88 Age: 32 Bats: L Throws: R Height: 6'1" Weight: 196

YEAR	TEAM	LVL	AGE	PA	R	2B	3B	HR	RBI	BB	K	SB	CS	Whiff%	AVG/OBP/SLG	DRC+	BABIP	BRR	FRAA	WARP
2018	FKU	NPB	29	550	95	29	5	36	102	62	105	21	7		.352/.431/.661					
2019	FKU	NPB	30	157	17	6	1	7	23	28	28	4	1		.289/.420/.516					
2020	FKU	NPB	31	515	90	23	5	29	86	84	103	7	2		.342/.449/.623					

Not only did Yanagita come back from an injury-plagued 2019, he blew past the rest of the league with his stellar combination of power and on-base ability in 2020, mashing everything en route to his well-deserved second Pacific League MVP award. His exceptional strength enables him to drive the ball over the fence even when the pitcher fools him into an awkward, one-handed swing. When he gets all of it? Pitchers have a tough time not to bring out the Ted Lilly postseason glove smash on the mound. During the month of July, he slashed an astounding .433/.556/.800 in 117 trips to the plate. Limiting to those who exceeded 100 plate appearances, only three major-league hitters in this millennium have surpassed that streak in any month: Todd Helton in May 2000, Barry Bonds in August 2002, and Lance Berkman in May 2008. Unfortunately for fans in North America, the only way for them to watch the best player the NPB is to wake up at wee hours, as Yanagita has six more years left on his current contract, which will likely keep him in Fukuoka for the rest of his career.

Yoshida Masataka 吉田 正尚 **OF** Born: 07/15/93 Age: 27 Bats: L Throws: R Height: 5'8" Weight: 176

YEAR	TEAM	LVL	AGE	PA	R	2B	3B	HR	RBI	BB	K	SB	CS	Whiff%	AVG/OBP/SLG	DRC+	BABIP	BRR	FRAA	WARP
2018	ORX	NPB	24	598	77	37	2	26	86	69	74	3	1		.321/.403/.553					
2019	ORX	NPB	25	610	92	24	2	29	85	79	64	5	1		.322/.413/.543					
2020	ORX	NPB	26	492	55	22	1	14	64	72	29	8	5		.350/.453/.512					

In one sense, Yoshida's 2020 was Bondsian. The last MLB hitter with a single-season K/BB north of two in at least 400 plate appearances was Barry Bonds in 2007, and Yoshida nearly reached 2.5. However, his contact-avoidance came at the expense of power, as his ISO slipped from .226 in the previous two years combined to .162 in 2020, and his AB/HR from 18.8 to 29.1. In that sense, Yoshida's 2020 more resembled Luis Castillo, the only other player in this millenium to notch a single-season BB/K ratio in the twos. Going forward, he needs to get his power back without sacrificing much of his newfound feel for contact, which he is capable of. That is, if he even gets strikes to swing at: The Orix lineup around him is likely to remain too futile to carry on his back for the foreseeable future.

PITCHERS

Raúl Alcántara **RHP** Born: 12/04/92 Age: 28 Bats: R Throws: R Height: 6'4" Weight: 220 Origin: International Free Agent, 2009

YEAR	TEAM	LVL	AGE	W	L	SV	G	GS	IP	H	HR	BB/9	K/9	K	GB%	BABIP	WHIP	ERA	DRA-	WARP	MPH	FA%	Whiff%	CSP
2018	NAS	AAA	25	5	7	5	32	10	83¹	100	10	1.5	5.7	53	38.0%	.319	1.37	5.29	102	0.5				
2019	KT	NPB	26	11	11	0	27	27	172²	189	15	1.0	5.2	100			1.25	4.01						
2020	DOO	NPB	27	20	1	0	31	31	198²	174	12	1.0	8.2	182			1.03	2.54						

Comparables: Jake Faria, Keury Mella, David Paulino

The list of players booted off of a roster to make room for Odrisamer Despaigne is as long as it is undistinguished—at least, it was until the KT Wiz sent Alcantara packing. The right-hander didn't pitch *badly* in 2019, but his performance fell short of the standard expected from foreign signings, and thus Doosan's decision to sign him for 2020 came as a surprise. But Alcantara thoroughly justified the Bears' faith, finishing with 20 wins and a 2.54 ERA across 198 innings, a herculean effort that netted him the Choi Dong-won award for the league's best pitcher. The mystery here isn't that he succeeded, as good control and the best velocity in the league is a pretty reliable formula. No, the real question is what happened in 2019, when all of those attributes produced a mediocre ERA and a 5.2 K/9? We may never know, but whatever the case, it sure seems like Alcantara is a big-league player wearing a KBO jersey.

Robbie Erlin LHP   Born: 10/08/90   Age: 30   Bats: R   Throws: L   Height: 5'11"   Weight: 200   Origin: Round 3, 2009 Draft (#93 overall)

YEAR	TEAM	LVL	AGE	W	L	SV	G	GS	IP	H	HR	BB/9	K/9	K	GB%	BABIP	WHIP	ERA	DRA-	WARP	MPH	FA%	Whiff%	CSP
2018	SD	MLB	27	4	7	0	39	12	109	112	12	1.0	7.3	88	46.3%	.309	1.14	4.21	68	2.6	91.8	59.2%	20.9%	52.1%
2019	ELP	AAA	28	0	1	1	10	0	15¹	26	2	1.2	8.2	14	47.3%	.462	1.83	8.80	119	0.1				
2019	SD	MLB	28	0	1	0	37	1	55¹	72	6	2.4	8.5	52	44.8%	.375	1.57	5.37	106	0.1	91.9	50.7%	23.6%	46.4%
2020	ATL	MLB	29	0	0	0	9	5	26²	33	8	2.4	8.4	25	28.4%	.312	1.50	8.10	156	-0.6	91.1	56.6%	19.3%	48.1%

Comparables: Kevin Gausman, Erasmo Ramírez, Alex Wood

A good sign of how badly the Braves' rotation was torn apart by injuries is that they claimed Robbie Erlin off waivers after he'd been designated for assignment by the *Pirates*. One team's trash didn't turn into another's treasure, as the veteran lefty was lit up over five brutal starts and subsequently let go in mid-September. The Pirates did not retrieve him.

Fujinami Shintaro 藤浪 晋太郎 RHP   Born: 04/12/94   Age: 27   Bats: R   Throws: R   Height: 6'0"   Weight: 180

YEAR	TEAM	LVL	AGE	W	L	SV	G	GS	IP	H	HR	BB/9	K/9	K	GB%	BABIP	WHIP	ERA	DRA-	WARP	MPH	FA%	Whiff%	CSP
2018	HNS	NPB	24	5	3	0	13	13	71	70	5	6.0	8.9	70			1.65	5.32						
2019	HNS	NPB	25	0	0	0	1		4¹	4	0	12.0	6.2	3			2.31	2.08						
2020	HNS	NPB	26	1	6	0	24		76¹	71	5	4.0	10.0	85			1.45	4.01						

The tall right-hander remains an enigma. Fujinami's electric pure stuff makes you want to tune in to the Tigers game every time he takes the mound. And yet, he possesses the worst command of his pitches since Vince Neil after he rejoined Mötley Crüe. He can strike a hitter out with nasty sliders and splitters to start an inning, then go on to walk the next three batters on 12 pitches, each one further away from the zone than the last. It's painful—sometimes even torturous—to watch, but you can't turn it off because you want to believe in his stuff and dream on him rediscovering his true self: the dominant starter he was in his first four professional seasons.

Imanaga Shota 今永 昇太 LHP   Born: 09/01/93   Age: 27   Bats: L   Throws: L   Height: 5'8"   Weight: 176

YEAR	TEAM	LVL	AGE	W	L	SV	G	GS	IP	H	HR	BB/9	K/9	K	GB%	BABIP	WHIP	ERA	DRA-	WARP	MPH	FA%	Whiff%	CSP
2018	YKO	NPB	24	1	2	0	6		20²	18	0	3.0	8.7	20			1.26	3.05						
2019	YKO	NPB	25	13	7	0	25		170	128	18	3.0	9.8	186			1.08	2.91						
2020	YKO	NPB	26	5	3	0	9		53	47	2	2.0	10.7	63			1.21	3.23						

In the winter of 2018-2019, coming off of his worst professional campaign, Imanaga had a stellar stint in the Australian Baseball League, striking out 57 while walking just one in 35 innings for Canberra. While it's uncertain whether Australia made him a better pitcher, like it made Eleanor, Chidi, Tahani, and Jason better people in the altered timeline, the southpaw has performed like the ace of the BayStars rotation ever since, at least when he's been healthy enough to take the mound every seven days. Imanaga has dealt with nagging shoulder soreness, which kept him sidelined for the better part of 2020, since his college days. Hopefully, we hope to see him at full strength in 2021 and beyond, now that he went under the knife in October to fix the issues.

Raidel Martinez RHP   Born: 10/11/96   Age: 24   Bats: R   Throws: R   Height: 5'9"   Weight: 176

YEAR	TEAM	LVL	AGE	W	L	SV	G	GS	IP	H	HR	BB/9	K/9	K	GB%	BABIP	WHIP	ERA	DRA-	WARP	MPH	FA%	Whiff%	CSP
2018	CHU	NPB	21	1	3	0	7	4	21²	28	4	3.0	5.8	14			1.66	6.65						
2019	CHU	NPB	22	1	4	8	43		40²	34	2	3.0	10.6	48			1.18	2.66						
2020	CHU	NPB	23	2	0	21	40		40	24	2	2.0	11.0	49			0.90	1.13						

In his first season as the full-time closer for the Dragons, the flamethrowing Cuban ranked second in the Central League in saves, trailing only fellow hard-throwing righty Robert Suárez. Martínez's upper-90s fastball is a dominant presence in a league where the average fastball velocity is a hair over 90 mph. In addition to the blazing heater, (he became the first Dragons pitcher ever to hit 100 mph on the stadium gun), his arsenal consists of a slider, splitter and changeup. For Chunichi, a team that has struggled to find a closer lasting more than one season since the all-time NPB saves leader Hitoki Iwase's last good season, Martínez seems to be capable of anchoring the role for the near future.

Livan Moinelo LHP   Born: 12/08/95   Age: 25   Bats: L   Throws: L   Height: 5'7"   Weight: 139

YEAR	TEAM	LVL	AGE	W	L	SV	G	GS	IP	H	HR	BB/9	K/9	K	GB%	BABIP	WHIP	ERA	DRA-	WARP	MPH	FA%	Whiff%	CSP
2018	FKU	NPB	22	5	1	0	49	0	45²	31	6	4.0	11.2	57			1.20	4.53						
2019	FKU	NPB	23	3	1	4	60		59¹	37	4	3.0	13.0	86			1.04	1.52						
2020	FKU	NPB	24	2	3	1	50		48	26	1	4.0	14.4	77			1.06	1.69						

Moinelo may have recorded a mere six saves in his 193 appearances with the Hawks, but the Cuban lefty is a superior fireman to their incumbent closer Yuito Mori. In his four-year NPB career, Moinelo has struck out a third of the hitters he has faced, and in 2020 led all NPB arms with at least 40 innings in strikeout percentage and contact allowed, both by wide margins. Thanks to his lethal four-pitch mix consisting of a 93 mph fastball, devastating slider, curve and changeup, he can neutralize platoon splits. The blemish on his profile is his inability to prevent walks, but it's never hurt anyone to have an occasional runner standing on first when the side is retired.

Matt Moore LHP   Born: 06/18/89   Age: 32   Bats: L   Throws: L   Height: 6'3"   Weight: 210   Origin: Round 8, 2007 Draft (#245 overall)

YEAR	TEAM	LVL	AGE	W	L	SV	G	GS	IP	H	HR	BB/9	K/9	K	GB%	BABIP	WHIP	ERA	DRA-	WARP	MPH	FA%	Whiff%	CSP
2018	TEX	MLB	29	3	8	0	39	12	102	128	19	3.6	7.6	86	38.1%	.342	1.66	6.79	156	-2.2	94.5	58.6%	22.0%	52.5%
2019	DET	MLB	30	0	0	0	2	2	10	3	0	0.9	8.1	9	56.5%	.130	0.40	0.00	91	0.1	94.6	53.8%	31.7%	53.0%
2020	FKU	NPB	31	6	3	0	13	0	78	64	7	2.0	10.3	89			1.10	2.65						

Comparables: Jake Odorizzi, Jhoulys Chacín, Dan Straily

A former top prospect, Moore churned out a pair of gems in two of his three postseason starts in his career: seven scoreless in the 2011 ALDS opener and an eight-inning, 10-strikeout masterpiece in Game 4 of the 2016 NLDS, allowing just a pair of hits in each of those outings. Defying all prediction, he added another to his collection by tossing seven no-hit innings in his Japan Series Game 3 start, contributing to the Hawks' second consecutive sweep of Yomiuri. During the regular season, the southpaw struck out 27.8 percent of opposing hitters while walking just 6.9 percent, his best marks in both areas in a season in which he logged more than 10 innings, albeit against less talented competition. Looking at his entire career, it's easy to understand why he wound up in Japan; after last year, it's equally easy to argue that he probably still belongs in his native USA as some team's fifth starter.

Morishita Masato 森下 暢仁 RHP Born: 08/25/97 Age: 23 Bats: R Throws: R Height: 5'10" Weight: 167

YEAR	TEAM	LVL	AGE	W	L	SV	G	GS	IP	H	HR	BB/9	K/9	K	GB%	BABIP	WHIP	ERA	DRA-	WARP	MPH	FA%	Whiff%	CSP
2020	HRO	NPB	22	10	3	0	18		122²	102	6	2.0	9.1	124			1.09	1.91						

One of the most polished college arms in this century, the right-hander Morishita withstood the high expectations in his rookie campaign, headlining the Hiroshima Carp pitching staff after his dominant four-year college career at Meiji University. He wields a four-seam fastball that averages 92 mph, a 84 mph slider (though some call it a cutter), and a 81 mph changeup, a slow, show-me hooker and double-plus command of all of the four pitches. The Carp's first-round pick in the 2019 NPB Draft punched out more than a quarter of the hitters he faced, well above the Central League average of 20 percent, while walking just 6.6 percent. Morishita's ability suggests that he should be a stalwart in the Hiroshima rotation for the years to come, although given his heavy workload in college, where he regularly threw 130-plus-pitch outings and occasionally neared 160 in a start, and the usage he saw in his first pro season (he threw more than 120 pitches in a handful of starts), one might wonder how long his body and stuff will hold up.

Dovydas Neverauskas RHP Born: 01/14/93 Age: 28 Bats: R Throws: R Height: 6'3" Weight: 225

YEAR	TEAM	LVL	AGE	W	L	SV	G	GS	IP	H	HR	BB/9	K/9	K	GB%	BABIP	WHIP	ERA	DRA-	WARP	MPH	FA%	Whiff%	CSP
2018	IND	AAA	25	2	3	4	34	0	46¹	31	2	5.8	11.3	58	48.5%	.290	1.32	2.53	69	0.9				
2018	PIT	MLB	25	0	0	0	25	0	27	30	9	3.3	9.0	27	37.0%	.292	1.48	8.00	107	0.0	98.6	48.1%	27.4%	49.5%
2019	IND	AAA	26	3	4	9	36	0	52	51	8	3.8	12.6	73	37.2%	.358	1.40	5.02	89	0.9				
2019	PIT	MLB	26	0	0	0	10	0	9¹	15	2	6.8	9.6	10	35.3%	.406	2.36	10.61	129	-0.1	97.6	57.1%	28.0%	49.0%
2020	PIT	MLB	27	0	3	0	17	0	19	24	5	4.7	10.9	23	46.4%	.373	1.79	7.11	94	0.2	96.3	46.4%	32.5%	40.0%

Comparables: Jake Barrett, Yacksel Ríos, J.B. Wendelken

Fans of the global game of baseball have a soft spot for Neverauskas as the first Lithuanian-born MLB player, but a second straight year of underachieving numbers had even the most loyal yinzers rumbling. The Pirates, always happy to listen to their fanbase (when it involves cutting payroll), designated Nerverauskas this November. He soon found a home with NPB's Hiroshima Toyo Carp. His struggles are perplexing because the stuff looks fine on paper, a mid-90s fastball paired with a changing-speed cutter and a hard curve; however, batters have crushed said fastball, mostly thanks to his propensity to throw it right down the heart of the plate. To his credit, he did cut the usage of his four-seamer from 57 percent to 48, which in our opinion is still too high given that batters slugged 1.000 off of it, but hey, they never ask us.

Nishi Yuki 西 勇輝 RHP Born: 11/10/90 Age: 30 Bats: R Throws: R Height: 5'11" Weight: 176

YEAR	TEAM	LVL	AGE	W	L	SV	G	GS	IP	H	HR	BB/9	K/9	K	GB%	BABIP	WHIP	ERA	DRA-	WARP	MPH	FA%	Whiff%	CSP
2018	ORX	NPB	27	10	13	0	25		162¹	162	15	2.0	6.6	119			1.22	3.60						
2019	HNS	NPB	28	10	8	0	26	25	172¹	159	12	1.0	5.8	112			1.13	2.92						
2020	HNS	NPB	29	11	5	0	21		147²	116	15	1.0	7.0	115			0.98	2.26						

In the 2019 Draft, Hanshin selected Junya Nishi, Yuki's third cousin and fellow right-handed hurler, in the first round out of high school. In his second season as a Tiger and the first in the same organization as his distant relative, the elder Nishi proved that he's still the best pitcher in the extended family, both on the mound and in the batter's box. On Opening Day, he went 2-for-2 with a double and his first-career long ball, both off of Yomiuri ace Tomoyuki Sugano, driving in all of the runs Hanshin scored that day. Long live pitchers hitting, right? Although he added just three more base knocks over the rest of the season, his performance on the mound was on par with his career numbers, further cementing his status as one of the most consistent hurlers in the nation. With two more years on the contract, the Tigers may see a third of their six rotation spots occupied by Nishis come the second half of 2021.

Norimoto Takahiro 則本 昂大 RHP Born: 12/17/90 Age: 30 Bats: R Throws: R Height: 5'10" Weight: 178

YEAR	TEAM	LVL	AGE	W	L	SV	G	GS	IP	H	HR	BB/9	K/9	K	GB%	BABIP	WHIP	ERA	DRA-	WARP	MPH	FA%	Whiff%	CSP
2018	RAK	NPB	27	10	11	0	27		180¹	171	18	2.0	9.3	187			1.23	3.69						
2019	RAK	NPB	28	5	5	0	12		68	58	7	1.0	8.9	67			1.00	2.78						
2020	RAK	NPB	29	5	7	0	18		109	110	13	2.0	8.7	105			1.32	3.96						

Two years into his current seven-year contract, things for Norimoto have not gone as expected. He missed the first half of the season with a sore elbow in 2019, then sustained a hand injury when he fell down in the dugout, sidelining him for three weeks in 2020. The result was that he failed to qualify for the ERA title in consecutive seasons, in addition to the lowest strikeout rate and the highest walk rate since his rookie campaign. Despite the diminished performance, he is still as good as any Rakuten hurler when his health permits him to toe the rubber. If the traditional injuries of one's mid-30s replace the unlucky ones he's seen of late, it may be a rough denouement for that contract.

Ohno Yudai 大野 雄大 LHP Born: 09/26/88 Age: 32 Bats: L Throws: L Height: 6'0" Weight: 171

YEAR	TEAM	LVL	AGE	W	L	SV	G	GS	IP	H	HR	BB/9	K/9	K	GB%	BABIP	WHIP	ERA	DRA-	WARP	MPH	FA%	Whiff%	CSP
2018	CHU	NPB	29	4	7	0	20		77	95	13	2.0	8.0	93			1.22	3.80						
2019	CHU	NPB	30	9	8	0	26		181²	137	18	2.0	7.8	157			1.00	2.68						
2020	CHU	NPB	31	11	6	0	20		148²	106	13	1.0	9.0	148			0.87	1.82						

What does starting pitching usage look like in a country that never developed Kevin Cash? The southpaw's 2020 statline is one way to answer the question. In a year in which major-league pitchers threw a combined 14 nine-inning complete games, none with more than one, the Chunichi ace completed 10 starts by himself, including six in a row. He failed to log at least six innings in just three of his 20 starts, and averaged more than seven innings per start. Deservedly, he was the recipient of the 2020 Sawamura Award, the Japanese equivalent of the Cy Young Award, although the award lacks the prestige of its stateside equivalent. Perhaps the three-year extension Ohno signed at the end of the season, which will keep him in Nagoya through his age-34 campaign and keep him away from the major leagues, will work perfectly for both parties, considering his apparent desire to replicate Old Hoss Radbourn's workload.

Sawamura Hirokazu 澤村 拓一　RHP　Born: 04/03/88　Age: 33　Bats: R　Throws: R　Height: 6'0"　Weight: 212

YEAR	TEAM	LVL	AGE	W	L	SV	G	GS	IP	H	HR	BB/9	K/9	K	GB%	BABIP	WHIP	ERA	DRA-	WARP	MPH	FA%	Whiff%	CSP
2018	YOM	NPB	30	1	6	0	49	0	52¹	55	4	4.0	9.3	27			1.57	4.64						
2019	YOM	NPB	31	2	2	0	43	0	48¹	40	3	3.0	10.2	17			1.18	2.61						
2020	YOM	NPB	32	1	1	0	13		13¹	14	1	5.0	7.4	11			1.65	6.08						
2020	CHB	NPB	32	0	2	1	22		21	10	2	4.0	12.4	29			0.95	1.71						

Relievers are volatile. A month after making Yomiuri's Opening Day roster to start the 2020 season, Sawamura was demoted to the farm, where he lost all semblance of control before being traded to Lotte for a career up-and-down bench bat. At that point, seeking a major-league contract after the season seemed like a far-fetched dream. In two-plus months with the new team, he bounced back mightily and became one of the most dominant relievers in the Pacific League with his mid-90s fastball and devastating low-90s splitter. A potential move to the major leagues, which appears to have been his ultimate goal since his college days, doesn't seem like a farfetched idea now.

Senga Kodai 千賀 滉大　RHP　Born: 01/30/93　Age: 28　Bats: L　Throws: R　Height: 6'0"　Weight: 178

YEAR	TEAM	LVL	AGE	W	L	SV	G	GS	IP	H	HR	BB/9	K/9	K	GB%	BABIP	WHIP	ERA	DRA-	WARP	MPH	FA%	Whiff%	CSP
2018	FKU	NPB	25	13	7	0	22		141	116	21	3.0	10.4	163			1.23	3.51						
2019	FKU	NPB	26	13	8	0	20		180¹	134	19	3.0	11.3	227			1.16	2.79						
2020	FKU	NPB	27	11	6	0	18		121	90	4	4.0	11.1	149			1.22	2.16						

Twice in the entire 2010s, a major-league pitcher exceeded 140 pitches in a start: Edwin Jackson and Tim Lincecum in their respective no-hitters. Senga, the SoftBank ace, did it twice all by himself in a span of three weeks in 2020, not to mention four other occasions where he tossed more than 120 pitches. It seemed as if Hawks manager Kimiyasu Kudo was trying to have Senga, who was never a big-name prospect as an amateur, make up for the abuse many of top Japanese high school arms face. The 28-year-old is unquestionably one of the three best pitchers in Japan and possesses ultra-electric stuff, and should be on every major-league club's radar. Although considering the aforementioned usage and the nagging arm injuries he has suffered over the years, one wonders if he will remain a top-shelf starter by the time he hits the international market.

Cy Sneed　RHP　Born: 10/01/92　Age: 28　Bats: R　Throws: R　Height: 6'4"　Weight: 213　Origin: Round 3, 2014 Draft (#85 overall)

YEAR	TEAM	LVL	AGE	W	L	SV	G	GS	IP	H	HR	BB/9	K/9	K	GB%	BABIP	WHIP	ERA	DRA-	WARP	MPH	FA%	Whiff%	CSP
2018	FRE	AAA	25	10	6	0	26	20	127	120	6	3.8	8.1	114	43.5%	.317	1.36	3.83	103	1.0				
2019	RR	AAA	26	7	6	1	19	9	81²	71	13	2.6	7.8	71	38.3%	.266	1.16	4.19	59	2.9				
2019	HOU	MLB	26	0	1	0	8	0	21¹	26	5	2.1	9.7	23	44.6%	.356	1.45	5.48	107	0.0	94.6	70.3%	22.1%	50.7%
2020	HOU	MLB	27	0	3	0	18	0	17¹	22	3	5.2	10.9	21	28.8%	.404	1.85	5.71	105	0.1	95.5	69.6%	24.5%	48.7%

Comparables: Mike Mayers, Scott Barlow, Kyle McGowin

Sneed bears such a close resemblance to 1960s claymation prospector Yukon Cornelius that the right-hander had the nickname inscribed on his glove. The similarity ends there. Cornelius was the greatest prospector in the north, whereas Sneed struggles to get by in the south. There's no gold to be found in his numbers beyond an elevated strikeout rate, although you might find a little silver developing in his beard from a few too many baserunners and homers. The staunchest McKinseyite in the Astros org might've balked at banishing Sneed to the Island of Misfit Toys, but that didn't prevent him from joining the Yakult Swallows in early December.

Robert Suarez　RHP　Born: 03/01/91　Age: 30　Bats: R　Throws: R　Height: 6'2"　Weight: 210

YEAR	TEAM	LVL	AGE	W	L	SV	G	GS	IP	H	HR	BB/9	K/9	K	GB%	BABIP	WHIP	ERA	DRA-	WARP	MPH	FA%	Whiff%	CSP
2018	FKU	NPB	27	1	1	0	11	0	10	15	1	4.0	9.0	10			2.00	6.30						
2019	FKU	NPB	28	0	4	0	9	0	26²	28	6	6.0	9.1	27			1.80	5.74						
2020	HNS	NPB	29	3	1	25	51		52¹	36	2	3.0	8.6	50			1.05	2.24						

The Venezuelan right-hander fully recovered from a 2017 Tommy John surgery and threw the highest-octane fastball among all NPB hurlers, averaging 96.7 mph, while racking up a Central League-leading 25 saves. With two effective secondaries in a slider and a splitter, Suárez induced a higher chase rate than any other pitcher in the country with at least 30 innings. It's a shame for the Hawks, his original team, that they gave up on him just a year too early; Tommy John demands patience above all else. Hanshin elected not to repeat the mistake, rewarding the fireballer with a generous contract.

Sugano Tomoyuki 菅野 智之　RHP　Born: 10/11/89　Age: 31　Bats: R　Throws: R　Height: 6'1"　Weight: 183

YEAR	TEAM	LVL	AGE	W	L	SV	G	GS	IP	H	HR	BB/9	K/9	K	GB%	BABIP	WHIP	ERA	DRA-	WARP	MPH	FA%	Whiff%	CSP
2018	YOM	NPB	28	15	8	0	28	0	202	166	14	1.0	8.9	200			1.00	2.14						
2019	YOM	NPB	29	11	6	0	22	0	136¹	138	20	2.0	7.9	120			1.25	3.89						
2020	YOM	NPB	30	14	2	0	20	0	137¹	97	8	1.0	8.6	131			0.89	1.97						

In 2013, his last year in Japan, Masahiro Tanaka went an unprecedented 24-0, setting the world record for the most consecutive winning decisions to start a season. That's a tall order to match in a normal year, let alone in a pandemic-shortened campaign. Sugano's quest to break the record in 2020 ended at 13 wins before he took the first loss in his fourth-to-last start of the season. However, that doesn't mean Sugano's talent level is significantly behind that of Tanaka. The nephew of Yomiuri manager Tatsunori Hara was one of the very best arms in his native country in his eight professional seasons, with an ability to locate three plus-or-better pitches while logging innings. Though already in his thirties, Sugano has demonstrated no evidence of decline; the right-hander is ready to serve as the second or third member of a major-league rotation in 2021.

Taira Kaima 平良 海馬 RHP Born: 11/15/99 Age: 21 Bats: L Throws: R Height: 5'8" Weight: 209

YEAR	TEAM	LVL	AGE	W	L	SV	G	GS	IP	H	HR	BB/9	K/9	K	GB%	BABIP	WHIP	ERA	DRA-	WARP	MPH	FA%	Whiff%	CSP
2018	SEI	NPB	19	0	0	0	10		16²	11	2	9.0	11.3	21			1.68	5.40						
2019	SEI	NPB	20	3	1	1	33		40	38	2	3.0	10.1	45			1.35	2.48						
2020	SEI	NPB	21	1	0	1	54		53	22	2	4.0	10.5	62			0.96	1.87						

In an era every MLB bullpen employs multiple relievers who sit in the upper-90s and above with their fastballs, fans don't tune in to watch them sling one heater after another in particular. Rob Friedman's Twitter account has it covered for you as far as it doesn't get suspended by the powers that be. However, the climate is slightly different on the other side of the ocean. In a country where only a handful of relievers average 93, let alone 95 with their heaters, it's an appointment viewing when a fireballer like Taira takes the mound. Taira, who had drawn attention with his 24-inning cameo in 2019, made a national headline on July 19th, when he hit 160 KPH (99.4 MPH), becoming the sixth Japanese hurler to top the milestone. Armed with a five-pitch mix, including the aforementioned blazing heater, which averaged harder than all but two NPB pitchers who tossed at least 50 innings in 2020. His filled-out, 5'8", 220-pound frame suggests he's a reliever, but it's an arsenal that would work in a starting role, as far as he cuts down on his walk rate going forward.

Takahashi Kona 高橋 光成 RHP Born: 02/03/97 Age: 24 Bats: R Throws: R Height: 6'2" Weight: 198

YEAR	TEAM	LVL	AGE	W	L	SV	G	GS	IP	H	HR	BB/9	K/9	K	GB%	BABIP	WHIP	ERA	DRA-	WARP	MPH	FA%	Whiff%	CSP
2018	SEI	NPB	21	2	1	0	3		20	17	2	3.0	6.8	15			1.50	4.50						
2019	SEI	NPB	22	10	6	0	21		123²	144	13	3.0	6.5	90			1.54	4.51						
2020	SEI	NPB	23	8	8	0	20		120¹	100	9	3.0	7.5	100			1.20	3.74						

It was eons ago in baseball time when Takahashi rose to stardom in the summer of 2013, leading Maebashi Ikuei High School to a Summer Koshien championship as an underclassman ace. In his sixth season as a professional, the right-hander qualified for the ERA title for the first time in his career (albeit in a pandemic-shortened season), tossing at least six innings in 14 of his 20 starts. Takahashi, who spent the entirety of the 2020 campaign as a 23-year-old, has enough time to establish himself as one of the better hurlers in the country. If he does make another splash as a celebrity, this time as an adult, there's a possibility he'll ink an endorsement deal with a certain Hawaiian brewery.

Togo Shosei RHP Born: 04/04/00 Age: 21 Bats: R Throws: R Height: 6'1" Weight: 160

YEAR	TEAM	LVL	AGE	W	L	SV	G	GS	IP	H	HR	BB/9	K/9	K	GB%	BABIP	WHIP	ERA	DRA-	WARP	MPH	FA%	Whiff%	CSP
2019	YOM	NPB	19	5	1		13		50²	50	4	2.0	9.8	55			1.20	2.84						
2020	YOM	NPB	20	9	6		19		107²	87	12	3.0	8.9	106			1.20	2.76						

In 2020, amidst the COVID-19 pandemic, people's preference at restaurants and fast food joints around the world went from "for here" to "to go". Similarly, in 2020, after a winter in which they posted a key rotation piece to the big leagues, Yomiuri's number two starter went from Shun Yamaguchi to Togo. Despite turning just 20 shortly after the originally scheduled Opening Day, he missed bats at an above-league-average rate, inducing a 71.5 percent contact rate to go with a 23.8 percent K rate. With a low-90s fastball and two effective secondaries in a slider and a forkball and room for improvement, Togo is capable of headlining the post-Tomoyuki Sugano Yomiuri rotation.

Yamamoto Yoshinobu 山本 由伸 RHP Born: 08/17/98 Age: 22 Bats: R Throws: R Height: 5'10" Weight: 169

YEAR	TEAM	LVL	AGE	W	L	SV	G	GS	IP	H	HR	BB/9	K/9	K	GB%	BABIP	WHIP	ERA	DRA-	WARP	MPH	FA%	Whiff%	CSP
2018	ORX	NPB	18	4	2	1	54		53	40	4	2.0	7.8	46			1.06	2.89						
2019	ORX	NPB	19	8	6	0	20		143	101	8	2.0	8.0	127			0.96	1.95						
2020	ORX	NPB	20	8	4	0	18		126²	82	6	2.0	10.6	149			0.94	2.20						

In his four years as a pro, the former fourth-round pick has gone from a hard-throwing (relatively speaking for the NPB) prospect to key bullpen piece to arguably the best starter in the country. In 2020, his second season as a full-time starter and the bona-fide, capital A Ace of the Buffaloes, Yamamoto led all NPB hurlers with at least 50 innings in K%, K-BB%, and ranked second in contact% allowed, beating even some of the best relievers in the country. It's no coincidence he threw 31 consecutive scoreless innings in the second half of the season. The boatload of whiffs comes from his electric six-pitch mix, including a four-seam fastball that averages at 94 mph, a devastating forkball and the Ginoza curveball, his signature pitch. The only blemish in his profile so far seems to be durability, as he has missed time with upper body discomfort in each of his three full seasons. Despite the slight frame for a starter, Yamamoto has the potential to overcome his weakness and take another step to be the best pitcher in the NPB, and the cornerstone of a major-league rotation by his mid-20s.

KOREA BASEBALL ORGANIZATION

Essay by Brendan Gawlowski

Player comments by Brendan Gawlowski and BP staff

As fans stared down the dismal prospect of a spring without baseball, the KBO rose to fill the void. Days after spring training sites shuttered and the possibility of a major league season seemed a distant, childlike hope, Korean teams were just starting to get going. Better yet, they were putting their early-spring scrimmages on television. Only a moment of cultural stillness could make the prospect of an intersquad scrimmage played in Korea sound appealing. And yet, for a sports-starved audience, Chris Flexen was a sight for sore eyes.

Silly as it sounds now, those March and April scrimmages had an immensely soothing effect. Somehow, somewhere, Maslow's hierarchy of needs were sufficiently satisfied to permit a baseball game. For the first time since the United States effectively shut down, you could squint and see something normal. The KBO wasn't the only league going in MLB's absence (Taiwan's CPBL actually commenced a bit earlier) but it was a few enterprising clubs in Korea that first thought to stream their games on YouTube, and that first-mover advantage helped the league attract an audience craving baseball. For at least some fans, that outreach sparked an enduring attachment to the Korean game.

Last spring, the KBO sat atop baseball's throne. Guides to the league sprouted up on baseball sites large and small. Even Mookie Betts participated, uploading a video where he raved about the hitting talents of Lee Jung-hoo and Kang Baek-ho. After years of appealing to a niche audience, Dan Kurtz's Mykbostats.com saw such a surge in traffic that the website crashed. ESPN secured broadcasting rights for the KBO, and when Opening Day rolled around, Baseball Twitter had the glow of Christmas morning.

As with anything new, there was an acclimation period. Most American viewers could count the league's recognizable names on two hands, and the challenge of learning a whole new set of players was only magnified by a language barrier and unfamiliar naming convention. One early season game highlighted the challenge, as KT replaced starter Kim Min with Kim Min-soo while Kim Min-hyeok stood in left field. For the first time in decades, scorecards would have been handy.

But the joys outweighed the challenges. Between ESPN's telecasts and Korean broadcasts on Twitch, the product itself was accessible and the games entertaining. The KBO brought us bat flips and polite apologies for wayward beanballs, but also a more contact-oriented style of play that felt both familiar and refreshing.

The league also reanimated the way I watch the sport. I haven't entirely lost my fandom, as so many other longtime writers have, but after 10 years of covering the increasingly stale MLB, I watch much differently than I used to. The KBO allowed for a reset, a chance to enjoy the pleasures of backing a team from a new vantage point. They say the team chooses you, and it wasn't long before the KT Wiz came calling.

A daily tradition began. Late at night, with most of the west coast asleep, I settled in to watch the previous night's game. I soon came to appreciate an entirely new cast of characters: the incredible batting eye of Jo Yong-ho, the reliability of Ju Kwon, the endearingly stupid baserunning of Sim Woo-jun. In this most anxious of years, the Wiz were a refuge, if only for a few hours.

This isn't to sanitize the league entirely. Like any human enterprise, the KBO has its flaws and bad actors. The Kiwoom Heroes, already saddled with the league's bad-boy reputation, doubled down and signed Addison Russell. The kinds of financial contortions we're used to seeing from American owners aren't entirely absent in South Korea. And while the nation's masterful handling of the pandemic's early stages enabled a far more normal summer there than Americans experienced, Hanwha's minor league squad did suffer an outbreak.

Still, there was something delightfully unobtrusive about an entertainment able to proceed without recklessly risking a large-scale outbreak. The same could not be said of the league across the pond, as MLB never mustered any serious effort to operate safely at all. Perhaps that shouldn't have come as a surprise. The way MLB's unseemly and financially-motivated reluctance to play yielded to a runaway season barreling down the tracks come hell or high-COVID suggested as much. And if by some chance we forgot all of that for a moment, the additional advertisements plastered over empty seats and the pitcher's mound served as constant reminders of a league oozing with greed.

In the spring, I figured my KBO habit would fade swiftly, certainly once the big leagues were back in swing. A funny thing happened though: When MLB returned, I continued my evening ritual. I watched some MLB, sure, but less than normal. And one late October day, when it came down to the World Series or the Wiz, I picked the latter without a second thought. And why not? I liked my new friends.

I suspect that MLB is far too complacent to learn any lessons from a rocky 2020. This is an organization confident enough in its standing to gut the minor leagues, juice the ball beyond reason, brush aside a cheating scandal, dub the World Series trophy a "piece of metal," embrace a bitter labor dispute, endorse tanking, and utterly fail to grow the game's footprint without a care in the world for potential long-term damage.

The minor league contractions happened under the guise of a plan entitled "One Baseball." It is a darkly revealing monker for a monopolistic enterprise whose capricious indifference renders clear its belief that they have a captive audience of people with nowhere else to turn if they want to watch baseball. That, for all intents and purposes, MLB and baseball are synonymous. So what if a few seamheads turned their attention to Asia and liked what they saw? Nobody in ownership or the league's main office will lose a wink of sleep over it.

Perhaps they should. Major League Baseball owners may see themselves as gatekeepers to the only baseball worth consuming, but they're as out of touch here as anywhere else. For all that went wrong, 2020 revealed in perfect clarity that we live in a big world, and that it's very easy to be a baseball fan first and a Major League Baseball supporter a distant second. I'll be paying plenty of attention to the KBO next year, and the fact that you are reading this sentence suggests I won't be alone. Should the looming labor dispute delay (or worse) the 2020 season, I'll sleep soundly; there are other ways to enjoy this greatest of games.

The presence of compelling alternatives should be a sobering wakeup call for MLB. Because if you can lose me—someone who spent every waking childhood moment playing, watching and breathing baseball, someone who watches upwards of 100 games a year as an adult—you can lose anyone. ■

—Brendan Gawlowski is an author at FanGraphs.

HITTERS

Aaron Altherr CF Born: 01/14/91   Age: 30   Bats: R   Throws: R   Height: 6'5"   Weight: 215   Origin: Round 9, 2009 Draft (#287 overall)

YEAR	TEAM	LVL	AGE	PA	R	2B	3B	HR	RBI	BB	K	SB	CS	Whiff%	AVG/OBP/SLG	DRC+	BABIP	BRR	FRAA	WARP
2018	LHV	AAA	27	134	15	5	0	2	12	14	37	4	0		.244/.321/.336	90	.333	-0.6	CF(21): -0.6, LF(8): 2.7, RF(2): -0.2	0.2
2018	PHI	MLB	27	285	28	11	1	8	38	36	91	3	2	32.8%	.181/.295/.333	73	.247	-1.2	RF(68): -4.2, CF(11): -0.4, LF(6): 0.4	-0.8
2019	SYR	AAA	28	88	9	5	1	4	13	10	16	3	2		.270/.375/.527	114	.291	-0.8	CF(11): -0.7, RF(11): 2.1, LF(3): 0.9	0.5
2019	SF	MLB	28	1	0	0	0	0	0	0	1	0	0	100.0%	.000/.000/.000	28				0.0
2019	PHI	MLB	28	30	2	1	0	0	1	1	9	0	0	28.8%	.034/.067/.069	58	.050	0.0	CF(8): -0.3, RF(4): 0.2, LF(1): -0.0	-0.1
2019	NYM	MLB	28	35	6	1	0	1	2	2	15	0	0	40.0%	.129/.200/.258	42	.188	0.0	LF(13): -0.5, CF(8): -0.1, RF(2): -0.2	-0.2
2020	NC	KBO	29	546	90	20	7	31	108	44	149	22	3		.278/.352/.541					

Comparables: Jayson Werth, Byron Browne, Kevin Roberson

In the majors, Altherr's trouble with the slow stuff ran him out of the league, which made him a bit of an odd choice for a KBO signee. There's not much velo in the Korean game, but every hurler has a steady supply of junk, and after a terrible first couple of weeks, the Dinos had to have been at least a little worried about their import center fielder. Fortunately for all parties, he soon found his footing. While he nearly led the league in strikeout percentage, he also hit 30 bombs and played the circuit's best center field. Somewhat bizarrely, the early-season slump stuck him in the eight-hole for most of the season even as he grew into one of the team's toughest outs. His three-run shot in Game 1 of the Korean series was a vital part of the Dinos title run, and provided that a late-season mask controversy—he refused to wear it during a post-game press conference—is all water under the bridge, a return to Changwon seems to make sense for all parties.

Choi Hyeong-woo 최형우 OF Born: 12/04/89   Age: 31   Bats: L   Throws: L   Height: 6'0"   Weight: 190

YEAR	TEAM	LVL	AGE	PA	R	2B	3B	HR	RBI	BB	K	SB	CS	Whiff%	AVG/OBP/SLG	DRC+	BABIP	BRR	FRAA	WARP
2018	KIA	KBO	34	609	92	34	1	25	103	66	87	3	0		.339/.414/549.000					
2019	KIA	KBO	35	555	65	31	1	17	86	85	77	0	1		.300/.413/.485					
2020	KIA	KBO	36	600	93	37	1	28	115	70	101	0	0		.354/.433/.590					

Here we have a lefty who shrugged off a slow start to his career to become the game's best DH and maintain that title throughout his 30s: Who is this, David Ortiz? Ortiz is actually a fair cross-league comparison, as the personable and charismatic Choi is perhaps the game's least well-rounded star. He can't throw, doesn't play the field and he's slower than a tree, but dangit he can hit. His .354 average kept Mel Rojas Jr. from winning the Triple Crown, and he managed to post the league's second best OPS despite playing in a very tough park to hit. While he'll be 37 next year, there's no reason to suspect that Kia's best player has started his descent just yet.

Choi Jeong 최정 3B Born: 02/28/87   Age: 34   Bats: R   Throws: R   Height: 5'11"   Weight: 185

YEAR	TEAM	LVL	AGE	PA	R	2B	3B	HR	RBI	BB	K	SB	CS	Whiff%	AVG/OBP/SLG	DRC+	BABIP	BRR	FRAA	WARP
2018	SK	KBO	31	489	95	16	1	35	74	58	129	9	2		.244/.368/.547					
2019	SK	KBO	32	606	86	27	0	29	99	69	92	3	2		.292/.399/.519					
2020	SK	KBO	33	553	90	22	0	33	96	75	98	8	3		.270/.392/.538					

Choi captained what was easily the KBO's most disappointing outfit in 2020. Preseason title contenders, the Wyverns had an almost cartoonishly bad season. The club stumbled to a 1-13 start, their manager missed most of the season after collapsing from stress in the middle of a game, and they ultimately posted their worst-ever season. Yet there the Korean Miguel Cabrera was, stoically plying his trade, notching another .900 OPS season with 30 bombs and his trademark good defense at the hot corner. At 34, Choi has won titles and Gold medals. The KBO career home run record is in sight and given the league's friendly aging curve, it's probably his to lose. The question here is whether he wants to keep chasing that record now, or test his mettle at the highest level the sport can offer. He's spurned several opportunities to come stateside in the past, but with the Wyverns in the gutter and his career nearing an end, a pilgrimage must seem tempting.

Jose Miguel Fernandez 1B Born: 04/27/88 Age: 33 Bats: L Throws: R Height: 5'10" Weight: 185

YEAR	TEAM	LVL	AGE	PA	R	2B	3B	HR	RBI	BB	K	SB	CS	Whiff%	AVG/OBP/SLG	DRC+	BABIP	BRR	FRAA	WARP
2018	SL	AAA	30	394	66	19	1	17	59	33	34	2	2		.333/.396/.535	137	.333	-0.7	2B(33): 1.4, 1B(17): 1.9, 3B(16): -1.0	2.2
2018	LAA	MLB	30	123	9	8	0	2	11	6	14	1	0	15.9%	.267/.309/.388	97	.290	-2.5	1B(28): -3.0, 3B(2): -0.1, 2B(1): 0.0	-0.4
2019	DOO	KBO	31	645	87	34	0	15	88	61	54	1	2		.344/.409/.483					
2020	DOO	KBO	32	668	104	29	0	21	105	58	42	0	1		.340/.404/.497					

Comparables: Johnny Giavotella, Luis Antonio Rodriguez, Edgar Gonzalez

If you're looking to pull an elaborate heist in Seoul and need some video to patch into the closed circuit feed to fool the security guard, there's no better choice than Doosan's DH, flicking infinite liners into the hole for base hits. One of three Jose Fernandezes to appear in a big league game last decade, Jose Miguel has settled in to life in Korea as the league's Edgar Martinez. The batting title has narrowly eluded his grasp two years running, but after consecutive .340 campaigns, it's only a matter of time. He can't run and he's the only international player who doesn't play defense, but none of that matters here, as he's one of the five or so best hitters in the league.

Hwang Jae-gyun 황재균 3B Born: 07/28/87 Age: 33 Bats: R Throws: R Height: 6'0" Weight: 215

YEAR	TEAM	LVL	AGE	PA	R	2B	3B	HR	RBI	BB	K	SB	CS	Whiff%	AVG/OBP/SLG	DRC+	BABIP	BRR	FRAA	WARP
2018	KT	KBO	30	588	76	41	3	25	88	49	120	14	7		.296/.358/.526					
2019	KT	KBO	31	507	78	16	3	20	67	52	71	10	7		.283/.357/.467					
2020	KT	KBO	32	600	108	35	5	21	97	47	98	11	6		.312/.370/.512					

As Willie Bloomquist embodied the replacement-level big leaguer, Hwang is kind of a litmus test for any Korean who dreams of playing stateside. In the KBO, Hwang is among the 15 best position players in the league, a durable third baseman and a star on offense and defense. He's not quite an MVP candidate, but Hwang's power, arm strength, soft hands, and general athleticism make him stand out in a circuit where popups are often an adventure and benches overflow with players who could never hack it in Rookie ball. When San Francisco took a chance on him in 2017 though, Hwang barely clung to the Giants' 40-man roster. He was an average hitter in Triple-A, and while he got a midsummer cup of coffee, the Giants declined to take a longer look while they played out the string in September. That's no knock on Hwang; big leaguers are just really, really freaking good.

Kang Baek-ho 강백호 1B Born: 07/29/99 Age: 21 Bats: L Throws: R Height: 6'0" Weight: 215

YEAR	TEAM	LVL	AGE	PA	R	2B	3B	HR	RBI	BB	K	SB	CS	Whiff%	AVG/OBP/SLG	DRC+	BABIP	BRR	FRAA	WARP
2018	KT	KBO	18	585	108	32	2	29	84	52	124	3	5		.290/.356/.524					
2019	KT	KBO	19	505	72	29	1	13	65	61	87	9	5		.336/.416/.495					
2020	KT	KBO	20	574	95	36	1	23	89	66	93	7	2		.330/.411/.540					

Kang's game is probably the best advertisement the KBO could offer American audiences. Just 21, the big slugger is the most watchable player in the league. With a huge leg kick and the most violent swing you've ever seen—he regularly falls over from the effort—Kang smacks the absolute crap out of the ball. He's also a remarkably good contact hitter for how wildly he swings, as his ability to track pitches and adjust to spin is belied by the sheer effort in his cut. An outfielder before 2020, the adjustment to first somehow added another watchable dimension to his game, though not always to the benefit of his club. While he started to get the hang of it over the season, Kang had about a 50/50 shot of clanging a hard grounder early on, and in one more memorable May moment, he short-circuited a potential 3-6 putout by firing a one-hopper to his left fielder. No other player so routinely justifies the cost of admission all by himself.

Kim Hyun-soo 김현수 OF Born: 01/12/88 Age: 33 Bats: R Throws: L Height: 6'2" Weight: 210

YEAR	TEAM	LVL	AGE	PA	R	2B	3B	HR	RBI	BB	K	SB	CS	Whiff%	AVG/OBP/SLG	DRC+	BABIP	BRR	FRAA	WARP
2018	LG	KBO	30	511	95	39	2	20	101	47	61	1	3		.362/.415/.589					
2019	LG	KBO	31	595	75	37	0	11	82	54	52	3	1		.304/.370/.437					
2020	LG	KBO	32	619	98	35	2	22	119	63	53	0	2		.331/.397/.523					

You may recall Kim from his successful rookie season with the 2016 Orioles, when he won a starting job and notched a 110 DRC+ for Baltimore's last good team in the Jones-Machado era. What you may not know is that his time in the majors was must-see TV in Korea, where bleary-eyed baseball fans woke up in the middle of the night to watch their hero make his debut. A disappointing 2017 season has proven to be the anomaly of his baseball life, as he's done nothing but hit since returning to his native country. He remains one of the most fearsome sluggers in the league, and is on the shortlist of MVP candidates in 2021.

Koo Ja-wook 구자욱 OF Born: 02/12/93 Age: 28 Bats: R Throws: L Height: 6'2" Weight: 165

YEAR	TEAM	LVL	AGE	PA	R	2B	3B	HR	RBI	BB	K	SB	CS	Whiff%	AVG/OBP/SLG	DRC+	BABIP	BRR	FRAA	WARP
2018	SAM	KBO	25	529	100	26	5	20	84	43	110	10	0		.333/.392/.533					
2019	SAM	KBO	26	526	66	27	6	15	71	38	88	11	3		.267/.327/.444					
2020	SAM	KBO	27	510	70	27	2	15	78	51	91	19	5		.307/.385/.478					

Where are all the guys who hit .300 with doubles power? Not in the major leagues, these days, as the juiced ball and launch angle revolution has made them an endangered species. Over in Korea, Koo is carrying the torch. Undoubtedly, he has the strength and bat control to trade a bunch of singles and doubles for a few homers and a lot of strikeouts. Bless him for choosing a different path.

Lee Dae-ho 이대호 1B   Born: 06/21/82   Age: 39   Bats: R   Throws: R   Height: 6'4"   Weight: 250

YEAR	TEAM	LVL	AGE	PA	R	2B	3B	HR	RBI	BB	K	SB	CS	Whiff%	AVG/OBP/SLG	DRC+	BABIP	BRR	FRAA	WARP
2018	LOT	KBO	36	604	81	30	0	37	125	43	75	0	1		.333/.394/.593					
2019	LOT	KBO	37	549	48	23	1	16	88	47	65	0	0		.285/.355/.435					
2020	LOT	KBO	38	611	67	27	0	20	110	53	68	1	0		.292/.354/.452					

Last season, Lee's bat looked about as good as it did during his Seattle days. That's a problem for Lotte, as Lee is not only an aging first baseman with waning pop but also the highest-paid player in the league. It's a bit gauche to describe a player in the context of his salary these days, but the KBO isn't MLB: If you're making $2 million a year, you better be making the All-Star team, too. Lee didn't come particularly close, and while he remains a popular and lovable player, he's starting to look every bit of his 38 years.

Lee Jung-ho 이정후 OF   Born: 08/20/98   Age: 22   Bats: L   Throws: R   Height: 6'0"   Weight: 171

YEAR	TEAM	LVL	AGE	PA	R	2B	3B	HR	RBI	BB	K	SB	CS	Whiff%	AVG/OBP/SLG	DRC+	BABIP	BRR	FRAA	WARP
2018	KIW	KBO	19	459	81	34	2	6	57	42	58	11	4		.355/.412/.477					
2019	KIW	KBO	20	574	91	31	10	6	68	45	40	13	7		.336/.386/.456					
2020	KIW	KBO	21	544	85	49	5	15	101	59	47	12	2		.333/.397/.524					

Ichiro is a player you should never, ever use as a comp. The future Hall of Famer was far too distinct, and far too talented in the unique way he played the game, to be anything other than a unicorn. But if you had to mention another player in the same breath, it may as well be the L/R speedy outfielder who splits time between center and right while hitting .340 with a timing mechanism that can only work for the most preternaturally gifted of batsmen. That Lee is also a perfect baserunner who wears no. 51 feels almost gratuitous to include. Lee's teammate Kim Ha-seong is often considered the best prospect in the league, and perhaps deservedly so. But there's an argument to be made to take Lee. He has a very rare ability to track pitches, manipulate the barrel and hit anything you throw at him. He's also growing into more power and managed to raise his launch angle without sacrificing too much of his on-base ability. To watch him is to know you're seeing someone special; American audiences will likely have the privilege some time soon.

Dixon Machado SS   Born: 02/22/92   Age: 29   Bats: R   Throws: R   Height: 6'1"   Weight: 190   Origin: International Free Agent, 2008

YEAR	TEAM	LVL	AGE	PA	R	2B	3B	HR	RBI	BB	K	SB	CS	Whiff%	AVG/OBP/SLG	DRC+	BABIP	BRR	FRAA	WARP
2018	TOL	AAA	26	171	19	5	0	1	8	18	28	4	2		.224/.321/.279	82	.271	0.0	SS(25): -0.2, 2B(16): 3.2	0.4
2018	DET	MLB	26	233	20	13	1	1	21	14	41	1	1	19.2%	.206/.263/.290	70	.249	1.5	2B(64): 0.8	0.1
2019	IOW	AAA	27	393	53	19	1	17	65	54	79	0	2		.261/.371/.480	103	.295	0.0	SS(74): 4.0, 2B(16): 1.1, 1B(7): 0.4	2.2
2020	LOT	KBO	28	560	79	31	1	12	67	54	60	15	1		.280/.356/.422					

Comparables: Ryan Jackson, Mike Rouse, Edwin Maysonet

Limited by the rules to just one position player—at least until 2021—most KBO teams opt to sign a slugger to anchor the middle of their order. Lotte took a different tack, signing the glove-first Machado and hoping that his 2019 Triple-A numbers would translate to climes without such a juicy baseball. Good move. The former Tiger managed a better than league average line at the plate, but shone particularly brightly in the field. In a circuit where even the most routine grounders to short can't be taken for granted, the 28-year-old dazzled with a collection of highlight plays and provided the league's sturdiest defense at the six. By far the biggest difference in the quality of play between the KBO and the big leagues shows up on defense, and it's thus a little surprising that more teams haven't signed their own Dixon Machado. Perhaps his success in 2020 will spark a trend.

Na Sung-bom 나성범 RF   Born: 10/03/89   Age: 31   Bats: L   Throws: L   Height: 6'0"   Weight: 220

YEAR	TEAM	LVL	AGE	PA	R	2B	3B	HR	RBI	BB	K	SB	CS	Whiff%	AVG/OBP/SLG	DRC+	BABIP	BRR	FRAA	WARP
2018	NC	KBO	28	620	110	36	3	23	91	44	131	15	2		.318/.381/.518					
2019	NC	KBO	29	106	19	12	1	4	14	12	26	2	1		.366/.443/.645					
2020	NC	KBO	30	584	115	37	2	34	112	49	148	3	1		.324/.390/.596					

A gruesome leg injury delayed Na's MLB dreams, but after a healthy 2020, it's full speed ahead to the other side of the Pacific. Na's game is one that American audiences will recognize: He's a corner outfielder with legitimate plus raw power and a knack for getting it into games. He can hit the ball out to all fields, and while he's a fastball hitter at heart, he's far from helpless against the bendy stuff. The problem here is that even back breaking balls and changeups can lure him out of the zone, particularly below the knees; anyone running a 26 percent whiff rate in Korea will have one heck of an adjustment to make in the states. That's not to say Na can't carve a role for himself, but there are KBO stars with worse numbers who are better bets to crack a big-league lineup.

Roberto Ramos 1B   Born: 12/28/94   Age: 26   Bats: L   Throws: R   Height: 6'3"   Weight: 220   Origin: Round 16, 2014 Draft (#473 overall)

YEAR	TEAM	LVL	AGE	PA	R	2B	3B	HR	RBI	BB	K	SB	CS	Whiff%	AVG/OBP/SLG	DRC+	BABIP	BRR	FRAA	WARP
2018	LAN	HI-A	23	255	44	15	3	17	43	32	65	3	1		.304/.411/.640	159	.364	1.2	1B(42): -0.8	1.2
2018	HFD	AA	23	228	26	9	0	15	34	26	75	2	1		.231/.320/.503	116	.279	-1.1	1B(42): -0.4	0.2
2019	ABQ	AAA	24	503	77	27	0	30	105	61	141	0	1		.309/.400/.580	124	.390	-1.3	1B(104): -7.8, 3B(2): -0.1	1.4
2020	LG	KBO	25	494	74	17	2	38	86	55	136	2	0		.278/.362/.592					

Comparables: Chris Carter, Brad Eldred, Mat Gamel

It's not often that a big-league prospect (okay, fine, a *fringy* big-league prospect) will pack his bats and head overseas before reaching the show, but Ramos did just that in 2020. The timing was perfect, as smacking 38 homers and collecting half a million bucks for the pleasure sounds a lot better than getting stiffed at an alternate training site like his former Quad-A brethren. But if Ramos was hoping to parlay his time in Asia into an MLB deal, a la Eric Thames, he'll probably need to take another spin through the league. A torrid start oversells his overall line, as KBO pitchers soon found real holes in his swing and exploited his lack of bat speed. Wherever he goes, he's tracking to have Roberto Petagine's career. Perhaps he should call up Petagine—a former LG Twin himself—and ask which continent he enjoyed playing on more.

Jamie Romak RF Born: 09/30/85 Age: 35 Bats: R Throws: R Height: 6'2" Weight: 220 Origin: Round 4, 2003 Draft (#127 overall)

YEAR	TEAM	LVL	AGE	PA	R	2B	3B	HR	RBI	BB	K	SB	CS	Whiff%	AVG/OBP/SLG	DRC+	BABIP	BRR	FRAA	WARP
2018	SK	KBO	32	616	102	19	0	43	107	72	123	10	5		.316/.404/.597					
2019	SK	KBO	33	589	86	28	1	29	95	73	117	6	3		.276/.370/.508					
2020	SK	KBO	34	586	85	32	0	32	91	91	116	4	2		.282/.399/.546					

As SK slogged through a dreadful and disappointing season, Romak managed to endure the campaign without once changing facial expressions. Perhaps that natural stoicism goes some way toward explaining his extremely consistent production since joining the Wyverns back in 2017. Thirty-five years old now, Romak is too old to get another big league shot, but young enough to post a few more 130 OPS+ seasons in Korea before he hangs 'em up.

Addison Russell 2B Born: 01/23/94 Age: 27 Bats: R Throws: R Height: 6'0" Weight: 200 Origin: Round 1, 2012 Draft (#11 overall)

YEAR	TEAM	LVL	AGE	PA	R	2B	3B	HR	RBI	BB	K	SB	CS	Whiff%	AVG/OBP/SLG	DRC+	BABIP	BRR	FRAA	WARP
2018	CHC	MLB	24	465	52	21	1	5	38	40	99	4	0	27.1%	.250/.317/.340	80	.314	-0.8	SS(129): 1.2	1.0
2019	IOW	AAA	25	119	25	6	0	7	26	14	25	1	2		.281/.387/.562	113	.294	-0.1	SS(18): 0.4, 2B(7): 1.7	0.8
2019	CHC	MLB	25	241	25	4	1	9	23	20	58	2	0	30.3%	.237/.308/.391	83	.280	0.0	2B(63): 3.4, SS(21): -0.2	0.7
2020	KIW	KBO	26	271	22	14	0	2	31	22	37	2	0		.254/.317/.336					

Comparables: Jose Valentin, Jed Lowrie, Dansby Swanson

My, how the mighty have fallen.

Son Ah-seop 손광민 OF Born: 03/18/88 Age: 33 Bats: L Throws: R Height: 5'9" Weight: 190

YEAR	TEAM	LVL	AGE	PA	R	2B	3B	HR	RBI	BB	K	SB	CS	Whiff%	AVG/OBP/SLG	DRC+	BABIP	BRR	FRAA	WARP
2018	LOT	KBO	30	625	109	32	5	26	93	68	99	20	3		.329/.404/.546					
2019	LOT	KBO	31	568	78	22	1	10	63	52	92	13	8		.295/.360/.400					
2020	LOT	KBO	32	611	98	43	0	11	85	61	56	5	0		.352/.415/.493					

The first thing you'll notice about Son is his bat. Not his production with the bat—though there's much to write home about there—but the actual stick itself. In lieu of a traditional knob, Son uses an axe-bat (the handle looks how you'd expect from the name), which is unusual enough even before you factor in the strange, donut-like appendage attached to it that forces him to choke up. Hit .350, and they call you colorful.

Preston Tucker LF Born: 07/06/90 Age: 31 Bats: L Throws: L Height: 6'0" Weight: 210 Origin: Round 7, 2012 Draft (#219 overall)

YEAR	TEAM	LVL	AGE	PA	R	2B	3B	HR	RBI	BB	K	SB	CS	Whiff%	AVG/OBP/SLG	DRC+	BABIP	BRR	FRAA	WARP
2018	GWN	AAA	27	62	7	4	1	0	6	2	5	0	0		.250/.274/.350	72	.273	0.4	LF(14): 0.1	-0.1
2018	CIN	MLB	27	42	4	1	0	2	5	4	9	0	0	21.8%	.189/.286/.378	90	.192	-0.2	LF(10): -2.6	-0.2
2018	ATL	MLB	27	142	15	10	0	4	22	9	34	0	0	26.8%	.240/.303/.411	85	.293	0.4	LF(27): 1.2, RF(4): -0.2	0.3
2019	CHA	AAA	28	93	14	8	0	1	10	9	7	0	1		.277/.344/.410	98	.289	-0.6	LF(14): -0.4, RF(3): 0.0	0.1
2019	KIA	KBO	28	399	50	33	0	9	50	38	44	0	0		.311/.381/.479					
2020	KIA	KBO	29	631	100	40	0	32	113	76	67	0	2		.306/.398/.557					

Comparables: Mike Colangelo, Ryan Rua, Jon Knott

"Hit a car, win the car" is the rule of the game at Gwangju Kia Champions Field, and Tucker earned a bit of notoriety by denting the Kia Sorrento perched atop the right field pavilion last May. In his first full season in Tigers colors, Tucker and his amusingly tiny batting helmet torched the league. His OPS was good for fifth in the league, all the more impressive considering his cavernous home park. The 30-year-old has all of the physical skills you normally find in a big-league regular; his one fatal flaw is that he can't *not* swing at the high cheese. Major-league pitchers figured this out quickly enough, and ate him alive with heaters up, well out of the zone. But while he swung and missed at that pitch in the states, KBO pitchers don't throw quite so hard, and all of those empty hacks turned into foul balls over in Korea. Eventually they threw something else, often to their detriment. If he can keep from scratching the big-league itch, he'll rake in Asia for as long as he wants.

Yang Eui-je 양의지 C Born: 06/05/87 Age: 34 Bats: R Throws: R Height: 5'11" Weight: 188

YEAR	TEAM	LVL	AGE	PA	R	2B	3B	HR	RBI	BB	K	SB	CS	Whiff%	AVG/OBP/SLG	DRC+	BABIP	BRR	FRAA	WARP
2018	DOO	KBO	31	503	84	29	1	23	77	45	40	6	0		.358/.427/.585					
2019	NC	KBO	32	459	61	26	0	20	68	48	43	4	3		.354/.438/.574					
2020	NC	KBO	33	528	86	26	1	33	124	46	47	5	2		.328/.400/.603					

Review the list of KBO stars set to test their mettle in las ligas mayores, and an obvious question arises: Why isn't Yang one of them? As a player, Yang has many virtues. The Korean Series MVP walks more than he whiffs, regularly hits .300, slugs .600 and plays first on the days he's not in the bucket. Obviously, there would be drawbacks. He's not as good defensively as the Zuninos of the world, and you'd rather not have a big language barrier between your catcher and pitching staff. Still, the state of MLB catching is dire right now. Few can hit their weight, and increasingly, the defensive skills that clubs seem to prioritize are trainable. For teams who can't stomach J.T. Realmuto's contract but still needs help behind the plate, Yang could serve as a creative stopgap.

PITCHERS

Aaron Brooks RHP Born: 04/27/90 Age: 31 Bats: R Throws: R Height: 6'4" Weight: 230 Origin: Round 9, 2011 Draft (#276 overall)

YEAR	TEAM	LVL	AGE	W	L	SV	G	GS	IP	H	HR	BB/9	K/9	K	GB%	BABIP	WHIP	ERA	DRA-	WARP	MPH	FA%	Whiff%	CSP
2018	RMV	AAA	28	9	4	0	26	15	99¹	100	8	2.5	6.7	74	54.9%	.309	1.29	3.35	98	1.0				
2018	OAK	MLB	28	0	0	0	3	0	2²	1	0	6.8	3.4	1	71.4%	.143	1.12	0.00	105	0.0	94.1	45.2%	0.0%	43.4%
2019	BAL	MLB	29	4	5	0	14	12	59²	69	9	3.0	5.9	39	45.5%	.312	1.49	6.18	120	-0.1	93.7	50.3%	18.6%	48.0%
2019	OAK	MLB	29	2	3	0	15	6	50¹	49	12	2.5	7.7	43	40.3%	.261	1.25	5.01	130	-0.4	94.3	58.4%	20.8%	47.7%
2020	KIA	KBO	30	11	4	0	23	23	151¹	131	4	1.0	7.7	130			1.02	2.50						

Comparables: Chris Stratton, Jordan Lyles, Mike Wright

For four and a half months, Brooks was one of the best pitchers in the KBO. He had the league's top FIP and lowest home run rate, and was one of the main drivers behind a surprisingly decent Kia Tigers club as they battled for the playoffs. Then, real life intervened. Back home in Kansas, Brooks' wife and two children were involved in a serious car accident. Everyone survived, but two-year-old Westin was badly hurt and ultimately lost an eye; Brooks immediately flew back to the United States to be with his family. His departure effectively ended Brooks's season and with it any real chance Kia had of reaching the playoffs. In the wake of that disappointment, the ensuing support of the Brooks family from the Tigers, their fans, and the rest of the league speaks volumes about the Korean League's generosity of spirit and order of priorities. Everyone on the Tigers, and many other players from around the league, wrote Westin's initials on their caps. Kia started a "praying for the Brooks family" campaign and hung Aaron's jersey in the dugout for the remainder of the season. A continent away, the Brooks family regularly expressed the gratitude they felt toward the community in Gwangju. In lieu of testing big-league waters after a very successful season, Aaron immediately re-signed with the Tigers. In a year where baseball often seemed less important than ever, this was perhaps the finest example of the game's capacity to unify and uplift.

David Buchanan RHP Born: 05/11/89 Age: 32 Bats: R Throws: R Height: 6'3" Weight: 200 Origin: Round 7, 2010 Draft (#231 overall)

YEAR	TEAM	LVL	AGE	W	L	SV	G	GS	IP	H	HR	BB/9	K/9	K	GB%	BABIP	WHIP	ERA	DRA-	WARP	MPH	FA%	Whiff%	CSP
2018	YKL	NPB	29	10	11	0	28	28	174¹	186	17	2.0	4.9	95			1.37	4.03						
2019	YKL	NPB	30	4	6	0	18		99²	118	10	3.0	5.2	58			1.51	4.79						
2020	SAM	KBO	31	15	7	0	27	27	174²	172	16	2.0	6.2	121			1.27	3.45						

Been a while since you've thought about this guy, eh? The Lions took a bit of a gamble on Buchanan, signing him to a one-year deal after three pretty mediocre seasons in the NPB. But the competition in the KBO is a half-step below the Japanese league, and the right-hander found his footing immediately. While his peripherals don't look amazing, Buchanan is the kind of player who can break DIPS theory, at least in this circuit. One of the harder throwers in the league, KBO bats have a very hard time squaring up his low-to-mid 90s velocity. He's around the plate all the time, and taken together, you can understand why he was able to run a .292 BABIP—the 12th-best mark amongst starters in the league. He's probably not going to miss enough bats to ever be a top-five arm in this league, but for the Lions, Buchanan makes sense as a proven commodity who can hold down the fort while Samsung's very young rotation takes its lumps.

Ryan Carpenter LHP Born: 08/22/90 Age: 30 Bats: L Throws: L Height: 6'5" Weight: 230 Origin: Round 7, 2011 Draft (#240 overall)

YEAR	TEAM	LVL	AGE	W	L	SV	G	GS	IP	H	HR	BB/9	K/9	K	GB%	BABIP	WHIP	ERA	DRA-	WARP	MPH	FA%	Whiff%	CSP
2018	TOL	AAA	27	2	8	0	14	14	76¹	96	8	2.5	8.6	73	32.7%	.374	1.53	5.07	93	0.8				
2018	DET	MLB	27	1	2	0	6	5	22¹	34	8	1.6	6.0	15	34.1%	.338	1.70	7.25	129	-0.1	91.7	51.6%	20.9%	51.0%
2019	TOL	AAA	28	5	7	0	14	14	77	77	11	3.0	8.9	76	41.5%	.310	1.34	5.26	97	1.5				
2019	DET	MLB	28	1	6	0	9	9	40²	61	12	2.9	5.5	25	36.3%	.338	1.82	9.30	185	-1.4	91.9	45.2%	16.2%	51.9%
2020	RAK	CPBL	29	11	7	0	29	28	172²	194	14	1.8	8.9	170			1.33	3.81						

Comparables: Jerad Eickhoff, Matt Koch, Justin Haley

Even when they were the class of the league in the first month or two of the season, the Monkeys were never exactly known for their pitching. That being said, Carpenter added some stability to the Rakuten staff, leading their starters in ERA and strikeouts while effectively limiting walks and homers. The long-time Tigers farmhand appeared for some brief, unmemorable stints with the big league team in 2018 and 2019. But his solid work in 2020 reportedly turned some heads, as there were rumors in August that a KBO team was looking to lure Carpenter away from the Monkeys for their stretch run. That ticket finally arrived in the offseason; he'll move up—and down—to the KBO, and to its worst team, the Hanwha Eagles, in 2021.

William Cuevas RHP Born: 10/14/90 Age: 30 Bats: S Throws: R Height: 6'2" Weight: 215

YEAR	TEAM	LVL	AGE	W	L	SV	G	GS	IP	H	HR	BB/9	K/9	K	GB%	BABIP	WHIP	ERA	DRA-	WARP	MPH	FA%	Whiff%	CSP
2018	WOR	AAA	27	10	7	0	23	23	135¹	120	17	2.5	8.0	121	31.2%	.272	1.17	3.39	98	1.0				
2018	BOS	MLB	27	0	2	0	9	1	17	20	3	5.8	10.6	20	49.0%	.378	1.82	7.41	140	-0.3	92.6	39.0%	31.7%	41.6%
2019	KT	KBO	28	13	10	0	30	30	184	153	18	3.0	6.6	135			1.17	3.62						
2020	KT	KBO	29	10	8	0	27	27	158	152	16	2.0	6.3	110			1.25	4.10						

Comparables: Alec Mills, Austin Voth, Adam Plutko

Velocity, command and movement are the bedrocks of pitching. To hack it in the majors, you need at least two of those, and Cuevas only has the latter. A late season cameo with Boston in 2018 earned him a ring, and perhaps sensing that his big league luck could only run so much further, he repaired to Korea soon after. An extended dead arm period at the start of 2020 fluffed up his overall line, but upon his return to action in the summer, Cuevas was one of the better hurlers in the league. His pitch mix is best described as "slippery," as seemingly everything in his arsenal moves like it's covered in Crisco. When he's dealing, Korean hitters simply can't square him up. Between that and the joy he radiates in the dugout, hamming it up with teammates and goofing off whenever the camera finds him, it appears he's found his baseball home for as long as KT will have him.

Odrisamer Despaigne RHP   Born: 04/04/87   Age: 34   Bats: R   Throws: R   Height: 6'0"   Weight: 200   Origin: International Free Agent, 2014

YEAR	TEAM	LVL	AGE	W	L	SV	G	GS	IP	H	HR	BB/9	K/9	K	GB%	BABIP	WHIP	ERA	DRA-	WARP	MPH	FA%	Whiff%	CSP
2018	NO	AAA	31	2	3	2	13	4	43¹	52	0	2.5	8.3	40	43.1%	.380	1.48	4.36	82	0.7				
2018	MIA	MLB	31	2	0	0	11	1	20¹	22	1	3.5	8.0	18	39.1%	.339	1.48	5.31	103	0.1	94.1	71.6%	31.3%	43.3%
2018	LAA	MLB	31	0	3	0	8	4	18²	30	3	5.3	8.2	17	44.1%	.415	2.20	8.20	150	-0.4	95.0	67.2%	20.9%	48.9%
2019	CHA	AAA	32	5	4	0	16	14	83	83	6	3.0	9.1	84	47.7%	.335	1.34	3.25	90	1.8				
2019	LOU	AAA	32	3	2	0	8	8	41¹	40	5	3.5	8.7	40	50.8%	.310	1.35	3.92	105	0.6				
2019	CHW	MLB	32	0	2	0	3	3	13¹	24	3	4.7	4.7	7	28.3%	.420	2.33	9.45	205	-0.6	94.5	74.8%	13.6%	45.2%
2020	KT	KBO	33	15	8	0	35	34	207²	233	18	2.0	6.6	152			1.45	4.33						

Comparables: Trevor Cahill, Ross Ohlendorf, Josh A. Smith

At a glance, Despaigne's numbers aren't all that impressive, and the two statistics that best capture his importance to KT—games started and innings pitched—are usually afterthoughts. But unlike in MLB, where the third time through the order penalty reduces a team's incentive to push their starters, top arms in the KBO need to eat innings. Usually, they do so as part of a six-day rotation, as every Monday is an off-day in the KBO. KT took a different tack with Despaigne, using him on a five-day schedule all season long. Working with less rest than anybody else, the journeyman right-hander still posted a well-above average ERA and FIP, all while making five more starts and tossing 50 more innings than the typical foreign signing. Those extra starts and innings would have otherwise gone to one of three longmen, all of whom notched ERAs on the wrong side of six. In a year where KT snuck into second place, a single game ahead of fifth-place Kiwoom, two things are clear: Manager Lee Kang-chul deserves a tip of the cap, and Despaigne deserves a raise.

Wilmer Font RHP   Born: 05/24/90   Age: 31   Bats: R   Throws: R   Height: 6'4"   Weight: 255   Origin: International Free Agent, 2006

YEAR	TEAM	LVL	AGE	W	L	SV	G	GS	IP	H	HR	BB/9	K/9	K	GB%	BABIP	WHIP	ERA	DRA-	WARP	MPH	FA%	Whiff%	CSP
2018	LAD	MLB	28	0	2	0	6	0	10¹	18	5	0.9	6.1	7	42.5%	.371	1.84	11.32	157	-0.2	96.3	69.5%	16.1%	51.9%
2018	OAK	MLB	28	0	0	0	4	0	6²	13	5	5.4	12.2	9	33.3%	.421	2.55	14.85	84	0.1	96.9	68.5%	29.7%	41.7%
2018	TB	MLB	28	2	1	0	9	5	27	15	2	3.7	6.7	20	45.3%	.178	0.96	1.67	144	-0.4	97.5	63.6%	21.3%	49.0%
2019	TOR	MLB	29	2	3	0	23	14	39¹	34	7	2.5	12.1	53	35.1%	.300	1.14	3.66	73	0.8	96.8	61.8%	29.0%	47.3%
2019	NYM	MLB	29	1	2	0	15	3	31	29	8	3.8	7.0	24	35.8%	.241	1.35	4.94	134	-0.4	96.9	58.5%	24.7%	47.9%
2019	TB	MLB	29	1	0	0	10	0	14	15	2	3.2	11.6	18	43.2%	.371	1.43	5.79	103	0.1	96.5	50.9%	29.6%	46.9%
2020	TOR	MLB	30	1	3	0	21	0	16¹	28	2	5.0	8.3	15	35.0%	.448	2.27	9.92	110	0.1	97.1	70.1%	19.3%	46.8%

Comparables: Burch Smith, Matt Magill, Tyler Chatwood

Font was designated for assignment mere hours before the Jays clinched a playoff berth, which sums up how well this season went for him. Hints of competence were almost always followed by unmitigated disasters. Over Font's final three appearances for the Jays, he allowed five hits, five runs and five walks while recording just five outs; toward the end of the season, the mere announcement of his name, the sight of him jogging out of the bullpen, became enough to induce an overwhelming sense of despair. It was one of those seasons where absolutely nothing worked. The only comfort for Font is that it was a short one. He'll join the SK Wyverns, who have had no shortage of disappointment of late.

Eric Jokisch LHP   Born: 07/29/89   Age: 31   Bats: R   Throws: L   Height: 6'2"   Weight: 205   Origin: Round 11, 2010 Draft (#340 overall)

YEAR	TEAM	LVL	AGE	W	L	SV	G	GS	IP	H	HR	BB/9	K/9	K	GB%	BABIP	WHIP	ERA	DRA-	WARP	MPH	FA%	Whiff%	CSP
2018	NAS	AAA	28	5	11	1	26	23	148²	165	12	2.8	7.3	121	52.1%	.328	1.42	4.06	81	2.9				
2019	KIW	KBO	29	13	9	0	30	30	181¹	166	9	1.0	7.0	141			1.13	3.13						
2020	KIW	KBO	30	12	7	0	27	27	159²	144	6	1.0	6.5	115			1.06	2.14						

Comparables: Jerad Eickhoff, Casey Sadler, T.J. McFarland

Despite a half-decade of solid production in Triple-A, Jokisch never really got a fair look in the majors; his only big league action amounted to 14 September innings on the last Cubs team of the pre-Joe Maddon era. After yet another solid campaign in 2018 went unrewarded, the soft-tossing lefty decided his fortunes lied in the Far East and he's proved to be an excellent signing for Kiwoom. His glistening ERA (222 ERA+!) in 2020 oversells his ability, even as he's been plenty dominant. While he doesn't miss all that many bats, he spots everything in his four-pitch mix well, and he finished second in the KBO in BB% and HR%. In an era marked by the mistake hitter, teams really have to beat Jokisch three times to score a run. In contrast to his former American employers, Kiwoom seems to know what they have: Just two weeks after the season, the Heroes re-signed him for 2021 while nearly doubling his salary.

Casey Kelly RHP   Born: 10/04/89   Age: 31   Bats: R   Throws: R   Height: 6'3"   Weight: 215   Origin: Round 1, 2008 Draft (#30 overall)

YEAR	TEAM	LVL	AGE	W	L	SV	G	GS	IP	H	HR	BB/9	K/9	K	GB%	BABIP	WHIP	ERA	DRA-	WARP	MPH	FA%	Whiff%	CSP
2018	SAC	AAA	28	10	9	0	24	24	136	155	19	2.5	7.3	111	40.5%	.328	1.42	4.76	92	1.9				
2018	SF	MLB	28	0	3	0	7	3	23²	28	3	1.9	6.1	16	50.0%	.316	1.39	3.04	78	0.5	93.6	52.7%	22.8%	49.6%
2019	LG	KBO	29	14	12	0	29	29	180¹	164	7	2.0	6.3	126			1.14	2.55						
2020	LG	KBO	30	15	7	0	28	28	173¹	160	16	2.0	7.0	134			1.15	3.32						

Comparables: Jordan Lyles, Chris Stratton, Erasmo Ramírez

Kelly's comprehensive blandness has always made his game difficult to enjoy. Like Bon Iver, there's not any one flaw that stands out, but rather a collection of underwhelming traits and tools that leaves you wanting more. But while Kelly's stuff is a little light for MLB, it's plenty good in South Korea. He quickly emerged as LG's ace, and his collection of 45's on the scouting report made him one of the league's top starters. As with many other Quad-A talents, sometimes you just have to hit the road to find success.

Koo Chang-Mo 구창모 LHP Born: 02/17/97 Age: 24 Bats: L Throws: L Height: 6'0" Weight: 167

YEAR	TEAM	LVL	AGE	W	L	SV	G	GS	IP	H	HR	BB/9	K/9	K	GB%	BABIP	WHIP	ERA	DRA-	WARP	MPH	FA%	Whiff%	CSP
2018	NC	KBO	21	5	11	0	36	23	133	158	21	3.0	7.8	116			1.58	5.35						
2019	NC	KBO	22	10	7	0	23	19	107	85	10	3.0	9.6	114			1.18	3.36						
2020	NC	KBO	23	9	0	0	15	14	93¹	58	7	1.0	9.8	102			0.81	1.74						

Injuries are the only thing standing between Koo and a job in an MLB rotation. While the southpaw doesn't throw all that hard, scraping the low-90s but sitting in the upper-80s, everything else in his game stands out. He has elite command of two swing-and-miss offspeed pitches—a fading change with late sink, and a nasty slider that just falls off the table—and tremendous feel for the corners of the strike zone. A forearm strain, and the small fracture that accompanied his rehab, limited him to three months' work, though he was able to return for a triumphant Korean Series in which he gave up two earned runs in 13 innings. Pedestrian arm strength makes it hard to project Koo as more than a No. 3/4 type stateside, but provided that he stays healthy, it's just a matter of time before we see him in the majors.

Walker Lockett RHP Born: 05/03/94 Age: 27 Bats: R Throws: R Height: 6'5" Weight: 225 Origin: Round 4, 2012 Draft (#135 overall)

YEAR	TEAM	LVL	AGE	W	L	SV	G	GS	IP	H	HR	BB/9	K/9	K	GB%	BABIP	WHIP	ERA	DRA-	WARP	MPH	FA%	Whiff%	CSP
2018	ELP	AAA	24	5	9	0	23	23	133¹	145	17	2.2	8.0	118	45.8%	.327	1.33	4.72	86	2.3				
2018	SD	MLB	24	0	3	0	4	3	15	22	4	6.0	7.2	12	55.6%	.360	2.13	9.60	135	-0.1	94.3	55.5%	21.4%	44.6%
2019	STL	HI-A	25	1	0	0	2	2	7	8	1	0.0	7.7	6	52.2%	.318	1.14	5.14	85	0.1				
2019	SYR	AAA	25	3	3	0	11	10	59	75	5	1.7	5.9	39	54.5%	.343	1.46	3.66	91	1.3				
2019	NYM	MLB	25	1	1	0	9	4	22²	33	6	2.4	6.4	16	41.2%	.370	1.72	8.34	101	0.2	94.4	54.3%	16.0%	51.3%
2020	TOR	MLB	26	1	0	0	7	1	16¹	21	2	2.2	6.1	11	42.9%	.352	1.53	4.96	102	0.1	95.0	34.8%	20.7%	54.5%

Comparables: Drew Anderson, John Gant, Lucas Sims

When you're a sinkerballer with a 41.8 percent groundball rate, you tend to move around a lot. Lockett shuffled the deck in 2020, favoring his good curveball and abandoning his four-seamer for the aforementioned sinker, but he struggled to get it down in the zone, so it was really just a less-fast fastball. The Mariners claimed him off waivers in September, the Blue Jays in December, and the Doosan Bears of the KBO shortly after. He'll have one last chance to reinvent himself; the real tragedy is that there are only so many pitches one can learn.

Daniel Mengden RHP Born: 02/19/93 Age: 28 Bats: R Throws: R Height: 6'1" Weight: 215 Origin: Round 4, 2014 Draft (#106 overall)

YEAR	TEAM	LVL	AGE	W	L	SV	G	GS	IP	H	HR	BB/9	K/9	K	GB%	BABIP	WHIP	ERA	DRA-	WARP	MPH	FA%	Whiff%	CSP
2018	NAS	AAA	25	4	1	0	9	8	45¹	39	2	1.4	6.8	34	42.8%	.274	1.01	2.98	82	0.9				
2018	OAK	MLB	25	7	6	0	22	17	115²	103	18	2.0	5.6	72	38.9%	.241	1.12	4.05	120	-0.2	94.2	53.0%	18.2%	51.6%
2019	LV	AAA	26	4	3	0	13	10	64	56	8	2.8	8.6	61	52.9%	.268	1.19	4.22	49	2.6				
2019	OAK	MLB	26	5	2	1	13	9	59²	59	7	4.1	6.3	42	37.2%	.283	1.44	4.83	153	-1.1	93.5	52.6%	15.1%	48.5%
2020	OAK	MLB	27	0	1	0	4	1	12¹	14	2	5.1	7.3	10	40.0%	.316	1.70	3.65	120	0.0	92.2	51.5%	19.6%	45.2%

Comparables: Jeff Hoffman, Erick Fedde, Jakob Junis

DRA isn't a particular fan of Mengden's work, his resultant negative career WARP a swing of several wins from other value scales. Chalk this round up as a win for DRA, then, with Oakland designating the 30-year-old for assignment in September and ultimately outrighting him to Triple-A. Instead, he'll ply his trade with the Kia Tigers in 2021.

Aríel Miranda LHP Born: 01/10/89 Age: 32 Bats: L Throws: L Height: 6'2" Weight: 190 Origin: International Free Agent, 2015

YEAR	TEAM	LVL	AGE	W	L	SV	G	GS	IP	H	HR	BB/9	K/9	K	GB%	BABIP	WHIP	ERA	DRA-	WARP	MPH	FA%	Whiff%	CSP
2018	TAC	AAA	29	5	0	0	10	9	45¹	44	3	4.8	7.9	40	34.8%	.318	1.50	3.97	107	0.3				
2018	FKU	NPB	29	6	1	0	8	8	47²	28	3	5.0	7.6	40			1.15	1.89						
2018	SEA	MLB	29	0	0	0	1	1	5	6	0	7.2	9.0	5	40.0%	.400	2.00	1.80	132	0.0	93.0	59.8%	27.5%	51.2%
2019	FKU	NPB	30	7	5	0	18		86	80	13	5.0	6.1	58			1.49	4.19						
2020	CTB	CPBL	31	10	8	0	26	26	160¹	150	14	3.4	9.8	175			1.32	3.70						

Comparables: Nick Tropeano, Wily Peralta, Chad Bettis

A foreign southpaw like De Paula, Miranda was another new addition to the Brothers' rotation prior to the 2020 season. A veteran of the Cuban National Series before signing with the Orioles in 2015, Miranda's experience spans beyond the 200+ innings he threw for Baltimore and Seattle in the latter half of the 2010s, as well as parts of two seasons with the Fukuoka Softbank Hawks. With the Brothers last year he was able to step in and co-anchor the pitching staff with De Paula. Third in the league in ERA and second in strikeout rate among qualified starters, Miranda spun a gem in Game 3 of the Taiwan Series, throwing a three-hit complete game against the Lions. It was enough to earn him a promotion, as he'll spend 2021 with the Doosan Bears of the KBO.

Ricardo Pinto RHP Born: 01/20/94 Age: 27 Bats: R Throws: R Height: 6'0" Weight: 195

YEAR	TEAM	LVL	AGE	W	L	SV	G	GS	IP	H	HR	BB/9	K/9	K	GB%	BABIP	WHIP	ERA	DRA-	WARP	MPH	FA%	Whiff%	CSP
2018	WS	HI-A	24	1	0	0	3	3	10²	13	2	6.8	6.8	8	52.8%	.324	1.97	6.75	85	0.2				
2018	CHA	AAA	24	2	2	0	27	3	54¹	68	7	3.6	6.3	38	50.0%	.349	1.66	5.80	97	0.3				
2019	MTG	AA	25	2	1	0	4	2	18²	20	2	3.9	7.2	15	22.8%	.333	1.50	4.82	130	-0.4				
2019	DUR	AAA	25	10	5	0	24	4	104²	96	18	4.0	8.3	96	48.0%	.283	1.36	4.13	92	1.9				
2019	TB	MLB	25	0	0	0	2	0	2¹	4	1	7.7	0.0	0	45.5%	.300	2.57	15.43	135	0.0	97.1	66.7%	16.7%	55.2%
2020	SK	KBO	26	6	15	0	30	30	162	198	19	5.0	6.2	112			1.78	6.17						

Comparables: Chih-Wei Hu, Thyago Vieira, Miguel Almonte

Yikes. Former big leaguers are supposed to headline your rotation in the KBO, but in this case, the anchor was heavier than the ship. At one point in a dreadful stretch of 10 outings, he allowed four runs or more nine times, and his ERA in July and August was 8.95, a figure once thought to be only a theoretical possibility. You could chart Pinto's season by the shift in his facial reactions over the course of the year. Like a man navigating the stages of grief, spring smiles of disbelief soon gave way to visible frustration, then desperate pleas to the wind to push just one one of those soaring fly balls back into the yard. By early autumn, the collision of baseball and left field bleacher could do no more damage to Pinto's already cadaverous expression. As of this writing, he's still in the rotation, and his brow remains furrowed; the beatings will continue until morale improves.

Drew Rucinski RHP   Born: 12/30/88   Age: 32   Bats: R   Throws: R   Height: 6'2"   Weight: 190

YEAR	TEAM	LVL	AGE	W	L	SV	G	GS	IP	H	HR	BB/9	K/9	K	GB%	BABIP	WHIP	ERA	DRA-	WARP	MPH	FA%	Whiff%	CSP
2018	NO	AAA	29	0	0	0	14	0	25	27	0	2.2	7.6	21	57.3%	.365	1.32	2.52	56	0.7				
2018	MIA	MLB	29	4	2	0	32	0	35¹	34	2	3.3	6.9	27	47.3%	.299	1.33	4.33	92	0.3	95.2	48.1%	23.9%	47.9%
2019	NC	KBO	30	9	9	0	30	30	177¹	164	13	2.0	6.0	119			1.18	3.05						
2020	NC	KBO	31	19	5	0	30	30	183	173	14	2.0	8.2	167			1.26	3.05						

Comparables: César Ramos, Justin Grimm, Joe Biagini

Most of the international pitchers in the KBO are spot starters, or at the very least Triple-A workhorses. Rucinski was thus an odd choice for the Dinos to pursue, as the right-hander had barely started at all in his past five seasons. The gamble proved a masterstroke, as Rucinski quickly became one of the league's top arms and the driving force behind the club's Korean Series victory. The right-hander started twice, winning both games, and also pitched three innings of dominant relief in Game 4 to even the series at two apiece. He may not have planned to become Korea's Madison Bumgarner, but it's certainly not a bad life to stumble into.

Josh A. Smith RHP   Born: 08/07/87   Age: 33   Bats: R   Throws: R   Height: 6'2"   Weight: 210   Origin: Round 21, 2010 Draft (#637 overall)

YEAR	TEAM	LVL	AGE	W	L	SV	G	GS	IP	H	HR	BB/9	K/9	K	GB%	BABIP	WHIP	ERA	DRA-	WARP	MPH	FA%	Whiff%	CSP
2018	WOR	AAA	30	5	6	1	18	10	74	75	5	1.9	9.2	76	35.2%	.333	1.23	4.14	78	1.3				
2018	TAC	AAA	30	0	2	0	4	1	10¹	17	3	2.6	12.2	14	27.0%	.412	1.94	6.10	74	0.2				
2019	WOR	AAA	31	5	3	0	13	12	67¹	82	9	2.7	9.4	70	37.9%	.376	1.51	5.48	121	0.5				
2019	BOS	MLB	31	0	3	1	18	2	31	36	10	2.3	8.4	29	34.3%	.292	1.42	5.81	148	-0.6	93.1	38.8%	28.3%	44.0%
2020	MIA	MLB	32	1	1	1	16	1	26¹	33	3	3.8	6.2	18	42.9%	.345	1.67	6.84	109	0.1	91.8	35.2%	22.5%	43.7%

Comparables: Odrisamer Despaigne, Trevor Cahill, Chris Rusin

On June 28, 2018, Pawtucket lefty reliever Josh A. Smith had a three-inning courtesy save in a blowout behind righty starting pitcher Josh D. Smith's six scoreless innings. The Joshes Smith went their separate ways after the season, until they became 2020 Marlins. Their bond will be tested again, as the A version signed with Kiwoom.

Dan Straily RHP   Born: 12/01/88   Age: 32   Bats: R   Throws: R   Height: 6'2"   Weight: 220   Origin: Round 24, 2009 Draft (#723 overall)

YEAR	TEAM	LVL	AGE	W	L	SV	G	GS	IP	H	HR	BB/9	K/9	K	GB%	BABIP	WHIP	ERA	DRA-	WARP	MPH	FA%	Whiff%	CSP
2018	JUP	HI-A	29	1	1	0	2	2	7²	11	2	3.5	7.0	6	33.3%	.321	1.83	8.22	69	0.2				
2018	MIA	MLB	29	5	6	0	23	23	122¹	107	20	3.8	7.3	99	31.4%	.259	1.30	4.12	115	0.2	92.0	49.3%	24.0%	46.5%
2019	LHV	AAA	30	1	4	0	6	6	33	33	5	2.5	8.2	30	46.0%	.295	1.27	5.18	90	0.7				
2019	NOR	AAA	30	4	0	0	6	6	34	24	4	2.1	10.1	38	40.2%	.244	0.94	2.38	96	0.7				
2019	BAL	MLB	30	2	4	0	14	8	47²	73	22	4.2	6.2	33	26.8%	.325	1.99	9.82	228	-2.8	92.2	52.3%	18.4%	48.3%
2020	LOT	KBO	31	15	4	0	31	31	194²	148	10	2.0	9.5	205			1.02	2.50						

Comparables: Bud Norris, Dillon Gee, Jake Odorizzi

In 2019, Straily threw up one of the worst pitcher seasons of all time. Like an episode of the podcast Effectively Wild brought to real life, we all had the displeasure of seeing what would happen if you placed a fly ball pitcher on a bad team in a home run ballpark with the most hitter-friendly baseball of all time. To top it off, with the deck already stacked against him, Straily also just pitched like crap. He hung breaking balls, flubbed changeups, located badly and wound up so deep in a funk that the only thing to do was to put a nation and an ocean between himself and Camden Yards and start over. The thing to remember though, is that for as bad as he was, it was just 47 innings. And even 47 of the least inspiring innings of his life is still a pretty tiny sample. After an offseason in the gym and the tweak of a grip, Straily pretty much looked like the backend starter we all got to know over most of his big league career. A big-league no. 4 is a mismatch for the KBO, and with apologies to Koo Chang-mo and Aaron Brooks, Straily was the KBO's best pitcher. He's poised to retain that title after getting a nifty raise to remain with the Lotte Giants for 2021.

CHINESE PROFESSIONAL BASEBALL LEAGUE

Essay by Lucas Apostoleris

Player comments by Lucas Apostoleris and BP staff

At a time when virtually all professional sporting events had been put on hold, the seemingly endless stay-at-home weeks introduced many fans to the Chinese Professional Baseball League (CPBL) – the premier baseball league in Taiwan that, thanks to the country's swift handling of the novel coronavirus and the sport's rapid, well-executed attempt to translate the sport for an English-speaking audience, took center stage in mid-April. The CPBL season was only delayed a few weeks past its typical March starting point, and there were no issues completing the league's typical 120 game season. The league was even able to reintroduce spectators in the stands throughout the summer, an unusual sight compared to the rest of the sports landscape of 2020.

Four teams (a fifth, the Wei Chuan Dragons, is joining via expansion in 2021) battle through a split-schedule season. The reigning champion Uni-President Lions signed three North American pitchers at midseason to storm back and claim the Taiwan Series after falling behind three games to one. The CTBC Brothers rode a dominant rotation led by José de Paula to a dominant first half and a season that just fell short. In the second tier, the Rakuten Monkeys featured an excellent offense and little pitching, while the hitting-starved Fubon Guardians featured the demotion of team captain Chin-Lung Hu after allegations spread that he was trying to get his manager fired.

The vast majority of CPBL players are Taiwan-born, and the most common route to the league is through a yearly draft. Typically, the league's foreign players either have upper-minors experience or are a few years past the end of brief big-league careers; however, last season saw a modest uptick in players with more recent experience (Ryan Carpenter, Manny Bañuelos, Tim Melville, and Ryan Feierabend all made 2019 cameos in the majors). It wouldn't be a surprise to see that trend continue in the coming years, as a shrinking American minor league system and increased exposure for overseas play make the expatriate life an interesting second act for professional ballplayers.

Year	Foreign Players	MLB Experience	Prior Year MLB	Median Age
2015	25	14	1	30
2016	22	10	2	30
2017	18	7	0	31
2018	17	10	0	31
2019	22	10	2	32
2020	22	15	4	31

It's not a stretch to say that in some ways, the CPBL resembles previous eras of the American version of the sport. Not unlike the Korea Baseball Organization and Japan's Nippon Professional Baseball, you're going to see a lot more contact-hitting and action on the basepaths in Taiwan than you will these days in North America, two of the aspects of the game that many of the latter fans miss.

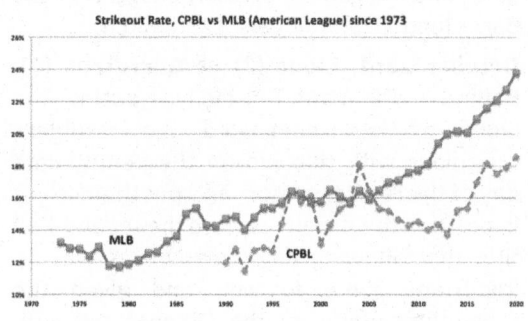

Strikeout Rate, CPBL vs MLB (American League) since 1973

Stolen Bases per Team Game, CPBL vs MLB (both leagues) since 1973

While both measures are not as extreme in the CPBL as they were earlier this century–in fact, the average strikeout rate was at its highest in the league's history this past year–the divergence from what we see in today's version of MLB is stark. There's another aspect of CPBL play that, when compared to professional baseball in the United States, seems to harken back to a previous era: the importance of the starting pitcher. Considering the fact that pitching roles have become increasingly amorphous in Major League Baseball, particularly over the past few years, the reliance on the starter in CPBL games provides a stark contrast. Let's take a look at a few specific examples from last season where the starting pitcher remained central to the game's storyline longer than you might expect.

- **June 6th, Guardians (9) at Monkeys (6).** The Monkeys appeared to have Sosa on the ropes, with a 6-4 lead over Fubon in the 4th inning. The Guardians chipped away, though, and took the lead for good in the 7th inning. When some extra insurance runs gave them a 9-6 cushion in the 8th inning, the Guardians didn't turn to their bullpen: they brought Sosa out for his 8th inning of work, and despite ultimately allowing 12 hits and six runs, Sosa was the winning pitcher after throwing 128 pitches.

- **September 5th, Guardians (0) at Brothers (1).** This was a good ol' fashioned pitcher's duel, with both the Guardians' Kuo-Hao Chiang and the Brothers' Esmil Rogers throwing complete games. Rogers really had to work for it: his team left him in the game despite letting the go-ahead run get to second base, and the game ultimately ended with the bases loaded after Rogers' 123rd pitch.

- **October 23rd, Lions (2) at Guardians (0).** Behind a dominant Tim Mellvile outing, the Lions officially eliminated the resurgent Guardians with this win on the penultimate day of the regular season, and put themselves in position to officially capture the second-half title the following day. Clearly, this was an important game to win, and given the scheduling quirks of the October make-up games, the Lions hadn't played in a full week—so, clearly, they had a fully rested bullpen to work with. But it was starter Melville who went the distance on 123 pitches, capping his outing off with a pair of perfect innings.

These are just three examples, but clearly, the starting pitcher is far more central to the plot of a CPBL game than in the majors: in the 480 CPBL games last season, the starting pitcher threw 100 or more pitches 229 times, or 48 percent of total starts. Compare that to the 1796 MLB games last year, in which the starter reached the century-mark only 14 percent of the time—an all-time low for a league that in recent years has been aggressively emphasizing short starts and infinite pitching changes.

This type of managing style is more prevalent in CPBL than the major leagues, for several reasons. The league's schedule makes it easier for starters to pitch deeper into games: CPBL teams usually have two off-days per week, putting a five-pitcher rotation on a once-a-week schedule. That gives starters more in the tank to work with, since they'll often be working on six days' rest. Foreign player roster spots are another factor; since 2015, there have only been five foreign position players in the league (and none since 2019, when third baseman Alex Liddi and outfielders Roger Bernadina and Eric Wood made cameos), and the vast majority of the pitchers brought in are starters appointed to anchor their team's staff. These foreign import starters are on higher-paying salaries than local players, and it makes sense that their teams are trying to milk them for all they're worth.

But a third reason might get at why the style of play in CPBL seems like a distant memory in the American game: much less of an emphasis is placed on data and "sabermetric principles" than there is in Major League Baseball. Sure, you will see glimmers of a data-centric approach given that there are Trackman cameras in the stadiums, and you might sometimes see an exit velocity reading flash on the broadcast. But on the whole, you're just not going to find the same kind of reliance on analytical evidence from CPBL teams as you will from pretty much any MLB club, particularly to the level of granularity that has led to so much erosion in the aesthetic aspect of the game.

Part of the appeal of CPBL play is how it gives us a window into how things might look if we didn't overthink everything. And at the same time, this must be recognized as a two-way street.

While we looked at where lengthy pitching efforts were rewarded, there are also instances when it backfires spectacularly. In Game 7 of the Taiwan Series, the Brothers began the 7th inning ahead 4-3, with Ariel Miranda returning to the mound having thrown exactly 100 pitches. The Brothers, of all teams, were best equipped to navigate such a situation with their excellent bullpen. Despite Miranda's apparent fatigue setting in, he was allowed to remain in the game and surrender the lead, while the Brothers' well-rested relievers (and helpless fans) could only watch.

But that's just part of the package. The era of shouting helplessly at the television screen, both in joy over a double steal and in horror over a managerial decision, is alive and well in Taiwan. While uncertainty yet again hangs over the start of the 2021 MLB season, the CPBL will kick off on March 13th, with a Taiwan Series rematch between the Brothers and the Lions. For American fans looking for something different than the homogenization within the league over the past decade, the CPBL provides its alternate interpretation of the sport, one built on scoring and energy and effort and, occasionally, hubris. It's almost exactly what sports were meant to deliver. ■

—Lucas Apostoleris is an author of Baseball Prospectus.

HITTERS

Chang Chih-Hao 張志豪 CF Born: 05/15/87 Age: 34 Bats: L Throws: R Height: 5'11" Weight: 179

YEAR	TEAM	LVL	AGE	PA	R	2B	3B	HR	RBI	BB	K	SB	CS	Whiff%	AVG/OBP/SLG	DRC+	BABIP	BRR	FRAA	WARP
2018	CTB	CPBL	31	416	65	21	3	22	61	25	110	4	4		.268/.322/.510		.320			
2019	CTB	CPBL	32	369	63	8	2	26	74	32	97	10	2		.257/.330/.532		.280			
2020	CTB	CPBL	33	418	66	17	0	27	88	36	78	4	0		.298/.373/.564		.311			

Typically regarded as a sure-handed defender in center, 2020 marked the first time in four seasons that Chang did not go home with the league's Gold Glove award. On the flip side, "Hollywood" yet again set a personal best in homers, the seventh time he's done so. Despite only tallying one in 107 games as a rookie back in 2010, Chang has actually hit more homers than any CPBL batter over the past five seasons. Keep in mind that the offensive environment over the past few years is drastically different than it was in the early 2010s, but you could argue that there's a Brett Gardner comparison to be made.

Chen Chen-Wei 陳晨威 2B Born: 12/12/97 Age: 23 Bats: L Throws: R Height: 5'11" Weight: 158

YEAR	TEAM	LVL	AGE	PA	R	2B	3B	HR	RBI	BB	K	SB	CS	Whiff%	AVG/OBP/SLG	DRC+	BABIP	BRR	FRAA	WARP
2018	LAM	CPBL	20	31	4	0	0	1	3	0	4	5	1		.355/.355/.452		.385			
2019	LAM	CPBL	21	423	68	8	11	5	33	37	56	24	7		.298/.364/.418		.338			
2020	RAK	CPBL	22	528	93	16	15	4	56	32	54	42	13		.289/.335/.409		.316			

If you take a look at Chen's triple-slash line, nothing's going to jump out at you. In a high-offense environment like the CPBL, his offensive contributions have amounted to an OPS approximately 20 percent lower than the league average. But what makes Chen a unique player–and incredibly fun to watch–is his blazing speed. Since 2019, when he became a full-time player, Chen has by far the most steals and triples of anyone in the league. His total of 64 steals is hardly challenged by the Guardians' Tsung-Hsien Lee and the Brothers' Wei-Chen Wang, at 44; his whopping 24 triples blows away teammate Li Lin's total of eight. So while he might not reach base as often as his peers, be prepared to watch him fly when he does.

Chen Chieh-Hsien 陳傑憲 OF Born: 01/07/94 Age: 27 Bats: R Throws: L Height: 5'9" Weight: 159

YEAR	TEAM	LVL	AGE	PA	R	2B	3B	HR	RBI	BB	K	SB	CS	Whiff%	AVG/OBP/SLG	DRC+	BABIP	BRR	FRAA	WARP
2018	UNI	CPBL	24	543	104	29	7	8	64	48	45	17	11		.353/.415/.494		.377			
2019	UNI	CPBL	25	88	17	3	0	2	15	8	5	5	2		.372/.432/.487		.375			
2020	UNI	CPBL	26	549	99	32	4	3	67	48	42	21	10		.360/.419/.461		.383			

Chen was the Lions' shortstop as recently as last April, but his continued defensive lapses left the team no choice but to find a new position for him. Fortunately, Chen's transition to the outfield was a seamless one, and he was the team's starting center fielder by mid-May. Which brings us to his offense: Chen was a potent table-setter atop the Lions' lineup in 2020, winning the CPBL batting title and leading qualified hitters with a miniscule strikeout rate of just 7.7 percent. This is nothing new for him, as last year's numbers are right in line with his career norms (.366 average and 7.6 percent strikeouts in 1811 career plate appearances). While Chen is hardly known for his power, his 7th inning two-run home run in Game 7 of the Taiwan Series (which extended the Lions' lead to 7-4) was undoubtedly one of the most important hits not just of the season, but of the many in his career.

Chou Szu-Chi 周思齊 OF Born: 10/26/81 Age: 39 Bats: L Throws: L Height: 5'10" Weight: 198

YEAR	TEAM	LVL	AGE	PA	R	2B	3B	HR	RBI	BB	K	SB	CS	Whiff%	AVG/OBP/SLG	DRC+	BABIP	BRR	FRAA	WARP
2018	CTB	CPBL	36	435	36	21	2	11	64	30	60	2	3		.305/.353/.452		.334			
2019	CTB	CPBL	37	212	30	7	2	6	33	16	28	3	4		.258/.313/.411		.269			
2020	CTB	CPBL	38	399	75	26	1	22	81	36	66	6	3		.324/.386/.589		.344			

A time-tested veteran and president of the CPBL players' union, Chou has been in the league since 2005 and celebrated his 39th birthday last October. His advanced age didn't stop him from putting together one of his finest campaigns, setting career highs in both home runs and slugging percentage. Perhaps most impressive is how he ended his season: Chou hit .382/.439/.781 in 82 September plate appearances, and was rewarded as the league's Player Of The Month.

Chu Yu-Hsien 朱育賢 1B Born: 11/26/91 Age: 29 Bats: L Throws: L Height: 6'2" Weight: 220

YEAR	TEAM	LVL	AGE	PA	R	2B	3B	HR	RBI	BB	K	SB	CS	Whiff%	AVG/OBP/SLG	DRC+	BABIP	BRR	FRAA	WARP
2018	LAM	CPBL	26	373	60	19	0	12	83	32	71	1	0		.325/.382/.491		.376			
2019	LAM	CPBL	27	507	93	26	1	30	105	38	105	0	0		.347/.394/.605		.393			
2020	RAK	CPBL	28	407	64	20	1	27	71	31	84	0	0		.352/.404/.631		.395			

Affectionately known by CPBL fans as "Dimple Cannon" for his smile and his propensity to hit home runs, Chu has, indeed, become one of the preeminent sluggers in the league since his debut in 2016. His aggressiveness at the plate, perhaps his only offensive weakness, only adds to his legend, as the slugger treats every pitch like an opportunity for a home run. He's often correct. He picked up the MVP in 2019, with his 30 homers leading the league. Proving that his award-winning campaign was no fluke, Chu got off to a blazing start in 2020, becoming the fastest player in league history to reach 10 homers in a season (51 at-bats). In total, 2020 was another stellar year for Chu: He finished first among qualifying batters in slugging percentage, and third in both batting average and on-base percentage.

Rosell Herrera OF Born: 10/16/92 Age: 28 Bats: S Throws: R Height: 6'3" Weight: 180

YEAR	TEAM	LVL	AGE	PA	R	2B	3B	HR	RBI	BB	K	SB	CS	Whiff%	AVG/OBP/SLG	DRC+	BABIP	BRR	FRAA	WARP
2018	OMA	AAA	25	41	8	3	2	1	5	5	7	4	1		.278/.366/.556	126	.321	0.5	CF(6): 0.4, RF(2): 0.2, LF(1): -0.3	0.3
2018	LOU	AAA	25	98	11	8	2	3	11	6	15	2	1		.267/.320/.500	123	.292	1.3	3B(7): -0.5, LF(6): -1.1, RF(4): -0.5	0.2
2018	CIN	MLB	25	13	0	0	0	0	0	0	5	0	1	22.7%	.154/.154/.154	69	.250	-0.1	LF(2): -0.1, 2B(1): -0.1	0.0
2018	KC	MLB	25	289	25	14	3	1	20	19	52	3	4	22.3%	.238/.292/.325	71	.290	1.7	RF(29): -0.4, 2B(17): 0.5, CF(12): -1.3	-0.2
2019	NO	AAA	26	180	21	11	1	5	24	14	32	2	1		.309/.367/.479	115	.359	0.5	3B(21): -1.4, LF(12): 0.0, 2B(11): -1.3	0.7
2019	MIA	MLB	26	119	10	6	0	2	11	11	27	4	1	32.9%	.200/.288/.314	71	.250	0.9	CF(25): -2.0, RF(15): -1.9, LF(13): -0.0	-0.3

Comparables: Mark Davidson, Bob Gallagher, Lee Lacy

Maybe it *feels* like longer ago (2020 had a way of aging us), but it hasn't even been a year since Herrera was turning heads in Yankees camp with a 1.044 OPS in his first 27 spring plate appearances. But Herrera's prospects of making the Bombers' squad vasnished along with the spring: He subsequently suffered injuries in both heels, and didn't factor into the team's plans when the season re-started in July. Herrera became a minor-league free agent and signed with the Dragons in December; he'll be the first foreign position player in the CPBL since 2019. His solid offensive performance in the upper minors–119 DRC+ in Triple-A in 2018-2019–and experience at second, third, shortstop and all three outfield positions gives the Dragons some choices in their lineup and around the diamond.

Jhang Jin-De 張進德 C Born: 05/17/93 Age: 28 Bats: L Throws: R Height: 5'9" Weight: 225

YEAR	TEAM	LVL	AGE	PA	R	2B	3B	HR	RBI	BB	K	SB	CS	Whiff%	AVG/OBP/SLG	DRC+	BABIP	BRR	FRAA	WARP
2018	ALT	AA	25	135	13	8	0	1	23	11	14	0	0		.320/.373/.410	123	.352	-0.3	C(22): 1.9	0.8
2019	GIB	ROK	26	50	5	1	1	1	7	6	4	1	0		.256/.340/.395	111	.256	-1.1	C(7): -0.1	0.1
2019	RIC	AA	26	100	1	1	0	1	7	6	15	0	0		.138/.190/.181	41	.154	-0.4	C(26): 4.2	0.3
2020	FUB	CPBL	27	321	49	22	0	14	47	28	30	2	2		.375/.429/.595		.385			

Comparables: Jhonatan Solano, Manny Piña, Francisco Arcia

YEAR	TEAM	P. COUNT	FRM RUNS	BLK RUNS	THRW RUNS	TOT RUNS
2018	ALT	2990	1.8	0.0	-0.3	1.5
2019	RIC	3129	2.8	0.0	0.8	3.5

Signed by the Pittsburgh Pirates in 2011 from Taiwan, Jhang spent much of the decade in their system, reaching Triple-A. Regarded as a solid defender behind the plate by prospect evaluators–backed up by his +12 FRAA across his MiLB career–Jhang had a journeyman backup catcher career path in front of him before injuries began to cut into his playing time. After spending a year in the Giants' system in 2019, he went back to Taiwan, entered the 2020 CPBL Draft, and signed with the Guardians. Marking his July 25 debut with a pair of doubles, Jhang provided the anemic Guardians' offense with a much-needed jolt in the second half of the season.

Kao Kuo-Hui 羅國輝 OF Born: 09/26/85 Age: 35 Bats: R Throws: R Height: 6'2" Weight: 209

YEAR	TEAM	LVL	AGE	PA	R	2B	3B	HR	RBI	BB	K	SB	CS	Whiff%	AVG/OBP/SLG	DRC+	BABIP	BRR	FRAA	WARP
2018	FUB	CPBL	32	293	31	14	0	12	54	46	62	3	1		.264/.382/.471		.304			
2019	FUB	CPBL	33	230	35	19	1	14	44	20	54	1	2		.327/.383/.630		.380			
2020	FUB	CPBL	34	403	63	28	0	27	76	35	89	3	0		.305/.363/.607		.332			

The 35-year-old Kao's stint with the team goes back to 2013, after leaving the Seattle Mariners' system (where he played from 2006 until 2011). He's been a prolific slugger: He holds the CPBL's single-season home run record, when he hit 39 in 2015, while playing in all 120 of his team's games. The second-highest home run season? His follow-up 2016, with 34. He was hampered by injuries for much of the 2017-2019 campaigns, but came back strong this year and received the league's Comeback Player Of The Year Award.

Kao Kuo-Lin 羅國麟 RF Born: 01/02/93 Age: 28 Bats: R Throws: R Height: 6'0" Weight: 202

YEAR	TEAM	LVL	AGE	PA	R	2B	3B	HR	RBI	BB	K	SB	CS	Whiff%	AVG/OBP/SLG	DRC+	BABIP	BRR	FRAA	WARP
2018	FUB	CPBL	25	210	31	11	2	5	27	21	50	2	1		.285/.375/.453		.365			
2019	FUB	CPBL	26	206	29	9	2	11	36	19	50	1	0		.258/.343/.517		.294			
2020	FUB	CPBL	27	343	45	16	0	16	50	30	74	1	4		.289/.367/.502		.333			

The younger Kao is eight years Kuo-Hui's junior, and 2020 marked the first time that they both played in the majority of their team's games together. Kuo-Lin doesn't have the pedigree of his older brother, but 2020 did mark something of a breakout for him. While his overall production tapered off after a hot start, he set career highs in homers and total bases while seeing regular playing time as the team's primary right-fielder. Also, it's worth noting that those home runs gave him more opportunities to showcase his bat-flip–certainly one of the most prolific in the league.

Liao Chien-Fu 廖健富 C Born: 09/28/98 Age: 22 Bats: L Throws: R Height: 5'10" Weight: 187

YEAR	TEAM	LVL	AGE	PA	R	2B	3B	HR	RBI	BB	K	SB	CS	Whiff%	AVG/OBP/SLG	DRC+	BABIP	BRR	FRAA	WARP
2018	LAM	CPBL	19	356	62	21	2	10	69	40	41	0	3		.383/.455/.567		.415			
2019	LAM	CPBL	20	336	42	12	0	6	49	39	34	1	1		.291/.381/.397		.306			
2020	RAK	CPBL	21	357	55	31	1	10	52	29	32	1	1		.346/.415/.548		.359			

Liao has already wrapped up his third full season in the CPBL, despite turning 22 last September. His talent has been apparent for a while: The first overall pick in the 2017 CPBL draft, he began his career by earning the CPBL MVP for March/April 2018, batting .434/.505/.639 over his first 26 games. After a sophomore slump in 2019 brought him back down to earth, Liao was again excellent in 2020 while continuing an impressive transition from a primary DH to primary catcher.

Lin An-Ko 林安可　RF　Born: 05/19/97　Age: 24　Bats: L　Throws: L　Height: 6'0"　Weight: 198

YEAR	TEAM	LVL	AGE	PA	R	2B	3B	HR	RBI	BB	K	SB	CS	Whiff%	AVG/OBP/SLG	DRC+	BABIP	BRR	FRAA	WARP
2019	UNI	CPBL	22	140	16	7	0	3	15	14	33	1	1		.264/.355/.397		.341			
2020	UNI	CPBL	23	503	90	23	1	32	99	52	113	10	1		.310/.395/.590		.351			

Lin's excellent offensive output – including a league-best 32 homers – is what made him an easy choice for the CPBL Rookie of the Year in 2020. But his story is much more than just that of a typical slugging outfielder, even one as precocious as he's shown himself to be. The half-Taiwanese, half-Argentinian Lin was actually a highly-regarded pitching prospect as an amateur, and as recently as Spring 2020 was being considered as a two-way player in CPBL before the Lions ultimately decided to utilize him purely as an outfielder. While it goes without saying that two-way players are extremely fun, the Lions surely are pleased with allowing Lin to focus the beam, given the results he's generated so far in his career.

Lin Li 林立　3B　Born: 01/01/96　Age: 25　Bats: R　Throws: R　Height: 5'11"　Weight: 165

YEAR	TEAM	LVL	AGE	PA	R	2B	3B	HR	RBI	BB	K	SB	CS	Whiff%	AVG/OBP/SLG	DRC+	BABIP	BRR	FRAA	WARP
2018	LAM	CPBL	22	335	62	18	2	7	38	16	82	12	3		.317/.352/.458		.409			
2019	LAM	CPBL	23	464	101	30	4	20	81	34	76	11	5		.382/.430/.623		.427			
2020	RAK	CPBL	24	471	94	23	4	25	86	39	107	22	6		.356/.417/.608		.430			

Lin is another product of Rakuten's fantastic 2017 CPBL draft, going as their second pick behind Liao. In a short time, he's become one of the offensive stars of the league: over 845 plate appearances since the start of 2019, Lin's OPS of 1.051 (with an eye-popping triple-slash of .373/.425/.626) is the highest in the league. His firepower has propelled the Monkeys' lineup, but it's worth noting that Lin has had his struggles on the other side of the ball: he made 25 errors last year split between third and second base, and his fielding percentage at the hot corner alone was just .886. It's not good if you can roll an error on a six-sided die. Lin's bat allows the Monkeys to live with his glove, but surely they'd like to see some defensive consistency.

Lin Yi-Chuan 林益全　3B　Born: 11/11/85　Age: 35　Bats: L　Throws: R　Height: 5'11"　Weight: 180

YEAR	TEAM	LVL	AGE	PA	R	2B	3B	HR	RBI	BB	K	SB	CS	Whiff%	AVG/OBP/SLG	DRC+	BABIP	BRR	FRAA	WARP
2018	FUB	CPBL	32	392	46	27	0	8	54	27	54	2	1		.317/.362/.462		.349			
2019	FUB	CPBL	33	484	71	26	0	27	108	37	58	1	1		.325/.373/.573		.319			
2020	FUB	CPBL	34	435	55	18	0	23	81	31	71	1	0		.314/.363/.533		.333			

Lin is the longest-tenured member of the Fubon organization, and one of the living legends of the league. Drafted as the top pick in the 2007 CPBL draft, his remarkable debut (.348/.388/.543 while playing all 120 games) in 2009 earned him not only the Rookie of the Year award, but MVP honors as well – he's since won the award twice more, and is the only player in CPBL history with three MVP wins. He's always been a consistent performer, with an OPS above league average and only once playing in fewer than 100 games (95 in 2018) over his 12 CPBL campaigns; among active players, he's second in both hits (1,717) and home runs (193).

Liu Chi-Hung 劉基鴻　3B　Born: 11/03/00　Age: 20　Bats: R　Throws: R　Height: 5'11"　Weight: 194

YEAR	TEAM	LVL	AGE	PA	R	2B	3B	HR	RBI	BB	K	SB	CS	Whiff%	AVG/OBP/SLG	DRC+	BABIP	BRR	FRAA	WARP
2020	WEI	CPBL	19	355	73	22	1	15	75	22	48	1	1		.343/.394/.562		.358			

Aside from Wei-Chung Wang, Dragons fans might be most eager to get a glimpse of Liu, who shares the pitcher's background as a recent first-overall pick in the CPBL draft. Their surrounding circumstances are quite different, though: While Wang already had plenty of experience under his belt, Liu was drafted right out of high school in 2019. He'll be 20 years old for the entirety of the 2021 season. Liu acquitted himself nicely in his professional debut, playing in 81 of the Dragons' 86 minor league games with 15 homers and a .975 OPS, an excellent mark even for the offense-heavy CPBL minors.

Su Chih-Chieh 蘇智傑　LF　Born: 07/28/94　Age: 26　Bats: L　Throws: R　Height: 5'11"　Weight: 194

YEAR	TEAM	LVL	AGE	PA	R	2B	3B	HR	RBI	BB	K	SB	CS	Whiff%	AVG/OBP/SLG	DRC+	BABIP	BRR	FRAA	WARP
2018	UNI	CPBL	23	290	47	3	2	17	50	31	61	14	2		.308/.390/.540		.345			
2019	UNI	CPBL	24	508	77	30	2	27	83	48	103	21	7		.282/.361/.541		.311			
2020	UNI	CPBL	25	511	104	31	4	28	98	57	115	13	6		.313/.394/.594		.360			

The other member of the Lions' dynamic outfield trio, Su looks like he's turning into an all-around player as he heads into his age-27 season. The power numbers may be the most notable–he's been the runner-up in homers in each of the last two seasons–but Su's 57 walks this past season led the league, while still collecting hits at an above-average rate. We haven't even mentioned his baserunning yet, as Su's 2019 season marked the first 20/20 campaign for any Lions player in their team's history (overall, there have been nine such seasons across all CPBL teams). Oh, and he's been a CPBL Gold Glove award winner the past two seasons as well.

Wu Tung-Jung 吳東融　SS　Born: 09/29/91　Age: 29　Bats: R　Throws: R　Height: 5'8"　Weight: 159

YEAR	TEAM	LVL	AGE	PA	R	2B	3B	HR	RBI	BB	K	SB	CS	Whiff%	AVG/OBP/SLG	DRC+	BABIP	BRR	FRAA	WARP
2018	CTB	CPBL	26	211	36	11	2	4	30	19	33	10	3		.297/.376/.445		.345			
2019	CTB	CPBL	27	371	65	12	2	4	34	24	52	11	7		.304/.400/.396		.353			
2020	CTB	CPBL	28	314	56	17	3	2	17	17	58	11	2		.301/.380/.409		.378			

In addition to garnering the top pick in the yearly draft, the Dragons were also able to obtain four players from other rosters as part of November's expansion draft. The highest-profile player selected was Wu, who had spent his career to that point as a member of the Brothers. Given that Wu had played in a majority of the games with the Brothers just last season, the fact that he wasn't protected from the expansion draft came as a surprise to many fans and analysts. Wu has been a capable hitter for a middle infielder, with an OPS about 10 percent below league average over his nearly 1000 plate appearances; his addition adds some stability to a very young and inexperienced squad.

PITCHERS

Jake Brigham RHP   Born: 02/10/88   Age: 33   Bats: R   Throws: R   Height: 6'3"   Weight: 210   Origin: Round 6, 2006 Draft (#178 overall)

YEAR	TEAM	LVL	AGE	W	L	SV	G	GS	IP	H	HR	BB/9	K/9	K	GB%	BABIP	WHIP	ERA	DRA-	WARP	MPH	FA%	Whiff%	CSP
2018	KIW	KBO	30	11	7	0	31	30	199	188	19	2.0	7.9	175			1.20	3.84						
2019	KIW	KBO	31	13	5	0	28	28	158¹	148	5	2.0	7.4	130			1.23	2.96						
2020	KIW	KBO	32	9	5	0	21	21	107	98	6	3.0	8.8	105			1.31	3.62						

In the KBO, where teams may only sign three non-Korean players, it's vital to use those roster spaces wisely. That applies double for contenders in a season like last year where the difference between fifth place (and two do-or-die games to advance) and second place (a bye until the semifinals) amounted to a single game in the standings. That brings us to Brigham, who has headlined Kiwoom's rotation for four years now. The former Atlanta Brave once again turned in a solid season, notching a 131 ERA+ while striking out nearly a batter per inning. Unfortunately, what he provided in quality he lacked in volume. Brigham strained his elbow in his first outing, and ultimately missed 10 starts. Oftentimes, such an injury will prompt KBO clubs to seek a replacement, as the penalty for replacing a former major leaguer with a long reliever in the rotation is very stiff in this league. But, given the pandemic and perhaps the equity Brigham had built up, the Heroes decided to keep him on the roster. All those missed starts added up in the end, as Kiwoom found themselves in the dreaded fifth slot for the playoffs. Sometimes, loyalty isn't cheap.

Chen Yun-Wen 陳韻文 RHP   Born: 11/28/95   Age: 25   Bats: R   Throws: R   Height: 6'0"   Weight: 214

YEAR	TEAM	LVL	AGE	W	L	SV	G	GS	IP	H	HR	BB/9	K/9	K	GB%	BABIP	WHIP	ERA	DRA-	WARP	MPH	FA%	Whiff%	CSP
2018	UNI	CPBL	22	3	1	19	51	0	48	35	3	3.9	12.2	65			1.17	3.56						
2019	UNI	CPBL	23	2	3	24	49	0	48²	51	5	3.5	10.5	57			1.44	2.96						
2020	UNI	CPBL	24	5	2	23	56	0	56	42	5	3.1	8.7	54			1.09	2.09						

He just turned 25 years old in November, but Chen is something of a CPBL veteran already. Since 2017, he's been the Lions' closer, and one of the more successful relievers in the league: Among pitchers with at least 100 games pitched in that timeframe, Chen ranks third in both ERA and strikeout rate. Chen throws harder than the average CPBL pitcher, reaching the mid-90s with his fastball and backing it up with a power-forkball that he uses as his main strikeout pitch. International teams have taken note of Chen's work; following the 2018 season, Chen filed for international free agency in order to negotiate playing opportunities outside of Taiwan. However, nothing materialized that time around, and Chen has remained the Lions' closer.

Jose De Paula LHP   Born: 03/04/88   Age: 33   Bats: R   Throws: L   Height: 6'1"   Weight: 170

YEAR	TEAM	LVL	AGE	W	L	SV	G	GS	IP	H	HR	BB/9	K/9	K	GB%	BABIP	WHIP	ERA	DRA-	WARP	MPH	FA%	Whiff%	CSP
2018	MTY	AAA	30	4	5	0	13	13	75¹	69	6	2.2	8.7	73	43.6%	.315	1.15	3.58						
2019	LEO	AAA	31	3	0	0	5	5	27²	33	1	3.3	6.5	20	48.9%	.364	1.55	4.55						
2019	MTY	AAA	31	3	1	0	13	13	62²	84	6	2.7	9.6	67	49.0%	.426	1.64	4.74						
2020	CTB	CPBL	32	17	9	0	28	27	179¹	161	18	2.5	9.9	198			1.18	3.21						

On June 21, 2015, De Paula came out of the Yankees bullpen and mopped up an eventual 12-4 loss to the Tigers, pitching the final 3⅓ innings of the game. To date, that was the only time he appeared in a major league game and, having signed his first professional contract with the Padres in 2007, essentially ended a chapter of his time in affiliated ball. But since then, De Paula has carved out a solid career for himself outside of the United States, highlighted by a few years in the Mexican League before joining the Brothers in January 2020. On a strong Brothers pitching staff, De Paula's performance was arguably the best of all, and his season was highlighted by a July 14 14-strikeout shutout of the Uni-Lions. That the game was actually suspended, and that he finished his own complete game on a different day, is what they like to call symbolism.

Ryan Feierabend LHP   Born: 08/22/85   Age: 35   Bats: L   Throws: L   Height: 6'3"   Weight: 225   Origin: Round 3, 2003 Draft (#86 overall)

YEAR	TEAM	LVL	AGE	W	L	SV	G	GS	IP	H	HR	BB/9	K/9	K	GB%	BABIP	WHIP	ERA	DRA-	WARP	MPH	FA%	Whiff%	CSP
2018	KT	KBO	32	8	8	0	27	26	163¹	186	24	2.0	7.1	141			1.54	4.30						
2019	BUF	AAA	33	6	5	0	14	12	68¹	77	19	2.8	7.0	53	37.4%	.287	1.43	5.53	119	0.6				
2019	TOR	MLB	33	0	1	0	2	1	5²	11	2	1.6	6.4	4	41.7%	.409	2.12	11.12	130	0.0	87.1	23.1%	23.3%	23.5%
2020	UNI	CPBL	34	2	3	0	11	10	57	67	5	3.2	8.7	55			1.53	4.74						

Comparables: Austin Bibens-Dirkx, Steven Wright, Chris Rusin

It's always fun to have a knuckleballer around, and the Lions enjoyed adding Feierabend to their squad prior to the 2020 season. His major league career split itself into three spread-out parts–2006-2008 with the Mariners, 2014 with the Rangers, and 2019 with the Blue Jays–but you could argue that the most important phase of his career was his four-year stay in the KBO, when the knuckler became an integral part of his pitching repertoire for the first time. Feierabend was a reliable member of the Lions' rotation from April to June while the team as a whole was struggling, but his stay with the team was short; his last game with the team was June 27th, as he returned home to be closer to family during the pandemic.

Huang En-Sih 黃恩賜 RHP   Born: 05/17/96   Age: 25   Bats: L   Throws: R   Height: 6'1"   Weight: 198

YEAR	TEAM	LVL	AGE	W	L	SV	G	GS	IP	H	HR	BB/9	K/9	K	GB%	BABIP	WHIP	ERA	DRA-	WARP	MPH	FA%	Whiff%	CSP
2019	CTB	CPBL	23	7	6	0	25	17	94²	127	13	2.8	6.5	68			1.65	5.89						
2020	CTB	CPBL	24	9	2	0	20	20	109¹	110	16	2.6	9.1	110			1.29	4.36						

Two years removed from Tommy John surgery, Huang's sophomore campaign marked his breakout as one of the league's finest local starters: For a stretch of six games in June and July, Huang maintained a 2.25 ERA with 52 strikeouts against seven walks, while averaging 6⅔ innings per start. Along the same lines, it's worth noting that he led local starting pitchers with 8.9 strikeouts per nine innings (min. 10 IP). Largely responsible for his strikeout prevalence is Huang's tumbling forkball, part of a deep repertoire of secondary pitches that he relied on throughout the year.

Lee Chen-Chang 李振昌 RHP Born: 10/21/86 Age: 34 Bats: R Throws: R Height: 5'11" Weight: 190

YEAR	TEAM	LVL	AGE	W	L	SV	G	GS	IP	H	HR	BB/9	K/9	K	GB%	BABIP	WHIP	ERA	DRA-	WARP	MPH	FA%	Whiff%	CSP
2018	OKC	AAA	31	2	2	0	22	0	25¹	17	3	3.2	14.6	41	42.3%	.286	1.03	3.91	19	1.2				
2018	CTB	CPBL	31	1	0	14	28	0	27¹	24	1	2.3	8.2	25			1.13	1.65						
2019	CTB	CPBL	32	3	1	10	54	0	52	43	2	0.9	11.4	66			0.92	1.21						
2020	CTB	CPBL	33	1	4	23	51	0	51¹	33	6	2.6	13.7	78			0.94	3.86						

Comparables: Miguel Socolovich, Preston Guilmet, Brandon Gomes

Lee has some big league experience under his belt, throwing 34 innings for Cleveland from 2013 to 2015 after being signed out of Taiwan in 2008. After bouncing around the minors for a few years, with a 2016 stint on NPB's Seibu Lions mixed in, Lee made the decision to return to back home in 2018, and was picked in the first round (third overall) by the Brothers in that year's CPBL draft. Since then, he's been a lights-out closer, and his 13.7 K/9 in 2020 was a league-best. His streaks of dominance earned him the nickname "Instant Noodles Timer" around the league: start your instant noodles when Lee starts the ninth inning, and they still won't be done in the time it takes him to finish the game.

Mike Loree RHP Born: 09/14/86 Age: 34 Bats: R Throws: R Height: 6'6" Weight: 226 Origin: Round 50, 2007 Draft (#1441 overall)

YEAR	TEAM	LVL	AGE	W	L	SV	G	GS	IP	H	HR	BB/9	K/9	K	GB%	BABIP	WHIP	ERA	DRA-	WARP	MPH	FA%	Whiff%	CSP
2018	FUB	CPBL	33	10	8	0	26	26	161	177	15	0.9	8.8	157			1.20	3.47						
2019	FUB	CPBL	34	13	10	0	28	28	179²	149	13	1.7	8.7	173			1.02	2.76						
2020	FUB	CPBL	35	6	12	0	25	25	144²	186	16	1.9	8.5	136			1.49	5.23						

In a league where foreign players rarely stick around for too long, Loree is an exception. Save for a pitstop in Korea in 2014, he's been a stalwart of the CPBL since 2012, making 2020 his eighth season in the league–the most for a foreign pitcher since the Domincan-born Osvaldo Martinez from 1997-2005. And it's not just his service time that makes him stand out, as Loree has consistently ranked among the best starters in the league for the better half of the past decade. Never a particularly hard thrower, Loree commands his tailing high-80s fastball impeccably, and CPBL batters are still baffled by his splitter. When it's all said and done for Loree–under contract to return to Fubon in 2021–he'll undoubtedly be viewed as one of the most accomplished pitchers in the league's history.

Shih Tzu-Chien 施子謙 RHP Born: 12/19/94 Age: 26 Bats: R Throws: R Height: 6'0" Weight: 198

YEAR	TEAM	LVL	AGE	W	L	SV	G	GS	IP	H	HR	BB/9	K/9	K	GB%	BABIP	WHIP	ERA	DRA-	WARP	MPH	FA%	Whiff%	CSP
2018	UNI	CPBL	23	11	5	0	21	20	114	148	5	2.8	4.6	58			1.61	3.95						
2019	UNI	CPBL	24	5	9	0	21	19	99²	131	18	2.0	5.3	59			1.54	6.41						
2020	UNI	CPBL	25	8	11	0	26	25	122²	192	29	2.8	5.4	74			1.88	7.56						

You can only have so many foreign players on your roster in the CPBL, and teams prefer to use that investment to bolster their pitching staffs (like a Henry Sosa, or an Aríel Miranda, etc). As such, someone like the Taiwan-native Shih fits the mold of a low-ceiling, back-of-the-rotation type hurler who's expected to take the ball every week and eat some innings. And that's what he's done: Since becoming a regular member of the Lions' staff in 2018, Shih ranks second (behind the Monkeys' Yi-Cheng Wang) among local pitchers in both games started (57) and innings pitched (310). Unfortunately for Shih, his actual results on the field have declined since a successful rookie campaign in 2018, when he was the CPBL Rookie of the Year.

Henry Sosa RHP Born: 07/28/85 Age: 35 Bats: R Throws: R Height: 6'1" Weight: 210

YEAR	TEAM	LVL	AGE	W	L	SV	G	GS	IP	H	HR	BB/9	K/9	K	GB%	BABIP	WHIP	ERA	DRA-	WARP	MPH	FA%	Whiff%	CSP
2018	LG	KBO	32	9	9	0	27	27	181¹	192	16	1.0	9.0	181			1.21	3.52						
2019	FUB	CPBL	33	8	2	0	12	12	86²	60	5	1.0	8.8	85			0.81	1.56						
2019	SK	KBO	33	9	3	0	16	16	94¹	85	15	2.0	9.2	96			1.14	3.82						
2020	FUB	CPBL	34	15	5	0	29	29	194¹	230	12	1.7	8.0	172			1.37	3.38						

You might remember Sosa from a lifetime or two ago, when he was a well-regarded prospect for the Giants (and earned himself a handful of mentions in BP Annuals of yesteryear). While he did briefly reach The Show on a miserable Astros team in 2011, Sosa's career is mostly defined by his fine work overseas, first in the KBO for much of the 2010s, and now in the CPBL. He joined the Guardians in 2019, but then returned to the KBO under some duress, as Korea had changed its income tax laws in 2015, and teams failed to notify players of the repercussions. Sosa found himself owing a signficant sum in back taxes, so his signing bonus paid off what he owed. He was glad to get back to Taiwan in 2020. Awarded the league's Pitcher of the Month award last September, the hard-throwing Sosa was the anchor of a resurgent Guardians team that played well down the stretch after a rough first half of the year. The Guardians weren't shy about relying on Sosa; his four complete games were the most in the league (only one other pitcher, Esmil Rogers, had as many as two), and he was also the league-leader in games started and innings pitched.

Wang Wei-Chung LHP Born: 04/25/92   Age: 29   Bats: L   Throws: L   Height: 6'1"   Weight: 160   Origin: International Free Agent, 2011

YEAR	TEAM	LVL	AGE	W	L	SV	G	GS	IP	H	HR	BB/9	K/9	K	GB%	BABIP	WHIP	ERA	DRA-	WARP	MPH	FA%	Whiff%	CSP
2019	LV	AAA	27	1	1	1	19	0	26¹	29	5	2.7	8.2	24	43.4%	.316	1.41	4.78	76	0.6				
2019	PIT	MLB	27	2	0	0	5	0	4	5	0	6.8	4.5	2	64.3%	.357	2.00	6.75	44	0.1	93.9	47.4%	11.4%	41.2%
2019	OAK	MLB	27	1	0	0	20	0	27	22	4	3.7	5.3	16	30.5%	.231	1.22	3.33	151	-0.6	94.0	43.1%	21.7%	47.4%

Comparables: Tyler Duffey, Brooks Pounders, Cory Mazzoni

The Dragons are joining the CPBL for the 2021 season, and their biggest splash to date was bringing aboard Wang, a recent big-leaguer who became a clear choice as the first pick of the 2020 CPBL draft after announcing his return to Taiwan. Following a few months of negotiation, the Dragons ultimately lured Wang with the most lucrative contract in the CPBL's history (a five-year deal worth slightly over $2 million USD). Wang and his four-pitch mix will still be just 28 at the start of the season, and stands to be the Dragons' clear-cut ace.

Ordinality in an Unordinary Year

by Jeffrey Paternostro, Jarrett Seidler and Keanan Lamb

When we started looking at player development during the pandemic, our first question was: what development even was there? We didn't see a whole lot with our own eyes. There was no minor-league season at all. Spring training was truncated right as players were ramping up.

Select prospects had time at the alternate training site, and teams took wildly different approaches in choosing who was on those rosters. At the extremes, Milwaukee and Oakland loaded up with extremely young talent, including recent draftees and international signees with little to no pro experience, figuring that simulated games against upper-level prospects and minor-league vets were a better developmental experience than nothing at all. Other teams, like the Mets and Astros, went heavy on Quad-A types and added the further-away kids later in the summer (and only a small handful at that). Most teams were somewhere in the middle.

Evaluating tools, skills and overall projection—and how those things change throughout a season—is the foundational aspect of how the Top 101 is assembled. A previous year's work is not torn up when it comes time to create a new one, as track record and trajectory play a substantial part. But why Julio Rodríguez thrived in leagues where he was nearly a half-decade younger than the average player, or why Dylan Carlson went from slugging .390 in A-ball to .542 in the upper-minors is a puzzle that needs to be assembled. The performance exists to be explained—good, bad or indifferent.

Rodríguez was not an unknown entering the 2019 season. He was a seven-figure IFA outfielder who had industry buzz based on his performance in the Dominican Summer League. We tend to be fairly cautious with ranking these prospects—international complex ball has wildly variant competition, and even reliable second-hand looks are hard to come by—and he wasn't one of our Top 101 Prospects entering the season. Rodríguez opened 2019 in the South Atlantic League as an 18-year-old—an extremely aggressive assignment. His arrival in full-season ball allowed our team to get live looks (our most-valued data point), and each one suggested he was among the top prospects in all of baseball: a potential five-tool outfielder with light-tower power. Similarly effervescent reports followed a late-season promotion to High-A and it was clear that Rodríguez had

established himself as a 70 OFP prospect—a potential all-star—by our evaluation system. He ranked as the no. 10 prospect in all of baseball going into 2020.

Every minor-league season provides us with new information about prospects. And every season a handful of them have this kind of breakout. Perhaps with Rodríguez it was merely a matter of our team getting eyes on him, but for teammate Jarred Kelenic, there was an obvious swing tweak that unlocked a new level for both his hit and power tools. That moved him from the no. 63 prospect in baseball to no. 7. Dodgers infielder Gavin Lux added loft and power and dominated the high-minors without losing his speed or infield range. The aforementioned Carlson started lifting the ball more consistently and took to center field better than expected.

Young players change rapidly and are reminders that development is not linear. As recently as 10 years ago, the widespread belief in baseball was that the most important thing you could do was identify talent at point of acquisition, whether it be in the draft and international market or through trade and free agency. For amateur talent especially, the idea was that you need to merely water the prospects and they would grow into whatever was preordained. Sure, that skinny Texas prep arm would add a couple miles an hour as he naturally filled out; that was foreseeable, mere extrapolation. But with the sheer amount of data teams now compile on their prospects, with the highly specialized technology that exists to measure every output from every baseball action, identifying what and how much you can change the players in your organization is paramount.

Baseball Prospectus doesn't have access to most of what goes behind the curtain, but we try to be front row when the stage lights go on. The backbone of our work is live looks. We might not know exactly what a team saw in a pitcher's arm stroke, release point and spin axis that suggested a new slider grip, but can evaluate the new pitch and how well it works in games. The end product is what we are both looking for anyway.

Yet whereas our evaluations are usually composed of hundreds and hundreds of live looks, we had a scant few dozen in 2020—some spring training and early-season college action, plus a few scattered amateur showcases in the summer and fall instructional league looks. And we weren't alone. Major League Baseball banned live amateur scouting from March until June, and kept professional scouts working from home all summer, only relenting for fall coverage.

Domestic instructional leagues varied wildly, too, ranging from the Royals running a longer program split between two locations to the Yankees and Cardinals running nothing at all. For many, fall instructs—normally a waystation for minor-leaguers to get in a little extra work and experimentation during informal games—were not just the best opportunity to get updated reports on players, but also the primary source of direct team instruction for the entire year.

So, what were the minor leaguers doing the rest of the time? For starters, they were dealing with the ugly ramifications of a worldwide pandemic. Players got sick. Players got hurt. Players got stuck thousands of miles away from their homes for months on end, at team complexes instead of with their families. Most did the best they could off the radar, working out on their own at home or informal private camps. A few even popped up in indy ball or collegiate summer leagues; Jake Burger and Colin Barber, for example, played well in those conditions and were later added to alternate site rosters. Communication with the team—and even sometimes training sessions—took place over Zoom and FaceTime. In some cases, team sources we talked to didn't even know for sure what their prospects were up to.

In what might sum up the overall weirdness of the season, and the conundrum of ranking players in this moment, *Baseball America* reported that many of the Cubs' top pitching prospects wouldn't be present at the fall instructs after not being assigned to the alternate site because they "accumulated their required innings through a virtual training program."

There were fewer opportunities for players to improve than in a normal year, and while we've concluded that there simply were fewer breakouts this year, it's possible, even likely, that some of them happened in places we couldn't see.

⚾ ⚾ ⚾

Our biggest problem in compiling lists wasn't a *lack* of information, but rather information asymmetry. While we were able to get responses on nearly every player we asked about, the amount of information available varied significantly depending on what the player was doing during the lack of minor-league season.

While the various levels of competition, environmental conditions and org-specific development goals make evaluations complicated to reconcile in a normal year, 2020 put into sharp relief how good we've had it. Some prospects produced an end product by pitching in the majors or in college. Others produced a partial product via alternate site reports and data generation—about two-thirds of the teams participated in the video and data share—or third-party live scouting reports from fall instructs. Still others had teams that didn't participate in data-sharing or reciprocal scouting

during instructs, and thus were even more nebulous. Consider the following five prospects, all pitchers ranked within the Top 25 who were born in 1998 or 1999:

- Ian Anderson — Made 10 brilliant major-league starts in the regular season and postseason, with all the video and Statcast data that comes with that.
- Luis Patiño — Thirteen major-league relief appearances and one start as an opener in the regular season and postseason; didn't look so hot, but was adjusting to a different role under difficult circumstances.
- MacKenzie Gore — Pitched all summer at the alternate site without getting called up even though the Padres really could have used him; San Diego was not in the data share, so third-party sources don't have much new information on him.
- Shane Baz — Pitched all summer at the alternate site; the Rays were in the data share, so pro scouts did updated work on him and we were able to get their opinions, and he also threw in televised exhibitions.
- Asa Lacy — Made four starts at Texas A&M before the college season was shut down and ended up at the alternate site and instructs toward the end of the summer; the Royals were also not in the data share.

Those are wildly different levels of information about each player, and it was hard to figure out how to weigh everything against prior reports. We do suspect there were Julio Rodríguezes or Dylan Carlsons making major skill improvements—prospects who should be jumping way up the list. We're pretty confident a few made skills leaps behind closed doors; prospects like Corbin Carroll and Edward Cabrera, but a constant question hung over the entire process like the sword of Damocles: how can we be sure?

A major-league track record provides the highest-confidence information. Anderson, for example, threw 51 innings between the regular season and playoffs. He was absolutely phenomenal in that stretch, and he has clearly surpassed not just his 2019 skill level but his projection as of a year ago. We thought his changeup might have above-average or even plus potential, yet he showed up in the majors with a regular plus-plus *cambio*, fully developed.

Admittedly, we have been bitten in the past by aggressively ranking pitchers based off huge late-season jumps in stuff. But Anderson has been on this list four times before. He was the no. 3 overall pick in the 2016 draft as a prep righty, which is a heck of a starting point. He's been on the edge of a 70 OFP grade for two cycles. Is it really that hard to believe he took a major step with his changeup development and got there in the calendar year we didn't see him?

In a normal season, a half-season of Anderson tormenting Triple-A batters would back up the major-league improvements—if he hadn't been called up earlier and lost prospect eligibility. This year, there is no safety net, no additional context against which to determine whether what was shown in the majors was real; not just on Anderson but also on Sixto Sánchez, Ke'Bryan Hayes, Ryan Mountcastle, Dane Dunning and Triston McKenzie. Similarly, we had to figure out whether Carlson, Casey Mize, Joey Bart, Spencer Howard and Tarik Skubal struggling in the majors were real downward profile shifts or just noise. In a few cases, like Shane McClanahan, Brailyn Marquez and Alex Kirilloff, there is only the tiniest bit of big-league action to try and glean changes off of. If minor-league evaluations and performance provide a safety net for major-league glimpses, 2020 was a Wallenda-level challenge.

Suffice to say, if you flip over a few pages, you'll see that we believe Anderson's changeup development is real, just like we believe that Hayes will sustain at least some of his sudden and similarly unexpected big jump with his in-game power. Both the data and our eyes support those conclusions. We're optimistic Carlson will still play back to his tools, which mostly showed up as expected even as he struggled mightily, but we're relatively less optimistic on Mize, who only flashed brief glimpses of the ace-in-waiting he'd shown prior to his 2019 injury.

⚾　　⚾　　⚾

As complicated as things were on the pro scene, the amateur side was not much better and possibly worse.

The 2020 draft was sliced from its customary 40 rounds down to only five, so there were far fewer players selected, even though 2020 was widely viewed as a strong draft class. Most teams executed pool-manipulation strategies, so the 160 players selected weren't precisely the best 160 players that would've been taken in a normal draft. While much of the scouting work for this past draft was already completed by the time things started shutting down in March, the scouting community surely missed some late risers from the high school and college seasons—Rangers second-rounder Evan Carter, for example, elicited a community reaction of "who is that?" when selected, but later shined during fall instructs. Even the top draft picks, like Lacy, didn't actually play much in their draft year.

The changes will continue rippling. The 2021 draft is likely to be shortened, even though it will have stronger depth than normal because of college players who would've signed in a normal 2020 draft now stampeding towards pro ball. The 2023 draft is likely to have a bumper crop of college talent because of all the preps that didn't have an opportunity to sign last year.

As part of the league's One Baseball initiative, MLB is getting more involved with draft showcases and wood bat summer leagues—and the all-important data output from those events. This funneling helps to filter the manpower needed for team decision-makers to see as many top prospects as possible. Not only is it more convenient, players will face competition closer to their own level, making for an easier assessment when comparing like prospects.

With a new CBA coming and minor-league reorganization reducing the number of players a team can have under contract, it's very possible that there won't be another 40-round draft. The draft process consolidation is already leading to staff reductions in amateur scouting departments, a trend we expect to continue as teams aggressively cut costs. Saying the quiet part out loud: we were already heading this way long before a worldwide pandemic provided a tidy excuse to begin implementation.

⚾　　⚾　　⚾

Baseball tried to look like itself in 2020. We've tried to present a Top 101 Prospects list that at least *looks* like the ones you're accustomed to. If you check under the hood, though, there's less movement than on lists in the past. Where there has been change for non-obvious reasons, there will be an accompanying explanation, be it a change in profile verified by sourcing, or something altogether different.

We will be back at the ballpark at some point, watching baseball from behind home plate in minor leagues that have been transformed by MLB in our absence. Hopefully, next year's 101 will reflect that. ▓

—Jeffrey Paternostro, Jarrett Seidler and Keanan Lamb are authors of Baseball Prospectus.

Top 101 Prospects

by Jeffrey Paternostro, Jarrett Seidler and Keanan Lamb

1. Wander Franco, SS, Tampa Bay Rays

Franco remains the top prospect in baseball in large part because there's no new evidence to suggest he isn't. What is known about Franco's 2020: 1) He was at the alternate site, and even made the playoff taxi squad. 2) As part of said taxi squad he appeared on the field after Tampa Bay clinched the AL pennant, showing off bigger arms in a cutoff t-shirt. 3) He went to the Dominican Winter League and looked more or less like you'd expect before those swole biceps started barking. Franco was shut down as a precautionary measure, but it's considered a minor injury. He's on the verge of taking his place in the middle of the Rays lineup and infield, where he should challenge for batting titles—in a world without Nick Madrigal, he'd have the best contact ability on this list—and bop 20-plus home runs. Sometimes no news isn't the worst news.

2. Adley Rutschman, C, Baltimore Orioles

How many cold-weather catchers, lightly followed out of high school and with a meager beginning to their college career, end up garnering consideration for the top overall spot just a few years later? Not many. Despite the geographical biases, or the iffy historical success rate for catchers, Rutschman is a well-rounded player on both sides of the ball, and he may ascend to the top spot next year—if he doesn't graduate first, anyway. There is power in the bat, plenty of contact ability and the discipline of a professional approach. (He sees the ball incredibly well from both sides of the plate, which isn't always true with switch hitters.) On the defensive side, he's nimble and athletic with at least a plus arm, and he also collaborates well with his pitching staff. You can't really build a potential franchise player much better than this.

3. Julio Rodríguez, OF, Seattle Mariners

If you wanted to make an argument for Rodríguez as the top prospect in baseball you can start with this: He hits the ball incredibly hard. Exit velocity can be a bit of a fun fact, or merely an expression of the obvious, but when a teenager is regularly showing the kind of hard contact that would garner a tip of the cap from Giancarlo Stanton, take notice. The on-field performance got Rodríguez into the top 10 last year—he slugged .540 at two A-ball levels as an 18-year-old—and the reports from the alternate site in 2020 did nothing to dampen our enthusiasm. Unlike the two players ahead of him, though, we can point out minor quibbles. It's still unclear how good the hit tool is—it projects as above-average, which could allow the elite raw to play to 40 home runs—or where he will stand in the outfield. (Right field currently looks more likely than center.) Rodríguez should be a plus defender in a corner, and given the present (and voluble) offensive tools, he may have the highest ceiling of any prospect on this list.

4. Sixto Sánchez, RHP, Miami Marlins

Sánchez's ascension turned out to be worth waiting another year for. The uber-talented righty has long tantalized with ace potential: triple-digit heat from a free and easy delivery and nearly every offspeed in the book. In 2020, one of the offspeeds—his hard changeup—revealed itself to be a fully-operational out pitch. That was the last ingredient Sánchez needed for major-league success, and he was splendid down the stretch for the Marlins. There are minor nitpicks: his health record is not clean, his fastball shape doesn't lead to as many swings-and-misses as the velocity would indicate and his command occasionally deserts him (most notably in the NLDS). But make no mistake, it's absolutely elite stuff and pitchability, and he has the best chance to be an ace of anyone on this list by a good margin. That makes him the best pitching prospect in baseball…

5. Ian Anderson, RHP, Atlanta Braves

… but it was actually a razor-close call. While Sánchez does have a better chance of being an ace, we think Anderson's probably the better pitcher right now. His changeup progressed even more than Sánchez's, jumping from a pitch with average-to-above-average projection to a straight present plus-plus offering that was baffling hitters deep into the playoffs. His fastball and curveball are good enough to overcome mediocre spin rates, and the back of his baseball card has been nearly spotless since he was the third-overall pick in 2016. Sure, he could use another half-grade of command improvement, but who couldn't? Anderson is a very good major-league pitcher, right now.

6. Jarred Kelenic, OF, Seattle Mariners

Kelenic unlocked his full offensive potential following his trade to Seattle two years ago. With an improved swing path, he now projects for both plus-or-better hit and plus-or-better power potential. The Wisconsin native has excellent barrel control and the ball just jumps off his bat. He has a very good shot to remain in center field all the way up the chain, with above-average speed at present and strong outfield instincts, although he could move to a corner as the natural aging progression takes its course. He's poised for a call-up in the near future; if the Mariners were a little more aggressive he might've gotten there already.

7. Ke'Bryan Hayes, 3B, Pittsburgh Pirates

Last year's blurb noted Hayes' loud contact, good approach and Gold Glove-quality defense at the hot corner. It specified that "the wait continues to see if he can adjust the launch angle on those laser beams off his bat." As you might be able to intuit from his current ranking, he did. The power breakout we'd finally been waiting for happened, as he smashed 14 extra-base hits in 24 games, including five home runs that all landed somewhere between the power alleys. He still doesn't hit the ball in the air as often as a typical 30-homer hitter should, but when he does they go an awful long way, and he's capable of putting on a plus-plus raw power show in batting practice. Hayes only needs to scrape 20 to be an All-Star caliber player given the rest of the profile. There's always some danger in moving a prospect this much off such a small sample, but this doesn't seem like an outlier, merely an inevitability.

8. Marco Luciano, SS, San Francisco Giants

Like Rodríguez, Luciano hits the ball *extremely* hard. He mashed a monstrous homer off Ryan Rolison during fall instructs that registered a bonkers 119 mph off the bat, the product of a lightning-fast swing (which he pairs with an equally intense bat flip). Unlike Rodríguez, Luciano doesn't have the solid 2019 foundation of torching both full-season A-ball levels; his entire pro experience has been in the complex, save a nine-game cup of coffee in short-season last year. The lack of a 2020 season cost him the opportunity to prove that he could make consistent quality contact against more advanced pitching, and that's the only thing stopping him from vaulting to the very top of this list.

9. Bobby Witt Jr., SS, Kansas City Royals

It's only natural that kids are attracted to following in the footsteps of their fathers. It's rarer when the progeny plays the same sport as Dad, but excels in a completely different way. The elder Witt pitched for 16 years in the big leagues, and while Junior does have a cannon for a right arm, he'll be terrorizing pitchers instead. The physicality, body control, plus power and makeup all point towards a future star in the making. As one of the younger members at the Royals' alternate site, he established himself as someone who not only belonged, but excelled against older competition. Every indication says he'll stay at shortstop, with the worst-case scenario being a plus defender at third base. Follow that up

with good wheels, and the only question mark remaining will be whether the bat will make enough contact to become a true five-tool player.

10. C.J. Abrams, SS, San Diego Padres

Abrams went sixth overall to the Padres in 2019, and he immediately dispelled any pre-draft concerns about his offensive tools by brutalizing the Arizona League. Okay, that's complex ball played across a series of launching pads, but the reports only got louder at instructs this past fall, when he raked against a much older level of competition. Okay, that's instructional ball across a series of launching pads. But it's unfair to hold that missing 2020 season where he might've dominated full-season ball against him. All we can do is look at the available information. Abrams is a top-of-the-scale runner who will land at a premium defensive position—if he doesn't quite have the arm for shortstop, center field should make for a soft landing given his tool set. He may never hit for a ton of over-the-fence power, but he is already capable of loud contact against plus velocity, and he has room to get stronger without losing his speed. Abrams will be able to hurt opposing teams in a variety of ways. He's better than the sum of his parts, albeit with some uncertainty—for good and ill—about the individual parts until we see him in a more normal prospect environment.

11. MacKenzie Gore, LHP, San Diego Padres

We waited all season for Gore to get the call to The Show. And then, when the Padres needed a live arm the most in the playoffs, they went instead to Ryan Weathers. This decision made little sense on the surface; Weathers had never pitched above Low-A while Gore had Double-A experience, and Gore is a much better prospect. Combined with reports that he didn't look sharp at the alternate site, we're left to infer that this probably wasn't a great season of development for the talented southpaw. Our 2019 looks were splendid; a four-pitch starter led by a mid-90s fastball and a dazzling curveball. He certainly could come out throwing seeds in 2021 and make us look foolish for doubting, even a little, but for now Sánchez and Anderson have passed him as the top pitching prospect in baseball.

12. Nick Madrigal, 2B, Chicago White Sox

Madrigal became an even more extreme version of himself in 109 major-league plate appearances in 2020, hitting .340 by making an extraordinarily large amount of contact and shooting the ball where they ain't. He also showed off next-to-no power, even less than expected—of his three extra-base hits, only one was actually hit over an outfielder's head, and he didn't have a single batted ball all season which Statcast rated as a barrel. It's possible that the complete lack of wattage was due to an early-season shoulder separation, which cost him just enough time to remain rookie-eligible, and that he had surgery after the season to fix. It's also possible that this is just who he is: a singles machine on par with The Beatles living in a world where Top 40 radio has given way to Spotify. That still has a lot of value, but it's not a superstar in the 2020s.

13. Spencer Torkelson, 3B/1B, Detroit Tigers

As ready-made as collegiate sluggers come, Torkelson toyed with the college ranks, biding his time before being selected first overall in the 2020 draft with little hesitation. While he may not be mentioned in the same breath as other recent slam-dunk college picks like Rutschman and Stephen Strasburg, there is a reasonable argument to make that he is one of the "safer" picks you can make in the amateur draft. So much is unknown at the time players are picked; Tork alleviates much of the guesswork. He has an above-average hit tool, a plus-plus eye to get on base, plus-or-better game power to all fields, a Statcast-friendly profile. Simply put: He is an offensive machine. So what if he's only a first baseman for a considerable amount of his career? The certainty he brings when dealing with probabilistic career outcomes for a franchise that can't mess around with missing on guys at the top of the draft is incalculable.

14. Andrew Vaughn, 1B, Chicago White Sox

Inevitably tied at the hip to Torkelson, Vaughn has a similar history and profile: a bat-first top-three pick that pummeled the Pac-12 and is likely to play mostly first base. The difference between the two is that Vaughn is shorter, and even a little undersized (6-feet tall) compared to what you'd expect out of a power hitter. Alas, his shorter stature does not give him an advantage in the athleticism department, where he is a below-average runner and lesser compared to Torkelson. Though there has been some experimentation with Vaughn, both in the outfield and at third base, in order to get his bat into an already stacked White Sox lineup, the fact remains that he will end up playing first base over the long haul. Regardless, Vaughn has a chance to hit for more average utilizing a line-drive swing that still produces a ton of power.

15. Kristian Robinson, OF, Arizona Diamondbacks

Let's Make a Deal, hosted by Hugh Everett

Behind Door #1: Robinson dominates the Midwest League in 2020, sending 400-plus foot shots through the frigid April night skies of Fort Wayne, Beloit and Lansing. He continues to mash in the Cal League after a midseason promotion and ranks up with the top outfield prospects in baseball. He certainly has that level of ceiling.

Behind Door #2: Robinson struggles to adjust to full-season arms as a 19-year-old. College pitchers who can spin a breaking ball when they're ahead give him fits, and a high strikeout rate eats into his game power, although it still shows up in flashes. He slashes something like .246/.304/.455, not bad given his age and experience level, but enough to knock him down the list a bit.

Behind Door #3: The 2020 minor league season is cancelled due to a pandemic. Robinson struggles at times at the alternate site against more advanced arms than he'd see in A-ball. The All-Star upside remains due to the power/speed combination. Likewise, the risk remains high given the swing-and-miss concerns. Nothing new is laid bare, nothing made obvious.

16. Dylan Carlson, OF, St. Louis Cardinals

After a 2019 breakout, Carlson got the call to St. Louis after the team's COVID-19 outbreak. He looked better than his .176/.233/.265 line in August, taking good at-bats and hitting a bunch of line drives right at some gloves. But as the team got healthy and found themselves in a playoff race, a sub-.500 OPS wasn't going to play. Perhaps Carlson found something back at the alternate site, perhaps he just had some better results on contact or perhaps he made those key secondary adjustments against major-league pitching. Back in The Show, he posted an .806 OPS in September and started all three games in the wild card round. There's little reason to think he isn't broadly the same prospect as last year, a plus hit/power/speed triple threat who can play all three outfield spots.

17. Deivi García, RHP, New York Yankees

García didn't get to prove he could handle a full starting workload given the abbreviated season and an August 30 call-up. He *did* get to prove that his stuff was plenty good enough to hang with the big boys. García's fastball is nothing special in terms of velocity or spin, but it plays extremely well off his go-to overhand curveball. The big, tumbling hook has been an obvious out-pitch for years, and he's developed better command to spot it where needed, often on the edges of the strike zone. He mixes in enough changeups and sliders to keep batters honest, and everything but his height (he's 5-foot-9) points to long-term success in the rotation. A couple decades ago, that almost certainly would've consigned him to the bullpen, but the Yankees are likely to give him every chance to start moving forward.

18. Cristian Pache, OF, Atlanta Braves

We got an appetizer portion's worth of Pache in late August during his brief call-up, followed by something closer to resembling an entrée during the Braves postseason run. Never in doubt were his elite fielding skills in center, featuring preternatural instincts off the bat with above-average speed and a 70-grade arm. Those traits alone would have him starting every day for most any team. The heights of his career arc will be determined by how much value comes from his offense. There is plus bat speed to go with an aggressive approach that hunts fastballs early in the count, showing there is some pop to go along with the glove. And during his 29 plate appearances there was some evidence of patience, something that had been lacking in previous years in the minors. If he can be a league-average hitter—the dessert of this 3-course meal—we're talking about 20-20 potential at a premium position.

19. Riley Greene, OF, Detroit Tigers

While the BP Prospect Team didn't get to see a lot of live baseball in 2020, among our handful of in-person looks was Tigers instructional league action. Taken one pick before C.J. Abrams in the 2019 draft, Greene has seen similar rapid maturation despite the atypical player development environs. If you would have predicted a Greene breakout last offseason, it would have looked a lot like this. He's added significant good weight and we're more confident the plus power part of the plus hit/power projection gets there. After looking tentative in the outfield in his first pro summer, additional reps on the grass have improved his center field defense. The reports from the alternate site—against better arms—back up our instructs looks. In a season where almost nothing went to plan in baseball, Greene's improvements seem comfortingly normal for a highly touted projectable prep outfielder.

20. Randy Arozarena, OF, Tampa Bay Rays

In a single shortened season, Arozarena advanced from an interesting-if-tweenerish outfield prospect with average pop to a true slugger with apparent plus-plus game power. If you're reading this book, you probably already know that he had one of the best postseasons in baseball history. He was quite difficult to rank on merit, because a two-grade jump in game power that has only shown up for a couple months is difficult to evaluate, and the new power came at the cost of significant swing-and-miss, especially within the zone. Some sources thought he should be in the top five of this list, and others wouldn't place him in the top half.

Arozarena was detained in Mexico in November after domestic violence allegations. His ex-partner declined to press charges.

21. Asa Lacy, LHP, Kansas City Royals

The power lefty out of Texas A&M dazzled during his limited spring season, striking out nearly two batters per inning and pairing improved strike-throwing ability with a tick in stuff. Lacy's fastball velocity comfortably sits in the mid 90s with an extra gear available when he needs it. There is effort to the delivery, which has caused control issues in the past, but the prominent head whack he had earlier in his college career was a touch more reserved of late. His nasty slider that is effective against both righties and lefties, and his curve and change are in the vicinity of average. Add it all up and he's got a starter's repertoire, a starter's body and frontline potential.

22. Austin Martin, SS, Toronto Blue Jays

What is an "Austin Martin?" Try defining him, and you end up with a bunch of different player comps, none of which aptly describes what he does in the game. There is enough varied defensive ability to play just about anywhere in the field,

but no obvious position where he fits best. He has a whippy, looping swing with plenty of energy and barrel control to collect hits of all varieties. The power is coming along, steadily advancing each year at Vanderbilt while maintaining his excellent control of the strike zone. He doesn't fit a particular cookie cutter profile, which shouldn't diminish anything he brings to the field each day. He is his own brand of player, one that should be a good regular in short order.

23. Nolan Gorman, 3B, St. Louis Cardinals

In a shade over a season's worth of plate appearances, Gorman has cracked 30-plus home runs and 40-plus doubles. He did this before turning 20 and with most of the games coming at full-season levels. Flash forward a few years, and a few levels, and that's what you are hoping to get from his bat in the majors. There's plus-plus raw power that might end up top of the scale as he gets stronger in his 20s. The swing has some stiffness and length, but there's plenty of bat speed and loft, and his hands work well enough to project an average hit tool. That's all he will need to be a middle-of-the-lineup force. He's not the rangiest third baseman, but he does enough there that he should stick at the hot corner, and his arm is strong enough to be an asset. Major League Equivalencies aren't as simple as made out above, and Double-A will be a stern test of the present profile. If he hits there, then Gorman could soon be bringing majestic dingers to a Cardinals game near you.

24. Shane Baz, RHP, Tampa Bay Rays

In *Kiss Me Deadly*, a rather loose adaptation of one of Mickey Spillane's Mike Hammer novels, our hard-boiled detective finds himself caught between a *femme fatale* and a bunch of hired goons, all searching for a mysterious box that his secretary (and occasional lover) Velda calls "the great whatsit." Baz is the great whatsit of this year's prospect list. Since being drafted 12th overall in 2017, he's been used awfully sparingly due to the conservative development proclivities of both the Pirates and Rays. When on the mound, he has routinely hit triple digits with his fastball and he can unleash a plus-plus slider as well. In *Kiss Me Deadly*, the mystery box is filled with radioactive material that immolates the *femme fatale*; in the movie version, the great whatsit is a metaphor for Cold War nihilism. In the prospect blurb version, one supposes it could be a metaphor for Baz's blazing fastball, or the control and command issues that keep him from being higher on the list. After all, any good film critic allows for the possibility of multiple meanings.

25. Luis Patiño, RHP, Tampa Bay Rays

It's easier to deal with a new, positive level of performance for prospects in the majors in 2020. There are more tools to identify what, if anything, changed in the profile and how sticky it might be going forward. But what about when a prospect struggles during our least favorite year? It's hard to hold Patiño's season against him. He had made a grand total of two starts above A-ball coming into the year and his role with the Padres would have been unfamiliar. He was asked to pitch out of the bullpen; to come in with runners on base. The stuff that made him the No. 15 prospect last year was still broadly present, with three potential plus offerings. He still missed plenty of bats swung by the best hitters in the world. Patiño's command and control weren't quite ready for the show, but was it fair to expect any different? Still, how a prospect fails can be useful information too, and Patiño clocks in at No. 24 this year, because those command and control issues—combined with his smaller frame—up the reliever risk in the profile. Is that fair? We're not sure. The Rays are betting on the 2019 version returning in force after making him the centerpiece of the Blake Snell deal.

26. Leody Taveras, OF, Texas Rangers

This marks Taveras' fifth consecutive entry on the 101, and he posted his best slugging percentage of his career in 2020.

"That's good!"

It was in the majors.

"That's even better!"

It was .395.

Tumbleweeds roll by as the BP Lead Prospect Writer stares off into the middle distance.

Taveras got handed the everyday center field job late in the season as the Rangers made their September roster into a mini-Arizona Fall League for many of their top prospects. He was as advertised defensively, looking like an immediate Gold Glove candidate. The plus-plus defense/speed combo makes him likely to have a long career, even if he only xeroxes his 2020 line going forward. But there's reason to be optimistic: He was jumping straight to the majors after only a half season of Double-A, and he's shown the ingredients for above-average hit and power tools while playing in some terrible home parks—including Globe Life Field which played like old school Petco in its debut season.

Okay, you may have noticed this also marks a fifth consecutive entry on the 101 handwaving Taveras posting a .700 OPS while ranking him in the Top 50, but he only has to hit a little bit more to be a plus regular.

27. Casey Mize, RHP, Detroit Tigers

Making a somewhat surprising debut in 2020 as the Tigers flirted with contention during a condensed season, Mize showed he was perhaps not quite ready for the bigs. The book on Mize since his draft year at Auburn, where he quickly pitched himself into the consensus first-overall pick, was one of a control pitcher who also happened to have plenty of juice on each of his four potential plus offerings. Often command is sacrificed for stuff—he had both. What was most surprising in his seven major-league starts was a dramatic uptick in walks. The mechanics appeared to be consistent; moreover, he seemed to be trying to be too fine with his locations, especially with his cutter and splitter that both move a fair amount. Instead of letting his pitches work for him, he was getting behind and unable to recover. Let him

get that extra seasoning in the minors in 2021 so he can rediscover his dominant form from before his arm injury in 2019, and work up to the big leagues with less pressure.

28. Ryan Mountcastle, OF, Baltimore Orioles

This will be more coda than prospect projection, as Mountcastle was a mere four at-bats from exhausting his list eligibility. He's long been a confounding prospect, but we always thought he'd get to the majors and hit. Sure enough, he got to the majors and hit. Mountcastle is not a true talent .333 hitter, mind you; the strikeout rate and underlying swing rates don't support that, but he should have a plus hit tool going forward. We'd expect him to show more extra-base pop as well, something in the range of 25 home runs and 35 doubles. Drafted as a prep shortstop who was never going to stick, he's settled in as a decent enough left fielder. He'll likely see some time at first base and DH as well.

29. Joey Bart, C, San Francisco Giants

In a perfect world, Bart would've spent 2020 conquering the high-minors, making up for time lost to injuries in 2019 and perhaps coming up for a cameo as part of a long-term passing of the torch with Buster Posey. In this one, Posey opted out of the season and Bart was called up in mid-August when the Chadwick Tromp/Tyler Heineman catching tandem went about as well as you'd expect. Contact was always an ephemeral concern for Bart, and in 2020 it proved to be an insurmountable one; staying productive while striking out nearly 37 percent of the time is a feat only Joey Gallo seems to be able to pull off, and while Bart has real power, he doesn't have *that* kind of power. Luckily Posey is back, so Bart can return to his own developmental timetable.

30. Grayson Rodriguez, RHP, Baltimore Orioles

Rodriguez made steady improvements over the course of the 2019 season, showing markedly better by the end of the campaign than he did at the beginning: velocity up, changeup sharpening, curveball and slider both flashing, command improving. He was invited to the alternate site and continued to pump mid-90s gas with strong reports on the overall development track, and all arrows seem to still be pointing up. If he ever gets the chance to throw 100 innings with that heat, there's a pretty good chance he'll be one of the best pitching prospects in baseball by the end of it—if he's not in the majors first. When you draft a prep pitcher in the top of half of the first round, this is exactly where you hope he'll be two-plus years in … well, except for the whole cancelled season part.

31. Royce Lewis, IF/OF, Minnesota Twins

Let's start with what's good about Lewis: he's got explosive actions and great lateral quickness, along with plenty of thunder in a bat that can catch up to velocity. What is holding him back, and what obviously held him back at the team's alternate site, is a swing that is not ready for high-caliber pitching. We were among the first to note in 2019 how his mechanics had become disjointed following a strong introduction to pro ball. His upper body and lower half were out of sync, failing to work in concert with each other except for the occasional ambushed early count fastball, and his strikeout rate ballooned as a result. Even after earning MVP honors of the Arizona Fall League, the underlying concerns remained, and were exacerbated as he began to see less and less time at shortstop. There is only so much that can be done with elite bat speed alone, and until he can figure out a way to quiet his timing down to match good pitching, we will remain bearish on his future.

32. Heliot Ramos, OF, San Francisco Giants

In a year where time passed more slowly than the event horizon of a black hole, prospect fatigue conversely accelerated. We are only three years removed from Ramos announcing himself on the national prospect stage by mashing in Arizona as a 17-year-old. He's been on quite the *bildungsroman* as a player since, adding some bad weight and struggling at full-season ball as an 18-year-old, reshaping his body and reaffirming potential plus hit and power tools in the California and Eastern Leagues as a 19-year-old. As a 20-year-old his season was bookended by a pair of oblique strains, one that hampered him during spring training, and one that cut his time short at Giants instructs. In between he spent time at the alternate site, where he still looked like a quality major-leaguer, albeit one that will spend more time in right field than center.

33. JJ Bleday, OF, Miami Marlins

The Marlins boast one of the best farm systems in all of baseball. One piece of their embarrassment of riches is Bleday, the former Vandy standout and the fourth-overall pick in 2019, who is likely to make his big-league debut in 2021. He is well-rounded offensively, displaying power and contact to all fields with a keen eye of the strike zone. He's also the type of player who is nearly impervious to streaks, never too high or too low. He'll never wow you with his speed, which might be the only deficiency to his game, but he'll make up for it in right with a plus arm. Regardless, his track record of performance and proximity to a call-up make him one of the safer prospects on the list.

34. Corbin Carroll, OF, Arizona Diamondbacks

Every year we lament leaving a prospect off the list, only to see them break out during the season. Carroll served as that prospect in 2020, which is impressive given the whole lack of a season thing. There has to be a good reason to jump a prospect this much, especially without on-field performance to point to. There are two factors working in concert here: 1) We probably underrated Carroll coming off the draft last year because he's an undersized prep outfielder; despite how hard he hits the ball, there's limited physical projection in the offensive tools when you are listed at 5-foot-10. And, 2) Carroll, really, really mashed at the alternate site, doing so against significantly more advanced pitching. Some

prospects make the leap every year, and Carroll sure seemed to amid tough circumstances. He's an above-average center fielder with a plus hit tool and at least average power. You could even argue he should be in the next tier of outfielders up with Taveras, Pache and Greene.

35. Nate Pearson, RHP, Toronto Blue Jays

More than 20 prospects on this list made their big-league debuts in 2020, including Pearson. Starting strong in his first game versus the Nats, he found a comfortable release point to amp up his 80-grade heat late in the outing. However, finding that release point wasn't always easy. He struggled in other starts, failing to land the fastball for strikes while his secondaries didn't fare much better. His entire game is predicated off velocity, speeding up the hitter's bats so he can break off his plus-plus power slider and other offspeed varieties. Pearson's frustration later turned to injury, and he missed a month with a strained elbow, only to return late in the season to produce better results in a bullpen role. Don't worry (yet) about a potential full-time move to the 'pen—as with most pitchers of his size and mechanics, he just needs to find a routine he can settle into and find his groove.

36. Garrett Crochet, LHP, Chicago White Sox

Tell me if you've read this script before: the White Sox drafted a spindly college lefty with questionable mechanics who throws a huge fastball and a hellacious slider, and then brought him to the majors the same year as a dominant reliever. Crochet has an enormous ceiling as a starting pitcher—if you saw him on the right day as an amateur, he looked like a potential ace—but he only made 13 collegiate starts at Tennessee between injuries, use as a reliever and the pandemic. Chicago brought him straight to the majors for its playoff run and he was sitting 100 mph, touching 102 out of the bullpen and generally looking unhittable ... right up until his velocity tanked in the playoffs and he was diagnosed with a flexor strain. If this all works out, Crochet could turn into an ace, but there's a ton of bullpen risk evident with his command, changeup and arm health. At least the proof of concept for a dominant relief outcome is already there.

37. Michael Kopech, RHP, Chicago White Sox

After spending all of 2019 recovering from Tommy John surgery, Kopech opted out of the 2020 season; James Fegan of *The Athletic* reported he was concerned about the short ramp-up to game action and the uncertainty about his role and the pandemic season at large. He hasn't seen official game action since September 2018, although he has pitched in instructs and threw a spring inning before the league shut down. In that frame, he looked phenomenal, sitting 100-101 mph and mixing in his best breaking balls. Kopech's command was a work-in-progress before he got hurt, and this ranking is a pure dart throw given how much developmental time he's missed.

38. Logan Gilbert, RHP, Seattle Mariners

The first of a trio of right-handed Mariners pitchers on this list, you'll notice a pattern within the group. Gilbert separates himself from the pack as he is further along the developmental track. Although he's a strong-bodied 6-foot-5 hurler, he's not known for throwing gas. In fact, his fastball velocity has ebbed and flowed over the last several years, at times averaging in the mid 90s, and at other times a bit lower. Reports from camp have the fastball pendulum swinging back toward the positive side, to go along with a plus snapping curveball and advanced control.

39. Nick Gonzales, 2B, Pittsburgh Pirates

There are few instances of diminutive players surpassing all the obstacles and biases placed in front of them to be taken as high as Gonzales was in the most recent draft. While 5-foot-10 might be a generous listing, his work ethic and video-game numbers are unmistakable. He maximizes his height thanks to fast hands and sound lower-half mechanics, which adds loft to his swing path. Yes, the aforementioned stats may have been helped by extremely friendly home field conditions, but he also raked and earned MVP honors at the Cape in 2019. He's going to need to keep hitting, because he's likely to be limited to second base by so-so range and an arm that wouldn't play at shortstop.

40. Drew Waters, OF, Atlanta Braves

Twenty-year-olds who win batting titles in Double-A are to be celebrated, even as we await the arrival of their power and have concerns about an overly aggressive plate approach. The power was an area of focus at the alternate site this summer for Waters, with Atlanta hoping his hard-hit line drives would gain the carry needed to get over the fences. Even with an advanced hit tool from both sides of the plate, he's a conundrum to predict based upon his pro performance thus far and the potential for the best pitchers in the world to better exploit the holes in his game. You want to believe in it, yet you remain hesitant because you haven't seen it with your own eyes.

41. Jordan Groshans, SS, Toronto Blue Jays

Good news: Groshans is fully recovered from the foot injury that cost him most of 2019, and the reports from the alternate site indicate the same strong offensive tools that propelled him up our rankings to begin with.

Bad news: He lost even more developmental time since his "season" didn't get going until summer camp commenced in July.

Groshans is a better prospect than he was two years ago, though he only has 96 real plate appearances in the time since, making this a real outlier situation, in a season filled with them. He hit the ball hard against good pitching at Toronto's alternate site, and that's promising given his general lack of professional experience. The bet here is that he's going to come out in 2021 and rip up Double-A, but that's still a gamble—not just that he'll reach that level and perform, but that there will be a Double-A season for him to tear up at all.

42. Ronny Mauricio, SS, New York Mets

Mauricio's gap year is a tricky one to evaluate. Signed as a switch-hitting shortstop out of the Dominican Republic in 2017, Mauricio has been pushed aggressively throughout his career. He kept his head above water for the most part, showcasing a potential plus hit/power combination—especially from the left side—though he'd go through periods where it was all he could do just to make contact. We ranked him as aggressively as he was pushed last year, slotting him into the Top 50, with the wager that he'd get stronger, gain experience and hit a bit more at a new level. Our bet never got a chance to play out, as Mauricio had only brief stints at the alternate site and instructs (Mets camp was shut down early due to a COVID-19 outbreak). We don't know what we don't know, so this has become a bit of a parlay on last year's gamble.

43. Matthew Liberatore, LHP, St. Louis Cardinals

When one franchise known for its player dev voodoo trades a prospect to another org also known for its developmental witchcraft, who ends up getting the better end of the deal? That's where we stand with Liberatore, a highly regarded prep pitching prospect who fell into Tampa Bay's lap thanks to pre-draft nitpicking, then proceeded to pitch well before being shipped to St. Louis. A tall lefty with a good frame and an easy arm action, he doesn't have the kind of backspin on his fastball that would pair well with his curveball. The breaker instead stands alone as an elite pitch, with his sinking fastball working independently. For someone his age and size, he's a surprisingly good strike-thrower, relying more on pitchability than the pure stuff potential he possesses. It's this dichotomy—command/control artist or swing-and-miss butcher—that has evaluators flummoxed.

44. Brandon Marsh, OF, Los Angeles Angels

Imagine an outfield with Mike Trout, Jo Adell and Marsh. Pretty good, right? That image in your head is close to becoming a reality. While Marsh's in-game power hasn't quite manifested to the point you'd expect from a 6-foot-4 23-year-old, he's played in some pitcher-friendly environments in the minors. One scout had predicted before the shutdown he could hit 30 homers in the Pacific Coast League with an improved ability to lift the ball. His is an impressive overall package, and he moves incredibly well despite his hulking frame. He would be a center fielder on most teams, but, given the current state of the Angels, he'll be repositioned as an above-average defender in one of the corner-outfield spots.

45. Edward Cabrera, RHP, Miami Marlins

The Marlins already feature a mononymous pitcher in their system, because when you're great and your name is uniquely memorable you can do that, like Cher or Madonna or Prince. Sliding under the radar, yet routinely referenced by sources as having stuff just as good as Sixto's, is Edward Cabrera. He hasn't received the hype that comes with being the centerpiece of a blockbuster deal, but with a fastball in the upper-90s and two secondary pitches that both flash plus, there is a palpable reason for excitement. Cabrera has a more ideal starter's body than Sixto does, and he has shown an ability to make adjustments to his mechanics at the request of pitching coaches. Minor injuries have dogged him the past two years, and the hope is that he can avoid those nicks as he approaches a role in Miami's rotation in 2021.

46. Matt Manning, RHP, Detroit Tigers

The Tigers called up two of their three notable pitching prospects in 2020—Casey Mize and Tarik Skubal. Both struggled to various degrees. You could argue that struggling in the majors is better than "dealing with a mild forearm strain," which caused Manning to be shut down at the alternate site. (On the other hand, we haven't seen Manning struggle yet.) Since overhauling his delivery in the low minors, he's routinely hit 95 with big extension and plane from his 6-foot-6 frame. He pairs it with a curve that flashes plus, or even better some starts, and an improving changeup that has a chance to be more than just a show-me pitch against lefties. It's never all come together for him, but he remains a good mid-rotation prospect. We'd say "safe" mid-rotation prospect, but there's really no such thing as a "mild" forearm strain.

47. Alek Thomas, CF, Arizona Diamondbacks

The third of three Diamondbacks center fielders in the Top 50, Thomas puts on a pretty good show himself. He is more likely to stick in center and be above-average there than Robinson, though perhaps less so than Carroll. While he doesn't have Robinson's projection and physicality, he's bigger than Carroll, and he arguably has the most advanced hit tool of the three. Thomas sprays hard line drives all over the field, showing plus bat speed despite noisy hands as he sets up. He doesn't lift the ball enough at present to get his plus raw power into games, and while Thomas is likely to be an above-average regular for a long time, he lacks the upside of his organization mates. There's no real shame in coming in third among this trio of prospects though.

48. George Valera, OF, Cleveland

Player value can be reduced to a simple sum of discrete parts. Offensive runs created + defensive runs prevented + positional value + replacement level. Valera has played mostly center field as a professional, but he's spent enough time in a corner in the low minors to suggest he's likely to operate there long term. He should be fine, but he won't be a real asset with the glove there. That means the lion's share of his value will have to come from his bat. His swing is even noisier than Thomas', and it's not the loose, rotational, aesthetically pleasing lefty swing prospect writers dream about. Even so, he has a ton of bat speed and is able to generate an impressive amount of in-game power. We think he's going to hit for average as well, making him one to watch.

49. Zac Veen, OF, Colorado Rockies

Veen provided about as much data as possible for a high school pick prior to the shutdown. After a solid summer where he entered first-round consideration, the early beginning to Florida baseball allowed scouts to see him against top competition. Lean and with long levers, he displayed a gliding-sort of athleticism rare for his 6-foot-4 size. The swing, like the rest of his movements, is smooth and effortless and packs plenty of power potential to go along with good contact skills. Unlike a lot of players of his age and ilk, he has an advanced approach at the plate and he is content with being patient, unafraid to take a pitch while he works the pitcher. It was moderately shocking to see a different high school outfielder (Robert Hassell III) taken ahead of him. Veen's ranking reflects the difference between the two.

50. Emerson Hancock, RHP, Seattle Mariners

Before the college season began, Hancock was among a select shortlist of players vying to be the first-overall pick. A rough first start short-circuited that argument, but his final three outings went more to plan: he threw 20 innings, allowing 13 hits and two walks while punching out 30. Like his other Mariners brethren found in the 101, he's blessed with an ideal starting pitcher's body. He has an advanced feel for, and command of, his arsenal. The fastball rests comfortably in the 94-96 mph range and at times he can dial it up into the upper 90s while working all quadrants of the zone. His best secondary is a hard-biting slider, with the changeup not far behind; a passable curve rounds out his repertoire. There may not be the unlimited ceiling so many scouting directors scour for in the draft, though the appeal of Hancock and the other M's recent high pitching picks is the elevated floors that offer plenty of mid-rotation depth.

51. Max Meyer, RHP, Miami Marlins

Meyer, listed at an even 6-feet tall, is a gifted athlete who maximizes every movement in his delivery to generate blistering velocity. He even eclipsed the 100-mph mark in some outings. His downward breaking slider, meanwhile, is one of the best out-pitches seen in years by amateur scouts. He's shown a propensity for using it as both a chase offering and a pitch that he can throw for strikes. Meyer may have two plus-plus pitches, but he needs the changeup to be at least a show-me pitch for him to stick in the rotation. At worst, his present traits profile to an elite closer; at best, if he can prove he can hold up against the rigors of a starter's schedule and develop that third pitch, it checks the boxes of a no. 2 starter, and perhaps even better.

52. Nolan Jones, 3B, Cleveland

Jones has plus-plus raw power and an excellent plate approach, producing elite offensive performance driven by walks and extra-base hits up and down the minor-league chain (he's posted a 150 DRC+ or better at every full-season stop so far). Of course, if you scratch a little deeper under the surface, there's some warts, too; otherwise, he'd be higher on this list. Jones has struck out a high clip, and we're concerned that his approach is too pull-heavy to maintain a decent average at the highest level. His defense at third base is rough despite a plus-plus arm, and he might end up at a corner-outfield spot or first base down the road (especially given José Ramírez's presence). Even if he doesn't totally iron out the defense or contact, Jones stands a pretty good chance to be a fun Three True Outcomes slugger regardless.

53. DL Hall, LHP, Baltimore Orioles

We've finally reached the mid-rotation starter or late-inning reliever tier, a Top 101 tradition like no other. A review of the ground rules: the pitcher must have a plus fastball, one plus secondary (it's most often a breaking ball) and questions about his command and third pitch (usually the *cambio*). This template isn't as cut and dry as it used to be, as teams figure out ways to maximize the best part of their arms' arsenals, but it's a useful descriptor for our purposes. Hall tops this group because the fastball isn't merely plus; a 2020 velocity jump had him sitting in the upper 90s and touching 99. He has the requisite plus breaker, and his changeup improved as well. He's not in the "number two starter" tier because the questions about his command are along the lines of "uh, didn't he walk six per nine in Advanced-A last we saw him?" Yes reader, yes he did.

54. Mick Abel, RHP, Philadelphia Phillies

It was a widely-held belief within the industry that with a shortage of both picks and information before the draft that teams would ration both to be more risk averse. This "go with what you know" rationale created a recency bias working against some prospects who had little-to-no game action. Abel, the presumptive best prep pitcher in the class and one of only two first-round selections from that group, was one such instance of that dynamic at play. Scouts weren't able to see him in the spring with Oregon's late start to games, so they instead turned to his social media and devoured workout videos of bullpen sessions where he was touching 99. In a normal year, he likely would have pitched his way into a higher pick than 15th overall. Reports out of Clearwater suggest he has already added strength to his highly projectable frame. He might be a monster in the making.

55. Josiah Gray, RHP, Los Angeles Dodgers

Gray went from a Division II college shortstop to a mid-rotation pitching prospect in the space of about three years. He's on the shorter side at only 6-foot-1, but his delivery is fluid and repeatable with only moderate effort. There's the issue of limited reps on the mound, but that cuts both ways, as there's limited wear and tear as well. The idea with position-player converts is often "they have big arm strength, try to teach them a slider and then let them rip." Gray was a full-time starter by his junior year at LeMoyne College, and he tossed 130 effective innings across three levels in 2019. He does have the big arm strength, sitting mid-90s, but he has also shown a feel for both a slider and change as a pro. Sure, everything might play up in short bursts, but perhaps Gray is just a mid-rotation starter, full stop.

56. Josh Jung, 3B, Texas Rangers

Calling Jung's scouting report dry is a little unfair, but it's not the most interesting nor the loudest collection of tools. He was a productive three-year starter at Texas Tech, torching the Big 12 his sophomore and junior years. But his tools don't pop as loud as his slash line. He's a solid third baseman, but one limited by fringy range and instincts. He's an above-average hitter, but he's unlikely to challenge for batting titles. He has plus raw strength, but a swing plane on the flatter side, which might make his power play merely to average. Jung also has a quality approach that makes the offensive side of his game play up. Reports from the alternate site rumor a swing change that has him unlocking more of his raw pop. If that's true, then it works contrary to what a different Jung proposed: there is linear evolution, not merely a circumambulation of the self.

57. Nick Lodolo, LHP, Cincinnati Reds

Nothing is flashy when it comes to Lodolo. You'd think that a big 6-foot-6 lefty with good downward plane on his fastball would be cruising in the mid-to-upper 90s with minimal effort. Instead, it's mostly 92-94 with some sink. His breaking ball and changeup don't serve as your typical "fool me" pitches, either, and he uses them to throw strikes and get ahead in the count. It sounds all too overly simplistic, but he's been able to strike out as many batters as he has and limit walks simply by pounding the zone using excellent command. Maybe there is more to coax out of the arm in the form of added spin, but it's hard to tamper with a good thing when you know you have a mid-rotation starter in hand.

58. Jazz Chisholm, SS, Miami Marlins

As recent, highly-anticipated Jazz debuts go, Chisholm's late season call-up for the Marlins failed to reach the critical heights of Kamasi Washington's *The Epic*, but the Christgaus on the BP Prospect Team still foresee a *Heaven-and-Earth*-quality follow-up in his near future. Jumping from Double-A—where he struck out 32 percent of the time in 2019—to the majors would be a heavy ask in normal circumstances; the Marlins did Chisholm no favors, as he received inconsistent playing time behind Jon Berti and Miguel Rojas. Despite tempering his aggressive approach some, he struggled badly against high-quality offspeed stuff. Chisholm still flashed his plus power and plus glove enough in 2020 to keep us on the hook. Elvis Costello once said "you have 20 years to write your first album and you have six months to write your second one." We'll see if that's enough time for Chisholm to find the right chord.

59. Jasson Dominguez, OF, New York Yankees

In the nature of full disclosure, we don't know much more about where Dominguez should be on this list than we did a year ago. He was briefly stateside for spring training, but the Yankees didn't invite him to the alternate site, and they were one of two teams who didn't hold domestic fall instructs. Dominguez spent his summer training in his native Dominican Republic. By reputation, he is one of the most hyped and talented prospects around, a potential five-tool center fielder, but he's never faced a real professional pitch and we do like seeing these things for ourselves (or, at least, talking to unbiased sources who have). Hopefully, the reality of Dominguez meets the hype, because he'll be a hell of a prospect if everything we've heard is true.

60. Dane Dunning, RHP, Texas Rangers

Dunning made his major-league debut opposite Casey Mize's, and frankly outshined the former no. 1 pick. He continued to play the part of a present mid-rotation arm throughout the season, looking like exactly the pitcher he looked to be *before* spring 2019 Tommy John surgery. Dunning is perfectly typecast for the role: he's a four-pitch starter with a low-90s fastball and solid command, yet he's missing an out-pitch. The White Sox flipped him to the Rangers for Lance Lynn this offseason, trading the likelihood of solid pitching for a year of potential greatness as they loaded up for a pennant run.

61. Luis Campusano, C, San Diego Padres

Campusano made an unexpected major-league debut in 2020, and homered in his first game. He was then scratched from his planned start a day later and missed the rest of the season with a sprained wrist. When right, he's an offense-first catching prospect with the potential to hit for both average and power. Defensively, he's got a big arm, but he remains a work-in-progress as a receiver.

In October, he was charged with felony marijuana possession after a traffic stop in Georgia. It is patently absurd that possession of slightly less than three ounces of weed constitutes a felony, to say nothing of broader systemic racial bias in the criminal justice system. At the time of publication, Campusano was still facing these ridiculous charges.

62. Kyle Muller, LHP, Atlanta Braves

The 2020 Braves had Josh Tomlin, Robbie Erlin and Tommy Milone toe the rubber, while Muller—a former second-round pick with a full-season of Double-A under his belt—hung out at the alternate site. The fact that he never made a start for a team struggling to find enough starting pitching while making a playoff push is a piece of actionable data, especially in a season where we'd have been happy to find a prospect's TikTok montage from instructs. Reports from Gwinnett suggested that while Muller's command and control were improving over his 2019—where he walked almost 15 percent of the batters he faced—it was still a bit of an issue. That's also actionable data. But so is the fact that Muller is regularly touching 100 now. Six-foot-seven lefties who throw that hard are rare commodities, and he isn't a mere arm-strength prospect either, as both his change and breaking ball should end up as above-average offerings.

63. Brailyn Marquez, LHP, Chicago Cubs

The Cubs called Marquez up at the very end of the season for a look-see, since it cost them next-to-nothing in service time and he had to be added to the 40-man roster this offseason anyway. He was absolutely dreadful, allowing five runs in less than an inning, and he had major trouble throwing strikes. But we did see the promising parts too: the easy upper-90s heat, the big-breaking slider. Marquez focused on nursing his changeup at the alternate site, and he reportedly made major strides there. That changeup development is going to be the key in whether he sticks as a starting pitcher over the longer term. There's big potential in his power arm regardless of role, provided he can throw enough strikes.

64. Robert Hassell III, OF, San Diego Padres

One of the best pure hitters in the class, Hassell made a late jump into the top 10 thanks to a sweet swing the Padres couldn't bear to pass on. (There was even a thought that he could be a two-way player with a fastball up to 93 off the mound.) His hit tool projection and present ability to play in center field are the focus, though he may end up in a corner spot where his plus arm can be featured. The swing itself is balanced and level, showing good barrel control that sacrifices outright power for line-drive hard contact. Not to worry, there's still plenty of juice in the bat and has been known to show off rare oppo power. With other young position players in their system, it will be interesting to see how aggressively he is pushed in his first year in the minors.

65. Spencer Howard, RHP, Philadelphia Phillies

Howard is the best example of a class of players that flummoxed this season: he wasn't just bad in the majors, but was bad in ways that didn't seem promising for the future. Ranked 36 last year under the expectation that he was a major-league-ready pitcher with substantial upside, he came up and it was just all a little less than anticipated—a tick or two less on the radar gun; a less-than-plus slider and changeup; homers by the bushel. Pitchers were especially compromised by having to ramp up twice this year, so it's quite possible some of this is not representative of the future. We're kind of middling it, dropping Howard a bit since the high-end stuff isn't there, but also recognizing there's a real chance his 2019 stuff shows back up with a more normal schedule.

66. Heston Kjerstad, OF, Baltimore Orioles

The first "wow" moment of the draft saw the Orioles selecting Kjerstad second overall. It's not as if he was a complete unknown, entering the night with a distinct possibility of going in the first dozen picks. It was a calculated tactic, as they chose to add an offensive-minded player with SEC pedigree in order to spread their bonus pool around to others. A perennial terror during his two years and change with Arkansas, he somehow found another gear during their abbreviated season. His innate barrel control allowed him to find the ball anywhere in the zone—oftentimes not in the zone at all—and suggests a potential above-average hit tool. There is plus power as well, and even when he's fooled on outside offerings he can keep the hands back with strong wrists to elevate to the opposite field. His defense and overall athleticism don't rise to the level his hitting prowess does, and that's fine, since the stick is largely where his value will be coming from.

67. Vidal Brujan, 2B, Tampa Bay Rays

Brujan is a much better fantasy prospect than real life one. Steals are far, far more valuable to your dynasty team than to a major-league team. Conversely your fantasy team doesn't care as much about position or defense. Brujan is a good real-life prospect, too. Those steals are borne of his plus-plus speed, and he has good feel for contact and a solid approach that should allow for something like a .280 average and a .350 OBP. As for slugging, Brujan is not going to hit for much power—he may scrape 10 or so homers at the Trop, limiting the upside of the offensive game. He's an above-average defender at second base, and played a little center field in winter ball, adding to his positional versatility. The total package is more above-average regular than star, but Brujan could reach that designation as soon as the 2021 season.

68. George Kirby, RHP, Seattle Mariners

The last of the Mariners pitchers on this list, Kirby might be the most unique of the trio. He also presents one of the most uncommon skill sets you'll find on the 101. Top-of-the-scale grades aren't thrown around often, and for good reason, as they measure something truly special. His individual pitch grades and velocity are average-to-better, but what is incredible is the level of command he bestows on each pitch. He has a strikeout-to-walk ratio exceeding 6.00 dating back to his college career, including stints in the Cape Cod League and his first 23 professional innings. Kirby arrived at spring training with added muscle that propelled his fastball velocity into the mid-90s and higher, and reports indicate the stuff may have gone up without requiring that he sacrifice his precious command. Watch out for Kirby in 2021; he's someone who could take a big leap forward.

69. Forrest Whitley, RHP, Houston Astros

2017: Establishes himself as one of the best pitching prospects in baseball, throwing 92 1/3 innings between Low-A, High-A and Double-A.

2018: Suspended for the first 50 games for a banned stimulant. Makes six great starts in Double-A, misses a month-and-a-half with an oblique strain, ramps back up to the Arizona Fall League and looks like the best pitching prospect in baseball again in front of half the scouts and prospect writers in the known universe.

2019: Posts an airplane ERA in the high-minors sandwiched around missed time for vague shoulder fatigue, repeatedly showing up without his best stuff. Once again looks great in the AFL.

2020: Feels arm discomfort ramping up at summer camp, never really gets going and doesn't officially pitch anywhere. (There's no AFL for him to star in, of course.)

Whitley needs to make 20 healthy starts at some level this year, badly.

70. Daniel Lynch, LHP, Kansas City Royals

The fastball now sits mid-nineties or more
Slider has always had plus two-plane bite
His pro career has been all you'd ask for
Changeup improved at the alternate site
His name should be in the prospect limelight
Command and injuries still leave some doubts
But lefties with stuff will always get chances
So Lynch will soon extract major-league outs
Worse comes to worst, your pen he enhances
But third-starter role, that's what our stance is

71. Alex Kirilloff, OF, Minnesota Twins

Kirilloff is now immortalized as the answer to a bit of trivia: Who was the first position player to make their major-league debut in the playoffs? His first big-league hit, after a 1-for-4 day at the plate, won't be recognized as his first official hit, since postseason stats are recorded separately from the regular season. We expect many more hits from the free-swinging lefty, who has been a tough one to evaluate during his minor-league career. Tommy John surgery caused him to lose what would have been his first full professional season, and nagging injuries affected his 2019 progression in Double-A. Kirilloff has plus hit potential, although he's altered his lower half to open up his hips on virtually every swing, pulling off to sell out for more power. This has caused an uptick in strikeouts since he's more vulnerable to pitches away. The physical traits are still there to be a well-above-average offensive player.

72. Taylor Trammell, OF, Seattle Mariners

How many top prospects have been dealt twice before reaching the majors?* We often say to watch what organizations do with a player, not what they say about them. That's going to be even more true until things return to normal. The Padres dealt Trammell to the Mariners at the deadline for a 30-year-old catcher with fewer than a season's worth of games under his belt (albeit one that showed signs of being a first-division starter). In an era where front offices hold their prospects close, two teams have seen Trammell as excess. (Conversely, you could argue two teams have made it a priority to acquire him.) He remains a divisive prospect for us as well, and it doesn't help that he didn't get to change our opinions last season. Some of us see Trammell as a bench outfielder with a swing that won't work consistently and an arm best suited for left field. Others see a potential five-tool center fielder. We don't feel too bad, since it seems major-league teams aren't even that confident either.

If you want to take the game of half-full/half-empty to its logical conclusion, the four prospects that jumped to mind immediately were Gio Gonzalez, Anthony Rizzo, Jake Odorizzi and Lewis Brinson.

73. Triston McKenzie, RHP, Cleveland

McKenzie dominated the minors off a low-90s fastball that played up due to the deception and extension in his delivery, and a plus curveball he could manipulate in and out of the zone. He then missed a chunk of 2018 with a forearm strain and all of 2019 with a back injury. We began to wonder if his projectable, but downright thin frame, was sturdy enough to handle the rigors of a starting pitcher's workload. He was healthy by 2020 spring training, but it was a surprise to see him make his first pro start in two years for Cleveland's big-league team. It was a shock to see him come out pumping 95 and showing a new slider with above-average projection. He had a dominant debut, making us wonder if the last two years weren't some sort of Mandela Effect we had all collectively imagined. His velocity backslid in subsequent starts, a reasonable result given he hadn't pitched in game conditions in two years. Still, it's fair to have the same concerns about his fastball and overall durability. Even back working in the low-90s, McKenzie might be a present mid-rotation starter.

74. Keibert Ruiz, C, Los Angeles Dodgers

Ruiz's evaluation has seen ups and downs thanks to inconsistent quality of contact. The underlying profile hasn't changed much—he's shown a strong feel for hitting, and there's always been above-average raw power and defensive abilities. He's been consistently young for the levels he's played at, but our live looks haven't always resulted in a strong hit tool projection. Ruiz debuted in 2020 and homered in his first at-bat, but it was only a two-game fill-in, leaving questions about his offensive consistency unanswered. He's currently stuck behind emerging star Will Smith, and the Dodgers have several notable catching prospects coming up behind him. Naturally, he has been rumored in trade talks, although that might not be necessary given Smith's positional versatility and how the org has tended to split catching playing time over the past few years.

75. Hunter Bishop, OF, San Francisco Giants

Bishop set perhaps unrealistic expectations for himself as a prospect by challenging Barry Bonds' junior-year triple crown stats at Arizona State. He further followed in Bonds' footsteps by donning the orange and black after getting popped 10th overall in 2019. There's little to be learned since, as Bishop generated pedestrian numbers with an elevated strikeout rate in 85 short-season at-bats following the draft and lost an entire minor-league season to COVID-19. The pressure, a bit unfairly, will be on Bishop to come out of the gates hitting the next chance he gets, given that he'll be 23 heading into next season. As it stands the 6-foot-5 outfielder remains a power/speed dual-threat outfielder with some risk in the hit tool due to his 6-foot-5 frame and lengthy swing.

76. Jordyn Adams, OF, Los Angeles Angels

Adams is a sure shot center fielder who could develop into one of the best outfield defenders in the game because of his plus speed and advanced route running (the reasons he was also a highly-regarded wide receiver recruit out of high school). His bat lags behind, especially in the power department, but both offensive tools project to be above-average at peak. His .704 OPS in Burlington in 2019 actually grades out as 22 percent better than average accounting for how tough that park and league is on offense. So, in a reversal of expectations, this prep outfielder might be the safer bet when compared to the collegiate prospect ranked directly ahead of him.

77. Miguel Vargas, 3B, Los Angeles Dodgers

Vargas tends to fly under the radar. He wasn't a big bonus recipient out of Cuba, signing for just $300,000 after defecting as a 16-year-old. He's a third baseman without notable physical tools, and there's some risk he grows off the position. But he's hit .300 each of his professional seasons while dealing with aggressive assignments for his age. His swing and approach both support a plus-or-better hit tool. If his current doubles power turns into home run power as Vargas moves through his early 20s, he will be an offensive force. And while the body might be high maintenance, he's presently a fine defender at third, with more than enough arm for the left side.

78. Brennen Davis, OF, Chicago Cubs

Limited to just 50 games in 2019 because of a broken finger, the stage seemed set for a 2020 breakout for the former second-round pick. Davis got stuck in a round of Q2Q rehearsals at the alternate site instead. There he showed off a stronger frame and harder contact against more advanced arms. We will have to wait for the curtain to rise in 2021 before we know for sure if an all-star is born. We won't tell him to "break a leg"— that idiom should probably stay in the theater world, since durability may be the only hurdle between Davis and the top half of this list.

79. Matthew Allan, RHP, New York Mets

Allan has a fine starting kit for a pitching prospect—mid-90s fastball with good shape, excellent feel for a curveball, developing changeup, you know the drill. Allan possesses the type of velocity and spin rate that tends to show up nicely on a TrackMan readout, which is how teams were doing the majority of their professional scouting in 2020. Correspondingly, reports from his alternate site work were quite strong. We still need to see this in full-season ball, but Allan might shoot up this list pretty quickly with increased exposure.

80. Shane McClanahan, LHP, Tampa Bay Rays

McClanahan became the first pitcher to make his major-league debut in the postseason, as the Rays managed to get the benefit of his electric arm on their postseason roster without granting him any service time. The upper-90s fastball and mid-80s breaking ball both flashed huge in four outings. He was also wild, inconsistent with his mechanics (which haven't always been great) and barely threw his changeup. While the top two pitches are electric, nothing that we saw in the majors or heard about his work earlier in the summer increased our confidence that McClanahan has a great shot to remain in the rotation. With every year that passes without the necessary improvements to his command and changeup, the relief risk inches up.

81. Shea Langeliers, C, Atlanta Braves

Langeliers is in some ways a throwback catching prospect. He has a good arm and gets high marks for handling his pitching staff, and he's a switch-hitter with big raw power, although it's unclear how much of that will find its way into games against better velocity. You saw a lot of these types in the 90s: Todd Hundley, Darren Daulton, Mike Lieberthal, etc. Catcher evaluation has changed markedly since then with a focus on framing, but Langeliers also grades out well there. There's little doubt the glove will make him a major-leaguer, but the track record of non-elite catching prospects without a high offensive floor has just as many Dan Wilsons in the mix as well. Catchers are weird, so by extension catching prospects are weird.

82. Jeremy Peña, SS, Houston Astros

I had no choice but to bump you
You stated your case, time and again
I thought about it

You showed up late to Corpus Christi
I'm not used to scouting LIDOM tape
You flashed improved bat speed

You've already won me over, in spite of me
And don't be alarmed if I fall glove over cleats
I won't be surprised if you're big league, with all that you are
I couldn't help it, you could go far

83. Trevor Larnach, OF, Minnesota Twins

Larnach's bat has some of the easiest game power you'll find. Utilizing an up-the-middle approach, the power mostly manifests to the pull-side with a growing ability to distribute to all fields. This has been the case since his draft year at Oregon State. Hit the ball, hit the ball hard, get on base and try not to do anything too bad on defense. He's a big, lumbering guy that should be hidden in left field so the bat can be in the lineup on an everyday basis. There isn't much left to prove on the minor-league side of things.

84. Francisco Alvarez, C, New York Mets

Alvarez was sent stateside as soon as he was eligible and it took only a week in the Gulf Coast League to show that he was too good for complex ball. He then more than held his own in the Appalachian League as a 17-year-old. Alvarez spent a few weeks at the Mets alternate site in 2020, and then a few more in the St. Lucie and Dominican complexes, but the only trace of him you'll easily find this year was from a team-affiliated prospect account posting video of him at instructs. We can discern the Mets have tweaked his stance and setup, as he has a much wider base with minimal lower half engagement compared to 2019. What does this mean for his advanced contact ability and above-average power projection? How have his raw defensive skills progressed? Tune in next year to find out!

85. Triston Casas, 1B, Boston Red Sox

As the Red Sox begin the arduous task of rebuilding a depleted farm system following the closing of their championship window, Casas is the type of player that opens the next championship window when he's ready. Boasting one of the best raw power tools in the prep ranks over the last several years, he's been working to try and cut down on the amount of swing-and-miss to his game. Hitting instructors in the org noted their desire to get him to avoid being so pull-happy, believing the use of all fields will make him a more well-rounded hitter and assist with the strikeout numbers. He has seen time at third base thanks to an above-average arm, yet it seems like a forgone conclusion that the body will move him to exclusively first base, which is perfectly fine for a left-handed swinging slugger.

86. Reid Detmers, LHP, Los Angeles Angels

It has been no secret that the Angels have prioritized multi-sport athletes in recent drafts, hoping to plug holes in the pitching staff with rentals and cast-offs at discounted prices. Detmers' selection bucked that trend. A star lefty at Louisville who carries very little risk of becoming a reliever, his polished starter attributes include a fastball that lacks upper tier velocity but that can be commanded around the plate and a snapdragon curveball that was nearly untouchable in college. With fluid mechanics and feel to pitch, the one piece of polish that is noticeably missing is a clear third pitch. A changeup might be the obvious answer, although a short slider/cutter could also provide utility.

87. Gabriel Arias, SS, Cleveland

Arias was the prospect centerpiece sent to Cleveland in the Padres deadline deal for Mike Clevinger. There likely wasn't room for him on the left side of the San Diego infield for the next decade or so, and Cleveland might have a Francisco-Lindor-shaped hole at shortstop by the time this book is in your hands. It's not fair to ask any prospect to replace Lindor, but Arias is capable of making the kind of plays at shortstop that might make fans reminisce. He's a potential plus-plus defender whose bat broke out in High-A in 2019. Many prospects have shined in the launching pads of the California League and then taken a step back in more normal environs against advanced pitching—we raise a glass to you, Lars Anderson. Until it's clear the bat will play under typical conditions, we're going to say he's more steady than stratospheric.

88. Ed Howard, SS, Chicago Cubs

Widely considered the best prep shortstop in the draft, the South Side kid landed crosstown in what could amount to a steal. His game is built around elite hands that offer loose actions from the shortstop position and excellent bat-to-ball skills. Missing from the profile is a sense of where the power will eventually go, with the prevailing thought being that his projectable frame will add the needed muscle to get to at least average grades. He's a long ways away, but the Cubbies can afford to be patient.

89. Miguel Amaya, C, Chicago Cubs

Amaya remains a solid two-way catching prospect, where you can dream on above-average hit and power tools and a still-developing, but potentially solid defensive profile as well. His arm is ahead of his receiving, but both project to at least average. Amaya still needs to conquer the upper minors without the bat stagnating—a common malady for catchers first identified by John Sickels—but his overall balanced skill set should keep him on these lists until he arrives.

90. Geraldo Perdomo, SS, Arizona Diamondbacks

While we are in a bit of a golden era for major league shortstops, there still aren't that many players that do enough things well enough to stick at the 6. Perdomo will do more than stick, he has a chance to be a good defensive shortstop. Combine that with an advanced approach and a chance for double-digit home run power as he fills out in his 20s, and you will get a (relatively) safe future major leaguer.

91. Michael Busch, 2B, Los Angeles Dodgers

It's always wise to bet on the player you think is going to hit. Busch hit for average and power and walked more than he struck out his sophomore year at UNC, that summer on the Cape, and then again his junior year. Okay, he didn't hit in 10 games post-draft, but every report we got on him from the alternate site and instructs suggests he has above-average hit and power tools and a good approach. If that's the case, teams will find a place for you to stand in the field. Busch was primarily a first baseman and corner outfielder as an amateur, but so far he's primarily played second base. He's fringy but playable there. Also, being as it is the Dodgers, Busch will probably see time all over the diamond, because they'll want to get that bat in the lineup as much as possible.

92. Jordan Walker, 3B, St. Louis Cardinals

This placement might exaggerate the gap between Walker and Nolan Gorman at this point in time; there is just more of a track record on Gorman. After being drafted 21st overall in 2020, Walker immediately started matching his organization mate's prodigious power potential at the alternate site. A divisive draft prospect, who some thought might end up in the outfield due to his 6-foot-5 frame, Walker has quelled a lot of doubts with his post-draft performance. His upside matches Gorman's, and his OFP might soon as well. Just have that pesky need to see him in some games first to feel more confident that he's a .270, 30-home-run third baseman. Of course, if the bat gets there, it doesn't really matter whether he's a third baseman either.

93. Xavier Edwards, SS/2B, Tampa Bay Rays

Edwards' potential carrying weapon is his hit tool; he has strong bat-to-ball skills, an advanced plate approach and decent bat speed. Most of our live reports on Edwards point to a plus hit outcome, and he's going to leg out a few extra singles a year with his elite speed. He's going to need to hit for a high average, because his game power is currently negligible and it doesn't project out. He might have even less raw power than Nick Madrigal. He's not likely to stay at shortstop full-time, either, and long-term he might find his best fit as a slash-and-burn multi-positional type. He's certainly made his way to the right organization for that.

94. Trevor Rogers, LHP, Miami Marlins

Rogers showed better stuff in the majors than he'd ever shown as a prospect, continuing a gradual glow-up dating back to the 2017 draft. His fastball sat around 94 mph, up a few ticks from past readings, and it's a high-spin offering that induced good swing-and-miss. His diving changeup has developed into exactly the kind of out pitch that so many of the prospects you've read about here need to reach, and his slider is a solid pitch as well. The topline results in terms of runs allowed weren't there (owing to one disastrous outing), but the underlying rate metrics were quite promising. Rogers' development is why teams will constantly bet on projectable prep lefties high in the draft—he was the No. 13 overall pick because his frame portended velocity and secondary pitches would come—even though the house tends to win that particular game of chance.

95. Jackson Kowar, RHP, Kansas City Royals

Kowar is the third and final Royals pitcher on this year's 101. Last year's edition included Brady Singer and Kris Bubic, both of whom got just enough service time to graduate. That makes a full starting rotation of young, quality pitching prospects. It rarely works out so neatly in the end, but if you collect enough quality arms, one or two might break out past their mid-rotation projection. Kowar isn't a bad bet in that regard. He's continued to gain velocity as a pro, and now sits mid-90s and was touching 99 at the alternate site. His breaking ball has improved to the point that it's an average offering and his change remains a bat-misser he can throw with confidence to both lefties and righties. It would be nice to see him truly dominate a level in the minors given the stuff, and his command will need to improve another grade or so for that to happen, but everything is trending positively.

96. Clarke Schmidt, RHP, New York Yankees

Schmidt tore through the Grapefruit League with two distinct mid-90s fastballs and a hellacious breaking ball that has the best properties of a curve and slider. Though he pitched poorly in the majors, we now have some additional context on that breaking ball: The average spin rate was 3,085 rpm, which makes it one of the highest-spin breaking balls in the majors. It's likely to be an elite swing-and-miss pitch in any role, though he's going to need substantial development on his changeup and command to stay in the rotation.

97. Erick Peña, OF, Kansas City Royals

Peña's stock has been steadily rising as a pro—and he signed for the fourth-highest signing bonus in the 2019 international class, so he wasn't exactly a low-profile prospect to begin with. We started hearing impressive buzz from pro scouts when he came stateside for 2019 fall instructs (where he roomed with Bobby Witt Jr.), and that steam kept building last offseason. Instead of making his pro debut in the summer, the Royals sent him to both sets of fall camps they ran. While he struggled adjusting to the advanced pitching prospects who were at the alternate site, he later shined against more age-appropriate competition in Arizona. Like Jasson Dominguez, we're going to need to see Peña hit in real games to truly buy in, but we can already tell there's a sweet swing with hit and power potential present.

98. Sam Huff, C, Texas Rangers

If Shea Langeliers is one type of throwback catching prospect, Sam Huff is a different kind of throwback: a huge dude with light-tower power and a big arm. Huff had only 20 batted balls in the majors, but he absolutely murdered the ball when he made contact, with a superlative 95.7 mph average exit velocity. He arrived ahead of schedule, with no experience above High-A, and looked fine. There are approach contact issues here to be sure—he struck out 154

times in A-ball in 2019, and in the small sample in the majors he was still swinging at, and through, too many pitches. There's some risk he's going to have to move off catcher to a corner eventually. But there is also big upside if everything clicks and he stays behind the dish.

99. Tarik Skubal, LHP, Detroit Tigers

Skubal made eight appearances (seven starts) for the Tigers in 2020, and even that allows for a wealth of data on his arsenal and its relative effectiveness. The problem here is his pitch mix *wasn't* effective. Skubal's mid-90s fastball produced a .547 slugging against, and he threw his changeup—his clear third pitch—more often than his potential plus-plus slider. The heater is high-spin and comes from a deceptive angle, but can run a bit true, and Skubal wasn't fine enough with his command the first go-round against major-league hitters. So, when he wasn't missing bats, he got hit hard. The Tigers have every reason to keep giving him a chance to start, but given the health track record and early returns, he might be best suited as a late-inning multi-inning force where the fastball velocity might play up and he can throw the wipeout slider more.

100. Daniel Espino, RHP, Cleveland

High-school hurlers who touch 100, have advanced secondaries and an athletic body rarely make it to the tail-end of the first round, where Espino was selected. Of concern was an elongated arm action that whips through the delivery giving a less-than-pleasing visual. It is unorthodox, sure, but so is an 18-year-old who throws that hard. After entering the system, he has received high praise for his ability to retain information, being receptive to coaching on his mechanics and working hard in the weight room to fill out his thin frame. We received strong reports on his development this summer and fall, and with so many explosive qualities, file Espino under the category of players who we're dying to see take a big step in 2021.

101. Alejandro Kirk, C, Toronto Blue Jays

The short-and-stout backstop was one of the more surprising call-ups of the 2020 season. We were in on Kirk's hit tool and improving defense some coming into the season, but 21-year-old catchers who haven't played above A-ball aren't traditional call-ups. (Then again, 2020 wasn't a traditional season.) Kirk didn't look out of place in the majors, scorching the ball when he got into games and looking perfectly fine behind the dish. We still aren't sold on his ability to lift the ball for game power, but he sure seems like he's going to hit a bunch and be able to catch. That the Blue Jays thought he was one of their best options during a pennant chase—even DHing him in a playoff game against Blake Snell—is a vote of confidence, too.

MLB Managers

Joe Girardi   wRM+: 111

TEAM	YEAR	W	L	Pythag +/-	Avg PC	100+ P	120+ P	QS	BQS	REL	REL w Zero R	IBB	PH	PH Avg	PH HR	SB2	CS2	SB3	CS3	SAC Att	SAC %	POS SAC	Squeeze	Swing	In Play
NYY	2014	84	78	7	93.26	54	0	83	6	475	399	23	95	.244	2	97	23	13	3	45	81	27	0	311	85
NYY	2015	87	75	-1	92.45	42	0	72	9	497	400	16	111	.250	3	60	23	3	2	33	72	24	1	231	75
NYY	2016	84	78	6	91.48	40	0	31	5	483	383	15	75	.191	3	64	21	5	1	38	77	19	0	215	65
NYY	2017	91	71	-11	90.70	38	0	52	2	477	392	18	104	.161	4	85	21	5	1	28	80	16	0	285	74
PHI	2020	28	32	-1	91.00	12	0	20	4	189	91	12	40	.300	0	32	8	3	0	16	50	16	1	62	12

Ron Gardenhire   wRM+: 110

TEAM	YEAR	W	L	Pythag +/-	Avg PC	100+ P	120+ P	QS	BQS	REL	REL w Zero R	IBB	PH	PH Avg	PH HR	SB2	CS2	SB3	CS3	SAC Att	SAC %	POS SAC	Squeeze	Swing	In Play
MIN	2013	66	96	5	91.09	44	0	62	6	511	415	31	97	.163	1	50	31	1	2	40	61	26	0	292	93
MIN	2014	70	92	-4	91.56	36	0	66	8	491	378	24	90	.210	0	84	33	15	2	34	73	25	0	307	98
DET	2018	64	98	2	86.29	20	0	29	2	542	415	20	66	.155	1	66	28	4	1	29	70	13	0	249	70
DET	2019	47	114	1	84.01	20	0	18	2	577	380	24	52	.286	2	54	20	3	0	20	74	9	0	248	64
DET	2020	23	35	-4	94.00	1	0	9	3	218	112	2	29	.241	0	16	6	3	0	1	100	1	0	63	7

Craig Counsell   wRM+: 106

TEAM	YEAR	W	L	Pythag +/-	Avg PC	100+ P	120+ P	QS	BQS	REL	REL w Zero R	IBB	PH	PH Avg	PH HR	SB2	CS2	SB3	CS3	SAC Att	SAC %	POS SAC	Squeeze	Swing	In Play
MIL	2016	73	89	-1	90.31	30	0	31	1	513	393	33	282	.178	7	144	46	35	10	87	76	21	2	371	76
MIL	2017	86	76	1	88.10	30	0	39	0	550	435	45	284	.219	8	98	32	30	7	68	76	12	3	336	94
MIL	2018	96	67	4	85.67	18	0	18	1	559	440	34	282	.246	10	96	25	28	7	48	79	6	0	331	74
MIL	2019	89	73	8	84.22	16	0	17	0	588	429	28	314	.190	8	79	18	22	5	32	80	5	1	297	76
MIL	2020	29	31	1	102.00	7	0	15	2	189	83	1	59	.271	1	14	10	1	1	1	0	1	0	110	16

Terry Francona   wRM+: 106

TEAM	YEAR	W	L	Pythag +/-	Avg PC	100+ P	120+ P	QS	BQS	REL	REL w Zero R	IBB	PH	PH Avg	PH HR	SB2	CS2	SB3	CS3	SAC Att	SAC %	POS SAC	Squeeze	Swing	In Play
CLE	2016	94	67	2	92.04	60	0	63	4	504	428	34	106	.143	1	104	25	29	6	48	81	27	0	294	71
CLE	2017	102	60	-8	93.73	72	1	60	4	497	430	15	86	.145	2	79	21	9	2	39	79	22	0	266	78
CLE	2018	91	71	-9	96.85	78	2	79	2	508	401	29	87	.234	2	118	32	15	3	45	79	23	0	344	78
CLE	2019	93	69	-1	93.48	75	3	54	3	522	409	19	91	.222	2	92	28	10	5	62	75	38	0	286	69
CLE	2020	35	25	1	101.00	22	0	37	12	181	96	8	32	.188	0	23	7	2	2	17	41	17	1	53	6

Bud Black   wRM+: 104

TEAM	YEAR	W	L	Pythag +/-	Avg PC	100+ P	120+ P	QS	BQS	REL	REL w Zero R	IBB	PH	PH Avg	PH HR	SB2	CS2	SB3	CS3	SAC Att	SAC %	POS SAC	Squeeze	Swing	In Play
SD	2015	32	35	0	97.69	33	0	43	0	206	160	16	119	.170	1	44	10	2	1	29	81	11	0	106	36
COL	2017	87	75	-1	89.98	28	1	34	1	549	424	20	261	.208	6	51	32	8	2	87	63	20	2	297	94
COL	2018	91	72	6	92.44	42	0	55	0	518	398	24	272	.242	8	91	33	4	0	76	74	11	1	267	71
COL	2019	71	91	1	87.79	24	0	26	2	590	422	33	296	.189	13	63	31	8	0	73	70	10	3	268	72
COL	2020	26	34	-2	88.00	9	0	28	10	189	98	5	43	.186	1	37	8	5	0	12	58	12	0	97	8

Brandon Hyde   wRM+: 104

TEAM	YEAR	W	L	Pythag +/-	Avg PC	100+ P	120+ P	QS	BQS	REL	REL w Zero R	IBB	PH	PH Avg	PH HR	SB2	CS2	SB3	CS3	SAC Att	SAC %	POS SAC	Squeeze	Swing	In Play
BAL	2019	54	108	-4	84.98	17	0	20	0	533	341	11	120	.194	2	73	24	10	5	43	74	19	2	248	67
BAL	2020	25	35	-5	83.00	0	0	10	4	207	76	2	38	.184	2	17	11	2	1	18	83	18	0	74	7

Scott Servais   wRM+: 103

TEAM	YEAR	W	L	Pythag +/-	Avg PC	100+ P	120+ P	QS	BQS	REL	REL w Zero R	IBB	PH	PH Avg	PH HR	SB2	CS2	SB3	CS3	SAC Att	SAC %	POS SAC	Squeeze	Swing	In Play
SEA	2016	86	76	-2	92.09	43	0	48	6	477	379	30	146	.254	4	48	26	8	1	43	67	21	0	268	83
SEA	2017	78	84	-1	88.22	32	0	31	0	526	405	28	87	.189	0	83	31	6	4	27	72	11	0	236	65
SEA	2018	89	73	12	86.41	31	0	40	1	537	417	21	97	.232	2	69	34	10	2	47	68	27	1	225	65
SEA	2019	68	94	0	75.77	20	0	32	1	537	354	25	69	.183	1	104	42	10	3	18	71	11	0	341	82
SEA	2020	27	33	0	92.00	7	0	25	4	189	89	7	19	.211	0	48	15	2	1	5	60	5	0	49	4

David Bell   wRM+: 102

TEAM	YEAR	W	L	Pythag +/-	Avg PC	100+ P	120+ P	QS	BQS	REL	REL w Zero R	IBB	PH	PH Avg	PH HR	SB2	CS2	SB3	CS3	SAC Att	SAC %	POS SAC	Squeeze	Swing	In Play
CIN	2019	75	87	-5	91.61	47	0	29	2	535	407	31	311	.173	8	73	33	7	4	45	68	2	2	309	88
CIN	2020	31	29	0	99.00	20	0	26	8	168	92	6	57	.228	3	27	8	2	1	1	0	1	0	105	13

Luis Rojas   wRM+: 101

TEAM	YEAR	W	L	Pythag +/-	Avg PC	100+ P	120+ P	QS	BQS	REL	REL w Zero R	IBB	PH	PH Avg	PH HR	SB2	CS2	SB3	CS3	SAC Att	SAC %	POS SAC	Squeeze	Swing	In Play
NYM	2020	26	34	-4	90.00	12	0	17	7	197	110	7	33	.182	1	19	9	1	1	3	33	3	0	79	6

Kevin Cash   wRM+: 101

TEAM	YEAR	W	L	Pythag +/-	Avg PC	100+ P	120+ P	QS	BQS	REL	REL w Zero R	IBB	PH	PH Avg	PH HR	SB2	CS2	SB3	CS3	SAC Att	SAC %	POS SAC	Squeeze	Swing	In Play
TB	2016	68	94	-8	96.20	67	1	41	5	485	369	25	92	.128	1	48	33	12	3	31	62	18	1	306	86
TB	2017	80	82	0	93.83	74	1	43	4	511	403	37	103	.191	2	66	28	22	5	35	72	14	1	292	72
TB	2018	90	72	1	63.04	21	0	21	1	553	403	34	97	.200	1	116	44	11	4	53	72	28	5	371	107
TB	2019	96	66	2	69.79	22	0	26	0	603	434	27	117	.219	3	82	30	10	4	15	72	8	1	343	107
TB	2020	40	20	0	100.00	6	0	7	3	219	170	4	54	.259	0	42	8	6	1	1	0	1	0	92	14

Rick Renteria   wRM+: 101

TEAM	YEAR	W	L	Pythag +/-	Avg PC	100+ P	120+ P	QS	BQS	REL	REL w Zero R	IBB	PH	PH Avg	PH HR	SB2	CS2	SB3	CS3	SAC Att	SAC %	POS SAC	Squeeze	Swing	In Play
CHC	2014	73	89	3	93.64	48	1	79	0	537	446	37	272	.185	1	58	37	7	3	93	62	25	3	246	82
CHW	2017	67	95	-2	93.16	52	0	32	1	520	397	36	77	.183	1	61	25	10	3	62	70	33	3	291	76
CHW	2018	62	100	1	92.92	49	0	47	0	553	430	25	79	.159	1	79	37	19	3	38	71	23	4	274	75
CHW	2019	72	89	4	88.97	50	0	24	1	536	401	30	72	.209	4	54	23	9	4	49	69	34	7	250	68
CHW	2020	35	25	1	92.00	13	0	19	7	224	96	6	19	.263	0	19	8	1	0	3	33	3	0	34	5

Brian Snitker   wRM+: 100

TEAM	YEAR	W	L	Pythag +/-	Avg PC	100+ P	120+ P	QS	BQS	REL	REL w Zero R	IBB	PH	PH Avg	PH HR	SB2	CS2	SB3	CS3	SAC Att	SAC %	POS SAC	Squeeze	Swing	In Play
ATL	2016	59	65	4	89.91	40	0	25	1	456	371	40	212	.226	4	48	21	11	3	78	71	14	1	208	74
ATL	2017	72	90	0	93.57	45	1	45	3	530	406	39	270	.234	10	64	29	13	2	87	71	18	0	312	92
ATL	2018	90	72	-3	90.84	41	1	28	3	552	427	43	247	.202	7	75	28	13	7	76	71	13	3	277	84
ATL	2019	97	65	5	88.25	27	0	30	0	575	433	33	260	.252	9	81	24	8	3	34	76	9	2	281	77
ATL	2020	35	25	3	86.00	2	0	13	3	228	151	13	25	.200	1	21	4	2	0	3	33	3	0	52	5

Rocco Baldelli   wRM+: 100

TEAM	YEAR	W	L	Pythag +/-	Avg PC	100+ P	120+ P	QS	BQS	REL	REL w Zero R	IBB	PH	PH Avg	PH HR	SB2	CS2	SB3	CS3	SAC Att	SAC %	POS SAC	Squeeze	Swing	In Play
MIN	2019	101	61	3	89.51	33	0	28	3	524	419	10	75	.271	2	27	20	1	0	18	57	7	0	171	60
MIN	2020	36	24	3	94.00	4	0	16	3	202	75	0	28	.250	0	14	7	0	0	5	40	5	1	56	7

David Ross   wRM+: 100

TEAM	YEAR	W	L	Pythag +/-	Avg PC	100+ P	120+ P	QS	BQS	REL	REL w Zero R	IBB	PH	PH Avg	PH HR	SB2	CS2	SB3	CS3	SAC Att	SAC %	POS SAC	Squeeze	Swing	In Play
CHC	2020	34	26	2	93.00	11	0	30	6	188	116	7	44	.114	1	21	10	2	0	2	50	2	0	84	5

Joe Maddon   wRM+: 100

TEAM	YEAR	W	L	Pythag +/-	Avg PC	100+ P	120+ P	QS	BQS	REL	REL w Zero R	IBB	PH	PH Avg	PH HR	SB2	CS2	SB3	CS3	SAC Att	SAC %	POS SAC	Squeeze	Swing	In Play
CHC	2016	103	59	-7	94.52	56	1	66	2	502	407	24	234	.215	2	57	30	9	1	78	66	14	8	264	93
CHC	2017	92	70	-2	91.09	40	0	32	0	531	413	29	295	.241	5	56	25	5	6	65	67	22	5	263	75
CHC	2018	95	68	0	90.70	40	1	28	1	600	503	33	277	.242	6	53	31	11	6	71	63	14	4	280	85
CHC	2019	84	78	-7	90.38	40	0	38	0	576	444	16	240	.217	6	38	17	7	3	50	65	7	1	211	58
LAA	2020	26	34	0	90.00	12	0	15	3	228	104	8	19	.211	0	20	8	1	0	9	67	9	1	38	4

Aaron Boone wRM+: 100

TEAM	YEAR	W	L	Pythag +/-	Avg PC	100+ P	120+ P	QS	BQS	REL	REL w Zero R	IBB	PH	PH Avg	PH HR	SB2	CS2	SB3	CS3	SAC Att	SAC %	POS SAC	Squeeze	Swing	In Play
NYY	2018	100	62	0	88.09	33	0	27	3	508	408	9	63	.208	1	54	19	9	1	19	75	10	0	264	77
NYY	2019	103	59	3	79.15	20	0	25	1	545	404	12	54	.224	3	46	20	9	1	20	71	6	2	241	77
NYY	2020	33	27	1	86.00	11	0	18	4	175	80	5	30	.233	1	23	6	4	1	5	20	5	0	48	7

Don Mattingly wRM+: 99

TEAM	YEAR	W	L	Pythag +/-	Avg PC	100+ P	120+ P	QS	BQS	REL	REL w Zero R	IBB	PH	PH Avg	PH HR	SB2	CS2	SB3	CS3	SAC Att	SAC %	POS SAC	Squeeze	Swing	In Play
MIA	2016	79	82	2	90.84	46	0	32	1	559	443	62	277	.215	6	61	25	10	3	76	72	15	2	240	74
MIA	2017	77	85	0	87.46	29	0	22	0	580	435	59	270	.262	6	82	22	9	6	84	75	15	3	275	80
MIA	2018	63	98	7	88.43	32	0	27	0	546	407	73	281	.177	6	40	29	5	2	58	59	12	0	251	80
MIA	2019	57	105	-2	91.76	36	0	31	1	539	389	52	290	.214	9	49	25	6	1	53	65	8	2	236	67
MIA	2020	31	29	2	85.00	5	0	16	7	215	126	14	30	.233	0	41	10	7	4	9	67	9	1	53	7

Ron Roenicke wRM+: 99

TEAM	YEAR	W	L	Pythag +/-	Avg PC	100+ P	120+ P	QS	BQS	REL	REL w Zero R	IBB	PH	PH Avg	PH HR	SB2	CS2	SB3	CS3	SAC Att	SAC %	POS SAC	Squeeze	Swing	In Play
MIL	2012	83	79	-3	97.10	84	0	85	3	512	370	20	315	.223	4	134	32	24	5	129	80	45	8	356	90
MIL	2013	74	88	-1	91.60	45	0	82	3	501	399	29	265	.210	4	120	40	21	4	106	74	35	10	352	101
MIL	2014	82	80	2	97.64	76	1	103	5	478	395	20	246	.222	4	83	41	19	2	110	70	27	3	265	72
MIL	2015	7	18	-1	92.44	6	0	10	0	72	59	6	47	.233	0	5	4	3	2	18	57	7	0	34	6
BOS	2020	24	36	0	107.00	0	0	9	4	232	98	4	16	.125	0	24	7	7	2	5	80	5	0	35	2

Mike Shildt wRM+: 99

TEAM	YEAR	W	L	Pythag +/-	Avg PC	100+ P	120+ P	QS	BQS	REL	REL w Zero R	IBB	PH	PH Avg	PH HR	SB2	CS2	SB3	CS3	SAC Att	SAC %	POS SAC	Squeeze	Swing	In Play
STL	2018	41	29	0	88.21	14	0	12	3	251	181	26	113	.206	3	25	9	5	1	36	75	6	1	140	50
STL	2019	91	71	-2	90.16	30	1	39	1	542	422	41	266	.218	10	93	24	23	5	62	80	9	0	308	107
STL	2020	30	28	-1	92.00	4	1	18	5	177	92	8	29	.034	0	16	8	2	2	5	80	5	0	49	1

Derek Shelton wRM+: 98

TEAM	YEAR	W	L	Pythag +/-	Avg PC	100+ P	120+ P	QS	BQS	REL	REL w Zero R	IBB	PH	PH Avg	PH HR	SB2	CS2	SB3	CS3	SAC Att	SAC %	POS SAC	Squeeze	Swing	In Play
PIT	2020	19	41	-5	88.00	7	0	9	4	210	84	3	25	.160	0	14	9	2	2	9	78	9	0	49	4

Gabe Kapler wRM+: 98

TEAM	YEAR	W	L	Pythag +/-	Avg PC	100+ P	120+ P	QS	BQS	REL	REL w Zero R	IBB	PH	PH Avg	PH HR	SB2	CS2	SB3	CS3	SAC Att	SAC %	POS SAC	Squeeze	Swing	In Play
PHI	2018	80	82	5	87.72	37	0	46	4	596	467	35	295	.207	5	64	20	3	5	53	73	6	0	198	50
PHI	2019	81	81	2	89.20	42	0	37	4	564	430	38	308	.202	9	65	15	12	1	55	81	11	1	261	55
SF	2020	29	31	-1	88.00	14	0	11	5	236	131	2	60	.267	4	19	7	0	1	4	100	4	0	109	16

Dave Roberts wRM+: 98

TEAM	YEAR	W	L	Pythag +/-	Avg PC	100+ P	120+ P	QS	BQS	REL	REL w Zero R	IBB	PH	PH Avg	PH HR	SB2	CS2	SB3	CS3	SAC Att	SAC %	POS SAC	Squeeze	Swing	In Play
LAD	2016	91	71	0	87.65	29	0	32	2	606	503	50	323	.189	6	40	22	5	2	62	63	5	2	254	84
LAD	2017	104	58	1	86.63	21	0	38	1	536	428	33	341	.243	8	60	24	15	2	51	73	4	1	237	70
LAD	2018	92	71	-11	86.52	22	0	35	1	593	465	39	354	.238	9	57	20	18	1	65	76	9	3	248	63
LAD	2019	106	56	-4	85.78	24	0	50	1	545	413	24	302	.235	13	52	10	4	0	64	85	3	3	228	74
LAD	2020	43	17	4	88.00	0	0	18	6	249	222	4	36	.194	1	24	6	4	1	6	50	2	2	65	7

Jayce Tingler wRM+: 97

TEAM	YEAR	W	L	Pythag +/-	Avg PC	100+ P	120+ P	QS	BQS	REL	REL w Zero R	IBB	PH	PH Avg	PH HR	SB2	CS2	SB3	CS3	SAC Att	SAC %	POS SAC	Squeeze	Swing	In Play
SD	2020	37	23	4	89.00	3	0	22	6	218	188	2	39	.256	1	45	10	10	3	19	63	19	1	73	10

Charlie Montoyo wRM+: 97

TEAM	YEAR	W	L	Pythag +/-	Avg PC	100+ P	120+ P	QS	BQS	REL	REL w Zero R	IBB	PH	PH Avg	PH HR	SB2	CS2	SB3	CS3	SAC Att	SAC %	POS SAC	Squeeze	Swing	In Play
TOR	2019	67	95	-3	75.92	19	0	15	0	591	409	25	70	.172	2	40	16	10	3	19	72	14	1	239	76
TOR	2020	32	28	5	87.00	2	0	11	2	226	77	7	30	.133	0	23	6	10	0	11	73	11	0	48	4

Dave Martinez   wRM+: 96

TEAM	YEAR	W	L	Pythag +/-	Avg PC	100+ P	120+ P	QS	BQS	REL	REL w Zero R	IBB	PH	PH Avg	PH HR	SB2	CS2	SB3	CS3	SAC Att	SAC %	POS SAC	Squeeze	Swing	In Play
WAS	2018	82	80	-9	94.04	68	1	49	2	562	440	37	293	.176	4	98	31	20	2	78	78	13	0	299	68
WAS	2019	93	69	-3	94.83	66	0	44	3	530	384	41	252	.261	5	97	26	18	3	84	80	20	2	279	73
WAS	2020	26	34	-3	89.00	18	0	16	7	202	93	22	28	.321	0	28	10	5	1	12	42	12	0	65	9

Bob Melvin   wRM+: 96

TEAM	YEAR	W	L	Pythag +/-	Avg PC	100+ P	120+ P	QS	BQS	REL	REL w Zero R	IBB	PH	PH Avg	PH HR	SB2	CS2	SB3	CS3	SAC Att	SAC %	POS SAC	Squeeze	Swing	In Play
OAK	2016	69	93	0	87.24	40	0	40	2	492	403	28	113	.185	2	44	23	6	0	24	68	10	1	205	61
OAK	2017	75	87	3	90.57	40	0	36	2	525	388	17	120	.217	1	47	20	9	2	23	72	9	1	226	59
OAK	2018	97	65	1	80.46	15	0	37	0	578	474	19	126	.239	3	31	20	3	1	10	63	6	0	225	75
OAK	2019	97	65	-1	88.55	30	1	36	0	547	435	19	107	.228	4	43	20	6	1	11	70	6	0	247	81
OAK	2020	36	24	3	87.00	7	0	19	1	181	79	6	29	.103	1	25	2	1	1	3	67	3	0	50	3

Torey Lovullo   wRM+: 96

TEAM	YEAR	W	L	Pythag +/-	Avg PC	100+ P	120+ P	QS	BQS	REL	REL w Zero R	IBB	PH	PH Avg	PH HR	SB2	CS2	SB3	CS3	SAC Att	SAC %	POS SAC	Squeeze	Swing	In Play
ARI	2017	93	69	-5	96.17	73	1	52	2	513	424	45	251	.223	7	77	24	25	6	56	77	8	0	265	73
ARI	2018	82	80	-5	92.42	36	0	44	2	574	474	43	256	.203	5	61	22	18	3	64	76	10	0	252	82
ARI	2019	85	77	-3	88.98	32	0	36	2	557	431	38	254	.218	12	84	12	3	1	51	86	5	2	248	85
ARI	2020	25	35	-2	96.00	3	0	13	3	200	98	20	22	.000	0	22	6	1	1	4	25	4	0	46	7

Mike Matheny   wRM+: 95

TEAM	YEAR	W	L	Pythag +/-	Avg PC	100+ P	120+ P	QS	BQS	REL	REL w Zero R	IBB	PH	PH Avg	PH HR	SB2	CS2	SB3	CS3	SAC Att	SAC %	POS SAC	Squeeze	Swing	In Play
STL	2015	100	62	2	94.47	64	0	106	1	515	434	37	270	.218	4	62	33	7	5	64	64	12	1	297	100
STL	2016	86	76	-2	91.17	39	1	47	4	481	381	35	274	.333	17	33	19	2	6	67	57	13	0	207	76
STL	2017	83	79	-4	92.23	49	1	39	5	546	420	50	290	.301	5	66	27	15	4	79	72	14	2	299	95
STL	2018	47	45	-1	93.45	18	0	26	0	314	232	23	135	.181	2	32	19	1	2	37	60	8	2	131	48
KC	2020	26	34	-2	90.00	11	0	11	3	232	124	7	45	.200	3	38	17	11	3	19	42	19	0	80	9

Chris Woodward   wRM+: 94

TEAM	YEAR	W	L	Pythag +/-	Avg PC	100+ P	120+ P	QS	BQS	REL	REL w Zero R	IBB	PH	PH Avg	PH HR	SB2	CS2	SB3	CS3	SAC Att	SAC %	POS SAC	Squeeze	Swing	In Play
TEX	2019	78	84	4	86.89	60	1	38	3	499	335	11	79	.206	4	107	34	20	4	25	78	16	0	319	69
TEX	2020	22	38	-2	98.00	18	0	17	7	204	76	3	24	.208	0	40	13	8	1	8	25	8	0	44	5

Dusty Baker   wRM+: 92

TEAM	YEAR	W	L	Pythag +/-	Avg PC	100+ P	120+ P	QS	BQS	REL	REL w Zero R	IBB	PH	PH Avg	PH HR	SB2	CS2	SB3	CS3	SAC Att	SAC %	POS SAC	Squeeze	Swing	In Play
CIN	2012	97	65	6	97.39	74	1	98	6	425	365	33	201	.269	2	73	24	14	2	119	76	28	2	310	97
CIN	2013	90	72	-5	95.31	61	2	94	6	461	389	28	232	.248	5	61	32	6	2	118	66	37	2	314	111
WAS	2016	95	67	-4	97.40	79	1	68	2	508	419	43	218	.207	12	102	37	18	2	69	76	11	5	330	93
WAS	2017	97	65	0	99.72	96	4	64	2	487	372	39	244	.215	5	91	24	17	6	62	78	15	0	245	75
HOU	2020	29	31	-1	92.00	9	0	25	10	193	114	7	24	.208	0	20	10	2	1	8	75	8	0	53	5

Team Codes

CODE	TEAM	LG	AFF	NAME
ABD	Aberdeen	NYP	Orioles	IronBirds
AKR	Akron	EAS	Cleveland	RubberDucks
ABQ	Albuquerque	PCL	Rockies	Isotopes
ALT	Altoona	EAS	Pirates	Curve
AMA	Amarillo	TEX	Padres	Sod Poodles
ARI	Arizona	NL	-	D-backs
ARK	Arkansas	TEX	Mariners	Travelers
ART	Artemisa	CNS	-	-
ASH	Asheville	SAL	Rockies	Tourists
ATL	Atlanta	NL	-	Braves
AUB	Auburn	NYP	Nationals	Doubledays
AUG	Augusta	SAL	Giants	GreenJackets
ANG	AZL Angels	AZL	Angels	-
ASGO	AZL Athletics Gold	AZL	Athletics	-
ASGR	AZL Athletics Green	AZL	Athletics	-
BRB	AZL Brewers Blue	AZL	Brewers	-
BRG	AZL Brewers Gold	AZL	Brewers	-
CLT	AZL Cleveland Blue	AZL	Cleveland	-
CLE	AZL Cleveland Red	AZL	Cleveland	-
CUBB	AZL Cubs 1	AZL	Cubs	-
CUBR	AZL Cubs 2	AZL	Cubs	-
DIA	AZL D-backs	AZL	D-backs	-
DOD1	AZL Dodgers 1	AZL	Dodgers	-
DOD2	AZL Dodgers 2	AZL	Dodgers	-
GIB	AZL Giants Black	AZL	Giants	-
GIO	AZL Giants Orange	AZL	Giants	-
MAR	AZL Mariners	AZL	Mariners	-
SD1	AZL Padres 1	AZL	Padres	-
SD2	AZL Padres 2	AZL	Padres	-
RAN	AZL Rangers	AZL	Rangers	-
RED	AZL Reds	AZL	Reds	-
ROY	AZL Royals	AZL	Royals	-
WSX	AZL White Sox	AZL	White Sox	-
BAL	Baltimore	AL	-	Orioles
BAT	Batavia	NYP	Marlins	Muckdogs
BEL	Beloit	MID	Athletics	Snappers
BIL	Billings	PIO	Reds	Mustangs
BLX	Biloxi	SOU	Brewers	Shuckers
BNG	Binghamtom	EAS	Mets	Rumble Ponies
BIR	Birmingham	SOU	White Sox	Barons
BLU	Bluefield	APP	Blue Jays	Blue Jays
BOI	Boise	NWL	Rockies	Hawks
BOS	Boston	AL	-	Red Sox
BOW	Bowie	EAS	Orioles	Baysox
BG	Bowling Green	MID	Rays	Hot Rods
BRD	Bradenton	FSL	Pirates	Marauders
BRS	Bristol	APP	Pirates	Pirates
BRK	Brooklyn	NYP	Mets	Cyclones
BUF	Buffalo	INT	Blue Jays	Bisons
BUR	Burlington	APP	Royals	Royals
BUR	Burlington	MID	Angels	Bees
CAR	Carolina	CAR	Brewers	Mudcats
CR	Cedar Rapids	MID	Twins	Kernels
CSC	Charleston	SAL	Yankees	RiverDogs
CHA	Charlotte	FSL	Rays	Stone Crabs

CODE	TEAM	LG	AFF	NAME
CHA	Charlotte	INT	White Sox	Knights
CHA	Chattanooga	SOU	Reds	Lookouts
CHB	Chiba Lotte	NPB	-	Marines
CHW	Chicago	AL	-	White Sox
CHC	Chicago	NL	-	Cubs
CHU	Chunichi	NPB	-	Dragons
CFG	Cienfuegos	CNS	-	-
CIN	Cincinnati	NL	-	Reds
CLR	Clearwater	FSL	Phillies	Threshers
CLE	Cleveland	AL	-	-
INDB	Cleveland Blue	AZL	Cleveland	-
INDR	Cleveland Red	AZL	Cleveland	-
CLI	Clinton	MID	Marlins	LumberKings
COL	Columbia	SAL	Mets	Fireflies
COL	Columbus	INT	Cleveland	Clippers
COH	Columbus	INT	Cleveland	Clippers
ONE	Connecticut	NYP	Tigers	Tigers
CC	Corpus Christi	TEX	Astros	Hooks
DAN	Danville	APP	Braves	Braves
DYT	Dayton	MID	Reds	Dragons
DAY	Daytona	FSL	Reds	Tortugas
DEL	Delmarva	SAL	Orioles	Shorebirds
DET	Detroit	AL	-	Tigers
DE	Down East	CAR	Rangers	Wood Ducks
DUN	Dunedin	FSL	Blue Jays	Blue Jays
DUR	Durham	INT	Rays	Bulls
ELP	El Paso	PCL	Padres	Chihuahuas
ELZ	Elizabethton	APP	Twins	Twins
ERI	Erie	EAS	Tigers	SeaWolves
EUG	Eugene	NWL	Cubs	Emeralds
EVE	Everett	NWL	Mariners	AquaSox
FAY	Fayetteville	CAR	Astros	Woodpeckers
BRV	Florida	FSL	Braves	Fire Frogs
FTM	Fort Myers	FSL	Twins	Miracle
FW	Fort Wayne	MID	Padres	TinCaps
FRE	Frederick	CAR	Orioles	Keys
FRE	Fresno	PCL	Nationals	Grizzlies
FRI	Frisco	TEX	Rangers	RoughRiders
FKU	Fukuoka	NPB	-	Hawks
AST	GCL Astros	GCL	Astros	-
BLJ	GCL Blue Jays	GCL	Blue Jays	-
BRA	GCL Braves	GCL	Braves	-
CRD	GCL Cardinals	GCL	Cardinals	-
MRL	GCL Marlins	GCL	Marlins	-
MTS	GCL Mets	GCL	Mets	-
NAT	GCL Nationals	GCL	Nationals	-
ORI	GCL Orioles	GCL	Orioles	-
PHE	GCL Phillies East	GCL	Phillies	-
PHW	GCL Phillies West	GCL	Phillies	-
PIR	GCL Pirates	GCL	Pirates	-
RAY	GCL Rays	GCL	Rays	-
RSX	GCL Red Sox	GCL	Red Sox	-
TIG	GCL Tigers East	GCL	Tigers	-
TIW	GCL Tigers West	GCL	Tigers	-
TWI	GCL Twins	GCL	Twins	-

CODE	TEAM	LG	AFF	NAME
YAE	GCL Yankees East	GCL	Yankees	-
YAW	GCL Yankees West	GCL	Yankees	-
GJ	Grand Junction	PIO	Rockies	Rockies
GTF	Great Falls	PIO	White Sox	Voyagers
GL	Great Lakes	MID	Dodgers	Loons
GRN	Greeneville	APP	Reds	Reds
GBO	Greensboro	SAL	Pirates	Grasshoppers
GVL	Greenville	SAL	Red Sox	Drive
GWN	Gwinnett	INT	Braves	Stripers
HAG	Hagerstown	SAL	Nationals	Suns
HNS	Hanshin	NPB	-	Tigers
HBG	Harrisburg	EAS	Nationals	Senators
HFD	Hartford	EAS	Rockies	Yard Goats
HIC	Hickory	SAL	Rangers	Crawdads
HIL	Hillsboro	NWL	D-backs	Hops
HRO	Hiroshima Toyo	NPB	-	Carp
HOU	Houston	AL	-	Astros
HV	Hudson Valley	NYP	Rays	Renegades
IDF	Idaho Falls	PIO	Royals	Chukars
IND	Indianapolis	INT	Pirates	Indianapolis
IE	Inland Empire	CAL	Angels	66ers
IOW	Iowa	PCL	Cubs	Cubs
JXN	Jackson	SOU	D-backs	Generals
JAX	Jacksonville	SOU	Marlins	Jumbo Shrimp
JC	Johnson City	APP	Cardinals	Cardinals
JUP	Jupiter	FSL	Marlins	Hammerheads
KNC	Kane County	MID	D-backs	Cougars
KAN	Kannapolis	SAL	White Sox	Intimidators
KC	Kansas City	AL	-	Royals
KNG	Kingsport	APP	Mets	Mets
HAB	La Habana	CNS	-	
LC	Lake Country	MID	Cleveland	Captains
LE	Lake Elsinore	CAL	Padres	Storm
LAK	Lakeland	FSL	Tigers	Flying Tigers
JS	Lakewood	SAL	Phillies	BlueClaws
LNC	Lancaster	CAL	Rockies	JetHawks
LAN	Lansing	MID	Blue Jays	Lugnuts
LTU	Las Tunas	CNS	-	
LV	Las Vegas	PCL	Athletics	Aviators
LHV	Lehigh Valley	INT	Phillies	IronPigs
LEX	Lexington	SAL	Royals	Legends
LAA	Los Angeles	AL	-	Angels
LAD	Los Angeles	NL	-	Dodgers
LOU	Louisville	INT	Reds	Bats
LOW	Lowell	NYP	Red Sox	Spinners
LYN	Lynchburg	CAR	Cleveland	Hillcats
MV	Mahoning Valley	NYP	Cleveland	Scrappers
MEM	Memphis	PCL	Cardinals	Redbirds
MIA	Miami	NL	-	Marlins
MID	Midland	TEX	Athletics	RockHounds
MIL	Milwaukee	NL	-	Brewers
MIN	Minnesota	AL	-	Twins
MIS	Mississippi	SOU	Braves	Braves
MIS	Missoula	PIO	D-backs	Osprey
MOB	Mobile	SOU	Angels	BayBears
MOD	Modesto	CAL	Mariners	Nuts
MTG	Montgomery	SOU	Rays	Biscuits
MB	Myrtle Beach	CAR	Cubs	Pelicans
NAS	Nashville	PCL	Rangers	Sounds
NH	New Hampsire	EAS	Blue Jays	Fisher Cats
NO	New Orleans	PCL	Marlins	Baby Cakes
NYY	New York	AL	-	Yankees
NYM	New York	NL	-	Mets
NIP	Nippon Ham	NPB	-	Fighters

CODE	TEAM	LG	AFF	NAME
NOR	Norfolk	INT	Orioles	Tides
NWA	NW Arkansas	TEX	Royals	Naturals
OAK	Oakland	AL	-	Athletics
OGD	Ogden	PIO	Dodgers	Raptors
OKC	Oklahoma City	PCL	Dodgers	Dodgers
OMA	Omaha	PCL	Royals	Storm Chasers
ORM	Orem	PIO	Angels	Owiz
ORX	Orix	NPB	-	Buffaloes
PMB	Palm Beach	FSL	Cardinals	Cardinals
WOR	Pawtucket	INT	Red Sox	Red Sox
PNS	Pensacola	SOU	Twins	Blue Wahoos
PEO	Peoria	MID	Cardinals	Chiefs
PHI	Philadelphia	NL	-	Phillies
PIT	Pittsburgh	NL	-	Pirates
POR	Portland	EAS	Red Sox	Sea Dogs
FBG	Potomac	CAR	Nationals	Nationals
PRN	Princeton	APP	Rays	Rays
PUL	Pulaski	APP	Yankees	Yankees
QC	Quad Cities	MID	Astros	River Bandits
RAK	Rakuten	NPB	-	Golden Eagles
RC	Rancho Cucamongo	CAL	Dodgers	Quakes
REA	Reading	EAS	Phillies	Fightin Phils
RNO	Reno	PCL	D-backs	Aces
RIC	Richmond	EAS	Giants	Flying Squirrels
ROC	Rochester	INT	Twins	Red Wings
COL	Rockies	NL	-	Rockies
RMV	Rocky Mountain	PIO	Brewers	Vibes
ROM	Rome	SAL	Braves	Braves
RR	Round Rock	PCL	Astros	Express
SAC	Sacramento	PCL	Giants	River Cats
SAL	Salem	CAR	Red Sox	Red Sox
SK	Salem-Keizer	NWL	Giants	Volcanoes
SL	Salt Lake	PCL	Angels	Bees
SA	San Antonio	PCL	Brewers	Missions
SD	San Diego	NL	-	Padres
SF	San Francisco	NL	-	Giants
SJ	San Jose	CAL	Giants	Giants
SWB	Scranton/WB	INT	Yankees	RailRiders
SEA	Seattle	AL	-	Mariners
SEI	Seibu	NPB	-	Lions
SB	South Bend	MID	Cubs	Cubs
SPO	Spokane	NWL	Rangers	Spokane
SPR	Springfield	TEX	Cardinals	Cardinals
SL	St. Louis	NL	-	Cardinals
SLU	St. Lucie	FSL	Mets	Mets
SCO	State College	NYP	Cardinals	Spikes
SI	Staten Island	NYP	Yankees	Yankees
STK	Stockton	CAL	Athletics	Ports
SYR	Syracuse	INT	Mets	Mets
TAC	Tacoma	PCL	Mariners	Rainiers
TAM	Tampa	FSL	Yankees	Tarpons
TB	Tampa Bay	AL	-	Rays
TNS	Tennessee	SOU	Cubs	Smokies
TEX	Texas	AL	-	Rangers
TOL	Toledo	INT	Tigers	Mud Hens
TOR	Toronto	AL	-	Blue Jays
TRN	Trenton	EAS	Yankees	Thunder
TCV	Tri-City	NYP	Astros	ValleyCats
TRI	Tri-City	NWL	Padres	Dust Devils
TUL	Tulsa	TEX	Dodgers	Drillers
VAN	Vancouver	NWL	Blue Jays	Canadians
VER	Vermont	NYP	Athletics	Lake Monsters
VIS	Visalia	CAL	D-backs	Rawhide
WAS	Washington	NL	-	Nationals

CODE	TEAM	LG	AFF	NAME
WEV	West Virginia	NYP	Pirates	Black Bears
WV	West Virginia (PIT)	SAL	Mariners	Power
WM	Western Michican	MID	Tigers	Whitecaps
WIL	Williamsport	NYP	Phillies	Crosscutters
WIL	Wilmington	CAR	Royals	Blue Rocks
WS	Winston-Salem	CAR	White Sox	Dash
WIS	Wisconsin	MID	Brewers	Timber Rattlers
YKL	Yakult	NPB	-	Swallows
YKO	Yokohama DeNa	NPB	-	BayStars
YOM	Yomiuri	NPB	-	Giants

Contributors

Nathalie Alonso is an editorial producer and reporter at LasMayores.com, MLB's Spanish-language website, where she began her career as an intern in 2006. A graduate of Columbia University, she lives in Queens, N.Y., where she was born and raised.

R.J. Anderson has been a staff writer at CBS Sports since 2016. Previously, he contributed to Baseball Prospectus (and five Annuals) as an author. He lives in Washington, D.C., where he's developed disdain for the GEICO Gecko who resides at Nationals Park.

Lucas Apostoleris lives in Miami, Florida, with his wife and their two cats. He is a full-time musician and released his first album last June. He is also a baseball analyst, and he joined Baseball Prospectus as a writer and researcher in 2019. He has been published at a variety of outlets, including ESPN and FanGraphs.

Rob Arthur is a Chicago-based journalist and data science consultant. In addition to a weekly column at Baseball Prospectus, he has written for FiveThirtyEight, VICE News, the Wall Street Journal, and many other publications. He enjoys baseball and thanks to the pandemic has developed an inordinate fondness for the entire 90 Day Fiancé family of shows.

Robert Au is the Director of Operations at Baseball Prospectus. He has been fortunate enough to shelter in place in the San Francisco Bay Area with three humans, three cats, and a grand piano, the latter of which somehow needed five string replacements in 2020.

Darius Austin is a fantasy writer and depth chart administrator at Baseball Prospectus. In the rare moments when he isn't thinking about Farhan Zaidi's latest transaction, he writes the occasional article for Banished to the Pen and podcasts for Bat Flips & Nerds and Friends with Fantasy Benefits.

Emma Baccellieri is a staff writer at *Sports Illustrated*, where she primarily covers (surprise!) baseball. She lives in Washington, D.C.

Bill Baer is a freelance writer from the Philadelphia area. A veteran of the industry since 2007, he has had bylines with ESPN, NBC Sports, and Baseball Prospectus, among others. He's currently writing newsletter jawns about baseball at baerinmind.substack.com.

Mark Barry is an author and fantasy writer at Baseball Prospectus. He lives in Los Angeles with his wife and two cats, and still dreams of a day (although this time wistfully) spent playing catch and talking about life with Francisco Lindor. Carlos Santana is there too. And maybe Joey Votto.

Sydney Bergman is an educator, podcaster, and writer living in the D.C. area. She worked as a high school science teacher for nine years before getting into the world of teacher education. Yell with her about player ejection data on Twitter at @sydrpfp.

Nathan Bishop has written at Baseball Prospectus and Lookout Landing. He currently writes and podcasts his doubts of the Seattle Mariners at the blog Dome and Bedlam, which is the internet's foremost resource for semi-annual proofs of life from yours truly.

Grant Brisbee (born 3 December 1948)[2] is an English singer, songwriter, and television personality. He rose to prominence during the 1970s as the lead vocalist of the heavy metal band Black Sabbath, during which period he adopted the nickname "Prince of Darkness".[3]

Craig Brown lives in Kansas City and has spent the last 17 seasons writing about the adventures of the Royals. Along the way, he has contributed to Baseball Prospectus, ESPN, Beyond the Boxscore, Sports on Earth, SB Nation and The Hardball Times. If you are fortunate enough to attend a ballgame in 2021, keep score.

Adrian Burgos, Jr. is a Professor of History at the University of Illinois who has authored three books on Latinos and baseball. His work has appeared in MLB.com, SportingNews.com, and Memories and Dreams, among others. He was also the founding editor-in-chief of La Vida Baseball, a multiplatform digital brand on baseball and Latinos.

Craig Calcaterra is the writer and editor of the daily baseball and culture newsletter, Cup of Coffee. Before that he was the national baseball writer for NBC Sports. He has also written for Esquire, Bloomberg News, MSNBC, Yahoo, Bleacher Report, and The Hardball Times and has appeared on National Public Radio a lot because he loves to stay on brand. He lives in New Albany, Ohio with his wife, children, and many cats.

Russell A. Carleton has technically been an author of Baseball Prospectus for three decades, minus the couple of times he snuck out the window to consult for a couple of

MLB teams. He lives in Atlanta, Georgia with his wife (who is awesome) and five kids. He is the author of The Shift: The Next Evolution in Baseball Thinking.

Ben Carsley is a Senior Author at Baseball Prospectus. When he's not writing about baseball, Ben is generally cooking, drinking IPAs, losing NFL parlays or ignoring Malinowski's Law on Twitter. By day, he manages a team of SEO analysts and content writers who are fairly convinced he's Ron Swanson. He is a lifelong fan of the Padres, a team he has always loved.

Alexis Collins is a contributor to the R&D and Prospect teams at Baseball Prospectus. Outside of baseball she works as a systems analyst. In her free time she enjoys weightlifting and taking walks with her dogs.

Zach Crizer is the baseball editor at Yahoo Sports and a former Baseball Prospectus columnist. He lives in New York City.

Bradford William Davis is a columnist at the New York Daily News. He misses daps.

Patrick Dubuque is an accountant with political science and teaching degrees. He's also an editor and writer for Baseball Prospectus. His hobbies include sighing, having opinions about commas, and failing to monetize his hobbies.

James Fegan is a staff writer for The Athletic. His work has appeared in Baseball Prospectus, ESPN SweetSpot, NBC Sports Chicago, FanSided and Athlete's Quarterly. He lives and works in his hometown of Chicago with his wife Jacqueline Restrepo.

Noah Frank is a contributing writer for Baseball Prospectus and a writer and editor in Washington, D.C. He is a veteran of professional baseball front offices at both the major and minor league level. He believes there is a small, but passionate market for Sean Manaea/Matt Olson mustache buddy cop fan-fiction.

Bailey Freeman is the creator of the Youtube channel Foolish Baseball, where he produces a flagship video essay series called Baseball Bits. His whereabouts are unknown to this day.

Ken Funck has contributed to the Baseball Prospectus annual each year since 2009, during which time saplings became trees, children blossomed into adults and baseball analytics grew from nerdy outsider subculture to core organizational competency. Ken designs and manages Business Intelligence systems and lives outside Madison, Wisconsin with his wife and ideal travel companion Stephanie, a terrier named Jack and an enduring belief that his favorite literary affectation—the em-dash—is sadly underutilized.

Brendan Gawlowski is an author at FanGraphs and an editor at TheBestSchools.org. He lives in Seattle with his wife, Sierra, and his dog Yukon; she is part of the family.

Mike Gianella has written about baseball—fantasy and otherwise—at Baseball Prospectus since 2013. He is an avid fantasy baseball player and has won (among other things) the League of Alternative Baseball Reality (LABR), Tout Wars, and Tout Wars DFS in 2020. He lives in suburban Philadelphia with his wife, two children, two cats and works in the healthcare field to help improve patient outcomes when he isn't working to help improve your fantasy team.

Steven Goldman, former BP editor-in-chief and current consulting editor, edited, co-edited, as well as contributed to multiple volumes of this book and was also responsible for BP's books Mind Game, It Ain't Over 'Til It's Over, and Extra Innings: More Baseball Between the Numbers. He's also the author of the Casey Stengel biography Forging Genius. His work has appeared in numerous other places ranging from Deadspin (original formula) to The Daily Beast. He's also the host of the long-running Infinite Inning podcast, which sits at the crossroads of baseball, history, politics, and culture, cohosts the Bob Dylan career retrospective podcast Everything is Broken, and is one of the panelists on the ongoing baseball and politics podcast Say It Ain't Contagious. All of the above originates from New Jersey, where he resides with his wife, son, occasionally his daughter, three cats, and an unmanageable number of books.

Craig Goldstein is the editor-in-chief of Baseball Prospectus. His work has appeared in Sports Illustrated, Vice Sports, Fox Sports MLB/JABO and SB Nation MLB. He lives in Maryland, where he spends just the right amount of time thinking of good ideas and standing by them.

Bryan Grosnick is an author of Baseball Prospectus and has consulted for an MLB franchise. This is his seventh consecutive appearance in the Annual, for which he is extremely grateful. He lives in New England with his death-defying, semi-vegan, and hotel carpet-obsessed wife, as well as his Pokémon-trainer son and two dogs.

Jon Hegglund is one of possibly 10-20 Giants fans currently residing in the state of Idaho. When he's not writing and podcasting about fantasy baseball, he thinks a lot about tacos, beer, the weather, cognitive narratology, late-stage capitalism, the end of the world and what comes after.

Kamila Hinkson is a Montreal-based journalist who works for the Canadian Broadcasting Corporation. She has won several RTDNA Canada awards for sports feature writing, but her crowning achievement is that she's been to 17 major-league parks and counting.

Kendra James is a writer whose work has appeared in Elle, Marie Claire, Harpers Bazaar, The Daily Beast, Cosmopolitan, espnW, and Shondaland, where she was a senior editor. She lives in Los Angeles, where she is working on her first book and memoir, Congratulations on Your Acceptance: A Black Girl's Guide to Attending a New England Boarding School.

Alex Kirshner is a writer in Washington, D.C. His work has appeared at The Ringer, Slate, SB Nation, and elsewhere. He hosts a college football podcast called Split Zone Duo, and he considers himself lucky in every way other than that he was born to care about the Pittsburgh Pirates.

Justin Klugh is a writer for Baseball Prospectus. His work has appeared on FanGraphs, The Athletic, SB Nation, and various billboards in Pennsylvania and Maryland. He hosts "The Dirty Inning," a podcast about the dumbest, funniest, or most obscure innings in Phillies history.

Keanan Lamb is the Senior MLB Draft Writer for Baseball Prospectus. This is his first year writing for the annual, after previously working for the Toronto Blue Jays and Miami Marlins. He resides in Jacksonville, Florida.

Tom Ley is a co-founder of Defector, a worker-owned sports blog and media company.

Rob Mains is a writer at Baseball Prospectus, where his career in finance is distressingly handy in discussing the game today. He lives in a redoubt in upstate New York, surrounded by Finger Lakes wine, waging a lonely battle to preserve the Chicago Manual of Style usage of the word only.

Rachael McDaniel is still updating. Please don't turn off your computer.

Kelsey McKinney is a co-owner at Defector.com, a very good sports blog, and the author of the novel GOD SPARE THE GIRLS, out in June 2021. Her work has appeared in the New York Times, Cosmopolitan, New York Mag, and many other places. She lives in Washington, D.C. with her husband and her dumb dog.

Jake Mintz is a baseball tweeter, podcaster, word-vomit creator, life-long Orioles supporter and the less intelligent half of Céspedes Family BBQ. He co-hosts a podcast for The Ringer Podcast Network and formerly worked at MLB.com and DAZN. Jake resides in New York City where he spends the majority of his time biking around Central Park, where he makes phone calls that are impossible to hear because he's on a damn bike and it's windy.

Emily Nemens's debut novel, The Cactus League, is a finalist for the 2020 Casey Award and one of NPR's Best Books of 2020. She lives and works in New York, where she edits The Paris Review, draws the occasional political portrait, and defends MLB expansion teams.

Marc Normandin is the former MLB Editor of SB Nation, current writer and editor at Baseball Prospectus, and writes on baseball's labor issues and more for Patreon subscribers at marcnormandin.com. His baseball writing has appeared at Deadspin, Sports Illustrated, ESPN, Sports on Earth, The Guardian, The Nation and TalkPoverty, among others.

Eric Nusbaum is the author of "Stealing Home: Los Angeles, the Dodgers, and the Lives Caught in Between." He lives in Tacoma, Washington with his family.

Robert O'Connell is a writer and relay-throw aficionado whose work has appeared in The Atlantic, the New York Times, the Guardian, Deadspin, Sports Illustrated, and elsewhere.

Sridhar Pappu is the author of The Year of The Pitcher: Bob Gibson, Denny McLain and the End of Baseball's Golden Age. A former columnist with The New York Times, he's also worked as a correspondent for The Atlantic and staff writer for the New York Observer, Sports Illustrated and The

Washington Post. Born and raised in Oxford, Ohio, he lives in Brooklyn, still trying to determine why there's a photo of George Brett in his bathroom.

Jeffrey Paternostro is the Lead Prospect Writer and Multimedia Production Manager for Baseball Prospectus. Before that he was the Minor League Editor at SBNation's Amazin' Avenue. Before that he sat in New Britain Stadium trying to figure out why Brian Bannister looked like a major leaguer despite a fastball in the high-80s. Eventually he will be back behind home plate.

Harry Pavlidis is the Director of R&D for Baseball Prospectus.

Amy Pircher is a software engineer in Los Angeles, who helps send stuff to space by day, works for Baseball Prospectus at night, and is #1 cat mom at all times.

Kate Preusser is a contributor at Baseball Prospectus and editor in chief at SB Nation's Lookout Landing, where she writes about the Mariners and spends too much time considering the hip-size-to-power ratio of Dylan Moore. After writing these comments, she is now, also, regrettably, a Pirates fan, and begs Rob Manfred not to add any more seafaring teams in future expansions, as those two are quite enough to be getting on with.

Tommy Rancel a.k.a. Pen Griffey Jr a.k.a Flow DiMaggio a.k.a The One Marichal a.k.a Drip Shumaker is a writer for ESPN and The Athletic. He has previously written for FanGraphs as well as contributing to the Baseball Prospectus Annual. He lives in the Tampa Bay area with his wife Jamie and their five children.

David Roth is an editor and co-owner at Defector and the co-host of the affiliated podcast The Distraction. His writing has appeared in The New Republic, The New Yorker, Columbia Journalism Review, and the previous six Baseball Prospectus Annuals. He is from New Jersey and lives in New York.

Bret Sayre is the President of Baseball Prospectus. By day, he tells investment professionals what not to do. By night, he is a full-time family man and part-time nurse, cook, dynasty ranker, copy editor, musician and dog whisperer. As an eight-year-old boy, he was knocked over by a man in his thirties as he tried to catch a dead ball thrown by Kevin Mitchell at Shea Stadium. Now, he lives in New Jersey with his wife, Carolyn, their two children, Aly and Josh, a big-eyed bear named Hobbes, a fridge full of wine and more LEGOs than a Target.

Ginny Searle is a writer and associate editor for Baseball Prospectus. Her work has previously appeared in SB Nation, Deadspin (RIP), and Allure. She lives in Southern California and spends her free time reading dead authors and developing backstories for stuffed animals.

Jarrett Seidler is the Senior Prospect Writer and Evaluation Coordinator for Baseball Prospectus. He also co-hosts For All You Kids Out There, a weekly BP podcast that is occasionally about the Mets. As a lifelong New Jersey resident, he reluctantly admits that the Bleachers/Bruce Springsteen collaboration "chinatown" is a million times better than any recent E Street Band work.

Adam Sobsey has been writing for Baseball Prospectus since 2011. He is the lead author of Bull City Summer (Daylight Books, 2014), and Chrissie Hynde: A Musical Biography (University of Texas Press, 2017). He spends his free time thinking up limericks that start, "There once was a team from Pawtucket."

Stephanie Springer is an analyst of organic chemistry, patents, pharmaceuticals, and life in general. She can usually be found reading while sipping on a cup of coffee or an IPA.

Elizabeth Strom is a writer and editor for DRaysBay. A native of Brooklyn, she can recall the entire starting lineup of the first Mets game she attended in 1968 but can never remember where she left her glasses. She has lived in Tampa, FL since 2005.

Matt Sussman lives in Toledo, Ohio. His hobbies include baseball writing, curling, and strict chronological lists (though not necessarily in that order).

Jon Tayler is an editor at FanGraphs and was formerly a staff writer at Sports Illustrated who spends too much time thinking about and getting mad at the Mookie Betts trade. He lives in New York City and is available for birthdays, weddings and bar mitzvahs.

Luis Torres is a medicinal chemist with nearly 15 years of experience in the pharmaceutical industry. He is the son of two amazing Puerto Rican parents and grew up in New Jersey. While not in the lab, he has been a baseball blogger since 2014, including a four-year stint at Beyond the Box Score as a Featured Writer before leaving in July 2020, and he has also contributed to the Hardball Times. Even though he has lived in the Boston area since 2007, he is still a Mets fan for some reason, but he was still as mad as any Red Sox fan over the Mookie Betts trade.

Matt Trueblood writes for Baseball Prospectus, Minnesota Twins site Twins Daily, the Athlon and Lindy's MLB Preview magazines, and for subscribers to his newsletter, Penning Bull. He lives in the North Metro of the Twin Cities.

Collin Whitchurch is an editor at Action Network, former associate editor at Baseball Prospectus, and newspaper industry expat who has been writing about baseball in some form or another since 2013. A native Midwesterner, he lives and works in Austin, TX, and does not miss the snow in any way, shape, or form.

Randy Wilkins is a three-time Emmy award winning filmmaker from the Bronx, NY. His work has appeared on ESPN, Apple+, HBO, and Netflix. Randy is a co-founder and writer for the Yankees blog, Views From 314ft.

Jasmyn Wimbish is a writer for CBS Sports where she covers the NBA and WNBA. She lives and works in Chicago, IL where she works tirelessly to explain to those from the midwest that the dry heat of Phoenix summers is far worse than the humidity in Chicago.

Jeff Wiser is a contributor to Baseball Prospectus. He has previously had work published at The Athletic AZ, BeerAdvocate, ESPN, SB Nation, and other outlets. Jeff lives in Portland, Oregon, works professionally in education and fly fishes as much as possible.

Kazuto Yamazaki is a professional pitch tagger and failing amateur stand-up comedian/guitarist based in Tokyo. He spends most of his waking hours looking for images of pitch grips and while blasting heavy metal tunes.

Clinton Yates is a columnist for The Undefeated and ESPN Los Angeles, and a regular panelist on the ESPN show Around the Horn. He's previously written for The Washington Post, Washington Post Express, and Washington Top News.

Acknowledgements

Nathalie Alonso: Many thanks to my colleague Do-Hyoung Park, the Twins' beat writer for MLB.com, who answered questions about his team and helped me brainstorm; and to fellow BP contributor Sydney Bergman, for her encouragement when writer's block set in. A big thank you also to Craig Goldstein, whose insightful suggestions and edits helped make this an essay I'm proud of.

R.J. Anderson: Emma Baccellieri, Craig Goldstein, Bret Sayre, Patrick Dubuque, Tommy Rancel, Adam Sobsey, and his CBS Sports colleagues. My parents and the rest of my family, forever and always.

Lucas Apostoleris: I owe plenty to my family—most especially my parents and my wife, Kathleen—for their continued support in every facet of my life. I also need to thank my editors—Craig Goldstein, Patrick Dubuque, and R.J. Anderson—for making me a better writer. And I also have a lot of appreciation for those on the BP Stats team—Harry Pavlidis, Robert Au, Cory Frontin, among many others—who have answered my questions and helped me understand complicated things. And this year, I need to mention in particular: Jacky Bing Sheng Lee, Jean An, and Rob Liu, who have all been so kind and immensely helpful to me over the course of the 2020 CPBL season.

Rob Arthur: Thanks to Dan Hirsch for the invaluable Baseball Gauge, my editors for improving my work, my colleagues in the BP Stats Group for discussion, and my family for their love.

Robert Au: Thank you to Laura, Alexei, and Henry for everything, and to my mother, for her patience and love. Harry Pavlidis has been a wonderful partner in data crime. Thanks to everyone on the BP stats team for making it through an extremely difficult year together, and to Kathy Woolner and Rob Mains for taking care of so many unsung jobs. Rob McQuown somehow continues to provide answers even though he's no longer with us. I'm dedicating my work on the annual to the memory of my uncle.

Darius Austin: The Bat Flips & Nerds podcast crew, a wonderful set of lockdown companions: John McGee, Tom Pringle, Ben Carter, Russell Eassom, Rob Noverraz & Rachel Steinberg. J.P. Breen, for his excellent editing and advice.

The indispensable Depth Charts team, for their hard work in a season that could not have been more complicated: Kaz Yamazaki, Brian Duricy, Derek Albin, Daniel Epstein, Randy Holt and Scott Orgera. Rob Mains, for his consistent support and invaluable insight.

Emma Baccellieri: All the friends, readers, and flavored seltzers that made sure baseball writing was still a worthwhile pursuit over the last year.

Bill Baer: Craig Goldstein, Patrick Dubuque, Craig Calcaterra. (Who are three people who have never been in my kitchen?)

Mark Barry: To the people that have given me a chance, most specifically Bret Sayre. To Craig Goldstein, Mike Gianella, JP Breen, Patrick Dubuque and R.J. Anderson. To my family most of all, Amanda, Kristen, Mom and Dad. You're all the best and the coolest.

Sydney Bergman: I couldn't have done this without my mishpacha group chat or the fine folks at Nats twitter and BP, particularly Jarrett. A shout-out to my husband, parents, and sister—the world's biggest Willie Harris fan. And lastly, this writing year wouldn't have been what it was without Nathalie as a publishing buddy, or Laura, the finest book midwife in any galaxy.

Nathan Bishop: My friend and editor Patrick Dubuque, who treats me with more patience, good humor, and gentle rebukes than I deserve. Thanks to all my friends at D&B, Mariners Twitter, and of course my absurdly wonderful wife and children, who ask so little of me in return for all the wonder and joy they give.

Grant Brisbee: To my wife and two daughters: When I turned to you and said, "None of you seem to understand. I'm not locked in here with you. You're locked in here with me," you laughed, and then I didn't, and then you stopped laughing and then we stared at each other and it became really uncomfortable for a year or so. But I love you all more than you could possibly know. Thanks for being you.

Craig Brown: Thanks to R.J. Anderson, Patrick Dubuque, Craig Goldstein and Bret Sayre for inviting me back. A tip of the cap to Jeffrey Flanagan, Alec Lewis, Jeff Passan, Sam Mellinger and Lynn Worthy for the exceptional coverage behind closed doors in 2020. And of course thanks to my family who continues to indulge my baseball whims.

Adrian Burgos, Jr.: Thanks to my family who indulge my passion for talking and writing about baseball, and to Patrick Dubuque and Craig Goldstein for their feedback in writing this piece.

Ben Carsley: My Red Sox-crazed family, the ever-patient Allyson Clancy, Bret Sayre, Craig Goldstein, Sam Miller, R.J. Anderson, Patrick Dubuque, Xander Bogaerts, Eli Fredman, Mary Donovan, Daniel Ohman and the C-4 Content Team.

Zach Crizer: Thanks to Craig Goldstein, R.J. Anderson and Patrick Dubuque. And to Hannah Keyser, Stein, Jason Catania, Jefe, Stin and Steph.

Bradford William Davis: L, G, and D—no one I'd rather be locked inside an 850 square foot apartment with than my big three. Thank you for believing in me.

Patrick Dubuque: Thanks to R.J. Anderson, Craig Goldstein, and Bret Sayre for dealing with all my organization, to Craig Brown, Harry Pavlidis, Robert Au, Alexis Collins, and Amy Pircher for their help making these words into a book, to Sam Miller and Jason Wojciechowski for getting us to this book, to all the writers and friends over a decade of happy semi-professionalism, to Jeffrey Leonard, but most of all thanks to Kjersten for her support and to Sylvie and Felix for tempering their disappointment at Dad having such boring jobs.

Noah Frank: Thanks to the BP staff, especially Craig, for both the opportunity and the support this year. To my wife Micah, for knowingly signing up to be a part of this life and doing it anyway. And to my mom, who took me to my first game, and who would have been the proudest person to see my name in this book.

Bailey Freeman: Thank you to my parents for supporting my non-traditional career, as well as Jeff Mathis for being Jeff Mathis.

Ken Funck: R.J. Anderson, Steph Bee, Patrick Dubuque, Aaron Gleeman, Steven Goldman, Craig Goldstein, Christina Kahrl, King Kaufman, Ben Lindbergh, Sam Miller, John Perrotto, Bret Sayre, Cecilia Tan, Jason Wojciechowski and anyone else who has worked their editorial magic on my behalf.

Brendan Gawlowski: Thank you to Dan Kurtz and Ben Howell for the amazing KBO statistical work that helped the Korean chapters come to life. Thank you to the scouts who prefer to remain anonymous, and to Jeffrey Paternostro for sanity checking my Royce Lewis impressions. Thanks to Patrick Dubuque, R.J. Anderson and Craig Goldstein for their thoughtful editing. And finally, thank you Rich and Sierra Gawlowski for your inspiration and understanding.

Mike Gianella: My wife Colleen and my children Lucy and Elise, three amazing human beings who made an awful and unbearable year much less so. Bret Sayre, Craig Goldstein, J.P. Breen, Mark Barry and so many others at Baseball Prospectus who allow my words to appear on the virtual page and make them sound much better than they do in my initial drafts. Jon Hegglund and Samuel Hale, my podcast partners-in-crime and friends who I hope to meet in person someday. Darius Austin, Kevin Jebens, Jesse Roche and Tim McCullough, the rest of the greatest fantasy baseball squad ever assembled. Alex Patton and Peter Kreutzer, two fantasy baseball giants who I am privileged to call friends. Tristan Cockcroft, Eric Karabell, Steve Gardner, Jeff Erickson, Gray Albright, Rudy Gamble, Derek Van Riper and Doug Dennis, just some of the many talented people in this industry who never stop making me more competitive or pushing me to improve what I do.

Steve Goldman: The usual forever-gratitude to Stefanie, Sarah, Clemens, Reuven, Eliane, Ilana, Andy, Rick, Cliff, Mickey, Raven, Charity, Christine, Mike, Craig, the SAIC gang, and a special note of appreciation to Bret and Craig G for the fruitful return engagement.

Craig Goldstein: Katherine and Charlie Pappas, Laurie Gross, Harvey Goldstein, Alexis Goldstein, R.J. Anderson, Patrick Dubuque, Bret Sayre, Jason Wojciechowski, Sam Miller, Ginny Searle, Collin Whitchurch, Rob McQuown, Ben Carsley, Jacob Raim, Lucas Apostoleris, Harry Pavlidis, Jonathan Judge, Rob Mains, Jeffrey Paternostro, Jason Parks, Ben Lindbergh, The BP Prospect Team, Jarrett Seidler, Marc Normandin, Zach Mortimer, Tucker Blair, Ethan Purser, Mike Ferrin, Spike Lundberg, Tommy Rancel, Michael Baumann, Meg Rowley, James Fegan, Emma Baccellieri, Bradford William Davis, Mauricio Rubio, Shakeia Taylor, J.P. Breen, Wilson Karaman, Zach Crizer, Jeffrey Wiser.

Bryan Grosnick: Sarah Grosnick, Luke Grosnick, Phil and Debbie Grosnick, Bret Sayre, Craig Goldstein, R.J. Anderson, Patrick Dubuque, Jarrett Seidler, Jeffrey Paternostro, Jason Wojciechowski, Sam Miller, Kate Feldman, Jonathan Judge, bubble tea, the staff of Amazin' Avenue, the BP Stats team, and the data providers at Baseball Prospectus, FanGraphs, Baseball-Reference, and Brooks Baseball.

Kamila Hinkson: Thank you to Sydney Bergman, who read an early version of this essay and provided invaluable feedback, and to the editing team at BP who helped turn my jumbled thoughts into something coherent.

Kendra James: It wouldn't have been possible without the dad who raised me in Cubs fandom, the women who brought me back to it in college, the friends who suffered with me on the road to the World Series, and the man who married me even after I barfed on him in a cab after my boys clinched league title on October 22, 2016.

Alex Kirshner: Miles Kirshner.

Justin Klugh: I'd like to thank my loving family, in particular my wife, Aviva.

Tom Ley: Ian Stewart.

Rob Mains: My mother, Rhoda Mains, for instilling a love of the game and my wife, Amy Durland, for encouraging me to pursue it and often not regretting having done so. Martín Alonso, José Hernández, Marco Gámez, Pepe Latorre, and Carlos Pérez for making BP en español, our daily Spanish-language content, a reality. My editors, Craig Goldstein, Ginny Searle, and Collin Whitchurch, for putting up with my overuse of charts and tables. Everyone at BP who helped us survive 2020. AM and PM, for who they are.

Rachael McDaniel: My gay family, my mom, and Patrick for making me do this again.

Kelsey McKinney: Thank you to Trey, for everything, to my perfect dog for keeping me sane. Thank you to Defector.com, a bright light in a very dark year, and thank you to the Washington Nationals who were so terrible in 2020, I didn't even feel bad about being too depressed to watch them play.

Jake Mintz: Jordan Shusterman first and foremost because he's held my ass in check for almost a decade now. Shouts to Craig Goldstein, Kevin Brown, Connor Newcomb, Hannah Broder, Matt Ritchie, Jason Cole and Eric Longenhagen for chatting through the merits of various Orioles with me. Joon Lee, Bradford William Davis, Sarah Langs, Brent Honeywell, Lucas Giolito, Ryan Spilborghs, Rhea Butcher, Clinton Yates, José Gómez, Russ Dorsey, Bob Kendrick, Arlenis Peña, Lindsey Adler and Bobby Wagner are each my favorite person to talk about baseball with, but Clinton is actually No. 1. Thanks, to my lovely girlfriend Tamar Eisen for accommodating a living situation that involves 80 shirseys and 50 baseball hats. General thanks to Abby Mintz, Cal Ripken, my parents, Adam Jones, Lanterne Rouge, Lachlan Morton, earth's moral compass Gemma Kaneko, Lail Wilcox, Daniel Geanon and Jack Besser. And thanks to Max Cormier, the best human being and pitching mind I know, for always being a phone call away.

Emily Nemens: Thanks to Craig Goldstein, Patrick Dubuque, R.J. Anderson, and everyone at BPA for letting a story writer into the building. Friends, family, Mariners fans: thank you for your perseverance.

Eric Nusbaum: Many thanks to the Volcanoes family for letting me tell a small piece of their story, and to Janelle, Clay, and Marco for, well, everything.

Sridhar Pappu: I'd like to thank my very patient family, particularly my father, Rama Rao Pappu, for providing the support and encouragement to take on new challenges in what can be an emotionally crippling career, even in the best of times. Early in 2020, Joey Votto was gracious enough to spend time talking with me, forever transforming the way I viewed the game. For a decade, Brian Lin and Joseph Squance have helped me dissect almost every single game the Reds have played and our conversations provided the underpinning for the piece. As always, C. Trent Rosencrans was generous to share his time and expertise with me before I started writing, and Jack Greiner and Charlie Michael provided invaluable insight as I worked through various drafts. Finally, thanks to Craig Goldstein, Patrick Dubuque and R.J. Anderson, for both the opportunity to write but in helping shape the work. To count myself amongst this group of writers is an unforgettable honor.

Jeffrey Paternostro: My wife Jess for staying in a quarantine pod that involved many many 2020 Mets games. My daughter Evelyn whose screen time will remain limited to 15 minutes of Sixto Sánchez for a while longer. Jarrett Seidler who can never stay limited to 15 minutes about Sixto Sánchez. The Prospect Team for knocking it out of the the park even when we couldn't go to the park. And of course the readers, listeners, well-wishers, group DMs, and slack channels that got me through 2020 somehow.

Harry Pavlidis: This book is made possible by the entire R&D staff, with a special thanks to Shawn Brody and Andrew Koo for their contributions. Thanks to Alan Nathan and Barton Smith for their endless patience and willingness to teach.

Amy Pircher: Juan—thank you for dealing with all my bullshit, and making sure I eat.

Kate Preusser: I would like to acknowledge the work of Pirates beat writer Jason Mackey, and encourage burgeoning Pirates fans and baseball fans alike to subscribe to the Pittsburgh Post-Gazette in order to read his work and keep up with a team on the upswing.

Tommy Rancel: Jamie, Alexis, Vincent, Jarek, Brooklyn, Dakota, Rebecca Basse, Carlos Alvarez, R.J. Anderson, Erik Hahmann, Craig Goldstein, Andrew Schulz, Alex Media, Akaash Singh, Mark Gagnon, Nandor Relentless, Laszlo Cravensworth, Nadja Cravensworth, Not Guillermo De La Cruz, Keith Law, Joel Martinez, Daniel Baker, LaJethro Jenkins, Dragonfly Jonez, Joset Kamali, Randy Lemery, Grant Jackson, Carl Reed, Daniel Levy, Jackie Daytona and Colin Robinson.

David Roth: I would like to thank everyone at BP for continuing to invite me back to the annual and tormenting me by assigning essays on depressing or baffling or otherwise upsetting teams. I would also like to thank everyone who helped me barely hold it together in 2020: Kate and everyone else I care about, Kate whom I have spent all my time with and somehow only enjoyed more and all the rest of which I miss dearly; everyone at Defector, who helped make my only real work-related aspiration a reality; the far-flung family of former collaborators from SB Nation and Vice and Deadspin and The Classical, who give me hope for a less stupid and more humane future, or at least a better internet.

Bret Sayre: Carolyn, for not only being better than me at everything, but not holding it against me. Aly and Josh for always making me smile. Lynn and Peter Sayre. Team DIY. Craig Goldstein, Ben Carsley, Patrick Dubuque, R.J. Anderson, Mike Gianella. The Heights Heat. Annie Young. Rob McQuown.

Ginny Searle: Thanks to so many people from BP, including but not limited to: Craig Goldstein, Patrick Dubuque, Collin Whitchurch, Rob Mains, Steven Goldman. Trans people: You are loved, you are wanted. To Tori: Thank you for you; IOU bones.

Jarrett Seidler: In memory of Meryl Sabat, who was one of more than 335,000 Americans to pass away from COVID-19 in 2020. I love you, Grandmom.

Adam Sobsey: R.J. Anderson, Patrick Dubuque, Heather Mallory, Fernando Perez, Leonard Fisher.

Stephanie Springer: I would like to thank the staff at BP for being fantastic folks to work with, and I'd like to thank Stu, famed Kai and Hobie wrangler.

Elizabeth Strom: Thanks to Danny Russell for giving me the opportunity to write about baseball and helping me write meaningfully about baseball. Also thanks to the whole DRaysBay crew, but especially Ian Malinowski and Joshua Morgan, who have taught me that relievers are gonna reliever and clutch probably isn't a thing. Finally, I thank my Papa Willie and Uncle Arnie for taking me to that first Mets game in 1968 and making me memorize that starting lineup.

Matt Sussman: To the only three people I've seen for the past several Marches: Brit, Max, Mom.

Jon Tayler: Shouts to all the nerds putting and interpreting stats online so that I can have informed opinions about Luke Jackson's pitch arsenal. Thanks to the fine folks at BP for letting me be part of the Annual for a second straight year and giving me a safe space to have feelings about Ryan Zimmerman. Much love to the friends and family (and dog) who kept me sane in 2020. Caring about each other is all we've got.

Luis Torres: First and foremost, special thanks goes to my amazing, beautiful wife Katie, who has always been supportive of my baseball writing. Thanks also goes to all my managing editors at Beyond the Box Score: Neil Weinberg and Kevin Ruprecht for bringing me aboard, and Ryan Romano, Henry Druschel, Matt Provenzano, and Kenny Kelly. I'd also like to acknowledge and thank Keith Law, Mark Simon, and Eric Karabell, because without their old Baseball Today podcast I probably never would have taken up baseball writing in the first place.

Matt Trueblood: Thanks to Maria, who talks me out of quitting baseball writing every December (so far); to Emerson, who inspires me and shames me when I ponder giving up on anything, even now; to Sorkin, whose baserunning makes Javy Báez's look tame and kindles my love of the game; to Lincoln, whose hilarious irreverence reminds me not to take this appallingly serious business that seriously; to Anna, who asks me to tell her more about the 1993 Giants every night while she falls asleep; to my parents, who didn't rat me out when a neighbor at a park association meeting mentioned a lefty taking aim at their playhouse with fungo flies; and to my colleagues and editors, at BP, Twins Daily, and other places, in this dreadful year and in much better previous ones, for being steadier, more generous, and wiser than me.

Collin Whitchurch: I would like to thank Craig Goldstein, Ginny Searle, and Patrick Dubuque for the many hours of late-night banter about mundane grammar minutiae. And earnestly for making me a better editor and writer, and for their friendship and camaraderie. I'd also like to thank my parents for supporting the hell out of what I do, even if they don't entirely understand what the hell I do.

Randy Wilkins: I would like to thank Eljon for her never ending support and love. Thank you to Bobby, Derek, Matt, Steven, and Jay for helping me find my baseball writing voice. Thank you to Shakeia and Bradford for being inspirations and voices of courage. And as always, sending love to my mother, grandmother, and sister for being my foundation.

Jasmyn Wimbish: I want to first thank R.J. Anderson for even thinking of me to write for this book, as well as my editor Craig Goldstein for helping me along the way in this process and making me feel comfortable in taking on this challenge. I also want to thank my parents, Shanda and Keith, for supporting me not just in this endeavor but in everything I do. Lastly, I want to thank my girlfriend Laura

Cebrij for allowing me to spend hours and hours for a few nights straight to write, and keeping me focused to finish this when all I wanted to do was watch movies.

Jeff Wiser: I would like to thank his wife, Annie, and their pup, Simcoe, for being patient supporters of his baseball work. I'd also like to thank my BP teammates for their

inspiration, his friends and family for their ongoing love and support, and the great craft brewers of PDX for the endless supply of liquid goodies.

Kaz Yamazaki: R.J. Anderson, Lucas Apostoleris, Patrick Dubuque, Dani Esparza, Dan Evans, Mr. Fujimoto, Ben Lindbergh, the late great Rob McQuown, Jeffrey Paternostro, Harry Pavlidis, Bret Sayre, Jarrett Seidler, and the rest of my colleagues at Baseball Prospectus.

Index of Names

For the Joy of Keeping Score

THIRTY81 Project is an ongoing graphic design project focused on the ballparks of baseball. Since being established in 2013, scorecards have been a fundemantal part of the effort. Each two-page card is uniquely ballpark-centric — there are 30 variants — and designed with both beginning and veteran scorekeepers in mind. Evolving over the years with suggestions from fans, broadcasters, and official scorers, the sheets are freely available to everyone as printable letter-size PDFs at the project webshop: www.THIRTY81Project.com

Download, Print, Score, Repeat ...

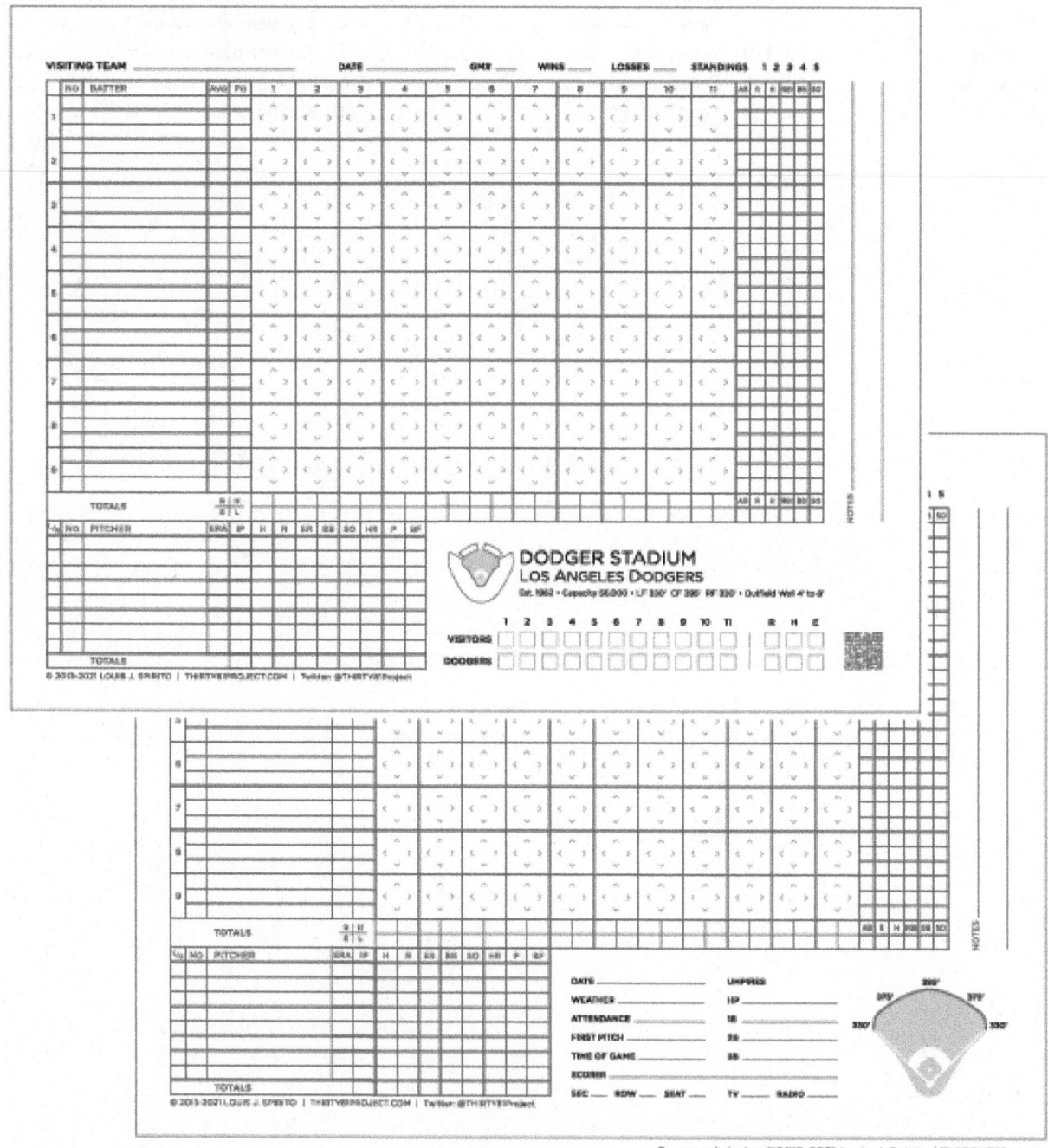

Scorecard design ©2013-2021 Louis J. Spirito | THIRTY81Project